The Sporting News

BASEBALL GUIDE

2000 EDITION

Editors

CRAIG CARTER
DAVE SLOAN

The Sporting News

Efrem Zimbalist III, President and Chief Executive Officer, Times Mirror Magazines; James H. Nuckols, President, The Sporting News; Francis X. Farrell, Senior Vice President, Publisher; John D. Rawlings, Senior Vice President, Editorial Director; John Kastberg, Vice President, General Manager; Kathy Kinkeade, Vice President, Operations; Steve Meyerhoff, Executive Editor; Joe Hoppel, Senior Editor; Sean Stewart, Associate Editor; Brendan Roberts and David Walton, Assistant Editors; Marilyn Kasal, Production Director; Terry Shea, Database Analyst; Bob Parajon, Prepress Director; Michael Behrens, Art Director, Special Projects; Christen Webster, Production Artist.

A Times Mirror
Company

EXPLANATION OF STATISTICAL ABBREVIATIONS

A: assists. **AB:** at-bats. **Avg.:** batting average (hits divided by at-bats). **BB:** bases on balls. **Bk.:** balks. **CG:** complete games. **CS:** caught stealing. **E:** errors. **ER:** earned runs. **ERA:** earned-run average (earned runs times nine divided by innings pitched). **G:** games. **GB:** games behind. **GF:** games finished. **GDP:** grounding into double plays. **GS:** games started. **H:** hits. **HB:** hit batsmen. **HP:** hit by pitches. **HR:** home runs. **IBB:** intentional bases on balls. **IP:** innings pitched. **L:** losses. **OBP:** on-base percentage (hits plus bases on balls plus hit by pitches divided by at-bats plus bases on balls plus hit by pitches plus sacrifice flies). **Pct.:** winning percentage. **PO:** putouts. **Pos.:** position. **R:** runs. **RBI:** runs batted in. **SB:** stolen bases. **SF:** sacrifice flies (run-scoring flyouts). **SH:** sacrifice hits (bunts that advance one or more runners but result in the batter being retired at first base or reaching first on an error). **ShO:** shutouts. **Slg.:** slugging percentage (total bases divided by at-bats). **SO:** strikeouts. **Sv.:** saves. **TB:** total bases (hits plus doubles plus two times the number of triples plus three times the number of home runs). **TBF:** total batters faced. **TC:** total chances (putouts plus assists plus errors). **TPA:** total plate appearances (at-bats plus bases on balls plus sacrifice hits plus sacrifice flies plus hit by pitches plus times reaching base on catcher's interference). **W:** wins. **WP:** wild pitches. **2B:** doubles. **3B:** triples.

World Series, A.L. Championship Series, N.L. Championship Series, A.L. Division Series, N.L. Division Series and All-Star Game highlights written by Joe Hoppel, Brendan Roberts and Ron Smith of THE SPORTING NEWS.

Major league statistics compiled by STATS, Inc., Lincolnwood, Ill.

Minor league statistics compiled by Howe Sportsdata International Inc., Boston.

ISBN: 0-89204-628-7

10 9 8 7 6 5 4 3 2 1

CONTENTS

ON THE COVER: The New York Yankees celebrate their victory in the 1999 World Series. (Photo by Albert Dickson/THE SPORTING NEWS.)

Spine photo of Mike Piazza by Bob Leverone/THE SPORTING NEWS.

2000 SEASON

Major League Baseball directories

Team by team

MAJOR LEAGUE BASEBALL

Address
245 Park Avenue
New York, NY 10167
Telephone
212-931-7800
FAX
212-949-5654
Commissioner of baseball
Allan H. "Bud" Selig
Chief operating officer
Paul Beeston
Executive v.p., baseball operations
Sandy Alderson

Executive vice president, administration
Robert DuPuy
Executive v.p., labor relations and human resources
Robert Manfred
Vice president, marketing
Kathleen Francis
Exec. dir., security/facility management
Kevin Hallinan
Executive director, public relations
Richard Levin
Executive director, baseball operations
William Murray

General counsel
Thomas J. Ostertag
Exec. director, minor league relations
Jimmie Lee Solomon
Chief financial officer
Jeffrey White
V.p., broadcasting and new media dev.
Leslie Sullivan
Sr. v.p., domestic and int'l properties
Timothy Brosnan

AMERICAN LEAGUE

Address
245 Park Avenue
New York, NY 10167
Telephone
212-931-7600
Vice president
Carl R. Pohlad
Executive director of umpiring
Martin J. Springstead

Senior vice president
Phyllis Merhige
Director, waivers and player records
Brian Small
Coordinator, baseball information
Jason Carr
Administrator of umpires/travel
Tess Basta-Marino

Administrative assistants
Carolyn Coen
Angelica Cintron

NATIONAL LEAGUE

Address
245 Park Avenue
New York, NY 10167
Telephone
212-931-7700
Senior vice president and secretary
Katy Feeney

V.p, media relations and market dev.
Ricky Clemons
Executive director, player records
Nancy Crofts
Executive secretary
Rita Aughavin

Administrative assistant, umpires
Cathy Davis
Asst., media rel. and player records
Moises Rodriguez

OTHER ORGANIZATIONS

LABOR RELATIONS COMMITTEE
Address
245 Park Avenue
New York, NY 10167
Telephone
212-931-7401
212-949-5690 (FAX)
Executive vice president of labor and human resources and labor counsel
Robert D. Manfred Jr.
General labor counsel
Francis Coonelly
Associate counsels
Louis Melendez
John Westhoff
Supervisor, salary and contract admin.
John Ricco
Attorney
Derek Jackson

NATIONAL ASSOCIATION OF PROFESSIONAL BASEBALL LEAGUES
Address
P.O. Box A
St. Petersburg, FL 33731
Telephone
727-822-6937
727-821-5819 (FAX)

President
Mike Moore
Vice president/administration
Pat O'Conner
Executive director of development
Rob Dlugozima
General counsel
Ben Hayes
Director/licensing
Brian Earle
Director/media relations
Jim Ferguson
Director of baseball operations
Tim Brunswick
Director of marketing
Rod Meadows
Director of business/finance
Eric Krupa
Director of Professional Baseball Umpire Corporation
Mike Fitzpatrick
Director of Professional Baseball Employment Opportunities
Ann Perkins

ASSOCIATION OF PROFESSIONAL BASEBALL PLAYERS OF AMERICA
Address
12062 Valley View, Suite 211
Garden Grove, CA 92645
Telephone
714-892-9900
714-897-0233 (FAX)
President
John J. McHale
Vice presidents
Arthur Richman
Robert Kennedy
Secretary/treasurer
Dick Beverage

BASEBALL ASSISTANCE TEAM INC.
Address
245 Park Avenue
New York, NY 10167
Telephone
212-931-7821
Chairman
Ralph Branca
President
Joe Garagiola

Vice presidents
Joe Black
Earl Wilson
Executive director
James J. Martin
Secretary/treasurer
Tom Ostertag

NATIONAL BASEBALL HALL OF FAME AND MUSEUM

Address
P.O. Box 590
Cooperstown, NY 13326
Telephone
607-547-7200
607-547-2044 (FAX)
Chairman of Hall of Fame
Edward W. Stack
V.p. of business and administration
Frank Simio
V.p. and chief curator
William T. Spencer Jr.
Curator of collections
Peter P. Clark
Executive director of retail marketing
Barbara Shinn
Controller
Frances L. Althiser
Librarian
James L. Gates
Executive director of communications and education
Jeff Idelson
Executive director of communications and museum programs
John Ralph

MAJOR LEAGUE SCOUTING BUREAU

Address
3500 Porsche Way, Suite 100
Ontario, CA 91764
Telephone
909-980-1881
909-980-7794 (FAX)
Director
Frank Marcos

MAJOR LEAGUE BASEBALL PLAYERS ASSOCIATION

Address
12 E. 49th St., 24th Floor
New York, NY 10017
Telephone
212-826-0808
212-752-3649 (FAX)
Executive director and general counsel
Donald M. Fehr
Special assistants
Tony Bernazard
Steve Rogers
Associate general counsel
Eugene D. Orza
Assistant general counsel
Doyle R. Pryor
Michael Weiner
Counsel
Robert Leneghan
Director of licensing
Judy Heeter
Director of communications
Greg Bouris

MAJOR LEAGUE BASEBALL PLAYERS ALUMNI ASSOC.

Address
1631 Mesa Ave., Suite C
Colorado Springs, CO 80906
Telephone
719-477-1870
719-477-1875 (FAX)
President
Brooks Robinson
Vice presidents
Bob Boone
George Brett
Mike Hegan
Chuck Hinton
Al Kaline
Carl Erskine
Rusty Staub
Robin Yount
Secretary/treasurer
Fred Valentine

ELIAS SPORTS BUREAU

Address
500 Fifth Ave.
New York, NY 10110
Telephone
212-869-1530
212-354-0980 (FAX)
General manager
Seymour Siwoff

MAJOR LEAGUE UMPIRES ASSOCIATION

Address
1735 Market St., Suite 3420
Philadelphia, PA 19103
Telephone
215-979-3220
215-979-3201 (FAX)
General counsel
Richard G. Phillips

BASEBALL WRITERS' ASSOCIATION OF AMERICA

President
Charles Scoggins, Lowell (Mass.) Sun
Vice president
Ian MacDonald, Montreal Gazette
Secretary/treasurer
Jack O'Connell, Hartford Courant

HOWE SPORTSDATA INTERNATIONAL INC.

Address
Boston Fish Pier
West Building No. 1, Suite 302
Boston, MA 02210
Telephone
617-951-0070
617-951-1379 (stats request)
617-737-9960 (FAX)
President
Jay Virshbo
Historical consultant
William Weiss

ANAHEIM ANGELS
AMERICAN LEAGUE WEST DIVISION

2000 Angels Schedule
Home games shaded. *—All-Star Game at Turner Field (Atlanta).

March
SUN	MON	TUE	WED	THU	FRI	SAT
26	27	28	29	30	31	

April
SUN	MON	TUE	WED	THU	FRI	SAT
						1
2	3 NYY	4 NYY	5 NYY	6	7 BOS	8 BOS
9 BOS	10 TOR	11 TOR	12 TOR	13	14 CWS	15 CWS
16 CWS	17 TOR	18 TOR	19 TOR	20 TOR	21 TB	22 TB
23 TB	24 DET	25 DET	26 DET	27 TB	28 TB	29 TB
30 TB						

May
SUN	MON	TUE	WED	THU	FRI	SAT
	1	2 BAL	3 BAL	4 BAL	5 SEA	6 SEA
7 SEA	8 OAK	9 OAK	10 OAK	11 TEX	12 TEX	13 TEX
14 TEX	15	16 BAL	17 BAL	18	19 KC	20 KC
21 KC	22	23 MIN	24 MIN	25 MIN	26 KC	27 KC
28 KC	29 CLE	30 CLE	31 CLE			

June
SUN	MON	TUE	WED	THU	FRI	SAT
				1	2 LA	3 LA
4 LA	5 SF	6 SF	7 SF	8	9 ARI	10 ARI
11 ARI	12	13 TB	14 TB	15 TB	16 BAL	17 BAL
18 BAL	19	20 KC	21 KC	22 KC	23 MIN	24 MIN
25 MIN	26	27 SEA	28 SEA	29 SEA	30 OAK	

July
SUN	MON	TUE	WED	THU	FRI	SAT
						1 OAK
2 OAK	3 SEA	4 SEA	5 SEA	6 SEA	7 COL	8 COL
9 COL	10	11	* 12	13 LA	14 LA	15 LA
16 SD	17 SD	18 SD	19	20 TEX	21 OAK	22 OAK
23 OAK	24 TEX	25 TEX	26 TEX	27 TEX	28 CWS	29 CWS
30 CWS	31 DET					

August
SUN	MON	TUE	WED	THU	FRI	SAT
		1 DET	2 DET	3	4 CLE	5 CLE
6 CLE	7 BOS	8 BOS	9 BOS	10	11 NYY	12 NYY
13 NYY	14	15 TOR	16 TOR	17 TOR	18 NYY	19 NYY
20 NYY	21 BOS	22 BOS	23 BOS	24	25 CLE	26 CLE
27 CLE	28 TOR	29 TOR	30 TOR	31		

September
SUN	MON	TUE	WED	THU	FRI	SAT
					1 CWS	2 CWS
3 CWS	4 DET	5 DET	6 DET	7 DET	8 BAL	9 BAL
10 BAL	11	12	13	14	15 MIN	16 MIN
17 MIN	18	19 KC	20 KC	21 KC	22 TEX	23 TEX
24 TEX	25 OAK	26 OAK	27 OAK	28 OAK	29 SEA	30 SEA

October
SUN	MON	TUE	WED	THU	FRI	SAT
1 SEA	2	3	4	5	6	7

2000 SEASON
CLUB DIRECTORY

Owner
The Walt Disney Company
Chairman and CEO, The Walt Disney Co.
Michael Eisner
President
Tony Tavares
Vice president and general manager
Bill Stoneman
Vice president of finance/administation
Andy Roundtree
V.p., advertising sales and broadcasting
Bob Wagner
Vice president, sales and marketing
Ron Minegar
Vice president, communications
Tim Mead
Vice president, ballpark operations
Kevin Uhlich
V.p., business and legal affairs
Rick Schlesinger
Assistant general manager
Ken Forsch
Special assistant to general manager
Preston Gomez
Legal counsel/contract negotiations
Mark Rosenthal
Director, scouting
Donny Rowland
Director, player development
Darrell Miller
Manager, baseball operations
Tony Reagins
Equipment manager
Ken Higdon
Visiting clubhouse manager
Brian Harkins
Senior video coordinator
Diego Lopez
Manager, baseball information
Larry Babcock

Manager, media services
Nancy Mazmanian
Manager, publications
Doug Ward
Manager, community relations
To be announced
Media services/travel coordinator
Tom Taylor
Dir., ticket sales and customer service
Lawrence Cohen
Director, marketing
Lisa Manning
Manager, ticket operations
Sheila Brazelton
Equipment manager
Ken Higdon
Medical director
Dr. Lewis Yocum
Team physician
Dr. Craig Milhouse
Head athletic trainer
Ned Bergert
Scouts
Don Archer, John Burden, Tom Burns, Todd Claus, Pete Coachman, David Crowson, Clay Daniel, Tom Davis, Jose Gomez, Steve Gruwell, Felipe Gutierrez, Kevin Ham, Rick Ingalls, Tim Kelly, Tom Kotchman, George Lauzerique, Jose Leiva, Guy Mader, Ron Marigny, Mario Mendoza, Tom Osowski, Paul Robinson, Rick Schroeder, Jack Uhey, Victor Villa
Major league scouts
Jay Hankins, Jon Niederer, Rich Schlenker, Moose Stubing, Dale Sutherland, Gary Sutherland, John Van Ornum

MINOR LEAGUE AFFILIATES

Class	Team	League	Manager
AAA	Edmonton	Pacific Coast	Carney Lansford
AA	Erie	Eastern	Garry Templeton
A	Boise	Northwest	Tom Kotchman
A	Cedar Rapids	Midwest	Mitch Seoane
A	Lake Elsinore	California	Mario Mendoza
Rookie	Butte	Pioneer	Joe Urso

BROADCAST INFORMATION
Radio: KLAC-AM (570).
TV: KCAL-TV (Channel 9).
Cable TV: Fox Sports West.

SPRING TRAINING
Ballpark (city): Tempe Diablo Stadium (Tempe, Ariz.).
Ticket information: 602-254-3300, 800-326-0331.

SPRING TRAINING ROSTER

Manager—Mike Scioscia (14).
Coaches—Bud Black (24), Alfredo Griffin (4), Mickey Hatcher (2), Joe Maddon (70), Orlando Mercado (88), Bobby Ramos (13), Ron Roenicke (12).

No.	PITCHERS	B/T	Ht./Wt.	Born	1999 clubs
18	Alvarez, Juan	L/L	6-0/175	8-9-73	Erie, Edmonton, Anaheim
41	Belcher, Tim	R/R	6-3/235	10-19-61	Anaheim
45	Cooper, Brian	R/R	6-1/185	8-19-74	Erie, Edmonton, Anaheim
19	Dickson, Jason	L/R	6-0/195	3-30-73	DID NOT PLAY
27	Fyhrie, Michael	R/R	6-2/203	12-9-69	Edmonton, Anaheim
21	Hasegawa, Shigetoshi	R/R	5-11/178	8-1-68	Anaheim
44	Hill, Ken	R/R	6-2/215	12-14-65	Anaheim
65	Holtz, Mike	L/L	5-9/188	10-10-72	Anaheim, Edmonton
43	Levine, Al	R/R	6-3/198	5-22-68	Anaheim
59	Nina, Elvin	R/R	6-0/185	11-25-75	Modesto, Midland, Erie
36	Ortiz, Ramon	R/R	6-0/175	5-23-76	Erie, Edmonton, Anaheim
40	Percival, Troy	R/R	6-3/238	8-9-69	Anaheim
34	Petkovsek, Mark	R/R	6-0/198	11-18-65	Anaheim
58	Pote, Lou	R/R	6-3/208	8-27-71	Edmonton, Anaheim
60	Schoeneweis, Scott	L/L	6-0/186	10-2-73	Anaheim, Edmonton
62	Shields, Scot	R/R	6-1/175	7-22-75	Lake Elsinore, Erie
54	Turnbow, Derrick	R/R	6-3/180	1-25-78	Piedmont
56	Washburn, Jarrod	L/L	6-1/198	8-13-74	Edmonton, Anaheim
64	Wise, Matt	R/R	6-4/190	11-18-75	Erie

No.	CATCHERS	B/T	Ht./Wt.	Born	1999 clubs
61	Dewey, Jason	R/R	6-1/190	4-18-77	Erie, Lake Elsinore
8	Hemphill, Bret	B/R	6-2/200	12-17-71	Edmonton, Anaheim
63	Molina, Benjie	R/R	5-11/207	7-20-74	Edmonton, Anaheim
6	Walbeck, Matt	B/R	5-11/188	10-2-69	Anaheim

No.	INFIELDERS	B/T	Ht./Wt.	Born	1999 clubs
37	Barnes, Larry	L/L	6-1/195	7-23-74	Erie
9	DiSarcina, Gary	R/R	6-2/194	11-19-67	Lake Elsinore, Erie, Anaheim
20	Durrington, Trent	R/R	5-10/188	8-27-75	Erie, Anaheim
28	Glaus, Troy	R/R	6-5/229	8-3-76	Anaheim
42	Vaughn, Mo	L/R	6-1/268	12-15-67	Anaheim

No.	OUTFIELDERS	B/T	Ht./Wt.	Born	1999 clubs
16	Anderson, Garret	L/L	6-3/220	6-30-72	Anaheim
10	Colangelo, Mike	R/R	6-1/185	10-22-76	Erie, Edmonton, Anaheim
55	DaVanon, Jeff	B/R	6-0/185	12-8-73	Midland, Edmonton, Anaheim
25	Edmonds, Jim	L/L	6-1/212	6-27-70	Lake Elsinore, Anaheim
17	Erstad, Darin	L/L	6-2/212	6-4-74	Anaheim
22	Greene, Todd	R/R	5-10/208	5-8-71	Anaheim, Edmonton
48	Guzman, Elpidio	L/L	6-0/165	2-24-79	Cedar Rapids
35	Hutchins, Norm	B/L	5-11/198	11-20-75	Edmonton
3	Palmeiro, Orlando	L/L	5-11/175	1-19-69	Anaheim
15	Salmon, Tim	R/R	6-3/221	8-24-68	Anaheim, Lake Elsinore

BALLPARK INFORMATION

Ballpark (capacity, surface)
Edison International Field of Anaheim (45,050, grass)
Address
2000 Gene Autry Way
Anaheim, CA 92806
Business phone
714-940-2000
Ticket information
714-663-9000
Ticket prices
$19 (field box)
$17.50 (terrace box, terrace disabled MVP)
$13 (lower view MVP)
$11 (lower view box)
$10 (upper value box, terrace disabled box)
$8 (terrace/club pavilion-adult)
$6 (left field pavilion-adult)
$5.50 (terrace/club pavilion-child)
$3 (left field pavilion-child)
Field dimensions (from home plate)
To left field at foul line, 330 feet
To center field, 400 feet
To right field at foul line, 330 feet
First game played
April 19, 1966 (White Sox 3, Angels 1)

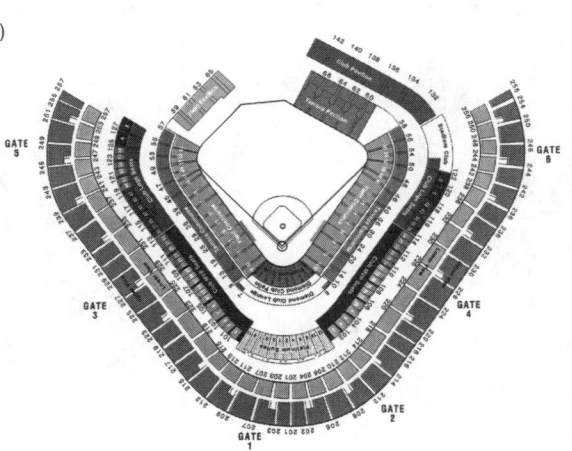

2000 SEASON *Anaheim Angels*

Date	Opp.	Res.	Score	(inn.*)	Hits	Opp. hits	Winning pitcher	Losing pitcher	Save	Record	Pos.	GB
4-7	Cle.	L	1-9		4	13	Burba	Hill		1-1	2nd	0.5
4-8	Cle.	L	1-9		4	13	Colon	Sparks		1-2	T2nd	1.0
4-9	At Tex.	W	8-4		12	10	Finley	Burkett		2-2	T1st	
4-10	At Tex.	W	10-0		19	3	Olivares	Helling		3-2	1st	+1.0
4-11	At Tex.	L	3-6		6	12	Sele	Belcher	Wetteland	3-3	T1st	...
4-12	At Tex.	W	13-5		20	7	Magnante	Clark		4-3	T1st	...
4-13	At Oak.	L	2-3		9	7	Oquist	Sparks	Taylor	4-4	T1st	...
4-14	At Oak.	L	5-6		9	7	Mathews	Finley	Taylor	4-5	T2nd	1.0
4-15	At Oak.	W	12-1		18	5	Olivares	Heredia		5-5	2nd	1.0
4-16	Sea.	W	9-5		14	5	Belcher	Moyer		6-5	T1st	...
4-17	Sea.	L	3-4	(10)	8	7	Paniagua	Percival	Mesa	6-6	T1st	...
4-18	Sea.	L	5-8		10	10	Cloude	Sparks	Mesa	6-7	T2nd	1.0
4-20	At Tor.	L	1-5		8	7	Escobar	Finley		6-8	T2nd	1.0
4-21	At Tor.	L	2-3		8	10	Carpenter	Olivares	Person	6-9	T2nd	1.0
4-22	At Tor.	L	7-8		8	13	Davey	Petkovsek	Lloyd	6-10	4th	2.0
4-23	At K.C.	W	4-2		6	4	Hasegawa	Montgomery	Percival	7-10	4th	2.0
4-24	At K.C.	L	3-4		6	8	Santiago	Hasegawa		7-11	4th	3.0
4-26	Tor.	W	4-3	(11)	10	8	Percival	Rodriguez		8-11	T3rd	3.0
4-27	Tor.	L	1-10		5	13	Hentgen	Olivares		8-12	T3rd	3.0
4-28	Tor.	W	12-10		14	15	Petkovsek	Lloyd	Percival	9-12	T2nd	3.0
4-29	Tor.	W	17-1		15	4	Hill	Halladay		10-12	T2nd	2.0
4-30	Chi.	W	3-1		5	5	Petkovsek	Navarro	Percival	11-12	T2nd	2.0
5-1	Chi.	L	5-8		13	14	Lundquist	Percival	Howry	11-13	T2nd	2.0
5-2	Chi.	W	6-3		11	5	Olivares	Parque		12-13	T2nd	2.0
5-3	Chi.	L	1-8		4	12	Snyder	Belcher		12-14	T2nd	2.0
5-4	At Det.	L	1-3		8	9	Brocail	Holtz	Jones	12-15	4th	2.5
5-5	At Det.	W	4-1		6	3	Sparks	Weaver	Percival	13-15	4th	2.5
5-6	At Det.	L	2-4		7	10	Florie	Finley	Jones	13-16	4th	2.5
5-7	At Bos.	L	0-6		6	10	Martinez	Olivares		13-17	4th	2.5
5-8	At Bos.	L	1-6		4	12	Pena	Belcher	Lowe	13-18	4th	3.5
5-9	At Bos.	L	2-4		10	10	Portugal	Hill	Wakefield	13-19	4th	4.5
5-11	At N.Y.	W	9-7		14	8	Petkovsek	Mendoza	Percival	14-19	4th	4.0
5-12	At N.Y.	W	1-0		6	3	Finley	Cone	Percival	15-19	T3rd	3.5
5-13	At N.Y.	W	2-0		9	6	Olivares	Irabu	Percival	16-19	3rd	3.5
5-14	T.B.	W	8-3		10	5	Belcher	Witt		17-19	3rd	3.5
5-15	T.B.	L	1-3		3	7	Saunders	Hill	Hernandez	17-20	3rd	4.5
5-16	T.B.	L	4-7		10	13	Alvarez	Sparks		17-21	3rd	4.5
5-18	At Bal.	L	3-5		7	8	Mussina	Finley	Timlin	17-22	4th	4.0
5-19	At Bal.	W	5-4		8	11	Levine	Timlin	Percival	18-22	4th	4.0
5-20	At Bal.	W	6-4		9	9	Belcher	Johnson	Percival	19-22	4th	3.5
5-21	At T.B.	L	9-10		14	12	White	Magnante	Hernandez	19-23	4th	3.5
5-22	At T.B.	W	8-6		16	9	Petkovsek	Newman	Percival	20-23	4th	3.5
5-23	At T.B.	W	4-0	(10)	4	3	Finley	Hernandez		21-23	T3rd	2.5
5-25	Bal.	W	4-1		6	6	Olivares	Erickson	Percival	22-23	T2nd	3.0
5-26	Bal.	L	2-3		4	4	Ponson	Belcher	Rhodes	22-24	4th	4.0
5-27	Bal.	L	3-6		7	12	Guzman	Hill	Timlin	22-25	4th	4.5
5-28	K.C.	L	4-11		10	12	Appier	Finley		22-26	4th	5.5
5-29	K.C.	W	4-3		7	6	Sparks	Fussell	Percival	23-26	4th	5.5
5-30	K.C.	W	4-3		7	6	Olivares	Rosado	Percival	24-26	4th	5.5
5-31	Min.	L	2-3		10	8	Hawkins	Hasegawa	Trombley	24-27	4th	6.5
6-1	Min.	W	5-1		7	5	Hill	Lincoln		25-27	4th	6.5
6-2	Min.	W	2-1		9	5	Finley	Radke	Percival	26-27	4th	6.5
6-4	At L.A.	L	4-5		10	11	Brown	Olivares	Shaw	26-28	4th	6.5
6-5	At L.A.	L	4-7		7	12	Masaoka	Belcher	Shaw	26-29	4th	7.5
6-6	At L.A.	W	7-5		11	9	Hill	Perez	Percival	27-29	4th	6.5
6-7	At S.F	L	2-5		7	5	Ortiz	Finley	Nen	27-30	4th	7.5
6-8	At S.F	L	2-6		5	12	Estes	Sparks		27-31	4th	8.5
6-9	At S.F	W	2-1		7	4	Belcher	Brock		28-31	4th	7.5
6-11	Ari.	L	2-12		8	18	Reynoso	Hill		28-32	4th	8.5
6-12	Ari.	W	4-3		10	6	Petkovsek	Benes	Percival	29-32	4th	7.5
6-13	Ari.	L	1-3	(13)	9	9	Nunez	Petkovsek	Olson	29-33	4th	7.5
6-15	At Tor.	L	2-13		6	18	Wells	Belcher		29-34	4th	7.0
6-16	At Tor.	L	2-3		6	8	Lloyd	Schoeneweis	Koch	29-35	4th	8.0
6-17	At Tor.	L	0-3		8	5	Escobar	Hill	Koch	29-36	4th	9.0
6-18	At N.Y.	L	1-4		5	8	Pettitte	Finley	Rivera	29-37	4th	10.0
6-19	At N.Y.	L	2-6		3	11	Irabu	Olivares	Mendoza	29-38	4th	10.0
6-20	At N.Y.	W	4-2		8	7	Belcher	Cone	Percival	30-38	4th	9.0
6-22	At Sea.	W	4-2		8	6	Petkovsek	Garcia	Percival	31-38	4th	7.5
6-23	At Sea.	L	3-8		10	10	Halama	Hill	Rodriguez	31-39	4th	8.5
6-24	At Sea.	W	12-7		16	9	Schoeneweis	Mesa	Petkovsek	32-39	4th	8.5
6-25	Oak.	W	4-3		8	9	Percival	Jones		33-39	4th	8.5
6-26	Oak.	W	5-4		10	7	Magnante	Rigby	Percival	34-39	4th	7.5

Date	Opp.	Res.	Score	(inn.*)	Hits	Opp. hits	Winning pitcher	Losing pitcher	Save	Record	Pos.	GB
6-27	Oak.	W	4-3		12	7	Sparks	Rogers	Percival	35-39	4th	6.5
6-28	Tex.	L	1-9		7	9	Morgan	Finley		35-40	4th	7.5
6-29	Tex.	L	0-5		1	13	Burkett	Olivares		35-41	4th	8.5
6-30	Tex.	L	4-18		10	20	Glynn	Hill		35-42	4th	9.5
7-2	At Oak.	W	10-6		14	10	Petkovsek	Harville		36-42	4th	9.5
7-3	At Oak.	L	7-9		13	12	Heredia	Finley	Taylor	36-43	4th	9.5
7-4	At Oak.	W	5-2		12	5	Olivares	Oquist		37-43	4th	8.5
7-5	Sea.	L	0-10		3	14	Fassero	Hasegawa		37-44	4th	8.5
7-6	Sea.	W	8-2		9	7	Petkovsek	Rodriguez		38-44	4th	7.5
7-7	Sea.	W	10-3		16	13	Sparks	Moyer		39-44	4th	7.5
7-9	At Col.	W	9-6		15	12	Finley	Kile	Percival	40-44	4th	7.5
7-10	At Col.	W	9-3		13	6	Olivares	Astacio		41-44	4th	6.5
7-11	At Col.	L	2-8		5	11	Dipoto	Fyhrie		41-45	4th	6.5
7-15	L.A.	W	7-6	(10)	10	12	Petkovsek	Mills		42-45	3rd	6.5
7-16	L.A.	L	1-3		5	5	Valdes	Olivares	Shaw	42-46	3rd	7.5
7-17	L.A.	L	3-13		7	14	Park	Sparks		42-47	4th	7.5
7-18	S.D.	L	3-6		10	14	Boehringer	Fyhrie	Hoffman	42-48	4th	8.5
7-19	S.D.	L	1-4	(10)	9	8	Miceli	Hasegawa	Hoffman	42-49	4th	9.5
7-20	S.D.	L	1-2		6	5	Ashby	Petkovsek	Hoffman	42-50	4th	10.5
7-21	At Tex.	L	5-9		10	13	Sele	Olivares	Zimmerman	42-51	4th	11.5
7-22	At Tex.	L	7-9		15	10	Burkett	Sparks	Zimmerman	42-52	4th	12.5
7-23	At Bal.	L	0-1		6	7	Guzman	McDowell	Timlin	42-53	4th	13.5
7-24	At Bal.	L	4-8		6	17	Johnson	Hill		42-54	4th	14.5
7-25	At Bal.	L	7-8	(11)	6	11	Kamieniecki	Holtz		42-55	4th	15.5
7-26	At T.B.	L	0-7		4	11	Witt	Olivares		42-56	4th	16.0
7-27	At T.B.	W	10-5		12	13	Magnante	Callaway		43-56	4th	16.0
7-28	At T.B.	L	1-4		6	11	Rupe	McDowell	Hernandez	43-57	4th	16.0
7-30	Min.	L	1-3		7	9	Radke	Hill		43-58	4th	17.5
7-31	Min.	L	0-8		3	11	Milton	Finley		43-59	4th	17.5
8-1	Min.	W	2-1		7	2	Sparks	Mays	Percival	44-59	4th	17.5
8-2	K.C.	L	4-12		11	17	Rosado	McDowell		44-60	4th	18.5
8-3	K.C.	L	0-7		5	10	Suppan	Fyhrie		44-61	4th	19.5
8-4	K.C.	W	4-3		10	6	Hill	Witasick	Percival	45-61	4th	19.5
8-5	Bos.	W	8-0		14	4	Finley	Rose		46-61	4th	19.0
8-6	Bos.	L	1-5		8	10	Saberhagen	Sparks		46-62	4th	19.0
8-7	Bos.	L	3-14		8	19	Rapp	Belcher		46-63	4th	20.0
8-8	Bos.	L	3-9		6	13	Martinez	McDowell		46-64	4th	20.0
8-9	Cle.	L	0-4		7	9	Colon	Hill		46-65	4th	20.0
8-10	Cle.	L	1-2	(10)	4	7	Rincon	Petkovsek	Jackson	46-66	4th	21.0
8-11	Cle.	L	3-4		10	10	Burba	Sparks	Jackson	46-67	4th	22.0
8-13	At Det.	L	7-8	(10)	10	9	Jones	Hasegawa		46-68	4th	21.0
8-14	At Det.	W	7-4		12	10	Magnante	Moehler	Percival	47-68	4th	20.0
8-15	At Det.	W	10-2		14	7	Finley	Thompson		48-68	4th	20.0
8-16	At Chi.	L	1-6		6	10	Sirotka	Washburn		48-69	4th	21.0
8-17	At Chi.	L	3-4	(12)	12	7	Howry	Holtz		48-70	4th	22.0
8-18	At Chi.	L	3-4		6	6	Baldwin	Magnante	Howry	48-71	4th	23.0
8-19	At Chi.	W	9-2		14	6	Ortiz	Parque		49-71	4th	22.0
8-20	Det.	W	5-1		7	5	Finley	Moehler		50-71	4th	22.0
8-21	Det.	L	0-5		4	9	Weaver	Washburn		50-72	4th	23.0
8-22	Det.	L	3-12		8	17	Mlicki	Sparks		50-73	4th	24.0
8-23	Det.	W	6-5		9	11	Percival	Brocail		51-73	4th	23.0
8-24	Tor.	L	1-5		6	10	Hentgen	Ortiz	Koch	51-74	4th	23.0
8-25	Tor.	L	2-7		6	9	Hamilton	Finley		51-75	4th	24.0
8-27	At Bos.	L	3-4		6	5	Garces	Percival	Lowe	51-76	4th	25.0
8-28	At Bos.	L	6-7		10	8	Lowe	Pote		51-77	4th	26.0
8-29	At Bos.	L	4-7		11	10	Rapp	Belcher	Lowe	51-78	4th	27.0
8-30	At Cle.	L	5-7		7	7	Colon	Levine	Jackson	51-79	4th	27.0
8-31	At Cle.	L	12-14		14	19	Poole	Percival	Shuey	51-80	4th	27.0
9-1	At Cle.	L	1-8		8	12	Burba	Washburn		51-81	4th	28.0
9-2	At Cle.	L	5-6		11	10	Nagy	Sparks	Jackson	51-82	4th	28.0
9-3	N.Y.	W	8-2		15	10	Belcher	Pettitte		52-82	4th	28.0
9-4	N.Y.	L	6-9		6	10	Watson	Alvarez	Rivera	52-83	4th	28.0
9-5	N.Y.	L	3-8		6	13	Yarnall	Fyhrie		52-84	4th	28.5
9-6	N.Y.	W	5-3		6	5	Washburn	Clemens	Percival	53-84	4th	29.0
9-7	Chi.	W	14-1		12	4	Cooper	Sirotka		54-84	4th	29.0
9-8	Chi.	W	6-5	(10)	10	7	Percival	Simas		55-84	4th	29.0
9-10	At Min.	W	4-2		13	4	Finley	Radke	Percival	56-84	4th	28.0
9-11	At Min.	L	0-7		0	10	Milton	Ortiz		56-85	4th	28.0
9-12	At Min.	W	6-3		9	5	Washburn	Mays		57-85	4th	27.0
9-13	At Min.	W	6-5		10	10	Magnante	Hawkins	Hasegawa	58-85	4th	27.0
9-14†	At K.C.	W	8-6		12	15	Pote	Morman	Hasegawa	59-85		
9-14‡	At K.C.	W	6-5		9	5	Hasegawa	Byrdak	Percival	60-85	4th	26.5
9-15	At K.C.	W	1-0		7	3	Finley	Carter	Percival	61-85	4th	26.5
9-16	At K.C.	L	1-7		6	12	Suppan	Ortiz		61-86	4th	27.0
9-17	Bal.	L	2-4		6	12	Erickson	Washburn	Timlin	61-87	4th	27.0
9-18	Bal.	L	3-6		8	5	Ponson	Cooper	Timlin	61-88	4th	28.0

Date	Opp.	Res.	Score	(inn.*)	Hits	Opp. hits	Winning pitcher	Losing pitcher	Save	Record	Pos.	GB
9-19	Bal.	L	4-5		9	11	Molina	Percival	Timlin	61-89	4th	28.0
9-20	T.B.	W	10-5		11	13	Finley	Alvarez		62-89	4th	27.5
9-21	T.B.	W	7-5		9	7	Ortiz	Eiland	Percival	63-89	4th	26.5
9-22	T.B.	W	8-5		11	11	Washburn	Wheeler		64-89	4th	25.5
9-24	At Sea.	L	3-4	(10)	5	8	Mesa	Percival		64-90	4th	26.5
9-25	At Sea.	W	7-3		6	4	Finley	Moyer		65-90	4th	26.5
9-26	At Sea.	L	2-3		6	8	Davey	Hasegawa		65-91	4th	27.5
9-28	Oak.	L	3-9		4	14	Hudson	Washburn	Mahay	65-92	4th	29.0
9-29	Oak.	W	7-4		12	4	Hasegawa	Mathews	Pote	66-92	4th	28.0
9-30	Oak.	W	5-4		10	13	Petkovsek	Isringhausen	Pote	67-92	4th	28.0
10-1	Tex.	W	7-6		9	8	Holtz	Morgan		68-92	4th	27.0
10-2	Tex.	W	15-3		14	9	Hasegawa	Helling		69-92	4th	26.0
10-3	Tex.	W	1-0		3	5	Washburn	Morgan	Pote	70-92	4th	25.0

Monthly records: April (11-12), May (13-15), June (11-15), July (8-17), August (8-21), September (16-12), October (3-0).
*Innings, if other than nine. † First game of a doubleheader. ‡ Second game of a doubleheader.

HIGHLIGHTS

High point: The Angels, despite losing outfielders Tim Salmon and Jim Edmonds and pitcher Tim Belcher to injury, won six of eight games against the A's, Mariners and Rockies just before the All-Star break, trimming their 9.5-game deficit in the A.L. West race to 6.5 and fueling optimism.

Low point: Interim manager Joe Maddon gave almost all of his starters the day off on September 11, and the Angels were no-hit by Minnesota's Eric Milton, who entered the game with a 6-11 record.

Turning point: After beating the Dodgers in their first game after the All-Star break, the Angels lost 11 straight, falling 16 games behind division-leading Texas. While the bats cooled, tensions heated up in the clubhouse. The on-field collapse and off-field turmoil led to the resignations of manager Terry Collins (in early September) and general manager Bill Bavasi (the last weekend of the season).

Most valuable player: The Angels didn't really have one, but their most consistent and productive player was second baseman Randy Velarde, who in 95 games hit .306 with nine homers, 48 RBIs and 13 stolen bases and also played superb defense. Velarde's reward: He was traded to the A's on July 29.

Most valuable pitcher: Lefthander Chuck Finley rebounded from a horrendous slump to go 7-1 with a 2.16 ERA in his last 11 starts. The veteran finished with a 12-11 record and 4.43 ERA and struck out 200 batters for the third time in four years.

Most improved player: After a sizzling start, third baseman Troy Glaus struggled for a month and there were rumblings he might be banished to Class AAA. But he regained a more consistent stroke and finished with 29 homers and 79 RBIs. His .240 average was a minus, though.

Most pleasant surprise: Pitcher Omar Olivares, who again had to win a rotation spot in spring training. He developed a nice cut fastball to go with his sinker and went 8-9 with a 4.05 ERA before being dispatched to Oakland with Velarde.

Biggest disappointment: Outfielder Darin Erstad drove in fewer runs all season (53) than he did in the first half of 1998 (59). Pitchers Tim Belcher (6.73 ERA), Ken Hill

(4-11 record) and Steve Sparks (5-11) also stumbled. And DH Todd Greene didn't provide the thump expected of him, hitting 14 homers in 321 at-bats.

Key injuries: Shortstop Gary DiSarcina (broken forearm) and Edmonds (torn cartilage in his shoulder) suffered spring-training injuries that sidelined them for 12 weeks and four months, respectively. First baseman Mo Vaughn incurred a severe sprain of his left ankle on opening night, an injury that hampered him all season, and Salmon sprained his left wrist in early May and was out for 2.5 months.

Notable: Barely able to run at times, Vaughn hit .281 with a team-high 33 homers and 108 RBIs. ... Salmon, despite his lengthy absence, knocked in 69 runs in only 98 games. ... The Angels had the fifth-best team ERA (4.79) and tied for the third-best team fielding percentage (.983) in the American League.

—MIKE DiGIOVANNA

RECORDS

1999 regular-season record: 70-92 (4th in A.L. West); 37-44 at home; 33-48 on road; 20-36 vs. East; 24-28 vs. Central; 26-28 vs. A.L. West; 6-12 vs. N.L.; 19-19 vs. lefthanded starters; 51-73 vs. righthanded starters; 62-81 on grass; 8-11 on turf; 17-28 in daytime; 53-64 at night; 23-25 in one-run games; 1-0-0 in doubleheaders.

Team record past five years: 387-405 (.489, ranks 8th in league in that span).

TEAM LEADERS

Batting average: Garret Anderson (.303).
At-bats: Garret Anderson (620).
Runs: Garret Anderson (88).
Hits: Garret Anderson (188).
Total Bases: Garret Anderson (291).
Doubles: Garret Anderson (36).
Triples: Darin Erstad (5).
Home runs: Mo Vaughn (33).
Runs batted in: Mo Vaughn (108).
Stolen bases: Darin Erstad, Randy Velarde (13).
Slugging percentage: Mo Vaughn (.508).
On-base percentage: Mo Vaughn (.358).

Wins: Chuck Finley (12).
Earned-run average: Chuck Finley (4.43).
Complete games: Omar Olivares (3).
Shutouts: None.
Saves: Troy Percival (31).
Innings pitched: Chuck Finley (213.1).
Strikeouts: Chuck Finley (200).

GAMES BY POSITION

Catcher: Matt Walbeck 97, Ben Molina 30, Charlie O'Brien 27, Steve Decker 17, Todd Greene 12, Bret Hemphill 12.
First base: Darin Erstad 78, Mo Vaughn 72, Chris Pritchett 15, Jeff Huson 8, Steve Decker 6, Matt Luke 4, Jim Edmonds 2.
Second base: Randy Velarde 95, Jeff Huson 41, Trent Durrington 41, Andy Sheets 7, Dave Silvestri 1, Tim Unroe 1.
Third base: Troy Glaus 153, Jeff Huson 9, Tim Unroe 3, Andy Sheets 1.
Shortstop: Gary DiSarcina 81, Andy Sheets 76, Jeff Huson 22, Dave Silvestri 1.
Outfield: Garret Anderson 153, Orlando Palmeiro 92, Tim Salmon 89, Darin Erstad 69, Jim Edmonds 42, Todd Greene 30, Reggie Williams 24, Tim Unroe 12, Matt Luke 6, Jeff DaVanon 5, Jeff Huson 2, Dave Silvestri 1.
Designated hitter: Mo Vaughn 67, Todd Greene 44, Orlando Palmeiro 10, Jim Edmonds 9, Tim Unroe 8, Jeff Huson 7, Tim Salmon 7, Chris Pritchett 5, Garret Anderson 4, Steve Decker 3, Reggie Williams 3, Darin Erstad 2, Jeff DaVanon 2, Matt Walbeck 1, Steve Sparks 1, Troy Glaus 1, Trent Durrington 1.

TOP DRAFT CHOICES

1. None
2. **John Lackey,** RHP, Grayson County (Tex.) C.C.
3. **Phil Wilson,** RHP, Poway (Calif.) H.S.
4. **Stan Bukowski,** RHP, Dunedin (Fla.) H.S.
5. **Vince LaCorte,** RHP, San Jose State U.
6. **Dusty Bergman,** LHP, U. of Hawaii
7. **Alan Wawrzyniak,** RHP, Philadelphia College of Textiles
8. **Aaron Franke,** RHP, Owens (Ohio) C.C.
9. **Brian Specht,** SS/2B, Doherty H.S., Colorado Springs
10. **Robb Quinlan,** 1B, U. of Minnesota

BALTIMORE ORIOLES
AMERICAN LEAGUE EAST DIVISION

2000 Orioles Schedule

Home games shaded. *—All-Star Game at Turner Field (Atlanta).

March

SUN	MON	TUE	WED	THU	FRI	SAT
26	27	28	29	30	31	

April

SUN	MON	TUE	WED	THU	FRI	SAT
						1
2	3 CLE	4	5 CLE	6 CLE	7 DET	8 DET
9 DET	10	11 KC	12 KC	13 KC	14 MIN	15 MIN
16 MIN	17 TB	18 TB	19 TB	20	21 OAK	22 OAK
23 OAK	24 CWS	25 CWS	26 CWS	27 CWS	28 TEX	29 TEX
30 TEX						

May

SUN	MON	TUE	WED	THU	FRI	SAT
	1 ANA	2 ANA	3 ANA	4 ANA	5 NYY	6 NYY
7 NYY	8 TOR	9 TOR	10 TOR	11 BOS	12 BOS	13 BOS
14 BOS	15	16 ANA	17 ANA	18 TEX	19 TEX	20 TEX
21 TEX	22	23 SEA	24 SEA	25 SEA	26 OAK	27 OAK
28 OAK	29 TB	30 TB	31 TB			

June

SUN	MON	TUE	WED	THU	FRI	SAT
				1 TB	2 MON	3 MON
4 MON	5 NYM	6 NYM	7 NYM	8	9 PHI	10 PHI
11 PHI	12	13 TEX	14 TEX	15 TEX	16 ANA	17 ANA
18 ANA	19 OAK	20 OAK	21 OAK	22 SEA	23 SEA	24 SEA
25 SEA	26	27 BOS	28 BOS	29 BOS	30 TOR	

July

SUN	MON	TUE	WED	THU	FRI	SAT
						1 TOR
2 TOR	3 TOR	4 NYY	5 NYY	6 NYY	7 PHI	8 PHI
9 PHI	10	11 *	12	13 ATL	14 ATL	15 ATL
16 FLA	17 FLA	18 FLA	19 BOS	20 BOS	21 TOR	22 TOR
23 TOR	24 NYY	25 NYY	26 NYY	27	28 CLE	29 CLE
30 CLE	31 MIN					

August

SUN	MON	TUE	WED	THU	FRI	SAT
		1 MIN	2 MIN	3	4 TB	5 TB
6 TB	7 DET	8 DET	9 DET	10 DET	11 KC	12 KC
13 KC	14	15 CWS	16 CWS	17 CWS	18 CWS	19 KC
20 KC	21 KC	22	23 CWS	24 CWS	25 TB	26 TB
27 TB	28	29 DET	30 DET	31 DET		

September

SUN	MON	TUE	WED	THU	FRI	SAT
					1 CLE	2 CLE
3 CLE	4 MIN	5 MIN	6 MIN	7	8 ANA	9 ANA
10 ANA	11 ANA	12 TEX	13 TEX	14	15 SEA	16 SEA
17 SEA	18 OAK	19 OAK	20 OAK	21	22 BOS	23 BOS
24 BOS	25	26 TOR	27 TOR	28 TOR	29 NYY	30 NYY

October

SUN	MON	TUE	WED	THU	FRI	SAT
1 NYY	2	3	4	5	6	7

2000 SEASON
CLUB DIRECTORY

Chairman/chief executive officer
Peter Angelos

Vice chairman, chief operating officer
Joe Foss

Executive vice president
John Angelos

Vice president/chief financial officer
Robert Ames

V.p., marketing & broadcasting
Mike Lehr

Vice president, baseball operations
Syd Thrift

Director, minor league operations
Don Buford

Director of scouting
Tony DeMacio

Dir., major and minor league instruction
Tom Trebelhorn

Special assistants to the V.P., baseball operations
Bruce Manno, Bob Schaeffer

Assistant dir., minor league operations
Tripp Norton

Traveling secretary
Philip Itzoe

Director, public relations
Bill Stetka

Public relations assistant
Kevin Behan

Director, ballpark operations
Roger Hayden

Director, community relations
Julie Wagner

Director, computer services
James Kline

Director, ballpark entertainment
To be announced

Director, publishing and advertising
Christina Palmisano

Director, fan and ticket services
Donald Grove

Director, sales
Matthew Dryer

Head athletic trainer
Richard Bancells

Assistant athletic trainer
Brian Ebel

Strength and conditioning
Tim Bishop

Advance scout
Deacon Jones

Professional scouts
Danny Garcia, Curt Motton, Fred Uhlman Sr.

National cross-checker
Mike Ledna

Regional supervisors
Shawn Pender, Logan White

Full-time scouts
Dean Decillis, John Gillette, Troy Hoerner, Jim Howard, Ray Kraczyk, Gil Kubski, Jeff Morris, Lamar North, Deron Rombach, Harry Shelton, Ed Sprague, Marc Tramuta, Mike Tullier, Dominic Viola, Marc Ziegler

Director, Latin American scouting
Carlos Bernhardt

Caribbean & S. American supervisor
Jesus Halabi

International scouts
Ubaldo Heredia, Salvator Ramirez, Arturo Sanchez, Brett Ward

MINOR LEAGUE AFFILIATES

Class	Team	League	Manager
AAA	Rochester	International	Marv Foley
AA	Bowie	Eastern	Andy Etchebarren
A	Frederick	Carolina	Dave Machemer
A	Delmarva	South Atlantic	Joe Ferguson
Rookie	Bluefield	Appalachian	Duffy Dyer
Rookie	Gulf Coast Orioles	Gulf Coast	Jesus Alfaro

BROADCAST INFORMATION

Radio: WBAL-AM (1090).
TV: WJZ (Channel 13), WNUV (Channel 54), WFTY (Channel 50).
Cable TV: Home Team Sports.

SPRING TRAINING

Ballpark (city): Ft. Lauderdale Stadium (Ft. Lauderdale, Fla.).
Ticket information: 954-523-3309, 305-358-5885, 561-776-9116.

SPRING TRAINING ROSTER

Manager—Mike Hargrove.
Coaches—Terry Crowley, Sammy Ellis, Brian Graham, Elrod Hendricks (44), Eddie Murray (33), Jeff Newman, Sam Perlozzo (2).

No.	PITCHERS	B/T	Ht./Wt.	Born	1999 clubs
	Aracena, Juan	R/R	6-0/190	12-17-76	Columbus, Kinston, Frederick
28	Dykhoff, Radhames	L/L	6-0/200	9-27-74	Rochester
19	Erickson, Scott	R/R	6-4/230	2-2-68	Baltimore
51	Falkenborg, Brian	R/R	6-6/195	1-18-78	Bowie, Gulf Coast Orioles, Baltimore
	Groom, Buddy	L/L	6-2/207	7-10-65	Oakland
	Guzman, Juan	R/R	6-2/184	3-4-78	Delmarva
	Hamilton, Jimmy	L/L	6-3/190	8-1-75	Akron, Buffalo, Rochester
41	Johnson, Jason	R/R	6-6/235	10-27-73	Rochester, Baltimore
	Maduro, Calvin	R/R	6-0/188	9-5-74	Rochester
	McElroy, Chuck	L/L	6-0/205	10-1-67	Colorado, New York N.L.
45	Molina, Gabe	R/R	5-11/207	5-3-75	Rochester, Baltimore
35	Mussina, Mike	B/R	6-2/183	12-8-68	Baltimore
	Negrette, Richard	R/R	6-2/173	3-6-76	Akron, West Tenn
43	Ponson, Sidney	R/R	6-1/225	11-2-76	Baltimore
32	Reyes, Al	R/R	6-1/208	4-10-71	Louisville, Milwaukee, Baltimore
25	Riley, Matt	L/L	6-1/201	8-2-79	Frederick, Bowie, Baltimore
52	Ryan, B.J.	L/L	6-6/230	12-28-75	Chattanooga, Indianapolis, Cincinnati, Rochester, Baltimore
40	Timlin, Mike	R/R	6-4/210	3-10-66	Baltimore
	Trombley, Mike	R/R	6-2/210	4-14-67	Minnesota

No.	CATCHERS	B/T	Ht./Wt.	Born	1999 clubs
21	Johnson, Charles	R/R	6-2/220	7-20-71	Baltimore
	Myers, Greg	L/R	6-2/225	4-14-66	San Diego, Rancho Cucamonga, Atlanta

No.	INFIELDERS	B/T	Ht./Wt.	Born	1999 clubs
14	Bordick, Mike	R/R	5-11/175	7-21-65	Baltimore
80	Casimiro, Carlos	R/R	5-11/170	11-8-76	Bowie
23	Clark, Will	L/L	6-1/200	3-13-64	Baltimore
65	Coffie, Ivanon	L/R	6-1/182	5-16-77	Bowie, Frederick
18	Conine, Jeff	R/R	6-1/220	6-27-66	Baltimore
11	DeShields, Delino	L/R	6-1/175	1-15-69	Bowie, Baltimore, Delmarva, Frederick
1	Garcia, Jesse	R/R	5-10/171	9-24-73	Baltimore, Rochester
13	Hairston, Jerry	R/R	5-10/173	5-29-76	Rochester, Baltimore
	Martinez, Eddy	R/R	6-2/173	10-23-77	Frederick
10	Minor, Ryan	R/R	6-7/245	1-5-74	Rochester, Baltimore
39	Pickering, Calvin	L/L	6-5/278	9-29-76	Rochester, Baltimore
8	Ripken, Cal	R/R	6-4/220	8-24-60	Baltimore

No.	OUTFIELDERS	B/T	Ht./Wt.	Born	1999 clubs
6	Amaral, Rich	R/R	6-0/175	4-1-62	Baltimore
9	Anderson, Brady	L/L	6-1/202	1-18-64	Baltimore
3	Baines, Harold	L/L	6-2/195	3-15-59	Baltimore, Cleveland
88	Belle, Albert	R/R	6-2/210	8-25-66	Baltimore
33	Kingsale, Gene	B/R	6-3/194	8-20-76	Bowie, Rochester, Baltimore
	Matos, Luis	L/R	6-0/179	10-30-78	Frederick, Bowie
17	Surhoff, B.J.	L/R	6-1/200	8-4-64	Baltimore

BALLPARK INFORMATION

Ballpark (capacity, surface)
Oriole Park at Camden Yards (48,876, grass)
Address
333 W. Camden St.
Baltimore, MD 21201
Business phone
410-685-9800
Ticket information
410-481-SEAT
Ticket prices
$35 (club box)
$30 (field box sec. 20-54)
$27 (field box sec. 14-18, 56-58)
$23 (terrace box sec. 19-53)
$22 (left field club, lower box)
$20 (terrace box sec. 1-17, 55-65)
$18 (left field lower box, upper box)
$16 (left field upper box; lower reserve sec. 19-53)
$13 (upper reserve; lower reserve sec. 4, 7-17, 55-87)
$11 (left field upper reserve)
$9 (bleacher)
$7 (standing room)
Field dimensions (from home plate)
To left field at foul line, 333 feet
To center field, 400 feet
To right field at foul line, 318
First game played
April 6, 1992 (Orioles 2, Indians 0)

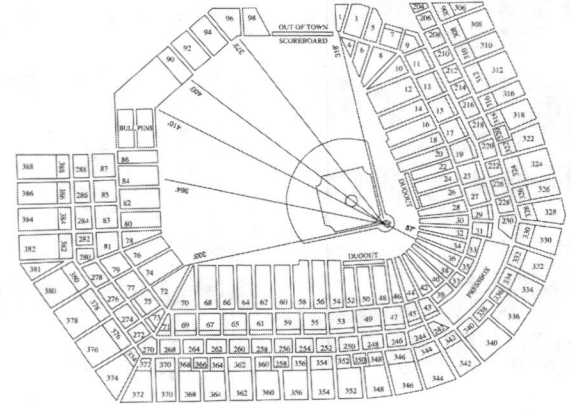

DAY BY DAY

Baltimore Orioles

2000 SEASON

Date	Opp.	Res.	Score	(inn.*)	Hits	Opp. hits	Winning pitcher	Losing pitcher	Save	Record	Pos.	GB
4-7	T.B.	L	5-8		13	14	Saunders	Guzman	Hernandez	1-1	T3rd	1.0
4-8	T.B.	L	3-6		9	10	Witt	Erickson		1-2	T4th	2.0
4-9	Tor.	L	4-7		6	8	Escobar	Ponson		1-3	5th	3.0
4-10	Tor.	W	1-0		6	6	Mussina	Carpenter	Timlin	2-3	T3rd	3.0
4-11	Tor.	L	5-9		8	10	Halladay	Orosco		2-4	5th	3.0
4-13	At N.Y.	L	3-6		10	7	Nelson	Rhodes		2-5	5th	4.0
4-14	At N.Y.	L	7-14		9	17	Cone	Erickson		2-6	5th	5.0
4-15	At N.Y.	W	9-7		18	10	Rhodes	Rivera	Timlin	3-6	5th	4.0
4-16	At Tor.	L	6-7		12	10	Lloyd	Bones	Person	3-7	5th	4.0
4-17	At Tor.	L	4-7		7	10	Wells	Linton	Lloyd	3-8	5th	4.5
4-18	At Tor.	L	0-6		3	7	Halladay	Guzman		3-9	5th	5.5
4-20	At T.B.	L	3-5		6	12	Santana	Erickson	Hernandez	3-10	5th	6.5
4-21	At T.B.	L	8-14		11	17	Rekar	Mussina		3-11	5th	7.5
4-22	At T.B.	L	0-1		1	4	Saunders	Ponson	Hernandez	3-12	5th	8.5
4-23	Oak.	W	7-4		8	9	Fetters	Haynes		4-12	5th	7.5
4-24	Oak.	L	0-3		4	6	Oquist	Erickson	Taylor	4-13	5th	7.5
4-25	Oak.	L	10-11		9	10	Rigby	Timlin	Taylor	4-14	5th	8.5
4-27	K.C.	W	8-4		12	10	Mussina	Appier	Timlin	5-14	5th	8.5
4-28	K.C.	L	2-8		5	10	Rosado	Guzman		5-15	5th	8.5
4-29	K.C.	L	5-15		7	15	Suppan	Erickson	Santiago	5-16	5th	9.5
4-30	Min.	W	7-1		8	4	Ponson	Hawkins		6-16	5th	8.5
5-1	Min.	L	2-7		8	11	Radke	Coppinger		6-17	5th	9.5
5-2	Min.	W	6-0		9	6	Mussina	Milton		7-17	5th	9.5
5-4	Chi.	W	9-5	(10)	10	9	Timlin	Lundquist		8-17	5th	8.0
5-5	Chi.	W	8-0		7	6	Guzman	Navarro		9-17	5th	8.0
5-6	Chi.	W	4-2		5	8	Ponson	Baldwin	Timlin	10-17	5th	8.0
5-7	At Det.	W	9-4		12	10	Mussina	Thompson		11-17	5th	8.0
5-8	At Det.	L	6-7		8	5	Blair	Kamieniecki	Jones	11-18	5th	8.0
5-9	At Det.	W	5-0		7	5	Erickson	Mlicki		12-18	5th	8.0
5-10	At Cle.	L	4-6		7	8	Burba	Guzman	Jackson	12-19	5th	8.5
5-11	At Cle.	L	6-11		11	12	Colon	Ponson		12-20	5th	8.5
5-12	At Cle.	L	5-6		9	10	Assenmacher	Timlin	Shuey	12-21	5th	8.5
5-13	At Tex.	L	7-15		13	13	Morgan	Kamieniecki		12-22	5th	8.5
5-14	At Tex.	L	6-7		15	11	Crabtree	Rhodes	Wetteland	12-23	5th	8.5
5-15	At Tex.	L	1-8		7	14	Helling	Johns		12-24	5th	8.5
5-16	At Tex.	W	16-5		24	11	Ponson	Sele		13-24	5th	8.5
5-18	Ana.	W	5-3		8	7	Mussina	Finley	Timlin	14-24	5th	8.0
5-19	Ana.	L	4-5		11	8	Levine	Timlin	Percival	14-25	5th	9.0
5-20	Ana.	L	4-6		9	9	Belcher	Johnson	Percival	14-26	5th	9.0
5-21	Tex.	W	3-2		7	6	Ponson	Helling		15-26	5th	9.0
5-22	Tex.	L	7-8		14	7	Crabtree	Timlin	Wetteland	15-27	5th	10.0
5-23	Tex.	W	15-6		15	14	Mussina	Morgan		16-27	5th	10.0
5-25	At Ana.	L	1-4		6	6	Olivares	Erickson	Percival	16-28	5th	11.0
5-26	At Ana.	W	3-2		4	4	Ponson	Belcher	Rhodes	17-28	5th	10.0
5-27	At Ana.	W	6-3		12	7	Guzman	Hill	Timlin	18-28	5th	9.0
5-28	At Oak.	L	1-2		4	6	Candiotti	Mussina	Taylor	18-29	5th	10.0
5-29	At Oak.	W	7-5		13	10	Johns	Mathews	Rhodes	19-29	5th	10.0
5-30	At Oak.	L	5-11		10	16	Rigby	Erickson		19-30	5th	11.0
5-31	At Sea.	L	6-10		12	13	Moyer	Ponson	Mesa	19-31	5th	12.0
6-1	At Sea.	W	14-11		14	14	Johns	Garcia		20-31	5th	12.0
6-2	At Sea.	L	2-4		12	6	Paniagua	Mussina	Mesa	20-32	5th	12.0
6-4	Phi.	L	5-9		9	18	Ogea	Erickson		20-33	5th	13.0
6-5	Phi.	W	7-6	(10)	12	7	Timlin	Montgomery		21-33	5th	12.0
6-6	Phi.	L	7-11		14	19	Bennett	Bones		21-34	5th	12.0
6-8†	At Fla.	L	1-2		6	6	Edmondson	Timlin		21-35		
6-8‡	At Fla.	L	3-5		11	11	Alfonseca	Kamieniecki	Mantei	21-36	5th	12.0
6-9	At Fla.	W	4-2		12	5	Erickson	Springer	Rhodes	22-36	5th	11.5
6-11	At Atl.	W	6-2		12	5	Ponson	Maddux		23-36	5th	11.5
6-12	At Atl.	W	5-0		13	6	Guzman	Millwood		24-36	5th	11.5
6-13	At Atl.	W	22-1		25	6	Mussina	Smoltz		25-36	4th	10.5
6-14	K.C.	W	7-1		12	9	Erickson	Appier		26-36	4th	10.5
6-15	K.C.	W	6-5	(10)	13	11	Timlin	Service		27-36	4th	10.5
6-16	K.C.	W	2-1		7	9	Ponson	Rosado		28-36	4th	9.5
6-17	At Chi.	L	3-9		12	11	Sirotka	Guzman	Foulke	28-37	4th	9.5
6-18	At Chi.	W	3-2		8	7	Mussina	Navarro		29-37	4th	9.5
6-19	At Chi.	W	11-9	(11)	12	17	Rhodes	Foulke	Kamieniecki	30-37	4th	9.5
6-20	At Chi.	W	8-4		12	10	Johnson	Baldwin	Timlin	31-37	4th	8.5
6-22	Bos.	W	5-3		7	9	Rhodes	Guthrie	Timlin	32-37	4th	8.5
6-23	Bos.	L	0-5		8	9	Saberhagen	Guzman		32-38	4th	9.5
6-24	Bos.	L	1-2		7	7	Portugal	Mussina	Wakefield	32-39	4th	10.5
6-25	N.Y.	L	8-9		13	16	Naulty	Timlin	Rivera	32-40	4th	11.5

Date	Opp.	Res.	Score	(inn.*)	Hits	Opp. hits	Winning pitcher	Losing pitcher	Save	Record	Pos.	GB
6-26	N.Y.	L	4-7		8	11	Cone	Johnson	Rivera	32-41	4th	12.5
6-27	N.Y.	L	2-6		7	12	Hernandez	Ponson		32-42	4th	13.5
6-29	At Tor.	L	5-6	(10)	12	10	Frascatore	Rhodes		32-43	4th	14.5
6-30	At Tor.	L	9-10	(10)	16	12	Frascatore	Orosco		32-44	5th	14.5
7-1	At Tor.	L	6-8		9	10	Frascatore	Timlin	Koch	32-45	5th	15.5
7-2	At N.Y.	L	1-2		8	7	Cone	Johnson	Rivera	32-46	5th	16.5
7-3	At N.Y.	L	5-6		6	9	Grimsley	Rhodes		32-47	5th	17.5
7-4	At N.Y.	W	7-3		9	9	Guzman	Mendoza	Kamieniecki	33-47	5th	16.5
7-5	At N.Y.	W	9-1		13	7	Mussina	Pettitte		34-47	5th	15.5
7-6	Tor.	L	3-4	(10)	8	7	Lloyd	Timlin	Koch	34-48	5th	16.5
7-7	Tor.	L	6-7		13	6	Spoljaric	Molina	Koch	34-49	5th	16.5
7-8	Tor.	L	6-11		14	15	Escobar	Ponson		34-50	5th	17.5
7-9	At Phi.	L	2-4		8	5	Schilling	Guzman		34-51	5th	17.5
7-10	At Phi.	W	8-4		13	6	Mussina	Byrd		35-51	5th	16.5
7-11	At Phi.	W	6-2		12	6	Erickson	Ogea		36-51	5th	16.5
7-15	Mon.	W	8-2		9	11	Ponson	Thurman		37-51	5th	15.5
7-16	Mon.	W	9-4		17	9	Mussina	Smith		38-51	5th	14.5
7-17	Mon.	W	2-1		4	6	Erickson	Hermanson		39-51	5th	14.5
7-18	N.Y. (NL)	L	6-8		12	12	Yoshii	Guzman	Benitez	39-52	5th	15.5
7-19	N.Y. (NL)	L	1-4		4	9	Dotel	Johnson	Benitez	39-53	5th	15.5
7-20	N.Y. (NL)	W	4-1		9	6	Ponson	Leiter		40-53	5th	15.5
7-21	At Bos.	W	6-1		11	6	Mussina	Saberhagen		41-53	4th	15.5
7-22	At Bos.	W	5-2		12	8	Erickson	Cho	Timlin	42-53	4th	15.5
7-23	Ana.	W	1-0		7	6	Guzman	McDowell	Timlin	43-53	4th	15.5
7-24	Ana.	W	8-4		17	6	Johnson	Hill		44-53	4th	15.5
7-25	Ana.	W	8-7	(11)	11	6	Kamieniecki	Holtz		45-53	4th	15.5
7-27	Tex.	L	6-8		11	14	Sele	Mussina	Wetteland	45-54	4th	16.5
7-28	Tex.	W	8-6		13	8	Erickson	Burkett	Timlin	46-54	4th	15.5
7-29	Tex.	L	1-3		3	6	Morgan	Guzman	Wetteland	46-55	4th	15.5
7-30	At Sea.	L	4-7		7	7	Meche	Johnson	Mesa	46-56	4th	16.5
7-31	At Sea.	L	2-5		8	9	Moyer	Ponson	Mesa	46-57	4th	16.5
8-1	At Sea.	L	1-3		8	3	Abbott	Mussina	Mesa	46-58	4th	16.5
8-2	At Oak.	L	1-7		4	9	Appier	Erickson		46-59	4th	17.5
8-3	At Oak.	L	2-12		9	12	Hudson	Bones		46-60	4th	17.5
8-4	At Oak.	W	9-5		14	8	Johnson	Haynes		47-60	4th	17.5
8-5	Det.	W	6-3		11	9	Ponson	Weaver	Timlin	48-60	4th	17.5
8-6	Det.	L	3-4		7	11	Mlicki	Mussina	Jones	48-61	4th	18.5
8-7	Det.	W	5-4		9	7	Erickson	Borkowski	Timlin	49-61	4th	18.5
8-8	Det.	L	2-5	(11)	10	8	Brocail	Kamieniecki	Jones	49-62	4th	19.5
8-9	At T.B.	L	9-10		12	15	Rupe	Johnson	Hernandez	49-63	4th	20.5
8-10	At T.B.	W	17-1		20	6	Ponson	Eiland		50-63	4th	19.5
8-11	At T.B.	W	4-2		13	10	Mussina	Arrojo	Timlin	51-63	4th	19.5
8-13	At Cle.	L	3-6		9	8	Rincon	Erickson	Jackson	51-64	4th	20.5
8-14	At Cle.	L	1-7		4	6	Karsay	Johnson		51-65	4th	20.5
8-15	At Cle.	L	1-5		5	13	Colon	Ponson		51-66	4th	20.5
8-17	Min.	W	8-3		13	10	Mussina	Mays		52-66	4th	21.0
8-18	Min.	W	2-0		5	5	Erickson	Hawkins		53-66	4th	20.0
8-19	Min.	W	9-3		11	6	Johnson	Perkins		54-66	4th	19.0
8-21†	Chi.	L	3-4		7	14	Simas	Reyes	Howry	54-67		
8-21‡	Chi.	L	5-8	(10)	14	13	Howry	Johns	Foulke	54-68	4th	20.0
8-22	Chi.	W	9-4		16	7	Johns	Navarro		55-68	4th	20.0
8-23	At K.C.	W	4-2		10	8	Erickson	Reichert	Timlin	56-68	4th	20.0
8-24	At K.C.	W	5-3	(10)	10	7	Kamieniecki	Wallace	Timlin	57-68	4th	20.0
8-25	At K.C.	L	6-8		11	14	Suppan	Linton	Montgomery	57-69	4th	20.0
8-26	At K.C.	L	0-6		4	11	Witasick	Ponson		57-70	4th	20.5
8-27	At Det.	L	4-5		5	11	Weaver	Reyes	Jones	57-71	4th	21.5
8-28	At Det.	L	3-4		10	7	Mlicki	Erickson	Jones	57-72	4th	22.5
8-29	At Det.	W	11-4		13	7	Johnson	Nitkowski		58-72	4th	22.5
8-31	T.B.	L	0-3		3	11	Rupe	Ponson	Hernandez	58-73	5th	23.0
9-1	T.B.	W	3-1		5	5	Johns	Wheeler	Timlin	59-73	4th	22.0
9-2	T.B.	W	11-6		13	14	Erickson	Arrojo		60-73	4th	22.0
9-3	Cle.	L	6-7		10	9	Assenmacher	Reyes	Jackson	60-74	4th	22.0
9-4	Cle.	W	3-1		9	6	Linton	Colon	Timlin	61-74	4th	22.0
9-5	Cle.	L	7-15		11	12	Brower	Ponson		61-75	4th	23.0
9-6	Cle.	L	6-7		9	8	Burba	Johns	Jackson	61-76	4th	23.0
9-7	At Min.	W	5-0		10	3	Erickson	Mays		62-76	4th	22.0
9-8	At Min.	W	10-0		14	6	Johnson	Hawkins		63-76	4th	22.0
9-9	At Min.	W	6-5		12	7	Reyes	Miller	Timlin	64-76	4th	21.5
9-10	Sea.	W	5-4	(12)	9	9	Reyes	Ramsay		65-76	4th	20.5
9-11	Sea.	W	4-2		12	4	Johns	Garcia	Timlin	66-76	4th	19.5
9-12	Sea.	W	4-1		9	5	Erickson	Halama		67-76	4th	18.5
9-13	Sea.	W	5-4	(10)	9	11	Ryan	Mesa		68-76	4th	17.5
9-14	Oak.	W	13-6		16	11	Mussina	Oquist		69-76	4th	17.5
9-17	At Ana.	W	4-2		12	6	Erickson	Washburn	Timlin	70-76	4th	18.5
9-18	At Ana.	W	6-3		5	8	Ponson	Cooper	Timlin	71-76	4th	17.5

Date	Opp.	Res.	Score	(inn.*)	Hits	Opp. hits	Winning pitcher	Losing pitcher	Save	Record	Pos.	GB
9-19	At Ana.	W	5-4		11	9	Molina	Percival	Timlin	72-76	4th	17.5
9-21	At Tex.	W	4-2		7	6	Johnson	Loaiza	Timlin	73-76	4th	17.5
9-22	At Tex.	W	7-4		9	10	Erickson	Helling	Timlin	74-76	4th	17.5
9-23†	Oak.	L	6-9		8	15	Mathews	Molina	Isringhausen	74-77		
9-23‡	Oak.	W	12-4		12	8	Johns	Olivares		75-77	4th	18.0
9-24	At Bos.	W	1-0		8	6	Mussina	Saberhagen	Timlin	76-77	4th	18.0
9-25	At Bos.	L	1-4		4	6	Martinez	Linton	Garces	76-78	4th	18.0
9-26	At Bos.	W	8-5		5	8	Johnson	Wakefield	Orosco	77-78	4th	17.0
9-27	At Bos.	L	3-5		8	8	Martinez	Erickson	Lowe	77-79	4th	17.0
9-28	N.Y.	L	5-9		10	10	Mendoza	Ponson		77-80	4th	18.0
9-30†	N.Y.	W	5-0		5	8	Mussina	Clemens		78-80		
9-30‡	N.Y.	L	5-12		12	17	Hernandez	Corsi		78-81	4th	18.0
10-1	Bos.	L	2-6		8	12	Ohka	Linton		78-82	4th	19.0
10-2	Bos.	L	0-8		3	12	Martinez	Johns		78-83	4th	20.0
10-3	Bos.	L	0-1	(10)	6	5	Rose	Timlin	Wakefield	78-84	4th	20.0

Monthly records: April (6-16), May (13-15), June (13-13), July (14-13), August (12-16), September (20-8), October (0-3). *Innings, if other than nine. † First game of a doubleheader. ‡ Second game of a doubleheader.

HIGHLIGHTS

High point: The Orioles defeated the Rangers, 7-4, on September 22 for their 13th consecutive victory. The win improved their record to 74-76, the closest they had been to .500 since the first week of the season.

Low point: On July 3, the Yankees defeated the Orioles, 6-5, extending Baltimore's losing streak to a season-worst 10 games. The Orioles already were well out of contention by then, but the streak-lengthening loss to New York was particularly galling because the O's were expected to be the Yanks' chief A.L. East rival.

Turning point: The Orioles appeared in position to overcome a horrible start when they reeled off five straight victories in early May, but the club soon went into a six-game skid (May 10-15) that dropped it 12 games under .500 (12-24).

Most valuable player: Left fielder B.J. Surhoff established career highs with 104 runs, 28 home runs and 107 RBIs. Though Albert Belle's run-production numbers were higher, Surhoff was the more consistent presence in the lineup.

Most valuable pitcher: Staff ace Mike Mussina had another strong year, finishing 18-7 with a 3.50 ERA. Once again, an injury hurt the righthander's chances of reaching 20 victories—he missed four starts after getting struck in the shoulder by a line drive.

Most improved player: Mike Bordick, already a strong defensive infielder with decent offensive skills, had a terrific year with the glove and stepped up to career highs in runs (93) and RBIs (77).

Most pleasant surprise: The Orioles didn't expect too much when they acquired righthander Jason Johnson in a late-spring trade with the Devil Rays, but he won a spot in the rotation and wound up 8-7 despite a 5.46 ERA.

Biggest disappointment: Cal Ripken was outstanding when he was able to play, but the Orioles' great was knocked out of action three times by back spasms, the last time when he was just nine hits away from reaching 3,000 for his career.

Key injuries: Ripken went on the D.L. twice and was shut down for the final 13 games of the season. First baseman Will Clark missed time early in the season

with a broken left thumb and eventually cut his season short to undergo surgery on his left elbow. He was limited to only 77 games. And second baseman Delino DeShields was in and out of the lineup with a series of injuries and appeared in just 96 games.

Notable: Ripken hit his 400th career home run on September 2 against Tampa Bay. ... Ripken went 6-for-6 with 13 total bases on June 13 when the Orioles punished the Braves, 22-1. ... Belle hit three home runs on July 25 against the Angels. ... Bordick led the league in total chances and fielding percentage at shortstop.

—PETER SCHMUCK

RECORDS

1999 regular-season record: 78-84 (4th in A.L. East); 41-40 at home; 37-44 on road; 15-34 vs. A.L. East; 27-22 vs. Central; 25-21 vs. West; 11-7 vs. N.L.; 12-15 vs. lefthanded starters; 66-69 vs. righthanded starters; 70-71 on grass; 8-13 on turf; 24-28 in daytime; 54-56 at night; 16-26 in one-run games; 8-6 in extra-inning games; 0-2-2 in doubleheaders. **Team record past five years:** 414-378 (.523, ranks 5th in league in that span).

TEAM LEADERS

Batting average: B.J. Surhoff (.308).
At-bats: B.J. Surhoff (673).
Runs: Brady Anderson (109).
Hits: B.J. Surhoff (207).
Total Bases: B.J. Surhoff (331).
Doubles: B.J. Surhoff (38).
Triples: Mike Bordick (7).
Home runs: Albert Belle (37).
Runs batted in: Albert Belle (117).
Stolen bases: Brady Anderson (36).
Slugging percentage: Albert Belle (.541).
On-base percentage: Brady Anderson (.404).
Wins: Mike Mussina (18).
Earned-run average: Mike Mussina (3.50).
Complete games: Scott Erickson, Sidney Ponson (6).
Shutouts: Scott Erickson (3).
Saves: Mike Timlin (27).
Innings pitched: Scott Erickson (230.1).
Strikeouts: Mike Mussina (172).

GAMES BY POSITION

Catcher: Charles Johnson 135, Mike Figga 41, Lenny Webster 12, Tommy Davis 4.
First base: Jeff Conine 99, Will Clark 63, Calvin Pickering 8, Willis Otanez 5, Rich Amaral 2, Ryan Minor 1, Tommy Davis 1.
Second base: Delino DeShields 93, Jerry Hairston Jr. 50, Jeff Reboulet 36, Jesse Garcia 6, Rich Amaral 2.
Third base: Cal Ripken Jr. 85, Jeff Reboulet 56, Ryan Minor 45, Willis Otanez 22, Jeff Conine 4, B.J. Surhoff 2, Jesse Garcia 2, Rich Amaral 1.
Shortstop: Mike Bordick 159, Jeff Reboulet 10, Jesse Garcia 7.
Outfield: Albert Belle 154, B.J. Surhoff 148, Brady Anderson 136, Rich Amaral 50, Gene Kingsale 24, Jeff Conine 13, Derrick May 5.
Designated hitter: Harold Baines 96, Jeff Conine 19, Rich Amaral 18, B.J. Surhoff 13, Brady Anderson 10, Derrick May 9, Albert Belle 7, Calvin Pickering 7, Will Clark 3, Willis Otanez 3, Lenny Webster 2, Gene Kingsale 2, Jesse Garcia 1.

TOP DRAFT CHOICES

1a. **Mike Paradis,** RHP, Clemson Univ.
1b. **Richard Stahl,** LHP, Newton H.S., Covington, Ga.
1c. **Larry Bigbie,** OF, Ball State University
1d. **Keith Reed,** OF, Providence College
1e. **Josh Cenate,** LHP, Jefferson H.S., Shenandoah Junction, W.Va.
1f. **Scott Rice,** LHP, Royal H.S., Simi Valley, Calif.
1g. **Brian Roberts,** SS, U. of S. Carolina
2. None
3. **Jon Kessick,** C, Ball State University
4. None
5. None
6. **Erik Bedard,** LHP, Norwalk (Conn.) C.C.
7. **David Farren,** RHP, Texas H.S., Texarkana, Tex.
8. **Matthew Tate,** RHP, Holmes County H.S., Bonifay, Fla.
9. **Pete Shier,** SS, Hilliard H.S., Columbus, Ohio
10. **Octavio Martinez,** C, Bakersfield (Calif.) J.C.

BOSTON RED SOX
AMERICAN LEAGUE EAST DIVISION

2000 Red Sox Schedule
Home games shaded. "*—All-Star Game at Turner Field (Atlanta).

March
SUN	MON	TUE	WED	THU	FRI	SAT
26	27	28	29	30	31	

April
SUN	MON	TUE	WED	THU	FRI	SAT
						1
2	3 SEA	4 SEA	5 SEA	6	7 ANA	8 ANA
9 ANA	10	11 MIN	12 MIN	13 MIN	14 OAK	15 OAK
16 OAK	17 OAK	18 DET	19 DET	20 DET	21 CLE	22 CLE
23 CLE	24 TEX	25 TEX	26 TEX	27	28 CLE	29 CLE
30 CLE						

May
SUN	MON	TUE	WED	THU	FRI	SAT
	1 DET	2 DET	3 DET	4	5 TB	6 TB
7 TB	8 CWS	9 CWS	10 CWS	11 BAL	12 BAL	13 BAL
14 BAL	15 TOR	16 TOR	17 TOR	18	19 DET	20 DET
21 DET	22	23 TOR	24 TOR	25 TOR	26 NYY	27 NYY
28 NYY	29	30 KC	31 KC			

June
SUN	MON	TUE	WED	THU	FRI	SAT
				1 KC	2 PHI	3 PHI
4 PHI	5 FLA	6 FLA	7 FLA	8	9 ATL	10 ATL
11 ATL	12 NYY	13 NYY	14 NYY	15	16 TOR	17 TOR
18 TOR	19 NYY	20 NYY	21 NYY	22 NYY	23 TOR	24 TOR
25 TOR	26	27 BAL	28 BAL	29 BAL	30 CWS	

July
SUN	MON	TUE	WED	THU	FRI	SAT
						1 CWS
2 CWS	3 MIN	4 MIN	5 MIN	6	7 ATL	8 ATL
9 ATL	10	11	* 12	13 NYM	14 NYM	15 NYM
16 MON	17 MON	18 MON	19 BAL	20 BAL	21 CWS	22 CWS
23 CWS	24 MIN	25 MIN	26 MIN	27 OAK	28 OAK	29 OAK
30 OAK	31 SEA					

August
SUN	MON	TUE	WED	THU	FRI	SAT
		1 SEA	2 SEA	3	4 KC	5 KC
6 KC	7 ANA	8 ANA	9 ANA	10	11 TEX	12 TEX
13 TEX	14 TB	15 TB	16 TB	17 TB	18 TEX	19 TEX
20 TEX	21 ANA	22 ANA	23 ANA	24 KC	25 KC	26 KC
27 KC	28 TB	29 TB	30 TB	31		

September
SUN	MON	TUE	WED	THU	FRI	SAT
					1 SEA	2 SEA
3 SEA	4 SEA	5 OAK	6 OAK	7	8 NYY	9 NYY
10 NYY	11	12 CLE	13 CLE	14 CLE	15 DET	16 DET
17 DET	18	19 CLE	20 CLE	21 CLE	22 BAL	23 BAL
24 BAL	25	26 CWS	27 CWS	28 CWS	29 TB	30 TB

October
SUN	MON	TUE	WED	THU	FRI	SAT
1 TB	2	3	4	5	6	7

2000 SEASON
CLUB DIRECTORY

Chief executive officer
John L. Harrington
Exec. v.p. and general manager
Daniel F. Duquette
Exec. vice president, administration
John S. Buckley
V.p. and chief financial officer
Robert C. Furbush
Vice president, baseball operations
Michael D. Port
V.p., broadcasting and technology
James P. Healey
Vice president, public affairs
Richard L. Bresciani
Vice president, sales and marketing
Lawrence C. Cancro
Vice president, stadium operations
Joseph F. McDermott
Vice president, assistant g.m. and legal counsel
Elaine W. Steward
Assistant general manager
Edward P. Kenney
Dir. of com. and baseball information
Kevin J. Shea
Dir. of human resources and office mgmt.
Michele Julian
Vice president, scouting
W. Wayne Britton
Exec. dir. of int'l baseball operations
R. Ray Poitevint
Director of minor league operations
Kent A. Qualls
Coordinator of Florida operations
Ryan Richeal
Traveling secretary
John F. McCormick
Special asst. for player development
John M. Pesky
Major league scout
Frank J. Malzone
Major league special assignment scout
G. Edwin Haas
Baseball administration coordinator
Marci Blacker
Assistant scouting director
Tom Moore
Technology manager
Clay Rendon
Director of sales
Michael Schetzel
Group sales manager
Corey Bowdre
Telephone sales manager
Amy McCarthy
Property maintenance manager
John Caron
600 Club and suites manager
Dan Lyons
Food service manager
Ed Pistorino
Premium seating sales manager
Jeff Connors

Medical director
Arthur M. Pappas, M.D.
Trainer
James W. Rowe Jr.
Physical therapist
Richard M. Zawacki
Strength and conditioning coordinator
Merle V. "B.J." Baker III
Baseball information coordinator
Glenn Wilburn
Instructors
Theodore S. Williams, Carl M. Yastrzemski
Executive administrative assistant
Lorraine Leong
Equip. manager and clubhouse operations
J. Joseph Cochran
Controller
Stanley H. Tran
Director of advertising and sponsorships
Jeffrey E. Goldenberg
Director of facilities management
Thomas L. Queenan Jr.
Director of food services
Patricia T. Flanagan
Director of ticket operations
Joseph P. Helyar
Executive consultant, public affairs
James "Lou" Gorman
Superintendent of grounds and maint.
Joseph P. Mooney
Box office manager
Richard J. Beaton Jr.
Broadcasting manager
James E. Shannahan
Community relations manager
Ronald E. Burton Jr.
Customer relations manager
Ann Marie C. Starzyk
Ground crew manager
Casey Erven
Promotions manager
Marcita Thompson
Publications manager
Debra A. Matson
Scouts
Raymond Boone, Buzz Bowers, Kevin Burrell, Ben Cherington, Edwin Correa, Ray Crone Jr., George Digby, Johnny DiPuglia, Danny Doyle, William Enos, Ray Fagnant, Steve Flores, Eddie Haas, Matt Haas, Ernie Jacobs, Wally Komatsubara, Chuck Koney, Kenneth Lee, Don Lenhardt, Frank Malzone, Joe Mason, Steve McAllister, Gary Rajsich, Eddie Robinson, Jim Robinson, Ed Roebuck, Edward Scott, Mathew Sczesny, Dick Sorkin, Jerry Stephenson, Joseph Stephenson, Lee Thomas, Fay Thompson, Charles Wagner, Jeffrey Zona
International scouts
Mark Garcia, Jon Kodama, Ray Poitevint, Lee Sigman
Latin American scouts
Julian Camilo, Robinson Garcia, Luis Marin, Sebastian Martinez, Jose Maza, Levy Ochoa, Carlos Ramirez, Michael Victoria

MINOR LEAGUE AFFILIATES

Class	Team	League	Manager
AAA	Pawtucket	International	Gary Jones
AA	Trenton	Eastern	Billy Gardner Jr.
A	Sarasota	Florida State	Ron Johnson
A	Augusta	South Atlantic	Mike Boulanger
A	Lowell	New York-Pennsylvania	Luis Aguayo
Rookie	Gulf Coast Red Sox	Gulf Coast	John Sanders

BROADCAST INFORMATION
Radio: WEEI-AM (680).
TV: WFXT-TV (Fox 25).
Cable TV: New England Sports Network.

SPRING TRAINING
Ballpark (city): City of Palms Park (Fort Myers, Fla.).
Ticket information: 941-334-4700.

Manager—Jimy Williams (22).
Coaches—Buddy Bailey, John Cumberland, Joe Kerrigan (16), Wendell Kim (31), Jim Rice (14).

No.	PITCHERS	B/T	Ht./Wt.	Born	1999 clubs
47	Beck, Rod	R/R	6-1/235	8-3-68	Chicago N.L., Iowa, Boston
61	Cho, Jin Ho	R/R	6-3/220	8-16-75	Pawtucket, Boston
37	Cormier, Rheal	L/L	5-10/187	4-23-67	Boston
13	Fassero, Jeff	L/L	6-1/195	1-5-63	Seattle, Texas
39	Florie, Bryce	R/R	5-11/192	5-21-70	Lakeland, Detroit, Boston
34	Garces, Richard	R/R	6-0/215	5-18-71	Pawtucket, Boston
36	Gordon, Tom	R/R	5-9/190	11-18-67	Boston
	Lee, Sang-Hoon	L/L	—	3-11-71	Chunichi Dragons
32	Lowe, Derek	R/R	6-6/200	6-1-73	Boston
45	Martinez, Pedro J.	R/R	5-11/170	10-25-71	Boston
48	Martinez, Ramon J.	R/R	6-4/184	3-22-68	Lowell, Gulf Coast Red Sox, Sarasota, Pawtucket, Boston
53	Ohka, Tomokazu	R/R	6-1/179	3-18-76	Trenton, Pawtucket, Boston
	Pena, Juan	R/R	6-5/215	6-27-77	Pawtucket, Boston, Gulf Coast Red Sox, Sarasota
19	Rose, Brian	R/R	6-3/215	2-13-76	Pawtucket, Boston
17	Saberhagen, Bret	R/R	6-1/200	4-11-64	Boston, Trenton
	Sekany, Jason	R/R	6-4/214	7-20-75	Trenton, Pawtucket
49	Wakefield, Tim	R/R	6-2/210	8-2-66	Boston
46	Wasdin, John	R/R	6-2/195	8-5-72	Pawtucket, Boston, Gulf Coast Red Sox
	Young, Tim	L/L	5-9/170	10-15-73	Trenton

No.	CATCHERS	B/T	Ht./Wt.	Born	1999 clubs
10	Hatteberg, Scott	L/R	6-1/205	12-14-69	Boston, Pawtucket, Gulf Coast Red Sox, Sarasota
56	Lomasney, Steve	R/R	6-0/195	8-29-77	Sarasota, Trenton, Boston
33	Varitek, Jason	R/R	6-2/220	4-11-72	Boston

No.	INFIELDERS	B/T	Ht./Wt.	Born	1999 clubs
24	Alexander, Manny	R/R	5-10/180	3-20-71	Chicago N.L.
23	Daubach, Brian	L/R	6-1/201	2-11-72	Boston, Pawtucket
3	Frye, Jeff	R/R	5-9/170	8-31-66	Boston, Gulf Coast Red Sox, Pawtucket
5	Garciaparra, Nomar	R/R	6-0/175	7-23-73	Boston
30	Offerman, Jose	B/R	6-0/190	11-8-68	Boston
15	Sadler, Donnie	R/R	5-6/175	6-17-75	Boston, Pawtucket, Gulf Coast Red Sox
24	Stanley, Mike	R/R	6-0/205	6-25-63	Boston
	Stenson, Dernell	L/L	6-1/232	6-17-78	Pawtucket, Gulf Coast Red Sox
13	Valentin, John	R/R	6-0/185	2-18-67	Boston
38	Veras, Wilton	R/R	6-2/198	1-19-78	Trenton, Boston

No.	OUTFIELDERS	B/T	Ht./Wt.	Born	1999 clubs
	Allensworth, Jermaine	R/R	6-0/190	1-11-72	New York N.L., Norfolk
44	Coleman, Michael	R/R	5-11/215	8-16-75	Pawtucket, Boston
3	Everett, Carl	B/R	6-0/190	6-3-71	Houston
20	Lewis, Darren	R/R	6-0/190	8-28-67	Boston
7	Nixon, Trot	L/L	6-2/200	4-11-74	Boston
25	O'Leary, Troy	L/L	6-0/200	8-4-69	Boston

BALLPARK INFORMATION

Ballpark (capacity, surface)
Fenway Park (33,455; grass)
Address
4 Yawkey Way
Boston, MA 02215-3496
Business phone
617-267-9440
Ticket information
617-267-1700, 617-482-4769
Ticket prices
$45 (field box)
$40 (loge box and infield roof)
$28 (reserved grandstand)
$27 (right-field boxes and right-field roof)
$20 (outfield grandstand)
$16 (lower bleachers)
$14 (upper bleachers)
Field dimensions (from home plate)
To left field at foul line, 310 feet
To center field, 420 feet
To right field at foul line, 302 feet
First game played
April 20, 1912
(Red Sox 7, New York Highlanders 6)

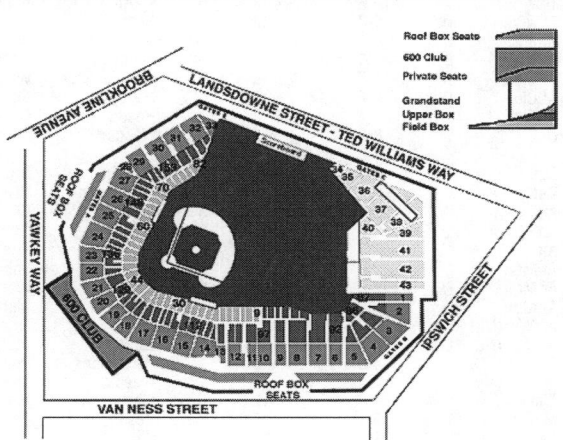

2000 SEASON   Boston Red Sox

2000 SEASON · *Boston Red Sox*

Date	Opp.	Res.	Score	(inn.*)	Hits	Opp. hits	Winning pitcher	Losing pitcher	Save	Record	Pos.	GB
4-7	At K.C.	W	6-0		13	4	Saberhagen	Rosado		2-0	1st	+0.5
4-8	At K.C.	W	4-1		10	4	Wakefield	Suppan	Gordon	3-0	1st	+1.0
4-9	At T.B.	W	4-1		11	4	Portugal	Arrojo		4-0	1st	+1.0
4-10	At T.B.	W	5-3		6	7	Martinez	Santana	Gordon	5-0	1st	+1.0
4-11	At T.B.	L	4-5		8	7	Aldred	Lowe	Hernandez	5-1	T1st	...
4-13	Chi.	W	6-0		7	7	Saberhagen	Parque		6-1	T1st	...
4-15	Chi.	L	0-4		6	8	Snyder	Martinez		6-2	2nd	0.5
4-16	T.B.	L	2-6		7	13	Rekar	Wakefield		6-3	2nd	0.5
4-17	T.B.	W	8-5		11	9	Portugal	Saunders		7-3	1st	...
4-18	T.B.	L	1-5		5	7	Witt	Rapp		7-4	2nd	1.0
4-19	T.B.	L	1-4		6	9	Arrojo	Saberhagen	Hernandez	7-5	T2nd	1.5
4-20	At Det.	W	1-0		3	3	Martinez	Weaver	Lowe	8-5	T2nd	1.5
4-21	At Det.	L	2-9		8	15	Moehler	Wakefield		8-6	3rd	2.5
4-22	At Det.	L	0-1		2	3	Thompson	Portugal	Jones	8-7	4th	3.5
4-23	Cle.	L	6-7		7	9	Karsay	Corsi	Jackson	8-8	4th	3.5
4-24	Cle.	W	9-4		13	12	Harikkala	DeLucia		9-8	4th	2.5
4-25	Cle.	W	3-2		12	7	Martinez	Shuey		10-8	3rd	2.5
4-26	At Min.	L	2-6		10	9	Radke	Wakefield	Trombley	10-9	4th	3.0
4-27	At Min.	L	5-6		11	9	Guardado	Corsi	Aguilera	10-10	4th	4.0
4-28	At Min.	W	9-4		11	13	Rapp	Lincoln		11-10	3rd	3.0
4-30	At Oak.	L	9-13		12	10	Mathews	Lowe		11-11	T3rd	3.5
5-1	At Oak.	W	7-2		15	6	Martinez	Heredia		12-11	3rd	3.5
5-2	At Oak.	L	5-7		12	9	Jones	Harikkala	Taylor	12-12	T3rd	4.5
5-3	At Oak.	L	11-12	(10)	13	11	Mathews	Gross		12-13	4th	4.5
5-5	Tex.	L	3-8		8	12	Helling	Rapp		12-14	4th	5.0
5-6	Tex.	W	3-2		10	10	Cormier	Sele	Wakefield	13-14	4th	5.0
5-7	Ana.	W	6-0		10	6	Martinez	Olivares		14-14	4th	5.0
5-8	Ana.	W	6-1		12	4	Pena	Belcher	Lowe	15-14	3rd	4.0
5-9	Ana.	W	4-2		10	10	Portugal	Hill	Wakefield	16-14	2nd	4.0
5-10	Sea.	W	12-4		10	9	Wasdin	Hinchliffe		17-14	2nd	3.5
5-11	Sea.	L	5-8		10	14	Moyer	Wakefield		17-15	2nd	3.5
5-12	Sea.	W	9-2		11	6	Martinez	Suzuki		18-15	2nd	2.5
5-14	At Tor.	W	5-0		11	6	Pena	Wells		19-15	2nd	1.0
5-15	At Tor.	W	6-5		14	10	Wasdin	Plesac	Gordon	20-15	T1st	...
5-16	At Tor.	L	6-9		12	11	Lloyd	Gross		20-16	2nd	1.0
5-17	At Tor.	W	8-7		13	13	Wasdin	Lloyd		21-16	2nd	0.5
5-18	N.Y.	W	6-3		10	13	Martinez	Cone	Gordon	22-16	1st	+0.5
5-19	N.Y.	W	6-0		15	8	Rose	Irabu		23-16	1st	+1.5
5-20	N.Y.	L	1-3		3	5	Hernandez	Portugal	Rivera	23-17	1st	+0.5
5-21	Tor.	W	5-2		5	4	Rapp	Escobar		24-17	1st	+1.0
5-22	Tor.	W	6-4		14	6	Wakefield	Carpenter	Gordon	25-17	1st	+1.5
5-23	Tor.	W	10-8		13	15	Martinez	Hentgen	Gordon	26-17	1st	+1.5
5-25	At N.Y.	W	5-2		10	6	Rose	Irabu	Gordon	27-17	1st	+2.5
5-26	At N.Y.	L	3-8		8	11	Hernandez	Portugal	Rivera	27-18	1st	+1.5
5-27	At N.Y.	L	1-4		2	9	Clemens	Rapp	Rivera	27-19	1st	+0.5
5-28	At Cle.	W	12-5		18	9	Wakefield	Wright	Lowe	28-19	1st	+0.5
5-29	At Cle.	W	4-2		8	5	Martinez	Colon	Gordon	29-19	1st	+0.5
5-30	At Cle.	W	4-2		9	3	Rose	Gooden	Gordon	30-19	1st	+0.5
5-31	Det.	W	8-7		12	12	Wasdin	Anderson	Gordon	31-19	1st	+1.5
6-1	Det.	W	5-4		9	12	Wasdin	Brocail	Lowe	32-19	1st	+1.5
6-2	Det.	L	2-4		6	7	Thompson	Wakefield	Jones	32-20	1st	+1.5
6-4	Atl.	W	5-1		9	3	Martinez	Glavine		33-20	1st	+1.5
6-5	Atl.	L	5-6		11	9	Maddux	Gordon	Rocker	33-21	1st	+0.5
6-6	Atl.	L	2-3	(10)	3	6	Seanez	Portugal	Rocker	33-22	1st	+0.5
6-7	At Mon.	L	2-8		6	13	Pavano	Saberhagen		33-23	1st	+0.5
6-8	At Mon.	L	1-5		4	9	Smith	Wakefield		33-24	1st	+0.5
6-9	At Mon.	L	1-13		5	14	Thurman	Martinez		33-25	2nd	0.5
6-11	At N.Y. (NL)	W	3-2	(12)	11	8	Corsi	Franco	Wasdin	34-25	2nd	0.5
6-12	At N.Y. (NL)	L	2-4		7	8	Leiter	Rapp	Franco	34-26	2nd	1.5
6-13	At N.Y. (NL)	L	4-5		8	11	Hershiser	Portugal	Wendell	34-27	2nd	1.5
6-14	Min.	W	4-3		11	7	Wasdin	Trombley		35-27	2nd	1.5
6-15	Min.	W	4-2		12	6	Martinez	Milton	Wakefield	36-27	2nd	1.5
6-16	Min.	W	5-1		7	8	Rose	Perkins	Guthrie	37-27	2nd	0.5
6-17	Min.	L	7-8		12	11	Hawkins	Rapp	Trombley	37-28	2nd	0.5
6-18	Tex.	L	1-4		3	8	Morgan	Portugal	Zimmerman	37-29	2nd	1.5
6-19	Tex.	W	7-4		15	6	Cho	Clark	Wakefield	38-29	2nd	1.5
6-20	Tex.	W	5-2		12	8	Martinez	Glynn	Wakefield	39-29	2nd	0.5
6-21	Tex.	W	5-4		10	9	Wasdin	Helling	Wakefield	40-29	2nd	...
6-22	At Bal.	L	3-5		9	7	Rhodes	Guthrie	Timlin	40-30	2nd	1.0
6-23	At Bal.	W	5-0		9	8	Saberhagen	Guzman		41-30	2nd	1.0
6-24	At Bal.	W	2-1		7	7	Portugal	Mussina	Wakefield	42-30	2nd	1.0

Date	Opp.	Res.	Score	(inn.*)	Hits	Opp. hits	Winning pitcher	Losing pitcher	Save	Record	Pos.	GB
6-25	Chi.	W	6-1		13	7	Cho	Snyder	Guthrie	43-30	2nd	1.0
6-26	Chi.	W	17-1		14	3	Martinez	Baldwin	Wasdin	44-30	2nd	1.0
6-27	Chi.	L	6-7		9	8	Simas	Wakefield	Howry	44-31	2nd	2.0
6-28	Chi.	W	14-1		21	8	Saberhagen	Sirotka		45-31	2nd	1.5
6-30	T.B.	L	10-11	(10)	12	14	Hernandez	Wasdin		45-32	2nd	2.0
7-1	T.B.	L	3-12		7	16	Alvarez	Cho		45-33	2nd	3.0
7-2	At Chi.	W	6-1		10	7	Martinez	Parque		46-33	2nd	3.0
7-3	At Chi.	L	2-11		9	16	Sirotka	Rose		46-34	2nd	4.0
7-4	At Chi.	W	5-2		10	6	Saberhagen	Navarro	Wakefield	47-34	2nd	3.0
7-5	At T.B.	W	4-2		9	9	Portugal	Rekar	Wakefield	48-34	2nd	2.0
7-6	At T.B.	L	4-6		9	7	Lopez	Wasdin	Hernandez	48-35	2nd	3.0
7-7	At T.B.	L	2-3		7	7	Eiland	Martinez	Hernandez	48-36	2nd	4.0
7-8	At T.B.	L	2-3		9	8	Witt	Rose	Hernandez	48-37	2nd	4.0
7-9	At Atl.	W	5-4		5	8	Saberhagen	Chen	Wakefield	49-37	2nd	3.0
7-10	At Atl.	L	1-2	(11)	6	10	Seanez	Wasdin		49-38	2nd	4.0
7-11	At Atl.	L	1-8		6	8	Maddux	Cho		49-39	2nd	4.0
7-15	Phi.	W	6-4		12	9	Rose	Byrd	Wakefield	50-39	2nd	3.0
7-16	Phi.	L	4-5		8	10	Person	Saberhagen	Gomes	50-40	2nd	3.0
7-17	Phi.	L	3-11		7	18	Wolf	Portugal		50-41	2nd	4.0
7-18	Fla.	W	11-9		12	14	Lowe	Nunez	Wakefield	51-41	2nd	4.0
7-19	Fla.	L	7-10		15	16	Meadows	Ohka	Alfonseca	51-42	2nd	4.0
7-20	Fla.	W	7-1		12	5	Rose	Hernandez		52-42	2nd	4.0
7-21	Bal.	L	1-6		6	11	Mussina	Saberhagen		52-43	2nd	5.0
7-22	Bal.	L	2-5		8	12	Erickson	Cho	Timlin	52-44	T2nd	6.0
7-23	At Det.	L	5-14		8	15	Moehler	Ohka		52-45	3rd	7.0
7-24	At Det.	W	11-4		13	10	Portugal	Weaver	Lowe	53-45	3rd	7.0
7-25	At Det.	L	1-9		6	10	Mlicki	Rose		53-46	3rd	8.0
7-27	At Tor.	W	11-9		18	14	Guthrie	Halladay	Wakefield	54-46	3rd	8.0
7-28	At Tor.	W	8-0		11	2	Rapp	Hamilton		55-46	3rd	7.0
7-30	N.Y.	L	3-13		7	16	Irabu	Portugal		55-47	3rd	7.5
7-31	N.Y.	W	6-5		12	15	Lowe	Mendoza		56-47	3rd	6.5
8-1	N.Y.	W	5-4		9	9	Saberhagen	Hernandez	Wakefield	57-47	3rd	5.5
8-2	Cle.	L	5-7		10	8	Karsay	Garces	Jackson	57-48	3rd	6.5
8-3	Cle.	L	4-5		7	6	Shuey	Wakefield	Jackson	57-49	3rd	6.5
8-4	Cle.	W	7-2		10	10	Portugal	Colon		58-49	3rd	6.5
8-5	At Ana.	L	0-8		4	14	Finley	Rose		58-50	3rd	7.5
8-6	At Ana.	W	5-1		10	8	Saberhagen	Sparks		59-50	3rd	7.5
8-7	At Ana.	W	14-3		19	8	Rapp	Belcher		60-50	3rd	7.5
8-8	At Ana.	W	9-3		13	6	Martinez	McDowell		61-50	2nd	7.5
8-9	At K.C.	L	2-5		4	9	Suppan	Portugal		61-51	3rd	8.5
8-10	At K.C.	W	9-6	(10)	16	13	Wakefield	Whisenant	Garces	62-51	3rd	7.5
8-11	At K.C.	W	9-3		12	5	Saberhagen	Rosado		63-51	3rd	7.5
8-13	Sea.	W	11-6		10	8	Lowe	Fassero		64-51	3rd	7.5
8-14	Sea.	W	13-2		19	8	Martinez	Halama		65-51	2nd	6.5
8-15	Sea.	L	3-4		6	8	Meche	Portugal	Mesa	65-52	2nd	6.5
8-16	Oak.	W	6-5		11	7	Lowe	Jones		66-52	2nd	6.5
8-17	Oak.	L	1-12		10	17	Heredia	Saberhagen		66-53	2nd	7.5
8-18	Oak.	W	7-4		13	3	Garces	Appier	Lowe	67-53	2nd	6.5
8-19	Oak.	L	2-6		4	12	Hudson	Martinez	Mathews	67-54	2nd	6.5
8-20	At Tex.	L	3-4		6	10	Loaiza	Portugal	Wetteland	67-55	2nd	7.5
8-21	At Tex.	L	2-9		9	12	Helling	Rose		67-56	2nd	7.5
8-22	At Tex.	L	0-6		8	10	Sele	Wakefield		67-57	2nd	8.5
8-23	At Min.	W	4-1		10	10	Rapp	Hawkins	Lowe	68-57	2nd	8.5
8-24	At Min.	W	7-1		11	5	Martinez	Ryan		69-57	2nd	8.5
8-25	At Min.	L	3-6		5	8	Radke	Portugal		69-58	2nd	8.5
8-27	Ana.	W	4-3		5	6	Garces	Percival	Lowe	70-58	2nd	8.5
8-28	Ana.	W	7-6		8	10	Lowe	Pote		71-58	2nd	8.5
8-29	Ana.	W	7-4		10	11	Rapp	Belcher	Lowe	72-58	2nd	8.5
8-30	K.C.	W	9-1		14	5	Martinez	Suppan		73-58	2nd	8.5
8-31	K.C.	W	6-3		11	4	Garces	Witasick	Lowe	74-58	2nd	7.5
9-1	K.C.	W	4-3		6	3	Mercker	Rosado	Beck	75-58	2nd	6.5
9-2	K.C.	L	2-4		7	9	Suzuki	Martinez	Fussell	75-59	2nd	7.5
9-3	At Sea.	L	1-2		3	9	Moyer	Lowe		75-60	2nd	7.5
9-4	At Sea.	W	4-0		6	3	Martinez	Abbott		76-60	2nd	7.5
9-5	At Sea.	W	9-7		13	12	Garces	Paniagua	Lowe	77-60	2nd	7.5
9-6	At Sea.	W	3-2		10	5	Florie	Halama	Lowe	78-60	2nd	6.5
9-7	At Oak.	W	5-3		10	6	Wakefield	Heredia	Lowe	79-60	2nd	5.5
9-8	At Oak.	L	2-6		5	8	Appier	Rapp		79-61	2nd	6.5
9-10	At N.Y.	W	3-1		12	1	Martinez	Pettitte		80-61	2nd	5.5
9-11	At N.Y.	W	11-10		10	12	Garces	Irabu	Beck	81-61	2nd	4.5
9-12	At N.Y.	W	4-1		7	5	Cormier	Clemens	Beck	82-61	2nd	3.5
9-13	At Cle.	L	7-11		10	12	Nagy	Wakefield	Shuey	82-62	2nd	3.5
9-14	At Cle.	W	12-3		16	4	Lowe	Gooden		83-62	2nd	3.5
9-15	At Cle.	W	6-4	(13)	10	12	Wasdin	Brower		84-62	2nd	3.5
9-17	Det.	W	14-3		16	8	Florie	Blair		85-62	2nd	4.0
9-18	Det.	W	9-1		13	7	Saberhagen	Weaver		86-62	2nd	3.0

Date	Opp.	Res.	Score	(inn.*)	Hits	Opp. hits	Winning pitcher	Losing pitcher	Save	Record	Pos.	GB
9-19	Det.	W	7-3		11	5	Wakefield	Mlicki	Lowe	87-62	2nd	3.0
9-21	Tor.	W	3-0		11	3	Martinez	Hentgen		88-62	2nd	3.0
9-22	Tor.	L	9-14		10	22	Escobar	Rapp		88-63	2nd	4.0
9-23	Tor.	L	5-7		12	11	Wells	Beck	Koch	88-64	2nd	5.0
9-24	Bal.	L	0-1		6	8	Mussina	Saberhagen	Timlin	88-65	2nd	6.0
9-25	Bal.	W	4-1		6	4	Martinez	Linton	Garces	89-65	2nd	5.0
9-26	Bal.	L	5-8		8	5	Johnson	Wakefield	Orosco	89-66	2nd	5.0
9-27	Bal.	W	5-3		8	8	Martinez	Erickson	Lowe	90-66	2nd	4.0
9-29†	At Chi.	W	6-2		10	10	Mercker	Parque		91-66		
9-29‡	At Chi.	L	2-4		7	6	Foulke	Gordon	Howry	91-67	2nd	4.5
9-30	At Chi.	L	2-5		8	9	Lowe	Rose	Howry	91-68	2nd	5.0
10-1	At Bal.	W	6-2		12	8	Ohka	Linton		92-68	2nd	5.0
10-2	At Bal.	W	8-0		12	3	Martinez	Johns		93-68	2nd	5.0
10-3	At Bal.	W	1-0	(10)	5	6	Rose	Timlin	Wakefield	94-68	2nd	4.0

Monthly records: April (11-11), May (20-8), June (14-13), July (11-15), August (18-11), September (17-10), October (3-0).
*Innings, if other than nine. † First game of a doubleheader. ‡ Second game of a doubleheader.

HIGHLIGHTS

High point: With Pedro Martinez pitching six hitless innings, the Red Sox completed a division series comeback with a 12-8 victory over the Indians in Game 5. After losing the first two games, the Red Sox showed their resiliency and season-long ability to overachieve by winning three in a row (one game by a 23-7 score).

Low point: Boston went quickly in the ALCS, winning only one game against the Yankees (when they hammered Roger Clemens and got more great pitching from Martinez).

Turning point: The Red Sox were in a tight wild-card race when they began a 12-game, two-week, four-city trip in early September. They went 9-3 against the Mariners, A's, Yankees and Indians, sealing a postseason spot.

Most valuable player: Nomar Garciaparra, who won the A.L. batting title with a .357 average. The shortstop had 42 doubles, 27 homers, 104 RBIs and 14 stolen bases.

Most valuable pitcher: Martinez, who posted one of the most dominant seasons in decades. He went 23-4 with a 2.07 ERA and had 313 strikeouts and only 37 walks in 213.1 innings. Martinez pitched a 17-strikeout, one-hit game against the Yankees and had a 16-strikeout, three-hit performance against the Braves.

Most improved player: Jason Varitek established himself as one of the game's top young catchers, a take-charge player who hit .269 with 10 homers and 76 RBIs. His most eye-popping offensive number: 39 doubles.

Most pleasant surprise: Rookie Brian Daubach. He wasn't expected to make the team after signing a minor league contract, and even after earning a roster spot in spring training, he was demoted in April. But he returned to fill a void in the middle of the lineup, finishing with a .294 average, 21 homers and 73 RBIs in 381 at-bats.

Biggest disappointment: Third baseman John Valentin continued his downward spiral, hitting .253 with 12 homers and 70 RBIs in 113 games of an injury-plagued year. He did excel in the postseason.

Key injuries: Closer Tom Gordon, who had 46 saves in 1998, missed a large portion of the season because of an elbow injury. Bret Saberhagen was limited to 22 starts because of three stints on the D.L. Valentin was beaned in June and went on the D.L., and he missed three weeks in September with tendinitis in his left knee. Catcher Scott Hatteberg was out three months with an elbow injury, and second baseman Jeff Frye was sidelined 2.5 months with a knee strain. The team also lost rookie pitcher Juan Pena, who missed the final four months with tendinitis in his right shoulder after going 2-0 with a 0.69 ERA in two May starts.

Notable: The Red Sox made back-to-back postseason appearances for the first time since 1915-1916. ... Pedro Martinez became the second pitcher in major league history (Randy Johnson is the other) to record 300 or more strikeouts in each league.

—PAUL DOYLE

RECORDS

1999 regular-season record: 94-68 (2nd in A.L. East); 49-32 at home; 45-36 on road; 28-21 vs. A.L. East; 36-20 vs. Central; 24-15 vs. West; 6-12 vs. N.L.; 18-17 vs. lefthanded starters; 76-51 vs. righthanded starters; 83-57 on grass; 11-11 on turf; 38-22 in daytime; 56-46 at night; 21-20 in one-run games; 4-4 in extra-inning games; 0-0-1 in doubleheaders.

Team record past five years: 435-357 (.549, ranks 3rd in league in that span).

TEAM LEADERS

Batting average: Nomar Garciaparra (.357).
At-bats: Troy O'Leary (596).
Runs: Jose Offerman (107).
Hits: Nomar Garciaparra (190).
Total Bases: Nomar Garciaparra (321).
Doubles: Nomar Garciaparra (42).
Triples: Jose Offerman (11).
Home runs: Troy O'Leary (28).
Runs batted in: Nomar Garciaparra (104).
Stolen bases: Jose Offerman (18).
Slugging percentage: Nomar Garciaparra (.603).
On-base percentage: Nomar Garciaparra (.418).
Wins: Pedro Martinez (23).
Earned-run average: Pedro Martinez (2.07).

Complete games: Pedro Martinez (5).
Shutouts: Pedro Martinez (1).
Saves: Derek Lowe, Tim Wakefield (15).
Innings pitched: Pedro Martinez (213.1).
Strikeouts: Pedro Martinez (313).

GAMES BY POSITION

Catcher: Jason Varitek 140, Scott Hatteberg 23, Creighton Gubanich 14, Lenny Webster 6, Steve Lomasney 1.
First base: Mike Stanley 111, Brian Daubach 61, Jose Offerman 8, Reggie Jefferson 2, Lou Merloni 1.
Second base: Jose Offerman 128, Jeff Frye 26, Donnie Sadler 10, Lou Merloni 8, Chad Fonville 2.
Third base: John Valentin 111, Wilton Veras 35, Donnie Sadler 9, Lou Merloni 9, Jeff Frye 7, Butch Huskey 2, Brian Daubach 1, Creighton Gubanich 1.
Shortstop: Nomar Garciaparra 134, Lou Merloni 24, Donnie Sadler 14, Jeff Frye 2.
Outfield: Troy O'Leary 157, Darren Lewis 130, Trot Nixon 121, Damon Buford 84, Donnie Sadler 8, Butch Huskey 4, Jon Nunnally 2, Michael Coleman 2, Brian Daubach 2, Lou Merloni 1.
Designated hitter: Reggie Jefferson 58, Brian Daubach 43, Butch Huskey 37, Mike Stanley 20, Jose Offerman 17, Scott Hatteberg 6, Damon Buford 5, Donnie Sadler 4, Jon Nunnally 3, Lou Merloni 3, Darren Lewis 2, Jeff Frye 2, Jason Varitek 2, Creighton Gubanich 2, John Valentin 1.

TOP DRAFT CHOICES

1a. **Rick Asadoorian,** OF, Northbridge H.S., Whitinsville, Mass.
1b. **Brad Baker,** RHP, Pioneer Valley H.S., Leyden, Mass.
1c. **Casey Fossum,** LHP, Texas A&M University
2. **Mat Thompson,** RHP, Timberline H.S., Boise, Ida.
3a. **Richard Rundles,** LHP, Jefferson County H.S., New Market, Tenn.
3b. **Antron Seiber,** OF, Independence (La.) H.S.
4. **Rory Shortell,** RHP, Madison H.S., Portland, Ore.
5. **Greg Montalbano,** LHP, Northeastern U.
6. **Jon Kail,** OF, Baldwin H.S., Pittsburgh
7. **Richard Carroll,** 1B, Venice (Fla.) H.S.
8. **Andrew Heimbach,** RHP, Mount Vernon Nazarene (Ohio) College
9. **Hank Thoms,** RHP, Mississippi St. U.
10. **Brian Wiese,** OF, Mississippi State U.

CHICAGO WHITE SOX
AMERICAN LEAGUE CENTRAL DIVISION

2000 White Sox Schedule
Home games shaded. *—All-Star Game at Turner Field (Atlanta).

March
SUN	MON	TUE	WED	THU	FRI	SAT
26	27	28	29	30	31	

April
SUN	MON	TUE	WED	THU	FRI	SAT
						1
2	3 TEX	4 TEX	5 TEX	6 TEX	7 OAK	8 OAK
9 OAK	10	11 TB	12 TB	13 TB	14 ANA	15 ANA
16 ANA	17 SEA	18 SEA	19 SEA	20	21 DET	22 DET
23 DET	24 BAL	25 BAL	26 BAL	27 BAL	28 DET	29 DET
30 DET						

May
SUN	MON	TUE	WED	THU	FRI	SAT
	1 TOR	2 TOR	3 TOR	4	5 KC	6 KC
7 KC	8 BOS	9 BOS	10 BOS	11	12 MIN	13 MIN
14 MIN	15	16 NYY	17 NYY	18	19 TOR	20 TOR
21 TOR	22 NYY	23 NYY	24 NYY	25 NYY	26 CLE	27 CLE
28 CLE	29 SEA	30 SEA	31 SEA			

June
SUN	MON	TUE	WED	THU	FRI	SAT
				1	2 HOU	3 HOU
4 HOU	5 CIN	6 CIN	7 CIN	8	9 CUB	10 CUB
11 CUB	12 CLE	13 CLE	14 CLE	15 NYY	16 NYY	17 NYY
18 NYY	19 CLE	20 CLE	21 CLE	22 CLE	23 NYY	24 NYY
25 NYY	26	27 MIN	28 MIN	29 MIN	30 BOS	

July
SUN	MON	TUE	WED	THU	FRI	SAT
						1 BOS
2 BOS	3 KC	4 KC	5 KC	6	7 CUB	8 CUB
9 CUB	10	11	*12	13 STL	14 STL	15 STL
16 MIL	17 MIL	18 MIN	19 MIN	20 MIN	21 BOS	22 BOS
23 BOS	24 KC	25 KC	26 KC	27 ANA	28 ANA	29 ANA
30 ANA	31					

August
SUN	MON	TUE	WED	THU	FRI	SAT
		1 TEX	2 TEX	3	4 OAK	5 OAK
6 OAK	7	8 SEA	9 SEA	10 SEA	11 TB	12 TB
13 TB	14 BAL	15 BAL	16 BAL	17 BAL	18 TB	19 TB
20 TB	21 TB	22	23 BAL	24 BAL	25 SEA	26 SEA
27 SEA	28 OAK	29 OAK	30 OAK	31		

September
SUN	MON	TUE	WED	THU	FRI	SAT
					1 ANA	2 ANA
3 ANA	4 TEX	5 TEX	6 TEX	7 TEX	8 CLE	9 CLE
10 CLE	11 DET	12 DET	13 DET	14	15 TOR	16 TOR
17 TOR	18 DET	19 DET	20 DET	21 MIN	22 MIN	23 MIN
24 MIN	25	26 BOS	27 BOS	28 BOS	29 KC	30 KC

October
SUN	MON	TUE	WED	THU	FRI	SAT
1 KC	2	3	4	5	6	7

2000 SEASON
CLUB DIRECTORY

Chairman
Jerry Reinsdorf
Vice chairman
Eddie Einhorn
Executive vice president
Howard Pizer
Senior v.p., major league operations
Ron Schueler
Sr. v.p., marketing and broadcasting
Rob Gallas
Senior vice president, baseball
Jack Gould
V.p., administration and finance
Tim Buzard
Vice president, stadium operations
Terry Savarise
V.p., free agent and major league scouting
Larry Monroe
Vice president, player development
Ken Williams
Dir. of baseball operations/asst. g.m.
Dan Evans
Special assistants to Ron Schueler
Ed Brinkman
Dave Yoakum
Special assignment
Mike Pazik
Director of scouting
Duane Shaffer
Director of minor league instruction
Jim Snyder
Manager of team travel
Ed Cassin
Asst. dir. of min. league & scouting admin.
Grace Guerrero Zwit
Asst. dir. of scouting & min. league op.
Daniel Fabian
Director of marketing and broadcasting
Bob Grim
Director of community relations
Christine Makowski
Director of sales
Jim Muno
Director of ticket operations
Bob Devoy

Dir. of management information services
Don Brown
Director of human resources
Moira Foy
Controller
Bill Waters
Director of public relations
Scott Reifert
Trainers
Herm Schneider
Mark Anderson
Director of conditioning
Steve Odgers
Team physicians
Dr. James Boscardin
Dr. Hugo Cuadros
Dr. Bernard Feldman
Dr. David Orth
Dr. Scott Price
Dr. Lowell Scott Weil
Scouting national cross-checker
Doug Laumann
Scouting supervisors
Bob Fontaine
Ed Pebley
Ken Stauffer
Professional scouts
George Bradley
Gary Pellant
Full-time scouts
Joe Butler, Hernan Cortes, Alex Cosmidis, Nathan Durst, Roberto Espinoza, Denny Gonzalez, Larry Grefer, Warren Hughes, Miguel Ibarra, George Kachigian, John Kazanas, Jose Ortega, Paul Provas, Mark Salas, Mike Sgobba, John Tumminia
Part-time scouts
Darrell Brown, Tommy Butler, Javier Centeno, Jaime Correa, Curt Daniels, Mike Davenport, Mariano DeLeon, John Doldoorian, James Ellison, Matt Hattabaugh, Joe Ingalls, Jack Jolly, Robert Jones, Dario Lodigiani, Don Metzger, Glenn Murdock, Paul Murphy, Al Otto, Mike Paris, Jose Ponce, Wuarnner Rincones, Tony Rodriguez, Joe Rudi, Oswaldo Salazar, Alex Slattery, Keith Staab, Fermin Urbi

MINOR LEAGUE AFFILIATES

Class	Team	League	Manager
AAA	Charlotte	International	Nick Leyva
AA	Birmingham	Southern	To be announced
A	Burlington	Midwest	Nick Capra
A	Winston-Salem	Carolina	Jerry Terrell
Rookie	Bristol	Appalachian	R.J. Reynolds
Rookie	Tucson	Arizona	Jerry Hairston

BROADCAST INFORMATION
Radio: ESPN-AM (1000).
TV: WGN-TV (Channel 9).
Cable TV: Fox Sports Chicago.

SPRING TRAINING
Ballpark (city): Tucson Electric Park (Tucson, Ariz.).
Ticket information: 888-683-3900.

SPRING TRAINING ROSTER

Manager—Jerry Manuel (7).
Coaches—Nardi Contreras (54), Wallace Johnson (18), Von Joshua (48), Art Kusyner (53), Bryan Little (20), Joe Nossek (23).

No.	PITCHERS	B/T	Ht./Wt.	Born	1999 clubs
37	Baldwin, James	R/R	6-3/235	7-15-71	Chicago A.L.
	Barcelo, Lorenzo	R/R	6-4/220	8-10-77	Arizona White Sox, Burlington, Birmingham
57	Beirne, Kevin	L/R	6-4/210	1-1-74	Charlotte
44	Bradford, Chad	R/R	6-5/205	9-14-74	Charlotte, Chicago A.L.
43	Castillo, Carlos	R/R	6-2/250	4-21-75	Charlotte, Chicago A.L.
51	Daneker, Pat	R/R	6-3/195	1-14-76	Charlotte, Chicago A.L., Birmingham
60	Davenport, Joe	R/R	6-5/225	3-24-76	Birmingham, Chicago A.L., Charlotte
36	Eyre, Scott	L/L	6-1/200	5-30-72	Charlotte, Chicago A.L.
29	Foulke, Keith	R/R	6-0/200	10-19-72	Chicago A.L.
46	Howry, Bobby	L/R	6-5/220	8-4-73	Chicago A.L.
50	Lowe, Sean	R/R	6-2/205	3-29-71	Chicago A.L.
62	Myette, Aaron	R/R	6-4/195	9-26-77	Birmingham, Chicago A.L.
38	Navarro, Jaime	R/R	6-4/250	3-27-68	Chicago A.L.
40	Parque, Jim	L/L	5-11/165	2-8-76	Chicago A.L.
61	Pena, Jesus	L/L	6-0/170	3-8-75	Birmingham, Chicago A.L.
41	Simas, Bill	L/R	6-3/235	11-28-71	Chicago A.L.
33	Sirotka, Mike	L/L	6-1/200	5-13-71	Chicago A.L.
59	Snyder, John	R/R	6-3/200	8-16-74	Chicago A.L., Charlotte
47	Sturtze, Tanyon	R/R	6-5/205	10-12-70	Charlotte, Chicago A.L.
32	Wells, Kip	R/R	6-3/196	4-21-77	Winston-Salem, Birmingham, Chicago A.L.

No.	CATCHERS	B/T	Ht./Wt.	Born	1999 clubs
8	Fordyce, Brook	R/R	6-0/190	5-7-70	Chicago A.L.
10	Johnson, Mark	L/R	6-0/185	9-12-75	Chicago A.L.
15	Paul, Josh	R/R	6-1/185	5-19-75	Birmingham, Chicago A.L.

No.	INFIELDERS	B/T	Ht./Wt.	Born	1999 clubs
17	Caruso, Mike	L/R	6-0/172	5-27-77	Chicago A.L.
21	Crede, Joe	R/R	6-3/195	4-26-78	Birmingham
34	Dellaero, Jason	B/R	6-2/195	12-17-76	Winston-Salem, Birmingham, Chicago A.L.
5	Durham, Ray	B/R	5-8/180	11-30-71	Chicago A.L.
14	Konerko, Paul	R/R	6-3/211	3-5-76	Chicago A.L.
39	Liefer, Jeff	L/R	6-3/195	8-17-74	Chicago A.L., Charlotte
31	Norton, Greg	B/R	6-1/205	7-6-72	Chicago A.L.
28	Wilson, Craig	R/R	6-0/185	9-3-70	Chicago A.L.

No.	OUTFIELDERS	B/T	Ht./Wt.	Born	1999 clubs
25	Abbott, Jeff	R/L	6-2/200	8-17-72	Chicago A.L., Charlotte
26	Christensen, McKay	L/L	5-11/180	8-14-75	Chicago A.L., Birmingham, Charlotte
45	Lee, Carlos	R/R	6-2/220	6-20-76	Charlotte, Chicago A.L.
30	Ordonez, Magglio	R/R	6-0/200	1-28-74	Chicago A.L.
27	Simmons, Brian	B/R	6-2/190	9-4-73	Chicago A.L., Charlotte
12	Singleton, Chris	L/L	6-2/195	8-15-72	Chicago A.L.
35	Thomas, Frank	R/R	6-5/270	5-27-68	Chicago A.L.

BALLPARK INFORMATION

Ballpark (capacity, surface)
Comiskey Park (44,321, grass)
Address
333 W. 35th St.
Chicago, IL 60616
Business phone
312-674-1000
Ticket information
312-674-1000
Ticket prices
$22 (lower deck box, club level)
$17 (lower deck reserved)
$15 (upper deck box)
$14 (bleacher reserved)
$10 (upper deck reserved)
Field dimensions (from home plate)
To left field at foul line, 347 feet
To center field, 400 feet
To right field at foul line, 347 feet
First game played
April 18, 1991 (Tigers 16, White Sox 0)

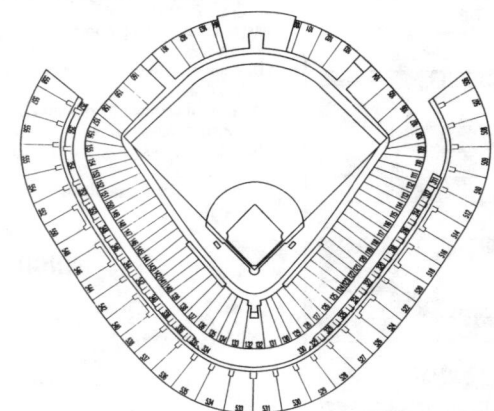

2000 SEASON Chicago White Sox

Date	Opp.	Res.	Score	(inn.*)	Hits	Opp. hits	Winning pitcher	Losing pitcher	Save	Record	Pos.	GB
4-6	At Sea.	W	11-3		15	6	Parque	Moyer		2-0	T1st	+0.5
4-7	At Sea.	L	3-7		10	10	Garcia	Snyder	Mesa	2-1	1st	+0.5
4-9	K.C.	L	5-10		9	13	Barber	Sirotka		2-2	T2nd	1.0
4-10	K.C.	L	4-9		7	15	Pittsley	Navarro	Service	2-3	T2nd	2.0
4-11	K.C.	L	1-3		5	8	Appier	Baldwin	Montgomery	2-4	T3rd	3.0
4-13	At Bos.	L	0-6		7	7	Saberhagen	Parque		2-5	4th	4.0
4-15	At Bos.	W	4-0		8	6	Snyder	Martinez		3-5	T3rd	4.0
4-16	At K.C.	L	2-7		9	8	Appier	Sirotka		3-6	4th	4.5
4-17	At K.C.	W	6-5		11	7	Lowe	Montgomery	Howry	4-6	T3rd	4.0
4-18	At K.C.	W	7-5		12	11	Baldwin	Barber	Howry	5-6	2nd	4.0
4-20	Sea.	W	3-1		8	5	Parque	Fassero	Howry	6-6	T2nd	4.0
4-21	Sea.	W	2-1		5	6	Snyder	Paniagua	Howry	7-6	2nd	4.0
4-23	Det.	W	5-0		9	5	Sirotka	Blair		8-6	2nd	3.5
4-24	Det.	W	3-1		4	6	Navarro	Mlicki	Howry	9-6	2nd	2.5
4-25	Det.	L	4-9		6	12	Weaver	Baldwin		9-7	2nd	2.5
4-28†	T.B.	W	10-7		14	8	Parque	Rekar	Howry	10-7		
4-28‡	T.B.	W	9-1		10	9	Snyder	Saunders		11-7	2nd	3.0
4-29	T.B.	L	1-4		4	9	Alvarez	Sirotka	Hernandez	11-8	2nd	4.0
4-30	At Ana.	L	1-3		5	5	Petkovsek	Navarro	Percival	11-9	2nd	4.0
5-1	At Ana.	W	8-5		14	13	Lundquist	Percival	Howry	12-9	2nd	4.0
5-2	At Ana.	L	3-6		5	11	Olivares	Parque		12-10	2nd	4.0
5-3	At Ana.	W	8-1		12	4	Snyder	Belcher		13-10	2nd	4.0
5-4	At Bal.	L	5-9	(10)	9	10	Timlin	Lundquist		13-11	2nd	4.5
5-5	At Bal.	L	0-8		6	7	Guzman	Navarro		13-12	2nd	4.5
5-6	At Bal.	L	2-4		8	5	Ponson	Baldwin	Timlin	13-13	2nd	5.5
5-7	Oak.	W	7-1		10	7	Parque	Candiotti		14-13	2nd	5.5
5-8	Oak.	W	5-3		11	8	Snyder	Haynes	Howry	15-13	2nd	4.5
5-9	Oak.	L	0-3		4	8	Oquist	Sirotka	Jones	15-14	2nd	5.5
5-10	Tex.	W	5-2		12	6	Navarro	Helling		16-14	2nd	5.5
5-11	Tex.	L	5-11		12	15	Zimmerman	Howry		16-15	2nd	6.5
5-14	At N.Y.	W	8-2		9	6	Parque	Hernandez	Simas	17-15	2nd	7.0
5-15	At N.Y.	W	12-4		17	13	Snyder	Mendoza		18-15	2nd	7.0
5-16	At N.Y.	L	1-2		8	8	Pettitte	Sirotka	Rivera	18-16	2nd	7.0
5-17	Cle.	L	9-13		12	17	Colon	Navarro		18-17	2nd	8.0
5-18	Cle.	L	0-13		2	13	Gooden	Baldwin		18-18	3rd	9.0
5-19	Cle.	L	7-13		9	18	Nagy	Parque		18-19	3rd	10.0
5-22†	N.Y.	L	2-10		7	13	Clemens	Snyder		18-20		
5-22‡	N.Y.	W	2-1		6	2	Sirotka	Pettitte	Simas	19-20	3rd	9.0
5-23	N.Y.	L	7-8	(10)	12	9	Rivera	Simas		19-21	3rd	10.0
5-24	At Cle.	W	10-3		15	10	Lowe	Gooden		20-21	3rd	9.0
5-25	At Cle.	L	1-3		6	8	Nagy	Parque	Jackson	20-22	3rd	10.0
5-26	At Cle.	L	2-6		8	11	Burba	Sirotka	Shuey	20-23	3rd	11.0
5-27	At Det.	L	5-10		9	14	Weaver	Snyder		20-24	3rd	11.5
5-28	At Det.	W	9-1		15	7	Navarro	Thompson		21-24	3rd	10.5
5-29	At Det.	W	7-1		13	5	Baldwin	Moehler		22-24	3rd	9.5
5-30	At Det.	L	2-3		9	11	Mlicki	Parque	Jones	22-25	3rd	9.5
6-1	At Tor.	W	6-2		13	7	Sirotka	Escobar		23-25	2nd	9.0
6-2	At Tor.	L	7-9		15	15	Carpenter	Snyder	Koch	23-26	2nd	10.0
6-3	At Tor.	W	10-3		16	7	Navarro	Hentgen		24-26	2nd	9.5
6-4	Pit.	L	3-6	(11)	10	9	Wilkins	Simas		24-27	2nd	9.5
6-5	Pit.	W	6-5		15	8	Parque	Benson	Foulke	25-27	2nd	9.5
6-6	Pit.	W	4-3		8	8	Sirotka	Silva	Howry	26-27	2nd	9.5
6-7	Hou.	L	2-8		8	17	Lima	Snyder		26-28	2nd	10.0
6-8	Hou.	W	4-3		7	9	Navarro	Reynolds	Howry	27-28	2nd	9.0
6-9	Hou.	L	4-13		9	17	Hampton	Baldwin		27-29	2nd	10.0
6-11	At Chi. (NL)	W	5-3	(6)	11	5	Parque	Lieber		28-29	2nd	9.5
6-12	At Chi. (NL)	W	8-2		18	8	Sirotka	Trachsel		29-29	2nd	9.5
6-13	At Chi. (NL)	W	6-4		12	7	Simas	Aguilera	Foulke	30-29	2nd	9.5
6-14	T.B.	W	9-7		9	11	Snyder	Alvarez	Howry	31-29	2nd	9.0
6-15	T.B.	L	2-3		12	6	Rupe	Baldwin	Hernandez	31-30	2nd	10.0
6-16	T.B.	W	3-2	(11)	8	8	Lowe	Charlton		32-30	2nd	10.0
6-17	Bal.	W	9-3		11	12	Sirotka	Guzman	Foulke	33-30	2nd	10.0
6-18	Bal.	L	2-3		7	8	Mussina	Navarro		33-31	2nd	10.0
6-19	Bal.	L	9-11	(11)	17	12	Rhodes	Foulke	Kamieniecki	33-32	2nd	11.0
6-20	Bal.	L	4-8		10	12	Johnson	Baldwin	Timlin	33-33	2nd	12.0
6-22	Min.	W	6-1		12	8	Parque	Hawkins		34-33	2nd	11.5
6-23	Min.	L	10-12		16	19	Sampson	Sirotka	Trombley	34-34	2nd	12.5
6-24	Min.	W	5-3		13	14	Navarro	Radke	Howry	35-34	2nd	11.5
6-25	At Bos.	L	1-6		7	13	Cho	Snyder	Guthrie	35-35	2nd	11.5
6-26	At Bos.	L	1-17		3	14	Martinez	Baldwin	Wasdin	35-36	2nd	11.5
6-27	At Bos.	W	7-6		8	9	Simas	Wakefield	Howry	36-36	2nd	11.5

Date	Opp.	Res.	Score	(inn.*)	Hits	Opp. hits	Winning pitcher	Losing pitcher	Save	Record	Pos.	GB
6-28	At Bos.	L	1-14		8	21	Saberhagen	Sirotka		36-37	2nd	12.5
6-29	At K.C.	L	4-7		10	11	Appier	Navarro	Service	36-38	2nd	13.5
6-30	At K.C.	W	10-9	(10)	16	14	Howry	Service		37-38	2nd	12.5
7-1	At K.C.	W	6-2		8	7	Baldwin	Pisciotta		38-38	2nd	12.5
7-2	Bos.	L	1-6		7	10	Martinez	Parque		38-39	2nd	12.5
7-3	Bos.	W	11-2		16	9	Sirotka	Rose		39-39	2nd	13.0
7-4	Bos.	L	2-5		6	10	Saberhagen	Navarro	Wakefield	39-40	2nd	13.0
7-6	K.C.	L	7-8	(10)	16	14	Whisenant	Foulke		39-41	2nd	14.0
7-7	K.C.	W	7-1		10	10	Parque	Suzuki		40-41	2nd	13.0
7-8	K.C.	W	6-5		10	10	Foulke	Byrdak		41-41	2nd	13.0
7-9	Chi. (NL)	W	3-2		9	9	Howry	Adams		42-41	2nd	12.0
7-10	Chi. (NL)	L	2-10		8	12	Lieber	Navarro		42-42	2nd	13.0
7-11	Chi. (NL)	L	3-6		6	7	Trachsel	Baldwin	Adams	42-43	2nd	13.0
7-15	At StL.	L	2-3	(13)	8	10	Croushore	Rizzo		42-44	2nd	14.0
7-16	At StL.	W	9-8		15	11	Navarro	Acevedo	Howry	43-44	2nd	13.0
7-17	At StL.	L	6-8		8	9	Stephenson	Ward	Bottalico	43-45	2nd	13.0
7-18	At Mil.	L	4-5		9	13	Plunk	Rizzo		43-46	2nd	13.0
7-19	At Mil.	W	10-8	(12)	18	11	Simas	Coppinger	Foulke	44-46	2nd	12.0
7-20	At Mil.	L	4-5		9	10	Plunk	Lowe	Wickman	44-47	2nd	13.0
7-21	At Min.	W	6-3	(10)	13	11	Simas	Carrasco	Howry	45-47	2nd	12.0
7-22	At Min.	L	0-3		5	11	Mays	Baldwin	Trombley	45-48	2nd	12.0
7-23	Tor.	L	1-2		7	8	Hamilton	Parque	Koch	45-49	2nd	12.0
7-24	Tor.	W	6-5		6	9	Eyre	Escobar	Howry	46-49	2nd	11.0
7-25	Tor.	L	3-11		5	17	Carpenter	Sirotka		46-50	2nd	11.0
7-26	Tor.	L	3-4	(11)	13	9	Frascatore	Howry	Koch	46-51	2nd	12.0
7-27	N.Y.	L	3-5		10	10	Hernandez	Baldwin	Rivera	46-52	2nd	13.0
7-28	N.Y.	W	11-3		19	11	Castillo	Pettitte		47-52	2nd	13.0
7-29	N.Y.	W	5-1		9	5	Snyder	Cone	Foulke	48-52	2nd	12.5
7-30	At Cle.	L	2-10		6	17	Colon	Sirotka		48-53	2nd	13.5
7-31	At Cle.	L	10-13		18	13	Shuey	Castillo	Jackson	48-54	2nd	14.5
8-1	At Cle.	W	6-3		11	6	Baldwin	Nagy	Howry	49-54	2nd	13.5
8-2	At Det.	W	6-2		11	7	Wells	Moehler		50-54	2nd	13.5
8-3	At Det.	W	9-6		15	9	Snyder	Thompson	Howry	51-54	2nd	13.5
8-5	At Oak.	L	6-7	(11)	11	11	Mathews	Eyre		51-55	2nd	13.5
8-6	At Oak.	L	1-9		5	15	Heredia	Navarro		51-56	2nd	13.5
8-7	At Oak.	L	1-11		6	14	Appier	Parque		51-57	2nd	14.5
8-8	At Oak.	L	5-7		11	9	Jones	Foulke		51-58	2nd	14.5
8-9	At Sea.	L	4-6		6	7	Meche	Snyder	Mesa	51-59	2nd	15.5
8-10	At Sea.	L	3-4		8	9	Moyer	Howry		51-60	2nd	16.5
8-11	At Sea.	L	2-11		6	10	Abbott	Navarro		51-61	2nd	17.5
8-13†	Tex.	W	4-2		11	6	Wells	Burkett	Howry	52-61		
8-13‡	Tex.	W	7-4		9	14	Baldwin	Glynn		53-61	2nd	17.0
8-14	Tex.	W	8-7		16	11	Howry	Zimmerman		54-61	2nd	17.0
8-15	Tex.	L	0-10		6	16	Loaiza	Snyder		54-62	2nd	18.0
8-16	Ana.	W	6-1		10	6	Sirotka	Washburn		55-62	2nd	17.0
8-17	Ana.	W	4-3	(12)	7	12	Howry	Holtz		56-62	2nd	16.0
8-18	Ana.	W	4-3		6	6	Baldwin	Magnante	Howry	57-62	2nd	15.0
8-19	Ana.	L	2-9		6	14	Ortiz	Parque		57-63	2nd	16.0
8-21†	At Bal.	W	4-3		14	7	Simas	Reyes	Howry	58-63		
8-21‡	At Bal.	W	8-5	(10)	13	14	Howry	Johns	Foulke	59-63	2nd	16.0
8-22	At Bal.	L	4-9		7	16	Johns	Navarro		59-64	2nd	17.0
8-23	At T.B.	W	10-2		13	8	Baldwin	Witt		60-64	2nd	16.0
8-24	At T.B.	L	5-6		5	11	Alvarez	Parque	Hernandez	60-65	2nd	16.0
8-25	At T.B.	W	6-1		12	7	Foulke	Rupe		61-65	2nd	16.0
8-26	At T.B.	L	7-9		14	13	White	Snyder	Hernandez	61-66	2nd	16.5
8-27	Oak.	L	6-9		13	10	Olivares	Sirotka	Isringhausen	61-67	2nd	17.5
8-28	Oak.	L	5-7		7	10	Heredia	Navarro	Jones	61-68	2nd	18.5
8-29	Oak.	W	7-2		10	10	Baldwin	Appier	Foulke	62-68	2nd	17.5
8-30†	Sea.	L	2-5		9	12	Garcia	Parque	Mesa	62-69		
8-30‡	Sea.	L	6-14		11	15	Cloude	Castillo	Rodriguez	62-70	2nd	19.0
8-31	Sea.	L	4-11		9	15	Halama	Snyder		62-71	2nd	20.0
9-1	Sea.	L	2-3		8	10	Meche	Sirotka	Mesa	62-72	2nd	21.0
9-3	At Tex.	L	4-10		10	15	Burkett	Baldwin		62-73	2nd	22.5
9-4	At Tex.	W	12-3		15	11	Castillo	Loaiza		63-73	2nd	21.5
9-6†	At Tex.	L	6-8		10	9	Helling	Parque	Wetteland	63-74		
9-6‡	At Tex.	L	3-6		12	8	Fassero	Snyder	Wetteland	63-75	2nd	23.5
9-7	At Ana.	L	1-14		4	12	Cooper	Sirotka		63-76	2nd	23.5
9-8	At Ana.	L	5-6	(10)	7	10	Percival	Simas		63-77	2nd	23.5
9-10	Cle.	L	6-14		5	14	Colon	Wells		63-78	2nd	24.5
9-11	Cle.	L	3-4		7	10	Burba	Parque	Jackson	63-79	2nd	25.5
9-12	Cle.	W	4-3		12	11	Sirotka	Wright	Howry	64-79	2nd	24.5
9-13	Det.	L	2-3		4	9	Mlicki	Snyder	Jones	64-80	2nd	25.5
9-14	Det.	L	0-7		4	11	Nitkowski	Myette		64-81	2nd	25.5
9-15	Det.	W	3-1		10	3	Baldwin	Moehler	Foulke	65-81	2nd	24.5
9-17	At Tor.	W	7-3		14	8	Wells	Escobar		66-81	2nd	23.0

Date	Opp.	Res.	Score	(inn.*)	Hits	Opp. hits	Winning pitcher	Losing pitcher	Save	Record	Pos.	GB
9-18	At Tor.	W	7-4		13	10	Navarro	Quantrill	Howry	67-81	2nd	23.0
9-19	At Tor.	W	3-2		5	6	Sirotka	Halladay	Howry	68-81	2nd	22.0
9-21	At N.Y.	L	1-3		6	10	Pettitte	Baldwin	Rivera	68-82	2nd	22.5
9-22	At N.Y.	L	4-5		9	9	Rivera	Navarro		68-83	2nd	23.5
9-23	At N.Y.	L	2-5		7	12	Clemens	Parque	Rivera	68-84	2nd	23.5
9-24	At Min.	L	2-6		2	7	Mays	Myette		68-85	2nd	24.5
9-25	At Min.	W	13-4		18	6	Sirotka	Hawkins		69-85	2nd	24.5
9-26	At Min.	W	3-0		12	6	Baldwin	Ryan	Howry	70-85	2nd	24.5
9-27	At Min.	W	3-1		5	5	Simas	Wells	Foulke	71-85	2nd	24.0
9-29†	Bos.	L	2-6		10	10	Mercker	Parque		71-86		
9-29‡	Bos.	W	4-2		6	7	Foulke	Gordon	Howry	72-86	2nd	24.0
9-30	Bos.	W	5-2		9	8	Lowe	Rose	Howry	73-86	2nd	24.0
10-1	Min.	W	9-8		13	12	Baldwin	Ryan	Howry	74-86	2nd	23.0
10-2	Min.	W	6-1		11	8	Wells	Perkins		75-86	2nd	22.0
10-3	Min.	T	1-1	(7)	4	6				75-86	2nd	21.5

Monthly records: April (11-9), May (11-16), June (15-13), July (11-16), August (14-17), September (11-15), October (2-0).
*Innings, if other than nine. † First game of a doubleheader. ‡ Second game of a doubleheader.

HIGHLIGHTS

High point: On June 13, Mike Caruso hit a rare home run—and it was well-timed. His two-run drive off Rick Aguilera snapped a 4-4 tie in the eighth inning and lifted the White Sox to a three-game sweep of the Cubs at Wrigley Field.

Low point: On August 8, Frank Thomas made a costly error at first base at Oakland and the A's went on to complete a four-game sweep. An angry Thomas said, "I bleeping booted it. That's why I'm a DH. I'm not a first baseman." After showing excellent leadership in the first half of the season, Thomas unraveled after the All-Star break.

Turning point: In their first game of the second half, at St. Louis, the White Sox lost, 3-2, in 13 innings. Ahead 2-1, the Sox thought they were victims of a bad call in the ninth on what appeared to be a game-ending double play. The tying run scored on the play. The defeat set the tone for a 33-43 record after the break for a Sox team that went 42-43 in the first half.

Most valuable player: In just his second full season in the majors, Magglio Ordonez established himself as an elite player. The right fielder batted .301 and led the team in home runs (30) and RBIs (117).

Most valuable pitcher: Keith Foulke had a dominant season, posting a team-low 2.22 ERA and limiting hitters to a .188 average. A setup man who also saw work as a closer, he used a nasty changeup to great effect in striking out 123 batters in 105.1 innings.

Most improved player: Young Paul Konerko was a minor league star but a major league bust until coming to the White Sox. As the 1999 season progressed, the first baseman/DH got into a groove and finished with 24 home runs and 81 RBIs.

Most pleasant surprise: Center fielder Chris Singleton, who was given a shot to start in mid-May. He went on to bat .300, hit 17 homers, drive in 72 runs and play solid defense.

Biggest disappointment: After making a remarkable jump from Class A to the Sox in 1998 and batting .306, shortstop Caruso experienced a major drop-off. His average plummeted 50 points and his on-base percentage was an awful .280 (compared with .331 in '98). His defense, a minus as a rookie, was shaky again.

Key injuries: Thomas didn't play after September 6 and underwent surgery to remove a bone spur from his right ankle. John Snyder, who was sensational early in the season (6-1 with a 2.00 ERA), tailed off badly and wound up having elbow surgery in September.

Notable: The White Sox finished second in the A.L. Central for the fourth consecutive year. ... Thomas, limited to a 135-game season, failed to hit 20 homers and drive in 100 runs for the first time in his career. He had 15 homers and 77 RBIs. ... Ray Durham became the first player in Sox history to score 100 runs and steal 30 bases in three consecutive seasons.

—SCOT GREGOR

RECORDS

1999 regular-season record: 75-86 (2nd in A.L. Central); 38-42 at home; 37-44 on road; 25-29 vs. East; 24-23 vs. A.L. Central; 17-25 vs. West; 9-9 vs. N.L.; 16-11 vs. lefthanded starters; 59-75 vs. righthanded starters; 62-80 on grass; 13-6 on turf; 24-29 in daytime; 51-57 at night; 20-19 in one-run games; 6-9 in extra-inning games; 3-2-2 in doubleheaders.
Team record past five years: 388-402 (.491, ranks 7th in league in that span).

TEAM LEADERS

Batting average: Frank Thomas (.305).
At-bats: Magglio Ordonez (624).
Runs: Ray Durham (109).
Hits: Magglio Ordonez (188).
Total Bases: Magglio Ordonez (318).
Doubles: Frank Thomas (36).
Triples: Ray Durham (8).
Home runs: Magglio Ordonez (30).
Runs batted in: Magglio Ordonez (117).
Stolen bases: Ray Durham (34).
Slugging percentage: Paul Konerko (.511).
On-base percentage: Frank Thomas (.414).
Wins: James Baldwin (12).

Earned-run average: Mike Sirotka (4.00).
Complete games: Mike Sirotka (3).
Shutouts: Mike Sirotka (1).
Saves: Bob Howry (28).
Innings pitched: Mike Sirotka (209.0).
Strikeouts: Mike Sirotka (125).

GAMES BY POSITION

Catcher: Brook Fordyce 103, Mark Johnson 72, Josh Paul 6, Brian Simmons 1.
First base: Paul Konerko 92, Frank Thomas 49, Greg Norton 26, Jeff Liefer 15, Carlos Lee 5, Craig Wilson 1.
Second base: Ray Durham 148, Liu Rodriguez 22, Craig Wilson 7.
Third base: Greg Norton 120, Craig Wilson 72, Paul Konerko 1, Liu Rodriguez 1.
Shortstop: Mike Caruso 132, Craig Wilson 22, Liu Rodriguez 14, Jason Dellaero 11.
Outfield: Magglio Ordonez 153, Chris Singleton 127, Carlos Lee 105, Darrin Jackson 64, Brian Simmons 46, McKay Christensen 27, Jeff Abbott 17, Jeff Liefer 17.
Designated hitter: Frank Thomas 82, Paul Konerko 46, Carlos Lee 16, Jeff Liefer 7, Ray Durham 4, Darrin Jackson 3, Brian Simmons 3, Magglio Ordonez 2, Mike Caruso 2, Chris Singleton 2, Liu Rodriguez 2, Greg Norton 1, Craig Wilson 1, Mark L. Johnson 1.

TOP DRAFT CHOICES

1a. **Jason Stumm,** RHP, Centralia (Wash.) H.S.
1b. **Matt Ginter,** RHP, Mississippi State U.
1c. **Brian West,** RHP, West Monroe H.S., Monroe, La.
1d. **Rob Purvis,** RHP, Bradley University
2a. **Danny Wright,** RHP, U. of Arkansas
2b. **Bobby Hill,** SS, Univ. of Miami
3. **Jon Rauch,** RHP, Morehead State U.
4. **Brandon Sloan,** RHP, Wichita State U.
5. **Josh Stewart,** LHP, Univ. of Memphis
6. **David Sanders,** LHP, Barton County (Kan.) C.C.
7. **Scott Patten,** RHP, Tecumseh (Okla.) H.S.
8. **Dennis Ulacia,** LHP, Monsignor Pace H.S., Opa Locka, Fla.
9. **Corwin Malone,** LHP, Thomasville (Ala.) H.S.
10. **Matt Guerrier,** RHP, Kent University

CLEVELAND INDIANS
AMERICAN LEAGUE CENTRAL DIVISION

2000 Indians Schedule
Home games shaded. *—All-Star Game at Turner Field (Atlanta).

March

SUN	MON	TUE	WED	THU	FRI	SAT
26	27	28	29	30	31	

April

SUN	MON	TUE	WED	THU	FRI	SAT
						1
2	3 BAL	4	5 BAL	6 BAL	7 TB	8 TB
9 TB	10 OAK	11 OAK	12 OAK	13	14 TEX	15 TEX
16 TEX	17	18 OAK	19 OAK	20 OAK	21 BOS	22 BOS
23 BOS	24 SEA	25 SEA	26 SEA	27	28 BOS	29 BOS
30 BOS						

May

SUN	MON	TUE	WED	THU	FRI	SAT
	1 NYY	2 NYY	3 NYY	4 TOR	5 TOR	6 TOR
7 TOR	8 MIN	9 MIN	10 MIN	11 KC	12 KC	13 KC
14 KC	15	16 DET	17 DET	18 DET	19 NYY	20 NYY
21 NYY	22	23 DET	24 DET	25 DET	26 CWS	27 CWS
28 CWS	29 ANA	30 ANA	31 ANA			

June

SUN	MON	TUE	WED	THU	FRI	SAT
				1	2 STL	3 STL
4 STL	5 MIL	6 MIL	7 MIL	8	9 CIN	10 CIN
11 CIN	12 CWS	13 CWS	14 CWG	15	16 DET	17 DET
18 DET	19 CWS	20 CWS	21 CWS	22 CWS	23 DET	24 DET
25 DET	26 KC	27 KC	28 KC	29 KC	30 MIN	

July

SUN	MON	TUE	WED	THU	FRI	SAT
						1 MIN
2 MIN	3	4 TOR	5 TOR	6 TOR	7 CIN	8 CIN
9 CIN	10	11	* 12	13 PIT	14 PIT	15 PIT
16 HOU	17 HOU	18 HOU	19 KC	20 KC	21 MIN	22 MIN
23 MIN	24	25 TOR	26 TOR	27	28 BAL	29 BAL
30 BAL	31					

August

SUN	MON	TUE	WED	THU	FRI	SAT
		1 TB	2 TB	3 TB	4 ANA	5 ANA
6 ANA	7 TEX	8 TEX	9 TEX	10	11 SEA	12 SEA
13 SEA	14 OAK	15 OAK	16 OAK	17	18 SEA	19 SEA
20 SEA	21	22 OAK	23 OAK	24 OAK	25 ANA	26 ANA
27 ANA	28 TEX	29 TEX	30 TEX	31 TEX		

September

SUN	MON	TUE	WED	THU	FRI	SAT
					1 BAL	2 BAL
3 BAL	4 TB	5 TB	6 TB	7 TB	8 CWS	9 CWS
10 CWS	11	12 BOS	13 BOS	14 BOS	15 NYY	16 NYY
17 NYY	18 NYY	19 BOS	20 BOS	21 BOS	22 KC	23 KC
24 KC	25 MIN	26 MIN	27 MIN	28 MIN	29 TOR	30 TOR

October

SUN	MON	TUE	WED	THU	FRI	SAT
1 TOR	2	3	4	5	6	7

2000 SEASON
CLUB DIRECTORY

Owner/CEO/chairman of the board
Richard E. Jacobs

Executive vice president, general manager
John Hart

Executive vice president, business
Dennis Lehman

Vice president of baseball operations/asst. general manager
Mark Shapiro

Director, player development
Neal Huntington

Director, scouting
John Mirabelli

Vice president, public relations
Bob DiBiasio

V.p., marketing and communications
Jeff Overton

Vice president, finance
Ken Stefanov

Director, media relations
Bart Swain

Manager, media relations, administrations & credentials
Susie Giuliano

Coordinator, media relations
Curtis Danburg

Director of team travel
Mike Seghi

Head trainer
Paul Spicuzza

Assistant trainer
Jim Warfield

Clubhouse manager
Ted Walsh

Visiting clubhouse
Cy Buynak

Groundskeeper
Brandon Koehnke

National cross-checker, West Coast supervisor
Jesse Flores

National cross-checker, East Coast supervisor
Jerry Jordan

Midwest supervisor
Bob Mayer

Full-time scouts
Steve Abney, Scott Anderson, Doug Baker, Keith Boeck, Jim Bretz, Paul Cogan, Henry Cruz, Dan Durst, Jim Gabella, Rene Gayo, Mark Germann, Chris Jefts, Tim Kissner, Chad MacDonald, Dave Miller, Chuck Ricci, Bill Schudlich

MINOR LEAGUE AFFILIATES

Class	Team	League	Manager
AAA	Buffalo	International	Joel Skinner
AA	Akron	Eastern	Eric Wedge
A	Kinston	Carolina	Brad Komminsk
A	Columbus	South Atlantic	Ricky Gutierrez
A	Mahoning Valley	New York-Pennsylvania	Ted Kubiak
Rookie	Burlington	Appalachian	Dave Turgeon

BROADCAST INFORMATION

Radio: WTAM (1100 AM).
TV: WUAB-TV (Channel 43).
Cable TV: Fox Sports Ohio.

SPRING TRAINING

Ballpark (city): Chain O'Lakes (Winter Haven, Fla.).
Ticket information: 941-293-3900.

SPRING TRAINING ROSTER

Manager—Charlie Manuel (32).
Coaches—Luis Isaac, Clarence Jones, Grady Little, Dick Pole, Jim Riggleman, Ted Uhlaender, Dan Williams.

No.	PITCHERS	B/T	Ht./Wt.	Born	1999 clubs
	Baez, Denys	R/R	6-4/225	9-10-77	DID NOT PLAY
	Vargas, Martin	R/R	6-0/155	2-22-78	Columbus, Kinston
64	Brammer, J.D.	R/R	6-4/235	1-30-75	Akron
50	Brower, Jim	R/R	6-2/205	12-29-72	Buffalo, Cleveland
34	Burba, Dave	R/R	6-4/240	7-7-66	Cleveland
40	Colon, Bartolo	R/R	6-0/225	5-24-75	Cleveland
56	DePaula, Sean	R/R	6-4/215	11-7-73	Kinston, Akron, Buffalo, Cleveland
73	Rincon, Ricardo	L/L	5-10/187	4-13-70	Cleveland, Akron
31	Finley, Chuck	L/L	6-6/226	11-26-62	Anaheim
	Kamienicki, Scott	R/R	6-0/200	4-19-64	Bowie, Frederick, Baltimore, Rochester
20	Karsay, Steve	R/R	6-3/205	3-24-72	Cleveland
36	Martin, Tom	L/L	6-1/200	5-21-70	Akron, Cleveland, Buffalo
71	Martinez, Willie	R/R	6-2/185	1-4-78	Akron, Buffalo
41	Nagy, Charles	L/R	6-3/200	5-5-67	Cleveland
39	Reed, Steve	R/R	6-2/212	3-11-66	Cleveland
54	Riske, Dave	R/R	6-2/175	10-23-76	Akron, Buffalo, Cleveland
53	Shuey, Paul	R/R	6-3/215	9-16-70	Cleveland, Buffalo
	Speier, Justin	R/R	6-4/205	11-6-73	Richmond, Atlanta
27	Wright, Jaret	R/R	6-2/230	12-29-75	Cleveland, Buffalo, Akron

No.	CATCHERS	B/T	Ht./Wt.	Born	1999 clubs
15	Alomar, Sandy	R/R	6-5/215	6-18-66	Cleveland, Akron, Buffalo
2	Diaz, Einar	R/R	5-10/165	12-28-72	Cleveland

No.	INFIELDERS	B/T	Ht./Wt.	Born	1999 clubs
12	Alomar, Roberto	B/R	6-0/185	2-5-68	Cleveland
66	Branyan, Russell	L/R	6-3/195	12-19-75	Buffalo, Cleveland
6	Cabrera, Jolbert	R/R	6-0/177	12-8-72	Cleveland, Buffalo
17	Fryman, Travis	R/R	6-1/195	3-25-69	Cleveland, Akron, Buffalo
72	McDonald, John	R/R	5-11/175	9-24-74	Akron, Buffalo, Cleveland
68	Peoples, Danny	R/R	6-1/225	1-20-75	Akron
44	Sexson, Richie	R/R	6-7/206	12-29-74	Cleveland
25	Thome, Jim	L/R	6-4/220	8-27-70	Cleveland
13	Vizquel, Omar	B/R	5-9/175	4-24-67	Cleveland
35	Wilson, Enrique	B/R	5-11/160	7-27-75	Cleveland

No.	OUTFIELDERS	B/T	Ht./Wt.	Born	1999 clubs
51	Cruz, Jacob	L/L	6-0/179	1-28-73	Cleveland, Buffalo
23	Justice, David	L/L	6-3/200	4-14-66	Cleveland
7	Lofton, Kenny	L/L	6-0/180	5-31-67	Cleveland
62	Morgan, Scott	R/R	6-7/230	7-19-73	Akron, Buffalo
61	Ramirez, Alex	R/R	5-11/176	10-3-74	Buffalo, Cleveland
24	Ramirez, Manny	R/R	6-0/205	5-30-72	Cleveland
52	Roberts, Dave	L/L	5-10/175	5-31-72	Buffalo, Cleveland

BALLPARK INFORMATION

Ballpark (capacity, surface)
Jacobs Field (43,368, grass)
Address
2401 Ontario St.
Cleveland, OH 44115
Business phone
216-420-4200
Ticket information
216-241-8888
Ticket prices
$35 (field box)
$32 (club seating)
$24 (lower box & view box)
$19 (lower reserved, upper box
& mezzanine seating)
$16 (bleachers)
$12 (upper reserved)
$7 (reserved general admission)
$6 (standing room only)
Field dimensions (from home plate)
To left field at foul line, 325 feet
To center field, 405 feet
To right field at foul line, 325 feet
First game played
April 4, 1994
(Indians 4, Mariners 3, 11 innings)

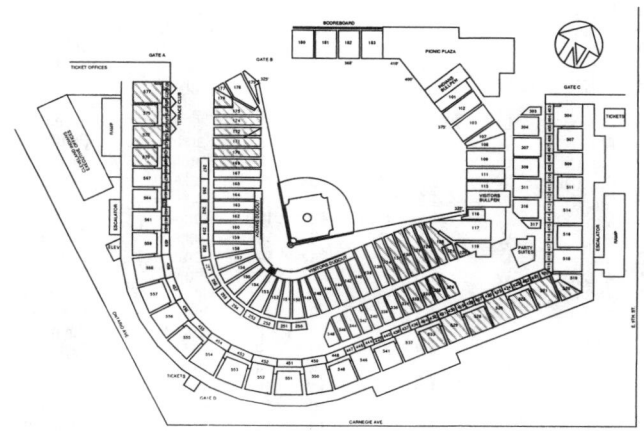

2000 SEASON *Cleveland Indians*

Date	Opp.	Res.	Score	(inn.*)	Hits	Opp. hits	Winning pitcher	Losing pitcher	Save	Record	Pos.	GB
4-7	At Ana.	W	9-1		13	4	Burba	Hill		1-1	T2nd	0.5
4-8	At Ana.	W	9-1		13	4	Colon	Sparks		2-1	T1st	...
4-9	At Min.	W	14-5		20	8	Nagy	Hawkins		3-1	1st	+1.0
4-10	At Min.	W	12-7		16	11	Karsay	Lincoln		4-1	1st	+2.0
4-11	At Min.	W	9-8		17	9	Wright	Radke	Jackson	5-1	1st	+2.0
4-12	K.C.	W	5-2	(10)	11	8	Shuey	Santiago		6-1	1st	+3.0
4-14	K.C.	W	11-4		14	10	Colon	Suppan		7-1	1st	+4.0
4-17†	Min.	W	5-1		10	5	Nagy	Radke		8-1		
4-17‡	Min.	L	8-13	(11)	12	16	Aguilera	Jackson		8-2	1st	+3.5
4-18	Min.	W	3-2		8	9	Shuey	Wells	Jackson	9-2	1st	+4.0
4-20	Oak.	W	5-1		9	3	Colon	Rogers		10-2	1st	+4.0
4-21	Oak.	W	5-4		14	8	Reed	Taylor		11-2	1st	+4.0
4-22	Oak.	L	1-4		3	8	Candiotti	Nagy	Taylor	11-3	1st	+3.5
4-23	At Bos.	W	7-6		9	7	Karsay	Corsi	Jackson	12-3	1st	+3.5
4-24	At Bos.	L	4-9		12	13	Harikkala	DeLucia		12-4	1st	+2.5
4-25	At Bos.	L	2-3		7	12	Martinez	Shuey		12-5	1st	+2.5
4-26	At Oak.	W	5-4	(10)	9	10	Karsay	Taylor	Jackson	13-5	1st	+3.0
4-27	At Oak.	W	8-5		12	11	Nagy	Candiotti	Jackson	14-5	1st	+3.5
4-28	At Oak.	W	4-1		6	6	Wright	Haynes	Jackson	15-5	1st	+3.0
4-29	At Oak.	W	8-3		9	4	Burba	Oquist		16-5	1st	+4.0
4-30	At Tex.	L	5-7		11	13	Helling	Colon	Wetteland	16-6	1st	+4.0
5-1	At Tex.	W	5-3		8	9	Gooden	Sele	Jackson	17-6	1st	+4.0
5-2	At Tex.	L	6-8		8	11	Clark	Nagy	Wetteland	17-7	1st	+4.0
5-3	At Tex.	W	10-4		16	6	Wright	Morgan		18-7	1st	+4.0
5-5	Sea.	L	5-6		10	10	Fassero	Burba	Mesa	18-8	1st	+4.5
5-6	Sea.	W	8-4		8	7	Colon	Weaver		19-8	1st	+5.5
5-7	T.B.	W	20-11		21	13	Wagner	Mecir		20-8	1st	+5.5
5-8	T.B.	L	6-7		12	14	Rekar	Nagy	Hernandez	20-9	1st	+4.5
5-9	T.B.	W	5-4		6	11	Wright	Alvarez	Jackson	21-9	1st	+5.5
5-10	Bal.	W	6-4		8	7	Burba	Guzman	Jackson	22-9	1st	+5.5
5-11	Bal.	W	11-6		12	11	Colon	Ponson		23-9	1st	+6.5
5-12	Bal.	W	6-5		10	9	Assenmacher	Timlin	Shuey	24-9	1st	+7.0
5-14	At Det.	W	4-2		6	8	Karsay	Brocail	Shuey	25-9	1st	+7.0
5-15	At Det.	W	12-7		12	10	Burba	Mlicki		26-9	1st	+7.0
5-16	At Det.	L	3-9		7	10	Weaver	Wright	Kida	26-10	1st	+7.0
5-17	At Chi.	W	13-9		17	12	Colon	Navarro		27-10	1st	+8.0
5-18	At Chi.	W	13-0		13	2	Gooden	Baldwin		28-10	1st	+8.5
5-19	At Chi.	W	13-7		18	9	Nagy	Parque		29-10	1st	+8.5
5-21	Det.	L	6-9		10	11	Nitkowski	Shuey	Jones	29-11	1st	+8.0
5-22	Det.	L	2-6		7	10	Weaver	Wright		29-12	1st	+8.0
5-23	Det.	W	7-4		10	8	Shuey	Jones		30-12	1st	+8.0
5-24	Chi.	L	3-10		10	15	Lowe	Gooden		30-13	1st	+7.5
5-25	Chi.	W	3-1		8	6	Nagy	Parque	Jackson	31-13	1st	+8.5
5-26	Chi.	W	6-2		11	8	Burba	Sirotka	Shuey	32-13	1st	+9.5
5-28	Bos.	L	5-12		9	18	Wakefield	Wright	Lowe	32-14	1st	+9.0
5-29	Bos.	L	2-4		5	8	Martinez	Colon	Gordon	32-15	1st	+9.0
5-30	Bos.	L	2-4		3	9	Rose	Gooden	Gordon	32-16	1st	+9.0
5-31	At N.Y.	W	7-1		7	7	Nagy	Hernandez		33-16	1st	+10.0
6-1	At N.Y.	L	5-11		9	13	Clemens	Burba		33-17	1st	+9.0
6-2	At N.Y.	W	10-7		15	9	Karsay	Pettitte	Jackson	34-17	1st	+10.0
6-4	Chi. (NL)	L	4-5		8	8	Aguilera	Jackson	Adams	34-18	1st	+9.5
6-5	Chi. (NL)	W	8-7	(11)	16	11	Jackson	Sanders		35-18	1st	+9.5
6-6	Chi. (NL)	W	4-2		8	8	Nagy	Trachsel	Shuey	36-18	1st	+9.5
6-8	Mil.	L	1-2	(10)	13	10	Roque	Assenmacher	Wickman	36-19	1st	+9.0
6-9	Mil.	W	6-5	(10)	9	9	Jackson	Roque		37-19	1st	+10.0
6-10	Mil.	L	9-15		14	14	Nomo	Colon		37-20	1st	+9.5
6-11	At Cin.	W	8-6		7	13	Shuey	Williamson	Jackson	38-20	1st	+9.5
6-12	At Cin.	W	4-3		9	5	Nagy	Harnisch	Jackson	39-20	1st	+9.5
6-13	At Cin.	W	7-3		9	10	Burba	Avery	Karsay	40-20	1st	+9.5
6-15	Oak.	W	8-3		12	8	Wright	Haynes		41-20	1st	+10.0
6-16	Oak.	W	9-8		10	9	Karsay	Taylor		42-20	1st	+10.0
6-17	Oak.	W	10-6		18	9	Shuey	Worrell		43-20	1st	+10.0
6-18	Sea.	L	4-9		11	10	Halama	Nagy		43-21	1st	+9.0
6-19	Sea.	W	10-6		10	12	Burba	Watson	Jackson	44-21	1st	+11.0
6-20	Sea.	W	13-5		14	11	Wright	Rodriguez		45-21	1st	+12.0
6-21	Sea.	W	4-3	(12)	12	10	Karsay	Mesa		46-21	1st	+12.5
6-22	At Tor.	L	3-4		8	6	Escobar	Gooden	Koch	46-22	1st	+11.5
6-23	At Tor.	W	9-6		12	10	Nagy	Quantrill		47-22	1st	+12.5
6-24	At Tor.	L	0-3		3	5	Halladay	Burba	Koch	47-23	1st	+11.5
6-25	At K.C.	L	2-8		6	12	Suppan	Wright		47-24	1st	+11.5
6-26	At K.C.	L	7-11		6	8	Montgomery	Rincon		47-25	1st	+11.5

Date	Opp.	Res.	Score	(inn.*)	Hits	Opp. hits	Winning pitcher	Losing pitcher	Save	Record	Pos.	GB
6-27	At K.C.	W	6-5		9	13	Reed	Byrdak	Jackson	48-25	1st	+11.5
6-28	At K.C.	W	6-1		12	7	Nagy	Witasick		49-25	1st	+12.5
6-29	Min.	W	5-4		9	7	Reed	Trombley		50-25	1st	+13.5
6-30	Min.	L	3-5		5	9	Milton	Wright	Trombley	50-26	1st	+12.5
7-1	Min.	W	7-5		9	12	Colon	Carrasco	Jackson	51-26	1st	+12.5
7-2	K.C.	L	7-9	(10)	8	12	Whisenant	Shuey		51-27	1st	+12.5
7-3†	K.C.	W	9-8		11	10	Candiotti	Pisciotta	Jackson	52-27		
7-3‡	K.C.	W	9-5		10	10	Langston	Wengert	Jackson	53-27	1st	+13.0
7-4	K.C.	L	9-10		12	13	Appier	Burba	Byrdak	53-28	1st	+13.0
7-6	At Min.	W	3-1		8	6	Wright	Milton	Jackson	54-28	1st	+14.0
7-7	At Min.	L	3-4		8	6	Trombley	Reed		54-29	1st	+13.0
7-8	At Min.	W	9-2		16	10	Nagy	Lincoln		55-29	1st	+13.0
7-9	Cin.	L	2-3		4	5	Avery	Burba	Williamson	55-30	1st	+12.0
7-10	Cin.	W	11-10		15	10	Jackson	Williamson		56-30	1st	+13.0
7-11	Cin.	L	4-9		9	14	Graves	Shuey		56-31	1st	+13.0
7-15	At Pit.	W	2-0		7	3	Colon	Schmidt	Jackson	57-31	1st	+14.0
7-16	At Pit.	L	3-11		12	13	Cordova	Burba		57-32	1st	+13.0
7-17	At Pit.	L	10-13		16	16	Benson	Nagy	Williams	57-33	1st	+13.0
7-18	At Hou.	L	0-2		4	4	Hampton	Wright		57-34	1st	+13.0
7-19	At Hou.	L	2-3	(11)	6	4	Cabrera	Candiotti		57-35	1st	+12.0
7-20	At Hou.	W	7-1		12	6	Colon	Reynolds		58-35	1st	+13.0
7-21	Tor.	L	3-4		8	6	Frascatore	Jackson	Koch	58-36	1st	+12.0
7-22	Tor.	L	3-4		10	7	Wells	Nagy	Koch	58-37	1st	+12.0
7-23	At N.Y.	L	8-9	(10)	10	13	Grimsley	Jackson		58-38	1st	+12.0
7-24	At N.Y.	L	1-21		9	21	Irabu	Langston		58-39	1st	+11.0
7-25	At N.Y.	L	1-2		6	6	Mendoza	Rincon		58-40	1st	+11.0
7-26	Det.	W	6-3		12	10	Burba	Thompson	Jackson	59-40	1st	+12.0
7-27	Det.	W	14-5		19	9	Nagy	Borkowski		60-40	1st	+13.0
7-28	Det.	W	7-2		11	5	Gooden	Moehler		61-40	1st	+13.0
7-30	Chi.	W	10-2		17	6	Colon	Sirotka		62-40	1st	+13.5
7-31	Chi.	W	13-10		13	18	Shuey	Castillo	Jackson	63-40	1st	+14.5
8-1	Chi.	L	3-6		6	11	Baldwin	Nagy	Howry	63-41	1st	+13.5
8-2	At Bos.	W	7-5		8	10	Karsay	Garces	Jackson	64-41	1st	+13.5
8-3	At Bos.	W	5-4		6	7	Shuey	Wakefield	Jackson	65-41	1st	+13.5
8-4	At Bos.	L	2-7		10	10	Portugal	Colon		65-42	1st	+13.0
8-6	At T.B.	L	2-4		7	7	Yan	Burba	Hernandez	65-43	1st	+13.5
8-7	At T.B.	W	15-10		19	14	Nagy	Witt		66-43	1st	+14.5
8-8	At T.B.	L	3-5		6	11	Alvarez	Wright	Hernandez	66-44	1st	+14.5
8-9	At Ana.	W	4-0		9	7	Colon	Hill		67-44	1st	+15.5
8-10	At Ana.	W	2-1	(10)	7	4	Rincon	Petkovsek	Jackson	68-44	1st	+16.5
8-11	At Ana.	W	4-3		10	10	Burba	Sparks	Jackson	69-44	1st	+17.5
8-13	Bal.	W	6-3		8	9	Rincon	Erickson	Jackson	70-44	1st	+17.0
8-14	Bal.	W	7-1		6	4	Karsay	Johnson		71-44	1st	+17.0
8-15	Bal.	W	5-1		13	5	Colon	Ponson		72-44	1st	+18.0
8-16	Tex.	L	5-13		10	16	Munoz	Rincon		72-45	1st	+17.0
8-17	Tex.	L	4-15		9	19	Sele	Langston		72-46	1st	+16.0
8-18	Tex.	L	1-6		7	9	Burkett	Nagy		72-47	1st	+15.0
8-19	Tex.	W	8-0		11	7	Karsay	Morgan		73-47	1st	+16.0
8-20	At Sea.	W	7-4		8	9	Colon	Halama	Jackson	74-47	1st	+16.5
8-21	At Sea.	W	6-0		9	6	Burba	Meche		75-47	1st	+16.0
8-22	At Sea.	W	7-4	(10)	11	7	Riske	Mesa	Jackson	76-47	1st	+17.0
8-23	At Sea.	L	1-4		5	6	Abbott	Nagy	Mesa	76-48	1st	+16.0
8-24	At Oak.	L	10-11		8	12	Mathews	Shuey		76-49	1st	+16.0
8-25	At Oak.	W	12-4		15	6	Colon	Oquist		77-49	1st	+16.0
8-27	T.B.	W	2-1		9	6	Burba	Arrojo	Jackson	78-49	1st	+17.5
8-28	T.B.	W	3-0		7	4	Nagy	Witt	Jackson	79-49	1st	+18.5
8-29	T.B.	L	4-6		10	11	Alvarez	Haney	Hernandez	79-50	1st	+17.5
8-30	Ana.	W	7-5		7	7	Colon	Levine	Jackson	80-50	1st	+19.0
8-31	Ana.	W	14-12		19	14	Poole	Percival	Shuey	81-50	1st	+20.0
9-1	Ana.	W	8-1		12	8	Burba	Washburn		82-50	1st	+21.0
9-2	Ana.	W	6-5		10	11	Nagy	Sparks	Jackson	83-50	1st	+21.5
9-3	At Bal.	W	7-6		9	10	Assenmacher	Reyes	Jackson	84-50	1st	+22.5
9-4	At Bal.	L	1-3		6	9	Linton	Colon	Timlin	84-51	1st	+21.5
9-5	At Bal.	W	15-7		12	11	Brower	Ponson		85-51	1st	+22.0
9-6	At Bal.	W	7-6		8	9	Burba	Johns	Jackson	86-51	1st	+23.5
9-7	At Tex.	L	3-4		6	10	Sele	Reed	Wetteland	86-52	1st	+23.5
9-8	At Tex.	L	0-3		8	7	Burkett	Haney	Wetteland	86-53	1st	+23.5
9-10	At Chi.	W	14-6		14	5	Colon	Wells		87-53	1st	+24.5
9-11	At Chi.	W	4-3		10	7	Burba	Parque	Jackson	88-53	1st	+25.5
9-12	At Chi.	L	3-4		11	12	Sirotka	Wright	Howry	88-54	1st	+24.5
9-13	Bos.	W	11-7		12	10	Nagy	Wakefield	Shuey	89-54	1st	+25.5
9-14	Bos.	L	3-12		4	16	Lowe	Gooden		89-55	1st	+25.5
9-15	Bos.	L	4-6	(13)	12	10	Wasdin	Brower		89-56	1st	+24.5
9-16	N.Y.	L	5-9		10	12	Irabu	Burba		89-57	1st	+24.0

Date	Opp.	Res.	Score	(inn.*)	Hits	Opp. hits	Winning pitcher	Losing pitcher	Save	Record	Pos.	GB
9-17	N.Y.	L	4-9		5	9	Clemens	Wright		89-58	1st	+23.0
9-18	N.Y.	W	5-4		8	12	Nagy	Hernandez	Jackson	90-58	1st	+23.0
9-19	N.Y.	L	7-11		9	18	Watson	Martin		90-59	1st	+22.0
9-20	At Det.	L	3-4	(10)	9	9	Jones	Riske		90-60	1st	+21.5
9-21	At Det.	W	6-1		8	4	Burba	Borkowski		91-60	1st	+22.5
9-22	At Det.	W	9-1		16	2	Wright	Moehler		92-60	1st	+23.5
9-23	At Det.	L	5-7		6	11	Blair	Nagy	Jones	92-61	1st	+23.5
9-24	At Tor.	W	18-4		15	9	Brower	Munro		93-61	1st	+24.5
9-25	At Tor.	W	9-6		13	9	Colon	Spoljaric	Jackson	94-61	1st	+24.5
9-26	At Tor.	W	11-7		14	9	Shuey	Koch		95-61	1st	+24.5
9-28	At K.C.	W	2-1		8	3	Brower	Witasick	Jackson	96-61	1st	+24.5
9-29	At K.C.	L	2-5		4	9	Rosado	Nagy		96-62	1st	+24.0
9-30	Tor.	W	9-2		8	9	Colon	Spoljaric		97-62	1st	+24.0
10-1	Tor.	L	6-8		11	12	Quantrill	Karsay	Koch	97-63	1st	+23.0
10-2	Tor.	L	3-7		8	14	Hentgen	Wright	Koch	97-64	1st	+22.0
10-3	Tor.	L	2-9		10	9	Wells	Burba		97-65	1st	+21.5

Monthly records: April (16-6), May (17-10), June (17-10), July (13-14), August (18-10), September (16-12), October (0-3).
*Innings, if other than nine. † First game of a doubleheader. ‡ Second game of a doubleheader.

HIGHLIGHTS

High point: The Indians rolled to their fifth consecutive A.L. Central title against overmatched divisional opposition. The championship continued the most successful run in franchise history.

Low point: Losing a best-of-five division series after seemingly having it won. The collapse cost Mike Hargrove his job, even though he was only eight wins short of becoming the winningest manager in team history.

Turning point: One victory away from sweeping the division series, the Indians tied the Red Sox 3-3 in the top of seventh of Game 3 but yielded six runs to Boston in its half of the inning. The Red Sox won, 9-3, and then erupted for 23-7 and 12-8 victories.

Most valuable player: Manny Ramirez led the majors with 165 RBIs, but this honor goes to second baseman Roberto Alomar. Signed as a free agent in the off-season, Alomar was the A.L.'s best all-around player. He batted .323 with 138 runs, 24 homers, 120 RBIs and 37 stolen bases. He made only six errors.

Most valuable pitcher: Righthander Bartolo Colon, who took steps toward becoming a long-sought No. 1 pitcher. He went 18-5 with a 3.95 ERA. Colon was dominant in the second half, going 11-2 with a 2.60 ERA. At age 24, he's on the verge of becoming one of the league's top starters.

Most improved player: Richie Sexson. Despite playing in only 134 games, he finished third on the team in home runs (31) and RBIs (116).

Most pleasant surprise: Steve Karsay, who made the team as the last man on the pitching staff. Pitching mostly in a setup role, he was 10-2 with a 2.97 ERA.

Biggest disappointment: Jaret Wright, who continues to regress after a strong rookie year in 1997. He went 8-10 with a 6.06 ERA and was on the disabled list twice.

Key injuries: The Indians were able to field their projected opening-day lineup only four times all season. Sandy Alomar Jr. tore a knee ligament in May and missed four months. Travis Fryman tore a knee ligament in July and missed two months. Wil Cordero broke his wrist in June and missed three months. Kenny Lofton pulled a hamstring in July and missed six weeks. Jacob Cruz tore a ligament in his thumb in August and missed the rest of the season.

Notable: The Indians scored a club-record 1,009 runs in the regular season. ... Ramirez became the first major leaguer to top the 160-RBI mark since Jimmie Foxx drove in 175 runs in 1938. ... The Indians went a combined 10-22 against New York, Boston and Texas, the A.L.'s other playoff teams. ... The Indians hit 12 grand slams, tying a major league record.

—STEVE HERRICK

RECORDS

1999 regular-season record: 97-65 (1st in A.L. Central); 47-34 at home; 50-31 on road; 26-27 vs. East; 33-16 vs. A.L. Central; 29-13 vs. West; 9-9 vs. N.L.; 28-15 vs. lefthanded starters; 69-50 vs. righthanded starters; 82-56 on grass; 15-9 on turf; 28-22 in daytime; 69-43 at night; 26-19 in one-run games; 7-7 in extra-inning games; 1-0-1 in doubleheaders.
Team record past five years: 471-319 (.596, ranks 2nd in league in that span).

TEAM LEADERS

Batting average: Manny Ramirez (.333).
At-bats: Omar Vizquel (574).
Runs: Roberto Alomar (138).
Hits: Omar Vizquel (191).
Total Bases: Manny Ramirez (346).
Doubles: Roberto Alomar (40).
Triples: Richie Sexson (7).
Home runs: Manny Ramirez (44).
Runs batted in: Manny Ramirez (165).
Stolen bases: Omar Vizquel (42).
Slugging percentage: Manny Ramirez (.663).
On-base percentage: Manny Ramirez (.442).
Wins: Bartolo Colon (18).
Earned-run average: Bartolo Colon (3.95).

Complete games: Dave Burba, Bartolo Colon, Charles Nagy (1).
Shutouts: Bartolo Colon (1).
Saves: Mike Jackson (39).
Innings pitched: Dave Burba (220.0).
Strikeouts: Dave Burba (174).

GAMES BY POSITION

Catcher: Einar Diaz 119, Sandy Alomar Jr. 35, Chris Turner 12, Jesse Levis 9, Pat Borders 5, Tyler Houston 1.
First base: Jim Thome 111, Richie Sexson 61, Jeff Manto 1.
Second base: Roberto Alomar 156, Enrique Wilson 21, John McDonald 7, Carlos Baerga 6, Jolbert Cabrera 6.
Third base: Travis Fryman 85, Enrique Wilson 61, Carlos Baerga 15, Jeff Manto 10, Tyler Houston 10, Russ Branyan 8, Pat Borders 1.
Shortstop: Omar Vizquel 143, Enrique Wilson 35, John McDonald 6.
Outfield: Manny Ramirez 146, Kenny Lofton 119, David Justice 93, Richie Sexson 49, David Roberts 39, Wil Cordero 29, Alex Ramirez 29, Jacob Cruz 24, Jolbert Cabrera 16, Mark Whiten 7, Omar Vizquel 1.
Designated hitter: David Justice 34, Jim Thome 34, Harold Baines 25, Richie Sexson 24, Wil Cordero 23, Alex Ramirez 14, Jolbert Cabrera 5, Russ Branyan 3, Roberto Alomar 2, Manny Ramirez 2, Jacob Cruz 2, Sandy Alomar Jr. 1, Carlos Baerga 1, Kenny Lofton 1, Enrique Wilson 1.

TOP DRAFT CHOICES

1. None
2. **Will Hartley,** C, Bradford County H.S., Stark, Fla.
3. **Eric Johnson,** OF, Western Carolina U.
4. **Jeff Baker,** SS, Garfield H.S., Woodbridge, Va.
5. **Curtis Gay,** 1B, Oklahoma City Univ.
6. **Shane Wallace,** LHP, Newman Smith H.S., Carrollton, Tex.
7. **Daylon Monette,** OF, Miller H.S., Fontana, Calif.
8. **Devin Rogers,** RHP, Nicholls State U.
9. **Stephen Cowie,** RHP, Duke University
10. **Fernando Cabrera,** RHP, Discipulus de Cristo H.S., Bayamon, P.R.

DETROIT TIGERS
AMERICAN LEAGUE CENTRAL DIVISION

2000 Tigers Schedule
Home games shaded. *—All-Star Game at Turner Field (Atlanta).

March

SUN	MON	TUE	WED	THU	FRI	SAT
26	27	28	29	30	31	

April

SUN	MON	TUE	WED	THU	FRI	SAT
						1
2	3 OAK	4 OAK	5 OAK	6	7 BAL	8 BAL
9 BAL	10	11 SEA	12 SEA	13 SEA	14 TB	15 TB
16 TB	17	18 BOS	19 BOS	20 BOS	21 CWS	22 CWS
23 CWS	24 ANA	25 ANA	26 ANA	27	28 CWS	29 CWS
30 CWS						

May

SUN	MON	TUE	WED	THU	FRI	SAT
	1 BOS	2 BOS	3 BOS	4 MIN	5 MIN	6 MIN
7 MIN	8 KC	9 KC	10 KC	11	12 NYY	13 NYY
14 NYY	15	16 CLE	17 CLE	18 CLE	19 BOS	20 BOS
21 BOS	22	23 CLE	24 CLE	25 CLE	26 TOR	27 TOR
28 TOR	29 TEX	30 TEX	31 TEX			

June

SUN	MON	TUE	WED	THU	FRI	SAT
				1	2 CUB	3 CUB
4 CUB	5 PIT	6 PIT	7 PIT	8	9 STL	10 STL
11 STL	12 TOR	13 TOR	14 TOR	15	16 CLE	17 CLE
18 CLE	19	20 TOR	21 TOR	22 TOR	23 CLE	24 CLE
25 CLE	26 CLE	27 NYY	28 NYY	29 NYY	30 KC	

July

SUN	MON	TUE	WED	THU	FRI	SAT
						1 KC
2 KC	3 TB	4 TB	5 TB	6	7 MIL	8 MIL
9 MIL	10	11 *	12	13 HOU	14 HOU	15 HOU
16 CIN	17 CIN	18 CIN	19 NYY	20 NYY	21 KC	22 KC
23 KC	24 TB	25 TB	26 TB	27 TEX	28 TEX	29 TEX
30 TEX	31 ANA					

August

SUN	MON	TUE	WED	THU	FRI	SAT
		1 ANA	2 ANA	3	4 MIN	5 MIN
6 MIN	7 BAL	8 BAL	9 BAL	10 BAL	11 OAK	12 OAK
13 OAK	14 SEA	15 SEA	16 SEA	17	18 SEA	19 SEA
20 OAK	21 OAK	22 OAK	23 SEA	24 SEA	25 MIN	26 MIN
27 MIN	28	29 BAL	30 BAL	31 BAL		

September

SUN	MON	TUE	WED	THU	FRI	SAT
					1 TEX	2 TEX
3 TEX	4 ANA	5 ANA	6 ANA	7 ANA	8 TOR	9 TOR
10 TOR	11 CWS	12 CWS	13 CWS	14	15 BOS	16 BOS
17 BOS	18 CWS	19 CWS	20	21	22 NYY	23 NYY
24 NYY	25 NYY	26 KC	27 KC	28 KC	29 MIN	30 MIN

October

SUN	MON	TUE	WED	THU	FRI	SAT
1 MIN	2	3	4	5	6	7

2000 SEASON
CLUB DIRECTORY

Owners
Michael Ilitch
President, chief executive officer
John McHale Jr.
Vice president, baseball operations/g.m.
Randy Smith
Vice president, business operations
David H. Glazier
Assistant general manager
Steve Lubratich
Assistants to baseball operations
Ricky Bennett, Hiroshi Yoshimura
Asst., bb operations, foreign affairs
Ramon Pena
Special assistants to the g.m.
Al Hargesheimer, Randy Johnson
Director of scouting
Greg Smith
Latin American liaison
Luis Mayoral
Director minor league operations
Dave Miller
Traveling secretary
Bill Brown
Director of public relations
Tyler Barnes
Assistant director of public relations
David Matheson
Manager, community relations
Celia Bobrowsky
Coordinator, community relations
Fred Feliciano
Coordinator, public relations
Giovanni Loria
Coordinator, public relations
Melanie Waters
Coordinator, community relations
Masico Brown
Marketing manager
Ellen Hill

Director of park operations
Tom Folk
Special assistant to the president
Gary Vitto
Director of corporate sales
Dan Sinagoga
Director of finance
Jennifer Marosso
Director of ticket services
Ken Marchetti
Director of ticket sales
Barry Gibson
Director of merchandise
Kayla French
Manager, home clubhouse
Jim Schmakel
Assistant manager, visiting clubhouse
John Nelson
Team physicians
David J. Collon, M.D., Terry Lock, M.D., Louis Saco, M.D., Michael Workings, M.D.
Medical director/head trainer
Russ Miller
Assistant trainer
Steve Carter
Strength and conditioning coach
Denny Taft
Scouts
Scott Bream, Bill Buck, Jerome Cochran, Tim Grieve, Rob Guzik, Jack Hays, Mike Herbert, Joe Hodges, Lou Laslo, Dennis Lieberthal, Jeff Malinoff, Mark Monahan, Pat Murtaugh, Steve Nichols, Jim Olander, Frank Paine, Derrick Ross, Mike Stafford, Steve Taylor, Clyde Weir, Jeff Wetherby, Rob Wilfong, Ellis Williams, Steve Williams, Gary York, Harold Zonder

MINOR LEAGUE AFFILIATES

Class	Team	League	Manager
AAA	Toledo	International	Dave Anderson
AA	Jacksonville	Southern	Gene Roof
A	Lakeland	Florida State	Skeeter Barnes
A	West Michigan	Midwest	Bruce Fields
A	Oneonta	New York-Pennsylvania	Kevin Bradshaw
Rookie	Gulf Coast Tigers	Gulf Coast	Gary Green

BROADCAST INFORMATION

Radio: WJR-AM (760).
TV: WKBD (Channel 50).
Cable TV: FOX Sports Detroit.

SPRING TRAINING

Ballpark (city): Marchant Stadium (Lakeland, Fla.).
Ticket information: 941-603-6278 or 941-603-6279.

SPRING TRAINING ROSTER

Manager—Phil Garner (33).
Coaches—Bill Madlock, Doug Mansolino, Bob Melvin, Lance Parrish (13), Juan Samuel (10), Dan Warthen.

No.	PITCHERS	B/T	Ht./Wt.	Born	1999 clubs
14	Anderson, Matt	R/R	6-4/200	8-17-76	Detroit, Toledo
20	Blair, Willie	R/R	6-1/185	12-18-65	Detroit
45	Borkowski, Dave	R/R	6-1/200	2-7-77	Toledo, Detroit
26	Brocail, Doug	L/R	6-5/235	5-16-67	Detroit
50	Greisinger, Seth	R/R	6-3/200	7-29-75	Lakeland, Toledo
	Heams, Shane	R/R	6-1/175	9-29-75	West Michigan
35	Hiljus, Erik	R/R	6-5/230	12-25-72	Lakeland, Jacksonville, Toledo, Detroit
	Johnson, Mark	R/R	6-3/226	5-2-75	Norwich, Gulf Coast Yankees, Tampa
59	Jones, Todd	L/R	6-3/230	4-24-68	Detroit
	Keller, Kris	R/R	6-2/225	3-1-78	West Michigan
41	Kida, Masao	R/R	6-2/210	9-12-68	Detroit, Toledo
30	Mlicki, Dave	R/R	6-4/205	6-8-68	Los Angeles, Detroit
38	Moehler, Brian	R/R	6-3/235	12-31-71	Detroit
49	Nitkowski, C.J.	L/L	6-3/205	3-9-73	Detroit
	Patterson, Danny	R/R	6-0/225	2-17-71	Texas, Oklahoma
	Roberts, Willis	R/R	6-3/175	6-19-75	Toledo, Detroit
44	Runyan, Sean	L/L	6-3/210	6-21-74	Toledo
	Santos, Victor	R/R	6-3/175	10-2-76	Jacksonville
	Tatis, Ramon	L/L	6-3/205	2-5-73	Durham
	Villafuerte, Brandon	R/R	5-11/165	12-17-75	Portland, Jacksonville
36	Weaver, Jeff	R/R	6-5/200	8-22-76	Detroit, Jacksonville

No.	CATCHERS	B/T	Ht./Wt.	Born	1999 clubs
12	Ausmus, Brad	R/R	5-11/195	4-14-69	Detroit
	Cardona, Javier	R/R	6-1/185	9-15-75	Jacksonville
31	Fick, Robert	L/R	6-1/189	3-15-74	Gulf Coast Tigers, West Michigan, Toledo, Detroit
	Munson, Eric	L/R	6-3/220	10-3-77	Lakeland, West Michigan
	Zaun, Gregg	B/R	5-10/190	4-14-71	Texas

No.	INFIELDERS	B/T	Ht./Wt.	Born	1999 clubs
25	Alvarez, Gabe	R/R	6-1/205	3-6-74	Toledo, Detroit
17	Clark, Tony	B/R	6-7/245	6-15-72	Detroit, Toledo
8	Cruz, Deivi	R/R	6-0/184	11-6-75	Detroit
9	Easley, Damion	R/R	5-11/185	11-11-69	Detroit
7	Palmer, Dean	R/R	6-1/210	12-27-68	Detroit
	Santana, Pedro	R/R	5-11/160	9-21-76	Jacksonville
	Sasser, Rob	R/R	6-3/205	3-9-75	Tulsa, Jacksonville

No.	OUTFIELDERS	B/T	Ht./Wt.	Born	1999 clubs
34	Encarnacion, Juan	R/R	6-3/187	3-8-76	Detroit
24	Garcia, Karim	L/L	6-0/172	10-29-75	Detroit
19	Gonzalez, Juan	R/R	6-3/220	10-16-69	Texas
4	Higginson, Bobby	L/R	5-11/195	8-18-70	Detroit
21	Jefferies, Gregg	B/R	5-10/185	8-1-67	Detroit, Toledo
29	Polonia, Luis	L/L	5-8/150	10-27-64	Toledo, Detroit
	Wakeland, Chris	L/L	6-0/185	6-15-74	Jacksonville, Gulf Coast Tigers, Lakeland

BALLPARK INFORMATION

Ballpark (capacity, surface)
Comerica Park (40,000, grass)

Address
2100 Woodward
Detroit, MI 48201

Business phone
313-962-4000

Ticket information
313-471-BALL

Ticket prices
$30 and $25 (box seats)
$20, $15, $14 and $12 (reserved seats)
$8 (Fan stands)

Field dimensions (from home plate)
To left field at foul line, 345 feet
To center field, 420 feet
To right field at foul line, 330 feet

First game played
Scheduled for April 11, 2000 vs. Mariners

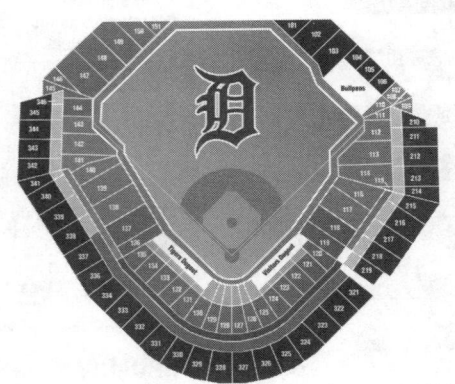

Date	Opp.	Res.	Score	(inn.*)	Hits	Opp. hits	Winning pitcher	Losing pitcher	Save	Record	Pos.	GB
4-6	At Tex.	L	0-6		7	12	Sele	Thompson		1-1	3rd	1.0
4-7	At Tex.	L	7-10		12	18	Morgan	Blair	Wetteland	1-2	4th	1.0
4-9	At N.Y.	L	3-12	(7)	3	9	Cone	Graterol		1-3	T4th	2.0
4-10	At N.Y.	L	0-5		3	10	Clemens	Moehler		1-4	5th	3.0
4-11	At N.Y.	L	2-11		5	9	Hernandez	Thompson		1-5	5th	4.0
4-12	Min.	L	0-1	(12)	3	6	Aguilera	Runyan		1-6	5th	5.0
4-14	Min.	W	7-1		13	3	Weaver	Hawkins		2-6	5th	5.0
4-15	Min.	L	6-8		11	10	Wells	Moehler	Aguilera	2-7	5th	5.5
4-16	N.Y.	W	8-1		5	7	Thompson	Hernandez		3-7	5th	5.0
4-17	N.Y.	W	3-1		10	6	Anderson	Nelson	Jones	4-7	5th	4.5
4-18	N.Y.	W	5-1		9	6	Mlicki	Mendoza		5-7	T3rd	4.5
4-20	Bos.	L	0-1		3	3	Martinez	Weaver	Lowe	5-8	4th	5.5
4-21	Bos.	W	9-2		15	8	Moehler	Wakefield		6-8	4th	5.5
4-22	Bos.	W	1-0		3	2	Thompson	Portugal	Jones	7-8	3rd	4.5
4-23	At Chi.	L	0-5		5	9	Sirotka	Blair		7-9	3rd	5.5
4-24	At Chi.	L	1-3		6	4	Navarro	Mlicki	Howry	7-10	3rd	5.5
4-25	At Chi.	W	9-4		12	6	Weaver	Baldwin		8-10	3rd	4.5
4-26	At Sea.	W	7-0		15	7	Moehler	Moyer		9-10	3rd	4.5
4-27	At Sea.	W	5-1		10	9	Thompson	Hinchliffe		10-10	3rd	4.5
4-28	At Sea.	L	6-8		8	10	Garcia	Blair		10-11	3rd	5.5
4-29	At Sea.	L	6-22		15	19	Cloude	Nitkowski		10-12	3rd	6.5
4-30	At T.B.	W	7-5		12	7	Weaver	Arrojo	Jones	11-12	3rd	5.5
5-1	At T.B.	L	3-4		4	7	Witt	Moehler	Hernandez	11-13	3rd	6.5
5-2	At T.B.	W	8-2		12	10	Thompson	Santana		12-13	3rd	5.5
5-3	At T.B.	L	6-14		12	12	Yan	Blair		12-14	3rd	6.5
5-4	Ana.	W	3-1		9	8	Brocail	Holtz	Jones	13-14	3rd	6.0
5-5	Ana.	L	1-4		3	6	Sparks	Weaver	Percival	13-15	3rd	6.0
5-6	Ana.	W	4-2		10	7	Florie	Finley	Jones	14-15	3rd	6.0
5-7	Bal.	L	4-9		10	12	Mussina	Thompson		14-16	3rd	7.0
5-8	Bal.	W	7-6		5	8	Blair	Kamieniecki	Jones	15-16	3rd	6.0
5-9	Bal.	L	0-5		5	7	Erickson	Mlicki		15-17	4th	7.0
5-11	Oak.	L	2-6		6	10	Rigby	Weaver		15-18	4th	8.5
5-12	Oak.	L	1-2		4	4	Heredia	Thompson	Taylor	15-19	4th	9.5
5-14	Cle.	L	2-4		8	6	Karsay	Brocail	Shuey	15-20	4th	10.5
5-15	Cle.	L	7-12		10	12	Burba	Mlicki		15-21	4th	11.5
5-16	Cle.	W	9-3		10	7	Weaver	Wright	Kida	16-21	4th	10.5
5-18	At Tor.	L	5-7		9	8	Hentgen	Thompson	Koch	16-22	4th	12.0
5-19	At Tor.	W	7-3		11	6	Moehler	Wells		17-22	4th	12.0
5-20	At Tor.	L	0-7		7	14	Halladay	Mlicki		17-23	4th	12.5
5-21	At Cle.	W	9-6		11	10	Nitkowski	Shuey	Jones	18-23	4th	11.5
5-22	At Cle.	W	6-2		10	7	Weaver	Wright		19-23	4th	10.5
5-23	At Cle.	L	4-7		8	10	Shuey	Jones		19-24	4th	11.5
5-24	Tor.	L	6-12		10	8	Wells	Moehler		19-25	4th	11.5
5-25	Tor.	L	3-5		11	8	Halladay	Mlicki	Koch	19-26	4th	12.5
5-26	Tor.	L	5-9		7	12	Escobar	Blair	Lloyd	19-27	4th	13.5
5-27	Chi.	W	10-5		14	9	Weaver	Snyder		20-27	4th	13.0
5-28	Chi.	L	1-9		7	15	Navarro	Thompson		20-28	4th	13.0
5-29	Chi.	L	1-7		5	13	Baldwin	Moehler		20-29	4th	13.0
5-30	Chi.	W	3-2		11	9	Mlicki	Parque	Jones	21-29	4th	12.0
5-31	At Bos.	L	7-8		12	12	Wasdin	Anderson	Gordon	21-30	4th	13.0
6-1	At Bos.	L	4-5		12	9	Wasdin	Brocail	Lowe	21-31	4th	13.0
6-2	At Bos.	W	4-2		7	6	Thompson	Wakefield	Jones	22-31	4th	13.0
6-4	StL.	W	4-1		7	4	Moehler	Jimenez	Jones	23-31	4th	12.0
6-5	StL.	L	2-7		5	15	Bottenfield	Blair	Bottalico	23-32	4th	13.0
6-6	StL.	L	4-8		9	14	Croushore	Nitkowski	Aybar	23-33	4th	14.0
6-7	Pit.	W	9-4		10	8	Brunson	Schmidt		24-33	3rd	13.5
6-8	Pit.	W	11-4		15	7	Cruz	Ritchie		25-33	3rd	12.5
6-9	Pit.	L	3-15		10	17	Cordova	Moehler		25-34	4th	13.5
6-11	At StL.	W	8-2		7	10	Mlicki	Bottenfield		26-34	4th	13.0
6-12	At StL.	L	7-8	(14)	8	17	Radinsky	Blair		26-35	4th	14.0
6-13	At StL.	W	3-1	(10)	11	9	Jones	Bottalico	Brocail	27-35	3rd	14.0
6-14	Sea.	W	8-7		10	13	Kida	Cloude		28-35	3rd	13.5
6-15	Sea.	L	4-5		9	6	Rodriguez	Moehler	Mesa	28-36	3rd	14.5
6-16	Sea.	L	1-7		9	13	Moyer	Mlicki		28-37	3rd	15.5
6-17	Sea.	L	3-4		7	7	Garcia	Jones	Mesa	28-38	3rd	16.5
6-18	Oak.	W	8-3		10	3	Thompson	Oquist		29-38	3rd	15.5
6-19	Oak.	L	1-13		11	16	Hudson	Cruz		29-39	3rd	16.5
6-20	Oak.	L	5-6		6	8	Haynes	Moehler	Taylor	29-40	3rd	17.5
6-21	Oak.	W	13-11		12	13	Brocail	Rigby	Jones	30-40	3rd	17.5
6-22	At K.C.	L	2-4		8	9	Rosado	Florie	Service	30-41	3rd	17.5
6-23	At K.C.	L	1-10		5	15	Witasick	Thompson		30-42	4th	18.5

Date	Opp.	Res.	Score	(inn.*)	Hits	Opp. hits	Winning pitcher	Losing pitcher	Save	Record	Pos.	GB
6-24	At K.C.	W	6-4		9	13	Cruz	Mathews	Jones	31-42	3rd	17.5
6-25	Min.	W	2-0		6	6	Moehler	Milton		32-42	3rd	16.5
6-26	Min.	L	0-1		5	6	Mays	Mlicki	Trombley	32-43	4th	16.5
6-27	Min.	L	7-12		11	17	Hawkins	Weaver		32-44	4th	17.5
6-29	At N.Y.	L	0-3		8	6	Clemens	Thompson		32-45	4th	19.0
6-30	At N.Y.	W	8-2		11	12	Moehler	Pettitte		33-45	3rd	18.0
7-1	At N.Y.	L	0-6		3	11	Irabu	Mlicki		33-46	3rd	19.0
7-2	At Min.	L	4-11		7	13	Hawkins	Weaver		33-47	4th	19.0
7-3	At Min.	L	2-7		5	13	Lincoln	Cruz		33-48	4th	20.5
7-4	At Min.	W	15-5		19	8	Thompson	Perkins		34-48	4th	19.5
7-6	N.Y.	L	8-9	(10)	9	17	Rivera	Jones	Mendoza	34-49	4th	20.5
7-7	N.Y.	W	6-4		12	10	Mlicki	Cone	Brocail	35-49	4th	19.5
7-8	N.Y.	L	2-3		8	9	Hernandez	Nitkowski	Rivera	35-50	4th	20.5
7-9	Mil.	L	1-4		6	9	Woodard	Cruz	Wickman	35-51	4th	20.5
7-10	Mil.	W	9-3		14	6	Thompson	Abbott		36-51	3rd	20.5
7-11	Mil.	L	2-3		9	6	Nomo	Moehler	Wickman	36-52	3rd	20.5
7-15	At Hou.	L	6-8		12	9	Miller	Blair	Wagner	36-53	4th	21.5
7-16	At Hou.	L	1-2		4	8	Cabrera	Brocail		36-54	4th	21.5
7-17	At Hou.	L	2-3	(10)	9	10	Wagner	Jones		36-55	4th	21.5
7-18	At Cin.	W	9-8	(10)	9	11	Brocail	Graves	Jones	37-55	4th	20.5
7-19	At Cin.	W	7-6		11	10	Nitkowski	Sullivan	Jones	38-55	4th	19.5
7-20	At Cin.	L	2-5		7	8	Parris	Mlicki	Graves	38-56	4th	20.5
7-21	K.C.	W	10-5		12	11	Thompson	Appier		39-56	3rd	19.5
7-22	K.C.	W	9-8		8	15	Florie	Rosado	Jones	40-56	3rd	18.5
7-23	Bos.	W	14-5		15	8	Moehler	Ohka		41-56	3rd	17.5
7-24	Bos.	L	4-11		10	13	Portugal	Weaver	Lowe	41-57	3rd	17.5
7-25	Bos.	W	9-1		10	6	Mlicki	Rose		42-57	3rd	16.5
7-26	At Cle.	L	3-6		10	12	Burba	Thompson	Jackson	42-58	3rd	17.5
7-27	At Cle.	L	5-14		9	19	Nagy	Borkowski		42-59	T3rd	18.5
7-28	At Cle.	L	2-7		5	11	Gooden	Moehler		42-60	5th	19.5
7-30	At Tor.	L	2-8		6	10	Escobar	Weaver		42-61	5th	20.5
7-31	At Tor.	L	6-7		15	12	Halladay	Mlicki	Koch	42-62	5th	21.5
8-1	At Tor.	L	5-8		9	10	Hentgen	Borkowski	Koch	42-63	5th	21.5
8-2	Chi.	L	2-6		7	11	Wells	Moehler		42-64	5th	22.5
8-3	Chi.	L	6-9		9	15	Snyder	Thompson	Howry	42-65	5th	23.5
8-5	At Bal.	L	3-6		9	11	Ponson	Weaver	Timlin	42-66	5th	23.5
8-6	At Bal.	W	4-3		11	7	Mlicki	Mussina	Jones	43-66	5th	22.5
8-7	At Bal.	L	4-5		7	9	Erickson	Borkowski	Timlin	43-67	5th	23.5
8-8	At Bal.	W	5-2	(11)	8	10	Brocail	Kamieniecki	Jones	44-67	5th	22.5
8-10	At Tex.	L	3-4	(12)	11	8	Patterson	Cruz		44-68	5th	24.0
8-11	At Tex.	L	2-8		6	12	Helling	Blair		44-69	5th	25.0
8-12	At Tex.	W	3-1		8	5	Mlicki	Sele	Jones	45-69	5th	24.5
8-13	Ana.	W	8-7	(10)	9	10	Jones	Hasegawa		46-69	5th	24.5
8-14	Ana.	L	4-7		10	12	Magnante	Moehler	Percival	46-70	5th	25.5
8-15	Ana.	L	2-10		7	14	Finley	Thompson		46-71	5th	26.5
8-16	T.B.	L	1-9		8	13	Arrojo	Weaver		46-72	5th	26.5
8-17	T.B.	W	3-1		8	6	Mlicki	Witt	Jones	47-72	5th	25.5
8-18	T.B.	L	0-4		1	8	Alvarez	Borkowski	Lopez	47-73	5th	25.5
8-20	At Ana.	L	1-5		5	7	Finley	Moehler		47-74	5th	27.0
8-21	At Ana.	W	5-0		9	4	Weaver	Washburn		48-74	5th	27.0
8-22	At Ana.	W	12-3		17	8	Mlicki	Sparks		49-74	T4th	27.0
8-23	At Ana.	L	5-6		11	9	Percival	Brocail		49-75	T4th	27.0
8-24	At Sea.	L	0-5		6	7	Garcia	Blair		49-76	T4th	27.0
8-25	At Sea.	L	2-3		9	7	Halama	Moehler	Mesa	49-77	5th	28.0
8-27	Bal.	W	5-4		11	5	Weaver	Reyes	Jones	50-77	5th	28.0
8-28	Bal.	W	4-3		7	10	Mlicki	Erickson	Jones	51-77	4th	28.0
8-29	Bal.	L	4-11		7	13	Johnson	Nitkowski		51-78	4th	28.0
8-30	Tex.	W	1-0		10	3	Moehler	Loaiza		52-78	4th	28.0
8-31	Tex.	W	14-6		16	11	Cordero	Kolb		53-78	4th	28.0
9-1	Tex.	L	7-14		12	15	Helling	Weaver	Wetteland	53-79	4th	29.0
9-2	Tex.	W	8-7		15	13	Mlicki	Zimmerman	Jones	54-79	4th	29.0
9-3	At Oak.	L	4-7		9	9	Appier	Cruz	Isringhausen	54-80	4th	30.0
9-4	At Oak.	L	1-2		4	9	Hudson	Cordero		54-81	4th	30.0
9-5	At Oak.	W	5-4		10	8	Blair	Haynes	Jones	55-81	4th	30.0
9-6	At Oak.	W	9-7		13	13	Borkowski	Olivares	Jones	56-81	4th	30.0
9-8	At T.B.	W	5-1		10	7	Mlicki	Witt		57-81	4th	28.5
9-9	At T.B.	L	3-5		13	8	Arrojo	Nitkowski	Hernandez	57-82	4th	29.0
9-10	Tor.	W	7-6		12	12	Jones	Frascatore		58-82	T3rd	29.0
9-11	Tor.	L	5-9		11	11	Spoljaric	Cordero		58-83	4th	30.0
9-12	Tor.	L	3-5		8	10	Escobar	Weaver	Koch	58-84	4th	30.0
9-13	At Chi.	W	3-2		9	4	Mlicki	Snyder	Jones	59-84	T3rd	30.0
9-14	At Chi.	W	7-0		11	4	Nitkowski	Myette		60-84	3rd	29.0
9-15	At Chi.	L	1-3		3	10	Baldwin	Moehler	Foulke	60-85	3rd	29.0
9-17	At Bos.	L	3-14		8	16	Florie	Blair		60-86	3rd	28.5
9-18	At Bos.	L	1-9		7	13	Saberhagen	Weaver		60-87	3rd	29.5
9-19	At Bos.	L	3-7		5	11	Wakefield	Mlicki	Lowe	60-88	T3rd	29.5

Date	Opp.	Res.	Score	(inn.*)	Hits	Opp. hits	Winning pitcher	Losing pitcher	Save	Record	Pos.	GB
9-20	Cle.	W	4-3	(10)	9	9	Jones	Riske		61-88	T3rd	28.5
9-21	Cle.	L	1-6		4	8	Burba	Borkowski		61-89	T3rd	29.5
9-22	Cle.	L	1-9		2	16	Wright	Moehler		61-90	4th	30.5
9-23	Cle.	W	7-5		11	6	Blair	Nagy	Jones	62-90	4th	29.5
9-24	K.C.	L	3-7		7	9	Rosado	Mlicki		62-91	4th	30.5
9-25	K.C.	W	11-3		10	8	Nitkowski	Suzuki		63-91	4th	30.5
9-26	K.C.	W	6-1		8	4	Borkowski	Stein		64-91	3rd	30.5
9-27	K.C.	W	8-2		11	11	Moehler	Suppan		65-91	3rd	30.0
9-28	At Min.	W	7-4		9	9	Anderson	Trombley	Jones	66-91	3rd	30.0
9-29	At Min.	W	6-3		7	9	Mlicki	Mays	Jones	67-91	3rd	29.0
9-30	At Min.	W	6-5		14	8	Cordero	Wells	Jones	68-91	3rd	29.0
10-1	At K.C.	L	5-9		14	9	Suzuki	Borkowski		68-92	3rd	29.0
10-2	At K.C.	W	4-3	(10)	10	8	Weaver	Suppan	Jones	69-92	3rd	28.0

Monthly records: April (11-12), May (10-18), June (12-15), July (9-17), August (11-16), September (15-13), October (1-1).
*Innings, if other than nine. † First game of a doubleheader. ‡ Second game of a doubleheader.

HIGHLIGHTS

High point: The Tigers closed their 88-season run at Tiger Stadium with an 8-2 victory over the Royals on September 27. Rookie Rob Fick hit a game-clinching grand slam off the right field roof—the final hit at the stadium. In an emotional postgame ceremony, players from past teams ran to their old positions in uniform.
Low point: The team fell to a 49-77 record with a season-defining 3-2 loss in Seattle on August 25. Kimera Bartee hit an inning-opening triple in that game, but he was tagged out on a one-hopper to third baseman Russ Davis, who then threw to first for a double play. That turn of events summed up the team's penchant for finding ways to fail.
Turning point: The club had rallied to a 15-16 mark after a 1-6 start, but a 5-0 defeat to the Orioles on May 9 began a five-game losing streak. The Tigers' slump reached 15 losses in 21 games, and they permanently fell out of contention.
Most valuable player: Catcher Brad Ausmus, the team's only All-Star Game participant, had a solid year offensively and defensively after being reacquired from Houston. He hit .275 and was one of the club's better contact hitters, even batting leadoff occasionally. Defensively, Ausmus helped keep opposing running games in check and drew raves from pitchers for the rapport he developed with them.
Most valuable pitcher: Righthander Dave Mlicki paid dividends after being obtained from Los Angeles, compiling a staff-high 14 victories that included wins in eight consecutive starts. He posted a 2.88 ERA during the streak and provided a much-needed anchor in his rotation.
Most improved player: Shortstop Deivi Cruz. Aided by a weight-transfer batting tip by coach Alan Trammell, Cruz emerged from the doldrums and finished at .284 with 13 homers and 58 RBIs—all career highs. Three weeks into May, Cruz was hitting .223 with no homers and three RBIs.
Most pleasant surprise: Veteran outfielder Luis Polonia, who had played the previous two years in the Mexican League. Recalled from Class AAA Toledo in late May, he provided a spark at leadoff. Polonia hit in the .400 range for several

weeks and finished at .324 with a career-high 10 homers in 87 games.
Biggest disappointment: Outfielder Bobby Higginson, who never got going and seemed to lose his trademark aggressiveness. Entering the season with a career .284 average, he slipped to .239 and hit only 12 homers with 46 RBIs.
Key injuries: Higginson missed a month with a toe injury. Righthander Seth Greisinger, a certain starter and perhaps the team's future ace, missed the entire season after surgery on his elbow. Lefthanded reliever Sean Runyan, who pitched in a club-record-tying 88 games in 1998, developed a career-threatening shoulder injury and made only 12 appearances for the Tigers. Lefthander Justin Thompson made his last start on August 15 before going on the D.L. with shoulder and neck injuries.
Notable: The Tigers experienced their sixth consecutive losing season. ... Third baseman Dean Palmer, signed as a free agent in November 1998, put up strong numbers (38 homers, 100 RBIs). ... The club went the entire decade without a Gold Glove winner.

—REID CREAGER

RECORDS

1999 regular-season record: 69-92 (3rd in A.L. Central); 38-43 at home; 31-49 on road; 21-34 vs. East; 23-25 vs. A.L. Central; 17-23 vs. West; 8-10 vs. N.L.; 15-14 vs. lefthanded starters; 54-78 vs. righthanded starters; 57-76 on grass; 12-16 on turf; 26-30 in daytime; 43-62 at night; 19-22 in one-run games; 5-5 in extra-inning games; 0-0-0 in doubleheaders.
Team record past five years: 326-465 (.412, ranks 13th in league in that span).

TEAM LEADERS

Batting average: Deivi Cruz (.284).
At-bats: Dean Palmer (560).
Runs: Dean Palmer (92).
Hits: Tony Clark (150).
Total Bases: Dean Palmer (290).
Doubles: Deivi Cruz (35).
Triples: Luis Polonia (8).
Home runs: Dean Palmer (38).
Runs batted in: Dean Palmer (100).

Stolen bases: Juan Encarnacion (33).
Slugging percentage: Dean Palmer (.518).
On-base percentage: Brad Ausmus (.365).
Wins: Dave Mlicki (14).
Earned-run average: Dave Mlicki (4.60).
Complete games: Dave Mlicki, Brian Moehler (2).
Shutouts: Brian Moehler (2).
Saves: Todd Jones (30).
Innings pitched: Brian Moehler (196.1).
Strikeouts: Dave Mlicki (119).

GAMES BY POSITION

Catcher: Brad Ausmus 127, Bill Haselman 39, Robert Fick 4.
First base: Tony Clark 132, Frank Catalanotto 32, Jason Wood 5, Gregg Jefferies 3.
Second base: Damion Easley 147, Frank Catalanotto 32, Gregg Jefferies 2, Jason Wood 1, Luis Garcia 1, Jose Macias 1.
Third base: Dean Palmer 141, Frank Catalanotto 21, Jason Wood 9, Gabe Alvarez 2.
Shortstop: Deivi Cruz 155, Damion Easley 19, Jason Wood 9, Luis Garcia 7.
Outfield: Juan Encarnacion 131, Gabe Kapler 128, Bob Higginson 88, Karim Garcia 81, Luis Polonia 40, Kimera Bartee 38, Brian L. Hunter 18, Gabe Alvarez 5, Gregg Jefferies 2.
Designated hitter: Gregg Jefferies 45, Luis Polonia 43, Bob Higginson 17, Gabe Alvarez 12, Tony Clark 11, Dean Palmer 9, Bill Haselman 9, Frank Catalanotto 9, Robert Fick 8, Karim Garcia 7, Gabe Kapler 2, C.J. Nitkowski 1, Kimera Bartee 1, Jason Wood 1.

TOP DRAFT CHOICES

1. **Eric Munson**, C, U. of Southern Calif.
2. None
3. **Neil Jenkins**, 3B, Dwyer H.S., Jupiter, Fla.
4. **Cody Ross**, OF, Carlsbad (N.M.) H.S.
5. **Dayle Campbell**, OF, Los Angeles Pierce J.C.
6. **Brant Ust**, 3B, U. of Notre Dame
7. **Tim Kalita**, LHP, U. of Notre Dame
8. **Anthony Ware**, 3B, Hamilton H.S., Los Angeles
9. **Casey Rowe**, RHP, Fresno State Univ.
10. **Jerrod Fuell**, RHP, Palo Verde H.S., Tucson, Ariz.

KANSAS CITY ROYALS
AMERICAN LEAGUE CENTRAL DIVISION

2000 Royals Schedule

Home games shaded. *—All-Star Game at Turner Field (Atlanta).

March

SUN	MON	TUE	WED	THU	FRI	SAT
26	27	28	29	30	31	

April

SUN	MON	TUE	WED	THU	FRI	SAT
						1
2	3 TOR	4 TOR	5 TOR	6 TOR	7 MIN	8 MIN
9 MIN	10 MIN	11 BAL	12 BAL	13 BAL	14 NYY	15 NYY
16 NYY	17	18 MIN	19 MIN	20 MIN	21 SEA	22 SEA
23 SEA	24	25 TB	26 TB	27	28 SEA	29 SEA
30 SEA						

May

SUN	MON	TUE	WED	THU	FRI	SAT
	1	2 OAK	3 OAK	4	5 CWS	6 CWS
7 CWS	8 DET	9 DET	10 DET	11 CLE	12 CLE	13 CLE
14 CLE	15 OAK	16 OAK	17 OAK	18	19 ANA	20 ANA
21 ANA	22	23 TEX	24 TEX	25 TEX	26 ANA	27 ANA
28 ANA	29	30 BOS	31 BOS			

June

SUN	MON	TUE	WED	THU	FRI	SAT
				1 BOS	2 PIT	3 PIT
4 PIT	5 STL	6 STL	7 STL	8	9 PIT	10 PIT
11 PIT	12 SEA	13 SEA	14 SEA	15	16 OAK	17 OAK
18 OAK	19	20 ANA	21 ANA	22 ANA	23 OAK	24 OAK
25 OAK	26	27 CLE	28 CLE	29 CLE	30 DET	

July

SUN	MON	TUE	WED	THU	FRI	SAT
						1 DET
2 DET	3 CWS	4 CWS	5 CWS	6	7 HOU	8 HOU
9 HOU	10	11	* 12	13 MIL	14 MIL	15 MIL
16 CUB	17 CUB	18 CUB	19 CLE	20 CLE	21 DET	22 DET
23 DET	24 CWS	25 CWS	26 CWS	27 TB	28 TB	29 TB
30 TB	31					

August

SUN	MON	TUE	WED	THU	FRI	SAT
		1 NYY	2 NYY	3 NYY	4 BOS	5 BOS
6 BOS	7 TOR	8 TOR	9 TOR	10 TOR	11 BAL	12 BAL
13 BAL	14 MIN	15 MIN	16 MIN	17 MIN	18 BAL	19 BAL
20 BAL	21 BAL	22 TOR	23 TOR	24 BOS	25 BOS	26 BOS
27 BOS	28	29 MIN	30 MIN	31 TB		

September

SUN	MON	TUE	WED	THU	FRI	SAT
					1 TB	2 TB
3 TB	4 NYY	5 NYY	6 NYY	7 NYY	8 TEX	9 TEX
10 TEX	11 SEA	12 SEA	13 SEA	14 TEX	15 TEX	16 TEX
17 TEX	18	19 ANA	20 ANA	21 ANA	22 ANA	23 ANA
24 CLE	25	26 DET	27 DET	28 DET	29 CWS	30 CWS

October

SUN	MON	TUE	WED	THU	FRI	SAT
1 CWS	2	3	4	5	6	7

2000 SEASON
CLUB DIRECTORY

Board of directors
David Glass, Richard Green, Mike Herman, Julia I. Kauffman, Janice Kreamer, Joseph McGuff, Louis Smith

Chairman of the board & CEO
David Glass

President
Mike Herman

Exec. v.p. and general manager
Herk Robinson

Sr. v.p., business operations & admin.
Art Chaudry

V.p. and asst. g.m. baseball operations
Allard Baird

Vice president, baseball operations
George Brett

V.p., marketing and communications
Mike Levy

V.p., finance & information systems
Dale Rohr

General counsel and assistant secretary
Jay Newcom

Senior director, minor league operations
Bob Hegman

Senior director, scouting
Terry Wetzel

Asst. general manager, baseball admin.
Muzzy Jackson

Sr. special assistant to general manager
Art Stewart

Director, team travel
David Witty

Minor league operations coordinator
Shaun McGinn

Scouting operations coordinator
Jin Wong

Sr. director, operations & administration
Jay Hinrichs

Dir., event ops. & revenue development
Chris Richardson

Director, stadium operations
Rodney Lewallen

Director, ticket operations
Christine Burgeson

Director, group sales
Michele Kammerer

Director, Royal Lancer program
Larry Sherrard

Director, season ticket services
Joe Grigoli

Senior director/controller
John Luther

Director, payroll and benefits accounting
Tom Pfannenstiel

Director, information systems
Jim Edwards

Director, marketing
Tonya Mangels

Publications/internet coordinator
Chad Rader

Senior director, communications
Jim Lachimia

Director, media relations
Steve Fink

Mgr., community rel. & special markets
Shani Tate

Media relations coordinator
Chris Stathos

Director, corporate sponsorships
Kevin Battle

Team physician
Dr. Steve Joyce

Athletic trainer
Nick Swartz

Assistant athletic trainer
Lee Kuntz

Strength & conditioning coordinator
Tim Maxey

Equipment manager
Mike Burkhalter

Visiting clubhouse manager
Chuck Hawke

Major league scout
Gail Henley

Advance scout
Ron Clark

Special assignment scout
John Wathan

National cross-checkers
Pat Jones, Jeff McKay, Earl Winn

Latin American scouting coordinator
Albert Gonzalez

Territorial scouts
Frank Baez, Bob Bishop, Jason Bryans, Albert Gonzalez, Dave Herrera, Keith Hughes, Phil Huttman, Gary Johnson, Cliff Pastornicky, Bill Price, Johnny Ramos, Sean Rooney, Chet Sergo, Greg Smith, Craig Struss, Gerald Turner, Junior Vizcaino, Mark Willoughby, Dennis Woody

MINOR LEAGUE AFFILIATES

Class	Team	League	Manager
AAA	Omaha	Pacific Coast	John Mizerock
AA	Wichita	Texas	Keith Bodie
A	Wilmington	Carolina	Jeff Garber
A	Charleston (WV)	Midwest	Joe Szekely
A	Spokane	Northwest	Tom Poquette
Rookie	Gulf Coast Royals	Gulf Coast	Ron Karkovice

BROADCAST INFORMATION

Radio: KMBZ-AM (980).
TV: KMBC (Channel 9), KCWB (Channel 29).
Cable TV: Fox Sports Midwest.

SPRING TRAINING

Ballpark (city): Baseball City Stadium (Davenport, Fla.).
Ticket information: 941-424-2500.

SPRING TRAINING ROSTER

Manager—Tony Muser (40).
Coaches—Tom Burgmeier (39), Rich Dauer (25), Lamar Johnson (23), Jamie Quirk (9), Brent Strom, Frank White (20).

No.	PITCHERS	B/T	Ht./Wt.	Born	1999 clubs
58	Byrdak, Tim	L/L	5-11/180	10-31-73	Omaha, Kansas City
53	Carter, Lance	R/R	6-1/190	12-18-74	Wichita, Kansas City
	D'Amico, Jeff	R/R	6-3/200	11-9-74	Midland, Vancouver, Omaha
49	Fussell, Chris	R/R	6-2/200	5-19-76	Omaha, Kansas City
	Green, Tyler	R/R	6-5/205	2-18-70	Scranton/Wilkes-Barre
	Lamber, Justin	R/L	6-0/210	5-22-76	Wilmington
	Lundquist, David	R/R	6-2/200	6-4-73	Chicago A.L., Charlotte
45	Moreno, Orber	R/R	6-2/190	4-27-77	Omaha, Kansas City, Gulf Coast Royals
57	Murray, Dan	R/R	6-1/195	11-21-73	Norfolk, New York N.L., Kansas City
	Rakers, Jason	R/R	6-2/200	6-29-73	Buffalo, Cleveland
54	Reichert, Dan	R/R	6-3/175	7-12-76	Omaha, Kansas City
30	Rigby, Brad	R/R	6-6/215	5-14-73	Oakland, Vancouver, Kansas City
50	Rosado, Jose	L/L	6-0/185	11-9-74	Kansas City
46	Santiago, Jose	R/R	6-3/215	11-5-74	Kansas City, Gulf Coast Royals, Wichita, Omaha
	Spradlin, Jerry	B/R	6-7/245	6-14-67	Cleveland, San Francisco
41	Stein, Blake	R/R	6-7/240	8-3-73	Vancouver, Oakland, Kansas City
37	Suppan, Jeff	R/R	6-2/210	1-2-75	Kansas City
55	Suzuki, Mac	R/R	6-3/205	5-31-75	Seattle, Kansas City
	Walker, Jamie	L/L	6-2/190	7-1-71	Omaha, Gulf Coast Royals
34	Wallace, Derek	R/R	6-3/215	9-1-71	Norfolk, Kansas City
47	Witasick, Jay	R/R	6-4/235	8-28-72	Kansas City

No.	CATCHERS	B/T	Ht./Wt.	Born	1999 clubs
13	Fasano, Sal	R/R	6-2/230	8-10-71	Omaha, Kansas City
	Johnson, Brian	R/R	6-2/210	1-8-68	Cincinnati, Indianapolis

No.	INFIELDERS	B/T	Ht./Wt.	Born	1999 clubs
3	Febles, Carlos	R/R	5-11/185	5-24-76	Kansas City
7	Giambi, Jeremy	L/L	6-0/200	9-30-74	Kansas City, Omaha
32	Holbert, Ray	R/R	6-0/185	9-25-70	Omaha, Gulf Coast Royals, Kansas City
19	Randa, Joe	R/R	5-11/190	12-18-69	Kansas City
	Reboulet, Jeff	R/R	6-0/175	4-30-64	Baltimore
1	Sanchez, Rey	R/R	5-9/175	10-5-67	Kansas City
29	Sweeney, Mike	R/R	6-2/215	7-22-73	Kansas City

No.	OUTFIELDERS	B/T	Ht./Wt.	Born	1999 clubs
36	Beltran, Carlos	B/R	6-1/190	4-24-77	Kansas City
27	Brown, Dee	L/R	6-0/215	3-27-78	Wilmington, Wichita, Kansas City
18	Damon, Johnny	L/L	6-2/190	11-5-73	Kansas City
	Dunwoody, Todd	L/L	6-1/195	4-11-75	Florida, Calgary
24	Dye, Jermaine	R/R	6-5/220	1-28-74	Kansas City
38	Pose, Scott	L/R	5-11/190	2-11-67	Kansas City
52	Quinn, Mark	R/R	6-1/195	5-21-74	Omaha, Kansas City
	Tomlinson, Goef	L/L	6-1/190	8-19-76	Wichita

BALLPARK INFORMATION

Ballpark (capacity, surface)
Kauffman Stadium (40,529, grass)

Address
P.O. Box 419969
Kansas City, MO 64141-6969

Business phone
816-921-8000

Ticket information
816-921-8000

Ticket prices
$17 (club box)
$15 (field box)
$13 (plaza reserved)
$12 (view upper box)
$11 (view upper reserved)
$7 (general admission)
$5.50 (Royal nights)

Field dimensions (from home plate)
To left field at foul line, 330 feet
To center field, 400 feet
To right field at foul line, 330 feet

First game played
April 10, 1973 (Royals 12, Rangers 1)

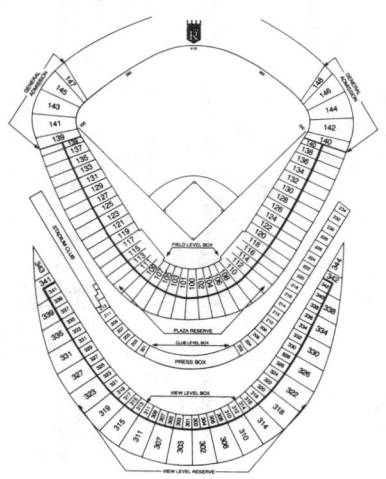

1999 REVIEW
DAY BY DAY

Date	Opp.	Res.	Score	(inn.*)	Hits	Opp. hits	Winning pitcher	Losing pitcher	Save	Record	Pos.	GB
4-7	Bos.	L	0-6		4	13	Saberhagen	Rosado		0-2	5th	1.5
4-8	Bos.	L	1-4		4	10	Wakefield	Suppan	Gordon	0-3	5th	2.0
4-9	At Chi.	W	10-5		13	9	Barber	Sirotka		1-3	T4th	2.0
4-10	At Chi.	W	9-4		15	7	Pittsley	Navarro	Service	2-3	T2nd	2.0
4-11	At Chi.	W	3-1		8	5	Appier	Baldwin	Montgomery	3-3	2nd	2.0
4-12	At Cle.	L	2-5	(10)	8	11	Shuey	Santiago		3-4	T2nd	3.0
4-14	At Cle.	L	4-11		10	14	Colon	Suppan		3-5	T2nd	4.0
4-16	Chi.	W	7-2		8	9	Appier	Sirotka		4-5	T2nd	3.5
4-17	Chi.	L	5-6		7	11	Lowe	Montgomery	Howry	4-6	T3rd	4.0
4-18	Chi.	L	5-7		11	12	Baldwin	Barber	Howry	4-7	5th	5.0
4-19	Min.	L	4-6		8	11	Hawkins	Suppan	Aguilera	4-8	5th	5.5
4-20	Min.	L	7-8	(13)	12	14	Aguilera	Witasick		4-9	5th	6.5
4-21	Min.	W	3-2	(10)	9	7	Mathews	Guardado		5-9	5th	6.5
4-23	Ana.	L	2-4		4	6	Hasegawa	Montgomery	Percival	5-10	5th	7.0
4-24	Ana.	W	4-3		8	6	Santiago	Hasegawa		6-10	5th	6.0
4-27	At Bal.	L	4-8		10	12	Mussina	Appier	Timlin	6-11	5th	7.0
4-28	At Bal.	W	8-2		10	5	Rosado	Guzman		7-11	5th	7.0
4-29	At Bal.	W	15-5		15	7	Suppan	Erickson	Santiago	8-11	4th	7.0
4-30	N.Y.	W	13-6		15	12	Morman	Pettitte		9-11	4th	6.0
5-1	N.Y.	L	4-8		7	13	Cone	Pittsley		9-12	4th	7.0
5-2	N.Y.	L	8-9		14	14	Grimsley	Santiago	Rivera	9-13	4th	7.0
5-3	N.Y.	W	9-3		8	7	Service	Hernandez		10-13	4th	7.0
5-4	At T.B.	W	5-3		7	11	Mathews	Hernandez	Montgomery	11-13	4th	6.5
5-5	At T.B.	L	7-10		9	17	White	Witasick	Hernandez	11-14	4th	6.5
5-6	At T.B.	L	4-5		11	8	Aldred	Morman	Hernandez	11-15	4th	7.5
5-7	At Min.	W	5-1		9	7	Appier	Milton		12-15	4th	7.5
5-8	At Min.	W	6-2		11	5	Rosado	Perkins	Santiago	13-15	4th	6.5
5-9	At Min.	W	7-2		9	9	Suppan	Lincoln		14-15	3rd	6.5
5-10	At Min.	W	8-4		14	8	Witasick	Hawkins		15-15	3rd	6.5
5-11	Tor.	L	2-8		10	14	Escobar	Pittsley		15-16	3rd	7.5
5-12	Tor.	W	7-1		11	3	Appier	Carpenter		16-16	3rd	7.5
5-13	Tor.	L	2-8		10	13	Hentgen	Rosado		16-17	3rd	8.0
5-14	At Sea.	W	12-7		19	10	Service	Fassero		17-17	3rd	8.0
5-15	At Sea.	W	11-10		17	8	Santiago	Paniagua	Montgomery	18-17	3rd	8.0
5-16	At Sea.	L	1-5		9	9	Moyer	Fussell		18-18	3rd	8.0
5-18	Oak.	W	13-3		17	6	Appier	Heredia		19-18	2nd	8.5
5-19	Oak.	W	14-3		13	6	Rosado	Candiotti	Mathews	20-18	2nd	8.5
5-20	Oak.	W	7-1		9	5	Suppan	Oquist		21-18	2nd	8.0
5-21	Sea.	L	2-5		11	12	Moyer	Witasick		21-19	2nd	8.0
5-22	Sea.	L	4-7		11	12	Carmona	Fussell	Mesa	21-20	2nd	8.0
5-23	Sea.	W	5-4		11	9	Whisenant	Paniagua	Montgomery	22-20	2nd	8.0
5-25	At Oak.	L	3-5		5	7	Oquist	Rosado	Jones	22-21	2nd	8.5
5-26	At Oak.	L	1-3		5	5	Haynes	Suppan	Taylor	22-22	2nd	9.5
5-27	At Oak.	L	1-6		6	8	Rogers	Witasick		22-23	2nd	10.0
5-28	At Ana.	W	11-4		12	10	Appier	Finley		23-23	2nd	9.0
5-29	At Ana.	L	3-4		6	7	Sparks	Fussell	Percival	23-24	2nd	9.0
5-30	At Ana.	L	3-4		6	7	Olivares	Rosado	Percival	23-25	2nd	9.0
5-31	At Tex.	L	3-4	(10)	9	7	Crabtree	Santiago		23-26	2nd	10.0
6-1	At Tex.	L	1-3		3	6	Zimmerman	Whisenant	Wetteland	23-27	3rd	10.0
6-2	At Tex.	L	4-7		10	6	Sele	Appier	Wetteland	23-28	3rd	11.0
6-5†	Cin.	L	4-9		9	13	Parris	Rosado		23-29		
6-5‡	Cin.	L	4-7	(10)	7	13	Williamson	Montgomery		23-30	3rd	12.0
6-6	Cin.	L	3-14		9	22	Sullivan	Witasick		23-31	3rd	13.0
6-7	StL.	L	5-7		7	12	Slocumb	Appier	Bottalico	23-32	4th	13.5
6-8	StL.	W	11-10		15	14	Service	Oliver	Montgomery	24-32	4th	12.5
6-9	StL.	W	17-13		19	18	Whisenant	Radinsky		25-32	4th	12.5
6-11	At Pit.	W	10-3		9	8	Rosado	Benson		26-32	3rd	12.0
6-12	At Pit.	L	8-9		13	17	Christiansen	Whisenant		26-33	3rd	13.0
6-13	At Pit.	L	4-8		9	8	Schmidt	Whisenant	Williams	26-34	4th	14.0
6-14	At Bal.	L	1-7		9	12	Erickson	Appier		26-35	4th	14.5
6-15	At Bal.	L	5-6	(10)	11	13	Timlin	Service		26-36	4th	15.5
6-16	At Bal.	L	1-2		9	7	Ponson	Rosado		26-37	4th	16.5
6-18	At Tor.	W	6-5		10	12	Witasick	Hentgen	Whisenant	27-37	4th	16.0
6-19	At Tor.	L	0-7		3	10	Halladay	Appier		27-38	4th	17.0
6-20	At Tor.	L	1-2		4	5	Wells	Service		27-39	4th	18.0
6-21	At Tor.	L	4-11		12	13	Hamilton	Fussell		27-40	4th	19.0
6-22	Det.	W	4-2		9	8	Rosado	Florie	Service	28-40	4th	18.0
6-23	Det.	W	10-1		15	5	Witasick	Thompson		29-40	3rd	18.0
6-24	Det.	L	4-6		13	9	Cruz	Mathews	Jones	29-41	4th	18.0
6-25	Cle.	W	8-2		12	6	Suppan	Wright		30-41	4th	17.0
6-26	Cle.	W	11-7		8	6	Montgomery	Rincon		31-41	3rd	16.0

Date	Opp.	Res.	Score	(inn.*)	Hits	Opp. hits	Winning pitcher	Losing pitcher	Save	Record	Pos.	GB
6-27	Cle.	L	5-6		13	9	Reed	Byrdak	Jackson	31-42	3rd	17.0
6-28	Cle.	L	1-6		7	12	Nagy	Witasick		31-43	4th	18.0
6-29	Chi.	W	7-4		11	10	Appier	Navarro	Service	32-43	3rd	18.0
6-30	Chi.	L	9-10	(10)	14	16	Howry	Service		32-44	4th	18.0
7-1	Chi.	L	2-6		7	8	Baldwin	Pisciotta		32-45	4th	19.0
7-2	At Cle.	W	9-7	(10)	12	8	Whisenant	Shuey		33-45	3rd	18.0
7-3†	At Cle.	L	8-9		10	11	Candiotti	Pisciotta	Jackson	33-46		
7-3‡	At Cle.	L	5-9		10	10	Langston	Wengert	Jackson	33-47	3rd	20.0
7-4	At Cle.	W	10-9		13	12	Appier	Burba	Byrdak	34-47	3rd	19.0
7-6	At Chi.	W	8-7	(10)	14	16	Whisenant	Foulke		35-47	3rd	19.0
7-7	At Chi.	L	1-7		10	10	Parque	Suzuki		35-48	3rd	19.0
7-8	At Chi.	L	5-6		10	10	Foulke	Byrdak		35-49	3rd	20.0
7-9	Hou.	L	5-6		12	9	Cabrera	Montgomery	Holt	35-50	3rd	20.0
7-10	Hou.	L	2-3		10	10	Hampton	Appier	Wagner	35-51	4th	21.0
7-11	Hou.	L	3-7		9	8	Lima	Suppan	Powell	35-52	4th	21.0
7-16†	At Mil.	L	0-2		4	9	Woodard	Appier	Wickman	35-53		
7-16‡	At Mil.	W	12-10		15	13	Ray	Pittsley	Service	36-53	3rd	21.0
7-17	At Mil.	L	3-11		7	17	Nomo	Rosado		36-54	3rd	21.0
7-18	At Chi. (NL)	W	5-4		8	11	Suppan	Tapani	Service	37-54	3rd	20.0
7-19	At Chi. (NL)	W	10-2		13	6	Witasick	Trachsel		38-54	3rd	19.0
7-20	At Chi. (NL)	L	7-8		14	15	Sanders	Barber	Adams	38-55	3rd	20.0
7-21	At Det.	L	5-10		11	12	Thompson	Appier		38-56	4th	20.0
7-22	At Det.	L	8-9		15	8	Florie	Rosado	Jones	38-57	5th	20.0
7-23	Oak.	W	12-7		15	10	Morman	Haynes	Barber	39-57	5th	19.0
7-24	Oak.	L	2-12		11	9	Oquist	Witasick		39-58	5th	19.0
7-25	Oak.	W	13-11	(10)	19	10	Service	Harville		40-58	5th	19.0
7-27	Sea.	W	9-7		15	15	Appier	Fassero	Service	41-58	T3rd	18.5
7-28	Sea.	W	5-3		9	8	Rosado	Garcia	Service	42-58	T3rd	18.5
7-29	Sea.	L	4-8		8	15	Halama	Suppan		42-59	4th	19.0
7-30	At Tex.	L	2-9		9	14	Loaiza	Witasick		42-60	4th	20.0
7-31	At Tex.	W	12-8		19	13	Reichert	Munoz	Service	43-60	4th	20.0
8-1	At Tex.	L	5-12		10	16	Sele	Barber		43-61	4th	20.0
8-2	At Ana.	W	12-4		17	11	Rosado	McDowell		44-61	4th	20.0
8-3	At Ana.	W	7-0		10	5	Suppan	Fyhrie		45-61	3rd	20.0
8-4	At Ana.	L	3-4		6	10	Hill	Witasick	Percival	45-62	3rd	20.0
8-6	Min.	L	8-9		14	17	Miller	Service	Trombley	45-63	4th	20.0
8-7	Min.	L	5-6		9	8	Wells	Rigby	Trombley	45-64	4th	21.0
8-8	Min.	L	3-7		7	11	Hawkins	Rigby	Carrasco	45-65	4th	21.0
8-9	Bos.	W	5-2		9	4	Suppan	Portugal		46-65	4th	21.0
8-10	Bos.	L	6-9	(10)	13	16	Wakefield	Whisenant	Garces	46-66	4th	22.0
8-11	Bos.	L	3-9		5	12	Saberhagen	Rosado		46-67	4th	23.0
8-12	T.B.	L	6-7		11	12	Witt	Reichert	Hernandez	46-68	4th	23.5
8-13	T.B.	W	2-1		10	6	Service	Yan		47-68	4th	23.5
8-14	T.B.	L	4-11		9	13	Rupe	Suppan		47-69	4th	24.5
8-15	T.B.	L	3-5		5	14	Eiland	Suzuki	Hernandez	47-70	4th	25.5
8-17	At N.Y.	L	2-5		7	7	Hernandez	Rosado	Rivera	47-71	4th	25.0
8-18	At N.Y.	W	3-0		8	6	Reichert	Pettitte	Montgomery	48-71	4th	24.0
8-19	At N.Y.	W	4-1	(11)	6	5	Rigby	Grimsley	Montgomery	49-71	4th	24.0
8-20	At T.B.	L	4-5		8	8	Hernandez	Service		49-72	4th	25.0
8-21	At T.B.	L	2-8		8	10	Eiland	Witasick		49-73	4th	26.0
8-22	At T.B.	L	1-2		6	3	Arrojo	Rosado		49-74	T4th	27.0
8-23	Bal.	L	2-4		8	10	Erickson	Reichert	Timlin	49-75	T4th	27.0
8-24	Bal.	L	3-5	(10)	7	10	Kamieniecki	Wallace	Timlin	49-76	T4th	27.0
8-25	Bal.	W	8-6		14	11	Suppan	Linton	Montgomery	50-76	4th	27.0
8-26	Bal.	W	6-0		11	4	Witasick	Ponson		51-76	4th	26.5
8-27	At Min.	L	1-4		7	10	Milton	Rosado	Trombley	51-77	4th	27.5
8-28	At Min.	L	3-4	(10)	6	10	Wells	Morman		51-78	5th	28.5
8-29	At Min.	L	2-6		8	7	Hawkins	Stein	Wells	51-79	5th	28.5
8-30	At Bos.	L	1-9		5	14	Martinez	Suppan		51-80	5th	29.5
8-31	At Bos.	L	3-6		4	11	Garces	Witasick	Lowe	51-81	5th	30.5
9-1	At Bos.	L	3-4		3	6	Mercker	Rosado	Beck	51-82	5th	31.5
9-2	At Bos.	W	4-2		9	7	Suzuki	Martinez	Fussell	52-82	5th	31.5
9-3	Tor.	L	4-5		14	9	Quantrill	Morman	Koch	52-83	5th	32.5
9-4	Tor.	L	3-6		4	13	Hentgen	Suppan	Frascatore	52-84	5th	32.5
9-5	Tor.	W	6-3		11	9	Witasick	Escobar	Fussell	53-84	5th	32.5
9-7	N.Y.	W	6-3		10	13	Rosado	Cone	Montgomery	54-84	5th	32.0
9-8	N.Y.	L	5-9		15	11	Hernandez	Rusch	Rivera	54-85	5th	32.0
9-10	Tex.	W	7-3		12	11	Stein	Loaiza	Montgomery	55-85	5th	32.0
9-11	Tex.	W	9-6		13	14	Suppan	Helling	Montgomery	56-85	5th	32.0
9-12	Tex.	W	6-3		9	9	Witasick	Sele	Morman	57-85	5th	31.0
9-13	Tex.	L	4-8	(10)	9	11	Wetteland	Santiago		57-86	5th	32.0
9-14†	Ana.	L	6-8		15	12	Pote	Morman	Hasegawa	57-87		
9-14‡	Ana.	L	5-6		5	9	Hasegawa	Byrdak	Percival	57-88	5th	32.5
9-15	Ana.	L	0-1		3	7	Finley	Carter	Percival	57-89	5th	32.5
9-16	Ana.	W	7-1		12	6	Suppan	Ortiz		58-89	5th	31.5
9-17	At Oak.	W	9-3		15	7	Witasick	Hudson		59-89	5th	30.5

Date	Opp.	Res.	Score	(inn.*)	Hits	Opp. hits	Winning pitcher	Losing pitcher	Save	Record	Pos.	GB
9-18	At Oak.	L	4-8		8	13	Olivares	Rosado	Isringhausen	59-90	5th	31.5
9-19	At Oak.	L	3-12		6	12	Heredia	Fussell		59-91	5th	31.5
9-20	At Sea.	W	10-9		15	9	Santiago	Hinchliffe	Montgomery	60-91	5th	30.5
9-21	At Sea.	L	3-13		13	15	Garcia	Suppan	Rodriguez	60-92	5th	31.5
9-22	At Sea.	W	12-6		14	13	Witasick	Halama		61-92	5th	31.5
9-24	At Det.	W	7-3		9	7	Rosado	Mlicki		62-92	5th	31.0
9-25	At Det.	L	3-11		8	10	Nitkowski	Suzuki		62-93	5th	32.0
9-26	At Det.	L	1-6		4	8	Borkowski	Stein		62-94	5th	33.0
9-27	At Det.	L	2-8		11	11	Moehler	Suppan		62-95	5th	33.5
9-28	Cle.	L	1-2		3	8	Brower	Witasick	Jackson	62-96	5th	34.5
9-29	Cle.	W	5-2		9	4	Rosado	Nagy		63-96	5th	33.5
10-1	Det.	W	9-5		9	14	Suzuki	Borkowski		64-96	4th	33.0
10-2	Det.	L	3-4		8	10	Weaver	Suppan	Jones	64-97	4th	33.0

Monthly records: April (9-11), May (14-15), June (9-18), July (11-16), August (8-21), September (12-15), October (1-1).
*Innings, if other than nine. † First game of a doubleheader. ‡ Second game of a doubleheader.

HIGHLIGHTS

High point: Jeff Suppan completed a May sweep of Oakland at home with a complete- game 7-1 triumph. With the three victories, Kansas City was 21-18 and in second place in the A.L. Central.

Low point: The Royals went from 22-20 on May 23 to 23-32 on June 7. The 1-12 stretch included a nine-game losing streak. They never recovered. In a loss at Texas, the Rangers' Lee Stevens hit a game-tying, three-run home run with two out in the ninth, foreshadowing Kansas City's chronic bullpen troubles.

Turning point: Jeff King's retirement on May 24. The Royals were two games over .500 on that date before embarking on a 1-8 road swing. A solid infield experienced a drop-off, with Kansas City quickly finding out that Mike Sweeney and Jeremy Giambi were below-average first basemen. And King's power was missed.

Most valuable player: Jermaine Dye stayed healthy and blossomed into a top defensive right fielder and a legitimate power threat with 27 homers and 119 RBIs. Center fielder Carlos Beltran was a force, too, winning A.L. Rookie of the Year honors.

Most valuable pitcher: Lefthander Jose Rosado established himself as the staff ace following Kevin Appier's departure. He owned the A.L.'s fifth-best ERA (3.85) and won 10 games for the first time.

Most improved player: Sweeney put together an impressive season after nearly being traded and changing positions (moving from catcher to first). He hit 44 doubles, had 102 RBIs and batted .322.

Most pleasant surprise: Shortstop Rey Sanchez arrived with a truckload of question marks, but he combined with rookie Carlos Febles for a potent double-play combination. Plus, he hit a solid .294.

Biggest disappointment: The bullpen was a disaster, blowing more saves (30) than it recorded (29).

Key injuries: King's back ailment was one factor in his retirement. Second baseman Febles was slowed at times by shoulder injuries, and a dislocated finger put him on the D.L. for three weeks. Closer Jeff Montgomery missed nearly a month with hip tendinitis. Rookie pitcher Dan Reichert missed two months' worth of starts because of a cracked bone in his elbow. Left fielder Johnny Damon's

rib-cage injury late in the year halted his team record of consecutive games played at 305.

Notable: Beltran became the first major league rookie in 24 years to reach 100 RBIs and 100 runs. ... Sweeney tied an American League record with at least one RBI in 13 consecutive games. He also had a 25-game hitting streak. ... Dye ranked in the A.L.'s top 10 in doubles, triples, RBIs and extra-base hits and tied for the league lead with 17 outfield assists. ... Mark Quinn became the fourth player in history to hit two homers in his first big-league game, accomplishing the feat against Anaheim on September 14. ... Kansas City's .398 winning percentage was the worst in club history.

—LUCIANA CHAVEZ

RECORDS

1999 regular-season record: 64-97 (4th in A.L. Central); 33-47 at home; 31-50 on road; 16-33 vs. East; 20-28 vs. A.L. Central; 22-24 vs. West; 6-12 vs. N.L.; 15-17 vs. lefthanded starters; 49-80 vs. righthanded starters; 55-83 on grass; 9-14 on turf; 14-35 in daytime; 50-62 at night; 11-32 in one-run games; 5-10 in extra-inning games; 0-3-1 in doubleheaders.
Team record past five years: 348-440 (.442, ranks 11th in league in that span).

TEAM LEADERS

Batting average: Mike Sweeney (.322).
At-bats: Carlos Beltran (663).
Runs: Carlos Beltran (112).
Hits: Joe Randa (197).
Total Bases: Jermaine Dye (320).
Doubles: Jermaine Dye, Mike Sweeney (44).
Triples: Johnny Damon, Carlos Febles (9).
Home runs: Jermaine Dye (27).
Runs batted in: Jermaine Dye (119).
Stolen bases: Johnny Damon (36).
Slugging percentage: Jermaine Dye (.526).
On-base percentage: Mike Sweeney (.387).
Wins: Jose Rosado, Jeff Suppan (10).
Earned-run average: Jose Rosado (3.85).
Complete games: Jose Rosado (5).
Shutouts: Jeff Suppan, Jay Witasick (1).

Saves: Jeff Montgomery (12).
Innings pitched: Jeff Suppan (208.2).
Strikeouts: Jose Rosado (141).

GAMES BY POSITION

Catcher: Chad Kreuter 101, Tim Spehr 59, Sal Fasano 23, Mike Sweeney 4.
First base: Mike Sweeney 74, Larry Sutton 30, Jeremy Giambi 26, Jeff King 20, Curt Leskanic 13, Steve Scarsone 12, Joe Vitiello 10, Jed Hansen 1.
Second base: Carlos Febles 122, Jed Hansen 21, Ray Holbert 11, Steve Scarsone 9, Mendy Lopez 6, Scott Leius 1, Felix Martinez 1.
Third base: Joe Randa 156, Scott Leius 10, Jed Hansen 4, Steve Scarsone 3, Ray Holbert 1.
Shortstop: Rey Sanchez 134, Ray Holbert 22, Steve Scarsone 16, Jed Hansen 10, Scott Leius 2, Felix Martinez 1, Mendy Lopez 1.
Outfield: Jermaine Dye 157, Carlos Beltran 154, Johnny Damon 140, Scott Pose 25, Mark Quinn 15, Jeremy Giambi 5, Dermal Brown 3, Jed Hansen 2, Larry Sutton 1.
Designated hitter: Mike Sweeney 71, Jeremy Giambi 48, Scott Pose 18, Scott Leius 6, Larry Sutton 5, Johnny Damon 4, Jed Hansen 3, Steve Scarsone 3, Joe Vitiello 2, Dermal Brown 2, Carlos Beltran 2, Chad Kreuter 1, Jeff King 1, Jermaine Dye 1, Mark Quinn 1.

TOP DRAFT CHOICES

1a. **Kyle Snyder,** RHP, U. of North Carolina
1b. **Mike MacDougal,** RHP, Wake Forest University
1c. **Jay Gehrke,** RHP, Pepperdine Univ.
1d. **Jimmy Gobble,** LHP, John Battle H.S., Bristol, Va.
2a. **Brian Sanches,** RHP, Lamar Univ.
2b. **Wes Obermueller,** RHP, U. of Iowa
3. **Kiki Bengochea,** RHP, Columbus H.S., Miami
4. **Mackeel Rodgers,** SS, Jackson H.S., Miami
5. **Ken Harvey,** 1B, U. of Nebraska
6. **Ryan Baerlocher,** RHP, Lewis-Clark State (Idaho) College
7. **James McAuley,** C, U. of Louisville
8. **Eric Nelson,** 2B, Baylor University
9. **Mark Ellis,** SS, U. of Florida
10. **Jesse Kurtz-Nicholl,** LHP, Rice U.

MINNESOTA TWINS
AMERICAN LEAGUE CENTRAL DIVISION

Minnesota Twins

2000 SEASON

2000 Twins Schedule
Home games shaded. *—All-Star Game at Turner Field (Atlanta).

March
SUN	MON	TUE	WED	THU	FRI	SAT
26	27	28	29	30	31	

April
SUN	MON	TUE	WED	THU	FRI	SAT
						1
2	3 TB	4 TB	5 TB	6 TB	7 KC	8 KC
9 KC	10 KC	11 BOS	12 BOS	13 BOS	14 BAL	15 BAL
16 BAL	17	18 KC	19 KC	20 KC	21 TEX	22 TEX
23 TEX	24 NYY	25 NYY	26 NYY	27	28 OAK	29 OAK
30 OAK						

May
SUN	MON	TUE	WED	THU	FRI	SAT
	1	2 SEA	3 SEA	4 DET	5 DET	6 DET
7 DET	8 CLE	9 CLE	10 CLE	11	12 CWS	13 CWS
14 CWS	15 SEA	16 SEA	17 SEA	18 OAK	19 OAK	20 OAK
21 OAK	22	23 ANA	24 ANA	25 ANA	26 TEX	27 TEX
28 TEX	29	30 TOR	31 TOR			

June
SUN	MON	TUE	WED	THU	FRI	SAT
				1 TOR	2 CIN	3 CIN
4 CIN	5 HOU	6 HOU	7 HOU	8	9 MIL	10 MIL
11 MIL	12 OAK	13 OAK	14 OAK	15 SEA	16 SEA	17 SEA
18 SEA	19	20 TEX	21 TEX	22 TEX	23 ANA	24 ANA
25 ANA	26 ANA	27 CWS	28 CWS	29 CWS	30 CLE	

July
SUN	MON	TUE	WED	THU	FRI	SAT
						1 CLE
2 CLE	3 BOS	4 BOS	5 BOS	6 BOS	7 PIT	8 PIT
9 PIT	10	11	*12	13 CUB	14 CUB	15 CUB
16 STL	17 STL	18 STL	19 CWS	20 CWS	21 CLE	22 CLE
23 CLE	24 BOS	25 BOS	26 BOS	27 NYY	28 NYY	29 NYY
30 NYY	31 BAL					

August
SUN	MON	TUE	WED	THU	FRI	SAT
		1 BAL	2 BAL	3	4 DET	5 DET
6 DET	7 TB	8 TB	9 TB	10 TB	11 TOR	12 TOR
13 TOR	14	15 KC	16 KC	17 KC	18 TOR	19 TOR
20 TOR	21	22 TB	23 TB	24	25 DET	26 DET
27 DET	28	29 KC	30 KC	31		

September
SUN	MON	TUE	WED	THU	FRI	SAT
					1 NYY	2 NYY
3 NYY	4 BAL	5 BAL	6 BAL	7	8 SEA	9 SEA
10 SEA	11 OAK	12 OAK	13 OAK	14	15 ANA	16 ANA
17 ANA	18 TEX	19 TEX	20 TEX	21 CWS	22 CWS	23 CWS
24 CWS	25 CLE	26 CLE	27 CLE	28 CLE	29 DET	30 DET

October
SUN	MON	TUE	WED	THU	FRI	SAT
1 DET	2	3	4	5	6	7

2000 SEASON
CLUB DIRECTORY

Owner
Carl R. Pohlad
President
Jerry Bell
Chairman of executive committee
Howard Fox
Directors
Carl R. Pohlad
Eloise Pohlad
James O. Pohlad
Robert C. Pohlad
William M. Pohlad
T. Geron (Jerry) Bell
Kirby Puckett
Chris Clouser
Vice president, general manager
Terry Ryan
Vice president, asst. general manager
Bill Smith
Assistant general manager
Wayne Krivsky
Executive vice president, baseball
Kirby Puckett
Vice president, operations
Matt Hoy
Director of minor leagues
Jim Rantz
Director of scouting
Mike Radcliff
Director of baseball operations
Rob Antony
Traveling secretary
Remzi Kiratli
Manager, media relations
Sean Harlin

Club physicians
Dr. Dan Buss
Dr. VeeJay Eyunni
Dr. Tom Jetzer
Dr. John Steubs
Scouts
Kevin Bootay
Ellsworth Brown
Larry Corrigan
Cal Ermer
Marty Esposito
Vern Followell (pro scouting supervisor)
Earl Frishman (east supervisor)
Bill Harford
Deron Johnson (west supervisor)
John Leavitt
Joel Lepel
Bill Lohr
Lee MacPhail
Joe McIlvaine
Bill Mele
Gregg Miller
Bill Milos
Tim O'Neil
Hector Otero
Mark Quimuyog
Mike Ruth (midwest supervisor)
Ricky Taylor
Brad Weitzel
John Wilson
International scouts
David Kim
Jose Leon
Howard Norsetter
Yoshi Okamoto
Johnny Sierra

MINOR LEAGUE AFFILIATES

Class	Team	League	Manager
AAA	Salt Lake	Pacific Coast	Phil Roof
AA	New Britain	Eastern	John Russell
A	Fort Myers	Florida State	Jose Marzan
A	Quad City	Midwest	Stan Cliburn
Rookie	Elizabethton	Appalachian	Jeff Carter
Rookie	Gulf Coast Twins	Gulf Coast	Al Newman

BROADCAST INFORMATION

Radio: WCCO-AM (830).
TV: KMSP-TV (Channel 9).
Cable TV: Midwest SportsChannel.

SPRING TRAINING

Ballpark (city): Lee County Sports Complex (Fort Myers, Fla.).
Ticket information: 800-33-TWINS.

SPRING TRAINING ROSTER

Manager—Tom Kelly (10).
Coaches—Ron Gardenhire (35), Paul Molitor (4), Rick Stelmaszek (43), Dick Such (44), Scott Ullger (45), Jerry White (13).

No.	PITCHERS	B/T	Ht./Wt.	Born	1999 clubs
38	Bergman, Sean	R/R	6-4/225	4-11-70	Houston, New Orleans, Atlanta
58	Carrasco, Hector	R/R	6-2/220	10-22-69	Fort Myers, Salt Lake, Minnesota
59	Cressend, Jack	R/R	6-1/190	5-13-75	Trenton, New Britain
18	Guardado, Eddie	R/L	6-0/194	10-2-70	Minnesota, New Britain
32	Hawkins, LaTroy	R/R	6-5/204	12-21-72	Minnesota
51	Kinney, Matt	R/R	6-4/200	12-16-76	New Britain, Gulf Coast Twins
40	Kusiewicz, Mike	R/L	6-2/190	11-1-76	Arizona Rockies
19	Lincoln, Mike	R/R	6-2/211	4-10-75	Minnesota, Salt Lake
53	Mays, Joe	B/R	6-1/185	12-10-75	Minnesota
20	Miller, Travis	R/L	6-3/209	11-2-72	Salt Lake, Minnesota
21	Milton, Eric	L/L	6-3/220	8-4-75	Minnesota
49	Perkins, Dan	R/R	6-2/193	3-15-75	Minnesota, Salt Lake
22	Radke, Brad	R/R	6-2/188	10-27-72	Minnesota
52	Randall, Scott	R/R	6-3/190	10-29-75	Colorado Springs, Carolina
55	Redman, Mark	L/L	6-5/220	1-5-74	Salt Lake, Minnesota
33	Romero, J.C.	B/L	5-11/195	6-4-76	New Britain, Salt Lake, Minnesota
54	Ryan, Jason	B/R	6-3/195	1-23-76	West Tenn, New Britain, Salt Lake, Minnesota
23	Sampson, Benj	L/L	6-2/210	4-27-75	Minnesota, Salt Lake
57	Santana, Johan	L/L	6-0/155	3-13-79	Michigan
37	Stentz, Brent	R/R	6-5/225	7-24-75	Salt Lake, New Britain
46	Wells, Bob	R/R	6-0/200	11-1-66	Minnesota

No.	CATCHERS	B/T	Ht./Wt.	Born	1999 clubs
39	Moeller, Chad	R/R	6-3/207	2-18-75	New Britain
9	Pierzynski, A.J.	L/R	6-3/220	12-30-76	Salt Lake, Minnesota
17	Valentin, Javier	B/R	5-10/192	9-19-75	Minnesota

No.	INFIELDERS	B/T	Ht./Wt.	Born	1999 clubs
8	Coomer, Ron	R/R	5-11/206	11-18-66	Minnesota
2	Davidson, Cleatus	B/R	5-10/170	11-1-76	New Britain, Minnesota
15	Guzman, Cristian	B/R	6-0/188	3-21-78	Minnesota
7	Hocking, Denny	B/R	5-10/183	4-2-70	Minnesota
47	Koskie, Corey	L/R	6-3/217	6-28-73	Minnesota
25	Mientkiewicz, Doug	L/R	6-2/193	6-19-74	Minnesota
27	Ortiz, David	L/L	6-4/237	11-18-75	Salt Lake, Minnesota
1	Rivas, Luis	R/R	5-10/175	8-30-79	New Britain
26	Valdez, Mario	L/R	6-2/190	11-19-74	Charlotte
12	Walker, Todd	L/R	6-0/181	5-25-73	Minnesota

No.	OUTFIELDERS	B/T	Ht./Wt.	Born	1999 clubs
31	Allen, Chad	R/R	6-1/195	2-6-75	Minnesota
30	Buchanan, Brian	R/R	6-4/230	7-21-73	Salt Lake
16	Cummings, Midre	L/R	6-0/195	10-14-71	New Britain, Salt Lake, Minnesota
48	Hunter, Torii	R/R	6-2/205	7-18-75	Minnesota
11	Jones, Jacque	L/L	5-10/176	4-25-75	Salt Lake, Minnesota
50	Lawton, Matt	L/R	5-10/186	11-3-71	Minnesota, Fort Myers, Gulf Coast Twins

BALLPARK INFORMATION

Ballpark (capacity, surface)
Hubert H. Humphrey Metrodome (48,678, artificial)

Address
34 Kirby Puckett Place
Minneapolis, MN 55415

Business phone
612-375-1366

Ticket information
1-800-338-9467

Ticket prices
$19 (VIP level, lower deck club level)
$17 (lower deck club)
$14 (lower deck reserved)
$12 (upper deck club level)
$9 (g.a., lower left field)
$4 (g.a., upper deck)

Field dimensions (from home plate)
To left field at foul line, 343 feet
To center field, 408 feet
To right field at foul line, 327 feet

First game played
April 6, 1982 (Mariners 11, Twins 7)

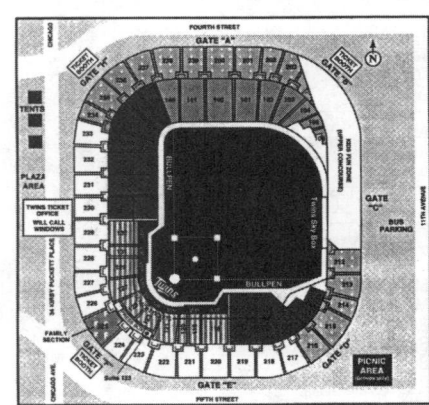

2000 SEASON Minnesota Twins

Date	Opp.	Res.	Score	(inn.*)	Hits	Opp. hits	Winning pitcher	Losing pitcher	Save	Record	Pos.	GB
4-7	Tor.	L	3-9		7	15	Wells	Lincoln	Halladay	1-1	T2nd	0.5
4-8	Tor.	W	11-9		15	13	Trombley	Hamilton	Aguilera	2-1	T1st	...
4-9	Cle.	L	5-14		8	20	Nagy	Hawkins		2-2	T2nd	1.0
4-10	Cle.	L	7-12		11	16	Karsay	Lincoln		2-3	T2nd	2.0
4-11	Cle.	L	8-9		9	17	Wright	Radke	Jackson	2-4	T3rd	3.0
4-12	At Det.	W	1-0	(12)	6	3	Aguilera	Runyan		3-4	T2nd	3.0
4-14	At Det.	L	1-7		3	13	Weaver	Hawkins		3-5	T2nd	4.0
4-15	At Det.	W	8-6		10	11	Wells	Moehler	Aguilera	4-5	2nd	3.5
4-17†	At Cle.	L	1-5		5	10	Nagy	Radke		4-6		
4-17‡	At Cle.	W	13-8	(11)	16	12	Aguilera	Jackson		5-6	2nd	3.5
4-18	At Cle.	L	2-3		9	8	Shuey	Wells	Jackson	5-7	T3rd	4.5
4-19	At K.C.	W	6-4		11	8	Hawkins	Suppan	Aguilera	6-7	2nd	4.0
4-20	At K.C.	W	8-7	(13)	14	12	Aguilera	Witasick		7-7	T2nd	4.0
4-21	At K.C.	L	2-3	(10)	7	9	Mathews	Guardado		7-8	3rd	5.0
4-22	Tex.	L	4-6		10	6	Sele	Milton	Wetteland	7-9	4th	5.0
4-23	Tex.	L	2-4		6	12	Clark	Lincoln	Wetteland	7-10	4th	6.0
4-24	Tex.	L	2-7		9	10	Morgan	Hawkins		7-11	4th	6.0
4-25	Tex.	L	5-9		10	11	Helling	Perkins		7-12	5th	6.0
4-26	Bos.	W	6-2		9	10	Radke	Wakefield	Trombley	8-12	4th	6.0
4-27	Bos.	W	6-5		9	11	Guardado	Corsi	Aguilera	9-12	4th	6.0
4-28	Bos.	L	4-9		13	11	Rapp	Lincoln		9-13	4th	7.0
4-30	At Bal.	L	1-7		4	8	Ponson	Hawkins		9-14	5th	7.5
5-1	At Bal.	W	7-2		11	8	Radke	Coppinger		10-14	5th	7.5
5-2	At Bal.	L	0-6		6	9	Mussina	Milton		10-15	5th	7.5
5-4	N.Y.	W	8-5		17	7	Lincoln	Mendoza	Aguilera	11-15	5th	7.5
5-5	N.Y.	L	3-5		5	11	Pettitte	Hawkins	Rivera	11-16	5th	7.5
5-6	N.Y.	L	3-4	(10)	7	14	Grimsley	Aguilera	Rivera	11-17	5th	8.5
5-7	K.C.	L	1-5		7	9	Appier	Milton		11-18	5th	9.5
5-8	K.C.	L	2-6		5	11	Rosado	Perkins	Santiago	11-19	5th	9.5
5-9	K.C.	L	2-7		9	9	Suppan	Lincoln		11-20	5th	10.5
5-10	K.C.	L	4-8		8	14	Witasick	Hawkins		11-21	5th	11.5
5-11	At T.B.	W	2-1		5	6	Radke	Rupe	Aguilera	12-21	5th	11.5
5-12	At T.B.	W	9-4		14	8	Milton	Arrojo	Trombley	13-21	5th	11.5
5-14	At Oak.	L	5-7		11	10	Worrell	Lincoln	Taylor	13-22	5th	12.5
5-15	At Oak.	L	5-6		10	8	Mathews	Guardado		13-23	5th	13.5
5-16	At Oak.	L	2-4		5	5	Haynes	Radke	Taylor	13-24	5th	13.5
5-17	At Sea.	L	5-15		9	16	Halama	Milton		13-25	5th	14.5
5-18	At Sea.	L	1-10		8	13	Garcia	Perkins		13-26	5th	15.5
5-19	At Sea.	L	0-7		5	11	Fassero	Lincoln		13-27	5th	16.5
5-21	Oak.	W	2-1	(15)	14	8	Miller	Jones		14-27	5th	15.5
5-22	Oak.	W	2-1	(10)	5	5	Wells	Rigby		15-27	5th	14.5
5-23	Oak.	W	8-3		15	7	Milton	Heredia		16-27	5th	14.5
5-24	Sea.	W	10-5		12	12	Perkins	Fassero		17-27	5th	13.5
5-25	Sea.	L	5-15		10	17	Halama	Rath		17-28	5th	14.5
5-26	Sea.	L	3-11		7	12	Moyer	Hawkins		17-29	5th	15.5
5-28	At Tex.	L	4-6		9	10	Sele	Radke	Wetteland	17-30	5th	15.5
5-29	At Tex.	L	3-4	(10)	12	11	Wetteland	Trombley		17-31	5th	15.5
5-30	At Tex.	L	2-3		6	9	Zimmerman	Mays	Wetteland	17-32	5th	15.5
5-31	At Ana.	W	3-2		8	10	Hawkins	Hasegawa	Trombley	18-32	5th	15.5
6-1	At Ana.	L	1-5		5	7	Hill	Lincoln		18-33	5th	15.5
6-2	At Ana.	L	1-2		5	9	Finley	Radke	Percival	18-34	5th	16.5
6-4	Hou.	L	6-7		6	14	Hampton	Trombley	Wagner	18-35	5th	16.5
6-5	Hou.	L	5-6		11	9	Elarton	Mays	Wagner	18-36	5th	17.5
6-6	Hou.	W	13-6		21	12	Sampson	Bergman		19-36	5th	17.5
6-7	Cin.	W	8-6		14	9	Lincoln	Avery	Trombley	20-36	5th	17.0
6-8	Cin.	W	5-2		12	5	Radke	Villone	Trombley	21-36	5th	16.0
6-9	Cin.	L	1-3		8	6	Tomko	Milton	Graves	21-37	5th	17.0
6-11	At Mil.	W	9-7		16	13	Wells	Weathers	Trombley	22-37	5th	16.5
6-12	At Mil.	W	8-6		15	15	Sampson	Eldred	Trombley	23-37	5th	16.5
6-14	At Bos.	L	3-4		7	11	Wasdin	Trombley		23-38	5th	17.5
6-15	At Bos.	L	2-4		6	12	Martinez	Milton	Wakefield	23-39	5th	18.5
6-16	At Bos.	L	1-5		8	7	Rose	Perkins	Guthrie	23-40	5th	19.5
6-17	At Bos.	W	8-7		11	12	Hawkins	Rapp	Trombley	24-40	5th	19.5
6-18	T.B.	W	8-5		12	10	Wells	Aldred	Trombley	25-40	5th	18.5
6-19	T.B.	L	3-4		10	10	Rekar	Radke	Hernandez	25-41	5th	19.5
6-20	T.B.	L	5-6	(11)	9	12	Newman	Trombley		25-42	5th	20.5
6-21	T.B.	L	2-3		5	9	Rupe	Radlosky	Hernandez	25-43	5th	21.5
6-22	At Chi.	L	1-6		8	12	Parque	Hawkins		25-44	5th	21.5
6-23	At Chi.	W	12-10		19	16	Sampson	Sirotka	Trombley	26-44	5th	21.5
6-24	At Chi.	L	3-5		14	13	Navarro	Radke	Howry	26-45	5th	21.5

Date	Opp.	Res.	Score	(inn.*)	Hits	Opp. hits	Winning pitcher	Losing pitcher	Save	Record	Pos.	GB
6-25	At Det.	L	0-2		6	6	Moehler	Milton		26-46	5th	21.5
6-26	At Det.	W	1-0		6	5	Mays	Mlicki	Trombley	27-46	5th	20.5
6-27	At Det.	W	12-7		17	11	Hawkins	Weaver		28-46	5th	20.5
6-29	At Cle.	L	4-5		7	9	Reed	Trombley		28-47	5th	22.0
6-30	At Cle.	W	5-3		9	5	Milton	Wright	Trombley	29-47	5th	21.0
7-1	At Cle.	L	5-7		12	9	Colon	Carrasco	Jackson	29-48	5th	22.0
7-2	Det.	W	11-4		13	7	Hawkins	Weaver		30-48	5th	21.0
7-3	Det.	W	7-2		13	5	Lincoln	Cruz		31-48	5th	21.5
7-4	Det.	L	5-15		8	19	Thompson	Perkins		31-49	5th	21.5
7-6	Cle.	L	1-3		6	8	Wright	Milton	Jackson	31-50	5th	22.5
7-7	Cle.	W	4-3		6	8	Trombley	Reed		32-50	5th	21.5
7-8	Cle.	L	2-9		10	16	Nagy	Lincoln		32-51	5th	22.5
7-9	Pit.	W	5-4		9	8	Radke	Silva	Trombley	33-51	5th	21.5
7-10	Pit.	W	5-4		10	12	Guardado	Williams		34-51	5th	21.5
7-11	Pit.	L	2-10		5	17	Ritchie	Mays		34-52	5th	21.5
7-15	At Chi. (NL)	L	3-9		9	17	Sanders	Radke	Adams	34-53	5th	22.5
7-16	At Chi. (NL)	L	10-11		15	16	Adams	Trombley		34-54	5th	22.5
7-17	At Chi. (NL)	W	8-0		14	3	Mays	Mulholland		35-54	5th	21.5
7-18	At StL.	W	5-2		7	9	Hawkins	Oliver		36-54	5th	20.5
7-19	At StL.	L	4-8		9	14	Mercker	Lincoln	Bottalico	36-55	5th	20.5
7-20	At StL.	W	4-2		7	7	Radke	Luebbers	Trombley	37-55	5th	20.5
7-21	Chi.	L	3-6	(10)	11	13	Simas	Carrasco	Howry	37-56	5th	20.5
7-22	Chi.	W	3-0		11	5	Mays	Baldwin	Trombley	38-56	4th	19.5
7-23	Sea.	W	5-4		13	7	Carrasco	Paniagua		39-56	4th	18.5
7-24	Sea.	W	10-3		12	6	Wells	Meche		40-56	4th	17.5
7-25	Sea.	L	3-4		7	9	Moyer	Radke	Mesa	40-57	4th	17.5
7-26	Oak.	L	7-14		12	16	Groom	Sampson		40-58	T4th	18.5
7-27	Oak.	W	3-2		6	5	Mays	Taylor	Guardado	41-58	T3rd	18.5
7-28	Oak.	W	5-3		9	8	Hawkins	Haynes	Trombley	42-58	T3rd	18.5
7-30	At Ana.	W	3-1		9	7	Radke	Hill		43-58	3rd	18.5
7-31	At Ana.	W	8-0		11	3	Milton	Finley		44-58	3rd	18.5
8-1	At Ana.	L	1-2		2	7	Sparks	Mays	Percival	44-59	3rd	18.5
8-2	At Tex.	L	4-5		9	8	Zimmerman	Guardado	Wetteland	44-60	3rd	19.5
8-3	At Tex.	L	5-9		14	13	Morgan	Sampson		44-61	4th	20.5
8-4	At Tex.	L	1-3		4	10	Loaiza	Radke	Wetteland	44-62	4th	20.5
8-6	At K.C.	W	9-8		17	14	Miller	Service	Trombley	45-62	3rd	19.5
8-7	At K.C.	W	6-5		8	9	Wells	Rigby	Trombley	46-62	3rd	19.5
8-8	At K.C.	W	7-3		11	7	Hawkins	Rigby	Carrasco	47-62	3rd	18.5
8-10	Tor.	L	6-10		11	15	Escobar	Radke		47-63	3rd	20.0
8-11	Tor.	L	3-6		7	12	Carpenter	Milton		47-64	3rd	21.0
8-12	Tor.	W	3-0		6	5	Mays	Hentgen	Trombley	48-64	3rd	20.5
8-13	At N.Y.	L	2-14		6	22	Pettitte	Hawkins		48-65	3rd	21.5
8-14	At N.Y.	W	6-3		8	9	Wells	Cone	Trombley	49-65	3rd	21.5
8-15	At N.Y.	W	5-3		10	12	Radke	Irabu	Trombley	50-65	3rd	21.5
8-16	At N.Y.	L	0-2		4	3	Clemens	Milton	Rivera	50-66	3rd	21.5
8-17	At Bal.	L	3-8		10	13	Mussina	Mays		50-67	3rd	21.5
8-18	At Bal.	L	0-2		5	5	Erickson	Hawkins		50-68	3rd	21.5
8-19	At Bal.	L	3-9		5	11	Johnson	Perkins		50-69	3rd	22.5
8-20	N.Y.	L	3-9		9	9	Irabu	Radke	Nelson	50-70	3rd	23.5
8-21	N.Y.	W	6-1		13	7	Milton	Clemens	Guardado	51-70	3rd	23.5
8-22	N.Y.	L	3-5		4	13	Hernandez	Mays	Rivera	51-71	3rd	24.5
8-23	Bos.	L	1-4		10	10	Rapp	Hawkins	Lowe	51-72	3rd	24.5
8-24	Bos.	L	1-7		5	11	Martinez	Ryan		51-73	3rd	24.5
8-25	Bos.	W	6-3		8	5	Radke	Portugal		52-73	3rd	24.5
8-27	K.C.	W	4-1		10	7	Milton	Rosado	Trombley	53-73	3rd	24.5
8-28	K.C.	W	4-3	(10)	10	6	Wells	Morman		54-73	3rd	24.5
8-29	K.C.	W	6-2		7	8	Hawkins	Stein	Wells	55-73	3rd	23.5
8-30	At Tor.	L	1-2		5	2	Hentgen	Ryan	Koch	55-74	3rd	24.5
8-31	At Tor.	W	14-3		20	9	Radke	Hamilton		56-74	3rd	24.5
9-1	At Tor.	L	0-4		5	5	Escobar	Milton		56-75	3rd	25.5
9-2	At Tor.	L	1-6		4	11	Wells	Mays		56-76	3rd	26.5
9-3	At T.B.	L	2-4		11	8	Charlton	Guardado	Hernandez	56-77	3rd	27.5
9-4	At T.B.	L	3-11		10	18	Lopez	Miller		56-78	3rd	27.5
9-5	At T.B.	W	4-1		10	5	Radke	Rupe		57-78	3rd	27.5
9-6	At T.B.	W	13-7		16	11	Carrasco	White		58-78	3rd	27.5
9-7	Bal.	L	0-5		3	10	Erickson	Mays		58-79	3rd	27.5
9-8	Bal.	L	0-10		6	14	Johnson	Hawkins		58-80	3rd	27.5
9-9	Bal.	L	5-6		7	12	Reyes	Miller	Timlin	58-81	3rd	28.0
9-10	Ana.	L	2-4		4	13	Finley	Radke	Percival	58-82	T3rd	29.0
9-11	Ana.	W	7-0		10	0	Milton	Ortiz		59-82	3rd	29.0
9-12	Ana.	L	3-6		5	9	Washburn	Mays		59-83	3rd	29.0
9-13	Ana.	L	5-6		10	10	Magnante	Hawkins	Hasegawa	59-84	T3rd	30.0
9-14	Tex.	L	4-5		10	10	Kolb	Guardado	Wetteland	59-85	4th	30.0
9-15	Tex.	L	3-8		9	12	Loaiza	Radke		59-86	4th	30.0

Date	Opp.	Res.	Score	(inn.*)	Hits	Opp. hits	Winning pitcher	Losing pitcher	Save	Record	Pos.	GB
9-17	At Sea.	L	3-4		6	7	Abbott	Trombley		59-87	4th	29.5
9-18	At Sea.	L	0-5		2	11	Meche	Mays		59-88	4th	30.5
9-19	At Sea.	W	2-1		6	5	Hawkins	Moyer	Trombley	60-88	T3rd	29.5
9-20	At Oak.	W	4-0		11	4	Ryan	Appier		61-88	T3rd	28.5
9-21	At Oak.	L	3-5		7	9	Mahay	Carrasco	Isringhausen	61-89	T3rd	29.5
9-22	At Oak.	W	5-4		7	8	Redman	Worrell	Trombley	62-89	3rd	29.5
9-24	Chi.	W	6-2		7	2	Mays	Myette		63-89	3rd	29.0
9-25	Chi.	L	4-13		6	18	Sirotka	Hawkins		63-90	3rd	30.0
9-26	Chi.	L	0-3		6	12	Baldwin	Ryan	Howry	63-91	4th	31.0
9-27	Chi.	L	1-3		5	5	Simas	Wells	Foulke	63-92	4th	31.5
9-28	Det.	L	4-7		9	9	Anderson	Trombley	Jones	63-93	4th	32.5
9-29	Det.	L	3-6		9	7	Mlicki	Mays	Jones	63-94	4th	32.5
9-30	Det.	L	5-6		8	14	Cordero	Wells	Jones	63-95	4th	33.5
10-1	At Chi.	L	8-9		12	13	Baldwin	Ryan	Howry	63-96	5th	33.5
10-2	At Chi.	L	1-6		8	11	Wells	Perkins		63-97	5th	33.5
10-3	At Chi.	T	1-1	(7)	6	4				63-97	5th	33.0

Monthly records: April (9-14), May (9-18), June (11-15), July (15-11), August (12-16), September (7-21), October (0-2).
*Innings, if other than nine. † First game of a doubleheader. ‡ Second game of a doubleheader.

HIGHLIGHTS

High point: Second-year pitcher Eric Milton threw a no-hitter against Anaheim on September 11. He struck out 13 batters in the game played at the Metrodome.

Low point: In its last game before the All-Star break, Minnesota lost to the Pirates, 10-2. Righthander Todd Ritchie, a former No. 1 draft pick of the Twins, was the winner in that July 11 game, which added insult to injury for a franchise with a long history of failing to develop pitchers.

Turning point: The fourth game of the year—really. The Twins had taken two of three from Toronto to open the season, looking competitive in the process, and they had some optimism entering a series with Cleveland. The Twins got their comeuppance—and a shot of reality—in the first game against the Indians, falling 14-5 (and then losing 12-7 and 9-8).

Most valuable player: Yes, the Twins cut him loose when the season ended, but designated hitter/outfielder Marty Cordova is the choice. He hit .285 with 14 home runs and 70 RBIs.

Most valuable pitcher: Brad Radke somehow went 12-14 with a 3.75 ERA, which would have allowed him to win 20 games with a good team.

Most improved player: Milton progressed from a pitcher who couldn't make it through the fifth inning to one who finished second on the team in innings pitched (206.1). He led Minnesota in complete games (five) and shutouts (two).

Most pleasant surprise: Shortstop Cristian Guzman was a raw rookie with supposedly no chance of hitting major league pitching. He proved to be one of the Twins' toughest players and one of the league's most promising fielders. And by season's end, there were indications he could hit big-league pitching (he batted .291 in July and .284 in August).

Biggest disappointment: The Twins keep waiting for LaTroy Hawkins to become a staff stalwart, and he keeps disappointing. Despite a few stretches in which he teased them again, Hawkins wound up with a 6.66 ERA. His 10-14 record was amazing, considering the fat ERA and the fact he allowed 238 hits in only 174.1 innings.

Key injuries: Right fielder Matt Lawton got beaned in early June, suffering a fracture of his right eye socket, and he never fully recovered. The injury killed what was projected to be his breakthrough season.

Notable: As bad as the Twins were—and figure to be in the future, considering their payroll isn't likely to grow—they finally found some semblance of decent starting pitching. Radke is a legitimate ace, Milton is progressing rapidly at age 24, Joe Mays had a stretch of brilliance during the middle of the season and, strangely, Hawkins, who has a nice array of pitches but fails to get results, could still make it.

—JIM SOUHAN

RECORDS

1999 regular-season record: 63-97 (5th in A.L. Central); 31-50 at home; 32-47 on road; 18-31 vs. East; 20-28 vs. A.L. Central; 15-31 vs. West; 10-7 vs. N.L.; 13-24 vs. lefthanded starters; 50-73 vs. righthanded starters; 27-39 on grass; 36-58 on turf; 21-25 in daytime; 42-72 at night; 19-26 in one-run games; 6-5 in extra-inning games; 0-0-1 in doubleheaders.

Team record past five years: 335-455 (.424, ranks 12th in league in that span).

TEAM LEADERS

Batting average: Todd Walker (.279).
At-bats: Todd Walker (531).
Runs: Chad Allen (69).
Hits: Todd Walker (148).
Total Bases: Todd Walker (211).
Doubles: Todd Walker (37).
Triples: Terry Steinbach, Todd Walker (4).
Home runs: Ron Coomer (16).
Runs batted in: Marty Cordova (70).
Stolen bases: Matt Lawton (26).
Slugging percentage: Todd Walker (.397).
On-base percentage: Todd Walker (.343).

Wins: Brad Radke (12).
Earned-run average: Brad Radke (3.75).
Complete games: Eric Milton (5).
Shutouts: Eric Milton (2).
Saves: Mike Trombley (24).
Innings pitched: Brad Radke (218.2).
Strikeouts: Eric Milton (163).

GAMES BY POSITION

Catcher: Terry Steinbach 96, Javier Valentin 76, A.J. Pierzynski 9.
First base: Doug Mientkiewicz 110, Ron Coomer 71, Brent Gates 5, Denny Hocking 2, David Ortiz 1.
Second base: Todd Walker 103, Denny Hocking 56, Brent Gates 47, Cleatus Davidson 6.
Third base: Corey Koskie 79, Brent Gates 61, Ron Coomer 57, Denny Hocking 6.
Shortstop: Cristian Guzman 131, Denny Hocking 61, Cleatus Davidson 4, Brent Gates 1.
Outfield: Chad Allen 133, Torii Hunter 130, Matt Lawton 109, Jacque Jones 93, Denny Hocking 38, Marty Cordova 29, Corey Koskie 25, Chris Latham 14, Midre Cummings 6, Ron Coomer 1.
Designated hitter: Marty Cordova 85, Todd Walker 34, Corey Koskie 12, Ron Coomer 7, Matt Lawton 6, Midre Cummings 5, David Ortiz 5, Chad Allen 2, Terry Steinbach 1, Brent Gates 1, Cleatus Davidson 1.

TOP DRAFT CHOICES

1. **B.J. Garbe,** OF, Moses Lake (Wash.) H.S.
2. **Rob Bowen,** C, Homestead H.S., Fort Wayne, Ind.
3. **Justin Morneau,** C, New Westminster (B.C.) SS.
4. **Jeff Randazzo,** LHP, Cardinal O'Hara H.S., Broomall, Pa.
5. **Brent Schoening,** RHP, Auburn Univ.
6. **Brian Wolfe,** RHP, Servite H.S., Anaheim
7. **Darren Ciraco,** OF, Pelham (N.Y.) Memorial H.S.
8. **Mike Scanlon,** 3B, U. of Minnesota
9. **Grant Gregg,** LHP, McLennan (Tex.) C.C.
10. **Jim Caine,** RHP, St. Charles (Ill.) H.S.

NEW YORK YANKEES
AMERICAN LEAGUE EAST DIVISION

2000 Yankees Schedule
Home games shaded. *—All-Star Game at Turner Field (Atlanta).

March
SUN	MON	TUE	WED	THU	FRI	SAT
26	27	28	29	30	31	

April
SUN	MON	TUE	WED	THU	FRI	SAT
						1
2	3 ANA	4 ANA	5 ANA	6	7 SEA	8 SEA
9 SEA	10	11 TEX	12 TEX	13 TEX	14 KC	15 KC
16 KC	17 TEX	18 TEX	19 TEX	20	21 TOR	22 TOR
23 TOR	24 MIN	25 MIN	26 MIN	27	28 TOR	29 TOR
30 TOR						

May
SUN	MON	TUE	WED	THU	FRI	SAT
1 CLE	2 CLE	3 CLE	4	5 BAL	6 BAL	
7 BAL	8 TB	9 TB	10 TB	11	12 DET	13 DET
14 DET	15	16 CWS	17 CWS	18	19 CLE	20 CLE
21 CLE	22	23 CHI	24 CHI	25 CHI	26 BOS	27 BOS
28 BOS	29 OAK	30 OAK	31 OAK			

June
SUN	MON	TUE	WED	THU	FRI	SAT
				1	2 ATL	3 ATL
4 ATL	5 MON	6 MON	7 MON	8	9 NYM	10 NYM
11 NYM	12 BOS	13 BOS	14 BOS	15 CWS	16 CWS	17 CWS
18 CWS	19 BOS	20 BOS	21 BOS	22 BOS	23 CHI	24 CHI
25 CHI	26	27 DET	28 DET	29 DET	30 TB	

July
SUN	MON	TUE	WED	THU	FRI	SAT
						1 TB
2 TB	3	4 BAL	5 BAL	6 BAL	7 NYM	8 NYM
9 NYM	10	11 *	12	13 FLA	14 FLA	15 FLA
16 PHI	17 PHI	18 PHI	19 DET	20 DET	21 TB	22 TB
23 TB	24 BAL	25 BAL	26 BAL	27 MIN	28 MIN	29 MIN
30 MIN	31					

August
SUN	MON	TUE	WED	THU	FRI	SAT
		1 KC	2 KC	3 KC	4 SEA	5 SEA
6 SEA	7 SEA	8 OAK	9 OAK	10 OAK	11 ANA	12 ANA
13 ANA	14 TEX	15 TEX	16 TEX	17 ANA	18 ANA	19 ANA
20 ANA	21	22 TEX	23 TEX	24 TEX	25 OAK	26 OAK
27 OAK	28 SEA	29 SEA	30 SEA	31		

September
SUN	MON	TUE	WED	THU	FRI	SAT
					1 MIN	2 MIN
3 MIN	4 KC	5 KC	6 KC	7 KC	8 BOS	9 BOS
10 BOS	11	12 TOR	13 TOR	14 TOR	15 CLE	16 CLE
17 CLE	18 CLE	19 TOR	20 TOR	21 TOR	22 DET	23 DET
24 DET	25 DET	26 TB	27 TB	28 TB	29 BAL	30 BAL

October
SUN	MON	TUE	WED	THU	FRI	SAT
1 BAL	2	3	4	5	6	7

2000 SEASON
CLUB DIRECTORY

Principal owner
George M. Steinbrenner III
General partners
Harold Z. Steinbrenner, Steven W. Swindal
President
Randy Levine
Executive v.p., general counsel
Lonn Trost
Vice president, ticket operations
Frank Swaine
Vice president, business development
Joseph M. Perello
Vice president, chief financial officer
Marty Greenspun
Controller
Robert Brown
Special advisory group
Clyde King, Dick Williams
Vice president, general manager
Brian Cashman
Vice president, baseball operations
Mark Newman
Vice president, scouting
Lin Garrett
Vice president, international and pro scouting
Gordon Blakeley
Vice president, player personnel
Billy Connors
Vice president, business development
Sonny Hight
Director of player development
Rob Thomson
Director of player personnel
Damon Oppenheimer
Director of baseball operations
Dan Matheson
Director of major league scouting
Gene Michael
Assistant general manager
Kim Ng
Major league administrator
Tom May
Traveling secretary
David Szen
Director of customer service
Joel White
Dir. of office administration and services
Harvey C. Winston
Manager, stadium operations
Kirk Randazzo
Assistant, stadium operations
Bob Pelegrino
Stadium superintendent
Bob Wilkinson
Head groundskeeper
Dan Cunningham
Director, video and broadcast operations
Doyal Martin
Asst. dir., video and broadcast operations
Joe Pullia
Public address announcer
Bob Sheppard
Stadium organist
Eddie Layton

Executive director of ticket operations
Jeff Kline
Senior ticket director
Ken Skrypek
Director of media relations and publicity
Rick Cerrone
Director, publications and multimedia
Dan Cahalane
Asst. dir. of media relations and publicity
Jason Zillo
Senior advisor
Arthur Richman
Director of marketing
Deborah A. Tymon
Dir. of community relations/special assistant to George M. Steinbrenner
Brian Smith
Director of Yankee Alumni Association
Jim Ogle
Director of entertainment
Stanley Kay
Special assistant
Joe Pepitone
Dir. of television and video production
Joe Violone
Manager of publications and multimedia
Kara McGovern
Team photographer
Steve Crandall
Assistant directors of baseball operations
Tommy Larsen, Rigo Garcia
Assistant director of scouting
Joe Caro
Coord. of Latin American player dev.
Ken Dominguez
Team physician
Dr. Stuart Hershon
Head trainer
Gene Monahan
Assistant trainer
Steve Donohue
Strength & conditioning coach
Jeff Mangold
Regional cross-checkers
Joe Arnold, Tim Kelly, Greg Orr
Pro scouts
Joe Caro, Bill Emslie, Mick Kelleher, Bob Miske, Mike Naples
Scouts
Mike Baker, Mark Batchko, Steve Boros, Bobby Dejardin, Dick Groch, Steve Lemke, Abe Martinez, Bob Miske, Scott Pleis, Cesar Presbott, Gus Quattlebaum, Joe Robison, Phil Rossi, Steve Swail, Leon Wurth, Bill Young
Coordinator of Pacific rim scouting
John Cox
Coordinator of Latin American scouting
Carlos Rios
Foreign scouts
Manuel Duran, Ricardo Finol, Karl Heron, Ricardo Heron, Rudy Jabalera, Victor Mata, Jim Patterson, Jose Quintero, Edgar Rodriguez, Arquimedes Rojas, Freddy Tiburcio
Special assignment scouts
Stump Merrill, Ket Barber

MINOR LEAGUE AFFILIATES

Class	Team	League	Manager
AAA	Columbus	International	Trey Hillman
AA	Norwich	Eastern	Dan Radison
A	Tampa	Florida State	Tom Nieto
A	Greensboro	South Atlantic	Stan Hough
A	Staten Island	New York-Pennsylvania	Joe Arnold
Rookie	Tampa	Gulf Coast	Derek Shelton

BROADCAST INFORMATION

Radio: WABC-AM (770).
TV: WNYW-TV (Channel 5).
Cable TV: Madison Square Garden Network.

SPRING TRAINING

Ballpark (city): Legends Field (Tampa, Fla.).
Ticket information: 813-879-2244, 813-287-8844.

SPRING TRAINING ROSTER

Manager—Joe Torre (6).
Coaches—Chris Chambliss (48), Tony Cloninger (41), Lee Mazzilli, Willie Randolph (30), Mel Stottlemyre (34), Don Zimmer (50).

No.	PITCHERS	B/T	Ht./Wt.	Born	1999 clubs
59	Bradley, Ryan	R/R	6-4/226	10-26-75	Columbus
41	Buddie, Mike	R/R	6-3/210	12-12-70	Columbus, New York A.L.
22	Clemens, Roger	R/R	6-4/230	8-4-62	New York A.L.
36	Cone, David	L/R	6-1/190	1-2-63	New York A.L.
64	De Los Santos, Luis	R/R	6-2/187	11-1-77	Columbus, Gulf Coast Yankees
67	Einertson, Chief	R/R	6-2/190	9-4-72	Gulf Coast Yankees, Tampa, Norwich
58	Erdos, Todd	R/R	6-1/190	11-21-73	Columbus, New York A.L.
	Ford, Ben	R/R	6-7/200	8-15-75	Columbus
38	Grimsley, Jason	R/R	6-3/180	8-7-67	New York A.L.
26	Hernandez, Orlando	R/R	6-2/190	10-11-65	New York A.L.
57	Juden, Jeff	B/R	6-8/265	1-19-71	Columbus, New York A.L.
55	Mendoza, Ramiro	R/R	6-2/155	6-15-72	New York A.L.
43	Nelson, Jeff	R/R	6-8/225	11-17-66	New York A.L., Gulf Coast Yankees, Tampa
46	Pettitte, Andy	L/L	6-5/225	6-15-72	Tampa, New York A.L.
42	Rivera, Mariano	R/R	6-2/170	11-29-69	New York A.L.
29	Stanton, Mike	L/L	6-1/215	6-2-67	New York A.L.
62	Tessmer, Jay	R/R	6-3/190	12-26-71	Columbus, New York A.L.
27	Watson, Allen	L/L	6-1/212	11-18-70	New York N.L., Seattle, Columbus, New York A.L.
	Westbrook, Jake	R/R	6-3/200	9-29-77	Harrisburg
52	Yarnall, Ed	L/L	6-3/234	12-4-75	Columbus, New York A.L.

No.	CATCHERS	B/T	Ht./Wt.	Born	1999 clubs
13	Leyritz, Jim	R/R	5-11/220	12-27-63	San Diego, Rancho Cucamonga, Las Vegas, New York A.L.
20	Posada, Jorge	B/R	6-2/205	8-17-71	New York A.L.

No.	INFIELDERS	B/T	Ht./Wt.	Born	1999 clubs
35	Bellinger, Clay	R/R	6-3/195	11-18-68	New York A.L., Columbus
18	Brosius, Scott	R/R	6-1/202	8-15-66	New York A.L., Tampa
2	Jeter, Derek	R/R	6-3/195	6-26-74	New York A.L.
59	Jimenez, D'Angelo	R/R	6-0/160	12-21-77	Columbus, New York A.L.
11	Knoblauch, Chuck	R/R	5-9/170	7-7-68	New York A.L.
24	Martinez, Tino	L/R	6-2/210	12-7-67	New York A.L.
58	Soriano, Alfonso	R/R	6-1/160	1-7-78	Norwich, Gulf Coast Yankees, Columbus, New York A.L.

No.	OUTFIELDERS	B/T	Ht./Wt.	Born	1999 clubs
	Jones, Terry	B/R	5-10/165	2-15-71	Ottawa, Montreal
17	Ledee, Ricky	L/L	6-1/160	11-22-73	New York A.L., Columbus
84	McDonald, Donzell	B/R	5-11/165	2-20-75	Norwich
21	O'Neill, Paul	L/L	6-4/215	2-25-63	New York A.L.
47	Spencer, Shane	R/R	5-11/210	2-20-72	New York A.L., Columbus
39	Strawberry, Darryl	L/L	6-6/215	3-12-62	Columbus, New York A.L.
51	Williams, Bernie	B/R	6-2/205	9-13-68	New York A.L.

BALLPARK INFORMATION

Ballpark (capacity, surface)
Yankee Stadium (57,546, grass)

Address
Yankee Stadium
E. 161 St. and River Ave.
Bronx, NY 10451

Business phone
718-293-4300

Ticket information
212-307-1212, 718-293-6013

Ticket prices
$35 (main-infield)
$32 (loge-infield)
$30 (main & loge-outfield, main reserved-infield)
$26 (main reserved-outfield)
$15 (tier)
$8 (bleachers)

Field dimensions (from home plate)
To left field at foul line, 318 feet
To center field, 408 feet
To right field at foul line, 314 feet

First game played
April 18, 1923 (Yankees 4, Red Sox 1)

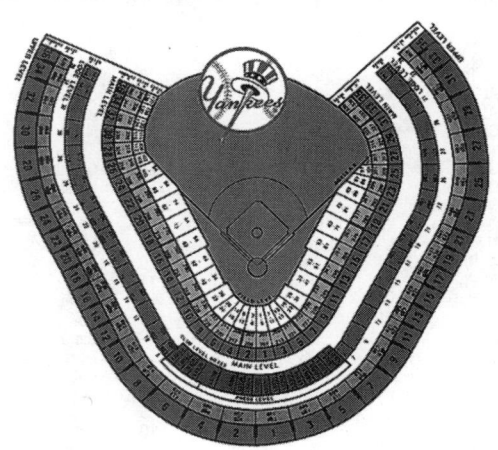

1999 REVIEW
DAY BY DAY

Date	Opp.	Res.	Score	(inn.*)	Hits	Opp. hits	Winning pitcher	Losing pitcher	Save	Record	Pos.	GB
4-6	At Oak.	W	7-4		12	5	Hernandez	Candiotti	Rivera	1-1	3rd	0.5
4-7	At Oak.	W	4-0		8	5	Mendoza	Haynes		2-1	2nd	0.5
4-9	Det.	W	12-3	(7)	9	3	Cone	Graterol		3-1	2nd	1.0
4-10	Det.	W	5-0		10	3	Clemens	Moehler		4-1	2nd	1.0
4-11	Det.	W	11-2		9	5	Hernandez	Thompson		5-1	T1st	...
4-13	Bal.	W	6-3		7	10	Nelson	Rhodes		6-1	T1st	...
4-14	Bal.	W	14-7		17	9	Cone	Erickson		7-1	1st	+0.5
4-15	Bal.	L	7-9		10	18	Rhodes	Rivera	Timlin	7-2	1st	+0.5
4-16	At Det.	L	1-8		7	5	Thompson	Hernandez		7-3	1st	+0.5
4-17	At Det.	L	1-3		6	10	Anderson	Nelson	Jones	7-4	3rd	0.5
4-18	At Det.	L	1-5		6	9	Mlicki	Mendoza		7-5	3rd	1.5
4-20	Tex.	W	4-0		13	4	Cone	Burkett		8-5	T2nd	1.5
4-21	Tex.	W	4-2		6	5	Clemens	Helling	Rivera	9-5	2nd	1.5
4-23	Tor.	W	6-4		9	10	Hernandez	Wells	Rivera	10-5	2nd	1.0
4-24	Tor.	W	7-4		9	9	Mendoza	Plesac	Rivera	11-5	1st	...
4-25	Tor.	W	4-3	(11)	9	5	Grimsley	Person		12-5	1st	+1.0
4-27	At Tex.	W	7-6		14	7	Stanton	Wetteland	Rivera	13-5	1st	+1.5
4-28	At Tex.	L	6-8		10	12	Munoz	Stanton	Wetteland	13-6	1st	+1.5
4-29	At Tex.	W	5-3		6	9	Mendoza	Morgan	Rivera	14-6	1st	+2.5
4-30	At K.C.	L	6-13		12	15	Morman	Pettitte		14-7	1st	+2.5
5-1	At K.C.	W	8-4		13	7	Cone	Pittsley		15-7	1st	+2.5
5-2	At K.C.	W	9-8		14	14	Grimsley	Santiago	Rivera	16-7	1st	+3.5
5-3	At K.C.	L	3-9		7	8	Service	Hernandez		16-8	1st	+2.5
5-4	At Min.	L	5-8		7	17	Lincoln	Mendoza	Aguilera	16-9	1st	+2.5
5-5	At Min.	W	5-3		11	5	Pettitte	Hawkins	Rivera	17-9	1st	+3.5
5-6	At Min.	W	4-3	(10)	14	7	Grimsley	Aguilera	Rivera	18-9	1st	+3.5
5-7	Sea.	W	10-1		10	5	Irabu	Suzuki		19-9	1st	+4.5
5-8	Sea.	L	5-14		8	19	Garcia	Hernandez		19-10	1st	+3.5
5-9	Sea.	W	6-1		9	3	Grimsley	Fassero		20-10	1st	+4.0
5-11	Ana.	L	7-9		8	14	Petkovsek	Mendoza	Percival	20-11	1st	+3.5
5-12	Ana.	L	0-1		3	6	Finley	Cone	Percival	20-12	1st	+2.5
5-13	Ana.	L	0-2		6	9	Olivares	Irabu	Percival	20-13	1st	+2.0
5-14	Chi.	L	2-8		6	9	Parque	Hernandez	Simas	20-14	1st	+1.0
5-15	Chi.	L	4-12		13	17	Snyder	Mendoza		20-15	T1st	...
5-16	Chi.	W	2-1		8	8	Pettitte	Sirotka	Rivera	21-15	1st	+1.0
5-18	At Bos.	L	3-6		13	10	Martinez	Cone	Gordon	21-16	2nd	0.5
5-19	At Bos.	L	0-6		8	15	Rose	Irabu		21-17	2nd	1.5
5-20	At Bos.	W	3-1		5	3	Hernandez	Portugal	Rivera	22-17	2nd	0.5
5-22†	At Chi.	W	10-2		13	7	Clemens	Snyder		23-17		
5-22‡	At Chi.	L	1-2		2	6	Sirotka	Pettitte	Simas	23-18	2nd	1.5
5-23	At Chi.	W	8-7	(10)	9	12	Rivera	Simas		24-18	2nd	1.5
5-25	Bos.	L	2-5		6	10	Rose	Irabu	Gordon	24-19	2nd	2.5
5-26	Bos.	W	8-3		11	8	Hernandez	Portugal	Rivera	25-19	2nd	1.5
5-27	Bos.	W	4-1		9	2	Clemens	Rapp	Rivera	26-19	2nd	0.5
5-28	At Tor.	W	10-6		16	9	Pettitte	Carpenter		27-19	2nd	0.5
5-29	At Tor.	W	8-3		12	7	Cone	Hentgen		28-19	2nd	0.5
5-30	At Tor.	W	8-3		9	8	Irabu	Wells		29-19	2nd	0.5
5-31	Cle.	L	1-7		7	7	Nagy	Hernandez		29-20	2nd	1.5
6-1	Cle.	W	11-5		13	9	Clemens	Burba		30-20	2nd	1.5
6-2	Cle.	L	7-10		9	15	Karsay	Pettitte	Jackson	30-21	2nd	1.5
6-4	N.Y. (NL)	W	4-3		5	7	Grimsley	Reed	Rivera	31-21	2nd	1.5
6-5	N.Y. (NL)	W	6-3		11	9	Hernandez	Yoshii	Rivera	32-21	2nd	0.5
6-6	N.Y. (NL)	L	2-7		6	8	Leiter	Clemens		32-22	2nd	0.5
6-7	At Phi.	L	5-6		7	9	Byrd	Pettitte		32-23	2nd	0.5
6-8	At Phi.	L	5-11		8	11	Perez	Grimsley		32-24	2nd	0.5
6-9	At Phi.	W	11-5		13	9	Cone	Ogea		33-24	1st	+0.5
6-11	At Fla.	W	8-4		11	6	Hernandez	Meadows	Rivera	34-24	1st	+0.5
6-12	At Fla.	W	5-4		6	9	Clemens	Hernandez	Rivera	35-24	1st	+1.5
6-13	At Fla.	L	2-8		5	13	Fernandez	Pettitte		35-25	1st	+1.5
6-14	Tex.	W	8-2		14	8	Irabu	Clark		36-25	1st	+1.5
6-15	Tex.	W	6-2		6	4	Cone	Glynn		37-25	1st	+1.5
6-16	Tex.	L	0-3		4	5	Helling	Hernandez	Wetteland	37-26	1st	+0.5
6-17	Tex.	L	2-4		7	10	Sele	Clemens	Wetteland	37-27	1st	+0.5
6-18	Ana.	W	4-1		8	5	Pettitte	Finley	Rivera	38-27	1st	+1.5
6-19	Ana.	W	6-2		11	3	Irabu	Olivares	Mendoza	39-27	1st	+1.5
6-20	Ana.	L	2-4		7	8	Belcher	Cone	Percival	39-28	1st	+0.5
6-22	At T.B.	W	7-0		12	3	Hernandez	Witt		40-28	1st	+1.0
6-23	At T.B.	W	12-4		19	11	Clemens	Eiland		41-28	1st	+1.0
6-24	At T.B.	W	7-3		13	7	Pettitte	Rekar	Mendoza	42-28	1st	+1.0
6-25	At Bal.	W	9-8		16	13	Naulty	Timlin	Rivera	43-28	1st	+1.0
6-26	At Bal.	W	7-4		11	8	Cone	Johnson	Rivera	44-28	1st	+1.0
6-27	At Bal.	W	6-2		12	7	Hernandez	Ponson		45-28	1st	+2.0

Date	Opp.	Res.	Score	(inn.*)	Hits	Opp. hits	Winning pitcher	Losing pitcher	Save	Record	Pos.	GB
6-29	Det.	W	3-0		6	8	Clemens	Thompson		46-28	1st	+2.0
6-30	Det.	L	2-8		12	11	Moehler	Pettitte		46-29	1st	+2.0
7-1	Det.	W	6-0		11	3	Irabu	Mlicki		47-29	1st	+3.0
7-2	Bal.	W	2-1		7	8	Cone	Johnson	Rivera	48-29	1st	+3.0
7-3	Bal.	W	6-5		9	6	Grimsley	Rhodes		49-29	1st	+4.0
7-4	Bal.	L	3-7		9	9	Guzman	Mendoza	Kamieniecki	49-30	1st	+3.0
7-5	Bal.	L	1-9		7	13	Mussina	Pettitte		49-31	1st	+2.0
7-6	At Det.	W	9-8	(10)	17	9	Rivera	Jones	Mendoza	50-31	1st	+3.0
7-7	At Det.	L	4-6		10	12	Mlicki	Cone	Brocail	50-32	1st	+3.0
7-8	At Det.	W	3-2		9	8	Hernandez	Nitkowski	Rivera	51-32	1st	+4.0
7-9	At N.Y. (NL)	L	2-5		5	12	Leiter	Clemens	Benitez	51-33	1st	+3.0
7-10	At N.Y. (NL)	L	8-9		11	9	Mahomes	Rivera		51-34	1st	+3.0
7-11	At N.Y. (NL)	W	6-3		13	8	Irabu	Hershiser	Rivera	52-34	1st	+4.0
7-15	Atl.	L	2-6		7	10	Glavine	Clemens		52-35	1st	+3.0
7-16	Atl.	L	7-10		14	12	Springer	Rivera	Rocker	52-36	1st	+3.0
7-17	Atl.	W	11-4		13	12	Pettitte	Perez	Grimsley	53-36	1st	+4.0
7-18	Mon.	W	6-0		8	0	Cone	Vazquez		54-36	1st	+4.0
7-19	Mon.	L	4-6		10	12	Kline	Mendoza	Urbina	54-37	1st	+4.0
7-20	Mon.	W	7-4		9	9	Clemens	Thurman	Rivera	55-37	1st	+4.0
7-21	T.B.	W	4-3		8	7	Hernandez	Witt	Rivera	56-37	1st	+5.0
7-22	T.B.	W	5-4		12	9	Pettitte	Rekar	Rivera	57-37	1st	+6.0
7-23	Cle.	W	9-8	(10)	13	10	Grimsley	Jackson		58-37	1st	+6.0
7-24	Cle.	W	21-1		21	9	Irabu	Langston		59-37	1st	+7.0
7-25	Cle.	W	2-1		6	6	Mendoza	Rincon		60-37	1st	+7.0
7-27	At Chi.	W	5-3		10	10	Hernandez	Baldwin	Rivera	61-37	1st	+7.5
7-28	At Chi.	L	3-11		11	19	Castillo	Pettitte		61-38	1st	+7.0
7-29	At Chi.	L	1-5		5	9	Snyder	Cone	Foulke	61-39	1st	+6.5
7-30	At Bos.	W	13-3		16	7	Irabu	Portugal		62-39	1st	+7.0
7-31	At Bos.	L	5-6		15	12	Lowe	Mendoza		62-40	1st	+6.0
8-1	At Bos.	L	4-5		9	9	Saberhagen	Hernandez	Wakefield	62-41	1st	+5.0
8-2	Tor.	W	3-1		7	7	Pettitte	Wells	Rivera	63-41	1st	+6.0
8-3	Tor.	L	1-3		5	11	Hamilton	Cone	Koch	63-42	1st	+5.0
8-4	Tor.	W	8-3		8	9	Irabu	Escobar		64-42	1st	+6.0
8-5	At Sea.	W	7-4		12	6	Clemens	Moyer	Rivera	65-42	1st	+6.5
8-6	At Sea.	W	11-8		15	13	Watson	Fassero	Rivera	66-42	1st	+6.5
8-7	At Sea.	W	1-0		3	4	Pettitte	Garcia	Rivera	67-42	1st	+7.5
8-8	At Sea.	W	9-3		11	6	Cone	Halama		68-42	1st	+7.5
8-9	At Oak.	W	12-8		9	13	Mendoza	Haynes		69-42	1st	+7.5
8-10	At Oak.	L	1-6		9	10	Olivares	Clemens	Jones	69-43	1st	+6.5
8-11	At Oak.	W	5-3		8	6	Watson	Jones	Rivera	70-43	1st	+6.5
8-13	Min.	W	14-2		22	6	Pettitte	Hawkins		71-43	1st	+7.5
8-14	Min.	L	3-6		9	8	Wells	Cone	Trombley	71-44	1st	+6.5
8-15	Min.	L	3-5		12	10	Radke	Irabu	Trombley	71-45	1st	+6.5
8-16	Min.	W	2-0		3	4	Clemens	Milton	Rivera	72-45	1st	+6.5
8-17	K.C.	W	5-2		7	7	Hernandez	Rosado	Rivera	73-45	1st	+7.5
8-18	K.C.	L	0-3		6	8	Reichert	Pettitte	Montgomery	73-46	1st	+6.5
8-19	K.C.	L	1-4	(11)	5	6	Rigby	Grimsley	Montgomery	73-47	1st	+6.5
8-20	At Min.	W	9-3		9	9	Irabu	Radke	Nelson	74-47	1st	+7.5
8-21	At Min.	L	1-6		7	13	Milton	Clemens	Guardado	74-48	1st	+7.5
8-22	At Min.	W	5-3		13	4	Hernandez	Mays	Rivera	75-48	1st	+8.5
8-23	At Tex.	W	21-3		23	10	Pettitte	Burkett		76-48	1st	+8.5
8-24	At Tex.	W	10-7	(11)	11	14	Mendoza	Lee	Rivera	77-48	1st	+8.5
8-25	At Tex.	L	3-7		8	12	Loaiza	Irabu		77-49	1st	+8.5
8-27	Sea.	W	8-0		12	5	Clemens	Meche		78-49	1st	+8.5
8-28	Sea.	W	2-1		8	4	Rivera	Paniagua		79-49	1st	+8.5
8-29	Sea.	W	11-5		12	10	Pettitte	Abbott	Rivera	80-49	1st	+8.5
8-30	Oak.	W	7-4		8	10	Nelson	Mathews	Rivera	81-49	1st	+8.5
8-31	Oak.	L	2-3	(11)	8	10	Jones	Mendoza	Isringhausen	81-50	1st	+7.5
9-1	Oak.	L	1-7		6	10	Olivares	Clemens		81-51	1st	+6.5
9-2	Oak.	W	9-3		14	8	Hernandez	Heredia		82-51	1st	+7.5
9-3	At Ana.	L	2-8		10	15	Belcher	Pettitte		82-52	1st	+7.5
9-4	At Ana.	W	9-6		10	6	Watson	Alvarez	Rivera	83-52	1st	+7.5
9-5	At Ana.	W	8-3		13	6	Yarnall	Fyhrie		84-52	1st	+7.5
9-6	At Ana.	L	3-5		5	6	Washburn	Clemens	Percival	84-53	1st	+6.5
9-7	At K.C.	L	3-6		13	10	Rosado	Cone	Montgomery	84-54	1st	+5.5
9-8	At K.C.	W	9-5		11	15	Hernandez	Rusch	Rivera	85-54	1st	+6.5
9-10	Bos.	L	1-3		1	12	Martinez	Pettitte		85-55	1st	+5.5
9-11	Bos.	L	10-11		12	10	Garces	Irabu	Beck	85-56	1st	+4.5
9-12	Bos.	L	1-4		5	7	Cormier	Clemens	Beck	85-57	1st	+3.5
9-13	At Tor.	L	1-2		4	5	Wells	Hernandez		85-58	1st	+3.5
9-14	At Tor.	W	10-6		9	11	Mendoza	Koch		86-58	1st	+3.5
9-15	At Tor.	W	6-4		7	8	Pettitte	Hentgen	Rivera	87-58	1st	+3.5
9-16	At Cle.	W	9-5		12	10	Irabu	Burba		88-58	1st	+4.0
9-17	At Cle.	W	9-4		9	5	Clemens	Wright		89-58	1st	+4.0
9-18	At Cle.	L	4-5		12	8	Nagy	Hernandez	Jackson	89-59	1st	+3.0
9-19	At Cle.	W	11-7		18	9	Watson	Martin		90-59	1st	+3.0

Date	Opp.	Res.	Score	(inn.*)	Hits	Opp. hits	Winning pitcher	Losing pitcher	Save	Record	Pos.	GB
9-21	Chi.	W	3-1		10	6	Pettitte	Baldwin	Rivera	91-59	1st	+3.0
9-22	Chi.	W	5-4		9	9	Rivera	Navarro		92-59	1st	+4.0
9-23	Chi.	W	5-2		12	7	Clemens	Parque	Rivera	93-59	1st	+5.0
9-24	T.B.	W	4-3	(11)	9	7	Stanton	Charlton		94-59	1st	+6.0
9-25	T.B.	L	1-2		5	11	Arrojo	Cone	Hernandez	94-60	1st	+5.0
9-26	T.B.	L	5-6		11	15	Lidle	Mendoza	Hernandez	94-61	1st	+5.0
9-27	T.B.	L	6-10		9	11	Duvall	Irabu	Sparks	94-62	1st	+4.0
9-28	At Bal.	W	9-5		10	10	Mendoza	Ponson		95-62	1st	+4.5
9-30†	At Bal.	L	0-5		8	5	Mussina	Clemens		95-63		
9-30‡	At Bal.	W	12-5		17	12	Hernandez	Corsi		96-63	1st	+5.0
10-1	At T.B.	W	11-7		14	9	Mendoza	Arrojo	Rivera	97-63	1st	+5.0
10-2	At T.B.	W	3-2		9	6	Cone	Alvarez	Rivera	98-63	1st	+5.0
10-3	At T.B.	L	2-6		6	6	Gaillard	Juden	Hernandez	98-64	1st	+4.0

Monthly records: April (14-7), May (15-13), June (17-9), July (16-11), August (19-10), September (15-13), October (2-1).
*Innings, if other than nine. † First game of a doubleheader. ‡ Second game of a doubleheader.

HIGHLIGHTS

High point: What else? The last out of the millennium, Keith Lockhart's pop fly to Chad Curtis in left field on October 27. With that, the Yankees swept the Braves and won their 25th World Series crown and third in four years under Joe Torre.
Low point: The spring. In March, news of Torre's cancer diagnosis stunned the club. Then, in April, the team was shaken by Darryl Strawberry's arrest in Florida on charges of cocaine possession and solicitation (he pleaded no contest to both).
Turning point: Stuck in a four-game losing streak and down 6-1 in the eighth inning of a September 14 game in Toronto, the Yankees rallied to win. Bernie Williams hit an eighth-inning, game-tying grand slam against Billy Koch, and Paul O'Neill homered with the bases loaded in the ninth for the victory. Not only did the dramatic win end the losing streak, it rejuvenated the Yankees and helped them stave off the tenacious Red Sox in the A.L. East.
Most valuable player: Derek Jeter. The always-improving Jeter, 25, set career highs in many offensive categories and improved his defense as well. While most teammates slumped in the first half of the season, the shortstop reached base safely in the club's first 53 games.
Most valuable pitcher: Mariano Rivera. Once the Yankees took a lead into the ninth inning, they were virtually certain of victory. The closer converted 45 of 49 save opportunities.
Most improved player: Andy Pettitte, who flashed some of his 1996 and 1997 form. Once the July 31 trading deadline passed, the lefthander seemed at ease and went 5-1 with a 1.76 ERA in six August starts. And he was 2-0 in postseason play (although he did get roughed up in Game 3 of the World Series).
Most pleasant surprise: Jason Grimsley. A non-roster invitee to spring training, Grimsley helped bridge the gap from the starters to Rivera and finished 7-2 with a 3.60 ERA. He was particularly effective in May (1.21 ERA in 13 games) and September (0.96 in seven games).
Biggest disappointment: Roger Clemens. When Clemens arrived in spring training, the Yankees thought they might challenge their 1998 A.L. record of 114 regular-season victories. They didn't come close, and Clemens contributed to the drop-off with a 14-10 record and a career-worst 4.60 ERA. The man for whom he was traded, David Wells, had gone 18-4 in '98 with a 3.49 ERA.
Key injuries: Really, the most significant absence was that of Torre. After being diagnosed with prostate cancer in March and then undergoing surgery, he missed the last three weeks of spring training and the first 36 games of the season. The Yankees were fortunate that they lost only one player—reliever Jeff Nelson—for an extended time because of injury. Nelson had two stints on the D.L. and underwent arthroscopic surgery on his elbow in June.
Notable: David Cone pitched a perfect game against the Expos on July 18. ... Bernie Williams, in the first season of his seven-year, $87.5 million contract, put up career highs in batting average (.342), hits (202), runs (116), RBIs (115), walks (100) and games (158).

—KEN DAVIDOFF

RECORDS

1999 regular-season record: 98-64 (1st in A.L. East); 48-33 at home; 50-31 on road; 31-18 vs. A.L. East; 31-22 vs. Central; 27-15 vs. West; 9-9 vs. N.L.; 19-14 vs. lefthanded starters; 79-50 vs. righthanded starters; 83-58 on grass; 15-6 on turf; 34-24 in daytime; 64-40 at night; 22-12 in one-run games; 7-2 in extra-inning games; 0-0-2 in doubleheaders.
Team record past five years: 479-313 (.605, ranks 1st in league in that span).

TEAM LEADERS

Batting average: Derek Jeter (.349).
At-bats: Derek Jeter (627).
Runs: Derek Jeter (134).
Hits: Derek Jeter (219).
Total Bases: Derek Jeter (346).
Doubles: Paul O'Neill (39).
Triples: Derek Jeter (9).
Home runs: Tino Martinez (28).
Runs batted in: Bernie Williams (115).
Stolen bases: Chuck Knoblauch (28).

Slugging percentage: Derek Jeter (.552).
On-base percentage: Derek Jeter (.438).
Wins: Orlando Hernandez (17).
Earned-run average: David Cone (3.44).
Complete games: Orlando Hernandez, Hideki Irabu (2).
Shutouts: Roger Clemens, David Cone, Orlando Hernandez, Hideki Irabu (1).
Saves: Mariano Rivera (45).
Innings pitched: Orlando Hernandez (214.1).
Strikeouts: David Cone (177).

GAMES BY POSITION

Catcher: Jorge Posada 109, Joe Girardi 65, Mike Figga 2, Jim Leyritz 1.
First base: Tino Martinez 158, Jim Leyritz 9, Clay Bellinger 8, Luis Sojo 4, Jeff Manto 3, Jorge Posada 1.
Second base: Chuck Knoblauch 150, Luis Sojo 16, Clay Bellinger 1, D'Angelo Jimenez 1.
Third base: Scott Brosius 132, Luis Sojo 20, Clay Bellinger 16, D'Angelo Jimenez 6, Jeff Manto 1, Jim Leyritz 1.
Shortstop: Derek Jeter 158, Luis Sojo 6, Alfonso Soriano 1, Clay Bellinger 1.
Outfield: Bernie Williams 155, Paul O'Neill 151, Chad Curtis 81, Ricky Ledee 77, Shane Spencer 64, Tony Tarasco 12, Clay Bellinger 2.
Designated hitter: Chili Davis 132, Darryl Strawberry 17, Jim Leyritz 14, Chad Curtis 14, Alfonso Soriano 6, Ricky Ledee 5, Clay Bellinger 4, Shane Spencer 3, Luis Sojo 2, Bernie Williams 2, Scott Brosius 1, Tony Tarasco 1, Jorge Posada 1.

TOP DRAFT CHOICES

1. **David Walling**, RHP, U. of Arkansas
2. **Tommy Winrow**, OF, Bishop Verot H.S., Fort Myers, Fla.
3. **Alex Graman**, LHP, Indiana State Univ.
4. **Robert Corrado**, RHP, Oakwood H.S., Dayton, Ohio
5. **Seth Taylor**, SS, U. of South Alabama
6. **Reggie Laplante**, RHP, Ahuntsic College, Montreal
7. **Andy Phillips**, 3B, U. of Alabama
8. **Scott Oliver**, RHP, College of Charleston
9. **Jeff Leaumont**, 1B, Louisiana State U.
10. **Brad Ticehurst**, OF, U. of Southern California

OAKLAND ATHLETICS
AMERICAN LEAGUE WEST DIVISION

2000 Athletics Schedule

Home games shaded. *—All-Star Game at Turner Field (Atlanta).

March
SUN	MON	TUE	WED	THU	FRI	SAT
26	27	28	29	30	31	

April
SUN	MON	TUE	WED	THU	FRI	SAT
						1
2	3 DET	4 DET	5	6	7 CWS	8 CWS
9 CWS	10 CLE	11 CLE	12 CLE	13	14 BOS	15 BOS
16 BOS	17 BOS	18 CLE	19 CLE	20 CLE	21 BAL	22 BAL
23 BAL	24 TOR	25 TOR	26 TOR	27	28 MIN	29 MIN
30 MIN						

May
SUN	MON	TUE	WED	THU	FRI	SAT
	1 KC	2 KC	3 KC	4	5 TEX	6 TEX
7 TEX	8 ANA	9 ANA	10 ANA	11 SEA	12 SEA	13 SEA
14 SEA	15 KC	16 KC	17 KC	18 MIN	19 MIN	20 MIN
21 MIN	22	23 TB	24 TB	25 TB	26 BAL	27 BAL
28 BAL	29 NYY	30 NYY	31 NYY			

June
SUN	MON	TUE	WED	THU	FRI	SAT
				1 SF	2 SF	3 SF
4 SF	5 SD	6 SD	7 SD	8	9 LA	10 LA
11 LA	12 MIN	13 MIN	14 MIN	15	16 KC	17 KC
18 KC	19 BAL	20 BAL	21 BAL	22	23 KC	24 KC
25 KC	26	27 TEX	28 TEX	29 TEX	30 ANA	

July
SUN	MON	TUE	WED	THU	FRI	SAT
						1 ANA
2 ANA	3 TEX	4 TEX	5 TEX	6	7 ARI	8 ARI
9 ARI	10	11 *	12	13 SF	14 SF	15 SF
16 COL	17 COL	18 COL	19 SEA	20 SEA	21 ANA	22 ANA
23 ANA	24 SEA	25 SEA	26 SEA	27 BOS	28 BOS	29 BOS
30 BOS	31 TOR					

August
SUN	MON	TUE	WED	THU	FRI	SAT
		1 TOR	2 TOR	3	4 CWS	5 CWS
6 CWS	7	8 NYY	9 NYY	10 NYY	11 DET	12 DET
13 DET	14 CLE	15 CLE	16 CLE	17	18 DET	19 DET
20 DET	21 DET	22 CLE	23 CLE	24 CLE	25 NYY	26 NYY
27 NYY	28 CWS	29 CWS	30 CWS	31		

September
SUN	MON	TUE	WED	THU	FRI	SAT
					1 TOR	2 TOR
3 TOR	4 TOR	5 BOS	6 BOS	7	8 TB	9 TB
10 TB	11 MIN	12 MIN	13	14	15 TB	16 TB
17 TB	18 BAL	19 BAL	20 BAL	21 SEA	22 SEA	23 SEA
24 SEA	25 ANA	26 ANA	27 ANA	28 ANA	29 TEX	30 TEX

October
SUN	MON	TUE	WED	THU	FRI	SAT
1 TEX	2	3	4	5	6	7

2000 SEASON
CLUB DIRECTORY

Owners
Stephen C. Schott
Ken Hofmann
President
Michael P. Crowley
General manager
Billy Beane
Assistant general manager
Paul DePodesta
Special assistant to general manager
Bill Rigney
Director of player development
Keith Lieppman
Director of player personnel
J.P. Ricciardi
Director of scouting
Grady Fuson
Director of minor league operations
Ted Polakowski
Director of baseball administration
Pam Pitts
Traveling secretary
Mickey Morabito
Scouting and player development asst.
Danny McCormack
Baseball operations assistant
Dave Forst
Senior director of broadcasting and communications
Ken Pries
Director of public relations
Jim Young
Baseball information manager
Mike Selleck
Broadcasting manager
Robert Buan
Sr. director of stadium operations
David Rinetti
Sr. director of sales and marketing
David Alioto

Director of corporate sales
Franklin Lowe
Dir. of promotions and special events
Susan Weiglein
Director of ticket sales
Dennis Murphy
Director of business services
David Lozow
Executive assistant
Carolyn Jones
Executive assistant, baseball operations
Betty Shinoda
Team physician
Dr. Allan Pont
Team orthopedist
Dr. Jerrald Goldman
Trainers
Larry Davis
Steven Sayles
Equipment manager
Steve Vucinich
Visiting clubhouse manager
Mike Thalblum
Special assignment scout
Dick Bogard
National cross-checkers
Ron Hopkins
Chris Pittaro
Major League advance scout
Bob Johnson
Supervisor of international scouting
Eric Kubota
Scouts
Steve Bowden, Tom Clark, Ruben Escalera, Kelly Heath, Bob Johnson, Tim Holt, John Kuehl, Rick Magnante, Gary McGraw, Billy Owens, John Poloni, Jim Pransky, Will Shock, Rich Sparks, Ron Vaughn

MINOR LEAGUE AFFILIATES

Class	Team	League	Manager
AAA	Sacramento	Pacific Coast	Bob Geren
AA	Midland	Texas	Tony DeFrancesco
A	Modesto	California	Greg Sparks
A	Visalia	California	Juan Navarette
A	Vancouver	Northwest	Dave Joppie
Rookie	Scottsdale A's	Arizona	John Kuehl

BROADCAST INFORMATION

Radio: KABL-AM (960).
TV: KICU-TV (Channel 36).
Cable TV: Fox Sports Bay Area.

SPRING TRAINING

Ballpark (city): Phoenix Municipal Stadium (Phoenix, Ariz.).
Ticket information: 602-392-0074.

2000 SEASON *Oakland Athletics*

Manager—Art Howe (18).
Coaches—Thad Bosley (41), Brad Fischer (35), Ken Macha (39), Rick Peterson (47), Mike Quede (45), Ron Washington (38).

No.	PITCHERS	B/T	Ht./Wt.	Born	1999 clubs
19	Appier, Kevin	R/R	6-2/200	12-6-67	Kansas City, Oakland
61	Vizcaino, Luis	R/R	5-11/169	6-1-77	Midland, Vancouver, Oakland
40	Dubose, Eric	L/L	6-3/215	5-15-76	Midland
49	Enochs, Chris	R/R	6-3/225	10-11-75	Midland, Visalia
62	Gregg, Kevin	R/R	6-5/203	6-20-78	Visalia, Midland, Vancouver
32	Harville, Chad	R/R	5-9/180	9-16-76	Midland, Vancouver, Oakland
31	Heredia, Gil	R/R	6-1/221	10-26-65	Oakland
15	Hudson, Tim	R/R	6-0/160	7-14-75	Midland, Vancouver, Oakland
45	Isringhausen, Jason	R/R	6-3/210	9-7-72	Norfolk, New York N.L., Oakland
24	Jones, Doug	R/R	6-2/224	6-24-57	Oakland
58	Kubinski, Tim	L/L	6-4/205	1-20-72	Vancouver, Oakland
59	Laxton, Brett	L/R	6-2/210	10-5-73	Vancouver, Oakland
52	Magnante, Mike	L/L	6-1/185	6-17-65	Anaheim
17	Mahay, Ron	L/L	6-2/190	6-28-71	Oakland, Vancouver
33	Mathews, T.J.	R/R	6-1/214	1-19-70	Oakland, Vancouver
	Olivares, Omar	R/R	6-0/205	7-6-67	Anaheim, Oakland
30	Prieto, Ariel	R/R	6-2/247	10-22-69	DID NOT PLAY
	Service, Scott	R/R	6-6/240	2-26-67	Kansas City
54	Vasquez, Leo	L/L	6-4/193	7-1-73	Binghamton, Midland, Vancouver

No.	CATCHERS	B/T	Ht./Wt.	Born	1999 clubs
7	Ardoin, Danny	R/R	6-0/218	7-8-74	Vancouver
55	Hernandez, Ramon	R/R	6-0/227	5-20-76	Vancouver, Oakland
23	Hinch, A.J.	R/R	6-1/207	5-15-74	Oakland, Vancouver

No.	INFIELDERS	B/T	Ht./Wt.	Born	1999 clubs
3	Chavez, Eric	L/R	6-0/204	12-7-77	Oakland
50	Espada, Josue	R/R	5-10/175	8-30-75	Midland, Vancouver
16	Giambi, Jason	L/R	6-3/235	1-8-71	Oakland
5	Jaha, John	R/R	6-1/217	5-27-66	Oakland
11	Menechino, Frank	R/R	5-9/175	1-7-71	Vancouver, Oakland
60	Ortiz, Jose	R/R	5-9/177	6-13-77	Vancouver
36	Piatt, Adam	R/R	6-2/195	2-8-76	Midland, Vancouver
9	Saenz, Olmedo	R/R	6-0/185	10-8-70	Oakland, Vancouver
4	Tejada, Miguel	R/R	5-9/188	5-25-76	Oakland
13	Velandia, Jorge	R/R	5-9/185	1-12-75	Oakland
8	Velarde, Randy	R/R	6-0/200	11-24-62	Anaheim, Oakland

No.	OUTFIELDERS	B/T	Ht./Wt.	Born	1999 clubs
	Becker, Rich	L/L	5-10/193	2-1-72	Milwaukee, Oakland
28	Christenson, Ryan	R/R	6-0/191	3-28-74	Oakland, Vancouver
23	Encarnacion, Mario	R/R	6-2/205	9-24-77	Midland, Vancouver
14	Grieve, Ben	L/R	6-4/230	5-4-76	Oakland
37	Long, Terrence	L/L	6-1/190	2-29-76	Norfolk, New York N.L., Vancouver
44	Porter, Bo	R/R	6-2/195	7-5-72	Iowa, Chicago N.L.
12	Stairs, Matt	L/R	5-9/217	2-27-68	Oakland

BALLPARK INFORMATION

Ballpark (capacity, surface)
Network Associates Coliseum (43,662, grass)

Address
Oakland Athletics
7677 Oakport St., Suite 200
Oakland, CA 94621

Business phone
510-638-4900

Ticket information
510-638-4627

Ticket prices
$24 (plaza club)
$22 (MVP infield)
$16 (field level-infield)
$15 (field level, plaza-infield)
$14 (plaza)
$5 (upper reserved)
$4 (bleachers)

Field dimensions (from home plate)
To left field at foul line, 330 feet
To center field, 400 feet
To right field at foul line, 330 feet

First game played
April 17, 1968 (Orioles 4, Athletics 1)

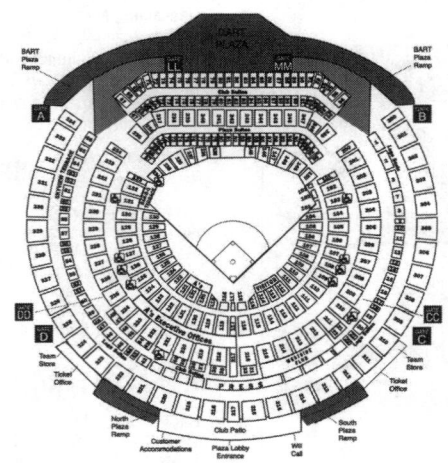

2000 SEASON Oakland Athletics

Date	Opp.	Res.	Score	(inn.*)	Hits	Opp. hits	Winning pitcher	Losing pitcher	Save	Record	Pos.	GB
4-6	N.Y.	L	4-7		5	12	Hernandez	Candiotti	Rivera	1-1	T2nd	0.5
4-7	N.Y.	L	0-4		5	8	Mendoza	Haynes		1-2	T3rd	1.0
4-9	At Sea.	L	1-6		3	10	Henry	Rogers		1-3	4th	1.0
4-10	At Sea.	W	11-4		17	9	Heredia	Fassero		2-3	T2nd	1.0
4-11	At Sea.	L	8-11		12	18	Moyer	Candiotti		2-4	4th	1.0
4-12	At Sea.	L	3-6		9	12	Garcia	Haynes	Mesa	2-5	4th	2.0
4-13	Ana.	W	3-2		7	9	Oquist	Sparks	Taylor	3-5	4th	1.0
4-14	Ana.	W	6-5		7	9	Mathews	Finley	Taylor	4-5	T2nd	1.0
4-15	Ana.	L	1-12		5	18	Olivares	Heredia		4-6	T3rd	2.0
4-16	Tex.	W	8-2		17	3	Candiotti	Sele		5-6	3rd	1.0
4-17	Tex.	W	11-3		13	6	Haynes	Clark		6-6	T1st	...
4-18	Tex.	L	2-6		7	15	Morgan	Oquist		6-7	T2nd	1.0
4-20	At Cle.	L	1-5		3	9	Colon	Rogers		6-8	T2nd	1.0
4-21	At Cle.	L	4-5		8	14	Reed	Taylor		6-9	T2nd	1.0
4-22	At Cle.	W	4-1		8	3	Candiotti	Nagy	Taylor	7-9	2nd	1.0
4-23	At Bal.	L	4-7		9	8	Fetters	Haynes		7-10	T2nd	2.0
4-24	At Bal.	W	3-0		6	4	Oquist	Erickson	Taylor	8-10	2nd	2.0
4-25	At Bal.	W	11-10		10	9	Rigby	Timlin	Taylor	9-10	2nd	2.0
4-26	Cle.	L	4-5	(10)	10	9	Karsay	Taylor	Jackson	9-11	2nd	2.5
4-27	Cle.	L	5-8		11	12	Nagy	Candiotti	Jackson	9-12	2nd	2.5
4-28	Cle.	L	1-4		6	6	Wright	Haynes	Jackson	9-13	4th	3.5
4-29	Cle.	L	3-8		4	9	Burba	Oquist		9-14	4th	3.5
4-30	Bos.	W	13-9		10	12	Mathews	Lowe		10-14	4th	3.5
5-1	Bos.	L	2-7		6	15	Martinez	Heredia		10-15	4th	3.5
5-2	Bos.	W	7-5		9	12	Jones	Harikkala	Taylor	11-15	4th	3.5
5-3	Bos.	W	12-11	(10)	11	13	Mathews	Gross		12-15	4th	2.5
5-4	At Tor.	W	13-4		13	11	Oquist	Halladay	Jones	13-15	2nd	2.0
5-5	At Tor.	W	8-2		15	5	Rogers	Escobar		14-15	2nd	2.0
5-6	At Tor.	W	3-2		6	10	Heredia	Carpenter	Taylor	15-15	2nd	1.0
5-7	At Chi.	L	1-7		7	10	Parque	Candiotti		15-16	2nd	1.0
5-8	At Chi.	L	3-5		8	11	Snyder	Haynes	Howry	15-17	2nd	2.0
5-9	At Chi.	W	3-0		8	4	Oquist	Sirotka	Jones	16-17	2nd	2.0
5-11	At Det.	W	6-2		10	6	Rigby	Weaver		17-17	2nd	1.5
5-12	At Det.	W	2-1		4	4	Heredia	Thompson	Taylor	18-17	2nd	1.0
5-14	Min.	W	7-5		10	11	Worrell	Lincoln	Taylor	19-17	2nd	1.5
5-15	Min.	W	6-5		8	10	Mathews	Guardado		20-17	2nd	1.5
5-16	Min.	W	4-2		5	5	Haynes	Radke	Taylor	21-17	2nd	0.5
5-18	At K.C.	L	3-13		6	17	Appier	Heredia		21-18	T1st	...
5-19	At K.C.	L	3-14		6	13	Rosado	Candiotti	Mathews	21-19	2nd	1.0
5-20	At K.C.	L	1-7		5	9	Suppan	Oquist		21-20	2nd	1.5
5-21	At Min.	L	1-2	(15)	8	14	Miller	Jones		21-21	2nd	1.5
5-22	At Min.	L	1-2	(10)	5	5	Wells	Rigby		21-22	2nd	2.5
5-23	At Min.	L	3-8		7	15	Milton	Heredia		21-23	T3rd	2.5
5-25	K.C.	W	5-3		7	5	Oquist	Rosado	Jones	22-23	T2nd	3.0
5-26	K.C.	W	3-1		5	5	Haynes	Suppan	Taylor	23-23	T2nd	3.0
5-27	K.C.	W	6-1		8	6	Rogers	Witasick		24-23	2nd	2.5
5-28	Bal.	W	2-1		6	4	Candiotti	Mussina	Taylor	25-23	2nd	2.5
5-29	Bal.	L	5-7		10	13	Johns	Mathews	Rhodes	25-24	3rd	3.5
5-30	Bal.	W	11-5		16	10	Rigby	Erickson		26-24	2nd	3.5
5-31	T.B.	W	10-7		7	11	Groom	Yan		27-24	2nd	3.5
6-1	T.B.	W	5-2		3	10	Rogers	Eiland	Taylor	28-24	2nd	3.5
6-2	T.B.	L	6-7		8	11	Yan	Mathews	Hernandez	28-25	2nd	4.5
6-4	At S.F	L	3-4	(15)	9	9	Spradlin	Taylor		28-26	2nd	4.5
6-5	At S.F	L	0-8		8	10	Rueter	Oquist		28-27	2nd	5.5
6-6	At S.F	W	7-6		8	12	Groom	Johnstone	Taylor	29-27	2nd	4.5
6-8	At S.D.	L	3-5		8	11	Wall	Groom	Hoffman	29-28	2nd	6.0
6-9	At S.D.	W	3-0		8	4	Haynes	Clement	Taylor	30-28	T2nd	5.0
6-10	At S.D.	L	1-2		4	7	Hitchcock	Heredia	Hoffman	30-29	3rd	5.5
6-11	L.A.	W	12-6		16	9	Oquist	Perez	Mathews	31-29	3rd	5.5
6-12	L.A.	W	4-3		8	12	Rogers	Valdes	Taylor	32-29	2nd	4.5
6-13	L.A.	W	9-3		8	10	Hudson	Dreifort		33-29	2nd	3.5
6-15	At Cle.	L	3-8		8	12	Wright	Haynes		33-30	2nd	3.0
6-16	At Cle.	L	8-9		9	10	Karsay	Taylor		33-31	T2nd	4.0
6-17	At Cle.	L	6-10		9	18	Shuey	Worrell		33-32	3rd	5.0
6-18	At Det.	L	3-8		3	10	Thompson	Oquist		33-33	3rd	6.0
6-19	At Det.	W	13-1		16	11	Hudson	Cruz		34-33	3rd	5.0
6-20	At Det.	W	6-5		8	6	Haynes	Moehler	Taylor	35-33	T2nd	4.0
6-21	At Det.	L	11-13		13	12	Brocail	Rigby	Jones	35-34	T2nd	4.0
6-22	At Tex.	W	5-3		11	11	Mathews	Wetteland	Taylor	36-34	2nd	3.0
6-23	At Tex.	L	6-7		7	13	Morgan	Oquist	Wetteland	36-35	T2nd	4.0
6-24	At Tex.	L	2-5		7	6	Burkett	Hudson	Wetteland	36-36	T2nd	5.0
6-25	At Ana.	L	3-4		9	8	Percival	Jones		36-37	T2nd	6.0

Date	Opp.	Res.	Score	(inn.*)	Hits	Opp. hits	Winning pitcher	Losing pitcher	Save	Record	Pos.	GB
6-26	At Ana.	L	4-5		7	10	Magnante	Rigby	Percival	36-38	3rd	6.0
6-27	At Ana.	L	3-4		7	12	Sparks	Rogers	Percival	36-39	3rd	6.0
6-29	Sea.	L	1-2	(12)	9	7	Paniagua	Mathews	Mesa	36-40	3rd	7.5
6-30	Sea.	W	14-5		14	12	Hudson	Fassero		37-40	3rd	7.5
7-1	Sea.	W	5-4		10	7	Taylor	Paniagua		38-40	3rd	7.0
7-2	Ana.	L	6-10		10	14	Petkovsek	Harville		38-41	3rd	8.0
7-3	Ana.	W	9-7		12	13	Heredia	Finley	Taylor	39-41	3rd	7.0
7-4	Ana.	L	2-5		5	12	Olivares	Oquist		39-42	3rd	7.0
7-5	Tex.	W	4-2		12	6	Hudson	Burkett	Taylor	40-42	3rd	6.0
7-6	Tex.	W	4-0		5	4	Haynes	Glynn		41-42	3rd	5.0
7-7	Tex.	L	4-7		7	10	Zimmerman	Rigby	Wetteland	41-43	3rd	6.0
7-9	At Ari.	W	5-2		8	12	Heredia	Benes	Taylor	42-43	T2nd	6.0
7-10	At Ari.	W	2-0		3	3	Hudson	Johnson	Taylor	43-43	2nd	5.0
7-11	At Ari.	L	4-7		6	7	Daal	Haynes	Mantei	43-44	2nd	5.0
7-15	S.F	W	11-9		12	10	Jones	Nen		44-44	2nd	5.0
7-16	S.F	W	4-2		5	5	Heredia	Ortiz	Taylor	45-44	2nd	5.0
7-17	S.F	L	2-7		6	10	Rueter	Groom		45-45	2nd	5.0
7-18	Col.	W	3-2		5	5	Haynes	Jones	Taylor	46-45	2nd	5.0
7-19	Col.	W	10-5		12	10	Worrell	Ramirez	Jones	47-45	2nd	5.0
7-20	Col.	W	4-3		5	6	Rogers	Kile	Taylor	48-45	2nd	5.0
7-21	At Sea.	W	13-3		15	7	Heredia	Fassero		49-45	2nd	5.0
7-22	At Sea.	L	4-5	(10)	4	10	Abbott	Jones		49-46	2nd	6.0
7-23	At K.C.	L	7-12		10	15	Morman	Haynes	Barber	49-47	2nd	7.0
7-24	At K.C.	W	12-2		9	11	Oquist	Witasick		50-47	2nd	7.0
7-25	At K.C.	L	11-13	(10)	10	19	Service	Harville		50-48	2nd	8.0
7-26	At Min.	W	14-7		16	12	Groom	Sampson		51-48	2nd	7.5
7-27	At Min.	L	2-3		5	6	Mays	Taylor	Guardado	51-49	2nd	8.5
7-28	At Min.	L	3-5		8	9	Hawkins	Haynes	Trombley	51-50	2nd	8.5
7-30	T.B.	W	4-1		8	5	Oquist	Eiland	Taylor	52-50	2nd	9.0
7-31	T.B.	W	5-1		5	7	Olivares	Arrojo	Jones	53-50	2nd	8.0
8-1	T.B.	W	10-6		12	12	Heredia	Witt	Mathews	54-50	2nd	8.0
8-2	Bal.	W	7-1		9	4	Appier	Erickson		55-50	2nd	8.0
8-3	Bal.	W	12-2		12	9	Hudson	Bones		56-50	2nd	8.0
8-4	Bal.	L	5-9		8	14	Johnson	Haynes		56-51	2nd	9.0
8-5	Chi.	W	7-6	(11)	11	11	Mathews	Eyre		57-51	2nd	8.5
8-6	Chi.	W	9-1		15	5	Heredia	Navarro		58-51	2nd	7.5
8-7	Chi.	W	11-1		14	6	Appier	Parque		59-51	2nd	7.5
8-8	Chi.	W	7-5		9	11	Jones	Foulke		60-51	2nd	6.5
8-9	N.Y.	L	8-12		13	9	Mendoza	Haynes		60-52	2nd	6.5
8-10	N.Y.	W	6-1		10	9	Olivares	Clemens	Jones	61-52	2nd	6.5
8-11	N.Y.	L	3-5		6	8	Watson	Jones	Rivera	61-53	2nd	7.5
8-13	At Tor.	W	9-8		12	8	Appier	Halladay	Jones	62-53	2nd	5.5
8-14	At Tor.	W	13-5		14	11	Hudson	Hamilton		63-53	2nd	4.5
8-15	At Tor.	W	9-5		15	10	Oquist	Escobar		64-53	2nd	4.5
8-16	At Bos.	L	5-6		7	11	Lowe	Jones		64-54	2nd	5.5
8-17	At Bos.	W	12-1		17	10	Heredia	Saberhagen		65-54	2nd	5.5
8-18	At Bos.	L	4-7		3	13	Garces	Appier	Lowe	65-55	2nd	6.5
8-19	At Bos.	W	6-2		12	4	Hudson	Martinez	Mathews	66-55	2nd	5.5
8-20	Tor.	L	0-11		4	13	Hamilton	Oquist		66-56	2nd	6.5
8-21	Tor.	W	8-4		9	8	Olivares	Carpenter		67-56	2nd	6.5
8-22	Tor.	W	4-3		8	12	Jones	Koch		68-56	2nd	6.5
8-23	Tor.	L	4-9		11	14	Wells	Appier		68-57	2nd	6.5
8-24	Cle.	W	11-10		12	8	Mathews	Shuey		69-57	2nd	5.5
8-25	Cle.	L	4-12		6	15	Colon	Oquist		69-58	2nd	6.5
8-27	At Chi.	W	9-6		10	13	Olivares	Sirotka	Isringhausen	70-58	2nd	6.5
8-28	At Chi.	W	7-5		10	7	Heredia	Navarro	Jones	71-58	2nd	6.5
8-29	At Chi.	L	2-7		10	10	Baldwin	Appier	Foulke	71-59	2nd	7.5
8-30	At N.Y.	L	4-7		10	8	Nelson	Mathews	Rivera	71-60	2nd	7.5
8-31	At N.Y.	W	3-2	(11)	10	8	Jones	Mendoza	Isringhausen	72-60	2nd	6.5
9-1	At N.Y.	W	7-1		10	6	Olivares	Clemens		73-60	2nd	6.5
9-2	At N.Y.	L	3-9		8	14	Hernandez	Heredia		73-61	2nd	6.5
9-3	Det.	W	7-4		9	9	Appier	Cruz	Isringhausen	74-61	2nd	6.5
9-4	Det.	W	2-1		9	4	Hudson	Cordero		75-61	2nd	5.5
9-5	Det.	L	4-5		8	10	Blair	Haynes	Jones	75-62	2nd	6.0
9-6	Det.	L	7-9		13	13	Borkowski	Olivares	Jones	75-63	2nd	7.5
9-7	Bos.	L	3-5		6	10	Wakefield	Heredia	Lowe	75-64	2nd	8.5
9-8	Bos.	W	6-2		8	5	Appier	Rapp		76-64	2nd	8.5
9-10	At T.B.	W	7-2		14	8	Hudson	Alvarez		77-64	2nd	7.5
9-11	At T.B.	W	5-4		6	8	Olivares	Rupe	Jones	78-64	2nd	6.5
9-12	At T.B.	W	4-3		6	6	Heredia	Wheeler	Isringhausen	79-64	2nd	5.5
9-13	At T.B.	W	8-3		13	7	Appier	Witt		80-64	2nd	5.5
9-14	At Bal.	L	6-13		11	16	Mussina	Oquist		80-65	2nd	6.5
9-17	K.C.	L	3-9		7	15	Witasick	Hudson		80-66	2nd	7.0
9-18	K.C.	W	8-4		13	8	Olivares	Rosado	Isringhausen	81-66	2nd	7.0
9-19	K.C.	W	12-3		12	6	Heredia	Fussell		82-66	2nd	6.0
9-20	Min.	L	0-4		7	11	Ryan	Appier		82-67	2nd	6.5

Date	Opp.	Res.	Score	(inn.*)	Hits	Opp. hits	Winning pitcher	Losing pitcher	Save	Record	Pos.	GB
9-21	Min.	W	5-3		9	7	Mahay	Carrasco	Isringhausen	83-67	2nd	5.5
9-22	Min.	L	4-5		8	7	Redman	Worrell	Trombley	83-68	2nd	5.5
9-23†	At Bal.	W	9-6		15	8	Mathews	Molina	Isringhausen	84-68		
9-23‡	At Bal.	L	4-12		8	12	Johns	Olivares		84-69	2nd	5.5
9-24	At Tex.	L	4-12		8	18	Sele	Heredia		84-70	2nd	6.5
9-25	At Tex.	L	4-10		6	9	Burkett	Appier		84-71	2nd	7.5
9-26	At Tex.	L	3-10		7	12	Loaiza	Jarvis		84-72	2nd	8.5
9-28	At Ana.	W	9-3		14	4	Hudson	Washburn	Mahay	85-72	2nd	9.0
9-29	At Ana.	L	4-7		4	12	Hasegawa	Mathews	Pote	85-73	2nd	9.0
9-30	At Ana.	L	4-5		13	10	Petkovsek	Isringhausen	Pote	85-74	2nd	10.0
10-1	Sea.	W	5-1		7	4	Appier	Ramsay	Jones	86-74	2nd	9.0
10-2	Sea.	L	2-10		8	12	Garcia	Laxton		86-75	2nd	9.0
10-3	Sea.	W	3-1		11	4	Mahay	Halama	Isringhausen	87-75	2nd	8.0

Monthly records: April (10-14), May (17-10), June (10-16), July (16-10), August (19-10), September (13-14), October (2-1).
*Innings, if other than nine. † First game of a doubleheader. ‡ Second game of a doubleheader.

HIGHLIGHTS

High point: The A's seized sole possession of the wild-card lead on August 22 when Randy Velarde delivered a two-out bloop single in the ninth inning against Toronto. The 4-3 victory moved the club 12 games over .500—exactly its standing at season's end.

Low point: Oakland, trailing the A.L. West-leading Rangers by 5.5 games and down 4.5 games to the Red Sox in the wild-card race, went to Texas for a three-game series in late September, just one day after playing a makeup doubleheader in Baltimore. The A's were swept by the Rangers—and outscored, 32-11. Texas clinched the division crown in the series finale.

Turning point: The A's vaulted into post-season contention after acquiring second baseman Randy Velarde and pitchers Omar Olivares, Kevin Appier and Jason Isringhausen in trading-deadline deals. Beginning July 30, Oakland won nine of 10 games.

Most valuable player: First baseman Jason Giambi, who had career highs in batting average (.315), home runs (33) and RBIs (123), one shy of the Oakland record, held by Jose Canseco. Also, he improved vastly in the field and played a key leadership role.

Most valuable pitcher: Tim Hudson jumped from Class AA to Class AAA to the big leagues by June. After going 7-0 in the minors, he compiled an 11-2 record and a 3.23 ERA for the A's. Hudson really opened eyes by winning against Randy Johnson and Pedro Martinez.

Most improved player: Gil Heredia, who emerged as Oakland's steadiest starter. He won a career-high 13 games and led the A.L. in fewest walks per nine innings pitched (1.5).

Most pleasant surprise: Signed to a minor league deal with an invitation to the A's camp, DH John Jaha made an amazing comeback at age 33 by hitting 35 home runs and driving in 111 runs. He was Oakland's lone representative at the All-Star Game.

Biggest disappointment: Entering the season, the A's envisioned Jimmy Haynes as their future ace. By season's end, he was in the bullpen, virtually unused. Despite showing glimpses of his old form, Haynes never got into a groove and finished 7-12 with a 6.34 ERA.

Key injuries: Sparkplug utility player Tony Phillips, a vocal leader, was sidelined for the final seven weeks of the season when he broke his left leg at Toronto on August 15. Another valuable veteran, outfielder Tim Raines, was diagnosed with lupus and didn't play after July 18. Rookie third baseman Eric Chavez missed a month with a heel injury, and T.J. Mathews, the team's top setup man, spent time on the D.L. with a sore elbow—an ailment that bothered him much of the season and required post-season surgery.

Notable: The A's notched their first winning season since 1992. ... The club's 13-game improvement from 1998 was the largest gain among American League clubs. ... Oakland's 4.69 ERA was third-best in the league. ... The A's drew 770 walks, the fifth-highest total in major league history. ... Isringhausen went 8-for-8 in save opportunities down the stretch.

—SUSAN SLUSSER

RECORDS

1999 regular-season record: 87-75 (2nd in A.L. West; 52-29 at home; 35-46 on road; 34-18 vs. East; 26-30 vs. Central; 15-21 vs. A.L. West; 12-6 vs. N.L.; 23-17 vs. lefthanded starters; 64-58 vs. righthanded starters; 75-67 on grass; 12-8 on turf; 33-27 in daytime; 54-48 at night; 22-19 in one-run games; 3-7 in extra-inning games; 0-0-1 in doubleheaders).
Team record past five years: 371-421 (.468, ranks 10th in league in that span).

TEAM LEADERS

Batting average: Jason Giambi (.315).
At-bats: Miguel Tejada (593).
Runs: Jason Giambi (115).
Hits: Jason Giambi (181).
Total Bases: Jason Giambi (318).
Doubles: Jason Giambi (36).
Triples: Tony Phillips, Miguel Tejada (4).
Home runs: Matt Stairs (38).
Runs batted in: Jason Giambi (123).
Stolen bases: Tony Phillips, Randy Velarde (11).

Slugging percentage: John Jaha (.556).
On-base percentage: Jason Giambi (.422).
Wins: Gil Heredia (13).
Earned-run average: Gil Heredia (4.81).
Complete games: Kenny Rogers (3).
Shutouts: None.
Saves: Billy Taylor (26).
Innings pitched: Gil Heredia (200.1).
Strikeouts: Tim Hudson (132).

GAMES BY POSITION

Catcher: Mike Macfarlane 79, A.J. Hinch 73, Ramon Hernandez 40.
First base: Jason Giambi 142, Olmedo Saenz 28, Scott Spiezio 10, John Jaha 8, Matt Stairs 1.
Second base: Tony Phillips 66, Randy Velarde 61, Jorge Velandia 52, Scott Spiezio 42, Jason McDonald 1.
Third base: Eric Chavez 105, Olmedo Saenz 56, Scott Spiezio 31, Tony Phillips 2, Jorge Velandia 2, Jason Giambi 1, Frank Menechino 1.
Shortstop: Miguel Tejada 159, Jorge Velandia 8, Frank Menechino 5, Eric Chavez 2, Tony Phillips 1.
Outfield: Matt Stairs 139, Ben Grieve 137, Ryan Christenson 104, Jason McDonald 89, Tony Phillips 62, Rich Becker 39, Tim Raines 38.
Designated hitter: John Jaha 121, Jason Giambi 15, Olmedo Saenz 8, Scott Spiezio 6, Matt Stairs 5, Jason McDonald 5, Ben Grieve 4, Tim Raines 3, Eric Chavez 3, Frank Menechino 3, Tim Hudson 2, Tony Phillips 1, Mike Macfarlane 1, Rich Becker 1, Jorge Velandia 1, Ryan Christenson 1.

TOP DRAFT CHOICES

1. **Barry Zito**, LHP, U. of Southern California
2. **Ryan Ludwick**, OF, U. of Nevada-Las Vegas
3. **Jorge Soto**, C/1B, Troy State Univ.
4. **Keith Surkont**, RHP, Williams (Mass.) College
5. **Darin Moore**, RHP, U. of the Pacific
6. **Mario Ramos**, LHP, Rice University
7. **Josh Hochgesang**, 3B, Stanford Univ.
8. **Justin Lehr**, RHP/C, U. of Southern California
9. **Kirk Asche**, OF, Jacksonville University
10. **Justin Sobchuk**, RHP, Sehome H.S., Bellingham, Wash.

SEATTLE MARINERS
AMERICAN LEAGUE WEST DIVISION

2000 Mariners Schedule
Home games shaded. "*"—All-Star Game at Turner Field (Atlanta).

March
SUN	MON	TUE	WED	THU	FRI	SAT
26	27	28	29	30	31	

April
SUN	MON	TUE	WED	THU	FRI	SAT
						1
2	3 BOS	4 BOS	5 BOS	6	7 NYY	8 NYY
9 NYY	10	11 DET	12 DET	13 DET	14 TOR	15 TOR
16 TOR	17 CWS	18 CWS	19 CWS	20	21 KC	22 KC
23 KC	24 CLE	25 CLE	26 CLE	27	28 KC	29 KC
30 KC						

May
SUN	MON	TUE	WED	THU	FRI	SAT
	1 MIN	2 MIN	3 MIN	4	5 ANA	6 ANA
7 ANA	8 TEX	9 TEX	10 TEX	11 OAK	12 OAK	13 OAK
14 OAK	15 MIN	16 MIN	17 MIN	18	19 TB	20 TB
21 TB	22	23 BAL	24 BAL	25 BAL	26 TB	27 TB
28 TB	29 CWS	30 CWS	31 CWS			

June
SUN	MON	TUE	WED	THU	FRI	SAT
				1	2 SD	3 SD
4 SD	5 COL	6 COL	7 COL	8	9 SF	10 SF
11 SF	12 KC	13 KC	14 KC	15	16 MIN	17 MIN
18 MIN	19 TB	20 TB	21 TB	22 BAL	23 BAL	24 BAL
25 BAL	26	27 ANA	28 ANA	29 ANA	30 TEX	

July
SUN	MON	TUE	WED	THU	FRI	SAT
						1 TEX
2 TEX	3 ANA	4 ANA	5 ANA	6 ANA	7 LA	8 LA
9 LA	10	11 *	12	13 SD	14 SD	15 SD
16 ARI	17 ARI	18 ARI	19 OAK	20 OAK	21 TEX	22 TEX
23 TEX	24 OAK	25 OAK	26 OAK	27 TOR	28 TOR	29 TOR
30 TOR	31 BOS					

August
SUN	MON	TUE	WED	THU	FRI	SAT
		1 BOS	2 BOS	3	4 NYY	5 NYY
6 NYY	7 NYY	8 CWS	9 CWS	10 CWS	11 CLE	12 CLE
13 CLE	14 DET	15 DET	16 DET	17	18 CLE	19 CLE
20 CLE	21 DET	22 DET	23 DET	24 DET	25 CWS	26 CWS
27 CWS	28 NYY	29 NYY	30 NYY	31		

September
SUN	MON	TUE	WED	THU	FRI	SAT
					1 BOS	2 BOS
3 BOS	4 BOS	5 TOR	6 TOR	7 TOR	8 MIN	9 MIN
10 MIN	11 KC	12 KC	13 KC	14	15 BAL	16 BAL
17 BAL	18 TB	19 TB	20 TB	21 OAK	22 OAK	23 OAK
24 OAK	25	26 TEX	27 TEX	28 TEX	29 ANA	30 ANA

October
SUN	MON	TUE	WED	THU	FRI	SAT
1 ANA	2	3	4	5	6	7

2000 SEASON
CLUB DIRECTORY

Chairman & chief executive officer
Howard Lincoln

Board of directors
Howard Lincoln, chairman; John Ellis, chairman emeritus; Minoru Arakawa; Chris Larson; John McCaw; Frank Shrontz; Craig Watjen

President and chief operating officer
Chuck Armstrong

Executive v.p., baseball operations
Pat Gillick

Executive v.p., business operations
Bob Aylward

Exec. v.p., finance and ballpark ops.
Kevin Mather

Vice president, baseball administration
Lee Pelekoudas

V.p., scouting and player development
Roger Jongewaard

Vice president, communications
Randy Adamack

Vice president, ballpark operations
Neil Campbell

V.p., ballpark planning and development
John Palmer

Controller
Tim Kornegay

Director, Pacific rim scouting
Jim Colborn

Director, player development
Benny Looper

Director, professional scouting
Ken Compton

Director, scouting
Frank Mattox

Director, team travel
Ron Spellecy

Director, baseball information
Tim Hevly

Dir., broadcasting & communications
Dave Aust

Director, public information
Rebecca Hale

Special assignment
Woody Woodward

Coord. of baseball technical information
Mike Kuharich

Coordinator of minor league instruction
Mike Goff

Medical director
Dr. Larry Pedegana

Trainers
Rick Griffin, Tom Newberg, Ken Roll

Team physician
Dr. Mitchel Storey

Team dentist
Dr. Robert Hughes

Home clubhouse manager
Scott Gilbert

Visiting clubhouse manager
Henry Genzale

Video coordinator
Carl Hamilton

Strength and conditioning coach
Allen Wirtala

Head groundskeeper
Steve Peeler

Assistant groundskeeper
Eddie Busque

Advance scout
Stan Williams

National cross-checker
Steve Jongewaard

Major League scouts
Brandy Davis, Bob Harrison, Bill Kearns, Steve Pope

Scouting supervisors
Curtis Dishman, Ken Madeja, John McMichen, Carroll Sembera

Scouts
Dave Alexander, Maximo Alvarez, Brian Ballentine, Jeff Brisson, Mark Brown, Jon Bunnell, Rodney Davis, Ramon de los Santos, Murray Gage-Cole, Pete Garcia, Phil Geisler, Ron Hafner, Des Hamilton, Larry Harper, Ted Heid, Jae Lee, Jay Lee, Stan Lewis, Mark Lummus, Tom McNamara, Wilmer Madera, Luis Martinez, Tom McNamara, Juan Marquez, John Martin, Luis Martinez, Mauro Mazzotti, Julio Molina, Omer Munoz Sr., Myron Pines, Phil Pote, Steve Rath, Eric Robinson, Jesus Salazar, Rafael Santana, Alex Smith, Jim Stewart, Harry Stricklett, Derek Valenzuela, Kyle Van Hook, Ray Vince, Curtis Wallace, Karel Williams, Selwyn Young

MINOR LEAGUE AFFILIATES

Class	Team	League	Manager
AAA	Tacoma	Pacific Coast	Dave Myers
AA	New Haven	Eastern	Dan Rohn
A	Lancaster	California	Mark Parent
A	Wisconsin	Midwest	Gary Thurman
A	Everett	Northwest	Terry Pollreisz
Rookie	Peoria Mariners	Arizona	Omer Munoz Jr.

BROADCAST INFORMATION
Radio: KIRO-AM (710).
TV: KIRO-TV (Channel 7).
Cable TV: Fox Sports Net Northwest.

SPRING TRAINING
Ballpark: Peoria Stadium (Peoria, Ariz.).
Ticket information: 480-784-4444.

SPRING TRAINING ROSTER

Manager—Lou Piniella (14).
Coaches—Larry Bowa, John McLaren (7), John Moses, Gerald Perry, Bryan Price, Matt Sinatro (15).

No.	PITCHERS	B/T	Ht./Wt.	Born	1999 clubs
45	Abbott, Paul	R/R	6-3/195	9-15-67	Tacoma, Seattle
26	Cloude, Ken	R/R	6-1/180	1-9-75	Tacoma, Seattle
43	Davey, Tom	R/R	6-7/230	9-11-73	Toronto, Syracuse, Seattle
	Franklin, Ryan	R/R	6-3/185	3-5-73	Tacoma, Seattle
	Fuentes, Brian	L/L	6-4/220	8-9-75	New Haven
34	Garcia, Freddy	R/R	6-4/235	10-6-76	Seattle
54	Halama, John	L/L	6-5/200	2-22-72	Seattle
32	Hinchliffe, Brett	R/R	6-5/190	7-21-74	Seattle, Tacoma
	Hodges, Kevin	R/R	6-4/200	6-24-73	Jackson, New Orleans, Tacoma
	Mears, Chris	R/R	6-4/180	1-20-78	Wisconsin, Lancaster
55	Meche, Gil	R/R	6-3/180	9-8-78	New Haven, Tacoma, Seattle
49	Mesa, Jose	R/R	6-3/225	5-22-66	Seattle
	Montane, Ivan	R/R	6-2/195	6-3-73	Wisconsin, New Haven
50	Moyer, Jamie	L/L	6-0/170	11-18-62	Seattle
30	Paniagua, Jose	R/R	6-2/185	8-20-73	Seattle
23	Ramsay, Robert	L/L	6-5/220	12-3-73	Pawtucket, Seattle, Tacoma
53	Rhodes, Arthur	L/L	6-2/205	10-24-69	Baltimore
33	Rodriguez, Frankie	R/R	6-0/210	12-11-72	Salt Lake, Seattle
	Sasaki, Kazuhiro	R/R	6-4/208	2-22-68	Yokohama BayStars
53	Sinclair, Steve	L/L	6-2/190	8-2-71	Syracuse, Toronto, Seattle, Tacoma
48	Spencer, Sean	L/L	5-11/185	5-29-75	Tacoma, Seattle
67	Stark, Dennis	R/R	6-2/210	10-27-74	New Haven, Seattle
31	Williams, Todd	R/R	6-3/210	2-13-71	Indianapolis, Tacoma, Seattle
46	Zimmerman, Jordan	R/L	6-0/200	4-28-75	New Haven, Seattle, Tacoma, Everett

No.	CATCHERS	B/T	Ht./Wt.	Born	1999 clubs
17	Lampkin, Tom	L/R	5-11/195	3-4-64	Seattle
6	Wilson, Dan	R/R	6-3/202	3-25-69	Seattle

No.	INFIELDERS	B/T	Ht./Wt.	Born	1999 clubs
25	Bell, David	R/R	5-10/175	9-14-72	Seattle
19	Buhner, Jay	R/R	6-3/215	8-13-64	Seattle
8	Guillen, Carlos	B/R	6-1/180	9-30-75	Seattle
11	Martinez, Edgar	R/R	5-11/200	1-2-63	Seattle
	McLemore, Mark	B/R	5-11/207	10-4-64	Texas
	Olerud, John	L/L	6-5/220	8-5-68	New York N.L.
3	Rodriguez, Alex	R/R	6-3/195	7-27-75	Seattle

No.	OUTFIELDERS	B/T	Ht./Wt.	Born	1999 clubs
	Alexander, Chad	R/R	6-1/195	5-22-74	Jackson, New Orleans
1	Gipson, Charles	R/R	6-2/180	12-16-72	Seattle, Tacoma, New Haven, Everett
24	Griffey Jr., Ken	L/L	6-3/205	11-21-69	Seattle
	Hunter, Brian	R/R	6-3/180	3-5-71	Detroit, Seattle
5	Ibanez, Raul	L/R	6-2/200	6-2-72	Seattle, Tacoma
	Javier, Stan	B/R	6-0/202	1-9-64	San Francisco, Houston
47	Mabry, John	L/R	6-4/195	10-17-70	Seattle
12	Monahan, Shane	L/R	6-0/195	8-12-74	Tacoma, Seattle

BALLPARK INFORMATION

Ballpark (capacity, surface)
SAFECO Field (47,116, grass).

Address
1st Avenue S & Atlantic
Seattle, WA 98104

Business phone
206-346-4001

Ticket information
206-346-4001

Ticket prices
$37 (terrace club infield)
$32 (lower box)
$29 (terrace club outfield)
$27 (field)
$18 (view box, lower outfield reserved)
$14 (view reserved)
$9 (left field bleachers)
$5 (center field bleachers)

Field dimensions (from home plate)
To left field at foul line, 331 feet
To center field, 405 feet
To right field at foul line, 326 feet

First game played
July 15, 1999 (Padres 3, Mariners 2)

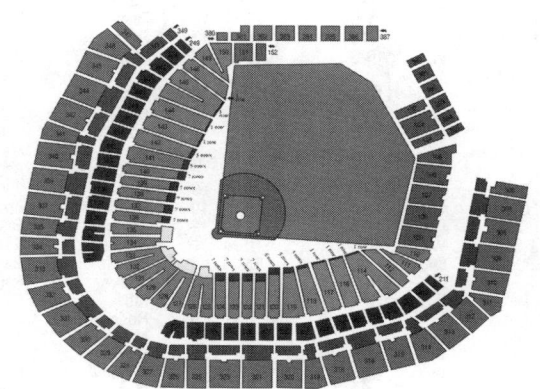

2000 SEASON *Seattle Mariners*

Date	Opp.	Res.	Score	(inn.*)	Hits	Opp. hits	Winning pitcher	Losing pitcher	Save	Record	Pos.	GB
4-6	Chi.	L	3-11		6	15	Parque	Moyer		0-2	4th	1.5
4-7	Chi.	W	7-3		10	10	Garcia	Snyder	Mesa	1-2	T3rd	1.0
4-9	Oak.	W	6-1		10	3	Henry	Rogers		2-2	T1st	...
4-10	Oak.	L	4-11		9	17	Heredia	Fassero		2-3	T2nd	...
4-11	Oak.	W	11-8		18	12	Moyer	Candiotti		3-3	T1st	...
4-12	Oak.	W	6-3		12	9	Garcia	Haynes	Mesa	4-3	T1st	...
4-13	Tex.	L	6-15		10	19	Morgan	Cloude		4-4	T1st	...
4-14	Tex.	L	6-9		11	17	Zimmerman	Paniagua	Wetteland	4-5	T2nd	1.0
4-15	Tex.	L	3-4	(10)	5	9	Crabtree	Halama	Wetteland	4-6	T3rd	2.0
4-16	At Ana.	L	5-9		5	14	Belcher	Moyer		4-7	4th	2.0
4-17	At Ana.	W	4-3	(10)	7	8	Paniagua	Percival	Mesa	5-7	4th	1.0
4-18	At Ana.	W	8-5		10	10	Cloude	Sparks	Mesa	6-7	T2nd	1.0
4-20	At Chi.	L	1-3		5	8	Parque	Fassero	Howry	6-8	T2nd	1.0
4-21	At Chi.	L	1-2		6	5	Snyder	Paniagua	Howry	6-9	T2nd	1.0
4-23	At T.B.	L	4-5		7	11	White	Halama	Hernandez	6-10	4th	2.5
4-24	At T.B.	W	9-4		12	8	Henry	Arrojo		7-10	3rd	2.5
4-25	At T.B.	W	6-4		12	6	Paniagua	Hernandez	Mesa	8-10	3rd	2.5
4-26	Det.	L	0-7		7	15	Moehler	Moyer		8-11	T3rd	3.0
4-27	Det.	L	1-5		9	10	Thompson	Hinchliffe		8-12	T3rd	3.0
4-28	Det.	W	8-6		10	8	Garcia	Blair		9-12	T2nd	3.0
4-29	Det.	W	22-6		19	15	Cloude	Nitkowski		10-12	T2nd	2.0
4-30	Tor.	W	11-9		10	12	Halama	Person	Mesa	11-12	T2nd	2.0
5-1	Tor.	L	3-9		11	13	Carpenter	Moyer	Davey	11-13	T2nd	2.0
5-2	Tor.	W	3-2		7	8	Cloude	Plesac		12-13	T2nd	2.0
5-3	Tor.	L	10-16		13	17	Wells	Garcia		12-14	T2nd	2.0
5-5	At Cle.	W	6-5		10	10	Fassero	Burba	Mesa	13-14	3rd	2.0
5-6	At Cle.	L	4-8		7	8	Colon	Weaver		13-15	3rd	2.0
5-7	At N.Y.	L	1-10		5	10	Irabu	Suzuki		13-16	3rd	2.0
5-8	At N.Y.	W	14-5		19	8	Garcia	Hernandez		14-16	3rd	2.0
5-9	At N.Y.	L	1-6		3	9	Grimsley	Fassero		14-17	3rd	3.0
5-10	At Bos.	L	4-12		9	10	Wasdin	Hinchliffe		14-18	3rd	3.0
5-11	At Bos.	W	8-5		14	10	Moyer	Wakefield		15-18	3rd	3.0
5-12	At Bos.	L	2-9		6	11	Martinez	Suzuki		15-19	T3rd	3.5
5-14	K.C.	L	7-12		10	19	Service	Fassero		15-20	4th	5.0
5-15	K.C.	L	10-11		8	17	Santiago	Paniagua	Montgomery	15-21	4th	6.0
5-16	K.C.	W	5-1		9	9	Moyer	Fussell		16-21	4th	5.0
5-17	Min.	W	15-5		16	9	Halama	Milton		17-21	T3rd	4.0
5-18	Min.	W	10-1		13	8	Garcia	Perkins		18-21	3rd	3.0
5-19	Min.	W	7-0		11	5	Fassero	Lincoln		19-21	3rd	3.0
5-21	At K.C.	W	5-2		12	11	Moyer	Witasick		20-21	3rd	2.0
5-22	At K.C.	W	7-4		12	11	Carmona	Fussell	Mesa	21-21	2nd	2.0
5-23	At K.C.	L	4-5		9	11	Whisenant	Paniagua	Montgomery	21-22	2nd	2.0
5-24	At Min.	L	5-10		12	12	Perkins	Fassero		21-23	T2nd	3.0
5-25	At Min.	W	15-5		17	10	Halama	Rath		22-23	T2nd	3.0
5-26	At Min.	W	11-3		12	7	Moyer	Hawkins		23-23	T2nd	3.0
5-28	T.B.	W	6-1		11	5	Garcia	Alvarez		24-23	3rd	3.0
5-29	T.B.	W	11-5		12	10	Fassero	Rupe		25-23	2nd	3.0
5-30	T.B.	L	7-15		15	17	Rekar	Cloude		25-24	3rd	4.0
5-31	Bal.	W	10-6		13	12	Moyer	Ponson	Mesa	26-24	3rd	4.0
6-1	Bal.	L	11-14		14	14	Johns	Garcia		26-25	3rd	5.0
6-2	Bal.	W	4-2		6	12	Paniagua	Mussina	Mesa	27-25	3rd	5.0
6-4	At S.D.	L	2-3		7	6	Wall	Paniagua	Hoffman	27-26	3rd	5.0
6-5	At S.D.	L	2-3	(10)	9	7	Reyes	Mesa		27-27	3rd	6.0
6-6	At S.D.	W	4-1		7	4	Garcia	Ashby	Paniagua	28-27	3rd	5.0
6-7	At Col.	W	4-2		8	9	Halama	Jones	Mesa	29-27	T2nd	5.0
6-8	At Col.	W	10-5		15	10	Rodriguez	Brownson	Cloude	30-27	2nd	5.0
6-9	At Col.	L	11-16		12	12	Bohanon	Fassero		30-28	T2nd	5.0
6-11	S.F	W	7-3		10	9	Moyer	Gardner	Mesa	31-28	2nd	5.0
6-12	S.F	L	11-15		15	22	Rueter	Garcia		31-29	3rd	5.0
6-13	S.F	L	4-8		7	13	Tavarez	Paniagua		31-30	3rd	5.0
6-14	At Det.	L	7-8		13	10	Kida	Cloude		31-31	3rd	5.0
6-15	At Det.	W	5-4		6	9	Rodriguez	Moehler	Mesa	32-31	3rd	4.0
6-16	At Det.	W	7-1		13	9	Moyer	Mlicki		33-31	T2nd	4.0
6-17	At Det.	W	4-3		7	7	Garcia	Jones	Mesa	34-31	2nd	4.0
6-18	At Cle.	W	9-4		10	11	Halama	Nagy		35-31	2nd	4.0
6-19	At Cle.	L	6-10		12	10	Burba	Watson	Jackson	35-32	2nd	4.0
6-20	At Cle.	L	5-13		11	14	Wright	Rodriguez		35-33	T2nd	4.0
6-21	At Cle.	L	3-4	(12)	10	12	Karsay	Mesa		35-34	T2nd	4.0
6-22	Ana.	L	2-4		6	8	Petkovsek	Garcia	Percival	35-35	3rd	4.0
6-23	Ana.	W	8-3		10	10	Halama	Hill	Rodriguez	36-35	T2nd	4.0
6-24	Ana.	L	7-12		9	16	Schoeneweis	Mesa	Petkovsek	36-36	T2nd	5.0
6-25	Tex.	L	4-14		6	18	Glynn	Rodriguez		36-37	T2nd	6.0

Date	Opp.	Res.	Score	(inn.*)	Hits	Opp. hits	Winning pitcher	Losing pitcher	Save	Record	Pos.	GB
6-26	Tex.	W	5-4		8	12	Paniagua	Venafro	Mesa	37-37	2nd	5.0
6-27	Tex.	W	5-2		10	6	Garcia	Sele	Mesa	38-37	2nd	4.0
6-29	At Oak.	W	2-1	(12)	7	9	Paniagua	Mathews	Mesa	39-37	2nd	4.5
6-30	At Oak.	L	5-14		12	14	Hudson	Fassero		39-38	2nd	5.5
7-1	At Oak.	L	4-5		7	10	Taylor	Paniagua		39-39	2nd	6.0
7-2	At Tex.	L	6-7		14	10	Wetteland	Cloude		39-40	2nd	7.0
7-3	At Tex.	W	13-12		15	15	Paniagua	Crabtree	Mesa	40-40	2nd	6.0
7-4	At Tex.	W	6-0		12	6	Halama	Morgan		41-40	2nd	5.0
7-5	At Ana.	W	10-0		14	3	Fassero	Hasegawa		42-40	2nd	4.0
7-6	At Ana.	L	2-8		7	9	Petkovsek	Rodriguez		42-41	2nd	4.0
7-7	At Ana.	L	3-10		13	16	Sparks	Moyer		42-42	2nd	5.0
7-9	At L.A.	L	0-5		7	11	Valdes	Garcia		42-43	T2nd	6.0
7-10	At L.A.	L	1-2		3	6	Shaw	Paniagua		42-44	3rd	6.0
7-11	At L.A.	L	3-14		6	15	Dreifort	Fassero	Masaoka	42-45	3rd	6.0
7-15	S.D.	L	2-3		8	7	Cunnane	Mesa	Miceli	42-46	4th	7.0
7-16	S.D.	L	1-2		9	8	Hitchcock	Fassero	Hoffman	42-47	4th	8.0
7-17	S.D.	W	9-1		11	5	Garcia	Williams		43-47	3rd	7.0
7-18	Ari.	W	8-7	(10)	10	11	Mesa	Kim		44-47	3rd	7.0
7-19	Ari.	W	7-5		11	8	Meche	Anderson		45-47	3rd	7.0
7-20	Ari.	L	0-6		8	15	Johnson	Marte		45-48	3rd	8.0
7-21	Oak.	L	3-13		7	15	Heredia	Fassero		45-49	3rd	9.0
7-22	Oak.	W	5-4	(10)	10	4	Abbott	Jones		46-49	3rd	9.0
7-23	At Min.	L	4-5		7	13	Carrasco	Paniagua		46-50	3rd	10.0
7-24	At Min.	L	3-10		6	12	Wells	Meche		46-51	3rd	11.0
7-25	At Min.	W	4-3		9	7	Moyer	Radke	Mesa	47-51	3rd	11.0
7-27	At K.C.	L	7-9		15	15	Appier	Fassero	Service	47-52	3rd	12.0
7-28	At K.C.	L	3-5		8	9	Rosado	Garcia	Service	47-53	3rd	12.0
7-29	At K.C.	W	8-4		15	8	Halama	Suppan		48-53	3rd	12.0
7-30	Bal.	W	7-4		7	7	Meche	Johnson	Mesa	49-53	3rd	12.0
7-31	Bal.	W	5-2		9	8	Moyer	Ponson	Mesa	50-53	3rd	11.0
8-1	Bal.	W	3-1		3	8	Abbott	Mussina	Mesa	51-53	3rd	11.0
8-2	T.B.	W	4-0		8	6	Garcia	Callaway	Paniagua	52-53	3rd	11.0
8-3	T.B.	W	5-2		10	9	Halama	Rupe	Mesa	53-53	3rd	11.0
8-4	T.B.	L	1-7		5	15	Eiland	Meche		53-54	3rd	12.0
8-5	N.Y.	L	4-7		6	12	Clemens	Moyer	Rivera	53-55	3rd	12.5
8-6	N.Y.	L	8-11		13	15	Watson	Fassero	Rivera	53-56	3rd	12.5
8-7	N.Y.	L	0-1		4	3	Pettitte	Garcia	Rivera	53-57	3rd	13.5
8-8	N.Y.	L	3-9		6	11	Cone	Halama		53-58	3rd	13.5
8-9	Chi.	W	6-4		7	6	Meche	Snyder	Mesa	54-58	3rd	12.5
8-10	Chi.	W	4-3		9	8	Moyer	Howry		55-58	3rd	12.5
8-11	Chi.	W	11-2		10	6	Abbott	Navarro		56-58	3rd	12.5
8-13	At Bos.	L	6-11		8	10	Lowe	Fassero		56-59	3rd	11.5
8-14	At Bos.	L	2-13		8	19	Martinez	Halama		56-60	3rd	11.5
8-15	At Bos.	W	4-3		8	6	Meche	Portugal	Mesa	57-60	3rd	11.5
8-16	At Tor.	W	7-5		11	10	Moyer	Carpenter	Mesa	58-60	3rd	11.5
8-17	At Tor.	W	8-5		12	7	Abbott	Hentgen	Mesa	59-60	3rd	11.5
8-18	At Tor.	W	5-1		10	6	Garcia	Wells	Paniagua	60-60	3rd	11.5
8-20	Cle.	L	4-7		9	8	Colon	Halama	Jackson	60-61	3rd	12.0
8-21	Cle.	L	0-6		6	9	Burba	Meche		60-62	3rd	13.0
8-22	Cle.	L	4-7	(10)	7	11	Riske	Mesa	Jackson	60-63	3rd	14.0
8-23	Cle.	W	4-1		6	5	Abbott	Nagy	Mesa	61-63	3rd	13.0
8-24	Det.	W	5-0		7	6	Garcia	Blair		62-63	3rd	12.0
8-25	Det.	W	3-2		7	9	Halama	Moehler	Mesa	63-63	3rd	12.0
8-27	At N.Y.	L	0-8		5	12	Clemens	Meche		63-64	3rd	13.0
8-28	At N.Y.	L	1-2		4	8	Rivera	Paniagua		63-65	3rd	14.0
8-29	At N.Y.	L	5-11		10	12	Pettitte	Abbott	Rivera	63-66	3rd	15.0
8-30†	At Chi.	W	5-2		12	9	Garcia	Parque	Mesa	64-66		
8-30‡	At Chi.	W	14-6		15	11	Cloude	Castillo	Rodriguez	65-66	3rd	13.5
8-31	At Chi.	W	11-4		15	9	Halama	Snyder		66-66	3rd	12.5
9-1	At Chi.	W	3-2		10	8	Meche	Sirotka	Mesa	67-66	3rd	12.5
9-3	Bos.	W	2-1		9	3	Moyer	Lowe		68-66	3rd	12.0
9-4	Bos.	L	0-4		3	6	Martinez	Abbott		68-67	3rd	12.0
9-5	Bos.	L	7-9		12	13	Garces	Paniagua	Lowe	68-68	3rd	12.5
9-6	Bos.	L	2-3		5	10	Florie	Halama	Lowe	68-69	3rd	14.0
9-7	Tor.	W	7-4		9	7	Meche	Wells	Mesa	69-69	3rd	14.0
9-8	Tor.	W	4-3		7	9	Mesa	Koch		70-69	3rd	14.0
9-10	At Bal.	L	4-5	(12)	9	9	Reyes	Ramsay		70-70	3rd	14.0
9-11	At Bal.	L	2-4		4	12	Johns	Garcia	Timlin	70-71	3rd	14.0
9-12	At Bal.	L	1-4		5	9	Erickson	Halama		70-72	3rd	14.0
9-13	At Bal.	L	4-5	(10)	11	9	Ryan	Mesa		70-73	3rd	15.0
9-14	At T.B.	W	5-1		7	7	Moyer	Arrojo		71-73	3rd	15.0
9-15	At T.B.	L	4-8		10	13	Lopez	Rodriguez		71-74	3rd	16.0
9-16	At T.B.	W	5-3		6	5	Garcia	Yan	Mesa	72-74	3rd	15.5
9-17	Min.	W	4-3		7	6	Abbott	Trombley		73-74	3rd	14.5
9-18	Min.	W	5-0		11	2	Meche	Mays		74-74	3rd	14.5
9-19	Min.	L	1-2		5	6	Hawkins	Moyer	Trombley	74-75	3rd	14.5

Date	Opp.	Res.	Score	(inn.*)	Hits	Opp. hits	Winning pitcher	Losing pitcher	Save	Record	Pos.	GB
9-20	K.C.	L	9-10		9	15	Santiago	Hinchliffe	Montgomery	74-76	3rd	15.0
9-21	K.C.	W	13-3		15	13	Garcia	Suppan	Rodriguez	75-76	3rd	14.0
9-22	K.C.	L	6-12		13	14	Witasick	Halama		75-77	3rd	14.0
9-24	Ana.	W	4-3	(10)	8	5	Mesa	Percival		76-77	3rd	14.0
9-25	Ana.	L	3-7		4	6	Finley	Moyer		76-78	3rd	15.0
9-26	Ana.	W	3-2		8	6	Davey	Hasegawa		77-78	3rd	15.0
9-27	At Tex.	L	2-3		7	10	Crabtree	Sinclair	Wetteland	77-79	3rd	16.0
9-28	At Tex.	L	0-10		5	15	Morgan	Halama		77-80	3rd	17.0
9-29	At Tex.	W	7-3		13	9	Meche	Sele		78-80	3rd	16.0
9-30	At Tex.	L	0-7		4	8	Burkett	Hinchliffe		78-81	3rd	17.0
10-1	At Oak.	L	1-5		4	7	Appier	Ramsay	Jones	78-82	3rd	17.0
10-2	At Oak.	W	10-2		12	8	Garcia	Laxton		79-82	3rd	16.0
10-3	At Oak.	L	1-3		4	11	Mahay	Halama	Isringhausen	79-83	3rd	16.0

Monthly records: April (11-12), May (15-12), June (13-14), July (11-15), August (16-13), September (12-15), October (1-2).
*Innings, if other than nine. † First game of a doubleheader. ‡ Second game of a doubleheader.

HIGHLIGHTS

High point: The final Mariners game in Kingdome history was the feel-good moment of the year, with a crowd of 56,530 attracted to festivities featuring the best players in franchise history. Fittingly, Ken Griffey Jr. hit a three-run home run in the June 27 game, a 5-2 Mariners victory over Texas.

Low point: The first home series in September, when the Mariners—trying to creep back into the wild-card race—played host to Boston for four games. Seattle won the first game, but Pedro Martinez shut down the Mariners the next day and the Red Sox took the next two games as well. By September 13, Seattle had lost seven of nine games and dropped out of postseason contention.

Turning point: On July 5, the Mariners won their third consecutive game, improving to 42-40, and were within four games of first-place Texas in the A.L. West. On July 6, Seattle began a seven-game losing streak that dropped the club eight games back—and the Mariners weren't two games above .500 again until September.

Most valuable player: Ken Griffey Jr. had another outstanding year. He won his 10th Gold Glove and was an All-Star Game selection for the 10th time. In 160 games, Griffey hit 48 home runs and drove in 134 runs.

Most valuable pitcher: Veteran Jamie Moyer was a coach between starts, but no one had a more consistent season than rookie Freddy Garcia. He led the team with 17 victories and never lost consecutive decisions.

Most improved player: After a tough 1998 season in which his 34 errors led the majors, third baseman Russ Davis played 124 games and committed just 12 errors. Offensively, he slumped to .245 but hit a career-high 21 homers.

Most pleasant surprise: David Bell left spring training as a reserve infielder. Five games later, the Mariners lost injured second baseman Carlos Guillen for the season. Bell stepped in and contributed career highs in homers (21) and RBIs (78).

Biggest disappointment: Veteran left-hander Jeff Fassero was the Mariners' opening-night starter, but it was a month before he won his first game. At the All-Star break, he was 4-9 with a 6.89 ERA—then went 0-5 before being traded

to Texas.

Key injuries: Veterans Butch Henry and Mark Leiter were acquired in the offseason to solidify a young pitching staff, but both went down early and combined for only 26.1 innings all season. Shortstop Alex Rodriguez missed 5.5 weeks because of knee surgery, outfielder Jay Buhner was limited to 87 games because of myriad injuries and Guillen went down with a torn ACL. Also, Davis broke a foot and John Mabry suffered a kneecap fracture.

Notable: The Mariners moved into Safeco Field on July 15 and wound up going 23-19 in their new ballpark. They were 20-19 at the Kingdome. ... Despite playing in only 129 games, Rodriguez hit 42 homers and knocked in 111 runs. ... Edgar Martinez batted .337, marking the fifth time in eight seasons he had hit at least .325.

—LARRY LaRUE

RECORDS

1999 regular-season record: 79-83 (3rd in A.L. West); 43-38 at home; 36-45 on road; 24-27 vs. East; 31-25 vs. Central; 17-20 vs. A.L. West; 7-11 vs. N.L.; 13-22 vs. lefthanded starters; 66-61 vs. righthanded starters; 49-59 on grass; 30-24 on turf; 24-23 in daytime; 55-60 at night; 20-23 in one-run games; 5-6 in extra-inning games; 1-0-0 in doubleheaders. **Team record past five years:** 409-382 (.517, ranks 6th in league in that span).

TEAM LEADERS

Batting average: Edgar Martinez (.337).
At-bats: Ken Griffey Jr. (606).
Runs: Ken Griffey Jr. (123).
Hits: Ken Griffey Jr. (173).
Total Bases: Ken Griffey Jr. (349).
Doubles: Edgar Martinez (35).
Triples: Brian L. Hunter (5).
Home runs: Ken Griffey Jr. (48).
Runs batted in: Ken Griffey Jr. (134).
Stolen bases: Brian L. Hunter (44).
Slugging percentage: Alex Rodriguez (.586).
On-base percentage: Edgar Martinez (.447).
Wins: Freddy Garcia (17).
Earned-run average: Jamie Moyer (3.87).
Complete games: Jamie Moyer (4).

Shutouts: Freddy Garcia, John Halama (1).
Saves: Jose Mesa (33).
Innings pitched: Jamie Moyer (228.0).
Strikeouts: Freddy Garcia (170).

GAMES BY POSITION

Catcher: Dan Wilson 121, Tom Lampkin 56, Raul Ibanez 1.
First base: David Segui 90, Ryan Jackson 29, Raul Ibanez 21, John Mabry 20, Mike Blowers 14, Butch Huskey 10, Edgar Martinez 5, Dan Wilson 5, David Bell 4, Jay Buhner 1, Ozzie Timmons 1.
Second base: David Bell 154, Rafael Bournigal 5, Charles Gipson 3, Carlos Guillen 2, Domingo Cedeno 1.
Third base: Russ Davis 124, John Mabry 24, Charles Gipson 17, Rafael Bournigal 8, Mike Blowers 4, Domingo Cedeno 1, Butch Huskey 1.
Shortstop: Alex Rodriguez 129, Rafael Bournigal 28, Domingo Cedeno 20, Giomar Guevara 9, Charles Gipson 3, Carlos Guillen 1, Russ Davis 2, David Bell 1.
Outfield: Ken Griffey Jr. 158, Brian L. Hunter 121, Jay Buhner 85, Raul Ibanez 57, Butch Huskey 53, John Mabry 43, Charles Gipson 28, Matt Mieske 20, Ozzie Timmons 17, Shane Monahan 9, Tom Lampkin 2, Rafael Bournigal 1, Ryan Jackson 1.
Designated hitter: Edgar Martinez 134, Butch Huskey 7, Ken Griffey Jr. 6, Ozzie Timmons 5, Charles Gipson 4, Shane Monahan 3, Tom Lampkin 2, Mike Blowers 1, Rafael Bournigal 1, Matt Mieske 1, John Mabry 1, Raul Ibanez 1.

TOP DRAFT CHOICES

1a. **Ryan Christianson**, C, Arlington H.S., Riverside, Calif.
1b. **Jeff Heaverlo**, RHP, U. of Washington
2. None
3a. **Willie Bloomquist**, SS, Arizona St. U.
3b. **Sheldon Fulse**, SS, George Jenkins H.S., Bartow, Fla.
4. **Vaughn Schill**, SS, Duke University
5. **Clint Nageotte**, RHP, Brooklyn (Ohio) H.S.
6. **J.J. Putz**, RHP, U. of Michigan
7. **Michael Davies**, LHP, Westview H.S., Beaverton, Ore.
8. **Terrmel Sledge**, OF, Long Beach State Univ.
9. **Steve Kent**, LHP, Florida International Univ.
10. **Justin Smith**, LHP, U. of Alabama

TAMPA BAY DEVIL RAYS
AMERICAN LEAGUE EAST DIVISION

2000 Devil Rays Schedule
Home games shaded. *—All-Star Game at Turner Field (Atlanta).

March
SUN	MON	TUE	WED	THU	FRI	SAT
26	27	28	29	30	31	

April
SUN	MON	TUE	WED	THU	FRI	SAT
						1
2	3 MIN	4 MIN	5 MIN	6 MIN	7 CLE	8 CLE
9 CLE	10	11 CWS	12 CWS	13 CWS	14 DET	15 DET
16 DET	17 BAL	18 BAL	19 BAL	20	21 ANA	22 ANA
23 ANA	24	25 KC	26 KC	27 ANA	28 ANA	29 ANA
30 ANA						

May
SUN	MON	TUE	WED	THU	FRI	SAT
	1	2 TEX	3 TEX	4 TEX	5 BOS	6 BOS
7 BOS	8 NYY	9 NYY	10 NYY	11	12 TOR	13 TOR
14 TOR	15 TEX	16 TEX	17 TEX	18	19 SEA	20 SEA
21 SEA	22	23 OAK	24 OAK	25 OAK	26 SEA	27 SEA
28 SEA	29 BAL	30 BAL	31 BAL			

June
SUN	MON	TUE	WED	THU	FRI	SAT
				1 BAL	2 NYM	3 NYM
4 NYM	5 PHI	6 PHI	7 PHI	8	9 FLA	10 FLA
11 FLA	12	13 ANA	14 ANA	15 ANA	16 TEX	17 TEX
18 TEX	19 SEA	20 SEA	21 SEA	22	23 TEX	24 TEX
25 TEX	26	27 TOR	28 TOR	29 TOR	30 NYY	

July
SUN	MON	TUE	WED	THU	FRI	SAT
						1 NYY
2 NYY	3 DET	4 DET	5 DET	6	7 FLA	8 FLA
9 FLA	10	*12	13 MON	14 MON	15 MON	
16 ATL	17 ATL	18	19 TOR	20 TOR	21 NYY	22 NYY
23 NYY	24 DET	25 DET	26 DET	27 KC	28 KC	29 KC
30 KC	31					

August
SUN	MON	TUE	WED	THU	FRI	SAT
		1 CLE	2 CLE	3 CLE	4 BAL	5 BAL
6 BAL	7 MIN	8 MIN	9 MIN	10 MIN	11 CWS	12 CWS
13 CWS	14 BOS	15 BOS	16 BOS	17	18 CWS	19 CWS
20 CWS	21 MIN	22 MIN	23 MIN	24	25 BAL	26 BAL
27 BAL	28 BOS	29 BOS	30 BOS	31 KC		

September
SUN	MON	TUE	WED	THU	FRI	SAT
					1 KC	2 KC
3 KC	4 CLE	5 CLE	6 CLE	7 CLE	8 OAK	9 OAK
10 OAK	11 OAK	12 ANA	13 ANA	14	15 OAK	16 OAK
17 OAK	18 SEA	19 SEA	20 SEA	21	22 TOR	23 TOR
24 TOR	25 TOR	26 NYY	27 NYY	28 NYY	29 BOS	30 BOS

October
SUN	MON	TUE	WED	THU	FRI	SAT
1 BOS	2	3	4	5	6	7

2000 SEASON
CLUB DIRECTORY

Managing General Partner/CEO
Vincent J. Naimoli
Sr. v.p.baseball operations/g.m.
Chuck LaMar
Sr. v.p.-admin. & general counsel
John P. Higgins
Vice president of sales & marketing
John Browne
Vice president of public relations
Rick Vaughn
Vice president of operations/facilities
Rick Nafe
Asst. general manager-baseball operations
Bart Braun
Assistant general manager-administration
Scott Proefrock
Special assistants to the general manager
Eddie Bane, Wade Boggs, Bill Livesey
Director of scouting
Dan Jennings
Special advisor for baseball operations
Frank Howard
Director of minor league operations
Tom Foley
Assistant to player development
Mitch Lukevics
Traveling secretary
Jeffrey Ziegler
Travel consultant
Dirk Smith
Controller
Patrick Smith
Director of human resources
Louise "Jeep" Weber
Director of business administration
Bill Wiener Jr.
Senior director of corporate sales & broadcasting
Larry McCabe
Manager of broadcast operations
Joe Ciaravino
Director of corporate sales
Tom Whaley
Managers of sponsorship coordination
Tammy Atmore, Kelly Davis
Manager of promotions & special events
Christopher Dean
Director of ticket operations
Robert Bennett
Assistant director of ticket operations
Ken Mallory
Director of ticket sales
Carola Ross

Assistant to the v.p. of public relations
Carmen Molina
Director of publications
Matt Lorenz
Media relations manager
Chris Costello
Assistant media relations manager
Greg Landy
Manager of community relations
Liz-Beth Lauck
Director of event productions & entertainment
John Franzone
Video producer
Jason Rundle
Video coordinator
Chris Fernandez
Head trainer
Jamie Reed
Assistant head trainer
Ken Crenshaw
Strength & conditioning and rehabilitation coordinator
Kevin Harmon
Medical director
Dr. James Andrews
Medical team physician
Dr. Michael Reilly
Orthopaedic team physician
Dr. Koco Eaton
Head groundskeeper
Mike Williams
Clubhouse operations-home
Carlos Ledezma
Clubhouse operations-visitor
Guy Gallagher
Major League scouts
Jerry Gardner, Bart Johnson, Matt Keough, Al LaMacchia, Don Lindeberg, Don Williams
Crosscheckers
Jack Gillis, R.J. Harrison, Stan Meek
Area scouts
Fernando Arango, Jonathan Bonifay, Todd Brown, Skip Bundy, Matt Dodd, Kevin Elfering, Steve Foster, Doug Gassaway, Matt Kinzer, Paul Kirsch, Edwin Rodriguez, Charles Scott, Mac Seibert, Craig F. Weissmann, Doug Witt
Part-time scouts
Jorge Calvo Lara Sr., Jorge Calvo Jr., Philip Elhage, Benny Latino, Daniel McConnon, Adrian T. Meagher, Jose Perez, Juan Pringle, Junior Ramirez, Gustavo Rodriguez, Freddy Torres, Mel Zitter

MINOR LEAGUE AFFILIATES

Class	Team	League	Manager
AAA	Durham	International	Bill Evers
AA	Orlando	Southern	To be announced
A	St. Petersburg	Florida State	Mike Ramsey
A	Charleston (S.C.)	South Atlantic	Charlie Montoyo
A	Hudson Valley	New York-Pennsylvania	To be announced
Rookie	Princeton	Appalachian	Edwin Rodriguez

BROADCAST INFORMATION
Radio: WFLA-AM (970).
TV: MORE-TV (Channel 32); WTSP (Channel 10).
Cable TV: SportsChannel Florida.

SPRING TRAINING
Ballpark (city): Al Lang Stadium (St. Petersburg, Fla.).
Ticket information: 727-825-3250.

SPRING TRAINING ROSTER

Manager—Larry Rothschild (11).
Coaches—Jose Cardenal, Orlando Gomez (23), Billy Hatcher (22), Leon Roberts (5), Bill Russell, Rick Williams (38).

No.	PITCHERS	B/T	Ht./Wt.	Born	1999 clubs
40	Alvarez, Wilson	L/L	6-1/235	3-24-70	Tampa Bay
47	Duvall, Mike	R/L	6-0/185	10-11-74	Tampa Bay, Durham
	Guzman, Juan	R/R	5-11/195	10-28-66	Baltimore, Cincinnati
39	Hernandez, Roberto	R/R	6-4/235	11-11-64	Tampa Bay
27	Lidle, Cory	R/R	5-11/180	3-22-72	St. Petersburg, Durham, Tampa Bay
32	Lopez, Albie	R/R	6-2/185	8-18-71	Tampa Bay, St. Petersburg
45	Mecir, Jim	B/R	6-1/195	5-16-70	Tampa Bay
63	Morris, Jim	L/L	6-3/215	1-19-64	Orlando, Durham, Tampa Bay
	Ogea, Chad	L/R	6-2/220	11-9-70	Philadelphia
	Reitsma, Chris	R/R	6-5/214	12-31-77	Sarasota
56	Rekar, Bryan	R/R	6-3/210	6-3-72	Durham, Tampa Bay
24	Rupe, Ryan	R/R	6-5/230	3-31-75	Orlando, Tampa Bay
31	Saunders, Tony	L/L	6-2/205	4-29-74	Tampa Bay, Durham
62	Sparks, Jeff	R/R	6-3/220	4-4-72	Nashville, Durham, Tampa Bay
34	Wheeler, Dan	R/R	6-3/222	12-10-77	Orlando, Durham, Tampa Bay
51	White, Rick	R/R	6-4/215	12-23-68	Tampa Bay
43	Yan, Esteban	R/R	6-4/230	6-22-74	Tampa Bay, St. Petersburg

No.	CATCHERS	B/T	Ht./Wt.	Born	1999 clubs
8	Difelice, Mike	R/R	6-2/205	5-28-69	Tampa Bay
6	Flaherty, John	R/R	6-1/200	10-21-67	Tampa Bay

No.	INFIELDERS	B/T	Ht./Wt.	Born	1999 clubs
13	Cairo, Miguel	R/R	6-1/160	5-4-74	Tampa Bay, Orlando, St. Petersburg
20	Castilla, Vinny	R/R	6-1/205	7-4-67	Colorado
71	Cox, Steve	L/L	6-4/222	10-31-74	Durham, Tampa Bay
26	Graffanino, Tony	R/R	6-1/195	6-6-72	Durham, Tampa Bay
15	Lamb, David	B/R	6-2/165	6-6-75	Tampa Bay, Durham
29	McGriff, Fred	L/L	6-3/215	10-31-63	Tampa Bay
	Rolls, Damian	R/R	6-2/205	9-15-77	Vero Beach
9	Smith, Robert	R/R	6-3/190	5-10-74	Tampa Bay, Durham
19	Stocker, Kevin	B/R	6-1/175	2-13-70	Tampa Bay, St. Petersburg

No.	OUTFIELDERS	B/T	Ht./Wt.	Born	1999 clubs
33	Canseco, Jose	R/R	6-4/240	7-2-64	Tampa Bay
11	Guillen, Jose	R/R	5-11/195	5-17-76	Pittsburgh, Nashville, Durham, Tampa Bay
14	Martinez, Dave	L/L	5-10/175	9-26-64	Tampa Bay
3	McCracken, Quinton	B/R	5-7/173	3-16-70	Tampa Bay
1	Sanchez, Alex	L/L	5-10/180	8-26-76	Orlando, Durham
21	Trammell, Bubba	R/R	6-2/220	11-6-71	Durham, Tampa Bay
23	Vaughn, Greg	R/R	6-0/202	7-3-65	Cincinnati
	Wilcox, Luke	L/R	6-4/225	11-15-73	Orlando, Durham
	Williams, Gerald	R/R	6-2/187	8-10-66	Atlanta
2	Winn, Randy	B/R	6-2/175	6-9-74	Tampa Bay, Durham

BALLPARK INFORMATION

Ballpark (capacity, surface)
Tropicana Field (43,819, artificial)
Address
One Tropicana Drive
St. Petersburg, FL 33607
Business phone
727-825-3137
Ticket information
727-825-3250
Ticket prices
$160 (home plate box)
$65 (field box)
$35 (lower club box)
$30 (diamond club box, diamond club reserved)
$22 (lower box)
$20 (lower reserved, terrace box)
$17 (upper box)
$14 (terrace reserved, outfield)
$10 (the beach, upper reserved)
$8 (upper general admission)
Field dimensions (from home plate)
To left field at foul line, 315 feet
To center field, 404 feet
To right field at foul line, 322 feet
First game played
March 31, 1998 (Tigers 11, Devil Rays 6)

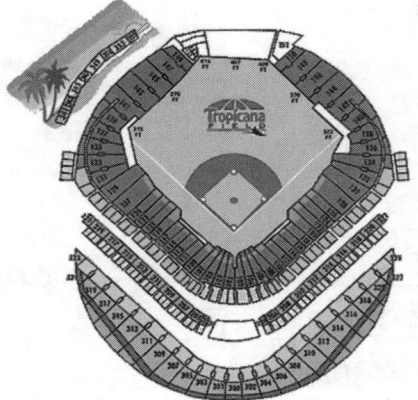

Date	Opp.	Res.	Score	(inn.*)	Hits	Opp. hits	Winning pitcher	Losing pitcher	Save	Record	Pos.	GB
4-7	At Bal.	W	8-5		14	13	Saunders	Guzman	Hernandez	1-1	T3rd	1.0
4-8	At Bal.	W	6-3		10	9	Witt	Erickson		2-1	T2nd	1.0
4-9	Bos.	L	1-4		4	11	Portugal	Arrojo		2-2	T3rd	2.0
4-10	Bos.	L	3-5		7	6	Martinez	Santana	Gordon	2-3	T3rd	3.0
4-11	Bos.	W	5-4		7	8	Aldred	Lowe	Hernandez	3-3	T3rd	2.0
4-12	At Tor.	L	1-7		6	12	Wells	Saunders		3-4	4th	2.5
4-13	At Tor.	W	8-5		15	11	White	Hamilton	Hernandez	4-4	4th	2.5
4-14	At Tor.	L	6-7	(11)	12	12	Lloyd	Lopez		4-5	4th	3.5
4-15	At Tor.	L	1-11		2	11	Carpenter	Santana		4-6	4th	3.5
4-16	At Bos.	W	6-2		13	7	Rekar	Wakefield		5-6	4th	2.5
4-17	At Bos.	L	5-8		9	11	Portugal	Saunders		5-7	4th	3.0
4-18	At Bos.	W	5-1		7	5	Witt	Rapp		6-7	4th	3.0
4-19	At Bos.	W	4-1		9	6	Arrojo	Saberhagen	Hernandez	7-7	4th	2.5
4-20	Bal.	W	5-3		12	6	Santana	Erickson	Hernandez	8-7	4th	2.5
4-21	Bal.	W	14-8		17	11	Rekar	Mussina		9-7	4th	2.5
4-22	Bal.	W	1-0		4	1	Saunders	Ponson	Hernandez	10-7	3rd	2.5
4-23	Sea.	W	5-4		11	7	White	Halama	Hernandez	11-7	3rd	1.5
4-24	Sea.	L	4-9		8	12	Henry	Arrojo		11-8	3rd	1.5
4-25	Sea.	L	4-6		6	12	Paniagua	Hernandez	Mesa	11-9	4th	2.5
4-28†	At Chi.	L	7-10		8	14	Parque	Rekar	Howry	11-10		
4-28‡	At Chi.	L	1-9		9	10	Snyder	Saunders		11-11	4th	3.5
4-29	At Chi.	W	4-1		9	4	Alvarez	Sirotka	Hernandez	12-11	4th	3.5
4-30	Det.	L	5-7		7	12	Weaver	Arrojo	Jones	12-12	T3rd	3.5
5-1	Det.	W	4-3		7	4	Witt	Moehler	Hernandez	13-12	4th	3.5
5-2	Det.	L	2-8		10	12	Thompson	Santana		13-13	T3rd	4.5
5-3	Det.	W	14-6		12	12	Yan	Blair		14-13	3rd	3.5
5-4	K.C.	L	3-5		11	7	Mathews	Hernandez	Montgomery	14-14	3rd	3.5
5-5	K.C.	W	10-7		17	9	White	Witasick	Hernandez	15-14	T2nd	3.5
5-6	K.C.	W	5-4		8	11	Aldred	Morman	Hernandez	16-14	2nd	3.5
5-7	At Cle.	L	11-20		13	21	Wagner	Mecir		16-15	T2nd	4.5
5-8	At Cle.	W	7-6		14	12	Rekar	Nagy	Hernandez	17-15	2nd	3.5
5-9	At Cle.	L	4-5		11	6	Wright	Alvarez	Jackson	17-16	3rd	4.5
5-11	Min.	L	1-2		6	5	Radke	Rupe	Aguilera	17-17	T3rd	4.5
5-12	Min.	L	4-9		8	14	Milton	Arrojo	Trombley	17-18	T3rd	4.5
5-14	At Ana.	L	3-8		5	10	Belcher	Witt		17-19	4th	4.0
5-15	At Ana.	W	3-1		7	3	Saunders	Hill	Hernandez	18-19	3rd	3.0
5-16	At Ana.	W	7-4		13	10	Alvarez	Sparks		19-19	3rd	3.0
5-17	At Tex.	W	13-3		15	6	Rupe	Burkett		20-19	3rd	2.5
5-18	At Tex.	W	5-4		10	14	Arrojo	Morgan	Hernandez	21-19	3rd	2.0
5-19	At Tex.	L	6-7		11	9	Zimmerman	Aldred	Wetteland	21-20	3rd	3.0
5-21	Ana.	W	10-9		12	14	White	Magnante	Hernandez	22-20	3rd	2.5
5-22	Ana.	L	6-8		9	16	Petkovsek	Newman	Percival	22-21	3rd	3.5
5-23	Ana.	L	0-4	(10)	3	4	Finley	Hernandez		22-22	3rd	4.5
5-24	Tex.	L	3-12		10	16	Clark	Arrojo		22-23	3rd	5.0
5-25	Tex.	L	2-7		9	11	Venafro	Witt		22-24	4th	6.0
5-26	Tex.	L	6-8		11	12	Helling	Santana	Wetteland	22-25	4th	6.0
5-28	At Sea.	L	1-6		5	11	Garcia	Alvarez		22-26	4th	6.5
5-29	At Sea.	L	5-11		10	12	Fassero	Rupe		22-27	4th	7.5
5-30	At Sea.	W	15-7		17	15	Rekar	Cloude		23-27	4th	7.5
5-31	At Oak.	L	7-10		11	7	Groom	Yan		23-28	4th	8.5
6-1	At Oak.	L	2-5		10	3	Rogers	Eiland	Taylor	23-29	4th	9.5
6-2	At Oak.	W	7-6		11	8	Yan	Mathews	Hernandez	24-29	4th	8.5
6-4	Fla.	L	0-10		7	11	Springer	Rupe		24-30	4th	9.5
6-5	Fla.	L	7-9		9	14	Meadows	Duvall	Mantei	24-31	4th	9.5
6-6	Fla.	L	6-11		9	17	Alfonseca	Yan		24-32	4th	9.5
6-7	At Atl.	L	5-9		13	10	Smoltz	Eiland	Rocker	24-33	4th	9.5
6-8	At Atl.	L	2-11		8	16	Perez	Alvarez		24-34	4th	10.0
6-9	At Atl.	L	3-4	(12)	10	13	McGlinchy	White		24-35	4th	10.0
6-11	At Mon.	L	4-5		9	9	Batista	Witt	Urbina	24-36	4th	11.0
6-12	At Mon.	W	5-3		14	9	Callaway	Hermanson	Hernandez	25-36	4th	11.0
6-13	At Mon.	L	0-4		3	8	Pavano	Rekar		25-37	5th	11.0
6-14	At Chi.	L	7-9		11	9	Snyder	Alvarez	Howry	25-38	5th	12.0
6-15	At Chi.	W	3-2		6	12	Rupe	Baldwin	Hernandez	26-38	5th	12.0
6-16	At Chi.	L	2-3	(11)	8	8	Lowe	Charlton		26-39	5th	12.0
6-18	At Min.	L	5-8		10	12	Wells	Aldred	Trombley	26-40	5th	12.5
6-19	At Min.	W	4-3		10	10	Rekar	Radke	Hernandez	27-40	5th	12.5
6-20	At Min.	W	6-5	(11)	12	9	Newman	Trombley		28-40	5th	11.5
6-21	At Min.	W	3-2		9	5	Rupe	Radlosky	Hernandez	29-40	5th	11.0
6-22	N.Y.	L	0-7		3	12	Hernandez	Witt		29-41	5th	12.0
6-23	N.Y.	L	4-12		11	19	Clemens	Eiland		29-42	5th	13.0
6-24	N.Y.	L	3-7		7	13	Pettitte	Rekar	Mendoza	29-43	5th	14.0
6-25	Tor.	W	11-4		14	6	Alvarez	Wells		30-43	5th	14.0

Date	Opp.	Res.	Score	(inn.*)	Hits	Opp. hits	Winning pitcher	Losing pitcher	Save	Record	Pos.	GB
6-26	Tor.	W	5-2		9	12	Rupe	Hamilton	Hernandez	31-43	5th	14.0
6-27	Tor.	W	8-0		10	3	Witt	Escobar		32-43	5th	14.0
6-28	Tor.	L	2-3		8	10	Carpenter	Eiland	Koch	32-44	5th	14.5
6-30	At Bos.	W	11-10	(10)	14	12	Hernandez	Wasdin		33-44	4th	14.0
7-1	At Bos.	W	12-3		16	7	Alvarez	Cho		34-44	4th	14.0
7-2	At Tor.	W	8-7		11	14	Aldred	Escobar	Hernandez	35-44	4th	14.0
7-3	At Tor.	L	0-5		3	13	Carpenter	Witt		35-45	4th	15.0
7-4	At Tor.	L	3-6		11	10	Hentgen	White	Koch	35-46	4th	15.0
7-5	Bos.	L	2-4		9	9	Portugal	Rekar	Wakefield	35-47	4th	15.0
7-6	Bos.	W	6-4		7	9	Lopez	Wasdin	Hernandez	36-47	4th	15.0
7-7	Bos.	W	3-2		7	7	Eiland	Martinez	Hernandez	37-47	4th	14.0
7-8	Bos.	W	3-2		8	9	Witt	Rose	Hernandez	38-47	4th	14.0
7-9	At Fla.	L	4-11		11	12	Hernandez	Rupe		38-48	4th	14.0
7-10	At Fla.	W	9-8		14	15	Rekar	Springer	Hernandez	39-48	4th	13.0
7-11	At Fla.	L	2-3		6	5	Fernandez	Alvarez	Alfonseca	39-49	4th	14.0
7-15	N.Y. (NL)	L	7-8	(10)	13	8	Benitez	Charlton		39-50	4th	14.0
7-16	N.Y. (NL)	L	7-9		11	15	Reed	Eiland	Cook	39-51	4th	14.0
7-17	N.Y. (NL)	W	3-2		8	8	Alvarez	Hershiser	Hernandez	40-51	4th	14.0
7-18	Phi.	L	2-3		4	7	Schilling	Lopez		40-52	4th	15.0
7-19	Phi.	L	3-16		7	22	Ogea	Rekar		40-53	4th	15.0
7-20	Phi.	W	5-4	(13)	12	10	Charlton	Schrenk		41-53	4th	15.0
7-21	At N.Y.	L	3-4		7	8	Hernandez	Witt	Rivera	41-54	5th	16.0
7-22	At N.Y.	L	4-5		9	12	Pettitte	Rekar	Rivera	41-55	5th	17.0
7-23	Tex.	L	8-11		17	13	Kolb	Rupe		41-56	5th	18.0
7-24	Tex.	L	3-5		5	11	Loaiza	Newman	Wetteland	41-57	5th	19.0
7-25	Tex.	L	3-4		7	8	Helling	Arrojo	Wetteland	41-58	5th	20.0
7-26	Ana.	W	7-0		11	4	Witt	Olivares		42-58	5th	19.5
7-27	Ana.	L	5-10		13	12	Magnante	Callaway		42-59	5th	20.5
7-28	Ana.	W	4-1		11	6	Rupe	McDowell	Hernandez	43-59	5th	19.5
7-30	At Oak.	L	1-4		5	8	Oquist	Eiland	Taylor	43-60	5th	20.0
7-31	At Oak.	L	1-5		7	5	Olivares	Arrojo	Jones	43-61	5th	20.0
8-1	At Oak.	L	6-10		12	12	Heredia	Witt	Mathews	43-62	5th	20.0
8-2	At Sea.	L	0-4		6	8	Garcia	Callaway	Paniagua	43-63	5th	21.0
8-3	At Sea.	L	2-5		9	10	Halama	Rupe	Mesa	43-64	5th	21.0
8-4	At Sea.	W	7-1		15	5	Eiland	Meche		44-64	5th	21.0
8-6	Cle.	W	4-2		7	7	Yan	Burba	Hernandez	45-64	5th	21.5
8-7	Cle.	L	10-15		14	19	Nagy	Witt		45-65	5th	22.5
8-8	Cle.	W	5-3		11	6	Alvarez	Wright	Hernandez	46-65	5th	22.5
8-9	Bal.	W	10-9		15	12	Rupe	Johnson	Hernandez	47-65	5th	22.5
8-10	Bal.	L	1-17		6	20	Ponson	Eiland		47-66	5th	22.5
8-11	Bal.	L	2-4		10	13	Mussina	Arrojo	Timlin	47-67	5th	23.5
8-12	At K.C.	W	7-6		12	11	Witt	Reichert	Hernandez	48-67	5th	23.0
8-13	At K.C.	L	1-2		6	10	Service	Yan		48-68	5th	24.0
8-14	At K.C.	W	11-4		13	9	Rupe	Suppan		49-68	5th	23.0
8-15	At K.C.	W	5-3		14	5	Eiland	Suzuki	Hernandez	50-68	5th	22.0
8-16	At Det.	W	9-1		13	8	Arrojo	Weaver		51-68	5th	22.0
8-17	At Det.	L	1-3		6	8	Mlicki	Witt	Jones	51-69	5th	23.0
8-18	At Det.	W	4-0		8	1	Alvarez	Borkowski	Lopez	52-69	5th	22.0
8-20	K.C.	W	5-4		8	8	Hernandez	Service		53-69	5th	21.5
8-21	K.C.	W	8-2		10	8	Eiland	Witasick		54-69	5th	20.5
8-22	K.C.	W	2-1		3	6	Arrojo	Rosado		55-69	5th	20.5
8-23	Chi.	L	2-10		8	13	Baldwin	Witt		55-70	5th	21.5
8-24	Chi.	W	6-5		11	5	Alvarez	Parque	Hernandez	56-70	5th	21.5
8-25	Chi.	L	1-6		7	12	Foulke	Rupe		56-71	5th	21.5
8-26	Chi.	W	9-7		13	14	White	Snyder	Hernandez	57-71	5th	21.0
8-27	At Cle.	L	1-2		6	9	Burba	Arrojo	Jackson	57-72	5th	22.0
8-28	At Cle.	L	0-3		4	7	Nagy	Witt	Jackson	57-73	5th	23.0
8-29	At Cle.	W	6-4		11	10	Alvarez	Haney	Hernandez	58-73	5th	23.0
8-31	At Bal.	W	3-0		11	3	Rupe	Ponson	Hernandez	59-73	4th	22.5
9-1	At Bal.	L	1-3		5	5	Johns	Wheeler	Timlin	59-74	5th	22.5
9-2	At Bal.	L	6-11		14	13	Erickson	Arrojo		59-75	5th	23.5
9-3	Min.	W	4-2		8	11	Charlton	Guardado	Hernandez	60-75	5th	22.5
9-4	Min.	W	11-3		18	10	Lopez	Miller		61-75	5th	22.5
9-5	Min.	L	1-4		5	10	Radke	Rupe		61-76	5th	23.5
9-6	Min.	L	7-13		11	16	Carrasco	White		61-77	5th	23.5
9-8	Det.	L	1-5		7	10	Mlicki	Witt		61-78	5th	24.0
9-9	Det.	W	5-3		8	13	Arrojo	Nitkowski	Hernandez	62-78	5th	23.5
9-10	Oak.	L	2-7		8	14	Hudson	Alvarez		62-79	5th	23.5
9-11	Oak.	L	4-5		8	6	Olivares	Rupe	Jones	62-80	5th	23.5
9-12	Oak.	L	3-4		6	6	Heredia	Wheeler	Isringhausen	62-81	5th	23.5
9-13	Oak.	L	3-8		7	13	Appier	Witt		62-82	5th	23.5
9-14	Sea.	L	1-5		7	7	Moyer	Arrojo		62-83	5th	24.5
9-15	Sea.	W	8-4		13	10	Lopez	Rodriguez		63-83	5th	24.5
9-16	Sea.	L	3-5		5	6	Garcia	Yan	Mesa	63-84	5th	25.5
9-17	At Tex.	W	7-5		13	16	Newman	Helling	Hernandez	64-84	5th	25.5
9-18	At Tex.	L	1-6		6	9	Sele	Witt		64-85	5th	25.5

Date	Opp.	Res.	Score	(inn.*)	Hits	Opp. hits	Winning pitcher	Losing pitcher	Save	Record	Pos.	GB
9-19	At Tex.	W	15-2		15	7	Arrojo	Burkett		65-85	5th	25.5
9-20	At Ana.	L	5-10		13	11	Finley	Alvarez		65-86	5th	26.0
9-21	At Ana.	L	5-7		7	9	Ortiz	Eiland	Percival	65-87	5th	27.0
9-22	At Ana.	L	5-8		11	11	Washburn	Wheeler		65-88	5th	28.0
9-24	At N.Y.	L	3-4	(11)	7	9	Stanton	Charlton		65-89	5th	29.5
9-25	At N.Y.	W	2-1		11	5	Arrojo	Cone	Hernandez	66-89	5th	28.5
9-26	At N.Y.	W	6-5		15	11	Lidle	Mendoza	Hernandez	67-89	5th	27.5
9-27	At N.Y.	W	10-6		11	9	Duvall	Irabu	Sparks	68-89	5th	26.5
9-28	Tor.	L	2-8		5	13	Wells	Wheeler		68-90	5th	27.5
9-29	Tor.	L	2-6		9	14	Escobar	Witt		68-91	5th	28.0
10-1	N.Y.	L	7-11		9	14	Mendoza	Arrojo	Rivera	68-92	5th	29.0
10-2	N.Y.	L	2-3		6	9	Cone	Alvarez	Rivera	68-93	5th	30.0
10-3	N.Y.	W	6-2		6	6	Gaillard	Juden	Hernandez	69-93	5th	29.0

Monthly records: April (12-12), May (11-16), June (10-16), July (10-17), August (16-12), September (9-18), October (1-2).
*Innings, if other than nine. † First game of a doubleheader. ‡ Second game of a doubleheader.

HIGHLIGHTS

High point: At a juncture when all was lost and most teams were scratching off the days until October, the Devil Rays went into Yankee Stadium on the next-to-last weekend of the season and won three of four, stalling the Yankees' division-clinching celebration. It marked their first-ever wins at the Stadium.
Low point: Trying to fight through a stretch of injuries, the Rays returned from the West Coast on June 4 and were shut out, 10-0, by the Marlins and former teammate Dennis Springer. The defeat touched off a seven-game losing streak, dropping Tampa Bay 12 games below .500.
Turning point: The Rays were cruising along at 22-20 when injuries ravaged their lineup, stalled their momentum and crushed their spirit. The result was a season-wrecking 2-16 stretch (capped by the seven consecutive defeats).
Most valuable player: In the final year of his contract, first baseman Fred McGriff played like his old self. He led the team in batting (.310), hits (164), doubles (30), total bases (292) and RBIs (104). The payoff: a new two-year deal.
Most valuable pitcher: Closer Roberto Hernandez, who recorded a career-high 43 saves (in 47 opportunities). Hernandez also won two games, giving him a hand in 45 of the Rays' 69 victories.
Most improved player: Catcher John Flaherty rebounded from a horrendous season with one of his best, raising his average 71 points to .278. He also had career highs in homers (14) and RBIs (71).
Most pleasant surprise: The Rays figured they would see Ryan Rupe pitch at some point in 1999—they just didn't know it would be so soon. A year out of Texas A&M, Rupe joined the rotation in early May from Class AA Orlando and compiled an 8-9 record.
Biggest disappointment: The plan was for Wade Boggs to get his 3,000th hit and Bobby Smith to slip into the job as the regular third baseman. Boggs did his part, but Smith wound up hitting .181 in 199 at-bats and spent two months of the season in the minors.
Key injuries: Tampa Bay made an astonishing 22 D.L. moves, and five of the injured players underwent season-ending

surgeries. The lowlights: Outfielder Quinton McCracken (torn ACL) and pitcher Tony Saunders (broken left arm) suffered brutal-to-watch on-field injuries two days apart in late May. And DH Jose Canseco was out six weeks after undergoing back surgery.
Notable: Boggs got his 3,000th hit on August 7 against Cleveland and reached the milestone in unprecedented fashion—with a home run. ... Canseco was having a big season—31 homers in 82 games—before being sidelined. He hit only three homers in 31 games after his return. ... Jim Morris, 35, made an amazing transformation from high school coach to major league pitcher after an impressive tryout. In five relief appearances, he held hitters to a .167 average. ... No Rays pitcher posted a double-figure victory total. Wilson Alvarez led the club with nine wins.

—MARC TOPKIN

RECORDS

1999 regular-season record: 69-93 (5th in A.L. East); 33-48 at home; 36-45 on road; 25-25 vs. A.L. East; 26-22 vs. Central; 14-32 vs. West; 4-14 vs. N.L.; 8-23 vs. lefthanded starters; 61-70 vs. righthanded starters; 29-35 on grass; 40-58 on turf; 23-22 in daytime; 46-71 at night; 27-20 in one-run games; 3-6 in extra-inning games; 0-1-0 in doubleheaders.
Team record past five years: 132-192 in two years (.407).

TEAM LEADERS

Batting average: Fred McGriff (.310).
At-bats: Fred McGriff (529).
Runs: Dave Martinez (79).
Hits: Fred McGriff (164).
Total Bases: Fred McGriff (292).
Doubles: Fred McGriff (30).
Triples: Miguel Cairo, Dave Martinez (5).
Home runs: Jose Canseco (34).
Runs batted in: Fred McGriff (104).
Stolen bases: Miguel Cairo (22).
Slugging percentage: Jose Canseco (.563).
On-base percentage: Fred McGriff (.405).
Wins: Wilson Alvarez (9).

Earned-run average: Bobby Witt (5.84).
Complete games: Bobby Witt (3).
Shutouts: Bobby Witt (2).
Saves: Roberto Hernandez (43).
Innings pitched: Bobby Witt (180.1).
Strikeouts: Wilson Alvarez (128).

GAMES BY POSITION

Catcher: John Flaherty 115, Mike DiFelice 51.
First base: Fred McGriff 125, Paul Sorrento 27, Herbert Perry 14, Wade Boggs 4, Aaron Ledesma 4, Steve Cox 4, Julio Franco 1.
Second base: Miguel Cairo 117, Aaron Ledesma 17, Tony Graffanino 17, David Lamb 15, Bobby Smith 13.
Third base: Wade Boggs 74, Bobby Smith 59, Herbert Perry 42, Aaron Ledesma 26, Tony Graffanino 1.
Shortstop: Kevin Stocker 76, Aaron Ledesma 50, David Lamb 35, Tony Graffanino 17.
Outfield: Dave Martinez 140, Randy Winn 77, Bubba Trammell 74, Terrell Lowery 60, Paul Sorrento 57, Jose Guillen 47, Quinton McCracken 40, Danny Clyburn 24, Jose Canseco 6, Herbert Perry 6, Rich Butler 6, Steve Cox 2.
Designated hitter: Jose Canseco 106, Fred McGriff 18, Paul Sorrento 9, Wade Boggs 7, Bubba Trammell 6, Herbert Perry 5, Danny Clyburn 4, David Lamb 3, Miguel Cairo 2, John Flaherty 1, Aaron Ledesma 1, Tony Graffanino 1, Terrell Lowery 1, Mickey Callaway 1.

TOP DRAFT CHOICES

1. **Josh Hamilton,** OF, Athens Drive H.S., Raleigh, N.C.
2. **Carl Crawford,** OF, Jefferson Davis H.S., Houston
3. **Doug Waechter,** RHP, Northeast H.S., St. Petersburg, Fla.
4. **Alex Santos,** RHP, U. of Miami
5. **Seth McClung,** RHP, Greenbrier East H.S., Lewisburg, W.Va.
6. **Eric Henderson,** LHP, Santa Fe (Fla.) C.C.
7. **Andrew Beinbrink,** 3B, Arizona St. U.
8. **Ryan Gloger,** LHP, Jesuit H.S., Tampa
9. **Dan Ortiz,** 1B, Hemet H.S., Nuevo, Calif.
10. **Nathan Cromer,** LHP, Lincoln H.S., Des Moines, Ia.

TEXAS RANGERS
AMERICAN LEAGUE WEST DIVISION

2000 Rangers Schedule
Home games shaded. *—All-Star Game at Turner Field (Atlanta).

March

SUN	MON	TUE	WED	THU	FRI	SAT
26	27	28	29	30	31	

April

SUN	MON	TUE	WED	THU	FRI	SAT
						1
2	3 CWS	4 CWS	5 CWS	6 CWS	7 TOR	8 TOR
9 TOR	10	11 NYY	12 NYY	13 NYY	14 CLE	15 CLE
16 CLE	17 NYY	18 NYY	19 NYY	20	21 MIN	22 MIN
23 MIN	24 BOS	25 BOS	26 BOS	27	28 BAL	29 BAL
30 BAL						

May

SUN	MON	TUE	WED	THU	FRI	SAT
	1	2 TB	3 TB	4 TB	5 OAK	6 OAK
7 OAK	8 SEA	9 SEA	10 SEA	11 ANA	12 ANA	13 ANA
14 ANA	15 TB	16 TB	17 TB	18 BAL	19 BAL	20 BAL
21 BAL	22	23 KC	24 KC	25 KC	26 MIN	27 MIN
28 MIN	29 DET	30 DET	31 DET			

June

SUN	MON	TUE	WED	THU	FRI	SAT
				1	2 ARI	3 ARI
4 ARI	5 LA	6 LA	7 LA	8	9 COL	10 COL
11 COL	12	13 LA	14 BAL	15 BAL	16 TB	17 TB
18 TB	19	20 MIN	21 MIN	22 MIN	23 TB	24 TB
25 TB	26	27 OAK	28 OAK	29 OAK	30 SEA	

July

SUN	MON	TUE	WED	THU	FRI	SAT
						1 SEA
2 SEA	3 OAK	4 OAK	5 OAK	6	7 SD	8 SD
9 SD	10	11	* 12	13 ARI	14 ARI	15 ARI
16 SF	17 SF	18 SF	19 ANA	20 ANA	21 SEA	22 SEA
23 SEA	24 ANA	25 ANA	26 ANA	27 DET	28 DET	29 DET
30 DET	31					

August

SUN	MON	TUE	WED	THU	FRI	SAT
		1 CWS	2 CWS	3 TOR	4 TOR	5 TOR
6 TOR	7	8 CLE	9 CLE	10 CLE	11 BOS	12 BOS
13 BOS	14 NYY	15 NYY	16 NYY	17 BOS	18 BOS	19 BOS
20 BOS	21	22 NYY	23 NYY	24 NYY	25 TOR	26 TOR
27 TOR	28 CLE	29 CLE	30 CLE	31 CLE		

September

SUN	MON	TUE	WED	THU	FRI	SAT
					1 DET	2 DET
3 DET	4 CWS	5 CWS	6 CWS	7 CWS	8 KC	9 KC
10 KC	11	12 BAL	13 BAL	14 KC	15 KC	16 KC
17 KC	18 MIN	19 MIN	20 MIN	21	22 ANA	23 ANA
24 ANA	25	26 SEA	27 SEA	28 SEA	29 OAK	30 OAK

October

SUN	MON	TUE	WED	THU	FRI	SAT
1 OAK	2	3	4	5	6	7

2000 SEASON
CLUB DIRECTORY

Chairman of the board and owner
Thomas O. Hicks
President
James R. Lites
Exec. v.p., general manager
Doug Melvin
Exec. v.p., finance and operations
John McMichael
Exec. v.p., broadcasting and sales
Bill Strong
Exec. v.p., marketing and communications
Jeff Cogen
Sr. vice president, communications
John Blake
V.p., community development/relations
Norm Lyons
Vice president, finance
Chip Sawicki
Vice president, facilities and construction
Billy Ray Johnson
Vice president, diversified operations
Rick McLaughlin
Vice president, information technology
Steve McNeill
Vice president, business operations
Geoff Moore
Vice president, event operations
Tim Murphy
Vice president, merchandising
Steve Shills
Vice president, corporate sales
Charlie Seraphin
Director, Legends of the Game Museum
Tom Smith
Director, human resources
Terry Turner
Corporate counsel
Lance Lankford
Assistant vice president, ticket sales
Brian Byrnes
Asst. vice president, corporate services
Jill Cogen
Asst. vice president, ticket operations
Augie Manfredo
Assistant vice president, marketing
Christy Martinez
Asst. vice president, advertising sales
David Peart
Controller
Kellie Fischer
Assistant general manager
Dan O'Brien

Director, Major League administration
Judy Johns
Director, scouting
Chuck McMichael
Director, player development
Reid Nichols
Asst. dir., professional and int'l scouting
Monty Clegg
Assistant to director of scouting
Debbie Bent
Asst. to director of player development
Debbie Bent
Director of travel
Chris Lyngos
Director, medical services
Dr. John Conway
Director, media relations
Kurt Daniels
Director, community relations
Taunee Paur Taylor
Director, community development
Rhonda Houston
Assistant director, communications
Dana Wilcox
Assistant director, media relations
Brad Horn
Senior director, events
Lee Gleiser
Senior director, entertainment
Chuck Morgan
Senior director, graphic design
Rainer Uhlir
Head trainer
Danny Wheat
Visiting clubhouse manager
Joe Macko
Equipment and home clubhouse manager
Zack Minasian
National cross-checkers
Tim Hallgren
David Klipstein
Jeff Taylor
Latin coordinator
Manny Batista
Scouts
Dave Birecki, Carl Cassell, Jim Cuthbert, Mike Daughtry, Jay Eddings, Kip Fagg, Jim Fairey, Tim Fortugno, Mark Giegler, Joel Grampietro, Mike Grouse, Todd Guggiana, Doug Harris, Zackary Hoyrst, Ray Jackson, Jim Lentine, Dennis Meeks, Sammy Melendez, Gary Neibauer, Mike Paustian, Javier Rodriguez, Randy Taylor, Ron Toenjes, Greg Whitworth, Jeff Wren

MINOR LEAGUE AFFILIATES

Class	Team	League	Manager
AAA	Oklahoma	Pacific Coast	DeMarlo Hale
AA	Tulsa	Texas	Bobby Jones
A	Charlotte	Florida State	Jim Byrd
A	Savannah	South Atlantic	Paul Carey
Rookie	Pulaski	Appalachian	Bruce Crabbe
Rookie	Gulf Coast Rangers	Gulf Coast	Darryl Kennedy

BROADCAST INFORMATION

Radio: KRLD-AM (1080); KESS (1270), Spanish.
TV: KXAS-TV (Channel 5); KXTX-TV (Channel 39).
Cable TV: Fox Sports Net.

SPRING TRAINING

Ballpark (city): Charlotte County Stadium (Port Charlotte, Fla.).
Ticket information: 941-625-9500.

SPRING TRAINING ROSTER

Manager—Johnny Oates (26).
Coaches—Dick Bosman (17), Bucky Dent (20), Larry Hardy (48), Rudy Jaramillo (8), Ed Napoleon (12), Jerry Narron (5).

No.	PITCHERS	B/T	Ht./Wt.	Born	1999 clubs
53	Benoit, Joaquin	R/R	6-3/205	7-26-79	Charlotte
54	Clark, Mark	R/R	6-5/235	5-12-68	Texas, Savannah, Charlotte
33	Cordero, Francisco	R/R	6-2/200	8-11-77	Jacksonville, Detroit
23	Crabtree, Tim	R/R	6-4/220	10-13-69	Texas
46	Davis, Doug	R/L	6-3/190	9-21-75	Tulsa, Oklahoma, Texas
47	Elder, David	R/R	6-0/180	9-23-75	Charlotte, Tulsa
38	Glynn, Ryan	R/R	6-3/195	11-1-74	Oklahoma, Texas
32	Helling, Rick	R/R	6-3/220	12-15-70	Texas
50	Johnson, Jonathan	R/R	6-0/180	7-16-74	Oklahoma, Gulf Coast Rangers, Tulsa, Texas
52	Kolb, Danny	R/R	6-4/215	3-29-75	Tulsa, Oklahoma, Texas
36	Lee, Corey	B/L	6-2/185	12-26-74	Tulsa, Oklahoma, Texas
28	Loaiza, Esteban	R/R	6-3/210	12-31-71	Texas, Oklahoma
39	Moreno, Juan	L/L	6-1/205	2-28-75	Tulsa
51	Munoz, Mike	L/L	6-2/198	7-12-65	Texas
40	Perisho, Matt	L/L	6-0/205	6-8-75	Oklahoma, Texas
	Rogers, Kenny	L/L	6-1/205	11-10-64	Oakland, New York N.L.
49	Sikorski, Brian	R/R	6-1/190	7-27-74	New Orleans
45	Smith, Chuck	R/R	6-1/185	10-21-69	Oklahoma
22	Thompson, Justin	L/L	6-4/215	3-8-73	Detroit
43	Venafro, Mike	L/L	5-10/180	8-2-73	Oklahoma, Texas
35	Wetteland, John	R/R	6-2/215	8-21-66	Texas
59	Zimmerman, Jeff	R/R	6-1/200	8-9-72	Oklahoma, Texas

No.	CATCHERS	B/T	Ht./Wt.	Born	1999 clubs
37	Haselman, Bill	R/R	6-3/223	5-25-66	Detroit
2	King, Cesar	R/R	6-0/215	2-28-78	Tulsa
7	Rodriguez, Ivan	R/R	5-9/205	11-30-71	Texas

No.	INFIELDERS	B/T	Ht./Wt.	Born	1999 clubs
10	Alicea, Luis	B/R	5-9/176	7-29-65	Texas
27	Catalanotto, Frank	L/R	6-0/195	4-27-74	Detroit
11	Clayton, Royce	R/R	6-0/183	1-2-70	Texas, Oklahoma
44	Dransfeldt, Kelly	R/R	6-2/195	4-16-75	Oklahoma, Texas
53	Grabowski, Jason	L/R	6-3/200	5-24-76	Charlotte, Tulsa
14	Lamb, Mike	L/R	6-1/185	8-9-75	Tulsa, Oklahoma
25	Palmeiro, Rafael	L/L	6-0/190	9-24-64	Texas
4	Sheldon, Scott	R/R	6-3/215	11-20-68	Oklahoma, Texas
9	Stevens, Lee	L/L	6-4/235	7-10-67	Texas

No.	OUTFIELDERS	B/T	Ht./Wt.	Born	1999 clubs
3	Curtis, Chad	R/R	5-10/185	11-6-68	New York A.L.
41	Green, Scarborough	R/R	5-10/175	6-9-74	Texas, Oklahoma
29	Greer, Rusty	L/L	6-0/195	1-21-69	Texas
18	Kapler, Gabe	R/R	6-2/208	8-31-75	Detroit, Toledo
38	Mateo, Ruben	R/R	6-0/185	2-10-78	Texas, Oklahoma
16	Simms, Mike	R/R	6-4/230	1-12-67	Charlotte, Oklahoma, Texas

BALLPARK INFORMATION

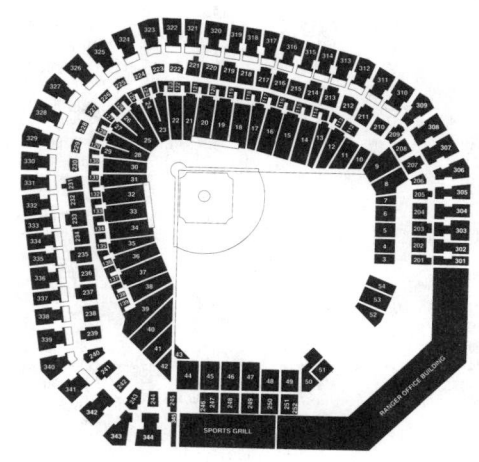

Ballpark (capacity, surface)
The Ballpark in Arlington (49,166, grass)
Address
1000 Ballpark Way
Arlington, TX 76011
Business phone
817-273-5222
Ticket information
817-273-5100
Ticket prices
$37.50 (lower box)
$35 (club box)
$30 (club reserved)
$25 (corner box)
$20 (terrace club box)
$17.50 (left field reserved; lower home run porch)
$14 (upper box)
$12 (upper home run porch)
$10 (upper reserved; bleachers)
$6 (grandstand reserved)
$5 (grandstand)
Field dimensions (from home plate)
To left field at foul line, 334 feet
To center field, 400 feet
To right field at foul line, 325 feet
First game played
April 11, 1994 (Brewers 4, Rangers 3)

2000 SEASON *Texas Rangers*

Date	Opp.	Res.	Score	(inn.*)	Hits	Opp. hits	Winning pitcher	Losing pitcher	Save	Record	Pos.	GB
4-6	Det.	W	6-0		12	7	Sele	Thompson		1-1	T2nd	0.5
4-7	Det.	W	10-7		18	12	Morgan	Blair	Wetteland	2-1	1st	+0.5
4-9	Ana.	L	4-8		10	12	Finley	Burkett		2-2	T1st	...
4-10	Ana.	L	0-10		3	19	Olivares	Helling		2-3	T2nd	1.0
4-11	Ana.	W	6-3		12	6	Sele	Belcher	Wetteland	3-3	T1st	...
4-12	Ana.	L	5-13		7	20	Magnante	Clark		3-4	3rd	1.0
4-13	At Sea.	W	15-6		19	10	Morgan	Cloude		4-4	T1st	...
4-14	At Sea.	W	9-6		17	11	Zimmerman	Paniagua	Wetteland	5-4	1st	+1.0
4-15	At Sea.	W	4-3	(10)	9	5	Crabtree	Halama	Wetteland	6-4	1st	+1.0
4-16	At Oak.	L	2-8		3	17	Candiotti	Sele		6-5	T1st	...
4-17	At Oak.	L	3-11		6	13	Haynes	Clark		6-6	T1st	...
4-18	At Oak.	W	6-2		15	7	Morgan	Oquist		7-6	1st	+1.0
4-20	At N.Y.	L	0-4		4	13	Cone	Burkett		7-7	1st	+1.0
4-21	At N.Y.	L	2-4		5	6	Clemens	Helling	Rivera	7-8	1st	+1.0
4-22	At Min.	W	6-4		6	10	Sele	Milton	Wetteland	8-8	1st	+1.0
4-23	At Min.	W	4-2		12	6	Clark	Lincoln	Wetteland	9-8	1st	+2.0
4-24	At Min.	W	7-2		10	9	Morgan	Hawkins		10-8	1st	+2.0
4-25	At Min.	W	9-5		11	10	Helling	Perkins		11-8	1st	+2.0
4-27	N.Y.	L	6-7		7	14	Stanton	Wetteland	Rivera	11-9	1st	+2.5
4-28	N.Y.	W	8-6		12	10	Munoz	Stanton	Wetteland	12-9	1st	+3.0
4-29	N.Y.	L	3-5		9	6	Mendoza	Morgan	Rivera	12-10	1st	+2.0
4-30	Cle.	W	7-5		13	11	Helling	Colon	Wetteland	13-10	1st	+2.0
5-1	Cle.	L	3-5		9	8	Gooden	Sele	Jackson	13-11	1st	+2.0
5-2	Cle.	W	8-6		11	8	Clark	Nagy	Wetteland	14-11	1st	+2.0
5-3	Cle.	L	4-10		6	16	Wright	Morgan		14-12	1st	+2.0
5-5	At Bos.	W	8-3		12	8	Helling	Rapp		15-12	1st	+2.0
5-6	At Bos.	L	2-3		10	10	Cormier	Sele	Wakefield	15-13	1st	+1.0
5-7	At Tor.	L	6-9		7	17	Hentgen	Clark	Koch	15-14	1st	+1.0
5-8	At Tor.	W	4-3		7	7	Morgan	Wells	Wetteland	16-14	1st	+2.0
5-9	At Tor.	W	11-6		20	8	Patterson	Munro		17-14	1st	+2.0
5-10	At Chi.	L	2-5		6	12	Navarro	Helling		17-15	1st	+1.5
5-11	At Chi.	W	11-5		15	12	Zimmerman	Howry		18-15	1st	+1.5
5-13	Bal.	W	15-7		13	13	Morgan	Kamieniecki		19-15	1st	+1.5
5-14	Bal.	W	7-6		11	15	Crabtree	Rhodes	Wetteland	20-15	1st	+1.5
5-15	Bal.	W	8-1		14	7	Helling	Johns		21-15	1st	+1.5
5-16	Bal.	L	5-16		11	24	Ponson	Sele		21-16	1st	+0.5
5-17	T.B.	L	3-13		6	15	Rupe	Burkett		21-17	T1st	...
5-18	T.B.	L	4-5		14	10	Arrojo	Morgan	Hernandez	21-18	T1st	...
5-19	T.B.	W	7-6		9	11	Zimmerman	Aldred	Wetteland	22-18	1st	+1.0
5-21	At Bal.	L	2-3		6	7	Ponson	Helling		22-19	1st	+1.5
5-22	At Bal.	W	8-7		7	14	Crabtree	Timlin	Wetteland	23-19	1st	+2.0
5-23	At Bal.	L	6-15		14	15	Mussina	Morgan		23-20	1st	+2.0
5-24	At T.B.	W	12-3		16	10	Clark	Arrojo		24-20	1st	+3.0
5-25	At T.B.	W	7-2		11	9	Venafro	Witt		25-20	1st	+3.0
5-26	At T.B.	W	8-6		12	11	Helling	Santana	Wetteland	26-20	1st	+3.0
5-28	Min.	W	6-4		10	9	Sele	Radke	Wetteland	27-20	1st	+2.5
5-29	Min.	W	4-3	(10)	11	12	Wetteland	Trombley		28-20	1st	+3.0
5-30	Min.	W	3-2		9	6	Zimmerman	Mays	Wetteland	29-20	1st	+3.5
5-31	K.C.	W	4-3	(10)	7	9	Crabtree	Santiago		30-20	1st	+3.5
6-1	K.C.	W	3-1		6	3	Zimmerman	Whisenant	Wetteland	31-20	1st	+3.5
6-2	K.C.	W	7-4		6	10	Sele	Appier	Wetteland	32-20	1st	+4.5
6-4	At Ari.	L	3-11		4	12	Johnson	Clark		32-21	1st	+4.5
6-5	At Ari.	W	9-8		9	7	Venafro	Holmes	Wetteland	33-21	1st	+5.5
6-6	At Ari.	L	2-4		7	6	Benes	Helling	Olson	33-22	1st	+4.5
6-7	At L.A.	W	3-2		10	6	Sele	Valdes	Wetteland	34-22	1st	+5.0
6-8	At L.A.	W	7-6	(13)	16	11	Zimmerman	Mills	Munoz	35-22	1st	+5.0
6-9	At L.A.	L	2-7		5	11	Brown	Clark		35-23	1st	+5.0
6-11	Col.	W	3-2		8	6	Zimmerman	McElroy	Wetteland	36-23	1st	+5.0
6-12	Col.	L	7-8		13	13	Astacio	Sele	Veres	36-24	1st	+4.5
6-13	Col.	L	2-4		7	8	Jones	Morgan	Veres	36-25	1st	+3.5
6-14	At N.Y.	L	2-8		8	14	Irabu	Clark		36-26	1st	+3.0
6-15	At N.Y.	L	2-6		4	6	Cone	Glynn		36-27	1st	+3.0
6-16	At N.Y.	W	3-0		5	4	Helling	Hernandez	Wetteland	37-27	1st	+4.0
6-17	At N.Y.	W	4-2		10	7	Sele	Clemens	Wetteland	38-27	1st	+4.0
6-18	At Bos.	W	4-1		8	3	Morgan	Portugal	Zimmerman	39-27	1st	+4.0
6-19	At Bos.	L	4-7		6	15	Cho	Clark	Wakefield	39-28	1st	+4.0
6-20	At Bos.	L	2-5		8	12	Martinez	Glynn	Wakefield	39-29	1st	+4.0
6-21	At Bos.	L	4-5		9	10	Wasdin	Helling	Wakefield	39-30	1st	+4.0
6-22	Oak.	L	3-5		11	11	Mathews	Wetteland	Taylor	39-31	1st	+3.0
6-23	Oak.	W	7-6		13	7	Morgan	Oquist	Wetteland	40-31	1st	+4.0
6-24	Oak.	W	5-2		6	7	Burkett	Hudson	Wetteland	41-31	1st	+5.0
6-25	At Sea.	W	14-4		18	6	Glynn	Rodriguez		42-31	1st	+6.0

Date	Opp.	Res.	Score	(inn.*)	Hits	Opp. hits	Winning pitcher	Losing pitcher	Save	Record	Pos.	GB
6-26	At Sea.	L	4-5		12	8	Paniagua	Venafro	Mesa	42-32	1st	+5.0
6-27	At Sea.	L	2-5		6	10	Garcia	Sele	Mesa	42-33	1st	+4.0
6-28	At Ana.	W	9-1		9	7	Morgan	Finley		43-33	1st	+4.5
6-29	At Ana.	W	5-0		13	1	Burkett	Olivares		44-33	1st	+4.5
6-30	At Ana.	W	18-4		20	10	Glynn	Hill		45-33	1st	+5.5
7-2	Sea.	W	7-6		10	14	Wetteland	Cloude		46-33	1st	+7.0
7-3	Sea.	L	12-13		15	15	Paniagua	Crabtree	Mesa	46-34	1st	+6.0
7-4	Sea.	L	0-6		6	12	Halama	Morgan		46-35	1st	+5.0
7-5	At Oak.	L	2-4		6	12	Hudson	Burkett	Taylor	46-36	1st	+4.0
7-6	At Oak.	L	0-4		4	5	Haynes	Glynn		46-37	1st	+4.0
7-7	At Oak.	W	7-4		10	7	Zimmerman	Rigby	Wetteland	47-37	1st	+5.0
7-9	At S.D.	W	7-2		8	9	Sele	Williams		48-37	1st	+6.0
7-10	At S.D.	L	4-5		9	8	Wall	Wetteland		48-38	1st	+5.0
7-11	At S.D.	L	2-6		4	11	Miceli	Loaiza		48-39	1st	+5.0
7-15	Ari.	W	3-2		7	5	Venafro	Mantei		49-39	1st	+5.0
7-16	Ari.	W	9-8		14	10	Wetteland	Chouinard		50-39	1st	+5.0
7-17	Ari.	L	6-8	(10)	11	13	Plesac	Wetteland	Mantei	50-40	1st	+5.0
7-18	S.F	W	5-4		7	9	Morgan	Gardner	Wetteland	51-40	1st	+5.0
7-19	S.F	W	14-7		17	10	Loaiza	Brock		52-40	1st	+5.0
7-20	S.F	W	6-3		10	7	Helling	Estes		53-40	1st	+5.0
7-21	Ana.	W	9-5		13	10	Sele	Olivares	Zimmerman	54-40	1st	+5.0
7-22	Ana.	W	9-7		10	15	Burkett	Sparks	Zimmerman	55-40	1st	+6.0
7-23	At T.B.	W	11-8		13	17	Kolb	Rupe		56-40	1st	+7.0
7-24	At T.B.	W	5-3		11	5	Loaiza	Newman	Wetteland	57-40	1st	+7.0
7-25	At T.B.	W	4-3		8	7	Helling	Arrojo	Wetteland	58-40	1st	+8.0
7-27	At Bal.	W	8-6		14	11	Sele	Mussina	Wetteland	59-40	1st	+8.5
7-28	At Bal.	L	6-8		8	13	Erickson	Burkett	Timlin	59-41	1st	+8.5
7-29	At Bal.	W	3-1		6	3	Morgan	Guzman	Wetteland	60-41	1st	+9.0
7-30	K.C.	W	9-2		14	9	Loaiza	Witasick		61-41	1st	+9.0
7-31	K.C.	L	8-12		13	19	Reichert	Munoz	Service	61-42	1st	+8.0
8-1	K.C.	W	12-5		16	10	Sele	Barber		62-42	1st	+8.0
8-2	Min.	W	5-4		8	9	Zimmerman	Guardado	Wetteland	63-42	1st	+8.0
8-3	Min.	W	9-5		13	14	Morgan	Sampson		64-42	1st	+8.0
8-4	Min.	W	3-1		10	4	Loaiza	Radke	Wetteland	65-42	1st	+9.0
8-6	Tor.	L	4-5		11	10	Carpenter	Zimmerman	Koch	65-43	1st	+7.5
8-7	Tor.	W	6-0		13	6	Sele	Hentgen		66-43	1st	+7.5
8-8	Tor.	L	7-8		11	11	Frascatore	Venafro	Koch	66-44	1st	+6.5
8-9	Tor.	L	4-19		7	25	Hamilton	Morgan		66-45	1st	+6.5
8-10	Det.	W	4-3	(12)	8	11	Patterson	Cruz		67-45	1st	+6.5
8-11	Det.	W	8-2		12	6	Helling	Blair		68-45	1st	+7.5
8-12	Det.	L	1-3		5	8	Mlicki	Sele	Jones	68-46	1st	+7.0
8-13†	At Chi.	L	2-4		6	11	Wells	Burkett	Howry	68-47		
8-13‡	At Chi.	L	4-7		14	9	Baldwin	Glynn		68-48	1st	+5.5
8-14	At Chi.	L	7-8		11	16	Howry	Zimmerman		68-49	1st	+4.5
8-15	At Chi.	W	10-0		16	6	Loaiza	Snyder		69-49	1st	+4.5
8-16	At Cle.	W	13-5		16	10	Munoz	Rincon		70-49	1st	+5.5
8-17	At Cle.	W	15-4		19	9	Sele	Langston		71-49	1st	+5.5
8-18	At Cle.	W	6-1		9	7	Burkett	Nagy		72-49	1st	+6.5
8-19	At Cle.	L	0-8		7	11	Karsay	Morgan		72-50	1st	+5.5
8-20	Bos.	W	4-3		10	6	Loaiza	Portugal	Wetteland	73-50	1st	+6.5
8-21	Bos.	W	9-2		12	9	Helling	Rose		74-50	1st	+6.5
8-22	Bos.	W	6-0		10	8	Sele	Wakefield		75-50	1st	+6.5
8-23	N.Y.	L	3-21		10	23	Pettitte	Burkett		75-51	1st	+6.5
8-24	N.Y.	L	7-10	(11)	14	11	Mendoza	Lee	Rivera	75-52	1st	+5.5
8-25	N.Y.	W	7-3		12	8	Loaiza	Irabu		76-52	1st	+6.5
8-27	At Tor.	W	8-2		14	6	Helling	Carpenter		77-52	1st	+6.5
8-28	At Tor.	W	9-7		14	14	Sele	Wells	Wetteland	78-52	1st	+6.5
8-29	At Tor.	W	4-2		11	9	Burkett	Halladay	Wetteland	79-52	1st	+7.5
8-30	At Det.	L	0-1		3	10	Moehler	Loaiza		79-53	1st	+7.5
8-31	At Det.	L	6-14		11	16	Cordero	Kolb		79-54	1st	+6.5
9-1	At Det.	W	14-7		15	12	Helling	Weaver	Wetteland	80-54	1st	+6.5
9-2	At Det.	L	7-8		13	15	Mlicki	Zimmerman	Jones	80-55	1st	+6.5
9-3	Chi.	W	10-4		15	10	Burkett	Baldwin		81-55	1st	+6.5
9-4	Chi.	L	3-12		11	15	Castillo	Loaiza		81-56	1st	+5.5
9-6†	Chi.	W	8-6		9	10	Helling	Parque	Wetteland	82-56		
9-6‡	Chi.	W	6-3		8	12	Fassero	Snyder	Wetteland	83-56	1st	+7.5
9-7	Cle.	W	4-3		10	6	Sele	Reed	Wetteland	84-56	1st	+8.5
9-8	Cle.	W	3-0		7	8	Burkett	Haney	Wetteland	85-56	1st	+8.5
9-10	At K.C.	L	3-7		11	12	Stein	Loaiza	Montgomery	85-57	1st	+7.5
9-11	At K.C.	L	6-9		14	13	Suppan	Helling	Montgomery	85-58	1st	+6.5
9-12	At K.C.	L	3-6		9	9	Witasick	Sele	Morman	85-59	1st	+5.5
9-13	At K.C.	W	8-4	(10)	11	9	Wetteland	Santiago		86-59	1st	+5.5
9-14	At Min.	W	5-4		10	10	Kolb	Guardado	Wetteland	87-59	1st	+6.5
9-15	At Min.	W	8-3		12	9	Loaiza	Radke		88-59	1st	+7.0
9-17	T.B.	L	5-7		16	13	Newman	Helling	Hernandez	88-60	1st	+7.0
9-18	T.B.	W	6-1		9	6	Sele	Witt		89-60	1st	+7.0

Date	Opp.	Res.	Score	(inn.*)	Hits	Opp. hits	Winning pitcher	Losing pitcher	Save	Record	Pos.	GB
9-19	T.B.	L	2-15		7	15	Arrojo	Burkett		89-61	1st	+6.0
9-21	Bal.	L	2-4		6	7	Johnson	Loaiza	Timlin	89-62	1st	+5.5
9-22	Bal.	L	4-7	10		9	Erickson	Helling	Timlin	89-63	1st	+5.5
9-24	Oak.	W	12-4		18	8	Sele	Heredia		90-63	1st	+6.5
9-25	Oak.	W	10-4		9	6	Burkett	Appier		91-63	1st	+7.5
9-26	Oak.	W	10-3		12	7	Loaiza	Jarvis		92-63	1st	+8.5
9-27	Sea.	W	3-2	10		7	Crabtree	Sinclair	Wetteland	93-63	1st	+9.0
9-28	Sea.	W	10-0		15	5	Morgan	Halama		94-63	1st	+9.0
9-29	Sea.	L	3-7		9	13	Meche	Sele		94-64	1st	+9.0
9-30	Sea.	W	7-0		8	4	Burkett	Hinchliffe		95-64	1st	+10.0
10-1	At Ana.	L	6-7		8	9	Holtz	Morgan		95-65	1st	+9.0
10-2	At Ana.	L	3-15		9	14	Hasegawa	Helling		95-66	1st	+9.0
10-3	At Ana.	L	0-1		5	3	Washburn	Morgan	Pote	95-67	1st	+8.0

Monthly records: April (13-10), May (17-10), June (15-13), July (16-9), August (18-12), September (16-10), October (0-3).
*Innings, if other than nine. † First game of a doubleheader. ‡ Second game of a doubleheader.

HIGHLIGHTS

High point: September 30, when the Rangers set a franchise record with their 95th victory, a 7-0 win over Seattle that came in Texas' regular-season home finale. Four days earlier, the Rangers had clinched their third A.L. West title in four seasons.

Low point: October 9, when the Rangers went quietly in Game 3 of the division series against New York. With the 3-0 victory, the Yankees swept the Rangers out of the playoffs for the second consecutive season. In each series, the Rangers scored only one run.

Turning point: With two on and one out in the first inning of Game 1 of the division series, cleanup hitter Juan Gonzalez was overmatched against Yankees righthander Orlando Hernandez and struck out. The Rangers didn't score in that inning or in the game, and lost 8-0.

Most valuable player: Yes, catcher Ivan Rodriguez won the league MVP honor, but designated hitter Rafael Palmeiro is the choice here. Palmeiro hit .324 with 47 home runs and 148 RBIs and was the Rangers' top clutch hitter. He hit .358 with runners in scoring position and .500 with the bases loaded. Rodriguez had one of the best offensive seasons by a catcher in major league history, batting .332 with 35 home runs, 113 RBIs and 116 runs scored. He also threw out a major league-record 54.2 percent of runners trying to steal.

Most valuable pitcher: With a shaky rotation in place, Texas added rookie righthander Jeff Zimmerman from the minors eight days into the season to strengthen the bullpen. Zimmerman won his first nine decisions and had a sub-2.00 ERA for most of the year.

Most improved player: By mid-May, Esteban Loaiza was sidelined with a broken hand and all but written out of the Rangers' long-term plans. But the righthander stood out upon his return, going 9-4 with a 3.72 ERA after the All-Star break, and now looms large in Texas' future.

Most pleasant surprise: Zimmerman, who went from being "just another body" to one of the top setup men in the majors.

Biggest disappointment: After missing out on Randy Johnson, the Rangers signed Mark Clark as a consolation prize. He went 3-7 with an 8.60 ERA through mid-June, then was sidelined for the season because of a partially torn ligament in his elbow.

Key injuries: Palmeiro was limited to 28 games at first base because of two off-season arthroscopic knee surgeries. Mike Simms, one of Palmeiro's backups, underwent heel surgery and had exactly two at-bats. Rookie center fielder Ruben Mateo broke a bone in his right wrist on August 4 and didn't return.

Notable: Right fielder Gonzalez had another big season (.326 average, 39 homers and 128 RBIs), but fell out of favor because of a questionable attitude. ... The Rangers had four 100-RBI men— Palmeiro, Gonzalez, Rodriguez and left fielder Rusty Greer. Third baseman Todd Zeile wound up at 98. ... Aaron Sele, a 19-game winner in 1998 (his first season with Texas), won 18 times in '99. ... John Wetteland's 43 saves moved him within four of 300 for his career.

—EVAN GRANT

RECORDS

1999 regular-season record: 95-67 (1st in A.L. West); 51-30 at home; 44-37 on road; 29-26 vs. East; 35-17 vs. Central; 21-16 vs. A.L. West; 10-8 vs. N.L.; 20-10 vs. left-handed starters; 75-57 vs. righthanded starters; 74-64 on grass; 21-3 on turf; 17-18 in daytime; 78-49 at night; 24-16 in one-run games; 6-2 in extra-inning games; 1-1-0 in doubleheaders.
Team record past five years: 424-368 (.535, ranks 4th in league in that span).

TEAM LEADERS

Batting average: Ivan Rodriguez (.332).
At-bats: Ivan Rodriguez (600).
Runs: Ivan Rodriguez (116).
Hits: Ivan Rodriguez (199).
Total Bases: Rafael Palmeiro (356).
Doubles: Rusty Greer, Todd Zeile (41).
Triples: Mark McLemore (7).
Home runs: Rafael Palmeiro (47).
Runs batted in: Rafael Palmeiro (148).
Stolen bases: Tom Goodwin (39).
Slugging percentage: Rafael Palmeiro (.630).
On-base percentage: Rafael Palmeiro (.420).

Wins: Aaron Sele (18).
Earned-run average: Aaron Sele (4.79).
Complete games: Rick Helling (3).
Shutouts: Aaron Sele (2).
Saves: John Wetteland (43).
Innings pitched: Rick Helling (219.1).
Strikeouts: Aaron Sele (186).

GAMES BY POSITION

Catcher: Ivan Rodriguez 141, Gregg Zaun 37.
First base: Lee Stevens 133, Rafael Palmeiro 28, Jon Shave 9, Todd Zeile 1, Mike Simms 1.
Second base: Mark McLemore 135, Luis Alicea 37, Jon Shave 1.
Third base: Todd Zeile 155, Luis Alicea 10, Jon Shave 6, Scott Sheldon 2.
Shortstop: Royce Clayton 133, Jon Shave 24, Kelly Dransfeldt 16.
Outfield: Rusty Greer 145, Juan Gonzalez 131, Tom Goodwin 107, Roberto Kelly 85, Ruben Mateo 31, Mark McLemore 11, Scarborough Green 9, Luis Alicea 1, Mike Simms 1.
Designated hitter: Rafael Palmeiro 128, Juan Gonzalez 14, Lee Stevens 8, Luis Alicea 7, Scarborough Green 4, Jon Shave 3, Mike Simms 2, Gregg Zaun 2, Mark McLemore 1, Todd Zeile 1, Ivan Rodriguez 1, Rusty Greer 1, Ruben Mateo 1.

TOP DRAFT CHOICES

1a. **Colby Lewis,** RHP, Bakersfield (Calif.) J.C.
1b. **David Mead,** RHP, Soddy Daisy H.S., Chattanooga, Tenn.
2. **Nick Regilio,** RHP, Jacksonville University
3. **Hank Blalock,** SS, Rancho Bernardo H.S., San Diego
4a. **Kevin Mench,** OF, U. of Delaware
4b. **Chris Jaile,** C, Columbus H.S., Miami
5a. **Andy Cavazos,** RHP, Brazoswood H.S., Clute, Tex.
5b. **Victor Hillaert,** RHP, Shippensburg (Pa.) Univ.
6. **Aaron Harang,** RHP, San Diego St. U.
7. **Luz Portobanco,** RHP, Miami Senior H.S.
8. **John Rahrer,** RHP, Emmett (Ida.) H.S.
9. **Brett Cadiente,** OF, Arizona State Univ.
10. **Jason Bryan,** OF, New Utrecht H.S., Brooklyn

TORONTO BLUE JAYS
AMERICAN LEAGUE EAST DIVISION

2000 Blue Jays Schedule
Home games shaded. *—All-Star Game at Turner Field (Atlanta).

March
SUN	MON	TUE	WED	THU	FRI	SAT
26	27	28	29	30	31	

April
SUN	MON	TUE	WED	THU	FRI	SAT
						1
2	3 KC	4 KC	5 KC	6	7 TEX	8 TEX
9 TEX	10 ANA	11 ANA	12 ANA	13	14 SEA	15 SEA
16 SEA	17 ANA	18 ANA	19 ANA	20 ANA	21 NYY	22 NYY
23 NYY	24 OAK	25 OAK	26 OAK	27	28 NYY	29 NYY
30 NYY						

May
SUN	MON	TUE	WED	THU	FRI	SAT
	1 CWS	2 CWS	3 CWS	4 CLE	5 CLE	6 CLE
7 CLE	8 BAL	9 BAL	10 BAL	11	12 TB	13 TB
14 TB	15 BOS	16 BOS	17 BOS	18	19 CWS	20 CWS
21 CWS	22 CWS	23 BOS	24 BOS	25 BOS	26 DET	27 DET
28 DET	29	30 MIN	31 MIN			

June
SUN	MON	TUE	WED	THU	FRI	SAT
				1 MIN	2 FLA	3 FLA
4 FLA	5 ATL	6 ATL	7 ATL	8	9 MON	10 MON
11 MON	12 DET	13 DET	14 DET	15	16 BOS	17 BOS
18 BOS	19	20 DET	21 DET	22 DET	23 BOS	24 BOS
25 BOS	26	27 TB	28 TB	29 TB	30 BAL	

July
SUN	MON	TUE	WED	THU	FRI	SAT
						1 BAL
2 BAL	3 BAL	4 CLE	5 CLE	6 CLE	7 MON	8 MON
9 MON	10	11	* 12	13 PHI	14 PHI	15 PHI
16 NYM	17 NYM	18 NYM	19 TB	20 TB	21 BAL	22 BAL
23 BAL	24	25 CLE	26 CLE	27 SEA	28 SEA	29 SEA
30 SEA	31 OAK					

August
SUN	MON	TUE	WED	THU	FRI	SAT
		1 OAK	2 OAK	3 TEX	4 TEX	5 TEX
6 TEX	7 KC	8 KC	9 KC	10 KC	11 MIN	12 MIN
13 MIN	14	15 ANA	16 ANA	17	18 MIN	19 MIN
20 MIN	21	22 KC	23 KC	24	25 TEX	26 TEX
27 TEX	28 ANA	29 ANA	30 ANA	31		

September
SUN	MON	TUE	WED	THU	FRI	SAT
					1 OAK	2 OAK
3 OAK	4 OAK	5 SEA	6 SEA	7 SEA	8 DET	9 DET
10 DET	11	12 NYY	13 NYY	14 NYY	15 CWS	16 CWS
17 CWS	18	19 NYY	20 NYY	21 NYY	22 TB	23 TB
24 TB	25 TB	26 BAL	27 BAL	28 BAL	29 CLE	30 CLE

October
SUN	MON	TUE	WED	THU	FRI	SAT
1 CLE	2	3	4	5	6	7

2000 SEASON
CLUB DIRECTORY

President, baseball operations
Gord Ash
Vice president, sales and marketing
Terry Zuk
Vice president, finance and operations
Stu Hutcheson
Vice president, baseball
Bob Mattick
Vice president, baseball operations
Tim McCleary
Asst. g.m. and dir., player personnel
Dave Stewart
Special assistants to president and g.m.
Wayne Morgan
Mel Queen
Al Widmar
Vice president, media relations
Howard Starkman
V.p., finance and administration
Susan Brioux
Director, scouting
Tim Wilken
Assistant director, scouting
Chris Buckley
Director, player development
Jim Hoff
Director, Canadian scouting
Bill Byckowski
Director, minor leagues
Bob Nelson
Director, Florida operations
Ken Carson
Director, operations
Mario Coutinho

Director, marketing
Peter Cosentino
Director, corporate partnerships
Mark Lemmon
Box office manager
Randy Low
General manager, TBJ merchandising
Michael Andrejak
Manager, team travel
John Brioux
Trainers
George Poulis
Scott Shannon
Strength and conditioning coordinator
Jeff Krushell
Team physicians
Dr. Allan Gross
Dr. Steve Mirabello
Dr. Ron Taylor
Advance scout
Sal Butera
Scouts
Charles Aliano, Tony Arias, Andy
Beene, David Blume, Chris Bourjos,
Bus Campbell, Rick Cerrone, Jeff
Cornell, Ellis Dungan, Joe Ford, Tom
Hinkle, Tim Huff, Jim Hughes,
Duane Larson, Ted Lekas, Mike
Mangan, Ben McLure, Marty Miller,
Bill Moore, Ty Nichols, Andy
Pienovi, Denerius Pittman, Jorge
Rivera, Marteese Robinson, Joe
Siers, Mark Snipp, Ron Tostenson

MINOR LEAGUE AFFILIATES

Class	Team	League	Manager
AAA	Syracuse	International	Pat Kelly
AA	Tennessee	Southern	Rocket Wheeler
A	Dunedin	Florida State	Marty Pevey
A	Hagerstown	South Atlantic	Rolando Pino
A	St. Catharines	New York-Penn	Eddie Rodriguez
Rookie	Medicine Hat	Pioneer	Paul Elliott

BROADCAST INFORMATION

Radio: CHUM (1050).
TV: CBC-TV.
Cable TV: The Sports Network, CTV
SportsNet.

SPRING TRAINING

Ballpark (city): Dunedin Stadium at
Grant Field (Dunedin, Fla.).
Ticket information: 800-707-8269;
727-733-0429.

SPRING TRAINING ROSTER

Manager—Jim Fregosi (11).
Coaches—Lee Elia (3), Cito Gaston (41), Bobby Knoop (29), Roly de Armas (56), Rick Lankford (22), Terry Bevington (35).

No.	PITCHERS	B/T	Ht./Wt.	Born	1999 clubs
34	Andrews, Clayton	R/L	6-0/180	5-15-78	Knoxville, Syracuse
49	Bale, John	L/L	6-4/205	5-22-74	Knoxville, Syracuse, Toronto
36	Borbon, Pedro	L/L	6-1/205	11-15-67	Los Angeles
26	Carpenter, Chris	R/R	6-6/225	4-27-75	Toronto, St. Catharines
53	Coco, Pasqual	R/R	6-1/185	9-24-77	Hagerstown, Dunedin
45	DeWitt, Matt	R/R	6-3/210	9-4-77	Arkansas
45	Escobar, Kelvim	R/R	6-1/195	4-11-76	Toronto
66	Estrella, Leo	R/R	6-1/185	2-20-75	Dunedin
52	Frascatore, John	R/R	6-1/223	2-4-70	Arizona, Toronto
51	Glover, Gary	R/R	6-5/205	12-3-76	Knoxville, Syracuse, Toronto
32	Halladay, Roy	R/R	6-6/225	5-14-77	Toronto
50	Hamilton, Joey	R/R	6-4/230	9-9-70	Toronto, Syracuse
44	Koch, Billy	R/R	6-3/205	12-14-74	Syracuse, Toronto
13	Munro, Peter	R/R	6-2/210	6-14-75	Toronto, Syracuse
40	Painter, Lance	L/L	6-1/200	7-21-67	St. Louis, Arkansas
48	Quantrill, Paul	L/R	6-1/190	11-3-68	Dunedin, Syracuse, Toronto
39	Rodriguez, Nerio	R/R	6-1/205	3-22-73	Syracuse, Toronto
46	Sneed, John	L/R	6-6/250	6-30-76	Dunedin, Knoxville
33	Wells, David	L/L	6-4/235	5-20-63	Toronto

No.	CATCHERS	B/T	Ht./Wt.	Born	1999 clubs
30	Castillo, Alberto	R/R	6-0/185	2-10-70	St. Louis
9	Fletcher, Darrin	L/R	6-2/205	10-3-66	Toronto, Syracuse
17	Phelps, Josh	R/R	6-3/220	5-12-78	Dunedin

No.	INFIELDERS	B/T	Ht./Wt.	Born	1999 clubs
7	Batista, Tony	R/R	6-0/185	12-9-73	Arizona, Toronto
28	Blake, Casey	R/R	6-2/200	8-23-73	Syracuse, Toronto, St. Catharines
16	Bush, Homer	R/R	5-10/180	11-12-72	Toronto, Dunedin
25	Delgado, Carlos	L/R	6-3/225	6-25-72	Toronto
8	Gonzalez, Alex	R/R	6-0/200	4-8-73	Toronto
4	Grebeck, Craig	R/R	5-7/155	12-29-64	Toronto, Syracuse
6	Lawrence, Joe	R/R	6-2/200	2-13-77	Knoxville
19	Segui, David	B/L	6-1/202	7-19-66	Seattle, Toronto
12	Witt, Kevin	L/R	6-4/210	1-5-76	Syracuse, Toronto
31	Woodward, Chris	R/R	6-0/173	6-27-76	Syracuse, Toronto

No.	OUTFIELDERS	B/T	Ht./Wt.	Born	1999 clubs
23	Cruz, Jose	B/R	6-0/200	4-19-74	Toronto, Syracuse
43	Mondesi, Raul	R/R	5-11/215	3-12-71	Los Angeles
27	Sanders, Anthony	R/R	6-2/205	3-2-74	Syracuse, Toronto
24	Stewart, Shannon	R/R	6-1/205	2-25-74	Toronto
16	Thompson, Andy	R/R	6-3/215	10-8-75	Knoxville, Syracuse
10	Wells, Vernon	R/R	6-1/210	12-8-78	Dunedin, Knoxville, Syracuse, Toronto

BALLPARK INFORMATION

Ballpark (capacity, surface)
SkyDome (45,100, artificial)

Address
One Blue Jays Way
Suite 3200
Toronto, Ontario M5V 1J1

Business phone
416-341-1000

Ticket information
416-341-1234

Ticket prices
$42 (premium dugout level)
$39 (field level-infield)
$33.50 (field level-bases)
$30.75 (field level-baselines; Skyclub outfield)
$23 (100 level-outfield; Skyclub-infield;
       Skyclub bleachers)
$16 (Skydeck-bases)
$7 (Skydeck-baselines)

Field dimensions (from home plate)
To left field at foul line, 330 feet
To center field, 400 feet
To right field at foul line, 330 feet

First game played
June 5, 1989 (Brewers 5, Blue Jays 3)

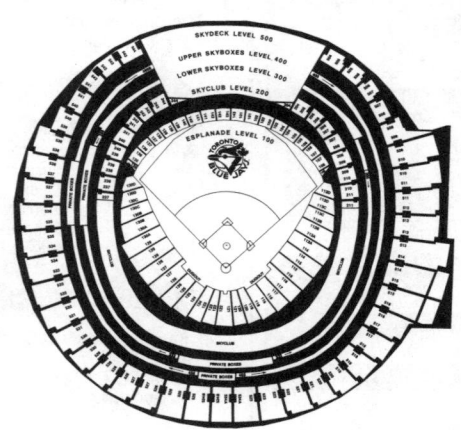

Date	Opp.	Res.	Score	(inn.*)	Hits	Opp. hits	Winning pitcher	Losing pitcher	Save	Record	Pos.	GB
4-7	At Min.	W	9-3		15	7	Wells	Lincoln	Halladay	1-1	T3rd	1.0
4-8	At Min.	L	9-11		13	15	Trombley	Hamilton	Aguilera	1-2	T4th	2.0
4-9	At Bal.	W	7-4		8	6	Escobar	Ponson		2-2	T3rd	2.0
4-10	At Bal.	L	0-1		6	6	Mussina	Carpenter	Timlin	2-3	T3rd	3.0
4-11	At Bal.	W	9-5		10	8	Halladay	Orosco		3-3	T3rd	2.0
4-12	T.B.	W	7-1		12	6	Wells	Saunders		4-3	3rd	1.5
4-13	T.B.	L	5-8		11	15	White	Hamilton	Hernandez	4-4	T3rd	2.5
4-14	T.B.	W	7-6	(11)	12	12	Lloyd	Lopez		5-4	3rd	2.5
4-15	T.B.	W	11-1		11	2	Carpenter	Santana		6-4	3rd	1.5
4-16	Bal.	W	7-6		10	12	Lloyd	Bones	Person	7-4	3rd	0.5
4-17	Bal.	W	7-4		10	7	Wells	Linton	Lloyd	8-4	2nd	...
4-18	Bal.	W	6-0		7	3	Halladay	Guzman		9-4	1st	+1.0
4-20	Ana.	W	5-1		7	8	Escobar	Finley		10-4	1st	+1.5
4-21	Ana.	W	3-2		10	8	Carpenter	Olivares	Person	11-4	1st	+1.5
4-22	Ana.	W	8-7		13	8	Davey	Petkovsek	Lloyd	12-4	1st	+2.0
4-23	At N.Y.	L	4-6		10	9	Hernandez	Wells	Rivera	12-5	1st	+1.0
4-24	At N.Y.	L	4-7		9	9	Mendoza	Plesac	Rivera	12-6	2nd	...
4-25	At N.Y.	L	3-4	(11)	5	9	Grimsley	Person		12-7	2nd	1.5
4-26	At Ana.	L	3-4	(11)	8	10	Percival	Rodriguez		12-8	2nd	1.5
4-27	At Ana.	W	10-1		13	5	Hentgen	Olivares		13-8	2nd	1.5
4-28	At Ana.	L	10-12		15	14	Petkovsek	Lloyd	Percival	13-9	2nd	1.5
4-29	At Ana.	L	1-17		4	15	Hill	Halladay		13-10	2nd	2.5
4-30	At Sea.	L	9-11		12	10	Halama	Person	Mesa	13-11	2nd	2.5
5-1	At Sea.	W	9-3		13	11	Carpenter	Moyer	Davey	14-11	2nd	2.5
5-2	At Sea.	L	2-3		8	7	Cloude	Plesac		14-12	2nd	3.5
5-3	At Sea.	W	16-10		17	13	Wells	Garcia		15-12	2nd	2.5
5-4	Oak.	L	4-13		11	13	Oquist	Halladay	Jones	15-13	2nd	2.5
5-5	Oak.	L	2-8		5	15	Rogers	Escobar		15-14	T2nd	3.5
5-6	Oak.	L	2-3		10	6	Heredia	Carpenter	Taylor	15-15	3rd	4.5
5-7	Tex.	W	9-6		17	7	Hentgen	Clark	Koch	16-15	T2nd	4.5
5-8	Tex.	L	3-4		7	7	Morgan	Wells	Wetteland	16-16	4th	4.5
5-9	Tex.	L	6-11		8	20	Patterson	Munro		16-17	4th	5.5
5-11	At K.C.	W	8-2		14	10	Escobar	Pittsley		17-17	T3rd	4.5
5-12	At K.C.	L	1-7		3	11	Appier	Carpenter		17-18	T3rd	4.5
5-13	At K.C.	W	8-2		13	10	Hentgen	Rosado		18-18	3rd	3.5
5-14	Bos.	L	0-5		6	11	Pena	Wells		18-19	3rd	3.5
5-15	Bos.	L	5-6		10	14	Wasdin	Plesac	Gordon	18-20	4th	3.5
5-16	Bos.	W	9-6		11	12	Lloyd	Gross		19-20	4th	3.5
5-17	Bos.	L	7-8		13	13	Wasdin	Lloyd		19-21	4th	4.0
5-18	Det.	W	7-5		8	9	Hentgen	Thompson	Koch	20-21	4th	3.5
5-19	Det.	L	3-7		6	11	Moehler	Wells		20-22	4th	4.5
5-20	Det.	W	7-0		14	7	Halladay	Mlicki		21-22	4th	3.5
5-21	At Bos.	L	2-5		4	5	Rapp	Escobar		21-23	4th	4.5
5-22	At Bos.	L	4-6		6	14	Wakefield	Carpenter	Gordon	21-24	4th	5.5
5-23	At Bos.	L	8-10		15	13	Martinez	Hentgen	Gordon	21-25	4th	6.5
5-24	At Det.	W	12-6		8	10	Wells	Moehler		22-25	4th	6.0
5-25	At Det.	W	5-3		8	11	Halladay	Mlicki	Koch	23-25	3rd	6.0
5-26	At Det.	W	9-5		12	7	Escobar	Blair	Lloyd	24-25	3rd	5.0
5-28	N.Y.	L	6-10		9	16	Pettitte	Carpenter		24-26	3rd	5.5
5-29	N.Y.	L	3-8		7	12	Cone	Hentgen		24-27	3rd	6.5
5-30	N.Y.	L	3-8		8	9	Irabu	Wells		24-28	3rd	7.5
6-1	Chi.	L	2-6		7	13	Sirotka	Escobar		24-29	3rd	9.0
6-2	Chi.	W	9-7		15	15	Carpenter	Snyder	Koch	25-29	3rd	8.0
6-3	Chi.	L	3-10		7	16	Navarro	Hentgen		25-30	3rd	8.5
6-4	Mon.	W	6-2		9	6	Wells	Ayala		26-30	3rd	8.5
6-5	Mon.	L	0-5		3	6	Batista	Hamilton		26-31	3rd	8.5
6-6	Mon.	W	9-2		13	8	Escobar	Hermanson		27-31	3rd	7.5
6-7	At N.Y. (NL)	L	2-8		8	14	Hershiser	Halladay		27-32	3rd	7.5
6-8	At N.Y. (NL)	L	3-11		4	14	Isringhausen	Hentgen		27-33	3rd	7.5
6-9	At N.Y. (NL)	L	3-4	(14)	15	11	Mahomes	Davey		27-34	3rd	8.0
6-11	At Phi.	L	4-8		9	9	Wolf	Hamilton		27-35	3rd	9.0
6-12	At Phi.	L	2-7		6	9	Byrd	Escobar		27-36	3rd	10.0
6-13	At Phi.	W	7-2		13	4	Hentgen	Schilling		28-36	3rd	9.0
6-15	Ana.	W	13-2		18	6	Wells	Belcher		29-36	3rd	9.5
6-16	Ana.	W	3-2		8	6	Lloyd	Schoeneweis	Koch	30-36	3rd	8.5
6-17	Ana.	W	3-0		5	8	Escobar	Hill	Koch	31-36	3rd	7.5
6-18	K.C.	L	5-6		12	10	Witasick	Hentgen	Whisenant	31-37	3rd	8.5
6-19	K.C.	W	7-0		10	3	Halladay	Appier		32-37	3rd	8.5
6-20	K.C.	W	2-1		5	4	Wells	Service		33-37	3rd	7.5
6-21	K.C.	W	11-4		13	12	Hamilton	Fussell		34-37	3rd	7.0
6-22	Cle.	W	4-3		6	8	Escobar	Gooden	Koch	35-37	3rd	7.0
6-23	Cle.	L	6-9		10	12	Nagy	Quantrill		35-38	3rd	8.0

Date	Opp.	Res.	Score	(inn.*)	Hits	Opp. hits	Winning pitcher	Losing pitcher	Save	Record	Pos.	GB
6-24	Cle.	W	3-0		5	3	Halladay	Burba	Koch	36-38	3rd	8.0
6-25	At T.B.	L	4-11		6	14	Alvarez	Wells		36-39	3rd	9.0
6-26	At T.B.	L	2-5		12	9	Rupe	Hamilton	Hernandez	36-40	3rd	10.0
6-27	At T.B.	L	0-8		3	10	Witt	Escobar		36-41	3rd	11.0
6-28	At T.B.	W	3-2		10	8	Carpenter	Eiland	Koch	37-41	3rd	10.5
6-29	Bal.	W	6-5	(10)	10	12	Frascatore	Rhodes		38-41	3rd	10.5
6-30	Bal.	W	10-9	(10)	12	16	Frascatore	Orosco		39-41	3rd	9.5
7-1	Bal.	W	8-6		10	9	Frascatore	Timlin	Koch	40-41	3rd	9.5
7-2	T.B.	L	7-8		14	11	Aldred	Escobar	Hernandez	40-42	3rd	10.5
7-3	T.B.	W	5-0		13	3	Carpenter	Witt		41-42	3rd	10.5
7-4	T.B.	W	6-3		10	11	Hentgen	White	Koch	42-42	3rd	9.5
7-6	At Bal.	W	4-3	(10)	7	8	Lloyd	Timlin	Koch	43-42	3rd	9.0
7-7	At Bal.	W	7-6		6	13	Spoljaric	Molina	Koch	44-42	3rd	8.0
7-8	At Bal.	W	11-6		15	14	Escobar	Ponson		45-42	3rd	8.0
7-9	At Mon.	L	3-4		9	16	Urbina	Lloyd		45-43	3rd	8.0
7-10	At Mon.	W	7-6		9	11	Quantrill	Telford	Koch	46-43	3rd	7.0
7-11	At Mon.	W	1-0		4	2	Wells	Pavano		47-43	3rd	7.0
7-15	Fla.	L	6-8		11	11	Looper	Koch	Alfonseca	47-44	3rd	7.0
7-16	Fla.	L	2-4		11	10	Springer	Hentgen	Alfonseca	47-45	3rd	7.0
7-17	Fla.	W	6-1		10	6	Wells	Edmondson		48-45	3rd	7.0
7-18	Atl.	W	3-2		10	6	Hamilton	Millwood	Koch	49-45	3rd	7.0
7-19	Atl.	W	8-7	(10)	9	10	Frascatore	Hudek		50-45	3rd	6.0
7-20	Atl.	W	11-6		15	13	Halladay	Glavine		51-45	3rd	6.0
7-21	At Cle.	W	4-3		6	8	Frascatore	Jackson	Koch	52-45	3rd	6.0
7-22	At Cle.	W	4-3		7	10	Wells	Nagy	Koch	53-45	T2nd	6.0
7-23	At Chi.	W	2-1		8	7	Hamilton	Parque	Koch	54-45	2nd	6.0
7-24	At Chi.	L	5-6		9	6	Eyre	Escobar	Howry	54-46	3rd	7.0
7-25	At Chi.	W	11-3		17	5	Carpenter	Sirotka		55-46	2nd	7.0
7-26	At Chi.	W	4-3	(11)	9	13	Frascatore	Howry	Koch	56-46	2nd	6.5
7-27	Bos.	L	9-11		14	18	Guthrie	Halladay	Wakefield	56-47	2nd	7.5
7-28	Bos.	L	0-8		2	11	Rapp	Hamilton		56-48	3rd	7.5
7-30	Det.	W	8-2		10	6	Escobar	Weaver		57-48	2nd	7.0
7-31	Det.	W	7-6		12	15	Halladay	Mlicki	Koch	58-48	2nd	6.0
8-1	Det.	W	8-5		10	9	Hentgen	Borkowski	Koch	59-48	2nd	5.0
8-2	At N.Y.	L	1-3		7	7	Pettitte	Wells	Rivera	59-49	2nd	6.0
8-3	At N.Y.	W	3-1		11	5	Hamilton	Cone	Koch	60-49	2nd	5.0
8-4	At N.Y.	L	3-8		9	8	Irabu	Escobar		60-50	2nd	6.0
8-6	At Tex.	W	5-4		10	11	Carpenter	Zimmerman	Koch	61-50	2nd	6.5
8-7	At Tex.	L	0-6		6	13	Sele	Hentgen		61-51	3rd	7.5
8-8	At Tex.	W	8-7		11	11	Frascatore	Venafro	Koch	62-51	3rd	7.5
8-9	At Tex.	W	19-4		25	7	Hamilton	Morgan		63-51	2nd	7.5
8-10	At Min.	W	10-6		15	11	Escobar	Radke		64-51	2nd	6.5
8-11	At Min.	W	6-3		12	7	Carpenter	Milton		65-51	2nd	6.5
8-12	At Min.	L	0-3		5	6	Mays	Hentgen	Trombley	65-52	2nd	7.0
8-13	Oak.	L	8-9		8	12	Appier	Halladay	Jones	65-53	3rd	8.0
8-14	Oak.	L	5-13		11	14	Hudson	Hamilton		65-54	3rd	8.0
8-15	Oak.	L	5-9		10	15	Oquist	Escobar		65-55	3rd	8.0
8-16	Sea.	L	5-7		10	11	Moyer	Carpenter	Mesa	65-56	3rd	9.0
8-17	Sea.	L	5-8		7	12	Abbott	Hentgen	Mesa	65-57	3rd	10.0
8-18	Sea.	L	1-5		6	10	Garcia	Wells	Paniagua	65-58	3rd	10.0
8-20	At Oak.	W	11-0		13	4	Hamilton	Oquist		66-58	3rd	9.5
8-21	At Oak.	L	4-8		8	9	Olivares	Carpenter		66-59	3rd	9.5
8-22	At Oak.	L	3-4		12	8	Jones	Koch		66-60	3rd	10.5
8-23	At Oak.	W	9-4		14	11	Wells	Appier		67-60	3rd	10.5
8-24	At Ana.	W	5-1		10	6	Hentgen	Ortiz	Koch	68-60	3rd	10.5
8-25	At Ana.	W	7-2		9	6	Hamilton	Finley		69-60	3rd	9.5
8-27	Tex.	L	2-8		6	14	Helling	Carpenter		69-61	3rd	10.5
8-28	Tex.	L	7-9		14	14	Sele	Wells	Wetteland	69-62	3rd	11.5
8-29	Tex.	L	2-4		9	11	Burkett	Halladay	Wetteland	69-63	3rd	12.5
8-30	Min.	W	2-1		2	5	Hentgen	Ryan	Koch	70-63	3rd	12.5
8-31	Min.	L	3-14		9	20	Radke	Hamilton		70-64	3rd	12.5
9-1	Min.	W	4-0		5	5	Escobar	Milton		71-64	3rd	11.5
9-2	Min.	W	6-1		11	4	Wells	Mays		72-64	3rd	11.5
9-3	At K.C.	W	5-4		9	14	Quantrill	Morman	Koch	73-64	3rd	10.5
9-4	At K.C.	W	6-3		13	4	Hentgen	Suppan	Frascatore	74-64	3rd	10.5
9-5	At K.C.	L	3-6		9	11	Witasick	Escobar	Fussell	74-65	3rd	11.5
9-7	At Sea.	L	4-7		7	9	Meche	Wells	Mesa	74-66	3rd	11.0
9-8	At Sea.	L	3-4		9	7	Mesa	Koch		74-67	3rd	12.0
9-10	At Det.	L	6-7		12	12	Jones	Frascatore		74-68	3rd	12.0
9-11	At Det.	W	9-5		11	11	Spoljaric	Cordero		75-68	3rd	11.0
9-12	At Det.	W	5-3		10	8	Escobar	Weaver	Koch	76-68	3rd	10.0
9-13	N.Y.	W	2-1		5	4	Wells	Hernandez		77-68	3rd	9.0
9-14	N.Y.	L	6-10		11	9	Mendoza	Koch		77-69	3rd	10.0
9-15	N.Y.	L	4-6		8	7	Pettitte	Hentgen	Rivera	77-70	3rd	11.0
9-17	Chi.	L	3-7		8	14	Wells	Escobar		77-71	3rd	12.5
9-18	Chi.	L	4-7		10	13	Navarro	Quantrill	Howry	77-72	3rd	12.5

Date	Opp.	Res.	Score	(inn.*)	Hits	Opp. hits	Winning pitcher	Losing pitcher	Save	Record	Pos.	GB
9-19	Chi.	L	2-3		6	5	Sirotka	Halladay	Howry	77-73	3rd	13.5
9-21	At Bos.	L	0-3		3	11	Martinez	Hentgen		77-74	3rd	14.5
9-22	At Bos.	W	14-9		22	10	Escobar	Rapp		78-74	3rd	14.5
9-23	At Bos.	W	7-5		11	12	Wells	Beck	Koch	79-74	3rd	14.5
9-24	Cle.	L	4-18		9	15	Brower	Munro		79-75	3rd	15.5
9-25	Cle.	L	6-9		9	13	Colon	Spoljaric	Jackson	79-76	3rd	15.5
9-26	Cle.	L	7-11		9	14	Shuey	Koch		79-77	3rd	15.5
9-28	At T.B.	W	8-2		13	5	Wells	Wheeler		80-77	3rd	15.0
9-29	At T.B.	W	6-2		14	9	Escobar	Witt		81-77	3rd	14.5
9-30	At Cle.	L	2-9		9	8	Colon	Spoljaric		81-78	3rd	15.0
10-1	At Cle.	W	8-6		12	11	Quantrill	Karsay	Koch	82-78	3rd	15.0
10-2	At Cle.	W	7-3		14	8	Hentgen	Wright	Koch	83-78	3rd	15.0
10-3	At Cle.	W	9-2		9	10	Wells	Burba		84-78	3rd	14.0

Monthly records: April (13-11), May (11-17), June (15-13), July (19-7), August (12-16), September (11-14), October (3-0).
*Innings, if other than nine. † First game of a doubleheader. ‡ Second game of a doubleheader.

HIGHLIGHTS

High point: With first baseman Carlos Delgado hitting his eighth homer in six games, the Blue Jays improved their record to 65-51 on August 11 with a victory over the Twins. They held a one-game lead on Boston in the wild-card race.
Low point: The Blue Jays lost all six games of a mid-August homestand against Oakland and Seattle, then got swept by Texas in late August for a nine-game losing streak at SkyDome. In between, assistant G.M. Dave Stewart questioned the players' commitment and intensity.
Turning point: When Toronto lost 10 of 13 games in a stretch ending September 21, shattering the club's wild-card hopes.
Most valuable player: Outfielder Shawn Green, followed closely by shortstop Tony Batista. Green followed his first 30-30 season by establishing career highs in batting average, runs, home runs and RBIs. Batista, obtained from Arizona in June, was a revelation. In 98 games, he had 26 homers and 79 RBIs.
Most valuable pitcher: Billy Koch, who had been a starter at Class AAA Syracuse before being called up in early May. Soon designated as the Jays' closer, he converted 31 of 35 save opportunities in his rookie season.
Most improved player: Coming off a solid 1998 season, catcher Darrin Fletcher bumped his numbers with a .291 average, 18 homers and 80 RBIs.
Most pleasant surprise: After coming over from the Yankees in the Roger Clemens trade, Homer Bush asked not to be compared with former Jays standout second baseman Roberto Alomar. Bush gave a good imitation, though, batting .320 and stealing 32 bases.
Biggest disappointment: Righthander Joey Hamilton, who had been obtained in a December trade with the Padres. Expected to be an innings eater and win 15 games, he went 7-8 with a 6.52 ERA and, hampered by shoulder problems, worked only 98 innings.
Key injuries: Shortstop Alex Gonzalez suffered a shoulder tear and didn't play after May 16. Bush was sidelined for a month with a ligament tear in a finger. Fletcher was out nearly a month after being struck in the eye by a ball that ricocheted off a batting cage. Setup man

Paul Quantrill, recovering from a broken leg incurred in a snowmobiling accident, missed the first 10 weeks. Hamilton was shut down for the season after an August 31 start against Minnesota. Starter Chris Carpenter was out most of June with elbow inflammation and underwent surgery in September. Middle reliever Bill Risley missed the entire season because of back problems.
Notable: Green established a franchise record with a 28-game hitting streak. ... David Wells led the A.L. in complete games with seven and topped all of the league's lefthanders in victories with 17. ... Delgado tied George Bell's club record of 134 RBIs despite missing the last 10 games because of injury. ... Delgado (44) and Green (42) combined for 86 homers.

—TOM MALONEY

RECORDS

1999 regular-season record: 84-78 (3rd in A.L. East); 40-41 at home; 44-37 on road; 24-25 vs. A.L. East; 34-20 vs. Central; 17-24 vs. West; 9-9 vs. N.L.; 13-15 vs. lefthanded starters; 71-63 vs. righthanded starters; 33-26 on grass; 51-52 on turf; 27-26 in daytime; 57-52 at night; 26-18 in one-run games; 6-3 in extra-inning games; 0-0-0 in doubleheaders.
Team record past five years: 378-414 (.477, ranks 9th in league in that span).

TEAM LEADERS

Batting average: Tony Fernandez (.328).
At-bats: Shawn Green (614).
Runs: Shawn Green (134).
Hits: Shawn Green (190).
Total Bases: Shawn Green (361).
Doubles: Shawn Green (45).
Triples: Homer Bush (4).
Home runs: Carlos Delgado (44).
Runs batted in: Carlos Delgado (134).
Stolen bases: Shannon Stewart (37).
Slugging percentage: Shawn Green (.588).
On-base percentage: Tony Fernandez (.427).
Wins: David Wells (17).
Earned-run average: Pat Hentgen (4.79).
Complete games: David Wells (7).
Shutouts: Chris Carpenter, Roy Halladay, David Wells (1).

Saves: Billy Koch (31).
Innings pitched: David Wells (231.2).
Strikeouts: David Wells (169).

GAMES BY POSITION

Catcher: Darrin Fletcher 113, Mike Matheny 57, Mark Dalesandro 8, Pat Borders 3, Kevin L. Brown 2.
First base: Carlos Delgado 147, Willis Otanez 13, David Segui 4.
Second base: Homer Bush 109, Pat Kelly 35, Craig Grebeck 17, Norberto Martin 8, Tony Fernandez 1.
Third base: Tony Fernandez 132, Willis Otanez 24, Casey Blake 14, Willie Greene 7, Craig Grebeck 2, Mark Dalesandro 2, Chris Woodward 2.
Shortstop: Tony Batista 98, Alex Gonzalez 37, Homer Bush 18, Chris Woodward 10, Craig Grebeck 4, Norberto Martin 1.
Outfield: Shawn Green 152, Shannon Stewart 142, Jose Cruz 106, Jacob Brumfield 53, Vernon Wells 24, Brian McRae 13, Patrick Lennon 8, Willie Greene 3, Geronimo Berroa 2, Rob Butler 2, Curtis Goodwin 2, Anthony Sanders 1.
Designated hitter: Willie Greene 51, David Segui 25, Dave Hollins 23, Geronimo Berroa 17, Brian McRae 15, Kevin Witt 11, Craig Grebeck 10, Tony Fernandez 9, Jacob Brumfield 6, Carlos Delgado 5, Mark Dalesandro 5, Pat Borders 3, Rob Butler 3, Pat Kelly 2, Shannon Stewart 2, Willis Otanez 2, Anthony Sanders 2, Alex Gonzalez 1.

TOP DRAFT CHOICES

1. **Alexis Rios**, 3B, San Pedro Martir H.S., Guaynabo, P.R.
2. **Michael Snyder**, 3B, Ayala H.S., Chino Hills, Calif.
3. **Matt Ford**, LHP, Taravella H.S., Tamarac, Fla.
4. **Brian Cardwell**, RHP, Sapulpa (Okla.) H.S.
5. **Scott Porter**, RHP, Jacksonville University
6. **David Hanson**, RHP, Richland (Wash.) H.S.
7. **Derrick Nunley**, RHP, Englewood H.S., Jacksonville, Fla.
8. **Ryan McCullem**, LHP, Hickman H.S., Columbia, Mo.
9. **Josh Holliday**, C/3B, Oklahoma State U.
10. **Robert Cosby**, SS, Academie Bautista, San Juan, P.R.

ARIZONA DIAMONDBACKS
NATIONAL LEAGUE WEST DIVISION

2000 Diamondbacks Schedule
Home games shaded. *—All-Star Game at Turner Field (Atlanta).

March
SUN	MON	TUE	WED	THU	FRI	SAT
26	27	28	29	30	31	

April
SUN	MON	TUE	WED	THU	FRI	SAT
						1
2	3	4 PHI	5 PHI	6 PHI	7 PIT	8 PIT
9 PIT	10 SD	11 SD	12 SD	13 SD	14 SF	15 SF
16 SF	17 COL	18 COL	19 COL	20 COL	21 SF	22 SF
23 SF	24	25 PHI	26 PHI	27 PHI	28 CUB	29 CUB
30 CUB						

May
SUN	MON	TUE	WED	THU	FRI	SAT
	1	2 MIL	3 MIL	4 MIL	5 SD	6 SD
7 SD	8 LA	9 LA	10 LA	11	12 SD	13 SD
14 SD	15	16 MON	17 MON	18 MON	19 NYM	20 NYM
21 NYM	22	23 PIT	24 PIT	25 PIT	26 MIL	27 MIL
28 MIL	29 STL	30 STL	31 STL			

June
SUN	MON	TUE	WED	THU	FRI	SAT
				1 STL	2 TEX	3 TEX
4 TEX	5 CUB	6 CUB	7 CUB	8	9 ANA	10 ANA
11 ANA	12 LA	13 LA	14 LA	15 LA	16 COL	17 COL
18 COL	19 SD	20 SD	21 SD	22	23 COL	24 COL
25 COL	26 HOU	27 HOU	28 HOU	29 HOU	30 CIN	

July
SUN	MON	TUE	WED	THU	FRI	SAT
						1 CIN
2 CIN	3 CIN	4 HOU	5 HOU	6 HOU	7 OAK	8 OAK
9 OAK	10	11 *	12 TEX	13 TEX	14 TEX	15 TEX
16 SEA	17 SEA	18 SEA	19 STL	20 STL	21 CIN	22 CIN
23 CIN	24	25 STL	26 STL	27 STL	28 FLA	29 FLA
30 FLA	31					

August
SUN	MON	TUE	WED	THU	FRI	SAT
		1 ATL	2 ATL	3 ATL	4 NYM	5 NYM
6 NYM	7 MON	8 MON	9 MON	10	11 PIT	12 PIT
13 PIT	14 PHI	15 PHI	16 PHI	17	18 CUB	19 CUB
20 CUB	21 MIL	22 MIL	23 MIL	24	25 NYM	26 NYM
27 NYM	28 MON	29 MON	30 MON	31		

September
SUN	MON	TUE	WED	THU	FRI	SAT
					1 FLA	2 FLA
3 FLA	4	5 ATL	6 ATL	7 ATL	8 FLA	9 FLA
10 FLA	11 LA	12 LA	13 LA	14	15 ATL	16 ATL
17 ATL	18 LA	19 LA	20 LA	21 SF	22 SF	23 SF
24 SF	25	26 COL	27 COL	28 COL	29 SF	30 SF

October
SUN	MON	TUE	WED	THU	FRI	SAT
1 SF	2	3	4	5	6	7

2000 SEASON
CLUB DIRECTORY

Managing general partner
Jerry Colangelo
President
Richard Dozer
Vice president and general manager
Joe Garagiola Jr.
Senior executive vice president, baseball operations
Roland Hemond
Sr. vice president, sales and marketing
Scott Brubaker
Vice president, finance
Thomas Harris
V.p., tickets and special services
Dianne Aguilar
Vice president, sales
Blake Edwards
Vice president, community affairs
Mark Fernandez
Senior assistant to the general manager
Mel Didier
Assistant to the general manager
Bryan Lambe
Director of Hispanic marketing
Richard Saenz
Director of Tucson operations
Rich Tomey
Director of public relations
Mike Swanson
Director of ballpark services
Russ Amaral
Director of suite services
Diney Mahoney
Director of team travel
Roger Riley
Director of minor league operations
Tommy Jones
Director of Pacific Rim operations
Jim Marshall
Trainer
Paul Lessard

Assistant trainer
Dave Edwards
Club physician
Dr. David Zeman
Director of scouting
Mike Rizzo
Assistant director of scouting
Bob Miller
National scouting supervisor
Kendall Carter
Scouting coordinators
Derek Bryant, Junior Noboa
Professional scouts
Bill Earnhart, Mike Piatnik
Special assistants to general manager
Mack (Shooty) Babitt, Ron Hassey, Bryan Lambe
Advance scout
Dick Scott
Regional scouting supervisors
Ed Durkin, Kris Kline, Steve Springer
Area scouting supervisors
Ray Blanco, Ray Corbett, Jason Goligoski, Brian Guinn, Scott Jaster, James Keller, Chris Knabenshue, Hal Kurtzman, Greg Lonigro, Howard McCullough, Louie Medina, Matt Merullo, Carlos Porte, Phillip Rizzo, Mike Valarezo, Brad Vaughn, Luke Wrenn
Scouts
Pablo Abreu, Juan Aguirre, Ossie Alvarez, Pete Carmona, John Cole, Luis Delgado, Leo Figueroa, Jose Martin, Tony Levato, Jonathan Leyba, David May, Rafael Mena, Jose Diaz Perez, Juan Salabarria, Joel Serna, Mark Smelko, Bob Sullivan, Jorge Urribari, Roberto Verdugo, John Wadsworth, Doyle Wilson, John Wright

MINOR LEAGUE AFFILIATES

Class	Team	League	Manager
AAA	Tucson	Pacific Coast	Tom Spencer
AA	El Paso	Texas	Don Wakamatsu
A	High Desert	California	Scott Coolbaugh
A	South Bend	Midwest	Dave Jorn
Rookie	Missoula	Pioneer	Chip Hale
Rookie	Tucson	Arizona	Roly de Armas

BROADCAST INFORMATION

Radio: KTAR-AM (620).
TV: KTVK (Channel 3).
Cable TV: Fox Sports Net Arizona.

SPRING TRAINING

Ballpark (city): Tucson Electric Park (Tucson, Ariz.).
Ticket information: 800-638-4253, 520-434-1111.

SPRING TRAINING ROSTER

Manager—Buck Showalter (11).
Coaches—Brian Butterfield (55), Mark Connor (52), Dwayne Murphy (21), Jim Presley (17), Glenn Sherlock (53), Carlos Tosca (14).

No.	PITCHERS	B/T	Ht./Wt.	Born	1999 clubs
34	Anderson, Brian	B/L	6-1/190	4-26-72	Arizona, Tucson
	Bierbroldt, Nick	L/L	6-5/190	5-16-78	El Paso, Tucson
	Brohawn, Troy	L/L	6-1/190	1-14-73	Tucson
41	Chouinard, Bobby	R/R	6-1/190	5-1-72	Tucson, Arizona
	Clontz, Brad	R/R	6-1/203	4-25-71	Nashville, Pittsburgh
37	Daal, Omar	L/L	6-3/185	3-1-72	Arizona
	Figueroa, Nelson	B/R	6-1/155	5-18-74	Tucson, Diamondbacks (Ariz. Lg.)
46	Holmes, Darren	R/R	6-0/202	4-25-66	Arizona, Diamondbacks (Ariz. Lg.), Tucson
51	Johnson, Randy	R/L	6-10/230	9-10-63	Arizona
49	Kim, Byung-Hyun	R/R	5-11/176	1-21-79	El Paso, Tucson, Arizona, Diamondbacks (Ariz. Lg.)
31	Mantei, Matt	R/R	6-1/190	7-7-73	Florida, Arizona
	Norris, Ben	B/L	6-3/185	12-6-77	High Desert, El Paso
19	Plesac, Dan	L/L	6-5/217	2-4-62	Toronto, Arizona
	Randolph, Steve	L/L	6-3/185	5-1-74	El Paso, Tucson, Diamondbacks (Ariz. Lg.)
27	Reynoso, Armando	R/R	6-0/204	5-1-66	Arizona
36	Springer, Russ	R/R	6-4/220	11-7-68	Richmond, Atlanta
32	Stottlemyre, Todd	L/R	6-3/200	5-20-65	Arizona, Diamondbacks (Ariz. Lg.)
22	Swindell, Greg	R/L	6-3/230	1-2-65	Arizona

No.	CATCHERS	B/T	Ht./Wt.	Born	1999 clubs
48	Barajas, Rod	R/R	6-2/220	9-5-75	El Paso, Arizona
26	Miller, Damian	R/R	6-2/190	10-13-69	Arizona
35	Stinnett, Kelly	R/R	5-11/195	2-4-70	Arizona

No.	INFIELDERS	B/T	Ht./Wt.	Born	1999 clubs
33	Bell, Jay	R/R	6-0/182	12-11-65	Arizona
44	Durazo, Erubiel	L/L	6-3/225	1-23-74	El Paso, Tucson, Arizona
28	Colbrunn, Greg	R/R	6-0/205	7-26-69	Arizona
6	Fox, Andy	L/R	6-4/205	1-12-71	Arizona
2	Frias, Hanley	B/R	6-0/165	12-5-73	Arizona, Tucson
29	Harris, Lenny	L/R	5-10/220	10-28-64	Colorado, Arizona
7	Klassen, Danny	R/R	6-0/175	9-22-75	Tucson, Diamondbacks (Ariz. Lg.), Arizona
	Ordaz, Luis	R/R	5-11/170	8-12-75	St. Louis, Memphis
	Spivey, Junior	R/R	6-0/185	1-28-75	El Paso
9	Williams, Matt	R/R	6-2/210	11-28-65	Arizona
5	Womack, Tony	L/R	5-9/159	9-25-69	Tucson, Arizona

No.	OUTFIELDERS	B/T	Ht./Wt.	Born	1999 clubs
63	Conti, Jason	L/R	5-11/180	1-27-75	Tucson
25	Dellucci, David	L/L	5-10/180	10-31-73	Arizona
12	Finley, Steve	L/L	6-2/180	3-12-65	Arizona
23	Gilkey, Bernard	R/R	6-0/200	9-24-66	Arizona
20	Gonzalez, Luis	L/R	6-2/190	9-2-67	Arizona
16	Lee, Travis	L/L	6-3/210	5-26-75	Arizona

BALLPARK INFORMATION

Ballpark (capacity, surface)
Bank One Ballpark (49,033)

Address
401 East Jefferson
Phoenix, AZ 85004

Business phone
602-462-6500

Ticket information
602-514-8400

Ticket prices
$10 to $22.50 (lower level)
$1 to $15.50 (upper level)
$35 to 55 (lower level premium seats)
$27 and $33 (Infiniti Diamond level)

Field dimensions (from home plate)
To left field at foul line, 330 feet
To center field, 407 feet
To right field at foul line, 334 feet

First game played
March 31, 1998 (Rockies 9, Diamondbacks 2)

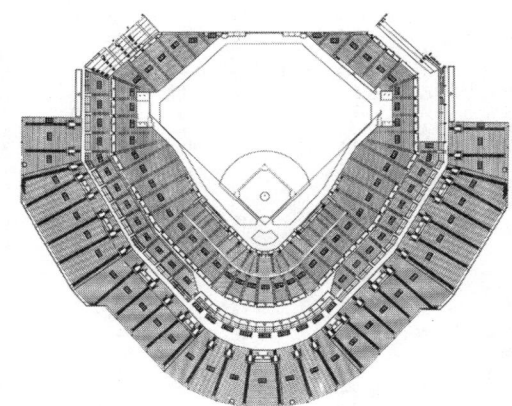

Arizona Diamondbacks

2000 SEASON

Date	Opp.	Res.	Score	(inn.*)	Hits	Opp. hits	Winning pitcher	Losing pitcher	Save	Record	Pos.	GB
4-6	At L.A.	L	2-3	(10)	5	10	Mills	Anderson		0-2	5th	2.0
4-7	At L.A.	L	4-6		7	12	Valdes	Benes	Shaw	0-3	5th	3.0
4-9	At Atl.	L	2-3	(10)	6	8	Rocker	Frascatore		0-4	5th	4.5
4-10	At Atl.	W	8-3		16	6	Johnson	Glavine		1-4	5th	3.5
4-11	At Atl.	L	2-3		7	5	McGlinchy	Olson		1-5	5th	4.5
4-12	L.A.	W	12-6		10	11	Benes	Park		2-5	T4th	4.0
4-13	L.A.	W	7-6	(16)	21	11	Chouinard	Mlicki		3-5	4th	3.0
4-14	L.A.	W	6-2		11	4	Daal	Perez		4-5	4th	2.0
4-15	L.A.	L	1-8		2	8	Dreifort	Johnson		4-6	4th	3.0
4-16	S.F	W	10-4		14	8	Stottlemyre	Gardner	Anderson	5-6	4th	2.0
4-17	S.F	L	5-8		10	9	Rueter	Benes		5-7	5th	3.0
4-18	S.F	W	12-3		11	6	Reynoso	Ortiz		6-7	4th	2.0
4-19	Phi.	W	3-2		8	4	Daal	Perez	Swindell	7-7	T2nd	2.0
4-20	Phi.	W	8-1		10	7	Johnson	Spoljaric		8-7	T2nd	1.0
4-21	Phi.	W	4-2		8	7	Stottlemyre	Schilling	Olson	9-7	2nd	1.0
4-23	At S.D.	W	10-6		11	10	Benes	Hitchcock		10-7	2nd	0.5
4-24	At S.D.	L	2-7		7	11	Williams	Daal		10-8	2nd	1.5
4-25	At S.D.	W	5-3	(11)	12	5	Swindell	Miceli	Olson	11-8	2nd	1.5
4-26	At Hou.	L	2-5		7	6	Lima	Stottlemyre	Wagner	11-9	2nd	2.0
4-27	At Hou.	L	0-11		6	14	Reynolds	Reynoso		11-10	2nd	3.0
4-28	At Hou.	W	10-6		14	7	Holmes	Wagner		12-10	2nd	3.0
4-29	At Hou.	L	2-5		4	12	Hampton	Daal	Wagner	12-11	3rd	4.0
4-30	At Mil.	W	3-2		10	7	Holmes	Myers	Olson	13-11	3rd	3.0
5-1	At Mil.	W	5-3		10	8	Stottlemyre	Abbott	Olson	14-11	3rd	2.0
5-2	At Mil.	L	5-6		8	13	Weathers	Olson	Wickman	14-12	3rd	2.0
5-3	At Cin.	L	3-4		8	9	Williamson	Holmes		14-13	3rd	2.0
5-4	At Cin.	L	4-6		9	7	Reyes	Daal	Graves	14-14	3rd	3.0
5-5	At Cin.	W	5-1		8	4	Johnson	Avery		15-14	3rd	2.0
5-7	N.Y.	W	14-7		15	12	Stottlemyre	Hershiser		16-14	3rd	2.0
5-8	N.Y.	L	2-4		6	11	Yoshii	Benes	Benitez	16-15	3rd	3.0
5-9	N.Y.	W	11-6		13	16	Daal	Reed		17-15	3rd	2.0
5-10	Mon.	W	7-6		11	13	Olson	Ayala		18-15	3rd	2.0
5-11	Mon.	W	4-3	(10)	7	9	Olson	Mota		19-15	2nd	1.0
5-12	Mon.	W	8-6		10	10	Telemaco	Smart		20-15	2nd	1.0
5-14	Col.	L	1-4		6	9	Bohanon	Benes		20-16	3rd	1.0
5-15	Col.	W	9-2		16	3	Johnson	Kile		21-16	T1st	...
5-16	Col.	L	1-5		7	6	Astacio	Daal		21-17	2nd	1.0
5-17	At S.F	W	12-1		13	4	Frascatore	Estes		22-17	T1st	...
5-18	At S.F	W	7-3		11	11	Reynoso	Brock		23-17	1st	+1.0
5-19	At S.F	L	3-8		6	9	Rueter	Benes		23-18	T1st	...
5-20	At Col.	L	4-8		7	10	Kile	Johnson		23-19	2nd	0.5
5-21	At Col.	L	7-8	(11)	16	14	Leskanic	Frascatore		23-20	2nd	1.5
5-22	At Col.	W	8-3		14	11	Daal	Jones		24-20	2nd	1.5
5-23	At Col.	L	6-7		11	11	McElroy	Olson		24-21	2nd	1.5
5-24	S.D.	W	6-5		13	13	Benes	Ashby	Olson	25-21	2nd	1.0
5-25	S.D.	W	4-0		6	6	Johnson	Hitchcock		26-21	2nd	1.0
5-26	S.D.	W	3-2	(11)	8	8	Olson	Miceli		27-21	2nd	1.0
5-28	At N.Y.	W	2-1		6	6	Daal	Reed	Olson	28-21	1st	+0.5
5-29	At N.Y.	W	8-7		13	11	Reynoso	Beltran	Kim	29-21	1st	+1.5
5-30	At N.Y.	W	10-1		15	6	Johnson	Yoshii		30-21	1st	+2.5
5-31	At Mon.	W	8-5	(10)	16	10	Holmes	Kline	Olson	31-21	1st	+3.5
6-1	At Mon.	L	8-10		14	12	Mota	Frascatore	Urbina	31-22	1st	+2.5
6-2	At Mon.	W	15-2		20	5	Daal	Vazquez		32-22	1st	+3.5
6-4	Tex.	W	11-3		12	4	Johnson	Clark		33-22	1st	+3.0
6-5	Tex.	L	8-9		7	9	Venafro	Holmes	Wetteland	33-23	1st	+2.0
6-6	Tex.	W	4-2		6	7	Benes	Helling	Olson	34-23	1st	+3.0
6-7	Chi.	L	6-7		12	13	Adams	Holmes		34-24	1st	+2.0
6-8	Chi.	L	3-5		6	5	Aguilera	Olson	Adams	34-25	1st	+1.0
6-9	Chi.	W	8-7		18	12	Johnson	Mulholland	Nunez	35-25	1st	+2.0
6-11	At Ana.	W	12-2		18	8	Reynoso	Hill		36-25	1st	+3.0
6-12	At Ana.	L	3-4		6	10	Petkovsek	Benes	Percival	36-26	1st	+2.0
6-13	At Ana.	W	3-1	(13)	9	9	Nunez	Petkovsek	Olson	37-26	1st	+2.0
6-14	Fla.	W	2-0		8	4	Johnson	Dempster	Olson	38-26	1st	+3.0
6-15	Fla.	W	4-3		8	12	Anderson	Springer	Olson	39-26	1st	+4.0
6-16	Fla.	W	12-6		17	12	Reynoso	Meadows		40-26	1st	+4.0
6-18	Atl.	L	0-6		6	12	Smoltz	Benes		40-27	1st	+2.5
6-19	Atl.	W	7-3		10	7	Daal	Perez		41-27	1st	+2.5
6-20	Atl.	L	4-10		10	12	Glavine	Johnson		41-28	1st	+1.5
6-21	Cin.	L	4-7	(10)	9	15	White	Nunez	Graves	41-29	1st	+1.5
6-22	Cin.	L	7-8		13	12	Reyes	Vosberg	Graves	41-30	1st	+1.5
6-23	Cin.	L	7-9		8	17	Avery	Benes	Williamson	41-31	1st	+1.5
6-24	StL.	W	8-7		11	14	Nunez	Bottalico		42-31	1st	+2.0

Date	Opp.	Res.	Score	(inn.*)	Hits	Opp. hits	Winning pitcher	Losing pitcher	Save	Record	Pos.	GB
6-25	StL.	L	0-1		0	5	Jimenez	Johnson		42-32	1st	+2.0
6-26	StL.	L	1-2	(10)	7	5	Aybar	Nunez		42-33	1st	+2.0
6-27	StL.	W	3-2	(10)	8	7	Nunez	Bottalico		43-33	1st	+2.0
6-29	At Cin.	L	4-5		5	7	Graves	Padilla		43-34	1st	+1.0
6-30	At Cin.	L	0-2		1	7	Villone	Johnson	Williamson	43-35	T1st	...
7-1	At Cin.	L	1-2	(10)	7	7	Williamson	Plesac		43-36	2nd	1.0
7-2	At StL.	W	9-5		15	9	Anderson	Oliver		44-36	2nd	1.0
7-3	At StL.	L	1-2	(10)	4	5	Painter	Kim		44-37	2nd	2.0
7-4	At StL.	W	17-5		19	13	Benes	Croushore		45-37	2nd	1.0
7-5	At StL.	L	0-1		2	4	Jimenez	Johnson		45-38	2nd	2.0
7-6	Hou.	L	1-3		5	7	Lima	Daal	Wagner	45-39	2nd	3.0
7-7	Hou.	W	13-7		14	11	Chouinard	Miller		46-39	2nd	2.0
7-8	Hou.	W	8-7	(11)	15	13	Olson	Williams		47-39	2nd	1.5
7-9	Oak.	L	2-5		12	8	Heredia	Benes	Taylor	47-40	2nd	2.5
7-10	Oak.	L	0-2		3	3	Hudson	Johnson	Taylor	47-41	2nd	3.5
7-11	Oak.	W	7-4		7	6	Daal	Haynes	Mantei	48-41	2nd	2.5
7-15	At Tex.	L	2-3		5	7	Venafro	Mantei		48-42	2nd	2.5
7-16	At Tex.	L	8-9		10	14	Wetteland	Chouinard		48-43	2nd	2.5
7-17	At Tex.	W	8-6	(10)	13	11	Plesac	Wetteland	Mantei	49-43	2nd	2.5
7-18	At Sea.	L	7-8	(10)	11	10	Mesa	Kim		49-44	2nd	2.5
7-19	At Sea.	L	5-7		8	11	Meche	Anderson		49-45	2nd	2.5
7-20	At Sea.	W	6-0		15	8	Johnson	Marte		50-45	2nd	1.5
7-21	At Hou.	W	7-4		10	8	Chouinard	Powell	Mantei	51-45	2nd	1.5
7-22	At Hou.	W	2-1		7	7	Benes	Lima	Mantei	52-45	2nd	0.5
7-23	L.A.	W	10-1		11	2	Daal	Perez		53-45	2nd	0.5
7-24	L.A.	W	3-0		7	6	Anderson	Dreifort	Mantei	54-45	1st	+0.5
7-25	L.A.	L	1-2		3	8	Brown	Johnson	Shaw	54-46	1st	+0.5
7-26	At S.D.	W	2-0		7	6	Reynoso	Hitchcock	Mantei	55-46	1st	+0.5
7-27	At S.D.	W	4-3		10	7	Olson	Reyes	Mantei	56-46	1st	+0.5
7-28	At S.D.	W	7-4		10	6	Daal	Boehringer	Plesac	57-46	1st	+1.5
7-30	At L.A.	W	6-5		9	11	Chouinard	Shaw	Mantei	58-46	1st	+2.5
7-31	At L.A.	W	4-2		9	6	Johnson	Valdes		59-46	1st	+2.5
8-1	At L.A.	L	2-4		9	11	Masaoka	Benes	Shaw	59-47	1st	+2.5
8-2	S.F	W	16-6		14	16	Reynoso	Rueter		60-47	1st	+3.5
8-3	S.F	L	1-3		3	6	Hernandez	Daal	Nen	60-48	1st	+2.5
8-4	S.F	W	8-4		10	8	Anderson	Nathan		61-48	1st	+3.5
8-6	At Phi.	L	2-4	(11)	6	8	Gomes	Chouinard		61-49	1st	+3.5
8-7	At Phi.	W	8-2		9	7	Benes	Schilling		62-49	1st	+4.5
8-8	At Phi.	W	7-4		13	10	Reynoso	Ogea	Mantei	63-49	1st	+4.5
8-9	At Chi.	W	10-7		15	8	Daal	Sanders		64-49	1st	+5.5
8-10	At Chi.	W	3-1		5	9	Swindell	Lieber	Olson	65-49	1st	+6.5
8-11	At Chi.	W	7-5	(11)	15	9	Plesac	Rain	Olson	66-49	1st	+7.5
8-13	Mil.	L	1-3		4	7	Nomo	Benes	Wickman	66-50	1st	+6.5
8-14	Mil.	L	2-4		10	6	Karl	Reynoso	Wickman	66-51	1st	+6.5
8-15	Mil.	W	4-0		7	7	Daal	Pulsipher		67-51	1st	+7.5
8-16	Chi.	W	10-3		14	7	Johnson	Lieber		68-51	1st	+7.5
8-17	Chi.	W	4-0		7	3	Anderson	Lorraine		69-51	1st	+8.5
8-18	Chi.	W	3-1		10	5	Benes	Tapani	Mantei	70-51	1st	+8.5
8-20	At Pit.	L	4-5		5	11	Ritchie	Stottlemyre	Williams	70-52	1st	+7.5
8-21	At Pit.	W	4-2		9	6	Johnson	Anderson		71-52	1st	+7.5
8-22	At Pit.	W	7-5		10	7	Daal	Schmidt	Mantei	72-52	1st	+7.5
8-23	At Pit.	W	2-1		8	7	Reynoso	Cordova	Mantei	73-52	1st	+8.0
8-24	At Fla.	W	5-4		6	4	Benes	Almanza	Mantei	74-52	1st	+8.0
8-25	At Fla.	W	7-2		8	7	Stottlemyre	Nunez		75-52	1st	+7.5
8-26	At Fla.	W	12-2		11	8	Johnson	Meadows		76-52	1st	+8.5
8-27	N.Y.	L	3-6		8	11	Dotel	Daal	Benitez	76-53	1st	+8.5
8-28	N.Y.	W	5-3		8	6	Reynoso	Cook	Mantei	77-53	1st	+8.5
8-29	N.Y.	W	8-4		12	10	Anderson	Leiter	Olson	78-53	1st	+8.5
8-30	Mon.	W	5-4		9	8	Chouinard	Batista	Mantei	79-53	1st	+8.5
8-31	Mon.	L	1-2		6	6	Thurman	Johnson	Urbina	79-54	1st	+7.5
9-1	Mon.	L	1-8		7	11	Hermanson	Daal		79-55	1st	+6.5
9-3	At Atl.	L	3-7		8	9	Millwood	Reynoso		79-56	1st	+5.0
9-4	At Atl.	W	5-4		10	5	Benes	Smoltz	Mantei	80-56	1st	+5.0
9-5	At Atl.	W	7-5		10	7	Olson	Rocker	Mantei	81-56	1st	+6.5
9-7	At Mil.	W	11-9		12	13	Holmes	Dale	Mantei	82-56	1st	+6.5
9-8	At Mil.	W	9-1		14	7	Daal	Nomo		83-56	1st	+7.5
9-9	At Mil.	L	8-9		11	14	Karl	Reynoso	Wickman	83-57	1st	+7.0
9-10	Phi.	W	3-1		7	6	Johnson	Person		84-57	1st	+8.0
9-11	Phi.	W	4-0		12	6	Benes	Wolf		85-57	1st	+8.0
9-12	Phi.	W	5-0		11	7	Stottlemyre	Grace		86-57	1st	+8.0
9-13	Pit.	W	5-1		8	10	Daal	Schmidt	Chouinard	87-57	1st	+8.5
9-14	Pit.	W	2-1		3	4	Swindell	Wilkins	Mantei	88-57	1st	+8.5
9-15	Pit.	L	1-5		7	7	Benson	Reynoso		88-58	1st	+7.5
9-17	Fla.	L	6-10		7	16	Burnett	Benes		88-59	1st	+6.0
9-18	Fla.	W	8-6	(10)	11	15	Swindell	Almonte		89-59	1st	+7.0
9-19	Fla.	W	8-7		15	11	Olson	Looper		90-59	1st	+8.0

Date	Opp.	Res.	Score	(inn.*)	Hits	Opp. hits	Winning pitcher	Losing pitcher	Save	Record	Pos.	GB
9-20	At Col.	L	7-12		12	15	Wright	Daal		90-60	1st	+8.0
9-21	At Col.	W	7-6		11	8	Olson	Ramirez	Mantei	91-60	1st	+9.0
9-22	At Col.	W	11-3		11	7	Benes	Hackman		92-60	1st	+9.0
9-24	At S.F	W	11-3		17	5	Johnson	Estes		93-60	1st	+10.5
9-25	At S.F	W	7-3		14	8	Olson	Nen		94-60	1st	+11.5
9-26	At S.F	W	7-1		14	6	Daal	Rueter		95-60	1st	+12.5
9-27	Col.	W	10-3		10	9	Anderson	Bohanon		96-60	1st	+13.0
9-28	Col.	W	9-3		15	6	Benes	Hackman		97-60	1st	+14.0
9-29	Col.	L	1-4		8	8	Astacio	Reynoso		97-61	1st	+13.0
9-30	S.D.	W	5-3		11	6	Johnson	Hitchcock	Mantei	98-61	1st	+14.0
10-1	S.D.	L	1-6		6	12	Williams	Stottlemyre		98-62	1st	+13.0
10-2	S.D.	W	7-5		7	7	Kim	Whisenant	Mantei	99-62	1st	+13.0
10-3	S.D.	W	10-3		11	7	Anderson	Murray		100-62	1st	+14.0

Monthly records: April (13-11), May (18-10), June (12-14), July (16-11), August (20-8), September (19-7), October (2-1).
*Innings, if other than nine. † First game of a doubleheader. ‡ Second game of a doubleheader.

HIGHLIGHTS

High point: Clinching its first division title on September 24 in San Francisco was easily the pinnacle of a remarkable season for the second-year Arizona franchise, which made a 35-game turnaround in the standings (from 65-97 in 1998 to 100-62).

Low point: Just one week into the season, the Diamondbacks suffered their third ninth-inning blown save, in a 3-2 loss at Atlanta on April 11. Gregg Olson, who had 30 saves in 1998, was pitching his way out of the closer role. And the D-backs were 1-5.

Turning point: July 11, the day Matt Mantei recorded his first save for the Diamondbacks after arriving in a trade from Florida. The club was backpedaling at the time, having lost 15 of its previous 22 games after improving to 40-26 on June 16. With Mantei on hand, Arizona had the final piece to its 1999 puzzle and sprinted to the N.L. West championship.

Most valuable player: After experiencing a '98 season that bordered on embarrassing, third baseman Matt Williams rebounded with a vengeance by hitting 35 home runs and driving in a career-high 142 runs.

Most valuable pitcher: Free-agent signee Randy Johnson proved he still ranked among the game's great pitchers. He led the league in complete games (12), ERA (2.48), strikeouts (364) and innings pitched (271.2) en route to winning the Cy Young Award.

Most improved player: Left fielder Luis Gonzalez, who at age 32 led the N.L. in hits with 206 and batted .336 (36 points higher than his previous career best). Gonzalez had a 30-game hitting streak, topped 100 RBIs for the first time and displayed extra-base power with 45 doubles and 26 homers.

Most pleasant surprise: First baseman Erubiel Durazo, who made a stunning climb up the ladder. After hitting .403 in 64 games in Class AA and then .407 in 30 games in Class AAA, the former Mexican Leaguer was promoted to the D-backs—and kept on hitting. Durazo contributed 11 homers, 30 RBIs and a .329 average in 52 games with Arizona.

Biggest disappointment: Travis Lee was projected to wind up the year entrenched at first base and on his way to stardom. By late July, he was mired in what turned out to be a season-long slump.

Key injuries: Starter Todd Stottlemyre, off to a 4-1 start, was diagnosed with a partial tear of his rotator cuff on May 17. Rejecting surgery, he began three months of intense rehabilitation and returned three weeks into August. He wound up notching Arizona's only postseason victory (against the Mets in the division series).

Notable: The Diamondbacks reached the playoffs quicker than any expansion team in history, surpassing the Rockies' feat of qualifying in only their third season. Their division title came six years faster than the previous expansion record (the Mets and Royals won divisional crowns in their eighth seasons of existence). ... Second baseman Jay Bell, who entered the season with a career high of 21 home runs, had 24 by the All-Star break and finished with 38. ... Arizona had four players reach 100 RBIs (Williams, Bell, Gonzalez and Steve Finley) and four score 100 runs (Bell, Gonzalez, Finley and Tony Womack).

—PEDRO GOMEZ

RECORDS

1999 regular-season record: 100-62 (1st in N.L. West); 52-29 at home; 48-33 on road; 33-12 vs. East; 27-24 vs. Central; 33-18 vs. N.L. West; 7-8 vs. A.L.; 32-16 vs. lefthanded starters; 68-46 vs. righthanded starters; 89-51 on grass; 11-11 on turf; 26-14 in daytime; 74-48 at night; 24-24 in one-run games; 11-10 in extra-inning games; 0-0-0 in doubleheaders.
Team record past five years: 165-159 in two years (.509).

TEAM LEADERS

Batting average: Luis Gonzalez (.336).
At-bats: Matt Williams (627).
Runs: Jay Bell (132).
Hits: Luis Gonzalez (206).
Total Bases: Luis Gonzalez (337).
Doubles: Luis Gonzalez (45).
Triples: Steve Finley, Tony Womack (10).

Home runs: Jay Bell (38).
Runs batted in: Matt Williams (142).
Stolen bases: Tony Womack (72).
Slugging percentage: Jay Bell (.557).
On-base percentage: Luis Gonzalez (.403).
Wins: Randy Johnson (17).
Earned-run average: Randy Johnson (2.48).
Complete games: Randy Johnson (12).
Shutouts: Randy Johnson (2).
Saves: Matt Mantei (22).
Innings pitched: Randy Johnson (271.2).
Strikeouts: Randy Johnson (364).

GAMES BY POSITION

Catcher: Kelly Stinnett 86, Damian Miller 86, Rod Barajas 5.
First base: Travis Lee 114, Erubiel Durazo 44, Greg Colbrunn 39.
Second base: Jay Bell 148, Tony Womack 19, Hanley Frias 8, Edwin Diaz 2.
Third base: Matt Williams 153, Andy Fox 12, Lenny Harris 5, Greg Colbrunn 2.
Shortstop: Andy Fox 82, Hanley Frias 53, Tony Batista 33, Tony Womack 19, Edwin Diaz 2, Jay Bell 1.
Outfield: Steve Finley 155, Luis Gonzalez 148, Tony Womack 123, Bernard Gilkey 53, David Dellucci 31, Dante Powell 15, Turner Ward 5, Rob Ryan 5, Ernie Young 4, Lenny Harris 2, Travis Lee 2.
Designated hitter: Luis Gonzalez 4, Jay Bell 2, Greg Colbrunn 2, Steve Finley 1, David Dellucci 1.

TOP DRAFT CHOICES

1a. **Corey Myers,** SS, Desert Vista H.S., Phoenix
1b. **Casey Daigle,** RHP, Sulphur (La.) H.S.
2. **Jeremy Ward,** RHP, Long Beach State University
3. None
4. None
5. None
6. **Justin Maureau,** LHP, Highlands Ranch (Colo.) H.S.
7. **Ryan Owens,** SS, Cal State Fullerton
8. **Chris Capuano,** LHP, Duke University
9. **Matt Kata,** SS, Vanderbilt University
10. **Matt Abram,** 3B, Chaparral H.S., Scottsdale, Ariz.

ATLANTA BRAVES
NATIONAL LEAGUE EAST DIVISION

2000 Braves Schedule
Home games shaded. *—All-Star Game at Turner Field (Atlanta).

March
SUN	MON	TUE	WED	THU	FRI	SAT
26	27	28	29	30	31	

April
SUN	MON	TUE	WED	THU	FRI	SAT
						1
2	3 COL	4 COL	5 COL	6	7 SF	8 SF
9 SF	10 CUB	11	12 CUB	13 CUB	14 MIL	15 MIL
16 MIL	17	18 PHI	19 PHI	20 PHI	21 PIT	22 PIT
23 PIT	24	25 LA	26 LA	27 LA	28 SD	29 SD
30 SD						

May
SUN	MON	TUE	WED	THU	FRI	SAT
	1 LA	2 LA	3 LA	4	5 PHI	6 PHI
7 PHI	8 FLA	9 FLA	10 FLA	11 FLA	12 PHI	13 PHI
14 PHI	15	16 SF	17 SF	18 SF	19 SD	20 SD
21 SD	22	23 MIL	24 MIL	25 MIL	26 HOU	27 HOU
28 HOU	29 CUB	30 CUB	31 CUB			

June
SUN	MON	TUE	WED	THU	FRI	SAT
				1	2 NYY	3 NYY
4 NYY	5 TOR	6 TOR	7 TOR	8	9 BOS	10 BOS
11 BOS	12 PIT	13 PIT	14 PIT	15 PHI	16 PHI	17 PHI
18 PHI	19 PHI	20 CUB	21 CUB	22 CUB	23 MIL	24 MIL
25 MIL	26 MON	27 MON	28	29 NYM	30 NYM	

July
SUN	MON	TUE	WED	THU	FRI	SAT
						1 NYM
2 NYM	3 MON	4 MON	5 MON	6 MON	7 BOS	8 BOS
9 BOS	10	11 *	12	13 BAL	14 BAL	15 BAL
16 TB	17 TB	18 TB	19 FLA	20 FLA	21 NYM	22 NYM
23 NYM	24	25 FLA	26 FLA	27 FLA	28 HOU	29 HOU
30 HOU	31					

August
SUN	MON	TUE	WED	THU	FRI	SAT
		1 ARI	2 ARI	3 ARI	4 STL	5 STL
6 STL	7 CIN	8 CIN	9 CIN	10	11 LA	12 LA
13 LA	14 SD	15 SD	16 SD	17	18 SF	19 SF
20 SF	21 COL	22 COL	23 COL	24 STL	25 STL	26 STL
27 STL	28 CIN	29 CIN	30 CIN	31 CIN		

September
SUN	MON	TUE	WED	THU	FRI	SAT
					1 HOU	2 HOU
3 HOU	4	5 ARI	6 ARI	7 ARI	8 MON	9 MON
10 MON	11	12 FLA	13 FLA	14 FLA	15 ARI	16 ARI
17 ARI	18 NYM	19 NYM	20 NYM	21	22 MON	23 MON
24 MON	25 MON	26 NYM	27 NYM	28 NYM	29 COL	30 COL

October
SUN	MON	TUE	WED	THU	FRI	SAT
1 COL	2	3	4	5	6	7

2000 SEASON
CLUB DIRECTORY

Owner
R.E. Turner III
Chairman of the board of directors
William C. Bartholomay
President
Stanley H. Kasten
Executive vice president and general manager
John Schuerholz
Senior v.p. and assistant to the president
Henry L. Aaron
Senior vice president, administration
Bob Wolfe
Vice president, assistant general manager
Frank Wren
V.p., director of marketing and broadcasting
Wayne Long
Vice president
Lee Douglas
Vice president of development
Janet Marie Smith
Vice president of human resources
Michelle Thomas
Assistant director of scouting
Dayton Moore
Special assistants to general manager
Bill Lajoie, Brian Murphy
Special assistant to g.m./player development
Jose Martinez
Special asst., scouting and player development
Guy Hansen
Director of team travel, equipment manager
Bill Acree
Director of player development
Dick Balderson
Director of scouting
Roy Clark
Asst. dir. of scouting and player development
Dayton Moore
Senior director of promotions and civic affairs
Miles McRea
Vice president/Controller
Chip Moore
Director of ticket sales
Paul Adams
Director of minor league business operations
Bruce Baldwin
Director of stadium operations and security
Larry Bowman
Director of Braves foundation
Danny Goodwin
Field director
Ed Mangan
Director of ticket operations
Ed Newman
Team counsel
David Payne

Director of stadium operations and security
Larry Bowman
Director of community relations
Cara Maglione
Director of special events
David Lee
Director of audio video operations
Jennifer Berger
Director of corporate sales
Jim Allen
Director of public relations
Jim Schultz
Media relations manager
Glen Serra
Public relations assistants
Steve Copses, Robert Gahagan, Kim Zieglar
Trainer
Dave Pursley
Club physician
Dr. David T. Watson
Associate physicians
Dr. William Barber, Dr. John Cantwell, Dr. Norman Elliott
Major league scouts
Dick Balderson, Scott Nethery, Bobby Wine
National supervisor
Tony LaCava
Regional supervisors
Harold Cronin, Paul Faulk, John Flannery, Bob Wadsworth
Area supervisors
Mike Baker, Dan Bates, Tyrone Brooks, Stu Cann, Rob English, Ralph Garr, Rod Gilbreath, John Hagemann, J. Harrison, J. Harrison, Kurt Kemp, Brian Kohlscheen, Jim Martz, Marco Paddy, Donnie Poplin, J.J. Picollo, John Ramey, John Stewart
Scouts
Nez Balelo, Jim Buchert, Joe Caputo, Todd Cook, Edgar Fernandez, Jose Figueroa, Pedro Flores, Bill Froberg, Ruben Garcia, Luis Herrera, Bob Isabelle, Rafael Josela, James Kane, Dewayne Kitts, Seong Yeol Kwak, Al Kubski, Duk Jung Lee, Jose Leon, Robert Lucas, William Marcot, Giorgio Moretti, Jose Mota, Dario Paulino, Ernie Pedersen, Elvis Pineda, Ubaldo Salinas, Olivio Sanasota, Charlie Smith, Miguel Teren, Ted Thornton, Marv Throneberry, Carlos Torres, Rip Tutor, Gary Wilson, Murray Zuk
International supervisors
Felix Francisco, Gil Garrido, Andres Lopez, Julian Perez, Rolando Petit, Fernando Villescusa
Eastern Rim coordinator
Phil Dale
Latin American coordinator
Rene Francisco

MINOR LEAGUE AFFILIATES
Class	Team	League	Manager
AAA	Richmond	International	Randy Ingle
AA	Greenville	Southern	Paul Runge
A	Myrtle Beach	Carolina	Brian Snitker
A	Macon	South Atlantic	Jeff Treadway
A	Jamestown	New York-Pennsylvania	Jim Saul
Rookie	Danville	Appalachian	J.J. Cannon
Rookie	Gulf Coast Braves	Gulf Coast	Rick Albert

BROADCAST INFORMATION
Radio: WSB-AM (750).
TV: TBS-TV (Channel 17).
Cable TV: Fox SportsSouth.

SPRING TRAINING
Ballpark (city): Disney's Wide World of Sports Baseball Stadium (Kissimmee, Fla.).
Ticket information: 407-839-3900, 407-939-1418.

SPRING TRAINING ROSTER

Manager—Bobby Cox (6).
Coaches—Pat Corrales (39), Bobby Dews (52), Glenn Hubbard (17), Leo Mazzone (54), Merv Rettenmund (16), Ned Yost (5).

No.	PITCHERS	B/T	Ht./Wt.	Born	1999 clubs
74	Abreu, Winston	R/R	6-2/155	4-5-77	Macon, Myrtle Beach
48	Chen, Bruce	B/L	6-1/180	6-19-77	Richmond, Atlanta
51	Cortes, David	R/R	5-11/195	10-15-73	Richmond, Atlanta
50	Ebert, Derrin	R/L	6-3/200	8-21-76	Atlanta, Richmond
47	Glavine, Tom	L/L	6-0/185	3-25-66	Atlanta
46	Ligtenberg, Kerry	R/R	6-2/215	5-11-71	DID NOT PLAY
31	Maddux, Greg	R/R	6-0/185	4-14-66	Atlanta
68	Marquis, Jason	L/R	6-1/185	8-21-78	Myrtle Beach, Greenville
30	McGlinchy, Kevin	R/R	6-5/220	6-28-77	Atlanta
36	Medina, Rafael	R/R	6-3/200	2-15-75	Calgary, Florida
34	Millwood, Kevin	R/R	6-4/220	12-24-74	Atlanta
61	Moss, Damian	R/L	6-0/187	11-24-76	Macon, Greenville
45	Mulholland, Terry	R/L	6-3/220	3-9-63	Chicago N.L., Atlanta
43	Perez, Odalis	L/L	6-0/150	6-7-78	Atlanta
37	Remlinger, Mike	L/L	6-1/210	3-23-66	Atlanta
72	Rivera, Luis	R/R	6-3/163	6-21-78	Myrtle Beach
49	Rocker, John	R/L	6-4/225	10-17-74	Atlanta
40	Seanez, Rudy	R/R	5-10/190	10-20-68	Atlanta
29	Smoltz, John	R/R	6-3/220	5-15-67	Atlanta, Greenville
56	Stull, Everett	R/R	6-3/200	8-24-71	Richmond, Atlanta
70	Villegas, Ismael	R/R	6-1/188	8-12-76	Richmond

No.	CATCHERS	B/T	Ht./Wt.	Born	1999 clubs
8	Lopez, Javy	R/R	6-3/200	11-5-70	Atlanta
11	Matos, Pascual	R/R	6-2/160	12-23-74	Richmond, Atlanta
12	Perez, Eddie	R/R	6-1/185	5-4-68	Atlanta

No.	INFIELDERS	B/T	Ht./Wt.	Born	1999 clubs
14	Galarraga, Andres	R/R	6-3/235	6-18-61	DID NOT PLAY
20	Garcia, Freddy	R/R	6-2/224	8-1-72	Pittsburgh, Nashville, Atlanta
13	Guillen, Ozzie	L/R	5-11/165	1-20-64	Atlanta
28	Helms, Wes	R/R	6-4/230	5-12-76	Gulf Coast Braves, Greenville
10	Jones, Chipper	B/R	6-4/210	4-24-72	Atlanta
22	Joyner, Wally	L/L	6-2/200	6-16-62	San Diego, Las Vegas
7	Lockhart, Keith	L/R	5-10/170	11-10-64	Atlanta
15	Simon, Randall	L/L	6-0/180	5-26-75	Atlanta, Richmond
4	Veras, Quilvio	B/R	5-10/183	4-3-71	San Diego
22	Weiss, Walt	B/R	6-0/168	11-28-63	Atlanta

No.	OUTFIELDERS	B/T	Ht./Wt.	Born	1999 clubs
57	Brignac, Junior	R/R	6-3/175	2-15-78	Macon, Myrtle Beach
25	Jones, Andruw	R/R	6-1/210	4-23-77	Atlanta
33	Jordan, Brian	R/R	6-1/206	3-29-67	Atlanta
26	Lombard, George	L/R	6-0/202	9-14-75	Richmond, Atlanta
16	Sanders, Reggie	R/R	6-1/185	12-1-67	San Diego

BALLPARK INFORMATION

Ballpark (capacity, surface)
Turner Field (50,062, grass)

Address
P.O. Box 4064
Atlanta, GA 30302

Business phone
404-522-7630

Ticket information
404-249-6400 or 800-326-4000

Ticket prices
$35 (dugout level)
$29 (club level)
$25 (field level, terrace level)
$17 (field pavilion, terrace pavilion)
$12 (upper level)
$5 (upper pavilion)
$1 (skyline)

Field dimensions (from home plate)
To left field at foul line, 335 feet
To center field, 401 feet
To right field at foul line, 330 feet

First game played
April 4, 1997 (Braves 5, Cubs 4)

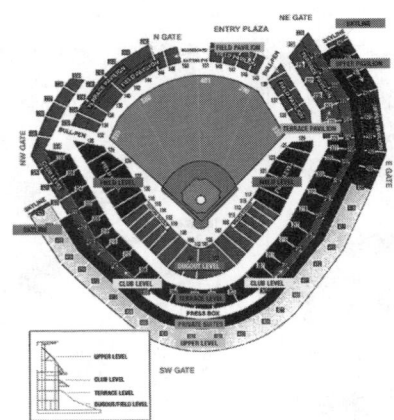

Date	Opp.	Res.	Score	(inn.*)	Hits	Opp. hits	Winning pitcher	Losing pitcher	Save	Record	Pos.	GB
4-6	Phi.	W	11-3		17	13	Maddux	Ogea	Ebert	1-1	T1st	...
4-7	Phi.	W	4-0		7	5	Smoltz	Loewer		2-1	T1st	...
4-8	Phi.	L	3-6		4	7	Byrd	Millwood	Brantley	2-2	T2nd	1.0
4-9	Ari.	W	3-2	(10)	8	6	Rocker	Frascatore		3-2	T1st	...
4-10	Ari.	L	3-8		6	16	Johnson	Glavine		3-3	T2nd	1.0
4-11	Ari.	W	3-2		5	7	McGlinchy	Olson		4-3	T2nd	1.0
4-12	At Phi.	W	8-6		9	10	Cather	Ryan	Seanez	5-3	2nd	1.0
4-14	At Phi.	W	10-4		12	9	Millwood	Byrd		6-3	2nd	1.0
4-17	At Col.	L	4-5		8	10	McElroy	Rocker		6-4	2nd	1.0
4-18	At Col.	W	20-5		24	10	Maddux	Astacio		7-4	1st	...
4-19	At L.A.	W	11-3		18	8	Smoltz	Perez		8-4	1st	+0.5
4-20	At L.A.	L	4-5		4	10	Dreifort	Millwood	Shaw	8-5	2nd	0.5
4-21	At L.A.	W	11-4	(12)	13	7	Remlinger	Kubenka		9-5	1st	+0.5
4-23	At Fla.	L	1-9		9	14	Hernandez	Glavine		9-6	2nd	1.0
4-24	At Fla.	W	8-7		13	12	Maddux	Edmondson	Rocker	10-6	1st	...
4-25	At Fla.	W	5-1		9	6	Smoltz	Meadows		11-6	1st	+1.0
4-26	At Fla.	W	5-3		9	5	Seanez	Alfonseca		12-6	1st	+1.5
4-27	Pit.	L	3-5		7	10	Schmidt	Perez	Williams	12-7	1st	+1.0
4-28	Pit.	W	5-4		9	8	Glavine	Christiansen		13-7	1st	+1.5
4-29	Pit.	W	8-1		10	11	Maddux	Silva		14-7	1st	+1.5
4-30	Cin.	W	3-0		6	1	Smoltz	Avery		15-7	1st	+1.5
5-1	Cin.	W	5-1		10	3	Millwood	Harnisch		16-7	1st	+1.5
5-2	Cin.	W	5-3		8	6	Perez	Neagle	Rocker	17-7	1st	+1.5
5-3	StL.	W	4-2		8	10	Remlinger	Jimenez	Rocker	18-7	1st	+1.5
5-4	StL.	L	1-9		4	16	Aybar	Maddux		18-8	1st	+1.5
5-5	StL.	W	12-3		16	7	Smoltz	Bottenfield		19-8	1st	+2.5
5-7	At S.D.	L	3-4		4	9	Boehringer	Rocker	Hoffman	19-9	1st	+2.5
5-8	At S.D.	W	11-1		14	8	Glavine	Ashby		20-9	1st	+2.5
5-9	At S.D.	L	0-5		5	12	Hitchcock	Maddux		20-10	1st	+2.5
5-10	At S.F	L	1-4		4	7	Ortiz	Smoltz	Nen	20-11	1st	+2.5
5-11	At S.F	W	9-8	(12)	10	9	Rocker	Rodriguez		21-11	1st	+3.0
5-12	At S.F	L	1-5		7	12	Brock	Millwood		21-12	1st	+2.0
5-14	At Chi.	L	0-9		7	10	Lieber	Glavine		21-13	1st	+1.5
5-15	At Chi.	L	1-5		6	15	Trachsel	Maddux		21-14	1st	+0.5
5-16	At Chi.	W	8-5		11	8	McGlinchy	Myers	Rocker	22-14	1st	+1.5
5-17	Pit.	W	2-1		7	5	Millwood	Ritchie	Rocker	23-14	1st	+2.0
5-18	Pit.	W	12-4		16	12	Perez	Schmidt		24-14	1st	+3.0
5-19	Pit.	W	7-3		6	6	Glavine	Cordova		25-14	1st	+4.0
5-20	Chi.	L	5-6	(12)	10	10	Serafini	McGlinchy		25-15	1st	+2.5
5-21	Chi.	L	4-8		8	9	Adams	McGlinchy		25-16	1st	+1.5
5-22	Chi.	W	4-2		7	7	Millwood	Tapani	Rocker	26-16	1st	+2.5
5-23	Chi.	L	1-5		5	6	Mulholland	Perez		26-17	1st	+1.5
5-24	At Mil.	L	7-10		13	13	Woodard	Glavine		26-18	1st	+1.5
5-25	At Mil.	W	5-2		12	8	Seanez	Wickman	Rocker	27-18	1st	+1.5
5-26	At Mil.	W	3-2	(10)	11	6	Seanez	Weathers	Rocker	28-18	1st	+1.5
5-27	At Mil.	W	8-7		11	13	Millwood	Karl	Seanez	29-18	1st	+2.0
5-28	L.A.	W	4-2		8	6	Perez	Dreifort	Rocker	30-18	1st	+3.0
5-29	L.A.	L	1-2		5	7	Perez	Glavine	Shaw	30-19	1st	+3.0
5-30	L.A.	L	4-5	(11)	8	9	Borbon	Remlinger	Shaw	30-20	1st	+3.0
5-31	Col.	W	3-1		8	8	Millwood	Astacio	Rocker	31-20	1st	+4.0
6-1	Col.	W	7-2		6	6	Smoltz	Jones		32-20	1st	+5.0
6-2	Col.	L	2-3	(11)	9	5	Dipoto	Springer		32-21	1st	+5.0
6-4	At Bos.	L	1-5		3	9	Martinez	Glavine		32-22	1st	+4.5
6-5	At Bos.	W	6-5		9	11	Maddux	Gordon	Rocker	33-22	1st	+5.5
6-6	At Bos.	W	3-2	(10)	6	3	Seanez	Portugal	Rocker	34-22	1st	+5.5
6-7	T.B.	W	9-5		10	13	Smoltz	Eiland	Rocker	35-22	1st	+5.5
6-8	T.B.	W	11-2		16	8	Perez	Alvarez		36-22	1st	+6.0
6-9	T.B.	W	4-3	(12)	13	10	McGlinchy	White		37-22	1st	+6.0
6-11	Bal.	L	2-6		5	12	Ponson	Maddux		37-23	1st	+5.5
6-12	Bal.	L	0-5		6	13	Guzman	Millwood		37-24	1st	+4.5
6-13	Bal.	L	1-22		6	25	Mussina	Smoltz		37-25	1st	+4.0
6-14	At Hou.	L	4-10		10	13	Hampton	Perez	Miller	37-26	1st	+4.0
6-15	At Hou.	W	4-3		7	6	Glavine	Elarton	Rocker	38-26	1st	+4.0
6-16	At Hou.	W	3-1		14	3	Maddux	Bergman	Rocker	39-26	1st	+4.0
6-17	At Hou.	W	8-5		13	6	Millwood	Lima	Seanez	40-26	1st	+4.0
6-18	At Ari.	W	6-0		12	6	Smoltz	Benes		41-26	1st	+4.0
6-19	At Ari.	L	3-7		7	10	Daal	Perez		41-27	1st	+4.0
6-20	At Ari.	W	10-4		12	10	Glavine	Johnson		42-27	1st	+4.0
6-22	Mon.	L	1-2		9	8	Thurman	Maddux	Urbina	42-28	1st	+3.0
6-23	Mon.	W	7-3		13	7	Millwood	Batista		43-28	1st	+3.0
6-24	Mon.	W	3-2	(11)	13	7	McGlinchy	Mota		44-28	1st	+3.0
6-25	N.Y.	L	2-10		8	13	Reed	Perez		44-29	1st	+2.0

2000 SEASON Atlanta Braves

Date	Opp.	Res.	Score	(inn.*)	Hits	Opp. hits	Winning pitcher	Losing pitcher	Save	Record	Pos.	GB
6-26	N.Y.	W	7-2		7	7	Glavine	Dotel		45-29	1st	+3.0
6-27	N.Y.	W	1-0		4	3	Maddux	Yoshii	Rocker	46-29	1st	+4.0
6-28	At Mon.	W	13-5		16	11	Millwood	Batista		47-29	1st	+4.0
6-29	At Mon.	L	5-6		10	10	Urbina	Rocker		47-30	1st	+3.0
6-30	At Mon.	L	5-7		8	10	Kline	McGlinchy	Urbina	47-31	1st	+3.0
7-1	At Mon.	W	4-1		12	7	Glavine	Smith		48-31	1st	+3.0
7-2	At N.Y.	W	16-0		15	3	Maddux	Yoshii		49-31	1st	+4.0
7-3	At N.Y.	W	3-0		7	3	Millwood	Leiter	Rocker	50-31	1st	+5.0
7-4	At N.Y.	L	6-7		8	11	Cook	Smoltz	Benitez	50-32	1st	+4.0
7-5	Fla.	W	6-5		11	8	McGlinchy	Alfonseca		51-32	1st	+4.0
7-6	Fla.	L	2-5		4	17	Fernandez	Glavine	Mantei	51-33	1st	+3.0
7-7	Fla.	W	7-3		8	6	Maddux	Dempster		52-33	1st	+4.0
7-8	Fla.	W	5-2		8	7	Millwood	Meadows		53-33	1st	+5.0
7-9	Bos.	L	4-5		8	5	Saberhagen	Chen	Wakefield	53-34	1st	+4.0
7-10	Bos.	W	2-1	(11)	10	6	Seanez	Wasdin		54-34	1st	+4.0
7-11	Bos.	W	8-1		8	6	Maddux	Cho		55-34	1st	+5.0
7-15	At N.Y. (AL)	W	6-2		10	7	Glavine	Clemens		56-34	1st	+5.0
7-16	At N.Y. (AL)	W	10-7		12	14	Springer	Rivera	Rocker	57-34	1st	+5.0
7-17	At N.Y. (AL)	L	4-11		12	13	Pettitte	Perez	Grimsley	57-35	1st	+5.0
7-18	At Tor.	L	2-3		6	10	Hamilton	Millwood	Koch	57-36	1st	+4.0
7-19	At Tor.	L	7-8	(10)	10	9	Frascatore	Hudek		57-37	1st	+3.0
7-20	At Tor.	L	6-11		13	15	Halladay	Glavine		57-38	1st	+3.0
7-21	At Fla.	L	0-2		7	9	Springer	Maddux		57-39	1st	+2.0
7-22	At Fla.	W	6-3		11	6	McGlinchy	Fernandez	Rocker	58-39	1st	+2.0
7-23†	At Phi.	L	5-6		9	7	Telemaco	Seanez	Gomes	58-40		
7-23‡	At Phi.	W	3-1		7	5	Chen	Shumaker	Rocker	59-40	1st	+1.5
7-24	At Phi.	L	3-4		6	11	Montgomery	Bowie	Gomes	59-41	1st	+0.5
7-25	At Phi.	W	5-4	(10)	12	8	Rocker	Montgomery		60-41	1st	+0.5
7-26	Mil.	W	6-1		8	6	Maddux	Karl		61-41	1st	+0.5
7-27	Mil.	W	10-2		14	6	Millwood	Nomo		62-41	1st	+1.5
7-28	Mil.	L	4-10		9	13	Pulsipher	Chen		62-42	1st	+0.5
7-30	Phi.	L	2-9		5	12	Byrd	Smoltz		62-43	2nd	0.5
7-31	Phi.	W	8-6		12	11	Glavine	Person	Rocker	63-43	1st	+0.5
8-1	Phi.	W	12-4		10	8	Maddux	Wolf		64-43	1st	+0.5
8-3	At Pit.	L	1-7		4	7	Benson	Millwood		64-44	2nd	1.0
8-4	At Pit.	L	2-3		5	5	Ritchie	Smoltz	Williams	64-45	2nd	2.0
8-5	At Pit.	W	6-3		9	7	Remlinger	Hansell	Rocker	65-45	2nd	1.5
8-6	S.F	W	7-3		10	11	Maddux	Estes		66-45	2nd	1.5
8-7	S.F	W	15-4		16	11	Mulholland	Ortiz		67-45	2nd	0.5
8-8	S.F	L	2-5		8	8	Rueter	Millwood	Nen	67-46	2nd	0.5
8-9	Hou.	W	5-3		10	14	Seanez	Henry	Rocker	68-46	1st	+0.5
8-10	Hou.	W	6-4		8	8	Glavine	Reynolds	Rocker	69-46	1st	+0.5
8-11	Hou.	W	8-5		10	11	Maddux	Lima	Rocker	70-46	1st	+0.5
8-13	At L.A.	W	7-3		12	5	Millwood	Dreifort		71-46	1st	+1.0
8-14	At L.A.	L	1-8		5	14	Brown	Smoltz		71-47	1st	...
8-15	At L.A.	W	5-4	(11)	10	12	Remlinger	Arnold	Rocker	72-47	T1st	...
8-16	At Col.	W	14-6		17	17	Maddux	Jones		73-47	T1st	...
8-17	At Col.	L	2-3		10	8	Lee	Mulholland	Veres	73-48	T1st	...
8-18	At Col.	L	1-4		8	3	Veres	Rocker		73-49	2nd	1.0
8-19	At Col.	W	9-7	(14)	13	11	Chen	Lee	Mulholland	74-49	2nd	0.5
8-20	S.D.	W	4-3	(11)	7	6	Remlinger	Reyes		75-49	2nd	...
8-21	S.D.	W	6-2		10	8	Maddux	Ashby		76-49	2nd	...
8-22	S.D.	W	3-2		9	6	Rocker	Miceli		77-49	1st	+0.5
8-23	Cin.	W	6-2		6	4	Millwood	Tomko	Springer	78-49	1st	+0.5
8-24	Cin.	W	6-4		10	5	Smoltz	Harnisch	Rocker	79-49	1st	+1.5
8-25	Cin.	W	5-2		7	8	Glavine	Neagle	Rocker	80-49	1st	+1.5
8-27	At StL.	W	2-1		8	8	Springer	Acevedo	Rocker	81-49	1st	+1.5
8-28	At StL.	W	3-0	(13)	7	4	Remlinger	Painter	Rocker	82-49	1st	+2.5
8-29	At StL.	W	4-3	(12)	9	8	McGlinchy	Acevedo		83-49	1st	+3.5
8-30	At Cin.	L	3-11		6	12	Neagle	Glavine		83-50	1st	+2.5
8-31	At Cin.	W	8-2		11	9	Maddux	Guzman		84-50	1st	+3.5
9-1	At Cin.	W	8-7		11	13	Mulholland	Villone	Rocker	85-50	1st	+3.5
9-3	Ari.	W	7-3		9	8	Millwood	Reynoso		86-50	1st	+4.5
9-4	Ari.	L	4-5		5	10	Benes	Smoltz	Mantei	86-51	1st	+3.5
9-5	Ari.	L	5-7		7	10	Olson	Rocker	Mantei	86-52	1st	+2.5
9-6	StL.	W	4-1		9	3	Maddux	Stephenson		87-52	1st	+2.5
9-7	StL.	W	3-2		9	6	Remlinger	Oliver		88-52	1st	+3.5
9-8	StL.	W	5-4		7	9	Millwood	Ankiel	Rocker	89-52	1st	+3.5
9-10	At S.F	W	4-2		10	8	Remlinger	Ortiz	Rocker	90-52	1st	+4.0
9-11	At S.F	L	2-3		7	8	Rueter	Glavine	Nen	90-53	1st	+3.0
9-12	At S.F	L	4-8		9	13	Nathan	Maddux		90-54	1st	+2.0
9-13	At S.D.	L	0-3		4	11	Williams	Mulholland	Hoffman	90-55	1st	+1.0
9-14	At S.D.	W	11-4		14	7	Millwood	Carlyle		91-55	1st	+2.0
9-15	At S.D.	L	1-4		4	9	Clement	Smoltz	Hoffman	91-56	1st	+1.0
9-17	Mon.	W	6-5	(10)	5	12	Remlinger	Kline		92-56	1st	+2.0
9-18	Mon.	L	3-4		11	8	Hermanson	Maddux	Urbina	92-57	1st	+1.0

Date	Opp.	Res.	Score	(inn.*)	Hits	Opp. hits	Winning pitcher	Losing pitcher	Save	Record	Pos.	GB
9-19	Mon.	W	5-1		7	7	Millwood	Lilly		93-57	1st	+1.0
9-21	N.Y.	W	2-1		8	6	Remlinger	Cook	Rocker	94-57	1st	+2.0
9-22	N.Y.	W	5-2		6	8	Glavine	Hershiser	Rocker	95-57	1st	+3.0
9-23	N.Y.	W	6-3		13	7	Maddux	Leiter	Rocker	96-57	1st	+4.0
9-24	At Mon.	W	4-3	(10)	9	4	Bergman	Mota	Remlinger	97-57	1st	+5.0
9-25	At Mon.	W	5-3		9	10	Mulholland	Vazquez	Rocker	98-57	1st	+6.0
9-26	At Mon.	W	10-0		13	6	Smoltz	Powell		99-57	1st	+7.0
9-28	At N.Y.	W	9-3		13	9	Glavine	Hershiser		100-57	1st	+8.0
9-29	At N.Y.	L	2-9		5	13	Leiter	Maddux		100-58	1st	+7.0
9-30	At N.Y.	W	4-3	(11)	8	6	Mulholland	Dotel		101-58	1st	+8.0
10-1	Fla.	W	4-1		8	6	Smoltz	Meadows	Rocker	102-58	1st	+8.0
10-2	Fla.	L	0-1	(10)	7	2	Looper	Ebert	Alfonseca	102-59	1st	+7.0
10-3	Fla.	W	18-0		21	5	Glavine	Springer		103-59	1st	+7.0

Monthly records: April (15-7), May (16-13), June (16-11), July (16-12), August (21-7), September (17-8), October (2-1).
*Innings, if other than nine. † First game of a doubleheader. ‡ Second game of a doubleheader.

HIGHLIGHTS

High point: The Braves won an unprecedented eighth consecutive division title. They also captured their fifth N.L. pennant in the 1990s and became the first team in nearly three decades to post three straight 100-win seasons. All this despite losing three key players—first baseman Andres Galarraga, closer Kerry Ligtenberg and catcher Javy Lopez.

Low point: August 4, when the Pirates beat the Braves and dropped Atlanta two games behind the Mets in the N.L. East. After building a six-game lead in early June, the Braves saw their division lead erode during July (when they went 16-12).

Turning point: The Braves swept the Mets in a three-game series in Atlanta September 21-23 to boost their division lead to four games. They then swept three in Montreal to clinch the N.L. East crown before arriving in New York for a rematch with the Mets.

Most valuable player: Third baseman Chipper Jones, who hit a career-best 45 home runs and reached 100 RBIs for the fourth year in a row. His homer total set an N.L. record for a switch hitter. He batted .319 and drew 126 walks—both career highs.

Most valuable pitcher: John Rocker had little experience as a closer when the role was thrust on him by Ligtenberg's season-ending injury in spring training. He responded with 38 saves, one shy of Mark Wohlers' club record, and struck out 104 batters in 72.1 innings.

Most improved player: Left fielder Gerald Williams, who was inserted into the lineup as the leadoff hitter in early August and ignited the club. He wound up with a career-high 17 homers and drove in 68 runs. The Braves went 39-14 once Williams was installed in the leadoff spot.

Most pleasant surprise: Kevin Millwood demonstrated his 17-win season of 1998 was no fluke. He finished with 18 victories, lowered his ERA from 4.08 to 2.68 and led the majors' starting pitchers by holding opponents to a .202 average.

Biggest disappointment: Second baseman Bret Boone followed up a 24-homer, 95-RBI season for the Reds with a 20-homer, 63-RBI performance for the Braves—which might have been acceptable if he

hadn't slipped on defense as well.

Key injuries: Galarraga missed the season after being diagnosed with lymphoma in spring training. Ligtenberg was lost after tearing an elbow ligament. Lopez went down with a knee injury in July and didn't return. Lefthander Odalis Perez tore a ligament in his elbow in July and was sidelined the rest of the season. Reliever Rudy Seanez didn't pitch after August 20 because of a stress fracture in his elbow. And John Smoltz, troubled by a sore elbow, had two stints on the disabled list and made only 29 starts.

Notable: Five Braves slugged 20 or more homers, with center fielder Andruw Jones finishing second to Chipper Jones with 26. ... Chipper's 87 extra-base hits established a club record. ... Free-agent acquisition Brian Jordan proved valuable, hitting 23 homers and knocking in 115 runs. ... Greg Maddux's ERA jumped from 2.22 to 3.57, but he still won 19 games. ... Atlanta scored a franchise-record 840 runs.

—BILL ZACK

RECORDS

1999 regular-season record: 103-59 (1st in N.L. East); 56-25 at home; 47-34 on road; 35-16 vs. N.L. East; 35-13 vs. Central; 24-21 vs. West; 9-9 vs. A.L.; 29-15 vs. lefthanded starters; 74-44 vs. righthanded starters; 88-48 on grass; 15-11 on turf; 29-17 in daytime; 74-42 at night; 29-21 in one-run games; 17-5 in extra-inning games; 0-0-1 in doubleheaders.

Team record past five years: 496-296 (.626, ranks 1st in league in that span).

TEAM LEADERS

Batting average: Chipper Jones (.319).
At-bats: Bret Boone (608).
Runs: Chipper Jones (116).
Hits: Chipper Jones (181).
Total Bases: Chipper Jones (359).
Doubles: Chipper Jones (41).
Triples: Andruw Jones (5).
Home runs: Chipper Jones (45).
Runs batted in: Brian Jordan (115).
Stolen bases: Otis Nixon (26).

Slugging percentage: Chipper Jones (.633).
On-base percentage: Chipper Jones (.441).
Wins: Greg Maddux (19).
Earned-run average: Kevin Millwood (2.68).
Complete games: Greg Maddux (4).
Shutouts: John Smoltz (1).
Saves: John Rocker (38).
Innings pitched: Tom Glavine (234.0).
Strikeouts: Kevin Millwood (205).

GAMES BY POSITION

Catcher: Eddie Perez 98, Javy Lopez 60, Greg Myers 31, Pascual Matos 5, Jorge Fabregas 4.
First base: Brian Hunter 101, Ryan Klesko 75, Randall Simon 70, Eddie Perez 2, Jose Hernandez 1, Jorge Fabregas 1.
Second base: Bret Boone 151, Keith Lockhart 25, Ozzie Guillen 1.
Third base: Chipper Jones 156, Keith Lockhart 10, Ozzie Guillen 6, Howard Battle 6.
Shortstop: Walt Weiss 102, Ozzie Guillen 53, Jose Hernandez 45, Mark DeRosa 2, Chipper Jones 1.
Outfield: Andruw Jones 162, Brian Jordan 150, Gerald Williams 139, Ryan Klesko 53, Otis Nixon 52, Brian Hunter 8, George Lombard 4, Jose Hernandez 1, Freddy Garcia 1.
Designated hitter: Javy Lopez 4, Keith Lockhart 4, Ryan Klesko 1.

TOP DRAFT CHOICES

1. None
2. **Matt Butler,** RHP, Hattiesburg (Miss.) H.S.
3. **Pat Manning,** SS, Mater Dei H.S., Anaheim Hills, Calif.
4. **Alec Zumwalt,** OF, East Forsyth H.S., Kernersville, N.C.
5. **Matt McClendon,** RHP, U. of Florida
6. **Andrew Brown,** RHP, Trinity Christian Academy, Deltona, Fla.
7. **Brett Evert,** RHP, North Salem H.S., Salem, Ore.
8. **Chris Spencer,** RHP, Humble (Texas) H.S.
9. **Angelo Burrows,** OF, Killian H.S., Miami
10. **Bryan Cetani,** LHP, Deep Valley Christian H.S., Ukiah, Calif.

CHICAGO CUBS
NATIONAL LEAGUE CENTRAL DIVISION

2000 Cubs Schedule

Home games shaded. ▲—All-Star Game at Turner Field (Atlanta).
† Game played in Tokyo.

March

SUN	MON	TUE	WED	THU	FRI	SAT
26	27	28	29 †	30 † NYM	1 NYM	31

April

SUN	MON	TUE	WED	THU	FRI	SAT
						1
2	3 STL	4	5 STL	6 STL	7 CIN	8 CIN
9 CIN	10	11	12 ATL	13 ATL	14 FLA	15 FLA
16 FLA	17 FLA	18 MON	19 MON	20 MON	21 NYM	22 NYM
23 NYM	24	25 HOU	26 HOU	27 HOU	28 ARIZ	29 ARIZ
30 ARIZ						

May

SUN	MON	TUE	WED	THU	FRI	SAT
	1	2 HOU	3 HOU	4 HOU	5 PIT	6 PIT
7 PIT	8 MIL	9 MIL	10 MIL	11	12 MON	13 MON
14 MON	15	16 LA	17 LA	18 LA	19 CIN	20 CIN
21 CIN	22	23 COL	24 COL	25 COL	26 SF	27 SF
28 SF	29 ATL	30 ATL	31 ATL			

June

SUN	MON	TUE	WED	THU	FRI	SAT
				1	2 DET	3 DET
4 DET	5 ARIZ	6 ARIZ	7 ARIZ	8	9 CWS	10 CWS
11 CWS	12	13 NYM	14 NYM	15	16 MON	17 MON
18 MON	19	20 ATL	21 ATL	22 ATL	23 FLA	24 FLA
25 FLA	26	27 PIT	28 PIT	29 PIT	30 MIL	

July

SUN	MON	TUE	WED	THU	FRI	SAT
						1 MIL
2 MIL	3 PIT	4 PIT	5 PIT	6	7 CWS	8 CWS
9 CWS	10	11 ▲	12	13 MIN	14 MIN	15 MIN
16 KC	17 KC	18 KC	19 PHI	20 PHI	21 MIL	22 MIL
23 MIL	24	25 PHI	26 PHI	27 PHI	28 SF	29 SF
30 SF	31 COL					

August

SUN	MON	TUE	WED	THU	FRI	SAT
		1 COL	2 COL	3 SD	4 SD	5 SD
6 SD	7 LA	8 LA	9 LA	10	11 CIN	12 CIN
13 CIN	14 STL	15 STL	16 STL	17	18 ARIZ	19 ARIZ
20 ARIZ	21 HOU	22 HOU	23 HOU	24	25 LA	26 LA
27 LA	28 SD	29 SD	30 SD	31 SD		

September

SUN	MON	TUE	WED	THU	FRI	SAT
					1 SF	2 SF
3 SF	4 COL	5 COL	6 COL	7	8 HOU	9 HOU
10 HOU	11 CIN	12 CIN	13 CIN	14 STL	15 STL	16 STL
17 STL	18 MIL	19 MIL	20 MIL	21	22 STL	23 STL
24 STL	25 PHI	26 PHI	27 PHI	28 PHI	29 PIT	30 PIT

October

SUN	MON	TUE	WED	THU	FRI	SAT
1 PIT	2	3	4	5	6	7

2000 SEASON
CLUB DIRECTORY

Board of directors
Dennis FitzSimons
Andrew B. MacPhail
Andrew McKenna
President and chief executive officer
Andrew B. MacPhail
Vice president/general manager
Ed Lynch
Dir., player development and scouting
Jim Hendry
Director, baseball operations
Scott Nelson
Special assistants to the g.m.
Keith Champion
Larry Himes
Ken Kravec
Major league advance scout
Terry Collins
Traveling secretary
Jimmy Bank
Executive v.p., business operations
Mark McGuire
Manager, information systems
Carl Rice
PC systems specialist
Kyle Hoker
Sr. legal counsel/corporate secretary
Crane Kenney
Controller
Jodi Norman
Director, human resources
Jenifer Surma
V.p., marketing and broadcasting
John McDonough
Director, promotions and advertising
Jay Blunk
Director, publications
Lena McDonagh
Manager, publications
Jay Rand
Director, stadium operations
Paul Rathje
Manager, event operations/security
Mike Hill

Head groundskeeper
Roger Baird
Director, ticket operations
Frank Maloney
Director, media relations
Sharon Pannozzo
Manager, media information
Chuck Wasserstrom
Media relations assistant
Benjamin de la Fuente
Team physician
Michael Schafer, M.D.
Head athletic trainer
David Tumbas
Assistant athletic trainer
Steve Melendez
Strength and conditioning coordinator
Mark Wilbert
Home clubhouse manager, emeritus
Yosh Kawano
Home clubhouse manager
Tom Hellmann
Visiting clubhouse manager
Dana Noeltner
Coordinator of scouting
John Stockstill
Pacific Rim coordinator
Leon Lee
Regional scouting supervisors
Joe Housey
Brad Kelley
Larry Maxie
Coordinator, Latin American operations
Oneri Fleita
Scouts
Mark Adair, Billy Blitzer, Tom Bourque, Jim Crawford, Steve Fuller, Al Geddes, John Gracio, Gene Handley, Bill Harford, Steve Hinton, Sam Hughes, Spider Jorgensen, Buzzy Keller, Scott May, Brian Milner, Hector Ortega, Fred Peterson, Ted Powers, Marc Russo, Jose Serra, Mark Servais, Tom Shafer, Mike Soper, Billy Swoope, Jose Trujillo, Glen Van Proyen

MINOR LEAGUE AFFILIATES

Class	Team	League	Manager
AAA	Iowa	Pacific Coast	Dave Trembley
AA	West Tenn	Southern	Dave Bialas
A	Daytona	Florida State	Richie Zisk
A	Lansing	Midwest	Steve McFarland
A	Eugene	Northwest	Danny Sheaffer
Rookie	Mesa Cubs	Arizona	Carmelo Martinez

BROADCAST INFORMATION

Radio: WGN-AM (720).
TV: WGN-TV (Channel 9); WCIU-TV (Channel 26).
Cable TV: Fox Sports Net Chicago.

SPRING TRAINING

Ballpark (city): HoHoKam Park (Mesa, Ariz.).
Ticket information: 800-638-4253.

SPRING TRANSTRAINING ROSTER

Manager—Don Baylor (25).
Coaches—Oscar Acosta, Sandy Alomar Sr., Gene Glynn, Rene Lachemann, Jeff Pentland (2), Billy Williams (26).

No.	PITCHERS	B/T	Ht./Wt.	Born	1999 clubs
38	Aguilera, Rick	R/R	6-5/210	12-31-61	Minnesota, Chicago N.L.
53	Bowie, Micah	L/L	6-4/210	11-10-74	Richmond, Atlanta, Chicago N.L.
	Downs, Scott	L/L	6-2/190	3-17-76	New Britain, Fort Myers, Daytona, West Tenn
44	Farnsworth, Kyle	B/R	6-4/215	4-14-76	Iowa, Chicago N.L.
	Gissell, Chris	R/R	6-5/200	1-4-78	West Tenn
54	Gonzalez, Jeremi	R/R	6-2/215	1-8-75	Daytona, West Tenn, Iowa
30	Guthrie, Mark	R/L	6-4/215	9-22-65	Boston, Pawtucket, Chicago N.L.
49	Heredia, Felix	L/L	6-0/180	6-18-76	Chicago N.L.
52	Karchner, Matt	R/R	6-4/220	6-28-67	Chicago N.L., Iowa
56	King, Ray	L/L	6-1/230	1-15-74	Iowa, Chicago N.L.
32	Lieber, Jon	L/R	6-3/225	4-2-70	Chicago N.L.
55	Lorraine, Andrew	L/L	6-3/200	8-11-72	Iowa, Chicago N.L.
33	McNichol, Brian	L/L	6-5/225	5-20-74	Iowa, Chicago N.L.
	Meyers, Mike	R/R	6-2/210	10-18-77	Daytona, West Tenn
59	Myers, Rodney	R/R	6-1/215	6-26-69	Iowa, Chicago N.L.
50	Norton, Phil	B/L	6-1/190	2-1-76	West Tenn, Iowa
	Quevedo, Ruben	R/R	6-1/230	1-5-79	Richmond, Iowa
41	Rain, Steve	R/R	6-6/260	6-2-75	West Tenn, Chicago N.L., Iowa
36	Tapani, Kevin	R/R	6-1/190	2-18-64	Chicago N.L.
	Valdes, Ismael	R/R	6-3/215	8-21-73	Los Angeles
	Williams, Brian	R/R	6-2/225	2-15-69	Houston
34	Wood, Kerry	R/R	6-5/230	6-16-77	DID NOT PLAY
	Young, Danny	R/L	6-4/210	11-3-71	West Tenn

No.	CATCHERS	B/T	Ht./Wt.	Born	1999 clubs
22	Cline, Pat	R/R	6-4/230	10-9-74	Iowa
	Girardi, Joe	R/R	5-11/200	10-14-64	New York A.L.
19	Molina, Jose	R/R	6-1/215	6-3-75	West Tenn, Iowa, Chicago N.L.
16	Reed, Jeff	L/R	6-2/200	11-12-62	Colorado, Chicago N.L.

No.	INFIELDERS	B/T	Ht./Wt.	Born	1999 clubs
7	Andrews, Shane	R/R	6-1/210	8-28-71	Montreal, Ottawa, Chicago N.L.
17	Grace, Mark	L/L	6-2/200	6-28-64	Chicago N.L.
	Gutierrez, Ricky	R/R	6-1/175	5-23-70	Houston, Jackson, New Orleans
18	Liniak, Cole	R/R	6-1/190	8-23-76	Pawtucket, Chicago N.L.
20	Meyers, Chad	R/R	6-0/190	8-8-75	West Tenn, Iowa, Chicago N.L.
11	Nieves, Jose	R/R	6-1/180	6-16-75	Iowa, Chicago N.L.
	Young, Eric	R/R	5-8/175	5-18-67	Los Angeles, San Bernardino
	Zuleta, Julio	R/R	6-6/230	3-28-75	West Tenn

No.	OUTFIELDERS	B/T	Ht./Wt.	Born	1999 clubs
28	Brown, Roosevelt	L/R	5-11/195	8-3-75	West Tenn, Chicago N.L., Iowa
	Buford, Damon	R/R	5-10/180	6-12-70	Boston
8	Hill, Glenallen	R/R	6-3/230	3-22-65	Chicago N.L.
40	Rodriguez, Henry	L/L	6-2/225	11-8-67	Chicago N.L.
21	Sosa, Sammy	R/R	6-0/220	11-12-68	Chicago N.L.

BALLPARK INFORMATION

Ballpark (capacity, surface)
Wrigley Field (39,056, grass)

Address
1060 W. Addison St.
Chicago, IL 60613-4397

Business phone
773-404-2827

Ticket information
773-404-2827

Ticket prices
$25 (club box, field box)
$20 (terrace box, upper deck box, family section)
$16 (terrace reserved)
$15 (bleachers)
$10 (adult upper deck reserved)
$6 (under 14 upper deck reserved)

Field dimensions (from home plate)
To left field at foul line, 355 feet
To center field, 400 feet
To right field at foul line, 353 feet

First game played
April 20, 1916 (Cubs 7, Reds 6)

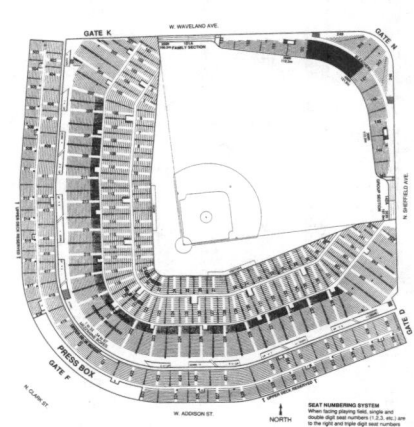

2000 SEASON *Chicago Cubs*

Date	Opp.	Res.	Score	(inn.*)	Hits	Opp. hits	Winning pitcher	Losing pitcher	Save	Record	Pos.	GB
4-7	At Hou.	W	9-2		12	5	Tapani	Hampton		1-1	T1st	...
4-8	At Hou.	W	2-1		6	6	Lieber	Lima	Beck	2-1	T1st	...
4-9	At Pit.	L	1-2		4	2	Benson	Sanders	Williams	2-2	T1st	...
4-10	At Pit.	L	3-9		5	9	Sauerbeck	Woodall		2-3	T3rd	1.0
4-11	At Pit.	L	6-9		13	12	Schmidt	Trachsel		2-4	T4th	2.0
4-12	Cin.	L	2-7		6	13	Avery	Tapani		2-5	6th	2.5
4-14	Cin.	W	5-4		6	9	Lieber	Harnisch	Beck	3-5	T4th	2.0
4-16	At Mil.	W	9-4		13	8	Heredia	Pulsipher		4-5	T3rd	2.0
4-17	At Mil.	L	4-5		9	8	Myers	Beck		4-6	T5th	3.0
4-18	At Mil.	W	6-5	(10)	13	11	Beck	de los Santos	Serafini	5-6	4th	2.0
4-20	Hou.	L	4-10		9	16	Lima	Lieber	Elarton	5-7	4th	3.5
4-21	Hou.	L	3-10		10	13	Reynolds	Sanders		5-8	T5th	3.5
4-23	N.Y.	L	5-6		8	13	Cook	Beck	Franco	5-9	6th	4.5
4-24	N.Y.	W	2-0		5	8	Mulholland	Watson	Beck	6-9	5th	3.5
4-25	N.Y.	W	8-4		8	11	Myers	Hershiser		7-9	5th	3.5
4-27	At Fla.	L	0-8		6	14	Edmondson	Sanders		7-10	5th	4.5
4-28	At Fla.	W	6-1		16	3	Trachsel	Hernandez		8-10	5th	3.5
4-29	At Fla.	W	5-2		12	10	Farnsworth	Sanchez	Beck	9-10	3rd	2.5
4-30	S.D.	W	6-5		9	10	Mulholland	Spencer	Beck	10-10	3rd	2.0
5-1	S.D.	W	2-1		7	3	Tapani	Clement	Heredia	11-10	3rd	2.0
5-2	S.D.	W	3-2		12	6	Myers	Rivera	Beck	12-10	3rd	2.0
5-3	Col.	L	1-6		6	12	Bohanon	Trachsel		12-11	3rd	2.0
5-4	Col.	W	13-12		14	17	Beck	Dipoto		13-11	3rd	2.0
5-5	Col.	L	6-13		10	18	Astacio	Mulholland		13-12	3rd	3.0
5-7	At Cin.	L	2-3		6	13	Graves	Beck		13-13	T3rd	4.0
5-8	At Cin.	W	7-4		11	11	Lieber	Neagle	Beck	14-13	3rd	3.0
5-9	At Cin.	L	5-8		7	13	Williamson	Adams	Graves	14-14	4th	3.0
5-10	At L.A.	L	3-4		12	7	Valdes	Trachsel	Shaw	14-15	4th	4.0
5-11	At L.A.	W	10-5		11	9	Farnsworth	Perez		15-15	T3rd	4.0
5-12	At L.A.	L	2-3		5	8	Arnold	Beck		15-16	4th	5.0
5-14	Atl.	W	9-0		10	7	Lieber	Glavine		16-16	T2nd	5.0
5-15	Atl.	W	5-1		15	6	Trachsel	Maddux		17-16	2nd	5.0
5-16	Atl.	L	5-8		8	11	McGlinchy	Myers	Rocker	17-17	4th	5.0
5-17	At Fla.	W	8-1		12	4	Tapani	Dempster		18-17	3rd	4.5
5-18	At Fla.	W	4-1	(11)	10	3	Heredia	Springer	Sanders	19-17	3rd	4.5
5-19	At Fla.	W	8-7		12	11	Myers	Mantei	Adams	20-17	2nd	3.5
5-20	At Atl.	W	6-5	(12)	10	10	Serafini	McGlinchy		21-17	2nd	3.5
5-21	At Atl.	W	8-4		9	8	Adams	McGlinchy		22-17	2nd	2.5
5-22	At Atl.	L	2-4		7	7	Millwood	Tapani	Rocker	22-18	2nd	2.5
5-23	At Atl.	W	5-1		6	5	Mulholland	Perez		23-18	2nd	2.5
5-24	Fla.	L	5-7		9	12	Mantei	Aguilera		23-19	T2nd	3.5
5-25	Fla.	L	3-6		8	8	Meadows	Trachsel		23-20	T3rd	4.5
5-26	Fla.	W	6-4		11	7	Aguilera	Looper		24-20	2nd	4.5
5-28	StL.	W	6-3		14	7	Tapani	Painter	Aguilera	25-20	2nd	3.0
5-29	StL.	W	4-3		8	9	Heredia	Bottalico		26-20	2nd	2.0
5-30	StL.	W	7-4		12	10	Lieber	Jimenez		27-20	2nd	1.0
6-1	S.D.	L	0-1	(6)	3	4	Ashby	Trachsel		27-21	2nd	2.0
6-2	S.D.	W	9-8		14	11	Sanders	Hoffman		28-21	2nd	2.0
6-3	S.D.	W	7-2		7	10	Tapani	Clement		29-21	2nd	1.0
6-4	At Cle.	W	5-4		8	8	Aguilera	Jackson	Adams	30-21	2nd	1.0
6-5	At Cle.	L	7-8	(11)	11	16	Jackson	Sanders		30-22	2nd	2.0
6-6	At Cle.	L	2-4		8	8	Nagy	Trachsel	Shuey	30-23	3rd	2.0
6-7	At Ari.	W	7-6		13	12	Adams	Holmes		31-23	2nd	2.0
6-8	At Ari.	W	5-3		5	6	Aguilera	Olson	Adams	32-23	2nd	1.0
6-9	At Ari.	L	7-8		12	18	Johnson	Mulholland	Nunez	32-24	2nd	2.0
6-11	Chi. (AL)	L	3-5	(6)	5	11	Parque	Lieber		32-25	2nd	3.0
6-12	Chi. (AL)	L	2-8		8	18	Sirotka	Trachsel		32-26	2nd	4.0
6-13	Chi. (AL)	L	4-6		7	12	Simas	Aguilera	Foulke	32-27	2nd	4.5
6-14	At Mil.	L	1-5		9	11	Woodard	Farnsworth		32-28	3rd	5.5
6-15	At Mil.	W	7-4		9	10	Lieber	Abbott	Adams	33-28	2nd	4.5
6-16	At Mil.	L	4-11		6	12	Nomo	Trachsel		33-29	2nd	4.5
6-17	At S.F	L	2-3		4	10	Nen	Serafini		33-30	4th	4.5
6-18	At S.F	L	5-8		8	10	Ortiz	Tapani	Nen	33-31	4th	5.5
6-19	At S.F	L	5-11		6	9	Estes	Farnsworth		33-32	4th	6.5
6-20	At S.F	L	6-7		11	9	Embree	Aguilera		33-33	4th	7.5
6-22	At Col.	W	13-12		14	15	Sanders	DeJean	Aguilera	34-33	3rd	6.0
6-23	At Col.	L	1-10		7	19	Astacio	Mulholland		34-34	4th	7.0
6-24	At Col.	W	12-10		15	18	Tapani	Jones		35-34	3rd	6.0
6-25	Phi.	L	2-3		3	6	Ogea	Lieber	Gomes	35-35	4th	6.0
6-26	Phi.	L	2-6		8	11	Person	Trachsel		35-36	5th	6.0
6-27	Phi.	W	13-7		15	11	Mulholland	Grace		36-36	4th	5.0
6-29	Mil.	L	6-17		9	21	Woodard	Tapani		36-37	4th	6.0
6-30	Mil.	W	5-4		7	10	Karchner	Weathers	Aguilera	37-37	4th	6.0

Date	Opp.	Res.	Score	(inn.*)	Hits	Opp. hits	Winning pitcher	Losing pitcher	Save	Record	Pos.	GB
7-1	Mil.	L	12-19		11	21	Myers	Trachsel		37-38	4th	7.0
7-2	At Phi.	L	1-14		6	17	Wolf	Mulholland		37-39	4th	7.0
7-3	At Phi.	L	8-21		11	21	Byrd	Farnsworth		37-40	6th	8.0
7-4	At Phi.	L	2-6		7	12	Schilling	Tapani		37-41	6th	8.0
7-5	At Pit.	W	5-2		9	11	Lieber	Schmidt	Aguilera	38-41	6th	8.0
7-6	At Pit.	L	1-6		9	8	Ritchie	Trachsel		38-42	6th	8.0
7-7	At Pit.	L	1-4		5	8	Cordova	Mulholland		38-43	6th	8.0
7-8	At Pit.	W	9-4		11	5	Serafini	Benson	Sanders	39-43	6th	8.0
7-9	At Chi. (AL)	L	2-3		9	9	Howry	Adams		39-44	6th	9.0
7-10	At Chi. (AL)	W	10-2		12	8	Lieber	Navarro		40-44	6th	8.0
7-11	At Chi. (AL)	W	6-3		7	6	Trachsel	Baldwin	Adams	41-44	6th	8.0
7-15	Min.	W	9-3		17	9	Sanders	Radke	Adams	42-44	T4th	8.0
7-16	Min.	W	11-10		16	15	Adams	Trombley		43-44	T3rd	8.0
7-17	Min.	L	0-8		3	14	Mays	Mulholland		43-45	6th	9.0
7-18	K.C.	L	4-5		11	8	Suppan	Tapani	Service	43-46	6th	10.0
7-19	K.C.	L	2-10		6	13	Witasick	Trachsel		43-47	6th	11.0
7-20	K.C.	W	8-7		15	14	Sanders	Barber	Adams	44-47	6th	10.0
7-21	Pit.	W	2-1		9	6	Aguilera	Christiansen		45-47	T4th	9.0
7-22	Pit.	W	5-3		10	8	Mulholland	Benson	Adams	46-47	4th	8.0
7-23	At N.Y.	L	4-5		7	9	Cook	Tapani	Benitez	46-48	5th	9.5
7-24	At N.Y.	L	1-2		6	5	Dotel	Trachsel	Benitez	46-49	T5th	10.5
7-25	At N.Y.	L	1-5		8	5	Leiter	Serafini		46-50	6th	11.5
7-26	At Mon.	L	1-6		9	9	Smith	Lieber		46-51	6th	12.5
7-27	At Mon.	W	4-2		8	10	Mulholland	Hermanson	Adams	47-51	5th	13.0
7-28	At Mon.	L	2-8		3	10	Vazquez	Tapani		47-52	6th	13.5
7-30	N.Y.	L	9-10		13	14	Mahomes	Farnsworth	Benitez	47-53	6th	14.0
7-31	N.Y.	W	17-10		14	18	Serafini	Isringhausen		48-53	6th	14.0
8-1	N.Y.	L	4-5	(13)	10	10	Mahomes	Sanders		48-54	6th	14.0
8-2	Mon.	L	1-5		6	7	Hermanson	Tapani	Urbina	48-55	6th	14.5
8-3	Mon.	L	4-9		12	13	Vazquez	Bowie		48-56	6th	15.5
8-4	Mon.	W	5-1		7	5	Trachsel	Powell		49-56	5th	14.5
8-5	Mon.	L	2-5		10	10	Thurman	Lieber	Urbina	49-57	T5th	15.5
8-6†	Hou.	L	1-6		8	10	Lima	Farnsworth	Powell	49-58		
8-6‡	Hou.	W	6-0		9	3	Lorraine	Bergman		50-58	5th	15.5
8-7	Hou.	L	4-10		5	14	Elarton	Tapani		50-59	6th	16.5
8-8	Hou.	L	2-6		7	14	Hampton	Bowie		50-60	6th	17.5
8-9	Ari.	L	7-10		8	15	Daal	Sanders		50-61	6th	17.5
8-10	Ari.	L	1-3		9	5	Swindell	Lieber	Olson	50-62	6th	17.5
8-11	Ari.	L	5-7	(11)	9	15	Plesac	Rain	Olson	50-63	6th	17.5
8-13	At StL.	L	1-7		8	7	Bottenfield	Farnsworth		50-64	6th	17.5
8-14	At StL.	W	9-7		10	10	Adams	Slocumb		51-64	6th	17.5
8-15	At StL.	L	5-6		9	13	Bottalico	Adams		51-65	6th	17.5
8-16	At Ari.	L	3-10		7	14	Johnson	Lieber		51-66	6th	18.5
8-17	At Ari.	L	0-4		3	7	Anderson	Lorraine		51-67	6th	19.5
8-18	At Ari.	L	1-3		5	10	Benes	Tapani	Mantei	51-68	6th	20.5
8-20	Col.	L	3-11		7	14	Astacio	Farnsworth		51-69	6th	21.0
8-21	Col.	W	8-6		10	12	Bowie	Thomson	Adams	52-69	6th	21.0
8-22	Col.	L	2-3		6	5	Wright	Trachsel	Veres	52-70	6th	21.5
8-24	S.F	L	4-12		9	18	Estes	Lorraine		52-71	6th	22.0
8-25†	S.F	L	5-11		7	14	Ortiz	Tapani		52-72		
8-25‡	S.F	L	5-6		10	9	Rueter	Lieber	Nen	52-73	6th	22.5
8-26	S.F	W	11-10		16	11	Adams	Nen		53-73	6th	22.0
8-27	At L.A.	L	0-9		7	13	Valdes	Trachsel		53-74	6th	22.5
8-28	At L.A.	L	3-4		8	7	Park	Lorraine	Shaw	53-75	6th	22.5
8-29	At L.A.	W	6-0		9	2	Farnsworth	Dreifort		54-75	6th	22.5
8-30	At S.D.	L	4-8		11	10	Wall	Heredia		54-76	6th	22.5
8-31	At S.D.	L	3-7		5	9	Ashby	Bowie		54-77	6th	23.5
9-1	At S.D.	W	1-0		2	4	Trachsel	Hitchcock	Adams	55-77	6th	22.5
9-3	L.A.	L	6-8		12	9	Park	Sanders	Shaw	55-78	6th	23.5
9-4	L.A.	L	0-6		2	11	Brown	Farnsworth		55-79	6th	24.5
9-5	L.A.	L	1-4		7	6	Dreifort	Lieber	Shaw	55-80	6th	25.5
9-6	Cin.	L	3-6		7	7	Guzman	Bowie	Graves	55-81	6th	26.5
9-7†	Cin.	W	2-1		5	4	Trachsel	Villone	Adams	56-81		
9-7‡	Cin.	L	3-10		10	16	Tomko	McNichol		56-82	6th	27.0
9-8	Cin.	L	4-6		9	9	Parris	Lorraine	Graves	56-83	6th	28.0
9-9	Cin.	L	3-5		9	14	Sullivan	Farnsworth	Graves	56-84	6th	29.0
9-10	At Hou.	L	4-6	(13)	9	12	Wagner	Ayala		56-85	6th	30.0
9-11	At Hou.	L	3-5		7	7	Lima	Bowie	Wagner	56-86	6th	31.0
9-12	At Hou.	L	1-7		6	12	Holt	Trachsel		56-87	6th	32.0
9-14	At Cin.	W	4-3		6	9	Farnsworth	Harnisch	Adams	57-87	6th	32.5
9-15	At Cin.	L	4-5		12	10	Neagle	Lieber	Graves	57-88	6th	32.5
9-16	At Cin.	W	7-6		9	8	Adams	Graves	Aguilera	58-88	6th	32.0
9-17	Mil.	W	6-5	(10)	7	11	Aguilera	Peterson		59-88	6th	31.0
9-18	Mil.	L	4-7	(14)	10	9	Peterson	Guthrie		59-89	6th	31.0
9-19	Mil.	W	8-7	(10)	12	10	Aguilera	Ramirez		60-89	6th	31.0
9-20	StL.	L	2-7		8	9	Thompson	Lieber		60-90	6th	31.0

Date	Opp.	Res.	Score	(inn.*)	Hits	Opp. hits	Winning pitcher	Losing pitcher	Save	Record	Pos.	GB
9-21	StL.	L	2-7		3	8	Bottenfield	Lorraine		60-91	6th	32.0
9-22	StL.	W	5-3		8	7	Trachsel	Stephenson	Aguilera	61-91	6th	31.0
9-23	Pit.	W	8-5		13	7	Bowie	Peters	Aguilera	62-91	6th	30.5
9-24	Pit.	W	9-0		14	5	Farnsworth	Schmidt		63-91	6th	30.5
9-25	Pit.	W	3-1		5	3	Lieber	Cordova		64-91	6th	29.5
9-26	Pit.	L	4-8	(11)	8	15	Sauerbeck	Guthrie		64-92	6th	29.5
9-28	At Phi.	W	8-2		10	9	Trachsel	Wolf		65-92	6th	29.5
9-29	At Phi.	L	0-5		4	12	Brewer	Bowie		65-93	6th	29.5
9-30	At Phi.	L	1-2		3	7	Person	McNichol	Montgomery	65-94	6th	30.0
10-1	At StL.	W	3-2		7	7	Lieber	Thompson		66-94	6th	29.0
10-2	At StL.	W	6-3		10	6	Lorraine	Stephenson	Aguilera	67-94	6th	29.0
10-3	At StL.	L	5-9	(5)	6	10	Luebbers	Trachsel	Ankiel	67-95	6th	30.0

Monthly records: April (10-10), May (17-10), June (10-17), July (11-16), August (6-24), September (11-17), October (2-1).
*Innings, if other than nine. † First game of a doubleheader. ‡ Second game of a doubleheader.

HIGHLIGHTS

High point: The Cubs finished a 9-3 run on June 8 when they won at Arizona. The victory gave Chicago a 32-23 record and put the Cubs one game out of first place in the N.L. Central. At that point, Chicago's starting pitching was among the league's best.

Low point: The Cubs tumbled 30 games below .500 at 56-86 when they lost at Houston on September 11. It took a monumental collapse—63 defeats in 87 games—to sink to that level.

Turning point: Four days in June. First, down 8-1 to the Diamondbacks' Randy Johnson, the Cubs closed within 8-7 before Lance Johnson was picked off first base to end the June 9 game. Then the club came home and was swept in three games by the White Sox, effectively torpedoing the Cubs' season.

Most valuable player: In an otherwise dismal season, right fielder Sammy Sosa was a shining light with 63 home runs and 141 RBIs. Though he finished second to the Cardinals' Mark McGwire in the homer race, Sosa became the first man to hit 60 homers in consecutive seasons when he connected off Milwaukee's Jason Bere on September 18.

Most valuable pitcher: Righthander Jon Lieber was the only Cubs pitcher to win 10 games. Lieber started the season 8-3 but didn't capture his ninth victory until September 25 (a drought of 2.5 months). He established career highs in strikeouts (186) and innings pitched (203.1) and ranked among the N.L.'s top 10 in strikeouts, strikeouts per nine innings and fewest walks per nine innings.

Most improved player: Kyle Farnsworth came up in late April and won his first two decisions before suffering through massive growing pains (he twice was sent back to Class AAA Iowa). But the righthander finished up well, winning three of his last five decisions.

Most pleasant surprise: Veteran left fielder Glenallen Hill hit an even .300 with 20 home runs and 55 RBIs as a part-timer. Plus, he was a positive force in the clubhouse amid the losing.

Biggest disappointment: Second baseman Mickey Morandini saw his batting average fall from a career-best .296 in 1998 to .241. He committed only five

errors in 1999, the same as in '98, but the club thought his range diminished markedly.

Key injuries: Kerry Wood, the 1998 rookie sensation, missed the entire season because of major surgery after blowing out his right elbow in spring training. Righthander Jeremi Gonzalez suffered a setback in his recovery from '98 elbow surgery and, like Wood, underwent "Tommy John surgery." He hasn't pitched for the Cubs since July 1998. Pitchers Lieber, Farnsworth, Kevin Tapani, Terry Adams and Rick Aguilera spent time on the disabled list, as did center fielder Johnson. Overall, the Cubs placed 13 players on the D.L. in '99.

Notable: After winning the wild card in '98, the Cubs hoped to post their first back-to-back winning seasons since 1971-1972—but failed miserably. ... The team ERA of 5.27 was the worst in club history, as were the number of homers allowed (221) and runs given up (920). ... Mark Grace led the majors in hits (1,754) and doubles (364) in the 1990s. Third baseman Gary Gaetti became the 40th player in big-league history to play in 2,500 games.

—BRUCE MILES

RECORDS

1999 regular-season record: 67-95 (6th in N.L. Central); 34-47 at home; 33-48 on road; 18-23 vs. East; 28-34 vs. N.L. Central; 15-29 vs. West; 6-9 vs. A.L.; 5-22 vs. lefthanded starters; 42-73 vs. righthanded starters; 58-76 on grass; 9-19 on turf; 41-49 in daytime; 26-46 at night; 26-24 in one-run games; 5-6 in extra-inning games; 0-1-2 in doubleheaders.
Team record past five years: 374-419 (.472, ranks 10th in league in that span).

TEAM LEADERS

Batting average: Mark Grace (.309).
At-bats: Sammy Sosa (625).
Runs: Sammy Sosa (114).
Hits: Mark Grace (183).
Total Bases: Sammy Sosa (397).
Doubles: Mark Grace (44).
Triples: Lance Johnson (6).
Home runs: Sammy Sosa (63).

Runs batted in: Sammy Sosa (141).
Stolen bases: Lance Johnson (13).
Slugging percentage: Sammy Sosa (.635).
On-base percentage: Mark Grace (.390).
Wins: Jon Lieber (10).
Earned-run average: Jon Lieber (4.07).
Complete games: Steve Trachsel (4).
Shutouts: Kyle Farnsworth, Jon Lieber, Andrew Lorraine (1).
Saves: Terry Adams (13).
Innings pitched: Steve Trachsel (205.2).
Strikeouts: Jon Lieber (186).

GAMES BY POSITION

Catcher: Benito Santiago 107, Jeff Reed 49, Tyler Houston 18, Sandy Martinez 12, Jose Molina 10.
First base: Mark Grace 160, Gary Gaetti 8, Tyler Houston 2, Benito Santiago 1, Jose Hernandez 1, Shane Andrews 1.
Second base: Mickey Morandini 132, Chad Meyers 32, Jeff Blauser 25, Manny Alexander 17.
Third base: Gary Gaetti 81, Tyler Houston 63, Manny Alexander 22, Shane Andrews 19, Jeff Blauser 18, Cole Liniak 10, Jeff Reed 1.
Shortstop: Jose Hernandez 92, Jose Nieves 52, Manny Alexander 30, Jeff Blauser 22, Gary Gaetti 1.
Outfield: Sammy Sosa 162, Henry Rodriguez 122, Lance Johnson 91, Curtis Goodwin 76, Glenallen Hill 62, Bo Porter 21, Jose Hernandez 20, Roosevelt Brown 18, Chad Meyers 14, Manny Alexander 2, Jeff Blauser 1, Tyler Houston 1.
Designated hitter: Glenallen Hill 4, Henry Rodriguez 2.

TOP DRAFT CHOICES

1. **Ben Christensen,** RHP, Wichita St. U.
2. **Michael Mallory,** OF, Dinwiddie County H.S., Dinwiddie, Va.
3. **Ryan Gripp,** 3B, Creighton University
4. **Steve Smyth,** LHP, U. of Southern California
5. **Todd Deininger,** RHP, Joliet Township (Ill.) H.S.
6. **Ben Shaffar,** RHP, U. of Kentucky
7. **Mike Dzurilla,** 2B, St. John's Univ.
8. **Dustin Pate,** RHP, Daniel H.S., Clemson, S.C.
9. **Chris Curry,** C, Mississippi State Univ.
10. **Jim Deschaine,** SS, Brandeis (Mass.) University

CINCINNATI REDS
NATIONAL LEAGUE CENTRAL DIVISION

2000 Reds Schedule

Home games shaded. *—All-Star Game at Turner Field (Atlanta).

March

SUN	MON	TUE	WED	THU	FRI	SAT
26	27	28	29	30	31	

April

SUN	MON	TUE	WED	THU	FRI	SAT
						1
2	3 MIL	4	5 MIL	6	7 CUB	8 CUB
9 CUB	10 COL	11 COL	12 COL	13	14 LA	15 LA
16 LA	17	18 SF	19 SF	20 SF	21 LA	22 LA
23 LA	24	25 NYM	26 NYM	27 NYM	28 PIT	29 PIT
30 PIT						

May

SUN	MON	TUE	WED	THU	FRI	SAT
	1 PIT	2 PHI	3 PHI	4 PHI	5 STL	6 STL
7 STL	8	9 SD	10 SD	11 SD	12 HOU	13 HOU
14 HOU	15 HOU	16 PIT	17 PIT	18 PIT	19 CUB	20 CUB
21 CUB	22 LA	23 LA	24 LA	25	26 FLA	27 FLA
28 FLA	29	30 MON	31 MON			

June

SUN	MON	TUE	WED	THU	FRI	SAT
				1 MON	2 MIN	3 MIN
4 MIN	5 CWS	6 CWS	7 CWS	8	9 CLE	10 CLE
11 CLE	12 SF	13 SF	14 SF	15	16 SD	17 SD
18 SD	19	20 COL	21 COL	22 COL	23 SD	24 SD
25 SD	26 STL	27 STL	28 STL	29 STL	30 ARI	

July

SUN	MON	TUE	WED	THU	FRI	SAT
						1 ARI
2 ARI	3 ARI	4 STL	5 STL	6 STL	7 CLE	8 CLE
9 CLE	10	11	12 *	13 COL	14 COL	15 COL
16 DET	17 DET	18 DET	19 HOU	20 HOU	21 ARI	22 ARI
23 ARI	24 HOU	25 HOU	26 HOU	27	28 MON	29 MON
30 MON	31 NYM					

August

SUN	MON	TUE	WED	THU	FRI	SAT
		1 NYM	2 NYM	3	4 FLA	5 FLA
6 FLA	7 ATL	8 ATL	9 ATL	10	11 CUB	12 CUB
13 CUB	14 MIL	15 MIL	16 MIL	17	18 PHI	19 PHI
20 PIT	21 PHI	22 PHI	23 PHI	24	25 FLA	26 FLA
27 FLA	28 ATL	29 ATL	30 ATL	31 ATL		

September

SUN	MON	TUE	WED	THU	FRI	SAT
					1 MON	2 MON
3 MON	4 NYM	5 NYM	6 NYM	7	8 PIT	9 PIT
10 PIT	11 CUB	12 CUB	13 CUB	14 MIL	15 MIL	16 MIL
17 MIL	18 SF	19 SF	20 SF	21	22 HOU	23 HOU
24 HOU	25	26 MIL	27 MIL	28 MIL	29 STL	30 STL

October

SUN	MON	TUE	WED	THU	FRI	SAT
1 STL	2	3	4	5	6	7

2000 SEASON
CLUB DIRECTORY

Chief executive officer
Carl H. Lindner
Chief operating officer
John Allen
General manager
James G. Bowden IV
Assistant general manager
Darrell "Doc" Rodgers
Sr. dir. of player development/scouting
Leland Maddox
Special asst. to the g.m./advance scout
Gene Bennett
Special assistants to the g.m.
Bob Boone, Larry Barton Jr., Johnny Bench, Al Goldis
Director of baseball administration
Brad Kullman
Major league scout/nat. cross-checker
Kasey McKeon
Executive assistant to the g.m.
Lois Schneider
Senior advisor, player development
Chief Bender
Admin. assistant, player development
Lois Hudson
Director of scouting
De Jon Watson
Senior advisor, scouting
Bob Zuk
Director of scouting administration
Wilma Mann
Traveling secretary
Gary Wahoff
Director of media relations
Rob Butcher
Public relations assistant
Larry Herms
Controller
Anthony Ward
Director, stadium operations
Jody Pettyjohn
Director, ticket department
John O'Brien
Director of season/group sales
Pat McCaffrey
Director of communications
Mike Ringering
Assistant director of communications
Ralph Mitchell

Director of new stadium development
Jenny Gardner
Marketing consultant
Cal Levy
Legal counsel
Robert C. Martin
Director, group sales
Brad Blettner
Assistant director, media relations
Michael Vassallo
Exec. assistant to chief operating officer
Joyce Pfarr
Business and broadcast administrator
Ginny Kamp
Head trainer
Greg Lynn
Assistant trainer
Mark Mann
Conditioning coordinator
Lance Sewell
Field superintendent
Jeff Guilkey
Sr. clubhouse & equipment manager
Bernie Stowe
Reds clubhouse & equipment manager
Rick Stowe
Visiting clubhouse & equip. manager
Mark Stowe
Director of international scouting
Jorge Oquendo
Cross-checkers
Johnny Almaraz, Alvin Rittman, Ross Sapp, Bill Scherrer
Scouting supervisors
Terry Abbott, Butch Baccala, Howard Bowens, John Brickley, Mark Corey, Robert Filotei, Jerry Flowers, Jimmy Gonzales, David Jennings, Robert Koontz, Craig Kornfeld, Steve Kring, Brian Mejia, Cotton Nye, Tom Severtson, Perry Smith, Brian Wilson, Greg Zunino
Scouts
Amador Arias, John Bellino, Fred Blair, Kevin Carcamo, Felix Delgado, Jim Grief, Don Gust, Frank Henderson, Don Hill, Thomas Herrera, Juan Linares, Anthony Lowe, Victor Mateo, Denny Nagel, Rafael Nava, Everett Renteria, Glenn Serviente, Marlon Styles, Lee Toole, Ruben Vargas

MINOR LEAGUE AFFILIATES

Class	Team	League	Manager
AAA	Louisville	International	Dave Miley
AA	Chattanooga	Southern	Michael Rojas
A	Clinton	Midwest	Jay Sorg
A	Dayton	Midwest	Freddie Benavides
Rookie	Billings	Pioneer	Russ Nixon
Rookie	Gulf Coast Reds	Gulf Coast	Luis Quinones

BROADCAST INFORMATION

Radio: WLW-AM (700).
Cable TV: Fox Sports Net.

SPRING TRAINING

Ballpark (city): Ed Smith Stadium (Sarasota, Fla.).
Ticket information: 941-954-4101.

SPRING TRAINING ROSTER

Manager—Jack McKeon (31).
Coaches—Dave Collins (22), Harry Dunlop (2), Ken Griffey Sr. (30), Don Gullett (35), Tom Hume (47), Denis Menke (19), Ron Oester (16), Mark Berry (55).

No.	PITCHERS	B/T	Ht./Wt.	Born	1999 clubs
50	Bell, Rob	R/R	6-5/226	1-17-77	Chattanooga, Gulf Coast Reds
60	Burnside, Adrian	R/L	6-3/168	3-15-77	San Bernardino
72	Flury, Patrick	R/R	6-1/220	3-14-73	Chattanooga, Indianapolis
59	Gaillard, Eddie	R/R	6-2/195	8-13-70	Durham, Tampa Bay
32	Graves, Danny	R/R	5-11/185	8-7-73	Cincinnati
38	Harnisch, Pete	R/R	6-0/228	9-23-66	Cincinnati
63	Dessens, Elmer	R/R	6-0/187	1-13-72	Yomiuri Giants
67	Murray, Heath	L/L	6-4/215	4-19-73	Las Vegas, San Diego
15	Neagle, Denny	L/L	6-3/225	9-13-68	Indianapolis, Cincinnati
58	Parris, Steve	R/R	6-0/195	12-17-67	Indianapolis, Cincinnati
49	Reyes, Dennys	L/L	6-3/246	4-19-77	Cincinnati
46	Riedling, John	R/R	5-11/190	8-29-75	Chattanooga, Indianapolis
56	Sullivan, Scott	R/R	6-3/210	3-13-71	Cincinnati
40	Tomko, Brett	R/R	6-4/216	4-7-73	Cincinnati, Indianapolis
41	Villone, Ron	L/L	6-3/237	1-16-70	Indianapolis, Cincinnati
36	White, Gabe	L/L	6-2/200	11-20-71	Cincinnati
48	Williamson, Scott	R/R	6-0/185	2-17-76	Cincinnati
51	Winchester, Scott	R/R	6-2/210	4-20-73	Rockford

No.	CATCHERS	B/T	Ht./Wt.	Born	1999 clubs
26	LaRue, Jason	R/R	5-11/200	3-19-74	Indianapolis, Cincinnati
10	Taubensee, Eddie	L/R	6-3/230	10-31-68	Cincinnati

No.	INFIELDERS	B/T	Ht./Wt.	Born	1999 clubs
17	Boone, Aaron	R/R	6-2/200	3-9-73	Cincinnati, Indianapolis
21	Casey, Sean	L/R	6-4/226	7-2-74	Cincinnati
69	Cromer, D.T.	L/L	6-2/190	3-19-71	Indianapolis
6	Dawkins, Travis	R/R	6-1/180	5-12-79	Rockford, Chattanooga, Cincinnati
11	Larkin, Barry	R/R	6-0/185	4-28-64	Cincinnati
75	Larson, Brandon	R/R	6-0/210	5-24-76	Rockford, Chattanooga
28	Lewis, Mark	R/R	6-1/195	11-30-69	Cincinnati
23	Morris, Hal	L/L	6-2/195	4-9-65	Cincinnati
3	Reese, Pokey	R/R	5-11/180	6-10-73	Cincinnati
23	Stynes, Chris	R/R	5-10/185	1-19-73	Cincinnati
68	Wright, Ron	R/R	6-1/230	1-21-76	Altoona

No.	OUTFIELDERS	B/T	Ht./Wt.	Born	1999 clubs
46	Bartee, Kimera	R/R	6-0/200	7-21-72	Toledo, Detroit
9	Bichette, Dante	R/R	6-3/238	11-18-63	Colorado
44	Cameron, Mike	R/R	6-2/190	1-8-73	Cincinnati
66	Clark, Brady	R/R	6-2/195	4-18-73	Chattanooga
73	Frank, Mike	L/L	6-2/195	1-14-75	Indianapolis
33	Sweeney, Mark	L/L	6-1/195	10-26-69	Cincinnati, Indianapolis
34	Tucker, Michael	L/R	6-2/185	6-25-71	Cincinnati
25	Young, Dmitri	B/R	6-2/235	10-11-73	Cincinnati

BALLPARK INFORMATION

Ballpark (capacity, surface)
Cinergy Field (52,953, artificial)

Address
100 Cinergy Field
Cincinnati, OH 45202

Business phone
513-421-4510

Ticket information
513-421-7337, 1-800-829-5353

Ticket prices
$21, $18 (blue level box seats)
$16, $14 (green level box seats)
$13 (yellow level box seats)
$12 (red level box seats)
$11 (green level reserved seats)
$8 (red level reserved seats)
$5 ("top six" reserved seats)

Field dimensions (from home plate)
To left field at foul line, 330 feet
To center field, 404 feet
To right field at foul line, 330 feet

First game played
June 30, 1970 (Braves 8, Reds 2)

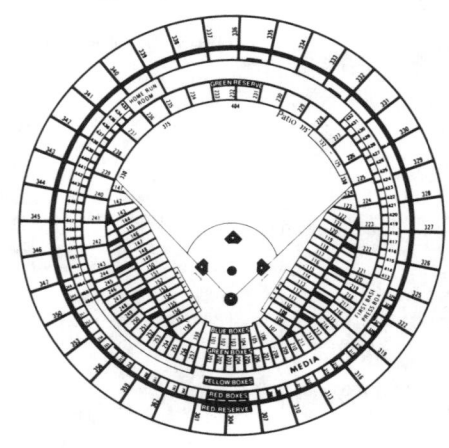

Date	Opp.	Res.	Score	(inn.*)	Hits	Opp. hits	Winning pitcher	Losing pitcher	Save	Record	Pos.	GB
4-6	S.F	L	6-7		11	11	Tavarez	Graves	Nen	0-2	T4th	1.5
4-7	S.F	L	3-8		6	7	Ortiz	Avery		0-3	6th	1.5
4-9	At StL.	W	3-0		5	6	Harnisch	Oliver		1-3	T5th	1.0
4-10	At StL.	L	2-4		7	6	Acevedo	Williamson		1-4	6th	2.0
4-11	At StL.	W	4-2		6	10	Bere	Osborne	Graves	2-4	T4th	2.0
4-12	At Chi.	W	7-2		13	6	Avery	Tapani		3-4	4th	1.5
4-14	At Chi.	L	4-5		9	6	Lieber	Harnisch	Beck	3-5	T4th	2.0
4-16	Pit.	W	6-5		9	9	Graves	Christiansen		4-5	T3rd	2.0
4-17	Pit.	L	6-7	(10)	9	11	Christiansen	White		4-6	T5th	3.0
4-18	Pit.	L	2-4		7	8	Loiselle	Graves	Williams	4-7	6th	3.0
4-20	N.Y.	L	2-3		8	8	Cook	Harnisch	Franco	4-8	6th	4.5
4-21	N.Y.	W	7-4		7	3	Sullivan	Yoshii	Graves	5-8	T5th	3.5
4-22	N.Y.	L	1-4		6	7	Leiter	Tomko	Franco	5-9	6th	4.0
4-23	Hou.	W	7-5		10	11	Sullivan	Holt	Graves	6-9	5th	4.0
4-24	Hou.	L	3-4		5	6	Elarton	Graves	Wagner	6-10	6th	4.0
4-25	Hou.	W	7-6		10	8	Harnisch	Henry	Williamson	7-10	6th	4.0
4-27	At Phi.	L	0-1	(10)	5	7	Brantley	White		7-11	6th	5.0
4-28	At Phi.	W	12-8		13	13	Williamson	Brantley		8-11	6th	4.0
4-29	At Phi.	W	7-3		13	8	Bere	Loewer		9-11	T4th	3.0
4-30	At Atl.	L	0-3		1	6	Smoltz	Avery		9-12	T4th	3.5
5-1	At Atl.	L	1-5		3	10	Millwood	Harnisch		9-13	5th	4.5
5-2	At Atl.	L	3-5		6	8	Perez	Neagle	Rocker	9-14	6th	5.5
5-3	Ari.	W	4-3		9	8	Williamson	Holmes		10-14	6th	4.5
5-4	Ari.	W	6-4		7	9	Reyes	Daal	Graves	11-14	6th	4.5
5-5	Ari.	L	1-5		4	8	Johnson	Avery		11-15	6th	5.5
5-7	Chi.	W	3-2		13	6	Graves	Beck		12-15	6th	5.5
5-8	Chi.	L	4-7		11	11	Lieber	Neagle	Beck	12-16	6th	5.5
5-9	Chi.	W	8-5		13	7	Williamson	Adams	Graves	13-16	6th	4.5
5-11	Mil.	W	9-1		12	4	Avery	Eldred		14-16	5th	5.0
5-12	Mil.	L	7-8		12	15	Karl	Harnisch	Wickman	14-17	6th	6.0
5-14	S.D.	L	3-7		9	8	Ashby	Neagle	Hoffman	14-18	6th	7.0
5-15	S.D.	W	6-2		4	8	Parris	Hitchcock	Williamson	15-18	6th	7.0
5-16	S.D.	W	3-0		6	4	Tomko	Williams	Williamson	16-18	5th	6.0
5-17	At Col.	W	7-2		10	6	Harnisch	Jones		17-18	5th	5.5
5-18	At Col.	W	5-3		10	6	Graves	Leskanic	Williamson	18-18	T4th	5.5
5-19	At Col.	W	24-12		28	15	Parris	Dipoto	Villone	19-18	4th	4.5
5-21	At S.D.	L	4-5		10	10	Williams	Tomko	Hoffman	19-19	4th	5.0
5-22	At S.D.	W	3-0		9	3	Harnisch	Murray		20-19	4th	4.0
5-23	At S.D.	W	6-2		7	2	Avery	Clement	Williamson	21-19	4th	4.0
5-25	L.A.	W	3-2		5	7	Parris	Brown	Graves	22-19	2nd	4.5
5-26	L.A.	L	3-9		7	10	Park	Tomko		22-20	3rd	5.5
5-27	L.A.	L	3-4		7	8	Valdes	Harnisch	Shaw	22-21	4th	5.5
5-28	At Fla.	L	1-8		9	8	Dempster	Avery		22-22	4th	5.5
5-29	At Fla.	W	8-1		17	7	Bere	Fernandez		23-22	3rd	4.5
5-30	At Fla.	W	6-4		12	10	Graves	Edmondson		24-22	3rd	3.5
5-31	At N.Y.	W	5-3		8	6	Villone	Leiter	Williamson	25-22	3rd	3.0
6-1	At N.Y.	W	4-0		10	7	Harnisch	Hershiser		26-22	3rd	3.0
6-2	At N.Y.	W	8-7		11	8	Williamson	Franco	Sullivan	27-22	3rd	3.0
6-5†	At K.C.	W	9-4		13	9	Parris	Rosado		28-22		
6-5‡	At K.C.	W	7-4	(10)	13	7	Williamson	Montgomery		29-22	3rd	2.5
6-6	At K.C.	W	14-3		22	9	Sullivan	Witasick		30-22	2nd	1.5
6-7	At Min.	L	6-8		9	14	Lincoln	Avery	Trombley	30-23	3rd	2.5
6-8	At Min.	L	2-5		5	12	Radke	Villone	Trombley	30-24	3rd	2.5
6-9	At Min.	W	3-1		6	8	Tomko	Milton	Graves	31-24	3rd	2.5
6-11	Cle.	L	6-8		13	7	Shuey	Williamson	Jackson	31-25	3rd	3.5
6-12	Cle.	L	3-4		5	9	Nagy	Harnisch	Jackson	31-26	3rd	4.5
6-13	Cle.	L	3-7		10	9	Burba	Avery	Karsay	31-27	3rd	5.0
6-14	N.Y.	W	8-4		10	5	Williamson	McMichael		32-27	2nd	5.0
6-15	N.Y.	L	3-11		9	12	Reed	Tomko		32-28	3rd	5.0
6-16	N.Y.	L	2-5		8	10	Yoshii	Parris	Franco	32-29	T3rd	5.0
6-17	Mil.	W	2-0		8	4	Harnisch	Karl	Williamson	33-29	2nd	4.0
6-18	Mil.	W	7-1		11	3	Avery	Roque		34-29	2nd	4.0
6-19	Mil.	L	1-10		4	12	Woodard	Villone		34-30	2nd	5.0
6-20	Mil.	L	4-7		9	10	Weathers	Reyes	Wickman	34-31	2nd	6.0
6-21	At Ari.	W	7-4	(10)	15	9	White	Nunez	Graves	35-31	2nd	5.0
6-22	At Ari.	W	8-7		12	13	Reyes	Vosberg	Graves	36-31	2nd	4.0
6-23	At Ari.	W	9-7		17	8	Avery	Benes	Williamson	37-31	2nd	4.0
6-24	At Hou.	W	3-0		5	1	Villone	Hampton	Graves	38-31	2nd	3.0
6-25	At Hou.	W	10-7		12	10	Tomko	Holt	Williamson	39-31	2nd	2.0
6-26	At Hou.	W	8-1		11	2	Parris	Bergman		40-31	2nd	1.0
6-27	At Hou.	W	5-2		12	5	Harnisch	Lima		41-31	1st	...
6-29	Ari.	W	5-4		7	5	Graves	Padilla		42-31	1st	...
6-30	Ari.	W	2-0		7	1	Villone	Johnson	Williamson	43-31	1st	...

Date	Opp.	Res.	Score	(inn.*)	Hits	Opp. hits	Winning pitcher	Losing pitcher	Save	Record	Pos.	GB
7-1	Ari.	W	2-1	(10)	7	7	Williamson	Plesac		44-31	1st	+1.0
7-2	Hou.	L	5-7		11	15	Powell	Belinda	Wagner	44-32	1st	...
7-3	Hou.	W	10-0		13	5	Harnisch	Elarton	Reyes	45-32	1st	+1.0
7-4	Hou.	L	3-5		12	8	Reynolds	Avery	Wagner	45-33	1st	...
7-5	Hou.	W	5-2		11	6	Villone	Holt	Graves	46-33	1st	+1.0
7-6	At StL.	L	5-6		9	10	Bottenfield	Tomko	Bottalico	46-34	1st	...
7-7	At StL.	L	1-2		9	7	Croushore	Williamson		46-35	1st	...
7-8	At StL.	W	8-5		11	10	Harnisch	Mercker	Graves	47-35	1st	+1.0
7-9	At Cle.	W	3-2		5	4	Avery	Burba	Williamson	48-35	1st	+1.0
7-10	At Cle.	L	10-11		10	15	Jackson	Williamson		48-36	1st	...
7-11	At Cle.	W	9-4		14	9	Graves	Shuey		49-36	1st	...
7-15	Col.	W	10-7		12	12	Parris	Kile	Graves	50-36	1st	...
7-16	Col.	L	2-6		4	11	Astacio	Villone	Veres	50-37	2nd	1.0
7-17	Col.	W	3-2		3	8	Williamson	Dipoto		51-37	2nd	1.0
7-18	Det.	L	8-9	(10)	11	9	Brocail	Graves	Jones	51-38	2nd	2.0
7-19	Det.	L	6-7		10	11	Nitkowski	Sullivan	Jones	51-39	2nd	3.0
7-20	Det.	W	5-2		8	7	Parris	Mlicki	Graves	52-39	2nd	2.0
7-21	StL.	W	1-0		3	1	Villone	Jimenez	Williamson	53-39	2nd	1.0
7-22	StL.	L	5-6		8	5	Painter	Graves	Bottalico	53-40	2nd	1.0
7-23	At S.F	L	5-6		9	7	Spradlin	Sullivan	Nen	53-41	2nd	2.5
7-24	At S.F	W	7-6		6	8	Williamson	Nen	Graves	54-41	2nd	2.5
7-25	At S.F	W	2-1	(14)	5	4	Belinda	Nen		55-41	2nd	2.5
7-26	At L.A.	W	5-3	(10)	13	8	Belinda	Shaw		56-41	2nd	2.5
7-27	At L.A.	W	5-3	(10)	15	10	Graves	Mills	Williamson	57-41	2nd	2.5
7-28	At L.A.	L	1-9		7	13	Checo	Reyes	Arnold	57-42	2nd	3.5
7-29	At L.A.	W	7-5		14	9	Harnisch	Dreifort	Williamson	58-42	2nd	2.5
7-30	S.F	W	7-4		10	9	Neagle	Gardner	Williamson	59-42	2nd	2.5
7-31	S.F	L	1-11		8	15	Estes	Villone		59-43	2nd	3.5
8-1	S.F	W	9-1		12	6	Tomko	Ortiz		60-43	2nd	2.5
8-3	Col.	W	2-1		8	6	Williamson	DeJean		61-43	2nd	2.5
8-4	Col.	W	6-3		12	7	Neagle	Kile	Graves	62-43	2nd	1.5
8-5	Col.	L	1-2		4	10	Astacio	Guzman		62-44	2nd	2.5
8-6	At Mil.	W	9-2		15	4	Villone	Woodard	Sullivan	63-44	2nd	2.0
8-7	At Mil.	L	4-6		9	11	Weathers	Graves	Wickman	63-45	2nd	3.0
8-8	At Mil.	W	8-2		11	7	Harnisch	Nomo	Belinda	64-45	2nd	3.0
8-9	At Pit.	W	4-2		7	2	Neagle	Ritchie	Williamson	65-45	2nd	2.0
8-10	At Pit.	W	6-1		13	6	Guzman	Schourek		66-45	2nd	1.0
8-11	At Pit.	L	4-5		9	9	Williams	Williamson		66-46	2nd	1.0
8-13	Phi.	W	5-4		11	13	Williamson	Schrenk		67-46	1st	...
8-14	Phi.	W	4-1		14	4	Harnisch	Ogea	Graves	68-46	1st	...
8-15	Phi.	L	3-9		7	10	Person	Neagle		68-47	1st	...
8-16	Pit.	W	9-2		10	5	Guzman	Schourek		69-47	1st	...
8-17	Pit.	W	7-4	(12)	7	8	Graves	Williams		70-47	1st	...
8-18	Pit.	L	6-12		11	13	Cordova	Tomko		70-48	2nd	1.0
8-19	Pit.	W	1-0		7	1	Harnisch	Benson	Williamson	71-48	1st	...
8-20	Mon.	L	3-5		8	9	Batista	Sullivan	Urbina	71-49	2nd	1.0
8-21	Mon.	W	9-3		11	8	Guzman	Thurman		72-49	2nd	1.0
8-22	Mon.	W	4-3	(11)	12	11	Sullivan	Urbina		73-49	2nd	0.5
8-23	At Atl.	L	2-6		4	6	Millwood	Tomko	Springer	73-50	2nd	0.5
8-24	At Atl.	L	4-6		5	10	Smoltz	Harnisch	Rocker	73-51	2nd	1.5
8-25	At Atl.	L	2-5		8	7	Glavine	Neagle	Rocker	73-52	2nd	1.5
8-26	At Mon.	W	10-4		14	8	Guzman	Thurman	Williamson	74-52	2nd	1.0
8-27	At Mon.	W	4-1		10	4	Villone	Hermanson	Graves	75-52	2nd	0.5
8-28	At Mon.	L	6-8		9	11	Kline	Williamson		75-53	2nd	0.5
8-29	At Mon.	L	6-8		10	8	Mota	Harnisch	Urbina	75-54	2nd	1.5
8-30	Atl.	W	11-3		12	6	Neagle	Glavine		76-54	2nd	0.5
8-31	Atl.	L	2-8		9	11	Maddux	Guzman		76-55	2nd	1.5
9-1	Atl.	L	7-8		13	11	Mulholland	Villone	Rocker	76-56	2nd	1.5
9-3	At Phi.	L	2-10		6	12	Schilling	Parris		76-57	2nd	2.5
9-4	At Phi.	W	22-3		19	11	Harnisch	Byrd	Belinda	77-57	2nd	2.5
9-5	At Phi.	W	9-7		13	7	Neagle	Person	Sullivan	78-57	2nd	2.5
9-6	At Chi.	W	6-3		7	7	Guzman	Bowie	Graves	79-57	2nd	2.5
9-7†	At Chi.	L	1-2		4	5	Trachsel	Villone	Adams	79-57		
9-7‡	At Chi.	W	10-3		16	10	Tomko	McNichol		80-58	2nd	3.0
9-8	At Chi.	W	6-4		9	9	Parris	Lorraine	Graves	81-58	2nd	3.0
9-9	At Chi.	W	5-3		14	9	Sullivan	Farnsworth	Graves	82-58	2nd	3.0
9-10	Fla.	W	4-2		5	7	Neagle	Springer	Graves	83-58	2nd	3.0
9-11	Fla.	W	12-4		9	9	Guzman	Nunez		84-58	2nd	3.0
9-12	Fla.	W	11-5		13	9	Villone	Burnett		85-58	2nd	3.0
9-13	Fla.	W	7-4		8	10	Parris	Sanchez	Graves	86-58	2nd	3.0
9-14	Chi.	L	3-4		9	6	Farnsworth	Harnisch	Adams	86-59	2nd	4.0
9-15	Chi.	W	5-4		10	12	Neagle	Lieber	Graves	87-59	2nd	3.0
9-16	Chi.	L	6-7		8	9	Adams	Graves	Aguilera	87-60	2nd	3.5
9-17	At Pit.	L	1-3		7	4	Ritchie	Villone	Sauerbeck	87-61	2nd	3.5
9-18	At Pit.	W	3-0		7	6	Parris	Peters		88-61	2nd	2.5

Date	Opp.	Res.	Score	(inn.*)	Hits	Opp. hits	Winning pitcher	Losing pitcher	Save	Record	Pos.	GB
9-19	At Pit.	L	5-8		9	8	Schmidt	Harnisch	Clontz	88-62	2nd	3.5
9-20	At S.D.	W	12-1		15	3	Neagle	Carlyle		89-62	2nd	2.5
9-21	At S.D.	L	2-6		7	9	Clement	Williamson		89-63	2nd	3.5
9-22	At S.D.	W	4-3		8	9	Villone	Ashby	Graves	90-63	2nd	2.5
9-24	StL.	W	5-4		10	7	Parris	Croushore	Graves	91-63	2nd	2.5
9-25	StL.	W	6-1		9	4	Neagle	Jimenez	Graves	92-63	2nd	1.5
9-26	StL.	W	7-5	(12)	10	9	Williamson	Mohler		93-63	2nd	0.5
9-27	StL.	W	9-7		14	8	Belinda	Croushore	Reyes	94-63	T1st	...
9-28	At Hou.	W	4-1		8	4	Harnisch	Lima	Williamson	95-63	1st	+1.0
9-29	At Hou.	L	1-4		7	7	Hampton	Parris	Wagner	95-64	T1st	...
10-1	At Mil.	L	3-4	(10)	5	10	Coppinger	Sullivan		95-65	T1st	...
10-2	At Mil.	L	6-10		12	14	Peterson	Guzman		95-66	2nd	1.0
10-3	At Mil.	W	7-1		12	6	Harnisch	Eldred	Villone	96-66	2nd	1.0
10-4	N.Y.	L	0-5		2	9	Leiter	Parris		96-67	2nd	1.5

Monthly records: April (9-12), May (16-10), June (18-9), July (16-12), August (17-12), September (19-9), October (1-3).
*Innings, if other than nine. † First game of a doubleheader. ‡ Second game of a doubleheader.

HIGHLIGHTS

High point: Sore shoulder and all, Pete Harnisch pitched a four-hit, eight-inning gem on September 28 at Houston. The Reds beat 20-game winner Jose Lima, 4-1, and seized a one-game lead over the Astros in the N.L. Central with four games to play.
Low point: An 8-5 loss at Pittsburgh on September 19 dropped the Reds 3.5 games behind Houston in the Central and four games behind New York in the wild-card race with 12 games left.
Turning point: Leading 3-0 at Milwaukee on October 1, the Reds had a chance to strengthen their grip on a postseason berth but instead lost, 4-3, in 10 innings. A Cincinnati victory and a New York loss would have clinched a wild-card berth. Instead, the Reds would be forced into a one-game playoff three days later against New York, and the Mets won that game, 5-0, to advance to the postseason.
Most valuable player: Playing his first full season at second base, Pokey Reese sparkled on defense (he won a Gold Glove) and also provided robust offense (a .285 batting average, 37 doubles, 38 steals).
Most valuable pitcher: Harnisch (16-10) and Danny Graves (27 saves) deserve consideration, but the Reds would have been in trouble in the first half without rookie Scott Williamson, who set the tone for the bullpen's season-long excellence. Williamson had 11 saves and a 1.66 ERA at the All-Star break, and he finished 12-7 with 19 saves and a 2.41 ERA. He held hitters to a .171 average in 1999.
Most improved player: Sean Casey had been projected as a potential batting champion, but no one thought he would emerge so quickly. Casey didn't top the N.L. in hitting, but he did wind up fourth at .332 (60 points higher than his 1998 figure). He also slammed 25 homers.
Most pleasant surprise: Ron Villone began the season in Class AAA. He finished it as a key member of the pitching staff. After spending all of his major league career as a reliever, Villone found a niche in Cincinnati's rotation, going 9-7 (the Reds won 13 of his 22 starts) and

allowing only 114 hits in 142.2 innings.
Biggest disappointment: Opening-day starter Brett Tomko, who went on to a 5-7 season that included a brief demotion to the minors and removal from the rotation.
Key injuries: Denny Neagle missed essentially half of the season because of weakened muscles in his left shoulder. Steve Avery, the team's best pitcher in April, was finished in July with a strained left shoulder. And Harnisch pitched through pain in the final four months.
Notable: Vaughn tied Frank Robinson's franchise record for home runs in one month with 14 in September. ... Cincinnati won nine consecutive series from July 23 through August 22. ... The Reds were a major league-best 51-30 on the road. ... The bullpen led the majors in ERA (3.37) and opponents' batting average (.225), and it tied Atlanta for the big-league lead with 33 victories. ... The Reds set an N.L. record by hitting nine homers in one game—on September 4, at Philadelphia. A major league record eight different Reds players homered during the contest. The next day they added five homers for a big league record 14 in two consecutive games.
—CHRIS HAFT

RECORDS

1999 regular-season record: 96-67 (2nd in N.L. Central); 45-37 at home; 51-30 on road; 22-20 vs. East; 38-25 vs. N.L. Central; 29-14 vs. West; 7-8 vs. A.L.; 27-17 vs. lefthanded starters; 69-50 vs. right-handed starters; 36-20 on grass; 60-47 on turf; 33-24 in daytime; 63-43 at night; 21-24 in one-run games; 9-4 in extra-inning games; 1-0-1 in doubleheaders.
Team record past five years: 415-378 (.523, ranks 4th in league in that span).

TEAM LEADERS

Batting average: Sean Casey (.332).
At-bats: Sean Casey (594).
Runs: Barry Larkin (108).
Hits: Sean Casey (197).
Total Bases: Sean Casey (320).

Doubles: Sean Casey (42).
Triples: Mike Cameron (9).
Home runs: Greg Vaughn (45).
Runs batted in: Greg Vaughn (118).
Stolen bases: Mike Cameron, Pokey Reese (38).
Slugging percentage: Sean Casey (.539).
On-base percentage: Sean Casey (.399).
Wins: Pete Harnisch (16).
Earned-run average: Pete Harnisch (3.68).
Complete games: Pete Harnisch, Steve Parris (2).
Shutouts: Pete Harnisch (2).
Saves: Danny Graves (27).
Innings pitched: Pete Harnisch (198.1).
Strikeouts: Brett Tomko (132).

GAMES BY POSITION

Catcher: Eddie Taubensee 124, Brian Johnson 39, Jason LaRue 35.
First base: Sean Casey 148, Hal Morris 25, Dmitri Young 9, Mark Sweeney 1.
Second base: Pokey Reese 146, Chris Stynes 43, Mark Lewis 2.
Third base: Aaron Boone 136, Mark Lewis 52, Chris Stynes 8.
Shortstop: Barry Larkin 161, Pokey Reese 16, Travis Dawkins 7, Aaron Boone 6.
Outfield: Mike Cameron 146, Greg Vaughn 144, Michael Tucker 114, Jeffrey Hammonds 106, Dmitri Young 91, Hal Morris 4, Chris Stynes 4, Kerry Robinson 2, Mark Sweeney 1.
Designated hitter: Greg Vaughn 6, Hal Morris 1, Dmitri Young 1, Sean Casey 1.

TOP DRAFT CHOICES

1. **Ty Howington**, LHP, Hudson's Bay H.S., Vancouver, Wash.
2. **Ben Broussard**, 1B, McNeese State U.
3. **Brandon Love**, RHP, Viola (Ark.) H.S.
4. **Ken Lutz**, RHP, Collinsville H.S., Caseyville, Ill.
5. **Mike Esposito**, RHP, Cimarron-Memorial H.S., Las Vegas
6. **Ron LeFlore**, OF, Pinellas Park (Fla.) H.S.
7. **Okorie Barrow**, OF, Clarke Central H.S., Athens, Ga.
8. **Ryan Lundquist**, C, U. of Arkansas
9. **Casey Bookout**, 1B, U. of Oklahoma
10. **Scott Dunn**, RHP, U. of Texas

COLORADO ROCKIES
NATIONAL LEAGUE WEST DIVISION

2000 Rockies Schedule
Home games shaded. *—All-Star Game at Turner Field (Atlanta).

March
SUN	MON	TUE	WED	THU	FRI	SAT
26	27	28	29	30	30	

April
SUN	MON	TUE	WED	THU	FRI	SAT
						1
2	3 ATL	4 ATL	5 ATL	6	7 FLA	8 FLA
9 FLA	10 CIN	11 CIN	12 CIN	13 STL	14 STL	15 STL
16 STL	17 ARI	18 ARI	19 ARI	20 ARI	21 STL	22 STL
23 STL	24 STL	25 MON	26 MON	27	28 NYM	29 NYM
30 NYM						

May
SUN	MON	TUE	WED	THU	FRI	SAT
	1 MON	2 MON	3 MON	4	5 SF	6 SF
7 SF	8 HOU	9 HOU	10 HOU	11	12 SF	13 SF
14 SF	15	16 NYM	17 NYM	18 NYM	19 PHI	20 PHI
21 PHI	22	23 CUB	24 CUB	25 CUB	26 PIT	27 PIT
28 PIT	29 HOU	30 HOU	31 HOU			

June
SUN	MON	TUE	WED	THU	FRI	SAT
				1	2 MIL	3 MIL
4 MIL	5 SEA	6 SEA	7 SEA	8	9 TEX	10 TEX
11 TEX	12	13 HOU	14 HOU	15 HOU	16 ARI	17 ARI
18 ARI	19	20 CIN	21 CIN	22 CIN	23 ARI	24 ARI
25 ARI	26 SF	27 SF	28 SF	29 SF	30 SD	

July
SUN	MON	TUE	WED	THU	FRI	SAT
						1 SD
2 SD	3 SD	4 SF	5 SF	6 SF	7 ANA	8 ANA
9 ANA	10	11	* 12	13 CIN	14 CIN	15 CIN
16 OAK	17 OAK	18 OAK	19 LA	20 LA	21 SD	22 SD
23 SD	24 LA	25 LA	26 LA	27 LA	28 MIL	29 MIL
30 MIL	31 CUB					

August
SUN	MON	TUE	WED	THU	FRI	SAT
		1 CUB	2 CUB	3		5 PHI
	7 PIT	8 PIT	9 PIT	10	11 MON	12 MON
13 MON	14 MON	15 NYM	16 NYM	17 NYM	18 FLA	19 FLA
20 FLA	21 ATL	22 ATL	23 ATL	24	25 PIT	26 PIT
27 PIT	28 PHI	29 PHI	30 PHI	31		

September
SUN	MON	TUE	WED	THU	FRI	SAT
					1 MIL	2 MIL
3 MIL	4 CUB	5 CUB	6 CUB	7	8 LA	9 LA
10 LA	11 SD	12 SD	13 SD	14 LA	15 LA	16 LA
17 LA	18	19 SD	20 SD	21 SD	22 FLA	23 FLA
24 FLA	25	26 ARI	27 ARI	28 ARI	29 ATL	30 ATL

October
SUN	MON	TUE	WED	THU	FRI	SAT
1 ATL	2	3	4	5	6	

2000 SEASON
CLUB DIRECTORY

Chairman, president and CEO
Jerry McMorris
Vice chairmen
Charles Monfort
Richard Monfort
Executive v.p., business operations
Keli McGregor
Executive v.p., general manager
Dan O'Dowd
Senior v.p., chief financial officer
Hal Roth
Senior v.p., corporate counsel
Clark Weaver
Vice president, finance
Michael Kent
Vice president, sales and marketing
Greg Feasel
V.p., ticket operations & sales
Sue Ann McClaren
Sr. dir., baseball ops. and asst. g.m.
Josh Byrnes
Senior director, player personnel
Mark Wiley
Special assistant to the g.m.
Pat Daugherty
Sr. dir., public rel. & communications
Jay Alves
Senior director, Coors Field operations
Kevin Kahn
Sr. director, personnel & administration
Liz Stecklein
Sr. director, corporate sales
Marcy English Glasser
Director, player development
Michael Hill
Director, minor league operations
Paul Egins
Director, scouting
Bill Schmidt
Director, baseball administration
Tony Siegle
Director, broadcasting
Eric Brummond
Director, community affairs
Roger Kinney

Director, information systems
Mary Bruns
Director, merchandising
Jim Kellogg
Dir., promotions and special events
Alan Bossart
Director, team travel
Brandy Lay
Director, ticket sales
Jill Roberts
Dir., ticket services & spring training business operations
Chuck Javernick
Head groundskeeper
Mark Razum
Coordinator of instruction
Rick Mathews
National cross-checkers
Bill Gayton
Dave Holliday
Regional cross-checkers
Jay Darnell
Robyn Lynch
Danny Montgomery
Major league scouts
Pat Daugherty, Jim Fregosi Jr., Dave Garcia, Will George, Milt May, Mark Wiley
Professional scouts
Joe McDonald, Art Pontarelli, Steve Schryver
Scouts
John Cedarburg, Ty Coslow, Dar Cox, Mike Ericson, Abe Flores, Mike Garlatti, Bert Holt, Greg Hopkins, Bill Hughes, Damon Iannelli, Eric Johnson, Bill Mackenzie, Jay Matthews, Lance Nichols, Sean O'Connor, Brooks Roybal, Ed Santa, Nick Venuto, Tom Wheeler
International scouts
Phil Allen, Dario Arias, Francisco Cartaya, Cristobal A. Giron, Tim Ireland, Alexander Marquez, Oscar Martinez, Brian McRobie, Atanacio Mendez, Jorge Moreno, Ramon Pena, Jorge Posada, Jesus Rizales, Reed Spencer, Ron Steele

MINOR LEAGUE AFFILIATES

Class	Team	League	Manager
AAA	Colorado Springs	Pacific Coast	Chris Cron
AA	Carolina	Southern	Ron Gideon
A	Salem	Carolina	Alan Cockrell
A	Asheville	South Atlantic	Joe Mikulik
A	Portland	Northwest	Billy White
Rookie	Rockies	Arizona	P.J. Carey

BROADCAST INFORMATION
Radio: KOA-AM (850), KCUV-AM (1150).
TV: KWGN-TV (Channel 2).
Cable TV: Fox Sports Rocky Mountain.

SPRING TRAINING
Ballpark (city): Hi Corbett Field (Tucson, Ariz.).
Ticket information: 1-800-388-ROCK.

2000 SEASON *Colorado Rockies*

Manager—Buddy Bell (25).
Coaches—Rich Donnelly, Toby Harrah, Clint Hurdle, Fred Kendall, Marcel Lachemann, Dallas Williams

No.	PITCHERS	B/T	Ht./Wt.	Born	1999 clubs
30	Arrojo, Rolando	R/R	6-4/220	7-18-68	Tampa Bay, St. Petersburg
34	Astacio, Pedro	R/R	6-2/208	11-28-69	Colorado
38	Aybar, Manny	R/R	6-2/208	11-28-69	St. Louis
37	Belinda, Stan	R/R	6-3/215	8-6-66	Indianapolis, Cincinnati
43	Beltran, Rigo	L/L	5-11/185	11-13-69	Norfolk, New York N.L., Colorado Springs, Colorado
41	Bohanon, Brian	L/L	6-2/240	8-1-68	Colorado
	Croushore, Rick	R/R	6-4/210	8-7-70	Memphis, St. Louis
44	DeJean, Mike	R/R	6-2/212	9-28-70	Colorado, Colorado Springs
45	Dipoto, Jerry	R/R	6-2/205	5-24-68	Colorado
38	Gonzalez, Lariel	R/R	6-4/228	5-25-76	Colorado Springs, Carolina
	Jimenez, Jose	R/R	6-3/190	7-7-73	St. Louis, Memphis
36	Jones, Bobby	R/L	6-0/178	4-11-72	Colorado, Colorado Springs
	Karl, Scott	L/L	6-2/209	8-9-71	Milwaukee
	Lee, David	R/R	6-1/202	3-12-73	Carolina, Colorado, Colorado Springs
	Myers, Mike	L/L	6-4/214	6-26-69	Milwaukee
51	Shoemaker, Steve	L/R	6-1/214	2-3-73	Colorado Springs
	Tavarez, Julian	L/R	6-2/190	5-22-73	San Francisco, Fresno, San Jose
52	Thomson, John	R/R	6-3/187	10-1-73	Colorado, Colorado Springs, Salem

No.	CATCHERS	B/T	Ht./Wt.	Born	1999 clubs
	Mayne, Brent	L/R	6-1/192	4-19-68	San Francisco
7	Petrick, Ben	R/R	6-0/199	4-7-77	Carolina, Colorado Springs, Colorado

No.	INFIELDERS	B/T	Ht./Wt.	Born	1999 clubs
	Butler, Brent	R/R	6-0/180	2-11-78	Arkansas
26	Cirillo, Jeff	R/R	6-1/195	9-23-69	Milwaukee
17	Helton, Todd	L/L	6-2/206	8-20-73	Colorado
3	Lansing, Mike	R/R	6-0/195	4-3-68	Colorado
	Ledesma, Aaron	R/R	6-2/210	6-3-71	St. Petersburg, Durham, Tampa Bay
5	Perez, Neifi	B/R	6-0/175	6-2-75	Colorado
29	Shumpert, Terry	R/R	6-2/195	8-16-66	Colorado Springs, Colorado
	Sosa, Juan	R/R	6-1/175	8-19-75	Carolina, Colorado Springs, Colorado

No.	OUTFIELDERS	B/T	Ht./Wt.	Born	1999 clubs
11	Echevarria, Angel	R/R	6-3/226	5-25-71	Colorado
24	Gibson, Derrick	R/R	6-2/244	2-5-75	Colorado Springs, Colorado
	Goodwin, Tom	L/R	6-1/175	7-27-68	Texas, Charlotte
	Hammonds, Jeffrey	R/R	6-0/195	3-5-71	Cincinnati
28	Latham, Chris	B/R	6-0/198	5-26-73	Minnesota, Salt Lake
19	Clemente, Edgard	R/R	5-11/188	12-15-75	Colorado Springs, Colorado
33	Walker, Larry	L/R	6-3/237	12-1-66	Colorado

BALLPARK INFORMATION

Ballpark (capacity, surface)
Coors Field (50,381, grass)
Address
2001 Blake St.
Denver, CO 80205-2000
Business phone
303-292-0200
Ticket information
800-388-7625
Ticket prices
$32 (club level, infield)
$30 (club level, outfield)
$27 (infield box)
$21.50 (outfield box)
$16 (lower reserved, infield)
$13 (lower reserved, outfield)
$12 (upper reserved infield, RF box)
$11 (lower reserved corner)
$10 (RF mezzanine)
$9 (upper reserved, outfield; lower pavilion)
$8 (lower pavilion)
$7 (upper reserved corner)
$6 (lower RF reserved)
$5 (upper RF reserved)
$4 (rockpile)
$1 (rockpile)
Field dimensions (from home plate)
To left field at foul line, 347 feet
To center field, 415 feet
To right field at foul line, 350
First game played
April 26, 1995 (Rockies 11, Mets 9, 14 innings)

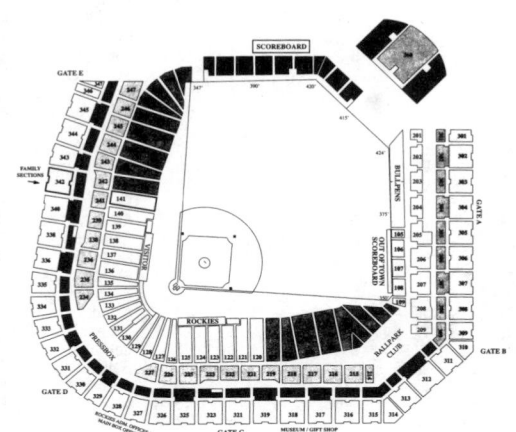

2000 SEASON *Colorado Rockies*

Date	Opp.	Res.	Score	(inn.*)	Hits	Opp. hits	Winning pitcher	Losing pitcher	Save	Record	Pos.	GB
4-4	At S.D.§	W	8-2		18	6	Kile	Ashby		1-0	1st	+0.5
4-6	At S.D.	L	3-4		9	9	Hitchcock	Astacio	Hoffman	1-1	T3rd	1.0
4-7	At S.D.	L	1-2		8	8	Rivera	Jones		1-2	4th	2.0
4-8	At L.A.	W	4-2		5	5	Bohanon	Perez	Veres	2-2	T3rd	2.0
4-9	At L.A.	L	6-9		9	17	Dreifort	Thomson	Shaw	2-3	T3rd	3.0
4-10	At L.A.	L	0-2		3	5	Brown	Kile	Shaw	2-4	4th	3.0
4-12	S.D.	L	5-8	(11)	10	13	Wall	Veres	Reyes	2-5	T4th	4.0
4-15	S.D.	W	6-4		10	4	Bohanon	Clement	Veres	3-5	5th	3.0
4-17	Atl.	W	5-4		10	8	McElroy	Rocker		4-5	4th	2.5
4-18	Atl.	L	5-20		10	24	Maddux	Astacio		4-6	5th	2.5
4-19	Mon.	W	11-10		11	20	Veres	Urbina		5-6	5th	2.5
4-22	At S.F	W	8-5		13	9	Bohanon	Rueter	Veres	6-6	T3rd	1.5
4-23	At S.F	L	2-7		6	10	Ortiz	Kile		6-7	4th	2.5
4-24	At S.F	L	4-8		4	11	Estes	Astacio		6-8	5th	3.5
4-25	At S.F	L	6-7		9	10	Embree	DeJean	Nen	6-9	5th	4.5
4-27	At StL.	L	5-7		10	8	Oliver	Thomson	Radinsky	6-10	5th	5.5
4-28	At StL.	W	9-7		11	14	Bohanon	Jimenez	Veres	7-10	5th	5.5
4-29	At StL.	W	6-2		11	8	Kile	Mercker		8-10	4th	5.5
4-30	At Pit.	W	7-2		8	8	Astacio	Schourek		9-10	4th	4.5
5-1	At Pit.	L	3-9		8	9	Ritchie	Wright		9-11	4th	4.5
5-2	At Pit.	L	5-8		8	12	Schmidt	Thomson	Williams	9-12	4th	4.5
5-3	At Chi.	W	6-1		12	6	Bohanon	Trachsel		10-12	4th	3.5
5-4	At Chi.	L	12-13		17	14	Beck	Dipoto		10-13	4th	4.5
5-5	At Chi.	W	13-6		18	10	Astacio	Mulholland		11-13	4th	3.5
5-7	Phi.	L	1-8		7	14	Schilling	Thomson		11-14	4th	4.5
5-8	Phi.	L	2-7		9	12	Bennett	Bohanon		11-15	4th	5.5
5-9	Phi.	L	8-10		12	17	Ryan	Veres	Gomes	11-16	4th	5.5
5-10	N.Y.	W	10-3		12	7	Astacio	Leiter		12-16	4th	5.5
5-11	N.Y.	W	8-5		12	11	Jones	Jones		13-16	4th	4.5
5-12	N.Y.	L	5-10		10	15	Reed	Thomson		13-17	4th	5.5
5-14	At Ari.	W	4-1		9	6	Bohanon	Benes		14-17	4th	4.5
5-15	At Ari.	L	2-9		3	16	Johnson	Kile		14-18	4th	4.5
5-16	At Ari.	W	5-1		6	7	Astacio	Daal		15-18	4th	4.5
5-17	Cin.	L	2-7		6	10	Harnisch	Jones		15-19	4th	4.5
5-18	Cin.	L	3-5		6	10	Graves	Leskanic	Williamson	15-20	4th	5.5
5-19	Cin.	L	12-24		15	28	Parris	Dipoto	Villone	15-21	5th	5.5
5-20	Ari.	W	8-4		10	7	Kile	Johnson		16-21	4th	5.0
5-21	Ari.	W	8-7	(11)	14	16	Leskanic	Frascatore		17-21	4th	5.0
5-22	Ari.	L	3-8		11	14	Daal	Jones		17-22	4th	6.0
5-23	Ari.	W	7-6		11	11	McElroy	Olson		18-22	4th	5.0
5-24	At Hou.	L	2-5		9	8	Reynolds	Bohanon		18-23	4th	5.5
5-25	At Hou.	L	1-2	(12)	5	9	Elarton	DeJean		18-24	4th	6.5
5-26	At Hou.	L	2-3		7	9	Powell	Astacio		18-25	4th	7.5
5-27	At Hou.	W	4-3		7	4	Dipoto	Miller	Veres	19-25	4th	6.5
5-28	At Phi.	W	5-3		7	12	Leskanic	Byrd	Veres	20-25	4th	6.0
5-29	At Phi.	L	0-2		4	4	Schilling	Bohanon		20-26	4th	7.0
5-30	At Phi.	W	1-0		7	5	Kile	Poole	Veres	21-26	4th	7.0
5-31	At Atl.	L	1-3		8	8	Millwood	Astacio	Rocker	21-27	4th	8.0
6-1	At Atl.	L	2-7		6	6	Smoltz	Jones		21-28	4th	8.0
6-2	At Atl.	W	3-2	(11)	5	9	Dipoto	Springer		22-28	4th	8.0
6-4	Mil.	W	9-8	(10)	17	17	Veres	Wickman		23-28	4th	8.0
6-5	Mil.	W	12-11		13	14	DeJean	Plunk	Dipoto	24-28	4th	7.0
6-6	Mil.	W	10-5		14	9	Astacio	Karl		25-28	4th	7.0
6-7	Sea.	L	2-4		9	8	Halama	Jones	Mesa	25-29	4th	7.0
6-8	Sea.	L	5-10		10	15	Rodriguez	Brownson	Cloude	25-30	4th	7.0
6-9	Sea.	W	16-11		12	12	Bohanon	Fassero		26-30	4th	7.0
6-11	At Tex.	L	2-3		6	8	Zimmerman	McElroy	Wetteland	26-31	4th	8.0
6-12	At Tex.	W	8-7		13	13	Astacio	Sele	Veres	27-31	4th	7.0
6-13	At Tex.	W	4-2		8	7	Jones	Morgan	Veres	28-31	4th	7.0
6-14	S.F	W	5-4		7	8	Leskanic	Johnstone	Veres	29-31	3rd	7.0
6-15	S.F	W	15-6		16	15	Bohanon	Brock		30-31	3rd	7.0
6-16	S.F	L	2-15		6	19	Gardner	Kile		30-32	3rd	8.0
6-18	Fla.	W	11-10		18	13	McElroy	Mantei		31-32	3rd	7.0
6-19	Fla.	W	10-2		15	7	Jones	Fernandez		32-32	3rd	7.0
6-20	Fla.	W	8-7		11	15	Bohanon	Dempster	Veres	33-32	3rd	6.0
6-22	Chi.	L	12-13		15	14	Sanders	DeJean	Aguilera	33-33	3rd	5.5
6-23	Chi.	W	10-1		19	7	Astacio	Mulholland		34-33	3rd	4.5
6-24	Chi.	L	10-12		18	15	Tapani	Jones		34-34	3rd	5.5
6-25	At S.D.	L	1-10		7	10	Boehringer	Bohanon		34-35	3rd	5.5
6-26	At S.D.	L	6-13		10	9	Clement	Brownson		34-36	3rd	5.5
6-27	At S.D.	L	3-5		7	8	Hitchcock	Kile	Hoffman	34-37	3rd	6.5
6-28	At S.D.	L	7-8		14	10	Williams	Astacio	Hoffman	34-38	4th	7.0
6-29	At S.F	L	1-10		6	13	Rueter	Jones		34-39	4th	7.0
6-30	At S.F	L	1-4		7	8	Ortiz	Bohanon	Nen	34-40	4th	7.0

Date	Opp.	Res.	Score	(inn.*)	Hits	Opp. hits	Winning pitcher	Losing pitcher	Save	Record	Pos.	GB
7-1	At S.F	L	1-7		6	9	Estes	Kile		34-41	4th	8.0
7-2	S.D.	L	3-15		8	19	Hitchcock	Astacio		34-42	4th	9.0
7-3†	S.D.	W	12-10		17	13	Ramirez	Williams	Veres	35-42		
7-3‡	S.D.	W	8-6		15	9	Jones	Murray	Veres	36-42	4th	8.5
7-4	S.D.	L	0-11		6	17	Ashby	Bohanon		36-43	4th	8.5
7-5	L.A.	W	8-4		14	11	Kile	Brown		37-43	4th	8.5
7-6	L.A.	W	5-2		10	6	Astacio	Dreifort		38-43	4th	8.5
7-7	L.A.	W	7-5		14	11	DeJean	Arnold	Veres	39-43	4th	7.5
7-8	L.A.	L	8-11		12	12	Park	Bohanon	Shaw	39-44	4th	8.0
7-9	Ana.	L	6-9		12	15	Finley	Kile	Percival	39-45	4th	9.0
7-10	Ana.	L	3-9		6	13	Olivares	Astacio		39-46	4th	10.0
7-11	Ana.	W	8-2		11	5	Dipoto	Fyhrie		40-46	4th	9.0
7-15	At Cin.	L	7-10		12	12	Parris	Kile	Graves	40-47	4th	9.0
7-16	At Cin.	W	6-2		11	4	Astacio	Villone	Veres	41-47	4th	8.0
7-17	At Cin.	L	2-3		8	3	Williamson	Dipoto		41-48	T4th	9.0
7-18	At Oak.	L	2-3		5	5	Haynes	Jones	Taylor	41-49	T4th	9.0
7-19	At Oak.	L	5-10		10	12	Worrell	Ramirez	Jones	41-50	5th	9.0
7-20	At Oak.	L	3-4		6	5	Rogers	Kile	Taylor	41-51	5th	9.0
7-21	At L.A.	W	5-4		13	8	Astacio	Valdes	Veres	42-51	5th	9.0
7-22†	At L.A.	W	4-1		8	3	Jones	Park	Veres	43-51		
7-22‡	At L.A.	W	12-11		13	15	Lee	Masaoka	Veres	44-51	4th	7.5
7-23	StL.	L	4-6		12	11	Oliver	Ramirez	Slocumb	44-52	4th	8.5
7-24	StL.	L	2-10		11	15	Mercker	Kile		44-53	4th	9.0
7-25	StL.	L	4-6		9	8	Luebbers	Astacio	Aybar	44-54	T4th	9.0
7-26	Hou.	L	5-8		10	17	Williams	Veres	Wagner	44-55	T4th	10.0
7-27	Hou.	L	3-6		10	12	Lima	Bohanon	Wagner	44-56	T4th	11.0
7-28	Hou.	L	8-16		18	21	Hampton	Ramirez		44-57	5th	12.0
7-29	Hou.	W	4-2		11	9	Kile	Holt	Veres	45-57	T4th	11.5
7-30	At StL.	W	5-4		9	7	Astacio	Aybar	Veres	46-57	4th	11.5
7-31	At StL.	L	5-6		11	10	Painter	Leskanic	Bottalico	46-58	4th	12.5
8-1	At StL.	W	5-4		13	10	Bohanon	Jimenez	Veres	47-58	4th	11.5
8-3	At Cin.	L	1-2		6	8	Williamson	DeJean		47-59	4th	12.0
8-4	At Cin.	L	3-6		7	12	Neagle	Kile	Graves	47-60	T4th	13.0
8-5	At Cin.	W	2-1		10	4	Astacio	Guzman		48-60	4th	12.5
8-6	At Fla.	L	1-9		3	13	Fernandez	Jones		48-61	4th	12.5
8-7	At Fla.	L	1-4		7	7	Meadows	Bohanon	Alfonseca	48-62	T4th	13.5
8-8	At Fla.	L	1-2		4	4	Dempster	Wright	Alfonseca	48-63	5th	14.5
8-9	At Mil.	L	6-7		9	11	Wickman	Veres		48-64	5th	15.5
8-10	At Mil.	L	1-2	(10)	6	3	Coppinger	Veres		48-65	5th	16.5
8-11	At Mil.	W	8-5		14	10	Jones	Woodard		49-65	5th	16.5
8-13†	Mon.	L	13-14	(10)	15	14	Urbina	Dipoto	Telford	49-66		
8-13‡	Mon.	L	6-8		11	13	Vazquez	Bohanon	Urbina	49-67	5th	17.0
8-14	Mon.	W	11-8		18	11	Kile	Powell	Veres	50-67	5th	16.0
8-15†	Mon.	W	8-2		9	7	Thomson	Thurman	Ramirez	51-67		
8-15‡	Mon.	W	12-4		14	12	Astacio	Bennett		52-67	5th	15.5
8-16	Atl.	L	6-14		17	17	Maddux	Jones		52-68	5th	16.5
8-17	Atl.	W	3-2		8	10	Lee	Mulholland	Veres	53-68	5th	16.5
8-18	Atl.	W	4-1		3	8	Veres	Rocker		54-68	5th	16.5
8-19	Atl.	L	7-9	(14)	11	13	Chen	Lee	Mulholland	54-69	5th	17.0
8-20	At Chi.	W	11-3		14	7	Astacio	Farnsworth		55-69	5th	16.0
8-21	At Chi.	L	6-8		12	10	Bowie	Thomson	Adams	55-70	5th	17.0
8-22	At Chi.	W	3-2		5	6	Wright	Trachsel	Veres	56-70	4th	17.0
8-24	At Pit.	W	3-2		8	7	Leskanic	Williams	Veres	57-70	4th	17.5
8-25	At Pit.	L	3-9		7	14	Peters	Kile		57-71	4th	18.5
8-26	At Pit.	L	4-8		8	15	Anderson	Astacio		57-72	5th	19.5
8-28†	Phi.	W	11-6		15	9	Lee	Aldred		58-72		
8-28‡	Phi.	W	4-0		11	4	Bohanon	Grahe		59-72	4th	18.5
8-29	Phi.	W	6-5		14	9	Kile	Byrd	Veres	60-72	4th	18.5
8-30	Pit.	L	8-11		16	16	Peters	Ramirez	Williams	60-73	5th	19.5
8-31	Pit.	L	8-9	(10)	18	14	Williams	Lee	Silva	60-74	5th	19.5
9-1	Pit.	L	8-9		12	12	Sauerbeck	Veres	Clontz	60-75	5th	19.5
9-3	At N.Y.	W	5-2	(10)	8	10	Leskanic	Wendell	Veres	61-75	5th	18.5
9-4	At N.Y.	L	2-4		11	5	Leiter	Bohanon	Benitez	61-76	5th	19.5
9-5	At N.Y.	L	2-6		9	9	Yoshii	Kile		61-77	5th	20.5
9-6	At Mon.	W	5-3		10	9	Astacio	Thurman	Veres	62-77	5th	20.0
9-7	At Mon.	L	1-4		6	5	Hermanson	Thomson	Urbina	62-78	5th	21.0
9-8	At Mon.	W	5-1		7	6	Wright	Smith		63-78	5th	21.0
9-10	Mil.	W	15-3		14	9	Bohanon	Pulsipher		64-78	5th	20.5
9-11	Mil.	W	7-6		12	8	Dipoto	Coppinger	Veres	65-78	5th	20.5
9-12	Mil.	L	9-12		13	16	Plunk	Veres	Wickman	65-79	5th	21.5
9-13	N.Y.	L	5-6		13	9	Wendell	Veres	Benitez	65-80	5th	22.5
9-14	N.Y.	W	7-2		10	7	Wright	Dotel		66-80	5th	22.5
9-15	N.Y.	L	5-10		11	13	Wendell	Dipoto	Benitez	66-81	5th	22.5
9-17	L.A.	W	18-10		20	11	Hackman	Checo		67-81	5th	21.5
9-18	L.A.	L	4-5		10	9	Park	Astacio	Shaw	67-82	5th	22.5
9-19	L.A.	L	2-5	(8)	7	8	Brown	Thomson	Borbon	67-83	5th	23.5
9-20	Ari.	W	12-7		15	12	Wright	Daal		68-83	5th	22.5

Date	Opp.	Res.	Score	(inn.*)	Hits	Opp. hits	Winning pitcher	Losing pitcher	Save	Record	Pos.	GB
9-21	Ari.	L	6-7		8	11	Olson	Ramirez	Mantei	68-84	5th	23.5
9-22	Ari.	L	3-11		7	11	Benes	Hackman		68-85	5th	24.5
9-24	At Fla.	W	5-3		8	9	Astacio	Edmondson	Veres	69-85	5th	24.5
9-25	At Fla.	L	2-8		6	13	Dempster	Thomson		69-86	5th	25.5
9-26	At Fla.	W	8-6		8	12	Leskanic	Medina	Veres	70-86	5th	25.5
9-27	At Ari.	L	3-10		9	10	Anderson	Bohanon		70-87	5th	26.5
9-28	At Ari.	L	3-9		6	15	Benes	Hackman		70-88	5th	27.5
9-29	At Ari.	W	4-1		8	8	Astacio	Reynoso		71-88	5th	26.5
10-1	S.F	L	4-9		7	11	Ortiz	Thomson		71-89	5th	27.0
10-2	S.F	L	7-16		13	18	Rueter	Wright		71-90	5th	28.0
10-3	S.F	W	9-8		11	12	Veres	Embree		72-90	5th	28.0

Monthly records: April (9-10), May (12-17), June (13-13), July (12-18), August (14-16), September (11-14), October (1-2).
*Innings, if other than nine. † First game of a doubleheader. ‡ Second game of a doubleheader. §At Monterrey, Mex.

HIGHLIGHTS

High point: On June 23, the Rockies beat the Cubs, 10-1, for their eighth win in 10 games. The victory improved Colorado's record to 34-33—only the second time the team had been over .500 since winning on opening day—and pulled it within 4.5 games of first place.

Low point: The Rockies lost 18 of their final 30 games to finish last in the N.L. West for the first time in their seven-year existence, and their .444 winning percentage was the second-lowest in club history.

Turning point: The Rockies dropped a 12-10 game to the Cubs on June 24, beginning a nine-game losing streak that dropped them nine games from the top and out of contention. During the losing streak (which included all seven games of a trip to San Diego and San Francisco), the Rockies were outscored 84-33.

Most valuable player: Right fielder Larry Walker, who hit .379 with 37 home runs and 115 RBIs. Besides winning his second consecutive National League batting title, Walker also led the N.L. in slugging percentage (.710) and on-base percentage (.458). He became the first major leaguer to lead his league in those three percentage categories since the Royals' George Brett did it in the A.L. in 1980 and the first National Leaguer to accomplish the feat since the Cardinals' Stan Musial turned the trick in 1948.

Most valuable pitcher: Pedro Astacio, who tied the franchise record for victories (17) and set Rockies marks for complete games (seven), strikeouts (210) and innings pitched (232). He went 7-2 in his final 12 starts and pitched at least seven innings in 12 of his 15 outings after the All-Star break.

Most improved player: After spending the first two months of the season in Class AAA, veteran handyman Terry Shumpert hit .347 with 26 doubles and 10 homers in 92 games. He was 14-for-14 in steal attempts.

Most pleasant surprise: Dave Veres, who before the 1999 season never had been a full-time closer and had only 15 career saves. He set a Rockies record with 31 saves and pitched in a career-high 73 games.

Biggest disappointment: Darryl Kile, who didn't experience the turnaround season the Rockies wanted. The righthander slipped to an 8-13 record with a 6.61 ERA (7.44 at Coors Field), and he even struggled on the road (3-10, 5.89 ERA).

Key injuries: Second baseman Mike Lansing didn't play after May 20 and underwent back surgery. Walker had only 438 at-bats, missing time because of assorted injuries (including soreness in both knees and a strained rib cage). Versatile Kurt Abbott was sidelined a month overall with a mild concussion and a groin strain. And catcher Kirt Manwaring missed all of May with a broken finger.

Notable: Walker hit an astonishing .461 at home. ... Rockies pitchers set an N.L. record by allowing 737 walks. They also yielded 1,028 runs—no N.L. team had permitted 1,000 since the Phillies gave up a major league-record 1,199 in 1930. ... First baseman Todd Helton hit for the cycle on June 19 against Florida. ... Colorado scored in every inning of its May 5 game against the Cubs, winning 13-6 at Wrigley Field. No big-league team had achieved that feat in 35 years.
—JACK ETKIN

RECORDS

1999 regular-season record: 72-90 (5th in N.L. West); 39-42 at home; 33-48 on road; 24-21 vs. East; 21-32 vs. Central; 23-29 vs. N.L. West; 4-8 vs. A.L.; 23-28 vs. lefthanded starters; 49-62 vs. righthanded starters; 63-77 on grass; 9-13 on turf; 30-38 in daytime; 42-52 at night; 24-23 in one-run games; 4-6 in extra-inning games; 4-1-0 in doubleheaders.
Team record past five years: 392-400 (.495, ranks 8th in league in that span).

TEAM LEADERS

Batting average: Larry Walker (.379).
At-bats: Neifi Perez (690).
Runs: Todd Helton (114).
Hits: Neifi Perez (193).
Total Bases: Todd Helton (339).
Doubles: Todd Helton (39).
Triples: Neifi Perez (11).
Home runs: Larry Walker (37).

Runs batted in: Dante Bichette (133).
Stolen bases: Terry Shumpert (14).
Slugging percentage: Larry Walker (.710).
On-base percentage: Larry Walker (.458).
Wins: Pedro Astacio (17).
Earned-run average: Pedro Astacio (5.04).
Complete games: Pedro Astacio (7).
Shutouts: Brian Bohanon (1).
Saves: Dave Veres (31).
Innings pitched: Pedro Astacio (232.0).
Strikeouts: Pedro Astacio (210).

GAMES BY POSITION

Catcher: Henry Blanco 86, Kirt Manwaring 44, Jeff Reed 36, Ben Petrick 19.
First base: Todd Helton 156, Angel Echevarria 10, Kurt Abbott 8, J.R. Phillips 4.
Second base: Kurt Abbott 66, Terry Shumpert 54, Mike Lansing 35, Lenny Harris 24, Chris Sexton 10, Chris Petersen 6.
Third base: Vinny Castilla 157, Terry Shumpert 14, Lenny Harris 2.
Shortstop: Neifi Perez 157, Chris Sexton 6, Kurt Abbott 3, Terry Shumpert 2, Juan Sosa 2, Chris Petersen 1.
Outfield: Dante Bichette 144, Larry Walker 114, Darryl Hamilton 82, Jeff Barry 56, Angel Echevarria 49, Edgard Clemente 49, Terry Shumpert 19, Lenny Harris 14, Chris Sexton 13, Pat Watkins 10, Derrick Gibson 10, Brian McRae 7, J.R. Phillips 7, Juan Sosa 6, Kurt Abbott 4, John Cangelosi 1, Mike Kelly 1, Henry Blanco 1.
Designated hitter: Dante Bichette 2, Lenny Harris 2, Jeff Reed 1, Kirt Manwaring 1, Larry Walker 1.

TOP DRAFT CHOICES

1. **Jason Jennings,** RHP, Baylor University
2. **Ryan Kibler,** RHP, King H.S., Tampa
3. **Josh Bard,** C, Texas Tech
4. **Chuck Crowder,** LHP, Georgia Tech
5. **Chris Testa,** OF, Palmdale (Calif.) H.S.
6. **Roney Johnson,** RHP, Woodcreek H.S., Antelope, Calif.
7. **Carlos Figueroa,** SS, Gilberto Concepcion H.S., Carolina, P.R.
8. **Greg Catalanotte,** OF, U. of Florida
9. **Colin Young,** LHP, Fordham University
10. **Sean Daly,** C, Golden West H.S., Visalia, Calif.

FLORIDA MARLINS
NATIONAL LEAGUE EAST DIVISION

2000 Marlins Schedule
Home games shaded. "*"—All-Star Game at Turner Field (Atlanta).

March
SUN	MON	TUE	WED	THU	FRI	SAT
26	27	28	29	30	31	

April
SUN	MON	TUE	WED	THU	FRI	SAT
						1
2	3 SF	4 SF	5 SF	6 SF	7 COL	8 COL
9 COL	10 MIL	11	12 MIL	13 MIL	14 CUB	15 CUB
16 CUB	17 CUB	18 PIT	19 PIT	20 PIT	21 PHI	22 PHI
23 PHI	24 PHI	25 SF	26 SF	27	28 LA	29 LA
30 LA						

May
SUN	MON	TUE	WED	THU	FRI	SAT
	1 SD	2 SD	3 SD	4	5 NYM	6 NYM
7 NYM	8 ATL	9 ATL	10 ATL	11 ATL	12 NYM	13 NYM
14 NYM	15	16 SD	17 SD	18 SD	19 LA	20 LA
21 LA	22	23 STL	24 STL	25 STL	26 CIN	27 CIN
28 CIN	29 PIT	30 PIT	31 PIT			

June
SUN	MON	TUE	WED	THU	FRI	SAT
				1	2 TOR	3 TOR
4 TOR	5 BOS	6 BOS	7 BOS	8	9 TB	10 TB
11 TB	12 PHI	13 PHI	14 PHI	15	16 PIT	17 PIT
18 PIT	19 MIL	20 MIL	21 MIL	22 MIL	23 CUB	24 CUB
25 CUB	26 NYM	27 NYM	28 NYM	29	30 MON	

July
SUN	MON	TUE	WED	THU	FRI	SAT
						1 MON
2 MON	3 NYM	4 NYM	5 NYM	6	7 TB	8 TB
9 TB	10	11 *	12 NYY	13 NYY	14 NYY	15 NYY
16 BAL	17 BAL	18 BAL	19 ATL	20 ATL	21 ATL	22 MON
23 MON	24	25 ATL	26 ATL	27 ATL	28 ARI	29 ARI
30 ARI	31 HOU					

August
SUN	MON	TUE	WED	THU	FRI	SAT
		1 HOU	2 HOU	3 HOU	4 CIN	5 CIN
6 CIN	7 STL	8 STL	9 STL	10	11 SD	12 SD
13 SD	14 LA	15 LA	16 LA	17	18 COL	19 COL
20 COL	21 SF	22 SF	23 SF	24	25 CIN	26 CIN
27 CIN	28 STL	29 STL	30 STL	31		

September
SUN	MON	TUE	WED	THU	FRI	SAT
					1 ARI	2 ARI
3 ARI	4 HOU	5 HOU	6 HOU	7 HOU	8 ARI	9 ARI
10 ARI	11	12 ATL	13 ATL	14 ATL	15 PHI	16 PHI
17 PHI	18 MON	19 MON	20 MON	21 MON	22 COL	23 COL
24 COL	25	26 MON	27 MON	28 MON	29 PHI	30 PHI

October
SUN	MON	TUE	WED	THU	FRI	SAT
1 PHI	2	3	4	5	6	7

2000 SEASON
CLUB DIRECTORY

Chairman
John W. Henry
Vice chairman
David Ginsberg
Exec. vice president and general manager
David Dombrowski
Exec. vice president of CFO
Jonathan D. Mariner
Sr. v.p., sales, communications and marketing
Julio G. Rebull
V.p., communications and broadcasting
Ron Colangelo
Vice president, sales
Lou DePaoli
Assistant general manager
Dave Littlefield
Dir., scouting and Latin Am. operations
Al Avila
Director, Major League administration
Dan Lunetta
Special assistants to the g.m.
Andre Dawson, Orrin Freeman, Tony Perez, Scott Reid
Director, field operations
Rob Leary
Director, team travel
Bill Beck
Video coordinator
Cullen McRae
Manager, scouting administration
Cheryl Evans
Manager, minor league administration
Kim-Lee Carkeek Luchs
Manager, player development
Mike Parkinson
Manager, baseball information systems
David Kuan
Director, media relations
Eric M. Carrington
Assistant director, media relations
Julio C. Sarmiento
Coordinator, media relations
Jonathan Jensen
Manager, broadcasting
Sandra van Meek
Manager, community affairs
Israel Negron
Dir., creative services and in-game entertainment
Leslie Riguero
Mgr., publications and creative services
Renee Torguson
Director, marketing
John Pierce
Marketing manager
Liz Capra
Director, marketing partnerships
Jim Frevola

Director, season and group sales
Pat McNamara
Director, finance/controller
Susan Jaison
Director, information technology
Esther Fleming
Coordinator, information technology
Ken Strand
Director, administration
Mike Whittle
Director, legal affairs
Lucinda Treat
Director, public affairs
Susan Budd
Vice president, ticket operations
Bill Galante
Team physician
Dr. Dan Kanell
Head athletic trainer
Larry Starr
Strength and conditioning director
Rick Slate
Equipment manager
Mike Wallace
Visiting clubhouse manager
Matt Rosenthal
Major league scouts and special asst. to the g.m.
Orrin Freeman, Scott Reid
Manager of scouting administration
Cheryl Evans
Scouting assistant
James Orr
National crosscheckers
Bill Singer, Murray Cook, David Chedd, Mike Russell, Tim Schmidt
Scouts
John Booker, Dick Egan, Manny Estrada, Kelvin Bowles, Lou Fitzgerald, Charlie Silvers, Ty Brown, John Castleberry, John Deeble, Brad Del Barba, Louis Eljaua, David Finley, Bob Laurie, Steve Minor, Steve Mondile, Jax Robertson, Cucho Rodriguez, Jimmy Rough, Dennis Sheehan, Keith Snider, Stan Zielinski
Director Dominican Republic operations
Jesus Alou
Dominican Republic scouts
Pablo Lantigua, Cesar Santiago
Puerto Rico scouts
Cucho Rodriguez, Pedro Cintron
Venezuela scout
Miguel Angel Garcia
Colombia scout
Holbert Cabrera
Panama scout
Ramon Webster
Latin America scout
Hubert Silva

MINOR LEAGUE AFFILIATES

Class	Team	League	Manager
AAA	Calgary	Pacific Coast	Lynn Jones
AA	Portland	Eastern	Rick Renteria
A	Brevard County	Florida State	Dave Huppert
A	Kane County	Midwest	Russ Morman
A	Utica	New York-Pennsylvania	Jon Deeble
Rookie	Gulf Coast Marlins	Gulf Coast	Kevin Boles

BROADCAST INFORMATION

Radio: WQAM-AM (560); WQBA-AM (1140, Spanish language).
TV: WAMI (Channel 69).
Cable TV: Sports Channel Florida.

SPRING TRAINING

Ballpark (city): Space Coast Stadium (Melbourne, Fla.).
Ticket information: 321-633-9200.

SPRING TRAINING ROSTER

Manager—John Boles (13).
Coaches—Joe Breeden (12), Rich Dubee (31), Fredi Gonzalez (9), Rusty Kuntz (22), Jack Maloof (16), Tony Taylor (8).

No.	PITCHERS	B/T	Ht./Wt.	Born	1999 clubs
57	Alfonseca, Antonio	R/R	6-5/235	4-16-72	Florida
56	Almanza, Armando	L/L	6-3/205	10-26-72	Calgary, Portland, Florida
59	Almonte, Hector	R/R	6-2/190	10-17-75	Portland, Florida
61	Beckett, Josh	R/R	6-4/190	5-15-80	
43	Burnett, A.J.	R/R	6-5/205	1-3-77	Portland, Florida
47	Camp, Jared	R/R	6-2/195	5-4-75	Kinston, Akron, Buffalo
38	Cornelius, Reid	R/R	6-0/200	6-2-70	Calgary, Florida
40	Darensbourg, Vic	L/L	5-10/165	11-13-70	Florida, Calgary
46	Dempster, Ryan	R/R	6-1/201	5-3-77	Calgary, Florida
20	Edmondson, Brian	R/R	6-2/175	1-29-73	Florida
32	Fernandez, Alex	R/R	6-1/225	8-13-69	Florida
54	Fontenot, Joe	R/R	6-2/185	3-20-77	Calgary
53	Lara, Nelson	R/R	6-4/185	7-15-78	Kane County
41	Looper, Braden	R/R	6-5/225	10-28-74	Florida
33	Miceli, Dan	R/R	6-0/216	9-9-70	San Diego
36	Nunez, Vladimir	R/R	6-4/224	3-15-75	Tucson, Arizona, Florida
21	Sanchez, Jesus	L/L	5-10/155	10-11-74	Florida, Calgary
58	Tejera, Michael	L/L	5-9/175	10-18-76	Portland, Calgary, Florida

No.	CATCHERS	B/T	Ht./Wt.	Born	1999 clubs
6	Castro, Ramon	R/R	6-3/225	3-1-76	Calgary, Florida
52	Redmond, Mike	R/R	6-1/185	5-5-71	Florida

No.	INFIELDERS	B/T	Ht./Wt.	Born	1999 clubs
10	Berg, David	R/R	5-11/185	9-3-70	Florida
1	Castillo, Luis	B/R	5-11/175	9-12-75	Florida
45	Garcia, Amaury	R/R	5-10/160	5-20-75	Calgary, Florida
11	Gonzalez, Alex	R/R	6-0/170	2-15-77	Florida
25	Lee, Derrek	R/R	6-5/225	9-6-75	Florida, Calgary
19	Lowell, Mike	R/R	6-4/205	2-24-74	Calgary, Florida
15	Millar, Kevin	R/R	6-0/185	9-24-71	Calgary, Florida
3	Ozuna, Pablo	R/R	6-0/160	8-25-78	Portland
26	Rolison, Nate	L/R	6-5/240	3-27-77	Portland

No.	OUTFIELDERS	B/T	Ht./Wt.	Born	1999 clubs
23	Bautista, Danny	R/R	5-11/170	5-24-72	Calgary, Florida
37	Brown, Brant	L/L	6-3/220	6-22-71	Pittsburgh
30	Floyd, Cliff	L/R	6-4/240	12-5-72	Florida, Calgary
7	Kotsay, Mark	L/L	6-0/190	12-2-75	Florida
14	Ramirez, Julio	R/R	5-11/170	8-10-77	Portland, Florida
44	Wilson, Preston	R/R	6-2/193	7-19-74	Florida

BALLPARK INFORMATION

Ballpark (capacity, surface)
Pro Player Stadium (42,530, grass)
Address
2267 N.W. 199th St.
Miami, Fla. 33056
Business phone
305-626-7400
Ticket information
305-350-5050
Ticket prices
$28 (club level section A)
$21 (infield box)
$20 (club level section B)
$15 (club level section C)
$12.50 (terrace box, mezzanine box)
$10 (club level-senior citizens)
$9 (outfield reserved, adult)
$7 (mezzanine reserved, adult)
$4 (outfield reserved, children)
$2 (mezzanine)
Field dimensions (from home plate)
To left field at foul line, 330 feet
To center field, 434 feet
To right field at foul line, 345 feet
First game played
April 5, 1993 (Marlins 6, Dodgers 3)

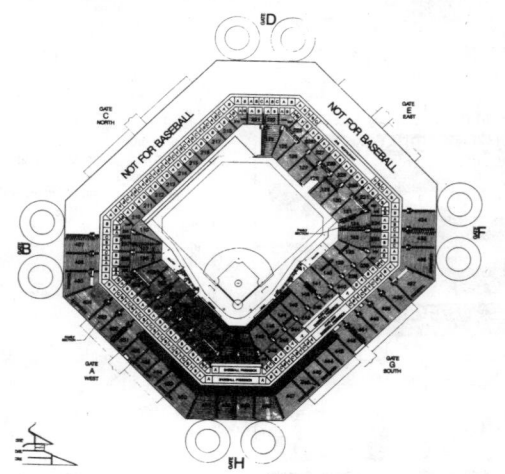

2000 SEASON *Florida Marlins*

Date	Opp.	Res.	Score	(inn.*)	Hits	Opp. hits	Winning pitcher	Losing pitcher	Save	Record	Pos.	GB
4-6	N.Y.	L	3-12		8	13	Reed	Hernandez	Watson	1-1	T1st	...
4-7	N.Y.	L	0-6		6	13	Jones	Sanchez		1-2	T4th	1.0
4-9	Phi.	W	7-4		9	5	Meadows	Spoljaric		2-2	4th	0.5
4-10	Phi.	L	2-5		6	8	Schilling	Springer	Brantley	2-3	5th	1.5
4-11	Phi.	L	1-2		5	6	Ogea	Fernandez	Brantley	2-4	5th	2.5
4-12	At N.Y.	L	1-8		5	9	Jones	Hernandez		2-5	5th	3.5
4-14	At N.Y.	L	1-4		5	3	Hershiser	Sanchez	Franco	2-6	5th	4.5
4-15	At N.Y.	W	11-4		18	9	Meadows	Yoshii		3-6	5th	3.5
4-16	At Phi.	L	3-17		7	16	Schilling	Springer		3-7	5th	3.5
4-17	At Phi.	L	1-2		7	7	Gomes	Alfonseca		3-8	5th	4.5
4-18	At Phi.	L	2-7		8	14	Loewer	Ojala		3-9	5th	4.5
4-19	At S.F	L	4-5		7	5	Johnstone	Alfonseca	Nen	3-10	5th	5.5
4-20	At S.F	W	7-2		11	7	Meadows	Brock	Edmondson	4-10	5th	5.0
4-21	At S.F	L	0-4		5	5	Nathan	Springer		4-11	5th	5.5
4-23	Atl.	W	9-1		14	9	Hernandez	Glavine		5-11	5th	5.5
4-24	Atl.	L	7-8		12	13	Maddux	Edmondson	Rocker	5-12	5th	5.5
4-25	Atl.	L	1-5		6	9	Smoltz	Meadows		5-13	5th	6.5
4-26	Atl.	L	3-5		5	9	Seanez	Alfonseca		5-14	5th	7.5
4-27	Chi.	W	8-0		14	6	Edmondson	Sanders		6-14	5th	6.5
4-28	Chi.	L	1-6		3	16	Trachsel	Hernandez		6-15	5th	7.5
4-29	Chi.	L	2-5		10	12	Farnsworth	Sanchez	Beck	6-16	5th	8.5
4-30	Hou.	L	1-8		9	9	Bergman	Meadows		6-17	5th	9.5
5-1	Hou.	L	4-6		11	10	Lima	Springer	Wagner	6-18	5th	10.5
5-2	Hou.	L	2-3		9	13	Reynolds	Fernandez	Wagner	6-19	5th	11.5
5-3	Mil.	L	4-6	(13)	11	12	Wickman	Corbin		6-20	5th	12.5
5-4	Mil.	L	1-8		7	10	Eldred	Sanchez		6-21	5th	12.5
5-5	Mil.	L	0-2		8	7	Karl	Meadows	Wickman	6-22	5th	13.5
5-7	At L.A.	W	6-3		8	9	Springer	Dreifort	Mantei	7-22	5th	12.5
5-8	At L.A.	L	1-8		3	14	Brown	Hernandez		7-23	5th	13.5
5-9	At L.A.	W	6-4		7	6	Edmondson	Borbon	Mantei	8-23	5th	12.5
5-10	At S.D.	L	5-7		8	12	Miceli	Alfonseca	Hoffman	8-24	5th	12.5
5-11	At S.D.	W	5-4		15	10	Dempster	Spencer	Mantei	9-24	5th	12.5
5-12	At S.D.	L	7-8		15	10	Wall	Edmondson	Hoffman	9-25	5th	12.5
5-14	At Mil.	W	14-6		14	8	Sanchez	Roque	Mantei	10-25	5th	11.5
5-15	At Mil.	L	2-7		4	11	Woodard	Meadows		10-26	5th	11.5
5-16	At Mil.	W	3-2		9	14	Hernandez	Nomo	Mantei	11-26	4th	11.5
5-17	Chi.	L	1-8		4	12	Tapani	Dempster		11-27	4th	12.5
5-18	Chi.	L	1-4	(11)	3	10	Heredia	Springer	Sanders	11-28	5th	13.5
5-19	Chi.	L	7-8		11	12	Myers	Mantei	Adams	11-29	5th	14.5
5-20	Pit.	W	4-3	(14)	12	12	Alfonseca	Williams		12-29	5th	13.5
5-21	Pit.	W	8-1		10	4	Hernandez	Schourek		13-29	4th	12.5
5-22	Pit.	L	4-11		8	14	Ritchie	Springer		13-30	5th	13.5
5-23	Pit.	L	5-6		11	10	Wallace	Darensbourg	Williams	13-31	5th	13.5
5-24	At Chi.	W	7-5		12	9	Mantei	Aguilera		14-31	4th	12.5
5-25	At Chi.	W	6-3		8	8	Meadows	Trachsel		15-31	4th	12.5
5-26	At Chi.	L	4-6		7	11	Aguilera	Looper		15-32	5th	13.5
5-28	Cin.	W	8-1		8	9	Dempster	Avery		16-32	5th	14.0
5-29	Cin.	L	1-8		7	17	Bere	Fernandez		16-33	5th	14.0
5-30	Cin.	L	4-6		10	12	Graves	Edmondson		16-34	5th	14.0
5-31	StL.	L	2-5		10	11	Bottenfield	Meadows	Bottalico	16-35	5th	15.0
6-1	StL.	L	4-8		8	11	Acevedo	Hernandez		16-36	5th	16.0
6-2	StL.	W	10-2		14	8	Dempster	Painter		17-36	5th	15.0
6-3	StL.	W	4-2		5	8	Looper	Oliver	Mantei	18-36	5th	14.5
6-4	At T.B.	W	10-0		11	7	Springer	Rupe		19-36	5th	13.5
6-5	At T.B.	W	9-7		14	9	Meadows	Duvall	Mantei	20-36	5th	13.5
6-6	At T.B.	W	11-6		17	9	Alfonseca	Yan		21-36	5th	13.5
6-8†	Bal.	W	2-1		6	6	Edmondson	Timlin		22-36		
6-8‡	Bal.	W	5-3		11	11	Alfonseca	Kamieniecki	Mantei	23-36	5th	13.5
6-9	Bal.	L	2-4		5	12	Erickson	Springer	Rhodes	23-37	5th	14.5
6-11	N.Y. (AL)	L	4-8		6	11	Hernandez	Meadows	Rivera	23-38	5th	14.5
6-12	N.Y. (AL)	L	4-5		9	6	Clemens	Hernandez	Rivera	23-39	5th	14.5
6-13	N.Y. (AL)	W	8-2		13	5	Fernandez	Pettitte		24-39	5th	13.5
6-14	At Ari.	L	0-2		4	8	Johnson	Dempster	Olson	24-40	5th	13.5
6-15	At Ari.	L	3-4		12	8	Anderson	Springer	Olson	24-41	5th	14.5
6-16	At Ari.	L	6-12		12	17	Reynoso	Meadows		24-42	5th	15.5
6-18	At Col.	L	10-11		13	18	McElroy	Mantei		24-43	5th	17.0
6-19	At Col.	L	2-10		7	15	Jones	Fernandez		24-44	5th	17.0
6-20	At Col.	L	7-8		15	11	Bohanon	Dempster	Veres	24-45	5th	18.0
6-22	At N.Y.	L	2-8		4	14	McMichael	Springer	Benitez	24-46	5th	18.0
6-23	At N.Y.	L	3-6		7	8	Leiter	Meadows	Franco	24-47	5th	19.0
6-24	At N.Y.	L	2-3		9	8	Cook	Hernandez	Franco	24-48	5th	20.0
6-25	At Mon.	L	3-4		5	12	Pavano	Fernandez	Urbina	24-49	5th	20.0

Date	Opp.	Res.	Score	(inn.*)	Hits	Opp. hits	Winning pitcher	Losing pitcher	Save	Record	Pos.	GB
6-26	At Mon.	W	9-3		12	8	Dempster	Smith		25-49	5th	20.0
6-27	At Mon.	W	4-3		6	8	Springer	Thurman	Mantei	26-49	5th	20.0
6-28	N.Y.	L	4-10		11	14	Leiter	Meadows		26-50	5th	21.0
6-29	N.Y.	L	1-5		5	9	Hershiser	Hernandez		26-51	5th	21.0
6-30	N.Y.	W	4-3	(10)	9	8	Alfonseca	Benitez		27-51	5th	20.0
7-1	N.Y.	L	8-12		13	12	Dotel	Dempster		27-52	5th	21.0
7-3	Mon.	W	6-1		9	7	Meadows	Batista		28-52	5th	21.5
7-4	Mon.	W	5-1		8	8	Hernandez	Powell		29-52	5th	20.5
7-5	At Atl.	L	5-6		8	11	McGlinchy	Alfonseca		29-53	5th	21.5
7-6	At Atl.	W	5-2		17	4	Fernandez	Glavine	Mantei	30-53	5th	20.5
7-7	At Atl.	L	3-7		6	8	Maddux	Dempster		30-54	5th	21.5
7-8	At Atl.	L	2-5		7	8	Millwood	Meadows		30-55	5th	22.5
7-9	T.B.	W	11-4		12	11	Hernandez	Rupe		31-55	5th	21.5
7-10	T.B.	L	8-9		15	14	Rekar	Springer	Hernandez	31-56	5th	22.5
7-11	T.B.	W	3-2		5	6	Fernandez	Alvarez	Alfonseca	32-56	5th	22.5
7-15	At Tor.	W	8-6		11	11	Looper	Koch	Alfonseca	33-56	5th	22.5
7-16	At Tor.	W	4-2		10	11	Springer	Hentgen	Alfonseca	34-56	5th	22.5
7-17	At Tor.	L	1-6		6	10	Wells	Edmondson		34-57	5th	22.5
7-18	At Bos.	L	9-11		14	12	Lowe	Nunez	Wakefield	34-58	5th	22.5
7-19	At Bos.	W	10-7		16	15	Meadows	Ohka	Alfonseca	35-58	5th	21.5
7-20	At Bos.	L	1-7		5	12	Rose	Hernandez		35-59	5th	21.5
7-21	Atl.	W	2-0		9	7	Springer	Maddux		36-59	4th	20.5
7-22	Atl.	L	3-6		6	11	McGlinchy	Fernandez	Rocker	36-60	4th	21.5
7-23	Mil.	W	5-4		13	8	Nunez	Wickman		37-60	4th	21.0
7-24	Mil.	W	4-1		9	6	Meadows	Peterson	Alfonseca	38-60	4th	20.0
7-25	Mil.	W	4-3		10	8	Sanchez	Weathers	Alfonseca	39-60	4th	20.0
7-26	At Phi.	L	1-9		7	15	Person	Nunez		39-61	4th	21.0
7-27	At Phi.	W	6-2		12	7	Fernandez	Wolf	Alfonseca	40-61	4th	21.0
7-28	At Phi.	L	4-9		8	13	Schrenk	Dempster		40-62	4th	21.0
7-29	At Phi.	L	1-12		6	13	Ogea	Meadows		40-63	4th	21.5
7-30	At Pit.	W	8-7		14	11	Edmondson	Hansell	Alfonseca	41-63	4th	21.0
7-31	At Pit.	L	2-4		8	5	Schmidt	Edmondson	Williams	41-64	4th	21.5
8-1	At Pit.	L	1-2		5	10	Cordova	Fernandez		41-65	4th	22.5
8-3	Phi.	L	5-6		9	12	Telemaco	Edmondson	Gomes	41-66	5th	23.5
8-4	Phi.	L	1-4		10	9	Byrd	Springer	Schrenk	41-67	5th	24.5
8-5	Phi.	L	3-9		10	12	Person	Nunez		41-68	5th	25.0
8-6	Col.	W	9-1		13	3	Fernandez	Jones		42-68	5th	25.0
8-7	Col.	W	4-1		7	7	Meadows	Bohanon	Alfonseca	43-68	5th	24.0
8-8	Col.	W	2-1		4	4	Dempster	Wright	Alfonseca	44-68	5th	23.0
8-9	S.F	W	5-4		12	12	Sanchez	Johnstone		45-68	5th	22.5
8-10	S.F	W	8-7	(12)	13	13	Edmondson	Rodriguez		46-68	5th	22.5
8-11	S.F	W	6-5	(10)	12	9	Sanchez	Nen		47-68	5th	22.5
8-13	At S.D.	W	4-3		13	10	Meadows	Boehringer	Alfonseca	48-68	5th	22.5
8-14	At S.D.	L	4-6		9	10	Clement	Sanchez	Hoffman	48-69	5th	22.5
8-15	At S.D.	L	6-7		10	15	Ashby	Springer	Hoffman	48-70	5th	23.5
8-16	At L.A.	W	7-5		8	11	Nunez	Park		49-70	4th	23.5
8-17	At L.A.	W	6-1		11	7	Burnett	Judd	Springer	50-70	4th	22.5
8-18	At L.A.	L	0-7		7	11	Dreifort	Meadows		50-71	4th	23.5
8-20	Hou.	L	4-6	(16)	15	7	Miller	Sanchez	Wagner	50-72	5th	24.0
8-21	Hou.	L	4-5		8	8	Henry	Edmondson	Wagner	50-73	5th	25.0
8-24	Ari.	L	4-5		4	6	Benes	Almanza	Mantei	50-74	5th	27.0
8-25	Ari.	L	2-7		7	8	Stottlemyre	Nunez		50-75	5th	28.0
8-26	Ari.	L	2-12		8	11	Johnson	Meadows		50-76	5th	28.5
8-27†	At Hou.	L	2-3		9	8	Lima	Springer	Wagner	50-77		
8-27‡	At Hou.	W	3-1		11	7	Dempster	Holt	Alfonseca	51-77	5th	29.0
8-28	At Hou.	W	5-2		10	7	Burnett	Elarton	Alfonseca	52-77	5th	29.0
8-29	At Hou.	L	4-10		10	14	Hampton	Fernandez		52-78	5th	30.0
8-30	At StL.	W	4-2		13	5	Nunez	Bottenfield	Alfonseca	53-78	5th	29.0
8-31	At StL.	L	1-8		5	12	Luebbers	Meadows		53-79	5th	30.0
9-1	At StL.	L	3-9		9	10	Stephenson	Dempster		53-80	5th	31.0
9-3	S.D.	L	3-6		8	9	Williams	Burnett	Hoffman	53-81	5th	32.0
9-4	S.D.	W	6-4		6	3	Fernandez	Carlyle	Alfonseca	54-81	5th	31.0
9-5	S.D.	L	2-5		6	9	Clement	Nunez	Hoffman	54-82	5th	31.0
9-6	L.A.	W	8-6		15	10	Meadows	Valdes	Alfonseca	55-82	5th	31.0
9-7	L.A.	W	2-1		6	7	Sanchez	Herges	Alfonseca	56-82	5th	31.0
9-8	L.A.	W	5-4	(13)	12	13	Medina	Masaoka		57-82	5th	31.0
9-10	At Cin.	L	2-4		7	5	Neagle	Springer	Graves	57-83	5th	32.0
9-11	At Cin.	L	4-12		9	9	Guzman	Nunez		57-84	5th	32.0
9-12	At Cin.	L	5-11		9	13	Villone	Burnett		57-85	5th	32.0
9-13	At Cin.	L	4-7		10	8	Parris	Sanchez	Graves	57-86	5th	32.0
9-14	At S.F	L	0-3		4	8	Estes	Dempster		57-87	5th	33.0
9-15	At S.F	L	3-4		5	9	Ortiz	Springer	Nen	57-88	5th	33.0
9-16	At S.F	L	5-6		9	9	Patrick	Nunez	Nen	57-89	5th	33.5
9-17	At Ari.	W	10-6		16	7	Burnett	Benes		58-89	5th	33.5
9-18	At Ari.	L	6-8	(10)	15	11	Swindell	Almonte		58-90	5th	33.5

Date	Opp.	Res.	Score	(inn.*)	Hits	Opp. hits	Winning pitcher	Losing pitcher	Save	Record	Pos.	GB
9-19	At Ari.	L	7-8		11	15	Olson	Looper		58-91	5th	34.5
9-21†	Mon.	W	5-3		8	11	Springer	Telford	Alfonseca	59-91		
9-21‡	Mon.	W	4-0		8	7	Cornelius	Powell		60-91	5th	34.0
9-22	Mon.	L	3-5		7	7	Batista	Nunez	Urbina	60-92	5th	35.0
9-23	Mon.	W	2-1		4	9	Burnett	Hermanson	Alfonseca	61-92	5th	35.0
9-24	Col.	L	3-5		9	8	Astacio	Edmondson	Veres	61-93	5th	36.0
9-25	Col.	W	8-2		13	6	Dempster	Thomson		62-93	5th	36.0
9-26	Col.	L	6-8		12	8	Leskanic	Medina	Veres	62-94	5th	37.0
9-27	At Mon.	L	4-8		8	7	Telford	Almonte		62-95	5th	37.5
9-28	At Mon.	W	5-3		11	8	Nunez	Hermanson	Alfonseca	63-95	5th	37.5
9-29	At Mon.	L	3-5		6	8	Kline	Looper	Urbina	63-96	5th	37.5
10-1	At Atl.	L	1-4		6	8	Smoltz	Meadows	Rocker	63-97	5th	39.0
10-2	At Atl.	W	1-0	(10)	2	7	Looper	Ebert	Alfonseca	64-97	5th	38.0
10-3	At Atl.	L	0-18		5	21	Glavine	Springer		64-98	5th	39.0

Monthly records: April (6-17), May (10-18), June (11-16), July (14-13), August (12-15), September (10-17), October (1-2).
*Innings, if other than nine. † First game of a doubleheader. ‡ Second game of a doubleheader.

HIGHLIGHTS

High point: It didn't get a lot better than opening day, when Alex Fernandez, making his first start since undergoing rotator-cuff surgery in October 1997, pitched five strong innings and defeated the Mets, 6-2. It went downhill from there for the Marlins.
Low point: On May 5, Florida lost to Milwaukee, 2-0, completing a 2-11 homestand (the Marlins scored only 26 runs in those 11 defeats) that dropped the team's overall record to 6-22.
Turning point: The Marlins won seven consecutive games August 6-13, sweeping home series against the Rockies and Giants and winning a trip opener at San Diego. Coming on the heels of a 14-13 July that was Florida's first winning month since August 1997, the streak built some confidence in a young team that badly needed it.
Most valuable player: Second baseman Luis Castillo, who finally emerged as a legitimate major leaguer and was one of the National League's best leadoff hitters in the second half of the season. Castillo ended up with a .302 batting average and 50 stolen bases despite missing the final 23 games with a shoulder injury.
Most valuable pitcher: Fernandez made only 24 starts and worked just 141 innings, but he gave the club a chance to win virtually every time he took the ball—and the righthander provided expert guidance for the Marlins' young pitchers, too. His record: 7-8, with a 3.38 ERA.
Most improved player: Antonio Alfonseca, who took over the closer's role July 9 after Matt Mantei was traded to Arizona. From that point on, the hard-throwing righthander was 21-for-23 in save opportunities.
Most pleasant surprise: Righthander A.J. Burnett put up poor numbers (6-12 record, 5.52 ERA) at Class AA Portland, but Florida played a hunch and brought up its best pitching prospect in mid-August. The precocious Burnett made seven starts for the Marlins, going 4-2 with a 3.48 ERA.
Biggest disappointment: The Marlins expected right fielder Mark Kotsay to blossom into a .300 hitter, but he finished at

.271. The team now wonders if its 1996 No. 1 draft pick has enough speed or power to be an everyday major leaguer.
Key Injuries: Cliff Floyd, the big left fielder with the big contract, injured his knee in spring training and then went down with an ankle injury at midseason. Expected to provide a threat in the middle of the order, Floyd played in only 69 games. The still-recuperating Fernandez missed sizable chunks of time, as was expected. Armando Almanza was sidelined for the final month with a shoulder injury, depriving the team of its top left-handed reliever.
Notable: Florida did something no other major league club did in 1999—it pounded Red Sox ace Pedro Martinez. Five days after Martinez's scintillating performance in the All-Star Game, the Marlins hammered him for 12 hits and seven earned runs in 3.2 innings. ... Center fielder Preston Wilson led all major league rookies with 26 home runs. ... Brian Meadows was the only double-figure winner on the pitching staff, posting 11 victories. ... The Marlins lost a total of 206 games in 1998 and 1999.
—DAN GRAZIANO

RECORDS

1999 regular-season record: 64-98 (5th in N.L. East); 35-45 at home; 29-53 on road; 17-34 vs. N.L. East; 17-31 vs. Central; 19-26 vs. West; 11-7 vs. A.L.; 18-21 vs. lefthanded starters; 46-77 vs. righthanded starters; 53-80 on grass; 11-18 on turf; 17-30 in daytime; 47-68 at night; 19-25 in one-run games; 6-4 in extra-inning games; 2-0-1 in doubleheaders.
Team record past five years: 357-434 (.451, ranks T12th in league in that span).

TEAM LEADERS

Batting average: Luis Castillo (.302).
At-bats: Alex Gonzalez (560).
Runs: Alex Gonzalez (81).
Hits: Alex Gonzalez (155).
Total Bases: Preston Wilson (242).
Doubles: Alex Gonzalez (28).
Triples: Mark Kotsay (9).

Home runs: Preston Wilson (26).
Runs batted in: Preston Wilson (71).
Stolen bases: Luis Castillo (50).
Slugging percentage: Preston Wilson (.502).
On-base percentage: Luis Castillo (.384).
Wins: Brian Meadows (11).
Earned-run average: Dennis Springer (4.86).
Complete games: Dennis Springer (3).
Shutouts: Dennis Springer (2).
Saves: Antonio Alfonseca (21).
Innings pitched: Dennis Springer (196.1).
Strikeouts: Ryan Dempster (126).

GAMES BY POSITION

Catcher: Mike Redmond 82, Jorge Fabregas 78, Ramon Castro 24, Guillermo Garcia 3, John Roskos 1.
First base: Kevin Millar 94, Derrek Lee 66, Mark Kotsay 19, Tim Hyers 14, Kevin Orie 1.
Second base: Luis Castillo 126, Dave Berg 29, Craig Counsell 12, Amaury Garcia 8, Chris Clapinski 2.
Third base: Mike Lowell 83, Kevin Orie 64, Dave Berg 19, Chris Clapinski 9, Kevin Millar 1.
Shortstop: Alex Gonzalez 135, Dave Berg 37, Chris Clapinski 6.
Outfield: Preston Wilson 136, Mark Kotsay 129, Bruce Aven 102, Cliff Floyd 62, Danny Bautista 60, Todd Dunwoody 55, Tim Hyers 15, Julio Ramirez 11, Chris Clapinski 3, Dave Berg 3, Kevin Millar 1.
Designated hitter: Bruce Aven 6, Cliff Floyd 3, Tim Hyers 1, Chris Clapinski 1.

TOP DRAFT CHOICES

1. **Josh Beckett**, RHP, Spring (Texas) H.S.
2. **Terry Byron**, RHP, Indian River (Fla.) J.C.
3. **Josh Wilson**, SS, Mt. Lebanon H.S., Pittsburgh
4. **Dominic Woody**, C, U. of Washington
5. **Nate Robertson**, LHP, Wichita State U.
6. **Charlie Frazier**, OF, Toms River (N.J.) South H.S.
7. **Jake Laidlaw**, SS, Cheyenne H.S., Las Vegas
8. **Kevin Hooper**, 2B, Wichita State Univ.
9. **Ben Hickman**, RHP, Louisiana Tech
10. **Scott Goodman**, OF, Arizona State U.

HOUSTON ASTROS
NATIONAL LEAGUE CENTRAL DIVISION

2000 Astros Schedule
Home games shaded. *—All-Star Game at Turner Field (Atlanta).

March
SUN	MON	TUE	WED	THU	FRI	SAT
26	27	28	29	30	31	

April
SUN	MON	TUE	WED	THU	FRI	SAT
						1
2	3 PIT	4	5 PIT	6 PIT	7 PHI	8 PHI
9 PHI	10 STL	11 STL	12 STL	13	14 SD	15 SD
16 SD	17 LA	18 LA	19 LA	20	21 SD	22 SD
23 SD	24	25 CUB	26 CUB	27 CUB	28 MIL	29 MIL
30 MIL						

May
SUN	MON	TUE	WED	THU	FRI	SAT
	1 MIL	2 CUB	3 CUB	4 CUB	5 LA	6 LA
7 LA	8 COL	9 COL	10 COL	11	12 CIN	13 CIN
14 CIN	15 CIN	16 MIL	17 MIL	18 MIL	19 MON	20 MON
21 MON	22	23 PHI	24 PHI	25 PHI	26 ATL	27 ATL
28 ATL	29 COL	30 COL	31 COL			

June
SUN	MON	TUE	WED	THU	FRI	SAT
				1	2 CWS	3 CWS
4 CWS	5 MIN	6 MIN	7 MIN	8	9 SD	10 SD
11 SD	12	13 COL	14 COL	15 COL	16 SF	17 SF
18 SF	19	20 LA	21 LA	22 LA	23 SF	24 SF
25 SF	26 ARIZ	27 ARIZ	28 ARIZ	29 ARIZ	30 STL	

July
SUN	MON	TUE	WED	THU	FRI	SAT
						1 STL
2 STL	3	4 ARIZ	5 ARIZ	6 ARIZ	7 KC	8 KC
9 KC	10	11	*12	13 DET	14 DET	15 DET
16 CLE	17 CLE	18 CLE	19 CIN	20 CIN	21 STL	22 STL
23 STL	24 CIN	25 CIN	26 CIN	27	28 ATL	29 ATL
30 ATL	31 FLA					

August
SUN	MON	TUE	WED	THU	FRI	SAT
		1 FLA	2 FLA	3 FLA	4 MON	5 MON
6 MON	7 NYM	8 NYM	9 NYM	10 NYM	11 PHI	12 PHI
13 PHI	14 PIT	15 PIT	16 PIT	17	18 MIL	19 MIL
20 MIL	21 CUB	22 CUB	23 CUB	24	25 MON	26 MON
27 MON	28 NYM	29 NYM	30 NYM	31		

September
SUN	MON	TUE	WED	THU	FRI	SAT
					1 ATL	2 ATL
3 ATL	4 FLA	5 FLA	6 FLA	7 FLA	8 CUB	9 CUB
10 CUB	11 SF	12 SF	13 SF	14 PIT	15 PIT	16 PIT
17 PIT	18	19 STL	20 STL	21 STL	22 CIN	23 CIN
24 CIN	25	26 PIT	27 PIT	28 PIT	29 MIL	30 MIL

October
SUN	MON	TUE	WED	THU	FRI	SAT
1 MIL	2	3	4	5	6	7

2000 SEASON
CLUB DIRECTORY

Chairman and chief executive officer
Drayton McLane Jr.
President
Tal Smith
Sr. vice president, business operations
Bob McClaren
Sr. vice president, sales and marketing
Pam Gardner
General manager
Gerry Hunsicker
Assistant general manager
Tim Purpura
Special assistant to the general manager for international scouting
Andres Reiner
Director of scouting
David Lakey
Director of baseball administration
Barry Waters
Vice president, finance
Robert McBurnett
Vice president, sales and broadcasting
Jamie Hildreth
V.p., ticket sales and services
John Sorrentino
V.p., community development
Marian Harper
Vice president, market development
Rosi Hernandez
Vice president, communications
Rob Matwick
Director of media relations
Warren Miller
Assistant director of media relations
Alyson Footer

Communications manager
Todd Fedewa
Professional scouts
Leo Labossiere, Kimball Crossley, Joe Pittman, Tom Romenesko, Scipio Spinks
Major league scouts
Stan Benjamin, Walt Matthews, Tom Mooney, Fred Nelson, Bob Skinner, Paul Weaver, Tom Wiedenbauer
Full-time scouts
Bob Blair, Joe Bogar, Ralph Bratton, Chuck Carlson, Gerry Craft, Doug Deutsch, James Farrar, David Henderson, Dan Huston, Marc Johnson, Brian Keegan, Bill Kelso, Bob King, Mike Maggart, Jerry Marik, Tom McCormack, Mel Nelson, Joe Robinson, Tad Slowik, Frankie Thon, Tim Tolman, Danny Watkins, Gene Wellman
Foreign scouts
Ricardo Aponte, Jesus Aristimuno, Sergio A. Beltre, Rafael Cariel, Alexis Corro, Arnold Elles, Mario Gonzalez, Julio Linares, Rodney Linares, Omar Lopez, Carlos Maldonado, Ramon Morales, Oscar Padron, Guillermo Ramirez, Rafael Ramirez, Wolfgang Ramos, Anibal Reluz, Adriano Rodriguez, Dr. Lester Storey, Pablo Torrealba, Calixto Vargas, Mark Van Zanten

MINOR LEAGUE AFFILIATES

Class	Team	League	Manager
AAA	New Orleans	Pacific Coast	Tony Pena
AA	Round Rock	Texas	Jackie Moore
A	Kissimmee	Florida State	Manny Acta
A	Michigan	Midwest	Al Pedrique
A	Auburn	New York-Pennsylvania	To be announced
Rookie	Martinsville	Appalachian	Brad Wellman

BROADCAST INFORMATION

Radio: KTRH-AM (740); KXYZ-AM (1320, Spanish language).
TV: KNWS-TV (Channel 51).
Cable TV: Fox Sports Southwest.

SPRING TRAINING

Ballpark (city): Osceola County Stadium (Kissimmee, Fla.).
Ticket information: 407-839-3900.

SPRING TRAINING ROSTER

Manager—Larry Dierker (49).
Coaches—Jose Cruz (25), Mike Cubbage (24), Matt Galante (8), Tom McCraw (16), Vern Ruhle (48), John Tamargo.

No.	PITCHERS	B/T	Ht./Wt.	Born	1999 clubs
51	Cabrera, Jose	R/R	6-0/180	3-24-72	New Orleans, Houston
29	Dotel, Octavio	R/R	6-0/175	11-25-75	Norfolk, New York N.L.
50	Elarton, Scott	R/R	6-7/240	2-23-76	Houston
60	Franklin, Wayne	L/L	6-2/195	3-9-74	Kissimmee, Jackson
54	Green, Jason	R/R	6-1/205	6-5-75	Jackson
19	Henry, Doug	R/R	6-4/205	12-10-63	Houston, New Orleans, Jackson
44	Holt, Chris	R/R	6-4/205	9-18-71	Houston
55	Ireland, Eric	R/R	6-1/170	3-11-77	Kissimmee, Jackson
42	Lima, Jose	R/R	6-2/205	9-30-72	Houston
59	McKnight, Tony	R/R	6-5/205	6-29-77	Jackson
46	Miller, Trever	R/L	6-4/195	5-29-73	Houston
52	Miller, Wade	R/R	6-2/185	9-13-76	New Orleans, Houston
44	Powell, Brian	R/R	6-2/205	10-10-73	New Orleans
39	Powell, Jay	R/R	6-4/225	1-9-72	Houston
37	Reynolds, Shane	R/R	6-3/210	3-26-68	Houston
56	Robertson, Jeromie	L/L	6-1/190	3-30-77	Jackson
66	Rodriguez, Wilfredo	L/L	6-3/180	3-20-79	Kissimmee
13	Wagner, Billy	L/L	5-11/180	7-25-71	Houston

No.	CATCHERS	B/T	Ht./Wt.	Born	1999 clubs
6	Bako, Paul	L/R	6-2/205	6-20-72	New Orleans, Houston
20	Eusebio, Tony	R/R	6-2/210	4-27-67	Houston
21	Meluskey, Mitch	B/R	6-0/185	9-18-73	Houston

No.	INFIELDERS	B/T	Ht./Wt.	Born	1999 clubs
5	Bagwell, Jeff	R/R	6-0/195	5-27-68	Houston
7	Biggio, Craig	R/R	5-11/180	12-14-65	Houston
27	Bogar, Tim	R/R	6-2/198	10-28-66	Houston
11	Caminiti, Ken	B/R	6-0/200	4-21-63	Houston, New Orleans
	Everett, Adam	R/R	6-0/156	2-2-77	Trenton
4	Hernandez, Carlos	R/R	5-9/175	12-12-75	New Orleans, Houston
9	Johnson, Russ	R/R	5-10/180	2-22-73	New Orleans, Houston
68	Lugo, Julio	R/R	6-1/165	11-16-75	Jackson
62	McNeal, Aaron	R/R	6-3/230	4-28-78	Michigan
28	Spiers, Bill	L/R	6-2/190	6-5-66	Houston
64	Truby, Chris	R/R	6-2/190	12-9-73	Jackson
31	Ward, Daryle	L/L	6-2/230	6-27-75	New Orleans, Houston

No.	OUTFIELDERS	B/T	Ht./Wt.	Born	1999 clubs
18	Alou, Moises	R/R	6-3/195	7-3-66	DID NOT PLAY
29	Barker, Glen	R/R	5-10/180	5-10-71	Houston
22	Berkman, Lance	B/L	6-1/205	2-10-76	New Orleans, Houston
19	Cedeno, Roger	R/R	6-1/205	8-16-74	New York N.L.
15	Hidalgo, Richard	R/R	6-3/190	7-2-75	Houston
23	Mieske, Matt	R/R	6-0/194	2-13-68	Seattle, Houston

BALLPARK INFORMATION

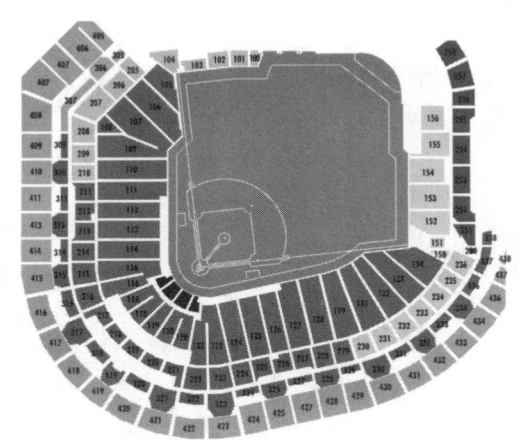

Ballpark (capacity, surface)
Enron Field (42,000, grass)

Address
P.O. Box 288
Houston, TX 77001-0288

Business phone
713-799-9500

Ticket information
713-799-9567; 1-800-ASTROS-2

Ticket prices
$29 (dugout)
$28 (club)
$25 (field level)
$24 (club)
$17 (Crawford box)
$15 (bullpen box)
$12 (mezzanine, terrace deck)
$10 (upper deck)
$5-$1 (outfield deck)

Field dimensions (from home plate)
To left field at foul line, 315 feet
To center field, 435 feet
To right field at foul line, 326 feet

First game played
Scheduled for April 7, 2000 vs. Phillies

Date	Opp.	Res.	Score	(inn.*)	Hits	Opp. hits	Winning pitcher	Losing pitcher	Save	Record	Pos.	GB
4-7	Chi.	L	2-9		5	12	Tapani	Hampton		1-1	T1st	...
4-8	Chi.	L	1-2		6	6	Lieber	Lima	Beck	1-2	T3rd	1.0
4-9	Mil.	W	3-2		7	5	Elarton	Wickman	Wagner	2-2	T1st	...
4-10	Mil.	L	2-8		7	13	Pulsipher	Holt	Weathers	2-3	T3rd	1.0
4-11	Mil.	W	5-2		13	8	Reynolds	Roque	Wagner	3-3	T2nd	1.0
4-13	At S.F	W	7-3		12	6	Hampton	Ortiz	Powell	4-3	T1st	...
4-14	At S.F	W	6-3		14	8	Lima	Estes	Wagner	5-3	T1st	...
4-15	At S.F	L	2-5		6	9	Brock	Bergman	Nen	5-4	2nd	0.5
4-16	StL.	L	3-5		11	9	Oliver	Reynolds	Bottalico	5-5	2nd	1.5
4-17	StL.	L	5-8		11	10	Jimenez	Holt		5-6	T3rd	2.5
4-18	StL.	W	8-4		16	9	Powell	Painter		6-6	3rd	1.5
4-20	At Chi.	W	10-4		16	9	Lima	Lieber	Elarton	7-6	3rd	2.0
4-21	At Chi.	W	10-3		13	10	Reynolds	Sanders		8-6	T2nd	1.0
4-23	At Cin.	L	5-7		11	10	Sullivan	Holt	Graves	8-7	T2nd	2.0
4-24	At Cin.	W	4-3		6	5	Elarton	Graves	Wagner	9-7	2nd	1.0
4-25	At Cin.	L	6-7		8	10	Harnisch	Henry	Williamson	9-8	2nd	2.0
4-26	Ari.	W	5-2		6	7	Lima	Stottlemyre	Wagner	10-8	2nd	1.5
4-27	Ari.	W	11-0		14	6	Reynolds	Reynoso		11-8	2nd	1.5
4-28	Ari.	L	6-10		7	14	Holmes	Wagner		11-9	2nd	1.5
4-29	Ari.	W	5-2		12	4	Hampton	Daal	Wagner	12-9	2nd	0.5
4-30	At Fla.	W	8-1		9	9	Bergman	Meadows		13-9	1st	+0.5
5-1	At Fla.	W	6-4		10	11	Lima	Springer	Wagner	14-9	1st	+0.5
5-2	At Fla.	W	3-2		13	9	Reynolds	Fernandez	Wagner	15-9	1st	+0.5
5-3	At N.Y.	L	3-5		6	9	Reed	Holt	Franco	15-10	1st	+0.5
5-4	At N.Y.	W	6-1		13	3	Hampton	Leiter		16-10	1st	+0.5
5-5	At N.Y.	W	5-4		8	11	Powell	Benitez	Wagner	17-10	1st	+1.5
5-7	Mon.	W	5-2		8	9	Lima	Batista		18-10	1st	+2.0
5-8	Mon.	L	5-6		9	12	Hermanson	Reynolds	Urbina	18-11	1st	+2.0
5-9	Mon.	L	2-4		9	13	Pavano	Holt	Urbina	18-12	1st	+2.0
5-10	Pit.	W	6-0		13	5	Hampton	Schourek		19-12	1st	+2.0
5-11	Pit.	W	19-8		18	14	Bergman	Ritchie		20-12	1st	+3.0
5-12	Pit.	W	6-2		10	8	Lima	Schmidt		21-12	1st	+4.0
5-14	S.F	W	7-4		14	7	Reynolds	Rueter	Wagner	22-12	1st	+5.0
5-15	S.F	W	10-5		12	9	Hampton	Gardner		23-12	1st	+5.0
5-16	S.F	L	4-5	(11)	9	10	Nen	Elarton	Nathan	23-13	1st	+4.0
5-18	At L.A.	W	11-3		12	9	Lima	Perez		24-13	1st	+4.0
5-19	At L.A.	L	2-5		5	8	Brown	Reynolds		24-14	1st	+3.5
5-20	At L.A.	W	4-3	(10)	6	9	Wagner	Shaw		25-14	1st	+3.5
5-21	At S.F	L	3-4		7	12	Johnstone	Powell	Nen	25-15	1st	+2.5
5-22	At S.F	L	1-3		4	7	Ortiz	Holt	Nen	25-16	1st	+2.5
5-23	At S.F	W	4-1		5	4	Lima	Nathan	Wagner	26-16	1st	+2.5
5-24	Col.	W	5-2		8	9	Reynolds	Bohanon		27-16	1st	+3.5
5-25	Col.	W	2-1	(12)	9	5	Elarton	DeJean		28-16	1st	+4.5
5-26	Col.	W	3-2		9	7	Powell	Astacio		29-16	1st	+4.5
5-27	Col.	L	3-4		4	7	Dipoto	Miller	Veres	29-17	1st	+4.0
5-28	At Pit.	L	5-6		6	9	Ritchie	Lima	Williams	29-18	1st	+3.0
5-29	At Pit.	L	1-5		5	8	Cordova	Reynolds		29-19	1st	+2.0
5-30	At Pit.	L	3-7		4	11	Benson	Hampton		29-20	1st	+1.0
6-1	At Mil.	W	3-0	(8)	5	6	Bergman	Karl		30-20	1st	+2.0
6-2	At Mil.	W	9-1		9	4	Lima	Eldred		31-20	1st	+2.0
6-3	At Mil.	L	1-4		7	10	Woodard	Reynolds	Wickman	31-21	1st	+1.0
6-4	At Min.	W	7-6		14	6	Hampton	Trombley	Wagner	32-21	1st	+1.0
6-5	At Min.	W	6-5		9	11	Elarton	Mays	Wagner	33-21	1st	+2.0
6-6	At Min.	L	6-13		12	21	Sampson	Bergman		33-22	1st	+1.5
6-7	At Chi. (AL)	W	8-2		17	8	Lima	Snyder		34-22	1st	+2.0
6-8	At Chi. (AL)	L	3-4		9	7	Navarro	Reynolds	Howry	34-23	1st	+1.0
6-9	At Chi. (AL)	W	13-4		17	9	Hampton	Baldwin		35-23	1st	+2.0
6-11	S.D.	W	2-1		5	4	Bergman	Williams	Wagner	36-23	1st	+3.0
6-12	S.D.	W	3-2		7	7	Lima	Wall	Wagner	37-23	1st	+4.0
6-13	S.D.	W	4-3		9	8	Reynolds	Murray	Wagner	38-23	1st	+4.5
6-14	Atl.	W	10-4		13	10	Hampton	Perez	Miller	39-23	1st	+5.0
6-15	Atl.	L	3-4		6	7	Glavine	Elarton	Rocker	39-24	1st	+4.5
6-16	Atl.	L	1-3		3	14	Maddux	Bergman	Rocker	39-25	1st	+4.5
6-17	Atl.	L	5-8		6	13	Millwood	Lima	Seanez	39-26	1st	+4.0
6-18	Mon.	W	5-0		6	6	Reynolds	Hermanson		40-26	1st	+4.0
6-19	Mon.	W	5-2		10	8	Hampton	Pavano	Wagner	41-26	1st	+5.0
6-20	Mon.	W	11-3		9	11	Holt	Smith		42-26	1st	+6.0
6-21	At StL.	L	3-5		5	10	Bottenfield	Bergman	Bottalico	42-27	1st	+5.0
6-22	At StL.	L	3-4	(14)	11	13	Mohler	McCurry		42-28	1st	+4.0
6-23	At StL.	W	8-4		12	14	Reynolds	Acevedo		43-28	1st	+4.0
6-24	Cin.	L	0-3		1	5	Villone	Hampton	Graves	43-29	1st	+3.0

Date	Opp.	Res.	Score	(inn.*)	Hits	Opp. hits	Winning pitcher	Losing pitcher	Save	Record	Pos.	GB
6-25	Cin.	L	7-10		10	12	Tomko	Holt	Williamson	43-30	1st	+2.0
6-26	Cin.	L	1-8		2	11	Parris	Bergman		43-31	1st	+1.0
6-27	Cin.	L	2-5		5	12	Harnisch	Lima		43-32	2nd	...
6-29	StL.	W	5-4		7	8	Elarton	Aybar	Wagner	44-32	2nd	...
6-30	StL.	W	11-3		13	8	Hampton	Jimenez		45-32	2nd	...
7-1	StL.	L	4-10		10	12	Bottenfield	Holt		45-33	2nd	1.0
7-2	At Cin.	W	7-5		15	11	Powell	Belinda	Wagner	46-33	2nd	...
7-3	At Cin.	L	0-10		5	13	Harnisch	Elarton	Reyes	46-34	2nd	1.0
7-4	At Cin.	W	5-3		8	12	Reynolds	Avery	Wagner	47-34	2nd	...
7-5	At Cin.	L	2-5		6	11	Villone	Holt	Graves	47-35	2nd	1.0
7-6	At Ari.	W	3-1		7	5	Lima	Daal	Wagner	48-35	2nd	...
7-7	At Ari.	L	7-13		11	14	Chouinard	Miller		48-36	2nd	...
7-8	At Ari.	L	7-8	(11)	13	15	Olson	Williams		48-37	2nd	1.0
7-9	At K.C.	W	6-5		9	12	Cabrera	Montgomery	Holt	49-37	2nd	1.0
7-10	At K.C.	W	3-2		10	10	Hampton	Appier	Wagner	50-37	2nd	...
7-11	At K.C.	W	7-3		8	9	Lima	Suppan	Powell	51-37	2nd	...
7-15	Det.	W	8-6		9	12	Miller	Blair	Wagner	52-37	2nd	...
7-16	Det.	W	2-1		8	4	Cabrera	Brocail		53-37	1st	+1.0
7-17	Det.	W	3-2	(10)	10	9	Wagner	Jones		54-37	1st	+1.0
7-18	Cle.	W	2-0		4	4	Hampton	Wright		55-37	1st	+2.0
7-19	Cle.	W	3-2	(11)	4	6	Cabrera	Candiotti		56-37	1st	+3.0
7-20	Cle.	L	1-7		6	12	Colon	Reynolds		56-38	1st	+2.0
7-21	Ari.	L	4-7		8	10	Chouinard	Powell	Mantei	56-39	1st	+1.0
7-22	Ari.	L	1-2		7	7	Benes	Lima	Mantei	56-40	1st	+1.0
7-23	S.D.	W	7-4		7	8	Hampton	Wall		57-40	1st	+2.5
7-24	S.D.	W	5-2		10	8	Holt	Clement	Wagner	58-40	1st	+2.5
7-25	S.D.	W	5-2		11	8	Reynolds	Ashby		59-40	1st	+2.5
7-26	At Col.	W	8-5		17	10	Williams	Veres	Wagner	60-40	1st	+2.5
7-27	At Col.	W	6-3		12	10	Lima	Bohanon	Wagner	61-40	1st	+2.5
7-28	At Col.	W	16-8		21	18	Hampton	Ramirez		62-40	1st	+3.5
7-29	At Col.	L	2-4		9	11	Kile	Holt	Veres	62-41	1st	+2.5
7-30	At S.D.	W	5-1		8	6	Reynolds	Clement		63-41	1st	+2.5
7-31	At S.D.	W	8-5		10	7	Henry	Miceli		64-41	1st	+3.5
8-1	At S.D.	L	3-10		6	15	Hitchcock	Lima		64-42	1st	+2.5
8-3	L.A.	W	7-2		10	6	Hampton	Dreifort		65-42	1st	+2.5
8-4	L.A.	L	1-2		4	4	Brown	Holt		65-43	1st	+1.5
8-5	L.A.	W	7-0		11	5	Reynolds	Valdes		66-43	1st	+2.5
8-6†	At Chi.	W	6-1		10	8	Lima	Farnsworth	Powell	67-43		
8-6‡	At Chi.	L	0-6		3	9	Lorraine	Bergman		67-44	1st	+2.0
8-7	At Chi.	W	10-4		14	5	Elarton	Tapani		68-44	1st	+3.0
8-8	At Chi.	W	6-2		14	7	Hampton	Bowie		69-44	1st	+3.0
8-9	At Atl.	L	3-5		14	10	Seanez	Henry	Rocker	69-45	1st	+2.0
8-10	At Atl.	L	4-6		8	8	Glavine	Reynolds	Rocker	69-46	1st	+1.0
8-11	At Atl.	L	5-8		11	10	Maddux	Lima	Rocker	69-47	1st	+1.0
8-13	Pit.	L	5-6	(13)	11	8	Clontz	Miller	Williams	69-48	2nd	...
8-14	Pit.	W	7-1		6	6	Holt	Benson		70-48	2nd	...
8-15	Pit.	L	0-2		7	5	Ritchie	Reynolds	Williams	70-49	2nd	...
8-16	Mil.	W	2-0		8	2	Lima	Peterson	Wagner	71-49	2nd	...
8-17	Mil.	W	8-6		9	11	Elarton	Eldred	Wagner	72-49	2nd	...
8-18	Mil.	W	6-4		9	8	Williams	Plunk	Wagner	73-49	1st	+1.0
8-19	Mil.	L	5-6		10	17	Coppinger	Powell	Wickman	73-50	2nd	...
8-20	At Fla.	W	6-4	(16)	7	15	Miller	Sanchez	Wagner	74-50	1st	+1.0
8-21	At Fla.	W	5-4		8	8	Henry	Edmondson	Wagner	75-50	1st	+1.0
8-23	At N.Y.	L	2-3		10	8	Benitez	Powell		75-51	1st	+0.5
8-24	At N.Y.	W	5-1	(10)	8	5	Wagner	Cook		76-51	1st	+1.5
8-25	At N.Y.	L	0-4		7	12	Rogers	Reynolds	Cook	76-52	1st	+1.5
8-27†	Fla.	W	3-2		8	9	Lima	Springer	Wagner	77-52		
8-27‡	Fla.	L	1-3		7	11	Dempster	Holt	Alfonseca	77-53	1st	+0.5
8-28	Fla.	L	2-5		7	10	Burnett	Elarton	Alfonseca	77-54	1st	+0.5
8-29	Fla.	W	10-4		14	10	Hampton	Fernandez		78-54	1st	+1.5
8-30	N.Y.	L	1-17		5	21	Yoshii	Reynolds		78-55	1st	+0.5
8-31	N.Y.	W	6-2		7	7	Lima	Wendell		79-55	1st	+1.5
9-1	N.Y.	L	5-9		7	18	Dotel	Holt		79-56	1st	+1.5
9-3	At Mon.	W	8-1		11	7	Hampton	Smith		80-56	1st	+2.5
9-4	At Mon.	W	5-2	(10)	6	8	Cabrera	Urbina		81-56	1st	+2.5
9-5	At Mon.	W	6-2		12	9	Elarton	Telford		82-56	1st	+2.5
9-6	At Phi.	W	6-5		6	12	Lima	Wolf	Wagner	83-56	1st	+2.5
9-7	At Phi.	W	8-6		12	10	Powell	Gomes	Henry	84-56	1st	+3.0
9-8	At Phi.	W	10-2		12	6	Hampton	Schilling		85-56	1st	+3.0
9-9	At Phi.	W	3-1		9	4	Reynolds	Montgomery	Wagner	86-56	1st	+3.0
9-10	Chi.	W	6-4	(13)	12	9	Wagner	Ayala		87-56	1st	+3.0
9-11	Chi.	W	5-3		7	7	Lima	Bowie	Wagner	88-56	1st	+3.0
9-12	Chi.	W	7-1		12	6	Holt	Trachsel		89-56	1st	+3.0
9-13	Phi.	W	13-2		10	6	Hampton	Grahe		90-56	1st	+3.0

Date	Opp.	Res.	Score	(inn.*)	Hits	Opp. hits	Winning pitcher	Losing pitcher	Save	Record	Pos.	GB
9-14	Phi.	W	12-2		16	8	Reynolds	Byrd		91-56	1st	+4.0
9-15	Phi.	L	6-8	(10)	12	14	Gomes	Henry	Brewer	91-57	1st	+3.0
9-17	At StL.	L	8-11		8	18	Stephenson	Lima	Bottalico	91-58	1st	+3.5
9-18	At StL.	L	6-13		11	13	Oliver	Hampton		91-59	1st	+2.5
9-19	At StL.	W	4-3		10	7	Holt	Croushore	Wagner	92-59	1st	+3.5
9-20	At Pit.	L	5-11		9	14	Schourek	Reynolds		92-60	1st	+2.5
9-21	At Pit.	W	6-3		8	10	Elarton	Benson	Henry	93-60	1st	+3.5
9-22	At Pit.	L	2-3		6	5	Ritchie	Lima		93-61	1st	+2.5
9-24	At Mil.	W	9-4		7	8	Miller	Plunk	Powell	94-61	1st	+2.5
9-25	At Mil.	L	2-3	(10)	9	9	Karl	Reynolds	Wickman	94-62	1st	+1.5
9-26	At Mil.	L	3-11		9	16	Peterson	Elarton		94-63	1st	+0.5
9-28	Cin.	L	1-4		4	8	Harnisch	Lima	Williamson	94-64	2nd	1.0
9-29	Cin.	W	4-1		7	7	Hampton	Parris	Wagner	95-64	T1st	...
10-1	L.A.	L	1-5		7	9	Gagne	Reynolds		95-65	T1st	...
10-2	L.A.	W	3-0		6	9	Lima	Park	Wagner	96-65	1st	+1.0
10-3	L.A.	W	9-4		8	7	Hampton	Checo		97-65	1st	+1.0

Monthly records: April (13-9), May (16-11), June (16-12), July (19-9), August (15-14), September (16-9), October (2-1).
*Innings, if other than nine. † First game of a doubleheader. ‡ Second game of a doubleheader.

HIGHLIGHTS

High point: Entering the final two days of the season tied with Cincinnati for first place in the N.L. Central, the Astros turned to their two 20-game winners, Jose Lima and Mike Hampton. The staff standouts beat the Dodgers, 3-0 and 9-4, while the Reds split two games in Milwaukee. The Sunday division clincher—in which Hampton ran his record to 22-4—was the final regular-season game in Astrodome history.

Low point: The darkest day was June 13 when manager Larry Dierker suffered a grand mal seizure in the dugout during a game against San Diego. He underwent brain surgery two days later and missed 27 games (Houston was 13-14 during his absence).

Turning point: When the Astros asserted themselves and won a franchise-record 12 consecutive games from September 3 through September 14. Hampton won three times in that stretch.

Most valuable player: First baseman Jeff Bagwell, who hit .304 with 42 homers, 126 RBIs and 30 stolen bases. It was the second 30-30 season of Bagwell's career.

Most valuable pitcher: Lefthander Hampton, who shed his label of inconsistency in a compelling manner. He fashioned a 2.90 ERA and worked at least seven innings in 28 of his 34 starts. The Astros were 29-5 when Hampton took the mound.

Most improved player: Closer Billy Wagner actually got better in 1999, adding a slider to his repertoire and becoming virtually unhittable. He held opponents to a .135 average, averaged 14.9 strikeouts per nine innings, saved a career-high 39 games and posted a 1.57 ERA.

Most pleasant surprise: Injuries having ravaged the Astros' outfield, converted first baseman Daryle Ward became the everyday left fielder down the stretch and acquitted himself well. In 150 at-bats, he hit .273 with eight homers and 30 RBIs.

Biggest disappointment: Right fielder Derek Bell saw his numbers drop in nearly every offensive category. His average plummeted 78 points, to .236, and he had only 12 homers and 66 RBIs. Also, he struck out 129 times in 128 games.

Key injuries: Left fielder Moises Alou, who hit 38 homers and drove in 124 runs in 1998, missed the entire season after undergoing surgery for a knee injury incurred in pre-camp workouts. Third baseman Ken Caminiti was sidelined 79 games because of a torn muscle in his right calf. Shortstop Ricky Gutierrez spent two stints on the disabled list because of broken bones in his hands, and outfielder Richard Hidalgo had his season shortened because of knee surgery.

Notable: Houston's 97 victories marked the second-highest total in franchise history. ... Hampton and Wagner established club records for wins and saves, respectively. ... Center fielder Carl Everett had a breakthrough season. He finished tied for seventh in the N.L. batting race with a .325 mark, hit 25 homers, knocked in 108 runs and stole 27 bases. ... The 1999 season was the Astros' 35th and last at the Astrodome. They will move to Enron Field in 2000.

—CARLTON THOMPSON

RECORDS

1999 regular-season record: 97-65 (1st in N.L. Central); 50-32 at home; 47-33 on road; 25-16 vs. East; 31-31 vs. N.L. Central; 29-15 vs. West; 12-3 vs. A.L.; 27-16 vs. lefthanded starters; 70-49 vs. righthanded starters; 34-23 on grass; 63-42 on turf; 27-19 in daytime; 70-46 at night; 22-18 in one-run games; 8-5 in extra-inning games; 0-0-2 in doubleheaders.
Team record past five years: 441-351 (.557, ranks 2nd in league in that span).

TEAM LEADERS

Batting average: Carl Everett (.325).
At-bats: Craig Biggio (639).
Runs: Jeff Bagwell (143).
Hits: Craig Biggio (188).
Total Bases: Jeff Bagwell (332).
Doubles: Craig Biggio (56).
Triples: Ricky Gutierrez, Bill Spiers (5).
Home runs: Jeff Bagwell (42).
Runs batted in: Jeff Bagwell (126).
Stolen bases: Jeff Bagwell (30).
Slugging percentage: Jeff Bagwell (.591).

On-base percentage: Jeff Bagwell (.454).
Wins: Mike Hampton (22).
Earned-run average: Mike Hampton (2.90).
Complete games: Shane Reynolds (4).
Shutouts: Mike Hampton, Shane Reynolds (2).
Saves: Billy Wagner (39).
Innings pitched: Jose Lima (246.1).
Strikeouts: Shane Reynolds (197).

GAMES BY POSITION

Catcher: Tony Eusebio 98, Paul Bako 71, Randy Knorr 11, Mitch Meluskey 10.
First base: Jeff Bagwell 161, Daryle Ward 10, Jack Howell 5, Bill Spiers 1, Lance Berkman 1.
Second base: Craig Biggio 155, Russ Johnson 15, Carlos E. Hernandez 7, Bill Spiers 4, Tim Bogar 1.
Third base: Ken Caminiti 75, Bill Spiers 71, Russ Johnson 36, Tim Bogar 12, Jack Howell 3, Ricky Gutierrez 1, Jose Lima 1.
Shortstop: Tim Bogar 90, Ricky Gutierrez 80, Bill Spiers 13, Russ Johnson 2, Carlos E. Hernandez 2.
Outfield: Derek Bell 126, Carl Everett 121, Richard Hidalgo 108, Glen Barker 57, Matt Mieske 37, Bill Spiers 31, Daryle Ward 31, Lance Berkman 27, Stan Javier 18, Ryan Thompson 10, Alex Diaz 8, Craig Biggio 6, Scott Elarton 1.
Designated hitter: Daryle Ward 3, Jack Howell 2, Craig Biggio 2, Jeff Bagwell 2, Carl Everett 2, Glen Barker 1.

TOP DRAFT CHOICES

1. **Michael Rosamond**, OF, U. of Mississippi
2a. **Jay Perez**, C, Seymour (Conn.) H.S.
2b. **Travis Anderson**, RHP, U. of Washington
3. **Jim Barrett**, RHP, Fort Hill H.S., Cumberland, Md.
4. **Jon Topolski**, OF, Baylor University
5. **Mike Gallo**, LHP, Long Beach State U.
6. **Jason Lane**, OF, U. of Southern California
7. **Nick Roberts**, RHP, U. of Southern Utah
8. **Chris Sampson**, SS, Texas Tech
9. **Jonathan Helquist**, SS, University Christian H.S., Jacksonville, Fla.
10. **Greg Dobbs**, 3B, Long Beach State U.

LOS ANGELES DODGERS
NATIONAL LEAGUE WEST DIVISION

2000 Dodgers Schedule
Home games shaded. *—All-Star Game at Turner Field (Atlanta).

March

SUN	MON	TUE	WED	THU	FRI	SAT
26	27	28	29	30	31	

April

SUN	MON	TUE	WED	THU	FRI	SAT
						1
2	3 MON	4 MON	5 MON	6 MON	7 NYM	8 NYM
9 NYM	10	11 SF	12 SF	13 SF	14 CIN	15 CIN
16 CIN	17 HOU	18 HOU	19 HOU	20	21 CIN	22 CIN
23 CIN	24	25 ATL	26 ATL	27 ATL	28 FLA	29 FLA
30 FLA						

May

SUN	MON	TUE	WED	THU	FRI	SAT
	1 ATL	2 ATL	3 ATL	4	5 HOU	6 HOU
7 HOU	8 ARI	9 ARI	10 ARI	11	12 STL	13 STL
14 STL	15	16 CUB	17 CUB	18 CUB	19 FLA	20 FLA
21 FLA	22 CIN	23 CIN	24 CIN	25	26 PHI	27 PHI
28 PHI	29 NYM	30 NYM	31 NYM			

June

SUN	MON	TUE	WED	THU	FRI	SAT
				1	2 ANA	3 ANA
4 ANA	5 TEX	6 TEX	7 TEX	8	9 OAK	10 OAK
11 OAK	12 ARI	13 ARI	14 ARI	15 STL	16 STL	17 STL
18 STL	19	20 HOU	21 HOU	22 HOU	23 STL	24 STL
25 STL	26 SD	27 SD	28 SD	29 SD	30 SF	

July

SUN	MON	TUE	WED	THU	FRI	SAT
						1 SF
2 SF	3	4 SD	5 SD	6 SD	7 SEA	8 SEA
9 SEA	10	11	*12	13 ANA	14 ANA	15 ANA
16 PIT	17 PIT	18 PIT	19 COL	20 COL	21 SF	22 SF
23 SF	24 COL	25 COL	26 COL	27 COL	28 PHI	29 PHI
30 PHI	31 PIT					

August

SUN	MON	TUE	WED	THU	FRI	SAT
		1 PIT	2 PIT	3	4 MIL	5 MIL
6 MIL	7 CUB	8 CUB	9 CUB	10	11 ATL	12 ATL
13 ATL	14 FLA	15 FLA	16 FLA	17	18 NYM	19 NYM
20 NYM	21 MON	22 MON	23 MON	24 MON	25 CUB	26 CUB
27 CUB	28 MIL	29 MIL	30 MIL	31 MIL		

September

SUN	MON	TUE	WED	THU	FRI	SAT
				1 PHI	2 PHI
3 PHI	4 PIT	5 PIT	6 PIT	7	8 COL	9 COL
10 COL	11 ARI	12 ARI	13 ARI	14 COL	15 COL	16 COL
17 COL	18 ARI	19 ARI	20 ARI	21	22 SD	23 SD
24 SD	25	26 SF	27 SF	28 SF	29 SD	30 SD

October

SUN	MON	TUE	WED	THU	FRI	SAT
1 SD	2	3	4	5	6	7

2000 SEASON
CLUB DIRECTORY

Chairman and CEO
Bob Daly
President and COO
Bob Graziano
Board of directors
Chase Carey, Peter Chernin, Peter O'Malley, Bob Graziano, Sam Fernandez
Executive vice president and g.m.
Kevin Malone
Executive vice president and CMO
Kris Rone
Senior vice president, communications
Derrick Hall
Senior vice president
Tommy Lasorda
Vice president, communications
Tommy Hawkins
Traveling secretary
Billy DeLury
Asst. secretary and general counsel
Santiago Fernandez
Managing director, Dodgertown
Craig Callan
Asst. general manager, minor leagues
Bill Geivett
Director, Finance and CFO
Christine Hurley
Dir. of management info. services
Mike Mularky
Director of ticket marketing
Bob Wymbs
Director, media relations
To be announced
Assistant director, media relations
Shaun Rachau
Dir., broadcasting and new media
Brent Shyer
Director, community relations
Don Newcombe
Director, public affairs
Monique Brandon
Director, stadium operations
Doug Duennes
Director, ticket operations
Billy Hunter
Director, human resources and admin.
Gina Galasso
Assistant to general manager, scouting
Ed Creech
Assistant director of scouting
Matt Slater
Head trainer
Stan Johnston
Assistant trainer
Matt Wilson
Physical therapist
Pat Screnar
Strength and conditioning
Todd Clausen
Club physicians
Dr. Frank Jobe, Dr. Michael Mellman, Dr. Herndon Harding
Special asst. to the general manager
Jeff Schugel
Senior scouting advisor
Don Welke
Pro scouts
Phil Favia, Dan Freed, Carl Loewenstine, Marty Maier, Terry Reynolds, Ron Rizzi, Mark Weidemaier
Full-time scouts
John Barr, Gib Bodet, Mike Brito, Ray Brown, Doug Carpenter, Jim Chapman, Bob Darwin, Joe Ferrone, Scott Groot, Mike Hankins, Hanke Jones, Lon Joyce, John Kosciak, Marty Lamb, Jimmy Lester, Mike Leuzinger, Bump Merriweather, Camilo Pascual, Bill Pleis, Willie Powell, Scott Sharp, Mark Sheehy, Chris Smith, Bob Szymkowski, Tom Thomas, Mitch Webster

MINOR LEAGUE AFFILIATES

Class	Team	League	Manager
AAA	Albuquerque	Pacific Coast	Tom Gamboa
AA	San Antonio	Texas	Rick Burleson
A	San Bernardino	California	Dino Ebel
A	Vero Beach	Florida State	John Shoemaker
A	Yakima	Northwest	Butch Hughes
Rookie	Great Falls	Pioneer	Juan Bustabad

BROADCAST INFORMATION

Radio: XTRA-AM (1150); KWKW-AM (1330, Spanish language).
TV: KTLA-TV (Channel 5)
Cable TV: Fox Sports Net 2.

SPRING TRAINING

Ballpark (city): Holman Stadium (Vero Beach, Fla.).
Ticket information: 561-569-6858.

SPRING TRAINING ROSTER

Manager—Davey Johnson.
Coaches—Rick Dempsey (26), Rick Down (44), Glenn Hoffman (35), Claude Osteen (38), John Shelby (31), Jim Tracy (12).

No.	PITCHERS	B/T	Ht./Wt.	Born	1999 clubs
	Adams, Terry	R/R	6-3/205	3-6-73	West Tenn, Chicago N.L.
52	Arnold, Jamie	R/R	6-2/188	3-24-74	Albuquerque, Los Angeles
27	Brown, Kevin	R/R	6-4/200	3-14-65	Los Angeles
37	Dreifort, Darren	R/R	6-2/211	5-3-72	Los Angeles
46	Gagne, Eric	R/R	6-2/195	1-7-76	San Antonio, Los Angeles
	Garcia, Apostol	R/R	6-0/155	8-3-76	Jacksonville, San Antonio
49	Herges, Matt	L/R	6-0/200	4-1-70	Albuquerque, Los Angeles
	Hershiser, Orel	R/R	6-3/195	9-16-58	New York N.L.
60	Judd, Mike	R/R	6-1/217	6-30-75	Albuquerque, Los Angeles
65	Masaoka, Onan	R/L	6-0/180	10-27-77	Los Angeles
75	Mills, Alan	R/R	6-1/195	10-18-66	Los Angeles
	Naulty, Dan	R/R	6-6/224	1-6-70	New York A.L., Columbus
	Olson, Gregg	R/R	6-4/210	10-11-66	Arizona
13	Osuna, Antonio	R/R	5-11/206	4-12-73	San Bernardino, Los Angeles
61	Park, Chan Ho	R/R	6-2/204	6-30-73	Los Angeles
33	Perez, Carlos	L/L	6-3/210	1-14-71	Los Angeles, Albuquerque
	Ricketts, Chad	R/R	6-5/225	2-12-75	West Tenn
41	Shaw, Jeff	R/R	6-2/200	7-7-66	Los Angeles
54	Williams, Jeff	R/L	6-0/185	6-6-72	Albuquerque, Los Angeles

No.	CATCHERS	B/T	Ht./Wt.	Born	1999 clubs
9	Hundley, Todd	B/R	5-11/199	5-27-69	Los Angeles
16	LoDuca, Paul	R/R	5-10/185	4-12-72	Los Angeles, Albuquerque
63	Pena, Angel	R/R	5-10/228	2-16-75	Albuquerque, Los Angeles

No.	INFIELDERS	B/T	Ht./Wt.	Born	1999 clubs
29	Beltre, Adrian	R/R	5-11/170	4-7-78	Los Angeles
66	Bocachica, Hiram	R/R	5-11/165	3-4-76	San Antonio
17	Castro, Juan	R/R	5-10/187	6-20-72	Albuquerque, Los Angeles
3	Cora, Alex	L/R	6-0/180	10-18-75	Albuquerque, Los Angeles
8	Grudzielanek, Mark	R/R	6-1/185	6-30-70	Los Angeles, San Bernardino
25	Hansen, Dave	L/R	6-0/195	11-24-68	Los Angeles
23	Karros, Eric	R/R	6-4/226	11-4-67	Los Angeles
	Orie, Kevin	R/R	6-4/215	9-1-72	Florida, Calgary
	Santangelo, F.P.	B/R	5-10/190	10-24-67	San Francisco
5	Vizcaino, Jose	B/R	6-1/180	3-26-68	Los Angeles

No.	OUTFIELDERS	B/T	Ht./Wt.	Born	1999 clubs
57	Gibbs, Kevin	B/R	6-2/185	4-3-74	Albuquerque
15	Green, Shawn	L/L	6-4/200	11-10-72	Toronto
28	Hollandsworth, Todd	L/L	6-2/215	4-20-73	San Bernardino, Los Angeles
47	Hubbard, Trenidad	R/R	5-9/185	5-11-66	Albuquerque, Los Angeles
10	Sheffield, Gary	R/R	5-11/205	11-18-68	Los Angeles
22	White, Devon	B/R	6-2/190	12-29-62	Los Angeles

BALLPARK INFORMATION

Ballpark (capacity, surface)
  Dodger Stadium (56,000, grass)
Address
  1000 Elysian Park Ave.
  Los Angeles, CA 90012
Business phone
  323-224-1500
Ticket information
  323-224-1448
Ticket prices
  $17 (field box)
  $15 (inner reserve)
  $13 (loge box)
  $10 (outer reserve)
  $6 (top deck, left and right pavilion)
Field dimensions (from home plate)
  To left field at foul line, 330 feet
  To center field, 395 feet
  To right field at foul line, 330 feet
First game played
  April 10, 1962 (Reds 6, Dodgers 3)

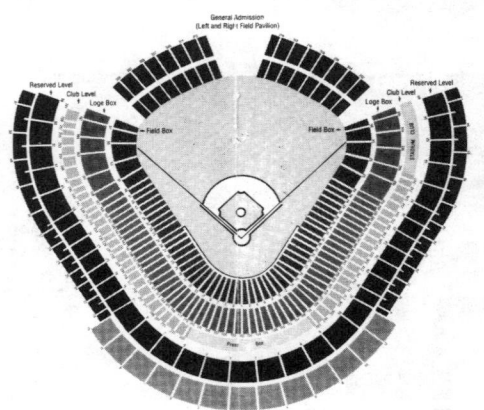

2000 SEASON *Los Angeles Dodgers*

Date	Opp.	Res.	Score	(inn.*)	Hits	Opp. hits	Winning pitcher	Losing pitcher	Save	Record	Pos.	GB
4-6	Ari.	W	3-2	(10)	10	5	Mills	Anderson		2-0	T1st	...
4-7	Ari.	W	6-4		12	7	Valdes	Benes	Shaw	3-0	T1st	...
4-8	Col.	L	2-4		5	5	Bohanon	Perez	Veres	3-1	2nd	1.0
4-9	Col.	W	9-6		17	9	Dreifort	Thomson	Shaw	4-1	2nd	1.0
4-10	Col.	W	2-0		5	3	Brown	Kile	Shaw	5-1	T1st	...
4-12	At Ari.	L	6-12		11	10	Benes	Park		5-2	2nd	1.0
4-13	At Ari.	L	6-7	(16)	11	21	Chouinard	Mlicki		5-3	2nd	1.0
4-14	At Ari.	L	2-6		4	11	Daal	Perez		5-4	2nd	1.0
4-15	At Ari.	W	8-1		8	2	Dreifort	Johnson		6-4	2nd	1.0
4-16	At S.D.	L	0-3		5	11	Ashby	Brown		6-5	2nd	1.0
4-17	At S.D.	W	7-3		8	9	Park	Reyes		7-5	2nd	1.0
4-18	At S.D.	L	3-4		8	8	Miceli	Masaoka	Hoffman	7-6	2nd	1.0
4-19	Atl.	L	3-11		8	18	Smoltz	Perez		7-7	T2nd	2.0
4-20	Atl.	W	5-4		10	4	Dreifort	Millwood	Shaw	8-7	T2nd	1.0
4-21	Atl.	L	4-11	(12)	7	13	Remlinger	Kubenka		8-8	3rd	2.0
4-23	StL.	L	5-12		11	11	Jimenez	Park		8-9	3rd	2.5
4-24	StL.	W	6-1		8	6	Valdes	Osborne		9-9	3rd	2.5
4-25	StL.	L	4-6		8	9	Bottenfield	Dreifort	Acevedo	9-10	3rd	3.5
4-27	At Mil.	W	3-2		7	6	Brown	Roque	Shaw	10-10	3rd	3.5
4-28	At Mil.	W	3-2		10	11	Park	Woodard	Shaw	11-10	3rd	3.5
4-29	At Mil.	W	10-4		13	8	Valdes	Eldred		12-10	3rd	3.5
4-30	At Phi.	W	4-3		8	9	Perez	Byrd	Shaw	13-10	2nd	2.5
5-1	At Phi.	W	12-6		12	13	Dreifort	Spoljaric		14-10	2nd	1.5
5-2	At Phi.	L	3-12		8	13	Schilling	Brown		14-11	2nd	1.5
5-3	At Mon.	W	7-0		13	7	Park	Hermanson		15-11	2nd	0.5
5-4	At Mon.	L	1-2		4	7	Pavano	Valdes	Urbina	15-12	2nd	1.5
5-5	At Mon.	W	8-2		13	4	Arnold	Vazquez		16-12	2nd	0.5
5-7	Fla.	L	3-6		9	8	Springer	Dreifort	Mantei	16-13	2nd	1.5
5-8	Fla.	W	8-1		14	3	Brown	Hernandez		17-13	2nd	1.5
5-9	Fla.	L	4-6		6	7	Edmondson	Borbon	Mantei	17-14	2nd	1.5
5-10	Chi.	W	4-3		7	12	Valdes	Trachsel	Shaw	18-14	2nd	1.5
5-11	Chi.	L	5-10		9	11	Farnsworth	Perez		18-15	3rd	1.5
5-12	Chi.	W	3-2		8	5	Arnold	Beck		19-15	3rd	1.5
5-14	At StL.	W	7-3		10	8	Brown	Jimenez		20-15	2nd	0.5
5-15	At StL.	L	5-8		12	12	Bottenfield	Park		20-16	3rd	0.5
5-16	At StL.	L	4-5		9	8	Bottalico	Shaw		20-17	3rd	1.5
5-18	Hou.	L	3-11		9	12	Lima	Perez		20-18	3rd	2.0
5-19	Hou.	W	5-2		8	5	Brown	Reynolds		21-18	3rd	1.0
5-20	Hou.	L	3-4	(10)	9	6	Wagner	Shaw		21-19	3rd	1.5
5-21	StL.	L	6-10		7	10	Acevedo	Valdes	Aybar	21-20	3rd	2.5
5-22	StL.	W	10-7		14	12	Dreifort	Sodowsky	Shaw	22-20	3rd	2.5
5-23	StL.	L	3-8		11	14	Oliver	Perez		22-21	3rd	2.5
5-25	At Cin.	L	2-3		7	5	Parris	Brown	Graves	22-22	3rd	3.5
5-26	At Cin.	W	9-3		10	7	Park	Tomko		23-22	3rd	3.5
5-27	At Cin.	W	4-3		8	7	Valdes	Harnisch	Shaw	24-22	3rd	2.5
5-28	At Atl.	L	2-4		6	8	Perez	Dreifort	Rocker	24-23	3rd	3.0
5-29	At Atl.	W	2-1		7	5	Perez	Glavine	Shaw	25-23	3rd	3.0
5-30	At Atl.	W	5-4	(11)	9	8	Borbon	Remlinger	Shaw	26-23	3rd	3.0
5-31	At Pit.	L	4-5		9	7	Wilkins	Arnold	Williams	26-24	3rd	4.0
6-1	At Pit.	L	2-4		7	8	Schmidt	Valdes	Williams	26-25	3rd	4.0
6-2	At Pit.	L	4-8		8	11	Ritchie	Dreifort		26-26	3rd	5.0
6-4	Ana.	W	5-4		11	10	Brown	Olivares	Shaw	27-26	3rd	5.0
6-5	Ana.	W	7-4		12	7	Masaoka	Belcher	Shaw	28-26	3rd	4.0
6-6	Ana.	L	5-7		9	11	Hill	Perez	Percival	28-27	3rd	5.0
6-7	Tex.	L	2-3		6	10	Sele	Valdes	Wetteland	28-28	3rd	5.0
6-8	Tex.	L	6-7	(13)	11	16	Zimmerman	Mills	Munoz	28-29	3rd	5.0
6-9	Tex.	W	7-2		11	5	Brown	Clark		29-29	3rd	5.0
6-11	At Oak.	L	6-12		9	16	Oquist	Perez	Mathews	29-30	3rd	6.0
6-12	At Oak.	L	3-4		12	8	Rogers	Valdes	Taylor	29-31	3rd	6.0
6-13	At Oak.	L	3-9		10	8	Hudson	Dreifort		29-32	3rd	7.0
6-15	Pit.	L	1-11		7	14	Ritchie	Brown		29-33	4th	8.5
6-16	Pit.	W	6-5		12	11	Borbon	Clontz	Shaw	30-33	4th	8.5
6-17	Pit.	L	3-8		5	14	Benson	Park		30-34	4th	9.0
6-18	Phi.	L	1-2		4	6	Schilling	Valdes	Gomes	30-35	4th	9.0
6-19	Phi.	W	8-1		13	7	Dreifort	Person		31-35	4th	9.0
6-20	Phi.	W	3-2		6	5	Brown	Ogea	Shaw	32-35	4th	8.0
6-22	S.D.	L	1-4		7	7	Hitchcock	Park	Hoffman	32-36	4th	7.5
6-23	S.D.	L	2-6		5	7	Williams	Valdes	Hoffman	32-37	4th	7.5
6-24	S.D.	L	1-2		5	6	Ashby	Dreifort	Miceli	32-38	4th	8.5
6-25	At S.F	W	4-2		9	6	Brown	Estes	Shaw	33-38	4th	7.5
6-26	At S.F	W	7-6		15	11	Mills	Nen	Shaw	34-38	4th	6.5
6-27	At S.F	L	7-8		12	14	Gardner	Park	Nen	34-39	5th	7.5

Date	Opp.	Res.	Score	(inn.*)	Hits	Opp. hits	Winning pitcher	Losing pitcher	Save	Record	Pos.	GB
6-29	At S.D.	L	3-4	(12)	5	13	Wall	Maddux		34-40	5th	7.5
6-30	At S.D.	L	2-11		8	14	Boehringer	Brown		34-41	5th	7.5
7-1	At S.D.	L	3-6		5	10	Clement	Dreifort	Hoffman	34-42	5th	8.5
7-2	S.F	L	3-6		9	8	Brock	Perez	Nen	34-43	5th	9.5
7-3	S.F	L	1-9		4	12	Gardner	Park		34-44	5th	10.5
7-4	S.F	W	7-1		11	5	Valdes	Rueter		35-44	5th	9.5
7-5	At Col.	L	4-8		11	14	Kile	Brown		35-45	5th	10.5
7-6	At Col.	L	2-5		6	10	Astacio	Dreifort		35-46	5th	11.5
7-7	At Col.	L	5-7		11	14	DeJean	Arnold	Veres	35-47	5th	11.5
7-8	At Col.	W	11-8		12	12	Park	Bohanon	Shaw	36-47	5th	11.0
7-9	Sea.	W	5-0		11	7	Valdes	Garcia		37-47	5th	11.0
7-10	Sea.	W	2-1		6	3	Shaw	Paniagua		38-47	5th	11.0
7-11	Sea.	W	14-3		15	6	Dreifort	Fassero	Masaoka	39-47	5th	10.0
7-15	At Ana.	L	6-7	(10)	12	10	Petkovsek	Mills		39-48	5th	10.0
7-16	At Ana.	W	3-1		5	5	Valdes	Olivares	Shaw	40-48	5th	9.0
7-17	At Ana.	W	13-3		14	7	Park	Sparks		41-48	T4th	9.0
7-18	At Pit.	L	5-6	(10)	14	11	Sauerbeck	Mills		41-49	5th	9.0
7-19	At Pit.	W	12-7		14	6	Dreifort	Silva		42-49	4th	8.0
7-20	At Pit.	W	8-4		13	7	Brown	Clontz		43-49	4th	7.0
7-21	Col.	L	4-5		8	13	Astacio	Valdes	Veres	43-50	4th	8.0
7-22†	Col.	L	1-4		3	8	Jones	Park	Veres	43-51		
7-22‡	Col.	L	11-12		15	13	Lee	Masaoka	Veres	43-52	5th	8.5
7-23	At Ari.	L	1-10		2	11	Daal	Perez		43-53	5th	9.5
7-24	At Ari.	L	0-3		6	7	Anderson	Dreifort	Mantei	43-54	5th	10.0
7-25	At Ari.	W	2-1		8	3	Brown	Johnson	Shaw	44-54	T4th	9.0
7-26	Cin.	L	3-5	(10)	8	13	Belinda	Shaw		44-55	T4th	10.0
7-27	Cin.	L	3-5	(10)	10	15	Graves	Mills	Williamson	44-56	T4th	11.0
7-28	Cin.	W	9-1		13	7	Checo	Reyes	Arnold	45-56	4th	11.0
7-29	Cin.	L	5-7		9	14	Harnisch	Dreifort	Williamson	45-57	T4th	11.5
7-30	Ari.	L	5-6		11	9	Chouinard	Shaw	Mantei	45-58	5th	12.5
7-31	Ari.	L	2-4		6	9	Johnson	Valdes		45-59	5th	13.5
8-1	Ari.	W	4-2		11	9	Masaoka	Benes	Shaw	46-59	5th	12.5
8-3	At Hou.	L	2-7		6	10	Hampton	Dreifort		46-60	5th	13.0
8-4	At Hou.	W	2-1		4	4	Brown	Holt		47-60	T4th	13.0
8-5	At Hou.	L	0-7		5	11	Reynolds	Valdes		47-61	5th	13.5
8-6	At N.Y.	L	1-2		5	4	Dotel	Park	Benitez	47-62	5th	13.5
8-7	At N.Y.	W	7-6		13	11	Borbon	Taylor	Shaw	48-62	T4th	13.5
8-8	At N.Y.	W	14-3		14	7	Dreifort	Reed		49-62	4th	13.5
8-9	At N.Y.	W	9-2		13	6	Brown	Hershiser		50-62	4th	13.5
8-10	At Mon.	L	4-6		7	8	Thurman	Valdes	Urbina	50-63	4th	14.5
8-11	At Mon.	W	9-7		11	15	Maddux	Ayala	Shaw	51-63	4th	14.5
8-12	At Mon.	W	10-5		11	10	Judd	Hermanson		52-63	T3rd	14.0
8-13	Atl.	L	3-7		5	12	Millwood	Dreifort		52-64	T3rd	14.0
8-14	Atl.	W	8-1		14	5	Brown	Smoltz		53-64	T3rd	13.0
8-15	Atl.	L	4-5	(11)	12	10	Remlinger	Arnold	Rocker	53-65	4th	14.0
8-16	Fla.	L	5-7		11	8	Nunez	Park		53-66	4th	15.0
8-17	Fla.	L	1-6		7	11	Burnett	Judd	Springer	53-67	4th	16.0
8-18	Fla.	W	7-0		11	7	Dreifort	Meadows		54-67	4th	16.0
8-20	At Phi.	W	8-5	(10)	5	12	Mills	Gomes		55-67	T3rd	15.0
8-21	At Phi.	L	5-6	(11)	12	10	Gomes	Masaoka		55-68	T3rd	16.0
8-22	At Phi.	W	9-7		12	9	Park	Shumaker	Shaw	56-68	3rd	16.0
8-23	At Mil.	W	8-4		8	9	Dreifort	Nomo	Shaw	57-68	3rd	16.0
8-24	At Mil.	W	5-2		11	4	Judd	Karl	Shaw	58-68	3rd	16.0
8-25	At Mil.	L	7-9		9	9	Plunk	Borbon	Wickman	58-69	3rd	17.0
8-27	Chi.	W	9-0		13	7	Valdes	Trachsel		59-69	3rd	16.5
8-28	Chi.	W	4-3		7	8	Park	Lorraine	Shaw	60-69	3rd	16.5
8-29	Chi.	L	0-6		2	9	Farnsworth	Dreifort		60-70	3rd	17.5
8-30	Mil.	W	6-1		8	9	Brown	Pulsipher		61-70	3rd	17.5
8-31	Mil.	W	5-3		12	8	Judd	Peterson	Shaw	62-70	3rd	16.5
9-1	Mil.	L	4-5		7	8	Eldred	Valdes	Wickman	62-71	3rd	16.5
9-3	At Chi.	W	8-6		9	12	Park	Sanders	Shaw	63-71	3rd	15.5
9-4	At Chi.	W	6-0		11	2	Brown	Farnsworth		64-71	3rd	15.5
9-5	At Chi.	W	4-1		6	7	Dreifort	Lieber	Shaw	65-71	3rd	15.5
9-6	At Fla.	L	6-8		10	15	Meadows	Valdes	Alfonseca	65-72	3rd	16.0
9-7	At Fla.	L	1-2		7	6	Sanchez	Herges	Alfonseca	65-73	3rd	17.0
9-8	At Fla.	L	4-5	(13)	13	12	Medina	Masaoka		65-74	3rd	18.0
9-9	N.Y.	L	1-3		2	7	Hershiser	Brown	Benitez	65-75	4th	18.0
9-10	N.Y.	W	3-1		6	6	Dreifort	Leiter	Shaw	66-75	4th	18.0
9-11	N.Y.	L	2-6		7	11	Yoshii	Valdes		66-76	4th	19.0
9-12	N.Y.	L	3-10		14	12	Rogers	Gagne		66-77	4th	20.0
9-13	Mon.	W	12-4		15	10	Park	Smith		67-77	4th	20.0
9-14	Mon.	L	0-3		1	9	Vazquez	Brown		67-78	4th	21.0
9-15	Mon.	L	7-10		14	12	Powell	Arnold	Urbina	67-79	4th	21.0
9-17	At Col.	L	10-18		11	20	Hackman	Checo		67-80	4th	21.0
9-18	At Col.	W	5-4		9	10	Park	Astacio	Shaw	68-80	4th	21.0
9-19	At Col.	W	5-2	(8)	8	7	Brown	Thomson	Borbon	69-80	4th	21.0

Date	Opp.	Res.	Score	(inn.*)	Hits	Opp. hits	Winning pitcher	Losing pitcher	Save	Record	Pos.	GB
9-20	S.F	W	6-5		7	7	Borbon	Embree		70-80	4th	20.0
9-21	S.F	W	9-4		11	6	Williams	Rueter		71-80	4th	20.0
9-22	S.F	L	4-5		6	8	Gardner	Borbon	Nen	71-81	4th	21.0
9-23	S.F	W	5-3		9	5	Park	Hernandez	Shaw	72-81	T3rd	20.5
9-24	S.D.	W	5-1		10	6	Brown	Hitchcock		73-81	3rd	20.5
9-25	S.D.	L	2-3		5	5	Williams	Herges	Hoffman	73-82	T3rd	21.5
9-26	S.D.	W	10-7		13	6	Checo	Miceli		74-82	3rd	21.5
9-28	At S.F	W	6-3		12	5	Park	Nathan		75-82	3rd	22.0
9-29	At S.F	L	1-5		12	7	Hernandez	Brown	Patrick	75-83	3rd	22.0
9-30	At S.F	W	9-4		15	8	Williams	Estes		76-83	3rd	22.0
10-1	At Hou.	W	5-1		9	7	Gagne	Reynolds		77-83	3rd	21.0
10-2	At Hou.	L	0-3		9	6	Lima	Park	Wagner	77-84	3rd	22.0
10-3	At Hou.	L	4-9		7	8	Hampton	Checo		77-85	3rd	23.0

Monthly records: April (13-10), May (13-14), June (8-17), July (11-18), August (17-11), September (14-13), October (1-2).
*Innings, if other than nine. † First game of a doubleheader. ‡ Second game of a doubleheader.

HIGHLIGHTS

High point: The Dodgers won five of their first six games. Raul Mondesi was powering the club with his bat, and the pitching staff appeared to be as good as advertised—maybe better. Fans thought the Dodgers might be back on track.
Low point: When Mondesi blasted manager Davey Johnson and general manager Kevin Malone in an expletive-filled tirade on August 11 at Montreal. The right fielder said Johnson and Malone treated him unfairly, and he demanded to be traded. The comments rocked the organization.
Turning point: After the 5-1 start, the Dodgers went 3-7 against the Diamondbacks, Padres and Braves. Their many deficiencies were exposed during that span, including catcher Todd Hundley's ineffectiveness against baserunners. Still bothered by late-1997 surgery on his right elbow, Hundley threw out only 18 percent of basestealers in 1999.
Most valuable player: Outfielder Gary Sheffield. He made a successful switch from right field to left and had an outstanding offensive season, batting .301 with 34 home runs and 101 RBIs. He became the second player in Dodgers history to bat at least .300 with 30 homers, 100 RBIs, 100 runs and 100 walks (the other: Duke Snider, who did it for Brooklyn in 1955).
Most valuable pitcher: Righthander Kevin Brown. The Dodgers got their money's worth after making Brown the game's highest-paid player with a seven-year, $105 million contract. Brown went 18-9 with a 3.00 ERA, and he struck out 221 batters (while walking only 59) in 252.1 innings.
Most improved player: Third baseman Adrian Beltre. Predictably, he had struggled the year because he was rushed to the big leagues from Class AA. But Beltre didn't disappoint after Dodgers officials committed to him as the everyday third baseman for 1999—he batted .275 with 15 homers, 27 doubles and 67 RBIs.
Most pleasant surprise: Rookie righthander Eric Gagne had a 2.10 ERA in five starts after being promoted from Class AA (where he was 12-4 and named the organization's minor league pitcher of the year). On the strength of his late-season audition, Gagne will open spring training as the Dodgers' fifth starter.
Biggest disappointment: Pitcher Carlos Perez. The lefthander was a bust after signing a three-year, $15.6 million contract extension. He went 2-10 with a 7.43 ERA in 17 games (16 starts) before being demoted to Class AAA. He also struggled with Albuquerque.
Key injuries: Outfielder Todd Hollandsworth missed three weeks because of a strained right hamstring. Pitcher Robinson Checo was sidelined two months because of a strained right groin. Second baseman Eric Young was out a month because of various leg injuries. Pitcher Darren Dreifort missed the final 2.5 weeks because of shoulder stiffness.
Notable: First baseman Eric Karros established career highs in batting (.304), hits (176), RBIs (112) and doubles (40). He also matched his career best in homers with 34. ... Mark Grudzielanek finished the season with a team-high .326 average, the highest mark for a shortstop in franchise history. ... Manager Johnson used 109 lineups.
—JASON REID

RECORDS

1999 regular-season record: 77-85 (3rd in N.L. West); 37-44 at home; 40-41 on road; 21-23 vs. East; 26-26 vs. Central; 22-29 vs. N.L. West; 8-7 vs. A.L.; 24-25 vs. lefthanded starters; 53-60 vs. righthanded starters; 63-72 on grass; 14-13 on turf; 25-21 in daytime; 52-64 at night; 21-27 in one-run games; 4-12 in extra-inning games; 0-1-0 in doubleheaders.
Team record past five years: 416-376 (.525, ranks 3rd in league in that span).

TEAM LEADERS

Batting average: Mark Grudzielanek (.326).
At-bats: Raul Mondesi (601).
Runs: Gary Sheffield (103).
Hits: Eric Karros (176).
Total Bases: Eric Karros (318).
Doubles: Eric Karros (40).
Triples: Adrian Beltre, Mark Grudzielanek, Raul Mondesi (5).
Home runs: Eric Karros, Gary Sheffield (34).
Runs batted in: Eric Karros (112).
Stolen bases: Eric Young (51).
Slugging percentage: Eric Karros (.550).
On-base percentage: Gary Sheffield (.407).
Wins: Kevin Brown (18).
Earned-run average: Kevin Brown (3.00).
Complete games: Kevin Brown (5).
Shutouts: Kevin Brown, Darren Dreifort, Ismael Valdes (1).
Saves: Jeff Shaw (34).
Innings pitched: Kevin Brown (252.1).
Strikeouts: Kevin Brown (221).

GAMES BY POSITION

Catcher: Todd Hundley 108, Angel Pena 43, Paul LoDuca 34, Rick Wilkins 1, Trenidad Hubbard 1.
First base: Eric Karros 151, Dave Hansen 20, Todd Hollandsworth 13, Tripp Cromer 1.
Second base: Eric Young 117, Craig Counsell 38, Jose Vizcaino 30, Tripp Cromer 9, Alex Cora 3, Chance Sanford 2, Trenidad Hubbard 1, Juan Castro 1.
Third base: Adrian Beltre 152, Dave Hansen 13, Jose Vizcaino 9, Tripp Cromer 2.
Shortstop: Mark Grudzielanek 119, Jose Vizcaino 44, Tripp Cromer 9, Alex Cora 8, Craig Counsell 2, Juan Castro 1.
Outfield: Raul Mondesi 158, Gary Sheffield 145, Devon White 128, Todd Hollandsworth 67, Trenidad Hubbard 51, Jacob Brumfield 11, Brent Cookson 3, Dave Hansen 2, Tripp Cromer 2, Jose Vizcaino 1.
Designated hitter: Gary Sheffield 3, Dave Hansen 2, Devon White 1.

TOP DRAFT CHOICES

1. **Jason Repko,** SS/OF, Hanford H.S., West Richland, Wash.
2a. **Brennan King,** SS, Oakland H.S., Murfreesboro, Tenn.
2b. **Drew Meyer,** SS/OF, Bishop England H.S., Charleston, S.C.
3. None
4. **Joe Thurston,** SS, Sacramento C.C.
5. **Phil Devey,** LHP, U. of Southwestern Louisiana
6. **Shane Victorino,** OF, St. Anthony's H.S., Wailuku, Haw.
7. **Jose Escalera,** OF, Carlos Escobar Lopez H.S., Loiza, P.R.
8. **T.J. Nall,** RHP, Schaumburg (Ill.) H.S.
9. **Jonathan Berry,** RHP, Newberry (S.C.) College.
10. **Lamont Matthews,** OF, Oklahoma State U.

MILWAUKEE BREWERS
NATIONAL LEAGUE CENTRAL DIVISION

2000 Brewers Schedule
Home games shaded. *—All-Star Game at Turner Field (Atlanta).

March
SUN	MON	TUE	WED	THU	FRI	SAT
26	27	28	29	30	31	

April
SUN	MON	TUE	WED	THU	FRI	SAT
						1
2	3 CIN	4	5 CIN	6 CIN	7 STL	8 STL
9 STL	10	11	12 FLA	13 FLA	14 ATL	15 ATL
16 ATL	17	18 NYM	19 NYM	20 NYM	21 MON	22 MON
23 MON	24	25 STL	26 STL	27 STL	28 HOU	29 HOU
30 HOU						

May
SUN	MON	TUE	WED	THU	FRI	SAT
	1 HOU	2 ARI	3 ARI	4 ARI	5 MON	6 MON
7 MON	8 CUB	9 CUB	10 CUB	11 CUB	12 PIT	13 PIT
14 PIT	15	16 HOU	17 HOU	18 HOU	19 SF	20 SF
21 SF	22	23 ATL	24 ATL	25 ATL	26 ARI	27 ARI
28 ARI	29 SD	30 SD	31 SD			

June
SUN	MON	TUE	WED	THU	FRI	SAT
				1	2 COL	3 COL
4 COL	5 CLE	6 CLE	7 CLE	8	9 MIN	10 MIN
11 MIN	12 MON	13 MON	14 MON	15	16 NYM	17 NYM
18 NYM	19 FLA	20 FLA	21 FLA	22 FLA	23 ATL	24 ATL
25 ATL	26	27 PHI	28 PHI	29 PHI	30 CUB	

July
SUN	MON	TUE	WED	THU	FRI	SAT
						1 CUB
2 CUB	3 PHI	4 PHI	5 PHI	6 PHI	7 DET	8 DET
9 DET	10	11	*	12 KC	13 KC	14 KC	15 KC
16 CWS	17 CWS	18 CWS	19 PIT	20 PIT	21 CUB	22 CUB
23 CUB	24	25 PIT	26 PIT	27 PIT	28 COL	29 COL
30 COL	31 SF					

August
SUN	MON	TUE	WED	THU	FRI	SAT
		1 SF	2 SF	3	4 LA	5 LA
6 LA	7 SF	8 SF	9 SF	10	11 STL	12 STL
13 STL	14 CIN	15 CIN	16 CIN	17	18 HOU	19 HOU
20 HOU	21 ARI	22 ARI	23 ARI	24	25 SD	26 SD
27 SD	28 LA	29 LA	30 LA	31 LA		

September
SUN	MON	TUE	WED	THU	FRI	SAT
					1 COL	2 COL
3 COL	4 SD	5 SD	6 SD	7	8 STL	9 STL
10 STL	11 NYM	12 NYM	13 NYM	14 CIN	15 CIN	16 CIN
17 CIN	18 CUB	19 CUB	20 CUB	21 PIT	22 PIT	23 PIT
24 PIT	25	26 CIN	27 CIN	28 CIN	29 HOU	30 HOU

October
SUN	MON	TUE	WED	THU	FRI	SAT
1 HOU	2	3	4	5	6	7

2000 SEASON
CLUB DIRECTORY

President and chief executive officer
Wendy Selig-Prieb

Sr. vice president and general manager
Dean Taylor

Vice president & general counsel
Tom Gausden

Assistant general counsel
Eugene (Pepi) Randolph

Special assistant to the president
Sal Bando

V.p., new ballpark development
Michael Bucek

Vice president, stadium operations
Scott Jenkins

Vice president, corporate affairs
Laurel Prieb

Vice president, finance
Paul Baniel

Vice president, ticket sales
Bob Voight

Vice president, player personnel
David Wilder

Director, community relations
Michael Downs

Director, event services
Steve Ethier

Director, grounds
Gary Vanden Berg

Director, media relations
Jon Greenberg

Director, player development
Greg Riddoch

Director, Brewers Gold Club & Baseball for Wisconsin
Mike Harlan

Director of publications
Mario Ziino

Director of ticket operations
John Barnes

Director, scouting
Jack Zduriencik

Director, clubhouse operations
Tony Migliaccio

Traveling secretary
Dan Larrea

Trainers
John Adam
Roger Caplinger

Strength and conditioning coach
Phil Falco

Team physicians
Dr. Richard Franklin
Dr. Angelo Mattalino

Southwest supervisor/cross-checker
Ric Wilson

Midwest supervisor/cross-checker
Tom Allison

International supervisor/cross-checker
Epy Guerrero

East coast supervisor/cross-checker
Bobby Heck

Professional scouts
Carl Blando, Alan Regier, Daranka Shaheed, Elanis Westbrooks

Major League scouts
Russ Bove, Ken Califano, Larry Haney, Al Monchak, Chuck Tanner, Dick Wiencek

Scouts
Larry Aaron, Fred Beane, Jeff Brookens, Kevin Christman, Steve Connelly, Felix Delgado, Mike Farrell, Dick Foster, Mike Gibbons, Manolo Hernandez, Elvio Jimenez, Brian Johnson, Tim Johnson, Harvey Kuenn Jr., John Logan, Demie Mainieri, Alex Morales, Douglas Reynolds, Corey Rodriguez, Bruce Seid, Jonathan Story, Tom Tanous, John Viney, Red Whitsett, Walter Youse

MINOR LEAGUE AFFILIATES

Class	Team	League	Manager
AAA	Indianapolis	International	Steve Smith
AA	Huntsville	Southern	Carlos Lezcano
A	Mudville	California	Barry Moss
A	Beloit	Midwest	Don Money
Rookie	Helena	Pioneer	Dan Norman
Rookie	Ogden	Pioneer	Ed Sedar

BROADCAST INFORMATION
Radio: WTMJ-AM (620).
TV: WCGV-TV (Channel 24).
Cable TV: Midwest Sports Channel.

SPRING TRAINING
Ballpark (city): Maryvale Baseball Park (Phoenix, Ariz.).
Ticket information: 602-245-5500.

SPRING TRAINING ROSTER

Manager—Davey Lopes (30).
Coaches—Gary Allenson (45), Bob Apodaca (36), Rod Carew (29), Bill Castro (35), Jerry Royster (3), Chris Speier (43).

No.	PITCHERS	B/T	Ht./Wt.	Born	1999 clubs
53	Acevedo, Juan	R/R	6-2/220	5-5-70	St. Louis
47	Bere, Jason	R/R	6-4/189	5-26-71	Cincinnati, Indianapolis, Louisville, Milwaukee
32	Coppinger, Rocky	R/R	6-5/240	3-19-74	Baltimore, Milwaukee
13	D'Amico, Jeff	R/R	6-7/250	12-27-75	Beloit, Huntsville, Louisville, Milwaukee
28	De Los Santos, Valerio	L/L	6-2/180	10-6-75	Milwaukee
21	Eldred, Cal	R/R	6-4/237	11-24-67	Huntsville, Louisville, Milwaukee
48	Estrada, Horacio	L/L	6-0/160	10-19-75	Louisville, Milwaukee
40	Fox, Chad	R/R	6-3/190	9-3-70	Milwaukee
51	Haynes, Jimmy	R/R	6-4/203	9-5-72	Oakland
39	Leskanic, Curtis	R/R	6-0/186	4-2-68	Colorado
26	Peterson, Kyle	R/R	6-3/215	4-9-76	Louisville, Milwaukee
46	Pulsipher, Bill	L/L	6-3/200	10-9-73	Milwaukee, Louisville
52	Roque, Rafael	L/L	6-4/189	10-27-73	Milwaukee, Louisville
49	Weathers, Dave	R/R	6-3/230	9-25-69	Milwaukee
27	Wickman, Bob	R/R	6-1/227	2-6-69	Milwaukee
41	Williams, Matt	B/L	6-0/175	4-12-71	Norwich, Columbus
37	Woodard, Steve	L/R	6-4/217	5-15-75	Milwaukee
38	Wright, Jamey	R/R	6-5/221	12-24-74	Colorado, Colorado Springs

No.	CATCHERS	B/T	Ht./Wt.	Born	1999 clubs
25	Banks, Brian	B/R	6-3/208	9-28-70	Milwaukee, Louisville
12	Blanco, Henry	R/R	5-11/190	8-29-71	Colorado Springs, Colorado
50	Cancel, Robinson	R/R	6-0/195	5-4-76	Huntsville, Louisville, Milwaukee
31	Hughes, Bobby	R/R	6-4/229	4-10-71	Milwaukee

No.	INFIELDERS	B/T	Ht./Wt.	Born	1999 clubs
22	Barker, Kevin	R/R	6-3/205	7-26-75	Louisville, Milwaukee
10	Belliard, Ron	R/R	5-8/180	7-4-76	Louisville, Milwaukee
7	Berry, Sean	R/R	5-11/200	3-22-66	Milwaukee
16	Collier, Lou	R/R	5-10/182	8-21-73	Milwaukee, Louisville
18	Hernandez, Jose	R/R	6-1/180	7-14-69	Chicago N.L., Atlanta
8	Loretta, Mark	R/R	6-0/190	8-14-71	Milwaukee
57	Perez, Santiago	B/R	6-2/150	12-30-75	Louisville
2	Valentin, Jose	L/R	5-10/173	10-12-69	Milwaukee, Louisville

No.	OUTFIELDERS	B/T	Ht./Wt.	Born	1999 clubs
20	Burnitz, Jeromy	L/R	6-0/205	4-15-69	Milwaukee
61	Green, Chad	B/R	5-10/180	6-28-75	Huntsville
9	Grissom, Marquis	R/R	5-11/188	4-17-67	Milwaukee
5	Jenkins, Geoff	L/R	6-1/204	7-21-74	Milwaukee
33	Mouton, Lyle	R/R	6-4/230	5-13-69	Rochester, Louisville, Milwaukee
24	Ochoa, Alex	R/R	6-0/195	3-29-72	Milwaukee

BALLPARK INFORMATION

Ballpark (capacity, surface)
County Stadium (53,192, grass)

Address
County Stadium
P.O. Box 3099
Milwaukee, WI 53201-3099

Business phone
414-933-4114

Ticket information
414-933-9000, 800-933-7890

Ticket prices
$28 (diamond box)
$20 (lower box)
$16 (lower grandstand)
$14 (upper box)
$8 (upper grandstand)
$7 (general admission)
$5 (bleachers)

Field dimensions (from home plate)
To left field at foul line, 315 feet
To center field, 402 feet
To right field at foul line, 315 feet

First game played
April 7, 1970 (Angels 12, Brewers 0)

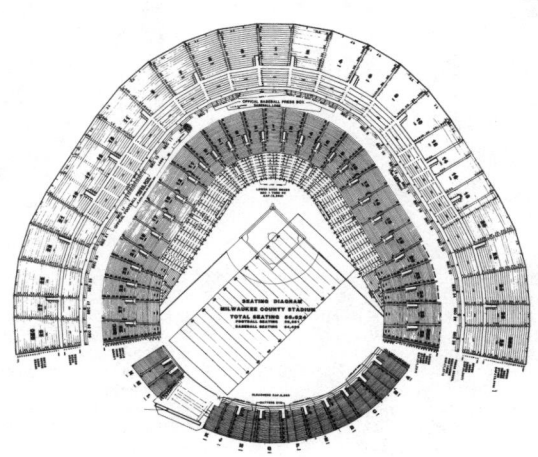

2000 SEASON *Milwaukee Brewers*

Date	Opp.	Res.	Score	(inn.*)	Hits	Opp. hits	Winning pitcher	Losing pitcher	Save	Record	Pos.	GB
4-7	At StL.	L	1-4		5	7	Bottenfield	Woodard	Acevedo	1-1	T1st	...
4-8	At StL.	L	4-9		13	8	Mercker	Abbott		1-2	T3rd	1.0
4-9	At Hou.	L	2-3		5	7	Elarton	Wickman	Wagner	1-3	T5th	1.0
4-10	At Hou.	W	8-2		13	7	Pulsipher	Holt	Weathers	2-3	T3rd	1.0
4-11	At Hou.	L	2-5		8	13	Reynolds	Roque	Wagner	2-4	T4th	2.0
4-13	At Mon.	W	8-4		14	12	Woodard	Vazquez		3-4	T4th	1.0
4-14	At Mon.	L	1-15		6	17	Batista	Abbott		3-5	T4th	2.0
4-15	At Mon.	W	9-4		11	12	Karl	Ayala		4-5	4th	1.5
4-16	Chi.	L	4-9		8	13	Heredia	Pulsipher		4-6	6th	2.5
4-17	Chi.	W	5-4		8	9	Myers	Beck		5-6	T3rd	2.5
4-18	Chi.	L	5-6	(10)	11	13	Beck	de los Santos	Serafini	5-7	5th	2.5
4-19	StL.	L	2-6		7	12	Bottenfield	Abbott		5-8	5th	3.5
4-20	StL.	L	3-8		6	12	Mercker	Karl		5-9	5th	4.5
4-21	StL.	W	2-1		5	6	Reyes	Painter	Wickman	6-9	4th	3.5
4-23	At Pit.	W	9-1		13	8	Woodard	Peters		7-9	4th	3.5
4-24	At Pit.	W	5-3		7	6	Reyes	Ritchie	Wickman	8-9	4th	2.5
4-25	At Pit.	W	4-2		10	8	Karl	Benson	Wickman	9-9	3rd	2.5
4-27	L.A.	L	2-3		6	7	Brown	Roque	Shaw	9-10	4th	3.5
4-28	L.A.	L	2-3		11	10	Park	Woodard	Shaw	9-11	4th	3.5
4-29	L.A.	L	4-10		8	13	Valdes	Eldred		9-12	6th	3.5
4-30	Ari.	L	2-3		7	10	Holmes	Myers	Olson	9-13	6th	4.0
5-1	Ari.	L	3-5		8	10	Stottlemyre	Abbott	Olson	9-14	6th	5.0
5-2	Ari.	W	6-5		13	8	Weathers	Olson	Wickman	10-14	5th	5.0
5-3	At Fla.	W	6-4	(13)	12	11	Wickman	Corbin		11-14	5th	4.0
5-4	At Fla.	W	8-1		10	7	Eldred	Sanchez		12-14	5th	4.0
5-5	At Fla.	W	2-0		7	8	Karl	Meadows	Wickman	13-14	5th	4.0
5-7	At S.F	L	3-4		8	7	Brock	Roque	Nen	13-15	5th	5.0
5-8	At S.F	L	4-6		7	13	Rueter	Woodard	Nen	13-16	5th	5.0
5-9	At S.F	W	3-2		7	7	Nomo	Gardner	Wickman	14-16	5th	4.0
5-11	At Cin.	L	1-9		4	12	Avery	Eldred		14-17	5th	5.5
5-12	At Cin.	W	8-7		15	12	Karl	Harnisch	Wickman	15-17	5th	5.5
5-14	Fla.	L	6-14		8	14	Sanchez	Roque	Mantei	15-18	5th	6.5
5-15	Fla.	W	7-2		11	4	Woodard	Meadows		16-18	5th	6.5
5-16	Fla.	L	2-3		14	9	Hernandez	Nomo	Mantei	16-19	6th	6.5
5-17	At N.Y.	W	7-6		13	11	Karl	Jones	Wickman	17-19	6th	6.0
5-18	At N.Y.	W	4-2		8	11	Weathers	Cook	Wickman	18-19	6th	6.0
5-20†	At N.Y.	L	10-11		13	12	Leiter	Abbott	Franco	18-20		
5-20‡	At N.Y.	L	1-10		9	12	Yoshii	Woodard		18-21	6th	7.0
5-21	At Mon.	W	5-3	(11)	9	6	Wickman	Ayala		19-21	5th	6.0
5-22	At Mon.	L	4-12		7	14	Vazquez	Karl	Telford	19-22	6th	6.0
5-23	At Mon.	W	13-4		13	7	Weathers	Urbina		20-22	6th	6.0
5-24	Atl.	W	10-7		13	13	Woodard	Glavine		21-22	6th	6.0
5-25	Atl.	L	2-5		8	12	Seanez	Wickman	Rocker	21-23	6th	7.0
5-26	Atl.	L	2-3	(10)	6	11	Seanez	Weathers	Rocker	21-24	6th	8.0
5-27	Atl.	L	7-8		13	11	Millwood	Karl	Seanez	21-25	6th	8.0
5-28	S.D.	L	8-10		11	13	Reyes	Eldred	Hoffman	21-26	6th	8.0
5-29	S.D.	L	3-12		10	15	Clement	Woodard		21-27	6th	8.0
5-30	S.D.	W	10-3		11	10	Abbott	Hitchcock		22-27	6th	7.0
5-31	S.D.	W	8-2		14	5	Nomo	Williams		23-27	6th	6.5
6-1	Hou.	L	0-3	(8)	6	5	Bergman	Karl		23-28	6th	7.5
6-2	Hou.	L	1-9		4	9	Lima	Eldred		23-29	6th	8.5
6-3	Hou.	W	4-1		10	7	Woodard	Reynolds	Wickman	24-29	6th	7.5
6-4	At Col.	L	8-9	(10)	17	17	Veres	Wickman		24-30	6th	8.5
6-5	At Col.	L	11-12		14	13	DeJean	Plunk	Dipoto	24-31	6th	9.5
6-6	At Col.	L	5-10		9	14	Astacio	Karl		24-32	6th	9.5
6-8	At Cle.	W	2-1	(10)	10	13	Roque	Assenmacher	Wickman	25-32	6th	9.0
6-9	At Cle.	L	5-6	(10)	9	9	Jackson	Roque		25-33	6th	10.0
6-10	At Cle.	W	15-9		14	14	Nomo	Colon		26-33	6th	9.5
6-11	Min.	L	7-9		13	16	Wells	Weathers	Trombley	26-34	6th	10.5
6-12	Min.	L	6-8		15	15	Sampson	Eldred	Trombley	26-35	6th	11.5
6-14	Chi.	W	5-1		11	9	Woodard	Farnsworth		27-35	6th	11.5
6-15	Chi.	L	4-7		10	9	Lieber	Abbott	Adams	27-36	6th	11.5
6-16	Chi.	W	11-4		12	6	Nomo	Trachsel		28-36	6th	10.5
6-17	At Cin.	L	0-2		4	8	Harnisch	Karl	Williamson	28-37	6th	10.5
6-18	At Cin.	L	1-7		3	11	Avery	Roque		28-38	6th	11.5
6-19	At Cin.	W	10-1		12	4	Woodard	Villone		29-38	6th	11.5
6-20	At Cin.	W	7-4		10	9	Weathers	Reyes	Wickman	30-38	6th	11.5
6-21	At S.F	W	8-1		11	7	Nomo	Gardner		31-38	6th	10.5
6-22	At S.F	W	5-1		13	8	Karl	Rueter		32-38	6th	9.5
6-23	At S.F	W	9-6		12	13	Woodard	Ortiz	Wickman	33-38	6th	9.5
6-25	Pit.	L	3-5		10	11	Schmidt	Abbott	Christiansen	33-39	6th	9.0

Date	Opp.	Res.	Score	(inn.*)	Hits	Opp. hits	Winning pitcher	Losing pitcher	Save	Record	Pos.	GB
6-26	Pit.	W	7-4		11	10	Nomo	Ritchie	Wickman	34-39	6th	8.0
6-27	Pit.	L	5-6		9	7	Cordova	Karl	Christiansen	34-40	6th	8.0
6-29	At Chi.	W	17-6		21	9	Woodard	Tapani		35-40	6th	8.0
6-30	At Chi.	L	4-5		10	7	Karchner	Weathers	Aguilera	35-41	6th	9.0
7-1	At Chi.	W	19-12		21	11	Myers	Trachsel		36-41	6th	9.0
7-2	At Pit.	W	5-2		11	9	Karl	Cordova	Wickman	37-41	6th	8.0
7-3	At Pit.	W	9-4		11	11	Pulsipher	Benson		38-41	5th	8.0
7-4	At Pit.	W	4-3		8	6	Weathers	Clontz	Wickman	39-41	4th	7.0
7-5	At Phi.	W	5-0		10	6	Abbott	Ogea	Roque	40-41	T3rd	7.0
7-6	At Phi.	L	0-1		5	4	Person	Nomo	Gomes	40-42	5th	7.0
7-7	At Phi.	L	4-5		8	10	Gomes	Wickman		40-43	5th	7.0
7-9	At Det.	W	4-1		9	6	Woodard	Cruz	Wickman	41-43	T4th	7.5
7-10	At Det.	L	3-9		6	14	Thompson	Abbott		41-44	5th	7.5
7-11	At Det.	W	3-2		6	9	Nomo	Moehler	Wickman	42-44	T4th	7.5
7-16†	K.C.	W	2-0		9	4	Woodard	Appier	Wickman	43-44		
7-16‡	K.C.	L	10-12		13	15	Ray	Pittsley	Service	43-45	6th	8.5
7-17	K.C.	W	11-3		17	7	Nomo	Rosado		44-45	T4th	8.5
7-18	Chi. (AL)	W	5-4		13	9	Plunk	Rizzo		45-45	4th	8.5
7-19	Chi. (AL)	L	8-10	(12)	11	18	Simas	Coppinger	Foulke	45-46	T4th	9.5
7-20	Chi. (AL)	W	5-4		10	9	Plunk	Lowe	Wickman	46-46	3rd	8.5
7-21	Phi.	L	0-7		7	15	Person	Karl	Poole	46-47	3rd	8.5
7-22	Phi.	W	5-0		6	5	Nomo	Wolf		47-47	3rd	7.5
7-23	At Fla.	L	4-5		8	13	Nunez	Wickman		47-48	T3rd	9.0
7-24	At Fla.	L	1-4		6	9	Meadows	Peterson	Alfonseca	47-49	4th	10.0
7-25	At Fla.	L	3-4		8	10	Sanchez	Weathers	Alfonseca	47-50	5th	11.0
7-26	At Atl.	L	1-6		6	8	Maddux	Karl		47-51	5th	12.0
7-27	At Atl.	L	2-10		6	14	Millwood	Nomo		47-52	6th	13.0
7-28	At Atl.	W	10-4		13	9	Pulsipher	Chen		48-52	5th	13.0
7-30	Mon.	W	1-0		7	5	Peterson	Powell	Wickman	49-52	4th	12.5
7-31	Mon.	L	2-4		5	12	Telford	Plunk	Urbina	49-53	5th	13.5
8-1	Mon.	L	4-10		7	13	Smith	Karl		49-54	5th	13.5
8-2	N.Y.	L	2-7		8	12	Reed	Nomo		49-55	5th	14.0
8-3	N.Y.	L	3-10		6	13	Hershiser	Pulsipher		49-56	5th	15.0
8-4	N.Y.	L	5-9		7	17	Rogers	Peterson		49-57	6th	15.0
8-6	Cin.	L	2-9		4	15	Villone	Woodard	Sullivan	49-58	6th	16.0
8-7	Cin.	W	6-4		11	9	Weathers	Graves	Wickman	50-58	5th	16.0
8-8	Cin.	L	2-8		7	11	Harnisch	Nomo	Belinda	50-59	5th	17.0
8-9	Col.	W	7-6		11	9	Wickman	Veres		51-59	5th	16.0
8-10	Col.	W	2-1	(10)	3	6	Coppinger	Veres		52-59	5th	15.0
8-11	Col.	L	5-8		10	14	Jones	Woodard		52-60	5th	15.0
8-13	At Ari.	W	3-1		7	4	Nomo	Benes	Wickman	53-60	5th	14.0
8-14	At Ari.	W	4-2		6	10	Karl	Reynoso	Wickman	54-60	5th	14.0
8-15	At Ari.	L	0-4		7	7	Daal	Pulsipher		54-61	5th	14.0
8-16	At Hou.	L	0-2		2	8	Lima	Peterson	Wagner	54-62	5th	15.0
8-17	At Hou.	L	6-8		11	9	Elarton	Eldred	Wagner	54-63	5th	16.0
8-18	At Hou.	L	4-6		8	9	Williams	Plunk	Wagner	54-64	5th	17.0
8-19	At Hou.	W	6-5		17	10	Coppinger	Powell	Wickman	55-64	5th	16.0
8-20	S.F	L	3-10		9	14	Rueter	Pulsipher		55-65	5th	17.0
8-21	S.F	L	1-5		7	7	Hernandez	Peterson		55-66	5th	18.0
8-22	S.F	L	3-7		12	12	Nathan	Eldred		55-67	5th	18.5
8-23	L.A.	L	4-8		9	8	Dreifort	Nomo	Shaw	55-68	5th	18.5
8-24	L.A.	L	2-5		4	11	Judd	Karl	Shaw	55-69	5th	19.5
8-25	L.A.	W	9-7		9	9	Plunk	Borbon	Wickman	56-69	5th	18.5
8-26	At S.D.	L	3-4		8	8	Ashby	Coppinger	Hoffman	56-70	5th	19.0
8-27	At S.D.	L	7-8		15	9	Whiteside	Wickman		56-71	5th	19.5
8-28	At S.D.	W	6-4		11	9	Nomo	Williams	Wickman	57-71	5th	18.5
8-29	At S.D.	L	4-5	(10)	3	10	Hoffman	Wickman		57-72	5th	19.5
8-30	At L.A.	L	1-6		9	8	Brown	Pulsipher		57-73	5th	19.5
8-31	At L.A.	L	3-5		8	12	Judd	Peterson	Shaw	57-74	5th	20.5
9-1	At L.A.	W	5-4		8	7	Eldred	Valdes	Wickman	58-74	5th	19.5
9-2	StL.	L	3-4		8	9	Painter	Ramirez	Bottalico	58-75	5th	20.0
9-3	StL.	W	5-4	(11)	12	12	Coppinger	Acevedo		59-75	5th	20.0
9-4	StL.	W	4-2		6	3	Pulsipher	Thompson	Wickman	60-75	5th	20.0
9-5	StL.	L	9-13	(10)	12	18	Bottalico	Wickman		60-76	5th	21.0
9-7	Ari.	L	9-11		13	12	Holmes	Dale	Mantei	60-77	5th	22.5
9-8	Ari.	L	1-9		7	14	Daal	Nomo		60-78	5th	23.5
9-9	Ari.	W	9-8		14	11	Karl	Reynoso	Wickman	61-78	5th	23.5
9-10	At Col.	L	3-15		9	14	Bohanon	Pulsipher		61-79	5th	24.5
9-11	At Col.	L	6-7		8	12	Dipoto	Coppinger	Veres	61-80	5th	25.5
9-12	At Col.	W	12-9		16	13	Plunk	Veres	Wickman	62-80	5th	25.5
9-13	At StL.	W	4-3		9	8	Nomo	Thompson	Wickman	63-80	5th	25.5
9-14	At StL.	W	4-1		7	8	Karl	Aybar	Wickman	64-80	5th	25.5
9-15	At StL.	W	10-8	(12)	15	13	Ramirez	Acevedo		65-80	5th	24.5
9-17	At Chi.	L	5-6	(10)	11	7	Aguilera	Peterson		65-81	5th	24.5
9-18	At Chi.	W	7-4	(14)	9	10	Peterson	Guthrie		66-81	5th	23.5

Date	Opp.	Res.	Score	(inn.*)	Hits	Opp. hits	Winning pitcher	Losing pitcher	Save	Record	Pos.	GB
9-19	At Chi.	L	7-8	(10)	10	12	Aguilera	Ramirez		66-82	5th	24.5
9-20	Phi.	W	5-4		8	14	Coppinger	Loewer	Wickman	67-82	5th	23.5
9-21	Phi.	W	8-6		11	9	Pulsipher	Shumaker	Wickman	68-82	5th	23.5
9-19	At Col.	W	5-2	(8)	8	7	Brown	Thomson	Borbon	69-80	4th	21.0
9-22	Phi.	L	3-12		4	16	Telemaco	Peterson		68-83	5th	23.5
9-23	Phi.	W	11-6		12	8	Bere	Grace		69-83	5th	23.0
9-24	Hou.	L	4-9		8	7	Miller	Plunk	Powell	69-84	5th	24.0
9-25	Hou.	W	3-2		9	10	Karl	Reynolds	Wickman	70-84	5th	23.0
9-26	Hou.	W	11-3		16	9	Peterson	Elarton		71-84	5th	22.0
9-29†	Pit.	L	5-7		9	11	Ritchie	Woodard	Williams	71-85		
9-29‡	Pit.	W	5-2		7	7	Bere	Peters	Wickman	72-85	5th	22.0
9-30	Pit.	L	2-3		5	8	Garcia	Nomo	Sauerbeck	72-86	5th	22.5
10-1	Cin.	W	4-3	(10)	10	5	Coppinger	Sullivan		73-86	5th	21.5
10-2	Cin.	W	10-6		14	12	Peterson	Guzman		74-86	T4th	21.5
10-3	Cin.	L	1-7		6	12	Harnisch	Eldred	Villone	74-87	5th	22.5

Monthly records: April (9-13), May (14-14), June (12-14), July (14-12), August (8-21), September (15-12), October (2-1).
*Innings, if other than nine. † First game of a doubleheader. ‡ Second game of a doubleheader.

HIGHLIGHTS

High point: After falling 10 games below .500 on June 18 in Cincinnati, the Brewers won five consecutive road games to ignite a 17-7 run that enabled them to reach the break-even mark on July 18.

Low point: On July 14, the day before the second half of the season was to start, a crane collapsed at the Miller Park construction site, killing three ironworkers and severely damaging the new stadium. After several weeks, officials determined that the opening of the new ballpark—scheduled for 2000—would be set back a full year.

Turning point: With a 47-47 record and hopes of climbing back into the wild-card race, the team went to Florida for a three-game series July 23 and was swept by the lowly Marlins. The pratfall kicked off a stretch in which the Brewers lost 11 of 13 games and waved goodbye to the .500 mark for the rest of the season.

Most valuable player: Despite missing more than a month with a hand fracture, right fielder Jeromy Burnitz led the club in homers (33), RBIs (103), walks (91) and on-base percentage (.402). Plus, he played in the All-Star Game.

Most valuable pitcher: Bob Wickman, who managed a franchise-record 37 saves despite blowing eight opportunities.

Most improved player: After playing just 84 games as a rookie in 1998, left fielder Geoff Jenkins emerged with a .313 average, 21 homers, 43 doubles and 82 RBIs. He also improved his defense, recording 14 assists.

Most pleasant surprise: Plucked off the scrap heap, righthander Hideo Nomo joined the team May 9 and revived his career. He was 12-8 in 28 starts, with bad luck and shaky run support costing him a chance for more victories.

Biggest disappointment: Signed to provide righthanded-hitting run production, first baseman Sean Berry was a bust. He batted just .228 with two homers and 23 RBIs. He was so lost at the plate that by midseason he was buried on the bench.

Key injuries: Second baseman Fernando Vina injured his right knee in early May and was sidelined for most of the season. Righthander Steve Woodard broke his left wrist July 25 and was out for nearly a month. Catcher David Nilsson missed most of the last month with a broken right thumb.

Notable: After 7.5 years as manager, Phil Garner was fired August 12 and replaced by Jim Lefebvre. With a 563-617 record, Garner is the winningest and losingest manager in club history. ... General manager Sal Bando was reassigned within the organization on the day Garner was fired. ... The club was 42-39 on the road but a horrendous 32-48 at home. ... Jeff Cirillo's .326 batting average tied for fifth in the N.L. ... The team turned a triple play against the Cubs in the April 16 home opener. ... The team allowed 177 stolen bases, the most in the major leagues. ... Shortstop Jose Valentin hit two-run homers from both sides of the plate in a 19-12 victory over the Cubs on July 1 at Wrigley Field.

—DREW OLSON

RECORDS

1999 regular-season record: 74-87 (5th in N.L. Central); 32-48 at home; 42-39 on road; 18-23 vs. East; 32-30 vs. N.L. Central; 16-28 vs. West; 8-6 vs. A.L.; 21-27 vs. lefthanded starters; 53-60 vs. righthanded starters; 58-75 on grass; 16-12 on turf; 31-28 in daytime; 43-59 at night; 22-27 in one-run games; 8-9 in extra-inning games; 0-1-2 in doubleheaders.

Team record past five years: 371-419 (.470).

TEAM LEADERS

Batting average: Jeff Cirillo (.326).
At-bats: Jeff Cirillo (607).
Runs: Jeff Cirillo (98).
Hits: Jeff Cirillo (198).
Total Bases: Jeff Cirillo (280).
Doubles: Geoff Jenkins (43).
Triples: Mark Loretta, Jose Valentin (5).
Home runs: Jeromy Burnitz (33).
Runs batted in: Jeromy Burnitz (103).
Stolen bases: Marquis Grissom (24).

Slugging percentage: Jeromy Burnitz (.561).
On-base percentage: Jeromy Burnitz (.402).
Wins: Hideo Nomo (12).
Earned-run average: Steve Woodard (4.52).
Complete games: Steve Woodard (2).
Shutouts: None.
Saves: Bob Wickman (37).
Innings pitched: Scott Karl (197.2).
Strikeouts: Hideo Nomo (161).

GAMES BY POSITION

Catcher: Dave Nilsson 101, Bobby Hughes 44, Brian Banks 40, Charlie Greene 31, Robinson Cancel 15.
First base: Mark Loretta 66, Sean Berry 64, Brian Banks 44, Kevin Barker 31.
Second base: Ron Belliard 119, Fernando Vina 37, Mark Loretta 17, Lou Collier 4, Eddie Zosky 2.
Third base: Jeff Cirillo 155, Mark Loretta 14, Lou Collier 7, Eddie Zosky 4, Ron Belliard 1.
Shortstop: Jose Valentin 85, Mark Loretta 74, Lou Collier 31, Ron Belliard 1.
Outfield: Marquis Grissom 149, Geoff Jenkins 128, Jeromy Burnitz 127, Alex Ochoa 85, Rich Becker 50, Lou Collier 10, Brian Banks 5, Lyle Mouton 3.
Designated hitter: Jeromy Burnitz 3, Rich Becker 2, Dave Nilsson 1, Alex Ochoa 1, Bobby Hughes 1.

TOP DRAFT CHOICES

1. **Ben Sheets,** RHP, NE Louisiana U.
2. **Kade Johnson,** C, Seminole State (Okla.) J.C.
3. **Ruddy Lugo,** RHP, Xaverian H.S., Brooklyn, N.Y.
4. **Travis Horne,** LHP, First Coast H.S., Jacksonville, Fla.
5. **Dustin Lansford,** RHP, McLennan C.C.
6. **Mark Ernster,** 2B, Arizona State Univ.
7. **Jeff Robinson,** RHP, U. of Southwestern Louisiana
8. **David Pember,** RHP, Western Carolina Univ.
9. **Matt Tindell,** RHP, Avon Park (Fla.) H.S.
10. **Ben Hendrickson,** RHP, Jefferson H.S., Bloomington, Min.

MONTREAL EXPOS
NATIONAL LEAGUE EAST DIVISION

2000 Expos Schedule
Home games shaded. *—All-Star Game at Turner Field (Atlanta).

March
SUN	MON	TUE	WED	THU	FRI	SAT
26	27	28	29	30	31	

April
SUN	MON	TUE	WED	THU	FRI	SAT
						1
2	3 LA	4 LA	5 LA	6 LA	7 SD	8 SD
9 SD	10	11 PIT	12 PIT	13 PIT	14 PHI	15 PHI
16 PHI	17 PHI	18 CUB	19 CUB	20 CUB	21 MIL	22 MIL
23 MIL	24	25 COL	26 COL	27	28 SF	29 SF
30 SF						

May
SUN	MON	TUE	WED	THU	FRI	SAT
	1 COL	2 COL	3 COL	4	5 MIL	6 MIL
7 MIL	8	9 PHI	10 PHI	11 PHI	12 CUB	13 CUB
14 CUB	15	16 ARI	17 ARI	18 ARI	19 HOU	20 HOU
21 HOU	22	23 SF	24 SF	25 SF	26 SD	27 SD
28 SD	29	30 CIN	31 CIN			

June
SUN	MON	TUE	WED	THU	FRI	SAT
				1 CIN	2 BAL	3 BAL
4 BAL	5 NYY	6 NYY	7 NYY	8	9 TOR	10 TOR
11 TOR	12 MIL	13 MIL	14 MIL	15	16 CUB	17 CUB
18 CUB	19 PIT	20 PIT	21 PIT	22	23 PHI	24 PHI
25 PHI	26	27 ATL	28 ATL	29	30 FLA	

July
SUN	MON	TUE	WED	THU	FRI	SAT
						1 FLA
2 FLA	3 ATL	4 ATL	5 ATL	6 TGR	7 TGR	8 TGR
9 TGR	10	11 *	12	13 TB	14 TB	15 TB
16 BOS	17 BOS	18 BOS	19 NYM	20 NYM	21 FLA	22 FLA
23 FLA	24	25 NYM	26 NYM	27 NYM	28 CIN	29 CIN
30 CIN	31 STL					

August
SUN	MON	TUE	WED	THU	FRI	SAT
		1 STL	2 STL	3	4 HOU	5 HOU
6 HOU	7 ARI	8 ARI	9 ARI	10	11 COL	12 COL
13 COL	14 COL	15 SF	16 SF	17 SF	18 SD	19 SD
20 SD	21 LA	22 LA	23 LA	24 LA	25 HOU	26 HOU
27 HOU	28 ARI	29 ARI	30 ARI	31		

September
SUN	MON	TUE	WED	THU	FRI	SAT
					1 CIN	2 CIN
3 CIN	4 STL	5 STL	6 STL	7 STL	8 ATL	9 ATL
10 ATL	11	12 PHI	13 PHI	14 NYM	15 NYM	16 NYM
17 NYM	18 FLA	19 FLA	20 FLA	21 ATL	22 ATL	23 ATL
24 ATL	25 FLA	26 FLA	27 FLA	28 FLA	29 NYM	30 NYM

October
SUN	MON	TUE	WED	THU	FRI	SAT
1 NYM	2	3	4	5	6	7

2000 SEASON
CLUB DIRECTORY

Chairman and CEO
Jeffrey Loria
Executive vice president
David Samson
Chairman of the partnership committee
L. Jacques Menard
Vice president and general manager
Jim Beattie
Assistant general manager
Larry Beinfest
V.p. and dir. of international operations
Fred Ferreira
Director, scouting
Jim Fleming
Director, player development
Don Reynolds
Assistant director, scouting
Gregg Leonard
Vice president, finance and treasurer
Michel Bussiere
Vice president, stadium operations
Claude Delorme
Director, media relations
P.J. Loyello
Director, media services
Monique Giroux

Director, Olympic Stadium ticket office
Hubert Richard
Director, stadium operations
Denis Pare
Directors, advertising sales
Luigi Carola
John Di Terlizzi
Danielle La Roche
Director, season ticket sales
Gilles Beauregard
Director, business development
Real Sureau
Club physician
Dr. Mike Thomassin
Club orthopedist
Dr. Larry Coughlin
Scouts
Alex Agostino, Matt Anderson, Mark Baca, Mike Berger, Bob Cluck, Dennis Cardoza, Robby Corsaro, Dave Dangler, Marc Del Piano, Dan Freed, Scott Goldby, John Hughes, Joe Jordan, Mark Leavit, Dave Malpass, Darryl Monroe, Bob Oldis, Scott Stanley, Len Strelitz, Tommy Thompson

MINOR LEAGUE AFFILIATES

Class	Team	League	Manager
AAA	Ottawa	International	Jeff Cox
AA	Harrisburg	Eastern	Doug Sisson
A	Jupiter	Florida State	Luis Dorante
A	Cape Fear	South Atlantic	Bill Masse
A	Vermont	New York-Pennsylvania	To be announced
Rookie	Gulf Coast Expos	Gulf Coast	Steve Phillips

BROADCAST INFORMATION

Radio: To be announced.
TV: To be announced.
Cable TV: To be announced..

SPRING TRAINING

Ballpark (city): Roger Dean Stadium (Jupiter, Fla.).
Ticket information: 561-775-1818.

SPRING TRAINING ROSTER

Manager—Felipe Alou (17).

Coaches—Brad Arnsberg, Pierre Arsenault (67), Bobby Cuellar (26), Perry Hill, Pete Mackanin (25), Luis Pujols (55), Pat Roessler.

No.	PITCHERS	B/T	Ht./Wt.	Born	1999 clubs
51	Armas Jr., Tony	R/R	6-4/205	4-29-78	Harrisburg, Montreal
48	Batista, Miguel	R/R	6-2/195	2-19-71	Ottawa, Montreal
	Billingsley, Brent	L/L	6-2/200	4-19-75	Calgary, Florida
	Blank, Matt	L/L	6-2/195	4-5-76	Jupiter, Harrisburg
30	Hermanson, Dustin	R/R	6-2/200	12-21-72	Montreal
14	Irabu, Hideki	R/R	6-4/240	5-5-69	New York A.L.
47	Johnson, Mike	L/R	6-2/170	10-3-75	Ottawa, Montreal
44	Kline, Steve	B/L	6-1/215	8-22-72	Montreal
28	Lilly, Ted	L/L	6-0/185	1-4-76	Ottawa, Montreal
27	Lloyd, Graeme	L/L	6-7/234	4-9-67	Toronto
	McLeary, Marty	R/R	6-5/212	10-26-74	Sarasota, Augusta
29	Moore, Trey	L/L	6-0/190	10-2-72	DID NOT PLAY
40	Mota, Guillermo	R/R	6-4/205	7-25-73	Ottawa, Montreal
45	Pavano, Carl	R/R	6-5/230	1-8-76	Montreal, Ottawa
49	Powell, Jeremy	R/R	6-5/230	6-18-76	Ottawa, Montreal
56	Smart, J.D.	R/R	6-2/180	11-12-73	Montreal, Ottawa
51	Strickland, Scott	R/R	5-11/180	4-26-76	Jupiter, Harrisburg, Ottawa, Montreal
32	Telford, Anthony	R/R	6-0/195	3-6-66	Montreal
35	Thurman, Mike	R/R	6-5/210	7-22-73	Montreal
41	Urbina, Ugueth	R/R	6-0/205	2-15-74	Montreal
23	Vazquez, Javier	R/R	6-2/195	7-25-76	Montreal, Ottawa

No.	CATCHERS	B/T	Ht./Wt.	Born	1999 clubs
13	Henley, Bob	R/R	6-2/205	1-30-73	Gulf Coast Expos
63	Schneider, Brian	L/R	6-1/200	11-26-76	Harrisburg
16	Widger, Chris	R/R	6-2/215	5-21-71	Montreal

No.	INFIELDERS	B/T	Ht./Wt.	Born	1999 clubs
5	Barrett, Michael	R/R	6-2/200	10-22-76	Montreal, Ottawa
50	Blum, Geoff	B/R	6-3/195	4-26-73	Ottawa, Montreal
18	Cabrera, Orlando	R/R	5-10/175	11-2-74	Montreal
53	Coquillette, Trace	R/R	5-11/185	6-4-74	Ottawa, Montreal
	De La Rosa, Tomas	R/R	5-10/165	1-28-78	Harrisburg
20	Fullmer, Brad	L/R	6-0/215	1-17-75	Montreal, Ottawa
4	Guerrero, Wilton	B/R	6-0/175	10-24-74	Montreal
12	Mordecai, Mike	R/R	5-10/185	12-13-67	Montreal
	Nunnari, Talmadge	L/L	6-1/200	4-9-75	Jupiter, Harrisburg
33	Seguignol, Fernando	B/R	6-5/230	1-19-75	Ottawa, Montreal
3	Vidro, Jose	B/R	5-11/190	8-27-74	Montreal

No.	OUTFIELDERS	B/T	Ht./Wt.	Born	1999 clubs
33	Bergeron, Peter	L/R	6-0/185	11-9-77	Harrisburg, Ottawa, Montreal
	Bradley, Milton	B/R	6-0/180	4-15-78	Harrisburg
27	Guerrero, Vladimir	R/R	6-3/205	2-9-76	Montreal
40	Martinez, Manny	R/R	6-0/180	10-3-70	Montreal
22	White, Rondell	R/R	6-0/210	2-23-72	Montreal

BALLPARK INFORMATION

Ballpark (capacity, surface)
Olympic Stadium (46,500, artificial)

Address
P.O. Box 500, Station M
Montreal, Que. H1V 3P2

Business phone
514-253-3434

Ticket information
800-GO-EXPOS

Ticket prices
$36 (VIP box seats)
$26 (box seats)
$16 (terrace)
$8 (general admission)

Field dimensions (from home plate)
To left field at foul line, 325 feet
To center field, 404 feet
To right field at foul line, 325 feet

First game played
April 15, 1977 (Phillies 7, Expos 2)

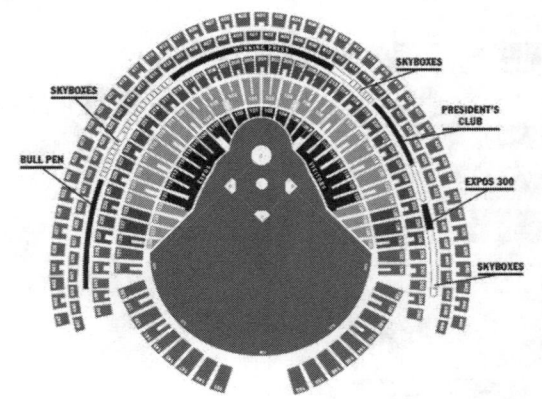

2000 SEASON *Montreal Expos*

Date	Opp.	Res.	Score	(inn.*)	Hits	Opp. hits	Winning pitcher	Losing pitcher	Save	Record	Pos.	GB
4-6	At Pit.	L	2-8		3	10	Schmidt	Pavano		1-1	T1st	...
4-7	At Pit.	W	4-3		7	11	Urbina	Loiselle		2-1	T1st	...
4-8	N.Y.	W	5-1		10	6	Batista	Hershiser	Urbina	3-1	1st	+1.0
4-9	N.Y.	L	3-10		5	11	Yoshii	Thurman		3-2	T1st	...
4-10	N.Y.	L	3-4	(11)	7	8	Cook	Telford	Franco	3-3	T2nd	1.0
4-11	N.Y.	L	3-6		7	14	Watson	Pavano	Franco	3-4	4th	2.0
4-13	Mil.	L	4-8		12	14	Woodard	Vazquez		3-5	4th	3.0
4-14	Mil.	W	15-1		17	6	Batista	Abbott		4-5	T3rd	3.0
4-15	Mil.	L	4-9		12	11	Karl	Ayala		4-6	4th	3.0
4-16	At N.Y.	W	6-4		7	7	Hermanson	Leiter	Urbina	5-6	4th	2.0
4-17	At N.Y.	L	2-3		7	6	Jones	Pavano	Franco	5-7	4th	3.0
4-18	At N.Y.	W	4-2		11	6	Vazquez	Watson	Urbina	6-7	4th	2.0
4-19	At Col.	L	10-11		20	11	Veres	Urbina		6-8	4th	3.0
4-23	Phi.	L	2-6		6	10	Ogea	Hermanson		6-9	4th	4.0
4-24	Phi.	L	5-6		12	11	Grace	Ayala	Gomes	6-10	4th	4.0
4-25	Phi.	L	6-8		8	10	Byrd	Urbina		6-11	4th	5.0
4-27	S.F	L	2-3	(10)	10	6	Johnstone	Kline	Nen	6-12	4th	5.5
4-28	S.F	L	3-4		9	7	Nathan	Hermanson	Nen	6-13	4th	6.5
4-29	S.F	L	5-6		9	13	Ortiz	Pavano	Nen	6-14	4th	7.5
4-30	StL.	W	3-2		8	6	Urbina	Acevedo		7-14	4th	7.5
5-1	StL.	L	5-16		8	19	Osborne	Thurman	Mohler	7-15	4th	8.5
5-2	StL.	L	7-8	(10)	14	11	Acevedo	Urbina	Radinsky	7-16	4th	9.5
5-3	L.A.	L	0-7		7	13	Park	Hermanson		7-17	4th	10.5
5-4	L.A.	W	2-1		7	4	Pavano	Valdes	Urbina	8-17	4th	9.5
5-5	L.A.	L	2-8		4	13	Arnold	Vazquez		8-18	4th	10.5
5-7	At Hou.	L	2-5		9	8	Lima	Batista		8-19	4th	10.5
5-8	At Hou.	W	6-5		12	9	Hermanson	Reynolds	Urbina	9-19	4th	10.5
5-9	At Hou.	W	4-2		13	9	Pavano	Holt	Urbina	10-19	4th	9.5
5-10	At Ari.	L	6-7		13	11	Olson	Ayala		10-20	4th	9.5
5-11	At Ari.	L	3-4	(10)	9	7	Olson	Mota		10-21	4th	10.5
5-12	At Ari.	L	6-8		10	10	Telemaco	Smart		10-22	4th	10.5
5-14	At Pit.	L	3-5		5	10	Benson	Hermanson	Williams	10-23	4th	10.5
5-15	At Pit.	L	6-17		11	17	Silva	Pavano		10-24	4th	10.5
5-16	At Pit.	L	4-9		10	8	Schourek	Vazquez		10-25	5th	11.5
5-17	Phi.	L	3-4		9	8	Schilling	Thurman		10-26	5th	12.5
5-18	Phi.	W	7-4		9	9	Batista	Bennett	Urbina	11-26	4th	12.5
5-19	Phi.	W	10-9		13	8	Kline	Brantley		12-26	4th	12.5
5-21	Mil.	L	3-5	(11)	6	9	Wickman	Ayala	Weathers	12-27	5th	12.0
5-22	Mil.	W	12-4		14	7	Vazquez	Karl	Telford	13-27	4th	12.0
5-23	Mil.	L	4-13		7	13	Weathers	Urbina		13-28	4th	12.0
5-24	At Phi.	L	4-5		7	7	Perez	Batista	Gomes	13-29	5th	12.0
5-25	At Phi.	W	4-2	(11)	10	6	Urbina	Montgomery		14-29	5th	12.0
5-26	At Phi.	W	5-2		8	6	Pavano	Loewer	Urbina	15-29	4th	12.0
5-28	S.F	W	4-2		9	6	Telford	Ortiz	Urbina	16-29	4th	12.5
5-29	S.F	W	7-4		11	7	Thurman	Estes	Urbina	17-29	4th	11.5
5-30	S.F	W	6-4		12	10	Batista	Brock	Urbina	18-29	4th	10.5
5-31	Ari.	L	5-8	(10)	10	16	Holmes	Kline	Olson	18-30	4th	11.5
6-1	Ari.	W	10-8		12	14	Mota	Frascatore	Urbina	19-30	4th	11.5
6-2	Ari.	L	2-15		5	20	Daal	Vazquez		19-31	4th	11.5
6-4	At Tor.	L	2-6		6	9	Wells	Ayala		19-32	4th	11.5
6-5	At Tor.	W	5-0		6	3	Batista	Hamilton		20-32	4th	11.5
6-6	At Tor.	L	2-9		8	13	Escobar	Hermanson		20-33	4th	12.5
6-7	Bos.	W	8-2		13	6	Pavano	Saberhagen		21-33	4th	12.5
6-8	Bos.	W	5-1		9	4	Smith	Wakefield		22-33	4th	12.5
6-9	Bos.	W	13-1		14	5	Thurman	Martinez		23-33	4th	12.5
6-11	T.B.	W	5-4		9	9	Batista	Witt	Urbina	24-33	4th	11.5
6-12	T.B.	L	3-5		9	14	Callaway	Hermanson	Hernandez	24-34	4th	11.5
6-13	T.B.	W	4-0		8	3	Pavano	Rekar		25-34	4th	10.5
6-14	At StL.	W	7-5		11	9	Telford	Oliver	Urbina	26-34	4th	9.5
6-15	At StL.	L	2-3		5	5	Jimenez	Thurman	Bottalico	26-35	4th	10.5
6-16	At StL.	L	4-5		6	9	Bottenfield	Batista	Bottalico	26-36	4th	11.5
6-18	At Hou.	L	0-5		6	6	Reynolds	Hermanson		26-37	4th	13.0
6-19	At Hou.	L	2-5		8	10	Hampton	Pavano	Wagner	26-38	4th	13.0
6-20	At Hou.	L	3-11		11	9	Holt	Smith		26-39	4th	14.0
6-22	At Atl.	W	2-1		8	9	Thurman	Maddux	Urbina	27-39	4th	13.0
6-23	At Atl.	L	3-7		7	13	Millwood	Batista		27-40	4th	14.0
6-24	At Atl.	L	2-3	(11)	7	13	McGlinchy	Mota		27-41	4th	15.0
6-25	Fla.	W	4-3		12	5	Pavano	Fernandez	Urbina	28-41	4th	14.0
6-26	Fla.	L	3-9		8	12	Dempster	Smith		28-42	4th	15.0
6-27	Fla.	L	3-4		8	6	Springer	Thurman	Mantei	28-43	4th	16.0
6-28	Atl.	L	5-13		11	16	Millwood	Batista		28-44	4th	17.0
6-29	Atl.	W	6-5		10	10	Urbina	Rocker		29-44	4th	16.0
6-30	Atl.	W	7-5		10	8	Kline	McGlinchy	Urbina	30-44	4th	15.0

Date	Opp.	Res.	Score	(inn.*)	Hits	Opp. hits	Winning pitcher	Losing pitcher	Save	Record	Pos.	GB
7-1	Atl.	L	1-4		7	12	Glavine	Smith		30-45	4th	16.0
7-3	At Fla.	L	1-6		7	9	Meadows	Batista		30-46	4th	17.5
7-4	At Fla.	L	1-5		8	8	Hernandez	Powell		30-47	4th	17.5
7-5	At N.Y.	L	1-2		6	9	Wendell	Mota	Benitez	30-48	4th	18.5
7-6	At N.Y.	L	0-10		6	13	Hershiser	Pavano	Isringhausen	30-49	4th	18.5
7-7	At N.Y.	W	3-1		8	7	Kline	Wendell	Urbina	31-49	4th	18.5
7-8	At N.Y.	W	4-3		6	6	Ayala	Cook	Urbina	32-49	4th	18.5
7-9	Tor.	W	4-3		16	9	Urbina	Lloyd		33-49	4th	17.5
7-10	Tor.	L	6-7		11	9	Quantrill	Telford	Koch	33-50	4th	18.5
7-11	Tor.	L	0-1		2	4	Wells	Pavano		33-51	4th	19.5
7-15	At Bal.	L	2-8		11	9	Ponson	Thurman		33-52	4th	20.5
7-16	At Bal.	L	4-9		9	17	Mussina	Smith		33-53	4th	21.5
7-17	At Bal.	L	1-2		6	4	Erickson	Hermanson		33-54	4th	21.5
7-18	At N.Y. (AL)	L	0-6		0	8	Cone	Vazquez		33-55	4th	21.5
7-19	At N.Y. (AL)	W	6-4		12	10	Kline	Mendoza	Urbina	34-55	4th	20.5
7-20	At N.Y. (AL)	L	4-7		9	9	Clemens	Thurman	Rivera	34-56	4th	20.5
7-21	N.Y.	L	3-7		12	12	Reed	Smith		34-57	5th	20.5
7-22	N.Y.	L	4-7		9	12	Hershiser	Hermanson		34-58	5th	21.5
7-23	Pit.	W	5-1		9	4	Vazquez	Ritchie		35-58	5th	21.0
7-24	Pit.	L	2-7		7	11	Schourek	Powell		35-59	5th	21.0
7-25	Pit.	L	1-6		4	11	Schmidt	Kline		35-60	5th	22.0
7-26	Chi.	W	6-1		9	9	Smith	Lieber		36-60	5th	22.0
7-27	Chi.	L	2-4		10	8	Mulholland	Hermanson	Adams	36-61	5th	23.0
7-28	Chi.	W	8-2		10	3	Vazquez	Tapani		37-61	5th	22.0
7-30	At Mil.	L	0-1		5	7	Peterson	Powell	Wickman	37-62	5th	22.5
7-31	At Mil.	W	4-2		12	5	Telford	Plunk	Urbina	38-62	5th	22.0
8-1	At Mil.	W	10-4		13	7	Smith	Karl		39-62	5th	22.0
8-2	At Chi.	W	5-1		7	6	Hermanson	Tapani	Urbina	40-62	4th	21.5
8-3	At Chi.	W	9-4		13	12	Vazquez	Bowie		41-62	4th	21.5
8-4	At Chi.	L	1-5		5	7	Trachsel	Powell		41-63	4th	22.5
8-5	At Chi.	W	5-2		10	10	Thurman	Lieber	Urbina	42-63	4th	22.0
8-6	S.D.	L	10-12		9	17	Hitchcock	Smith	Hoffman	42-64	4th	23.0
8-7	S.D.	W	3-1		8	4	Hermanson	Williams	Urbina	43-64	4th	22.0
8-8	S.D.	W	4-2		13	7	Kline	Reyes	Urbina	44-64	4th	21.0
8-9	S.D.	W	8-0		11	7	Powell	Clement		45-64	4th	20.5
8-10	L.A.	W	6-4		8	7	Thurman	Valdes	Urbina	46-64	4th	20.5
8-11	L.A.	L	7-9		15	11	Maddux	Ayala	Shaw	46-65	4th	21.5
8-12	L.A.	L	5-10		10	11	Judd	Hermanson		46-66	4th	22.0
8-13†	At Col.	W	14-13	(10)	14	15	Urbina	Dipoto	Telford	47-66		
8-13‡	At Col.	W	8-6		13	11	Vazquez	Bohanon	Urbina	48-66	4th	21.5
8-14	At Col.	L	8-11		11	18	Kile	Powell	Veres	48-67	4th	21.5
8-15†	At Col.	L	2-8		7	9	Thomson	Thurman	Ramirez	48-68		
8-15‡	At Col.	L	4-12		12	14	Astacio	Bennett		48-69	4th	23.0
8-16	At S.F	L	4-7		8	12	Nathan	Armas Jr.	Nen	48-70	5th	24.0
8-17	At S.F	W	2-1	(12)	10	7	Smith	Johnstone	Urbina	49-70	5th	23.0
8-18	At S.F	L	4-5		12	7	Ortiz	Vazquez	Nen	49-71	5th	24.0
8-20	At Cin.	W	5-3		9	8	Batista	Sullivan	Urbina	50-71	4th	23.5
8-21	At Cin.	L	3-9		8	11	Guzman	Thurman		50-72	4th	24.5
8-22	At Cin.	L	3-4	(11)	11	12	Sullivan	Urbina		50-73	T4th	25.5
8-23	StL.	W	11-7		14	11	Telford	Croushore		51-73	4th	25.5
8-24	StL.	W	8-4		12	10	Vazquez	Bottenfield	Urbina	52-73	4th	25.5
8-25	StL.	W	4-1		8	7	Powell	Luebbers	Urbina	53-73	4th	25.5
8-26	Cin.	L	4-10		8	14	Guzman	Thurman	Williamson	53-74	4th	26.0
8-27	Cin.	L	1-4		4	10	Villone	Hermanson	Graves	53-75	4th	27.0
8-28	Cin.	W	8-6		11	9	Kline	Williamson		54-75	4th	27.0
8-29	Cin.	W	8-6		8	10	Mota	Harnisch	Urbina	55-75	4th	27.0
8-30	At Ari.	L	4-5		8	9	Chouinard	Batista	Mantei	55-76	4th	27.0
8-31	At Ari.	W	2-1		6	6	Thurman	Johnson	Urbina	56-76	4th	27.0
9-1	At Ari.	W	8-1		11	7	Hermanson	Daal		57-76	4th	27.0
9-3	Hou.	L	1-8		7	11	Hampton	Smith		57-77	4th	28.0
9-4	Hou.	L	2-5	(10)	8	6	Cabrera	Urbina		57-78	4th	28.0
9-5	Hou.	L	2-6		9	12	Elarton	Telford		57-79	4th	28.0
9-6	Col.	L	3-5		9	10	Astacio	Thurman	Veres	57-80	4th	29.0
9-7	Col.	W	4-1		5	6	Hermanson	Thomson	Urbina	58-80	4th	29.0
9-8	Col.	L	1-5		6	7	Wright	Smith		58-81	4th	30.0
9-9	At S.D.	L	3-10		6	17	Carlyle	Vazquez		58-82	4th	30.5
9-10	At S.D.	L	3-10		8	10	Clement	Powell		58-83	4th	31.5
9-11	At S.D.	W	5-4		7	10	Thurman	Ashby	Urbina	59-83	4th	30.5
9-12	At S.D.	W	8-4		12	12	Hermanson	Hitchcock	Urbina	60-83	4th	29.5
9-13	At L.A.	L	4-12		10	15	Park	Smith		60-84	4th	29.5
9-14	At L.A.	W	3-0		9	1	Vazquez	Brown		61-84	4th	29.5
9-15	At L.A.	W	10-7		12	14	Powell	Arnold	Urbina	62-84	4th	28.5
9-17	At Atl.	L	5-6	(10)	12	5	Remlinger	Kline		62-85	4th	29.5
9-18	At Atl.	W	4-3		8	11	Hermanson	Maddux	Urbina	63-85	4th	28.5
9-19	At Atl.	L	1-5		7	7	Millwood	Lilly		63-86	4th	29.5
9-21†	At Fla.	L	3-5		11	8	Springer	Telford	Alfonseca	63-87		
9-21‡	At Fla.	L	0-4		7	8	Cornelius	Powell		63-88	4th	31.0

Date	Opp.	Res.	Score	(inn.*)	Hits	Opp. hits	Winning pitcher	Losing pitcher	Save	Record	Pos.	GB
9-22	At Fla.	W	5-3		7	7	Batista	Nunez	Urbina	64-88	4th	31.0
9-23	At Fla.	L	1-2		9	4	Burnett	Hermanson	Alfonseca	64-89	4th	32.0
9-24	Atl.	L	3-4	(10)	4	9	Bergman	Mota	Remlinger	64-90	4th	33.0
9-25	Atl.	L	3-5		10	9	Mulholland	Vazquez	Rocker	64-91	4th	34.0
9-26	Atl.	L	0-10		6	13	Smoltz	Powell		64-92	4th	35.0
9-27	Fla.	W	8-4		7	8	Telford	Almonte		65-92	4th	34.5
9-28	Fla.	L	3-5		8	11	Nunez	Hermanson	Alfonseca	65-93	4th	35.5
9-29	Fla.	W	5-3		8	6	Kline	Looper	Urbina	66-93	4th	34.5
10-1	At Phi.	W	7-4		13	11	Vazquez	Grahe	Urbina	67-93	4th	35.0
10-2	At Phi.	W	13-3		14	8	Powell	Byrd	Batista	68-93	4th	34.0
10-3	At Phi.	L	5-6		8	9	Politte	Strickland	Montgomery	68-94	4th	35.0

Monthly records: April (7-14), May (11-16), June (12-14), July (8-18), August (18-14), September (10-17), October (2-1).
*Innings, if other than nine. † First game of a doubleheader. ‡ Second game of a doubleheader.

HIGHLIGHTS

High point: A three-game sweep of the Red Sox June 7-9 at Olympic Stadium. The Expos defeated Bret Saberhagen, Tim Wakefield and former Expos stand-out Pedro Martinez, prevailing by a cumulative score of 26-4.

Low point: David Cone's perfect game for the Yankees against the Expos on July 18 came on a Sunday afternoon after the club had played in sapping heat in Baltimore the night before. The Expos might have been dragging that day at Yankee Stadium, but comments minimizing Cone's achievement still had to hurt. The oft-heard line: It wasn't much of an accomplishment to shut down lowly Montreal.

Turning point: A draining five-game series against the Rockies in Colorado August 13-15 (including two double-headers in three days) was made necessary by the April postponement of two games in the aftermath of the Columbine High School shootings in suburban Denver. The Expos swept the first dou-bleheader, but lost the remaining three games and then tumbled into last place on August 16.

Most valuable player: Vladimir Guerrero solved many of his early fielding prob-lems and again proved why he's the play-er the team is building around. Guerrero set eight single-season Expos offensive records, including highs in home runs (42) and RBIs (131). His 31-game hitting streak was the longest in the National League since 1987.

Most valuable pitcher: Ugueth Urbina led the N.L. in saves with 41 despite playing for a team that lost 94 games. In 75.2 innings, he struck out 100 batters and yielded only 59 hits.

Most improved player: Jose Vidro worked on his hitting in winter ball—and it showed. Despite a poor September, he finished with a .304 average and 45 dou-bles. The second baseman went back to winter ball after the 1999 season to work on his defense—hopefully with similar results.

Most pleasant surprise: Javier Vazquez was 5-15 with a 6.06 ERA in his rookie season of 1998, and he was struggling again when he was sent to the minors in June. Upon his return in July, he was the loser in Cone's perfect game but then pitched complete-game victories in his next two starts. He finished with a 9-8 record.

Biggest disappointment: No. 1 starter Dustin Hermanson had a terrible first half, then rallied (a 2.95 ERA after the All-Star break). First baseman Brad Fullmer was sent to Class AAA Ottawa twice during the season.

Key injuries: The loss of shortstop Orlando Cabrera (ankle sprain) for the final two months was a setback. Righthanded starter Carl Pavano (elbow problems) made only one appearance after the All-Star break—and that was in relief.

Notable: Lefthanded reliever Steve Kline led the majors in appearances with 82, and righthander Anthony Telford worked 79 times out of the bullpen. ... Guerrero again was a constant in the lineup (159 games in 1998, 160 in 1999), avoiding injuries despite his aggressive play. ... Guerrero had 13 errors by June 30 but only six thereafter. ... Rondell White, who split time between left and center field, batted .312 with 22 homers. ... Michael Barrett managed 433 at-bats and a .293 average while trying to master two posi-tions (third base, catcher).

—STEPHANIE MYLES

RECORDS

1999 regular-season record: 68-94 (4th in N.L. East); 35-46 at home; 33-48 on road; 19-31 vs. N.L. East; 22-28 vs. Central; 19-25 vs. West; 8-10 vs. A.L.; 18-21 vs. lefthanded starters; 50-73 vs. right-handed starters; 23-35 on grass; 45-59 on turf; 14-32 in daytime; 54-62 at night; 16-28 in one-run games; 3-11 in extra-inning games; 1-2-0 in doubleheaders.
Team record past five years: 365-427 (.461, ranks 11th in league in that span).

TEAM LEADERS

Batting average: Vladimir Guerrero (.316).
At-bats: Vladimir Guerrero (610).
Runs: Vladimir Guerrero (102).
Hits: Vladimir Guerrero (193).
Total Bases: Vladimir Guerrero (366).
Doubles: Jose Vidro (45).
Triples: Wilton Guerrero, Manny Martinez (7).
Home runs: Vladimir Guerrero (42).
Runs batted in: Vladimir Guerrero (131).
Stolen bases: Manny Martinez (19).
Slugging percentage: Vladimir Guerrero (.600).

On-base percentage: Vladimir Guerrero (.378).
Wins: Dustin Hermanson, Javier Vazquez (9).
Earned-run average: Dustin Hermanson (4.20).
Complete games: Javier Vazquez (3).
Shutouts: Miguel Batista, Carl Pavano, Javier Vazquez (1).
Saves: Ugueth Urbina (41).
Innings pitched: Dustin Hermanson (216.1).
Strikeouts: Dustin Hermanson (145).

GAMES BY POSITION

Catcher: Chris Widger 118, Michael Barrett 59, Robert Machado 17, Darron Cox 14.
First base: Brad Fullmer 94, Ryan McGuire 58, Fernando Seguignol 23, Shane Andrews 18, Jose Vidro 14, Orlando Merced 7, Mike Mordecai 1.
Second base: Jose Vidro 121, Wilton Guerrero 54, Mike Mordecai 38, Trace Coquillette 6, Geoff Blum 2.
Third base: Shane Andrews 82, Michael Barrett 66, Mike Mordecai 32, Trace Coquillette 11, Jose Fernandez 6, Jose Vidro 2.
Shortstop: Orlando Cabrera 102, Geoff Blum 42, Mike Mordecai 38, Michael Barrett 2.
Outfield: Vladimir Guerrero 160, Rondell White 135, Manny Martinez 126, James Mouton 56, Orlando Merced 44, Ryan McGuire 23, Wilton Guerrero 22, Terry Jones 17, Peter Bergeron 13, Fernando Seguignol 8, Jose Vidro 4, Chris Stowers 2.
Designated hitter: Wilton Guerrero 5, Orlando Merced 2, James Mouton 1, Shane Andrews 1.

TOP DRAFT CHOICES

1. **Josh Girdley,** LHP, Jasper (Texas) H.S.
2. **Brandon Phillips,** SS, Redan H.S., Stone Mountain, Ga.
3. **Drew McMillan,** C, El Dorado H.S., Placentia, Calif.
4. **Matt Cepicky,** OF, Southwest Missouri State University
5. **Pat Collins,** RHP, St. John's University
6. **Dom Ambrosini,** OF, Connetquot H.S., Ronkonkoma, N.Y.
7. **Cletis Boyer,** SS, Largo (Fla.) H.S.
8. **Luke Lockwood,** LHP, Silverado H.S., Victorville, Calif.
9. **Brandon Watson,** 2B, Westchester H.S., Los Angeles
10. **Grant Dorn,** RHP, North Carolina State University

NEW YORK METS
NATIONAL LEAGUE EAST DIVISION

2000 Yankees Schedule
Home games shaded. *—All-Star Game at Turner Field (Atlanta).

March

SUN	MON	TUE	WED	THU	FRI	SAT
26	27	28	29	30	31	

April

SUN	MON	TUE	WED	THU	FRI	SAT
						1
2	3 ANA	4 ANA	5 ANA	6	7 SEA	8 SEA
9 SEA	10	11 TEX	12 TEX	13 TEX	14 KC	15 KC
16 KC	17 TEX	18 TEX	19 TEX	20	21 TOR	22 TOR
23 TOR	24 MIN	25 MIN	26 MIN	27	28 TOR	29 TOR
30 TOR						

May

SUN	MON	TUE	WED	THU	FRI	SAT
	1 CLE	2 CLE	3 CLE	4	5 BAL	6 BAL
7 BAL	8 TB	9 TB	10	11	12 DET	13 DET
14 DET	15	16 CWS	17 CWS	18	19 CLE	20 CLE
21 CLE	22	23 CHI	24 CHI	25 CHI	26 BOS	27 BOS
28 BOS	29 OAK	30 OAK				

June

SUN	MON	TUE	WED	THU	FRI	SAT
				1	2 ATL	3 ATL
4 ATL	5 MON	6 MON	7 MON	8	9 NYM	10 NYM
11 NYM	12 BOS	13 BOS	14 BOS	15 CWS	16 CWS	17 CWS
18 CWS	19 BOS	20 BOS	21 BOS	22 BOS	23 CHI	24 CHI
25 CHI	26	27 DET	28 DET	29 DET	30 TB	

July

SUN	MON	TUE	WED	THU	FRI	SAT
						1 TB
2 TB	3	4 BAL	5 BAL	6 BAL	7 NYM	8 NYM
9 NYM	10	11 *	12	13 FLA	14 FLA	15 FLA
16 PHI	17 PHI	18 DET	19 DET	20 DET	21 TB	22 TB
23 TB	24 BAL	25 BAL	26 BAL	27 MIN	28 MIN	29 MIN
30 MIN	31					

August

SUN	MON	TUE	WED	THU	FRI	SAT
		1 KC	2 KC	3 KC	4 SEA	5 SEA
6 SEA	7 OAK	8 OAK	9 OAK	10 ANA	11 ANA	12 ANA
13 ANA	14 TEX	15 TEX	16 TEX	17 ANA	18 ANA	19 ANA
20 ANA	21	22 TEX	23 TEX	24 TEX	25 OAK	26 OAK
27 OAK	28 SEA	29 SEA	30 SEA	31		

September

SUN	MON	TUE	WED	THU	FRI	SAT
					1 MIN	2 MIN
3 MIN	4 KC	5 KC	6 KC	7 KC	8 BOS	9 BOS
10 BOS	11	12 TOR	13 TOR	14 TOR	15 CLE	16 CLE
17 CLE	18 TOR	19 TOR	20 TOR	21 TOR	22 DET	23 DET
24 DET	25 DET	26 TB	27 TB	28 TB	29 BAL	30 BAL

October

SUN	MON	TUE	WED	THU	FRI	SAT
1 BAL	2	3	4	5	6	7

2000 SEASON
CLUB DIRECTORY

Chairman of the board
Nelson Doubleday

President and chief executive officer
Fred Wilpon

Directors
Nelson Doubleday, Fred Wilpon, Saul B. Katz, Steve Phillips, Marvin B. Tepper

Special advisor to the board of directors
Richard Cummins

Senior v.p., general manager
Steve Phillips

Sr. asst. g.m./international scouting dir.
Omar Minaya

Assistant g.m./player personnel
Jim Duquette

Assistant g.m./amateur scouting
Gary LaRocque

Assistant g.m./professional scouting
Carmen Fusco

Special assistants to the g.m.
Harry Minor, Darrell Johnson, Larry Doughty

Assistant directors of amateur scouting
Jack Bowen, Fred Wright

Assistant director of player personnel
Kevin Morgan

Senior v.p. and treasurer
Harold W. O'Shaughnessy

Senior v.p. of business & legal affairs
David Howard

Vice president, marketing
Mark Bingham

V.p., purchasing and special projects
Bob Mandt

Vice president, ticket sales and services
Bill Ianniciello

Senior v.p. and consultant
J. Frank Cashen

Director of marketing
Kit Geis

Director of marketing production
Tim Gunkel

Director of human resources
To be announced

General counsel
David Cohen

Dir., admin. and data processing
Russ Richardson

Director, community outreach
Jill Knee

Director of corporate sales
Paul Danforth

Director of corporate sales
Paul Danforth

Controller
Lennie Labita

Director of media relations
Jay Horwitz

Director, ticket operations
Dan DeMato

Manager, customer relations
Joann Galardy

Director of stadium operations
Kevin McCarthy

Club physicians
Dr. David Altchek

Club psychologist/E.A.P.
Dr. Allan Lans

Team trainers
Fred Hina, Scott Lawrenson

Special assignment scouts
Buddy Kerr, Darrell Johnson

Professional scouts
Bruce Benedict, Edwin Bryant, Howard Johnson, Roland Johnson, Bill Latham, Mike Toomey, Tim Teufel

Regional scouting supervisors
Paul Fryer, Gene Kerns, Terry Tripp

Scouting supervisors
Kevin Blankenship, Quincy Boyd, Larry Chase, Joe DelliCarri, Kevin Frady, Chuck Hensley Jr., Dave Lottsfeldt, Fred Mazuca, Marlin McPhail, Randy Milligan, Bob Minor, Greg Morhardt, Joe Morlan, Joe Nigro, Jim Reeves, Junior Roman, Bob Rossi, Joe Salermo, Greg Tubbs

MINOR LEAGUE AFFILIATES

Class	Team	League	Manager
AAA	Norfolk	International	John Gibbons
AA	Binghamton	Eastern	Doug Davis
A	St. Lucie	Florida State	Dave Engle
A	Capital City	South Atlantic	John Stephenson
A	Pittsfield	New York-Pennsylvania	Tony Tijerina
Rookie	Kingsport	Appalachian	Edgar Alfonzo

BROADCAST INFORMATION

Radio: WFAN-AM (660).
TV: WPIX-TV (Channel 11).
Cable TV: Fox Sports New York.

SPRING TRAINING

Ballpark (city): Thomas J. White Stadium (Port St. Lucie, Fla.).
Ticket information: 561-871-2115.

SPRING TRAINING ROSTER

Manager—Bobby Valentine (2).
Coaches—Al Jackson (54), Tom Robson (53), Cookie Rojas (8), John Stearns (12), Dave Wallace (52), Mookie Wilson (1).

No.	PITCHERS	B/T	Ht./Wt.	Born	1999 clubs
49	Benitez, Armando	R/R	6-4/229	11-3-72	New York N.L.
	Cammack, Eric	R/R	6-1/180	8-14-75	Binghamton, Norfolk
27	Cook, Dennis	L/L	6-3/190	10-4-62	New York N.L.
45	Franco, John	L/L	5-10/185	9-17-60	New York N.L., Binghamton
	Gonzalez, Dicky	R/R	5-11/170	10-21-78	St. Lucie, Norfolk
10	Hampton, Mike	R/L	5-10/180	9-9-72	Houston
28	Jones, Bobby	R/R	6-4/225	2-10-70	New York N.L., Binghamton, Norfolk
22	Leiter, Al	L/L	6-3/220	10-23-65	New York N.L.
23	Mahomes, Pat	R/R	6-4/212	8-9-70	Norfolk, New York N.L.
	Mann, Jim	R/R	6-3/225	11-17-74	Knoxville, Syracuse
	Orosco, Jesse	R/L	6-2/205	4-21-57	Baltimore
35	Reed, Rick	R/R	6-1/195	8-16-65	New York N.L., Norfolk, Binghamton
	Roberts, Grant	R/R	6-3/205	9-13-77	Binghamton, Norfolk
48	Rusch, Glendon	L/L	6-1/200	11-7-74	Omaha, Gulf Coast Royals, Kansas City, New York N.L.
99	Wendell, Turk	L/R	6-2/205	5-19-67	New York N.L.
32	Wilson, Paul	R/R	6-5/235	3-28-73	DID NOT PLAY
21	Yoshii, Masato	R/R	6-2/210	4-20-65	New York N.L.

No.	CATCHERS	B/T	Ht./Wt.	Born	1999 clubs
31	Piazza, Mike	R/R	6-3/215	9-4-68	New York N.L.
7	Pratt, Todd	R/R	6-3/230	2-9-67	New York N.L.
3	Wilson, Vance	R/R	5-11/190	3-17-73	Norfolk, New York N.L.

No.	INFIELDERS	B/T	Ht./Wt.	Born	1999 clubs
13	Alfonzo, Edgardo	R/R	5-11/187	11-8-73	New York N.L.
15	Franco, Matt	L/R	6-1/210	8-19-69	New York N.L.
11	Halter, Shane	R/R	6-0/180	11-8-69	Norfolk, New York N.L.
33	Kinkade, Mike	R/R	6-1/210	5-6-73	New York N.L., Norfolk
17	Lopez, Luis	B/R	5-11/166	9-4-70	New York N.L.
10	Ordonez, Rey	R/R	5-9/159	11-11-72	New York N.L.
30	Toca, Jorge	R/R	6-3/220	1-7-75	Binghamton, Norfolk, New York N.L.
4	Ventura, Robin	L/R	6-1/198	7-14-67	New York N.L.
	Zeile, Todd	R/R	6-1/200	9-9-65	Texas

No.	OUTFIELDERS	B/T	Ht./Wt.	Born	1999 clubs
50	Agbayani, Benny	R/R	5-11/225	12-28-71	Norfolk, New York N.L.
14	Bell, Derek	R/R	6-2/215	12-11-68	Houston
	Escobar, Alex	R/R	6-1/180	9-6-78	Gulf Coast Mets, St. Lucie
18	Hamilton, Darryl	L/R	6-1/192	12-3-64	Colorado, New York N.L.
24	Henderson, Rickey	R/L	5-10/190	12-25-58	New York N.L.
	LeBron, Juan	R/R	6-6/205	6-7-77	DID NOT PLAY
6	Mora, Melvin	R/R	5-10/180	2-2-72	Norfolk, New York N.L.
22	Nunnally, Jon	L/R	5-10/190	11-9-71	Pawtucket, Boston
44	Payton, Jay	R/R	5-10/185	11-22-72	St. Lucie, Norfolk, New York N.L.

BALLPARK INFORMATION

Ballpark (capacity, surface)
Shea Stadium (56,521, grass)

Address
123-01 Roosevelt Ave.
Flushing, NY 11368

Business phone
718-507-METS

Ticket information
718-507-TIXX

Ticket prices
$57 (Metropolitan Club gold)
$54 (Metropolitan Club)
$37 (inner field box, inner loge box)
$33 (middle field box)
$30 (outer field box, outer loge box, mezzanine box)
$26 (loge reserved)
$21 (mezzanine reserved, upper box)
$12 (upper reserved, back rows loge and mezzanine)
$1 (senior citizen-designated dates)

Field dimensions (from home plate)
To left field at foul line, 338 feet
To center field, 410 feet
To right field at foul line, 338 feet

First game played
April 17, 1964 (Pirates 4, Mets 3)

2000 SEASON *New York Mets*

Date	Opp.	Res.	Score	(inn.*)	Hits	Opp. hits	Winning pitcher	Losing pitcher	Save	Record	Pos.	GB
4-6	At Fla.	W	12-3		13	8	Reed	Hernandez	Watson	1-1	T1st	...
4-7	At Fla.	W	6-0		13	6	Jones	Sanchez		2-1	T1st	...
4-8	At Mon.	L	1-5		6	10	Batista	Hershiser	Urbina	2-2	T2nd	1.0
4-9	At Mon.	W	10-3		11	5	Yoshii	Thurman		3-2	T1st	...
4-10	At Mon.	W	4-3	(11)	8	7	Cook	Telford	Franco	4-2	1st	+1.0
4-11	At Mon.	W	6-3		14	7	Watson	Pavano	Franco	5-2	1st	+1.0
4-12	Fla.	W	8-1		9	5	Jones	Hernandez		6-2	1st	+1.0
4-14	Fla.	W	4-1		3	5	Hershiser	Sanchez	Franco	7-2	1st	+1.0
4-15	Fla.	L	4-11		9	18	Meadows	Yoshii		7-3	1st	+0.5
4-16	Mon.	L	4-6		7	7	Hermanson	Leiter	Urbina	7-4	2nd	...
4-17	Mon.	W	3-2		6	7	Jones	Pavano	Franco	8-4	1st	+1.0
4-18	Mon.	L	2-4		6	11	Vazquez	Watson	Urbina	8-5	2nd	...
4-20	At Cin.	W	3-2		8	8	Cook	Harnisch	Franco	9-5	1st	+0.5
4-21	At Cin.	L	4-7		3	7	Sullivan	Yoshii	Graves	9-6	2nd	0.5
4-22	At Cin.	W	4-1		7	6	Leiter	Tomko	Franco	10-6	2nd	...
4-23	At Chi.	W	6-5		13	8	Cook	Beck	Franco	11-6	1st	+1.0
4-24	At Chi.	L	0-2		8	5	Mulholland	Watson	Beck	11-7	2nd	...
4-25	At Chi.	L	4-8		11	8	Myers	Hershiser		11-8	2nd	1.0
4-27	S.D.	L	2-6		5	8	Ashby	Yoshii		11-9	3rd	1.5
4-28	S.D.	W	4-3		11	6	Wendell	Hoffman		12-9	2nd	1.5
4-29	S.D.	W	8-5		6	11	Cook	Boehringer	Franco	13-9	2nd	1.5
4-30	S.F	W	7-2		14	6	Watson	Estes	Wendell	14-9	2nd	1.5
5-1	S.F	W	9-4		12	7	Hershiser	Brock		15-9	2nd	1.5
5-2	S.F	W	2-0		5	7	Cook	Johnstone	Franco	16-9	2nd	1.5
5-3	Hou.	W	5-3		9	6	Reed	Holt	Franco	17-9	2nd	1.5
5-4	Hou.	L	1-6		3	13	Hampton	Leiter		17-10	2nd	1.5
5-5	Hou.	L	4-5		11	8	Powell	Benitez	Wagner	17-11	2nd	2.5
5-7	At Ari.	L	7-14		12	15	Stottlemyre	Hershiser		17-12	2nd	2.5
5-8	At Ari.	W	4-2		11	6	Yoshii	Benes	Benitez	18-12	2nd	2.5
5-9	At Ari.	L	6-11		16	13	Daal	Reed		18-13	2nd	2.5
5-10	At Col.	L	3-10		7	12	Astacio	Leiter		18-14	2nd	2.5
5-11	At Col.	L	5-8		11	12	Jones	Jones		18-15	3rd	3.5
5-12	At Col.	W	10-5		15	10	Reed	Thomson		19-15	3rd	2.5
5-14	At Phi.	W	7-3		9	5	Yoshii	Ogea		20-15	2nd	1.5
5-15	At Phi.	W	9-7		12	13	Mahomes	Ryan	Franco	21-15	2nd	0.5
5-16	At Phi.	L	2-5		8	10	Byrd	Hershiser	Brantley	21-16	2nd	1.5
5-17	Mil.	L	6-7		11	13	Karl	Jones	Wickman	21-17	3rd	2.5
5-18	Mil.	L	2-4		11	8	Weathers	Cook	Wickman	21-18	3rd	3.5
5-20†	Mil.	W	11-10		12	13	Leiter	Abbott	Franco	22-18		
5-20‡	Mil.	W	10-1		12	9	Yoshii	Woodard		23-18	2nd	2.5
5-21	Phi.	W	7-5		13	10	Hershiser	Loewer	Franco	24-18	2nd	1.5
5-22	Phi.	L	3-9		7	13	Byrd	Jones		24-19	2nd	2.5
5-23	Phi.	W	5-4		12	9	Beltran	Schilling		25-19	2nd	1.5
5-24	At Pit.	L	4-7		7	8	Silva	Isringhausen	Williams	25-20	2nd	1.5
5-25	At Pit.	W	8-3		11	6	Yoshii	Benson		26-20	2nd	1.5
5-26	At Pit.	W	5-2		10	5	Hershiser	Schourek	Franco	27-20	2nd	1.5
5-28	Ari.	L	1-2		6	6	Daal	Reed	Olson	27-21	2nd	3.0
5-29	Ari.	L	7-8		11	13	Reynoso	Beltran	Kim	27-22	2nd	3.0
5-30	Ari.	L	1-10		6	15	Johnson	Yoshii		27-23	2nd	3.0
5-31	Cin.	L	3-5		6	8	Villone	Leiter	Williamson	27-24	2nd	4.0
6-1	Cin.	L	0-4		7	10	Harnisch	Hershiser		27-25	2nd	5.0
6-2	Cin.	L	7-8		8	11	Williamson	Franco	Sullivan	27-26	3rd	5.0
6-4	At N.Y. (AL)	L	3-4		7	5	Grimsley	Reed	Rivera	27-27	3rd	5.0
6-5	At N.Y. (AL)	L	3-6		9	11	Hernandez	Yoshii	Rivera	27-28	3rd	6.0
6-6	At N.Y. (AL)	W	7-2		8	6	Leiter	Clemens		28-28	3rd	6.0
6-7	Tor.	W	8-2		14	8	Hershiser	Halladay		29-28	3rd	6.0
6-8	Tor.	W	11-3		14	4	Isringhausen	Hentgen		30-28	3rd	6.0
6-9	Tor.	W	4-3	(14)	11	15	Mahomes	Davey		31-28	2nd	6.0
6-11	Bos.	L	2-3	(12)	8	11	Corsi	Franco	Wasdin	31-29	3rd	6.0
6-12	Bos.	W	4-2		8	7	Leiter	Rapp	Franco	32-29	3rd	5.0
6-13	Bos.	W	5-4		11	8	Hershiser	Portugal	Wendell	33-29	2nd	4.0
6-14	At Cin.	L	4-8		5	10	Williamson	McMichael		33-30	T2nd	4.0
6-15	At Cin.	W	11-3		12	9	Reed	Tomko		34-30	2nd	4.0
6-16	At Cin.	W	5-2		10	8	Yoshii	Parris	Franco	35-30	2nd	4.0
6-17	At StL.	W	4-3		10	6	Leiter	Mercker	Cook	36-30	2nd	4.0
6-18	At StL.	W	6-2		14	3	Hershiser	Acevedo	Benitez	37-30	2nd	4.0
6-19	At StL.	L	6-7		9	10	Aybar	Isringhausen	Bottalico	37-31	2nd	4.0
6-20	At StL.	W	9-6		12	10	Reed	Croushore	Franco	38-31	2nd	4.0
6-22	Fla.	W	8-2		14	4	McMichael	Springer	Benitez	39-31	2nd	3.0
6-23	Fla.	W	6-3		8	7	Leiter	Meadows	Franco	40-31	2nd	3.0
6-24	Fla.	W	3-2		8	9	Cook	Hernandez	Franco	41-31	2nd	3.0
6-25	At Atl.	W	10-2		13	8	Reed	Perez		42-31	2nd	2.0

Date	Opp.	Res.	Score	(inn.*)	Hits	Opp. hits	Winning pitcher	Losing pitcher	Save	Record	Pos.	GB
6-26	At Atl.	L	2-7		7	7	Glavine	Dotel		42-32	2nd	3.0
6-27	At Atl.	L	0-1		3	4	Maddux	Yoshii	Rocker	42-33	2nd	4.0
6-28	At Fla.	W	10-4		14	11	Leiter	Meadows		43-33	2nd	4.0
6-29	At Fla.	W	5-1		9	5	Hershiser	Hernandez		44-33	2nd	3.0
6-30	At Fla.	L	3-4	(10)	8	9	Alfonseca	Benitez		44-34	2nd	3.0
7-1	At Fla.	W	12-8		12	13	Dotel	Dempster		45-34	2nd	3.0
7-2	Atl.	L	0-16		3	15	Maddux	Yoshii		45-35	2nd	4.0
7-3	Atl.	L	0-3		3	7	Millwood	Leiter	Rocker	45-36	2nd	5.0
7-4	Atl.	W	7-6		11	8	Cook	Smoltz	Benitez	46-36	2nd	4.0
7-5	Mon.	W	2-1		9	6	Wendell	Mota	Benitez	47-36	2nd	4.0
7-6	Mon.	W	10-0		13	6	Hershiser	Pavano	Isringhausen	48-36	2nd	3.0
7-7	Mon.	L	1-3		7	8	Kline	Wendell	Urbina	48-37	2nd	4.0
7-8	Mon.	L	3-4		6	6	Ayala	Cook	Urbina	48-38	2nd	5.0
7-9	N.Y. (AL)	W	5-2		12	5	Leiter	Clemens	Benitez	49-38	2nd	4.0
7-10	N.Y. (AL)	W	9-8		9	11	Mahomes	Rivera		50-38	2nd	4.0
7-11	N.Y. (AL)	L	3-6		8	13	Irabu	Hershiser	Rivera	50-39	2nd	5.0
7-15	At T.B.	W	8-7	(10)	8	13	Benitez	Charlton		51-39	2nd	5.0
7-16	At T.B.	W	9-7		15	11	Reed	Eiland	Cook	52-39	2nd	5.0
7-17	At T.B.	L	2-3		8	8	Alvarez	Hershiser	Hernandez	52-40	2nd	5.0
7-18	At Bal.	W	8-6		12	12	Yoshii	Guzman	Benitez	53-40	2nd	4.0
7-19	At Bal.	W	4-1		9	4	Dotel	Johnson	Benitez	54-40	2nd	3.0
7-20	At Bal.	L	1-4		6	9	Ponson	Leiter		54-41	2nd	3.0
7-21	At Mon.	W	7-3		12	12	Reed	Smith		55-41	2nd	2.0
7-22	At Mon.	W	7-4		12	9	Hershiser	Hermanson		56-41	2nd	2.0
7-23	Chi.	W	5-4		9	7	Cook	Tapani	Benitez	57-41	2nd	1.5
7-24	Chi.	W	2-1		5	6	Dotel	Trachsel	Benitez	58-41	2nd	0.5
7-25	Chi.	W	5-1		5	8	Leiter	Serafini		59-41	2nd	0.5
7-26	Pit.	W	7-5		9	10	Reed	Cordova	Wendell	60-41	2nd	0.5
7-27	Pit.	L	1-5		6	9	Benson	Hershiser		60-42	2nd	1.5
7-28	Pit.	W	9-2		10	3	Cook	Wilkins		61-42	2nd	0.5
7-30	At Chi.	W	10-9		14	13	Mahomes	Farnsworth	Benitez	62-42	1st	+0.5
7-31	At Chi.	L	10-17		18	14	Serafini	Isringhausen		62-43	2nd	0.5
8-1	At Chi.	W	5-4	(13)	10	10	Mahomes	Sanders		63-43	2nd	0.5
8-2	At Mil.	W	7-2		12	8	Reed	Nomo		64-43	T1st	...
8-3	At Mil.	W	10-3		13	6	Hershiser	Pulsipher		65-43	1st	+1.0
8-4	At Mil.	W	9-5		17	7	Rogers	Peterson		66-43	1st	+2.0
8-6	L.A.	W	2-1		4	5	Dotel	Park	Benitez	67-43	1st	+1.5
8-7	L.A.	L	6-7		11	13	Borbon	Taylor	Shaw	67-44	1st	+0.5
8-8	L.A.	L	3-14		7	14	Dreifort	Reed		67-45	1st	+0.5
8-9	L.A.	L	2-9		6	13	Brown	Hershiser		67-46	2nd	0.5
8-10	S.D.	W	4-3		15	9	Wendell	Ashby	Benitez	68-46	2nd	0.5
8-11	S.D.	W	12-5		14	6	Mahomes	Hitchcock		69-46	2nd	0.5
8-12	S.D.	W	9-3		11	5	Leiter	Williams		70-46	T1st	...
8-13	At S.F	L	2-3		9	5	Ortiz	Yoshii	Nen	70-47	2nd	1.0
8-14	At S.F	W	6-1		16	5	Hershiser	Rueter		71-47	T1st	...
8-15	At S.F	W	12-5		16	12	Rogers	Hernandez		72-47	T1st	...
8-16	At S.D.	W	4-3	(10)	10	2	Cook	Cunnane	Benitez	73-47	T1st	...
8-17	At S.D.	L	2-3		5	5	Williams	Leiter	Hoffman	73-48	T1st	...
8-18	At S.D.	W	9-1		15	6	Yoshii	Spencer		74-48	1st	+1.0
8-21	StL.	W	7-4		9	8	Mahomes	Mercker	Benitez	75-48	1st	...
8-22†	StL.	W	8-7		11	12	Benitez	Bottalico		76-48		
8-22‡	StL.	L	5-7		11	10	Stephenson	Hershiser	Acevedo	76-49	2nd	0.5
8-23	Hou.	W	3-2		8	10	Benitez	Powell		77-49	2nd	0.5
8-24	Hou.	L	1-5	(10)	5	8	Wagner	Cook		77-50	2nd	1.5
8-25	Hou.	W	4-0		12	7	Rogers	Reynolds	Cook	78-50	2nd	1.5
8-27	At Ari.	W	6-3		11	8	Dotel	Daal	Benitez	79-50	2nd	1.5
8-28	At Ari.	L	3-5		6	8	Reynoso	Cook	Mantei	79-51	2nd	2.5
8-29	At Ari.	L	4-8		10	12	Anderson	Leiter	Olson	79-52	2nd	3.5
8-30	At Hou.	W	17-1		21	5	Yoshii	Reynolds		80-52	2nd	2.5
8-31	At Hou.	L	2-6		7	7	Lima	Wendell		80-53	2nd	3.5
9-1	At Hou.	W	9-5		18	7	Dotel	Holt		81-53	2nd	3.5
9-3	Col.	L	2-5	(10)	10	8	Leskanic	Wendell	Veres	81-54	2nd	4.5
9-4	Col.	W	4-2		5	11	Leiter	Bohanon	Benitez	82-54	2nd	3.5
9-5	Col.	W	6-2		9	9	Yoshii	Kile		83-54	2nd	2.5
9-6	S.F	W	3-0		4	4	Rogers	Gardner		84-54	2nd	2.5
9-7	S.F	L	4-7		4	12	Rodriguez	Wendell	Nen	84-55	2nd	3.5
9-8	S.F	W	7-5		10	7	Dotel	Estes	Benitez	85-55	2nd	3.5
9-9	At L.A.	W	3-1		7	2	Hershiser	Brown	Benitez	86-55	2nd	3.0
9-10	At L.A.	L	1-3		6	6	Dreifort	Leiter	Shaw	86-56	2nd	4.0
9-11	At L.A.	W	6-2		11	7	Yoshii	Valdes		87-56	2nd	3.0
9-12	At L.A.	W	10-3		12	14	Rogers	Gagne		88-56	2nd	2.0
9-13	At Col.	W	6-5		9	13	Wendell	Veres	Benitez	89-56	2nd	1.0
9-14	At Col.	L	2-7		7	10	Wright	Dotel		89-57	2nd	2.0
9-15	At Col.	W	10-5		13	11	Wendell	Dipoto	Benitez	90-57	2nd	1.0
9-17	Phi.	L	5-8		9	11	Wolf	Leiter	Brewer	90-58	2nd	2.0
9-18	Phi.	W	11-1		15	5	Yoshii	Grace		91-58	2nd	1.0

Date	Opp.	Res.	Score	(inn.*)	Hits	Opp. hits	Winning pitcher	Losing pitcher	Save	Record	Pos.	GB
9-19	Phi.	W	8-6		9	9	Dotel	Byrd	Benitez	92-58	2nd	1.0
9-21	At Atl.	L	1-2		6	8	Remlinger	Cook	Rocker	92-59	2nd	2.0
9-22	At Atl.	L	2-5		8	6	Glavine	Hershiser	Rocker	92-60	2nd	3.0
9-23	At Atl.	L	3-6		7	13	Maddux	Leiter	Rocker	92-61	2nd	4.0
9-24	At Phi.	L	2-3		9	6	Grahe	Benitez	Aldred	92-62	2nd	5.0
9-25	At Phi.	L	2-4		4	6	Person	Rogers	Gomes	92-63	2nd	6.0
9-26	At Phi.	L	2-3		6	4	Byrd	Reed	Montgomery	92-64	2nd	7.0
9-28	Atl.	L	3-9		9	13	Glavine	Hershiser		92-65	2nd	8.0
9-29	Atl.	W	9-2		13	5	Leiter	Maddux		93-65	2nd	7.0
9-30	Atl.	L	3-4	(11)	6	8	Mulholland	Dotel		93-66	2nd	8.0
10-1	Pit.	W	3-2	(11)	10	7	Mahomes	Sauerbeck		94-66	2nd	8.0
10-2	Pit.	W	7-0		9	3	Reed	Cordova		95-66	2nd	7.0
10-3	Pit.	W	2-1		9	3	Benitez	Hansell		96-66	.2nd	7.0
10-4	At Cin.	W	5-0		9	2	Leiter	Parris		97-66	2nd	6.5

Monthly records: April (14-9), May (13-15), June (17-10), July (18-9), August (18-10), September (13-13), October (4-0).
*Innings, if other than nine. † First game of a doubleheader. ‡ Second game of a doubleheader.

HIGHLIGHTS

High point: It was a grand slam that turned into a grand single. Robin Ventura drove a Kevin McGlinchy pitch over the wall in right- center at Shea Stadium to cap a 15th-inning comeback against the Braves in Game 5 of the NLCS. The bases were loaded, but Ventura was credited with a run-scoring single when Todd Pratt raised him in celebration before he reached second base. The Mets won, 4-3, to force Game 6 in Atlanta, where their season ended.

Low point: Kenny Rogers' high-and-out-side fastball to Andruw Jones may have been his last pitch as a Met. It forced home Gerald Williams with the winning run in the 11th inning of Game 6 of the NLCS, sending the Braves to the World Series and the Mets home.

Turning point: Al Leiter's win over the Yankees and Roger Clemens on June 6 at Yankee Stadium. The victory, which ended an eight-game losing streak and came on the heels of the messy firing of three Mets coaches, ignited a 40-15 run that vaulted the club from a 27-28 record to a 67-43 mark, the best in the majors.

Most valuable player: Third baseman Robin Ventura. (Any "most valuable" honor really should go to G.M. Steve Phillips, whose signing of Ventura was a masterstroke in itself and also triggered the move of Edgardo Alfonzo from third to second base, thereby creating one of baseball's best-ever infields.) Ventura won his sixth Gold Glove, batted .301 with 32 homers and 120 RBIs and provided protection for Mike Piazza in the lineup.

Most valuable pitcher: Armando Benitez, who quickly emerged as one of the N.L.'s most overpowering relievers and then replaced John Franco as the closer after an injury sidelined Franco for two months. Benitez had 22 saves and a 1.85 ERA.

Most improved player: Alfonzo. He handled the move to second without a problem, teaming with shortstop Rey Ordonez to form a dazzling double-play combination. Alfonzo also continued to mature as a power hitter, posting career highs with 27 homers and 108 RBIs.

Most pleasant surprise: Roger Cedeno, who was targeted as a fourth outfielder but made 82 starts in right and appeared in 155 games overall. He batted .313 and blossomed as a basestealer, setting a Mets record with 66 steals.

Biggest disappointment: Bobby Bonilla. He engaged in two confrontations with manager Bobby Valentine and hit .160 in a limited role after incurring an injury in spring training.

Key injuries: Franco's absence because of a torn tendon in his middle finger cost the Mets bullpen depth. And Bonilla, who had only 119 at-bats, was hobbled by a bad knee.

Notable: The Mets set a major league record for fewest errors in a season, 68. ... Ventura became the first player in major league history to hit a grand slam in each game of a doubleheader, connecting against the Brewers on May 20. ... Piazza had his second 40-homer season in three years. ... The Mets made the postseason for the first time since 1988.

—**RAFAEL HERMOSO**

RECORDS

1999 regular-season record: 97-66 (2nd in N.L. East); 49-32 at home; 48-34 on road; 27-23 vs. N.L. East; 33-18 vs. Central; 25-19 vs. West; 12-6 vs. A.L.; 22-18 vs. lefthanded starters; 75-48 vs. right-handed starters; 79-56 on grass; 18-10 on turf; 33-23 in daytime; 64-43 at night; 27-19 in one-run games; 6-5 in extra-inning games; 1-0-1 in doubleheaders.
Team record past five years: 413-380 (.521, ranks 5th in league in that span).

TEAM LEADERS

Batting average: Rickey Henderson (.315).
At-bats: Edgardo Alfonzo (628).
Runs: Edgardo Alfonzo (123).
Hits: Edgardo Alfonzo (191).
Total Bases: Edgardo Alfonzo (315).
Doubles: Edgardo Alfonzo (41).
Triples: Roger Cedeno (4).
Home runs: Mike Piazza (40).
Runs batted in: Mike Piazza (124).
Stolen bases: Roger Cedeno (66).
Slugging percentage: Mike Piazza (.575).
On-base percentage: John Olerud (.427).

Wins: Orel Hershiser, Al Leiter (13).
Earned-run average: Al Leiter (4.23).
Complete games: Kenny Rogers (2).
Shutouts: Al Leiter, Rick Reed, Kenny Rogers (1).
Saves: Armando Benitez (22).
Innings pitched: Al Leiter (213.0).
Strikeouts: Al Leiter (162).

GAMES BY POSITION

Catcher: Mike Piazza 137, Todd Pratt 52, Vance Wilson 1, Mike Kinkade 1.
First base: John Olerud 160, Matt Franco 19, Bobby Bonilla 4, Robin Ventura 1, Todd Pratt 1, Mike Kinkade 1, Jorge Toca 1.
Second base: Edgardo Alfonzo 158, Luis Lopez 16, Melvin Mora 4, Roger Cedeno 1.
Third base: Robin Ventura 160, Matt Franco 12, Luis Lopez 9, Mike Kinkade 3, Melvin Mora 3, Shawon Dunston 1.
Shortstop: Rey Ordonez 154, Luis Lopez 33, Shane Halter 1, Melvin Mora 1.
Outfield: Roger Cedeno 149, Rickey Henderson 116, Brian McRae 87, Benny Agbayani 80, Darryl Hamilton 52, Melvin Mora 45, Jermaine Allensworth 33, Shawon Dunston 27, Bobby Bonilla 25, Matt Franco 19, Mike Kinkade 17, Jay Payton 6, Shane Halter 2, Rick Reed 1, Chuck McElroy 1, Todd Pratt 1.
Designated hitter: Matt Franco 4, Bobby Bonilla 3, Benny Agbayani 2, Rickey Henderson 1, Mike Piazza 1.

TOP DRAFT CHOICES

1. None
2a. **Neal Musser,** LHP, Benton Central H.S., Otterbein, Ind.
2b. **Jake Joseph,** RHP, Cosumnes River (Calif.) J.C.
3. **Jeremy Griffiths,** RHP, U. of Toledo
4. **Angel Pagan,** OF, Republica De Colombia H.S., Rio Piedras, P.R.
5. **Nick James,** RHP, Hancock (Calif.) J.C.
6. **Tyler Parker,** C, Lassiter H.S., Marietta, Ga.
7. **Rodney Nye,** 3B, U. of Arkansas
8. **Forrest Lawson,** OF, Rogers H.S., Puyallup, Wash.
9. **Wayne Lydon,** OF, Valley View H.S., Jessup, Pa.
10. **Prentice Redman,** OF, Bevill State (Ala.) C.C.

PHILADELPHIA PHILLIES
NATIONAL LEAGUE EAST DIVISION

2000 Phillies Schedule
Home games shaded. *—All-Star Game at Turner Field (Atlanta).

March
SUN	MON	TUE	WED	THU	FRI	SAT
26	27	28	29	30	31	

April
SUN	MON	TUE	WED	THU	FRI	SAT
						1
2	3	4 ARI	5 ARI	6 ARI	7 HOU	8 HOU
9 HOU	10 NYM	11	12 NYM	13 NYM	14 MON	15 MON
16 MON	17 ATL	18 ATL	19 ATL	20 ATL	21 FLA	22 FLA
23 FLA	24 FLA	25 ARI	26 ARI	27 ARI	28 STL	29 STL
30 STL						

May
SUN	MON	TUE	WED	THU	FRI	SAT
	1	2 CIN	3 CIN	4 CIN	5 ATL	6 ATL
7 ATL	8	9 MON	10 MON	11 MON	12 ATL	13 ATL
14 ATL	15	16 STL	17 STL	18 STL	19 COL	20 COL
21 COL	22	23 HOU	24 HOU	25 HOU	26 LA	27 LA
28 LA	29 SF	30 SF	31 SF			

June
SUN	MON	TUE	WED	THU	FRI	SAT
				1	2 BOS	3 BOS
4 BOS	5 TB	6 TB	7 TB	8	9 BAL	10 BAL
11 BAL	12 FLA	13 FLA	14 FLA	15	16 ATL	17 ATL
18 ATL	19 NYM	20 NYM	21 NYM	22 NYM	23 MON	24 MON
25 MON	26	27 MIL	28 MIL	29 MIL	30 PIT	

July
SUN	MON	TUE	WED	THU	FRI	SAT
						1 PIT
2 PIT	3	4 MIL	5 MIL	6 MIL	7 BAL	8 BAL
9 BAL	10	11	*12	13 TOR	14 TOR	15 TOR
16 NYY	17 NYY	18 NYY	19 CUB	20 CUB	21 PIT	22 PIT
23 PIT	24	25 CUB	26 CUB	27 CUB	28 LA	29 LA
30 LA	31 SD					

August
SUN	MON	TUE	WED	THU	FRI	SAT
	1 SD	2 SD	3	4 COL	5 COL	
6 COL	7 SD	8 SD	9 SD	10 SD	11 HOU	12 HOU
13 HOU	14 ARI	15 ARI	16 ARI	17	18 STL	19 STL
20 STL	21 CIN	22 CIN	23 CIN	24 CIN	25 SF	26 SF
27 SF	28 COL	29 COL	30 COL	31		

September
SUN	MON	TUE	WED	THU	FRI	SAT
					1 LA	2 LA
3 LA	4 SF	5 SF	6 SF	7	8 NYM	9 NYM
10 NYM	11	12 MON	13 MON	14	15 FLA	16 FLA
17 FLA	18 PIT	19 PIT	20 PIT	21 NYM	22 NYM	23 NYM
24 NYM	25 CUB	26 CUB	27 CUB	28 CUB	29 FLA	30 FLA

October
SUN	MON	TUE	WED	THU	FRI	SAT
1 FLA	2	3	4	5	6	7

2000 SEASON
CLUB DIRECTORY

Managing gen. partner, president, CEO
David Montgomery
Chairman, general partner
Bill Giles
Partners
Claire S. Betz, Tri-Play Associates (Alexander K. Buck, J. Mahlon Buck Jr., William C. Buck), Double Play, Inc. (John Middleton, chairman), Fitz Eugene Dixon Jr.
Secretary and general counsel
Bill Webb
Senior v.p., finance and planning
Jerry Clothier
Special assistant to the president
Sharon Swainson
Director, business development
Joe Giles
Vice president and general manager
Ed Wade
Assistant general manager
Ruben Amaro Jr.
Controller
John Fusco
Director, scouting
Mike Arbuckle
Senior advisors to general manager
Dallas Green, Paul Owens
Dir., minor league field ops./instruction
Gary Ruby
Director, minor league operations
Steve Noworyta
Executive asst. to the general manager
Susan Ingersoll
Traveling secretary
Eddie Ferenz
Vice president, public relations
Larry Shenk
Manager, publicity
Leigh Tobin
Manager, media relations
Gene Dias
Vice president, advertising sales
Dave Buck
Director, information systems
Brian Lamoreaux

Vice president, ticket operations
Richard Deats
Director, ticket department
Dan Goroff
Director, sales
John Weber
Director, broadcasting and video services
Rory McNeil
Director, stadium operations
Mike DiMuzio
Club physician
Dr. Michael Ciccotti
Club trainers
Jeff Cooper, Mark Andersen
Mgr., equipment and home clubhouse
Frank Coppenbarger
Manager, visiting clubhouse
Kevin Steinhour
National supervisor
Marti Wolever
Director, Florida operations
John Timberlake
Director, Latin American operations
Sal Artiaga
Director, Major League scouts
Gordon Lakey
Major League scout
Jimmy Stewart
Advance scout, Major Leagues
Hank King
Special assignment scout
Dean Jongewaard
Coordinator, professional coverage
Dick Lawlor
Regular scouts
Sal Agostinelli, Emil Belich, Steve Gillispie, Bill Harper, Ken Hultzapple, Marlon Jones, Jerry Lafferty, Matt Lundin, Miguel Machado, Lloyd Merritt, Venice Murray, Dave Owen, Arthur Parrack, Scott Ramsay, Mitch Sokol, Doug Takaragawa, Roy Tanner

MINOR LEAGUE AFFILIATES

Class	Team	League	Manager
AAA	Scranton/Wilkes-Barre	International	Marc Bombard
AA	Reading	Eastern	Gary Varsho
A	Clearwater	Florida State	Ken Oberkfell
A	Piedmont	South Atlantic	Greg Legg
A	Batavia	New York-Pennsylvania	Frank Klebe
Rookie	Gulf Coast Phillies	Gulf Coast	Ramon Aviles

BROADCAST INFORMATION
Radio: WPHT Talk Radio 1210.
TV: UPN 57.
Cable TV: Comcast SportsNet.

SPRING TRAINING
Ballpark (city): Jack Russell Stadium (Clearwater, Fla.).
Ticket information: 215-463-1000 or 727-442-8496.

SPRING TRAINING ROSTER

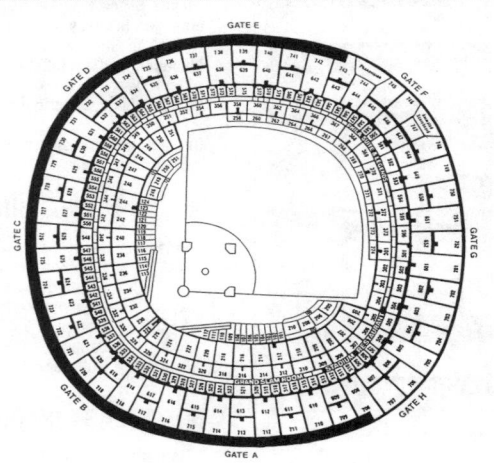

2000 SEASON *Philadelphia Phillies*

Manager—Terry Francona (7).
Coaches—Galen Cisco (40), Chuck Cottier (3), Ramon Henderson (59), Hal McRae (56), Brad Mills (9), John Vukovich (18).

No.	PITCHERS	B/T	Ht./Wt.	Born	1999 clubs
30	Aldred, Scott	L/L	6-4/220	6-12-68	Tampa Bay, Philadelphia
43	Ashby, Andy	R/R	6-1/202	7-11-67	San Diego
46	Barrios, Manuel	R/R	6-0/185	9-21-74	Indianapolis
45	Brantley, Jeff	R/R	5-10/197	9-5-63	Philadelphia
62	Brester, Jason	L/L	6-3/190	12-7-76	Carolina, Reading
55	Brock, Chris	R/R	6-0/185	2-5-70	San Francisco
49	Brownson, Mark	L/R	6-2/185	6-17-75	Colorado Springs, Colorado
34	Byrd, Paul	R/R	6-1/184	12-3-70	Philadelphia
72	Coggin, Dave	R/R	6-4/205	10-30-76	Reading
61	Gomes, Wayne	R/R	6-2/227	1-15-73	Philadelphia
42	Jackson, Mike	R/R	6-2/225	12-22-64	Cleveland
78	Nickle, Doug	R/R	6-4/210	10-2-74	Clearwater
31	Person, Robert	R/R	6-0/194	10-6-69	Dunedin, Toronto, Philadelphia
35	Politte, Cliff	R/R	5-11/185	2-27-74	Reading, Philadelphia
44	Reyes, Carlos	B/R	6-0/190	4-4-69	San Diego
38	Schilling, Curt	R/R	6-4/231	11-14-66	Philadelphia
52	Schrenk, Steve	R/R	6-3/215	11-20-68	Scranton/Wilkes-Barre, Philadelphia
37	Shumaker, Anthony	L/L	6-5/219	5-14-73	Reading, Scranton/Wilkes-Barre, Philadelphia
47	Telemaco, Amaury	R/R	6-3/222	1-19-74	Tucson, Arizona, Philadelphia
54	Wolf, Randy	L/L	6-0/194	8-22-76	Scranton/Wilkes-Barre, Philadelphia

No.	CATCHERS	B/T	Ht./Wt.	Born	1999 clubs
14	Bennett, Gary	R/R	6-0/208	4-17-72	Philadelphia
24	Lieberthal, Mike	R/R	6-0/190	1-18-72	Philadelphia
12	Prince, Tom	R/R	5-11/206	8-13-64	Gulf Coast Phillies, Clearwater, Scranton/Wilkes-Barre, Philadelphia

No.	INFIELDERS	B/T	Ht./Wt.	Born	1999 clubs
16	Anderson, Marlon	L/R	5-11/198	1-6-74	Philadelphia
26	Arias, Alex	R/R	6-3/202	11-20-67	Philadelphia
2	Brogna, Rico	L/L	6-2/203	4-18-70	Philadelphia
33	Burrell, Pat	R/R	6-4/225	10-10-76	Reading, Scranton/Wilkes-Barre
67	Duncan, Carlos	R/R	6-1/185	6-30-77	Piedmont
23	Jordan, Kevin	R/R	6-1/201	10-9-69	Philadelphia
19	Martinez, Felix	B/R	6-0/180	5-18-74	Wichita, Omaha, Kansas City
8	Relaford, Desi	B/R	5-9/174	9-16-73	Philadelphia, Clearwater
17	Rolen, Scott	R/R	6-4/226	4-4-75	Philadelphia
68	Rollins, Jimmy	B/R	5-8/154	11-27-78	Reading, Scranton/Wilkes-Barre

No.	OUTFIELDERS	B/T	Ht./Wt.	Born	1999 clubs
53	Abreu, Bobby	L/R	6-0/197	3-11-74	Philadelphia
25	Ducey, Rob	L/R	6-2/183	5-24-65	Philadelphia
5	Gant, Ron	R/R	6-0/196	3-2-65	Philadelphia
6	Glanville, Doug	R/R	6-2/172	8-25-70	Philadelphia
29	Magee, Wendell	R/R	6-0/220	8-3-72	Scranton/Wilkes-Barre, Philadelphia
11	Sefcik, Kevin	R/R	5-10/182	2-10-71	Philadelphia
63	Taylor, Reggie	L/R	6-1/178	1-12-77	Reading

BALLPARK INFORMATION

Ballpark (capacity, surface)
Veterans Stadium (62,411, artificial)

Address
P.O. Box 7575
Philadelphia, PA 19101

Business phone
215-463-6000

Ticket information
215-463-1000

Ticket prices
$22.50 (field box)
$19 (sections 258-201)
$19 (terrace box)
$17 (loge box)
$13 (reserved, 600 level)
$7 (reserved, 700 level, adult gen. admission)
$5 (children's general admission)

Field dimensions (from home plate)
To left field at foul line, 330 feet
To center field, 408 feet
To right field at foul line, 330 feet

First game played
April 10, 1971 (Phillies 4, Expos 1)

Date	Opp.	Res.	Score	(inn.*)	Hits	Opp. hits	Winning pitcher	Losing pitcher	Save	Record	Pos.	GB
4-6	At Atl.	L	3-11		13	17	Maddux	Ogea	Ebert	1-1	T1st	...
4-7	At Atl.	L	0-4		5	7	Smoltz	Loewer		1-2	T4th	1.0
4-8	At Atl.	W	6-3		7	4	Byrd	Millwood	Brantley	2-2	T2nd	1.0
4-9	At Fla.	L	4-7		5	9	Meadows	Spoljaric		2-3	5th	1.0
4-10	At Fla.	W	5-2		8	6	Schilling	Springer	Brantley	3-3	T2nd	1.0
4-11	At Fla.	W	2-1		6	5	Ogea	Fernandez	Brantley	4-3	T2nd	1.0
4-12	Atl.	L	6-8		10	9	Cather	Ryan	Seanez	4-4	3rd	2.0
4-14	Atl.	L	4-10		9	12	Millwood	Byrd		4-5	T3rd	3.0
4-16	Fla.	W	17-3		16	7	Schilling	Springer		5-5	3rd	1.5
4-17	Fla.	W	2-1		7	7	Gomes	Alfonseca		6-5	3rd	1.5
4-18	Fla.	W	7-2		14	8	Loewer	Ojala		7-5	3rd	0.5
4-19	At Ari.	L	2-3		4	8	Daal	Perez	Swindell	7-6	3rd	1.5
4-20	At Ari.	L	1-8		7	10	Johnson	Spoljaric		7-7	3rd	2.0
4-21	At Ari.	L	2-4		7	8	Stottlemyre	Schilling	Olson	7-8	3rd	2.5
4-23	At Mon.	W	6-2		10	6	Ogea	Hermanson		8-8	3rd	2.5
4-24	At Mon.	W	6-5		11	12	Grace	Ayala	Gomes	9-8	3rd	1.5
4-25	At Mon.	W	8-6		10	8	Byrd	Urbina		10-8	3rd	1.5
4-27	Cin.	W	1-0	(10)	7	5	Brantley	White		11-8	2nd	1.0
4-28	Cin.	L	8-12		13	13	Williamson	Brantley		11-9	3rd	2.0
4-29	Cin.	L	3-7		8	13	Bere	Loewer		11-10	3rd	3.0
4-30	L.A.	L	3-4		9	8	Perez	Byrd	Shaw	11-11	3rd	4.0
5-1	L.A.	L	6-12		13	12	Dreifort	Spoljaric		11-12	3rd	5.0
5-2	L.A.	W	12-3		13	8	Schilling	Brown		12-12	3rd	5.0
5-3	S.D.	L	3-9		13	14	Hitchcock	Ogea		12-13	3rd	6.0
5-4	S.D.	W	3-0		4	5	Loewer	Williams		13-13	3rd	5.0
5-5	S.D.	W	11-1		14	3	Byrd	Spencer		14-13	3rd	5.0
5-7	At Col.	W	8-1		14	7	Schilling	Thomson		15-13	3rd	4.0
5-8	At Col.	W	7-2		12	9	Bennett	Bohanon		16-13	3rd	4.0
5-9	At Col.	W	10-8		17	12	Ryan	Veres	Gomes	17-13	3rd	3.0
5-10	At StL.	L	2-5		7	9	Bottenfield	Loewer	Radinsky	17-14	3rd	3.0
5-11	At StL.	W	9-4		13	7	Byrd	Mercker		18-14	2nd	3.0
5-12	At StL.	W	8-4		12	7	Schilling	Oliver		19-14	2nd	2.0
5-14	N.Y.	L	3-7		5	9	Yoshii	Ogea		19-15	3rd	2.0
5-15	N.Y.	L	7-9		13	12	Mahomes	Ryan	Franco	19-16	3rd	2.0
5-16	N.Y.	W	5-2		10	8	Byrd	Hershiser	Brantley	20-16	3rd	2.0
5-17	At Mon.	W	4-3		8	9	Schilling	Thurman		21-16	2nd	2.0
5-18	At Mon.	L	4-7		9	9	Batista	Bennett	Urbina	21-17	2nd	3.0
5-19	At Mon.	L	9-10		8	13	Kline	Brantley		21-18	T2nd	4.0
5-21	At N.Y.	L	5-7		10	13	Hershiser	Loewer	Franco	21-19	3rd	3.5
5-22	At N.Y.	W	9-3		13	7	Byrd	Jones		22-19	3rd	3.5
5-23	At N.Y.	L	4-5		9	12	Beltran	Schilling		22-20	3rd	3.5
5-24	Mon.	W	5-4		7	7	Perez	Batista	Gomes	23-20	3rd	2.5
5-25	Mon.	L	2-4	(11)	6	10	Urbina	Montgomery		23-21	3rd	3.5
5-26	Mon.	L	2-5		6	8	Pavano	Loewer	Urbina	23-22	3rd	4.5
5-28	Col.	L	3-5		12	7	Leskanic	Byrd	Veres	23-23	3rd	6.0
5-29	Col.	W	2-0		4	4	Schilling	Bohanon		24-23	3rd	5.0
5-30	Col.	L	0-1		5	7	Kile	Poole	Veres	24-24	3rd	5.0
5-31	S.F	W	4-3		9	12	Perez	Johnstone	Gomes	25-24	3rd	5.0
6-1	S.F	L	5-6	(12)	13	8	Nen	Gomes		25-25	3rd	6.0
6-2	S.F	W	7-6		11	10	Byrd	Ortiz	Gomes	26-25	2nd	5.0
6-3	S.F	L	4-7		5	11	Spradlin	Schilling	Nen	26-26	3rd	5.5
6-4	At Bal.	W	9-5		18	9	Ogea	Erickson		27-26	2nd	4.5
6-5	At Bal.	L	6-7	(10)	7	12	Timlin	Montgomery		27-27	2nd	5.5
6-6	At Bal.	W	11-7		19	14	Bennett	Bones		28-27	2nd	5.5
6-7	N.Y. (AL)	W	6-5		9	7	Byrd	Pettitte		29-27	2nd	5.5
6-8	N.Y. (AL)	W	11-5		11	8	Perez	Grimsley		30-27	2nd	5.5
6-9	N.Y. (AL)	L	5-11		9	13	Cone	Ogea		30-28	3rd	6.5
6-11	Tor.	W	8-4		9	9	Wolf	Hamilton		31-28	2nd	5.5
6-12	Tor.	W	7-2		9	6	Byrd	Escobar		32-28	2nd	4.5
6-13	Tor.	L	2-7		4	13	Hentgen	Schilling		32-29	3rd	4.5
6-15	At S.D.	L	1-6		6	11	Clement	Ogea		32-30	3rd	5.0
6-16	At S.D.	W	4-2		9	7	Wolf	Hitchcock	Gomes	33-30	3rd	5.0
6-17	At S.D.	W	7-5		12	12	Byrd	Williams	Gomes	34-30	3rd	5.0
6-18	At L.A.	W	2-1		6	4	Schilling	Valdes	Gomes	35-30	3rd	5.0
6-19	At L.A.	L	1-8		7	13	Dreifort	Person		35-31	3rd	5.0
6-20	At L.A.	L	2-3		5	6	Brown	Ogea	Shaw	35-32	3rd	6.0
6-22	Pit.	W	3-2		7	6	Wolf	Cordova	Gomes	36-32	3rd	5.0
6-23	Pit.	L	6-8		11	12	Benson	Byrd	Williams	36-33	3rd	6.0
6-24	Pit.	W	7-5		10	10	Schilling	Silva	Gomes	37-33	3rd	6.0
6-25	At Chi.	W	3-2		6	3	Ogea	Lieber	Gomes	38-33	3rd	5.0
6-26	At Chi.	W	6-2		11	8	Person	Trachsel		39-33	3rd	5.0

Date	Opp.	Res.	Score	(inn.*)	Hits	Opp. hits	Winning pitcher	Losing pitcher	Save	Record	Pos.	GB
6-27	At Chi.	L	7-13		11	15	Mulholland	Grace		39-34	3rd	6.0
6-28	At Pit.	L	2-3	(10)	6	7	Hansell	Montgomery		39-35	3rd	7.0
6-29	At Pit.	W	7-4		11	7	Schilling	Silva		40-35	3rd	6.0
6-30	At Pit.	L	1-9		9	12	Schmidt	Ogea		40-36	3rd	6.0
7-1	At Pit.	L	7-12		9	14	Ritchie	Person		40-37	3rd	7.0
7-2	Chi.	W	14-1		17	6	Wolf	Mulholland		41-37	3rd	7.0
7-3	Chi.	W	21-8		21	11	Byrd	Farnsworth		42-37	3rd	7.0
7-4	Chi.	W	6-2		12	7	Schilling	Tapani		43-37	3rd	6.0
7-5	Mil.	L	0-5		6	10	Abbott	Ogea	Roque	43-38	3rd	7.0
7-6	Mil.	W	1-0		4	5	Person	Nomo	Gomes	44-38	3rd	6.0
7-7	Mil.	W	5-4		10	8	Gomes	Wickman		45-38	3rd	6.0
7-9	Bal.	W	4-2		5	8	Schilling	Guzman		46-38	3rd	5.5
7-10	Bal.	L	4-8		6	13	Mussina	Byrd		46-39	3rd	6.5
7-11	Bal.	L	2-6		6	12	Erickson	Ogea		46-40	3rd	7.5
7-15	At Bos.	L	4-6		9	12	Rose	Byrd	Wakefield	46-41	3rd	8.5
7-16	At Bos.	W	5-4		10	8	Person	Saberhagen	Gomes	47-41	3rd	8.5
7-17	At Bos.	W	11-3		18	7	Wolf	Portugal		48-41	3rd	7.5
7-18	At T.B.	W	3-2		7	4	Schilling	Lopez		49-41	3rd	6.5
7-19	At T.B.	W	16-3		22	7	Ogea	Rekar		50-41	3rd	5.5
7-20	At T.B.	L	4-5	(13)	10	12	Charlton	Schrenk		50-42	3rd	5.5
7-21	At Mil.	W	7-0		15	7	Person	Karl	Poole	51-42	3rd	4.5
7-22	At Mil.	L	0-5		5	6	Nomo	Wolf		51-43	3rd	5.5
7-23†	Atl.	W	6-5		7	9	Telemaco	Seanez	Gomes	52-43		
7-23‡	Atl.	L	1-3		5	7	Chen	Shumaker	Rocker	52-44	3rd	5.5
7-24	Atl.	W	4-3		11	6	Montgomery	Bowie	Gomes	53-44	3rd	4.5
7-25	Atl.	L	4-5	(10)	8	12	Rocker	Montgomery		53-45	3rd	5.5
7-26	Fla.	W	9-1		15	9	Person	Nunez		54-45	3rd	5.5
7-27	Fla.	L	2-6		7	12	Fernandez	Wolf	Alfonseca	54-46	3rd	6.5
7-28	Fla.	W	9-4		13	8	Schrenk	Dempster		55-46	3rd	5.5
7-29	Fla.	W	12-1		13	6	Ogea	Meadows		56-46	3rd	5.0
7-30	At Atl.	W	9-2		12	5	Byrd	Smoltz		57-46	3rd	4.5
7-31	At Atl.	L	6-8		11	12	Glavine	Person	Rocker	57-47	3rd	5.0
8-1	At Atl.	L	4-12		8	10	Maddux	Wolf		57-48	3rd	6.0
8-3	At Fla.	W	6-5		12	9	Telemaco	Edmondson	Gomes	58-48	3rd	6.0
8-4	At Fla.	W	4-1		9	10	Byrd	Springer	Schrenk	59-48	3rd	6.0
8-5	At Fla.	W	9-3		12	10	Person	Nunez		60-48	3rd	5.5
8-6	Ari.	W	4-2	(11)	8	6	Gomes	Chouinard		61-48	3rd	5.5
8-7	Ari.	L	2-8		7	9	Benes	Schilling		61-49	3rd	5.5
8-8	Ari.	L	4-7		10	13	Reynoso	Ogea	Mantei	61-50	3rd	5.5
8-9	StL.	L	6-12		11	15	Mercker	Schrenk		61-51	3rd	6.0
8-10	StL.	W	7-5		6	10	Poole	Bottalico	Gomes	62-51	3rd	6.0
8-11	StL.	L	1-5		6	9	Stephenson	Wolf	Slocumb	62-52	3rd	7.0
8-13	At Cin.	L	4-5		13	11	Williamson	Schrenk		62-53	3rd	8.0
8-14	At Cin.	L	1-4		4	14	Harnisch	Ogea	Graves	62-54	3rd	8.0
8-15	At Cin.	W	9-3		10	7	Person	Neagle		63-54	3rd	8.0
8-16	At StL.	L	3-4		9	4	Mercker	Wolf	Bottalico	63-55	3rd	9.0
8-17	At StL.	L	5-6		10	10	Acevedo	Gomes		63-56	3rd	9.0
8-18	At StL.	W	6-5		17	8	Aldred	Croushore	Gomes	64-56	3rd	9.0
8-20	L.A.	L	5-8	(10)	12	5	Mills	Gomes		64-57	3rd	9.5
8-21	L.A.	W	6-5	(11)	10	12	Gomes	Masaoka		65-57	3rd	9.5
8-22	L.A.	L	7-9		9	12	Park	Shumaker	Shaw	65-58	3rd	10.5
8-23	S.D.	L	6-7		9	12	Williams	Ogea	Hoffman	65-59	3rd	11.5
8-24	S.D.	W	18-2		22	9	Byrd	Spencer		66-59	3rd	11.5
8-25	S.D.	W	15-1		14	6	Person	Clement		67-59	3rd	11.5
8-28†	At Col.	L	6-11		9	15	Lee	Aldred		67-60		
8-28‡	At Col.	L	0-4		4	11	Bohanon	Grahe		67-61	3rd	13.5
8-29	At Col.	L	5-6		9	14	Kile	Byrd	Veres	67-62	3rd	14.5
8-30	At S.F	L	4-6	(10)	9	9	Rodriguez	Brewer		67-63	3rd	14.5
8-31	At S.F	L	1-8		7	11	Rueter	Wolf		67-64	3rd	15.5
9-1	At S.F	L	3-5	(11)	6	11	Rodriguez	Gomes		67-65	3rd	16.5
9-2	At S.F	L	2-3		7	8	Nathan	Grahe	Nen	67-66	3rd	17.0
9-3	Cin.	W	10-2		12	6	Schilling	Parris		68-66	3rd	17.0
9-4	Cin.	L	3-22		11	19	Harnisch	Byrd	Belinda	68-67	3rd	17.0
9-5	Cin.	L	7-9		7	13	Neagle	Person	Sullivan	68-68	3rd	17.0
9-6	Hou.	L	5-6		12	6	Lima	Wolf	Wagner	68-69	3rd	18.0
9-7	Hou.	L	6-8		10	12	Powell	Gomes	Henry	68-70	3rd	19.0
9-8	Hou.	L	2-10		8	12	Hampton	Schilling		68-71	3rd	20.0
9-9	Hou.	L	1-3		4	9	Reynolds	Montgomery	Wagner	68-72	3rd	20.5
9-10	At Ari.	L	1-3		6	7	Johnson	Person		68-73	3rd	21.5
9-11	At Ari.	L	0-4		6	12	Benes	Wolf		68-74	3rd	21.5
9-12	At Ari.	L	0-5		7	11	Stottlemyre	Grace		68-75	3rd	21.5
9-13	At Hou.	L	2-13		6	10	Hampton	Grahe		68-76	3rd	21.5
9-14	At Hou.	L	2-12		8	16	Reynolds	Byrd		68-77	3rd	22.5
9-15	At Hou.	W	8-6	(10)	14	12	Gomes	Henry	Brewer	69-77	3rd	21.5
9-17	At N.Y.	W	8-5		11	9	Wolf	Leiter	Brewer	70-77	3rd	21.5

Date	Opp.	Res.	Score	(inn.*)	Hits	Opp. hits	Winning pitcher	Losing pitcher	Save	Record	Pos.	GB
9-18	At N.Y.	L	1-11		5	15	Yoshii	Grace		70-78	3rd	21.5
9-19	At N.Y.	L	6-8		9	9	Dotel	Byrd	Benitez	70-79	3rd	22.5
9-20	At Mil.	L	4-5		14	8	Coppinger	Loewer	Wickman	70-80	3rd	23.0
9-21	At Mil.	L	6-8		9	11	Pulsipher	Shumaker	Wickman	70-81	3rd	24.0
9-22	At Mil.	W	12-3		16	4	Telemaco	Peterson		71-81	3rd	24.0
9-23	At Mil.	L	6-11		8	12	Bere	Grace		71-82	3rd	25.0
9-24	N.Y.	W	3-2		6	9	Grahe	Benitez	Aldred	72-82	3rd	25.0
9-25	N.Y.	W	4-2		6	4	Person	Rogers	Gomes	73-82	3rd	25.0
9-26	N.Y.	W	3-2		4	6	Byrd	Reed	Montgomery	74-82	3rd	25.0
9-28	Chi.	L	2-8		9	10	Trachsel	Wolf		74-83	3rd	26.0
9-29	Chi.	W	5-0		12	4	Brewer	Bowie		75-83	3rd	25.0
9-30	Chi.	W	2-1		7	3	Person	McNichol	Montgomery	76-83	3rd	25.0
10-1	Mon.	L	4-7		11	13	Vazquez	Grahe	Urbina	76-84	3rd	26.0
10-2	Mon.	L	3-13		8	14	Powell	Byrd	Batista	76-85	3rd	26.0
10-3	Mon.	W	6-5		9	8	Politte	Strickland	Montgomery	77-85	3rd	26.0

Monthly records: April (11-11), May (14-13), June (15-12), July (17-11), August (10-17), September (9-19), October (1-2).
*Innings, if other than nine. † First game of a doubleheader. ‡ Second game of a doubleheader.

HIGHLIGHTS

High point: On August 6, the Phillies climbed a season-best 13 games over .500 with a victory over eventual N.L. West champion Arizona. At 61-48, the team also was in the thick of the N.L. East race. The rest of the season was a disaster, however, as the Phils won just 16 of their last 53 games and tumbled to 77-85.
Low point: When a doubleheader loss to the Rockies triggered a slid of 18 defeats in 19 games. Included in the stretch was a 22-3 loss to the Reds, who went on a nine-homer barrage against Phillies pitching.
Turning point: Third baseman Scott Rolen wrenched his lower back during a hard slide at Milwaukee on July 21. He was on a tear at the time, having had back-to-back two-homer games at Tampa Bay in the previous series. He played only 23 games after the injury before being shut down for the season.
Most valuable player: Right fielder Bobby Abreu, who emerged as a contender for the batting title and wound up hitting .335. He tied for the N.L. lead in triples with 11 and also contributed 118 runs, 109 walks, 35 doubles, 20 home runs and 93 RBIs. Abreu reached base in 52 of his last 54 games.
Most valuable pitcher: Curt Schilling. He started the All-Star Game and seemed to be a lock for his first 20-win season—until biceps tendinitis limited him to a total of three starts after July 23. Schilling finished with a 15-6 record and eight complete games, but his 152 strikeouts were barely half of his total in 1998.
Most improved player: Catcher Mike Lieberthal became the first Phillies player to bat .300 with 30 homers since Mike Schmidt accomplished the feat in 1981. Lieberthal drove in 96 runs and committed just three errors in 143 games behind the plate. He also had a 100-game errorless streak.
Most pleasant surprise: All-Star Paul Byrd, who won 15 games and came within one-third of an inning of reaching his spring goal of 200 innings pitched. Byrd allowed 34 home runs and tied a league-high 17 hit batsmen, but he tied Schilling for the team victory lead.

Biggest disappointment: Chad Ogea was acquired from Cleveland to be the No. 2 starter. He went 6-12, compiled a 5.63 ERA and allowed 36 homers. Ogea was moved to the bullpen in September.
Key injuries: Shortstop Desi Relaford, who underwent wrist surgery in late June, played only 65 games. Rolen missed almost one-third of the season, and Schilling had only 24 starts after making 35 in 1997 and 1998. Closer Jeff Brantley recorded just five saves before undergoing season-ending shoulder surgery in late May.
Notable: With 204 hits, center fielder Doug Glanville was the first Phillie to reach 200 since Pete Rose did it in 1979. ... Glanville stole 34 bases in 36 attempts. ... Rico Brogna became the first Philadelphia first baseman to record consecutive 100-RBI seasons (102 in '99, 104 in '98). ... The team established a franchise record with only 100 errors. ... Five players— Brogna, Lieberthal, Abreu, Rolen and Ron Gant—had 75 or more RBIs, and Glanville just missed with 73.

—CHRIS EDWARDS

RECORDS

1999 regular-season record: 77-85 (3rd in N.L. East); 41-40 at home; 36-45 on road; 28-22 vs. N.L. East; 22-28 vs. Central; 16-28 vs. West; 11-7 vs. A.L.; 19-22 vs. lefthanded starters; 58-63 vs. righthanded starters; 27-35 on grass; 50-50 on turf; 25-25 in daytime; 52-60 at night; 25-19 in one-run games; 4-9 in extra-inning games; 0-1-1 in doubleheaders.
Team record past five years: 356-436 (.449, ranks 14th in league in that span).

TEAM LEADERS

Batting average: Bobby Abreu (.335).
At-bats: Doug Glanville (628).
Runs: Bobby Abreu (118).
Hits: Doug Glanville (204).
Total Bases: Bobby Abreu (300).
Doubles: Doug Glanville (38).
Triples: Bobby Abreu (11).

Home runs: Mike Lieberthal (31).
Runs batted in: Rico Brogna (102).
Stolen bases: Doug Glanville (34).
Slugging percentage: Mike Lieberthal (.551).
On-base percentage: Bobby Abreu (.446).
Wins: Paul Byrd, Curt Schilling (15).
Earned-run average: Curt Schilling (3.54).
Complete games: Curt Schilling (8).
Shutouts: Carlton Loewer, Curt Schilling (1).
Saves: Wayne Gomes (19).
Innings pitched: Paul Byrd (199.2).
Strikeouts: Curt Schilling (152).

GAMES BY POSITION

Catcher: Mike Lieberthal 143, Gary Bennett 32, Bobby Estalella 7, Tom Prince 4.
First base: Rico Brogna 157, Kevin Jordan 13, Torey Lovullo 6.
Second base: Marlon Anderson 121, David Doster 77, Kevin Jordan 33, Kevin Sefcik 15, Torey Lovullo 6, Alex Arias 1, Domingo Cedeno 1.
Third base: Scott Rolen 112, Kevin Jordan 62, David Doster 6, Alex Arias 2.
Shortstop: Alex Arias 95, Desi Relaford 63, Domingo Cedeno 19, David Doster 5.
Outfield: Doug Glanville 148, Bobby Abreu 146, Ron Gant 133, Kevin Sefcik 64, Rob Ducey 58, Wendell Magee 4.
Designated hitter: Bobby Abreu 5, Rob Ducey 2, Ron Gant 2.

TOP DRAFT CHOICES

1. **Brett Myers,** RHP, Englewood H.S., Jacksonville, Fla.
2. **Jason Cooper,** OF, Moses Lake (Wash.) H.S.
3. **Russ Jacobson,** C, U. of Miami
4. **Brad Pautz,** RHP, U. of Minnesota
5. **Joe Saunders,** LHP, West Springfield H.S., Springfield, Va.
6. **Daniel Tosca,** C, Durant H.S., Seffner, Fla.
7. **David Gil,** RHP, U. of Miami
8. **Jesse Thrasher,** RHP, Benton H.S., St. Joseph, Mo.
9. **Julio Collazo,** SS, Mississippi Delta J.C.
10. **Marlon Byrd,** OF, Georgia Perimeter J.C.

PITTSBURGH PIRATES
NATIONAL LEAGUE CENTRAL DIVISION

2000 Pirates Schedule
Home games shaded. *—All-Star Game at Turner Field (Atlanta).

March
SUN	MON	TUE	WED	THU	FRI	SAT
26	27	28	29	30	31	

April
SUN	MON	TUE	WED	THU	FRI	SAT
						1
2	3 HOU	4	5 HOU	6 HOU	7 ARI	8 ARI
9 ARI	10	11 MON	12 MON	13 MON	14 NYM	15 NYM
16 NYM	17	18 FLA	19 FLA	20 FLA	21 ATL	22 ATL
23 ATL	24	25 SD	26 SD	27 SD	28	29 CIN
30 CIN						

May
SUN	MON	TUE	WED	THU	FRI	SAT
	1 CIN	2 STL	3 STL	4 STL	5 CUB	6 CUB
7 CUB	8	9 NYM	10 NYM	11 NYM	12 MIL	13 MIL
14 MIL	15	16 CIN	17 CIN	18 CIN	19 STL	20 STL
21 STL	22	23 ARI	24 ARI	25 ARI	26 COL	27 COL
28 COL	29 FLA	30 FLA	31 FLA			

June
SUN	MON	TUE	WED	THU	FRI	SAT
				1	2 KC	3 KC
4 KC	5 DET	6 DET	7 DET	8	9 KC	10 KC
11 KC	12 ATL	13 ATL	14 ATL	15 ATL	16 FLA	17 FLA
18 FLA	19 MON	20 MON	21 MON	22 MON	23 NYM	24 NYM
25 NYM	26	27 CUB	28 CUB	29 CUB	30 PHI	

July
SUN	MON	TUE	WED	THU	FRI	SAT
						1 PHI
2 PHI	3 CUB	4 CUB	5 CUB	6	7 MIN	8 MIN
9 MIN	10	11 *	12	13 CLE	14 CLE	15 CLE
16 LA	17 LA	18 LA	19 MIL	20 MIL	21 PHI	22 PHI
23 PHI	24	25 MIL	26 MIL	27 MIL	28 SD	29 SD
30 SD	31 LA					

August
SUN	MON	TUE	WED	THU	FRI	SAT
		1 LA	2 LA	3 SF	4 SF	5 SF
6 SF	7 COL	8 COL	9 COL	10	11 ARI	12 ARI
13 ARI	14 HOU	15 HOU	16 HOU	17	18 CIN	19 CIN
20 CIN	21 STL	22 STL	23 STL	24	25 COL	26 COL
27 COL	28 SF	29 SF	30 SF	31 SF		

September
SUN	MON	TUE	WED	THU	FRI	SAT
					1 SD	2 SD
3 SD	4 LA	5 LA	6 LA	7	8 CIN	9 CIN
10 CIN	11 STL	12 STL	13 STL	14 HOU	15 HOU	16 HOU
17 HOU	18 PHI	19 PHI	20 PHI	21 MIL	22 MIL	23 MIL
24 MIL	25	26 HOU	27 HOU	28 HOU	29 CUB	30 CUB

October
SUN	MON	TUE	WED	THU	FRI	SAT
1 CUB	2	3	4	5	6	7

2000 SEASON
CLUB DIRECTORY

General partner
Kevin S. McClatchy
Board of directors
William B. Allen
Donald Beaver
Frank Brenner
Chip Ganassi
Kevin S. McClatchy
Mayor Tom Murphy
G. Ogden Nutting
William E. Springer
Chief operating officer
Dick Freeman
Sr. v.p. and general manager
Cam Bonifay
Assistant g.m./baseball operations
John Sirignano
Assistant g.m./player personnel
Roy Smith
Sr. advisor/player personnel
Lenny Yochim
Special assistants to the g.m.
Chet Montgomery
Ken Parker
Willie Stargell
V.p., finance and administration
Jim Plake
V.p., broadcasting and marketing
Vic Gregovits
V.p., communications and new ballpark dev.
Steven N. Greenberg
Vice president, operations
Dennis DaPra
Vice president, special events
Nellie Briles
Controller
David Bowman
Director of finance
Patti Mistick
Traveling secretary
Greg Johnson
Dir. of corporate sales & broadcasting
Mark Ferraco
Director of Florida baseball operations
Mike Kennedy
Director of human resources
Sarah Tarosky

Director of information systems
Terry Zeigler
Director of marketing communications
Mike Gordon
Director of in-game entertainment
Eric Wolff
Director of media relations
Jim Trdinich
Director of merchandising
Joe Billetdeaux
Director of player development
Paul Tinnell
Dir. of community & player relations
Kathy Guy
Dir. of promotions and advertising
Rick Orienza
Director of sales
Jim Alexander
Club physician
Dr. Joseph Coroso
Team orthopedist
Dr. Jack Failla
Head trainer
Kent Biggerstaff
Equipment manager
Roger Wilson
Director of scouting
Mickey White
Scouting coordinators
Tom Barnard, Dana Brown, Mark McKnight
Special assignment scout
Jim Guinn
Latin America coordinators
Pablo Cruz (advisor), Jose Luna
Scouting supervisors
Jason Angel, Russell Bowen, Grant Brittain, Dan Durst, Duane Gustavson, James House, Mike Kendall, Jose Luna, Greg McClain, John Mercurio, Jack Powell, Everett Russell, Delvy Santiago, Rob Sidwell, Charlie Sullivan, Mike Williams, Ted Williams

MINOR LEAGUE AFFILIATES

Class	Team	League	Manager
AAA	Nashville	Pacific Coast	Trent Jewett
AA	Altoona	Eastern	Marty Brown
A	Lynchburg	Carolina	Tracy Woodson
A	Hickory	South Atlantic	Jay Loviglio
A	Williamsport	New York-Pennsylvania	Curtis Wilkerson
Rookie	Gulf Coast Pirates	Gulf Coast	Woody Huyke

BROADCAST INFORMATION
Radio: KDKA-AM (1020).
Cable TV: Fox Sports Pittsburgh.

SPRING TRAINING
Ballpark (city): McKechnie Field (Bradenton, Fla.).
Ticket information: 941-748-4610.

SPRING TRAINING ROSTER

Manager—Gene Lamont (32).
Coaches—Jeff Banister (70), Joe Jones (27), Jack Lind (45), Lloyd McClendon (23), Rick Renick (44), Pete Vuckovich (50), Spin Williams (54).

No.	PITCHERS	B/T	Ht./Wt.	Born	1999 clubs
55	Anderson, Jimmy	L/L	6-1/207	1-22-76	Nashville, Pittsburgh
69	Arroyo, Bronson	R/R	6-5/180	2-24-77	Altoona, Nashville
34	Benson, Kris	R/R	6-4/188	11-7-74	Pittsburgh
60	Boyd, Jason	R/R	6-3/173	2-23-73	Tucson, Nashville, Pittsburgh
41	Christiansen, Jason	R/L	6-5/241	9-21-69	Pittsburgh, Altoona, Nashville
67	Cordova, Francisco	R/R	6-1/197	4-26-72	Pittsburgh, Nashville, Altoona
64	Garcia, Mike	R/R	6-2/220	5-11-68	Mexico City Red Devils, Nashville, Pittsburgh
51	Loiselle, Rich	R/R	6-5/253	1-12-72	Pittsburgh
58	O'Connor, Brian	L/L	6-2/190	1-4-77	Altoona
53	Pena, Alex	R/R	6-2/205	9-9-77	Hickory, Altoona
31	Peters, Chris	L/L	6-1/170	1-28-72	Pittsburgh, Nashville
48	Ritchie, Todd	R/R	6-3/222	11-7-71	Nashville, Pittsburgh
47	Sauerbeck, Scott	R/L	6-3/197	11-9-71	Pittsburgh
22	Schmidt, Jason	R/R	6-5/213	1-29-73	Pittsburgh
46	Schourek, Pete	L/L	6-5/220	5-10-69	Pittsburgh
56	Silva, Jose	R/R	6-5/235	12-19-73	Nashville, Pittsburgh
39	Wallace, Jeff	L/L	6-2/238	4-12-76	Nashville, Pittsburgh
35	Wilkins, Marc	R/R	5-11/212	10-21-70	Altoona, Nashville, Pittsburgh
43	Williams, Mike	R/R	6-2/204	7-29-68	Pittsburgh

No.	CATCHERS	B/T	Ht./Wt.	Born	1999 clubs
7	Haad, Yamid	R/R	6-2/204	9-2-77	Lynchburg, Altoona, Pittsburgh
18	Kendall, Jason	R/R	6-0/195	6-26-74	Pittsburgh
15	Osik, Keith	R/R	6-0/192	10-22-68	Pittsburgh, Nashville

No.	INFIELDERS	B/T	Ht./Wt.	Born	1999 clubs
10	Nunez, Abraham	B/R	5-11/185	3-16-76	Pittsburgh, Nashville
6	Benjamin, Mike	R/R	6-0/172	11-22-65	Pittsburgh
12	Cordero, Wil	R/R	6-2/200	10-3-71	Cleveland, Akron
25	Cruz, Ivan	L/L	6-2/219	5-3-68	Nashville, Pittsburgh, Altoona
2	Meares, Pat	R/R	6-0/187	9-6-68	Pittsburgh, Nashville
30	Morris, Warren	L/R	5-11/179	1-11-74	Pittsburgh
16	Ramirez, Aramis	R/R	6-1/219	6-25-78	Nashville, Pittsburgh
29	Young, Kevin	R/R	6-3/222	6-16-69	Pittsburgh

No.	OUTFIELDERS	B/T	Ht./Wt.	Born	1999 clubs
37	Aven, Bruce	R/R	5-9/180	3-4-72	Florida
13	Brown, Adrian	B/R	6-0/185	2-7-74	Pittsburgh, Nashville
19	Brown, Emil	R/R	6-2/193	12-29-74	Nashville, Pittsburgh
24	Giles, Brian	L/L	5-10/200	1-20-71	Pittsburgh
3	Hermansen, Chad	R/R	6-2/185	9-10-77	Nashville, Pittsburgh
52	Hernandez, Alex	L/L	6-4/186	5-28-77	Altoona
28	Martin, Al	L/L	6-2/214	11-24-67	Pittsburgh

BALLPARK INFORMATION

Ballpark (capacity, surface)
Three Rivers Stadium (47,972, artificial)

Address
600 Stadium Circle
Pittsburgh, PA 15212

Business phone
412-323-5000

Ticket information
800-BUY-BUCS

Ticket prices
$20 (field box-infield)
$19 (field box-outfield)
$18 (club box-infield)
$17 (club box-outfield)
$13 (terrace box; family box)
$10 (reserved seats)
$3 (g.a., children 14 and under)

Field dimensions (from home plate)
To left field at foul line, 335 feet
To center field, 400 feet
To right field at foul line, 335 feet

First game played
July 16, 1970 (Reds 3, Pirates 2)

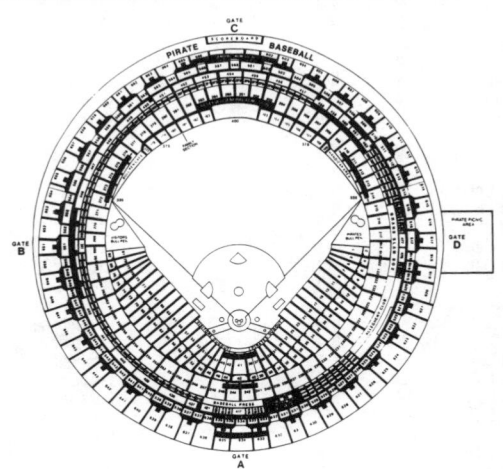

2000 SEASON *Pittsburgh Pirates*

Date	Opp.	Res.	Score	(inn.*)	Hits	Opp. hits	Winning pitcher	Losing pitcher	Save	Record	Pos.	GB
4-6	Mon.	W	8-2		10	3	Schmidt	Pavano		1-1	3rd	0.5
4-7	Mon.	L	3-4		11	7	Urbina	Loiselle		1-2	5th	0.5
4-9	Chi.	W	2-1		2	4	Benson	Sanders	Williams	2-2	T1st	...
4-10	Chi.	W	9-3		9	5	Sauerbeck	Woodall		3-2	T1st	...
4-11	Chi.	W	9-6		12	13	Schmidt	Trachsel		4-2	1st	+1.0
4-13	StL.	L	2-4		10	9	Bottenfield	Schourek	Acevedo	4-3	T1st	...
4-14	StL.	L	5-9		14	12	Aybar	Benson		4-4	3rd	1.0
4-16	At Cin.	L	5-6		9	9	Graves	Christiansen		4-5	T3rd	2.0
4-17	At Cin.	W	7-6	(10)	11	9	Christiansen	White		5-5	2nd	2.0
4-18	At Cin.	W	4-2		8	7	Loiselle	Graves	Williams	6-5	2nd	1.0
4-19	At S.D.	W	3-0		6	5	Schourek	Spencer	Christiansen	7-5	2nd	1.0
4-20	At S.D.	W	7-3	(10)	10	8	Williams	Hoffman		8-5	2nd	1.0
4-21	At S.D.	L	0-2		3	8	Ashby	Schmidt	Hoffman	8-6	T2nd	1.0
4-23	Mil.	L	1-9		8	13	Woodard	Peters		8-7	T2nd	2.0
4-24	Mil.	L	3-5		6	7	Reyes	Ritchie	Wickman	8-8	3rd	2.0
4-25	Mil.	L	2-4		8	10	Karl	Benson	Wickman	8-9	4th	3.0
4-27	At Atl.	W	5-3		10	7	Schmidt	Perez	Williams	9-9	3rd	3.0
4-28	At Atl.	L	4-5		8	9	Glavine	Christiansen		9-10	3rd	3.0
4-29	At Atl.	L	1-8		11	10	Maddux	Silva		9-11	T4th	3.0
4-30	Col.	L	2-7		8	8	Astacio	Schourek		9-12	T4th	3.5
5-1	Col.	W	9-3		9	8	Ritchie	Wright		10-12	4th	3.5
5-2	Col.	W	8-5		12	8	Schmidt	Thomson	Williams	11-12	4th	3.5
5-3	S.F	W	9-8		13	13	Loiselle	Nen		12-12	4th	2.5
5-4	S.F	L	4-7		10	13	Ortiz	Silva		12-13	4th	3.5
5-5	S.F	W	4-3	(12)	8	7	Loiselle	Rodriguez		13-13	4th	3.5
5-6	At StL.	W	13-3		15	7	Ritchie	Osborne		14-13	4th	3.0
5-7	At StL.	L	2-4		13	6	Radinsky	Loiselle		14-14	T3rd	4.0
5-8	At StL.	W	7-0		10	4	Benson	Jimenez		15-14	4th	3.0
5-9	At StL.	W	12-9		15	9	Peters	Aybar	Williams	16-14	T2nd	2.0
5-10	At Hou.	L	0-6		5	13	Hampton	Schourek		16-15	3rd	3.0
5-11	At Hou.	L	8-19		14	18	Bergman	Ritchie		16-16	T3rd	4.0
5-12	At Hou.	L	2-6		8	10	Lima	Schmidt		16-17	3rd	5.0
5-14	Mon.	W	5-3		10	5	Benson	Hermanson	Williams	17-17	T2nd	5.0
5-15	Mon.	W	17-6		17	11	Silva	Pavano		18-17	T3rd	5.0
5-16	Mon.	W	9-4		8	10	Schourek	Vazquez		19-17	T2nd	4.0
5-17	At Atl.	L	1-2		5	7	Millwood	Ritchie	Rocker	19-18	4th	4.5
5-18	At Atl.	L	4-12		12	16	Perez	Schmidt		19-19	T4th	5.5
5-19	At Atl.	L	3-7		6	6	Glavine	Cordova		19-20	5th	5.5
5-20	At Fla.	L	3-4	(14)	12	12	Alfonseca	Williams		19-21	5th	6.5
5-21	At Fla.	L	1-8		4	10	Hernandez	Schourek		19-22	6th	6.5
5-22	At Fla.	W	11-4		14	8	Ritchie	Springer		20-22	5th	5.5
5-23	At Fla.	W	6-5		10	11	Wallace	Darensbourg	Williams	21-22	5th	5.5
5-24	N.Y.	W	7-4		8	7	Silva	Isringhausen	Williams	22-22	5th	5.5
5-25	N.Y.	L	3-8		6	11	Yoshii	Benson		22-23	5th	6.5
5-26	N.Y.	L	2-5		5	10	Hershiser	Schourek	Franco	22-24	5th	7.5
5-28	Hou.	W	6-5		9	6	Ritchie	Lima	Williams	23-24	5th	6.0
5-29	Hou.	W	5-1		8	5	Cordova	Reynolds		24-24	5th	5.0
5-30	Hou.	W	7-3		11	4	Benson	Hampton		25-24	4th	4.0
5-31	L.A.	W	5-4		7	9	Wilkins	Arnold	Williams	26-24	4th	3.5
6-1	L.A.	W	4-2		8	7	Schmidt	Valdes	Williams	27-24	4th	3.5
6-2	L.A.	W	8-4		11	8	Ritchie	Dreifort		28-24	4th	3.5
6-4	At Chi. (AL)	W	6-3	(11)	9	10	Wilkins	Simas		29-24	4th	3.0
6-5	At Chi. (AL)	L	5-6		8	15	Parque	Benson	Foulke	29-25	4th	4.0
6-6	At Chi. (AL)	L	3-4		8	8	Sirotka	Silva	Howry	29-26	4th	4.0
6-7	At Det.	L	4-9		8	10	Brunson	Schmidt		29-27	T4th	5.0
6-8	At Det.	L	4-11		7	15	Cruz	Ritchie		29-28	T4th	5.0
6-9	At Det.	W	15-3		17	10	Cordova	Moehler		30-28	4th	5.0
6-11	K.C.	L	3-10		8	9	Rosado	Benson		30-29	4th	6.0
6-12	K.C.	W	9-8		17	13	Christiansen	Whisenant		31-29	4th	6.0
6-13	K.C.	W	8-4		9	9	Schmidt	Whisenant	Williams	32-29	4th	5.5
6-15	At L.A.	W	11-1		14	7	Ritchie	Brown		33-29	4th	5.0
6-16	At L.A.	L	5-6		11	12	Borbon	Clontz	Shaw	33-30	T3rd	5.0
6-17	At L.A.	W	8-3		14	5	Benson	Park		34-30	3rd	4.0
6-18	At S.D.	L	2-4		8	8	Boehringer	Silva	Hoffman	34-31	3rd	5.0
6-19	At S.D.	L	4-5		5	10	Cunnane	Schmidt	Hoffman	34-32	3rd	6.0
6-20	At S.D.	L	3-6		8	12	Clement	Ritchie	Hoffman	34-33	3rd	7.0
6-22	At Phi.	L	2-3		6	7	Wolf	Cordova	Gomes	34-34	T4th	6.5
6-23	At Phi.	W	8-6		12	11	Benson	Byrd	Williams	35-34	3rd	6.5
6-24	At Phi.	L	5-7		10	10	Schilling	Silva	Gomes	35-35	4th	6.5
6-25	At Mil.	W	5-3		11	10	Schmidt	Abbott	Christiansen	36-35	3rd	5.5
6-26	At Mil.	L	4-7		10	11	Nomo	Ritchie	Wickman	36-36	T3rd	5.5
6-27	At Mil.	W	6-5		7	9	Cordova	Karl	Christiansen	37-36	3rd	4.5

Date	Opp.	Res.	Score	(inn.*)	Hits	Opp. hits	Winning pitcher	Losing pitcher	Save	Record	Pos.	GB
6-28	Phi.	W	3-2	(10)	7	6	Hansell	Montgomery		38-36	3rd	4.0
6-29	Phi.	L	4-7		7	11	Schilling	Silva		38-37	3rd	5.0
6-30	Phi.	W	9-1		12	9	Schmidt	Ogea		39-37	3rd	5.0
7-1	Phi.	W	12-7		14	9	Ritchie	Person		40-37	3rd	5.0
7-2	Mil.	L	2-5		9	11	Karl	Cordova	Wickman	40-38	3rd	5.0
7-3	Mil.	L	4-9		11	11	Pulsipher	Benson		40-39	3rd	6.0
7-4	Mil.	L	3-4		6	8	Weathers	Clontz	Wickman	40-40	3rd	6.0
7-5	Chi.	L	2-5		11	9	Lieber	Schmidt	Aguilera	40-41	T3rd	7.0
7-6	Chi.	W	6-1		8	9	Ritchie	Trachsel		41-41	3rd	6.0
7-7	Chi.	W	4-1		8	5	Cordova	Mulholland		42-41	3rd	5.0
7-8	Chi.	L	4-9		5	11	Serafini	Benson	Sanders	42-42	3rd	6.0
7-9	At Min.	L	4-5		8	9	Radke	Silva	Trombley	42-43	3rd	7.0
7-10	At Min.	L	4-5		12	10	Guardado	Williams		42-44	3rd	7.0
7-11	At Min.	W	10-2		17	5	Ritchie	Mays		43-44	3rd	7.0
7-15	Cle.	L	0-2		3	7	Colon	Schmidt	Jackson	43-45	T4th	8.0
7-16	Cle.	W	11-3		13	12	Cordova	Burba		44-45	T3rd	8.0
7-17	Cle.	W	13-10		16	16	Benson	Nagy	Williams	45-45	3rd	8.0
7-18	L.A.	W	6-5	(10)	11	14	Sauerbeck	Mills		46-45	3rd	8.0
7-19	L.A.	L	7-12		6	14	Dreifort	Silva		46-46	3rd	9.0
7-20	L.A.	L	4-8		7	13	Brown	Clontz		46-47	4th	9.0
7-21	At Chi.	L	1-2		6	9	Aguilera	Christiansen		46-48	T4th	9.0
7-22	At Chi.	L	3-5		8	10	Mulholland	Benson	Adams	46-49	6th	9.0
7-23	At Mon.	L	1-5		4	9	Vazquez	Ritchie		46-50	6th	10.5
7-24	At Mon.	W	7-2		11	7	Schourek	Powell		47-50	T5th	10.5
7-25	At Mon.	W	6-1		11	4	Schmidt	Kline		48-50	4th	10.5
7-26	At N.Y.	L	5-7		10	9	Reed	Cordova	Wendell	48-51	4th	11.5
7-27	At N.Y.	W	5-1		9	6	Benson	Hershiser		49-51	4th	11.5
7-28	At N.Y.	L	2-9		3	10	Cook	Wilkins		49-52	4th	12.5
7-30	Fla.	L	7-8		11	14	Edmondson	Hansell	Alfonseca	49-53	5th	13.0
7-31	Fla.	W	4-2		5	8	Schmidt	Edmondson	Williams	50-53	4th	13.0
8-1	Fla.	W	2-1		10	5	Cordova	Fernandez		51-53	4th	12.0
8-3	Atl.	W	7-1		7	4	Benson	Millwood		52-53	4th	12.0
8-4	Atl.	W	3-2		5	5	Ritchie	Smoltz	Williams	53-53	4th	11.0
8-5	Atl.	L	3-6		7	9	Remlinger	Hansell	Rocker	53-54	4th	12.0
8-6†	StL.	W	5-1		10	6	Anderson	Jimenez	Silva	54-54		
8-6‡	StL.	L	1-5		3	10	Stephenson	Schmidt	Croushore	54-55	4th	12.0
8-7	StL.	W	3-1		11	7	Cordova	Bottenfield	Williams	55-55	T3rd	12.0
8-8	StL.	W	5-1		8	4	Benson	Oliver		56-55	3rd	12.0
8-9	Cin.	L	2-4		2	7	Neagle	Ritchie	Williamson	56-56	T3rd	12.0
8-10	Cin.	L	1-6		6	13	Guzman	Schourek		56-57	T3rd	12.0
8-11	Cin.	W	5-4		9	9	Williams	Williamson		57-57	T3rd	11.0
8-13	At Hou.	W	6-5	(13)	8	11	Clontz	Miller	Williams	58-57	T3rd	10.0
8-14	At Hou.	L	1-7		6	6	Holt	Benson		58-58	T3rd	11.0
8-15	At Hou.	W	2-0		5	7	Ritchie	Reynolds	Williams	59-58	3rd	10.0
8-16	At Cin.	L	2-9		5	10	Guzman	Schourek		59-59	4th	11.0
8-17	At Cin.	L	4-7	(12)	8	7	Graves	Williams		59-60	4th	12.0
8-18	At Cin.	W	12-6		13	11	Cordova	Tomko		60-60	4th	12.0
8-19	At Cin.	L	0-1		1	7	Harnisch	Benson	Williamson	60-61	4th	12.0
8-20	Ari.	W	5-4		11	5	Ritchie	Stottlemyre	Williams	61-61	4th	11.0
8-21	Ari.	L	2-4		6	9	Johnson	Anderson		61-62	4th	13.0
8-22	Ari.	L	5-7		7	10	Daal	Schmidt	Mantei	61-63	4th	13.5
8-23	Ari.	L	1-2		7	8	Reynoso	Cordova	Mantei	61-64	4th	13.5
8-24	Col.	L	2-3		7	8	Leskanic	Williams	Veres	61-65	4th	14.5
8-25	Col.	W	9-3		14	7	Peters	Kile		62-65	4th	13.5
8-26	Col.	W	8-4		15	8	Anderson	Astacio		63-65	T3rd	13.0
8-27	At S.F	W	4-1		9	6	Schmidt	Nathan	Williams	64-65	3rd	12.5
8-28	At S.F	L	2-6		4	13	Gardner	Cordova		64-66	3rd	12.5
8-29	At S.F	L	3-5		7	7	Estes	Benson	Nen	64-67	3rd	13.5
8-30	At Col.	W	11-8		16	16	Peters	Ramirez	Williams	65-67	3rd	12.5
8-31	At Col.	W	9-8	(10)	14	18	Williams	Lee	Silva	66-67	3rd	12.5
9-1	At Col.	W	9-8		12	12	Sauerbeck	Veres	Clontz	67-67	3rd	11.5
9-3	S.F	L	2-12		7	10	Estes	Cordova		67-68	3rd	12.5
9-4	S.F	L	2-9		5	9	Ortiz	Benson		67-69	3rd	13.5
9-5	S.F	W	8-4		10	8	Peters	Rueter		68-69	3rd	13.5
9-6	S.D.	L	3-4		8	6	Ashby	Ritchie	Hoffman	68-70	3rd	14.5
9-7	S.D.	W	3-1		7	4	Schmidt	Hitchcock	Silva	69-70	3rd	14.5
9-8	S.D.	L	4-7	(10)	10	11	Hoffman	Wilkins		69-71	3rd	15.5
9-10	At StL.	L	5-11		10	13	Bottenfield	Benson		69-72	3rd	17.0
9-11	At StL.	W	8-5		11	10	Peters	Jimenez	Silva	70-72	3rd	17.0
9-13	At Ari.	L	1-5		10	8	Daal	Schmidt	Chouinard	70-73	3rd	18.5
9-14	At Ari.	L	1-2		4	3	Swindell	Wilkins	Mantei	70-74	3rd	19.5
9-15	At Ari.	W	5-1		7	7	Benson	Reynoso		71-74	3rd	18.5
9-17	Cin.	W	3-1		4	7	Ritchie	Villone	Sauerbeck	72-74	3rd	17.5
9-18	Cin.	L	0-3		6	7	Parris	Peters		72-75	3rd	17.5
9-19	Cin.	W	8-5		8	9	Schmidt	Harnisch	Clontz	73-75	3rd	17.5

Date	Opp.	Res.	Score	(inn.*)	Hits	Opp. hits	Winning pitcher	Losing pitcher	Save	Record	Pos.	GB
9-20	Hou.	W	11-5		14	9	Schourek	Reynolds		74-75	3rd	16.5
9-21	Hou.	L	3-6		10	8	Elarton	Benson	Henry	74-76	3rd	17.5
9-22	Hou.	W	3-2		5	6	Ritchie	Lima		75-76	3rd	16.5
9-23	At Chi.	L	5-8		7	13	Bowie	Peters	Aguilera	75-77	3rd	17.0
9-24	At Chi.	L	0-9		5	14	Farnsworth	Schmidt		75-78	3rd	18.0
9-25	At Chi.	L	1-3		3	5	Lieber	Cordova		75-79	3rd	18.0
9-26	At Chi.	W	8-4	(11)	15	8	Sauerbeck	Guthrie		76-79	3rd	17.0
9-29†	At Mil.	W	7-5		11	9	Ritchie	Woodard	Williams	77-79		
9-29‡	At Mil.	L	2-5		7	7	Bere	Peters	Wickman	77-80	3rd	17.0
9-30	At Mil.	W	3-2		8	5	Garcia	Nomo	Sauerbeck	78-80	3rd	16.5
10-1	At N.Y.	L	2-3	(11)	7	10	Mahomes	Sauerbeck		78-81	3rd	16.5
10-2	At N.Y.	L	0-7		3	9	Reed	Cordova		78-82	3rd	17.5
10-3	At N.Y.	L	1-2		3	9	Benitez	Hansell		78-83	3rd	18.5

Monthly records: April (9-12), May (17-12), June (13-13), July (11-16), August (16-14), September (12-13), October (0-3).
*Innings, if other than nine. † First game of a doubleheader. ‡ Second game of a doubleheader.

HIGHLIGHTS

High point: The Pirates won seven consecutive games from May 28 through June 4, which put them a season-best five games over .500 (29-24) and three games behind N.L. Central-leading Houston. It was the closest they would get to first place in the final four months of the season.

Low point: Beginning July 2, Pittsburgh dropped seven of nine games—and it lost catcher Jason Kendall for the season on July 4. Any hope the team had of contending was dashed.

Turning point: Kendall's gruesome ankle dislocation changed the season, robbing the team of a vital component. The Pirates were 38-43 in the 81 games without Kendall, and the catcher's primary replacements (Keith Osik and Joe Oliver) combined for a sub-.200 batting average. Kendall had batted .327 in 1998 and was hitting .332 when he went down.

Most valuable player: Outfielder Brian Giles, who had been obtained from the Indians. He became a force, clubbing 39 home runs, knocking in 115 runs and batting .315. His career highs entering the season were 17 homers and 66 RBIs. Giles also played well in center field after Brant Brown faltered defensively.

Most valuable pitcher: Todd Ritchie, who was signed as a minor league free agent after pitching without distinction in the Twins' bullpen. The righthander won a staff-high 15 games, and his 3.49 ERA was the sixth-best figure in the N.L.

Most improved player: Left fielder Al Martin rebounded from a career-worst season, thanks to laser eye surgery and a reworked batting stance. Martin batted .277 with 24 homers and 20 stolen bases. He also became an adequate defensive player.

Most pleasant surprise: Ritchie was supposed to work in relief in Class AAA, but injuries helped change all that. After one start at Nashville, he was summoned by Pittsburgh in mid-April and soon won a spot in the rotation. Scott Sauerbeck rates mention, too. A Rule 5 draftee, he emerged as a highly dependable reliever (2.00 ERA in 65 appearances).

Biggest disappointment: The Pirates traded starter Jon Lieber to get Brown, thinking the former Cub would thrive as the starting center fielder. He wound up a bench player with some power and a lot of strikeouts.

Key injuries: Kendall's ankle injury headed the list. Shortstop Pat Meares played in only 21 games because of a hand injury that required surgery. Reliever Rich Loiselle needed elbow surgery and was lost for much of the season. Reliever Jason Christiansen was on the disabled list three times with neck and back problems. Giles missed the final 11 games with a broken finger. And starters Francisco Cordova and Chris Peters spent time on the D.L.

Notable: The Pirates hit 171 home runs, breaking the team record of 158 set in 1966. ... For the first time in franchise history, four players had at least 20 home runs: Giles (39), Kevin Young (26), Martin (24) and Ed Sprague (22). ... Righthander Kris Benson led N.L. rookie pitchers in ERA (4.07), innings pitched (196.2) and strikeouts (139). ... First baseman Young became the second Pirate to have 40 doubles in consecutive seasons. Paul Waner reached or surpassed that figure in three straight years (1927 through 1929).

—JOHN MEHNO

RECORDS

1999 regular-season record: 78-83 (3rd in N.L. Central); 45-36 at home; 33-47 on road; 19-22 vs. East; 30-32 vs. N.L. Central; 22-21 vs. West; 7-8 vs. A.L.; 17-30 vs. lefthanded starters; 61-53 vs. righthanded starters; 24-34 on grass; 54-49 on turf; 25-22 in daytime; 53-61 at night; 20-22 in one-run games; 9-4 in extra-inning games; 0-0-2 in doubleheaders.
Team record past five years: 357-434 (.451, ranks T12th in league in that span).

TEAM LEADERS

Batting average: Brian Giles (.315).
At-bats: Kevin Young (584).
Runs: Brian Giles (109).
Hits: Kevin Young (174).
Total Bases: Brian Giles (320).
Doubles: Kevin Young (41).
Triples: Al Martin (8).
Home runs: Brian Giles (39).
Runs batted in: Brian Giles (115).

Stolen bases: Jason Kendall, Kevin Young (22).
Slugging percentage: Brian Giles (.614).
On-base percentage: Brian Giles (.418).
Wins: Todd Ritchie (15).
Earned-run average: Todd Ritchie (3.50).
Complete games: Kris Benson, Francisco Cordova, Todd Ritchie, Jason Schmidt (2).
Shutouts: None.
Saves: Mike Williams (23).
Innings pitched: Jason Schmidt (212.2).
Strikeouts: Jason Schmidt (148).

GAMES BY POSITION

Catcher: Jason Kendall 75, Keith Osik 50, Joe Oliver 44, Chris Tremie 8, Tim Laker 2.
First base: Kevin Young 155, Brant Brown 7, Dale Sveum 4, Freddy Garcia 1, Ivan Cruz 1.
Second base: Warren Morris 144, Abraham Nunez 14, Mike Benjamin 12, Dale Sveum 2, John Wehner 1.
Third base: Ed Sprague 134, Aramis Ramirez 17, Dale Sveum 12, Freddy Garcia 9, Mike Benjamin 6, John Wehner 2.
Shortstop: Mike Benjamin 93, Abraham Nunez 65, Pat Meares 21, Dale Sveum 4, John Wehner 2.
Outfield: Brian Giles 138, Al Martin 134, Adrian Brown 96, Brant Brown 82, Jose Guillen 37, Turner Ward 34, Freddy Garcia 24, Chad Hermansen 18, John Wehner 17, Emil Brown 6, Dale Sveum 1, Ivan Cruz 1.
Designated hitter: Brant Brown 6, Brian Giles 3, Freddy Garcia 2.

TOP DRAFT CHOICES

1. **Bobby Bradley,** RHP, Wellington (Fla.) H.S.
2. **Ryan Doumit,** C, Moses Lake (Wash.) H.S.
3. **Aron Weston,** OF, Solon (Ohio) H.S.
4. **Justin Reid,** RHP, U. of California-Davis
5. **J.R. House,** C, Seabreeze H.S., Ormond Beach, Fla.
6. **B.J. Barns,** OF, Duquesne University
7. **Matt Schneider,** OF, U. of N. Florida
8. **Jonathan Searles,** RHP, Huntington (N.Y.) H.S.
9. **Shane Wright,** RHP, Texas Tech
10. **Jeremy Sickles,** C, Cal State Northridge

ST. LOUIS CARDINALS
NATIONAL LEAGUE CENTRAL DIVISION

2000 Cardinals Schedule
Home games shaded. *—All-Star Game at Turner Field (Atlanta).

March
SUN	MON	TUE	WED	THU	FRI	SAT
26	27	28	29	30	31	

April
SUN	MON	TUE	WED	THU	FRI	SAT
						1
2	3 CUB	4	5 CUB	6 CUB	7 MIL	8 MIL
9 MIL	10 HOU	11 HOU	12 HOU	13 COL	14 COL	15 COL
16 COL	17	18 SD	19 SD	20 SD	21 COL	22 COL
23 COL	24 COL	25 MIL	26 MIL	27 MIL	28 PHI	29 PHI
30 PHI						

May
SUN	MON	TUE	WED	THU	FRI	SAT
	1	2 PIT	3 PIT	4 PIT	5 CIN	6 CIN
7 CIN	8 SF	9 SF	10 SF	11	12 LA	13 LA
14 LA	15	16 PHI	17 PHI	18 PHI	19 PIT	20 PIT
21 PIT	22	23 FLA	24 FLA	25 FLA	26 NYM	27 NYM
28 NYM	29 ARI	30 ARI	31 ARI			

June
SUN	MON	TUE	WED	THU	FRI	SAT
				1 ARI	2 CLE	3 CLE
4 CLE	5 KC	6 KC	7 KC	8	9 DET	10 DET
11 DET	12 SD	13 SD	14 SD	15	16 LA	17 LA
18 LA	19	20 SF	21 SF	22 SF	23 HOU	24 HOU
25 LA	26 CIN	27 CIN	28 CIN	29 CIN	30 HOU	

July
SUN	MON	TUE	WED	THU	FRI	SAT
						1 HOU
2 HOU	3	4 CIN	5 CIN	6 SF	7 SF	8 SF
9 SF	10	11 *	12	13 CWS	14 CWS	15 CWS
16 MIN	17 MIN	18 MIN	19 ARI	20 ARI	21 HOU	22 HOU
23 HOU	24	25 ARI	26 ARI	27 ARI	28 NYM	29 NYM
30 NYM	31 MON					

August
SUN	MON	TUE	WED	THU	FRI	SAT
		1 MON	2 MON	3	4 ATL	5 ATL
6 ATL	7 FLA	8 FLA	9 FLA	10	11 MIL	12 MIL
13 MIL	14 CUB	15 CUB	16 CUB	17	18 PHI	19 PHI
20 PHI	21 PIT	22 PIT	23 PIT	24 ATL	25 ATL	26 ATL
27 ATL	28 FLA	29 FLA	30 FLA	31		

September
SUN	MON	TUE	WED	THU	FRI	SAT
					1 NYM	2 NYM
3 NYM	4 MON	5 MON	6 MON	7 MON	8 MIL	9 MIL
10 MIL	11 PIT	12 PIT	13 PIT	14	15 CUB	16 CUB
17 CUB	18	19 HOU	20 HOU	21 HOU	22 CUB	23 CUB
24 CUB	25	26 SD	27 SD	28 SD	29 CIN	30 CIN

October
SUN	MON	TUE	WED	THU	FRI	SAT
1 CIN	2	3	4	5	6	7

2000 SEASON
CLUB DIRECTORY

Chairman of the board/general partner
William O. DeWitt Jr.
Chairman
Frederick O. Hanser
Secretary-treasurer
Andrew N. Baur
President
Mark C. Lamping
Vice president, general manager
Walt Jocketty
Admin. assistant to the president
Julie Laningham
Sr. exec. asst. to v.p., general manager
Judy Carpenter-Barada
Vice president/player personnel
Jerry Walker
Special asst. to the general manager
Bob Gebhard
Senior v.p., sales and marketing
Dan Farrell
Vice president, controller
Brad Wood
Vice president, community relations
Marty Hendin
Vice president, business development
Bill DeWitt III
Vice president, stadium operations
Joe Abernathy
Vice president, ticket operations
Josie Arnold
Vice president, sales
Kevin Wade
Director, group sales
Joe Strohm
Manager, ticket sales
Mark Murray
Director, corporate sales/marketing
Thane van Breusegen
Group director, community outreach/ Cardinals Care
Tim Hanser
Director, target marketing
Ted Savage
Director, media relations
Brian Bartow

Mgr., media relations & publications
Steve Zesch
Assistant to director, media relations
Brad Hainje
Traveling secretary
C.J. Cherre
Director, player development
Mike Jorgensen
Director, player procurement
Jeff Scott
Director, scouting operations
John Mozeliak
Director, minor league operations
Scott Smulczenski
Mgr., baseball info./player development
John Vuch
Major league trainer
Barry Weinberg
Assistant major league trainer
Brad Henderson
Medical/rehabilitation coordinator
Mark O'Neal
Equipment manager
Buddy Bates
Assistant equipment manager
Rip Rowan
Special assignment scouts
Bing Devine, Marty Keough, Jim Leyland, Fred McAlister, Joe Sparks (advance scout), Mike Squires
National cross-checker
Mike Roberts
Regional cross-checkers
Tim Conroy
Clark Crist
Scouts
Randy Benson, Jorge Brito, Roberto Diaz, Chuck Fick, Ben Galante, Steve Grilli, Manny Guerra, Dave Karaff, Scott Melvin, Scott Nichols, Jay North, Dan Ontiveros, Joe Rigoli, Tommy Shields, Roger Smith, Steve Turco, Dane Walker

MINOR LEAGUE AFFILIATES

Class	Team	League	Manager
AAA	Memphis	Pacific Coast	Gaylen Pitts
AA	Arkansas	Texas	Chris Maloney
A	Potomac	Carolina	Joe Cunningham
A	Peoria	Midwest	Tom Lawless
A	New Jersey	New York-Pennsylvania	Jeff Shireman
Rookie	Johnson City	Appalachian	To be announced

BROADCAST INFORMATION

Radio: KMOX-AM (1120).
TV: KPLR-TV (Channel 11).
Cable TV: Fox Sports Midwest.

SPRING TRAINING

Ballpark (city): Roger Dean Stadium (Jupiter, Fla.).
Ticket information: 561-966-3309.

2000 SEASON *St. Louis Cardinals*

Manager—Tony La Russa (10).
Coaches—Mark DeJohn (34), Dave Duncan (18), Mike Easler (4), Marty Mason (38), Dave McKay (39), Jose Oquendo (11).

No.	PITCHERS	B/T	Ht./Wt.	Born	1999 clubs
77	Ambrose, John	R/R	6-5/180	11-1-74	Arkansas
30	Ankiel, Rick	L/L	6-1/210	7-19-79	Arkansas, Memphis, St. Louis
31	Benes, Alan	R/R	6-5/235	1-21-72	Arkansas, Potomac, Memphis, St. Louis
	Benes, Andy	R/R	6-6/245	8-20-67	Arizona
37	Bottenfield, Kent	R/R	6-3/240	11-14-68	St. Louis
66	Brunette, Justin	L/L	6-2/200	10-7-75	Peoria, Arkansas
63	Hackman, Luther	R/R	6-4/195	10-10-74	Carolina, Colorado Springs, Colorado
62	Heiserman, Rick	R/R	6-7/225	2-22-73	Memphis, St. Louis
40	Hentgen, Pat	R/R	6-2/195	11-13-68	Toronto
65	Hutchinson, Chad	R/R	6-5/230	2-21-77	Arkansas, Memphis
57	Kile, Darryl	R/R	6-5/212	12-2-68	Colorado
70	Matthews, Mike	L/L	6-2/175	10-24-73	Buffalo, Akron, Trenton, Arkansas
32	Mohler, Mike	R/L	6-2/208	7-26-68	St. Louis, Memphis
35	Morris, Matt	R/R	6-5/210	8-9-74	DID NOT PLAY
36	Radinsky, Scott	L/L	6-3/215	3-3-68	St. Louis
58	Slocumb, Heathcliff	R/R	6-3/220	6-7-66	Baltimore, Memphis, St. Louis
50	Spoljaric, Paul	R/L	6-3/210	9-24-70	Philadelphia, Toronto
55	Stephenson, Garrett	R/R	6-5/208	1-2-72	Memphis, Arkansas, St. Louis
43	Thompson, Mark	R/R	6-2/212	4-7-71	Indianapolis, Memphis, St. Louis
46	Veres, Dave	R/R	6-2/220	10-19-66	Colorado

No.	CATCHERS	B/T	Ht./Wt.	Born	1999 clubs
26	Marrero, Eli	R/R	6-1/180	11-17-73	St. Louis
22	Matheny, Mike	R/R	6-3/205	9-22-70	Toronto

No.	INFIELDERS	B/T	Ht./Wt.	Born	1999 clubs
61	Haas, Chris	L/R	6-1/205	10-15-76	Memphis
8	Kennedy, Adam	L/R	6-2/180	1-10-76	Memphis, St. Louis
47	McEwing, Joe	R/R	5-11/170	10-19-72	St. Louis
25	McGwire, Mark	R/R	6-5/250	10-1-63	St. Louis
21	Paquette, Craig	R/R	6-0/190	3-28-69	Norfolk, St. Louis
27	Polanco, Placido	R/R	5-10/168	10-10-75	St. Louis, Memphis
3	Renteria, Edgar	R/R	6-1/180	8-7-75	St. Louis
68	Richard, Chris	L/L	6-2/185	6-7-74	Arkansas, Memphis
28	Sutton, Larry	L/L	6-0/185	5-14-70	Kansas City, Gulf Coast Royals, Omaha
23	Tatis, Fernando	R/R	5-10/175	1-1-75	St. Louis
1	Vina, Fernando	L/R	5-9/170	4-16-69	Milwaukee, Beloit
64	Woolf, Jason	B/R	6-1/170	6-6-77	Arkansas

No.	OUTFIELDERS	B/T	Ht./Wt.	Born	1999 clubs
24	Davis, Eric	R/R	6-3/185	5-29-62	St. Louis
7	Drew, J.D.	L/R	6-1/195	11-20-75	St. Louis, Memphis
22	Howard, Thomas	B/R	6-2/205	12-11-64	Memphis, St. Louis
16	Lankford, Ray	L/L	5-11/200	6-5-67	St. Louis
15	Powell, Dante	R/R	6-2/185	8-25-73	Arizona, Tucson
76	Saturria, Luis	R/R	6-2/165	7-21-76	Arkansas

BALLPARK INFORMATION

Ballpark (capacity, surface)
Busch Stadium (49,738, grass)
Address
250 Stadium Plaza
St. Louis, MO 63102
Business phone
314-421-3060
Ticket information
314-421-2400
Ticket prices
$30 (field boxes-infield)
$28 (loge boxes-infield)
$25 (field boxes-outfield)
$24 (loge boxes-outfield)
$20 (terrace boxes-infield, loge reserved-infield)
$18 (terrace boxes-outfield, loge reserved-outfield)
$15 (terrace reserved-adults)
$8 (bleachers)
$7 (ter. reserved-children, upper ter. reserved-adults)
$3 (upper terrace reserved-children)
Field dimensions (from home plate)
To left field at foul line, 330 feet
To center field, 402 feet
To right field at foul line, 330 feet
First game played
May 12, 1966 (Cardinals 4, Braves 3)

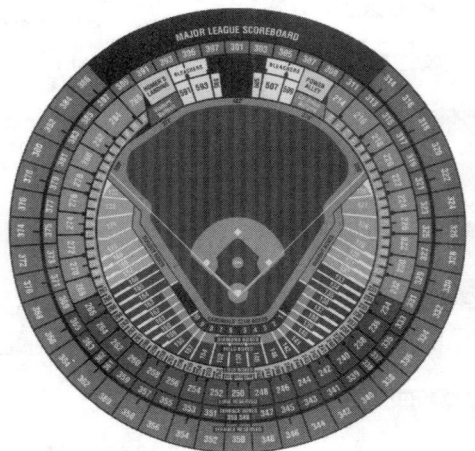

2000 SEASON *St. Louis Cardinals*

Date	Opp.	Res.	Score	(inn.*)	Hits	Opp. hits	Winning pitcher	Losing pitcher	Save	Record	Pos.	GB
4-7	Mil.	W	4-1		7	5	Bottenfield	Woodard	Acevedo	1-1	T1st	...
4-8	Mil.	W	9-4		8	13	Mercker	Abbott		2-1	T1st	...
4-9	Cin.	L	0-3		6	5	Harnisch	Oliver		2-2	T1st	...
4-10	Cin.	W	4-2		6	7	Acevedo	Williamson		3-2	T1st	...
4-11	Cin.	L	2-4		10	6	Bere	Osborne	Graves	3-3	T2nd	1.0
4-13	At Pit.	W	4-2		9	10	Bottenfield	Schourek	Acevedo	4-3	T1st	...
4-14	At Pit.	W	9-5		12	14	Aybar	Benson		5-3	T1st	...
4-16	At Hou.	W	5-3		9	11	Oliver	Reynolds	Bottalico	6-3	1st	+1.5
4-17	At Hou.	W	8-5		10	11	Jimenez	Holt		7-3	1st	+2.0
4-18	At Hou.	L	4-8		9	16	Powell	Painter		7-4	1st	+1.0
4-19	At Mil.	W	6-2		12	7	Bottenfield	Abbott		8-4	1st	+1.0
4-20	At Mil.	W	8-3		12	6	Mercker	Karl		9-4	1st	+1.0
4-21	At Mil.	L	1-2		6	5	Reyes	Painter	Wickman	9-5	1st	+1.0
4-23	At L.A.	W	12-5		11	11	Jimenez	Park		10-5	1st	+2.0
4-24	At L.A.	L	1-6		6	8	Valdes	Osborne		10-6	1st	+1.0
4-25	At L.A.	W	6-4		9	8	Bottenfield	Dreifort	Acevedo	11-6	1st	+2.0
4-27	Col.	W	7-5		8	10	Oliver	Thomson	Radinsky	12-6	1st	+1.5
4-28	Col.	L	7-9		14	11	Bohanon	Jimenez	Veres	12-7	1st	+1.5
4-29	Col.	L	2-6		8	11	Kile	Mercker		12-8	1st	+0.5
4-30	At Mon.	L	2-3		6	8	Urbina	Acevedo		12-9	2nd	0.5
5-1	At Mon.	W	16-5		19	8	Osborne	Thurman	Mohler	13-9	2nd	0.5
5-2	At Mon.	W	8-7	(10)	11	14	Acevedo	Urbina	Radinsky	14-9	2nd	0.5
5-3	At Atl.	L	2-4		10	8	Remlinger	Jimenez	Rocker	14-10	2nd	0.5
5-4	At Atl.	W	9-1		16	4	Aybar	Maddux		15-10	2nd	0.5
5-5	At Atl.	L	3-12		7	16	Smoltz	Bottenfield		15-11	2nd	1.5
5-6	Pit.	L	3-13		7	15	Ritchie	Osborne		15-12	2nd	2.0
5-7	Pit.	W	4-2		6	13	Radinsky	Loiselle		16-12	2nd	2.0
5-8	Pit.	L	0-7		4	10	Benson	Jimenez		16-13	2nd	2.0
5-9	Pit.	L	9-12		9	15	Peters	Aybar	Williams	16-14	T2nd	2.0
5-10	Phi.	W	5-2		9	7	Bottenfield	Loewer	Radinsky	17-14	2nd	2.0
5-11	Phi.	L	4-9		7	13	Byrd	Mercker		17-15	2nd	3.0
5-12	Phi.	L	4-8		7	12	Schilling	Oliver		17-16	2nd	4.0
5-14	L.A.	L	3-7		8	10	Brown	Jimenez		17-17	T2nd	5.0
5-15	L.A.	W	8-5		12	12	Bottenfield	Park		18-17	T3rd	5.0
5-16	L.A.	W	5-4		8	9	Bottalico	Shaw		19-17	T2nd	4.0
5-18	At S.D.	W	5-2		9	4	Oliver	Clement	Bottalico	20-17	2nd	4.0
5-19	At S.D.	L	6-7		9	8	Boehringer	Bottalico		20-18	3rd	4.0
5-20	At S.D.	W	6-4		9	9	Bottenfield	Hitchcock	Bottalico	21-18	3rd	4.0
5-21	At L.A.	W	10-6		10	7	Acevedo	Valdes	Aybar	22-18	3rd	3.0
5-22	At L.A.	L	7-10		12	14	Dreifort	Sodowsky	Shaw	22-19	3rd	3.0
5-23	At L.A.	W	8-3		14	11	Oliver	Perez		23-19	3rd	3.0
5-25	S.F	L	1-17		5	17	Brock	Jimenez		23-20	T3rd	4.5
5-26	S.F	L	6-7		9	12	Rueter	Bottenfield	Nen	23-21	4th	5.5
5-27	S.F	W	3-2	(12)	6	8	Slocumb	Spradlin		24-21	4th	4.5
5-28	At Chi.	L	3-6		7	14	Tapani	Painter	Aguilera	24-22	3rd	4.5
5-29	At Chi.	L	3-4		9	8	Heredia	Bottalico		24-23	4th	4.5
5-30	At Chi.	L	4-7		10	12	Lieber	Jimenez		24-24	5th	4.5
5-31	At Fla.	W	5-2		11	10	Bottenfield	Meadows	Bottalico	25-24	5th	4.0
6-1	At Fla.	W	8-4		11	8	Acevedo	Hernandez		26-24	5th	4.0
6-2	At Fla.	L	2-10		8	14	Dempster	Painter		26-25	5th	5.0
6-3	At Fla.	L	2-4		8	5	Looper	Oliver	Mantei	26-26	5th	5.0
6-4	At Det.	L	1-4		4	7	Moehler	Jimenez	Jones	26-27	5th	6.0
6-5	At Det.	W	7-2		15	5	Bottenfield	Blair	Bottalico	27-27	5th	6.0
6-6	At Det.	W	8-4		14	9	Croushore	Nitkowski	Aybar	28-27	5th	5.0
6-7	At K.C.	W	7-5		12	7	Slocumb	Appier	Bottalico	29-27	T4th	5.0
6-8	At K.C.	L	10-11		14	15	Service	Oliver	Montgomery	29-28	T4th	5.0
6-9	At K.C.	L	13-17		18	19	Whisenant	Radinsky		29-29	5th	6.0
6-11	Det.	L	2-8		10	7	Mlicki	Bottenfield		29-30	5th	7.0
6-12	Det.	W	8-7	(14)	17	8	Radinsky	Blair		30-30	5th	7.0
6-13	Det.	L	1-3	(10)	9	11	Jones	Bottalico	Brocail	30-31	5th	7.5
6-14	Mon.	L	5-7		9	11	Telford	Oliver	Urbina	30-32	5th	8.5
6-15	Mon.	W	3-2		5	5	Jimenez	Thurman	Bottalico	31-32	5th	7.5
6-16	Mon.	W	5-4		9	6	Bottenfield	Batista	Bottalico	32-32	5th	6.5
6-17	N.Y.	L	3-4		6	10	Leiter	Mercker	Cook	32-33	5th	6.5
6-18	N.Y.	L	2-6		3	14	Hershiser	Acevedo	Benitez	32-34	5th	7.5
6-19	N.Y.	W	7-6		10	9	Aybar	Isringhausen	Bottalico	33-34	5th	7.5
6-20	N.Y.	L	6-9		10	12	Reed	Croushore	Franco	33-35	5th	8.5
6-21	Hou.	W	5-3		10	5	Bottenfield	Bergman	Bottalico	34-35	5th	7.5
6-22	Hou.	W	4-3	(14)	13	11	Mohler	McCurry		35-35	T4th	6.5
6-23	Hou.	L	4-8		14	12	Reynolds	Acevedo		35-36	5th	7.5
6-24	At Ari.	L	7-8		14	11	Nunez	Bottalico		35-37	5th	7.5
6-25	At Ari.	W	1-0		5	0	Jimenez	Johnson		36-37	5th	6.5

Date	Opp.	Res.	Score	(inn.*)	Hits	Opp. hits	Winning pitcher	Losing pitcher	Save	Record	Pos.	GB
6-26	At Ari.	W	2-1	(10)	5	7	Aybar	Nunez		37-37	T3rd	5.5
6-27	At Ari.	L	2-3	(10)	7	8	Nunez	Bottalico		37-38	5th	5.5
6-29	At Hou.	L	4-5		8	7	Elarton	Aybar	Wagner	37-39	5th	6.5
6-30	At Hou.	L	3-11		8	13	Hampton	Jimenez		37-40	5th	7.5
7-1	At Hou.	W	10-4		12	10	Bottenfield	Holt		38-40	5th	7.5
7-2	Ari.	L	5-9		9	15	Anderson	Oliver		38-41	5th	7.5
7-3	Ari.	W	2-1	(10)	5	4	Painter	Kim		39-41	4th	7.5
7-4	Ari.	L	5-17		13	19	Benes	Croushore		39-42	5th	7.5
7-5	Ari.	W	1-0		4	2	Jimenez	Johnson		40-42	5th	7.5
7-6	Cin.	W	6-5		10	9	Bottenfield	Tomko	Bottalico	41-42	4th	6.5
7-7	Cin.	W	2-1		7	9	Croushore	Williamson		42-42	4th	5.5
7-8	Cin.	L	5-8		10	11	Harnisch	Mercker	Graves	42-43	4th	6.5
7-9	At S.F	L	4-5	(11)	11	9	Rodriguez	Aybar		42-44	T4th	7.5
7-10	At S.F	L	2-4		7	7	Ortiz	Jimenez	Johnstone	42-45	4th	7.5
7-11	At S.F	W	5-4		7	8	Bottenfield	Gardner	Bottalico	43-45	T4th	7.5
7-15	Chi. (AL)	W	3-2	(13)	10	8	Croushore	Rizzo		44-45	3rd	7.5
7-16	Chi. (AL)	L	8-9		11	15	Navarro	Acevedo	Howry	44-46	4th	8.5
7-17	Chi. (AL)	W	8-6		9	8	Stephenson	Ward	Bottalico	45-46	T4th	8.5
7-18	Min.	L	2-5		9	7	Hawkins	Oliver		45-47	5th	9.5
7-19	Min.	W	8-4		14	9	Mercker	Lincoln	Bottalico	46-47	T4th	9.5
7-20	Min.	L	2-4		7	7	Radke	Luebbers	Trombley	46-48	5th	9.5
7-21	At Cin.	L	0-1		1	3	Villone	Jimenez	Williamson	46-49	6th	9.5
7-22	At Cin.	W	6-5		5	8	Painter	Graves	Bottalico	47-49	5th	8.5
7-23	At Col.	W	6-4		11	12	Oliver	Ramirez	Slocumb	48-49	T3rd	9.0
7-24	At Col.	W	10-2		15	11	Mercker	Kile		49-49	3rd	9.0
7-25	At Col.	W	6-4		8	9	Luebbers	Astacio	Aybar	50-49	3rd	9.0
7-26	At S.F	L	8-10		11	14	Rodriguez	Slocumb	Nen	50-50	3rd	10.0
7-27	At S.F	L	1-2		4	7	Rueter	Bottenfield	Johnstone	50-51	3rd	11.0
7-28	At S.F	W	6-3		7	7	Oliver	Hernandez	Bottalico	51-51	3rd	11.0
7-30	Col.	L	4-5		7	9	Astacio	Aybar	Veres	51-52	3rd	11.5
7-31	Col.	W	6-5		10	11	Painter	Leskanic	Bottalico	52-52	3rd	11.5
8-1	Col.	L	4-5		10	13	Bohanon	Jimenez	Veres	52-53	3rd	11.5
8-2	S.D.	W	6-5		9	10	Bottenfield	Williams	Croushore	53-53	3rd	11.0
8-3	S.D.	W	6-0		9	4	Oliver	Boehringer		54-53	3rd	11.0
8-4	S.D.	W	7-6		13	6	Slocumb	Wall	Croushore	55-53	3rd	10.0
8-5	S.D.	L	3-10		6	10	Ashby	Luebbers	Hoffman	55-54	3rd	11.0
8-6†	At Pit.	L	1-5		6	10	Anderson	Jimenez	Silva	55-55		
8-6‡	At Pit.	W	5-1		10	3	Stephenson	Schmidt	Croushore	56-55	3rd	11.0
8-7	At Pit.	L	1-3		7	11	Cordova	Bottenfield	Williams	56-56	T3rd	12.0
8-8	At Pit.	L	1-5		4	8	Benson	Oliver		56-57	4th	13.0
8-9	At Phi.	W	12-6		15	11	Mercker	Schrenk		57-57	T3rd	12.0
8-10	At Phi.	L	5-7		10	6	Poole	Bottalico	Gomes	57-58	T3rd	12.0
8-11	At Phi.	W	5-1		9	6	Stephenson	Wolf	Slocumb	58-58	T3rd	11.0
8-13	Chi.	W	7-1		7	8	Bottenfield	Farnsworth		59-58	T3rd	10.0
8-14	Chi.	L	7-9		10	10	Adams	Slocumb		59-59	T3rd	11.0
8-15	Chi.	W	6-5		13	9	Bottalico	Adams		60-59	4th	10.0
8-16	Phi.	W	4-3		4	9	Mercker	Wolf	Bottalico	61-59	3rd	10.0
8-17	Phi.	W	6-5		10	10	Acevedo	Gomes		62-59	3rd	10.0
8-18	Phi.	L	5-6		8	17	Aldred	Croushore	Gomes	62-60	3rd	11.0
8-21	At N.Y.	L	4-7		8	9	Mahomes	Mercker	Benitez	62-61	3rd	12.0
8-22†	At N.Y.	L	7-8		12	11	Benitez	Bottalico		62-62		
8-22‡	At N.Y.	W	7-5		10	11	Stephenson	Hershiser	Acevedo	63-62	3rd	12.0
8-23	At Mon.	L	7-11		11	14	Telford	Croushore		63-63	3rd	12.0
8-24	At Mon.	L	4-8		10	12	Vazquez	Bottenfield	Urbina	63-64	3rd	13.0
8-25	At Mon.	L	1-4		7	8	Powell	Luebbers	Urbina	63-65	3rd	13.0
8-27	Atl.	L	1-2		8	8	Springer	Acevedo	Rocker	63-66	4th	13.5
8-28	Atl.	L	0-3	(13)	4	7	Remlinger	Painter	Rocker	63-67	4th	13.5
8-29	Atl.	L	3-4	(12)	8	9	McGlinchy	Acevedo		63-68	4th	14.5
8-30	Fla.	L	2-4		5	13	Nunez	Bottenfield	Alfonseca	63-69	4th	14.5
8-31	Fla.	W	8-1		12	5	Luebbers	Meadows		64-69	4th	14.5
9-1	Fla.	W	9-3		10	9	Stephenson	Dempster		65-69	4th	13.5
9-2	At Mil.	W	4-3		9	8	Painter	Ramirez	Bottalico	66-69	4th	13.0
9-3	At Mil.	L	4-5	(11)	12	12	Coppinger	Acevedo		66-70	4th	14.0
9-4	At Mil.	L	2-4		3	6	Pulsipher	Thompson	Wickman	66-71	4th	15.0
9-5	At Mil.	W	13-9	(10)	18	12	Bottalico	Wickman		67-71	4th	15.0
9-6	At Atl.	L	1-4		3	9	Maddux	Stephenson		67-72	4th	16.0
9-7	At Atl.	L	2-3		6	9	Remlinger	Oliver		67-73	4th	17.0
9-8	At Atl.	L	4-5		9	7	Millwood	Ankiel	Rocker	67-74	4th	18.0
9-10	Pit.	W	11-5		13	10	Bottenfield	Benson		68-74	4th	18.5
9-11	Pit.	L	5-8		10	11	Peters	Jimenez	Silva	68-75	4th	19.5
9-13	Mil.	L	3-4		8	9	Nomo	Thompson	Wickman	68-76	4th	21.0
9-14	Mil.	L	1-4		8	7	Karl	Aybar	Wickman	68-77	4th	22.0
9-15	Mil.	L	8-10	(12)	13	15	Ramirez	Acevedo		68-78	4th	22.0
9-17	Hou.	W	11-8		18	8	Stephenson	Lima	Bottalico	69-78	4th	21.0
9-18	Hou.	W	13-6		13	11	Oliver	Hampton		70-78	4th	20.0
9-19	Hou.	L	3-4		7	10	Holt	Croushore	Wagner	70-79	4th	21.0

Date	Opp.	Res.	Score	(inn.*)	Hits	Opp. hits	Winning pitcher	Losing pitcher	Save	Record	Pos.	GB
9-20	At Chi.	W	7-2		9	8	Thompson	Lieber		71-79	4th	20.0
9-21	At Chi.	W	7-2		8	3	Bottenfield	Lorraine		72-79	4th	20.0
9-22	Chi.	L	3-5		7	8	Trachsel	Stephenson	Aguilera	72-80	4th	20.0
9-24	At Cin.	L	4-5		7	10	Parris	Croushore	Graves	72-81	4th	21.0
9-25	At Cin.	L	1-6		4	9	Neagle	Jimenez	Graves	72-82	4th	21.0
9-26	At Cin.	L	5-7	(12)	9	10	Williamson	Mohler		72-83	4th	21.0
9-27	At Cin.	L	7-9		8	14	Belinda	Croushore	Reyes	72-84	4th	21.5
9-29†	S.D.	W	4-3		8	5	Oliver	Wall	Painter	73-84		
9-29‡	S.D.	W	6-5	(10)	9	10	Acevedo	Guzman		74-84	4th	20.5
10-1	Chi.	L	2-3		7	7	Lieber	Thompson		74-85	4th	20.5
10-2	Chi.	L	3-6		6	10	Lorraine	Stephenson	Aguilera	74-86	T4th	21.5
10-3	Chi.	W	9-5	(5)	10	6	Luebbers	Trachsel	Ankiel	75-86	4th	21.5

Monthly records: April (12-9), May (13-15), June (12-16), July (15-12), August (12-17), September (10-15), October (1-2).
*Innings, if other than nine. † First game of a doubleheader. ‡ Second game of a doubleheader.

HIGHLIGHTS

High point: Mark McGwire had another monster season, finishing only five home runs short of his record total of 70. He hit 50 or more homers for a record fourth consecutive season and reached the 500-mark faster than anyone in history. Also, he won his first RBI crown, driving in 147 runs.
Low point: After being two games over .500 at 62-60 on August 20, the Cardinals lost 26 of their last 39 games.
Turning point: The season went downhill in spring training. Emerging staff ace Matt Morris went down with an elbow injury and had to undergo Tommy John surgery, which cost him the season and dealt the rotation a crippling blow.
Most valuable player: McGwire, although the Cardinals hit just 24 of the 56 games in which he homered and, almost unbelievably, were 2-7 in games in which he homered twice. His run-production exploits nonetheless were extraordinary—and his presence spurred the Cardinals to a record attendance of 3.23 million.
Most valuable pitcher: Entering the season with only 18 victories in his major league career, Kent Bottenfield matched that in one season as he developed into the Cardinals' No. 1 pitcher.
Most improved player: Bottenfield. The righthander had been only mediocre in his career as a longtime reliever and spot starter, but he prospered when installed in the rotation and left there. He lost a chance at 20 wins when, because of shoulder fatigue, he was shut down with 10 days left in the season.
Most pleasant surprise: The Cardinals knew third baseman Fernando Tatis was a promising player, but they never envisioned he'd have such a standout season. Tatis hit .298 with 34 homers and 107 RBIs, and he stole 21 bases. Plus, he displayed superior quickness and range at third base.
Biggest disappointment: Catcher Eli Marrero, a year removed from thyroid cancer surgery, batted just .192. Much-heralded center fielder J.D. Drew hit only .242 and showed defensive deficiencies, and lefthanded starter Donovan Osborne had more injury problems and pitched in only six games.
Key injuries: Morris was joined on the sidelines by Osborne (shoulder surgery

after one win), starter Alan Benes (just two innings after shoulder problems), outfielder Eric Davis (shoulder surgery, missed three months), outfielder Darren Bragg (knee surgery, out two months) and reliever Scott Radinsky (elbow surgery, sidelined two months).
Notable: Tatis became the first player in major league history to hit two grand slams in one inning, accomplishing the feat on April 23 in Los Angeles. ... Righthander Jose Jimenez pitched a no-hit game—at Arizona on June 25—in his first full season in the majors. ... Bottenfield was the staff's lone double-figure winner. ... Garrett Stephenson made only 12 starts, but he tied for third on the club with six wins. ... Utilityman Joe McEwing set a club rookie record with a 25-game hitting streak and was a constant spark. ... Benes has pitched in just two games for the Cardinals in the past two years.

—RICK HUMMEL

RECORDS

1999 regular-season record: 75-86 (4th in N.L. Central); 38-42 at home; 37-44 on road; 16-25 vs. East; 27-34 vs. N.L. Central; 25-19 vs. West; 7-8 vs. A.L.; 17-29 vs. lefthanded starters; 58-57 vs. righthanded starters; 64-70 on grass; 11-16 on turf; 25-28 in daytime; 50-58 at night; 26-27 in one-run games; 9-8 in extra-inning games; 1-0-2 in doubleheaders.
Team record past five years: 381-409 (.482, ranks 9th in league in that span).

TEAM LEADERS

Batting average: Fernando Tatis (.298).
At-bats: Edgar Renteria (585).
Runs: Mark McGwire (118).
Hits: Edgar Renteria (161).
Total Bases: Mark McGwire (363).
Doubles: Edgar Renteria (36).
Triples: J.D. Drew (6).
Home runs: Mark McGwire (65).
Runs batted in: Mark McGwire (147).
Stolen bases: Edgar Renteria (37).
Slugging percentage: Mark McGwire (.697).
On-base percentage: Mark McGwire (.424).
Wins: Kent Bottenfield (18).

Earned-run average: Kent Bottenfield (3.97).
Complete games: Jose Jimenez, Darren Oliver (2).
Shutouts: Jose Jimenez (2).
Saves: Ricky Bottalico (20).
Innings pitched: Darren Oliver (196.1).
Strikeouts: Kent Bottenfield (124).

GAMES BY POSITION

Catcher: Eli Marrero 96, Alberto Castillo 91, Marcus Jensen 14.
First base: Mark McGwire 151, Eli Marrero 20, David Howard 9, Shawon Dunston 8, Craig Paquette 6, Eduardo Perez 5, Willie McGee 3, Joe McEwing 2.
Second base: Joe McEwing 96, Placido Polanco 66, Adam Kennedy 29, David Howard 9, Craig Paquette 7, Luis Ordaz 1.
Third base: Fernando Tatis 147, Craig Paquette 10, Placido Polanco 9, Joe McEwing 6, Shawon Dunston 5, David Howard 4, Luis Ordaz 1.
Shortstop: Edgar Renteria 151, David Howard 13, Placido Polanco 9, Luis Ordaz 8, Shawon Dunston 7, Joe McEwing 1.
Outfield: Ray Lankford 106, J.D. Drew 98, Willie McGee 89, Darren Bragg 88, Joe McEwing 66, Eric Davis 51, Thomas Howard 48, Craig Paquette 27, Shawon Dunston 23, Eduardo Perez 6, David Howard 5.
Designated hitter: Eric Davis 2, Shawon Dunston 2, Thomas Howard 1, Ray Lankford 1.

TOP DRAFT CHOICES

1a. **Chance Caple,** RHP, Texas A&M U.
1b. **Nick Stocks,** RHP, Florida State Univ.
1c. **Chris Duncan,** 1B, Canyon del Oro H.S., Tucson, Ariz.
2. **Josh Pearce,** RHP, U. of Arizona
3. **B.R. Cook,** RHP, Oregon State U.
4a. **Ben Johnson,** OF, Germantown (Tenn.) H.S.
4b. **Jim Journell,** RHP, U. of Illinois
5. **Charles Williams,** OF, Rice University
6. **Josh Teekel,** RHP, Belaire H.S., Greenwell Springs, La.
7. **Covelli Crisp,** 2B, Los Angeles Pierce J.C.
8. **Shawn Schumacher,** C/3B, Texas A&M University
9. **Damon Thames,** SS, Rice University
10. **Kevin Sprague,** LHP, McNeese State University

SAN DIEGO PADRES
NATIONAL LEAGUE WEST DIVISION

2000 Padres Schedule
Home games shaded. *—All-Star Game at Turner Field (Atlanta).

March
SUN	MON	TUE	WED	THU	FRI	SAT
26	27	28	29	30	31	

April
SUN	MON	TUE	WED	THU	FRI	SAT
						1
2	3 NYM	4	5 NYM	6 NYM	7 MON	8 MON
9 MON	10 ARI	11 ARI	12 ARI	13 ARI	14 HOU	15 HOU
16 HOU	17	18 STL	19 STL	20 STL	21 HOU	22 HOU
23 HOU	24	25 PIT	26 PIT	27 PIT	28 ATL	29 ATL
30 ATL						

May
SUN	MON	TUE	WED	THU	FRI	SAT
	1 FLA	2 FLA	3 FLA	4	5 ARI	6 ARI
7 ARI	8	9 CIN	10 CIN	11 CIN	12 ARI	13 ARI
14 ARI	15	16 FLA	17 FLA	18 FLA	19 ATL	20 ATL
21 ATL	22 NYM	23 NYM	24 NYM	25	26 MON	27 MON
28 MON	29 MIL	30 MIL	31 MIL			

June
SUN	MON	TUE	WED	THU	FRI	SAT
				1	2 SEA	3 SEA
4 SEA	5 OAK	6 OAK	7 OAK	8	9 HOU	10 HOU
11 HOU	12 STL	13 STL	14 STL	15	16 CIN	17 CIN
18 CIN	19 ARI	20 ARI	21 ARI	22	23 CIN	24 CIN
25 CIN	26 LA	27 LA	28 LA	29 LA	30 COL	

July
SUN	MON	TUE	WED	THU	FRI	SAT
						1 COL
2 COL	3 COL	4 LA	5 LA	6 LA	7 TEX	8 TEX
9 TEX	10	11	12 *	13 SEA	14 SEA	15 SEA
16 ANA	17 ANA	18 ANA	19 SF	20 SF	21 COL	22 COL
23 COL	24 SF	25 SF	26 SF	27	28 PIT	29 PIT
30 PIT	31 PHI					

August
SUN	MON	TUE	WED	THU	FRI	SAT
		1 PHI	2	3 CUB	4 CUB	5 CUB
6 CUB	7 PHI	8 PHI	9 PHI	10 PHI	11 FLA	12 FLA
13 FLA	14 ATL	15 ATL	16 ATL	17	18 MON	19 MON
20 MON	21 NYM	22 NYM	23 NYM	24	25 MIL	26 MIL
27 MIL	28 CUB	29 CUB	30 CUB	31 CUB		

September
SUN	MON	TUE	WED	THU	FRI	SAT
					1 PIT	2 PIT
3 PIT	4 MIL	5 MIL	6 MIL	7 SF	8 SF	9 SF
10 SF	11 COL	12 COL	13 COL	14	15 SF	16 SF
17 SF	18	19 COL	20 COL	21 COL	22 LA	23 LA
24 LA	25	26 STL	27 STL	28 STL	29 LA	30 LA

October
SUN	MON	TUE	WED	THU	FRI	SAT
1 LA	2	3	4	5	6	7

2000 SEASON
CLUB DIRECTORY

Chairman
John Moores
President & chief executive officer
Larry Lucchino
Executive v.p./chief operating officer
Jack McGrory
Executive vice president/public affairs
Charles Steinberg
Sr. v.p./baseball operations and g.m.
Kevin Towers
Sr. v.p./corporate development
Michael Dee
Vice president/special counsel
Bob Vizas
Vice president/finance
Bob Wells
Vice president/community relations
Michele Anderson
V.p./Hispanic & multicultural marketing
Enrique Morones
Assistant general manager
Fred Uhlman Jr.
Director/merchandising
Michael Babida
Controller
Steve Fitch
Director/administrative services
Lucy Freeman
Director/ticket operations & services
Dave Gilmore
Director/stadium operations
Mark Guglielmo
Director/player development
Tye Waller
Director/minor league operations
Priscilla Oppenheimer
Director/team travel
Brian Prilaman
Director/public relations
Glenn Geffner

Director/fan services
Tim Katzman
Director/scouting
Brad Sloan
Trainer
Todd Hutcheson
Assistant trainer
Jim Daniel
Strength and conditioning coach
Sam Gannelli
Club physicians
Cliff Colwell
Jan Fronek
Paul Hirshman
Blaine Phillips
Director of professional scouting
Gary Nickels
Major league scouts
Ken Bracey, Ray Crone, Moose Johnson
Advance scout
Jeff Gardner
International supervisor
Bill Clark
Professional scouts
Chas Bolton, Rich Hacker, Ben McLure, Gary Roenicke, Van Smith
Full-time scouts
Miguel Blanco, Joe Bochy, Rich Bordi, Bob Buob, Julio Coronado, Bob Cummings, Takeo Daigo, Lane Decker, Jimmy Dreyer, Leroy Dreyer, Ronquito Garcia, Robert Gutierrez, Chris Gwynn, Andy Hancock, Timothy Harkness, Mike Keenan, William Killian, Steve Leavitt, Don Lyle, Jose Martinez, Tim McWilliam, Juan Melo, Darryl Milne, Rene Mons, Gary Nickels, Chuck Pierce, Jack Pierce, Gene Thompson, Mark Wasinger, Jim Woodward

MINOR LEAGUE AFFILIATES

Class	Team	League	Manager
AAA	Las Vegas	Pacific Coast	Duane Espy
AA	Mobile	Southern	Mike Basso
A	Rancho Cucamonga	California	Tom Le Vasseur
A	Fort Wayne	Midwest	Craig Colbert
Rookie	Idaho Falls	Pioneer	Don Werner
Rookie	Peoria Padres	Arizona	Howard Bushong

BROADCAST INFORMATION

Radio: KOGO-AM (600), KURS-AM (1040, Spanish)
TV: KUSI (Channel 9).
Cable TV: Channel 4 Padres.

SPRING TRAINING

Ballpark (city): Peoria Stadium (Peoria, Ariz.).
Ticket information: 623-878-4337, 800-409-1511.

SPRING TRAINING ROSTER

Manager—Bruce Bochy (15).
Coaches—Greg Booker (38), Tim Flannery (11), Ben Oglivie (24), Rob Picciolo (5), Dave Smith (45), Alan Trammell (3).

No.	PITCHERS	B/T	Ht./Wt.	Born	1999 clubs
40	Almanzar, Carlos	R/R	6-2/200	11-6-73	Las Vegas, San Diego
37	Boehringer, Brian	B/R	6-2/190	1-8-70	San Diego
58	Carlyle, Buddy	L/R	6-3/175	12-21-77	Las Vegas, San Diego
31	Clement, Matt	R/R	6-3/195	8-12-74	San Diego
39	Cunnane, Will	R/R	6-2/175	4-24-74	Las Vegas, San Diego
43	Guzman, Domingo	R/R	6-0/210	4-5-75	Mobile, San Diego
41	Hitchcock, Sterling	L/L	6-1/192	4-29-71	San Diego
51	Hoffman, Trevor	R/R	6-0/205	10-13-67	San Diego
46	Loewer, Carlton	R/R	6-6/211	9-24-73	Philadelphia, Gulf Coast Phillies, Clearwater
60	Lopez, Rodrigo	R/R	6-1/180	12-14-75	Mobile
34	Meadows, Brian	R/R	6-4/200	11-21-75	Florida
27	Montgomery, Steve	R/R	6-4/200	12-25-70	Scranton/Wilkes-Barre, Philadelphia
48	Myers, Randy	L/L	6-1/210	9-19-62	DID NOT PLAY
55	Serafini, Daniel	R/L	6-3/210	1-25-74	Chicago N.L., Iowa
64	Serrano, Wascar	R/R	6-2/178	6-2-78	Rancho Cucamonga, Mobile
36	Wall, Donne	R/R	6-1/205	7-11-67	San Diego
50	Whisenant, Matt	R/L	6-3/215	6-8-71	Kansas City, San Diego
18	Williams, Woody	R/R	6-1/195	8-19-66	San Diego

No.	CATCHERS	B/T	Ht./Wt.	Born	1999 clubs
13	Davis, Ben	B/R	6-4/215	3-10-77	Las Vegas, San Diego
7	Gonzalez, Wiki	R/R	5-11/184	5-17-74	Mobile, Las Vegas, San Diego
9	Hernandez, Carlos	R/R	5-11/215	5-24-67	DID NOT PLAY

No.	INFIELDERS	B/T	Ht./Wt.	Born	1999 clubs
29	Boone, Bret	R/R	5-10/180	4-6-69	Atlanta
10	Gomez, Chris	R/R	6-1/195	6-16-71	San Diego, Las Vegas
2	Jackson, Damian	R/R	5-11/185	8-6-73	San Diego
12	Magadan, Dave	L/R	6-4/215	9-30-62	San Diego
23	Nevin, Phil	R/R	6-2/231	1-19-71	Las Vegas, San Diego
14	Newhan, David	L/R	5-10/180	9-7-73	Las Vegas, San Diego

No.	OUTFIELDERS	B/T	Ht./Wt.	Born	1999 clubs
26	Darr, Mike	L/R	6-3/205	3-21-76	Las Vegas, San Diego
25	DeHaan, Kory	L/R	6-2/187	7-16-76	Lynchburg, Altoona
19	Gwynn, Tony	L/L	5-11/203	5-9-60	San Diego
30	Klesko, Ryan	L/L	6-3/220	6-12-71	Atlanta
21	Matthews, Gary	B/R	6-3/200	8-25-74	Las Vegas, San Diego
8	Owens, Eric	R/R	6-0/198	2-3-71	San Diego
28	Rivera, Ruben	R/R	6-3/200	11-14-73	San Diego
53	Tucci, Peter	R/R	6-2/205	10-8-75	Mobile
29	Vander Wal, John	L/L	6-2/197	4-29-66	San Diego

BALLPARK INFORMATION

Ballpark (capacity, surface)
Qualcomm Stadium (56,133, grass)

Address
P.O. Box 2000
San Diego, CA 92112-2000

Business phone
619-881-6500

Ticket information
888-723-7379

Ticket prices
$18 (club level, field level, IF)
$16 (plaza level/IF)
$14 (plaza level, loge level)
$11 (press level)
$8 (grandstand)
$7 (view level/IF)
$6 (view level)
$5 (RF & LF bleachers, view level)

Field dimensions (from home plate)
To left field at foul line, 327 feet
To center field, 405 feet
To right field at foul line, 330 feet

First game played
April 8, 1969 (Padres 2, Astros 1)

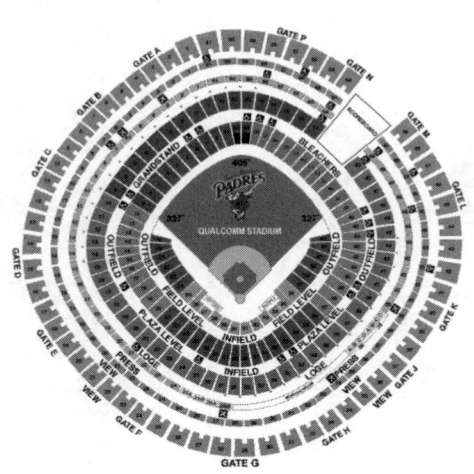

1999 REVIEW
DAY BY DAY

Date	Opp.	Res.	Score	(inn.*)	Hits	Opp. hits	Winning pitcher	Losing pitcher	Save	Record	Pos.	GB
4-4	Col.§	L	2-8		6	18	Kile	Ashby		0-1	5th	1.0
4-6	Col.	W	4-3		9	9	Hitchcock	Astacio	Hoffman	1-1	T3rd	1.0
4-7	Col.	W	2-1		8	8	Rivera	Jones		2-1	3rd	1.0
4-8	At S.F	L	4-12		9	16	Estes	Spencer		2-2	T3rd	2.0
4-9	At S.F	L	3-8		8	11	Brock	Clement		2-3	T3rd	3.0
4-10	At S.F	W	11-1		12	7	Ashby	Gardner		3-3	3rd	2.0
4-11	At S.F	L	6-8		8	11	Johnstone	Rivera	Nen	3-4	3rd	3.0
4-12	At Col.	W	8-5	(11)	13	10	Wall	Veres	Reyes	4-4	3rd	2.5
4-15	At Col.	L	4-6		4	10	Bohanon	Clement	Veres	4-5	3rd	2.5
4-16	L.A.	W	3-0		11	5	Ashby	Brown		5-5	3rd	1.5
4-17	L.A.	L	3-7		9	8	Park	Reyes		5-6	3rd	2.5
4-18	L.A.	W	4-3		8	8	Miceli	Masaoka	Hoffman	6-6	3rd	1.5
4-19	Pit.	L	0-3		5	6	Schourek	Spencer	Christiansen	6-7	4th	2.5
4-20	Pit.	L	3-7	(10)	8	10	Williams	Hoffman		6-8	5th	2.5
4-21	Pit.	W	2-0		8	3	Ashby	Schmidt	Hoffman	7-8	4th	2.5
4-23	Ari.	L	6-10		10	11	Benes	Hitchcock		7-9	5th	3.0
4-24	Ari.	W	7-2		11	7	Williams	Daal		8-9	4th	3.0
4-25	Ari.	L	3-5	(11)	5	12	Swindell	Miceli	Olson	8-10	4th	4.0
4-27	At N.Y.	W	6-2		8	5	Ashby	Yoshii		9-10	4th	4.0
4-28	At N.Y.	L	3-4		6	11	Wendell	Hoffman		9-11	4th	5.0
4-29	At N.Y.	L	5-8		11	6	Cook	Boehringer	Franco	9-12	5th	6.0
4-30	At Chi.	L	5-6		10	9	Mulholland	Spencer	Beck	9-13	5th	6.0
5-1	At Chi.	L	1-2		3	7	Tapani	Clement	Heredia	9-14	5th	6.0
5-2	At Chi.	L	2-3		6	12	Myers	Rivera	Beck	9-15	5th	6.0
5-3	At Phi.	W	9-3		14	13	Hitchcock	Ogea		10-15	5th	5.0
5-4	At Phi.	L	0-3		5	4	Loewer	Williams		10-16	5th	6.0
5-5	At Phi.	L	1-11		3	14	Byrd	Spencer		10-17	5th	6.0
5-7	Atl.	W	4-3		9	4	Boehringer	Rocker	Hoffman	11-17	5th	6.0
5-8	Atl.	L	1-11		8	14	Glavine	Ashby		11-18	5th	7.0
5-9	Atl.	W	5-0		12	5	Hitchcock	Maddux		12-18	5th	6.0
5-10	Fla.	W	7-5		12	8	Miceli	Alfonseca	Hoffman	13-18	5th	6.0
5-11	Fla.	L	4-5		10	15	Dempster	Spencer	Mantei	13-19	5th	6.0
5-12	Fla.	W	8-7		10	15	Wall	Edmondson	Hoffman	14-19	5th	6.0
5-14	At Cin.	W	7-3		8	9	Ashby	Neagle	Hoffman	15-19	5th	5.0
5-15	At Cin.	L	2-6		8	4	Parris	Hitchcock	Williamson	15-20	5th	5.0
5-16	At Cin.	L	0-3		4	6	Tomko	Williams	Williamson	15-21	5th	6.0
5-18	StL.	L	2-5		4	9	Oliver	Clement	Bottalico	15-22	5th	6.5
5-19	StL.	W	7-6		8	9	Boehringer	Bottalico		16-22	4th	5.5
5-20	StL.	L	4-6		9	9	Bottenfield	Hitchcock	Bottalico	16-23	5th	6.0
5-21	Cin.	W	5-4		10	10	Williams	Tomko	Hoffman	17-23	5th	6.0
5-22	Cin.	L	0-3		3	9	Harnisch	Murray		17-24	5th	7.0
5-23	Cin.	L	2-6		2	7	Avery	Clement	Williamson	17-25	5th	7.0
5-24	At Ari.	L	5-6		13	13	Benes	Ashby	Olson	17-26	5th	7.5
5-25	At Ari.	L	0-4		6	6	Johnson	Hitchcock		17-27	5th	8.5
5-26	At Ari.	L	2-3	(11)	8	8	Olson	Miceli		17-28	5th	9.5
5-28	At Mil.	W	10-8		13	11	Reyes	Eldred	Hoffman	18-28	5th	8.5
5-29	At Mil.	W	12-3		15	10	Clement	Woodard		19-28	5th	8.5
5-30	At Mil.	L	3-10		10	11	Abbott	Hitchcock		19-29	5th	9.5
5-31	At Mil.	L	2-8		5	14	Nomo	Williams		19-30	5th	10.5
6-1	At Chi.	W	1-0	(6)	4	3	Ashby	Trachsel		20-30	5th	9.5
6-2	At Chi.	L	8-9		11	14	Sanders	Hoffman		20-31	5th	10.5
6-3	At Chi.	L	2-7		10	7	Tapani	Clement		20-32	5th	11.0
6-4	Sea.	W	3-2		6	7	Wall	Paniagua	Hoffman	21-32	5th	11.0
6-5	Sea.	W	3-2	(10)	7	9	Reyes	Mesa		22-32	5th	10.0
6-6	Sea.	L	1-4		4	7	Garcia	Ashby	Paniagua	22-33	5th	11.0
6-8	Oak.	W	5-3		11	8	Wall	Groom	Hoffman	23-33	5th	9.5
6-9	Oak.	L	0-3		4	8	Haynes	Clement	Taylor	23-34	5th	10.5
6-10	Oak.	W	2-1		7	4	Hitchcock	Heredia	Hoffman	24-34	5th	10.0
6-11	At Hou.	L	1-2		4	5	Bergman	Williams	Wagner	24-35	5th	11.0
6-12	At Hou.	L	2-3		7	7	Lima	Wall	Wagner	24-36	5th	11.0
6-13	At Hou.	L	3-4		8	9	Reynolds	Murray	Wagner	24-37	5th	11.5
6-15	Phi.	W	6-1		11	6	Clement	Ogea		25-37	5th	12.0
6-16	Phi.	L	2-4		7	9	Wolf	Hitchcock	Gomes	25-38	5th	13.0
6-17	Phi.	L	5-7		12	12	Byrd	Williams	Gomes	25-39	5th	13.5
6-18	Pit.	W	4-2		8	8	Boehringer	Silva	Hoffman	26-39	5th	12.5
6-19	Pit.	W	5-4		10	5	Cunnane	Schmidt	Hoffman	27-39	5th	12.5
6-20	Pit.	W	6-3		12	8	Clement	Ritchie	Hoffman	28-39	5th	11.5
6-22	At L.A.	W	4-1		7	7	Hitchcock	Park	Hoffman	29-39	5th	10.0
6-23	At L.A.	W	6-2		7	5	Williams	Valdes	Hoffman	30-39	5th	9.0
6-24	At L.A.	W	2-1		6	5	Ashby	Dreifort	Miceli	31-39	5th	9.0
6-25	Col.	W	10-1		10	7	Boehringer	Bohanon		32-39	5th	8.0
6-26	Col.	W	13-6		9	10	Clement	Brownson		33-39	5th	7.0
6-27	Col.	W	5-3		8	7	Hitchcock	Kile	Hoffman	34-39	4th	7.0

Date	Opp.	Res.	Score	(inn.*)	Hits	Opp. hits	Winning pitcher	Losing pitcher	Save	Record	Pos.	GB
6-28	Col.	W	8-7		10	14	Williams	Astacio	Hoffman	35-39	3rd	6.5
6-29	L.A.	W	4-3	(12)	13	5	Wall	Maddux		36-39	3rd	5.5
6-30	L.A.	W	11-2		14	8	Boehringer	Brown		37-39	3rd	4.5
7-1	L.A.	W	6-3		10	5	Clement	Dreifort	Hoffman	38-39	3rd	4.5
7-2	At Col.	W	15-3		19	8	Hitchcock	Astacio		39-39	3rd	4.5
7-3†	At Col.	L	10-12		13	17	Ramirez	Williams	Veres	39-40		
7-3‡	At Col.	L	6-8		9	15	Jones	Murray	Veres	39-41	3rd	6.0
7-4	At Col.	W	11-0		17	6	Ashby	Bohanon		40-41	3rd	5.0
7-5	S.F	L	1-4		6	9	Ortiz	Boehringer		40-42	3rd	6.0
7-6	S.F	L	9-10		15	10	Estes	Clement	Johnstone	40-43	3rd	7.0
7-7	S.F	W	5-2		7	10	Hitchcock	Brock	Hoffman	41-43	3rd	6.0
7-9	Tex.	L	2-7		9	8	Sele	Williams		41-44	3rd	7.0
7-10	Tex.	W	5-4		8	9	Wall	Wetteland		42-44	3rd	7.0
7-11	Tex.	W	6-2		11	4	Miceli	Loaiza		43-44	3rd	6.0
7-15	At Sea.	W	3-2		7	8	Cunnane	Mesa	Miceli	44-44	3rd	5.0
7-16	At Sea.	W	2-1		8	9	Hitchcock	Fassero	Hoffman	45-44	3rd	4.0
7-17	At Sea.	L	1-9		5	11	Garcia	Williams		45-45	3rd	5.0
7-18	At Ana.	W	6-3		14	10	Boehringer	Fyhrie	Hoffman	46-45	3rd	4.0
7-19	At Ana.	W	4-1	(10)	8	9	Miceli	Hasegawa	Hoffman	47-45	3rd	3.0
7-20	At Ana.	W	2-1		5	6	Ashby	Petkovsek	Hoffman	48-45	3rd	2.0
7-21	At S.F	L	2-10		7	12	Ortiz	Hitchcock		48-46	3rd	3.0
7-22	At S.F	W	8-7		11	7	Williams	Rueter	Hoffman	49-46	3rd	2.0
7-23	At Hou.	L	4-7		8	7	Hampton	Wall		49-47	3rd	3.5
7-24	At Hou.	L	2-5		8	10	Holt	Clement	Wagner	49-48	3rd	4.0
7-25	At Hou.	L	2-5		8	11	Reynolds	Ashby		49-49	3rd	4.0
7-26	Ari.	L	0-2		6	7	Reynoso	Hitchcock	Mantei	49-50	3rd	5.0
7-27	Ari.	L	3-4		7	10	Olson	Reyes	Mantei	49-51	3rd	6.0
7-28	Ari.	L	4-7		6	10	Daal	Boehringer	Plesac	49-52	3rd	7.0
7-30	Hou.	L	1-5		6	8	Reynolds	Clement		49-53	3rd	8.0
7-31	Hou.	L	5-8		7	10	Henry	Miceli		49-54	3rd	9.0
8-1	Hou.	W	10-3		15	6	Hitchcock	Lima		50-54	3rd	8.0
8-2	At StL.	L	5-6		10	9	Bottenfield	Williams	Croushore	50-55	3rd	9.0
8-3	At StL.	L	0-6		4	9	Oliver	Boehringer		50-56	3rd	9.0
8-4	At StL.	L	6-7		6	13	Slocumb	Wall	Croushore	50-57	3rd	10.0
8-5	At StL.	W	10-3		10	6	Ashby	Luebbers	Hoffman	51-57	3rd	9.5
8-6	At Mon.	W	12-10		17	9	Hitchcock	Smith	Hoffman	52-57	3rd	8.5
8-7	At Mon.	L	1-3		4	8	Hermanson	Williams	Urbina	52-58	3rd	9.5
8-8	At Mon.	L	2-4		7	13	Kline	Reyes	Urbina	52-59	3rd	10.5
8-9	At Mon.	L	0-8		7	11	Powell	Clement		52-60	3rd	11.5
8-10	At N.Y.	L	3-4		9	15	Wendell	Ashby	Benitez	52-61	3rd	12.5
8-11	At N.Y.	L	5-12		6	14	Mahomes	Hitchcock		52-62	3rd	13.5
8-12	At N.Y.	L	3-9		5	11	Leiter	Williams		52-63	T3rd	14.0
8-13	Fla.	L	3-4		10	13	Meadows	Boehringer	Alfonseca	52-64	T3rd	14.0
8-14	Fla.	W	6-4		10	9	Clement	Sanchez	Hoffman	53-64	3rd	13.0
8-15	Fla.	W	7-6		15	10	Ashby	Springer	Hoffman	54-64	3rd	13.0
8-16	N.Y.	L	3-4	(10)	2	10	Cook	Cunnane	Benitez	54-65	3rd	14.0
8-17	N.Y.	W	3-2		5	5	Williams	Leiter	Hoffman	55-65	3rd	14.0
8-18	N.Y.	L	1-9		6	15	Yoshii	Spencer		55-66	3rd	15.0
8-20	At Atl.	L	3-4	(11)	6	7	Remlinger	Reyes		55-67	T3rd	15.0
8-21	At Atl.	L	2-6		8	10	Maddux	Ashby		55-68	T3rd	16.0
8-22	At Atl.	L	2-3		6	9	Rocker	Miceli		55-69	5th	17.0
8-23	At Phi.	W	7-6		12	9	Williams	Ogea	Hoffman	56-69	5th	17.0
8-24	At Phi.	L	2-18		5	22	Byrd	Spencer		56-70	5th	18.0
8-25	At Phi.	L	1-15		6	14	Person	Clement		56-71	5th	19.0
8-26	Mil.	W	4-3		8	8	Ashby	Coppinger	Hoffman	57-71	4th	19.0
8-27	Mil.	W	8-7		9	15	Whiteside	Wickman		58-71	4th	18.0
8-28	Mil.	L	4-6		9	11	Nomo	Williams	Wickman	58-72	5th	19.0
8-29	Mil.	W	5-4	(10)	10	3	Hoffman	Wickman		59-72	5th	19.0
8-30	Chi.	W	8-4		10	11	Wall	Heredia		60-72	4th	19.0
8-31	Chi.	W	7-3		9	5	Ashby	Bowie		61-72	4th	18.0
9-1	Chi.	L	0-1		4	2	Trachsel	Hitchcock	Adams	61-73	4th	18.0
9-3	At Fla.	W	6-3		9	8	Williams	Burnett	Hoffman	62-73	4th	17.0
9-4	At Fla.	L	4-6		3	6	Fernandez	Carlyle	Alfonseca	62-74	4th	18.0
9-5	At Fla.	W	5-2		9	6	Clement	Nunez	Hoffman	63-74	4th	18.0
9-6	At Pit.	W	4-3		6	8	Ashby	Ritchie	Hoffman	64-74	4th	17.5
9-7	At Pit.	L	1-3		4	7	Schmidt	Hitchcock	Silva	64-75	4th	18.5
9-8	At Pit.	W	7-4	(10)	11	10	Hoffman	Wilkins		65-75	4th	18.5
9-9	Mon.	W	10-3		17	6	Carlyle	Vazquez		66-75	3rd	17.5
9-10	Mon.	W	10-3		10	8	Clement	Powell		67-75	3rd	17.5
9-11	Mon.	L	4-5		10	7	Thurman	Ashby	Urbina	67-76	3rd	18.5
9-12	Mon.	L	4-8		12	12	Hermanson	Hitchcock	Urbina	67-77	3rd	19.5
9-13	Atl.	W	3-0		11	4	Williams	Mulholland	Hoffman	68-77	3rd	19.5
9-14	Atl.	L	4-11		7	14	Millwood	Carlyle		68-78	3rd	20.5
9-15	Atl.	W	4-1		9	4	Clement	Smoltz	Hoffman	69-78	3rd	19.5
9-17	S.F	L	2-4		8	8	Nathan	Ashby	Nen	69-79	3rd	19.5
9-18	S.F	W	11-5		13	8	Hitchcock	Gardner		70-79	3rd	19.5

Date	Opp.	Res.	Score	(inn.*)	Hits	Opp. hits	Winning pitcher	Losing pitcher	Save	Record	Pos.	GB
9-19	S.F	W	6-3		9	9	Williams	Estes	Hoffman	71-79	3rd	19.5
9-20	Cin.	L	1-12		3	15	Neagle	Carlyle		71-80	3rd	19.5
9-21	Cin.	W	6-2		9	7	Clement	Williamson		72-80	3rd	19.5
9-22	Cin.	L	3-4		9	8	Villone	Ashby	Graves	72-81	3rd	20.5
9-24	At L.A.	L	1-5		6	10	Brown	Hitchcock		72-82	4th	21.5
9-25	At L.A.	W	3-2		5	5	Williams	Herges	Hoffman	73-82	T3rd	21.5
9-26	At L.A.	L	7-10		6	13	Checo	Miceli		73-83	4th	22.5
9-29†	At StL.	L	3-4		5	8	Oliver	Wall	Painter	73-84		
9-29‡	At StL.	L	5-6	(10)	10	9	Acevedo	Guzman		73-85	4th	24.0
9-30	At Ari.	L	3-5		6	11	Johnson	Hitchcock	Mantei	73-86	4th	25.0
10-1	At Ari.	W	6-1		12	6	Williams	Stottlemyre		74-86	4th	24.0
10-2	At Ari.	L	5-7		7	7	Kim	Whisenant	Mantei	74-87	4th	25.0
10-3	At Ari.	L	3-10		7	11	Anderson	Murray		74-88	4th	26.0

Monthly records: April (9-13), May (10-17), June (18-9), July (12-15), August (12-18), September (12-14), October (1-2).
*Innings, if other than nine. † First game of a doubleheader. ‡ Second game of a doubleheader. §At Monterrey, Mex.

HIGHLIGHTS

High point: A franchise-record 14-game winning streak from June 18 through July 2. Eleven of the victories were against division rivals Los Angeles and Colorado.

Low point: Rather than begin the season at home, where San Diegans wanted to celebrate the franchise's World Series season of 1998, the club agreed to play its opener in Monterrey, Mexico. Pitcher Andy Ashby never got a good feel for the mound in Monterrey and was quickly knocked out in an 8-2 loss to the Rockies.

Turning point: When catcher Carlos Hernandez ruptured an Achilles' tendon in an exhibition game on March 17. The Padres lost an inspirational leader, a competent hitter and a solid defender. Also, after closing within two games of first place on July 22, the Padres lost twice on July 23 at Houston, touching off a nine-game losing streak.

Most valuable player: Trevor Hoffman, who converted 40 of 43 save chances. The intimidating righthander was 31-for-31 to finish the season.

Most valuable pitcher: Hoffman. After signing a four-year, $32 million contract in spring training, Hoffman held opponents to a .197 batting average and finished second in the league in saves. He earned a win or a save in 57 percent of the team's victories.

Most improved player: Third baseman Phil Nevin. Acquired from the Angels in March, he hit .269 with 27 doubles, 24 home runs and 85 RBIs. Batting in the cleanup spot, he hit 18 homers in 72 games.

Most pleasant surprise: Lefthanded reliever Matt Whisenant, who was signed as a free agent on August 20. He posted a 2.03 ERA in his first 17 appearances.

Biggest disappointment: Signed in the offseason to a guarantee worth about $7 million, veteran first baseman Wally Joyner, bothered by a bad shoulder, batted .195 on the road and only .248 overall.

Key injuries: Hernandez missed the entire season. Leadoff man Quilvio Veras sat out 30 games because of leg ailments. Shortstop Chris Gomez, who had arthroscopic surgery on both knees in June, appeared in only 76 games. A pulled calf muscle twice sent eight-time batting champion Tony Gwynn to the disabled list.

Notable: Gwynn became the 22nd player in major league history to get 3,000 hits, reaching the milestone on August 6 in Montreal. By season's end, he was 18th on the all-time list with 3,067. ... The team's 28-53 road record was the worst in the majors. ... Ruben Rivera had the dubious distinction of batting less than .200 in a season in which he had more than 400 at-bats. Finishing at .195, the outfielder did contribute 23 homers. ... Outfielder Reggie Sanders, who hadn't reached the 20-homer plateau since 1995 (when he was with the Reds), hit a club-high 26. ... Ashby achieved the second-best victory total of his career, winning 14 games. He won a career-high 17 in 1998. ... The Padres' .252 team batting average was the lowest in the majors.
—TOM KRASOVIC

RECORDS

1999 regular-season record: 74-88 (4th in N.L. West); 46-35 at home; 28-53 on road; 18-26 vs. East; 20-33 vs. Central; 25-25 vs. N.L. West; 11-4 vs. A.L.; 15-32 vs. lefthanded starters; 59-56 vs. righthanded starters; 68-72 on grass; 6-16 on turf; 24-32 in daytime; 50-56 at night; 28-25 in one-run games; 6-6 in extra-inning games; 0-2-0 in doubleheaders.

Team record past five years: 409-383 (.516, ranks 6th in league in that span).

TEAM LEADERS

Batting average: Reggie Sanders (.285).
At-bats: Reggie Sanders (478).
Runs: Quilvio Veras (95).
Hits: Tony Gwynn (139).
Total Bases: Reggie Sanders (252).
Doubles: Tony Gwynn, Phil Nevin (27).
Triples: Reggie Sanders (7).
Home runs: Reggie Sanders (26).
Runs batted in: Phil Nevin (85).
Stolen bases: Reggie Sanders (36).
Slugging percentage: Reggie Sanders (.527).
On-base percentage: Reggie Sanders (.376).
Wins: Andy Ashby (14).
Earned-run average: Andy Ashby (3.80).
Complete games: Andy Ashby (4).
Shutouts: Andy Ashby (3).
Saves: Trevor Hoffman (40).

Innings pitched: Woody Williams (208.1).
Strikeouts: Sterling Hitchcock (194).

GAMES BY POSITION

Catcher: Ben Davis 74, Greg Myers 41, Phil Nevin 31, Jim Leyritz 24, Wiki Gonzalez 17.
First base: Wally Joyner 105, Dave Magadan 42, John Vander Wal 28, Jim Leyritz 19, Eric Owens 12, Phil Nevin 11, Carlos Baerga 2, Carlos Garcia 1.
Second base: Quilvio Veras 119, Damian Jackson 21, Ed Giovanola 19, David Newhan 19, Carlos Baerga 13, Eric Owens 1.
Third base: Phil Nevin 67, Dave Magadan 52, George Arias 50, Ed Giovanola 25, Carlos Baerga 13, Carlos Garcia 4, Eric Owens 4, Jim Leyritz 1, David Newhan 1.
Shortstop: Damian Jackson 100, Chris Gomez 75, Ed Giovanola 7.
Outfield: Ruben Rivera 143, Reggie Sanders 129, Eric Owens 116, Tony Gwynn 104, John Vander Wal 48, Mike Darr 22, Gary Matthews Jr. 17, Phil Nevin 13, Damian Jackson 3.
Designated hitter: Tony Gwynn 2, Wally Joyner 1, Carlos Baerga 1, Reggie Sanders 1, John Vander Wal 1, Phil Nevin 1.

TOP DRAFT CHOICES

1a. **Vince Faison**, OF, Toombs County H.S., Lyons, Ga.
1b. **Gerik Baxter**, RHP, Edmonds-Woodway H.S., Edmonds, Wash.
1c. **Omar Ortiz**, RHP, U. of Texas-Pan American
1d. **Casey Burns**, RHP, U. of Richmond
1e. **Mike Bynum**, LHP, U. of North Carolina
1f. **Nick Trzesniak**, C, Andrew H.S., Tinley Park, Ill.
2. **Alberto Concepcion**, C, El Segundo (Calif.) H.S.
3. **Josh Vitek**, RHP, Fayetteville (Tex.) H.S.
4. **Jason Moore**, SS, U. of Texas
5a. **Chris Heck**, LHP, Clemson University
5b. **Mike Thompson**, RHP, Lamar (Colo.) H.S.
6. **Blair DeHart**, RHP, James Madison U.
7. **John Scheschuk**, 1B, Texas A&M U.
8. **Todd Donovan**, OF, Siena College
9. **John Puccinelli**, SS/3B, Notre Dame H.S., Toluca Lake, Calif.
10. **Todd Shiyuk**, LHP, U. of Alabama-Huntsville

SAN FRANCISCO GIANTS
NATIONAL LEAGUE WEST DIVISION

2000 Giants Schedule
Home games shaded. | —All-Star Game at Turner Field (Atlanta).

March
SUN	MON	TUE	WED	THU	FRI	SAT
26	27	28	29	30	31	

April
SUN	MON	TUE	WED	THU	FRI	SAT
						1
2	3 FLA	4 FLA	5 FLA	6 FLA	7 ATL	8 ATL
9 ATL	10	11 LA	12 LA	13 LA	14 ARI	15 ARI
16 ARI	17	18 CIN	19 CIN	20 CIN	21 ARI	22 ARI
23 ARI	24	25 FLA	26 FLA	27	28 MON	29 MON
30 MON						

May
SUN	MON	TUE	WED	THU	FRI	SAT
	1 NYM	2 NYM	3 NYM	4 NYM	5 COL	6 COL
7 COL	8 STL	9 STL	10 STL	11	12 COL	13 COL
14 COL	15	16 ATL	17 ATL	18 ATL	19 MIL	20 MIL
21 MIL	22	23 MON	24 MON	25 MON	26 CUB	27 CUB
28 CUB	29 PHI	30 PHI	31 PHI			

June
SUN	MON	TUE	WED	THU	FRI	SAT
				1	2 OAK	3 OAK
4 OAK	5 ANA	6 ANA	7 ANA	8	9 SEA	10 SEA
11 SEA	12 CIN	13 CIN	14 CIN	15	16 HOU	17 HOU
18 HOU	19	20 STL	21 STL	22 STL	23 HOU	24 HOU
25 HOU	26 COL	27 COL	28 COL	29 COL	30 LA	

July
SUN	MON	TUE	WED	THU	FRI	SAT
						1 LA
2 LA	3	4 COL	5 COL	6 COL	7 STL	8 STL
9 STL	10	11	* 12	13 OAK	14 OAK	15 OAK
16 TEX	17 TEX	18 TEX	19 SD	20 SD	21 LA	22 LA
23 LA	24 SD	25 SD	26 SD	27	28 CUB	29 CUB
30 CUB	31 MIL					

August
SUN	MON	TUE	WED	THU	FRI	SAT
		1 MIL	2 MIL	3 PIT	4 PIT	5 PIT
6 PIT	7 MIL	8 MIL	9 MIL	10	11 NYM	12 NYM
13 NYM	14 NYM	15 MON	16 MON	17 MON	18 ATL	19 ATL
20 ATL	21 FLA	22 FLA	23 FLA	24	25 PHI	26 PHI
27 PHI	28 PIT	29 PIT	30 PIT	31 PIT		

September
SUN	MON	TUE	WED	THU	FRI	SAT
					1 CUB	2 CUB
3 CUB	4 PHI	5 PHI	6 PHI	7 SD	8 SD	9 SD
10 SD	11 HOU	12 HOU	13 HOU	14	15 SD	16 SD
17 SD	18 CIN	19 CIN	20 CIN	21 ARI	22 ARI	23 ARI
24 ARI	25	26 LA	27 LA	28 LA	29 ARI	30 ARI

October
SUN	MON	TUE	WED	THU	FRI	SAT
1 ARI	2	3	4	5	6	7

2000 SEASON
CLUB DIRECTORY

President and managing general partner
Peter A. Magowan
Executive vice president/COO
Larry Baer
Senior v.p. and general manager
Brian Sabean
Special assistant to the general manager
Ron Perranoski
Vice president and assistant g.m.
Ned Colletti
Vice president of player personnel
Dick Tidrow
Director of player development
Jack Hiatt
Coordinator of international operations
Rick Ragazzo
Sr. v.p. and chief financial officer
John Yee
Sr. v.p., ballpark operations/security
Jorge Costa
Vice president, communications
Bob Rose
Sr. vice president, corporate marketing
Mario Alioto
Sr. v.p., consumer marketing
Tom McDonald
General manager, retail
Connie Kullberg
Director of ballpark operations
Gene Telucci
Vice president, ticket services
Russ Stanley

Director of travel
Reggie Younger Jr.
Sr. vice president and general counsel
Jack Bair
Media relations manager
Jim Moorehead
National cross-checker
Randy Waddill
Eastern cross-checker
Paul Turco
Western cross-checker
Doug Mapson
Major league advance scout
Pat Dobson
Major league scout
Cal Emery
Special assignment scouts
Joe DiCarlo, Stan Saleski, Bob Hartsfield
Scouts
Mateo Alou, Steve Arnieri, Jose Cassino, Dick Cole, Joe DiCarlo, Pat Dobson, Charlie Gonzales, Tom Korenek, Doug Mapson, Alan Marr, Doug McMillan, Bobby Myrick, Matt Nerland, Bo Osborne, Luis Pena, Carlos Ramirez, Stan Saleski, Bienvenido Sanchez, John Shafer, Joe Strain, Todd Thomas, Alex Torres, Glenn Tufts, Paul Turco, Ciro Villalobos, Randy Waddill, Darren Wittcke, Tom Zimmer

MINOR LEAGUE AFFILIATES

Class	Team	League	Manager
AAA	Fresno	Pacific Coast	Shane Turner
AA	Shreveport	Texas	Bill Hayes
A	San Jose	California	Keith Comstock
A	Bakersfield	California	Lenn Sakata
Rookie	Salem-Keizer	Northwest	Fred Stanley
Rookie	Giants	Arizona	To be announced

BROADCAST INFORMATION

Radio: KNBR-AM (680).
TV: KTVU-TV (Channel 2).
Cable TV: FOX Sports Net.

SPRING TRAINING

Ballpark (city): Scottsdale Stadium (Scottsdale, Ariz.).
Ticket information: 602-990-7972 or 602-784-4444.

SPRING TRAINING ROSTER

Manager— Dusty Baker (12).
Coaches—Gene Clines (20), Sonny Jackson (16), Juan Lopez (59), Dave Righetti (19), Robby Thompson (9), Ron Wotus (10).

No.	PITCHERS	B/T	Ht./Wt.	Born	1999 clubs
37	Del Toro, Miguel	R/R	6-1/180	6-22-72	San Francisco, Fresno
56	Embree, Alan	L/L	6-2/190	1-23-70	San Francisco
55	Estes, Shawn	L/L	6-2/192	2-18-73	San Francisco
26	Gardner, Mark	R/R	6-1/220	3-1-62	San Francisco, San Jose
61	Hernandez, Livan	R/R	6-2/225	2-20-75	Florida, San Francisco
49	Johnstone, John	R/R	6-3/210	11-25-68	San Francisco
	Maurer, David	R/L	6-2/205	2-23-75	Mobile
36	Nathan, Joe	R/R	6-4/195	11-22-74	Shreveport, San Francisco, Fresno
31	Nen, Robb	R/R	6-5/215	11-28-69	San Francisco
48	Ortiz, Russ	R/R	6-1/210	6-5-74	San Francisco
	Ray, Ken	R/R	6-2/200	11-27-74	Wichita, Omaha, Kansas City
47	Rodriguez, Felix	R/R	6-1/190	12-5-72	San Francisco
46	Rueter, Kirk	L/L	6-3/205	12-1-70	San Francisco

No.	CATCHERS	B/T	Ht./Wt.	Born	1999 clubs
5	Estalella, Robert	R/R	6-1/205	8-23-74	Clearwater, Scranton/Wilkes-Barre, Philadelphia
33	Mirabelli, Doug	R/R	6-1/218	10-18-70	Fresno, San Francisco
51	Torrealba, Yorvit	R/R	5-11/180	7-19-78	Shreveport, Fresno, San Jose

No.	INFIELDERS	B/T	Ht./Wt.	Born	1999 clubs
35	Aurilia, Rich	R/R	6-1/185	9-2-71	San Francisco
18	Canizaro, Jay	R/R	5-9/178	7-4-73	Fresno, San Francisco
52	Castro, Nelson	R/R	5-10/190	6-4-76	Lake Elsinore
57	Crespo, Felipe	B/R	5-11/200	3-5-73	Fresno
62	Delgado, Wilson	B/R	5-11/160	7-15-75	Fresno, San Francisco
53	Feliz, Pedro	R/R	6-1/195	4-27-77	Shreveport
21	Kent, Jeff	R/R	6-1/205	3-7-68	San Francisco
34	Martinez, Ramon E.	R/R	6-1/187	10-10-72	San Francisco, Fresno
22	Minor, Damon	L/L	6-7/230	1-9-75	Shreveport
32	Mueller, Bill	B/R	5-10/180	3-17-71	San Francisco, Fresno
6	Snow, J.T.	L/L	6-2/205	2-26-68	San Francisco

No.	OUTFIELDERS	B/T	Ht./Wt.	Born	1999 clubs
7	Benard, Marvin	L/L	5-9/185	1-20-70	San Francisco
25	Bonds, Barry	L/L	6-2/210	7-24-64	San Francisco
23	Burks, Ellis	R/R	6-2/205	9-11-64	San Francisco
8	Murray, Calvin	R/R	5-11/190	7-30-71	Fresno, San Francisco
1	Rios, Armando	L/L	5-9/185	9-13-71	Fresno, San Francisco

BALLPARK INFORMATION

Ballpark (capacity, surface)
Pacific Bell Park (40,800, grass)

Address
24 Willie Mays Plaza
San Francisco, CA 94107

Business phone
415-972-2000

Ticket information
To be announced

Ticket prices
$23 (lower box)
$18 (view box)
$18 (arcade)
$15 (view reserved)
$10 (bleachers)

Field dimensions (from home plate)
To left field at foul line, 335 feet
To center field, 400 feet
To right field at foul line, 328 feet

First game played
Scheduled for April 11, 2000 vs. Dodgers

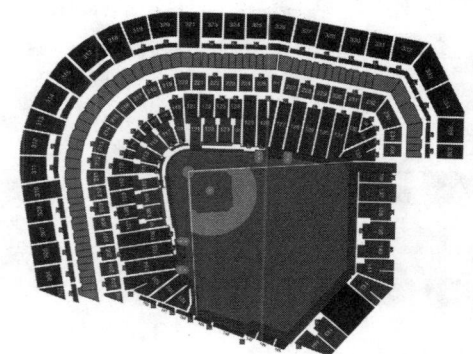

Date	Opp.	Res.	Score	(inn.*)	Hits	Opp. hits	Winning pitcher	Losing pitcher	Save	Record	Pos.	GB
4-6	At Cin.	W	7-6		11	11	Tavarez	Graves	Nen	2-0	T1st	...
4-7	At Cin.	W	8-3		7	6	Ortiz	Avery		3-0	T1st	...
4-8	S.D.	W	12-4		16	9	Estes	Spencer		4-0	1st	+1.0
4-9	S.D.	W	8-3		11	8	Brock	Clement		5-0	1st	+1.0
4-10	S.D.	L	1-11		7	12	Ashby	Gardner		5-1	T1st	...
4-11	S.D.	W	8-6		11	8	Johnstone	Rivera	Nen	6-1	1st	+0.5
4-13	Hou.	L	3-7		6	12	Hampton	Ortiz	Powell	6-2	1st	+1.0
4-14	Hou.	L	3-6		8	14	Lima	Estes	Wagner	6-3	1st	+1.0
4-15	Hou.	W	5-2		9	6	Brock	Bergman	Nen	7-3	1st	+1.0
4-16	At Ari.	L	4-10		8	14	Stottlemyre	Gardner	Anderson	7-4	1st	+1.0
4-17	At Ari.	W	8-5		9	10	Rueter	Benes		8-4	1st	+1.0
4-18	At Ari.	L	3-12		6	11	Reynoso	Ortiz		8-5	1st	+1.0
4-19	Fla.	W	5-4		5	7	Johnstone	Alfonseca	Nen	9-5	1st	+2.0
4-20	Fla.	L	2-7		7	11	Meadows	Brock	Edmondson	9-6	1st	+1.0
4-21	Fla.	W	4-0		5	5	Nathan	Springer		10-6	1st	+1.0
4-22	Col.	L	5-8		9	13	Bohanon	Rueter	Veres	10-7	1st	+0.5
4-23	Col.	W	7-2		10	6	Ortiz	Kile		11-7	1st	+0.5
4-24	Col.	W	8-4		11	4	Estes	Astacio		12-7	1st	+1.5
4-25	Col.	W	7-6		10	9	Embree	DeJean	Nen	13-7	1st	+1.5
4-27	At Mon.	W	3-2	(10)	6	10	Johnstone	Kline	Nen	14-7	1st	+3.0
4-28	At Mon.	W	4-3		7	9	Nathan	Hermanson	Nen	15-7	1st	+3.0
4-29	At Mon.	W	6-5		13	9	Ortiz	Pavano	Nen	16-7	1st	+3.5
4-30	At N.Y.	L	2-7		6	14	Watson	Estes	Wendell	16-8	1st	+2.5
5-1	At N.Y.	L	4-9		7	12	Hershiser	Brock		16-9	1st	+1.5
5-2	At N.Y.	L	0-2		7	5	Cook	Johnstone	Franco	16-10	1st	+1.5
5-3	At Pit.	L	8-9		13	13	Loiselle	Nen		16-11	1st	+0.5
5-4	At Pit.	W	7-4		13	10	Ortiz	Silva		17-11	1st	+1.5
5-5	At Pit.	L	3-4	(12)	7	8	Loiselle	Rodriguez		17-12	1st	+0.5
5-7	Mil.	W	4-3		7	8	Brock	Roque	Nen	18-12	1st	+1.5
5-8	Mil.	W	6-4		13	7	Rueter	Woodard	Nen	19-12	1st	+1.5
5-9	Mil.	L	2-3		7	7	Nomo	Gardner	Wickman	19-13	1st	+1.5
5-10	Atl.	W	4-1		7	4	Ortiz	Smoltz	Nen	20-13	1st	+1.5
5-11	Atl.	L	8-9	(12)	9	10	Rocker	Rodriguez		20-14	1st	+1.0
5-12	Atl.	W	5-1		12	7	Brock	Millwood		21-14	1st	+1.0
5-14	At Hou.	L	4-7		7	14	Reynolds	Rueter	Wagner	21-15	1st	+0.5
5-15	At Hou.	L	5-10		9	12	Hampton	Gardner		21-16	T1st	...
5-16	At Hou.	W	5-4	(11)	10	9	Nen	Elarton	Nathan	22-16	1st	+1.0
5-17	Ari.	L	1-12		4	13	Frascatore	Estes		22-17	T1st	...
5-18	Ari.	L	3-7		11	11	Reynoso	Brock		22-18	2nd	1.0
5-19	Ari.	W	8-3		9	6	Rueter	Benes		23-18	T1st	...
5-21	Hou.	W	4-3		12	7	Johnstone	Powell	Nen	24-18	1st	+1.5
5-22	Hou.	W	3-1		7	4	Ortiz	Holt	Nen	25-18	1st	+1.5
5-23	Hou.	L	1-4		4	5	Lima	Nathan	Wagner	25-19	1st	+1.5
5-25	At StL.	W	17-1		17	5	Brock	Jimenez		26-19	1st	+1.0
5-26	At StL.	W	7-6		12	9	Rueter	Bottenfield	Nen	27-19	1st	+1.0
5-27	At StL.	L	2-3	(12)	8	6	Slocumb	Spradlin		27-20	1st	+0.5
5-28	At Mon.	L	2-4		6	9	Telford	Ortiz	Urbina	27-21	2nd	0.5
5-29	At Mon.	L	4-7		7	11	Thurman	Estes	Urbina	27-22	2nd	1.5
5-30	At Mon.	L	4-6		10	12	Batista	Brock	Urbina	27-23	2nd	2.5
5-31	At Phi.	L	3-4		12	9	Perez	Johnstone	Gomes	27-24	2nd	3.5
6-1	At Phi.	W	6-5	(12)	8	13	Nen	Gomes		28-24	2nd	2.5
6-2	At Phi.	L	6-7		10	11	Byrd	Ortiz	Gomes	28-25	2nd	3.5
6-3	At Phi.	W	7-4		11	5	Spradlin	Schilling	Nen	29-25	2nd	3.0
6-4	Oak.	W	4-3	(15)	9	9	Spradlin	Taylor		30-25	2nd	3.0
6-5	Oak.	W	8-0		10	8	Rueter	Oquist		31-25	2nd	2.0
6-6	Oak.	L	6-7		12	8	Groom	Johnstone	Taylor	31-26	2nd	3.0
6-7	Ana.	W	5-2		5	7	Ortiz	Finley	Nen	32-26	2nd	2.0
6-8	Ana.	W	6-2		12	5	Estes	Sparks		33-26	2nd	1.0
6-9	Ana.	L	1-2		4	7	Belcher	Brock	Percival	33-27	2nd	2.0
6-11	At Sea.	L	3-7		9	10	Moyer	Gardner	Mesa	33-28	2nd	3.0
6-12	At Sea.	W	15-11		22	15	Rueter	Garcia		34-28	2nd	2.0
6-13	At Sea.	W	8-4		13	7	Tavarez	Paniagua		35-28	2nd	2.0
6-14	At Col.	L	4-5		8	7	Leskanic	Johnstone	Veres	35-29	2nd	3.0
6-15	At Col.	L	6-15		15	16	Bohanon	Brock		35-30	2nd	4.0
6-16	At Col.	W	15-2		19	6	Gardner	Kile		36-30	2nd	4.0
6-17	Chi.	W	3-2		10	4	Nen	Serafini		37-30	2nd	3.5
6-18	Chi.	W	8-5		10	8	Ortiz	Tapani	Nen	38-30	2nd	2.5
6-19	Chi.	W	11-5		9	6	Estes	Farnsworth		39-30	2nd	2.5
6-20	Chi.	W	7-6		9	11	Embree	Aguilera		40-30	2nd	1.5
6-21	Mil.	L	1-8		7	11	Nomo	Gardner		40-31	2nd	1.5
6-22	Mil.	L	1-5		8	13	Karl	Rueter		40-32	2nd	1.5
6-23	Mil.	L	6-9		13	12	Woodard	Ortiz	Wickman	40-33	2nd	1.5

Date	Opp.	Res.	Score	(inn.*)	Hits	Opp. hits	Winning pitcher	Losing pitcher	Save	Record	Pos.	GB
6-25	L.A.	L	2-4		6	9	Brown	Estes	Shaw	40-34	2nd	2.0
6-26	L.A.	L	6-7		11	15	Mills	Nen	Shaw	40-35	2nd	2.0
6-27	L.A.	W	8-7		14	12	Gardner	Park	Nen	41-35	2nd	2.0
6-29	Col.	W	10-1		13	6	Rueter	Jones		42-35	2nd	1.0
6-30	Col.	W	4-1		8	7	Ortiz	Bohanon	Nen	43-35	T1st	...
7-1	Col.	W	7-1		9	6	Estes	Kile		44-35	1st	+1.0
7-2	At L.A.	W	6-3		8	9	Brock	Perez	Nen	45-35	1st	+1.0
7-3	At L.A.	W	9-1		12	4	Gardner	Park		46-35	1st	+2.0
7-4	At L.A.	L	1-7		5	11	Valdes	Rueter		46-36	1st	+1.0
7-5	At S.D.	W	4-1		9	6	Ortiz	Boehringer		47-36	1st	+2.0
7-6	At S.D.	W	10-9		10	15	Estes	Clement	Johnstone	48-36	1st	+3.0
7-7	At S.D.	L	2-5		10	7	Hitchcock	Brock	Hoffman	48-37	1st	+2.0
7-9	StL.	W	5-4	(11)	9	11	Rodriguez	Aybar		49-37	1st	+2.5
7-10	StL.	W	4-2		7	2	Ortiz	Jimenez	Johnstone	50-37	1st	+3.5
7-11	StL.	L	4-5		8	7	Bottenfield	Gardner	Bottalico	50-38	1st	+2.5
7-15	At Oak.	L	9-11		10	12	Jones	Nen		50-39	1st	+2.5
7-16	At Oak.	L	2-4		5	5	Heredia	Ortiz	Taylor	50-40	1st	+2.5
7-17	At Oak.	W	7-2		10	6	Rueter	Groom		51-40	1st	+2.5
7-18	At Tex.	L	4-5		9	7	Morgan	Gardner	Wetteland	51-41	1st	+2.5
7-19	At Tex.	L	7-14		10	17	Loaiza	Brock		51-42	1st	+2.5
7-20	At Tex.	L	3-6		7	10	Helling	Estes		51-43	1st	+1.5
7-21	S.D.	W	10-2		12	7	Ortiz	Hitchcock		52-43	1st	+1.5
7-22	S.D.	L	7-8		7	11	Williams	Rueter	Hoffman	52-44	1st	+0.5
7-23	Cin.	W	6-5		7	9	Spradlin	Sullivan	Nen	53-44	1st	+0.5
7-24	Cin.	L	6-7		8	6	Williamson	Nen	Graves	53-45	2nd	0.5
7-25	Cin.	L	1-2	(14)	4	5	Belinda	Nen		53-46	2nd	0.5
7-26	StL.	W	10-8		14	11	Rodriguez	Slocumb	Nen	54-46	2nd	0.5
7-27	StL.	W	2-1		7	4	Rueter	Bottenfield	Johnstone	55-46	2nd	0.5
7-28	StL.	L	3-6		7	7	Oliver	Hernandez	Bottalico	55-47	2nd	1.5
7-30	At Cin.	L	4-7		9	10	Neagle	Gardner	Williamson	55-48	2nd	2.5
7-31	At Cin.	W	11-1		15	8	Estes	Villone		56-48	2nd	2.5
8-1	At Cin.	L	1-9		6	12	Tomko	Ortiz		56-49	2nd	2.5
8-2	At Ari.	L	6-16		16	14	Reynoso	Rueter		56-50	2nd	3.5
8-3	At Ari.	W	3-1		6	3	Hernandez	Daal	Nen	57-50	2nd	2.5
8-4	At Ari.	L	4-8		8	10	Anderson	Nathan		57-51	2nd	3.5
8-6	At Atl.	L	3-7		11	10	Maddux	Estes		57-52	2nd	3.5
8-7	At Atl.	L	4-15		11	16	Mulholland	Ortiz		57-53	2nd	4.5
8-8	At Atl.	W	5-2		8	8	Rueter	Millwood	Nen	58-53	2nd	4.5
8-9	At Fla.	L	4-5		12	12	Sanchez	Johnstone		58-54	2nd	5.5
8-10	At Fla.	L	7-8	(12)	13	13	Edmondson	Rodriguez		58-55	2nd	6.5
8-11	At Fla.	L	5-6	(10)	9	12	Sanchez	Nen		58-56	2nd	7.5
8-13	N.Y.	W	3-2		5	9	Ortiz	Yoshii	Nen	59-56	2nd	6.5
8-14	N.Y.	L	1-6		5	16	Hershiser	Rueter		59-57	2nd	6.5
8-15	N.Y.	L	5-12		12	16	Rogers	Hernandez		59-58	2nd	7.5
8-16	Mon.	W	7-4		12	8	Nathan	Armas Jr.	Nen	60-58	2nd	7.5
8-17	Mon.	L	1-2	(12)	7	10	Smith	Johnstone	Urbina	60-59	2nd	8.5
8-18	Mon.	W	5-4		7	12	Ortiz	Vazquez	Nen	61-59	2nd	8.5
8-20	At Mil.	W	10-3		14	9	Rueter	Pulsipher		62-59	2nd	7.5
8-21	At Mil.	W	5-1		7	7	Hernandez	Peterson		63-59	2nd	7.5
8-22	At Mil.	W	7-3		12	12	Nathan	Eldred		64-59	2nd	7.5
8-24	At Chi.	W	12-4		18	9	Estes	Lorraine		65-59	2nd	8.0
8-25†	At Chi.	W	11-5		14	7	Ortiz	Tapani		66-59		
8-25‡	At Chi.	W	6-5		9	10	Rueter	Lieber	Nen	67-59	2nd	7.5
8-26	At Chi.	L	10-11		11	16	Adams	Nen		67-60	2nd	8.5
8-27	Pit.	L	1-4		6	9	Schmidt	Nathan	Williams	67-61	2nd	8.5
8-28	Pit.	W	6-2		13	4	Gardner	Cordova		68-61	2nd	8.5
8-29	Pit.	W	5-3		7	7	Estes	Benson	Nen	69-61	2nd	8.5
8-30	Phi.	W	6-4	(10)	9	9	Rodriguez	Brewer		70-61	2nd	8.5
8-31	Phi.	W	8-1		11	7	Rueter	Wolf		71-61	2nd	7.5
9-1	Phi.	W	5-3	(11)	11	6	Rodriguez	Gomes		72-61	2nd	6.5
9-2	Phi.	W	3-2		8	7	Nathan	Grahe	Nen	73-61	2nd	6.0
9-3	At Pit.	W	12-2		10	7	Estes	Cordova		74-61	2nd	5.0
9-4	At Pit.	W	9-2		9	5	Ortiz	Benson		75-61	2nd	5.0
9-5	At Pit.	L	4-8		8	10	Peters	Rueter		75-62	2nd	6.0
9-6	At N.Y.	L	0-3		4	4	Rogers	Gardner		75-63	2nd	6.5
9-7	At N.Y.	W	7-4		12	4	Rodriguez	Wendell	Nen	76-63	2nd	6.5
9-8	At N.Y.	L	5-7		7	10	Dotel	Estes	Benitez	76-64	2nd	7.5
9-10	Atl.	L	2-4		8	10	Remlinger	Ortiz	Rocker	76-65	2nd	8.0
9-11	Atl.	W	3-2		8	7	Rueter	Glavine	Nen	77-65	2nd	8.0
9-12	Atl.	W	8-4		13	9	Nathan	Maddux		78-65	2nd	8.0
9-14	Fla.	W	3-0		8	4	Estes	Dempster		79-65	2nd	8.5
9-15	Fla.	W	4-3		9	5	Ortiz	Springer	Nen	80-65	2nd	7.5
9-16	Fla.	W	6-5		9	9	Patrick	Nunez	Nen	81-65	2nd	7.0
9-17	At S.D.	W	4-2		8	8	Nathan	Ashby	Nen	82-65	2nd	6.0
9-18	At S.D.	L	5-11		8	13	Hitchcock	Gardner		82-66	2nd	7.0

Date	Opp.	Res.	Score	(inn.*)	Hits	Opp. hits	Winning pitcher	Losing pitcher	Save	Record	Pos.	GB
9-19	At S.D.	L	3-6		9	9	Williams	Estes	Hoffman	82-67	2nd	8.0
9-20	At L.A.	L	5-6		7	7	Borbon	Embree		82-68	2nd	8.0
9-21	At L.A.	L	4-9		6	11	Williams	Rueter		82-69	2nd	9.0
9-22	At L.A.	W	5-4		8	6	Gardner	Borbon	Nen	83-69	2nd	9.0
9-23	At L.A.	L	3-5		5	9	Park	Hernandez	Shaw	83-70	2nd	9.5
9-24	Ari.	L	3-11		5	17	Johnson	Estes		83-71	2nd	10.5
9-25	Ari.	L	3-7		8	14	Olson	Nen		83-72	2nd	11.5
9-26	Ari.	L	1-7		6	14	Daal	Rueter		83-73	2nd	12.5
9-28	L.A.	L	3-6		5	12	Park	Nathan		83-74	2nd	14.0
9-29	L.A.	W	5-1		7	12	Hernandez	Brown	Patrick	84-74	2nd	13.0
9-30	L.A.	L	4-9		8	15	Williams	Estes		84-75	2nd	14.0
10-1	At Col.	W	9-4		11	7	Ortiz	Thomson		85-75	2nd	13.0
10-2	At Col.	W	16-7		18	13	Rueter	Wright		86-75	2nd	13.0
10-3	At Col.	L	8-9		12	11	Veres	Embree		86-76	2nd	14.0

Monthly records: April (16-8), May (11-16), June (16-11), July (13-13), August (15-13), September (13-14), October (2-1).
*Innings, if other than nine. †First game of a doubleheader. ‡Second game of a doubleheader.

HIGHLIGHTS

High point: With Russ Ortiz giving up only two hits over 8.2 innings, the Giants beat St. Louis, 4-2, on July 10 and took a 3.5-game lead in the N.L. West. It was a sizable accomplishment, considering Barry Bonds' 47-game absence after elbow surgery in April.

Low point: Reality came on September 17, when the Giants won for the 22nd time in 28 games but still trailed Arizona by six games in the division race. The club had gained only 2.5 games on the Diamondbacks despite the impressive surge, dashing hopes of overtaking the front-runners.

Turning point: On August 9-11, the Giants ended a 3-9 trip in horrific fashion, blowing four-run leads in three consecutive losses to the lowly Marlins. When the Giants started the trip, they were 1.5 games out of first place; when they ended it, they were 7.5 behind.

Most valuable player: Despite being hobbled by a bad toe, second baseman Jeff Kent finished with a .290 average, 23 homers and 101 RBIs. He had one of his best months in May (.304, four homers, 20 RBIs) even though Bonds wasn't in the lineup to protect him.

Most valuable pitcher: In his first full season in the majors, righthander Ortiz emerged as one of the league's best. Displaying great stuff, he finished 18-9. One negative: He had control problems after the All-Star break, walking 66 batters in 88.1 innings.

Most improved player: First baseman J.T. Snow. Batting only from the left side, the former switch hitter improved his overall average by 26 points, to .274, from the year before. Also, he hit .231 against lefthanders compared to his abysmal .164 figure of 1998, and that improvement helped keep him—and his Gold Glove—in the lineup against lefties.

Most pleasant surprise: Rookie righthander Joe Nathan, who shored up San Francisco's rotation by going 7-4 with a 4.18 ERA.

Biggest disappointment: Starter Mark Gardner, who won 37 games in the three previous seasons and was supposed to be the staff ace. Gardner was a bust, going 5-11 with a 6.47 ERA, and he needed postseason shoulder surgery.

Key injuries: Just two weeks into the season, left fielder Bonds went down with his elbow injury and didn't return until June 9. The injury bothered him even after he returned. Third baseman Bill Mueller suffered a toe fracture in his first at-bat of the season and was out for six weeks. Rookie outfielder Armando Rios, projected as a key reserve, hurt his shoulder in June and was sidelined nearly 2.5 months. And Chris Brock, an effective fifth starter, suffered a season-ending knee injury in late July.

Notable: The Giants closed out 40 years at Candlestick/3Com Park by drawing 2 million-plus fans for only the third time in franchise history. The final game at Candlestick: a 9-4 loss to the Dodgers on September 30. ... Bonds collected his 2,000th career hit against Atlanta's Tom Glavine on September 11. ... Five Giants hit at least 20 homers—Bonds, Kent, Snow, Rich Aurilia and Ellis Burks. ... Snow and Burks had 98 and 96 RBIs, respectively. ... Snow won a Gold Glove for the fifth consecutive season.

—HENRY SCHULMAN

RECORDS

1999 regular-season record: 86-76 (2nd in N.L. West); 49-32 at home; 37-44 on road; 23-21 vs. East; 32-21 vs. Central; 24-26 vs. N.L. West; 7-8 vs. A.L.; 18-28 vs. lefthanded starters; 68-48 vs. righthanded starters; 71-63 on grass; 15-13 on turf; 40-34 in daytime; 46-42 at night; 27-23 in one-run games; 7-7 in extra-inning games; 1-0-0 in doubleheaders.
Team record past five years: 400-393 (.504, ranks 7th in league in that span).

TEAM LEADERS

Batting average: Marvin Benard (.290).
At-bats: J.T. Snow (570).
Runs: Marvin Benard (100).
Hits: Marvin Benard (163).
Total Bases: Jeff Kent (261).
Doubles: Jeff Kent (40).
Triples: Marvin Benard (5).
Home runs: Barry Bonds (34).

Runs batted in: Jeff Kent (101).
Stolen bases: Marvin Benard (27).
Slugging percentage: Jeff Kent (.511).
On-base percentage: J.T. Snow (.370).
Wins: Russ Ortiz (18).
Earned-run average: Russ Ortiz (3.81).
Complete games: Russ Ortiz (3).
Shutouts: Shawn Estes (1).
Saves: Robb Nen (37).
Innings pitched: Russ Ortiz (207.2).
Strikeouts: Russ Ortiz (164).

GAMES BY POSITION

Catcher: Brent Mayne 105, Scott Servais 62, Doug Mirabelli 30, Edwards Guzman 1.
First base: J.T. Snow 160, Charlie Hayes 20, Scott Servais 1, Jeff Kent 1.
Second base: Jeff Kent 133, Ramon E. Martinez 27, Wilson Delgado 15, F.P. Santangelo 11, Jay Canizaro 4, Bill Mueller 3.
Third base: Bill Mueller 108, Charlie Hayes 55, Ramon E. Martinez 11, Edwards Guzman 5, F.P. Santangelo 3.
Shortstop: Rich Aurilia 150, Wilson Delgado 20, Ramon E. Martinez 12, F.P. Santangelo 1.
Outfield: Marvin Benard 142, Ellis Burks 107, Barry Bonds 96, Stan Javier 94, F.P. Santangelo 81, Armando Rios 53, Calvin Murray 9, Charlie Hayes 1.
Designated hitter: Barry Bonds 4, Ellis Burks 3, Charlie Hayes 2, Stan Javier 1, Ramon E. Martinez 1.

TOP DRAFT CHOICES

1a. **Kurt Ainsworth,** RHP, Louisiana State Univ.
1b. **Jerome Williams,** RHP, Waipahu H.S., Honolulu
2a. **John Thomas,** LHP, Righetti H.S., Orcutt, Calif.
2b. **Jack Taschner,** LHP, U. of Wisconsin-Oshkosh
3. **Sean McGowan,** 1B, Boston College
4. **Jeremy Cunningham,** RHP, Cal Poly San Luis Obispo
5. **Ryan Cox,** RHP, Southern Illinois U.-Edwardsville
6. **Ryan Pene,** OF, Dixie (Utah) J.C.
7. **Joe Jester,** SS, U. of Arkansas
8. **Kevin Vent,** RHP, U. of Arkansas
9. **Josh Cook,** SS, Yuba (Calif.) C.C.
10. **Anthony Yacco,** RHP, Mahopac (N.Y.) H.S.

1999 REVIEW

Year in review

American League Division Series

National League Division Series

American League Championship Series

National League Championship Series

World Series

All-Star Game

Notable Performances

Transactions

Award Winners

Miscellaneous

Necrology

By STEVE GIETSCHIER

TSN Archivist

Baseball approached the end of the century and the millennium with celebrations and an exciting season. Tight division races highlighted by several individual achievements, including another assault on the single-season home run record, and a memorable postseason were augmented by a nostalgic ceremony prior to the All-Star Game and complementary festivities during the World Series. The good feelings engendered by these events were tempered by a nasty journalistic tempest surrounding the continued Hall of Fame ineligibility of Pete Rose, the closing of three historic ballparks and an explosive confrontation between the two leagues and the Major League Umpires Association.

When the New York Yankees swept the Atlanta Braves to win the World Series, the suddenness of their triumph put a quick end to the debate over which team should be dubbed baseball's "Team of the Decade." The Braves, at or near the top of the National League since winning the West Division in 1991, could make a strong case, but the Yankees' efficient victory, playing the kind of baseball that has earned them widespread admiration even from stalwart Yankee-haters, preempted lengthy argument. By finishing first in the American League East for the fourth time in six years and winning their third Series in four years, twice over an Atlanta team that won the Series but once, New York earned the decade's honors easily. For the way the Yankees played the game and for their tenacity in overcoming a host of adversity, THE SPORTING NEWS honored them as 1999's Sportsmen of the Year.

McGWIRE HITS 65 AND SOSA 63

For the second year in a row, Mark McGwire of the St. Louis Cardinals and Sammy Sosa of the Chicago Cubs cracked the 60-home run standard. No player had ever hit 60 or more twice, and only Babe Ruth (1920-21 and 1927-28), Ken Griffey (1997-98) and McGwire himself (1996-99) had hit 50 or more in consecutive seasons. Sosa reached 60 on September 18 in Chicago's 148th game. McGwire did so on September 26 in the Cardinals' 155th game and thereafter hit five more to Sosa's three to retain the single-season home run championship.

McGwire also hit his 500th career home run on August 5, doing so in only 5,487 career at-bats, the fewest ever needed to reach 500. He wound up the year with 522 homers, passing 10 players during the 1999 season to reach 10th place on the all-time list. Along the way, McGwire set records for most homers in five, four, three and two consecutive seasons. He also became the oldest player (age 35) to hit 50 home runs, the 15th player to hit 100 or more homers in both leagues, the third player to hit 400 in a decade and the third player to hit a homer out of Dodger Stadium. He set a N.L. record for most homers in July

(16) and a major league record for most homers by a first baseman, surpassing Lou Gehrig.

ROSE AND THE ALL-CENTURY TEAM

Pregame festivities before the 70th All-Star Game, played in Fenway Park, were highlighted by the introduction of 41 of the game's greatest stars, including 22 members of the Hall of Fame. The occasion was the start of fan balloting to determine the MasterCard MLB All-Century Team. A panel of media members, baseball executives and historians had selected 100 players for inclusion on the ballot, including the 41 present in Boston. Fans were asked to vote for a roster of 25: Two infielders at each position, two catchers, six pitchers and nine outfielders. Another panel was empowered to add up to five additional players, if the voting went awry, with the results to be announced at the World Series.

The legends who gathered in Boston turned their appearance into a spine-tingling homage to 80-year-old Ted Williams, who threw out the ceremonial first pitch while seated in a golf cart. Conspicuous by their presence on the ballot were the names of Pete Rose and Joe Jackson, both on baseball's permanently ineligible list. About this seeming contradiction, Commissioner Allan H. (Bud) Selig said, "They were great players; they're entitled to be on the ballot. It doesn't in any way affect their status with Major League Baseball."

But Rose, on the ineligible list since 1989 and not present in Boston, sought to use his inclusion on the ballot and his later election by the fans as a wedge to reopen discussion of his status. His case was given an unwitting boost immediately after the All-Century Team was introduced on television prior to Game 2 of the World Series. NBC reporter Jim Gray interviewed Rose as the presentation was ending and asked him persistently whether he was now willing to admit that he had, in fact, bet on baseball, the allegations about which formed the basis for the agreement Rose signed making him ineligible. Rose denied the allegations heatedly and retorted that he was surprised to be hassled about them during a celebratory occasion.

Viewer reaction to the interview criticized Gray's approach and timing, and media commentary was mixed at best. Reaction to the incident reaffirmed that a wide segment of the public would like to see Rose reinstated and elected to the Hall of Fame, regardless of his past conduct. In the following weeks, Rose indicated that his team of attorneys had exchanged correspondence with baseball's attorneys that might lead to some sort of reconsideration for him.

FOUR BALLPARKS CLOSE; ONE OPENS

On June 27, the Seattle Mariners played their final game in the Kingdome, defeating the Texas Rangers, 5-2. Generally considered one of the worst ballparks in the majors, the Kingdome had been

Seattle's only home, having opened on April 6, 1977. The Mariners opened their their new ballpark, Safeco Field, on July 15, losing to the San Diego Padres, 3-2.

The Detroit Tigers, San Francisco Giants and Houston Astros closed their old ballparks at the end of the season. On September 27, Detroit said good-bye to Tiger Stadium, the team's home since April 20, 1912. Along with Fenway Park, Tiger Stadium had been one of the two oldest ballparks in the majors. The Tigers beat the Kansas City Royals, 8-2. The Giants played their last game in 3Com Park (formerly Candlestick Park), their home since April 12, 1960, on September 30, losing to the Los Angeles Dodgers, 9-4, before 61,389 fans, the largest regular-season crowd in the park's history. Game 4 of the N.L. Division Series, won by the Braves, 7-5, was the last game played in the Astrodome, opened on April 12, 1965.

Construction on Miller Park, the new home of the Milwaukee Brewers, was suspended following the collapse on July 14 of a 567-foot crane lifting a 400-ton section of the park's retractable roof in a 30-mph wind. Three people died in the accident, and damage was estimated at $50 to 75 million. The delay postponed the anticipated opening of the park until Opening Day of 2001.

22 UMPIRES TERMINATED

Years of acrimony and ill will came to a head on July 14 when Richie Phillips, general counsel of the umpires union, announced a mass resignation of umpires, effective September 2. The union was reacting not only to a prolonged period of hostility between umpires and players and between umpires and baseball's administration, but also to a series of incidents in 1999, all of which the union interpreted as disrespectful: MLB's announced intention to switch authority over umpires from the two leagues to the Office of the Commissioner; renewed attempts by MLB to standardize the precise size and location of the strike zone; release in March of a survey commissioned by the Major League Baseball Players Association ranking umpires best-to-worst in eight performance categories; and the three-day suspension imposed July 2 on umpire Tom Hallion for bumping a player during an argument.

The resignations, eventually submitted by 55 of the 68 umpires, were also a strategic move by the union, barred from striking, to force baseball to begin negotiating a new contract before expiration of the current agreement on December 31. The union's stance got very little public or media support and did not force management to the bargaining table. Within a week, news stories indicated that there was dissension within the union, with some umpires favoring the resignation strategy and others hoping to rescind the resignations and perhaps remove Phillips from his leadership position. Baseball officials suggested that resignations, once offered, could not be rescinded and announced a plan to promote umpires from the minor leagues to fill vacancies.

On July 26, the union, clearly divided within its ranks, sued baseball for the right to withdraw the resignations. While most N.L. umpires were stand-

ing firm behind Phillips and the resignation plan, all but nine A.L. umpires had bailed out on both, resurrecting an earlier idea to replace Phillips with a more conciliatory leader. A.L. President Eugene Budig informed the nine A.L. umps who had not rescinded their resignations that they would lose their jobs on September 2. The next day, when the 33 N.L. umpires who had remained firm attempted to withdraw their resignations, N.L. President Leonard Coleman said that there were only 20 openings available.

Thus, 22 umpires were scheduled to lose their jobs on September 2: From the A.L., Drew Coble, Jim Evans, Dale Ford, Rich Garcia, Ed Hickox, Mark Johnson, Ken Kaiser, Greg Kosc and Larry McCoy; and from the N.L., Gary Darling, Bob Davidson, Bruce Dreckman, Eric Gregg, Tom Hallion, Bill Hohn, Sam Holbrook, Paul Nauert, Larry Poncino, Frank Pulli, Terry Tata, Larry Vanover and Joe West.

On August 3, the union filed unfair labor charges with the National Labor Relations Board, contending that the leagues were discharging its members unlawfully. The leagues countered by filing a grievance against the mass resignation strategy. The union filed a new lawsuit on August 30 and asked for an injunction against the dismissals. Two days later, both sides agreed to drop all legal action in exchange for having the dismissals submitted to arbitration with the terminated umpires being paid full salaries and benefits through the rest of the year. Hearings before arbitrator Alan Symonette were continued until January.

Meanwhile, the dissident movement within the union to remove Phillips continued. A group calling itself the Major League Umpires Independent Organizing Committee, with advice from attorney and players' agent Ron Shapiro, began collecting signatures to petition the NLRB to hold a decertification election. The NLRB accepted the petition, and when the results of the mail ballot were tabulated on November 30, the dissidents had won, 57 to 35, with one ballot voided because it was signed. The MLUA filed an objection to this election, but asked in December to have the hearing on its objection postponed until January. Thus, as the MLUA's contract expired, the fate of the discharged umpires had not been decided, and it was unclear which union would represent the umpires in negotiations yet to be commenced.

SEASON OPENER IN MEXICO

Following a three-games series in 1996 between the Padres and the New York Mets in Monterrey, Mexico, baseball continued to expand its international presence. The 1999 season opened in Monterrey on April 4, with the Colorado Rockies beating the "home-team" Padres, 8-2, before a capacity crowd of 27,104. Perhaps more significantly, the Baltimore Orioles played a two-game exhibition series against the Cuban National Team as part of a U.S. initiative to build ties with Cuba. The Orioles won the first game, 3-2 in 11 innings, played March 28 at Havana's Estadio Latinamericano, and the Cubans won the return engagement, 12-6, played May 3 at Oriole Park at Camden Yards.

In October commissioner Selig and Donald Fehr, executive director of the players union, announced plans to have the Mets and the Cubs open the 2000 season with a two-game series at the Tokyo Dome in Japan. Prior to these games, both teams will play exhibition games against the Yomiuri Giants and the Seibu Lions.

INTERLEAGUE PLAY IN THIRD YEAR

One of baseball's other gestures toward modernity, interleague play—regular-season games between A.L. clubs and N.L. clubs—continued for the third consecutive year. The '99 schedule called for two periods of interleague play: June 4-13 and July 9-20, surrounding the All-Star break. Once again, each team played its interleague games against the corresponding division of the other league. All A.L. teams and teams in the N.L. East played 18 games. All others played 15, except for the Rockies, who played 12.

Overall, N.L. teams won 135 interleague games and lost 116. The Oakland A's compiled the best interleague record among A.L. teams (12-6), and the Tampa Bay Devil Rays had the worst (4-14). In the N.L., Houston finished best (12-3) while the Rockies were worst (4-8). Despite some concern that the novelty of interleague play was wearing thin, attendance at these games averaged 33,482, up 6 percent from 1998's 31,447, and 22 percent higher than the average for intraleague games played prior to the interleague periods.

ATLANTA WINS DIVISION AGAIN

The Braves began their bid to win unofficial recognition as the team of the decade by winning the N.L. East title for the fifth year in a row. Leaving aside the incomplete 1994 season, Atlanta has now won an unprecedented eight straight division titles, the first three in the N.L. West before the divisional realignment of 1994. In contrast to previous seasons, the Braves were dogged persistently by the Mets, who took over the division lead for a period in late July and early August. Atlanta regained first place for good on August 22 and clinched the pennant on September 26, defeating the Montreal Expos, 10-0. Bobby Cox was named TSN's N.L. Manager of the Year.

The Braves offense was led by Chipper Jones, who hit .319 with 45 home runs and 110 RBIs. Brian Jordan hit 23 homers and drove in 115 runs. Javy Lopez batted .317 before being injured, and Andruw Jones added 26 homers.

Atlanta's pitching staff led the league in ERA (3.63). Greg Maddux won 19 games, Kevin Millwood won 18 and Tom Glavine 14. Millwood finished second in the league in ERA (2.68), John Smoltz was fifth and Maddux eighth. Millwood finished fourth in strikeouts, and Glavine led the league in most hits allowed. John Rocker recorded 38 saves, fourth in the league.

METS WIN WILD CARD PLAYOFF

New York defeated the Cincinnati Reds, 5-0, to win a one-game playoff for the N.L. wild-card berth. The Mets had battled the Braves for most of the season and were only one game out of first place on September 19. They then lost seven games in a row to fall out of the race for first and jeopardize their wild card chance as well. A three-game sweep of the Pittsburgh Pirates on the season's last weekend allowed New York to catch the Reds, losers of two of three to the Brewers.

New York was sparked by Mike Piazza (.303, 40, 124) and by its infield, John Olerud (.298, 19, 96), Edgardo Alfonzo (.304, 27, 108), Rey Ordonez and Robin Ventura (.301, 32, 120), the four of whom made only 27 errors. Rickey Henderson batted .315 and stole 37 bases. Roger Cedeno hit .313 and stole 66, second in the league.

No Mets pitcher won more than 13 games, but the New York bullpen performed well. John Franco became the second player, after Lee Smith, to record 400 career saves, doing so on April 14 against the Florida Marlins.

The Cubs, the N.L.'s 1998 wild-card team, finished in last place in the N.L. Central with a record of 67-95.

HOUSTON WINS THIRD N.L. CENTRAL TITLE

The Astros won the N.L. Central title for the third straight season, nipping the Reds by 1.5 games. Houston occupied first place most of the year, but with four games to play, the Astros found themselves a game behind the Reds. Houston beat Cincinnati, 4-1, to tie for first and then took two of three games from the Dodgers while the Reds were losing two of three to Milwaukee. Manager Larry Dierker missed 27 games after collapsing in the dugout on June 13 and undergoing brain surgery.

Jeff Bagwell led the Astros offense, hitting .304 with 42 home runs (tied for fifth in the league) and 126 RBIs (sixth). Carl Everett .325 (tied for seventh in the league) with 25 homers and 108 RBIs.

Houston's pitching staff lost Randy Johnson to free agency but still had an outstanding season. Mike Hampton won a league-leading 22 games against only four losses (with a 2.90 ERA) and was named TSN's N.L. Pitcher of the Year. Jose Lima added 21 wins, and Shane Reynolds had 16. Houston's staff led the league in strikeouts (1,204). Reynolds was fifth (197), Lima seventh (187) and Hampton ninth (177). Billy Wagner recorded 39 saves (third in the league) and struck out 124 batters in 74.2 innings.

ARIZONA WINS FIRST N.L. WEST FLAG

The Arizona Diamondbacks set a record for the greatest turnaround in modern baseball, going from 65 wins in their inaugural season to 100 wins in their second year. They took the N.L. West, winning a division title quicker than any other expansion team. They won the division by 14 games over San Francisco, the largest margin in the N.L. West since 1975, and clinched the pennant on September 24 with an 11-3 win over the Giants.

Four Arizona players recorded more than 100 RBIs. Matt Williams had 142, Jay Bell 112, Luis Gonzalez 111 and Steve Finley 103. Gonzalez finished second in the league in batting (.336) and hit 26 home runs. Williams hit .303 with 35 home runs. Bell hit 38 homers, and Finley added 34. Tony Womack stole 72 bases to lead the league.

Randy Johnson won 17 games, struck out a league-leading 364 batters and had an ERA of 2.48, also best in the league. Omar Daal had 16 wins, and Andy Benes added 13. Matt Mantei, acquired from Florida in mid-July, saved 22 games for Arizona.

NEW YORK WINS A.L. EAST

While not nearly as dominant as they were in 1998, the Yankees still won the A.L. East by a comfortable margin over the Boston Red Sox. After seeing a lead of 4.5 games in early May disappear, New York regained first place on June 9 and was never headed. They led the Red Sox by four games at the All-Star break, 7.5 games at the end of August and clinched the flag on September 30 by winning the second game of a doubleheader against the Orioles, 12-5.

The Yankees offense was led by Derek Jeter, who batted .349 (second in the league) with 24 home runs and 102 RBIs. He also led the league in hits (219) and tied for second in runs (134). Tino Martinez hit 28 homers, and Bernie Williams added 25. Williams had 115 RBIs, Paul O'Neill 110 and Martinez 105.

Orlando Hernandez led New York with 17 wins. Roger Clemens and Andy Pettitte added 14 each, and David Cone had 12, including a 6-0 perfect game against Montreal on July 18 at Yankee Stadium. Mariano Rivera led the league in saves with 45.

BOSTON TAKES WILD CARD AGAIN

The Red Sox won 94 games but had to settle for the A.L. wild-card spot for the second year in a row. Boston held off a sustained challenge from surprising Oakland and clinched a playoff spot on September 29, beating the Chicago White Sox in the first game of a doubleheader. The Red Sox were led by TSN's A.L. Pitcher of the Year, Pedro Martinez, who won the pitcher's triple crown with 23 wins, a 2.07 earned run average and 313 strikeouts; Nomar Garciaparra, who batted .357 (to lead the league) with 27 home runs and 104 RBIs, and Troy O'Leary (.280, 28, 103). Jimy Williams was named TSN's A.L. Manager of the Year.

INDIANS WIN FIFTH STRAIGHT CENTRAL TITLE

The Cleveland Indians won the A.L. Central Division title for the fifth straight year, romping over the White Sox by 21.5 games. The Indians spent all but the first two days of the season in first place. They led Chicago by 13 games at the All-Star break and clinched the title on September 8 while losing to Texas.

Cleveland's offense rebounded from a sluggish 1998 by scoring a franchise-record 1,009 runs, the first time any team had scored more than 1,000 since 1950. The Indians finished second in the league in batting and sixth in home runs, and they tied the major league record for grand slams in a season with 12. Five Indians scored 100 or more runs, and four drove in 100 or more, both franchise marks. Manny Ramirez led the league with 165 RBIs, also a team record, batted .333 and hit 44 home runs. Jim Thome hit 33 homers and had 108 RBIs. Richie Sexson added 31 homers and 116 RBIs. Roberto Alomar hit .323 and led the league in runs

with 138. Omar Vizquel had 191 hits, stole 42 bases and batted .333.

Bartolo Colon won 18 games, Charles Nagy won 17 and Dave Burba 15. Mike Jackson added 39 saves, fourth best in the league.

RANGERS WIN A.L. WEST AGAIN

Texas won the A.L. West for the second straight season and the third time in four years. The Rangers never relinquished at least a share of first place after April 13. They had a five-game lead at the All-Star break and finished eight games ahead of the A's, clinching the division on September 26 with a 10-3 win over Oakland. The Rangers' 95 wins set a franchise record.

Texas led the league in batting (.293, a club record), hits, total bases and slugging average. The club scored 10 or more runs 21 times. The Rangers offense was led by TSN's Major League Player of the Year, Rafael Palmeiro (.324, 47 home runs, 148 RBIs), Juan Gonzalez (.326, 39, 128) and Ivan Rodriguez (.332, 35, 113). Todd Zeile and Lee Stevens each added 24 home runs, and Rusty Greer drove in 101 runs.

Aaron Sele won 18 games, and Rick Helling and Mike Morgan won 13 each. John Wetteland recorded 43 saves, tied for second in the league. The Rangers' team ERA was 5.07, 11th in the league and the second-highest ever for a team advancing to postseason play.

DIVISION SERIES WINNERS

Only one of the four division series went to a fifth game. In the N.L., the Braves lost the opening game to the Astros, but came back to win three in a row, and the wild-card Mets ousted the Diamondbacks, three games to one. In the A.L., the Yankees swept the Rangers for the second straight year (and gave up only one run for the second straight year), and the Red Sox came back from a 2-0 deficit to defeat the Indians, winning the last two games, 23-7 and 12-8.

BRAVES OUST METS IN SIX

In the N.L. Championship Series, the Braves picked up where they had left off in September when they had defeated the Mets in five games out of six. Atlanta won Game 1, 4-2, behind seven strong innings from Maddux and a home run by Eddie Perez. Millwood beat Kenny Rogers, 4-3, in Game 2 as Jordan and Perez hit back-to-back homers in a four-run sixth inning. As the series moved to New York, Glavine and two relievers shut out the Mets, 1-0, on an unearned run in the first inning.

Like the Braves of the season before, the Mets faced the daunting task of coming back from a three-games-to-none deficit, and like those same Braves, New York won Games 4 and 5. In Game 4, Atlanta took a 2-1 lead in the top of the eighth inning on home runs by Ryan Klesko and Jordan, but the Mets got a two-run single from Olerud in the bottom of the eighth to win, 3-2. New York won Game 5, 4-3, in 15 innings on a most unusual play. With the Braves having scored the go-ahead run in the top of the inning, the Mets loaded the bases and tied the game on a walk. Ventura then hit a ball over the right-field fence for an apparent game-winning grand slam.

But Ventura's teammates mobbed him between first and second, and he never got to touch second base. The umpires ruled that Ventura be credited with a single, and only one run counted.

The series returned to Atlanta for Game 6, and the Braves prevailed, 10-9, in 11 innings. The Mets trailed, 5-0, after the first inning but they rallied to take the lead twice. In the bottom of the 11th, the Braves loaded the bases with one out, and Rogers walked Andruw Jones to force in the winning run. Thus, Atlanta returned to the World Series after failing to survive the championship series in the previous two years.

YANKEES BOUNCE RED SOX IN FIVE

Boston fans seeking to reverse eight decades of postseason futility and to undo what is colloquially known as "The Curse of the Bambino" saw their hopes quickly extinguished. New York won Game 1 of the A.L. Championship Series, 4-3 in 10 innings, on a leadoff home run by Bernie Williams and Game 2, 3-2, as the Red Sox left 13 runners on base, including a pair in the ninth.

Boston cut the Yankees' lead in half by winning Game 3 in Fenway Park, 13-1, with Pedro Martinez besting Clemens. The Yankees then won Game 4, 9-2, as the Red Sox were victimized by four errors and a controversial call by second base umpire Tim Tschida in the eighth inning. When another call went against Boston in the ninth, manager Williams argued and was ejected. Fans threw bottles and other objects onto the field, and the game was delayed for eight minutes. Umpires threatened a forfeit before order was restored.

The Yankees closed out the Red Sox in Game 6, 6-1, behind the pitching of Hernandez and a pair of two-run homers by Jeter and Jorge Posada. New York thus returned to the World Series for the second consecutive season.

YANKEES SWEEP BRAVES

The World Series opened in Atlanta with the Yankees winning Game 1, 4-1. Hernandez yielded only one run, a home run by Chipper Jones, through seven innings, and New York tallied four times in the eighth with key hits by Jeter and O'Neill. The Yankees took Game 2, 7-2, behind Cone's seven scoreless innings and a barrage of 14 hits. New York scored three runs in the first on five singles and two runs in the third on two hits and an error.

New York completed the sweep when the Series moved to Yankee Stadium. The Braves built a 5-1 lead in Game 3, but couldn't hold it. Chad Curtis homered in the fifth, Martinez homered in the seventh and Chuck Knoblauch hit a two-run homer in the eighth to tie the score. Curtis' second homer of the game in the 10th inning gave the Yankees a 6-5 win. In Game 4, New York scored three runs in the third inning while Clemens and two relievers held the Braves to five hits for a 4-1 win.

Each member of the Yankees voted a full World Series share received $307,808.70, a slight decrease from last year's record of $312,042.41. Atlanta's full shares came to $203,542.49, also down slightly from '98. Television ratings for the Series rose 13 percent from 1998 but were still the second lowest on record.

OTHER FEATS AND EVENTS

The 1999 season was not "The Year of the Home Run" like 1998, but it was nearly "The Year of the Grand Slam." A.L. batters hit 79 slams, just two short of the league record set in 1996, and batters in the 16-club N.L. hit 60, equalling 1996's league high, set in a 14-club circuit. On April 23, Fernando Tatis of the Cardinals became the first major leaguer to hit two grand slams in the same inning (both against righthander Chan Ho Park), doing it in an 11-run third inning in a 12-5 win over the Dodgers. On May 3, Boston's Creighton Gubanich became the fourth player to hit a grand slam for his first big-league hit. Ventura became the first major leaguer to hit grand slams in both ends of a doubleheader, doing so on May 20 against Milwaukee. On August 9, major leaguers hit five grand slams, also a first. Connecting were Tatis, Jose Vidro of the Expos, the Marlins' Mike Lowell, Bernie Williams of the Yankees and Jay Buhner of the Mariners.

A.L. batters hit 2,635 homers, and N.L. batters hit 2,893, far in excess of the 1998 record of 2,565. The major league total, 5,528, was also a record. For the first time since 1995, no one hit 50 homers for the first time. Ken Griffey led the A.L. with 48. Four players hit 40 for the first time, 10 hit 30 for the first time and 29 hit 20 for the first time, a record.

Tony Gwynn of the Padres and Tampa Bay's Wade Boggs both reached the 3,000-hit plateau. Gwynn got his 3,000th, a single, on August 6 against the Expos' Dan Smith. Boggs got three hits against Cleveland on August 7, the last of them a home run for No. 3,000.

Larry Walker of the Rockies led the N.L. in batting (.379) for the second straight year, and McGwire led the league in RBIs (147). Ugueth Urbina of Montreal paced the league in saves with 41. On June 25, the Cardinals' Jose Jimenez pitched a no-hitter against Randy Johnson and the Diamondbacks, winning 1-0. Eric Milton of the Minnesota Twins no-hit the Angels, 7-0, on September 11. Cone's July 18 perfect game was the second at Yankee Stadium in as many seasons.

Despite continuing efforts to speed up play, the average game time in the N.L. rose eight minutes to 2:51, and the average time in the A.L. rose four minutes to 2:56. The overall average of 2:53 was up six minutes from 1998 and just one minute short of the 1994 high.

CONFLICT WITH ESPN RESOLVED

Determined to protect its position in the television market, MLB went to court over ESPN's decision to shift several Sunday night telecasts in September from ESPN to ESPN2, a cable channel with about 10 million fewer subscribers. This dispute followed an earlier scuffle in 1998 when ESPN announced its intention to shift three games, and MLB revoked the network's right to telecast those games at all. In April, absent an agreement, MLB moved to terminate the cable network's contract that was supposed to run through 2002.

ESPN sued, contending that the contract allowed it to move up to 10 games for events of significant interest, presumably including regular-season NFL games, the programming it wanted to air in September in place of baseball. MLB argued that the contract prohibited pre-empting any baseball games without prior approval and that entering into conflicting arrangements was a contract violation.

On December 6, the day the ESPN suit was to go to trial, the two parties announced that they had reached a new agreement replacing the contract that MLB had voided. Under the terms of the new, six-year, $800 million contract, ESPN and ESPN2 will televise more than 800 hours of regular season games and studio programming each year from 2000 through 2005. The two channels will telecast up to 108 regular season games with expanded broadcasts of "Baseball Tonight," expanded highlights on "SportsCenter" and a new Sunday afternoon recap-preview show to be called "Baseball 2Day." In addition, for at least the first two years of the contract, Sunday night telecasts in September will be eliminated with ESPN2 showing two games for every Sunday night formerly devoted to baseball on ESPN. One of these games will be aired on Fridays in September and the other will be shown on Sunday nights earlier in the year, creating a simultaneous ESPN/ESPN2 "double play" on those nights.

ATTENDANCE DECLINES

Major league attendance for 1999 totalled 70,139,380, a decline of 0.3 percent from the previous year. The 16 N.L. teams outdrew the 14 A.L. teams, 38,322,848 to 31,816,532. Average attendance was 29,164.

Eight teams drew more than three million fans: Colorado (which led both leagues with 3,481,065, exceeding the three-million mark for a record seventh consecutive year), Atlanta, St. Louis, Los Angeles and Arizona in the N.L. and Cleveland, Baltimore and New York in the A.L. Twelve other clubs exceeded the two-million mark, and all clubs except Montreal drew at least one million.

The Tigers showed the greatest increase, up 617,050 to 2,026,441 in the final year of Tiger Stadium, while the Diamondbacks—despite winning a division title—declined the most, down 580,758 to 3,019,654.

EIGHT MANAGERIAL CHANGES

One team changed its manager before the season began, two made changes during the season and five others made changes afterward.

In a rare spring training occurrence, the Toronto Blue Jays fired Tim Johnson on March 17 and replaced him with Jim Fregosi. Johnson damaged his credibility during the 1998 season when he fabricated stories about his service in the Marines during the Vietnam War. Johnson had apologized to his players, but general manager Gord Ash decided in the spring that the continuing controversy was interfering with the team's ability to focus on playing baseball.

The Brewers fired Phil Garner on August 12 with the team in fifth place in the N.L. Central with a record of 52-60. Hitting coach Jim Lefebvre served as interim manager for the balance of the season (22-27), and former infielder Davey Lopes was hired on November 4. Terry Collins resigned as manager of the Anaheim Angels on September 3 with the

team in fourth place in the A.L. West with a record of 51-82. Bench coach Joe Maddon served as interim manager for the balance of the season (19-10), and the Angels hired former Dodgers catcher Mike Scioscia on November 18.

Colorado manager Jim Leyland announced his resignation on September 1, effective at the end of the season. The Rockies, after finishing fifth in the N.L. West (72-90), hired former Tigers manager Buddy Bell on October 20. The Cubs fired Jim Riggleman on October 4, the day after the season ended with the team last in the N.L. Central (67-95). Riggleman was replaced by Don Baylor, hitting coach for the Braves and former manager of the Rockies, on November 1. The Tigers fired Larry Parrish on October 14 after the team finished third in the A.L. Central (69-92) and named Garner to replace him the same day. The Orioles fired Ray Miller on October 7 after his team finished fourth in the A.L. East (78-84), and the Indians fired Mike Hargrove on October 15 after Cleveland had been eliminated from postseason play. Hargrove had managed the Indians for nine seasons, winning five consecutive division titles and losing two World Series. Cleveland named hitting instructor Charlie Manuel to replace Hargrove on November 1, and Baltimore named Hargrove as Miller's replacement November 3.

LUXURY TAX IN SECOND YEAR

In January, clubs received their bills for the second year of the three-year luxury tax on salaries adopted as part of the settlement to the 1994-95 work stoppage. Under this plan, teams with the five highest payrolls pay a 35 percent tax on the difference between their payrolls and the midpoint between the fifth and sixth highest payrolls.

For 1998, Baltimore was assessed the highest tax, $3,138,621. The Red Sox paid $2,184,734, followed by the Yankees ($684,390), the Braves ($495,625) and the Dodgers ($49,561). The monies collected go to baseball's industry growth fund and can be distributed to the sport's disadvantaged franchises.

LEAGUES AND OWNERS

On January 13, owners approved the sale of the Marlins from H. Wayne Huizenga to commodities trader John Henry for $150 million. Later in the year, Henry proposed to build a 42,000-seat ballpark with a retractable roof in Miami or Fort Lauderdale. In exchange for public funding of 75 percent of the estimated $400 million cost, Henry offered back to the public 90 percent of the team's operating profits or profits on the sale of the team.

Meeting on September 15, owners voted on a plan to change significantly the way the sport is governed and voted on three proposals to buy franchises. They voted unanimously to approve a resolution calling for a redraft of the Major League Agreement, the document that governs the two leagues, for the purpose of merging the leagues in all areas except the games on the field. Day-to-day control of such matters as scheduling, umpires and discipline now fall to Sandy Alderson, executive vice president for baseball operations.

Owners also approved the sale of Marge Schott's controlling interest in the Reds to three of her limited partners for $67 million. Carl Lindner, owner of the Great American Insurance Company, assumed control of the team on October 1. The sale followed a prolonged period during which Schott had been banned from any direct participation in most team operations. The ban, first imposed in June 1996 for remarks she had made that were deemed insensitive and offensive to minorities, had been most recently extended in October 1998 to last through the end of the year, and then again in December 1998 to last through March, giving Schott a chance to find suitable buyers.

In addition, owners agreed to table a proposal from New York attorney Miles Prentice to buy the Royals from the foundation established by the team's late owner, Ewing Kauffman, for $75 million. Owners told Prentice that there were too many investors—almost 50—in his ownership group. In December, David Glass, chairman of the Royals since Kauffman's death in 1993, announced his intention to try to buy the team.

Owners also voted, 28-2, to postpone approval of the proposed sale of the A's from Steve Schott and Ken Hoffman to a group headed by supermarket owner Bob Piccinini for $122.4 million. The group subsequently withdrew its $12 million deposit.

Underlying the refusal to approve these sales was the owners' intention to postpone all action on the ownership of so-called small-market clubs until receipt of the report from the Blue Ribbon Task Force on Baseball Economics, established in January. The committee, composed of high-ranking club officials plus four outsiders with Selig as chair, was due to make its report very late in the year.

In October, Carl Pohlad came to an agreement to sell the Twins for $120 million to Glen Taylor, owner of the NBA's Minnesota Timberwolves, and Robert Naegele Jr, managing partner of the NHL's Minnesota Wild, pending approval by the voters of St. Paul of a half-cent sales tax increase to finance one-third the cost of a new stadium, with the other two-thirds to come from the Twins and the state. But St. Paul voters rejected the referendum on November 2.

On November 4, Richard Jacobs announced his intention to sell the Indians to attorney Larry Dolan and the Dolan family trusts for a record $320 million, $9 million more than the 1998 selling price for the Dodgers. Dolan promised to keep the Indians in Cleveland, which was one of Jacobs' goals when he put the team up for sale. Jacobs had offered 4,000,000 shares of stock in the Indians to the public in 1998 at $15 a share. Dolan will pay approximately $22.50 per share if the sale is approved.

On November 30, owners approved what amounted to a merger between the business operations of the Yankees and those of the NBA's New Jersey Nets, whose owners paid more than $200 million to become equal partners in YankeeNets, a holding company. They also approved transfer of control of the Expos to a group composed of local interests and New York art dealer Jeffrey Loria, who would hold a 39 percent interest in the club. At year's end, the group was negotiating with the Province of Quebec on constructing a new ballpark.

ELEVEN ARBITRATION CASES

Sixty-two players filed for salary arbitration, but only 11 cases proceeded through the hearing and decision stage. A total of 38 players exchanged figures with their teams. Rick Helling, who settled with the Rangers before exchanging figures, won the largest percentage increase ever, 1,517 percent. His salary increased from $216,000 in 1998 to an average of $3.5 million for 1999-2001.

Only two players (Derek Jeter and Mariano Rivera) won their cases, while nine (Shane Andrews, Midre Cummings, Johnny Damon, Mark Grudzielanek, John Hudek, Brian L. Hunter, Charles Johnson, Matt Lawton and Darren Oliver) lost theirs. These decisions gave owners a 236-181 record since arbitration began in 1974, but the 62 players who filed earned increases that averaged a record 169 percent. Average salaries of those who filed went from $781,780 in 1998 to $2,099,790, also a record.

Forty-four players doubled their salaries, 26 tripled theirs, 17 got fivefold increases and 11 got sixfold increases. Terrell Wade of the Devil Rays, on the disabled list most of the previous season, got the smallest increase, 12 percent, from $222,500 to $250,000.

SALARIES RISE

According to figures distributed at a meeting of general managers in November and released by the Associated Press, the average major league salary in 1999 was $1,567,873, up 13.2 percent over 1998's $1,384,530. (Salary figures, it should be noted, differ slightly, depending on what factors are included.) Of the players listed on opening day rosters, a record 348, or 41.9 percent, earned $1 million or more while 254 earned $2 million or more and 91 earned $5 million or more. Sixty-eight players were paid at the new minimum, $200,000. The Yankees had the highest payroll, a record $91.99 million, and the Marlins had the lowest, $14.65 million.

In response to these numbers, Alderson said the commissioner's office would be committed in 2000 to making some recommendations on salaries. Of particular concern was the fact that all eight playoff teams were among the top 10 teams in total payroll and that, in the period since the 1994-95 work stoppage, only one team not among the top half in total payroll, the 1997 Astros, had advanced to the postseason. Many observers shared the view expressed by Padres manager Bruce Bochy, "It's more a case today where clubs know they don't have a chance to compete." But in January, Don Fehr told the Sports Summit, an annual meeting of sports advertising and marketing executives, that baseball players would resist both individual and team salary caps.

FREE AGENTS

In the weeks following the end of the season, several prominent players changed teams via free agency and others signed new deals with their old clubs. The Mariners signed John Olerud (three years, $20 million); the Orioles reacquired Harold Baines (one year, $2 million) and re-signed Jeff Conine (two years, $5.5 million); Tom Goodwin left Texas for Colorado (three years, $10.75) and the Philadelphia Phillies signed Mike Jackson (one year, $3 million). The Yankees retained Mike Stanton (three years, $7.35 million) and David Cone (one year, $12 million), the Astros extended the contract of Craig Biggio (three years, $28 million), and the Blue Jays re-signed Carlos Delgado (three years, $36 million). The Indians signed Chuck Finley (three years, $27 million), Tampa Bay signed Greg Vaughn (four years, $34 million), the Cubs signed Joe Girardi (three years, $5.5 million) and the Mets signed Todd Zeile (three years, $18 million).

RETIREMENTS

Wade Boggs retired after the season, having played 18 years in the majors with three teams.

Boggs finished with 3,010 hits and a career batting average of .328. The Devil Rays named him a special assistant to the general manager.

CONCLUSION

On July 15, A.L. umpire Tim McClelland, commenting on his union's decision to have its members submit mass resignations, said, "It's not going to be pretty. Obviously, we think we're an integral part of the game, and we give a big part to the game. If they bring up umpires to take our place, the quality of the games would be going down."

That may be so, but here is how the game on the field ended up in 1999:

FINAL STANDINGS

AMERICAN LEAGUE

EAST DIVISION

Team	N.Y.	Bos	Tor.	Bal.	T.B.	Cle.	Chi.	Det.	K.C.	Min.	Tex.	Oak.	Sea.	Ana.	Atl.	N.Y.	Phi.	Mon.	Fla.	W	L	Pct.	GB
New York	....	4	10	9	8	7	7	7	4	6	8	6	9	4	1-2	3-3	1-2	2-1	2-1	98	64	.605	....
Boston	8	....	9	7	4	8	7	7	8	6	4	4	7	9	2-4	1-2	1-2	0-3	2-1	94	68	.580	4.0
Toronto	2	3	....	11	8	7	4	10	7	6	4	2	2	9	3-0	0-3	1-2	4-2	1-2	84	78	.519	14.0
Baltimore	4	5	1	....	5	1	7	5	6	8	6	5	5	9	3-0	1-2	3-3	3-0	1-2	78	84	.481	20.0
Tampa Bay	4	9	5	7	....	4	4	5	8	5	4	1	4	5	0-3	1-2	1-2	1-2	1-5	69	93	.426	29.0

CENTRAL DIVISION

Team	Cle.	Chi.	Det.	K.C.	Min.	N.Y.	Bos.	Tor.	Bal.	T.B.	Tex.	Oak.	Sea.	Ana.	Hou.	Cin.	Pit.	St.L.	Mil.	Chi.	W	L	Pct.	GB
Cleveland	....	9	8	7	9	3	4	5	9	5	3	10	7	9	1-2	4-2	1-2	....	1-2	2-1	97	65	.599	....
Chicago	3	....	7	6	8	5	5	6	3	6	5	3	4	5	1-2	....	2-1	1-2	1-2	4-2	75	86	.466	21.5
Detroit	5	5	....	7	6	5	5	2	5	4	5	4	3	5	0-3	2-1	2-1	3-3	1-2	....	69	92	.429	27.5
Kansas City	5	6	4	....	5	5	2	3	4	2	4	6	7	5	0-3	0-3	1-2	2-1	1-2	2-1	64	97	.398	32.5
Minnesota	3	3	6	8	....	4	4	4	1	5	0	7	4	4	1-2	2-1	2-1	2-1	2-0	1-2	63	97	.394	33.0

WEST DIVISION

Team	Tex.	Oak.	Sea.	Ana.	N.Y.	Bos.	Tor.	Bal.	T.B.	Cle.	Chi.	Det.	K.C.	Min.	Ari.	S.F.	L.A.	S.D.	Col.	W	L	PCT	GB
Texas	....	7	8	6	4	5	6	6	8	7	5	6	6	12	3-3	3-0	2-1	1-2	1-2	95	67	.586	....
Oakland	5	....	6	4	4	6	8	7	9	2	7	6	6	5	2-1	3-3	3-0	1-2	3-0	87	75	.537	8.0
Seattle	5	6	....	6	1	3	7	5	8	3	8	7	5	8	2-1	1-2	0-3	2-4	2-1	79	83	.488	16.0
Anaheim	6	8	6	....	6	1	3	3	7	1	5	5	7	6	1-2	1-2	2-4	0-3	2-1	70	92	.432	25.0

Tie game—Minnesota at Chicago A.L., October 3 (6.5 innings).

NOTE: Read across for wins, down for losses.

Clinching dates: New York (East)—September 30, second game; Cleveland (Central)—September 8; Texas (West)—September 26; Boston (wild card)—September 30.

NATIONAL LEAGUE

EAST DIVISION

Team	Atl.	N.Y.	Phi.	Mon.	Fla.	Hou.	Cin.	Pit.	St.L.	Mil.	Chi.	Ari.	S.F.	L.A.	S.D.	Col.	N.Y.	Bos.	Tor.	Bal.	T.B.	W	L	PCT	GB
Atlanta	....	9	8	9	9	6	8	6	8	5	2	5	4	5	5	5	2-1	4-2	0-3	0-3	3-0	103	59	.636	....
New York	3	....	6	8	10	3	5	7	5	5	6	2	7	4	7	5	3-3	2-1	3-0	2-1	2-1	97	66	.595	6.5
Philadelphia	5	6	....	6	11	1	3	3	4	4	7	1	2	3	6	4	2-1	2-1	2-1	3-3	2-1	77	85	.475	26.0
Montreal	4	5	6	....	4	2	3	3	5	4	5	3	4	4	5	3	1-2	3-0	2-4	0-3	2-1	68	94	.420	35.0
Florida	4	3	2	8	....	2	1	3	3	5	3	1	4	7	3	4	1-2	1-2	2-1	2-1	5-1	64	98	.395	39.0

CENTRAL DIVISION

Team	Hou.	Cin.	Pit.	St.L.	Mil.	Chi.	Atl.	N.Y.	Phi.	Mon.	Fla.	Ari.	S.F.	L.A.	S.D.	Col.	Cle.	Chi.	Det.	K.C.	Min.	W	L	PCT	GB
Houston	....	4	5	5	8	9	1	4	6	7	7	4	5	6	8	6	2-1	2-1	3-0	3-0	2-1	97	65	.599	....
Cincinnati	9	....	7	8	6	8	1	5	6	4	6	8	4	4	5	7	2-4	....	1-2	3-0	2-1	96	67	.589	1.5
Pittsburgh	7	6	....	7	4	6	3	2	4	6	4	2	4	6	3	7	2-1	1-2	1-2	2-1	1-2	78	83	.484	18.5
St. Louis	7	4	5	....	6	5	1	2	5	4	4	4	3	6	7	5	....	2-1	3-3	1-2	1-2	75	86	.466	21.5
Milwaukee	5	6	8	7	....	6	2	2	5	5	4	4	2	3	3		2-1	2-1	2-1	0-2	1-2	74	87	.460	22.5
Chicago	3	5	7	7	6	....	5	3	2	6	2	1	2	6	4		2-1	2-4	....	1-2	2-1	67	95	.414	30.0

WEST DIVISION

Team	Ari.	S.F.	L.A.	S.D.	Col.	Atl.	N.Y.	Phi.	Mon.	Fla.	Hou.	Cin.	Pit.	St.L.	Mil.	Chi.	Tex.	Oak.	Sea.	Ana.	W	L	PCT	GB
Arizona	....	9	7	11	6	4	7	8	6	8	5	1	5	4	5	7	3-3	1-2	1-2	2-1	100	62	.617	....
San Fran.	3	....	5	7	9	5	2	6	5	5	4	5	5	6	5	7	0-3	3-3	2-1	2-1	86	76	.531	14.0
Los Angeles	6	8	....	3	5	4	4	6	5	2	3	3	3	7			1-2	0-3	3-0	4-2	77	85	.475	23.0
San Diego	2	5	9	....	9	4	2	3	6	1	3	6	2	5	3		2-1	2-1	4-2	3-0	74	88	.457	26.0
Colorado	7	4	8	4	....	4	4	5	6	5	2	2	4	6	5		2-1	0-3	1-2	1-2	72	90	.444	28.0

NOTE: Read across for wins, down for losses.

Clinching dates: Atlanta (East)—September 26, second game; Houston (Central)—October 3; Arizona (West)—September 24; New York (wild card)—October 4.

A.L. DIVISION SERIES
BOSTON VS. CLEVELAND

HIGHLIGHTS

The bottom line: The Boston Red Sox avenged last year's Division Series loss to the Cleveland Indians with a stunning five-game series victory. Not only did they beat a team that won 97 games in the regular season, they beat them three consecutive times with the series on the brink. After the Indians drubbed the Red Sox 11-1 at Jacobs Field in Game 2 for a 2-0 series lead, Boston's morale and shear firepower appeared diminished as they went home to Fenway Park for Game 3. But the team responded impressively, ending a five-series losing streak and sending the team to the A.L. Championship Series for the first time since 1986.

Why the Red Sox won: In their most critical time of need, ace righthander Pedro Martinez came through, pitching six innings of no-hit relief in the 12-8 series-clinching win. Martinez, baseball's most dominant pitcher during the regular season, had not pitched in the series after he was forced out of Game 1 with a sore back after working four shutout innings. It looked doubtful that he would pitch again in 1999, but he did—masterfully. After Boston forged an 8-8 tie in Game 5, Martinez came in and helped settle down a series that had become a slugfest.

The turning points:

Game 1: The Red Sox led, 2-0, after four innings when Martinez was forced to leave, and the Indians took advantage of his successors. Righthander Derek Lowe retired Cleveland in order in the fifth and got two outs in the sixth before trouble erupted. Manny Ramirez hit a grounder to third that John Valentin fielded cleanly, but his throw went into the dirt at first, and Ramirez was safe. Cleanup hitter Jim Thome then crushed Lowe's next pitch 434 feet for a home run that tied the game. That was the score when Travis Fryman singled with one out and the bases loaded in the ninth inning, giving Cleveland a 3-2 win.

Game 2: Although Thome's grand slam in the fourth inning made the highlight shows, the biggest hit belonged to 40-year-old DH Harold Baines, a late-season acquisition from Baltimore. After Boston starter Bret Saberhagen, working with a 1-0 lead, walked Fryman leading off the third inning, second baseman Jose Offerman botched a potential double-play grounder by Sandy Alomar, pulling first baseman Mike Stanley off the bag with a poor relay throw. Kenny Lofton walked, and Omar Vizquel drove in two runs with a triple. Roberto Alomar doubled in a run, and Thome walked, setting the stage for Baines' three-run blast that gave the Indians a 6-1 lead. Thome's grand slam was the icing on an 11-1 triumph.

Game 3: With star shortstop Nomar Garciaparra sidelined with a bruised right wrist and the Indians primed for a sweep, the Red Sox kept the series alive with a 9-3 victory. Boston broke open a 3-3 game with six runs in the seventh inning. The big blows were a two-run double by Valentin and a three-run homer by Brian Daubach. Just as Martinez's early exit proved pivotal in Game 1, an early departure by Cleveland righthander Dave Burba—who retired the first nine batters he faced before leaving with numbness in his pitching arm—affected Game 3. Burba's replacement, Jaret Wright, gave up two runs and three hits in the fifth inning, then a solo home run to Valentin in the sixth.

Game 4: A cynic might say there's not much of a turning point after the national anthem in a 23-7 game, but the biggest blow might have been Offerman's two-run homer into the screen above Fenway Park's Green Monster with no outs in the second inning. Offerman's blast increased Boston's lead to 7-2 and chased ineffective Cleveland starter Bartolo Colon, pitching on three days rest for the first time in his career. It was the first of two five-run innings for Boston.

Game 5: With the score tied 8-8 in the seventh, Indians manager Mike Hargrove elected to walk Garciaparra and pitch to Troy O'Leary with one out and one on. The strategy backfired as O'Leary—who in the third inning had clubbed the first postseason grand slam in Red Sox history after an intentional pass to Garciaparra—drove righthander Paul Shuey's first pitch over the right field wall, giving Boston an 11-8 lead. That was more than enough support for Martinez, who held Cleveland hitless the remainder of the game. The Indians gave up leads of 5-2 and 8-7.

Notable:

Indians: Cleveland's Game 1 victory snapped a streak of eight consecutive losses in playoff openers. ... Thome ended the series with 16 postseason home runs, third on the all-time list behind Reggie Jackson (18) and Mickey Mantle (18). He passed Babe Ruth (15). ... Thome's two postseason grand slams are the most of any player. ... The Indians and Red Sox combined for 79 runs in the five-game series, three shy of the record for one postseason series, set by the Yankees and Pirates in seven games in the 1960 World Series. That series lasted seven games. ... Nagy had been 3-0 with a 1.23 ERA against the Red Sox in postseason play before getting tagged for eight runs in three innings in Game 5.

Red Sox: Boston became the second team (after the 1995 Mariners) to rebound from a two-games-to-none deficit and win a Division Series. The Red Sox became just the fifth team to come from two down in any best-of-five playoff series. ... Before their Game

3 win, the Red Sox had lost 18 of 19 postseason games, beginning with Bill Buckner's infamous error in Game 6 of the 1986 World Series. ... The 11-1 loss in Game 2 was the most lopsided in Red Sox playoffs history. ... Boston's 23 runs and 24 hits in Game 4 were the most in postseason history for any team. So was the 16-run margin of victory.

Quotable:

Indians: Travis Fryman, after Martinez's exit in Game 1: "We got a break with Pedro getting hurt. Any time you face Pedro, he's tough. He's the best pitcher I ever faced. You look up there in the sixth inning and you don't see him out there, it gives you a little pick-me-up." ... Thome, on the same subject: "We were excited. Pedro was pitching a real good game. To get him out of the game like that, it livened us up." ...Thome, on his Game 1 homer off Derek Lowe: "I figured he wasn't going to start me off with a fastball over the plate. So I looked for a changeup and there it was." ... Hargrove, after Game 2: "I don't think there is any danger of being overconfident. We have a tremendous amount of respect for the Red Sox. We know that we still have a fight on our hands. We haven't finished the job by any stretch of the imagination." ... Roberto Alomar, after Game 2: "Teams have been down 2-0 and come back before." ... Burba, after being forced to leave Game 3 with an injury and the Indians thinking sweep: "What frustrated me is that I felt I let my team down. I felt I let the air out of the balloon." ... Sandy Alomar, after the 23-7 loss in Game 4: "It was embarrassing. It was humiliating. But the good part about it is that none of those runs mean anything tomorrow." ... Hargrove, on Martinez's Game 5 performance: "He was outstanding. His velocity wasn't used to what we were seeing, but his off-speed pitches were good. He pitched. He made his pitches when he needed to."

Red Sox: Manager Jimy Williams, on Martinez telling him he felt pain in his back after the fourth inning of Game 1: "He never says anything, so for him to say something, we knew it meant something was wrong." ... Bret Saberhagen, on Harold Baines' big hit in Game 2: "I thought I made a real good pitch on Baines—down and away—and he deposited it in the right-field seats. It's going to be a long flight home." ... Red Sox outfielder Trot Nixon, after Game 5: "There ain't no scale that can measure the heart of this team. Whether we're down two games or three games, there is no quit in this team." ... Saberhagen, after Game 5: "You might say we're celebrating a little too hard. But after a series like this, you have to kick off your shoes a little bit."

GAME 1 BOX SCORE

CLEVELAND 3, BOSTON 2

WEDNESDAY, OCTOBER 6, AT CLEVELAND

Boston	AB	R	H	RBI	PO	A
Offerman, 2b	2	0	0	0	3	5
Valentin, 3b	4	0	0	0	1	3
Varitek, c	4	0	0	0	7	0
Garciaparra, ss	3	2	2	1	0	1
O'Leary, lf	4	0	0	0	1	0
Stanley, 1b	4	0	3	1	9	1
Daubach, dh	3	0	0	0	0	0
Lewis, cf	3	0	0	0	3	0
Nixon, rf	3	0	0	0	0	0
P. Martinez, p	0	0	0	0	1	0
Lowe, p	0	0	0	0	0	2
Cormier, p	0	0	0	0	0	0
Garces, p	0	0	0	0	0	0
Totals	30	2	5	2	25	12

Cleveland	AB	R	H	RBI	PO	A
Lofton, cf	3	0	0	0	1	0
Vizquel, ss	4	0	0	0	1	2
R. Alomar, 2b	4	0	2	0	3	4
Ramirez, rf	3	2	0	0	0	0
Thome, 1b	4	1	1	2	7	0
Baines, dh	3	0	1	0	0	0
Cordero, ph-dh	1	0	1	0	0	0
Justice, lf	3	0	0	0	3	1
Sexson, ph	0	0	0	0	0	0
Fryman, 3b	4	0	1	1	0	2
S. Alomar, c	3	0	0	0	12	0
Colon, p	0	0	0	0	0	0
Shuey, p	0	0	0	0	0	0
Totals	32	3	6	3	27	9

Boston	0	1	0		1	0	0		0	0	0—2
Cleveland	0	0	0		0	0	2		0	0	1—3

One out when winning run scored.

Boston	IP	H	R	ER	BB	SO
P. Martinez	4.0	3	0	0	1	3
Lowe (L)	*4.0	1	3	1	0	4
Cormier	0.1	1	0	0	0	0
Garces	0.0	1	0	0	1	0

Cleveland	IP	H	R	ER	BB	SO
Colon	8.0	5	2	2	3	11
Shuey (W)	1.0	0	0	0	0	1

*Pitched to one batter in ninth.

E—Valentin, R. Alomar. DP—Cleveland 2. LOB—Boston 4, Cleveland 7. 2B—Garciaparra. HR—Garciaparra, Thome. SB—R. Alomar. HBP—By Lowe (Ramirez). T—2:53. A—45,182. U—Roe, plate; Young, first; Hirschbeck, second; Brinkman, third; Reilly, left field; Cousins, right field.

GAME 2 BOX SCORE

CLEVELAND 11, BOSTON 1

THURSDAY, OCTOBER 7, AT CLEVELAND

Boston	AB	R	H	RBI	PO	A
Offerman, 2b	4	0	2	1	2	1
Valentin, 3b	4	0	0	0	1	0
Varitek, c	4	0	0	0	9	0
Garciaparra, ss	3	0	0	0	2	3
Merloni, ss	1	0	0	0	0	0
O'Leary, lf	3	0	1	0	3	0
Stanley, 1b	3	0	2	0	2	1
Huskey, dh	3	0	0	0	0	0
Nixon, rf	2	1	1	0	1	0
Buford, cf	3	0	0	0	3	0
Saberhagen, p	0	0	0	0	0	0
Wasdin, p	0	0	0	0	0	0
Wakefield, p	0	0	0	0	0	0
Gordon, p	0	0	0	0	0	0
Beck, p	0	0	0	0	1	0
Totals	30	1	6	1	24	5

Cleveland	AB	R	H	RBI	PO	A
Lofton, cf	3	2	0	0	4	0
Vizquel, ss	4	2	2	2	1	2
R. Alomar, 2b	4	1	3	2	3	1
Wilson, 2b	0	0	0	0	2	0

Cleveland	AB	R	H	RBI	PO	A
Ramirez, rf	4	1	0	0	1	1
Thome, 1b	3	2	1	4	5	4
Sexson, 1b	1	0	0	0	0	0
Baines, dh	4	1	2	3	0	0
Justice, lf	4	0	0	0	3	0
Fryman, 3b	0	1	0	0	0	2
S. Alomar, c	4	1	0	0	5	1
Diaz, c	0	0	0	0	0	0
Nagy, p	0	0	0	0	3	0
Karsay, p	0	0	0	0	0	0
Jackson, p	0	0	0	0	0	0
Totals	31	11	8	11	27	11

```
Boston.............. 0   0  1    0  0  0    0  0  0— 1
Cleveland.......... 0   0  6    5  0  0    0  0  x—11
```

Boston	IP	H	R	ER	BB	SO
Saberhagen (L)	2.2	5	6	6	3	2
Wasdin	1.1	2	5	5	3	1
Wakefield	2.0	1	0	0	2	4
Gordon	1.0	0	0	0	1	2
Beck	1.0	0	0	0	0	1

Cleveland	IP	H	R	ER	BB	SO
Nagy (W)	7.0	5	1	1	0	4
Karsay	1.0	1	0	0	1	1
Jackson	1.0	0	0	0	0	0

DP—Boston 1, Cleveland 1. LOB—Boston 3, Cleveland 7. 2B—R. Alomar 2, Nixon, Stanley. 3B—Vizquel. HR—Baines, Thome. SF—R. Alomar. SB—Fryman. CS—Offerman. HBP—By Gordon (Fryman). PB—Varitek. T—2:47. A—45,184. U—Young, plate; Hirschbeck, first; Brinkman, second; Reilly, third; Cousins, left field; Roe, right field.

GAME 3 BOX SCORE

BOSTON 9, CLEVELAND 3

SATURDAY, OCTOBER 9, AT BOSTON

Cleveland	AB	R	H	RBI	PO	A
Lofton, cf	5	1	1	0	4	0
Vizquel, ss	5	0	2	0	1	2
R. Alomar, 2b	4	1	1	0	3	3
Ramirez, rf	5	0	0	0	5	0
Thome, 1b	3	1	1	0	7	0
Baines, dh	4	0	2	0	0	0
Justice, lf	1	0	0	1	1	1
Fryman, 3b	4	0	1	0	0	2
S. Alomar, c	4	0	1	0	3	0
Burba, p	0	0	0	0	0	1
Wright, p	0	0	0	0	0	1
Rincon, p	0	0	0	0	0	0
DePaula, p	0	0	0	0	0	0
Reed, p	0	0	0	0	0	0
Totals	35	3	9	2	24	10

Boston	AB	R	H	RBI	PO	A
Offerman, 2b	3	1	1	0	2	1
Valentin, 3b	5	2	2	3	2	4
Huskey, dh	2	0	1	0	0	0
Daubach, ph-dh	2	1	1	3	0	0
Stanley, 1b	3	1	0	0	9	2
O'Leary, lf	4	0	1	0	1	0
Merloni, ss	3	1	2	1	3	1
Varitek, c	3	2	1	0	8	0
Lewis, cf	4	1	2	1	1	0
Nixon, rf	3	0	0	1	1	0
R. Martinez, p	0	0	0	0	0	1
Lowe, p	0	0	0	0	0	1
Beck, p	0	0	0	0	0	0
Totals	32	9	11	9	27	10

```
Cleveland.......... 0   0  0    1  0  1    1  0  0—3
Boston.............. 0   0  0    0  2  1    6  0  x—9
```

Cleveland	IP	H	R	ER	BB	SO
Burba	4.0	1	0	0	1	0
Wright (L)	*2.0	4	5	5	1	1

Cleveland	IP	H	R	ER	BB	SO
Rincon	0.2	2	3	3	1	1
DePaula	0.1	2	1	1	1	0
Reed	1.0	2	0	0	0	0

Boston	IP	H	R	ER	BB	SO
R. Martinez	5.2	5	2	2	3	6
Lowe (W)	2.1	2	1	0	1	1
Beck	1.0	2	0	0	0	1

*Pitched to two batters in seventh.

E—Lofton, Merloni, Valentin. DP—Cleveland 1, Boston 1. LOB—Cleveland 10, Boston 5. 2B—R. Alomar, Varitek, Valentin, Offerman. HR—Valentin, Daubach. SF—Justice, Nixon. SB—Lofton. HBP—By Wright (Varitek). T—3:08. A—33,539. U—Welke, plate; McKean, first; Shulock, second; Merrill, third; Joyce, left field; Meriwether, right field.

GAME 4 BOX SCORE

BOSTON 23, CLEVELAND 7

SUNDAY, OCTOBER 10, AT BOSTON

Cleveland	AB	R	H	RBI	PO	A
Lofton, cf	3	1	1	1	4	0
Roberts, ph-cf	1	0	0	0	0	0
Vizquel, ss	3	0	0	0	2	2
R. Alomar, 2b	3	1	0	1	2	1
Wilson, 2b	1	0	0	0	1	0
Ramirez, rf	3	1	0	0	1	0
Cordero, dh	4	2	3	2	0	0
Sexson, lf	5	1	1	1	1	0
Thome, 1b	3	1	1	0	2	3
Fryman, 3b	3	0	1	1	0	2
S. Alomar, c	1	0	1	1	6	0
Diaz, ph-c	1	0	0	0	3	1
Colon, p	0	0	0	0	1	0
Karsay, p	0	0	0	0	0	0
Reed, p	0	0	0	0	0	0
DePaula, p	0	0	0	0	0	0
Assenmacher, p	0	0	0	0	1	0
Shuey, p	0	0	0	0	0	0
Totals	31	7	8	7	24	9

Boston	AB	R	H	RBI	PO	A
Offerman, 2b	5	3	3	5	2	1
Valentin, 3b	5	2	4	7	1	2
Sadler, ph-3b	2	0	1	0	1	1
Daubach, dh-1b	6	0	0	0	1	0
Garciaparra, ss	3	1	1	0	1	3
Merloni, ph-ss	2	0	0	0	0	1
O'Leary, lf	5	2	0	0	2	0
Stanley, 1b	6	3	5	1	8	1
Gordon, p	0	0	0	0	0	0
Varitek, c	5	5	4	3	6	0
Hatteberg, c	1	1	1	1	2	0
Lewis, cf	5	3	3	1	2	0
Nixon, rf	3	3	2	5	0	0
Mercker, p	0	0	0	0	0	1
Garces, p	0	0	0	0	1	0
Wakefield, p	0	0	0	0	0	0
Wasdin, p	0	0	0	0	0	0
Cormier, p	0	0	0	0	0	0
Totals	48	23	24	23	27	10

```
Cleveland.......... 1   1  0    0  4  0    0  0  1— 7
Boston.............. 2   5  3    5  3  0    3  2  x—23
```

Cleveland	IP	H	R	ER	BB	SO
Colon (L)	*1.0	6	7	7	1	1
Karsay	2.0	4	3	3	0	2
Reed	1.1	7	8	8	1	1
DePaula	1.2	0	0	0	0	3
Assenmacher	1.0	5	3	3	0	0
Shuey	1.0	2	2	2	3	2

Boston	IP	H	R	ER	BB	SO
Mercker	1.2	3	2	2	3	1
Garces (W)	†2.1	1	1	1	2	2

Boston	IP	H	R	ER	BB	SO
Wakefield	‡0.0	2	3	3	2	0
Wasdin	0.1	0	0	0	1	0
Cormier	3.2	1	0	0	1	4
Gordon	1.0	1	1	1	0	1

*Pitched to five batters in second. †Pitched to one batter in fifth.
‡Pitched to four batters in fifth.

DP—Boston 1. LOB—Cleveland 9, Boston 9. 2B—Nixon 2, Varitek 2, Lofton, Valentin, Sadler, Stanley. 3B—Stanley. HR—Valentin 2, Cordero, Offerman, Varitek. SH—Vizquel. SF—S. Alomar, Fryman, Nixon. SB—R. Alomar, Lewis. HBP—By Reed (Garciaparra, Lewis). WP—Karsay 2. PB—Varitek 2. T—3:49. A—33,898. U—McKean, plate; Shulock, first; Merrill, second; Joyce, third; Meriwether, left field; Welke, right field.

Cleveland	AB	R	H	RBI	PO	A
Lofton, cf	2	1	0	0	1	0
Roberts, cf	2	0	0	0	3	0
Vizquel, ss	5	1	1	1	2	1
R. Alomar, 2b	4	1	1	0	2	5
Ramirez, rf	3	1	1	1	1	0
Thome, 1b	4	2	2	4	8	0
Baines, dh	3	0	0	0	0	0
Cordero, lf	4	1	1	0	3	0
Fryman, 3b	4	1	1	2	0	2
S. Alomar, c	2	0	0	0	7	0
Wilson, ph	1	0	0	0	0	0
Nagy, p	0	0	0	0	0	1
DePaula, p	0	0	0	0	0	0
Shuey, p	0	0	0	0	0	0
Jackson, p	0	0	0	0	0	0
Totals	34	8	7	8	27	9

Boston	2	0	5	1	0	0	3	0	1—12
Cleveland	3	2	3	0	0	0	0	0	0— 8

Boston	IP	H	R	ER	BB	SO
Saberhagen	*1.0	4	5	5	1	0
Lowe	2.0	3	3	3	0	2
P. Martinez (W)	6.0	0	0	0	3	8

Cleveland	IP	H	R	ER	BB	SO
Nagy	†3.0	6	8	7	2	2
DePaula	3.0	0	0	0	2	2
Shuey (L)	2.0	2	3	3	1	2
Jackson	1.0	2	1	1	1	1

*Pitched to two batters in second. †Pitched to one batter in fourth.
E—S. Alomar. LOB—Boston 4, Cleveland 3. 2B—Daubach 2, Lewis, Garciaparra, Vizquel, R. Alomar, Ramirez. HR—O'Leary 2, Thome 2, Garciaparra, Fryman. SF—Valentin. SB—Lofton. T—3:12. A—45,114. U—Shulock, plate; Merrill, first; Joyce, second; Meriwether, third; Welke, left field; McKean, right field.

GAME 5 BOX SCORE

BOSTON 12, CLEVELAND 8

MONDAY, OCTOBER 11, AT CLEVELAND

Boston	AB	R	H	RBI	PO	A
Offerman, 2b	4	0	1	0	2	1
Valentin, 3b	4	2	1	2	0	2
Daubach, dh	5	2	3	0	0	0
Sadler, pr-dh	0	1	0	0	0	0
Garciaparra, ss	3	3	2	3	2	4
O'Leary, lf	4	2	2	7	0	0
Stanley, 1b	4	0	0	0	10	0
Varitek, c	5	0	0	0	10	0
Lewis, cf	4	1	1	0	1	0
Nixon, rf	3	1	0	0	1	0
Saberhagen, p	0	0	0	0	0	0
Lowe, p	0	0	0	0	0	0
P. Martinez, p	0	0	0	0	1	0
Totals	36	12	10	12	27	8

STATISTICS

BOSTON RED SOX'S BATTING AND FIELDING AVERAGES

					BATTING										FIELDING		
Player, position	G	AB	R	H	TB	2B	3B	HR	RBI	BB	IBB	SO	Avg.	PO	A	E	Avg.
Hatteberg, c	1	1	1	1	1	0	0	0	1	0	0	0	1.000	2	0	0	1.000
Stanley, 1b	5	20	4	10	14	2	1	0	2	2	0	3	.500	38	6	0	1.000
Sadler, ph-3b-pr-dh	2	2	1	1	2	1	0	0	0	0	0	1	.500	1	1	0	1.000
Garciaparra, ss	4	12	6	5	13	2	0	2	4	3	2	3	.417	5	11	0	1.000
Offerman, 2b	5	18	4	7	11	1	0	1	6	7	0	0	.389	11	9	0	1.000
Lewis, cf	4	16	5	6	7	1	0	0	2	0	0	2	.375	7	0	0	1.000
Merloni, ss-ph	3	6	1	2	2	0	0	0	1	1	0	1	.333	3	2	1	.833
Valentin, 3b	5	22	6	7	18	2	0	3	12	0	0	4	.318	5	11	2	.889
Daubach, dh-ph-1b	4	16	3	4	9	2	0	1	3	0	0	7	.250	1	0	0	1.000
Varitek, c	5	21	7	5	11	3	0	1	3	0	0	4	.238	40	0	0	1.000
Nixon, rf	5	14	5	3	6	3	0	0	6	4	0	5	.214	3	0	0	1.000
O'Leary, lf	5	20	4	4	10	0	0	2	7	2	1	3	.200	7	0	0	1.000
Huskey, dh	2	5	0	1	1	0	0	0	0	0	0	1	.200	0	0	0	.000
Lowe, p	3	0	0	0	0	0	0	0	0	0	0	0	.000	0	3	0	1.000
Beck, p	2	0	0	0	0	0	0	0	0	0	0	0	.000	1	0	0	1.000
Cormier, p	2	0	0	0	0	0	0	0	0	0	0	0	.000	0	0	0	.000
Garces, p	2	0	0	0	0	0	0	0	0	0	0	0	.000	1	0	0	1.000
Gordon, p	2	0	0	0	0	0	0	0	0	0	0	0	.000	0	0	0	.000
P. Martinez, p	2	0	0	0	0	0	0	0	0	0	0	0	.000	2	0	0	1.000
Saberhagen, p	2	0	0	0	0	0	0	0	0	0	0	0	.000	0	0	0	.000
Wakefield, p	2	0	0	0	0	0	0	0	0	0	0	0	.000	0	0	0	.000
Wasdin, p	2	0	0	0	0	0	0	0	0	0	0	0	.000	0	1	0	1.000
R. Martinez, p	1	0	0	0	0	0	0	0	0	0	0	0	.000	0	1	0	1.000
Mercker, p	1	0	0	0	0	0	0	0	0	0	0	0	.000	0	1	0	1.000
Buford, cf	1	3	0	0	0	0	0	0	0	0	0	1	.000	3	0	0	.000
Totals	5	176	47	56	105	17	1	10	47	19	3	35	.318	130	45	3	.983

CLEVELAND INDIANS' BATTING AND FIELDING AVERAGES

					BATTING										FIELDING		
Player, position	G	AB	R	H	TB	2B	3B	HR	RBI	BB	IBB	SO	Avg.	PO	A	E	Avg.
Cordero, ph-dh-lf	3	9	3	5	8	0	0	1	2	1	0	2	.556	3	0	0	1.000

Player, position	G	AB	R	H	TB	2B	3B	HR	RBI	BB	IBB	SO	Avg.	PO	A	E	Avg.
R. Alomar, 2b	5	19	4	7	11	4	0	0	3	2	0	3	.368	13	14	1	.964
Baines, dh	4	14	1	5	8	0	0	1	4	2	0	1	.357	0	0	0	.000
Thome, 1b	5	17	7	6	18	0	0	4	10	4	0	5	.353	29	7	0	1.000
Fryman, 3b	5	15	2	4	7	0	0	1	4	3	0	2	.267	0	10	0	1.000
Vizquel, ss	5	21	3	5	8	1	1	0	3	2	0	3	.238	7	9	0	1.000
Sexson, ph-1b-lf	3	6	1	1	1	0	0	0	1	1	0	3	.167	1	0	0	1.000
S. Alomar, c	5	14	1	2	2	0	0	0	1	2	0	6	.143	33	1	1	.971
Lofton, cf	5	16	5	2	3	1	0	0	1	5	0	6	.125	14	0	1	.933
Ramirez, rf	5	18	5	1	2	1	0	0	1	4	0	8	.056	8	1	0	1.000
DePaula, p	3	0	0	0	0	0	0	0	0	0	0	0	.000	0	0	0	.000
Shuey, p	3	0	0	0	0	0	0	0	0	0	0	0	.000	0	0	0	.000
Colon, p	2	0	0	0	0	0	0	0	0	0	0	0	.000	1	0	0	1.000
Jackson, p	2	0	0	0	0	0	0	0	0	0	0	0	.000	0	0	0	.000
Karsay, p	2	0	0	0	0	0	0	0	0	0	0	0	.000	0	0	0	.000
Nagy, p	2	0	0	0	0	0	0	0	0	0	0	0	.000	3	1	0	1.000
Reed, p	2	0	0	0	0	0	0	0	0	0	0	0	.000	0	0	0	.000
Assenmacher, p	1	0	0	0	0	0	0	0	0	0	0	0	.000	1	0	0	1.000
Burba, p	1	0	0	0	0	0	0	0	0	0	0	0	.000	0	1	0	1.000
Rincon, p	1	0	0	0	0	0	0	0	0	0	0	0	.000	0	0	0	.000
Wright, p	1	0	0	0	0	0	0	0	0	0	0	0	.000	0	1	0	1.000
Diaz, c-ph	2	1	0	0	0	0	0	0	0	0	0	0	.000	3	1	0	1.000
Wilson, 2b-ph	3	2	0	0	0	0	0	0	0	0	0	0	.000	3	0	0	1.000
Roberts, ph-cf	2	3	0	0	0	0	0	0	0	0	0	2	.000	3	0	0	1.000
Justice, lf	3	8	0	0	0	0	0	0	1	2	1	2	.000	7	2	0	1.000
Totals	5	163	32	38	68	7	1	7	31	28	1	43	.233	129	48	3	.983

BOSTON RED SOX'S PITCHING RECORDS

Pitcher	G	GS	CG	IP	H	R	ER	HR	BB	IBB	SO	HB	WP	W	L	Pct.	ERA
P. Martinez	2	1	0	10.0	3	0	0	0	4	0	11	0	0	1	0	1.000	0.00
Cormier	2	0	0	4.0	2	0	0	0	1	0	4	0	0	0	0	.000	0.00
Beck	2	0	0	2.0	2	0	0	0	0	0	2	0	0	0	0	.000	0.00
R. Martinez	1	1	0	5.2	5	2	2	0	3	1	6	0	0	0	0	.000	3.18
Garces	2	0	0	2.1	2	1	1	0	3	0	2	0	0	1	0	1.000	3.86
Lowe	3	0	0	8.1	6	7	4	2	1	0	7	1	0	1	1	.500	4.32
Gordon	2	0	0	2.0	1	1	1	1	1	0	3	1	0	0	0	.000	4.50
Mercker	1	1	0	1.2	3	2	2	0	3	0	1	0	0	0	0	.000	10.80
Wakefield	2	0	0	2.0	3	3	3	0	4	0	4	0	0	0	0	.000	13.50
Saberhagen	2	2	0	3.2	9	11	11	3	4	0	2	0	0	0	1	.000	27.00
Wasdin	2	0	0	1.2	2	5	5	1	4	0	1	0	0	0	0	.000	27.00
Totals	5	5	0	43.1	38	32	29	7	28	1	43	2	0	3	2	.600	6.02

No shutouts or saves.

CLEVELAND INDIANS' PITCHING RECORDS

Pitcher	G	GS	CG	IP	H	R	ER	HR	BB	IBB	SO	HB	WP	W	L	Pct.	ERA
Burba	1	1	0	4.0	1	0	0	0	1	0	0	0	0	0	0	.000	0.00
DePaula	3	0	0	5.0	2	1	1	0	3	0	5	0	0	0	0	.000	1.80
Jackson	2	0	0	2.0	2	1	1	0	1	1	1	0	0	0	0	.000	4.50
Nagy	2	2	0	10.0	11	9	8	2	2	1	6	0	0	1	0	1.000	7.20
Colon	2	2	0	9.0	11	9	9	3	4	0	12	0	0	0	1	.000	9.00
Karsay	2	0	0	3.0	5	3	3	1	1	0	3	0	2	0	0	.000	9.00
Shuey	3	0	0	4.0	4	5	5	1	4	1	5	0	0	1	1	.500	11.25
Wright	1	0	0	2.0	4	5	5	1	1	0	1	1	0	0	1	.000	22.50
Assenmacher	1	0	0	1.0	5	3	3	0	0	0	0	0	0	0	0	.000	27.00
Reed	2	0	0	2.1	9	8	8	1	1	0	1	2	0	0	0	.000	30.86
Rincon	1	0	0	0.2	2	3	3	1	1	0	1	0	0	0	0	.000	40.50
Totals	5	5	0	43.0	56	47	46	10	19	3	35	3	2	2	3	.400	9.63

No shutouts or saves.

SCORE BY INNINGS

Boston	4	6	9	7	5	1	12	2	1—47
Cleveland	4	3	9	6	4	3	1	0	2—32

MISCELLANEOUS STATISTICS

Sacrifice hit—Vizquel.
Sacrifice flies—Nixon 2, R. Alomar, S. Alomar, Fryman, Justice, Valentin.
Stolen bases—R. Alomar, Lofton 2, Fryman, Lewis.
Caught stealing—Offerman.
Double plays—Fryman, R. Alomar and Thome 2; Valentin, Offerman and Stanley 2; Burba, R. Alomar and Thome; Justice, R. Alomar and Thome; Offerman, Garciaparra and Stanley.

Left on bases—Boston 4, 3, 5, 9, 4—25; Cleveland 7, 7,10, 9, 3—36.
Hit by pitcher—By Reed 2 (Garciaparra, Lewis), by Lowe (Ramirez), by Gordon (Fryman), by Wright (Varitek).
Passed balls—Varitek 3.
Balks—None.
Time of games—First game, 2:53; second game, 2:47; third game, 3:08; fourth game, 3:49; fifth game, 3:12.
Attendance—First game, 45,182; second game, 45,184; third game, 33,539; fourth game, 33,898; fifth game, 45,114.
Umpires—Roe, Young, Hirschbeck, Brinkman, Reilly, Cousins, Welke, McKean, Shulock, Merrill, Joyce and Meriwether.
Official scorers—Bruce Guindon, Hank Kozloski.

NEW YORK VS. TEXAS

HIGHLIGHTS

The bottom line: Going into the playoffs, baseball experts were saying the '99 version of the New York Yankees wasn't nearly as strong as the miraculous 125-win championship team of 1998. While that may be true, the Yankees appeared every bit as good, if not better, in the 3-0 A.L. Division Series sweep of the Texas Rangers. For the second year in a row, Yankees pitching was far superior to the mighty Rangers offense, holding a team that scored more than 5.8 runs a game during the regular season to just one run in three playoff games. The Yankees sparkled with the bats, the gloves and the arms, certainly turning it up a notch from a so-so final month of the regular season and putting themselves one step closer to their major league record 36th pennant and 25th World Series victory.

Why the Yankees won: Pitching, pitching, pitching. It was Orlando Hernandez's gem in Game 1, Andy Pettitte's in Game 2 and Roger Clemens' in Game 3. The Rangers appeared befuddled—a solo homer by Juan Gonzalez in the fourth inning of Game 2 was the only run the team scored. They couldn't hit the ball solidly, and when they did, Yankee heroes such as Bernie Williams and Derek Jeter found a way to put a glove around it. The Rangers hit .293 with plenty of power in the regular season, but they managed just a .152 average (14-for-92, three extra-base hits) against Yankees hurlers in the three games. This on the heels of a similar performance in the 1998 season—a .141 mark in a 3-0 sweep. The Yankees got clutch performances from their veteran players. Williams had a six-RBI performance in Game 1 and Darryl Strawberry a three-run homer in the first inning of Game 3 that gave Roger Clemens plenty to work with.

The turning points:

Game 1: Bernie Williams lined Aaron Sele's 3-2 fastball off the base of the centerfield wall, scoring Derek Jeter and Paul O'Neill, in a two-run fifth inning that paced the Yankees to an 8-0 win at Yankee Stadium. Williams not only took over the game offensively, but defensively. In the third inning, he made a sliding grab of Juan Gonzalez's liner in right-center with two runners on, then hauled in Rafael Palmeiro's deep fly one batter later, preserving the Yankees 1-0 lead. Then he got busy at the plate, roping a two-run double over Tom Goodwin's head in the fifth; hammering a three-run homer to right off Rangers rookie reliever Mike Venafro in the sixth, and adding an RBI single off Jeff Fassero in the eighth for a six-RBI night. Yankees Game 1 starter Orlando Hernandez really didn't need that much offense. Hernandez continued the playoffs dominance of Yankees pitchers over the Rangers with an eight-inning, two-hit outing. The Rangers didn't get a runner past first base after Williams' defensive gems in the third inning.

Game 2: When Lee Stevens' double put runners on second and third with nobody out in the fifth inning, the Rangers threatened to blow the game open. Juan Gonzalez had homered an inning earlier and Rick Helling had the Yankees in check for a 1-0 lead. But Yankees hurler Andy Pettitte took care of the situation. After falling behind 3-0, he came back to strike out contact-hitting Mark McLemore, then he coaxed Royce Clayton into a weak groundout to third and struck out Rusty Greer. Killing the rally—which prompted a hard fist-pump from Pettitte as he walked off the mound—appeared to energize the Yankees and their raucous fans. The Rangers did not threaten again, and the Yankees finally got to Helling with three runs in the next four innings for a 3-1 win in Yankee Stadium. Another crucial moment came in the New York seventh inning. With two runners on and one out, rookie outfielder Ricky Ledee lined a ball to right-center. Roberto Kelly, starting in place of speedy centerfielder Tom Goodwin against the left-handed Pettitte, appeared to give up on the ball early, letting it drop in front of him in the gap for an RBI double. That knocked out Helling and gave the Yankees a one-run lead they did not lose.

Game 3: The Yankees turned to a pair of 37-year-old veterans for heroics in Game 3. Five-time Cy Young Award winner Roger Clemens fired seven shutout innings and Darryl Strawberry clouted a three-run homer in the first inning for a 3-0 game—and series—victory at The Ballpark in Arlington. It was sweet vindication for both players. Clemens had a below-normal 1999 season, posting a career-high 4.60 ERA during the regular season. Against the Rangers he allowed just five runners (three hits, two walks) to reach base. Meanwhile, Strawberry, who hadn't joined the team until September because of a March arrest and suspension, hammered an Esteban Loaiza offering 415 feet over the left-center-field wall for the decisive total.

Notable:

Rangers: Since beating the Yankees in the A.L. Division Series opener in 1996, the Rangers have lost nine straight postseason games, scoring just two runs in their last 60 innings. After leading the A.L. in hitting in 1998 and 1999, the team was a combined .147 (27-for-184) in the two Division Series sweeps, going just 1-for-30 with runners in scoring position. ... Aaron Sele threw Bernie Williams seven straight curveballs before Williams lined a 3-2 fastball to center for the two-run double in the fifth inning of Game 1. Sele hopped off the mound, expecting a strikeout, after Williams took a 1-2 curveball, but the call didn't go the Rangers' way. ... Rangers outfielders had trouble with the Yankee Stadium lighting. Left fielder Rusty Greer lost Ricky Ledee's liner in Game 1, and it went past him for an RBI double. He also lost a high drive by Scott Brosius, also an RBI double, in Game 2. Roberto Kelly claimed he had trouble picking up Ledee's RBI double in Game 2. ... In the days leading up to Game 3, Esteban Loaiza was quoted saying he would use his fastball to beat the Yankees. While that theory worked for him in six of his seven innings of work, it was a fastball that Strawberry hit for the first-inning homer.

Yankees: Don Zimmer sustained cuts to the left jaw and ear when he was hit by Chuck Knoblauch's liner into the Yankees dugout in the fifth inning of Game 1. The 68-year-old Zimmer slumped to the dugout floor and appeared wobbly as he left the dugout, but he returned before the inning concluded. In Game 2, he wore a military helmet with a Yankees logo for a gag. ... Bernie Williams' Game 1 heroics were a redemption of sorts. He was 0-for-11 against Texas in the 1998 A.L. Division Series. ... Orlando Hernandez improved to 3-0 with a 0.41 ERA in postseason play. ... The Yankees' sweep gave them victories in 10 straight postseason games. ... Clemens' Game 3 win was just his second in 10 postseason starts; the other was in 1986 with Boston. He made the start after not pitching for 12 days. ... Paul O'Neill missed the final game of the series with a side injury he suffered late in the regular season. He found out later he had a small displaced rib fracture.

Quotable:

Rangers: Manager Johnny Oates, frustrated after the Rangers bats again were quiet in Game 1: "I don't care, Yankee Stadium, Yellowstone Park, it doesn't matter. We can score more runs than this by accident." ... Oates, again, recapping his team's miserable offense in the series: "I've got a few months to analyze what happened in this playoff and see how we can score at will pretty much in the season and then in three games not even smell home plate." ... Mark McLemore, with the same frustration: "This is very hard to take. We came in this year with a better ball club, and the same thing happened." ... Tom Goodwin, about Yankees pitching: "They make other teams look not as good as they really are."

Yankees: Hernandez, after holding the Rangers hitters to just two hits in eight innings in Game 1: "I like to have pressure when I pitch." ... Bernie Williams, after his Game 1 heroics: "I thought I was going to have a terrible night. I was sleepy and dragging, and it was cold. Something happened when they said the lineups. Something inside of me just woke up, said it's time to play." ... Darryl Strawberry, speaking of Williams' Game 1 performance: "Tonight's an example of the type of team we have. You don't look to any one person. Tonight it was Bernie. Next time it could be anyone else." ... Torre, on deciding to start Andy Pettitte over Roger Clemens and David Cone in Game 2: "I've seen Andy do it before. When you need him, he doesn't disappoint. He makes big plays, he makes big pitches."

GAME 1 BOX SCORE

NEW YORK 8, TEXAS 0

TUESDAY, OCTOBER 5, AT NEW YORK

Texas	AB	R	H	RBI	PO	A
McLemore, 2b	3	0	0	0	1	3
Rodriguez, c	4	0	2	0	5	0
Greer, lf	2	0	0	0	3	0
Gonzalez, rf	3	0	0	0	1	0
Palmeiro, dh	3	0	0	0	0	0
Zeile, 3b	3	0	0	0	0	2
Stevens, 1b	3	0	0	0	8	1
Clayton, ss	3	0	0	0	2	3
Goodwin, cf	3	0	0	0	3	0
Sele, p	0	0	0	0	1	0
Crabtree, p	0	0	0	0	0	0
Venafro, p	0	0	0	0	0	0
Patterson, p	0	0	0	0	0	0
Fassero, p	0	0	0	0	0	0
Totals	27	0	2	0	24	9

New York	AB	R	H	RBI	PO	A
Knoblauch, 2b	4	1	2	0	0	2
Jeter, ss	3	2	1	0	2	2
O'Neill, rf	4	2	1	0	3	0
Curtis, lf	0	0	0	0	0	0
Williams, cf	5	1	3	6	7	0
Martinez, 1b	4	0	1	0	7	0
Strawberry, dh	2	1	0	0	0	0
Leyritz, ph-dh	2	0	0	0	0	0
Posada, c	4	0	1	0	5	0
Ledee, lf-rf	3	1	1	1	3	0
Brosius, 3b	3	0	0	0	0	1
Hernandez, p	0	0	0	0	0	0
Nelson, p	0	0	0	0	0	0
Totals	34	8	10	7	27	6

Texas	0	0	0	0	0	0	0	0	0—0
New York	0	1	0	2	4	0	1	x—8	

Texas	IP	H	R	ER	BB	SO
Sele (L)	*5.0	6	4	3	5	3
Crabtree	0.2	0	1	0	1	1
Venafro	0.1	1	2	0	0	0
Patterson	1.0	1	0	0	0	0
Fassero	1.0	2	1	1	1	1

New York	IP	H	R	ER	BB	SO
Hernandez (W)	8.0	2	0	0	6	4
Nelson	1.0	0	0	0	1	1

*Pitched to one batter in sixth.

E—Zeile. DP—New York 2. LOB—Texas 7, New York 10. 2B—Rodriguez, Ledee, Williams, Posada. HR—Williams. SH—Brosius. SB—Rodriguez. WP—Sele. T—3:37. A—57,099. U—Joyce, plate; Meriwether, first; Welke, second; McKean, third; Shulock, left field; Merrill, right field.

GAME 2 BOX SCORE

NEW YORK 3, TEXAS 1

THURSDAY, OCTOBER 7, AT NEW YORK

Texas	AB	R	H	RBI	PO	A
Clayton, ss	4	0	0	0	1	3
Greer, lf	4	0	0	0	4	0
Rodriguez, c	4	0	1	0	10	0
Gonzalez, rf	4	1	1	1	2	0
Palmeiro, dh	4	0	2	0	0	0
Zeile, 3b	4	0	1	0	1	1
Kelly, cf	3	0	1	0	1	0
Goodwin, cf	1	0	0	0	0	0
Stevens, 1b	3	0	1	0	5	1
McLemore, 2b	3	0	0	0	0	0
Helling, p	0	0	0	0	0	0
Crabtree, p	0	0	0	0	0	1
Venafro, p	0	0	0	0	0	1
Totals	34	1	7	1	24	7

New York	AB	R	H	RBI	PO	A
Knoblauch, 2b	4	0	0	0	1	5
Jeter, ss	4	0	2	0	2	4
O'Neill, rf	4	0	1	0	1	0
Curtis, pr-lf	0	1	0	0	0	0
Williams, cf	3	0	0	0	4	0
Martinez, 1b	3	2	1	0	8	0
Davis, dh	3	0	1	0	0	0
Bellinger, pr-dh	0	0	0	1	0	0
Ledee, lf-rf	4	0	1	1	2	0
Brosius, 3b	3	0	1	1	0	1
Girardi, c	3	0	0	0	9	0
Pettitte, p	0	0	0	0	0	0
Nelson, p	0	0	0	0	0	0
Rivera, p	0	0	0	0	0	0
Totals	31	3	7	3	27	10

Texas	0	0	0		1	0	0		0	0	0—1
New York	0	0	0		0	1	0		1	1	x—3

Texas	IP	H	R	ER	BB	SO
Helling (L)	6.1	5	2	2	1	8
Crabtree	1.0	1	1	1	0	0
Venafro	0.2	1	0	0	1	0

New York	IP	H	R	ER	BB	SO
Pettitte (W)	7.1	7	1	1	0	5
Nelson	0.2	0	0	0	0	2
Rivera (S)	1.0	0	0	0	0	2

E—Martinez, Knoblauch. DP—New York 2. LOB—Texas 6, New York 7. 2B—Stevens, Jeter, Brosius, Ledee. HR—Gonzalez. HBP—By Venafro (Williams). T—3:32. A—57,485. U—Meriwether, plate; Welke, first; McKean, second; Shulock, third; Merrill, left field; Joyce, right field.

GAME 3 BOX SCORE

NEW YORK 3, TEXAS 0

SATURDAY, OCTOBER 9, AT TEXAS

New York	AB	R	H	RBI	PO	A
Knoblauch, 2b	4	0	0	0	1	4
Jeter, ss	4	1	2	0	1	4
Williams, cf	3	1	1	0	4	0
Martinez, 1b	4	0	0	0	14	1
Strawberry, dh	4	1	2	3	0	0
Ledee, rf	4	0	1	0	1	0
Brosius, 3b	4	0	0	0	2	1
Curtis, lf	3	0	0	0	0	0
Girardi, c	3	0	0	0	3	0
Clemens, p	0	0	0	0	1	3
Nelson, p	0	0	0	0	0	0
Rivera, p	0	0	0	0	0	0
Totals	33	3	6	3	27	13

Texas	AB	R	H	RBI	PO	A
McLemore, 2b	4	0	1	0	1	6
Rodriguez, c	4	0	0	0	6	0
Greer, lf	3	0	1	0	2	0
Gonzalez, rf	4	0	1	0	2	0
Palmeiro, dh	4	0	1	0	0	0
Zeile, 3b	3	0	0	0	0	1
Stevens, 1b	3	0	0	0	12	0
Clayton, ss	3	0	0	0	1	4
Goodwin, cf	3	0	1	0	3	0
Loaiza, p	0	0	0	0	0	0
Zimmerman, p	0	0	0	0	0	0
Wetteland, p	0	0	0	0	0	0
Totals	31	0	5	0	27	11

New York	3	0	0		0	0	0		0	0	0—3
Texas	0	0	0		0	0	0		0	0	0—0

New York	IP	H	R	ER	BB	SO
Clemens (W)	7.0	3	0	0	2	2
Nelson	*0.0	1	0	0	0	0
Rivera (S)	2.0	1	0	0	0	1

Texas	IP	H	R	ER	BB	SO
Loaiza (L)	7.0	5	3	3	1	4
Zimmerman	1.0	1	0	0	0	1
Wetteland	1.0	0	0	0	0	1

*Pitched to one batter in eighth.

E—Zeile. DP—New York 1, Texas 1. LOB—New York 4, Texas 6. 3B—Jeter. HR—Strawberry. WP—Rivera. T—3:00. A—50,269. U—Hirschbeck, plate; Brinkman, first; Reilly, second; Cousins, third; Roe, left field; Young, right field.

STATISTICS

NEW YORK YANKEES' BATTING AND FIELDING AVERAGES

Player, position	G	AB	R	H	TB	2B	3B	HR	RBI	BB	IBB	SO	Avg.	PO	A	E	Avg.
Jeter, ss	3	11	3	5	8	1	1	0	0	2	0	3	.455	5	10	0	1.000
Williams, cf	3	11	2	4	8	1	0	1	6	1	0	2	.364	15	0	0	1.000
Strawberry, dh	2	6	2	2	5	0	0	1	3	1	1	1	.333	0	0	0	.000
Davis, dh	1	3	0	1	1	0	0	0	0	0	0	2	.333	0	0	0	.000
Ledee, lf-rf	3	11	1	3	5	2	0	0	2	1	0	5	.273	6	0	0	1.000
O'Neill, rf	2	8	2	2	2	0	0	0	0	1	0	1	.250	4	0	0	1.000
Posada, c	1	4	0	1	2	1	0	0	0	0	0	0	.250	5	0	0	1.000
Martinez, 1b	3	11	2	2	2	0	0	0	0	2	1	2	.182	29	1	1	.968
Knoblauch, 2b	3	12	1	2	2	0	0	0	0	1	0	3	.167	2	11	1	.929
Brosius, 3b	3	10	0	1	2	1	0	0	1	0	0	0	.100	2	3	0	1.000
Nelson, p	3	0	0	0	0	0	0	0	0	0	0	0	.000	0	0	0	.000
Rivera, p	2	0	0	0	0	0	0	0	0	0	0	0	.000	0	0	0	.000
Bellinger, pr-dh	1	0	1	0	0	0	0	0	0	0	0	0	.000	0	0	0	.000
Clemens, p	1	0	0	0	0	0	0	0	0	0	0	0	.000	1	3	0	1.000
Hernandez, p	1	0	0	0	0	0	0	0	0	0	0	0	.000	0	1	0	1.000

Player, position	G	AB	R	H	TB	2B	3B	HR	RBI	BB	IBB	SO	Avg.	PO	A	E	Avg.
Pettitte, p	1	0	0	0	0	0	0	0	0	0	0	0	.000	0	0	0	.000
Leyritz, ph-dh	2	2	0	0	0	0	0	0	1	1	0	0	.000	0	0	0	.000
Curtis, lf-pr	3	3	1	0	0	0	0	0	0	0	0	0	.000	0	0	0	.000
Girardi, c	2	6	0	0	0	0	0	0	0	0	0	1	.000	12	0	0	1.000
Totals	3	98	14	23	37	6	1	2	13	10	2	19	.235	81	29	2	.982

TEXAS RANGERS' BATTING AND FIELDING AVERAGES

Player, position	G	AB	R	H	TB	2B	3B	HR	RBI	BB	IBB	SO	Avg.	PO	A	E	Avg.
Kelly, cf	1	3	0	1	1	0	0	0	0	0	0	2	.333	1	0	0	1.000
Palmeiro, dh	3	11	0	3	3	0	0	0	0	1	0	1	.273	0	0	0	.000
Rodriguez, c	3	12	0	3	4	1	0	0	0	0	0	2	.250	21	0	0	1.000
Gonzalez, rf	3	11	1	2	5	0	0	1	1	1	0	3	.182	5	0	0	1.000
Goodwin, cf	3	7	0	1	1	0	0	0	0	0	0	1	.143	6	0	0	1.000
Greer, lf	3	9	0	1	1	0	0	0	0	3	0	1	.111	9	0	0	1.000
Stevens, 1b	3	9	0	1	2	1	0	0	0	1	0	2	.111	25	2	0	1.000
McLemore, 2b	3	10	0	1	1	0	0	0	0	1	0	3	.100	2	9	0	1.000
Zeile, 3b	3	10	0	1	1	0	0	0	0	2	0	1	.100	1	4	2	.714
Crabtree, p	2	0	0	0	0	0	0	0	0	0	0	0	.000	0	1	0	1.000
Venafro, p	2	0	0	0	0	0	0	0	0	0	0	0	.000	0	1	0	1.000
Fassero, p	1	0	0	0	0	0	0	0	0	0	0	0	.000	0	0	0	.000
Helling, p	1	0	0	0	0	0	0	0	0	0	0	0	.000	0	0	0	.000
Loaiza, p	1	0	0	0	0	0	0	0	0	0	0	0	.000	0	0	0	.000
Patterson, p	1	0	0	0	0	0	0	0	0	0	0	0	.000	0	0	0	.000
Sele, p	1	0	0	0	0	0	0	0	0	0	0	0	.000	1	0	0	1.000
Wetteland, p	1	0	0	0	0	0	0	0	0	0	0	0	.000	0	0	0	.000
Zimmerman, p	1	0	0	0	0	0	0	0	0	0	0	0	.000	0	0	0	.000
Clayton, ss	3	10	0	0	0	0	0	0	0	0	0	1	.000	4	10	0	1.000
Totals	3	92	1	14	19	2	0	1	1	9	0	17	.152	75	27	2	.981

NEW YORK YANKEES' PITCHING RECORDS

Pitcher	G	GS	CG	IP	H	R	ER	HR	BB	IBB	SO	HB	WP	W	L	Pct.	ERA
Hernandez	1	1	0	8.0	2	0	0	0	6	0	4	0	0	1	0	1.000	0.00
Clemens	1	1	0	7.0	3	0	0	0	2	0	2	0	0	1	0	1.000	0.00
Rivera	2	0	0	3.0	1	0	0	0	0	0	3	0	1	0	0	.000	0.00
Nelson	3	0	0	1.2	1	0	0	0	1	0	3	0	0	0	0	.000	0.00
Pettitte	1	1	0	7.1	7	1	1	1	0	0	5	0	0	1	0	1.000	1.23
Totals	3	3	0	27.0	14	1	1	1	9	0	17	0	1	3	0	1.000	0.33

Shutouts—Hernandez and Nelson (combined); Clemens, Nelson and Rivera (combined). Saves—Rivera 2.

TEXAS RANGERS' PITCHING RECORDS

Pitcher	G	GS	CG	IP	H	R	ER	HR	BB	IBB	SO	HB	WP	W	L	Pct.	ERA
Patterson	1	0	0	1.0	0	0	0	0	0	0	0	0	0	0	0	.000	0.00
Venafro	2	0	0	1.0	2	2	0	1	1	0	0	1	0	0	0	.000	0.00
Wetteland	1	0	0	1.0	0	0	0	0	0	0	1	0	0	0	0	.000	0.00
Zimmerman	1	0	0	1.0	1	0	0	0	0	0	1	0	0	0	0	.000	0.00
Helling	1	1	0	6.1	5	2	2	0	1	0	8	0	0	0	1	.000	2.84
Loaiza	1	1	0	7.0	5	3	3	1	1	0	4	0	0	0	1	.000	3.86
Sele	1	1	0	5.0	6	4	3	0	5	2	3	0	1	0	1	.000	5.40
Crabtree	2	0	0	1.2	1	2	1	0	1	0	1	0	0	0	0	.000	5.40
Fassero	1	0	0	1.0	2	1	1	0	1	0	1	0	0	0	0	.000	9.00
Totals	3	3	0	25.0	23	14	10	2	10	2	19	1	1	0	3	.000	3.60

No shutouts or saves.

SCORE BY INNINGS

New York	3	1	0		0	3	4		1	2	0—14
Texas	0	0	0		1	0	0		0	0	0— 1

MISCELLANEOUS STATISTICS

Sacrifice hit—Brosius.
Sacrifice flies—None.
Stolen base—Rodriguez.
Caught stealing—None.
Double plays—Brosius and Martinez; Clayton, McLemore and Stevens; Jeter, Knoblauch and Martinez; Knoblauch, Jeter and Martinez; Martinez (unassisted).
Left on bases—New York 10, 7, 4—21; Texas 7, 6, 6—19.

Hit by pitcher—By Venafro (Williams).
Passed balls—None.
Balks—None.
Time of games—First game, 3:37; second game, 3:32; third game, 3:00.
Attendance—First game, 57,099; second game, 57,485; third game, 50,269.
Umpires—Joyce, Meriwether, Welke, McKean, Shulock, Merrill, Hirschbeck, Brinkman, Reilly, Cousins, Roe and Young.
Official scorers—Joe Donnelly, Curt Iverson, Howie Karpin.

HIGHLIGHTS

The bottom line: Both franchises were fresh on the playoffs scene. The wild-card New York Mets hadn't been to the postseason since 1988, and the Arizona Diamondbacks, with the best one-year turnaround for a team, won the N.L. West in just their second year of existence. The big reason for the Mets' resurgence? All-Star catcher Mike Piazza's bat in the line-up. The big reason for Arizona's turnaround? They had the one pitcher no one in the National League wanted to face: Randy Johnson. But neither player was a factor in the series, as the Mets proved it takes a team effort to win in the postseason. The club shellacked Johnson in Game 1, then relied on standouts such as John Olerud and Edgardo Alfonzo to fill the void with Piazza on the bench because of an injury in Game 3 and the series-clinching Game 4. Not bad for a team that was all but out of the playoffs picture when the final weekend of the season began. Then the Mets won their final three games, forcing a one-game playoff with the Cincinnati Reds. They shut out the Reds, advancing into the postseason.

Why the Mets won: Timely hitting and a different hero each game. In Game 1, Edgardo Alfonzo provided the heroics. In Game 3, it was a combination of Rickey Henderson and John Olerud, and in Game 4 it was backup catcher Todd Pratt. Outside of Kenny Rogers' shaky outing in Game 2, the starting pitchers outperformed an outstanding Diamondbacks rotation. Costly errors by Tony Womack, one each in Games 3 and 4, cost the Diamondbacks a chance to win each game and take the momentum back from the Mets at Shea Stadium. The Diamondbacks had a plethora of veteran players, but at times in this series, they played like a second-year franchise.

The turning points:

Game 1: Edgardo Alfonzo's ninth-inning grand slam off Arizona reliever Bobby Chouinard broke a 4-4 tie and gave the Mets an 8-4 victory in Phoenix. Surprisingly, seven of the eight runs were charged to Randy Johnson, who led the NL with a 2.48 ERA in the regular season. Johnson allowed singles by Robin Ventura and Rey Ordonez before walking young Melvin Mora, which loaded the bases with one out in the ninth. Chouinard got one out on a sparkling defensive play by Matt Williams on Rickey Henderson's grounder which forced Ventura at the plate, but Alfonzo clocked his second homer of the game just inside the left field foul pole. Mets reliever Turk Wendell followed a hitless eighth inning with a perfect ninth for a save in his first postseason appearance.

Game 2: With the bases loaded in the bottom of the third inning, Steve Finley, a career .091 hitter in Division Series games, singled in two runs off Mets starter Kenny Rogers, giving the Diamondbacks a 3-1 lead. Finley added a two-run double in the fifth inning and a bases-loaded walk in the seventh inning for a five-RBI game. Todd Stottlemyre didn't need any more than the three third-inning runs, pitching 6.2 strong innings in Arizona's 7-1 victory.

Game 3: John Olerud's two-run single in the sixth inning broke open the game, propelling the Mets to a 9-2 victory at Shea Stadium. With the Mets leading 4-2 and one out in the sixth, Arizona manager Buck Showalter played the odds, bringing in lefty reliever Dan Plesac to face the lefthanded-hitting Olerud. Plesac specialized all season in getting out lefthanded hitters—they hit just .186 against him. But Olerud lined a two-run single to right, Roger Cedeno followed with an RBI single, and lefthanded Darryl Hamilton added a two-run single to center. The Mets were without catcher Mike Piazza, who was nursing an injured thumb.

Game 4: Todd Pratt hit a 10th-inning pitch from Matt Mantei that just cleared Finley's glove and the center field wall for a game-winning and series-ending homer. Pratt, replacing Piazza behind the plate, lifted Mantei's fastball to center field where Finley, a two-time Gold Glove winner, nearly made a leaping grab. The 4-3 win kept the Mets from traveling back to Arizona for Game 5. Defense made a difference earlier in the game. Mora, a rookie left fielder, gunned down Jay Bell at the plate in the top of the eighth inning as the Diamondbacks tried to add to a 3-2 lead. Then in the bottom of the frame, Tony Womack missed catching Olerud's fly ball, setting up the game-tying sacrifice fly by Cedeno.

Notable:

Mets: John Olerud's Game 1 homer was the first homer by a lefthander off Randy Johnson since September 23, 1997. In fact, the only two lefthanders in the Mets lineup, Olerud and Robin Ventura, went a combined 4-for-8 in Game 1 against Johnson, who allowed just nine hits to lefties during the regular season. ... Rickey Henderson, 40, batted .400 in the Division Series and broke a Division Series record with six stolen bases. ... Kenny Rogers is winless in four career postseason starts. ... John Franco broke a string of 878 career games played with no postseason appearances, a major league record, with his Game 2 appearance. His Game 4 win was his first since September 13, 1997. ... Todd Pratt was 0-for-7 in the series before hitting the series-clinching home run. He was only the fourth player to end a postseason series with a home run, the most recent being Toronto's Joe Carter in the 1993 World Series.

Diamondbacks: The Diamondbacks had won seven of the nine games against the Mets during the regular season. ... Johnson lost a major league record sixth straight postseason decision. ... The

Diamondbacks compiled a 32-16 record against left-handed starters during the regular season. That didn't bode well for Kenny Rogers in Game 2. ... Todd Stottlemyre improved to 2-1 with a 1.69 ERA in three career Division Series starts. ... The Diamondbacks committed three errors and walked eight batters in Game 3. Of those eight walks, three came in the sixth inning, and all three runners scored in the six-run inning. ... Matt Mantei gave up Pratt's homer in his first postseason appearance. ... Arizona hadn't lost consecutive road games since July 18 and 19 at Seattle. ... During the regular season, Womack made only two errors in 258 chances while playing in the outfield. He equalled that total with an error each in Games 3 and 4.

Quotable:

Mets: Mike Piazza, who had a hit and two strike-outs in four at-bats against Randy Johnson in Game 1: "Maybe he threw his best pitches to me and made some mistakes to the other guys. In that case, I'll be the whipping boy. It's no problem." ... Rogers on his pitching performance in Game 2: "With the stuff I had, pretty much from the first inning, I knew I'd have to battle." ... Todd Pratt on replacing Mike Piazza in Game 3: "I'm not Mike. I can handle the bat. I can handle myself defensively. But I'm not Mike. We all know that." ... Orel Hershiser, on Rickey Henderson's performance in the Division Series: "I think he's genetically blessed in the same way that Nolan Ryan was genetically blessed." ... Pratt again, on the Division Series win: "It was a team effort, and we really haven't done anything yet." ... John Franco, on winning Game 4: "Growing up as a Mets fan, getting the win in probably the biggest game here in 11 years . . . I am ecstatic right now."

Diamondbacks: Bobby Chouinard, on giving up the game-winning grand slam in Game 1: "I was trying to throw too hard. I threw a 3-1 fastball right down the middle. I fell behind and paid for it." ... Stottlemyre, on how he is pitching with a 70 percent tear of his rotator cuff: "Regardless of what people think, my arm feels good. I consider myself healthy, although medically I have two tears in my shoulder." ... Buck Showalter talking about his team's three-error, eight-walk performance in Game 3: "It certainly wasn't characteristic of the way we've been playing." ... Showalter again, on Tony Womack's second error in as many games, "He's one of the big reasons we're here today. It would be very unfeeling for me or anybody to forget that."

GAME 1 BOX SCORE

NEW YORK 8, ARIZONA 4

TUESDAY, OCTOBER 5, AT ARIZONA

New York	AB	R	H	RBI	PO	A
Henderson, lf	3	2	0	0	1	1
Benitez, p	0	0	0	0	0	0
Alfonzo, 2b	5	2	2	5	2	2
Olerud, 1b	5	1	3	2	5	0
Piazza, c	5	0	1	0	4	0
Agbayani, rf	4	0	0	0	2	0
Wendell, p	0	0	0	0	0	0

New York	AB	R	H	RBI	PO	A
Hamilton, cf	0	0	0	0	1	0
Ventura, 3b	4	1	2	0	2	0
Dunston, cf	3	0	1	0	5	0
Cook, p	0	0	0	0	1	0
Cedeno, rf	1	0	0	0	1	0
Ordonez, ss	3	1	1	1	2	2
Yoshii, p	2	0	0	0	0	1
Mora, cf-lf	1	1	0	0	1	0
Totals	**36**	**8**	**10**	**8**	**27**	**6**

Arizona	AB	R	H	RBI	PO	A
Womack, rf	4	1	1	0	3	0
Bell, 2b	3	1	1	1	0	3
Gonzalez, lf	3	1	2	2	0	0
Williams, 3b	4	0	0	0	1	3
Durazo, 1b	4	1	1	1	7	0
Finley, cf	3	0	1	0	3	0
Frias, ss	4	0	0	0	0	0
Stinnett, c	3	0	0	0	12	0
Johnson, p	3	0	1	0	1	2
Chouinard, p	0	0	0	0	0	0
Totals	**31**	**4**	**7**	**4**	**27**	**8**

New York	1	0	2	1	0	0	0	0	4—8
Arizona	0	0	1	1	0	2	0	0	0—4

New York	IP	H	R	ER	BB	SO
Yoshii	5.1	6	4	4	0	3
Cook	1.2	1	0	0	1	1
Wendell (W)	1.0	0	0	0	1	0
Benitez	1.0	0	0	0	0	0

Arizona	IP	H	R	ER	BB	SO
Johnson (L)	8.1	8	7	7	3	11
Chouinard	0.2	2	1	1	0	0

DP—New York 2. LOB—New York 5, Arizona 3. 2B—Ventura, Gonzalez, Johnson. 3B—Womack. HR—Alfonzo 2, Olerud, Durazo, Gonzalez. SH—Ordonez. SF—Bell. SB—Henderson 2. T—2:53. A—49,584. U—Gorman, plate; Bell, first; Hirschbeck, second; DeMuth, third; Marsh, left field; Schrieber, right field.

GAME 2 BOX SCORE

ARIZONA 7, NEW YORK 1

WEDNESDAY, OCTOBER 6, AT ARIZONA

New York	AB	R	H	RBI	PO	A
Henderson, lf	3	1	2	0	2	0
Alfonzo, 2b	4	0	0	0	1	2
Olerud, 1b	3	0	0	1	8	1
Piazza, c	4	0	1	0	9	0
Ventura, 3b	2	0	0	0	0	4
Hamilton, cf	2	0	0	0	2	0
Agbayani, ph-rf	1	0	0	0	0	0
Cedeno, rf-cf	3	0	1	0	0	0
Dunston, ph	1	0	0	0	0	0
Ordonez, ss	4	0	1	0	1	2
Rogers, p	2	0	0	0	0	2
Mahomes, p	0	0	0	0	0	0
Bonilla, ph	1	0	0	0	0	0
Dotel, p	0	0	0	0	0	0
J. Franco, p	0	0	0	0	1	0
Pratt, ph	1	0	0	0	0	0
Totals	**31**	**1**	**5**	**1**	**24**	**11**

Arizona	AB	R	H	RBI	PO	A
Womack, ss-rf	5	0	0	0	1	3
Bell, 2b	5	2	2	0	3	4
Gonzalez, lf	1	2	0	0	1	0
Williams, 3b	4	3	3	0	1	3
Colbrunn, 1b	2	0	1	1	12	0
Finley, cf	3	0	2	5	0	0
Gilkey, rf	3	0	0	0	2	0
Ward, ph	1	0	0	1	0	0
Swindell, p	0	0	0	0	0	1
Stinnett, c	4	0	1	0	7	1
Stottlemyre, p	3	0	0	0	0	0
Olson, p	0	0	0	0	0	0
Frias, ss	1	0	0	0	0	1
Totals	**32**	**7**	**9**	**7**	**27**	**13**

New York	0	0	1	0	0	0	0	0	0—1
Arizona	0	0	3	0	2	0	2	0	x—7

New York	IP	H	R	ER	BB	SO
Rogers (L)	4.1	5	4	4	2	6
Mahomes	1.2	3	1	1	0	1
Dotel	0.1	1	2	2	2	0
J. Franco	1.2	0	0	0	0	1
Arizona	**IP**	**H**	**R**	**ER**	**BB**	**SO**
Stottlemyre (W)	6.2	4	1	1	5	6
Olson	0.1	0	0	0	0	0
Swindell	2.0	1	0	0	0	1

E—Bell. DP—New York 1, Arizona 1. LOB—New York 8, Arizona 7. 2B—Ordonez, Colbrunn, Finley, Williams. SB—Henderson 3, Ordonez. HBP—By Rogers (Gonzalez), by Dotel (Colbrunn). T—3:13. A—49,328. U—Bell, plate; Hirschbeck, first; DeMuth, second; Marsh, third; Schrieber, left field; Gorman, right field.

GAME 3 BOX SCORE

NEW YORK 9, ARIZONA 2

FRIDAY, OCTOBER 8, AT NEW YORK

Arizona	AB	R	H	RBI	PO	A
Womack, rf	4	0	0	0	0	0
Bell, 2b	4	0	0	0	4	0
Gonzalez, lf	3	0	0	0	1	0
Williams, 3b	4	0	2	0	0	1
Durazo, 1b	3	0	0	0	8	0
Finley, cf	3	0	1	0	3	0
Fox, ss	3	0	0	0	1	2
Plesac, p	0	0	0	0	0	0
Chouinard, p	0	0	0	0	0	0
Swindell, p	0	0	0	0	0	0
Harris, ph	1	0	0	0	0	0
Stinnett, c	3	1	1	0	5	1
Daal, p	1	0	0	0	0	0
Ward, ph	1	1	1	2	0	0
Holmes, p	0	0	0	0	0	0
Frias, ss	1	0	0	0	2	0
Totals	**31**	**2**	**5**	**2**	**24**	**9**
New York	**AB**	**R**	**H**	**RBI**	**PO**	**A**
Henderson, lf	5	1	3	1	1	0
Mora, lf	0	0	0	0	0	0
Alfonzo, 2b	3	2	1	0	1	5
Olerud, 1b	4	2	2	3	10	3
Agbayani, rf	2	1	2	0	1	0
Cedeno, ph-rf	2	1	1	1	2	0
Ventura, 3b	4	0	0	1	1	0
Dunston, cf	2	0	0	0	2	0
Hamilton, ph-cf	3	0	1	2	2	0
Pratt, c	2	1	0	0	3	0
Ordonez, ss	3	0	1	1	2	4
Reed, p	1	0	0	0	2	1
Bonilla, ph	0	1	0	0	0	0
Wendell, p	1	0	0	0	0	0
J. Franco, p	0	0	0	0	0	0
Hershiser, p	0	0	0	0	0	0
Totals	**32**	**9**	**11**	**9**	**27**	**13**

Arizona	0	0	0		0	2	0		0	0	0—2
New York	0	1	2		0	0	6		0	0	x—9

Arizona	IP	H	R	ER	BB	SO
Daal (L)	4.0	6	3	3	3	4
Holmes	1.1	1	4	4	3	0
Plesac	0.1	3	2	2	0	0
Chouinard	1.1	1	0	0	0	1
Swindell	1.0	0	0	0	2	0
New York	**IP**	**H**	**R**	**ER**	**BB**	**SO**
Reed (W)	6.0	4	2	2	3	2
Wendell	1.0	0	0	0	1	0

New York	IP	H	R	ER	BB	SO
J. Franco	1.0	1	0	0	0	0
Hershiser	1.0	0	0	0	0	1

E—Fox, Daal, Womack. DP—Arizona 1, New York 1. LOB—Arizona 6, New York 9. 2B—Stinnett, Alfonzo. HR—Ward. SH—Reed, Ordonez. SB—Henderson, Cedeno. WP—Reed. T—3:05. A—56,180. U—Rieker, plate; Davis, first; Froemming, second; Meals, third; Winters, left field; Williams, right field.

GAME 4 BOX SCORE

NEW YORK 4, ARIZONA 3 (10 INNINGS)

SATURDAY, OCTOBER 9, AT NEW YORK

Arizona	AB	R	H	RBI	PO	A
Womack, ss-rf	5	1	1	0	1	2
Bell, 2b	2	0	1	2	1	1
Gonzalez, lf	3	0	0	0	4	0
Williams, 3b	4	0	1	0	1	2
Mantei, p	0	0	0	0	1	1
Colbrunn, 1b	3	1	1	1	5	0
Finley, cf	4	0	1	0	4	0
Gilkey, rf	3	0	0	0	3	0
Frias, ss	1	0	0	0	2	0
Stinnett, c	4	0	0	0	5	0
Anderson, p	2	0	0	0	1	1
Ward, ph	0	1	0	0	0	0
Olson, p	0	0	0	0	0	0
Swindell, p	0	0	0	0	0	0
Harris, 3b	1	0	0	0	0	0
Totals	**32**	**3**	**5**	**3**	**28**	**7**
New York	**AB**	**R**	**H**	**RBI**	**PO**	**A**
Henderson, lf	4	1	1	0	3	0
Mora, lf	0	0	0	0	1	1
Alfonzo, 2b	4	2	1	1	1	2
Olerud, 1b	4	0	2	0	8	0
Agbayani, rf	3	0	1	1	2	0
Cedeno, rf	1	0	0	1	1	0
Ventura, 3b	4	0	1	0	1	4
Pratt, c	5	1	1	1	8	1
Hamilton, cf	3	0	0	0	4	0
Ordonez, ss	4	0	1	0	2	1
Leiter, p	3	0	0	0	0	1
Benitez, p	0	0	0	0	0	0
M. Franco, ph	0	0	0	0	0	0
Dunston, p	0	0	0	0	0	0
J. Franco, p	0	0	0	0	0	1
Totals	**35**	**4**	**8**	**4**	**30**	**11**

Arizona	0	0	0		0	1	0		0	2	0	0—3
New York	0	0	0		1	0	1		0	1	0	1—4

One out when winning run scored.

Arizona	IP	H	R	ER	BB	SO
Anderson	7.0	7	2	2	0	4
Olson	*0.0	0	1	0	1	0
Swindell	0.1	0	0	0	1	0
Mantei (L)	2.0	1	1	1	3	1
New York	**IP**	**H**	**R**	**ER**	**BB**	**SO**
Leiter	7.2	3	3	3	3	4
Benitez	1.1	2	0	0	1	2
J. Franco (W)	1.0	0	0	0	0	1

*Pitched to one batter in eighth.

E—Womack. DP—New York 1. LOB—Arizona 4, New York 10. 2B—Bell, Ventura, Agbayani. HR—Colbrunn, Alfonzo, Pratt. SH—Mora. SF—Cedeno. CS—Bell. HBP—By Leiter (Bell). T—3:23. A—56,177. U—Davis, plate; Froemming, first; Meals, second; Winters, third; Williams, left field; Rieker, right field.

STATISTICS

NEW YORK METS' BATTING AND FIELDING AVERAGES

Player, position	G	AB	R	H	TB	2B	3B	HR	RBI	BB	IBB	SO	Avg.	PO	A	E	Avg.
Olerud, 1b	4	16	3	7	10	0	0	1	6	3	1	2	.438	31	4	0	1.000
Henderson, lf	4	15	5	6	6	0	0	1	3	0	1	1	.400	7	1	0	1.000
Agbayani, rf-ph	4	10	1	3	4	1	0	0	1	0	0	3	.300	5	0	0	1.000
Ordonez, ss	4	14	1	4	5	1	0	0	2	0	0	5	.286	7	9	0	1.000

Player, position	G	AB	R	H	TB	2B	3B	HR	RBI	BB	IBB	SO	Avg.	PO	A	E	Avg.
Cedeno, rf-cf-ph	4	7	1	2	2	0	0	0	2	1	0	1	.286	4	0	0	1.000
Alfonzo, 2b	4	16	6	4	14	1	0	3	6	3	1	2	.250	5	11	0	1.000
Piazza, c	2	9	0	2	2	0	0	0	0	0	0	4	.222	13	0	0	1.000
Ventura, 3b	4	14	1	3	5	2	0	0	1	4	1	2	.214	3	8	0	1.000
Dunston, cf-ph-pr	4	6	0	1	1	0	0	0	0	0	0	1	.167	7	0	0	1.000
Hamilton, cf-ph	4	8	0	1	1	0	0	0	2	2	0	0	.125	9	0	0	1.000
Pratt, ph-c	3	8	2	1	4	0	0	1	1	2	0	1	.125	11	1	0	1.000
Bonilla, ph	2	1	1	0	0	0	0	0	0	1	0	0	.000	0	0	0	.000
Mora, cf-lf	3	1	1	0	0	0	0	0	0	1	0	0	.000	2	1	0	1.000
Benitez, p	2	0	0	0	0	0	0	0	0	0	0	0	.000	0	0	0	.000
Cook, p	1	0	0	0	0	0	0	0	0	0	0	0	.000	1	0	0	1.000
Dotel, p	1	0	0	0	0	0	0	0	0	0	0	0	.000	0	0	0	.000
M. Franco, ph	1	0	0	0	0	0	0	0	0	1	0	0	.000	0	0	0	.000
J. Franco, p	3	0	0	0	0	0	0	0	0	0	0	0	.000	1	1	0	1.000
Hershiser, p	1	0	0	0	0	0	0	0	0	0	0	0	.000	0	0	0	.000
Mahomes, p	1	0	0	0	0	0	0	0	0	0	0	0	.000	0	0	0	.000
Reed, p	1	1	0	0	0	0	0	0	0	0	0	1	.000	2	1	0	1.000
Wendell, p	2	1	0	0	0	0	0	0	0	0	0	1	.000	0	0	0	.000
Rogers, p	1	2	0	0	0	0	0	0	0	0	0	1	.000	0	2	0	1.000
Yoshii, p	1	2	0	0	0	0	0	0	0	0	0	1	.000	0	1	0	1.000
Leiter, p	1	3	0	0	0	0	0	0	0	0	0	2	.000	0	1	0	1.000
Totals	4	134	22	34	54	5	0	5	22	21	3	28	.254	108	41	0	1.000

ARIZONA DIAMONDBACKS' BATTING AND FIELDING AVERAGES

Player, position	G	AB	R	H	TB	2B	3B	HR	RBI	BB	IBB	SO	Avg.	PO	A	E	Avg.
Ward, ph	3	2	2	1	4	0	0	1	3	1	0	0	.500	0	0	0	.000
Colbrunn, 1b	2	5	1	2	6	1	0	1	2	2	0	2	.400	17	0	0	1.000
Finley, cf	4	13	0	5	6	1	0	0	5	3	0	1	.385	10	0	0	1.000
Williams, 3b	4	16	3	6	7	1	0	0	0	0	0	1	.375	3	9	0	1.000
Johnson, p	1	3	0	1	2	1	0	0	0	0	0	1	.333	1	2	0	1.000
Bell, 2b	4	14	3	4	5	1	0	0	3	1	0	0	.286	8	11	1	.950
Gonzalez, lf	4	10	3	2	6	1	0	1	2	5	1	1	.200	6	0	0	1.000
Stinnett, c	4	14	1	2	3	1	0	0	0	1	0	4	.143	29	2	0	1.000
Durazo, 1b	2	7	1	1	4	0	0	1	1	1	0	0	.143	15	1	0	1.000
Womack, rf-ss	4	18	2	2	4	0	1	0	0	0	0	6	.111	5	5	2	.833
Chouinard, p	2	0	0	0	0	0	0	0	0	0	0	0	.000	0	0	0	.000
Holmes, p	1	0	0	0	0	0	0	0	0	0	0	0	.000	0	0	0	.000
Mantei, p	1	0	0	0	0	0	0	0	0	0	0	0	.000	1	1	0	1.000
Olson, p	2	0	0	0	0	0	0	0	0	0	0	0	.000	0	0	0	.000
Plesac, p	1	0	0	0	0	0	0	0	0	0	0	0	.000	0	0	0	.000
Swindell, p	3	0	0	0	0	0	0	0	0	0	0	0	.000	0	1	0	1.000
Daal, p	1	1	0	0	0	0	0	0	0	0	0	1	.000	0	1	1	.500
Anderson, p	1	2	0	0	0	0	0	0	0	0	0	0	.000	1	1	0	1.000
Harris, ph-3b	2	2	0	0	0	0	0	0	0	0	0	0	.000	0	0	0	.000
Fox, ss	1	3	0	0	0	0	0	0	0	0	0	1	.000	1	2	1	.750
Stottlemyre, p	1	3	0	0	0	0	0	0	0	0	0	1	.000	0	0	0	.000
Gilkey, rf	2	6	0	0	0	0	0	0	0	0	0	0	.000	5	0	0	1.000
Frias, ss	4	7	0	0	0	0	0	0	0	0	0	3	.000	4	1	0	1.000
Totals	4	126	16	26	47	7	1	4	16	14	1	22	.206	106	37	5	.966

NEW YORK METS' PITCHING RECORDS

Pitcher	G	GS	CG	IP	H	R	ER	HR	BB	IBB	SO	HB	WP	W	L	Pct.	ERA
J. Franco	3	0	0	3.2	1	0	0	0	0	0	2	0	0	1	0	1.000	0.00
Benitez	2	0	0	2.1	2	0	0	0	1	1	2	0	0	0	0	.000	0.00
Wendell	2	0	0	2.0	0	0	0	0	2	0	0	0	0	1	0	1.000	0.00
Cook	1	0	0	1.2	1	0	0	0	1	0	1	0	0	0	0	.000	0.00
Hershiser	1	0	0	1.0	0	0	0	0	0	0	1	0	0	0	0	.000	0.00
Reed	1	1	0	6.0	4	2	2	1	3	0	2	0	1	1	0	1.000	3.00
Leiter	1	1	0	7.2	3	3	3	1	3	0	4	1	0	0	0	.000	3.52
Mahomes	1	0	0	1.2	3	1	1	0	0	0	1	0	0	0	0	.000	5.40
Yoshii	1	1	0	5.1	6	4	4	2	0	0	3	0	0	0	0	.000	6.75
Rogers	1	1	0	4.1	5	4	4	0	2	0	6	1	0	0	1	.000	8.31
Dotel	1	0	0	0.1	1	2	2	0	2	0	0	1	0	0	0	.000	54.00
Totals	4	4	0	36.0	26	16	16	4	14	1	22	3	1	3	1	.750	4.00

No shutouts or saves.

ARIZONA DIAMONDBACKS' PITCHING RECORDS

Pitcher	G	GS	CG	IP	H	R	ER	HR	BB	IBB	SO	HB	WP	W	L	Pct.	ERA
Swindell	3	0	0	3.1	1	0	0	0	3	1	1	0	0	0	0	.000	0.00
Olson	2	0	0	0.1	0	1	0	0	1	0	0	0	0	0	0	.000	0.00

Pitcher	G	GS	CG	IP	H	R	ER	HR	BB	IBB	SO	HB	WP	W	L	Pct.	ERA
Stottlemyre	1	1	0	6.2	4	1	1	0	5	0	6	0	0	1	0	1.000	1.35
Anderson	1	1	0	7.0	7	2	2	1	0	0	4	0	0	0	0	.000	2.57
Chouinard	2	0	0	2.0	3	1	1	1	0	0	1	0	0	0	0	.000	4.50
Mantei	1	0	0	2.0	1	1	1	1	3	1	1	0	0	0	1	.000	4.50
Daal	1	1	0	4.0	6	3	3	0	3	0	4	0	0	0	1	.000	6.75
Johnson	1	1	0	8.1	8	7	7	2	3	0	11	0	0	0	1	.000	7.56
Holmes	1	0	0	1.1	1	4	4	0	3	1	0	0	0	0	0	.000	27.00
Plesac	1	0	0	0.1	3	2	2	0	0	0	0	0	0	0	0	.000	54.00
Totals	4	4	0	35.1	34	22	21	5	21	3	28	0	0	1	3	.250	5.35

No shutouts or saves.

SCORE BY INNINGS

New York .... 1 1 5   2 0 7   0 1 4   1—22

Arizona .... 0 0 4   1 5 2   2 2 0   0—16

MISCELLANEOUS STATISTICS

Sacrifice hits—Ordonez 2, Mora, Reed.
Sacrifice flies—Bell, Cedeno.
Stolen bases—Henderson 6, Cedeno, Ordonez.
Caught stealing—Bell.
Double plays—Alfonzo, Ordonez and Olerud 2; Bell and Colbrunn; Fox, Bell and Durazo; Henderson and Alfonzo; Ordonez, Alfonzo and Olerud; Ventura, Ordonez and Alfonzo.
Left on bases—New York 5, 8, 9, 10—32; Arizona 3, 7, 6, 4—20.
Hit by pitcher—By Rogers (Gonzalez), by Dotel (Colbrunn), by Leiter (Bell).
Passed balls—None.
Balks—None.
Time of games—First game, 2:53; second game, 3:13; third game, 3:05; fourth game, 3:23.
Attendance—First game, 49,584; second game, 49,328; third game, 56,180; fourth game, 56,177.
Umpires—Gorman, Bell, Hirschbeck, DeMuth, Marsh, Schreiber, Rieker, Davis, Froemming, Meals, Winters and Williams.
Official scorers—Bob Eger, Joe Donnelly.

ATLANTA VS. HOUSTON

HIGHLIGHTS

The bottom line: What figured to be an outstanding series between two similar teams turned out to be something very different—a relatively easy 3-1 victory for the Atlanta Braves. For the sixth time, Houston failed to get its first postseason series victory, and Atlanta advanced to its eighth consecutive National League Championship Series. On paper, the Astros' starting rotation looked every bit as strong as the Braves' heralded rotation. The three-man heart of the Astros' rotation—Shane Reynolds, Jose Lima and Mike Hampton—won 59 games during the regular season, only three fewer than Atlanta's four stalwarts, Greg Maddux, Kevin Millwood, Tom Glavine and John Smoltz. But it was Atlanta, as it has all decade, that continually made the big pitches and kept the big hitters off the bases. The Braves also got the necessary timely hitting for a victory. The Braves were relatively subdued after the Division Series victory. They realized that this was just a first step—the Braves had just one championship to show for their decade of dominance. And they wanted that to change.

Why the Braves won: The Braves continually kept the top two Astros hitters off the bases. Craig Biggio and Jeff Bagwell combined for a .299 batting average, 149 extra-base hits and 199 RBIs during the regular season. In this series, the two combined for a .125 average and no RBIs or extra-base hits. Ken Caminiti had the only productive series at the plate for Houston, batting .471 with three home runs and eight RBIs. The Braves got plenty of production from the center of their lineup. Brian Jordan led the way, batting .471 with seven RBIs, and Ryan Klesko had a .333 average. In addition, No. 2 hitter Bret Boone batted .474. National League MVP Chipper Jones hit just .231, but he was pitched around and walked much of the series, setting up RBI opportunities for Jordan and Klesko. The Braves bullpen also was tough in the crunch, allowing just two runs in eight innings in the final two games of the series.

The turning points:

Game 1: Shane Reynolds struck out Ryan Klesko swinging with the bases loaded and two outs in the fifth inning, killing a Braves rally and keeping the game tied 1-1. Daryle Ward's booming homer to right an inning later gave the Astros a 2-1 lead and sent them toward a 6-1 victory in Atlanta. Reynolds and Maddux locked into a pitching duel, with both pitchers getting out of several jams. The Braves' only serious threat was the fifth inning, tying the game on an RBI single from Gerald Williams with two outs. But Reynolds' lone strikeout of the game kept the Braves from scoring more.

Game 2: After giving up a solo home run to Ken Caminiti in the second inning, Atlanta starter Kevin Millwood dominated the Astros lineup. Millwood didn't allow another runner to reach base until Chipper Jones' error in the seventh, and he faced just two batters over the minimum and pitched a one-hit complete game. It was the first complete game one-hitter in the postseason since Jim Lonborg of the Red Sox pitched a one-hitter against the Cardinals in the 1967 World Series. Brian Jordan continued his strong play in the series with two RBIs in the 5-1 victory.

Game 3: The Astros were one deep fly ball or a seeing-eye single or even a soft grounder from winning Game 3. Braves reliever John Rocker didn't allow it. With the bases loaded and no outs and the game tied 3-3 in the bottom of the tenth, Rocker came in and shut down the Astros. The first batter, Carl Everett, grounded to Klesko who threw to catcher Eddie Perez for the first out. Next, Tony Eusebio grounded a ball up the middle, but Walt Weiss made a diving stab, scrambled to his feet and threw another runner out at home. Then Rocker struck out Ricky Gutierrez, ending the inning and leaving Astros fans in agony. Brian Jordan picked up where he left off in Game 2 by driving in the winning run with a two-run double in the 12th inning, giving the Braves a 5-3 victory. It was Jordan's fifth RBI of the day and seventh in the last two games.

Game 4: The Astros, just as they had in their two previous losses, had a chance to win this game—as late as the bottom of the ninth inning. Down 7-5 in the final frame with a runner on and nobody out, John Rocker struck out National League MVP runner-up Jeff Bagwell and streaky hitter Carl Everett, then he coaxed hot-hitting Ken Caminiti, who had homered earlier, to hit a fly ball to center field for the series-clinching out. Two-run singles by Eddie Perez and Gerald Williams in the sixth inning put the Braves in front 7-0 before Houston rallied.

Notable:

Astros: The Astros surpassed their entire run total —five—from their 1997 Division Series loss to the Braves by scoring six runs in Game 1. ... Jose Lima, pitching on three days rest, gave up four runs on nine hits in 6.2 innings of Game 2. This was his first start with three days rest all season. ... The Astros left 12 runners on base in Game 3. ... There was not a sellout in the series at either place. ... The Astros have never hit above .233 in any postseason appearance.

Braves: The Braves had been 12-1, with 10 straight wins in Division Series play going into Game 1. ... In losing Game 1 the Braves had lost four straight home playoff games, only scoring three runs in that span. ... There were 20,024 unsold tickets for Games 1 and 2 at Turner Field. ... Tom Glavine had not lost at the Astrodome since June 25, 1991. True to form, he didn't lose Game 3 either; the Braves won in extra innings. ... Both Game 1 starter Greg Maddux and Game 2 starter Kevin Millwood pitched in Game 3 out of the bullpen. ... Atlanta became the first team to win a Division Series after losing Game 1. (Boston matched the feat two days later with a series win over Cleveland.)

Quotable:

Astros: Shane Reynolds on his decision to walk Chipper Jones to load the bases in the fifth: "If there are runners in scoring position, if it's a crucial situation, don't give him anything to hit. If you get behind in the count, take a chance on walking him and get-

ting the next guy." ... Manager Larry Dierker, speaking to whether the Braves had momentum going into Game 3: "I don't know what momentum is. (Twins manager) Tom Kelly said it's your next game's starting pitcher and our next starting pitcher is Mike Hampton. So I feel pretty good about our chances." ... Tony Eusebio, on Walt Weiss's game-saving stab in the bottom of the tenth: "There's no way he should have made that play. He made a heck of a play. When I saw the ball go past the pitcher, I thought it was a hit for sure." ... Jeff Bagwell, on losing the series: "We had a chance, but it wasn't enough. It just goes to show how big Game 3 is." ... Craig Biggio, also on losing the series: "It's frustrating beyond belief. We really didn't start playing relaxed until it was too late."

Braves: Chipper Jones on the Astros' decision to pitch around him: "It's frustrating. I hope to go up there in situations where they have to pitch to me. Other teams have been doing this for awhile now and mostly the guys behind me have made them pay." ... Kevin Millwood on Caminiti's home run, the only hit Millwood allowed in Game 2: "That pitch was a mistake. I was trying to go away and threw it right over the middle of the plate. But it was one of the few mistakes I made all day." ... Braves closer John Rocker about his being brought in with the bases loaded and no outs in the bottom of the tenth: "If you can think of a tougher situation than that, let me know." ... John Smoltz, on Tony Eusebio's ground ball in the tenth inning: "When he hit it, I got up and started to walk out of the dugout." ... John Smoltz on Ken Caminiti's Division Series performance: "He's just got me baffled when it comes to this time of the year. He almost won the game single-handedly."

GAME 1 BOX SCORE

HOUSTON 6, ATLANTA 1

TUESDAY, OCTOBER 5, AT ATLANTA

Houston	AB	R	H	RBI	PO	A
Biggio, 2b	5	0	1	0	4	6
Spiers, rf-lf	4	0	2	0	2	0
Javier, ph-lf	1	0	1	0	0	0
Bagwell, 1b	4	1	1	0	14	1
Everett, cf-rf	3	1	1	1	2	0
Caminiti, 3b	4	1	3	3	0	3
Ward, lf	3	1	1	1	2	0
Barker, cf	1	0	0	0	0	0
Eusebio, c	4	0	2	1	3	0
Gutierrez, ss	2	0	0	0	0	6
Reynolds, p	3	0	1	0	0	0
Miller, p	0	0	0	0	0	0
Henry, p	0	0	0	0	0	0
Mieske, ph	0	1	0	0	0	0
Wagner, p	0	0	0	0	0	0
Totals	34	6	13	6	27	16
Atlanta	**AB**	**R**	**H**	**RBI**	**PO**	**A**
Williams, lf	4	0	2	1	0	0
Boone, 2b	4	0	1	0	2	4
C. Jones, 3b	2	0	0	0	2	0
Klesko, 1b	4	0	0	0	9	0
Jordan, rf	4	0	2	0	2	1
A. Jones, cf	4	0	0	0	4	0
Perez, c	4	0	1	0	7	1
Hernandez, ss	4	1	1	0	1	4

Atlanta	AB	R	H	RBI	PO	A
Maddux, p	1	0	0	0	0	1
Lockhart, ph	0	0	0	0	0	0
Battle, ph	1	0	0	0	0	0
Remlinger, p	0	0	0	0	0	2
Totals	32	1	7	1	27	13

Houston	0	1 0	0 0 1	0 0	4—6
Atlanta	0	0 0	0 1 0	0 0	x—1

Houston	IP	H	R	ER	BB	SO
Reynolds (W)	6.0	7	1	1	2	1
Miller	0.1	0	0	0	0	0
Henry	1.2	0	0	0	0	0
Wagner	1.0	0	0	0	0	1

Atlanta	IP	H	R	ER	BB	SO
Maddux (L)	7.0	10	2	2	4	5
Remlinger	2.0	3	4	4	2	2

DP—Houston 1, Atlanta 2. LOB—Houston 9, Atlanta 7. HR—Ward, Caminiti. SH—Barker, Maddux. SF—Everett. SB—Spiers, Hernandez. CS—Caminiti. T—3:03. A—39,119. U—Winters, plate; Williams, first; Rieker, second; Davis, third; Froemming, left field; Meals, right field.

GAME 2 BOX SCORE

ATLANTA 5, HOUSTON 1

WEDNESDAY, OCTOBER 6, AT ATLANTA

Houston	AB	R	H	RBI	PO	A
Biggio, 2b	4	0	0	0	2	1
Javier, rf	4	0	0	0	1	0
Bagwell, 1b	3	0	0	0	7	1
Everett, cf	3	0	0	0	5	0
Caminiti, 3b	3	1	1	1	0	2
Ward, lf	3	0	0	0	1	0
Eusebio, c	3	0	0	0	5	0
Gutierrez, ss	3	0	0	0	2	4
Lima, p	2	0	0	0	0	0
Elarton, p	0	0	0	0	0	0
Powell, p	0	0	0	0	1	0
Spiers, ph	1	0	0	0	0	0
Totals	29	1	1	1	24	9

Atlanta	AB	R	H	RBI	PO	A
Williams, lf	5	1	1	0	3	0
Boone, 2b	4	1	2	0	2	3
C. Jones, 3b	3	1	1	0	0	1
Jordan, rf	3	0	1	2	2	0
Klesko, 1b	4	2	3	1	8	0
Hunter, 1b	0	0	0	0	1	1
A. Jones, cf	4	0	2	1	0	0
Perez, c	3	0	0	1	8	0
Hernandez, ss	2	0	0	0	2	2
Weiss, ss	1	0	0	0	0	0
Millwood, p	4	0	1	0	1	4
Totals	33	5	11	5	27	11

Houston	0	1 0	0 0 0	0 0	0—1
Atlanta	1	0 0	0 0 1	3 0	x—5

Houston	IP	H	R	ER	BB	SO
Lima (L)	6.2	9	4	4	2	4
Elarton	0.1	2	1	1	0	0
Powell	1.0	0	0	0	0	1

Atlanta	IP	H	R	ER	BB	SO
Millwood (W)	9.0	1	1	1	0	8

E—Ward, C. Jones. LOB—Houston 1, Atlanta 8. 2B—A. Jones, Boone. HR—Caminiti. SF—Perez, Jordan. SB—Williams. WP—Elarton 2. T—2:13. A—41,913. U—Williams, plate; Rieker, first; Davis, second; Froemming, third; Meals, left field; Winters, right field.

GAME 3 BOX SCORE

ATLANTA 5, HOUSTON 3 (12 INNINGS)

FRIDAY, OCTOBER 8, AT HOUSTON

Atlanta	AB	R	H	RBI	PO	A
Williams, lf	5	0	2	0	0	0
Nixon, pr-lf	1	1	1	0	0	0
Boone, 2b	6	2	3	0	3	6
C. Jones, 3b	4	1	1	0	1	1
Jordan, rf	5	1	3	5	4	0

Atlanta	AB	R	H	RBI	PO	A
A. Jones, cf	5	0	1	0	2	0
Hunter, 1b	3	0	0	0	9	0
Lockhart, ph	1	0	0	0	0	0
Springer, p	0	0	0	0	0	0
Rocker, p	0	0	0	0	0	0
Guillen, ph	1	0	0	0	0	0
Millwood, p	0	0	0	0	0	0
Perez, c	5	0	1	0	14	0
Hernandez, ss	3	0	0	0	2	3
Mulholland, p	0	0	0	0	0	0
Maddux, p	0	0	0	0	0	0
Remlinger, p	0	0	0	0	0	0
Klesko, ph-1b	2	0	0	0	1	1
Glavine, p	2	0	0	0	0	0
Weiss, ph-ss	3	0	0	0	0	3
Totals	46	5	12	5	36	14

Houston	AB	R	H	RBI	PO	A
Biggio, 2b	5	1	1	0	4	1
Bell, rf	3	0	1	0	1	0
Spiers, ph-lf	2	0	1	1	0	0
Henry, p	0	0	0	0	0	0
Bogar, ph	0	0	0	0	0	0
Powell, p	0	0	0	0	0	0
Bagwell, 1b	2	1	0	0	10	1
Caminiti, 3b	6	0	3	1	0	4
Mieske, lf	4	0	0	0	0	0
Cabrera, p	0	0	0	0	0	0
Javier, lf	2	0	1	0	2	0
Everett, cf-rf	5	0	1	0	0	0
Eusebio, c	4	0	0	1	16	2
Gutierrez, ss	5	0	0	0	2	6
Hampton, p	2	0	0	0	0	1
Johnson, ph	1	0	1	0	0	0
Barker, pr-cf	2	1	0	0	1	0
Totals	43	3	9	3	36	15

Atlanta	0 0 0	0 0 3	0 0 0	2—5
Houston	2 0 0	0 0 1	0 0 0	0—3

Atlanta	IP	H	R	ER	BB	SO
Glavine	6.0	5	2	2	3	6
Mulholland	0.1	1	1	1	0	0
Maddux	*0.0	0	0	0	1	0
Remlinger	1.2	1	0	0	1	2
Springer	†1.0	2	0	0	1	1
Rocker (W)	2.0	0	0	0	1	2
Millwood (S)	1.0	0	0	0	0	0

Houston	IP	H	R	ER	BB	SO
Hampton	7.0	6	3	3	1	9
Cabrera	2.0	2	0	0	6	6
Henry	2.0	1	0	0	3	2
Powell (L)	1.0	3	2	2	1	1

*Pitched to one batter in seventh. †Pitched to three batters in 10th.
E—Gutierrez, Eusebio. DP—Atlanta 2, Houston 2. LOB—Atlanta 10, Houston 12. 2B—Jordan, Johnson. HR—Jordan. SB—Nixon, Barker. HBP—By Glavine (Bagwell). WP—Hampton. T—4:19. A—48,625. U—Hirschbeck, plate; DeMuth, first; Marsh, second; Schrieber, third; Gorman, left field; Bell, right field.

GAME 4 BOX SCORE

ATLANTA 7, HOUSTON 5

SATURDAY, OCTOBER 9, AT HOUSTON

Atlanta	AB	R	H	RBI	PO	A
Williams, lf	4	1	2	2	1	0
Boone, 2b	5	0	3	1	4	2
Rocker, p	0	0	0	0	0	0
C. Jones, 3b	4	0	1	1	0	2
Jordan, rf	5	1	2	0	4	0
Klesko, 1b	2	1	1	0	4	1
Hunter, 1b	1	0	0	0	1	0
A. Jones, cf	5	1	1	1	6	0
Perez, c	4	1	2	2	6	0
Hernandez, ss	2	0	0	0	1	0
Weiss, ss	2	1	1	0	0	2
Smoltz, p	3	1	2	0	0	1
Mulholland, p	0	0	0	0	0	0
McGlinchy, p	0	0	0	0	0	0
Lockhart, 2b	0	0	0	0	0	0
Totals	37	7	15	7	27	8

Houston	AB	R	H	RBI	PO	A
Biggio, 2b	5	0	0	0	4	2
Javier, rf	4	0	1	0	1	0
Bagwell, 1b	4	1	1	0	5	0
Everett, cf	4	1	0	0	1	0
Caminiti, 3b	4	1	1	3	1	1
Spiers, lf	4	0	0	0	1	0
Eusebio, c	4	2	2	1	10	1
Bogar, ss	4	0	3	1	4	4
Reynolds, p	1	0	0	0	0	1
Holt, p	0	0	0	0	0	0
Elarton, p	0	0	0	0	0	1
Johnson, ph	0	0	0	0	0	0
Miller, p	0	0	0	0	0	0
Bell, ph	0	0	0	0	0	0
Ward, ph	1	0	0	0	0	0
Powell, p	0	0	0	0	0	0
Totals	35	5	8	5	27	10

Atlanta	IP	H	R	ER	BB	SO
Smoltz (W)	‡7.0	6	4	4	3	3
Mulholland	0.1	2	1	1	0	0
McGlinchy	0.1	0	0	0	0	0
Rocker (S)	1.1	0	0	0	1	3

Houston	IP	H	R	ER	BB	SO
Reynolds (L)	*5.0	9	4	4	1	4
Holt	†0.0	3	3	3	0	0
Elarton	2.0	2	0	0	1	3
Miller	1.0	1	0	0	0	2
Powell	1.0	0	0	0	0	1

Atlanta	1 0 1	0 0 5	0 0 0	—7
Houston	0 0 0	0 0 0	1 4 0	—5

*Pitched to two batters in sixth. †Pitched to three batters in sixth. ‡Pitched to three batters in eighth.

E—Hernandez, Spiers. DP—Houston 1. LOB—Atlanta 8, Houston 9. 2B—Williams, Smoltz, Bogar. HR—Eusebio, Caminiti. SH—Williams, Smoltz, Reynolds. SF—C. Jones. SB—Boone, Everett. CS—Jordan. HBP—By Smoltz (Everett). WP—Miller, Rocker. T—3:12. A—48,553. U—DeMuth, plate; Marsh, first; Schrieber, second; Gorman, third; Bell, left field; Hirschbeck, right field.

STATISTICS

ATLANTA BRAVES' BATTING AND FIELDING AVERAGES

Player, position	G	AB	R	H	TB	2B	3B	HR	RBI	BB	IBB	SO	Avg.	PO	A	E	Avg.
Nixon, pr-lf	1	1	1	1	1	0	0	0	0	0	0	0	1.000	0	0	0	.000
Smoltz, p	1	3	1	2	3	1	0	0	0	0	0	1	.667	0	1	0	1.000
Boone, 2b	4	19	3	9	10	1	0	0	1	0	0	4	.474	11	15	0	1.000
Jordan, rf	4	17	2	8	12	1	0	1	7	1	0	2	.471	12	1	0	1.000
Williams, lf	4	18	2	7	8	1	0	0	3	0	0	3	.389	4	0	0	1.000
Klesko, 1b-ph	4	12	3	4	4	0	0	0	1	1	0	4	.333	22	2	0	1.000
Perez, c	4	16	1	4	4	0	0	0	3	0	0	3	.250	35	1	0	1.000
Millwood, p	2	4	0	1	1	0	0	0	0	0	0	3	.250	1	4	0	1.000
C. Jones, 3b	4	13	2	3	3	0	0	0	1	5	2	2	.231	3	4	1	.875
A. Jones, cf	4	18	1	4	5	1	0	0	2	1	1	3	.222	12	0	0	1.000
Weiss, ss-ph	3	6	1	1	1	0	0	0	0	0	0	2	.167	0	5	0	1.000
Hernandez, ss	4	11	1	1	1	0	0	0	0	1	1	3	.091	6	9	1	.938
McGlinchy, p	1	0	0	0	0	0	0	0	0	0	0	0	.000	0	0	0	.000
Mulholland, p	2	0	0	0	0	0	0	0	0	0	0	0	.000	0	0	0	.000
Remlinger, p	2	0	0	0	0	0	0	0	0	0	0	0	.000	0	2	0	1.000
Rocker, p	2	0	0	0	0	0	0	0	0	1	0	0	.000	0	0	0	.000
Springer, p	1	0	0	0	0	0	0	0	0	0	0	0	.000	0	0	0	.000
Battle, ph	1	1	0	0	0	0	0	0	0	0	0	0	.000	0	0	0	.000
Guillen, ph	1	1	0	0	0	0	0	0	0	0	0	0	.000	0	0	0	.000
Lockhart, ph-2b	3	1	0	0	0	0	0	0	0	0	0	1	.000	0	0	0	.000
Maddux, p	2	1	0	0	0	0	0	0	0	0	0	0	.000	0	1	0	1.000
Glavine, p	1	2	0	0	0	0	0	0	0	0	0	1	.000	0	0	0	.000
Hunter, 1b	3	4	0	0	0	0	0	0	0	1	0	3	.000	11	1	0	1.000
Totals	4	148	18	45	53	5	0	1	18	11	4	35	.304	117	46	2	.988

HOUSTON ASTROS' BATTING AND FIELDING AVERAGES

Player, position	G	AB	R	H	TB	2B	3B	HR	RBI	BB	IBB	SO	Avg.	PO	A	E	Avg.
Johnson, ph	2	1	0	1	2	1	0	0	0	0	1	0	1.000	0	0	0	.000
Bogar, ph-ss	2	4	0	3	4	1	0	0	1	1	0	0	.750	4	4	0	1.000
Caminiti, 3b	4	17	3	8	17	0	0	3	8	2	0	1	.471	1	10	0	1.000
Bell, rf-ph	2	3	0	1	1	0	0	0	0	0	0	0	.333	1	0	0	1.000
Javier, ph-lf-rf	4	11	1	3	3	0	0	0	0	1	0	1	.273	4	0	0	1.000
Spiers, rf-lf-ph	4	11	0	3	3	0	0	0	1	0	0	1	.273	3	0	1	.750
Eusebio, c	4	15	2	4	7	0	0	1	3	1	0	2	.267	34	3	1	.974
Reynolds, p	2	4	0	1	1	0	0	0	0	0	0	0	.250	0	1	0	1.000
Bagwell, 1b	4	13	3	2	2	0	0	0	0	5	2	4	.154	36	3	0	1.000
Ward, lf-ph	3	7	1	1	4	0	0	1	1	0	0	2	.143	3	0	1	.750
Everett, cf-rf	4	15	2	2	2	0	0	0	1	2	1	8	.133	8	0	0	1.000
Biggio, 2b	4	19	1	2	2	0	0	0	0	1	0	5	.105	14	10	0	1.000
Cabrera, p	1	0	0	0	0	0	0	0	0	0	0	0	.000	0	0	0	.000
Elarton, p	2	0	0	0	0	0	0	0	0	0	0	0	.000	0	1	0	1.000
Henry, p	2	0	0	0	0	0	0	0	0	0	0	0	.000	0	0	0	.000
Holt, p	1	0	0	0	0	0	0	0	0	0	0	0	.000	0	0	0	.000
Miller, p	2	0	0	0	0	0	0	0	0	0	0	0	.000	0	0	0	.000
Powell, p	3	0	0	0	0	0	0	0	0	0	0	0	.000	1	0	0	1.000
Wagner, p	1	0	0	0	0	0	0	0	0	0	0	0	.000	0	0	0	.000

1999 REVIEW N.L. Division Series

Player, position	G	AB	R	H	TB	2B	3B	HR	RBI	BB	IBB	SO	Avg.	PO	A	E	Avg.
Hampton, p	1	2	0	0	0	0	0	0	0	0	0	1	.000	0	1	0	1.000
Lima, p	1	2	0	0	0	0	0	0	0	0	0	1	.000	0	1	0	1.000
Barker, cf-pr	2	3	1	0	0	0	0	0	0	0	0	2	.000	1	0	0	1.000
Mieske, ph-lf	2	4	1	0	0	0	0	0	0	1	0	0	.000	0	0	0	.000
Gutierrez, ss	3	10	0	0	0	0	0	0	0	2	1	5	.000	4	16	1	.952
Totals	4	141	15	31	48	2	0	5	15	17	4	33	.220	114	50	4	.976

ATLANTA BRAVES' PITCHING RECORDS

Pitcher	G	GS	CG	IP	H	R	ER	HR	BB	IBB	SO	HB	WP	W	L	Pct.	ERA
Rocker	2	0	0	3.1	0	0	0	0	2	0	5	0	1	1	0	1.000	0.00
Springer	1	0	0	1.0	2	0	0	0	1	0	1	0	0	0	0	.000	0.00
McGlinchy	1	0	0	0.1	0	0	0	0	0	0	0	0	0	0	0	.000	0.00
Millwood	2	1	1	10.0	1	1	1	1	0	0	9	0	0	1	0	1.000	0.90
Maddux	2	1	0	7.0	10	2	2	1	5	2	5	0	0	0	1	.000	2.57
Glavine	1	1	0	6.0	5	2	2	0	3	0	6	1	0	0	0	.000	3.00
Smoltz	1	1	0	7.0	6	4	4	2	3	0	3	1	0	1	0	1.000	5.14
Remlinger	2	0	0	3.2	4	4	4	1	3	2	4	0	0	0	0	.000	9.82
Mulholland	2	0	0	0.2	3	2	2	0	0	0	0	0	0	0	0	.000	27.00
Totals	4	4	1	39.0	31	15	15	5	17	4	33	2	1	3	1	.750	3.46

No shutouts. Saves—Millwood, Rocker.

HOUSTON ASTROS' PITCHING RECORDS

Pitcher	G	GS	CG	IP	H	R	ER	HR	BB	IBB	SO	HB	WP	W	L	Pct.	ERA
Henry	2	0	0	3.2	1	0	0	0	3	1	2	0	0	0	0	.000	0.00
Cabrera	1	0	0	2.0	2	0	0	0	0	0	6	0	0	0	0	.000	0.00
Miller	2	0	0	1.1	1	0	0	0	0	0	2	0	1	0	0	.000	0.00
Wagner	1	0	0	1.0	0	0	0	0	0	0	1	0	0	0	0	.000	0.00
Hampton	1	1	0	7.0	6	3	3	1	1	0	9	0	1	0	0	.000	3.86
Elarton	2	0	0	2.1	4	1	1	0	1	0	3	0	2	0	0	.000	3.86
Reynolds	2	2	0	11.0	16	5	5	0	3	0	5	0	1	1	1	.500	4.09
Lima	1	1	0	6.2	9	4	4	0	2	2	4	0	0	0	1	.000	5.40
Powell	3	0	0	3.0	3	2	2	0	1	1	3	0	0	0	1	.000	6.00
Holt	1	0	0	0.0	3	3	3	0	0	0	0	0	0	0	0	.000	Inf.
Totals	4	4	0	38.0	45	18	18	1	11	4	35	0	4	1	3	.250	4.26

No shutouts or saves.

SCORE BY INNINGS

Atlanta ....2 0 1   0 1 9   3 0 0   0 0 2 —18
Houston ....2 2 0   0 0 1   2 4 4   0 0 0 —15

MISCELLANEOUS STATISTICS

Sacrifice hits—Barker, Maddux, Reynolds, Smoltz, Williams.
Sacrifice flies—Everett, C. Jones, Jordan, Perez.
Stolen bases—Barker, Boone, Everett, Hernandez, Nixon, Spiers, Williams.
Caught stealing—Caminiti, Jordan.
Double plays—Boone, Hernandez and Hunter 2; Bagwell, Gutierrez and Biggio; Biggio, Bogar and Bagwell; Biggio, Gutierrez and Bagwell; Boone, Hernandez and Klesko; Gutierrez, Biggio and Bagwell; Hernandez, Boone and Klesko.
Left on bases—Atlanta 7, 8, 10, 8—33; Houston 9, 1, 12, 9—31.
Hit by pitcher—By Glavine (Bagwell), by Smoltz (Everett).
Passed balls—None.
Balks—None.
Time of games—First game, 3:03; second game, 2:13; third game, 4:19; fourth game, 3:12.
Attendance—First game, 39,119; second game, 41,913; third game, 48,625; fourth game, 48,553.
Umpires—Winters, Williams, Rieker, Davis, Froemming, Meals, Hirschbeck, DeMuth, Marsh, Schrieber, Gorman and Bell.
Official scorers—Rick Blount, Mike Stamus.

A.L. CHAMPIONSHIP SERIES

The bottom line: Much of the drama for the Yankees-Red Sox championship series was rooted in events that took place long before any of the players were born. The so-called "Curse of the Bambino" claims that the Red Sox were cursed after selling Babe Ruth to the Yankees before the 1920 season. Indeed, Boston has not won a World Series since, and the Yankees now have won 25. That history, coupled with the proximity of the two division foes, has fueled one of the fiercest rivalries in sports. For the first time, the teams met in a postseason series. The Yankees, the A.L. East champs, were seeking a return trip to the World Series, and the scrappy Red Sox, the American League wild-card winners, were going for their first World Series appearance in 13 years. But except for their surreal, 13-1 victory in Game 3 at Fenway Park, it was curses for the Red Sox. Again.

Why the Yankees won: They did little wrong. They had depth at the plate and on the mound, and they were flawless in the field. And, they allowed the Red Sox to sink themselves with mistakes and missed opportunities. Boston stranded 45 runners and made 10 errors in the five games, failures that seemed to happen at the most opportune times for the Yankees. The Yankees, sparked by Bernie Williams' 10th-inning, game-winning home run in Game 1, got strong starting pitching from Orlando Hernandez, David Cone and Andy Pettitte. Shortstop Derek Jeter hit .350 in the series, and the Yankees' short relievers did not allow a run in nine innings.

The turning points:

Game 1: All-Star center fielder Bernie Williams hit the second pitch from Red Sox reliever Rod Beck for a home run to center field in the bottom of the 10th inning, capping the Yankees' 4-3 comeback win at Yankee Stadium. The Red Sox jumped out to a 2-0 lead in the first and added a run in the second inning, but in both innings they wasted one-out, first-and-second opportunities against Yankees hurler Orlando Hernandez. Hernandez got stronger as the game continued, and the Red Sox had just five hits and no runs the rest of the way. After a two-run home run by Scott Brosius in the second, the Yankees tied it in the seventh when Brosius scored on a single by Derek Jeter, despite a perfect throw from right fielder Trot Nixon that catcher Jason Varitek could not handle.

Game 2: Yankees lefthander Paul O'Neill, who had struggled against lefthanded pitching all season, faced Boston lefty Rheal Cormier in the seventh inning with the score 2-2, and came through with a game-winning single that scored Chuck Knoblauch. New York again used a late-inning rally to snuff the Red Sox at Yankee Stadium, 3-2. Boston starter Ramon Martinez, who missed most of the last two seasons recovering from shoulder surgery, pitched

6.2 innings, but he was outdone by David Cone of the Yankees, who struck out nine in seven innings. The Red Sox led, 2-1, on Nomar Garciaparra's home run, but the Yankees got a run in the seventh on Knoblauch's double before O'Neill's single.

Game 3: John Valentin's first-inning home run after Jose Offerman's leadoff triple set the tone for the Red Sox. With ace Pedro Martinez as their anchor on the mound, the Red Sox breezed to a 13-1 win as the series moved to Fenway Park. Oozing with subplots, it was among the most heavily hyped games in Championship Series history. There was Martinez, a shoo-in for the Cy Young Award, the hero of the Red Sox's series win over the Indians. There was pitcher Roger Clemens, who won three Cy Young Awards in 13 seasons as the Red Sox ace, returning to Fenway Park in a crucial playoff game—now as a member of the Yankees. Clemens flopped, though, giving up five runs in two-plus innings, helping the Red Sox on their way to a rout.

Game 4: With the Yankees ahead, 3-2, in the bottom of the eighth, Jose Offerman of the Red Sox was called out on a tag play that umpire Tim Tschida later admitted was the wrong call. It was the second time in the series an umpire admitted a call that went against Boston was incorrect, and the Red Sox did not recover. They allowed six runs in the top of the ninth, losing 9-2. In that inning, Offerman threw away a double-play ball that could have ended the Yankees threat, and the next batter, Ricky Ledee, hit a grand slam that sealed the win.

Game 5: After Derek Jeter put the Yankees ahead, 2-0, with a home run, series MVP Orlando Hernandez again defused some early Boston rallies. He held the Red Sox to one run over seven innings, and the Yankees closed out the series with a 6-1 victory. The Red Sox had runners on first and third with no outs in the first inning, then had runners on first and second in the second, but Hernandez held them scoreless both times. The Yankees secured the game with two runs in the seventh, getting three hits and some help from three Red Sox errors.

Notable:

Yankees: The Yankees were outscored, 11-5, in the first three innings over the five games, but they outscored the Red Sox, 15-5, from the seventh inning on. ... New York turned seven double plays, and Boston turned none. ... Closer Mariano Rivera made three appearances, getting a win and two saves. He threw 74 pitches—only 21 were balls. ... Series MVP Orlando Hernandez's brother, Livan, was the 1997 NLCS MVP for the Marlins. ... The Yankees finished the century with a 1,011-826 advantage against the rival Red Sox. ... Paul O'Neill was a standout in the series despite playing with a broken rib.

Red Sox: Boston's 10 errors—in just five games—were a League Championship Series record. Five of the 23 runs allowed by Red Sox pitchers were unearned. ... After manager Jimy Williams was ejected arguing a call in the ninth inning of Game 4, fans at Fenway Park threw debris onto the field, causing the players to be cleared from the Yankees bullpen. A forfeit was threatened over stadium loudspeakers. ... Babe Ruth's daughter threw out the first pitch for Game 5 at Fenway Park. ... In their Game 3 win, the Red Sox were 7-for-17 (.412) with runners in scoring position. In the other four games, Boston was 6-for 36 (.167). ... The Red Sox had lost 10 straight ALCS games before winning Game 3.

Quotable:

Red Sox: Rod Beck, after allowing Bernie Williams' game-winning home run in Game 1: "It was a bad time for a bad pitch." ... Umpire Rick Reed, whose missed call in the top of the 10th inning in Game 1 blunted a Red Sox rally: "As an umpire, it was my job to get it right. I didn't. I feel awful." ... Boston's Game 2 starter Ramon Martinez, after the Yankees' 3-2 win: "This is one of the greatest teams. That is the reason why they are here. I know I am going to have a tough game. I did the best that I could." ... John Valentin, after the Red Sox's Game 3 win: "We had to win today. Going down 3-0 against the New York Yankees would have been almost impossible to come back from. It would have been like going down 2-0 to Cleveland." ... Darren Lewis, after umpire Tim Tschida admittedly made a bad call, ending a Red Sox threat, in the eighth inning of Game 4: "We made some mistakes. But at the same time, they're taking away something we've worked for all year. With calls like this, we feel like we're being cheated."

Yankees: Bernie Williams after his game-winning, 10th-inning home run in Game 1: "If it took a break like that to get us going, it is welcomed." ... Yankee manager Joe Torre after Boston's Pedro Martinez struck out 12 in seven innings in Game 3: "He is an artist out there, except he has a baseball instead of a paint brush." ... Torre, after frustrated fans threw debris on the field at Fenway Park during Game 4: "The sad part about it is you have a ballclub, the Boston Red Sox, who have busted their butts to give this city something to be proud of. I think it's inexcusable." ... MVP Orlando Hernandez, after the series-ending Game 5: "This is a beautiful moment."

GAME 1 BOX SCORE

NEW YORK 4, BOSTON 3 (10 INNINGS)

WEDNESDAY, OCTOBER 13, AT NEW YORK

Boston	AB	R	H	RBI	PO	A
Offerman, 2b	5	1	3	1	5	2
Valentin, 3b	5	1	1	0	0	2
Daubach, dh	5	0	1	1	0	0
Garciaparra, ss	4	0	0	0	2	3
O'Leary, lf	3	0	0	0	1	0
Stanley, 1b	4	0	1	0	8	0
Varitek, c	4	0	1	0	7	0
Lewis, cf	3	1	0	0	2	0
Nixon, rf	4	0	1	0	2	0
Mercker, p	0	0	0	0	0	2
Garces, p	0	0	0	0	0	1
Lowe, p	0	0	0	0	0	1
Cormier, p	0	0	0	0	0	1

Boston	AB	R	H	RBI	PO	A
Beck, p	0	0	0	0	0	0
Totals	37	3	8	2	27	12

New York	AB	R	H	RBI	PO	A
Knoblauch, 2b	3	0	1	0	2	1
Jeter, ss	4	0	2	1	4	1
O'Neill, rf	5	0	1	0	4	0
Williams, cf	5	1	2	1	5	0
Davis, dh	4	0	0	0	0	0
T. Martinez, 1b	4	0	0	0	5	1
Posada, c	4	0	0	0	6	1
Spencer, lf	4	1	1	0	3	0
Brosius, 3b	4	2	3	2	1	1
Hernandez, p	0	0	0	0	0	0
Rivera, p	0	0	0	0	0	2
Totals	37	4	10	4	30	7

Boston	2	1	0	0 0 0	0 0 0	0—3
New York	0	2	0	0 0 0	1 0 0	1—4

None out when winning run scored.

Boston	IP	H	R	ER	BB	SO
Mercker	4.0	6	2	2	2	2
Garces	2.0	0	0	0	0	1
Lowe	2.2	3	1	1	0	4
Cormier	0.1	0	0	0	0	0
Beck (L)	0.0	1	1	1	0	0

New York	IP	H	R	ER	BB	SO
Hernandez	8.0	7	3	2	2	4
Rivera (W)	2.0	1	0	0	0	1

E—Garciaparra 2, Varitek. DP—New York 2. LOB—Boston 6, New York 9. 2B—Jeter, Valentin. 3B—Brosius. HR—Brosius, Williams. SH—Knoblauch. SB—Williams, Lewis. CS—Lewis. T—3:39. A—57,181. U—McClelland, plate; Morrison, first; Reed, second; Clark, third; Scott, left field; Tschida, right field.

GAME 2 BOX SCORE

NEW YORK 3, BOSTON 2

THURSDAY, OCTOBER 14, AT NEW YORK

Boston	AB	R	H	RBI	PO	A
Offerman, 2b	5	1	2	0	4	0
Valentin, 3b	3	0	0	0	1	1
Daubach, dh-1b	5	0	0	0	0	0
Garciaparra, ss	4	1	3	2	0	1
O'Leary, lf	5	0	3	0	1	0
Stanley, 1b	3	0	0	0	5	0
Buford, pr-cf	1	0	0	0	2	0
Varitek, c	3	0	2	0	6	1
Lewis, cf	3	0	0	0	1	0
Hatteberg, ph	0	0	0	0	0	0
Merloni, ph	0	0	0	0	0	0
Sadler, pr-rf	0	0	0	0	0	0
Nixon, rf	3	0	0	0	4	0
Huskey, ph-dh	1	0	0	0	0	0
R. Martinez, p	0	0	0	0	0	2
Gordon, p	0	0	0	0	0	0
Cormier, p	0	0	0	0	0	0
Totals	36	2	10	2	24	5

New York	AB	R	H	RBI	PO	A
Knoblauch, 2b	4	1	1	1	1	1
Jeter, ss	3	0	1	0	2	0
O'Neill, rf	3	0	1	1	5	0
Williams, cf	3	0	0	0	3	0
T. Martinez, 1b	3	1	1	1	3	0
Strawberry, dh	3	0	0	0	0	0
Davis, ph-dh	1	0	0	0	0	0
Ledee, lf	3	1	1	0	2	0
Brosius, 3b	3	0	0	0	0	0
Girardi, c	3	0	2	0	11	1
Cone, p	0	0	0	0	0	0
Stanton, p	0	0	0	0	0	0
Nelson, p	0	0	0	0	0	1
Watson, p	0	0	0	0	0	0
Mendoza, p	0	0	0	0	0	0
Rivera, p	0	0	0	0	0	0
Totals	29	3	7	3	27	3

Boston	0 0 0	0 2 0	0 0 0—2
New York	0 0 0	1 0 0	2 0 x—3

Boston	IP	H	R	ER	BB	SO
R. Martinez (L)	6.2	6	3	3	3	5
Gordon	*0.0	0	0	0	1	0
Cormier	1.1	1	0	0	1	1

New York	IP	H	R	ER	BB	SO
Cone (W)	7.0	7	2	2	3	9
Stanton	†0.0	1	0	0	0	0
Nelson	0.1	0	0	0	0	0
Watson	†0.0	0	0	0	1	0
Mendoza	0.2	0	0	0	0	1
Rivera (S)	1.0	2	0	0	0	1

*Pitched to one batter in seventh. †Pitched to one batter in eighth.
LOB—Boston 13, New York 8. 2B—Varitek, Knoblauch, O'Leary. 3B—Varitek. HR—T. Martinez, Garciaparra. SH—Varitek, Brosius. SB—Offerman, Knoblauch. CS—Ledee. HBP—By Nelson (Stanley). PB—Girardi. T—3:46. A—57,180. U—Morrison, plate; Reed, first; Clark, second; Scott, third; Tschida, left field; McClelland, right field.

GAME 3 BOX SCORE

BOSTON 13, NEW YORK 1

SATURDAY, OCTOBER 16, AT BOSTON

New York	AB	R	H	RBI	PO	A
Knoblauch, 2b	2	0	0	0	1	2
Sojo, ph-2b	1	0	0	0	1	1
Jeter, ss	3	0	1	0	2	4
Bellinger, ph-ss	1	0	0	0	0	1
O'Neill, rf	3	0	0	0	0	0
Curtis, lf-cf	1	0	0	0	0	0
Williams, cf	3	0	0	0	3	0
Spencer, lf	0	0	0	0	0	0
T. Martinez, 1b	4	0	1	0	7	3
Davis, dh	3	0	0	0	0	0
Ledee, lf-rf	4	0	0	0	1	0
Brosius, 3b	3	1	1	1	1	0
Girardi, c	1	0	0	0	2	0
Posada, c	2	0	0	0	4	0
Clemens, p	0	0	0	0	0	0
Irabu, p	0	0	0	0	2	0
Stanton, p	0	0	0	0	0	1
Watson, p	0	0	0	0	0	0
Totals	31	1	3	1	24	12

Boston	AB	R	H	RBI	PO	A
Offerman, 2b	6	2	3	0	1	1
Valentin, 3b	6	2	3	5	1	1
Varitek, c	4	0	0	0	13	0
Hatteberg, c	0	0	0	0	0	0
Garciaparra, ss	5	1	4	3	1	0
O'Leary, lf	5	2	2	0	2	0
Stanley, 1b	4	1	2	1	5	0
Daubach, ph-dh	4	2	2	2	0	0
Huskey, ph-dh	1	0	0	0	0	0
Lewis, cf-rf	5	1	2	1	3	0
Nixon, rf	4	2	3	0	1	0
Buford, ph-cf	1	0	0	0	0	0
P. Martinez, p	0	0	0	0	0	0
Gordon, p	0	0	0	0	0	1
Rapp, p	0	0	0	0	0	0
Totals	45	13	21	12	27	3

New York											
New York	0	0	0		0	0	0		0	1	0— 1
Boston	2	2	2		0	2	1		4	0	x—13

New York	IP	H	R	ER	BB	SO
Clemens (L)	*2.0	6	5	5	2	2
Irabu	4.2	13	8	7	0	3
Stanton	0.1	0	0	0	0	0
Watson	1.0	2	0	0	0	1

Boston	IP	H	R	ER	BB	SO
P. Martinez (W)	7.0	2	0	0	2	12
Gordon	1.0	1	1	1	0	1
Rapp	1.0	0	0	0	1	0

*Pitched to one batter in third.
E—Knoblauch, Posada, Ledee, Garciaparra. DP—New York 2. LOB—New York 6, Boston 10. 2B—Nixon 2, Garciaparra, Daubach, Lewis, O'Leary. 3B—Offerman. HR—Valentin, Daubach, Garciaparra, Brosius. T—3:14. A—33,190. U—Reed, plate; Clark, first; Scott, second; Tschida, third; McClelland, left field; Morrison, right field.

GAME 4 BOX SCORE

NEW YORK 9, BOSTON 2

SUNDAY, OCTOBER 17, AT BOSTON

New York	AB	R	H	RBI	PO	A
Knoblauch, 2b	4	1	2	0	3	5
Jeter, ss	5	1	1	0	2	5
O'Neill, rf	5	1	2	0	5	0
Williams, cf	5	2	3	1	0	1
T. Martinez, 1b	4	2	1	1	10	0
Strawberry, dh	2	1	1	1	0	0
Davis, ph	0	0	0	0	0	0
Bellinger, pr-dh	0	0	0	0	0	0
Ledee, lf	1	1	1	4	0	0
Brosius, 3b	5	0	0	0	0	1
Curtis, lf	5	0	0	0	0	0
Girardi, c	4	0	0	0	7	0
Pettitte, p	0	0	0	0	0	0
Rivera, p	0	0	0	0	0	0
Totals	40	9	11	7	27	12

Boston	AB	R	H	RBI	PO	A
Offerman, 2b	4	0	2	1	4	2
Valentin, 3b	4	0	2	0	0	1
Garciaparra, ss	3	0	0	0	2	4
Stanley, 1b	4	0	1	0	9	1
Huskey, dh	3	1	1	0	0	0
Daubach, ph-dh	1	0	0	0	0	0
O'Leary, lf	4	0	2	1	2	0
Varitek, c	4	0	0	0	7	0
Lewis, rf	3	0	0	0	1	0
Buford, rf	3	1	2	0	2	0
Saberhagen, p	0	0	0	0	0	2
Lowe, p	0	0	0	0	0	0
Cormier, p	0	0	0	0	0	0
Garces, p	0	0	0	0	0	0
Beck, p	0	0	0	0	0	0
Totals	33	2	10	2	27	10

New York											
New York	0	1	0		2	0	0		0	0	6—9
Boston	0	1	1		0	0	0		0	0	0—2

New York	IP	H	R	ER	BB	SO
Pettitte (W)	7.1	8	2	2	1	5
Rivera (S)	1.2	2	0	0	0	1

Boston	IP	H	R	ER	BB	SO
Saberhagen (L)	6.0	5	3	1	1	5
Lowe	*1.0	2	0	0	1	0
Cormier	0.1	0	0	0	1	0
Garces	1.0	3	5	4	1	1
Beck	0.2	1	1	1	0	1

*Pitched to two batters in eighth.
E—Garciaparra, Saberhagen, Offerman, Lewis. DP—New York 3. LOB—New York 8, Boston 5. 2B—Huskey, Valentin, T. Martinez, Williams, O'Leary. HR—Strawberry, Ledee. SB—Buford. T—3:39. A—33,586. U—Clark, plate; Scott, first; Tschida, second; McClelland, third; Morrison, left field; Reed, right field.

GAME 5 BOX SCORE

NEW YORK 6, BOSTON 1

MONDAY, OCTOBER 18, AT BOSTON

New York	AB	R	H	RBI	PO	A
Knoblauch, 2b	5	1	2	0	1	1
Sojo, 2b	0	0	0	0	0	0
Jeter, ss	5	2	2	2	0	0
O'Neill, rf	5	1	2	0	4	0
Williams, cf	4	0	0	0	2	0
Davis, dh	3	0	1	1	0	0
Bellinger, pr-dh	0	0	0	0	0	0
Strawberry, ph	1	0	1	0	0	0
Curtis, pr-dh	0	1	0	0	0	0
T. Martinez, 1b	4	0	2	1	4	1
Posada, c	4	1	1	2	10	0
Spencer, lf	5	0	0	0	2	0
Brosius, 3b	3	0	0	0	3	2
Hernandez, p	0	0	0	0	0	0
Stanton, p	0	0	0	0	0	0
Nelson, p	0	0	0	0	0	0

New York	AB	R	H	RBI	PO	A
Watson, p	0	0	0	0	0	0
Mendoza, p	0	0	0	0	1	0
Totals	39	6	11	6	27	4

Boston	AB	R	H	RBI	PO	A
Offerman, 2b	4	0	1	0	1	1
Valentin, 3b	5	0	2	0	2	2
Varitek, c	5	1	1	1	11	0
Garciaparra, ss	4	0	1	0	2	5
O'Leary, lf	3	0	0	0	1	0
Stanley, 1b	3	0	0	0	8	1
Daubach, dh	2	0	0	0	0	0
Huskey, ph	0	0	0	0	0	0
Sadler, pr-dh	0	0	0	0	0	0
Lewis, cf	3	0	0	0	1	0
Hatteberg, ph	1	0	0	0	0	0
Buford, cf	0	0	0	0	0	0
Nixon, rf	3	0	0	0	0	0
Mercker, p	0	0	0	0	1	1
Lowe, p	0	0	0	0	0	0
Cormier, p	0	0	0	0	0	0
Gordon, p	0	0	0	0	0	0
Totals	33	1	5	1	27	10

New York...... 2 0 0 0 0 0 2 0 2—6
Boston......... 0 0 0 0 0 0 0 1 0—1

New York	IP	H	R	ER	BB	SO
Hernandez (W)	*7.0	5	1	1	4	9
Stanton	†0.0	0	0	0	1	0
Nelson	0.1	0	0	0	0	0
Watson	†0.0	0	0	0	1	0
Mendoza (S)	1.2	0	0	0	0	1

Boston	IP	H	R	ER	BB	SO
Mercker (L)	3.2	6	2	2	2	3
Lowe	2.2	1	2	0	1	3
Cormier	1.2	2	0	0	1	3
Gordon	1.0	2	2	2	0	2

*Pitched to two batters in eighth. †Pitched to one batter in eighth.
E—Jeter, Stanley, Offerman. LOB—New York 11, Boston 11. 2B—Garciaparra. HR—Jeter, Varitek, Posada. SB—Curtis, Garciaparra. HBP—By Mercker (T. Martinez). U—Scott, plate; Tschida, first; McClelland, second; Morrison, third; Reed, left field; Clark, right field. T—4:09. A—33,589.

STATISTICS

NEW YORK YANKEES' BATTING AND FIELDING AVERAGES

Player, position	G	AB	R	H	TB	2B	3B	HR	RBI	BB	IBB	SO	Avg.	PO	A	E	Avg.
Jeter, ss	5	20	3	7	11	1	0	1	3	2	0	3	.350	10	10	1	.952
Knoblauch, 2b	5	18	3	6	7	1	0	0	1	3	0	0	.333	8	10	1	.947
Strawberry, dh-ph	3	6	1	2	5	0	0	1	1	1	1	2	.333	0	0	0	.000
O'Neill, rf	5	21	2	6	6	0	0	0	1	1	0	5	.286	18	0	0	1.000
T. Martinez, 1b	5	19	3	5	9	1	0	1	3	2	1	4	.263	29	5	0	1.000
Williams, cf	5	20	3	5	9	1	0	1	2	2	0	5	.250	13	1	0	1.000
Girardi, c	3	8	0	2	2	0	0	0	0	0	0	2	.250	20	1	0	1.000
Ledee, lf-rf-ph-dh	3	8	2	2	5	0	0	1	4	1	0	4	.250	3	0	1	.750
Brosius, 3b	5	18	3	4	12	0	1	2	3	1	0	4	.222	5	4	0	1.000
Spencer, lf	3	9	1	1	1	0	0	0	0	1	0	6	.111	5	0	0	1.000
Posada, c	3	10	1	1	4	0	0	1	2	1	0	2	.100	20	1	1	.955
Davis, dh-ph	5	11	0	1	1	0	0	0	1	3	1	4	.091	0	0	0	.000
Clemens, p	1	0	0	0	0	0	0	0	0	0	0	0	.000	0	0	0	.000
Cone, p	1	0	0	0	0	0	0	0	0	0	0	0	.000	0	0	0	.000
Hernandez, p	2	0	0	0	0	0	0	0	0	0	0	0	.000	0	0	0	.000
Irabu, p	1	0	0	0	0	0	0	0	0	0	0	0	.000	2	0	0	1.000
Mendoza, p	2	0	0	0	0	0	0	0	0	0	0	0	.000	1	0	0	1.000
Nelson, p	2	0	0	0	0	0	0	0	0	0	0	0	.000	0	1	0	1.000
Pettitte, p	1	0	0	0	0	0	0	0	0	0	0	0	.000	0	0	0	.000
Rivera, p	3	0	0	0	0	0	0	0	0	0	0	0	.000	0	2	0	1.000
Stanton, p	3	0	0	0	0	0	0	0	0	0	0	0	.000	0	1	0	1.000
Watson, p	3	0	0	0	0	0	0	0	0	0	0	0	.000	0	0	0	.000
Bellinger, ph-ss-pr-dh	3	1	0	0	0	0	0	0	0	0	0	1	.000	0	0	0	.000
Sojo, ph-2b	2	1	0	0	0	0	0	0	0	0	0	0	.000	1	1	0	1.000
Curtis, lf-cf-pr-dh	3	6	1	0	0	0	0	0	0	0	0	2	.000	0	0	0	.000
Totals	5	176	23	42	72	4	1	8	21	18	3	44	.239	135	38	4	.977

BOSTON RED SOX'S BATTING AND FIELDING AVERAGES

Player, position	G	AB	R	H	TB	2B	3B	HR	RBI	BB	IBB	SO	Avg.	PO	A	E	Avg.
Offerman, 2b	5	24	4	11	13	0	1	0	2	1	0	3	.458	15	6	2	.913
Garciaparra, ss	5	20	2	8	16	2	0	2	5	2	0	2	.400	7	13	4	.833
Buford, pr-cf-ph	4	5	1	2	2	0	0	0	0	0	0	2	.400	4	0	0	1.000
O'Leary, lf	5	20	2	7	10	3	0	0	1	2	0	5	.350	7	0	0	1.000
Valentin, 3b	5	23	3	8	13	2	0	1	5	2	0	4	.348	4	7	0	1.000
Nixon, rf	4	14	2	4	6	2	0	0	0	1	0	5	.286	7	0	0	1.000
Stanley, 1b	5	18	1	4	4	0	0	0	1	2	0	4	.222	35	2	1	.974
Varitek, c	5	20	1	4	10	1	1	1	1	1	0	4	.200	44	1	1	.978
Huskey, ph-dh	4	5	1	1	2	1	0	0	0	1	0	1	.200	0	0	0	.000
Daubach, dh-1b-ph	5	17	2	3	7	1	0	1	3	1	0	4	.176	0	0	0	.000
Lewis, cf-rf	5	17	2	2	3	1	0	0	1	1	0	3	.118	8	0	1	.889
Beck, p	2	0	0	0	0	0	0	0	0	0	0	0	.000	0	0	0	.000
Cormier, p	4	0	0	0	0	0	0	0	0	0	0	0	.000	0	1	0	1.000
Garces, p	2	0	0	0	0	0	0	0	0	0	0	0	.000	0	1	0	1.000

Player, position	G	AB	R	H	TB	2B	3B	HR	RBI	BB	IBB	SO	Avg.	PO	A	E	Avg.
								BATTING								FIELDING	
Gordon, p	3	0	0	0	0	0	0	0	0	0	0	0	.000	0	1	0	1.000
Lowe, p	3	0	0	0	0	0	0	0	0	0	0	0	.000	0	1	0	1.000
P. Martinez, p	1	0	0	0	0	0	0	0	0	0	0	0	.000	0	0	0	.000
R. Martinez, p	1	0	0	0	0	0	0	0	0	0	0	0	.000	0	2	0	1.000
Mercker, p	2	0	0	0	0	0	0	0	0	0	0	0	.000	1	3	0	1.000
Merloni, ph	1	0	0	0	0	0	0	0	0	1	1	0	.000	0	0	0	.000
Rapp, p	1	0	0	0	0	0	0	0	0	0	0	0	.000	0	0	0	.000
Saberhagen, p	1	0	0	0	0	0	0	0	0	0	0	0	.000	0	2	1	.667
Sadler, pr-rf-dh	2	0	0	0	0	0	0	0	0	0	0	0	.000	0	0	0	.000
Hatteberg, ph-c	3	1	0	0	0	0	0	0	0	0	0	1	.000	0	0	0	.000
Totals	5	184	21	54	86	13	2	5	19	15	1	38	.293	132	40	10	.945

NEW YORK YANKEES' PITCHING RECORDS

Pitcher	G	GS	CG	IP	H	R	ER	HR	BB	IBB	SO	HB	WP	W	L	Pct.	ERA
Stanton	3	0	0	0.1	1	0	0	0	1	0	0	0	0	0	0	.000	0.00
Nelson	2	0	0	0.2	0	0	0	0	0	0	0	1	0	0	0	.000	0.00
Watson	3	0	0	1.0	2	0	0	0	2	1	1	0	0	0	0	.000	0.00
Mendoza	2	0	0	2.1	0	0	0	0	0	0	2	0	0	0	0	.000	0.00
Rivera	3	0	0	4.2	5	0	0	0	0	0	3	0	0	1	0	1.000	0.00
Hernandez	2	2	0	15.0	12	4	3	1	6	0	13	0	0	1	0	1.000	1.80
Pettitte	1	1	0	7.1	8	2	2	0	1	0	5	0	0	1	0	1.000	2.45
Cone	1	1	0	7.0	7	2	2	1	3	0	9	0	0	1	0	1.000	2.57
Irabu	1	0	0	4.2	13	8	7	2	0	0	3	0	0	0	0	.000	13.50
Clemens	1	1	0	2.0	6	5	5	1	2	0	2	0	0	0	1	.000	22.50
Totals	5	5	0	45.0	54	21	19	5	15	1	38	1	0	4	1	.800	3.80

No shutouts. Saves—Rivera 2, Mendoza.

BOSTON RED SOX'S PITCHING RECORDS

Pitcher	G	GS	CG	IP	H	R	ER	HR	BB	IBB	SO	HB	WP	W	L	Pct.	ERA
Cormier	4	0	0	3.2	3	0	0	0	3	1	4	0	0	0	0	.000	0.00
P. Martinez	1	1	0	7.0	2	0	0	0	2	0	12	0	0	1	0	1.000	0.00
Rapp	1	0	0	1.0	0	0	0	0	1	0	0	0	0	0	0	.000	0.00
Lowe	3	0	0	6.1	6	3	1	0	2	0	7	0	0	0	0	.000	1.42
Saberhagen	1	1	0	6.0	5	3	1	1	1	1	5	0	0	0	1	.000	1.50
R. Martinez	1	1	0	6.2	6	3	3	1	3	0	5	0	0	0	1	.000	4.05
Mercker	2	2	0	7.2	12	4	4	2	4	0	5	1	0	0	1	.000	4.70
Garces	2	0	0	3.0	3	5	4	0	1	1	2	0	0	0	0	.000	12.00
Gordon	3	0	0	2.0	3	3	3	2	1	0	3	0	0	0	0	.000	13.50
Beck	2	0	0	0.2	2	2	2	2	0	0	1	0	0	0	1	.000	27.00
Totals	5	5	0	44.0	42	23	18	8	18	3	44	1	0	1	4	.200	3.68

No shutouts or saves.

SCORE BY INNINGS

New York	2	3	0	3	0	0	5	1	8	1—23
Boston	4	4	3	0	4	1	4	1	0	0—21

MISCELLANEOUS STATISTICS

Sacrifice hits—Brosius, Knoblauch, Varitek.
Sacrifice flies—None.
Stolen bases—Buford, Curtis, Garciaparra, Knoblauch, Lewis, Offerman, Williams.
Caught stealing—Ledee, Lewis.
Double plays—Bellinger, Sojo and Martinez; Jeter, Knoblauch and Martinez; Jeter and Martinez; Knoblauch, Jeter and Martinez; Knoblauch and Martinez; Posada and Jeter; Rivera, Jeter and Martinez.
Left on bases—New York 9, 8, 6, 8, 11—42; Boston 6, 13, 10, 5, 11—45.
Hit by pitcher—By Mercker (Martinez), by Nelson (Stanley).
Passed ball—Girardi.
Balks—None.
Time of games—First game, 3:39; second game, 3:46; third game, 3:14; fourth game, 3:39; fifth game, 4:09.
Attendance—First game, 57,181; second game, 57,180; third game, 33,190; fourth game, 33,586; fifth game, 33,589.
Umpires—McClelland, Morrison, Reed, Clark, Scott and Tschida.
Official scorers—Howie Karpin, Charlie Scoggins, Bill Shannon.

N.L. CHAMPIONSHIP SERIES

HIGHLIGHTS

The bottom line: The Braves dominated the Mets in the regular season (winning nine of 12 games) on their way to their eighth straight division title. Atlanta continued that domination by taking the first three games of the NLCS, getting clutch hitting from unexpected sources and great pitching performances from their reliable starters and bullpen. But the wild-card Mets made a series of it, winning the final two games in New York before losing a 10-9, 11-inning Game 6 in Atlanta. This heated rivalry between division foes was entertaining—close games, off-the-field trash talk, unlikely heroes—as Atlanta gained its fifth trip to the World Series in the '90s.

Why the Braves won: No surprise here, but Atlanta won this series with its superior pitching. The Braves continually got outs when they needed to, and the Mets gave up big hits to generally light-hitting players such as Eddie Perez and Keith Lockhart in the series. The Braves won three games by one run, and the fourth by two runs. John Rocker's 6.2 scoreless innings (he appeared in all six games), including two saves, may have been the difference on the mound. Eddie Perez's .500 average with two homers and five RBIs was the difference at the plate. The Mets, who committed a major league low 68 errors during the regular season, didn't help themselves with eight errors in the series. As the season displayed, the Mets had the firepower and talent to hang with the Braves, they just didn't have the big-game experience.

The turning points:

Game 1: When you're facing Greg Maddux, a four-time Cy Young winner, you must score every chance you have runners in scoring position. And though it was just the third inning, the Mets botched their best opportunity of the night. After Roger Cedeno advanced to third after a double and Gerald Williams' throwing error, the Braves' 1-0 lead appeared in jeopardy. But Rey Ordonez's weak groundout to third and starting pitcher Masato Yoshii's failed suicide squeeze attempt (Cedeno was trapped and tagged out) got the Braves out of the mess. The Mets were able to get only a run off Maddux in his seven innings of work, and weren't able to overcome a 3-1 lead in a 4-2 loss.

Game 2: Though Kenny Rogers already had given up a two-run homer to Brian Jordan and a single to Andruw Jones in the sixth inning, Mets manager Bobby Valentine inexplicably decided to stay with Rogers over reliever Turk Wendell against hot-hitting Eddie Perez. The move backfired as Perez homered into the left field bleachers, giving the Braves a 4-2 lead. Chipper Jones' eighth-inning error opened the door for a Mets rally, but John Rocker struck out both John Olerud and Robin Ventura, preserving the Braves' 4-3 victory.

Game 3: The Mets hadn't committed two errors in the same inning all season until Game 3—and it was the first inning. They paid for it, too. Throwing errors by Al Leiter and Mike Piazza led to an unearned Braves run, the only run Tom Glavine needed. Glavine was brilliant, hitting spot after spot and inducing groundout after groundout in his seven innings of work. The Mets scattered seven hits, but never really got a good scoring chance.

Game 4: After back-to-back homers by Jordan and Ryan Klesko gave the Braves a 2-1 lead in the top of the eighth inning, the Mets' season appeared to be over, especially given the dominant Braves bullpen. But Olerud's single up the middle off the outstretched glove of Atlanta reserve shortstop Ozzie Guillen drove in the tying and game-winning runs in the bottom of the inning and kept the Mets alive in the best-of-7 series. The two-out single followed a well-executed double steal by Cedeno and Melvin Mora.

Game 5: Robin Ventura sent the exhausted Mets fans home happy and the series back to Atlanta with a game-ending grand slam in the 15th inning off Kevin McGlinchy. The grand slam officially was a single, making it a 4-3 Mets victory, because Ventura was not able to complete his trip around the basepaths. He was mobbed after rounding first base by his teammates, who were relieved still to be in the series. Nobody was more relieved than Ventura, who was 1-for-18 in the series to that point. The Mets tied the scored 3-3 earlier in the inning when McGlinchy issue a bases-loaded walk to Todd Pratt.

Game 6: Andruw Jones drew a bases-loaded walk from Kenny Rogers in the 11th inning, giving the Braves a 10-9 victory and a berth in the World Series. What started as a Braves fan's dream and a Mets fan's worst nightmare, ended in the same fashion. But there were plenty of twists and turns along the way. The Braves jumped out to early 5-0 and 7-3 leads, highlighted by two-run singles by Perez and Jose Hernandez. But the Mets came back, eventually tying the game 8-8 and knocking around dependable hurlers Kevin Millwood and John Smoltz in the process. Each team scored a 10th-inning run before the 11th-inning game-winner with one out.

Notable:

Braves: The Braves were appearing in their eighth straight National League Championship Series. ... Series MVP Eddie Perez, who hadn't homered all season at Turner Field, had two in three games there. Perez batted .500 in the NLCS after batting .249 during the regular season. ... John Smoltz made his first career postseason relief appearance in Game 2, picking up his first career save. ... John Rocker set a record in every game he appeared. He now has appeared in 12 consecutive NLCS games, six each from the '98 and '99 seasons. ... During the regular season, the Braves were 74-8 when leading after seven innings. They were 3-0 in this series. ... The

Braves left 19 runners on base in Game 5, a postseason record. ... Turner Field's Game 6 attendance of 52,335 was the first sellout of the '99 postseason for the Braves and set a Turner Field record. ... Atlanta was 14-for-17 in stolen bases during the series. The 14 stolen bases is an NLCS record. The previous record was 11 by the Cincinnati Reds in 1975.

Mets: Melvin Mora homered for the first time in his major league career in Game 2. ... In six career postseason starts, Kenny Rogers has given up 20 runs in 19 innings. ... Before getting the game-winning hit in the eighth inning of Game 4, Olerud had been hitless in nine at-bats against Rocker. ... The Mets were trying to become the first team ever to come back from a 3-0 deficit in a playoff series. ... The Mets have been involved in two of the longest postseason games in history. They were involved in a 16-inning game in 1986 against the Astros and in Game 5, which lasted 15 innings and took five hours and 46 minutes to complete. ... As a team, the Mets batted .340 in Game 6. In Games 1-5, the Mets batted .188. ... Mike Piazza's home run in Game 6 was his only extra-base hit of the series.

Quotable:

Braves: Eddie Perez, on the Braves' winning Game 1: "I think winning the first game is important. I remember the Padres won the first game and went on to win the series. Two years ago the Marlins won the first game and then won the series." ... Manager Bobby Cox, on John Rocker's verbal sparring with Mets fans throughout the series: "He's a great pitcher, a great competitor, but he needs to work on his player-fan relationships." ... Rocker's take on the Mets fans: "A majority of Mets fans aren't human. The bottom line is that 80 percent of Mets fans are Neanderthal." ... Bobby Cox, on John Olerud's two-run single that was the eventual game-winning hit in Game 4: "I don't think any of our shortstops catch that ball. It ends up the same way." ... Cox again, on Kevin McGlinchy's struggle to get batters out in the bottom of the 15th: "McGlinchy is a big leaguer. He should be able to throw strikes and get them out. We thought he would." ... Rocker, on pitching in the high-intensity Game 6: "When I went out for my second inning, I really didn't have much mentally. I was so mentally exhausted from just being in a nail-biting game every single day. It was two weeks of just constant mental anguish and torture. Games hinging on one pitch night after night. Without ever stepping on the field, you walk out there exhausted already."

Mets: Bobby Valentine, on his decision not to pull Kenny Rogers from Game 2: "I should have done it. No doubt about that. I had no reason to keep him in, and it was absolutely the wrong move." ... Valentine, on the Braves pitching staff: "I don't think we have to wait for any historians. The Braves pitchers are as good as there is—in any era, in any decade." ... Al Leiter, on his costly first-inning error in Game 3: "I was thinking I should be throwing to second while I was throwing to first. To think that my bonehead mistake, a poor throw, was the difference between a

win and a loss. It was a total brain cramp." ... Robin Ventura, after notified he only was awarded a single, despite hitting the ball over the fence to end Game 5: "As long as I touch first, we won. That's fine with me." ... Valentine, on what he told his players after Game 6, "I told them they played like champions. We don't have a trophy, but they did everything they had to." ... Rogers, about giving up the Game 6 winning run on a bases-loaded walk: "I'm a big boy. I can handle it. God thinks I can handle a lot. He can lay off me now."

GAME 1 BOX SCORE

ATLANTA 4, NEW YORK 2

TUESDAY, OCTOBER 12, AT ATLANTA

New York	AB	R	H	RBI	PO	A
Henderson, lf	4	0	0	0	2	0
Alfonzo, 2b	4	1	2	0	2	1
Olerud, 1b	4	0	1	0	8	0
Piazza, c	4	0	0	1	5	0
Ventura, 3b	3	0	0	0	0	2
Hamilton, cf	3	0	0	0	2	0
Dunston, ph	1	1	0	0	0	0
Cedeno, rf	3	0	2	0	3	0
Pratt, ph	1	0	1	1	0	0
Ordonez, ss	4	0	0	0	1	3
Yoshii, p	2	0	0	0	0	3
Mahomes, p	0	0	0	0	0	1
Cook, p	0	0	0	0	0	0
M. Franco, ph	0	0	0	0	0	0
Mora, ph	0	0	0	0	0	0
Wendell, p	0	0	0	0	1	0
Totals	33	2	6	2	24	10

Atlanta	AB	R	H	RBI	PO	A
Williams, lf	5	1	2	1	2	0
Boone, 2b	4	0	1	1	0	3
C. Jones, 3b	1	0	0	0	3	5
Jordan, rf	3	0	0	0	0	0
Klesko, 1b	3	0	0	0	12	0
Battle, ph-1b	1	0	0	0	0	0
Remlinger, p	0	0	0	0	0	1
Rocker, p	0	0	0	0	0	0
A. Jones, cf	3	1	0	0	2	0
Perez, c	3	1	2	1	5	1
Weiss, ss	4	1	3	1	0	1
Maddux, p	2	0	0	0	1	4
Hunter, 1b	1	0	0	0	4	0
Totals	30	4	8	4	27	15

New York	0	0 0		1 0 0		0 0	1—2
Atlanta	1	0 0		0 1 1		0 1	x—4

New York	IP	H	R	ER	BB	SO
Yoshii (L)	4.2	5	2	2	2	1
Mahomes	1.1	2	1	1	0	1
Cook	1.0	0	0	0	2	1
Wendell	1.0	1	1	1	1	2

Atlanta	IP	H	R	ER	BB	SO
Maddux (W)	7.0	5	1	1	1	2
Remlinger	0.2	0	0	0	1	0
Rocker (S)	1.1	1	1	0	0	2

E—Henderson, Olerud, Williams, C. Jones. DP—New York 1. LOB—New York 6, Atlanta 9. 2B—Alfonzo 2, Perez, Cedeno, Weiss. HR—Perez. SH—Maddux, Perez. SB—Williams, C. Jones, Weiss. CS—Cedeno. WP—Rocker. T—3:09. A—44,172. U—Montague, plate; Kellogg, first; Reliford, second; Rapuano, third; Layne, left field; Crawford, right field.

GAME 2 BOX SCORE

ATLANTA 4, NEW YORK 3

WEDNESDAY, OCTOBER 13, AT ATLANTA

New York	AB	R	H	RBI	PO	A
Henderson, lf	2	0	0	0	0	0
Mora, lf	2	2	1	1	1	0

New York	AB	R	H	RBI	PO	A
Alfonzo, 2b	4	0	2	1	3	3
Olerud, 1b	4	0	0	0	12	1
Piazza, c	3	0	0	0	4	0
Ventura, 3b	3	1	0	0	1	1
Hamilton, cf	3	0	1	0	2	0
Dunston, ph	1	0	0	0	0	0
Cedeno, rf	4	0	1	1	1	0
Ordonez, ss	3	0	0	0	0	7
Bonilla, ph	1	0	0	0	0	0
Rogers, p	1	0	0	0	0	4
Wendell, p	0	0	0	0	0	0
M. Franco, ph	1	0	0	0	0	0
Benitez, p	0	0	0	0	0	0
Totals	32	3	5	3	24	16

Atlanta	AB	R	H	RBI	PO	A
Williams, lf	4	0	1	0	1	0
Boone, 2b	4	0	1	0	0	2
C. Jones, 3b	2	1	0	0	0	0
Jordan, rf	4	1	1	2	5	0
A. Jones, cf	4	1	3	0	3	0
Perez, c	4	1	2	2	7	0
Hunter, 1b	3	0	0	0	7	1
Weiss, ss	3	0	1	0	2	1
Millwood, p	2	0	0	0	2	2
Rocker, p	0	0	0	0	0	0
Smoltz, p	0	0	0	0	0	0
Totals	30	4	9	4	27	6

New York	0 1 0	0 1 0	0 1 0—3
Atlanta	0 0 0	0 0 4	0 0 0—4

New York	IP	H	R	ER	BB	SO
Rogers (L)	5.1	9	4	4	3	1
Wendell	1.2	0	0	0	1	1
Benitez	1.0	0	0	0	0	2

Atlanta	IP	H	R	ER	BB	SO
Millwood (W)	7.1	5	3	2	1	4
Rocker	0.2	0	0	0	1	2
Smoltz (S)	1.0	0	0	0	0	1

E—Alfonzo, C. Jones. DP—New York 2. LOB—New York 5, Atlanta 6. 2B—Alfonzo. HR—Mora, Jordan, Perez. SH—Rogers. CS—A. Jones. T—2:42. A—44,624. U—Kellogg, plate; Reliford, first; Rapuano, second; Layne, third; Crawford, left field; Montague, right field.

GAME 3 BOX SCORE

ATLANTA 1, NEW YORK 0
FRIDAY, OCTOBER 15, AT NEW YORK

Atlanta	AB	R	H	RBI	PO	A
Williams, lf	3	1	0	0	0	0
Boone, 2b	4	0	0	0	3	3
C. Jones, 3b	4	0	1	0	0	0
Jordan, rf	4	0	0	0	4	0
A. Jones, cf	3	0	0	0	3	0
Perez, c	3	0	2	0	9	1
Hunter, 1b	2	0	0	0	6	0
Weiss, ss	2	0	0	0	2	2
Glavine, p	2	0	0	0	0	1
Remlinger, p	0	0	0	0	0	0
Rocker, p	0	0	0	0	0	0
Totals	27	1	3	0	27	7

New York	AB	R	H	RBI	PO	A
Henderson, lf	4	0	1	0	2	2
Olerud, 1b	3	0	1	0	6	0
Alfonzo, 2b	4	0	0	0	5	2
Piazza, c	4	0	2	0	8	0
Agbayani, rf	4	0	0	0	0	0
Ventura, 3b	3	0	0	0	1	1
Pratt, ph	1	0	0	0	0	0
Mora, cf	4	0	2	0	3	1
Ordonez, ss	4	0	1	0	2	4
Leiter, p	2	0	0	0	0	1
Dunston, ph	1	0	0	0	0	0
J. Franco, p	0	0	0	0	0	1
Benitez, p	0	0	0	0	0	0
Totals	34	0	7	0	27	12

Atlanta	1 0 0	0 0 0	0 0 0—1
New York	0 0 0	0 0 0	0 0 0—0

Atlanta	IP	H	R	ER	BB	SO
Glavine (W)	7.0	7	0	0	1	8
Remlinger	1.0	0	0	0	0	1
Rocker (S)	1.0	0	0	0	0	1

New York	IP	H	R	ER	BB	SO
Leiter (L)	7.0	3	1	0	3	5
J. Franco	0.1	0	0	0	1	0
Benitez	1.2	0	0	0	0	3

E—Weiss, Leiter, Piazza. DP—Atlanta 1, New York 2. LOB—Atlanta 4, New York 8. SH—Glavine. SB—Williams, Boone. CS—Dunston. WP—Leiter. PB—Perez. T—3:04. A—55,911. U—Reliford, plate; Rapuano, first; Layne, second; Crawford, third; Montague, left field; Kellogg, right field.

GAME 4 BOX SCORE

NEW YORK 3, ATLANTA 2
SATURDAY, OCTOBER 16, AT NEW YORK

Atlanta	AB	R	H	RBI	PO	A
Williams, lf	4	0	0	0	4	0
Boone, 2b	3	0	1	0	1	1
Lockhart, ph	1	0	0	0	0	0
C. Jones, 3b	3	0	0	0	1	0
Jordan, rf	3	1	1	1	1	0
Klesko, 1b	3	1	1	1	5	1
Hunter, 1b	0	0	0	0	1	0
A. Jones, cf	3	0	0	0	1	0
Perez, c	3	0	0	0	9	0
Weiss, ss	3	0	0	0	0	2
Rocker, p	0	0	0	0	0	0
Smoltz, p	2	0	0	0	1	0
Remlinger, p	0	0	0	0	0	0
Guillen, ss	1	0	0	0	0	0
Totals	29	2	3	2	24	4

New York	AB	R	H	RBI	PO	A
Henderson, lf	3	0	0	0	0	0
Mora, lf	0	1	0	0	0	0
Olerud, 1b	4	1	2	3	10	0
Alfonzo, 2b	4	0	0	0	0	3
Piazza, c	3	0	0	0	7	1
Ventura, 3b	3	0	0	0	1	4
Hamilton, cf	3	0	0	0	1	0
Cedeno, rf	3	1	3	0	6	0
Ordonez, ss	3	0	0	0	1	3
Reed, p	2	0	0	0	0	0
Wendell, p	0	0	0	0	0	0
M. Franco, ph	0	0	0	0	0	0
Agbayani, ph	1	0	0	0	0	0
Benitez, p	0	0	0	0	0	0
Totals	29	3	5	3	27	11

Atlanta	0 0 0	0 0 0	0 2 0—2
New York	0 0 0	0 0 1	0 2 x—3

Atlanta	IP	H	R	ER	BB	SO
Smoltz	7.1	4	2	2	0	7
Remlinger (L)	0.1	0	1	1	1	1
Rocker	0.1	1	0	0	1	0

New York	IP	H	R	ER	BB	SO
Reed	*7.0	3	2	2	0	5
Wendell (W)	1.0	0	0	0	0	0
Benitez (S)	1.0	0	0	0	0	0

*Pitched to two batters in eighth.
LOB—Atlanta 0, New York 3. HR—Olerud, Jordan, Klesko. SB—Cedeno 2, Mora. CS—Boone. T—2:20. A—55,872. U—Rapuano, plate; Layne, first; Crawford, second; Montague, third; Kellogg, left field; Reliford, right field.

GAME 5 BOX SCORE

NEW YORK 4, ATLANTA 3 (15 INNINGS)
SUNDAY, OCTOBER 17, AT NEW YORK

Atlanta	AB	R	H	RBI	PO	A
Williams, lf	7	0	1	0	2	0
Boone, 2b	3	1	1	0	0	3
Nixon, pr	0	0	0	0	0	0
Lockhart, 2b	4	0	2	1	1	3
C. Jones, 3b	6	1	3	1	2	2
Jordan, rf	7	0	2	1	4	0

Atlanta	AB	R	H	RBI	PO	A
Klesko, 1b	2	0	0	0	8	1
Hunter, ph-1b	3	0	0	0	7	0
A. Jones, cf	5	0	0	0	2	0
Perez, c	4	0	2	0	7	0
Battle, pr	0	0	0	0	0	0
Myers, c	1	0	0	0	7	0
Weiss, ss	6	1	2	0	2	7
Maddux, p	3	0	0	0	1	0
Hernandez, ph	1	0	0	0	0	0
Mulholland, p	0	0	0	0	0	0
Guillen, ph	1	0	0	0	0	0
Remlinger, p	0	0	0	0	0	0
Springer, p	0	0	0	0	0	0
Fabregas, ph	1	0	0	0	0	0
Rocker, p	0	0	0	0	0	0
McGlinchy, p	1	0	0	0	0	1
Totals	55	3	13	3	43	17

New York	AB	R	H	RBI	PO	A
Henderson, lf	5	1	1	0	2	0
Rogers, p	0	0	0	0	0	0
Bonilla, ph	1	0	0	0	0	0
Dotel, p	0	0	0	0	0	0
M. Franco, ph	0	0	0	0	0	0
Cedeno, pr	0	1	0	0	0	0
Alfonzo, 2b	6	0	1	0	2	5
Olerud, 1b	6	1	2	2	12	1
Piazza, c	6	0	1	0	16	2
Pratt, c	0	0	0	1	4	0
Ventura, 3b	7	0	2	1	0	7
Mora, rf-cf-rf	6	0	1	0	3	1
Hamilton, cf	3	0	2	0	2	0
Agbayani, ph-rf-lf	1	0	0	0	1	0
Ordonez, ss	6	0	1	0	1	2
Yoshii, p	1	0	0	0	0	0
Hershiser, p	1	0	0	0	2	0
Wendell, p	0	0	0	0	0	0
Cook, p	0	0	0	0	0	0
Mahomes, p	1	0	0	0	0	0
J. Franco, p	0	0	0	0	0	0
Benitez, p	0	0	0	0	0	0
Dunston, ph-cf	3	1	1	0	0	0
Totals	53	4	11	4	45	18

Atlanta....... 0 0 0 2 0 0 0 0 0 0 0 1—3
New York... 2 0 0 0 0 0 0 0 0 0 0 2—4
One out when winning run scored.

Atlanta	IP	H	R	ER	BB	SO
Maddux	7.0	7	2	2	0	5
Mulholland	2.0	1	0	0	0	2
Remlinger	2.0	1	0	0	0	2
Springer	1.0	0	0	0	1	1
Rocker	1.1	0	0	0	0	2
McGlinchy (L)	1.0	2	2	2	4	1

New York	IP	H	R	ER	BB	SO
Yoshii	*3.0	4	2	2	1	3
Hershiser	3.1	1	0	0	3	5
Wendell	0.1	0	0	0	1	1
Cook	0.0	0	0	0	0	0
Mahomes	1.0	1	0	0	2	1
J. Franco	1.1	1	0	0	0	2
Benitez	1.0	1	0	0	0	1
Rogers	2.0	1	0	0	1	0
Dotel (W)	3.0	4	1	1	2	5

*Pitched to four batters in fourth.

E—Klesko 2, Olerud. DP—Atlanta 2, New York 2. LOB—Atlanta 19, New York 12. 2B—C. Jones 2, Hamilton, Perez, Boone, Williams, Weiss. 3B—Lockhart. HR—Olerud. SH—A. Jones, Alfonzo. SB—Nixon, Battle, Weiss, Agbayani, Dunston. CS—Klesko. HBP—By Hershiser (Boone). T—5:46. A—55,723. U—Layne, plate; Crawford, first; Montague, second; Kellogg, third; Reliford, left field; Rapuano, right field.

GAME 6 BOX SCORE

ATLANTA 10, NEW YORK 9 (11 INNINGS)

TUESDAY, OCTOBER 19, AT ATLANTA

New York	AB	R	H	RBI	PO	A
Henderson, lf	5	1	2	1	1	0
J. Franco, p	0	0	0	0	0	1
Pratt, c	0	0	0	1	2	0
Alfonzo, 2b	5	1	1	0	2	4
Olerud, 1b	6	2	2	1	11	2
Piazza, c	4	1	1	3	4	0
Benitez, p	0	0	0	0	0	0
Dunston, ph	1	0	0	0	0	0
Rogers, p	0	0	0	0	0	0
Ventura, 3b	6	1	1	0	2	1
Hamilton, cf	5	0	3	2	1	0
Cedeno, rf	2	0	0	0	2	0
Agbayani, ph-rf-lf	1	2	1	0	3	0
Ordonez, ss	4	0	0	0	2	5
Leiter, p	0	0	0	0	0	0
Mahomes, p	1	0	0	0	1	1
Bonilla, ph	1	0	1	0	0	0
Wendell, p	0	0	0	0	0	0
Cook, p	0	0	0	0	0	0
M. Franco, ph	1	1	1	0	0	0
Hershiser, p	0	0	0	0	0	0
Mora, ph-rf	2	0	2	1	0	1
Totals	44	9	15	9	31	15

Atlanta	AB	R	H	RBI	PO	A
Williams, lf	5	2	1	0	3	0
Boone, 2b	4	1	1	0	1	2
C. Jones, 3b	3	1	1	1	1	1
Jordan, rf	4	1	1	1	3	0
A. Jones, cf	5	3	2	1	6	0
Perez, c	3	0	2	2	5	0
Nixon, pr	0	1	0	0	0	0
Myers, c	1	0	0	0	1	0
Hunter, 1b	1	1	1	2	6	1
Klesko, ph-1b	0	0	0	0	2	0
Weiss, ss	3	0	0	0	3	1
Guillen, ph-ss	1	0	1	1	0	0
Millwood, p	2	0	0	0	1	0
Mulholland, p	0	0	0	0	0	0
Lockhart, ph	0	0	0	0	0	0
Hernandez, ph	1	0	1	2	0	0
Smoltz, p	0	0	0	0	0	0
Remlinger, p	0	0	0	0	1	0
Battle, ph	1	0	0	0	0	0
Rocker, p	0	0	0	0	0	1
Fabregas, ph	1	0	0	0	0	0
Springer, p	0	0	0	0	0	0
Totals	35	10	10	9	33	6

New York .... 0 0 0 0 0 3 4 1 0 1 0— 9
Atlanta.............. 5 0 0 0 0 2 0 1 0 1 1—10
One out when winning run scored.

New York	IP	H	R	ER	BB	SO
Leiter	*0.0	2	5	5	1	0
Mahomes	4.0	1	0	0	1	1
Wendell	1.2	1	2	2	1	1
Cook	0.1	1	0	0	0	0
Hershiser	1.0	0	0	0	0	0
J. Franco	1.0	2	1	1	0	1
Benitez	2.0	2	1	1	2	2
Rogers (L)	0.1	1	1	1	3	0

Atlanta	IP	H	R	ER	BB	SO
Millwood	5.1	8	3	3	0	5
Mulholland	0.2	0	0	0	1	0
Smoltz	0.1	4	4	4	0	0
Remlinger	1.2	2	1	1	1	0
Rocker	2.0	1	1	0	1	1
Springer (W)	1.0	0	0	0	0	0

*Pitched to six batters in first.

E—Piazza 2, Hunter. DP—New York 2, Atlanta 1. LOB—New York 8, Atlanta 9. 2B—Alfonzo, Ventura, M. Franco, Henderson, Williams. HR—Piazza. SH—Ordonez, Perez, Weiss, Boone. SF—Piazza, Pratt, Hunter. SB—C. Jones 2, Henderson, Mora, Williams, Boone, Hunter, Nixon. CS—Agbayani. HBP—Leiter 2 (Williams, C. Jones), Wendell (Jordan). T—4:25. A—52,335. U—Crawford, plate; Montague, first; Kellogg, second; Reliford, third; Rapuano, left field; Layne, right field.

ATLANTA BRAVES' BATTING AND FIELDING AVERAGES

Player, position	G	AB	R	H	TB	2B	3B	HR	RBI	BB	IBB	SO	Avg.	PO	A	E	Avg.
Perez, c	6	20	2	10	18	2	0	2	5	1	1	3	.500	42	2	0	1.000
Hernandez, ph	2	2	0	1	1	0	0	0	2	0	0	1	.500	0	0	0	.000
Lockhart, ph-2b	3	5	0	2	4	0	1	0	1	0	0	2	.400	1	3	0	1.000
Guillen, ss-ph	3	3	0	1	1	0	0	0	1	0	0	0	.333	0	0	0	.000
Weiss, ss	6	21	2	6	8	2	0	0	1	2	0	4	.286	9	14	1	.958
C. Jones, 3b	6	19	3	5	7	2	0	0	1	9	4	7	.263	5	8	2	.867
A. Jones, cf	6	23	5	5	5	0	0	0	1	4	0	3	.217	17	0	0	1.000
Jordan, rf	6	25	3	5	11	0	0	2	5	3	3	5	.200	17	0	0	1.000
Boone, 2b	6	22	2	4	5	1	0	0	1	1	0	7	.182	5	14	0	1.000
Williams, lf	6	28	4	5	7	2	0	0	1	2	1	2	.179	12	0	1	.923
Klesko, 1b-ph	4	8	1	1	4	0	0	1	1	2	0	1	.125	27	2	2	.935
Hunter, 1b-ph	6	10	1	1	1	0	0	0	2	5	1	2	.100	31	2	1	.971
Mulholland, p	2	0	0	0	0	0	0	0	0	0	0	0	.000	0	0	0	.000
Nixon, pr	2	0	1	0	0	0	0	0	0	0	0	0	.000	0	0	0	.000
Remlinger, p	5	0	0	0	0	0	0	0	0	0	0	0	.000	1	1	0	1.000
Rocker, p	6	0	0	0	0	0	0	0	0	0	0	0	.000	0	1	0	1.000
Springer, p	2	0	0	0	0	0	0	0	0	0	0	0	.000	0	0	0	.000
McGlinchy, p	1	1	0	0	0	0	0	0	0	0	0	1	.000	0	1	0	1.000
Battle, ph-1b-pr	3	2	0	0	0	0	0	0	0	0	0	2	.000	0	0	0	.000
Fabregas, ph	2	2	0	0	0	0	0	0	0	0	0	1	.000	0	0	0	.000
Glavine, p	1	2	0	0	0	0	0	0	0	0	0	1	.000	0	1	0	1.000
Myers, c	2	2	0	0	0	0	0	0	0	1	0	1	.000	8	0	0	1.000
Smoltz, p	3	2	0	0	0	0	0	0	0	0	0	0	.000	1	0	0	1.000
Millwood, p	2	4	0	0	0	0	0	0	0	1	0	0	.000	3	2	0	1.000
Maddux, p	2	5	0	0	0	0	0	0	0	0	0	4	.000	2	4	0	1.000
Totals	6	206	24	46	72	9	1	5	22	31	10	47	.223	181	55	7	.971

NEW YORK METS' BATTING AND FIELDING AVERAGES

Player, position	G	AB	R	H	TB	2B	3B	HR	RBI	BB	IBB	SO	Avg.	PO	A	E	Avg.
Cedeno, rf-pr	5	12	2	6	7	1	0	0	1	0	0	1	.500	12	0	0	1.000
M. Franco, ph	5	2	1	1	2	1	0	0	0	1	0	0	.500	0	0	0	.000
Pratt, ph-c	4	2	0	1	1	0	0	0	3	1	0	1	.500	6	0	0	1.000
Mora, ph-lf-cf-rf	6	14	3	6	9	0	0	1	2	2	0	2	.429	7	3	0	1.000
Hamilton, cf	5	17	0	6	7	1	0	0	2	0	0	4	.353	8	0	0	1.000
Bonilla, ph	3	3	0	1	1	0	0	0	0	0	0	2	.333	0	0	0	.000
Olerud, 1b	6	27	4	8	14	0	0	2	6	2	1	3	.296	59	4	2	.969
Alfonzo, 2b	6	27	2	6	10	4	0	0	1	1	0	9	.222	15	18	1	.971
Henderson, lf	6	23	2	4	5	1	0	0	1	0	0	5	.174	7	2	1	.900
Piazza, c	6	24	1	4	7	0	0	1	4	1	1	6	.167	44	3	3	.940
Agbayani, rf-ph-lf	4	7	2	1	1	0	0	0	0	4	0	2	.143	4	0	0	1.000
Dunston, ph-cf	5	7	2	1	1	0	0	0	0	0	0	2	.143	0	0	0	.000
Ventura, 3b	6	25	2	3	4	1	0	0	1	2	0	5	.120	5	16	0	1.000
Ordonez, ss	6	24	0	1	1	0	0	0	0	0	0	2	.042	7	24	0	1.000
Benitez, p	5	0	0	0	0	0	0	0	0	0	0	0	.000	0	0	0	.000
Cook, p	3	0	0	0	0	0	0	0	0	0	0	0	.000	0	0	0	.000
Dotel, p	1	0	0	0	0	0	0	0	0	0	0	0	.000	0	0	0	.000
J. Franco, p	3	0	0	0	0	0	0	0	0	0	0	0	.000	0	2	0	1.000
Wendell, p	5	0	0	0	0	0	0	0	0	0	0	0	.000	1	0	0	1.000
Hershiser, p	2	1	0	0	0	0	0	0	0	0	0	0	.000	2	0	0	1.000
Rogers, p	3	1	0	0	0	0	0	0	0	0	0	1	.000	0	4	0	1.000
Leiter, p	2	2	0	0	0	0	0	0	0	0	0	0	.000	0	1	1	.500
Mahomes, p	3	2	0	0	0	0	0	0	0	0	0	2	.000	1	2	0	1.000
Reed, p	1	2	0	0	0	0	0	0	0	0	0	0	.000	0	0	0	.000
Yoshii, p	2	3	0	0	0	0	0	0	0	0	0	1	.000	0	3	0	1.000
Totals	6	225	21	49	70	9	0	4	21	14	2	49	.218	178	82	8	.970

ATLANTA BRAVES' PITCHING RECORDS

Pitcher	G	GS	CG	IP	H	R	ER	HR	BB	IBB	SO	HB	WP	W	L	Pct.	ERA
Glavine	1	1	0	7.0	7	0	0	0	1	0	8	0	0	1	0	1.000	0.00
Rocker	6	0	0	6.2	3	2	0	0	2	1	9	0	1	0	0	.000	0.00
Mulholland	2	0	0	2.2	1	0	0	0	1	0	2	0	0	0	0	.000	0.00
Springer	2	0	0	2.0	0	0	0	0	1	0	1	0	0	1	0	1.000	0.00
Maddux	2	2	0	14.0	12	3	3	1	1	0	7	0	0	1	0	1.000	1.93
Remlinger	5	0	0	5.2	3	2	2	0	3	0	4	0	0	0	1	.000	3.18
Millwood	2	2	0	12.2	13	6	5	1	1	0	9	0	0	1	0	1.000	3.55

Pitcher	G	GS	CG	IP	H	R	ER	HR	BB	IBB	SO	HB	WP	W	L	Pct.	ERA
Smoltz	3	1	0	8.2	8	6	6	2	0	0	8	0	0	0	0	.000	6.23
McGlinchy	1	0	0	1.0	2	2	2	0	4	1	1	0	0	0	1	.000	18.00
Totals	6	6	0	60.1	49	21	18	4	14	2	49	0	1	4	2	.667	2.69

Shutout—Glavine, Remlinger and Rocker (combined). Saves—Rocker 2, Smoltz.

NEW YORK METS' PITCHING RECORDS

Pitcher	G	GS	CG	IP	H	R	ER	HR	BB	IBB	SO	HB	WP	W	L	Pct.	ERA
Hershiser	2	0	0	4.1	1	0	0	0	3	2	5	1	0	0	0	.000	0.00
Cook	3	0	0	1.1	1	0	0	0	2	1	1	0	0	0	0	.000	0.00
Benitez	5	0	0	6.2	3	1	1	0	2	0	9	0	0	0	0	.000	1.35
Mahomes	3	0	0	6.1	4	1	1	1	3	1	3	0	0	0	0	.000	1.42
Reed	1	1	0	7.0	3	2	2	2	0	0	5	0	0	0	0	.000	2.57
Dotel	1	0	0	3.0	4	1	1	0	2	1	5	0	0	1	0	1.000	3.00
J. Franco	3	0	0	2.2	3	1	1	0	1	0	3	0	0	0	0	.000	3.38
Yoshii	2	2	0	7.2	9	4	4	0	3	1	4	0	0	0	1	.000	4.70
Wendell	5	0	0	5.2	2	3	3	0	4	2	5	1	0	1	0	1.000	4.76
Rogers	3	1	0	7.2	11	5	5	2	7	2	2	0	0	0	2	.000	5.87
Leiter	2	2	0	7.0	5	6	5	0	4	0	5	2	1	0	1	.000	6.43
Totals	6	6	0	59.1	46	24	23	5	31	10	47	4	1	2	4	.333	3.49

No shutouts. Save—Benitez.

SCORE BY INNINGS

Atlanta	7	0	0	2	1	7	0	4	0	1	1	0	0	0	1—24
New York	2	1	0	1	1	4	4	4	1	1	0	0	0	0	2—21

MISCELLANEOUS STATISTICS

Sacrifice hits—Perez 2, Alfonzo, Boone, Glavine, A. Jones, Maddux, Ordonez, Rogers, Weiss.

Sacrifice flies—Hunter, Piazza, Pratt.

Stolen bases—C. Jones 3, Williams 3, Boone 2, Cedeno 2, Mora 2, Nixon 2, Weiss 2, Agbayani, Battle, Dunston, Henderson, Hunter.

Caught stealing—Agbayani, Boone, Cedeno, Dunston, A. Jones, Klesko.

Double plays—Alfonzo, Ordonez and Olerud; Lockhart, Weiss and Hunter; Mahomes, Alfonzo, Ordonez and Olerud; Mahomes and Ventura; Mora and Piazza; Ordonez, Alfonzo and Olerud; Piazza, Ventura and Hershiser; Rogers, Ordonez, Alfonzo and Olerud; Ventura and Alfonzo; Ventura, Alfonzo and Olerud; Weiss (unassisted); Weiss, Boone and Hunter; Weiss and Klesko.

Left on bases—Atlanta 9, 6, 4, 0, 19, 9—47; New York 6, 5, 8, 3, 12, 8—42.

Hit by pitcher—By Leiter 2 (Williams, C. Jones), by Hershiser (Boone), by Wendell (Jordan).

Passed ball—Perez.

Balks—None.

Time of games—First game, 3:09; second game, 2:42; third game, 3:04; fourth game, 2:20; fifth game, 5:46; sixth game, 4:25.

Attendance—First game, 44,172; second game, 44,624; third game, 55,911; fourth game, 55,872; fifth game, 55,723; sixth game, 52,335.

Umpires—Montague, Kellogg, Reliford, Rapuano, Layne and Crawford.

Official scorers—Red Foley, Mark Frederickson, Bill Shannon.

WORLD SERIES

NEW YORK 4, ATLANTA 1

Why the Yankees won: Starting pitcher Orlando Hernandez threw seven innings of one-hit ball, showing off a dazzling assortment of pitches and arm angles that kept the Braves off-stride. Hernandez is 5-0 in six career playoff starts.

Why the Braves lost: Their inability to make what should be routine plays, a must in the postseason, proved costly late in the game. Brian Hunter, inserted into the lineup as a defensive replacement at first base for Ryan Klesko, committed two errors in the eighth inning as the Yankees turned a 1-0 deficit into a 4-1 lead.

The turning point: Braves starter Greg Maddux had given up only three singles going into the eighth. With the bases loaded and no outs (thanks in part to Hunter's dropping Chuck Knoblauch's bunt) in the eighth, Maddux got ahead of Derek Jeter, 0-2. Jeter singled to left, tying the score, 1-1. After John Rocker relieved, Paul O'Neill singled through a drawn-in infield that would have been playing back had Hunter gotten an out on Knoblauch's bunt.

Notable: Tom Glavine was scheduled to open the series for Atlanta, but he came down with the flu, forcing scheduled Game 2 starter Maddux to step in. ... Hernandez's postseason ERA stands at 1.02 ERA, trailing only Sandy Koufax and teammate Mariano Rivera among players with at least 40 postseason innings. ... Hunter made four errors in 114 regular-season games, but became the first player to commit two in one World Series inning since the Milwaukee Braves' Frank Torre (Joe's brother) did it in 1958 against, yep, the Yankees. ... Though Yankees catcher Jorge Posada was envisioning a 1-0, one-hit loss because of Chipper Jones' home run, Atlanta managed only one other hit, Bret Boone's ninth-inning single. You couldn't even pin the problem on the top, middle or bottom of the order. No one hit, thus no one scored.

Quotable: "You don't want to come in for defense and make errors," Atlanta's Hunter said. "That makes you look stupid." ... Joe Torre, marveling over the two-run, eighth-inning single by O'Neill, a lefthanded hitter who had batted .190 against lefthanders in the regular season: "Rocker is tough on righthanders, much less lefthanders." ... Atlanta's Cox, on why he left Maddux in as long as he did: "Maddux was still throwing well. The only ball that was hit well was Jeter's. Even when I took him out, he was still throwing well. He didn't get a whole lot of help, that's for sure. I thought he was as good as he's ever been." ... Torre, on Hernandez: "He con-

tinues to make you shake your head. He took control early, as did Maddux." ... Cox, on Glavine's coming down with the flu: "There's absolutely nothing you can do to prevent it except keep Tommy home for a day or two and hope nobody else gets it."

BOX SCORE

SATURDAY, OCTOBER 23, AT ATLANTA

New York	AB	R	H	RBI	PO	A
Knoblauch, 2b	4	1	0	0	1	1
Jeter, ss	4	1	2	1	1	1
O'Neill, rf	4	0	1	2	3	0
B. Williams, cf	2	0	0	0	0	0
Martinez, 1b	3	0	0	0	4	0
Posada, c	4	0	0	0	13	0
Ledee, lf	3	0	0	0	0	0
‡Leyritz, ph	0	0	0	1	0	0
Nelson, p	0	0	0	0	0	0
Stanton, p	0	0	0	0	0	0
Rivera, p	0	0	0	0	0	0
Brosius, 3b	4	1	3	0	3	0
O. Hernandez, p	1	0	0	0	2	1
*Strawberry, ph	0	0	0	0	0	0
†Curtis, pr-lf	1	1	0	0	0	0
Totals	30	4	6	4	27	5

Atlanta	AB	R	H	RBI	PO	A
G. Williams, lf	4	0	0	0	3	0
Boone, 2b	4	0	1	0	1	5
C. Jones, 3b	2	1	1	1	0	2
Jordan, rf	4	0	0	0	2	0
Klesko, 1b	3	0	0	0	7	0
Hunter, 1b	0	0	0	0	1	1
■Myers, ph	1	0	0	0	0	0
A. Jones, cf	2	0	0	0	1	0
Perez, c	2	0	0	0	7	1
Weiss, ss	2	0	0	0	3	1
§Guillen, ph	0	0	0	0	0	0
∞J. Hernandez, ph-ss	1	0	0	0	1	0
Maddux, p	2	0	0	0	1	0
Rocker, p	0	0	0	0	0	0
▲Battle, ph	0	0	0	0	0	0
◆Lockhart, ph	1	0	0	0	0	0
Remlinger, p	0	0	0	0	0	1
Totals	28	1	2	1	27	11

New York	0	0 0		0 0 0		0	4	0—4
Atlanta	0	0 0		1 0 0		0	0	0—1

New York	IP	H	R	ER	BB	SO
O. Hernandez (W)	7.0	1	1	1	2	10
Nelson	0.1	0	0	0	1	1
Stanton	0.1	0	0	0	0	1
Rivera (S)	0.1	1	0	0	1	1

Atlanta	IP	H	R	ER	BB	SO
Maddux (L)	*7.0	5	4	2	3	5
Rocker	1.0	1	0	0	2	3
Remlinger	1.0	0	0	0	1	0

*Pitched to four batters in eighth.

Bases on balls—Off O. Hernandez 2 (A. Jones, C. Jones), off Nelson 1 (Perez), off River 1 (C. Jones), off Maddux 3 (Martinez, B. Williams, Strawberry), off Rocker 2 (B. Williams, Leyritz), off Remlinger 1 (Jeter).

Strikeouts—By O. Hernandez 10 (G. Williams 2, Boone 2, Perez 2, Maddux 2, C. Jones, Weiss), by Nelson 1 (A. Jones), by Stanton 1 (J. Hernandez), by Rivera 1 (Jordan), by Maddux 5 (B. Williams, O'Neill, Jeter, Martinez, Ledee), by Rocker 3 (Martinez, Posada, Brosius).

*Walked for O. Hernandez in eighth. †Ran for Strawberry in eighth. ‡Walked for Ledee in eighth. §Announced for Weiss in eighth. ∞Struck out for Guillen in eighth. ▲Announced for Rocker in eighth. ◆Grounded out for Battle in eighth. ■Fouled out for Hunter in ninth. E—Hunter 2. DP—Atlanta 1. LOB—New York 7, Atlanta 4. HR—C. Jones. SH—O. Hernandez, Knoblauch. SB—Jeter, B. Williams. T—2:57. A—51,342. U—Marsh (N.L.), plate; Roe (A.L.), first; Rippley (N.L.), second; Cousins (N.L.), third; Davis (N.L.), left field; Joyce (A.L.), right field.

FIRST INNING

New York—Knoblauch flied to Jordan. Jeter singled to center. O'Neill flied to G. Williams. Jeter stole second. B. Williams struck out.

Atlanta—G. Williams, Boone and C. Jones struck out.

SECOND INNING

New York—Martinez walked. Posada grounded into a double play, Boone to Weiss to Klesko. Ledee flied to G. Williams.

Atlanta—Jordan and Klesko flied to O'Neill. A. Jones walked. Perez struck out.

THIRD INNING

New York—Brosius singled to right. O. Hernandez sacrificed, C. Jones to Boone, as Brosius went to second. Knoblauch flied to A. Jones. Jeter grounded out, Boone to Klesko.

Atlanta—Weiss, Maddux and G. Williams struck out.

FOURTH INNING

New York—O'Neill struck out. B. Williams lined to Klesko. Martinez flied to G. Williams.

Atlanta—Boone struck out. C. Jones homered to right. Jordan flied to O'Neill. Klesko grounded out, O. Hernandez to Martinez. **Atl. 1, N.Y. 0**

FIFTH INNING

New York—Posada grounded out, Boone to Klesko. Ledee popped to Weiss. Brosius singled to center. O. Hernandez grounded out, Boone to Klesko.

Atlanta—A. Jones lined to Brosius. Perez struck out. Weiss grounded out, Martinez to O. Hernandez.

SIXTH INNING

New York—Knoblauch grounded out, C. Jones to Klesko. Jeter struck out. O'Neill grounded to Maddux.

Atlanta—Maddux struck out. G. Williams grounded to O. Hernandez. Boone grounded out, Jeter to Martinez.

SEVENTH INNING

New York—B. Williams walked and stole second. Martinez struck out, Perez threw to Klesko on the dropped third strike. Posada popped to Weiss. Ledee struck out.

Atlanta—C. Jones walked. Jordan popped to Jeter. Klesko popped to Brosius. C. Jones caught stealing, Posada to Knoblauch.

EIGHTH INNING

New York—Hunter now at first. Brosius singled to left. Strawberry, pinch-hitting for O. Hernandez, walked. Curtis now pinch-running for Strawberry. Knoblauch sacrificed, but was safe at first on an error by Hunter, as Brosius went to third and Curtis to second. Jeter singled to left, scoring Brosius as Curtis went to third and Knoblauch to second. Rocker now pitching. O'Neill singled to right and reached second on a wild throw error by Hunter, as Curtis and Knoblauch scored and Jeter went to third. B. Williams was walked intentionally. Martinez and Posada struck out. Leyritz, pinch-hitting for Ledee, walked, scoring Jeter. Brosius struck out. **N.Y. 4, Atl. 1.**

Atlanta—Curtis now in left field and Nelson pitching. A. Jones struck out. Perez walked. Guillen was announced as a pinch-hitter for Weiss. Stanton now pitching. J. Hernandez, pinch-hitting for Guillen, struck out. Battle was announced as a pinch-hitter for Rocker. Rivera now pitching. Lockhart, pinch-hitting for Battle, grounded to Martinez.

NINTH INNING

New York—J. Hernandez now at shortstop and Remlinger pitching. Curtis flied to Jordan. Knoblauch grounded out, Boone to Hunter. Jeter walked. Jeter caught stealing, Remlinger to Hunter to J. Hernandez. **Final score: N.Y. 4, Atl. 1.**

NEW YORK 7, ATLANTA 2

Why the Yankees won: Pitching continued to be the key for New York. David Cone, who had a roller-coaster season, had a roller-coaster game. He didn't give up a hit until the fifth, but allowed a baserunner in every inning until retiring the Braves in order in the sixth. He walked more (five) than he struck out (four), but Greg Myers' fifth-inning single to center was Atlanta's only hit off Cone in his seven innings, and Myers was erased in a double play.

Why the Braves lost: Starting pitcher Kevin Millwood allowed five runs in two-plus innings in his first World Series start, taking the Braves out of the game before they were ever in it. Millwood, who had been scheduled to start Game 3 but was moved up because of the ripple effect of Tom Glavine's flu, allowed eight hits and walked two, and, again, shoddy defense didn't help.

The turning point: Up-the-middle run-scoring singles by Tino Martinez and Scott Brosius with two outs in the first inning just eluded shortstop Ozzie Guillen, starting instead of Walt Weiss. The Yankees put together five singles and a walk in the first to build a 3-0 lead. Guillen also missed a soft flare right to him in the third, allowing a run to score on the error.

Notable: In Cone's last two Series starts against the Braves (1999 and 1996), he allowed no runs on five hits. ... Seventeen of the Yankees' 20 hits in the first two games were singles. ... Braves manager Bobby Cox shuffled his lineup (Guillen for Weiss at short and Keith Lockhart for Bret Boone at second) in hopes of injecting some life into the order that got only one run on two hits in Game 1. The result: no runs on two hits . ... Having fallen behind 3-0 after one inning and 5-0 after two, the Braves needed to be patient at the plate, work the count and get baserunners. That's not the strong suit of an Atlanta lineup littered with free swingers. That trait was all the more evident against a veteran pitcher like the Yankees' Cone.

Quotable: "You run into good pitching," Atlanta's Cox said of his team's offensive struggles, "you're not going to score no matter who you run out there." ... "Everyone talks about the Braves' pitchers, and rightly so," New York's Chuck Knoblauch said. "But I think our pitching staff is very comparable, or even, with the Braves." ... "We've had periods of inconsistency with our at-bats before," Braves batting coach Don Baylor said. "But right now is the one that counts the most. You can get by in the season, but right now they're halfway to the World Series title. We've had minimal hits and runs, and that had better change quickly." ... "They've got a lot of veteran hitters who work the count and make you throw the ball over the plate," Atlanta's Millwood said. "I just threw it over the middle, instead of the corners. My job is to go out and give us a chance to win, and I didn't do that." ... "This is the way we score runs, keep pounding away, get a break here or there and make them pay," the Yankees' Paul O'Neill said. "We don't have guys who hit 40 or 50 homers, but we have a team full of guys who scrap and claw and get on base." ... "The pitching pretty much sets the tone for what we do, and David Cone was terrific," New York manager Joe Torre said. ... "I thought I caught a break on that one," Cone said of Brian Jordan's drive caught on the warning track in the first inning. "That's easily a home run on a warmer day."

BOX SCORE

SUNDAY, OCTOBER 24, AT ATLANTA

New York	AB	R	H	RBI	PO	A
Knoblauch, 2b	4	1	2	1	3	4
Jeter, ss	5	2	2	0	3	4
O'Neill, rf	4	0	1	1	3	0
B. Williams, cf	4	1	3	0	1	0
Martinez, 1b	5	2	2	2	9	1
Ledee, lf	4	0	2	1	1	0
Brosius, 3b	5	1	2	1	2	2
Girardi, c	4	0	0	0	4	0
Cone, p	4	0	0	0	1	0
Mendoza, p	1	0	0	0	0	1
Nelson, p	0	0	0	0	0	0
Totals	40	7	14	6	27	12

Atlanta	AB	R	H	RBI	PO	A
G. Williams, lf	4	0	0	0	1	0
Guillen, ss	4	0	0	0	4	3
C. Jones, 3b	3	1	1	0	0	2
Jordan, rf	3	0	0	0	0	0
Klesko, 1b	4	0	0	0	8	0
Lockhart, 2b	2	1	0	0	1	2
Myers, c	3	0	2	1	8	0
A. Jones, cf	3	0	0	0	4	0
McGlinchy, p	0	0	0	0	0	0
†Boone, ph	1	0	1	1	0	0
Millwood, p	0	0	0	0	0	0
Mulholland, p	0	0	0	0	1	0
*Fabregas, ph	1	0	0	0	0	0
Springer, p	0	0	0	0	0	1
Nixon, cf	2	0	1	0	0	0
Totals	30	2	5	2	27	8

New York	3	0	2	1	1	0	0	0	0—7
Atlanta	0	0	0	0	0	0	0	0	2—2

New York	IP	H	R	ER	BB	SO
Cone (W)	7.0	1	0	0	5	4
Mendoza	1.2	3	2	2	1	0
Nelson	0.1	1	0	0	0	0

Atlanta	IP	H	R	ER	BB	SO
Millwood (L)	*2.0	8	5	4	2	2
Mulholland	3.0	3	2	2	1	3
Springer	2.0	1	0	0	0	1
McGlinchy	2.0	2	0	0	1	2

*Pitched to three batters in third.
Bases on balls—Off Cone 5 (Myers, Mulholland, C. Jones, Jordan, Lockhart), off Mendoza 1 (Lockhart), off Millwood 2 (Ledee, Knoblauch), off Mulholland 1 (B. Williams), off McGlinchy 1 (O'Neill).
Strikeouts—By Cone 4 (Klesko, Fabregas, G. Williams, A. Jones), by Millwood 2 (Girardi, Jeter), by Mulholland 3 (Brosius, Knoblauch, Ledee), by Springer 1 (Ledee), by McGlinchy 2 (Martinez, Brosius).
*Struck out for Mulholland in fifth. †Doubled for McGlinchy in ninth. E—Cone, Guillen. DP—New York 3, Atlanta 1. LOB—New York 11, Atlanta 7. 2B—Jeter, Ledee, Brosius, Boone. SH—Girardi. SB—Knoblauch. T—3:14. A—51,226. U—Roe (A.L.), plate; Rippley (N.L.), first; Cousins (A.L.), second; Davis (N.L.), third; Joyce (A.L.), left field; Marsh (N.L.), right field.

PLAY BY PLAY

FIRST INNING
New York—Knoblauch singled to left-center. Jeter singled to left as Knoblauch went to second. O'Neill singled to center, scor-

ing Knoblauch as Jeter went to second. B. Williams grounded into a double play, Guillen to Klesko, as Jeter went to third. Martinez singled to center, scoring Jeter. Ledee walked. Brosius singled to center, scoring Martinez as Ledee went to second. Girardi struck out. **N.Y. 3, Atl. 0.**
Atlanta—G. Williams grounded out, Jeter to Martinez. Guillen went to second on a throwing error by Cone. C. Jones grounded out, Knoblauch to Martinez, as Guillen went to third. Jordan flied to Ledee.

SECOND INNING
New York—Cone grounded to Klesko. Knoblauch walked. Jeter struck out as Knoblauch stole second. O'Neill grounded out, C. Jones to Klesko.
Atlanta—Klesko grounded out, Martinez to Cone. Lockhart popped to Brosius. Myers walked. A. Jones popped to Jeter.

THIRD INNING
New York—B. Williams singled to center. Martinez singled to left as B. Williams went to second. Ledee doubled to left-center, scoring B. Williams as Martinez went to third. Mulholland now pitching. Brosius struck out. Girardi grounded out, Guillen to Klesko. Cone reached on an error by Guillen, as Martinez scored and Ledee went to third. Knoblauch struck out. **N.Y. 5, Atl. 0.**
Atlanta—Mulholland walked. G. Williams flied to O'Neill. Guillen grounded into a double play, Jeter to Martinez.

FOURTH INNING
New York—Jeter doubled to left-center. O'Neill flied to A. Jones as Jeter went to third. B. Williams was walked intentionally. Martinez forced B. Williams at second, Guillen to Lockhart, as Jeter scored. Ledee struck out. **N.Y. 6, Atl. 0.**
Atlanta—C. Jones walked. Jordan flied to O'Neill. Klesko struck out. Lockhart grounded out, Knoblauch to Martinez.

FIFTH INNING
New York—Brosius doubled to right. Girardi sacrificed Brosius to third, Mulholland made the unassisted putout. Cone popped to Guillen. Knoblauch singled to left, scoring Brosius. Jeter forced Knoblauch at second, Lockhart to Guillen. **N.Y. 7, Atl. 0.**
Atlanta—Myers singled to center. A. Jones grounded into a double play, Brosius to Knoblauch to Martinez. Fabregas, pinch-hitting for Mulholland, struck out.

SIXTH INNING
New York—Springer now pitching. O'Neill flied to G. Williams. B. Williams singled to right. Martinez forced B. Williams at second, Springer to Guillen. Ledee struck out.
Atlanta—G. Williams struck out. Guillen lined to Knoblauch. C. Jones popped to Brosius.

SEVENTH INNING
New York—Brosius, Girardi and Cone flied to A. Jones.
Atlanta—Jordan walked. Klesko popped to Knoblauch. Lockhart walked. Myers flied to B. Williams as Jordan went to third. A. Jones struck out.

EIGHTH INNING
New York—Nixon now in center field and McGlinchy pitching. Knoblauch popped foul to Klesko. Jeter grounded to Klesko. O'Neill walked. B. Williams singled to center as O'Neill went to second. Martinez struck out.
Atlanta—Mendoza now pitching. Nixon singled to second. G. Williams grounded into a double play, Knoblauch to Jeter to Martinez. Guillen grounded out, Mendoza to Martinez.

NINTH INNING
New York—Ledee singled to right. Brosius struck out. Girardi grounded out, C. Jones to Klesko, as Ledee went to second. Mendoza grounded out, Lockhart to Klesko.
Atlanta—C. Jones singled to center. Jordan grounded out, Brosius to Martinez, as C. Jones went to second. Klesko flied to O'Neill. Lockhart walked. Myers singled to center, scoring C. Jones, as Lockhart went to second. Boone now pinch-hitting for McGlinchy. Nelson now pitching. Boone doubled to left, scoring Lockhart, as Myers went to third. Nixon grounded out, Jeter to Martinez. **Final score: N.Y. 7, Atl. 2.**

GAME 3
HIGHLIGHTS

NEW YORK 6, ATLANTA 5 (10 INNINGS)

Why the Yankees won: Journeyman Chad Curtis etched his name in Yankees and World Series lore with two home runs after hitting five all season. His second was the game-winner, coming in the bottom of the 10th off Braves reliever Mike Remlinger.

Why the Braves lost: Atlanta built a 5-1 lead by the fifth inning, with every batter getting at least one hit in that span, but the Braves lineup went silent from there. Down 0-2 in the Series, Atlanta jumped on New York starter Andy Pettitte and needed to pour it on for a convincing road victory.

The turning point: Braves manager Bobby Cox, who was looking for seven strong innings from starter Tom Glavine, got it. But Cox pushed his and Atlanta's luck by letting Glavine, pushed back from a scheduled Game 1 start because of the flu, come out for the eighth inning after the Yankees had cut the lead to two, 5-3. Joe Girardi singled to start the eighth, and Chuck Knoblauch sent a tying two-run homer over the short porch in right, ending Glavine's night.

Notable: The victory was the Yankees' 200th in World Series play; the Cardinals rank second with 96 Series wins. ... If New York relievers Jason Grimsley, Jeff Nelson and winner Mariano Rivera hadn't shut down the Braves' offense, holding Atlanta scoreless after New York starter Andy Pettitte gave up five runs in 3.2 innings, then a comeback would have been impossible. ... Although this Yankees team wasn't known for its power, Glavine allowed three home runs in only 76 pitches. Of course, that was a better number than loser Remlinger, who gave up one home run in three pitches. ... The Series victory was the 11th in a row for Yankees manager Joe Torre, breaking the record set by Joe McCarthy of the Yankees.

Quotable: "I'm still amazed, and yet I'm not amazed," New York's Torre said of the come-from-behind victory. "We go out there and play nine innings, and good things happen." ... Said Torre's counterpart, Atlanta's Bobby Cox: "It would've been nice to have won. It would have gotten us going real good. This was a big one to lose." ... "I have a tendency when I get up there in that situation, I try to hit a home run," Curtis said of game-winner in the 10th. "So I went up there and tried to hit it up the middle, and I hit a home run." ... Cox on Curtis, the Yankees' unlikely hero: "Always someone you don't expect. You never know where it's going to come from." ... "It was a changeup," Atlanta's Remlinger said of the 10th-inning pitch Curtis hit. "It looked like it got too much of the plate." ... "I never stepped on the field," Curtis said, recalling not having played in the 1998 World Series victory over the Padres. "I wasn't pouting; we won the World Series. By the

same token, I felt like I was more congratulating my teammates than celebrating with them." ... "Every time Joe Torre takes a guy out of the game when we're losing, he tells the new pitcher to hold them here and get a win," the Yankees' Knoblauch said. "That's the way we have to think. It's not cockiness. It's having a great deal of confidence in the guys we have on our team to come back." ... "When we saw Andy struggle a little bit, we knew it was going to be one of those games we were going to need a lot of middle relief," said Yankees reliever Jeff Nelson, who pitched two perfect innings.

BOX SCORE

TUESDAY, OCTOBER 26, AT NEW YORK

Atlanta	AB	R	H	RBI	PO	A
G. Williams, lf	5	2	2	0	2	0
Boone, 2b	5	1	4	1	1	2
*Nixon, pr	0	0	0	0	0	0
Lockhart, 2b	0	0	0	0	0	0
C. Jones, 3b	4	0	1	1	1	0
Jordan, rf	3	1	1	1	4	0
A. Jones, cf	5	1	1	0	4	0
J. Hernandez, dh	4	0	1	2	0	0
†Guillen, ph-dh	1	0	0	0	0	0
Perez, c	4	0	1	0	5	0
‡Klesko, ph-1b	1	0	1	0	0	0
Hunter, 1b	4	0	1	0	8	1
§Myers, ph-c	1	0	0	0	0	0
Weiss, ss	4	0	1	0	2	3
Glavine, p	0	0	0	0	0	2
Rocker, p	0	0	0	0	0	0
Remlinger, p	0	0	0	0	0	0
Totals	41	5	14	5	27	8

New York	AB	R	H	RBI	PO	A
Knoblauch, 2b	4	2	2	2	2	2
Jeter, ss	4	0	1	0	2	4
O'Neill, rf	4	0	1	1	0	0
B. Williams, cf	4	0	0	0	1	0
Davis, dh	4	0	0	0	0	0
Martinez, 1b	4	1	1	1	12	0
Brosius, 3b	4	0	0	0	2	2
Curtis, lf	4	2	2	2	4	0
Girardi, c	3	1	2	0	5	2
Pettitte, p	0	0	0	0	0	3
Grimsley, p	0	0	0	0	0	0
Nelson, p	0	0	0	0	0	1
Rivera, p	0	0	0	0	0	0
Totals	35	6	9	6	30	14

Atlanta	1	0	3		1	0	0		0	0	0	0—5
New York	1	0	0		0	1	0		1	2	0	1—6

Atlanta	IP	H	R	ER	BB	SO
Glavine	*7.0	7	5	4	0	3
Rocker	2.0	1	0	0	0	1
Remlinger (L)	0.0	1	1	1	0	0

New York	IP	H	R	ER	BB	SO
Pettitte	3.2	10	5	5	1	1
Grimsley	2.1	2	0	0	2	0
Nelson	2.0	0	0	0	0	2
Rivera (W)	2.0	2	0	0	0	2

*Pitched to two batters in eighth.

Bases on balls—Off Pettitte 1 (Jordan), off Grimsley 2 (Jordan, C. Jones). Strikeouts—By Glavine 3 (Jeter, Brosius, Davis), by Rocker 1 (Davis), by Pettitte 1 (Perez), by Nelson 2 (J. Hernandez, Hunter), by Rivera 2 (C. Jones, Guillen).

*Ran for Boone in ninth. †Struck out for J. Hernandez in 10th. ‡Singled for Perez in 10th. §Grounded out for Hunter in 10th. E—Jordan. DP—Atlanta 2, New York 1. LOB—Atlanta 9, New York 2. 2B—Boone 3, J. Hernandez, Knoblauch. 3B—G. Williams. HR—Curtis 2, Knoblauch, Martinez. SB—J. Hernandez. WP—Pettitte. T—3:16. A—56,794. U—Rippley (N.L.), plate; Cousins (A.L.), first; Davis (N.L.), second; Joyce (A.L.), third; Marsh (N.L.), left field; Roe (A.L.), right field.

PLAY BY PLAY

FIRST INNING

Atlanta—G. Williams singled to right. Boone doubled to right as G. Williams went to third. C. Jones grounded out, Brosius to Martinez, as G. Williams scored. Jordan walked. A. Jones grounded out, Pettitte to Martinez, as Boone went to third and Jordan to second. J. Hernandez grounded out, Jeter to Martinez. **Atl. 1, N.Y. 0.**

New York—Knoblauch reached second on an error by Jordan. Jeter flied to Jordan as Knoblauch went to third. O'Neill singled to left, scoring Knoblauch. B. Williams lined to Hunter, who doubled O'Neill off first, unassisted. **Atl. 1, N.Y. 1.**

SECOND INNING

Atlanta—Perez struck out. Hunter singled to left and went to second on a wild pitch. Weiss grounded out, Knoblauch to Martinez, as Hunter went to third. G. Williams grounded out, Pettitte to Martinez.

New York—Davis grounded out, Weiss to Hunter. Martinez and Brosius flied to A. Jones.

THIRD INNING

Atlanta—Boone doubled to right-center. C. Jones grounded out, Jeter to Martinez, as Boone went to third. Jordan singled to right, scoring Boone. A. Jones singled to left, as Jordan went to second. J. Hernandez doubled to left, scoring Jordan and A. Jones. Perez flied to Curtis. J. Hernandez stole third. Hunter flied to O'Neill. **Atl. 4, N.Y. 1.**

New York—Curtis flied to G. Williams. Girardi flied to Jordan. Knoblauch doubled to left. Jeter struck out.

FOURTH INNING

Atlanta—Weiss grounded out, Pettitte to Martinez. G. Williams tripled to center. Boone doubled to left, scoring G. Williams. Boone caught stealing third, Girardi to Brosius. C. Jones singled to center. Grimsley now pitching. Jordan walked. A. Jones popped to Knoblauch. **Atl. 5, N.Y. 1.**

New York—O'Neill grounded to Perez. B. Williams grounded out, Boone to Hunter. Davis flied to Jordan.

FIFTH INNING

Atlanta—J. Hernandez flied to O'Neill. Perez singled to center. Hunter forced Perez at second, Brosius to Knoblauch. Weiss singled to right as Hunter went to second. G. Williams flied to Curtis.

New York—Martinez grounded out, Boone to Hunter. Brosius struck out. Curtis homered to right. Girardi singled to left-center. Knoblauch grounded out, Glavine to Hunter. **Atl. 5, N.Y. 2.**

SIXTH INNING

Atlanta—Boone flied to B. Williams, C. Jones walked. Jordan grounded into a double play, Jeter to Martinez.

New York—Jeter flied to G. Williams. O'Neill grounded out, Glavine to Hunter. B. Williams flied to Jordan.

SEVENTH INNING

Atlanta—Nelson now pitching. A. Jones popped to Brosius. J. Hernandez struck out. Perez grounded out, Nelson to Martinez.

New York—Davis struck out. Martinez homered to right. Brosius flied to A. Jones. Curtis grounded out, Weiss to Hunter. **Atl. 5, N.Y. 3.**

EIGHTH INNING

Atlanta—Hunter struck out. Weiss and G. Williams flied to Curtis.

New York—Girardi singled to right. Knoblauch homered to right, scoring Girardi. Rocker now pitching. Jeter singled to center. O'Neill bunted into a double play, Hunter to Weiss to Boone. B. Williams flied to A. Jones. **Atl. 5, N.Y. 5.**

NINTH INNING

Atlanta—Rivera now pitching. Boone singled to right. Nixon now pinch-running for Boone. Nixon caught stealing second, Girardi to Jeter. C. Jones struck out. Jordan grounded out, Jeter to Martinez.

New York—Lockhart now at second. Davis struck out. Martinez popped foul to C. Jones. Brosius popped to Weiss.

10TH INNING

Atlanta—A. Jones grounded out, Knoblauch to Martinez. Guillen, pinch-hitting for J. Hernandez, struck out. Klesko, pinch-hitting for Perez, singled to right. Myers, pinch-hitting for Hunter, grounded to Martinez.

New York—Klesko now at first, Myers catching and Remlinger pitching. Curtis homered to left. **Final score: N.Y. 6, Atl. 5.**

GAME 4
HIGHLIGHTS

NEW YORK 4, ATLANTA 1

Why the Yankees won: Roger Clemens, 37, put to rest any talk of his being a postseason bust (247 lifetime victories, but none in the World Series) by looking like "The Rocket" of his prime. He hit 96 mph on the radar gun and allowed one run on four hits in 7.2 innings. In fact, if he hadn't gotten hurt while covering first base on an eighth-inning play, Clemens might have gone the distance.

Why the Braves lost: Defense wins championships, and Atlanta's inability to make plays—routine and otherwise—hurt again. Singles off Walt Weiss' and Ryan Klesko's gloves set up the Yankees' three-run third and proved that when the box scores showed only four errors charged to the Braves in the four-game series, it was deceiving.

The turning point: Braves starter John Smoltz intentionally walked Bernie Williams, loading the bases with one out in the third inning. Tino Martinez's sharp grounder to Klesko's right could have become the inning-ending double play the Braves needed, but the ball ricocheted off Klesko's arm, allowing two runs to score. One batter later, Jorge Posada lined a single to right, knocking in the third Yankees run of the inning.

Notable: The Yankees became the first team in 60 years to sweep consecutive World Series. ... Only No. 2 hitter Bret Boone (1-for-3 in Game 4, but .538 for the Series) hit the ball with any regularity for Atlanta. The Braves got 26 hits in four games, and few of those were in key situations. That spelled trouble against a team as effective and opportunistic as the Yankees. ... With a record-tying 12-game World Series winning streak intact, the Yankees' most visible constant was manager Joe Torre, who not only has the perfect personality to buffer his clubhouse from principal owner George Steinbrenner, but he also has outmanaged Bobby Cox twice (1996 and '99) and Bruce Bochy once (1998) in winning three championships in four years. ... New York's Jim Leyritz hit the 18th pinch-hit home run in World Series play, the first since Ed Sprague did it for the Blue Jays in Game 2 of the '92 Series against Atlanta. ... The Braves joined the New York Giants (1910-9) as the only teams to have lost four World Series in a decade. ... New York's Derek Jeter extended his postseason hitting streak to 17 games, tying the Yankees' Hank Bauer for the longest ever; Bauer's streak was in World Series games from 1956-58. Jeter has hit in nine consecutive World Series games.

Quotable: Afterward, New York's Clemens, acquired in February recalled seeing teammates receive their 1998 Series rings in spring training: "I was sitting there watching them receive them. They said, 'We're going to get you one.' " ... "It seemed like a perfect setup," New York's Torre said of Clemens' opportunity to complete the sweep, "I couldn't see it *not* happening, not with the way his career had gone." ... Series MVP Mariano Rivera, who pitched 12.1 scoreless innings in eight postseason appearances, on the first repeat championship since Toronto in 1992-93: "Everybody talked about last year, but this is unbelievable, back-to-back." ... "I think they think in their minds that they had a tremendous year with all the ballclub went through," the Braves' Cox said of his team. "They're disappointed just like I am." ... "The best team won," said Atlanta's Smoltz, who fell to 12-4 in postseason play. "The Yankees are head and shoulders above most when it comes to this time of the year. We lost to the best team. The Yankees are a model of how to win." ... The Yankees' Jeter on his team's place in history: "I'd have to rank it at the top. Three tiers of playoffs doesn't make it twice as hard or three times as hard, it makes it five times as hard." ... "To win three in four years," Yankees principal owner George Steinbrenner said, "these guys have to be put up there with the old, great Yankees teams."

BOX SCORE

WEDNESDAY, OCTOBER 27, AT NEW YORK

Atlanta	AB	R	H	RBI	PO	A
G. Williams, lf	4	0	1	0	0	0
Boone, 2b	3	0	1	1	2	2
C. Jones, 3b	4	0	0	0	0	1
Jordan, rf	3	0	0	0	2	0
Klesko, 1b	4	0	1	0	6	0
Lockhart, dh	4	0	1	0	0	0
Perez, c	2	0	0	0	11	0
*Myers, ph-c	1	0	0	0	1	0
A. Jones, cf	3	0	0	0	1	0
Weiss, ss	3	1	1	0	1	1
Smoltz, p	0	0	0	0	0	0
Mulholland, p	0	0	0	0	0	0
Springer, p	0	0	0	0	0	0
Totals	31	1	5	1	24	4

New York	AB	R	H	RBI	PO	A
Knoblauch, 2b	4	1	1	0	4	3
Sojo, 2b	0	0	0	0	1	1
Jeter, ss	4	1	1	0	6	6
O'Neill, rf	3	0	0	0	0	0
B. Williams, cf	3	1	0	0	0	0
Martinez, 1b	3	0	1	2	16	0
Strawberry, dh	3	0	1	0	0	0
†Leyritz, ph-dh	1	1	1	1	0	0
Posada, c	4	0	2	1	4	0
Ledee, lf	3	0	0	0	0	0
‡Curtis, ph-lf	1	0	0	0	1	0
Brosius, 3b	3	0	1	0	1	3
Clemens, p	0	0	0	0	0	3
Nelson, p	0	0	0	0	0	0
Rivera, p	0	0	0	0	0	1
Totals	32	4	8	4	27	17

Atlanta	0	0	0	0	0	0	0 1	0—1
New York	0	0	3	0	0	0	0 1	x—4

Atlanta	IP	H	R	ER	BB	SO
Smoltz (L)	7.0	6	3	3	3	11
Mulholland	0.2	2	1	1	0	0
Springer	0.1	0	0	0	0	0

New York	IP	H	R	ER	BB	SO
Clemens (W)	7.2	4	1	1	2	4
Nelson	*0.0	1	0	0	0	0
Rivera (S)	1.1	0	0	0	0	0

*Pitched to one batter in eighth.
Bases on balls—Off Smoltz 3 (O'Neill, Martinez, B. Williams), off Clemens 2 (Jordan, Boone).
Strikeouts—By Smoltz 11 (Knoblauch 2, Posada 2, Strawberry 2, Ledee, Brosius, O'Neill, B. Williams, Martinez), by Clemens 4 (G. Williams, Boone, A. Jones, Jordan).
*Grounded out for Perez in eighth. †Homered for Strawberry in eighth. ‡Fouled out for Ledee in eighth. DP—New York 1. LOB—Atlanta 5, New York 7. 2B—Posada. HR—Leyritz. SB—Jeter 2. T—2:58. A—56,752. U—Cousins (A.L.), plate; Davis (N.L.), first; Joyce (A.L.), second; Marsh (N.L.), third; Roe (A.L.), left field; Rippley (N.L.), right field.

PLAY BY PLAY

FIRST INNING
Atlanta—G. Williams struck out. Boone and C. Jones grounded out, Jeter to Martinez.

New York—Knoblauch struck out. Jeter grounded to Klesko. O'Neill walked. B. Williams grounded out, Boone to Klesko.

SECOND INNING
Atlanta—Jordan grounded out, Knoblauch to Martinez. Klesko singled to right-center. Lockhart forced Klesko at second, Brosius to Knoblauch. Perez forced Lockhart at second, Jeter to Knoblauch.

New York—Martinez walked. Strawberry singled to left as Martinez went to second. Posada, Ledee and Brosius struck out.

THIRD INNING
Atlanta—A. Jones grounded out, Jeter to Martinez. Weiss grounded to Martinez. G. Williams popped to Knoblauch.

New York—Knoblauch singled to short. Jeter singled to right as Knoblauch went to third. O'Neill struck out as Jeter stole second. B. Williams was walked intentionally. Martinez singled to first, scoring Knoblauch and Jeter, as B. Williams went to third. Strawberry struck out. Posada singled to right, scoring B. Williams, as Martinez went to third. Ledee popped to Weiss. **N.Y. 3, Atl. 0.**

FOURTH INNING
Atlanta—Boone struck out. C. Jones grounded out, Clemens to Martinez. Jordan walked. Klesko grounded to Martinez.

New York—Brosius and Knoblauch flied to Jordan. Jeter grounded out, C. Jones to Klesko.

FIFTH INNING
Atlanta—Lockhart singled to center. Perez grounded into a double play, Brosius to Knoblauch to Martinez. A. Jones struck out.

New York—O'Neill grounded out, Boone to Klesko. B. Williams and Martinez struck out.

SIXTH INNING
Atlanta—Weiss grounded out, Clemens to Martinez. G. Williams grounded out, Jeter to Martinez. Boone walked. C. Jones grounded out, Brosius to Martinez.

New York—Strawberry and Posada struck out. Ledee grounded to Klesko.

SEVENTH INNING
Atlanta—Jordan struck out. Klesko grounded out, Knoblauch to Martinez. Lockhart popped to Brosius.

New York—Brosius singled to right-center. Knoblauch struck out. Jeter forced Brosius at second, Weiss to Boone. Jeter stole second. O'Neill flied to A. Jones.

EIGHTH INNING
Atlanta—Sojo now at second. Myers, pinch-hitting for Perez, grounded out, Clemens to Martinez. A. Jones grounded out, Jeter

to Martinez. Weiss singled to first. G. Williams singled to left as Weiss went to second. Nelson now pitching. Boone singled to center, scoring Weiss, as G. Williams went to third. Rivera now pitching. C. Jones grounded out, Sojo to Martinez. **N.Y. 3, Atl. 1.**

New York—Myers now catching and Mulholland pitching. B. Williams popped to Boone. Martinez popped foul to Myers. Leyritz, pinch-hitting for Strawberry, homered to left. Posada doubled to center. Curtis was announced as a pinch-hitter for Ledee. Springer now pitching. Curtis popped foul to Klesko. **N.Y. 4, Atl. 1.**

NINTH INNING

Atlanta—Curtis now in left field. Jordan grounded out, Rivera to Martinez. Klesko popped to Sojo. Lockhart flied to Curtis. **Final score: N.Y. 4, Atl. 1.**

STATISTICS

NEW YORK YANKEES' BATTING AND FIELDING AVERAGES

Player, position	G	AB	R	H	TB	2B	3B	HR	RBI	BB	IBB	SO	Avg.	PO	A	E	Avg.
Leyritz, ph-dh	2	1	1	1	4	0	0	1	2	1	0	0	1.000	0	0	0	.000
Brosius, 3b	4	16	2	6	7	1	0	0	1	0	0	5	.375	8	7	0	1.000
Jeter, ss	4	17	4	6	7	1	0	0	1	1	0	3	.353	6	15	0	1.000
Curtis, pr-lf-ph	3	6	3	2	8	0	0	2	2	0	0	0	.333	5	0	0	1.000
Strawberry, ph-dh	2	3	0	1	1	0	0	0	0	1	0	2	.333	0	0	0	.000
Knoblauch, 2b	4	16	5	5	9	1	0	1	3	1	0	3	.313	10	10	0	1.000
Girardi, c	2	7	1	2	2	0	0	0	0	0	0	1	.286	9	2	0	1.000
Martinez, 1b	4	15	3	4	7	0	0	1	5	2	0	4	.267	41	2	0	1.000
Posada, c	2	8	0	2	3	1	0	0	1	0	0	3	.250	17	1	0	1.000
B. Williams, cf	4	13	2	3	3	0	0	0	0	4	3	2	.231	2	0	0	1.000
Ledee, lf	3	10	0	2	3	1	0	0	1	1	0	4	.200	1	0	0	1.000
O'Neill, rf	4	15	0	3	3	0	0	0	4	2	0	2	.200	8	0	0	1.000
Clemens, p	1	0	0	0	0	0	0	0	0	0	0	0	.000	0	3	0	1.000
Grimsley, p	1	0	0	0	0	0	0	0	0	0	0	0	.000	0	0	0	.000
Nelson, p	4	0	0	0	0	0	0	0	0	0	0	0	.000	0	1	0	1.000
Pettitte, p	1	0	0	0	0	0	0	0	0	0	0	0	.000	0	3	0	1.000
Rivera, p	3	0	0	0	0	0	0	0	0	0	0	0	.000	0	1	0	1.000
Sojo, 2b	1	0	0	0	0	0	0	0	0	0	0	0	.000	1	1	0	1.000
Stanton, p	1	0	0	0	0	0	0	0	0	0	0	0	.000	0	0	0	.000
O. Hernandez, p	1	1	0	0	0	0	0	0	0	0	0	0	.000	2	1	0	1.000
Mendoza, p	1	1	0	0	0	0	0	0	0	0	0	0	.000	0	1	0	1.000
Davis, dh	1	4	0	0	0	0	0	0	0	0	0	2	.000	0	0	0	.000
Cone, p	1	4	0	0	0	0	0	0	0	0	0	0	.000	1	0	1	.500
Totals	4	137	21	37	57	5	0	5	20	13	3	31	.270	111	48	1	.994

ATLANTA BRAVES' BATTING AND FIELDING AVERAGES

Player, position	G	AB	R	H	TB	2B	3B	HR	RBI	BB	IBB	SO	Avg.	PO	A	E	Avg.
Boone, 2b-ph	4	13	1	7	11	4	0	0	3	1	0	3	.538	4	9	0	1.000
Nixon, cf-pr	2	2	0	1	1	0	0	0	0	0	0	0	.500	0	0	0	.000
Myers, ph-c	4	6	0	2	2	0	0	0	1	1	0	0	.333	9	0	0	1.000
Hunter, 1b	2	4	0	1	1	0	0	0	0	0	0	1	.250	9	2	2	.846
Weiss, ss	3	9	1	2	2	0	0	0	0	0	0	1	.222	6	5	0	1.000
J. Hernandez, ph-ss-dh	2	5	0	1	2	1	0	0	2	0	0	2	.200	1	0	0	1.000
C. Jones, 3b	4	13	2	3	6	0	0	1	2	4	0	2	.231	1	5	0	1.000
G. Williams, lf	4	17	2	3	5	0	1	0	0	0	0	4	.176	6	0	0	1.000
Klesko, 1b-ph	4	12	0	2	2	0	0	0	0	0	0	1	.167	21	0	0	1.000
Lockhart, ph-2b-dh	4	7	1	1	1	0	0	0	0	2	0	0	.143	1	2	0	1.000
Perez, c	3	8	0	1	1	0	0	0	0	1	0	3	.125	23	1	0	1.000
A. Jones, cf	4	13	1	1	1	0	0	0	0	1	0	3	.077	10	0	0	1.000
Jordan, rf	4	13	1	1	1	0	0	0	1	4	0	2	.077	8	0	1	.889
Battle, ph	1	0	0	0	0	0	0	0	0	0	0	0	.000	0	0	0	.000
Glavine, p	1	0	0	0	0	0	0	0	0	0	0	0	.000	0	2	0	1.000
McGlinchy, p	1	0	0	0	0	0	0	0	0	0	0	0	.000	0	0	0	.000
Millwood, p	1	0	0	0	0	0	0	0	0	0	0	0	.000	0	0	0	.000
Mulholland, p	2	0	0	0	0	0	0	0	1	0	0	0	.000	1	0	0	1.000
Remlinger, p	2	0	0	0	0	0	0	0	0	0	0	0	.000	0	1	0	1.000
Rocker, p	2	0	0	0	0	0	0	0	0	0	0	0	.000	0	0	0	.000
Smoltz, p	1	0	0	0	0	0	0	0	0	0	0	0	.000	0	0	0	.000
Springer, p	2	0	0	0	0	0	0	0	0	0	0	0	.000	0	1	0	1.000
Fabregas, ph	1	1	0	0	0	0	0	0	0	0	0	0	.000	0	0	0	.000
Maddux, p	1	2	0	0	0	0	0	0	0	0	0	0	.000	1	0	0	1.000
Guillen, ph-ss-dh	3	5	0	0	0	0	0	0	0	0	0	1	.000	4	3	1	.875
Totals	4	130	9	26	36	5	1	1	9	15	0	26	.200	105	31	4	.971

NEW YORK YANKEES' PITCHING RECORDS

Pitcher	G	GS	CG	IP	H	R	ER	HR	BB	IBB	SO	HB	WP	W	L	Pct.	ERA
Cone	1	1	0	7.0	1	0	0	0	5	0	4	0	0	1	0	1.000	0.00
Rivera	3	0	0	4.2	3	0	0	0	1	0	3	0	0	1	0	1.000	0.00

Pitcher	G	GS	CG	IP	H	R	ER	HR	BB	IBB	SO	HB	WP	W	L	Pct.	ERA
Nelson	4	0	0	2.2	2	0	0	0	1	0	3	0	0	0	0	.000	0.00
Grimsley	1	0	0	2.1	2	0	0	0	2	0	0	0	0	0	0	.000	0.00
Stanton	1	0	0	0.1	0	0	0	0	0	0	1	0	0	0	0	.000	0.00
Clemens	1	1	0	7.2	4	1	1	0	2	0	4	0	0	1	0	1.000	1.17
O. Hernandez	1	1	0	7.0	1	1	1	1	2	0	10	0	0	1	0	1.000	1.29
Mendoza	1	0	0	1.2	3	2	2	0	1	0	0	0	0	0	0	.000	10.80
Pettitte	1	1	0	3.2	10	5	5	0	1	0	1	0	1	0	0	.000	12.27
Totals	4	4	0	37.0	26	9	9	1	15	0	26	0	1	4	0	1.000	2.19

Shutouts—None. Saves—Rivera 2.

ATLANTA BRAVES' PITCHING RECORDS

Pitcher	G	GS	CG	IP	H	R	ER	HR	BB	IBB	SO	HB	WP	W	L	Pct.	ERA
Rocker	2	0	0	3.0	2	0	0	0	2	1	4	0	0	0	0	.000	0.00
Springer	2	0	0	2.1	1	0	0	0	0	0	1	0	0	0	0	.000	0.00
McGlinchy	1	0	0	2.0	2	0	0	0	1	0	2	0	0	0	0	.000	0.00
Maddux	1	1	0	7.0	5	4	2	0	3	0	5	0	0	0	1	.000	2.57
Smoltz	1	1	0	7.0	6	3	3	0	3	1	11	0	0	0	1	.000	3.86
Glavine	1	1	0	7.0	7	5	4	3	0	0	3	0	0	0	0	.000	5.14
Mulholland	2	0	0	3.2	5	3	3	1	1	1	3	0	0	0	0	.000	7.36
Remlinger	2	0	0	1.0	1	1	1	1	1	0	0	0	0	0	1	.000	9.00
Millwood	1	1	0	2.0	8	5	4	0	2	0	2	0	0	0	1	.000	18.00
Totals	4	4	0	35.0	37	21	17	5	13	3	31	0	0	0	4	.000	4.37

No shutouts or saves.

SCORE BY INNINGS

New York	4	0	5	1	2	0	1	7	0	1	—	21
Atlanta	1	0	3	2	0	0	0	1	2	0	—	9

MISCELLANEOUS STATISTICS

Sacrifice hits—Girardi, O. Hernandez, Knoblauch.
Sacrifice flies—None.
Stolen bases—Jeter 3, J. Hernandez, Knoblauch, B. Williams.
Caught stealing—Boone, Jeter, C. Jones, Nixon.
Double plays—Brosius, Knoblauch and Martinez 2; Jeter and Martinez 2; Boone, Weiss and Klesko; Guillen and Klesko; Hunter (unassisted); Hunter, Weiss and Boone; Knoblauch, Jeter and Martinez.
Left on bases—New York 7, 11, 2, 7—27; Atlanta 4, 7, 9, 5—25.
Hit by pitcher—None.
Passed balls—None.
Balks—None.
Time of games—First game, 2:57; second game, 3:14; third game, 3:16; fourth game, 2:58.
Attendance—First game, 51,342; second game, 51,226; third game, 56,794; fourth game, 56,752.
Umpires—Marsh, Roe, Rippley, Cousins, Davis and Joyce.
Official scorers—Bob Elliott, Red Foley, Mark Frederickson, Jack O'Connell.

ALL-STAR GAME

HIGHLIGHTS

AMERICAN LEAGUE 4, NATIONAL LEAGUE 1

Why the American League won: Its pitchers, led by starter and MVP Pedro Martinez, held N.L. batters at bay while its own hitters came up with timely hits and its defense turned three double plays and made a couple of sparkling plays. Martinez, Boston's star righthander and the winningest pitcher in the majors (15) in the first half of 1999, set an All-Star Game record by striking out the first four batters he faced. Five of the six outs he recorded were by strikeout.

Why the National League lost: It never could mount a sustained offensive attack. Seven A.L. pitchers scattered seven hits, just two that went for extra bases (both doubles). Sluggers Mark McGwire of the Cardinals and Sammy Sosa of the Cubs combined for four strikeouts in five at-bats. All told, the N.L. left eight runners on base, five of them in scoring position with two out, and struck out 12 times.

The turning points:

1. After Martinez struck out the side in the top of the first, the A.L. scored two runs against N.L. starter Curt Schilling of Philadelphia in the bottom of the inning. Cleveland's Kenny Lofton led off with an infield single and, two outs later, stole second. Indians teammate Manny Ramirez walked, but yet another Cleveland player, Jim Thome, singled to drive home Lofton. Baltimore's Cal Ripken then singled home Ramirez.

2. After the N.L. halved the deficit with a run in the third, the A.L. bounced back with two runs in the fourth inning against Cardinals righthander Kent Bottenfield. Thome led off with a walk and Bottenfield then hit Ripken with a pitch. The next batter, Rafael Palmeiro of the Rangers, singled to right to drive home Thome. Bottenfield struck out Texas' Ivan Rodriguez but N.L. third baseman Matt Williams of the Diamondbacks was unable to backhand a grounder by Cleveland's Roberto Alomar, scoring Ripken.

3. With runners at second and third with one out in the fifth, the N.L.'s last, best scoring opportunity ends as Baltimore righthander Mike Mussina strikes out Sosa and McGwire in successive at-bats.

Notable: The pregame ceremonies included the appearance of 41 baseball legends walking in from the outfield at Fenway Park, a la the scene from Field of Dreams. Former Red Sox outfielder Ted Williams, 80, shook hands and shared hugs with many past and current players before throwing out the first pitch. . . . There were no homers in the game despite the fact the 16 non-pitching starters had hit a combined 363 home runs in the first half of the season. . . . The two teams combined to strike out 22 times, an All-Star record. . . . Alomar became

the fifth player to appear in the All-Star Game with four different teams. He previously represented the Padres, Blue Jays and Orioles, joining Walker Cooper, Rich "Goose" Gossage, George Kell and Lee Smith as four-club All-Stars. . . . Martinez became only the third starting pitcher to win an All-Star Game in his home park, joining Johnny Vander Meer of the 1938 Reds (Crosley Field) and Steve Rogers of the 1982 Expos (Olympic Stadium). . . . The All-Star win was the A.L.'s third straight, ninth in 12 games and cut the N.L.'s all-time advantage in the midsummer classic to 40-29-1.

Quotable: A.L. shortstop Nomar Garciaparra of Boston, on the delayed start of the game due to the emotion-packed pregame ceremonies: "Nobody wanted to leave. What time was the first pitch? Nobody cared.". . . A.L. catcher Rodriguez, on the overpowering Martinez: "He's the best in the game. His first two pitches (were so hard), I wasn't able to even see them.". . . A.L. manager Joe Torre of the Yankees: "When you have a guy like Pedro Martinez out there, it's like hitting in a darkroom.". . . . McGwire, who now is four for 20 in All-Star competition with no home runs and eight strikeouts: "I have my two strikeouts every All-Star Game.". . . Milwaukee outfielder Jeromy Burnitz, on the pregame festivities: "It was a pretty awesome experience. It was something I'll remember a long, long time."

BOX SCORE

National League	AB	R	H	RBI	PO	A
Larkin, ss (Reds)	3	0	1	1	1	1
‡A. Gonzalez, ph-ss (Marlins)....	1	0	0	0	1	0
Walker, rf (Rockies)	2	0	0	0	1	0
L. Gonzalez, lf (D'backs)	2	0	1	0	0	0
Sosa, cf (Cubs)	3	0	0	0	1	0
Guerrero, rf (Expos)	1	0	0	0	1	0
McGwire, 1b (Cardinals)	2	0	0	0	3	0
Casey, 1b (Reds)	1	0	0	0	4	0
M. Williams, 3b (D'backs)	3	0	1	0	1	0
Sprague, 3b (Pirates).............	1	0	0	0	0	0
Bagwell, dh (Astros)	3	0	1	0	0	0
§Sheffield, ph-dh (Dodgers)	1	0	0	0	0	0
Piazza, c (Mets)	2	0	1	0	6	0
Lieberthal, c (Phillies)	1	0	0	0	1	0
Nilsson, c (Brewers)	1	0	0	0	3	0
Burnitz, lf (Brewers).............	2	1	1	0	0	0
Jordan, cf (Braves)	1	0	1	0	0	0
Bell, 2b (Diamondbacks)........	1	0	0	0	0	1
Kent, 2b (Giants).................	1	0	0	0	1	2
Schilling, p (Phillies).............	0	0	0	0	0	0
Johnson, p (D'backs)	0	0	0	0	0	0
Bottenfield, p (Cardinals)	0	0	0	0	0	0
Lima, p (Astros)	0	0	0	0	0	0
Millwood, p (Braves)	0	0	0	0	0	1
Ashby, p (Padres)	0	0	0	0	0	0
Hampton, p (Astros)	0	0	0	0	0	0
Hoffman, p (Padres)	0	0	0	0	0	0
Wagner, p (Astros)...............	0	0	0	0	0	0
Totals.................................	**32**	**1**	**7**	**1**	**24**	**5**

American League	AB	R	H	RBI	PO	A
Lofton, lf-cf (Indians)............	3	1	1	0	0	0
B. Williams, cf (Yankees)	1	0	0	0	0	0
Garciaparra, ss (Red Sox)......	2	0	0	0	0	0
Jeter, ss (Yankees)	1	0	0	0	1	0

American League	AB	R	H	RBI	PO	A
Vizquel, ss (Indians)	1	0	0	0	1	4
Griffey, cf (Mariners)..............	2	0	0	0	0	0
Surhoff, lf (Orioles)...............	2	0	0	0	0	0
Ramirez, rf (Indians)...............	1	1	0	0	0	0
Green, rf (Blue Jays)	1	0	1	0	0	0
Ordonez, rf (White Sox)	1	0	0	0	0	0
Thome, 1b (Indians)	2	1	1	1	4	0
Coomer, 1b (Twins)	1	0	0	0	4	0
Ripken, 3b (Orioles)..............	1	1	1	1	0	0
Fernandez, 3b (Blue Jays)......	2	0	0	0	0	2
Palmeiro, dh (Rangers)	2	0	1	1	0	0
*Baines, ph-dh (Orioles)........	1	0	1	0	0	0
∞Jaha, ph-dh (Athletics)........	1	0	0	0	0	0
Rodriguez, c (Rangers)	2	0	0	0	10	1
Ausmus, c (Tigers)	1	0	0	0	2	1
R. Alomar, 2b (Indians).........	2	0	0	1	2	2
†Offerman, ph-2b (Red Sox)....	1	0	0	0	3	0
Martinez, p (Red Sox)	0	0	0	0	0	0
Cone, p (Yankees)	0	0	0	0	0	1
Mussina, p (Orioles)	0	0	0	0	0	0
Rosado, p (Royals)	0	0	0	0	0	0
Zimmerman, p (Rangers)	0	0	0	0	0	0
Hernandez, p (Devil Rays)	0	0	0	0	0	0
Wetteland, p (Rangers)	0	0	0	0	0	1
Totals................................	31	4	6	4	27	12

National League	0	0	1		0	0	0		0	0	0—1
American League	2	0	0		2	0	0		0	0	x—4

National League	IP	H	R	ER	BB	SO
Schilling (Phillies)	2.0	3	2	2	1	3
Johnson (Diamondbacks)	1.0	0	0	0	0	1
Bottenfield (Cardinals)	1.0	1	2	2	1	2
Lima (Astros)	1.0	0	0	0	0	0
Millwood (Braves)..................	1.0	1	0	0	0	1
Ashby (Padres)	0.1	0	0	0	0	0
Hampton (Astros)	0.2	0	0	0	0	0
Hoffman (Padres)	0.1	0	0	0	0	1
Wagner (Astros)	0.2	0	0	0	0	2

American League	IP	H	R	ER	BB	SO
Martinez (Red Sox)	2.0	0	0	0	0	5
Cone (Yankees).....................	2.0	4	1	1	1	3
Mussina (Orioles)	1.0	1	0	0	1	2
Rosado (Royals)	1.0	1	0	0	0	1
Zimmerman (Rangers)...........	1.0	0	0	0	2	0
Hernandez (Devil Rays)	1.0	0	0	0	0	0
Wetteland (Rangers)	1.0	1	0	0	0	1

Winning pitcher—Martinez. Losing pitcher—Schilling. Save—Wetteland. *Singled for Palmeiro in sixth. †Grounded out for Alomar in sixth. ‡Popped out for Larkin in seventh. §Grounded out for Bagwell in eighth. ∞Struck out for Baines in eighth. DP—A.L. 3. LOB—N.L. 8, A.L. 6. 2B—L. Gonzalez, Burnitz. SB—Lofton. CS—M. Williams, Jordan. HBP—By Bottenfield (Ripken). BB—Off Schilling 1 (Ramirez), off Bottenfield 1 (Thome), off Cone 1 (McGwire), off Mussina 1 (Bell), off Zimmerman 2 (Jordan, Kent). SO—By Schilling 3 (Griffey, R. Alomar, Lofton), by Johnson 1 (Ramirez), by Bottenfield 2 (Rodriguez, Jeter), by Millwood 1 (B. Williams), by Hoffman 1 (Coomer), by Wagner 2 (Fernandez, Jaha), by Martinez 5 (Larkin, Walker, Sosa, McGwire, Bagwell), by Cone 3 (Piazza, Bell, M. Williams), by Mussina 2 (Sosa, McGwire), by Rosado 1 (Bagwell), by Wetteland 1 (Nilsson). T—2:53. A—34,187. U—Evans (A.L.), plate; Tata (N.L.), first; Ford (A.L.), second; Hernandez (N.L.), third; Johnson (A.L.), left field; Vanover (N.L.), right field. Official scorers—Bob Elliott, Dave O'Hara and Charlie Scoggins.

Players listed on rosters but not used: N.L.—Byrd (Phillies), Williamson (Reds); A.L.—Nagy (Indians), Percival (Angels).

PLAY BY PLAY

FIRST INNING

N.L.—Larkin, Walker and Sosa struck out.

A.L.—Lofton singled to first. Garciaparra flied to Walker. Griffey struck out. With Ramirez batting, Lofton stole second. Ramirez walked. Thome singled to center, scoring Lofton as Ramirez went to second. Ripken singled to right, scoring Ramirez as Thome went to second. Palmeiro grounded to McGwire. A.L. 2, N.L. 0.

SECOND INNING

N.L.—McGwire struck out. M. Williams reached first on an error by R. Alomar. Bagwell struck out as M. Williams was caught stealing, Rodriguez to R. Alomar, to complete a double play.

A.L.—Rodriguez grounded out, Bell to McGwire. R. Alomar and Lofton struck out.

THIRD INNING

N.L.—Cone now pitching. Piazza struck out. Burnitz doubled to right. Bell struck out. Larkin singled to center, scoring Burnitz. Walker grounded out, Cone to Thome. A.L. 2, N.L. 1.

A.L.—Johnson now pitching. Garciaparra popped to Sosa. Griffey grounded to McGwire. Ramirez struck out.

FOURTH INNING

N.L.—Jeter now at short, Surhoff in left field, Lofton in center field and Green in right field. Sosa popped to Thome. McGwire walked. M. Williams struck out. Bagwell singled to right as McGwire went to second. Piazza singled to right as McGwire went to third and Bagwell to second. Burnitz grounded to Thome.

A.L.—Bottenfield now pitching, L. Gonzalez in left field and Burnitz in right field. Thome walked. Ripken was hit by a pitch. Palmeiro singled to right, scoring Thome as Ripken went to third. Rodriguez struck out. Alomar reached first on an error by M. Williams as Ripken scored and Palmeiro went to second. Lofton popped to M. Williams in foul territory. Jeter struck out. A.L. 4, N.L. 1.

FIFTH INNING

N.L.—Mussina now pitching and Fernandez at third. Bell walked. Larkin forced Bell at second, R. Alomar to Jeter. L. Gonzalez doubled to left as Larkin went to third. Sosa and McGwire struck out.

A.L.—Lima now pitching, Jordan in center field, V. Guerrero in right field, Casey at first, Kent at second and Lieberthal catching. Surhoff grounded to Casey. Green singled to second. Thome flied to V. Guerrero. Fernandez grounded out, Kent to Larkin.

SIXTH INNING

N.L.—Rosado now pitching, B. Williams now in center field and Ausmus now catching. M. Williams singled to left. Bagwell struck out. Lieberthal grounded into a double play, Fernandez to R. Alomar to Thome.

A.L.—Millwood now pitching and Sprague at third. Baines, pinch-hitting for Palmeiro, singled to left. Ausmus forced Baines at second, Larkin to Kent. Offerman, pinch-hitting for R. Alomar, grounded out, Millwood to Casey, as Ausmus went to second. B. Williams struck out.

SEVENTH INNING

N.L.—Zimmerman now pitching, Coomer at first, Offerman at second, Vizquel at shortstop and Ordonez in right field. Jordan walked. Jordan caught stealing, Ausmus to Jordan. Kent walked. A. Gonzalez, pinch-hitting for Larkin, popped to Offerman. L. Gonzalez reached first base on a throwing error by Offerman. Guerrero grounded out, Vizquel to Offerman.

A.L.—Ashby now pitching and A. Gonzalez at shortstop. Vizquel grounded to Casey. Hampton now pitching. Surhoff grounded out, Kent to A. Gonzalez. Ordonez flied to A. Gonzalez.

EIGHTH INNING

N.L.—Hernandez now pitching. Casey grounded out, Vizquel to Coomer. Sprague grounded out, Fernandez to Coomer. Sheffield, pinch-hitting for Bagwell, grounded out, Vizquel to Coomer.

A.L.—Hoffman now pitching and Nilsson catching. Coomer struck out. Wagner now pitching. Fernandez struck out. Jaha, pinch-hitting for Baines, struck out.

NINTH INNING

N.L.—Wetteland now pitching. Nilsson struck out. Jordan singled to right. Kent grounded into a double play, Wetteland to Vizquel to Coomer. **Final score: A.L. 4, N.L. 1.**

NOTABLE PERFORMANCES

BOX SCORES OF NO-HIT GAMES

JOSE JIMENEZ
JUNE 25

St. Louis 1, Arizona 0 (N)

ST. LOUIS	AB	R	H	RBI	ARIZONA	AB	R	H	RBI
McEwing, 2b	4	0	1	0	Womack, rf	4	0	0	0
Bragg, cf-lf	2	1	0	0	Bell, 2b	3	0	0	0
McGwire, 1b	3	0	0	0	Gonzalez, lf	2	0	0	0
Davis, rf	4	0	0	0	Williams, 3b	3	0	0	0
T. Howard, lf	4	0	1	1	Finley, cf	2	0	0	0
Lankford, cf	0	0	0	0	Lee, 1b	3	0	0	0
Renteria, ss	3	0	1	0	Miller, c	3	0	0	0
Castillo, c	3	0	1	0	Fox, ss	2	0	0	0
D. Howard, 3b	3	0	1	0	Johnson, p	2	0	0	0
Jimenez, p	3	0	0	0	Dellucci, ph	1	0	0	0
TOTALS	29	1	5	1	TOTALS	25	0	0	0

```
St. Louis .........    0  0  0     0  0  0     0  0  1—1
Arizona ...........    0  0  0     0  0  0     0  0  0—0
```

DP—St. Louis 2, Arizona 1. LOB—St. Louis 4, Arizona 1. 2B—McEwing, Renteria, D. Howard. SH—Bragg.

ST. LOUIS	IP	H	R	ER	BB	SO
Jimenez (W, 4-7)	9.0	0	0	0	2	8
ARIZONA	IP	H	R	ER	BB	SO
Johnson (L, 9-4)	9.0	5	1	1	2	14

HBP—By Jimenez (Fox). T—2:10. A—45,540. Umpires—HP, Froemming; 1B, Nelson; 2B, Wegner; 3B, Bell.

DAVID CONE (PERFECT GAME)
JULY 18

New York 6, Montreal 0 (D)

MONTREAL	AB	R	H	RBI	NEW YORK	AB	R	H	RBI
W. Guerrero, dh	3	0	0	0	Knoblauch, 2b	2	1	1	0
Jones, cf	2	0	0	0	Jeter, ss	4	1	1	2
Mouton, cf	1	0	0	0	O'Neill, rf	4	1	1	0
White, lf	3	0	0	0	Williams, cf	4	0	1	1
V. Guerrero, rf	3	0	0	0	Martinez, 1b	4	0	1	0
Vidro, 2b	3	0	0	0	Davis, dh	3	1	1	0
Fullmer, 1b	3	0	0	0	Ledee, lf	4	1	1	2
Widger, c	3	0	0	0	Brosius, 3b	2	1	0	0
Andrews, 3b	2	0	0	0	Girardi, c	3	0	1	1
McGuire, ph	1	0	0	0					
Cabrera, ss	3	0	0	0					
TOTALS	27	0	0	0	TOTALS	30	6	8	6

```
Montreal ...........    0  0  0     0  0  0     0  0  0—0
New York ...........    0  5  0     0  0  0     0  1  x—6
```

DP—Montreal 1. LOB—Montreal 0, New York 4. 2B—Girardi, O'Neill. HR—Ledee, Jeter.

MONTREAL	IP	H	R	ER	BB	SO
Vazquez (L, 2-5)	*7.0	7	6	6	2	3
Ayala	1.0	1	0	0	0	0
NEW YORK	IP	H	R	ER	BB	SO
Cone (W, 10-4)	9.0	0	0	0	0	10

*Pitched to two batters in eighth.

HBP—By Vazquez 2 (Knoblauch, Brosius).T—2:16. A—41,930. Umpires—HP, Barrett; 1B, McCoy; 2B, Evans; 3B, Meriwether.

ERIC MILTON
SEPTEMBER 11

Minnesota 7, Anaheim 0 (D)

ANAHEIM	AB	R	H	RBI	MINNESOTA	AB	R	H	RBI
Davanon, rf	3	0	0	0	Jones, cf	4	1	1	0
Palmeiro, cf	2	0	0	0	Hocking, ss	4	1	2	3
Greene, lf	3	0	0	0	Lawton, rf	3	1	1	0
Glaus, 3b	3	0	0	0	Steinbach, c	4	1	2	1
Decker, dh	3	0	0	0	Walker, dh	3	0	0	0
Luke, 1b	3	0	0	0	Koskie, 3b	4	1	2	1
Hemphill, c	3	0	0	0	Hunter, lf	4	1	1	0
Durrington, 2b	3	0	0	0	Mientkiewicz, 1b	3	1	1	0
Sheets, ss	3	0	0	0	Davidson, 2b	3	0	0	1
TOTALS	26	0	0	0	TOTALS	32	7	10	6

```
Anaheim ...........    0  0  0     0  0  0     0  0  0—0
Minnesota ...........   1  3  0     0  2  0     0  1  x—7
```

E—Hemphill. DP—Anaheim 1. LOB—Anaheim 1, Minnesota 4. 2B—Mientkiewicz, Steinbach, Koskie. 3B—Steinbach, Jones. HR—Hocking. SB—Lawton. CS—Davanon, Hocking.

ANAHEIM	IP	H	R	ER	BB	SO
Ortiz (L, 1-2)	4.1	7	6	6	1	3
Levine	1.2	0	0	0	0	0
Holtz	1.0	1	0	0	0	1
Mintz	1.0	2	1	1	1	1
MINNESOTA	IP	H	R	ER	BB	SO
Milton (W, 7-11)	9.0	0	0	0	2	13

HBP—By Ortiz (Lawton). WP—Holtz. Balk—Ortiz. T—2:28. A—11,222. Umpires—HP, Welke; 1B, Tschida; 2B, Craft; 3B, Joyce.

LOW-HIT GAMES
AMERICAN LEAGUE

ONE-HIT GAMES

Date — Pitcher(s), Team, Opponent, Result—Player with hit

4-22 — Tony Saunders (7.2 inn.), Jim Mecir (0.1 inn.) and Roberto Hernandez (1 inn.), Tampa Bay vs. Baltimore, W 1-0—Mike Bordick (single in eighth)

6-29 — John Burkett (7 inn.), Jeff Zimmerman (1 inn.) and John Wetteland (1 inn.), Texas at Anaheim, W 5-0—Matt Walbeck (double in third)

Date	Pitcher(s), Team, Opponent, Result—Player with hit
8-18	Wilson Alvarez (6 inn.) and Albie Lopez (3 inn.), Tampa Bay at Detroit, W 4-0—Gabe Kapler (triple in third)
9-10	Pedro Martinez, Boston at New York, W 3-1—Chili Davis (home run in second)

TWO-HIT GAMES

Date	Pitcher(s), Team, Opponent, Result—Player(s) with hit(s)
4-15	Chris Carpenter, Toronto vs. Tampa Bay, W 11-1—Fred McGriff (home run in second), Mike DiFelice (double in sixth)
4-22	Justin Thompson (8 inn.) and Todd Jones (1 inn.), Detroit vs. Boston, W 1-0—Damon Buford (single in fifth), Donnie Sadler (single in ninth)
5-18	Dwight Gooden (7 inn.), Ricky Rincon (1 inn.) and Paul Assenmacher (1 inn.), Cleveland at Chicago, W 13-0—Mike Caruso (single in ninth), Chris Singleton (single in third)
5-22	Mike Sirotka (8 inn.), Bob Howry (0.2 inn.) and Bill Simas (0.1 inn.), Chicago vs. New York, W 2-1—Chad Curtis (single in first and single in fourth)
5-27	Roger Clemens (7 inn.), Mike Stanton (0.2 inn.), Jeff Nelson (0.1 inn.) and Mariano Rivera (1 inn.), New York vs. Boston, W 4-1—John Valentin (single in first and single in sixth)
7-11	David Wells, Toronto at Montreal N.L., W 1-0—James Mouton (double in first), Shane Andrews (single in eighth)
7-28	Pat Rapp (8 inn.) and Tim Wakefield (1 inn.), Boston at Toronto, W 8-0—Shawn Green (single in first), Homer Bush (single in third)
8-1	Steve Sparks (8 inn.) and Troy Percival (1 inn.), Anaheim vs. Minnesota, W 2-1—Terry Steinbach (single in seventh), Chad Allen (single in eighth)
8-30	Jason Ryan, Minnesota at Toronto, L 1-2—Tony Fernandez (single in first), Tony Batista (home run in second)
9-18	Gil Meche (6.1 inn.) and Paul Abbott (2.2 inn.), Seattle vs. Minnesota, W 5-0—Ron Coomer (single in second), Doug Mientkiewicz (single in fifth)
9-22	Jaret Wright (7 inn.), Steve Karsay (1 inn.) and Ricky Rincon (1 inn.), Cleveland at Detroit, W 9-1—Dean Palmer (single in second), Karim Garcia (single in fifth)
9-24	Joe Mays (8 inn.) and Bob Wells (1 inn.), Minnesota vs. Chicago, W 6-2—Greg Norton (double in sixth), Josh Paul (single in sixth)

NATIONAL LEAGUE

ONE-HIT GAMES

Date	Pitcher(s), Team, Opponent, Result—Player with hit
4-30	John Smoltz, Atlanta vs. Cincinnati, W 3-0—Eddie Taubensee (single in fifth)
6-24	Ron Villone (7 inn.) and Danny Graves (2 inn.), Cincinnati at Houston, W 3-0—Tony Eusebio (single in seventh)
6-30	Ron Villone (8 inn.) and Scott Williamson (1 inn.), Cincinnati vs. Arizona, W 2-0—Tony Womack (single in sixth)
7-21	Ron Villone (8 inn.) and Scott Williamson (1 inn.), Cincinnati vs. St. Louis, W 1-0—J.D. Drew (double in first)
8-19	Pete Harnisch (8 inn.) and Scott Williamson (1 inn.), Cincinnati vs. Pittsburgh, W 1-0—Mike Benjamin (single in seventh)
9-14	Javier Vazquez, Montreal at Los Angeles, W 3-0—Mark Grudzielanek (single in fourth)

TWO-HIT GAMES

Date	Pitcher(s), Team, Opponent, Result—Player(s) with hit(s)
4-9	Scott Sanders (5.1 inn.), Matt Karchner (1.2 inn.) and Terry Mulholland (1 inn.), Chicago at Pittsburgh, L 1-2—Warren Morris (home run in third), Kevin Young (double in ninth)
4-15	Darren Dreifort (7 inn.) and Pedro Borbon (2 inn.), Los Angeles at Arizona, W 8-1—Luis Gonzalez (triple in fourth), Damian Miller (single in fifth)
5-23	Steve Avery (6 inn.) and Scott Williamson (3 inn.), Cincinnati at San Diego, W 6-2—Reggie Sanders (single in first and single in sixth)
6-26	Steve Parris (7 inn.), Stan Belinda (1 inn.) and Gabe White (1 inn.), Cincinnati at Houston, W 8-1—Carl Everett (single in first), Ricky Gutierrez (single in ninth)
7-5	Jose Jimenez, St. Louis vs. Arizona, W 1-0—Steve Finley (double in fifth), Andy Fox (single in sixth)
7-10	Russ Ortiz (8.2 inn.) and John Johnstone (0.1 inn.), San Francisco vs. St. Louis, W 4-2—Mark McGwire (home run in first), Fernando Tatis (home run in seventh)
7-23	Omar Daal (7 inn.) and Byung-Hyun Kim (2 inn.), Arizona vs. Los Angeles, W 10-1—Eric Young (single in fifth), Gary Sheffield (home run in sixth)
8-9	Denny Neagle (7 inn.) and Scott Williamson (2 inn.), Cincinnati at Pittsburgh, W 4-2—Abraham Nunez (single in ninth), Warren Morris (home run in fifth)
8-16	Jose Lima (8 inn.) and Billy Wagner (1 inn.), Houston vs. Milwaukee, W 2-0—Rich Becker (double in third), Dave Nilsson (single in fourth)
8-16	Octavio Dotel (7 inn.), Turk Wendell (1 inn.), Dennis Cook (1 inn.) and Armando Benitez (1 inn.), New York at San Diego, W 4-3—Phil Nevin (home run in seventh), Wally Joyner (single in ninth)
8-29	Kyle Farnsworth, Chicago at Los Angeles, W 6-0—Mark Grudzielanek (single in ninth), Todd Hollandsworth (single in fourth)
9-1	Sterling Hitchcock (7 inn.) and Dan Miceli (2 inn.), San Diego vs. Chicago, L 0-1—Sammy Sosa (home run in fourth), Glenallen Hill (single in seventh)
9-4	Kevin Brown, Los Angeles at Chicago, W 6-0—Jeff Reed (single in second and single in fifth)
9-9	Orel Hershiser (8 inn.) and Armando Benitez (1 inn.), New York at Los Angeles, W 3-1—Mark Grudzielanek (single in fourth), Gary Sheffield (home run in first)
10-2	Bruce Chen (6 inn.), Kevin McGlinchy (2 inn.), Sean Bergman (1 inn.) and Derrin Ebert (1 inn.), Atlanta vs. Florida, L 0-1—Cliff Floyd (single in first and home run in tenth)
10-4	Al Leiter, New York at Cincinnati, W 5-0—Pokey Reese (double in ninth), Jeffrey Hammonds (single in second)

15-STRIKEOUT GAMES

AMERICAN LEAGUE

Date	Pitcher, Team, Opponent	IP	H	R	ER	BB	SO	Result
5-7	Pedro Martinez, Boston vs. Anaheim	8	6	0	0	0	15	W 6-0
5-12	Pedro Martinez, Boston vs. Seattle	8	4	2	2	1	15	W 9-2
6-4	Pedro Martinez, Boston vs. Atlanta N.L.	9	3	1	1	2	16	W 5-1
8-24	Pedro Martinez, Boston at Minnesota	8	4	1	0	1	15	W 7-1

Date	Pitcher, Team, Opponent	IP	H	R	ER	BB	SO	Result
9-4	Pedro Martinez, Boston at Seattle	8	2	0	0	3	15	W 4-0
9-10	Pedro Martinez, Boston at New York	9	1	1	1	0	17	W 3-1

NATIONAL LEAGUE

Date	Pitcher, Team, Opponent	IP	H	R	ER	BB	SO	Result
4-10	Randy Johnson, Arizona at Atlanta	9	6	3	3	2	15	W 8-3
6-30	Randy Johnson, Arizona at Cincinnati	8	7	2	2	0	17	L 0-2
8-1	Al Leiter, New York at Chicago	7	7	2	2	2	15	W 5-4

10-STRIKEOUT GAMES

AMERICAN LEAGUE

Team	No.	Pitchers
Boston	19	Pedro Martinez 19.
New York	7	David Cone 3, Roger Clemens 1, Andy Pettitte 1, Hideki Irabu 1, Orlando Hernandez 1.
Seattle	6	Freddy Garcia 4, Paul Abbott 1, Jeff Fassero 1.
Texas	6	Aaron Sele 3, Rick Helling 2, Matt Perisho 1.
Baltimore	4	Mike Mussina 4.
Cleveland	3	Dave Burba 3.
Minnesota	3	Eric Milton 3.
Anaheim	2	Chuck Finley 2.
Detroit	2	C.J. Nitkowski 1, Justin Thompson 1.
Oakland	2	Tim Hudson 2.
Tampa Bay	2	Wilson Alvarez 1, Dan Wheeler 1.
Kansas City	1	Jay Witasick 1.
Chicago	0	None.
Toronto	0	None.

NATIONAL LEAGUE

Team	No.	Pitchers
Arizona	26	Randy Johnson 23, Andy Benes 2, Omar Daal 1.
Houston	7	Shane Reynolds 3, Jose Lima 3, Scott Elarton 1.
Atlanta	6	Kevin Millwood 4, Greg Maddux 1, John Smoltz 1.
Philadelphia	6	Curt Schilling 2, Robert Person 2, Randy Wolf 2.
Colorado	6	Pedro Astacio 5, Brian Bohanon 1.
New York	4	Kenny Rogers 1, Al Leiter 1, Rick Reed 1, Octavio Dotel 1.
Pittsburgh	4	Francisco Cordova 2, Jason Schmidt 1, Todd Ritchie 1.
Los Angeles	3	Ismael Valdes 2, Kevin Brown 1.
San Francisco	3	Russ Ortiz 2, Kirk Rueter 1.
Milwaukee	2	Hideo Nomo 1, Steve Woodard 1.
Chicago	2	Jon Lieber 2.
Cincinnati	2	Pete Harnisch 1, Brett Tomko 1.
St. Louis	2	Kent Bottenfield 1, Darren Oliver 1.
Montreal	1	Javier Vazquez 1.
San Diego	1	Woody Williams 1.
Florida	1	Ryan Dempster 1.

1-0 GAMES
AMERICAN LEAGUE

Date	Winner	Loser	Inn.*	Site
4-10	†Mike Mussina, Baltimore	†Chris Carpenter, Toronto	1	Baltimore
4-12	†Rick Aguilera, Minnesota	†Sean Runyan, Detroit	12	Detroit
4-20	†Pedro Martinez, Boston	†Jeff Weaver, Detroit	4	Detroit
4-22	†Justin Thompson, Detroit	Mark Portugal, Boston	8	Detroit
4-22	†Tony Saunders, Tampa Bay	†Sidney Ponson, Baltimore	4	Tampa Bay
5-12	†Chuck Finley, Anaheim	†David Cone, New York	7	New York
6-26	†Joe Mays, Minnesota	Dave Mlicki, Detroit	6	Detroit
7-11	David Wells, Toronto	†Carl Pavano, Montreal N.L.	4	Montreal
7-23	†Juan Guzman, Baltimore	†Jack McDowell, Anaheim	4	Baltimore
8-7	†Andy Pettitte, New York	Freddy Garcia, Seattle	5	Seattle
8-30	Brian Moehler, Detroit	†Esteban Loaiza, Texas	7	Detroit
9-15	†Chuck Finley, Anaheim	†Lance Carter, Kansas City	9	Kansas City
9-24	†Mike Mussina, Baltimore	†Bret Saberhagen, Boston	4	Boston
10-3	†Brian Rose, Boston	†Mike Timlin, Baltimore	10	Baltimore
10-3	†Jarrod Washburn, Anaheim	†Mike Morgan, Texas	7	Anaheim

PLAYERS HITTING HOME RUNS IN 1-0 GAMES: 4-12—Todd Walker, Minnesota; 4-20—Troy O'Leary, Boston; 4-22—Brad Ausmus, Detroit; 8-30—Gabe Kapler, Detroit; 9-15—Darin Erstad, Anaheim; 10-3—Tim Salmon, Anaheim.

*Inning in which run scored. †Did not pitch complete game. Note: Interleague 1-0 games are listed in the winning club's league.

NATIONAL LEAGUE

Date	Winner	Loser	Inn.*	Site
4-27	†Jeff Brantley, Philadelphia	†Gabe White, Cincinnati	10	Philadelphia
5-30	†Darryl Kile, Colorado	†Jim Poole, Philadelphia	8	Philadelphia
6-1	Andy Ashby, San Diego	Steve Trachsel, Chicago	4	Chicago
6-25	Jose Jimenez, St. Louis	Randy Johnson, Arizona	9	Arizona
6-27	†Greg Maddux, Atlanta	†Masato Yoshii, New York	3	Atlanta
7-5	Jose Jimenez, St. Louis	Randy Johnson, Arizona	4	St. Louis
7-6	†Robert Person, Philadelphia	†Hideo Nomo, Milwaukee	3	Philadelphia
7-21	†Ron Villone, Cincinnati	†Jose Jimenez, St. Louis	4	Cincinnati
7-30	†Kyle Peterson, Milwaukee	†Jeremy Powell, Montreal	2	Milwaukee
8-19	†Pete Harnisch, Cincinnati	Kris Benson, Pittsburgh	8	Cincinnati
9-1	†Steve Trachsel, Chicago	†Sterling Hitchcock, San Diego	4	San Diego
10-2	†Braden Looper, Florida	†Derrin Ebert, Atlanta	10	Atlanta

PLAYERS HITTING HOME RUNS IN 1-0 GAMES: 6-1—John Vander Wal, San Diego; 7-21—Pokey Reese, Cincinnati; 7-30—Alex Ochoa, Milwaukee; 8-19—Sean Casey, Cincinnati; 9-1—Sammy Sosa, Chicago; 10-2—Cliff Floyd, Florida.

*Inning in which run scored. †Did not pitch complete game. Note: Interleague 1-0 games are listed in the winning club's league.

FOUR OR MORE HITS IN ONE GAME
AMERICAN LEAGUE

Team	No.	Hitters
Baltimore	22	Albert Belle 4, B.J. Surhoff 3, Mike Bordick 3, Jeff Conine 3, Jerry Hairston Jr. 3, Cal Ripken Jr. 2, Charles Johnson 2, Harold Baines 1, Will Clark 1.
Kansas City	22	Joe Randa 5, Carlos Beltran 5, Jermaine Dye 3, Mike Sweeney 2, Carlos Febles 2, Chad Kreuter 1, Rey Sanchez 1, Ray Holbert 1, Johnny Damon 1, Jeremy Giambi 1.
New York	22	Bernie Williams 7, Chuck Knoblauch 4, Tino Martinez 3, Chili Davis 2, Jorge Posada 2, Joe Girardi 1, Scott Brosius 1, Derek Jeter 1, D'Angelo Jimenez 1.
Texas	20	Ivan Rodriguez 6, Todd Zeile 4, Rafael Palmeiro 3, Juan Gonzalez 2, Mark McLemore 1, Lee Stevens 1, Tom Goodwin 1, Rusty Greer 1, Ruben Mateo 1.
Toronto	19	Tony Fernandez 5, Shannon Stewart 3, Craig Grebeck 2, Carlos Delgado 2, Shawn Green 2, Jacob Brumfield 1, Willie Greene 1, Alex Gonzalez 1, Homer Bush 1, Vernon Wells 1.
Chicago	18	Chris Singleton 5, Ray Durham 4, Brook Fordyce 3, Frank Thomas 2, Magglio Ordonez 2, Darrin Jackson 1, Paul Konerko 1.
Boston	17	Jose Offerman 5, Nomar Garciaparra 5, Mike Stanley 1, Jeff Frye 1, John Valentin 1, Troy O'Leary 1, Trot Nixon 1, Jason Varitek 1, Brian Daubach 1.
Anaheim	17	Randy Velarde 4, Garret Anderson 4, Mo Vaughn 3, Tim Salmon 2, Jim Edmonds 2, Darin Erstad 1, Troy Glaus 1.
Tampa Bay	13	Fred McGriff 3, Jose Canseco 2, Dave Martinez 1, Paul Sorrento 1, Kevin Stocker 1, Herbert Perry 1, Aaron Ledesma 1, Miguel Cairo 1, Mike DiFelice 1, Randy Winn 1.
Cleveland	11	Omar Vizquel 2, Kenny Lofton 2, Manny Ramirez 2, Roberto Alomar 1, David Justice 1, Jim Thome 1, Einar Diaz 1, Richie Sexson 1.
Detroit	11	Luis Polonia 4, Karim Garcia 2, Frank Catalanotto 2, Damion Easley 1, Brad Ausmus 1, Juan Encarnacion 1.
Minnesota	10	Denny Hocking 2, Matt Lawton 2, Ron Coomer 1, Marty Cordova 1, Todd Walker 1, Corey Koskie 1, Doug Mientkiewicz 1, Chad Allen 1.
Oakland	8	Jason Giambi 3, Tony Phillips 1, Mike Macfarlane 1, Randy Velarde 1, John Jaha 1, Ramon Hernandez 1.
Seattle	7	Ken Griffey Jr. 2, Jay Buhner 1, Edgar Martinez 1, Butch Huskey 1, John Mabry 1, Alex Rodriguez 1.

NATIONAL LEAGUE

Team	No.	Hitters
Colorado	24	Dante Bichette 6, Larry Walker 4, Neifi Perez 4, Darryl Hamilton 2, Vinny Castilla 2, Todd Helton 2, Kirt Manwaring 1, Mike Lansing 1, Kurt Abbott 1, Angel Echevarria 1.
Philadelphia	21	Bobby Abreu 4, Rico Brogna 3, Mike Lieberthal 3, Doug Glanville 3, Rob Ducey 2, Scott Rolen 2, Marlon Anderson 2, Ron Gant 1, Kevin Jordan 1.
Florida	19	Dave Berg 4, Preston Wilson 3, Luis Castillo 2, Derrek Lee 2, Bruce Aven 2, Alex Gonzalez 2, Danny Bautista 1, Tim Hyers 1, Todd Dunwoody 1, Mike Redmond 1.
Houston	18	Carl Everett 5, Craig Biggio 4, Derek Bell 3, Ricky Gutierrez 3, Matt Mieske 1, Russ Johnson 1, Paul Bako 1.
New York	18	Rickey Henderson 3, Mike Piazza 3, Edgardo Alfonzo 2, John Olerud 2, Robin Ventura 2, Rey Ordonez 2, Darryl Hamilton 1, Roger Cedeno 1, Benny Agbayani 1.
Arizona	18	Steve Finley 4, Jay Bell 3, Luis Gonzalez 3, Tony Womack 3, Matt Williams 1, Lenny Harris 1, Tony Batista 1, David Dellucci 1, Travis Lee 1.
San Francisco	15	Brent Mayne 3, Jeff Kent 3, Marvin Benard 3, Rich Aurilia 2, Stan Javier 1, Barry Bonds 1, Ellis Burks 1, J.T. Snow 1.
Milwaukee	14	Marquis Grissom 3, Jeff Cirillo 3, Mark Loretta 3, Jeromy Burnitz 2, Dave Nilsson 1, Brian Banks 1, Ron Belliard 1.
Cincinnati	13	Sean Casey 4, Eddie Taubensee 2, Pokey Reese 2, Barry Larkin 1, Hal Morris 1, Mark Lewis 1, Jeffrey Hammonds 1, Aaron Boone 1.
Atlanta	12	Ryan Klesko 2, Javy Lopez 2, Eddie Perez 2, Ozzie Guillen 1, Bret Boone 1, Gerald Williams 1, Chipper Jones 1, Andruw Jones 1, Randall Simon 1.
Los Angeles	9	Devon White 2, Raul Mondesi 2, Mark Grudzielanek 2, Jose Vizcaino 1, Eric Karros 1, Adrian Beltre 1.
Montreal	9	Wilton Guerrero 2, Jose Vidro 2, Rondell White 1, Chris Widger 1, Brad Fullmer 1.
San Diego	9	Tony Gwynn 2, Reggie Sanders 2, Wally Joyner 1, Dave Magadan 1, Chris Gomez 1, Quilvio Veras 1, Ben Davis 1.
Chicago	7	Glenallen Hill 2, Sammy Sosa 2, Lance Johnson 1, Mark Grace 1, Mickey Morandini 1.
Pittsburgh	7	Jason Kendall 2, Al Martin 1, Pat Meares 1, Brian S. Giles 1, Brant Brown 1, Warren Morris 1.
St. Louis	7	Edgar Renteria 2, Eric Davis 1, Thomas Howard 1, Darren Bragg 1, Fernando Tatis 1, Adam Kennedy 1.

FIVE- AND SIX-HIT GAMES
AMERICAN LEAGUE

Date	Player, Team, Opponent	AB	R	H	2B	3B	HR	RBI	Result
4-14	Chuck Knoblauch, New York vs. Baltimore	6	2	5	0	0	1	2	W 14-7
4-27	B.J. Surhoff, Baltimore vs. Kansas City	5	2	5	2	0	1	3	W 8-4
5-7	Tony Fernandez, Toronto vs. Texas	5	3	5	3	0	0	2	W 9-6
5-8	John Mabry, Seattle at New York	6	2	5	1	0	0	1	W 14-5
5-27	Luis Polonia, Detroit vs. Chicago	5	4	5	2	0	0	1	W 10-5
6-9	Joe Randa, Kansas City vs. St. Louis N.L.	5	4	5	2	0	0	2	W 17-13
6-13	Cal Ripken Jr., Baltimore at Atlanta N.L.	6	5	6	1	0	2	6	W 22-1

Date	Player, Team, Opponent	AB	R	H	2B	3B	HR	RBI	Result
6-24	Randy Velarde, Anaheim at Seattle	6	3	5	0	0	1	4	W 12-7
6-24	Mo Vaughn, Anaheim at Seattle	6	2	5	1	0	2	6	W 12-7
6-27	Denny Hocking, Minnesota at Detroit	6	2	5	3	0	0	0	W 12-7
7-6	Chris Singleton, Chicago vs. Kansas City	6	3	5	1	1	1	4	L 7-8
7-9	Joe Randa, Kansas City vs. Houston N.L.	5	2	5	0	1	0	1	L 5-6
7-19	Chris Singleton, Chicago at Milwaukee N.L.	6	2	5	0	0	1	2	W 10-8
7-24	Chili Davis, New York vs. Cleveland	6	3	5	1	0	1	6	W 21-1
7-30	Chuck Knoblauch, New York at Boston	6	2	5	1	0	1	4	W 13-3
8-1	Ivan Rodriguez, Texas vs. Kansas City	6	1	5	0	0	1	4	W 12-5
8-14	Brian Daubach, Boston vs. Seattle	5	2	5	0	0	1	6	W 13-2

NATIONAL LEAGUE

Date	Player, Team, Opponent	AB	R	H	2B	3B	HR	RBI	Result
4-10	Tony Batista, Arizona at Atlanta	5	2	5	0	0	1	4	W 8-3
4-11	Glenallen Hill, Chicago at Pittsburgh	5	1	5	1	0	1	2	L 6-9
4-18	Andruw Jones, Atlanta at Colorado	6	2	5	0	1	1	6	W 20-5
4-18	Eddie Perez, Atlanta at Colorado	6	1	5	0	0	0	1	W 20-5
5-3	Jeff Kent, San Francisco at Pittsburgh	5	2	5	1	1	1	5	L 8-9
5-3	Jason Kendall, Pittsburgh vs. San Francisco	5	0	5	2	0	0	0	W 9-8
5-9	Pat Meares, Pittsburgh at St. Louis	6	3	5	1	0	0	2	W 12-9
6-6	Sean Casey, Cincinnati at Kansas City A.L.	6	3	5	1	0	0	2	W 14-3
6-9	Brant Brown, Pittsburgh at Detroit A.L.	5	4	5	1	0	1	5	W 15-3
6-9	Travis Lee, Arizona vs. Chicago	5	2	5	1	1	0	0	W 8-7
6-12	Jeff Kent, San Francisco at Seattle A.L.	5	3	5	2	0	1	4	W15-11
6-22	Pokey Reese, Cincinnati at Arizona	6	3	5	1	1	0	1	W 8-7
7-3	Marlon Anderson, Philadelphia vs. Chicago	6	4	5	1	0	1	2	W 21-8
7-3	Jeff Cirillo, Milwaukee at Pittsburgh	5	3	5	1	0	1	3	W 9-4
7-17	Mark Loretta, Milwaukee vs. Kansas City A.L.	6	3	5	1	0	1	4	W 11-3
7-22†	Mark Grudzielanek, Los Angeles vs. Colorado	5	4	5	0	0	0	0	L11-12
8-8	Bobby Abreu, Philadelphia vs. Arizona	5	1	5	1	0	0	2	L 4-7
8-24	Rob Ducey, Philadelphia vs. San Diego	6	4	5	1	0	0	2	W 18-2
8-27	Jeff Cirillo, Milwaukee at San Diego	5	1	5	1	0	0	2	L 7-8
8-30	Edgardo Alfonzo, New York at Houston	6	6	6	1	0	3	5	W 17-1
9-15	Doug Glanville, Philadelphia at Houston	6	3	5	1	0	1	2	W 8-6
10-2	Marvin Benard, San Francisco at Colorado	6	3	5	1	0	0	0	W 16-7

†Second game of doubleheader.

HITTING STREAKS OF 15 OR MORE GAMES

AMERICAN LEAGUE

G	Player, Team	Span of streak
28	Shawn Green, Toronto	June 29-July 31
26	Shannon Stewart, Toronto	Aug. 1-Aug. 29
25	Mike Sweeney, Kansas City	July 18-Aug. 13
21	Frank Thomas, Chicago	May 24-June 15
	B.J. Surhoff, Baltimore	May 29-June 20
20	Ivan Rodriguez, Texas	May 8-June 1
19	Tony Clark, Detroit	July 10-Aug. 1
18	Joe Randa, Kansas City	July 1-July 21
	Jason Giambi, Oakland	July 23-Aug. 10
17	Nomar Garciaparra, Boston	June 13-July 2
	Bernie Williams, New York	June 18-July 6
	Todd Zeile, Texas	June 21-July 10
	Tony Batista, Toronto	July 30-Aug. 16
	Garret Anderson, Anaheim	Aug. 30-Sept. 17
16	Nomar Garciaparra, Boston	Apr. 26-May 14
	Johnny Damon, Kansas City	Apr. 27-May 12
	Derek Jeter, New York	May 4-May 22
	Ken Griffey Jr., Seattle	May 10-May 28
	Luis Polonia, Detroit	May 31-June 21
	Shannon Stewart, Toronto	June 15-June 30
	Mike Sweeney, Kansas City	June 22-July 7
	Garret Anderson, Anaheim	July 6-July 25
15	B.J. Surhoff, Baltimore	May 9-May 25
	David Segui, Seattle	May 10-May 29
	Troy O'Leary, Boston	July 30-Aug. 14
	Carlos Lee, Chicago	Aug. 23-Sept. 6
	Albert Belle, Baltimore	Sept. 1-Sept. 17

NATIONAL LEAGUE

G	Player, Team	Span of streak
31	Vladimir Guerrero, Montreal	July 27-Aug. 26
30	Luis Gonzalez, Arizona	Apr. 11-May 18
25	Joe McEwing, St. Louis	June 8-July 4
24	Mike Piazza, New York	May 25-June 22
22	Luis Castillo, Florida	Aug. 9-Sept. 3
21	Larry Walker, Colorado	Apr. 25-May 21
20	Al Martin, Pittsburgh	June 20-July 11
19	Matt Williams, Arizona	May 26-June 18
18	Sammy Sosa, Chicago	May 26-June 15
	Larry Walker, Colorado	June 14-July 3
	Eric Owens, San Diego	June 17-July 6
17	Tony Batista, Toronto	July 30-Aug. 16
16	Jason Kendall, Pittsburgh	May 20-June 7
	Eddie Taubensee, Cincinnati	May 22-June 13
	Barry Larkin, Cincinnati	June 20-July 6
	Brad Fullmer, Montreal	Aug. 7-Aug. 22
	Luis Gonzalez, Arizona	Aug. 16-Sept. 1
	Tony Gwynn, San Diego	Sept. 5-Sept. 21
15	Kevin Young, Pittsburgh	Apr. 23-May 8
	Gerald Williams, Atlanta	July 23-Aug. 13
	Henry Rodriguez, Chicago	July 31-Aug. 14
	Al Martin, Pittsburgh	Aug. 25-Sept. 11

MULTI-HOMER GAMES
AMERICAN LEAGUE

Team	No.	Hitters
Seattle	18	Alex Rodriguez 6, Edgar Martinez 4, Ken Griffey Jr. 4, Russ Davis 2, Butch Huskey 1, John Mabry 1.
Texas	17	Juan Gonzalez 5, Ivan Rodriguez 5, Rafael Palmeiro 3, Rusty Greer 2, Roberto Kelly 1, Lee Stevens 1.
Toronto	15	Carlos Delgado 6, Shawn Green 3, Darrin Fletcher 2, Pat Kelly 2, Tony Batista 1, Willis Otanez 1.
Baltimore	14	Albert Belle 4, Brady Anderson 3, Cal Ripken 2, Charles Johnson 2, Harold Baines 1, B.J. Surhoff 1, Jeff Conine 1.
Kansas City	14	Jermaine Dye 4, Joe Randa 3, Mike Sweeney 3, Mark Quinn 2, Sal Fasano 1, Carlos Beltran 1.
Oakland	13	John Jaha 5, Jason Giambi 4, Randy Velarde 1, Matt Stairs 1, Miguel Tejada 1, Ben Grieve 1.
Detroit	12	Tony Clark 3, Bob Higginson 2, Dean Palmer 1, Damion Easley 1, Karim Garcia 1, Deivi Cruz 1, Juan Encarnacion 1, Frank Catalanotto 1, Gabe Kapler 1.
Cleveland	11	Manny Ramirez 4, Roberto Alomar 2, Richie Sexson 2, David Justice 1, Travis Fryman 1, Jim Thome 1.
Boston	10	Nomar Garciaparra 5, Jason Varitek 2, Jose Offerman 1, Butch Huskey 1, Trot Nixon 1.
New York	10	Tino Martinez 3, Bernie Williams 3, Paul O'Neill 2, Scott Brosius 1, Jorge Posada 1.
Chicago	9	Greg Norton 3, Magglio Ordonez 2, Ray Durham 1, Paul Konerko 1, Craig Wilson 1, Chris Singleton 1.
Anaheim	8	Tim Salmon 3, Mo Vaughn 2, Troy Glaus 2, Garret Anderson 1.
Tampa Bay	7	Fred McGriff 2, Jose Canseco 2, John Flaherty 2, Herbert Perry 1.
Minnesota	3	Ron Coomer 2, Corey Koskie 1.

NATIONAL LEAGUE

Team	No.	Hitters
Colorado	23	Todd Helton 6, Dante Bichette 4, Larry Walker 4, Vinny Castilla 3, Terry Shumpert 1, Angel Echevarria 1, Henry Blanco 1, Edgard Clemente 1, Derrick Gibson 1, Ben Petrick 1.
Arizona	19	Steve Finley 7, Jay Bell 3, Matt Williams 2, Luis Gonzalez 2, Bernard Gilkey 1, Kelly Stinnett 1, Damian Miller 1, Travis Lee 1, Erubiel Durazo 1.
St. Louis	18	Mark McGwire 9, Fernando Tatis 4, Ray Lankford 3, Darren Bragg 1, Edgar Renteria 1.
Atlanta	17	Chipper Jones 6, Bret Boone 2, Ryan Klesko 2, Javy Lopez 2, Andruw Jones 2, Brian Jordan 1, Gerald Williams 1, Eddie Perez 1.
Los Angeles	15	Raul Mondesi 5, Gary Sheffield 4, Eric Karros 4, Todd Hundley 2.
San Francisco	15	Barry Bonds 7, Ellis Burks 3, Stan Javier 1, Jeff Kent 1, Rich Aurilia 1, Marvin Benard 1, Armando Rios 1.
Pittsburgh	14	Brian S. Giles 5, Kevin Young 3, Al Martin 3, Dale Sveum 1, Ed Sprague 1, Brant Brown 1.
Chicago	12	Sammy Sosa 6, Glenallen Hill 2, Henry Rodriguez 2, Benito Santiago 1, Mickey Morandini 1.
Houston	12	Jeff Bagwell 4, Carl Everett 4, Ken Caminiti 2, Matt Mieske 1, Lance Berkman 1.
Cincinnati	11	Jeffrey Hammonds 3, Greg Vaughn 2, Mike Cameron 2, Sean Casey 2, Eddie Taubensee 1, Aaron Boone 1.
Milwaukee	10	Dave Nilsson 3, Jeromy Burnitz 2, Marquis Grissom 1, Jose Valentin 1, Rich Becker 1, Alex Ochoa 1, Geoff Jenkins 1.
Philadelphia	9	Mike Lieberthal 3, Scott Rolen 3, Ron Gant 1, Rico Brogna 1, Bobby Abreu 1.
Montreal	8	Vladimir Guerrero 3, Orlando Merced 1, Rondell White 1, Shane Andrews 1, Chris Widger 1, Geoff Blum 1.
New York	8	Rickey Henderson 2, Robin Ventura 2, Benny Agbayani 2, John Olerud 1, Edgardo Alfonzo 1.
San Diego	6	Reggie Sanders 2, Tony Gwynn 2, Phil Nevin 1, Ruben Rivera 1, George Arias 1.
Florida	4	Tim Hyers 1, Bruce Aven 1, Preston Wilson 1, Mike Lowell 1.

THREE-HOMER GAMES
AMERICAN LEAGUE

Date	Player, Team, Opponent	AB	R	H	2B	3B	HR	RBI	Result
5-10	Nomar Garciaparra, Boston vs. Seattle	4	3	3	0	0	3	10	W 12-4
5-18	Edgar Martinez, Seattle vs. Minnesota	5	3	3	0	0	3	4	W 10-1
6-11	Miguel Tejada, Oakland vs. Los Angeles N.L.	4	3	3	0	0	3	5	W 12-6
7-24	Trot Nixon, Boston vs. Detroit	4	3	3	0	0	3	5	W 11-4
7-25	Albert Belle, Baltimore vs. Anaheim	4	3	4	0	0	3	6	W 8-7
8-6	Carlos Delgado, Toronto at Texas	4	3	3	0	0	3	3	W 5-4
8-25	Manny Ramirez, Cleveland at Oakland	5	4	4	1	0	3	4	W 12-4
9-24	Juan Gonzalez, Texas vs. Oakland	5	3	4	0	0	3	5	W 12-4

NATIONAL LEAGUE

Date	Player, Team, Opponent	AB	R	H	2B	3B	HR	RBI	Result
4-21	Jeff Bagwell, Houston at Chicago	5	3	3	0	0	3	6	W 10-3
4-28	Larry Walker, Colorado at St. Louis	5	3	4	0	0	3	8	W 9-7
5-19	Jeffrey Hammonds, Cincinnati at Colorado	6	5	4	1	0	3	5	W 24-12
6-5	Vinny Castilla, Colorado vs. Milwaukee	5	3	4	0	0	3	5	W 12-11
6-9	Jeff Bagwell, Houston at Chicago A.L.	6	3	3	0	0	3	6	W 13-4
8-30	Edgardo Alfonzo, New York at Houston	6	6	6	1	0	3	5	W 17-1
9-7†	Greg Vaughn, Cincinnati at Chicago	4	4	3	0	0	3	5	W 10-3
9-8	Steve Finley, Arizona at Milwaukee	5	3	3	0	0	3	6	W 9-1

†Second game of doubleheader.

GRAND SLAMS
AMERICAN LEAGUE

Date	Batter, Team	Pitcher, Team	Inn.*	Site
4-9	Chili Davis, New York	Beiker Graterol, Detroit	3	New York
4-13	Ivan Rodriguez, Texas	Makoto Suzuki, Seattle	3	Seattle
4-15	Tim Salmon, Anaheim	Kevin Jarvis, Oakland	6	Oakland
4-16	Todd Greene, Anaheim	Jamie Moyer, Seattle	7	Anaheim
4-17‡	Matt Lawton, Minnesota	Jerry Spradlin, Cleveland	8	Cleveland
4-25	Jason Giambi, Oakland	Ricky Bones, Baltimore	2	Baltimore
4-26	Torii Hunter, Minnesota	Tim Wakefield, Boston	4	Minnesota
4-28‡	Magglio Ordonez, Chicago	Tony Saunders, Tampa Bay	3	Chicago
4-29	Andy Sheets, Anaheim	Roy Halladay, Toronto	1	Anaheim
4-29	Ken Griffey Jr., Seattle	Mel Rojas, Detroit	5	Seattle
4-30	Matt Stairs, Oakland	Kip Gross, Boston	1	Oakland
4-30	Ken Griffey Jr., Seattle	Graeme Lloyd, Toronto	8	Seattle
5-1	Larry Sutton, Kansas City	Tony Fossas, New York	8	Kansas City
5-3	Creighton Gubanich, Boston	Jimmy Haynes, Oakland	1	Oakland
5-4	Harold Baines, Baltimore	David Lundquist, Chicago	10	Baltimore
5-7	Roberto Alomar, Cleveland	Eddie Gaillard, Tampa Bay	8	Cleveland
5-10	Nomar Garciaparra, Boston	Brett Hinchliffe, Seattle	1	Boston
5-10	Nomar Garciaparra, Boston	Eric Weaver, Seattle	8	Boston
5-11	Rusty Greer, Texas	Bryan Ward, Chicago	9	Chicago
5-13	Roberto Kelly, Texas	Scott Kamieniecki, Baltimore	4	Texas
5-14	Mo Vaughn, Anaheim	Bobby Witt, Tampa Bay	6	Anaheim
5-14	Mike Sweeney, Kansas City	Jeff Fassero, Seattle	5	Seattle
5-15	David Justice, Cleveland	Dave Mlicki, Detroit	3	Detroit
5-17	Carlos Lee, Chicago	Bartolo Colon, Cleveland	1	Chicago
5-17	Butch Huskey, Seattle	Joe Mays, Minnesota	6	Seattle
5-18	Manny Ramirez, Cleveland	James Baldwin, Chicago	2	Chicago
5-19	Richie Sexson, Cleveland	Bryan Ward, Chicago	5	Chicago
5-22	John Valentin, Boston	Chris Carpenter, Toronto	3	Boston
5-23	Omar Vizquel, Cleveland	Todd Jones, Detroit	9	Cleveland
5-26	Edgar Martinez, Seattle	LaTroy Hawkins, Minnesota	5	Minnesota
5-26	Tino Martinez, New York	John Wasdin, Boston	5	New York
5-27	Brady Anderson, Baltimore	Mike Magnante, Anaheim	7	Anaheim
5-31	Jim Thome, Cleveland	Orlando Hernandez, New York	2	New York
6-4	Denny Hocking, Minnesota	Mike Hampton, Houston N.L.	2	Minnesota
6-5	Matt Walbeck, Anaheim	Chan Ho Park, Los Angeles N.L.	4	Los Angeles
6-5	Rafael Palmeiro, Texas	Darren Holmes, Arizona N.L.	7	Arizona
6-11	Juan Encarnacion, Detroit	Manny Aybar, St. Louis N.L.	9	St. Louis
6-17	Paul Konerko, Chicago	Jesse Orosco, Baltimore	7	Chicago
6-20	Dean Palmer, Detroit	T.J. Mathews, Oakland	8	Detroit
6-28	Jose Offerman, Boston	Bryan Ward, Chicago	7	Boston
7-4	B.J. Surhoff, Baltimore	Ramiro Mendoza, New York	7	New York
7-17	Raul Ibanez, Seattle	Carlos Reyes, San Diego N.L.	7	Seattle
7-17	Magglio Ordonez, Chicago	Kent Bottenfield, St. Louis N.L.	5	St. Louis
7-19	Alex Rodriguez, Seattle	Vicente Padilla, Arizona N.L.	6	Seattle
7-19	Shawn Green, Toronto	Bruce Chen, Atlanta N.L.	3	Toronto
7-20	Darrin Fletcher, Toronto	Mike Remlinger, Atlanta N.L.	6	Toronto
7-21	Eric Chavez, Oakland	Ken Cloude, Seattle	8	Seattle
7-22	Rafael Palmeiro, Texas	Steve Sparks, Anaheim	3	Texas
7-23	Jason Giambi, Oakland	Makoto Suzuki, Kansas City	3	Kansas City
7-23	Roberto Alomar, Cleveland	David Cone, New York	4	New York
7-24	Corey Koskie, Minnesota	Frank Rodriguez, Seattle	5	Minnesota
7-25	John Jaha, Oakland	Brian Barber, Kansas City	4	Kansas City
7-28	Butch Huskey, Boston	Joey Hamilton, Toronto	6	Toronto
7-30	Alex Rodriguez, Seattle	Arthur Rhodes, Baltimore	5	Seattle
8-9	Bernie Williams, New York	Mike Oquist, Oakland	2	Oakland
8-9	Jay Buhner, Seattle	John Snyder, Chicago	6	Seattle
8-13	Chuck Knoblauch, New York	Benj Sampson, Minnesota	6	New York
8-13	Matt Stairs, Oakland	Paul Spoljaric, Toronto	5	Toronto
8-14	Jim Thome, Cleveland	Jason Johnson, Baltimore	1	Cleveland
8-14	A.J. Hinch, Oakland	Joey Hamilton, Toronto	1	Toronto
8-18	Terrell Lowery, Tampa Bay	Dave Borkowski, Detroit	2	Detroit
8-20	Ricky Ledee, New York	Brad Radke, Minnesota	1	Minnesota
8-24	Jim Thome, Cleveland	Tim Hudson, Oakland	1	Oakland
8-24	John Jaha, Oakland	Steve Karsay, Cleveland	3	Oakland
8-30‡	Edgar Martinez, Seattle	Bill Simas, Chicago	8	Chicago
9-6†	Todd Zeile, Texas	Jim Parque, Chicago	1	Texas
9-10	David Justice, Cleveland	Carlos Castillo, Chicago	4	Chicago
9-14	Paul O'Neill, New York	Paul Spoljaric, Toronto	9	Toronto
9-14	Bernie Williams, New York	Billy Koch, Toronto	8	Toronto
9-16	Alex Rodriguez, Seattle	Esteban Yan, Tampa Bay	8	Tampa Bay
9-24	Manny Ramirez, Cleveland	Mike Romano, Toronto	5	Toronto

Date	Batter, Team	Pitcher, Team	Inn.*	Site
9-24	David Roberts, Cleveland	John Hudek, Toronto	8	Toronto
9-25	Todd Zeile, Texas	Kevin Appier, Oakland	2	Texas
9-26	Rafael Palmeiro, Texas	Tim Kubinski, Oakland	6	Texas
9-27	Robert Fick, Detroit	Jeff Montgomery, Kansas City	8	Detroit
10-1	Carlos Lee, Chicago	Jason Ryan, Minnesota	1	Chicago
10-2	Damon Buford, Boston	Gabe Molina, Baltimore	9	Baltimore
10-3	Tony Batista, Toronto	Mike Jackson, Cleveland	8	Cleveland
10-3	Randy Winn, Tampa Bay	Jeff Juden, New York	4	Tampa Bay

*Inning in which grand slam was hit. †First game of doubleheader. ‡Second game of doubleheader.

NATIONAL LEAGUE

Date	Batter, Team	Pitcher, Team	Inn.*	Site
4-10	Ed Sprague, Pittsburgh	Kurt Miller, Chicago	5	Pittsburgh
4-12	Travis Lee, Arizona	Chan Ho Park, Los Angeles	3	Arizona
4-16	Bobby Abreu, Philadelphia	Rafael Medina, Florida	4	Philadelphia
4-23	Fernando Tatis, St. Louis	Chan Ho Park, Los Angeles	3	Los Angeles
4-23	Fernando Tatis, St. Louis	Chan Ho Park, Los Angeles	3	Los Angeles
4-23	Matt Williams, Arizona	Brian Boehringer, San Diego	7	San Diego
5-1	Brian McRae, New York	Jerry Spradlin, San Francisco	7	New York
5-4	Mark McGwire, St. Louis	Greg Maddux, Atlanta	2	Atlanta
5-4	Mark Grace, Chicago	Darryl Kile, Colorado	3	Chicago
5-7	Bruce Aven, Florida	Alan Mills, Los Angeles	7	Los Angeles
5-8	Brian S. Giles, Pittsburgh	Jose Jimenez, St. Louis	2	St. Louis
5-9	Shawon Dunston, St. Louis	Jose Silva, Pittsburgh	1	St. Louis
5-10	Steve Finley, Arizona	Javier Vazquez, Montreal	1	Arizona
5-18	Travis Lee, Arizona	Rich Rodriguez, San Francisco	7	San Francisco
5-19	Brian Jordan, Atlanta	Francisco Cordova, Pittsburgh	6	Atlanta
5-19	Mike Lieberthal, Philadelphia	Dustin Hermanson, Montreal	5	Montreal
5-20†	Robin Ventura, New York	Jim Abbott, Milwaukee	1	New York
5-20‡	Robin Ventura, New York	Horacio Estrada, Milwaukee	4	New York
5-21	Gary Gaetti, Chicago	Bruce Chen, Atlanta	1	Atlanta
5-25	Bill Mueller, San Francisco	Kent Mercker, St. Louis	5	St. Louis
6-5	Devon White, Los Angeles	Tim Belcher, Anaheim A.L.	6	Los Angeles
6-6	Bruce Aven, Florida	Julio Santana, Tampa Bay A.L.	8	Tampa Bay
6-13	Derek Bell, Houston	Heath Murray, San Diego	6	Houston
6-18	Armando Rios, San Francisco	Doug Creek, Chicago	6	San Francisco
6-20	Carl Everett, Houston	Ugueth Urbina, Montreal	8	Houston
6-27	Jeromy Burnitz, Milwaukee	Scott Sauerbeck, Pittsburgh	8	Milwaukee
7-3	Scott Rolen, Philadelphia	Scott Sanders, Chicago	4	Philadelphia
7-3‡	Neifi Perez, Colorado	Heath Murray, San Diego	2	Colorado
7-11	Jay Bell, Arizona	Jimmy Haynes, Oakland A.L.	6	Arizona
7-19	Todd Hundley, Los Angeles	Jose Silva, Pittsburgh	3	Pittsburgh
7-21	Tony Womack, Arizona	Billy Wagner, Houston	8	Houston
7-21	Ellis Burks, San Francisco	Sterling Hitchcock, San Diego	3	San Francisco
7-23	Matt Mieske, Houston	Donne Wall, San Diego	8	Houston
7-28	Jeff Bagwell, Houston	Mike Porzio, Colorado	6	Colorado
7-31	Gary Gaetti, Chicago	Octavio Dotel, New York	1	Chicago
8-1	Gerald Williams, Atlanta	Randy Wolf, Philadelphia	4	Atlanta
8-4	Tony Gwynn, San Diego	Kent Mercker, St. Louis	5	St. Louis
8-9	Jose Vidro, Montreal	Carlos Almanzar, San Diego	6	Montreal
8-9	Fernando Tatis, St. Louis	Billy Brewer, Philadelphia	4	Philadelphia
8-9	Mike Lowell, Florida	John Johnstone, San Francisco	8	Florida
8-11	Eric Karros, Los Angeles	Anthony Telford, Montreal	7	Montreal
8-15	Robin Ventura, New York	Livan Hernandez, San Francisco	5	San Francisco
8-16	Preston Wilson, Florida	Mike Maddux, Los Angeles	8	Los Angeles
8-21	Eddie Taubensee, Cincinnati	Bobby Ayala, Montreal	7	Cincinnati
8-21	Aaron Boone, Cincinnati	Mike Thurman, Montreal	6	Cincinnati
8-22	Gary Sheffield, Los Angeles	Steve Montgomery, Philadelphia	6	Philadelphia
8-22†	John Olerud, New York	Rich Croushore, St. Louis	8	New York
8-25	Jose Valentin, Milwaukee	Kevin Brown, Los Angeles	6	Milwaukee
8-26	Damian Miller, Arizona	Brent Billingsley, Florida	9	Florida
8-31	Ken Caminiti, Houston	Turk Wendell, New York	8	Houston
8-31	Kevin Young, Pittsburgh	Dave Veres, Colorado	9	Colorado
9-3	Jeff Kent, San Francisco	Francisco Cordova, Pittsburgh	5	Pittsburgh
9-5	Darryl Hamilton, New York	Darryl Kile, Colorado	5	New York
9-6	Mark Kotsay, Florida	Ismael Valdes, Los Angeles	1	Florida
9-7	Matt Williams, Arizona	Eric Plunk, Milwaukee	6	Milwaukee
9-17	Mark McGwire, St. Louis	Jose Lima, Houston	4	St. Louis
9-17	Dante Bichette, Colorado	Robinson Checo, Los Angeles	5	Colorado
9-18	Rey Ordonez, New York	Carlton Loewer, Philadelphia	6	New York
9-29	John Olerud, New York	Greg Maddux, Atlanta	4	New York
10-2	Wilton Guerrero, Montreal	Paul Byrd, Philadelphia	2	Philadelphia

*Inning in which grand slam was hit. †First game of doubleheader. ‡Second game of doubleheader.

TRANSACTIONS

JANUARY 1, 1999-DECEMBER 31, 1999

JANUARY 4
Twins organization signed 3B Brian Richardson.
Athletics organization signed P Kevin Jarvis.

JANUARY 5
Red Sox organization signed P Rheal Cormier, P Kip Gross.
Indians organization signed P Dave Telgheder, P Mike Walker, 3B Jeff Manto, SS Orlando Miller and C Chris Turner.

JANUARY 6
Blue Jays organization signed OF Wayne Kirby and OF Jimmy Hurst.
Reds traded OF Pat Watkins to Marlins for P Pedro Minaya.
Dodgers organization signed P Chris Haney, P Pedro Borbon, P Jaime Arnold, 3B Pete Rose Jr., C Tim Laker and C Hector Ortiz.

JANUARY 7
Athletics organization signed OF Marc Newfield.
Expos claimed P Roberto Duran on waivers from Tigers.

JANUARY 8
Giants claimed P Steve Connelly on waivers from Red Sox.

JANUARY 11
Red Sox signed P Pat Rapp.
Indians organization signed P Jim Brower and C Angelo Encarnacion.
Athletics signed P Doug Jones.
Reds signed C Brian Johnson.
Dodgers signed 3B Dave Hansen.
Brewers signed OF Rick Becker.

JANUARY 12
Angels signed OF Matt Luke.
Red Sox organization signed OF Pedro Valdes.
Dodgers traded P Darren Hall to White Sox for C Joe Sutton.
Indians organization signed P Jeff Schmidt.
Diamondbacks organization signed P Frank Castillo.
Dodgers signed P Greg Cadaret.
Mets organization signed C-IF-OF Jerry Brooks.
Cardinals signed OF Darren Bragg.

JANUARY 13
Expos organization signed C Darron Cox.
Devil Rays organization signed OF Billy Ashley.
Rangers organization signed C John Marzano.

JANUARY 14
Reds signed 1B Hal Morris
Astros traded C Brad Ausmus and P C.J. Nitkowski to Tigers for C Paul Bako, P Dean Crow, P Mark Persails, P Brian Powell and 3B Carlos Villalobos.
Royals signed P Terry Mathews.

JANUARY 15
Angels organization signed SS-2B Luis Rivera.
Orioles signed P Heathcliff Slocumb.
Dodgers signed P Carlos Perez, 3B Scott Livingstone and P Ricardo Jordan.
Cardinals signed P Mike Mohler.

JANUARY 17
Giants signed C Scott Servais.

JANUARY 18
Rangers organization signed P Joe Hudson to a minor league contract.
Blue Jays signed 2B Joey Cora and 3B Willie Greene.

JANUARY 19
Twins signed P Bob Wells.
Blue Jays signed P Vincente Palacios.
Mets signed P Allen Watson.

JANUARY 20
Mariners organization signed P Brien Taylor.
Devil Rays organization signed P Bobby Witt, P Steve Ontiveros, P Marc Valdes, P Steve Cooke and P Norm Charlton.
Twins announced retirement of P Bob Tewksbury.

JANUARY 21
Astros organization signed P Brian Williams, P Jeff McCurry, C Randy Knorr, IF-OF Casey Candaele, OF Alex Diaz and OF Ryan Thompson.

JANUARY 22
Athletics organization signed 1B Jeff Ball.
Mets organization signed 2B Mariano Duncan.

JANUARY 25
Angels organization signed IF Andy Stankiewicz, P Christian Michalak and P Stephen Mintz.
Royals organization signed P Pete Smith, OF Tony Tarasco and IF Steve Scarsone.
Athletics signed OF Tim Raines.
Astros organization signed P Xavier Hernandez.

JANUARY 26
Red Sox organization signed 1B-DH Bob Hamelin. White Sox organization signed OF John Cangelosi and OF Darrin Jackson.
Indians organization signed P Dave Stevens and P Scott Klingenbeck.
Royals organization signed P Tim Scott.
Rangers organization signed P Mike Morgan.

JANUARY 27
Angels signed P Mike Magnante.
Brewers signed P Jim Abbott.
Cardinals signed 2B Carlos Baerga.

JANUARY 28
Tigers claimed P Mike Grzanich on waivers from Astros.
Expos signed OF Orlando Merced.

JANUARY 29
Cubs organization signed P Doug Creek.
Orioles announced retirement of P Jimmy Key.

FEBRUARY 1
Twins traded P Chris Cumberland to Red Sox for cash considerations.
Yankees traded 3B Mike Lowell to Marlins for P Ed Yarnall, P Mark Johnson and P Todd Noel.
Padres organization signed OF Chris Jones.

FEBRUARY 2
Red Sox organization signed P Seung Jun Song.
Expos organization signed P Mike Maddux.
Phillies organization signed P Joe Grahe.
Padres traded OF Greg Vaughn and 1B-OF Mark Sweeney to Reds for OF Reggie Sanders, SS Damian Jackson and P Josh Harris.

FEBRUARY 3
Indians signed IF-OF Wil Cordero, IF Bill Selby, P Jamie Brewington and P Paul Wagner.
Devil Rays organization signed C Joe Oliver.
Cubs organization signed OF Tarrik Brock.

FEBRUARY 4
Orioles organization signed P Mike Fetters.
Mets traded IF Ralph Milliard to Reds for P Mark Corey.
Padres organization signed P Carlos Reyes.

FEBRUARY 7
Braves announced retirement of P Dennis Martinez.

FEBRUARY 8
Blue Jays organization signed 1B-DH Cecil Fielder.

FEBRUARY 9
Cubs organization signed C Danny Sheaffer.
Cardinals traded P Sean Lowe to White Sox for P John Ambrose.

FEBRUARY 12
Blue Jays released OF Patrick Lennon.
Expos organization signed P Jose Bautista.
Padres organization signed C Mark Parent.

FEBRUARY 16
Cardinals signed SS Shawon Dunston.
Cardinals organization signed 1B Eduardo Perez.

FEBRUARY 17
Athletics signed 1B John Jaha.
Blue Jays announced retirement of P Dave Stieb.

FEBRUARY 18
Yankees traded P David Wells, P Graeme Lloyd and 2B Homer Bush to Blue Jays for P Roger Clemens.
Devil Rays organization signed P Ben McDonald.

FEBRUARY 19
Devil Rays organization signed 1B-DH Julio Franco.
Diamondbacks organization signed P Byung-Hyun Kim.

FEBRUARY 20
Indians signed P Orel Hershiser.
Pirates signed SS Pat Meares.

FEBRUARY 24
Royals organization signed OF Curtis Pride.

FEBRUARY 25
Pirates traded 2B Tony Womack to Diamondbacks for OF Paul Weichard and a player to be named; Diamondbacks sent P Jason Boyd to complete deal (August 25).

FEBRUARY 27
Reds organization signed 3B Tim Naehring.

MARCH 3
Dodgers organization signed C Rick Wilkins.

MARCH 4
Royals released OF Curtis Pride.

MARCH 7
Angels announced retirement of INF Craig Shipley.

MARCH 11
Red Sox organization signed P Ramon Martinez.
Reds released P Joey Eischen and SS Pat Listach.
Blue Jays announced retirement of 2B Joey Cora.

MARCH 12
Royals released P Jamie Walker, P Allen McDill, P John Cummings and P Brian Bevil.

MARCH 16
Giants released P Trevor Wilson.

MARCH 17
Red Sox released 1B-DH Bob Hamelin.
Reds released P Todd Williams.
Mets released P Oscar Henriquez.
Cardinals released 2B Carlos Baerga.

MARCH 18
Royals released OF Tony Tarasco.

•MARCH 19
Royals sold contract of P Ricky Pickett to Rangers.

MARCH 20
Tigers organization signed 1B-DH Bob Hamelin.

Twins sold contract of OF Melvin Nieves to Daiei of Japanese Pacific League.

MARCH 22
Mets organization signed P Oscar Henriquez. Mets traded OF Jonathan Guzman to Royals for SS Shane Halter.

MARCH 23
Indians traded OF Jim Betzhold to Astros for a player to be named.
Royals released P Pete Smith.
Yankees organization signed P Trevor Wilson.
Reds organization signed 2B Carlos Baerga.

MARCH 24
Tigers claimed IF Jason Maxwell on waivers from Cubs.
Rangers released P Tony Fossas.
Phillies released P Chris Eddy, P Greg Whiteman and C-3B James Fritz.

MARCH 25
Reds traded OF Jon Nunnally to Red Sox for P Pat Flury.
Reds traded C Brook Fordyce to White Sox for P Jake Meyer.
Yankees organization signed P Tony Fossas.
Astros traded C Marc Ronan to Phillies for future considerations.
Mets signed P Orel Hershiser.

MARCH 26
Royals released P Tim Scott and P Dario Veras.
Mariners released IF Randy Jorgensen, P Rafael Batista, P Albert Derenches, P Jose Gonzalez, P Orin Kawahara, P Dallas Mahan, P Matt Massimi, P Kristofer Totten, OF Anton French, IF David Dallospedale, IF Chris Dean, IF Kip Garcia, IF Domingo Pacheco and IF Felix Rosario.
Dodgers traded C Tim Laker to Pirates for a player to be named.
Mets released P Hideo Nomo.

MARCH 27
Yankees released OF Jerome Walton.
Expos released P Erik Bennett, OF Ed Brady, OF Dax Jones, C Luis Rivera, OF Mo Blakeney, OF Jermaine Swinton, OF Trovin Valdez, P Jason Woodring, P Andrew Frierson and P Raymond Plummer.
Mets released 2B Mariano Duncan.
Pirates released IF Rafael Bournigal.

MARCH 29
Royals released 1B Cary Coffee, P Scott Taylor and P Roland De La Maza.
Mariners released P Bill Swift.
Orioles traded OF Danny Clyburn and a player to be named to Devil Rays for P Jason Johnson; Orioles sent SS Angel Bolivar Volquez to complete deal (April 22).
Cubs claimed OF Curtis Goodwin on waivers from Colorado.
Marlins traded OF Pat Watkins to Rockies for a player to be named; Rockies sent P Kevin Gordon to complete deal (July 16).
Astros released P Xavier Hernandez and OF Dave Clark.
Angels traded C Phil Nevin and P Keith Volkman to Padres for IF Andy Sheets and OF Gus Kennedy.
Padres released C Mark Parent and OF Chris Jones.
Angels announced retirement of INF Luis Rivera.
Padres announced retirement of P Mark Langston.

MARCH 30
Angels organization released IF Andy Stankiewicz and P Rich DeLucia.
Red Sox released OF Midre Cummings.
White Sox released OF John Cangelosi.
Indians released P John Burke.
Indians released 1B Mike Glavine to Braves for future considerations.
Yankees traded P Darren Holmes and cash to Diamondbacks for C Izzy Molina and P Ben Ford.
Athletics claimed P Ron Mahay on waivers from Red Sox.
Athletics traded P Jay Witasick to Royals for a player to be named and cash.
Rangers organization signed IF Rafael Bournigal.
Angels traded 3B-1B Dave Hollins and cash Blue Jays for SS Tomas Perez.

Cardinals traded P John Frascatore to Diamondbacks for P Clint Sodowsky.
Diamondbacks released P Aaron Small.
Cubs released P Marc Pisciotta.

MARCH 31
Royals released P Erik Hanson and P A.J. Sager.
Twins traded P Dan Serafini to Cubs for cash.
Devil Rays released OF Mike Kelly, P Steve Cooke, P Larry Casian, P Mark Hutton, P Steve Ontiveros, P Mark Sievert and OF Billy Ashley.
Blue Jays released 1B-DH Cecil Fielder.
Braves released OF Danny Bautista and 2B Tony Graffanino.
Cubs claimed P Brad Woodall on waivers from Brewers.
Brewers released P William Van Landingham.

APRIL 1
Yankees released P Tony Fossas and P Jim Bruske.
Athletics released P Mark Holzemer.
Blue Jays organization signed P Doug Bochtler.
Marlins traded P Justin Speier to Braves for a player to be named; Braves sent P Matthew Targac to complete deal (June 11).
Cubs organization signed P Hideo Nomo.
Padres released P Mark Langston.

APRIL 2
Angels claimed P Al Levine on waivers from Rangers.
Royals traded 1B-OF Jeff Conine to Orioles for P Chris Fussell.
Orioles released C-1B Chris Hoiles.
Orioles organization signed OF Jose Herrera. Indians released P Ron Villone.
Mariners claimed 1B-OF Ryan Jackson on waivers from Marlins.
Ranngers claimed 3B Tom Evans on waivers from Blue Jays.
Braves organization signed P Marc Pisciotta. Rockies organization signed OF Mike Kelly.

APRIL 3
Indians organization signed P Mark Langston.
Yankees organization signed P Tony Fossas.
Mariners traded P Bobby Ayala to Expos for P Jimmy Turman.

APRIL 5
Indians organization signed P Rich DeLucia.
Reds organization signed P Ron Villone.
Expos released OF Terry Jones.

APRIL 6
Indians organization signed P Chris Haney.
Reds organization signed P A.J. Sager.

APRIL 8
Expos released OF Derrick May.

APRIL 9
Devil Rays organization signed 2B Tony Graffanino.
Devil Rays released SS Dave Silvestri.

APRIL 10
Mariners signed 2B-SS Domingo Cedeno.

APRIL 15
Tigers claimed 3B Rob Sasser on waivers from Rangers.
Blue Jays signed 2B Pat Kelly.

APRIL 16
Braves traded P Mark Wohlers and cash to Reds for P John Hudek.
Marlins claimed P Eric Ludwick on waivers from Blue Jays.
Dodgers traded P Dave Mlicki and P Mel Rojas to Tigers for P Robinson Checo, P Aposto Garcia and P Richard Roberts.

APRIL 20
Reds purchased contract of C Guillermo Garcia from Marlins.

APRIL 22
Twins claimed P Jack Cressend on waivers from Red Sox.
Indians traded P Jerry Spradlin to Giants for OF Dan McKinley and a player to be named; Giants sent P Josh Santos to complete deal (June 27).

APRIL 23
Cubs released P Hideo Nomo.

APRIL 25
Dodgers organization signed P Mike Maddux.

APRIL 27
Rangers traded IF Rafael Bournigal to Mariners for cash.

APRIL 28
Tigers traded OF Brian Hunter to Mariners for two players to be named; Mariners sent P Andrew Vanhekken (June 27) and OF Jerry Amador (August 26) to complete deal.

APRIL 29
Brewers signed P Hideo Nomo.

APRIL 30
Orioles released P Heathcliff Slocumb.

MAY 3
Expos organization signed P Charles Debuc.

MAY 5
Phillies traded P Paul Spoljaric to Blue Jays for P Robert Person.

MAY 7
Blue Jays claimed OF Jacob Brumfield on waivers from Dodgers.

MAY 11
Tigers released P Mel Rojas.

MAY 12
Blue Jays traded P Luis Arroya to Marlins for a player to be named.

MAY 14
Mets organization signed P Xavier Hernandez.

MAY 15
Cardinals organization signed P Heathcliff Slocumb.

MAY 17
Expos organization signed P Mel Rojas.
Pirates organization signed IF Dale Sveum.

MAY 19
Blue Jays traded P Doug Bochtler to Dodgers for cash considerations.

MAY 21
Twins traded P Rick Aguilera and P Scott Downs to Cubs for P Kyle Lohse and P Jason Ryan.

MAY 23
Brewers claimed P Jim Pittsley on waivers from Royals.
Expos organization released P Jose Bautista.
Royals announced retirement of 1B Jeff King.

MAY 26
Mariners claimed P Frankie Rodriguez on waivers from Twins.

MAY 28
Yankees claimed P Greg McCarthy on waivers from Mariners.
Blue Jays claimed 3B Willis Otanez on waivers from Orioles.

JUNE 1
Orioles traded OF Lyle Mouton to Brewers for OF Todd Dunn.

JUNE 3
Orioles claimed C Mike Figga on waivers from Yankees.

JUNE 4
Reds released 2B Carlos Baerga.
Mets organization signed P Jose Bautista.

JUNE 5
Padres organization released P Ed Vosberg. Padres organization signed 2B Carlos Baerga and OF Wayne Kirby.

JUNE 8
Phillies claimed P Amaury Telemaco on waivers from Diamondbacks.

JUNE 10
Expos claimed OF Scott Hunter on waivers from Mets.

JUNE 11
Expos sold P Rick DeHart to the Hiroshima Carp of Japan League.

JUNE 12
Blue Jays traded P Dan Plesac to Diamondbacks for SS Tony Batista and P John Frascatore.

JUNE 14
Phillies claimed P Jason Brester on waivers from Rockies.

JUNE 15
Marlins traded IF Craig Counsell to Dodgers for a player to be named; Dodgers sent P Ryan Moskau to complete deal (July 15).

JUNE 16
Athletics released P Tom Candiotti.

JUNE 18
Indians claimed P Jeff Tam on waivers from Mets.
Indians traded P Tony Dougherty to Pirates for a player to be named.
Indians organization signed P Paul Menhart.
Royals traded IF Jose Cepada to Braves for P Marc Pisciotta.
Mariners traded P Mac Suzuki and a player to be named to Mets for P Allen Watson and cash; Mariners sent P Justin Dunning to complete deal (September 14).

JUNE 19
Mariners traded OF Matt Mieske to Astros for P Kevin Hodges.

JUNE 21
Indians released P Dave Stevens.
Blue Jays released 1B-3B Dave Hollins.

JUNE 22
Royals claimed P Mac Suzuki on waivers from the Mets.

JUNE 23
Red Sox claimed P Travis Baptist on waivers from Twins.

JUNE 27
Mariners released P Brien Taylor.

JUNE 28
Mariners released P Allen Watson.
Diamondbacks traded OF Mike Stoner to Angels for OF Jason Herrick.

JUNE 29
Indians signed P Tom Candiotti.

JULY 2
Orioles organization signed P Jim Corsi.
Yankees claimed 3B Jeff Manto on waivers from Indians.

JULY 3
Yankees signed P Allen Watson.
Rockies released C Jeff Reed.

JULY 6
Devil Rays released P Roger Bailey.
Expos released P Mel Rojas.

JULY 7
Mariners traded 2B-SS Domingo Cedeno to Phillies for IF Jose Flores.

JULY 8
Blue Jays traded P Isabel Giron to Padres for SS Juan Melo.

JULY 9
Marlins traded P Matt Mantei to Diamondbacks for P Vladimir Nunez, P Brad Penny and a player to be named; Diamondbacks sent OF Abraham Nunez to complete deal (December 13).

JULY 16
Orioles traded P Rocky Coppinger to the Milwaukee Brewers for a player to be named; Brewers sent P Al Reyes to complete deal (July 21).
Royals released P Don Wengert.

JULY 17
Mariners organization signed C Ryan Christianson.

JULY 20
Phillies traded P Marty Barnett to Devil Rays for a player to be named; Devil Ray sent P Scott Aldred to complete deal (July 25).
Marlins organization signed P Paul Menhart and 2B Mariano Duncan.

JULY 21
Devil Rays traded P Julio Santana to Red Sox for a player to be named.

JULY 22
Mariners traded OF Kerry Robinson to Reds for P Todd Williams.

JULY 23
Angels released 1B-3B Tim Unroe.
Brewers released P Jim Abbott.
Athletics traded P Kenny Rogers to Mets for OF Terrence Long and P Leo Vasquez.
Pirates traded OF Jose Guillen and P Jeff Sparks to Devil Rays for C Joe Oliver and C Humberto Cota.

JULY 25
Marlins traded P Livan Hernandez to San Francisco for P Jason Grilli and P Nathan Bump.

JULY 26
Mariners traded OF Butch Huskey to Boston for P Robert Ramsay.
Braves traded P Doug Dent to San Diego for C Greg Myers.
Rockies traded 3B Tal Light to the Brewers for a player to be named.

JULY 27
Mets organization signed 3B Scott Livingstone and P Jimmy Myers.

JULY 28
Red Sox signed C Lenny Webster.
Mariners traded 1B David Segui to Blue Jays for P Tom Davey and P Steve Sinclair.

JULY 29
White Sox traded P Mario Iglesias to Orioles for IF Esteban Beltre.
Angels traded 2B Randy Velarde and P Omar Olivares to Athletics for P Elvin Nina, OF Jeff DaVanon and OF Nathan Haynes.

JULY 30
Indians organization signed C Jesse Levis.
Mets organization signed P Vicente Palacios.
Red Sox traded C Mandy Romero to Mets for a player to be named.

JULY 31
Orioles traded P Juan Guzman and cash to Reds for P B.J. Ryan and P Jacobo Sequea. Tigers traded P Bryce Florie to Red Sox for P Mike Maroth.
Royals traded P Kevin Appier to Athletics for P Blake Stein, P Jeff D'Amico and P Brad Rigby.
Athletics traded P Billy Taylor to Mets for P Jason Isringhausen and P Greg McMichael.
Blue Jays organization signed P John Hudek.
Cubs traded P Terry Mulholland and IF Jose Hernandez to Braves for P Micah Bowie, P Ruben Quevedo and a minor league player to be named; Braves sent P Joey Nation to complete deal (August 24).
Marlins traded P Brandon Villafuerte to Tigers for P Mike Drumright.

Mets traded OF Brian McRae, P Rigo Beltran and OF Thomas Johnson to Rockies for OF Darryl Hamilton and P Chuck McElroy. Cardinals traded IF Shawon Dunston to Mets for IF Craig Paquette.
Padres traded C-1B Jim Leyritz to Yankees for P Geraldo Padua.

AUGUST 4
Reds released P Jason Bere.

AUGUST 6
Angels released C Charlie O'Brien.
Blue Jays claimed OF Curtis Goodwin on waivers from Cubs.

AUGUST 9
Angels released P Jack McDowell.
Rockies traded OF Brian McRae to Blue Jays for a player to be named; Blue Jays sent P Pat Lynch to complete deal (August 23).

AUGUST 11
Mets claimed P Jeff Tam on waivers from Indians.
Pirates released OF Turner Ward.

AUGUST 12
Blue Jays announced retirement of OF Curtis Goodwin.

AUGUST 13
Indians organization signed 3B Jeff Manto. Royals traded P Jeremy Jackson to the Mets for P Derek Wallace.
Brewers organization signed P Jason Bere.

AUGUST 15
Royals released P Matt Whisenant and P Terry Mathews.

AUGUST 16
Padres traded 2B Carlos Baerga to Indians for cash.

AUGUST 18
Brewers traded OF Rich Becker to Athletics for a player to be named; Athletics sent P Carl Dale to complete deal (August 20).

AUGUST 20
Orioles released P Ricky Bones.
Padres signed P Matt Whisenant.

AUGUST 24
Cardinals traded P Kent Mercker to Red Sox for P Mike Matthews and C David Benham.

AUGUST 26
Indians organization signed P Jim Poole.
Marlins released C Jorge Fabregas.

AUGUST 27
Orioles traded DH Harold Baines to Indians for P Juan Aracena and a player to be named; Indians sent P Jimmy Hamilton to complete deal (August 31).
Mariners traded P Jeff Fassero to Rangers for a player to be named; Rangers sent OF Adrian Myers to complete deal (September 22).
Expos released P Bobby Ayala.

AUGUST 30
Blue Jays released OF Geronimo Berroa.

AUGUST 31
Angels released OF Reggie Williams.
Red Sox traded P Mark Guthrie to Cubs for P Rod Beck and a player to named; Red Sox sent 3B Cole Liniak to complete deal (September 1).
Cubs traded C Tyler Houston to Indians for P Richard Negrette.
Blue Jays signed C Pat Borders.
Rockies traded IF Lenny Harris to Diamondbacks for IF Belvani Martinez.
Braves signed C Jorge Fabregas.
Astros released OF Alex Diaz and P Sean Bergman.
Astros traded P Joe Messman to Giants for OF Stan Javier.

SEPTEMBER 5
Braves organization signed P Sean Bergman.
Expos released 3B Shane Andrews.

SEPTEMBER 9
Pirates traded IF Freddy Garcia to Braves for P Greg Dukeman.
Cubs signed 3B Shane Andrews.

SEPTEMBER 10
Dodgers claimed P Dwayne Jacobs on waivers from White Sox.

SEPTEMBER 12
Royals released IF Steve Scarsone.
Phillies released 2B-SS Domingo Cedeno.

SEPTEMBER 14
Royals traded P Glendon Rusch to Mets for P Dan Murray.

SEPTEMBER 20
Diamondbacks claimed P Jeff Kubenka on waivers from Dodgers.

SEPTEMBER 24
Red Sox released P Mark Portugal.
Rockies announced retirement of OF John Cangelosi.

SEPTEMBER 29
Twins claimed 1B Mario Valdez on waivers from White Sox.
Phillies released P Matt Beech.

OCTOBER 1
Athletics announced retirement of C Mike Macfarlane.

OCTOBER 5
Marlins organization signed IF Chris Clapinski.

OCTOBER 6
Cubs released OF Lance Johnson.
Reds claimed P Heath Murray on waivers from Padres.
Phillies claimed SS Felix Martinez on waivers from Royals.
Phillies claimed P Carlos Reyes on waivers from Padres.
Padres claimed IF Jed Hanson on waivers from Royals.

OCTOBER 8
Twins released OF Marty Cordova and IF Brent Gates.
Reds released C Brian Johnson.

OCTOBER 13
Padres organization signed OF Ethan Faggett, P Brian Doughty, P Len Hart and P Ryan Lynch.
Giants claimed SS Nelson Castro on waivers from Angels.

OCTOBER 14
Reds claimed 1B Ron Wright on waivers from Pirates.

OCTOBER 15
Cardinals organization signed P Mike James and OF Steve Bieser.

OCTOBER 18
Royals claimed P David Lundquist on waivers from White Sox.
Cubs released 3B Gary Gaetti.

OCTOBER 20
Blue Jays released P John Hudek.

OCTOBER 22
Dodgers organization signed P Kris Foster.
Phillies claimed P Manny Barrios on waivers from Reds.

OCTOBER 25
Padres organization signed P Matt Whiteside.

OCTOBER 26
Indians organization signed P Jamie Brewington, P Cameron Cairncross and P Roy Padilla.

OCTOBER 28
Rangers released P Eric Gunderson and INF Jon Shave.
Phillies claimed P Hideo Nomo on waivers from Brewers.

OCTOBER 30
Rockies traded OF Dante Bichette and cash to Reds for OF Jeffrey Hammonds and P Stan Belinda.

NOVEMBER 2

Rangers traded OF Juan Gonzalez, P Danny Patterson and C Gregg Zaun to Tigers for P Justin Thompson, P Francisco Cordero, OF Gabe Kapler, C Bill Haselman, 2B Frank Catalanotto and P Alan Webb.

Marlins organization signed C Chris Tremie and P Jake Benz.

NOVEMBER 3

Reds organization signed INF Mike Bell, INF Chris Sexton and OF Pat Watkins.

NOVEMBER 4

Padres organization signed P Oscar Henriquez, P Luis Andujar, P Eric Moody, P Vicente Palacios, P Anthony Runion, P Derek Root, P Matt Dunbar, OF Ryan Radmanovich and INF Ralph Milliard.

NOVEMBER 7

Indians signed P Danys Baez.

NOVEMBER 8

Blue Jays traded OF Shawn Green and 2B Jorge Nunez to Dodgers for OF Raul Mondesi and P Pedro Borbon.

NOVEMBER 9

Rangers claimed P Brian Sikorski on waivers from Astros.

NOVEMBER 10

Tigers claimed INF Carlos Villalobos on waivers from Astros.
Padres traded P Andy Ashby to Phillies for P Carlton Loewer, P Steve Montgomery and P Adam Eaton.

NOVEMBER 11

Devil Rays announced retirement of 3B Wade Boggs.
Blue Jays traded P Pat Hentgen and P Paul Spoljaric to Cardinals for P Lance Painter, C Alberto Castillo and P Matt DeWitt.
Dodgers organization signed INF Dave Hansen.

NOVEMBER 12

Marlins traded INF Kevin Orie to Dodgers for a minor league player to be named.
Red Sox traded OF Jon Nunnally to Mets for OF Jermaine Allensworth.

NOVEMBER 15

Padres traded P Dan Miceli to Marlins for P Brian Meadows.
Pirates organization signed P Pep Harris and 3B Jarrod Patterson.

NOVEMBER 16

Twins announced retirement of C Terry Steinbach.
Reds organization signed P Larry Luebbers, P Neil Weber, P Tom Fordham, P Bobby Munoz, P Terrell Wade, P Joe Borowski and INF Brooks Kieschnick.
Rockies claimed P Julian Tavarez on waivers from Giants.
Rockies traded P Darryl Kile, RHP Dave Veres and RHP Luther Hackman to Cardinals for RHP Jose Jimenez, RHP Manny Aybar, RHP Rick Croushore and INF Brent Butler.

NOVEMBER 17

Orioles signed P Mike Trombley.
Royals claimed P Jason Rakers on waivers from Indians.
Mariners organization signed OF Rich Butler, C Robert Machada, INF Steven Goodell and INF Robert Gandolfo.
Blue Jays released C Mike Matheny.
Rockies traded P Curtis Leskanic to Brewers for P Mike Myers.
Mets organization signed INF Maurice Bruce.

NOVEMBER 18

Twins claimed P Sean Bergman on waivers from Braves.
Twins claimed P Mike Kusiewicz on waivers from Rockies
Twins claimed 1B Mario Valdez on waivers from Cubs.
Athletics signed P Mike Magnante.
Devil Rays claimed C Mike Figga on waivers from Orioles.
Expos claimed P Brent Billingsley on waivers from Marlins.
Phillies claimed P Mark Brownson on waivers from Rockies.

NOVEMBER 22

Cubs organization signed P Todd Van Poppel, P Daniel Garibay, P Dave Zancanaro, P Mike Heathcott, P Kerry Lacy, C Angelo Encarnacion, C Alan Zinter, INF Chris Peterson, OF Tarrik Brock, OF Raul Gonzalez and OF Chris Hatcher.
Padres organization signed 1B Joe Vitiello, P Jayson Durocher, P Stan Spencer, C George Williams and C John Roskos.

NOVEMBER 23

Indians claimed P Justin Speier on waivers from Braves.
Tigers organization signed P Chad Ogea.
Athletics organization signed P Frank Lankford, P Jon Ratliff, P Jeff Tam, P Will Brunson, P Terry Burrows, P Rich Sauveur, C Chris Norton, OF Greg Martinez and OF David McCarty.
Diamondbacks signed P Russ Springer.

NOVEMBER 24

Tigers claimed P Ramon Tatis on waivers from Devil Rays.
Reds claimed P Eddie Gaillard on waivers from Devil Rays.

NOVEMBER 29

Tigers organization signed P Mike Oquist.
Rockies sold the contract of P Roberto Ramirez to Hanshin Tigers of Japan Central League.

DECEMBER 1

Yankees released DH Chili Davis.
Brewers organization signed P Rod Bolton, P Ricardo Jordan, 1B Kurt Bierek, SS Norberto Martin, OF Damon Hollins, OF Matt Luke and OF Brad Tyler.
Phillies signed P Mike Jackson.

DECEMBER 2

White Sox announced retirement of OF Darrin Jackson.
Indians signed P Scott Kamieniecki.
Mets signed OF Mike Kelly, INF Orlando Miller, P Brian Shouse and P Jim Baron.

DECEMBER 3

Indians organization signed P Brian Barber.

DECEMBER 6

Braves claimed P Rafael Medina on waivers from Marlins.

DECEMBER 7

Rockies traded P Scott Randall to Twins for OF Chris Latham.
Mariners signed 1B John Olerud.
Brewers organization signed P Michael Busby, P Mike Iglesias, P Greg Mix, P Mike Rossiter, P Travis Smith, P Eric Ludwick, P Greg McCarthy, P David West, P Joe Crawford and C Kade Johnson.
Pirates organization signed OF Adam Hyzdu, INF Jason Wood, P Jose Lopez and OF Daren Hooper.
Pirates released P Michael Chaney, P Mario Cordoba, P Danny Crawford, P Manuel Helena, C David Diaz, C Jose Sanchez, C Alvaro Zambrano, 3B Victor Araujo, SS Digno Delarosa, OF Santos Cortez, OF Mo Douglas, OF Juan Hernandez and OF Alvin Hidalgo. Pirates sold contract of P Greg Hansell to Hanshin Tigers of Japanese Central League.

DECEMBER 8

Orioles released P Doug Linton.
Twins signed P Sean Bergman.
Rockies signed OF Tom Goodwin.
Cardinals signed 1B/OF Larry Sutton.

DECEMBER 9

Orioles signed DH Harold Baines.
Rockies signed C Brent Mayne.

DECEMBER 10

Cubs organization signed C Kweon Yoon-min.
Reds released INF Juan Melo.
Mets traded P Chuck McElroy to Orioles for P Jesse Orosco.

DECEMBER 12

Red Sox traded OF Damon Buford to Cubs for INF Manny Alexander.

Orioles traded INF Jeff Reboulet to Royals for a player to be named.

Rangers organization signed P Koichi Taniguchi.

Dodgers traded P Ismael Valdes and 2B Eric Young to Cubs for P Terry Adams, P Chad Ricketts and a player to be named; Cubs sent P Brian Stephenson to complete deal (December 16).

Rockies organization signed P Butch Henry.

Tigers traded OF Kimera Bartee to Reds for a player to be named or cash.

Reds released C Guillermo Garcia.

Mets signed 3B Todd Zeile.

Giants traded P Chris Brock to Phillies for C Bobby Estalella.

DECEMBER 13

Giants traded P Jerry Spradlin to Royals for a player to be named.

Marlins traded P Johan Santana to Twins for P Jared Camp and cash.

Yankees traded OF Chad Curtis to Rangers for P Brandon Knight and P Sam Marsonek.

Devil Rays signed OF Greg Vaughn.

Reds organization signed P Elmer Dessens.

Cubs traded P Richard Negrette to Orioles for SS Augie Ojeda.

Rockies traded 3B Vinny Castilla to Devil Rays for P Rolando Arrojo and INF Aaron Ledesma.

Athletics traded P Jimmy Haynes to Brewers. Rockies traded C Henry Blanco and P Jamey Wright to Brewers for 3B Jeff Cirillo, P Scott Karl and cash.

Rockies traded P Justin Miller and cash to Athletics.

Brewers organization signed OF James Mouton.

Expos released INF Jose Fernandez.

Mets organization signed 1B Ryan McGuire, P Johan Lopez and OF Juan Moreno.

Pirates traded P Brad Clontz to Diamondbacks for a player to be named; Diamondbacks sent P Robert Manzueta to complete deal (December 15).

Pirates traded OF Brant Brown to Marlins for OF Bruce Aven.

DECEMBER 14

Reds traded 1B Stephen Larkin to Orioles for a player to be named.

Royals signed C Brian Johnson.

Yankees traded P Dan Naulty to Dodgers for 1B Nicholas Leach.

Pirates signed OF-INF Wil Cordero.

DECEMBER 15

Diamondbacks traded OF Dante Powell to Cardinals for SS Luis Ordaz.

Cubs signed C Joe Girardi.

Marlins traded OF Todd Dunwoody to Royals for INF Sean McNally.

Astros traded OF Carl Everett to Red Sox for SS Adam Everett and P Greg Miller.

Dodgers organization signed P Mike Fetters.

DECEMBER 16

Indians signed P Chuck Finley.

Tigers organization signed P Allen McDill, P Anthony Chavez, P Edgar Ramos, P Danny Rios, INF Jesus Azuaje, INF Tilson Brito and INF Carlos Mendez.

Rangers organization signed OF David Hulse and C Reed Secrist.

Brewers signed INF Jose Hernandez.

Cardinals signed C Mike Matheny.

DECEMBER 17

Orioles signed C Greg Myers.

Cubs organization signed P Andy Larkin.

Rockies organization signed C Scott Servais.

Dodgers signed P Orel Hershiser.

DECEMBER 19

Mariners signed P Kazuhiro Sasaki on a two-year contract.

Devil Rays signed OF Gerald Williams.

DECEMBER 20

Tigers organization signed P Jim Poole, INF Marty Malloy, INF Kevin Polcovich, P Bart Evans, P Douglas Walls and INF Giomar Guevara.

Twins signed LHP Todd Rizzo.

Mariners signed 2B Mark McLemore and OF Stan Javier.

Rangers organization signed C B.J. Waszgis and INF Edwin Diaz.

Diamondbacks organization signed 1B Alex Cabrera, P David Evans, P Alfredo Garcia, SS Cesar Morillo and 3B Bryant Nelson.

Cubs signed SS Ricky Gutierrez.

Expos signed P Graeme Lloyd.

Cardinals traded P Juan Acevedo and two minor leaguers to be named to Brewers for 2B Fernando Vina.

DECEMBER 21

Orioles signed P Buddy Groom.

Mariners signed P Arthur Rhodes.

Blue Jays organizations signed P Frank Castillo.

Astros organization signed INF Tripp Cromer.

DECEMBER 22

Red Sox signed P Jeff Fassero.

Indians organization signed P Kane Davis, C Mandy Romero, C Kevin Lidle, INF Ryan Jones and P Ernie Delgado.

Yankees traded P Hideki Irabu to Expos for P Jake Westbrook and two players to be named.

Cubs traded P Dan Serafini to Padres for OF Brandon Pernell.

Marlins organization signed P Ricardo Bones.

Braves traded 1B Ryan Klesko, 2B Bret Boone and P Jason Shiell to Padres for 2B Quilvio Veras, 1B Wally Joyner and OF Reggie Sanders.

DECEMBER 23

Red Sox signed P Sang Lee.

Indians organization signed OF Ruben Sierra, INF Bill Selby, P Jim Dedrick, P Jose Pett and P Joey Eischen.

Astros traded P Mike Hampton and OF Derek Bell to Mets for OF Roger Cedeno, P Octavio Dotel and P Kyle Kessel.

DECEMBER 29

Rangers signed P Kenny Rogers.

DECEMBER 30

Athletics signed P Scott Service.

AWARD WINNERS

THE SPORTING NEWS

AMERICAN LEAGUE

Pitcher of the Year: Pedro Martinez, Boston
Rookie Player of the Year: Carlos Beltran, Kansas City, OF
Rookie Pitcher of the Year: Tim Hudson, Oakland
Fireman of the Year: Mariano Rivera, New York
Comeback Player of the Year: John Jaha, Oakland
Manager of the Year: Jimy Williams, Boston

NATIONAL LEAGUE

Pitcher of the Year: Mike Hampton, Houston
Rookie Player of the Year: Preston Wilson, Florida
Rookie Pitcher of the Year: Scott Williamson, Cincinnati
Fireman of the Year: Ugueth Urbina, Montreal
Comeback Player of the Year: Rickey Henderson, New York
Manager of the Year: Bobby Cox, Atlanta

MAJOR LEAGUE

Player of the Year: Rafael Palmeiro, Texas
Executive of the Year: Billy Beane, Oakland

MINOR LEAGUE

Player of the Year: Rick Ankiel, Arkansas, Texas; Memphis, Pacific Coast
Manager of the Year: DeMarlo Hale, Trenton, Eastern
Executive of the Year: Ben Mondor, Pawtucket, International

BASEBALL WRITERS' ASSOCIATION OF AMERICA

AMERICAN LEAGUE

MOST VALUABLE PLAYER

Player, Team	1	2	3	4	5	6	7	8	9	10	Pts.
Ivan Rodriguez, Texas	7	6	7	-	5	2	1	-	-	-	252
Pedro Martinez, Boston	8	6	4	1	2	2	3	-	-	-	239
Roberto Alomar, Cleveland	4	7	6	4	4	-	1	1	-	-	226
Manny Ramirez, Cleveland	4	4	5	9	1	5	-	-	-	-	226
Rafael Palmeiro, Texas	4	1	2	4	8	4	3	1	-	1	193
Derek Jeter, New York	1	2	2	9	3	7	2	1	1	-	177
Nomar Garciaparra, Boston	-	2	2	-	5	5	10	2	1	-	137
Jason Giambi, Oakland	-	-	-	1	-	1	2	6	3	5	49
Shawn Green, Toronto	-	-	-	-	-	1	-	4	10	7	44
Ken Griffey Jr., Seattle	-	-	-	-	-	-	2	6	6	4	42
Bernie Williams, New York	-	-	-	-	-	1	1	2	2	2	21
Carlos Delgado, Toronto	-	-	-	-	-	-	2	1	1	3	16
Juan Gonzalez, Texas	-	-	-	-	-	-	1	1	1	1	10
Mariano Rivera, New York	-	-	-	-	-	-	-	2	1	1	9
Alex Rodriguez, Seattle	-	-	-	-	-	-	-	-	1	2	4
Omar Vizquel, Cleveland	-	-	-	-	-	-	-	1	-	-	3
Matt Stairs, Oakland	-	-	-	-	-	-	-	-	1	-	2
John Jaha, Oakland	-	-	-	-	-	-	-	-	-	1	1
B.J. Surhoff, Baltimore	-	-	-	-	-	-	-	-	-	1	1

Fourteen points awarded for a first-place vote, nine for second and down to one for 10th.

ROOKIE OF THE YEAR

Player, Team	1	2	3	Pts.
Carlos Beltran, Kansas City	26	1	-	133
Freddy Garcia, Seattle	1	12	4	45
Jeff Zimmerman, Texas	-	6	9	27
Brian Daubach, Boston	1	3	2	16
Tim Hudson, Oakland	-	3	4	13
Chris Singleton, Chicago	-	2	3	9
Carlos Lee, Chicago	-	1	1	4
Billy Koch, Toronto	-	-	4	4
Trot Nixon, Boston	-	-	1	1

Five points awarded for a first-place vote, three for second and one for third.

MANAGER OF THE YEAR

Manager, Team	1	2	3	Pts.
Jimy Williams, Boston	20	5	-	115
Art Howe, Oakland	5	19	3	85
Joe Torre, New York	-	4	9	21
Johnny Oates, Texas	1	-	13	18
Mike Hargrove, Cleveland	2	-	3	13

Five points awarded for a first-place vote, three for second and one for third.

CY YOUNG AWARD

Pitcher, Team	1	2	3	Pts.
Pedro Martinez, Boston	28	-	-	140
Mike Mussina, Baltimore	-	16	6	54
Mariano Rivera, New York	-	6	9	27
Bartolo Colon, Cleveland	-	3	5	14
Aaron Sele, Texas	-	-	4	4
David Cone, New York	-	1	-	3
Jamie Moyer, Seattle	-	1	-	3
John Wetteland, Texas	-	1	-	3
Freddy Garcia, Seattle	-	-	2	2
Keith Foulke, Chicago	-	-	1	1
Roberto Hernandez, Tampa Bay	-	-	1	1

Five points awarded for a first-place vote, three for second and one for third.

MOST VALUABLE PLAYER

Player, Team	1	2	3	4	5	6	7	8	9	10	Pts.
Chipper Jones, Atlanta	29	2	1	-	-	-	-	-	-	-	432
Jeff Bagwell, Houston	1	20	6	4	1	-	-	-	-	-	276
Matt Williams, Arizona	2	7	21	-	1	-	1	-	-	-	269
Greg Vaughn, Cincinnati	-	1	2	7	2	3	3	2	1	-	121
Mark McGwire, St. Louis	-	1	1	3	1	3	6	5	7	3	115
Robin Ventura, New York	-	1	-	4	5	7	2	1	-	-	113
Mike Piazza, New York	-	-	-	5	7	2	3	1	3	1	109
Edgardo Alfonzo, New York	-	-	1	6	4	2	-	1	-	1	88
Sammy Sosa, Chicago	-	-	-	-	3	5	2	6	5	8	87
Larry Walker, Colorado	-	-	-	-	-	1	4	-	5	4	35
Vladimir Guerrero, Montreal	-	-	-	1	-	-	2	4	1	5	34
Craig Biggio, Houston	-	-	-	1	2	1	1	-	2	-	32
Jay Bell, Arizona	-	-	-	-	1	2	2	1	2	-	31
Sean Casey, Cincinnati	-	-	-	-	1	2	1	-	-	3	23
Randy Johnson, Arizona	-	-	-	-	2	1	-	1	-	1	21
Billy Wagner, Houston	-	-	-	-	1	-	2	1	-	2	19
Carl Everett, Houston	-	-	-	-	-	-	-	4	1	1	15
Luis Gonzalez, Arizona	-	-	-	-	-	-	1	1	2	1	12
Brian Jordan, Atlanta	-	-	-	-	1	1	-	-	-	-	11
Brian Giles, Pittsburgh	-	-	-	-	-	2	-	-	-	1	11
Mike Hampton, Houston	-	-	-	-	-	-	1	2	-	-	10
Barry Larkin, Cincinnati	-	-	-	1	-	-	-	-	-	-	7
Bobby Abreu, Philadelphia	-	-	-	-	-	-	1	-	1	-	6
Barry Bonds, San Francisco	-	-	-	-	-	-	-	1	-	-	3
Matt Mantei, Florida-Arizona	-	-	-	-	-	-	-	1	-	-	3
Jeff Kent, San Francisco	-	-	-	-	-	-	-	-	1	-	2
Kevin Millwood, Atlanta	-	-	-	-	-	-	-	-	1	-	2
Trevor Hoffman, San Diego	-	-	-	-	-	-	-	-	-	1	1

Fourteen points awarded for a first-place vote, nine for second and down to one for 10th.

MANAGER OF THE YEAR

Manager, Team	1	2	3	Pts.
Jack McKeon, Cincinnati	17	9	3	115
Bobby Cox, Atlanta	10	14	6	98
Larry Dierker, Houston	4	6	10	48
Buck Showalter, Arizona	1	1	9	17
Bobby Valentine, New York	-	2	4	10

Five points awarded for a first-place vote, three for second and one for third.

ROOKIE OF THE YEAR

Player, Team	1	2	3	Pts.
Scott Williamson, Cincinnati	17	9	6	118
Preston Wilson, Florida	9	11	10	88
Warren Morris, Pittsburgh	6	10	9	69
Kris Benson, Pittsburgh	-	1	2	5
Alex Gonzalez, Florida	-	1	1	4
Joe McEwing, St. Louis	-	-	3	3
Kevin McGlinchy, Atlanta	-	-	1	1

Five points awarded for a first-place vote, three for second and one for third.

CY YOUNG AWARD

Pitcher, Team	1	2	3	Pts.
Randy Johnson, Arizona	20	11	1	134
Mike Hampton, Houston	11	17	4	110
Kevin Millwood, Atlanta	1	4	19	36
Jose Lima, Houston	-	-	3	3
Billy Wagner, Houston	-	-	3	3
Kevin Brown, Los Angeles	-	-	1	1
Trevor Hoffman, San Diego	-	-	1	1

Five points awarded for a first-place vote, three for second and one for third.

MISCELLANEOUS

ATTENDANCE

AMERICAN LEAGUE

	Home	Road
Cleveland	3,468,456	2,449,537
Baltimore	3,433,150	2,199,081
New York	3,292,736	2,679,089
Seattle	2,916,346	2,441,959
Texas	2,771,469	2,070,648
Boston	2,446,162	2,395,593
Anaheim	2,253,123	2,203,406
Toronto	2,163,464	2,161,286
Detroit	2,026,441	2,151,140
Tampa Bay	1,562,827	2,207,280
Kansas City	1,506,068	2,208,840
Oakland	1,434,610	2,238,111
Chicago	1,338,851	2,311,582
Minnesota	1,202,829	2,245,944
Totals	**31,816,532**	**31,963,496**

NATIONAL LEAGUE

	Home	Road
Colorado	3,481,065	2,273,665
Atlanta	3,284,897	2,479,052
St. Louis	3,225,334	2,820,564
Los Angeles	3,095,346	2,621,265
Arizona	3,019,654	2,446,063
Chicago	2,813,854	2,795,628
New York	2,725,668	2,593,748
Houston	2,706,017	2,056,636
San Diego	2,523,538	2,447,634
San Francisco	2,078,399	2,430,406
Cincinnati	2,061,222	2,243,015
Philadelphia	1,825,337	2,289,949
Milwaukee	1,701,796	2,056,547
Pittsburgh	1,638,023	2,170,366
Florida	1,369,421	2,149,065
Montreal	773,277	2,302,281
Totals	**38,322,848**	**38,175,884**

DEBUTS

Player	Pos.	Team	Birth date	Birthplace	Debut
Allen, John Chad	LF	Minnesota	2-6-75	Dallas, Texas	4-6
Almanza, Armando	P	Florida	10-26-72	El Paso, Texas	7-29
Almonte, Hector	P	Florida	10-17-75	Santo Domingo, Dominican Rep.	7-26
Alvarez, Juan	P	Anaheim	8-9-73	Coral Gables, Florida	9-1
Anderson, Jimmy	P	Pittsburgh	1-22-76	Portsmouth, Virginia	7-4
Ankiel, Richard Alexand	P	St. Louis	7-19-79	Fort Pierce, Florida	8-23
Armas Jr., Antonio Jose	P	Montreal	4-29-78	Puerto Piritu, Venezuela	8-16
Arnold, Jamie	P	Los Angeles	3-24-74	Dearborn, Michigan	4-20
Bale, John Robert	P	Toronto	5-22-74	Cheverly, Maryland	9-30
Barajas, Rodrigo Richard	C	Arizona	9-5-75	Ontario, California	9-25
Barker, Glen F.	PH	Houston	5-10-71	Albany, New York	4-7
Barker, Richard Frank	P	Chicago N.L.	10-29-72	Revere, Massachusetts	4-25
Barker, Kevin	1B	Milwaukee	7-26-75	Bristol, Virginia	8-19
Bellinger, Clayton Daniel	PH	New York A.L.	11-18-68	Oneonta, New York	4-9
Benson, Kris	P	Pittsburgh	11-7-74	Superior, Wisconsin	4-9
Bergeron, Peter	LF	Montreal	11-9-77	Greenfield, Massachusetts	9-7
Berkman, William	PH	Houston	2-10-76	Waco, Texas	7-16
Billingsley, Brent Aaron	P	Florida	4-19-75	Downey, California	5-20
Blake, William Casey	3B	Toronto	8-23-73	Des Moines, Iowa	8-14
Blum, Geoffrey E.	SS	Montreal	4-26-73	Redwood City, California	8-9
Borkowski, Dave	P	Detroit	2-7-77	Detroit, Michigan	7-17
Bowie, Micah Andrew	P	Atlanta	11-10-74	Humble, Texas	7-24
Boyd, Jason	P	Pittsburgh	2-23-73	St. Clair, Illinois	9-10
Brower, James Robert	P	Cleveland	12-29-72	Edina, Minnesota	9-5
Brown, Roosevelt Laway	PH	Chicago N.L.	8-3-75	Vicksburg, Mississippi	5-18
Burnett, Allan James	P	Florida	1-3-77	North Little Rock, Arkansas	8-17
Callaway, Mickey	P	Tampa Bay	5-13-75	Memphis, Tennessee	6-12
Cancel, Robinson Castro	C	Milwaukee	5-4-76	Lajas, Puerto Rico	9-3
Carlyle, Earl L.	P	San Diego	12-21-77	Omaha, Nebraska	8-29
Carter, Lance	P	Kansas City	12-18-74	Bradenton, Florida	9-15
Castro, Ramon A.	C	Florida	3-1-76	Vega Baja, Puerto Rico	8-27
Christensen, McKay A.	CF	Chicago A.L.	8-14-75	Upland, California	4-6
Clapinski, Christopher	PH	Florida	8-20-71	Buffalo, New York	7-17
Colangelo, Mike	LF	Anaheim	10-22-76	Teaneck, New Jersey	6-13
Cooper, Brian John	P	Anaheim	8-19-74	Hollywood, California	9-7
Coquillette, Trace	3B	Montreal	6-4-74	Carmichael, California	9-7
Cordero, Francisco Javie	P	Detroit	8-11-77	Santo Domingo, Dominican Rep.	8-2
Cortes, David	P	Atlanta	10-15-73	Mexicali, Mexico	8-30
Cox, Darron	C	Montreal	11-21-67	Oklahoma City, Oklahoma	4-6
Cox, Steve	PH	Tampa Bay	10-31-74	Delano, California	9-19
Dale, Carl	P	Milwaukee	12-7-72	Indianapolis, Indiana	9-7
Daneker, Pat	P	Chicago A.L.	1-14-76	Williamsport, Pennsylvania	7-2
Darr, Mike	PH	San Diego	3-21-76	Corona, California	5-23
DaVanon, Jeffrey Graham	RF	Anaheim	12-8-73	San Diego, California	9-7

Player	Pos.	Team	Birth date	Birthplace	Debut
Davenport, Joe	P	Chicago A.L.	3-24-76	Chicago, Illinois	7-20
Davey, Thomas Joseph	P	Toronto	9-11-73	Garden City, Michigan	4-6
Davidson, Cleatus Lavon	PR	Minnesota	11-1-76	Bartow, Florida	5-30
Davis, Douglas	P	Texas	9-21-75	Sacramento, California	8-9
Davis, Tommy	C	Baltimore	5-21-73	Mobile, Alabama	5-14
Dawkins, Travis Sentell	SS	Cincinnati	5-12-79	Newberry, South Carolina	9-3
Dellaero, Jason Christopher	SS	Chicago A.L.	12-17-76	Mt. Kisco, New York	9-7
del Toro, Miguel Alfonso	P	San Francisco	6-22-72	Sonora, Mexico	4-6
DePaula, Sean	P	Cleveland	11-7-73	Newton, Massachusetts	8-31
Dotel, Octavio Eduardo	P	New York N.L.	11-25-75	Santo Domingo, Dominican Rep.	6-26
Dransfeldt, Kelly Daniel	SS	Texas	4-16-75	Joliet, Illinois	5-1
Durazo, Erubiel Cardena	PH	Arizona	1-23-74	Hermosillo, Mexico	7-26
Durbin, Chad	P	Kansas City	12-3-77	Spring Valley, Illinois	9-26
Durrington, Trent John	2B	Anaheim	8-27-75	Sydney, Australia	8-6
Ebert, Derrin Lee	P	Atlanta	8-21-76	Anaheim, California	4-6
Estrada, Horacio Jimene	P	Milwaukee	10-19-75	San Joaquin, Venezuela	5-4
Falkenborg, Brian Thomas	P	Baltimore	1-18-78	Newport Beach, California	10-1
Farnsworth, Kyle Lynn	P	Chicago N.L.	4-14-76	Wichita, Kansas	4-29
Fernandez, Jose Mayobanex	3B	Montreal	11-2-74	La Vega, Dominican Rep.	7-3
Franklin, Ryan Ray	P	Seattle	3-5-73	Fort Smith, Arkansas	5-15
Gagne, Eric Serge	P	Los Angeles	1-7-76	Montreal, Canada	9-7
Garcia, Amaury Miguel	PH	Florida	5-20-75	Santo Domingo, Dominican Rep.	7-5
Garcia, Freddy Antonio	P	Seattle	10-6-76	Caracas, Venezuela	4-7
Garcia, Jesus Jesse	2B	Baltimore	9-24-73	Corpus Christi, Texas	4-5
Garcia, Luis Rafael	SS	Detroit	5-20-75	San Francisco de Macoris, Dom. Rep.	4-5
Garcia, Michael	P	Pittsburgh	5-11-68	Riverside, California	9-10
Glover, John Gary	P	Toronto	12-3-76	Cleveland, Ohio	9-30
Glynn, Ryan David	P	Texas	11-1-74	Portsmouth, Virginia	5-16
Gonzalez, Wiklenman	C	San Diego	5-17-74	Aragua, Venezuela	8-14
Graterol, Beiker	P	Detroit	11-9-74	Edo Lara, Dominican Rep.	4-9
Greene, Rick	P	Cincinnati	1-2-71	Ft. Knox, Kentucky	6-19
Gubanich, Creighton Wade	C	Boston	3-27-72	Belleville, New Jersey	4-16
Guzman, Cristian Antonio	SS	Minnesota	3-21-78	Santo Domingo, Dominican Rep.	4-6
Guzman, Domingo Serrano	P	San Diego	4-5-75	San Cristobal, Dominican Rep.	9-9
Guzman, Edwards	PH	San Francisco	9-11-76	Bayamon, Puerto Rico	4-6
Haad, Yamid Salcedo	PH	Pittsburgh	9-2-77	Cartagena, Colombia	7-5
Hackman, Luther	P	Colorado	10-10-74	Lawndale, Mississippi	9-1
Harville, Chad	P	Oakland	9-16-76	Selmer, Tennessee	6-23
Heiserman, Richard Michael	P	St. Louis	2-22-73	Atlantic, Iowa	5-23
Hemphill, Bret	C	Anaheim	12-17-71	Santa Clara, California	6-28
Herges, Matthew	P	Los Angeles	4-1-70	Champaign, Illinois	8-3
Hermansen, Chad B.	LF	Pittsburgh	9-10-77	Salt Lake City, Utah	9-7
Hernandez, Carlos Eduardo	PR	Houston	12-12-75	Caracas, Venezuela	5-26
Hernandez, Ramon Jose	C	Oakland	5-20-76	Caracas, Venezuela	6-29
Hiljus, Erik	P	Detroit	12-25-72	Panorama City, California	9-10
Hinchliffe, Brett	P	Seattle	7-21-74	Detroit, Michigan	4-5
Hudson, Timothy Adam	P	Oakland	7-14-75	Columbus, Georgia	6-8
Jimenez, D'Angelo	3B	New York A.L.	12-21-77	Santo Domingo, Dominican Rep.	9-15
Jones, Jacque	RF	Minnesota	4-25-75	San Diego, California	6-9
Kennedy, Adam	2B	St. Louis	1-10-76	Riverside, California	8-21
Kida, Masao	P	Detroit	9-12-68	Tokyo, Japan	4-5
Kim, Byung-Hyun	P	Arizona	1-21-79	Kwangju, South Korea	5-29
King, Raymond Keith	P	Chicago N.L.	1-15-74	Chicago, Illinois	5-21
Koch, William Christopher	P	Toronto	12-14-74	Rockville Center, New York	5-5
Kolb, Danny Lee	P	Texas	3-29-75	Sterling, Illinois	6-4
Lamb, David Christian	SS	Tampa Bay	6-6-75	West Hills, California	4-12
LaRue, Michael Jason	C	Cincinnati	3-19-74	Houston, Texas	6-15
Laxton, Brett	P	Oakland	10-5-73	Stratford, New Jersey	6-21
Lee, Carlos Noriel	LF	Chicago A.L.	6-20-76	Aguadulce, Panama	5-7
Lee, Corey Wayne	P	Texas	12-26-74	Raleigh, North Carolina	8-24
Lee, David Emmer	P	Colorado	3-12-73	Pittsburgh, Pennsylvania	5-22
Liefer, Jeffrey David	1B	Chicago A.L.	8-17-74	Fontana, California	4-7
Lilly, Theodore Roosev	P	Montreal	1-4-76	Lemeta, California	5-14
Lincoln, Michael George	P	Minnesota	4-10-75	Carmichael, California	4-7
Liniak, Cole Edward	3B	Chicago N.L.	8-23-76	Encinitas, California	9-3
Lomasney, Steven James	C	Boston	8-29-77	Melrose, Massachusetts	10-3
Long, Terrence Deon	PH	New York N.L.	2-29-76	Montgomery, Alabama	4-14
Lundquist, David	P	Chicago A.L.	6-4-73	Beverly, Massachusetts	4-6
Macias, Jose Prade	2B	Detroit	1-25-74	Panama City, Panama	5-12
Marte, Damaso Sabinon	P	Seattle	2-14-75	Santo Domingo, Dominican Rep.	6-30
Masaoka, Onan Kainoa	P	Los Angeles	10-27-77	Hilo, Hawaii	4-5
Mateo, Ruben Amaurys	CF	Texas	2-10-78	San Cristobal, Dominican Rep.	6-12
Matos, Pascual Cuevas	PH	Atlanta	12-23-74	Barahona, Dominican Rep.	5-11
Matthews Jr., Gary Nathaniel	RF	San Diego	8-25-74	San Francisco, California	6-4

Player	Pos.	Team	Birth date	Birthplace	Debut
Mays, Joseph E.	P	Minnesota	12-10-75	Flint, Michigan	4-7
McDonald, John Joseph	PH	Cleveland	9-24-74	New London, Connecticut	7-4
McGlinchy, Kevin Michael	P	Atlanta	6-28-77	Malden, Massachusetts	4-5
McNichol, Brian	P	Chicago N.L.	5-20-74	Fairfax, Virginia	9-7
Meche, Gil	P	Seattle	9-8-78	Lafayette, Louisiana	7-6
Menechino, Frank	SS	Oakland	1-7-71	Staten Island, New York	9-6
Meyers, Chad	CF	Chicago N.L.	8-8-75	Omaha, Nebraska	8-6
Miller, Wade	P	Houston	9-13-76	Reading, Pennsylvania	7-7
Molina, Cruz Gabriel	P	Baltimore	5-3-75	Denver, Colorado	5-1
Molina, Jose Benjamin	C	Chicago N.L.	6-3-75	Bayamon, Puerto Rico	9-6
Mora, Melvin	SS	New York N.L.	2-2-72	Agua Negar, Venezuela	5-30
Moreno, Orber Aguiles	P	Kansas City	4-27-77	Caracas, Venezuela	5-25
Morris, Warren	2B	Pittsburgh	1-11-74	Alexandria, Louisiana	4-5
Morris, Jim	P	Tampa Bay	1-19-64	Brownwood, Texas	9-18
Mota, Guillermo	P	Montreal	7-25-73	San Pedro de Macoris, Dom. Rep.	5-2
Munro, Peter Daniel	P	Toronto	6-14-75	Flushing, New York	4-6
Murray, Calvin Duane	PH	San Francisco	7-30-71	Dallas, Texas	6-22
Murray, Dan	P	New York N.L.	11-21-73	Los Alamitos, California	8-9
Myette, Aaron K.	P	Chicago A.L.	9-26-77	New Westminster, Canada	9-7
Nathan, Joseph Michael	P	San Francisco	11-22-74	Houston, Texas	4-21
Newhan, David Matthew	PR	San Diego	9-7-73	Fullerton, California	6-4
Newman, Alan Spencer	P	Tampa Bay	10-2-69	La Habra, California	5-14
Ohka, Tomokazu	P	Boston	3-18-76	Kyoto, Japan	7-19
Ortiz, Ramon	P	Anaheim	5-23-76	Las Matas Cotui, Dominican Rep.	8-19
Padilla, Vicente D.	P	Arizona	9-27-77	Chinandega, Nicaragua	6-29
Paul, Josh	C	Chicago A.L.	5-19-75	Evanston, Illinois	9-7
Pena, Juan Francisco	P	Boston	6-27-77	Santo Domingo, Dominican Rep.	5-8
Pena, Jesus	P	Chicago A.L.	3-8-75	Santo Domingo, Dominican Rep.	8-7
Perkins, Daniel Lee	P	Minnesota	3-15-75	Miami, Florida	4-7
Petersen, Christopher Ron	SS	Colorado	11-6-70	Boston, Massachusetts	5-25
Peterson, Kyle J.	P	Milwaukee	4-9-76	Elkhorn, Nebraska	7-19
Petrick, Benjamin Wayne	C	Colorado	4-7-77	Salem, Oregon	9-1
Phillips, Jason Charles	P	Pittsburgh	3-22-74	Williamsport, Pennsylvania	4-5
Porter, Marquis D.	PH	Chicago N.L.	7-5-72	Newark, New Jersey	5-9
Porzio, Lawrence Michael	P	Colorado	8-20-72	Waterbury, Connecticut	7-9
Pote, Lou	P	Anaheim	8-27-71	Evergreen Park, Illinois	8-11
Quinn, Mark David	DH	Kansas City	5-21-74	La Miranda, California	9-14
Radlosky, Rob	P	Minnesota	1-7-74	West Palm Beach, Florida	5-25
Rain, Steve Nicholas	P	Chicago N.L.	6-2-75	Los Angeles, California	7-17
Ramirez, Julio Caesar	PR	Florida	8-10-77	San Juan de la Maguana, Dom. Rep.	9-10
Ramirez, Hector	P	Milwaukee	12-15-71	El Seybo, Dominican Rep.	8-28
Ramsay, Robert Arthur	P	Seattle	12-3-73	Vancouver, Washington	8-27
Ray, Ken	P	Kansas City	11-27-74	Atlanta, Georgia	7-10
Redman, Mark	P	Minnesota	1-5-74	San Diego, California	7-24
Reichert, Dan	P	Kansas City	7-12-76	Monterey, California	7-16
Riley, Matt	P	Baltimore	8-2-79	Antioch, California	9-9
Riske, David	P	Cleveland	10-23-76	Renton, Washington	8-14
Roberts, David Ray	CF	Cleveland	5-31-72	Okinawa, Japan	8-7
Roberts, Willis	P	Detroit	6-19-75	San Cristobal, Dominican Rep.	7-2
Rodriguez, Liubiemithz	SS	Chicago A.L.	11-5-76	Caracas, Venezuela	6-9
Romano, Michael	P	Toronto	3-3-72	Largo, Illinois	9-5
Romero, Juan C.	P	Minnesota	6-4-76	Rio Piedras, Puerto Rico	9-15
Rupe, Ryan Kittman	P	Tampa Bay	3-31-75	Houston, Texas	5-5
Ryan, Jason Paul	P	Minnesota	1-23-76	Long Branch, New Jersey	8-24
Ryan, Robert James	PH	Arizona	6-24-73	Havre, Montana	8-20
Ryan, Robert Victor	P	Cincinnati	12-28-75	Bossier City, Louisiana	7-28
Sabel, Erik Douglas	P	Arizona	10-14-74	West Lafayette, Indiana	7-9
Sanders, Anthony Marcus	DH	Toronto	3-2-74	Tucson, Arizona	4-26
Sauerbeck, Scott	P	Pittsburgh	11-9-71	Cincinnati, Ohio	4-5
Scheffer, Aaron	P	Seattle	10-15-75	Ypsilanti, Michigan	6-13
Schoeneweis, Scott David	P	Anaheim	10-2-73	Long Branch, New Jersey	4-7
Schrenk, Steven Wayne	P	Philadelphia	11-20-68	Great Lakes, Illinois	7-3
Sexton, Christopher Phi	LF	Colorado	8-3-71	Cincinnati, Ohio	5-3
Shumaker, Anthony Warren	P	Philadelphia	5-14-73	Tucson, Arizona	7-23
Singleton, Christopher Verdell	PH	Chicago A.L.	8-15-72	Martinez, California	4-10
Smart, Jon David	P	Montreal	11-12-73	San Saba, Texas	4-6
Smith, Daniel Charles	P	Montreal	9-15-75	Flemington, New Jersey	6-8
Soriano, Alfonso	PR	New York A.L.	1-7-78	San Pedro de Macoris, Dom. Rep.	9-14
Sosa, Juan Luis	PH	Colorado	8-19-75	San Francisco de Macoris, Dom. Rep.	9-10
Sparks, Jeff	P	Tampa Bay	4-4-72	Houston, Texas	9-12
Spencer, Sean James	P	Seattle	5-29-75	Seattle, Washington	5-6
Stark, Dennis	P	Seattle	10-27-74	Hicksville, Ohio	9-15
Stowers, Chris	PH	Montreal	8-18-74	St. Louis, Missouri	7-10
Strickland, Scott	P	Montreal	4-26-76	Houston, Texas	8-14

Player	Pos.	Team	Birth date	Birthplace	Debut
Tejera, Michael	P	Florida	10-18-76	Havana, Cuba	9-8
Toca, Jorge Luis	PH	New York N.L.	1-7-75	Villaclara, Cuba	9-12
Venafro, Michael Robert	P	Texas	8-2-73	Takoma Park, Maryland	4-24
Veras, Wilton Andres	3B	Boston	1-19-78	Monte Cristy, Dominican Rep.	7-1
Vizcaino, Luis	P	Oakland	6-1-77	Bani, Dominican Rep.	7-23
Weaver, Jeffrey Charles	P	Detroit	8-22-76	Northridge, California	4-14
Wells, Robert Kip	P	Chicago A.L.	4-21-77	Houston, Texas	8-2
Wells, Vernon	CF	Toronto	12-8-78	Shreveport, Louisiana	8-30
Wheeler, Dan	P	Tampa Bay	12-10-77	Providence, Rhode Island	9-1
Williams, Jeffrey	P	Los Angeles	6-6-72	Canberra, Australia	9-12
Williamson, Scott Ryan	P	Cincinnati	2-17-76	Ft. Polk, Louisiana	4-5
Wilson, Vance A.	C	New York N.L.	3-17-73	Mesa, Arizona	4-24
Winkelsas, Joseph	P	Atlanta	9-14-73	Buffalo, New York	4-10
Wolf, Randall C.	P	Philadelphia	8-22-76	Canoga Park, California	6-11
Woodward, Chris	SS	Toronto	6-27-76	Covina, California	6-7
Yarnall, Ed	P	New York A.L.	12-4-75	Lima, Pennsylvania	7-15
Zimmerman, Jeffrey Ross	P	Texas	8-9-72	Kelowna, Canada	4-13
Zimmerman, Jordan William	P	Seattle	4-28-75	Kelowna, Canada	5-17

SALARY ARBITRATION RESULTS

WINNERS

Player, Team	Salary awarded	Team's offer
Derek Jeter, New York A.L.	$5,000,000	$3,200,000
Mariano Rivera, New York A.L.	$4,250,000	$3,000,000

LOSERS

Player, Team	Salary awarded	Player's request
Charles Johnson, Baltimore	$3,600,000	$5,100,000
Darren Oliver, St. Louis	$3,550,000	$4,150,000
Johnny Damon, Kansas City	$2,100,000	$3,200,000
Mark Grudzielanek, Los Angeles	$1,900,000	$2,600,000
Brian Hunter, Detroit	$1,750,000	$2,750,000
Matt Lawton, Minnesota	$1,600,000	$2,400,000
Shane Andrews, Montreal	$1,250,000	$2,300,000
John Hudek, Cincinnati	$800,000	$1,300,000
Midre Cummings, Boston	$450,000	$725,000

1999 FREE-AGENT FILINGS

AMERICAN LEAGUE

Anaheim: Chuck Finley, Jeff Huson, Mike Magnante.
Baltimore: Jeff Conine, Jim Corsi, Mike Fetters, Scott Kamieniecki, Arthur Rhodes.
Boston: Reggie Jefferson, Kent Mercker, Pat Rapp.
Chicago: Darrin Jackson.
Cleveland: Paul Assenmacher, Carlos Baerga, Harold Baines, Wil Cordero, Dwight Gooden, Chris Haney, Mike Jackson, Mark Langston.
Detroit: Luis Polonia.
Kansas City: Chad Krueter, Scott Leius, Jeff Montgomery, Hipolito Pichardo, Rey Sanchez, Tim Spehr.
Minnesota: Terry Steinbach, Mike Trombley.
New York: David Cone, Joe Girardi, Luis Sojo, Mike Stanton, Allen Watson.
Oakland: Buddy Groom, Mike Macfarlane, Greg McMichael, Omar Olivares, Tony Phillips, Tim Raines, Tim Worrell.
Seattle: Mike Blowers, Jay Buhner, Butch Henry, Mark Leiter.
Tampa Bay: Norm Charlton, Paul Sorrento, Bobby Witt.
Texas: Luis Alicea, John Burkett, Jeff Fassero, Tom Goodwin, Roberto Kelly, Mark McLemore, Mike Morgan, Mike Munoz, Aaron Sele, Todd Zeile.
Toronto: Pat Borders, Tony Fernandez, Graeme Lloyd, Brian McRae, Bill Risley, David Segui.

NATIONAL LEAGUE

Arizona: Andy Benes, Gregg Olson, Turner Ward.
Atlanta: Jose Hernandez, Brian R. Hunter, Greg Myers, Otis Nixon, Rudy Seanez, Russ Springer, Gerald Williams.
Chicago: Bobby Ayala, Jeff Glauser, Mickey Morandini, Benito Santiago, Steve Trachsel.
Cincinnati: Steve Avery, Juan Guzman, Mark Lewis, Greg Vaughn, Mark Wohlers.
Colorado: Kurt Abbott, Kirt Manwaring, Kevin Ritz, Terry Shumpert.
Florida: None
Houston: Tony Eusebio, Ricky Gutierrez, Doug Henry, Jack Howell, Stan Javier, Brian Williams.
Los Angeles: None.
Milwaukee: Jason Bere, David Nilsson, Eric Plunk, David Weathers.
Montreal: None.
New York: Shawon Dunston, Orel Hershiser, John Olerud, Kenny Rogers.
Philadelphia: Jeff Brantley.
Pittsburgh: Joe Oliver, Ed Sprague, Doug Strange, Dale Sveum.
St. Louis: David Howard, Thomas Howard, Willie McGee, Darren Oliver, Donovan Osborne, Heathcliff Slocumb.
San Diego: None.
San Francisco: Charlie Hayes, Brent Mayne, Rich Rodriguez, Scott Servais.

(Listed in order of selection)

Player	Pos.	Drafted by	Drafted from (major league organization)
Jared Camp	P	Minnesota	Buffalo, International League (Indians)
Johan Santana	P	Florida	New Orleans, Pacific Coast League (Astros)
Damian Rolls	3B	Kansas City	Albuquerque, Pacific Coast League (Dodgers)
Chad Ogea	P	Tampa Bay	Toledo, International League (Tigers)
Marty McLeary	P	Montreal	Pawtucket, International League (Red Sox)
Mark Johnson	P	Detroit	Columbus, International League (Yankees)
Thomas Turnbow	P	Anaheim	Scranton/Wilkes-Barre, International League (Phillies)
Korwin Dehaan	OF	San Diego	Nashville, Pacific Coast League (Pirates)
Matt Williams	P	Milwaukee	Columbus, International League (Yankees)
Chad Alexander	OF	Seattle	New Orleans, Pacific Coast League (Astros)
Dwayne Wise	P	Toronto	Indianapolis, International League (Reds)
Bo Porter	OF	Oakland	Iowa, Pacific Coast League (Cubs)
Randall Smith	P	Pittsburgh	Syracuse, International League (Blue Jays)
David Maurer	P	San Francisco	Las Vegas, Pacific Coast League (Padres)
Adrian Burnside	P	Cincinnati	Albuquerque, Pacific Coast League (Dodgers)
Jim Mann	P	New York N.L.	Syracuse, International League (Blue Jays)
Chris Reitsma	P	Tampa Bay	Pawtucket, International League (Red Sox)

NECROLOGY

Joe Adcock, 71, at Coushatta, La., on May 3. A key member of standout Milwaukee Braves teams, he hit a record-tying four home runs in one game in 1954 and finished his 17-year major league career with 336 homers. When Pittsburgh's Harvey Haddix pitched 12 perfect innings against the Braves in 1959, it was first baseman Adcock who won the game in the 13th with Milwaukee's only hit. Adcock managed the Indians in 1967.

Gene Baker, 74, at Davenport, Iowa, on December 1. Second baseman Baker, a reserve for the 1960 World Series champion Pirates, hit .265 in eight seasons in the majors. He was the second black player in Cubs history, making his debut with the club in 1953— three days after Ernie Banks broke in. He and Banks were a double-play combination for the Cubs for three seasons.

Dick Bertell, 64, at Mission Viejo, Calif., on December 20. Bertell, a big-league catcher for seven seasons, played 422 of his 444 games with the Cubs and batted .250. In 77 games with Chicago in 1962, he hit .302.

Clay Bryant, 87, at Boca Raton, Fla., on April 9. Righthander Bryant compiled a 9-3 record for the 1937 Cubs and was a 19-game winner in 1938 for Chicago's N.L. championship club. He was the Cubs' starter and loser in Game 3 of the '38 World Series against the Yankees.

Paul Calvert, 81, at Sherbrooke, Quebec, on February 1. Primarily a reliever, he was thrust into a starting role for a 1949 Senators team that lost 104 games. Calvert was 5-15 as a starter that year and 6-17 overall.

Joe DiMaggio, 84, at Hollywood, Fla., on March 8. Hall of Famer DiMaggio, whose grace on and off the field helped make him an American icon, established one of baseball's most notable records in 1941 when he hit safely in 56 consecutive games. The Yankee Clipper had a career .325 batting average and hit 361 home runs. A three-time MVP, the center fielder extraordinaire played on nine World Series championship teams for the Yankees in his 13 seasons in the majors.

Len Dondero, 95, at Fremont, Calif., on January 1. Infielder Dondero appeared in 19 games for the 1929 St. Louis Browns.

Dutch Dotterer, 67, at Syracuse, N.Y., on October 9. Dotterer saw duty as a reserve catcher for the Reds from 1957 through 1960 and played briefly for the Senators in 1961.

Jimmy Dudley, 89, at Tucson, Ariz., on February 12. Inducted into the broadcasters' wing of the Hall of Fame in 1997, he broadcast Indians games for two decades beginning in 1948 and also did Seattle Pilots games in that franchise's only season (1969).

James (Red) Dunn, 67, at Gadsden, Ala., on January 6. Dunn made three relief appearances for the 1952 Pirates.

Jim Dyck, 76, at Cheney, Wash., on January 11. A six-year major leaguer, outfielder/third baseman Dyck had his best season in 1952 when he hit 15 home runs and drove in 64 runs for the St. Louis Browns.

Arnold Earley, 66, at Flint, Mich., on September 29. Lefthander Earley pitched in 223 big-league games, 208 of them for the Red Sox. A reliever, he appeared in 53 games for Boston in 1963 and 57 games for the A.L. club in 1965.

John "Red" Flaherty, 81, at Falmouth, Mass., on April 1. Flaherty was an American League umpire from 1953 through 1973.

Dee Fondy, 74, at Redlands, Calif., on August 19. A .286 hitter over eight big-league seasons, first baseman Fondy had his best season in 1953 when he batted .309 and hit 18 home runs for the Cubs.

Bob Garber, 70, at Redwood, Calif., on June 7. Garber pitched in two games for the 1956 Pirates.

Greek George, 86, at Metairie, La., on August 15. George was Bob Feller's batterymate on August 23, 1936, when the Indians' Feller, 17, struck out 15 St. Louis Browns in his first major league start. George played in 118 games over five big-league seasons.

Oscar Georgy, 82, at New Orleans on January 15. At age 21, Georgy pitched one inning for the 1938 Giants—and never again appeared in the majors.

George Gill, 90, at Jackson, Miss., on February 21. Gill spent three years in the majors, compiling 11-4 and 12-9 records for the Tigers in 1937 and 1938 before plummeting to a 1-13 mark for Detroit and the St. Louis Browns in 1939.

Paul Gregory, 91, at Southaven, Miss., on September 16. Pitching for the White Sox in 1932 and 1933, righthander Gregory went 9-14 overall.

Calvin Griffith, 87, at Melbourne, Fla., on October 20. Griffith's family owned the Washington Senators/Minnesota Twins franchise for more than six decades. Griffith moved the Senators to Minnesota after the 1960 season and retained ownership of the team for a quarter-century.

Howie Haak, 87, at Palm Springs, Calif., on February 22. A protege of Branch Rickey, Haak was a pioneer of scouting in Latin America and signed scores of players for the Pirates.

Doug Hansen, 70, at Orem, Utah, on September 16. Infielder Hansen made three pinch-running appearances for the 1951 Indians and scored two runs.

Wally Hebert, 92, at Westlake, La., on December 8. After a 10-year absence from the majors, Hebert won 10 games and had a 2.98 ERA for the Pirates in 1943. The lefthander once suffered through a 1-12 season (with the Browns, in 1932).

Randy Heflin, 80, at Fredericksburg, Va., on August 17. Heflin pitched for the Red Sox in 1945 and 1946, compiling a 4-11 record overall. He had two shutouts in '45.

Clarence Heise, 91, at Winter Park, Fla., on May 30. Heise pitched in one game for the Gas House Gang Cardinals of 1934.

Jerry Hoffberger, 80, at Baltimore on April 9. Hoffberger was owner of the Orioles from 1965 through 1979, a time frame in which the club won five pennants and two World Series.

Earl Huckleberry, 88, at Seminole, Okla., on February 25. Huckleberry pitched in one big-league game—for the 1935 Athletics—and won it despite allowing seven runs in 6.2 innings. The A's defeated the White Sox, 19-7.

Jim "Catfish" Hunter, 53, at Hertford, N.C., on September 9. Hall of Famer Hunter won more than 20 games in five consecutive seasons, pitched in six World Series and finished his 15-year career with the A's and Yankees with 224 victories. He pitched a perfect game for the A's in 1968 and won the Cy Young Award with Oakland in 1974. After the '74 season, in which he won 25 games, Hunter claimed the A's had breached his contract and gained free-agent status. Center stage in baseball's first free-agent bidding war, Hunter signed with the Yankees. In his first season with New York, he won 23 games and pitched 30 complete games.

Warren Huston, 85, at Wareham, Mass., on August 30. Infielder Huston played 38 games for the 1937 Athletics and 33 games for the 1944 Braves.

Ike Kahdot, 97, at Oklahoma City on March 31. The infielder appeared in four games for the 1922 Indians.

Ray Katt, 72, at New Braunfels, Texas, on October 19. Katt, the No. 2 catcher for the 1954 World Series champion New York Giants, had two stints with the Giants and two with the Cardinals during eight years in the majors.

Eddie Kazak, 79, at Austin, Texas, on December 15. Kazak played 185 of his 218 big-league games for the Cardinals in 1949 and 1950. As a rookie in '49, he batted .304 in 92 games and went 2-for-2 as the N.L.'s starting third baseman in the All-Star Game.

Henry Kimbro, 87, at Nashville, Tenn., on July 11. Kimbro was regarded as one of the best outfielders in Negro leagues history.

Whitey Kurowski, 81, at Sinking Spring, Pa., on December 9. A fixture at third base for the Cardinals for much of the 1940s, Kurowski hit a ninth-inning home run in Game 5 of the 1942 World Series against the Yankees that clinched the championship for St. Louis. Overcoming a longtime arm injury, Kurowski played nine seasons and batted .286. He twice drove in more than 100 runs, and he hit 27 homers in 1947.

Tim Layana, 35, in an auto accident at Bakersfield, Calif., on June 26. Layana made 78 relief appearances over three big-league seasons—55 for a 1990 Reds team that won the World Series.

Bill Lohrman, 86, at Poughkeepsie, N.Y., on September 13. Righthander Lohrman went 60-59 in nine major league seasons. Pitching for the Giants in 1940, he shared the N.L. lead in shutouts with five. After starting the 1942 season with the Cardinals, he returned to the Giants in May and finished the season with a 14-5 record overall and a 2.48 ERA.

Doc Marshall, 93, at Lake San Marcos, Calif., on September 1. A reserve infielder, Marshall played in 219 games for the Giants from 1929 through 1932.

Pat McLaughlin, 89, at Houston on November 1. He pitched in 12 major leagues games—10 of them for the 1937 Tigers.

Vinegar Bend Mizell, 68, at Kerrville, Texas, on February 21. Lefthander Mizell was a double-figure winner six times in his nine years in the majors. A Cardinals pitcher for six-plus seasons, he was traded to Pittsburgh in late May of 1960 and went 13-5 for a Pirates team that went on to win the World Series. Mizell started Game 3 of the '60 Series against the Yankees and was knocked out in the first inning.

Pat Mullin, 81, at Brownsville, Pa., on August 14. Outfielder Mullin played all 10 of his major league seasons with the Tigers. In 1948, he batted .288 with 23 home runs.

Max Patkin, 79, at Paoli, Pa., on October 30. Patkin, dressed in a baggy uniform with a question mark on the back, entertained baseball fans for nearly half a century with his comedy routines and contortions before and during games.

Bob Patrick, 81, at Fort Smith, Ark., on October 6. Outfielder Patrick appeared in a total of nine games for the Tigers in 1941 and 1942.

Bill Peterman, 77, at Philadelphia on March 13. Peterman, a catcher, singled in his only major league at-bat, which came with the Phillies in 1942.

Boots Poffenberger, 84, at Williamsport, Md., on September 1. Righthander Poffenberger went 10-5 for the 1937 Tigers and was 16-12 overall in three seasons in the majors.

Dave Pope, 74, at Cleveland on August 28. Outfielder Pope played a total of 230 games for the Indians and Orioles over four seasons, hitting .265 with 12 home runs. He appeared in three games for Cleveland in the 1954 World Series.

Carl Powis, 71, at Houston on May 10. Outfielder Powis played 15 games for the 1957 Orioles. He had only two RBIs as a major leaguer, but one (on a sacrifice fly) was an opening-day game-winner at Washington.

Pee Wee Reese, 81, at Louisville, Ky., on August 14. Reese, a Hall of Fame shortstop, was the leader of Brooklyn teams that won seven pennants and one World Series in a 16-year stretch. He batted .269 in 2,166 big-league games, collected 2,170 hits and stole 232 bases. Reese is the only man to play in all 44 of the Subway Series games between the Dodgers and Yankees (those New York clubs having met in the World Series in 1941, 1947, 1949, 1952, 1953, 1955, 1956).

Cal Ripken Sr., 63, at Baltimore on March 26. Ripken was a long-time Orioles coach who also served as the team's manager for one entire season, 1987. Father of major leaguers Cal Jr. and Billy, he was a hands-on instructor credited with teaching the "Oriole way" beginning in his days as a manager in Baltimore's farm system.

Ken Robinson, 29, in an automobile accident at Tucson, Ariz., on February 28. A pitcher in the Diamondbacks' organization at the time of his death, Robinson appeared in a total of 29 games for the Blue Jays and Royals from 1995 through 1997.

Buck Rogers, 86, at Winston-Salem, N.C., on February 20. Lefthander Rogers made two appearances for the 1935 Senators.

Cliff Ross, 70, at Philadelphia on April 13. Lefthander Ross made four relief appearances for the 1954 Reds.

Joe Rossi, 75, at Oakland on February 20. Rossi, a catcher, batted .221 in 55 games with the 1952 Reds.

Fred Saigh, 94, at Chesterfield, Mo., on December 29. Saigh was owner of the Cardinals when, in 1953, he sold the club to Anheuser-Busch Inc., headed by August A. Busch Jr. Saigh, who had owned the club since 1948, reportedly received higher offers from out-of-town interests, but he sold the franchise to Busch to ensure that the team would remain in St. Louis.

A. Ray Smith, 84, at Tulsa, Okla., on June 28. Smith was owner of the Louisville franchise when, in 1983, the American Association club became the first minor league team to draw one million fans in a season.

Bernie Snyder, 85, at Havertown, Pa., on April 15. Infielder Snyder went 11-for-32 (.344) at the plate in a 10-game stint with the 1935 Athletics.

Eddie Stanky, 82, at Fairhope, Ala., on June 6. An 11-year major league player, the scrappy Stanky was the second baseman on three pennant-winning teams—the 1947 Dodgers, 1948 Braves and 1951 Giants. He managed the Cardinals for three-plus seasons in the 1950s, the White Sox for 2.5 seasons in the '60s and the Rangers for one game in 1977 as a midseason replacement before deciding, at age 60, that he really didn't want to resume the big-league managerial grind.

Carl Sumner, 90, at Chatham, Mass., on February 8. Outfielder Sumner batted .276 in 16 games for the 1928 Red Sox.

Ben Taylor, 71, at Alma, Okla., on May 11. First baseman Taylor played a total of 52 games for the 1951 Browns, 1952 Tigers and 1955 Braves.

Paul Toth, 63, at Anaheim on March 20. Righthander Toth, who began his three-year major league career with the Cardinals and was traded back to St. Louis in 1964 as part of the Cubs' Lou Brock-for-Ernie Broglio deal, was 9-12 in the majors.

Birdie Tebbetts, 86, at Bradenton, Fla., on March 24. Tebbetts, a big-league catcher for 14 seasons, managed in the majors for 11 years. His 1956 Reds finished 91-63 and only two games out of first place in the N.L. Tebbetts later was acknowledged as one of game's top scouts.

Earl Turner, 76, at Lee, Mass., on October 20. Catcher Turner appeared in 40 games for the Pirates in 1950 and played briefly for the club two years earlier.

Harry "The Hat" Walker, 82, at Birmingham, Ala., on August 8. Walker hit .296 over 11 big-league seasons. He batted .412 for the Cardinals in the 1946 World Series, delivering the Series-winning hit (a double) on which Enos Slaughter scored from first base on his "Mad Dash." Traded to the Phillies in May 1947, outfielder Walker won the N.L. batting title that year with a .363 average. A manager in the majors for nine years, he guided the Pirates to 90- and 92-victory seasons in 1965 and 1966.

Johnnie Wittig, 84, at Nassawadox, Va., on February 24. Wittig appeared in 40 games for the 1943 Giants and went 5-15. His five-season record in the majors was 10-25.

William Wrigley, 66, at Chicago on March 8. Following his grandfather and father as owner of the Cubs, he sold the club to the Tribune Co. in 1981.

Whitlow Wyatt, 91, at Buchanan, Ga., on July 16. A 26-43 pitcher in his first nine big-league seasons, all in the A.L., Wyatt evolved into a standout pitcher after joining the Dodgers in 1939. He reeled off 8-3, 15-14, 22-10, 19-7 and 14-5 records in his first five years with Brooklyn. In his 22-victory season of 1941, he threw seven shutouts and posted an ERA of 2.34. He accounted for the Dodgers' only win in the '41 World Series with a complete-game triumph against the Yankees in Game 2.

Early Wynn, 79, at Venice, Fla., on April 4. A fierce competitor, Hall of Famer Wynn compiled a 300-244 record in 23 big-league seasons. He was a 20-game winner five times, all of the milestone seasons coming in a nine-year stretch. Although most of his banner seasons were with the Indians (he helped Cleveland reach the 1954 World Series), he had a Cy Young Award-winning year with the A.L. champion White Sox in 1959.

Norm Zauchin, 69, at Birmingham, Ala., on January 31. After a five-game stint with the Red Sox in 1951, first baseman Zauchin returned to the club in 1955 and, despite batting only .239, hit 27 home runs with 93 RBIs. He had a memorable night against the Senators on May 27, 1955, hitting three home runs and a double and driving in 10 runs. Zauchin had only 23 homers in the next four seasons, though, and was out of the majors at age 29.

1999 A.L. STATISTICS

Batting

Designated hitting

Pinch-hitting

Pitching

Fielding

Miscellaneous

BATTING

TEAM

Team	Avg.	G	TPA	AB	R	H	TB	2B	3B	HR	RBI	SH	SF	HP	BB	IBB	SO	SB	CS	GDP	LOB	ShO	Slg.	OBP
Texas	.293	162	6388	5651	945	1653	2705	304	29	230	897	35	62	29	611	41	937	111	54	147	1176	7	.479	.361
Cleveland	.289	162	6553	5634	1009	1629	2629	309	32	209	960	54	67	55	743	41	1099	147	50	136	1234	3	.467	.373
Kansas City	.282	161	6325	5624	856	1584	2435	294	52	151	800	46	56	64	535	25	932	127	39	156	1165	4	.433	.348
New York	.282	162	6416	5568	900	1568	2521	302	36	193	855	22	53	55	718	47	978	104	57	137	1244	6	.453	.366
Toronto	.280	162	6369	5642	883	1580	2581	337	14	212	856	28	45	76	578	29	1077	119	48	129	1177	8	.457	.352
Baltimore	.279	162	6409	5637	851	1572	2522	299	21	203	804	41	55	61	615	34	890	107	46	146	1241	8	.447	.353
Boston	.278	162	6321	5579	836	1551	2497	334	42	176	808	34	56	55	597	27	928	67	39	131	1213	5	.448	.350
Chicago	.277	162	6262	5644	777	1563	2421	298	37	162	742	40	45	34	499	22	810	110	50	138	1157	7	.429	.337
Tampa Bay	.274	162	6272	5586	772	1531	2296	272	29	145	728	30	48	64	544	24	1042	73	49	157	1169	7	.411	.343
Seattle	.269	162	6310	5572	859	1499	2536	263	21	244	825	38	48	42	610	38	1095	130	45	114	1147	9	.455	.343
Minnesota	.264	161	6124	5495	686	1450	2110	285	30	105	643	24	56	49	500	28	978	118	60	151	1118	10	.384	.328
Detroit	.261	162	6095	5481	747	1433	2426	289	34	212	704	35	39	82	458	16	1049	108	70	108	1061	12	.443	.326
Oakland	.259	162	6440	5519	893	1430	2462	287	20	235	845	39	41	71	770	32	1129	70	37	129	1246	4	.446	.355
Anaheim	.256	162	6131	5494	711	1404	2170	248	22	158	673	41	42	43	511	24	1022	71	45	135	1097	11	.395	.322
Totals	.275	1133	88415	78126	11725	21447	34311	4121	419	2635	11140	507	713	780	8289	431	13966	1462	689	1914	16445	101	.439	.347

INDIVIDUAL

TOP QUALIFIERS FOR BATTING CHAMPIONSHIP

Minimum 502 plate appearances. *Lefthanded batter. †Switch-hitter.

Player, Team	Avg.	G	TPA	AB	R	H	TB	2B	3B	HR	RBI	SH	SF	HP	BB	IBB	SO	SB	CS	GDP	Slg.	OBP
Garciaparra, Nomar, Bos.	.357	135	595	532	103	190	321	42	4	27	104	0	4	8	51	7	39	14	3	11	.603	.418
Jeter, Derek, N.Y.	.349	158	739	627	134	219	346	37	9	24	102	3	6	12	91	5	116	19	8	12	.552	.438
Williams, Bernie, N.Y.†	.342	158	697	591	116	202	317	28	6	25	115	0	5	1	100	17	95	9	10	11	.536	.435
Martinez, Edgar, Sea.	.337	142	608	502	86	169	278	35	1	24	86	0	3	6	97	6	99	7	2	12	.554	.447
Ramirez, Manny, Cle.	.333	147	640	522	131	174	346	34	3	44	165	0	9	13	96	9	131	2	4	12	.663	.442
Vizquel, Omar, Cle.†	.333	144	664	574	112	191	250	36	4	5	66	17	7	1	65	0	50	42	9	8	.436	.397
Rodriguez, Ivan, Tex.	.332	144	630	600	116	199	335	29	1	35	113	0	5	1	24	2	64	25	12	31	.558	.356
Fernandez, Tony, Tor.†	.328	142	576	485	73	159	218	41	0	6	75	0	4	10	77	11	62	6	7	10	.449	.427
Gonzalez, Juan, Tex.	.326	144	629	562	114	183	338	36	1	39	128	0	12	4	51	7	105	3	3	10	.601	.378
Palmeiro, Rafael, Tex.*	.324	158	674	565	96	183	356	30	1	47	148	0	9	3	97	14	69	2	4	13	.630	.420
Alomar, Roberto, Cle.†	.323	159	694	563	138	182	300	40	3	24	120	12	13	7	99	3	96	37	6	13	.533	.422
Sweeney, Mike, K.C.	.322	150	643	575	101	185	299	44	2	22	102	0	4	10	54	0	48	6	1	21	.520	.387
Bush, Homer, Tor.	.320	128	523	485	69	155	204	26	4	5	55	8	3	6	21	0	82	32	8	9	.421	.353
Velarde, Randy, Ana.-Oak.	.317	156	711	631	105	200	287	25	7	16	76	4	0	6	70	2	98	24	8	19	.455	.390
Giambi, Jason, Oak.*	.315	158	695	575	115	181	318	36	1	33	123	0	8	7	105	6	106	1	1	11	.553	.422

DEPARTMENTAL LEADERS: G—Surhoff, Bal., 162; AB—Surhoff, Bal., 673; R—R. Alomar, Cle., 138; H—Jeter, N.Y., 219; TB—Green, Tor., 361; 1B—Velarde, Ana.-Oak., 152; 2B—Green, Tor., 45; 3B—Offerman, Bos., 11; HR—Griffey, Sea., 48; RBI—M. Ramirez, Cle., 165; SH—Vizquel, Cle., 17; SF—Alomar, Cle., 13; HP—Anderson, Bal., 24; BB—Thome, Cle., 127; IBB—Griffey, Sea., 17; SO—Thome, Cle., 171; SB—Hunter, Det.-Sea., 44; CS—Caruso, Chi., Stewart, Tor., 14; GIDP—Rodriguez, Tex., 32; Slg. Pct.—M. Ramirez, Cle., .663; OB Pct.—Martinez, Sea., .447.

ALL PLAYERS

*Lefthanded batter. †Switch-hitter.

Player, Team	Avg.	G	TPA	AB	R	H	TB	2B	3B	HR	RBI	SH	SF	HP	BB	IBB	SO	SB	CS	GDP	Slg.	OBP
Abbott, Jeff, Chi.	.158	17	64	57	5	9	15	0	0	2	6	1	1	0	5	0	12	1	1	4	.263	.222
Alicea, Luis, Tex.†	.201	68	196	164	33	33	52	10	0	3	17	3	1	0	28	0	32	2	1	4	.317	.316
Allen, Chad, Min.	.277	137	523	481	69	133	190	21	3	10	46	1	2	2	37	1	89	14	7	10	.395	.330
Alomar, Roberto, Cle.†	.323	159	694	563	138	182	300	40	3	24	120	12	13	7	99	3	96	37	6	13	.533	.422
Alomar, Sandy, Cle.	.307	37	144	137	19	42	73	13	0	6	25	1	2	0	4	0	23	0	1	1	.533	.322
Alvarez, Gabe, Det.	.208	22	56	53	5	11	20	3	0	2	4	0	0	0	3	0	9	0	0	1	.377	.250
Amaral, Rich, Bal.	.277	91	156	137	21	38	48	8	1	0	11	1	2	1	15	0	20	9	6	1	.350	.348
Anderson, Brady, Bal.*	.282	150	692	564	109	159	269	28	5	24	81	1	7	24	96	7	105	36	7	6	.477	.404
Anderson, Garret, Ana.*	.303	157	660	620	88	188	291	36	2	21	80	0	6	0	34	8	81	3	4	15	.469	.336
Ausmus, Brad, Det.	.275	127	527	458	62	126	190	25	6	9	54	3	1	14	51	0	71	12	9	11	.415	.365
Baerga, Carlos, Cle.†	.228	22	63	57	4	13	16	0	0	1	5	1	1	0	4	1	10	1	1	3	.281	.274
Baines, Harold, Bal.-Cle.*	.312	135	486	430	62	134	229	18	1	25	103	0	2	0	54	3	48	1	2	16	.533	.387
Baldwin, James, Chi.	.500	35	2	2	1	1	3	1	0	1	1	0	0	0	0	0	1	0	0	0	1.500	.500
Bartee, Kimera, Det.	.195	41	89	77	11	15	22	1	3	0	3	3	0	0	9	0	20	3	3	2	.286	.279
Batista, Tony, Tor.	.285	98	409	375	61	107	212	25	1	26	79	3	5	4	22	1	79	2	0	11	.565	.328
Becker, Rich, Oak.*	.264	40	153	125	21	33	39	3	0	1	10	1	0	2	25	0	43	3	2	3	.312	.395
Bell, David, Sea.	.268	157	667	590	92	160	258	31	2	21	78	3	7	2	58	0	90	7	4	7	.432	.331
Belle, Albert, Bal.	.297	161	722	610	108	181	330	36	1	37	117	0	4	7	101	15	82	17	3	19	.541	.400
Bellinger, Clay, N.Y.	.200	32	46	45	12	9	14	2	0	1	2	0	0	1	0	0	10	1	0	1	.311	.217
Beltran, Carlos, K.C.†	.293	156	723	663	112	194	301	27	7	22	108	0	10	4	46	2	123	27	8	17	.454	.337
Berroa, Geronimo, Tor.	.194	22	73	62	11	12	18	3	0	1	6	0	0	2	9	0	15	0	0	5	.290	.315
Blake, Casey, Tor.	.256	14	41	39	6	10	15	2	0	1	1	0	0	0	2	0	7	0	0	1	.385	.293
Blowers, Mike, Sea.	.239	19	50	46	2	11	18	1	0	2	7	0	0	0	4	0	12	0	0	2	.391	.300
Boggs, Wade, T.B.*	.301	90	334	292	40	88	110	14	1	2	29	0	4	0	38	2	23	1	0	14	.377	.377
Bones, Ricky, Bal.	.000	31	0	0	1	0	0	0	0	0	0	0	0	0	0	0	0	0	0	0	.000	.000
Borders, Pat, Cle.-Tor.	.265	12	35	34	3	9	14	0	1	1	6	0	0	0	1	0	5	0	1	0	.412	.286
Bordick, Mike, Bal.	.277	160	708	631	93	175	254	35	7	10	77	8	10	5	54	1	102	14	4	25	.403	.334
Bournigal, Rafael, Sea.	.274	55	108	95	16	26	37	5	0	2	14	4	2	0	7	0	6	0	0	5	.389	.317

Player, Team	Avg.	G	TPA	AB	R	H	TB	2B	3B	HR	RBI	SH	SF	HP	BB	IBB	SO	SB	CS	GDP	Slg.	OBP
Branyan, Russell, Cle.*	.211	11	42	38	4	8	13	2	0	1	6	0	0	1	3	0	19	0	0	0	.342	.286
Brosius, Scott, N.Y.	.247	133	529	473	64	117	196	26	1	17	71	2	9	6	39	2	74	9	3	13	.414	.307
Brown, Dee, K.C.*	.080	12	27	25	1	2	2	0	0	0	0	0	0	0	2	0	7	0	0	0	.080	.148
Brown, Kevin, Tor.	.444	2	9	9	1	4	6	2	0	0	1	0	0	0	0	0	3	0	0	0	.667	.444
Brumfield, Jacob, Tor.	.235	62	195	170	25	40	60	8	3	2	19	3	3	0	19	0	39	1	2	2	.353	.307
Buford, Damon, Bos.	.242	91	324	297	39	72	109	15	2	6	38	1	3	2	21	0	74	9	2	5	.367	.294
Buhner, Jay, Sea.	.222	87	343	266	37	59	112	11	0	14	38	0	3	5	69	0	100	0	0	6	.421	.388
Bush, Homer, Tor.	.320	128	523	485	69	155	204	26	4	5	55	8	3	6	21	0	82	32	8	9	.421	.353
Butler, Rich, T.B.*	.150	7	22	20	2	3	4	1	0	0	0	0	0	0	2	0	4	0	0	0	.200	.227
Butler, Rob, Tor.*	.143	8	8	7	1	1	1	0	0	0	1	0	0	1	0	0	0	0	0	0	.143	.250
Byrdak, Tim, K.C.*	.500	33	2	2	1	1	2	1	0	0	0	0	0	0	0	0	0	0	0	0	1.000	.500
Cabrera, Jolbert, Cle.	.189	30	39	37	6	7	8	1	0	0	0	0	1	1	0	0	8	3	0	1	.216	.231
Cairo, Miguel, T.B.	.295	120	508	465	61	137	171	15	5	3	36	7	5	7	24	0	46	22	7	13	.368	.335
Canseco, Jose, T.B.	.279	113	502	430	75	120	242	18	1	34	95	0	7	7	58	3	135	3	0	14	.563	.369
Caruso, Mike, Chi.*	.250	136	564	529	60	132	157	11	4	2	35	11	1	3	20	0	36	12	14	6	.297	.280
Catalanotto, Frank, Det.*	.276	100	315	286	41	79	131	19	0	11	35	0	5	5	15	1	49	3	4	5	.458	.327
Cedeno, Domingo, Sea.†	.214	21	48	42	4	9	17	2	0	2	8	0	0	1	5	0	9	1	1	1	.405	.313
Chavez, Eric, Oak.*	.247	115	402	356	47	88	152	21	2	13	50	0	0	0	46	4	56	1	1	7	.427	.333
Christensen, McKay, Chi.*	.226	28	60	53	10	12	16	1	0	1	6	1	2	0	4	0	7	2	1	1	.302	.271
Christenson, Ryan, Oak.	.209	106	319	268	41	56	82	12	1	4	24	8	4	1	38	0	58	7	5	6	.306	.305
Clark, Tony, Det.†	.280	143	609	536	74	150	272	29	0	31	99	0	3	6	64	7	133	2	1	14	.507	.361
Clark, Will, Bal.*	.303	77	294	251	40	76	121	15	0	10	29	0	3	2	38	2	42	2	2	5	.482	.395
Clayton, Royce, Tex.	.288	133	520	465	69	134	207	21	5	14	52	9	3	4	39	1	100	8	6	6	.445	.346
Clyburn, Danny, T.B.	.198	28	89	81	8	16	29	4	0	3	5	0	0	1	7	0	21	0	0	5	.358	.270
Coleman, Michael, Bos.	.200	2	6	5	1	1	1	0	0	0	0	0	0	0	0	0	1	0	0	0	.200	.333
Cone, David, N.Y.*	.333	31	3	3	1	1	2	1	0	0	1	0	0	0	0	0	0	0	0	1	.667	.333
Conine, Jeff, Bal.	.291	139	485	444	54	129	201	31	1	13	75	1	7	3	30	0	40	0	3	12	.453	.335
Coomer, Ron, Min.	.263	127	501	467	53	123	198	25	1	16	65	0	3	1	30	1	69	2	1	16	.424	.307
Cordero, Wil, Cle.	.299	54	217	194	35	58	97	15	0	8	32	0	2	6	15	0	37	2	0	7	.500	.364
Cordova, Marty, Min.	.285	124	488	425	62	121	197	28	3	14	70	0	6	9	48	2	96	13	4	22	.464	.365
Cruz, Deivi, Det.	.284	155	553	518	64	147	221	35	0	13	58	14	5	4	12	0	57	1	4	10	.427	.302
Cruz, Jacob, Cle.*	.330	32	96	88	14	29	45	5	1	3	17	1	1	1	5	0	13	0	2	4	.511	.368
Cruz, Jose, Tor.†	.241	106	414	349	63	84	151	19	3	14	45	1	0	0	64	5	91	14	4	6	.433	.358
Cummings, Midre, Min.*	.263	16	42	38	1	10	13	0	0	1	9	0	1	0	3	0	7	2	0	0	.342	.310
Curtis, Chad, N.Y.	.262	96	245	195	37	51	72	6	0	5	24	1	3	3	43	0	35	8	4	6	.369	.398
Dalesandro, Mark, Tor.	.185	16	29	27	3	5	5	0	0	0	1	0	1	1	0	0	2	1	0	1	.185	.207
Damon, Johnny, K.C.*	.307	145	660	583	101	179	278	39	9	14	77	3	4	3	67	5	50	36	6	13	.477	.379
Daubach, Brian, Bos.*	.294	110	420	381	61	112	214	33	3	21	73	0	0	3	36	0	92	0	1	5	.562	.360
DaVanon, Jeff, Ana.†	.200	7	22	20	4	4	9	0	1	1	4	0	0	0	2	0	7	0	1	0	.450	.273
Davidson, Cleatus, Min.†	.136	12	24	22	3	3	3	0	0	0	3	2	0	0	0	0	4	2	0	2	.136	.136
Davis, Chili, N.Y.†	.269	146	554	476	59	128	212	25	1	19	78	0	3	2	73	7	100	4	1	12	.445	.366
Davis, Russ, Sea.	.245	124	478	432	55	106	188	17	1	21	59	7	2	5	32	1	111	3	3	13	.435	.304
Decker, Steve, Ana.	.238	28	79	63	5	15	21	6	0	0	5	1	1	1	13	0	9	0	0	4	.333	.372
Delgado, Carlos, Tor.*	.272	152	681	573	113	156	327	39	0	44	134	0	7	15	86	7	141	1	1	11	.571	.377
Dellaero, Jason, Chi.†	.091	11	35	33	1	3	3	0	0	0	2	1	0	1	0	0	13	0	0	0	.091	.114
DeShields, Delino, Bal.*	.264	96	374	330	46	87	120	11	2	6	34	5	1	1	37	0	52	11	8	5	.364	.339
Diaz, Einar, Cle.	.281	119	427	392	43	110	142	21	1	3	32	6	1	5	23	0	41	11	4	10	.362	.328
DiFelice, Mike, T.B.	.307	51	191	179	21	55	84	11	0	6	27	0	1	3	8	0	23	0	0	1	.469	.346
DiSarcina, Gary, Ana.	.229	81	298	271	32	62	74	7	1	1	29	9	1	2	15	0	32	2	2	8	.273	.273
Dransfeldt, Kelly, Tex.	.189	16	57	53	3	10	14	1	0	1	5	1	0	0	3	0	12	0	0	2	.264	.232
Durham, Ray, Chi.†	.296	153	694	612	109	181	266	30	8	13	60	3	2	4	73	1	105	34	11	9	.435	.373
Durrington, Trent, Ana.	.180	43	136	122	14	22	24	2	0	0	5	0	0	9	0	28	4	3	1	.197	.237
Dye, Jermaine, K.C.	.294	158	673	608	96	179	320	44	0	27	119	0	6	1	58	4	119	2	3	17	.526	.354
Easley, Damion, Det.	.266	151	627	549	83	146	238	30	1	20	65	2	6	19	51	2	124	11	3	15	.434	.346
Edmonds, Jim, Ana.*	.250	55	233	204	34	51	87	17	2	5	23	0	1	0	28	0	45	5	4	3	.426	.339
Encarnacion, Juan, Det.	.255	132	538	509	62	130	229	30	6	19	74	4	2	9	14	1	113	33	12	12	.450	.287
Erstad, Darin, Ana.*	.253	142	638	585	84	148	219	22	5	13	53	2	3	1	47	3	101	13	7	16	.374	.308
Fasano, Sal, K.C.	.233	23	75	60	11	14	31	2	0	5	16	0	1	7	7	0	17	0	1	1	.517	.373
Febles, Carlos, K.C.	.256	123	524	453	71	116	186	22	9	10	53	12	3	9	47	0	91	20	4	16	.411	.336
Fernandez, Tony, Tor.†	.328	142	576	485	73	159	218	41	0	6	75	0	4	10	77	11	62	6	7	10	.449	.427
Fick, Robert, Det.*	.220	15	49	41	6	9	18	0	0	3	10	0	1	0	7	0	6	1	0	1	.439	.327
Figga, Mike, N.Y.-Bal.	.221	43	91	86	12	19	26	4	0	1	5	2	1	0	2	0	27	0	2	1	.302	.236
Flaherty, John, T.B.	.278	117	482	446	53	124	185	19	0	14	71	1	10	6	19	0	64	0	2	14	.415	.313
Fletcher, Darrin, Tor.*	.291	115	448	412	48	120	200	26	0	18	80	0	4	6	26	0	47	0	0	16	.485	.339
Fonville, Chad, Bos.†	.000	3	4	2	1	0	0	0	0	0	0	0	0	0	2	0	1	0	0	0	.000	.500
Fordyce, Brook, Chi.	.297	105	362	333	36	99	153	25	1	9	49	3	2	3	21	0	48	2	0	5	.459	.343
Frye, Jeff, Bos.	.281	41	131	114	14	32	38	3	0	1	12	1	1	1	14	1	11	2	2	2	.333	.362
Fryman, Travis, Cle.	.255	85	350	322	45	82	132	16	2	10	48	0	2	1	25	1	57	2	1	13	.410	.309
Garcia, Jesse, Bal.	.207	17	34	29	6	6	12	0	0	2	3	2	0	0	2	0	3	0	0	1	.414	.258
Garcia, Karim, Det.*	.240	96	309	288	38	69	127	10	3	14	32	0	1	0	20	1	67	2	4	2	.441	.288
Garciaparra, Nomar, Bos.	.357	135	595	532	103	190	321	42	4	27	104	0	4	8	51	7	39	14	3	11	.603	.418
Gates, Brent, Min.†	.255	110	346	306	40	78	104	13	2	3	38	2	3	1	34	1	56	1	3	11	.340	.328
Giambi, Jason, Oak.*	.315	158	695	575	115	181	318	36	1	33	123	0	8	7	105	6	106	1	1	11	.553	.422
Giambi, Jeremy, K.C.*	.285	90	336	288	34	82	106	13	1	3	34	1	4	3	40	5	67	0	0	7	.368	.373
Gipson, Charles, Sea.	.225	55	89	80	16	18	27	5	2	0	9	2	0	1	6	0	13	3	4	2	.338	.287
Girardi, Joe, N.Y.	.239	65	229	209	23	50	74	16	1	2	27	8	2	0	10	0	26	3	1	16	.354	.271
Glaus, Troy, Ana.	.240	154	631	551	85	132	248	29	0	29	79	0	3	6	71	1	143	5	1	9	.450	.331
Gonzalez, Alex, Tor.	.292	38	173	154	22	45	64	13	0	2	12	0	0	3	16	0	23	4	2	4	.416	.370
Gonzalez, Juan, Tex.	.326	144	629	562	114	183	338	36	1	39	128	0	12	4	51	7	105	3	3	10	.601	.378
Gooden, Dwight, Cle.	.500	26	3	2	1	1	4	0	0	1	2	0	0	0	1	0	1	0	0	0	2.000	.667
Goodwin, Tom, Tex.*	.259	109	455	405	63	105	138	12	6	3	33	7	3	0	40	0	61	39	11	7	.341	.324
Graffanino, Tony, T.B.	.315	39	142	130	20	41	64	9	4	2	19	2	0	1	9	0	22	3	2	1	.492	.364

Player, Team	Avg.	G	TPA	AB	R	H	TB	2B	3B	HR	RBI	SH	SF	HP	BB	IBB	SO	SB	CS	GDP	Slg.	OBP
Grebeck, Craig, Tor.	.363	34	134	113	18	41	48	7	0	0	10	3	1	2	15	0	13	0	0	2	.425	.443
Green, Scarborough, Tex.	.308	18	14	13	4	4	4	0	0	0	0	0	0	1	0	0	2	0	1	0	.308	.357
Green, Shawn, Tor.*	.309	153	696	614	134	190	361	45	0	42	123	0	5	11	66	4	117	20	7	13	.588	.384
Greene, Todd, Ana.	.243	97	338	321	36	78	140	20	0	14	42	0	2	3	12	0	63	1	4	8	.436	.275
Greene, Willie, Tor.*	.204	81	248	226	22	46	89	7	0	12	41	0	2	0	20	0	56	0	0	1	.394	.266
Greer, Rusty, Tex.*	.300	147	662	556	107	167	274	41	3	20	101	0	5	5	96	2	67	2	2	17	.493	.405
Grieve, Ben, Oak.*	.265	148	558	486	80	129	234	21	0	28	86	0	1	8	63	2	108	4	0	17	.481	.358
Griffey, Ken, Sea.*	.285	160	706	606	123	173	349	26	3	48	134	0	2	7	91	17	108	24	7	8	.576	.384
Gubanich, Creighton, Bos.	.277	18	52	47	4	13	20	2	1	1	11	0	0	2	3	0	13	0	0	3	.426	.346
Guevara, Giomar, Sea.	.250	10	12	12	2	3	5	2	0	0	2	0	0	0	0	0	2	0	0	0	.417	.250
Guillen, Carlos, Sea.†	.158	5	21	19	2	3	6	0	0	1	3	1	0	0	1	0	6	0	0	1	.316	.200
Guillen, Jose, T.B.	.244	47	186	168	24	41	57	10	0	2	13	0	1	7	10	1	36	0	0	9	.339	.312
Guzman, Cristian, Min.†	.226	131	456	420	47	95	116	12	3	1	26	7	4	3	22	0	90	9	7	5	.276	.267
Hairston, Jerry, Bal.	.269	50	193	175	26	47	73	12	1	4	17	4	0	3	11	0	24	9	4	2	.417	.323
Halama, John, Sea.*	.200	38	6	5	1	1	2	1	0	0	0	0	0	0	1	0	2	0	0	0	.400	.333
Hansen, Jed, K.C.	.203	49	94	79	16	16	26	1	0	3	5	4	1	0	10	0	32	0	1	0	.329	.289
Haselman, Bill, Det.	.273	48	153	143	13	39	59	8	0	4	14	0	0	0	10	1	26	2	0	4	.413	.320
Hatteberg, Scott, Bos.*	.275	30	100	80	12	22	30	5	0	1	11	0	1	1	18	0	14	0	0	2	.375	.410
Hemphill, Bret, Ana.†	.143	12	27	21	3	3	3	0	0	0	2	1	1	0	4	0	4	0	0	1	.143	.269
Hernandez, Orlando, N.Y.	.333	33	3	3	1	1	1	0	0	0	0	0	0	0	0	0	0	0	0	0	.333	.333
Hernandez, Ramon, Oak.	.279	40	158	136	13	38	54	7	0	3	21	1	2	1	18	0	11	1	0	5	.397	.363
Higginson, Bobby, Det.*	.239	107	445	377	51	90	144	18	0	12	46	0	2	2	64	2	66	4	6	2	.382	.351
Hinch, A.J., Oak.	.215	76	228	205	26	44	71	4	1	7	24	9	1	2	11	0	41	6	2	4	.346	.260
Hocking, Denny, Min.†	.267	136	421	386	47	103	146	18	2	7	41	4	6	3	22	1	54	11	7	10	.378	.307
Holbert, Ray, K.C.	.280	34	115	100	14	28	31	3	0	0	5	6	1	0	8	0	20	7	4	4	.310	.330
Hollins, Dave, Tor.†	.222	27	104	99	12	22	33	5	0	2	6	0	0	0	5	0	22	0	0	2	.333	.260
Houston, Tyler, Cle.*	.148	13	30	27	2	4	8	1	0	1	3	0	0	0	3	0	11	0	0	0	.296	.233
Hunter, Brian, Det.-Sea.	.232	139	589	539	79	125	162	13	6	4	34	4	7	2	37	0	91	44	8	8	.301	.280
Hunter, Torii, Min.	.255	135	422	384	52	98	146	17	2	9	35	1	5	6	26	1	72	10	6	9	.380	.309
Huskey, Butch, Sea.-Bos.	.282	119	423	386	62	109	190	15	0	22	77	0	3	0	34	1	65	3	1	9	.492	.338
Huson, Jeff, Ana.*	.262	97	245	225	21	59	68	7	1	0	18	1	3	0	16	0	27	10	1	9	.302	.314
Ibanez, Raul, Sea.*	.258	87	227	209	23	54	88	7	0	9	27	0	1	0	17	1	32	5	1	4	.421	.313
Jackson, Darrin, Chi.	.275	73	155	149	22	41	64	9	1	4	16	2	1	0	3	0	20	4	1	4	.430	.288
Jackson, Ryan, Sea.*	.235	32	77	68	4	16	19	3	0	0	10	0	2	1	6	0	19	3	3	3	.279	.299
Jaha, John, Oak.	.276	142	570	457	93	126	254	23	0	35	111	0	3	9	101	2	129	2	0	14	.556	.414
Jefferies, Gregg, Det.†	.200	70	225	205	22	41	67	8	0	6	18	0	3	4	13	1	11	3	4	9	.327	.258
Jefferson, Reggie, Bos.*	.277	83	225	206	21	57	87	13	1	5	17	0	0	2	17	0	54	0	0	9	.422	.338
Jeter, Derek, N.Y.	.349	158	739	627	134	219	346	37	9	24	102	3	6	12	91	5	116	19	8	12	.552	.438
Jimenez, D'Angelo, N.Y.†	.400	7	23	20	3	8	10	2	0	0	4	0	0	0	3	0	4	0	0	0	.500	.478
Johnson, Charles, Bal.	.251	135	492	426	58	107	176	19	1	16	54	4	3	4	55	2	107	0	0	13	.413	.340
Johnson, Mark, Chi.*	.227	73	248	207	27	47	70	11	0	4	16	1	2	2	36	0	58	3	1	2	.338	.344
Jones, Jacque, Min.*	.289	95	347	322	54	93	148	24	2	9	44	1	3	4	17	1	63	3	4	7	.460	.329
Justice, David, Cle.*	.287	133	530	429	75	123	204	18	0	21	88	0	5	2	94	11	90	1	3	14	.476	.413
Kapler, Gabe, Det.	.245	130	468	416	60	102	186	22	4	18	49	4	4	2	42	0	74	11	5	7	.447	.315
Kelly, Pat, Tor.	.267	37	130	116	17	31	56	7	0	6	20	1	3	0	10	0	23	0	1	1	.483	.318
Kelly, Roberto, Tex.	.300	87	318	290	41	87	130	17	1	8	37	0	2	5	21	0	57	6	1	5	.448	.355
King, Jeff, K.C.	.236	21	91	72	14	17	28	2	0	3	11	0	1	3	15	1	10	2	0	1	.389	.385
Kingsale, Eugene, Bal.†	.247	28	95	85	9	21	23	2	0	0	7	2	1	2	5	0	13	1	3	3	.271	.301
Knoblauch, Chuck, N.Y.	.292	150	715	603	120	176	274	36	4	18	68	3	5	21	83	0	57	28	9	7	.454	.393
Konerko, Paul, Chi.	.294	142	564	513	71	151	262	31	4	24	81	1	3	2	45	0	68	1	0	19	.511	.352
Koskie, Corey, Min.*	.310	117	392	342	42	106	160	21	0	11	58	2	3	5	40	4	72	4	4	6	.468	.387
Kreuter, Chad, K.C.†	.225	107	368	324	31	73	103	15	0	5	35	2	2	4	34	1	65	0	0	16	.318	.309
Lamb, David, T.B.†	.226	55	134	124	18	28	38	5	1	1	13	0	0	0	10	0	18	0	1	4	.306	.284
Lampkin, Tom, Sea.*	.291	76	227	206	29	60	102	11	2	9	34	1	2	5	13	1	32	1	3	2	.495	.345
Latham, Chris, Min.†	.091	14	24	22	1	2	2	0	0	0	3	0	2	0	0	0	13	0	0	0	.091	.083
Lawton, Matt, Min.*	.259	118	476	406	58	105	144	18	0	7	54	0	7	6	57	7	42	26	4	11	.355	.353
Ledee, Ricky, N.Y.*	.276	88	280	250	45	69	119	13	5	9	40	0	2	0	28	5	73	4	3	2	.476	.346
Ledesma, Aaron, T.B.	.265	93	312	294	32	78	93	15	0	0	30	1	0	3	14	1	35	1	1	14	.316	.305
Lee, Carlos, Chi.	.293	127	517	492	66	144	228	32	2	16	84	1	7	4	13	0	72	4	2	11	.463	.312
Leius, Scott, K.C.	.203	37	82	74	8	15	19	1	0	1	10	0	3	1	4	0	8	1	0	1	.257	.244
Lennon, Patrick, Tor.	.207	9	32	29	3	6	11	2	0	1	6	0	0	1	2	0	12	0	0	0	.379	.281
Lewis, Darren, Bos.	.240	135	538	470	63	113	145	14	6	2	40	14	4	5	45	0	52	16	10	5	.309	.311
Leyritz, Jim, N.Y.	.227	31	79	66	8	15	21	4	1	0	5	0	0	0	13	1	17	0	0	3	.318	.354
Liefer, Jeff, Chi.*	.248	45	122	113	8	28	37	7	1	0	14	0	1	0	8	0	28	2	0	3	.327	.316
Lofton, Kenny, Cle.*	.301	120	540	465	110	140	201	28	6	7	39	5	5	6	79	2	84	25	6	6	.432	.405
Lopez, Mendy, K.C.	.400	7	21	20	2	8	10	0	1	0	3	0	0	1	0	0	5	0	0	0	.500	.429
Lowery, Terrell, T.B.	.259	66	206	185	25	48	71	15	1	2	17	0	1	1	19	0	53	0	2	1	.384	.330
Luke, Matt, Ana.*	.300	18	32	30	4	9	18	0	0	3	6	0	0	0	2	0	9	0	0	2	.600	.344
Mabry, John, Sea.*	.244	87	285	262	34	64	105	14	0	9	33	2	1	0	20	1	60	2	1	6	.401	.297
Macfarlane, Mike, Oak.	.243	81	246	226	24	55	84	17	0	4	31	1	5	1	13	0	52	0	0	7	.372	.282
Macias, Jose, Det.†	.250	5	4	4	2	1	4	0	0	1	2	0	0	0	0	0	0	0	0	0	1.000	.250
Manto, Jeff, Cle.-N.Y.	.182	18	47	33	5	6	9	0	0	1	2	1	0	0	13	0	15	0	0	0	.273	.413
Martin, Norberto, Tor.	.222	9	33	27	3	6	8	2	0	0	0	1	0	0	4	0	4	0	0	2	.296	.324
Martinez, Tino, N.Y.*	.263	159	665	589	95	155	270	27	2	28	105	0	4	3	69	7	86	3	4	14	.458	.341
Martinez, Dave, T.B.*	.284	143	594	514	79	146	199	25	5	6	66	10	5	3	60	3	76	13	6	6	.387	.361
Martinez, Edgar, Sea.	.337	142	608	502	86	169	278	35	1	24	86	0	3	6	97	6	99	7	2	12	.554	.447
Martinez, Felix, K.C.†	.143	6	7	7	1	1	1	0	0	0	0	0	0	0	0	0	2	0	0	1	.143	.143
Mateo, Ruben, Tex.	.238	32	127	122	16	29	55	9	1	5	18	0	1	4	0	0	28	3	0	2	.451	.266
Matheny, Mike, Tor.	.215	57	179	163	16	35	50	6	0	3	17	2	1	1	12	0	37	0	0	3	.307	.271
May, Derrick, Bal.*	.265	26	54	49	5	13	25	0	0	4	12	0	1	0	4	0	9	0	0	2	.510	.315
McCracken, Quinton, T.B.†	.250	40	165	148	20	37	48	6	1	1	18	1	1	1	14	0	23	6	5	7	.324	.317
McDonald, Jason, Oak.†	.209	100	220	187	26	39	52	2	1	3	8	4	1	3	25	0	48	6	3	2	.278	.310

Player, Team	Avg.	G	TPA	AB	R	H	TB	2B	3B	HR	RBI	SH	SF	HP	BB	IBB	SO	SB	CS	GDP	Slg.	OBP
McDonald, John, Cle.	.333	18	21	21	2	7	7	0	0	0	0	0	0	0	0	0	3	0	1	2	.333	.333
McGriff, Fred, T.B.*	.310	144	620	529	75	164	292	30	1	32	104	0	4	1	86	11	107	1	0	12	.552	.405
McLemore, Mark, Tex.†	.274	144	664	566	105	155	207	20	7	6	45	9	6	0	83	2	79	16	8	8	.366	.363
McRae, Brian, Tor.†	.195	31	101	82	11	16	30	3	1	3	11	1	0	2	16	1	22	0	1	2	.366	.340
Merloni, Lou, Bos.	.254	43	140	126	18	32	42	7	0	1	13	3	1	2	8	0	16	0	0	6	.333	.307
Mientkiewicz, Doug, Min.*	.229	118	379	327	34	75	108	21	3	2	32	3	2	4	43	3	51	1	1	13	.330	.324
Mieske, Matt, Sea.	.366	24	43	41	11	15	27	0	0	4	7	0	0	0	2	1	9	0	0	0	.659	.395
Minor, Ryan, Bal.	.194	46	133	124	13	24	40	7	0	3	10	0	1	0	8	0	43	1	0	1	.323	.241
Molina, Ben, Ana.	.257	31	109	101	8	26	34	5	0	1	10	0	0	2	6	0	6	0	1	5	.337	.312
Monahan, Shane, Sea.*	.133	16	15	15	3	2	2	0	0	0	0	0	0	0	0	0	6	0	0	0	.133	.133
Mussina, Mike, Bal.*	.273	31	11	11	1	3	4	1	0	0	4	0	0	0	0	0	1	0	0	0	.364	.273
Nixon, Trot, Bos.*	.270	124	447	381	67	103	180	22	5	15	52	2	8	3	53	1	75	3	1	7	.472	.357
Norton, Greg, Chi.†	.255	132	510	436	62	111	185	26	0	16	50	1	2	2	69	3	93	4	4	11	.424	.358
Nunnally, Jon, Bos.*	.286	10	14	14	4	4	5	1	0	0	1	0	0	0	0	0	6	0	0	0	.357	.286
O'Brien, Charlie, Ana.	.097	27	67	62	3	6	9	0	0	1	4	1	1	2	1	0	12	0	0	1	.145	.136
Offerman, Jose, Bos.†	.294	149	693	586	107	172	255	37	11	8	69	2	7	2	96	5	79	18	12	11	.435	.391
O'Leary, Troy, Bos.*	.280	157	661	596	84	167	295	36	4	28	103	0	5	4	56	5	91	1	2	21	.495	.343
O'Neill, Paul, N.Y.*	.285	153	675	597	70	170	274	39	4	19	110	0	10	2	66	1	89	11	9	24	.459	.353
Ordonez, Magglio, Chi.	.301	157	677	624	100	188	318	34	3	30	117	0	5	1	47	4	64	13	6	24	.510	.349
Ortiz, David, Min.*	.000	10	25	20	1	0	0	0	0	0	0	0	0	0	5	0	12	0	0	2	.000	.200
Otanez, Willis, Bal.-Tor.	.237	71	226	207	28	49	81	11	0	7	24	1	1	2	15	0	46	0	0	6	.391	.293
Palmeiro, Orlando, Ana.*	.278	109	371	317	46	88	105	12	1	1	23	6	3	6	39	1	30	5	5	4	.331	.364
Palmeiro, Rafael, Tex.*	.324	158	674	565	96	183	356	30	1	47	148	0	9	3	97	14	69	2	4	13	.630	.420
Palmer, Dean, Det.	.263	150	631	560	92	147	290	25	2	38	100	0	4	10	57	3	153	3	3	12	.518	.339
Paul, Josh, Chi.	.222	6	18	18	2	4	5	1	0	0	1	0	0	0	0	0	4	0	0	0	.278	.222
Perry, Herbert, T.B.	.254	66	239	209	29	53	83	10	1	6	32	0	4	10	16	1	42	0	0	13	.397	.331
Phillips, Tony, Oak.†	.244	106	484	406	76	99	176	24	4	15	49	0	2	5	71	3	94	11	3	7	.433	.362
Pickering, Calvin, Bal.*	.125	23	51	40	4	5	9	1	0	1	5	0	0	0	11	0	16	0	0	1	.225	.314
Pierzynski, A.J., Min.*	.273	9	24	22	3	6	8	2	0	0	3	0	0	1	1	0	4	0	0	0	.364	.333
Polonia, Luis, Det.*	.324	87	355	333	46	108	175	21	8	10	32	2	2	2	16	0	32	17	9	2	.526	.357
Posada, Jorge, N.Y.†	.245	112	437	379	50	93	152	19	2	12	57	0	2	3	53	2	91	1	0	9	.401	.341
Pose, Scott, K.C.*	.285	86	160	137	27	39	42	3	0	0	12	1	1	0	21	1	22	6	2	3	.307	.377
Pritchett, Chris, Ana.*	.156	20	49	45	3	7	11	1	0	1	2	1	1	0	2	0	9	1	1	0	.244	.188
Quinn, Mark, K.C.	.333	17	65	60	11	20	44	4	1	6	18	0	0	1	4	0	11	1	0	1	.733	.385
Raines, Tim, Oak.†	.215	58	164	135	20	29	46	5	0	4	17	1	2	0	26	1	17	4	1	5	.341	.337
Ramirez, Alex, Cle.	.299	48	102	97	11	29	46	6	1	3	18	1	0	1	3	0	26	1	1	1	.474	.327
Ramirez, Manny, Cle.	.333	147	640	522	131	174	346	34	3	44	165	0	9	13	96	9	131	2	4	12	.663	.442
Randa, Joe, K.C.	.314	156	689	628	92	197	297	36	8	16	84	1	7	3	50	4	80	5	4	15	.473	.363
Reboulet, Jeff, Bal.	.162	99	192	154	25	25	29	4	0	0	4	3	0	2	33	0	29	1	0	1	.188	.317
Ripken, Cal, Bal.	.340	86	354	332	51	113	194	27	0	18	57	3	3	3	13	3	31	0	1	14	.584	.368
Roberts, Dave, Cle.*	.238	41	156	143	26	34	44	4	0	2	12	3	1	0	9	0	16	11	3	0	.308	.281
Rodriguez, Alex, Sea.	.285	129	572	502	110	143	294	25	0	42	111	1	8	5	56	2	109	21	7	12	.586	.357
Rodriguez, Frankie, Sea.	.333	30	3	3	1	1	1	0	0	0	1	0	0	0	0	0	0	0	0	0	.333	.333
Rodriguez, Ivan, Tex.	.332	144	630	600	116	199	335	29	1	35	113	0	5	1	24	2	64	25	12	31	.558	.356
Rodriguez, Liu, Chi.†	.237	39	111	93	8	22	31	2	2	1	12	3	0	3	12	0	11	0	0	5	.333	.343
Sadler, Donnie, Bos.	.280	49	115	107	18	30	37	5	1	0	4	3	0	0	5	0	20	2	1	1	.346	.313
Saenz, Olmedo, Oak.	.275	97	295	255	41	70	121	18	0	11	41	0	3	15	22	1	47	1	1	6	.475	.363
Salmon, Tim, Ana.	.266	98	422	353	60	94	173	24	2	17	69	0	6	0	63	2	82	4	1	7	.490	.372
Sanchez, Rey, K.C.	.294	134	518	479	66	141	177	18	6	2	56	10	3	4	22	2	48	11	5	14	.370	.329
Sanders, Anthony, Tor.	.286	3	7	7	1	2	3	1	0	0	2	0	0	0	0	0	2	0	0	1	.429	.286
Scarsone, Steve, K.C.	.206	46	79	68	2	14	19	5	0	0	6	1	1	0	9	0	24	1	0	0	.279	.295
Segui, David, Sea.-Tor.†	.298	121	486	440	57	131	206	27	3	14	52	1	4	1	40	4	60	1	2	10	.468	.355
Sexson, Richie, Cle.	.255	134	525	479	72	122	246	17	7	31	116	0	8	4	34	0	117	3	3	19	.514	.305
Shave, Jon, Tex.	.288	43	83	73	10	21	25	4	0	0	9	3	0	2	5	0	17	1	0	0	.342	.350
Sheets, Andy, Ana.	.197	87	269	244	22	48	67	10	0	3	29	6	5	0	14	0	59	1	2	6	.275	.236
Simmons, Brian, Chi.†	.230	54	135	126	14	29	50	3	3	4	17	0	0	0	9	0	30	4	0	3	.397	.281
Singleton, Chris, Chi.*	.300	133	529	496	72	149	243	31	6	17	72	4	6	1	22	1	45	20	5	10	.490	.328
Sirotka, Mike, Chi.*	.250	32	8	8	1	2	2	0	0	0	0	0	0	0	0	0	3	0	0	1	.250	.250
Smith, Bobby, T.B.	.181	68	219	199	18	36	51	4	1	3	19	2	1	1	16	0	64	4	4	8	.256	.244
Sojo, Luis, N.Y.	.252	49	133	127	20	32	44	6	0	2	16	2	0	0	4	0	17	1	0	4	.346	.275
Soriano, Alfonso, N.Y.	.125	9	8	8	2	1	4	0	0	1	1	0	0	0	0	0	3	0	1	0	.500	.125
Sorrento, Paul, T.B.*	.235	99	348	294	40	69	118	14	1	11	42	0	1	4	49	1	101	1	1	4	.401	.351
Spehr, Tim, K.C.	.206	60	187	155	26	32	66	7	0	9	26	2	2	6	22	0	47	1	0	2	.426	.324
Spencer, Shane, N.Y.	.234	71	226	205	25	48	80	8	0	8	20	0	1	2	18	0	51	0	4	1	.390	.301
Spiezio, Scott, Oak.†	.243	89	282	247	31	60	108	24	0	8	33	1	3	2	29	3	36	0	0	5	.437	.324
Stairs, Matt, Oak.*	.258	146	623	531	94	137	283	26	3	38	102	0	1	2	89	6	124	2	7	8	.533	.366
Stanley, Mike, Bos.	.281	136	512	427	59	120	199	22	0	19	72	0	4	11	70	3	94	0	0	8	.466	.393
Steinbach, Terry, Min.	.284	101	380	338	35	96	132	16	4	4	42	0	2	2	38	1	54	2	2	10	.391	.358
Stevens, Lee, Tex.*	.282	146	576	517	76	146	251	31	1	24	81	0	7	0	52	10	132	2	3	19	.485	.344
Stewart, Shannon, Tor.	.304	145	682	608	102	185	250	28	2	11	67	3	4	8	59	0	83	37	14	12	.411	.371
Stocker, Kevin, T.B.†	.299	79	286	254	39	76	94	11	2	1	27	4	0	4	24	0	41	9	7	4	.370	.369
Strawberry, Darryl, N.Y.*	.327	24	66	49	10	16	30	5	0	3	6	0	0	0	17	0	16	2	0	0	.612	.500
Surhoff, B.J., Bal.*	.308	162	727	673	104	207	331	38	1	28	107	1	8	2	43	1	78	5	1	15	.492	.347
Sutton, Larry, K.C.*	.225	43	118	102	14	23	35	6	0	2	15	1	2	0	13	0	17	1	0	4	.343	.308
Sweeney, Mike, K.C.	.322	150	643	575	101	185	299	44	2	22	102	0	4	10	54	0	48	6	1	21	.520	.387
Tarasco, Tony, N.Y.*	.161	14	35	31	5	5	7	2	0	0	3	0	1	0	3	0	5	1	0	1	.226	.229
Tejada, Miguel, Oak.	.251	159	674	593	93	149	253	33	4	21	84	9	5	10	57	3	94	8	7	11	.427	.325
Thomas, Frank, Chi.	.305	135	590	486	74	148	229	36	0	15	77	0	8	9	87	13	66	3	3	15	.471	.414
Thome, Jim, Cle.*	.277	146	629	494	101	137	267	27	2	33	108	0	4	4	127	13	171	0	0	6	.540	.426
Timmons, Ozzie, Sea.	.114	26	48	44	4	5	10	2	0	1	3	0	0	0	4	0	12	0	1	0	.227	.188
Trammell, Bubba, T.B.	.290	82	328	283	49	82	143	19	0	14	39	0	1	1	43	1	37	0	2	7	.505	.384
Turner, Chris, Cle.	.190	12	22	21	3	4	4	0	0	0	0	0	0	0	1	0	8	1	0	0	.190	.227

Player, Team	Avg.	G	TPA	AB	R	H	TB	2B	3B	HR	RBI	SH	SF	HP	BB	IBB	SO	SB	CS	GDP	Slg.	OBP
Unroe, Tim, Ana.	.241	27	59	54	5	13	18	2	0	1	6	0	0	1	4	0	16	0	0	0	.333	.305
Valentin, John, Bos.	.253	113	503	450	58	114	179	27	1	12	70	1	8	4	40	2	68	0	1	11	.398	.315
Valentin, Javier, Min.†	.248	78	247	218	22	54	83	12	1	5	28	1	5	1	22	0	39	0	0	2	.381	.313
Varitek, Jason, Bos.†	.269	144	544	483	70	130	233	39	2	20	76	5	8	2	46	2	85	1	2	13	.482	.330
Vaughn, Mo, Ana.*	.281	139	592	524	63	147	266	20	0	33	108	0	3	11	54	7	127	0	0	11	.508	.358
Velandia, Jorge, Oak.	.188	63	51	48	4	9	10	1	0	0	2	0	0	1	2	0	13	2	0	0	.208	.235
Velarde, Randy, Ana.-Oak.	.317	156	711	631	105	200	287	25	7	16	76	4	0	6	70	2	98	24	8	19	.455	.390
Veras, Wilton, Bos.	.288	36	127	118	14	34	47	5	1	2	13	0	2	2	5	0	14	0	2	5	.398	.323
Vitiello, Joe, K.C.	.146	13	45	41	4	6	10	1	0	1	4	0	0	2	2	0	9	0	0	2	.244	.222
Vizquel, Omar, Cle.†	.333	144	664	574	112	191	250	36	4	5	66	17	7	1	65	0	50	42	9	8	.436	.397
Walbeck, Matt, Ana.†	.240	107	321	288	26	69	88	8	1	3	22	3	1	3	26	1	46	2	3	12	.306	.308
Walker, Todd, Min.*	.279	143	586	531	62	148	211	37	4	6	46	0	2	1	52	5	83	18	10	15	.397	.343
Weaver, Jeff, Det.	.500	31	5	4	2	2	3	1	0	0	0	1	0	0	0	0	1	0	0	0	.750	.500
Webster, Lenny, Bal.-Bos.	.120	22	62	50	1	6	7	1	0	0	4	0	0	2	10	0	7	0	0	1	.140	.290
Wells, Vernon, Tor.	.261	24	92	88	8	23	31	5	0	1	8	0	0	0	4	0	18	1	1	6	.352	.293
Whiten, Mark, Cle.†	.160	8	28	25	2	4	8	1	0	1	4	0	0	0	3	0	4	0	0	1	.320	.250
Williams, Bernie, N.Y.†	.342	158	697	591	116	202	317	28	6	25	115	0	5	1	100	17	95	9	10	11	.536	.435
Williams, Reggie, Ana.†	.222	30	71	63	8	14	22	1	2	1	6	1	1	1	5	0	21	2	1	3	.349	.286
Wilson, Craig, Chi.	.238	98	282	252	28	60	82	8	1	4	26	6	1	0	23	0	22	1	1	5	.325	.301
Wilson, Dan, Sea.	.266	123	457	414	46	110	158	23	2	7	38	10	2	2	29	4	83	5	0	10	.382	.315
Wilson, Enrique, Cle.†	.262	113	368	332	41	87	117	22	1	2	24	4	6	1	25	1	41	5	4	12	.352	.310
Winn, Randy, T.B.†	.267	79	324	303	44	81	111	16	4	2	24	1	2	1	17	0	63	9	9	3	.366	.307
Witt, Kevin, Tor.*	.206	15	37	34	3	7	11	1	0	1	5	1	0	0	2	0	9	0	0	0	.324	.250
Wood, Jason, Det.	.159	27	47	44	5	7	11	1	0	1	8	1	0	0	2	0	13	0	0	0	.250	.196
Woodward, Chris, Tor.	.231	14	29	26	1	6	7	1	0	0	2	0	1	0	2	0	6	0	0	1	.269	.276
Zaun, Gregg, Tex.†	.247	43	106	93	12	23	30	2	1	1	12	1	2	0	10	0	7	1	0	2	.323	.314
Zeile, Todd, Tex.	.293	156	656	588	80	172	287	41	1	24	98	1	7	4	56	3	94	1	2	20	.488	.354

AWARDED FIRST BASE ON OBSTRUCTION OR CATCHER'S INTERFERENCE—K. Garcia, Detroit (Varitek); Grebeck, Toronto (Piazza); Kelly, Texas (Wilson); Lee, Chicago (DiFelice); Lofton, Cleveland (Flaherty); Palmeiro, Anaheim (DiFelice); Saenz, Oakland (Davis); Singleton, Chicago (Figga); Spiezio, Oakland (Varitek).

PLAYERS WITH TWO OR MORE TEAMS

Player, Team	Avg.	G	TPA	AB	R	H	TB	2B	3B	HR	RBI	SH	SF	HP	BB	IBB	SO	SB	CS	GDP	Slg.	OBP
Baines, Harold, Bal.*	.322	107	390	345	57	111	201	16	1	24	81	0	2	0	43	3	38	1	2	14	.583	.395
Baines, Harold, Cle.*	.271	28	96	85	5	23	28	2	0	1	22	0	0	0	11	0	10	0	0	2	.329	.354
Borders, Pat, Cle.	.300	6	20	20	2	6	8	0	1	0	3	0	0	0	0	0	3	0	1	0	.400	.300
Borders, Pat, Tor.	.214	6	15	14	1	3	6	0	0	1	3	0	0	0	1	0	2	0	0	0	.429	.267
Figga, Mike, N.Y.	.000	2	0	0	0	0	0	0	0	0	0	0	0	0	0	0	0	0	0	0	.000	.000
Figga, Mike, Cle.	.221	41	91	86	12	19	26	4	0	1	5	2	1	0	2	0	27	0	2	1	.302	.236
Hunter, Brian, Det.	.236	18	62	55	8	13	17	2	1	0	1	0	1	0	5	0	11	0	3	0	.309	.311
Hunter, Brian, Sea.	.231	121	527	484	71	112	145	11	5	4	34	3	7	1	32	0	80	44	5	8	.300	.277
Huskey, Butch, Sea.	.290	74	292	262	44	76	130	9	0	15	49	0	3	0	27	0	45	3	1	3	.496	.353
Huskey, Butch, Bos.	.266	45	131	124	18	33	60	6	0	7	28	0	0	0	7	1	20	0	0	6	.484	.305
Manto, Jeff, Cle.	.200	12	37	25	5	5	8	0	0	1	2	1	0	0	11	0	11	0	0	0	.320	.444
Manto, Jeff, N.Y.	.125	6	10	8	0	1	1	0	0	0	0	0	0	0	2	0	4	0	0	0	.125	.300
Otanez, Willis, Bal.	.213	29	89	80	7	17	26	3	0	2	11	1	1	1	6	0	16	0	0	3	.325	.273
Otanez, Willis, Tor.	.252	42	137	127	21	32	55	8	0	5	13	0	0	1	9	0	30	0	0	3	.433	.307
Segui, David, Sea.†	.293	90	382	345	43	101	156	22	3	9	39	1	3	1	32	4	43	1	2	9	.452	.352
Segui, David, Tor.†	.316	31	104	95	14	30	50	5	0	5	13	0	1	0	8	0	17	0	0	1	.526	.365
Velarde, Randy, Ana.	.306	95	425	376	57	115	165	15	4	9	48	2	0	4	43	1	56	13	4	8	.439	.383
Velarde, Randy, Oak.	.333	61	286	255	48	85	122	10	3	7	28	2	0	2	27	1	42	11	4	11	.478	.401
Webster, Lenny, Bal.	.167	16	45	36	1	6	7	1	0	0	3	0	0	1	8	0	5	0	0	1	.194	.333
Webster, Lenny, Bos.	.000	6	17	14	0	0	0	0	0	0	1	0	0	1	2	0	2	0	0	0	.000	.176

DESIGNATED HITTING

TEAM

Team	Avg.	G	TPA	AB	R	H	TB	2B	3B	HR	RBI	SH	SF	HP	BB	IBB	SO	SB	CS	GDP	Slg.	OBP
Texas	.323	153	671	566	104	183	342	28	1	43	138	1	8	2	94	14	79	5	4	15	.604	.416
Seattle	.318	153	671	556	99	177	292	38	1	25	95	1	4	6	104	8	113	9	2	11	.525	.428
Baltimore	.303	153	668	588	93	178	302	38	1	28	115	1	6	7	66	4	76	2	5	19	.514	.376
Kansas City	.296	152	665	577	94	171	257	30	1	18	97	2	7	11	68	3	93	7	2	19	.445	.377
Boston	.281	153	675	612	83	172	292	43	7	21	91	0	1	7	55	2	138	1	0	18	.477	.347
Chicago	.281	153	668	573	80	161	257	40	1	18	93	0	9	9	77	12	83	7	0	20	.449	.370
New York	.275	153	665	561	87	154	257	32	1	23	84	0	3	2	99	8	124	9	1	13	.458	.383
Oakland	.274	153	690	562	117	154	304	30	0	40	125	0	2	12	114	4	155	2	0	17	.541	.406
Cleveland	.265	153	662	566	82	150	255	31	1	24	114	1	4	4	87	5	130	4	2	19	.451	.365
Minnesota	.259	153	655	572	79	148	235	35	5	14	82	0	6	10	67	5	123	14	7	28	.411	.344
Anaheim	.258	153	651	590	66	152	268	29	0	29	106	1	2	7	51	4	118	5	1	13	.454	.323
Tampa Bay	.257	153	681	588	92	151	289	19	1	39	109	0	7	8	78	4	166	3	2	26	.491	.348
Detroit	.252	153	666	603	79	152	262	39	4	21	68	1	6	6	50	2	86	14	10	10	.434	.313
Toronto	.249	153	669	610	80	152	251	27	0	24	81	3	4	6	46	4	130	0	1	13	.411	.306
Totals	.278	1195	9357	8124	1235	2255	3863	459	24	367	1398	11	69	97	1056	79	1614	82	37	241	.476	.365

TOP DESIGNATED HITTERS

Minimum 100 at-bats. *Lefthanded batter. †Switch-hitter.

Player, Team	Avg.	G	TPA	AB	R	H	TB	2B	3B	HR	RBI	SH	SF	HP	BB	IBB	SO	SB	CS	GDP	Slg.	OBP
Polonia, Luis, Det.*	.337	43	187	172	26	58	98	14	4	6	20	1	2	1	11	0	19	11	5	1	.570	.376
Martinez, Edgar, Sea.	.333	134	585	483	82	161	260	34	1	21	82	0	3	6	93	6	96	7	1	11	.538	.444
Sweeney, Mike, K.C.	.333	71	309	273	50	91	147	17	0	13	53	0	1	7	28	0	28	2	0	11	.538	.408
Daubach, Brian, Bos.*	.329	43	167	149	25	49	89	12	2	8	32	0	0	1	17	0	36	0	0	2	.597	.401
Palmeiro, Rafael, Tex.*	.321	128	547	458	75	147	284	24	1	37	115	0	6	2	81	11	54	2	4	12	.620	.420
Baines, Harold, Bal.-Cle.*	.316	121	473	418	61	132	227	18	1	25	96	0	2	0	53	3	45	1	2	15	.543	.391
Konerko, Paul, Chi.	.311	46	177	167	24	52	91	12	0	9	30	0	2	0	8	0	21	1	0	7	.545	.339
Thome, Jim, Cle.*	.298	34	148	114	21	34	66	5	0	9	30	0	0	4	34	2	31	0	0	1	.579	.459
Vaughn, Mo, Ana.*	.292	67	289	260	31	76	150	11	0	21	64	0	1	4	24	4	53	0	0	4	.577	.360
Jaha, John, Oak.	.285	121	534	431	93	123	250	22	0	35	105	0	1	9	93	2	123	2	0	14	.580	.421
Giambi, Jeremy, K.C.*	.283	48	201	173	21	49	63	9	1	1	22	1	3	2	22	2	37	0	0	5	.364	.365
Thomas, Frank, Chi.	.281	82	369	295	43	83	125	21	0	7	45	0	5	6	63	12	41	2	0	13	.424	.412
Cordova, Marty, Min.	.272	85	370	320	47	87	140	20	3	9	48	0	4	9	37	2	73	9	4	19	.438	.359
Jefferson, Reggie, Bos.*	.272	58	202	184	20	50	76	12	1	4	15	0	0	2	16	0	48	0	0	7	.413	.337
Canseco, Jose, T.B.	.271	106	476	406	70	110	222	14	1	32	91	0	7	6	57	3	126	3	0	14	.547	.363

ALL DESIGNATED HITTERS

*Lefthanded batter. †Switch-hitter.

Player, Team	Avg.	G	TPA	AB	R	H	TB	2B	3B	HR	RBI	SH	SF	HP	BB	IBB	SO	SB	CS	GDP	Slg.	OBP
Alicea, Luis, Tex.†	.222	7	13	9	6	2	2	0	0	0	0	1	0	0	3	0	3	1	0	0	.222	.417
Allen, Chad, Min.	.000	2	1	1	0	0	0	0	0	0	0	0	0	0	0	0	0	0	0	0	.000	.000
Alomar, Roberto, Cle.†	.250	2	5	4	1	1	2	1	0	0	0	0	0	0	1	0	1	0	0	0	.500	.400
Alomar, Sandy, Cle.	.400	1	5	5	1	2	3	1	0	0	1	0	0	0	0	0	1	0	0	0	.600	.400
Alvarez, Gabe, Det.	.152	12	36	33	3	5	10	2	0	1	2	0	0	0	3	0	5	0	0	0	.303	.222
Amaral, Rich, Bal.	.296	18	32	27	5	8	11	3	0	0	5	1	1	0	3	0	2	0	2	0	.407	.355
Anderson, Brady, Bal.*	.235	10	41	34	6	8	20	3	0	3	9	0	1	3	3	0	5	1	0	0	.588	.341
Anderson, Garret, Ana.*	.500	4	18	16	1	8	10	2	0	0	1	0	0	0	2	0	1	0	0	1	.625	.556
Baerga, Carlos, Cle.†	.000	1	2	2	0	0	0	0	0	0	0	0	0	0	0	0	2	0	0	0	.000	.000
Baines, Harold, Bal.-Cle.*	.316	121	473	418	61	132	227	18	1	25	96	0	2	0	53	3	45	1	2	15	.543	.391
Bartee, Kimera, Det.	.000	1	0	0	0	0	0	0	0	0	0	0	0	0	0	0	0	1	0	0	.000	.000
Becker, Rich, Oak.*	.000	1	0	0	0	0	0	0	0	0	0	0	0	0	0	0	0	0	0	0	.000	.000
Belle, Albert, Bal.	.414	7	33	29	5	12	19	7	0	0	6	0	0	0	4	1	4	0	0	1	.655	.485
Bellinger, Clay, N.Y.	.000	4	1	1	2	0	0	0	0	0	0	0	0	0	0	0	1	0	0	0	.000	.000
Beltran, Carlos, K.C.†	.500	2	6	4	1	2	2	0	0	0	2	0	0	1	1	0	1	0	0	0	.500	.500
Berroa, Geronimo, Tor.	.226	17	61	53	11	12	18	3	0	1	4	0	0	1	7	0	12	0	0	4	.340	.328
Blowers, Mike, Sea.	.000	1	2	2	0	0	0	0	0	0	0	0	0	0	0	0	1	0	0	0	.000	.000
Boggs, Wade, T.B.*	.200	7	27	25	2	5	6	1	0	0	1	0	0	0	2	0	2	0	0	2	.240	.259
Borders, Pat, Tor.	.333	3	9	9	1	3	6	3	0	0	1	2	0	0	0	0	0	0	0	0	.667	.333
Bournigal, Rafael, Sea.	.000	1	1	1	0	0	0	0	0	0	0	0	0	0	0	0	0	0	0	0	.000	.000
Branyan, Russell, Cle.*	.333	3	13	12	1	4	6	2	0	0	3	0	0	0	1	0	4	0	0	0	.500	.385
Brosius, Scott, N.Y.	.000	1	1	1	0	0	0	0	0	0	0	0	0	0	0	0	1	0	0	0	.000	.000
Brown, Dee, K.C.*	.143	2	8	7	1	1	1	0	0	0	0	0	0	0	1	0	2	0	0	0	.143	.250
Brumfield, Jacob, Tor.	.000	6	3	3	0	0	0	0	0	0	0	0	0	0	0	0	1	0	0	0	.000	.000
Buford, Damon, Bos.	.000	5	4	4	0	0	0	0	0	0	0	0	0	0	0	0	2	0	0	0	.000	.000
Butler, Rob, Tor.*	1.000	3	2	1	1	1	1	0	0	0	0	0	0	0	1	0	0	0	0	0	1.000	1.000
Cabrera, Jolbert, Cle.	.000	5	0	0	0	0	0	0	0	0	0	0	0	0	0	0	0	0	0	0	.000	.000
Cairo, Miguel, T.B.	.000	2	2	2	2	0	0	0	0	0	0	0	0	0	0	0	0	0	0	0	.000	.000
Callaway, Mickey, T.B.	.000	1	1	1	0	0	0	0	0	0	0	0	0	0	0	0	0	0	0	0	.000	.000
Canseco, Jose, T.B.	.271	106	476	406	70	110	222	14	1	32	91	0	7	6	57	3	126	3	0	14	.547	.363
Caruso, Mike, Chi.*	.000	2	0	0	1	0	0	0	0	0	0	0	0	0	0	0	0	0	0	0	.000	.000
Catalanotto, Frank, Det.*	.179	9	31	28	2	5	10	2	0	1	2	0	0	0	3	0	3	0	0	0	.357	.258
Chavez, Eric, Oak.*	.500	3	2	2	2	1	2	1	0	0	1	0	0	0	0	0	0	0	0	0	1.000	.500
Christenson, Ryan, Oak.	.000	1	0	0	1	0	0	0	0	0	0	0	0	0	0	0	0	0	0	0	.000	.000

Player, Team	Avg.	G	TPA	AB	R	H	TB	2B	3B	HR	RBI	SH	SF	HP	BB	IBB	SO	SB	CS	GDP	Slg.	OBP
Clark, Tony, Det.†	.293	11	49	41	8	12	23	5	0	2	7	0	0	1	7	1	12	0	0	0	.561	.408
Clark, Will, Bal.*	.000	3	13	12	0	0	0	0	0	0	1	0	0	1	0	0	2	0	0	0	.000	.077
Clyburn, Danny, T.B.	.333	4	14	12	2	4	5	1	0	0	0	0	0	1	1	0	2	0	0	0	.417	.429
Conine, Jeff, Bal.	.244	20	46	41	2	10	15	5	0	0	7	0	1	1	3	0	4	0	0	1	.366	.304
Coomer, Ron, Min.	.240	7	29	25	4	6	10	1	0	1	6	0	1	0	3	0	5	0	0	1	.400	.310
Cordero, Wil, Cle.	.291	23	91	79	15	23	36	4	0	3	12	0	0	3	9	0	14	1	0	4	.456	.385
Cordova, Marty, Min.	.272	85	370	320	47	87	140	20	3	9	48	0	4	9	37	2	73	9	4	19	.438	.359
Cruz, Jacob, Cle.*	.333	2	3	3	0	1	1	0	0	0	0	0	0	0	0	0	0	0	0	0	.333	.333
Cummings, Midre, Min.*	.316	5	21	19	0	6	6	0	0	0	4	0	1	0	1	0	2	1	0	0	.316	.333
Curtis, Chad, N.Y.	.500	14	4	4	2	2	3	1	0	0	1	0	0	0	0	0	0	2	0	0	.750	.500
Dalesandro, Mark, Tor.	.154	5	15	13	2	2	2	0	0	0	1	0	1	1	0	0	4	0	0	1	.154	.200
Damon, Johnny, K.C.*	.267	4	18	15	3	4	9	2	0	1	4	1	0	0	2	0	2	1	0	0	.600	.353
Daubach, Brian, Bos.*	.329	43	167	149	25	49	89	12	2	8	32	0	0	1	17	0	36	0	0	2	.597	.401
DaVanon, Jeff, Ana.†	.000	2	3	3	1	0	0	0	0	0	0	0	0	0	0	0	0	0	0	0	.000	.000
Davidson, Cleatus, Min.†	.000	1	0	0	0	0	0	0	0	0	0	0	0	0	0	0	0	0	0	0	.000	.000
Davis, Chili, N.Y.†	.270	132	540	463	59	125	208	24	1	19	73	0	3	2	72	7	97	4	1	12	.449	.369
Decker, Steve, Ana.	.143	3	8	7	0	1	1	0	0	0	0	0	0	0	1	0	2	0	0	0	.143	.250
Delgado, Carlos, Tor.*	.421	5	21	19	5	8	20	0	0	4	5	0	0	1	1	0	2	0	0	0	1.053	.476
Durham, Ray, Chi.†	.235	4	18	17	1	4	4	0	0	0	1	0	0	1	0	0	2	1	0	0	.235	.278
Durrington, Trent, Ana.	.000	1	0	0	0	0	0	0	0	0	0	0	0	0	0	0	0	0	0	0	.000	.000
Dye, Jermaine, K.C.	.000	1	4	4	0	0	0	0	0	0	0	0	0	0	0	0	2	0	0	0	.000	.000
Edmonds, Jim, Ana.*	.250	9	38	36	6	9	13	4	0	0	3	0	0	0	2	0	8	3	0	0	.361	.289
Erstad, Darin, Ana.*	.000	2	9	8	0	0	0	0	0	0	0	0	0	0	1	0	2	1	0	0	.000	.111
Fernandez, Tony, Tor.†	.250	9	27	24	3	6	8	2	0	0	2	0	0	0	3	3	7	0	0	1	.333	.333
Fick, Robert, Det.*	.172	8	34	29	5	5	14	0	0	3	9	0	1	0	4	0	3	0	0	0	.483	.265
Flaherty, John, T.B.	.333	1	4	3	0	1	1	0	0	0	0	0	0	0	1	0	0	0	1	1	.333	.500
Frye, Jeff, Bos.	.000	2	5	5	0	0	0	0	0	0	0	0	0	0	0	0	0	0	0	0	.000	.000
Garcia, Jesse, Bal.	.000	1	0	0	1	0	0	0	0	0	0	0	0	0	0	0	0	0	0	0	.000	.000
Garcia, Karim, Det.*	.250	7	8	8	1	2	3	1	0	0	0	0	0	0	0	0	3	0	0	0	.375	.250
Gates, Brent, Min.†	.250	1	5	4	1	1	2	1	0	0	3	0	0	0	1	0	0	0	0	0	.500	.400
Giambi, Jason, Oak.*	.351	15	72	57	13	20	37	5	0	4	14	0	1	1	13	1	12	0	0	1	.649	.472
Giambi, Jeremy, K.C.*	.283	48	201	173	21	49	63	9	1	1	22	1	3	2	22	2	37	0	0	5	.364	.365
Gipson, Charles, Sea.	.000	4	0	0	2	0	0	0	0	0	0	0	0	0	0	0	1	0	0	0	.000	.000
Glaus, Troy, Ana.	.000	1	5	4	1	0	0	0	0	0	0	0	0	0	1	0	1	0	0	0	.000	.200
Gonzalez, Alex, Tor.	.000	1	5	4	0	0	0	0	0	0	0	0	0	0	1	0	1	0	0	0	.000	.200
Gonzalez, Juan, Tex.	.393	14	65	56	10	22	34	3	0	3	16	0	1	0	8	3	10	2	0	2	.607	.462
Graffanino, Tony, T.B.	.000	1	0	0	0	0	0	0	0	0	0	0	0	0	0	0	0	0	0	0	.000	.000
Grebeck, Craig, Tor.	.417	10	42	36	5	15	16	1	0	0	1	1	0	1	4	0	2	0	0	1	.444	.488
Green, Scarborough, Tex.	.000	4	0	0	1	0	0	0	0	0	0	0	0	0	0	0	0	0	0	0	.000	.000
Greene, Todd, Ana.	.236	44	169	161	18	38	69	10	0	7	25	0	1	1	6	0	33	0	0	4	.429	.266
Greene, Willie, Tor.*	.212	51	197	184	17	39	73	7	0	9	33	0	0	0	13	0	46	0	0	4	.397	.264
Greer, Rusty, Tex.*	.000	1	0	0	1	0	0	0	0	0	0	0	0	0	0	0	0	0	0	0	.000	.000
Grieve, Ben, Oak.*	.083	4	14	12	1	1	1	0	0	0	0	0	0	0	2	0	4	0	0	0	.083	.214
Griffey, Ken, Sea.*	.292	6	28	24	6	7	12	2	0	1	4	0	0	0	4	2	5	1	0	0	.500	.393
Gubanich, Creighton, Bos.	.444	2	9	9	1	4	7	1	1	0	3	0	0	0	0	0	2	0	0	1	.778	.444
Hansen, Jed, K.C.	.000	3	0	0	2	0	0	0	0	0	0	0	0	0	0	0	0	0	0	0	.000	.000
Haselman, Bill, Det.	.294	9	18	17	1	5	9	1	0	1	3	0	0	0	1	0	2	0	0	1	.529	.333
Hatteberg, Scott, Bos.*	.381	6	23	21	2	8	10	2	0	0	3	0	0	1	1	0	7	0	0	0	.476	.435
Higginson, Bobby, Det.*	.239	17	72	67	9	16	29	4	0	3	5	0	0	0	5	0	14	0	0	1	.433	.292
Hollins, Dave, Tor.†	.211	23	100	95	11	20	31	5	0	2	6	0	0	0	5	0	22	0	0	2	.326	.250
Hudson, Tim, Oak.	.000	2	0	0	0	0	0	0	0	0	0	0	0	0	0	0	0	0	0	0	.000	.000
Huskey, Butch, Sea.-Bos.	.230	44	138	126	17	29	63	7	0	9	27	0	1	0	11	1	24	0	0	5	.500	.290
Huson, Jeff, Ana.*	.273	7	11	11	2	3	4	1	0	0	4	0	0	0	0	0	4	0	0	1	.364	.273
Ibanez, Raul, Sea.*	.000	1	1	1	0	0	0	0	0	0	0	0	0	0	0	0	1	0	0	0	.000	.000
Jackson, Darrin, Chi.	.000	3	2	2	0	0	0	0	0	0	0	0	0	0	0	0	2	0	0	0	.000	.000
Jaha, John, Oak.	.285	121	534	431	93	123	250	22	0	35	105	0	1	9	93	2	123	2	0	14	.580	.421
Jefferies, Gregg, Det.†	.199	45	188	171	18	34	53	7	0	4	15	0	2	3	12	1	10	3	4	6	.310	.261
Jefferson, Reggie, Bos.*	.272	58	202	184	20	50	76	12	1	4	15	0	2	0	16	0	48	0	0	7	.413	.337
Johnson, Mark, Chi.*	.000	1	1	1	0	0	0	0	0	0	0	0	0	0	0	0	0	0	0	0	.000	.000
Justice, David, Cle.*	.240	34	143	121	21	29	56	6	0	7	25	0	1	0	21	3	25	1	1	7	.463	.350
Kapler, Gabe, Det.	.000	2	1	1	1	0	0	0	0	0	0	0	0	0	0	0	0	0	0	0	.000	.000
Kelly, Pat, Tor.	.200	2	6	5	1	1	2	1	0	0	1	0	1	0	0	0	1	0	0	0	.400	.167
King, Jeff, K.C.	1.000	1	2	1	1	1	1	0	0	0	0	0	0	0	1	0	0	0	0	0	1.000	1.000
Kingsale, Eugene, Bal.†	.000	2	3	2	1	0	0	0	0	0	0	0	0	0	1	0	0	0	1	0	.000	.333
Konerko, Paul, Chi.	.311	46	177	167	24	52	91	12	0	9	30	0	2	0	8	0	21	1	0	7	.545	.339
Koskie, Corey, Min.*	.267	12	50	45	6	12	24	3	0	3	10	0	0	1	4	2	9	0	1	0	.533	.340
Kreuter, Chad, K.C.†	.000	1	4	2	1	0	0	0	0	0	0	0	0	0	2	0	1	0	0	1	.000	.500
Lamb, David, T.B.†	.000	3	1	1	1	0	0	0	0	0	0	0	0	0	0	0	0	0	0	0	.000	.000
Lampkin, Tom, Sea.*	.333	2	6	6	1	2	2	0	0	0	1	0	0	0	0	0	2	0	0	0	.333	.333
Lawton, Matt, Min.*	.238	6	24	21	4	5	5	0	0	0	2	0	0	0	3	0	2	1	0	0	.238	.333
Ledee, Ricky, N.Y.*	1.000	5	1	1	3	1	1	0	0	0	1	0	0	0	0	0	0	1	0	0	1.000	1.000
Ledesma, Aaron, T.B.	.250	1	4	4	0	1	1	0	0	0	0	0	0	0	0	0	2	0	0	1	.250	.250
Lee, Carlos, Chi.	.190	16	68	63	7	12	24	4	1	2	11	0	2	2	1	0	13	1	0	0	.381	.221
Leius, Scott, K.C.	.087	6	23	23	1	2	5	0	0	1	4	0	0	0	0	0	3	0	0	1	.217	.087
Lewis, Darren, Bos.	.000	2	0	0	1	0	0	0	0	0	0	0	0	0	0	0	0	0	0	0	.000	.000
Leyritz, Jim, N.Y.	.241	14	38	29	5	7	9	2	0	0	1	0	0	0	9	0	8	0	0	0	.310	.421
Liefer, Jeff, Chi.*	.333	7	18	15	1	5	6	1	0	0	4	0	0	0	3	0	2	0	0	0	.400	.444
Lofton, Kenny, Cle.*	.000	1	4	2	1	0	0	0	0	0	0	0	0	0	1	0	0	0	0	0	.000	.500
Lowery, Terrell, T.B.	.000	1	0	0	0	0	0	0	0	0	0	0	0	0	0	0	0	0	0	0	.000	.000
Mabry, John, Sea.*	.000	1	4	4	0	0	0	0	0	0	0	0	0	0	0	0	1	0	0	1	.000	.000
Macfarlane, Mike, Oak.	.000	1	1	1	0	0	0	0	0	0	0	0	0	0	0	0	0	0	0	0	.000	.000
Martinez, Edgar, Sea.	.333	134	585	483	82	161	260	34	1	21	82	0	3	6	93	6	96	7	1	11	.538	.444

Player, Team	Avg.	G	TPA	AB	R	H	TB	2B	3B	HR	RBI	SH	SF	HP	BB	IBB	SO	SB	CS	GDP	Slg.	OBP
Mateo, Ruben, Tex.	.000	1	0	0	0	0	0	0	0	0	0	0	0	0	0	0	0	0	0	0	.000	.000
May, Derrick, Bal.*	.214	9	29	28	1	6	9	0	0	1	2	0	0	0	1	0	6	0	0	1	.321	.241
McDonald, Jason, Oak.†	.000	5	1	1	0	0	0	0	0	0	0	0	0	0	0	0	1	0	0	0	.000	.000
McGriff, Fred, T.B.*	.229	18	76	70	6	16	27	2	0	3	9	0	0	0	6	1	14	0	0	4	.386	.289
McLemore, Mark, Tex.†	.000	1	0	0	0	0	0	0	0	0	0	0	0	0	0	0	0	0	0	0	.000	.000
McRae, Brian, Tor.†	.219	15	38	32	3	7	12	2	0	1	7	1	0	0	5	1	6	0	0	1	.375	.324
Menechino, Frank, Oak.	.000	3	0	0	0	0	0	0	0	0	0	0	0	0	0	0	0	0	0	0	.000	.000
Merloni, Lou, Bos.	.000	3	3	1	1	0	0	0	0	0	1	0	1	0	1	0	0	0	0	1	.000	.333
Mieske, Matt, Sea.	.000	1	3	3	0	0	0	0	0	0	0	0	0	0	0	0	1	0	0	0	.000	.000
Monahan, Shane, Sea.*	.000	3	1	1	1	0	0	0	0	0	0	0	0	0	0	0	1	0	0	0	.000	.000
Nitkowski, C.J., Det.*	.000	1	0	0	0	0	0	0	0	0	0	0	0	0	0	0	0	0	0	0	.000	.000
Norton, Greg, Chi.†	.250	1	4	4	0	1	1	0	0	0	1	0	0	0	0	0	1	0	0	0	.250	.250
Nunnally, Jon, Bos.*	.333	3	6	6	2	2	2	0	0	0	0	0	0	0	0	0	3	0	0	0	.333	.333
Offerman, Jose, Bos.†	.246	17	74	69	7	17	31	8	3	0	5	0	0	1	4	1	8	1	0	2	.449	.297
Ordonez, Magglio, Chi.	.400	2	6	5	0	2	3	1	0	0	0	0	0	0	1	0	1	0	0	0	.600	.500
Ortiz, David, Min.*	.000	5	19	15	1	0	0	0	0	0	0	0	0	0	4	0	10	0	0	2	.000	.211
Otanez, Willis, Bal.-Tor.	.333	5	14	12	5	4	4	0	0	0	1	0	0	1	1	0	4	0	0	1	.333	.429
Palmeiro, Orlando, Ana.*	.303	10	40	33	1	10	11	1	0	0	2	1	0	1	5	0	1	1	1	1	.333	.410
Palmeiro, Rafael, Tex.*	.321	128	547	458	75	147	284	24	1	37	115	0	6	2	81	11	54	2	4	12	.620	.420
Palmer, Dean, Det.	.303	9	39	33	5	10	13	3	0	0	5	0	1	1	4	0	12	0	0	1	.394	.385
Perry, Herbert, T.B.	.238	5	22	21	3	5	8	0	0	1	2	0	0	0	1	0	3	0	0	2	.381	.273
Phillips, Tony, Oak.†	.000	1	5	4	1	0	0	0	0	0	0	0	0	0	1	0	0	0	0	0	.000	.200
Pickering, Calvin, Bal.*	.071	7	20	14	1	1	1	0	0	0	1	0	0	0	6	0	7	0	0	1	.071	.350
Polonia, Luis, Det.*	.337	43	187	172	26	58	98	14	4	6	20	1	2	1	11	0	19	11	5	1	.570	.376
Posada, Jorge, N.Y.†	.000	1	4	3	0	0	0	0	0	0	0	0	0	0	1	0	2	0	0	0	.000	.250
Pose, Scott, K.C.*	.280	18	60	50	11	14	14	0	0	0	6	0	1	0	9	1	8	4	2	1	.280	.383
Pritchett, Chris, Ana.*	.167	5	13	12	0	2	2	0	0	0	0	0	0	0	1	0	1	0	0	0	.167	.231
Quinn, Mark, K.C.	.750	1	4	4	2	3	10	1	0	2	4	0	0	0	0	0	0	0	0	0	2.500	.750
Raines, Tim, Oak.†	.222	3	10	9	0	2	2	0	0	0	2	0	0	0	1	0	1	0	0	0	.222	.300
Ramirez, Alex, Cle.	.260	14	53	50	4	13	19	3	0	1	6	1	0	0	2	0	17	1	1	1	.380	.288
Ramirez, Manny, Cle.	1.000	2	4	3	2	3	5	2	0	0	0	0	0	0	1	0	0	0	0	0	1.667	1.000
Rodriguez, Ivan, Tex.	.000	1	4	4	0	0	0	0	0	0	0	0	0	0	0	0	1	0	0	0	.000	.000
Rodriguez, Liu, Chi.†	.000	2	0	0	0	0	0	0	0	0	0	0	0	0	0	0	0	0	0	0	.000	.000
Sadler, Donnie, Bos.	.000	4	0	0	2	0	0	0	0	0	0	0	0	0	0	0	0	0	0	0	.000	.000
Saenz, Olmedo, Oak.	.190	8	24	21	3	4	7	0	0	1	3	0	0	2	1	0	3	0	0	1	.333	.292
Salmon, Tim, Ana.	.042	7	31	24	3	1	4	0	0	1	5	0	0	0	7	0	6	0	0	2	.167	.258
Sanders, Anthony, Tor.	.500	2	4	4	1	2	3	1	0	0	2	0	0	0	0	0	1	0	0	0	.750	.500
Scarsone, Steve, K.C.	.000	2	3	2	0	0	0	0	0	0	0	0	0	0	1	0	2	0	0	0	.000	.333
Segui, David, Tor.†	.310	25	89	84	13	26	45	4	0	5	12	0	1	0	4	0	16	0	0	0	.536	.337
Sexson, Richie, Cle.	.205	24	97	88	10	18	34	5	1	3	17	0	3	0	6	0	25	1	0	4	.386	.247
Shave, Jon, Tex.	1.000	3	1	1	1	1	1	0	0	0	0	0	0	0	0	0	0	0	0	0	1.000	1.000
Simmons, Brian, Chi.†	.500	3	4	4	1	2	3	1	0	0	1	0	0	0	0	0	2	0	0	0	.750	.500
Simms, Mike, Tex.	.500	2	2	2	0	1	1	0	0	0	0	0	0	0	0	0	1	0	0	0	.500	.500
Singleton, Chris, Chi.*	.000	2	0	0	1	0	0	0	0	0	0	0	0	0	0	0	0	0	0	0	.000	.000
Sojo, Luis, N.Y.	.000	2	0	0	1	0	0	0	0	0	0	0	0	0	0	0	0	0	0	0	.000	.000
Soriano, Alfonso, N.Y.	.333	6	3	3	2	1	4	0	0	1	1	0	0	0	0	0	0	0	0	0	1.333	.333
Sorrento, Paul, T.B.*	.143	9	33	28	3	4	7	0	0	1	2	0	0	1	4	0	14	0	1	2	.250	.273
Sparks, Steve, Ana.	.000	1	0	0	0	0	0	0	0	0	0	0	0	0	0	0	0	0	0	0	.000	.000
Spencer, Shane, N.Y.	.333	3	9	9	3	3	4	1	0	0	2	0	0	0	0	0	2	0	0	0	.444	.333
Spiezio, Scott, Oak.†	.125	6	9	8	0	1	1	0	0	0	1	0	0	0	1	0	4	0	0	0	.125	.222
Stairs, Matt, Oak.*	.125	5	18	16	1	2	4	2	0	0	0	0	0	0	2	1	7	0	0	1	.250	.222
Stanley, Mike, Bos.	.288	20	65	52	8	15	23	2	0	2	9	0	0	2	11	0	13	0	0	1	.442	.431
Steinbach, Terry, Min.	.000	1	1	1	0	0	0	0	0	0	0	0	0	0	0	0	1	0	0	0	.000	.000
Stevens, Lee, Tex.*	.250	8	34	32	6	8	15	1	0	2	5	0	1	0	1	0	9	0	0	1	.469	.265
Stewart, Shannon, Tor.	.250	2	9	8	1	2	2	0	0	0	1	0	1	0	0	0	2	0	1	0	.250	.222
Strawberry, Darryl, N.Y.*	.310	17	59	42	10	13	25	3	0	3	5	0	0	0	17	0	13	2	0	0	.595	.508
Surhoff, B.J., Bal.*	.357	13	61	56	12	20	24	4	0	0	6	0	1	0	4	0	3	0	0	1	.429	.393
Sutton, Larry, K.C.*	.231	5	14	13	0	3	4	1	0	0	2	0	1	0	0	0	4	0	0	1	.308	.214
Sweeney, Mike, K.C.	.333	71	309	273	50	91	147	17	0	13	53	0	1	7	28	0	28	2	0	11	.538	.408
Tarasco, Tony, N.Y.*	.000	1	0	0	0	0	0	0	0	0	0	0	0	0	0	0	0	0	0	0	.000	.000
Thomas, Frank, Chi.	.281	82	369	295	43	83	125	21	0	7	45	0	5	6	63	12	41	2	0	13	.424	.412
Thome, Jim, Cle.*	.298	34	148	114	21	34	66	5	0	9	30	0	0	0	34	2	31	0	0	1	.579	.459
Timmons, Ozzie, Sea.	.222	5	9	9	2	2	3	1	0	0	1	0	0	0	0	0	1	0	0	0	.333	.222
Trammell, Bubba, T.B.	.313	6	22	16	3	5	12	1	0	2	4	0	0	0	6	0	3	0	0	0	.750	.500
Unroe, Tim, Ana.	.222	8	10	9	1	2	2	0	0	0	1	0	0	1	0	0	2	0	0	0	.222	.300
Valentin, John, Bos.	.200	1	5	5	1	1	1	0	0	0	0	0	0	0	0	0	0	0	0	0	.200	.200
Varitek, Jason, Bos.†	.500	2	5	4	1	2	5	0	0	1	2	0	0	0	1	0	0	0	0	0	1.250	.600
Vaughn, Mo, Ana.*	.292	67	289	260	31	76	150	11	0	21	64	0	1	4	24	1	53	0	0	6	.577	.360
Velandia, Jorge, Oak.	.000	1	0	0	1	0	0	0	0	0	0	0	0	0	0	0	0	0	0	0	.000	.000
Vitiello, Joe, K.C.	.167	2	9	6	1	1	1	0	0	0	0	0	0	1	2	0	3	0	0	0	.167	.444
Walbeck, Matt, Ana.†	.500	1	3	2	1	1	1	0	0	0	0	0	0	0	1	0	0	0	0	0	.500	.667
Walker, Todd, Min.*	.256	34	135	121	16	31	48	10	2	1	9	0	0	0	14	1	21	3	2	6	.397	.333
Webster, Lenny, Bal.	.333	2	4	3	0	1	1	0	0	0	1	0	0	0	1	0	0	0	0	1	.333	.500
Williams, Bernie, N.Y.†	.400	2	5	5	0	2	3	1	0	0	0	0	0	0	0	0	1	0	0	0	.600	.400
Williams, Reggie, Ana.†	.250	3	4	4	0	1	1	0	0	0	1	0	0	0	0	0	2	0	0	0	.250	.250
Wilson, Craig, Chi.	.000	1	1	0	1	0	0	0	0	0	0	0	0	0	1	0	0	0	0	0	.000	1.000
Wilson, Enrique, Cle.†	.000	1	1	1	0	0	0	0	0	0	0	0	0	0	0	0	0	0	0	0	.000	.000
Witt, Kevin, Tor.*	.200	11	33	30	3	6	10	1	0	1	3	1	0	0	2	0	8	0	0	0	.333	.250
Wood, Jason, Det.	.000	1	3	3	0	0	0	0	0	0	0	0	0	0	0	0	0	0	0	0	.000	.000
Zaun, Gregg, Tex.†	1.000	2	1	1	2	1	1	0	0	0	0	0	0	0	0	0	0	0	0	0	1.000	1.000
Zeile, Todd, Tex.	.333	1	4	3	2	1	4	0	0	1	2	0	0	0	1	0	1	0	0	0	1.333	.500

Player, Team	Avg.	G	TPA	AB	R	H	TB	2B	3B	HR	RBI	SH	SF	HP	BB	IBB	SO	SB	CS	GDP	Slg.	OBP
Baines, Harold, Bal.*	.327	96	380	336	56	110	200	16	1	24	76	0	2	0	42	3	35	1	2	13	.595	.400
Baines, Harold, Cle.*	.268	25	93	82	5	22	27	2	0	1	20	0	0	0	11	0	10	0	0	2	.329	.355
Huskey, Butch, Sea.	.217	7	31	23	5	5	15	1	0	3	6	0	1	0	7	0	5	0	0	0	.652	.387
Huskey, Butch, Bos.	.233	37	107	103	12	24	48	6	0	6	21	0	0	0	4	1	19	0	0	5	.466	.262
Otanez, Willis, Bal.	.333	3	6	6	3	2	2	0	0	0	1	0	0	0	0	0	2	0	0	1	.333	.333
Otanez, Willis, Tor.	.333	2	8	6	2	2	2	0	0	0	0	0	0	1	1	0	2	0	0	0	.333	.500

The following designated hitters, each of whom appeared in at least one game, had no plate appearances, runs scored or stolen base attempts: Cabrera, Jolbert, Cleveland (5); Menechino, Frank, Oakland (3); Hudson, Tim, Oakland (2); Rodriguez, Liu, Chicago (2); Becker, Rich, Oakland; Callaway, Mickey, Tampa Bay; Davidson, Cleatus, Minnesota; Durrington, Trent, Anaheim; Graffanino, Tony, Tampa Bay; Lowery, Terrell, Tampa Bay; Mateo, Ruben, Texas; McLemore, Mark, Texas; Nitkowski, C.J., Detroit; Sparks, Steve, Anaheim; Tarasco, Tony, New York.

PINCH-HITTING

TEAM

Team	Avg.	G	TPA	AB	R	H	TB	2B	3B	HR	RBI	SH	SF	HP	BB	IBB	SO	SB	CS	GDP	Slg.	OBP
Boston	.287	80	120	101	12	29	46	5	0	4	22	0	3	1	15	2	28	2	0	8	.455	.375
Baltimore	.276	94	141	123	15	34	51	3	1	4	25	1	2	2	13	1	31	1	0	4	.415	.350
Oakland	.270	91	144	115	17	31	39	8	0	0	22	2	2	2	23	3	31	1	0	2	.339	.394
Cleveland	.267	67	99	86	12	23	33	7	0	1	14	1	2	1	9	0	21	0	0	3	.384	.337
Anaheim	.255	72	117	98	15	25	37	6	0	2	11	0	2	0	17	0	30	0	1	3	.378	.359
Chicago	.250	56	78	72	7	18	22	4	0	0	11	1	0	0	5	1	11	0	0	4	.306	.299
Minnesota	.250	94	162	132	15	33	46	5	1	2	26	1	4	2	23	3	29	2	0	4	.348	.360
Texas	.244	40	56	45	9	11	16	2	0	1	6	0	1	1	9	0	10	0	0	1	.356	.375
Toronto	.238	70	92	84	9	20	36	4	0	4	13	1	2	0	5	2	23	0	0	2	.429	.275
New York	.234	75	112	94	5	22	29	4	0	1	17	0	1	0	17	4	30	0	0	2	.309	.348
Detroit	.194	73	101	98	9	19	33	6	1	2	10	0	0	1	2	0	24	0	0	0	.337	.218
Seattle	.182	73	118	99	7	18	27	3	0	2	12	3	0	1	15	3	17	0	0	3	.273	.296
Kansas City	.156	77	111	96	8	15	17	2	0	0	10	1	3	0	11	0	24	1	0	2	.177	.253
Tampa Bay	.145	50	65	55	7	8	14	4	1	0	1	0	0	2	8	1	15	0	0	0	.255	.277
Totals	.236	1012	1516	1298	147	306	446	63	4	23	200	11	22	13	172	20	324	7	1	38	.344	.326

TOP PINCH-HITTERS

Minimum 20 at-bats. *Lefthanded batter. †Switch-hitter.

Player, Team	Avg.	G	TPA	AB	R	H	TB	2B	3B	HR	RBI	SH	SF	HP	BB	IBB	SO	SB	CS	GDP	Slg.	OBP
Conine, Jeff, Bal.	.360	28	27	25	2	9	16	1	0	2	8	0	0	1	1	0	3	0	0	1	.640	.407
Greene, Willie, Tor.*	.300	24	22	20	3	6	15	0	0	3	6	0	1	0	1	0	6	0	0	0	.750	.318
Jefferson, Reggie, Bos.*	.296	30	28	27	1	8	12	1	0	1	2	0	0	0	1	0	8	0	0	4	.444	.321
Catalanotto, Frank, Det.*	.292	25	25	24	4	7	14	4	0	1	6	0	0	0	1	0	3	0	0	0	.583	.320
Amaral, Rich, Bal.	.286	25	25	21	4	6	7	1	0	0	1	0	0	1	3	0	4	1	0	0	.333	.400
Huson, Jeff, Ana.*	.259	33	33	27	4	7	9	2	0	0	3	0	1	0	5	0	7	0	0	0	.333	.364
Gates, Brent, Min.†	.200	31	31	25	2	5	7	0	1	0	4	0	1	0	5	1	4	0	0	2	.280	.323
Saenz, Olmedo, Oak.	.200	23	23	20	1	4	6	2	0	0	2	0	0	2	1	1	7	0	0	1	.300	.304
Ibanez, Raul, Sea.*	.182	26	25	22	0	4	5	1	0	0	2	0	0	0	3	0	1	0	0	1	.227	.280
Pose, Scott, K.C.*	.179	50	46	39	7	7	8	1	0	0	4	0	0	0	7	0	9	1	0	2	.205	.304
Hocking, Denny, Min.†	.130	23	23	23	1	3	4	1	0	0	2	0	0	0	0	0	6	0	0	0	.174	.130
Lampkin, Tom, Sea.*	.130	24	24	23	1	3	4	1	0	0	4	0	0	1	0	0	4	0	0	0	.174	.167

ALL PINCH-HITTERS

*Lefthanded batter. †Switch-hitter.

Player, Team	Avg.	G	TPA	AB	R	H	TB	2B	3B	HR	RBI	SH	SF	HP	BB	IBB	SO	SB	CS	GDP	Slg.	OBP
Alicea, Luis, Tex.†	.143	17	17	14	3	2	3	1	0	0	0	0	0	0	3	0	3	0	0	0	.214	.294
Allen, Chad, Min.	.000	4	3	2	0	0	0	0	0	0	0	0	0	0	1	1	0	0	0	0	.000	.333
Alomar, Roberto, Cle.†	.500	3	3	2	1	1	1	0	0	0	0	0	0	0	1	0	1	0	0	0	.500	.667
Alomar, Sandy, Cle.	.000	1	1	1	0	0	0	0	0	0	0	1	0	0	0	0	0	0	0	0	.000	.000
Alvarez, Gabe, Det.	.250	8	8	8	0	2	3	1	0	0	0	0	0	0	0	0	1	0	0	0	.375	.250
Amaral, Rich, Bal.	.286	25	25	21	4	6	7	1	0	0	1	0	0	1	3	0	4	1	0	0	.333	.400
Anderson, Brady, Bal.*	.167	7	7	6	1	1	1	0	0	0	0	0	0	0	1	0	3	0	0	0	.167	.286
Ausmus, Brad, Det.	1.000	1	1	1	0	1	1	0	0	0	1	0	0	0	0	0	0	0	0	0	1.000	1.000
Baerga, Carlos, Cle.†	.000	1	1	1	0	0	0	0	0	0	0	0	0	0	0	0	1	0	0	0	.000	.000
Baines, Harold, Bal.-Cle.*	.313	18	17	16	2	5	7	0	1	0	8	0	0	1	0	0	3	0	0	1	.438	.353
Bartee, Kimera, Det.	.333	4	4	3	3	1	3	0	1	0	0	0	0	0	1	0	1	0	0	0	1.000	.500
Becker, Rich, Oak.*	.400	5	5	5	0	2	2	0	0	0	1	0	0	0	0	0	2	0	0	0	.400	.400
Bell, David, Sea.	.500	2	2	2	0	1	1	0	0	0	0	0	0	0	0	0	0	0	0	0	.500	.500
Bellinger, Clay, N.Y.	.000	3	3	3	0	0	0	0	0	0	0	0	0	0	0	0	1	0	0	0	.000	.000
Berroa, Geronimo, Tor.	.250	4	4	4	1	1	2	1	0	0	0	0	0	0	0	0	1	0	0	1	.500	.250
Blowers, Mike, Sea.	.250	5	5	4	0	1	1	0	0	0	0	0	0	0	1	0	2	0	0	0	.250	.400
Boggs, Wade, T.B.*	.000	7	7	6	0	0	0	0	0	0	0	0	0	0	1	1	1	0	0	0	.000	.143
Bordick, Mike, Bal.	.000	1	1	1	0	0	0	0	0	0	0	0	0	0	0	0	1	0	0	0	.000	.000
Bournigal, Rafael, Sea.	.000	5	5	5	0	0	0	0	0	0	0	0	0	0	0	0	0	0	0	0	.000	.000
Brosius, Scott, N.Y.	.000	1	1	1	0	0	0	0	0	0	0	0	0	0	0	0	1	0	0	0	.000	.000
Brown, Dee, K.C.*	.000	7	6	5	0	0	0	0	0	0	0	0	0	0	1	0	0	0	0	0	.000	.167
Brumfield, Jacob, Bos.	.143	7	7	7	1	1	4	0	0	1	2	0	0	0	0	0	2	0	0	0	.571	.143
Buford, Damon, Bos.	.500	9	9	8	1	4	5	1	0	0	2	0	0	0	1	0	3	2	0	0	.625	.556
Buhner, Jay, Sea.	.000	3	3	1	1	0	0	0	0	0	0	0	1	0	2	0	0	0	0	0	.000	.667
Butler, Rich, T.B.*	1.000	1	1	1	0	1	1	0	0	0	0	0	0	0	0	0	0	0	0	0	1.000	1.000
Butler, Rob, Tor.*	.000	2	2	2	0	0	0	0	0	0	0	0	0	0	0	0	0	0	0	0	.000	.000
Cabrera, Jolbert, Cle.	.143	7	7	7	1	1	1	0	0	0	0	0	0	0	0	0	2	0	0	1	.143	.143
Cairo, Miguel, T.B.	.000	2	2	2	1	0	0	0	0	0	0	0	0	0	0	0	1	0	0	0	.000	.000
Canseco, Jose, T.B.	.000	1	1	1	0	0	0	0	0	0	0	0	0	0	0	0	1	0	0	0	.000	.000
Caruso, Mike, Chi.*	.667	3	3	3	1	2	2	0	0	0	0	0	0	0	0	0	0	0	0	0	.667	.667
Catalanotto, Frank, Det.*	.292	25	25	24	4	7	14	4	0	1	6	0	0	0	1	0	3	0	0	0	.583	.320
Cedeno, Domingo, Sea.†	.000	1	1	1	0	0	0	0	0	0	0	0	0	0	0	0	0	0	0	0	.000	.000
Chavez, Eric, Oak.*	.462	14	14	13	4	6	9	3	0	0	6	0	0	0	1	0	0	0	0	0	.692	.500
Christensen, McKay, Chi.*	.000	1	1	1	0	0	0	0	0	0	0	0	0	0	0	0	0	0	0	0	.000	.000
Christenson, Ryan, Oak.	.500	6	6	4	0	2	2	0	0	0	1	1	0	0	1	0	1	0	0	0	.500	.600
Clark, Tony, Det.†	.000	1	1	1	0	0	0	0	0	0	0	0	0	0	0	0	0	0	0	0	.000	.000
Clark, Will, Bal.*	.455	12	12	11	1	5	6	1	0	0	0	0	0	0	1	0	2	0	0	0	.545	.500

Player, Team	Avg.	G	TPA	AB	R	H	TB	2B	3B	HR	RBI	SH	SF	HP	BB	IBB	SO	SB	CS	GDP	Slg.	OBP
Clyburn, Danny, T.B.	.333	3	3	3	0	1	2	1	0	0	0	0	0	0	0	0	1	0	0	0	.667	.333
Coleman, Michael, Bos.	.000	1	1	1	0	0	0	0	0	0	0	0	0	0	0	0	0	0	0	0	.000	.000
Conine, Jeff, Bal.	.360	28	27	25	2	9	16	1	0	2	8	0	0	1	1	0	3	0	0	1	.640	.407
Coomer, Ron, Min.	.500	9	9	8	0	4	5	1	0	0	3	0	0	1	0	0	2	0	0	0	.625	.556
Cordero, Wil, Cle.	.250	6	6	4	2	1	2	1	0	0	1	0	0	0	2	0	1	0	0	0	.500	.500
Cordova, Marty, Min.	.357	16	16	14	1	5	6	1	0	0	3	0	0	0	2	0	1	1	0	1	.429	.438
Cox, Steve, T.B.*	1.000	1	1	1	0	1	2	1	0	0	0	0	0	0	0	0	0	0	0	0	2.000	1.000
Cruz, Jacob, Cle.*	.000	10	9	7	0	0	0	0	0	0	0	0	0	0	2	0	1	0	0	0	.000	.222
Cruz, Jose, Tor.†	.000	2	2	2	0	0	0	0	0	0	0	0	0	0	0	0	0	0	0	0	.000	.000
Cummings, Midre, Min.*	.167	7	7	6	1	1	4	0	0	1	4	0	0	0	1	0	3	0	0	0	.667	.286
Curtis, Chad, N.Y.	.357	17	17	14	1	5	6	1	0	0	4	0	0	0	3	0	2	0	0	1	.429	.471
Dalesandro, Mark, Tor.	.000	4	3	3	0	0	0	0	0	0	0	0	0	0	0	0	0	0	0	0	.000	.000
Daubach, Brian, Bos.*	.100	12	12	10	1	1	1	0	0	0	0	0	0	0	2	0	4	0	0	1	.100	.250
Davidson, Cleatus, Min.†	.000	1	1	0	0	0	0	0	0	0	0	0	1	0	0	0	0	0	0	0	.000	.000
Davis, Chili, N.Y.†	.250	19	19	16	0	4	5	1	0	0	5	0	0	0	3	1	4	0	0	0	.313	.368
Davis, Russ, Sea.	.000	1	1	1	0	0	0	0	0	0	0	0	0	0	0	0	0	0	0	0	.000	.000
Decker, Steve, Ana.	.000	3	2	0	0	0	0	0	0	0	0	0	0	0	2	0	0	0	0	0	.000	1.000
DeShields, Delino, Bal.*	.143	9	9	7	1	1	1	0	0	0	2	0	1	0	1	0	3	0	0	0	.143	.222
Diaz, Einar, Cle.	.000	2	2	2	0	0	0	0	0	0	0	0	0	0	0	0	0	0	0	0	.000	.000
Durham, Ray, Chi.†	.500	2	2	2	0	1	1	0	0	0	1	0	0	0	0	0	0	0	0	0	.500	.500
Durrington, Trent, Ana.	.333	3	3	3	0	1	1	0	0	0	0	0	0	0	0	0	1	0	0	0	.333	.333
Edmonds, Jim, Ana.*	1.000	2	2	1	1	1	1	0	0	0	0	0	0	0	1	0	0	0	0	0	1.000	1.000
Encarnacion, Juan, Det.	.000	2	2	2	0	0	0	0	0	0	0	0	0	0	0	0	1	0	0	0	.000	.000
Fernandez, Tony, Tor.†	.500	5	5	4	0	2	2	0	0	0	0	0	0	0	1	1	1	0	0	0	.500	.600
Fick, Robert, Det.*	.000	3	3	3	0	0	0	0	0	0	0	0	0	0	0	0	2	0	0	0	.000	.000
Flaherty, John, T.B.	.000	1	1	1	0	0	0	0	0	0	0	0	0	0	0	0	0	0	0	0	.000	.000
Fletcher, Darrin, Tor.*	.500	4	4	4	0	2	2	0	0	0	0	0	0	0	0	0	1	0	0	0	.500	.500
Fordyce, Brook, Chi.	.300	11	11	10	1	3	5	2	0	0	2	0	0	0	1	0	1	0	0	0	.500	.364
Franco, Julio, T.B.	.000	1	1	1	0	0	0	0	0	0	0	0	0	0	0	0	0	0	0	0	.000	.000
Frye, Jeff, Bos.	.000	2	2	1	1	0	0	0	0	0	0	0	0	0	1	0	0	0	0	0	.000	.500
Garcia, Freddy, Sea.	.000	1	1	1	0	0	0	0	0	0	0	0	0	0	0	0	1	0	0	0	.000	.000
Garcia, Jesse, Bal.	.000	1	1	1	0	0	0	0	0	0	0	0	0	0	0	0	1	0	0	0	.000	.000
Garcia, Karim, Det.*	.071	15	14	14	0	1	1	0	0	0	0	0	0	0	0	0	5	0	0	0	.071	.071
Garcia, Luis, Det.	.000	1	1	1	0	0	0	0	0	0	0	0	0	0	0	0	0	0	0	0	.000	.000
Garciaparra, Nomar, Bos.	.000	1	1	1	0	0	0	0	0	0	0	0	0	0	0	0	1	0	0	0	.000	.000
Gates, Brent, Min.†	.200	31	31	25	2	5	7	0	1	0	4	0	1	0	5	1	4	0	0	2	.280	.323
Giambi, Jason, Oak.*	.500	2	2	2	0	1	1	0	0	0	1	0	0	0	0	0	0	0	0	0	.500	.500
Giambi, Jeremy, K.C.*	.200	11	11	10	0	2	2	0	0	0	1	0	0	0	1	0	4	0	0	0	.200	.273
Gipson, Charles, Sea.	.500	2	2	2	1	1	2	1	0	0	2	0	0	0	0	0	0	0	0	0	1.000	.500
Girardi, Joe, N.Y.	.000	1	1	1	0	0	0	0	0	0	0	0	0	0	0	0	0	0	0	0	.000	.000
Goodwin, Tom, Tex.*	.000	2	2	2	0	0	0	0	0	0	0	0	0	0	0	0	0	0	0	0	.000	.000
Grebeck, Craig, Tor.	.000	5	5	5	0	0	0	0	0	0	0	0	0	0	0	0	1	0	0	0	.000	.000
Green, Scarborough, Tex.	.333	5	4	3	0	1	1	0	0	0	0	0	0	0	1	0	0	0	0	0	.333	.500
Greene, Todd, Ana.	.273	14	13	11	2	3	8	2	0	1	4	0	0	0	2	0	3	0	0	0	.727	.385
Greene, Willie, Tor.*	.300	24	22	20	3	6	15	0	0	3	6	0	1	0	1	0	6	0	0	1	.750	.318
Greer, Rusty, Tex.*	.000	1	1	0	1	0	0	0	0	0	0	0	0	0	1	0	0	0	0	0	.000	1.000
Grieve, Ben, Oak.*	.375	9	9	8	1	3	4	1	0	0	3	0	0	0	1	0	1	0	0	0	.500	.444
Gubanich, Creighton, Bos.	.000	1	1	1	0	0	0	0	0	0	0	0	0	0	0	0	1	0	0	0	.000	.000
Hansen, Jed, K.C.	.333	3	3	3	1	1	1	0	0	0	0	0	0	0	0	0	1	0	0	0	.333	.333
Haselman, Bill, Det.	.167	6	6	6	0	1	1	0	0	0	0	0	0	0	0	0	1	0	0	0	.167	.167
Hatteberg, Scott, Bos.*	.333	4	4	3	0	1	1	0	0	0	1	0	0	0	1	0	1	0	0	0	.333	.500
Higginson, Bobby, Det.*	.000	3	3	3	0	0	0	0	0	0	0	0	0	0	0	0	3	0	0	0	.000	.000
Hinch, A.J., Oak.	.000	1	1	0	0	0	0	0	0	0	0	0	1	0	0	0	0	0	0	0	.000	.000
Hocking, Denny, Min.†	.130	23	23	23	1	3	4	1	0	0	2	0	0	0	0	0	6	0	0	0	.174	.130
Holbert, Ray, K.C.	.000	2	2	2	0	0	0	0	0	0	0	0	0	0	0	0	1	0	0	0	.000	.000
Hollins, Dave, Tor.†	.500	4	4	4	1	2	2	0	0	0	0	0	0	0	0	0	0	0	0	0	.500	.500
Houston, Tyler, Cle.*	.000	3	3	3	0	0	0	0	0	0	0	0	0	0	0	0	0	0	0	0	.000	.000
Hunter, Brian, Sea.	.500	2	2	2	1	1	1	0	0	0	0	0	0	0	0	0	0	0	0	0	.500	.500
Hunter, Torii, Min.	.000	8	8	8	0	0	0	0	0	0	0	0	0	0	0	0	1	0	0	1	.000	.000
Huskey, Butch, Sea.-Bos.	.353	22	21	17	4	6	10	1	0	1	5	0	0	0	4	0	2	0	0	1	.588	.476
Huson, Jeff, Ana.*	.259	33	33	27	4	7	9	2	0	0	3	0	1	0	5	0	7	0	0	1	.333	.364
Ibanez, Raul, Sea.*	.182	26	25	22	0	4	5	1	0	0	2	0	0	0	3	0	1	0	0	1	.227	.280
Jackson, Darrin, Chi.	.250	14	13	12	1	3	3	0	0	0	2	1	0	0	0	0	1	0	0	2	.250	.250
Jackson, Ryan, Sea.*	.000	4	4	4	0	0	0	0	0	0	0	0	0	0	0	0	3	0	0	0	.000	.000
Jaha, John, Oak.	.091	16	16	11	0	1	1	0	0	0	4	0	2	0	3	0	4	0	0	0	.091	.250
Jefferies, Gregg, Det.†	.158	20	20	19	0	3	3	0	0	0	0	0	0	1	0	0	1	0	0	0	.158	.200
Jefferson, Reggie, Bos.*	.296	30	28	27	1	8	12	1	0	1	2	0	0	0	1	0	8	0	0	4	.444	.321
Jimenez, D'Angelo, N.Y.†	.000	1	1	1	0	0	0	0	0	0	0	0	0	0	0	0	0	0	0	0	.000	.000
Johnson, Charles, Bal.	.000	4	4	3	1	0	0	0	0	0	0	0	0	0	1	0	2	0	0	0	.000	.250
Jones, Jacque, Min.*	.333	5	5	3	1	1	1	0	0	0	0	0	0	0	2	1	1	0	0	0	.333	.600
Justice, David, Cle.*	.400	7	7	5	1	2	5	0	0	1	2	0	1	0	1	0	1	0	0	0	1.000	.429
Kapler, Gabe, Det.	.000	2	2	2	0	0	0	0	0	0	0	0	0	0	0	0	1	0	0	0	.000	.000
Kelly, Pat, Tor.	.000	2	2	1	0	0	0	0	0	0	1	0	1	0	0	0	1	0	0	0	.000	.000
Kelly, Roberto, Tex.	.143	8	8	7	1	1	1	0	0	0	1	0	0	1	0	0	3	0	0	0	.143	.250
Kingsale, Eugene, Bal.†	.500	2	2	2	0	1	1	0	0	0	0	0	0	0	0	0	1	0	0	0	.500	.500
Konerko, Paul, Chi.	.333	9	9	9	0	3	3	0	0	0	2	0	0	0	0	0	0	0	0	1	.333	.333
Koskie, Corey, Min.*	.600	15	15	10	5	6	7	1	0	0	1	0	0	2	3	0	2	0	0	0	.700	.733
Kreuter, Chad, K.C.†	.000	7	7	7	0	0	0	0	0	0	0	0	0	0	0	0	3	0	0	0	.000	.000
Lamb, David, T.B.†	.000	6	6	6	0	0	0	0	0	0	0	0	0	0	0	0	0	0	0	0	.000	.000
Lampkin, Tom, Sea.*	.130	24	24	23	1	3	4	1	0	0	4	0	0	1	0	0	4	0	0	0	.174	.167
Latham, Chris, Min.†	.000	1	1	1	0	0	0	0	0	0	0	0	0	0	0	0	1	0	0	0	.000	.000
Lawton, Matt, Min.*	.333	9	9	6	2	2	5	0	0	1	7	0	2	0	1	0	1	1	0	0	.833	.333

Player, Team	Avg.	G	TPA	AB	R	H	TB	2B	3B	HR	RBI	SH	SF	HP	BB	IBB	SO	SB	CS	GDP	Slg.	OBP
Ledee, Ricky, N.Y.*	.286	10	10	7	0	2	2	0	0	0	4	0	1	0	2	1	1	0	0	0	.286	.400
Ledesma, Aaron, T.B.	.000	4	4	3	1	0	0	0	0	0	1	0	1	0	1	0	1	0	0	0	.000	.250
Lee, Carlos, Chi.	1.000	2	2	2	0	2	2	0	0	0	0	0	0	0	0	0	0	0	0	0	1.000	1.000
Leius, Scott, K.C.	.111	13	11	9	0	1	1	0	0	0	3	0	2	0	0	0	0	0	0	0	.111	.091
Lennon, Patrick, Tor.	.000	1	1	1	0	0	0	0	0	0	0	0	0	0	0	0	1	0	0	0	.000	.000
Levis, Jesse, Cle.*	.000	1	1	1	0	0	0	0	0	0	0	0	0	0	0	0	1	0	0	0	.000	.000
Lewis, Darren, Bos.	.000	1	1	1	0	0	0	0	0	0	0	0	0	0	0	0	0	0	0	0	.000	.000
Leyritz, Jim, N.Y.	.250	13	12	8	1	2	2	0	0	0	1	0	0	0	4	1	2	0	0	0	.250	.500
Liefer, Jeff, Chi.*	.222	9	9	9	1	2	3	1	0	0	3	0	0	0	0	0	1	0	0	0	.333	.222
Lofton, Kenny, Cle.*	1.000	2	2	1	0	1	2	1	0	0	1	0	0	0	0	0	0	0	0	0	2.000	1.000
Lowery, Terrell, T.B.	.000	5	4	4	0	0	0	0	0	0	0	0	0	0	0	0	1	0	0	0	.000	.000
Luke, Matt, Ana.*	.143	10	8	7	2	1	4	0	0	1	2	0	0	0	1	0	4	0	0	1	.571	.250
Mabry, John, Sea.*	.167	7	7	6	0	1	1	0	0	0	0	0	0	0	1	0	2	0	0	0	.167	.286
Macfarlane, Mike, Oak.	.333	6	6	6	1	2	3	1	0	0	1	0	0	0	0	0	1	0	0	0	.500	.333
Macias, Jose, Det.†	.500	2	2	2	1	1	4	0	0	1	2	0	0	0	0	0	1	0	0	0	2.000	.500
Manto, Jeff, Cle.-N.Y.	.000	6	6	4	1	0	0	0	0	0	0	0	0	0	2	0	2	0	0	0	.000	.333
Martinez, Dave, T.B.*	.000	2	2	1	0	0	0	0	0	0	0	0	0	1	0	0	0	0	0	0	.000	.500
Martinez, Edgar, Sea.	.500	3	3	2	1	1	4	0	0	1	1	0	0	0	1	0	0	0	0	1	2.000	.667
Martinez, Tino, N.Y.*	.333	4	4	3	1	1	1	0	0	0	0	0	0	0	1	1	0	0	0	0	.333	.500
May, Derrick, Bal.*	.308	16	14	13	1	4	7	0	0	1	5	0	1	0	0	0	2	0	0	1	.538	.286
McCracken, Quinton, T.B.†	.000	1	1	1	0	0	0	0	0	0	0	0	0	0	0	0	1	0	0	0	.000	.000
McDonald, Jason, Oak.†	.125	12	12	8	3	1	1	0	0	0	0	0	0	0	4	0	3	0	0	0	.125	.417
McDonald, John, Cle.	.400	5	5	5	1	2	2	0	0	0	0	0	0	0	0	0	2	0	0	0	.400	.400
McGriff, Fred, T.B.*	.000	2	2	2	0	0	0	0	0	0	0	0	0	0	0	0	0	0	0	0	.000	.000
McLemore, Mark, Tex.†	.333	3	3	3	1	1	1	0	0	0	0	0	0	0	0	0	0	0	0	0	.333	.333
McRae, Brian, Tor.†	.200	13	13	10	2	2	3	1	0	0	2	1	0	0	2	1	5	0	0	0	.300	.333
Menechino, Frank, Oak.	1.000	1	1	1	0	1	1	0	0	0	0	0	0	0	0	0	0	0	0	0	1.000	1.000
Merloni, Lou, Bos.	.500	4	4	2	2	1	2	1	0	0	3	0	1	0	1	0	0	0	0	1	1.000	.500
Mientkiewicz, Doug, Min.*	.182	14	13	11	1	2	3	1	0	0	0	0	0	0	2	0	3	0	0	0	.273	.308
Mieske, Matt, Sea.	.500	7	5	4	1	2	5	0	0	1	1	0	0	0	1	1	0	0	0	0	1.250	.600
Minor, Ryan, Bal.	.000	1	1	1	0	0	0	0	0	0	0	0	0	0	0	0	1	0	0	0	.000	.000
Molina, Ben, Ana.	.000	1	1	1	0	0	0	0	0	0	0	0	0	0	0	0	0	0	0	0	.000	.000
Monahan, Shane, Sea.*	.000	3	3	3	0	0	0	0	0	0	0	0	0	0	0	0	1	0	0	0	.000	.000
Nixon, Trot, Bos.*	.000	3	3	3	0	0	0	0	0	0	0	0	0	0	0	0	1	0	0	0	.000	.000
Norton, Greg, Chi.†	.000	6	6	6	0	0	0	0	0	0	0	0	0	0	0	0	2	0	0	1	.000	.000
Nunnally, Jon, Bos.*	.250	4	4	4	0	1	2	1	0	0	1	0	0	0	0	0	3	0	0	0	.500	.250
O'Brien, Charlie, Ana.	.000	1	1	1	0	0	0	0	0	0	0	0	0	0	0	0	0	0	0	0	.000	.000
O'Neill, Paul, N.Y.*	.000	3	3	3	0	0	0	0	0	0	0	0	0	0	0	0	2	0	0	0	.000	.000
Offerman, Jose, Bos.†	.000	1	1	1	0	0	0	0	0	0	0	0	0	0	0	0	0	0	0	0	.000	.000
Ordonez, Magglio, Chi.	.000	2	2	1	0	0	0	0	0	0	0	0	0	0	1	1	0	0	0	0	.000	.500
Ortiz, David, Min.*	.000	5	5	3	0	0	0	0	0	0	0	0	0	0	2	0	1	0	0	0	.000	.400
Otanez, Willis, Bal.-Tor.	.125	9	9	8	0	1	2	1	0	0	0	0	0	0	1	0	2	0	0	1	.250	.222
Palmeiro, Orlando, Ana.*	.333	13	13	12	3	4	5	1	0	0	0	0	0	0	1	0	1	0	0	1	.417	.385
Palmeiro, Rafael, Tex.*	1.000	2	2	1	1	1	4	0	0	1	3	0	0	0	1	0	0	0	0	0	4.000	1.000
Perry, Herbert, T.B.	.400	7	7	5	2	2	4	0	1	0	4	0	0	0	2	0	1	0	0	0	.800	.571
Phillips, Tony, Oak.†	.000	3	3	3	0	0	0	0	0	0	0	0	0	0	0	0	0	0	0	0	.000	.000
Pickering, Calvin, Bal.*	.111	11	11	9	0	1	1	0	0	0	0	0	0	0	2	0	4	0	0	0	.111	.273
Polonia, Luis, Det.*	.333	6	6	6	1	2	3	1	0	0	1	0	0	0	0	0	0	2	0	0	.500	.333
Posada, Jorge, N.Y.†	.182	12	12	11	0	2	2	0	0	0	0	0	0	0	0	0	5	0	0	1	.182	.250
Pose, Scott, K.C.*	.179	50	46	39	7	7	8	1	0	0	4	0	0	0	7	0	9	1	0	2	.205	.304
Pritchett, Chris, Ana.*	1.000	3	3	2	0	2	2	0	0	0	1	0	1	0	0	0	0	0	0	0	1.000	.667
Quinn, Mark, K.C.	.000	1	1	1	0	0	0	0	0	0	0	0	0	0	0	0	1	0	0	0	.000	.000
Raines, Tim, Oak.†	.333	25	25	18	6	6	7	1	0	0	3	0	0	0	7	1	2	1	0	1	.389	.520
Ramirez, Alex, Cle.	.375	9	9	8	2	3	4	1	0	0	1	0	0	1	0	0	4	0	0	0	.500	.444
Ramirez, Manny, Cle.	.000	1	1	1	0	0	0	0	0	0	0	0	0	0	0	0	1	0	0	0	.000	.000
Reboulet, Jeff, Bal.	.000	4	4	1	1	0	0	0	0	0	0	1	0	0	2	0	0	0	0	0	.000	.667
Ripken, Cal, Bal.	1.000	1	1	1	0	1	1	0	0	0	0	0	0	0	0	0	0	0	0	0	1.000	1.000
Roberts, Dave, Cle.*	.000	2	2	2	0	0	0	0	0	0	1	0	0	0	0	0	1	0	0	0	.000	.000
Rodriguez, Ivan, Tex.	.500	2	2	2	0	1	1	0	0	0	0	0	0	0	0	0	1	0	0	0	.500	.500
Rodriguez, Liu, Chi.†	.000	3	3	3	0	0	0	0	0	0	0	0	0	0	0	0	1	0	0	0	.000	.000
Sadler, Donnie, Bos.	.000	1	1	1	0	0	0	0	0	0	0	0	0	0	0	0	1	0	0	0	.000	.000
Saenz, Olmedo, Oak.	.200	23	23	20	1	4	6	2	0	0	2	0	0	2	1	1	7	0	0	1	.300	.304
Salmon, Tim, Ana.	.000	2	2	0	0	0	0	0	0	0	0	0	0	0	2	0	0	0	0	0	.000	1.000
Sanders, Anthony, Tor.	.000	1	0	0	0	0	0	0	0	0	0	0	0	0	0	0	0	0	0	0	.000	.000
Scarsone, Steve, K.C.	.167	7	7	6	0	1	2	1	0	0	0	0	0	0	1	0	4	0	0	0	.333	.286
Segui, David, Sea.-Tor.†	.333	7	7	6	0	2	3	1	0	0	0	0	0	0	1	0	1	0	0	1	.500	.429
Sexson, Richie, Cle.	.100	11	11	10	0	1	1	0	0	0	3	0	1	0	0	0	3	0	0	1	.100	.091
Shave, Jon, Tex.	.000	1	1	1	0	0	0	0	0	0	0	0	0	0	0	0	1	0	0	0	.000	.000
Sheets, Andy, Ana.	.143	7	7	7	0	1	1	0	0	0	0	0	0	0	0	0	2	0	1	1	.143	.143
Simmons, Brian, Chi.†	.400	5	5	5	1	2	3	1	0	0	1	0	0	0	0	0	1	0	0	0	.600	.400
Simms, Mike, Tex.	.500	2	2	2	0	1	1	0	0	0	0	0	0	0	0	0	1	0	0	0	.500	.500
Singleton, Chris, Chi.*	.000	4	4	4	0	0	0	0	0	0	0	0	0	0	0	0	0	0	0	0	.000	.000
Smith, Bobby, T.B.	.000	1	1	1	0	0	0	0	0	0	0	0	0	0	0	0	1	0	0	0	.000	.000
Sojo, Luis, N.Y.	.000	4	4	4	0	0	0	0	0	0	0	0	0	0	0	0	0	0	0	0	.000	.000
Sorrento, Paul, T.B.*	.100	11	11	10	0	1	2	1	0	0	0	0	0	0	1	0	5	0	0	0	.200	.182
Spehr, Tim, K.C.	.000	1	1	1	0	0	0	0	0	0	0	0	0	0	0	0	0	0	0	0	.000	.000
Spencer, Shane, N.Y.	.286	8	8	7	2	2	5	0	0	1	1	0	0	0	1	0	3	0	0	0	.714	.375
Spiezio, Scott, Oak.†	.100	14	14	10	1	1	1	0	0	0	0	0	0	0	4	1	3	0	0	0	.100	.357
Stairs, Matt, Oak.*	.000	3	3	2	0	0	0	0	0	0	0	0	0	0	1	0	0	0	0	0	.000	.333
Stanley, Mike, Bos.	.214	23	23	14	1	3	6	0	0	1	6	0	2	1	6	2	1	0	0	1	.429	.435
Steinbach, Terry, Min.	.500	5	5	4	0	2	2	0	0	0	1	0	0	0	1	0	1	0	0	0	.500	.600
Stevens, Lee, Tex.*	.200	6	6	5	1	1	2	1	0	0	1	0	0	0	1	0	0	0	0	1	.400	.333

Player, Team	Avg.	G	TPA	AB	R	H	TB	2B	3B	HR	RBI	SH	SF	HP	BB	IBB	SO	SB	CS	GDP	Slg.	OBP
Stocker, Kevin, T.B.†	.000	3	3	2	1	0	0	0	0	0	0	0	0	0	1	0	0	0	0	0	.000	.333
Strawberry, Darryl, N.Y.*	.375	9	9	8	0	3	5	2	0	0	1	0	0	0	1	0	4	0	0	0	.625	.444
Surhoff, B.J., Bal.*	1.000	1	1	1	1	1	4	0	0	1	1	0	0	0	0	0	0	0	0	0	4.000	1.000
Sutton, Larry, K.C.*	.250	11	11	8	0	2	2	0	0	0	1	1	1	0	1	0	1	0	0	0	.250	.300
Sweeney, Mike, K.C.	.250	4	4	4	0	1	1	0	0	0	0	0	0	0	0	0	0	0	0	0	.250	.250
Tarasco, Tony, N.Y.*	.000	1	1	1	0	0	0	0	0	0	0	0	0	0	0	0	0	0	0	0	.000	.000
Tejada, Miguel, Oak.	.000	1	1	1	0	0	0	0	0	0	0	0	0	0	0	0	0	0	0	0	.000	.000
Thomas, Frank, Chi.	.000	3	3	3	0	0	0	0	0	0	0	0	0	0	0	0	2	0	0	0	.000	.000
Thome, Jim, Cle.*	1.000	3	3	2	0	2	3	1	0	0	1	0	0	0	1	0	0	0	0	0	1.500	1.000
Timmons, Ozzie, Sea.	.000	9	9	8	0	0	0	0	0	0	0	0	0	0	1	0	2	0	0	0	.000	.111
Trammell, Bubba, T.B.	.500	5	5	2	2	1	2	1	0	0	0	0	0	0	3	0	1	0	0	0	1.000	.800
Unroe, Tim, Ana.	.000	7	6	5	0	0	0	0	0	0	0	0	0	0	1	0	2	0	0	0	.000	.167
Valentin, Javier, Min.†	.000	3	3	3	0	0	0	0	0	0	0	0	0	0	0	0	1	0	0	0	.000	.000
Valentin, John, Bos.	1.000	1	1	1	0	1	1	0	0	0	0	0	0	0	0	0	0	0	0	0	1.000	1.000
Varitek, Jason, Bos.†	.375	8	8	8	2	3	6	0	0	1	2	0	0	0	0	0	2	0	0	0	.750	.375
Velandia, Jorge, Oak.	.333	3	3	3	0	1	1	0	0	0	0	0	0	0	0	0	1	0	0	0	.333	.333
Veras, Wilton, Bos.	1.000	1	1	1	0	1	1	0	0	0	0	0	0	0	0	0	0	0	0	0	1.000	1.000
Vitiello, Joe, K.C.	.000	1	1	1	0	0	0	0	0	0	0	0	0	0	0	0	0	0	0	0	.000	.000
Vizquel, Omar, Cle.†	1.000	2	2	2	1	2	3	1	0	0	0	0	0	0	0	0	0	0	0	0	1.500	1.000
Walbeck, Matt, Ana.†	.250	18	18	16	3	4	5	1	0	0	0	0	0	0	2	0	6	0	0	0	.313	.333
Walker, Todd, Min.*	.400	9	8	5	1	2	2	0	0	0	1	0	1	0	2	0	1	0	0	0	.400	.500
Webster, Lenny, Bal.	.250	4	4	4	0	1	1	0	0	0	1	0	0	0	0	0	0	0	0	0	.250	.250
Whiten, Mark, Cle.†	.000	1	1	1	0	0	0	0	0	0	0	0	0	0	0	0	0	0	0	0	.000	.000
Williams, Bernie, N.Y.†	.333	4	4	3	0	1	1	0	0	0	0	1	0	0	1	0	0	0	0	0	.333	.500
Williams, Reggie, Ana.†	.200	5	5	5	0	1	1	0	0	0	1	0	0	0	0	0	3	0	0	0	.200	.200
Wilson, Craig, Chi.	.000	5	5	2	2	0	0	0	0	0	0	0	0	0	3	0	2	0	0	0	.000	.600
Wilson, Dan, Sea.	.200	7	7	5	0	1	1	0	0	0	1	0	0	0	2	1	1	0	0	1	.200	.429
Wilson, Enrique, Cle.†	.313	16	16	16	2	5	7	2	0	0	1	0	0	0	0	0	1	0	0	1	.438	.313
Winn, Randy, T.B.†	.500	2	2	2	0	1	1	0	0	0	0	0	0	0	0	0	1	0	0	0	.500	.500
Witt, Kevin, Tor.*	.125	8	8	8	0	1	1	0	0	0	2	0	0	0	0	0	2	0	0	0	.125	.125
Wood, Jason, Det.	.000	3	3	3	0	0	0	0	0	0	0	0	0	0	0	0	2	0	0	0	.000	.000
Woodward, Chris, Tor.	1.000	1	1	1	1	1	1	0	0	0	0	0	0	0	0	0	0	0	0	0	1.000	1.000
Zaun, Gregg, Tex.†	.400	8	8	5	1	2	2	0	0	0	1	0	1	0	2	0	0	0	0	0	.400	.500

PINCH-HITTERS WITH TWO OR MORE TEAMS

Player, Team	Avg.	G	TPA	AB	R	H	TB	2B	3B	HR	RBI	SH	SF	HP	BB	IBB	SO	SB	CS	GDP	Slg.	OBP
Baines, Harold, Bal.*	.250	14	13	12	2	3	5	0	1	0	6	0	0	0	1	0	3	0	0	1	.417	.308
Baines, Harold, Cle.*	.500	4	4	4	0	2	2	0	0	0	2	0	0	0	0	0	0	0	0	0	.500	.500
Huskey, Butch, Sea.	.250	6	6	4	1	1	1	0	0	0	0	0	0	0	2	0	0	0	0	0	.250	.500
Huskey, Butch, Bos.	.385	16	15	13	3	5	9	1	0	1	5	0	0	0	2	0	2	0	0	1	.692	.467
Manto, Mike, Cle.	.000	3	3	1	1	0	0	0	0	0	0	0	0	0	2	0	0	0	0	0	.000	.667
Manto, Mike, N.Y.	.000	3	3	3	0	0	0	0	0	0	0	0	0	0	0	0	2	0	0	0	.000	.000
Otanez, Willis, Bal.	.000	4	4	4	0	0	0	0	0	0	0	0	0	0	0	0	1	0	0	1	.000	.000
Otanez, Willis, Tor.	.250	5	5	4	0	1	2	1	0	0	0	0	0	0	1	0	1	0	0	0	.500	.400
Segui, David, Sea.†	.500	3	3	2	0	1	1	0	0	0	0	0	0	0	1	0	0	0	0	0	.500	.667
Segui, David, Tor.†	.250	4	4	4	0	1	2	1	0	0	0	0	0	0	0	0	1	0	0	1	.500	.250

PITCHING

TEAM

Team	W	L	Pct.	ERA	G	ShO	Rel.	Sv.	IP	H	TBF	R	ER	HR	SH	SF	HB	BB	IBB	SO	WP	Bk.
Boston	94	68	.580	4.00	162	12	412	50	1436.2	1396	6120	718	638	160	27	43	55	469	25	1131	28	0
New York	98	64	.605	4.13	162	10	359	50	1439.2	1402	6233	731	661	158	42	47	57	581	27	1111	49	4
Oakland	87	75	.537	4.69	162	5	406	48	1438.1	1537	6309	846	750	160	34	39	54	569	45	967	57	8
Baltimore	78	84	.481	4.77	162	11	393	33	1435.0	1468	6259	815	760	198	47	49	49	647	34	982	55	6
Anaheim	70	92	.432	4.79	162	7	400	37	1431.1	1472	6258	826	762	177	36	65	56	624	17	877	65	5
Cleveland	97	65	.599	4.89	162	6	466	46	1450.1	1503	6374	860	788	197	41	39	54	634	55	1120	54	3
Chicago	75	86	.466	4.92	162	3	409	39	1438.1	1608	6452	870	786	210	39	56	61	596	31	968	60	9
Toronto	84	78	.519	4.92	162	9	377	39	1439.0	1582	6368	862	787	191	39	57	53	575	25	1009	55	4
Minnesota	63	97	.394	5.00	161	8	417	34	1423.1	1591	6216	845	791	208	32	48	28	487	22	927	57	6
Tampa Bay	69	93	.426	5.06	162	5	453	45	1433.0	1606	6482	913	805	172	42	53	79	695	25	1055	52	5
Texas	95	67	.586	5.07	162	9	439	47	1436.1	1626	6313	859	809	186	34	52	40	509	23	979	50	2
Detroit	69	92	.429	5.17	161	6	421	33	1421.0	1528	6286	882	817	209	39	60	70	583	26	976	43	4
Seattle	79	83	.488	5.24	162	6	346	40	1433.2	1613	6471	905	834	191	34	54	71	684	39	980	63	3
Kansas City	64	97	.398	5.35	161	3	416	29	1420.2	1607	6387	921	844	202	44	53	68	643	34	831	60	6
Totals	1122	1141	.496	4.86	1133	100	5714	570	20076.2	21539	88528	11853	10832	2619	530	715	795	8296	428	13913	748	65

NOTE—Totals for earned runs for several clubs do not agree with composite total for all pitchers of each respective club due to instances in which provisions of Section 10.18(i) of the Scoring Rules were applied. The following differences are to be noted: New York pitchers add to 665; Oakland pitchers add to 761; Baltimore pitchers add to 761; Cleveland pitchers add to 792; Chicago pitchers add to 787; Toronto pitchers add to 788; Minnesota pitchers add to 795; Detroit pitchers add to 824; Seattle pitchers add to 836; Kansas City pitchers add to 845.

INDIVIDUAL

TOP QUALIFIERS FOR EARNED-RUN AVERAGE TITLE

Minimum 162 innings. *Throws lefthanded.

Pitcher, Team	W	L	Pct.	ERA	G	GS	CG	ShO	GF	Sv.	IP	H	TBF	R	ER	HR	SH	SF	HB	BB	IBB	SO	WP	Bk.
Martinez, Pedro, Bos.	23	4	.852	2.07	31	29	5	1	1	0	213.1	160	835	56	49	9	3	6	9	37	1	313	6	0
Cone, David, N.Y.	12	9	.571	3.44	31	31	1	1	0	0	193.1	164	827	84	74	21	5	6	11	90	2	177	7	1
Mussina, Mike, Bal.	18	7	.720	3.50	31	31	4	0	0	0	203.1	207	842	88	79	16	9	7	1	52	0	172	2	0
Radke, Brad, Min.	12	14	.462	3.75	33	33	4	0	0	0	218.2	239	900	97	91	28	5	5	1	44	0	121	4	0
Rosado, Jose, K.C.*	10	14	.417	3.85	33	33	5	0	0	0	208.0	197	882	103	89	24	8	4	5	72	1	141	9	0
Moyer, Jamie, Sea.*	14	8	.636	3.87	32	32	4	0	0	0	228.0	235	945	108	98	23	6	2	9	48	1	137	3	0
Colon, Bartolo, Cle.	18	5	.783	3.95	32	32	1	1	0	0	205.0	185	858	97	90	24	5	4	7	76	5	161	4	0
Sirotka, Mike, Chi.*	11	13	.458	4.00	32	32	3	1	0	0	209.0	236	909	108	93	24	5	9	3	57	2	125	4	0
Garcia, Freddy, Sea.	17	8	.680	4.07	33	33	2	1	0	0	201.1	205	888	96	91	18	3	6	10	90	4	170	12	3
Hernandez, Orlando, N.Y.	17	9	.654	4.12	33	33	2	1	0	0	214.1	187	910	108	98	24	3	11	8	87	2	157	4	0
Olivares, Omar, Ana.-Oak.	15	11	.577	4.16	32	32	4	0	0	0	205.2	217	885	105	95	19	3	7	9	81	0	85	6	0
Halama, John, Sea.*	11	10	.524	4.22	38	24	1	1	7	0	179.0	193	763	88	84	20	5	9	7	56	3	105	4	0
Burba, Dave, Cle.	15	9	.625	4.25	34	34	1	0	0	0	220.0	211	940	113	104	30	2	3	8	96	3	174	13	0
Mays, Joe, Min.	6	11	.353	4.37	49	20	2	1	8	0	171.0	179	746	92	83	24	7	6	2	67	2	115	6	0
Finley, Chuck, Ana.*	12	11	.522	4.43	33	33	1	0	0	0	213.1	197	913	117	105	23	7	3	8	94	2	200	15	0

DEPARTMENTAL LEADERS: W—P. Martinez, Bos., 23; L—Moehler, Det., 16; G—Groom, Oak., Wells, Min., 76; GS—Helling, Tex., 35; CG—D. Wells, Tor., 7; ShO—Erickson, Bal., 3; GF—Hernandez, T.B., 66; Sv.—Rivera, N.Y., 45; IP—D. Wells, Tor., 231; H—D. Wells, Tor., 246; TBF—Erickson, Bal., 995; R—Hawkins, Min., 136; ER—Hawkins, Min., 129; HR—Helling, Tex., 41; SH—Clemens, N.Y., 10; SF—Hentgen, Tor., Hernandez, N.Y., 11; HB—Weaver, Det., 17; TBB—Erickson, Bal., 99; IBB—Service, K.C., 8; SO—P. Martinez, Bos., 313; WP—Finley, Ana., 15; BK—Garcia, Sea., Nitkowski, Det., 3.

ALL PITCHERS

*Throws lefthanded.

Pitcher, Team	W	L	Pct.	ERA	G	GS	CG	ShO	GF	Sv.	IP	H	TBF	R	ER	HR	SH	SF	HB	BB	IBB	SO	WP	Bk.
Abbott, Paul, Sea.	6	2	.750	3.10	25	7	0	0	8	0	72.2	50	298	31	25	9	3	4	0	32	3	68	2	0
Aguilera, Rick, Min.	3	1	.750	1.27	17	0	0	0	16	6	21.1	10	76	3	3	2	0	0	2	0	13	1	1	
Aldred, Scott, T.B.*	3	2	.600	5.18	37	0	0	0	9	0	24.1	26	114	15	14	1	2	1	2	14	0	22	1	0
Alvarez, Juan, Ana.*	0	1	.000	3.00	8	0	0	0	1	0	3.0	1	14	1	1	0	1	0	0	4	0	4	1	0
Alvarez, Wilson, T.B.*	9	9	.500	4.22	28	28	1	0	0	0	160.0	159	703	92	75	22	3	3	6	79	1	128	3	0
Anderson, Matt, Det.	2	1	.667	5.68	37	0	0	0	9	0	38.0	33	180	27	24	8	0	2	1	35	1	32	3	0
Appier, Kevin, K.C.-Oak.	16	14	.533	5.17	34	34	1	0	0	0	209.0	230	926	131	120	27	7	5	7	84	4	131	10	1
Arrojo, Rolando, T.B.	7	12	.368	5.18	24	24	2	0	0	0	140.2	162	630	84	81	23	5	3	14	60	2	107	2	0
Assenmacher, Paul, Cle.*	2	1	.667	8.18	55	0	0	0	8	0	33.0	50	165	32	30	6	1	2	1	17	5	29	1	1
Baldwin, James, Chi.	12	13	.480	5.10	35	33	1	0	0	0	199.1	219	886	119	113	34	4	7	7	81	1	123	11	1
Bale, John, Tor.*	0	0	.000	13.50	1	0	0	0	1	0	2.0	2	10	3	3	1	0	0	0	2	0	4	0	0
Barber, Brian, K.C.	0	3	.250	9.64	8	3	0	0	1	1	18.2	31	95	20	20	6	1	1	2	10	2	7	0	0
Beck, Rod, Bos.	0	1	.000	1.93	12	0	0	0	8	3	14.0	9	55	3	3	0	0	0	1	5	0	12	0	0
Belcher, Tim, Ana.	6	8	.429	6.73	24	24	0	0	0	0	132.1	168	600	104	99	27	6	9	5	46	0	52	7	1
Blair, Willie, Det.	3	11	.214	6.85	39	16	0	0	4	0	134.0	169	604	107	102	29	3	4	4	44	0	82	5	0
Boggs, Wade, T.B.	0	0	.000	6.75	1	0	0	0	1	0	1.1	3	7	1	1	0	0	0	0	0	0	0	1	0
Bones, Ricky, Bal.	0	3	.000	5.98	30	2	0	0	7	0	43.2	59	207	29	29	7	2	1	2	19	0	26	3	0
Borkowski, Dave, Det.	2	6	.250	6.10	17	12	0	0	2	0	76.2	86	351	58	52	10	1	2	4	40	0	50	3	0
Bradford, Chad, Chi.	0	0	.000	19.64	3	0	0	0	1	0	3.2	9	24	8	8	1	0	0	0	5	0	1	0	0
Brocail, Doug, Det.	4	4	.500	2.52	70	0	0	0	22	2	82.0	60	326	23	23	7	4	2	4	25	1	78	4	1
Brower, Jim, Cle.	3	1	.750	4.56	9	2	0	0	1	0	25.2	27	113	13	13	8	1	1	1	10	1	18	0	0
Brunson, Will, Det.*	1	0	1.000	6.00	17	0	0	0	1	0	12.0	18	58	9	8	3	1	2	0	6	1	9	0	0
Buddie, Mike, N.Y.	0	0	.000	4.50	2	0	0	0	0	0	2.0	3	9	1	1	1	0	0	0	0	0	0	0	0
Bullinger, Kirk, Bos.	0	0	.000	4.50	4	0	0	0	0	0	2.0	2	9	1	1	0	0	0	0	2	0	0	0	0

Pitcher, Team	W	L	Pct.	ERA	G	GS	CG	ShO	GF	Sv.	IP	H	TBF	R	ER	HR	SH	SF	HB	BB	IBB	SO	WP	Bk.
Bunch, Melvin, Sea.	0	0	.000	11.70	5	1	0	0	4	0	10.0	20	55	13	13	3	0	1	0	7	0	4	0	0
Burba, Dave, Cle.	15	9	.625	4.25	34	34	1	0	0	0	220.0	211	940	113	104	30	2	3	8	96	3	174	13	0
Burkett, John, Tex.	9	8	.529	5.62	30	25	0	0	1	0	147.1	184	656	95	92	18	5	3	3	46	1	96	4	0
Byrdak, Tim, K.C.*	0	3	.000	7.66	33	0	0	0	5	1	24.2	32	128	24	21	5	3	0	1	20	2	17	3	1
Callaway, Mickey, T.B.	1	2	.333	7.45	5	4	0	0	0	0	19.1	30	99	20	16	2	0	1	0	14	1	11	1	0
Candiotti, Tom, Oak.-Cle.	4	6	.400	7.32	18	13	0	0	1	0	71.1	86	326	64	58	14	2	4	3	30	0	41	13	0
Carmona, Rafael, Sea.	1	0	1.000	7.94	9	0	0	0	3	0	11.1	18	57	11	10	3	2	2	0	9	1	0	0	0
Carpenter, Chris, Tor.	9	8	.529	4.38	24	24	4	1	0	0	150.0	177	663	81	73	16	4	6	3	48	1	106	9	1
Carrasco, Hector, Min.	2	3	.400	4.96	39	0	0	0	10	1	49.0	48	204	29	27	3	0	1	1	18	0	35	4	0
Carter, Lance, K.C.	0	1	.000	5.06	6	0	0	0	3	0	5.1	3	21	3	3	2	0	0	0	3	0	3	0	0
Castillo, Carlos, Chi.	2	2	.500	5.71	18	2	0	0	6	0	41.0	45	178	26	26	10	0	0	0	14	1	23	0	2
Charlton, Norm, T.B.*	2	3	.400	4.44	42	0	0	0	9	0	50.2	49	233	29	25	4	2	3	1	36	0	45	4	0
Cho, Jin Ho, Bos.	2	3	.400	5.72	9	7	0	0	1	0	39.1	45	171	26	25	7	1	3	2	8	0	16	0	0
Clark, Mark, Tex.	3	7	.300	8.60	15	15	0	0	0	0	74.1	103	353	73	71	17	1	4	1	34	1	44	7	0
Clemens, Roger, N.Y.	14	10	.583	4.60	30	30	1	1	0	0	187.2	185	822	101	96	20	10	5	9	90	0	163	8	0
Cloude, Ken, Sea.	4	4	.500	7.96	31	6	0	0	8	1	72.1	106	362	67	64	10	1	4	5	46	5	35	8	0
Colon, Bartolo, Cle.	18	5	.783	3.95	32	32	1	1	0	0	205.0	185	858	97	90	24	5	4	7	76	5	161	4	0
Cone, David, N.Y.	12	9	.571	3.44	31	31	1	1	0	0	193.1	164	827	84	74	21	5	6	11	90	2	177	7	1
Cooper, Brian, Ana.	1	1	.500	4.88	5	5	0	0	0	0	27.2	23	124	15	15	3	0	1	4	18	0	15	0	0
Coppinger, Rocky, Bal.	0	1	.000	8.31	11	2	0	0	7	0	21.2	25	105	21	20	8	0	1	0	19	0	17	0	0
Cordero, Francisco, Det.	2	2	.500	3.32	20	0	0	0	4	0	19.0	19	91	7	7	2	2	4	0	18	2	19	1	0
Cormier, Rheal, Bos.*	2	0	1.000	3.69	60	0	0	0	7	0	63.1	61	275	34	26	4	1	3	5	18	2	39	1	0
Corsi, Jim, Bos.-Bal.	1	3	.250	4.34	36	0	0	0	8	0	37.1	40	166	19	18	6	4	1	2	20	3	22	0	0
Crabtree, Tim, Tex.	5	1	.833	3.46	68	0	0	0	21	0	65.0	71	275	26	25	4	1	1	1	18	1	54	5	0
Cruz, Nelson, Det.	1	5	.286	5.67	29	6	0	0	10	0	66.2	74	295	44	42	11	2	4	3	23	1	46	2	0
Daneker, Pat, Chi.	0	0	.000	4.20	3	2	0	0	1	0	15.0	14	64	8	7	1	2	1	0	6	0	5	0	0
Davenport, Joe, Chi.	0	0	.000	0.00	3	0	0	0	2	0	1.2	1	7	0	0	0	0	0	0	2	0	0	0	0
Davey, Tom, Tor.-Sea.	2	1	.667	4.71	45	0	0	0	15	1	65.0	62	298	41	34	5	1	2	7	40	1	59	6	0
Davis, Doug, Tex.*	0	0	.000	33.75	2	0	0	0	0	0	2.2	12	20	10	10	3	0	0	0	6	0	3	0	0
DeLucia, Rich, Cle.	0	1	.000	6.75	6	0	0	0	2	0	9.1	13	50	7	7	4	0	0	0	9	2	7	1	0
DePaula, Sean, Cle.	0	0	.000	4.63	11	0	0	0	4	0	11.2	8	45	6	6	0	2	0	0	3	0	18	0	0
Durbin, Chad, K.C.	0	0	.000	0.00	1	0	0	0	0	0	2.1	1	9	0	0	0	0	0	0	1	0	3	1	0
Duvall, Mike, T.B.*	1	1	.500	4.05	40	0	0	0	7	0	40.0	46	188	21	18	5	1	1	2	27	1	18	4	1
Eiland, Dave, T.B.	4	8	.333	5.60	21	15	0	0	0	0	80.1	98	369	59	50	8	2	4	3	27	1	53	2	1
Erdos, Todd, N.Y.	0	0	.000	3.86	4	0	0	0	1	0	7.0	5	31	4	3	2	0	1	0	4	0	4	1	0
Erickson, Scott, Bal.	15	12	.556	4.81	34	34	6	3	0	0	230.1	244	995	127	123	27	7	6	11	99	4	106	10	0
Escobar, Kelvim, Tor.	14	11	.560	5.69	33	30	1	0	2	0	174.0	203	795	118	110	19	2	8	10	81	2	129	6	1
Eyre, Scott, Chi.*	1	1	.500	7.56	21	0	0	0	8	0	25.0	38	129	22	21	6	0	1	1	15	2	17	1	0
Falkenborg, Brian, Bal.	0	0	.000	0.00	2	0	0	0	0	0	3.0	2	12	0	0	0	0	0	0	2	0	1	0	0
Fassero, Jeff, Sea.-Tex.*	5	14	.263	7.20	37	27	0	0	2	0	156.1	208	751	135	125	35	2	7	4	83	3	114	9	0
Fetters, Mike, Bal.	1	0	1.000	5.81	27	0	0	0	10	0	31.0	35	151	23	20	5	1	0	2	22	2	22	1	1
Finley, Chuck, Ana.*	12	11	.522	4.43	33	33	1	0	0	0	213.1	197	913	117	105	23	7	3	8	94	2	200	15	0
Florie, Bryce, Det.-Bos.	4	1	.800	4.65	41	5	0	0	10	0	81.1	94	368	50	42	8	3	2	2	35	5	65	8	0
Fossas, Tony, N.Y.*	0	0	.000	36.00	5	0	0	0	0	0	1.0	6	10	4	4	1	0	0	0	1	0	1	0	0
Foulke, Keith, Chi.	3	3	.500	2.22	67	0	0	0	31	9	105.1	72	411	28	26	11	3	0	3	21	4	123	1	0
Franklin, Ryan, Sea.	0	0	.000	4.76	6	0	0	0	2	0	11.1	10	51	6	6	2	0	0	1	8	1	6	0	0
Frascatore, John, Tor.	7	1	.875	3.41	33	0	0	0	14	1	37.0	42	161	16	14	5	2	1	9	4	2	22	5	0
Fussell, Chris, K.C.	0	5	.000	7.39	17	8	0	0	3	2	56.0	72	265	51	46	9	1	4	5	36	3	37	6	0
Fyhrie, Mike, Ana.	0	4	.000	5.05	16	7	0	0	5	0	51.2	61	235	32	29	8	0	1	0	21	1	26	0	0
Gaillard, Eddie, T.B.	1	0	1.000	2.08	8	0	0	0	1	0	8.2	12	43	9	2	1	1	0	1	4	0	7	0	0
Garces, Rich, Bos.	5	1	.833	1.55	30	0	0	0	4	2	40.2	25	164	9	7	1	0	0	0	18	1	33	0	0
Garcia, Freddy, Sea.	17	8	.680	4.07	33	33	2	1	0	0	201.1	205	888	96	91	18	3	6	10	90	4	170	12	3
Glover, Gary, Tor.	0	0	.000	0.00	1	0	0	0	0	0	1.0	0	3	0	0	0	0	0	0	1	0	0	0	0
Glynn, Ryan, Tex.	2	4	.333	7.24	13	10	0	0	2	0	54.2	71	262	46	44	10	0	1	1	35	0	39	3	1
Gooden, Dwight, Cle.	3	4	.429	6.26	26	22	0	0	0	0	115.0	127	532	90	80	18	1	4	9	67	3	88	4	0
Gordon, Tom, Bos.	0	2	.000	5.60	21	0	0	0	15	11	17.2	17	82	11	11	2	0	1	2	12	2	24	0	0
Graterol, Beiker, Det.	0	1	.000	15.75	1	1	0	0	0	0	4.0	4	20	7	7	3	0	0	0	4	1	2	0	0
Grimsley, Jason, N.Y.	7	2	.778	3.60	55	0	0	0	25	1	75.0	66	336	39	30	7	3	4	40	5	49	8	0	
Groom, Buddy, Oak.*	3	2	.600	5.09	76	0	0	0	6	0	46.0	48	196	29	26	1	2	0	1	18	5	32	2	1
Gross, Kip, Bos.	0	2	.000	7.82	11	1	0	0	7	0	12.2	15	64	11	11	3	1	1	3	8	2	9	1	0
Guardado, Eddie, Min.*	2	5	.286	4.50	63	0	0	0	13	2	48.0	37	197	24	24	6	2	1	2	25	4	50	0	0
Gunderson, Eric, Tex.*	0	0	.000	7.20	11	0	0	0	3	0	10.0	20	51	8	8	1	0	1	0	2	0	6	3	0
Guthrie, Mark, Bos.*	1	1	.500	5.83	46	0	0	0	15	2	46.1	50	207	32	30	9	0	3	2	20	3	36	2	0
Guzman, Juan, Bal.	5	9	.357	4.18	21	21	1	1	0	0	122.2	124	544	63	57	18	4	3	6	65	3	95	7	2
Halama, John, Sea.*	11	10	.524	4.22	38	24	1	1	7	0	179.0	193	763	88	84	20	5	9	7	56	3	105	4	0
Halladay, Roy, Tor.	8	7	.533	3.92	36	18	1	1	2	1	149.1	156	668	76	65	19	3	4	4	79	1	82	6	0
Hamilton, Joey, Tor.	7	8	.467	6.52	22	18	0	0	1	0	98.0	118	440	73	71	13	0	2	3	39	0	56	4	1
Haney, Chris, Cle.*	0	2	.000	4.69	13	4	0	0	1	0	40.1	43	178	22	21	3	0	0	3	16	0	22	0	0
Harikkala, Tim, Bos.	1	1	.500	6.23	7	0	0	0	2	0	13.0	15	58	9	9	0	2	0	1	6	1	7	1	0
Harville, Chad, Oak.	0	2	.000	6.91	15	0	0	0	8	0	14.1	18	69	11	11	2	0	1	0	10	1	15	3	1
Hasegawa, Shigetoshi, Ana.	4	6	.400	4.91	64	1	0	0	26	2	77.0	80	333	45	42	14	3	4	2	34	2	44	4	0
Hawkins, LaTroy, Min.	10	14	.417	6.66	33	33	1	0	0	0	174.1	238	803	136	129	29	1	5	1	60	2	103	9	0
Haynes, Jimmy, Oak.	7	12	.368	6.34	30	25	0	0	2	0	142.0	158	652	112	100	21	4	5	2	80	3	93	7	2
Helling, Rick, Tex.	13	11	.542	4.84	35	35	3	0	0	0	219.1	228	943	127	118	41	5	10	6	85	5	131	8	0
Henry, Butch, Sea.*	2	0	1.000	5.04	7	4	0	0	0	0	25.0	30	112	15	14	1	0	1	2	10	0	15	0	0
Hentgen, Pat, Tor.	11	12	.478	4.79	34	34	1	0	0	0	199.0	225	869	115	106	32	3	11	3	65	1	118	8	1
Heredia, Gil, Oak.	13	8	.619	4.81	33	33	1	0	0	0	200.1	228	852	114	109	27	3	8	3	34	4	117	2	1
Hernandez, Orlando, N.Y.	17	9	.654	4.12	33	33	2	1	0	0	214.1	187	910	108	98	24	3	11	8	87	2	157	4	0
Hernandez, Roberto, T.B.	2	3	.400	3.07	72	0	0	0	66	43	73.1	68	321	27	25	1	2	3	4	33	1	69	3	0
Hiljus, Erik, Det.	0	0	.000	5.19	6	0	0	0	2	0	8.2	7	35	5	5	2	0	1	0	5	0	1	0	0
Hill, Ken, Ana.	4	11	.267	4.77	26	22	0	0	2	0	128.1	129	569	72	68	14	3	8	4	76	1	76	5	0
Hinchliffe, Brett, Sea.	0	4	.000	8.80	11	4	0	0	2	0	30.2	41	153	31	30	10	1	0	4	21	0	14	2	0

Pitcher, Team	W	L	Pct.	ERA	G	GS	CG	ShO	GF	Sv.	IP	H	TBF	R	ER	HR	SH	SF	HB	BB	IBB	SO	WP	Bk.
Holtz, Mike, Ana.*	2	3	.400	8.06	28	0	0	0	9	0	22.1	26	106	20	20	3	1	0	2	15	1	17	3	0
Howry, Bobby, Chi.	5	3	.625	3.59	69	0	0	0	54	28	67.2	58	298	34	27	8	3	1	3	38	3	80	3	1
Hudek, John, Tor.	0	0	.000	12.27	3	0	0	0	1	0	3.2	8	19	5	5	1	0	1	0	1	0	2	0	0
Hudson, Tim, Oak.	11	2	.846	3.23	21	21	1	0	0	0	136.1	121	580	56	49	8	1	2	4	62	2	132	6	0
Irabu, Hideki, N.Y.	11	7	.611	4.84	32	27	2	1	2	0	169.1	180	733	98	91	26	2	4	6	46	0	133	7	0
Isringhausen, Jason, Oak.	0	1	.000	2.13	20	0	0	0	18	8	25.1	21	107	6	6	2	0	0	1	12	2	20	2	0
Jackson, Mike, Cle.	3	4	.429	4.06	72	0	0	0	65	39	68.2	60	291	32	31	11	2	2	2	26	1	55	0	1
Jarvis, Kevin, Oak.	0	1	.000	11.57	4	1	0	0	0	0	14.0	28	75	19	18	6	0	1	1	6	0	11	0	0
Johns, Doug, Bal.*	6	4	.600	4.47	32	5	0	0	2	0	86.2	81	368	45	43	9	1	7	8	25	2	50	1	0
Johnson, Jason, Bal.	8	7	.533	5.46	22	21	0	0	0	0	115.1	120	515	74	70	16	2	4	3	55	0	71	5	1
Johnson, Jonathan, Tex.	0	0	.000	15.00	1	0	0	0	0	0	3.0	9	21	5	5	0	0	1	1	2	0	3	0	0
Jones, Doug, Oak.	5	5	.500	3.55	70	0	0	0	35	10	104.0	106	430	43	41	10	3	3	3	24	3	63	2	0
Jones, Todd, Det.	4	4	.500	3.80	65	0	0	0	62	30	66.1	64	287	30	28	7	3	1	1	35	1	64	2	0
Juden, Jeff, N.Y.	0	1	.000	1.59	2	1	0	0	0	0	5.2	5	29	1	1	0	0	1	0	3	0	9	0	0
Kamieniecki, Scott, Bal.	2	4	.333	4.95	43	3	0	0	18	2	56.1	52	248	32	31	4	4	3	4	29	2	39	4	0
Karsay, Steve, Cle.	10	2	.833	2.97	50	3	0	0	13	1	78.2	71	324	29	26	6	2	3	2	30	3	68	5	0
Kida, Masao, Det.	1	0	1.000	6.26	49	0	0	0	21	1	64.2	73	292	48	45	6	1	4	4	30	3	50	7	0
Koch, Billy, Tor.	0	5	.000	3.39	56	0	0	0	48	31	63.2	55	272	26	24	5	4	1	3	30	5	57	0	0
Kolb, Danny, Tex.	2	1	.667	4.65	16	0	0	0	6	0	31.0	33	139	18	16	2	0	0	1	15	0	15	2	0
Kubinski, Tim, Oak.*	0	0	.000	5.84	14	0	0	0	4	0	12.1	14	57	8	8	3	0	1	1	5	1	7	0	0
Langston, Mark, Cle.*	1	2	.333	5.25	25	5	0	0	2	0	61.2	69	274	40	36	9	3	2	0	29	6	43	2	0
Laxton, Brett, Oak.	0	1	.000	7.45	3	2	0	0	0	0	9.2	12	50	12	8	1	0	3	2	7	1	9	3	0
Lee, Corey, Tex.*	0	1	.000	27.00	1	0	0	0	1	0	1.0	2	6	3	3	1	0	0	0	1	0	0	0	0
Leiter, Mark, Sea.	0	0	.000	6.75	2	0	0	0	0	0	1.1	2	6	1	1	0	0	0	0	0	0	1	0	0
Levine, Al, Ana.	1	1	.500	3.39	50	1	0	0	12	0	85.0	76	349	40	32	13	2	7	3	29	2	37	3	0
Lidle, Cory, T.B.	1	0	1.000	7.20	5	1	0	0	1	0	5.0	8	24	4	4	0	0	0	0	2	0	4	0	0
Lincoln, Mike, Min.	3	10	.231	6.84	18	15	0	0	0	0	76.1	102	353	59	58	11	2	6	1	26	0	27	4	0
Linton, Doug, Bal.	1	4	.200	5.95	14	8	0	0	1	0	59.0	69	264	41	39	14	4	0	2	25	1	31	4	0
Lira, Felipe, Det.	0	0	.000	10.80	2	0	0	0	0	0	3.1	7	20	5	4	2	0	0	0	2	0	3	0	0
Lloyd, Graeme, Tor.*	5	3	.625	3.63	74	0	0	0	25	3	72.0	68	301	36	29	11	1	1	4	23	4	47	1	0
Loaiza, Esteban, Tex.	9	5	.643	4.56	30	15	0	0	4	0	120.1	128	517	65	61	10	7	4	0	40	2	77	2	0
Lopez, Albie, T.B.	3	2	.600	4.64	51	0	0	0	14	1	64.0	66	281	40	33	8	1	4	1	24	2	37	3	0
Lowe, Derek, Bos.	6	3	.667	2.63	74	0	0	0	32	15	109.1	84	436	35	32	7	1	2	4	25	1	80	1	0
Lowe, Sean, Chi.	4	1	.800	3.67	64	0	0	0	13	0	95.2	90	406	39	39	10	3	9	4	46	1	62	4	0
Ludwick, Eric, Tor.	0	0	.000	27.00	1	0	0	0	0	0	1.0	3	8	3	3	0	0	0	0	2	0	0	0	0
Lundquist, David, Chi.	1	1	.500	8.59	17	0	0	0	7	0	22.0	28	106	21	21	3	2	2	1	12	0	18	0	0
Magnante, Mike, Ana.*	5	2	.714	3.38	53	0	0	0	13	0	69.1	68	299	30	26	2	0	7	3	29	4	44	3	1
Mahay, Ron, Oak.*	2	0	1.000	1.86	6	1	0	0	2	1	19.1	8	68	4	4	2	0	0	0	3	0	15	0	0
Marte, Damaso, Sea.*	0	1	.000	9.35	5	0	0	0	2	0	8.2	16	47	9	9	3	0	0	0	6	0	3	0	0
Martin, Tom, Cle.*	0	1	.000	8.68	42	0	0	0	0	0	9.1	13	44	9	9	2	1	0	1	3	1	8	0	0
Martinez, Pedro, Bos.	23	4	.852	2.07	31	29	5	1	1	0	213.1	160	835	56	49	9	3	6	9	37	1	313	6	0
Martinez, Ramon, Bos.	2	1	.667	3.05	4	4	0	0	0	0	20.2	14	84	8	7	2	0	1	2	8	0	15	0	0
Mathews, Terry, K.C.	2	1	.667	4.38	24	1	0	0	7	1	39.0	44	175	21	19	4	0	4	2	17	1	19	0	0
Mathews, T.J., Oak.	9	5	.643	3.81	50	0	0	0	15	3	59.0	46	242	28	25	9	5	1	2	20	4	42	2	0
Mays, Joe, Min.	6	11	.353	4.37	49	20	2	1	8	0	171.0	179	746	92	83	24	7	6	2	67	2	115	6	0
McDowell, Jack, Ana.	0	4	.000	8.05	4	4	0	0	0	0	19.0	31	93	17	17	4	1	1	2	5	0	12	0	0
McMichael, Greg, Oak.	0	0	.000	5.40	17	0	0	0	4	0	15.0	15	69	9	9	3	1	1	2	12	2	3	0	0
Meche, Gil, Sea.	8	4	.667	4.73	16	15	0	0	0	0	85.2	73	375	48	45	9	5	3	2	57	1	47	1	0
Mecir, Jim, T.B.	0	1	.000	2.61	17	0	0	0	3	0	20.2	15	91	7	6	0	0	2	1	14	0	15	0	0
Mendoza, Ramiro, N.Y.	9	9	.500	4.29	53	6	0	0	15	3	123.2	141	536	68	59	13	6	4	3	27	3	80	2	0
Mercker, Kent, Bos.*	2	0	1.000	3.51	5	5	0	0	0	0	25.2	23	113	12	10	0	1	1	3	13	0	17	0	0
Mesa, Jose, Sea.	3	6	.333	4.98	68	0	0	0	60	33	68.2	84	325	42	38	11	2	4	4	40	4	42	7	0
Miller, Travis, Min.*	2	2	.500	2.72	52	0	0	0	12	0	49.2	55	214	19	15	3	2	0	0	16	3	40	6	0
Milton, Eric, Min.*	7	11	.389	4.49	34	34	5	2	0	0	206.1	190	858	111	103	28	3	6	3	63	2	163	2	0
Mintz, Steve, Ana.	3	0	.000	3.60	3	0	0	0	2	0	5.0	8	23	2	2	1	0	0	0	2	0	2	0	0
Mlicki, Dave, Det.	14	12	.538	4.60	31	31	2	0	0	0	191.2	209	850	108	98	24	3	8	12	70	1	119	0	0
Moehler, Brian, Det.	10	16	.385	5.04	32	32	2	2	0	0	196.1	229	859	116	110	22	8	5	7	59	5	106	4	0
Molina, Gabe, Bal.	1	2	.333	6.65	20	0	0	0	7	0	23.0	22	102	19	17	4	0	0	16	1	14	4	0	0
Montgomery, Jeff, K.C.	1	4	.200	6.84	49	0	0	0	36	12	51.1	72	237	40	39	7	2	2	2	23	3	27	1	0
Moreno, Orber, K.C.	0	0	.000	5.63	7	0	0	0	3	0	8.0	4	34	5	5	1	0	0	6	0	7	0	0	0
Morgan, Mike, Tex.	13	10	.565	6.24	34	25	1	0	1	0	140.0	184	632	108	97	25	3	5	7	48	2	61	3	1
Morman, Alvin, K.C.*	2	4	.333	4.05	49	0	0	0	2	1	53.1	66	246	27	24	6	0	4	4	23	0	31	1	0
Morris, Jim, T.B.*	0	0	.000	5.79	5	0	0	0	3	0	4.2	3	21	3	3	1	0	0	1	2	0	3	0	0
Moyer, Jamie, Sea.*	14	8	.636	3.87	32	32	4	0	0	0	228.0	235	945	108	98	23	6	2	9	48	1	137	3	0
Munoz, Mike, Tex.*	2	1	.667	3.93	56	0	0	0	11	1	52.2	52	221	24	23	5	1	3	1	18	2	27	2	0
Munro, Peter, Tor.	0	2	.000	6.02	31	2	0	0	9	0	55.1	70	250	38	37	6	1	4	2	23	0	38	3	0
Murray, Dan, K.C.	0	0	.000	6.48	4	0	0	0	1	0	8.1	9	39	8	6	4	0	0	1	4	0	8	0	0
Mussina, Mike, Bal.	18	7	.720	3.50	31	31	4	0	0	0	203.1	207	842	88	79	16	9	7	1	52	0	172	2	0
Myette, Aaron, Chi.	0	2	.000	6.32	4	3	0	0	0	0	15.2	17	80	11	11	2	0	0	2	14	1	11	2	0
Nagy, Charles, Cle.	17	11	.607	4.95	33	32	1	0	0	0	202.0	238	887	120	111	26	5	4	6	59	4	126	3	0
Naulty, Dan, N.Y.	1	0	1.000	4.38	33	0	0	0	20	0	49.1	40	206	24	24	8	1	1	4	22	2	35	3	0
Navarro, Jaime, Chi.	8	13	.381	6.09	32	27	0	0	1	0	159.2	206	748	126	108	29	3	4	11	71	1	74	9	0
Nelson, Jeff, N.Y.	2	1	.667	4.15	39	0	0	0	8	1	30.1	27	139	14	14	2	2	3	22	2	35	2	1	0
Newman, Alan, T.B.*	2	2	.500	6.89	18	0	0	0	5	0	15.2	22	76	12	12	2	0	0	1	9	0	20	2	1
Nitkowski, C.J., Det.*	4	5	.444	4.30	68	7	0	0	7	0	81.2	63	349	44	39	11	1	4	3	45	3	66	4	3
Ohka, Tomo, Bos.	1	2	.333	6.23	8	2	0	0	3	0	13.0	21	65	12	9	2	0	1	0	6	0	8	0	0
Olivares, Omar, Ana.-Oak.	15	11	.577	4.16	32	32	4	0	0	0	205.2	217	885	105	95	19	3	7	9	81	0	85	6	0
Oquist, Mike, Oak.	9	10	.474	5.37	28	24	0	0	1	0	140.2	158	629	86	84	18	3	1	2	64	5	89	2	0
Orosco, Jesse, Bal.*	0	2	.000	5.34	65	0	0	0	12	1	32.0	28	144	21	19	5	2	3	2	20	3	35	2	0
Ortiz, Ramon, Ana.	2	2	.500	6.52	9	9	0	0	0	0	48.1	50	218	35	35	7	0	2	2	25	0	44	2	2
Paniagua, Jose, Sea.	6	11	.353	4.06	59	0	0	0	16	3	77.2	75	350	37	35	6	4	3	7	52	4	74	6	0
Parque, Jim, Chi.*	9	15	.375	5.13	31	30	1	0	0	0	173.2	210	804	111	99	23	5	8	10	79	2	111	3	2

Pitcher, Team	W	L	Pct.	ERA	G	GS	CG	ShO	GF	Sv.	IP	H	TBF	R	ER	HR	SH	SF	HB	BB	IBB	SO	WP	Bk.
Patterson, Danny, Tex.	2	0	1.000	5.67	53	0	0	0	18	0	60.1	77	275	38	38	5	0	2	1	19	3	43	2	0
Pena, Jesus, Chi.*	0	0	.000	5.31	26	0	0	0	1	0	20.1	21	106	15	12	3	1	0	1	23	5	20	3	0
Pena, Juan, Bos.	2	0	1.000	0.69	2	2	0	0	0	0	13.0	9	49	1	1	0	0	0	0	3	0	15	0	0
Percival, Troy, Ana.	4	6	.400	3.79	60	0	0	0	50	31	57.0	38	230	24	24	9	0	1	3	22	0	58	3	0
Perisho, Matt, Tex.*	0	0	.000	2.61	4	1	0	0	3	0	10.1	8	40	3	3	0	0	0	0	2	1	17	1	0
Perkins, Dan, Min.	1	7	.125	6.54	29	12	0	0	7	0	86.2	117	413	69	63	14	2	4	5	43	0	44	6	2
Person, Robert, Tor.	0	2	.000	9.82	11	0	0	0	7	2	11.0	9	60	12	12	1	0	2	4	15	1	12	2	0
Petkovsek, Mark, Ana.	10	4	.714	3.47	64	0	0	0	18	1	83.0	85	349	37	32	6	5	5	2	21	2	43	3	1
Pettitte, Andy, N.Y.*	14	11	.560	4.70	31	31	0	0	0	0	191.2	216	851	105	100	20	6	6	3	89	3	121	3	1
Pisciotta, Marc, K.C.	0	2	.000	8.64	8	0	0	0	3	0	8.1	9	42	8	8	1	0	0	0	10	0	3	1	1
Pittsley, Jim, K.C.	1	2	.333	6.94	5	5	0	0	0	0	23.1	33	115	22	18	2	0	1	1	15	0	7	2	0
Plesac, Dan, Tor.*	0	3	.000	8.34	30	0	0	0	5	0	22.2	28	104	21	21	4	3	1	0	9	1	26	2	0
Ponson, Sidney, Bal.	12	12	.500	4.71	32	32	6	0	0	0	210.0	227	897	118	110	35	4	7	1	80	2	112	4	0
Poole, Jim, Cle.*	1	0	1.000	18.00	3	0	0	0	0	0	1.0	2	7	2	2	0	0	1	0	3	1	0	0	0
Portugal, Mark, Bos.	7	12	.368	5.51	31	27	1	0	1	0	150.1	179	667	100	92	28	3	6	4	41	1	79	2	0
Pote, Lou, Ana.	1	1	.500	2.15	20	0	0	0	10	3	29.1	23	118	9	7	1	1	0	0	12	1	20	1	0
Quantrill, Paul, Tor.	3	2	.600	3.33	41	0	0	0	13	0	48.2	53	212	19	18	5	1	2	4	17	1	28	0	0
Radke, Brad, Min.	12	14	.462	3.75	33	33	4	0	0	0	218.2	239	910	97	91	28	5	5	1	44	0	121	4	0
Radlosky, Rob, Min.	0	1	.000	12.46	7	0	0	0	2	0	8.2	15	45	12	12	7	0	0	1	4	0	3	1	0
Rakers, Jason, Cle.	0	0	.000	4.50	1	0	0	0	0	0	2.0	2	9	1	1	1	0	0	0	1	0	0	0	0
Ramsay, Robert, Sea.*	0	2	.000	6.38	6	3	0	0	1	0	18.1	23	81	13	13	3	0	1	0	9	1	11	1	0
Rapp, Pat, Bos.	6	7	.462	4.12	37	26	0	0	3	0	146.1	147	638	78	67	13	3	0	7	69	1	90	5	0
Rath, Gary, Min.*	0	1	.000	11.57	5	1	0	0	1	0	4.2	6	25	6	6	1	0	0	0	5	0	1	2	1
Ray, Ken, K.C.	1	0	1.000	8.74	13	0	0	0	4	0	11.1	23	57	12	11	2	0	0	1	6	0	0	0	0
Redman, Mark, Min.*	1	0	1.000	8.53	5	1	0	0	0	0	12.2	17	65	13	12	3	0	0	1	7	0	11	0	0
Reed, Steve, Cle.	3	2	.600	4.23	63	0	0	0	15	0	61.2	69	274	33	29	10	4	5	3	20	5	44	2	0
Reichert, Dan, K.C.	2	2	.500	9.08	8	8	0	0	0	0	36.2	48	183	38	37	2	1	1	2	32	1	20	1	0
Rekar, Bryan, T.B.	6	6	.500	5.80	27	12	0	0	2	0	94.2	121	437	68	61	14	3	2	5	41	2	55	4	0
Reyes, Al, Bal.	2	3	.400	4.85	27	0	0	0	6	0	29.2	23	126	16	16	4	3	2	3	16	2	28	1	0
Rhodes, Arthur, Bal.*	3	4	.429	5.43	43	0	0	0	11	0	53.0	43	244	37	32	9	2	2	0	45	6	59	4	0
Rigby, Brad, Oak.-K.C.	4	6	.400	5.06	49	0	0	0	11	0	83.2	102	382	51	47	11	2	5	7	31	7	36	6	0
Riley, Matt, Bal.*	0	0	.000	7.36	3	3	0	0	0	0	11.0	17	59	9	9	4	0	1	0	13	0	6	0	2
Rincon, Ricardo, Cle.*	2	3	.400	4.43	59	0	0	0	14	0	44.2	41	193	22	22	6	2	1	1	24	5	30	2	1
Riske, David, Cle.	1	1	.500	8.36	12	0	0	0	3	0	14.0	20	68	15	13	2	1	1	0	6	0	16	0	0
Rivera, Mariano, N.Y.	4	3	.571	1.83	66	0	0	0	63	45	69.0	43	268	15	14	2	0	2	3	18	3	52	2	1
Rizzo, Todd, Chi.*	0	2	.000	6.75	3	0	0	0	2	0	1.1	4	12	2	1	0	1	0	0	3	1	2	0	0
Roberts, Willi, Det.	0	0	.000	13.50	1	0	0	0	0	0	1.1	3	8	4	2	0	0	1	1	0	0	0	0	0
Rodriguez, Frankie, Sea.	2	4	.333	5.65	28	5	0	0	10	3	73.1	94	334	47	46	11	0	1	4	30	2	47	1	0
Rodriguez, Nerio, Tor.	0	1	.000	13.50	2	0	0	0	1	0	2.0	2	10	3	3	2	0	0	0	2	0	2	0	0
Rogers, Kenny, Oak.*	5	3	.625	4.30	19	19	3	0	0	0	119.1	135	528	66	57	8	4	6	9	41	0	68	3	1
Rojas, Mel, Det.	3	0	.000	22.74	5	0	0	0	2	0	6.1	12	39	16	16	3	0	1	3	4	0	6	0	0
Romano, Mike, Tor.	0	0	.000	11.81	3	0	0	0	1	0	5.1	8	28	8	7	1	0	1	0	5	0	3	1	0
Romero, J.C., Min.*	0	0	.000	3.72	5	0	0	0	3	0	9.2	13	39	4	4	0	0	0	0	4	0	4	0	0
Rosado, Jose, K.C.*	10	14	.417	3.85	33	33	5	0	0	0	208.0	197	882	103	89	24	8	4	5	72	1	141	9	0
Rose, Brian, Bos.	7	6	.538	4.87	22	18	0	0	1	0	98.0	112	433	59	53	19	2	0	2	29	2	51	0	0
Runyan, Sean, Det.*	0	1	.000	3.38	12	0	0	0	2	0	10.2	9	45	4	4	2	1	2	1	3	1	6	2	0
Rupe, Ryan, T.B.	8	9	.471	4.55	24	24	0	0	0	0	142.1	136	614	81	72	17	1	7	12	57	2	97	4	1
Rusch, Glendon, K.C.*	0	1	.000	15.75	3	0	0	0	1	0	4.0	7	23	7	7	1	0	0	1	3	0	4	0	0
Ryan, Jay, Min.	1	4	.200	4.87	8	8	1	0	0	0	40.2	46	182	23	22	9	0	1	3	17	0	15	0	0
Ryan, B.J., Bal.*	1	0	1.000	2.95	13	0	0	0	3	0	18.1	9	73	6	6	0	0	1	0	12	1	28	1	0
Saberhagen, Bret, Bos.	10	6	.625	2.95	22	22	0	0	0	0	119.0	122	480	43	39	11	4	2	11	0	81	1	0
Sampson, Benj., Min.*	3	2	.600	8.11	30	4	0	0	7	0	71.0	107	345	65	64	17	1	5	0	34	3	56	2	2
Santana, Julio, T.B.	1	4	.200	7.32	22	5	0	0	7	0	55.1	66	261	49	45	10	1	1	7	32	0	34	0	0
Santana, Marino, Bos.	0	0	.000	15.75	3	0	0	0	1	0	4.0	8	22	7	7	3	0	1	0	3	0	4	1	0
Santiago, Jose, K.C.	3	4	.429	3.42	34	0	0	0	15	2	47.1	46	203	23	18	7	1	3	2	14	2	15	2	1
Saunders, Tony, T.B.*	3	3	.500	6.43	9	9	0	0	0	0	42.0	53	204	39	30	6	1	2	4	29	0	30	3	0
Scheffer, Aaron, Sea.	0	0	.000	1.93	4	0	0	0	3	0	4.2	6	24	5	1	0	0	3	1	3	0	4	0	0
Schoeneweis, Scott, Ana.*	1	1	.500	5.49	31	0	0	0	6	0	39.1	47	175	27	24	4	0	1	0	14	1	22	1	0
Sele, Aaron, Tex.	18	9	.667	4.79	33	33	2	2	0	0	205.0	244	920	115	109	21	1	3	12	70	3	186	4	0
Service, Scott, K.C.	5	5	.500	6.09	68	0	0	0	29	8	75.1	87	352	51	51	13	4	7	3	42	8	68	3	0
Shuey, Paul, Cle.	8	5	.615	3.53	72	0	0	0	28	6	81.2	68	351	37	32	8	4	1	1	40	7	103	8	0
Simas, Bill, Chi.	6	3	.667	3.75	70	0	0	0	21	2	72.0	73	324	36	30	6	4	4	6	32	6	41	4	1
Sinclair, Steve, Tor.-Sea.*	0	1	.000	6.52	21	0	0	0	6	0	19.1	22	95	16	14	5	0	0	2	14	2	18	0	0
Sirotka, Mike, Chi.*	11	13	.458	4.00	32	32	3	1	0	0	209.0	236	909	108	93	24	9	3	3	57	2	125	4	0
Slocumb, Heathcliff, Bal.	0	0	.000	12.46	10	0	0	0	7	0	8.2	15	49	12	12	2	0	0	2	9	2	12	1	0
Snyder, John, Chi.	9	12	.429	6.68	25	25	1	0	0	0	129.1	167	602	103	96	27	3	7	6	49	0	67	11	0
Sparks, Jeff, T.B.	0	0	.000	5.40	8	0	0	0	2	1	10.0	6	49	6	6	1	0	1	1	12	1	17	1	0
Sparks, Steve, Ana.	5	11	.313	5.42	28	26	0	0	1	0	147.2	165	688	101	89	21	2	8	9	82	0	73	8	0
Spencer, Sean, Sea.*	0	0	.000	21.60	2	0	0	0	0	0	1.2	5	12	4	4	0	0	0	0	3	0	2	0	0
Spoljaric, Paul, Tor.*	2	2	.500	4.65	37	2	0	0	7	0	62.0	62	282	41	32	9	5	3	2	32	2	63	1	0
Spradlin, Jerry, Cle.	0	0	.000	18.00	4	0	0	0	1	0	3.0	6	18	6	6	1	0	0	0	3	0	2	0	0
Stanton, Mike, N.Y.*	2	2	.500	4.33	73	1	0	0	10	0	62.1	71	271	30	30	5	4	2	1	18	4	59	2	0
Stark, Dennis, Sea.	0	0	.000	9.95	5	0	0	0	2	0	6.1	10	31	8	7	0	0	0	0	4	0	4	0	0
Stein, Blake, Oak.-K.C.	1	2	.333	4.56	13	12	0	0	0	0	73.0	65	327	38	37	11	2	1	7	47	1	47	3	0
Stevens, Dave, Cle.	0	0	.000	10.00	5	0	0	0	4	0	9.0	10	44	10	10	1	0	1	0	8	1	6	1	0
Sturtze, Tanyon, Chi.	0	0	.000	0.00	1	1	0	0	0	0	6.0	4	22	0	0	0	0	0	0	2	0	2	0	0
Suppan, Jeff, K.C.	10	12	.455	4.53	32	32	4	1	0	0	208.2	222	887	113	105	28	7	5	3	62	4	103	5	1
Suzuki, Mac, Sea.-K.C.	2	5	.286	6.79	38	13	0	0	6	0	110.0	124	510	92	83	16	2	3	7	64	3	68	11	0
Tam, Jeff, Cle.	0	0	.000	81.00	1	0	0	0	0	0	0.1	3	4	3	3	0	1	0	0	1	1	0	0	0
Taylor, Billy, Oak.	1	5	.167	3.48	43	0	0	0	38	26	43.0	48	189	23	19	3	4	2	2	14	3	38	1	1
Tessmer, Jay, N.Y.	0	0	.000	14.85	6	0	0	0	4	0	6.2	16	41	11	11	1	0	0	1	4	2	3	0	0
Thompson, Justin, Det.*	9	11	.450	5.11	24	24	0	0	0	0	142.2	152	626	85	81	24	1	7	4	59	1	83	2	0

Pitcher, Team	W	L	Pct.	ERA	G	GS	CG	ShO	GF	Sv.	IP	H	TBF	R	ER	HR	SH	SF	HB	BB	IBB	SO	WP	Bk.
Timlin, Mike, Bal.	3	9	.250	3.57	62	0	0	0	52	27	63.0	51	261	30	25	9	1	1	5	23	3	50	1	0
Trombley, Mike, Min.	2	8	.200	4.33	75	0	0	0	56	24	87.1	93	377	42	42	15	2	3	2	28	2	82	6	0
Venafro, Mike, Tex.*	3	2	.600	3.29	65	0	0	0	11	0	68.1	63	283	29	25	4	5	2	3	22	0	37	0	0
Vizcaino, Luis, Oak.	0	0	.000	5.40	1	0	0	0	1	0	3.1	3	16	2	2	1	0	0	0	3	0	2	1	0
Wagner, Paul, Cle.	1	0	1.000	4.15	3	0	0	0	1	0	4.1	5	24	4	2	0	0	0	2	3	0	0	0	0
Wakefield, Tim, Bos.	6	11	.353	5.08	49	17	0	0	28	15	140.0	146	635	93	79	19	1	8	5	72	2	104	1	0
Wallace, Derek, K.C.	0	1	.000	3.24	8	0	0	0	4	0	8.1	7	34	4	3	2	1	1	0	5	0	5	0	0
Ward, Bryan, Chi.*	0	1	.000	7.55	40	0	0	0	8	0	39.1	63	183	36	33	10	0	1	0	11	1	35	2	0
Wasdin, John, Bos.	8	3	.727	4.12	45	0	0	0	17	2	74.1	66	302	38	34	14	2	2	0	18	0	57	2	0
Washburn, Jarrod, Ana.*	4	5	.444	5.25	16	10	0	0	3	0	61.2	61	264	36	36	6	1	2	1	26	0	39	2	0
Watson, Allen, Sea.-N.Y.*	4	1	.800	2.89	24	0	0	0	8	0	37.1	36	156	17	12	8	0	1	0	13	0	32	2	0
Weaver, Eric, Sea.	0	1	.000	10.61	8	0	0	0	2	0	9.1	14	52	12	11	2	0	0	0	8	1	14	5	0
Weaver, Jeff, Det.	9	12	.429	5.55	30	29	0	0	1	0	163.2	176	717	104	101	27	5	5	17	56	2	114	0	1
Wells, David, Tor.*	17	10	.630	4.82	34	34	7	1	0	0	231.2	246	987	132	124	32	6	6	6	62	2	169	1	0
Wells, Kip, Chi.	4	1	.800	4.04	7	7	0	0	0	0	35.2	33	153	17	16	2	0	2	3	15	0	29	1	2
Wells, Bob, Min.	8	3	.727	3.81	76	0	0	0	18	1	87.1	79	364	41	37	8	5	3	5	28	4	44	4	0
Wengert, Don, K.C.	0	1	.000	9.25	11	1	0	0	2	0	24.1	41	116	26	25	6	0	2	0	5	0	10	0	0
Wetteland, John, Tex.	4	4	.500	3.68	62	0	0	0	59	43	66.0	67	281	30	27	9	1	5	0	19	1	60	0	0
Wheeler, Dan, T.B.	0	4	.000	5.87	6	6	0	0	0	0	30.2	35	136	20	20	7	1	0	0	13	1	32	1	0
Whisenant, Matt, K.C.*	4	4	.500	6.35	48	0	0	0	21	1	39.2	40	184	28	28	4	1	0	7	26	1	27	1	0
White, Rick, T.B.	5	3	.625	4.08	63	1	0	0	11	0	108.0	132	480	56	49	8	2	5	1	38	5	81	3	0
Williams, Todd, Sea.	0	0	.000	4.66	13	0	0	0	7	0	9.2	11	47	5	5	1	1	0	1	7	0	7	0	0
Witasick, Jay, K.C.	9	12	.429	5.57	32	28	1	1	2	0	158.1	191	732	108	98	23	4	8	8	83	1	102	5	2
Witt, Bobby, T.B.	7	15	.318	5.84	32	32	3	2	0	0	180.1	213	815	130	117	23	7	8	3	96	1	123	9	1
Wolcott, Bob, Bos.	0	0	.000	8.10	4	0	0	0	1	0	6.2	8	29	6	6	1	0	1	1	3	0	2	0	0
Worrell, Tim, Oak.	2	2	.500	4.15	53	0	0	0	17	0	69.1	69	309	38	32	6	1	1	3	34	1	62	1	0
Wright, Jaret, Cle.	8	10	.444	6.06	26	26	0	0	0	0	133.2	144	609	99	90	18	3	3	7	77	1	91	4	0
Yan, Esteban, T.B.	3	4	.429	5.90	50	1	0	0	15	0	61.0	77	286	41	40	8	6	3	9	32	4	46	2	0
Yarnall, Ed, N.Y.*	1	0	1.000	3.71	5	2	0	0	2	0	17.0	17	77	8	7	1	0	0	0	10	0	13	0	0
Zimmerman, Jeff, Tex.	9	3	.750	2.36	65	0	0	0	14	3	87.2	50	336	24	23	9	3	6	2	23	1	67	2	0
Zimmerman, Jordan, Tex.	0	0	.000	7.88	12	0	0	0	2	0	8.0	14	41	8	7	0	0	1	0	4	0	3	0	0

COMBINATION SHUTOUTS: **Anaheim (7)**—Olivares, Magnante and Hasegawa; Finley and Percival; Olivares, Schoeneweis, Hasegawa and Percival; Finley and Percival; Finley and Levine; Finley and Percival; Washburn and Pote. **Baltimore (7)**—Mussina, Rhodes and Timlin; Mussina, Rhodes and Timlin; Guzman and Molina; Guzman, Orosco and Timlin; J. Johnson, Molina and Ryan; Mussina, Kamieniecki and Timlin; Mussina and Kamieniecki. **Boston (11)**—Saberhagen, Guthrie, Corsi and Gordon; Saberhagen, Lowe and Guthrie; P. Martinez, Cormier and Lowe; P. Martinez and Wakefield; Saberhagen, Lowe and Cormier; Pena, Lowe and Cormier; Rapp and Wakefield; Rose, Guthrie and Corsi; P. Martinez and Beck; R. Martinez, P. Martinez, Wasdin and Wakefield; Rapp, Cormier, Garces, Lowe, Gordon, Beck, Rose and Wakefield. **Chicago (2)**—Snyder, Foulke and Howry; Baldwin and Howry. **Cleveland (5)**—Colon and Jackson; Gooden, Rincon and Assenmacher; Karsay, Reed, Shuey and Jackson; Burba and Rincon; Nagy and Jackson. **Detroit (4)**—Thompson and Jones; Moehler, Brocail and Rojas; Weaver, Brocail and Jones; Nitkowski, Anderson and N. Cruz. **Kansas City (1)**—Reichert, Wallace and Montgomery. **Minnesota (5)**—Milton, Trombley and Aguilera; Mays, Wells and Trombley; Mays and Trombley; Mays, Wells and Trombley; Ryan, Miller, Wells, Guardado and Trombley. **New York (6)**—Mendoza and Irabu; Clemens and Nelson; Cone and Rivera; Pettitte, Stanton and Rivera; Clemens and Rivera; Clemens and Nelson. **Oakland (5)**—Haynes, Mathews and Taylor; Oquist, Mathews, Groom and Taylor; Oquist and Jones; Haynes, Worrell, Groom and Taylor; Hudson and Taylor. **Seattle (4)**—Fassero and Abbott; Garcia, Sinclair and Paniagua; Fassero and Paniagua; Meche and Abbott. **Tampa Bay (3)**—Saunders, Mecir and Hernandez; Alvarez and Lopez; Rupe, Lopez and Hernandez. **Texas (7)**—Sele, Crabtree and Patterson; Burkett, Zimmerman and Wetteland; Loaiza and Kolb; Burkett, Venafro, Crabtree and Wetteland; Helling, Zimmerman and Wetteland; Fassero, Morgan, Patterson and Kolb; Burkett, Crabtree, Zimmerman and Venafro. **Toronto (6)**—Escobar, Lloyd and Koch; Halladay and Munro; Halladay, Lloyd and Quantrill; Halladay and Koch; Hamilton, Lloyd, Quantrill and Escobar; Escobar, Lloyd and Koch.

PITCHERS WITH TWO OR MORE TEAMS

Pitcher, Team	W	L	Pct.	ERA	G	GS	CG	ShO	GF	Sv.	IP	H	TBF	R	ER	HR	SH	SF	HB	BB	IBB	SO	WP	Bk.
Appier, Kevin, K.C.	9	9	.500	4.87	22	22	1	0	0	0	140.1	153	613	81	76	18	5	3	6	51	3	78	5	0
Appier, Kevin, Oak.	7	5	.583	5.77	12	12	0	0	0	0	68.2	77	313	50	44	9	2	2	1	33	1	53	5	1
Candiotti, Tom, Oak.	3	5	.375	6.35	11	11	0	0	0	0	56.2	67	254	46	40	11	0	4	2	23	0	30	9	0
Candiotti, Tom, Cle.	1	1	.500	11.05	7	2	0	0	1	0	14.2	19	72	18	18	3	2	0	1	7	0	11	4	0
Corsi, Jim, Bos.	1	2	.333	5.25	23	0	0	0	5	0	24.0	25	113	15	14	4	3	1	2	19	3	14	0	0
Corsi, Jim, Bal.	0	1	.000	2.70	13	0	0	0	3	0	13.1	15	53	4	4	2	1	0	0	1	0	8	0	0
Davey, Tom, Tor.	1	1	.500	4.70	29	0	0	0	10	1	44.0	40	198	28	23	5	1	2	3	26	0	42	6	0
Davey, Tom, Sea.	1	0	1.000	4.71	16	0	0	0	5	0	21.0	22	100	13	11	0	0	0	4	14	1	17	0	0
Fassero, Jeff, Sea.*	4	14	.222	7.38	30	24	0	0	1	0	139.0	188	669	123	114	34	1	6	4	73	3	101	7	0
Fassero, Jeff, Tex.*	1	0	1.000	5.71	7	3	0	0	1	0	17.1	20	82	12	11	1	1	1	0	10	0	13	2	0
Florie, Bryce, Det.	2	1	.667	4.56	27	3	0	0	6	0	51.1	61	234	31	26	6	3	1	1	20	2	40	4	0
Florie, Bryce, Bos.	2	0	1.000	4.80	14	2	0	0	4	0	30.0	33	134	19	16	2	0	1	1	15	3	25	4	0
Olivares, Omar, Ana.	8	9	.471	4.05	20	20	3	0	0	0	131.0	135	558	62	59	11	3	5	6	49	0	49	4	0
Olivares, Omar, Oak.	7	2	.778	4.34	12	12	1	0	0	0	74.2	82	327	43	36	8	0	2	3	32	0	36	2	0
Rigby, Brad, Oak.	3	4	.429	4.33	29	0	0	0	5	0	62.1	69	278	31	30	5	1	3	5	26	7	26	3	0
Rigby, Brad, K.C.	1	2	.333	7.17	20	0	0	0	6	0	21.1	33	104	20	17	6	1	2	2	5	0	10	3	0
Sinclair, Steve, Tor.*	0	0	.000	12.71	3	0	0	0	1	0	5.2	7	28	8	8	4	0	0	1	4	0	3	0	0
Sinclair, Steve, Sea.*	0	1	.000	3.95	18	0	0	0	5	0	13.2	15	67	8	6	1	0	0	1	10	2	15	0	0
Stein, Blake, Oak.	0	0	.000	16.88	1	1	0	0	0	0	2.2	6	19	5	5	1	0	0	0	6	0	4	1	0
Stein, Blake, K.C.	1	2	.333	4.09	12	11	0	0	0	0	70.1	59	308	33	32	10	2	1	7	41	1	43	2	0
Suzuki, Mac, Sea.	0	2	.000	9.43	16	4	0	0	3	0	42.0	47	207	47	44	7	0	3	4	34	2	32	2	0
Suzuki, Mac, K.C.	2	3	.400	5.16	22	9	0	0	3	0	68.0	77	303	45	39	9	2	0	3	30	1	36	9	0
Watson, Allen, Sea.*	0	1	.000	12.00	3	0	0	0	2	0	3.0	6	19	4	4	5	0	1	0	3	0	2	1	0
Watson, Allen, N.Y.*	4	0	1.000	2.10	21	0	0	0	6	0	34.1	30	137	8	8	3	0	0	0	10	0	30	1	0

FIELDING

TEAM

Team	Pct.	G	PO	A	E	TC	DP	TP	PB
Baltimore	.986	162	4305	1781	89	6175	191	0	5
Minnesota	.985	161	4270	1613	92	5975	150	0	12
Cleveland	.983	162	4351	1739	106	6196	154	0	8
Anaheim	.983	162	4294	1723	106	6123	156	0	20
Toronto	.983	162	4317	1664	106	6087	165	0	13
Detroit	.982	161	4263	1623	106	5992	156	0	12
New York	.982	162	4319	1577	111	6007	132	0	18
Seattle	.981	162	4301	1690	113	6104	182	0	8
Texas	.981	162	4309	1730	119	6158	169	1	2
Oakland	.980	162	4315	1700	122	6137	166	0	18
Kansas City	.980	161	4262	1727	125	6114	188	0	10
Boston	.979	162	4310	1548	127	5985	132	0	31
Tampa Bay	.978	162	4299	1776	135	6210	198	0	12
Chicago	.977	162	4315	1563	136	6014	149	0	14
Totals	.981	1133	60230	23454	1593	85277	2288	1	183

INDIVIDUAL

FIRST BASEMEN

NOTE: All caps denotes fielding-percentage leader based on 81 games for catchers, 108 for all other non-pitchers and 162 innings for pitchers. *Throws lefthanded.

Player, Team	Pct.	G	PO	A	E	TC	DP
Amaral, Rich, Bal.	1.000	2	4	2	0	6	1
Bell, David, Sea.	1.000	4	15	1	0	16	2
Bellinger, Clay, N.Y.	1.000	8	7	1	0	8	1
Blowers, Mike, Sea.	1.000	14	72	6	0	78	14
Boggs, Wade, T.B.	1.000	4	32	0	0	32	3
Buhner, Jay, Sea.	1.000	1	9	0	0	9	1
Catalanotto, Frank, Det.	1.000	32	219	11	0	230	29
Clark, Tony, Det.	.992	132	1126	85	10	1221	111
Clark, Will, Bal.*	.995	63	575	42	3	620	54
Conine, Jeff, Bal.	.993	99	831	52	6	889	108
Coomer, Ron, Min.	.996	71	518	47	2	567	57
Cox, Steve, T.B.*	1.000	4	19	1	0	20	5
Daubach, Brian, Bos.	.983	61	418	35	8	461	35
Davis, Tommy, Bal.	1.000	1	2	0	0	2	0
Decker, Steve, Ana.	1.000	6	30	4	0	34	2
Delgado, Carlos, Tor.	.990	147	1306	84	14	1404	134
Edmonds, Jim, Ana.*	1.000	2	19	1	0	20	2
Erstad, Darin, Ana.*	.999	78	669	41	1	711	59
Franco, Julio, T.B.	1.000	1	2	0	0	2	0
Gates, Brent, Min.	1.000	5	27	0	0	27	2
Giambi, Jason, Oak.	.995	142	1251	45	7	1303	128
Giambi, Jeremy, K.C.*	.991	26	208	8	2	218	22
Hansen, Jed, K.C.	.000	1	0	0	0	0	0
Hocking, Denny, Min.	1.000	2	7	0	0	7	0
Huskey, Butch, Sea.	.988	10	76	3	1	80	10
Huson, Jeff, Ana.	1.000	8	25	1	0	26	3
Ibanez, Raul, Sea.	.987	21	147	7	2	156	18
Jackson, Ryan, Sea.*	.989	29	167	11	2	180	19
Jaha, John, Oak.	1.000	8	42	4	0	46	3
Jefferies, Gregg, Det.	1.000	3	19	4	0	23	1
Jefferson, Reggie, Bos.*	1.000	2	8	1	0	9	0
King, Jeff, K.C.	.990	20	188	15	2	205	21
Konerko, Paul, Chi.	.995	92	740	58	4	802	72
Ledesma, Aaron, T.B.	1.000	4	27	6	0	33	4
Lee, Carlos, Chi.	.966	5	24	4	1	29	3
Leius, Scott, K.C.	.971	13	61	6	2	69	13
Leyritz, Jim, N.Y.	.986	9	60	8	1	69	6
Liefer, Jeff, Chi.	1.000	15	96	11	0	107	11
Luke, Matt, Ana.*	1.000	4	20	4	0	24	5
Mabry, John, Sea.	.992	20	120	10	1	131	11
Manto, Jeff, Cle.-N.Y.	1.000	4	19	1	0	20	1
Martinez, Edgar, Sea.	1.000	5	29	2	0	31	2
Martinez, Tino, N.Y.	.995	158	1297	106	7	1410	110
McGriff, Fred, T.B.*	.989	125	1037	88	13	1138	132
Merloni, Lou, Bos.	.909	1	9	1	1	11	0
MIENTKIEWICZ, Doug, Min.	.997	110	882	50	3	935	75
Minor, Ryan, Bal.	.917	1	10	1	1	12	1
Norton, Greg, Chi.	.972	26	67	3	2	72	9
Offerman, Jose, Bos.	1.000	8	48	3	0	51	7
Ortiz, David, Min.*	1.000	1	7	0	0	7	1
Otanez, Willis, Bal.-Tor.	1.000	18	95	7	0	102	11
Palmeiro, Rafael, Tex.*	.996	28	261	13	1	275	23
Perry, Herbert, T.B.	1.000	14	77	4	0	81	13
Pickering, Calvin, Bal.*	.960	8	46	2	2	50	8
Posada, Jorge, N.Y.	1.000	1	4	1	0	5	1
Pritchett, Chris, Ana.	.990	15	96	8	1	105	8
Saenz, Olmedo, Oak.	.994	28	153	12	1	166	11
Scarsone, Steve, K.C.	1.000	12	69	9	0	78	8

Player, Team	Pct.	G	PO	A	E	TC	DP
Segui, David, Sea.-Tor.*	.995	94	719	63	4	786	89
Sexson, Richie, Cle.	.988	61	517	51	7	575	48
Shave, Jon, Tex.	1.000	9	43	1	0	44	7
Simms, Mike, Tex.	1.000	1	0	1	0	1	0
Sojo, Luis, N.Y.	1.000	4	8	0	0	8	0
Sorrento, Paul, T.B.	.995	27	203	9	1	213	19
Spiezio, Scott, Oak.	1.000	10	51	1	0	52	6
Stairs, Matt, Oak.	1.000	1	2	0	0	2	0
Stanley, Mike, Bos.	.988	111	830	60	11	901	71
Stevens, Lee, Tex.*	.994	133	1228	60	8	1296	128
Sutton, Larry, K.C.*	.987	30	215	13	3	231	19
Sweeney, Mike, K.C.	.981	74	584	41	12	637	76
Thomas, Frank, Chi.	.990	49	385	18	4	407	40
Thome, Jim, Cle.	.994	111	930	83	6	1019	93
Timmons, Ozzie, Sea.	1.000	1	1	0	0	1	0
Vaughn, Mo, Ana.	.995	72	584	35	3	622	62
Vitiello, Joe, K.C.	1.000	10	65	7	0	72	11
Wilson, Craig, Chi.	1.000	1	4	0	0	4	0
Wilson, Dan, Sea.	1.000	5	10	2	0	12	1
Wood, Jason, Det.	.972	5	35	0	1	36	3
Zeile, Todd, Tex.	1.000	1	1	0	0	1	0

TRIPLE PLAY: Stevens, Tex.

FIRST BASEMEN WITH TWO OR MORE TEAMS

Player, Team	Pct.	G	PO	A	E	TC	DP
Manto, Jeff, Cle.	1.000	1	5	0	0	5	0
Manto, Jeff, N.Y.	1.000	3	14	1	0	15	1
Otanez, Willis, Bal.	1.000	5	6	0	0	6	0
Otanez, Willis, Tor.	1.000	13	89	7	0	96	11
Segui, David, Sea.*	.996	90	700	61	3	764	86
Segui, David, Tor.*	.955	4	19	2	1	22	3

SECOND BASEMEN

Player, Team	Pct.	G	PO	A	E	TC	DP
Alicea, Luis, Tex.	.980	37	60	87	3	150	19
ALOMAR, Roberto, Cle.	.992	156	270	466	6	742	102
Amaral, Rich, Bal.	.000	2	0	0	0	0	0
Baerga, Carlos, Cle.	1.000	6	5	9	0	14	3
Bell, David, Sea.	.978	154	313	426	17	756	118
Bellinger, Clay, N.Y.	.000	1	0	0	0	0	0
Bournigal, Rafael, Sea.	.983	17	26	33	1	60	10
Bush, Homer, Tor.	.984	109	220	350	9	579	81
Cabrera, Jolbert, Cle.	1.000	6	4	4	0	8	1
Cairo, Miguel, T.B.	.986	117	251	377	9	637	102
Catalanotto, Frank, Det.	.966	32	24	61	3	88	7
Cedeno, Domingo, Sea.	1.000	1	1	2	0	3	0
Davidson, Cleatus, Min.	.973	6	13	23	1	37	7
DeShields, Delino, Bal.	.977	93	178	249	10	437	54
Durham, Ray, Chi.	.974	148	305	412	19	736	100
Durrington, Trent, Ana.	.966	41	73	98	6	177	19
Easley, Damion, Det.	.989	147	302	421	8	731	111
Febles, Carlos, K.C.	.979	122	272	375	14	661	101
Fernandez, Tony, Tor.	1.000	1	0	2	0	2	0
Fonville, Chad, Bos.	.900	2	6	3	1	10	1
Frye, Jeff, Bos.	.980	26	41	56	2	99	9
Garcia, Jesse, Bal.	1.000	6	7	8	0	15	3
Garcia, Luis, Det.	.000	1	0	0	0	0	0
Gates, Brent, Min.	1.000	47	44	95	0	139	19
Gipson, Charles, Sea.	1.000	3	1	1	0	2	1
Graffanino, Tony, T.B.	.990	17	38	65	1	104	14
Grebeck, Craig, Tor.	.959	17	32	39	3	74	7
Guillen, Carlos, Sea.	1.000	2	6	6	0	12	5

Player, Team	Pct.	G	PO	A	E	TC	DP
Hairston, Jerry, Bal.	1.000	50	115	154	0	269	47
Hansen, Jed, K.C.	.989	21	44	44	1	89	18
Hocking, Denny, Min.	.994	56	77	85	1	163	22
Holbert, Ray, K.C.	.978	11	14	30	1	45	4
Huson, Jeff, Ana.	.993	41	53	92	1	146	20
Jefferies, Gregg, Det.	1.000	2	0	1	0	1	0
Jimenez, D'Angelo, N.Y.	1.000	1	1	1	0	2	0
Kelly, Pat, Tor.	.962	35	60	92	6	158	17
Knoblauch, Chuck, N.Y.	.963	150	254	425	26	705	67
Lamb, David, T.B.	.949	15	12	25	2	39	6
Ledesma, Aaron, T.B.	.990	17	43	56	1	100	18
Leius, Scott, K.C.	.000	1	0	0	0	0	0
Lopez, Mendy, K.C.	1.000	6	11	16	0	27	5
Macias, Jose, Det.	1.000	1	1	6	0	7	0
Martin, Norberto, Tor.	.974	8	9	29	1	39	8
Martinez, Felix, K.C.	1.000	1	1	2	0	3	1
McDonald, Jason, Oak.	1.000	1	1	0	0	1	0
McDonald, John, Cle.	1.000	7	7	11	0	18	4
McLemore, Mark, Tex.	.983	135	261	433	12	706	93
Merloni, Lou, Bos.	.949	8	17	20	2	39	4
Offerman, Jose, Bos.	.975	128	237	318	14	569	70
Phillips, Tony, Oak.	.974	66	96	164	7	267	41
Reboulet, Jeff, Bal.	.993	36	54	83	1	138	21
Rodriguez, Liu, Chi.	.985	22	25	41	1	67	6
Sadler, Donnie, Bos.	.935	10	7	22	2	31	4
Scarsone, Steve, K.C.	.938	9	17	13	2	32	3
Shave, Jon, Tex.	1.000	1	1	1	0	2	1
Sheets, Andy, Ana.	.929	7	6	7	1	14	0
Silvestri, Dave, Ana.	1.000	1	0	3	0	3	0
Smith, Bobby, T.B.	.964	13	22	32	2	56	7
Sojo, Luis, N.Y.	.986	16	30	40	1	71	12
Spiezio, Scott, Oak.	.984	42	57	127	3	187	25
Unroe, Tim, Ana.	.000	1	0	0	0	0	0
Velandia, Jorge, Oak.	.989	52	36	57	1	94	13
Velarde, Randy, Ana.-Oak.	.983	156	298	493	14	805	104
Walker, Todd, Min.	.984	103	168	270	7	445	54
Wilson, Craig, Chi.	.938	7	6	9	1	16	1
Wilson, Enrique, Cle.	1.000	21	16	19	0	35	2
Wood, Jason, Det.	1.000	1	0	1	0	1	0

TRIPLE PLAY: McLemore, Tex.

SECOND BASEMEN WITH TWO OR MORE TEAMS

Player, Team	Pct.	G	PO	A	E	TC	DP
Velarde, Randy, Ana.	.986	95	191	307	7	505	61
Velarde, Randy, Oak.	.977	61	107	186	7	300	43

THIRD BASEMEN

Player, Team	Pct.	G	PO	A	E	TC	DP
Alicea, Luis, Tex.	.905	10	6	13	2	21	3
Alvarez, Gabe, Det.	1.000	2	0	1	0	1	0
Amaral, Rich, Bal.	.000	1	0	0	0	0	0
Baerga, Carlos, Cle.	.964	15	8	19	1	28	1
Bellinger, Clay, N.Y.	1.000	16	12	16	0	28	1
Blake, Casey, Tor.	1.000	14	12	23	0	35	4
Blowers, Mike, Sea.	.875	4	2	5	1	8	1
Boggs, Wade, T.B.	.942	74	45	100	9	154	14
Borders, Pat, Cle.	.000	1	0	0	0	0	0
Bournigal, Rafael, Sea.	.900	8	5	4	1	10	0
Branyan, Russ, Cle.	.960	8	6	18	1	25	0
BROSIUS, Scott, N.Y.	.962	132	87	239	13	339	20
Catalanotto, Frank, Det.	.946	21	9	26	2	37	4
Cedeno, Domingo, Sea.	.000	1	0	0	0	0	0
Chavez, Eric, Oak.	.961	105	69	155	9	233	13
Conine, Jeff, Bal.	.000	4	0	0	1	1	0
Coomer, Ron, Min.	.969	57	24	101	4	129	9
Dalesandro, Mark, Tor.	1.000	2	0	1	0	1	0
Daubach, Brian, Bos.	.000	1	0	0	0	0	0
Davis, Russ, Sea.	.959	124	71	207	12	290	17
Fernandez, Tony, Tor.	.939	132	65	212	18	295	21
Frye, Jeff, Bos.	.882	7	5	10	2	17	0
Fryman, Travis, Cle.	.969	85	41	146	6	193	12
Garcia, Jesse, Bal.	1.000	2	0	1	0	1	0
Gates, Brent, Min.	.972	61	27	79	3	109	10
Giambi, Jason, Oak.	.000	1	0	0	0	0	0
Gipson, Charles, Sea.	.983	17	13	45	1	59	4
Glaus, Troy, Ana.	.954	153	114	277	19	410	25
Graffanino, Tony, T.B.	.000	1	0	0	0	0	0
Grebeck, Craig, Tor.	1.000	2	1	0	0	1	0
Greene, Willie, Tor.	.917	7	4	7	1	12	0
Gubanich, Creighton, Bos.	1.000	1	1	3	0	4	0
Hansen, Jed, K.C.	1.000	4	2	1	0	3	0

Player, Team	Pct.	G	PO	A	E	TC	DP
Hocking, Denny, Min.	1.000	6	1	5	0	6	1
Holbert, Ray, K.C.	.000	1	0	0	0	0	0
Houston, Tyler, Cle.	1.000	10	3	11	0	14	1
Huskey, Butch, Sea.-Bos.	1.000	3	1	1	0	2	0
Huson, Jeff, Ana.	.971	9	11	22	1	34	4
Jimenez, D'Angelo, N.Y.	1.000	6	2	8	0	10	2
Konerko, Paul, Chi.	.000	1	0	0	0	0	0
Koskie, Corey, Min.	.962	79	33	143	7	183	8
Ledesma, Aaron, T.B.	.907	26	11	28	4	43	1
Leius, Scott, K.C.	1.000	10	7	14	0	21	3
Leyritz, Jim, N.Y.	.800	1	2	2	1	5	0
Mabry, John, Sea.	.873	24	21	34	8	63	1
Manto, Jeff, Cle.-N.Y.	1.000	11	7	16	0	23	2
Menechino, Frank, Oak.	1.000	1	1	1	0	2	0
Merloni, Lou, Bos.	.885	9	6	17	3	26	1
Minor, Ryan, Bal.	.963	45	26	79	4	109	8
Norton, Greg, Chi.	.922	120	93	201	25	319	17
Otanez, Willis, Bal.-Tor.	.934	46	32	53	6	91	8
Palmer, Dean, Det.	.945	141	89	240	19	348	24
Perry, Herbert, T.B.	.955	42	32	75	5	112	11
Phillips, Tony, Oak.	.000	2	0	0	0	0	0
Randa, Joe, K.C.	.952	156	119	314	22	455	28
Reboulet, Jeff, Bal.	.987	56	19	56	1	76	4
Ripken, Cal, Bal.	.932	85	36	142	13	191	11
Rodriguez, Liu, Chi.	.000	1	0	0	0	0	0
Sadler, Donnie, Bos.	.813	9	7	6	3	16	0
Saenz, Olmedo, Oak.	.938	56	27	79	7	113	12
Scarsone, Steve, K.C.	.000	3	0	0	0	0	0
Shave, Jon, Tex.	.889	6	2	6	1	9	1
Sheets, Andy, Ana.	.500	1	0	1	1	2	0
Sheldon, Scott, Tex.	1.000	2	2	3	0	5	0
Smith, Bobby, T.B.	.933	59	26	100	9	135	13
Sojo, Luis, N.Y.	.974	20	15	23	1	39	3
Spiezio, Scott, Oak.	.927	31	16	35	4	55	1
Surhoff, B.J., Bal.	1.000	2	1	5	0	6	0
Unroe, Tim, Ana.	1.000	3	1	2	0	3	0
Valentin, John, Bos.	.954	111	84	208	14	306	16
Velandia, Jorge, Oak.	1.000	2	1	1	0	2	0
Veras, Wilton, Bos.	.929	35	23	56	6	85	7
Wilson, Craig, Chi.	.969	72	47	108	5	160	10
Wilson, Enrique, Cle.	.965	61	24	86	4	114	2
Wood, Jason, Det.	.909	9	5	5	1	11	0
Woodward, Chris, Tor.	1.000	2	0	3	0	3	0
Zeile, Todd, Tex.	.941	155	104	294	25	423	23

THIRD BASEMEN WITH TWO OR MORE TEAMS

Player, Team	Pct.	G	PO	A	E	TC	DP
Huskey, Butch, Sea.	.000	1	0	0	0	0	0
Huskey, Butch, Bos.	1.000	2	1	1	0	2	0
Manto, Jeff, Cle.	1.000	10	7	16	0	23	2
Manto, Jeff, N.Y.	.000	1	0	0	0	0	0
Otanez, Willis, Bal.	.917	22	16	28	4	48	2
Otanez, Willis, Tor.	.953	24	16	25	2	43	6

SHORTSTOPS

Player, Team	Pct.	G	PO	A	E	TC	DP
Batista, Tony, Tor.	.975	98	165	308	12	485	72
Bell, David, Sea.	1.000	1	1	0	0	1	0
Bellinger, Clay, N.Y.	1.000	1	2	1	0	3	0
BORDICK, Mike, Bal.	.989	159	277	511	9	797	132
Bournigal, Rafael, Sea.	.987	28	28	47	1	76	13
Bush, Homer, Tor.	.920	18	26	54	7	87	5
Caruso, Mike, Chi.	.957	132	183	348	24	555	86
Cedeno, Domingo, Sea.	.941	20	17	47	4	68	11
Chavez, Eric, Oak.	.000	2	0	0	0	0	0
Clayton, Royce, Tex.	.961	133	204	406	25	635	91
Cruz, Deivi, Det.	.983	155	230	453	12	695	106
Davidson, Cleatus, Min.	1.000	4	5	5	0	10	1
Davis, Russ, Sea.	.000	2	0	0	0	0	0
Dellaero, Jason, Chi.	.917	11	16	28	4	48	5
DiSarcina, Gary, Ana.	.963	81	138	249	15	402	62
Dransfeldt, Kelly, Tex.	.966	16	31	54	3	88	13
Easley, Damion, Det.	1.000	19	16	24	0	40	5
Frye, Jeff, Bos.	1.000	2	6	5	0	11	1
Garcia, Jesse, Bal.	1.000	7	9	13	0	22	5
Garcia, Luis, Det.	1.000	7	3	2	0	5	0
Garciaparra, Nomar, Bos.	.972	134	232	357	17	606	72
Gates, Brent, Min.	.000	1	0	0	0	0	0
Gipson, Charles, Sea.	.750	3	2	1	1	4	0
Gonzalez, Alex, Tor.	.980	37	69	132	4	205	34
Graffanino, Tony, T.B.	.951	17	28	49	4	81	14

Player, Team	Pct.	G	PO	A	E	TC	DP
Grebeck, Craig, Tor.	.882	4	9	6	2	17	3
Guevara, Giomar, Sea.	.870	9	6	14	3	23	2
Guillen, Carlos, Sea.	.938	3	6	9	1	16	1
Guzman, Cristian, Min.	.959	131	196	363	24	583	82
Hansen, Jed, K.C.	1.000	10	11	22	0	33	3
Hocking, Denny, Min.	.987	61	62	95	2	159	22
Holbert, Ray, K.C.	.987	22	31	46	1	78	16
Huson, Jeff, Ana.	.939	22	14	32	3	49	7
Jeter, Derek, N.Y.	.978	158	230	391	14	635	87
Lamb, David, T.B.	.945	35	46	75	7	128	28
Ledesma, Aaron, T.B.	.978	50	83	135	5	223	37
Leius, Scott, K.C.	.000	2	0	0	0	0	0
Lopez, Mendy, K.C.	.000	1	0	0	0	0	0
Martin, Norberto, Tor.	.000	1	0	0	0	0	0
Martinez, Felix, K.C.	.000	2	0	0	0	0	0
McDonald, John, Cle.	.917	6	1	10	1	12	1
Menechino, Frank, Oak.	1.000	5	3	6	0	9	2
Merloni, Lou, Bos.	.956	24	36	50	4	90	12
Phillips, Tony, Oak.	.000	1	0	0	0	0	0
Reboulet, Jeff, Bal.	1.000	10	6	13	0	19	0
Rodriguez, Alex, Sea.	.977	129	213	382	14	609	104
Rodriguez, Liu, Chi.	.958	14	20	26	2	48	6
Sadler, Donnie, Bos.	.930	14	18	22	3	43	5
Sanchez, Rey, K.C.	.982	134	242	452	13	707	111
Scarsone, Steve, K.C.	.977	16	15	27	1	43	7
Shave, Jon, Tex.	.953	24	26	55	4	85	14
Sheets, Andy, Ana.	.966	76	107	174	10	291	37
Silvestri, Dave, Ana.	.833	1	2	3	1	6	0
Sojo, Luis, N.Y.	1.000	6	12	9	0	21	2
Soriano, Alfonso, N.Y.	.500	1	0	1	1	2	1
Stocker, Kevin, T.B.	.957	76	137	216	16	369	55
Tejada, Miguel, Oak.	.973	159	292	471	21	784	110
Velandia, Jorge, Oak.	.938	8	9	21	2	32	4
Vizquel, Omar, Cle.	.976	143	221	396	15	632	88
Wilson, Craig, Chi.	.985	22	29	38	1	68	8
Wilson, Enrique, Cle.	.960	35	37	58	4	99	21
Wood, Jason, Det.	.818	9	2	7	2	11	1
Woodward, Chris, Tor.	.939	10	8	23	2	33	2

TRIPLE PLAY: Clayton, Tex.

OUTFIELDERS

Player, Team	Pct.	G	PO	A	E	TC	DP
Abbott, Jeff, Chi.*	.962	17	25	0	1	26	0
Alicea, Luis, Tex.	.000	1	0	0	0	0	0
Allen, Chad, Min.	.975	133	267	9	7	283	3
Alvarez, Gabe, Det.	1.000	5	3	0	0	3	0
Amaral, Rich, Bal.	1.000	50	66	0	0	66	0
Anderson, Brady, Bal.*	.997	136	308	3	1	312	1
Anderson, Garret, Ana.*	.993	153	406	7	3	416	1
Bartee, Kimera, Det.	.985	38	67	0	1	68	0
Becker, Rich, Oak.*	.986	39	66	4	1	71	1
Belle, Albert, Bal.	.985	154	252	17	4	273	2
Bellinger, Clay, N.Y.	1.000	2	2	0	0	2	0
Beltran, Carlos, K.C.	.972	154	395	16	12	423	2
Berroa, Geronimo, Tor.	1.000	2	4	0	0	4	0
Bournigal, Rafael, Sea.	.000	1	0	0	0	0	0
Brown, Dee, K.C.	.929	3	12	1	1	14	0
Brumfield, Jacob, Tor.	.978	53	126	5	3	134	0
Buford, Damon, Bos.	.985	84	189	6	3	198	2
Buhner, Jay, Sea.	.993	85	127	7	1	135	2
Butler, Rich, T.B.	1.000	6	8	0	0	8	0
Butler, Rob, Tor.*	1.000	2	1	0	0	1	0
Cabrera, Jolbert, Cle.	.957	16	22	0	1	23	0
Canseco, Jose, T.B.	1.000	6	7	1	0	8	0
Christensen, McKay, Chi.*	.943	27	50	0	3	53	0
Christenson, Ryan, Oak.	.969	104	213	3	7	223	1
Clyburn, Danny, T.B.	1.000	24	39	3	0	42	1
Colangelo, Mike, Ana.	1.000	1	1	1	0	2	1
Coleman, Michael, Bos.	.000	2	0	0	0	0	0
Conine, Jeff, Bal.	1.000	13	17	1	0	18	0
Coomer, Ron, Min.	.000	1	0	0	0	0	0
Cordero, Wil, Cle.	.981	29	51	0	1	52	0
Cordova, Marty, Min.	.927	29	38	0	3	41	0
Cox, Steve, T.B.*	1.000	2	1	0	0	1	0
Cruz, Jacob, Cle.*	1.000	24	48	0	0	48	0
Cruz, Jose, Tor.	.990	106	277	8	3	288	2
Cummings, Midre, Min.	1.000	5	5	0	0	5	0
Curtis, Chad, N.Y.	.990	81	98	2	1	101	0
Damon, Johnny, K.C.*	.987	140	301	8	4	313	0
Daubach, Brian, Bos.	1.000	2	2	0	0	2	0
DaVanon, Jeff, Ana.	1.000	5	5	0	0	5	0

Player, Team	Pct.	G	PO	A	E	TC	DP
Dye, Jermaine, K.C.	.984	157	362	17	6	385	6
Edmonds, Jim, Ana.*	.992	42	119	4	1	124	1
Encarnacion, Juan, Det.	.968	131	264	10	9	283	2
Erstad, Darin, Ana.*	1.000	69	185	7	0	192	1
Garcia, Karim, Det.*	.958	81	152	7	7	166	1
Giambi, Jeremy, K.C.*	1.000	5	5	0	0	5	0
Gipson, Charles, Sea.	.960	28	19	5	1	25	0
Gonzalez, Juan, Tex.	.983	131	223	7	4	234	3
Goodwin, Curtis, Tor.*	1.000	2	7	1	0	8	0
Goodwin, Tom, Tex.	.989	107	258	4	3	265	0
Green, Scarborough, Tex.	1.000	9	6	0	0	6	0
Green, Shawn, Tor.*	.997	152	340	5	1	346	1
Greene, Todd, Ana.	.974	30	36	1	1	38	0
Greene, Willie, Tor.	1.000	3	3	0	0	3	0
Greer, Rusty, Tex.*	.983	145	286	3	5	294	1
Grieve, Ben, Oak.	.988	137	232	6	3	241	2
Griffey, Ken, Sea.*	.978	158	387	10	9	406	5
Guillen, Jose, T.B.	.966	47	80	5	3	88	0
Hansen, Jed, K.C.	.000	2	0	0	0	0	0
Higginson, Bob, Det.	.983	88	175	2	3	180	0
Hocking, Denny, Min.	1.000	38	46	5	0	51	0
Hunter, Brian L., Det.-Sea.	.988	139	301	15	4	320	3
Hunter, Torii, Min.	.997	130	284	7	1	292	3
Huskey, Butch, Sea.-Bos.	1.000	57	105	2	0	107	0
Huson, Jeff, Ana.	1.000	2	1	0	0	1	0
Ibanez, Raul, Sea.	.988	57	83	1	1	85	0
Jackson, Darrin, Chi.	.972	64	103	2	3	108	0
Jackson, Ryan, Sea.*	.000	1	0	0	0	0	0
Jefferies, Gregg, Det.	1.000	2	2	0	0	2	0
Jones, Jacque, Min.*	.980	93	231	9	5	245	2
Justice, David, Cle.*	.977	93	161	7	4	172	3
Kapler, Gabe, Det.	.981	128	302	4	6	312	2
Kelly, Roberto, Tex.	.981	85	155	4	3	162	2
Kingsale, Gene, Bal.	.980	24	48	1	1	50	0
Koskie, Corey, Min.	.962	25	25	0	1	26	0
Lampkin, Tom, Sea.	.000	2	0	0	0	0	0
Latham, Chris, Min.	1.000	14	13	0	0	13	0
Lawton, Matt, Min.	.982	109	213	3	4	220	0
Ledee, Ricky, N.Y.*	.942	77	143	3	9	155	0
Lee, Carlos, Chi.	.981	105	201	3	4	208	0
Lennon, Patrick, Tor.	1.000	8	23	1	0	24	1
Lewis, Darren, Bos.	.994	130	309	4	2	315	2
Liefer, Jeff, Chi.	1.000	17	28	1	0	29	1
Lofton, Kenny, Cle.*	.989	119	255	11	3	269	3
Lowery, Terrell, T.B.	.971	60	97	4	3	104	1
Luke, Matt, Ana.*	1.000	6	8	0	0	8	0
Mabry, John, Sea.	.989	43	80	6	1	87	1
Martinez, Dave, T.B.*	.985	140	253	8	4	265	1
Mateo, Ruben, Tex.	1.000	31	62	3	0	65	0
May, Derrick, Bal.	1.000	5	7	1	0	8	1
McCracken, Quinton, T.B.	.988	40	80	1	1	82	0
McDonald, Jason, Oak.	.993	89	149	3	1	153	1
McLemore, Mark, Tex.	1.000	11	15	0	0	15	0
McRae, Brian, Tor.	1.000	13	28	1	0	29	1
Merloni, Lou, Bos.	.000	1	0	0	0	0	0
Mieske, Matt, Sea.	1.000	20	25	1	0	26	0
Monahan, Shane, Sea.	1.000	9	7	0	0	7	0
Nixon, Trot, Bos.*	.968	121	209	3	7	219	1
Nunnally, Jon, Bos.	.000	2	0	0	0	0	0
O'Leary, Troy, Bos.*	.993	157	296	9	2	307	3
O'Neill, Paul, N.Y.*	.974	151	291	10	8	309	3
Ordonez, Magglio, Chi.	.991	153	331	12	3	346	4
Palmeiro, Orlando, Ana.*	.994	92	154	6	1	161	0
Perry, Herbert, T.B.	1.000	6	4	0	0	4	0
Phillips, Tony, Oak.	.937	62	85	4	6	95	1
Polonia, Luis, Det.*	.986	40	68	4	1	73	0
Pose, Scott, K.C.	.970	25	29	3	1	33	1
Quinn, Mark, K.C.	.964	15	25	2	1	28	0
Raines, Tim, Oak.	1.000	38	61	0	0	61	0
Ramirez, Alex, Cle.	.920	29	22	1	2	25	0
Ramirez, Manny, Cle.	.975	145	267	7	7	281	2
Roberts, David, Cle.*	1.000	39	87	0	0	87	0
Sadler, Donnie, Bos.	.941	8	14	2	1	17	1
Salmon, Tim, Ana.	.981	89	204	7	4	215	1
Sanders, Anthony, Tor.	1.000	1	1	0	0	1	0
Sexson, Richie, Cle.	1.000	49	66	3	0	69	0
Silvestri, Dave, Ana.	1.000	1	1	0	0	1	0
Simmons, Brian, Chi.	.976	46	79	2	2	83	1
Simms, Mike, Tex.	1.000	1	0	0	0	0	0
Singleton, Chris, Chi.*	.990	127	376	9	4	389	3
Sorrento, Paul, T.B.	.957	57	87	2	4	93	1
Spencer, Shane, N.Y.	1.000	64	108	5	0	113	3

Player, Team	Pct.	G	PO	A	E	TC	DP
Stairs, Matt, Oak.	.981	139	245	13	5	263	1
Stewart, Shannon, Tor.	.981	142	257	4	5	266	1
SURHOFF, B.J., Bal.	1.000	148	282	16	0	298	5
Sutton, Larry, K.C.*	.000	1	0	0	0	0	0
Tarasco, Tony, N.Y.	1.000	12	11	0	0	11	0
Timmons, Ozzie, Sea.	1.000	17	12	0	0	12	0
Trammell, Bubba, T.B.	.993	74	142	2	1	145	1
Unroe, Tim, N.Y.	1.000	12	13	1	0	14	0
Vizquel, Omar, Cle.	.000	1	0	0	0	0	0
Wells, Vernon, Tor.	1.000	24	50	4	0	54	1
Whiten, Mark, Cle.	1.000	7	11	1	0	12	0
Williams, Bernie, N.Y.	.987	155	381	9	5	395	3
Williams, Reggie, Ana.	.974	24	34	3	1	38	3
Winn, Randy, T.B.	.995	77	180	4	1	185	0

OUTFIELDERS WITH TWO OR MORE TEAMS

Player, Team	Pct.	G	PO	A	E	TC	DP
Hunter, Brian L., Det.	1.000	18	49	1	0	50	0
Hunter, Brian L., Sea.	.985	121	252	14	4	270	3
Huskey, Butch, Sea.	1.000	53	101	1	0	102	0
Huskey, Butch, Bos.	1.000	4	4	1	0	5	0

CATCHERS

Player, Team	Pct.	G	PO	A	E	TC	DP	PB
Alomar, Sandy, Cle.	.974	35	257	10	7	274	2	1
AUSMUS, Brad, Det.	.998	127	754	56	2	812	5	7
Borders, Pat, Cle.-Tor.	.955	8	39	3	2	44	0	2
Brown, Kevin L., Tor.	1.000	2	10	1	0	11	0	0
Dalesandro, Mark, Tor.	1.000	8	22	2	0	24	2	1
Davis, Tommy, Bal.	.909	4	9	1	1	11	0	0
Decker, Steve, Ana.	.987	17	73	4	1	78	0	5
Diaz, Einar, Cle.	.988	119	751	81	10	842	8	5
DiFelice, Mike, T.B.	.987	51	344	28	5	377	5	8
Fasano, Sal, K.C.	1.000	23	143	8	0	151	0	1
Fick, Robert, Det.	1.000	4	24	1	0	25	0	1
Figga, Mike, N.Y.-Bal.	.973	43	171	12	5	188	1	2
Flaherty, John, T.B.	.993	115	726	87	6	819	12	4
Fletcher, Darrin, Tor.	.997	113	638	42	2	682	4	10
Fordyce, Brook, Chi.	.987	103	561	30	8	599	5	4
Girardi, Joe, N.Y.	.984	65	452	34	8	494	5	1
Greene, Todd, Ana.	.984	12	55	7	1	63	0	5
Gubanich, Creighton, Bos.	.979	14	39	8	1	48	1	3
Haselman, Bill, Det.	.996	39	231	13	1	245	0	4
Hatteberg, Scott, Bos.	.993	23	128	14	1	143	1	2
Hemphill, Bret, Ana.	.955	12	36	6	2	44	1	1
Hernandez, Ramon, Oak.	.980	40	274	19	6	299	5	2
Hinch, A.J., Oak.	.987	73	368	26	5	399	4	10
Houston, Tyler, Cle.	1.000	1	4	0	0	4	0	0
Ibanez, Raul, Sea.	1.000	1	4	0	0	4	0	0
Johnson, Charles, Bal.	.994	135	770	66	5	841	14	3
Johnson, Mark L., Chi.	.993	72	413	33	3	449	6	10
Kreuter, Chad, K.C.	.994	101	460	44	3	507	8	6
Lampkin, Tom, Sea.	.985	56	292	27	5	324	5	5
Levis, Jesse, Cle.	1.000	9	53	3	0	56	0	0
Leyritz, Jim, N.Y.	.000	1	0	0	0	0	0	0
Lomasney, Steve, Bos.	1.000	1	7	2	0	9	0	0
Macfarlane, Mike, Oak.	.997	79	351	43	1	395	8	6
Matheny, Mike, Tor.	.995	57	346	33	2	381	8	2
Molina, Ben, Ana.	.991	30	192	19	2	213	2	3
O'Brien, Charlie, Ana.	.993	27	140	11	1	152	2	0
Paul, Josh, Chi.	1.000	6	40	2	0	42	0	0
Pierzynski, A.J., Min.	1.000	9	35	2	0	37	1	1
Posada, Jorge, N.Y.	.993	109	705	46	5	756	7	17
Rodriguez, Ivan, Tex.	.993	141	850	83	7	940	13	1
Spehr, Tim, K.C.	.990	59	274	11	3	288	4	3
Steinbach, Terry, Min.	.991	96	539	30	5	574	5	5
Sweeney, Mike, K.C.	1.000	4	4	2	0	6	0	0
Turner, Chris, Cle.	.964	12	50	3	2	55	0	0
Valentin, Javier, Min.	.998	76	387	27	1	415	4	6
Varitek, Jason, Bos.	.990	140	972	66	11	1049	8	25
Walbeck, Matt, Ana.	.989	97	407	46	5	458	9	6
Webster, Lenny, Bal.-Bos.	.990	18	92	9	1	102	3	1
Wilson, Dan, Sea.	.995	121	743	46	4	793	7	3
Zaun, Gregg, Tex.	.984	37	165	15	3	183	0	1

CATCHERS WITH TWO OR MORE TEAMS

Player, Team	Pct.	G	PO	A	E	TC	DP	PB
Borders, Pat, Cle.	.943	5	32	1	2	35	0	2
Borders, Pat, Tor.	1.000	3	7	2	0	9	0	0
Figga, Mike, N.Y.	1.000	2	3	0	0	3	0	0

Player, Team	Pct.	G	PO	A	E	TC	DP	PB
Figga, Mike, Bal.	.973	41	168	12	5	185	1	2
Webster, Lenny, Bal.	.986	12	67	6	1	74	2	0
Webster, Lenny, Bos.	1.000	6	25	3	0	28	1	1

PITCHERS

Player, Team	Pct.	G	PO	A	E	TC	DP
Abbott, Paul, Sea.	1.000	25	7	8	0	15	1
Aguilera, Rick, Min.	1.000	17	2	1	0	3	0
Aldred, Scott, T.B.*	1.000	37	0	2	0	2	0
Alvarez, Juan, Ana.*	1.000	8	0	2	0	2	0
Alvarez, Wilson, T.B.*	.897	28	2	24	3	29	1
Anderson, Matt, Det.	1.000	37	0	1	0	1	0
Appier, Kevin, K.C.-Oak..	.971	34	13	21	1	35	2
Arrojo, Rolando, T.B.	1.000	24	13	19	0	32	3
Assenmacher, Paul, Cle.*	1.000	55	1	4	0	5	1
Baldwin, James, Chi.	.943	35	12	21	2	35	0
Bale, John, Tor.*	.000	1	0	0	0	0	0
Barber, Brian, K.C.	1.000	8	1	3	0	4	0
Beck, Rod, Bos.	1.000	12	1	2	0	3	0
Belcher, Tim, Ana.	.929	24	11	15	2	28	1
Blair, Willie, Det.	1.000	39	6	15	0	21	0
Boggs, Wade, T.B.	.000	1	0	0	0	0	0
Bones, Ricky, Bal.	1.000	30	2	2	0	4	0
Borkowski, Dave, Det.	.810	17	7	10	4	21	1
Bradford, Chad, Chi.	1.000	3	1	3	0	4	0
Brocail, Doug, Det.	1.000	70	11	6	0	17	1
Brower, Jim, Cle.	1.000	9	1	2	0	3	0
Brunson, Will, Det.*	1.000	17	0	3	0	3	1
Buddie, Mike, N.Y.	1.000	2	1	0	0	1	0
Bullinger, Kirk, Bos.	1.000	4	1	2	0	3	1
Bunch, Mel, Sea.	1.000	5	0	2	0	2	0
Burba, Dave, Cle.	.980	34	20	29	1	50	4
Burkett, John, Tex.	1.000	30	7	18	0	25	2
Byrdak, Tim, K.C.*	1.000	33	2	6	0	8	1
Callaway, Mickey, T.B.	1.000	5	0	4	0	4	0
Candiotti, Tom, Oak.-Cle.	.929	18	1	12	1	14	1
Carmona, Rafael, Sea.	.500	9	1	0	1	2	0
Carpenter, Chris, Tor.	.962	24	10	15	1	26	3
Carrasco, Hector, Min.	.833	39	5	0	1	6	0
Carter, Lance, K.C.	1.000	6	0	1	0	1	0
Castillo, Carlos, Chi.	1.000	18	1	5	0	6	0
Charlton, Norm, T.B.*	.889	42	2	6	1	9	0
Cho, Jin Ho, Bos.	1.000	9	1	5	0	6	1
Clark, Mark, Tex.	.875	15	3	4	1	8	1
Clemens, Roger, N.Y.	.979	30	16	30	1	47	2
Cloude, Ken, Sea.	1.000	31	3	9	0	12	0
Colon, Bartolo, Cle.	.962	32	20	31	2	53	4
Cone, David, N.Y.	.950	31	7	12	1	20	1
Cooper, Brian, Ana.	1.000	5	2	5	0	7	2
Coppinger, Rocky, Bal.	1.000	11	3	1	0	4	0
Cordero, Francisco, Det.	1.000	20	2	5	0	7	1
Cormier, Rheal, Bos.*	.889	60	1	7	1	9	1
Corsi, Jim, Bos.-Bal.	1.000	36	3	8	0	11	0
Crabtree, Tim, Tex.	1.000	68	6	4	0	10	0
Cruz, Nelson, Det.	.926	29	8	17	2	27	0
Daneker, Pat, Chi.	1.000	3	0	3	0	3	0
Davenport, Joe, Chi.	1.000	3	0	1	0	1	0
Davey, Tom, Tor.-Sea.	.833	45	4	6	2	12	1
Davis, Doug, Tex.*	1.000	2	0	1	0	1	0
DeLucia, Rich, Cle.	.000	6	0	0	0	0	0
DePaula, Sean, Cle.	1.000	11	0	2	0	2	0
Durbin, Chad, K.C.	.000	1	0	0	0	0	0
Duvall, Mike, T.B.*	.900	40	5	4	1	10	2
Eiland, Dave, T.B.	1.000	21	5	15	0	20	1
Erdos, Todd, N.Y.	1.000	4	0	1	0	1	0
Erickson, Scott, Bal.	.971	34	24	42	2	68	5
Escobar, Kelvim, Tor.	.944	33	6	11	1	18	1
Eyre, Scott, Chi.*	1.000	21	0	1	0	1	0
Falkenborg, Brian, Bal.	1.000	2	1	0	0	1	0
Fassero, Jeff, Sea.-Tex.*	1.000	37	4	29	0	33	2
Fetters, Mike, Bal.	.667	27	2	4	3	9	0
Finley, Chuck, Ana.*	.921	33	7	28	3	38	1
Florie, Bryce, Det.-Bos.	.824	41	2	12	3	17	1
Fossas, Tony, N.Y.*	.000	5	0	0	0	0	0
Foulke, Keith, Chi.	.947	67	5	13	1	19	0
Franklin, Ryan, Sea.	1.000	6	1	1	0	2	1
Frascatore, John, Tor.	1.000	33	2	6	0	8	0
Fussell, Chris, K.C.	.727	17	2	6	3	11	3
Fyhrie, Mike, Ana.	1.000	16	2	3	0	5	0
Gaillard, Eddie, T.B.	1.000	8	0	3	0	3	0
Garces, Rich, Bos.	1.000	30	5	6	0	11	0

Player, Team	Pct.	G	PO	A	E	TC	DP
Garcia, Freddy, Sea.	.953	33	13	28	2	43	1
Glover, Gary, Tor.	.000	1	0	0	0	0	0
Glynn, Ryan, Tex.	1.000	13	2	3	0	5	0
Gooden, Dwight, Cle.	1.000	26	5	16	0	21	1
Gordon, Tom, Bos.	1.000	21	0	1	0	1	0
Graterol, Beiker, Det.	1.000	1	0	1	0	1	0
Grimsley, Jason, N.Y.	1.000	55	8	13	0	21	0
Groom, Buddy, Oak.*	1.000	76	1	13	0	14	1
Gross, Kip, Bos.	1.000	11	0	1	0	1	0
Guardado, Eddie, Min.*	.900	63	0	9	1	10	1
Gunderson, Eric, Tex.*	1.000	11	0	1	0	1	0
Guthrie, Mark, Bos.*	1.000	46	1	6	0	7	0
Guzman, Juan, Bal.	.895	21	2	15	2	19	5
Halama, John, Sea.*	.951	38	7	32	2	41	5
Halladay, Roy, Tor.	1.000	36	8	16	0	24	3
Hamilton, Joey, Tor.	1.000	22	4	10	0	14	0
Haney, Chris, Cle.*	.875	13	4	3	1	8	1
Harikkala, Tim, Bos.	1.000	7	0	2	0	2	0
Harville, Chad, Oak.	.000	15	0	0	0	0	0
Hasegawa, Shigetoshi, Ana.	1.000	64	5	14	0	19	1
Hawkins, LaTroy, Min.	.962	33	7	18	1	26	3
Haynes, Jimmy, Oak.	.800	30	1	19	5	25	1
Helling, Rick, Tex.	.903	35	4	24	3	31	2
Henry, Butch, Sea.*	1.000	7	0	2	0	2	0
Hentgen, Pat, Tor.	.925	34	15	22	3	40	4
Heredia, Gil, Oak.	.975	33	10	29	1	40	2
Hernandez, Orlando, N.Y.	.955	33	17	25	2	44	3
Hernandez, Roberto, T.B.	.933	72	4	10	1	15	1
Hiljus, Erik, Det.	1.000	6	0	1	0	1	0
Hill, Ken, Ana.	1.000	26	6	25	0	31	3
Hinchliffe, Brett, Sea.	.875	11	5	2	1	8	0
Holtz, Mike, Ana.*	1.000	28	2	5	0	7	0
Howry, Bob, Chi.	1.000	69	2	3	0	5	0
Hudek, John, Tor.	.000	3	0	0	0	0	0
Hudson, Tim, Oak.	.970	21	10	22	1	33	3
Irabu, Hideki, N.Y.	1.000	32	2	13	0	15	0
Isringhausen, Jason, Oak.	1.000	20	1	4	0	5	0
Jackson, Mike, Cle.	.947	72	2	16	1	19	1
Jarvis, Kevin, Tex.	1.000	4	2	1	0	3	0
Johns, Doug, Bal.*	1.000	32	10	11	0	21	0
Johnson, Jason, Bal.	.882	22	4	11	2	17	1
Johnson, Jonathan, Tex.	.000	1	0	0	0	0	0
Jones, Doug, Oak.	.895	70	5	12	2	19	2
Jones, Todd, Det.	.875	65	2	5	1	8	0
Juden, Jeff, N.Y.	1.000	2	0	1	0	1	0
Kamieniecki, Scott, Bal.	1.000	43	5	16	0	21	1
Karsay, Steve, Cle.	.857	50	8	10	3	21	1
Kida, Masao, Det.	1.000	49	2	7	0	9	0
Koch, Billy, Tor.	1.000	56	3	12	0	15	0
Kolb, Danny, Tex.	1.000	16	1	7	0	8	0
Kubinski, Tim, Oak.*	1.000	14	0	4	0	4	0
Langston, Mark, Cle.*	.882	25	7	8	2	17	1
Laxton, Brett, Oak.	.500	3	0	1	1	2	0
Lee, Corey, Tex.*	.000	1	0	0	0	0	0
Leiter, Mark, Sea.	.000	2	0	0	0	0	0
Levine, Al, Ana.	.895	50	5	12	2	19	3
Lidle, Cory, T.B.	1.000	5	0	2	0	2	0
Lincoln, Mike, Min.	1.000	18	5	12	0	17	0
Linton, Doug, Bal.	1.000	14	5	8	0	13	0
Lira, Felipe, Det.	1.000	2	1	0	0	1	0
Lloyd, Graeme, Tor.*	1.000	74	1	4	0	5	0
Loaiza, Esteban, Tex.	1.000	30	8	17	0	25	0
Lopez, Albie, T.B.	.909	51	3	7	1	11	1
Lowe, Derek, Bos.	1.000	74	8	14	0	22	1
Lowe, Sean, Chi.	1.000	64	5	14	0	19	1
Ludwick, Eric, Tor.	1.000	1	1	0	0	1	0
Lundquist, David, Chi.	1.000	17	1	2	0	3	0
Magnante, Mike, Ana.*	1.000	53	3	13	0	16	3
Mahay, Ron, Oak.*	1.000	6	0	2	0	2	0
Marte, Damaso, Sea.*	1.000	5	0	1	0	1	0
Martin, Tom, Cle.*	.000	6	0	0	0	0	0
Martinez, Pedro, Bos.	.966	31	13	15	1	29	0
Martinez, Ramon, Bos.	1.000	4	1	2	0	3	1
Mathews, T.J., Oak.	1.000	50	6	7	0	13	0
Mathews, Terry, K.C.	1.000	24	4	4	0	8	0
Mays, Joe, Min.	.976	49	17	23	1	41	2
McDowell, Jack, Ana.	1.000	4	0	6	0	6	0
McMichael, Greg, Oak.	1.000	17	0	1	0	1	0
Meche, Gil, Sea.	1.000	16	10	8	0	18	0
Mecir, Jim, T.B.	1.000	17	1	4	0	5	0
Mendoza, Ramiro, N.Y.	.971	53	11	23	1	35	1
Mercker, Kent, Bos.*	.900	5	1	8	1	10	0
Mesa, Jose, Sea.	.947	68	11	7	1	19	2
Miller, Travis, Min.*	1.000	52	3	8	0	11	0
Milton, Eric, Min.*	.889	34	8	16	3	27	1
Mintz, Steve, Ana.	.000	3	0	0	0	0	0
Mlicki, Dave, Det.	.917	31	14	19	3	36	2
Moehler, Brian, Det.	1.000	32	18	31	0	49	2
Molina, Gabe, Bal.	1.000	20	1	2	0	3	0
Montgomery, Jeff, K.C.	1.000	49	3	9	0	12	2
Moreno, Orber, K.C.	1.000	7	1	1	0	2	0
Morgan, Mike, Tex.	.943	34	7	26	2	35	3
Morman, Alvin, K.C.*	.933	49	4	10	1	15	1
Morris, Jim, T.B.*	.000	5	0	0	0	0	0
Moyer, Jamie, Sea.*	.969	32	15	47	2	64	9
Munoz, Mike, Tex.*	.923	56	3	9	1	13	2
Munro, Peter, Tor.	1.000	31	3	8	0	11	0
Murray, Dan, K.C.	1.000	4	2	0	0	2	0
Mussina, Mike, Bal.	.984	31	14	46	1	61	3
Myette, Aaron, Chi.	1.000	4	0	1	0	1	0
Nagy, Charles, Cle.	.982	33	21	33	1	55	3
Naulty, Dan, N.Y.	1.000	33	2	9	0	11	0
Navarro, Jaime, Chi.	.923	32	9	15	2	26	2
Nelson, Jeff, N.Y.	.889	39	3	5	1	9	2
Newman, Alan, T.B.*	.500	18	0	1	1	2	0
Nitkowski, C.J., Det.*	.880	68	5	17	3	25	0
Ohka, Tomokazu, Bos.	1.000	8	0	3	0	3	0
Olivares, Omar, Ana.-Oak.	.944	32	13	38	3	54	4
Oquist, Mike, Oak.	.947	28	1	17	1	19	3
Orosco, Jesse, Bal.*	.875	65	2	5	1	8	0
Ortiz, Ramon, Ana.	1.000	9	4	6	0	10	0
Paniagua, Jose, Sea.	.923	59	7	5	1	13	0
Parque, Jim, Chi.*	.964	31	6	21	1	28	1
Patterson, Danny, Tex.	1.000	53	3	6	0	9	1
Pena, Jesus, Chi.*	1.000	26	0	5	0	5	0
Pena, Juan, Bos.	1.000	2	3	1	0	4	0
Percival, Troy, Ana.	1.000	60	3	1	0	4	0
Perisho, Matt, Tex.*	1.000	4	0	2	0	2	0
Perkins, Dan, Min.	.938	29	7	8	1	16	0
Person, Robert, Tor.	.000	11	0	0	0	0	0
Petkovsek, Mark, Ana.	.955	64	5	16	1	22	1
Pettitte, Andy, N.Y.*	.956	31	5	38	2	45	3
Pisciotta, Marc, K.C.	.667	8	0	2	1	3	0
Pittsley, Jim, K.C.	.857	5	0	6	1	7	0
Plesac, Dan, Tor.*	1.000	30	0	2	0	2	0
Ponson, Sidney, Bal.	.950	32	12	26	2	40	6
Poole, Jim, Cle.*	.000	3	0	0	0	0	0
Portugal, Mark, Bos.	1.000	31	9	22	0	31	1
Pote, Lou, Ana.	1.000	20	0	5	0	5	1
Quantrill, Paul, Tor.	1.000	41	2	9	0	11	1
RADKE, Brad, Min.	1.000	33	21	36	0	57	5
Radlosky, Rob, Min.	.667	7	1	1	1	3	0
Rakers, Jason, Cle.	1.000	1	0	0	0	0	0
Ramsay, Rob, Sea.*	1.000	6	0	1	0	1	0
Rapp, Pat, Bos.	1.000	37	7	15	0	22	2
Rath, Gary, Min.*	1.000	5	0	1	0	1	0
Ray, Ken, K.C.	1.000	13	1	3	0	4	2
Redman, Mark, Min.*	1.000	5	2	0	0	2	0
Reed, Steve, Cle.	.933	63	4	10	1	15	0
Reichert, Dan, K.C.	1.000	8	3	3	0	6	1
Rekar, Bryan, T.B.	.950	27	6	13	1	20	2
Reyes, Al, Bal.	1.000	27	0	5	0	5	1
Rhodes, Arthur, Bal.*	1.000	43	0	6	0	6	0
Rigby, Brad, Oak.-K.C.	.636	49	2	5	4	11	1
Riley, Matt, Bal.*	1.000	3	0	2	0	2	0
Rincon, Ricky, Cle.*	1.000	59	1	10	0	11	1
Riske, David, Cle.	.750	12	1	2	1	4	0
Rivera, Mariano, N.Y.	1.000	66	12	10	0	22	2
Rizzo, Todd, Chi.*	.000	3	0	0	0	0	0
Roberts, Willis, Det.	.500	1	0	1	1	2	0
Rodriguez, Frank, Sea.	.950	28	6	13	1	20	2
Rodriguez, Nerio, Tor.	.000	2	0	0	0	0	0
Rogers, Kenny, Oak.*	.942	19	6	43	3	52	2
Rojas, Mel, Det.	1.000	5	0	1	0	1	0
Romano, Mike, Tor.	1.000	3	1	0	0	1	0
Romero, J.C., Min.*	.667	5	1	1	1	3	1
Rosado, Jose, K.C.*	.944	33	7	27	2	36	1
Rose, Brian, Bos.	.960	22	6	18	1	25	2
Runyan, Sean, Det.*	1.000	12	1	3	0	4	0
Rupe, Ryan, T.B.	.850	24	5	12	3	20	5
Rusch, Glendon, K.C.*	.000	3	0	0	0	0	0
Ryan, B.J., Bal.*	1.000	13	0	1	0	1	0
Ryan, Jason, Min.	1.000	8	3	4	0	7	1

Player, Team	Pct.	G	PO	A	E	TC	DP
Saberhagen, Bret, Bos.	1.000	22	5	18	0	23	0
Sampson, Benj, Min.*	1.000	30	3	4	0	7	0
Santana, Julio, T.B.	.889	22	3	5	1	9	1
Santana, Marino, Bos.	1.000	3	0	1	0	1	0
Santiago, Jose, K.C.	1.000	34	4	4	0	8	0
Saunders, Tony, T.B.*	.900	9	4	5	1	10	0
Scheffer, Aaron, Sea.	.000	4	0	0	1	1	0
Schoeneweis, Scott, Ana.*	1.000	31	1	10	0	11	1
Sele, Aaron, Tex.	.950	33	8	30	2	40	2
Service, Scott, K.C.	.833	68	2	3	1	6	0
Shuey, Paul, Cle.	1.000	72	3	10	0	13	1
Simas, Bill, Chi.	1.000	70	7	6	0	13	1
Sinclair, Steve, Tor.-Sea.*	1.000	21	0	1	0	1	0
Sirotka, Mike, Chi.*	.879	32	5	24	4	33	0
Slocumb, Heathcliff, Bal.	.000	10	0	0	0	0	0
Snyder, John, Chi.	1.000	25	10	16	0	26	1
Sparks, Jeff, T.B.	.000	8	0	0	0	0	0
Sparks, Steve, Ana.	.933	28	7	35	3	45	4
Spencer, Sean, Sea.*	.000	2	0	0	0	0	0
Spoljaric, Paul, Tor.*	.889	37	0	8	1	9	0
Spradlin, Jerry, Cle.	.000	4	0	0	0	0	0
Stanton, Mike, N.Y.*	.889	73	2	6	1	9	0
Stark, Dennis, Sea.	.000	5	0	0	0	0	0
Stein, Blake, Oak.-K.C.	1.000	13	2	4	0	6	0
Stevens, Dave, Cle.	1.000	5	0	1	0	1	0
Sturtze, Tanyon, Chi.	1.000	1	0	1	0	1	1
Suppan, Jeff, K.C.	.977	32	16	27	1	44	0
Suzuki, Makoto, Sea.-K.C.	.944	38	6	11	1	18	0
Tam, Jeff, Cle.	1.000	1	0	1	0	1	0
Taylor, Billy, Oak.	1.000	43	1	5	0	6	0
Tessmer, Jay, N.Y.	1.000	6	0	1	0	1	0
Thompson, Justin, Det.*	.941	24	5	11	1	17	1
Timlin, Mike, Bal.	.813	62	5	8	3	16	1
Trombley, Mike, Min.	1.000	75	8	9	0	17	0
Venafro, Mike, Tex.*	1.000	65	2	18	0	20	0
Vizcaino, Luis, Oak.	.000	1	0	0	0	0	0
Wagner, Paul, Cle.	1.000	3	1	0	0	1	0
Wakefield, Tim, Bos.	.950	49	7	12	1	20	1
Wallace, Derek, K.C.	.500	8	0	1	1	2	0
Ward, Bryan, Chi.*	1.000	40	0	6	0	6	0
Wasdin, John, Bos.	.889	45	3	5	1	9	0
Washburn, Jarrod, Ana.*	1.000	16	2	5	0	7	3
Watson, Allen, Sea.-N.Y.*	.857	24	1	5	1	7	0
Weaver, Eric, Sea.	.500	8	0	1	1	2	0
Weaver, Jeff, Det.	1.000	30	9	18	0	27	3

Player, Team	Pct.	G	PO	A	E	TC	DP
Wells, Bob, Min.	.923	76	3	9	1	13	0
Wells, David, Tor.*	1.000	34	7	30	0	37	2
Wells, Kip, Chi.	.778	7	4	3	2	9	0
Wengert, Don, K.C.	1.000	11	0	3	0	3	0
Wetteland, John, Tex.	.875	62	2	5	1	8	0
Wheeler, Dan, T.B.	1.000	6	1	2	0	3	0
Whisenant, Matt, K.C.*	.875	48	2	5	1	8	0
White, Rick, T.B.	.917	63	6	16	2	24	1
Williams, Todd, Sea.	1.000	13	0	1	0	1	0
Witasick, Jay, K.C.	.889	32	4	12	2	18	0
Witt, Bobby, T.B.	.929	32	12	27	3	42	4
Wolcott, Bob, Bos.	.000	4	0	0	0	0	0
Worrell, Tim, Oak.	1.000	53	1	3	0	4	0
Wright, Jaret, Cle.	.903	26	13	15	3	31	0
Yan, Esteban, T.B.	1.000	50	8	9	0	17	2
Yarnall, Ed, N.Y.*	1.000	5	1	4	0	5	0
Zimmerman, Jeff, Tex.	1.000	65	3	7	0	10	0
Zimmerman, Jordan, Sea.*	1.000	12	0	1	0	1	0

PITCHERS WITH TWO OR MORE TEAMS

Player, Team	Pct.	G	PO	A	E	TC	DP
Appier, Kevin, K.C.	.958	22	10	13	1	24	2
Appier, Kevin, Oak.	1.000	12	3	8	0	11	0
Candiotti, Tom, Oak.	.889	11	1	7	1	9	1
Candiotti, Tom, Cle.	1.000	7	0	5	0	5	0
Corsi, Jim, Bos.	1.000	23	2	3	0	5	0
Corsi, Jim, Bal.	1.000	13	1	5	0	6	0
Davey, Tom, Tor.	.778	29	4	3	2	9	1
Davey, Tom, Sea.	1.000	16	0	3	0	3	0
Fassero, Jeff, Sea.*	1.000	30	4	27	0	31	2
Fassero, Jeff, Tex.*	1.000	7	0	2	0	2	0
Florie, Bryce, Det.	.667	27	1	5	3	9	0
Florie, Bryce, Bos.	1.000	14	1	7	0	8	1
Olivares, Omar, Ana.	.941	20	6	26	2	34	2
Olivares, Omar, Oak.	.950	12	7	12	1	20	2
Rigby, Brad, Oak.	.714	29	1	4	2	7	1
Rigby, Brad, K.C.	.500	20	1	1	2	4	0
Sinclair, Steve, Tor.*	.000	3	0	0	0	0	0
Sinclair, Steve, Sea.*	1.000	18	0	1	0	1	0
Stein, Blake, Oak.	.000	1	0	0	0	0	0
Stein, Blake, K.C.	1.000	12	2	4	0	6	0
Suzuki, Makoto, Sea.	1.000	16	1	5	0	6	0
Suzuki, Makoto, K.C.	.917	22	5	6	1	12	0
Watson, Allen, Sea.*	1.000	3	0	1	0	1	0
Watson, Allen, N.Y.*	.833	21	1	4	1	6	0

SHUTOUT GAMES

Read across for wins, down for losses.

Team	Bos.	Cle.	N.Y.	Bal.	Tex.	Oak.	Tor.	Min.	K.C.	T.B.	Sea.	Ana.	Det.	Chi.	N.L.	W	L	Pct.
Boston	..	0	1	3	0	0	3	0	1	0	1	1	1	1	0	12	5	.706
Cleveland	0	..	0	0	1	0	0	0	0	1	1	1	1	0	1	6	3	.667
New York	0	0	..	0	1	1	0	1	0	1	2	0	3	0	1	10	6	.625
Baltimore	1	0	1	..	0	0	1	4	0	0	0	1	1	1	1	11	8	.579
Texas	1	1	1	0	..	0	1	0	0	0	0	2	1	1	0	9	7	.563
Oakland	0	0	0	1	1	..	0	0	0	0	0	0	0	1	2	5	4	.556
Toronto	0	1	0	1	0	1	..	1	1	1	0	1	1	0	1	9	8	.529
Minnesota	0	0	0	0	0	1	1	..	0	0	0	2	2	1	1	8	10	.444
Kansas City	0	0	1	1	0	0	0	0	..	0	0	1	0	0	0	3	4	.429
Tampa Bay	0	0	0	2	0	0	1	0	0	..	0	1	1	0	0	5	7	.417
Seattle	0	0	0	0	1	0	0	2	0	1	..	1	1	0	0	6	9	.400
Anaheim	1	0	2	0	2	0	0	0	1	1	0	..	0	0	0	7	11	.389
Detroit	1	0	0	0	1	0	1	1	0	0	1	1	..	1	0	6	12	.333
Chicago	1	0	0	0	0	0	0	0	0	0	0	0	1	..	0	3	7	.300
N.L. Clubs	0	1	0	0	0	1	1	0	1	2	2	0	0	0	..	..	..	..
Lost	5	3	6	8	7	4	8	10	4	7	9	11	12	7	..	100	101	.498

A.L. shutouts vs. N.L. clubs (7): Baltimore vs. Atlanta; Cleveland vs. Pittsburgh; Minnesota vs. Chicago N.L.; New York A.L. vs. Montreal; Oakland vs. San Diego and Arizona; Toronto vs. Montreal.

HOME RECORD

Read across for home wins, down for road losses.

Team	Oak.	Tex.	Bos.	N.Y.	Cle.	Sea.	Bal.	Tor.	Chi.	Det.	Ana.	K.C.	T.B.	Min.	N.L.	W	L	Pct.
Oakland	..	4	4	2	1	4	4	2	4	2	3	5	5	4	8	52	29	.642
Texas	5	..	3	2	4	4	3	1	3	4	3	5	2	6	6	51	30	.630
Boston	2	4	..	4	3	4	2	4	4	5	6	3	1	3	4	49	32	.605
New York	2	4	2	..	4	5	4	5	4	5	2	1	3	2	5	48	33	.593
Cleveland	5	1	1	1	..	4	6	1	4	4	4	4	4	4	4	47	34	.580
Seattle	4	2	1	0	1	..	5	4	4	4	3	2	4	5	4	43	38	.531
Baltimore	3	3	1	1	1	4	..	1	4	2	4	4	3	5	5	41	40	.506
Toronto	0	1	1	1	2	0	6	..	1	5	6	3	5	3	6	40	41	.494
Chicago	3	4	3	3	1	2	1	1	..	3	3	2	4	4	4	38	42	.475
Detroit	2	3	4	4	3	1	3	1	2	..	3	5	1	2	4	38	43	.469
Anaheim	5	3	1	2	1	3	1	3	4	2	..	3	4	3	2	37	44	.457
Kansas City	5	3	1	3	3	3	2	2	2	3	2	..	1	1	2	33	47	.413
Tampa Bay	0	0	4	1	2	2	4	3	2	3	3	5	..	2	2	33	48	.407
Minnesota	5	0	3	2	1	3	0	3	2	2	1	3	1	..	5	31	50	.383
N.L. clubs	5	5	7	5	4	6	3	6	4	5	5	5	7	3	..	..	..	..
Lost	46	37	36	31	31	45	44	37	44	49	48	50	45	47	..	581	551	.513

HOME RECORDS IN INTERLEAGUE GAMES

Team	Atl.	Fla.	Mon.	N.Y.	Phi.
Baltimore	..	..	3-0	1-2	1-2
Boston	1-2	2-1	..	..	1-2
New York	1-2	..	2-1	2-1	..
Tampa Bay	..	0-3	..	1-2	1-2
Toronto	3-0	1-2	2-1	..	..

Team	Chi.	Cin.	Hou.	Mil.	Pit.	St.L.
Chicago	1-2	..	1-2	..	..	2-1
Cleveland	2-1	1-2	..	1-2	..	..
Detroit	..	..	..	1-2	2-1	1-2
Kansas City	..	0-3	0-3	..	..	2-1
Minnesota	..	2-1	1-2	..	2-1	..

Team	Ariz.	Col.	L.A.	S.D.	S.F.
Anaheim	1-2	..	1-2	0-3	..
Oakland	..	3-0	3-0	..	2-1
Seattle	2-1	..	..	1-2	1-2
Texas	2-1	1-2	..	..	3-0

ROAD RECORD

Read across for road wins, down for home losses.

Team	Cle.	N.Y.	Bos.	Tex.	Tor.	Bal.	Chi.	Sea.	T.B.	Oak.	Ana.	Min.	Det.	K.C.	N.L.	W	L	Pct.
Cleveland	..	2	3	2	4	3	5	3	1	5	5	5	4	3	5	50	31	.617
New York	3	..	2	4	5	5	3	4	5	4	2	4	2	3	4	50	31	.617
Boston	5	4	..	0	5	5	3	3	3	2	3	3	2	5	2	45	36	.556
Texas	3	2	2	..	5	3	2	4	6	2	3	6	1	1	4	44	37	.543
Toronto	5	1	2	3	..	5	3	2	3	2	3	5	4	3	4	44	37	.543
Baltimore	0	3	4	3	0	..	3	1	2	2	5	3	3	2	6	37	44	.457
Chicago	2	2	2	1	5	2	..	2	2	0	2	4	4	4	5	37	44	.457
Seattle	2	1	2	3	3	0	4	..	4	2	3	3	3	3	3	36	45	.444
Tampa Bay	2	3	5	4	2	3	2	2	..	1	2	3	2	3	2	36	45	.444
Oakland	1	2	2	1	6	3	3	2	4	..	1	1	4	1	4	35	46	.432
Anaheim	0	4	0	3	0	2	1	3	3	3	..	3	4	4	3	32	48	.407
Minnesota	2	2	1	0	1	1	1	1	4	2	3	..	4	5	5	32	47	.405
Detroit	2	1	2	1	2	2	3	2	3	2	2	4	..	2	4	31	49	.388
Kansas City	2	2	1	1	1	2	4	4	1	1	3	4	1	..	4	31	50	.383
N.L. clubs	5	4	5	3	3	4	5	5	7	1	7	4	5	7	..	..	..	..
Lost	34	33	32	30	41	40	42	38	48	29	44	50	43	47	..	541	590	.478

1999 A.L. STATISTICS Miscellaneous

PITCHING AGAINST EACH CLUB

ANAHEIM—70-92

Pitcher	Bal. W-L	Bos. W-L	Chi. W-L	Cle. W-L	Det. W-L	K.C. W-L	Min. W-L	N.Y. W-L	Oak. W-L	Sea. W-L	T.B. W-L	Tex. W-L	Tor. W-L	N.L. W-L	Total W-L
Alvarez, Juan	0-0	0-0	0-0	0-0	0-0	0-0	0-0	0-1	0-0	0-0	0-0	0-0	0-0	0-0	0-1
Belcher, Tim	1-1	0-3	0-1	0-0	0-0	0-0	0-0	2-0	0-0	1-0	1-0	0-1	0-1	1-1	6-8
Cooper, Brian	0-1	0-0	1-0	0-0	0-0	0-0	0-0	0-0	0-0	0-0	0-0	0-0	0-0	0-0	1-1
Finley, Chuck	0-1	1-0	0-0	0-0	2-1	1-1	2-1	1-1	0-2	1-0	2-0	1-1	0-2	1-1	12-11
Fyhrie, Mike	0-0	0-0	0-0	0-0	0-0	0-1	0-0	0-1	0-0	0-0	0-0	0-0	0-0	0-2	0-4
Hasegawa, Shigetoshi	0-0	0-0	0-0	0-0	0-1	2-1	0-1	0-0	1-0	0-2	0-0	1-0	0-0	0-1	4-6
Hill, Ken	0-2	0-1	0-0	0-2	0-0	1-0	1-1	0-0	0-0	0-1	0-1	0-1	1-1	1-1	4-11
Holtz, Mike	0-1	0-0	0-1	1-0	0-1	0-0	0-0	0-0	0-0	0-0	0-0	1-0	0-0	0-0	2-3
Levine, Al	1-0	0-0	0-0	0-1	0-0	0-0	0-0	0-0	0-0	0-0	0-0	0-0	0-0	0-0	1-1
Magnante, Mike	0-0	0-0	0-1	0-0	1-0	0-0	1-0	0-0	1-0	0-0	1-1	1-0	0-0	0-0	5-2
McDowell, Jack	0-1	0-1	0-0	0-0	0-0	0-1	0-0	0-0	0-0	0-0	0-1	0-0	0-0	0-0	0-4
Mintz, Steve	0-0	0-0	0-0	0-0	0-0	0-0	0-0	0-0	0-0	0-0	0-0	0-0	0-0	0-0	0-0
Olivares, Omar	1-0	0-1	1-0	0-0	0-0	1-0	0-0	1-1	2-0	0-0	0-1	1-2	0-2	1-2	8-9
Ortiz, Ramon	0-0	0-0	1-0	0-0	0-0	0-1	0-1	0-0	0-0	0-0	1-0	0-0	0-1	0-0	2-3
Percival, Troy	0-1	0-1	1-1	0-1	1-0	0-0	0-0	0-0	1-0	0-2	0-0	0-0	1-0	0-0	4-6
Petkovsek, Mark	0-0	0-0	1-0	0-1	0-0	0-0	0-0	1-0	2-0	2-0	1-0	0-0	1-1	2-2	10-4
Pote, Lou	0-1	0-0	0-0	0-0	0-0	1-0	0-0	0-0	0-0	0-0	0-0	0-0	0-0	0-0	1-1
Schoeneweis, Scott	0-0	0-0	0-0	0-0	0-0	0-0	0-0	0-0	0-0	1-0	0-0	0-0	0-1	0-0	1-1
Sparks, Steve	0-0	0-1	0-0	0-3	1-1	1-0	1-0	0-0	1-1	1-1	0-1	0-1	0-0	0-2	5-11
Washburn, Jarrod	0-1	0-0	0-1	0-1	0-1	0-0	1-0	1-0	0-0	1-0	1-0	1-0	0-0	0-0	4-5
Totals	3-9	1-9	5-5	1-9	5-5	7-5	6-4	6-4	8-4	6-6	7-5	6-6	3-9	6-12	70-92

INTERLEAGUE BREAKDOWN: Petkovsek 1-0, Hill 1-0, Olivares 0-2, Belcher 0-1, Sparks 0-1 vs. Dodgers; Fyhrie 0-1, Petkovsek 0-1, Hasegawa 0-1 vs. Padres; Belcher 1-0, Finley 0-1, Sparks 0-1 vs. Giants; Finley 1-0, Olivares 1-0, Fyhrie 0-1 vs. Rockies; Petkovsek 1-1, Hill 0-1 vs. Diamondbacks. Total: 6-12.

BALTIMORE—78-84

Pitcher	Ana. W-L	Bos. W-L	Chi. W-L	Cle. W-L	Det. W-L	K.C. W-L	Min. W-L	N.Y. W-L	Oak. W-L	Sea. W-L	T.B. W-L	Tex. W-L	Tor. W-L	N.L. W-L	Total W-L
Bones, Ricky	0-0	0-0	0-0	0-0	0-0	0-0	0-0	0-0	0-1	0-0	0-0	0-0	0-1	0-1	0-3
Coppinger, Rocky	0-0	0-0	0-0	0-0	0-0	0-0	0-1	0-0	0-0	0-0	0-0	0-0	0-0	0-0	0-1
Corsi, Jim	0-0	0-0	0-0	0-0	0-0	0-0	0-1	0-0	0-0	0-0	0-0	0-0	0-0	0-0	0-1
Erickson, Scott	1-1	1-1	0-0	0-1	2-1	2-1	2-0	0-1	0-3	1-0	1-2	2-0	0-0	3-1	15-12
Falkenborg, Brian	0-0	0-0	0-0	0-0	0-0	0-0	0-0	0-0	0-0	0-0	0-0	0-0	0-0	0-0	0-0
Fetters, Mike	0-0	0-0	0-0	0-0	0-0	0-0	0-0	0-0	1-0	0-0	0-0	0-0	0-0	0-0	1-0
Guzman, Juan	2-0	0-1	1-1	0-1	0-0	0-1	0-0	1-0	0-0	0-0	0-1	0-1	0-1	1-2	5-9
Johns, Doug	0-0	0-1	1-1	0-1	0-0	0-0	0-0	0-0	2-0	2-0	1-0	0-1	0-0	0-0	6-4
Johnson, Jason	1-1	1-0	1-0	0-1	1-0	0-0	2-0	0-2	0-1	0-1	0-1	1-0	0-0	0-1	8-7
Kamieniecki, Scott	1-0	0-0	0-0	0-0	0-2	1-0	0-0	0-0	0-0	0-0	0-0	0-1	0-0	0-1	2-4
Linton, Doug	0-0	0-2	0-0	1-0	0-0	0-1	0-0	0-0	0-0	0-0	0-0	0-0	0-1	0-0	1-4
Molina, Gabe	1-0	0-0	0-0	0-0	0-0	0-0	0-0	0-0	0-1	0-0	0-0	0-0	0-1	0-0	1-2
Mussina, Mike	1-0	2-1	1-0	0-0	1-1	1-0	2-0	2-0	1-1	0-2	2-1	1-1	1-0	3-0	18-7
Orosco, Jesse	0-0	0-0	0-0	0-0	0-0	0-0	0-0	0-0	0-0	0-0	0-0	0-2	0-0	0-0	0-2
Ponson, Sidney	2-0	0-0	1-0	0-3	1-0	1-1	1-0	0-2	0-0	0-2	1-2	2-0	0-2	3-0	12-12
Reyes, Al	0-0	0-0	0-1	0-0	0-1	0-0	1-0	0-0	0-0	1-0	0-0	0-0	0-0	0-0	2-3
Rhodes, Arthur	0-0	1-0	1-0	0-0	0-0	0-0	1-2	0-0	0-0	0-0	0-1	0-1	0-0	0-0	3-4
Riley, Matt	0-0	0-0	0-0	0-0	0-0	0-0	0-0	0-0	0-0	0-0	0-0	0-0	0-0	0-0	0-0
Ryan, B.J.	0-0	0-0	0-0	0-0	0-0	0-0	0-0	0-0	0-0	1-0	0-0	0-0	0-0	0-0	1-0
Slocumb, Heathcliff	0-0	0-0	0-0	0-0	0-0	0-0	0-0	0-0	0-0	0-0	0-0	0-0	0-0	0-0	0-0
Timlin, Mike	0-1	0-1	1-0	0-1	0-0	1-0	0-0	0-1	0-1	0-0	0-0	0-1	0-2	1-1	3-9
Totals	9-3	5-7	7-3	1-9	5-5	6-4	8-1	4-9	5-7	5-5	5-7	6-6	1-11	11-7	78-84

INTERLEAGUE BREAKDOWN: Ponson 1-0, Guzman 1-0, Mussina 1-0 vs. Braves; Ponson 1-0, Mussina 1-0, Erickson 1-0 vs. Expos; Ponson 1-0, Guzman 0-1, Johnson 0-1 vs. Mets; Erickson 1-1, Timlin 1-0, Mussina 1-0, Bones 0-1, Guzman 0-1 vs. Phillies; Erickson 1-0, Timlin 0-1, Kamieniecki 0-1 vs. Marlins. Total: 11-7.

BOSTON—94-68

Pitcher	Ana. W-L	Bal. W-L	Chi. W-L	Cle. W-L	Det. W-L	K.C. W-L	Min. W-L	N.Y. W-L	Oak. W-L	Sea. W-L	T.B. W-L	Tex. W-L	Tor. W-L	N.L. W-L	Total W-L
Beck, Rod	0-0	0-0	0-0	0-0	0-0	0-0	0-0	0-0	0-0	0-0	0-0	0-0	0-1	0-0	0-1
Bullinger, Kirk	0-0	0-0	0-0	0-0	0-0	0-0	0-0	0-0	0-0	0-0	0-0	0-0	0-0	0-0	0-0
Cho, Jin Ho	0-0	0-1	1-0	0-0	0-0	0-0	0-0	0-0	0-0	0-1	1-0	0-0	0-0	0-1	2-3
Cormier, Rheal	0-0	0-0	0-0	0-0	0-0	0-0	1-0	0-0	0-0	0-0	1-0	0-0	0-0	0-0	2-0
Corsi, Jim	0-0	0-0	0-0	0-1	0-0	0-0	0-1	0-0	0-0	0-0	0-0	0-0	0-0	1-0	1-2
Florie, Bryce	0-0	0-0	0-0	0-0	1-0	0-0	0-0	0-0	1-0	0-0	0-0	0-0	0-0	0-0	2-0
Garces, Rich	1-0	0-0	0-0	0-1	0-0	1-0	0-0	1-0	1-0	1-0	0-0	0-0	0-0	0-0	5-1
Gordon, Tom	0-0	0-0	0-1	0-0	0-0	0-0	0-0	0-0	0-0	0-0	0-0	0-0	0-0	0-1	0-2
Gross, Kip	0-0	0-0	0-0	0-0	0-0	0-0	0-0	0-1	0-0	0-0	0-0	0-1	0-0	0-0	0-2
Guthrie, Mark	0-0	0-1	0-0	0-0	0-0	0-0	0-0	0-0	0-0	0-0	0-0	1-0	0-0	0-0	1-1
Harikkala, Tim	0-0	0-0	0-0	1-0	0-0	0-0	0-0	0-1	0-0	0-0	0-0	0-0	0-0	0-0	1-1
Lowe, Derek	1-0	0-0	0-0	1-0	0-0	0-0	0-0	1-1	1-1	0-1	0-0	0-0	0-0	1-0	6-3
Martinez, Pedro	2-0	1-0	2-1	2-0	1-0	2-0	2-0	2-0	1-1	3-0	1-1	1-0	2-0	1-1	23-4
Martinez, Ramon	0-0	2-0	0-0	0-0	0-0	0-1	0-0	0-0	0-0	0-0	0-0	0-0	0-0	0-0	2-1
Mercker, Kent	0-0	0-0	1-0	0-0	0-0	1-0	0-0	0-0	0-0	0-0	0-0	0-0	0-0	0-0	2-0
Ohka, Tomokazu	0-0	1-0	0-0	0-0	0-1	0-0	0-0	0-0	0-0	0-0	0-0	0-0	0-0	0-1	1-2
Pena, Juan	1-0	0-0	0-0	0-0	0-0	0-0	0-0	0-0	0-0	0-0	0-0	0-0	1-0	0-0	2-0
Portugal, Mark	1-0	1-0	0-0	1-0	1-1	0-1	0-0	0-3	0-0	0-1	3-0	0-2	0-0	0-3	7-12

Pitcher	Ana. W-L	Bal. W-L	Chi. W-L	Cle. W-L	Det. W-L	K.C. W-L	Min. W-L	N.Y. W-L	Oak. W-L	Sea. W-L	T.B. W-L	Tex. W-L	Tor. W-L	N.L. W-L	Total W-L
Rapp, Pat....................	2-0	0-0	0-0	0-0	0-0	0-0	2-1	0-1	0-1	0-0	0-1	0-1	2-1	0-1	6-7
Rose, Brian.................	0-1	1-0	0-2	1-0	0-1	0-0	1-0	2-0	0-0	0-0	0-1	0-1	0-0	2-0	7-6
Saberhagen, Bret..........	1-0	1-2	3-0	0-1	1-0	2-0	0-0	1-0	0-1	0-0	0-1	0-0	0-0	1-2	10-6
Santana, Marino	0-0	0-0	0-0	0-0	0-0	0-0	0-0	0-0	0-0	0-0	0-0	0-0	0-0	0-0	0-0
Wakefield, Tim..........	0-0	0-1	0-1	1-2	1-2	2-0	0-1	0-0	1-0	0-1	0-1	0-1	1-0	0-1	6-11
Wasdin, John	0-0	0-0	0-0	1-0	2-0	0-0	1-0	0-0	0-0	1-0	0-2	1-0	2-0	0-1	8-3
Wolcott, Bob................	0-0	0-0	0-0	0-0	0-0	0-0	0-0	0-0	0-0	0-0	0-0	0-0	0-0	0-0	0-0
Totals	9-1	7-5	7-5	8-4	7-5	8-2	6-4	8-4	4-6	7-3	4-9	4-5	9-3	6-12	94-68

INTERLEAGUE BREAKDOWN: Martinez 1-0, Saberhagen 1-0, Gordon 0-1, Portugal 0-1, Wasdin 0-1, Cho 0-1 vs. Braves; Saberhagen 0-1, Wakefield 0-1, Martinez 0-1 vs. Expos; Corsi 1-0, Rapp 0-1, Portugal 0-1 vs. Mets; Rose 1-0, Saberhagen 0-1, Portugal 0-1 vs. Phillies; Lowe 1-0, Rose 1-0, Ohka 0-1 vs. Marlins. Total: 6-12.

CHICAGO—75-86

Pitcher	Ana. W-L	Bal. W-L	Bos. W-L	Cle. W-L	Det. W-L	K.C. W-L	Min. W-L	N.Y. W-L	Oak. W-L	Sea. W-L	T.B. W-L	Tex. W-L	Tor. W-L	N.L. W-L	Total W-L
Baldwin, James	1-0	0-2	0-1	1-1	2-1	2-1	2-1	0-2	1-0	1-0	1-1	1-1	0-0	0-2	12-13
Bradford, Chad	0-0	0-0	0-0	0-0	0-0	0-0	0-0	0-0	0-0	0-0	0-0	0-0	0-0	0-0	0-0
Castillo, Carlos	0-0	0-0	0-0	0-1	0-0	0-0	0-0	1-0	0-0	0-1	0-0	1-0	0-0	0-0	2-2
Daneker, Pat	0-0	0-0	0-0	0-0	0-0	0-0	0-0	0-0	0-0	0-0	0-0	0-0	0-0	0-0	0-0
Davenport, Joe	0-0	0-0	0-0	0-0	0-0	0-0	0-0	0-0	0-0	0-0	0-0	0-0	0-0	0-0	0-0
Eyre, Scott....................	0-0	0-0	0-0	0-0	0-0	0-0	0-0	0-1	0-0	0-0	0-0	0-0	1-0	0-0	1-1
Foulke, Keith...............	0-0	0-1	1-0	0-0	0-0	1-1	0-0	0-0	0-1	0-0	1-0	0-0	0-0	0-0	3-3
Howry, Bob....................	1-0	1-0	0-0	0-0	0-0	1-0	0-0	0-0	0-1	0-0	0-0	1-1	0-1	1-0	5-3
Lowe, Sean...................	0-0	0-0	1-0	1-0	0-0	0-0	0-0	0-0	0-0	0-0	1-0	0-0	0-0	0-1	4-1
Lundquist, David	1-0	0-1	0-0	0-0	0-0	0-0	0-0	0-0	0-0	0-0	0-0	0-0	0-0	0-0	1-1
Myette, Aaron	0-0	0-0	0-0	0-0	0-1	0-0	0-1	0-0	0-0	0-0	0-0	0-0	0-0	0-0	0-2
Navarro, Jaime	0-1	0-3	0-1	0-1	2-0	0-2	0-2	1-0	0-1	0-2	0-1	1-0	2-0	2-1	8-13
Parque, Jim	0-2	0-0	0-3	0-3	0-1	1-0	1-0	1-1	1-1	2-1	1-1	0-1	0-1	2-0	9-15
Pena, Jesus	0-0	0-0	0-0	0-0	0-0	0-0	0-0	0-0	0-0	0-0	0-0	0-0	0-0	0-0	0-0
Rizzo, Todd	0-0	0-0	0-0	0-0	0-0	0-0	0-0	0-0	0-0	0-0	0-0	0-0	0-2	0-2	0-2
Simas, Bill	0-1	1-0	1-0	0-0	0-0	0-0	2-0	0-1	0-0	0-0	0-0	0-0	2-1	0-0	6-3
Sirotka, Mike	1-1	1-0	1-1	1-2	1-0	0-2	1-1	1-1	0-2	0-1	0-1	0-0	2-1	2-0	11-13
Snyder, John	1-0	0-0	1-1	0-0	1-2	0-0	0-0	2-1	1-0	1-3	2-1	0-2	0-1	0-1	9-12
Sturtze, Tanyon.............	0-0	0-0	0-0	0-0	0-0	0-0	0-0	0-0	0-0	0-0	0-0	0-0	0-0	0-0	0-0
Ward, Bryan	0-0	0-0	0-0	0-0	0-0	0-0	0-0	0-0	0-0	0-0	0-0	0-0	0-1	0-1	0-1
Wells, Kip	0-0	0-0	0-0	0-1	1-0	0-0	1-0	0-0	0-0	0-0	0-0	1-0	1-0	0-0	4-1
Totals	5-5	3-7	5-7	3-9	7-5	6-6	8-3	5-7	3-7	4-8	6-4	5-5	6-4	9-9	75-86

INTERLEAGUE BREAKDOWN: Simas 1-0, Rizzo 0-1, Lowe 0-1 vs. Brewers; Parque 1-0, Sirotka 1-0, Howry 1-0, Simas 1-0, Navarro 0-1, Baldwin 0-1 vs. Cubs; Navarro 1-0, Snyder 0-1, Baldwin 0-1 vs. Astros; Parque 1-0, Sirotka 1-0, Simas 0-1 vs. Pirates; Navarro 1-0, Ward 0-1, Rizzo 0-1 vs. Cardinals. Total: 9-9.

CLEVELAND—97-65

Pitcher	Ana. W-L	Bal. W-L	Bos. W-L	Chi. W-L	Det. W-L	K.C. W-L	Min. W-L	N.Y. W-L	Oak. W-L	Sea. W-L	T.B. W-L	Tex. W-L	Tor. W-L	N.L. W-L	Total W-L
Assenmacher, Paul	0-0	2-0	0-0	0-0	0-0	0-0	0-0	0-0	0-0	0-0	0-0	0-0	0-0	0-1	2-1
Brower, Jim	0-0	1-0	0-1	0-0	0-0	1-0	0-0	0-0	0-0	0-0	0-0	0-0	1-0	0-0	3-1
Burba, Dave..................	3-0	2-0	0-0	2-0	3-0	0-1	0-0	0-2	1-0	2-1	1-1	0-0	0-2	1-2	15-9
Candiotti, Tom	0-0	0-0	0-0	0-0	0-0	1-0	0-0	0-0	0-0	0-0	0-0	0-0	0-0	0-1	1-1
Colon, Bartolo	3-0	2-1	0-2	3-0	0-0	1-0	1-0	0-0	2-0	2-0	0-0	0-1	2-0	2-1	18-5
De Paula, Sean	0-0	0-0	0-0	0-0	0-0	0-0	0-0	0-0	0-0	0-0	0-0	0-0	0-0	0-0	0-0
DeLucia, Rich	0-0	0-0	0-1	0-0	0-0	0-0	0-0	0-0	0-0	0-0	0-0	0-0	0-0	0-0	0-1
Gooden, Dwight.............	0-0	0-0	0-2	1-1	1-0	0-0	0-0	0-0	0-0	0-0	0-0	1-0	0-1	0-0	3-4
Haney, Chris	0-0	0-0	0-0	0-0	0-0	0-0	0-0	0-0	0-0	0-0	0-1	0-1	0-0	0-0	0-2
Jackson, Mike	0-0	0-0	0-0	0-0	0-0	0-0	0-1	0-1	0-0	0-0	0-0	0-0	0-1	3-1	3-4
Karsay, Steve	0-1	1-0	2-0	0-0	1-0	0-0	1-0	1-0	2-0	1-0	0-0	0-1	0-0	1-0	10-2
Langston, Mark	0-0	0-0	0-0	0-0	0-0	1-0	0-0	0-1	0-0	0-1	0-0	0-0	0-0	0-0	1-2
Martin, Tom	0-0	0-0	0-0	0-0	0-0	0-0	0-0	0-1	0-0	0-0	0-0	0-0	0-0	0-0	0-1
Nagy, Charles	1-0	0-0	1-0	2-1	1-1	1-1	3-0	2-0	1-1	0-2	2-1	0-2	1-1	2-1	17-11
Poole, Jim	1-0	0-0	0-0	0-0	0-0	0-0	0-0	0-0	0-0	0-0	0-0	0-0	0-0	0-0	1-0
Rakers, Jason	0-0	0-0	0-0	0-0	0-0	0-0	0-0	0-0	0-0	0-0	0-0	0-0	0-0	0-0	0-0
Reed, Steve	0-0	0-0	0-0	0-0	0-0	1-0	1-1	0-0	1-0	0-0	0-1	0-0	0-0	0-0	3-2
Rincon, Ricky	1-0	1-0	0-0	0-0	0-0	0-1	0-0	0-1	0-0	0-0	0-1	0-0	0-0	0-0	2-3
Riske, David	0-0	0-0	0-0	0-0	0-1	0-0	0-0	0-0	0-0	1-0	0-0	0-0	0-0	0-0	1-1
Shuey, Paul	0-0	0-0	1-1	1-0	1-1	1-1	1-0	0-0	1-1	0-0	0-0	0-0	1-0	1-1	8-5
Spradlin, Jerry..............	0-0	0-0	0-0	0-0	0-0	0-0	0-0	0-0	0-0	0-0	0-0	0-0	0-0	0-0	0-0
Stevens, Dave	0-0	0-0	0-0	0-0	0-0	0-0	0-0	0-0	0-0	0-0	0-0	0-0	0-0	0-0	0-0
Tam, Jeff	0-0	0-0	0-0	0-0	0-0	0-0	0-0	0-0	0-0	0-0	0-0	0-0	0-0	0-0	0-0
Wagner, Paul	0-0	0-0	0-0	0-0	0-0	0-0	0-0	0-0	0-0	0-0	1-0	0-0	0-0	0-0	1-0
Wright, Jaret	0-0	0-0	0-0	0-0	1-2	0-1	2-1	0-1	2-0	1-0	1-1	1-0	0-1	0-1	8-10
Totals	9-1	9-1	4-8	9-3	8-5	7-5	9-3	3-7	10-2	7-3	5-4	3-7	5-7	9-9	97-65

INTERLEAGUE BREAKDOWN: Jackson 1-0, Assenmacher 0-1, Colon 0-1 vs. Brewers; Jackson 1-1, Nagy 1-0 vs. Cubs; Shuey 1-1, Burba 1-1, Jackson 1-0, Nagy 1-0 vs. Reds; Colon 1-0, Wright 0-1, Candiotti 0-1 vs. Astros; Colon 1-0, Burba 0-1, Nagy 0-1 vs. Pirates. Total: 9-9.

DETROIT—69-92

Pitcher	Ana. W-L	Bal. W-L	Bos. W-L	Chi. W-L	Cle. W-L	K.C. W-L	Min. W-L	N.Y. W-L	Oak. W-L	Sea. W-L	T.B. W-L	Tex. W-L	Tor. W-L	N.L. W-L	Total W-L
Anderson, Matt..............	0-0	0-0	0-1	0-0	0-0	0-0	1-0	1-0	0-0	0-0	0-0	0-0	0-0	0-0	2-1
Blair, Willie	0-0	1-0	0-1	0-1	1-0	0-0	0-0	0-0	1-0	0-2	0-1	0-2	0-1	0-3	3-11
Borkowski, Dave...........	0-0	0-1	0-0	0-0	0-2	1-1	0-0	0-0	1-0	0-0	0-1	0-0	0-1	0-0	2-6

Pitcher	Ana. W-L	Bal. W-L	Bos. W-L	Chi. W-L	Cle. W-L	K.C. W-L	Min. W-L	N.Y. W-L	Oak. W-L	Sea. W-L	T.B. W-L	Tex. W-L	Tor. W-L	N.L. W-L	Total W-L
Brocail, Doug	1-1	1-0	0-1	0-0	0-1	0-0	0-0	0-0	1-0	0-0	0-0	0-0	0-0	1-1	4-4
Brunson, Will	0-0	0-0	0-0	0-0	0-0	0-0	0-0	0-0	0-0	0-0	0-0	0-0	0-0	1-0	1-0
Cordero, Francisco	0-0	0-0	0-0	0-0	0-0	0-0	1-0	0-0	0-1	0-0	0-0	1-0	0-1	0-0	2-2
Cruz, Nelson	0-0	0-0	0-0	0-0	0-0	1-0	0-1	0-0	0-2	0-0	0-0	0-1	0-0	1-1	2-5
Florie, Bryce	1-0	0-0	0-0	0-0	0-0	1-1	0-0	0-0	0-0	0-0	0-0	0-0	0-0	0-0	2-1
Graterol, Beiker	0-0	0-0	0-0	0-0	0-0	0-0	0-0	0-1	0-0	0-0	0-0	0-0	0-0	0-0	0-1
Hiljus, Erik	0-0	0-0	0-0	0-0	0-0	0-0	0-0	0-0	0-0	0-0	0-0	0-0	0-0	0-0	0-0
Jones, Todd	1-0	0-0	0-0	0-0	1-1	0-0	0-0	0-1	0-0	0-1	0-0	0-0	1-0	1-1	4-4
Kida, Masao	0-0	0-0	0-0	0-0	0-0	0-0	0-0	0-0	0-0	1-0	0-0	0-0	0-0	0-0	1-0
Lira, Felipe	0-0	0-0	0-0	0-0	0-0	0-0	0-0	0-0	0-0	0-0	0-0	0-0	0-0	0-0	0-0
Mlicki, Dave	1-0	2-1	1-1	2-1	0-1	0-1	1-1	2-1	0-0	0-1	2-0	2-0	0-3	1-1	14-12
Moehler, Brian	0-2	0-0	2-0	0-3	0-2	1-0	1-1	1-1	0-1	1-2	0-1	2-0	1-1	1-2	10-16
Nitkowski, C.J.	0-0	0-1	0-0	1-0	1-0	1-0	0-0	0-1	0-0	0-1	0-1	0-0	0-0	1-1	4-5
Roberts, Willis	0-0	0-0	0-0	0-0	0-0	0-0	0-0	0-0	0-0	0-0	0-0	0-0	0-0	0-0	0-0
Rojas, Mel	0-0	0-0	0-0	0-0	0-0	0-0	0-0	0-0	0-0	0-0	0-0	0-0	0-0	0-0	0-0
Runyan, Sean	0-0	0-0	0-0	0-0	0-0	0-0	0-1	0-0	0-0	0-0	0-0	0-0	0-0	0-0	0-1
Thompson, Justin	0-1	0-1	2-0	0-2	0-1	1-1	0-1	1-2	1-1	1-0	1-0	0-1	0-1	1-0	9-11
Weaver, Jeff	1-1	1-1	0-3	2-0	2-0	1-0	1-2	0-0	0-1	0-0	1-1	0-1	0-2	0-0	9-12
Totals	5-5	5-5	5-7	5-7	5-8	7-4	6-6	5-7	4-6	3-7	4-5	5-5	2-10	8-10	69-92

INTERLEAGUE BREAKDOWN: Thompson 1-0, Cruz 0-1, Moehler 0-1 vs. Brewers; Brocail 1-0, Nitkowski 1-0, Mlicki 0-1 vs. Reds; Blair 0-1, Brocail 0-1, Jones 0-1 vs. Astros; Brunson 1-0, Cruz 1-0, Moehler 0-1 vs. Pirates; Moehler 1-0, Jones 1-0, Mlicki 1-0, Blair 0-2, Nitkowski 0-1 vs. Cardinals. Total: 8-10.

KANSAS CITY—64-97

Pitcher	Ana. W-L	Bal. W-L	Bos. W-L	Chi. W-L	Cle. W-L	Det. W-L	Min. W-L	N.Y. W-L	Oak. W-L	Sea. W-L	T.B. W-L	Tex. W-L	Tor. W-L	N.L. W-L	Total W-L
Appier, Kevin	1-0	0-2	0-1	3-0	1-0	0-1	1-0	0-0	1-0	1-0	0-0	0-1	1-1	0-3	9-9
Barber, Brian	0-0	0-0	0-0	1-1	0-0	0-0	0-0	0-0	0-0	0-0	0-1	0-0	0-1	0-0	1-3
Byrdak, Tim	0-1	0-0	0-0	0-1	0-1	0-0	0-0	0-0	0-0	0-0	0-0	0-0	0-0	0-0	0-3
Carter, Lance	0-1	0-0	0-0	0-0	0-0	0-0	0-0	0-0	0-0	0-0	0-0	0-0	0-0	0-0	0-1
Durbin, Chad	0-0	0-0	0-0	0-0	0-0	0-0	0-0	0-0	0-0	0-0	0-0	0-0	0-0	0-0	0-0
Fussell, Chris	0-1	0-0	0-0	0-0	0-0	0-0	0-0	0-0	0-1	0-2	0-0	0-0	0-1	0-0	0-5
Mathews, Terry	0-0	0-0	0-0	0-0	0-0	0-1	1-0	0-0	0-0	0-0	1-0	0-0	0-0	0-0	2-1
Montgomery, Jeff	0-1	0-0	0-0	0-1	1-0	0-0	0-0	0-0	0-0	0-0	0-0	0-0	0-0	0-2	1-4
Moreno, Orber	0-0	0-0	0-0	0-0	0-0	0-0	0-0	0-0	0-0	0-0	0-0	0-0	0-0	0-0	0-0
Morman, Alvin	0-1	0-0	0-0	0-0	0-0	0-0	0-0	0-1	1-0	1-0	0-0	0-1	0-0	0-1	2-4
Murray, Dan	0-0	0-0	0-0	0-0	0-0	0-0	0-0	0-0	0-0	0-0	0-0	0-0	0-0	0-0	0-2
Pisciotta, Marc	0-0	0-0	0-0	0-1	0-1	0-0	0-0	0-0	0-0	0-0	0-0	0-0	0-0	0-0	0-2
Pittsley, Jim	0-0	0-0	0-0	1-0	0-0	0-0	0-0	0-1	0-0	0-0	0-0	0-0	0-1	0-0	1-2
Ray, Ken	0-0	0-0	0-0	0-0	0-0	0-0	0-0	0-0	0-0	0-0	0-0	0-0	0-0	1-0	1-0
Reichert, Dan	0-0	0-1	0-0	0-0	0-0	0-0	0-0	1-0	0-0	0-0	0-1	1-0	0-0	0-0	2-2
Rigby, Brad	0-0	0-0	0-0	0-0	0-0	0-0	0-2	0-0	0-0	0-0	0-0	0-0	0-0	0-0	1-2
Rosado, Jose	1-1	1-1	0-3	0-0	1-0	2-1	1-1	1-1	1-2	1-0	0-1	0-0	0-1	1-2	10-14
Rusch, Glendon	0-0	0-0	0-0	0-0	0-0	0-0	0-0	0-1	0-0	0-0	0-0	0-0	0-0	0-0	0-1
Santiago, Jose	1-0	0-0	0-0	0-0	0-1	0-0	0-1	0-0	2-0	0-0	0-2	0-0	0-0	0-0	3-4
Service, Scott	0-0	0-1	0-0	0-1	0-0	0-0	0-1	1-0	1-0	1-0	1-1	0-0	0-1	1-0	5-5
Stein, Blake	0-0	0-0	0-0	0-0	0-0	0-1	0-1	0-0	0-0	0-0	1-0	0-0	0-0	0-0	1-2
Suppan, Jeff	2-0	2-0	1-2	0-0	1-1	0-2	1-1	0-0	1-1	0-2	0-1	1-0	0-1	1-1	10-12
Suzuki, Makoto	0-0	0-0	1-0	0-1	0-0	1-1	0-0	0-0	0-0	0-0	0-1	0-0	0-0	0-0	2-3
Wallace, Derek	0-0	0-1	0-0	0-0	0-0	0-0	0-0	0-0	0-0	0-0	0-0	0-0	0-0	0-0	0-1
Wengert, Don	0-0	0-0	0-0	0-0	0-1	0-0	0-0	0-0	0-0	0-0	0-0	0-0	0-0	0-0	0-1
Whisenant, Matt	0-0	0-0	0-1	1-0	1-0	0-0	0-0	0-0	0-0	0-0	1-0	0-0	0-1	1-2	4-4
Witasick, Jay	0-1	0-0	0-0	0-0	0-2	1-0	1-1	0-0	0-1	2-1	1-1	0-2	1-1	2-0	9-12
Totals	5-7	4-6	2-8	6-6	5-7	4-7	5-8	5-4	6-6	7-5	2-8	4-6	3-7	6-12	64-97

INTERLEAGUE BREAKDOWN: Ray 1-0, Appier 0-1, Rosado 0-1 vs. Brewers; Suppan 1-0, Witasick 1-0, Barber 0-1 vs. Cubs; Rosado 0-1, Montgomery 0-1, Witasick 0-1 vs. Reds; Montgomery 0-1, Appier 0-1, Suppan 0-1 vs. Astros; Rosado 1-0, Whisenant 0-2 vs. Pirates; Whisenant 1-0, Service 1-0, Appier 0-1 vs. Cardinals. Total: 6-12.

MINNESOTA—63-97

Pitcher	Ana. W-L	Bal. W-L	Bos. W-L	Chi. W-L	Cle. W-L	Det. W-L	K.C. W-L	N.Y. W-L	Oak. W-L	Sea. W-L	T.B. W-L	Tex. W-L	Tor. W-L	N.L. W-L	Total W-L
Aguilera, Rick	0-0	0-0	0-0	0-0	1-0	1-0	1-0	0-1	0-0	0-0	0-0	0-0	0-0	0-0	3-1
Carrasco, Hector	0-0	0-0	0-0	0-1	0-1	0-0	0-0	0-0	0-1	1-0	1-0	0-0	0-0	0-0	2-3
Guardado, Eddie	0-0	0-0	1-0	0-0	0-0	0-0	0-1	0-0	0-1	0-0	0-1	0-2	0-0	1-0	2-5
Hawkins, LaTroy	1-1	0-3	1-1	0-2	0-1	2-1	3-1	0-2	1-0	1-1	0-0	0-1	0-0	1-0	10-14
Lincoln, Mike	0-1	0-0	0-1	0-0	0-2	1-0	0-1	1-0	0-1	0-0	0-1	0-1	0-1	1-1	3-10
Mays, Joe	0-2	0-2	0-0	2-0	0-0	1-1	0-0	0-0	1-0	0-1	0-0	0-1	1-1	1-2	6-11
Miller, Travis	0-0	0-1	0-0	0-0	0-0	0-0	1-0	0-0	1-0	0-0	0-1	0-0	0-0	0-0	2-2
Milton, Eric	2-0	0-1	0-1	0-0	1-1	0-1	1-1	1-1	1-0	0-1	1-0	0-2	0-1	0-1	7-11
Perkins, Dan	0-0	0-1	0-1	0-1	0-0	0-1	0-1	0-0	1-1	0-0	0-1	0-0	0-0	0-0	1-7
Radke, Brad	1-2	1-0	2-0	0-1	0-2	0-0	0-0	1-1	0-1	0-1	2-1	0-3	2-1	3-1	12-14
Radlosky, Rob	0-0	0-0	0-0	0-0	0-0	0-0	0-0	0-0	0-0	0-0	0-0	0-0	0-1	0-0	0-1
Rath, Gary	0-0	0-0	0-0	0-0	0-0	0-0	0-0	0-0	0-0	0-0	0-1	0-0	0-0	0-0	0-1
Redman, Mark	0-0	0-0	0-0	0-0	0-0	0-0	0-0	0-0	1-0	0-0	0-0	0-0	0-0	0-0	1-0
Romero, J.C.	0-0	0-0	0-0	0-0	0-0	0-0	0-0	0-0	0-0	0-0	0-0	0-0	0-0	0-0	0-0
Ryan, Jason	0-0	0-0	0-1	0-2	0-0	0-0	0-0	0-0	1-0	0-0	0-0	0-1	0-0	0-0	1-4
Sampson, Benj	0-0	0-0	0-0	1-0	0-0	0-0	0-0	0-0	0-0	0-0	0-0	0-1	0-0	2-0	3-2
Trombley, Mike	0-0	0-0	0-0	0-0	0-1	1-0	0-0	0-0	0-0	0-0	0-1	0-1	1-0	0-2	2-8
Wells, Bob	0-0	0-0	0-0	0-1	0-1	1-1	2-0	1-0	1-0	1-0	1-0	0-0	0-0	1-0	8-3
Totals	4-6	1-8	4-6	3-8	3-9	6-6	8-5	4-6	7-5	4-8	5-5	0-12	4-6	10-7	63-97

1999 A.L. STATISTICS Miscellaneous

INTERLEAGUE BREAKDOWN: Wells 1-0, Sampson 1-0 vs. Brewers; Mays 1-0, Radke 0-1, Trombley 0-1 vs. Cubs; Lincoln 1-0, Radke 0-1, Milton 0-1 vs. Reds; Sampson 1-0, Trombley 0-1, Mays 0-1 vs. Astros; Radke 1-0, Guardado 1-0, Mays 0-1 vs. Pirates; Hawkins 1-0, Radke 1-0, Lincoln 0-1 vs. Cardinals. Total: 10-7.

NEW YORK—98-64

Pitcher	Ana. W-L	Bal. W-L	Bos. W-L	Chi. W-L	Cle. W-L	Det. W-L	K.C. W-L	Min. W-L	Oak. W-L	Sea. W-L	T.B. W-L	Tex. W-L	Tor. W-L	N.L. W-L	Total W-L
Buddie, Mike	0-0	0-0	0-0	0-0	0-0	0-0	0-0	0-0	0-0	0-0	0-0	0-0	0-0	0-0	0-0
Clemens, Roger	0-1	0-1	1-1	2-0	2-0	2-0	0-0	1-1	0-2	2-0	1-0	1-1	0-0	2-3	14-10
Cone, David	0-2	3-0	0-1	0-1	0-0	1-1	1-1	0-1	0-0	1-0	1-1	2-0	1-1	2-0	12-9
Erdos, Todd	0-0	0-0	0-0	0-0	0-0	0-0	0-0	0-0	0-0	0-0	0-0	0-0	0-0	0-0	0-0
Fossas, Tony	0-0	0-0	0-0	0-0	0-0	0-0	0-0	0-0	0-0	0-0	0-0	0-0	0-0	0-0	0-0
Grimsley, Jason	0-0	1-0	0-0	0-0	1-0	0-0	1-1	1-0	0-0	1-0	0-0	0-0	1-0	1-1	7-2
Hernandez, Orlando	0-0	2-0	2-1	1-1	0-2	2-1	2-1	1-0	2-0	0-1	2-0	0-1	1-1	2-0	17-9
Irabu, Hideki	1-1	0-0	1-3	0-0	2-0	1-0	0-0	1-1	0-0	1-0	0-1	1-1	2-0	1-0	11-7
Juden, Jeff	0-0	0-0	0-0	0-0	0-0	0-0	0-0	0-0	0-0	0-0	0-1	0-0	0-0	0-0	0-1
Mendoza, Ramiro	0-1	1-1	0-1	0-1	1-0	0-1	0-0	0-1	2-1	0-0	1-1	2-0	2-0	0-1	9-9
Naulty, Dan	0-0	1-0	0-0	0-0	0-0	0-0	0-0	0-0	0-0	0-0	0-0	0-0	0-0	0-0	1-0
Nelson, Jeff	0-0	1-0	0-0	0-0	0-0	0-0	0-0	1-0	0-0	0-0	0-0	0-0	0-0	0-0	2-0
Pettitte, Andy	1-1	0-1	0-1	2-2	0-1	0-1	0-2	2-0	0-0	2-0	2-0	1-0	3-0	1-2	14-11
Rivera, Mariano	0-0	0-1	0-0	2-0	0-0	1-0	0-0	0-0	0-0	1-0	0-0	0-0	0-0	0-2	4-3
Stanton, Mike	0-0	0-0	0-0	0-0	0-0	0-0	0-0	0-1	0-0	0-0	1-0	1-1	0-0	0-0	2-2
Tessmer, Jay	0-0	0-0	0-0	0-0	0-0	0-0	0-0	0-0	0-0	0-0	0-0	0-0	0-0	0-0	0-0
Watson, Allen	1-0	0-0	0-0	0-0	1-0	0-0	0-0	1-0	0-0	1-0	0-0	0-0	0-0	0-0	4-0
Yarnall, Ed	1-0	0-0	0-0	0-0	0-0	0-0	0-0	0-0	0-0	0-0	0-0	0-0	0-0	0-0	1-0
Totals	4-6	9-4	4-8	7-5	7-3	7-5	4-5	6-4	6-4	9-1	8-4	8-4	10-2	9-9	98-64

INTERLEAGUE BREAKDOWN: Pettitte 1-0, Clemens 0-1, Rivera 0-1 vs. Braves; Cone 1-0, Clemens 1-0, Mendoza 0-1 vs. Expos; Grimsley 1-0, Hernandez 1-0, Irabu 1-0, Clemens 0-2, Rivera 0-1 vs. Mets; Cone 1-0, Pettitte 0-1, Grimsley 0-1 vs. Phillies; Hernandez 1-0, Clemens 1-0, Pettitte 0-1 vs. Marlins. Total: 9-9.

OAKLAND—87-75

Pitcher	Ana. W-L	Bal. W-L	Bos. W-L	Chi. W-L	Cle. W-L	Det. W-L	K.C. W-L	Min. W-L	N.Y. W-L	Sea. W-L	T.B. W-L	Tex. W-L	Tor. W-L	N.L. W-L	Total W-L
Appier, Kevin	0-0	1-0	1-1	1-1	0-0	1-0	0-0	0-1	0-0	1-0	1-0	0-1	1-1	0-0	7-5
Candiotti, Tom	0-0	1-0	0-0	0-1	1-1	0-0	0-1	0-0	0-1	0-1	1-0	0-0	0-0	0-0	3-5
Groom, Buddy	0-0	0-0	0-0	0-0	0-0	0-0	1-0	0-0	0-0	0-0	1-0	0-0	0-0	1-2	3-2
Harville, Chad	0-1	0-0	0-0	0-0	0-0	0-0	0-1	0-0	0-0	0-0	0-0	0-0	0-0	0-0	0-2
Haynes, Jimmy	0-0	0-2	0-1	0-2	0-2	1-1	1-1	1-1	0-2	0-1	0-0	2-0	0-0	2-1	7-12
Heredia, Gil	1-1	0-0	1-2	2-0	0-0	1-0	1-1	0-1	0-1	2-0	2-0	0-1	1-0	2-1	13-8
Hudson, Tim	1-0	1-0	1-0	0-0	0-0	2-0	0-0	1-0	0-0	1-0	1-0	1-1	1-0	2-1	11-2
Isringhausen, Jason	0-1	0-0	0-0	0-0	0-0	0-0	0-0	0-0	0-0	0-0	0-0	0-0	0-0	0-0	0-1
Jarvis, Kevin	0-0	0-0	0-0	0-0	0-0	0-0	0-0	0-0	0-0	0-0	0-1	0-0	0-0	0-0	0-1
Jones, Doug	0-1	0-0	1-1	1-0	0-0	0-0	0-0	0-1	1-1	0-1	0-0	0-0	1-0	1-0	5-5
Kubinski, Tim	0-0	0-0	0-0	0-0	0-0	0-0	0-0	0-0	0-0	0-0	0-0	0-0	0-0	0-0	0-0
Laxton, Brett	0-0	0-0	0-0	0-0	0-0	0-0	0-0	0-0	0-0	0-0	0-0	0-0	0-1	0-0	0-1
Mahay, Ron	0-0	0-0	0-0	0-0	0-0	0-0	0-0	1-0	0-0	1-0	0-0	0-0	0-0	0-0	2-0
Mathews, T.J.	1-1	1-1	2-0	1-0	1-0	0-0	1-0	1-1	0-1	0-1	1-0	0-0	0-0	0-0	9-5
McMichael, Greg	0-0	0-0	0-0	0-0	0-0	0-0	0-0	0-0	0-0	0-0	0-0	0-0	0-0	0-0	0-0
Olivares, Omar	0-0	0-1	0-0	1-0	0-0	0-1	1-0	0-0	2-0	0-0	0-0	1-0	0-0	1-0	7-2
Oquist, Mike	1-1	1-1	0-0	1-0	0-2	0-1	2-1	0-0	0-0	0-0	1-0	0-2	2-1	1-1	9-10
Rigby, Brad	0-1	2-0	0-0	0-0	0-0	1-1	0-0	0-1	0-0	0-0	0-1	0-0	0-0	0-0	3-4
Rogers, Kenny	0-1	0-0	0-0	0-0	0-1	0-0	1-0	0-0	0-0	0-1	0-0	0-0	1-0	2-0	5-3
Stein, Blake	0-0	0-0	0-0	0-0	0-0	0-0	0-0	0-0	0-0	0-0	0-0	0-0	0-0	0-0	0-0
Taylor, Billy	0-0	0-0	0-0	0-0	0-3	0-0	0-0	0-1	0-0	1-0	0-0	0-0	0-0	0-1	1-5
Vizcaino, Luis	0-0	0-0	0-0	0-0	0-0	0-0	0-0	0-0	0-0	0-0	0-0	0-0	0-0	0-0	0-0
Worrell, Tim	0-0	0-0	0-0	0-0	0-1	0-0	0-0	1-1	0-0	0-0	0-0	0-0	0-0	1-0	2-2
Totals	4-8	7-5	6-4	7-3	2-10	6-4	6-6	5-7	4-6	6-6	9-1	5-7	8-2	12-6	87-75

INTERLEAGUE BREAKDOWN: Oquist 1-0, Rogers 1-0, Hudson 1-0 vs. Dodgers; Haynes 1-0, Groom 0-1, Heredia 0-1 vs. Padres; Groom 1-1, Heredia 1-0, Jones 1-0, Taylor 0-1, Oquist 0-1 vs. Giants; Haynes 1-0, Worrell 1-0, Rogers 1-0 vs. Rockies; Heredia 1-0, Hudson 1-0, Haynes 0-1 vs. Diamondbacks. Total: 12-6.

SEATTLE—79-83

Pitcher	Ana. W-L	Bal. W-L	Bos. W-L	Chi. W-L	Cle. W-L	Det. W-L	K.C. W-L	Min. W-L	N.Y. W-L	Oak. W-L	T.B. W-L	Tex. W-L	Tor. W-L	N.L. W-L	Total W-L
Abbott, Paul	0-0	1-0	0-1	1-0	1-0	0-0	0-0	1-0	0-1	1-0	0-0	0-0	1-0	0-0	6-2
Bunch, Mel	0-0	0-0	0-0	0-0	0-0	0-0	0-0	0-0	0-0	0-0	0-0	0-0	0-0	0-0	0-0
Carmona, Rafael	0-0	0-0	0-0	0-0	0-0	0-0	1-0	0-0	0-0	0-0	0-0	0-0	0-0	0-0	1-0
Cloude, Ken	1-0	0-0	0-0	1-0	0-0	1-1	0-0	0-0	0-0	0-1	0-2	1-0	0-0	0-0	4-4
Davey, Tom	1-0	0-0	0-0	0-0	0-0	0-0	0-0	0-0	0-0	0-0	0-0	0-0	0-0	0-0	1-0
Fassero, Jeff	1-0	0-0	0-1	0-2	1-0	0-0	0-2	1-1	0-2	0-3	1-0	0-0	0-0	0-3	4-14
Franklin, Ryan	0-0	0-0	0-0	0-0	0-0	0-0	0-0	0-0	0-0	0-0	0-0	0-0	0-0	0-0	0-0
Garcia, Freddy	0-1	0-2	0-0	2-0	0-0	3-0	1-1	1-0	1-1	2-0	3-0	1-0	1-1	2-2	17-8
Halama, John	1-0	0-1	0-2	1-0	1-1	1-0	1-1	2-0	0-1	0-1	1-1	1-2	0-1	1-0	11-10
Henry, Butch	0-0	0-0	0-0	0-0	0-0	0-0	0-0	0-0	0-0	1-0	1-0	0-0	0-0	0-0	2-0
Hinchliffe, Brett	0-0	0-0	0-1	0-0	0-0	0-1	0-1	0-0	0-0	0-0	0-1	0-0	0-0	0-0	0-4
Leiter, Mark	0-0	0-0	0-0	0-0	0-0	0-0	0-0	0-0	0-0	0-0	0-0	0-0	0-0	0-0	0-0
Marte, Damaso	0-0	0-0	0-0	0-0	0-0	0-0	0-0	0-0	0-0	0-0	0-0	0-0	0-0	0-1	0-1
Meche, Gil	0-0	1-0	1-0	2-0	0-1	0-0	0-0	1-1	0-1	0-0	0-1	1-0	1-0	1-0	8-4
Mesa, Jose	1-1	0-1	0-0	0-0	0-2	0-0	0-0	0-0	0-0	0-0	0-0	0-0	0-0	1-2	3-6
Moyer, Jamie	0-3	2-0	2-0	1-1	0-0	1-1	2-0	2-1	0-1	1-0	1-0	0-0	1-1	1-0	14-8
Paniagua, Jose	1-0	1-0	0-1	0-1	0-0	0-0	0-2	0-1	0-1	1-1	1-0	2-1	0-0	0-3	6-11
Ramsay, Robert	0-0	0-1	0-0	0-0	0-0	0-0	0-0	0-0	0-0	0-0	0-1	0-0	0-0	0-0	0-2
Rodriguez, Frank	0-1	0-0	0-0	0-0	0-1	0-0	0-0	0-0	0-0	0-0	0-1	0-1	0-0	1-0	2-4

Pitcher	Ana. W-L	Bal. W-L	Bos. W-L	Chi. W-L	Cle. W-L	Det. W-L	K.C. W-L	Min. W-L	N.Y. W-L	Oak. W-L	T.B. W-L	Tex. W-L	Tor. W-L	N.L. W-L	Total W-L
Scheffer, Aaron	0-0	0-0	0-0	0-0	0-0	0-0	0-0	0-0	0-0	0-0	0-0	0-0	0-0	0-0	0-0
Sinclair, Steve	0-0	0-0	0-0	0-0	0-0	0-0	0-0	0-0	0-0	0-0	0-0	0-1	0-0	0-0	0-1
Spencer, Sean	0-0	0-0	0-0	0-0	0-0	0-0	0-0	0-0	0-0	0-0	0-0	0-0	0-0	0-0	0-0
Stark, Dennis	0-0	0-0	0-0	0-0	0-0	0-0	0-0	0-0	0-0	0-0	0-0	0-0	0-0	0-0	0-0
Suzuki, Makoto	0-0	0-0	0-1	0-0	0-0	0-0	0-0	0-0	0-1	0-0	0-0	0-0	0-0	0-0	0-2
Watson, Allen	0-0	0-0	0-0	0-0	0-1	0-0	0-0	0-0	0-0	0-0	0-0	0-0	0-0	0-0	0-1
Weaver, Eric	0-0	0-0	0-0	0-0	0-1	0-0	0-0	0-0	0-0	0-0	0-0	0-0	0-0	0-0	0-1
Williams, Todd	0-0	0-0	0-0	0-0	0-0	0-0	0-0	0-0	0-0	0-0	0-0	0-0	0-0	0-0	0-0
Zimmerman, Jordan	0-0	0-0	0-0	0-0	0-0	0-0	0-0	0-0	0-0	0-0	0-0	0-0	0-0	0-0	0-0
Totals	6-6	5-5	3-7	8-4	3-7	7-3	5-7	8-4	1-9	6-6	8-4	5-8	7-2	7-11	79-83

INTERLEAGUE BREAKDOWN: Garcia 0-1, Paniagua 0-1, Fassero 0-1 vs. Dodgers; Garcia 2-0, Mesa 0-2, Fassero 0-1, Paniagua 0-1 vs. Padres; Moyer 1-0, Paniagua 0-1, Garcia 0-1 vs. Giants; Halama 1-0, Rodriguez 1-0, Fassero 0-1 vs. Rockies; Mesa 1-0, Meche 1-0, Marte 0-1 vs. Diamondbacks. Total: 7-11.

TAMPA BAY—69-93

Pitcher	Ana. W-L	Bal. W-L	Bos. W-L	Chi. W-L	Cle. W-L	Det. W-L	K.C. W-L	Min. W-L	N.Y. W-L	Oak. W-L	Sea. W-L	Tex. W-L	Tor. W-L	N.L. W-L	Total W-L
Aldred, Scott	0-0	0-0	1-0	0-0	0-0	0-0	1-0	0-1	0-0	0-0	0-0	0-1	1-0	0-0	3-2
Alvarez, Wilson	1-1	0-1	1-0	2-1	2-1	1-0	0-0	0-0	0-1	0-1	0-1	0-0	1-0	1-2	9-9
Arrojo, Rolando	0-0	0-2	1-1	0-0	0-1	2-1	1-0	0-1	1-1	0-1	0-2	2-2	0-0	0-0	7-12
Boggs, Wade	0-0	0-0	0-0	0-0	0-0	0-0	0-0	0-0	0-0	0-0	0-0	0-0	0-0	0-0	0-0
Callaway, Mickey	0-1	0-0	0-0	0-0	0-0	0-0	0-0	0-0	0-0	0-0	0-1	0-0	0-0	1-0	1-2
Charlton, Norm	0-0	0-0	0-0	0-1	0-0	0-0	0-0	1-0	0-1	0-0	0-0	0-0	0-0	1-1	2-3
Duvall, Mike	0-0	0-0	0-0	0-0	0-0	0-0	0-0	0-0	1-0	0-0	0-0	0-0	0-0	0-1	1-1
Eiland, Dave	0-1	0-1	1-0	0-0	0-0	0-0	2-0	0-0	0-1	0-2	1-0	0-0	0-1	0-2	4-8
Gaillard, Eddie	0-0	0-0	0-0	0-0	0-0	0-0	0-0	1-0	0-0	0-0	0-0	0-0	0-0	0-0	1-0
Hernandez, Roberto	0-1	0-0	1-0	0-0	0-0	0-0	1-1	0-0	0-0	0-0	0-1	0-0	0-0	0-0	2-3
Lidle, Cory	0-0	0-0	0-0	0-0	0-0	0-0	0-0	1-0	0-0	0-0	0-0	0-0	0-0	0-0	1-0
Lopez, Albie	0-0	0-0	1-0	0-0	0-0	0-0	0-0	1-0	0-0	0-0	1-0	0-0	0-1	0-1	3-2
Mecir, Jim	0-0	0-0	0-0	0-0	0-1	0-0	0-0	0-0	0-0	0-0	0-0	0-0	0-0	0-0	0-1
Morris, Jim	0-0	0-0	0-0	0-0	0-0	0-0	0-0	0-0	0-0	0-0	0-0	0-0	0-0	0-0	0-0
Newman, Alan	0-1	0-0	0-0	0-0	0-0	0-0	1-0	0-0	0-0	0-0	0-0	1-1	0-0	0-0	2-2
Rekar, Bryan	0-0	1-0	1-1	0-1	1-0	0-0	0-0	1-0	0-2	0-0	1-0	0-0	0-0	1-2	6-6
Rupe, Ryan	1-0	2-0	0-0	1-1	0-0	0-0	1-0	1-2	0-0	0-1	0-2	1-1	1-0	0-2	8-9
Santana, Julio	0-0	1-0	0-1	0-0	0-0	0-1	0-0	0-0	0-0	0-0	0-0	0-1	0-1	0-0	1-4
Saunders, Tony	1-0	2-0	0-1	0-1	0-0	0-0	0-0	0-0	0-0	0-0	0-0	0-0	0-1	0-0	3-3
Sparks, Jeff	0-0	0-0	0-0	0-0	0-0	0-0	0-0	0-0	0-0	0-0	0-0	0-0	0-0	0-0	0-0
Wheeler, Daniel	0-1	0-1	0-0	0-0	0-0	0-0	0-0	0-0	0-0	0-1	0-0	0-0	0-1	0-0	0-4
White, Rick	1-0	0-0	0-0	1-0	0-0	0-0	1-0	0-0	0-1	0-0	1-0	0-0	1-1	0-1	5-3
Witt, Bobby	1-1	1-0	2-0	0-0	0-2	1-2	1-0	0-0	0-2	0-2	0-0	0-2	1-2	0-1	7-15
Yan, Esteban	0-0	0-0	0-0	0-0	1-0	1-0	0-1	0-0	0-0	1-1	0-1	0-0	0-0	0-1	3-4
Totals	5-7	7-5	9-4	4-6	4-5	5-4	8-2	5-5	4-8	1-9	4-8	4-8	5-8	4-14	69-93

INTERLEAGUE BREAKDOWN: Eiland 0-1, White 0-1, Alvarez 0-1 vs. Braves; Callaway 1-0, Witt 0-1, Rekar 0-1 vs. Expos; Alvarez 1-0, Charlton 0-1, Eiland 0-1 vs. Mets; Charlton 1-0, Lopez 0-1, Rekar 0-1 vs. Phillies; Rekar 1-0, Rupe 0-2, Duvall 0-1, Yan 0-1, Alvarez 0-1 vs. Marlins. Total: 4-14.

TEXAS—95-67

Pitcher	Ana. W-L	Bal. W-L	Bos. W-L	Chi. W-L	Cle. W-L	Det. W-L	K.C. W-L	Min. W-L	N.Y. W-L	Oak. W-L	Sea. W-L	T.B. W-L	Tor. W-L	N.L. W-L	Total W-L
Burkett, John	2-1	0-1	0-0	1-1	2-0	0-0	0-0	0-0	0-2	2-1	1-0	0-2	1-0	0-0	9-8
Clark, Mark	0-1	0-0	0-1	0-0	1-0	0-0	0-0	1-0	0-1	0-1	0-0	1-0	0-1	0-2	3-7
Crabtree, Tim	0-0	2-0	0-0	0-0	0-0	0-0	1-0	0-0	0-0	0-0	2-1	0-0	0-0	0-0	5-1
Davis, Doug	0-0	0-0	0-0	0-0	0-0	0-0	0-0	0-0	0-0	0-0	0-0	0-0	0-0	0-0	0-0
Fassero, Jeff	0-0	0-0	0-0	1-0	0-0	0-0	0-0	0-0	0-0	0-0	0-0	0-0	0-0	0-0	1-0
Glynn, Ryan	1-0	0-0	0-1	0-1	0-0	0-0	0-0	0-0	0-1	0-1	1-0	0-0	0-0	0-0	2-4
Gunderson, Eric	0-0	0-0	0-0	0-0	0-0	0-0	0-0	0-0	0-0	0-0	0-0	0-0	0-0	0-0	0-0
Helling, Rick	0-2	1-2	2-1	1-1	1-0	2-1	0-1	1-0	1-1	0-0	0-0	2-1	1-0	1-1	13-11
Johnson, Jonathan	0-0	0-0	0-0	0-0	0-0	0-0	0-0	1-0	0-0	0-0	1-0	0-0	0-0	0-0	2-1
Kolb, Danny	0-0	0-0	0-0	0-0	0-0	0-1	0-0	1-0	0-0	0-0	0-0	1-0	0-0	0-0	2-1
Lee, Corey	0-0	0-0	0-0	0-0	0-0	0-0	0-0	0-0	0-1	0-0	0-0	0-0	0-0	0-0	0-1
Loaiza, Esteban	0-0	0-1	1-0	1-1	0-0	0-1	1-1	2-0	1-0	1-0	0-0	1-0	0-0	1-1	9-5
Morgan, Mike	1-2	2-1	1-0	0-0	0-2	1-0	0-0	2-0	0-1	2-0	2-1	0-1	1-1	1-1	13-10
Munoz, Mike	0-0	0-0	0-0	0-0	1-0	0-0	0-1	0-0	1-0	0-0	0-0	0-0	0-0	0-0	2-1
Patterson, Danny	0-0	0-0	0-0	0-0	0-0	1-0	0-0	0-0	0-0	0-0	0-0	0-0	1-0	0-0	2-0
Perisho, Matt	0-0	0-0	0-0	0-0	0-0	0-0	0-0	0-0	0-0	0-0	0-0	0-0	0-0	0-0	0-0
Sele, Aaron	2-0	1-1	1-1	0-0	2-1	1-1	2-1	0-0	1-0	0-2	1-0	2-0	2-1	2-1	18-9
Venafro, Mike	0-0	0-0	0-0	0-0	0-0	0-0	0-0	0-0	0-1	0-0	1-0	0-1	0-0	2-0	3-2
Wetteland, John	0-0	0-0	0-0	0-0	0-0	0-0	1-0	1-0	0-1	0-1	1-0	0-0	0-0	1-2	4-4
Zimmerman, Jeff	0-0	0-0	0-0	1-1	0-0	0-1	1-0	2-0	0-0	1-0	1-0	1-0	0-1	2-0	9-3
Totals	6-6	6-6	5-4	5-5	7-3	5-5	6-4	12-0	4-8	7-5	8-5	8-4	6-4	10-8	95-67

INTERLEAGUE BREAKDOWN: Sele 1-0, Zimmerman 1-0, Clark 0-1 vs. Dodgers; Sele 1-0, Wetteland 0-1, Loaiza 0-1 vs. Padres; Morgan 1-0, Loaiza 1-0, Helling 1-0 vs. Giants; Zimmerman 1-0, Sele 0-1, Morgan 0-1 vs. Rockies; Venafro 2-0, Wetteland 1-1, Clark 0-1, Helling 0-1 vs. Diamondbacks. Total: 10-8.

TORONTO—84-78

Pitcher	Ana. W-L	Bal. W-L	Bos. W-L	Chi. W-L	Cle. W-L	Det. W-L	K.C. W-L	Min. W-L	N.Y. W-L	Oak. W-L	Sea. W-L	Tex. W-L	T.B. W-L	N.L. W-L	Total W-L
Bale, John	0-0	0-0	0-0	0-0	0-0	0-0	0-0	0-0	0-0	0-0	0-0	0-0	0-0	0-0	0-0
Carpenter, Chris	1-0	0-1	0-1	2-0	0-0	0-0	0-1	1-0	0-1	0-2	1-1	3-0	1-1	0-0	9-8
Davey, Tom	1-0	0-0	0-0	0-0	0-0	0-0	0-0	0-0	0-0	0-0	0-0	0-0	0-0	0-1	1-1
Escobar, Kelvim	2-0	2-0	1-1	0-3	1-0	3-0	1-1	2-0	0-1	0-2	0-0	1-2	0-0	1-1	14-11

Pitcher	Ana. W-L	Bal. W-L	Bos. W-L	Chi. W-L	Cle. W-L	Det. W-L	K.C. W-L	Min. W-L	N.Y. W-L	Oak. W-L	Sea. W-L	Tex. W-L	T.B. W-L	N.L. W-L	Total W-L
Frascatore, John	0-0	3-0	0-0	1-0	1-0	0-1	0-0	0-0	0-0	0-0	0-0	0-0	0-0	1-0	7-1
Glover, Gary	0-0	0-0	0-0	0-0	0-0	0-0	0-0	0-0	0-0	0-0	0-0	0-0	0-0	0-0	0-0
Halladay, Roy	0-1	2-0	0-1	0-1	1-0	3-0	1-0	0-0	0-0	0-2	0-0	0-0	0-1	1-1	8-7
Hamilton, Joey	1-0	0-0	0-1	1-0	0-0	0-0	1-0	0-2	1-0	1-1	0-0	0-2	1-0	1-2	7-8
Hentgen, Pat	2-0	0-0	0-2	0-1	1-0	2-0	2-1	1-2	0-2	0-0	0-1	1-0	1-1	1-2	11-12
Hudek, John	0-0	0-0	0-0	0-0	0-0	0-0	0-0	0-0	0-0	0-0	0-0	0-0	0-0	0-0	0-0
Koch, Billy	0-0	0-0	0-0	0-0	0-1	0-0	0-0	0-0	0-1	0-1	0-1	0-0	0-0	0-1	0-5
Lloyd, Graeme	1-1	2-0	1-1	0-0	0-0	0-0	0-0	0-0	0-0	0-0	0-0	1-0	0-0	0-1	5-3
Ludwick, Eric	0-0	0-0	0-0	0-0	0-0	0-0	0-0	0-0	0-0	0-0	0-0	0-0	0-0	0-0	0-0
Munro, Peter	0-0	0-0	0-0	0-0	0-1	0-0	0-0	0-0	0-0	0-0	0-0	0-0	0-1	0-0	0-2
Person, Robert	0-0	0-0	0-0	0-0	0-0	0-0	0-0	0-0	0-1	0-0	0-1	0-0	0-0	0-0	0-2
Plesac, Dan	0-0	0-0	0-1	0-0	0-0	0-0	1-0	0-0	0-0	0-0	0-1	0-0	0-0	0-0	0-3
Quantrill, Paul	0-0	0-0	0-0	1-1	0-0	0-0	1-0	0-0	0-0	0-0	0-0	0-0	0-0	1-0	3-2
Rodriguez, Nerio	0-1	0-0	0-0	0-0	0-0	0-0	0-0	0-0	0-0	0-0	0-0	0-0	0-0	0-0	0-1
Romano, Mike	0-0	0-0	0-0	0-0	0-0	0-0	0-0	0-0	0-0	0-0	0-0	0-0	0-0	0-0	0-0
Sinclair, Steve	0-0	0-0	0-0	0-0	0-0	0-0	0-0	0-0	0-0	0-0	0-0	0-0	0-0	0-0	0-0
Spoljaric, Paul	0-0	1-0	0-0	0-0	0-2	1-0	0-0	0-0	0-0	0-0	0-0	0-0	0-0	0-0	2-2
Wells, David	1-0	1-0	1-1	0-0	2-0	1-1	1-0	2-0	1-3	1-0	0-0	1-2	2-1	3-0	17-10
Totals	9-3	11-1	3-9	4-6	7-5	10-2	7-3	6-4	2-10	2-8	2-7	8-5	4-6	9-9	84-78

INTERLEAGUE BREAKDOWN: Hamilton 1-0, Frascatore 1-0, Halladay 1-0 vs. Braves; Wells 2-0, Escobar 1-0, Quantrill 1-0, Hamilton 0-1, Lloyd 0-1 vs. Expos; Halladay 0-1, Davey 0-1, Hentgen 0-1 vs. Mets; Hentgen 1-0, Hamilton 0-1, Escobar 0-1 vs. Phillies; Wells 1-0, Koch 0-1, Hentgen 0-1 vs. Marlins. Total: 9-9.

HOME RUNS BY PARKS

	At Ana.	At Bal.	At Bos.	At Chi.	At Cle.	At Det.	At K.C.	At Min.	At N.Y.	At Oak.	At Sea.	At T.B.	At Tex.	At Tor.	At N.L. Parks	Totals 1999	Totals 1998	HR Allow.
Anaheim	74	6	0	5	8	11	8	4	6	4	7	2	8	5	10	158	147	177
Baltimore	7	98	2	11	4	12	4	6	9	8	2	5	13	9	13	203	214	198
Boston	6	10	80	2	13	9	9	8	9	4	6	5	1	7	7	176	205	160
Chicago	7	3	7	77	4	11	5	6	6	4	8	3	3	5	13	162	198	210
Cleveland	5	5	8	10	110	8	4	6	7	12	5	3	8	8	10	209	198	197
Detroit	3	5	8	5	6	118	7	9	3	4	7	7	8	6	16	212	165	209
Kansas City	7	4	1	12	8	5	74	3	0	3	12	4	4	2	12	151	134	202
Minnesota	2	3	2	4	8	7	7	47	2	3	1	6	2	3	8	105	115	208
New York	7	10	6	6	6	4	3	8	84	9	8	10	12	6	14	193	207	158
Oakland	8	14	5	6	6	14	10	6	4	112	11	6	8	15	10	235	149	160
Seattle	17	6	8	8	9	4	9	14	6	3	122	13	7	5	13	244	234	191
Tampa Bay	3	3	11	7	5	2	5	1	4	3	6	66	15	7	5	145	111	172
Texas	8	12	5	13	10	10	3	13	4	5	9	12	103	10	13	230	201	186
Toronto	10	11	1	4	11	11	7	13	3	5	14	5	10	96	11	212	221	191
N.L. clubs	15	9	8	13	11	9	15	12	11	7	7	10	10	5	....	142	123	....
1999 Totals	179	199	152	183	219	235	170	156	158	186	*227	157	212	189	155	2635	....	2619
1998 Totals	141	191	176	200	187	205	186	144	171	154	218	163	184	189	....	....	2499	....

*There were 134 home runs hit at the Kingdome and 93 hit at Safeco Field in 1999.

AT ANAHEIM (179):

Anaheim (74)—Vaughn 16, Glaus 12, Anderson 10, Erstad 7, Greene 7, Salmon 7, Velarde 4, Edmonds 3, Sheets 3, DaVanon 1, DiSarcina 1, Pritchett 1, Unroe 1, Walbeck 1. **Arizona (6)**—Bell 2, Fox 1, Finley 1, Stinnett 1, Williams 1. **Baltimore (7)**—Baines 2, Anderson 1, Belle 1, Bordick 1, May 1, Surhoff 1. **Boston (6)**—Daubach 3, O'Leary 2, Stanley 1. **Chicago (7)**—Singleton 2, Abbott 1, Durham 1, Fordyce 1, Norton 1, Ordonez 1. **Cleveland (5)**—R. Alomar 2, M. Ramirez 2, Vizquel 1. **Detroit (5)**—Easley 1, Encarnacion 1, K. Garcia 1, Kelly 1. **Kansas City (7)**—Dye 3, Beltran 1, Febles, Randa 1, Spehr 1. **Los Angeles (6)**—Karros 2, Hollandsworth 1, Mondesi 1, Pena 1, White 1. **Minnesota (2)**—Hunter 1, Koskie 1. **New York (7)**—Martinez 2, Davis 1, Jeter 1, Posada 1, Spencer 1, Strawberry 1. **Oakland (8)**—Giambi 3, Grieve 2, Jaha 1, McDonald 1, Stairs 1. **San Diego (3)**—Davis 1, R. Rivera 1, Vander Wal 1. **Seattle (17)**—A. Rodriguez 4, Martinez 2, Griffey 2, Huskey 2, Mabry 2, Davis 2, Buhner 1, Segui 1, Cedeno 1. **Tampa Bay (3)**—Canseco 1, Martinez 1, Flaherty 1. **Texas (8)**—Gonzalez 2, Clayton 2, McLemore 1, Palmeiro 1, Rodriguez 1, Goodwin 1. **Toronto (10)**—Green 3, Delgado 2, Kelly 1, Brumfield 1, Gonzalez 1, Stewart 1, Witt 1.

AT BALTIMORE (199):

Anaheim (6)—Velarde 3, Greene 2, O'Brien 1. **Baltimore (98)**—Belle 19, Baines 12, Ripken 12, Anderson 10, Surhoff 9, C. Johnson 8, Conine 7, Clark 5, DeShields 4, Bordick 3, Minor 3, May 2, Otanez 1, Pickering 1, Hairston 1, Garcia 1. **Boston (10)**—O'Leary 2, Varitek 2, Stanley 1, Offerman 1, Jefferson 1, Valentin 1, Buford 1, Merloni 1. **Chicago (2)**—Konerko 2, Durham 1. **Cleveland (5)**—M. Ramirez 2, R. Alomar 1, Sexson 1. **Detroit (5)**—Encarnacion 2, Palmer 1, D. Cruz 1, Catalanotto 1. **Kansas City (4)**—Spehr 1, Damon 1, Febles 1, Beltran 1. **Minnesota (3)**—Coomer 2, Hocking 1. **Montreal (1)**—V. Guerrero 1. **New York A.L.(10)**—Spencer 3, Martinez 2, Williams 2, Brosius 2, Sojo 1. **New York N.L. (3)**—Henderson 1, Ventura 1, Alfonzo 1. **Oakland (14)**—Stairs 5, Phillips 2, Macfarlane 1, Velarde 1, Jaha 1, Giambi 1, Spiezio 1, Tejada 1, Grieve 1. **Philadelphia (5)**—Lieberthal 3, Ducey 1, Rolen 1. **Seattle (6)**—Bell 2, Martinez 1, Blowers 1, Davis 1, A. Rodriguez 1. **Tampa Bay (3)**—Canseco 1, Martinez 1, Flaherty 1. **Texas (12)**—Palmeiro 2, Gonzalez 2, Rodriguez 2, McLemore 1, Kelly 1, Alicea 1, Zeile 1, Clayton 1, Mateo 1. **Toronto (11)**—Batista 3, Stewart 2, Otanez 2, Fletcher 1, Greene 1, Delgado 1, Green 1.

AT BOSTON (152):

Atlanta (2)—Jordan 1, Klesko 1. **Baltimore (2)**—Belle 2. **Boston (80)**—Garciaparra 14, O'Leary 13, Varitek 12, Daubach 11, Stanley 8, Offerman 5, Valentin 5, Buford 3, Nixon 3, Huskey 2, Lewis 1, Jefferson 1, Frye 1, Hatteberg 1. **Chicago (7)**—Ordonez 2, Wilson 2, Thomas 2, Norton 1, Singleton 1. **Cleveland (8)**—Thome 3, Justice 1, Fryman 1, Lofton 1, Cordero 1, Sexson 1. **Detroit (8)**—Palmer 2, Encarnacion 2, Ausmus 1, Higginson 1, Fick 1, Kapler 1. **Florida (1)**—Wilson 1. **Kansas City (1)**—Fasano 1. **Minnesota (2)**—Hunter 1, Allen 1. **New York (6)**—Knoblauch 2, O'Neill 1, Williams 1, Jeter 1, Posada 1. **Oakland (5)**—Tejada 2, Spiezio 1, Grieve 1, Hinch 1. **Philadelphia (5)**—Gant 1, Glanville 1, Rolen 1, Abreu 1. **Seattle (8)**—A. Rodriguez 4, Bell 2, Buhner 1, Lampkin 1, Huskey 1. **Tampa Bay (11)**—Canseco 4, Boggs 1, Martinez 1, Sorrento 1, Flaherty 1, Cairo 1, Trammell 1, Clyburn 1, Smith 1. **Texas (5)**—Rodriguez 2, Zeile 1, Gonzalez 1, Stevens 1. **Toronto (1)**—Green 1.

AT CHICAGO (183):

Anaheim (5)—Vaughn 3, Molina 1, Glaus 1. **Baltimore (11)**—Surhoff 3, Baines 2, Belle 2, Ripken 1, Clark 1, Anderson 1, Bordick 1. **Boston (2)**—O'Leary 1, Garciaparra 1. **Chicago A.L.(77)**—Ordonez 16, Konerko 16, Lee 10, Thomas 9, Durham 7, Fordyce 5, Norton 5, Singleton 5, Johnson 2, Jackson 1, Christensen 1. **Chicago N.L. (4)**—Hill 2, Hernandez 1, Houston 1. **Cleveland (10)**—Justice 3, Sexson 3, Lofton 2, M. Ramirez 2. **Detroit (5)**—K. Garcia 2, Palmer 1, Fick 1, Kapler 1. **Houston (6)**—Bagwell 3, Everett 2, Bogar 1. **Kansas City (12)**—Randa 3, Sweeney 2, Beltran 2, King 1, Leius 1, Sanchez 1, Damon

1, Dye 1. **Minnesota (4)**—Coomer 1, Cordova 1, Lawton 1, Jones 1. **New York (6)**—Martinez 1, Williams 1, Brosius 1, Curtis 1, Jeter 1, Posada 1. **Oakland (6)**—Phillips 1, Stairs 1, Jaha 1, Saenz 1, Tejada 1, Grieve 1. **Pittsburgh (3)**—F. Garcia 1, Kendall 1, Morris 1. **Seattle (8)**—Martinez 3, A. Rodriguez 2, Buhner 1, Lampkin 1, Ibanez 1. **Tampa Bay (7)**—Canseco 3, McGriff 2, Smith 1, Lamb 1. **Texas (13)**—Greer 5, Gonzalez 2, Stevens 2, Rodriguez 2, Palmeiro 1, Zeile 1. **Toronto (4)**—Batista 2, Green 1, Matheny 1.

AT CLEVELAND (219):

Anaheim (8)—Salmon 2, Anderson 2, Glaus 2, Vaughn 1, Edmonds 1. **Baltimore (4)**—Conine 3, Surhoff 1. **Boston (13)**—Garciaparra 4, Nixon 3, Varitek 2, Stanley 1, Offerman 1, O'Leary 1, Daubach 1. **Chicago A.L. (4)**—Fordyce 1, Ordonez 1, Johnson 1, Simmons 1. **Chicago N.L. (2)**—Gaetti 1, Hill 1. **Cincinnati (3)**—Vaughn 1, Taubensee 1, Cameron 1. **Cleveland (110)**—M. Ramirez 21, Thome 19, Sexson 18, R. Alomar 12, Justice 11, Fryman 6, S. Alomar 4, Vizquel 3, Cordero 3, Cruz 3, Diaz 2, A. Ramirez 2, Baines 1, Baerga 1, Manto 1, Lofton 1, Wilson 1, Roberts 1. **Detroit (6)**—Catalanotto 2, Palmer 1, K. Garcia 1, Clark 1, D. Cruz 1. **Kansas City (8)**—Dye 6, Sweeney 1, Febles 1. **Milwaukee (6)**—Nilsson 2, Jenkins 2, Burnitz 1, Loretta 1. **Minnesota (8)**—Steinbach 1, Hocking 1, Coomer 1, Lawton 1, Hunter 1, Valentin 1, Koskie 1, Allen 1. **New York (6)**—O'Neill 3, Jeter 2, Ledee 1. **Oakland (6)**—Phillips 2, Grieve 2, Spiezio 1, Chavez 1. **Seattle (9)**—Griffey 3, Huskey 2, Wilson 1, Mabry 1, Davis 1, Bell 1. **Tampa Bay (5)**—McGriff 2, Canseco 1, Sorrento 1, Clyburn 1. **Texas (10)**—Palmeiro 3, Rodriguez 2, Clayton 2, McLemore 1, Alicea 1, Gonzalez 1. **Toronto (11)**—Green 2, Batista 2, Otanez 2, Segui 1, Greene 1, Delgado 1, Cruz 1, Blake 1.

AT DETROIT (235):

Anaheim (11)—Salmon 2, Anderson 2, Greene 2, Glaus 2, Vaughn 1, Walbeck 1, Erstad 1. **Baltimore (12)**—C. Johnson 4, Baines 1, Surhoff 1, Anderson 1, Belle 1, DeShields 1, Bordick 1, May 1, Conine 1. **Boston (9)**—Nixon 3, O'Leary 2, Garciaparra 2, Offerman 1, Daubach 1. **Chicago (11)**—Norton 5, Thomas 1, Durham 1, Fordyce 1, Konerko 1, Wilson 1, Singleton 1. **Cleveland (8)**—R. Alomar 2, Thome 2, Justice 1, Fryman 1, Cordero 1, M. Ramirez 1. **Detroit (118)**—Palmer 24, Easley 12, Clark 12, Kapler 12, D. Cruz 9, Polonia 8, Higginson 8, Encarnacion 6, Catalanotto 6, Jefferies 5, Ausmus 5, K. Garcia 4, Haselman 2, Alvarez 2, Wood 1, Fick 1, Macias 1. **Kansas City (5)**—Sweeney 2, Damon 1, Febles 1, Quinn 1. **Milwaukee (3)**—Burnitz 2, Jenkins 1. **Minnesota (7)**—Koskie 2, Gates 1, Coomer 1, Walker 1, Hunter 1, Allen 1. **New York (4)**—Davis 1, Martinez 1, Brosius 1, Jeter 1. **Oakland (14)**—Jaha 5, Giambi 3, Grieve 2, Raines 1, Stairs 1, Tejada 1, Chavez 1. **Pittsburgh (5)**—Sprague 2, Giles 1, B. Brown 1, Guillen 1. **St. Louis (1)**—Davis 1. **Seattle (4)**—Griffey 1, Wilson 1, Hunter 1, A. Rodriguez 1. **Tampa Bay (2)**—McGriff 1, Lowery 1. **Texas (10)**—Gonzalez 2, Greer 2, Palmeiro 2, Alicea 1, Zeile 1, Rodriguez 1, Clayton 1, Zaun 1. **Toronto (11)**—Delgado 3, Fletcher 2, Green 2, Lennon 1, Hollins 1, Segui 1, Batista 1.

AT KANSAS CITY (170):

Anaheim (8)—Salmon 3, Vaughn 1, Edmonds 1, Luke 1, Erstad 1, Glaus 1. **Baltimore (4)**—Anderson 2, Belle 1, Figga 1. **Boston (9)**—Valentin 2, O'Leary 2, Nixon 2, Stanley 1, Huskey 1, Daubach 1. **Chicago (5)**—Ordonez 3, Thomas 1, Rodriguez 1. **Cincinnati (7)**—Vaughn 2, Hammonds 2, Casey 2, Larkin 1. **Cleveland (4)**—Justice 1, Whiten 1, Sexson 1, Wilson 1. **Detroit (7)**—Clark 3, Kapler 2, Polonia 1, Encarnacion 1. **Houston (2)**—Howell 1, Bagwell 1. **Kansas City (74)**—Dye 15, Beltran 12, Sweeney 10, Randa 7, Damon 5, Febles 5, Spehr 4, Hansen 3, Kreuter 2, King 2, Fasano 2, Sutton 2, Giambi 2, Quinn 2, Sanchez 1. **Minnesota (7)**—Cordova 2, Allen 2, Coomer 1, Lawton 1, Hunter 1. **New York (3)**—Martinez 1, Williams 1, Brosius 1. **Oakland (10)**—Stairs 3, Giambi 3, Jaha 2, Tejada 1, Christenson 1. **St. Louis (6)**—McGwire 2, Dunston 1, Renteria 1, Tatis 1, Marrero 1. **Seattle (9)**—Davis 2, Buhner 1, Martinez 1, Griffey 1, Hunter 1, A. Rodriguez 1, Bell 1, Ibanez 1. **Tampa Bay (5)**—Trammell 2, Sorrento 1, Flaherty 1, Graffanino 1. **Texas (3)**—Palmeiro 1, Gonzalez 1, Rodriguez 1. **Toronto (7)**—Green 3, Segui 1, Greene 1, Delgado 1, Bush 1.

AT MINNESOTA (156):

Anaheim (4)—Vaughn 3, Glaus 1. **Baltimore (6)**—Anderson 3, Surhoff 1, Belle 1, Hairston 1. **Boston (8)**—Nixon 3, Jefferson 2, Lewis 1, Buford 1, O'Leary 1. **Chicago (6)**—Konerko 2, Singleton 2, Ordonez 1, Simmons 1. **Cincinnati (3)**—Taubensee 1, Reese 1, Boone 1. **Cleveland (6)**—Thome 2, M. Ramirez 2, Cordero 1, Sexson 1. **Detroit (9)**—Palmer 2, Polonia 1, Haselman 1, K. Garcia 1, Clark 1, Encarnacion 1, Catalanotto 1, Kapler 1. **Houston (5)**—Bagwell 2, Hidalgo 2, Johnson 1. **Kansas City (3)**—Damon 2, Beltran 1. **Minnesota (47)**—Cordova 9, Coomer 6, Jones 5, Walker 4, Koskie 4, Allen 4, Steinbach 3, Gates 2, Hocking 1, Lawton 2, Hunter 2, Valentin 2, Cummings 1, Guzman 1. **New York (4)**—Davis 2, Williams 2, Brosius 2, Posada 1, Ledee 1. **Oakland (6)**—Stairs 3, Macfarlane 1, Jaha 1, Spiezio 1. **Pittsburgh (4)**—Giles 2, Martin 1, A. Brown 1. **Seattle (14)**—Griffey 5, A. Rodriguez 3, Martinez 1, Mieske 1, Huskey 1, Hunter 1, Davis 1, Timmons 1. **Tampa Bay (1)**—Canseco 1. **Texas (4)**—Palmeiro 3, Stevens 3, Kelly 2, Zeile 2, Rodriguez 2, Gonzalez 1. **Toronto (13)**—Delgado 5, Stewart 2, Fernandez 1, Fletcher 1, Green 1, Batista 1, Bush 1, Cruz 1.

AT NEW YORK (158):

Anaheim (6)—Vaughn 2, Anderson 1, Greene 1, Luke 1, Glaus 1. **Atlanta (7)**—Klesko 2, A. Jones 2, Jordan 1, Williams 1, C. Jones 1. **Baltimore (9)**—Belle 3, Baines 2, Surhoff 2, Ripken 1, Clark 1. **Boston (9)**—Garciaparra 3, Stanley 2, O'Leary 1, Huskey 1, Nixon 1, Daubach 1. **Chicago (6)**—Singleton 3, Norton 1, Caruso 1, Lee 1. **Cleveland (7)**—R. Alomar 1, Fryman 1, Thome 1, Cordero 1, M. Ramirez 1, Sexson 1, Branyan 1. **Detroit (3)**—Haselman 1, Higginson 1, Clark 1. **Minnesota (2)**—Valentin 1, Mientkiewicz 1. **Montreal (2)**—Andrews 1, Fullmer 1. **New York A.L. (84)**—Jeter 15, Davis 12, Knoblauch 11, Williams 11, O'Neill 9, Martinez 7, Brosius 4, Posada 4, Ledee 4, Spencer 2, Strawberry 1, Girardi 1, Sojo 1, Soriano 1, Bellinger 1. **New York N.L. (2)**—McRae 1, Piazza 1. **Oakland (4)**—Stairs 1, Saenz 1, Spiezio 1, Tejada 1. **Seattle (6)**—Buhner 1, Lampkin 1, Griffey 1, Davis 1, Bell 1, Ibanez 1. **Tampa Bay (4)**—McGriff 2, Trammell 2. **Texas (4)**—Gonzalez 2, Zeile 1, Stevens 1. **Toronto (3)**—Segui 1, Green 1, Batista 1.

AT OAKLAND (186):

Anaheim (4)—Salmon 2, Greene 1, Glaus 1. **Baltimore (8)**—Baines 2, Surhoff 2, Bordick 2, Anderson 1, Belle 1. **Boston (4)**—Valentin 1, O'Leary 1, Gubanich 1. **Chicago (4)**—Thomas 1, Norton 1, Ordonez 1, Konerko 1. **Cleveland (12)**—M. Ramirez 5, Thome 3, Justice 2, Vizquel 1, Fryman 1. **Colorado (3)**—Bichette 1, Walker 1, Blanco 1. **Detroit (4)**—Clark 2, Palmer 1, K. Garcia 1. **Kansas City (3)**—Sweeney 1, Fasano 1, Quinn 1. **Los Angeles (2)**—Karros 2. **Minnesota (3)**—Coomer 2, Lawton 1. **New York (9)**—Williams 2, Curtis 2, Jeter 2, Davis 1, Knoblauch 1, Ledee 1. **Oakland (112)**—Jaha 18, Giambi 17, Stairs 15, Grieve 13, Tejada 12, Saenz 10, Chavez 8, Phillips 5, Velarde 4, Spiezio 3, Hinch 3, Raines 2, Christenson 2, Becker 1, Hernandez 1. **San Francisco (2)**—Snow 1, Aurilia 1. **Seattle (3)**—A. Rodriguez 1, Bell 1, Ibanez 1. **Tampa Bay (3)**—Canseco 1, Graffanino 1, Lowery 1. **Texas (5)**—Stevens 2, Palmeiro 2, Zeile 1, Rodriguez 1. **Toronto (5)**—Batista 2, Fletcher 1, McRae 1, Greene 1.

AT SEATTLE (227):

Anaheim (7)—Vaughn 3, Erstad 2, Velarde 1, Luke 1. **Arizona (4)**—Stinnett 2, Gilkey 1, Gonzalez 1. **Baltimore (2)**—Ripken 1, Anderson 1. **Boston (6)**—Garciaparra 3, Varitek 3. **Chicago (8)**—Jackson 2, Thomas 1, Durham 1, Norton 1, Abbott 1, Konerko 1, Lee 1. **Cleveland (5)**—Sexson 2, R. Alomar 1, M. Ramirez 1, Diaz 1. **Detroit (7)**—Easley 2, K. Garcia 2, Ausmus 1, Clark 1, Encarnacion 1. **Kansas City (12)**—Beltran 2, Quinn 2, Kreuter 2, Spehr 1, Vitiello 1, Damon 1, Sweeney 1, Fasano 1, Dye 1, Febles 1. **Minnesota (1)**—Lawton 1. **New York (8)**—Martinez 2, Brosius 2, O'Neill 2, Knoblauch 1, Williams 1, Curtis 1. **Oakland (11)**—Jaha 4, Phillips 2, Stairs 1, Hinch 1, Christenson 1, Chavez 1, Hernandez 1. **San Francisco (3)**—Kent 1, Snow 1, Benard 1. **Seattle (122)**—Griffey 39, A. Rodriguez 20, Martinez 12, Davis 12, Bell 11, Huskey 7, Buhner 5, Lampkin 5, Mabry 5, Segui 4, Wilson 3, Mieske 3, Ibanez 3, Bournigal 2, Blowers 1, Cedeno 1, Guillen 1. **Tampa Bay (8)**—McGriff 2, Canseco 2, Sorrento 2, Flaherty 1, Perry 1, Cairo 1, DiFelice 1. **Texas (9)**—Rodriguez 4, Gonzalez 2, Stevens 2, Greer 1. **Toronto (14)**—Delgado 6, Green 3, Cruz 2, Berroa 1, Matheny 1, Batista 1. **Note:** Figures include 134 home runs at Kingdome as follows: **Anaheim (5)**—Vaughn 2, Erstad 1, Velarde 1, Luke 1. **Baltimore (2)**—Ripken 1, Anderson 1. **Chicago (5)**—Jackson 2, Durham 1, Abbott 1, Konerko 1. **Detroit (6)**—Easley 2, K. Garcia 2, Ausmus 1, Encarnacion 1. **Kansas City (5)**—Beltran 1, Kreuter 1, Damon 1, Sweeney 1, Febles 1. **Minnesota (1)**—Lawton 1. **Oakland (7)**—Jaha 2, Phillips 2, Stairs 1, Hinch 1, Christenson 1. **San Francisco (3)**—Kent 1, Snow 1, Benard 1. **Seattle (75)**—Griffey 13, Davis 10, Bell 9, Martinez 9, A. Rodriguez 7, Huskey 7, Mabry 4, Segui 4, Mieske 3, Buhner 2, Wilson 2, Bournigal 2, Cedeno 1, Guillen 1, Lampkin 1. **Tampa Bay (6)**—McGriff 1, Canseco 1, Sorrento 1, Flaherty 1, Perry 1, Cairo 1. **Texas (9)**—Rodriguez 4, Gonzalez 2, Stevens 2, Greer 1. **Toronto (10)**—Delgado 4, Green 2, Cruz 2, Berroa 1, Matheny 1.

AT TAMPA BAY (157):

Anaheim (2)—Vaughn 1, Anderson 1. **Baltimore (5)**—Surhoff 2, Baines 1, Belle 1, Otanez 1. **Boston (5)**—Stanley 2, Valentin 1, O'Leary 1, Veras 1. **Chicago (3)**—Jackson 1, Fordyce 1, Lee 1. **Cleveland (3)**—R. Alomar 1, Thome 1, M. Ramirez 1. **Detroit (7)**—Jefferies 1, Palmer 1, Easley 1, K. Garcia 1, Clark 1, D. Cruz 1, Kapler 1. **Florida (5)**—Hyers 2, Aven 2, Wilson 1. **Kansas City (4)**—Sweeney 2, Kreuter 1, Damon 1. **Minnesota (6)**—Koskie 2, Walker 1, Hunter 1,

Mientkiewicz 1, Jones 1. **New York A.L. (10)**—Martinez 3, Davis 2, Strawberry 1, Girardi 1, Williams 1, Brosius 1, Spencer 1. **New York N.L. (1)**—M. Franco 1. **Oakland (6)**—Giambi 3, Velarde 1, Stairs 1, Saenz 1. **Philadelphia (4)**—Rolen 4. **Seattle (13)**—Buhner 3, Griffey 3, Segui 2, Wilson 1, Mabry 1, A. Rodriguez 1, Bell 1, Ibanez 1. **Tampa Bay (66)**—McGriff 18, Canseco 12, Sorrento 6, Trammell 6, Perry 5, DiFelice 5, Flaherty 3, Martinez 2, Winn 2, Boggs 1, Stocker 1, McCracken 1, Cairo 1, Guillen 1, Clyburn 1, Smith 1. **Texas (12)**—Rodriguez 3, Zeile 2, Gonzalez 2, Stevens 2, Palmeiro 1, Kelly 1, Greer 1. **Toronto (5)**—Batista 2, McRae 1, Green 1, Stewart 1.

AT TEXAS (212):

Anaheim (8)—Glaus 3, Vaughn 1, Salmon 1, Anderson 1, Palmeiro 1, Greene 1. **Arizona (5)**—Bell 3, Finley 1, Stinnett 1. **Baltimore (13)**—Belle 4, C. Johnson 3, Anderson 2, Baines 1, Ripken 1, DeShields 1, Garcia 1. **Boston (1)**—Huskey 1. **Chicago (3)**—Wilson 1, Lee 1, Singleton 1. **Cleveland (8)**—R. Alomar 2, Lofton 2, Sexson 2, S. Alomar 1, M. Ramirez 1. **Colorado (2)**—Bichette 1, Abbott 1. **Detroit (8)**—Easley 2, Clark 2, Encarnacion 2, Ausmus 1, Higginson 1. **Kansas City (4)**—Sweeney 2, Kreuter 1, Beltran 1. **Minnesota (2)**—Hocking 1, Valentin 1. **New York (12)**—Martinez 6, Knoblauch 2, O'Neill 1, Brosius 1, Curtis 1, Posada 1. **Oakland (8)**—Grieve 3, Jaha 2, Macfarlane 1, Stairs 1, Chavez 1. **San Francisco (3)**—Bonds 2, Snow 1. **Seattle (7)**—A. Rodriguez 2, Martinez 1, Wilson 1, Hunter 1, Davis 1, Ibanez 1. **Tampa Bay (15)**—Flaherty 5, Canseco 4, McGriff 3, Sorrento 1, Trammell 1, Guillen 1. **Texas (103)**—Palmeiro 28, Gonzalez 14, Zeile 13, Rodriguez 12, Stevens 10, Greer 10, Clayton 6, Kelly 4, McLemore 2, Mateo 2, Goodwin 1, Dransfeldt 1. **Toronto (10)**—Delgado 5, Green 2, Fletcher 1, Batista 1, Bush 1.

AT TORONTO (189):

Anaheim (5)—Anderson 2, Velarde 1, Vaughn 1, Erstad 1. **Atlanta (1)**—C. Jones 1. **Baltimore (9)**—Surhoff 3, Baines 1, Anderson 1, Belle 1, Bordick 1, Conine 1, Hairston 1. **Boston (7)**—Huskey 2, Stanley 1, Jefferson 1, Valentin 1, Varitek 1, Daubach 1. **Chicago (5)**—Ordonez 2, Simmons 2, Lee 1. **Cleveland (8)**—M. Ramirez 2, S. Alomar 1, Justice 1, Cordero 1, Houston 1, Sexson 1, Roberts 1. **Detroit (6)**—Palmer 1, Ausmus 1, Higginson 1, K. Garcia 1, Clark 1, Encarnacion 1. **Florida (2)**—Millar 1, Lowell 1. **Kansas City (2)**—Randa 1, Giambi 1. **Minnesota (3)**—Coomer 1, Cordova 1, Jones 1. **Montreal (2)**—Merced 1, White 1. **New York (6)**—Williams 2, O'Neill 1, Martinez 1, Brosius 1, Spencer 1. **Oakland (15)**—Stairs 3, Giambi 2, Tejada 2, Grieve 2, Hinch 2, Phillips 1, Velarde 1, McDonald 1, Chavez 1. **Seattle (5)**—Martinez 2, Buhner 1, Griffey 1, A. Rodriguez 1. **Tampa Bay (7)**—Canseco 4, McGriff 1, Martinez 1, Trammell 1. **Texas (10)**—Gonzalez 3, McLemore 1, Palmeiro 1, Zeile 1, Stevens 1, Rodriguez 1, Goodwin 1, Greer 1. **Toronto (96)**—Green 20, Delgado 17, Fletcher 10, Batista 9, Greene 8, Cruz 8, Fernandez 5, Kelly 5, Stewart 4, Bush 2, Borders 1, Hollins 1, Segui 1, McRae 1, Gonzalez 1, Matheny 1, Otanez 1, V. Wells 1.

1999 N.L. STATISTICS

Batting

Designated hitting

Pinch-hitting

Pitching

Fielding

Miscellaneous

BATTING

TEAM

Team	Avg.	G	TPA	AB	R	H	TB	2B	3B	HR	RBI	SH	SF	HP	BB	IBB	SO	SB	CS	GDP	LOB	ShO	Slg.	OBP
Colorado	.288	162	6368	5717	906	1644	2696	305	39	223	863	54	46	43	508	31	863	70	43	125	1144	3	.472	.348
New York	.279	163	6454	5572	853	1553	2421	297	14	181	814	63	54	48	717	53	994	150	61	149	1267	5	.434	.363
Arizona	.277	162	6415	5658	908	1566	2595	289	46	216	865	61	60	48	588	52	1045	137	39	94	1169	6	.459	.347
Philadelphia	.275	162	6386	5598	841	1539	2412	302	44	161	797	70	41	46	631	37	1081	125	35	127	1221	7	.431	.351
Milwaukee	.273	161	6433	5582	815	1524	2378	299	30	165	777	87	51	55	658	44	1065	81	33	110	1276	6	.426	.353
Cincinnati	.272	163	6377	5649	865	1536	2549	312	37	209	820	70	44	45	569	37	1026	164	54	107	1168	3	.451	.341
San Francisco	.271	162	6448	5563	872	1507	2414	307	18	188	828	87	42	60	696	40	1028	109	56	129	1230	2	.434	.356
Houston	.267	162	6402	5485	823	1463	2306	293	23	168	784	79	58	52	728	57	1138	166	75	127	1252	5	.420	.355
Atlanta	.266	162	6351	5569	840	1481	2427	309	23	197	791	74	47	53	608	62	962	148	66	120	1155	6	.436	.341
Los Angeles	.266	162	6338	5567	793	1480	2340	253	23	187	761	74	51	52	594	34	1030	167	68	109	1173	6	.420	.339
Montreal	.265	162	6149	5559	718	1473	2376	320	47	163	680	71	28	53	438	39	939	70	51	138	1094	8	.427	.323
Florida	.263	162	6216	5578	691	1465	2203	266	44	128	655	44	56	59	479	30	1145	92	46	119	1159	7	.395	.325
St. Louis	.262	161	6353	5570	809	1461	2371	274	27	194	763	75	44	51	613	51	1202	134	48	110	1188	4	.426	.338
Pittsburgh	.259	161	6322	5488	775	1417	2292	282	40	171	735	87	45	60	573	40	1197	112	44	111	1157	7	.419	.334
Chicago	.257	162	6201	5482	747	1411	2303	255	35	189	717	65	44	39	571	38	1170	60	44	120	1130	7	.420	.329
San Diego	.252	162	6136	5394	710	1360	2119	256	22	153	671	36	40	35	631	31	1169	174	67	132	1139	10	.393	.332
Totals	.268	1296	101260	89011	12966	23880	38202	4619	512	2893	12321	1097	751	799	9602	676	17153	1959	830	1927	18922	92	.429	.342

INDIVIDUAL

TOP QUALIFIERS FOR BATTING CHAMPIONSHIP

Minimum 502 plate appearances. *Lefthanded batter. †Switch-hitter.

Player, Team	Avg.	G	TPA	AB	R	H	TB	2B	3B	HR	RBI	SH	SF	HP	BB	IBB	SO	SB	CS	GDP	Slg.	OBP
Walker, Larry, Col.*	.379	127	513	438	108	166	311	26	4	37	115	0	6	12	57	8	52	11	4	12	.710	.458
Gonzalez, Luis, Ari.*	.336	153	693	614	112	206	337	45	4	26	111	1	5	7	66	6	63	9	5	13	.549	.403
Abreu, Bobby, Phi.*	.335	152	662	546	118	183	300	35	11	20	93	0	4	3	109	8	113	27	9	13	.549	.446
Casey, Sean, Cin.*	.332	151	669	594	103	197	320	42	3	25	99	0	5	9	61	13	88	0	2	15	.539	.399
Cirillo, Jeff, Mil.	.326	157	697	607	98	198	280	35	1	15	88	3	7	5	75	4	83	7	4	15	.461	.401
Grudzielanek, Mark, L.A.	.326	123	534	488	72	159	213	23	5	7	46	2	3	10	31	1	65	6	6	13	.436	.376
Everett, Carl, Hou.†	.325	123	535	464	86	151	265	33	3	25	108	2	8	11	50	5	94	27	7	5	.571	.398
Glanville, Doug, Phi.	.325	150	692	628	101	204	287	38	6	11	73	5	5	6	48	1	82	34	2	9	.457	.376
Helton, Todd, Col.*	.320	159	656	578	114	185	339	39	5	35	113	0	4	6	68	6	77	7	6	14	.587	.395
Jones, Chipper, Atl.†	.319	157	701	567	116	181	359	41	1	45	110	0	6	2	126	18	94	25	3	20	.633	.441
Guerrero, Vladimir, Mon.	.316	160	674	610	102	193	366	37	5	42	131	0	2	7	55	14	62	14	7	18	.600	.378
Henderson, Rickey, N.Y.	.315	121	526	438	89	138	204	30	0	12	42	1	3	2	82	1	82	37	14	4	.466	.423
Hamilton, Darryl, Col.-N.Y.*	.315	146	568	505	82	159	213	19	4	9	45	3	1	2	57	0	39	6	8	9	.422	.386
Giles, Brian, Pit.*	.315	141	627	521	109	164	320	33	3	39	115	0	8	3	95	7	80	6	2	14	.614	.418
Cedeno, Roger, N.Y.†	.313	155	525	453	90	142	185	23	4	4	36	7	2	3	60	3	100	66	17	5	.408	.396

DEPARTMENTAL LEADERS: G—Bagwell, Hou., A. Jones, Atl., Olerud, N.Y., Sosa, Chi., 162; AB—Perez, Col., 690; R—Bagwell, Hou., 143; H—Gonzalez, Ari., 206; TB—Sosa, Chi., 397; 1B—Glanville, Phi., 149; 2B—Biggio, Hou., 56; 3B—Abreu, Phi., Perez, Col., 11; HR—McGwire, St.L., 65; RBI—McGwire, St.L., 147; SH—Reynolds, Hou., 17; SF—Bichette, Col., Grace, Chi., 10; HP—Sprague, Pit., 17; BB—Bagwell, Hou., 149; IBB—McGwire, St.L., 21; SO—Sosa, Chi., 171; SB—Womack, Ari., 72; CS—Young, L.A., 22; GIDP—Piazza, N.Y., 27; Slg. Pct.—Walker, Col., .710; OB. Pct.—Walker, Col., .458.

ALL PLAYERS

*Lefthanded batter. †Switch-hitter.

Player, Team	Avg.	G	TPA	AB	R	H	TB	2B	3B	HR	RBI	SH	SF	HP	BB	IBB	SO	SB	CS	GDP	Slg.	OBP
Abbott, Kurt, Col.	.273	96	305	286	41	78	123	17	2	8	41	2	1	0	16	0	69	3	2	4	.430	.310
Abreu, Bobby, Phi.*	.335	152	662	546	118	183	300	35	11	20	93	0	4	3	109	8	113	27	9	13	.549	.446
Agbayani, Benny, N.Y.	.286	101	314	276	42	79	145	18	3	14	42	0	3	3	32	4	60	6	4	8	.525	.363
Alexander, Manny, Chi.	.271	90	189	177	17	48	63	11	2	0	15	1	1	0	10	0	38	4	0	1	.356	.309
Alfonzo, Edgardo, N.Y.	.304	158	726	628	123	191	315	41	1	27	108	1	9	3	85	2	85	9	2	14	.502	.385
Allensworth, Jermaine, N.Y.	.219	40	86	73	14	16	27	2	0	3	9	2	1	1	9	0	23	2	1	1	.370	.310
Anderson, Brian, Ari.†	.132	32	42	38	4	5	10	0	1	1	2	1	1	0	2	0	10	1	0	1	.263	.171
Anderson, Jimmy, Pit.*	.333	13	9	9	2	3	4	1	0	0	1	0	0	0	0	0	2	0	0	0	.444	.333
Anderson, Marlon, Phi.*	.252	129	484	452	48	114	163	26	4	5	54	4	2	2	24	1	61	13	2	6	.361	.292
Andrews, Shane, Mon.-Chi.	.195	117	404	348	41	68	128	12	0	16	51	0	5	1	50	3	109	1	1	10	.368	.295
Arias, Alex, Phi.	.303	118	390	347	43	105	139	20	1	4	48	1	2	4	36	6	31	2	2	12	.401	.373
Arias, George, S.D.	.244	55	170	164	20	40	69	8	0	7	20	0	0	0	6	0	54	0	0	6	.421	.271
Arnold, Jamie, L.A.	.200	36	11	10	1	2	2	0	0	0	1	1	0	0	0	0	3	0	0	0	.200	.200
Ashby, Andy, S.D.	.129	31	72	62	3	8	10	2	0	0	2	7	0	0	3	0	25	0	0	1	.161	.169
Astacio, Pedro, Col.	.233	37	94	86	5	20	24	2	1	0	7	7	0	0	1	0	24	0	0	0	.279	.241
Aurilia, Rich, S.F.	.281	152	614	558	68	157	248	23	1	22	80	3	5	5	43	3	71	2	3	16	.444	.336
Aven, Bruce, Fla.	.289	137	440	381	57	110	169	19	2	12	70	0	6	9	44	1	82	3	0	6	.444	.370
Avery, Steve, Cin.*	.077	19	28	26	1	2	2	0	0	0	1	2	0	0	0	0	11	0	0	0	.077	.077
Baerga, Carlos, S.D.†	.250	33	89	80	6	20	27	1	0	2	5	1	0	2	6	0	14	1	0	2	.338	.318
Bagwell, Jeff, Hou.	.304	162	729	562	143	171	332	35	0	42	126	0	7	11	149	16	127	30	11	18	.591	.454
Bako, Paul, Hou.*	.256	73	247	215	16	55	77	14	1	2	17	3	3	0	26	3	57	1	1	4	.358	.332
Banks, Brian, Mil.†	.242	105	249	219	34	53	77	5	1	5	22	3	2	0	25	5	59	6	1	2	.352	.317
Barajas, Rod, Ari.	.250	5	16	16	3	4	8	1	0	1	3	1	0	0	1	0	0	0	0	0	.500	.294
Barker, Glen, Hou.†	.288	81	90	73	23	21	26	2	0	1	11	4	1	1	11	0	19	17	6	0	.356	.384
Barker, Kevin, Mil.*	.282	18	127	117	13	33	45	3	0	3	23	0	1	0	9	1	19	1	0	0	.385	.331
Barrett, Michael, Mon.	.293	126	469	433	42	127	189	32	3	8	52	0	1	3	32	4	39	0	2	18	.436	.345

Player, Team	Avg.	G	TPA	AB	R	H	TB	2B	3B	HR	RBI	SH	SF	HP	BB	IBB	SO	SB	CS	GDP	Slg.	OBP
Barry, Jeff, Col.†	.268	74	192	168	19	45	76	16	0	5	26	0	3	2	19	1	29	0	4	4	.452	.344
Batista, Miguel, Mon.	.200	39	41	35	6	7	11	1	0	1	3	4	0	0	2	0	19	0	0	0	.314	.243
Batista, Tony, Ari.	.257	44	164	144	16	37	57	5	0	5	21	0	2	2	16	3	17	2	0	1	.396	.335
Battle, Howard, Atl.	.353	15	19	17	2	6	9	0	0	1	5	0	0	0	2	0	3	0	0	1	.529	.421
Bautista, Danny, Fla.	.288	70	211	205	32	59	86	10	1	5	24	0	1	1	4	0	30	3	0	5	.420	.303
Becker, Rich, Mil.*	.252	89	174	139	15	35	59	5	2	5	16	2	0	0	33	0	38	5	0	4	.424	.395
Bell, Derek, Hou.	.236	128	568	509	61	120	178	22	0	12	66	0	5	4	50	1	129	18	6	20	.350	.306
Bell, Jay, Ari.	.289	151	688	589	132	170	328	32	6	38	112	4	9	4	82	2	132	7	4	9	.557	.374
Belliard, Ron, Mil.	.295	124	531	457	60	135	196	29	4	8	58	6	4	0	64	0	59	4	5	16	.429	.379
Beltre, Adrian, L.A.	.275	152	614	538	84	148	230	27	5	15	67	4	5	6	61	12	105	18	7	4	.428	.352
Benard, Marvin, S.F.*	.290	149	625	562	100	163	257	36	5	16	64	1	1	6	55	2	97	27	14	5	.457	.359
Benes, Andy, Ari.	.155	33	73	58	6	9	12	0	0	1	5	10	0	1	4	0	17	0	0	1	.207	.222
Benjamin, Mike, Pit.	.247	110	404	368	42	91	134	26	7	1	37	11	3	2	20	3	90	10	1	3	.364	.288
Bennett, Gary, Phi.	.273	36	94	88	7	24	31	4	0	1	21	0	2	0	4	0	11	0	0	7	.352	.298
Bennett, Joel, Phi.	.000	5	6	4	1	0	0	0	0	0	0	1	0	0	1	0	1	0	0	0	.000	.200
Benson, Kris, Pit.	.154	31	74	65	7	10	13	3	0	0	7	6	0	0	3	0	24	0	0	1	.200	.191
Bere, Jason, Cin.-Mil.	.318	17	27	22	3	7	7	0	0	0	1	2	0	1	2	0	9	0	0	0	.318	.400
Berg, Dave, Fla.	.286	109	336	304	42	87	116	18	1	3	25	3	0	2	27	0	59	2	2	7	.382	.348
Bergeron, Peter, Mon.*	.244	16	55	45	12	11	13	2	0	0	1	1	0	0	9	0	5	0	0	0	.289	.370
Bergman, Sean, Hou.-Atl.	.107	25	29	28	4	3	9	0	0	2	2	1	0	0	0	0	12	0	0	0	.321	.107
Berkman, Lance, Hou.†	.237	34	106	93	10	22	36	2	0	4	15	0	1	0	12	0	21	5	1	2	.387	.321
Berry, Sean, Mil.	.228	106	281	259	26	59	78	11	1	2	23	0	2	3	17	0	50	0	0	4	.301	.281
Bichette, Dante, Col.	.298	151	659	593	104	177	321	38	2	34	133	0	10	2	54	3	84	6	6	15	.541	.354
Biggio, Craig, Hou.	.294	160	749	639	123	188	292	56	0	16	73	0	5	6	88	9	107	28	14	5	.457	.386
Blanco, Henry, Col.	.232	88	303	263	30	61	97	12	3	6	28	3	2	1	34	1	38	1	1	4	.369	.320
Blauser, Jeff, Chi.	.240	104	238	200	41	48	84	5	2	9	26	2	2	8	26	0	52	2	2	0	.420	.347
Blum, Geoff, Mon.†	.241	45	153	133	21	32	67	7	2	8	18	3	0	0	17	3	25	1	0	3	.504	.327
Bogar, Tim, Hou.	.239	106	354	309	44	74	106	16	2	4	31	0	3	4	38	5	52	3	5	10	.343	.328
Bohanon, Brian, Col.*	.197	34	81	71	6	14	19	2	0	1	7	5	0	0	5	0	20	0	0	2	.268	.250
Bonds, Barry, S.F.*	.262	102	434	355	91	93	219	20	2	34	83	0	3	3	73	9	62	15	2	6	.617	.389
Bonilla, Bobby, N.Y.†	.160	60	141	119	12	19	36	5	0	4	18	0	2	1	19	1	16	0	1	4	.303	.277
Boone, Aaron, Cin.	.280	139	520	472	56	132	210	26	5	14	72	5	5	8	30	2	79	17	6	6	.445	.330
Boone, Bret, Atl.	.252	152	671	608	102	153	253	38	1	20	63	9	2	5	47	0	112	14	9	11	.416	.310
Bottenfield, Kent, St.L.	.148	31	70	61	4	9	12	3	0	0	5	8	0	0	1	0	26	0	0	0	.197	.161
Bragg, Darren, St.L.*	.260	93	325	273	38	71	103	12	1	6	26	5	0	3	44	1	67	3	0	5	.377	.369
Brock, Chris, S.F.	.200	19	42	35	4	7	7	0	0	0	4	4	0	0	3	0	8	0	0	0	.200	.263
Brogna, Rico, Phi.*	.278	157	679	619	90	172	281	29	4	24	102	0	4	2	54	7	132	8	5	19	.454	.336
Brown, Adrian, Pit.†	.270	116	267	226	34	61	82	5	2	4	17	6	1	1	33	2	39	5	3	5	.363	.364
Brown, Brant, Pit.*	.232	130	371	341	49	79	153	20	3	16	58	0	4	4	22	3	114	3	4	4	.449	.283
Brown, Kevin, L.A.	.064	35	94	78	1	5	5	0	0	0	3	13	1	0	2	0	24	0	0	0	.064	.086
Brown, Roosevelt, Chi.*	.219	33	70	64	6	14	25	6	1	1	10	3	1	0	2	0	14	1	0	2	.391	.239
Brownson, Mark, Col.*	.111	7	11	9	1	1	1	0	0	0	0	2	0	0	0	0	2	0	0	0	.111	.111
Brumfield, Jacob, L.A.	.294	18	17	17	4	5	7	0	1	0	1	0	0	0	0	0	5	0	0	0	.412	.294
Burks, Ellis, S.F.	.282	120	469	390	73	110	222	19	0	31	96	0	4	6	69	2	86	7	5	11	.569	.394
Burnett, A.J., Fla.	.118	7	17	17	1	2	2	0	0	0	0	0	0	0	0	0	10	0	0	0	.118	.118
Burnitz, Jeromy, Mil.*	.270	130	580	467	87	126	262	33	2	33	103	0	6	16	91	7	124	7	3	11	.561	.402
Byrd, Paul, Phi.	.127	32	71	55	6	7	7	0	0	0	4	11	0	0	5	0	11	0	0	2	.127	.200
Cabrera, Orlando, Mon.	.254	104	407	382	48	97	154	23	5	8	39	4	0	3	18	4	38	2	2	9	.403	.293
Cameron, Mike, Cin.	.256	146	636	542	93	139	254	34	9	21	66	5	3	6	80	2	145	38	12	4	.469	.357
Caminiti, Ken, Hou.†	.286	78	329	273	45	78	130	11	1	13	56	0	7	3	46	4	58	6	2	7	.476	.386
Cancel, Robinson, Mil.	.182	15	48	44	5	8	10	2	0	0	5	1	0	1	2	0	12	0	0	0	.227	.234
Canizaro, Jay, S.F.	.444	12	19	18	5	8	13	2	0	1	9	0	0	1	0	0	2	1	0	0	.722	.474
Carlyle, Buddy, S.D.*	.222	7	11	9	1	2	2	0	0	0	1	0	0	0	2	0	3	0	0	1	.222	.364
Casey, Sean, Cin.*	.332	151	669	594	103	197	320	42	3	25	99	0	5	9	61	13	88	0	2	15	.539	.399
Castilla, Vinny, Col.	.275	158	674	615	83	169	294	24	1	33	102	0	5	1	53	7	75	2	3	15	.478	.331
Castillo, Alberto, St.L.	.263	93	290	255	21	67	87	8	0	4	31	5	4	2	24	1	48	0	0	6	.341	.326
Castillo, Luis, Fla.†	.302	128	563	487	76	147	178	23	4	0	28	6	3	0	67	0	85	50	17	3	.366	.384
Castro, Ramon, Fla.	.179	24	78	67	4	12	22	4	0	2	4	0	1	0	10	3	14	0	0	1	.328	.282
Cedeno, Domingo, Phi.†	.152	32	72	66	5	10	17	4	0	1	5	1	0	0	5	0	22	0	1	2	.258	.211
Cedeno, Roger, N.Y.†	.313	155	525	453	90	142	185	23	4	4	36	7	2	3	60	3	100	66	17	5	.408	.396
Cirillo, Jeff, Mil.	.326	157	697	607	98	198	280	35	1	15	88	3	7	5	75	4	83	7	4	15	.461	.401
Clapinski, Chris, Fla.†	.232	36	66	56	6	13	18	1	2	0	2	0	0	1	9	0	12	1	0	1	.321	.348
Clement, Matt, S.D.	.077	31	62	52	7	4	4	0	0	0	1	6	0	0	4	0	28	0	0	1	.077	.143
Clemente, Edgard, Col.	.253	57	171	162	24	41	79	10	2	8	25	1	1	0	7	0	46	0	0	4	.488	.282
Colbrunn, Greg, Ari.	.326	67	153	135	20	44	70	5	3	5	24	0	2	4	12	0	23	1	1	3	.519	.392
Collier, Lou, Mil.	.259	74	152	135	18	35	50	9	0	2	21	1	2	0	14	0	32	3	2	2	.370	.325
Coquillette, Trace, Mon.	.265	17	55	49	2	13	16	3	0	0	4	1	0	1	4	0	7	1	0	3	.327	.333
Cora, Alex, L.A.*	.167	11	31	30	2	5	6	1	0	0	3	0	0	0	1	0	4	0	0	1	.200	.194
Cordova, Francisco, Pit.	.163	27	56	49	2	8	8	0	0	0	2	5	0	0	2	0	15	0	0	0	.163	.196
Counsell, Craig, Fla.-L.A.*	.218	87	195	174	24	38	45	7	0	0	11	5	2	0	14	0	24	1	0	2	.259	.274
Cox, Darron, Mon.	.240	15	27	25	2	6	10	1	0	1	2	0	0	0	2	0	5	0	0	0	.400	.296
Cromer, Tripp, L.A.	.192	33	57	52	5	10	16	0	0	2	8	0	0	0	5	0	10	0	0	4	.308	.263
Croushore, Rick, St.L.	.333	59	4	3	1	1	1	0	0	0	0	0	0	0	1	0	1	0	0	0	.333	.500
Cruz, Ivan, Pit.*	.400	5	10	10	3	4	7	0	0	1	2	0	0	0	0	0	2	0	0	0	.700	.400
Daal, Omar, Ari.*	.232	32	77	69	8	16	18	2	0	0	4	6	0	0	2	0	10	0	0	2	.261	.254
Darr, Mike, S.D.*	.271	25	53	48	6	13	20	1	0	2	3	0	0	0	5	0	18	2	1	1	.417	.340
Davis, Eric, St.L	.257	58	223	191	27	49	77	9	2	5	30	0	1	1	30	1	49	5	4	1	.403	.359
Davis, Ben, S.D.†	.244	76	293	266	29	65	96	14	1	5	30	0	2	0	25	3	70	2	1	9	.361	.307
Dawkins, Travis, Cin.	.143	7	8	7	1	1	1	0	0	0	0	0	0	0	0	0	4	0	0	0	.143	.250
Delgado, Wilson, S.F.†	.254	35	78	71	7	18	22	2	1	0	3	1	0	1	5	0	9	1	0	2	.310	.312
Dellucci, David, Ari.*	.394	63	123	109	27	43	55	7	1	1	15	0	0	3	11	0	24	2	0	3	.505	.463
Dempster, Ryan, Fla.	.102	26	51	49	5	5	6	1	0	0	2	1	0	0	1	0	22	0	0	1	.122	.120

Player, Team	Avg.	G	TPA	AB	R	H	TB	2B	3B	HR	RBI	SH	SF	HP	BB	IBB	SO	SB	CS	GDP	Slg.	OBP
Diaz, Alex, Hou.†	.220	30	53	50	3	11	16	2	0	1	7	0	0	0	3	0	13	2	2	0	.320	.264
Diaz, Edwin, Ari.	.400	4	8	5	2	2	4	2	0	0	1	0	0	0	3	1	1	0	0	0	.800	.625
Doster, David, Phi.	.196	99	112	97	9	19	30	2	0	3	10	2	1	0	12	1	23	1	0	2	.309	.282
Dotel, Octavio, N.Y.	.125	19	30	24	2	3	3	0	0	0	1	1	0	1	4	0	17	0	0	0	.125	.276
Dreifort, Darren, L.A.	.210	30	69	62	7	13	20	4	0	1	9	4	0	0	3	0	23	1	0	2	.323	.246
Drew, J.D., St.L.*	.242	104	430	368	72	89	156	16	6	13	39	3	3	6	50	0	77	19	3	4	.424	.340
Ducey, Rob, Phi.*	.261	104	227	188	29	49	87	10	2	8	33	0	1	0	38	1	57	2	1	1	.463	.383
Dunston, Shawon, St.L-N.Y.	.321	104	255	243	35	78	110	11	3	5	41	3	2	5	2	0	39	10	4	8	.453	.337
Dunwoody, Todd, Fla.*	.220	64	200	186	20	41	59	6	3	2	20	0	1	1	12	0	41	3	4	1	.317	.270
Durazo, Erubiel, Ari.*	.329	52	185	155	31	51	92	4	2	11	30	0	3	1	26	1	43	1	1	1	.594	.422
Echevarria, Angel, Col.	.293	102	211	191	28	56	96	7	0	11	35	0	0	3	17	0	34	1	3	11	.503	.360
Elarton, Scott, Hou.	.192	43	33	26	1	5	5	0	0	0	1	7	0	0	0	0	10	0	0	0	.192	.192
Eldred, Cal, Mil.	.083	23	30	24	3	2	3	1	0	0	2	4	0	0	2	0	13	0	0	0	.125	.154
Estalella, Bobby, Phi.	.167	9	22	18	2	3	3	0	0	0	1	0	0	0	4	0	7	0	1	0	.167	.318
Estes, Shawn, S.F.	.164	42	75	61	8	10	14	4	0	0	5	10	0	1	3	0	21	0	1	0	.230	.215
Eusebio, Tony, Hou.	.272	103	363	323	31	88	115	15	0	4	33	0	0	0	40	4	67	0	0	9	.356	.353
Everett, Carl, Hou.*	.325	123	535	464	86	151	265	33	3	25	108	2	8	11	50	5	94	27	7	5	.571	.398
Fabregas, Jorge, Fla.-Atl.*	.199	88	268	231	20	46	69	10	2	3	21	4	5	2	26	6	27	0	0	9	.299	.280
Falteisek, Steve, Mil.	.000	11	1	1	1	0	0	0	0	0	0	0	0	0	0	0	1	0	0	0	.000	.000
Farnsworth, Kyle, Chi.	.086	27	44	35	3	3	3	0	0	0	2	6	0	1	2	0	10	0	0	0	.086	.158
Fernandez, Alex, Fla.	.233	25	46	43	3	10	20	1	0	3	7	3	0	0	0	0	5	0	0	1	.465	.233
Finley, Steve, Ari.*	.264	156	663	590	100	156	310	32	10	34	103	2	5	3	63	0	94	8	4	4	.525	.336
Floyd, Cliff, Fla.*	.303	69	285	251	37	76	130	19	1	11	49	0	2	2	30	5	47	5	6	8	.518	.379
Fox, Andy, Ari.*	.255	99	320	274	34	70	104	12	2	6	33	1	3	9	33	10	61	4	1	4	.380	.351
Franco, Matt, N.Y.*	.235	122	161	132	18	31	48	5	0	4	21	0	1	0	28	3	21	0	0	9	.364	.366
Frias, Hanley, Ari.†	.273	69	180	150	27	41	51	3	2	1	16	1	0	0	29	2	18	4	3	2	.340	.391
Fullmer, Brad, Mon.*	.277	100	374	347	38	96	161	34	2	9	47	0	3	2	22	6	35	2	3	14	.464	.321
Gaetti, Gary, Chi.	.204	113	308	280	22	57	95	9	1	9	46	0	5	2	21	0	51	0	1	5	.339	.260
Gagne, Eric, L.A.	.200	5	10	10	1	2	2	0	0	0	1	0	0	0	0	0	3	0	0	0	.200	.200
Gant, Ron, Phi.	.260	138	605	516	107	134	222	27	5	17	77	0	3	1	85	0	112	13	3	6	.430	.364
Garcia, Amaury, Fla.	.250	10	27	24	6	6	14	0	1	2	2	0	0	0	3	0	11	0	0	0	.583	.333
Garcia, Carlos, S.D.	.182	6	12	11	1	2	2	0	0	0	0	0	0	0	1	0	3	0	0	2	.182	.250
Garcia, Freddy, Pit.-Atl.	.235	57	138	132	17	31	57	5	0	7	24	0	1	0	5	0	42	0	0	3	.432	.261
Gardner, Mark, S.F.	.103	29	44	39	2	4	7	0	0	1	3	6	0	0	3	0	15	0	0	3	.179	.167
Gibson, Derrick, Col.	.179	10	29	28	2	5	12	1	0	2	6	0	0	1	0	0	7	0	0	2	.429	.207
Giles, Brian, Pit.*	.315	141	627	521	109	164	320	33	3	39	115	0	8	3	95	7	80	6	2	14	.614	.418
Gilkey, Bernard, Ari.	.294	94	241	204	28	60	102	16	1	8	39	1	5	2	29	2	42	2	2	7	.500	.379
Giovanola, Ed, S.D.*	.190	56	69	58	10	11	13	0	1	0	3	1	1	0	9	0	8	2	0	1	.224	.294
Glanville, Doug, Phi.	.325	150	692	628	101	204	287	38	6	11	73	5	5	6	48	1	82	34	2	9	.457	.376
Glavine, Tom, Atl.*	.138	36	77	65	3	9	10	1	0	0	4	7	0	0	5	0	17	0	0	0	.154	.200
Gomez, Chris, S.D.	.252	76	265	234	20	59	72	8	1	1	15	2	1	1	27	3	49	1	2	6	.308	.331
Gonzalez, Alex, Fla.	.277	136	591	560	81	155	241	28	8	14	59	1	3	12	15	0	113	3	5	13	.430	.308
Gonzalez, Luis, Ari.*	.336	153	693	614	112	206	337	45	4	26	111	1	5	7	66	6	63	9	5	13	.549	.403
Gonzalez, Wiki, S.D.	.253	30	85	83	7	21	34	2	1	3	12	0	0	1	0	0	8	0	0	5	.410	.271
Goodwin, Curtis, Chi.*	.242	89	175	157	15	38	46	6	1	0	9	4	1	0	13	1	38	2	4	7	.293	.298
Grace, Mark, Chi.*	.309	161	688	593	107	183	285	44	5	16	91	0	10	2	83	4	44	3	4	14	.481	.390
Grace, Mike, Phi.	.000	27	11	7	1	0	0	0	0	0	0	3	0	0	1	0	4	0	0	0	.000	.125
Grahe, Joe, Phi.	.143	13	8	7	1	1	1	0	0	0	0	0	0	0	1	0	3	0	0	0	.143	.250
Greene, Charlie, Mil.	.190	32	49	42	4	8	9	1	0	0	1	1	1	0	5	0	11	0	0	0	.214	.191
Grissom, Marquis, Mil.	.267	154	661	603	92	161	250	27	1	20	83	4	5	0	49	4	109	24	6	12	.415	.320
Grudzielanek, Mark, L.A.	.326	123	534	488	72	159	213	23	5	7	46	2	3	10	31	1	65	6	6	13	.436	.376
Guerrero, Vladimir, Mon.	.316	160	674	610	102	193	366	37	5	42	131	0	2	7	55	14	62	14	7	18	.600	.378
Guerrero, Wilton, Mon.†	.292	132	340	315	42	92	127	15	7	2	31	10	0	2	13	0	38	7	6	4	.403	.324
Guillen, Jose, Pit.	.267	40	132	120	18	32	41	6	0	1	18	1	1	0	10	1	21	1	0	7	.342	.321
Guillen, Ozzie, Atl.*	.241	92	255	232	21	56	75	16	0	1	20	5	3	0	15	2	17	4	2	6	.323	.284
Gutierrez, Ricky, Hou.	.261	85	311	268	33	70	90	7	5	1	25	3	1	2	37	4	45	2	5	9	.336	.354
Guzman, Juan, Cin.	.115	12	30	26	1	3	3	0	0	0	2	3	0	0	1	0	10	0	0	0	.115	.148
Gwynn, Tony, S.D.*	.338	111	446	411	59	139	196	27	0	10	62	0	4	2	29	5	14	7	2	15	.477	.381
Hackman, Luther, Col.	.200	5	5	5	1	1	1	0	0	0	0	0	0	0	0	0	3	0	0	0	.200	.200
Hamilton, Darryl, Col.-N.Y.*	.315	146	568	505	82	159	213	19	4	9	45	3	1	2	57	0	39	6	8	9	.422	.386
Hammonds, Jeffrey, Cin.	.279	123	293	262	43	73	137	13	0	17	41	2	1	1	27	0	64	3	6	4	.523	.347
Hampton, Mike, Hou.	.311	34	88	74	10	23	32	3	3	0	10	5	1	1	7	0	18	0	0	2	.432	.373
Hansen, Dave, L.A.*	.252	100	136	107	14	27	43	8	1	2	17	0	1	2	26	0	20	0	0	2	.402	.404
Harnisch, Pete, Cin.	.152	33	75	66	6	10	17	4	0	1	5	8	0	0	1	0	20	0	0	1	.258	.164
Harris, Lenny, Col.-Ari.*	.310	110	194	187	17	58	74	13	0	1	20	0	1	0	6	0	7	2	1	7	.396	.330
Hayes, Charlie, S.F.	.205	95	301	264	33	54	83	9	1	6	48	0	3	1	33	0	41	3	1	8	.314	.292
Helton, Todd, Col.*	.320	159	656	578	114	185	339	39	5	35	113	0	4	6	68	6	77	7	6	14	.587	.395
Henderson, Rickey, N.Y.	.315	121	526	438	89	138	204	30	0	12	42	1	3	2	82	1	82	37	14	4	.466	.423
Hermansen, Chad, Pit.	.233	19	69	60	5	14	20	3	0	1	1	1	0	1	7	1	19	2	2	0	.333	.324
Hermanson, Dustin, Mon.	.047	34	75	64	1	3	3	0	0	0	2	8	0	0	3	0	39	0	0	0	.047	.090
Hernandez, Carlos E., Hou.	.143	16	15	14	4	2	2	0	0	0	1	1	0	0	0	0	3	1	0	1	.143	.143
Hernandez, Livan, Fla.-S.F.	.270	31	73	63	6	17	25	2	0	2	8	7	1	1	1	0	18	1	0	2	.397	.333
Hernandez, Jose, Chi.-Atl.	.266	147	568	508	79	135	216	20	2	19	62	2	1	5	52	6	145	11	3	10	.425	.339
Hershiser, Orel, N.Y.	.145	32	68	62	3	9	10	1	0	0	3	3	2	0	1	0	18	1	0	3	.161	.154
Hidalgo, Richard, Hou.	.227	108	448	383	49	87	161	25	2	15	56	0	5	4	56	2	73	8	5	5	.420	.328
Hill, Glenallen, Chi.	.300	99	278	253	43	76	147	9	1	20	55	0	3	0	22	1	61	5	1	7	.581	.353
Hitchcock, Sterling, S.D.*	.082	33	71	61	4	5	5	0	0	0	2	6	0	0	3	0	34	0	0	1	.082	.125
Hollandsworth, Todd, L.A.*	.284	92	287	261	39	74	117	12	2	9	32	0	1	1	24	1	61	5	2	2	.448	.345
Holt, Chris, Hou.	.067	32	55	45	3	3	3	0	0	0	2	7	0	0	3	0	14	0	0	1	.067	.125
Houston, Tyler, Chi.*	.233	100	279	249	26	58	96	9	1	9	27	1	1	0	28	4	67	1	1	7	.386	.326
Howard, David, St.L†	.207	52	92	82	3	17	24	4	0	1	6	1	0	2	7	3	27	0	2	0	.293	.286
Howard, Thomas, St.L†	.292	98	215	195	16	57	85	10	0	6	28	0	1	2	17	0	26	1	1	3	.436	.353

Player, Team	Avg.	G	TPA	AB	R	H	TB	2B	3B	HR	RBI	SH	SF	HP	BB	IBB	SO	SB	CS	GDP	Slg.	OBP
Howell, Jack, Hou.*	.212	37	41	33	2	7	12	2	0	1	1	0	0	0	8	0	9	0	0	1	.364	.366
Hubbard, Trenidad, L.A.	.314	82	120	105	23	33	41	5	0	1	13	1	1	0	13	1	24	4	3	2	.390	.387
Hughes, Bobby, Mil.	.257	48	106	101	10	26	37	2	0	3	8	0	0	0	5	0	28	0	0	3	.366	.292
Hundley, Todd, L.A.*	.207	114	428	376	49	78	164	14	0	24	55	1	3	4	44	3	113	3	0	5	.436	.295
Hunter, Brian, Atl.	.249	114	223	181	28	45	77	12	1	6	30	5	2	4	31	1	40	0	1	6	.425	.367
Hyers, Tim, Fla.*	.222	58	96	81	8	18	30	4	1	2	12	0	1	0	14	0	11	0	0	1	.370	.333
Isringhausen, Jason, N.Y.	.083	13	13	12	2	1	2	1	0	0	1	1	0	0	0	0	4	0	0	0	.167	.083
Jackson, Damian, S.D.	.224	133	447	388	56	87	138	20	2	9	39	0	3	3	53	3	105	34	10	2	.356	.320
Javier, Stan, S.F.-Hou.†	.285	132	446	397	61	113	145	19	2	3	34	8	2	1	38	4	63	16	7	6	.365	.347
Jenkins, Geoff, Mil.*	.313	135	493	447	70	140	252	43	3	21	82	3	1	7	35	7	87	5	1	10	.564	.371
Jensen, Marcus, St.L†	.235	12	42	34	5	8	16	5	0	1	1	2	0	0	6	1	12	0	0	1	.471	.350
Jimenez, Jose, St.L.	.094	31	55	53	5	5	7	0	1	0	2	2	0	0	0	0	22	0	0	1	.132	.094
Johnson, Brian, Cin.	.231	45	127	117	12	27	49	7	0	5	18	1	0	0	9	0	31	0	0	2	.419	.286
Johnson, Lance, Chi.*	.260	95	377	335	46	87	113	11	6	1	21	4	1	0	37	0	20	13	3	6	.337	.332
Johnson, Mike, Mon.*	.250	3	4	4	1	1	1	0	0	0	0	0	0	0	0	0	1	0	0	0	.250	.250
Johnson, Randy, Ari.	.124	35	104	97	1	12	16	4	0	0	6	7	0	0	0	0	46	0	0	1	.165	.124
Johnson, Russ, Hou.	.282	83	183	156	24	44	69	10	0	5	23	4	3	0	20	0	31	2	3	3	.442	.358
Jones, Andruw, Atl.	.275	162	679	592	97	163	286	35	5	26	84	0	2	9	76	11	103	24	12	12	.483	.365
Jones, Chipper, Atl.†	.319	157	701	567	116	181	359	41	1	45	110	0	6	2	126	18	94	25	3	20	.633	.441
Jones, Bobby J., N.Y.	.313	12	17	16	1	5	8	0	0	1	1	1	0	0	0	0	4	0	0	0	.500	.313
Jones, Bobby M., Col.	.148	30	34	27	3	4	5	1	0	0	4	4	1	0	2	0	7	0	0	0	.185	.200
Jones, Terry, Mon.†	.270	17	66	63	4	17	20	1	1	0	3	0	0	0	3	0	14	1	2	0	.317	.303
Jordan, Brian, Atl.	.283	153	645	576	100	163	268	28	4	23	115	0	9	9	51	2	81	13	8	9	.465	.346
Jordan, Kevin, Phi.	.285	120	380	347	36	99	134	17	3	4	51	0	3	6	24	1	34	0	0	12	.386	.339
Joyner, Wally, S.D.*	.248	110	386	323	34	80	113	14	2	5	43	0	3	2	58	6	54	0	1	8	.350	.363
Karl, Scott, Mil.*	.183	33	76	60	5	11	19	2	0	2	7	12	1	0	3	0	17	0	0	1	.317	.219
Karros, Eric, L.A.	.304	153	639	578	74	176	318	40	0	34	112	0	6	2	53	0	119	8	5	18	.550	.362
Kendall, Jason, Pit.	.332	78	334	280	61	93	143	20	3	8	41	0	4	12	38	3	32	22	3	8	.511	.428
Kennedy, Adam, St.L*	.255	33	110	102	12	26	41	10	1	1	16	1	1	2	3	0	8	0	1	1	.402	.284
Kent, Jeff, S.F.	.290	138	585	511	86	148	261	40	2	23	101	0	8	5	61	3	112	13	6	12	.511	.366
Kile, Darryl, Col.	.135	32	64	52	3	7	7	0	0	0	4	8	0	0	4	0	20	0	0	3	.135	.196
Kinkade, Mike, N.Y.	.196	28	51	46	3	9	19	2	1	2	6	0	0	2	3	0	9	1	0	1	.413	.275
Klesko, Ryan, Atl.*	.297	133	466	404	55	120	215	28	2	21	80	0	7	2	53	8	69	5	2	6	.532	.376
Knorr, Randy, Hou.	.167	13	31	30	2	5	6	1	0	0	0	0	0	0	1	0	8	0	0	1	.200	.194
Kotsay, Mark, Fla.*	.271	148	535	495	57	134	199	23	9	8	50	2	9	0	29	5	50	7	6	11	.402	.306
Kubenka, Jeff, L.A.*	1.000	6	1	1	1	1	1	0	0	0	0	0	0	0	0	0	0	0	0	0	1.000	1.000
Lankford, Ray, St.L*	.306	122	476	422	77	129	208	32	1	15	63	0	2	3	49	3	110	14	4	6	.493	.380
Lansing, Mike, Col.	.310	35	155	145	24	45	66	9	0	4	15	1	1	1	7	0	22	2	0	3	.455	.344
Larkin, Barry, Cin.	.293	161	687	583	108	171	245	30	4	12	75	5	4	2	93	5	57	30	8	12	.420	.390
LaRue, Jason, Cin.	.211	36	103	90	12	19	35	7	0	3	12	0	2	0	11	1	32	4	1	4	.389	.311
Lee, David, Col.	.200	36	5	5	1	1	1	0	0	0	0	0	0	0	0	0	2	0	0	0	.200	.200
Lee, Derrek, Fla.	.206	70	236	218	21	45	71	9	1	5	20	0	1	0	17	1	70	2	1	3	.326	.263
Lee, Travis, Ari.*	.237	120	436	375	57	89	136	16	2	9	50	0	3	0	58	4	50	17	3	10	.363	.337
Leiter, Al, N.Y.*	.105	32	70	57	1	6	8	2	0	0	5	11	0	0	2	0	29	0	0	1	.140	.136
Leskanic, Curtis, Col.	.500	63	4	4	1	2	5	0	0	1	3	0	0	0	0	0	2	0	0	0	1.250	.500
Lewis, Mark, Cin.	.254	88	184	173	18	44	78	16	0	6	28	2	2	0	7	1	24	0	0	8	.451	.280
Leyritz, Jim, S.D.	.239	50	154	134	17	32	61	5	0	8	21	0	1	4	15	1	37	0	0	4	.455	.331
Lieber, Jon, Chi.*	.121	31	71	58	8	7	8	1	0	0	2	7	1	0	5	0	23	0	0	1	.138	.188
Lieberthal, Mike, Phi.	.300	145	574	510	84	153	281	33	1	31	96	1	8	11	44	7	86	0	0	15	.551	.363
Lima, Jose, Hou.	.080	36	91	75	4	6	6	0	0	0	2	13	0	0	3	0	24	0	0	3	.080	.115
Liniak, Cole, Chi.	.241	12	30	29	3	7	9	2	0	0	2	0	0	0	1	0	4	0	1	2	.310	.267
Lockhart, Keith, Atl.*	.261	108	184	161	20	42	50	3	1	1	21	0	3	1	19	0	21	3	1	2	.311	.337
LoDuca, Paul, L.A.	.232	36	110	95	11	22	32	1	0	3	11	1	2	2	10	4	9	1	2	3	.337	.312
Lombard, George, Atl.*	.333	6	7	6	1	2	2	0	0	0	0	0	0	0	1	0	2	2	0	0	.333	.429
Lopez, Javy, Atl.	.317	65	269	246	34	78	131	18	1	11	45	0	3	0	20	2	41	0	3	6	.533	.375
Lopez, Luis, N.Y.†	.212	68	121	104	11	22	32	4	0	2	13	1	1	3	12	0	33	1	1	1	.308	.308
Loretta, Mark, Mil.	.290	153	664	587	93	170	229	34	5	5	67	9	6	10	52	1	59	4	1	14	.390	.354
Lorraine, Andrew, Chi.*	.133	12	20	15	1	2	3	1	0	0	0	4	0	0	1	0	9	0	0	0	.200	.188
Lovullo, Torey, Phi.†	.211	17	41	38	3	8	14	0	0	2	5	0	0	0	3	0	11	0	0	1	.368	.268
Lowell, Mike, Fla.	.253	97	344	308	32	78	129	15	0	12	47	0	5	5	26	1	69	0	0	8	.419	.317
Luebbers, Larry, St.L	.125	8	18	16	1	2	2	0	0	0	0	1	0	0	1	0	2	0	0	0	.125	.176
Machado, Robert, Mon.	.182	17	24	22	3	4	5	1	0	0	0	0	0	0	2	0	6	0	0	0	.227	.250
Maddux, Greg, Atl.	.172	33	79	64	7	11	20	1	1	2	7	13	0	1	0	0	18	0	0	5	.313	.197
Magadan, Dave, S.D.*	.274	116	300	248	20	68	88	12	1	2	30	0	7	0	45	2	36	1	3	10	.355	.377
Magee, Wendell, Phi.	.357	12	15	14	4	5	12	1	0	2	5	0	0	0	1	0	4	0	0	1	.857	.400
Mahomes, Pat, N.Y.	.313	41	16	16	2	5	8	3	0	0	3	0	0	0	0	0	6	0	0	0	.500	.313
Manwaring, Kirt, Col.	.299	48	155	137	17	41	56	7	1	2	14	0	1	5	12	1	23	0	0	4	.409	.374
Marrero, Eli, St.L	.192	114	343	317	32	61	94	13	1	6	34	4	3	1	18	4	56	11	2	14	.297	.236
Martin, Al, Pit.*	.277	143	593	541	97	150	274	36	8	24	63	0	2	1	49	5	119	20	3	8	.506	.337
Martinez, Sandy, Chi.*	.167	17	30	30	1	5	8	3	0	0	1	0	0	0	0	0	11	0	0	0	.267	.167
Martinez, Manny, Mon.	.245	137	357	331	48	81	113	12	7	2	26	6	3	0	17	0	51	19	6	4	.341	.279
Martinez, Ramon, S.F.	.264	61	165	144	21	38	59	6	0	5	19	6	1	0	14	0	17	1	2	2	.410	.327
Matthews, Gary, S.D.†	.222	23	45	36	4	8	8	0	0	0	7	0	0	0	9	0	9	2	0	1	.222	.378
Mayne, Brent, S.F.*	.301	117	374	322	39	97	135	32	0	2	39	1	3	5	43	5	65	2	2	16	.419	.389
McEwing, Joe, St.L	.275	152	574	513	65	141	204	28	4	9	44	9	5	6	41	8	87	7	4	3	.398	.333
McGee, Willie, St.L†	.251	132	290	271	25	68	75	7	0	0	20	0	2	0	17	3	60	7	4	5	.277	.293
McGuire, Ryan, Mon.*	.221	88	170	140	17	31	48	7	2	2	18	3	0	0	27	0	33	1	1	9	.343	.347
McGwire, Mark, St.L	.278	153	661	521	118	145	363	21	1	65	147	0	5	2	133	21	141	0	0	12	.697	.424
McRae, Brian, N.Y.-Col.†	.224	103	371	321	36	72	115	14	1	9	37	0	2	7	41	1	64	2	6	6	.358	.323
Meadows, Brian, Fla.	.140	31	59	50	6	7	10	3	0	0	1	7	0	0	2	0	21	0	0	0	.200	.173
Meares, Pat, Pit.	.308	21	104	91	15	28	32	4	0	0	7	2	0	2	9	0	20	0	0	1	.352	.382
Meluskey, Mitch, Hou.†	.212	10	38	33	4	7	11	1	0	1	3	0	0	0	5	1	6	1	0	1	.333	.316

– 271 –

Player, Team	Avg.	G	TPA	AB	R	H	TB	2B	3B	HR	RBI	SH	SF	HP	BB	IBB	SO	SB	CS	GDP	Slg.	OBP
Merced, Orlando, Mon.*	.268	93	221	194	25	52	90	12	1	8	26	0	1	0	26	0	27	2	1	5	.464	.353
Mercker, Kent, St.L*	.179	26	34	28	5	5	6	1	0	0	2	4	0	0	2	0	10	0	0	0	.214	.233
Meyers, Chad, Chi.	.232	43	156	142	17	33	42	9	0	0	4	2	0	3	9	1	27	4	2	5	.296	.292
Mieske, Matt, Hou.	.284	54	118	109	13	31	51	5	0	5	22	1	2	0	6	1	22	0	0	4	.468	.316
Millar, Kevin, Fla.	.285	105	407	351	48	100	152	17	4	9	67	1	8	7	40	2	64	1	0	7	.433	.362
Miller, Damian, Ari.	.270	86	320	296	35	80	132	19	0	11	47	0	3	2	19	3	78	0	0	6	.446	.316
Millwood, Kevin, Atl.	.154	33	86	78	4	12	17	2	0	1	6	6	0	0	2	0	29	0	0	2	.218	.175
Mirabelli, Doug, S.F.	.253	33	98	87	10	22	31	6	0	1	10	0	1	1	9	1	25	0	0	1	.356	.327
Molina, Jose, Chi.	.263	10	21	19	3	5	6	1	0	0	1	0	0	0	2	1	4	0	0	0	.316	.333
Mondesi, Raul, L.A.	.253	159	680	601	98	152	290	29	5	33	99	0	5	3	71	6	134	36	9	3	.483	.332
Montgomery, Steve, Phi.	1.000	53	1	1	1	1	1	0	0	0	0	0	0	0	0	0	0	0	0	0	1.000	1.000
Mora, Melvin, N.Y.	.161	66	39	31	6	5	5	0	0	0	1	3	0	1	4	0	7	2	1	0	.161	.278
Morandini, Mickey, Chi.*	.241	144	521	456	60	110	150	18	5	4	37	7	4	6	48	2	61	6	6	10	.329	.319
Mordecai, Mike, Mon.	.235	109	250	226	29	53	82	10	2	5	25	1	2	1	20	0	31	2	5	1	.363	.297
Morris, Warren, Pit.*	.288	147	581	511	65	147	218	20	3	15	73	4	5	2	59	3	88	3	7	12	.427	.360
Morris, Hal, Cin.*	.284	80	112	102	10	29	38	9	0	0	16	0	0	0	10	0	21	0	0	1	.373	.348
Mota, Guillermo, Mon.	1.000	51	1	1	1	1	4	0	0	1	3	0	0	0	0	0	0	0	0	0	4.000	1.000
Mouton, James, Mon.	.262	95	146	122	18	32	45	5	1	2	13	3	1	2	18	1	31	6	2	2	.369	.364
Mouton, Lyle, Mon.	.176	14	19	17	2	3	7	1	0	1	3	0	0	0	2	0	3	0	0	0	.412	.263
Mueller, Bill, S.F.†	.290	116	492	414	61	120	150	24	0	2	36	8	2	3	65	1	52	4	2	11	.362	.388
Mulholland, Terry, Chi.-Atl.	.104	42	55	48	2	5	5	0	0	0	3	5	0	0	2	0	21	0	0	1	.104	.140
Murray, Calvin, S.F.	.263	15	21	19	1	5	7	2	0	0	5	0	0	0	2	0	4	1	0	0	.368	.333
Murray, Heath, S.D.	.154	22	15	13	1	2	2	0	0	0	0	1	0	0	1	0	9	0	0	0	.154	.214
Myers, Greg, S.D.-Atl.*	.265	84	227	200	19	53	74	6	0	5	24	0	1	0	26	4	30	0	0	6	.370	.348
Myers, Rodney, Chi.	.429	46	7	7	2	3	4	1	0	0	1	0	0	0	0	0	0	0	0	0	.571	.429
Nathan, Joe, S.F.	.179	19	35	28	1	5	6	1	0	0	1	5	0	0	2	0	6	0	0	0	.214	.233
Neagle, Denny, Cin.*	.162	20	43	37	1	6	7	1	0	0	2	5	0	0	1	0	9	0	0	0	.189	.184
Nevin, Phil, S.D.	.269	128	441	383	52	103	202	27	0	24	85	1	5	1	51	1	82	1	0	7	.527	.352
Newhan, David, S.D.*	.140	32	44	43	7	6	13	1	0	2	6	0	0	0	1	0	11	2	1	0	.302	.159
Nieves, Jose, Chi.	.249	54	199	181	16	45	62	9	1	2	18	3	3	4	8	0	25	0	2	5	.343	.291
Nilsson, David, Mil.*	.309	115	404	343	56	106	190	19	1	21	62	2	4	2	53	6	64	1	2	7	.554	.400
Nixon, Otis, Atl.†	.205	84	176	151	31	31	35	2	1	0	8	1	1	0	23	1	15	26	7	1	.232	.309
Nomo, Hideo, Mil.	.214	29	64	56	3	12	16	2	1	0	5	7	0	0	1	0	22	0	0	0	.286	.228
Nunez, Abraham, Pit.†	.220	90	301	259	25	57	65	8	0	0	17	13	0	1	28	0	54	9	1	2	.251	.299
Ochoa, Alex, Mil.	.300	119	329	277	47	83	129	16	3	8	40	0	2	5	45	2	43	6	4	4	.466	.404
Ogea, Chad, Phi.	.091	36	55	44	1	4	4	0	0	0	0	7	0	0	4	0	25	0	0	1	.091	.167
Olerud, John, N.Y.*	.298	162	723	581	107	173	269	39	0	19	96	0	6	11	125	6	66	3	0	22	.463	.427
Oliver, Darren, St.L	.274	35	84	73	7	20	24	4	0	0	6	8	0	0	3	0	23	0	0	1	.329	.303
Oliver, Joe, Pit.	.201	45	146	134	10	27	38	8	0	1	13	0	2	0	10	0	33	2	0	4	.284	.253
Ordaz, Luis, St.L	.111	10	11	9	3	1	1	0	0	0	2	1	0	0	1	0	2	1	0	0	.111	.200
Ordonez, Rey, N.Y.	.258	154	588	520	49	134	165	24	2	1	60	11	7	1	49	12	59	8	4	16	.317	.319
Orie, Kevin, Fla.	.254	77	267	240	26	61	95	16	0	6	29	0	2	3	22	1	43	1	0	8	.396	.322
Ortiz, Russ, S.F.	.197	33	81	71	7	14	19	2	0	1	8	7	0	0	3	0	17	0	0	1	.268	.230
Osborne, Donovan, St.L*	.100	6	11	10	1	1	2	1	0	0	0	1	0	0	0	0	2	0	0	0	.200	.100
Osik, Keith, Pit.	.186	66	181	167	12	31	42	3	1	2	13	1	1	1	11	0	30	0	0	8	.251	.239
Owens, Eric, S.D.	.266	149	485	440	55	117	172	22	3	9	61	2	3	3	38	2	50	33	7	12	.391	.327
Paquette, Craig, St.L	.287	48	166	157	21	45	81	6	0	10	37	1	2	0	6	0	38	1	0	6	.516	.309
Park, Chan Ho, L.A.	.153	33	69	59	4	9	11	2	0	0	6	6	2	0	2	0	26	0	0	1	.186	.175
Parris, Steve, Cin.	.158	22	43	38	1	6	6	0	0	0	4	5	0	0	0	0	11	0	0	1	.158	.158
Pavano, Carl, Mon.	.061	19	39	33	1	2	2	0	0	0	2	5	0	0	1	0	14	0	0	0	.061	.088
Payton, Jay, N.Y.	.250	13	9	8	1	2	3	1	0	0	1	0	0	1	0	0	2	1	2	0	.375	.333
Pena, Angel, L.A.	.208	43	135	120	14	25	43	6	0	4	21	1	2	0	12	0	24	0	1	6	.358	.276
Perez, Carlos, L.A.*	.296	17	32	27	2	8	13	2	0	1	2	3	0	0	2	0	8	0	0	0	.481	.345
Perez, Eddie, Atl.	.249	104	339	309	30	77	115	17	0	7	30	4	3	6	17	4	40	0	1	9	.372	.299
Perez, Eduardo, St.L	.344	21	39	32	6	11	16	2	0	1	9	0	0	1	7	0	6	0	0	1	.500	.462
Perez, Neifi, Col.†	.280	157	732	690	108	193	278	27	11	12	70	9	4	1	28	0	54	13	5	4	.403	.307
Perez, Odalis, Atl.*	.133	19	34	30	1	4	4	0	0	0	3	4	0	0	0	0	10	0	0	0	.133	.133
Person, Robert, Phi.	.073	31	47	41	3	3	3	0	0	0	1	4	0	1	1	0	23	0	0	0	.073	.116
Peters, Chris, Pit.*	.273	19	25	22	5	6	6	0	0	0	1	1	0	0	2	0	10	1	0	1	.273	.333
Petersen, Chris, Col.	.154	7	15	13	1	2	2	0	0	0	2	0	0	0	2	0	3	0	0	0	.154	.267
Peterson, Kyle, Mil.*	.136	17	25	22	2	3	3	0	0	0	1	2	0	0	1	0	9	0	0	0	.136	.174
Petrick, Ben, Col.	.323	19	72	62	13	20	35	3	0	4	12	0	0	0	10	0	13	1	0	1	.565	.417
Phillips, J.R., Col.*	.231	25	40	39	5	9	19	4	0	2	4	0	1	0	0	0	13	0	0	0	.487	.250
Piazza, Mike, N.Y.	.303	141	593	534	100	162	307	25	0	40	124	0	7	1	51	11	70	2	2	27	.575	.361
Polanco, Placido, St.L	.277	88	240	220	24	61	79	9	3	1	19	3	2	0	15	1	24	1	3	7	.359	.323
Porter, Bo, Chi.	.192	24	29	26	2	5	6	1	0	0	0	1	0	0	2	0	13	0	0	1	.231	.250
Powell, Jeremy, Mon.	.133	17	34	30	2	4	5	1	0	0	3	0	0	1	0	0	3	0	0	0	.167	.212
Powell, Dante, Ari.	.160	22	28	25	4	4	7	3	0	0	1	1	0	0	2	0	6	2	1	0	.280	.222
Pratt, Todd, N.Y.	.293	71	160	140	18	41	54	4	0	3	21	0	2	3	15	0	32	2	0	0	.386	.369
Prince, Tom, Phi.	.167	4	7	6	1	1	1	0	0	0	0	0	0	0	1	0	1	0	0	1	.167	.286
Pulsipher, Bill, Mil.*	.143	19	29	21	1	3	3	0	0	0	0	8	0	0	0	0	14	0	0	1	.143	.143
Ramirez, Aramis, Pit.	.179	18	64	56	2	10	14	2	1	0	7	1	1	0	6	0	9	0	0	0	.250	.254
Ramirez, Julio, Fla.	.143	15	22	21	3	3	4	1	0	0	2	0	0	0	1	0	6	0	1	0	.190	.182
Ramirez, Roberto, Col.	.143	32	9	7	1	1	1	0	0	0	0	1	0	0	1	0	6	0	0	0	.143	.250
Redmond, Mike, Fla.	.302	84	278	242	22	73	85	9	0	1	27	5	0	5	26	2	34	0	0	8	.351	.381
Reed, Jeff, Col.-Chi.*	.258	103	306	256	29	66	95	16	2	3	28	0	2	3	45	1	58	1	2	7	.371	.373
Reed, Rick, N.Y.	.244	27	54	45	2	11	13	2	0	0	5	8	0	0	1	0	14	0	0	0	.289	.261
Reese, Pokey, Cin.	.285	149	636	585	85	167	244	37	5	10	52	5	5	6	35	3	81	38	7	9	.417	.330
Relaford, Desi, Phi.†	.242	65	242	211	31	51	69	11	2	1	26	6	0	6	19	2	34	4	3	5	.327	.322
Remlinger, Mike, Atl.*	.000	73	4	2	1	0	0	0	0	0	0	2	0	0	0	0	2	0	0	0	.000	.000
Renteria, Edgar, St.L	.275	154	653	585	92	161	234	36	2	11	63	6	7	2	53	0	82	37	8	16	.400	.334
Reynolds, Shane, Hou.	.167	35	86	66	4	11	16	2	0	1	14	17	1	0	2	0	27	0	0	1	.242	.188

Player, Team	Avg.	G	TPA	AB	R	H	TB	2B	3B	HR	RBI	SH	SF	HP	BB	IBB	SO	SB	CS	GDP	Slg.	OBP
Reynoso, Armando, Ari.	.163	31	58	49	3	8	10	2	0	0	2	8	0	0	1	0	26	0	0	0	.204	.180
Rios, Armando, S.F.*	.327	72	177	150	32	49	79	9	0	7	29	1	1	1	24	1	35	7	4	3	.527	.420
Ritchie, Todd, Pit.	.151	29	62	53	3	8	9	1	0	0	1	8	0	0	1	0	16	0	0	1	.170	.167
Rivera, Ruben, S.D.	.195	147	475	411	65	80	167	16	1	23	48	0	4	5	55	1	143	18	7	9	.406	.295
Robinson, Kerry, Cin.*	.000	9	1	1	4	0	0	0	0	0	0	0	0	0	0	0	1	0	1	0	.000	.000
Rodriguez, Felix, S.F.	.333	47	8	6	3	2	6	1	0	1	3	1	0	1	0	0	1	0	0	0	1.000	.429
Rodriguez, Henry, Chi.*	.304	130	504	447	72	136	243	29	0	26	87	0	1	0	56	6	113	2	4	9	.544	.381
Rodriguez, Rich, S.F.*	1.000	62	2	1	1	1	1	0	0	0	1	1	0	0	0	0	0	0	0	0	1.000	1.000
Rogers, Kenny, N.Y.*	.120	12	30	25	2	3	3	0	0	0	1	3	0	0	2	0	10	0	0	0	.120	.185
Rolen, Scott, Phi.	.268	112	497	421	74	113	221	28	1	26	77	0	6	3	67	2	114	12	2	8	.525	.368
Rueter, Kirk, S.F.*	.155	33	70	58	6	9	11	2	0	0	5	8	1	0	3	0	6	0	0	3	.190	.194
Ryan, Robert, Ari.*	.241	20	30	29	4	7	14	1	0	2	5	0	0	0	1	0	8	0	0	0	.483	.267
Sanders, Reggie, S.D.	.285	133	550	478	92	136	252	24	7	26	72	0	1	6	65	1	108	36	13	10	.527	.376
Sanford, Chance, L.A.*	.250	5	8	8	1	2	2	0	0	0	2	0	0	0	0	0	1	0	0	0	.250	.250
Santangelo, F.P., S.F.†	.260	113	325	254	49	66	98	17	3	3	26	5	2	11	53	0	54	12	4	1	.386	.406
Santiago, Benito, Chi.	.249	109	386	350	28	87	132	18	3	7	36	0	2	2	32	6	71	1	1	12	.377	.313
Schilling, Curt, Pit.	.100	24	66	50	5	5	8	1	1	0	3	9	0	0	7	0	28	0	0	0	.160	.211
Schmidt, Jason, Pit.	.083	33	77	60	2	5	5	0	0	0	1	12	0	0	5	0	33	0	0	0	.083	.154
Schourek, Pete, Pit.*	.000	30	31	25	1	0	0	0	0	0	1	3	0	0	3	0	13	0	0	1	.000	.107
Seanez, Rudy, Atl.	.000	56	2	1	1	0	0	0	0	0	0	0	0	0	1	0	1	0	0	0	.000	.500
Sefcik, Kevin, Phi.	.278	111	242	209	28	58	82	15	3	1	11	3	0	1	29	0	24	9	4	4	.392	.368
Seguignol, Fernando, Mon.†.	.257	35	119	105	14	27	51	9	0	5	10	0	2	7	5	1	33	0	0	1	.486	.328
Serafini, Dan, Chi.	.083	42	16	12	1	1	1	0	0	0	0	1	0	0	3	0	7	0	0	0	.083	.267
Servais, Scott, S.F.	.273	69	217	198	21	54	79	10	0	5	21	3	0	3	13	2	31	0	0	7	.399	.327
Sexton, Chris, Col.	.237	35	70	59	9	14	19	0	1	1	7	0	0	0	11	1	10	4	2	2	.322	.357
Sheffield, Gary, L.A.	.301	152	663	549	103	165	287	20	0	34	101	0	9	4	101	4	64	11	5	10	.523	.407
Shumpert, Terry, Col.	.347	92	304	262	58	91	153	26	3	10	37	4	5	2	31	2	41	14	0	2	.584	.413
Simon, Randall, Atl.*	.317	90	237	218	26	69	100	16	0	5	25	0	1	1	17	6	25	2	2	10	.459	.367
Smith, Dan, Mon.	.083	20	30	24	3	2	2	0	0	0	1	3	0	0	3	0	15	0	0	1	.083	.185
Smoltz, John, Atl.	.274	29	72	62	11	17	24	4	0	1	7	4	0	1	5	0	28	0	0	0	.387	.338
Snow, J.T., S.F.*	.274	161	668	570	93	156	257	25	2	24	98	1	6	5	86	7	121	0	4	16	.451	.370
Sosa, Juan, Col.	.222	11	11	9	3	2	2	0	0	0	0	0	0	0	2	0	2	0	0	0	.222	.364
Sosa, Sammy, Chi.	.288	162	712	625	114	180	397	24	2	63	141	0	6	3	78	8	171	7	8	17	.635	.367
Spiers, Bill, Hou.*	.288	127	464	393	56	113	153	18	5	4	39	3	1	0	47	2	45	10	5	6	.389	.363
Sprague, Ed, Pit.	.267	137	564	490	71	131	228	27	2	22	81	1	6	17	50	6	93	3	6	12	.465	.352
Springer, Dennis, Fla.	.120	38	54	50	2	6	7	1	0	0	2	3	1	0	0	0	17	0	0	0	.140	.118
Stephenson, Garrett, St.L.	.074	18	30	27	1	2	3	1	0	0	0	3	0	0	0	0	5	0	0	2	.111	.074
Stinnett, Kelly, Ari.	.232	88	317	284	36	66	121	13	0	14	38	2	2	5	24	1	83	2	1	4	.426	.302
Stynes, Chris, Cin.	.239	73	129	113	18	27	34	1	0	2	14	3	1	0	12	1	13	5	2	2	.301	.310
Sullivan, Scott, Cin.	.000	79	15	15	1	0	0	0	0	0	0	0	0	0	0	0	11	0	0	0	.000	.000
Sveum, Dale, Pit.†	.211	49	80	71	7	15	31	5	1	3	13	1	1	0	7	1	28	0	0	0	.437	.278
Sweeney, Mark, Cin.*	.355	37	35	31	6	11	20	3	0	2	7	0	0	0	4	1	9	0	0	2	.645	.429
Tapani, Kevin, Chi.	.051	23	47	39	1	2	3	1	0	0	3	5	0	0	3	0	21	0	0	0	.077	.119
Tatis, Fernando, St.L.	.298	149	639	537	104	160	297	31	2	34	107	0	4	16	82	4	128	21	9	11	.553	.404
Taubensee, Eddie, Cin.*	.311	126	461	424	58	132	221	22	2	21	87	1	5	1	30	1	67	0	2	12	.521	.354
Thompson, Ryan, Hou.	.200	12	22	20	2	4	8	1	0	1	5	0	0	0	2	0	7	0	0	1	.400	.273
Thomson, John, Col.	.167	14	20	18	1	3	4	1	0	0	1	0	0	0	2	0	7	0	0	0	.222	.250
Thurman, Mike, Mon.	.025	29	46	40	1	1	1	0	0	0	0	4	0	1	1	0	31	0	0	0	.025	.071
Tomko, Brett, Cin.	.213	33	58	47	3	10	12	2	0	0	2	8	0	0	3	0	17	0	0	0	.255	.260
Trachsel, Steve, Chi.	.111	34	71	63	4	7	8	1	0	0	0	7	0	0	1	0	25	1	0	0	.127	.125
Tremie, Chris, Pit.	.071	9	16	14	1	1	1	0	0	0	1	0	0	0	2	0	4	0	0	1	.071	.188
Tucker, Michael, Cin.*	.253	133	340	296	55	75	126	8	5	11	44	0	4	3	37	3	81	11	4	5	.426	.338
Valdes, Ismael, L.A.	.086	32	69	58	1	5	5	0	0	0	2	10	0	0	1	0	18	1	0	2	.086	.102
Valentin, Jose, Mil.†	.227	89	313	256	45	58	107	9	5	10	38	2	5	2	48	1	52	3	2	3	.418	.347
Vander Wal, John, S.D.*	.272	132	288	246	26	67	103	18	0	6	41	0	3	2	37	1	59	2	1	5	.419	.368
Vaughn, Greg, Cin.	.245	153	643	550	104	135	280	20	2	45	118	0	5	3	85	3	137	15	2	9	.535	.347
Vazquez, Javier, Mon.	.286	26	53	42	4	12	14	2	0	0	5	8	0	0	3	0	8	0	0	1	.333	.333
Ventura, Robin, N.Y.*	.301	161	671	588	88	177	311	38	0	32	120	1	5	3	74	10	109	1	1	14	.529	.379
Veras, Quilvio, S.D.†	.280	132	545	475	95	133	180	25	2	6	41	1	2	2	65	0	88	30	17	7	.379	.368
Vidro, Jose, Mon.†	.304	140	531	494	67	150	235	45	2	12	59	2	2	4	29	2	51	0	4	12	.476	.346
Vina, Fernando, Mil.*	.266	37	177	154	17	41	51	7	0	1	16	3	2	4	14	0	6	5	2	1	.331	.339
Vizcaino, Jose, L.A.†	.252	94	299	266	27	67	79	9	0	1	29	9	2	1	20	0	23	2	1	9	.297	.304
Walker, Larry, Col.*	.379	127	513	438	108	166	311	26	4	37	115	0	6	12	57	8	52	11	4	12	.710	.458
Ward, Daryle, Hou.*	.273	64	161	150	11	41	71	6	0	8	30	0	2	0	9	0	31	0	0	3	.473	.311
Ward, Turner, Pit.-Ari.†	.237	59	135	114	8	27	36	3	0	2	15	3	2	1	15	0	15	2	2	2	.316	.326
Watkins, Pat, Col.	.053	16	22	19	2	1	1	0	0	0	0	1	0	0	2	0	5	0	0	1	.053	.143
Weathers, David, Mil.	.143	63	8	7	1	1	1	0	0	0	0	0	0	0	1	0	4	0	0	0	.143	.250
Wehner, John, Pit.	.185	39	75	65	6	12	17	2	0	1	4	3	0	0	7	0	12	1	0	1	.262	.264
Weiss, Walt, Atl.†	.226	110	327	279	38	63	90	13	4	2	29	6	4	3	35	1	48	7	3	1	.323	.315
White, Devon, L.A.†	.268	134	526	474	60	127	193	20	2	14	68	0	2	11	39	2	88	19	5	10	.407	.337
White, Rondell, Mon.	.312	138	588	539	83	168	272	26	6	22	64	0	6	11	32	2	85	10	6	17	.505	.359
Widger, Chris, Mon.	.264	124	419	383	42	101	169	24	1	14	56	0	1	7	28	0	86	1	4	5	.441	.325
Williams, Gerald, Atl.	.275	143	467	422	76	116	193	24	1	17	68	4	2	6	33	1	67	19	11	8	.457	.335
Williams, Woody, S.D.*	.178	34	80	73	4	13	17	4	0	0	6	4	1	0	2	0	19	0	1	0	.233	.197
Williams, Jeff, L.A.	.200	5	7	5	2	1	1	0	0	0	0	1	0	0	1	0	4	0	0	0	.200	.333
Williams, Matt, Ari.	.303	154	678	627	98	190	336	37	2	35	142	0	8	2	41	9	93	2	0	17	.536	.344
Wilson, Preston, Fla.	.280	149	543	482	67	135	242	21	4	26	71	0	6	9	46	3	156	11	4	15	.502	.350
Wolf, Randy, Phi.*	.233	22	39	30	2	7	8	1	0	0	0	7	0	0	2	0	8	0	0	0	.267	.281
Womack, Tony, Ari.*	.277	144	684	614	111	170	227	25	10	4	41	9	7	2	52	0	68	72	13	4	.370	.332
Woodard, Steve, Mil.*	.132	31	69	53	5	7	8	1	0	0	0	10	0	0	6	0	16	0	0	1	.151	.220
Yoshii, Masato, N.Y.	.164	31	61	55	1	9	9	0	0	0	2	6	0	0	0	0	16	0	1	3	.164	.164
Young, Dmitri, Cin.†	.300	127	409	373	63	112	188	30	2	14	56	0	4	2	30	1	71	3	1	11	.504	.352

Player, Team	Avg.	G	TPA	AB	R	H	TB	2B	3B	HR	RBI	SH	SF	HP	BB	IBB	SO	SB	CS	GDP	Slg.	OBP
Young, Eric, L.A.	.281	119	534	456	73	128	162	24	2	2	41	6	4	5	63	0	26	51	22	12	.355	.371
Young, Ernie, Ari.	.182	6	15	11	1	2	2	0	0	0	0	0	0	1	3	0	2	0	0	0	.182	.400
Young, Kevin, Pit.	.298	156	675	584	103	174	305	41	6	26	106	0	4	12	75	5	124	22	10	13	.522	.387
Zosky, Eddie, Mil.	.143	8	8	7	1	1	1	0	0	0	0	0	0	0	1	0	2	0	0	0	.143	.250

AWARDED FIRST BASE ON OBSTRUCTION OR CATCHER'S INTERFERENCE—Benson, Pittsburgh (Hughes); Blum, Montreal (Petrick); Boone, Cincinnati (Castillo); Helton, Colorado (Taubensee); Hidalgo, Houston (Taubensee); McEwing, St. Louis (Manwaring); McGuire, Montreal (Marrero); Santangelo, San Francisco (Reed).

PLAYERS WITH TWO OR MORE TEAMS

Player, Team	Avg.	G	TPA	AB	R	H	TB	2B	3B	HR	RBI	SH	SF	HP	BB	IBB	SO	SB	CS	GDP	Slg.	OBP
Andrews, Shane, Mon.	.181	98	328	281	28	51	92	8	0	11	37	0	4	0	43	2	88	1	0	10	.327	.287
Andrews, Shane, Chi.	.254	19	76	67	13	17	36	4	0	5	14	0	1	1	7	1	21	0	1	0	.537	.329
Bere, Jason, Cin.	.286	12	17	14	2	4	4	0	0	0	1	2	0	1	0	0	7	0	0	0	.286	.333
Bere, Jason, Mil.	.375	5	10	8	1	3	3	0	0	0	0	1	0	0	2	0	2	0	0	0	.375	.500
Bergman, Sean, Atl.	.000	6	0	0	0	0	0	0	0	0	0	0	0	0	0	0	0	0	0	0	.000	.000
Bergman, Sean, Hou.	.107	19	29	28	4	3	9	0	0	2	2	1	0	0	0	0	12	0	0	0	.321	.107
Counsell, Craig, Fla.*	.152	37	73	66	4	10	11	1	0	0	2	2	0	0	5	0	10	0	0	1	.167	.211
Counsell, Craig, L.A.*	.259	50	122	108	20	28	34	6	0	0	9	3	2	0	9	0	14	1	0	1	.315	.331
Dunston, Shawon, St.L	.307	62	158	150	23	46	70	5	2	5	25	2	1	3	2	0	23	6	3	4	.467	.327
Dunston, Shawon, N.Y.	.344	42	97	93	12	32	40	6	1	0	16	1	1	2	0	0	16	4	1	4	.430	.354
Fabregas, Jorge, Atl.*	.000	6	8	8	0	0	0	0	0	0	0	0	0	0	0	0	0	0	0	2	.000	.000
Fabregas, Jorge, Fla.*	.206	82	260	223	20	46	69	10	2	3	21	4	5	2	26	6	27	0	0	7	.309	.289
Garcia, Freddy, Pit.	.231	55	135	130	16	30	53	5	0	6	23	0	1	0	4	0	41	0	0	3	.408	.252
Garcia, Freddy, Atl.	.500	2	3	2	1	1	4	0	0	1	1	0	0	0	1	0	1	0	0	0	2.000	.667
Hamilton, Darryl, Col.*	.303	91	379	337	63	102	131	11	3	4	24	2	1	1	38	0	21	4	5	7	.389	.374
Hamilton, Darryl, N.Y.*	.339	55	189	168	19	57	82	8	1	5	21	1	0	1	19	0	18	2	3	2	.488	.410
Harris, Lenny, Col.*	.297	91	164	158	15	47	59	12	0	0	13	0	0	0	6	0	6	1	1	7	.373	.323
Harris, Lenny, Ari.*	.379	19	30	29	2	11	15	1	0	1	7	0	1	0	0	0	1	1	0	0	.517	.367
Hernandez, Livan, Fla.	.289	20	47	45	5	13	21	2	0	2	7	1	1	0	0	0	5	0	0	2	.467	.283
Hernandez, Livan, S.F.	.222	11	26	18	1	4	4	0	0	0	1	6	0	1	1	0	5	0	0	0	.222	.300
Hernandez, Jose, Chi.	.272	99	388	342	57	93	154	12	2	15	43	1	0	5	40	3	101	7	2	5	.450	.357
Hernandez, Jose, Atl.	.253	48	180	166	22	42	62	8	0	4	19	1	1	0	12	3	44	4	1	5	.373	.302
Javier, Stan, S.F.†	.276	112	371	333	49	92	118	15	1	3	30	7	1	1	29	4	55	13	6	4	.354	.335
Javier, Stan, Hou.†	.328	20	75	64	12	21	27	4	1	0	4	1	1	0	9	0	8	3	1	2	.422	.405
McRae, Brian, N.Y.†	.221	96	344	298	35	66	104	12	1	8	36	0	2	5	39	1	57	2	6	6	.349	.320
McRae, Brian, Col.†	.261	7	27	23	1	6	11	2	0	1	1	0	0	2	2	0	7	0	0	0	.478	.370
Mulholland, Terry, Chi.	.094	26	35	32	0	3	3	0	0	0	3	3	0	0	0	0	17	0	0	0	.094	.094
Mulholland, Terry, Atl.	.125	16	20	16	2	2	2	0	0	0	0	2	0	0	2	0	4	0	0	1	.125	.222
Myers, Greg, S.D.*	.289	50	141	128	9	37	50	4	0	3	15	0	0	0	13	2	14	0	0	5	.391	.355
Myers, Greg, Atl.*	.222	34	86	72	10	16	24	2	0	2	9	0	1	0	13	2	16	0	0	1	.333	.337
Reed, Jeff, Col.*	.255	46	125	106	11	27	38	5	0	2	17	0	1	1	17	1	24	0	1	3	.358	.360
Reed, Jeff, Chi.*	.260	57	181	150	18	39	57	11	2	1	17	0	1	2	28	0	34	1	1	4	.380	.381
Ward, Turner, Pit.†	.209	49	109	91	2	19	21	2	0	0	8	3	1	1	13	0	9	2	2	2	.231	.311
Ward, Turner, Ari.†	.348	10	26	23	6	8	15	1	0	2	7	0	1	0	2	0	6	0	0	0	.652	.385

DESIGNATED HITTING

TEAM

Team	Avg.	G	TPA	AB	R	H	TB	2B	3B	HR	RBI	SH	SF	HP	BB	IBB	SO	SB	CS	GDP	Slg.	OBP
Houston	.387	9	41	31	6	12	16	4	0	0	8	0	0	1	9	0	6	2	2	0	.516	.537
Philadelphia	.359	9	43	39	10	14	19	2	0	1	6	0	0	0	4	0	5	0	0	0	.487	.419
Florida	.325	9	45	40	8	13	17	4	0	0	5	0	0	1	4	1	4	0	1	0	.425	.400
St. Louis	.320	6	28	25	4	8	10	2	0	0	3	1	0	0	2	0	6	0	1	0	.400	.370
Atlanta	.289	9	40	38	6	11	16	2	0	1	9	0	0	0	2	0	6	1	0	2	.421	.325
Cincinnati	.289	9	41	38	6	11	18	1	0	2	8	0	0	0	3	0	8	1	0	0	.474	.341
Arizona	.263	9	45	38	5	10	17	1	0	2	4	0	0	0	7	0	8	0	0	0	.447	.378
Pittsburgh	.243	9	40	37	4	9	18	3	0	2	6	0	0	0	3	0	9	0	0	1	.486	.300
Montreal	.242	9	36	33	4	8	12	1	0	1	4	1	0	0	2	0	5	0	1	1	.364	.286
Chicago	.227	6	26	22	4	5	9	1	0	1	2	0	1	0	3	0	7	0	0	2	.409	.308
San Diego	.208	6	28	24	1	5	9	1	0	1	2	0	0	0	4	0	5	0	0	0	.375	.321
New York	.194	9	40	31	7	6	11	2	0	1	5	0	1	0	8	0	8	0	0	2	.355	.350
San Francisco	.167	9	41	36	4	6	9	0	0	1	7	0	0	0	5	1	7	1	0	0	.250	.268
Milwaukee	.148	6	28	27	4	4	8	1	0	1	3	0	0	0	1	0	11	0	0	0	.296	.179
Los Angeles	.143	6	26	21	4	3	3	0	0	0	0	0	0	1	4	0	3	0	0	0	.143	.308
Colorado	.143	6	26	21	2	3	6	0	0	1	2	0	0	0	5	1	4	0	0	0	.286	.308
Totals	.255	126	574	501	79	128	198	25	0	15	74	2	2	3	66	3	102	5	5	9	.395	.344

TOP DESIGNATED HITTERS

Minimum 15 at-bats. *Lefthanded batter. †Switch-hitter.

Player, Team	Avg.	G	TPA	AB	R	H	TB	2B	3B	HR	RBI	SH	SF	HP	BB	IBB	SO	SB	CS	GDP	Slg.	OBP
Lockhart, Keith, Atl.*	.353	4	18	17	5	6	7	1	0	0	4	0	0	0	1	0	0	1	0	0	.412	.389
Abreu, Bobby, Phi.*	.320	5	25	25	4	8	9	1	0	0	3	0	0	0	0	0	5	0	0	0	.360	.320
Gonzalez, Luis, Ari.*	.313	4	20	16	2	5	5	0	0	0	2	0	0	0	4	0	2	0	0	0	.313	.450
Guerrero, Wilton, Mon.†	.300	5	21	20	3	6	7	1	0	0	1	1	0	0	0	0	2	0	1	0	.350	.300
Aven, Bruce, Fla.	.296	6	27	27	3	8	10	2	0	0	2	0	0	0	0	0	3	0	0	0	.370	.296
Vaughn, Greg, Cin.	.269	7	28	26	4	7	13	0	0	2	8	0	0	0	2	0	7	1	0	0	.500	.321
Hill, Glenallen, Chi.	.250	4	17	16	1	4	8	1	0	1	2	0	1	0	0	0	5	0	0	2	.500	.235
Lopez, Javy, Atl.	.211	4	19	19	0	4	5	1	0	0	4	0	0	0	0	0	5	0	0	2	.263	.211
Brown, Brant, Pit.*	.100	6	20	20	1	2	4	2	0	0	0	0	0	0	0	0	5	0	0	0	.200	.100

ALL DESIGNATED HITTERS

*Lefthanded batter. †Switch-hitter.

Player, Team	Avg.	G	TPA	AB	R	H	TB	2B	3B	HR	RBI	SH	SF	HP	BB	IBB	SO	SB	CS	GDP	Slg.	OBP
Abreu, Bobby, Phi.*	.320	5	25	25	4	8	9	1	0	0	3	0	0	0	0	0	5	0	0	0	.360	.320
Agbayani, Benny, N.Y.	.250	2	4	4	1	1	2	1	0	0	0	0	0	0	0	0	2	0	0	0	.500	.250
Andrews, Shane, Mon.	.000	1	3	2	0	0	0	0	0	0	0	0	0	0	1	0	1	0	0	1	.000	.333
Aven, Bruce, Fla.	.296	6	27	27	3	8	10	2	0	0	2	0	0	0	0	0	3	0	0	0	.370	.296
Baerga, Carlos, S.D.†	.000	1	2	2	0	0	0	0	0	0	0	0	0	0	0	0	1	0	0	0	.000	.000
Bagwell, Jeff, Hou.	.333	2	8	3	3	1	2	1	0	0	0	0	0	1	4	0	1	1	1	1	.667	.750
Barker, Glen, Hou.†	.000	1	0	0	0	0	0	0	0	0	0	0	0	0	0	0	0	1	1	0	.000	.000
Becker, Rich, Mil.*	.000	2	5	5	0	0	0	0	0	0	0	0	0	0	0	0	5	0	0	0	.000	.000
Bell, Jay, Ari.	.300	2	11	10	2	3	10	1	0	2	2	0	0	0	1	0	1	0	0	0	1.000	.364
Bichette, Dante, Col.	.286	2	8	7	1	2	5	0	0	1	2	0	0	0	1	0	1	0	0	0	.714	.375
Biggio, Craig, Hou.	.333	2	10	9	2	3	4	1	0	0	2	0	0	0	1	0	1	0	0	0	.444	.400
Bonds, Barry, S.F.*	.091	4	15	11	2	1	4	0	0	1	3	0	0	0	4	1	1	0	0	0	.364	.333
Bonilla, Bobby, N.Y.†	.222	3	12	9	2	2	3	1	0	0	3	0	1	0	2	0	3	0	0	0	.333	.333
Brown, Brant, Pit.*	.100	6	20	20	1	2	4	2	0	0	0	0	0	0	0	0	5	0	0	0	.200	.100
Burks, Ellis, S.F.	.182	3	12	11	1	2	2	0	0	0	1	0	0	0	1	0	3	0	0	0	.182	.250
Burnitz, Jeromy, Mil.*	.214	3	14	14	3	3	7	1	0	1	3	0	0	0	0	0	2	0	0	0	.500	.214
Casey, Sean, Cin.*	.600	1	5	5	1	3	3	0	0	0	0	0	0	0	0	0	1	0	0	0	.600	.600
Clapinski, Chris, Fla.†	1.000	1	1	1	0	1	1	0	0	0	0	0	0	0	0	0	0	0	0	0	1.000	1.000
Colbrunn, Greg, Ari.	.167	2	8	6	1	1	1	0	0	0	0	0	0	0	2	0	2	0	0	0	.167	.375
Davis, Eric, St.L.	.429	2	9	7	2	3	3	0	0	0	1	0	0	0	2	0	2	0	0	0	.429	.556
Dellucci, David, Ari.*	.000	1	1	1	0	0	0	0	0	0	0	0	0	0	0	0	1	0	0	0	.000	.000
Ducey, Rob, Phi.*	.400	2	8	5	2	2	6	1	0	1	2	0	0	0	3	0	0	0	0	0	1.200	.625
Dunston, Shawon, St.L.	.400	2	11	10	2	4	6	2	0	0	1	1	0	0	0	0	2	0	1	0	.600	.400
Everett, Carl, Hou.†	1.000	2	2	2	0	2	3	1	0	0	4	0	0	0	0	0	0	0	0	0	1.500	1.000
Finley, Steve, Ari.*	.200	1	5	5	0	1	1	0	0	0	0	0	0	0	0	0	2	0	0	0	.200	.200
Floyd, Cliff, Fla.*	.364	3	16	11	5	4	6	2	0	0	3	0	0	1	4	1	1	0	1	0	.545	.563
Franco, Matt, N.Y.*	.182	4	15	11	3	2	5	0	0	1	2	0	0	0	4	0	1	0	0	2	.455	.400
Gant, Ron, Phi.	.444	2	10	9	4	4	4	0	0	0	1	0	0	0	1	0	0	0	0	0	.444	.500
Garcia, Freddy, Pit.	.500	2	6	6	1	3	6	0	0	1	3	0	0	0	0	0	1	0	0	0	1.000	.500
Giles, Brian S., Pit.*	.364	3	14	11	2	4	8	1	0	1	3	0	0	0	3	0	3	0	0	1	.727	.500
Gonzalez, Luis, Ari.*	.313	4	20	16	2	5	5	0	0	0	2	0	0	0	4	0	2	0	0	0	.313	.450
Guerrero, Wilton, Mon.†	.300	5	21	20	3	6	7	1	0	0	1	1	0	0	0	0	2	0	1	0	.350	.300
Gwynn, Tony, S.D.*	.125	2	10	8	0	1	2	1	0	0	0	0	0	0	2	0	1	0	0	0	.250	.300
Hansen, Dave, L.A.*	.143	2	8	7	1	1	1	0	0	0	0	0	0	1	0	0	2	0	0	0	.143	.250
Harris, Lenny, Col.*	.000	2	5	4	1	0	0	0	0	0	0	0	0	0	1	0	0	0	0	0	.000	.200
Hayes, Charlie, S.F.	.143	2	7	7	0	1	1	0	0	0	1	0	0	0	0	0	2	0	0	0	.143	.143
Henderson, Rickey, N.Y.	.250	1	5	4	1	1	1	0	0	0	0	0	0	0	1	0	1	0	0	0	.250	.400
Hill, Glenallen, Chi.	.250	4	17	16	1	4	8	1	0	1	2	0	1	0	0	0	5	0	0	2	.500	.235

Player, Team	Avg.	G	TPA	AB	R	H	TB	2B	3B	HR	RBI	SH	SF	HP	BB	IBB	SO	SB	CS	GDP	Slg.	OBP
Howard, Thomas, St.L.†	.000	1	3	3	0	0	0	0	0	0	0	0	0	0	0	0	0	0	0	0	.000	.000
Howell, Jack, Hou.*	.200	2	7	5	0	1	1	0	0	0	0	0	0	0	2	0	0	0	0	0	.200	.429
Hughes, Bobby, Mil.	.000	1	3	3	0	0	0	0	0	0	0	0	0	0	0	0	2	0	0	0	.000	.000
Hyers, Tim, Fla.*	.000	1	1	1	0	0	0	0	0	0	0	0	0	0	0	0	0	0	0	0	.000	.000
Javier, Stan, S.F.†	.333	1	6	6	1	2	2	0	0	0	2	0	0	0	0	0	1	1	0	0	.333	.333
Joyner, Wally, S.D.*	.000	1	4	3	0	0	0	0	0	0	0	0	0	0	1	0	2	0	0	0	.000	.250
Klesko, Ryan, Atl.*	.500	1	3	2	1	1	4	0	0	1	1	0	0	0	1	0	1	0	0	0	2.000	.667
Lankford, Ray, St.L.*	.200	1	5	5	0	1	1	0	0	0	1	0	0	0	0	0	2	0	0	0	.200	.200
Lockhart, Keith, Atl.*	.353	4	18	17	5	6	7	1	0	0	4	0	0	0	1	0	0	1	0	0	.412	.389
Lopez, Javy, Atl.	.211	4	19	19	0	4	5	1	0	0	4	0	0	0	0	0	5	0	0	2	.263	.211
Manwaring, Kirt, Col.	.000	1	3	3	0	0	0	0	0	0	0	0	0	0	0	0	1	0	0	0	.000	.000
Martinez, Ramon E., S.F.	.000	1	1	1	0	0	0	0	0	0	0	0	0	0	0	0	0	0	0	0	.000	.000
Merced, Orlando, Mon.*	.286	2	8	7	1	2	5	0	0	1	3	0	0	0	1	0	2	0	0	0	.714	.375
Morris, Hal, Cin.*	.000	1	3	3	0	0	0	0	0	0	0	0	0	0	0	0	0	0	0	0	.000	.000
Mouton, James, Mon.	.000	1	4	4	0	0	0	0	0	0	0	0	0	0	0	0	0	0	0	0	.000	.000
Nevin, Phil, S.D.	.500	1	4	4	0	2	2	0	0	0	1	0	0	0	0	0	1	0	0	0	.500	.500
Nilsson, Dave, Mil.*	.250	1	5	4	1	1	1	0	0	0	0	0	0	0	1	0	1	0	0	0	.250	.400
Ochoa, Alex, Mil.	.000	1	1	1	0	0	0	0	0	0	0	0	0	0	0	0	1	0	0	0	.000	.000
Piazza, Mike, N.Y.	.000	1	4	3	0	0	0	0	0	0	0	0	0	0	1	0	1	0	0	0	.000	.250
Reed, Jeff, Col.*	.200	1	5	5	0	1	1	0	0	0	0	0	0	0	0	0	2	0	0	0	.200	.200
Rodriguez, Henry, Chi.*	.167	2	9	6	3	1	1	0	0	0	0	0	0	0	3	0	2	0	0	0	.167	.444
Sanders, Reggie, S.D.	.000	1	5	4	0	0	0	0	0	0	0	0	0	0	1	0	0	0	0	0	.000	.200
Sheffield, Gary, L.A.	.167	3	14	12	3	2	2	0	0	0	0	0	0	0	2	0	1	0	0	1	.167	.286
Vander Wal, John, S.D.*	.667	1	3	3	1	2	5	0	0	1	1	0	0	0	0	0	0	0	0	0	1.667	.667
Vaughn, Greg, Cin.	.269	7	28	26	4	7	13	0	0	2	8	0	0	0	2	0	7	1	0	0	.500	.321
Walker, Larry, Col.*	.000	1	5	2	0	0	0	0	0	0	0	0	0	0	3	1	0	0	0	0	.000	.600
Ward, Daryle, Hou.*	.417	3	14	12	1	5	6	1	0	0	2	0	0	0	2	0	4	0	0	0	.500	.500
White, Devon, L.A.†	.000	1	4	2	0	0	0	0	0	0	0	0	0	1	1	0	0	0	0	0	.000	.500
Young, Dmitri, Cin.†	.250	1	5	4	1	1	2	1	0	0	0	0	0	0	1	0	0	0	0	0	.500	.400

PINCH-HITTING

TEAM

Team	Avg.	G	TPA	AB	R	H	TB	2B	3B	HR	RBI	SH	SF	HP	BB	IBB	SO	SB	CS	GDP	Slg.	OBP
Arizona	.319	126	217	188	29	60	87	10	1	5	41	1	3	5	20	2	47	3	1	7	.463	.394
Colorado	.278	141	292	259	36	72	113	14	0	9	45	3	2	4	24	0	61	3	1	10	.436	.346
Los Angeles	.271	130	231	188	22	51	76	9	2	4	32	6	2	4	31	0	42	2	2	4	.404	.382
Cincinnati	.257	125	244	214	25	55	84	11	0	6	37	4	1	0	25	3	56	3	0	4	.393	.333
Philadelphia	.255	133	237	204	31	52	84	13	2	5	29	3	1	0	29	4	50	3	0	6	.412	.346
Montreal	.254	124	241	205	21	52	77	8	4	3	34	4	2	0	30	0	37	1	2	4	.376	.346
Houston	.234	129	241	209	22	49	77	11	1	5	30	5	0	0	27	2	65	5	2	2	.368	.322
Pittsburgh	.229	121	238	210	21	48	77	7	2	6	25	0	1	2	25	4	76	2	1	6	.367	.315
Milwaukee	.227	137	282	247	22	56	77	7	1	4	30	0	2	2	31	3	69	3	1	5	.312	.316
San Francisco	.216	130	232	194	21	42	62	8	0	4	29	4	1	5	28	2	47	3	1	3	.320	.329
Chicago	.211	136	309	270	28	57	89	8	0	8	28	2	3	4	30	0	88	2	0	9	.330	.296
Atlanta	.208	137	265	226	16	47	64	8	0	3	30	6	5	2	26	3	51	7	0	9	.283	.290
St. Louis	.208	127	260	231	14	48	66	9	0	3	26	2	1	2	24	3	56	2	1	7	.286	.287
Florida	.205	126	255	229	21	47	83	12	0	8	26	0	3	0	23	0	64	0	0	2	.362	.275
San Diego	.203	137	290	251	21	51	80	8	0	7	41	1	4	1	33	1	69	2	1	4	.319	.294
New York	.198	148	308	257	26	51	74	15	1	2	24	1	3	5	42	5	82	3	3	7	.288	.319
Totals	.234	2107	4142	3582	376	838	1270	158	14	82	507	42	34	36	448	32	960	44	16	90	.355	.322

INDIVIDUAL
TOP PINCH-HITTERS

Minimum 20 at-bats.   *Lefthanded batter.   †Switch-hitter.

Player, Team	Avg.	G	TPA	AB	R	H	TB	2B	3B	HR	RBI	SH	SF	HP	BB	IBB	SO	SB	CS	GDP	Slg.	OBP
Arias, Alex, Phi.	.545	23	23	22	5	12	17	3	1	0	9	0	1	0	0	0	0	2	0	1	.773	.522
Harris, Lenny, Col.-Ari.*	.382	73	70	68	6	26	32	6	0	0	12	0	0	0	2	0	3	2	0	2	.471	.400
Colbrunn, Greg, Ari.	.375	28	28	24	5	9	15	3	0	1	8	0	2	2	0	0	4	0	0	0	.625	.393
Sweeney, Mark, Cin.*	.355	36	35	31	6	11	20	3	0	2	7	0	0	0	4	1	9	0	0	2	.645	.429
Vizcaino, Jose, L.A.†	.350	24	24	20	3	7	8	1	0	0	7	2	0	0	2	0	3	0	1	0	.400	.409
Spiers, Bill, Hou.*	.348	24	24	23	2	8	11	1	1	0	7	0	0	0	1	0	5	2	0	0	.478	.375
Young, Dmitri, Cin.†	.345	33	32	29	7	10	16	3	0	1	8	0	0	0	3	0	8	0	0	0	.552	.406
Johnson, Russ, Hou.	.343	42	42	35	7	12	18	3	0	1	6	3	0	0	4	0	13	2	1	0	.514	.410
Guerrero, Wilton, Mon.†	.340	58	58	50	7	17	22	1	2	0	7	2	0	0	6	0	4	1	2	0	.440	.411
Gilkey, Bernard, Ari.	.333	43	43	39	5	13	18	2	0	1	9	0	1	0	3	1	8	1	0	3	.462	.372
Mouton, James, Mon.	.324	40	40	34	2	11	13	2	0	0	6	0	0	0	6	0	9	0	0	0	.382	.425
Sveum, Dale, Pit.†	.321	32	32	28	4	9	15	3	0	1	7	0	1	0	3	1	7	0	0	0	.536	.375
Ward, Daryle, Hou.*	.320	26	26	25	2	8	15	1	0	2	4	0	0	0	1	0	8	0	0	0	.600	.346
Echevarria, Angel, Col.	.319	52	52	47	8	15	28	1	0	4	14	0	0	1	4	0	10	0	0	4	.596	.385
Tucker, Michael, Cin.*	.318	25	24	22	3	7	10	0	0	1	3	0	0	0	2	1	6	1	0	0	.455	.375

ALL PINCH-HITTERS

*Lefthanded batter.   †Switch-hitter.

Player, Team	Avg.	G	TPA	AB	R	H	TB	2B	3B	HR	RBI	SH	SF	HP	BB	IBB	SO	SB	CS	GDP	Slg.	OBP
Abbott, Kurt, Col.	.308	16	16	13	3	4	7	0	0	1	4	0	0	0	3	0	6	0	0	0	.538	.438
Abreu, Bobby, Phi.*	.000	2	2	1	0	0	0	0	0	0	0	0	0	0	1	1	0	0	0	0	.000	.500
Agbayani, Benny, N.Y.	.150	28	26	20	5	3	6	3	0	0	0	0	0	2	4	1	10	0	0	0	.300	.346
Alexander, Manny, Chi.	.293	46	46	41	2	12	16	4	0	0	2	1	0	0	4	0	9	0	0	1	.390	.356
Allensworth, Jermaine, N.Y.	.333	9	8	6	1	2	5	0	0	1	3	0	1	0	1	0	1	0	0	0	.833	.375
Anderson, Marlon, Phi.*	.000	6	6	5	0	0	0	0	0	0	0	0	0	0	1	0	1	0	0	1	.000	.167
Andrews, Shane, Mon.-Chi.	.400	10	9	5	1	2	2	0	0	0	1	0	1	0	3	0	2	0	0	0	.400	.556
Arias, Alex, Phi.	.545	23	23	22	5	12	17	3	1	0	9	0	1	0	0	0	0	2	0	1	.773	.522
Arias, George, S.D.	.375	8	8	8	1	3	4	1	0	0	0	0	0	0	0	0	5	0	0	0	.500	.375
Astacio, Pedro, Col.	.000	2	2	2	0	0	0	0	0	0	0	0	0	0	0	0	2	0	0	0	.000	.000
Aurilia, Rich, S.F.	.333	4	4	3	0	1	1	0	0	0	2	0	0	0	1	1	1	0	0	1	.333	.500
Aven, Bruce, Fla.	.269	34	34	26	4	7	14	1	0	2	10	0	1	0	7	0	11	0	0	0	.538	.412
Baerga, Carlos, S.D.†	.167	15	14	12	2	2	5	0	0	1	1	1	0	1	0	0	5	0	0	0	.417	.231
Bagwell, Jeff, Hou.	.000	2	2	0	0	0	0	0	0	0	0	0	0	0	2	0	0	0	0	0	.000	1.000
Bako, Paul, Hou.*	.500	2	2	2	1	1	1	0	0	0	0	0	0	0	0	0	0	0	0	0	.500	.500
Banks, Brian, Mil.†	.200	29	29	25	2	5	5	0	0	0	1	0	0	0	4	0	7	0	0	0	.200	.310
Barker, Glen, Hou.†	.083	14	14	12	1	1	1	0	0	0	0	0	0	0	2	0	3	0	0	0	.083	.214
Barker, Kevin, Mil.*	.143	8	7	7	0	1	1	0	0	0	0	0	0	0	0	0	3	0	0	0	.143	.143
Barrett, Michael, Mon.	.000	6	6	5	0	0	0	0	0	0	0	0	0	0	1	0	1	0	0	0	.000	.167
Barry, Jeff, Col.†	.211	21	21	19	2	4	8	1	0	1	2	0	0	0	2	0	5	0	0	1	.421	.286
Batista, Tony, Ari.	.250	4	4	4	0	1	1	0	0	0	1	0	0	0	0	0	2	0	0	0	.250	.250
Battle, Howard, Atl.	.375	10	10	8	1	3	3	0	0	0	2	0	0	0	2	0	2	0	0	1	.375	.500
Bautista, Danny, Fla.	.400	10	10	10	1	4	8	1	0	1	3	0	0	0	0	0	2	0	0	0	.800	.400
Becker, Rich, Mil.*	.263	47	46	38	4	10	16	1	1	1	4	0	0	0	8	0	10	1	0	2	.421	.391
Bell, Derek, Hou.	.000	4	4	3	0	0	0	0	0	0	0	0	0	0	1	1	1	0	0	0	.000	.250
Bell, Jay, Ari.	.333	4	4	3	0	1	1	0	0	0	0	0	0	0	1	0	1	0	0	0	.333	.500
Belliard, Ron, Mil.	.500	6	6	4	0	2	3	1	0	0	0	0	0	0	2	0	0	0	0	1	.750	.667
Beltran, Rigo, Col.*	.000	1	1	1	0	0	0	0	0	0	0	0	0	0	0	0	0	0	0	0	.000	.000
Beltre, Adrian, L.A.	.000	1	1	0	0	0	0	0	0	0	0	0	0	0	1	0	0	0	0	0	.000	1.000
Benard, Marvin, S.F.*	.364	11	11	11	1	4	5	1	0	0	2	0	0	0	0	0	2	2	0	0	.455	.364
Benjamin, Mike, Pit.	.429	7	7	7	1	3	3	0	0	0	1	0	0	0	0	0	2	0	0	0	.429	.429

Player, Team	Avg.	G	TPA	AB	R	H	TB	2B	3B	HR	RBI	SH	SF	HP	BB	IBB	SO	SB	CS	GDP	Slg.	OBP
Bennett, Gary, Phi.	.571	7	7	7	1	4	5	1	0	0	0	0	0	0	0	0	2	0	0	1	.714	.571
Berg, Dave, Fla.	.174	26	26	23	2	4	5	1	0	0	0	0	0	0	3	0	7	0	0	0	.217	.269
Bergeron, Peter, Mon.*	.000	3	3	3	0	0	0	0	0	0	0	0	0	0	0	0	0	0	0	0	.000	.000
Berkman, Lance, Hou.†	.000	10	10	9	0	0	0	0	0	0	0	0	0	0	1	0	3	0	0	1	.000	.100
Berry, Sean, Mil.	.190	47	45	42	4	8	9	1	0	0	3	0	1	1	1	0	15	0	0	0	.214	.222
Bichette, Dante, Col.	.000	5	5	3	1	0	0	0	0	0	0	0	0	0	2	0	1	0	0	0	.000	.400
Biggio, Craig, Hou.	.000	2	2	2	0	0	0	0	0	0	0	0	0	0	0	0	1	0	0	0	.000	.000
Blanco, Henry, Col.	.333	4	4	3	0	1	1	0	0	0	1	1	0	0	0	0	1	0	0	0	.333	.333
Blauser, Jeff, Chi.	.250	49	49	44	6	11	20	0	0	3	7	0	2	1	2	0	18	0	0	0	.455	.286
Blum, Geoff, Mon.†	.000	3	3	2	0	0	0	0	0	0	0	0	0	0	1	0	0	0	0	0	.000	.333
Bogar, Tim, Hou.	.000	7	6	4	0	0	0	0	0	0	0	0	0	0	2	0	1	0	0	0	.000	.333
Bohanon, Brian, Col.*	.000	1	1	1	0	0	0	0	0	0	0	0	0	0	0	0	0	0	0	0	.000	.000
Bonds, Barry, S.F.*	.000	3	3	1	1	0	0	0	0	0	0	1	0	0	0	2	0	0	0	0	.000	.667
Bonilla, Bobby, N.Y.†	.192	31	31	26	0	5	9	4	0	0	1	0	0	0	5	0	3	0	1	1	.346	.323
Boone, Aaron, Cin.	.000	2	2	2	0	0	0	0	0	0	0	0	0	0	0	0	0	0	0	0	.000	.000
Boone, Bret, Atl.	.250	4	4	4	0	1	1	0	0	0	0	0	0	0	0	0	1	0	0	0	.250	.250
Bragg, Darren, St.L*	.222	10	10	9	1	2	5	0	0	1	3	0	0	1	0	0	3	0	0	1	.556	.300
Brogna, Rico, Phi.*	.000	2	2	1	0	0	0	0	0	0	0	0	0	0	1	1	1	0	0	0	.000	.500
Brown, Adrian, Pit.†	.250	31	31	24	2	6	8	0	1	0	2	0	0	0	7	0	9	0	1	0	.333	.419
Brown, Brant, Pit.*	.114	41	38	35	1	4	7	0	0	1	1	0	0	1	2	1	19	0	0	0	.200	.184
Brown, Emil, Pit.	1.000	1	1	1	0	1	2	1	0	0	0	0	0	0	0	0	0	0	0	0	2.000	1.000
Brown, Roosevelt, Chi.*	.077	16	15	13	0	1	1	0	0	0	1	0	1	0	1	0	2	1	0	1	.077	.133
Brumfield, Jacob, L.A.	.250	4	4	4	1	1	3	0	1	0	0	0	0	0	0	0	1	0	0	0	.750	.250
Burks, Ellis, S.F.	.222	11	11	9	2	2	3	1	0	0	3	0	0	1	1	0	2	0	0	1	.333	.364
Cabrera, Orlando, Mon.	.000	1	1	1	0	0	0	0	0	0	0	0	0	0	0	0	0	0	0	0	.000	.000
Caminiti, Ken, Hou.†	.000	4	4	3	0	0	0	0	0	0	0	0	0	0	1	0	0	0	0	0	.000	.250
Cangelosi, John, Col.†	.167	6	6	6	0	1	2	1	0	0	0	0	0	0	0	0	4	0	0	0	.333	.167
Canizaro, Jay, S.F.	.500	9	9	8	4	4	9	2	0	1	2	0	0	0	1	0	1	0	0	0	1.125	.556
Casey, Sean, Cin.*	.500	3	3	2	0	1	1	0	0	0	0	0	0	1	0	1	1	0	0	0	.500	.667
Castilla, Vinny, Col.	.000	2	2	2	0	0	0	0	0	0	0	0	0	0	0	0	0	0	0	0	.000	.000
Castillo, Alberto, St.L	.250	5	5	4	0	1	1	0	0	0	0	0	0	0	1	0	0	0	0	0	.250	.400
Castillo, Luis, Fla.†	.500	2	2	2	0	1	2	1	0	0	0	0	0	0	0	0	0	0	0	0	1.000	.500
Cedeno, Domingo, Phi.†	.067	15	15	15	2	1	1	0	0	0	1	0	0	0	0	0	7	0	0	0	.067	.067
Cedeno, Roger, N.Y.†	.222	19	19	18	3	4	4	0	0	0	0	0	0	0	1	0	5	3	0	0	.222	.263
Cirillo, Jeff, Mil.	.500	2	2	2	1	1	1	0	0	0	0	0	0	0	0	0	1	0	0	0	.500	.500
Clapinski, Chris, Fla.†	.231	15	15	13	1	3	4	1	0	0	0	0	0	0	2	0	3	0	0	0	.308	.333
Clemente, Edgard, Col.	.167	8	8	6	0	1	2	1	0	0	1	1	1	0	0	0	3	0	0	0	.333	.143
Colbrunn, Greg, Ari.	.375	28	28	24	5	9	15	3	0	1	8	0	2	2	0	0	4	0	0	0	.625	.393
Collier, Lou, Mil.	.250	30	30	24	5	6	13	1	0	2	6	0	1	0	5	0	6	0	0	0	.542	.367
Cora, Alex, L.A.*	.500	2	2	2	0	1	1	0	0	0	0	0	0	0	0	0	0	0	0	0	.500	.500
Counsell, Craig, Fla.-L.A.*	.176	41	40	34	3	6	6	0	0	0	1	3	0	0	3	0	5	0	0	1	.176	.243
Cox, Darron, Mon.	.000	2	2	2	0	0	0	0	0	0	0	0	0	0	0	0	0	0	0	0	.000	.000
Cromer, Tripp, L.A.	.231	15	15	13	1	3	6	0	0	1	2	0	0	0	2	0	5	0	0	1	.462	.333
Cruz, Ivan, Pit.*	.250	4	4	4	1	1	4	0	0	1	1	0	0	0	0	0	2	0	0	0	1.000	.250
Darr, Mike, S.D.*	.000	5	5	5	0	0	0	0	0	0	0	0	0	0	0	0	4	0	0	0	.000	.000
Davis, Ben, S.D.†	1.000	2	2	2	1	2	2	0	0	0	0	0	0	0	0	0	0	0	0	0	1.000	1.000
Davis, Eric, St.L	.600	5	5	5	0	3	4	1	0	0	0	0	0	0	0	0	1	0	0	0	.800	.600
Dawkins, Travis, Cin.	.000	3	3	3	0	0	0	0	0	0	0	0	0	0	0	0	2	0	0	0	.000	.000
Delgado, Wilson, S.F.†	.333	6	6	6	0	2	2	0	0	0	0	0	0	0	0	0	1	0	0	0	.333	.333
Dellucci, David, Ari.*	.278	40	39	36	4	10	12	2	0	0	6	0	0	1	2	0	11	0	0	2	.333	.333
DeRosa, Mark, Atl.	.000	6	6	6	0	0	0	0	0	0	0	0	0	0	0	0	2	0	0	0	.000	.000
Diaz, Alex, Hou.†	.190	22	22	21	2	4	8	1	0	1	3	0	0	0	1	0	8	0	1	0	.381	.227
Diaz, Edwin, Ari.	1.000	1	1	1	0	1	2	1	0	0	0	0	0	0	0	0	0	0	0	0	2.000	1.000
Doster, David, Phi.	.235	18	18	17	1	4	7	0	0	1	3	0	0	0	1	0	3	0	0	0	.412	.278
Drew, J.D., St.L*	.167	8	8	6	0	1	2	1	0	0	2	0	0	0	2	0	2	0	0	1	.333	.375
Ducey, Rob, Phi.*	.186	51	49	43	5	8	16	2	0	2	4	0	0	0	6	1	11	0	0	1	.372	.286
Dunston, Shawon, St.L-N.Y.	.195	42	41	41	1	8	9	1	0	0	3	0	0	0	0	0	12	1	1	2	.220	.195
Dunwoody, Todd, Fla.*	.250	9	9	8	1	2	3	1	0	0	1	0	0	0	1	0	2	0	0	0	.375	.333
Durazo, Erubiel, Ari.*	.375	10	10	8	2	3	6	0	0	1	4	0	0	0	2	0	2	0	0	1	.750	.500
Echevarria, Angel, Col.	.319	52	52	47	8	15	28	1	0	4	14	0	0	1	4	0	10	0	0	4	.596	.385
Estalella, Bobby, Phi.	.000	2	2	2	0	0	0	0	0	0	0	0	0	0	0	0	2	0	0	0	.000	.000
Estes, Shawn, S.F.	.000	2	2	2	0	0	0	0	0	0	0	0	0	0	0	0	1	0	0	0	.000	.000
Eusebio, Tony, Hou.	.083	14	13	12	1	1	2	1	0	0	0	0	0	1	0	0	4	0	0	0	.167	.154
Everett, Carl, Hou.†	1.000	2	2	2	0	2	3	1	0	0	4	0	0	0	0	0	0	0	0	0	1.500	1.000
Fabregas, Jorge, Fla.-Atl.*	.111	9	9	9	1	1	1	0	0	0	0	0	0	0	0	0	1	0	0	1	.111	.111
Fernandez, Alex, Fla.	.000	1	1	1	0	0	0	0	0	0	0	0	0	0	0	0	0	0	0	0	.000	.000
Fernandez, Jose, Mon.	.000	2	2	2	0	0	0	0	0	0	0	0	0	0	0	0	1	0	0	0	.000	.000
Finley, Steve, Ari.*	.000	3	3	2	0	0	0	0	0	0	0	0	0	0	1	0	1	0	0	0	.000	.333
Floyd, Cliff, Fla.*	.000	5	5	5	0	0	0	0	0	0	0	0	0	0	0	0	3	0	0	0	.000	.000
Fox, Andy, Ari.*	.143	11	11	7	0	1	1	0	0	0	1	0	0	2	2	0	3	0	0	0	.143	.455
Franco, Matt, N.Y.*	.237	88	80	59	8	14	20	3	0	1	11	0	1	0	20	3	15	0	0	2	.339	.425
Frias, Hanley, Ari.†	.429	13	13	7	4	3	5	0	1	0	1	1	0	0	5	1	2	0	0	0	.714	.667
Fullmer, Brad, Mon.*	.000	7	6	6	0	0	0	0	0	0	1	0	0	0	0	0	0	0	0	0	.000	.000
Gaetti, Gary, Chi.	.111	31	31	27	1	3	4	1	0	0	1	0	0	0	4	0	7	0	0	1	.148	.226
Gant, Ron, Phi.	.000	4	4	1	1	0	0	0	0	0	0	0	0	0	3	0	1	0	0	0	.000	.750
Garcia, Amaury, Fla.	.000	2	2	2	1	0	0	0	0	0	0	0	0	0	0	0	1	0	0	0	.000	.000
Garcia, Carlos, S.D.	1.000	1	1	1	0	1	1	0	0	0	0	0	0	0	0	0	0	0	0	0	1.000	1.000
Garcia, Freddy, Pit.-Atl.	.050	21	21	20	0	1	1	0	0	0	1	0	0	0	1	0	11	0	0	0	.050	.095
Garcia, Guillermo, Fla.	.333	3	3	3	0	1	1	0	0	0	0	0	0	0	0	0	2	0	0	0	.333	.333
Gibson, Derrick, Col.	.000	2	2	1	0	0	0	0	0	0	0	0	0	0	1	0	0	0	0	0	.000	.500
Gilkey, Bernard, Ari.	.333	43	43	39	5	13	18	2	0	1	9	0	1	0	3	1	8	1	0	3	.462	.372
Giovanola, Ed, S.D.*	.167	10	9	6	0	1	1	0	0	0	1	0	0	0	2	0	1	0	0	0	.167	.333

Player, Team	Avg.	G	TPA	AB	R	H	TB	2B	3B	HR	RBI	SH	SF	HP	BB	IBB	SO	SB	CS	GDP	Slg.	OBP
Glanville, Doug, Phi.	.000	2	2	1	1	0	0	0	0	0	0	0	0	0	1	0	1	0	0	0	.000	.500
Glavine, Tom, Atl.*	.000	1	1	0	0	0	0	0	0	0	0	1	0	0	0	0	0	0	0	0	.000	.000
Gomez, Chris, S.D.	.000	1	1	1	0	0	0	0	0	0	0	0	0	0	0	0	1	0	0	0	.000	.000
Gonzalez, Alex, Fla.	.000	1	1	1	0	0	0	0	0	0	0	0	0	0	0	0	0	0	0	0	.000	.000
Gonzalez, Luis, Ari.*	.000	1	1	1	0	0	0	0	0	0	0	0	0	0	0	0	0	0	0	0	.000	.000
Gonzalez, Wiki, S.D.	.333	13	13	12	1	4	7	0	0	1	4	0	0	1	0	2	0	0	0	.583	.385
Goodwin, Curtis, Chi.*	.133	17	17	15	0	2	3	1	0	0	1	0	0	2	0	9	0	0	0	.200	.235
Grace, Mark, Chi.*	.500	2	2	2	1	1	1	0	0	0	0	0	0	0	0	0	0	0	0	.500	.500
Greene, Charlie, Mil.	.000	1	1	1	0	0	0	0	0	0	0	0	0	0	0	0	0	0	0	.000	.000
Grissom, Marquis, Mil.	.500	9	9	8	2	4	8	1	0	1	4	0	0	0	1	1	2	0	1	1.000	.556
Grudzielanek, Mark, L.A.	.250	5	4	4	1	1	1	0	0	0	0	0	0	0	0	1	0	0	0	.250	.250
Guerrero, Vladimir, Mon.	1.000	1	1	1	1	1	3	0	1	0	1	0	0	0	0	0	0	0	0	3.000	1.000
Guerrero, Wilton, Mon.†	.340	58	58	50	7	17	22	1	2	0	7	2	0	0	6	0	4	1	2	0	.440	.411
Guillen, Jose, Pit.	.000	4	4	4	0	0	0	0	0	0	0	0	0	0	0	2	0	0	0	.000	.000
Guillen, Ozzie, Atl.*	.226	34	34	31	2	7	9	2	0	0	3	2	0	1	0	4	0	0	2	.290	.250
Gutierrez, Ricky, Hou.	.000	5	5	3	0	0	0	0	0	0	0	1	0	0	1	0	0	0	0	.000	.250
Guzman, Edwards, S.F.*	.000	8	8	7	0	0	0	0	0	0	0	0	1	0	0	4	0	0	0	.000	.000
Gwynn, Tony, S.D.*	.250	5	5	4	0	1	1	0	0	0	1	0	1	0	0	1	0	0	0	.250	.200
Haad, Yamid, Pit.	.000	1	1	1	0	0	0	0	0	0	0	0	0	0	0	0	0	0	0	.000	.000
Hamilton, Darryl, Col.-N.Y.*	.071	16	16	14	2	1	3	0	1	0	1	0	0	0	2	0	3	0	1	.214	.188
Hammonds, Jeffrey, Cin.	.158	23	22	19	1	3	6	0	0	1	4	0	0	0	3	0	9	1	0	1	.316	.273
Hansen, Dave, L.A.*	.271	69	66	48	6	13	22	4	1	1	8	0	1	1	16	0	10	0	0	2	.458	.455
Harris, Lenny, Col.-Ari.*	.382	73	70	68	6	26	32	6	0	0	12	0	0	0	2	0	3	2	0	2	.471	.400
Hayes, Charlie, S.F.	.105	23	22	19	2	2	2	0	0	0	4	0	0	0	3	0	4	0	0	1	.105	.227
Helton, Todd, Col.*	.333	6	6	6	1	2	2	0	0	0	3	0	0	0	0	0	2	0	0	0	.333	.333
Henderson, Rickey, N.Y.	.500	5	5	2	2	1	1	0	0	0	0	0	0	0	3	1	0	0	1	0	.500	.800
Hermansen, Chad, Pit.	.000	2	2	2	0	0	0	0	0	0	0	0	0	0	0	1	0	0	0	.000	.000
Hernandez, Carlos, Hou.	.000	6	6	5	1	0	0	0	0	0	0	0	1	0	0	0	0	0	0	.000	.000
Hernandez, Jose, Atl.	.333	3	3	3	1	1	1	0	0	0	0	0	0	0	0	2	0	0	0	.333	.333
Hernandez, Livan, S.F.	.000	1	1	1	0	0	0	0	0	0	0	0	0	0	0	1	0	0	0	.000	.000
Hidalgo, Richard, Hou.	1.000	2	2	2	0	2	2	0	0	0	0	0	0	0	0	0	0	0	0	1.000	1.000
Hill, Glenallen, Chi.	.235	39	39	34	6	8	20	0	0	4	8	0	0	0	5	0	9	0	0	2	.588	.333
Hollandsworth, Todd, L.A.*	.304	26	26	23	4	7	12	2	0	1	4	0	0	0	3	0	7	0	1	0	.522	.385
Houston, Tyler, Chi.*	.077	28	28	26	2	2	5	0	0	1	3	0	0	0	2	0	10	0	0	1	.192	.143
Howard, David, St.L†	.077	14	14	13	1	1	4	0	0	1	1	0	0	0	1	0	9	0	0	0	.308	.143
Howard, Thomas, St.L†	.255	52	51	47	4	12	17	2	0	1	8	0	0	0	4	0	5	0	0	1	.362	.314
Howell, Jack, Hou.*	.250	29	25	20	1	5	7	2	0	0	0	0	0	0	5	0	7	0	0	0	.350	.400
Hubbard, Trenidad, L.A.	.222	31	31	27	1	6	6	0	0	0	3	0	0	0	4	0	8	2	0	0	.222	.323
Hughes, Bobby, Mil.	.286	7	7	7	0	2	2	0	0	0	0	0	0	0	0	0	1	0	0	0	.286	.286
Hundley, Todd, L.A.*	.222	12	12	9	0	2	3	1	0	0	3	0	0	2	1	0	2	0	0	0	.333	.417
Hunter, Brian, Atl.	.261	30	29	23	0	6	8	2	0	0	3	2	1	2	1	0	4	0	0	0	.348	.333
Hyers, Tim, Fla.*	.192	32	32	26	1	5	6	1	0	0	1	0	1	0	5	0	7	0	0	0	.231	.313
Jackson, Damian, S.D.	.143	7	7	7	0	1	2	1	0	0	0	0	0	0	0	0	4	0	0	0	.286	.143
Javier, Stan, S.F.-Hou.†	.143	24	24	21	2	3	4	1	0	0	1	0	0	0	3	0	2	0	0	0	.190	.250
Jenkins, Geoff, Mil.*	.250	12	12	12	0	3	4	1	0	0	2	0	0	0	0	0	4	0	0	0	.333	.250
Jennings, Robin, Chi.*	.200	5	5	5	0	1	1	0	0	0	0	0	0	0	0	0	1	0	0	0	.200	.200
Jensen, Marcus, St.L†	.000	4	4	2	0	0	0	0	0	0	0	0	0	0	2	0	0	0	0	0	.000	.500
Johnson, Brian, Cin.	.167	14	14	12	1	2	3	1	0	0	1	0	0	0	2	0	4	0	0	0	.250	.286
Johnson, Lance, Chi.*	.333	8	8	6	2	2	2	0	0	0	0	0	0	0	2	0	1	0	0	0	.333	.500
Johnson, Russ, Hou.	.343	42	42	35	7	12	18	3	0	1	6	3	0	0	4	0	13	2	1	0	.514	.410
Jones, Terry, Mon.†	.000	1	1	1	0	0	0	0	0	0	0	0	0	0	0	0	0	0	0	0	.000	.000
Jordan, Brian, Atl.	.000	2	2	1	0	0	0	0	0	0	0	0	0	0	1	0	1	1	0	0	.000	.500
Jordan, Kevin, Phi.	.200	29	29	25	4	5	6	1	0	0	2	0	0	0	4	1	7	0	0	0	.240	.310
Joyner, Wally, S.D.*	.000	8	8	8	0	0	0	0	0	0	0	0	0	0	0	0	1	0	0	0	.000	.000
Karros, Eric, L.A.	.500	2	2	2	0	1	2	1	0	0	0	0	0	0	0	0	0	0	0	0	1.000	.500
Kelly, Mike, Col.	1.000	1	1	1	0	1	2	1	0	0	1	0	0	0	0	0	0	0	0	0	2.000	1.000
Kendall, Jason, Pit.	.000	3	3	1	1	0	0	0	0	0	0	0	0	2	1	0	1	0	0	0	.000	.667
Kennedy, Adam, St.L*	.200	6	5	5	0	1	1	0	0	0	0	0	0	0	0	0	1	0	0	0	.200	.200
Kent, Jeff, S.F.	.000	5	5	5	0	0	0	0	0	0	0	0	0	0	0	0	4	0	0	0	.000	.000
Kinkade, Mike, N.Y.	.111	11	11	9	0	1	2	1	0	0	2	0	0	1	1	0	1	0	0	0	.222	.273
Klassen, Danny, Ari.	1.000	1	1	1	0	1	1	0	0	0	0	0	0	0	0	0	0	0	0	0	1.000	1.000
Klesko, Ryan, Atl.*	.250	15	14	8	0	2	2	0	0	0	3	0	2	0	4	3	5	0	0	0	.250	.429
Knorr, Randy, Hou.	.000	3	3	3	0	0	0	0	0	0	0	0	0	0	0	0	2	0	0	0	.000	.000
Kotsay, Mark, Fla.*	.538	13	13	13	4	7	12	2	0	1	1	0	0	0	0	0	1	0	0	0	.923	.538
Laker, Tim, Pit.	.400	5	5	5	0	2	2	0	0	0	0	0	0	0	0	0	1	0	0	0	.400	.400
Lankford, Ray, St.L*	.154	15	14	13	1	2	4	2	0	0	0	0	0	0	1	0	5	0	0	0	.308	.214
Lee, Derrek, Fla.	.000	5	5	4	0	0	0	0	0	0	0	0	0	0	1	0	2	0	0	0	.000	.200
Lee, Travis, Ari.*	.222	12	12	9	2	2	2	0	0	0	1	0	0	0	3	0	3	1	0	0	.222	.417
Lewis, Mark, Cin.	.172	36	34	29	1	5	6	1	0	0	3	2	1	0	2	0	4	0	0	0	.207	.219
Leyritz, Jim, S.D.	.364	15	14	11	3	4	10	0	0	2	3	0	0	0	3	0	3	0	0	0	.909	.500
Lieberthal, Mike, Phi.	.000	4	4	4	0	0	0	0	0	0	0	0	0	0	0	0	1	0	0	0	.000	.000
Liniak, Cole, Chi.	.500	2	2	2	0	1	1	0	0	0	0	0	0	0	0	0	1	0	0	0	.500	.500
Lockhart, Keith, Atl.*	.246	74	71	61	4	15	19	1	0	1	12	0	1	0	9	0	11	1	0	2	.311	.338
LoDuca, Paul, L.A.	.500	4	4	2	1	1	1	0	0	0	0	0	0	0	1	0	0	0	0	0	.500	.667
Lombard, George, Atl.*	.000	1	1	0	0	0	0	0	0	0	0	0	0	0	1	0	0	0	0	0	.000	1.000
Long, Terrence, N.Y.*	.000	3	3	3	0	0	0	0	0	0	0	0	0	0	0	0	2	0	0	1	.000	.000
Lopez, Javy, Atl.	.200	5	5	5	1	1	4	0	0	1	2	0	0	0	0	0	1	0	0	0	.800	.200
Lopez, Luis, N.Y.†	.107	30	30	28	1	3	4	1	0	0	0	0	0	1	1	0	13	0	0	0	.143	.167
Loretta, Mark, Mil.	.000	8	8	6	0	0	0	0	0	0	0	0	0	1	1	0	0	0	0	0	.000	.250
Lovullo, Torey, Phi.†	.000	6	6	5	0	0	0	0	0	0	0	0	0	0	1	0	2	0	0	0	.000	.167
Lowell, Mike, Fla.	.133	15	15	15	1	2	5	0	0	1	3	0	0	0	0	0	2	0	0	1	.333	.133
Machado, Robert, Mon.	.500	2	2	2	1	1	2	1	0	0	0	0	0	0	0	0	1	0	0	0	1.000	.500

Player, Team	Avg.	G	TPA	AB	R	H	TB	2B	3B	HR	RBI	SH	SF	HP	BB	IBB	SO	SB	CS	GDP	Slg.	OBP
Magadan, Dave, S.D.*	.219	41	40	32	1	7	7	0	0	0	3	0	1	0	7	0	4	0	0	0	.219	.350
Magee, Wendell, Phi.	.333	10	10	9	3	3	9	0	0	2	5	0	0	0	1	0	2	0	0	1	1.000	.400
Mahomes, Pat, N.Y.	.000	1	1	1	0	0	0	0	0	0	0	0	0	0	0	0	1	0	0	0	.000	.000
Manwaring, Kirt, Col.	.333	4	4	3	0	1	1	0	0	0	0	0	0	0	1	0	0	0	0	0	.333	.500
Marrero, Eli, St.L.	.143	7	7	7	0	1	1	0	0	0	1	0	0	0	0	0	3	0	0	0	.143	.143
Martin, Al, Pit.*	.600	13	13	10	1	6	7	1	0	0	1	0	0	0	3	0	2	1	0	0	.700	.692
Martinez, Manny, Mon.	.000	9	8	7	1	0	0	0	0	0	0	0	0	0	1	0	2	0	0	0	.000	.125
Martinez, Ramon, S.F.	.133	16	16	15	0	2	2	0	0	0	0	1	0	0	0	0	1	0	0	0	.133	.133
Martinez, Sandy, Chi.*	.167	6	6	6	0	1	1	0	0	0	0	0	0	0	0	0	4	0	0	0	.167	.167
Matos, Pascual, Atl.	.000	2	2	2	0	0	0	0	0	0	0	0	0	0	0	0	1	0	0	0	.000	.000
Matthews, Gary, S.D.†	.000	8	8	6	0	0	0	0	0	0	1	0	0	0	2	0	3	0	0	0	.000	.250
Mayne, Brent, S.F.*	.389	24	24	18	2	7	9	2	0	0	4	0	1	0	5	1	5	0	0	0	.500	.500
McEwing, Joe, St.L.	.333	12	12	9	0	3	3	0	0	0	0	1	0	0	2	0	0	0	0	0	.333	.455
McGee, Willie, St.L†	.160	55	55	50	1	8	10	2	0	0	5	0	0	0	5	2	13	0	0	3	.200	.236
McGuire, Ryan, Mon.*	.154	19	18	13	1	2	4	0	1	0	2	1	0	0	4	0	4	0	0	2	.308	.353
McGwire, Mark, St.L	.000	2	2	1	0	0	0	0	0	0	0	0	0	0	1	1	1	0	0	0	.000	.500
McRae, Brian, N.Y.†	.182	13	13	11	1	2	3	1	0	0	1	0	0	0	2	0	5	0	0	0	.273	.308
Merced, Orlando, Mon.*	.286	43	41	35	5	10	18	2	0	2	10	0	1	0	5	0	3	0	0	2	.514	.366
Meyers, Chad, Chi.	1.000	1	1	1	1	1	1	0	0	0	0	0	0	0	0	0	0	0	0	0	1.000	1.000
Mieske, Matt, Hou.	.235	20	19	17	2	4	5	1	0	0	5	0	0	0	2	1	7	0	0	1	.294	.316
Millar, Kevin, Fla.	.000	9	9	8	0	0	0	0	0	0	0	0	1	0	1	0	1	0	0	0	.000	.111
Miller, Damian, Ari.	.000	1	1	1	0	0	0	0	0	0	0	0	0	0	0	0	1	0	0	0	.000	.000
Mirabelli, Doug, S.F.	.200	5	5	5	0	1	1	0	0	0	1	0	0	0	0	0	1	0	0	0	.200	.200
Mondesi, Raul, L.A.	.333	3	3	3	0	1	1	0	0	0	0	0	0	0	0	0	0	0	0	0	.333	.333
Mora, Melvin, N.Y.	.167	17	16	12	0	2	2	0	0	0	0	1	0	1	2	0	4	0	0	0	.167	.333
Morandini, Mickey, Chi.*	.158	25	25	19	3	3	3	0	0	0	2	0	0	1	5	0	6	0	0	0	.158	.360
Mordecai, Mike, Mon.	.000	10	10	7	0	0	0	0	0	0	1	1	0	0	2	0	2	0	0	0	.000	.222
Morris, Hal, Cin.*	.222	53	52	45	2	10	12	2	0	0	6	0	0	0	7	0	10	0	0	1	.267	.327
Morris, Warren, Pit.*	.000	5	5	3	1	0	0	0	0	0	0	0	0	1	1	0	1	0	0	0	.000	.400
Mouton, James, Mon.	.324	40	40	34	2	11	13	2	0	0	6	0	0	0	6	0	9	0	0	0	.382	.425
Mouton, Lyle, Mil.	.000	11	11	10	0	0	0	0	0	0	2	0	0	0	1	0	3	0	0	0	.000	.091
Mueller, Bill, S.F.†	.000	8	8	6	0	0	0	0	0	0	0	0	0	0	2	0	1	0	0	0	.000	.250
Murray, Calvin, S.F.	.143	7	7	7	0	1	2	1	0	0	2	0	0	0	0	0	3	0	0	0	.286	.143
Myers, Greg, S.D.-Atl.*	.154	16	16	13	2	2	5	0	0	1	2	0	0	0	3	0	8	0	0	0	.385	.313
Myers, Rodney, Chi.	1.000	1	1	1	0	1	2	1	0	0	0	0	0	0	0	0	0	0	0	0	2.000	1.000
Nevin, Phil, S.D.	.300	23	22	20	3	6	13	1	0	2	8	0	0	0	2	0	3	0	0	0	.650	.364
Newhan, David, S.D.*	.000	5	5	5	0	0	0	0	0	0	0	0	0	0	0	0	2	0	0	0	.000	.000
Nieves, Jose, Chi.	.000	2	2	1	0	0	0	0	0	0	0	0	0	1	0	0	0	0	0	1	.000	.000
Nilsson, David, Mil.*	.071	18	16	14	1	1	1	0	0	0	0	0	0	0	2	1	2	0	0	2	.071	.188
Nixon, Otis, Atl.†	.133	17	17	15	3	2	3	1	0	0	0	0	0	0	2	0	2	5	0	1	.200	.235
Nunez, Abraham, Pit.†	.100	10	10	10	1	1	2	1	0	0	0	0	0	0	0	0	3	0	0	0	.200	.100
Ochoa, Alex, Mil.	.270	42	42	37	2	10	11	1	0	0	5	0	0	0	5	1	11	2	0	1	.297	.357
Olerud, John, N.Y.*	.000	2	2	2	0	0	0	0	0	0	0	0	0	0	0	0	1	0	0	1	.000	.000
Oliver, Darren, St.L.	.000	5	5	4	0	0	0	0	0	0	0	0	1	0	0	0	1	0	0	0	.000	.000
Oliver, Joe, Pit.	.000	1	1	1	0	0	0	0	0	0	0	0	0	0	0	0	0	0	0	0	.000	.000
Orie, Kevin, Fla.	.091	12	12	11	1	1	2	1	0	0	1	0	1	0	0	0	4	0	0	0	.182	.083
Osik, Keith, Pit.	.267	16	16	15	1	4	6	0	1	0	4	0	0	0	1	0	4	0	0	2	.400	.313
Owens, Eric, S.D.	.154	27	27	26	1	4	5	1	0	0	3	0	0	0	1	0	3	1	0	2	.192	.185
Paquette, Craig, St.L	.400	6	6	5	0	2	2	0	0	0	1	0	0	0	1	0	1	0	0	1	.400	.500
Payton, Jay, N.Y.	.400	5	5	5	0	2	3	1	0	0	1	0	0	0	0	0	1	0	1	0	.600	.400
Pena, Angel, L.A.	.000	1	1	1	0	0	0	0	0	0	0	0	0	0	0	0	0	0	0	0	.000	.000
Perez, Eddie, Atl.	.000	6	6	6	0	0	0	0	0	0	0	0	0	0	0	0	0	0	0	0	.000	.000
Perez, Eduardo, St.L	.375	11	10	8	2	3	3	0	0	0	1	0	0	0	2	0	1	0	0	0	.375	.500
Petersen, Chris, Col.	.000	1	1	1	1	0	0	0	0	0	0	0	0	0	0	0	0	0	0	0	.000	.000
Phillips, J.R., Col.*	.250	17	17	16	3	4	12	2	0	2	3	0	0	1	0	0	6	0	0	1	.750	.294
Piazza, Mike, N.Y.	.250	4	4	4	0	1	1	0	0	0	2	0	0	0	0	0	1	0	0	0	.250	.250
Polanco, Placido, St.L	.308	14	14	13	3	4	5	1	0	0	1	0	0	0	1	0	1	0	0	0	.385	.357
Porter, Bo, Chi.	.167	6	6	6	0	1	1	0	0	0	0	0	0	0	0	0	3	0	0	0	.167	.167
Powell, Dante, Ari.	.250	4	4	4	0	1	1	0	0	0	0	0	0	0	0	0	0	0	1	0	.250	.250
Pratt, Todd, N.Y.	.208	27	25	24	3	5	5	0	0	0	0	0	0	0	1	0	10	0	0	0	.208	.240
Ramirez, Aramis, Pit.	.000	1	1	1	0	0	0	0	0	0	0	0	0	0	0	0	0	0	0	0	.000	.000
Redmond, Mike, Fla.	.000	3	3	3	0	0	0	0	0	0	0	0	0	0	0	0	0	0	0	0	.000	.000
Reed, Jeff, Col.-Chi.*	.280	29	29	25	1	7	7	0	0	0	5	0	0	0	3	0	8	0	1	1	.280	.379
Renteria, Edgar, St.L	.000	8	8	5	1	0	0	0	0	0	1	0	1	1	1	0	2	1	0	0	.000	.250
Rios, Armando, S.F.*	.333	22	22	18	2	6	12	0	0	2	3	0	0	0	4	0	6	0	0	0	.667	.455
Ritchie, Todd, Pit.	.000	1	1	1	0	0	0	0	0	0	0	0	0	0	0	0	1	0	0	0	.000	.000
Rivera, Ruben, S.D.	.111	11	11	9	1	1	1	0	0	0	1	0	0	0	2	0	2	1	0	0	.111	.273
Rodriguez, Henry, Chi.*	.400	7	6	5	2	2	3	1	0	0	2	0	0	0	1	0	2	0	0	0	.600	.500
Rolen, Scott, Phi.	1.000	1	1	1	0	1	1	0	0	0	0	0	0	0	0	0	0	0	0	0	1.000	1.000
Roskos, John, Fla.	.182	12	12	11	0	2	4	2	0	0	1	0	0	0	1	0	7	0	0	0	.364	.250
Ryan, Robert, Ari.*	.200	16	15	15	2	3	4	1	0	0	2	0	0	0	0	0	4	0	0	0	.267	.200
Sanders, Reggie, S.D.	.000	3	3	3	0	0	0	0	0	0	0	0	0	0	0	0	0	0	0	0	.000	.000
Sanford, Chance, L.A.*	.250	4	4	4	0	1	1	0	0	0	0	0	0	0	0	0	0	0	0	0	.250	.250
Santangelo, F.P., S.F.†	.167	29	29	18	4	3	3	0	0	0	1	2	0	3	6	0	4	1	1	0	.167	.444
Santiago, Benito, Chi.	.167	8	7	6	0	1	1	0	0	0	1	0	0	1	0	0	2	0	0	1	.167	.286
Sefcik, Kevin, Phi.	.311	57	57	45	8	14	22	6	1	0	5	3	0	0	9	1	9	1	0	1	.489	.426
Seguignol, Fernando, Mon.†.	.333	6	6	6	0	2	2	0	0	0	0	0	0	0	0	0	1	0	0	0	.333	.333
Servais, Scott, S.F.	.364	12	12	11	1	4	7	0	0	1	3	0	0	1	0	0	2	0	0	0	.636	.417
Sexton, Chris, Col.	.375	10	10	8	1	3	3	0	0	0	0	0	0	0	2	0	1	0	0	0	.375	.500
Sheffield, Gary, L.A.	.000	4	4	3	0	0	0	0	0	0	0	0	1	0	1	0	0	0	0	0	.000	.000
Shumpert, Terry, Col.	.313	21	21	16	5	5	7	2	0	0	1	1	0	1	3	0	3	2	0	0	.438	.450
Simon, Randall, Atl.*	.105	23	21	19	0	2	3	1	0	0	2	0	1	0	1	0	3	0	0	2	.158	.143

Player, Team	Avg.	G	TPA	AB	R	H	TB	2B	3B	HR	RBI	SH	SF	HP	BB	IBB	SO	SB	CS	GDP	Slg.	OBP
Snow, J.T., S.F.*	.000	5	5	4	0	0	0	0	0	0	0	0	0	0	1	0	1	0	0	0	.000	.200
Sosa, Juan, Col.	.500	5	5	4	2	2	2	0	0	0	0	0	0	0	1	0	1	0	0	0	.500	.600
Spiers, Bill, Hou.*	.348	24	24	23	2	8	11	1	1	0	7	0	0	0	1	0	5	2	0	0	.478	.375
Sprague, Ed, Pit.	.500	5	5	4	2	2	5	0	0	1	1	0	0	0	1	1	1	0	0	0	1.250	.600
Stinnett, Kelly, Ari.	.500	4	4	4	1	2	5	0	0	1	2	0	0	0	0	0	2	0	0	0	1.250	.500
Stowers, Chris, Mon.*	.000	1	1	1	0	0	0	0	0	0	0	0	0	0	0	0	0	0	0	0	.000	.000
Stynes, Chris, Cin.	.364	13	13	11	3	4	7	0	0	1	3	2	0	0	0	0	1	1	0	0	.636	.364
Sveum, Dale, Pit.†	.321	32	32	28	4	9	15	3	0	1	7	0	1	0	3	1	7	0	0	0	.536	.375
Sweeney, Mark, Cin.*	.355	36	35	31	6	11	20	3	0	2	7	0	0	0	4	1	9	0	0	2	.645	.429
Tatis, Fernando, St.L	.000	2	2	2	0	0	0	0	0	0	0	0	0	0	0	0	1	0	0	0	.000	.000
Taubensee, Eddie, Cin.*	.286	7	7	7	0	2	3	1	0	0	2	0	0	0	0	0	1	0	0	0	.429	.286
Thompson, Ryan, Hou.	.200	6	6	5	2	1	4	0	0	1	1	0	0	0	1	0	2	0	0	0	.800	.333
Toca, Jorge, N.Y.	.333	3	3	3	0	1	1	0	0	0	0	0	0	0	0	0	2	0	0	0	.333	.333
Tremie, Chris, Pit.	.000	1	1	1	0	0	0	0	0	0	0	0	0	0	0	0	1	0	0	0	.000	.000
Tucker, Michael, Cin.*	.318	25	24	22	3	7	10	0	0	1	3	0	0	0	2	1	6	1	0	0	.455	.375
Valentin, Jose, Mil.†	.500	6	6	6	1	3	3	0	0	0	3	0	0	0	0	0	2	0	0	0	.500	.500
Vander Wal, John, S.D.*	.231	66	63	52	5	12	16	4	0	0	12	0	1	0	10	1	14	0	1	2	.308	.349
Vaughn, Greg, Cin.	.000	3	3	2	1	0	0	0	0	0	0	0	0	0	1	0	1	0	0	0	.000	.333
Ventura, Robin, N.Y.*	.000	2	2	1	0	0	0	0	0	0	1	0	1	0	0	0	0	0	0	0	.000	.000
Veras, Quilvio, S.D.†	.000	13	13	13	0	0	0	0	0	0	0	0	0	0	0	0	6	0	0	0	.000	.000
Vidro, Jose, Mon.†	.357	15	15	14	2	5	9	1	0	1	5	0	0	0	1	0	4	0	0	0	.643	.400
Vizcaino, Jose, L.A.†	.350	24	24	20	3	7	8	1	0	0	7	2	0	0	2	0	3	0	1	0	.400	.409
Walker, Larry, Col.*	.286	15	15	14	2	4	7	0	0	1	5	0	1	0	0	0	5	0	0	1	.500	.267
Ward, Daryle, Hou.*	.320	26	26	25	2	8	15	1	0	2	4	0	0	0	1	0	8	0	0	0	.600	.346
Ward, Turner, Pit.-Ari.†	.190	23	23	21	3	4	7	0	0	1	2	0	0	0	2	0	8	0	0	1	.333	.261
Watkins, Pat, Col.	.000	7	7	6	1	0	0	0	0	0	0	0	0	0	1	0	2	0	0	0	.000	.143
Weathers, David, Mil.	.000	1	1	1	0	0	0	0	0	0	0	0	0	0	0	0	1	0	0	0	.000	.000
Wehner, John, Pit.	.400	18	18	15	4	6	10	1	0	1	2	0	0	0	3	0	3	0	0	1	.667	.500
Weiss, Walt, Atl.†	.400	7	7	5	0	2	3	1	0	0	1	0	0	1	0	1	0	0	0	0	.600	.500
White, Devon, L.A.†	.250	9	9	8	1	2	5	0	0	1	4	0	0	1	0	0	1	0	0	0	.625	.333
White, Rondell, Mon.	.000	3	3	2	0	0	0	0	0	0	0	0	0	0	1	0	1	0	0	0	.000	.333
Widger, Chris, Mon.	.167	6	6	6	1	1	2	1	0	0	0	0	0	0	0	0	2	0	0	0	.333	.167
Wilkins, Rick, L.A.*	.000	3	3	3	0	0	0	0	0	0	0	0	0	0	0	0	1	0	0	0	.000	.000
Williams, Gerald, Atl.	.227	24	24	22	4	5	8	0	0	1	3	0	0	0	2	0	4	0	0	0	.364	.292
Williams, Matt, Ari.	.000	1	1	1	0	0	0	0	0	0	0	0	0	0	0	0	0	0	0	1	.000	.000
Wilson, Preston, Fla.	.385	13	13	13	3	5	14	0	0	3	4	0	0	0	0	0	4	0	0	0	1.077	.385
Womack, Tony, Ari.*	.000	2	2	2	0	0	0	0	0	0	0	0	0	0	0	0	0	0	0	0	.000	.000
Young, Dmitri, Cin.†	.345	33	32	29	7	10	16	3	0	1	8	0	0	0	3	0	8	0	0	0	.552	.406
Young, Eric, L.A.	.000	2	2	2	0	0	0	0	0	0	0	0	0	0	0	0	0	0	0	1	.000	.000
Young, Ernie, Ari.	.000	2	2	1	0	0	0	0	0	0	0	0	0	0	1	0	1	0	0	0	.000	.500
Young, Kevin, Pit.	.500	2	2	2	1	1	4	0	0	1	4	0	0	0	0	0	1	0	0	0	2.000	.500
Zosky, Eddie, Mil.	.000	4	4	3	0	0	0	0	0	0	0	0	0	0	1	0	1	0	0	0	.000	.250

PINCH-HITTERS WITH TWO OR MORE TEAMS

Player, Team	Avg.	G	TPA	AB	R	H	TB	2B	3B	HR	RBI	SH	SF	HP	BB	IBB	SO	SB	CS	GDP	Slg.	OBP
Andrews, Shane, Mon.	.400	9	8	5	0	2	2	0	0	0	1	0	1	0	2	0	2	0	0	0	.400	.500
Andrews, Shane, Chi.	.000	1	1	0	1	0	0	0	0	0	0	0	0	0	1	0	0	0	0	0	.000	1.000
Counsell, Craig, Fla.*	.083	26	26	24	0	2	2	0	0	0	1	0	0	0	2	0	2	0	0	1	.083	.154
Counsell, Craig, L.A.*	.400	15	14	10	3	4	4	0	0	0	0	3	0	0	1	0	3	0	0	0	.400	.455
Dunston, Shawon, St.L	.174	23	23	23	0	4	4	0	0	0	2	0	0	0	0	0	6	1	1	0	.174	.174
Dunston, Shawon, N.Y.	.222	19	18	18	1	4	5	1	0	0	1	0	0	0	0	0	6	0	0	2	.278	.222
Fabregas, Jorge, Fla.*	.143	7	7	7	1	1	1	0	0	0	0	0	0	0	0	0	1	0	0	0	.143	.143
Fabregas, Jorge, Atl.*	.000	2	2	2	0	0	0	0	0	0	0	0	0	0	0	0	0	0	0	1	.000	.000
Garcia, Freddy, Pit.	.050	20	20	20	0	1	1	0	0	0	1	0	0	0	0	0	11	0	0	2	.050	.050
Garcia, Freddy, Atl.	.000	1	1	0	0	0	0	0	0	0	0	0	0	0	1	0	0	0	0	0	.000	1.000
Hamilton, Darryl, Col.*	.000	10	10	9	1	0	0	0	0	0	0	0	0	0	1	0	2	0	0	1	.000	.100
Hamilton, Darryl, N.Y.*	.200	6	6	5	1	1	3	0	1	0	1	0	0	0	1	0	1	0	0	0	.600	.333
Harris, Lenny, Col.*	.357	60	58	56	5	20	25	5	0	0	8	0	0	0	2	0	3	1	0	2	.446	.379
Harris, Lenny, Ari.*	.500	13	12	12	1	6	7	1	0	0	4	0	0	0	0	0	1	0	0	0	.583	.500
Javier, Stan, S.F.†	.150	22	22	20	2	3	4	1	0	0	1	0	0	0	2	0	2	0	0	0	.200	.227
Javier, Stan, Hou.†	.000	2	2	1	0	0	0	0	0	0	0	0	0	0	1	0	0	0	0	0	.000	.500
Myers, Greg, S.D.*	.250	11	11	8	2	2	5	0	0	1	2	0	0	0	3	0	3	0	0	0	.625	.455
Myers, Greg, Atl.*	.000	5	5	5	0	0	0	0	0	0	0	0	0	0	0	0	5	0	0	0	.000	.000
Reed, Jeff, Col.*	.267	17	17	15	0	4	4	0	0	0	2	0	0	0	2	0	4	0	1	0	.267	.353
Reed, Jeff, Chi.*	.300	12	12	10	1	3	3	0	0	0	1	0	0	1	1	0	4	0	0	1	.300	.417
Ward, Turner, Pit.†	.067	17	17	15	0	1	1	0	0	0	1	0	0	0	2	0	6	0	0	1	.067	.176
Ward, Turner, Ari.†	.500	6	6	6	3	3	6	0	0	1	2	0	0	0	0	0	2	0	0	0	1.000	.500

PITCHING

1999 N.L. STATISTICS Pitching

TEAM

Team	W	L	Pct.	ERA	G	ShO	Rel.	Sv.	IP	H	TBF	R	ER	HR	SH	SF	HB	BB	IBB	SO	WP	Bk.
Atlanta	103	59	.636	3.63	162	9	394	45	1471.0	1398	6218	661	593	142	74	41	26	507	55	1197	34	3
Arizona	100	62	.617	3.77	162	9	382	42	1467.1	1387	6233	676	615	176	46	30	49	543	48	1198	39	10
Houston	97	65	.599	3.83	162	8	339	48	1458.2	1485	6199	675	620	128	60	49	40	478	17	1204	54	0
Cincinnati	96	67	.589	3.98	163	11	381	55	1462.0	1309	6221	711	647	190	71	43	45	636	46	1081	65	3
New York	97	66	.595	4.27	163	7	439	47	1456.2	1372	6232	711	691	167	57	51	52	617	53	1172	38	4
Pittsburgh	78	83	.484	4.33	161	3	425	34	1433.1	1444	6271	782	689	160	59	45	51	633	54	1083	54	10
Los Angeles	77	85	.475	4.45	162	6	399	37	1453.0	1438	6317	787	718	192	56	34	62	594	26	1077	53	9
San Diego	74	88	.457	4.47	162	6	403	43	1420.1	1454	6147	781	705	193	70	44	35	529	48	1078	73	5
Montreal	68	94	.420	4.69	162	4	432	44	1434.1	1505	6321	853	748	152	74	50	60	572	39	1043	46	8
San Francisco	86	76	.531	4.71	162	3	450	42	1456.1	1486	6430	831	762	194	71	39	51	655	41	1076	62	7
St. Louis	75	86	.466	4.74	161	3	454	38	1445.1	1519	6427	838	761	161	85	48	63	667	38	1025	60	9
Florida	64	98	.395	4.90	162	5	453	33	1435.2	1560	6389	852	781	171	69	69	54	655	54	943	46	12
Philadelphia	77	85	.475	4.92	162	6	441	44	1438.1	1494	6348	846	787	212	69	44	58	627	24	1030	67	10
Milwaukee	74	87	.460	5.07	161	5	453	40	1442.2	1618	6477	886	813	213	60	44	51	616	42	987	64	10
Chicago	67	95	.414	5.27	162	6	441	42	1430.2	1619	6359	920	837	221	79	66	27	529	48	980	59	9
Colorado	72	90	.444	6.01	162	2	420	33	1429.0	1700	6574	1028	955	237	74	52	60	737	46	1032	70	4
Totals	1305	1286	.504	4.56	1296	93	6706	647	23134.2	23788	101163	12838	11722	2909	1074	749	784	9595	679	17206	884	112

NOTE—Totals for earned runs for several clubs do not agree with composite total for all pitchers of each respective club due to instances in which provisions of Section 10.18(i) of the Scoring Rules were applied. The following differences are to be noted: Atlanta pitchers add to 596; Pittsburgh pitchers add to 692; St. Louis pitchers add to 764; Philadelphia pitchers add to 788; Milwaukee pitchers add to 815; Colorado pitchers add to 957.

INDIVIDUAL
TOP QUALIFIERS FOR EARNED-RUN AVERAGE TITLE

Minimum 162 innings. *Throws lefthanded.

Pitcher, Team	W	L	Pct.	ERA	G	GS	CG	ShO	GF	Sv.	IP	H	TBF	R	ER	HR	SH	SF	HB	BB	IBB	SO	WP	Bk.
Johnson, Randy, Ari.*	17	9	.654	2.48	35	35	12	2	0	0	271.2	207	1079	86	75	30	4	3	9	70	3	364	4	2
Millwood, Kevin, Atl.	18	7	.720	2.68	33	33	2	0	0	0	228.0	168	906	80	68	24	9	3	4	59	2	205	5	0
Hampton, Mike, Hou.*	22	4	.846	2.90	34	34	3	2	0	0	239.0	206	979	86	77	12	10	9	5	101	2	177	9	0
Brown, Kevin, L.A.	18	9	.667	3.00	35	35	5	1	0	0	252.1	210	1018	99	84	19	7	1	7	59	1	221	4	1
Smoltz, John, Atl.	11	8	.579	3.19	29	29	1	1	0	0	186.1	168	746	70	66	14	10	5	4	40	2	156	2	0
Ritchie, Todd, Pit.	15	9	.625	3.49	28	26	2	0	0	0	172.2	169	716	79	67	17	3	2	4	54	3	107	7	0
Schilling, Curt, Phi.	15	6	.714	3.54	24	24	8	1	0	0	180.1	159	735	74	71	25	11	3	5	44	0	152	4	0
Maddux, Greg, Atl.	19	9	.679	3.57	33	33	4	0	0	0	219.1	258	940	103	87	16	15	5	4	37	8	136	1	0
Lima, Jose, Hou.	21	10	.677	3.58	35	35	3	0	0	0	246.1	256	1024	108	98	30	5	7	2	44	2	187	8	0
Daal, Omar, Ari.*	16	9	.640	3.65	32	32	2	1	0	0	214.2	188	895	92	87	21	4	7	7	79	3	148	3	2
Harnisch, Pete, Cin.	16	10	.615	3.68	33	33	2	0	0	0	198.1	190	833	86	81	25	10	6	5	57	2	120	3	0
Ashby, Andy, S.D.	14	10	.583	3.80	31	31	4	3	0	0	206.0	204	862	95	87	26	10	1	7	54	4	132	6	0
Ortiz, Russ, S.F.	18	9	.667	3.81	33	33	3	0	0	0	207.2	189	922	109	88	24	11	6	6	125	5	164	13	0
Reynolds, Shane, Hou.	16	14	.533	3.85	35	35	4	2	0	0	231.2	250	963	108	99	23	11	5	1	37	0	197	4	0
Bottenfield, Kent, St.L	18	7	.720	3.97	31	31	0	0	0	0	190.1	197	843	91	84	21	11	9	5	89	3	124	1	0

DEPARTMENTAL LEADERS: W—Hampton, Hou., 22; L—Trachsel, Chi., 18; G—Kline, Mon., 82; GS—Brown, L.A., Glavine, Atl., Johnson, Ari., Lima, Hou., Reynolds, Hou., 35; CG—Johnson, Ari., 12; ShO—Ashby, S.D., 3; GF—Nen, S.F., 64; Sv.—Urbina, Mon., 41; IP—Johnson, Ari., 271; H—Glavine, Atl., 259; TBF—Johnson, Ari., 1079; R—Kile, Col., 150; ER—Kile, Col., 140; HR—Astacio, Col., 38; SH—Glavine, Atl., 22; SF—Trachsel, Chi., 14; HB—Byrd, Phi., 17; TBB—Ortiz, S.F., 125; IBB—Glavine, Atl., 14; SO—Johnson, Ari., 364; WP—Estes, S.F., Hitchcock, S.D., 15; BK—Dreifort, L.A., Schmidt, Pit., 4.

ALL PITCHERS

*Throws lefthanded.

Pitcher, Team	W	L	Pct.	ERA	G	GS	CG	ShO	GF	Sv.	IP	H	TBF	R	ER	HR	SH	SF	HB	BB	IBB	SO	WP	Bk.
Abbott, Jim, Mil.*	2	8	.200	6.91	20	15	0	0	3	0	82.0	110	394	71	63	14	2	1	2	42	3	37	7	0
Acevedo, Juan, St.L	6	8	.429	5.89	50	12	0	0	21	4	102.1	115	457	71	67	17	6	4	6	48	3	52	5	0
Adams, Terry, Chi.	6	3	.667	4.02	52	0	0	0	38	13	65.0	60	277	33	29	9	1	3	0	28	2	57	6	0
Aguilera, Rick, Chi.	3	3	.667	3.69	44	0	0	0	25	8	46.1	44	191	22	19	6	4	2	2	10	1	32	3	0
Aldred, Scott, Phi.*	1	1	.500	3.90	29	0	0	0	5	1	32.1	33	140	15	14	1	1	5	0	15	3	19	3	0
Alfonseca, Antonio, Fla.	4	5	.444	3.24	73	0	0	0	49	21	77.2	79	325	28	28	4	3	1	4	29	6	46	1	0
Almanza, Armando, Fla.*	0	1	.000	1.72	14	0	0	0	2	0	15.2	8	64	4	3	1	1	1	1	9	2	20	0	1
Almanzar, Carlos, S.D.	0	0	.000	7.47	28	0	0	0	11	0	37.1	48	173	32	31	6	2	1	3	15	2	30	2	0
Almonte, Hector, Fla.	0	2	.000	4.20	15	0	0	0	6	0	15.0	20	67	7	7	1	1	0		6	2	8	2	0
Anderson, Brian, Ari.*	8	2	.800	4.57	31	19	2	1	4	1	130.0	144	549	69	66	18	4	0	1	28	3	75	0	2
Anderson, Jimmy, Pit.*	2	1	.667	3.99	13	4	0	0	2	0	29.1	25	127	15	13	2	2	1	1	16	2	13	4	0
Ankiel, Rick, St.L*	0	1	.000	3.27	9	5	0	0	1	1	33.0	26	137	12	12	2	1	0	1	14	0	39	2	0
Armas, Tony, Mon.	1	1	.000	1.00	1	1	0	0	0	0	6.0	8	28	4	1	0	0	1	0	2	1	2	2	0
Arnold, Jamie, L.A.	2	4	.333	5.48	36	3	0	0	18	1	69.0	81	313	50	42	6	3	0	6	34	2	26	3	0
Ashby, Andy, S.D.	14	10	.583	3.80	31	31	4	3	0	0	206.0	204	862	95	87	26	10	1	7	54	4	132	6	0
Astacio, Pedro, Col.	17	11	.607	5.04	34	34	7	0	0	0	232.0	258	1008	140	130	38	6	10	11	75	6	210	5	0
Avery, Steve, Cin.*	6	7	.462	5.16	19	19	0	0	0	0	96.0	75	426	62	55	11	3	6	1	78	0	51	4	1
Ayala, Bobby, Mon.-Chi.	1	7	.125	3.51	66	0	0	0	21	0	82.0	71	365	43	32	10	5	3	6	39	2	79	5	0
Aybar, Manny, St.L	5	4	.444	5.47	65	1	0	0	26	1	97.0	104	430	67	59	13	4	3	4	36	3	74	1	2
Barker, Richard, Chi.	0	0	.000	7.20	5	0	0	0	0	0	5.0	6	25	4	4	0	0	1	0	4	1	3	1	0
Batista, Miguel, Mon.	8	7	.533	4.88	39	17	2	1	3	1	134.2	146	606	88	73	10	8	11	7	58	2	95	6	0
Beck, Rod, Chi.	2	4	.333	7.80	31	0	0	0	19	7	30.0	41	141	26	26	5	2	0	2	13	3	13	1	0
Belinda, Stan, Cin.	3	1	.750	5.27	29	0	0	0	12	0	42.2	42	185	26	25	11	2	1	1	18	3	40	3	0

Pitcher, Team	W	L	Pct.	ERA	G	GS	CG	ShO	GF	Sv.	IP	H	TBF	R	ER	HR	SH	SF	HB	BB	IBB	SO	WP	Bk.
Beltran, Rigo, N.Y.-Col.*	1	1	.500	4.50	33	0	0	0	12	0	42.0	50	195	24	21	7	3	0	1	19	3	50	7	0
Benes, Alan, St.L	0	0	.000	0.00	2	0	0	0	2	0	2.0	2	7	0	0	0	0	0	0	0	0	2	0	0
Benes, Andy, Ari.	13	12	.520	4.81	33	32	0	0	0	0	198.1	216	886	117	106	34	6	3	4	82	3	141	10	0
Benitez, Armando, N.Y.	4	3	.571	1.85	77	0	0	0	42	22	78.0	40	312	17	16	4	0	0	0	41	4	128	2	0
Bennett, Joel, Phi.	2	1	.667	9.00	5	3	0	0	0	0	17.0	26	83	17	17	10	2	0	0	7	0	13	0	0
Bennett, Shayne, Mon.	0	1	.000	14.29	5	1	0	0	1	0	11.1	24	59	18	18	4	0	1	1	3	0	4	0	0
Benson, Kris, Pit.	11	14	.440	4.07	31	31	2	0	0	0	196.2	184	840	105	89	16	6	7	6	83	5	139	2	1
Bere, Jason, Cin.-Mil.	5	0	1.000	6.08	17	14	0	0	0	0	66.2	79	322	52	45	9	6	2	2	50	3	47	6	0
Bergman, Sean, Hou.-Atl.	5	6	.455	5.21	25	16	2	1	2	0	105.1	135	455	62	61	9	4	4	3	29	1	44	3	0
Billingsley, Brent, Fla.*	0	0	.000	16.43	8	0	0	0	3	0	7.2	11	42	14	14	3	0	1	2	10	0	3	1	0
Bochtler, Doug, L.A.	0	0	.000	5.54	12	0	0	0	4	0	13.0	11	58	8	8	3	1	1	1	6	1	7	1	0
Boehringer, Brian, S.D.	6	5	.545	3.24	33	11	0	0	8	0	94.1	97	409	38	34	10	6	4	1	35	4	64	2	0
Bohanon, Brian, Col.*	12	12	.500	6.20	33	33	3	1	0	0	197.1	236	903	146	136	30	18	3	14	92	1	120	6	0
Borbon, Pedro, L.A.*	4	3	.571	4.09	70	0	0	0	11	1	50.2	39	220	23	23	5	0	3	1	29	1	33	1	0
Bottalico, Ricky, St.L	3	7	.300	4.91	68	0	0	0	40	20	73.1	83	347	45	40	8	3	0	3	49	1	66	6	0
Bottenfield, Kent, St.L	18	7	.720	3.97	31	31	0	0	0	0	190.1	197	843	91	84	21	11	9	5	89	5	124	1	0
Bowie, Micah, Atl.-Chi.*	2	7	.222	10.24	14	11	0	0	2	0	51.0	81	265	60	58	9	3	3	2	34	2	41	4	2
Boyd, Jason, Pit.	0	0	.000	3.38	4	0	0	0	0	0	5.1	5	24	2	2	0	0	1	1	2	0	4	1	0
Brantley, Jeff, Phi.	1	2	.333	5.19	10	0	0	0	9	5	8.2	5	40	6	5	0	0	1	0	8	0	11	0	0
Brewer, Billy, Phi.*	1	1	.500	7.01	25	0	0	0	8	2	25.2	30	118	20	20	4	1	1	0	14	1	28	1	0
Brock, Chris, S.F.	6	8	.429	5.48	19	19	0	0	0	0	106.2	124	479	69	65	18	5	3	4	41	2	76	8	2
Brown, Kevin, L.A.	18	9	.667	3.00	35	35	5	1	0	0	252.1	210	1018	99	84	19	7	1	7	59	1	221	4	1
Brownson, Mark, Col.	0	2	.000	7.89	7	7	0	0	0	0	29.2	42	139	26	26	8	4	0	1	8	0	21	2	0
Burnett, A.J., Fla.	4	2	.667	3.48	7	7	0	0	0	0	41.1	37	182	23	16	3	1	3	0	25	2	33	0	0
Busby, Mike, St.L	0	1	.000	7.13	15	0	0	0	3	0	17.2	21	86	15	14	2	0	0	2	14	0	7	1	0
Byrd, Paul, Phi.	15	11	.577	4.60	32	32	1	0	0	0	199.2	205	872	119	102	34	5	6	17	70	2	106	11	3
Cabrera, Jose, Hou.	4	0	1.000	2.15	26	0	0	0	11	0	29.1	21	119	7	7	3	0	3	0	9	2	28	4	0
Carlson, Dan, Ari.	0	0	.000	9.00	2	0	0	0	1	0	4.0	5	18	4	4	0	0	0	0	3	0	3	0	0
Carlyle, Buddy, S.D.	1	3	.250	5.97	7	7	0	0	0	0	37.2	36	162	28	25	7	1	2	2	17	0	29	1	0
Cather, Mike, Atl.	1	0	1.000	10.13	4	0	0	0	2	0	2.2	5	13	3	3	2	0	0	0	1	0	0	0	0
Checo, Robinson, L.A.	2	2	.500	10.34	9	2	0	0	1	0	15.2	24	85	20	18	5	0	0	0	13	1	11	2	0
Chen, Bruce, Atl.*	2	2	.500	5.47	16	7	0	0	3	0	51.0	38	214	32	31	11	1	1	2	27	3	45	0	0
Chouinard, Bobby, Ari.	5	2	.714	2.68	32	0	0	0	9	1	40.1	31	161	16	12	3	4	4	0	12	2	23	1	0
Christiansen, Jason, Pit.*	2	3	.400	4.06	39	0	0	0	17	3	37.2	26	158	17	17	2	2	1	2	22	4	35	0	0
Clement, Matt, S.D.	10	12	.455	4.48	31	31	0	0	0	0	180.2	190	803	106	90	18	7	6	9	86	2	135	11	0
Clontz, Brad, Pit.	1	3	.250	2.74	56	0	0	0	16	2	49.1	49	223	21	15	6	2	1	3	24	5	40	2	0
Cook, Dennis, N.Y.*	10	5	.667	3.86	71	0	0	0	12	3	63.0	50	262	27	27	11	1	2	1	27	1	68	0	0
Coppinger, Rocky, Mil.	5	3	.625	3.68	29	0	0	0	10	0	36.2	35	164	16	15	5	0	1	0	23	3	39	1	0
Corbin, Archie, Fla.	0	1	.000	7.29	17	0	0	0	4	0	21.0	25	104	20	17	2	1	1	1	15	0	30	3	0
Cordova, Francisco, Pit.	8	10	.444	4.43	27	27	2	0	0	0	160.2	166	682	83	79	16	7	4	4	59	6	98	5	0
Cornelius, Reid, Fla.	1	0	1.000	3.26	5	2	0	0	0	0	19.1	16	76	7	7	1	0	0	5	1	12	1	0	
Cortes, Dave, Atl.	0	0	.000	4.91	4	0	0	0	4	0	3.2	3	18	3	2	0	0	0	0	4	2	2	0	
Creek, Doug, Chi.*	0	0	.000	10.50	3	0	0	0	2	0	6.0	6	32	7	7	1	0	1	0	8	1	6	1	0
Croushore, Rick, St.L	3	7	.300	4.14	59	0	0	0	12	3	71.2	68	329	42	33	9	7	1	3	43	4	88	9	0
Cunnane, Will, S.D.	2	1	.667	5.23	24	0	0	0	10	0	31.0	34	130	19	18	8	2	0	0	12	3	22	3	0
Daal, Omar, Ari.*	16	9	.640	3.65	32	32	2	1	0	0	214.2	188	895	92	87	21	4	7	7	79	3	148	3	2
Dale, Carl, Mil.	0	0	.000	20.25	4	0	0	0	1	0	4.0	8	27	9	9	2	0	0	0	6	0	4	0	0
D'Amico, Jeff, Mil.	0	0	.000	0.00	1	0	0	0	1	0	1.0	1	4	0	0	0	0	0	0	0	0	1	0	0
Darensbourg, Vic, Fla.*	0	1	.000	8.83	56	0	0	0	5	0	34.2	50	180	36	34	3	5	2	5	21	1	16	1	3
DeHart, Rick, Mon.*	0	0	.000	21.60	3	0	0	0	1	0	1.2	6	14	4	4	2	0	0	3	1	1	0	0	
DeJean, Mike, Col.	2	4	.333	8.41	56	0	0	0	17	0	61.0	83	288	61	57	13	3	3	2	32	8	31	3	0
De Los Santos, Valerio, Mil.*	0	1	.000	6.48	7	0	0	0	3	0	8.1	12	43	6	6	1	0	1	7	0	5	1	0	
Del Toro, Miguel, S.F.	0	0	.000	4.18	14	0	0	0	2	0	23.2	24	102	11	11	5	0	0	0	11	0	20	0	0
Dempster, Ryan, Fla.	7	8	.467	4.71	25	25	0	0	0	0	147.0	146	666	77	77	21	3	6	6	93	2	126	8	0
Dipoto, Jerry, Col.	4	5	.444	4.26	63	0	0	0	18	1	86.2	91	379	44	41	10	1	5	3	44	4	69	6	0
Dotel, Octavio, N.Y.	8	3	.727	5.38	19	14	0	0	1	0	85.1	69	368	52	51	12	3	5	6	49	1	85	3	2
Dougherty, Jim, Pit.	0	0	.000	9.00	2	0	0	0	0	0	2.0	3	12	3	2	0	0	0	0	3	0	1	0	0
Dreifort, Darren, L.A.	13	13	.500	4.79	30	29	1	1	0	0	178.2	177	773	105	95	20	8	2	7	76	2	140	9	4
Ebert, Derrin, Atl.*	0	1	.000	5.63	5	0	0	0	3	1	8.0	9	35	5	5	2	0	0	0	5	1	4	0	0
Edmondson, Brian, Fla.	5	8	.385	5.84	68	0	0	0	14	1	94.0	106	428	65	61	11	6	7	6	44	5	58	5	0
Elarton, Scott, Hou.	9	5	.643	3.48	42	15	0	0	8	1	124.0	111	524	55	48	8	7	4	4	43	0	121	3	0
Eldred, Cal, Mil.	2	8	.200	7.79	20	15	0	0	2	0	82.0	101	392	75	71	19	2	1	46	0	60	8	1	
Embree, Alan, S.F.*	3	2	.600	3.38	68	0	0	0	13	0	58.2	42	244	22	22	6	3	2	3	26	2	53	3	0
Estes, Shawn, S.F.*	11	11	.500	4.92	32	32	1	1	0	0	203.0	209	914	121	111	21	14	3	5	112	2	159	15	1
Estrada, Horacio, Mil.*	0	0	.000	7.36	4	0	0	0	2	0	7.1	10	36	6	6	4	0	0	0	4	0	5	0	0
Falteisek, Steve, Mil.	0	0	.000	7.50	10	0	0	0	3	0	12.0	18	52	10	10	3	0	1	0	3	0	5	0	0
Farnsworth, Kyle, Chi.	5	9	.357	5.05	27	21	1	1	1	0	130.0	140	579	80	73	28	6	2	3	52	1	70	7	1
Fernandez, Alex, Fla.	7	8	.467	3.38	24	24	1	0	0	0	141.0	135	590	60	53	10	3	6	4	41	1	91	2	0
Fox, Chad, Mil.	0	0	.000	10.80	6	0	0	0	2	0	6.2	11	36	8	8	1	0	1	4	1	12	1	1	
Franco, John, N.Y.*	0	2	.000	2.88	46	0	0	0	34	19	40.2	40	182	14	13	1	3	1	2	19	1	41	0	0
Franco, Matt, N.Y.	0	0	.000	13.50	2	0	0	0	1	0	1.1	3	10	2	2	1	0	0	0	3	0	2	0	0
Frascatore, John, Ari.	1	4	.200	4.09	26	0	0	0	10	0	33.0	31	136	16	15	6	1	1	1	12	4	15	0	0
Gaetti, Gary, Chi.	0	0	.000	18.00	1	0	0	0	1	0	1.0	2	6	2	2	1	0	0	1	0	1	0	0	
Gagne, Eric, L.A.	1	1	.500	2.10	5	5	0	0	0	0	30.0	18	119	8	7	3	1	0	0	15	0	30	1	0
Garcia, Mike, Pit.	1	0	1.000	1.29	7	0	0	0	2	0	7.0	2	25	1	1	1	0	0	3	0	9	0	0	
Gardner, Mark, S.F.	5	11	.313	6.47	29	21	1	0	2	0	139.0	142	613	103	100	27	6	10	8	57	2	86	3	1
Giovanola, Ed, S.D.	0	0	.000	0.00	1	0	0	0	1	0	1.1	1	7	0	0	0	0	0	0	2	0	0	0	0
Glavine, Tom, Atl.*	14	11	.560	4.12	35	35	2	0	0	0	234.0	259	1023	115	107	18	22	10	4	83	14	138	2	0
Gomes, Wayne, Phi.	5	5	.500	4.26	73	0	0	0	58	19	74.0	70	341	38	35	5	5	3	2	56	2	58	3	1
Grace, Mike, Phi.	1	4	.200	7.69	27	5	0	1	0	0	55.0	80	273	48	47	5	3	3	6	30	0	28	4	0
Grahe, Joe, Phi.	1	4	.200	3.86	13	5	0	0	4	0	32.2	40	153	16	14	1	0	3	3	17	0	16	2	1
Graves, Danny, Cin.	8	7	.533	3.08	75	0	0	0	56	27	111.0	90	454	42	38	10	5	2	2	49	4	69	3	0

Pitcher, Team	W	L	Pct.	ERA	G	GS	CG	ShO	GF	Sv.	IP	H	TBF	R	ER	HR	SH	SF	HB	BB	IBB	SO	WP	Bk.
Greene, Rick, Cin.	0	0	.000	4.76	1	0	0	0	0	0	5.2	7	25	4	3	2	0	0	0	1	0	3	0	0
Guthrie, Mark, Chi.*	0	2	.000	3.65	11	0	0	0	0	0	12.1	7	47	6	5	1	2	0	0	4	2	9	1	0
Guzman, Domingo, S.D.	0	1	.000	21.60	7	0	0	0	2	0	5.0	13	33	12	12	1	2	0	0	3	2	4	0	0
Guzman, Juan, Cin.	6	3	.667	3.03	12	12	1	0	0	0	77.1	70	320	33	26	10	3	1	1	21	3	60	5	0
Hackman, Luther, Col.	1	2	.333	10.69	5	3	0	0	0	0	16.0	26	84	19	19	5	2	0	0	12	0	10	0	0
Hampton, Mike, Hou.*	22	4	.846	2.90	34	34	3	2	0	0	239.0	206	979	86	77	12	10	9	5	101	2	177	9	0
Hansell, Greg, Pit.	1	3	.250	3.89	33	0	0	0	9	0	39.1	42	168	20	17	5	3	1	3	11	3	34	2	0
Harnisch, Pete, Cin.	16	10	.615	3.68	33	33	2	2	0	0	198.1	190	833	86	81	25	10	6	5	57	2	120	3	0
Harris, Reggie, Mil.	0	0	.000	3.00	8	0	0	0	2	0	12.0	8	53	4	4	1	0	1	2	7	0	11	2	0
Heiserman, Rick, St.L	0	0	.000	8.31	3	0	0	0	0	0	4.1	8	24	4	4	2	0	0	0	4	0	4	2	0
Henry, Doug, Hou.	2	3	.400	4.65	35	0	0	0	17	2	40.2	45	188	24	21	8	1	0	3	24	0	36	0	0
Heredia, Felix, Chi.*	3	1	.750	4.85	69	0	0	0	15	1	52.0	56	237	35	28	7	1	4	1	25	2	50	2	0
Herges, Matt, L.A.	0	2	.000	4.07	17	0	0	0	9	0	24.1	24	104	13	11	5	1	0	1	8	0	18	0	0
Hermanson, Dustin, Mon.	9	14	.391	4.20	34	34	0	0	0	0	216.1	225	928	110	101	20	16	7	7	69	4	145	4	1
Hernandez, Livan, Fla.-S.F.	8	12	.400	4.64	30	30	2	0	0	0	199.2	227	886	110	103	23	7	6	2	76	5	144	2	2
Hershiser, Orel, N.Y.	13	12	.520	4.58	32	32	0	0	0	0	179.0	175	776	92	91	14	6	8	11	77	2	89	6	0
Hitchcock, Sterling, S.D.*	12	14	.462	4.11	33	33	1	0	0	0	205.2	202	892	99	94	29	9	6	5	76	6	194	15	2
Hoffman, Trevor, S.D.	2	3	.400	2.14	64	0	0	0	54	40	67.1	48	263	23	16	5	1	3	0	15	2	73	4	0
Holmes, Darren, Ari.	4	3	.571	3.70	44	0	0	0	9	0	48.2	50	219	21	20	3	2	0	1	25	8	35	0	2
Holt, Chris, Hou.	5	13	.278	4.66	32	26	0	0	2	1	164.0	193	720	92	85	12	9	8	8	57	1	115	5	0
Hudek, John, Cin.-Atl.	0	2	.000	7.64	17	0	0	0	12	0	17.2	25	93	17	15	2	0	1	1	14	0	18	0	0
Isringhausen, Jason, N.Y.	1	3	.250	6.41	13	5	0	0	2	1	39.1	43	179	29	28	7	0	1	2	22	2	31	2	0
Jimenez, Jose, St.L	5	14	.263	5.85	29	28	2	2	0	0	163.0	173	727	114	106	16	10	6	11	71	2	113	10	1
Johnson, Mike, Mon.	0	0	.000	8.64	3	1	0	0	0	0	8.1	12	44	8	8	2	0	0	0	7	1	6	2	0
Johnson, Randy, Ari.*	17	9	.654	2.48	35	35	12	2	0	0	271.2	207	1079	86	75	30	4	3	9	70	3	364	4	2
Johnstone, John, S.F.	4	6	.400	2.60	62	0	0	0	11	3	65.2	48	262	24	19	8	4	0	1	20	5	56	2	1
Jones, Bobby J., N.Y.	3	3	.500	5.61	12	9	0	0	0	0	59.1	69	253	37	37	3	3	3	2	11	0	31	0	0
Jones, Bobby M., Col.*	6	10	.375	6.33	30	20	0	0	1	0	112.1	132	546	91	79	24	7	4	6	77	0	74	4	0
Judd, Mike, L.A.	3	1	.750	5.46	7	4	0	0	0	0	28.0	30	120	17	17	4	0	0	1	12	0	22	3	0
Karchner, Matt, Chi.	1	0	1.000	2.50	16	0	0	0	2	0	18.0	16	80	5	5	3	1	0	2	9	0	9	1	0
Karl, Scott, Mil.*	11	11	.500	4.78	33	33	0	0	0	0	197.2	246	885	121	105	21	12	7	8	69	4	74	4	2
Kile, Darryl, Col.	8	13	.381	6.61	32	32	1	0	0	0	190.2	225	888	150	140	33	9	9	6	109	5	116	13	1
Kim, Byung-Hyun, Ari.	1	2	.333	4.61	25	0	0	0	10	1	27.1	20	121	15	14	2	1	0	5	20	2	31	4	1
King, Curtis, St.L	0	0	.000	18.00	2	0	0	0	1	0	1.0	3	6	2	2	0	0	0	0	0	0	1	0	1
King, Ray, Chi.*	0	0	.000	5.91	10	0	0	0	0	0	10.2	11	50	8	7	2	1	0	1	10	0	5	1	0
Kline, Steve, Mon.*	7	4	.636	3.75	82	0	0	0	18	0	69.2	56	297	32	29	8	3	1	3	33	6	69	2	0
Kubenka, Jeff, L.A.*	0	1	.000	11.74	6	0	0	0	2	0	7.2	13	42	12	10	1	2	1	0	4	0	2	0	0
Lee, David, Col.	3	2	.600	3.67	36	0	0	0	11	0	49.0	43	212	21	20	4	3	2	4	29	1	38	3	1
Leiter, Al, N.Y.*	13	12	.520	4.23	32	32	1	1	0	0	213.0	209	923	107	100	19	13	10	9	93	8	162	4	1
Leskanic, Curtis, Col.	6	2	.750	5.08	63	0	0	0	5	0	85.0	87	382	54	48	7	5	3	5	49	4	77	5	0
Lieber, Jon, Chi.	10	11	.476	4.07	31	31	3	1	0	0	203.1	226	875	107	92	28	7	11	1	46	6	186	2	2
Lilly, Ted, Mon.*	0	1	.000	7.61	9	3	0	0	1	0	23.2	30	110	20	20	7	0	1	3	9	0	28	1	0
Lima, Jose, Hou.	21	10	.677	3.58	35	35	3	0	0	0	246.1	256	1024	108	98	30	5	7	2	44	2	187	8	0
Loewer, Carlton, Phi.	2	6	.250	5.12	20	13	2	1	2	0	89.2	100	385	54	51	9	5	6	0	26	0	48	3	0
Loiselle, Rich, Pit.	3	2	.600	5.28	13	0	0	0	6	0	15.1	16	69	9	9	2	1	0	2	9	2	14	1	0
Looper, Braden, Fla.	3	3	.500	3.80	72	0	0	0	22	0	83.0	96	370	43	35	7	5	5	1	31	6	50	2	2
Lorraine, Andrew, Chi.*	2	5	.286	5.55	11	11	2	1	0	0	61.2	71	272	42	38	9	6	2	0	22	3	40	3	0
Luebbers, Larry, St.L	3	3	.500	5.12	8	8	1	0	0	0	45.2	46	199	27	26	8	4	0	3	16	0	16	1	1
Maddux, Greg, Atl.	19	9	.679	3.57	33	33	4	0	0	0	219.1	258	940	103	87	16	15	5	4	37	8	136	1	0
Maddux, Mike, Mon.-L.A.	1	1	.500	3.77	53	0	0	0	21	0	59.2	63	260	26	25	6	2	2	5	22	2	45	1	0
Mahomes, Pat, N.Y.	8	0	1.000	3.68	39	0	0	0	12	0	63.2	44	265	26	26	7	1	2	2	37	5	51	2	0
Mantei, Matt, Fla.-Ari.	1	3	.250	2.76	65	0	0	0	60	32	65.1	44	284	21	20	5	1	1	5	44	1	99	2	0
Manzanillo, Josias, N.Y.	0	0	.000	5.79	12	0	0	0	1	0	18.2	19	80	12	12	5	1	1	2	4	1	25	0	0
Masaoka, Onan, L.A.*	2	4	.333	4.32	54	0	0	0	12	1	66.2	55	300	33	32	8	1	2	2	47	3	61	3	0
McCurry, Jeff, Hou.	0	1	.000	15.75	5	0	0	0	1	0	4.0	11	25	8	7	1	0	0	0	2	0	3	0	0
McElroy, Chuck, Col.-N.Y.*	3	1	.750	5.50	56	0	0	0	19	0	54.0	60	251	34	33	9	1	3	1	36	4	44	5	0
McGlinchy, Kevin, Atl.	7	3	.700	2.82	64	0	0	0	21	0	70.1	66	298	25	22	6	4	4	1	30	7	67	1	0
McMichael, Greg, N.Y.	1	1	.500	4.82	19	0	0	0	4	0	18.2	20	84	10	10	3	1	1	0	8	3	18	4	0
McNichol, Brian, Chi.*	0	2	.000	6.75	4	2	0	0	1	0	10.2	15	54	8	8	4	0	1	1	7	0	12	0	0
Meadows, Brian, Fla.	11	15	.423	5.60	31	31	0	0	0	0	178.1	214	795	117	111	31	16	8	5	57	5	72	4	1
Medina, Rafael, Fla.	1	1	.500	5.79	20	0	0	0	4	0	23.1	20	110	15	15	3	1	0	1	20	2	16	2	1
Mercker, Kent, St.L*	6	5	.545	5.12	25	18	0	0	2	0	103.2	125	476	73	59	16	8	3	2	51	3	64	3	1
Miceli, Dan, S.D.	4	5	.444	4.46	66	0	0	0	28	2	68.2	67	296	39	34	7	4	2	2	36	5	59	2	0
Miller, Kurt, Chi.	0	0	.000	18.00	4	0	0	0	1	0	3.0	6	17	6	6	1	1	0	0	3	0	1	0	0
Miller, Trever, Hou.*	3	2	.600	5.07	47	0	0	0	11	1	49.2	58	232	29	28	6	2	2	5	29	1	37	4	0
Miller, Wade, Hou.	0	1	.000	9.58	5	1	0	0	2	0	10.1	17	52	11	11	4	0	0	0	5	0	8	0	0
Mills, Alan, L.A.	3	4	.429	3.73	68	0	0	0	18	0	72.1	70	322	33	30	10	3	4	4	43	4	49	3	0
Millwood, Kevin, Atl.	18	7	.720	2.68	33	33	2	0	0	0	228.0	168	906	80	68	24	9	3	4	59	2	205	5	0
Mlicki, Dave, L.A.	0	1	.000	4.91	2	0	0	0	0	0	7.1	10	33	4	4	1	0	0	0	2	0	1	1	0
Mohler, Mike, St.L*	1	1	.500	4.38	48	0	0	0	16	1	49.1	47	211	26	24	3	1	1	1	23	2	31	1	0
Montgomery, Steve, Phi.	1	5	.167	3.34	53	0	0	0	21	3	64.2	54	268	25	24	10	1	0	0	31	3	55	4	0
Mota, Guillermo, Mon.	2	4	.333	2.93	51	0	0	0	18	0	55.1	54	243	24	18	5	3	3	2	25	3	27	1	1
Mulholland, Terry, Chi.-Atl.*	10	8	.556	4.39	42	24	0	0	7	1	170.1	201	736	95	83	21	9	4	1	45	6	83	3	0
Murray, Dan, N.Y.	0	0	.000	13.50	1	0	0	0	1	0	2.0	4	12	3	3	0	0	1	0	2	0	1	1	0
Murray, Heath, S.D.*	0	4	.000	5.76	22	8	0	0	1	0	50.0	60	234	33	32	7	3	2	1	26	4	25	1	1
Myers, Mike, Mil.*	2	1	.667	5.23	71	0	0	0	14	0	41.1	46	179	24	24	7	5	0	3	13	1	35	1	0
Myers, Rodney, Chi.	3	1	.750	4.38	46	0	0	0	5	0	63.2	71	278	34	31	10	4	2	1	25	2	41	2	0
Nathan, Joe, S.F.	7	4	.636	4.18	19	14	0	0	2	1	90.1	84	395	45	42	17	2	0	1	46	0	54	2	0
Neagle, Denny, Cin.*	9	5	.643	4.27	20	19	0	0	0	0	111.2	95	467	54	53	23	3	5	4	40	3	76	4	0
Nen, Robb, S.F.	3	8	.273	3.98	72	0	0	0	64	37	72.1	79	320	36	32	8	5	1	0	27	3	77	5	0
Nomo, Hideo, Mil.	12	8	.600	4.54	28	28	0	0	0	0	176.1	173	767	96	89	27	5	5	3	78	2	161	10	1
Nunez, Vladimir, Ari.-Fla.	7	10	.412	4.06	44	12	0	0	12	1	108.2	95	463	63	49	11	7	6	4	54	6	86	8	1

Pitcher, Team	W	L	Pct.	ERA	G	GS	CG	ShO	GF	Sv.	IP	H	TBF	R	ER	HR	SH	SF	HB	BB	IBB	SO	WP	Bk.
Ogea, Chad, Phi.	6	12	.333	5.63	36	28	0	0	3	0	168.0	192	746	110	105	36	10	4	4	61	1	77	5	2
Ojala, Kirt, Fla.*	0	1	.000	14.34	8	1	0	0	2	0	10.2	21	56	17	17	1	0	2	0	6	0	5	0	0
Oliver, Darren, St.L*	9	9	.500	4.26	30	30	2	1	0	0	196.1	197	842	96	93	16	11	4	11	74	4	119	6	2
Olson, Gregg, Ari.	9	4	.692	3.71	61	0	0	0	36	14	60.2	54	257	28	25	9	1	2	2	25	2	45	1	0
Ortiz, Russ, S.F.	18	9	.667	3.81	33	33	3	0	0	0	207.2	189	922	109	88	24	11	6	6	125	5	164	13	0
Osborne, Donovan, St.L*	1	3	.250	5.52	6	6	0	0	0	0	29.1	34	130	18	18	4	3	1	2	10	0	21	1	0
Osik, Keith, Pit.	0	0	.000	36.00	1	0	0	0	1	0	1.0	2	8	4	4	0	0	0	1	2	0	1	0	0
Osuna, Antonio, L.A.	0	0	.000	7.71	5	0	0	0	1	0	4.2	4	22	5	4	0	0	0	1	3	0	5	1	0
Padilla, Vicente, Ari.	0	1	.000	16.88	5	0	0	0	2	0	2.2	7	19	5	5	1	1	0	0	3	0	0	0	0
Painter, Lance, St.L*	4	5	.444	4.83	56	4	0	0	10	1	63.1	63	272	37	34	6	4	3	2	25	1	56	4	0
Park, Chan Ho, L.A.	13	11	.542	5.23	33	33	0	0	0	0	194.1	208	883	120	113	31	10	5	14	100	4	174	11	1
Parris, Steve, Cin.	11	4	.733	3.50	22	21	2	1	0	0	128.2	124	545	59	50	16	7	3	6	52	4	86	3	0
Patrick, Bronswell, S.F.	1	0	1.000	10.13	6	0	0	0	2	1	5.1	9	28	7	6	1	0	1	0	3	0	6	0	0
Pavano, Carl, Mon.	6	8	.429	5.63	19	18	1	1	0	0	104.0	117	457	66	65	8	5	2	4	35	1	70	1	3
Perez, Carlos, L.A.*	2	10	.167	7.43	17	16	0	0	0	0	89.2	116	420	77	74	23	6	3	6	39	1	40	2	3
Perez, Odalis, Atl.*	4	6	.400	6.00	18	17	0	0	0	0	93.0	100	424	65	62	12	3	4	1	53	2	82	5	3
Perez, Yorkis, Phi.*	3	1	.750	3.94	35	0	0	0	4	0	32.0	29	137	15	14	4	2	1	0	15	1	26	5	0
Person, Robert, Phi.	10	5	.667	4.27	31	22	0	0	1	0	137.0	130	599	72	65	23	7	4	2	70	1	127	3	1
Peters, Chris, Pit.*	5	4	.556	6.59	19	11	0	0	2	0	71.0	98	343	59	52	11	4	4	4	27	0	46	2	1
Peterson, Kyle, Mil.	4	7	.364	4.56	17	12	0	0	2	0	77.0	87	341	46	39	3	4	3	4	25	2	34	1	0
Phillips, Jason, Pit.	0	0	.000	11.57	6	0	0	0	0	0	7.0	11	37	9	9	2	2	1	0	6	1	7	2	0
Pittsley, Jim, Mil.	0	1	.000	4.82	15	0	0	0	5	0	18.2	20	85	12	10	3	0	1	1	10	0	13	2	0
Plesac, Dan, Ari.*	2	1	.667	3.32	34	0	0	0	6	1	21.2	22	94	9	8	3	1	0	0	8	1	27	1	0
Plunk, Eric, Mil.	4	4	.500	5.02	68	0	0	0	13	0	75.1	71	338	44	42	15	5	2	5	43	5	63	5	1
Politte, Cliff, Phi.	1	0	1.000	7.13	13	0	0	0	0	0	17.2	19	85	14	14	2	1	0	0	15	0	15	2	0
Poole, Jim, Phi.*	1	1	.500	4.33	51	0	0	0	12	1	35.1	48	166	20	17	3	1	0	3	15	1	22	4	1
Porzio, Mike, Col.*	0	0	.000	8.59	16	0	0	0	3	0	14.2	21	75	14	14	5	1	0	0	10	0	10	0	0
Powell, Jay, Hou.	5	4	.556	4.32	67	0	0	0	26	4	75.0	82	341	38	36	3	5	2	3	40	4	77	5	0
Powell, Jeremy, Mon.	4	8	.333	4.73	17	17	0	0	0	0	97.0	113	438	60	51	14	9	3	8	44	2	44	4	1
Pulsipher, Bill, Mil.*	5	6	.455	5.98	19	16	0	0	1	0	87.1	100	398	65	58	19	6	4	2	36	2	42	4	0
Radinsky, Scott, St.L*	2	1	.667	4.88	43	0	0	0	13	3	27.2	27	126	16	15	2	2	5	1	18	3	17	3	1
Rain, Steve, Chi.	0	1	.000	9.20	16	0	0	0	5	0	14.2	28	79	17	15	1	3	1	1	7	0	12	1	0
Ramirez, Hector, Mil.	1	2	.333	3.43	15	0	0	0	5	0	21.0	19	88	8	8	1	0	0	0	11	2	9	0	1
Ramirez, Roberto, Col.*	1	5	.167	8.26	32	4	0	0	6	1	40.1	68	209	42	37	8	2	0	0	22	2	32	4	0
Reed, Rick, N.Y.	11	5	.688	4.58	26	26	1	1	0	0	149.1	163	637	77	76	23	6	3	1	47	2	104	1	0
Remlinger, Mike, Atl.*	10	1	.909	2.37	73	0	0	0	14	0	83.2	66	346	24	22	9	2	1	1	35	5	81	5	0
Reyes, Carlos, S.D.	2	4	.333	3.72	65	0	0	0	23	1	77.1	76	331	38	32	11	5	3	0	24	4	57	7	1
Reyes, Dennys, Cin.*	2	2	.500	3.79	65	1	0	0	12	2	61.2	53	277	30	26	5	4	3	3	39	1	72	5	1
Reyes, Al, Mil.	2	0	1.000	4.25	26	0	0	0	6	0	36.0	27	161	17	17	5	1	1	3	25	1	39	2	0
Reynolds, Shane, Hou.	16	14	.533	3.85	35	35	4	2	0	0	231.2	250	963	108	99	23	11	5	1	37	0	197	4	0
Reynoso, Armando, Ari.	10	6	.625	4.37	31	27	0	0	1	0	167.0	178	730	90	81	20	6	6	7	59	7	79	7	1
Ritchie, Todd, Pit.	15	9	.625	3.49	28	26	2	0	0	0	172.2	169	716	79	67	17	3	2	4	54	3	107	7	0
Rivera, Roberto, S.D.*	1	2	.333	3.86	12	0	0	0	3	0	7.0	6	30	4	3	1	1	1	0	3	0	3	1	0
Rocker, John, Atl.*	4	5	.444	2.49	74	0	0	0	61	38	72.1	47	301	24	20	5	2	0	1	37	4	104	7	0
Rodriguez, Felix, S.F.	2	3	.400	3.80	47	0	0	0	26	0	66.1	67	292	32	28	6	2	3	2	29	2	55	2	0
Rodriguez, Rich, S.F.*	3	0	1.000	5.24	62	0	0	0	8	0	56.2	60	255	33	33	8	5	2	1	28	5	44	1	0
Rogers, Kenny, N.Y.*	5	1	.833	4.03	12	12	2	1	0	0	76.0	71	317	35	34	8	3	1	4	28	1	58	1	0
Rojas, Mel, L.A.-Mon.	0	0	.000	14.09	8	0	0	0	3	0	7.2	10	40	12	12	3	0	1	2	5	1	4	1	0
Roque, Rafael, Mil.*	1	6	.143	5.34	43	9	0	0	7	1	84.1	96	386	52	50	16	1	3	4	42	1	66	4	1
Rueter, Kirk, S.F.*	15	10	.600	5.41	33	33	1	0	0	0	184.2	219	804	118	111	28	6	4	2	55	2	94	2	0
Rusch, Glendon, N.Y.*	0	0	.000	0.00	1	0	0	0	1	0	1.0	1	3	0	0	0	0	0	0	0	0	0	0	0
Ryan, Ken, Phi.	1	2	.333	6.32	15	0	0	0	5	0	15.2	16	71	11	11	2	0	0	0	11	2	9	1	0
Ryan, B.J., Cin.*	0	0	.000	4.50	1	0	0	0	1	0	2.0	4	9	1	1	0	0	0	0	1	0	1	0	0
Sabel, Erik, Ari.	0	0	.000	6.52	7	0	0	0	1	0	9.2	12	48	7	7	1	0	0	2	6	2	6	1	0
Sanchez, Jesus, Fla.*	5	7	.417	6.01	59	10	0	0	8	0	76.1	84	362	53	51	16	2	7	4	60	11	62	5	2
Sanders, Scott, Chi.	4	7	.364	5.52	67	6	0	0	16	2	104.1	112	469	69	64	19	8	3	0	53	8	89	5	1
Sauerbeck, Scott, Pit.*	4	1	.800	2.00	65	0	0	0	16	2	67.2	53	287	19	15	6	4	0	4	38	5	55	3	0
Schilling, Curt, Phi.	15	6	.714	3.54	24	24	8	1	0	0	180.1	159	735	74	71	25	11	3	5	44	0	152	4	0
Schmidt, Jason, Pit.	13	11	.542	4.19	33	33	2	0	0	0	212.2	219	937	110	99	24	7	7	3	85	4	148	6	4
Schourek, Pete, Pit.*	4	7	.364	5.34	30	17	0	0	2	0	113.0	128	511	75	67	20	3	8	5	49	5	94	0	0
Schrenk, Steve, Phi.	1	3	.250	4.29	32	2	0	0	8	1	50.1	41	209	24	24	6	3	1	7	14	4	36	2	0
Seanez, Rudy, Atl.	6	1	.857	3.35	56	0	0	0	13	0	53.2	47	225	21	20	3	1	2	1	21	1	41	3	0
Serafini, Dan, Chi.*	3	2	.600	6.93	42	4	0	0	8	1	62.1	86	302	51	48	9	8	3	1	32	3	17	3	0
Shaw, Jeff, L.A.	2	4	.333	2.78	64	0	0	0	56	34	68.0	64	284	25	21	6	1	2	1	15	1	43	1	0
Shumaker, Anthony, Phi.*	0	3	.000	5.96	8	4	0	0	2	0	22.2	23	105	17	15	3	2	0	1	14	0	17	1	1
Silva, Jose, Pit.	2	8	.200	5.73	34	12	0	0	9	4	97.1	108	433	70	62	10	3	3	3	39	0	77	4	3
Slocumb, Heathcliff, St.L	3	2	.600	2.36	40	0	0	0	12	2	53.1	49	238	16	14	3	4	1	1	30	5	48	3	0
Slusarski, Joe, Hou.	0	0	.000	0.00	3	0	0	0	1	0	3.2	1	15	0	0	0	0	0	3	1	3	0	0
Smart, J.D., Mon.	0	1	.000	5.02	29	0	0	0	6	0	52.0	56	223	30	29	4	2	1	0	17	0	21	0	0
Smith, Dan, Mon.*	4	9	.308	6.02	20	17	0	0	0	0	89.2	104	407	64	60	12	7	2	4	39	0	72	3	0
Smoltz, John, Atl.	11	8	.579	3.19	29	29	1	1	0	0	186.1	168	746	70	66	14	10	5	4	40	2	156	2	0
Sodowsky, Clint, St.L	0	1	.000	15.63	3	1	0	0	0	0	6.1	15	39	11	11	1	0	0	0	6	0	2	0	0
Speier, Justin, Atl.	0	0	.000	5.65	19	0	0	0	8	0	28.2	28	127	18	18	8	0	1	0	13	1	22	0	0
Spencer, Stan, S.D.	0	7	.000	9.16	9	8	0	0	1	0	38.1	56	183	44	39	11	4	0	1	11	1	36	1	1
Spoljaric, Paul, Phi.*	0	3	.000	15.09	5	3	0	0	1	0	11.1	23	64	24	19	1	1	1	1	7	0	10	0	0
Spradlin, Jerry, S.F.	3	1	.750	4.19	59	0	0	0	14	0	58.0	59	268	31	27	4	1	0	10	29	6	52	2	0
Springer, Dennis, Fla.	6	16	.273	4.86	38	29	3	2	3	1	196.1	231	855	121	106	23	12	10	7	64	4	83	2	0
Springer, Russ, Atl.	1	2	.667	3.42	49	0	0	0	8	1	47.1	31	194	20	18	5	0	2	2	22	2	49	0	0
Stephenson, Garrett, St.L	6	3	.667	4.22	18	12	0	0	1	0	85.1	90	371	43	40	11	5	5	1	29	1	59	0	0
Stottlemyre, Todd, Ari.	6	3	.667	4.09	17	17	0	0	0	0	101.1	106	446	51	46	12	3	1	6	40	1	74	2	0
Strickland, Scott, Mon.	0	1	.000	4.50	17	0	0	0	5	0	18.0	15	78	10	9	3	2	0	0	11	0	23	0	0
Stull, Everett, Atl.	0	0	.000	13.50	1	0	0	0	0	0	0.2	2	7	3	1	0	0	1	0	2	0	0	0	0

Pitcher, Team	W	L	Pct.	ERA	G	GS	CG	ShO	GF	Sv.	IP	H	TBF	R	ER	HR	SH	SF	HB	BB	IBB	SO	WP	Bk.
Sullivan, Scott, Cin.	5	4	.556	3.01	79	0	0	0	16	3	113.2	88	470	41	38	10	4	4	8	47	4	78	6	1
Swindell, Greg, Ari.*	4	0	1.000	2.51	63	0	0	0	15	1	64.2	54	261	19	18	8	4	0	1	21	1	51	0	0
Tam, Jeff, N.Y.	0	0	.000	3.18	9	0	0	0	3	0	11.1	6	43	4	4	3	0	0	0	3	0	8	0	0
Tapani, Kevin, Chi.	6	12	.333	4.83	23	23	1	0	0	0	136.0	151	591	81	73	12	8	7	4	33	2	73	3	0
Tavarez, Julian, S.F.	2	0	1.000	5.93	47	0	0	0	12	0	54.2	65	258	38	36	7	3	2	8	25	3	33	4	1
Taylor, Billy, N.Y.	0	1	.000	8.10	18	0	0	0	5	0	13.1	20	68	12	12	2	1	0	0	9	5	14	0	0
Tejera, Michael, Fla.*	0	0	.000	11.37	3	1	0	0	1	0	6.1	10	31	8	8	1	0	0	0	5	0	7	0	0
Telemaco, Amaury, Ari.-Phi.	4	0	1.000	5.77	49	0	0	0	10	0	53.0	52	234	34	34	10	4	1	2	26	4	43	5	0
Telford, Anthony, Mon.	5	4	.556	3.94	79	0	0	0	21	2	96.0	112	429	52	42	3	3	5	3	38	3	69	3	1
Thompson, Mark, St.L.	1	3	.250	2.76	5	5	0	0	0	0	29.1	26	130	12	9	1	3	0	2	17	1	22	1	0
Thomson, John, Col.	1	10	.091	8.04	14	13	1	0	1	0	62.2	85	305	62	56	11	4	2	1	36	1	34	2	0
Thurman, Mike, Mon.	7	11	.389	4.05	29	27	0	0	1	0	146.2	140	627	84	66	17	8	3	7	52	4	85	4	1
Tomko, Brett, Cin.	5	7	.417	4.92	33	26	1	0	1	0	172.0	175	744	103	94	31	9	5	4	60	10	132	8	0
Trachsel, Steve, Chi.	8	18	.308	5.56	34	34	4	0	0	0	205.2	226	894	133	127	32	6	14	3	64	4	149	8	3
Urbina, Ugueth, Mon.	6	6	.500	3.69	71	0	0	0	62	41	75.2	59	323	35	31	6	1	2	0	36	6	100	6	0
Valdes, Ismael, L.A.	9	14	.391	3.98	32	32	2	1	0	0	203.1	213	871	97	90	32	9	8	6	58	2	143	6	0
Vazquez, Javier, Mon.	9	8	.529	5.00	26	26	3	1	0	0	154.2	154	667	98	86	20	3	3	4	52	4	113	2	0
Veres, Dave, Col.	4	8	.333	5.14	73	0	0	0	63	31	77.0	88	349	46	44	14	5	2	2	37	7	71	8	1
Villone, Ron, Cin.*	9	7	.563	4.23	29	22	0	0	2	2	142.2	114	610	70	67	8	9	3	5	73	2	97	6	0
Vosberg, Ed, S.D.-Ari.*	0	1	.000	8.18	19	0	0	0	3	0	11.0	22	60	12	10	1	2	2	2	3	0	8	1	0
Wagner, Billy, Hou.*	4	1	.800	1.57	66	0	0	0	55	39	74.2	35	286	14	13	5	2	1	1	23	1	124	2	0
Wainhouse, David, Col.	0	0	.000	6.91	19	0	0	0	11	0	28.2	37	131	22	22	6	0	3	0	16	0	18	1	0
Wall, Donne, S.D.	7	4	.636	4.08	55	0	0	0	12	0	70.1	58	290	31	24	11	1	1	0	23	3	53	6	0
Wallace, Jeff, Pit.*	1	0	1.000	3.69	41	0	0	0	7	0	39.0	26	176	17	16	2	4	1	0	38	1	41	5	0
Watson, Allen, N.Y.*	2	2	.500	4.08	14	4	0	0	6	1	39.2	36	173	18	18	5	3	4	1	22	3	32	2	0
Weathers, David, Mil.	7	4	.636	4.65	63	0	0	0	14	2	93.0	102	414	49	48	14	4	4	2	38	3	74	1	1
Wendell, Turk, N.Y.	4	4	.556	3.05	80	0	0	0	14	3	85.2	80	369	31	29	9	2	1	2	37	8	77	2	1
Whisenant, Matt, S.D.*	0	1	.000	3.68	19	0	0	0	4	0	14.2	10	60	6	6	0	0	0	0	10	1	10	0	0
White, Gabe, Cin.*	1	2	.333	4.43	50	0	0	0	18	0	61.0	68	261	31	30	13	2	1	2	14	1	61	0	0
Whiteside, Matt, S.D.	1	0	1.000	13.91	10	0	0	0	4	0	11.0	19	55	17	17	1	1	1	0	5	0	9	1	0
Wickman, Bob, Mil.	3	8	.273	3.39	71	0	0	0	63	37	74.1	75	331	31	28	6	3	2	2	38	6	60	2	0
Wilkins, Marc, Pit.	2	3	.400	4.24	46	0	0	0	14	0	51.0	49	227	28	24	3	4	2	4	26	1	44	4	1
Williams, Brian, Hou.	2	1	.667	4.41	50	0	0	0	15	0	67.1	69	303	35	33	4	5	4	5	35	2	53	7	0
Williams, Jeff, L.A.*	2	0	1.000	4.08	5	3	0	0	1	0	17.2	12	73	10	8	2	1	0	0	9	0	7	0	0
Williams, Mike, Pit.	3	4	.429	5.09	58	0	0	0	50	23	58.1	63	269	36	33	9	2	1	1	37	7	76	4	0
Williams, Woody, S.D.	12	12	.500	4.41	33	33	0	0	0	0	208.1	213	887	106	102	33	9	9	2	73	5	137	9	0
Williamson, Scott, Cin.	12	7	.632	2.41	62	0	0	0	40	19	93.1	54	366	29	25	8	5	2	1	43	6	107	13	0
Winkelsas, Joe, Atl.	0	0	.000	54.00	1	0	0	0	1	0	0.1	4	6	2	2	1	0	0	0	1	0	0	0	0
Wohlers, Mark, Atl.	0	0	.000	27.00	2	0	0	0	0	0	0.2	1	10	2	2	0	1	0	0	6	0	0	0	0
Wolf, Randy, Phi.*	6	9	.400	5.55	22	21	0	0	0	0	121.2	126	552	78	75	20	5	1	5	67	0	116	4	0
Woodall, Brad, Chi.*	0	1	.000	5.63	6	3	0	0	3	0	16.0	17	71	12	10	5	0	1	1	6	0	7	1	0
Woodard, Steve, Mil.	11	8	.579	4.52	31	29	2	0	0	0	185.0	219	801	101	93	23	9	4	6	36	7	119	4	1
Wright, Jamey, Col.	4	3	.571	4.87	16	16	0	0	0	0	94.1	110	423	52	51	10	3	4	4	54	3	49	3	0
Yoshii, Masato, N.Y.	12	8	.600	4.40	31	29	1	0	1	0	174.0	168	723	86	85	25	7	6	6	58	3	105	1	0

COMBINATION SHUTOUTS (5)—**Arizona (5)**—Johnson, Kim, Plesac and Olson; Anderson and Mantei; Reynoso and Mantei; Benes and Swindell; Stottlemyre, Swindell, Plesac, Olson and Mantei. **Atlanta (8)**—Smoltz, Seanez and Rocker; Smoltz, McGlinchy and Rocker; Maddux and Rocker; Millwood, Remlinger and Rocker; Smoltz and Chen; Maddux, Springer and Hudek; Millwood and Rocker; Glavine, Springer, Mulholland, Remlinger and Rocker. **Chicago (3)**—Mulholland, Serafini, Myers, Heredia and Beck; Trachsel and Adams; Farnsworth, Heredia and Sanders. **Cincinnati (8)**—Tomko and Williamson; Harnisch and Williamson; Villone and Graves; Villone and Williamson; Harnisch and Sullivan; Harnisch and Williamson; Harnisch and Reyes; Villone and Williamson. **Colorado (1)**—Kile, DeJean and Veres. **Florida (3)**—Fernandez, Edmondson, Darensbourg and Looper; Cornelius, Looper and Edmondson; Dempster, Looper and Alfonseca. **Houston (3)**—Reynolds and Williams; Lima and Wagner; Lima and Wagner. **Los Angeles (3)**—Brown and Shaw; Park and Mills; Valdes, Borbon and Mills. **Milwaukee (5)**—Karl and Wickman; Abbott and Roque; Nomo and Coppinger; Peterson and Wickman; Woodard and Wickman. **Montreal (1)**—Powell, Mota and Telford. **New York (4)**—Jones, Cook, Benitez and J. Franco; Yoshii, Cook and J. Franco; Rogers and Cook; Hershiser, McMichael and Isringhausen. **Philadelphia (4)**—Schilling, Poole and Brantley; Person, Montgomery and Gomes; Person and Poole; Loewer, Brewer, Ogea and Montgomery. **Pittsburgh (3)**—Schourek, Loiselle, Wallace, Williams and Christiansen; Benson, Sauerbeck and Williams; Ritchie and Williams. **St. Louis (0)**—None. **San Diego (3)**—Hitchcock and Boehringer; Ashby and Hoffman; Williams and Hoffman. **San Francisco (2)**—Nathan, Johnstone and Nen; Rueter, R. Rodriguez and Tavarez.

PITCHERS WITH TWO OR MORE TEAMS

Pitcher, Team	W	L	Pct.	ERA	G	GS	CG	ShO	GF	Sv.	IP	H	TBF	R	ER	HR	SH	SF	HB	BB	IBB	SO	WP	Bk.
Ayala, Bobby, Mon.	1	6	.143	3.68	53	0	0	0	17	0	66.0	60	300	36	27	6	4	3	4	34	1	64	4	0
Ayala, Bobby, Chi.	0	1	.000	2.81	13	0	0	0	4	0	16.0	11	65	7	5	4	1	0	2	5	1	15	1	0
Beltran, Rigo, N.Y.*	1	1	.500	3.48	21	0	0	0	10	0	31.0	30	134	15	12	5	2	0	0	12	2	35	6	0
Beltran, Rigo, Col.*	0	0	.000	7.36	12	0	0	0	2	0	11.0	20	61	9	9	2	1	0	1	7	1	15	1	0
Bere, Jason, Cin.	3	0	1.000	6.85	12	10	0	0	0	0	43.1	56	220	37	33	6	5	1	2	40	3	28	2	0
Bere, Jason, Mil.	2	0	1.000	4.63	5	4	0	0	0	0	23.1	23	102	15	12	3	1	1	0	10	0	19	4	0
Bergman, Sean, Hou.	4	6	.400	5.36	19	16	2	1	1	0	99.0	130	428	60	59	9	3	4	3	26	1	38	3	0
Bergman, Sean, Atl.	1	0	1.000	2.84	6	0	0	0	1	0	6.1	5	27	2	2	0	1	0	0	3	0	6	0	0
Bowie, Micah, Atl.*	1	0	1.000	13.50	3	0	0	0	2	0	4.0	8	23	6	6	1	0	0	0	4	0	2	0	0
Bowie, Micah, Chi.*	2	6	.250	9.96	11	11	0	0	0	0	47.0	73	242	54	52	8	3	3	2	30	2	39	4	2
Hernandez, Livan, Fla.	5	9	.357	4.76	20	20	2	0	0	0	136.0	161	612	78	72	17	3	4	2	55	3	97	2	1
Hernandez, Livan, S.F.	3	3	.500	4.38	10	10	0	0	0	0	63.2	66	274	32	31	6	4	2	0	21	2	47	0	1
Hudek, John, Cin.	0	1	.000	27.00	2	0	0	0	1	0	1.0	4	9	3	3	1	0	0	0	3	0	0	0	0
Hudek, John, Atl.	1	0	1.000	6.48	15	0	0	0	12	0	16.2	21	84	14	12	1	0	1	1	11	0	18	0	0
Maddux, Mike, Mon.	0	0	.000	9.00	4	0	0	0	2	0	5.0	9	26	5	5	1	0	0	1	3	0	4	0	0
Maddux, Mike, L.A.	1	1	.500	3.29	49	0	0	0	19	0	54.2	54	234	21	20	5	2	4	2	19	2	41	1	0
Mantei, Matt, Fla.	1	2	.333	2.79	35	0	0	0	32	10	36.1	24	157	11	11	4	0	1	2	25	1	50	0	0
Mantei, Matt, Ari.	1	1	.500	2.79	30	0	0	0	28	22	29.0	20	127	10	9	1	1	0	3	19	0	49	2	0
McElroy, Chuck, Col.*	3	1	.750	6.20	41	0	0	0	12	0	40.2	48	192	29	28	9	2	0	3	22	3	37	4	0
McElroy, Chuck, N.Y.*	0	0	.000	3.38	15	0	0	0	7	0	13.1	12	59	5	5	0	1	1	1	8	1	7	1	0
Mulholland, Terry, Chi.*	6	6	.500	5.15	26	16	0	0	4	0	110.0	137	485	71	63	16	6	3	1	32	4	44	2	0
Mulholland, Terry, Atl.*	4	2	.667	2.98	8	8	0	0	3	1	60.1	64	251	24	20	5	3	1	0	13	2	39	1	0

Pitcher, Team	W	L	Pct.	ERA	G	GS	CG	ShO	GF	Sv.	IP	H	TBF	R	ER	HR	SH	SF	HB	BB	IBB	SO	WP	Bk.
Nunez, Vladimir, Ari.	3	2	.600	2.91	27	0	0	0	11	1	34.0	29	146	15	11	2	2	3	1	20	5	28	3	0
Nunez, Vladimir, Fla.	4	8	.333	4.58	17	12	0	0	1	0	74.2	66	317	48	38	9	5	3	3	34	1	58	5	1
Rojas, Mel, L.A.	0	0	.000	12.60	5	0	0	0	2	0	5.0	5	23	7	7	3	0	0	0	3	1	3	0	0
Rojas, Mel, Mon.	0	0	.000	16.88	3	0	0	0	1	0	2.2	5	17	5	5	0	0	1	2	2	0	1	1	0
Telemaco, Amaury, Ari.	1	0	1.000	7.50	5	0	0	0	3	0	6.0	7	28	5	5	2	1	0	0	6	1	2	0	0
Telemaco, Amaury, Phi.	3	0	1.000	5.55	44	0	0	0	7	0	47.0	45	206	29	29	8	3	1	2	20	3	41	5	0
Vosberg, Ed, S.D.*	0	0	.000	9.72	15	0	0	0	3	0	8.1	16	47	11	9	1	2	2	2	3	0	6	1	0
Vosberg, Ed, Ari.*	0	1	.000	3.38	4	0	0	0	0	0	2.2	6	13	1	1	0	0	0	0	0	0	2	0	0

FIELDING

TEAM

Team	Pct.	G	PO	A	E	TC	DP	TP	PB
New York	.989	163	4370	1607	68	6045	147	0	10
Philadelphia	.983	162	4315	1598	100	6013	144	1	13
Houston	.983	162	4376	1732	106	6214	175	0	9
Arizona	.983	162	4402	1590	104	6096	132	0	17
San Francisco	.983	162	4369	1630	105	6104	155	1	8
Cincinnati	.983	163	4386	1551	105	6042	139	0	11
Atlanta	.982	162	4413	1658	111	6182	127	0	10
Colorado	.981	162	4287	1737	118	6142	189	0	9
Milwaukee	.979	161	4328	1669	127	6124	146	1	13

Team	Pct.	G	PO	A	E	TC	DP	TP	PB
Florida	.979	162	4307	1687	127	6121	150	0	10
San Diego	.979	162	4261	1633	129	6023	151	0	15
St. Louis	.978	161	4336	1634	132	6102	163	0	8
Los Angeles	.978	162	4359	1725	137	6221	137	0	13
Chicago	.977	162	4292	1597	139	6028	135	0	14
Pittsburgh	.976	161	4300	1746	147	6193	179	0	9
Montreal	.974	162	4303	1618	160	6081	125	0	16
Totals	.980	1296	69404	26412	1915	97731	2394	3	185

INDIVIDUAL

FIRST BASEMEN

NOTE: All caps denotes fielding-percentage leader based on 81 games for catchers, 108 for all other non-pitchers and 162 innings for pitchers. *Throws lefthanded.

Player, Team	Pct.	G	PO	A	E	TC	DP
Abbott, Kurt, Col.	1.000	8	57	3	0	60	6
Andrews, Shane, Mon.-Chi.	.985	19	122	7	2	131	12
Baerga, Carlos, S.D.	.000	2	0	0	0	0	0
Bagwell, Jeff, Hou.	.994	161	1336	107	8	1451	141
Banks, Brian, Mil.	.992	44	221	20	2	243	18
Barker, Kevin, Mil.	.996	31	254	18	1	273	19
Berkman, Lance, Hou.*	1.000	1	1	0	0	1	1
Berry, Sean, Mil.	.989	64	438	27	5	470	50
Bonilla, Bobby, N.Y.	.962	4	23	2	1	26	2
Brogna, Rico, Phi.*	.995	157	1240	123	7	1370	119
Brown, Brant, Pit.*	1.000	7	37	3	0	40	2
Casey, Sean, Cin.	.995	148	1189	55	6	1250	109
Colbrunn, Greg, Ari.	.996	39	203	19	1	223	21
Cromer, Tripp, L.A.	1.000	1	1	0	0	1	0
Cruz, Ivan, Pit.*	1.000	1	13	1	0	14	3
Dunston, Shawon, St.L.	1.000	8	37	2	0	39	3
Durazo, Erubiel, Ari.*	1.000	44	324	20	0	344	25
Echevarria, Angel, Col.	1.000	10	58	4	0	62	6
Fabregas, Jorge, Atl.	1.000	1	0	1	0	1	0
Franco, Matt, N.Y.	1.000	19	41	5	0	46	8
Fullmer, Brad, Mon.	.991	94	700	41	7	748	48
Gaetti, Gary, Chi.	.957	8	39	6	2	47	6
Garcia, Carlos, S.D.	1.000	1	2	0	0	2	0
Garcia, Freddy, Pit.	.000	1	0	0	0	0	0
Grace, Mark, Chi.*	.994	160	1335	93	8	1436	115
Hansen, Dave, L.A.	.982	20	52	4	1	57	6
Hayes, Charlie, S.F.	1.000	20	103	8	0	111	9
Helton, Todd, Col.*	.993	156	1243	103	9	1355	152
Hernandez, Jose, Chi.-Atl.	1.000	2	3	0	0	3	0
Hollandsworth, Todd, L.A.*	.990	13	91	9	1	101	12
Houston, Tyler, Chi.	1.000	2	1	0	0	1	0
Howard, David, St.L.	1.000	9	33	1	0	34	4
Howell, Jack, Hou.	1.000	5	9	2	0	11	4
Hunter, Brian, Atl.*	.991	101	425	36	4	465	37
Hyers, Tim, Fla.*	1.000	14	71	3	0	74	6
Jordan, Kevin, Phi.	1.000	13	55	4	0	59	6
Joyner, Wally, S.D.*	.995	105	731	66	4	801	83
Karros, Eric, L.A.	.991	151	1291	126	13	1430	108
Kent, Jeff, S.F.	1.000	1	7	2	0	9	2
Kinkade, Mike, N.Y.	.000	1	0	0	0	0	0
Klesko, Ryan, Atl.*	.989	75	493	30	6	529	37
Kotsay, Mark, Fla.*	1.000	19	104	8	0	112	9
Lee, Derrek, Fla.	.994	66	463	47	3	513	44
LEE, Travis, Ari.*	.997	114	802	62	3	867	65
Leyritz, Jim, S.D.	.984	19	116	7	2	125	10
Loretta, Mark, Mil.	.994	66	474	31	3	508	44
Lovullo, Torey, Phi.	1.000	6	22	5	0	27	3
Magadan, Dave, S.D.	.985	42	186	15	3	204	19
Marrero, Eli, St.L.	1.000	20	47	5	0	52	2
McEwing, Joe, St.L.	1.000	2	5	0	0	5	0
McGee, Willie, St.L.	1.000	3	9	0	0	9	0
McGuire, Ryan, Mon.*	.997	58	267	37	1	305	19
McGwire, Mark, St.L.	.990	151	1180	80	13	1273	119
Merced, Orlando, Mon.	.917	7	21	1	2	24	2
Millar, Kevin, Fla.	.995	94	719	53	4	776	80
Mordecai, Mike, Mon.	1.000	1	2	0	0	2	0

Player, Team	Pct.	G	PO	A	E	TC	DP
Morris, Hal, Cin.*	.991	25	107	6	1	114	10
Nevin, Phil, S.D.	.988	11	74	9	1	84	5
Newhan, David, S.D.	.000	1	0	0	0	0	0
Olerud, John, N.Y.*	.994	160	1344	105	9	1458	127
Orie, Kevin, Fla.	1.000	1	1	0	0	1	1
Owens, Eric, S.D.	1.000	12	77	4	0	81	7
Paquette, Craig, St.L.	1.000	6	19	3	0	22	1
Perez, Eddie, Atl.	1.000	2	4	0	0	4	0
Perez, Eduardo, St.L.	.952	5	18	2	1	21	2
Phillips, J.R., Col.*	1.000	4	3	0	0	3	1
Pratt, Todd, N.Y.	.000	1	0	0	0	0	0
Santiago, Benito, Chi.	1.000	1	2	0	0	2	0
Seguignol, Fernando, Mon.	.989	23	172	11	2	185	20
Servais, Scott, S.F.	1.000	1	1	0	0	1	0
Simon, Randall, Atl.*	.994	70	462	27	3	492	38
Snow, J.T., S.F.*	.996	160	1221	122	6	1349	123
Spiers, Bill, Hou.	1.000	1	3	0	0	3	0
Sveum, Dale, Pit.	1.000	4	23	2	0	25	5
Sweeney, Mark, Cin.*	1.000	1	2	0	0	2	1
Toca, Jorge, N.Y.	1.000	1	2	0	0	2	0
Vander Wal, John, S.D.*	.994	28	156	8	1	165	14
Ventura, Robin, N.Y.	1.000	1	1	0	0	1	0
Vidro, Jose, Mon.	.970	14	59	5	2	66	7
Ward, Daryle, Hou.*	1.000	10	36	2	0	38	6
Young, Dmitri, Cin.	1.000	9	56	1	0	57	5
Young, Kevin, Pit.	.985	155	1413	97	23	1533	148

TRIPLE PLAYS: Berry, Mil.; Snow, S.F.

FIRST BASEMEN WITH TWO OR MORE TEAMS

Player, Team	Pct.	G	PO	A	E	TC	DP
Andrews, Shane, Mon.	.985	18	122	7	2	131	12
Andrews, Shane, Chi.	.000	1	0	0	0	0	0
Hernandez, Jose, Chi.	1.000	1	2	0	0	2	0
Hernandez, Jose, Atl.	1.000	1	1	0	0	1	0

SECOND BASEMEN

Player, Team	Pct.	G	PO	A	E	TC	DP
Abbott, Kurt, Col.	.989	66	124	145	3	272	34
Alexander, Manny, Chi.	.927	17	21	17	3	41	4
ALFONZO, Edgardo, N.Y.	.993	158	298	409	5	712	98
Anderson, Marlon, Phi.	.979	121	234	284	11	529	59
Arias, Alex, Phi.	.000	1	0	0	0	0	0
Baerga, Carlos, S.D.	1.000	13	16	20	0	36	7
Bell, Jay, Ari.	.968	148	320	340	22	682	86
Belliard, Ron, Mil.	.978	119	247	330	13	590	75
Benjamin, Mike, Pit.	1.000	12	21	31	0	52	5
Berg, Dave, Fla.	1.000	29	51	80	0	131	16
Biggio, Craig, Hou.	.985	155	359	430	12	801	117
Blauser, Jeff, Chi.	.961	25	41	32	3	76	9
Blum, Geoff, Mon.	1.000	2	0	2	0	2	0
Bogar, Tim, Hou.	1.000	1	1	2	0	3	1
Boone, Bret, Atl.	.982	151	270	424	13	707	78
Canizaro, Jay, S.F.	1.000	4	2	5	0	7	1
Castillo, Luis, Fla.	.976	126	257	343	15	615	75
Castro, Juan, L.A.	1.000	1	4	0	0	5	1
Cedeno, Domingo, Phi.	1.000	1	1	2	0	3	0
Cedeno, Roger, N.Y.	.000	1	0	0	0	0	0
Clapinski, Chris, Fla.	1.000	2	0	2	0	2	0
Collier, Lou, Mil.	1.000	4	7	0	0	7	0
Coquillette, Trace, Mon.	1.000	6	10	14	0	24	4

Player, Team	Pct.	G	PO	A	E	TC	DP
Cora, Alex, L.A.	.857	3	3	9	2	14	2
Counsell, Craig, Fla.-L.A.	.989	50	74	114	2	190	17
Cromer, Tripp, L.A.	1.000	9	7	18	0	25	5
Delgado, Wilson, S.F.	.963	15	17	9	1	27	2
Diaz, Edwin, Ari.	1.000	2	0	3	0	3	0
Doster, David, Phi.	.993	77	69	72	1	142	21
Frias, Hanley, Ari.	1.000	8	4	6	0	10	2
Garcia, Amaury, Fla.	.932	8	15	26	3	44	5
Giovanola, Ed, S.D.	.982	19	26	28	1	55	9
Guerrero, Wilton, Mon.	.931	54	65	98	12	175	17
Guillen, Ozzie, Atl.	1.000	1	1	0	0	1	0
Harris, Lenny, Col.	.924	24	46	51	8	105	19
Hernandez, Carlos E., Hou.	1.000	7	5	11	0	16	3
Howard, David, St.L.	1.000	9	10	16	0	26	4
Hubbard, Trenidad, L.A.	.000	1	0	0	0	0	0
Jackson, Damian, S.D.	.988	21	37	44	1	82	13
Johnson, Russ, Hou.	.960	15	16	32	2	50	6
Jordan, Kevin, Phi.	.984	33	56	67	2	125	22
Kennedy, Adam, St.L.	.971	29	68	64	4	136	14
Kent, Jeff, S.F.	.984	133	279	326	10	615	90
Lansing, Mike, Col.	.990	35	91	98	2	191	40
Lewis, Mark, Cin.	.500	2	0	1	1	2	0
Lockhart, Keith, Atl.	1.000	25	26	58	0	84	11
Lopez, Luis, N.Y.	.966	16	8	20	1	29	5
Loretta, Mark, Mil.	.956	17	28	37	3	68	8
Lovullo, Torey, Phi.	1.000	6	14	8	0	22	0
Martinez, Ramon E., S.F.	.992	27	50	68	1	119	15
McEwing, Joe, St.L.	.980	96	202	238	9	449	51
Meyers, Chad, Chi.	.983	32	49	69	2	120	13
Mora, Melvin, N.Y.	1.000	4	1	1	0	2	1
Morandini, Mickey, Chi.	.991	132	239	319	5	563	72
Mordecai, Mike, Mon.	.962	38	17	33	2	52	11
Morris, Warren, Pit.	.979	144	263	403	14	680	102
Mueller, Bill, S.F.	1.000	3	2	0	0	2	0
Newhan, David, S.D.	.970	19	28	36	2	66	10
Nunez, Abraham, Pit.	.985	14	24	42	1	67	13
Ordaz, Luis, St.L.	1.000	1	0	1	0	1	0
Owens, Eric, S.D.	1.000	1	1	0	0	1	0
Paquette, Craig, St.L.	.962	7	10	15	1	26	4
Petersen, Chris, Col.	.955	6	9	12	1	22	5
Polanco, Placido, St.L.	.979	66	116	122	5	243	32
Reese, Pokey, Cin.	.991	146	325	409	7	741	91
Sanford, Chance, L.A.	1.000	2	1	1	0	2	0
Santangelo, F.P., S.F.	1.000	11	13	21	0	34	1
Sefcik, Kevin, Phi.	.979	15	25	17	1	43	4
Sexton, Chris, Col.	.949	10	19	18	2	39	3
Shumpert, Terry, Col.	.988	54	102	151	3	256	35
Spiers, Bill, Hou.	1.000	4	5	10	0	15	0
Stynes, Chris, Cin.	.956	43	48	60	5	113	11
Sveum, Dale, Pit.	1.000	2	1	2	0	3	1
Veras, Quilvio, S.D.	.981	118	271	334	12	617	78
Vidro, Jose, Mon.	.982	121	208	291	9	508	61
Vina, Fernando, Mil.	.995	37	84	104	1	189	31
Vizcaino, Jose, L.A.	.991	30	36	70	1	107	9
Wehner, John, Pit.	1.000	1	4	2	0	6	2
Womack, Tony, Ari.	.971	19	30	36	2	68	6
Young, Eric, L.A.	.984	116	216	321	9	546	62
Zosky, Eddie, Mil.	1.000	2	1	3	0	4	0

TRIPLE PLAYS: Jordan, Phi.; Kent, S.F.; Vina, Mil.

SECOND BASEMEN WITH TWO OR MORE TEAMS

Player, Team	Pct.	G	PO	A	E	TC	DP
Counsell, Craig, Fla.	.980	12	20	29	1	50	4
Counsell, Craig, L.A.	.993	38	54	85	1	140	13

THIRD BASEMEN

Player, Team	Pct.	G	PO	A	E	TC	DP
Alexander, Manny, Chi.	.893	22	8	17	3	28	0
Andrews, Shane, Mon.-Chi.	.936	101	45	161	14	220	15
Arias, Alex, Phi.	1.000	2	1	1	0	2	0
Arias, George, S.D.	.941	50	35	93	8	136	4
Baerga, Carlos, S.D.	.882	13	5	10	2	17	2
Barrett, Michael, Mon.	.943	66	45	104	9	158	4
Battle, Howard, Atl.	1.000	6	2	4	0	6	0
Belliard, Ron, Mil.	1.000	1	1	0	0	1	0
Beltre, Adrian, L.A.	.932	152	121	274	29	424	24
Benjamin, Mike, Pit.	1.000	6	1	5	0	6	0
Berg, Dave, Fla.	.911	19	13	28	4	45	3
Blauser, Jeff, Chi.	.897	18	7	19	3	29	0
Bogar, Tim, Hou.	1.000	12	6	20	0	26	0
Boone, Aaron, Cin.	.958	136	86	253	15	354	17
Caminiti, Ken, Hou.	.932	75	52	139	14	205	17

Player, Team	Pct.	G	PO	A	E	TC	DP
Castilla, Vinny, Col.	.954	157	96	298	19	413	32
Cirillo, Jeff, Mil.	.967	155	124	312	15	451	35
Clapinski, Chris, Fla.	.882	9	6	9	2	17	1
Colbrunn, Greg, Ari.	.000	2	0	0	0	0	0
Collier, Lou, Mil.	.800	7	0	4	1	5	0
Coquillette, Trace, Mon.	.944	11	3	14	1	18	1
Cromer, Tripp, L.A.	1.000	2	2	1	0	3	0
Doster, David, Phi.	1.000	6	3	7	0	10	1
Dunston, Shawon, St.L.-N.Y.	.923	6	3	9	1	13	2
Fernandez, Jose, Mon.	.889	6	7	9	2	18	0
Fox, Andy, Ari.	.909	12	5	15	2	22	2
Franco, Matt, N.Y.	.950	12	1	18	1	20	1
Gaetti, Gary, Chi.	.962	81	35	140	7	182	8
Garcia, Carlos, S.D.	.778	4	4	3	2	9	0
Garcia, Freddy, Pit.	.938	9	1	14	1	16	1
Giovanola, Ed, S.D.	.938	25	4	11	1	16	0
Guillen, Ozzie, Atl.	1.000	6	3	9	0	12	1
Gutierrez, Ricky, Hou.	1.000	1	0	1	0	1	0
Guzman, Edwards, S.F.	1.000	5	2	7	0	9	0
Hansen, Dave, L.A.	.900	13	5	13	2	20	0
Harris, Lenny, Col.-Ari.	1.000	7	5	5	0	10	2
Hayes, Charlie, S.F.	.940	55	27	83	7	117	3
Houston, Tyler, Chi.	.901	63	35	83	13	131	7
Howard, David, St.L.	1.000	4	3	6	0	9	1
Howell, Jack, Hou.	1.000	3	1	3	0	4	0
Johnson, Russ, Hou.	.944	36	16	52	4	72	8
Jones, Chipper, Atl.	.950	156	88	238	17	343	10
Jordan, Kevin, Phi.	.943	62	40	93	8	141	10
Kinkade, Mike, N.Y.	1.000	3	1	1	0	2	0
Lewis, Mark, Cin.	.938	52	21	54	5	80	7
Leyritz, Jim, S.D.	.000	1	0	0	0	0	0
Liniak, Cole, Chi.	1.000	10	8	8	0	16	1
Lockhart, Keith, Atl.	.875	10	1	6	1	8	1
Lopez, Luis, N.Y.	.857	9	3	3	1	7	1
Loretta, Mark, Mil.	.900	14	11	16	3	30	2
Lowell, Mike, Fla.	.981	83	59	143	4	206	12
Magadan, Dave, S.D.	.969	52	23	70	3	96	5
Martinez, Ramon E., S.F.	1.000	11	5	9	0	14	0
McEwing, Joe, St.L.	.875	6	2	5	1	8	2
Millar, Kevin, Fla.	1.000	1	0	2	0	2	0
Mora, Melvin, N.Y.	1.000	3	2	5	0	7	1
Mordecai, Mike, Mon.	.984	32	15	48	1	64	4
Mueller, Bill, S.F.	.958	108	81	195	12	288	17
Nevin, Phil, S.D.	.982	67	36	131	3	170	12
Newhan, David, S.D.	.000	1	0	0	0	0	0
Ordaz, Luis, St.L.	.000	1	0	0	0	0	0
Orie, Kevin, Fla.	.961	64	51	120	7	178	8
Owens, Eric, S.D.	.714	4	1	4	2	7	0
Paquette, Craig, St.L.	1.000	10	4	24	0	28	0
Polanco, Placido, St.L.	.889	9	0	8	1	9	0
Ramirez, Aramis, Pit.	.930	17	11	29	3	43	2
Reed, Jeff, Chi.	.000	1	0	0	0	0	0
Rolen, Scott, Phi.	.960	112	111	227	14	352	21
Santangelo, F.P., S.F.	1.000	3	1	0	0	1	0
Shumpert, Terry, Col.	.947	14	6	12	1	19	3
Spiers, Bill, Hou.	.958	71	40	143	8	191	11
Sprague, Ed, Pit.	.920	134	79	254	29	362	22
Stynes, Chris, Cin.	.929	8	2	11	1	14	0
Sveum, Dale, Pit.	.944	12	2	15	1	18	0
Tatis, Fernando, St.L.	.958	147	101	267	16	384	30
VENTURA, Robin, N.Y.	.980	160	123	320	9	452	33
Vidro, Jose, Mon.	1.000	2	1	0	0	1	0
Vizcaino, Jose, L.A.	1.000	9	2	13	0	15	2
Wehner, John, Pit.	1.000	2	1	1	0	2	0
Williams, Matt, Ari.	.977	153	123	299	10	432	30
Zosky, Eddie, Mil.	1.000	4	0	1	0	1	0

TRIPLE PLAYS: Cirillo, Mil.; Mueller, S.F.

THIRD BASEMEN WITH TWO OR MORE TEAMS

Player, Team	Pct.	G	PO	A	E	TC	DP
Andrews, Shane, Mon.	.932	82	37	127	12	176	9
Andrews, Shane, Chi.	.955	19	8	34	2	44	6
Dunston, Shawon, St.L.	.909	5	2	8	1	11	2
Dunston, Shawon, N.Y.	1.000	1	1	1	0	2	0
Harris, Lenny, Col.	1.000	2	2	0	0	2	0
Harris, Lenny, Ari.	1.000	5	3	5	0	8	2

SHORTSTOPS

Player, Team	Pct.	G	PO	A	E	TC	DP
Abbott, Kurt, Col.	.857	3	3	3	1	7	2
Alexander, Manny, Chi.	.988	30	27	54	1	82	9
Arias, Alex, Phi.	.988	95	119	207	4	330	43

Player, Team	Pct.	G	PO	A	E	TC	DP
Aurilia, Rich, S.F.	.957	150	218	411	28	657	97
Barrett, Michael, Mon.	1.000	2	0	1	0	1	0
Batista, Tony, Ari.	.979	43	60	130	4	194	27
Bell, Jay, Ari.	.000	1	0	0	0	0	0
Belliard, Ron, Mil.	1.000	1	2	3	0	5	0
Benjamin, Mike, Pit.	.982	93	140	298	8	446	77
Berg, Dave, Fla.	.969	37	39	87	4	130	12
Blauser, Jeff, Chi.	.985	22	21	43	1	65	7
Blum, Geoff, Mon.	.928	42	47	82	10	139	11
Bogar, Tim, Hou.	.977	90	123	255	9	387	65
Boone, Aaron, Cin.	1.000	6	1	5	0	6	2
Cabrera, Orlando, Mon.	.979	102	186	289	10	485	61
Castro, Juan, L.A.	.000	1	0	0	0	0	0
Cedeno, Domingo, Phi.	.982	19	19	35	1	55	6
Clapinski, Chris, Fla.	.955	6	9	12	1	22	4
Collier, Lou, Mil.	.948	31	21	52	4	77	7
Cora, Alex, L.A.	1.000	8	10	11	0	21	2
Counsell, Craig, L.A.	1.000	2	0	1	0	1	0
Cromer, Tripp, L.A.	1.000	9	10	17	0	27	4
Dawkins, Travis, Cin.	1.000	7	2	4	0	6	1
Delgado, Wilson, S.F.	.932	20	22	33	4	59	10
DeRosa, Mark, Atl.	1.000	2	2	2	0	4	0
Diaz, Edwin, Ari.	1.000	2	4	2	0	6	0
Doster, David, Phi.	1.000	5	6	9	0	15	3
Dunston, Shawon, St.L.	.929	7	1	12	1	14	3
Fox, Andy, Ari.	.958	82	95	181	12	288	33
Frias, Hanley, Ari.	.965	53	42	95	5	142	16
Gaetti, Gary, Chi.	1.000	1	0	1	0	1	0
Giovanola, Ed, S.D.	1.000	7	6	8	0	14	2
Gomez, Chris, S.D.	.961	75	101	195	12	308	48
Gonzalez, Alex, Fla.	.955	135	237	339	27	603	85
Grudzielanek, Mark, L.A.	.973	119	171	306	13	490	66
Guillen, Ozzie, Atl.	.965	53	54	137	7	198	29
Gutierrez, Ricky, Hou.	.971	80	102	202	9	313	37
Halter, Shane, N.Y.	.000	1	0	0	0	0	0
Hernandez, Carlos E., Hou.	.667	2	2	0	1	3	0
Hernandez, Jose, Chi.-Atl.	.969	137	162	363	17	542	75
Howard, David, St.L.	.966	13	10	18	1	29	2
Jackson, Damian, S.D.	.940	100	136	258	25	419	57
Johnson, Russ, Hou.	.833	2	1	4	1	6	1
Jones, Chipper, Atl.	1.000	1	0	1	0	1	0
Larkin, Barry, Cin.	.978	161	220	401	14	635	77
Lopez, Luis, N.Y.	.971	33	23	45	2	70	8
Loretta, Mark, Mil.	.986	74	112	176	4	292	40
Martinez, Ramon E., S.F.	.878	12	11	25	5	41	4
McEwing, Joe, St.L.	.000	1	0	0	0	0	0
Meares, Pat, Pit.	.939	21	26	67	6	99	13
Mora, Melvin, N.Y.	1.000	1	0	1	0	1	0
Mordecai, Mike, Mon.	.966	38	38	75	4	117	20
Nieves, Jose, Chi.	.935	52	67	162	16	245	29
Nunez, Abraham, Pit.	.953	65	89	172	13	274	37
Ordaz, Luis, St.L.	.786	8	4	7	3	14	4
ORDONEZ, Rey, N.Y.	.994	154	220	416	4	640	91
Perez, Neifi, Col.	.981	157	260	481	14	755	124
Petersen, Chris, Col.	1.000	1	3	4	0	7	1
Polanco, Placido, St.L.	.931	9	7	20	2	29	5
Reese, Pokey, Cin.	1.000	16	15	16	0	31	4
Relaford, Desi, Phi.	.952	63	97	182	14	293	43
Renteria, Edgar, St.L.	.959	151	219	393	26	638	88
Santangelo, F.P., S.F.	.000	1	0	0	0	0	0
Sexton, Chris, Col.	1.000	6	3	7	0	10	1
Shumpert, Terry, Col.	1.000	2	1	2	0	3	1
Sosa, Juan, Col.	.875	2	4	3	1	8	1
Spiers, Bill, Hou.	1.000	13	22	23	0	45	7
Sveum, Dale, Pit.	1.000	4	1	5	0	6	1
Valentin, Jose, Mil.	.937	85	113	214	22	349	38
Vizcaino, Jose, L.A.	.966	44	60	109	6	175	20
Wehner, John, Pit.	1.000	2	0	1	0	1	0
Weiss, Walt, Atl.	.963	102	108	203	12	323	41
Womack, Tony, Ari.	.982	19	16	40	1	57	5

TRIPLE PLAYS: Arias, Phi.

SHORTSTOPS WITH TWO OR MORE TEAMS

Player, Team	Pct.	G	PO	A	E	TC	DP
Hernandez, Jose, Chi.	.971	92	114	249	11	374	51
Hernandez, Jose, Atl.	.964	45	48	114	6	168	24

OUTFIELDERS

Player, Team	Pct.	G	PO	A	E	TC	DP
Abbott, Kurt, Col.	1.000	4	4	0	0	4	0
Abreu, Bobby, Phi.	.989	146	260	8	3	271	0

Player, Team	Pct.	G	PO	A	E	TC	DP
Agbayani, Benny, N.Y.	.984	80	121	2	2	125	0
Alexander, Manny, Chi.	.000	2	0	0	0	0	0
Allensworth, Jermaine, N.Y.	1.000	33	47	1	0	48	1
Aven, Bruce, Fla.	.984	102	181	4	3	188	1
Banks, Brian, Mil.	1.000	5	1	0	0	1	0
Barker, Glen, Hou.	.981	57	50	2	1	53	1
Barry, Jeff, Col.	1.000	56	90	4	0	94	0
Bautista, Danny, Fla.	.979	60	140	3	3	146	0
Becker, Rich, Mil.*	.970	50	62	3	2	67	1
Bell, Derek, Hou.	.985	126	192	4	3	199	1
Benard, Marvin, S.F.*	.988	142	323	5	4	332	1
Berg, Dave, Fla.	.000	3	0	0	0	0	0
Bergeron, Peter, Mon.	.967	13	27	2	1	30	1
Berkman, Lance, Hou.*	.955	27	42	0	2	44	0
Bichette, Dante, Col.	.951	144	238	17	13	268	3
Biggio, Craig, Hou.	1.000	6	6	1	0	7	0
Blanco, Henry, Col.	.000	1	0	0	0	0	0
Blauser, Jeff, Chi.	1.000	1	1	0	0	1	0
Bonds, Barry, S.F.*	.984	96	177	4	3	184	2
Bonilla, Bobby, N.Y.	.974	25	36	2	1	39	0
Bragg, Darren, St.L.	.982	88	155	7	3	165	1
Brown, Adrian, Pit.	.966	96	111	3	4	118	2
Brown, Brant, Pit.*	.981	82	150	4	3	157	0
Brown, Emil, Pit.	1.000	6	8	0	0	8	0
Brown, Roosevelt, Chi.	.955	18	20	1	1	22	0
Brumfield, Jacob, L.A.	1.000	11	11	0	0	11	0
Burks, Ellis, S.F.	.991	107	210	3	2	215	2
Burnitz, Jeromy, Mil.	.982	127	262	8	5	275	2
Cameron, Mike, Cin.	.979	146	372	7	8	387	3
Cangelosi, John, Col.*	1.000	1	1	0	0	1	0
Cedeno, Roger, N.Y.	.989	149	256	9	3	268	2
Clapinski, Chris, Fla.	1.000	3	2	0	0	2	0
Clemente, Edgard, Col.	.972	49	101	2	3	106	1
Collier, Lou, Mil.	1.000	10	14	0	0	14	0
Cookson, Brent, L.A.	1.000	3	4	0	0	4	0
Cromer, Tripp, L.A.	1.000	2	1	0	0	1	0
Cruz, Ivan, Pit.*	.000	1	0	0	0	0	0
Darr, Mike, S.D.	1.000	22	28	0	0	28	0
Davis, Eric, St.L.	1.000	51	93	4	0	97	0
Dellucci, David, Ari.*	1.000	31	37	1	0	38	0
Diaz, Alex, Hou.	.900	8	8	1	1	10	0
Drew, J.D., St.L.	.972	98	235	9	7	251	6
Ducey, Rob, Phi.	1.000	58	89	1	0	90	0
Dunston, Shawon, St.L.-N.Y.	.988	50	81	2	1	84	0
Dunwoody, Todd, Fla.*	.981	55	102	3	2	107	0
Echevarria, Angel, Col.	.985	49	64	3	1	68	1
Everett, Carl, Hou.	.978	121	256	11	6	273	4
Finley, Steve, Ari.*	.995	155	397	5	2	404	0
Floyd, Cliff, Fla.	.952	62	115	4	6	125	0
Franco, Matt, N.Y.	1.000	18	13	0	0	13	0
Gant, Ron, Phi.	.993	133	260	7	2	269	2
Garcia, Freddy, Pit.-Atl.	.977	25	43	0	1	44	0
Gibson, Derrick, Col.	.944	10	15	2	1	18	1
Giles, Brian S., Pit.*	.990	138	294	8	3	305	2
Gilkey, Bernard, Ari.	.969	53	90	3	3	96	0
Glanville, Doug, Phi.	.980	148	385	13	8	406	3
Gonzalez, Luis, Ari.	.983	148	271	10	5	286	1
Goodwin, Curtis, Chi.*	.983	76	115	3	2	120	2
Grissom, Marquis, Mil.	.987	149	374	1	5	380	2
Guerrero, Vladimir, Mon.	.948	160	332	15	19	366	3
Guerrero, Wilton, Mon.	1.000	22	21	0	0	21	0
Guillen, Jose, Pit.	.952	37	58	1	3	62	1
Gwynn, Tony, S.D.*	.993	104	147	4	1	152	0
Halter, Shane, N.Y.	.000	2	0	0	0	0	0
HAMILTON, Darryl, Col.-N.Y.	1.000	134	305	3	0	308	0
Hammonds, Jeffrey, Cin.	1.000	106	157	5	0	162	2
Hansen, Dave, L.A.	1.000	2	1	0	0	1	0
Harris, Lenny, Col.-Ari.	.944	16	15	2	1	18	1
Hayes, Charlie, S.F.	.000	1	0	0	0	0	0
Henderson, Rickey, N.Y.*	.988	116	168	0	2	170	0
Hermansen, Chad, Pit.	1.000	18	29	0	0	29	0
Hernandez, Jose, Chi.-Atl.	1.000	21	29	0	0	29	0
Hidalgo, Richard, Hou.	.991	108	214	15	2	231	3
Hill, Glenallen, Chi.	.955	62	81	3	4	88	0
Hollandsworth, Todd, L.A.*	.984	67	120	2	2	124	0
Houston, Tyler, Chi.	.000	1	0	0	0	0	0
Howard, David, St.L.	1.000	5	3	0	0	3	0
Howard, Thomas, St.L.	.987	48	77	0	1	78	0
Hubbard, Trenidad, L.A.	.980	51	49	1	1	51	0
Hunter, Brian, Atl.*	1.000	8	10	0	0	10	0
Hyers, Tim, Fla.*	1.000	15	15	0	0	15	0
Jackson, Damian, S.D.	1.000	3	1	1	0	2	0

Player, Team	Pct.	G	PO	A	E	TC	DP
Javier, Stan, S.F.-Hou.	.980	112	189	5	4	198	3
Jenkins, Geoff, Mil.	.974	128	250	14	7	271	4
Johnson, Lance, Chi.*	.988	91	235	6	3	244	1
Jones, Andruw, Atl.	.981	162	492	13	10	515	1
Jones, Terry, Mon.	1.000	17	47	2	0	49	0
Jordan, Brian, Atl.	.990	150	295	9	3	307	3
Kelly, Mike, Col.	.000	1	0	0	0	0	0
Kinkade, Mike, N.Y.	1.000	17	14	1	0	15	0
Klesko, Ryan, Atl.*	1.000	53	61	2	0	63	0
Kotsay, Mark, Fla.*	.981	129	245	19	5	269	5
Lankford, Ray, St.L.*	.987	106	214	6	3	223	0
Lee, Travis, Ari.*	1.000	2	3	0	0	3	0
Lombard, George, Atl.	1.000	4	4	0	0	4	0
Magee, Wendell, Phi.	1.000	4	5	0	0	5	0
Martin, Al, Pit.*	.952	133	196	3	10	209	0
Martinez, Manny, Mon.	.968	126	234	10	8	252	1
Matthews, Gary, S.D.	1.000	17	22	0	0	22	0
McElroy, Chuck, N.Y.*	1.000	1	1	0	0	1	0
McEwing, Joe, St.L.	.991	66	111	3	1	115	1
McGee, Willie, St.L.	.972	89	103	2	3	108	1
McGuire, Ryan, Mon.*	.960	23	23	1	1	25	0
McRae, Brian, N.Y.-Col.	.994	94	166	1	1	168	0
Merced, Orlando, Mon.	.963	44	74	3	3	80	0
Meyers, Chad, Chi.	1.000	14	27	0	0	27	0
Mieske, Matt, Hou.	1.000	36	54	1	0	55	0
Millar, Kevin, Fla.	1.000	1	1	0	0	1	0
Mondesi, Raul, L.A.	.982	158	315	7	6	328	5
Mora, Melvin, N.Y.	1.000	45	18	0	0	18	0
Morris, Hal, Cin.*	1.000	4	3	0	0	3	0
Mouton, James, Mon.	.981	56	50	2	1	53	1
Mouton, Lyle, Mil.	1.000	3	1	0	0	1	0
Murray, Calvin, S.F.	1.000	9	6	0	0	6	0
Nevin, Phil, S.D.	1.000	13	11	0	0	11	0
Nixon, Otis, Atl.	.981	52	52	0	1	53	0
Ochoa, Alex, Mil.	.979	85	133	5	3	141	0
Owens, Eric, S.D.	.990	116	199	4	2	205	1
Paquette, Craig, St.L.	.955	27	42	0	2	44	0
Payton, Jay, N.Y.	1.000	6	3	0	0	3	0
Perez, Eduardo, St.L.	1.000	6	11	1	0	12	1
Phillips, J.R., Col.*	.933	7	11	3	1	15	2
Porter, Bo, Chi.	.941	21	16	0	1	17	0
Powell, Dante, Ari.	.929	15	13	0	1	14	0
Pratt, Todd, N.Y.	1.000	1	1	0	0	1	0
Ramirez, Julio, Fla.	.950	11	19	0	1	20	0
Reed, Rick, N.Y.	.000	1	0	0	0	0	0
Rios, Armando, S.F.*	.978	53	84	5	2	91	1
Rivera, Ruben, S.F.	.976	143	312	8	8	328	2
Robinson, Kerry, Cin.*	.000	2	0	0	0	0	0
Rodriguez, Henry, Chi.*	.974	122	222	7	6	235	1
Ryan, Rob, Ari.*	1.000	5	7	0	0	7	0
Sanders, Reggie, S.D.	.975	129	233	4	6	243	0
Santangelo, F.P., S.F.	.993	81	130	4	1	135	1
Sefcik, Kevin, Phi.	.986	64	68	1	1	70	0
Seguignol, Fernando, Mon.	1.000	8	11	0	0	11	0
Sexton, Chris, Col.	1.000	13	12	1	0	13	0
Sheffield, Gary, L.A.	.972	145	235	7	7	249	1
Shumpert, Terry, Col.	.952	19	20	0	1	21	0
Sosa, Juan, Col.	1.000	6	2	0	0	2	0
Sosa, Sammy, Chi.	.978	162	399	8	9	416	3
Spiers, Bill, Hou.	.976	31	40	0	1	41	0
Stowers, Chris, Mon.*	1.000	2	1	0	0	1	0
Stynes, Chris, Cin.	.000	4	0	0	0	0	0
Sveum, Dale, Pit.	1.000	1	2	0	0	2	0
Sweeney, Mark, Cin.*	1.000	1	1	0	0	1	0
Thompson, Ryan, Hou.	.800	10	3	1	1	5	1
Tucker, Michael, Cin.	.990	114	182	8	2	192	0
Vander Wal, John, S.D.*	1.000	48	71	2	0	73	1
Vaughn, Greg, Cin.	.986	144	264	8	4	276	2
Vidro, Jose, Mon.	1.000	3	2	0	0	2	0
Vizcaino, Jose, L.A.	.000	1	0	0	0	0	0
Walker, Larry, Col.	.982	114	204	13	4	221	3
Ward, Daryle, Hou.*	.944	31	33	1	2	36	0
Ward, Turner, Pit.-Ari.	.964	39	52	1	2	55	0
Watkins, Pat, Col.	1.000	10	10	0	0	10	0
Wehner, John, Pit.	.958	17	23	0	1	24	0
White, Devon, L.A.	.986	128	273	3	4	280	1
White, Rondell, Mon.	.964	135	286	7	11	304	2
Williams, Gerald, Atl.	.985	139	188	9	3	200	2
Wilson, Preston, Fla.	.973	136	320	10	9	339	1
Womack, Tony, Ari.	.992	123	247	9	2	258	2
Young, Dmitri, Cin.	.976	91	160	4	4	168	0
Young, Ernie, Ari.	1.000	4	10	1	0	11	1

OUTFIELDERS WITH TWO OR MORE TEAMS

Player, Team	Pct.	G	PO	A	E	TC	DP
Dunston, Shawon, St.L.	1.000	23	38	1	0	39	0
Dunston, Shawon, N.Y.	.978	27	43	1	1	45	0
Garcia, Freddy, Pit.	.977	24	43	0	1	44	0
Garcia, Freddy, Atl.	.000	1	0	0	0	0	0
Hamilton, Darryl, Col.	1.000	82	205	1	0	206	0
Hamilton, Darryl, N.Y.	1.000	52	100	2	0	102	0
Harris, Lenny, Col.	.933	14	12	2	1	15	1
Harris, Lenny, Ari.	1.000	2	3	0	0	3	0
Hernandez, Jose, Chi.	1.000	20	24	0	0	24	0
Hernandez, Jose, Atl.	1.000	1	5	0	0	5	0
Javier, Stan, S.F.	.976	94	158	4	4	166	3
Javier, Stan, Hou.	1.000	18	31	1	0	32	0
McRae, Brian, N.Y.	.994	87	152	1	1	154	0
McRae, Brian, Col.	1.000	7	14	0	0	14	0
Ward, Turner, Pit.	.955	34	41	1	2	44	0
Ward, Turner, Ari.	1.000	5	11	0	0	11	0

CATCHERS

Player, Team	Pct.	G	PO	A	E	TC	DP	PB
Bako, Paul, Hou.	.988	71	461	35	6	502	10	4
Banks, Brian, Mil.	.982	40	148	14	3	165	3	5
Barajas, Rod, Ari.	1.000	5	30	1	0	31	0	1
Barrett, Michael, Mon.	.986	59	329	25	5	359	2	7
Bennett, Gary, Phi.	.971	32	129	6	4	139	0	2
Blanco, Henry, Col.	.992	86	562	58	5	625	12	5
Cancel, Robinson, Mil.	.980	15	84	12	2	98	2	0
Castillo, Alberto, St.L.	.991	91	514	38	5	557	10	5
Castro, Ramon, Fla.	.992	24	105	17	1	123	1	3
Cox, Darron, Mon.	.963	14	48	4	2	54	1	0
Davis, Ben, S.D.	.986	74	471	29	7	507	7	4
Estalella, Bobby, Phi.	.976	7	38	2	1	41	0	0
Eusebio, Tony, Hou.	.994	98	657	37	4	693	3	4
Fabregas, Jorge, Fla.-Atl.	.990	82	425	52	5	482	2	4
Garcia, Guillermo, Fla.	1.000	3	5	0	0	5	0	0
Gonzalez, Wiki, S.D.	.992	17	109	15	1	125	2	1
Greene, Charlie, Mil.	.991	31	104	8	1	113	0	1
Guzman, Edwards, S.F.	1.000	1	0	0	0	1	0	0
Houston, Tyler, Chi.	.952	18	73	6	4	83	1	1
Hubbard, Trenidad, L.A.	1.000	1	1	0	0	1	0	0
Hughes, Bobby, Mil.	.988	44	149	15	2	166	2	5
Hundley, Todd, L.A.	.979	108	681	51	16	748	5	7
Jensen, Marcus, St.L.	.988	14	71	9	1	81	1	1
Johnson, Brian, Cin.	.995	39	201	11	1	213	2	4
Kendall, Jason, Pit.	.988	75	505	48	7	560	13	6
Kinkade, Mike, N.Y.	1.000	1	3	0	0	3	0	0
Knorr, Randy, Hou.	1.000	11	54	3	0	57	0	1
Laker, Tim, Pit.	1.000	2	9	0	0	9	0	0
LaRue, Jason, Cin.	.990	35	179	15	2	196	0	2
Leyritz, Jim, S.D.	.994	24	150	16	1	167	0	6
LIEBERTHAL, Mike, Phi.	.997	143	881	62	3	946	12	11
LoDuca, Paul, L.A.	.990	34	178	21	2	201	3	0
Lopez, Javy, Atl.	.991	60	413	29	4	446	3	6
Machado, Robert, Mon.	1.000	17	33	3	0	36	0	1
Manwaring, Kirt, Col.	.981	44	243	21	5	269	4	1
Marrero, Eli, St.L.	.987	96	490	42	7	539	12	2
Martinez, Sandy, Chi.	.959	12	45	2	2	49	0	0
Matos, Pascual, Atl.	1.000	5	13	1	0	14	0	0
Mayne, Brent, S.F.	.995	105	597	47	3	647	9	2
Meluskey, Mitch, Hou.	1.000	10	62	6	0	68	1	0
Miller, Damian, Ari.	.991	86	622	61	6	689	9	11
Mirabelli, Doug, S.F.	1.000	30	156	11	0	167	2	0
Molina, Jose, Chi.	1.000	10	44	5	0	49	1	1
Myers, Greg, S.D.-Atl.	.990	72	365	26	4	395	2	0
Nevin, Phil, S.D.	.994	31	155	14	1	170	0	4
Nilsson, Dave, Mil.	.991	101	531	44	5	580	3	2
Oliver, Joe, Pit.	.993	44	285	12	2	299	4	1
Osik, Keith, Pit.	.997	50	289	22	1	312	4	1
Pena, Angel, L.A.	.989	43	233	26	3	262	5	6
Perez, Eddie, Atl.	.993	98	616	48	5	669	7	4
Petrick, Ben, Col.	.982	19	100	7	2	109	1	3
Piazza, Mike, N.Y.	.989	137	953	47	11	1011	5	7
Pratt, Todd, N.Y.	.996	52	262	13	1	276	1	3
Prince, Tom, Phi.	1.000	4	13	1	0	14	0	0
Redmond, Mike, Fla.	.992	82	444	45	4	493	5	3
Reed, Jeff, Col.-Chi.	.985	85	442	32	7	481	4	2
Roskos, John, Fla.	1.000	1	5	0	0	5	0	0
Santiago, Benito, Chi.	.990	107	560	43	6	609	8	10
Servais, Scott, S.F.	.992	62	362	23	3	388	5	6
Stinnett, Kelly, Ari.	.990	86	549	37	6	592	7	5

Player, Team	Pct.	G	PO	A	E	TC	DP	PB
Taubensee, Eddie, Cin.	.989	124	733	48	9	790	8	5
Tremie, Chris, Pit.	1.000	8	29	2	0	31	0	1
Widger, Chris, Mon.	.992	117	662	54	6	722	6	8
Wilkins, Rick, L.A.	1.000	1	1	0	0	1	0	0
Wilson, Vance, N.Y.	.000	1	0	0	0	0	0	0

CATCHERS WITH TWO OR MORE TEAMS

Player, Team	Pct.	G	PO	A	E	TC	DP	PB
Fabregas, Jorge, Fla.	.989	78	404	52	5	461	2	4
Fabregas, Jorge, Atl.	1.000	4	21	0	0	21	0	0
Myers, Greg, S.D.	.986	41	199	14	3	216	0	0
Myers, Greg, Atl.	.994	31	166	12	1	179	2	0
Reed, Jeff, Col.	.983	36	160	15	3	178	1	0
Reed, Jeff, Chi.	.987	49	282	17	4	303	3	2

PITCHERS

Player, Team	Pct.	G	PO	A	E	TC	DP
Abbott, Jim, Mil.*	.963	20	3	23	1	27	1
Acevedo, Juan, St.L.	.857	50	5	7	2	14	0
Adams, Terry, Chi.	.933	52	8	6	1	15	0
Aguilera, Rick, Chi.	1.000	44	4	6	0	10	1
Aldred, Scott, Phi.*	1.000	29	2	6	0	8	0
Alfonseca, Antonio, Fla.	1.000	73	5	14	0	19	2
Almanza, Armando, Fla.*	1.000	14	0	2	0	2	1
Almanzar, Carlos, S.D.	.714	28	2	3	2	7	1
Almonte, Hector, Fla.	1.000	15	1	3	0	4	1
Anderson, Brian, Ari.*	.958	31	10	36	2	48	1
Anderson, Jimmy, Pit.*	1.000	13	1	5	0	6	2
Ankiel, Rick, St.L.*	1.000	9	2	0	0	2	0
Armas, Tony, Mon.	1.000	1	1	0	0	1	0
Arnold, Jamie, L.A.	.917	36	4	18	2	24	5
Ashby, Andy, S.D.	.961	31	14	35	2	51	4
Astacio, Pedro, Col.	.911	34	16	25	4	45	3
Avery, Steve, Cin.*	.952	19	4	16	1	21	0
Ayala, Bobby, Mon.-Chi.	.833	66	8	12	4	24	1
Aybar, Manny, St.L.	1.000	65	5	11	0	16	0
Barker, Richie, Cin.	1.000	5	1	0	0	1	0
Batista, Miguel, Mon.	.926	39	5	20	2	27	1
Beck, Rod, Chi.	1.000	31	4	4	0	8	0
Belinda, Stan, Cin.	1.000	29	0	5	0	5	0
Beltran, Rigo, N.Y.-Col.*	1.000	33	3	7	0	10	1
Benes, Alan, St.L.	1.000	2	1	0	0	1	0
Benes, Andy, Ari.	.933	33	13	15	2	30	1
Benitez, Armando, N.Y.	1.000	77	2	6	0	8	0
Bennett, Joel, Phi.	1.000	5	2	3	0	5	0
Bennett, Shayne, Mon.	ʻ.000	5	0	0	0	0	0
Benson, Kris, Pit.	.955	31	15	27	2	44	6
Bere, Jason, Cin.-Mil.	.900	17	1	8	1	10	1
Bergman, Sean, Hou.-Atl.	1.000	25	4	10	0	14	1
Billingsley, Brent, Fla.*	1.000	8	1	0	0	1	1
Bochtler, Doug, L.A.	1.000	12	1	3	0	4	0
Boehringer, Brian, S.D.	.944	33	8	9	1	18	0
Bohanon, Brian, Col.*	.973	33	7	29	1	37	2
Borbon, Pedro, L.A.*	1.000	70	2	6	0	8	0
Bottalico, Ricky, St.L.	1.000	68	4	9	0	13	2
Bottenfield, Kent, St.L.	1.000	31	10	30	0	40	3
Bowie, Micah, Atl.-Chi.*	.857	14	0	6	1	7	0
Boyd, Jason, Pit.	1.000	4	1	0	0	1	0
Brantley, Jeff, Phi.	1.000	10	0	1	0	1	0
Brewer, Billy, Phi.*	1.000	25	0	1	0	1	0
Brock, Chris, S.F.	.952	19	11	9	1	21	2
Brown, Kevin, L.A.	.935	35	41	46	6	93	2
Brownson, Mark, Col.	.857	7	1	5	1	7	0
Burnett, A.J., Fla.	.875	7	2	5	1	8	0
Busby, Mike, St.L.	1.000	15	1	2	0	3	1
Byrd, Paul, Phi.	.854	32	10	25	6	41	3
Cabrera, Jose, Hou.	1.000	26	0	2	0	2	0
Carlson, Dan, Ari.	.000	2	0	0	0	0	0
Carlyle, Buddy, S.D.	1.000	7	0	3	0	3	1
Cather, Mike, Atl.	1.000	4	0	1	0	1	0
Checo, Robinson, L.A.	.000	9	0	0	0	0	0
Chen, Bruce, Atl.*	.750	16	0	3	1	4	0
Chouinard, Bobby, Ari.	.889	32	2	6	1	9	1
Christiansen, Jason, Pit.*	1.000	39	0	7	0	7	1
Clement, Matt, S.D.	.923	31	12	12	2	26	0
Clontz, Brad, Pit.	1.000	56	1	7	0	8	0
Cook, Dennis, N.Y.*	1.000	71	2	8	0	10	0
Coppinger, Rocky, Mil.	.667	29	2	0	1	3	0
Corbin, Archie, Fla.	1.000	17	0	1	0	1	0
Cordova, Francisco, Pit.	.975	27	14	25	1	40	2
Cornelius, Reid, Fla.	1.000	5	0	5	0	5	0

Player, Team	Pct.	G	PO	A	E	TC	DP
Cortes, David, Atl.	.500	4	0	1	1	2	0
Creek, Doug, Chi.*	.000	3	0	0	0	0	0
Croushore, Rich, St.L.	.750	59	2	4	2	8	0
Cunnane, Will, S.D.	1.000	24	1	4	0	5	0
D'Amico, Jeff, Mil.	.000	1	0	0	0	0	0
Daal, Omar, Ari.*	.959	32	13	34	2	49	2
Dale, Carl, Mil.	.000	4	0	0	0	0	0
Darensbourg, Vic, Fla.*	1.000	56	1	4	0	5	0
de los Santos, Valerio, Mil.*	1.000	7	0	2	0	2	0
DeHart, Rick, Mon.*	.000	3	0	0	0	0	0
DeJean, Mike, Col.	1.000	56	4	11	0	15	2
del Toro, Miguel, S.F.	1.000	14	1	3	0	4	2
Dempster, Ryan, Fla.	.962	25	10	15	1	26	4
Dipoto, Jerry, Col.	.938	63	4	11	1	16	0
Dotel, Octavio, N.Y.	.944	19	8	9	1	18	0
Dougherty, Jim, Pit.	.000	2	0	0	0	0	0
Dreifort, Darren, L.A.	.936	30	18	26	3	47	2
Ebert, Derrin, Atl.*	1.000	5	0	2	0	2	0
Edmondson, Brian, Fla.	1.000	68	6	15	0	21	1
Elarton, Scott, Hou.	1.000	42	4	8	0	12	0
Eldred, Cal, Mil.	1.000	20	5	3	0	8	0
Embree, Alan, S.F.*	1.000	68	2	3	0	5	0
Estes, Shawn, S.F.*	.980	32	18	31	1	50	1
Estrada, Horacio, Mil.*	1.000	4	0	1	0	1	0
Falteisek, Steve, Mil.	.000	10	0	0	0	0	0
Farnsworth, Kyle, Chi.	.846	27	9	13	4	26	1
Fernandez, Alex, Fla.	.971	24	7	27	1	35	3
Fox, Chad, Mil.	1.000	6	2	0	0	2	0
Franco, John, N.Y.*	1.000	46	4	4	0	8	0
Franco, Matt, N.Y.	.000	2	0	0	0	0	0
Frascatore, John, Ari.	1.000	26	1	2	0	3	0
Gaetti, Gary, Chi.	.000	1	0	0	0	0	0
Gagne, Eric, L.A.	1.000	5	2	0	0	2	0
Garcia, Mike, Pit.	.000	7	0	0	0	0	0
Gardner, Mark, S.F.	1.000	29	7	18	0	25	1
Giovanola, Ed, S.D.	.000	1	0	0	0	0	0
Glavine, Tom, Atl.*	.986	35	12	59	1	72	6
Gomes, Wayne, Phi.	1.000	73	4	5	0	9	0
Grace, Mike, Phi.	1.000	27	5	5	0	10	0
Grahe, Joe, Phi.	1.000	13	3	5	0	8	1
Graves, Danny, Cin.	1.000	75	7	21	0	28	3
Greene, Rick, Cin.	.000	1	0	0	0	0	0
Guthrie, Mark, Chi.*	1.000	11	0	1	0	1	0
Guzman, Domingo, S.D.	.800	7	1	3	1	5	0
Guzman, Juan, Cin.	.929	12	5	8	1	14	1
Hackman, Luther, Col.	1.000	5	2	4	0	6	0
Hampton, Mike, Hou.*	.946	34	12	41	3	56	4
Hansell, Greg, Pit.	1.000	33	1	5	0	6	1
Harnisch, Pete, Cin.	.893	33	7	18	3	28	1
Harris, Reggie, Mil.	1.000	8	1	0	0	1	1
Heiserman, Rick, St.L.	1.000	3	1	0	0	1	1
Henry, Doug, Hou.	.889	35	2	6	1	9	0
Heredia, Felix, Chi.*	1.000	69	1	4	0	5	0
Herges, Matt, L.A.	1.000	17	2	2	0	4	0
Hermanson, Dustin, Mon.	1.000	34	20	21	0	41	1
Hernandez, Livan, Fla.-S.F.	.981	30	18	34	1	53	2
Hershiser, Orel, N.Y.	.947	32	19	35	3	57	1
Hitchcock, Sterling, S.D.*	.969	33	7	24	1	32	0
Hoffman, Trevor, S.D.	1.000	64	3	5	0	8	0
Holmes, Darren, Ari.	.917	44	6	5	1	12	1
Holt, Chris, Hou.	.968	32	14	16	1	31	2
Hudek, John, Cin.-Atl.	1.000	17	1	2	0	3	0
Isringhausen, Jason, N.Y.	.889	13	3	5	1	9	1
Jimenez, Jose, St.L.	.975	29	10	29	1	40	2
Johnson, Mike, Mon.	1.000	3	1	1	0	2	0
Johnson, Randy, Ari.*	.865	35	4	28	5	37	2
Johnstone, John, S.F.	1.000	62	5	8	0	13	0
Jones, Bobby, N.Y.	1.000	12	4	7	0	11	0
Jones, Bobby M., Col.*	.875	30	4	10	2	16	0
Judd, Mike, L.A.	1.000	7	0	4	0	4	1
Karchner, Matt, Chi.	1.000	16	1	1	0	2	0
Karl, Scott, Mil.*	.931	33	10	44	4	58	4
Kile, Darryl, Col.	.971	32	10	24	1	35	2
Kim, Byung-Hyun, Ari.	1.000	25	2	7	0	9	0
King, Curtis, St.L.	.000	2	0	0	0	0	0
King, Ray, Chi.*	1.000	10	0	1	0	1	0
Kline, Steve, Mon.*	.957	82	5	17	1	23	2
Kubenka, Jeff, L.A.*	1.000	6	0	3	0	3	0
Lee, David, Col.	1.000	36	3	7	0	10	0
Leiter, Al, N.Y.*	.840	32	3	18	4	25	1
Leskanic, Curt, Col.	.864	63	6	13	3	22	1
Lieber, Jon, Chi.	.946	31	18	17	2	37	1

Player, Team	Pct.	G	PO	A	E	TC	DP
Lilly, Ted, Mon.*	1.000	9	0	3	0	3	0
Lima, Jose, Hou.	.951	35	18	21	2	41	1
Loewer, Carlton, Phi.	.929	20	3	10	1	14	0
Loiselle, Rich, Pit.	1.000	13	2	3	0	5	1
Looper, Braden, Fla.	1.000	72	3	8	0	11	0
Lorraine, Andrew, Chi.*	.909	11	2	8	1	11	0
Luebbers, Larry, St.L.	1.000	8	4	7	0	11	0
Maddux, Greg, Atl.	.956	33	29	58	4	91	3
Maddux, Mike, Mon.-L.A.	.917	53	5	6	1	12	1
Mahomes, Pat, N.Y.	1.000	39	2	6	0	8	0
Mantei, Matt, Fla.-Ari.	.909	65	3	7	1	11	0
Manzanillo, Josias, N.Y.	1.000	12	2	2	0	4	0
Masaoka, Onan, L.A.*	.833	54	1	4	1	6	0
McCurry, Jeff, Hou.	.000	5	0	0	0	0	0
McElroy, Chuck, Col.-N.Y.*	1.000	56	2	8	0	10	1
McGlinchy, Kevin, Atl.	.833	64	4	6	2	12	0
McMichael, Greg, N.Y.	1.000	19	2	1	0	3	0
McNichol, Brian, Chi.*	.000	4	0	0	0	0	0
Meadows, Brian, Fla.	.943	31	12	21	2	35	1
Medina, Rafael, Fla.	1.000	20	1	1	0	2	0
Mercker, Kent, St.L.*	.810	25	1	16	4	21	1
Miceli, Dan, S.D.	.909	66	4	6	1	11	0
Miller, Kurt, Chi.	.000	4	0	0	0	0	0
Miller, Trever, Hou.*	1.000	47	3	7	0	10	0
Miller, Wade, Hou.	1.000	5	0	2	0	2	0
Mills, Alan, L.A.	.833	68	3	7	2	12	2
Millwood, Kevin, Atl.	.943	33	13	20	2	35	0
Mlicki, Dave, L.A.	1.000	2	1	0	0	1	0
Mohler, Mike, St.L.*	1.000	48	0	4	0	4	0
Montgomery, Steve, Phi.	1.000	53	1	6	0	7	0
Mota, Guillermo, Mon.	1.000	51	4	10	0	14	1
Mulholland, Terry, Chi.-Atl.*	.884	42	8	30	5	43	1
Murray, Dan, N.Y.	1.000	1	1	0	0	1	0
Murray, Heath, S.D.*	1.000	22	0	8	0	8	0
Myers, Mike, Mil.*	1.000	71	5	7	0	12	0
Myers, Rodney, Chi.	.857	46	2	4	1	7	0
Nathan, Joe, S.F.	1.000	19	3	11	0	14	0
Neagle, Denny, Cin.*	1.000	20	2	5	0	7	1
Nen, Robb, S.F.	.857	72	2	10	2	14	1
Nomo, Hideo, Mil.	1.000	28	11	11	0	22	3
Nunez, Vladimir, Ari.-Fla.	.929	44	7	19	2	28	1
Ogea, Chad, Phi.	.960	36	8	16	1	25	1
Ojala, Kirt, Fla.*	.000	8	0	0	0	0	0
Oliver, Darren, St.L.*	.952	30	7	33	2	42	1
Olson, Gregg, Ari.	1.000	61	4	9	0	13	0
Ortiz, Russ, S.F.	1.000	33	13	31	0	44	2
Osborne, Donovan, St.L.*	.889	6	1	7	1	9	0
Osik, Keith, Pit.	.000	1	0	0	0	0	0
Osuna, Antonio, L.A.	1.000	5	0	1	0	1	0
Padilla, Vicente, Ari.	.000	5	0	0	0	0	0
Painter, Lance, St.L.*	.938	56	3	12	1	16	1
Park, Chan Ho, L.A.	1.000	33	15	33	0	48	4
Parris, Steve, Cin.	.962	22	8	17	1	26	6
Patrick, Bronswell, S.F.	.500	6	0	1	1	2	0
Pavano, Carl, Mon.	1.000	19	10	24	0	34	0
Perez, Carlos, L.A.*	.905	17	4	15	2	21	0
Perez, Odalis, Atl.*	1.000	18	4	17	0	21	1
Perez, Yorkis, Pit.*	1.000	35	1	0	0	1	0
Person, Robert, Phi.	.955	31	8	13	1	22	0
Peters, Chris, Pit.*	1.000	19	5	14	0	19	0
Peterson, Kyle, Mil.	.833	17	3	7	2	12	0
Phillips, Jason, Pit.	1.000	6	0	2	0	2	0
Pittsley, Jim, Mil.	1.000	15	3	3	0	6	0
Plesac, Dan, Ari.*	1.000	34	1	4	0	5	0
Plunk, Eric, Mil.	.857	68	0	6	1	7	0
Politte, Cliff, Phi.	1.000	13	1	1	0	2	0
Poole, Jim, Phi.*	.800	51	1	3	1	5	0
Porzio, Mike, Col.*	1.000	16	0	3	0	3	0
Powell, Jay, Hou.	.800	67	1	7	2	10	0
Powell, Jeremy, Mon.	.957	17	9	13	1	23	0
Pulsipher, Bill, Mil.*	1.000	19	2	19	0	21	1
Radinsky, Scott, St.L.*	.833	43	1	4	1	6	1
Rain, Steve, Chi.	1.000	16	3	3	0	6	0
Ramirez, Hector, Mil.	1.000	15	2	1	0	3	0
Ramirez, Roberto, Col.*	1.000	32	2	5	0	7	1
Reed, Rick, N.Y.	.976	26	11	29	1	41	4
Remlinger, Mike, Atl.*	.933	73	4	10	1	15	1
Reyes, Al, Mil.	1.000	26	1	3	0	4	0
Reyes, Carlos, S.D.	1.000	65	3	15	0	18	2
Reyes, Dennys, Cin.*	.833	65	0	5	1	6	0
REYNOLDS, Shane, Hou.	1.000	35	18	41	0	59	3
Reynoso, Armando, Ari.	.930	31	12	28	3	43	4
Ritchie, Todd, Pit.	1.000	28	9	25	0	34	0
Rivera, Roberto, S.D.*	1.000	12	0	3	0	3	0
Rocker, John, Atl.*	1.000	74	1	10	0	11	0
Rodriguez, Felix, S.F.	1.000	47	5	11	0	16	1
Rodriguez, Rich, S.F.*	1.000	62	6	11	0	17	1
Rogers, Kenny, N.Y.*	.958	12	4	19	1	24	2
Rojas, Mel, L.A.-Mon.	1.000	8	0	2	0	2	0
Roque, Rafael, Mil.*	.895	43	3	14	2	19	0
Rueter, Kirk, S.F.*	.978	33	15	30	1	46	5
Rusch, Glendon, N.Y.*	.000	1	0	0	0	0	0
Ryan, B.J., Cin.*	.000	1	0	0	0	0	0
Ryan, Ken, Phi.	1.000	15	2	2	0	4	0
Sabel, Erik, Ari.	1.000	7	0	2	0	2	1
Sanchez, Jesus, Fla.*	1.000	59	7	8	0	15	1
Sanders, Scott, Chi.	.850	67	5	12	3	20	2
Sauerbeck, Scott, Pit.*	1.000	65	4	8	0	12	1
Schilling, Curt, Phi.	1.000	24	11	19	0	30	1
Schmidt, Jason, Pit.	.929	33	10	16	2	28	0
Schourek, Pete, Pit.	.900	30	3	15	2	20	0
Schrenk, Steve, Phi.	1.000	32	4	7	0	11	1
Seanez, Rudy, Atl.	1.000	56	4	5	0	9	0
Serafini, Dan, Chi.*	1.000	42	3	5	0	8	0
Shaw, Jeff, L.A.	1.000	64	10	4	0	14	1
Shumaker, Anthony, Phi.*	.833	8	0	5	1	6	0
Silva, Jose, Pit.	1.000	34	6	16	0	22	2
Slocumb, Heathcliff, St.L.	1.000	40	4	7	0	11	0
Slusarski, Joe, Hou.	.000	3	0	0	0	0	0
Smart, J.D., Mon.	1.000	29	2	8	0	10	0
Smith, Dan, Mon.	.846	20	4	7	2	13	0
Smoltz, John, Atl.	.975	29	9	30	1	40	3
Sodowsky, Clint, St.L.	1.000	3	1	0	0	1	0
Speier, Justin, Atl.	1.000	19	5	2	0	7	0
Spencer, Stan, S.D.	1.000	9	3	2	0	5	0
Spoljaric, Paul, Phi.*	.667	5	1	1	1	3	0
Spradlin, Jerry, S.F.	.750	59	2	4	2	8	1
Springer, Dennis, Fla.	.913	38	12	30	4	46	5
Springer, Russ, Atl.	1.000	49	1	4	0	5	0
Stephenson, Garrett, St.L.	1.000	18	6	9	0	15	1
Stottlemyre, Todd, Ari.	.952	17	8	12	1	21	1
Strickland, Scott, Mon.	1.000	17	0	4	0	4	0
Stull, Everett, Atl.	.000	1	0	0	0	0	0
Sullivan, Scott, Cin.	.842	79	6	10	3	19	0
Swindell, Greg, Ari.*	1.000	63	3	10	0	13	2
Tam, Jeff, N.Y.	1.000	9	3	1	0	4	0
Tapani, Kevin, Chi.	1.000	23	2	18	0	20	0
Tavarez, Julian, S.F.	.929	47	7	6	1	14	1
Taylor, Billy, N.Y.	1.000	18	0	2	0	2	0
Tejera, Michael, Fla.*	1.000	3	1	3	0	4	2
Telemaco, Amaury, Ari.-Phi.	.929	49	5	8	1	14	0
Telford, Anthony, Mon.	.862	79	10	15	4	29	0
Thompson, Mark, St.L.	1.000	5	3	4	0	7	0
Thomson, John, Col.	1.000	14	9	10	0	19	1
Thurman, Mike, Mon.	.955	29	9	12	1	22	0
Tomko, Brett, Cin.	.938	33	10	20	2	32	2
Trachsel, Steve, Chi.	1.000	34	18	20	0	38	3
Urbina, Ugueth, Mon.	1.000	71	5	2	0	7	0
Valdes, Ismael, L.A.	.978	32	12	33	1	46	1
Vazquez, Javier, Mon.	1.000	26	9	33	0	42	1
Veres, Dave, Col.	1.000	73	7	5	0	12	0
Villone, Ron, Cin.*	.854	29	7	28	6	41	1
Vosberg, Ed, S.D.-Ari.*	.800	19	1	3	1	5	0
Wagner, Billy, Hou.*	1.000	66	2	5	0	7	1
Wainhouse, Dave, Col.	1.000	19	3	4	0	7	1
Wall, Donne, S.D.	.909	55	9	11	2	22	1
Wallace, Jeff, Pit.*	1.000	41	0	3	0	3	0
Watson, Allen, N.Y.*	1.000	14	3	2	0	5	0
Weathers, Dave, Mil.	1.000	63	6	13	0	19	0
Wendell, Turk, N.Y.	.833	80	4	6	2	12	0
Whisenant, Matt, S.D.*	1.000	19	2	2	0	4	0
White, Gabe, Cin.*	1.000	50	1	2	0	3	0
Whiteside, Matt, S.D.	1.000	10	0	3	0	3	0
Wickman, Bob, Mil.	.840	71	6	15	4	25	2
Wilkins, Marc, Pit.	1.000	46	2	11	0	13	0
Williams, Brian, Hou.	1.000	50	4	11	0	15	1
Williams, Jeff, L.A.*	1.000	5	1	3	0	4	1
Williams, Mike, Pit.	.765	58	4	9	4	17	1
Williams, Woody, S.D.	.966	33	11	17	1	29	0
Williamson, Scott, Cin.	.900	62	2	7	1	10	1
Winkelsas, Joe, Atl.	.000	1	0	0	0	0	0
Wohlers, Mark, Atl.	.000	2	0	0	1	1	0
Wolf, Randy, Phi.*	.889	22	3	13	2	18	2
Woodall, Brad, Chi.*	1.000	6	1	2	0	3	1

Player, Team	Pct.	G	PO	A	E	TC	DP
Woodard, Steve, Mil.	1.000	31	12	24	0	36	0
Wright, Jamey, Col.	.964	16	9	18	1	28	2
Yoshii, Masato, N.Y.	1.000	31	7	10	0	17	1

PITCHERS WITH TWO OR MORE TEAMS

Player, Team	Pct.	G	PO	A	E	TC	DP
Ayala, Bobby, Mon.	.810	53	7	10	4	21	1
Ayala, Bobby, Chi.	1.000	13	1	2	0	3	0
Beltran, Rigo, N.Y.*	1.000	21	2	6	0	8	1
Beltran, Rigo, Col.*	1.000	12	1	1	0	2	0
Bere, Jason, Cin.	.889	12	1	7	1	9	1
Bere, Jason, Mil.	1.000	5	0	1	0	1	0
Bergman, Sean, Hou.	1.000	19	4	8	0	12	1
Bergman, Sean, Atl.	1.000	6	0	2	0	2	0
Bowie, Micah, Atl.*	.000	3	0	0	0	0	0
Bowie, Micah, Chi.*	.857	11	0	6	1	7	0
Hernandez, Livan, Fla.	.971	20	12	21	1	34	1
Hernandez, Livan, S.F.	1.000	10	6	13	0	19	1
Hudek, John, Cin.	.000	2	0	0	0	0	0
Hudek, John, Atl.	1.000	15	1	2	0	3	0
Maddux, Mike, Mon.	.000	4	0	0	0	0	0
Maddux, Mike, L.A.	.917	49	5	6	1	12	1
Mantei, Matt, Fla.	.833	35	2	3	1	6	0
Mantei, Matt, Ari.	1.000	30	1	4	0	5	0
McElroy, Chuck, Col.*	1.000	41	1	8	0	9	1
McElroy, Chuck, N.Y.*	1.000	15	1	0	0	1	0
Mulholland, Terry, Chi.*	.852	26	6	17	4	27	1
Mulholland, Terry, Atl.*	.938	16	2	13	1	16	0
Nunez, Vladimir, Ari.	1.000	27	1	6	0	7	0
Nunez, Vladimir, Fla.	.905	17	6	13	2	21	1
Rojas, Mel, L.A.	1.000	5	0	1	0	1	0
Rojas, Mel, Mon.	1.000	3	0	1	0	1	0
Telemaco, Amaury, Ari.	1.000	5	0	1	0	1	0
Telemaco, Amaury, Phi.	.923	44	5	7	1	13	0
Vosberg, Ed, S.D.*	.800	15	1	3	1	5	0
Vosberg, Ed, Ari.*	.000	4	0	0	0	0	0

MISCELLANEOUS

SHUTOUT GAMES

Read across for wins, down for losses.

Team	Cin.	Hou.	Ari.	Atl.	S.F.	N.Y.	L.A.	Chi.	Phi.	Mil.	St.L.	Fla.	Col.	S.D.	Mon.	Pit.	A.L.	W	L	Pct.
Cincinnati	..	2	1	0	0	1	0	0	0	1	2	0	0	2	0	2	0	11	3	.786
Houston	0	..	1	0	0	0	2	0	0	2	0	0	0	0	1	1	1	8	5	.615
Arizona	0	0	..	0	0	0	1	1	2	1	0	1	0	2	0	0	1	9	6	.600
Atlanta	1	0	1	..	0	3	0	0	1	0	1	1	0	0	1	0	0	9	6	.600
San Francisco	0	0	0	0	..	0	0	0	0	0	0	0	2	0	0	0	1	3	2	.600
New York	1	1	0	0	2	..	0	0	0	0	0	1	0	0	1	1	0	7	5	.583
Los Angeles	0	0	0	0	0	0	..	0	2	0	0	0	1	1	0	0	1	6	6	.500
Chicago	0	1	0	1	0	1	1	..	0	0	0	0	0	1	0	1	0	6	7	.462
Philadelphia	1	0	0	0	0	0	0	1	..	2	0	0	1	1	0	0	0	6	7	.462
Milwaukee	0	0	0	0	0	0	0	0	0	..	0	1	0	0	1	0	1	5	6	.455
St. Louis	0	0	2	0	0	0	0	0	0	0	..	0	0	1	0	0	0	3	4	.429
Florida	0	0	0	2	0	0	0	1	0	0	0	..	0	0	1	0	1	5	7	.417
Colorado	0	0	0	0	0	0	0	0	0	2	0	0	..	0	0	0	0	2	3	.400
San Diego	0	0	0	2	0	0	1	1	0	0	0	0	1	..	0	1	0	6	10	.375
Montreal	0	0	0	0	0	0	1	0	0	0	0	0	0	1	..	0	2	4	8	.333
Pittsburgh	0	1	0	0	0	0	0	0	0	0	1	0	0	1	0	..	0	3	7	.300
A.L. clubs	0	0	1	1	0	0	0	1	0	0	0	0	0	1	2	1	..	..	..	..
Lost	3	5	6	6	2	5	6	7	7	6	4	7	3	10	8	7	..	93	92	.503

N.L. shutouts vs. A.L. clubs (8): Arizona vs. Seattle; Florida vs. Tampa Bay; Houston vs. Cleveland; Los Angeles vs. Seattle; Milwaukee vs. Kansas City; Montreal vs. Tampa Bay and Toronto; San Francisco vs. Oakland.

HOME RECORD

Read across for home wins, down for road losses.

Team	Atl.	Ari.	Hou.	N.Y.	S.F.	S.D.	Pit.	Cin.	Phi.	Col.	St.L.	L.A.	Fla.	Mon.	Chi.	Mil.	A.L.	W	L	Pct.
Atlanta	..	3	3	5	2	3	5	6	4	2	5	1	5	4	1	2	5	56	25	.691
Arizona	1	..	2	4	4	6	2	0	6	3	2	5	5	4	4	1	3	52	29	.642
Houston	1	3	..	1	2	6	4	1	2	3	3	4	2	4	4	5	5	50	32	.610
New York	2	0	3	..	5	5	5	0	4	2	2	1	5	3	3	2	7	49	32	.605
San Francisco	4	1	3	1	..	4	2	1	4	6	4	2	5	2	4	2	4	49	32	.605
San Diego	4	1	1	1	3	..	4	2	1	6	1	5	4	2	2	3	6	46	35	.568
Pittsburgh	2	1	5	1	3	1	..	3	3	4	3	4	2	4	5	0	4	45	36	.556
Cincinnati	1	5	4	2	2	2	4	..	2	4	5	1	4	2	3	3	1	45	37	.549
Philadelphia	2	1	0	4	2	4	2	2	..	1	1	2	6	2	5	2	5	41	40	.506
Colorado	3	4	1	3	3	3	0	0	3	..	0	4	3	4	1	5	2	39	42	.481
St. Louis	0	2	4	1	1	5	2	3	3	2	..	2	2	2	3	2	4	38	42	.475
Los Angeles	2	4	1	1	4	2	1	1	2	2	2	..	2	1	4	2	6	37	44	.457
Florida	2	0	0	2	3	1	2	1	1	4	2	3	..	5	1	3	5	35	45	.438
Montreal	2	1	0	1	3	3	1	2	2	1	4	2	3	..	2	2	6	35	46	.432
Chicago	2	0	1	3	1	5	5	2	1	2	4	0	1	1	..	3	3	34	47	.420
Milwaukee	1	2	3	0	0	2	2	3	4	2	3	1	1	1	3	..	4	32	48	.400
A.L. clubs	5	5	2	4	6	1	6	3	3	4	3	4	3	7	3	2	..	..	..	..
Lost	34	33	33	34	44	53	47	30	45	48	44	41	53	48	48	39	..	683	612	.527

HOME RECORDS IN INTERLEAGUE GAMES

Team	Bal.	Bos.	N.Y.	T.B.	Tor.
Atlanta	0-3	2-1	..	3-0	..
Florida	2-1	..	1-2	2-1	..
Montreal	..	3-0	..	2-1	1-2
New York	..	2-1	2-1	..	3-0
Philadelphia	1-2	..	2-1	..	2-1

Team	Chi.	Cle.	Det.	K.C.	Min.
Chicago	0-3	..	..	1-2	2-1
Cincinnati	..	0-3	1-2	..	..
Houston	..	2-1	3-0	..	..
Milwaukee	2-1	..	..	2-1	0-2
Pittsburgh	..	2-1	..	2-1	..
St. Louis	2-1	..	1-2	..	1-2

Team	Ana.	Oak.	Sea.	Tex.
Arizona	..	1-2	..	2-1
Colorado	1-2	..	1-2	..
Los Angeles	2-1	..	3-0	1-2
San Diego	..	2-1	2-1	2-1
San Francisco	2-1	2-1	..	..

ROAD RECORD

Read across for road wins, down for home losses.

Team	Cin.	Ari.	Hou.	N.Y.	Atl.	Mil.	L.A.	St.L.	S.F.	Phi.	Pit.	Chi.	Col.	Mon.	Fla.	S.D.	A.L.	W	L	Pct.
Cincinnati	..	3	5	3	0	3	3	3	2	4	3	5	3	2	2	4	6	51	30	.630
Arizona	1	..	3	3	3	4	2	2	5	2	3	3	3	2	3	5	4	48	33	.593
Houston	3	1	..	3	0	3	2	2	3	4	1	5	3	3	5	2	7	47	33	.588
New York	5	2	2	..	1	3	3	3	2	2	2	3	3	5	5	2	5	48	34	.585
Atlanta	2	2	3	4	..	3	4	3	2	4	1	1	3	5	4	2	4	47	34	.580
Milwaukee	3	2	2	2	1	..	1	4	4	1	6	3	1	4	3	1	4	42	39	.519
Los Angeles	2	2	3	2	2	5	..	1	4	4	2	3	4	0	1	2	2	40	41	.494
St. Louis	1	2	3	1	1	4	4	..	2	2	3	2	3	2	2	3	3	37	44	.457
San Francisco	4	2	1	1	1	3	3	2	..	2	3	3	3	0	3	3	4	37	44	.457
Philadelphia	1	0	1	2	3	4	2	1	3	..	0	1	3	4	5	2	6	36	45	.444
Pittsburgh	3	1	2	1	1	4	2	4	1	1	..	1	3	2	2	2	3	33	47	.413
Chicago	3	2	2	0	3	3	2	3	0	1	2	..	2	1	5	1	3	33	48	.407
Colorado	2	3	1	1	1	1	4	4	1	2	2	4	..	2	2	1	2	33	48	.407
Montreal	1	2	2	4	2	2	2	1	1	4	2	3	2	..	1	2	2	33	48	.407

Team	Cin.	Ari.	Hou.	N.Y.	Atl.	Mil.	L.A.	St.L.	S.F.	Phi.	Pit.	Chi.	Col.	Mon.	Fla.	S.D.	A.L.	W	L	Pct.
Florida	0	1	2	1	2	2	4	1	1	1	1	2	0	3	..	2	6	29	53	.354
San Diego	1	1	0	1	0	2	4	1	2	2	2	1	3	1	2	..	5	28	53	.346
A.L. clubs	5	3	1	2	4	4	3	5	2	4	2	6	4	3	4	3	..	..	..	..
Lost	37	29	32	32	25	48	44	42	32	40	36	47	42	46	45	35	..	622	674	.480

PITCHING AGAINST EACH CLUB

ARIZONA—100-62

Pitcher	Atl. W-L	Chi. W-L	Cin. W-L	Col. W-L	Fla. W-L	Hou. W-L	L.A. W-L	Mil. W-L	Mon. W-L	N.Y. W-L	Phi. W-L	Pit. W-L	St.L. W-L	S.D. W-L	S.F. W-L	A.L. W-L	Total W-L
Anderson, Brian	0-0	1-0	0-0	1-0	1-0	0-0	1-1	0-0	0-0	1-0	0-0	0-0	1-0	1-0	1-0	0-1	8-2
Benes, Andy	1-1	1-0	0-1	2-1	1-1	1-0	1-2	0-1	0-0	0-1	2-0	0-0	1-0	2-0	0-2	1-2	13-12
Carlson, Dan	0-0	0-0	0-0	0-0	0-0	0-0	0-0	0-0	0-0	0-0	0-0	0-0	0-0	0-0	0-0	0-0	0-0
Chouinard, Bobby	0-0	0-0	0-0	0-0	0-0	2-0	2-0	0-0	1-0	0-0	0-1	0-0	0-0	0-0	0-0	0-1	5-2
Daal, Omar	1-0	1-0	0-1	1-2	0-0	0-2	2-0	2-0	1-1	2-1	1-0	2-0	0-0	1-1	1-1	1-0	16-9
Frascatore, John	0-1	0-0	0-0	0-1	0-0	0-0	0-1	0-0	0-1	0-0	0-0	0-0	0-0	1-0	0-0	0-0	1-4
Holmes, Darren	0-0	0-1	0-1	0-0	0-0	1-0	0-0	2-0	1-0	0-0	0-0	0-0	0-0	0-0	0-0	0-1	4-3
Johnson, Randy	1-1	2-0	1-1	1-1	2-0	0-0	1-2	0-0	0-1	1-0	2-0	1-0	0-2	2-0	1-0	2-1	17-9
Kim, Byung-Hyun	0-0	0-0	0-0	0-0	0-0	0-0	0-0	0-0	0-0	0-0	0-0	0-0	0-1	1-0	0-0	0-1	1-2
Mantei, Matt	0-0	0-0	0-0	0-0	0-0	0-0	0-0	0-0	0-0	0-0	0-0	0-0	0-0	0-0	0-0	0-1	0-1
Nunez, Vladimir	0-0	0-0	0-1	0-0	0-0	0-0	0-0	0-0	0-0	0-0	0-0	2-1	0-0	0-0	0-0	1-0	3-2
Olson, Gregg	1-1	0-1	0-0	1-1	1-0	1-0	0-0	0-1	2-0	0-0	0-0	0-0	2-0	1-0	0-0	0-0	9-4
Padilla, Vicente	0-0	0-0	0-1	0-0	0-0	0-0	0-0	0-0	0-0	0-0	0-0	0-0	0-0	0-0	0-0	0-0	0-0
Plesac, Dan	0-0	1-0	0-1	0-0	0-0	0-0	0-0	0-0	0-0	0-0	0-0	0-0	0-0	0-0	0-0	1-0	2-1
Reynoso, Armando	0-1	0-0	0-0	0-1	1-0	0-1	0-0	0-2	0-0	2-0	1-0	1-1	0-0	1-0	3-0	1-0	10-6
Sabel, Erik	0-0	0-0	0-0	0-0	0-0	0-0	0-0	0-0	0-0	0-0	0-0	0-0	0-0	0-0	0-0	0-0	0-0
Stottlemyre, Todd	0-0	0-0	0-0	0-0	1-0	0-0	1-0	0-0	1-0	2-0	0-1	0-0	0-1	1-0	0-0	0-0	6-3
Swindell, Greg	0-0	1-0	0-0	0-0	0-0	0-0	0-0	0-0	0-0	0-0	0-0	1-0	0-0	1-0	0-0	0-0	4-0
Telemaco, Amaury	0-0	0-0	0-0	0-0	0-0	0-0	0-0	0-0	0-1	0-0	0-0	0-0	0-0	0-0	0-0	0-0	1-0
Vosberg, Ed	0-0	0-0	0-1	0-0	0-0	0-0	0-0	0-0	0-0	0-0	0-0	0-0	0-0	0-0	0-0	0-0	0-1
Totals	4-5	7-2	1-8	6-7	8-1	5-4	7-6	5-4	6-3	7-2	8-1	5-2	4-4	11-2	9-3	7-8	100-62

INTERLEAGUE BREAKDOWN: Daal 1-0, Benes 0-1, Johnson 0-1 vs. Athletics; Johnson 1-0, Kim 0-1, Anderson 0-1 vs. Mariners; Johnson 1-0, Benes 1-0, Plesac 1-0, Holmes 0-1, Mantei 0-1, Chouinard 0-1 vs. Rangers; Reynoso 1-0, Nunez 1-0, Benes 0-1 vs. Angels. Total: 7-8.

ATLANTA—103-59

Pitcher	Ari. W-L	Chi. W-L	Cin. W-L	Col. W-L	Fla. W-L	Hou. W-L	L.A. W-L	Mil. W-L	Mon. W-L	N.Y. W-L	Phi. W-L	Pit. W-L	St.L. W-L	S.D. W-L	S.F. W-L	A.L. W-L	Total W-L
Bergman, Sean	0-0	0-0	0-0	0-0	0-0	0-0	0-0	0-0	1-0	0-0	0-0	0-0	0-0	0-0	0-0	0-0	1-0
Bowie, Micah	0-0	0-0	0-0	0-0	0-0	0-0	0-0	0-0	0-0	0-1	0-0	0-0	0-0	0-0	0-0	0-0	0-1
Cather, Mike	0-0	0-0	0-0	0-0	0-0	0-0	0-0	0-0	0-0	1-0	0-0	0-0	0-0	0-0	0-0	0-0	1-0
Chen, Bruce	0-0	0-0	0-0	1-0	0-0	0-0	0-1	0-0	0-0	1-0	0-0	0-0	0-0	0-0	0-0	0-1	2-2
Cortes, David	0-0	0-0	0-0	0-0	0-0	0-0	0-0	0-0	0-0	0-0	0-0	0-0	0-0	0-0	0-0	0-0	0-0
Ebert, Derrin	0-0	0-0	0-0	0-0	0-1	0-0	0-0	0-0	0-0	0-0	0-0	0-0	0-0	0-0	0-0	0-0	0-1
Glavine, Tom	1-1	0-1	1-1	0-0	1-2	2-0	0-1	0-1	1-0	3-0	1-1	2-0	0-0	1-0	0-1	1-2	14-11
Hudek, John	0-0	0-0	0-0	0-0	0-0	0-0	0-0	0-0	0-0	0-0	0-0	0-0	0-0	0-0	0-0	0-1	0-1
Maddux, Greg	0-0	0-1	1-0	2-0	2-1	2-0	0-0	1-0	0-2	3-1	2-0	1-0	1-1	1-1	1-1	2-1	19-9
McGlinchy, Kevin	1-0	1-2	0-0	0-0	2-0	0-0	0-0	0-0	1-1	0-0	0-0	0-0	0-0	0-0	0-0	1-0	7-3
Millwood, Kevin	1-0	1-0	2-0	1-0	1-0	1-0	1-1	0-0	3-0	1-0	1-1	1-1	1-0	0-0	0-2	0-2	18-7
Mulholland, Terry	0-0	0-0	1-0	0-1	0-0	0-0	0-0	1-0	1-0	0-0	0-0	0-0	0-1	1-0	0-0	0-0	4-2
Perez, Odalis	0-1	0-1	1-0	0-0	0-0	0-1	1-0	0-0	0-1	0-0	1-1	0-0	0-0	0-0	0-0	1-1	4-6
Remlinger, Mike	0-0	0-0	0-0	0-0	0-0	2-1	0-0	1-0	1-0	0-0	1-0	3-0	1-0	0-0	0-0	1-0	10-1
Rocker, John	1-1	0-0	0-0	0-2	0-0	0-0	0-0	0-1	0-0	1-0	0-0	1-1	1-0	0-0	0-0	0-0	4-5
Seanez, Rudy	0-0	0-0	0-0	0-0	1-0	1-0	0-0	2-0	0-0	0-1	0-0	0-0	0-0	0-0	2-0	0-0	6-1
Smoltz, John	1-1	0-0	2-0	1-0	2-0	0-0	1-1	0-0	1-0	0-1	1-1	0-1	1-0	0-1	0-1	1-1	11-8
Speier, Justin	0-0	0-0	0-0	0-0	0-0	0-0	0-0	0-0	0-0	0-0	0-0	0-0	0-0	0-0	0-0	0-0	0-0
Springer, Russ	0-0	0-0	0-0	0-1	0-0	0-0	0-0	0-0	0-0	0-0	0-0	0-0	0-0	0-0	1-0	2-1
Stull, Everett	0-0	0-0	0-0	0-0	0-0	0-0	0-0	0-0	0-0	0-0	0-0	0-0	0-0	0-0	0-0	0-0	0-0
Winkelsas, Joe	0-0	0-0	0-0	0-0	0-0	0-0	0-0	0-0	0-0	0-0	0-0	0-0	0-0	0-0	0-0	0-0	0-0
Wohlers, Mark	0-0	0-0	0-0	0-0	0-0	0-0	0-0	0-0	0-0	0-0	0-0	0-0	0-0	0-0	0-0	0-0	0-0
Totals	5-4	2-5	8-1	5-4	9-4	6-1	5-4	5-2	9-4	9-3	8-5	6-3	8-1	5-4	4-5	9-9	103-59

INTERLEAGUE BREAKDOWN: Maddux 0-1, Millwood 0-1, Smoltz 0-1 vs. Orioles; Maddux 2-0, Seanez 2-0, Glavine 0-1, Chen 0-1 vs. Red Sox; Glavine 1-0, Springer 1-0, Perez 0-1 vs. Yankees; Millwood 0-1, Hudek 0-1, Glavine 0-1 vs. Blue Jays; Smoltz 1-0, McGlinchy 1-0, Perez 1-0 vs. Devil Rays. Total: 9-9.

CHICAGO—67-95

Pitcher	Ari. W-L	Atl. W-L	Cin. W-L	Col. W-L	Fla. W-L	Hou. W-L	L.A. W-L	Mil. W-L	Mon. W-L	N.Y. W-L	Phi. W-L	Pit. W-L	St.L. W-L	S.D. W-L	S.F. W-L	A.L. W-L	Total W-L
Adams, Terry	1-0	1-0	1-1	0-0	0-0	0-0	0-0	0-0	0-0	0-0	0-0	0-0	1-1	0-0	1-0	1-1	6-3
Aguilera, Rick	1-0	0-0	0-0	0-0	1-1	0-0	2-0	0-0	0-0	0-0	1-0	0-0	0-0	0-1	1-1	6-3
Ayala, Bobby	0-0	0-0	0-0	0-0	0-0	0-1	0-0	0-0	0-0	0-0	0-0	0-0	0-0	0-0	0-0	0-0	0-0
Barker, Richie	0-0	0-0	0-0	0-0	0-0	0-0	0-0	0-0	0-0	0-0	0-0	0-0	0-0	0-0	0-0	0-0	0-0
Beck, Rod	0-0	0-0	0-1	1-0	0-0	0-0	0-1	1-1	0-0	0-1	0-0	0-0	0-0	0-0	0-0	0-0	2-4
Bowie, Micah	0-0	0-0	0-1	1-0	0-0	0-2	0-0	0-0	0-1	0-0	0-1	1-0	0-0	0-1	0-0	0-0	2-6
Creek, Doug	0-0	0-0	0-0	0-0	0-0	0-0	0-0	0-0	0-0	0-0	0-0	0-0	0-0	0-0	0-0	0-0	0-0
Farnsworth, Kyle	0-0	0-0	1-1	0-1	1-0	0-0	2-1	0-0	0-1	0-1	0-0	0-1	0-0	0-1	0-1	0-0	5-9
Gaetti, Gary	0-0	0-0	0-0	0-0	0-0	0-0	0-0	0-0	0-0	0-0	0-0	0-0	0-0	0-0	0-0	0-0	0-0
Guthrie, Mark	0-0	0-0	0-0	0-0	0-0	0-0	0-1	0-0	0-0	0-0	0-0	0-1	0-0	0-0	0-0	0-0	0-2
Heredia, Felix	0-0	0-0	0-0	0-0	0-0	1-0	0-0	1-0	0-0	0-0	0-0	0-0	1-0	0-1	0-0	0-0	3-1
Karchner, Matt	0-0	0-0	0-0	0-0	0-0	0-0	0-0	0-0	1-0	0-0	0-0	0-0	0-0	0-0	0-0	0-0	1-0
King, Ray	0-0	0-0	0-0	0-0	0-0	0-0	0-0	0-0	0-0	0-0	0-0	0-0	0-0	0-0	0-0	0-0	0-0

Pitcher	Ari. W-L	Atl. W-L	Cin. W-L	Col. W-L	Fla. W-L	Hou. W-L	L.A. W-L	Mil. W-L	Mon. W-L	N.Y. W-L	Phi. W-L	Pit. W-L	St.L. W-L	S.D. W-L	S.F. W-L	A.L. W-L	Total W-L
Lieber, Jon	0-2	1-0	2-1	0-0	0-0	1-1	0-1	1-0	0-2	0-0	0-1	2-0	2-1	0-0	0-1	1-1	10-11
Lorraine, Andrew	0-1	0-0	0-1	0-0	0-0	1-0	0-1	0-0	0-0	0-0	0-0	0-0	1-1	0-0	0-1	0-0	2-5
McNichol, Brian	0-0	0-0	0-1	0-0	0-0	0-0	0-0	0-0	0-0	0-0	0-1	0-0	0-0	0-0	0-0	0-0	0-2
Miller, Kurt	0-0	0-0	0-0	0-0	0-0	0-0	0-0	0-0	0-0	0-0	0-0	0-0	0-0	0-0	0-0	0-0	0-0
Mulholland, Terry	0-1	1-0	0-0	0-2	0-0	0-0	0-0	0-0	1-0	1-0	1-1	1-1	0-0	1-0	0-0	0-1	6-6
Myers, Rodney	0-0	0-1	0-0	0-0	1-0	0-0	0-0	0-0	1-0	0-0	0-0	0-0	1-0	0-0	0-0	0-0	3-1
Rain, Steve	0-1	0-0	0-0	0-0	0-0	0-0	0-0	0-0	0-0	0-0	0-0	0-0	0-0	0-0	0-0	0-0	0-1
Sanders, Scott	0-1	0-0	0-0	1-0	0-1	0-1	0-1	0-0	0-0	0-1	0-0	0-1	0-0	1-0	0-0	2-1	4-7
Serafini, Dan	0-0	1-0	0-0	0-0	0-0	0-0	0-0	0-0	0-0	1-1	0-0	1-0	0-0	0-0	0-1	0-0	3-2
Tapani, Kevin	0-1	0-1	0-1	1-0	1-0	1-1	0-0	0-1	0-2	0-1	0-1	0-0	1-0	2-0	0-2	0-1	6-12
Trachsel, Steve	0-0	1-0	1-0	0-2	1-1	0-2	0-2	0-2	1-0	0-1	1-1	0-2	1-1	1-1	0-0	1-3	8-18
Woodall, Brad	0-0	0-0	0-0	0-0	0-0	0-0	0-0	0-0	0-0	0-0	0-0	0-0	0-1	0-0	0-0	0-0	0-0
Totals	2-7	5-2	5-8	4-5	6-3	3-9	2-7	6-6	2-5	3-6	2-7	7-6	7-5	6-3	1-7	6-9	67-95

INTERLEAGUE BREAKDOWN: Lieber 1-1, Trachsel 1-1, Aguilera 0-1, Adams 0-1 vs. White Sox; Aguilera 1-0, Sanders 0-1, Trachsel 0-1 vs. Indians; Sanders 1-0, Tapani 0-1, Trachsel 0-1 vs. Royals; Sanders 1-0, Adams 1-0, Mulholland 0-1 vs. Twins. Total: 6-9.

CINCINNATI—96-67

Pitcher	Ari. W-L	Atl. W-L	Chi. W-L	Col. W-L	Fla. W-L	Hou. W-L	L.A. W-L	Mil. W-L	Mon. W-L	N.Y. W-L	Phi. W-L	Pit. W-L	St.L. W-L	S.D. W-L	S.F. W-L	A.L. W-L	Total W-L
Avery, Steve	1-1	0-1	1-0	0-0	0-1	0-1	0-0	2-0	0-0	0-0	0-0	0-0	0-0	1-0	0-1	1-2	6-7
Belinda, Stan	0-0	0-0	0-0	0-0	0-0	0-1	0-0	0-0	0-0	0-0	0-0	0-0	1-0	0-0	1-0	0-0	3-1
Bere, Jason	0-0	0-0	0-0	0-0	1-0	0-0	0-0	0-0	0-0	1-0	0-0	1-0	0-0	0-0	0-0	0-0	3-0
Graves, Danny	1-0	0-0	1-1	1-0	1-0	0-1	1-0	0-1	0-0	0-0	0-0	2-1	0-1	0-0	0-1	1-1	8-7
Greene, Rick	0-0	0-0	0-0	0-0	0-0	0-0	0-0	0-0	0-0	0-0	0-0	0-0	0-0	0-0	0-0	0-0	0-0
Guzman, Juan	0-0	0-1	1-0	1-0	1-0	0-0	0-1	2-0	0-0	0-0	2-0	0-0	0-0	0-0	0-0	0-0	6-3
Harnisch, Pete	0-0	0-2	0-2	1-0	0-0	4-0	1-1	3-1	0-1	1-1	2-0	1-1	2-0	1-0	0-0	0-1	16-10
Hudek, John	0-0	0-0	0-0	0-0	0-0	0-0	0-0	0-0	0-0	0-0	0-0	0-0	0-0	0-1	0-0	0-0	0-1
Neagle, Denny	0-0	1-2	1-1	1-0	1-0	0-0	0-0	0-0	0-0	1-1	1-0	1-1	1-0	1-0	0-0	0-0	9-5
Parris, Steve	0-0	0-0	1-0	2-0	1-0	1-1	1-0	0-0	0-2	0-1	1-0	1-0	1-0	0-0	2-0	0-0	11-4
Reyes, Dennys	2-0	0-0	0-0	0-0	0-0	0-0	0-1	0-0	0-0	0-0	0-0	0-0	0-0	0-0	0-0	0-0	2-2
Ryan, B.J.	0-0	0-0	0-0	0-0	0-0	0-0	0-0	0-0	0-0	0-0	0-0	0-0	0-0	0-0	0-0	0-0	0-0
Sullivan, Scott	0-0	0-0	1-0	0-0	0-0	1-0	0-0	0-1	1-1	1-0	0-0	0-0	0-0	0-0	0-1	1-1	5-4
Tomko, Brett	0-0	0-1	1-0	0-0	0-0	1-0	0-1	0-0	0-0	0-2	0-0	0-1	0-1	1-1	1-0	1-0	5-7
Villone, Ron	1-0	0-1	0-1	0-1	1-0	2-0	0-1	0-0	1-1	1-0	0-0	0-1	0-0	0-1	0-1	0-0	9-7
White, Gabe	1-0	0-0	0-0	0-0	0-0	0-0	0-0	0-0	0-0	0-1	0-1	0-0	0-0	0-0	0-0	0-0	1-2
Williamson, Scott	2-0	0-0	1-0	0-0	0-0	0-0	1-0	0-0	0-1	0-0	2-0	0-1	1-2	0-1	1-0	1-2	12-7
Totals	8-1	1-8	8-5	7-2	6-1	9-4	4-3	6-6	4-3	5-5	6-3	7-6	8-4	6-3	4-5	7-8	96-67

INTERLEAGUE BREAKDOWN: Avery 1-1, Graves 1-0, Williamson 0-2, Harnisch 0-1 vs. Indians; Parris 1-0, Sullivan 0-1, Graves 0-1 vs. Tigers; Parris 1-0, Sullivan 1-0, Williamson 1-0 vs. Royals; Tomko 1-0, Avery 0-1, Villone 0-1 vs. Twins. Total: 7-8.

COLORADO—72-90

Pitcher	Ari. W-L	Atl. W-L	Chi. W-L	Cin. W-L	Fla. W-L	Hou. W-L	L.A. W-L	Mil. W-L	Mon. W-L	N.Y. W-L	Phi. W-L	Pit. W-L	St.L. W-L	S.D. W-L	S.F. W-L	A.L. W-L	Total W-L
Astacio, Pedro	2-0	0-2	3-0	2-0	1-0	0-1	2-1	1-0	2-0	1-0	0-0	0-1	1-1	1-1	0-3	1-1	17-11
Beltran, Rigo	0-0	0-0	0-0	0-0	0-0	0-0	0-0	0-0	0-0	0-0	0-0	0-0	0-0	0-0	0-0	0-0	0-0
Bohanon, Brian	1-1	0-0	1-0	0-0	1-1	0-2	1-1	1-0	0-1	0-1	1-2	0-0	2-0	1-2	2-1	1-0	12-12
Brownson, Mark	0-0	0-0	0-0	0-0	0-0	0-0	0-0	0-0	0-0	0-0	0-0	0-0	0-0	0-1	0-0	0-1	0-2
DeJean, Mike	0-0	1-0	0-1	0-1	0-0	0-1	1-0	1-0	0-0	0-0	0-0	0-0	0-0	0-0	0-1	0-0	2-4
Dipoto, Jerry	0-0	1-0	0-1	0-2	0-0	1-0	0-0	0-1	0-1	0-0	0-0	0-0	0-0	0-0	0-0	1-0	4-5
Hackman, Luther	0-2	0-0	0-0	0-0	0-0	0-0	1-0	0-0	0-0	0-0	0-0	0-0	0-0	0-0	0-0	0-0	1-2
Harris, Lenny	0-0	0-0	0-0	0-0	0-0	0-0	0-0	0-0	0-0	0-0	0-0	0-0	0-0	0-0	0-0	0-0	0-0
Jones, Bobby M.	0-1	0-2	0-1	0-1	1-1	0-0	1-0	0-0	1-0	0-0	0-0	0-0	0-0	1-1	0-1	1-2	6-10
Kile, Darryl	1-1	0-0	0-0	0-2	0-0	1-0	1-1	0-0	1-0	0-1	2-0	0-1	1-1	1-1	0-3	0-2	8-13
Lee, David	0-0	1-1	0-0	0-0	0-0	0-0	0-0	0-0	1-0	0-1	0-1	0-0	0-0	0-0	0-0	0-0	3-2
Leskanic, Curt	1-0	0-0	0-0	0-1	0-0	0-0	0-0	1-0	1-0	0-0	1-0	0-1	0-0	0-0	0-0	0-0	6-2
McElroy, Chuck	1-0	1-0	0-0	0-0	1-0	0-0	0-0	0-0	0-0	0-0	0-0	0-0	0-0	0-0	0-1	0-0	3-1
Porzio, Mike	0-0	0-0	0-0	0-0	0-0	0-0	0-0	0-0	0-0	0-0	0-0	0-0	0-0	0-0	0-0	0-0	0-0
Ramirez, Roberto	0-1	0-0	0-0	0-0	0-0	0-1	0-0	0-0	0-0	0-0	0-0	0-0	0-1	1-0	0-0	0-1	1-5
Thomson, John	0-0	0-0	0-1	0-0	0-1	0-0	0-2	0-0	1-1	0-1	0-1	0-1	0-1	0-0	0-1	0-0	1-10
Veres, Dave	0-0	1-0	0-0	0-0	0-0	0-0	1-3	1-0	0-1	0-1	0-1	0-0	0-1	1-0	0-0	0-0	4-8
Wainhouse, Dave	0-0	0-0	0-0	0-0	0-0	0-0	0-0	0-0	0-0	0-0	0-0	0-0	0-0	0-0	0-0	0-0	0-0
Wright, Jamey	1-0	0-0	1-0	0-0	0-1	0-0	0-0	1-0	1-0	0-0	0-1	0-0	0-0	0-0	0-1	0-0	4-3
Totals	7-6	4-5	5-4	2-7	5-4	2-6	8-5	6-3	6-3	4-5	5-4	2-7	4-5	4-9	4-9	4-8	72-90

INTERLEAGUE BREAKDOWN: Jones 0-1, Ramirez 0-1, Kile 0-1 vs. Athletics; Bohanon 1-0, Jones 0-1, Brownson 0-1 vs. Mariners; Astacio 1-0, Jones 1-0, McElroy 0-1 vs. Rangers; Dipoto 1-0, Kile 0-1, Astacio 0-1 vs. Angels. Total: 4-8.

FLORIDA—64-98

Pitcher	Ari. W-L	Atl. W-L	Chi. W-L	Cin. W-L	Col. W-L	Hou. W-L	L.A. W-L	Mil. W-L	Mon. W-L	N.Y. W-L	Phi. W-L	Pit. W-L	St.L. W-L	S.D. W-L	S.F. W-L	A.L. W-L	Total W-L
Alfonseca, Antonio	0-0	0-2	0-0	0-0	0-0	0-0	0-0	0-0	0-0	1-0	0-1	1-0	0-0	0-1	0-1	2-0	4-5
Almanza, Armando	0-1	0-0	0-0	0-0	0-0	0-0	0-0	0-0	0-0	0-0	0-0	0-0	0-0	0-0	0-0	0-0	0-1
Almonte, Hector	0-1	0-0	0-0	0-0	0-0	0-0	0-0	0-1	0-0	0-0	0-0	0-0	0-0	0-0	0-0	0-0	0-2
Billingsley, Brent	0-0	0-0	0-0	0-0	0-0	0-0	0-0	0-0	0-0	0-0	0-0	0-0	0-0	0-0	0-0	0-0	0-0
Burnett, A.J.	1-0	0-0	0-0	0-1	0-0	1-0	1-0	0-0	1-0	0-0	0-0	0-0	0-1	0-0	0-0	0-0	4-2
Corbin, Archie	0-0	0-0	0-0	0-0	0-0	0-0	0-0	0-1	0-0	0-0	0-0	0-0	0-0	0-0	0-0	0-0	0-1
Cornelius, Reid	0-0	0-0	0-0	0-0	0-0	0-0	0-0	0-0	1-0	0-0	0-0	0-0	0-0	0-0	0-0	0-0	1-0
Darensbourg, Vic	0-0	0-0	0-0	0-0	0-0	0-0	0-0	0-0	0-0	0-0	0-0	0-0	0-0	0-0	0-1	0-0	0-1
Dempster, Ryan	0-1	0-1	1-0	1-0	2-1	1-0	0-0	0-0	1-0	0-1	0-1	0-0	1-1	1-0	0-1	0-0	7-8

Pitcher	Ari. W-L	Atl. W-L	Chi. W-L	Cin. W-L	Col. W-L	Hou. W-L	L.A. W-L	Mil. W-L	Mon. W-L	N.Y. W-L	Phi. W-L	Pit. W-L	St.L. W-L	S.D. W-L	S.F. W-L	A.L. W-L	Total W-L
Edmondson, Brian.	0-0	0-1	1-0	0-1	0-1	0-1	1-0	0-0	0-0	0-0	0-1	1-1	0-0	0-1	1-0	1-1	5-8
Fernandez, Alex	0-0	1-1	0-0	0-1	1-1	0-2	0-0	0-0	0-1	1-0	0-1	0-0	1-0	0-0	2-0	7-8	
Hernandez, Livan	0-0	1-0	0-1	0-0	0-0	0-0	0-1	1-0	1-0	0-4	0-0	1-0	0-0	0-0	1-2	5-9	
Looper, Braden	0-1	1-0	0-1	0-0	0-0	0-0	0-0	0-0	0-1	0-0	0-0	1-0	0-0	0-0	1-0	3-3	
Mantei, Matt	0-0	0-0	1-1	0-0	0-1	0-0	0-0	0-0	0-0	0-0	0-0	0-0	0-0	0-0	0-0	1-2	
Meadows, Brian	0-2	0-3	1-0	0-0	1-0	0-1	1-1	1-2	1-0	1-2	1-1	0-0	0-2	1-0	1-0	2-1	11-15
Medina, Rafael	0-0	0-0	0-0	0-0	0-1	0-0	0-0	0-0	0-0	0-0	0-0	0-0	0-0	0-0	0-0	0-0	1-1
Nunez, Vladimir	0-1	0-0	0-0	0-1	0-0	0-0	1-0	1-0	0-0	0-2	0-0	1-0	0-1	0-1	0-1	4-8	
Ojala, Kirt	0-0	0-0	0-0	0-0	0-0	0-0	0-0	0-0	0-0	0-1	0-0	0-0	0-0	0-0	0-0	0-0	0-1
Sanchez, Jesus	0-0	0-0	0-1	0-1	0-0	0-1	1-0	2-1	0-0	0-2	0-0	0-0	0-1	2-0	0-0	5-7	
Springer, Dennis	0-1	1-1	0-1	0-1	0-0	0-2	1-0	0-0	2-0	0-1	0-3	0-0	0-0	0-1	0-2	2-2	6-16
Tejera, Michael	0-0	0-0	0-0	0-0	0-0	0-0	0-0	0-0	0-0	0-0	0-0	0-0	0-0	0-0	0-0	0-0	0-0
Totals	**1-8**	**4-9**	**3-6**	**1-6**	**4-5**	**2-7**	**7-2**	**5-4**	**8-4**	**3-10**	**2-11**	**3-4**	**3-4**	**3-6**	**4-5**	**11-7**	**64-98**

INTERLEAGUE BREAKDOWN: Edmondson 1-0, Alfonseca 1-0, Springer 0-1 vs. Orioles; Meadows 1-0, Nunez 0-1, Hernandez 0-1 vs. Red Sox; Fernandez 1-0, Meadows 0-1, Hernandez 0-1 vs. Yankees; Looper 1-0, Springer 1-0, Edmondson 0-1 vs. Blue Jays; Springer 1-1, Meadows 1-0, Hernandez 1-0, Alfonseca 1-0, Fernandez 1-0 vs. Devil Rays. Total: 11-7.

HOUSTON—97-65

Pitcher	Ari. W-L	Atl. W-L	Chi. W-L	Cin. W-L	Col. W-L	Fla. W-L	L.A. W-L	Mil. W-L	Mon. W-L	N.Y. W-L	Phi. W-L	Pit. W-L	St.L. W-L	S.D. W-L	S.F. W-L	A.L. W-L	Total W-L
Bergman, Sean	0-0	0-1	0-1	0-1	0-0	1-0	0-0	1-0	0-0	0-0	0-0	1-0	0-1	1-0	0-1	0-1	4-6
Cabrera, Jose	0-0	0-0	0-0	0-0	0-0	0-0	0-0	0-0	0-0	0-0	0-0	0-0	0-0	0-0	0-0	3-0	4-0
Elarton, Scott	0-0	0-0	1-0	1-1	1-0	0-1	0-0	2-1	1-0	0-0	0-0	1-0	1-0	0-0	0-1	1-0	9-5
Hampton, Mike	1-0	1-0	1-1	1-1	1-0	1-0	2-0	0-0	2-0	1-0	1-1	1-1	1-0	2-0	4-0	22-4	
Henry, Doug	0-0	0-0	0-0	0-1	0-0	0-0	1-0	0-0	0-0	0-1	0-0	0-0	1-0	0-0	0-0	0-0	2-3
Holt, Chris	0-0	0-0	1-0	0-3	0-1	0-1	0-1	1-1	1-1	0-2	0-0	1-0	1-2	1-0	0-1	0-0	5-13
Lima, Jose	2-1	0-2	3-1	0-2	1-0	2-0	2-0	2-0	1-0	1-0	1-0	1-2	0-1	1-1	2-0	2-0	21-10
McCurry, Jeff	0-0	0-0	0-0	0-0	0-0	0-0	0-0	0-0	0-0	0-0	0-0	0-1	0-0	0-0	0-0	0-0	0-1
Miller, Trever	0-0	0-0	0-0	0-0	0-1	1-0	0-0	1-0	0-0	0-0	0-0	0-1	0-0	0-0	0-0	1-0	3-2
Miller, Wade	0-1	0-0	0-0	0-0	0-0	0-0	0-0	0-0	0-0	0-0	0-1	0-0	0-0	0-0	0-0	0-0	0-1
Powell, Jay	0-1	0-0	0-0	1-0	1-0	0-0	0-0	0-1	0-0	1-1	1-0	0-0	1-0	0-0	0-0	0-0	5-4
Reynolds, Shane	1-0	0-1	2-0	1-0	1-0	1-0	1-2	1-2	1-1	0-2	2-0	0-3	1-1	3-0	1-0	0-2	16-14
Slusarski, Joe	0-0	0-0	0-0	0-0	0-0	0-0	0-0	0-0	0-0	0-0	0-0	0-0	0-0	0-0	0-0	0-0	0-0
Wagner, Billy	0-1	0-0	1-0	0-0	0-0	0-0	0-0	0-0	1-0	0-0	0-0	0-0	0-0	0-0	1-0	1-0	4-1
Williams, Brian	0-1	0-0	0-0	0-0	0-0	0-0	0-0	0-0	0-0	0-0	0-0	0-0	0-0	0-0	0-0	0-0	2-1
Totals	**4-5**	**1-6**	**9-3**	**4-9**	**6-2**	**7-2**	**6-3**	**8-5**	**7-2**	**4-5**	**6-1**	**5-7**	**5-7**	**8-1**	**5-4**	**12-3**	**97-65**

INTERLEAGUE BREAKDOWN: Lima 1-0, Hampton 1-0, Reynolds 0-1 vs. White Sox; Hampton 1-0, Cabrera 1-0, Reynolds 0-1 vs. Indians; Miller 1-0, Wagner 1-0, Cabrera 1-0 vs. Tigers; Cabrera 1-0, Hampton 1-0, Lima 1-0 vs. Royals; Hampton 1-0, Elarton 1-0, Bergman 0-1 vs. Twins. Total: 12-3.

LOS ANGELES—77-85

Pitcher	Ari. W-L	Atl. W-L	Chi. W-L	Cin. W-L	Col. W-L	Fla. W-L	Hou. W-L	Mil. W-L	Mon. W-L	N.Y. W-L	Phi. W-L	Pit. W-L	St.L. W-L	S.D. W-L	S.F. W-L	A.L. W-L	Total W-L
Arnold, Jamie	0-0	0-1	1-0	0-0	0-1	0-0	0-0	0-0	1-1	0-0	0-0	0-1	1-0	0-0	0-0	0-0	2-4
Bochtler, Doug	0-0	0-0	0-0	0-0	0-0	0-0	0-0	0-0	0-0	0-0	0-0	0-0	0-0	0-0	0-0	0-0	0-0
Borbon, Pedro	0-0	1-0	0-0	0-0	0-0	0-1	0-0	0-1	0-0	1-0	0-0	1-0	0-0	0-0	1-1	0-0	4-3
Brown, Kevin	1-0	1-0	1-0	0-1	2-1	1-0	2-0	2-0	0-1	1-1	1-1	1-0	1-2	1-1	2-0	18-9	
Checo, Robinson	0-0	0-0	0-0	1-0	0-1	0-0	0-1	0-0	0-0	0-0	0-0	1-0	0-0	0-0	0-0	2-2	
Dreifort, Darren	1-1	1-2	1-1	0-1	1-1	1-1	0-1	1-0	0-0	2-0	2-0	1-1	1-1	0-2	0-0	1-1	13-13
Gagne, Eric	0-0	0-0	0-0	0-0	0-0	0-0	1-0	0-0	0-0	0-1	0-0	0-0	0-0	0-0	0-0	0-0	1-1
Herges, Matt	0-0	0-0	0-0	0-0	0-0	0-1	0-0	0-0	0-0	0-0	0-0	0-1	0-0	0-0	0-0	0-0	0-2
Judd, Mike	0-0	0-0	0-0	0-0	0-0	0-0	0-0	2-0	1-0	0-0	0-0	0-0	0-0	0-0	0-0	0-0	3-1
Kubenka, Jeff	0-0	0-1	0-0	0-0	0-0	0-0	0-0	0-0	0-0	0-0	0-0	0-0	0-0	0-0	0-0	0-0	0-1
Maddux, Mike	0-0	0-0	0-0	0-0	0-0	0-0	0-0	1-0	0-0	0-0	0-0	0-0	0-0	0-0	0-0	0-0	1-1
Masaoka, Onan	1-0	0-0	0-0	0-0	0-1	0-0	0-0	0-0	0-0	0-0	0-1	0-0	0-0	0-1	0-0	1-0	2-4
Mills, Alan	1-0	0-0	0-0	0-1	0-0	0-0	0-0	0-0	0-0	1-0	0-1	0-0	0-0	1-0	0-2	3-4	
Mlicki, Dave	0-1	0-0	0-0	0-0	0-1	0-0	0-0	0-0	0-0	0-0	0-0	0-0	0-0	0-0	0-0	0-0	0-1
Osuna, Antonio	0-0	0-0	0-0	0-0	0-0	0-0	0-0	0-0	0-0	0-0	0-0	0-0	0-0	0-0	0-0	0-0	0-0
Park, Chan Ho	0-1	0-0	2-0	1-0	2-1	0-0	1-0	2-0	0-1	1-0	0-1	0-2	1-1	2-2	1-0	13-11	
Perez, Carlos	0-2	1-1	0-1	0-0	0-0	1-0	0-0	0-0	0-1	0-0	0-0	0-0	0-1	0-0	0-2	2-10	
Rojas, Mel	0-0	0-0	0-0	0-0	0-0	0-0	0-0	0-0	0-0	0-0	0-0	0-0	0-0	0-0	0-0	0-0	0-0
Shaw, Jeff	1-1	0-0	0-0	0-1	0-0	0-0	0-1	0-0	0-0	0-0	0-0	0-0	0-1	0-0	1-0	2-4	
Valdes, Ismael	1-1	0-0	2-0	1-0	0-1	0-1	0-1	1-1	0-2	0-1	0-1	0-1	1-1	0-1	1-0	2-2	9-14
Williams, Jeff	0-0	0-0	0-0	0-0	0-0	0-0	0-0	0-0	0-0	0-0	0-0	0-0	0-0	0-0	0-0	0-0	0-0
Totals	**6-7**	**4-5**	**7-2**	**3-4**	**5-8**	**2-7**	**3-6**	**7-2**	**5-4**	**4-4**	**6-3**	**3-6**	**3-6**	**3-9**	**8-5**	**8-7**	**77-85**

INTERLEAGUE BREAKDOWN: Perez 0-1, Valdes 0-1, Dreifort 0-1 vs. Athletics; Valdes 1-0, Shaw 1-0, Dreifort 1-0 vs. Mariners; Brown 1-0, Valdes 0-1, Mills 0-1 vs. Rangers; Brown 1-0, Park 1-0, Masaoka 1-0, Valdes 1-0, Mills 0-1, Perez 0-1 vs. Angels. Total: 8-7.

MILWAUKEE—74-87

Pitcher	Ari. W-L	Atl. W-L	Chi. W-L	Cin. W-L	Col. W-L	Fla. W-L	Hou. W-L	L.A. W-L	Mon. W-L	N.Y. W-L	Phi. W-L	Pit. W-L	St.L. W-L	S.D. W-L	S.F. W-L	A.L. W-L	Total W-L
Abbott, Jim	0-1	0-0	0-1	0-0	0-0	0-0	0-0	0-0	0-1	0-1	1-0	0-1	0-2	1-0	0-0	0-1	2-8
Bere, Jason	0-0	0-0	0-0	0-0	0-0	0-0	0-0	0-0	0-0	1-0	1-0	0-0	0-0	0-0	0-0	0-0	2-0
Coppinger, Rocky	0-0	0-0	0-0	1-0	1-1	0-0	1-0	0-0	0-0	0-0	0-0	1-0	0-1	1-0	0-1	0-1	5-3
Dale, Carl	0-1	0-0	0-0	0-0	0-0	0-0	0-0	0-0	0-0	0-0	0-0	0-0	0-0	0-0	0-0	0-0	0-1
D'Amico, Jeff	0-0	0-0	0-0	0-0	0-0	0-0	0-0	0-0	0-0	0-0	0-0	0-0	0-0	0-0	0-0	0-0	0-0
de los Santos, V.	0-0	0-0	0-1	0-0	0-0	0-0	0-0	0-0	0-0	0-0	0-0	0-0	0-0	0-0	0-0	0-0	0-1
Eldred, Cal	0-0	0-0	0-0	0-2	0-0	1-0	0-2	1-1	0-0	0-0	0-0	0-0	0-0	0-1	0-1	2-8	
Estrada, Horacio	0-0	0-0	0-0	0-0	0-0	0-0	0-0	0-0	0-0	0-0	0-0	0-0	0-0	0-0	0-0	0-0	0-0

Pitcher	Ari. W-L	Atl. W-L	Chi. W-L	Cin. W-L	Col. W-L	Fla. W-L	Hou. W-L	L.A. W-L	Mon. W-L	N.Y. W-L	Phi. W-L	Pit. W-L	St.L. W-L	S.D. W-L	S.F. W-L	A.L. W-L	Total W-L
Falteisek, Steve	0-0	0-0	0-0	0-0	0-0	0-0	0-0	0-0	0-0	0-0	0-0	0-0	0-0	0-0	0-0	0-0	0-0
Fox, Chad	0-0	0-0	0-0	0-0	0-0	0-0	0-0	0-0	0-0	0-0	0-0	0-0	0-0	0-0	0-0	0-0	0-0
Harris, Reggie	0-0	0-0	0-0	0-0	0-0	0-0	0-0	0-0	0-0	0-0	0-0	0-0	0-0	0-0	0-0	0-0	0-0
Karl, Scott	2-0	0-2	0-0	1-1	0-1	1-0	1-1	0-1	1-2	1-0	0-1	2-1	1-1	0-0	1-0	0-0	11-11
Myers, Mike	0-1	0-0	2-0	0-0	0-0	0-0	0-0	0-0	0-0	0-0	0-0	0-0	0-0	0-0	0-0	0-0	2-1
Nomo, Hideo	1-1	0-1	1-0	0-1	0-0	0-1	0-0	0-1	0-0	0-1	1-1	1-1	1-0	2-0	2-0	3-0	12-8
Peterson, Kyle	0-0	0-0	1-1	1-0	0-0	0-1	1-1	0-1	1-0	0-1	0-1	0-0	0-0	0-0	0-1	0-0	4-7
Pittsley, Jim	0-0	0-0	0-0	0-0	0-0	0-0	0-0	0-0	0-0	0-0	0-0	0-0	0-0	0-0	0-1		0-1
Plunk, Eric	0-0	0-0	0-0	0-0	1-1	0-0	0-2	1-0	0-1	0-0	0-0	0-0	0-0	0-0	2-0		4-4
Pulsipher, Bill	0-1	1-0	0-1	0-0	0-1	0-0	1-0	0-1	0-0	0-1	1-0	1-0	1-0	0-0	0-1	0-0	5-6
Ramirez, Hector	0-0	0-0	0-1	0-0	0-0	0-0	0-0	0-0	0-0	0-0	0-0	0-1	0-0	0-0	0-0		1-2
Reyes, Al	0-0	0-0	0-0	0-0	0-0	0-0	0-0	0-0	0-0	0-0	0-0	1-0	1-0	0-0	0-0	0-0	2-0
Roque, Rafael	0-0	0-0	0-0	0-1	0-0	0-1	0-1	0-1	0-0	0-0	0-0	0-0	0-0	0-0	0-1	1-1	1-6
Weathers, Dave	1-0	0-1	0-1	2-0	0-0	0-1	0-0	0-0	1-0	1-0	0-0	1-0	0-0	0-0	0-0	0-1	7-4
Wickman, Bob	0-0	0-1	0-0	0-0	1-1	1-1	0-1	1-0	0-0	0-1	0-0	0-1	0-2	0-0	0-0		3-8
Woodard, Steve	0-0	1-0	2-0	1-1	0-1	1-0	0-1	0-1	0-1		0-1	1-1	0-1	0-1	1-1	2-0	11-8
Totals	4-5	2-5	6-6	6-6	3-6	4-5	5-8	2-7	5-4	2-5	5-4	8-4	7-6	3-5	4-5	8-6	74-87

INTERLEAGUE BREAKDOWN: Plunk 2-0, Coppinger 0-1 vs. White Sox; Roque 1-1, Nomo 1-0 vs. Indians; Woodard 1-0, Nomo 1-0, Abbott 0-1 vs. Tigers; Woodard 1-0, Nomo 1-0, Pittsley 0-1 vs. Royals; Weathers 0-1, Eldred 0-1 vs. Twins. Total: 8-6.

MONTREAL—68-94

Pitcher	Ari. W-L	Atl. W-L	Chi. W-L	Cin. W-L	Col. W-L	Fla. W-L	Hou. W-L	L.A. W-L	Mil. W-L	N.Y. W-L	Phi. W-L	Pit. W-L	St.L. W-L	S.D. W-L	S.F. W-L	A.L. W-L	Total W-L
Armas, Tony	0-0	0-0	0-0	0-0	0-0	0-0	0-0	0-0	0-0	0-0	0-0	0-0	0-0	0-0	0-1		0-1
Ayala, Bobby	0-1	0-0	0-0	0-0	0-0	0-0	0-0	0-1	0-2	1-0	0-1	0-0	0-0	0-0	0-0	0-1	1-6
Batista, Miguel	0-1	0-2	0-0	1-0	0-0	1-1	0-1	0-0	1-0	1-1	0-0	0-1	0-0	1-0	2-0		8-7
Bennett, Shayne	0-0	0-0	0-0	0-0	0-1	0-0	0-0	0-0	0-0	0-0	0-0	0-0	0-0	0-0	0-0		0-1
DeHart, Rick	0-0	0-0	0-0	0-0	0-0	0-0	0-0	0-0	0-0	0-0	0-0	0-0	0-0	0-0	0-0		0-0
Hermanson, Dustin	1-0	1-0	1-1	0-1	1-0	0-2	1-1	0-2	0-0	1-1	0-1	1-1	0-0	2-0	0-1	0-3	9-14
Johnson, Mike	0-0	0-0	0-0	0-0	0-0	0-0	0-0	0-0	0-0	0-0	0-0	0-0	0-0	0-0	0-0		0-0
Kline, Steve	0-1	1-1	0-0	1-0	0-0	1-0	0-0	0-0	1-0	1-0	0-1	0-0	1-0	0-1	1-0		7-4
Lilly, Ted	0-0	0-1	0-0	0-0	0-0	0-0	0-0	0-0	0-0	0-0	0-0	0-0	0-0	0-0	0-0		0-1
Maddux, Mike	0-0	0-0	0-0	0-0	0-0	0-0	0-0	0-0	0-0	0-0	0-0	0-0	0-0	0-0	0-0		0-0
Mota, Guillermo	1-1	0-2	0-0	1-0	0-0	0-0	0-0	0-0	0-1	0-0	0-0	0-0	0-0	0-0	0-0		2-4
Pavano, Carl	0-0	0-0	0-0	0-0	0-0	0-0	1-0	1-1	1-0	0-3	1-0	0-2	0-0	0-0	0-1	2-1	6-8
Powell, Jeremy	0-0	0-1	0-1	0-0	0-1	0-2	0-0	1-0	0-1	0-0	0-1	1-0	1-1	0-0	0-0		4-8
Rojas, Mel	0-0	0-0	0-0	0-0	0-0	0-0	0-0	0-0	0-0	0-0	0-0	0-0	0-0	0-0	0-0		0-0
Smart, J.D.	0-1	0-0	0-0	0-0	0-0	0-0	0-0	0-0	0-0	0-0	0-0	0-0	0-0	0-0	0-0		0-1
Smith, Dan	0-0	0-1	1-0	0-0	0-1	0-1	0-2	0-1	1-0	0-1	0-0	0-0	0-1	1-0	1-1		4-9
Strickland, Scott	0-0	0-0	0-0	0-0	0-0	0-0	0-0	0-0	0-0	0-1	0-0	0-0	0-0	0-0	0-0		0-1
Telford, Anthony	0-0	0-0	0-0	0-0	0-0	1-1	0-0	1-0	0-1	0-0	0-0	2-0	0-0	1-0	0-1		5-4
Thurman, Mike	1-0	1-0	1-0	0-2	0-2	0-1	0-0	1-0	0-0	0-1	0-1	0-0	0-2	1-0	1-0	1-2	7-11
Urbina, Ugueth	0-0	1-0	0-0	0-1	1-1	0-0	0-1	0-0	0-1	0-0	1-1	1-0	1-1	0-0	1-0		6-6
Vazquez, Javier	0-1	0-1	2-0	0-0	1-0	0-0	0-0	1-1	1-1	1-0	1-0	1-1	1-0	0-1	0-1	0-1	9-8
Totals	3-6	4-9	5-2	3-4	3-6	4-8	2-7	4-5	4-5	5-8	6-6	3-6	5-4	5-3	4-5	8-10	68-94

INTERLEAGUE BREAKDOWN: Thurman 0-1, Smith 0-1, Hermanson 0-1 vs. Orioles; Pavano 1-0, Smith 1-0, Thurman 1-0 vs. Red Sox; Kline 1-0, Vazquez 0-1, Thurman 0-1 vs. Yankees; Batista 1-0, Urbina 1-0, Ayala 0-1, Telford 0-1, Hermanson 0-1, Pavano 0-1 vs. Blue Jays; Batista 1-0, Pavano 1-0, Hermanson 0-1 vs. Devil Rays. Total: 8-10.

NEW YORK—97-66

Pitcher	Ari. W-L	Atl. W-L	Chi. W-L	Cin. W-L	Col. W-L	Fla. W-L	Hou. W-L	L.A. W-L	Mil. W-L	Mon. W-L	Phi. W-L	Pit. W-L	St.L. W-L	S.D. W-L	S.F. W-L	A.L. W-L	Total W-L
Beltran, Rigo	0-1	0-0	0-0	0-0	0-0	0-0	0-0	0-0	0-0	0-0	1-0	0-0	0-0	0-0	0-0	0-0	1-1
Benitez, A.	0-0	0-0	0-0	0-0	0-0	0-1	1-1	0-0	0-0	0-0	0-1	1-0	1-0	0-0	0-0	1-0	4-3
Cook, Dennis	0-1	1-1	2-0	1-0	0-0	1-0	0-1	0-0	0-1	1-1	0-0	1-0	0-0	2-0	1-0	0-0	10-5
Dotel, Octavio	1-0	0-2	1-0	0-0	0-1	1-0	1-0	1-0	0-0	0-0	1-0	0-0	0-0	0-0	1-0		8-3
Franco, John	0-0	0-0	0-0	0-1	0-0	0-0	0-0	0-0	0-0	0-0	0-0	0-0	0-0	0-0	0-1		0-2
Franco, Matt	0-0	0-0	0-0	0-0	0-0	0-0	0-0	0-0	0-0	0-0	0-0	0-0	0-0	0-0	0-0		0-0
Hershiser, Orel	0-1	0-2	0-1	0-1	0-0	2-0	0-0	1-1	1-0	2-1	1-1	1-1	0-0	2-0	2-2		13-12
Isringhausen, J.	0-0	0-0	0-1	0-0	0-0	0-0	0-0	0-0	0-0	0-0	0-1	0-1	0-0	0-0	1-0		1-3
Jones, Bobby	0-0	0-0	0-0	0-0	0-1	2-0	0-0	0-0	0-1	1-0	0-1	0-0	0-0	0-0	0-0		3-3
Leiter, Al	0-1	1-2	1-0	2-1	1-1	2-1	0-1	0-1	1-0	0-1	0-1	0-1	1-0	1-1	3-1		13-12
Mahomes, Pat	0-0	0-0	2-0	0-0	0-0	0-0	0-0	0-0	1-0	1-0	1-0	1-0	0-0	2-0			8-0
Manzanillo, Josias	0-0	0-0	0-0	0-0	0-0	0-0	0-0	0-0	0-0	0-0	0-0	0-0	0-0	0-0	0-0		0-0
McElroy, Chuck	0-0	0-0	0-0	0-0	0-0	0-0	0-0	0-0	0-0	0-0	0-0	0-0	0-0	0-0	0-0		0-0
McMichael, Greg	0-0	0-0	0-0	0-1	0-0	1-0	0-0	0-0	0-0	0-0	0-0	0-0	0-0	0-0	0-0		1-1
Murray, Dan	0-0	0-0	0-0	0-0	0-0	0-0	0-0	0-0	0-0	0-0	0-0	0-0	0-0	0-0	0-0		0-0
Reed, Rick	0-2	1-0	0-0	1-0	1-0	0-0	0-0	0-1	1-0	1-0	0-1	2-0	1-0	0-0	1-1		11-5
Rogers, Kenny	0-0	0-0	0-0	0-0	0-0	0-0	1-0	1-0	1-0	0-1	0-0	0-0	0-0	2-0	0-0		5-1
Rusch, Glendon	0-0	0-0	0-0	0-0	0-0	0-0	0-0	0-0	0-0	0-0	0-0	0-0	0-0	0-0	0-0		0-0
Tam, Jeff	0-0	0-0	0-0	0-0	0-0	0-0	0-0	0-0	0-0	0-0	0-0	0-0	0-0	0-0	0-0		0-0
Taylor, Billy	0-0	0-0	0-0	0-0	0-0	0-0	0-1	0-0	0-0	0-0	0-0	0-0	0-0	0-0	0-0		0-1
Watson, Allen	0-0	0-0	0-1	0-0	0-0	0-0	0-0	0-0	1-1	0-0	0-0	0-0	0-0	1-0	0-0		2-2
Wendell, Turk	0-0	0-0	0-0	0-0	2-1	0-0	0-0	0-0	1-1	0-0	0-0	0-0	2-0	0-1	0-0		5-4
Yoshii, Masato	1-1	0-0	0-0	1-1	1-0	0-1	1-0	0-1	1-0	0-0	0-0	1-0	2-0	1-1	0-1	1-1	12-8
Totals	2-7	3-9	6-3	5-5	5-4	10-3	5-4	4-4	5-2	8-5	6-6	7-2	5-2	7-2	7-2	12-6	97-66

INTERLEAGUE BREAKDOWN: Yoshii 1-0, Dotel 1-0, Leiter 0-1 vs. Orioles; Leiter 1-0, Hershiser 1-0, Franco 0-1 vs. Red Sox; Leiter 2-0, Mahomes 1-0, Reed 0-1, Yoshii 0-1, Hershiser 0-1 vs. Yankees; Hershiser 1-0, Mahomes 1-0, Isringhausen 1-0 vs. Blue Jays; Benitez 1-0, Reed 1-0, Hershiser 0-1 vs. Devil Rays. Total: 12-6.

PHILADELPHIA—77-85

Pitcher	Ari. W-L	Atl. W-L	Chi. W-L	Cin. W-L	Col. W-L	Fla. W-L	Hou. W-L	L.A. W-L	Mil. W-L	Mon. W-L	N.Y. W-L	Pit. W-L	St.L. W-L	S.D. W-L	S.F. W-L	A.L. W-L	Total W-L
Aldred, Scott	0-0	0-0	0-0	0-0	0-1	0-0	0-0	0-0	0-0	0-0	0-0	0-0	1-0	0-0	0-0	0-0	1-1
Bennett, Joel	0-0	0-0	0-0	0-0	1-0	0-0	0-0	0-0	0-0	0-1	0-0	0-0	0-0	0-0	0-0	1-0	2-1
Brantley, Jeff	0-0	0-0	0-0	1-1	0-0	0-0	0-0	0-0	0-0	0-1	0-0	0-0	0-0	0-0	0-0	0-0	1-2
Brewer, Billy	0-0	0-0	1-0	0-0	0-0	0-0	0-0	0-0	0-0	0-0	0-0	0-0	0-0	0-0	0-1	0-0	1-1
Byrd, Paul	0-0	2-1	1-0	0-1	0-2	1-0	0-1	0-1	0-0	1-1	3-1	0-1	1-0	3-0	1-0	2-2	15-11
Gomes, Wayne	1-0	0-0	0-0	0-0	0-0	1-0	1-1	1-1	1-0	0-0	0-0	0-0	0-1	0-0	0-2	0-0	5-5
Grace, Mike	0-1	0-0	0-1	0-0	0-0	0-0	0-0	0-0	0-1	1-0	1-0	0-0	0-0	0-0	0-0	0-0	1-4
Grahe, Joe	0-0	0-0	0-0	0-0	0-1	0-0	0-1	0-0	0-0	0-1	1-0	0-0	0-0	0-0	0-1	0-0	1-4
Loewer, Carlton	0-0	0-1	0-0	0-1	0-0	1-0	0-0	0-0	0-1	0-1	0-1	0-0	0-1	1-0	0-0	0-0	2-6
Montgomery, Steve.	0-0	1-1	0-0	0-0	0-0	0-0	0-1	0-0	0-0	0-1	0-0	0-1	0-0	0-0	0-0	0-1	1-5
Ogea, Chad	0-1	0-1	1-0	0-1	0-0	2-0	0-0	0-0	0-1	1-0	0-1	0-1	0-0	0-3	0-0	2-2	6-12
Perez, Yorkis	0-1	0-0	0-0	0-0	0-0	0-0	0-0	0-0	1-0	0-0	1-0	0-0	0-0	1-0	1-0	0-0	3-1
Person, Robert	0-1	0-1	2-0	1-1	0-0	2-0	0-0	0-1	2-0	1-0	1-0	0-0	1-0	0-0	1-0	1-0	10-5
Politte, Cliff	0-0	0-0	0-0	0-0	0-0	0-0	0-0	0-0	0-0	1-0	0-0	0-0	0-0	0-0	0-0	0-0	1-0
Poole, Jim	0-0	0-0	0-0	0-0	0-1	0-0	0-0	0-0	0-0	0-0	0-0	1-0	0-0	0-0	0-0	0-0	1-1
Ryan, Ken	0-0	0-1	0-0	0-0	1-0	0-0	0-0	0-0	0-0	0-1	0-0	0-0	0-0	0-0	0-0	0-0	1-2
Schilling, Curt	0-2	1-0	1-0	1-0	2-0	2-0	1-0	0-0	2-0	0-0	1-0	0-1	2-0	1-0	0-0	0-1	15-6
Schrenk, Steve	0-0	0-0	0-0	0-1	0-0	1-0	0-0	0-0	0-0	0-0	0-0	0-1	0-0	0-0	0-0	0-1	1-3
Shumaker, Anthony	0-0	0-1	0-0	0-0	0-0	0-0	0-0	0-1	0-1	0-0	0-0	0-0	0-0	0-0	0-0	0-0	0-3
Spoljaric, Paul	0-1	0-0	0-0	0-0	0-0	0-1	0-0	0-1	0-0	0-1	0-0	0-0	0-0	0-0	0-0	0-0	0-3
Telemaco, Amaury.	0-0	1-0	0-0	0-0	0-0	1-0	0-0	0-0	1-0	0-0	0-0	0-0	0-0	0-0	0-0	0-0	3-0
Wolf, Randy	0-1	0-1	1-1	0-0	0-0	0-1	0-1	0-0	0-0	1-0	1-0	0-2	1-0	0-1	2-0	6-9
Totals	**1-8**	**5-8**	**7-2**	**3-6**	**4-5**	**11-2**	**1-6**	**3-6**	**4-5**	**6-6**	**6-6**	**3-4**	**4-5**	**6-3**	**2-6**	**11-7**	**77-85**

INTERLEAGUE BREAKDOWN: Ogea 1-1, Bennett 1-0, Schilling 1-0, Montgomery 0-1, Byrd 0-1 vs. Orioles; Person 1-0, Wolf 1-0, Byrd 0-1 vs. Red Sox; Byrd 1-0, Perez 1-0, Ogea 0-1 vs. Yankees; Wolf 1-0, Byrd 1-0, Schilling 0-1 vs. Blue Jays; Schilling 1-0, Ogea 1-0, Schrenk 0-1 vs. Devil Rays. Total: 11-7.

PITTSBURGH—78-83

Pitcher	Ari. W-L	Atl. W-L	Chi. W-L	Cin. W-L	Col. W-L	Fla. W-L	Hou. W-L	L.A. W-L	Mil. W-L	Mon. W-L	N.Y. W-L	Phi. W-L	St.L. W-L	S.D. W-L	S.F. W-L	A.L. W-L	Total W-L
Anderson, Jimmy	0-1	0-0	0-0	0-0	1-0	0-0	0-0	0-0	0-0	0-0	0-0	0-0	1-0	0-0	0-0	0-0	2-1
Benson, Kris	1-0	1-0	1-2	0-1	0-0	0-0	1-2	1-0	0-2	1-0	1-1	1-0	2-2	0-0	0-2	1-2	11-14
Boyd, Jason	0-0	0-0	0-0	0-0	0-0	0-0	0-0	0-0	0-0	0-0	0-0	0-0	0-0	0-0	0-0	0-0	0-0
Brown, Adrian	0-0	0-0	0-0	0-0	0-0	0-0	0-0	0-0	0-0	0-0	0-0	0-0	0-0	0-0	0-0	0-0	0-0
Christiansen, J.	0-0	0-1	0-1	1-1	0-0	0-0	0-0	0-0	0-0	0-0	0-0	0-0	0-0	0-0	0-0	0-0	2-3
Clontz, Brad	0-0	0-0	0-0	0-0	0-0	0-0	1-0	0-2	0-1	0-0	0-0	0-0	0-0	0-0	0-0	0-0	1-3
Cordova, Francisco.	0-1	0-1	1-1	1-0	0-0	1-0	1-0	0-0	1-1	0-1	0-2	0-1	1-0	0-0	0-2	2-0	8-10
Dougherty, Jim	0-0	0-0	0-0	0-0	0-0	0-0	0-0	0-0	0-0	0-0	0-0	0-0	0-0	0-0	0-0	0-0	0-0
Garcia, Mike	0-0	0-0	0-0	0-0	0-0	0-0	0-0	0-0	1-0	0-0	0-0	0-0	0-0	0-0	0-0	0-0	1-0
Hansell, Greg	0-0	0-1	0-0	0-0	0-0	0-1	0-0	0-0	0-0	0-1	1-0	0-0	0-0	0-0	0-0	0-0	1-3
Loiselle, Rich	0-0	0-0	0-0	1-0	0-0	0-0	0-0	0-0	0-1	0-0	0-0	0-0	0-1	2-0	0-0	0-0	3-2
Osik, Keith	0-0	0-0	0-0	0-0	0-0	0-0	0-0	0-0	0-0	0-0	0-0	0-0	0-0	0-0	0-0	0-0	0-0
Peters, Chris	0-0	0-0	0-1	0-1	2-0	0-0	0-0	0-0	0-2	0-0	0-0	0-0	2-0	0-0	1-0	0-0	5-4
Phillips, Jason	0-0	0-0	0-0	0-0	0-0	0-0	0-0	0-0	0-0	0-0	0-0	0-0	0-0	0-0	0-0	0-0	0-0
Ritchie, Todd	1-0	1-1	1-0	1-1	1-0	1-0	3-1	2-0	1-2	0-1	0-0	1-0	1-0	0-2	0-0	1-1	15-9
Sauerbeck, Scott	0-0	0-0	2-0	0-0	0-0	1-0	0-0	1-0	0-0	0-0	0-1	0-0	0-0	0-0	0-0	0-0	4-1
Schmidt, Jason	0-2	1-1	1-2	1-0	1-0	1-0	0-1	1-0	1-0	2-0	0-0	1-0	0-1	1-2	1-0	1-2	13-11
Schourek, Pete	0-0	0-0	0-0	0-2	0-1	0-1	1-1	0-0	0-0	2-0	0-1	0-0	0-1	1-0	0-0	0-0	4-7
Silva, Jose	0-0	0-1	0-0	0-0	0-0	0-0	0-0	0-1	0-0	1-0	1-0	0-2	0-0	0-1	0-1	0-2	2-8
Wallace, Jeff	0-0	0-0	0-0	0-0	0-0	1-0	0-0	0-0	0-0	0-0	0-0	0-0	0-0	0-0	0-0	0-0	1-0
Wilkins, Marc	0-1	0-0	0-0	0-0	0-0	0-0	0-0	1-0	0-0	0-0	0-0	0-0	0-1	0-0	1-0	0-0	2-3
Williams, Mike	0-0	0-0	0-0	1-1	1-1	0-0	0-0	0-0	0-0	0-0	0-0	0-0	0-0	0-0	1-0	0-1	3-4
Totals	**2-5**	**3-6**	**6-7**	**6-7**	**7-2**	**4-3**	**7-5**	**6-3**	**4-8**	**6-3**	**2-7**	**4-3**	**7-5**	**3-6**	**4-5**	**7-8**	**78-83**

INTERLEAGUE BREAKDOWN: Wilkins 1-0, Benson 0-1, Silva 0-1 vs. White Sox; Cordova 1-0, Benson 1-0, Schmidt 0-1 vs. Indians; Cordova 1-0, Schmidt 0-1, Ritchie 0-1 vs. Tigers; Christiansen 1-0, Schmidt 1-0, Benson 0-1 vs. Royals; Ritchie 1-0, Silva 0-1, Williams 0-1 vs. Twins. Total: 7-8.

ST. LOUIS—75-86

Pitcher	Ari. W-L	Atl. W-L	Chi. W-L	Cin. W-L	Col. W-L	Fla. W-L	Hou. W-L	L.A. W-L	Mil. W-L	Mon. W-L	N.Y. W-L	Phi. W-L	Pit. W-L	S.D. W-L	S.F. W-L	A.L. W-L	Total W-L
Acevedo, Juan	0-0	0-2	0-0	1-0	0-0	1-0	0-1	1-0	0-2	1-1	0-1	1-0	0-0	1-0	0-0	0-1	6-8
Ankiel, Rick	0-0	0-1	0-0	0-0	0-0	0-0	0-0	0-0	0-0	0-0	0-0	0-0	0-0	0-0	0-0	0-0	0-1
Aybar, Manny	1-0	1-0	0-0	0-0	0-1	0-0	0-1	0-0	0-1	0-0	0-0	0-0	1-1	0-0	0-1	0-0	4-5
Benes, Alan	0-0	0-0	0-0	0-0	0-0	0-0	0-0	0-0	0-0	0-0	0-0	0-0	0-0	0-0	0-0	0-0	0-0
Bottalico, Ricky	0-2	0-0	1-1	0-0	0-0	0-0	0-0	1-0	0-0	0-1	0-1	0-0	0-1	0-0	0-0	0-1	3-7
Bottenfield, Kent	0-0	0-1	2-0	1-0	0-0	1-1	2-0	2-0	2-0	1-1	0-0	1-0	2-1	2-0	1-2	1-1	18-7
Busby, Mike	0-0	0-0	0-0	0-0	0-0	0-0	0-0	0-0	0-1	0-0	0-0	0-0	0-0	0-0	0-0	0-0	0-1
Croushore, Rich	0-1	0-0	0-0	1-2	0-0	0-0	0-1	0-0	0-1	0-0	0-1	0-0	0-0	0-0	2-0	0-0	3-7
Heiserman, Rick	0-0	0-0	0-0	0-0	0-0	0-0	0-0	0-0	0-0	0-0	0-0	0-0	0-0	0-0	0-0	0-0	0-0
Jimenez, Jose	2-0	0-1	0-1	0-2	0-2	0-0	1-1	1-1	0-0	1-0	0-0	0-0	0-3	0-0	0-2	0-1	5-14
King, Curtis	0-0	0-0	0-0	0-0	0-0	0-0	0-0	0-0	0-0	0-0	0-0	0-0	0-0	0-0	0-0	0-0	0-0
Luebbers, Larry	0-0	0-0	1-0	0-0	1-0	1-0	0-0	0-0	0-1	0-0	0-0	0-0	0-1	0-0	0-1	3-3
Mercker, Kent	0-0	0-0	0-0	0-1	1-1	0-0	0-0	0-0	2-0	0-0	0-2	2-1	0-0	0-0	0-0	1-0	6-5
Mohler, Mike	0-0	0-0	0-0	0-0	0-0	0-0	0-0	0-0	0-0	0-0	0-0	0-0	0-0	0-0	1-0	0-0	1-1
Oliver, Darren	0-1	0-1	0-0	0-1	2-0	0-1	2-0	1-0	0-0	0-1	0-0	0-1	0-1	3-0	1-0	0-2	9-9
Osborne, Donovan	0-0	0-0	0-0	0-0	0-0	0-0	0-1	0-0	1-0	0-0	0-0	0-0	0-0	0-0	0-1	0-0	1-3
Painter, Lance	1-0	0-1	0-1	1-0	0-1	0-1	0-1	0-0	1-1	0-0	0-0	0-0	0-0	0-0	0-0	0-0	4-5
Radinsky, Scott	0-0	0-0	0-0	0-0	0-0	0-0	0-0	0-0	0-0	0-0	0-0	0-0	1-0	0-0	0-0	1-1	2-1
Slocumb, H.	0-0	0-0	0-1	0-0	0-0	0-0	0-0	0-0	0-0	0-0	0-0	0-0	0-0	1-0	1-1	1-0	3-2
Sodowsky, Clint	0-0	0-0	0-0	0-0	0-0	0-0	0-0	0-1	0-0	0-0	0-0	0-0	0-0	0-0	0-0	0-0	0-1

Pitcher	Ari. W-L	Atl. W-L	Chi. W-L	Cin. W-L	Col. W-L	Fla. W-L	Hou. W-L	L.A. W-L	Mil. W-L	Mon. W-L	N.Y. W-L	Phi. W-L	Pit. W-L	S.D. W-L	S.F. W-L	A.L. W-L	Total W-L
Stephenson, G.......	0-0	0-1	0-2	0-0	0-0	1-0	1-0	0-0	0-0	0-0	1-0	1-0	1-0	0-0	0-0	1-0	6-3
Thompson, Mark...	0-0	0-0	1-1	0-0	0-0	0-0	0-0	0-0	0-2	0-0	0-0	0-0	0-0	0-0	0-0	0-0	1-3
Totals	4-4	1-8	5-7	4-8	5-4	4-3	7-5	6-3	6-7	4-5	2-5	5-4	5-7	7-2	3-6	7-8	75-86

INTERLEAGUE BREAKDOWN: Croushore 1-0, Stephenson 1-0, Acevedo 0-1 vs. White Sox; Bottenfield 1-1, Croushore 1-0, Radinsky 1-0, Jimenez 0-1, Bottalico 0-1 vs. Tigers; Slocumb 1-0, Radinsky 0-1, Oliver 0-1 vs. Royals; Mercker 1-0, Oliver 0-1, Luebbers 0-1 vs. Twins. Total: 7-8.

SAN DIEGO—74-88

Pitcher	Ari. W-L	Atl. W-L	Chi. W-L	Cin. W-L	Col. W-L	Fla. W-L	Hou. W-L	L.A. W-L	Mil. W-L	Mon. W-L	N.Y. W-L	Phi. W-L	Pit. W-L	St.L. W-L	S.F. W-L	A.L. W-L	Total W-L
Almanzar, Carlos....	0-0	0-0	0-0	0-0	0-0	0-0	0-0	0-0	0-0	0-0	0-0	0-0	0-0	0-0	0-0	0-0	0-0
Ashby, Andy	0-1	0-2	2-0	1-1	1-1	1-0	0-1	2-0	1-0	0-1	1-1	0-0	2-0	1-0	1-1	1-1	14-10
Boehringer, Brian...	0-1	0-0	0-0	0-0	1-0	0-1	0-0	1-0	0-0	0-0	0-1	0-0	1-0	1-1	0-1	1-0	6-5
Carlyle, Buddy	0-0	0-1	0-0	0-1	0-0	0-1	0-0	0-0	0-0	1-0	0-0	0-0	0-0	0-0	0-0	0-0	1-3
Clement, Matt	0-0	1-0	0-2	1-1	1-1	2-0	0-2	1-0	1-0	1-1	0-0	1-1	1-0	0-1	0-2	0-1	10-12
Cunnane, Will	0-0	0-0	0-0	0-0	0-0	0-0	0-0	0-0	0-0	0-0	0-1	0-0	1-0	0-0	0-0	1-0	2-1
Giovanola, Ed	0-0	0-0	0-0	0-0	0-0	0-0	0-0	0-0	0-0	0-0	0-0	0-0	0-0	0-0	0-0	0-1	0-1
Guzman, Domingo.	0-0	0-0	0-0	0-0	0-0	0-0	0-0	0-0	0-0	0-0	0-0	0-0	0-0	0-0	0-0	0-0	0-0
Hitchcock, Sterling.	0-4	1-0	0-1	0-1	3-0	0-0	1-0	1-1	0-1	1-1	0-1	1-1	0-1	0-1	2-1	2-0	12-14
Hoffman, Trevor	0-0	0-0	0-1	0-0	0-0	0-0	0-0	0-0	1-0	0-0	0-1	0-0	1-1	0-0	0-0	0-0	2-3
Miceli, Dan	0-2	0-1	0-0	0-0	0-0	1-0	0-1	1-1	0-0	0-0	0-0	0-0	0-0	0-0	0-0	2-0	4-5
Murray, Heath........	0-1	0-0	0-0	0-1	0-1	0-0	0-0	0-0	0-0	0-0	0-0	0-0	0-0	0-0	0-0	0-0	0-4
Reyes, Carlos	0-1	0-1	0-0	0-0	0-0	0-0	0-0	0-0	1-0	0-1	0-0	0-0	0-0	0-0	0-0	1-0	2-4
Rivera, Roberto	0-0	0-0	0-1	0-0	1-0	0-0	0-0	0-0	0-0	0-0	0-0	0-0	0-0	0-0	0-0	0-0	1-2
Spencer, Stan	0-0	0-0	0-1	0-0	0-0	0-1	0-0	0-0	0-0	0-0	0-1	0-2	0-1	0-0	0-1	0-0	0-7
Vosberg, Ed	0-0	0-0	0-0	0-0	0-0	0-0	0-0	0-0	0-0	0-0	0-0	0-0	0-0	0-0	0-0	0-0	0-0
Wall, Donne...........	0-0	0-0	1-0	0-0	0-0	1-0	0-2	1-0	0-0	0-0	0-0	0-0	0-0	0-2	0-0	3-0	7-4
Whisenant, Matt	0-1	0-0	0-0	0-0	0-0	0-0	0-0	0-0	0-0	0-0	0-0	0-0	0-0	0-0	0-0	0-0	0-1
Whiteside, Matt	0-0	0-0	0-0	0-0	0-0	0-0	0-0	0-0	1-0	0-0	0-0	0-0	0-0	0-0	0-0	0-0	1-0
Williams, Woody ...	2-0	1-0	0-0	1-1	1-1	1-0	0-1	2-0	0-2	0-1	1-1	1-2	0-1	0-0	2-0	0-2	12-12
Totals 2-11		4-5	3-6	3-6	9-4	4-3	1-8	9-3	5-3	3-5	2-7	3-6	6-3	2-7	5-7	11-4	74-88

INTERLEAGUE BREAKDOWN: Wall 1-0, Hitchcock 1-0, Clement 0-1 vs. Athletics; Hitchcock 1-0, Wall 1-0, Cunnane 0-1, Reyes 1-0, Williams 0-1, Ashby 0-1 vs. Mariners; Miceli 1-0, Wall 1-0, Williams 0-1 vs. Rangers; Boehringer 1-0, Miceli 1-0, Ashby 1-0 vs. Angels. Total: 11-4.

SAN FRANCISCO—86-76

Pitcher	Ari. W-L	Atl. W-L	Chi. W-L	Cin. W-L	Col. W-L	Fla. W-L	Hou. W-L	L.A. W-L	Mil. W-L	Mon. W-L	N.Y. W-L	Phi. W-L	Pit. W-L	St.L. W-L	S.D. W-L	A.L. W-L	Total W-L
Brock, Chris...........	0-1	1-0	0-0	0-0	0-1	0-1	1-0	1-0	1-0	0-1	0-1	0-0	0-0	1-0	1-1	0-2	6-8
del Toro, Miguel	0-0	0-0	0-0	0-0	0-0	0-0	0-0	0-0	0-0	0-0	0-0	0-0	0-0	0-0	0-0	0-0	0-0
Embree, Alan	0-0	0-0	1-0	1-0	1-1	0-0	0-0	0-1	0-0	0-0	0-0	0-0	0-0	0-0	0-0	0-0	3-2
Estes, Shawn	0-2	0-1	2-0	1-0	2-0	1-0	0-1	0-2	0-0	0-1	0-2	0-0	2-0	0-0	2-1	1-1	11-11
Gardner, Mark........	0-1	0-0	0-0	0-1	1-0	0-0	0-1	3-0	0-2	0-0	0-1	0-0	0-1	0-1	0-2	0-2	5-11
Hernandez, Livan ...	1-0	0-0	0-0	0-0	0-0	0-0	0-0	1-1	1-0	0-0	0-1	0-0	0-0	0-1	0-0	0-1	3-3
Johnstone, John.....	0-0	0-0	0-0	0-0	0-1	1-1	1-0	0-0	0-0	1-1	0-1	0-1	0-0	0-0	0-0	0-1	4-6
Nathan, Joe	0-1	1-0	0-0	0-0	0-0	1-0	0-1	0-1	1-0	2-0	1-0	0-1	0-0	1-0	0-0	0-1	7-4
Nen, Robb	0-1	0-0	1-1	0-2	0-0	0-1	1-0	0-0	0-0	0-0	1-0	0-1	0-0	0-0	0-0	0-1	3-8
Ortiz, Russ.............	0-1	1-2	2-0	1-1	3-0	1-0	1-1	0-0	0-1	2-1	1-0	0-1	2-0	1-0	2-0	1-1	18-9
Patrick, Bronswell .	0-0	0-0	0-0	0-0	0-0	1-0	0-0	0-0	0-0	0-0	0-0	0-0	0-0	0-0	0-0	0-0	1-0
Rodriguez, Felix.....	0-0	0-1	0-0	0-0	0-1	0-0	0-0	0-0	0-0	0-0	0-0	0-1	2-0	0-0	0-0	0-0	2-3
Rodriguez, Rich.....	0-0	0-0	0-0	0-0	0-0	0-0	0-0	0-0	0-0	0-0	0-0	1-0	2-0	0-0	0-0	0-0	3-0
Rueter, Kirk............	2-2	2-0	1-0	1-0	2-1	0-0	0-1	0-2	2-1	0-0	0-1	1-0	0-1	2-0	0-1	3-0	15-10
Spradlin, Jerry	0-0	0-0	0-0	1-0	0-0	0-0	0-0	0-0	0-0	0-0	0-0	0-0	0-1	0-0	1-0	1-0	3-1
Tavarez, Julian	0-0	0-0	0-0	1-0	0-0	0-0	0-0	0-0	0-0	0-0	0-0	0-0	0-0	0-0	0-0	1-0	2-0
Totals	3-9	5-4	7-1	5-4	9-4	5-4	4-5	5-4	5-4	5-4	2-7	6-2	5-4	6-3	7-5	7-8	86-76

INTERLEAGUE BREAKDOWN: Rueter 2-0, Spradlin 1-0, Johnstone 0-1, Nen 0-1, Ortiz 0-1 vs. Athletics; Tavarez 1-0, Rueter 1-0, Gardner 0-1 vs. Mariners; Gardner 0-1, Brock 0-1, Estes 0-1 vs. Rangers; Ortiz 1-0, Estes 1-0, Brock 0-1 vs. Angels. Total: 7-8.

HOME RUNS BY PARKS

	At Ari.	At Atl.	At Chi.	At Cin.	At Col.	At Fla.	At Hou.	At L.A.	At Mil.	At Mon.	At N.Y.	At Phi.	At Pit.	At St.L.	At S.D.	At S.F.	At A.L. Parks	Totals 1999	1998	HR Allow.
Arizona..............	101	8	2	4	11	4	3	10	14	6	4	6	7	3	8	10	15	216	159	176
Atlanta..............	6	86	5	6	13	5	4	10	8	7	12	12	1	1	4	7	10	197	215	142
Chicago.............	6	8	98	8	8	6	4	6	10	2	2	7	6	6	2	4	6	189	212	221
Cincinnati	5	3	14	97	9	1	5	3	12	2	3	17	6	8	6	5	13	209	138	190
Colorado...........	5	3	6	5	144	4	0	8	2	4	1	3	8	9	*8	8	5	223	183	237
Florida..............	8	5	8	6	4	48	0	7	6	6	3	3	1	2	7	6	8	128	114	171
Houston	4	1	8	9	6	11	65	5	5	4	7	7	1	7	7	8	13	168	166	128
Los Angeles	6	3	7	5	11	3	3	92	4	8	5	5	0	7	10	8	8	187	159	192
Milwaukee.........	0	2	14	10	9	6	4	1	77	5	3	3	8	6	2	6	9	165	152	213
Montreal...........	6	5	5	3	15	1	1	3	1	84	5	13	6	2	4	4	5	163	147	152
New York	6	4	8	13	6	7	7	3	7	5	84	7	4	4	5	5	6	181	136	167
Philadelphia	2	7	5	4	14	7	1	2	3	7	4	77	2	6	4	2	14	161	126	212
Pittsburgh	3	2	2	8	9	1	6	7	8	0	6	4	91	5	3	4	12	171	107	160
St. Louis	1	6	11	8	4	5	3	13	4	4	5	4	5	104	4	6	7	194	223	161
San Diego	6	1	8	3	15	2	5	8	8	1	2	5	3	5	69	9	3	153	167	193
San Francisco ...	10	3	8	11	11	3	3	9	7	1	2	4	7	6	8	87	8	188	161	194
A.L. clubs.........	10	14	13	13	14	9	4	7	11	6	13	8	5	13	11	4	....	155	113	....
1999 Totals...	185	161	222	213	303	123	118	194	187	152	161	185	171	187	*159	185	142	2893	....	2909
1998 Totals...	176	162	199	149	212	142	153	143	160	131	134	160	124	196	142	172	....	....	2565	....

*There were actually 158 home runs hit at San Diego in 1999. The totals include one home run by the Rockies at Monterrey Stadium, Mexico.

AT ARIZONA (185):

Arizona (101)—Bell 21, Williams 17, Finley 17, Gonzalez 10, Lee 7, Gilkey 4, Fox 4, Durazo 4, Stinnett 3, Miller 3, Ward 2, Colbrunn 2, Harris 1, Anderson 1, Womack 1, Batista 1, Frias 1, Ryan 1, Barajas 1. **Atlanta (6)**—Lopez 3, Williams 2, A. Jones 1. **Chicago (6)**—Sosa 3, Rodriguez 2, Houston 1. **Cincinnati (5)**—Larkin 1, Vaughn 1, Taubensee 1, Hammonds 1, Casey 1. **Colorado (5)**—Bichette 2, Castilla 2, Perez 1. **Florida (8)**—Lowell 3, Floyd 2, Wilson 2, Orie 1. **Houston (4)**—Biggio 2, Bagwell 1, Hidalgo 1. **Los Angeles (8)**—Sheffield 3, Karros 2, Grudzielanek 1. **Montreal (6)**—Blum 2, White 1, W. Guerrero 1, V. Guerrero 1, Vidro 1. **New York (6)**—Olerud 1, Piazza 1, Alfonzo 1, M. Franco 1, Allensworth 1, Kinkade 1. **Oakland (5)**—Raines 1, Stairs 1, McDonald 1, Grieve 1, Hernandez 1. **Philadelphia (2)**—Gant 1, Rolen 1. **Pittsburgh (3)**—Young 1, Giles 1, B. Brown 1. **St. Louis (1)**—McGwire 1. **San Diego (6)**—Gwynn 1, Veras 1, Owens 1, Nevin 1, R. Rivera 1, Newhan 1. **San Francisco (10)**—Aurilia 3, Snow 2, Benard 2, Burks 1, Hayes 1, Servais 1. **Texas (5)**—Palmeiro 2, Gonzalez 2, Clayton 1.

AT ATLANTA (161):

Arizona (8)—Gonzalez 2, Durazo 2, Williams 1, Gilkey 1, Batista 1, Lee 1. **Atlanta (86)**—C. Jones 25, Klesko 12, Jordan 11, A. Jones 10, Boone 9, Williams 7, Maddux 2, Hunter 2, Simon 2, Myers 1, Smoltz 1, Hernandez 1, Lopez 1, Garcia 1, Battle 1. **Baltimore (8)**—Ripken 2, Clark 2, Surhoff 1, Anderson 1, Bordick 1, C. Johnson 1. **Boston (4)**—Stanley 2, Buford 1, Veras 1. **Chicago (8)**—Sosa 2, Rodriguez 2, Gaetti 1, Blauser 1, Grace 1, Hernandez 1. **Cincinnati (3)**—Tucker 1, Cameron 1, Boone 1. **Colorado (3)**—Reed 1, Castilla 1, Helton 1. **Florida (5)**—Bautista 1, Floyd 1, Millar 1, Wilson 1, Lowell 1. **Houston (1)**—Bagwell 1. **Los Angeles (3)**—White 1, Mondesi 1, Beltre 1. **Milwaukee (2)**—Cirillo 1, Jenkins 1. **Montreal (5)**—Merced 2, Seguignol 1, Barrett 1, Blum 1. **New York (4)**—Piazza 2, Olerud 1, Agbayani 1. **Philadelphia (7)**—Rolen 3, Brogna 2, Lieberthal 1, Anderson 1. **Pittsburgh (2)**—Sprague 1, Giles 1. **St. Louis (6)**—McGwire 1, Lankford 1, Paquette 1, Renteria 1, Tatis 1, Polanco 1. **San Diego (1)**—Nevin 1. **San Francisco (3)**—Burks 1, Hayes 1, Santangelo 1. **Tampa Bay (2)**—McGriff 1, Canseco 1.

AT CHICAGO (222):

Arizona (2)—Williams 1, Finley 1. **Atlanta (5)**—Boone 2, Jordan 1, C. Jones 1, A. Jones 1. **Chicago A.L. (4)**—Thomas 1, Norton 1, Caruso 1, Johnson 1. **Chicago N.L. (98)**—Sosa 33, Rodriguez 14, Hill 11, Grace 8, Blauser 7, Gaetti 6, Hernandez 5, Andrews 4, Morandini 3, Santiago 2, Houston 2, Nieves 2, Johnson 1. **Cincinnati (14)**—Vaughn 5, Cameron 3, Boone 3, Larkin 1, Taubensee 1, Young 1. **Colorado (6)**—Bichette 1, Walker 1, Castilla 1, Echevarria 1, Perez 1, Sexton 1. **Florida (8)**—Wilson 3, Fabregas 1, Kotsay 1, Berg 1, Millar 1, Gonzalez 1. **Houston (8)**—Bagwell 3, Everett 3, Hidalgo 1, Meluskey 1. **Kansas City (5)**—Randa 2, Spehr 1, Damon 1, Beltran 1. **Los Angeles (7)**—Hundley 2, Grudzielanek 2, Sheffield 1, Karros 1, Mondesi 1. **Milwaukee (4)**—Grissom 4, Valentin 2, Burnitz 2, Cirillo 2, Nilsson 1, Becker 1, Belliard 1, Barker 1. **Minnesota (4)**—Hocking 1, Coomer 1, Hunter 1, Allen 1. **Montreal (5)**—Widger 2, Andrews 1, V. Guerrero 1, Cabrera 1. **New York (8)**—Ventura 3, Henderson 2, Olerud 1, Piazza 1, Alfonzo 1. **Philadelphia (5)**—Lieberthal 2, Gant 1, Brogna 1, Abreu 1. **Pittsburgh (2)**—Young 1, Hermansen 1. **St. Louis (11)**—McGwire 2, T. Howard 2, Lankford 2, Jensen 1, Renteria 1, Tatis 1, Marrero 1, Drew 1. **San Diego (8)**—Nevin 2, R. Rivera 2, Arias 2, Vander Wal 1, Owens 1. **San Francisco (8)**—Bonds 3, Snow 2, Hayes 1, Kent 1, Benard 1.

AT CINCINNATI (213):

Arizona (4)—Bell 1, Williams 1, Womack 1, Miller 1. **Atlanta (6)**—Weiss 1, Hunter 1, Boone 1, C. Jones 1, E. Perez 1, A. Jones 1. **Chicago (8)**—Santiago 2, Rodriguez 2, Hill 1, Sosa 1, Hernandez 1, Andrews 1. **Cincinnati (97)**—Vaughn 20, Cameron 12, Casey 11, Young 9, Taubensee 8, Larkin 7, Boone 7, Hammonds 5, Tucker 5, Reese 5, Johnson 3, Lewis 2, Stynes 1, Sweeney 1, LaRue 1. **Cleveland (6)**—M. Ramirez 2, Gooden 1, R. Alomar 1, Lofton 1, Sexson 1. **Colorado (5)**—Manwaring 1, Walker 1, Hamilton 1, Echevarria 1, Perez 1. **Detroit (7)**—Clark 3, Easley 2, Palmer 1, Encarnacion 1. **Florida (6)**—Wilson 2, Lee 1, Berg 1, Gonzalez 1, A. Garcia 1. **Houston (9)**—Bagwell 2, Bell 2, Everett 2, Caminiti 1, Mieske 1, Hidalgo 1. **Los Angeles (5)**—Sheffield 1, Karros 1, Mondesi 1, Cromer 1, Beltre 1. **Milwaukee (10)**—Nilsson 3, Valentin 2, Burnitz 1, Cirillo 1, Banks 1, Belliard 1, Jenkins 1. **Montreal (3)**—White 1, V. Guerrero 1, Barrett 1. **New York (13)**—Henderson 3, Bonilla 2, Pratt 2, Alfonzo 2, Olerud 1, Ventura 1, Piazza 1, M. Franco 1. **Philadelphia (4)**—Ducey 1, Gant 1, Lieberthal 1, Rolen 1. **Pittsburgh (3)**—Sprague 1, Sveum 2, Martin 1, Giles 1. **St. Louis (8)**—Tatis 4, McGwire 3, Perez 1. **San Diego (3)**—Leyritz 1, Owens 1, Arias 1. **San Francisco (11)**—Bonds 5, Javier 1, Burks 1, Hayes 1, Kent 1, Aurilia 1, Martinez 1.

AT COLORADO (303):

Anaheim (6)—Glaus 3, Anderson 2, Williams 1. **Arizona (11)**—Bell 2, Williams 2, Stinnett 2, Miller 2, Finley 1, Gonzalez 1, Batista 1. **Atlanta (13)**—Hunter 2, Hernandez 2, Jordan 2, C. Jones 2, E. Perez 2, Williams 1, A. Jones 1, Simon 1. **Chicago (8)**—Sosa 3, Hernandez 2, Blauser 1, Grace 1, Rodriguez 1. **Cincinnati (9)**—Hammonds 3, Casey 3, Vaughn 1, Lewis 1, Johnson 1. **Colorado (144)**—Walker 26, Helton 23, Bichette 20, Castilla 20, Shumpert 8, Perez 8, Clemente 7, Abbott 6, Echevarria 5, Barry 4, Petrick 4, Blanco 3, Hamilton 2, Lansing 2, Gibson 2, Manwaring 1, Bohanon 1, Leskanic 1, Phillips 1. **Florida (4)**—Orie 1, Kotsay 1, Wilson 1, Gonzalez 1. **Houston (6)**—Mieske 2, Biggio 1, Bagwell 1, Johnson 1, Ward 1. **Los Angeles (11)**—Karros 3, Sheffield 2, White 1, Hundley 1, Mondesi 1, Perez 1, Beltre 1, Pena 1. **Milwaukee (9)**—Burnitz 3, Grissom 2, Nilsson 1, Karl 1, Belliard 1, Hughes 1. **Montreal (15)**—White 3, Andrews 3, V. Guerrero 3, Blum 3, Fullmer 2, Vidro 1. **New York (6)**—Agbayani 2, Henderson 1, Lopez 1, Alfonzo 1, Allensworth 1. **Philadelphia (14)**—Lieberthal 3, Ducey 2, Gant 2, Jordan 2, Brogna 1, Glanville 1, Relaford 1, Rolen 1, Abreu 1. **Pittsburgh (9)**—Giles 3, Martin 2, B. Brown 2, Young 1, Morris 1. **St. Louis (4)**—McGwire 2, McEwing 1, Drew 1. **San Diego (15)**—Nevin 3, Sanders 2, R. Rivera 2, Gwynn 1, Joyner 1, Baerga 1, Leyritz 1, Vander Wal 1, Owens 1, Arias 1, Jackson 1. **San Francisco (11)**—Snow 4, Kent 2, Aurilia 2, Rios 2, Burks 1. **Seattle (8)**—Griffey 3, Huskey 2, Segui 1, A. Rodriguez 1, Bell 1.

AT FLORIDA (123):

Arizona (4)—Durazo 2, Bell 1, Miller 1. **Atlanta (5)**—Jordan 2, A. Jones 2, Boone 1. **Baltimore (3)**—Surhoff 2, Conine 1, Chicago **(6)**—Sosa 3, Rodriguez 2, Grace 1. **Cincinnati (1)**—Hammonds 1. **Colorado (4)**—Helton 2, McRae 1, Phillips 1. **Florida (48)**—Wilson 8, Gonzalez 7, Lowell 7, Kotsay 5, Floyd 4, Fernandez 3, Aven 3, Millar 3, Bautista 2, Hernandez 2, Fabregas 1, Orie 1, Dunwoody 1, Berg 1. **Houston (11)**—Bagwell 3, Caminiti 2, Everett 2, Spiers 1, Bell 1, Hidalgo 1, Barker 1. **Los Angeles (3)**—Mondesi 2, Karros 1. **Milwaukee (6)**—Nilsson 1, Valentin 1, Vina 1, Burnitz 1, Hughes 1, Jenkins 1. **Montreal (1)**—V. Guerrero 1. **New York A.L. (4)**—O'Neill 1, Williams 1, Brosius 1, Posada 1. **New York N.L. (7)**—Henderson 2, Ventura 2, Olerud 1, Piazza 1, Alfonzo 1. **Philadelphia (7)**—Brogna 3, Lieberthal 2, G. Bennett 1, Rolen 1. **Pittsburgh (1)**—Giles 1. **St. Louis (5)**—McGwire 2, Renteria 1, Lankford 1. **San Diego (2)**—Gwynn 1, Davis 1. **San Francisco (3)**—Burks 2, Snow 1. **Tampa Bay (2)**—Flaherty 1, Trammell 1.

AT HOUSTON (118):

Arizona (3)—Williams 1, Benes 1, Womack 1. **Atlanta (4)**—Lopez 2, A. Jones 2. **Chicago (4)**—Hill 1, Grace 1, Hernandez 1, Rodriguez 1. **Cincinnati (5)**—Tucker 2, Casey 2, Taubensee 1. **Cleveland (2)**—R. Alomar 1, M. Ramirez 1. **Detroit (2)**—Palmer 1, Clark 1. **Houston (65)**—Bagwell 12, Everett 11, Biggio 10, Bell 5, Hidalgo 5, Caminiti 4, Eusebio 2, Bogar 2, Johnson 2, Bako 2, Ward 2, Berkman 2, Spiers 1, Reynolds 1, Diaz 1, Gutierrez 1, Mieske 1, Bergman 1. **Los Angeles (3)**—White 1, Sheffield 1, Beltre 1. **Milwaukee (4)**—Jenkins 1, Burnitz 1, Loretta 1. **Montreal (1)**—Andrews 1. **New York (7)**—Alfonzo 3, Hamilton 1, Olerud 1, Ventura 1, Piazza 1. **Philadelphia (1)**—Glanville 1. **Pittsburgh (6)**—Martin 2, Morris 2, Young 1, Giles 1. **St. Louis (3)**—McGwire 1, Tatis 1, Drew 1. **San Diego (5)**—R. Rivera 2, Myers 1, Sanders 1, Nevin 1. **San Francisco (3)**—Servais 1, Aurilia 1, Rios 1.

AT LOS ANGELES (194):

Anaheim (4)—Glaus 2, Walbeck 1, Erstad 1. **Arizona (10)**—Gonzalez 4, Williams 2, Gilkey 2, Bell 1, Finley 1. **Atlanta (10)**—C. Jones 4, Jordan 2, Lopez 2, Boone 1, A. Jones 1. **Chicago (6)**—Sosa 2, Houston 2, Grace 1, Hernandez 1. **Cincinnati (3)**—Taubensee 1, Young 1, Casey 1. **Colorado (8)**—Blanco 2, Helton 2, Bichette 1, Castilla 1, Abbott 1, Barry 1. **Florida (7)**—Aven 2, Wilson 2, Floyd 1, Dunwoody 1, Millar 1. **Houston (5)**—Bagwell 3, Eusebio 1, Everett 1. **Los Angeles (92)**—Mondesi 18, Karros 17, Sheffield 15, Hundley 10, White 8, Beltre 6, Hollandsworth 5, Grudzielanek 4, Hansen 2, Young 2, Pena 2, Vizcaino 1, Cromer 1, LoDuca 1. **Milwaukee (1)**—Burnitz 1. **Montreal (3)**—V. Guerrero 2, Blum 1. **New York (9)**—Piazza 2, Alfonzo 1. **Philadelphia (2)**—Brogna 1, Lieberthal 1. **Pittsburgh (7)**—B. Brown 3, Sprague 1, Young 1, Martin 1, Kendall 1. **St. Louis (13)**—Tatis 5, McGwire 3, Lankford 2, Davis 1, T. Howard 1, Marrero 1, Drew 1. **San Diego (8)**—Sanders 2, R. Rivera 2, Gonzalez 2, Joyner 1, Owens 1. **San Francisco (9)**—Bonds 4, Benard 2, Burks 1, Snow 1, Aurilia 1. **Seattle (2)**—Griffey 1, Segui 1. **Texas (1)**—Gonzalez 1.

AT MILWAUKEE (187):

Arizona (14)—Finley 5, Williams 3, Bell 2, Miller 2, Gonzalez 1, Durazo 1. **Atlanta (8)**—C. Jones 3, Weiss 1, Hunter 1, Klesko 1, Lopez 1, Lockhart 1. **Chicago A.L. (5)**—Durham 1, Ordonez 1, Konerko 1, Lee 1, Singleton 1. **Chicago N.L. (10)**—Santiago 1, Sosa 2, Gaetti 1, Hill 1, Grace 1, Morandini 1, Hernandez 1, Houston 1. **Cincinnati (12)**—Vaughn 4, Taubensee 2, Cameron 2, Tucker 1, Stynes 1, Young 1, Boone 1. **Colorado (2)**—Echevarria 1, Clemente 1. **Florida**

(6)—Orie 2, Floyd 1, Kotsay 1, Aven 1, Wilson 1. **Houston (5)**—Caminiti 1, Spiers 1, Bagwell 1, Everett 1, Hidalgo 1. **Kansas City (4)**—Spehr 1, Damon 1, Sweeney 1, Dye 1. **Los Angeles (4)**—Mondesi 1, Hubbard 1, LoDuca 1, Beltre 1. **Milwaukee (77)**—Burnitz 12, Jenkins 10, Grissom 9, Nilsson 9, Ochoa 8, Cirillo 6, Belliard 5, Becker 4, Banks 4, Valentin 3, Loretta 2, Collier 2, Karl 1, Mouton 1, Barker 1. **Minnesota (2)**—Cordova 1, Koskie 1. **Montreal (1)**—White 1. **New York (7)**—Ventura 3, Piazza 2, Hamilton 1, Alfonzo 1. **Philadelphia (3)**—Gant 1, Glanville 1, Magee 1. **Pittsburgh (8)**—Young 4, Sprague 1, Martin 1, A. Brown 1, Morris 1. **St. Louis (4)**—McGwire 2, Tatis 1, Drew 1. **San Diego (8)**—Sanders 2, R. Rivera 2, Magadan 1, Leyritz 1, Owens 1, Arias 1. **San Francisco (7)**—Bonds 3, Burks 2, Kent 1, Martinez 1.

AT MONTREAL (152):

Arizona (6)—Finley 2, Williams 1, Gonzalez 1, Colbrunn 1, Stinnett 1. **Atlanta (7)**—Williams 2, E. Perez 2, A. Jones 2, Guillen 1. **Boston (1)**—Daubach 1. **Chicago (2)**—Hill 1, Sosa 1. **Cincinnati (2)**—Hammonds 1, Tucker 1. **Colorado (4)**—Helton 2, Bichette 1, Walker 1. **Florida (6)**—Gonzalez 2, Bautista 1, Lee 1, Aven 1, A. Garcia 1. **Houston (4)**—Caminiti 2, Bell 1, Ward 1. **Los Angeles (8)**—Sheffield 3, Hundley 2, Beltre 2, Karros 1. **Milwaukee (5)**—Burnitz 2, Grissom 1, Nilsson 1, Loretta 1. **Montreal (84)**—V. Guerrero 23, Widger 11, White 10, Cabrera 6, Andrews 5, Vidro 5, Barrett 5, Mordecai 4, Fullmer 4, Merced 3, Seguignol 3, Mouton 1, Martinez 1, McGuire 1, Cox 1, Mota 1. **New York (5)**—Ventura 2, Piazza 2, Alfonzo 1. **Philadelphia (7)**—Lieberthal 2, Abreu 2, Gant 1, Brogna 1, Rolen 1. **St. Louis (4)**—Tatis 2, McGwire 1, Castillo 1. **San Diego (1)**—Nevin 1. **San Francisco (2)**—Aurilia 1. **Tampa Bay (1)**—Canseco 1. **Toronto (4)**—Delgado 1, Green 1, Stewart 1, Batista 1.

AT NEW YORK (161):

Arizona (4)—Finley 2, Bell 1, Batista 1. **Atlanta (12)**—C. Jones 3, Jordan 2, Boone 2, Williams 2, Klesko 1, E. Perez 1, Simon 1. **Boston (2)**—O'Leary 1, Daubach 1. **Chicago (2)**—Sosa 2. **Cincinnati (3)**—Vaughn 2, Reese 1. **Colorado (1)**—Castilla 1. **Florida (3)**—Orie 1, Aven 1, Wilson 1. **Houston (7)**—Bagwell 2, Everett 2, Bell 1, Mieske 1, Hidalgo 1. **Los Angeles (5)**—Mondesi 3, Sheffield 1, Dreifort 1, LoDuca 1. **Milwaukee (3)**—Grissom 1, Cirillo 1, Jenkins 1. **Montreal (5)**—White 2, V. Guerrero 1, Vidro 1, Cabrera 1. **New York A.L. (7)**—O'Neill 2, Posada 2, Ledee 2, Knoblauch 1. **New York N.L. (84)**—Piazza 18, Ventura 13, Olerud 11, Alfonzo 11, Agbayani 10, McRae 5, Cedeno 4, Hamilton 3, Bonilla 2, Henderson 1, Pratt 1, Jones 1, Lopez 1, Ordonez 1, Allensworth 1, Kinkade 1. **Philadelphia (4)**—Gant 1, Brogna 1, Lieberthal 1, Abreu 1. **Pittsburgh (6)**—Martin 2, B. Brown 2, Wehner 1, Young 1. **St. Louis (5)**—McGwire 2, Paquette 1, Castillo 1, McEwing 1. **San Diego (2)**—Sanders 1, Owens 1. **San Francisco (4)**—Cruz 2, Fletcher 1, Brumfield 1.

AT PHILADELPHIA (185):

Arizona (6)—Bell 1, Williams 1, Gonzalez 1, Colbrunn 1, Miller 1, Durazo 1. **Atlanta (12)**—Boone 2, Klesko 2, Lopez 2, C. Jones 2, A. Jones 2, Williams 1, Simon 1. **Baltimore (2)**—Clark 1, Hairston 1. **Chicago (7)**—Sosa 3, Hill 1, Grace 1, Hernandez 1, Martinez 1. **Cincinnati (17)**—Taubensee 4, Hammonds 3, Vaughn 2, Young 2, Lewis 1, Johnson 1, Sweeney 1, Reese 1, Boone 1, Casey 1. **Colorado (3)**—Reed 1, Castilla 1, Helton 1. **Florida (3)**—Lee 1, Millar 1, Wilson 1. **Houston (7)**—Ward 2, Caminiti 1, Biggio 1, Bagwell 1, Thompson 1, Johnson 1. **Los Angeles (5)**—Mondesi 2, Sheffield 1, Hundley 1, Karros 1. **Milwaukee (3)**—Nilsson 1, Burnitz 1, Cirillo 1. **Montreal (13)**—V. Guerrero 4, Merced 1, Batista 1, White 1, Mordecai 1, Martinez 1, W. Guerrero 1, McGuire 1, Vidro 1, Seguignol 1. **New York A.L. (3)**—Martinez 2, Jeter 1. **New York N.L. (7)**—Ventura 3, Olerud 2, McRae 1, Alfonzo 1. **Philadelphia (77)**—Brogna 14, Abreu 13, Lieberthal 10, Rolen 9, Gant 6, Glanville 5, Arias 4, Anderson 4, Ducey 3, Lovullo 2, Jordan 2, Doster 2, Cedeno 1, Sefcik 1, Magee 1. **Pittsburgh (4)**—Sprague 1, Giles 1, B. Brown 1, Morris 1. **St. Louis (4)**—Lankford 1, Paquette 1, Tatis 1, Drew 1. **San Diego (5)**—Sanders 2, Nevin 1, R. Rivera 1, Jackson 1. **San Francisco (4)**—Burks 1, Mayne 1, Servais 1, Snow 1. **Toronto (3)**—Delgado 2, Fletcher 1.

AT PITTSBURGH (171):

Arizona (7)—Gonzalez 3, Bell 1, Williams 1, Durazo 1, Ryan 1. **Atlanta (1)**—Myers 1. **Chicago (6)**—Santiago 1, Hill 1, Sosa 1, Hernandez 1, Rodriguez 1, Houston 1. **Cincinnati (6)**—Larkin 1, Vaughn 1, Hammonds 1, Cameron 1, Casey 1, LaRue 1. **Cleveland (2)**—Justice 1, Thome 1. **Colorado (8)**—Walker 3, Castilla 2, Shumpert 1, Echevarria 1, Helton 1. **Florida (1)**—Wilson 1. **Houston (1)**—Hidalgo 1. **Kansas City (3)**—Randa 2, Beltran 1. **Los Angeles (10)**—Hundley 4, Hollandsworth 2, Sheffield 1, Karros 1, Mondesi 1, Beltre 1. **Milwaukee (8)**—Cirillo 3, Burnitz 2, Grissom 1, Nilsson 1, Jenkins 1. **Montreal (6)**—V. Guerrero 3, Merced 1, Widger 1, Vidro 1. **New York (4)**—McRae 1, Piazza 1, M. Franco 1, Agbayani 1. **Philadelphia (2)**—Rolen 1, Abreu 1. **Pittsburgh (91)**—Giles 24, Young 16, Martin 12, Sprague 10, Morris 9, F. Garcia 5, Kendall 5, B. Brown 4, A. Brown 2, Benjamin 1, Oliver 1, Osik 1, Cruz 1. **St. Louis (5)**—McGwire 2, Bragg 2, McEwing 1. **San Diego (3)**—Gwynn 1, Sanders 1, Veras 1. **San Francisco (7)**—Kent 3, Burks 1, Servais 1, Snow 1, Aurilia 1.

AT ST. LOUIS (187):

Arizona (3)—Gonzalez 1, Fox 1, Dellucci 1. **Atlanta (1)**—C. Jones 1. **Chicago A.L. (4)**—Ordonez 2, Durham 1, Singleton 1. **Chicago N.L. (6)**—Sosa 4, Reed 1, Brown 1. **Cincinnati (8)**—Vaughn 3, Casey 2, Larkin 1, Cameron 1, Reese 1. **Colorado (9)**—Walker 3, Helton 2, Bichette 1, Shumpert 1, Castilla 1, Echevarria 1. **Detroit (7)**—Palmer 2, Clark 2, D. Cruz 1, Encarnacion 1, Catalanotto 1. **Florida (2)**—Bautista 1, Castro 1. **Houston (7)**—Bagwell 2, Caminiti 1, Biggio 1, Bell 1, Eusebio 1, Everett 1. **Milwaukee (6)**—Berry 1, Nilsson 1, Valentin 1, Burnitz 1, Hughes 1, Barker 1. **Minnesota (2)**—Hocking 1, Jones 1. **Montreal (2)**—Mouton 1, Vidro 1. **New York (4)**—Piazza 2, Henderson 1, Ventura 1. **Philadelphia (6)**—Lieberthal 3, Glanville 1, Doster 1, Rolen 1. **Pittsburgh (5)**—Sprague 1, Giles 1, Kendall 1, Osik 1, B. Brown 1. **St. Louis (104)**—McGwire 37, Tatis 16, Lankford 8, Paquette 7, Renteria 6, McEwing 5, Drew 5, Dunston 4, Bragg 4, T. Howard 3, Marrero 3, Davis 2, Castillo 2, D. Howard 1, Kennedy 1. **San Diego (5)**—Sanders 2, Gwynn 1, Nevin 1, Darr 1. **San Francisco (6)**—Snow 2, Burks 1, Kent 1, Aurilia 1, Mueller 1.

AT SAN DIEGO (159):

Arizona (8)—Bell 2, Williams 2, Finley 2, Stinnett 2. **Atlanta (4)**—Hernandez 1, Klesko 1, E. Perez 1, Millwood 1. **Chicago (2)**—Sosa 2. **Cincinnati (6)**—Vaughn 2, Harnisch 1, Taubensee 1, Lewis 1, Casey 1. **Colorado (8)**—Bichette 4, Castilla 2, Walker 1, Perez 1. **Note:** the Rockies hit 7 home runs at San Diego. One of Bichette's home runs was hit at Monterrey, Mex. **Florida (7)**—Aven 2, Gonzalez 2, Floyd 1, Fabregas 1, Lee 1. **Houston (7)**—Bagwell 2, Ward 2, Berkman 2, Bogar 1. **Los Angeles (7)**—Sheffield 2, Karros 2, White 1, Hundley 1, Mondesi 1. **Milwaukee (2)**—Grissom 1, Jenkins 1. **Montreal (4)**—White 1, V. Guerrero 1, Fullmer 1, Barrett 1. **New York (5)**—Piazza 2, Henderson 1, Ventura 1, Alfonzo 1. **Oakland (1)**—Phillips 1. **Philadelphia (4)**—Gant 1, Lieberthal 1, Glanville 1, Rolen 1. **Pittsburgh (3)**—Sprague 1, Martin 1, Giles 1. **St. Louis (4)**—McGwire 2, Davis 1, McEwing 1. **San Diego (69)**—Nevin 12, Sanders 11, R. Rivera 10, Jackson 6, Leyritz 4, Veras 4, Joyner 2, Myers 2, Vander Wal 2, Owens 2, Arias 2, Magadan 1, Baerga 1, Gomez 1, Davis 1, Darr 1, Newhan 1, Gonzalez 1. **San Francisco (8)**—Burks 2, Kent 2, Bonds 1, Aurilia 1, Benard 1, Canizaro 1. **Seattle (3)**—Martinez 1, Lampkin 1, A. Rodriguez 1. **Texas (7)**—Palmeiro 2, Mateo 2, Gonzalez 1, Rodriguez 1, Clayton 1.

AT SAN FRANCISCO (185):

Arizona (10)—Stinnett 2, Williams 1, Finley 1, Gonzalez 1, Colbrunn 1, Womack 1, Batista 1, Miller 1, Lee 1. **Atlanta (7)**—Boone 2, Jordan 1, Klesko 1, Williams 1, C. Jones 1, A. Jones 1. **Chicago (4)**—Grace 1, Sosa 1, Rodriguez 1, Houston 1. **Cincinnati (5)**—Vaughn 1, Lewis 1, Tucker 1, Reese 1, LaRue 1. **Colorado (8)**—Bichette 2, Lansing 2, Hamilton 1, Castilla 1, Echevarria 1, Helton 1. **Florida (6)**—Floyd 1, Lee 1, Millar 1, Wilson 1, Redmond 1, Castro 1. **Houston (8)**—Bagwell 2, Caminiti 1, Biggio 1, Spiers 1, Bell 1, Bergman 1, Hidalgo 1. **Los Angeles (10)**—Sheffield 3, Hundley 3, White 1, Mondesi 1, Hollandsworth 1, Beltre 1. **Milwaukee (6)**—Burnitz 3, Grissom 1, Berry 1, Valentin 1. **Montreal (4)**—White 1, Vidro 1, Fullmer 1, Blum 1. **New York (5)**—Piazza 3, Ventura 1, Alfonzo 1. **Oakland (4)**—Phillips 1, Macfarlane 1, Stairs 1, Giambi 1. **Philadelphia (2)**—Ducey 1, Lieberthal 1. **Pittsburgh (4)**—Sveum 1, Martin 1, Giles 1, B. Brown 1. **St. Louis (6)**—McGwire 3, Drew 2, Tatis 1. **San Diego (9)**—Sanders 2, Davis 2, Joyner 1, Leyritz 1, Vander Wal 1, Nevin 1, Jackson 1. **San Francisco (87)**—Bonds 16, Burks 16, Kent 11, Aurilia 9, Benard 9, Snow 7, Rios 4, Martinez 3, Javier 2, Hayes 2, Santangelo 2, Gardner 1, Mayne 1, F. Rodriguez 1, Mueller 1, Mirabelli 1, Ortiz 1.

HISTORY

All-time results

Award winners

Hall of Fame

Team by team

ALL-TIME RESULTS

AMERICAN LEAGUE CHAMPIONS

Year	Team	Manager
1901	Chicago	Clark Griffith
1902	Philadelphia	Connie Mack
1903	Boston	Jimmy Collins
1904	Boston	Jimmy Collins
1905	Philadelphia	Connie Mack
1906	Chicago	Fielder Jones
1907	Detroit	Hugh Jennings
1908	Detroit	Hugh Jennings
1909	Detroit	Hugh Jennings
1910	Philadelphia	Connie Mack
1911	Philadelphia	Connie Mack
1912	Boston	Jake Stahl
1913	Philadelphia	Connie Mack
1914	Philadelphia	Connie Mack
1915	Boston	Bill Carrigan
1916	Boston	Bill Carrigan
1917	Chicago	Pants Rowland
1918	Boston	Ed Barrow
1919	Chicago	Kid Gleason
1920	Cleveland	Tris Speaker
1921	New York	Miller Huggins
1922	New York	Miller Huggins
1923	New York	Miller Huggins
1924	Washington	Bucky Harris
1925	Washington	Bucky Harris
1926	New York	Miller Huggins
1927	New York	Miller Huggins
1928	New York	Miller Huggins
1929	Philadelphia	Connie Mack
1930	Philadelphia	Connie Mack
1931	Philadelphia	Connie Mack
1932	New York	Joe McCarthy
1933	Washington	Joe Cronin
1934	Detroit	Mickey Cochrane
1935	Detroit	Mickey Cochrane
1936	New York	Joe McCarthy
1937	New York	Joe McCarthy
1938	New York	Joe McCarthy
1939	New York	Joe McCarthy
1940	Detroit	Del Baker
1941	New York	Joe McCarthy
1942	New York	Joe McCarthy
1943	New York	Joe McCarthy
1944	St. Louis	Luke Sewell
1945	Detroit	Steve O'Neill
1946	Boston	Joe Cronin
1947	New York	Bucky Harris
1948	Cleveland*	Lou Boudreau
1949	New York	Casey Stengel
1950	New York	Casey Stengel
1951	New York	Casey Stengel
1952	New York	Casey Stengel
1953	New York	Casey Stengel
1954	Cleveland	Al Lopez
1955	New York	Casey Stengel
1956	New York	Casey Stengel
1957	New York	Casey Stengel
1958	New York	Casey Stengel
1959	Chicago	Al Lopez
1960	New York	Casey Stengel
1961	New York	Ralph Houk
1962	New York	Ralph Houk
1963	New York	Ralph Houk
1964	New York	Yogi Berra
1965	Minnesota	Sam Mele
1966	Baltimore	Hank Bauer
1967	Boston	Dick Williams
1968	Detroit	Mayo Smith
1969	Baltimore (East Division)	Earl Weaver
1970	Baltimore (East Division)	Earl Weaver
1971	Baltimore (East Division)	Earl Weaver
1972	Oakland (West Division)	Dick Williams
1973	Oakland (West Division)	Dick Williams
1974	Oakland (West Division)	Al Dark
1975	Boston (East Division)	Darrell Johnson
1976	New York (East Division)	Billy Martin
1977	New York (East Division)	Billy Martin
1978	New York (East Division)	Billy Martin, Bob Lemon
1979	Baltimore (East Division)	Earl Weaver
1980	Kansas City (West Division)	Jim Frey
1981	New York (East Division)	Gene Michael, Bob Lemon
1982	Milwaukee (East Division)	Buck Rodgers, Harvey Kuenn
1983	Baltimore (East Division)	Joe Altobelli
1984	Detroit (East Division)	Sparky Anderson
1985	Kansas City (West Division)	Dick Howser
1986	Boston (East Division)	John McNamara
1987	Minnesota (West Division)	Tom Kelly
1988	Oakland (West Division)	Tony La Russa
1989	Oakland (West Division)	Tony La Russa
1990	Oakland (West Division)	Tony La Russa
1991	Minnesota (West Division)	Tom Kelly
1992	Toronto (East Division)	Cito Gaston
1993	Toronto (East Division)	Cito Gaston
1994	None†	
1995	Cleveland (Central Division)	Mike Hargrove
1996	New York (East Division)	Joe Torre
1997	Cleveland (Central Division)	Mike Hargrove
1998	New York (East Division)	Joe Torre
1999	New York (East Division)	Joe Torre

*Defeated Boston in one-game playoff. †New York finished the strike-shortened season with the league's best record.

NATIONAL LEAGUE CHAMPIONS

Year	Team	Manager
1876	Chicago	Albert Spalding
1877	Boston	Harry Wright
1878	Boston	Harry Wright
1879	Providence	George Wright
1880	Chicago	Adrian Anson
1881	Chicago	Adrian Anson
1882	Chicago	Adrian Anson
1883	Boston	John Morrill
1884	Providence	Frank Bancroft
1885	Chicago	Adrian Anson
1886	Chicago	Adrian Anson
1887	Detroit	William Watkins
1888	New York	James Mutrie
1889	New York	James Mutrie
1890	Brooklyn	William McGunnigle
1891	Boston	Frank Selee
1892	Boston	Frank Selee
1893	Boston	Frank Selee
1894	Baltimore	Edward Hanlon
1895	Baltimore	Edward Hanlon
1896	Baltimore	Edward Hanlon
1897	Boston	Frank Selee
1898	Boston	Frank Selee
1899	Brooklyn	Edward Hanlon
1900	Brooklyn	Edward Hanlon
1901	Pittsburgh	Fred Clarke
1902	Pittsburgh	Fred Clarke
1903	Pittsburgh	Fred Clarke

Year	Team	Manager	Year	Team	Manager
1904—New York	John McGraw		1956—Brooklyn	Walter Alston	
1905—New York	John McGraw		1957—Milwaukee	Fred Haney	
1906—Chicago	Frank Chance		1958—Milwaukee	Fred Haney	
1907—Chicago	Frank Chance		1959—Los Angeles‡	Walter Alston	
1908—Chicago	Frank Chance		1960—Pittsburgh	Danny Murtaugh	
1909—Pittsburgh	Fred Clarke		1961—Cincinnati	Fred Hutchinson	
1910—Chicago	Frank Chance		1962—San Francisco§	Al Dark	
1911—New York	John McGraw		1963—Los Angeles	Walter Alston	
1912—New York	John McGraw		1964—St. Louis	Johnny Keane	
1913—New York	John McGraw		1965—Los Angeles	Walter Alston	
1914—Boston	George Stallings		1966—Los Angeles	Walter Alston	
1915—Philadelphia	Pat Moran		1967—St. Louis	Red Schoendienst	
1916—Brooklyn	Wilbert Robinson		1968—St. Louis	Red Schoendienst	
1917—New York	John McGraw		1969—New York (East Division)	Gil Hodges	
1918—Chicago	Fred Mitchell		1970—Cincinnati (West Division)	Sparky Anderson	
1919—Cincinnati	Pat Moran		1971—Pittsburgh (East Division)	Danny Murtaugh	
1920—Brooklyn	Wilbert Robinson		1972—Cincinnati (West Division)	Sparky Anderson	
1921—New York	John McGraw		1973—New York (East Division)	Yogi Berra	
1922—New York	John McGraw		1974—Los Angeles (West Division)	Walter Alston	
1923—New York	John McGraw		1975—Cincinnati (West Division)	Sparky Anderson	
1924—New York	John McGraw		1976—Cincinnati (West Division)	Sparky Anderson	
1925—Pittsburgh	Bill McKechnie		1977—Los Angeles (West Division)	Tommy Lasorda	
1926—St. Louis	Rogers Hornsby		1978—Los Angeles (West Division)	Tommy Lasorda	
1927—Pittsburgh	Donie Bush		1979—Pittsburgh (East Division)	Chuck Tanner	
1928—St. Louis	Bill McKechnie		1980—Philadelphia (East Division)	Dallas Green	
1929—Chicago	Joe McCarthy		1981—Los Angeles (West Division)	Tommy Lasorda	
1930—St. Louis	Gabby Street		1982—St. Louis (East Division)	Whitey Herzog	
1931—St. Louis	Gabby Street		1983—Philadelphia (East Division)	Pat Corrales, Paul Owens	
1932—Chicago	Charlie Grimm		1984—San Diego (West Division)	Dick Williams	
1933—New York	Bill Terry		1985—St. Loius (East Division)	Whitey Herzog	
1934—St. Louis	Frank Frisch		1986—New York (East Division)	Dave Johnson	
1935—Chicago	Charlie Grimm		1987—St. Louis (East Division)	Whitey Herzog	
1936—New York	Bill Terry		1988—Los Angeles (West Division)	Tommy Lasorda	
1937—New York	Bill Terry		1989—San Francisco (West Division)	Roger Craig	
1938—Chicago	Gabby Hartnett		1990—Cincinnati (West Division)	Lou Piniella	
1939—Cincinnati	Bill McKechnie		1991—Atlanta (West Division)	Bobby Cox	
1940—Cincinnati	Bill McKechnie		1992—Atlanta (West Division)	Bobby Cox	
1941—Brooklyn	Leo Durocher		1993—Philadelphia (East Division)	Jim Fregosi	
1942—St. Louis	Billy Southworth		1994—None∞		
1943—St. Louis	Billy Southworth		1995—Atlanta (East Division)	Bobby Cox	
1944—St. Louis	Billy Southworth		1996—Atlanta (East Division)	Bobby Cox	
1945—Chicago	Charlie Grimm		1997—Florida (East Division)	Jim Leyland	
1946—St. Louis*	Eddie Dyer		1998—San Diego (West Division)	Bruce Bochy	
1947—Brooklyn	Burt Shotton		1999—Atlanta (East Division)	Bobby Cox	
1948—Boston	Billy Southworth				
1949—Brooklyn	Burt Shotton				
1950—Philadelphia	Eddie Sawyer				
1951—New York†	Leo Durocher				
1952—Brooklyn	Charlie Dressen				
1953—Brooklyn	Charlie Dressen				
1954—New York	Leo Durocher				
1955—Brooklyn	Walter Alston				

*Defeated Brooklyn, two games to none, in playoff for pennant.
†Defeated Brooklyn, two games to one, in playoff for pennant.
‡Defeated Milwaukee, two games to none, in playoff for pennant.
§Defeated Los Angeles, two games to one, in playoff for pennant.
∞Montreal finished the strike-shortened season with the league's best record.

WORLD SERIES

Year	Winner	Loser	Games	Year	Winner	Loser	Games
1903—Boston A.L.	Pittsburgh N.L.	5-3		1922—New York N.L.	New York A.L.	*4-0	
1904—No Series				1923—New York A.L.	New York N.L.	4-2	
1905—New York N.L.	Philadelphia A.L.	4-1		1924—Washington A.L.	New York N.L.	4-3	
1906—Chicago A.L.	Chicago N.L.	4-2		1925—Pittsburgh N.L.	Washington A.L.	4-3	
1907—Chicago N.L.	Detroit A.L.	*4-0		1926—St. Louis N.L.	New York A.L.	4-3	
1908—Chicago N.L.	Detroit A.L.	4-1		1927—New York A.L.	Pittsburgh, N.L.	4-0	
1909—Pittsburgh N.L.	Detroit A.L.	4-3		1928—New York A.L.	St. Louis N.L.	4-0	
1910—Philadelphia A.L.	Chicago N.L.	4-1		1929—Philadelphia A.L.	Chicago N.L.	4-1	
1911—Philadelphia A.L.	New York N.L.	4-2		1930—Philadelphia A.L.	St. Louis N.L.	4-2	
1912—Boston A.L.	New York N.L.	*4-3		1931—St. Louis N.L.	Philadelphia A.L.	4-3	
1913—Philadelphia A.L.	New York N.L.	4-1		1932—New York A.L.	Chicago N.L.	4-0	
1914—Boston N.L.	Philadelphia A.L.	4-0		1933—New York N.L.	Washington A.L.	4-1	
1915—Boston A.L.	Philadelphia N.L.	4-1		1934—St. Louis N.L.	Detroit A.L.	4-3	
1916—Boston A.L.	Brooklyn N.L.	4-1		1935—Detroit A.L.	Chicago N.L.	4-2	
1917—Chicago A.L.	New York N.L.	4-2		1936—New York A.L.	New York N.L.	4-2	
1918—Boston A.L.	Chicago N.L.	4-2		1937—New York A.L.	New York N.L.	4-1	
1919—Cincinnati N.L.	Chicago A.L.	5-3		1938—New York A.L.	Chicago N.L.	4-0	
1920—Cleveland A.L.	Brooklyn N.L.	5-2		1939—New York A.L.	Cincinnati N.L.	4-0	
1921—New York N.L.	New York A.L.	5-3		1940—Cincinnati N.L.	Detroit A.L.	4-3	

Year	Winner	Loser	Games
1941—New York A.L.	Brooklyn N.L.	4-1
1942—St. Louis N.L.	New York A.L.	4-1
1943—New York A.L.	St. Louis N.L.	4-1
1944—St. Louis N.L.	St. Louis A.L.	4-2
1945—Detroit A.L.	Chicago N.L.	4-3
1946—St. Louis N.L.	Boston A.L.	4-3
1947—New York A.L.	Brooklyn N.L.	4-3
1948—Cleveland A.L.	Boston N.L.	4-2
1949—New York A.L.	Brooklyn N.L.	4-1
1950—New York A.L.	Philadelphia N.L.	4-0
1951—New York A.L.	New York N.L.	4-2
1952—New York A.L.	Brooklyn N.L.	4-3
1953—New York A.L.	Brooklyn N.L.	4-2
1954—New York N.L.	Cleveland A.L.	4-0
1955—Brooklyn N.L.	New York A.L.	4-3
1956—New York A.L.	Brooklyn N.L.	4-3
1957—Milwaukee N.L.	New York A.L.	4-3
1958—New York A.L.	Milwaukee N.L.	4-3
1959—Los Angeles N.L.	Chicago A.L.	4-2
1960—Pittsburgh N.L.	New York A.L.	4-3
1961—New York A.L.	Cincinnati N.L.	4-1
1962—New York A.L.	San Francisco N.L.	4-3
1963—Los Angeles N.L.	New York A.L.	4-0
1964—St. Louis N.L.	New York A.L.	4-3
1965—Los Angeles N.L.	Minnesota A.L.	4-3
1966—Baltimore A.L.	Los Angeles N.L.	4-0
1967—St. Louis N.L.	Boston A.L.	4-3
1968—Detroit A.L.	St. Louis N.L.	4-3
1969—New York N.L.	Baltimore A.L.	4-1
1970—Baltimore A.L.	Cincinnati N.L.	4-1
1971—Pittsburgh N.L.	Baltimore A.L.	4-3
1972—Oakland A.L.	Cincinnati N.L.	4-3
1973—Oakland A.L.	New York N.L.	4-3
1974—Oakland A.L.	Los Angeles N.L.	4-1
1975—Cincinnati N.L.	Boston A.L.	4-3
1976—Cincinnati N.L.	New York A.L.	4-0
1977—New York A.L.	Los Angeles N.L.	4-2
1978—New York A.L.	Los Angeles N.L.	4-2
1979—Pittsburgh N.L.	Baltimore A.L.	4-3
1980—Philadelphia N.L.	Kansas City A.L.	4-2
1981—Los Angeles N.L.	New York A.L.	4-2
1982—St. Louis N.L.	Milwaukee A.L.	4-3
1983—Baltimore A.L.	Philadelphia N.L.	4-1
1984—Detroit A.L.	San Diego N.L.	4-1
1985—Kansas City A.L.	St. Louis N.L.	4-3
1986—New York N.L.	Boston A.L.	4-3
1987—Minnesota A.L.	St. Louis N.L.	4-3
1988—Los Angeles N.L.	Oakland A.L.	4-1
1989—Oakland A.L.	San Francisco N.L.	4-0
1990—Cincinnati N.L.	Oakland A.L.	4-0
1991—Minnesota A.L.	Atlanta N.L.	4-3
1992—Toronto A.L.	Atlanta N.L.	4-2
1993—Toronto A.L.	Philadelphia N.L.	4-2
1994—No Series		
1995—Atlanta N.L.	Cleveland A.L.	4-2
1996—New York A.L.	Atlanta N.L.	4-2
1997—Florida N.L.	Cleveland A.L.	4-3
1998—New York A.L.	San Diego N.L.	4-0
1999—New York A.L.	Atlanta N.L.	4-0

*Includes tie game.

DIVISION SERIES

AMERICAN LEAGUE

Year	Winner (Division)	Loser (Division)	Games
1981—New York (East)	Milwaukee (East)	3-2
Oakland (West)	Kansas City (West)	3-0
1995—Cleveland (Central)	Boston (East)	3-0
Seattle (West)	New York* (East)	3-2
1996—New York (East)	Texas (West)	3-1
Baltimore (East)*	Cleveland (Central)	3-1
1997—Baltimore (East)	Seattle (West)	3-1
Cleveland (Central)	New York (East)*	3-2
1998—New York (East)	Texas (West)	3-0
Cleveland (Central)	Boston (East)*	3-1
1999—New York (East)	Texas (West)	3-0
Boston (East)*	Cleveland (Central)	3-2

NATIONAL LEAGUE

Year	Winner (Division)	Loser (Division)	Games
1981—Montreal (East)	Philadelphia (East)	3-2
Los Angeles (West)	Houston (West)	3-2
1995—Atlanta (East)	Colorado* (West)	3-1
Cincinnati (Central)	Los Angeles (West)	3-0
1996—Atlanta (East)	Los Angeles (West)*	3-0
St. Louis (Central)	San Diego (West)	3-0
1997—Atlanta (East)	Houston (Central)	3-0
Florida (East)*	San Francisco (West)	3-0
1998—Atlanta (East)	Chicago (Central)*	3-0
San Diego (West)	Houston (Central)	3-1
1999—Atlanta (East)	Houston (Central)	3-1
New York (East)*	Arizona (West)	3-1

*Wild-card team.

CHAMPIONSHIP SERIES

AMERICAN LEAGUE

Year	Winner (Division)	Loser (Division)	Games
1969—Baltimore (East)	Minnesota (West)	3-0
1970—Baltimore (East)	Minnesota (West)	3-0
1971—Baltimore (East)	Oakland (West)	3-0
1972—Oakland (West)	Detroit (East)	3-2
1973—Oakland (West)	Baltimore (East)	3-2
1974—Oakland (West)	Baltimore (East)	3-1
1975—Boston (East)	Oakland (West)	3-0
1976—New York (East)	Kansas City (West)	3-2
1977—New York (East)	Kansas City (West)	3-2
1978—New York (East)	Kansas City (West)	3-1
1979—Baltimore (East)	California (West)	3-1
1980—Kansas City (West)	New York (East)	3-0
1981—New York (East)	Oakland (West)	3-0
1982—Milwaukee (East)	California (West)	3-2
1983—Baltimore (East)	Chicago (West)	3-1
1984—Detroit (East)	Kansas City (West)	3-0
1985—Kansas City (West)	Toronto (East)	4-3
1986—Boston (East)	California (West)	4-3
1987—Minnesota (West)	Detroit (East)	4-1
1988—Oakland (West)	Boston (East)	4-0
1989—Oakland (West)	Toronto (East)	4-1
1990—Oakland (West)	Boston (East)	4-0
1991—Minnesota (West)	Toronto (East)	4-1
1992—Toronto (East)	Oakland (West)	4-2
1993—Toronto (East)	Chicago (West)	4-2
1994—No series		
1995—Cleveland (Central)	Seattle (West)	4-2
1996—New York (East)	Baltimore (East)*	4-1
1997—Cleveland (Central)	Baltimore (East)	4-2
1998—New York (East)	Cleveland (Central)	4-2
1999—New York (East)	Boston (East)*	4-1

NATIONAL LEAGUE

Year	Winner (Division)	Loser (Division)	Games
1969—New York (East)	Atlanta (West)	3-0
1970—Cincinnati (West)	Pittsburgh (East)	3-0
1971—Pittsburgh (East)	San Francisco (West)	3-1

Year Winner (Division)	Loser (Division)	Games	Year Winner (Division)	Loser (Division)	Games
1972—Cincinnati (West)	Pittsburgh (East)	3-2	1987—St. Louis (East)	San Francisco (West)	4-3
1973—New York (East)	Cincinnati (West)	3-2	1988—Los Angeles (West)	New York (East)	4-3
1974—Los Angeles (West)	Pittsburgh (East)	3-1	1989—San Francisco (West)	Chicago (East)	4-1
1975—Cincinnati (West)	Pittsburgh (East)	3-0	1990—Cincinnati (West)	Pittsburgh (East)	4-2
1976—Cincinnati (West)	Philadelphia (East)	3-0	1991—Atlanta (West)	Pittsburgh (East)	4-3
1977—Los Angeles (West)	Philadelphia (East)	3-1	1992—Atlanta (West)	Pittsburgh (East)	4-3
1978—Los Angeles (West)	Philadelphia (East)	3-1	1993—Philadelphia (East)	Atlanta (West)	4-2
1979—Pittsburgh (East)	Cincinnati (West)	3-0	1994—No series		
1980—Philadelphia (East)	Houston (West)	3-2	1995—Atlanta (East)	Cincinnati (Central)	4-0
1981—Los Angeles (West)	Montreal (East)	3-2	1996—Atlanta (East)	St. Louis (Central)	4-3
1982—St. Louis (East)	Atlanta (West)	3-0	1997—Florida (East)*	Atlanta (East)	4-2
1983—Philadelphia (East)	Los Angeles (West)	3-1	1998—San Diego (West)	Atlanta (East)	4-2
1984—San Diego (West)	Chicago (East)	3-2	1999—Atlanta (East)	New York (East)*	4-2
1985—St. Louis (East)	Los Angeles (West)	4-2	*Wild-card team.		
1986—New York (East)	Houston (West)	4-2			

ALL-STAR GAME

Date	Site	Score (Winner)	Winning pitcher (Losing pitcher)	Winning manager (Losing manager)	Att.
7-6-33	Comiskey Park Chicago	4-2 (A.L.)	Lefty Gomez, Yankees (Bill Hallahan, Cardinals)	Connie Mack, Athletics (John McGraw, Giants)	47,595
7-10-34	Polo Grounds New York	9-7 (A.L.)	Mel Harder, Indians (Van Mungo, Dodgers)	Joe Cronin, Senators (Bill Terry, Giants)	48,363
7-8-35	Municipal Stadium Cleveland	4-1 (A.L.)	Lefty Gomez, Yankees (Bill Walker, Cardinals)	Mickey Cochrane, Tigers (Frankie Frisch, Cardinals)	69,831
7-7-36	Braves Field Boston	4-3 (N.L.)	Dizzy Dean, Cardinals (Lefty Grove, Red Sox)	Charlie Grimm, Cubs (Joe McCarthy, Yankees)	25,556
7-7-37	Griffith Stadium Washington	8-3 (A.L.)	Lefty Gomez, Yankees (Dizzy Dean, Cardinals)	Joe McCarthy, Yankees (Bill Terry, Giants)	31,391
7-6-38	Crosley Field Cincinnati	4-1 (N.L.)	Johnny Vander Meer, Reds (Lefty Gomez, Yankees)	Bill Terry, Giants (Joe McCarthy, Yankees)	27,067
7-11-39	Yankee Stadium New York	3-1 (A.L.)	Tommy Bridges, Tigers (Bill Lee, Cubs)	Joe McCarthy, Yankees (Gabby Hartnett, Cubs)	62,892
7-9-40	Sportsman's Park St. Louis	4-0 (N.L.)	Paul Derringer, Reds (Red Ruffing, Yankees)	Bill McKechnie, Reds (Joe Cronin, Red Sox)	32,373
7-8-41	Briggs Stadium Detroit	7-5 (A.L.)	Ed Smith, White Sox (Claude Passeau, Cardinals)	Del Baker, Tigers (Bill McKechnie, Reds)	54,674
7-6-42	Polo Grounds New York	3-1 (A.L.)	Spud Chandler, Yankees (Mort Cooper, Cardinals)	Joe McCarthy, Yankees (Leo Durocher, Dodgers)	34,178
7-13-43	Shibe Park Philadelphia	5-3 (A.L.)	Dutch Leonard, Senators (Mort Cooper, Cardinals)	Joe McCarthy, Yankees (Billy Southworth, Cardinals)	31,938
7-11-44	Forbes Field Pittsburgh	7-1 (N.L.)	Ken Raffensberger, Phillies (Tex Hughson, Red Sox)	Billy Southworth, Cardinals (Joe McCarthy, Yankees)	29,589
1945	No game played.				
7-9-46	Fenway Park Boston	12-0 (A.L.)	Bob Feller, Indians (Claude Passeau, Cubs)	Steve O'Neill, Tigers (Charlie Grimm, Cubs)	34,906
7-8-47	Wrigley Field Chicago	2-1 (A.L.)	Frank Shea, Yankees (Johnny Sain, Braves)	Joe Cronin, Red Sox (Eddie Dyer, Cardinals)	41,123
7-13-48	Sportsman's Park St. Louis	5-2 (A.L.)	Vic Raschi, Yankees (Johnny Schmitz, Cubs)	Bucky Harris, Yankees (Leo Durocher, Dodgers)	34,009
7-12-49	Ebbets Field Brooklyn	11-7 (A.L.)	Virgil Trucks, Tigers (Don Newcombe, Dodgers)	Lou Boudreau, Indians (Billy Southworth, Braves)	32,577
7-11-50	Comiskey Park Chicago	4-3* (N.L.)	Ewell Blackwell, Reds (Ted Gray, Tigers)	Burt Shotton, Dodgers (Casey Stengel, Yankees)	46,127
7-10-51	Briggs Stadium Detroit	8-3 (N.L.)	Sal Maglie, Giants (Ed Lopat, Yankees)	Eddie Sawyer, Phillies (Casey Stengel, Yankees)	52,075
7-8-52	Shibe Park Philadelphia	3-2† (N.L.)	Bob Rush, Cubs (Bob Lemon, Indians)	Leo Durocher, Giants (Casey Stengel, Yankees)	32,785
7-14-53	Crosley Field Cincinnati	5-1 (N.L.)	Warren Spahn, Braves (Allie Reynolds, Yankees)	Chuck Dressen, Dodgers (Casey Stengel, Yankees)	30,846
7-13-54	Municipal Stadium Cleveland	11-9 (A.L.)	Dean Stone, Senators (Gene Conley, Braves)	Casey Stengel, Yankees (Walter Alston, Dodgers)	68,751
7-12-55	Milwaukee Co. Stadium Milwaukee	6-5‡ (N.L.)	Gene Conley, Braves (Frank Sullivan, Red Sox)	Leo Durocher, Giants (Al Lopez, Indians)	45,643
7-10-56	Griffith Stadium Washington	7-3 (N.L.)	Bob Friend, Pirates (Billy Pierce, White Sox)	Walter Alston, Dodgers (Casey Stengel, Yankees)	28,843
7-9-57	Busch Stadium St. Louis	6-5 (A.L.)	Jim Bunning, Tigers (Curt Simmons, Phillies)	Casey Stengel, Yankees (Walter Alston, Dodgers)	30,693
7-8-58	Memorial Stadium Baltimore	4-3 (A.L.)	Early Wynn, White Sox (Bob Friend, Pirates)	Casey Stengel, Yankees (Fred Haney, Braves)	48,829
7-7-59	Forbes Field Pittsburgh	5-4 (N.L.)	Johnny Antonelli, Giants (Whitey Ford, Yankees)	Fred Haney, Braves (Casey Stengel, Yankees)	35,277
8-3-59	Memorial Coliseum Los Angeles	5-3 (A.L.)	Jerry Walker, Orioles (Don Drysdale, Dodgers)	Casey Stengel, Yankees (Fred Haney, Braves)	55,105

Date	Site	Score (Winner)	Winning pitcher (Losing pitcher)	Winning manager (Losing manager)	Att.
7-11-60	Municipal Stadium Kansas City	5-3 (N.L.)	Bob Friend, Pirates (Bill Monbouquette, Red Sox)	Walter Alston, Dodgers (Al Lopez, White Sox)	30,619
7-13-60	Yankee Stadium New York	6-0 (N.L.)	Vernon Law, Pirates (Whitey Ford, Yankees)	Walter Alston, Dodgers (Al Lopez, White Sox)	38,362
7-11-61	Candlestick Park San Francisco	5-4§ (N.L.)	Stu Miller, Giants (Hoyt Wilhelm, Orioles)	Danny Murtaugh, Pirates (Paul Richards, Orioles)	44,115
7-31-61	Fenway Park Boston	1-1 (tie)		Paul Richards, Orioles (A.L.) Danny Murtaugh, Pirates (N.L.)	31,851
7-10-62	District of Col. Stad. Washington	3-1 (N.L.)	Juan Marichal, Giants (Camilo Pascual, Twins)	Fred Hutchinson, Reds (Ralph Houk, Yankees)	45,480
7-30-62	Wrigley Field Chicago	9-4 (A.L.)	Ray Herbert, White Sox (Art Mahaffey, Phillies)	Ralph Houk, Yankees (Fred Hutchinson, Reds)	38,359
7-9-63	Municipal Stadium Cleveland	5-3 (N.L.)	Larry Jackson, Cubs (Jim Bunning, Tigers)	Alvin Dark, Giants (Ralph Houk, Yankees)	44,160
7-7-64	Shea Stadium New York	7-4 (N.L.)	Juan Marichal, Giants (Dick Radatz, Red Sox)	Walter Alston, Dodgers (Al Lopez, White Sox)	50,850
7-13-65	Metropolitan Stadium Bloomington, Minn.	6-5 (N.L.)	Sandy Koufax, Dodgers (Sam McDowell, Indians)	Gene Mauch, Phillies (Al Lopez, White Sox)	46,706
7-12-66	Busch Stadium St. Louis	2-1§ (N.L.)	Gaylord Perry, Giants (Pete Richert, Senators)	Walter Alston, Dodgers (Sam Mele, Twins)	49,936
7-11-67	Anaheim Stadium Anaheim, Calif.	2-1∞ (N.L.)	Don Drysdale, Dodgers (Jim Hunter, Athletics)	Walter Alston, Dodgers (Hank Bauer, Orioles)	46,309
7-9-68	Astrodome Houston	1-0 (N.L.)	Don Drysdale, Dodgers (Luis Tiant, Indians)	Red Schoendienst, Cardinals (Dick Williams, Red Sox)	48,321
7-23-69	R.F.K. Stadium Washington	9-3 (N.L.)	Steve Carlton, Cardinals (Mel Stottlemyre, Yankees)	Red Schoendienst, Cardinals (Mayo Smith, Tigers)	45,259
7-14-70	Riverfront Stadium Cincinnati	5-4‡ (N.L.)	Claude Osteen, Dodgers (Clyde Wright, Angels)	Gil Hodges, Mets (Earl Weaver, Orioles)	51,838
7-13-71	Tiger Stadium Detroit	6-4 (A.L.)	Vida Blue, Athletics (Dock Ellis, Pirates)	Earl Weaver, Orioles (Sparky Anderson, Reds)	53,559
7-25-72	Atlanta Stadium Atlanta	4-3§ (N.L.)	Tug McGraw, Mets (Dave McNally, Orioles)	Danny Murtaugh, Pirates (Earl Weaver, Orioles)	53,107
7-24-73	Royals Stadium Kansas City	7-1 (N.L.)	Rick Wise, Cardinals (Bert Blyleven, Twins)	Sparky Anderson, Reds (Dick Williams, Athletics)	40,849
7-23-74	Three Rivers Stadium Pittsburgh	7-2 (N.L.)	Ken Brett, Pirates (Luis Tiant, Red Sox)	Yogi Berra, Mets (Dick Williams, Athletics)	50,706
7-15-75	Milwaukee Co. Stadium Milwaukee	6-3 (N.L.)	Jon Matlack, Mets (Jim Hunter, Yankees)	Walter Alston, Dodgers (Alvin Dark, Athletics)	51,480
7-13-76	Veterans Stadium Philadelphia	7-1 (N.L)	Randy Jones, Padres (Mark Fidrych, Tigers)	Sparky Anderson, Reds (Darrell Johnson, Red Sox)	63,974
7-19-77	Yankee Stadium New York	7-5 (N.L.)	Don Sutton, Dodgers (Jim Palmer, Orioles)	Sparky Anderson, Reds (Billy Martin, Yankees)	56,683
7-11-78	San Diego Stadium San Diego	7-3 (N.L.)	Bruce Sutter, Cubs (Rich Gossage, Yankees)	Tommy Lasorda, Dodgers (Billy Martin, Yankees)	51,549
7-17-79	Kingdome Seattle	7-6 (N.L.)	Bruce Sutter, Cubs (Jim Kern, Rangers)	Tommy Lasorda, Dodgers (Bob Lemon, Yankees)	58,905
7-8-80	Dodger Stadium Los Angeles	4-2 (N.L.)	Jerry Reuss, Dodgers (Tommy John, Yankees)	Chuck Tanner, Pirates (Earl Weaver, Orioles)	56,088
8-9-81	Municipal Stadium Cleveland	5-4 (N.L.)	Vida Blue, Giants (Rollie Fingers, Brewers)	Dallas Green, Phillies (Jim Frey, Royals)	72,086
7-13-82	Olympic Stadium Montreal	4-1 (N.L.)	Steve Rogers, Expos (Dennis Eckersley, Red Sox)	Tommy Lasorda, Dodgers (Billy Martin, Athletics)	59,057
7-6-83	Comiskey Park Chicago	13-3 (A.L.)	Dave Stieb, Blue Jays (Mario Soto, Reds)	Harvey Kuenn, Brewers (Whitey Herzog, Cardinals)	43,801
7-10-84	Candlestick Park San Francisco	3-1 (N.L.)	Charlie Lea, Expos (Dave Stieb, Blue Jays)	Paul Owens, Phillies (Joe Altobelli, Orioles)	57,756
7-16-85	Metrodome Minneapolis	6-1 (N.L.)	LaMarr Hoyt, Padres (Jack Morris, Tigers)	Dick Williams, Padres (Sparky Anderson, Tigers)	54,960
7-15-86	Astrodome Houston	3-2 (A.L.)	Roger Clemens, Red Sox (Dwight Gooden, Mets)	Dick Howser, Royals (Whitey Herzog, Cardinals)	45,774
7-14-87	Oak.-Alameda Co. Col. Oakland	2-0▲ (N.L.)	Lee Smith, Cubs (Jay Howell, Athletics)	Dave Johnson, Mets (John McNamara, Red Sox)	49,671
7-12-88	Riverfront Stadium Cincinnati	2-1 (A.L.)	Frank Viola, Twins (Dwight Gooden, Mets)	Tom Kelly, Twins (Whitey Herzog, Cardinals)	55,837
7-11-89	Anaheim Stadium Anaheim, Calif.	5-3 (A.L.)	Nolan Ryan, Rangers (John Smoltz, Braves)	Tony La Russa, Athletics (Tommy Lasorda, Dodgers)	64,036
7-10-90	Wrigley Field Chicago	2-0 (A.L.)	Bret Saberhagen, Royals (Jeff Brantley, Giants)	Tony La Russa, Athletics (Roger Craig, Giants)	39,071
7-9-91	SkyDome Toronto	4-2 (A.L.)	Jimmy Key, Blue Jays (Dennis Martinez, Expos)	Tony La Russa, Athletics (Lou Piniella, Reds)	52,383
7-14-92	Jack Murphy Stadium San Diego	13-6 (A.L.)	Kevin Brown, Rangers (Tom Glavine, Braves)	Tom Kelly, Twins (Bobby Cox, Braves)	59,372
7-13-93	Oriole Park at Camden Yards, Baltimore	9-3 (A.L.)	Jack McDowell, White Sox (John Burkett, Giants)	Cito Gaston, Blue Jays (Bobby Cox, Braves)	48,147

Date	Site	Score (Winner)	Winning pitcher (Losing pitcher)	Winning manager (Losing manager)	Att.
7-12-94	Three Rivers Stadium Pittsburgh	8-7§ (N.L.)	Doug Jones, Phillies (Jason Bere, White Sox)	Jim Fregosi, Phillies (Cito Gaston, Blue Jays)	59,568
7-11-95	Ballpark in Arlington Arlington, Texas	3-2 (N.L.)	Heathcliff Slocumb, Phillies (Steve Ontiveros, A's)	Felipe Alou, Expos (Buck Showalter, Yankees)	50,920
7-9-96	Veterans Stadium Philadelphia	6-0 (N.L.)	John Smoltz, Braves (Charles Nagy, Indians)	Bobby Cox, Braves (Mike Hargrove, Indians)	62,670
7-8-97	Jacobs Field Cleveland	3-1 (A.L.)	Jose Rosado, Royals (Shawn Estes, Giants)	Joe Torre, Yankees (Bobby Cox, Braves)	44,916
7-7-98	Coors Field Colorado	13-8 (A.L.)	Bartolo Colon, Indians (Ugueth Urbina, Expos)	Mike Hargrove, Indians (Jim Leyland, Marlins)	51,267
7-13-99	Fenway Park Boston	4-1 (A.L.)	Pedro Martinez, Red Sox (Curt Schilling, Phillies)	Joe Torre, Yankees (Bruce Bochy, Padres)	34,187

*14 innings. †5 innings (rain). ‡12 innings. §10 innings. ∞15 innings. ▲13 innings.

AWARD WINNERS

THE SPORTING NEWS
MOST VALUABLE PLAYER

AMERICAN LEAGUE

Year	Player	Team	Pos.	Points
1929—Al Simmons		Philadelphia	OF	40
1930—Joe Cronin		Washington	SS	52
1931—Lou Gehrig		New York	1B	40
1932—Jimmie Foxx		Philadelphia	1B	46
1933—Jimmie Foxx		Philadelphia	1B	49
1934—Lou Gehrig		New York	1B	51
1935—Hank Greenberg		Detroit	1B	64
1936—Lou Gehrig		New York	1B	55
1937—Charley Gehringer		Detroit	2B	78
1938—Jimmie Foxx		Boston	1B	304
1939—Joe DiMaggio		New York	OF	280
1940—Hank Greenberg		Detroit	OF	292
1941—Joe DiMaggio		New York	OF	291
1942—Joe Gordon		New York	2B	270
1943—Spud Chandler		New York	P	246
1944—Bobby Doerr		Boston	2B	
1945—Eddie Mayo		Detroit	2B	

NATIONAL LEAGUE

Year	Player	Team	Pos.	Points
1929—No selection				
1930—Bill Terry		New York	1B	47
1931—Chuck Klein		Philadelphia	OF	40
1932—Chuck Klein		Philadelphia	OF	46
1933—Carl Hubbell		New York	P	64
1934—Dizzy Dean		St. Louis	P	57
1935—Arky Vaughan		Pittsburgh	SS	42
1936—Carl Hubbell		New York	P	61
1937—Joe Medwick		St. Louis	OF	70
1938—Ernie Lombardi		Cincinnati	C	229
1939—Bucky Walters		Cincinnati	P	303
1940—Frank McCormick		Cincinnati	1B	274
1941—Dolf Camilli		Brooklyn	1B	300
1942—Mort Cooper		St. Louis	P	263
1943—Stan Musial		St. Louis	OF	267
1944—Marty Marion		St. Louis	SS	
1945—Tommy Holmes		Boston	OF	

PLAYER AND PITCHER OF THE YEAR

AMERICAN LEAGUE

Year	Player	Team	Pos.
1944—Bobby Doerr	Boston	2B
Hal Newhouser	Detroit	P
1945—Eddie Mayo	Detroit	2B
Hal Newhouser	Detroit	P
1946—No selections		
1947—No selections		
1948—Lou Boudreau	Cleveland	SS
Bob Lemon	Cleveland	P
1949—Ted Williams	Boston	OF
Ellis Kinder	Boston	P
1950—Phil Rizzuto	New York	SS
Bob Lemon	Cleveland	P
1951—Ferris Fain	Philadelphia	1B
Bob Feller	Cleveland	P
1952—Luke Easter	Cleveland	1B
Bobby Shantz	Philadelphia	P
1953—Al Rosen	Cleveland	3B
Bob Porterfield	Washington	P
1954—Bobby Avila	Cleveland	2B
Bob Lemon	Cleveland	P
1955—Al Kaline	Detroit	OF
Whitey Ford	New York	P
1956—Mickey Mantle	New York	OF
Billy Pierce	Chicago	P
1957—Ted Williams	Boston	OF
Billy Pierce	Chicago	P
1958—Jackie Jensen	Boston	OF
Bob Turley	New York	P
1959—Nellie Fox	Chicago	2B
Early Wynn	Chicago	P
1960—Roger Maris	New York	OF
Chuck Estrada	Baltimore	P
1961—Roger Maris	New York	OF
Whitey Ford	New York	P
1962—Mickey Mantle	New York	OF
Dick Donovan	Cleveland	P
1963—Al Kaline	Detroit	OF
Whitey Ford	New York	P
1964—Brooks Robinson	Baltimore	3B
Dean Chance	Los Angeles	P
1965—Tony Oliva	Minnesota	OF
Jim Grant	Minnesota	P
1966—Frank Robinson	Baltimore	OF
Jim Kaat	Minnesota	P

NATIONAL LEAGUE

Year	Player	Team	Pos.
1944—Marty Marion	St. Louis	SS
Bill Voiselle	New York	P
1945—Tommy Holmes	Boston	OF
Hank Borowy	Chicago	P
1946—No selections		
1947—No selections		
1948—Stan Musial	St. Louis	OF-1B
Johnny Sain	Boston	P
1949—Enos Slaughter	St. Louis	OF
Howard Pollet	St. Louis	P
1950—Ralph Kiner	Pittsburgh	OF
Jim Konstanty	Philadelphia	P
1951—Stan Musial	St. Louis	OF
Preacher Roe	Brooklyn	P
1952—Hank Sauer	Chicago	OF
Robin Roberts	Philadelphia	P
1953—Roy Campanella	Brooklyn	C
Warren Spahn	Milwaukee	P
1954—Willie Mays	New York	OF
Johnny Antonelli	New York	P
1955—Duke Snider	Brooklyn	OF
Robin Roberts	Philadelphia	P
1956—Hank Aaron	Milwaukee	OF
Don Newcombe	Brooklyn	P
1957—Stan Musial	St. Louis	1B
Warren Spahn	Milwaukee	P
1958—Ernie Banks	Chicago	SS
Warren Spahn	Milwaukee	P
1959—Ernie Banks	Chicago	SS
Sam Jones	San Francisco	P
1960—Dick Groat	Pittsburgh	SS
Vern Law	Pittsburgh	P
1961—Frank Robinson	Cincinnati	OF
Warren Spahn	Milwaukee	P
1962—Maury Wills	Los Angeles	SS
Don Drysdale	Los Angeles	P
1963—Hank Aaron	Milwaukee	OF
Sandy Koufax	Los Angeles	P
1964—Ken Boyer	St. Louis	3B
Sandy Koufax	Los Angeles	P
1965—Willie Mays	San Francisco	OF
Sandy Koufax	Los Angeles	P
1966—Roberto Clemente	Pittsburgh	OF
Sandy Koufax	Los Angeles	P

Year	Player	Team	Pos.	Year	Player	Team	Pos.
1967—	Carl Yastrzemski	Boston	OF	1967—	Orlando Cepeda	St. Louis	1B
	Jim Lonborg	Boston	P		Mike McCormick	San Francisco	P
1968—	Ken Harrelson	Boston	OF	1968—	Pete Rose	Cincinnati	OF
	Denny McLain	Detroit	P		Bob Gibson	St. Louis	P
1969—	Harmon Killebrew	Minnesota	1B-3B	1969—	Willie McCovey	San Francisco	1B
	Denny McLain	Detroit	P		Tom Seaver	New York	P
1970—	Harmon Killebrew	Minnesota	3B	1970—	Johnny Bench	Cincinnati	C
	Sam McDowell	Cleveland	P		Bob Gibson	St. Louis	P
1971—	Tony Oliva	Minnesota	OF	1971—	Joe Torre	St. Louis	3B
	Vida Blue	Oakland	P		Ferguson Jenkins	Chicago	P
1972—	Dick Allen	Chicago	1B	1972—	Billy Williams	Chicago	OF
	Wilbur Wood	Chicago	P		Steve Carlton	Philadelphia	P
1973—	Reggie Jackson	Oakland	OF	1973—	Bobby Bonds	San Francisco	OF
	Jim Palmer	Baltimore	P		Ron Bryant	San Francisco	P
1974—	Jeff Burroughs	Texas	OF	1974—	Lou Brock	St. Louis	OF
	Jim Hunter	Oakland	P		Mike Marshall	Los Angeles	P
1975—	Fred Lynn	Boston	OF	1975—	Joe Morgan	Cincinnati	2B
	Jim Palmer	Baltimore	P		Tom Seaver	New York	P
1976—	Thurman Munson	New York	C	1976—	George Foster	Cincinnati	OF
	Jim Palmer	Baltimore	P		Randy Jones	San Diego	P
1977—	Rod Carew	Minnesota	1B	1977—	George Foster	Cincinnati	OF
	Nolan Ryan	California	P		Steve Carlton	Philadelphia	P
1978—	Jim Rice	Boston	OF	1978—	Dave Parker	Pittsburgh	OF
	Ron Guidry	New York	P		Vida Blue	San Francisco	P
1979—	Don Baylor	California	OF	1979—	Keith Hernandez	St. Louis	1B
	Mike Flanagan	Baltimore	P		Joe Niekro	Houston	P
1980—	George Brett	Kansas City	3B	1980—	Mike Schmidt	Philadelphia	3B
	Steve Stone	Baltimore	P		Steve Carlton	Philadelphia	P
1981—	Tony Armas	Oakland	OF	1981—	Andre Dawson	Montreal	OF
	Jack Morris	Detroit	P		Fernando Valenzuela	Los Angeles	P
1982—	Robin Yount	Milwaukee	SS	1982—	Dale Murphy	Atlanta	OF
	Dave Stieb	Toronto	P		Steve Carlton	Philadelphia	P
1983—	Cal Ripken Jr.	Baltimore	SS	1983—	Dale Murphy	Atlanta	OF
	LaMarr Hoyt	Chicago	P		John Denny	Philadelphia	P
1984—	Don Mattingly	New York	1B	1984—	Ryne Sandberg	Chicago	2B
	Willie Hernandez	Detroit	P		Rick Sutcliffe	Chicago	P
1985—	Don Mattingly	New York	1B	1985—	Willie McGee	St. Louis	OF
	Bret Saberhagen	Kansas City	P		Dwight Gooden	New York	P
1986—	Don Mattingly	New York	1B	1986—	Mike Schmidt	Philadelphia	3B
	Roger Clemens	Boston	P		Mike Scott	Houston	P
1987—	George Bell	Toronto	OF	1987—	Andre Dawson	Chicago	OF
	Jimmy Key	Toronto	P		Rick Sutcliffe	Chicago	P
1988—	Jose Canseco	Oakland	OF	1988—	Andy Van Slyke	Pittsburgh	OF
	Frank Viola	Minnesota	P		Orel Hershiser	Los Angeles	P
1989—	Ruben Sierra	Texas	OF	1989—	Kevin Mitchell	San Francisco	OF
	Bret Saberhagen	Kansas City	P		Mark Davis	San Diego	P
1990—	Cecil Fielder	Detroit	1B	1990—	Barry Bonds	Pittsburgh	OF
	Bob Welch	Oakland	P		Doug Drabek	Pittsburgh	P
1991—	Cal Ripken Jr.	Baltimore	SS	1991—	Barry Bonds	Pittsburgh	OF
	Roger Clemens	Boston	P		Tom Glavine	Atlanta	P

PITCHER OF THE YEAR

AMERICAN LEAGUE

NATIONAL LEAGUE

Year	Pitcher	Team	Year	Pitcher	Team
1992—	Dennis Eckersley	Oakland	1992—	Greg Maddux	Chicago
1993—	Jack McDowell	Chicago	1993—	Greg Maddux	Atlanta
1994—	Jimmy Key	New York	1994—	Greg Maddux	Atlanta
1995—	Randy Johnson	Seattle	1995—	Greg Maddux	Atlanta
1996—	Pat Hentgen	Toronto	1996—	John Smoltz	Atlanta
1997—	Roger Clemens	Toronto	1997—	Pedro Martinez	Montreal
1998—	Roger Clemens	Toronto	1998—	Kevin Brown	San Diego
1999—	Pedro Martinez	Boston	1999—	Mike Hampton	Houston

ROOKIE OF THE YEAR

1946—Combined selection—Del Ennis, Philadelphia N.L., OF
1947—Combined selection—Jackie Robinson, Brooklyn N.L., 1B
1948—Combined selection—Richie Ashburn, Philadelphia N.L., OF

AMERICAN LEAGUE

NATIONAL LEAGUE

Year	Player	Team	Pos.	Year	Player	Team	Pos.
1949—	Roy Sievers	St. Louis	OF	1949—	Don Newcombe	Brooklyn	P
1950—	Whitey Ford	New York	P	1950—	Combined A.L.-N.L. selection		
1951—	Minnie Minoso	Chicago	OF	1951—	Willie Mays	New York	OF

Year	Player	Team	Pos.	Year	Player	Team	Pos.
1952—Clint Courtney	St. Louis	C		1952—Joe Black	Brooklyn	P	
1953—Harvey Kuenn	Detroit	SS		1953—Jim Gilliam	Brooklyn	2B	
1954—Bob Grim	New York	P		1954—Wally Moon	St. Louis	OF	
1955—Herb Score	Cleveland	P		1955—Bill Virdon	St. Louis	OF	
1956—Luis Aparicio	Chicago	SS		1956—Frank Robinson	Cincinnati	OF	
1957—Tony Kubek	New York	IF-OF		1957—Ed Bouchee	Philadelphia	1B	
(No pitcher named)				Jack Sanford	Philadelphia	P	
1958—Albie Pearson	Washington	OF		1958—Orlando Cepeda	San Francisco	1B	
Ryne Duren	New York	P		Carlton Willey	Milwaukee	P	
1959—Bob Allison	Washington	OF		1959—Willie McCovey	San Francisco	1B	
1960—Ron Hansen	Baltimore	SS		1960—Frank Howard	Los Angeles	OF	
1961—Dick Howser	Kansas City	SS		1961—Billy Williams	Chicago	OF	
Don Schwall	Boston	P		Ken Hunt	Cincinnati	P	
1962—Tom Tresh	New York	OF-SS		1962—Ken Hubbs	Chicago	2B	
1963—Pete Ward	Chicago	3B		1963—Pete Rose	Cincinnati	2B	
Gary Peters	Chicago	P		Ray Culp	Philadelphia	P	
1964—Tony Oliva	Minnesota	OF		1964—Dick Allen	Philadelphia	3B	
Wally Bunker	Baltimore	P		Billy McCool	Cincinnati	P	
1965—Curt Blefary	Baltimore	OF		1965—Joe Morgan	Houston	2B	
Marcelino Lopez	California	P		Frank Linzy	San Francisco	P	
1966—Tommie Agee	Chicago	OF		1966—Tommy Helms	Cincinnati	3B	
Jim Nash	Kansas City	P		Don Sutton	Los Angeles	P	
1967—Rod Carew	Minnesota	2B		1967—Lee May	Cincinnati	1B	
Tom Phoebus	Baltimore	P		Dick Hughes	St. Louis	P	
1968—Del Unser	Washington	OF		1968—Johnny Bench	Cincinnati	C	
Stan Bahnsen	New York	P		Jerry Koosman	New York	P	
1969—Carlos May	Chicago	OF		1969—Coco Laboy	Montreal	3B	
Mike Nagy	Boston	P		Tom Griffin	Houston	P	
1970—Roy Foster	Cleveland	OF		1970—Bernie Carbo	Cincinnati	OF	
Bert Blyleven	Minnesota	P		Carl Morton	Montreal	P	
1971—Chris Chambliss	Cleveland	1B		1971—Earl Williams	Atlanta	C	
Bill Parsons	Milwaukee	P		Reggie Cleveland	St. Louis	P	
1972—Carlton Fisk	Boston	C		1972—Dave Rader	San Francisco	C	
Dick Tidrow	Cleveland	P		Jon Matlack	New York	P	
1973—Al Bumbry	Baltimore	OF		1973—Gary Matthews	San Francisco	OF	
Steve Busby	Kansas City	P		Steve Rogers	Montreal	P	
1974—Mike Hargrove	Texas	1B		1974—Greg Gross	Houston	OF	
Frank Tanana	California	P		John D'Acquisto	San Francisco	P	
1975—Fred Lynn	Boston	OF		1975—Gary Carter	Montreal	OF-C	
Dennis Eckersley	Cleveland	P		John Montefusco	San Francisco	P	
1976—Butch Wynegar	Minnesota	C		1976—Larry Herndon	San Francisco	OF	
Mark Fidrych	Detroit	P		Butch Metzger	San Diego	P	
1977—Mitchell Page	Oakland	OF		1977—Andre Dawson	Montreal	OF	
Dave Rozema	Detroit	P		Bob Owchinko	San Diego	P	
1978—Paul Molitor	Milwaukee	2B		1978—Bob Horner	Atlanta	3B	
Rich Gale	Kansas City	P		Don Robinson	Pittsburgh	P	
1979—Pat Putnam	Texas	1B		1979—Jeff Leonard	Houston	OF	
Mark Clear	California	P		Rick Sutcliffe	Los Angeles	P	
1980—Joe Charboneau	Cleveland	OF		1980—Lonnie Smith	Philadelphia	OF	
Britt Burns	Chicago	P		Bill Gullickson	Montreal	P	
1981—Rich Gedman	Boston	C		1981—Tim Raines	Montreal	OF	
Dave Righetti	New York	P		Fernando Valenzuela	Los Angeles	P	
1982—Cal Ripken Jr.	Baltimore	SS-3B		1982—Johnny Ray	Pittsburgh	2B	
Ed Vande Berg	Seattle	P		Steve Bedrosian	Atlanta	P	
1983—Ron Kittle	Chicago	OF		1983—Darryl Strawberry	New York	OF	
Mike Boddicker	Baltimore	P		Craig McMurtry	Atlanta	P	
1984—Alvin Davis	Seattle	1B		1984—Juan Samuel	Philadelphia	2B	
Mark Langston	Seattle	P		Dwight Gooden	New York	P	
1985 Ozzie Guillen	Chicago	SS		1985—Vince Coleman	St. Louis	OF	
Teddy Higuera	Milwaukee	P		Tom Browning	Cincinnati	P	
1986—Jose Canseco	Oakland	OF		1986—Robby Thompson	San Francisco	2B	
Mark Eichhorn	Toronto	P		Todd Worrell	St. Louis	P	
1987—Mark McGwire	Oakland	1B		1987—Benito Santiago	San Diego	C	
Mike Henneman	Detroit	P		Mike Dunne	Pittsburgh	P	
1988—Walt Weiss	Oakland	SS		1988—Mark Grace	Chicago	1B	
Bryan Harvey	California	P		Tim Belcher	Los Angeles	P	
1989—Craig Worthington	Baltimore	3B		1989—Jerome Walton	Chicago	OF	
Tom Gordon	Kansas City	P		Andy Benes	San Diego	P	
1990—Sandy Alomar Jr.	Cleveland	C		1990—David Justice	Atlanta	OF	
Kevin Appier	Kansas City	P		Mike Harkey	Chicago	P	
1991—Chuck Knoblauch	Minnesota	2B		1991—Jeff Bagwell	Houston	1B	
Juan Guzman	Toronto	P		Al Osuna	Houston	P	
1992—Pat Listach	Milwaukee	SS		1992—Eric Karros	Los Angeles	1B	
Cal Eldred	Milwaukee	P		Tim Wakefield	Pittsburgh	P	
1993—Tim Salmon	California	OF		1993—Mike Piazza	Los Angeles	C	
Aaron Sele	Boston	P		Kirk Rueter	Montreal	P	

Year	Player	Team	Pos.		Year	Player	Team	Pos.
1994—Bob Hamelin	Kansas City	DH			1994—Raul Mondesi	Los Angeles	OF
Brian Anderson	California	P			Steve Trachsel	Chicago	P
1995—Garret Anderson	California	OF			1995—Chipper Jones	Atlanta	3B
Julian Tavarez	Cleveland	P			Hideo Nomo	Los Angeles	P
1996—Derek Jeter	New York	SS			1996—Jason Kendall	Pittsburgh	C
James Baldwin	Chicago	P			Alan Benes	St. Louis	P
1997—Nomar Garciaparra	Boston	SS			1997—Scott Rolen	Philadelphia	3B
Jason Dickson	Anaheim	P			Matt Morris	St. Louis	P
1998—Ben Grieve	Oakland	OF			1998—Todd Helton	Colorado	1B
Rolando Arrojo	Tampa Bay	P			Kerry Wood	Chicago	P
1999—Carlos Beltran	Kansas City	OF			1999—Preston Wilson	Florida	OF
Tim Hudson	Oakland	P			Scott Williamson	Cincinnati	P

FIREMAN OF THE YEAR

AMERICAN LEAGUE

Year	Pitcher	Team
1960—Mike Fornieles	Boston
1961—Luis Arroyo	New York
1962—Dick Radatz	Boston
1963—Stu Miller	Baltimore
1964—Dick Radatz	Boston
1965—Eddie Fisher	Chicago
1966—Jack Aker	Kansas City
1967—Minnie Rojas	California
1968—Wilbur Wood	Chicago
1969—Ron Perranoski	Minnesota
1970—Ron Perranoski	Minnesota
1971—Ken Sanders	Milwaukee
1972—Sparky Lyle	New York
1973—John Hiller	Detroit
1974—Terry Forster	Chicago
1975—Rich Gossage	Chicago
1976—Bill Campbell	Minnesota
1977—Bill Campbell	Boston
1978—Rich Gossage	New York
1979—Mike Marshall	Minnesota
Jim Kern	Texas
1980—Dan Quisenberry	Kansas City
1981—Rollie Fingers	Milwaukee
1982—Dan Quisenberry	Kansas City
1983—Dan Quisenberry	Kansas City
1984—Dan Quisenberry	Kansas City
1985—Dan Quisenberry	Kansas City
1986—Dave Righetti	New York
1987—Dave Righetti	New York
Jeff Reardon	Minnesota
1988—Dennis Eckersley	Oakland
1989—Jeff Russell	Texas
1990—Bobby Thigpen	Chicago
1991—Dennis Eckersley	Oakland
Bryan Harvey	California
1992—Dennis Eckersley	Oakland
1993—Jeff Montgomery	Kansas City
1994—Lee Smith	Baltimore
1995—Jose Mesa	Cleveland
1996—John Wetteland	New York
1997—Mariano Rivera	New York
1998—Tom Gordon	Boston
1999—Mariano Rivera	New York

NATIONAL LEAGUE

Year	Pitcher	Team
1960—Lindy McDaniel	St. Louis
1961—Stu Miller	San Francisco
1962—Roy Face	Pittsburgh
1963—Lindy McDaniel	Chicago
1964—Al McBean	Pittsburgh
1965—Ted Abernathy	Chicago
1966—Phil Regan	Los Angeles
1967—Ted Abernathy	Cincinnati
1968—Phil Regan	L.A.-Chicago
1969—Wayne Granger	Cincinnati
1970—Wayne Granger	Cincinnati
1971—Dave Giusti	Pittsburgh
1972—Clay Carroll	Cincinnati
1973—Mike Marshall	Montreal
1974—Mike Marshall	Los Angeles
1975—Al Hrabosky	St. Louis
1976—Rawly Eastwick	Cincinnati
1977—Rollie Fingers	San Diego
1978—Rollie Fingers	San Diego
1979—Bruce Sutter	Chicago
1980—Rollie Fingers	San Diego
Tom Hume	Cincinnati
1981—Bruce Sutter	St. Louis
1982—Bruce Sutter	St. Louis
1983—Al Holland	Philadelphia
Lee Smith	Chicago
1984—Bruce Sutter	St. Louis
1985—Jeff Reardon	Montreal
1986—Todd Worrell	St. Louis
1987—Steve Bedrosian	Philadelphia
1988—John Franco	Cincinnati
1989—Mark Davis	San Diego
1990—John Franco	New York
1991—Lee Smith	St. Louis
1992—Doug Jones	Houston
Lee Smith	St. Louis
1993—Randy Myers	Chicago
1994—John Franco	New York
1995—Randy Myers	Chicago
1996—Trevor Hoffman	San Diego
1997—Jeff Shaw	Cincinnati
1998—Trevor Hoffman	San Diego
1999—Ugueth Urbina	Montreal

MAJOR LEAGUE PLAYER OF THE YEAR

Year	Player	Team		Year	Player	Team		Year	Player	Team
1936—Carl Hubbell	New York N.L.			1943—Spud Chandler	New York A.L.			1950—Phil Rizzuto	New York A.L.
1937—Johnny Allen	Cleveland A.L.			1944—Marty Marion	St. Louis N.L.			1951—Stan Musial	St. Louis N.L.
1938—Johnny Vander Meer	Cincinnati N.L.			1945—Hal Newhouser	Detroit A.L.			1952—Robin Roberts	Philadelphia N.L.
1939—Joe DiMaggio	New York A.L.			1946—Stan Musial	St. Louis N.L.			1953—Al Rosen	Cleveland A.L.
1940—Bob Feller	Cleveland A.L.			1947—Ted Williams	Boston A.L.			1954—Willie Mays	New York N.L.
1941—Ted Williams	Boston A.L.			1948—Lou Boudreau	Cleveland A.L.			1955—Duke Snider	Brooklyn N.L.
1942—Ted Williams	Boston A.L.			1949—Ted Williams	Boston A.L.			1956—Mickey Mantle	New York A.L.

Year	Player	Team	Year	Player	Team	Year	Player	Team
1957—Ted Williams	Boston A.L.		1971—Joe Torre	St. Louis N.L.		1986—Roger Clemens	Boston A.L.
1958—Bob Turley	New York A.L.		1972—Billy Williams	Chicago N.L.		1987—George Bell	Toronto A.L.
1959—Early Wynn	Chicago A.L.		1973—Reggie Jackson	Oakland A.L.		1988—Orel Hershiser	Los Angeles N.L.
1960—Bill Mazeroski	Pittsburgh N.L.		1974—Lou Brock	St. Louis N.L.		1989—Kevin Mitchell	San Francisco N.L.
1961—Roger Maris	New York A.L.		1975—Joe Morgan	Cincinnati N.L.		1990—Barry Bonds	Pittsburgh N.L.
1962—Maury Wills	Los Angeles N.L.		1976—Joe Morgan	Cincinnati N.L.		1991—Cal Ripken Jr.	Baltimore A.L.
Don Drysdale	Los Angeles N.L.		1977—Rod Carew	Minnesota A.L.		1992—Gary Sheffield	San Diego N.L.
1963—Sandy Koufax	Los Angeles N.L.		1978—Ron Guidry	New York A.L.		1993—Frank Thomas	Chicago A.L.
1964—Ken Boyer	St. Louis N.L.		1979—Willie Stargell	Pittsburgh N.L.		1994—Jeff Bagwell	Houston N.L.
1965—Sandy Koufax	Los Angeles N.L.		1980—George Brett	Kansas City A.L.		1995—Albert Belle	Cleveland A.L.
1966—Frank Robinson	Baltimore A.L.		1981—Fernando Valenzuela	Los Angeles N.L.		1996—Alex Rodriguez	Seattle A.L.
1967—Carl Yastrzemski	Boston A.L.		1982—Robin Yount	Milwaukee A.L.		1997—Ken Griffey Jr.	Seattle A.L.
1968—Denny McLain	Detroit A.L.		1983—Cal Ripken Jr.	Baltimore A.L.		1998—Sammy Sosa	Chicago N.L.
1969—Willie McCovey	San Francisco N.L.		1984—Ryne Sandberg	Chicago N.L.		1999—Rafael Palmeiro	Texas A.L.
1970—Johnny Bench	Cincinnati N.L.		1985—Don Mattingly	New York A.L.			

MAJOR LEAGUE MANAGER OF THE YEAR

Year	Manager	Team	Year	Manager	Team	Year	Manager	Team
1936—Joe McCarthy	New York A.L.		1963—Walter Alston	Los Angeles N.L.		1988—Tony La Russa	Oakland A.L.
1937—Bill McKechnie	Boston N.L.		1964—Johnny Keane	St. Louis N.L.		Tom Lasorda	L.A. N.L. (tie)
1938—Joe McCarthy	New York A.L.		1965—Sam Mele	Minnesota A.L.		Jim Leyland	Pit. N.L. (tie)
1939—Leo Durocher	Brooklyn N.L.		1966—Hank Bauer	Baltimore A.L.		1989—Frank Robinson	Baltimore A.L.
1940—Bill McKechnie	Cincinnati N.L.		1967—Dick Williams	Boston A.L.		Don Zimmer	Chicago N.L.
1941—Billy Southworth	St. Louis N.L.		1968—Mayo Smith	Detroit A.L.		1990—Jeff Torborg	Chicago A.L.
1942—Billy Southworth	St. Louis N.L.		1969—Gil Hodges	New York N.L.		Jim Leyland	Pittsburgh N.L.
1943—Joe McCarthy	New York A.L.		1970—Danny Murtaugh	Pittsburgh N.L.		1991—Tom Kelly	Minnesota A.L.
1944—Luke Sewell	St. Louis A.L.		1971—Charlie Fox	San Francisco N.L.		Bobby Cox	Atlanta N.L.
1945—Ossie Bluege	Washington A.L.		1972—Chuck Tanner	Chicago A.L.		1992—Tony La Russa	Oakland A.L.
1946—Eddie Dyer	St. Louis N.L.		1973—Gene Mauch	Montreal N.L.		Jim Leyland	Pittsburgh N.L.
1947—Bucky Harris	New York A.L.		1974—Bill Virdon	New York A.L.		1993—Johnny Oates	Baltimore A.L.
1948—Bill Meyer	Pittsburgh N.L.		1975—Darrell Johnson	Boston A.L.		Bobby Cox	Atlanta N.L.
1949—Casey Stengel	New York A.L.		1976—Danny Ozark	Philadelphia N.L.		1994—Buck Showalter	New York A.L.
1950—Red Rolfe	Detroit A.L.		1977—Earl Weaver	Baltimore A.L.		Felipe Alou	Montreal N.L.
1951—Leo Durocher	New York A.L.		1978—George Bamberger	Milwaukee A.L.		1995—Mike Hargrove	Cleveland A.L.
1952—Eddie Stanky	St. Louis N.L.		1979—Earl Weaver	Baltimore A.L.		Don Baylor	Colorado N.L.
1953—Casey Stengel	New York A.L.		1980—Bill Virdon	Houston N.L.		1996—Johnny Oates	Texas A.L.
1954—Leo Durocher	New York N.L.		1981—Billy Martin	Oakland A.L.		Bruce Bochy	San Diego N.L.
1955—Walter Alston	Brooklyn N.L.		1982—Whitey Herzog	St. Louis N.L.		1997—Dave Johnson	Baltimore A.L.
1956—Birdie Tebbetts	Cincinnati N.L.		1983—Tony La Russa	Chicago A.L.		Dusty Baker	San Fran. N.L.
1957—Fred Hutchinson	St. Louis N.L.		1984—Jim Frey	Chicago A.L.		1998—Joe Torre	New York A.L.
1958—Casey Stengel	New York A.L.		1985—Bobby Cox	Toronto A.L.		Bruce Bochy	San Diego N.L.
1959—Walter A.L.ston	Los Angeles N.L.		1986—John McNamara	Boston A.L.		1999—Jimy Williams	Boston A.L.
1960—Danny Murtaugh	Pittsburgh N.L.		Hal Lanier	Houston N.L.		Bobby Cox	Atlanta N.L.
1961—Ralph Houk	New York A.L.		1987—Sparky Anderson	Detroit A.L.			
1962—Bill Rigney	Los Angeles A.L.		Buck Rodgers	Montreal N.L.			

MAJOR LEAGUE EXECUTIVE OF THE YEAR

Year	Executive	Team	Year	Executive	Team	Year	Executive	Team
1936—Branch Rickey	St. Louis N.L.		1958—Joe Brown	Pittsburgh N.L.		1980—Tal Smith	Houston N.L.
1937—Ed Barrow	New York A.L.		1959—Buzzie Bavasi	L.A. N.L.		1981—John McHale	Montreal N.L.
1938—Warren Giles	Cincinnati N.L.		1960—George Weiss	New York A.L.		1982—Harry Dalton	Milwaukee A.L.
1939—Larry MacPhail	Brooklyn N.L.		1961—Dan Topping	New York A.L.		1983—Hank Peters	Baltimore A.L.
1940—Walter Briggs Sr.	Detroit A.L.		1962—Fred Haney	Los Angeles A.L.		1984—Dallas Green	Chicago N.L.
1941—Ed Barrow	New York A.L.		1963—Bing Devine	St. Louis N.L.		1985—John Schuerholz	Kansas City A.L.
1942—Branch Rickey	St. Louis N.L.		1964—Bing Devine	St. Louis N.L.		1986—Frank Cashen	New York N.L.
1943—Clark Griffith	Washington A.L.		1965—Cal Griffith	Minnesota A.L.		1987—Al Rosen	San Francisco N.L.
1944—Billy DeWitt	St. Louis A.L.		1966—Lee MacPhail	Commissioner's Office		1988—Fred Claire	Los Angeles N.L.
1945—Phil Wrigley	Chicago N.L.		1967—Dick O'Connell	Boston A.L.		1989—Roland Hemond	Baltimore A.L.
1946—Tom Yawkey	Boston A.L.		1968—Jim Campbell	Detroit A.L.		1990—Bob Quinn	Cincinnati N.L.
1947—Branch Rickey	Brooklyn N.L.		1969—John Murphy	New York N.L.		1991—Andy MacPhail	Minnesota A.L.
1948—Bill Veeck	Cleveland A.L.		1970—Harry Dalton	Baltimore A.L.		1992—Dan Duquette	Montreal N.L.
1949—Bob Carpenter	Philadelphia N.L.		1971—Cedric Tallis	Kansas City A.L.		1993—Lee Thomas	Philadelphia N.L.
1950—George Weiss	New York A.L.		1972—Roland Hemond	Chicago A.L.		1994—John Hart	Cleveland A.L.
1951—George Weiss	New York A.L.		1973—Bob Howsam	Cincinnati N.L.		1995—John Hart	Cleveland A.L.
1952—George Weiss	New York A.L.		1974—Gabe Paul	New York A.L.		1996—Doug Melvin	Texas A.L.
1953—Lou Perini	Milwaukee N.L.		1975—Dick O'Connell	Boston A.L.		1997—Cam Bonifay	Pittsburgh N.L.
1954—Horace Stoneham	New York N.L.		1976—Joe Burke	Kansas City A.L.		1998—Gerry Hunsicker	Houston N.L.
1955—Walter O'Malley	Brooklyn N.L.		1977—Bill Veeck	Chicago A.L.		1999—Billy Beane	Oakland A.L.
1956—Gabe Paul	Cincinnati N.L.		1978—Spec Richardson	San Francisco N.L.			
1957—Frank Lane	St. Louis N.L.		1979—Hank Peters	Baltimore A.L.			

HISTORY *Award winners*

1925
1B— Jim Bottomley, St. Louis N.L.
2B— Rogers Hornsby, St. Louis N.L.
SS— Glenn Wright, Pittsburgh N.L.
3B— Pie Traynor, Pittsburgh N.L.
OF— Kiki Cuyler, Pittsburgh N.L.
OF— Max Carey, Pittsburgh N.L.
OF— Goose Goslin, Washington A.L.
C— Mickey Cochrane, Phil. A.L.
P— Walter Johnson, Washington A.L.
P— Ed Rommel, Philadelphia A.L.
P— Dazzy Vance, Brooklyn N.L.

1926
1B— George Burns, Cleveland A.L.
2B— Rogers Hornsby, St. Louis N.L.
SS— Joe Sewell, Cleveland A.L.
3B— Pie Traynor, Pittsburgh N.L.
OF— Goose Goslin, Washington A.L.
OF— John Mostil, Chicago A.L.
OF— Babe Ruth, New York A.L.
C— Bob O'Farrell, St. Louis N.L.
P— Herb Pennock, New York A.L.
P— George Uhle, Cleveland A.L.
P— Grover Alexander, St. Louis N.L.

1927
1B— Lou Gehrig, New York A.L.
2B— Rogers Hornsby, New York N.L.
SS— Travis Jackson, New York N.L.
3B— Pie Traynor, Pittsburgh N.L.
OF— Babe Ruth, New York A.L.
OF— Al Simmons, Philadelphia A.L.
OF— Paul Waner, Pittsburgh N.L.
C— Gabby Hartnett, Chicago N.L.
P— Charley Root, Chicago N.L.
P— Ted Lyons, Chicago A.L.

1928
1B— Lou Gehrig, New York A.L.
2B— Rogers Hornsby, Boston N.L.
SS— Travis Jackson, New York N.L.
3B— Fred Lindstrom, New York N.L.
OF— Babe Ruth, New York A.L.
OF— Heinie Manush, St. Louis A.L.
OF— Paul Waner, Pittsburgh N.L.
C— Mickey Cochrane, Phil. A.L.
P— Lefty Grove, Philadelphia A.L.
P— Waite Hoyt, New York A.L.

1929
1B— Jimmie Foxx, Philadelphia A.L.
2B— Rogers Hornsby, Chicago N.L.
SS— Travis Jackson, New York N.L.
3B— Pie Traynor, Pittsburgh, N.L.
OF— Al Simmons, Philadelphia A.L.
OF— Hack Wilson, Chicago N.L.
OF— Babe Ruth, New York A.L.
C— Mickey Cochrane, Phil. A.L.
P— Lefty Grove, Philadelphia A.L.
P— Burleigh Grimes, Pittsburgh N.L.

1930
1B— Bill Terry, New York N.L.
2B— Frank Frisch, St. Louis N.L.
SS— Joe Cronin, Washington A.L.
3B— Fred Lindstrom, New York N.L.
OF— Al Simmons, Philadelphia A.L.
OF— Hack Wilson, Chicago N.L.
OF— Babe Ruth, New York A.L.
C— Mickey Cochrane, Phil. A.L.
P— Lefty Grove, Philadelphia A.L.
P— Wes Ferrell, Cleveland A.L.

1931
1B— Lou Gehrig, New York A.L.
2B— Frank Frisch, St. Louis N.L.
SS— Joe Cronin, Washington A.L.

3B— Pie Traynor, Pittsburgh N.L.
OF— Al Simmons, Philadelphia A.L.
OF— Earl Averill, Cleveland A.L.
OF— Babe Ruth, New York A.L.
C— Mickey Cochrane, Phil. A.L.
P— Lefty Grove, Philadelphia A.L.
P— George Earnshaw, Phil. A.L.

1932
1B— Jimmie Foxx, Philadelphia A.L.
2B— Tony Lazzeri, New York A.L.
SS— Joe Cronin, Washington A.L.
3B— Pie Traynor, Pittsburgh N.L.
OF— Lefty O'Doul, Brooklyn N.L.
OF— Earl Averill, Cleveland A.L.
OF— Chuck Klein, Philadelphia N.L.
C— Bill Dickey, New York A.L.
P— Lefty Grove, Philadelphia A.L.
P— Lon Warneke, Chicago N.L.

1933
1B— Jimmie Foxx, Philadelphia A.L.
2B— Charley Gehringer, Detroit A.L.
SS— Joe Cronin, Washington A.L.
3B— Pie Traynor, Pittsburgh N.L.
OF— Al Simmons, Chicago A.L.
OF— Wally Berger, Boston N.L.
OF— Chuck Klein, Philadelphia N.L.
C— Bill Dickey, New York A.L.
P— Alvin Crowder, Washington A.L.
P— Carl Hubbell, New York N.L.

1934
1B— Lou Gehrig, New York A.L.
2B— Charley Gehringer, Detroit A.L.
SS— Joe Cronin, Washington A.L.
3B— Mike Higgins, Philadelphia A.L.
OF— Al Simmons, Chicago A.L.
OF— Earl Averill, Cleveland A.L.
OF— Mel Ott, New York N.L.
C— Mickey Cochrane, Detroit A.L.
P— Lefty Gomez, New York A.L.
P— Schoolboy Rowe, Detroit A.L.
P— Dizzy Dean, St. Louis N.L.

1935
1B— Hank Greenberg, Detroit A.L.
2B— Charley Gehringer, Detroit A.L.
SS— Arky Vaughan, Pittsburgh N.L.
3B— Pepper Martin, St. Louis N.L.
OF— Joe Medwick, St. Louis N.L.
OF— Doc Cramer, Philadelphia A.L.
OF— Mel Ott, New York N.L.
C— Mickey Cochrane, Detroit A.L.
P— Carl Hubbell, New York N.L.
P— Dizzy Dean, St. Louis N.L.

1936
1B— Lou Gehrig, New York A.L.
2B— Charley Gehringer, Detroit A.L.
SS— Luke Appling, Chicago A.L.
3B— Mike Higgins, Philadelphia A.L.
OF— Joe Medwick, St. Louis N.L.
OF— Earl Averill, Cleveland A.L.
OF— Mel Ott, New York N.L.
C— Bill Dickey, New York A.L.
P— Carl Hubbell, New York N.L.
P— Dizzy Dean, St. Louis N.L.

1937
1B— Lou Gehrig, New York A.L.
2B— Charley Gehringer, Detroit A.L.
SS— Dick Bartell, New York N.L.
3B— Red Rolfe, New York A.L.
OF— Joe Medwick, St. Louis N.L.
OF— Joe DiMaggio, New York A.L.
OF— Paul Waner, Pittsburgh N.L.
C— Gabby Hartnett, Chicago N.L.

P— Carl Hubbell, New York N.L.
P— Red Ruffing, New York A.L.

1938
1B— Jimmie Foxx, Boston A.L.
2B— Charley Gehringer, Detroit A.L.
SS— Joe Cronin, Boston A.L.
3B— Red Rolfe, New York A.L.
OF— Joe Medwick, St. Louis N.L.
OF— Joe DiMaggio, New York A.L.
OF— Mel Ott, New York N.L.
C— Bill Dickey, New York A.L.
P— Red Ruffing, New York A.L.
P— Lefty Gomez, New York A.L.
P— Johnny Vander Meer, Cin. N.L.

1939
1B— Jimmie Foxx, Boston A.L.
2B— Joe Gordon, New York A.L.
SS— Joe Cronin, Boston A.L.
3B— Red Rolfe, New York A.L.
OF— Joe Medwick, St. Louis N.L.
OF— Joe DiMaggio, New York A.L.
OF— Ted Williams, Boston A.L.
C— Bill Dickey, New York A.L.
P— Red Ruffing, New York A.L.
P— Bob Feller, Cleveland A.L.
P— Bucky Walters, Cincinnati N.L.

1940
1B— Frank McCormick, Cincinnati N.L.
2B— Joe Gordon, New York A.L.
SS— Luke Appling, Chicago A.L.
3B— Stan Hack, Chicago N.L.
OF— Hank Greenberg, Detroit A.L.
OF— Joe DiMaggio, New York A.L.
OF— Ted Williams, Boston A.L.
C— Harry Danning, New York A.L.
P— Bob Feller, Cleveland A.L.
P— Bucky Walters, Cincinnati N.L.
P— Paul Derringer, Cincinnati N.L.

1941
1B— Dolf Camilli, Brooklyn N.L.
2B— Joe Gordon, New York A.L.
SS— Cecil Travis, Washington A.L.
3B— Stan Hack, Chicago N.L.
OF— Ted Williams, Boston A.L.
OF— Joe DiMaggio, New York A.L.
OF— Pete Reiser, Brooklyn N.L.
C— Bill Dickey, New York A.L.
P— Bob Feller, Cleveland A.L.
P— Whitlow Wyatt, Brooklyn N.L.
P— Thornton Lee, Chicago A.L.

1942
1B— Johnny Mize, New York N.L.
2B— Joe Gordon, New York A.L.
SS— Johnny Pesky, Boston A.L.
3B— Stan Hack, Chicago N.L.
OF— Ted Williams, Boston A.L.
OF— Joe DiMaggio, New York A.L.
OF— Enos Slaughter, St. Louis N.L.
C— Mickey Owen, Brooklyn N.L.
P— Mort Cooper, St. Louis N.L.
P— Tiny Bonham, New York A.L.
P— Tex Hughson, Boston A.L.

1943
1B— Rudy York, Detroit A.L.
2B— Billy Herman, Brooklyn N.L.
SS— Luke Appling, Chicago A.L.
3B— Billy Johnson, New York A.L.
OF— Dick Wakefield, Detroit A.L.
OF— Stan Musial, St. Louis N.L.
OF— Bill Nicholson, Chicago N.L.
C— Walker Cooper, St. Louis N.L.
P— Spud Chandler, New York A.L.

P— Mort Cooper, St. Louis N.L.
P— Rip Sewell, Pittsburgh N.L.

1944
1B— Ray Sanders, St. Louis N.L.
2B— Bobby Doerr, Boston A.L.
SS— Marty Marion, St. Louis N.L.
3B— Bob Elliott, Pittsburgh N.L.
OF— Stan Musial, St. Louis N.L.
OF— Dick Wakefield, Detroit A.L.
OF— Dixie Walker, Brooklyn, N.L.
C— Walker Cooper, St. Louis N.L.
P— Hal Newhouser, Detroit A.L.
P— Mort Cooper, St. Louis N.L.
P— Dizzy Trout, Detroit A.L.

1945
1B— Phil Cavarretta, Chicago N.L.
2B— George Stirnweiss, N.Y. A.L.
SS— Marty Marion, St. Louis N.L.
3B— Whitey Kurowski, St. Louis N.L.
OF— Tommy Holmes, Boston N.L.
OF— Andy Pafko, Chicago N.L.
OF— Goody Rosen, Brooklyn N.L.
C— Paul Richards, Detroit A.L.
P— Hal Newhouser, Detroit A.L.
P— Boo Ferriss, Boston A.L.
P— Hank Borowy, Chicago N.L.

1946
1B— Stan Musial, St. Louis N.L.
2B— Bobby Doerr, Boston A.L.
SS— Johnny Pesky, Boston A.L.
3B— George Kell, Detroit A.L.
OF— Ted Williams, Boston A.L.
OF— Dom DiMaggio, Boston A.L.
OF— Enos Slaughter, St. Louis N.L.
C— Aaron Robinson, New York A.L.
P— Hal Newhouser, Detroit A.L.
P— Bob Feller, Cleveland A.L.
P— Boo Ferriss, Boston A.L.

1947
1B— Johnny Mize, New York N.L.
2B— Joe Gordon, Cleveland A.L.
SS— Lou Boudreau, Cleveland A.L.
3B— George Kell, Detroit A.L.
OF— Ted Williams, Boston A.L.
OF— Joe DiMaggio, New York A.L.
OF— Ralph Kiner, Pittsburgh N.L.
C— Walker Cooper, New York N.L.
P— Ewell Blackwell, Cincinnati N.L.
P— Bob Feller, Cleveland A.L.
P— Ralph Branca, Brooklyn N.L.

1948
1B— Johnny Mize, New York N.L.
2B— Joe Gordon, Cleveland A.L.
SS— Lou Boudreau, Cleveland A.L.
3B— Bob Elliott, Boston N.L.
OF— Ted Williams, Boston A.L.
OF— Joe DiMaggio, New York A.L.
OF— Stan Musial, St. Louis N.L.
C— Birdie Tebbetts, Boston A.L.
P— Johnny Sain, Boston N.L.
P— Bob Lemon, Cleveland A.L.
P— Harry Brecheen, St. Louis N.L.

1949
1B— Tommy Henrich, New York A.L.
2B— Jackie Robinson, Brooklyn N.L.
SS— Phil Rizzuto, New York A.L.
3B— George Kell, Detroit A.L.
OF— Ted Williams, Boston A.L.
OF— Stan Musial, St. Louis N.L.
OF— Ralph Kiner, Pittsburgh N.L.
C— Roy Campanella, Brooklyn N.L.
P— Mel Parnell, Boston A.L.
P— Ellis Kinder, Boston A.L.
P— Joe Page, New York A.L.

1950
1B— Walt Dropo, Boston A.L.
2B— Jackie Robinson, Brooklyn N.L.
SS— Phil Rizzuto, New York A.L.
3B— George Kell, Detroit A.L.
OF— Stan Musial, St. Louis N.L.
OF— Ralph Kiner, Pittsburgh N.L.
OF— Larry Doby, Cleveland A.L.
C— Yogi Berra, New York A.L.
P— Vic Raschi, New York A.L.
P— Bob Lemon, Cleveland A.L.
P— Jim Konstanty, Phil. N.L.

1951
1B— Ferris Fain, Philadelphia A.L.
2B— Jackie Robinson, Brooklyn N.L.
SS— Phil Rizzuto, New York A.L.
3B— George Kell, Detroit A.L.
OF— Stan Musial, St. Louis N.L.
OF— Ted Williams, Boston A.L.
OF— Ralph Kiner, Pittsburgh N.L.
C— Roy Campanella, Brooklyn N.L.
P— Sal Maglie, New York N.L.
P— Preacher Roe, Brooklyn N.L.
P— Allie Reynolds, New York A.L.

1952
1B— Ferris Fain, Philadelphia A.L.
2B— Jackie Robinson, Brooklyn N.L.
SS— Phil Rizzuto, New York A.L.
3B— George Kell, Boston A.L.
OF— Stan Musial, St. Louis N.L.
OF— Hank Sauer, Chicago N.L.
OF— Mickey Mantle, New York A.L.
C— Yogi Berra, New York A.L.
P— Robin Roberts, Philadelphia N.L.
P— Bobby Shantz, Philadelphia A.L.
P— Allie Reynolds, New York A.L.

1953
1B— Mickey Vernon, Washington A.L.
2B— Red Schoendienst, St. Louis N.L.
SS— Pee Wee Reese, Brooklyn N.L.
3B— Al Rosen, Cleveland A.L.
OF— Stan Musial, St. Louis N.L.
OF— Duke Snider, Brooklyn N.L.
OF— Carl Furillo, Brooklyn N.L.
C— Roy Campanella, Brooklyn N.L.
P— Robin Roberts, Philadelphia N.L.
P— Warren Spahn, Milwaukee N.L.
P— Bob Porterfield, Washington A.L.

1954
1B— Ted Kluszewski, Cincinnati N.L.
2B— Bobby Avila, Cleveland A.L.
SS— Alvin Dark, New York N.L.
3B— Al Rosen, Cleveland A.L.
OF— Willie Mays, New York N.L.
OF— Stan Musial, St. Louis N.L.
OF— Duke Snider, Brooklyn N.L.
C— Yogi Berra, New York A.L.
P— Bob Lemon, Cleveland A.L.
P— Johnny Antonelli, New York N.L.
P— Robin Roberts, Philadelphia N.L.

1955
1B— Ted Kluszewski, Cincinnati N.L.
2B— Nellie Fox, Chicago A.L.
SS— Ernie Banks, Chicago N.L.
3B— Ed Mathews, Milwaukee N.L.
OF— Duke Snider, Brooklyn N.L.
OF— Ted Williams, Boston A.L.
OF— Al Kaline, Detroit A.L.
C— Roy Campanella, Brooklyn N.L.
P— Robin Roberts, Philadelphia N.L.
P— Don Newcombe, Brooklyn N.L.
P— Whitey Ford, New York A.L.

1956
1B— Ted Kluszewski, Cincinnati N.L.
2B— Nellie Fox, Chicago A.L.

SS— Harvey Kuenn, Detroit A.L.
3B— Ken Boyer, St. Louis A.L.
OF— Mickey Mantle, New York A.L.
OF— Hank Aaron, Milwaukee N.L.
OF— Ted Williams, Boston A.L.
C— Yogi Berra, New York A.L.
P— Don Newcombe, Brooklyn N.L.
P— Whitey Ford, New York A.L.
P— Billy Pierce, Chicago A.L.

1957
1B— Stan Musial, St. Louis N.L.
2B— Red Schoendienst, N.Y.-Mil. N.L.
SS— Gil McDougald, New York A.L.
3B— Ed Mathews, Milwaukee N.L.
OF— Mickey Mantle, New York A.L.
OF— Ted Williams, Boston A.L.
OF— Willie Mays, New York N.L.
C— Yogi Berra, New York A.L.
P— Warren Spahn, Milwaukee N.L.
P— Billy Pierce, Chicago N.L.
P— Jim Bunning, Detroit A.L.

1958
1B— Stan Musial, St. Louis N.L.
2B— Nellie Fox, Chicago A.L.
SS— Ernie Banks, Chicago N.L.
3B— Frank Thomas, Pittsburgh N.L.
OF— Ted Williams, Boston A.L.
OF— Willie Mays, San Francisco N.L.
OF— Hank Aaron, Milwaukee N.L.
C— Del Crandall, Milwaukee N.L.
P— Bob Turley, New York A.L.
P— Warren Spahn, Milwaukee N.L.
P— Bob Friend, Pittsburgh N.L.

1959
1B— Orlando Cepeda, S.F. N.L.
2B— Nellie Fox, Chicago A.L.
SS— Ernie Banks, Chicago N.L.
3B— Ed Mathews, Milwaukee N.L.
OF— Minnie Minoso, Cleveland A.L.
OF— Willie Mays, San Francisco N.L.
OF— Hank Aaron, Milwaukee N.L.
C— Sherm Lollar, Chicago A.L.
P— Early Wynn, Chicago A.L.
P— Sam Jones, San Francisco N.L.
P— Johnny Antonelli, S.F. N.L.

1960
1B— Bill Skowron, New York A.L.
2B— Bill Mazeroski, Pittsburgh N.L.
SS— Ernie Banks, Chicago N.L.
3B— Ed Mathews, Milwaukee N.L.
OF— Minnie Minoso, Chicago A.L.
OF— Willie Mays, San Francisco N.L.
OF— Roger Maris, New York A.L.
C— Del Crandall, Milwaukee N.L.
P— Vernon Law, Pittsburgh N.L.
P— Warren Spahn, Milwaukee N.L.
P— Ernie Broglio, St. Louis N.L.

1961
AMERICAN LEAGUE
1B— Norm Cash, Detroit
2B— Bobby Richardson, New York
SS— Tony Kubek, New York
3B— Brooks Robinson, Baltimore
OF— Mickey Mantle, New York
OF— Roger Maris, New York
OF— Rocky Colavito, Detroit
C— Elston Howard, New York
P— Whitey Ford, New York
P— Frank Lary, Detroit

NATIONAL LEAGUE
1B— Orlando Cepeda, San Francisco
2B— Frank Bolling, Milwaukee
SS— Maury Wills, Los Angeles
3B— Ken Boyer, St. Louis
OF— Willie Mays, San Francisco

OF— Frank Robinson, Cincinnati
OF— Roberto Clemente, Pittsburgh
C— Smoky Burgess, Pittsburgh
P— Joey Jay, Cincinnati
P— Warren Spahn, Milwaukee

1962
AMERICAN LEAGUE
1B— Norm Siebern, Kansas City
2B— Bobby Richardson, New York
SS— Tom Tresh, New York
3B— Brooks Robinson, Baltimore
OF— Leon Wagner, Los Angeles
OF— Mickey Mantle, New York
OF— Al Kaline, Detroit
C— Earl Battey, Minnesota
P— Ralph Terry, New York
P— Dick Donovan, Cleveland

NATIONAL LEAGUE
1B— Orlando Cepeda, San Francisco
2B— Bill Mazeroski, Pittsburgh
SS— Maury Wills, Los Angeles
3B— Ken Boyer, St. Louis
OF— Tommy Davis, Los Angeles
OF— Willie Mays, San Francisco
OF— Frank Robinson, Cincinnati
C— Del Crandall, Milwaukee
P— Don Drysdale, Los Angeles
P— Bob Purkey, Cincinnati

1963
AMERICAN LEAGUE
1B— Joe Pepitone, New York
2B— Bobby Richardson, New York
SS— Luis Aparicio, Baltimore
3B— Frank Malzone, Boston
OF— Carl Yastrzemski, Boston
OF— Albie Pearson, Los Angeles
OF— Al Kaline, Detroit
C— Elston Howard, New York
P— Whitey Ford, New York
P— Gary Peters, Chicago

NATIONAL LEAGUE
1B— Bill White, St. Louis
2B— Jim Gilliam, Los Angeles
SS— Dick Groat, St. Louis
3B— Ken Boyer, St. Louis
OF— Tommy Davis, Los Angeles
OF— Willie Mays, San Francisco
OF— Hank Aaron, Milwaukee
C— John Edwards, Cincinnati
P— Sandy Koufax, Los Angeles
P— Juan Marichal, San Francisco

1964
AMERICAN LEAGUE
1B— Dick Stuart, Boston
2B— Bobby Richardson, New York
SS— Jim Fregosi, Los Angeles
3B— Brooks Robinson, Baltimore
OF— Harmon Killebrew, Minnesota
OF— Mickey Mantle, New York
OF— Tony Oliva, Minnesota
C— Elston Howard, New York
P— Dean Chance, Los Angeles
P— Gary Peters, Chicago

NATIONAL LEAGUE
1B— Bill White, St. Louis
2B— Ron Hunt, New York
SS— Dick Groat, St. Louis
3B— Ken Boyer, St. Louis
OF— Billy Williams, Chicago
OF— Willie Mays, San Francisco
OF— Roberto Clemente, Pittsburgh
C— Joe Torre, Milwaukee
P— Sandy Koufax, Los Angeles
P— Jim Bunning, Philadelphia

1965
AMERICAN LEAGUE
1B— Fred Whitfield, Cleveland
2B— Bobby Richardson, New York
SS— Zoilo Versalles, Minnesota
3B— Brooks Robinson, Baltimore
OF— Carl Yastrzemski, Boston
OF— Jimmie Hall, Minnesota
OF— Tony Oliva, Minnesota
C— Earl Battey, Minnesota
P— Jim Grant, Minnesota
P— Mel Stottlemyre, New York

NATIONAL LEAGUE
1B— Willie McCovey, San Francisco
2B— Pete Rose, Cincinnati
SS— Maury Wills, Los Angeles
3B— Deron Johnson, Cincinnati
OF— Willie Stargell, Pittsburgh
OF— Willie Mays, San Francisco
OF— Hank Aaron, Milwaukee
C— Joe Torre, Milwaukee
P— Sandy Koufax, Los Angeles
P— Juan Marichal, San Francisco

1966
AMERICAN LEAGUE
1B— Boog Powell, Baltimore
2B— Bobby Richardson, New York
SS— Luis Aparicio, Baltimore
3B— Brooks Robinson, Baltimore
OF— Frank Robinson, Baltimore
OF— Al Kaline, Detroit
OF— Tony Oliva, Minnesota
C— Paul Casanova, Washington
P— Jim Kaat, Minnesota
P— Earl Wilson, Detroit

NATIONAL LEAGUE
1B— Felipe Alou, Atlanta
2B— Pete Rose, Cincinnati
SS— Gene Alley, Pittsburgh
3B— Ron Santo, Chicago
OF— Willie Stargell, Pittsburgh
OF— Willie Mays, San Francisco
OF— Roberto Clemente, Pittsburgh
C— Joe Torre, Atlanta
P— Sandy Koufax, Los Angeles
P— Juan Marichal, San Francisco

1967
AMERICAN LEAGUE
1B— Harmon Killebrew, Minnesota
2B— Rod Carew, Minnesota
SS— Jim Fregosi, California
3B— Brooks Robinson, Baltimore
OF— Carl Yastrzemski, Boston
OF— Al Kaline, Detroit
OF— Frank Robinson, Baltimore
C— Bill Freehan, Detroit
P— Jim Lonborg, Boston
P— Earl Wilson, Detroit

NATIONAL LEAGUE
1B— Orlando Cepeda, St. Louis
2B— Bill Mazeroski, Pittsburgh
SS— Gene Alley, Pittsburgh
3B— Ron Santo, Chicago
OF— Hank Aaron, Atlanta
OF— Jim Wynn, Houston
OF— Roberto Clemente, Pittsburgh
C— Tim McCarver, St. Louis
P— Mike McCormick, San Francisco
P— Ferguson Jenkins, Chicago

1968
AMERICAN LEAGUE
1B— Boog Powell, Baltimore
2B— Rod Carew, Minnesota
SS— Luis Aparicio, Chicago
3B— Brooks Robinson, Baltimore

OF— Ken Harrelson, Boston
OF— Willie Horton, Detroit
OF— Frank Howard, Washington
C— Bill Freehan, Detroit
P— Dave McNally, Baltimore
P— Denny McLain, Detroit

NATIONAL LEAGUE
1B— Willie McCovey, San Francisco
2B— Tommy Helms, Cincinnati
SS— Don Kessinger, Chicago
3B— Ron Santo, Chicago
OF— Billy Williams, Chicago
OF— Curt Flood, St. Louis
OF— Pete Rose, Cincinnati
C— Johnny Bench, Cincinnati
P— Bob Gibson, St. Louis
P— Juan Marichal, San Francisco

1969
AMERICAN LEAGUE
1B— Boog Powell, Baltimore
2B— Rod Carew, Minnesota
SS— Rico Petrocelli, Boston
3B— Harmon Killebrew, Minnesota
OF— Frank Howard, Washington
OF— Paul Blair, Baltimore
OF— Reggie Jackson, Oakland
C— Bill Freehan, Detroit
RHP— Denny McLain, Detroit
LHP— Mike Cuellar, Baltimore

NATIONAL LEAGUE
1B— Willie McCovey, San Francisco
2B— Glenn Beckert, Chicago
SS— Don Kessinger, Chicago
3B— Ron Santo, Chicago
OF— Cleon Jones, New York
OF— Matty Alou, Pittsburgh
OF— Hank Aaron, Atlanta
C— Johnny Bench, Cincinnati
RHP— Tom Seaver, New York
LHP— Steve Carlton, St. Louis

1970
AMERICAN LEAGUE
1B— Boog Powell, Baltimore
2B— Dave Johnson, Baltimore
SS— Luis Aparicio, Chicago
3B— Harmon Killebrew, Minnesota
OF— Frank Howard, Washington
OF— Reggie Smith, Boston
OF— Tony Oliva, Minnesota
C— Ray Fosse, Cleveland
RHP— Jim Perry, Minnesota
LHP— Sam McDowell, Cleveland

NATIONAL LEAGUE
1B— Willie McCovey, San Francisco
2B— Glenn Beckert, Chicago
SS— Don Kessinger, Chicago
3B— Tony Perez, Cincinnati
OF— Billy Williams, Chicago
OF— Bobby Tolan, Cincinnati
OF— Hank Aaron, Atlanta
C— Johnny Bench, Cincinnati
RHP— Bob Gibson, St. Louis
LHP— Jim Merritt, Cincinnati

1971
AMERICAN LEAGUE
1B— Norm Cash, Detroit
2B— Cookie Rojas, Kansas City
SS— Leo Cardenas, Minnesota
3B— Brooks Robinson, Baltimore
OF— Merv Rettenmund, Baltimore
OF— Bobby Murcer, New York
OF— Tony Oliva, Minnesota
C— Bill Freehan, Detroit
RHP— Jim Palmer, Baltimore
LHP— Vida Blue, Oakland

NATIONAL LEAGUE
1B— Lee May, Cincinnati
2B— Glenn Beckett, Chicago
SS— Bud Harrelson, New York
3B— Joe Torre, St. Louis
OF— Willie Stargell, Pittsburgh
OF— Willie Davis, Los Angeles
OF— Hank Aaron, Atlanta
C— Manny Sanguillen, Pittsburgh
RHP— Ferguson Jenkins, Chicago
LHP— Steve Carlton, St. Louis

1972
AMERICAN LEAGUE
1B— Dick Allen, Chicago
2B— Rod Carew, Minnesota
SS— Luis Aparicio, Boston
3B— Brooks Robinson, Baltimore
OF— Joe Rudi, Oakland
OF— Bobby Murcer, New York
OF— Richie Scheinblum, Kansas City
C— Carlton Fisk, Boston
RHP— Gaylord Perry, Cleveland
LHP— Wilbur Wood, Chicago

NATIONAL LEAGUE
1B— Willie Stargell, Pittsburgh
2B— Joe Morgan, Cincinnati
SS— Chris Speier, San Francisco
3B— Ron Santo, Chicago
OF— Billy Williams, Chicago
OF— Cesar Cedeno, Houston
OF— Roberto Clemente, Pittsburgh
C— Johnny Bench, Cincinnati
RHP— Ferguson Jenkins, Chicago
LHP— Steve Carlton, Philadelphia

1973
AMERICAN LEAGUE
1B— John Mayberry, Kansas City
2B— Rod Carew, Minnesota
SS— Bert Campaneris, Oakland
3B— Sal Bando, Oakland
OF— Reggie Jackson, Oakland
OF— Amos Otis, Kansas City
OF— Bobby Murcer, New York
C— Thurman Munson, New York
RHP— Jim Palmer, Baltimore
LHP— Ken Holtzman, Oakland

NATIONAL LEAGUE
1B— Tony Perez, Cincinnati
2B— Dave Johnson, Atlanta
SS— Bill Russell, Los Angeles
3B— Darrell Evans, Atlanta
OF— Bobby Bonds, San Francisco
OF— Cesar Cedeno, Houston
OF— Pete Rose, Cincinnati
C— Johnny Bench, Cincinnati
RHP— Tom Seaver, New York
LHP— Ron Bryant, San Francisco

1974
AMERICAN LEAGUE
1B— Dick Allen, Chicago
2B— Rod Carew, Minnesota
SS— Bert Campaneris, Oakland
3B— Sal Bando, Oakland
OF— Joe Rudi, Oakland
OF— Paul Blair, Baltimore
OF— Jeff Burroughs, Texas
C— Thurman Munson, New York
DH— Tommy Davis, Baltimore
RHP— Jim Hunter, Oakland
LHP— Mike Cuellar, Baltimore

NATIONAL LEAGUE
1B— Steve Garvey, Los Angeles
2B— Joe Morgan, Cincinnati
SS— Dave Concepcion, Cincinnati
3B— Mike Schmidt, Philadelphia

OF— Lou Brock, St. Louis
OF— Jim Wynn, Los Angeles
OF— Richie Zisk, Pittsburgh
C— Johnny Bench, Cincinnati
RHP— Andy Messersmith, Los Angeles
LHP— Don Gullett, Cincinnati

1975
AMERICAN LEAGUE
1B— John Mayberry, Kansas City
2B— Rod Carew, Minnesota
SS— Toby Harrah, Texas
3B— Graig Nettles, New York
OF— Jim Rice, Boston
OF— Fred Lynn, Boston
OF— Reggie Jackson, Oakland
C— Thurman Munson, New York
DH— Willie Horton, Detroit
RHP— Jim Palmer, Baltimore
LHP— Jim Kaat, Chicago

NATIONAL LEAGUE
1B— Steve Garvey, Los Angeles
2B— Joe Morgan, Cincinnati
SS— Larry Bowa, Philadelphia
3B— Bill Madlock, Chicago
OF— Greg Luzinski, Philadelphia
OF— Al Oliver, Pittsburgh
OF— Dave Parker, Pittsburgh
C— Johnny Bench, Cincinnati
RHP— Tom Seaver, New York
LHP— Randy Jones, San Diego

1976
AMERICAN LEAGUE
1B— Chris Chambliss, New York
2B— Bobby Grich, Baltimore
3B— George Brett, Kansas City
SS— Mark Belanger, Baltimore
OF— Joe Rudi, Oakland
OF— Mickey Rivers, New York
OF— Reggie Jackson, Baltimore
C— Thurman Munson, New York
DH— Hal McRae, Kansas City
RHP— Jim Palmer, Baltimore
LHP— Frank Tanana, California

NATIONAL LEAGUE
1B— Willie Montanez, S.F.-Atl.
2B— Joe Morgan, Cincinnati
3B— Mike Schmidt, Philadelphia
SS— Dave Concepcion, Cincinnati
OF— George Foster, Cincinnati
OF— Cesar Cedeno, Houston
OF— Ken Griffey, Cincinnati
C— Bob Boone, Philadelphia
RHP— Don Sutton, Los Angeles
LHP— Randy Jones, San Diego

1977
AMERICAN LEAGUE
1B— Rod Carew, Minnesota
2B— Willie Randolph, New York
3B— Graig Nettles, New York
SS— Rick Burleson, Boston
OF— Jim Rice, Boston
OF— Larry Hisle, Minnesota
OF— Bobby Bonds, California
C— Carlton Fisk, Boston
DH— Hal McRae, Kansas City
RHP— Nolan Ryan, California
LHP— Frank Tanana, California

NATIONAL LEAGUE
1B— Steve Garvey, Los Angeles
2B— Joe Morgan, Cincinnati
3B— Mike Schmidt, Philadelphia
SS— Garry Templeton, St. Louis
OF— George Foster, Cincinnati
OF— Dave Parker, Pittsburgh
OF— Greg Luzinski, Philadelphia

C— Ted Simmons, St. Louis
RHP— Rick Reuschel, Chicago
LHP— Steve Carlton, Philadelphia

1978
AMERICAN LEAGUE
1B— Rod Carew, Minnesota
2B— Frank White, Kansas City
3B— Graig Nettles, New York
SS— Robin Yount, Milwaukee
OF— Jim Rice, Boston
OF— Larry Hisle, Milwaukee
OF— Fred Lynn, Boston
C— Jim Sundberg, Texas
DH— Rusty Staub, Detroit
RHP— Jim Palmer, Baltimore
LHP— Ron Guidry, New York

NATIONAL LEAGUE
1B— Steve Garvey, Los Angeles
2B— Dave Lopes, Los Angeles
3B— Pete Rose, Cincinnati
SS— Larry Bowa, Philadelphia
OF— George Foster, Cincinnati
OF— Dave Parker, Pittsburgh
OF— Jack Clark, San Francisco
C— Ted Simmons, St. Louis
RHP— Gaylord Perry, San Diego
LHP— Vida Blue, San Francisco

1979
AMERICAN LEAGUE
1B— Cecil Cooper, Milwaukee
2B— Bobby Grich, California
3B— George Brett, Kansas City
SS— Roy Smalley, Minnesota
OF— Jim Rice, Boston
OF— Fred Lynn, Boston
OF— Ken Singleton, Baltimore
C— Darrell Porter, Kansas City
DH— Don Baylor, California
RHP— Jim Kern, Texas
LHP— Mike Flanagan, Baltimore

NATIONAL LEAGUE
1B— Keith Hernandez, St. Louis
2B— Dave Lopes, Los Angeles
3B— Mike Schmidt, Philadelphia
SS— Garry Templeton, St. Louis
OF— Dave Kingman, Chicago
OF— Omar Moreno, Pittsburgh
OF— Dave Winfield, San Diego
C— Ted Simmons, St. Louis
RHP— Joe Niekro, Houston
LHP— Steve Carlton, Philadelphia

1980
AMERICAN LEAGUE
1B— Cecil Cooper, Milwaukee
2B— Willie Randolph, New York
3B— George Brett, Kansas City
SS— Robin Yount, Milwaukee
OF— Ben Oglivie, Milwaukee
OF— Al Bumbry, Baltimore
OF— Reggie Jackson, New York
DH— Reggie Jackson, New York
C— Rick Cerone, New York
RHP— Steve Stone, Baltimore
LHP— Tommy John, New York

NATIONAL LEAGUE
1B— Keith Hernandez, St. Louis
2B— Manny Trillo, Philadelphia
3B— Mike Schmidt, Philadelphia
SS— Garry Templeton, St. Louis
OF— Dusty Baker, Los Angeles
OF— Cesar Cedeno, Houston
OF— George Hendrick, St. Louis
C— Gary Carter, Montreal
RHP— Jim Bibby, Pittsburgh
LHP— Steve Carlton, Philadelphia

1981
AMERICAN LEAGUE
1B— Cecil Cooper, Milwaukee
2B— Bobby Grich, California
3B— Buddy Bell, Texas
SS— Rick Burleson, California
OF— Rickey Henderson, Oakland
OF— Dwayne Murphy, Oakland
OF— Tony Armas, Oakland
C— Jim Sundberg, Texas
DH— Richie Zisk, Seattle
RHP— Jack Morris, Detroit
LHP— Ron Guidry, New York

NATIONAL LEAGUE
1B— Pete Rose, Philadelphia
2B— Manny Trillo, Philadelphia
3B— Mike Schmidt, Philadelphia
SS— Dave Concepcion, Cincinnati
OF— George Foster, Cincinnati
OF— Andre Dawson, Montreal
OF— Pedro Guerrero, Los Angeles
C— Gary Carter, Montreal
RHP— Tom Seaver, Cincinnati
LHP— Fernando Valenzuela, Los Angeles

1982
AMERICAN LEAGUE
1B— Cecil Cooper, Milwaukee
2B— Damaso Garcia, Toronto
3B— Doug DeCinces, California
SS— Robin Yount, Milwaukee
OF— Dave Winfield, New York
OF— Gorman Thomas, Milwaukee
OF— Dwight Evans, Boston
C— Lance Parrish, Detroit
DH— Hal McRae, Kansas City
RHP— Dave Stieb, Toronto
LHP— Geoff Zahn, California

NATIONAL LEAGUE
1B— Al Oliver, Montreal
2B— Manny Trillo, Philadelphia
3B— Mike Schmidt, Philadelphia
SS— Ozzie Smith, St. Louis
OF— Lonnie Smith, St. Louis
OF— Dale Murphy, Atlanta
OF— Pedro Guerrero, Los Angeles
C— Gary Carter, Montreal
RHP— Steve Rogers, Montreal
LHP— Steve Carlton, Philadelphia

1983
AMERICAN LEAGUE
1B— Eddie Murray, Baltimore
2B— Lou Whitaker, Detroit
3B— Wade Boggs, Boston
SS— Cal Ripken, Baltimore
OF— Jim Rice, Boston
OF— Dave Winfield, New York
OF— Lloyd Moseby, Toronto
C— Carlton Fisk, Chicago
DH— Greg Luzinski, Chicago
RHP— LaMarr Hoyt, Chicago
LHP— Ron Guidry, New York

NATIONAL LEAGUE
1B— George Hendrick, St. Louis
2B— Glenn Hubbard, Atlanta
3B— Mike Schmidt, Philadelphia
SS— Dickie Thon, Houston
OF— Dale Murphy, Atlanta
OF— Andre Dawson, Montreal
OF— Tim Raines, Montreal
C— Tony Pena, Pittsburgh
RHP— John Denny, Philadelphia
LHP— Larry McWilliams, Pittsburgh

1984
AMERICAN LEAGUE
1B— Don Mattingly, New York
2B— Lou Whitaker, Detroit

3B— Buddy Bell, Texas
SS— Cal Ripken, Baltimore
OF— Tony Armas, Boston
OF— Dwight Evans, Boston
OF— Dave Winfield, New York
C— Lance Parrish, Detroit
DH— Dave Kingman, Oakland
RHP— Mike Boddicker, Baltimore
LHP— Willie Hernandez, Detroit

NATIONAL LEAGUE
1B— Keith Hernandez, New York
2B— Ryne Sandberg, Chicago
3B— Mike Schmidt, Philadelphia
SS— Ozzie Smith, St. Louis
OF— Dale Murphy, Atlanta
OF— Jose Cruz, Houston
OF— Tony Gwynn, San Diego
C— Gary Carter, Montreal
RHP— Rick Sutcliffe, Chicago
LHP— Mark Thurmond, San Diego

1985
AMERICAN LEAGUE
1B— Don Mattingly, New York
2B— Damaso Garcia, Toronto
3B— Wade Boggs, Boston
SS— Cal Ripken, Baltimore
OF— Rickey Henderson, New York
OF— Harold Baines, Chicago
OF— Phil Bradley, Seattle
C— Carlton Fisk, Chicago
DH— Don Baylor, New York
RHP— Bret Saberhagen, Kansas City
LHP— Ron Guidry, New York

NATIONAL LEAGUE
1B— Keith Hernandez, New York
2B— Tom Herr, St. Louis
3B— Tim Wallach, Montreal
SS— Ozzie Smith, St. Louis
OF— Dave Parker, Cincinnati
OF— Willie McGee, St. Louis
OF— Dale Murphy, Atlanta
C— Gary Carter, New York
RHP— Dwight Gooden, New York
LHP— John Tudor, St. Louis

1986
AMERICAN LEAGUE
1B— Don Mattingly, New York
2B— Tony Bernazard, Cleveland
3B— Wade Boggs, Boston
SS— Tony Fernandez, Toronto
OF— Jim Rice, Boston
OF— George Bell, Toronto
OF— Kirby Puckett, Minnesota
C— Rich Gedman, Boston
DH— Don Baylor, Boston
RHP— Roger Clemens, Boston
LHP— Teddy Higuera, Milwaukee

NATIONAL LEAGUE
1B— Keith Hernandez, New York
2B— Steve Sax, Los Angeles
3B— Mike Schmidt, Philadelphia
SS— Ozzie Smith, St. Louis
OF— Tim Raines, Montreal
OF— Tony Gwynn, San Diego
OF— Dave Parker, Cincinnati
C— Gary Carter, New York
RHP— Mike Scott, Houston
LHP— Fernando Valenzuela, Los Angeles

1987
AMERICAN LEAGUE
1B— Don Mattingly, New York
2B— Willie Randolph, New York
3B— Wade Boggs, Boston
SS— Alan Trammell, Detroit
OF— George Bell, Toronto
OF— Kirby Puckett, Minnesota

OF— Dwight Evans, Boston
C— Matt Nokes, Detroit
DH— Paul Molitor, Milwaukee
RHP— Roger Clemens, Boston
LHP— Jimmy Key, Toronto

NATIONAL LEAGUE
1B— Jack Clark, St. Louis
2B— Juan Samuel, Philadelphia
3B— Tim Wallach, Montreal
SS— Ozzie Smith, St. Louis
OF— Andre Dawson, Chicago
OF— Tony Gwynn, San Diego
OF— Eric Davis, Cincinnati
C— Benito Santiago, San Diego
RHP— Rick Sutcliffe, Chicago
LHP— Zane Smith, Atlanta

1988
AMERICAN LEAGUE
1B— George Brett, Kansas City
2B— Johnny Ray, California
3B— Wade Boggs, Boston
SS— Alan Trammell, Detroit
OF— Kirby Puckett, Minnesota
OF— Mike Greenwell, Boston
OF— Jose Canseco, Oakland
C— Ernie Whitt, Toronto
DH— Harold Baines, Chicago
RHP— Dave Stewart, Oakland
LHP— Frank Viola, Minnesota

NATIONAL LEAGUE
1B— Will Clark, San Francisco
2B— Ryne Sandberg, Chicago
3B— Bobby Bonilla, Pittsburgh
SS— Barry Larkin, Cincinnati
OF— Darryl Strawberry, New York
OF— Andy Van Slyke, Pittsburgh
OF— Kevin McReynolds, New York
C— Mike LaValliere, Pittsburgh
RHP— Orel Hershiser, Los Angeles
LHP— Danny Jackson, Cincinnati

1989
AMERICAN LEAGUE
1B— Fred McGriff, Toronto
2B— Julio Franco, Texas
3B— Carney Lansford, Oakland
SS— Cal Ripken, Baltimore
OF— Ruben Sierra, Texas
OF— Kirby Puckett, Minnesota
OF— Robin Yount, Milwaukee
C— Mickey Tettleton, Baltimore
DH— Harold Baines, Chi.-Tex.
RHP— Bret Saberhagen, Kansas City
LHP— Chuck Finley, California

NATIONAL LEAGUE
1B— Will Clark, San Francisco
2B— Ryne Sandberg, Chicago
3B— Howard Johnson, New York
SS— Shawon Dunston, Chicago
OF— Tony Gwynn, San Diego
OF— Kevin Mitchell, San Francisco
OF— Eric Davis, Cincinnati
C— Benito Santiago, San Diego
RHP— Mike Scott, Houston
LHP— Mark Davis, San Diego

1990
AMERICAN LEAGUE
1B— Cecil Fielder, Detroit
2B— Julio Franco, Texas
3B— Kelly Gruber, Toronto
SS— Alan Trammell, Detroit
OF— Rickey Henderson, Oakland
OF— Jose Canseco, Oakland
OF— Ellis Burks, Boston
C— Carlton Fisk, Chicago
DH— Dave Parker, Milwaukee
RHP— Bob Welch, Oakland
LHP— Chuck Finley, California

NATIONAL LEAGUE
1B— Eddie Murray, Los Angeles
2B— Ryne Sandberg, Chicago
3B— Matt Williams, San Francisco
SS— Barry Larkin, Cincinnati
OF— Barry Bonds, Pittsburgh
OF— Bobby Bonilla, Pittsburgh
OF— Darryl Strawberry, New York
C— Mike Scioscia, Los Angeles
RHP— Doug Drabek, Pittsburgh
LHP— Frank Viola, New York

1991
AMERICAN LEAGUE
1B— Cecil Fielder, Detroit
2B— Julio Franco, Texas
3B— Wade Boggs, Boston
SS— Cal Ripken, Baltimore
OF— Jose Canseco, Oakland
OF— Joe Carter, Toronto
OF— Ken Griffey Jr., Seattle
C— Mickey Tettleton, Detroit
RHP— Roger Clemens, Boston
LHP— Jim Abbott, California

NATIONAL LEAGUE
1B— Will Clark, San Francisco
2B— Ryne Sandberg, Chicago
3B— Terry Pendleton, Atlanta
SS— Barry Larkin, Cincinnati
OF— Barry Bonds, Pittsburgh
OF— Bobby Bonilla, Pittsburgh
OF— Ron Gant, Atlanta
C— Benito Santiago, San Diego
RHP— Jose Rijo, Cincinnati
LHP— Tom Glavine, Atlanta

1992
AMERICAN LEAGUE
1B— Mark McGwire, Oakland
2B— Roberto Alomar, Toronto
3B— Edgar Martinez, Seattle
SS— Travis Fryman, Detroit
OF— Joe Carter, Toronto
OF— Mike Devereaux, Baltimore
OF— Kirby Puckett, Minnesota
C— Mickey Tettleton, Detroit
RHP— Jack McDowell, Chicago
LHP— Dave Fleming, Seattle

NATIONAL LEAGUE
1B— Fred McGriff, San Diego
2B— Ryne Sandberg, Chicago
3B— Gary Sheffield, San Diego
SS— Barry Larkin, Cincinnati
OF— Barry Bonds, Pittsburgh
OF— Andy Van Slyke, Pittsburgh
OF— Larry Walker, Montreal
C— Darren Daulton, Philadelphia
RHP— Greg Maddux, Chicago
LHP— Tom Glavine, Atlanta

1993
AMERICAN LEAGUE
1B— Frank Thomas, Chicago
2B— Carlos Baerga, Cleveland
3B— Travis Fryman, Detroit
SS— Cal Ripken Jr., Baltimore
OF— Albert Belle, Cleveland
OF— Juan Gonzalez, Texas
OF— Ken Griffey Jr., Seattle
C— Mike Stanley, New York
DH— Paul Molitor, Toronto
RHP— Jack McDowell, Chicago
LHP— Jimmy Key, New York

NATIONAL LEAGUE
1B— Fred McGriff, S.D.-Atl.
2B— Robby Thompson, San Francisco
3B— Matt Williams, San Francisco

SS— Jay Bell, Pittsburgh
OF— Barry Bonds, San Francisco
OF— Lenny Dykstra, Philadelphia
OF— David Justice, Atlanta
C— Mike Piazza, Los Angeles
RHP— Greg Maddux, Atlanta
LHP— Steve Avery, Atlanta

1994
AMERICAN LEAGUE
1B— Frank Thomas, Chicago
2B— Chuck Knoblauch, Minnesota
3B— Wade Boggs, New York
SS— Cal Ripken Jr., Baltimore
OF— Albert Belle, Cleveland
OF— Ken Griffey Jr., Seattle
OF— Kirby Puckett, Minnesota
C— Ivan Rodriguez, Texas
DH— Paul Molitor, Toronto
RHP— David Cone, Kansas City
LHP— Jimmy Key, New York

NATIONAL LEAGUE
1B— Jeff Bagwell, Houston
2B— Craig Biggio, Houston
3B— Matt Williams, San Francisco
SS— Barry Larkin, Cincinnati
OF— Moises Alou, Montreal
OF— Barry Bonds, San Francisco
OF— Tony Gwynn, San Diego
C— Mike Piazza, Los Angeles
RHP— Greg Maddux, Atlanta
LHP— Danny Jackson, Philadelphia

1995
AMERICAN LEAGUE
1B— Mo Vaughn, Boston
2B— Carlos Baerga, Cleveland
3B— Jim Thome, Cleveland
SS— Cal Ripken Jr., Baltimore
OF— Albert Belle, Cleveland
OF— Tim Salmon, California
OF— Jim Edmonds, California
C— Ivan Rodriguez, Texas
DH— Edgar Martinez, Seattle
RHP— Mike Mussina, Baltimore
LHP— Randy Johnson, Seattle

NATIONAL LEAGUE
1B— Eric Karros, Los Angeles
2B— Craig Biggio, Houston
3B— Vinny Castilla, Colorado
SS— Barry Larkin, Cincinnati
OF— Reggie Sanders, Cincinnati
OF— Dante Bichette, Colorado
OF— Sammy Sosa, Chicago
C— Mike Piazza, Los Angeles
RHP— Greg Maddux, Atlanta
LHP— Pete Schourek, Cincinnati

1996
AMERICAN LEAGUE
1B— Mark McGwire, Oakland
2B— Roberto Alomar, Baltimore
3B— Jim Thome, Cleveland
SS— Alex Rodriguez, Seattle
OF— Albert Belle, Cleveland
OF— Juan Gonzalez, Texas
OF— Ken Griffey Jr., Seattle
C— Ivan Rodriguez, Texas
DH— Paul Molitor, Minnesota
RHP— Pat Hentgen, Toronto
LHP— Andy Pettitte, New York

NATIONAL LEAGUE
1B— Jeff Bagwell, Houston
2B— Eric Young, Colorado
3B— Ken Caminiti, San Diego
SS— Barry Larkin, Cincinnati
OF— Barry Bonds, San Francisco
OF— Ellis Burks, Colorado

OF— Gary Sheffield, Florida
C— Mike Piazza, Los Angeles
RHP— John Smoltz, Atlanta
LHP— Al Leiter, Florida

1997
AMERICAN LEAGUE
1B— Tino Martinez, New York
2B— Chuck Knoblauch, Minnesota
3B— Matt Williams, Cleveland
SS— Nomar Garciaparra, Boston
OF— Ken Griffey Jr., Seattle
OF— David Justice, Cleveland
OF— Tim Salmon, Anaheim
C— Ivan Rodriguez, Texas
DH— Edgar Martinez, Seattle
RHP— Roger Clemens, Toronto
LHP— Randy Johnson, Seattle

NATIONAL LEAGUE
1B— Jeff Bagwell, Houston
2B— Craig Biggio, Houston
3B— Vinny Castillo, Colorado
SS— Jeff Blauser, Atlanta
OF— Barry Bonds, San Francisco
OF— Tony Gwynn, San Diego
OF— Larry Walker, Colorado
C— Mike Piazza, Los Angeles
RHP— Pedro Martinez, Montreal
LHP— Denny Neagle, Atlanta

1998
AMERICAN LEAGUE
1B— Rafael Palmeiro, Baltimore
2B— Roberto Alomar, Baltimore
3B— Scott Brosius, New York
SS— Alex Rodriguez, Seattle
OF— Ken Griffey Jr., Seattle
OF— Juan Gonzalez, Texas
OF— Albert Belle, Chicago
C— Ivan Rodriguez, Texas
DH— Jose Canseco, Toronto
RHP— Pedro Martinez, Boston
LHP— David Wells, New York

NATIONAL LEAGUE
1B— Mark McGwire, St. Louis
2B— Craig Biggio, Houston
3B— Vinny Castillo, Colorado
SS— Barry Larkin, Cincinnati
OF— Sammy Sosa, Chicago
OF— Moises Alou, Houston
OF— Greg Vaughn, San Diego
C— Mike Piazza, L.A.-Fla.-N.Y.
RHP— Kevin Brown, San Diego
LHP— Tom Glavine, Atlanta

1999
AMERICAN LEAGUE
1B— Rafael Palmeiro, Texas
2B— Roberto Alomar, Cleveland
3B— Dean Palmer, Detroit
SS— Nomar Garciaparra, Boston
OF— Shawn Green, Toronto
OF— Ken Griffey Jr., Seattle
OF— Manny Ramirez, Cleveland
C— Ivan Rodriguez, Texas
RHP— Pedro Martinez, Boston
LHP— Jamie Moyer, Seattle

NATIONAL LEAGUE
1B— Jeff Bagwell, Houston
2B— Edgardo Alfonzo, New York
3B— Chipper Jones, Atlanta
SS— Barry Larkin, Cincinnati
OF— Sammy Sosa, Chicago
OF— Vladimir Guerrero, Montreal
OF— Larry Walker, Colorado
C— Mike Piazza, New York
RHP— Jose Lima, Houston
LHP— Mike Hampton, Houston

MINOR LEAGUE PLAYER OF THE YEAR

Year	Player, Team, League
1936	John Vander Meer, Durham, Piedmont
1937	Charlie Keller, Newark, International
1938	Fred Hutchinson, Seattle, Pacific Coast
1939	Lou Novikoff, Tulsa, Texas; Los Angeles, Pacific Coast
1940	Phil Rizzuto, Kansas City, American Association
1941	John Lindell, Newark, International
1942	Dick Barrett, Seattle, Pacific Coast
1943	Chet Covington, Scranton, Eastern
1944	Rip Collins, Albany, Eastern
1945	Gil Coan, Chattanooga, Southern
1946	Sibby Sisti, Indianapolis, American Association
1947	Hank Sauer, Syracuse, International
1948	Gene Woodling, San Francisco, Pacific Coast
1949	Orie Arntzen, Albany, Eastern
1950	Frank Saucier, San Antonio, Texas
1951	Gene Conley, Hartford, Eastern
1952	Bill Skowron, Kansas City, American Association
1953	Gene Conley, Toledo, American Association
1954	Herb Score, Indianapolis, American Association
1955	John Murff, Dallas, Texas
1956	Steve Bilko, Los Angeles, Pacific Coast
1957	Norm Siebern, Denver, American Association
1958	Jim O'Toole, Nashville, Southern
1959	Frank Howard, Victoria-Spokane
1960	Willie Davis, Spokane, Pacific Coast
1961	Howie Koplitz, Birmingham, Southern
1962	Bob Bailey, Columbus, International
1963	Don Buford, Indianapolis, International
1964	Mel Stottlemyre, Richmond, International
1965	Joe Foy, Toronto, International
1966	Mike Epstein, Rochester, International
1967	Johnny Bench, Buffalo, International
1968	Merv Rettenmund, Rochester, International
1969	Danny Walton, Oklahoma City, American Association

Year	Player, Team, League
1970	Don Baylor, Rochester, International
1971	Bobby Grich, Rochester, International
1972	Tom Paciorek, Albuquerque, Pacific Coast
1973	Steve Ontiveros, Phoenix, Pacific Coast
1974	Jim Rice, Pawtucket, International
1975	Hector Cruz, Tulsa, American Association
1976	Pat Putnam, Asheville, Western Carolina
1977	Ken Landreaux, S.L.C., Pacific Coast; El Paso, Texas
1978	Champ Summers, Indianapolis, American Association
1979	Mark Bomback, Vancouver, Pacific Coast
1980	Tim Raines, Denver, American Association
1981	Mike Marshall, Albuquerque, Pacific Coast
1982	Ron Kittle, Edmonton, Pacific Coast
1983	Kevin McReynolds, Las Vegas, Pacific Coast
1984	Alan Knicely, Wichita, American Association
1985	Jose Canseco, Hunt., Southern-Tac., Pacific Coast
1986	Tim Pyznarski, Las Vegas, Pacific Coast
1987	Randy Milligan, Tidewater, International
1988	Sandy Alomar Jr., Las Vegas, Pacific Coast
	Gary Sheffield, Denver, American Association (tie)
1989	Sandy Alomar Jr., Las Vegas, Pacific Coast
1990	Jose Offerman, Albuquerque, Pacific Coast
1991	Pedro Martinez, Albuquerque, Pacific Coast
1992	Tim Salmon, Edmonton, Pacific Coast
1993	Cliff Floyd, Harrisburg, Eastern
1994	Derek Jeter, Tampa, Florida State; Albany, Eastern; Columbus, International
1995	Karim Garcia, Albuquerque, Pacific Coast
1996	Vladimir Guerrero, West Palm Beach, Florida State; Harrisburg, Eastern
1997	Ben Grieve, Huntsville, Southern; Edmonton, Pacific Coast
1998	Gabe Kapler, Jacksonville, Southern
1999	Rick Ankiel, Arkansas, Texas; Memphis, Pacific Coast

MINOR LEAGUE MANAGER OF THE YEAR

Year	Manager, Team, League
1936	Al Sothoron, Milwaukee, American Association
1937	Jake Flowers, Salisbury, Eastern Shore
1938	Paul Richards, Atlanta, Southern
1939	Bill Meyer, Kansas City, American Association
1940	Larry Gilbert, Nashville, Southern
1941	Burt Shotton, Columbus, American Association
1942	Eddie Dyer, Columbus, American Association
1943	Nick Cullop, Columbus, American Association
1944	Al Thomas, Baltimore, International
1945	Lefty O'Doul, San Francisco, Pacific Coast
1946	Clay Hopper, Montreal, International
1947	Nick Cullop, Milwaukee, American Association
1948	Casey Stengel, Oakland, Pacific Coast
1949	Fred Haney, Hollywood, Pacific Coast
1950	Rollie Hemsley, Columbus, American Association
1951	Charlie Grimm, Milwaukee, American Association
1952	Luke Appling, Memphis, Southern
1953	Bobby Bragan, Hollywood, Pacific Coast
1954	Kerby Farrell, Indianapolis, American Association
1955	Bill Rigney, Minneapolis, American Association
1956	Kerby Farrell, Indianapolis, American Association
1957	Ben Geraghty, Wichita, American Association
1958	Cal Ermer, Birmingham, Southern
1959	Pete Reiser, Victoria, Texas
1960	Mel McGaha, Toronto, International
1961	Kerby Farrell, Buffalo, International
1962	Ben Geraghty, Jacksonville, International
1963	Rollie Hemsley, Indianapolis, International
1964	Harry Walker, Jacksonville, International
1965	Grady Hatton, Oklahoma City, Pacific Coast
1966	Bob Lemon, Seattle, Pacific Coast
1967	Bob Skinner, San Diego, Pacific Coast

Year	Manager, Team, League
1968	Jack Tighe, Toledo, International
1969	Clyde McCullough, Tidewater, International
1970	Tom Lasorda, Spokane, Pacific Coast
1971	Del Rice, Salt Lake City, Pacific Coast
1972	Hank Bauer, Tidewater, International
1973	Joe Morgan, Charleston, International
1974	Joe Altobelli, Rochester, International
1975	Joe Frazier, Tidewater, International
1976	Vern Rapp, Denver, American Association
1977	Tommy Thompson, Arkan., Texas
1978	Les Moss, Evansville, American Association
1979	Vern Benson, Syracuse, International
1980	Hal Lanier, Springfield, American Association
1981	Del Crandall, Albuquerque, Pacific Coast
1982	George Scherger, Indianapolis, American Association
1983	Bill Dancy, Reading, Eastern
1984	Bob Rodgers, Indianapolis, American Association
1985	Jim Fregosi, Louisville, American Association
1986	Joe Sparks, Indianapolis, American Association
1987	Terry Collins, Albuquerque, Pacific Coast
1988	Joe Sparks, Indianapolis, American Association
1989	Bob Bailor, Syracuse, International
1990	Sal Rende, Omaha, American Association
1991	Chris Chambliss, Greenville, Southern
1992	Grady Little, Greenville, Southern
1993	Jim Tracy, Harrisburg, Eastern
1994	Mike Jirschele, Wilmington, Carolina
1995	Pete Mackanin, Ottawa, International
1996	John Mizerock, Wilmington, Carolina
1997	Marv Foley, Rochester, International
1998	Doug Davis, Columbia, South Atlantic
1999	DeMarlo Hale, Trenton, Eastern

MINOR LEAGUE EXECUTIVE OF THE YEAR (HIGHER CLASSIFICATIONS, 1936-1992)

(Restricted to Class AAA starting in 1963)

Year	Executive, Team, League
1936	Earl Mann, Atlanta, Southern
1937	Robert LaMotte, Savannah, Sally
1938	Louis McKenna, St. Paul, American Association
1939	Bruce Dudley, Louisville, American Association
1940	Roy Hamey, Kansas City, American Association
1941	Emil Sick, Seattle, Pacific Coast
1942	Bill Veeck, Milwaukee, American Association
1943	Clarence Rowland, Los Angeles, Pacific Coast
1944	William Mulligan, Seattle, Pacific Coast
1945	Bruce Dudley, Louisville, American Association
1946	Earl Mann, Atlanta, Southern
1947	William Purnhage, Waterloo, I.I.I.
1948	Edward Glennon, Birmingham, Southern
1949	Ted Sullivan, Indianapolis, American Association
1950	Clearnce (Brick) Laws, Oakland, Pacific Coast
1951	Robert Howsam, Denver, West
1952	Jack Cooke, Toronto, International
1953	Richard Burnett, Dallas, Texas
1954	Edward Stumpf, Indianapolis, American Association
1955	Dewey Soriano, Seattle, Pacific Coast
1956	Robert Howsam, Denver American Association
1957	John Stiglmeier, Buffalo, International
1958	Edward Glennon, Birmingham, Southern
1959	Edward Leishman, Salt Lake City, Pacific Coast
1960	Ray Winder, Little Rock, Southern
1961	Elten Schiller, Omaha, American Association
1962	George Sisler Jr., Rochester, International
1963	Lewis Matlin, Hawaii, Pacific Coast
1964	Edward Leishman, San Diego, Pacific Coast
1965	Harold Cooper, Columbus, International
1966	John Quinn Jr., Hawaii, Pacific Coast
1967	Hillman Lyons, Richmond, International
1968	Gabe Paul Jr., Tulsa, Pacific Coast
1969	Bill Gardner, Louisville, International
1970	Dick King, Wichita, American Association
1971	Carl Steinfeldt Jr., Rochester, International
1972	Don Labbruzzo, Evansville, American Association
1973	Merle Miller, Tucson, Pacific Coast
1974	John Carbray, Sacramento, Pacific Coast
1975	Stan Naccarato, Tacoma, Pacific Coast
1976	Art Teece, Salt Lake City, Pacific Coast
1977	George Sisler Jr., Columbus, International
1978	Willie Sanchez, Albuquerque, Pacific Coast
1979	George Sisler Jr., Columbus, International
1980	Jim Burris, Denver, American Association
1981	Pat McKernan, Albuquerque, Pacific Coast
1982	A. Ray Smith, Louisville, American Association
1983	A. Ray Smith, Louisville, American Association
1984	Mike Tamburro, Pawtucket, International
1985	Patty Cox Hampton, Oklahoma City, American Association
1986	Bob Goughan, Rochester, International
1987	Stu Kehoe, Vancouver, Pacific Coast
1988	Bob Rich, Buffalo, American Association
1989	Larry Schmittou, Nashville, American Association
1990	Greg Corns, Phoenix, Pacific Coast
1991	Tom Maloney, Denver, American Association
1992	Lou Schwechheimer, Pawtucket, International

MINOR LEAGUE EXECUTIVE OF THE YEAR (LOWER CLASSIFICATIONS, 1950-1990)

(Separate awards for Class AA and Class A started in 1963; for Short Class A in 1988)

Year	Executive, Team, League
1950	H. Cooper, Hutchinson, Western Association
1951	O. W. (Bill) Hayes, Triple, B.S.
1952	Hillman Lyons, Danville, MOV
1953	Carl Roth, Peoria, I.I.I.
1954	James Meagham, Cedar Rapids, I.I.I.
1955	John Petrakis, Dubuque, MOV
1956	Marvin Milkes, Fresno, California
1957	Richard Wagner, Lincoln, West.
1958	Gerald Waring, Macon, Sally
1959	Clay Dennis, Des Moines, I.I.I.
1960	Hubert Kittle, Yakima, Northwest
1961	David Steele, Fresno, California
1962	John Quinn Jr., San Jose, California
1963	Hugh Finnerty, Tulsa, Texas
	Ben Jewell, M. Valley, Pioneer
1964	Glynn West, Birmingham, Southern
	James Bayens, Rock Hill, W. Carolina
1965	Dick Butler, Dallas-Ft. Worth, Texas
	Ken. Blackman, Quad Cities, Midwest
1966	Tom Fleming, Evansville, Southern
	Cappy Harada, Lodi, California
1967	Robert Quinn, Reading, Eastern
	Pat Williams, Spar'burg, W.C.
1968	Phil Howser, Charlotte, Southern
	Merle Miller, Burlington, Midwest
1969	Charlie Blaney, Albuquerque, Texas
	Bill Gorman, Visalia, California
1970	Carl Sawatski, Arkansas, Texas
	Bob Williams, Bakersfield, California
1971	Miles Wolff, Savannah, Dixie Association
	Ed Holtz, Appleton, Midwest
1972	John Begzos, S. Antonio, Texas
	Bob Piccinini, Modesto, California
1973	Dick Kravitz, Jacksonville, Southern
	Fritz Colschen, Clinton, Midwest
1974	Jim Paul, El Paso, Texas
	Bing Russell, Portland, Northwest
1975	Jim Paul, El Paso, Texas
	Cordy Jensen, Eugene, Northwest
1976	Woodrow Reid, Chattanooga, Southern
	Don Buchheister, Cedar Rapids, Midwest
1977	Jim Paul, El Paso, Texas
	Harry Pells, Quad Cities, Midwest
1978	Larry Schmittou, Nashville, Southern
	Dave Hersh, Appleton, Midwest
1979	Bill Rigney Jr., Midland, Texas
	Tom Romenesko, Greensboro, W.C.
1980	Frances Crockett, Charlotte, Southern
	Tom Romenesko, Greensboro, W.C.
1981	Allie Prescott, Memphis, Southern
	Dan Overstreet, Hagerstown, Caro.
1982	Art Clarkson, Birmingham, Southern
	Bob Carruesco, Stockton, California
1983	Edward Kenney, New Britain, Eastern
	Terry Reynolds, Vero Beach, Florida State
1984	Bruce Baldwin, Greenville, Southern
	Dave Tarrolly, Beloit, Midwest
1985	Ben Bernard, Albany-Colonie, Eastern
	Pete Vonachen, Peoria, Midwest
1986	Bill Davidson, Midland, Texas
	Rob Dlugozima, Durham, Carolina
1987	Joe Preseren, Tulsa, Texas
	Skip Weisman, Greensboro, South Atlantic
1988	Bill Valentine, Arkansas, Texas
	Dennis Bastien, Charleston (W.Va.), South Atlantic
	Bob Beban, Eugene, Northwest
1989	Chuck Domino, Reading, Eastern
	John Baxter, South Bend, Midwest
	Bill Pereira, Boise, Northwest
1990	Joe Preseren, Tulsa, Texas
	Dan Chapman, Stockton, California
	Dave Baggott, Salt Lake City, Pioneer

MINOR LEAGUE EXECUTIVE OF THE YEAR

Year	Executive, Team, League
1993	Todd Vander Woude, Harrisburg, Eastern (AA)
1994	Scott Lane, West Michigan, Midwest (A)
1995	Jack and Mary Cain, Portland, Northwest (A)
1996	Wayne Hodes, Trenton, Eastern (AA)

Year	Executive, Team, League
1997	Andy Milovich, Erie, New York-Pennsylvania (A)
1998	Chuck Domino, Reading, Eastern (AA)
1999	Ben Mondor, Pawtucket, International

RAWLINGS GOLD GLOVE TEAMS

1957
MAJORS
P— Bobby Shantz, New York A.L.
C— Sherm Lollar, Chicago A.L.
1B— Gil Hodges, Brooklyn N.L.
2B— Nellie Fox, Chicago A.L.
3B— Frank Malzone, Boston A.L.
SS— Roy McMillan, Cincinnati N.L.
OF— Minnie Minoso, Chicago A.L.
OF— Willie Mays, New York N.L.
OF— Al Kaline, Detroit A.L.

1958
AMERICAN LEAGUE
P— Bobby Shantz, New York
C— Sherm Lollar, Chicago
1B— Vic Power, Cleveland
2B— Frank Bolling, Detroit
3B— Frank Malzone, Boston
SS— Luis Aparicio, Chicago
OF— Norm Siebern, New York
OF— Jimmy Piersall, Boston
OF— Al Kaline, Detroit

NATIONAL LEAGUE
P— Harvey Haddix, Cincinnati
C— Del Crandall, Milwaukee
1B— Gil Hodges, Los Angeles
2B— Bill Mazeroski, Pittsburgh
3B— Ken Boyer, St. Louis
SS— Roy McMillan, Cincinnati
OF— Frank Robinson, Cincinnati
OF— Willie Mays, San Francisco
OF— Hank Aaron, Milwaukee

1959
AMERICAN LEAGUE
P— Bobby Shantz, New York
C— Sherm Lollar, Chicago
1B— Vic Power, Cleveland
2B— Nellie Fox, Chicago
3B— Frank Malzone, Boston
SS— Luis Aparicio, Chicago
OF— Minnie Minoso, Cleveland
OF— Al Kaline, Detroit
OF— Jackie Jensen, Boston

NATIONAL LEAGUE
P— Harvey Haddix, Pittsburgh
C— Del Crandall, Milwaukee
1B— Gil Hodges, Los Angeles
2B— Charley Neal, Los Angeles
3B— Ken Boyer, St. Louis
SS— Roy McMillan, Cincinnati
OF— Jackie Brandt, San Francisco
OF— Willie Mays, San Francisco
OF— Hank Aaron, Milwaukee

1960
AMERICAN LEAGUE
P— Bobby Shantz, New York
C— Earl Battey, Washington
1B— Vic Power, Cleveland
2B— Nellie Fox, Chicago
3B— Brooks Robinson, Baltimore
SS— Luis Aparicio, Chicago
OF— Minnie Minoso, Chicago
OF— Jim Landis, Chicago
OF— Roger Maris, New York

NATIONAL LEAGUE
P— Harvey Haddix, Pittsburgh
C— Del Crandall, Milwaukee
1B— Bill White, St. Louis
2B— Bill Mazeroski, Pittsburgh
3B— Ken Boyer, St. Louis
SS— Ernie Banks, Chicago
OF— Wally Moon, Los Angeles
OF— Willie Mays, San Francisco
OF— Hank Aaron, Milwaukee

1961
AMERICAN LEAGUE
P— Frank Lary, Detroit
C— Earl Battey, Minnesota
1B— Vic Power, Cleveland
2B— Bobby Richardson, New York
3B— Brooks Robinson, Baltimore
SS— Luis Aparicio, Chicago
OF— Jimmy Piersall, Cleveland
OF— Jim Landis, Chicago

NATIONAL LEAGUE
P— Bobby Shantz, Pittsburgh
C— John Roseboro, Los Angeles
1B— Bill White, St. Louis
2B— Bill Mazeroski, Pittsburgh
3B— Ken Boyer, St. Louis
SS— Maury Wills, Los Angeles
OF— Willie Mays, San Francisco
OF— Roberto Clemente, Pittsburgh
OF— Vada Pinson, Cincinnati

1962
AMERICAN LEAGUE
P— Jim Kaat, Minnesota
C— Earl Battey, Minnesota
1B— Vic Power, Minnesota
2B— Bobby Richardson, New York
3B— Brooks Robinson, Baltimore
SS— Luis Aparicio, Chicago
OF— Jim Landis, Chicago
OF— Mickey Mantle, New York
OF— Al Kaline, Detroit

NATIONAL LEAGUE
P— Bobby Shantz, St. Louis
C— Del Crandall, Milwaukee
1B— Bill White, St. Louis
2B— Ken Hubbs, Chicago
3B— Jim Davenport, San Francisco
SS— Maury Wills, Los Angeles
OF— Willie Mays, San Francisco
OF— Roberto Clemente, Pittsburgh
OF— Bill Virdon, Pittsburgh

1963
AMERICAN LEAGUE
P— Jim Kaat, Minnesota
C— Elston Howard, New York
1B— Vic Power, Minnesota
2B— Bobby Richardson, New York
3B— Brooks Robinson, Baltimore
SS— Zoilo Versalles, Minnesota
OF— Al Kaline, Detroit
OF— Carl Yastrzemski, Boston
OF— Jim Landis, Chicago

1964
AMERICAN LEAGUE
P— Jim Kaat, Minnesota
C— Elston Howard, New York
1B— Vic Power, Los Angeles
2B— Bobby Richardson, New York
3B— Brooks Robinson, Baltimore
SS— Luis Aparicio, Baltimore
OF— Al Kaline, Detroit
OF— Jim Landis, Chicago
OF— Vic Davalillo, Cleveland

NATIONAL LEAGUE
P— Bobby Shantz, Philadelphia
C— Johnny Edwards, Cincinnati
1B— Bill White, St. Louis
2B— Bill Mazeroski, Pittsburgh
3B— Ron Santo, Chicago
SS— Ruben Amaro, Philadelphia
OF— Willie Mays, San Francisco
OF— Roberto Clemente, Pittsburgh
OF— Curt Flood, St. Louis

1965
AMERICAN LEAGUE
P— Jim Kaat, Minnesota
C— Bill Freehan, Detroit
1B— Joe Pepitone, New York
2B— Bobby Richardson, New York
3B— Brooks Robinson, Baltimore
SS— Zoilo Versalles, Minnesota
OF— Al Kaline, Detroit
OF— Tom Tresh, New York
OF— Carl Yastrzemski, Boston

NATIONAL LEAGUE
P— Bob Gibson, St. Louis
C— Joe Torre, Atlanta
1B— Bill White, St. Louis
2B— Bill Mazeroski, Pittsburgh
3B— Ron Santo, Chicago
SS— Leo Cardenas, Cincinnati
OF— Willie Mays, San Francisco
OF— Roberto Clemente, Pittsburgh
OF— Curt Flood, St. Louis

1966
AMERICAN LEAGUE
P— Jim Kaat, Minnesota
C— Bill Freehan, Detroit
1B— Joe Pepitone, New York
2B— Bobby Knoop, California
3B— Brooks Robinson, Baltimore
SS— Luis Aparicio, Baltimore
OF— Al Kaline, Detroit
OF— Tommie Agee, Chicago
OF— Tony Oliva, Minnesota

NATIONAL LEAGUE
P— Bobby Shantz, St. Louis
C— Johnny Edwards, Cincinnati
1B— Bill White, St. Louis
2B— Bill Mazeroski, Pittsburgh
3B— Ken Boyer, St. Louis
SS— Bobby Wine, Philadelphia
OF— Willie Mays, San Francisco
OF— Roberto Clemente, Pittsburgh
OF— Curt Flood, St. Louis

NATIONAL LEAGUE
P— Harvey Haddix, Pittsburgh
C— Del Crandall, Milwaukee
1B— Bill White, St. Louis
2B— Bill Mazeroski, Pittsburgh
3B— Ken Boyer, St. Louis
SS— Ernie Banks, Chicago
OF— Wally Moon, Los Angeles
OF— Willie Mays, San Francisco
OF— Hank Aaron, Milwaukee

HISTORY *Award winners*

NATIONAL LEAGUE
P— Bob Gibson, St. Louis
C— John Roseboro, Los Angeles
1B— Bill White, Philadelphia
2B— Bill Mazeroski, Pittsburgh
3B— Ron Santo, Chicago
SS— Gene Alley, Pittsburgh
OF— Willie Mays, San Francisco
OF— Curt Flood, St. Louis
OF— Roberto Clemente, Pittsburgh

1967
AMERICAN LEAGUE
P— Jim Kaat, Minnesota
C— Bill Freehan, Detroit
1B— George Scott, Boston
2B— Bobby Knoop, California
3B— Brooks Robinson, Baltimore
SS— Jim Fregosi, California
OF— Carl Yastrzemski, Boston
OF— Paul Blair, Baltimore
OF— Al Kaline, Detroit

NATIONAL LEAGUE
P— Bob Gibson, St. Louis
C— Randy Hundley, Chicago
1B— Wes Parker, Los Angeles
2B— Bill Mazeroski, Pittsburgh
3B— Ron Santo, Chicago
SS— Gene Alley, Pittsburgh
OF— Roberto Clemente, Pittsburgh
OF— Curt Flood, St. Louis
OF— Willie Mays, San Francisco

1968
AMERICAN LEAGUE
P— Jim Kaat, Minnesota
C— Bill Freehan, Detroit
1B— George Scott, Boston
2B— Bobby Knoop, California
3B— Brooks Robinson, Baltimore
SS— Luis Aparicio, Chicago
OF— Mickey Stanley, Detroit
OF— Carl Yastrzemski, Boston
OF— Reggie Smith, Boston

NATIONAL LEAGUE
P— Bob Gibson, St. Louis
C— Johnny Bench, Cincinnati
1B— Wes Parker, Los Angeles
2B— Glenn Beckert, Chicago
3B— Ron Santo, Chicago
SS— Dal Maxvill, St. Louis
OF— Willie Mays, San Francisco
OF— Roberto Clemente, Pittsburgh
OF— Curt Flood, St. Louis

1969
AMERICAN LEAGUE
P— Jim Kaat, Minnesota
C— Bill Freehan, Detroit
1B— Joe Pepitone, New York
2B— Dave Johnson, Baltimore
3B— Brooks Robinson, Baltimore
SS— Mark Belanger, Baltimore
OF— Paul Blair, Baltimore
OF— Mickey Stanley, Detroit
OF— Carl Yastrzemski, Boston

NATIONAL LEAGUE
P— Bob Gibson, St. Louis
C— Johnny Bench, Cincinnati
1B— Wes Parker, Los Angeles
2B— Felix Millan, Atlanta
3B— Clete Boyer, Atlanta
SS— Don Kessinger, Chicago
OF— Roberto Clemente, Pittsburgh
OF— Curt Flood, St. Louis
OF— Pete Rose, Cincinnati

1970
AMERICAN LEAGUE
P— Jim Kaat, Minnesota
C— Ray Fosse, Cleveland
1B— Jim Spencer, California
2B— Dave Johnson, Baltimore
3B— Brooks Robinson, Baltimore
SS— Luis Aparicio, Chicago
OF— Mickey Stanley, Detroit
OF— Paul Blair, Baltimore
OF— Ken Berry, Chicago

NATIONAL LEAGUE
P— Bob Gibson, St. Louis
C— Johnny Bench, Cincinnati
1B— Wes Parker, Los Angeles
2B— Tommy Helms, Cincinnati
3B— Doug Rader, Houston
SS— Don Kessinger, Chicago
OF— Roberto Clemente, Pittsburgh
OF— Tommie Agee, New York
OF— Pete Rose, Cincinnati

1971
AMERICAN LEAGUE
P— Jim Kaat, Minnesota
C— Ray Fosse, Cleveland
1B— George Scott, Boston
2B— Dave Johnson, Baltimore
3B— Brooks Robinson, Baltimore
SS— Mark Belanger, Baltimore
OF— Paul Blair, Baltimore
OF— Amos Otis, Kansas City
OF— Carl Yastrzemski, Boston

NATIONAL LEAGUE
P— Bob Gibson, St. Louis
C— Johnny Bench, Cincinnati
1B— Wes Parker, Los Angeles
2B— Tommy Helms, Cincinnati
3B— Doug Rader, Houston
SS— Bud Harrelson, New York
OF— Roberto Clemente, Pittsburgh
OF— Bobby Bonds, San Francisco
OF— Willie Davis, Los Angeles

1972
AMERICAN LEAGUE
P— Jim Kaat, Minnesota
C— Carlton Fisk, Boston
1B— George Scott, Milwaukee
2B— Doug Griffin, Boston
3B— Brooks Robinson, Baltimore
SS— Ed Brinkman, Detroit
OF— Paul Blair, Baltimore
OF— Bobby Murcer, New York
OF— Ken Berry, California

NATIONAL LEAGUE
P— Bob Gibson, St. Louis
C— Johnny Bench, Cincinnati
1B— Wes Parker, Los Angeles
2B— Felix Millan, Atlanta
3B— Doug Rader, Houston
SS— Larry Bowa, Philadelphia
OF— Roberto Clemente, Pittsburgh
OF— Cesar Cedeno, Houston
OF— Willie Davis, Los Angeles

1973
AMERICAN LEAGUE
P— Jim Kaat, Chicago
C— Thurman Munson, New York
1B— George Scott, Milwaukee
2B— Bobby Grich, Baltimore
3B— Brooks Robinson, Baltimore
SS— Mark Belanger, Baltimore
OF— Paul Blair, Baltimore
OF— Amos Otis, Kansas City
OF— Mickey Stanley, Detroit

NATIONAL LEAGUE
P— Bob Gibson, St. Louis
C— Johnny Bench, Cincinnati
1B— Mike Jorgensen, Montreal
2B— Joe Morgan, Cincinnati
3B— Doug Rader, Houston
SS— Roger Metzger, Houston
OF— Bobby Bonds, San Francisco
OF— Cesar Cedeno, Houston
OF— Willie Davis, Los Angeles

1974
AMERICAN LEAGUE
P— Jim Kaat, Chicago
C— Thurman Munson, New York
1B— George Scott, Milwaukee
2B— Bobby Grich, Baltimore
3B— Brooks Robinson, Baltimore
SS— Mark Belanger, Baltimore
OF— Paul Blair, Baltimore
OF— Amos Otis, Kansas City
OF— Joe Rudi, Oakland

NATIONAL LEAGUE
P— Andy Messersmith, Los Angeles
C— Johnny Bench, Cincinnati
1B— Steve Garvey, Los Angeles
2B— Joe Morgan, Cincinnati
3B— Doug Rader, Houston
SS— Dave Concepcion, Cincinnati
OF— Cesar Cedeno, Houston
OF— Cesar Geronimo, Cincinnati
OF— Bobby Bonds, San Francisco

1975
AMERICAN LEAGUE
P— Jim Kaat, Chicago
C— Thurman Munson, New York
1B— George Scott, Milwaukee
2B— Bobby Grich, Baltimore
3B— Brooks Robinson, Baltimore
SS— Mark Belanger, Baltimore
OF— Paul Blair, Baltimore
OF— Joe Rudi, Oakland
OF— Fred Lynn, Boston

NATIONAL LEAGUE
P— Andy Messersmith, Los Angeles
C— Johnny Bench, Cincinnati
1B— Steve Garvey, Los Angeles
2B— Joe Morgan, Cincinnati
3B— Ken Reitz, St. Louis
SS— Dave Concepcion, Cincinnati
OF— Cesar Cedeno, Houston
OF— Cesar Geronimo, Cincinnati
OF— Garry Maddox, Philadelphia

1976
AMERICAN LEAGUE
P— Jim Palmer, Baltimore
C— Jim Sundberg, Texas
1B— George Scott, Milwaukee
2B— Bobby Grich, Baltimore
3B— Aurelio Rodriguez, Detroit
SS— Mark Belanger, Baltimore
OF— Joe Rudi, Oakland
OF— Dwight Evans, Boston
OF— Rick Manning, Cleveland

NATIONAL LEAGUE
P— Jim Kaat, Philadelphia
C— Johnny Bench, Cincinnati
1B— Steve Garvey, Los Angeles
2B— Joe Morgan, Cincinnati
3B— Mike Schmidt, Philadelphia
SS— Dave Concepcion, Cincinnati
OF— Cesar Cedeno, Houston
OF— Cesar Geronimo, Cincinnati
OF— Garry Maddox, Philadelphia

1977
AMERICAN LEAGUE
P— Jim Palmer, Baltimore
C— Jim Sundberg, Texas
1B— Jim Spencer, Chicago
2B— Frank White, Kansas City
3B— Graig Nettles, New York
SS— Mark Belanger, Baltimore
OF— Juan Beniquez, Texas
OF— Carl Yastrzemski, Boston
OF— Al Cowens, Kansas City

NATIONAL LEAGUE
P— Jim Kaat, Philadelphia
C— Johnny Bench, Cincinnati
1B— Steve Garvey, Los Angeles
2B— Joe Morgan, Cincinnati
3B— Mike Schmidt, Philadelphia
SS— Dave Concepcion, Cincinnati
OF— Cesar Geronimo, Cincinnati
OF— Garry Maddox, Philadelphia
OF— Dave Parker, Pittsburgh

1978
AMERICAN LEAGUE
P— Jim Palmer, Baltimore
C— Jim Sundberg, Texas
1B— Chris Chambliss, New York
2B— Frank White, Kansas City
3B— Graig Nettles, New York
SS— Mark Belanger, Baltimore
OF— Fred Lynn, Boston
OF— Dwight Evans, Boston
OF— Rick Miller, California

NATIONAL LEAGUE
P— Phil Niekro, Atlanta
C— Bob Boone, Philadelphia
1B— Keith Hernandez, St. Louis
2B— Dave Lopes, Los Angeles
3B— Mike Schmidt, Philadelphia
SS— Larry Bowa, Philadelphia
OF— Garry Maddox, Philadelphia
OF— Dave Parker, Pittsburgh
OF— Ellis Valentine, Montreal

1979
AMERICAN LEAGUE
P— Jim Palmer, Baltimore
C— Jim Sundberg, Texas
1B— Cecil Cooper, Milwaukee
2B— Frank White, Kansas City
3B— Buddy Bell, Texas
SS— Rick Burleson, Boston
OF— Dwight Evans, Boston
OF— Sixto Lezcano, Milwaukee
OF— Fred Lynn, Boston

NATIONAL LEAGUE
P— Phil Niekro, Atlanta
C— Bob Boone, Philadelphia
1B— Keith Hernandez, St. Louis
2B— Manny Trillo, Philadelphia
3B— Mike Schmidt, Philadelphia
SS— Dave Concepcion, Cincinnati
OF— Garry Maddox, Philadelphia
OF— Dave Parker, Pittsburgh
OF— Dave Winfield, San Diego

1980
AMERICAN LEAGUE
P— Mike Norris, Oakland
C— Jim Sundberg, Texas
1B— Cecil Cooper, Milwaukee
2B— Frank White, Kansas City
3B— Buddy Bell, Texas
SS— Alan Trammell, Detroit
OF— Fred Lynn, Boston
OF— Dwayne Murphy, Oakland
OF— Willie Wilson, Kansas City

NATIONAL LEAGUE
P— Phil Niekro, Atlanta
C— Gary Carter, Montreal
1B— Keith Hernandez, St. Louis
2B— Doug Flynn, New York
3B— Mike Schmidt, Philadelphia
SS— Ozzie Smith, San Diego
OF— Andre Dawson, Montreal
OF— Garry Maddox, Philadelphia
OF— Dave Winfield, San Diego

1981
AMERICAN LEAGUE
P— Mike Norris, Oakland
C— Jim Sundberg, Texas
1B— Mike Squires, Chicago
2B— Frank White, Kansas City
3B— Buddy Bell, Texas
SS— Alan Trammell, Detroit
OF— Dwayne Murphy, Oakland
OF— Dwight Evans, Boston
OF— Rickey Henderson, Oakland

NATIONAL LEAGUE
P— Steve Carlton, Philadelphia
C— Gary Carter, Montreal
1B— Keith Hernandez, St. Louis
2B— Manny Trillo, Philadelphia
3B— Mike Schmidt, Philadelphia
SS— Ozzie Smith, San Diego
OF— Andre Dawson, Montreal
OF— Garry Maddox, Philadelphia
OF— Dusty Baker, Los Angeles

1982
AMERICAN LEAGUE
P— Ron Guidry, New York
C— Bob Boone, California
1B— Eddie Murray, Baltimore
2B— Frank White, Kansas City
3B— Buddy Bell, Texas
SS— Robin Yount, Milwaukee
OF— Dwight Evans, Boston
OF— Dave Winfield, New York
OF— Dwayne Murphy, Oakland

NATIONAL LEAGUE
P— Phil Niekro, Atlanta
C— Gary Carter, Montreal
1B— Keith Hernandez, St. Louis
2B— Manny Trillo, Philadelphia
3B— Mike Schmidt, Philadelphia
SS— Ozzie Smith, St. Louis
OF— Andre Dawson, Montreal
OF— Dale Murphy, Atlanta
OF— Garry Maddox, Philadelphia

1983
AMERICAN LEAGUE
P— Ron Guidry, New York
C— Lance Parrish, Detroit
1B— Eddie Murray, Baltimore
2B— Lou Whitaker, Detroit
3B— Buddy Bell, Texas
SS— Alan Trammell, Detroit
OF— Dwight Evans, Boston
OF— Dave Winfield, New York
OF— Dwayne Murphy, Oakland

NATIONAL LEAGUE
P— Phil Niekro, Atlanta
C— Tony Pena, Pittsburgh
1B— Keith Hernandez, St.L.-N.Y.
2B— Ryne Sandberg, Chicago
3B— Mike Schmidt, Philadelphia
SS— Ozzie Smith, St. Louis
OF— Andre Dawson, Montreal
OF— Dale Murphy, Atlanta
OF— Willie McGee, St. Louis

1984
AMERICAN LEAGUE
P— Ron Guidry, New York
C— Lance Parrish, Detroit
1B— Eddie Murray, Baltimore
2B— Lou Whitaker, Detroit
3B— Buddy Bell, Texas
SS— Alan Trammell, Detroit
OF— Dwight Evans, Boston
OF— Dave Winfield, New York
OF— Dwayne Murphy, Oakland

NATIONAL LEAGUE
P— Joaquin Andujar, St. Louis
C— Tony Pena, Pittsburgh
1B— Keith Hernandez, New York
2B— Ryne Sandberg, Chicago
3B— Mike Schmidt, Philadelphia
SS— Ozzie Smith, St. Louis
OF— Dale Murphy, Atlanta
OF— Bob Dernier, Chicago
OF— Andre Dawson, Montreal

1985
AMERICAN LEAGUE
P— Ron Guidry, New York
C— Lance Parrish, Detroit
1B— Don Mattingly, New York
2B— Lou Whitaker, Detroit
3B— George Brett, Kansas City
SS— Alfredo Griffin, Oakland
OF— Gary Pettis, California
OF— Dave Winfield, New York
OF— Dwight Evans, Boston (tie)
     Dwayne Murphy, Oakland (tie)

NATIONAL LEAGUE
P— Rick Reuschel, Pittsburgh
C— Tony Pena, Pittsburgh
1B— Keith Hernandez, New York
2B— Ryne Sandberg, Chicago
3B— Tim Wallach, Montreal
SS— Ozzie Smith, St. Louis
OF— Willie McGee, St. Louis
OF— Dale Murphy, Atlanta
OF— Andre Dawson, Montreal

1986
AMERICAN LEAGUE
P— Ron Guidry, New York
C— Bob Boone, California
1B— Don Mattingly, New York
2B— Frank White, Kansas City
3B— Gary Gaetti, Minnesota
SS— Tony Fernandez, Toronto
OF— Gary Pettis, California
OF— Jesse Barfield, Toronto
OF— Kirby Puckett, Minnesota

NATIONAL LEAGUE
P— Fernando Valenzuela, Los Angeles
C— Jody Davis, Chicago
1B— Keith Hernandez, New York
2B— Ryne Sandberg, Chicago
3B— Mike Schmidt, Philadelphia
SS— Ozzie Smith, St. Louis
OF— Tony Gwynn, San Diego
OF— Dale Murphy, Atlanta
OF— Willie McGee, St. Louis

1987
AMERICAN LEAGUE
P— Mark Langston, Seattle
C— Bob Boone, California
1B— Don Mattingly, New York
2B— Frank White, Kansas City
3B— Gary Gaetti, Minnesota
SS— Tony Fernandez, Toronto
OF— Jesse Barfield, Toronto
OF— Kirby Puckett, Minnesota
OF— Dave Winfield, New York

NATIONAL LEAGUE
P— Rick Reuschel, Pit.-S.F.
C— Mike LaValliere, Pittsburgh
1B— Keith Hernandez, New York
2B— Ryne Sandberg, Chicago
3B— Terry Pendleton, St. Louis
SS— Ozzie Smith, St. Louis
OF— Eric Davis, Cincinnati
OF— Tony Gwynn, San Diego
OF— Andre Dawson, Chicago

1988
AMERICAN LEAGUE
P— Mark Langston, Seattle
C— Bob Boone, California
1B— Don Mattingly, New York
2B— Harold Reynolds, Seattle
3B— Gary Gaetti, Minnesota
SS— Tony Fernandez, Toronto
OF— Kirby Puckett, Minnesota
OF— Devon White, California
OF— Gary Pettis, Detroit

NATIONAL LEAGUE
P— Orel Hershiser, Los Angeles
C— Benito Santiago, San Diego
1B— Keith Hernandez, New York
2B— Ryne Sandberg, Chicago
3B— Tim Wallach, Montreal
SS— Ozzie Smith, St. Louis
OF— Andy Van Slyke, Pittsburgh
OF— Eric Davis, Cincinnati
OF— Andre Dawson, Chicago

1989
AMERICAN LEAGUE
P— Bret Saberhagen, Kansas City
C— Bob Boone, Kansas City
1B— Don Mattingly, New York
2B— Harold Reynolds, Seattle
3B— Gary Gaetti, Minnesota
SS— Tony Fernandez, Toronto
OF— Kirby Puckett, Minnesota
OF— Devon White, California
OF— Gary Pettis, Detroit

NATIONAL LEAGUE
P— Ron Darling, New York
C— Benito Santiago, San Diego
1B— Andres Galarraga, Montreal
2B— Ryne Sandberg, Chicago
3B— Terry Pendleton, St. Louis
SS— Ozzie Smith, St. Louis
OF— Andy Van Slyke, Pittsburgh
OF— Tony Gwynn, San Diego
OF— Eric Davis, Cincinnati

1990
AMERICAN LEAGUE
P— Mike Boddicker, Boston
C— Sandy Alomar Jr., Cleveland
1B— Mark McGwire, Oakland
2B— Harold Reynolds, Seattle
3B— Kelly Gruber, Toronto
SS— Ozzie Guillen, Chicago
OF— Ken Griffey Jr., Seattle
OF— Ellis Burks, Boston
OF— Gary Pettis, Texas

NATIONAL LEAGUE
P— Greg Maddux, Chicago
C— Benito Santiago, San Diego
1B— Andres Galarraga, Montreal
2B— Ryne Sandberg, Chicago
3B— Tim Wallach, Montreal
SS— Ozzie Smith, St. Louis
OF— Barry Bonds, Pittsburgh
OF— Andy Van Slyke, Pittsburgh
OF— Tony Gwynn, San Diego

1991
AMERICAN LEAGUE
P— Mark Langston, California
C— Tony Pena, Boston
1B— Don Mattingly, New York
2B— Roberto Alomar, Toronto
3B— Robin Ventura, Chicago
SS— Cal Ripken, Baltimore
OF— Ken Griffey Jr., Seattle
OF— Kirby Puckett, Minnesota
OF— Devon White, Toronto

NATIONAL LEAGUE
P— Greg Maddux, Chicago
C— Tom Pagnozzi, St. Louis
1B— Will Clark, San Francisco
2B— Ryne Sandberg, Chicago
3B— Matt Williams, San Francisco
SS— Ozzie Smith, St. Louis
OF— Barry Bonds, Pittsburgh
OF— Andy Van Slyke, Pittsburgh
OF— Tony Gwynn, San Diego

1992
AMERICAN LEAGUE
P— Mark Langston, California
C— Ivan Rodriguez, Texas
1B— Don Mattingly, New York
2B— Roberto Alomar, Toronto
3B— Robin Ventura, Chicago
SS— Cal Ripken, Baltimore
OF— Ken Griffey Jr., Seattle
OF— Kirby Puckett, Minnesota
OF— Devon White, Toronto

NATIONAL LEAGUE
P— Greg Maddux, Chicago
C— Tom Pagnozzi, St. Louis
1B— Mark Grace, Chicago
2B— Jose Lind, Pittsburgh
3B— Terry Pendleton, Atlanta
SS— Ozzie Smith, St. Louis
OF— Barry Bonds, Pittsburgh
OF— Andy Van Slyke, Pittsburgh
OF— Larry Walker, Montreal

1993
AMERICAN LEAGUE
P— Mark Langston, California
C— Ivan Rodriguez, Texas
1B— Don Mattingly, New York
2B— Roberto Alomar, Toronto
3B— Robin Ventura, Chicago
SS— Omar Vizquel, Seattle
OF— Ken Griffey Jr., Seattle
OF— Kenny Lofton, Cleveland
OF— Devon White, Toronto

NATIONAL LEAGUE
P— Greg Maddux, Atlanta
C— Kirt Manwaring, San Francisco
1B— Mark Grace, Chicago
2B— Robby Thompson, San Fran.
3B— Matt Williams, San Francisco
SS— Jay Bell, Pittsburgh
OF— Barry Bonds, San Francisco
OF— Marquis Grissom, Montreal
OF— Larry Walker, Montreal

1994
AMERICAN LEAGUE
P— Mark Langston, California
C— Ivan Rodriguez, Texas
1B— Don Mattingly, New York
2B— Roberto Alomar, Toronto
3B— Wade Boggs, New York
SS— Omar Vizquel, Cleveland
OF— Ken Griffey Jr., Seattle
OF— Kenny Lofton, Cleveland
OF— Devon White, Toronto

NATIONAL LEAGUE
P— Greg Maddux, Atlanta
C— Tom Pagnozzi, St. Louis
1B— Jeff Bagwell, Houston
2B— Craig Biggio, Houston
3B— Matt Williams, San Francisco
SS— Barry Larkin, Cincinnati
OF— Barry Bonds, San Francisco
OF— Marquis Grissom, Montreal
OF— Darren Lewis, San Francisco

1995
AMERICAN LEAGUE
P— Mark Langston, California
C— Ivan Rodriguez, Texas
1B— J.T. Snow, California
2B— Roberto Alomar, Toronto
3B— Wade Boggs, New York
SS— Omar Vizquel, Cleveland
OF— Ken Griffey Jr., Seattle
OF— Kenny Lofton, Cleveland
OF— Devon White, Toronto

NATIONAL LEAGUE
P— Greg Maddux, Atlanta
C— Charles Johnson, Florida
1B— Mark Grace, Chicago
2B— Craig Biggio, Houston
3B— Ken Caminiti, San Diego
SS— Barry Larkin, Cincinnati
OF— Raul Mondesi, Los Angeles
OF— Marquis Grissom, Atlanta
OF— Steve Finley, San Diego

1996
AMERICAN LEAGUE
P— Mike Mussina, Baltimore
C— Ivan Rodriguez, Texas
1B— J.T. Snow, California
2B— Roberto Alomar, Baltimore
3B— Robin Ventura, Chicago
SS— Omar Vizquel, Cleveland
OF— Jay Buhner, Seattle
OF— Ken Griffey Jr., Seattle
OF— Kenny Lofton, Cleveland

NATIONAL LEAGUE
P— Greg Maddux, Atlanta
C— Charles Johnson, Florida
1B— Mark Grace, Chicago
2B— Craig Biggio, Houston
3B— Ken Caminiti, San Diego
SS— Barry Larkin, Cincinnati
OF— Barry Bonds, San Francisco
OF— Marquis Grissom, Atlanta
OF— Steve Finley, San Diego

1997
AMERICAN LEAGUE
P— Mike Mussina, Baltimore
C— Ivan Rodriguez, Texas
1B— Rafael Palmeiro, Baltimore
2B— Chuck Knoblauch, Minnesota
3B— Matt Williams, Cleveland
SS— Omar Vizquel, Cleveland
OF— Jim Edmonds, Anaheim
OF— Ken Griffey Jr., Seattle
OF— Bernie Williams, New York

NATIONAL LEAGUE
P— Greg Maddux, Atlanta
C— Charles Johnson, Florida
1B— J.T. Snow, San Francisco
2B— Craig Biggio, Houston
3B— Ken Caminiti, San Diego
SS— Rey Ordonez, New York
OF— Barry Bonds, San Francisco
OF— Raul Mondesi, Los Angeles
OF— Larry Walker, Colorado

1998
AMERICAN LEAGUE
P— Mike Mussina, Baltimore
C— Ivan Rodriguez, Texas
1B— Rafael Palmeiro, Baltimore
2B— Roberto Alomar, Baltimore
3B— Robin Ventura, White Sox
SS— Omar Vizquel, Cleveland
OF— Jim Edmonds, Anaheim
OF— Ken Griffey Jr., Seattle
OF— Bernie Williams, New York

NATIONAL LEAGUE
P— Greg Maddux, Atlanta
C— Charles Johnson, Fla.-L.A.

1B— J.T. Snow, San Francisco
2B— Bret Boone, Cincinnati
3B— Scott Rolen, Philadelphia
SS— Rey Ordonez, New York
OF— Barry Bonds, San Francisco
OF— Andruw Jones, Atlanta
OF— Larry Walker, Colorado

1999
AMERICAN LEAGUE
P— Mike Mussina, Baltimore
C— Ivan Rodriguez, Texas
1B— Rafael Palmeiro, Texas
2B— Roberto Alomar, Cleveland
3B— Scott Brosius, New York

SS— Omar Vizquel, Cleveland
OF— Shawn Green, Toronto
OF— Ken Griffey Jr., Seattle
OF— Bernie Williams, New York

NATIONAL LEAGUE
P— Greg Maddux, Atlanta
C— Mike Lieberthal, Philadelphia
1B— J.T. Snow, San Francisco
2B— Pokey Reese, Cincinnati
3B— Robin Ventura, New York
SS— Rey Ordonez, New York
OF— Steve Finley, Arizona
OF— Andruw Jones, Atlanta
OF— Larry Walker, Colorado

HILLERICH & BRADSBY SILVER SLUGGER TEAMS

1980
AMERICAN LEAGUE
1B— Cecil Cooper, Milwaukee
2B— Willie Randolph, New York
3B— George Brett, Kansas City
SS— Robin Yount, Milwaukee
OF— Ben Oglivie, Milwaukee
OF— Al Oliver, Texas
OF— Willie Wilson, Kansas City
C— Lance Parrish, Detroit
DH— Reggie Jackson, New York

NATIONAL LEAGUE
1B— Keith Hernandez, St. Louis
2B— Manny Trillo, Philadelphia
3B— Mike Schmidt, Philadelphia
SS— Garry Templeton, St. Louis
OF— Dusty Baker, Los Angeles
OF— Andre Dawson, Montreal
OF— George Hendrick, St. Louis
C— Ted Simmons, St. Louis
P— Bob Forsch, St. Louis

1981
AMERICAN LEAGUE
1B— Cecil Cooper, Milwaukee
2B— Bobby Grich, California
3B— Carney Lansford, Boston
SS— Rick Burleson, California
OF— Rickey Henderson, Oakland
OF— Dwight Evans, Boston
OF— Dave Winfield, New York
C— Carlton Fisk, Chicago
DH— Al Oliver, Texas

NATIONAL LEAGUE
1B— Pete Rose, Philadelphia
2B— Manny Trillo, Philadelphia
3B— Mike Schmidt, Philadelphia
SS— Dave Concepcion, Cincinnati
OF— Andre Dawson, Montreal
OF— George Foster, Cincinnati
OF— Dusty Baker, Los Angeles
C— Gary Carter, Montreal
P— Fernando Valenzuela, Los Angeles

1982
AMERICAN LEAGUE
1B— Cecil Cooper, Milwaukee
2B— Damaso Garcia, Toronto
3B— Doug DeCinces, California
SS— Robin Yount, Milwaukee
OF— Dave Winfield, New York
OF— Willie Wilson, Kansas City
OF— Reggie Jackson, California
C— Lance Parrish, Detroit
DH— Hal McRae, Kansas City

NATIONAL LEAGUE
1B— Al Oliver, Montreal
2B— Joe Morgan, San Francisco

3B— Mike Schmidt, Philadelphia
SS— Dave Concepcion, Cincinnati
OF— Dale Murphy, Atlanta
OF— Pedro Guerrero, Los Angeles
OF— Leon Durham, Chicago
C— Gary Carter, Montreal
P— Don Robinson, Pittsburgh

1983
AMERICAN LEAGUE
1B— Eddie Murray, Baltimore
2B— Lou Whitaker, Detroit
3B— Wade Boggs, Boston
SS— Cal Ripken Jr., Baltimore
OF— Jim Rice, Boston
OF— Dave Winfield, New York
OF— Lloyd Moseby, Toronto
C— Lance Parrish, Detroit
DH— Don Baylor, New York

NATIONAL LEAGUE
1B— George Hendrick, St. Louis
2B— Johnny Ray, Pittsburgh
3B— Mike Schmidt, Philadelphia
SS— Dickie Thon, Houston
OF— Andre Dawson, Montreal
OF— Dale Murphy, Atlanta
OF— Jose Cruz, Houston
C— Terry Kennedy, San Diego
P— Fernando Valenzuela, Los Angeles

1984
AMERICAN LEAGUE
1B— Eddie Murray, Baltimore
2B— Lou Whitaker, Detroit
3B— Buddy Bell, Texas
SS— Cal Ripken Jr., Baltimore
OF— Tony Armas, Boston
OF— Jim Rice, Boston
OF— Dave Winfield, New York
C— Lance Parrish, Detroit
DH— Andre Thornton, Cleveland

NATIONAL LEAGUE
1B— Keith Hernandez, New York
2B— Ryne Sandberg, Chicago
3B— Mike Schmidt, Philadelphia
SS— Garry Templeton, San Diego
OF— Dale Murphy, Atlanta
OF— Jose Cruz, Houston
OF— Tony Gwynn, San Diego
C— Gary Carter, Montreal
P— Rick Rhoden, Pittsburgh

1985
AMERICAN LEAGUE
1B— Don Mattingly, New York
2B— Lou Whitaker, Detroit
3B— George Brett, Kansas City
SS— Cal Ripken Jr., Baltimore
OF— Rickey Henderson, New York

OF— Dave Winfield, New York
OF— George Bell, Toronto
C— Carlton Fisk, Chicago
DH— Don Baylor, New York

NATIONAL LEAGUE
1B— Jack Clark, St. Louis
2B— Ryne Sandberg, Chicago
3B— Tim Wallach, Montreal
SS— Hubie Brooks, Montreal
OF— Willie McGee, St. Louis
OF— Dale Murphy, Atlanta
OF— Dave Parker, Cincinnati
C— Gary Carter, New York
P— Rick Rhoden, Pittsburgh

1986
AMERICAN LEAGUE
1B— Don Mattingly, New York
2B— Frank White, Kansas City
3B— Wade Boggs, Boston
SS— Cal Ripken Jr., Baltimore
OF— George Bell, Toronto
OF— Kirby Puckett, Minnesota
OF— Jesse Barfield, Toronto
C— Lance Parrish, Detroit
DH— Don Baylor, Boston

NATIONAL LEAGUE
1B— Glenn Davis, Houston
2B— Steve Sax, Los Angeles
3B— Mike Schmidt, Philadelphia
SS— Hubie Brooks, Montreal
OF— Tony Gwynn, San Diego
OF— Tim Raines, Montreal
OF— Dave Parker, Cincinnati
C— Gary Carter, New York
P— Rick Rhoden, Pittsburgh

1987
AMERICAN LEAGUE
1B— Don Mattingly, New York
2B— Lou Whitaker, Detroit
3B— Wade Boggs, Boston
SS— Alan Trammell, Detroit
OF— George Bell, Toronto
OF— Dwight Evans, Boston
OF— Kirby Puckett, Minnesota
C— Matt Nokes, Detroit
DH— Paul Molitor, Milwaukee

NATIONAL LEAGUE
1B— Jack Clark, St. Louis
2B— Juan Samuel, Philadelphia
3B— Tim Wallach, Montreal
SS— Ozzie Smith, St. Louis
OF— Andre Dawson, Chicago
OF— Eric Davis, Cincinnati
OF— Tony Gwynn, San Diego
C— Benito Santiago, San Diego
P— Bob Forsch, St. Louis

HISTORY *Award winners*

1988

AMERICAN LEAGUE
1B— George Brett, Kansas City
2B— Julio Franco, Cleveland
3B— Wade Boggs, Boston
SS— Alan Trammell, Detroit
OF— Kirby Puckett, Minnesota
OF— Jose Canseco, Oakland
OF— Mike Greenwell, Boston
C— Carlton Fisk, Chicago
DH— Paul Molitor, Milwaukee

NATIONAL LEAGUE
1B— Andres Galarraga, Montreal
2B— Ryne Sandberg, Chicago
3B— Bobby Bonilla, Pittsburgh
SS— Barry Larkin, Cincinnati
OF— Darryl Strawberry, New York
OF— Andy Van Slyke, Pittsburgh
OF— Kirk Gibson, Los Angeles
C— Benito Santiago, San Diego
P— Tim Leary, Los Angeles

1989

AMERICAN LEAGUE
1B— Fred McGriff, Toronto
2B— Julio Franco, Texas
3B— Wade Boggs, Boston
SS— Cal Ripken Jr., Baltimore
OF— Kirby Puckett, Minnesota
OF— Ruben Sierra, Texas
OF— Robin Yount, Milwaukee
C— Mickey Tettleton, Baltimore
DH— Harold Baines, Chi.-Tex.

NATIONAL LEAGUE
1B— Will Clark, San Francisco
2B— Ryne Sandberg, Chicago
3B— Howard Johnson, New York
SS— Barry Larkin, Cincinnati
OF— Kevin Mitchell, San Francisco
OF— Tony Gwynn, San Diego
OF— Eric Davis, Cincinnati
C— Craig Biggio, Houston
P— Don Robinson, San Francisco

1990

AMERICAN LEAGUE
1B— Cecil Fielder, Detroit
2B— Julio Franco, Texas
3B— Kelly Gruber, Toronto
SS— Alan Trammell, Detroit
OF— Rickey Henderson, Oakland
OF— Jose Canseco, Oakland
OF— Ellis Burks, Boston
C— Lance Parrish, California
DH— Dave Parker, Milwaukee

NATIONAL LEAGUE
1B— Eddie Murray, Los Angeles
2B— Ryne Sandberg, Chicago
3B— Matt Williams, San Francisco
SS— Barry Larkin, Cincinnati
OF— Barry Bonds, Pittsburgh
OF— Bobby Bonilla, Pittsburgh
OF— Darryl Strawberry, New York
C— Benito Santiago, San Diego
P— Don Robinson, San Francisco

1991

AMERICAN LEAGUE
1B— Cecil Fielder, Detroit
2B— Julio Franco, Texas
3B— Wade Boggs, Boston
SS— Cal Ripken Jr., Baltimore
OF— Jose Canseco, Oakland
OF— Joe Carter, Toronto
OF— Ken Griffey Jr., Seattle
C— Mickey Tettleton, Detroit
DH— Frank Thomas, Chicago

NATIONAL LEAGUE
1B— Will Clark, San Francisco
2B— Ryne Sandberg, Chicago
3B— Howard Johnson, New York
SS— Barry Larkin, Cincinnati
OF— Barry Bonds, Pittsburgh
OF— Bobby Bonilla, Pittsburgh
OF— Ron Gant, Atlanta
C— Benito Santiago, San Diego
P— Tom Glavine, Atlanta

1992

AMERICAN LEAGUE
1B— Mark McGwire, Oakland
2B— Roberto Alomar, Toronto
3B— Edgar Martinez, Seattle
SS— Travis Fryman, Detroit
OF— Joe Carter, Toronto
OF— Juan Gonzalez, Texas
OF— Kirby Puckett, Minnesota
C— Mickey Tettleton, Detroit
DH— Dave Winfield, Toronto

NATIONAL LEAGUE
1B— Fred McGriff, San Diego
2B— Ryne Sandberg, Chicago
3B— Gary Sheffield, San Diego
SS— Barry Larkin, Cincinnati
OF— Barry Bonds, Pittsburgh
OF— Andy Van Slyke, Pittsburgh
OF— Larry Walker, Montreal
C— Darren Daulton, Philadelphia
P— Dwight Gooden, New York

1993

AMERICAN LEAGUE
1B— Frank Thomas, Chicago
2B— Carlos Baerga, Cleveland
3B— Wade Boggs, New York
SS— Cal Ripken Jr., Baltimore
OF— Albert Belle, Cleveland
OF— Juan Gonzalez, Texas
OF— Ken Griffey Jr., Seattle
C— Mike Stanley, New York
DH— Paul Molitor, Toronto

NATIONAL LEAGUE
1B— Fred McGriff, S.D.-Atl.
2B— Robby Thompson, San Fran.
3B— Matt Williams, San Francisco
SS— Jay Bell, Pittsburgh
OF— Barry Bonds, San Francisco
OF— Lenny Dykstra, Philadelphia
OF— David Justice, Atlanta
C— Mike Piazza, Los Angeles
P— Orel Hershiser, Los Angeles

1994

AMERICAN LEAGUE
1B— Frank Thomas, Chicago
2B— Carlos Baerga, Cleveland
3B— Wade Boggs, New York
SS— Cal Ripken Jr., Baltimore
OF— Albert Belle, Cleveland
OF— Ken Griffey Jr., Seattle
OF— Kirby Puckett, Minnesota
C— Ivan Rodriguez, Texas
DH— Julio Franco, Chicago

NATIONAL LEAGUE
1B— Jeff Bagwell, Houston
2B— Craig Biggio, Houston
3B— Matt Williams, San Francisco
SS— Wil Cordero, Montreal
OF— Moises Alou, Montreal
OF— Barry Bonds, San Francisco
OF— Tony Gwynn, San Diego
C— Mike Piazza, Los Angeles
P— Mark Portugal, San Francisco

1995

AMERICAN LEAGUE
1B— Mo Vaughn, Boston
2B— Chuck Knoblauch, Minnesota
3B— Gary Gaetti, Kansas City
SS— John Valentin, Boston
OF— Albert Belle, Cleveland
OF— Tim Salmon, California
OF— Manny Ramirez, Cleveland
C— Ivan Rodriguez, Texas
DH— Edgar Martinez, Seattle

NATIONAL LEAGUE
1B— Eric Karros, Los Angeles
2B— Craig Biggio, Houston
3B— Vinny Castilla, Colorado
SS— Barry Larkin, Cincinnati
OF— Dante Bichette, Colorado
OF— Tony Gwynn, San Diego
OF— Sammy Sosa, Chicago
C— Mike Piazza, Los Angeles
P— Tom Glavine, Atlanta

1996

AMERICAN LEAGUE
1B— Mark McGwire, Oakland
2B— Roberto Alomar, Baltimore
3B— Jim Thome, Cleveland
SS— Alex Rodriguez, Seattle
OF— Albert Belle, Cleveland
OF— Juan Gonzalez, Texas
OF— Ken Griffey Jr., Seattle
C— Ivan Rodriguez, Texas
DH— Paul Molitor, Minnesota

NATIONAL LEAGUE
1B— Andres Galarraga, Colorado
2B— Eric Young, Colorado
3B— Ken Caminiti, San Diego
SS— Barry Larkin, Cincinnati
OF— Barry Bonds, San Francisco
OF— Ellis Burks, Colorado
OF— Gary Sheffield, Florida
C— Mike Piazza, Los Angeles
P— Tom Glavine, Atlanta

1997

AMERICAN LEAGUE
1B— Tino Martinez, New York
2B— Chuck Knoblauch, Minnesota
3B— Matt Williams, Cleveland
SS— Nomar Garciaparra, Boston
OF— Juan Gonzalez, Texas
OF— Ken Griffey Jr., Seattle
OF— David Justice, Cleveland
C— Ivan Rodriguez, Texas
DH— Edgar Martinez, Seattle

NATIONAL LEAGUE
1B— Jeff Bagwell, Houston
2B— Craig Biggio, Houston
3B— Vinny Castilla, Colorado
SS— Jeff Blauser, Atlanta
OF— Barry Bonds, San Francisco
OF— Tony Gwynn, San Diego
OF— Larry Walker, Colorado
C— Mike Piazza, Los Angeles
P— John Smoltz, Atlanta

1998

AMERICAN LEAGUE
1B— Rafael Palmeiro, Baltimore
2B— Damion Easley, Detroit
3B— Dean Palmer, Kansas City
SS— Alex Rodriguez, Seattle
OF— Juan Gonzalez, Texas
OF— Ken Griffey Jr., Seattle
OF— Albert Belle, Chicago
C— Ivan Rodriguez, Texas
DH— Jose Canseco, Toronto

BASEBALL WRITERS' ASSOCIATION OF AMERICA
MOST VALUABLE PLAYER

AMERICAN LEAGUE

Year Player	Team	Pos.	Points
1931—Lefty Grove	Philadelphia	P	78
1932—Jimmie Foxx	Philadelphia	1B	75
1933—Jimmie Foxx	Philadelphia	1B	74
1934—Mickey Cochrane	Detroit	C	67
1935—Hank Greenberg	Detroit	1B	*80
1936—Lou Gehrig	New York	1B	73
1937—Charley Gehringer	Detroit	2B	78
1938—Jimmie Foxx	Boston	1B	305
1939—Joe DiMaggio	New York	OF	280
1940—Hank Greenberg	Detroit	OF	292
1941—Joe DiMaggio	New York	OF	291
1942—Joe Gordon	New York	2B	270
1943—Spud Chandler	New York	P	246
1944—Hal Newhouser	Detroit	P	236
1945—Hal Newhouser	Detroit	P	236
1946—Ted Williams	Boston	OF	224
1947—Joe DiMaggio	New York	OF	202
1948—Lou Boudreau	Cleveland	SS	324
1949—Ted Williams	Boston	OF	272
1950—Phil Rizzuto	New York	SS	284
1951—Yogi Berra	New York	C	184
1952—Bobby Shantz	Philadelphia	P	280
1953—Al Rosen	Cleveland	3B	*336
1954—Yogi Berra	New York	C	230
1955—Yogi Berra	New York	C	218
1956—Mickey Mantle	New York	OF	*336
1957—Mickey Mantle	New York	OF	233
1958—Jackie Jensen	Boston	OF	233
1959—Nellie Fox	Chicago	2B	295
1960—Roger Maris	New York	OF	225
1961—Roger Maris	New York	OF	202
1962—Mickey Mantle	New York	OF	234
1963—Elston Howard	New York	C	248
1964—Brooks Robinson	Baltimore	3B	269
1965—Zoilo Versalles	Minnesota	SS	275
1966—Frank Robinson	Baltimore	OF	*280
1967—Carl Yastrzemski	Boston	OF	275
1968—Denny McLain	Detroit	P	*280
1969—Harmon Killebrew	Minnesota	1B-3B	294
1970—Boog Powell	Baltimore	1B	234
1971—Vida Blue	Oakland	P	268
1972—Dick Allen	Chicago	1B	321
1973—Reggie Jackson	Oakland	OF	*336
1974—Jeff Burroughs	Texas	OF	248
1975—Fred Lynn	Boston	OF	326
1976—Thurman Munson	New York	C	304
1977—Rod Carew	Minnesota	1B	273
1978—Jim Rice	Boston	OF	352
1979—Don Baylor	California	OF	347
1980—George Brett	Kansas City	3B	335
1981—Rollie Fingers	Milwaukee	P	319
1982—Robin Yount	Milwaukee	SS	385
1983—Cal Ripken Jr.	Baltimore	SS	322
1984—Willie Hernandez	Detroit	P	306
1985—Don Mattingly	New York	1B	367
1986—Roger Clemens	Boston	P	339
1987—George Bell	Toronto	OF	332

NATIONAL LEAGUE

Year Player	Team	Pos.	Points
1931—Frank Frisch	St. Louis	2B	65
1932—Chuck Klein	Philadelphia	OF	78
1933—Carl Hubbell	New York	P	77
1934—Dizzy Dean	St. Louis	P	78
1935—Gabby Hartnett	Chicago	C	75
1936—Carl Hubbell	New York	P	60
1937—Joe Medwick	St. Louis	OF	70
1938—Ernie Lombardi	Cincinnati	C	229
1939—Bucky Walters	Cincinnati	P	303
1940—Frank McCormick	Cincinnati	1B	274
1941—Dolf Camilli	Brooklyn	1B	300
1942—Mort Cooper	St. Louis	P	263
1943—Stan Musial	St. Louis	OF	267
1944—Marty Marion	St. Louis	SS	190
1945—Phil Cavarretta	Chicago	1B	279
1946—Stan Musial	St. Louis	1B	319
1947—Bob Elliott	Boston	3B	205
1948—Stan Musial	St. Louis	OF	303
1949—Jackie Robinson	Brooklyn	2B	264
1950—Jim Konstanty	Philadelphia	P	286
1951—Roy Campanella	Brooklyn	C	243
1952—Hank Sauer	Chicago	OF	226
1953—Roy Campanella	Brooklyn	C	297
1954—Willie Mays	New York	OF	283
1955—Roy Campanella	Brooklyn	C	226
1956—Don Newcombe	Brooklyn	P	223
1957—Hank Aaron	Milwaukee	OF	239
1958—Ernie Banks	Chicago	SS	283
1959—Ernie Banks	Chicago	SS	232½
1960—Dick Groat	Pittsburgh	SS	276
1961—Frank Robinson	Cincinnati	OF	219
1962—Maury Wills	Los Angeles	SS	209
1963—Sandy Koufax	Los Angeles	P	237
1964—Ken Boyer	St. Louis	3B	243
1965—Willie Mays	San Francisco	OF	224
1966—Roberto Clemente	Pittsburgh	OF	218
1967—Orlando Cepeda	St. Louis	1B	*280
1968—Bob Gibson	St. Louis	P	242
1969—Willie McCovey	San Francisco	1B	265
1970—Johnny Bench	Cincinnati	C	326
1971—Joe Torre	St. Louis	3B	318
1972—Johnny Bench	Cincinnati	C	263
1973—Pete Rose	Cincinnati	OF	274
1974—Steve Garvey	Los Angeles	1B	270
1975—Joe Morgan	Cincinnati	2B	321½
1976—Joe Morgan	Cincinnati	2B	311
1977—George Foster	Cincinnati	OF	291
1978—Dave Parker	Pittsburgh	OF	320
1979—Willie Stargell	Pittsburgh	1B	216
Keith Hernandez	St. Louis	1B	216
1980—Mike Schmidt	Philadelphia	3B	*336
1981—Mike Schmidt	Philadelphia	3B	321
1982—Dale Murphy	Atlanta	OF	283
1983—Dale Murphy	Atlanta	OF	318
1984—Ryne Sandberg	Chicago	2B	326
1985—Willie McGee	St. Louis	OF	280
1986—Mike Schmidt	Philadelphia	3B	287
1987—Andre Dawson	Chicago	OF	269

HISTORY *Award winners*

Year	Player	Team	Pos.	Points	Year	Player	Team	Pos.	Points
1988—Jose Canseco	Oakland	OF	*392		1988—Kirk Gibson	Los Angeles	OF	272	
1989—Robin Yount	Milwaukee	OF	256		1989—Kevin Mitchell	San Francisco	OF	314	
1990—Rickey Henderson	Oakland	OF	317		1990—Barry Bonds	Pittsburgh	OF	331	
1991—Cal Ripken Jr.	Baltimore	SS	318		1991—Terry Pendleton	Atlanta	3B	274	
1992—Dennis Eckersley	Oakland	P	306		1992—Barry Bonds	Pittsburgh	OF	304	
1993—Frank Thomas	Chicago	1B	*392		1993—Barry Bonds	San Francisco	OF	372	
1994—Frank Thomas	Chicago	1B	372		1994—Jeff Bagwell	Houston	1B	*392	
1995—Mo Vaughn	Boston	1B	308		1995—Barry Larkin	Cincinnati	SS	281	
1996—Juan Gonzalez	Texas	OF	290		1996—Ken Caminiti	San Diego	3B	*392	
1997—Ken Griffey Jr.	Seattle	OF	*392		1997—Larry Walker	Colorado	OF	359	
1998—Juan Gonzalez	Texas	OF	357		1998—Sammy Sosa	Chicago	OF	438	
1999—Ivan Rodriguez	Texas	C	252		1999—Chipper Jones	Atlanta	3B	432	

*Unanimous selection.

CY YOUNG MEMORIAL AWARD

Year	Pitcher	Team	Votes	Year	Pitcher	Team	Votes
1956—Don Newcombe	Brooklyn	10		1981—A.L.—Rollie Fingers	Milwaukee	126	
1957—Warren Spahn	Milwaukee	15		N.L.—Fernando Valenzuela	Los Angeles	70	
1958—Bob Turley	New York A.L.	5		1982—A.L.—Pete Vuckovich	Milwaukee	87	
1959—Early Wynn	Chicago A.L.	13		N.L.—Steve Carlton	Philadelphia	112	
1960—Vernon Law	Pittsburgh	8		1983—A.L.—LaMarr Hoyt	Chicago	116	
1961—Whitey Ford	New York A.L.	9		N.L.—John Denny	Philadelphia	103	
1962—Don Drysdale	Los Angeles N.L.	14		1984—A.L.—Willie Hernandez	Detroit	88	
1963—Sandy Koufax	Los Angeles N.L.	*20		N.L.—Rick Sutcliffe	Chicago	*120	
1964—Dean Chance	Los Angeles A.L.	17		1985—A.L.—Bret Saberhagen	Kansas City	127	
1965—Sandy Koufax	Los Angeles N.L.	*20		N.L.—Dwight Gooden	New York	*120	
1966—Sandy Koufax	Los Angeles N.L.	*20		1986—A.L.—Roger Clemens	Boston	*140	
1967—A.L.—Jim Lonborg	Boston	18		N.L.—Mike Scott	Houston	98	
N.L.—Mike McCormick	San Francisco	18		1987—A.L.—Roger Clemens	Boston	124	
1968—A.L.—Denny McLain	Detroit	*20		N.L.—Steve Bedrosian	Philadelphia	57	
N.L.—Bob Gibson	St. Louis	*20		1988—A.L.—Frank Viola	Minnesota	138	
1969—A.L.—Denny McLain	Detroit	10		N.L.—Orel Hershiser	Los Angeles	*120	
Mike Cuellar	Baltimore	10		1989—A.L.—Bret Saberhagen	Kansas City	138	
N.L.—Tom Seaver	New York	23		N.L.—Mark Davis	San Diego	107	
1970—A.L.—Jim Perry	Minnesota	55		1990—A.L.—Bob Welch	Oakland	107	
N.L.—Bob Gibson	St. Louis	118		N.L.—Doug Drabek	Pittsburgh	118	
1971—A.L.—Vida Blue	Oakland	98		1991—A.L.—Roger Clemens	Boston	119	
N.L.—Fergie Jenkins	Chicago	97		N.L.—Tom Glavine	Atlanta	110	
1972—A.L.—Gaylord Perry	Cleveland	64		1992—A.L.—Dennis Eckersley	Oakland	107	
N.L.—Steve Carlton	Philadelphia	*120		N.L.—Greg Maddux	Chicago	112	
1973—A.L.—Jim Palmer	Baltimore	88		1993—A.L.—Jack McDowell	Chicago	124	
N.L.—Tom Seaver	New York	71		N.L.—Greg Maddux	Atlanta	119	
1974—A.L.—Jim Hunter	Oakland	90		1994—A.L.—David Cone	Kansas City	108	
N.L.—Mike Marshall	Los Angeles	96		N.L.—Greg Maddux	Atlanta	*140	
1975—A.L.—Jim Palmer	Baltimore	98		1995—A.L.—Randy Johnson	Seattle	136	
N.L.—Tom Seaver	New York	98		N.L.—Greg Maddux	Atlanta	*140	
1976—A.L.—Jim Palmer	Baltimore	108		1996—A.L.—Pat Hentgen	Toronto	110	
N.L.—Randy Jones	San Diego	96		N.L.—John Smoltz	Atlanta	136	
1977—A.L.—Sparky Lyle	New York	56 1/2		1997—A.L.—Roger Clemens	Toronto	134	
N.L.—Steve Carlton	Philadelphia	*104		N.L.—Pedro Martinez	Montreal	134	
1978—A.L.—Ron Guidry	New York	*140		1998—A.L.—Roger Clemens	Toronto	*140	
N.L.—Gaylord Perry	San Diego	116		N.L.—Tom Glavine	Atlanta	99	
1979—A.L.—Mike Flanagan	Baltimore	136		1999—A.L.—Pedro Martinez	Boston	*140	
N.L.—Bruce Sutter	Chicago	72		N.L.—Randy Johnson	Arizona	134	
1980—A.L.—Steve Stone	Baltimore	100		*Unanimous selection.			
N.L.—Steve Carlton	Philadelphia	118					

ROOKIE OF THE YEAR

1947—Combined selection—Jackie Robinson, Brooklyn N.L., 1B
1948—Combined selection—Alvin Dark, Boston N.L., SS

AMERICAN LEAGUE / NATIONAL LEAGUE

Year	Player	Team	Pos.	Votes	Year	Player	Team	Pos.	Votes
1949—Roy Sievers	St. Louis	OF	10		1949—Don Newcombe	Brooklyn	P	21	
1950—Walt Dropo	Boston	1B	15		1950—Sam Jethroe	Boston	OF	11	
1951—Gil McDougald	New York	3B	13		1951—Willie Mays	New York	OF	18	
1952—Harry Byrd	Philadelphia	P	9		1952—Joe Black	Brooklyn	P	19	
1953—Harvey Kuenn	Detroit	SS	23		1953—Jim Gilliam	Brooklyn	2B	11	
1954—Bob Grim	New York	P	15		1954—Wally Moon	St. Louis	OF	17	
1955—Herb Score	Cleveland	P	18		1955—Bill Virdon	St. Louis	OF	15	
1956—Luis Aparicio	Chicago	SS	22		1956—Frank Robinson	Cincinnati	OF	*24	
1957—Tony Kubek	New York	IF-OF	23		1957—Jack Sanford	Philadelphia	P	16	
1958—Albie Pearson	Washington	OF	14		1958—Orlando Cepeda	San Francisco	1B	*†21	

Year	Player	Team	Pos.	Votes	Year	Player	Team	Pos.	Votes
1959—Bob Allison	Washington	OF	18		1959—Willie McCovey	San Francisco	1B	*24
1960—Ron Hansen	Baltimore	SS	22		1960—Frank Howard	Los Angeles	OF	12
1961—Don Schwall	Boston	P	7		1961—Billy Williams	Chicago	OF	10
1962—Tom Tresh	New York	OF-SS	13		1962—Ken Hubbs	Chicago	2B	19
1963—Gary Peters	Chicago	P	10		1963—Pete Rose	Cincinnati	2B	17
1964—Tony Oliva	Minnesota	OF	19		1964—Dick Allen	Philadelphia	3B	18
1965—Curt Blefary	Baltimore	OF	12		1965—Jim Lefebvre	Los Angeles	2B	13
1966—Tommie Agee	Chicago	OF	16		1966—Tommy Helms	Cincinnati	3B	12
1967—Rod Carew	Minnesota	2B	19		1967—Tom Seaver	New York	P	11
1968—Stan Bahnsen	New York	P	17		1968—Johnny Bench	Cincinnati	C	10½
1969—Lou Piniella	Kansas City	OF	9		1969—Ted Sizemore	Los Angeles	2B	14
1970—Thurman Munson	New York	C	23		1970—Carl Morton	Montreal	P	11
1971—Chris Chambliss	Cleveland	1B	11		1971—Earl Williams	Atlanta	C	18
1972—Carlton Fisk	Boston	C	*24		1972—Jon Matlack	New York	P	19
1973—Al Bumbry	Baltimore	OF	13½		1973—Gary Matthews	San Francisco	OF	11
1974—Mike Hargrove	Texas	1B	16½		1974—Bake McBride	St. Louis	OF	16
1975—Fred Lynn	Boston	OF	23		1975—John Montefusco	San Francisco	P	12
1976—Mark Fidrych	Detroit	P	22		1976—Butch Metzger	San Diego	P	11
					Pat Zachry	Cincinnati	P	11
1977—Eddie Murray	Baltimore	DH-1B	12½		1977—Andre Dawson	Montreal	OF	10
1978—Lou Whitaker	Detroit	2B	21		1978—Bob Horner	Atlanta	3B	12½
1979—John Castino	Minnesota	3B	7		1979—Rick Sutcliffe	Los Angeles	P	20
Alfredo Griffin	Toronto	SS	7					
1980—Joe Charboneau	Cleveland	OF	103		1980—Steve Howe	Los Angeles	P	80
1981—Dave Righetti	New York	P	127		1981—Fernando Valenzuela	Los Angeles	P	107
1982—Cal Ripken	Baltimore	SS-3B	132		1982—Steve Sax	Los Angeles	2B	63
1983—Ron Kittle	Chicago	OF	104		1983—Darryl Strawberry	New York	OF	109
1984—Alvin Davis	Seattle	1B	134		1984—Dwight Gooden	New York	P	118
1985—Ozzie Guillen	Chicago	SS	101		1985—Vince Coleman	St. Louis	OF	*120
1986—Jose Canseco	Oakland	OF	110		1986—Todd Worrell	St. Louis	P	118
1987—Mark McGwire	Oakland	1B	*140		1987—Benito Santiago	San Diego	C	*120
1988—Walt Weiss	Oakland	SS	103		1988—Chris Sabo	Cincinnati	3B	79
1989—Gregg Olson	Baltimore	P	136		1989—Jerome Walton	Chicago	OF	116
1990—Sandy Alomar Jr.	Cleveland	C	*140		1990—Dave Justice	Atlanta	OF	118
1991—Chuck Knoblauch	Minnesota	2B	136		1991—Jeff Bagwell	Houston	1B	118
1992—Pat Listach	Milwaukee	SS	122		1992—Eric Karros	Los Angeles	1B	116
1993—Tim Salmon	California	OF	*140		1993—Mike Piazza	Los Angeles	C	*140
1994—Bob Hamelin	Kansas City	DH	134		1994—Raul Mondesi	Los Angeles	OF	*140
1995—Marty Cordova	Minnesota	3B	105		1995—Hideo Nomo	Los Angeles	P	118
1996—Derek Jeter	New York	SS	*140		1996—Todd Hollandsworth	Los Angeles	OF	105
1997—Nomar Garciaparra	Boston	SS	*140		1997—Scott Rolen	Philadelphia	3B	*140
1998—Ben Grieve	Oakland	OF	130		1998—Kerry Wood	Chicago	P	128
1999—Carlos Beltran	Kansas City	OF	133		1999—Scott Williamson	Cincinnati	P	118

*Unanimous selection. †Three writers did not vote.

MANAGER OF THE YEAR

AMERICAN LEAGUE

Year	Manager	Team	Points
1983—Tony La Russa	Chicago	17
1984—Sparky Anderson	Detroit	96
1985—Bobby Cox	Toronto	104
1986—John McNamara	Boston	95
1987—Sparky Anderson	Detroit	90
1988—Tony La Russa	Oakland	103
1989—Frank Robinson	Baltimore	125
1990—Jeff Torborg	Chicago	128
1991—Tom Kelly	Minnesota	138
1992—Tony La Russa	Oakland	132
1993—Gene Lamont	Chicago	72
1994—Buck Showalter	New York	132
1995—Lou Piniella	Seattle	86
1996—Johnny Oates	Texas	89
Joe Torre	New York	89
1997—Dave Johnson	Baltimore	88
1998—Joe Torre	New York	128
1999—Jimy Williams	Boston	115

NATIONAL LEAGUE

Year	Manager	Team	Points
1983— Tommy Lasorda	Los Angeles	10
1984— Jim Frey	Chicago	101
1985— Whitey Herzog	St. Louis	86
1986— Hal Lanier	Houston	108
1987— Buck Rodgers	Montreal	92
1988— Tommy Lasorda	Los Angeles	101
1989— Don Zimmer	Chicago	118
1990— Jim Leyland	Pittsburgh	99
1991— Bobby Cox	Atlanta	96
1992— Jim Leyland	Pittsburgh	109
1993— Dusty Baker	San Francisco	105
1994— Felipe Alou	Montreal	138
1995— Don Baylor	Colorado	122
1996— Bruce Bochy	San Diego	76
1997— Dusty Baker	San Francisco	110
1998— Larry Dierker	Houston	102
1999— Jack McKeon	Cincinnati	115

EARLY MOST VALUABLE PLAYER AWARDS

CHALMERS AWARD

AMERICAN LEAGUE

Year	Player	Team	Pos.	Points
1911—Ty Cobb	Detroit	OF	64
1912—Tris Speaker	Boston	OF	59
1913—Walter Johnson	Washington	P	54
1914—Eddie Collins	Philadelphia	2B	63

NATIONAL LEAGUE

Year	Player	Team	Pos.	Points
1911—Frank Schulte	Chicago	OF	29
1912—Larry Doyle	New York	2B	48
1913—Jake Daubert	Brooklyn	1B	50
1914—Johnny Evers	Boston	2B	50

LEAGUE AWARDS

AMERICAN LEAGUE

Year	Player	Team	Pos.	Points
1922—George Sisler	St. Louis	1B	59
1923—Babe Ruth	New York	OF	64
1924—Walter Johnson	Washington	P	55
1925—Roger Peckinpaugh	Washington	SS	45
1926—George Burns	Cleveland	1B	63
1927—Lou Gehrig	New York	1B	56
1928—Mickey Cochrane	Philadelphia	C	53
1929—No selection			

NATIONAL LEAGUE

Year	Player	Team	Pos.	Points
1922—No selection			
1923—No selection			
1924—Dazzy Vance	Brooklyn	P	74
1925—Rogers Hornsby	St. Louis	2B	73
1926—Bob O'Farrell	St. Louis	C	79
1927—Paul Waner	Pittsburgh	OF	72
1928—Jim Bottomley	St. Louis	1B	76
1929—Rogers Hornsby	Chicago	2B	60

HALL OF FAME

ROSTER OF MEMBERS

Name	Des.*	Elec. year	Votes rec.†	Votes cast‡	% of vote	Teams as player
Aaron, Hank	P	1982	406	415	97.8	Milwaukee NL, Atlanta NL, Milwaukee AL
Alexander, Grover C.	P	1938	212	262	80.9	Philadelphia NL, Chicago NL, St. Louis NL
Alston, Walter	M	1983	CV	—	—	St. Louis NL
Anson, Cap	P	1939	C1	—	—	Chicago NL
Aparicio, Luis	P	1984	341	403	84.6	Chicago AL, Baltimore AL, Boston AL
Appling, Luke	P	1964	189	225	84.0	Chicago AL
Ashburn, Richie	P	1995	CV	—	—	Philadelphia NL, Chicago NL, New York NL
Averill, Earl	P	1975	CV	—	—	Cleveland AL, Detroit AL, Boston AL
Baker, Home Run	P	1955	CV	—	—	Philadelphia AL, New York AL
Bancroft, Dave	P	1971	CV	—	—	Philadelphia NL, New York NL, Boston NL, Brooklyn NL
Banks, Ernie	P	1977	321	383	83.8	Chicago NL
Barlick, Al	U	1989	CV	—	—	
Barrow, Ed	E	1953	CV	—	—	
Beckley, Jake	P	1971	CV	—	—	Pittsburgh NL, Pittsburgh PL, New York NL, Cincinnati NL, St. Louis NL
Bell, Cool Papa	P	1974	SCNL	—	—	Negro Leagues
Bench, Johnny	P	1989	431	447	96.4	Cincinnati NL
Bender, Chief	P	1953	CV	—	—	Philadelphia AL, Philadelphia NL, Chicago AL
Berra, Yogi	P	1972	339	396	85.6	New York AL, New York NL
Bottomley, Jim	P	1974	CV	—	—	St. Louis NL, Cincinnati NL, St. Louis AL
Boudreau, Lou	P	1970	232	300	77.3	Cleveland AL, Boston AL
Bresnahan, Roger	P	1945	C2	—	—	Washington NL, Chicago NL, Baltimore AL, New York NL, St. Louis NL
Brett, George	P	1999	488	497	98.2	Kansas City AL
Brock, Lou	P	1985	315	395	79.7	Chicago NL, St. Louis NL
Brouthers, Dan	P	1945	C2	—	—	Troy NL, Buffalo NL, Detroit NL, Boston NL, Boston PL, Boston AA,Brooklyn NL, Baltimore NL,Louisville NL, Philadelphia NL, New York NL
Brown, Three Finger	P	1949	C2	—	—	St. Louis NL, Chicago NL, Cincinnati NL
Bulkeley, Morgan	E	1937	CC	—	—	
Bunning, Jim	P	1996	CV	—	—	Detroit AL, Philadelphia NL, Pittsburgh NL, Los Angeles NL
Burkett, Jesse	P	1946	C2	—	—	New York NL, Cleveland NL, St. Louis NL, St. Louis AL, Boston AL
Campanella, Roy	P	1969	270	340	79.4	Brooklyn NL
Carew, Rod	P	1991	401	443	90.5	Minnesota AL, California AL
Carey, Max	P	1961	CV	—	—	Pittsburgh NL, Brooklyn NL
Carlton, Steve	P	1994	436	455	95.8	St. Louis NL, Philadelphia NL, San Francisco NL, Chicago AL, Cleveland AL, Minnesota AL
Cartwright, Alexander	O	1938	CC	—	—	
Cepeda, Orlando	P	1999	CV	—	—	San Francisco NL, St. Louis NL, Atlanta NL, Oakland AL, Boston AL, Kansas City AL
Chadwick, Henry	O	1938	CC	—	—	
Chance, Frank	P	1946	C2	—	—	Chicago NL, New York AL
Chandler, Happy	E	1982	CV	—	—	
Charleston, Oscar	P	1976	SCNL	—	—	Negro Leagues
Chesbro, Jack	P	1946	C2	—	—	Pittsburgh NL, New York AL, Boston AL
Chylak, Nestor	U	1999	CV	—	—	
Clarke, Fred	P	1945	C2	—	—	Louisville NL, Pittsburgh NL
Clarkson, John	P	1963	CV	—	—	Worcester NL, Chicago NL, Boston NL, Cleveland NL
Clemente, Roberto	P	1973	393	424	92.7	Pittsburgh NL
Cobb, Ty	P	1936	222	226	98.2	Detroit AL, Philadelphia AL
Cochrane, Mickey	P	1947	128	161	79.5	Philadelphia AL, Detroit AL
Collins, Eddie	P	1939	213	274	77.7	Philadelphia AL, Chicago AL
Collins, Jimmy	P	1945	C2	—	—	Boston NL, Louisville NL, Boston AL, Philadelphia AL
Combs, Earle	P	1970	CV	—	—	New York AL
Comiskey, Charley	F/P	1939	C1	—	—	St. Louis AA, Chicago PL, Cincinnati NL
Conlan, Jocko	U	1974	CV	—	—	Chicago AL
Connolly, Tommy	U	1953	CV	—	—	
Connor, Roger	P	1976	CV	—	—	Troy NL, New York NL, New York PL, Philadelphia NL, St. Louis NL
Coveleski, Stan	P	1969	CV	—	—	Philadelphia AL, Cleveland AL, Washington AL, New York AL
Crawford, Sam	P	1957	CV	—	—	Cincinnati NL, Detroit AL
Cronin, Joe	P	1956	152	193	78.8	Pittsburgh NL, Washington AL, Boston AL
Cummings, Candy	P	1939	C1	—	—	Hartford NL, Cincinnati NL
Cuyler, Kiki	P	1968	CV	—	—	Pittsburgh NL, Chicago NL, Cincinnati NL, Brooklyn NL
Dandridge, Ray	P	1987	CV	—	—	Negro Leagues

Name	Des.*	Elec. year	Votes rec.†	Votes cast‡	% of vote	Teams as player
Davis, George S.	P	1998	CV	—	—	Cleveland NL, New York NL, Chicago AL
Day, Leon	P	1995	CV	—	—	Negro Leagues
Dean, Dizzy	P	1953	209	264	79.2	St. Louis NL, Chicago NL, St. Louis AL
Delahanty, Ed	P	1945	C2	—	—	Philadelphia NL, Cleveland PL, Washington AL
Dickey, Bill	P	1954	202	252	80.2	New York AL
Dihigo, Martin	P	1977	SCNL	—	—	Negro Leagues
DiMaggio, Joe	P	1955	223	251	88.8	New York AL
Doby, Larry	P	1998	CV	—	—	Cleveland AL, Chicago AL, Detroit AL
Doerr, Bobby	P	1986	CV	—	—	Boston AL
Drysdale, Don	P	1984	316	403	78.4	Brooklyn NL, Los Angeles NL
Duffy, Hugh	P	1945	C2	—	—	Chicago NL, Chicago PL, Boston AA, Boston NL, Milwaukee AL, Philadelphia NL
Durocher, Leo	M	1994	CV	—	—	New York AL, Cincinnati NL, St. Louis NL, Brooklyn NL
Evans, Billy	U	1973	CV	—	—	
Evers, Johnny	P	1946	C2	—	—	Chicago NL, Boston NL, Philadelphia NL, Chicago AL
Ewing, Buck	P	1939	C1	—	—	Troy NL, New York NL, New York PL, Cleveland NL, Cincinnati NL
Faber, Red	P	1964	CV	—	—	Chicago AL
Feller, Bob	P	1962	150	160	93.8	Cleveland AL
Ferrell, Rick	P	1984	CV	—	—	St. Louis AL, Boston AL, Washington AL
Fingers, Rollie	P	1992	349	430	81.2	Oakland AL, San Diego NL, Milwaukee AL
Fisk, Carlton	P	2000	397	499	79.6	Boston AL, Chicago AL
Flick, Elmer	P	1963	CV	—	—	Philadelphia NL, Philadelphia AL, Cleveland AL
Ford, Whitey	P	1974	284	365	77.8	New York AL
Foster, Bill	P	1996	CV	—	—	Negro Leagues
Foster, Rube	P	1981	CV	—	—	Negro Leagues
Fox, Nellie	P	1997	CV	—	—	Philadelphia AL, Chicago AL, Houston NL
Foxx, Jimmie	P	1951	179	226	79.2	Philadelphia AL, Boston AL, Chicago NL, Philadelphia NL
Frick, Ford	E	1970	CV	—	—	
Frisch, Frank	P	1947	136	161	84.5	New York NL, St. Louis NL
Galvin, Pud	P	1965	CV	—	—	Buffalo NL, Pittsburgh AA, Pittsburgh NL, Pittsburgh PL, St. Louis NL
Gehrig, Lou	P	1939	SE	—	—	New York AL
Gehringer, Charley	P	1949	159	187	85.0	Detroit AL
Gibson, Bob	P	1981	337	401	84.0	St. Louis NL
Gibson, Josh	P	1972	SCNL	—	—	Negro Leagues
Giles, Warren	E	1979	CV	—	—	
Gomez, Lefty	P	1972	CV	—	—	New York AL, Washington AL
Goslin, Goose	P	1968	CV	—	—	Washington AL, St. Louis AL, Detroit AL
Greenberg, Hank	P	1956	164	193	85.0	Detroit AL, Pittsburgh NL
Griffith, Clark	M	1946	C2	—	—	St. Louis AA, Boston AA, Chicago NL, Chicago AL, New York AL, Cincinnati NL, Washington AL
Grimes, Burleigh	P	1964	CV	—	—	Pittsburgh NL, Brooklyn NL, New York NL, Boston NL, St. Louis NL, Chicago NL, New York AL
Grove, Lefty	P	1947	123	161	76.4	Philadelphia AL, Boston AL
Hafey, Chick	P	1971	CV	—	—	St. Louis NL, Cincinnati NL
Haines, Jesse	P	1970	CV	—	—	Cincinnati NL, St. Louis NL
Hamilton, Billy	P	1961	CV	—	—	Kansas City AA, Philadelphia NL, Boston NL
Hanlon, Ned	M	1996	CV	—	—	Cleveland NL, Detroit NL, Pittsburgh NL, Pittsburgh PL, Baltimore NL
Harridge, Will	E	1972	CV	—	—	
Harris, Bucky	M	1975	CV	—	—	Washington AL, Detroit AL
Hartnett, Gabby	P	1955	195	251	77.7	Chicago NL, New York NL
Heilmann, Harry	P	1952	203	234	86.8	Detroit AL, Cincinnati NL
Herman, Billy	P	1975	CV	—	—	Chicago NL, Brooklyn NL, Boston NL, Pittsburgh NL
Hooper, Harry	P	1971	CV	—	—	Boston AL, Chicago AL
Hornsby, Rogers	P	1942	182	233	78.1	St. Louis NL, New York NL, Boston NL, Chicago NL, St. Louis AL
Hoyt, Waite	P	1969	CV	—	—	New York NL, Boston AL, New York AL, Detroit AL, Philadelphia AL, Brooklyn NL, Pittsburgh NL
Hubbard, Cal	U	1976	CV	—	—	
Hubbell, Carl	P	1947	140	161	87.0	New York NL
Huggins, Miller	M	1964	CV	—	—	Cincinnati NL, St. Louis NL
Hulbert, William	F	1995	CV	—	—	
Hunter, Catfish	P	1987	315	413	76.3	Kansas City AL, Oakland AL, New York AL
Irvin, Monte	P	1973	SCNL	—	—	New York NL, Chicago NL, Negro Leagues
Jackson, Reggie	P	1993	396	423	93.6	Kansas City AL, Oakland AL, Baltimore AL, New York AL, California AL
Jackson, Travis	P	1982	CV	—	—	New York NL
Jenkins, Ferguson	P	1991	334	443	75.4	Philadelphia NL, Chicago NL, Texas AL, Boston AL
Jennings, Hugh	P	1945	C2	—	—	Louisville AA, Louisville NL, Baltimore NL, Brooklyn NL, Philadelphia NL, Detroit AL
Johnson, Ban	E	1937	CC	—	—	
Johnson, Judy	P	1975	SCNL	—	—	Negro Leagues

Name	Des.*	Elec. year	Votes rec.†	Votes cast‡	% of vote	Teams as player
Johnson, Walter	P	1936	189	226	83.6	Washington AL
Joss, Addie	P	1978	CV	—	—	Cleveland AL
Kaline, Al	P	1980	340	385	88.3	Detroit AL
Keefe, Tim	P	1964	CV	—	—	Troy NL, New York AA, New York NL, New York PL, Philadelphia NL
Keeler, Willie	P	1939	207	274	75.5	New York NL, Brooklyn, NL, Baltimore NL, New York AL
Kell, George	P	1983	CV	—	—	Philadelphia AL, Detroit AL, Boston AL, Chicago AL, Baltimore AL
Kelley, Joe	P	1971	CV	—	—	Boston NL, Pittsburgh NL, Baltimore NL, Brooklyn NL, Baltimore AL, Cincinnati NL
Kelly, George	P	1973	CV	—	—	New York NL, Pittsburgh NL, Cincinnati NL, Chicago NL, Brooklyn NL
Kelly, Mike	P	1945	C2	—	—	Cincinnati NL, Chicago NL, Boston NL, Boston PL, Cincinnati AA, Boston AA, New York NL
Killebrew, Harmon	P	1984	335	403	83.1	Washington AL, Minnesota AL, Kansas City AL
Kiner, Ralph	P	1975	273	362	75.4	Pittsburgh NL, Chicago NL, Cleveland AL
Klein, Chuck	P	1980	CV	—	—	Philadelphia NL, Chicago NL, Pittsburgh NL
Klem, Bill	U	1953	CV	—	—	
Koufax, Sandy	P	1972	344	396	86.9	Brooklyn NL, Los Angeles NL
Lajoie, Nap	P	1937	168	201	83.6	Philadelphia NL, Philadelphia AL, Cleveland AL
Landis, Kenesaw M.	E	1944	C2	—	—	
Lasorda, Tom	M	1997	CV	—	—	Brooklyn NL, Kansas City AL
Lazzeri, Tony	P	1991	CV	—	—	New York AL, Chicago NL, Brooklyn NL, New York NL
Lemon, Bob	P	1976	305	388	78.6	Cleveland AL
Leonard, Buck	P	1972	SCNL	—	—	Negro Leagues
Lindstrom, Fred	P	1976	CV	—	—	New York NL, Pittsburgh NL, Chicago NL, Brooklyn NL
Lloyd, John Henry	P	1977	SCNL	—	—	Negro Leagues
Lombardi, Ernie	P	1986	CV	—	—	Brooklyn NL, Cincinnati NL, Boston NL, New York NL
Lopez, Al	M	1977	CV	—	—	Brooklyn NL, Boston NL, Pittsburgh NL, Cleveland AL
Lyons, Ted	P	1955	217	251	86.5	Chicago AL
Mack, Connie	M	1937	CC	—	—	Washington NL, Buffalo PL, Pittsburgh NL
MacPhail, Larry	E	1978	CV	—	—	
MacPhail, Lee	E	1998	CV	—	—	
Mantle, Mickey	P	1974	322	365	88.2	New York AL
Manush, Heinie	P	1964	CV	—	—	Detroit AL, St. Louis AL, Washington AL, Boston AL, Brooklyn NL, Pittsburgh NL
Maranville, Rabbit	P	1954	209	252	82.9	Boston NL, Pittsburgh NL, Chicago NL, Brooklyn NL, St. Louis NL
Marichal, Juan	P	1983	313	374	83.7	San Francisco NL, Boston AL, Los Angeles NL
Marquard, Rube	P	1971	CV	—	—	New York NL, Brooklyn NL, Cincinnati NL, Boston NL
Mathews, Eddie	P	1978	301	379	79.4	Boston NL, Milwaukee NL, Atlanta NL, Houston NL, Detroit AL
Mathewson, Christy	P	1936	205	226	90.7	New York NL, Cincinnati NL
Mays, Willie	P	1979	409	432	94.7	New York (Giants)NL, San Francisco NL, New York (Mets)NL
McCarthy, Joe	M	1957	CV	—	—	
McCarthy, Tommy	P	1946	C2	—	—	Boston UA, Boston NL, Philadelphia NL, St. Louis AA, Brooklyn NL
McCovey, Willie	P	1986	346	425	81.4	San Francisco NL, San Diego NL, Oakland AL
McGinnity, Joe	P	1946	C2	—	—	Baltimore NL, Brooklyn NL, Baltimore AL, New York NL
McGowan, Bill	U	1992	CV	—	—	
McGraw, John	M	1937	CC	—	—	Baltimore AA, Baltimore NL, St. Louis NL, Baltimore AL, New York NL
McKechnie, Bill	M	1962	CV	—	—	Pittsburgh NL, Boston NL, New York AL, New York NL, Cincinnati
Medwick, Joe	P	1968	240	283	84.8	St. Louis NL, Brooklyn NL, New York NL, Boston NL
Mize, Johnny	P	1981	CV	—	—	St. Louis NL, New York NL, New York AL
Morgan, Joe	P	1990	363	444	81.8	Houston NL, Cincinnati NL, San Francisco NL, Philadelphia NL, Oakland AL
Musial, Stan	P	1969	317	340	93.2	St. Louis NL
Newhouser, Hal	P	1992	CV	—	—	Detroit AL, Cleveland AL
Nichols, Kid	P	1949	C2	—	—	Boston NL, St. Louis NL, Philadelphia NL
Niekro, Phil	P	1997	380	473	80.3	Milwaukee NL, Atlanta NL, New York AL, Cleveland AL, Toronto AL
O'Rourke, Jim	P	1945	C2	—	—	Boston NL, Providence NL, Buffalo NL, New York NL, Washington NL, New York PL
Ott, Mel	P	1951	197	226	87.2	New York NL
Paige, Satchel	P	1971	SCNL	—	—	Cleveland AL, St. Louis AL, Kansas City AL, Negro Leagues
Palmer, Jim	P	1990	411	444	92.6	Baltimore AL
Pennock, Herb	P	1948	94	121	77.7	Philadelphia AL, Boston AL, New York AL
Tony Perez	P	2000	385	499	77.2	Cincinnati NL, Montreal NL, Boston AL, Philadelphia NL

Name	Des.*	Elec. year	Votes rec.†	Votes cast‡	% of vote	Teams as player
Perry, Gaylord	P	1991	342	443	77.2	San Francisco NL, Cleveland AL, Texas AL, San Diego NL, New York AL, Atlanta NL, Seattle AL, Kansas City AL
Plank, Eddie	P	1946	C2	—	—	Philadelphia AL, St. Louis AL
Radbourn, Hoss	P	1939	C1	—	—	Buffalo NL, Providence NL, Boston NL, Boston PL, Cincinnati NL
Reese, Pee Wee	P	1984	CV	—	—	Brooklyn NL, Los Angeles NL
Rice, Sam	P	1963	CV	—	—	Washington AL, Cleveland AL
Rickey, Branch	E	1967	CV	—	—	St. Louis AL, New York AL
Rixey, Eppa	P	1963	CV	—	—	Philadelphia NL, Cincinnati NL
Rizzuto, Phil	P	1994	CV	—	—	New York AL
Roberts, Robin	P	1976	337	388	86.9	Philadelphia NL, Baltimore AL, Houston NL, Chicago NL
Robinson, Brooks	P	1983	344	374	92.0	Baltimore AL
Robinson, Frank	P	1982	370	415	89.2	Cincinnati NL, Baltimore AL, Los Angeles NL, California AL, Cleveland AL
Robinson, Jackie	P	1962	124	160	77.5	Brooklyn NL
Robinson, Wilbert	M	1945	C2	—	—	Philadelphia AA, Baltimore AA, Baltimore NL, St. Louis NL, Baltimore AL
Rogan, Bullet Joe	P	1998	CV	—	—	
Roush, Edd	P	1962	CV	—	—	Chicago AL, New York NL, Cincinnati NL
Ruffing, Red	P	1967	266	306	86.9	Boston AL, New York AL, Chicago AL
Rusie, Amos	P	1977	CV	—	—	Indianapolis NL, New York NL, Cincinnati NL
Ruth, Babe	P	1936	215	226	95.1	Boston AL, New York AL, Boston NL
Ryan, Nolan	P	1999	491	497	98.8	New York NL, California AL, Houston NL, Texas AL
Schalk, Ray	P	1955	CV	—	—	Chicago AL, New York NL
Schmidt, Mike	P	1995	444	460	96.5	Philadelphia NL
Schoendienst, Red	P	1989	CV	—	—	St. Louis NL, New York (Giants) NL, Milwaukee NL
Seaver, Tom	P	1992	425	430	98.8	New York NL, Cincinnati NL, Chicago AL, Boston AL
Selee, Frank	M	1999	CV	—	—	
Sewell, Joe	P	1977	CV	—	—	Cleveland AL, New York AL
Simmons, Al	P	1953	199	264	75.4	Philadelphia AL, Chicago AL, Detroit AL, Washington AL, Boston AL, Cincinnati NL, Boston AL
Sisler, George	P	1939	235	274	85.8	St. Louis AL, Washington AL, Boston NL
Slaughter, Enos	P	1985	CV	—	—	St. Louis NL, New York AL, Kansas City AL, Milwaukee NL
Snider, Duke	P	1980	333	385	86.5	Brooklyn NL, Los Angeles NL, New York NL, San Francisco NL
Spahn, Warren	P	1973	316	380	83.2	Boston NL, Milwaukee NL, New York NL, San Francisco NL
Spalding, Al	P	1939	C1	—	—	Chicago NL
Speaker, Tris	P	1937	165	201	82.1	Boston AL, Cleveland AL, Washington AL, Philadelphia AL
Stargell, Willie	P	1988	352	427	82.4	Pittsburgh NL
Stengel, Casey	M	1966	CV	—	—	Brooklyn NL, Pittsburgh NL, Philadelphia NL, New York NL, Boston NL
Sutton, Don	P	1998	386	473	81.6	Los Angeles NL, Houston NL, Milwaukee AL, Oakland AL, California AL
Terry, Bill	P	1954	195	252	77.4	New York NL
Thompson, Sam	P	1974	CV	—	—	Detroit NL, Philadelphia NL, Detroit AL
Tinker, Joe	P	1946	C2	—	—	Chicago NL, Cincinnati NL
Traynor, Pie	P	1948	93	121	76.9	Pittsburgh NL
Vance, Dazzy	P	1955	205	251	81.7	Pittsburgh NL, New York AL, Brooklyn NL, St. Louis NL, Cincinnati NL
Vaughan, Arky	P	1985	CV	—	—	Pittsburgh NL, Brooklyn NL
Veeck, Bill	E	1991	CV	—	—	
Waddell, Rube	P	1946	C2	—	—	Louisville NL, Pittsburgh NL, Chicago NL, Philadelphia AL, St. Louis AL
Wagner, Honus	P	1936	215	226	95.1	Louisville NL, Pittsburgh NL
Wallace, Bobby	P	1953	CV	—	—	Cleveland NL, St. Louis NL, St. Louis AL
Walsh, Ed	P	1946	C2	—	—	Chicago AL, Boston NL
Waner, Lloyd	P	1967	CV	—	—	Pittsburgh NL, Boston NL, Cincinnati NL, Philadelphia NL, Brooklyn NL
Waner, Paul	P	1952	195	234	83.3	Pittsburgh NL, Brooklyn NL, Boston NL, New York AL
Ward, John Montgomery	P	1964	CV	—	—	Providence NL, New York NL, Brooklyn PL, Brooklyn NL
Weaver, Earl	M	1996	CV	—	—	
Weiss, George	E	1971	CV	—	—	
Welch, Mickey	P	1973	CV	—	—	Troy NL, New York NL
Wells, Willie	P	1997	CV	—	—	
Wheat, Zack	P	1959	CV	—	—	Brooklyn NL, Philadelphia AL
Wilhelm, Hoyt	P	1985	331	395	83.8	New York NL, St. Louis NL, Cleveland AL, Baltimore AL, Chicago AL California AL, Atlanta NL, Chicago NL, Los Angeles NL

Name	Des.*	Elec. year	Votes rec.†	Votes cast‡	% of vote	Teams as player
Williams, Billy	P	1987	354	413	85.7	Chicago NL, Oakland AL
Williams, Smokey Joe	P	1999	CV	—	—	Negro Leagues
Williams, Ted	P	1966	282	302	93.4	Boston AL
Willis, Vic	P	1995	CV	—	—	Boston NL, Pittsburgh NL, St. Louis NL
Wilson, Hack	P	1979	CV	—	—	New York NL, Chicago NL, Brooklyn NL, Philadelphia NL
Wright, George	M	1937	CC	—	—	Boston NL, Providence NL
Wright, Harry	M	1953	CV	—	—	Boston NL
Wynn, Early	P	1972	301	396	76.0	Washington AL, Cleveland AL, Chicago AL
Yastrzemski, Carl	P	1989	423	447	94.6	Boston AL
Yawkey, Tom	E	1980	CV	—	—	
Young, Cy	P	1937	153	201	76.1	Cleveland NL, St. Louis NL, Boston AL, Cleveland AL, Boston NL
Youngs, Ross	P	1972	CV	—	—	New York NL
Yount, Robin	P	1999	385	497	77.5	Milwaukee AL

*Designation for which he was honored. Abbreviations: E—executive; F—founder; M—manager; O—organizer; P—player; U—umpire.

†Where an abbreviation is listed rather than a vote total, the enshrinee was selected by one of the following groups: Centennial Commission (CC), committee of old-time players and writers (C1), committee on old-timers (C2), Committee on Veterans (CV), special election by Baseball Writers' Association of America (SE) or Special Committee on Negro Leagues (SCNL).

‡Votes cast by eligible members of the Baseball Writers' Association of America.

League abbreviations: AA—American Association; AL—American League; NL—National League; PL—Players League; UA—Union Association.

TEAM BY TEAM
AMERICAN LEAGUE

ANAHEIM ANGELS
YEARLY FINISHES

(Known as Los Angeles Angels through September 1, 1965 and California Angels through 1996)

Year	Position	W	L	Pct.	*GB	Manager	Attendance
1961	8th	70	91	.435	38.5	Bill Rigney	603,510
1962	3rd	86	76	.531	10.0	Bill Rigney	1,144,063
1963	9th	70	91	.435	34.0	Bill Rigney	821,015
1964	5th	82	80	.506	17.0	Bill Rigney	760,439
1965	7th	75	87	.463	27.0	Bill Rigney	566,727
1966	6th	80	82	.494	18.0	Bill Rigney	1,400,321
1967	5th	84	77	.522	7.5	Bill Rigney	1,317,713
1968	8th	67	95	.414	36.0	Bill Rigney	1,025,956

WEST DIVISION

Year	Position	W	L	Pct.	*GB	Manager	Attendance
1969	3rd	71	91	.438	26.0	Bill Rigney, Lefty Phillips	758,388
1970	3rd	86	76	.531	12.0	Lefty Phillips	1,077,741
1971	4th	76	86	.469	25.5	Lefty Phillips	926,373
1972	5th	75	80	.484	18.0	Del Rice	744,190
1973	4th	79	83	.488	15.0	Bobby Winkles	1,058,206
1974	6th	68	94	.420	22.0	Bobby Winkles, Dick Williams	917,269
1975	6th	72	89	.447	25.5	Dick Williams	1,058,163
1976	4th (tied)	76	86	.469	14.0	Dick Williams, Norm Sherry	1,006,774
1977	5th	74	88	.457	28.0	Norm Sherry, Dave Garcia	1,432,633
1978	2nd (tied)	87	75	.537	5.0	Dave Garcia, Jim Fregosi	1,755,386
1979	1st†	88	74	.543	+3.0	Jim Fregosi	2,523,575
1980	6th	65	95	.406	31.0	Jim Fregosi	2,297,327
1981	4th/7th	51	59	.464	‡	Jim Fregosi, Gene Mauch	1,441,545
1982	1st†	93	69	.574	+3.0	Gene Mauch	2,807,360
1983	5th (tied)	70	92	.432	29.0	John McNamara	2,555,016
1984	2nd (tied)	81	81	.500	3.0	John McNamara	2,402,997
1985	2nd	90	72	.556	1.0	Gene Mauch	2,567,427
1986	1st†	92	70	.568	+5.0	Gene Mauch	2,655,872
1987	6th (tied)	75	87	.463	10.0	Gene Mauch	2,696,299
1988	4th	75	87	.463	29.0	Cookie Rojas	2,340,925
1989	3rd	91	71	.562	8.0	Doug Rader	2,647,291
1990	4th	80	82	.494	23.0	Doug Rader	2,555,688
1991	7th	81	81	.500	14.0	Doug Rader, Buck Rodgers	2,416,236
1992	5th (tied)	72	90	.444	24.0	Buck Rodgers	2,065,444
1993	5th (tied)	71	91	.438	23.0	Buck Rodgers	2,057,460
1994	4th	47	68	.409	5.5	Buck Rodgers, Marcel Lachemann	1,512,622
1995	2nd§	78	67	.538	1.0	Marcel Lachemann	1,748,680
1996	4th	70	91	.435	19.5	Marcel Lachemann, John McNamara, Joe Maddon	1,820,521
1997	2nd	84	78	.519	6.0	Terry Collins	1,767,330
1998	2nd	85	77	.525	3.0	Terry Collins	2,519,210
1999	4th	70	92	.432	25.0	Terry Collins, Joe Maddon	2,253,123

*Games behind winner. †Lost championship series. ‡First half 31-29; second 20-30. §Lost division playoff.

MANAGERIAL RECORDS

Terry Collins 220-237, Jim Fregosi 237-249, Dave Garcia 60-66, Marcel Lachemann 161-170, Joe Maddon 27-24, Gene Mauch 379-332, John McNamara 161-191, Lefty Phillips 222-225, Doug Rader 232-216, Del Rice 75-80, Bill Rigney 625-707, Buck Rodgers 179-223, Cookie Rojas 75-87, Norm Sherry 76-71, Dick Williams 147-194, Bobby Winkles 109-127.

BALTIMORE ORIOLES
YEARLY FINISHES

(Known as Milwaukee Brewers in 1901 and St. Louis Browns through 1953)

Year	Position	W	L	Pct.	*GB	Manager	Attendance
1901	8th	48	89	.350	35.5	Hugh Duffy	139,034
1902	2nd	78	58	.574	5.0	Jimmy McAleer	272,283
1903	6th	65	74	.468	26.5	Jimmy McAleer	380,405
1904	6th	65	87	.428	29.0	Jimmy McAleer	318,108
1905	8th	54	99	.354	40.5	Jimmy McAleer	339,112
1906	5th	76	73	.510	16.0	Jimmy McAleer	389,157

Year	Position	W	L	Pct.	*GB	Manager	Attendance
1907	6th	69	83	.454	24.0	Jimmy McAleer	419,025
1908	4th	83	69	.546	6.5	Jimmy McAleer	618,947
1909	7th	61	89	.407	36.0	Jimmy McAleer	366,274
1910	8th	47	107	.305	57.0	John O'Connor	249,889
1911	8th	45	107	.296	56.5	Bobby Wallace	207,984
1912	7th	53	101	.344	53.0	Bobby Wallace, George Stovall	214,070
1913	8th	57	96	.373	39.0	George Stovall, Branch Rickey	250,330
1914	5th	71	82	.464	28.5	Branch Rickey	244,714
1915	6th	63	91	.409	39.5	Branch Rickey	150,358
1916	5th	79	75	.513	12.0	Fielder Jones	335,740
1917	7th	57	97	.370	43.0	Fielder Jones	210,486
1918	5th	58	64	.475	15.0	Fielder Jones, Jimmy Austin, Jimmy Burke	122,076
1919	5th	67	72	.482	20.5	Jimmy Burke	349,350
1920	4th	76	77	.497	21.5	Jimmy Burke	419,311
1921	3rd	81	73	.526	17.5	Lee Fohl	355,978
1922	2nd	93	61	.604	1.0	Lee Fohl	712,918
1923	5th	74	78	.487	24.0	Lee Fohl, Jimmy Austin	430,296
1924	4th	74	78	.487	17.0	George Sisler	533,349
1925	3rd	82	71	.536	15.0	George Sisler	462,898
1926	7th	62	92	.403	29.0	George Sisler	283,986
1927	7th	59	94	.336	50.5	Dan Howley	247,879
1928	3rd	82	72	.532	19.0	Dan Howley	339,497
1929	4th	79	73	.520	26.0	Dan Howley	280,697
1930	6th	64	90	.416	38.0	Bill Killefer	152,088
1931	5th	63	91	.409	45.0	Bill Killefer	179,126
1932	6th	63	91	.409	44.0	Bill Killefer	112,558
1933	8th	55	96	.364	43.5	Bill Killefer, Allen Sothoron, Rogers Hornsby	88,113
1934	6th	67	85	.441	33.0	Rogers Hornsby	115,305
1935	7th	65	87	.428	28.5	Rogers Hornsby	80,922
1936	7th	57	95	.375	44.5	Rogers Hornsby	93,267
1937	8th	46	108	.299	56.0	Rogers Hornsby, Jim Bottomley	123,121
1938	7th	55	97	.362	44.0	Gabby Street	130,417
1939	8th	43	111	.279	64.5	Fred Haney	109,159
1940	6th	67	87	.435	23.0	Fred Haney	239,591
1941	6th (tied)	70	84	.455	31.0	Fred Haney, Luke Sewell	176,240
1942	3rd	82	69	.543	19.5	Luke Sewell	255,617
1943	6th	72	80	.474	25.0	Luke Sewell	214,392
1944	1st	89	65	.578	+1.0	Luke Sewell	508,644
1945	3rd	81	70	.536	6.0	Luke Sewell	482,986
1946	7th	66	88	.429	38.0	Luke Sewell, Zack Taylor	526,435
1947	8th	59	95	.383	38.0	Muddy Ruel	320,474
1948	6th	59	94	.386	37.0	Zack Taylor	335,546
1949	7th	53	101	.344	44.0	Zack Taylor	270,936
1950	7th	58	96	.377	40.0	Zack Taylor	247,131
1951	8th	52	102	.338	46.0	Zack Taylor	293,790
1952	7th	64	90	.416	31.0	Rogers Hornsby, Marty Marion	518,796
1953	8th	54	100	.351	46.5	Marty Marion	297,238
1954	7th	54	100	.351	57.0	Jimmie Dykes	1,060,910
1955	7th	57	97	.370	39.0	Paul Richards	852,039
1956	6th	69	85	.448	28.0	Paul Richards	901,201
1957	5th	76	76	.500	21.0	Paul Richards	1,029,581
1958	6th	74	79	.484	17.5	Paul Richards	829,991
1959	6th	74	80	.481	20.0	Paul Richards	891,926
1960	2nd	89	65	.578	8.0	Paul Richards	1,187,849
1961	3rd	95	67	.586	14.0	Paul Richards, Luman Harris	951,089
1962	7th	77	85	.475	19.0	Billy Hitchcock	790,254
1963	4th	86	76	.531	18.5	Billy Hitchcock	774,343
1964	3rd	97	65	.599	2.0	Hank Bauer	1,116,215
1965	3rd	94	68	.580	8.0	Hank Bauer	781,649
1966	1st	97	63	.606	+9.0	Hank Bauer	1,203,366
1967	6th (tied)	76	85	.472	15.5	Hank Bauer	955,053
1968	2nd	91	71	.562	12.0	Hank Bauer, Earl Weaver	943,977

EAST DIVISION

Year	Position	W	L	Pct.	*GB	Manager	Attendance
1969	1st†	109	53	.673	+19.0	Earl Weaver	1,058,168
1970	1st†	108	54	.667	+15.0	Earl Weaver	1,057,069
1971	1st†	101	57	.639	+12.0	Earl Weaver	1,023,037
1972	3rd	80	74	.519	5.0	Earl Weaver	899,950
1973	1st‡	97	65	.599	+8.0	Earl Weaver	958,667
1974	1st‡	91	71	.562	+2.0	Earl Weaver	962,572
1975	2nd	90	69	.566	4.5	Earl Weaver	1,002,157
1976	2nd	88	74	.543	10.5	Earl Weaver	1,058,609
1977	2nd (tied)	97	64	.602	2.5	Earl Weaver	1,195,769
1978	4th	90	71	.559	9.0	Earl Weaver	1,051,724

Year	Position	W	L	Pct.	*GB	Manager	Attendance
1979	1st†	102	57	.642	+8.0	Earl Weaver	1,681,009
1980	2nd	100	62	.617	3.0	Earl Weaver	1,797,438
1981	2nd/4th	59	46	.562	§	Earl Weaver	1,024,652
1982	2nd	94	68	.580	1.0	Earl Weaver	1,613,031
1983	1st†	98	64	.605	+6.0	Joe Altobelli	2,042,071
1984	5th	85	77	.525	19.0	Joe Altobelli	2,045,784
1985	4th	83	78	.516	16.0	Joe Altobelli, Earl Weaver	2,132,387
1986	7th	73	89	.451	22.5	Earl Weaver	1,973,176
1987	6th	67	95	.414	31.0	Cal Ripken Sr.	1,835,692
1988	7th	54	107	.335	34.5	Cal Ripken Sr., Frank Robinson	1,660,738
1989	2nd	87	75	.537	2.0	Frank Robinson	2,535,208
1990	5th	76	85	.472	11.5	Frank Robinson	2,415,189
1991	6th	67	95	.414	24.0	Frank Robinson, Johnny Oates	2,552,753
1992	3rd	89	73	.549	7.0	Johnny Oates	3,567,819
1993	3rd (tied)	85	77	.525	10.0	Johnny Oates	3,644,965
1994	2nd	63	49	.563	6.5	Johnny Oates	2,535,359
1995	3rd	71	73	.493	15.0	Phil Regan	3,098,475
1996	2nd∞‡	88	74	.543	4.0	Dave Johnson	3,646,950
1997	1st∞‡	98	64	.605	+2.0	Dave Johnson	3,711,132
1998	4th	79	83	.488	35.0	Ray Miller	3,685,194
1999	4th	78	84	.481	20.0	Ray Miller	3,433,150

*Games behind winner. †Won championship series. ‡Lost championship series. §First half 31-23; second 28-23. ∞Won division series.

MANAGERIAL RECORDS

Joe Altobelli 212-167, Jimmy Austin 29-38, Hank Bauer 407-318, Jim Bottomley 21-56, Jimmy Burke 172-180, Hugh Duffy 48-89, Jimmie Dykes 54-100, Lee Fohl 226-183, Fred Haney 125-227, Lum Harris 17-10, Billy Hitchcock 163-161, Rogers Hornsby 255-381, Dan Howley 220-239, Dave Johnson 186-138, Fielder Jones 158-196, Bill Killefer 224-329, Marty Marion 96-161, Jimmy McAleer 551-632, Ray Miller 157-167, Johnny Oates 291-270, Jack O'Connor 47-107, Phil Regan 71-73, Paul Richards 517-539, Branch Rickey 139-179, Cal Ripken Sr. 67-101, Frank Robinson 230-285, Luke Sewell 432-410, George Sisler 218-241, Al Sothoron 2-6, George Stovall 91-158, Gabby Street 55-97, Zack Taylor 235-410, Bobby Wallace 57-134, Earl Weaver 1,481-1,060.

BOSTON RED SOX
YEARLY FINISHES

Year	Position	W	L	Pct.	*GB	Manager	Attendance
1901	2nd	79	57	.581	4.0	Jimmy Collins	289,448
1902	3rd	77	60	.562	6.5	Jimmy Collins	348,567
1903	1st	91	47	.659	+14.5	Jimmy Collins	379,338
1904	1st	95	59	.617	+1.5	Jimmy Collins	623,295
1905	4th	78	74	.513	16.0	Jimmy Collins	468,828
1906	8th	49	105	.318	45.5	Jimmy Collins, Chick Stahl	410,209
1907	7th	59	90	.396	32.5	George Huff, Bob Unglaub, Deacon McGuire	436,777
1908	5th	75	79	.487	15.5	Deacon McGuire, Fred Lake	473,048
1909	3rd	88	63	.583	9.5	Fred Lake	668,965
1910	4th	81	72	.529	22.5	Patsy Donovan	584,619
1911	5th	78	75	.510	24.0	Patsy Donovan	503,961
1912	1st	105	47	.691	+14.0	Jake Stahl	597,096
1913	4th	79	71	.527	15.5	Jake Stahl, Bill Carrigan	437,194
1914	2nd	91	62	.595	8.5	Bill Carrigan	481,359
1915	1st	101	50	.669	+2.5	Bill Carrigan	539,885
1916	1st	91	63	.591	+2.0	Bill Carrigan	496,397
1917	2nd	90	62	.592	9.0	Jack Barry	387,856
1918	1st	75	51	.595	+2.5	Ed Barrow	249,513
1919	6th	66	71	.482	20.5	Ed Barrow	417,291
1920	5th	72	81	.471	25.5	Ed Barrow	402,445
1921	5th	75	79	.487	23.5	Hugh Duffy	279,273
1922	8th	61	93	.396	33.0	Hugh Duffy	259,184
1923	8th	61	91	.401	37.0	Frank Chance	229,668
1924	7th	67	87	.435	25.0	Lee Fohl	448,556
1925	8th	47	105	.309	49.5	Lee Fohl	267,782
1926	8th	46	107	.301	44.5	Lee Fohl	285,155
1927	8th	51	103	.331	59.0	Bill Carrigan	305,275
1928	8th	57	96	.373	43.5	Bill Carrigan	396,920
1929	8th	58	96	.377	48.0	Bill Carrigan	394,620
1930	8th	52	102	.338	50.0	Heinie Wagner	444,045
1931	6th	62	90	.408	45.0	Shano Collins	350,975
1932	8th	43	111	.279	64.0	Shano Collins, Marty McManus	182,150
1933	7th	63	86	.423	34.5	Marty McManus	268,715
1934	4th	76	76	.500	24.0	Bucky Harris	610,640
1935	4th	78	75	.510	16.0	Joseph Cronin	558,568
1936	6th	74	80	.481	28.5	Joe Cronin	626,895
1937	5th	80	72	.526	21.0	Joe Cronin	559,659
1938	2nd	88	61	.591	9.5	Joe Cronin	646,459

– 342 –

Year	Position	W	L	Pct.	*GB	Manager	Attendance
1939	2nd	89	62	.589	17.0	Joe Cronin	573,070
1940	4th (tied)	82	72	.532	8.0	Joe Cronin	716,234
1941	2nd	84	70	.545	17.0	Joe Cronin	718,497
1942	2nd	93	59	.612	9.0	Joe Cronin	730,340
1943	7th	68	84	.447	29.0	Joe Cronin	358,275
1944	4th	77	77	.500	12.0	Joe Cronin	506,975
1945	7th	71	83	.461	17.5	Joe Cronin	603,794
1946	1st	104	50	.675	+12.0	Joe Cronin	1,416,944
1947	3rd	83	71	.539	14.0	Joe Cronin	1,427,315
1948	2nd†	96	59	.619	1.0	Joe McCarthy	1,558,798
1949	2nd	96	58	.623	1.0	Joe McCarthy	1,596,650
1950	3rd	94	60	.610	4.0	Joe McCarthy, Steve O'Neill	1,344,080
1951	3rd	87	67	.565	11.0	Steve O'Neill	1,312,282
1952	6th	76	78	.494	19.0	Lou Boudreau	1,115,750
1953	4th	84	69	.549	16.0	Lou Boudreau	1,026,133
1954	4th	69	85	.448	42.0	Lou Boudreau	931,127
1955	4th	84	70	.545	12.0	Pinky Higgins	1,203,200
1956	4th	84	70	.545	13.0	Pinky Higgins	1,137,158
1957	3rd	82	72	.532	16.0	Pinky Higgins	1,181,087
1958	3rd	79	75	.513	13.0	Pinky Higgins	1,077,047
1959	5th	75	79	.487	19.0	Pinky Higgins, Billy Jurges	984,102
1960	7th	65	89	.422	32.0	Billy Jurges, Pinky Higgins	1,129,866
1961	6th	76	86	.469	33.0	Pinky Higgins	850,589
1962	8th	76	84	.475	19.0	Pinky Higgins	733,080
1963	7th	76	85	.472	28.0	Johnny Pesky	942,642
1964	8th	72	90	.444	27.0	Johnny Pesky, Billy Herman	883,276
1965	9th	62	100	.383	40.0	Billy Herman	652,201
1966	9th	72	90	.444	26.0	Billy Herman, Pete Runnels	811,172
1967	1st	92	70	.568	+1.0	Dick Williams	1,727,832
1968	4th	86	76	.531	17.0	Dick Williams	1,940,788

EAST DIVISION

Year	Position	W	L	Pct.	*GB	Manager	Attendance
1969	3rd	87	75	.537	22.0	Dick Williams, Eddie Popowski	1,833,246
1970	3rd	87	75	.537	21.0	Eddie Kasko	1,595,278
1971	3rd	85	77	.525	18.0	Eddie Kasko	1,678,732
1972	2nd	85	70	.548	0.5	Eddie Kasko	1,441,718
1973	2nd	89	73	.549	8.0	Eddie Kasko	1,481,002
1974	3rd	84	78	.519	7.0	Darrell Johnson	1,556,411
1975	1st‡	95	65	.594	+4.5	Darrell Johnson	1,748,587
1976	3rd	83	79	.512	15.5	Darrell Johnson, Don Zimmer	1,895,846
1977	2nd (tied)	97	64	.602	2.5	Don Zimmer	2,074,549
1978	2nd§	99	64	.607	1.0	Don Zimmer	2,320,643
1979	3rd	91	69	.569	11.5	Don Zimmer	2,353,114
1980	4th	83	77	.519	19.0	Don Zimmer, Johnny Pesky	1,956,092
1981	5th/2nd (tied)	59	49	.546	∞	Ralph Houk	1,060,379
1982	3rd	89	73	.549	6.0	Ralph Houk	1,950,124
1983	6th	78	84	.481	20.0	Ralph Houk	1,782,285
1984	4th	86	76	.531	18.0	Ralph Houk	1,661,618
1985	5th	81	81	.500	18.5	John McNamara	1,786,633
1986	1st‡	95	66	.590	+5.5	John McNamara	2,147,641
1987	5th	78	84	.481	20.0	John McNamara	2,231,551
1988	1st▲	89	73	.549	+1.0	John McNamara, Joe Morgan	2,464,851
1989	3rd	83	79	.512	6.0	Joe Morgan	2,510,012
1990	1st▲	88	74	.543	+2.0	Joe Morgan	2,528,986
1991	2nd (tied)	84	78	.519	7.0	Joe Morgan	2,562,435
1992	7th	73	89	.451	23.0	Butch Hobson	2,468,574
1993	5th	80	82	.494	15.0	Butch Hobson	2,422,021
1994	4th	54	61	.470	17.0	Butch Hobson	1,775,818
1995	1st◆	86	58	.597	+7.0	Kevin Kennedy	2,164,410
1996	3rd	85	77	.525	7.0	Kevin Kennedy	2,315,231
1997	4th	78	84	.481	20.0	Jimy Williams	2,226,136
1998	2nd◆	92	70	.568	22.0	Jimy Williams	2,343,947
1999	2nd■▲	94	68	.580	4.0	Jimy Williams	2,446,162

*Games behind winner. †Lost pennant playoff. ‡Won championship series. §Lost division playoff. ∞First half 30-26; second 29-23. ▲Lost championship series. ◆Lost division series. ■Won division series.

MANAGERIAL RECORDS

Ed Barrow 213-203, Jack Barry 90-62, Lou Boudreau 229-232, Bill Carrigan 489-500, Frank Chance 61-91, Jimmy Collins 455-376, Shano Collins 73-134, Joe Cronin 1,071-916, Patsy Donovan 159-147, Hugh Duffy 136-172, Lee Fohl 160-299, Bucky Harris 76-76, Billy Herman 128-182, Pinky Higgins 560-556, Butch Hobson 207-232, Ralph Houk 312-282, George Huff 2-6, Darrell Johnson 220-188, Billy Jurges 59-63, Eddie Kasko 346-295, Kevin Kennedy 171-135, Fred Lake 110-80, Joe McCarthy 223-145, Deacon McGuire 98-123, Marty McManus 95-153, John McNamara 297-273, Joe Morgan 301-262, Steve O'Neill 150-99, Johnny Pesky 147-179, Eddie Popowski 5-4, Pete Runnels 8-8, Chick Stahl 14-26, Jake Stahl 144-88, Bob Unglaub 9-20, Heinie Wagner 52-102, Dick Williams 260-217, Jimy Williams 264-222, Don Zimmer 411-304.

Year	Position	W	L	Pct.	*GB	Manager	Attendance
1901	1st	83	53	.610	+4.0	Clark Griffith	354,350
1902	4th	74	60	.552	8.0	Clark Griffith	337,898
1903	7th	60	77	.438	30.5	Nixey Callahan	286,183
1904	3rd	89	65	.578	6.0	Nixey Callahan, Fielder Jones	557,123
1905	2nd	92	60	.605	2.0	Fielder Jones	687,419
1906	1st	93	58	.616	+3.0	Fielder Jones	585,202
1907	3rd	87	64	.576	5.5	Fielder Jones	666,307
1908	3rd	88	64	.579	1.5	Fielder Jones	636,096
1909	4th	78	74	.513	20.0	Billy Sullivan	478,400
1910	6th	68	85	.444	35.5	Hugh Duffy	552,084
1911	4th	77	74	.510	24.0	Hugh Duffy	583,208
1912	4th	78	76	.506	28.0	Nixey Callahan	602,241
1913	5th	78	74	.513	17.5	Nixey Callahan	644,501
1914	6th (tied)	70	84	.455	30.0	Nixey Callahan	469,290
1915	3rd	93	61	.604	9.5	Pants Rowland	539,461
1916	2nd	89	65	.578	2.0	Pants Rowland	679,923
1917	1st	100	54	.649	+9.0	Pants Rowland	684,521
1918	6th	57	67	.460	17.0	Pants Rowland	195,081
1919	1st	88	52	.629	+3.5	Kid Gleason	627,186
1920	2nd	96	58	.623	2.0	Kid Gleason	833,492
1921	7th	62	92	.403	36.5	Kid Gleason	543,650
1922	5th	77	77	.500	17.0	Kid Gleason	602,860
1923	7th	69	85	.448	30.0	Kid Gleason	573,778
1924	8th	66	87	.431	25.5	Johnny Evers	606,658
1925	5th	79	75	.513	18.5	Eddie Collins	832,231
1926	5th	81	72	.529	9.5	Eddie Collins	710,339
1927	5th	70	83	.458	29.5	Ray Schalk	614,423
1928	5th	72	82	.468	29.0	Ray Schalk, Lena Blackburne	494,152
1929	7th	59	93	.388	46.0	Lena Blackburne	426,795
1930	7th	62	92	.403	40.0	Donie Bush	406,123
1931	8th	56	97	.366	51.0	Donie Bush	403,550
1932	7th	49	102	.325	56.5	Lew Fonseca	233,198
1933	6th	67	83	.447	31.0	Lew Fonseca	397,789
1934	8th	53	99	.349	47.0	Lew Fonseca, Jimmie Dykes	236,559
1935	5th	74	78	.487	19.5	Jimmie Dykes	470,281
1936	3rd	81	70	.536	20.0	Jimmie Dykes	440,810
1937	3rd	86	68	.558	16.0	Jimmie Dykes	589,245
1938	6th	65	83	.439	32.0	Jimmie Dykes	338,278
1939	4th	85	69	.552	22.5	Jimmie Dykes	594,104
1940	4th (tied)	82	72	.532	8.0	Jimmie Dykes	660,336
1941	3rd	77	77	.500	24.0	Jimmie Dykes	677,077
1942	6th	66	82	.446	34.0	Jimmie Dykes	425,734
1943	4th	82	72	.532	16.0	Jimmie Dykes	508,962
1944	7th	71	83	.461	18.0	Jimmie Dykes	563,539
1945	6th	71	78	.477	15.0	Jimmie Dykes	657,981
1946	5th	74	80	.481	30.0	Jimmie Dykes, Ted Lyons	983,403
1947	6th	70	84	.455	27.0	Ted Lyons	876,948
1948	8th	51	101	.336	44.5	Ted Lyons	777,844
1949	6th	63	91	.409	34.0	Jack Onslow	937,151
1950	6th	60	94	.390	38.0	Jack Onslow, Red Corriden	781,330
1951	4th	81	73	.526	17.0	Paul Richards	1,328,234
1952	3rd	81	73	.526	14.0	Paul Richards	1,231,675
1953	3rd	89	65	.578	11.5	Paul Richards	1,191,353
1954	3rd	94	60	.610	17.0	Paul Richards, Marty Marion	1,231,629
1955	3rd	91	63	.591	5.0	Marty Marion	1,175,684
1956	3rd	85	69	.552	12.0	Marty Marion	1,000,090
1957	2nd	90	64	.584	8.0	Al Lopez	1,135,668
1958	2nd	82	72	.532	10.0	Al Lopez	797,451
1959	1st	94	60	.610	+5.0	Al Lopez	1,423,144
1960	3rd	87	67	.565	10.0	Al Lopez	1,644,460
1961	4th	86	76	.531	23.0	Al Lopez	1,146,019
1962	5th	85	77	.525	11.0	Al Lopez	1,131,562
1963	2nd	94	68	.580	10.5	Al Lopez	1,158,848
1964	2nd	98	64	.605	1.0	Al Lopez	1,250,053
1965	2nd	95	67	.586	7.0	Al Lopez	1,130,519
1966	4th	83	79	.512	15.0	Eddie Stanky	990,016
1967	4th	89	73	.549	3.0	Eddie Stanky	985,634
1968	8th (tied)	67	95	.414	36.0	Eddie Stanky, Al Lopez	803,775

HISTORY *Team by team*

WEST DIVISION

Year	Position	W	L	Pct.	*GB	Manager	Attendance
1969	5th	68	94	.420	29.0	Al Lopez, Don Gutteridge	589,546
1970	6th	56	106	.346	42.0	Don Gutteridge, Chuck Tanner	495,355
1971	3rd	79	83	.488	22.5	Chuck Tanner	833,891
1972	2nd	87	67	.565	5.5	Chuck Tanner	1,177,318
1973	5th	77	85	.475	17.0	Chuck Tanner	1,302,527
1974	4th	80	80	.500	9.0	Chuck Tanner	1,149,596
1975	5th	75	86	.466	22.5	Chuck Tanner	750,802
1976	6th	64	97	.398	25.5	Paul Richards	914,945
1977	3rd	90	72	.556	12.0	Bob Lemon	1,657,135
1978	5th	71	90	.441	20.5	Bob Lemon, Larry Doby	1,491,100
1979	5th	73	87	.456	14.0	Don Kessinger, Tony La Russa	1,280,702
1980	5th	70	90	.438	26.0	Tony La Russa	1,200,365
1981	3rd/6th	54	52	.509	†	Tony La Russa	946,651
1982	3rd	87	75	.537	6.0	Tony La Russa	1,567,787
1983	1st‡	99	63	.611	+20.0	Tony La Russa	2,132,821
1984	5th (tied)	74	88	.457	10.0	Tony La Russa	2,136,988
1985	3rd	85	77	.525	6.0	Tony La Russa	1,669,888
1986	5th	72	90	.444	20.0	Tony La Russa, Jim Fregosi	1,424,313
1987	5th	77	85	.475	8.0	Jim Fregosi	1,208,060
1988	5th	71	90	.441	32.5	Jim Fregosi	1,115,749
1989	7th	69	92	.429	29.5	Jeff Torborg	1,045,651
1990	2nd	94	68	.580	9.0	Jeff Torborg	2,002,357
1991	2nd	87	75	.537	8.0	Jeff Torborg	2,934,154
1992	3rd	86	76	.531	10.0	Gene Lamont	2,681,156
1993	1st‡	94	68	.580	+8.0	Gene Lamont	2,581,091

CENTRAL DIVISION

Year	Position	W	L	Pct.	*GB	Manager	Attendance
1994	1st	67	46	.593	+1.0	Gene Lamont	1,697,398
1995	3rd	68	76	.472	32.0	Gene Lamont, Terry Bevington	1,609,773
1996	2nd	85	77	.525	14.5	Terry Bevington	1,676,403
1997	2nd	80	81	.497	6.0	Terry Bevington	1,864,782
1998	2nd	80	82	.494	9.0	Jerry Manuel	1,391,146
1999	2nd	75	86	.466	21.5	Jerry Manuel	1,338,851

*Games behind winner. †First half 31-22; second 23-30. ‡Lost championship series.

MANAGERIAL RECORDS

Terry Bevington 222-214, Lena Blackburne 99-133, Donie Bush 118-189, Nixey Callahan 309-329, Eddie Collins 160-147, Red Corriden 52-72, Larry Doby 37-50, Hugh Duffy 145-159, Jimmie Dykes 899-940, Johnny Evers 66-87, Lew Fonseca 120-196, Jim Fregosi 193-226, Kid Gleason 392-364, Clark Griffith 157-113, Don Gutteridge 109-172, Fielder Jones 426-293, Don Kessinger 46-60, Tony La Russa 522-510, Gene Lamont 258-210, Bob Lemon 124-112, Al Lopez 840-650, Ted Lyons 185-245, Jerry Manuel 155-168, Marty Marion 179-138, Jack Onslow 71-133, Paul Richards 406-362, Pants Rowland 339-247, Ray Schalk 102-125, Eddie Stanky 206-197, Billy Sullivan 78-74, Chuck Tanner 401-414, Jeff Torborg 250-235.

CLEVELAND INDIANS
YEARLY FINISHES

Year	Position	W	L	Pct.	*GB	Manager	Attendance
1901	7th	54	82	.397	29.0	James McAleer	131,380
1902	5th	69	67	.507	14.0	Bill Armour	275,395
1903	3rd	77	63	.550	15.0	Bill Armour	311,280
1904	4th	86	65	.570	7.5	Bill Armour	264,749
1905	5th	76	78	.494	19.0	Nap Lajoie	316,306
1906	3rd	89	64	.582	5.0	Nap Lajoie	325,733
1907	4th	85	67	.559	8.0	Nap Lajoie	382,046
1908	2nd	90	64	.584	0.5	Nap Lajoie	422,242
1909	6th	71	82	.464	27.5	Nap Lajoie, Deacon McGuire	354,627
1910	5th	71	81	.467	32.0	Deacon McGuire	293,456
1911	3rd	80	73	.523	22.0	Deacon McGuire, George Stovall	406,296
1912	5th	75	78	.490	30.5	Harry Davis, J.L. Birmingham	336,844
1913	3rd	86	66	.566	9.5	J.L. Birmingham	541,000
1914	8th	51	102	.333	48.5	J.L. Birmingham	185,997
1915	7th	57	95	.375	44.5	J.L. Birmingham, Lee Fohl	159,285
1916	6th	77	77	.500	14.0	Lee Fohl	492,106
1917	3rd	88	66	.571	12.0	Lee Fohl	477,298
1918	2nd	73	54	.575	2.5	Lee Fohl	295,515
1919	2nd	84	55	.604	3.5	Lee Fohl, Tris Speaker	538,135
1920	1st	98	56	.636	+2.0	Tris Speaker	912,832
1921	2nd	94	60	.610	4.5	Tris Speaker	748,705
1922	4th	78	76	.507	16.0	Tris Speaker	528,145
1923	3rd	82	71	.536	16.5	Tris Speaker	558,856

Year	Position	W	L	Pct.	*GB	Manager	Attendance
1924	6th	67	86	.438	24.5	Tris Speaker	481,905
1925	6th	70	84	.455	27.5	Tris Speaker	419,005
1926	2nd	88	66	.571	3.0	Tris Speaker	627,426
1927	6th	66	87	.431	43.5	Jack McAllister	373,138
1928	7th	62	92	.403	39.0	Roger Peckinpaugh	375,907
1929	3rd	81	71	.533	24.0	Roger Peckinpaugh	536,210
1930	4th	81	73	.536	21.0	Roger Peckinpaugh	528,657
1931	4th	78	76	.506	30.0	Roger Peckinpaugh	483,027
1932	4th	87	65	.572	19.0	Roger Peckinpaugh	468,953
1933	4th	75	76	.497	23.5	Roger Peckinpaugh, Walter Johnson	387,936
1934	3rd	85	69	.552	16.0	Walter Johnson	391,338
1935	3rd	82	71	.536	12.0	Walter Johnson, Steve O'Neill	397,615
1936	5th	80	74	.519	22.5	Steve O'Neill	500,391
1937	4th	83	71	.539	19.0	Steve O'Neill	564,849
1938	3rd	86	66	.566	13.0	Ossie Vitt	652,006
1939	3rd	87	67	.565	20.5	Ossie Vitt	563,926
1940	2nd	89	65	.578	1.0	Ossie Vitt	902,576
1941	4th (tied)	75	79	.487	26.0	Roger Peckinpaugh	745,948
1942	4th	75	79	.487	28.0	Lou Boudreau	459,447
1943	3rd	82	71	.536	15.5	Lou Boudreau	438,894
1944	5th (tied)	72	82	.468	17.0	Lou Boudreau	475,272
1945	5th	73	72	.503	11.0	Lou Boudreau	558,182
1946	6th	68	86	.442	36.0	Lou Boudreau	1,057,289
1947	4th	80	74	.519	17.0	Lou Boudreau	1,521,978
1948	1st†	97	58	.626	+1.0	Lou Boudreau	2,620,627
1949	3rd	89	65	.578	8.0	Lou Boudreau	2,233,771
1950	4th	92	62	.597	6.0	Lou Boudreau	1,727,464
1951	2nd	93	61	.604	5.0	Al Lopez	1,704,984
1952	2nd	93	61	.604	2.0	Al Lopez	1,444,607
1953	2nd	92	62	.597	8.5	Al Lopez	1,069,176
1954	1st	111	43	.721	+8.0	Al Lopez	1,335,472
1955	2nd	93	61	.604	3.0	Al Lopez	1,221,780
1956	2nd	88	66	.571	9.0	Al Lopez	865,467
1957	6th	76	77	.497	21.5	Kerby Farrell	722,256
1958	4th	77	76	.503	14.5	Bobby Bragan, Joe Gordon	663,805
1959	2nd	89	65	.578	5.0	Joe Gordon	1,497,976
1960	4th	76	78	.494	21.0	Joe Gordon, Jimmie Dykes	950,985
1961	5th	78	83	.484	30.5	Jimmie Dykes	725,547
1962	6th	80	82	.494	16.0	Mel McGaha	716,076
1963	5th (tied)	79	83	.488	25.5	Birdie Tebbetts	562,507
1964	6th (tied)	79	83	.488	20.0	Birdie Tebbetts	653,293
1965	5th	87	75	.537	15.0	Birdie Tebbetts	934,786
1966	5th	81	81	.500	17.0	Birdie Tebbetts, George Strickland	903,359
1967	8th	75	87	.463	17.0	Joe Adcock	662,980
1968	3rd	86	75	.534	16.5	Alvin Dark	857,994

EAST DIVISION

Year	Position	W	L	Pct.	*GB	Manager	Attendance
1969	6th	62	99	.385	46.5	Alvin Dark	619,970
1970	5th	76	86	.469	32.0	Alvin Dark	729,752
1971	6th	60	102	.370	43.0	Alvin Dark, John Lipon	591,361
1972	5th	72	84	.462	14.0	Ken Aspromonte	626,354
1973	6th	71	91	.438	26.0	Ken Aspromonte	615,107
1974	4th	77	85	.475	14.0	Ken Aspromonte	1,114,262
1975	4th	79	80	.497	15.5	Frank Robinson	977,039
1976	4th	81	78	.509	16.0	Frank Robinson	948,776
1977	5th	71	90	.441	28.5	Frank Robinson, Jeff Torborg	900,365
1978	6th	69	90	.434	29.0	Jeff Torborg	800,584
1979	6th	81	80	.503	22.0	Jeff Torborg, Dave Garcia	1,011,644
1980	6th	79	81	.494	23.0	Dave Garcia	1,033,827
1981	6th/5th	52	51	.504	‡	Dave Garcia	661,395
1982	6th (tied)	78	84	.481	17.0	Dave Garcia	1,044,021
1983	7th	70	92	.432	28.0	Mike Ferraro, Pat Corrales	768,941
1984	6th	75	87	.463	29.0	Pat Corrales	734,079
1985	7th	60	102	.370	39.5	Pat Corrales	655,181
1986	5th	84	78	.519	11.5	Pat Corrales	1,471,805
1987	7th	61	101	.377	37.0	Pat Corrales, Doc Edwards	1,077,898
1988	6th	78	84	.481	11.0	Doc Edwards	1,411,610
1989	6th	73	89	.451	16.0	Doc Edwards, John Hart	1,285,542
1990	4th	77	85	.475	11.0	John McNamara	1,225,240
1991	7th	57	105	.352	34.0	John McNamara, Mike Hargrove	1,051,863
1992	4th (tied)	76	86	.469	20.0	Mike Hargrove	1,224,274
1993	6th	76	86	.469	19.0	Mike Hargrove	2,177,908

CENTRAL DIVISION

Year	Position	W	L	Pct.	*GB	Manager	Attendance
1994	2nd	66	47	.584	1.0	Mike Hargrove	1,995,174
1995	1st§∞	100	44	.694	+30.0	Mike Hargrove	2,842,745
1996	1st▲	99	62	.615	+14.5	Mike Hargrove	3,318,174
1997	1st§∞	86	75	.534	+6.0	Mike Hargrove	3,404,750
1998	1st§◆	89	73	.549	+9.0	Mike Hargrove	3,467,299
1999	1st▲	97	65	.599	+21.5	Mike Hargrove	3,468,456

*Games behind winner. †Won pennant playoff. ‡First half 26-24; second 26-27. §Won division series. ∞Won championship series. ▲Lost division series. ◆Lost championship series.

MANAGERIAL RECORDS

Joe Adcock 75-87, Bill Armour 232-195, Ken Aspromonte 220-260, Joe Birmingham 170-191, Lou Boudreau 728-649, Bobby Bragan 31-36, Pat Corrales 280-355, Alvin Dark 266-321, Harry Davis 54-71, Jimmie Dykes 103-115, Doc Edwards 173-207, Kerby Farrell 76-77, Mike Ferraro 40-60, Lee Fohl 327-310, Dave Garcia 247-244, Joe Gordon 184-151, Mike Hargrove 721-591, John Hart 8-11, Walter Johnson 179-168, Nap Lajoie 377-309, Johnny Lipon 18-41, Al Lopez 570-354, Jimmy McAleer 54-82, Jack McCallister 66-87, Mel McGaha 80-82, Deacon McGuire 91-117, John McNamara 102-137, Steve O'Neill 199-168, Roger Peckinpaugh 490-481, Frank Robinson 186-189, Tris Speaker 617-520, George Stovall 74-62, George Strickland 15-24, Birdie Tebbetts 269-298, Jeff Torborg 157-201, Oscar Vitt 262-198.

DETROIT TIGERS
YEARLY FINISHES

Year	Position	W	L	Pct.	*GB	Manager	Attendance
1901	3rd	74	61	.548	8.5	George Stallings	259,430
1902	7th	52	83	.385	30.5	Frank Dwyer	189,469
1903	5th	65	71	.478	25.0	Ed Barrow	224,523
1904	7th	62	90	.408	32.0	Ed Barrow, Bobby Lowe	177,796
1905	3rd	79	74	.516	15.5	Bill Armour	193,384
1906	6th	71	78	.477	21.0	Bill Armour	174,043
1907	1st	92	58	.613	+1.5	Hughey Jennings	297,079
1908	1st	90	63	.588	+.5	Hughey Jennings	436,199
1909	1st	98	54	.645	+3.5	Hughey Jennings	490,490
1910	3rd	86	68	.558	18.0	Hughey Jennings	391,288
1911	2nd	89	65	.578	13.5	Hughey Jennings	484,988
1912	6th	69	84	.451	36.5	Hughey Jennings	402,870
1913	6th	66	87	.431	30.0	Hughey Jennings	398,502
1914	4th	80	73	.523	19.5	Hughey Jennings	416,225
1915	2nd	100	54	.649	2.5	Hughey Jennings	476,105
1916	3rd	87	67	.565	4.0	Hughey Jennings	616,772
1917	4th	78	75	.510	21.5	Hughey Jennings	457,289
1918	7th	55	71	.437	20.0	Hughey Jennings	203,719
1919	4th	80	60	.571	8.0	Hughey Jennings	643,805
1920	7th	61	93	.396	37.0	Hughey Jennings	579,650
1921	6th	71	82	.464	27.0	Ty Cobb	661,527
1922	3rd	79	75	.513	15.0	Ty Cobb	861,206
1923	2nd	83	71	.539	16.0	Ty Cobb	911,377
1924	3rd	86	68	.558	6.0	Ty Cobb	1,015,136
1925	4th	81	73	.526	16.5	Ty Cobb	820,766
1926	6th	79	75	.513	12.0	Ty Cobb	711,914
1927	4th	82	71	.536	27.5	George Moriarty	773,716
1928	6th	68	86	.442	33.0	George Moriarty	474,323
1929	6th	70	84	.455	36.0	Bucky Harris	869,318
1930	5th	75	79	.487	27.0	Bucky Harris	649,450
1931	7th	61	93	.396	47.0	Bucky Harris	434,056
1932	5th	76	75	.503	29.5	Bucky Harris	397,157
1933	5th	75	79	.487	25.0	Del Baker	320,972
1934	1st	101	53	.656	+7.0	Mickey Cochrane	919,161
1935	1st	93	58	.616	+3.0	Mickey Cochrane	1,034,929
1936	2nd	83	71	.539	19.5	Mickey Cochrane	875,948
1937	2nd	89	65	.578	13.0	Mickey Cochrane	1,072,276
1938	4th	84	70	.545	16.0	Mickey Cochrane, Del Baker	799,557
1939	5th	81	73	.526	26.5	Del Baker	836,279
1940	1st	90	64	.584	+1.0	Del Baker	1,112,693
1941	4th (tied)	75	79	.487	26.0	Del Baker	684,915
1942	5th	73	81	.474	30.0	Del Baker	580,087
1943	5th	78	76	.506	20.0	Steve O'Neill	606,287
1944	2nd	88	66	.571	1.0	Steve O'Neill	923,176
1945	1st	88	65	.575	+1.5	Steve O'Neill	1,280,341
1946	2nd	92	62	.597	12.0	Steve O'Neill	1,722,590
1947	2nd	85	69	.552	12.0	Steve O'Neill	1,398,093
1948	5th	78	76	.506	18.5	Steve O'Neill	1,743,035
1949	4th	87	67	.565	10.0	Red Rolfe	1,821,204

– 347 –

Year	Position	W	L	Pct.	*GB	Manager	Attendance
1950	2nd	95	59	.617	3.0	Red Rolfe	1,951,474
1951	5th	73	81	.474	25.0	Red Rolfe	1,132,641
1952	8th	50	104	.325	45.0	Red Rolfe, Fred Hutchinson	1,026,846
1953	6th	60	94	.390	40.5	Fred Hutchinson	884,658
1954	5th	68	86	.442	43.0	Fred Hutchinson	1,079,847
1955	5th	79	75	.513	17.0	Bucky Harris	1,181,838
1956	5th	82	72	.532	15.0	Bucky Harris	1,051,182
1957	4th	78	76	.506	20.0	Jack Tighe	1,272,346
1958	5th	77	77	.500	15.0	Jack Tighe, Bill Norman	1,098,924
1959	4th	76	78	.494	18.0	Bill Norman, Jimmie Dykes	1,221,221
1960	6th	71	83	.461	26.0	Jimmie Dykes, Billy Hitchcock, Joe Gordon	1,167,669
1961	2nd	101	61	.623	8.0	Bob Scheffing	1,600,710
1962	4th	85	76	.528	10.5	Bob Scheffing	1,207,881
1963	5th (tied)	79	83	.488	25.5	Bob Scheffing, Charlie Dressen	821,952
1964	4th	85	77	.525	14.0	Charlie Dressen	816,139
1965	4th	89	73	.549	13.0	Charlie Dressen, Bob Swift	1,029,645
1966	3rd	88	74	.543	10.0	Charlie Dressen, Bob Swift, Frank Skaff	1,124,293
1967	2nd	91	71	.562	1.0	Mayo Smith	1,447,143
1968	1st	103	59	.636	+12.0	Mayo Smith	2,031,847

EAST DIVISION

Year	Position	W	L	Pct.	*GB	Manager	Attendance
1969	2nd	90	72	.556	19.0	Mayo Smith	1,577,481
1970	4th	79	83	.488	29.0	Mayo Smith	1,501,293
1971	2nd	91	71	.562	12.0	Billy Martin	1,591,073
1972	1st†	86	70	.551	+0.5	Billy Martin	1,892,386
1973	3rd	85	77	.525	12.0	Billy Martin, Joe Schultz	1,724,146
1974	6th	72	90	.444	19.0	Ralph Houk	1,243,080
1975	6th	57	102	.358	37.5	Ralph Houk	1,058,836
1976	5th	74	87	.460	24.0	Ralph Houk	1,467,020
1977	4th	74	88	.457	26.0	Ralph Houk	1,359,856
1978	5th	86	76	.531	13.5	Ralph Houk	1,714,893
1979	5th	85	76	.528	18.0	Les Moss, Dick Tracewski, Sparky Anderson	1,630,929
1980	5th	84	78	.519	19.0	Sparky Anderson	1,785,293
1981	4th/2nd (tied)	60	49	.550	‡	Sparky Anderson	1,149,144
1982	4th	83	79	.512	12.0	Sparky Anderson	1,636,058
1983	2nd	92	70	.568	6.0	Sparky Anderson	1,829,636
1984	1st§	104	58	.642	+15.0	Sparky Anderson	2,704,794
1985	3rd	84	77	.522	15.0	Sparky Anderson	2,286,609
1986	3rd	87	75	.537	8.5	Sparky Anderson	1,899,437
1987	1st†	98	64	.605	+2.0	Sparky Anderson	2,061,830
1988	2nd	88	74	.543	1.0	Sparky Anderson	2,081,162
1989	7th	59	103	.364	30.0	Sparky Anderson	1,543,656
1990	3rd	79	83	.488	9.0	Sparky Anderson	1,495,785
1991	2nd	84	78	.519	7.0	Sparky Anderson	1,641,661
1992	6th	75	87	.463	21.0	Sparky Anderson	1,423,963
1993	3rd (tied)	85	77	.525	10.0	Sparky Anderson	1,971,421
1994	5th	53	62	.461	18.0	Sparky Anderson	1,184,783
1995	4th	60	84	.417	26.0	Sparky Anderson	1,180,979
1996	5th	53	109	.327	39.0	Buddy Bell	1,168,610
1997	3rd	79	83	.488	19.0	Buddy Bell	1,365,157

CENTRAL DIVISION

Year	Position	W	L	Pct.	*GB	Manager	Attendance
1998	5th	65	97	.401	24.0	Buddy Bell, Larry Parrish	1,409,391
1999	3rd	69	92	.429	27.5	Larry Parrish	2,026,441

*Games behind winner. †Lost championship series. ‡First half 31-26; second 29-23. §Won championship series.

MANAGERIAL RECORDS

Sparky Anderson 1,431-1,248, Bill Armour 150-152, Del Baker 392-336, Ed Barrow 97-117, Buddy Bell 184-277, Ty Cobb 479-444, Mickey Cochrane 379-278, Chuck Dressen 221-189, Frank Dwyer 52-83, Jimmie Dykes 118-115, Joe Gordon 26-31, Bucky Harris 516-557, Ralph Houk 366-443, Fred Hutchinson 155-235, Hugh Jennings 1,131-972, Bobby Lowe 30-44, Billy Martin 248-204, George Moriarty 150-157, Les Moss 27-26, Bill Norman 58-64, Steve O'Neill 509-414, Larry Parrish 82-104, Red Rolfe 278-256, Bob Scheffing 210-173, Joe Schultz 14-14, Frank Skaff 40-39, Mayo Smith 363-285, George Stallings 74-61, Bob Swift 56-43, Jack Tighe 99-104.

KANSAS CITY ROYALS
YEARLY FINISHES
WEST DIVISION

Year	Position	W	L	Pct.	*GB	Manager	Attendance
1969	4th	69	93	.429	28	Joe Gordon	902,414
1970	4th (tied)	65	97	.401	33	Charlie Metro, Bob Lemon	693,047

Year	Position	W	L	Pct.	*GB	Manager	Attendance
1971	2nd	85	76	.528	16	Bob Lemon	910,784
1972	4th	76	78	.494	16.5	Bob Lemon	707,656
1973	2nd	88	74	.543	6	Jack McKeon	1,345,341
1974	5th	77	85	.475	13	Jack McKeon	1,173,292
1975	2nd	91	71	.562	7	Jack McKeon, Whitey Herzog	1,151,836
1976	1st†	90	72	.556	+2.5	Whitey Herzog	1,680,265
1977	1st†	102	60	.630	+8	Whitey Herzog	1,852,603
1978	1st†	92	70	.568	+5	Whitey Herzog	2,255,493
1979	2nd	85	77	.525	3	Whitey Herzog	2,261,845
1980	1st‡	97	65	.599	+14	Jim Frey	2,288,714
1981	5th/1st∞	50	53	.485	§	Jim Frey, Dick Howser	1,279,403
1982	2nd	90	72	.556	3	Dick Howser	2,284,464
1983	2nd	79	83	.488	20	Dick Howser	1,963,875
1984	1st†	84	78	.519	+3	Dick Howser	1,810,018
1985	1st‡	91	71	.562	+1	Dick Howser	2,162,717
1986	3rd (tied)	76	86	.469	16	Dick Howser, Mike Ferraro	2,320,794
1987	2nd	83	79	.512	2	Billy Gardner, John Wathan	2,392,471
1988	3rd	84	77	.522	19.5	John Wathan	2,350,181
1989	2nd	92	70	.568	7	John Wathan	2,477,700
1990	6th	75	86	.466	27.5	John Wathan	2,244,956
1991	6th	82	80	.506	13	John Wathan, Hal McRae	2,161,537
1992	5th (tied)	72	90	.444	24	Hal McRae	1,867,689
1993	3rd	84	78	.519	10	Hal McRae	1,934,578

CENTRAL DIVISION

Year	Position	W	L	Pct.	*GB	Manager	Attendance
1994	3rd	64	51	.557	4	Hal McRae	1,400,494
1995	2nd	70	74	.486	30	Bob Boone	1,233,530
1996	5th	75	86	.466	24	Bob Boone	1,435,997
1997	5th	67	94	.416	19	Bob Boone, Tony Muser	1,517,638
1998	3rd	72	89	.447	16.5	Tony Muser	1,494,875
1999	4th	64	97	.398	32.5	Tony Muser	1,506,068

*Games behind winner. †Lost championship series. ‡Won championship series. §First half 20-30; second 30-23. ∞Lost division series.

MANAGERIAL RECORDS

Bob Boone 181-206, Mike Ferraro 36-38, Jim Frey 127-105, Billy Gardner 62-64, Joe Gordon 69-93, Whitey Herzog 410-304, Dick Howser 404-365, Bob Lemon 207-218, Jack McKeon 215-205, Hal McRae 286-277, Charlie Metro 19-33, Tony Muser 167-234, John Wathan 288-270.

MINNESOTA TWINS
YEARLY FINISHES

(Known as original Washington Senators through 1960)

Year	Position	W	L	Pct.	*GB	Manager	Attendance
1901	6th	61	72	.459	20.5	Jimmy Manning	161,661
1902	6th	61	75	.449	22.0	Tom Loftus	188,158
1903	8th	43	94	.314	47.5	Tom Loftus	128,878
1904	8th	38	113	.251	55.5	Patsy Donovan	131,744
1905	7th	64	87	.421	29.5	Jake Stahl	252,027
1906	7th	55	95	.367	37.5	Jake Stahl	129,903
1907	8th	49	102	.325	43.5	Joe Cantillon	221,929
1908	7th	67	85	.441	22.5	Joe Cantillon	264,252
1909	8th	42	110	.276	56.0	Joe Cantillon	205,199
1910	7th	66	85	.437	36.5	Jimmy McAleer	254,591
1911	7th	64	90	.416	38.5	Jimmy McAleer	244,884
1912	2nd	91	61	.599	14.0	Clark Griffith	350,663
1913	2nd	90	64	.584	6.5	Clark Griffith	325,831
1914	3rd	81	73	.526	19.0	Clark Griffith	243,888
1915	4th	85	68	.556	17.0	Clark Griffith	167,332
1916	7th	76	77	.497	14.5	Clark Griffith	177,265
1917	5th	74	79	.484	25.5	Clark Griffith	89,682
1918	3rd	72	56	.563	4.0	Clark Griffith	182,122
1919	7th	56	84	.400	32.0	Clark Griffith	234,096
1920	6th	68	84	.447	29.0	Clark Griffith	359,260
1921	4th	80	73	.523	18.0	George McBride	456,069
1922	6th	69	85	.448	25.0	Clyde Milan	458,552
1923	4th	75	78	.490	23.5	Donie Bush	357,406
1924	1st	92	62	.597	+2.0	Bucky Harris	534,310
1925	1st†	96	55	.636	+8.5	Bucky Harris	817,199
1926	4th	81	69	.540	8.0	Bucky Harris	551,580
1927	3rd	85	69	.552	25.0	Bucky Harris	528,976
1928	4th	75	79	.487	26.0	Bucky Harris	378,501

Year	Position	W	L	Pct.	*GB	Manager	Attendance
1929	5th	71	81	.467	34.0	Walter Johnson	355,506
1930	2nd	94	60	.610	8.0	Walter Johnson	614,474
1931	3rd	92	62	.597	16.0	Walter Johnson	492,657
1932	3rd	93	61	.604	14.0	Walter Johnson	371,396
1933	1st	99	53	.651	+7.0	Joe Cronin	437,533
1934	7th	66	86	.434	34.0	Joe Cronin	330,074
1935	6th	67	86	.438	27.0	Bucky Harris	255,011
1936	4th	82	71	.536	20.0	Bucky Harris	379,525
1937	6th	73	80	.477	28.5	Bucky Harris	397,799
1938	5th	75	76	.497	23.5	Bucky Harris	522,694
1939	6th	65	87	.428	41.5	Bucky Harris	339,257
1940	7th	64	90	.416	26.0	Bucky Harris	381,241
1941	6th (tied)	70	84	.455	31.0	Bucky Harris	415,663
1942	7th	62	89	.411	39.5	Bucky Harris	403,493
1943	2nd	84	69	.549	13.5	Ossie Bluege	574,694
1944	8th	64	90	.416	25.0	Ossie Bluege	525,235
1945	2nd	87	67	.565	1.5	Ossie Bluege	652,660
1946	4th	76	78	.494	28.0	Ossie Bluege	1,027,216
1947	7th	64	90	.416	33.0	Ossie Bluege	850,758
1948	7th	56	97	.366	40.0	Joe Kuhel	795,254
1949	8th	50	104	.325	47.0	Joe Kuhel	770,745
1950	5th	67	87	.435	31.0	Bucky Harris	699,697
1951	7th	62	92	.403	36.0	Bucky Harris	695,167
1952	5th	78	76	.506	17.0	Bucky Harris	699,457
1953	5th	76	76	.500	23.5	Bucky Harris	595,594
1954	6th	66	88	.429	45.0	Bucky Harris	503,542
1955	8th	53	101	.344	43.0	Chuck Dressen	425,238
1956	7th	59	95	.383	38.0	Chuck Dressen	431,647
1957	8th	55	99	.357	43.0	Chuck Dressen, Cookie Lavagetto	457,079
1958	8th	61	93	.396	31.0	Cookie Lavagetto	475,288
1959	8th	63	91	.409	31.0	Cookie Lavagetto	615,372
1960	5th	73	81	.474	24.0	Cookie Lavagetto	743,404
1961	7th	70	90	.438	38.0	Cookie Lavagetto, Sam Mele	1,256,723
1962	2nd	91	71	.562	5.0	Sam Mele	1,433,116
1963	3rd	91	70	.565	13.0	Sam Mele	1,406,652
1964	6th (tied)	79	83	.488	20.0	Sam Mele	1,207,514
1965	1st	102	60	.630	+7.0	Sam Mele	1,463,258
1966	2nd	89	73	.549	9.0	Sam Mele	1,259,374
1967	2nd (tied)	91	71	.562	1.0	Sam Mele, Cal Ermer	1,483,547
1968	7th	79	83	.488	24.0	Cal Ermer	1,143,257

WEST DIVISION

Year	Position	W	L	Pct.	*GB	Manager	Attendance
1969	1st†	97	65	.599	+9.0	Billy Martin	1,349,328
1970	1st†	98	64	.605	+9.0	Bill Rigney	1,261,887
1971	5th	74	86	.463	26.5	Bill Rigney	940,858
1972	3rd	77	77	.500	15.5	Bill Rigney, Frank Quilici	797,901
1973	3rd	81	81	.500	13.0	Frank Quilici	907,499
1974	3rd	82	80	.506	8.0	Frank Quilici	662,401
1975	4th	76	83	.478	20.5	Frank Quilici	737,156
1976	3rd	85	77	.525	5.0	Gene Mauch	715,394
1977	4th	84	77	.522	17.5	Gene Mauch	1,162,727
1978	4th	73	89	.451	19.0	Gene Mauch	787,878
1979	4th	82	80	.506	6.0	Gene Mauch	1,070,521
1980	3rd	77	84	.478	19.5	Gene Mauch, Johnny Goryl	769,206
1981	7th/4th	41	68	.376	‡	Johnny Goryl, Billy Gardner	469,090
1982	7th	60	102	.370	33.0	Billy Gardner	921,186
1983	5th (tied)	70	92	.432	29.0	Billy Gardner	858,939
1984	2nd (tied)	81	81	.500	3.0	Billy Gardner	1,598,422
1985	4th (tied)	77	85	.475	14.0	Billy Gardner, Ray Miller	1,651,814
1986	6th	71	91	.438	21.0	Ray Miller, Tom Kelly	1,255,453
1987	1st§	85	77	.525	+2.0	Tom Kelly	2,081,976
1988	2nd	91	71	.562	13.0	Tom Kelly	3,030,672
1989	5th	80	82	.494	19.0	Tom Kelly	2,277,438
1990	7th	74	88	.457	29.0	Tom Kelly	1,751,584
1991	1st§	95	67	.586	+8.0	Tom Kelly	2,293,842
1992	2nd	90	72	.556	6.0	Tom Kelly	2,482,428
1993	5th (tied)	71	91	.438	23.0	Tom Kelly	2,048,673

CENTRAL DIVISION

Year	Position	W	L	Pct.	*GB	Manager	Attendance
1994	4th	53	60	.469	14.0	Tom Kelly	1,398,565
1995	5th	56	88	.389	44.0	Tom Kelly	1,057,667
1996	4th	78	84	.481	21.5	Tom Kelly	1,437,352

Year	Position	W	L	Pct.	*GB	Manager	Attendance
1997	4th...........................68	94		.420	18.5	Tom Kelly...1,411,064
1998	4th...........................70	92		.432	19.0	Tom Kelly...1,165,980
1999	5th...........................63	97		.394	33.0	Tom Kelly...1,202,829

*Games behind winner. †Lost championship series. ‡First half 17-39; second 24-29. §Won championship series.

MANAGERIAL RECORDS

Ossie Bluege 375-394, Donie Bush 75-78, Joe Cantillon 158-297, Joe Cronin 165-139, Patsy Donovan 38-113, Chuck Dressen 116-212, Cal Ermer 145-129, Billy Gardner 268-353, Johnny Goryl 34-38, Clark Griffith 693-646, Bucky Harris 1,336-1,416, Walter Johnson 350-264, Tom Kelly 986-1,074, Joe Kuhel 106-201, Cookie Lavagetto 271-384, Tom Loftus 104-169, Jimmy Manning 61-72, Billy Martin 97-65, Gene Mauch 378-394, Jimmy McAleer 130-175, George McBride 80-73, Sam Mele 524-436, Clyde Milan 69-85, Ray Miller 109-130, Frank Quilici 280-287, Bill Rigney 208-184, Jake Stahl 119-182.

NEW YORK YANKEES
YEARLY FINISHES

(Known as Baltimore Orioles through 1902)

Year	Position	W	L	Pct.	*GB	Manager	Attendance
1901	5th...........................68	65		.511	13.5	John McGraw 141,952
1902	8th...........................50	88		.362	34.0	John McGraw, Wilbert Robinson...............174,606
1903	4th...........................72	62		.537	17.0	Clark Griffith 211,808
1904	2nd..........................92	59		.609	1.5	Clark Griffith 438,919
1905	6th...........................71	78		.477	21.5	Clark Griffith 309,100
1906	2nd..........................90	61		.596	3.0	Clark Griffith 434,709
1907	5th...........................70	78		.473	21.0	Clark Griffith 350,020
1908	8th...........................51	103		.331	39.5	Clark Griffith, Kid Elberfeld.....................305,500
1909	5th...........................74	77		.490	23.5	George Stallings 501,000
1910	2nd..........................88	63		.583	14.5	George Stallings, Hal Chase....................355,857
1911	6th...........................76	76		.500	25.5	Hal Chase..302,444
1912	8th...........................50	102		.329	55.0	Harry Wolverton 242,194
1913	7th...........................57	94		.377	38.0	Frank Chance 357,551
1914	6th (tied)...................70	84		.455	30.0	Frank Chance, Roger Peckinpaugh............359,477
1915	5th...........................69	83		.454	32.5	Bill Donovan...256,035
1916	4th...........................80	74		.519	11.0	Bill Donovan...469,211
1917	6th...........................71	82		.464	28.5	Bill Donovan...330,294
1918	4th...........................60	63		.488	13.5	Miller Huggins.......................................282,047
1919	3rd..........................80	59		.576	7.5	Miller Huggins.......................................619,164
1920	3rd..........................95	59		.617	3.0	Miller Huggins....................................1,289,422
1921	1st...........................98	55		.641	+4.5	Miller Huggins....................................1,230,696
1922	1st...........................94	60		.610	+1.0	Miller Huggins....................................1,026,134
1923	1st...........................98	54		.645	+16.0	Miller Huggins....................................1,007,066
1924	2nd..........................89	63		.586	2.0	Miller Huggins....................................1,053,533
1925	7th...........................69	85		.448	30.0	Miller Huggins.......................................697,267
1926	1st...........................91	63		.591	+3.0	Miller Huggins....................................1,027,095
1927	1st..........................110	44		.714	+19.0	Miller Huggins....................................1,164,015
1928	1st..........................101	53		.656	+2.5	Miller Huggins....................................1,072,132
1929	2nd..........................88	66		.571	18.0	Miller Huggins, Art Fletcher......................960,148
1930	3rd..........................86	68		.558	16.0	Bob Shawkey.....................................1,169,230
1931	2nd..........................94	59		.614	13.5	Joe McCarthy..912,437
1932	1st..........................107	47		.695	+13.0	Joe McCarthy..962,320
1933	2nd..........................91	59		.607	7.0	Joe McCarthy..728,014
1934	2nd..........................94	60		.610	7.0	Joe McCarthy..854,682
1935	2nd..........................89	60		.597	3.0	Joe McCarthy..657,508
1936	1st..........................102	51		.667	+19.5	Joe McCarthy..976,913
1937	1st..........................102	52		.662	+13.0	Joe McCarthy..998,148
1938	1st...........................99	53		.651	+9.5	Joe McCarthy..970,916
1939	1st..........................106	45		.702	+17.0	Joe McCarthy..859,785
1940	3rd..........................88	66		.571	2.0	Joe McCarthy..988,975
1941	1st..........................101	53		.656	+17.0	Joe McCarthy..964,722
1942	1st..........................103	51		.669	+9.0	Joe McCarthy..988,251
1943	1st...........................98	56		.636	+13.5	Joe McCarthy..645,006
1944	3rd..........................83	71		.539	6.0	Joe McCarthy..822,864
1945	4th...........................81	71		.533	6.5	Joe McCarthy..881,846
1946	3rd..........................87	67		.565	17.0	Joe McCarthy, Bill Dickey, Johnny Neun....2,265,512
1947	1st...........................97	57		.630	+12.0	Bucky Harris......................................2,178,937
1948	3rd..........................94	60		.610	2.5	Bucky Harris......................................2,373,901
1949	1st...........................97	57		.630	+1.0	Casey Stengel 2,281,676
1950	1st...........................98	56		.636	+3.0	Casey Stengel 2,081,380
1951	1st...........................98	56		.636	+5.0	Casey Stengel 1,950,107
1952	1st...........................95	59		.617	+2.0	Casey Stengel 1,629,665
1953	1st...........................99	52		.656	+8.5	Casey Stengel 1,537,811
1954	2nd.........................103	51		.669	8.0	Casey Stengel 1,475,171
1955	1st...........................96	58		.623	+3.0	Casey Stengel 1,490,138

Year	Position	W	L	Pct.	*GB	Manager	Attendance
1956	1st	97	57	.630	+9.0	Casey Stengel	1,491,784
1957	1st	98	56	.636	+8.0	Casey Stengel	1,497,134
1958	1st	92	62	.597	+10.0	Casey Stengel	1,428,438
1959	3rd	79	75	.513	15.0	Casey Stengel	1,552,030
1960	1st	97	57	.630	+8.0	Casey Stengel	1,627,349
1961	1st	109	53	.673	+8.0	Ralph Houk	1,747,725
1962	1st	96	66	.593	+5.0	Ralph Houk	1,493,574
1963	1st	104	57	.646	+10.5	Ralph Houk	1,308,920
1964	1st	99	63	.611	+1.0	Yogi Berra	1,305,638
1965	6th	77	85	.475	25.0	Johnny Keane	1,213,552
1966	10th	70	89	.440	26.5	Johnny Keane, Ralph Houk	1,124,648
1967	9th	72	90	.444	20.0	Ralph Houk	1,259,514
1968	5th	83	79	.512	20.0	Ralph Houk	1,185,666

EAST DIVISION

Year	Position	W	L	Pct.	*GB	Manager	Attendance
1969	5th	80	81	.497	28.5	Ralph Houk	1,067,996
1970	2nd	93	69	.574	15.0	Ralph Houk	1,136,879
1971	4th	82	80	.506	21.0	Ralph Houk	1,070,771
1972	4th	79	76	.510	6.5	Ralph Houk	966,328
1973	4th	80	82	.494	17.0	Ralph Houk	1,262,103
1974	2nd	89	73	.549	2.0	Bill Virdon	1,273,075
1975	3rd	83	77	.519	12.0	Bill Virdon, Billy Martin	1,288,048
1976	1st†	97	62	.610	+10.5	Billy Martin	2,012,434
1977	1st†	100	62	.617	+2.5	Billy Martin	2,103,092
1978	1st‡†	100	63	.613	+1.0	Billy Martin, Bob Lemon	2,335,871
1979	4th	89	71	.556	13.5	Bob Lemon, Billy Martin	2,537,765
1980	1st§	103	59	.636	+3.0	Dick Howser	2,627,417
1981	1st/6th▲†	59	48	.551	∞	Gene Michael, Bob Lemon	1,614,533
1982	5th	79	83	.488	16.0	Bob Lemon, Gene Michael, Clyde King	2,041,219
1983	3rd	91	71	.562	7.0	Billy Martin	2,257,976
1984	3rd	87	75	.537	17.0	Yogi Berra	1,821,815
1985	2nd	97	64	.602	2.0	Yogi Berra, Billy Martin	2,214,587
1986	2nd	90	72	.556	5.5	Lou Piniella	2,268,030
1987	4th	89	73	.549	9.0	Lou Piniella	2,427,672
1988	5th	85	76	.528	3.5	Billy Martin, Lou Piniella	2,633,701
1989	5th	74	87	.460	14.5	Dallas Green, Bucky Dent	2,170,485
1990	7th	67	95	.414	21.0	Bucky Dent, Stump Merrill	2,006,436
1991	5th	71	91	.438	20.0	Stump Merrill	1,863,733
1992	4th (tied)	76	86	.469	20.0	Buck Showalter	1,748,733
1993	2nd	88	74	.543	7.0	Buck Showalter	2,416,965
1994	1st	70	43	.619	+6.5	Buck Showalter	1,675,556
1995	2nd◆	79	65	.549	7.0	Buck Showalter	1,705,263
1996	1st▲†	92	70	.568	+4.0	Joe Torre	2,250,877
1997	2nd◆	96	66	.593	2.0	Joe Torre	2,580,325
1998	1st▲†	114	48	.704	+22.0	Joe Torre	2,949,734
1999	1st▲†	98	64	.605	+4.0	Joe Torre	3,292,736

*Games behind winner. †Won championship series. ‡Won pennant playoff. §Lost championship series. ∞First half 34-22; second 25-26. ▲Won division series. ◆Lost division series.

MANAGERIAL RECORDS

Yogi Berra 192-148, Frank Chance 117-168, Hal Chase 86-80, Bucky Dent 36-53, Bill Dickey 57-48, Bill Donovan 220-239, Kid Elberfeld 27-71, Art Fletcher 6-5, Dallas Green 56-65, Clark Griffith 419-370, Bucky Harris 191-117, Ralph Houk 944-806, Dick Howser 103-59, Miller Huggins 1,067-719, Johnny Keane 81-101, Clyde King 29-33, Bob Lemon 99-73, Billy Martin 501-385, Joe McCarthy 1,460-867, John McGraw 94-96, Stump Merrill 120-155, Gene Michael 92-76, Johnny Neun 8-6, Roger Peckinpaugh 10-10, Lou Piniella 224-193, Wilbert Robinson 24-57, Bob Shawkey 86-68, Buck Showalter 311-268, George Stallings 152-136, Casey Stengel 1,149-696, Joe Torre 400-248, Bill Virdon 142-124, Harry Wolverton 50-102.

OAKLAND A'S
YEARLY FINISHES

(Known as Philadelphia A's through 1954 and Kansas City A's through 1967)

Year	Position	W	L	Pct.	*GB	Manager	Attendance
1901	4th	74	62	.544	9.0	Connie Mack	206,329
1902	1st	83	53	.610	+5.0	Connie Mack	442,473
1903	2nd	75	60	.556	14.5	Connie Mack	420,078
1904	5th	81	70	.536	12.5	Connie Mack	512,294
1905	1st	92	56	.622	+2.0	Connie Mack	554,576
1906	4th	78	67	.538	12.0	Connie Mack	489,129
1907	2nd	88	57	.607	1.5	Connie Mack	625,581
1908	6th	68	85	.444	22.0	Connie Mack	455,062
1909	2nd	95	58	.621	3.5	Connie Mack	674,915

Year	Position	W	L	Pct.	*GB	Manager	Attendance
1910	1st	102	48	.680	+14.5	Connie Mack	588,905
1911	1st	101	50	.669	+13.5	Connie Mack	605,749
1912	3rd	90	62	.592	15.0	Connie Mack	517,653
1913	1st	96	57	.627	+6.5	Connie Mack	571,896
1914	1st	99	53	.651	+8.5	Connie Mack	346,641
1915	8th	43	109	.283	58.5	Connie Mack	146,223
1916	8th	36	117	.235	54.5	Connie Mack	184,471
1917	8th	55	98	.359	44.5	Connie Mack	221,432
1918	8th	52	76	.406	24.0	Connie Mack	177,926
1919	8th	36	104	.257	52.0	Connie Mack	225,209
1920	8th	48	106	.312	50.0	Connie Mack	287,888
1921	8th	53	100	.346	45.0	Connie Mack	344,430
1922	7th	65	89	.422	29.0	Connie Mack	425,356
1923	6th	69	83	.454	29.0	Connie Mack	534,122
1924	5th	71	81	.467	20.0	Connie Mack	531,992
1925	2nd	88	64	.579	8.5	Connie Mack	869,703
1926	3rd	83	67	.553	6.0	Connie Mack	714,308
1927	2nd	91	63	.591	19.0	Connie Mack	605,529
1928	2nd	98	55	.641	2.5	Connie Mack	689,756
1929	1st	104	46	.693	+18.0	Connie Mack	839,176
1930	1st	102	52	.662	+8.0	Connie Mack	721,663
1931	1st	107	45	.704	+13.5	Connie Mack	627,464
1932	2nd	94	60	.610	13.0	Connie Mack	405,500
1933	3rd	79	72	.523	19.5	Connie Mack	297,138
1934	5th	68	82	.453	31.0	Connie Mack	305,847
1935	8th	58	91	.389	34.0	Connie Mack	233,173
1936	8th	53	100	.346	49.0	Connie Mack	285,173
1937	7th	54	97	.358	46.5	Connie Mack	430,733
1938	8th	53	99	.349	46.0	Connie Mack	385,357
1939	7th	55	97	.362	51.5	Connie Mack	395,022
1940	8th	54	100	.351	36.0	Connie Mack	432,145
1941	8th	64	90	.416	37.0	Connie Mack	528,894
1942	8th	55	99	.357	48.0	Connie Mack	423,487
1943	8th	49	105	.318	49.0	Connie Mack	376,735
1944	5th (tied)	72	82	.468	17.0	Connie Mack	505,322
1945	8th	52	98	.347	34.5	Connie Mack	462,631
1946	8th	49	105	.318	55.0	Connie Mack	621,793
1947	5th	78	76	.506	19.0	Connie Mack	911,566
1948	4th	84	70	.545	12.5	Connie Mack	945,076
1949	5th	81	73	.526	16.0	Connie Mack	816,514
1950	8th	52	102	.338	46.0	Connie Mack	309,805
1951	6th	70	84	.455	28.0	Jimmie Dykes	465,469
1952	4th	79	75	.513	16.0	Jimmie Dykes	627,100
1953	7th	59	95	.383	41.5	Jimmie Dykes	362,113
1954	8th	51	103	.331	60.0	Ed Joost	304,666
1955	6th	63	91	.409	33.0	Lou Boudreau	1,393,054
1956	8th	52	102	.338	45.0	Lou Boudreau	1,015,154
1957	7th	59	94	.386	38.5	Lou Boudreau, Harry Craft	901,067
1958	7th	73	81	.474	19.0	Harry Craft	925,090
1959	7th	66	88	.429	28.0	Harry Craft	963,683
1960	8th	58	96	.377	39.0	Bob Elliot	774,944
1961	9th (tied)	61	100	.379	47.5	Joe Gordon, Hank Bauer	683,817
1962	9th	72	90	.444	24.0	Hank Bauer	635,675
1963	8th	73	89	.451	31.5	Ed Lopat	762,364
1964	10th	57	105	.352	42.0	Ed Lopat, Mel McGaha	642,478
1965	10th	59	103	.364	43.0	Mel McGaha, Haywood Sullivan	528,344
1966	7th	74	86	.463	23.0	Alvin Dark	773,929
1967	10th	62	99	.385	29.5	Alvin Dark, Luke Appling	726,639
1968	6th	82	80	.506	21.0	Bob Kennedy	837,466

WEST DIVISION

Year	Position	W	L	Pct.	*GB	Manager	Attendance
1969	2nd	88	74	.543	9.0	Hank Bauer, John McNamara	778,232
1970	2nd	89	73	.549	9.0	John McNamara	778,355
1971	1st†	101	60	.627	+16.0	Dick Williams	914,993
1972	1st‡	93	62	.600	+5.5	Dick Williams	921,323
1973	1st‡	94	68	.580	+6.0	Dick Williams	1,000,763
1974	1st‡	90	72	.556	+5.0	Alvin Dark	845,693
1975	1st†	98	64	.605	+7.0	Alvin Dark	1,075,518
1976	2nd	87	74	.540	2.5	Chuck Tanner	780,593
1977	7th	63	98	.391	38.5	Jack McKeon, Bobby Winkles	495,599
1978	6th	69	93	.426	23.0	Bobby Winkles, Jack McKeon	526,999
1979	7th	54	108	.333	34.0	Jim Marshall	306,763
1980	2nd	83	79	.512	14.0	Billy Martin	842,259
1981	1st/2nd∞†	64	45	.587	§	Billy Martin	1,304,054
1982	5th	68	94	.420	25.0	Billy Martin	1,735,489

Year	Position	W	L	Pct.	*GB	Manager	Attendance
1983	4th	74	88	.457	25.0	Steve Boros	1,294,941
1984	4th	77	85	.475	7.0	Steve Boros, Jackie Moore	1,353,281
1985	4th (tied)	77	85	.475	14.0	Jackie Moore	1,334,599
1986	3rd (tied)	76	86	.469	16.0	Jackie Moore, Tony La Russa	1,314,646
1987	3rd	81	81	.500	4.0	Tony La Russa	1,678,921
1988	1st‡	104	58	.642	+13.0	Tony La Russa	2,287,335
1989	1st‡	99	63	.611	+7.0	Tony La Russa	2,667,225
1990	1st‡	103	59	.636	+9.0	Tony La Russa	2,900,217
1991	4th	84	78	.519	11.0	Tony La Russa	2,713,493
1992	1st†	96	66	.593	+6.0	Tony La Russa	2,494,160
1993	7th	68	94	.420	26.0	Tony La Russa	2,035,025
1994	2nd	51	63	.447	1.0	Tony La Russa	1,242,692
1995	4th	67	77	.465	11.5	Tony La Russa	1,174,310
1996	3rd	78	84	.481	12.0	Art Howe	1,148,380
1997	4th	65	97	.401	25.0	Art Howe	1,264,218
1998	4th	74	88	.457	14.0	Art Howe	1,232,339
1999	2nd	87	75	.537	8.0	Art Howe	1,434,610

*Games behind winner. †Lost championship series. ‡Won championship series. §First half 37-23; second 27-22. ∞Won division series.

MANAGERIAL RECORDS

Luke Appling 10-30, Hank Bauer 187-226, Steve Boros 94-112, Lou Boudreau 151-260, Harry Craft 162-196, Alvin Dark 314-291, Jimmie Dykes 198-254, Bob Elliott 58-96, Joe Gordon 26-33, Art Howe 304-344, Eddie Joost 51-103, Bob Kennedy 82-80, Tony La Russa 695-614, Eddie Lopat 90-124, Connie Mack 3,582-3,814, Jim Marshall 54-108, Billy Martin 215-218, Mel McGaha 45-91, Jack McKeon 71-105, John McNamara 97-78, Jackie Moore 163-190, Haywood Sullivan 54-82, Chuck Tanner 87-74, Dick Williams 288-190, Bobby Winkles 61-86.

SEATTLE MARINERS
YEARLY FINISHES
WEST DIVISION

Year	Position	W	L	Pct.	*GB	Manager	Attendance
1977	6th	64	98	.395	38.0	Darrell Johnson	1,338,511
1978	7th	56	104	.350	35.0	Darrell Johnson	877,440
1979	6th	67	95	.414	21.0	Darrell Johnson	844,447
1980	7th	59	103	.364	38.0	Darrell Johnson, Maury Wills	836,204
1981	6th/5th	44	65	.404	†	Maury Wills, Rene Lachemann	636,276
1982	4th	76	86	.469	17.0	Rene Lachemann	1,070,404
1983	7th	60	102	.370	39.0	Rene Lachemann, Del Crandall	813,537
1984	5th (tied)	74	88	.457	10.0	Del Crandall, Chuck Cottier	870,372
1985	6th	74	88	.457	17.0	Chuck Cottier	1,128,696
1986	7th	67	95	.414	25.0	Chuck Cottier, Marty Martinez, Dick Williams	1,029,045
1987	4th	78	84	.481	7.0	Dick Williams	1,134,255
1988	7th	68	93	.422	35.5	Dick Williams, Jim Snyder	1,022,398
1989	6th	73	89	.451	26.0	Jim Lefebvre	1,298,443
1990	5th	77	85	.475	26.0	Jim Lefebvre	1,509,727
1991	5th	83	79	.512	12.0	Jim Lefebvre	2,147,905
1992	7th	64	98	.395	32.0	Bill Plummer	1,651,398
1993	4th	82	80	.506	12.0	Lou Piniella	2,051,853
1994	3rd	49	63	.438	2.0	Lou Piniella	1,104,206
1995	1st‡§∞	79	66	.545	+1.0	Lou Piniella	1,643,203
1996	2nd	85	76	.528	4.5	Lou Piniella	2,723,850
1997	1st▲	90	72	.556	+6.0	Lou Piniella	3,192,237
1998	3rd	76	85	.472	11.5	Lou Piniella	2,644,166
1999	3rd	79	83	.488	16.0	Lou Piniella	2,916,346

*Games behind winner. †First half 21-36; second 23-29. ‡Won division playoff. §Won division series. ∞Lost championship series. ▲Lost division series.

MANAGERIAL RECORDS

Chuck Cottier 98-120, Del Crandall 93-141, Darrell Johnson 226-362, Rene Lachemann 140-180, Jim Lefebvre 233-253, Lou Piniella 540-525, Bill Plummer 64-98, Jimmy Snyder 45-60, Dick Williams 159-192, Maury Wills 26-56.

TAMPA BAY DEVIL RAYS
YEARLY FINISHES
EAST DIVISION

Year	Position	W	L	Pct.	*GB	Manager	Attendance
1998	5th	63	99	.389	51.0	Larry Rothschild	2,506,023
1999	5th	69	93	.426	29.0	Larry Rothschild	1,562,827

*Games behind winner.

Larry Rothschild 132-192.

TEXAS RANGERS
YEARLY FINISHES

(Known as second Washington Senators through 1971)

Year	Position	W	L	Pct.	*GB	Manager	Attendance
1961	9th (tied)	61	100	.379	47.5	Mickey Vernon	597,287
1962	10th	60	101	.373	35.5	Mickey Vernon	729,775
1963	10th	56	106	.346	48.5	Mickey Vernon, Gil Hodges	535,604
1964	9th	62	100	.383	37.0	Gil Hodges	600,106
1965	8th	70	92	.432	32.0	Gil Hodges	560,083
1966	8th	71	88	.447	25.5	Gil Hodges	576,260
1967	6th (tied)	76	85	.472	15.5	Gil Hodges	770,863
1968	10th	65	96	.404	37.5	Jim Lemon	546,661

EAST DIVISION

Year	Position	W	L	Pct.	*GB	Manager	Attendance
1969	4th	86	76	.531	23.0	Ted Williams	918,106
1970	6th	70	92	.432	38.0	Ted Williams	824,789
1971	5th	63	96	.396	38.5	Ted Williams	655,156

WEST DIVISION

Year	Position	W	L	Pct.	*GB	Manager	Attendance
1972	6th	54	100	.351	38.5	Ted Williams	662,974
1973	6th	57	105	.352	37.0	Whitey Herzog, Del Wilber, Billy Martin	686,085
1974	2nd	84	76	.525	5.0	Billy Martin	1,193,902
1975	3rd	79	83	.488	19.0	Billy Martin, Frank Lucchesi	1,127,924
1976	4th (tied)	76	86	.469	14.0	Frank Lucchesi	1,164,982
1977	2nd	94	68	.580	8.0	Frank Lucchesi, Eddie Stanky, Connie Ryan, Billy Hunter	1,250,722
1978	2nd (tied)	87	75	.537	5.0	Billy Hunter, Pat Corrales	1,447,963
1979	3rd	83	79	.512	5.0	Pat Corrales	1,519,671
1980	4th	76	85	.472	20.5	Pat Corrales	1,198,175
1981	2nd/3rd	57	48	.543	†	Don Zimmer	850,076
1982	6th	64	98	.395	29.0	Don Zimmer, Darrell Johnson	1,154,432
1983	3rd	77	85	.475	22.0	Doug Rader	1,363,469
1984	7th	69	92	.429	14.5	Doug Rader	1,102,471
1985	7th	62	99	.385	28.5	Doug Rader, Bobby Valentine	1,112,497
1986	2nd	87	75	.537	5.0	Bobby Valentine	1,692,002
1987	6th (tied)	75	87	.463	10.0	Bobby Valentine	1,763,053
1988	6th	70	91	.435	33.5	Bobby Valentine	1,581,901
1989	4th	83	79	.512	16.0	Bobby Valentine	2,043,993
1990	3rd	83	79	.512	20.0	Bobby Valentine	2,057,911
1991	3rd	85	77	.525	10.0	Bobby Valentine	2,297,720
1992	4th	77	85	.475	19.0	Bobby Valentine, Toby Harrah	2,198,231
1993	2nd	86	76	.531	8.0	Kevin Kennedy	2,244,616
1994	1st	52	62	.456	+1.0	Kevin Kennedy	2,503,198
1995	3rd	74	70	.514	4.5	Johnny Oates	1,985,910
1996	1st‡	90	72	.556	+4.5	Johnny Oates	2,889,020
1997	3rd	77	85	.475	13.0	Johnny Oates	2,945,228
1998	1st‡	88	74	.543	+3.0	Johnny Oates	2,927,409
1999	1st‡	95	67	.586	+8.0	Johnny Oates	2,771,469

*Games behind winner. †First half 33-22; second 24-26. ‡Lost division series.

MANAGERIAL RECORDS

Pat Corrales 160-164, Toby Harrah 32-44, Whitey Herzog 47-91, Gil Hodges 321-444, Billy Hunter 146-108, Darrell Johnson 26-40, Kevin Kennedy 138-138, Jim Lemon 65-96, Frank Lucchesi 142-149, Billy Martin 137-141, Johnny Oates 424-368, Doug Rader 155-200, Connie Ryan 2-4, Eddie Stanky 1-0, Bobby Valentine 581-605, Mickey Vernon 135-227, Del Wilber 1-0, Ted Williams 273-364, Don Zimmer 95-106.

TORONTO BLUE JAYS
YEARLY FINISHES
EAST DIVISION

Year	Position	W	L	Pct.	*GB	Manager	Attendance
1977	7th	54	107	.335	45.5	Roy Hartsfield	1,701,052
1978	7th	59	102	.366	40.0	Roy Hartsfield	1,562,585
1979	7th	53	109	.327	50.5	Roy Hartsfield	1,431,651
1980	7th	67	95	.414	36.0	Bobby Mattick	1,400,327
1981	7th/7th	37	69	.349	†	Bobby Mattick	755,083

HISTORY Team by team

Year	Position	W	L	Pct.	*GB	Manager	Attendance
1982	6th (tied)	78	84	.481	17.0	Bobby Cox	1,275,978
1983	4th	89	73	.549	9.0	Bobby Cox	1,930,415
1984	2nd	89	73	.549	15.0	Bobby Cox	2,110,009
1985	1st‡	99	62	.615	+2.0	Bobby Cox	2,468,925
1986	4th	86	76	.531	9.5	Jimy Williams	2,455,477
1987	2nd	96	66	.593	2.0	Jimy Williams	2,778,429
1988	3rd (tied)	87	75	.537	2.0	Jimy Williams	2,595,175
1989	1st‡	89	73	.549	+2.0	Jimy Williams, Cito Gaston	3,375,883
1990	2nd	86	76	.531	2.0	Cito Gaston	3,885,284
1991	1st‡	91	71	.562	+7.0	Cito Gaston	4,001,527
1992	1st§	96	66	.593	+4.0	Cito Gaston	4,028,318
1993	1st§	95	67	.586	+7.0	Cito Gaston	4,057,947
1994	3rd	55	60	.478	16.0	Cito Gaston	2,907,933
1995	5th	56	88	.389	30.0	Cito Gaston	2,826,483
1996	4th	74	88	.457	18.0	Cito Gaston	2,559,573
1997	5th	76	86	.469	22.0	Cito Gaston, Mel Queen	2,589,297
1998	3rd	88	74	.543	26.0	Tim Johnson	2,454,183
1999	3rd	84	78	.519	14.0	Jim Fregosi	2,163,464

*Games behind winner. †First half 16-42; second 21-27. ‡Lost championship series.§Won championship series.

MANAGERIAL RECORDS

Bobby Cox 355-292, Jim Fregosi 84-78, Cito Gaston 702-650, Roy Hartsfield 166-318, Tim Johnson 88-74, Bobby Mattick 104-164, Mel Queen 4-1, Jimy Williams 281-241.

NATIONAL LEAGUE

ARIZONA DIAMONDBACKS
YEARLY FINISHES
WEST DIVISION

Year	Position	W	L	Pct.	*GB	Manager	Attendance
1998	5th	65	97	.401	33.0	Buck Showalter	3,600,412
1999	1st†	100	62	.617	+14.0	Buck Showalter	3,019,654

*Games behind winner.

MANAGERIAL RECORDS

Buck Showalter 165-159.

ATLANTA BRAVES
YEARLY FINISHES

(Known as Boston Braves through 1952 and Milwaukee Braves through 1965)

Year	Position	W	L	Pct.	*GB	Manager	Attendance
1901	5th	69	69	.500	20.5	Frank Selee	146,502
1902	3rd	73	64	.533	29.0	Al Buckenberger	116,960
1903	6th	58	80	.420	32.0	Al Buckenberger	143,155
1904	7th	55	98	.359	51.0	Al Buckenberger	140,694
1905	7th	51	103	.331	54.5	Fred Tenney	150,003
1906	8th	49	102	.325	66.5	Fred Tenney	143,280
1907	7th	58	90	.392	47.0	Fred Tenney	203,221
1908	6th	63	91	.409	36.0	Joe Kelley	253,750
1909	8th	45	108	.294	65.5	Frank Bowerman, Harry Smith	195,188
1910	8th	53	100	.346	50.5	Fred Lake	149,027
1911	8th	44	107	.291	54.0	Fred Tenney	116,000
1912	8th	52	101	.340	52.0	Johnny Kling	121,000
1913	5th	69	82	.457	31.5	George Stallings	208,000
1914	1st	94	59	.614	+10.5	George Stallings	382,913
1915	2nd	83	69	.546	7.0	George Stallings	376,283
1916	3rd	89	63	.586	4.0	George Stallings	313,495
1917	6th	72	81	.471	25.5	George Stallings	174,253
1918	7th	53	71	.427	28.5	George Stallings	84,938
1919	6th	57	82	.410	38.5	George Stallings	167,401
1920	7th	62	90	.408	30.0	George Stallings	162,483
1921	4th	79	74	.516	15.0	Fred Mitchell	318,627
1922	8th	53	100	.346	39.5	Fred Mitchell	167,965
1923	7th	54	100	.351	41.5	Fred Mitchell	227,802
1924	8th	53	100	.346	40.0	Dave Bancroft	117,478
1925	5th	70	83	.458	25.0	Dave Bancroft	313,528
1926	7th	66	86	.434	22.0	Dave Bancroft	303,598

Year	Position	W	L	Pct.	*GB	Manager	Attendance
1927	7th	60	94	.390	34.0	Dave Bancroft	288,685
1928	7th	50	103	.327	44.5	Jack Slattery, Rogers Hornsby	227,001
1929	8th	56	98	.364	43.0	Emil Fuchs	372,351
1930	6th	70	84	.455	22.0	Bill McKechnie	464,835
1931	7th	64	90	.416	37.0	Bill McKechnie	515,005
1932	5th	77	77	.500	13.0	Bill McKechnie	507,606
1933	4th	83	71	.539	9.0	Bill McKechnie	517,803
1934	4th	78	73	.517	16.0	Bill McKechnie	303,205
1935	8th	38	115	.248	61.5	Bill McKechnie	232,754
1936	6th	71	83	.461	21.0	Bill McKechnie	340,585
1937	5th	79	73	.520	16.0	Bill McKechnie	385,339
1938	5th	77	75	.507	12.0	Casey Stengel	341,149
1939	7th	63	88	.417	32.5	Casey Stengel	285,994
1940	7th	65	87	.428	34.5	Casey Stengel	241,616
1941	7th	62	92	.403	38.0	Casey Stengel	263,680
1942	7th	59	89	.399	44.0	Casey Stengel	285,332
1943	6th	68	85	.444	36.5	Casey Stengel	271,289
1944	6th	65	89	.422	40.0	Bob Coleman	208,691
1945	6th	67	85	.441	30.0	Bob Coleman, Del Bissonette	374,178
1946	4th	81	72	.529	15.5	Billy Southworth	969,673
1947	3rd	86	68	.558	8.0	Billy Southworth	1,277,361
1948	1st	91	62	.595	+6.5	Billy Southworth	1,455,439
1949	4th	75	79	.487	22.0	Billy Southworth	1,081,795
1950	4th	83	71	.539	8.0	Billy Southworth	944,391
1951	4th	76	78	.494	20.5	Billy Southworth, Tommy Holmes	487,475
1952	7th	64	89	.418	32.0	Tommy Holmes, Charlie Grimm	281,278
1953	2nd	92	62	.597	13.0	Charlie Grimm	1,826,397
1954	3rd	89	65	.578	8.0	Charlie Grimm	2,131,388
1955	2nd	85	69	.552	13.5	Charlie Grimm	2,005,836
1956	2nd	92	62	.597	1.0	Charlie Grimm, Fred Haney	2,046,331
1957	1st	95	59	.617	+8.0	Fred Haney	2,215,404
1958	1st	92	62	.597	+8.0	Fred Haney	1,971,101
1959	2nd▲	86	70	.551	2.0	Fred Haney	1,749,112
1960	2nd	88	66	.571	7.0	Chuck Dressen	1,497,799
1961	4th	83	71	.539	10.0	Chuck Dressen, Birdie Tebbetts	1,101,441
1962	5th	86	76	.531	15.5	Birdie Tebbetts	766,921
1963	6th	84	78	.519	15.0	Bobby Bragan	773,018
1964	5th	88	74	.543	5.0	Bobby Bragan	910,911
1965	5th	86	76	.531	11.0	Bobby Bragan	555,584
1966	5th	85	77	.525	10.0	Bobby Bragan, Billy Hitchcock	1,539,801
1967	7th	77	85	.475	24.5	Billy Hitchcock, Ken Silvestri	1,389,222
1968	5th	81	81	.500	16.0	Lum Harris	1,126,540

WEST DIVISION

Year	Position	W	L	Pct.	*GB	Manager	Attendance
1969	1st†	93	69	.574	+3.0	Lum Harris	1,458,320
1970	5th	76	86	.469	26.0	Lum Harris	1,078,848
1971	3rd	82	80	.506	8.0	Lum Harris	1,006,320
1972	4th	70	84	.455	25.0	Lum Harris, Eddie Mathews	752,973
1973	5th	76	85	.472	22.5	Eddie Mathews	800,655
1974	3rd	88	74	.543	14.0	Eddie Mathews, Clyde King	981,085
1975	5th	67	94	.416	40.5	Clyde King, Connie Ryan	534,672
1976	6th	70	92	.432	32.0	Dave Bristol	818,179
1977	6th	61	101	.377	37.0	Dave Bristol, Ted Turner	872,464
1978	6th	69	93	.426	26.0	Bobby Cox	904,494
1979	6th	66	94	.413	23.5	Bobby Cox	769,465
1980	4th	81	80	.503	11.0	Bobby Cox	1,048,411
1981	4th/5th	50	56	.472	‡	Bobby Cox	535,418
1982	1st†	89	73	.549	+1.0	Joe Torre	1,801,985
1983	2nd	88	74	.543	3.0	Joe Torre	2,119,935
1984	2nd (tied)	80	82	.494	12.0	Joe Torre	1,724,892
1985	5th	66	96	.407	29.0	Eddie Haas, Bobby Wine	1,350,137
1986	6th	72	89	.447	23.5	Chuck Tanner	1,387,181
1987	5th	69	92	.429	20.5	Chuck Tanner	1,217,402
1988	6th	54	106	.338	39.5	Chuck Tanner, Russ Nixon	848,089
1989	6th	63	97	.394	28.0	Russ Nixon	984,930
1990	6th	65	97	.401	26.0	Russ Nixon, Bobby Cox	980,129
1991	1st§	94	68	.580	+1.0	Bobby Cox	2,140,217
1992	1st§	98	64	.605	+8.0	Bobby Cox	3,077,400
1993	1st†	104	58	.642	+1.0	Bobby Cox	3,884,725

EAST DIVISION

Year	Position	W	L	Pct.	*GB	Manager	Attendance
1994	2nd	68	46	.596	6.0	Bobby Cox	2,539,240
1995	1st∞§	90	54	.625	+21.0	Bobby Cox	2,561,831

Year	Position	W	L	Pct.	*GB	Manager	Attendance
1996	1st∞§	96	66	.593	+8.0	Bobby Cox	2,901,242
1997	1st∞†	101	61	.623	+9.0	Bobby Cox	3,464,488
1998	1st∞†	106	56	.654	+18.0	Bobby Cox	3,361,350
1999	1st∞§	103	59	.636	+6.5	Bobby Cox	3,284,897

*Games behind winner. †Lost championship series. ‡First half 25-29; second 25-27. §Won championship series. ∞Won division series. ▲Lost pennant playoff.

MANAGERIAL RECORDS

Dave Bancroft 249-363, Del Bissonette 25-34, Frank Bowerman 23-55, Bobby Bragan 310-287, Dave Bristol 131-192, Al Buckenberger 186-242, Bob Coleman 107-140, Bobby Cox 1,166-912, Chuck Dressen 159-124, Emil Fuchs 56-98, Charlie Grimm 341-285, Eddie Haas 50-71, Fred Haney 341-231, Lum Harris 379-373, Billy Hitchcock 110-100, Tommy Holmes 61-69, Rogers Hornsby 39-83, Joe Kelley 63-91, Clyde King 96-101, Johnny Kling 52-101, Fred Lake 53-100, Eddie Mathews 149-161, Bill McKechnie 560-666, Fred Mitchell 186-274, Russ Nixon 130-216, Connie Ryan 9-18, Frank Selee 69-69, Ken Silvestri 0-3, Jack Slattery 11-20, Harry Smith 22-53, Billy Southworth 424-358, George Stallings 579-597, Casey Stengel 394-516, Chuck Tanner 153-208, Birdie Tebbetts 98-89, Fred Tenney 202-402, Joe Torre 257-229, Ted Turner 0-1, Bobby Wine 16-25.

CHICAGO CUBS
YEARLY FINISHES

Year	Position	W	L	Pct.	*GB	Manager	Attendance
1901	6th	53	86	.381	37.0	Tom Loftus	205,071
1902	5th	68	69	.496	34.0	Frank Selee	263,700
1903	3rd	82	56	.594	8.0	Frank Selee	386,205
1904	2nd	93	60	.608	13.0	Frank Selee	439,100
1905	3rd	92	61	.601	13.0	Frank Selee, Frank Chance	509,900
1906	1st	116	36	.763	+20.0	Frank Chance	654,300
1907	1st	107	45	.704	+17.0	Frank Chance	422,550
1908	1st	99	55	.643	+1.0	Frank Chance	665,325
1909	2nd	104	49	.680	6.5	Frank Chance	633,480
1910	1st	104	50	.675	+13.0	Frank Chance	526,152
1911	2nd	92	62	.597	7.5	Frank Chance	576,000
1912	3rd	91	59	.607	11.5	Frank Chance	514,000
1913	3rd	88	65	.575	13.5	Johnny Evers	419,000
1914	4th	78	76	.506	16.5	Hank O'Day	202,516
1915	4th	73	80	.477	17.5	Roger Bresnahan	217,058
1916	5th	67	86	.438	26.5	Joe Tinker	453,685
1917	5th	74	80	.481	24.0	Fred Mitchell	360,218
1918	1st	84	45	.651	+10.5	Fred Mitchell	337,256
1919	3rd	75	65	.536	21.0	Fred Mitchell	424,430
1950	5th (tied)	75	79	.487	18.0	Fred Mitchell	480,783
1921	7th	64	89	.418	30.0	Johnny Evers, Bill Killefer	410,107
1922	5th	80	74	.519	13.0	Bill Killefer	542,283
1923	4th	83	71	.539	12.5	Bill Killefer	703,705
1924	5th	81	72	.529	12.0	Bill Killefer	716,922
1925	8th	68	86	.442	27.5	Bill Killefer, Rabbit Maranville, George Gibson	622,610
1926	4th	82	72	.532	7.0	Joe McCarthy	885,063
1927	4th	85	68	.556	8.5	Joe McCarthy	1,159,168
1928	3rd	91	63	.591	4.0	Joe McCarthy	1,143,740
1929	1st	98	54	.645	+10.5	Joe McCarthy	1,485,166
1930	2nd	90	64	.584	2.0	Joe McCarthy, Rogers Hornsby	1,463,624
1931	3rd	84	70	.545	17.0	Rogers Hornsby	1,086,422
1932	1st	90	64	.584	+4.0	Rogers Hornsby, Charlie Grimm	974,688
1933	3rd	86	68	.558	6.0	Charlie Grimm	594,112
1934	3rd	86	65	.570	8.0	Charlie Grimm	707,525
1935	1st	100	54	.649	+4.0	Charlie Grimm	692,604
1936	2nd (tied)	87	67	.565	5.0	Charlie Grimm	699,370
1937	2nd	93	61	.604	3.0	Charlie Grimm	895,020
1938	1st	89	63	.586	+2.0	Charlie Grimm, Gabby Hartnett	951,640
1939	4th	84	70	.545	13.0	Gabby Hartnett	726,663
1940	5th	75	79	.487	25.5	Gabby Hartnett	534,878
1941	6th	70	84	.455	30.0	Jimmy Wilson	545,159
1942	6th	68	86	.442	38.0	Jimmy Wilson	590,872
1943	5th	74	79	.484	30.5	Jimmy Wilson	508,247
1944	4th	75	79	.487	30.0	Jimmy Wilson, Charlie Grimm	640,110
1945	1st	98	56	.636	+3.0	Charlie Grimm	1,036,386
1946	3rd	82	71	.536	14.5	Charlie Grimm	1,342,970
1947	6th	69	85	.448	25.0	Charlie Grimm	1,364,039
1948	8th	64	90	.416	27.5	Charlie Grimm	1,237,792
1949	8th	61	93	.396	36.0	Charlie Grimm, Frankie Frisch	1,143,139
1950	7th	64	89	.418	26.5	Frankie Frisch	1,165,944
1951	8th	62	92	.403	34.5	Frankie Frisch, Phil Cavarretta	894,415
1952	5th	77	77	.500	19.5	Phil Cavarretta	1,024,826
1953	7th	65	89	.422	40.0	Phil Cavarretta	763,658

Year	Position	W	L	Pct.	*GB	Manager	Attendance
1954	7th	64	90	.416	33.0	Stan Hack	748,183
1955	6th	72	81	.471	26.0	Stan Hack	875,800
1956	8th	60	94	.390	33.0	Stan Hack	720,118
1957	7th (tied)	62	92	.403	33.0	Bob Scheffing	670,629
1958	5th (tied)	72	82	.468	20.0	Bob Scheffing	979,904
1959	5th (tied)	74	80	.481	13.0	Bob Scheffing	858,255
1960	7th	60	94	.390	35.0	Charlie Grimm, Lou Boudreau	809,770
1961	7th	64	90	.416	29.0	Vedie Himsl, Harry Craft, Elvin Tappe, Lou Klein	673,057
1962	9th	59	103	.364	42.5	Charlie Metro, Elvin Tappe, Lou Klein	609,802
1963	7th	82	80	.506	17.0	Bob Kennedy	979,551
1964	8th	76	86	.469	17.0	Bob Kennedy	751,647
1965	8th	72	90	.444	25.0	Bob Kennedy, Lou Klein	641,361
1966	10th	59	103	.364	36.0	Leo Durocher	635,891
1967	3rd	87	74	.540	14.0	Leo Durocher	977,226
1968	3rd	84	78	.519	13.0	Leo Durocher	1,043,409

EAST DIVISION

Year	Position	W	L	Pct.	*GB	Manager	Attendance
1969	2nd	92	70	.568	8.0	Leo Durocher	1,674,993
1970	2nd	84	78	.519	5.0	Leo Durocher	1,642,705
1971	3rd (tied)	83	79	.512	14.0	Leo Durocher	1,653,007
1972	2nd	85	70	.548	11.0	Leo Durocher, Whitey Lockman	1,299,163
1973	5th	77	84	.478	5.0	Whitey Lockman	1,351,705
1974	6th	66	96	.407	22.0	Whitey Lockman, Jim Marshall	1,015,378
1975	5th (tied)	75	87	.463	17.5	Jim Marshall	1,034,819
1976	4th	75	87	.463	26.0	Jim Marshall	1,026,217
1977	4th	81	81	.500	20.0	Herman Franks	1,439,834
1978	3rd	79	83	.488	11.0	Herman Franks	1,525,311
1979	5th	80	82	.494	18.0	Herman Franks, Joe Amalfitano	1,648,587
1980	6th	64	98	.395	27.0	Preston Gomez, Joe Amalfitano	1,206,776
1981	6th/5th	38	65	.369	†	Joe Amalfitano	565,637
1982	5th	73	89	.451	19.0	Lee Elia	1,249,278
1983	5th	71	91	.438	19.0	Lee Elia, Charlie Fox	1,479,717
1984	1st‡	96	65	.596	+6.5	Jim Frey	2,104,219
1985	4th	77	84	.478	23.5	Jim Frey	2,161,534
1986	5th	70	90	.438	37.0	Jim Frey, John Vukovich, Gene Michael	1,859,102
1987	6th	76	85	.472	18.5	Gene Michael, Frank Lucchesi	2,035,130
1988	4th	77	85	.475	24.0	Don Zimmer	2,089,034
1989	1st‡	93	69	.574	+6.0	Don Zimmer	2,491,942
1990	4th	77	85	.475	18.0	Don Zimmer	2,243,791
1991	4th	77	83	.481	20.0	Don Zimmer, Joe Altobelli, Jim Essian	2,314,250
1992	4th	78	84	.481	18.0	Jim Lefebvre	2,126,720
1993	4th	84	78	.519	13.0	Jim Lefebvre	2,653,763

CENTRAL DIVISION

Year	Position	W	L	Pct.	*GB	Manager	Attendance
1994	5th	49	64	.434	16.5	Tom Trebelhorn	1,845,208
1995	3rd	73	71	.507	12.0	Jim Riggleman	1,918,265
1996	4th	76	86	.469	12.0	Jim Riggleman	2,219,110
1997	5th	68	94	.420	16.0	Jim Riggleman	2,190,308
1998	2nd§∞	90	73	.552	12.5	Jim Riggleman	2,623,000
1999	6th	67	95	.414	30.0	Jim Riggleman	2,813,854

*Games behind winner. †First half 15-37; second 23-28. ‡Lost championship series. §Won wild-card playoff. ∞Lost division series.

MANAGERIAL RECORDS

Joe Amalfitano 66-116, Lou Boudreau 54-83, Roger Bresnahan 73-80, Phil Cavarretta 169-213, Frank Chance 753-379, Harry Craft 7-9, Leo Durocher 535-526, Lee Elia 127-158, Jim Essian 59-63, Johnny Evers 130-121, Charlie Fox 17-22, Herman Franks 238-241, Jim Frey 196-182, Frank Frisch 141-196, George Gibson 12-14, Preston Gomez 38-52, Charlie Grimm 946-784, Stan Hack 196-265, Gabby Hartnett 203-176, Vedie Himsl 10-21, Rogers Hornsby 141-114, Roy Johnson 0-1, Bob Kennedy 182-198, Bill Killefer 299-292, Lou Klein 65-83, Jim Lefebvre 162-162, Whitey Lockman 157-162, Tom Loftus 53-86, Frank Lucchesi 8-17, Rabbit Maranville 23-30, Jim Marshall 175-218, Joe McCarthy 442-321, Charlie Metro 43-69, Gene Michael 114-124, Fred Mitchell 308-269, Hank O'Day 78-76, Jim Riggleman 374-419, Bob Scheffing 208-254, Frank Selee 295-223, Elvin Tappe 46-69, Joe Tinker 67-86, Tom Trebelhorn 49-64, John Vukovich 1-1, Jimmy Wilson 213-258, Don Zimmer 265-259.

CINCINNATI REDS

YEARLY FINISHES

Year	Position	W	L	Pct.	*GB	Manager	Attendance
1901	8th	52	87	.374	38.0	Bid McPhee	205,728
1902	4th	70	70	.500	33.5	Bid McPhee, Frank Bancroft, Joe Kelley	217,300
1903	4th	74	65	.532	16.5	Joe Kelley	351,680
1904	3rd	88	65	.575	18.0	Joe Kelley	391,915
1905	5th	79	74	.516	26.0	Joe Kelley	313,927

Year	Position	W	L	Pct.	*GB	Manager	Attendance
1906	6th	64	87	.424	51.5	Ned Hanlon	330,056
1907	6th	66	87	.431	41.5	Ned Hanlon	317,500
1908	5th	73	81	.474	26.0	John Ganzel	399,200
1909	4th	77	76	.503	33.5	Clark Griffith	424,643
1910	5th	75	79	.487	29.0	Clark Griffith	380,622
1911	6th	70	83	.458	29.0	Clark Griffith	300,000
1912	4th	75	78	.490	29.0	Hank O'Day	344,000
1913	7th	64	89	.418	37.5	Joe Tinker	258,000
1914	8th	60	94	.390	34.5	Buck Herzog	100,791
1915	7th	71	83	.461	20.0	Buck Herzog	218,878
1916	7th (tied)	60	93	.392	33.5	Buck Herzog, Christy Mathewson	255,846
1917	4th	78	76	.506	20.0	Christy Mathewson	269,056
1918	3rd	68	60	.531	15.5	Christy Mathewson, Heinie Groh	163,009
1919	1st	96	44	.686	+9.0	Pat Moran	532,501
1920	3rd	82	71	.536	10.5	Pat Moran	568,107
1921	6th	70	83	.458	24.0	Pat Moran	311,227
1922	2nd	86	68	.558	7.0	Pat Moran	493,754
1923	2nd	91	63	.591	4.5	Pat Moran	575,063
1924	4th	83	70	.542	10.0	Jack Hendricks	437,707
1925	3rd	80	73	.523	15.0	Jack Hendricks	464,920
1926	2nd	87	67	.565	2.0	Jack Hendricks	672,987
1927	5th	75	78	.490	18.5	Jack Hendricks	442,164
1928	5th	78	74	.513	16.0	Jack Hendricks	490,490
1929	7th	66	88	.429	33.0	Jack Hendricks	295,040
1930	7th	59	95	.383	33.0	Dan Howley	386,727
1931	8th	58	96	.377	43.0	Dan Howley	263,316
1932	8th	60	94	.390	30.0	Dan Howley	356,950
1933	8th	58	94	.382	33.0	Donie Bush	218,281
1934	8th	52	99	.344	42.0	Bob O'Farrell, Chuck Dressen	206,773
1935	6th	68	85	.444	31.5	Chuck Dressen	448,247
1936	5th	74	80	.481	18.0	Chuck Dressen	466,245
1937	8th	56	98	.364	40.0	Chuck Dressen, Bobby Wallace	411,221
1938	4th	82	68	.547	6.0	Bill McKechnie	706,756
1939	1st	97	57	.630	+4.5	Bill McKechnie	981,443
1940	1st	100	53	.654	+12.0	Bill McKechnie	850,180
1941	3rd	88	66	.571	12.0	Bill McKechnie	643,513
1942	4th	76	76	.500	29.0	Bill McKechnie	427,031
1943	2nd	87	67	.565	18.0	Bill McKechnie	379,122
1944	3rd	89	65	.578	16.0	Bill McKechnie	409,567
1945	7th	61	93	.396	37.0	Bill McKechnie	290,070
1946	6th	67	87	.435	30.0	Bill McKechnie	715,751
1947	5th	73	81	.474	21.0	Johnny Neun	899,975
1948	7th	64	89	.418	27.0	Johnny Neun, Bucky Walters	823,386
1949	7th	62	92	.403	35.0	Bucky Walters	707,782
1950	6th	66	87	.431	24.5	Luke Sewell	538,794
1951	6th	68	86	.442	28.5	Luke Sewell	588,268
1952	6th	69	85	.448	27.5	Luke Sewell, Rogers Hornsby	604,197
1953	6th	68	86	.442	37.0	Rogers Hornsby, Buster Mills	548,086
1954	5th	74	80	.481	23.0	Birdie Tebbetts	704,167
1955	5th	75	79	.487	23.5	Birdie Tebbetts	693,662
1956	3rd	91	63	.591	2.0	Birdie Tebbetts	1,125,928
1957	4th	80	74	.519	15.0	Birdie Tebbetts	1,070,850
1958	4th	76	78	.494	16.0	Birdie Tebbetts, Jimmie Dykes	788,582
1959	5th (tied)	74	80	.481	13.0	Mayo Smith, Fred Hutchinson	801,289
1960	6th	67	87	.435	28.0	Fred Hutchinson	663,486
1961	1st	93	61	.604	+4.0	Fred Hutchinson	1,117,603
1962	3rd	98	64	.605	3.5	Fred Hutchinson	982,085
1963	5th	86	76	.531	13.0	Fred Hutchinson	858,805
1964	2nd (tied)	92	70	.549	1.0	Fred Hutchinson, Dick Sisler	862,466
1965	4th	89	73	.549	8.0	Dick Sisler	1,047,824
1966	7th	76	84	.475	18.0	Don Heffner, Dave Bristol	742,958
1967	4th	87	75	.537	14.5	Dave Bristol	958,300
1968	4th	83	79	.512	14.0	Dave Bristol	733,354

WEST DIVISION

Year	Position	W	L	Pct.	*GB	Manager	Attendance
1969	3rd	89	73	.549	4.0	Dave Bristol	987,991
1970	1st†	102	60	.630	+14.5	Sparky Anderson	1,803,568
1971	4th (tied)	79	83	.488	11.0	Sparky Anderson	1,501,122
1972	1st†	95	59	.617	+10.5	Sparky Anderson	1,611,459
1973	1st‡	99	63	.611	+3.5	Sparky Anderson	2,017,601
1974	2nd	98	64	.605	4.0	Sparky Anderson	2,164,307
1975	1st†	108	54	.667	+20.0	Sparky Anderson	2,315,603
1976	1st†	102	60	.630	+10.0	Sparky Anderson	2,629,708
1977	2nd	88	74	.543	10.0	Sparky Anderson	2,519,670

Year	Position	W	L	Pct.	*GB	Manager	Attendance
1978	2nd	92	69	.571	2.5	Sparky Anderson	2,532,497
1979	1st‡	90	71	.559	+1.5	John McNamara	2,356,933
1980	3rd	89	73	.549	3.5	John McNamara	2,022,450
1981	2nd/2nd	66	42	.611	§	John McNamara	1,093,730
1982	6th	61	101	.377	28.0	John McNamara, Russ Nixon	1,326,528
1983	6th	74	88	.457	17.0	Russ Nixon	1,190,419
1984	5th	70	92	.432	22.0	Vern Rapp, Pete Rose	1,275,887
1985	2nd	89	72	.553	5.5	Pete Rose	1,834,619
1986	2nd	86	76	.531	10.0	Pete Rose	1,692,432
1987	2nd	84	78	.519	6.0	Pete Rose	2,185,205
1988	2nd	87	74	.540	7.0	Pete Rose	2,072,528
1989	5th	75	87	.463	17.0	Pete Rose, Tommy Helms	1,979,320
1990	1st†	91	71	.562	+5.0	Lou Piniella	2,400,892
1991	5th	74	88	.457	20.0	Lou Piniella	2,372,377
1992	2nd	90	72	.556	8.0	Lou Piniella	2,315,946
1993	5th	73	89	.451	31.0	Tony Perez, Dave Johnson	2,453,232

CENTRAL DIVISION

Year	Position	W	L	Pct.	*GB	Manager	Attendance
1994	1st	66	48	.579	+0.5	Dave Johnson	1,897,681
1995	1st∞‡	85	59	.590	+9.0	Dave Johnson	1,837,649
1996	3rd	81	81	.500	7.0	Ray Knight	1,861,428
1997	3rd	76	86	.469	8.0	Ray Knight, Jack McKeon	1,785,788
1998	4th	77	85	.475	25.0	Jack McKeon	1,793,679
1999	2nd▲	96	67	.589	1.5	Jack McKeon	2,061,222

*Games behind winner. †Won championship series. ‡Lost championship series. §First half 35-21; second 31-21. ∞Won division series. ▲Lost wild-card playoff.

MANAGERIAL RECORDS

Sparky Anderson 863-586, Frank Bancroft 9-7, Dave Bristol 298-265, Donie Bush 58-94, Chuck Dressen 214-282, Jimmie Dykes 24-17, John Ganzel 73-81, Clark Griffith 222-238, Heinie Groh 7-3, Ned Hanlon 130-174, Don Heffner 37-46, Tommy Helms 14-21, Jack Hendricks 469-450, Buck Herzog 165-226, Rogers Hornsby 91-106, Dan Howley 177-285, Fred Hutchinson 443-372, Dave Johnson 204-172, Joe Kelley 275-230, Ray Knight 124-137, Christy Mathewson 164-176, Bill McKechnie 747-632, Jack McKeon 206-182, John McNamara 279-244, Bid McPhee 79-124, Buster Mills 4-4, Pat Moran 425-329, Johnny Neun 117-137, Russ Nixon 101-131, Hank O'Day 75-78, Bob O'Farrell 30-60, Tony Perez 20-24, Lou Piniella 255-231, Vern Rapp 51-70, Pete Rose 426-388, Luke Sewell 176-234, Dick Sisler 121-94, Mayo Smith 35-45, Birdie Tebbetts 372-357, Joe Tinker 64-89, Bobby Wallace 5-20, Bucky Walters 81-123.

COLORADO ROCKIES
YEARLY FINISHES
WEST DIVISION

Year	Position	W	L	Pct.	*GB	Manager	Attendance
1993	6th	67	95	.414	37.0	Don Baylor	4,483,350
1994	3rd	53	64	.453	6.5	Don Baylor	3,281,511
1995	2nd†	77	67	.535	1.0	Don Baylor	3,390,037
1996	3rd	83	79	.512	8.0	Don Baylor	3,891,014
1997	3rd	83	79	.512	7.0	Don Baylor	3,888,453
1998	4th	77	85	.475	21.0	Don Baylor	3,789,347
1999	5th	72	90	.444	28.0	Jim Leyland	3,481,065

*Games behind winner. †Lost division series.

MANAGERIAL RECORDS

Don Baylor 440-469, Jim Leyland 72-90.

FLORIDA MARLINS
YEARLY FINISHES
EAST DIVISION

Year	Position	W	L	Pct.	*GB	Manager	Attendance
1993	6th	64	98	.395	33.0	Rene Lachemann	3,064,847
1994	5th	51	64	.443	23.5	Rene Lachemann	1,937,467
1995	4th	67	76	.469	22.5	Rene Lachemann	1,700,466
1996	3rd	80	82	.494	16.0	Rene Lachemann, John Boles	1,746,767
1997	2nd†‡	92	70	.568	9.0	Jim Leyland	2,364,387
1998	5th	54	108	.333	52.0	Jim Leyland	1,750,395
1999	5th	64	98	.395	39.0	John Boles	1,369,421

*Games behind winner. †Won division series. ‡Won championship series.

MANAGERIAL RECORDS

John Boles 104-133, Rene Lachemann 222-285, Jim Leyland 146-178.

HOUSTON ASTROS
YEARLY FINISHES

(Known as Houston Colt .45s through 1964)

Year	Position	W	L	Pct.	*GB	Manager	Attendance
1962	8th	64	96	.400	36.5	Harry Craft	924,456
1963	9th	66	96	.407	33.0	Harry Craft	719,502
1964	9th	66	96	.407	27.0	Harry Craft, Luman Harris	725,773
1965	9th	65	97	.401	32.0	Luman Harris	2,151,470
1966	8th	72	90	.444	23.0	Grady Hatton	1,872,108
1967	9th	69	93	.426	32.5	Grady Hatton	1,348,303
1968	10th	72	90	.444	25.0	Grady Hatton, Harry Walker	1,312,887

WEST DIVISION

Year	Position	W	L	Pct.	*GB	Manager	Attendance
1969	5th	81	81	.500	12.0	Harry Walker	1,442,995
1970	4th	79	83	.488	23.0	Harry Walker	1,253,444
1971	4th (tied)	79	83	.488	11.0	Harry Walker	1,261,589
1972	2nd	84	69	.549	10.5	Harry Walker, Salty Parker, Leo Durocher	1,469,247
1973	4th	82	80	.506	17.0	Leo Durocher, Preston Gomez	1,394,004
1974	4th	81	81	.500	21.0	Preston Gomez	1,090,728
1975	6th	64	97	.398	43.5	Preston Gomez, Bill Virdon	858,002
1976	3rd	80	82	.494	22.0	Bill Virdon	886,146
1977	3rd	81	81	.500	17.0	Bill Virdon	1,109,560
1978	5th	74	88	.457	21.0	Bill Virdon	1,126,145
1979	2nd	89	73	.549	1.5	Bill Virdon	1,900,312
1980	1st†‡	93	70	.571	+1.0	Bill Virdon	2,278,217
1981	3rd/1st∞	61	49	.555	§	Bill Virdon	1,321,282
1982	5th	77	85	.475	12.0	Bill Virdon, Bob Lillis	1,558,555
1983	3rd	85	77	.525	6.0	Bob Lillis	1,351,962
1984	2nd (tied)	80	82	.494	12.0	Bob Lillis	1,229,862
1985	3rd (tied)	83	79	.512	12.0	Bob Lillis	1,184,314
1986	1st‡	96	66	.593	+10.0	Hal Lanier	1,734,276
1987	3rd	76	86	.469	14.0	Hal Lanier	1,909,902
1988	5th	82	80	.506	12.5	Hal Lanier	1,933,505
1989	3rd	86	76	.531	6.0	Art Howe	1,834,908
1990	4th (tied)	75	87	.463	16.0	Art Howe	1,310,927
1991	6th	65	97	.401	29.0	Art Howe	1,196,152
1992	4th	81	81	.500	17.0	Art Howe	1,211,412
1993	3rd	85	77	.525	19.0	Art Howe	2,084,546

CENTRAL DIVISION

Year	Position	W	L	Pct.	*GB	Manager	Attendance
1994	2nd	66	49	.574	0.5	Terry Collins	1,561,136
1995	2nd	76	68	.528	9.0	Terry Collins	1,363,801
1996	2nd	82	80	.506	6.0	Terry Collins	1,975,888
1997	1st∞	84	78	.519	+5.0	Larry Dierker	2,046,781
1998	1st∞	102	60	.630	+12.5	Larry Dierker	2,450,451
1999	1st∞	97	65	.599	+1.5	Larry Dierker	2,706,017

*Games behind winner. †Won division playoff. ‡Lost championship series. §First half 28-29; second 33-20. ∞Lost division series.

MANAGERIAL RECORDS

Terry Collins 224-197, Harry Craft 191-280, Larry Dierker 283-203, Leo Durocher 98-95, Preston Gomez 128-161, Lum Harris 70-105, Grady Hatton 164-221, Art Howe 392-418, Hal Lanier 254-232, Bob Lillis 276-261, Bill Virdon 544-522, Harry Walker 355-353.

LOS ANGELES DODGERS
YEARLY FINISHES

(Known as Brooklyn Dodgers through 1957)

Year	Position	W	L	Pct.	*GB	Manager	Attendance
1901	3rd	79	57	.581	9.5	Ned Hanlon	189,200
1902	2nd	75	63	.543	27.5	Ned Hanlon	199,868
1903	5th	70	66	.515	19.0	Ned Hanlon	224,670
1904	6th	56	97	.366	50.0	Ned Hanlon	214,600
1905	8th	48	104	.316	56.5	Ned Hanlon	227,924
1906	5th	66	86	.434	50.0	Patsy Donovan	227,400
1907	5th	65	83	.439	40.0	Patsy Donovan	312,500
1908	7th	53	101	.344	46.0	Patsy Donovan	275,600

Year	Position	W	L	Pct.	*GB	Manager	Attendance
1909	6th	55	98	.359	55.5	Harry Lumley	321,300
1910	6th	64	90	.416	40.0	Bill Dahlen	279,321
1911	7th	64	86	.427	33.5	Bill Dahlen	269,000
1912	7th	58	95	.379	46.0	Bill Dahlen	243,000
1913	6th	65	84	.436	34.5	Bill Dahlen	347,000
1914	5th	75	79	.487	19.5	Wilbert Robinson	122,671
1915	3rd	80	72	.526	10.0	Wilbert Robinson	297,766
1916	1st	94	60	.610	+2.5	Wilbert Robinson	447,747
1917	7th	70	81	.464	26.5	Wilbert Robinson	221,619
1918	5th	57	69	.452	25.5	Wilbert Robinson	83,831
1919	5th	69	71	.493	27.0	Wilbert Robinson	360,721
1920	1st	93	61	.604	+7.0	Wilbert Robinson	808,722
1921	5th	77	75	.507	16.5	Wilbert Robinson	613,245
1922	6th	76	78	.494	17.0	Wilbert Robinson	498,856
1923	6th	76	78	.494	19.5	Wilbert Robinson	564,666
1924	2nd	92	62	.597	1.5	Wilbert Robinson	818,883
1925	6th (tied)	68	85	.444	27.0	Wilbert Robinson	659,435
1926	6th	71	82	.464	17.5	Wilbert Robinson	650,819
1927	6th	65	88	.425	28.5	Wilbert Robinson	637,230
1928	6th	77	76	.503	17.5	Wilbert Robinson	664,863
1929	6th	70	83	.458	28.5	Wilbert Robinson	731,886
1930	4th	86	68	.558	6.0	Wilbert Robinson	1,097,339
1931	4th	79	73	.520	21.0	Wilbert Robinson	753,133
1932	3rd	81	73	.526	9.0	Max Carey	681,827
1933	6th	65	88	.425	26.5	Max Carey	526,815
1934	6th	71	81	.467	23.5	Casey Stengel	434,188
1935	5th	70	83	.458	29.5	Casey Stengel	470,517
1936	7th	67	87	.435	25.0	Casey Stengel	489,618
1937	6th	62	91	.405	33.5	Burleigh Grimes	482,481
1938	7th	69	80	.463	18.5	Burleigh Grimes	663,087
1939	3rd	84	69	.549	12.5	Leo Durocher	955,668
1940	2nd	88	65	.575	12.0	Leo Durocher	975,978
1941	1st	100	54	.649	+2.5	Leo Durocher	1,214,910
1942	2nd	104	50	.675	2.0	Leo Durocher	1,037,765
1943	3rd	81	72	.529	23.5	Leo Durocher	661,739
1944	7th	63	91	.409	42.0	Leo Durocher	605,905
1945	3rd	87	67	.565	11.0	Leo Durocher	1,059,220
1946	2nd‡	96	60	.615	2.0	Leo Durocher	1,796,824
1947	1st	94	60	.610	+5.0	Clyde Sukeforth, Burt Shotton	1,807,526
1948	3rd	84	70	.545	7.5	Leo Durocher, Burt Shotton	1,398,967
1949	1st	97	57	.630	+1.0	Burt Shotton	1,633,747
1950	2nd	89	65	.578	2.0	Burt Shotton	1,185,896
1951	2nd‡	97	60	.618	1.0	Chuck Dressen	1,282,628
1952	1st	96	57	.627	+4.5	Chuck Dressen	1,088,704
1953	1st	105	49	.682	+13.0	Chuck Dressen	1,163,419
1954	2nd	92	62	.597	5.0	Walter Alston	1,020,531
1955	1st§	98	55	.641	+13.5	Walter Alston	1,033,589
1956	1st	93	61	.604	+1.0	Walter Alston	1,213,562
1957	3rd	84	70	.545	11.0	Walter Alston	1,028,258
1958	7th	71	83	.461	21.0	Walter Alston	1,845,556
1959	1st†	88	68	.564	+2.0	Walter Alston	2,071,045
1960	4th	82	72	.532	13.0	Walter Alston	2,253,887
1961	2nd	89	65	.578	4.0	Walter Alston	1,804,250
1962	2nd‡	102	63	.618	1.0	Walter Alston	2,755,184
1963	1st	99	63	.611	+6.0	Walter Alston	2,538,602
1964	6th (tied)	80	82	.494	13.0	Walter Alston	2,228,751
1965	1st	97	65	.599	+2.0	Walter Alston	2,553,577
1966	1st	95	67	.586	+1.5	Walter Alston	2,617,029
1967	8th	73	89	.451	28.5	Walter Alston	1,664,362
1968	7th	76	86	.469	21.0	Walter Alston	1,581,093

WEST DIVISION

Year	Position	W	L	Pct.	*GB	Manager	Attendance
1969	4th	85	77	.525	8.0	Walter Alston	1,784,527
1970	2nd	87	74	.540	14.5	Walter Alston	1,697,142
1971	2nd	89	73	.549	1.0	Walter Alston	2,064,594
1972	3rd	85	70	.548	10.5	Walter Alston	1,860,858
1973	2nd	95	66	.590	3.5	Walter Alston	2,136,192
1974	1st§	102	60	.630	+4.0	Walter Alston	2,632,474
1975	2nd	88	74	.543	20.0	Walter Alston	2,539,349
1976	2nd	92	70	.568	10.0	Walter Alston, Tommy Lasorda	2,386,301
1977	1st§	98	64	.605	+10.0	Tommy Lasorda	2,955,087
1978	1st§	95	67	.586	+2.5	Tommy Lasorda	3,347,845
1979	3rd	79	83	.488	11.5	Tommy Lasorda	2,860,954
1980	2nd∞	92	71	.564	1.0	Tommy Lasorda	3,249,287

Year	Position	W	L	Pct.	*GB	Manager	Attendance
1981	1st/4th◆§	63	47	.573	▲	Tommy Lasorda	2,381,292
1982	2nd	88	74	.543	1.0	Tommy Lasorda	3,608,881
1983	1st■	91	71	.652	+3.0	Tommy Lasorda	3,510,313
1984	4th	79	83	.488	13.0	Tommy Lasorda	3,134,824
1985	1st■	95	67	.586	+5.5	Tommy Lasorda	3,264,593
1986	5th	73	89	.451	23.0	Tommy Lasorda	3,023,208
1987	4th	73	89	.451	17.0	Tommy Lasorda	2,797,409
1988	1st§	94	67	.584	+7.0	Tommy Lasorda	2,980,262
1989	4th	77	83	.481	14.0	Tommy Lasorda	2,944,653
1990	2nd	86	76	.531	5.0	Tommy Lasorda	3,002,396
1991	2nd	93	69	.574	1.0	Tommy Lasorda	3,348,170
1992	6th	63	99	.389	35.0	Tommy Lasorda	2,473,266
1993	4th	81	81	.500	23.0	Tommy Lasorda	3,170,392
1994	1st◆	58	56	.509	+3.5	Tommy Lasorda	2,279,355
1995	1st▼	78	66	.542	+1.0	Tommy Lasorda	2,766,251
1996	2nd▼	90	72	.556	1.0	Tommy Lasorda, Bill Russell	3,188,454
1997	2nd	88	74	.543	2.0	Bill Russell	3,319,504
1998	3rd	83	79	.512	15.0	Bill Russell, Glenn Hoffman	3,089,201
1999	3rd	77	85	.475	23.0	Dave Johnson	3,095,346

*Games behind winner. †Won pennant playoff. ‡Lost pennant playoff. §Won championship series. ∞Lost division playoff. ▲First half 36-21; second half 27-26. ◆Won division series. ■Lost championship series. ▼Lost division series.

MANAGERIAL RECORDS

Walter Alston 2,040-1,613, Max Carey 146-161, Bill Dahlen 251-355, Patsy Donovan 184-270, Chuck Dressen 298-166, Leo Durocher 738-565, Burleigh Grimes 131-171, Ned Hanlon 328-387, Glenn Hoffman 47-41, Dave Johnson 77-85, Tommy Lasorda 1,599-1,439, Harry Lumley 55-98, Wilbert Robinson 1,375-1,341, Bill Russell 173-149, Burt Shotton 326-215, Casey Stengel 208-251, Clyde Sukeforth 2-0.

MILWAUKEE BREWERS
YEARLY FINISHES

(Known as Seattle Pilots in 1969)

AMERICAN LEAGUE WEST DIVISION

Year	Position	W	L	Pct.	*GB	Manager	Attendance
1969	6th	64	98	.395	33	Joe Schultz	677,944
1970	4th	65	97	.401	33.0	Dave Bristol	933,690
1971	6th	69	92	.429	32.0	Dave Bristol	731,531

AMERICAN LEAGUE EAST DIVISION

Year	Position	W	L	Pct.	*GB	Manager	Attendance
1972	6th	65	91	.417	21.0	Dave Bristol, Del Crandall	600,440
1973	5th	74	88	.457	23.0	Del Crandall	1,092,158
1974	5th	76	86	.469	15.0	Del Crandall	955,741
1975	5th	68	94	.420	28.0	Del Crandall	1,213,357
1976	6th	66	95	.410	32.0	Alex Grammas	1,012,164
1977	6th	67	95	.414	33.0	Alex Grammas	1,114,938
1978	3rd	93	69	.574	6.5	George Bamberger	1,601,406
1979	2nd	95	66	.590	8.0	George Bamberger	1,918,343
1980	3rd	86	76	.531	17.0	George Bamberger, Buck Rodgers	1,857,408
1981	3rd/1st‡	62	47	.569	†	Buck Rodgers	878,432
1982	1st§	95	67	.586	+1.0	Buck Rodgers, Harvey Kuenn	1,978,896
1983	5th	87	75	.537	11.0	Harvey Kuenn	2,397,131
1984	7th	67	94	.416	36.5	Rene Lachemann	1,608,509
1985	6th	71	90	.441	28.0	George Bamberger	1,360,265
1986	6th	77	84	.478	18.0	George Bamberger, Tom Trebelhorn	1,265,041
1987	3rd	91	71	.562	7.0	Tom Trebelhorn	1,909,244
1988	3rd (tied)	87	75	.537	2.0	Tom Trebelhorn	1,923,238
1989	4th	81	81	.500	8.0	Tom Trebelhorn	1,970,735
1990	6th	74	88	.457	14.0	Tom Trebelhorn	1,752,900
1991	4th	83	79	.512	8.0	Tom Trebelhorn	1,478,729
1992	2nd	92	70	.568	4.0	Phil Garner	1,857,314
1993	7th	69	93	.426	26.0	Phil Garner	1,688,080

AMERICAN LEAGUE CENTRAL DIVISION

Year	Position	W	L	Pct.	*GB	Manager	Attendance
1994	5th	53	62	.461	15.0	Phil Garner	1,268,399
1995	4th	65	79	.451	35.0	Phil Garner	1,087,560
1996	3rd	80	82	.494	19.5	Phil Garner	1,327,155
1997	3rd	78	83	.484	8.0	Phil Garner	1,444,027

NATIONAL LEAGUE CENTRAL DIVISION

Year	Position	W	L	Pct.	*GB	Manager	Attendance
1998	5th	74	88	.457	28.0	Phil Garner	1,811,548
1999	5th	74	87	.460	22.5	Phil Garner, Jim Lefebvre	1,701,796

*Games behind winner. †First half 31-25; second 31-22. ‡Lost division series. §Won championship series.

MANAGERIAL RECORDS

George Bamberger 377-351, Dave Bristol 144-209, Del Crandall 271-338, Phil Garner 563-617, Alex Grammas 133-190, Harvey Kuenn 160-118, Rene Lachemann 67-94, Jim Lefebvre 22-27, Buck Rodgers 124-102, Joe Schultz 64-98, Tom Trebelhorn 422-397.

MONTREAL EXPOS
YEARLY FINISHES
EAST DIVISION

Year	Position	W	L	Pct.	*GB	Manager	Attendance
1969	6th	52	110	.321	48.0	Gene Mauch	1,212,608
1970	6th	73	89	.451	16.0	Gene Mauch	1,424,683
1971	5th	71	90	.441	25.5	Gene Mauch	1,290,963
1972	5th	70	86	.449	26.5	Gene Mauch	1,142,145
1973	4th	79	83	.488	3.5	Gene Mauch	1,246,863
1974	4th	79	82	.491	8.5	Gene Mauch	1,019,134
1975	5th (tied)	75	87	.463	17.5	Gene Mauch	908,292
1976	6th	55	107	.340	46.0	Karl Kuehl, Charlie Fox	646,704
1977	5th	75	87	.463	26.0	Dick Williams	1,433,757
1978	4th	76	86	.469	14.0	Dick Williams	1,427,007
1979	2nd	95	65	.594	2.0	Dick Williams	2,102,173
1980	2nd	90	72	.556	1.0	Dick Williams	2,208,175
1981	3rd/1st‡§	60	48	.556	†	Dick Williams, Jim Fanning	1,534,564
1982	3rd	86	76	.531	6.0	Jim Fanning	2,318,292
1983	3rd	82	80	.506	8.0	Bill Virdon	2,320,651
1984	5th	78	83	.484	18.0	Bill Virdon, Jim Fanning	1,606,531
1985	3rd	84	77	.522	16.5	Buck Rodgers	1,502,494
1986	4th	78	83	.484	29.5	Buck Rodgers	1,128,981
1987	3rd	91	71	.562	4.0	Buck Rodgers	1,850,324
1988	3rd	81	81	.500	20.0	Buck Rodgers	1,478,659
1989	4th	81	81	.500	12.0	Buck Rodgers	1,783,533
1990	3rd	85	77	.525	10.0	Buck Rodgers	1,373,087
1991	6th	71	90	.441	26.5	Buck Rodgers, Tom Runnells	934,742
1992	2nd	87	75	.537	9.0	Tom Runnells, Felipe Alou	1,669,077
1993	2nd	94	68	.580	3.0	Felipe Alou	1,641,437
1994	1st	74	40	.649	+6.0	Felipe Alou	1,276,250
1995	5th	66	78	.458	24.0	Felipe Alou	1,309,618
1996	2nd	88	74	.543	8.0	Felipe Alou	1,616,709
1997	4th	78	84	.481	23.0	Felipe Alou	1,497,609
1998	4th	65	97	.401	41.0	Felipe Alou	914,717
1999	4th	68	94	.420	35.0	Felipe Alou	773,277

*Games behind winner. †First half 30-25; second 30-23. ‡Won division series. §Lost championship series.

MANAGERIAL RECORDS

Felipe Alou 603-590, Jim Fanning 116-103, Charlie Fox 12-22, Karl Kuehl 43-85, Gene Mauch 499-627, Buck Rodgers 520-499, Tom Runnells 68-81, Bill Virdon 146-147, Dick Williams 380-347.

NEW YORK METS
YEARLY FINISHES

Year	Position	W	L	Pct.	*GB	Manager	Attendance
1962	10th	40	120	.250	60.5	Casey Stengel	922,530
1963	10th	51	111	.315	48.0	Casey Stengel	1,080,108
1964	10th	53	109	.327	40.0	Casey Stengel	1,732,597
1965	10th	50	112	.309	47.0	Casey Stengel, Wes Westrum	1,768,389
1966	9th	66	95	.410	28.5	Wes Westrum	1,932,693
1967	10th	61	101	.377	40.5	Wes Westrum, Salty Parker	1,565,492
1968	9th	73	89	.451	24.0	Gil Hodges	1,781,657

EAST DIVISION

Year	Position	W	L	Pct.	*GB	Manager	Attendance
1969	1st†	100	62	.617	+8.0	Gil Hodges	2,175,373
1970	3rd	83	79	.512	6.0	Gil Hodges	2,697,479
1971	3rd (tied)	83	79	.512	14.0	Gil Hodges	2,266,680
1972	3rd	83	73	.532	13.5	Yogi Berra	2,134,185

HISTORY *Team by team*

Year	Position	W	L	Pct.	*GB	Manager	Attendance
1973	1st†	82	79	.509	+1.5	Yogi Berra	1,912,390
1974	5th	71	91	.438	17.0	Yogi Berra	1,722,209
1975	3rd (tied)	82	80	.506	10.5	Yogi Berra, Roy McMillan	1,730,566
1976	3rd	86	76	.531	15.0	Joe Frazier	1,468,754
1977	6th	64	98	.395	37.0	Joe Frazier, Joe Torre	1,066,825
1978	6th	66	96	.407	24.0	Joe Torre	1,007,328
1979	6th	63	99	.389	35.0	Joe Torre	788,905
1980	5th	67	95	.414	24.0	Joe Torre	1,192,073
1981	5th/4th	41	62	.398	‡	Joe Torre	704,244
1982	6th	65	97	.401	27.0	George Bamberger	1,323,036
1983	6th	68	94	.420	22.0	George Bamberger, Frank Howard	1,112,774
1984	2nd	90	72	.556	6.5	Dave Johnson	1,842,695
1985	2nd	98	64	.605	3.0	Dave Johnson	2,761,601
1986	1st†	108	54	.667	+21.5	Dave Johnson	2,767,601
1987	2nd	92	70	.568	3.0	Dave Johnson	3,034,129
1988	1st§	100	60	.625	+15.0	Dave Johnson	3,055,445
1989	2nd	87	75	.537	6.0	Dave Johnson	2,918,710
1990	2nd	91	71	.562	4.0	Dave Johnson, Bud Harrelson	2,732,745
1991	5th	77	84	.478	20.5	Bud Harrelson, Mike Cubbage	2,284,484
1992	5th	72	90	.444	24.0	Jeff Torborg	1,779,534
1993	7th	59	103	.364	38.0	Jeff Torborg, Dallas Green	1,873,183
1994	3rd	55	58	.487	18.5	Dallas Green	1,151,471
1995	2nd (tied)	69	75	.479	21.0	Dallas Green	1,273,183
1996	4th	71	91	.438	25.0	Dallas Green, Bobby Valentine	1,588,323
1997	3rd	88	74	.543	13.0	Bobby Valentine	1,766,174
1998	2nd	88	74	.543	18.0	Bobby Valentine	2,287,942
1999	2nd∞§	97	66	.595	6.5	Bobby Valentine	2,725,668

*Games behind winner. †Won championship series. ‡First half 17-34; second 24-28. §Lost championship series. ∞Won wild-card playoff.

MANAGERIAL RECORDS

George Bamberger 81-127, Yogi Berra 292-296, Mike Cubbage 3-4, Joe Frazier 101-106, Dallas Green 229-283, Bud Harrelson 145-129, Gil Hodges 339-309, Frank Howard 52-64, Davey Johnson 595-417, Roy McMillan 26-27, Salty Parker 4-7, Casey Stengel 175-404, Jeff Torborg 85-115, Joe Torre 286-420, Bobby Valentine 285-233, Wes Westrum 142-237.

PHILADELPHIA PHILLIES
YEARLY FINISHES

Year	Position	W	L	Pct.	*GB	Manager	Attendance
1901	2nd	83	57	.593	7.5	Bill Shettsline	234,937
1902	7th	56	81	.409	46.0	Bill Shettsline	112,066
1903	7th	49	86	.363	39.5	Chief Zimmer	151,729
1904	8th	52	100	.342	53.5	Hugh Duffy	140,771
1905	4th	83	69	.546	21.5	Hugh Duffy	317,932
1906	4th	71	82	.464	45.5	Hugh Duffy	294,680
1907	3rd	83	64	.565	21.5	Bill Murray	341,216
1908	4th	83	71	.539	16.0	Bill Murray	420,660
1909	5th	74	79	.484	36.5	Bill Murray	303,177
1910	4th	78	75	.510	25.5	Red Dooin	296,597
1911	4th	79	73	.520	19.5	Red Dooin	416,000
1912	5th	73	79	.480	30.5	Red Dooin	250,000
1913	2nd	88	63	.583	12.5	Red Dooin	470,000
1914	6th	74	80	.481	20.5	Red Dooin	138,474
1915	1st	90	62	.592	+7.0	Pat Moran	449,898
1916	2nd	91	62	.595	2.5	Pat Moran	515,365
1917	2nd	87	65	.572	10.0	Pat Moran	354,428
1918	6th	55	68	.447	26.0	Pat Moran	122,266
1919	8th	47	90	.343	47.5	Jack Coombs, Gavvy Cravath	240,424
1920	8th	62	91	.405	30.5	Gavvy Cravath	330,998
1921	8th	51	103	.331	43.5	Bill Donovan, Kaiser Wilhelm	273,961
1922	7th	57	96	.373	35.5	Kaiser Wilhelm	232,471
1923	8th	50	104	.325	45.5	Art Fletcher	228,168
1924	7th	55	96	.364	37.0	Art Fletcher	299,818
1925	6th (tied)	68	85	.444	27.0	Art Fletcher	304,905
1926	8th	58	93	.384	29.5	Art Fletcher	240,600
1927	8th	51	103	.331	43.0	Stuffy McInnis	305,420
1928	8th	43	109	.283	51.0	Burt Shotton	182,168
1929	5th	71	82	.464	27.5	Burt Shotton	281,200
1930	8th	52	102	.338	40.0	Burt Shotton	299,007
1931	6th	66	88	.429	35.0	Burt Shotton	284,849
1932	4th	78	76	.506	12.0	Burt Shotton	268,914
1933	7th	60	92	.395	31.0	Burt Shotton	156,421
1934	7th	56	93	.376	37.0	Jimmy Wilson	169,885

Year	Position	W	L	Pct.	*GB	Manager	Attendance
1935	7th	64	89	.418	35.5	Jimmy Wilson	205,470
1936	8th	54	100	.351	38.0	Jimmy Wilson	249,219
1937	7th	61	92	.399	34.5	Jimmy Wilson	212,790
1938	8th	45	105	.300	43.0	Jimmy Wilson, Hans Lobert	166,111
1939	8th	45	106	.298	50.5	Doc Prothro	277,973
1940	8th	50	103	.327	50.0	Doc Prothro	207,177
1941	8th	43	111	.279	57.0	Doc Prothro	231,401
1942	8th	42	109	.278	62.5	Hans Lobert	230,183
1943	7th	64	90	.416	41.0	Bucky Harris, Fred Fitzsimmons	466,975
1944	8th	61	92	.399	43.5	Fred Fitzsimmons	369,586
1945	8th	46	108	.299	52.0	Fred Fitzsimmons, Ben Chapman	285,057
1946	5th	69	85	.448	28.0	Ben Chapman	1,045,247
1947	7th (tied)	62	92	.403	32.0	Ben Chapman	907,332
1948	6th	66	88	.429	25.5	Ben Chapman, Dusty Cooke, Eddie Sawyer	767,429
1949	3rd	81	73	.526	16.0	Eddie Sawyer	819,698
1950	1st	91	63	.591	+2.0	Eddie Sawyer	1,217,035
1951	5th	73	81	.474	23.5	Eddie Sawyer	937,658
1952	4th	87	67	.565	9.5	Eddie Sawyer, Steve O'Neill	775,417
1953	3rd (tied)	83	71	.539	22.0	Steve O'Neill	853,644
1954	4th	75	79	.487	22.0	Steve O'Neill, Terry Moore	738,991
1955	4th	77	77	.500	21.5	Mayo Smith	922,886
1956	5th	71	83	.461	22.0	Mayo Smith	934,798
1957	5th	77	77	.500	19.0	Mayo Smith	1,146,230
1958	8th	69	85	.448	23.0	Mayo Smith, Eddie Sawyer	931,110
1959	8th	64	90	.416	23.0	Eddie Sawyer	802,815
1960	8th	59	95	.383	36.0	Eddie Sawyer, Andy Cohen, Gene Mauch	862,205
1961	8th	47	107	.305	46.0	Gene Mauch	590,039
1962	7th	81	80	.503	20.0	Gene Mauch	762,034
1963	4th	87	75	.537	12.0	Gene Mauch	907,141
1964	2nd (tied)	92	70	.568	1.0	Gene Mauch	1,425,891
1965	6th	85	76	.528	11.5	Gene Mauch	1,166,376
1966 *	4th	87	75	.537	8.0	Gene Mauch	1,108,201
1967	5th	82	80	.506	19.5	Gene Mauch	828,888
1968	7th (tied)	76	86	.469	21.0	Gene Mauch, George Myatt, Bob Skinner	664,546

EAST DIVISION

Year	Position	W	L	Pct.	*GB	Manager	Attendance
1969	5th	63	99	.389	37.0	Bob Skinner, George Myatt	519,414
1970	5th	73	88	.453	15.5	Frank Lucchesi	708,247
1971	6th	67	95	.414	30.0	Frank Lucchesi	1,511,223
1972	6th	59	97	.378	37.5	Frank Lucchesi, Paul Owens	1,343,329
1973	6th	71	91	.438	11.5	Danny Ozark	1,475,934
1974	3rd	80	82	.494	8.0	Danny Ozark	1,808,648
1975	2nd	86	76	.531	6.5	Danny Ozark	1,909,233
1976	1st†	101	61	.623	+9.0	Danny Ozark	2,480,150
1977	1st†	101	61	.623	+5.0	Danny Ozark	2,700,070
1978	1st†	90	72	.556	+1.5	Danny Ozark	2,583,389
1979	4th	84	78	.519	14.0	Danny Ozark, Dallas Green	2,775,011
1980	1st‡	91	71	.562	+1.0	Dallas Green	2,651,650
1981	1st/3rd∞	59	48	.551	§	Dallas Green	1,638,752
1982	2nd	89	73	.549	3.0	Pat Corrales	2,376,394
1983	1st‡	90	72	.556	+6.0	Pat Corrales, Paul Owens	2,128,339
1984	4th	81	81	.500	15.5	Paul Owens	2,062,693
1985	5th	75	87	.463	26.0	John Felske	1,830,350
1986	2nd	86	75	.534	21.5	John Felske	1,933,335
1987	4th (tied)	80	82	.494	15.0	John Felske, Lee Elia	2,100,110
1988	6th	65	96	.404	35.5	Lee Elia, John Vukovich	1,990,041
1989	6th	67	95	.414	26.0	Nick Leyva	1,861,985
1990	4th (tied)	77	85	.475	18.0	Nick Leyva	1,992,484
1991	3rd	78	84	.481	20.0	Nick Leyva, Jim Fregosi	2,050,012
1992	6th	70	92	.432	26.0	Jim Fregosi	1,927,448
1993	1st‡	97	65	.599	+3.0	Jim Fregosi	3,137,674
1994	4th	54	61	.470	20.5	Jim Fregosi	2,290,971
1995	2nd (tied)	69	75	.479	21.0	Jim Fregosi	2,043,598
1996	5th	67	95	.414	29.0	Jim Fregosi	1,801,677
1997	5th	68	94	.420	33.0	Terry Francona	1,490,638
1998	3rd	75	87	.463	31.0	Terry Francona	1,715,702
1999	3rd	77	85	.475	26.0	Terry Francona	1,825,337

*Games behind winner. †Lost championship series. ‡Won championship series. §First half 34-21; second 25-27. ∞Lost division series.

MANAGERIAL RECORDS

Ben Chapman 197-277, Andy Cohen 1-0, Dusty Cooke 6-6, Jack Coombs 18-44, Pat Corrales 132-115, Gavvy Cravath 91-137, Bill Donovan 31-71, Red Dooin 392-370, Hugh Duffy 206-251, Lee Elia 111-142, John Felske 190-194, Fred Fitzsimmons 102-179, Art

Fletcher 231-378, Terry Francona 220-266, Jim Fregosi 431-463, Dallas Green 169-130, Bucky Harris 40-53, Nick Leyva 148-189, Hans Lobert 42-111, Frank Lucchesi 166-233, Gene Mauch 645-684, Stuffy McInnis 51-103, Terry Moore 35-42, Pat Moran 323-257, Bill Murray 240-214, George Myatt 21-35, Steve O'Neill 182-140, Paul Owens 161-158, Danny Ozark 594-510, Doc Prothro 138-320, Eddie Sawyer 390-424, Bill Shettsline 139-138, Burt Shotton 370-549, Bob Skinner 92-123, Mayo Smith 264-281, John Vukovich 5-4, Kaiser Wilhelm 77-128, Jimmy Wilson 280-477, Chief Zimmer 49-86.

PITTSBURGH PIRATES
YEARLY FINISHES

Year	Position	W	L	Pct.	*GB	Manager	Attendance
1901	1st	90	49	.647	+7.5	Fred Clarke	251,955
1902	1st	103	36	.741	+27.5	Fred Clarke	243,826
1903	1st	91	49	.650	+6.5	Fred Clarke	326,855
1904	4th	87	66	.569	19.0	Fred Clarke	340,615
1905	2nd	96	57	.627	9.0	Fred Clarke	369,124
1906	3rd	93	60	.608	23.5	Fred Clarke	394,877
1907	2nd	91	63	.591	17.0	Fred Clarke	319,506
1908	2nd	98	56	.636	1.0	Fred Clarke	382,444
1909	1st	110	42	.724	+6.5	Fred Clarke	534,950
1910	3rd	86	67	.562	17.5	Fred Clarke	436,586
1911	3rd	85	69	.552	14.5	Fred Clarke	432,000
1912	2nd	93	58	.616	10.0	Fred Clarke	384,000
1913	4th	78	71	.523	21.5	Fred Clarke	296,000
1914	7th	69	85	.448	25.5	Fred Clarke	139,620
1915	5th	73	81	.474	18.0	Fred Clarke	225,743
1916	6th	65	89	.422	29.0	Jimmy Callahan	289,132
1917	8th	51	103	.331	47.0	Jimmy Callahan, Honus Wagner, Hugo Bezdek	192,807
1918	4th	65	60	.520	17.0	Hugo Bezdek	213,610
1919	4th	71	68	.511	24.5	Hugo Bezdek	276,810
1920	4th	79	75	.513	14.0	George Gibson	429,037
1921	2nd	90	63	.588	4.0	George Gibson	701,567
1922	3rd (tied)	85	69	.552	8.0	George Gibson, Bill McKechnie	523,675
1923	3rd	87	67	.565	8.5	Bill McKechnie	611,082
1924	3rd	90	63	.588	3.0	Bill McKechnie	736,883
1925	1st	95	58	.621	+8.5	Bill McKechnie	804,354
1926	3rd	84	69	.549	4.5	Bill McKechnie	798,542
1927	1st	94	60	.610	+1.5	Donie Bush	869,720
1928	4th	85	67	.559	9.0	Donie Bush	495,070
1929	2nd	88	65	.575	10.5	Donie Bush, Jewel Ens	491,377
1930	5th	80	74	.519	12.0	Jewel Ens	357,795
1931	5th	75	79	.487	26.0	Jewel Ens	260,392
1932	2nd	86	68	.558	4.0	George Gibson	287,262
1933	2nd	87	67	.565	5.0	George Gibson	288,747
1934	5th	74	76	.493	19.5	George Gibson, Pie Traynor	322,622
1935	4th	86	67	.562	13.5	Pie Traynor	352,885
1936	4th	84	70	.545	8.0	Pie Traynor	372,524
1937	3rd	86	68	.558	10.0	Pie Traynor	459,679
1938	2nd	86	64	.573	2.0	Pie Traynor	641,033
1939	6th	68	85	.444	28.5	Pie Traynor	376,734
1940	4th	78	76	.506	22.5	Frankie Frisch	507,934
1941	4th	81	73	.526	19.0	Frankie Frisch	482,241
1942	5th	66	81	.449	36.5	Frankie Frisch	448,897
1943	4th	80	74	.519	25.0	Frankie Frisch	604,278
1944	2nd	90	63	.588	14.5	Frankie Frisch	498,740
1945	4th	82	72	.532	16.0	Frankie Frisch	604,694
1946	7th	63	91	.409	34.0	Frankie Frisch, Spud Davis	749,962
1947	7th (tied)	62	92	.403	32.0	Billy Herman, Bill Burwell	1,283,531
1948	4th	83	71	.539	8.5	Billy Meyer	1,517,021
1949	6th	71	83	.461	26.0	Billy Meyer	1,499,435
1950	8th	57	96	.373	33.5	Billy Meyer	1,166,267
1951	7th	64	90	.416	32.5	Billy Meyer	980,590
1952	8th	42	112	.273	54.5	Billy Meyer	686,673
1953	8th	50	104	.325	55.0	Fred Haney	572,757
1954	8th	53	101	.344	44.0	Fred Haney	475,494
1955	8th	60	94	.390	38.5	Fred Haney	469,397
1956	7th	66	88	.429	27.0	Bobby Bragan	949,878
1957	7th (tied)	62	92	.403	33.0	Bobby Bragan, Danny Murtaugh	850,732
1958	2nd	84	70	.545	8.0	Danny Murtaugh	1,311,988
1959	4th	78	76	.506	9.0	Danny Murtaugh	1,359,917
1960	1st	95	59	.617	+7.0	Danny Murtaugh	1,705,828
1961	6th	75	79	.487	18.0	Danny Murtaugh	1,199,128
1962	4th	93	68	.578	8.0	Danny Murtaugh	1,090,648
1963	8th	74	88	.457	25.0	Danny Murtaugh	783,648
1964	6th (tied)	80	82	.494	13.0	Danny Murtaugh	759,496
1965	3rd	90	72	.556	7.0	Harry Walker	909,279

Year	Position	W	L	Pct.	*GB	Manager	Attendance
1966	3rd	92	70	.568	3.0	Harry Walker	1,196,618
1967	6th	81	81	.500	20.5	Harry Walker, Danny Murtaugh	907,012
1968	6th	80	82	.494	17.0	Larry Shepard	693,485

EAST DIVISION

Year	Position	W	L	Pct.	*GB	Manager	Attendance
1969	3rd	88	74	.543	12.0	Larry Shepard, Alex Grammas	769,369
1970	1st†	89	73	.549	+5.0	Danny Murtaugh	1,341,947
1971	1st‡	97	65	.599	+7.0	Danny Murtaugh	1,501,132
1972	1st†	96	59	.619	+11.0	Bill Virdon	1,427,460
1973	3rd	80	82	.494	2.5	Bill Virdon, Danny Murtaugh	1,319,913
1974	1st†	88	74	.543	+1.5	Danny Murtaugh	1,110,552
1975	1st†	92	69	.571	+6.5	Danny Murtaugh	1,270,018
1976	2nd	92	70	.568	9.0	Danny Murtaugh	1,025,945
1977	2nd	96	66	.593	5.0	Chuck Tanner	1,237,349
1978	2nd	88	73	.547	1.5	Chuck Tanner	964,106
1979	1st‡	98	64	.605	+2.0	Chuck Tanner	1,435,454
1980	3rd	83	79	.512	8.0	Chuck Tanner	1,646,757
1981	4th/6th	46	56	.451	§.0	Chuck Tanner	541,789
1982	4th	84	78	.519	8.0	Chuck Tanner	1,024,106
1983	2nd	84	78	.519	6.0	Chuck Tanner	1,225,916
1984	6th	75	87	.463	21.5	Chuck Tanner	773,500
1985	6th	57	104	.354	43.5	Chuck Tanner	735,900
1986	6th	64	98	.395	44.0	Jim Leyland	1,000,917
1987	4th (tied)	80	82	.494	15.0	Jim Leyland	1,161,193
1988	2nd	85	75	.531	15.0	Jim Leyland	1,866,713
1989	5th	74	88	.457	19.0	Jim Leyland	1,374,141
1990	1st†	95	67	.586	+4.0	Jim Leyland	2,049,908
1991	1st†	98	64	.605	+14.0	Jim Leyland	2,065,302
1992	1st†	96	66	.593	+9.0	Jim Leyland	1,829,395
1993	5th	75	87	.463	22.0	Jim Leyland	1,650,593

CENTRAL DIVISION

Year	Position	W	L	Pct.	*GB	Manager	Attendance
1994	3rd (tied)	53	61	.465	13.0	Jim Leyland	1,222,520
1995	5th	58	86	.403	27.0	Jim Leyland	905,517
1996	5th	73	89	.451	15.0	Jim Leyland	1,332,150
1997	2nd	79	83	.488	5.0	Gene Lamont	1,657,022
1998	6th	69	93	.426	33.0	Gene Lamont	1,560,950
1999	3rd	78	83	.484	18.5	Gene Lamont	1,638,023

*Games behind winner. †Lost championship series. ‡Won championship series. §First half 25-23; second half 21-33.

MANAGERIAL RECORDS

Hugo Bezdek 166-187, Bobby Bragan 102-155, Bill Burwell 1-0, Donie Bush 246-178, Jimmy Callahan 85-129, Fred Clarke 1,343-909, Spud Davis 1-2, Jewel Ens 176-167, Frank Frisch 539-528, George Gibson 401-330, Alex Grammas 4-1, Fred Haney 163-299, Billy Herman 61-92, Gene Lamont 226-259, Jim Leyland 851-863, Bill McKechnie 409-293, Billy Meyer 317-452, Danny Murtaugh 1,115-950, Larry Shepard 164-155, Chuck Tanner 711-685, Pie Traynor 457-406, Bill Virdon 163-128, Honus Wagner 1-4, Harry Walker 224-184.

ST. LOUIS CARDINALS
YEARLY FINISHES

Year	Position	W	L	Pct.	*GB	Manager	Attendance
1901	4th	76	64	.543	14.5	Patsy Donovan	379,988
1902	6th	56	78	.418	44.5	Patsy Donovan	226,417
1903	8th	43	94	.314	46.5	Patsy Donovan	226,538
1904	5th	75	79	.487	31.5	Kid Nichols	386,750
1905	6th	58	96	.377	47.5	Kid Nichols, Jimmy Burke, Matt Robison	292,800
1906	7th	52	98	.347	63.0	John McCloskey	283,770
1907	8th	52	101	.340	55.5	John McCloskey	185,377
1908	8th	49	105	.318	50.0	John McCloskey	205,129
1909	7th	54	98	.355	56.0	Roger Bresnahan	299,982
1910	7th	63	90	.412	40.5	Roger Bresnahan	355,668
1911	5th	75	74	.503	22.0	Roger Bresnahan	447,768
1912	6th	63	90	.412	41.0	Roger Bresnahan	241,759
1913	8th	51	99	.340	49.0	Miller Huggins	203,531
1914	3rd	81	72	.529	13.0	Miller Huggins	256,099
1915	6th	72	81	.471	18.5	Miller Huggins	252,666
1916	7th (tied)	60	93	.392	33.5	Miller Huggins	224,308
1917	3rd	82	70	.539	15.0	Miller Huggins	288,491
1918	8th	51	78	.395	33.0	Jack Hendricks	110,599
1919	7th	54	83	.394	40.5	Branch Rickey	167,059
1920	5th (tied)	75	79	.487	18.0	Branch Rickey	326,836

Year	Position	W	L	Pct.	*GB	Manager	Attendance
1921	3rd	87	66	.569	7.0	Branch Rickey	384,773
1922	3rd (tied)	85	69	.552	8.0	Branch Rickey	536,998
1923	5th	79	74	.516	16.0	Branch Rickey	338,551
1924	6th	65	89	.422	28.5	Branch Rickey	272,885
1925	4th	77	76	.503	18.0	Branch Rickey, Rogers Hornsby	404,959
1926	1st	89	65	.578	+2.0	Rogers Hornsby	668,428
1927	2nd	92	61	.601	1.5	Bob O'Farrell	749,340
1928	1st	95	59	.617	+2.0	Bill McKechnie	761,574
1929	4th	78	74	.513	20.0	Bill McKechnie, Billy Southworth	399,887
1930	1st	92	62	.597	+2.0	Gabby Street	508,501
1931	1st	101	53	.656	+13.0	Gabby Street	608,535
1932	6th (tied)	72	82	.468	18.0	Gabby Street	279,219
1933	5th	82	71	.536	9.5	Gabby Street, Frankie Frisch	256,171
1934	1st	95	58	.621	+2.0	Frankie Frisch	325,056
1935	2nd	96	58	.623	4.0	Frankie Frisch	506,084
1936	2nd (tied)	87	67	.565	5.0	Frankie Frisch	448,078
1937	4th	81	73	.526	15.0	Frankie Frisch	430,811
1938	6th	71	80	.470	17.5	Frankie Frisch, Mike Gonzalez	291,418
1939	2nd	92	61	.601	4.5	Ray Blades	400,245
1940	3rd	84	69	.549	16.0	Ray Blades, Mike Gonzalez, Billy Southworth	324,078
1941	2nd	97	56	.634	2.5	Billy Southworth	633,645
1942	1st	106	48	.688	+2.0	Billy Southworth	553,552
1943	1st	105	49	.682	+18.0	Billy Southworth	517,135
1944	1st	105	49	.682	+14.5	Billy Southworth	461,968
1945	2nd	95	59	.617	3.0	Billy Southworth	594,630
1946	1st†	98	58	.628	+2.0	Eddie Dyer	1,061,807
1947	2nd	89	65	.578	5.0	Eddie Dyer	1,247,913
1948	2nd	85	69	.552	6.5	Eddie Dyer	1,111,440
1949	2nd	96	58	.623	1.0	Eddie Dyer	1,430,676
1950	5th	78	75	.510	12.5	Eddie Dyer	1,093,411
1951	3rd	81	73	.526	15.5	Marty Marion	1,013,429
1952	3rd	88	66	.571	8.5	Eddie Stanky	913,113
1953	3rd (tied)	83	71	.539	22.0	Eddie Stanky	880,242
1954	6th	72	82	.468	25.0	Eddie Stanky	1,039,698
1955	7th	68	86	.442	30.5	Eddie Stanky, Harry Walker	849,130
1956	4th	76	78	.494	17.0	Fred Hutchinson	1,029,773
1957	2nd	87	67	.565	8.0	Fred Hutchinson	1,183,575
1958	5th (tied)	72	82	.468	20.0	Fred Hutchinson, Stan Hack	1,063,730
1959	7th	71	83	.461	16.0	Solly Hemus	929,953
1960	3rd	86	68	.558	9.0	Solly Hemus	1,096,632
1961	5th	80	74	.519	13.0	Solly Hemus, Johnny Keane	855,305
1962	6th	84	78	.519	17.5	Johnny Keane	953,895
1963	2nd	93	69	.574	6.0	Johnny Keane	1,170,546
1964	1st	93	69	.574	+1.0	Johnny Keane	1,143,294
1965	7th	80	81	.497	16.5	Red Schoendienst	1,241,201
1966	6th	83	79	.512	12.0	Red Schoendienst	1,712,980
1967	1st	101	60	.627	+10.5	Red Schoendienst	2,090,145
1968	1st	97	65	.599	+9.0	Red Schoendienst	2,011,167

EAST DIVISION

Year	Position	W	L	Pct.	*GB	Manager	Attendance
1969	4th	87	75	.537	13.0	Red Schoendienst	1,682,783
1970	4th	76	86	.469	13.0	Red Schoendienst	1,629,736
1971	2nd	90	72	.556	7.0	Red Schoendienst	1,604,671
1972	4th	75	81	.481	21.5	Red Schoendienst	1,196,894
1973	2nd	81	81	.500	1.5	Red Schoendienst	1,574,046
1974	2nd	86	75	.534	1.5	Red Schoendienst	1,838,413
1975	3rd (tied)	82	80	.506	10.5	Red Schoendienst	1,695,270
1976	5th	72	90	.444	29.0	Red Schoendienst	1,207,079
1977	3rd	83	79	.512	18.0	Vern Rapp	1,659,287
1978	5th	69	93	.426	21.0	Vern Rapp, Jack Krol, Ken Boyer	1,278,215
1979	3rd	86	76	.531	12.0	Ken Boyer	1,627,256
1980	4th	74	88	.457	17.0	Ken Boyer, Jack Krol, Whitey Herzog, Red Schoendienst	1,385,147
1981	2nd/2nd	59	43	.578	‡	Whitey Herzog	1,010,247
1982	1st§	92	70	.568	+3.0	Whitey Herzog	2,111,906
1983	4th	79	83	.488	11.0	Whitey Herzog	2,317,914
1984	3rd	84	78	.519	12.5	Whitey Herzog	2,037,448
1985	1st§	101	61	.623	+3.0	Whitey Herzog	2,637,563
1986	3rd	79	82	.491	28.5	Whitey Herzog	2,471,974
1987	1st§	95	67	.586	+3.0	Whitey Herzog	3,072,122
1988	5th	76	86	.469	25.0	Whitey Herzog	2,892,799
1989	3rd	86	76	.531	7.0	Whitey Herzog	3,080,980
1990	6th	70	92	.432	25.0	Whitey Herzog, Red Schoendienst, Joe Torre	2,573,225
1991	2nd	84	78	.519	14.0	Joe Torre	2,448,699
1992	3rd	83	79	.512	13.0	Joe Torre	2,418,483
1993	3rd	87	75	.537	10.0	Joe Torre	2,844,328

CENTRAL DIVISION

Year	Position	W	L	Pct.	*GB	Manager	Attendance
1994	3rd (tied)	53	61	.465	13.0	Joe Torre	1,866,544
1995	4th	62	81	.434	22.5	Joe Torre, Mike Jorgensen	1,756,727
1996	1st∞▲	88	74	.543	+6.0	Tony La Russa	2,654,718
1997	4th	73	89	.451	11.0	Tony La Russa	2,634,014
1998	3rd	83	79	.512	19.0	Tony La Russa	3,194,092
1999	4th	75	86	.466	21.5	Tony La Russa	3,225,334

*Games behind winner. †Won pennant playoff. ‡First half 30-20; second 29-23. §Won championship series. ∞Won division series. ▲Lost championship series.

MANAGERIAL RECORDS

Ray Blades 106-85, Ken Boyer 166-190, Roger Bresnahan 255-352, Jimmy Burke 17-32, Patsy Donovan 175-236, Eddie Dyer 446-325, Frank Frisch 458-354, Mike Gonzalez 9-13, Stan Hack 3-7, Solly Hemus 190-192, Jack Hendricks 51-78, Whitey Herzog 835-739, Rogers Hornsby 153-116, Miller Huggins 346-415, Fred Hutchinson 232-220, Mike Jorgensen 42-54, Johnny Keane 317-249, Tony La Russa 319-328, Marty Marion 81-73, John McCloskey 153-304, Bill McKechnie 129-88, Kid Nichols 94-108, Bob O'Farrell 92-61, Vern Rapp 89-90, Branch Rickey 458-485, Stanley Robison 22-35, Red Schoendienst 1,028-944, Billy Southworth 620-346, Eddie Stanky 260-238, Gabby Street 312-242, Joe Torre 351-354, Harry Walker 51-67.

SAN DIEGO PADRES
YEARLY FINISHES
WEST DIVISION

Year	Position	W	L	Pct.	*GB	Manager	Attendance
1969	6th	52	110	.321	41.0	Preston Gomez	512,970
1970	6th	63	99	.389	39.0	Preston Gomez	643,679
1971	6th	61	100	.379	28.5	Preston Gomez	557,513
1972	6th	58	95	.379	36.5	Preston Gomez, Don Zimmer	644,273
1973	6th	60	102	.370	39.0	Don Zimmer	611,826
1974	6th	60	102	.370	42.0	John McNamara	1,075,399
1975	4th	71	91	.438	37.0	John McNamara	1,281,747
1976	5th	73	89	.451	29.0	John McNamara	1,458,478
1977	5th	69	93	.426	29.0	John McNamara, Bob Skinner, Alvin Dark	1,376,269
1978	4th	84	78	.519	11.0	Roger Craig	1,670,107
1979	5th	68	93	.422	22.0	Roger Craig	1,456,967
1980	6th	73	89	.451	19.5	Jerry Coleman	1,139,026
1981	6th/6th	41	69	.373	†	Frank Howard	519,161
1982	4th	81	81	.500	8.0	Dick Williams	1,607,516
1983	4th	81	81	.500	10.0	Dick Williams	1,539,815
1984	1st‡	92	70	.568	+12.0	Dick Williams	1,983,904
1985	3rd (tied)	83	79	.512	12.0	Dick Williams	2,210,352
1986	4th	74	88	.457	22.0	Steve Boros	1,805,716
1987	6th	65	97	.401	25.0	Larry Bowa	1,454,061
1988	3rd	83	78	.516	11.0	Larry Bowa, Jack McKeon	1,506,896
1989	2nd	89	73	.549	3.0	Jack McKeon	2,009,031
1990	4th (tied)	75	87	.463	16.0	Jack McKeon, Greg Riddoch	1,856,396
1991	3rd	84	78	.519	10.0	Greg Riddoch	1,804,289
1992	3rd	82	80	.506	16.0	Greg Riddoch, Jim Riggleman	1,722,102
1993	7th	61	101	.377	43.0	Jim Riggleman	1,375,432
1994	4th	47	70	.402	12.5	Jim Riggleman	953,857
1995	3rd	70	74	.486	8.0	Bruce Bochy	1,041,805
1996	1st§	91	71	.562	+1.0	Bruce Bochy	2,187,886
1997	4th	76	86	.469	14.0	Bruce Bochy	2,089,333
1998	1st∞	98	64	.605	+9.5	Bruce Bochy	2,555,901
1999	4th	74	88	.457	26.0	Bruce Bochy	2,523,538

*Games behind winner. †First half 23-33; second 18-36. ‡Won championship series. §Lost division series. ∞Won division series.

MANAGERIAL RECORDS

Bruce Bochy 409-383, Steve Boros 74-88, Larry Bowa 81-127, Jerry Coleman 73-89, Roger Craig 152-171, Alvin Dark 49-65, Preston Gomez 180-316, Frank Howard 41-69, Jack McKeon 193-164, John McNamara 224-310, Greg Riddoch 200-194, Jim Riggleman 112-179, Dick Williams 337-311, Don Zimmer 114-190.

SAN FRANCISCO GIANTS
YEARLY FINISHES

(Known as New York Giants through 1957)

Year	Position	W	L	Pct.	*GB	Manager	Attendance
1901	7th	52	85	.380	37.0	George Davis	297,650
1902	8th	48	88	.353	53.5	Horace Fogel, Heinie Smith, John McGraw	302,875
1903	2nd	84	55	.604	6.5	John McGraw	579,530

Year	Position	W	L	Pct.	*GB	Manager	Attendance
1904	1st	106	47	.693	+13.0	John McGraw	609,826
1905	1st	105	48	.686	+9.0	John McGraw	552,700
1906	2nd	96	56	.632	20.0	John McGraw	402,850
1907	4th	82	71	.536	25.5	John McGraw	538,350
1908	2nd (tied)	98	56	.636	1.0	John McGraw	910,000
1909	3rd	92	61	.601	18.5	John McGraw	783,700
1910	2nd	91	63	.591	13.0	John McGraw	511,785
1911	1st	99	54	.647	+7.5	John McGraw	675,000
1912	1st	103	48	.682	+10.0	John McGraw	638,000
1913	1st	101	51	.664	+12.5	John McGraw	630,000
1914	2nd	84	70	.545	10.5	John McGraw	364,313
1915	8th	69	83	.454	21.0	John McGraw	391,850
1916	4th	86	66	.566	7.0	John McGraw	552,056
1917	1st	98	56	.636	+10.0	John McGraw	500,264
1918	2nd	71	53	.573	10.5	John McGraw	256,618
1919	2nd	87	53	.621	9.0	John McGraw	708,857
1920	2nd	86	68	.558	7.0	John McGraw	929,609
1921	1st	94	59	.614	+4.0	John McGraw	773,477
1922	1st	93	61	.604	+7.0	John McGraw	945,809
1923	1st	95	58	.621	+4.5	John McGraw	820,780
1924	1st	93	60	.608	+1.5	John McGraw	844,068
1925	2nd	86	66	.566	8.5	John McGraw	778,993
1926	5th	74	77	.490	13.5	John McGraw	700,362
1927	3rd	92	62	.597	2.0	John McGraw	858,190
1928	2nd	93	61	.604	2.0	John McGraw	916,191
1929	3rd	84	67	.556	13.5	John McGraw	868,806
1930	3rd	87	67	.565	5.0	John McGraw	868,714
1931	2nd	87	65	.572	13.0	John McGraw	812,163
1932	6th (tied)	72	82	.468	18.0	John McGraw, Bill Terry	484,868
1933	1st	91	61	.599	+5.0	Bill Terry	604,471
1934	2nd	93	60	.608	2.0	Bill Terry	730,851
1935	3rd	91	62	.595	8.5	Bill Terry	748,748
1936	1st	92	62	.597	+5.0	Bill Terry	837,952
1937	1st	95	57	.625	+3.0	Bill Terry	926,887
1938	3rd	83	67	.553	5.0	Bill Terry	799,633
1939	5th	77	74	.510	18.5	Bill Terry	702,457
1940	6th	72	80	.474	27.5	Bill Terry	747,852
1941	5th	74	79	.484	25.5	Bill Terry	763,098
1942	3rd	85	67	.559	20.0	Mel Ott	779,621
1943	8th	55	98	.359	49.5	Mel Ott	466,095
1944	5th	67	87	.435	38.0	Mel Ott	674,083
1945	5th	78	74	.513	19.0	Mel Ott	1,016,468
1946	8th	61	93	.396	36.0	Mel Ott	1,219,873
1947	4th	81	73	.526	13.0	Mel Ott	1,600,793
1948	5th	78	76	.506	13.5	Mel Ott, Leo Durocher	1,459,269
1949	5th	73	81	.474	24.0	Leo Durocher	1,218,446
1950	3rd	86	68	.558	5.0	Leo Durocher	1,008,876
1951	1st (tied)†	98	59	.624	+1.0	Leo Durocher	1,059,539
1952	2nd	92	62	.597	4.5	Leo Durocher	984,940
1953	5th	70	84	.455	35.0	Leo Durocher	811,518
1954	1st	97	57	.630	+5.0	Leo Durocher	1,155,067
1955	3rd	80	74	.519	18.5	Leo Durocher	824,112
1956	6th	67	87	.435	26.0	Bill Rigney	629,179
1957	6th	69	85	.448	26.0	Bill Rigney	653,923
1958	3rd	80	74	.519	12.0	Bill Rigney	1,272,625
1959	3rd	83	71	.539	4.0	Bill Rigney	1,422,130
1960	5th	79	75	.513	16.0	Bill Rigney, Tom Sheehan	1,795,356
1961	3rd	85	69	.552	8.0	Alvin Dark	1,390,679
1962	1st†	103	62	.624	+1.0	Alvin Dark	1,592,594
1963	3rd	88	74	.543	11.0	Alvin Dark	1,571,306
1964	4th	90	72	.556	3.0	Alvin Dark	1,504,364
1965	2nd	95	67	.586	2.0	Herman Franks	1,546,075
1966	2nd	93	68	.578	1.5	Herman Franks	1,657,192
1967	2nd	91	71	.562	10.5	Herman Franks	1,242,480
1968	2nd	88	74	.543	9.0	Herman Franks	837,220

WEST DIVISION

Year	Position	W	L	Pct.	*GB	Manager	Attendance
1969	2nd	90	72	.556	3.0	Clyde King	873,603
1970	3rd	86	76	.531	16.0	Clyde King, Charlie Fox	740,720
1971	1st‡	90	72	.556	+1.0	Charlie Fox	1,106,043
1972	5th	69	86	.445	26.5	Charlie Fox	647,744
1973	3rd	88	74	.543	11.0	Charlie Fox	834,193
1974	5th	72	90	.444	30.0	Charlie Fox, Wes Westrum	519,987
1975	3rd	80	81	.497	27.5	Wes Westrum	522,919

Year	Position	W	L	Pct.	*GB	Manager	Attendance
1976	4th	74	88	.457	28.0	Bill Rigney	626,868
1977	4th	75	87	.463	23.0	Joe Altobelli	700,056
1978	3rd	89	73	.549	6.0	Joe Altobelli	1,740,477
1979	4th	71	91	.438	19.5	Joe Altobelli, Dave Bristol	1,456,402
1980	5th	75	86	.466	17.0	Dave Bristol	1,096,115
1981	5th/3rd	56	55	.505	§	Frank Robinson	632,274
1982	3rd	87	75	.537	2.0	Frank Robinson	1,200,948
1983	5th	79	83	.488	12.0	Frank Robinson	1,251,530
1984	6th	66	96	.407	26.0	Frank Robinson, Danny Ozark	1,001,545
1985	6th	62	100	.383	33.0	Jim Davenport, Roger Craig	818,697
1986	3rd	83	79	.512	13.0	Roger Craig	1,528,748
1987	1st‡	90	72	.556	+6.0	Roger Craig	1,917,168
1988	4th	83	79	.512	11.5	Roger Craig	1,785,297
1989	1st∞	92	70	.568	+3.0	Roger Craig	2,059,701
1990	3rd	85	77	.525	6.0	Roger Craig	1,975,528
1991	4th	75	87	.463	19.0	Roger Craig	1,737,478
1992	5th	72	90	.444	26.0	Roger Craig	1,561,987
1993	2nd	103	59	.636	1.0	Dusty Baker	2,606,354
1994	2nd	55	60	.478	3.5	Dusty Baker	1,704,608
1995	4th	67	77	.465	11.0	Dusty Baker	1,241,500
1996	4th	68	94	.420	23.0	Dusty Baker	1,413,922
1997	1st▲	90	72	.556	+2.0	Dusty Baker	1,690,869
1998	2nd◆	89	74	.546	9.5	Dusty Baker	1,925,634
1999	2nd	86	76	.531	14.0	Dusty Baker	2,078,399

*Games behind winner. †Won pennant playoff. ‡Lost championship series. §First half 27-32; second half 29-23. ∞Won championship series. ▲Lost division series. ◆Lost wild-card playoff.

MANAGERIAL RECORDS

Joe Altobelli 225-239, Dusty Baker 558-512, Dave Bristol 85-98, Roger Craig 586-566, Alvin Dark 366-277, Jim Davenport 56-88, George Davis 52-85, Leo Durocher 637-523, Horace Fogel 18-23, Charlie Fox 348-327, Herman Franks 367-280, Clyde King 109-95, John McGraw 2,604-1,801, Mel Ott 464-530, Danny Ozark 24-32, Bill Rigney 406-430, Frank Robinson 264-277, Tom Sheehan 46-50, Heinie Smith 5-27, Bill Terry 823-661, Wes Westrum 118-129.

MINOR LEAGUES

Farm systems

International League

Mexican League

Pacific Coast League

Eastern League

Southern League

Texas League

California League

Carolina League

Florida State League

Midwest League

New York-Pennsylvania League

Northwest League

South Atlantic League

Appalachian League

Arizona League

Gulf Coast League

Pioneer League

Minor league index

FARM SYSTEMS

AMERICAN LEAGUE

ANAHEIM (6): AAA—Edmonton. AA—Erie. A—Boise, Cedar Rapids, Lake Elsinore. Rookie—Butte.
BALTIMORE (6): AAA—Rochester. AA—Bowie. A—Delmarva, Frederick. Rookie—Bluefield, Gulf Coast Orioles.
BOSTON (6): AAA—Pawtucket. AA—Trenton. A—Augusta, Lowell, Sarasota. Rookie—Gulf Coast Red Sox.
CHICAGO (6): AAA—Charlotte. AA—Birmingham. A—Burlington, Winston-Salem. Rookie—Bristol, Tucson White Sox.
CLEVELAND (6): AAA—Buffalo. AA—Akron. A—Columbus (GA), Kinston, Mahoning Valley. Rookie—Burlington.
DETROIT (6): AAA—Toledo. AA—Jacksonville. A—Lakeland, Oneonta, West Michigan. Rookie—Gulf Coast Tigers.
KANSAS CITY (6): AAA—Omaha. AA—Wichita. A—Charleston (WV), Spokane, Wilmington. Rookie—Gulf Coast Royals.
MINNESOTA (6): AAA—Salt Lake. AA—New Britain. A—Fort Myers, Quad City. Rookie—Elizabethton, Gulf Coast Twins.
NEW YORK (6): AAA—Columbus (OH). AA—Norwich. A—Greensboro, Staten Island, Tampa. Rookie—Gulf Coast Yankees.
OAKLAND (6): AAA—Sacramento. AA—Midland. A—Modesto, Vancouver, Visalia. Rookie—Scottsdale A's.
SEATTLE (6): AAA—Tacoma. AA—New Haven. A—Everett, Lancaster, Wisconsin. Rookie—Peoria Mariners.
TAMPA BAY (6): AAA—Durham. AA—Orlando. A—Charleston (SC), Hudson Valley, St. Petersburg. Rookie—Princeton.
TEXAS (6): AAA—Oklahoma. AA—Tulsa. A—Charlotte, Savannah. Rookie—Gulf Coast Rangers, Pulaski.
TORONTO (6): AAA—Syracuse. AA—Tennessee. A—Dunedin, Hagerstown, St. Catharines. Rookie—Medicine Hat.

NATIONAL LEAGUE

ARIZONA (6): AAA—Tucson. AA—El Paso. A—High Desert, South Bend. Rookie—Missoula, Tucson.
ATLANTA (7): AAA—Richmond. AA—Greenville. A—Jamestown, Macon, Myrtle Beach. Rookie—Danville, Gulf Coast Braves.
CHICAGO (6): AAA—Iowa. AA—West Tenn. A—Daytona Beach, Eugene, Lansing. Rookie—Mesa Cubs.
CINCINNATI (6): AAA—Louisville. AA—Chattanooga. A—Clinton, Dayton. Rookie—Billings, Gulf Coast Reds.
COLORADO (6): AAA—Colorado Springs. AA—Carolina. A—Asheville, Portland (OR), Salem. Rookie—Arizona Rockies.
FLORIDA (6): AAA—Calgary. AA—Portland (ME). A—Brevard County, Kane County, Utica. Rookie—Gulf Coast Marlins.
HOUSTON (6): AAA—New Orleans. AA—Round Rock. A—Auburn, Kissimmee, Michigan. Rookie—Martinsville.
LOS ANGELES (6): AAA—Albuquerque. AA—San Antonio. A—San Bernardino, Vero Beach, Yakima. Rookie—Great Falls.
MILWAUKEE (6): AAA—Indianapolis. AA—Huntsville. A—Beloit, Mudville. Rookie—Helena, Ogden.
MONTREAL (6): AAA—Ottawa. AA—Harrisburg. A—Fayetteville, Jupiter, Vermont. Rookie—Gulf Coast Expos.
NEW YORK (7): AAA—Norfolk. AA—Binghamton. A—Capital City, Pittsfield, St. Lucie. Rookie—Gulf Coast Mets, Kingsport.
PHILADELPHIA (6): AAA—Scranton/Wilkes-Barre. AA—Reading. A—Batavia, Clearwater, Piedmont. Rookie—Gulf Coast Phillies.
PITTSBURGH (6): AAA—Nashville. AA—Altoona. A—Hickory, Lynchburg, Williamsport. Rookie—Gulf Coast Pirates.
ST. LOUIS (6): AAA—Memphis. AA—Arkansas. A—New Jersey, Peoria (IL), Potomac. Rookie—Johnson City.
SAN DIEGO (6): AAA—Las Vegas. AA—Mobile. A—Fort Wayne, Rancho Cucamonga. Rookie—Idaho Falls, Peoria (AZ) Padres.
SAN FRANCISCO (6): AAA—Fresno. AA—Shreveport. A—Bakersfield, San Jose. Rookie—Arizona Giants, Salem-Keizer,

INTERNATIONAL LEAGUE

LEAGUE OFFICE

President
Randy Mobley

Address
55 S. High St., Suite 202
Dublin, OH 43017

Phone
614-791-9300

TEAMS

BUFFALO BISONS

General manager
Mike Buczkowski
Manager
Joel Skinner
Ballpark (capacity, surface)
Dunn Tire Park (21,050, grass)
Affiliation
Indians
Address
P.O. Box 450
Buffalo, NY 14205
Phone
716-846-2000

CHARLOTTE KNIGHTS

General manager
Tim Newman
Manager
Nick Leyva
Ballpark (capacity, surface)
Knights Stadium (10,005, grass)
Affiliation
White Sox
Address
2280 Deerfield Drive
Fort Mill, SC 29715
Phone
704-357-8071

COLUMBUS CLIPPERS

General manager
Ken Schnacke
Manager
Trey Hillman
Ballpark (capacity, surface)
Cooper Stadium (15,000, grass)
Affiliation
Yankees
Address
1155 W. Mound St.
Columbus, OH 43223
Phone
614-462-5250

DURHAM BULLS

General manager
Peter Anlyan
Manager
Bill Evers
Ballpark (capacity, surface)
Durham Bulls Athletic Park
(10,000, grass)
Affiliation
Devil Rays
Address
P.O. Box 507
Durham, NC 27702
Phone
919-687-6500

INDIANAPOLIS INDIANS

General manager
Cal Burleson
Manager
Steve Smith
Ballpark (capacity, surface)
Victory Field (15,000, grass)
Affiliation
Brewers
Address
501 W. Maryland St.
Indianapolis, IN 46225
Phone
317-269-3542

LOUISVILLE RIVERBATS

General manager
Dale Owens
Manager
Dave Miley
Ballpark (capacity, surface)
Cardinal Stadium (33,000, artificial)
Affiliation
Reds
Address
P.O. Box 36407
Louisville, KY 40233
Phone
502-367-9121

NORFOLK TIDES

General manager
Dave Rosenfield
Manager
John Gibbons
Ballpark (capacity, surface)
Harbor Park (12,059, grass)
Affiliation
Mets
Address
150 Park Ave.
Norfolk, VA 23510
Phone
757-622-2222

OTTAWA LYNX

Director of baseball operations
Kevin Whalen
Manager
Jeff Cox
Ballpark (capacity, surface)
JetForm Park (10,332, grass)
Affiliation
Expos
Address
300 Coventry Rd.
Ottawa, Ontario K1K 4P5
Phone
613-747-5969

PAWTUCKET RED SOX

General manager
Mike Tamburro
Manager
Gary Jones
Ballpark (capacity, surface)
McCoy Stadium (10,000, grass)
Affiliation
Red Sox
Address
P.O. Box 2365
Pawtucket, RI 02861
Phone
401-724-7303

RICHMOND BRAVES

General manager
Bruce Baldwin
Manager
Randy Ingle
Ballpark (capacity, surface)
The Diamond (12,156, grass)
Affiliation
Braves
Address
P.O. Box 6667
Richmond, VA 23230
Phone
804-359-4444

ROCHESTER RED WINGS

General manager
Dan Mason
Manager
Marv Foley
Ballpark (capacity, surface)
Frontier Field (22,844, grass)
Affiliation
Orioles
Address
1 Morrie Silver Way
Rochester, NY 14608
Phone
716-454-1001

SCRANTON/WILKES-BARRE RED BARONS

General manager
Rick Muntean
Manager
Marc Bombard
Ballpark (capacity, surface)
Lackawanna County Multi-Purpose
Stadium (10,982, artificial)
Affiliation
Phillies
Address
P.O. Box 3449
Scranton, PA 18505
Phone
570-969-2255

CLASS AAA *International League*

SYRACUSE SKY CHIEFS

General manager
John Simone
Manager
Pat Kelly
Ballpark (capacity, surface)
P&C Stadium (11,100, artificial)
Affiliation
Blue Jays

Address
One Tex Simone
Syracuse, NY 13208
Phone
315-474-7833

TOLEDO MUD HENS

General manager
Joe Napoli
Manager
Dave Anderson

Ballpark (capacity, surface)
Ned Skeldon Stadium (10,025, grass)
Affiliation
Tigers
Address
2901 Key Street
Toledo, OH 43537
Phone
419-893-9483

1999 FINAL STANDINGS

NORTH DIVISION

Team	W	L	T	Pct.	GB
Scranton/Wilkes-Barre (Phillies)	78	66	0	.566	...
Pawtucket (Red Sox)	76	68	0	.563	2.0
Syracuse (Blue Jays)	73	71	0	.507	5.0
Buffalo (Indians)	72	72	0	.500	6.0
Rochester (Orioles)	61	83	0	.424	17.0
Ottawa (Expos)	59	85	0	.410	19.0

SOUTH DIVISION

Team	W	L	T	Pct.	GB
Durham (Devil Rays)	83	60	0	.580	...
Charlotte (White Sox)	82	62	0	.569	1.5
Norfolk (Mets)	77	63	0	.550	4.5
Richmond (Braves)	64	78	0	.451	18.5

WEST DIVISION

Team	W	L	T	Pct.	GB
Columbus (Yankees)	83	58	0	.589	...
Indianapolis (Reds)	75	69	0	.521	9.5
Louisville (Brewers)	63	81	0	.438	21.5
Toledo (Tigers)	57	87	0	.396	27.5

COMPOSITE

Team	Col.	Dur.	Char.	Nor.	SWB	Paw.	Ind.	Syr.	Buf.	Rich.	Lou.	Roch.	Ott.	Tol.	W	L	T	Pct.	GB
Columbus (Yankees)	...	6	7	5	5	5	10	3	2	10	11	5	5	9	83	58	0	.589	...
Durham (Devil Rays)	5	...	7	10	5	5	7	4	5	11	6	5	7	6	83	60	0	.580	1.0
Charlotte (White Sox)	5	9	...	8	7	5	4	6	6	11	7	3	4	7	82	62	0	.569	2.5
Norfolk (Mets)	5	6	8	...	4	4	9	5	3	5	8	5	5	10	77	63	0	.550	5.5
Scranton/Wilkes-Barre (Phillies)	3	3	1	4	...	7	2	9	11	3	6	13	10	6	78	66	0	.542	6.5
Pawtucket (Red Sox)	3	3	3	4	9	...	6	9	8	5	6	9	8	3	76	68	0	.528	8.5
Indianapolis (Reds)	6	5	8	3	6	2	...	5	2	6	9	7	6	10	75	69	0	.521	9.5
Syracuse (Blue Jays)	5	4	2	3	7	7	3	...	11	4	6	7	9	5	73	71	0	.507	11.5
Buffalo (Indians)	6	3	2	5	5	8	6	5	...	4	4	9	10	5	72	72	0	.500	12.5
Richmond (Braves)	2	5	5	9	5	3	6	4	4	...	5	5	4	7	64	78	0	.451	19.5
Louisville (Brewers)	5	6	5	4	2	2	7	2	4	7	...	7	4	8	63	81	0	.438	21.5
Rochester (Orioles)	3	3	5	3	3	7	1	9	7	3	1	...	12	4	61	83	0	.424	23.5
Ottawa (Expos)	3	1	4	3	6	8	2	7	6	4	4	4	...	7	59	85	0	.410	25.5
Toledo (Tigers)	2	6	5	2	2	5	6	3	3	5	8	4	1	...	57	87	0	.396	27.5

Major league affiliations in parentheses.

PLAYOFFS: Charlotte defeated Scranton/Wilkes-Barre, three games to two; Durham defeated Columbus, three games to none; Charlotte defeated Durham, three games to one to win league championship.

REGULAR-SEASON ATTENDANCE: Buffalo, 684,051; Charlotte, 344,491; Columbus, 460,923; Durham, 464,020; Indianapolis, 658,250; Louisville, 361,419; Norfolk, 486,727; Ottawa, 195,979; Pawtucket, 596,624; Richmond, 523,670; Rochester, 481,039; Scranton/Wilkes-Barre, 440,553; Syracuse, 446,025; Toledo, 295,173. Total—6,438,744. Playoffs (12 games)—40,006. Class AAA All-Star Game at Metairie, La.—8,895.

MANAGERS: Buffalo, Jeff Datz; Charlotte, Tom Spencer; Columbus, Trey Hillman; Durham, Bill Evers; Indianapolis, Dave Miley; Louisville, Gary Allenson; Norfolk, John Gibbons; Ottawa, Jeff Cox; Pawtucket, Gary Jones; Richmond, Randy Ingle; Rochester, Dave Machemer; Scranton/Wilkes-Barre, Marc Bombard; Syracuse, Pat Kelly; Toledo, Gene Roof.

ALL-STAR TEAM: 1B—Steve Cox, Durham; 2B—Brian Raabe, Columbus; 3B—Scott McClain, Durham; SS—D'Angelo Jimenez, Columbus; OF—Chad Mottola, Charlotte; D.T. Cromer, Indianapolis; Michael Coleman, Pawtucket; C—Jason LaRue, Indianapolis; DH—Luis Raven, Charlotte; Utility—Jason Hardtke, Indianapolis; Starting pitcher—Ed Yarnall, Columbus; Relief pitcher—Jay Tessmer, Columbus; Most Valuable Player—Steve Cox, Durham; Most Valuable Pitcher—Ed Yarnall, Columbus; Rookie of the Year—Kurt Bierek, Columbus; Manager of the Year—Tom Spencer, Charlotte.

1999 BATTING

TEAM

Team	Avg.	G	TPA	AB	R	H	TB	2B	3B	HR	RBI	SH	SF	HP	BB	IBB	SO	SB	CS	GDP	LOB	ShO	Slg.	OBP
Durham	.295	143	5673	4951	923	1460	2432	336	39	186	865	48	56	53	565	30	956	103	56	110	1019	4	.491	.369
Charlotte	.290	144	5519	4843	836	1405	2250	309	22	164	777	52	48	70	506	20	850	95	37	112	1028	4	.465	.362
Columbus	.289	141	5523	4816	879	1391	2277	305	34	171	825	25	57	49	576	25	853	96	60	114	986	5	.473	.367
Indianapolis	.284	144	5586	4977	788	1411	2235	296	36	156	748	28	51	51	479	23	878	83	41	132	1026	6	.449	.349
Norfolk	.280	140	5303	4688	675	1313	1998	258	32	121	631	50	45	52	468	23	782	115	73	110	986	3	.426	.349
Buffalo	.269	144	5502	4829	748	1301	2085	254	34	154	697	39	46	46	542	20	947	143	45	109	1015	4	.432	.346
Rochester	.269	144	5489	4931	668	1325	2006	277	31	114	615	48	46	50	414	18	880	91	58	132	972	15	.407	.329
Syracuse	.268	144	5502	4891	744	1311	2094	257	32	154	688	29	40	44	498	23	968	102	38	121	986	6	.428	.336
Louisville	.265	144	5515	4893	731	1299	2134	265	36	166	686	40	43	47	492	20	1003	168	47	104	947	5	.436	.336
Richmond	.265	142	5363	4774	661	1263	1938	249	24	126	617	42	48	44	455	17	956	132	66	78	983	6	.406	.331
Pawtucket	.263	144	5611	4897	776	1286	2168	265	28	187	726	34	34	53	593	20	1008	90	33	91	1053	6	.443	.346

Team	Avg.	G	TPA	AB	R	H	TB	2B	3B	HR	RBI	SH	SF	HP	BB	IBB	SO	SB	CS	GDP	LOB	ShO	Slg.	OBP
Toledo	.258	144	5456	4814	706	1241	2083	250	32	176	668	23	49	44	526	10	978	86	48	103	983	5	.433	.333
Ottawa............	.255	144	5410	4770	647	1216	1886	246	32	120	603	40	58	82	460	25	1057	146	78	101	961	6	.395	.327
Scranton/W.-B..	.254	144	5513	4799	728	1220	1964	290	29	132	674	31	47	53	583	29	1035	90	36	106	1059	9	.409	.339

INDIVIDUAL

TOP QUALIFIERS FOR BATTING CHAMPIONSHIP

Minimum 389 plate appearances. *Lefthanded batter. †Switch-hitter.

Player, Team	Avg.	G	TPA	AB	R	H	TB	2B	3B	HR	RBI	SH	SF	HP	BB	IBB	SO	SB	CS	GDP	Slg.	OBP
Cox, Steve, Dur.*	.341	134	613	534	107	182	314	49	4	25	127	0	6	5	67	11	74	3	3	12	.588	.415
Hardtke, Jason, Ind.†	.329	101	458	416	74	137	214	37	2	12	61	1	4	2	35	1	43	7	4	7	.514	.381
Jimenez, D'Angelo, Col.†	.327	126	598	526	97	172	259	32	5	15	88	6	6	1	59	1	75	26	14	8	.492	.392
Raabe, Brian, Col.	.327	130	563	493	93	161	239	35	5	11	77	0	8	14	48	2	19	5	7	18	.485	.396
Coquillette, Trace, Ott.	.326	98	408	334	56	109	189	32	3	14	55	0	6	24	44	1	68	10	4	6	.566	.434
Lopez, Luis, Syr.	.322	136	582	531	76	171	222	35	2	4	69	2	8	1	40	2	58	1	0	22	.418	.366
Mottola, Chad, Char.	.321	140	581	511	95	164	264	32	4	20	94	0	7	3	60	1	83	18	6	7	.517	.391
Brito, Tilson, Char.	.318	111	458	406	60	129	202	30	5	11	58	3	3	12	34	3	66	6	4	5	.498	.385
Powell, Alonzo, Col.	.315	130	560	470	97	148	245	23	1	24	90	0	6	2	82	3	110	1	3	14	.521	.414
Graffanino, Tony, Dur.	.313	87	393	345	66	108	172	25	6	9	58	3	5	3	37	0	46	16	9	9	.499	.379
Vinas, Julio, Roch.	.312	126	517	484	67	151	247	32	2	20	83	0	7	1	25	1	73	4	3	13	.510	.342
Holbert, Aaron, Dur.	.311	100	390	347	77	108	170	18	4	12	56	8	5	5	25	0	56	14	5	4	.490	.361
Sisco, Steve, Rich.	.311	128	545	495	80	154	248	36	2	18	76	3	8	1	38	0	74	13	7	7	.501	.356
Haney, Todd, Nor.	.311	122	530	447	82	139	191	25	6	5	48	0	6	3	73	1	43	7	9	10	.427	.406
Mouton, Lyle, Roch.-Lou.	.310	127	521	467	89	145	263	43	3	23	94	0	8	6	40	0	98	22	1	14	.563	.367
Cromer, D.T., Ind.*	.310	136	590	535	83	166	301	37	4	30	107	0	7	3	44	3	98	4	2	12	.563	.362

DEPARTMENTAL LEADERS: G—Magee, 142; AB—Magee, 566; R—S. Cox, 107; H—S. Cox, 182; TB—S. Cox, 314; 2B—S. Cox, 49; 3B—D. Roberts, 10; HR—Raven, 33; RBI—S. Cox, 127; SH—Halter, 17; SF—McMillon, 10; HP—Coquillette, 24; BB—Zuber, 86; IBB—S. Cox, 11; SO—Branyan, 187; SB—G. Martinez, 48; CS—Halter, 18; GIDP—L. Lopez, 22; Slg.—S. Cox, .588; OBP—Coquillette, .434.

ALL PLAYERS

*Lefthanded batter. †Switch-hitter.

Player, Team	Avg.	G	TPA	AB	R	H	TB	2B	3B	HR	RBI	SH	SF	HP	BB	IBB	SO	SB	CS	GDP	Slg.	OBP
Abad, Andy, Paw.*	.297	102	435	377	61	112	186	21	4	15	65	2	3	2	51	5	50	7	2	9	.493	.381
Abbott, Jeff, Char.	.318	67	299	277	42	88	141	24	1	9	37	2	4	0	16	1	27	2	3	6	.509	.350
Adolfo, Carlos, Ott.	.189	16	59	53	5	10	20	2	1	2	9	0	2	1	3	0	11	0	0	2	.377	.237
Agbayani, Benny, Nor.	.356	28	121	101	21	36	70	8	1	8	32	0	2	2	16	1	19	5	3	2	.693	.446
Alcantara, Israel, Paw.	.272	24	93	81	13	22	52	3	0	9	23	0	0	3	9	0	29	0	0	0	.642	.366
Allensworth, Jermaine, Nor. ...	.264	81	319	273	44	72	117	20	5	5	20	2	1	7	36	0	39	10	5	3	.429	.363
Alomar, Sandy, Buf.	.273	10	40	33	9	9	19	2	1	2	10	0	0	1	6	0	3	0	0	1	.576	.400
Alvarez, Clemente, S./W.B.	.250	9	31	28	4	7	11	4	0	0	6	0	0	0	3	0	9	0	0	1	.393	.323
Alvarez, Gabe, Tol.	.285	110	482	410	70	117	204	24	0	21	67	0	9	6	57	0	80	1	3	8	.498	.373
Andreopoulos, Alex, Lou.*	.264	71	232	201	19	53	76	8	0	5	31	3	1	2	25	4	21	1	0	5	.378	.349
Andrews, Shane, Ott.	.250	2	8	8	1	2	5	0	0	1	4	0	0	0	0	0	2	0	0	1	.625	.250
Ashby, Chris, Col.	.267	70	230	206	46	55	97	13	1	9	32	1	0	2	21	0	39	6	3	5	.471	.341
Ashley, Billy, Tol.	.286	29	121	112	19	32	68	9	0	9	25	0	0	0	9	0	32	0	0	5	.607	.339
Atchley, Justin, Ind.*	.250	5	8	8	3	2	2	0	0	0	0	0	0	0	0	0	1	0	0	0	.250	.250
Baerga, Carlos, Ind.†	.290	52	236	221	32	64	83	10	0	3	27	2	2	1	10	3	18	2	1	11	.376	.321
Baez, Kevin, Ind.-Nor.	.270	80	249	215	19	58	69	8	0	1	33	1	3	2	28	1	25	3	0	4	.321	.355
Baker, Jason, Ind.*	.000	11	1	1	0	0	0	0	0	0	0	0	0	0	0	0	1	0	0	0	.000	.000
Banks, Brian, Lou.†	.208	6	27	24	3	5	12	2	1	1	6	0	1	0	2	1	5	0	0	0	.500	.259
Barker, Kevin, Lou.*	.278	121	512	442	89	123	229	27	5	23	87	0	7	4	59	5	94	2	2	13	.518	.363
Barrett, Michael, Ott.	.429	2	8	7	1	3	3	0	0	0	2	0	0	0	1	0	0	1	0	0	.429	.500
Barrios, Manny, Ind.	.100	49	10	10	0	1	1	0	0	0	0	0	0	0	0	0	5	0	0	0	.100	.100
Bartee, Kimera, Tol.†	.286	104	462	416	64	119	184	13	8	12	43	5	3	0	38	0	76	21	9	3	.442	.344
Bass, Jayson, Rich.†	.209	59	178	153	20	32	41	4	1	1	10	2	2	2	19	0	46	9	2	5	.268	.301
Batista, Miguel, Ott.	.000	3	1	1	0	0	0	0	0	0	0	0	0	0	0	0	0	0	0	0	.000	.000
Battle, Howard, Rich.	.284	121	495	454	80	129	232	29	1	24	74	0	5	3	33	2	66	2	3	12	.511	.333
Bautista, Jose, Ott.-Nor.	.000	36	11	10	0	0	0	0	0	0	0	0	0	1	0	0	6	0	0	0	.000	.000
Beamon, Trey, Char.*	.259	18	57	54	11	14	22	5	0	1	6	0	0	0	3	0	10	4	0	2	.407	.298
Bell, Mike, Nor.	.274	39	148	135	11	37	53	11	1	1	25	0	2	2	9	1	23	4	2	5	.393	.324
Belliard, Ronnie, Syr.	.241	29	124	108	14	26	33	4	0	1	8	0	1	1	14	0	13	12	3	3	.306	.331
Bellinger, Clay, Col.	.234	40	160	141	19	33	51	10	1	2	14	0	4	2	13	0	32	6	0	1	.362	.300
Beltran, Rigo, Nor.*	.000	21	1	0	0	0	0	0	0	0	0	0	0	0	0	0	1	0	0	0	.000	1.000
Beltre, Esteban, Roch.-Char. .	.262	130	476	435	72	114	156	27	3	3	40	7	3	1	30	1	80	9	3	17	.359	.309
Benitez, Yamil, Lou.	.214	99	374	341	47	73	137	24	2	12	49	1	1	2	29	0	103	13	4	7	.402	.279
Bennett, Joel, S./W.B.	.100	20	11	10	2	1	2	1	0	0	0	0	0	0	1	0	3	0	0	0	.200	.182
Bennett, Shayne, Ott.	.750	38	4	4	0	3	3	0	0	0	0	0	0	0	0	0	1	0	0	0	.750	.750
Benz, Jake, Ott.*	.000	18	2	1	0	0	0	0	0	0	0	0	0	0	0	0	0	0	0	0	.000	.000
Bere, Jason, Ind.-Lou.	.400	10	13	10	1	4	5	1	0	0	9	0	0	0	0	0	5	0	0	0	.500	.538
Bergeron, Peter, Ott.*	.314	58	221	194	36	61	88	12	3	3	20	1	2	1	23	0	40	14	8	1	.454	.386
Berroa, Geronimo, Syr.	.273	10	41	33	7	9	18	0	0	3	8	0	0	0	8	1	5	0	0	2	.545	.415
Bierek, Kurt, Col.*	.280	135	594	532	84	149	268	42	4	23	95	1	7	6	48	1	99	5	3	14	.504	.342
Blake, Casey, Syr.	.245	110	458	387	69	95	181	16	2	22	75	1	2	7	61	2	82	9	5	10	.468	.357
Blum, Geoff, Ott.†	.265	77	319	268	43	71	117	14	1	10	37	3	7	2	37	1	39	6	1	5	.437	.350
Bochtler, Doug, Syr.	.000	14	1	1	0	0	0	0	0	0	0	0	0	0	0	0	1	0	0	0	.000	.000
Bolton, Rod, S./W.B.	.077	24	15	13	1	1	1	0	0	0	0	2	0	0	0	0	1	0	0	1	.077	.200
Bonilla, Bobby, Nor.†	.231	3	13	13	1	3	3	0	0	0	1	0	0	0	0	0	4	0	0	0	.231	.231
Bonnici, Jim, Tol.	.224	22	66	58	10	13	22	3	0	2	4	0	1	1	6	0	25	0	0	0	.379	.303
Boone, Aaron, Ind.	.341	11	49	41	6	14	18	2	1	0	7	0	3	2	3	0	4	2	2	1	.439	.388
Borders, Pat, Buf.	.237	55	216	198	17	47	69	7	0	5	23	2	1	3	12	2	31	0	1	5	.348	.290

CLASS AAA International League

Player, Team	Avg.	G	TPA	AB	R	H	TB	2B	3B	HR	RBI	SH	SF	HP	BB	IBB	SO	SB	CS	GDP	Slg.	OBP
Borowski, Joe, Lou.	.000	58	2	2	0	0	0	0	0	0	0	0	0	0	0	0	2	0	0	0	.000	.000
Bowie, Micah, Rich.*	.167	13	7	6	0	1	1	0	0	0	0	0	0	0	1	0	2	0	0	0	.167	.286
Bradshaw, Terry, Ott.*	.197	56	148	127	13	25	36	5	3	0	10	1	1	3	16	1	31	4	2	1	.283	.299
Branson, Jeff, Ind.*	.253	124	480	430	57	109	152	18	2	7	56	1	2	1	46	3	86	2	2	3	.353	.326
Branyan, Russell, Buf.*	.208	109	453	395	51	82	185	11	1	30	67	0	2	4	52	2	187	8	3	5	.468	.305
Brewer, Billy, S./W.B.*	.333	33	7	6	0	2	2	0	0	0	1	0	0	1	0	0	2	0	0	0	.333	.429
Brito, Jorge, Lou.	.056	4	18	18	0	1	1	0	0	0	0	0	0	0	0	0	9	0	0	1	.056	.056
Brito, Tilson, Char.	.318	111	458	406	60	129	202	30	5	11	58	3	3	12	34	3	66	6	4	5	.498	.385
Brooks, Antone, Rich.*	.400	43	5	5	2	2	2	0	0	0	0	0	0	0	0	0	1	0	0	0	.400	.400
Brooks, Jerry, Nor.	.237	79	278	241	32	57	99	13	1	9	27	0	1	2	34	2	50	0	2	3	.411	.335
Brown, Kevin, Syr.	.258	88	320	295	39	76	137	18	2	13	51	0	2	2	21	1	79	0	1	2	.464	.309
Buccheri, Jim, Dur.-Nor.	.220	38	109	100	11	22	26	4	0	0	7	2	1	0	6	0	15	6	1	5	.260	.262
Budzinski, Mark, Buf.*	.286	47	157	133	24	38	57	7	3	2	17	2	0	0	22	2	36	4	2	3	.429	.387
Burkhart, Lance, Ott.	.125	2	8	8	1	1	1	0	0	0	0	0	0	0	0	0	5	0	0	0	.125	.125
Burrell, Pat, S./W.B.	.152	10	38	33	4	5	8	0	0	1	4	0	0	1	4	0	8	0	1	0	.242	.263
Burton, Darren, S./W.B.†	.262	118	465	409	61	107	182	30	3	13	63	3	4	5	44	2	96	7	2	9	.445	.338
Butler, Rich, Dur.*	.289	90	382	332	52	96	158	28	2	10	63	3	3	3	41	4	70	2	5	4	.476	.369
Cabrera, Jolbert, Buf.	.265	71	319	279	44	74	95	13	4	0	27	7	5	2	26	0	43	20	4	8	.341	.327
Camilli, Jason, Ott.	.265	35	113	102	12	27	33	6	0	0	8	0	0	1	11	0	19	4	1	3	.324	.336
Cancel, Robinson, Lou.	.368	39	134	117	22	43	66	8	0	5	28	1	1	1	14	0	28	6	2	6	.564	.436
Carpenter, Bubba, Col.*	.283	101	409	325	78	92	182	20	2	22	81	1	4	4	75	7	68	7	3	4	.560	.419
Carrara, Giovanni, Ind.	.130	39	24	23	0	3	3	0	0	0	1	0	0	0	0	0	3	0	0	0	.130	.130
Carter, Mike, S./W.B.	.161	9	33	31	2	5	11	1	1	1	4	0	0	2	0	0	8	0	1	0	.355	.212
Carter, Shannon, Syr.*	.111	2	9	9	0	1	1	0	0	0	0	0	0	0	0	0	2	0	0	2	.111	.111
Carvajal, Jhonny, Ott.	.231	106	390	355	28	82	110	20	4	0	34	3	6	5	21	2	67	7	3	8	.310	.279
Carver, Steve, S./W.B.*	.236	98	325	288	33	68	121	18	1	11	38	2	0	1	34	3	101	2	0	8	.420	.319
Casanova, Raul, Tol.†	.206	44	169	160	21	33	60	9	0	6	23	0	1	1	7	0	28	0	0	8	.375	.243
Cather, Mike, Rich.	.000	45	3	3	0	0	0	0	0	0	0	0	0	0	0	0	1	0	0	0	.000	.000
Cedeno, Andujar, Col.	.293	62	235	215	27	63	101	14	3	6	38	2	1	3	11	0	31	1	1	11	.470	.335
Chamblee, James, Paw.	.274	127	527	464	84	127	226	21	3	24	88	4	3	13	43	2	126	5	3	4	.487	.350
Chen, Bruce, Rich.†	.111	14	12	9	1	1	1	0	0	0	0	3	0	0	0	0	0	0	0	0	.111	.111
Christensen, McKay, Char.*	.250	1	4	4	0	1	1	0	0	0	0	0	0	0	0	0	1	0	0	0	.250	.250
Christopherson, Eric, Char.	.314	63	223	188	36	59	85	17	0	3	27	4	1	0	30	1	39	4	0	7	.452	.406
Clark, Howie, Rich.*	.294	79	317	279	33	82	127	19	4	6	28	1	2	1	34	2	24	1	2	8	.455	.370
Clark, Tony, Tol.†	.000	1	4	3	0	0	0	0	0	0	0	0	0	1	0	0	1	0	0	0	.000	.250
Clyburn, Danny, Dur.	.234	82	334	303	38	71	111	11	1	9	33	0	6	6	19	2	74	2	0	7	.366	.287
Coleman, Michael, Paw.	.268	115	529	467	95	125	248	29	2	30	74	4	4	3	51	1	128	14	6	7	.531	.341
Collier, Lou, Lou.	.385	27	108	91	25	35	57	10	0	4	11	0	1	1	15	0	14	6	3	2	.626	.472
Converse, Jim, Lou.*	.000	30	6	6	0	0	0	0	0	0	0	0	0	0	0	0	1	0	0	0	.000	.000
Coolbaugh, Mike, Col.	.276	114	437	391	65	108	188	31	2	15	66	2	4	2	38	0	112	5	7	5	.481	.340
Coquillette, Trace, Ott.	.326	98	408	334	56	109	189	32	3	14	55	0	6	24	44	1	68	10	4	6	.566	.434
Cox, Darron, Ott.	.000	3	10	9	0	0	0	0	0	0	0	0	0	0	1	0	2	0	0	0	.000	.100
Cox, Steve, Dur.*	.341	134	613	534	107	182	314	49	4	25	127	0	6	5	67	11	74	3	3	12	.588	.415
Cradle, Rickey, Tol.	.239	110	402	348	57	83	144	27	2	10	52	1	5	6	42	1	82	11	6	6	.414	.327
Cromer, Brandon, Lou.*	.215	115	373	330	46	71	157	12	1	24	61	1	0	2	40	5	103	6	0	1	.476	.304
Cromer, D.T., Ind.*	.310	136	590	535	83	166	301	37	4	30	107	0	7	3	44	3	98	4	2	12	.563	.362
Cruz, Jacob, Buf.*	.272	54	227	202	29	55	87	7	2	7	31	0	1	3	21	1	39	4	2	7	.431	.348
Cruz, Jose, Syr.†	.184	31	132	103	17	19	33	3	1	3	14	0	1	0	28	3	20	5	0	3	.320	.356
Dalesandro, Mark, Syr.	.225	20	76	71	3	16	18	2	0	0	5	0	2	2	1	0	7	1	0	1	.254	.250
Darden, Tony, Nor.	.121	18	41	33	4	4	5	1	0	0	3	0	1	0	7	1	4	2	2	2	.152	.268
Daubach, Brian, Paw.*	.290	9	39	31	4	9	14	2	0	1	6	0	0	2	6	0	8	0	0	0	.452	.436
Davis, James, Ind.	.288	16	57	52	7	15	21	4	1	0	10	0	1	1	3	0	6	0	0	3	.404	.333
Davis, Tommy, Roch.	.257	110	443	413	49	106	157	18	0	11	56	2	4	0	24	2	65	1	4	11	.380	.295
Dawley, Joey, Rich.	.000	7	9	7	0	0	0	0	0	0	0	2	0	0	0	0	3	0	0	0	.000	.000
DeCinces, Tim, Roch.*	.264	16	53	53	7	14	25	5	0	2	8	0	0	0	0	0	12	0	0	2	.472	.264
DeHart, Rick, Ott.	.000	15	3	3	0	0	0	0	0	0	0	0	0	0	0	0	1	0	0	0	.000	.000
Delgado, Alex, Syr.	.206	37	126	107	11	22	35	7	0	2	12	1	0	4	14	0	14	0	0	4	.327	.320
Dent, Darrell, Roch.*	.133	9	35	30	4	4	10	0	0	2	5	1	1	0	3	0	8	4	0	0	.333	.206
Depastino, Joe, Paw.	.253	77	287	257	35	65	117	13	0	13	52	0	2	1	27	0	40	1	1	4	.455	.324
DeRosa, Mark, Rich.	.272	105	397	364	41	99	122	16	2	1	40	3	4	5	21	1	49	7	6	5	.335	.317
DeSilva, John, Ott.	.000	23	13	10	1	0	0	0	0	0	0	1	0	0	2	0	2	0	0	0	.000	.167
Dodd, Robert, S./W.B.*	.000	6	6	5	0	0	0	0	0	0	0	1	0	0	0	0	1	0	0	0	.000	.000
Donnelly, Brendan, Dur.-Syr.	1.000	42	1	1	0	1	1	0	0	0	0	0	0	0	0	0	0	0	0	0	1.000	1.000
Dotel, Octavio, Nor.	.000	13	5	5	0	0	0	0	0	0	0	0	0	0	0	0	3	0	0	0	.000	.000
Dunn, Todd, Lou.-Roch.	.196	70	232	204	22	40	69	6	1	7	31	1	1	4	22	0	67	3	3	11	.338	.286
Duran, Roberto, Ott.*	.000	5	1	1	0	0	0	0	0	0	0	0	0	0	0	0	0	0	0	0	.000	.000
Durocher, Jayson, Ott.	.000	17	2	2	0	0	0	0	0	0	0	0	0	0	0	0	1	0	0	0	.000	.000
Eaton, Adam, S./W.B.	.250	3	5	4	0	1	1	0	0	0	0	1	0	0	0	0	0	0	0	0	.250	.250
Ebert, Derrin, Rich.	.100	25	22	20	1	2	3	1	0	0	1	1	0	0	1	0	6	0	0	0	.150	.143
Eddie, Steve, Ind.-Char.	.273	43	158	143	17	39	51	6	0	2	15	2	5	0	8	0	20	0	0	5	.357	.301
Eldred, Cal, Lou.	.000	4	3	2	0	0	0	0	0	0	0	1	0	0	0	0	1	0	0	0	.000	.000
Estalella, Bobby, S./W.B.	.231	110	452	386	58	89	161	23	2	15	62	0	6	5	55	1	100	4	1	12	.417	.330
Estrada, Horacio, Lou.*	.143	25	23	21	0	3	3	0	0	0	1	1	0	0	1	0	7	0	0	0	.143	.182
Etler, Todd, Ind.	.000	26	3	2	1	0	0	0	0	0	0	1	0	0	0	0	2	0	0	0	.000	.000
Evans, Dave, Roch.	.000	60	1	1	0	0	0	0	0	0	0	0	0	0	0	0	1	0	0	0	.000	.000
Evans, Keith, Ind.	.111	24	11	9	0	1	1	0	0	0	2	0	0	0	0	0	4	0	0	0	.111	.111
Falteisek, Steve, Lou.	.333	43	3	3	0	1	2	1	0	0	0	0	0	0	0	0	1	0	0	0	.667	.333
Fernandez, Jose, Ott.	.271	124	505	465	73	126	202	30	2	14	68	1	3	5	31	0	136	14	7	11	.434	.321
Fesh, Sean, S./W.B.*	.000	45	2	2	0	0	0	0	0	0	0	0	0	0	0	0	0	0	0	0	.000	.000
Fick, Robert, Tol.*	.313	14	58	48	11	15	23	0	1	2	8	0	1	1	8	0	5	1	0	0	.479	.414
Finn, John, S./W.B.	.218	42	144	124	18	27	40	1	0	4	10	2	0	3	15	0	12	2	0	2	.323	.317
Fleetham, Ben, Nor.	.000	6	1	1	0	0	0	0	0	0	0	0	0	0	0	0	1	0	0	0	.000	.000

Player, Team	Avg.	G	TPA	AB	R	H	TB	2B	3B	HR	RBI	SH	SF	HP	BB	IBB	SO	SB	CS	GDP	Slg.	OBP
Fletcher, Darrin, Syr.*	.267	4	16	15	0	4	4	0	0	0	0	0	0	0	1	0	1	0	0	1	.267	.313
Flores, Jose, S./W.B.	.246	64	276	228	35	56	66	6	2	0	18	4	0	7	37	1	43	13	3	1	.289	.368
Fonville, Chad, Paw.†	.253	74	283	257	31	65	75	3	2	1	14	4	0	2	20	0	31	6	4	4	.292	.312
Forbes, P.J., Roch.	.264	88	391	349	49	92	110	16	1	0	19	11	2	3	26	0	40	5	0	1	.315	.318
Foster, Jim, Roch.	.229	35	130	118	6	27	32	3	1	0	11	0	0	0	12	1	19	4	2	2	.271	.300
Frank, Mike, Ind.*	.296	121	482	433	73	128	205	36	7	9	62	2	3	8	36	2	55	10	6	10	.473	.358
Fraraccio, Dan, Dur.	.267	15	35	30	5	8	14	3	0	1	4	0	0	1	4	0	4	2	0	1	.467	.371
Frazier, Lou, S./W.B.†	.247	89	359	308	54	76	124	16	7	6	32	4	1	2	44	1	79	21	3	5	.403	.344
Freel, Ryan, Syr.	.299	20	90	77	15	23	33	3	2	1	11	1	0	4	8	0	13	10	3	3	.429	.393
Frye, Jeff, Paw.	.333	3	11	9	0	3	3	0	0	0	2	0	0	0	2	0	1	0	0	0	.333	.455
Fryman, Travis, Buf.	.182	3	11	11	1	2	5	0	0	1	2	0	0	0	0	0	3	0	0	0	.455	.182
Fullmer, Brad, Ott.*	.317	39	158	142	31	45	87	9	0	11	32	0	1	3	12	1	16	2	2	5	.613	.380
Garcia, Guillermo, Ind.	.288	65	265	233	30	67	106	9	0	10	28	0	5	5	22	2	44	1	1	12	.455	.355
Garcia, Jesse, Roch.	.255	62	243	220	25	56	76	10	2	2	23	11	1	0	11	0	21	9	6	5	.345	.289
Garcia, Luis, Tol.	.266	89	323	308	30	82	112	19	1	3	34	3	5	1	5	0	41	3	3	12	.364	.276
Garcia, Neil, Dur.†	.091	12	36	33	1	3	7	1	0	1	2	0	1	0	2	0	8	1	0	1	.212	.139
Glass, Chip, Col.*	.277	53	186	159	32	44	63	7	3	2	30	3	1	1	22	1	32	5	4	2	.396	.366
Glauber, Keith, Ind.	.000	12	11	10	0	0	0	0	0	0	0	1	0	0	0	0	1	0	0	0	.000	.000
Gonzalez, Jose, Char.	.286	9	15	14	3	4	5	1	0	0	1	1	0	0	0	0	3	1	0	1	.357	.286
Gonzalez, Manny, Char.†	.310	48	142	129	14	40	51	6	1	1	25	8	0	0	5	1	20	1	4	1	.395	.336
Grace, Mike, S./W.B.	.000	10	4	3	0	0	0	0	0	0	0	1	0	0	0	0	1	0	0	0	.000	.250
Graffanino, Tony, Dur.	.313	87	393	345	66	108	172	25	6	9	58	3	5	3	37	0	46	16	9	9	.499	.379
Grahe, Joe, S./W.B.	.000	23	1	1	0	0	0	0	0	0	0	0	0	0	0	0	1	0	0	0	.000	.000
Grebeck, Craig, Syr.	.250	4	17	16	3	4	8	1	0	1	2	0	0	0	1	0	1	0	0	0	.500	.294
Green, Tyler, S./W.B.	.167	20	7	6	1	1	2	1	0	0	2	1	0	0	0	0	1	0	0	0	.333	.167
Greene, Charlie, Lou.	.211	56	168	161	16	34	54	8	0	4	15	0	0	0	7	1	26	0	0	2	.335	.244
Greene, Rick, Ind.	.500	61	2	2	0	1	1	0	0	0	0	0	0	0	0	0	0	0	0	0	.500	.500
Greene, Willie, Syr.*	.327	14	58	52	12	17	33	1	0	5	11	0	0	0	6	2	14	0	0	1	.635	.397
Grifol, Pedro, Nor.	.260	59	196	177	11	46	63	5	0	4	27	3	4	0	12	1	33	1	1	3	.356	.301
Gubanich, Creighton, Paw.	.283	27	99	92	12	26	44	3	0	5	10	0	1	0	6	0	23	0	0	4	.478	.323
Guerra, Mark, Nor.	.000	64	4	4	0	0	0	0	0	0	0	0	0	0	0	0	2	0	0	0	.000	.000
Guiliano, Matt, S./W.B.	.190	71	242	216	20	41	62	15	0	2	24	5	2	2	17	0	61	3	2	4	.287	.253
Guillen, Jose, Dur.	.382	9	42	34	8	13	23	1	0	3	12	0	1	0	7	0	7	0	1	2	.676	.476
Hairston, Jerry, Roch.	.291	107	469	413	65	120	175	24	5	7	48	4	3	19	30	0	50	19	10	9	.424	.363
Halter, Shane, Nor.	.274	127	554	474	77	130	176	22	3	6	35	17	3	0	60	0	90	19	18	10	.371	.354
Haltiwanger, Garrick, Nor.	.000	6	13	13	2	0	0	0	0	0	0	0	0	0	0	0	8	0	0	1	.000	.000
Hamelin, Bob, Tol.*	.221	46	178	149	20	33	57	9	0	5	20	0	2	3	24	2	29	4	1	3	.383	.337
Haney, Todd, Nor.	.311	122	530	447	82	139	191	25	6	5	48	0	6	3	73	1	43	7	9	10	.427	.406
Hardtke, Jason, Ind.†	.329	101	458	416	74	137	214	37	2	12	61	1	4	2	35	1	43	7	4	7	.514	.381
Harriger, Denny, Ind.	.083	28	16	12	1	1	1	0	0	0	1	3	0	0	1	0	3	0	0	0	.083	.154
Harriss, Robin, Buf.	.000	2	5	3	0	0	0	0	0	0	0	0	1	0	1	0	1	0	0	0	.000	.250
Hatteberg, Scott, Paw.*	.176	10	38	34	3	6	8	2	0	0	4	0	0	0	4	0	6	0	0	2	.235	.263
Henderson, Rod, Lou.	.214	28	17	14	0	3	4	1	0	0	1	3	0	0	0	0	5	0	0	0	.286	.214
Henderson, Ryan, Lou.-Nor.	.000	28	2	2	0	0	0	0	0	0	0	0	0	0	0	0	1	0	0	1	.000	.000
Herrera, Jose, Roch.*	.205	39	132	127	11	26	41	7	1	2	16	2	1	0	2	0	20	3	1	4	.323	.215
Hiatt, Phil, Ind.	.238	78	346	311	46	74	139	11	0	18	54	0	3	2	30	0	103	0	0	8	.447	.306
Holbert, Aaron, Dur.	.311	100	390	347	77	108	170	18	4	12	56	8	5	5	25	0	56	14	5	4	.490	.361
Hollins, Damon, Ind.	.262	106	361	328	58	86	132	19	0	9	43	1	0	1	31	1	44	11	2	13	.402	.328
Hollins, Dave, Syr.-Char.†	.308	67	266	214	51	66	109	19	0	8	34	0	4	14	34	2	42	5	1	4	.509	.429
Hosey, Dwayne, Ott.†	.181	33	117	94	16	17	25	3	1	1	11	1	3	4	15	1	26	6	4	1	.266	.310
Huff, Larry, S./W.B.	.235	9	23	17	4	4	6	2	0	0	1	0	0	1	5	0	2	0	0	0	.353	.435
Hughes, Bobby, Lou.	.188	10	35	32	5	6	11	2	0	1	2	0	0	1	2	0	7	0	0	0	.344	.257
Hunter, Scott, Nor.-Ott.	.226	128	505	460	42	104	169	17	0	16	64	3	7	6	29	0	106	8	11	3	.367	.277
Hurst, Jimmy, Syr.	.282	99	120	103	18	29	41	3	0	3	10	0	2	0	15	0	32	4	3	3	.398	.367
Hyzdu, Adam, Paw.	.229	12	39	35	4	8	11	0	0	1	6	0	0	0	4	0	13	0	0	1	.314	.308
Iapoce, Anthony, Lou.†	.169	26	91	83	6	14	16	2	0	0	0	1	0	0	7	1	30	6	3	3	.193	.233
Inglin, Jeff, Char.	.205	14	44	39	8	8	17	0	0	3	8	0	0	1	4	0	9	0	1	0	.436	.295
Ingram, Garey, Paw.	.247	85	326	296	49	73	121	15	3	9	39	7	2	3	17	0	52	11	2	5	.409	.292
Isom, Johnny, Roch.	.345	34	129	119	19	41	59	12	0	2	10	0	0	0	10	0	28	1	1	6	.496	.395
Isringhausen, Jason, Nor.	.182	13	11	11	0	2	2	0	0	0	0	0	0	0	0	0	3	0	0	0	.182	.182
Jackson, Gavin, Paw.	.164	49	168	140	17	23	26	3	0	0	5	1	0	0	27	0	32	2	0	4	.186	.299
Janzen, Marty, Ind.	.000	9	1	1	0	0	0	0	0	0	0	0	0	0	0	0	1	0	0	0	.000	.000
Jefferies, Gregg, Tol.†	.250	2	8	8	0	2	2	0	0	0	0	0	0	0	0	0	2	0	0	0	.250	.250
Jefferson, Reggie, Paw.*	.000	3	13	10	1	0	0	0	0	0	0	0	0	1	2	0	4	0	0	0	.000	.231
Jimenez, D'Angelo, Col.†	.327	126	598	526	97	172	259	32	5	15	88	6	6	1	59	1	75	26	14	8	.492	.392
Johnson, Adam, Rich.*	.333	14	46	42	7	14	19	2	0	1	6	1	0	1	2	0	5	1	1	0	.452	.378
Johnson, Barry, S./W.B.	.056	31	19	18	0	1	1	0	0	0	1	0	0	0	1	0	10	0	0	0	.056	.105
Johnson, Brian, Ind.	.211	6	20	19	2	4	7	3	0	0	4	0	0	0	1	0	3	0	0	4	.368	.250
Johnson, Mike, Ott.*	.240	29	27	25	3	6	6	0	0	0	2	2	0	0	0	0	8	0	0	0	.240	.240
Jones, Bobby, Nor.	.000	2	2	2	0	0	0	0	0	0	0	0	0	0	0	0	1	0	0	0	.000	.000
Jones, Chris, Syr.	.237	81	299	279	45	66	108	12	3	8	40	1	0	0	19	0	74	11	3	12	.387	.285
Jones, Terry, Ott.	.262	88	367	332	49	87	108	17	2	0	23	7	3	1	24	0	66	30	10	6	.325	.311
Kapler, Gabe, Tol.	.315	14	65	54	11	17	36	6	2	3	14	0	2	0	9	1	10	0	1	0	.667	.400
Kieschnick, Brooks, Dur.*	.200	23	80	75	6	15	23	5	0	1	5	0	0	0	5	0	14	0	0	3	.307	.250
Kingsale, Eugene, Roch.†	.309	48	211	191	31	59	74	9	0	2	20	3	1	3	13	0	23	10	9	2	.387	.361
Kinkade, Mike, Nor.	.308	84	340	312	53	96	141	20	2	7	49	0	2	5	21	2	31	7	1	9	.452	.359
Klingenbeck, Scott, Ind.	.000	14	6	6	0	0	0	0	0	0	0	0	0	0	0	0	3	0	0	0	.000	.000
Krause, Scott, Lou.	.277	133	560	499	57	138	223	26	7	15	89	7	8	13	33	2	104	10	6	13	.447	.333
Lamb, David, Dur.†	.233	7	35	30	7	7	10	3	0	0	7	2	1	0	2	0	4	0	1	0	.333	.273
LaRue, Jason, Ind.	.251	70	284	263	42	66	118	12	2	12	37	0	2	4	15	1	52	0	3	13	.449	.299
Ledee, Ricky, Col.*	.252	30	134	115	18	29	50	7	1	4	15	1	1	0	17	1	29	4	2	1	.435	.346
Ledesma, Aaron, Dur.	.100	2	10	10	0	1	1	0	0	0	0	0	0	0	0	0	1	0	0	1	.100	.100

Player, Team	Avg.	G	TPA	AB	R	H	TB	2B	3B	HR	RBI	SH	SF	HP	BB	IBB	SO	SB	CS	GDP	Slg.	OBP
Lee, Carlos, Char.	.351	25	106	94	16	33	50	5	0	4	20	0	3	1	8	1	14	2	1	3	.532	.396
Lennon, Pat, Syr.-Tol.	.287	111	474	414	75	119	232	21	1	30	83	0	2	3	55	0	106	4	5	12	.560	.373
Levis, Jesse, Dur.*	.330	27	112	94	20	31	39	5	0	1	8	0	1	2	15	1	9	0	0	4	.415	.429
Levrault, Allen, Lou.	.333	9	3	3	0	1	2	1	0	0	0	0	0	0	0	0	1	0	0	0	.667	.333
Lewis, Richie, Nor.	.267	25	17	15	1	4	4	0	0	0	0	2	0	0	0	0	4	1	1	0	.267	.267
LeBlanc, Eric, Ind.*	.750	14	6	4	2	3	4	1	0	0	0	1	0	0	1	0	1	0	0	0	1.000	.800
Liefer, Jeff, Char.*	.339	46	195	171	36	58	104	17	1	9	34	1	1	1	21	3	26	2	1	3	.608	.412
Lilly, Ted, Ott.*	.000	16	9	7	0	0	0	0	0	0	0	2	0	0	0	0	3	0	0	0	.000	.000
Liniak, Cole, Paw.	.264	95	393	348	55	92	153	25	0	12	42	3	1	1	40	1	57	0	5	7	.440	.341
Livingstone, Scott, Roch.-Nor.*	.318	50	174	157	15	50	64	11	0	1	27	1	2	0	14	2	13	3	0	11	.408	.370
Lombard, George, Rich.*	.206	74	271	233	25	48	86	11	3	7	29	0	0	3	35	2	98	21	6	2	.369	.317
Long, Terrence, Nor.*	.326	78	329	304	41	99	148	20	4	7	47	0	1	1	23	4	41	14	6	6	.487	.374
Looney, Brian, Tol.-S./W.B.*	.000	50	2	2	0	0	0	0	0	0	0	0	0	0	0	0	1	0	0	0	.000	.000
Lopez, Johan, Nor.	.267	34	16	15	2	4	4	0	0	0	1	1	0	0	0	0	2	0	0	0	.267	.267
Lopez, Luis, Syr.	.322	136	582	531	76	171	222	35	2	4	69	2	8	1	40	2	58	1	0	22	.418	.366
Lopez, Mickey, Lou.†	.320	49	223	181	43	58	94	17	2	5	31	2	1	2	37	0	25	11	7	1	.519	.439
Lovullo, Torey, S./W.B.†	.279	139	610	519	90	145	250	36	3	21	106	1	9	3	78	10	89	3	4	12	.482	.371
Lowery, Terrell, Dur.	.335	71	329	275	69	92	167	20	5	15	57	8	2	1	43	1	62	10	5	3	.607	.424
Lucca, Lou, S./W.B.	.268	136	569	533	61	143	216	33	2	12	70	0	5	9	22	0	94	4	6	15	.405	.306
Lydy, Scott, Char.	.212	19	76	66	11	14	22	2	0	2	13	0	2	0	8	0	15	1	0	2	.333	.289
Machado, Robert, Char.-Ott.	.217	37	138	129	10	28	42	8	0	2	10	1	0	4	4	0	26	0	1	5	.326	.263
Macias, Jose, Tol.†	.244	112	485	438	44	107	147	18	8	2	36	5	2	4	36	0	60	10	5	8	.336	.306
Magdaleno, Ricky, Char.	.235	27	91	81	7	19	26	5	1	0	7	2	1	0	7	1	20	0	1	0	.321	.292
Magee, Wendell, S./W.B.	.283	142	629	566	95	160	258	34	2	20	79	1	5	2	55	0	124	10	8	12	.456	.346
Mahomes, Pat, Nor.	.375	9	11	8	2	3	3	0	0	0	0	3	0	0	0	0	0	0	0	0	.375	.375
Mahoney, Mike, Rich.	.228	55	157	145	10	33	46	7	0	2	20	2	3	1	6	1	25	0	1	2	.317	.258
Malave, Jaime, Ott.	.250	3	9	8	2	2	2	0	0	0	0	0	0	0	1	0	4	0	0	0	.250	.333
Malloy, Marty, Rich.*	.292	114	469	407	58	119	165	23	1	7	36	4	3	2	53	2	52	19	15	2	.405	.374
Manto, Jeff, Buf.	.296	66	273	203	47	60	138	9	0	23	44	0	1	3	66	1	47	3	1	4	.680	.473
Martin, Chris, Dur.	.273	120	470	399	64	109	158	20	1	9	53	9	7	7	48	3	61	14	2	15	.396	.356
Martin, Norberto, Syr.	.295	81	338	319	45	94	124	11	2	5	34	3	2	2	12	0	33	14	1	9	.389	.322
Martinez, Gabby, Char.	.286	16	57	49	8	14	27	1	0	4	5	3	0	0	5	0	6	3	3	2	.551	.352
Martinez, Greg, Lou.†	.265	107	483	419	79	111	144	13	4	4	29	5	1	4	53	0	50	48	7	10	.344	.352
Martinez, Pablo, Rich.†	.194	63	222	186	18	36	52	7	3	1	18	7	1	3	25	1	42	13	3	1	.280	.298
Matos, Pascual, Rich.	.210	66	236	224	17	47	63	7	0	3	21	3	2	1	6	0	47	3	1	6	.281	.232
Maxwell, Jason, Tol.	.236	119	482	419	60	99	165	17	2	15	62	4	4	2	53	0	87	6	3	4	.394	.322
May, Derrick, Roch.*	.278	71	320	295	39	82	122	19	3	5	43	0	2	1	22	1	28	4	2	10	.414	.328
McCall, Rod, Ind.*	.259	47	175	139	21	36	61	7	0	6	28	0	3	1	32	0	49	1	0	1	.439	.394
McCarty, Dave, Tol.	.268	132	543	466	85	125	248	24	3	31	77	0	3	4	70	5	110	6	6	9	.532	.366
McClain, Scott, Dur.	.251	137	615	533	106	134	253	33	1	28	104	0	6	3	73	1	156	4	2	11	.475	.341
McCommon, Jason, Roch.	.333	29	3	3	1	1	4	0	0	1	1	0	0	0	0	0	0	0	0	0	1.333	.333
McDonald, John, Buf.	.316	66	257	237	30	75	89	12	1	0	25	5	2	2	11	0	23	6	3	5	.376	.349
McGuire, Ryan, Ott.*	.251	53	221	183	23	46	66	6	1	4	27	0	3	0	35	3	37	1	3	5	.361	.367
McKeel, Walt, Tol.	.242	67	248	215	21	52	84	9	1	7	37	1	2	4	26	0	32	2	2	6	.391	.332
McMillon, Billy, S./W.B.*	.304	132	552	464	97	141	235	38	4	16	85	1	10	6	65	4	79	11	2	10	.506	.389
McNabb, Buck, Rich.*	.229	17	54	48	8	11	14	0	0	1	8	0	0	0	6	1	9	0	1	3	.292	.315
Meacham, Rusty, Ind.	.000	16	2	2	0	0	0	0	0	0	0	0	0	0	0	0	1	0	0	0	.000	.000
Melhuse, Adam, Syr.†	.282	21	81	71	15	20	31	5	0	2	16	0	0	0	10	0	20	1	1	1	.437	.370
Melo, Juan, Syr.-Ind.†	.240	44	162	150	23	36	59	9	1	4	16	0	1	1	10	0	33	9	4	2	.393	.290
Mendoza, Carlos, Dur.*	.293	75	314	266	57	78	95	8	3	1	25	9	0	7	32	0	38	9	8	5	.357	.384
Mercado, Hector, Nor.*	.000	2	2	1	0	0	0	0	0	0	0	1	0	0	0	0	1	0	0	0	.000	.000
Mercedes, Jose, Nor.	.000	6	9	7	0	0	0	0	0	0	0	2	0	0	0	0	2	0	0	0	.000	.000
Merloni, Lou, Paw.	.279	66	269	229	45	64	101	14	1	7	36	0	1	9	30	0	38	1	1	4	.441	.383
Merrell, Phil, Ind.	1.000	3	1	1	0	1	1	0	0	0	0	0	0	0	0	0	0	0	0	0	1.000	1.000
Millan, Adan, S./W.B.	.000	1	3	2	0	0	0	0	0	0	0	0	0	0	1	0	2	0	0	0	.000	.333
Miller, David, Buf.*	.240	101	360	325	37	78	111	21	3	2	37	1	1	0	33	2	57	12	5	8	.342	.309
Miller, Orlando, Buf.	.258	68	251	233	27	60	98	17	0	7	33	1	0	5	12	1	52	5	0	6	.421	.308
Minor, Blas, Lou.	.125	21	9	8	0	1	1	0	0	0	1	1	0	0	0	0	3	0	0	0	.125	.125
Minor, Ryan, Roch.	.256	101	432	383	56	98	187	24	1	21	67	1	6	5	37	1	119	3	1	8	.488	.325
Mitchell, Keith, Paw.	.258	117	514	431	71	111	187	32	4	12	52	1	4	0	78	0	69	9	1	11	.434	.368
Mitchell, Scott, Ott.	.455	19	11	11	0	5	5	0	0	0	1	0	0	0	0	0	4	0	0	0	.455	.455
Mix, Greg, Paw.	.000	47	1	1	0	0	0	0	0	0	0	0	0	0	0	0	1	0	0	0	.000	.000
Molina, Izzy, Col.	.246	97	365	338	44	83	113	16	1	4	51	2	6	1	18	0	47	4	2	9	.334	.281
Moore, Brandon, Char.	.284	90	339	299	44	85	113	21	2	1	41	13	4	2	21	1	41	3	2	6	.378	.331
Mora, Melvin, Nor.	.303	82	360	304	55	92	137	17	2	8	36	4	4	7	41	0	54	18	8	8	.451	.393
Moraga, David, Ott.*	.000	4	2	2	0	0	0	0	0	0	0	0	0	0	0	0	0	0	0	0	.000	.000
Morales, Francisco, Ott.	.229	99	387	345	43	79	122	11	1	10	44	1	5	5	31	1	93	1	1	10	.354	.298
Morgan, Scott, Buf.	.257	48	195	171	32	44	77	9	0	8	31	0	3	3	18	0	38	2	3	2	.450	.333
Mottola, Chad, Char.	.321	140	581	511	95	164	264	32	4	20	94	0	7	3	60	1	83	18	6	7	.517	.391
Mouton, Lyle, Roch.-Lou.	.310	127	521	467	89	145	263	43	3	23	94	0	8	6	40	0	98	22	1	14	.563	.367
Mummau, Rob, Syr.	.242	123	480	433	52	105	155	29	3	5	58	6	7	6	28	1	61	2	1	7	.358	.293
Murphy, Mike, Roch.	.226	70	258	217	35	49	64	6	3	1	21	3	3	1	34	0	63	7	3	6	.295	.329
Murray, Dan, Nor.	.059	31	27	17	1	1	1	0	0	0	0	6	0	0	4	0	10	0	0	1	.059	.238
Neagle, Denny, Ind.*	1.000	3	3	2	0	2	3	1	0	0	0	0	0	0	1	0	0	0	0	0	1.500	1.000
Nelson, Joe, Rich.	.167	13	6	6	1	1	1	0	0	0	0	0	0	0	0	0	2	0	0	0	.167	.167
Neubart, Garrett, Nor.	.158	13	47	38	6	6	6	0	0	0	2	0	0	3	6	0	7	5	1	2	.158	.319
Nunnally, Jon, Paw.*	.267	133	590	494	90	132	231	24	3	23	76	1	7	3	85	5	103	26	4	7	.468	.374
Nye, Ryan, S./W.B.	.000	14	5	4	0	0	0	0	0	0	0	0	0	0	1	0	3	0	0	0	.000	.200
Ojeda, Augie, Roch.†	.000	1	1	1	1	0	0	0	0	0	0	0	0	0	0	0	0	0	0	0	.000	.000
Oliver, Joe, Dur.	.301	57	232	219	27	66	107	18	1	7	43	1	3	2	7	0	50	1	0	7	.489	.325
Ontiveros, Steve, Lou.	.000	8	2	2	0	0	0	0	0	0	0	0	0	0	0	0	1	0	0	0	.000	.000
Ortiz, Luis, Lou.	.263	96	331	304	36	80	124	11	0	11	33	0	4	0	23	0	41	0	2	8	.408	.311

Player, Team	Avg.	G	TPA	AB	R	H	TB	2B	3B	HR	RBI	SH	SF	HP	BB	IBB	SO	SB	CS	GDP	Slg.	OBP
Ortiz, Nick, Buf.	.255	22	54	51	7	13	17	4	0	0	1	0	0	0	3	0	10	0	0	2	.333	.296
Otero, Ricky, Roch.†	.231	53	222	199	16	46	77	11	4	4	21	4	2	1	16	1	23	5	5	3	.387	.289
Owens, Jayhawk, Ind.	.208	18	60	53	7	11	24	1	0	4	10	0	0	3	4	0	18	0	0	1	.453	.300
Pachot, John, Ott.	.214	17	64	56	7	12	16	4	0	0	6	1	1	0	6	1	9	0	0	2	.286	.286
Paquette, Craig, Nor.	.272	70	302	283	40	77	148	20	3	15	54	0	6	3	10	1	47	3	0	4	.523	.298
Parris, Steve, Ind.	.250	6	4	4	0	1	1	0	0	0	0	0	0	0	0	0	1	0	0	0	.250	.250
Passini, Brian, Lou.*	.500	6	6	6	0	3	3	0	0	0	2	0	0	0	0	0	2	0	0	0	.500	.500
Payton, Jay, Nor.	.389	38	158	144	27	56	97	13	2	8	35	0	1	1	12	1	13	2	2	2	.674	.437
Perez, Santiago, Lou.†	.263	108	447	407	57	107	167	23	8	7	38	2	5	2	31	1	94	21	4	7	.410	.315
Perry, Chan, Buf.	.282	79	305	273	44	77	124	17	0	10	59	3	7	3	19	0	34	5	1	9	.454	.328
Perry, Herbert, Dur.	.311	27	111	103	21	32	55	8	0	5	20	0	0	2	6	0	21	0	0	3	.534	.360
Peterson, Kyle, Lou.*	.000	18	13	7	1	0	0	0	0	0	0	5	0	0	1	0	1	0	0	1	.000	.125
Pickering, Calvin, Roch.*	.285	103	447	372	63	106	174	20	0	16	63	0	4	11	60	6	99	1	3	10	.468	.396
Pittsley, Jim, Lou.	.250	8	8	8	0	2	3	1	0	0	0	0	0	0	0	0	5	0	0	0	.375	.250
Pohle, Ike, Syr.	.200	2	6	5	0	1	1	0	0	0	0	0	0	1	0	0	2	0	0	0	.200	.333
Polonia, Luis, Tol.*	.323	42	171	161	20	52	70	7	1	3	22	0	0	0	10	1	28	13	3	2	.435	.363
Pontes, Dan, Nor.	.000	15	3	2	0	0	0	0	0	0	0	0	0	0	1	0	0	0	0	0	.000	.333
Post, Dave, Ott.	.259	108	422	375	49	97	148	17	2	10	36	2	3	8	34	3	56	12	8	9	.395	.331
Powell, Alonzo, Col.	.315	130	560	470	97	148	245	23	1	24	90	0	6	2	82	3	110	1	3	14	.521	.414
Powell, Jeremy, Ott.	.167	16	12	12	1	2	5	0	0	1	1	0	0	0	0	0	6	0	0	0	.417	.167
Priest, Eddie, Ind.	.222	18	10	9	1	2	2	0	0	0	0	1	0	0	0	0	5	0	0	0	.222	.222
Prince, Tom, S./W.B.	.091	7	27	22	2	2	5	0	0	1	1	1	0	1	3	0	5	1	0	1	.227	.231
Probst, Alan, Syr.	.220	23	64	59	6	13	18	2	0	1	5	0	1	0	4	0	18	0	0	1	.305	.266
Pulsipher, Bill, Lou.*	1.000	6	2	1	0	1	1	0	0	0	0	1	0	0	0	0	0	0	0	0	1.000	1.000
Quevedo, Ruben, Rich.	.000	21	15	13	0	0	0	0	0	0	0	2	0	0	0	0	7	0	0	0	.000	.000
Raabe, Brian, Col.	.327	130	563	493	93	161	239	35	5	11	77	0	8	14	48	2	19	5	7	18	.485	.396
Ramirez, Alex, Buf.	.305	75	330	305	50	93	153	20	2	12	50	0	4	4	17	2	52	5	5	10	.502	.345
Ramirez, Dan, Char.	.143	6	18	14	2	2	3	1	0	0	2	1	1	1	1	0	3	1	0	1	.214	.235
Ramirez, Hector, Lou.	.000	58	6	5	0	0	0	0	0	0	0	1	0	0	0	0	2	0	0	0	.000	.000
Ratliff, Jon, Rich.	.158	28	20	19	3	3	3	0	0	0	0	1	0	0	0	0	4	0	0	0	.158	.158
Raven, Luis, Char.	.282	139	592	532	97	150	289	32	4	33	125	1	6	3	50	0	127	5	0	19	.543	.343
Reyes, Al, Lou.	.000	6	1	1	0	0	0	0	0	0	0	0	0	0	0	0	0	0	0	0	.000	.000
Riedling, John, Ind.	.000	24	1	1	0	0	0	0	0	0	0	0	0	0	0	0	1	0	0	0	.000	.000
Roberts, David, Buf.*	.271	89	407	350	65	95	132	17	10	0	38	8	4	2	43	1	52	39	3	1	.377	.351
Roberts, Grant, Nor.	.000	5	5	4	0	0	0	0	0	0	0	1	0	0	0	0	2	0	0	1	.000	.000
Roberts, Lonell, Rich.†	.262	119	483	442	66	116	154	19	5	3	41	0	8	0	33	1	95	17	9	5	.348	.308
Robinson, Kerry, Ind.*	.264	34	141	129	24	34	44	3	2	1	14	4	3	1	4	0	12	14	4	2	.341	.285
Rodriguez, Luis, Paw.	.000	2	3	3	0	0	0	0	0	0	0	0	0	0	0	0	1	0	0	0	.000	.000
Rodriguez, Sammy, Nor.	.222	5	12	9	2	2	8	0	0	2	4	0	0	0	3	0	2	0	0	0	.889	.417
Rollins, Jimmy, S./W.B.†	.077	4	15	13	0	1	2	1	0	0	0	1	0	0	1	0	1	1	0	0	.154	.143
Romano, Mike, Syr.	.000	29	1	1	0	0	0	0	0	0	0	0	0	0	0	0	0	0	0	0	.000	.000
Romero, Mandy, Paw.-Nor.† ..	.233	74	268	240	15	56	81	13	0	4	31	3	2	1	22	0	44	0	0	11	.338	.298
Ronan, Marc, S./W.B.*	.165	38	125	115	14	19	30	5	0	2	10	0	1	1	8	1	28	1	2	4	.261	.224
Ruebel, Matt, Nor.*	.000	7	4	4	0	0	0	0	0	0	0	0	0	0	0	0	1	0	0	0	.000	.000
Rumfield, Toby, Rich.	.274	111	424	383	57	105	175	23	1	15	62	2	2	6	31	1	57	1	2	13	.457	.336
Rust, Brian, Roch.	.000	1	4	3	0	0	0	0	0	0	0	1	0	0	0	0	0	0	0	0	.000	.000
Ryan, Ken, S./W.B.	.000	31	1	1	0	0	0	0	0	0	0	0	0	0	0	0	0	0	0	0	.000	.000
Sadler, Donnie, Paw.	.291	43	193	172	23	50	73	12	4	1	17	2	0	3	16	1	36	4	2	3	.424	.361
Sager, A.J., Ind.	.429	24	8	7	1	3	4	1	0	0	0	1	0	0	0	0	0	0	0	0	.571	.429
Salzano, Jerry, Ind.	.091	7	12	11	0	1	1	0	0	0	2	0	1	0	0	0	6	0	0	0	.091	.083
Sanchez, Alex, Dur.*	.200	3	11	10	2	2	3	1	0	0	0	0	0	0	1	0	0	0	0	0	.300	.273
Sanders, Anthony, Syr.	.244	124	558	496	71	121	207	22	5	18	59	8	5	3	46	0	111	18	10	6	.417	.309
Schall, Gene, Ind.	.293	100	402	355	49	104	167	25	1	12	53	1	3	8	35	1	84	0	1	7	.470	.367
Schrenk, Steve, S./W.B.	.000	32	1	1	0	0	0	0	0	0	0	0	0	0	1	0	0	0	0	0	.000	.000
Scott, Darryl, S./W.B.	.000	57	4	4	0	0	0	0	0	0	0	0	0	0	0	0	0	0	0	0	.000	.000
Scutaro, Marcos, Buf.	.273	129	539	462	76	126	178	24	2	8	51	6	4	6	61	2	69	21	6	5	.385	.362
Seelbach, Chris, Rich.	.091	15	11	11	0	1	1	0	0	0	0	0	0	0	0	0	4	0	0	0	.091	.091
Seguignol, Fernando, Ott.†	.285	87	367	312	54	89	181	17	3	23	74	0	4	11	40	8	96	3	8	9	.580	.384
Selby, Bill, Buf.*	.295	122	514	447	75	132	234	32	5	20	85	0	8	2	57	3	63	4	3	11	.523	.372
Shumaker, Anthony, S./W.B.*	.071	14	17	14	2	1	2	1	0	0	1	3	0	0	0	0	6	0	0	0	.143	.071
Siddall, Joe, Tol.*	.193	84	285	244	29	47	86	15	0	8	33	4	1	2	34	0	74	4	1	6	.352	.295
Silvestri, Dave, Dur.	.000	1	3	3	0	0	0	0	0	0	0	0	0	0	0	0	0	0	0	0	.000	.000
Simmons, Brian, Char.†	.270	78	329	285	53	77	121	14	0	10	44	1	1	5	37	1	60	8	2	5	.425	.363
Simon, Randall, Rich.*	.271	15	63	59	7	16	23	4	0	1	8	0	1	0	3	2	10	0	1	0	.390	.302
Simons, Mitch, Char.	.289	119	538	474	85	137	192	32	1	7	52	6	2	11	45	0	67	22	6	10	.405	.363
Sisco, Steve, Rich.	.311	128	545	495	80	154	248	36	2	18	76	3	8	1	38	0	74	13	7	7	.501	.356
Small, Mark, Ott.	.000	42	3	2	0	0	0	0	0	0	0	1	0	0	0	0	1	0	0	0	.000	.000
Smith, Bobby, Dur.	.333	57	259	225	52	75	138	15	3	14	47	0	3	4	27	0	61	13	4	3	.613	.409
Smith, Dan, Ott.	.000	11	11	9	0	0	0	0	0	0	0	2	1	0	0	1	6	0	0	0	.000	.100
Snopek, Chris, Paw.-Ind.	.275	127	521	462	76	127	200	31	3	12	74	3	5	4	47	0	66	19	6	12	.433	.344
Snusz, Chris, Ott.	.286	21	65	63	6	18	30	3	0	3	9	1	0	0	1	0	18	0	0	2	.476	.297
Snyder, Matt, Roch.	.000	48	1	1	0	0	0	0	0	0	0	0	0	0	0	0	0	0	0	0	.000	.000
Solano, Fausto, Syr.	.214	9	31	28	4	6	9	0	0	1	3	0	1	1	1	0	2	0	1	3	.321	.258
Soliz, Steve, Buf.	.259	40	121	112	15	29	41	6	0	2	14	0	1	2	6	0	24	0	0	1	.366	.306
Soriano, Alfonso, Col.	.183	20	89	82	8	15	28	5	1	2	11	0	2	0	5	0	18	1	1	1	.341	.225
Soriano, Fred, Syr.	.389	5	18	18	3	7	7	0	0	0	2	0	0	0	0	0	1	0	0	0	.389	.389
Speier, Justin, Rich.	.000	27	1	0	0	0	0	0	0	0	0	1	0	0	0	0	0	0	0	0	.000	.000
Spencer, Shane, Col.	.360	14	59	50	17	18	26	2	0	2	9	0	0	0	9	0	8	0	0	3	.520	.458
Stankiewicz, Andy, Col.	.276	50	194	163	34	45	62	8	3	1	20	4	1	3	23	0	27	6	1	3	.380	.374
Staton, T.J., Ott.*	.190	14	53	42	5	8	13	3	1	0	5	0	1	0	10	0	11	2	0	1	.310	.340
Stenson, Dernell, Paw.*	.270	121	508	440	64	119	205	28	2	18	82	2	5	6	55	5	119	2	1	7	.466	.356
Stewart, Scott, Nor.	.000	35	10	8	0	0	0	0	0	0	0	2	0	0	0	0	4	0	0	0	.000	.000

Player, Team	Avg.	G	TPA	AB	R	H	TB	2B	3B	HR	RBI	SH	SF	HP	BB	IBB	SO	SB	CS	GDP	Slg.	OBP
Stowers, Chris, Ott.*	.237	118	479	431	60	102	142	17	4	5	37	3	2	4	39	2	92	28	9	10	.329	.305
Strange, Mike, Syr.	.156	15	44	32	4	5	8	3	0	0	2	3	0	1	8	0	13	1	0	0	.250	.341
Strawberry, Darryl, Col.*	.288	21	86	73	12	21	40	5	1	4	15	0	2	0	11	1	13	1	2	1	.548	.372
Strickland, Scott, Ott.	.000	19	1	1	0	0	0	0	0	0	0	0	0	0	0	0	1	0	0	0	.000	.000
Stull, Everett, Rich.	.167	31	13	12	2	2	3	1	0	0	0	1	0	0	0	0	5	0	0	0	.250	.167
Swann, Pedro, Tol.*	.259	103	379	332	51	86	134	14	2	10	37	0	5	6	36	0	67	3	1	7	.404	.338
Sweeney, Mark, Ind.*	.322	86	377	311	66	100	155	17	1	12	51	0	3	4	59	4	40	3	2	7	.498	.432
Tam, Jeff, Nor.-Buf.*	.500	32	2	2	1	1	1	0	0	0	0	0	0	0	0	0	0	0	0	0	.500	.500
Tarasco, Tony, Col.*	.295	95	400	346	72	102	182	23	0	19	61	0	3	2	49	6	39	9	5	10	.526	.383
Tebbs, Nate, Paw.†	.600	4	8	5	1	3	4	1	0	0	1	0	0	1	2	0	1	0	1	0	.800	.750
Therneau, Dave, Ind.	.000	7	4	4	0	0	0	0	0	0	0	0	0	0	0	0	1	0	0	0	.000	.000
Thompson, Andy, Syr.	.293	62	252	229	42	67	136	17	2	16	42	0	0	2	21	0	45	5	0	4	.594	.357
Thompson, Mark, Ind.	.000	11	7	5	0	0	0	0	0	0	0	2	0	0	0	0	1	0	0	0	.000	.000
Tinsley, Lee, Ind.†	.211	30	83	76	5	16	25	2	2	1	6	2	0	0	5	0	14	1	4	0	.329	.259
Toca, Jorge, Nor.	.335	49	185	176	25	59	88	12	1	5	29	0	2	1	6	0	23	0	3	9	.500	.357
Tolar, Kevin, Ind.	.000	8	2	2	0	0	0	0	0	0	0	0	0	0	0	0	0	0	0	0	.000	.000
Tomberlin, Andy, Nor.*	.310	97	352	303	60	94	165	21	1	16	61	0	2	7	40	5	74	2	1	4	.545	.401
Tomko, Brett, Ind.	.250	2	6	4	1	1	1	0	0	0	1	1	0	0	1	0	0	0	0	1	.250	.400
Toth, Dave, Char.	.245	79	289	261	36	64	96	14	0	6	33	1	0	3	24	0	38	1	2	6	.368	.316
Trammell, Bubba, Dur.	.269	47	205	186	25	50	83	12	0	7	31	0	4	0	15	1	36	0	0	1	.446	.317
Treadwell, Jody, Nor.	.667	11	3	3	0	2	2	0	0	0	3	0	0	0	0	0	1	0	0	0	.667	.667
Turner, Chris, Buf.	.273	69	271	231	36	63	99	9	0	9	33	3	2	1	34	0	45	2	2	10	.429	.366
Tyler, Brad, Rich.*	.286	122	490	413	73	118	205	20	2	21	79	2	2	4	69	1	99	18	3	4	.496	.391
Tyner, Jason, Nor.*	.000	3	8	8	0	0	0	0	0	0	0	0	0	0	0	0	5	0	0	0	.000	.000
Valdez, Mario, Char.*	.274	121	492	402	78	110	209	17	2	26	76	0	1	12	76	4	91	1	0	8	.520	.403
Valentin, Jose, Lou.*	.250	6	24	20	6	5	14	0	0	3	3	0	0	0	4	0	3	0	1	0	.700	.375
Valera, Yohanny, Nor.	.154	23	71	65	3	10	15	2	0	1	6	1	0	1	4	0	16	0	0	2	.231	.214
VanEgmond, Tim, Lou.	.000	8	5	5	0	0	0	0	0	0	0	0	0	0	0	0	0	0	0	0	.000	.000
Vazquez, Javier, Ott.	.000	7	2	2	0	0	0	0	0	0	0	0	0	0	0	0	0	0	0	0	.000	.000
Villegas, Ismael, Rich.	.111	44	10	9	0	1	1	0	0	0	0	1	0	0	0	0	3	0	0	1	.111	.111
Vinas, Julio, Roch.	.312	126	517	484	67	151	247	32	2	20	83	0	7	1	25	1	73	4	3	13	.510	.342
Wallace, Derek, Nor.	.000	36	3	3	0	0	0	0	0	0	0	0	0	0	0	0	1	0	0	0	.000	.000
Waszgis, B.J., Col.	.277	63	227	191	36	53	83	12	0	6	31	2	1	6	27	2	55	4	2	4	.435	.382
Webster, Lenny, Roch.	.302	13	48	43	8	13	27	5	0	3	9	0	1	0	4	0	8	0	0	1	.628	.354
Welch, Mike, S./W.B.-Nor.*	.000	37	4	4	0	0	0	0	0	0	0	0	0	0	0	0	2	0	0	0	.000	.000
Wells, Vernon, Syr.	.310	33	143	129	20	40	62	8	1	4	21	0	3	1	10	0	22	5	1	3	.481	.357
Whatley, Gabe, Rich.*	.271	82	297	251	35	68	110	14	2	8	34	1	3	4	38	1	65	8	4	3	.438	.372
Whiten, Mark, Buf.†	.280	48	197	175	32	49	77	10	0	6	19	0	0	2	22	1	38	3	1	6	.440	.360
Whitmore, Darrell, Ind.*	.282	83	268	238	39	67	116	17	1	10	42	0	3	2	24	2	64	2	1	8	.487	.351
Wilcox, Luke, Dur.*	.328	39	158	134	32	44	93	12	5	9	34	1	0	1	22	4	18	1	3	2	.694	.427
Williams, Jason, Ind.	.381	40	181	160	30	61	89	18	2	2	19	1	1	5	14	1	25	4	1	4	.556	.444
Williams, Todd, Ind.	.500	38	2	2	0	1	1	0	0	0	1	0	0	0	0	0	1	0	0	0	.500	.500
Williamson, Antone, Lou.*	.239	68	218	184	21	44	66	7	0	5	20	0	2	2	30	0	29	0	1	5	.359	.349
Wilson, Tom, Dur.	.279	67	266	215	41	60	127	19	0	16	44	1	1	0	49	1	59	0	2	9	.591	.411
Wilson, Vance, Nor.	.264	15	58	53	10	14	26	3	0	3	5	0	0	1	4	2	8	1	0	4	.491	.328
Winn, Randy, Dur.†	.353	46	226	207	38	73	108	20	3	3	30	2	0	1	16	1	27	9	6	2	.522	.402
Witt, Kevin, Syr.*	.278	114	492	421	72	117	219	24	3	24	71	2	2	3	64	10	109	0	0	11	.520	.376
Wolf, Randy, S./W.B.*	.154	12	13	13	1	2	5	0	0	1	1	0	0	0	0	0	5	0	0	0	.385	.154
Wood, Jason, Tol.	.286	48	210	185	34	53	82	11	0	6	24	0	2	1	22	0	43	0	2	6	.443	.362
Woodward, Chris, Syr.	.292	75	321	281	46	82	111	20	3	1	20	1	0	1	38	1	49	4	1	5	.395	.378
Wunsch, Kelly, Lou.*	.250	16	4	4	1	1	1	0	0	0	0	0	0	0	0	0	2	0	0	0	.250	.250
Zosky, Eddie, Lou.	.294	116	448	405	60	122	186	22	3	12	47	4	3	3	23	0	68	5	1	6	.448	.333
Zuber, Jon, S./W.B.*	.295	111	480	387	69	114	160	24	2	6	54	0	4	1	86	6	48	7	1	9	.413	.421

GRAND SLAMS: Branyan, Brito, Carpenter, Chamblee, B. Cromer, L. Lopez, Lovullo, McClain, C. Perry, Raven, Tarasco, Thompson, Turner, Tyler, Wilcox, Winn, 2 each; Alcantara, Bierek, Branson, Cancel, Coleman, Coolbaugh, Cradle, J. Cruz, Depastino, Fullmer, J. Garcia, M. Gonzalez, Graffanino, Holbert, Hollins, Hyzdu, Liefer, Lombard, Long, M. Lopez, Lowery, Mallory, Maxwell, McCall, McCarty, McKeel, McMillon, Mottola, H. Perry, Powell, Raabe, Sanders, Scataro, Schall, Sisco, Snopek, Stenson, Toth, Trammell, Whatley, Whiten, Witt, 1 each.

AWARDED FIRST BASE ON CATCHER'S INTERFERENCE: McMillon, 6 (Grifol, LaRue, Vinas, Romero, Gubanich, Snusz); A. Cedeno, 3 (C. Greene, Grifol, Toth); Blum, 2 (LaRue 2); Zuber, 2 (Borders, Turner); Haney (Morales); Valdez (Romero); L. Garcia (Soliz); D.T. Cromer (Kevin Brown); Ingram (Morales); G. Martinez (Toth); Cox (T. Davis).

PLAYERS WITH TWO OR MORE TEAMS

Player, Team	Avg.	G	TPA	AB	R	H	TB	2B	3B	HR	RBI	SH	SF	HP	BB	IBB	SO	SB	CS	GDP	Slg.	OBP
Baez, Kevin, Ind.	.300	20	52	40	4	12	15	3	0	0	7	1	0	0	11	0	4	1	0	2	.375	.451
Baez, Kevin, Nor.	.263	60	197	175	15	46	54	5	0	1	26	0	3	2	17	1	21	2	0	2	.309	.330
Bautista, Jose, Ott.	.000	16	1	1	0	0	0	0	0	0	0	0	0	0	0	0	0	0	0	0	.000	.000
Bautista, Jose, Nor.	.000	20	10	9	0	0	0	0	0	0	0	1	0	0	0	0	6	0	0	0	.000	.000
Beltre, Esteban, Roch.	.264	92	343	314	45	83	111	19	3	1	23	4	1	1	23	1	64	5	3	11	.354	.316
Beltre, Esteban, Char.	.256	38	133	121	27	31	45	8	0	2	17	3	2	0	7	0	16	4	0	6	.372	.292
Bere, Jason, Ind.	.667	5	5	3	1	2	3	1	0	0	0	0	0	0	2	0	1	0	0	0	1.000	.800
Bere, Jason, Lou.	.286	5	8	7	0	2	2	0	0	0	0	0	0	0	1	0	2	0	0	0	.286	.375
Buccheri, Jim, Ind.	.125	6	12	8	2	1	2	1	0	0	2	1	1	0	2	0	2	0	1	1	.250	.273
Buccheri, Jim, Nor.	.228	32	97	92	9	21	24	3	0	0	5	1	0	0	4	0	15	4	1	4	.261	.260
Donnelly, Brendan, Dur.	1.000	37	1	1	0	1	1	0	0	0	0	0	0	0	0	0	0	0	0	0	1.000	1.000
Donnelly, Brendan, Syr.	.000	5	0	0	0	0	0	0	0	0	0	0	0	0	0	0	0	0	0	0	.000	.000
Dunn, Todd, Lou.	.217	40	122	106	14	23	41	1	1	5	16	0	0	2	14	0	32	2	1	2	.387	.320
Dunn, Todd, Roch.	.173	30	110	98	8	17	28	5	0	2	15	1	1	2	8	0	35	1	2	9	.286	.248
Eddie, Steve, Ind.	.375	10	25	24	3	9	11	2	0	0	3	0	0	0	1	0	1	0	0	0	.458	.400
Eddie, Steve, Char.	.252	33	133	119	14	30	40	4	0	2	12	2	5	0	7	0	19	0	0	5	.336	.282
Henderson, Ryan, Lou.	.000	21	0	0	0	0	0	0	0	0	0	0	0	0	0	0	0	0	0	1	.000	.000
Henderson, Ryan, Nor.	.000	7	2	2	0	0	0	0	0	0	0	0	0	0	0	0	1	0	0	0	.000	.000

Player, Team	Avg.	G	TPA	AB	R	H	TB	2B	3B	HR	RBI	SH	SF	HP	BB	IBB	SO	SB	CS	GDP	Slg.	OBP
Hollins, Dave, Syr.†	.200	4	17	15	2	3	4	1	0	0	1	0	0	1	1	0	5	0	0	0	.267	.294
Hollins, Dave, Char.†	.317	63	249	199	49	63	105	18	0	8	33	0	4	13	33	2	37	5	1	4	.528	.438
Hunter, Scott, Nor.	.228	50	194	180	20	41	69	4	0	8	23	1	2	3	8	0	42	6	6	2	.383	.269
Hunter, Scott, Ott.	.225	78	311	280	22	63	100	13	0	8	41	2	5	3	21	0	64	2	5	1	.357	.282
Lennon, Pat, Syr.	.336	37	158	134	26	45	77	5	0	9	33	0	1	1	22	0	40	3	3	2	.575	.430
Lennon, Pat, Tol.	.264	74	316	280	49	74	155	16	1	21	50	0	1	2	33	0	66	1	2	10	.554	.345
Livingstone, Scott, Roch.*	.372	14	51	43	5	16	20	4	0	0	7	0	1	0	7	2	4	1	0	5	.465	.451
Livingstone, Scott, Nor.*	.298	36	123	114	10	34	44	7	0	1	20	1	1	0	7	0	9	2	0	6	.386	.336
Looney, Brian, Tol.*	.000	47	0	0	0	0	0	0	0	0	0	0	0	0	0	0	0	0	0	0	.000	.000
Looney, Brian, S./W.B.*	.000	3	2	2	0	0	0	0	0	0	0	0	0	0	0	0	1	0	0	0	.000	.000
Machado, Robert, Char.	.204	16	60	54	4	11	20	3	0	2	7	0	0	2	4	0	13	0	0	3	.370	.283
Machado, Robert, Ott.	.227	21	78	75	6	17	22	5	0	0	3	1	0	2	0	0	13	0	1	2	.293	.247
Melo, Juan, Syr.†	.234	41	153	141	21	33	53	9	1	3	13	0	1	1	10	0	31	8	4	2	.376	.288
Melo, Juan, Ind.†	.333	3	9	9	2	3	6	0	0	1	3	0	0	0	0	0	2	1	0	0	.667	.333
Mouton, Lyle, Roch.	.222	44	178	162	25	36	59	9	1	4	17	0	2	1	13	0	31	3	1	6	.364	.281
Mouton, Lyle, Lou.	.357	83	343	305	64	109	204	34	2	19	77	0	6	5	27	0	67	19	0	8	.669	.411
Romero, Mandy, Paw.†	.217	46	159	143	8	31	47	7	0	3	22	2	1	0	13	0	26	0	0	6	.329	.280
Romero, Mandy, Nor.†	.258	28	109	97	7	25	34	6	0	1	9	1	1	1	9	0	18	0	0	5	.351	.324
Snopek, Chris, Paw.	.247	24	87	81	10	20	36	7	0	3	10	1	0	0	5	0	15	2	0	2	.444	.291
Snopek, Chris, Ind.	.281	103	434	381	66	107	164	24	3	9	64	2	5	4	42	0	51	17	6	10	.430	.354
Tam, Jeff, Nor.	.500	16	2	2	1	1	1	0	0	0	0	0	0	0	0	0	0	0	0	1	.500	.500
Tam, Jeff, Buf.	.000	16	0	0	0	0	0	0	0	0	0	0	0	0	0	0	0	0	0	0	.000	.000
Welch, Mike, S./W.B.*	.000	13	3	3	0	0	0	0	0	0	0	0	0	0	1	0	0	0	0	0	.000	.000
Welch, Mike, Nor.*	.000	24	1	1	0	0	0	0	0	0	0	0	0	0	0	0	1	0	0	0	.000	.000

1999 PITCHING

TEAM

Team	W	L	Pct.	ERA	G	CG	ShO	Sv.	IP	H	TBF	R	ER	HR	SH	SF	HB	BB	IBB	SO	WP	Bk.
Pawtucket	76	68	.528	4.01	144	11	9	31	1266.2	1283	5455	682	565	161	42	41	54	393	16	900	51	14
Buffalo	72	72	.500	4.34	144	2	5	42	1246.2	1278	5453	706	601	137	43	53	47	491	34	818	64	13
Ottawa	59	85	.410	4.48	144	2	6	36	1254.2	1321	5542	725	624	148	52	41	59	531	17	954	66	6
Norfolk	77	63	.550	4.58	140	7	7	39	1219.2	1283	5412	712	620	156	45	28	47	532	50	984	66	13
Scranton/W.-B.	78	66	.542	4.60	144	9	11	40	1253.0	1363	5503	715	641	115	35	50	33	494	31	912	65	2
Richmond	64	78	.451	4.65	142	4	8	34	1232.0	1256	5316	693	637	131	55	52	24	466	22	1040	74	8
Rochester	61	83	.424	4.68	144	5	8	30	1274.1	1290	5559	740	662	174	28	47	54	511	14	1017	67	13
Columbus	83	58	.589	4.70	141	9	5	34	1230.0	1262	5355	725	643	150	29	49	67	470	9	986	82	12
Syracuse	73	71	.507	4.88	144	4	4	41	1258.0	1284	5596	752	682	165	34	48	49	618	19	974	66	10
Indianapolis	75	69	.521	4.95	144	4	6	47	1264.2	1386	5557	773	696	137	41	61	63	496	27	854	66	8
Charlotte	82	62	.569	4.97	144	12	4	42	1225.0	1378	5397	763	677	154	32	44	37	440	8	952	72	5
Durham	83	60	.580	5.20	143	2	2	39	1253.0	1370	5574	817	724	165	21	46	61	533	10	961	72	13
Louisville	63	81	.438	5.41	144	2	7	33	1271.2	1361	5707	868	765	171	41	53	65	586	23	929	70	5
Toledo	57	87	.396	5.46	144	11	2	22	1241.0	1327	5559	839	753	163	31	55	78	596	23	848	75	14

INDIVIDUAL

TOP QUALIFIERS FOR EARNED-RUN AVERAGE TITLE

Minimum 115 innings. *Lefthanded pitcher.

Pitcher, Team	W	L	Pct.	ERA	G	GS	CG	ShO	GF	Sv.	IP	H	TBF	R	ER	HR	SH	SF	HB	BB	IBB	SO	WP	Bk.
Yarnall, Ed, Col.*	13	4	.765	3.47	23	23	1	1	0	0	145.1	136	611	61	56	5	3	8	3	57	0	146	2	1
Carrara, Giovanni, Ind.	12	7	.632	3.47	39	21	2	1	7	0	158.0	144	660	68	61	20	7	2	7	58	3	114	3	1
Borkowski, David, Tol.	6	8	.429	3.50	19	19	3	0	0	0	126.0	119	530	59	49	16	0	3	10	43	0	94	10	0
Wolcott, Bob, Paw.	6	13	.316	3.59	26	16	2	0	5	2	125.1	131	538	67	50	17	7	4	8	28	3	69	3	0
Linton, Doug, Roch.	7	5	.583	3.65	18	18	1	0	0	0	118.1	120	510	58	48	13	3	4	10	27	1	97	3	0
Wagner, Paul, Buf.	8	4	.667	3.82	23	23	0	0	0	0	129.2	123	559	67	55	11	1	4	4	55	2	95	11	0
Bolton, Rod, S./W.B.	11	10	.524	3.82	24	24	4	2	0	0	153.0	161	655	76	65	10	5	1	1	52	3	85	6	0
Maduro, Calvin, Roch.	11	11	.500	3.99	29	28	2	1	0	0	169.0	179	735	88	75	23	1	7	5	60	0	149	4	1
Harriger, Denny, Ind.	14	6	.700	4.08	27	27	1	0	0	0	172.0	183	717	82	78	15	2	5	4	36	2	110	6	0
Romano, Mike, Syr.	12	8	.600	4.13	29	28	2	0	0	0	174.1	160	756	90	80	21	4	4	8	84	2	104	8	1
Fernandez, Jared, Paw.	12	9	.571	4.24	27	20	3	0	2	0	163.1	172	687	88	77	20	7	5	5	39	0	76	3	1
Ebert, Derrin, Rich.*	8	7	.533	4.30	25	24	2	1	0	0	150.2	173	646	79	72	13	5	6	2	44	0	82	7	0
Ratliff, Jon, Rich.	5	12	.294	4.45	27	27	0	0	0	0	157.2	154	660	88	78	24	3	6	3	44	2	129	5	0
Stull, Everett, Rich.	8	8	.500	4.47	30	22	0	0	5	0	139.0	124	603	75	69	17	4	7	8	73	0	126	12	2
Rodriguez, Nerio, Syr.	10	8	.556	4.54	27	27	1	1	0	0	162.2	161	688	84	82	17	3	5	7	53	0	137	5	2

DEPARTMENTAL LEADERS: W—Harriger, 14; L—Drews, 14; Pct.—Alan Newman, 1.000; G—Guerra, 63; GS—Tatis, 28; CG—Castillo, 5; ShO—Cruz, Bolton, 2 each; GF—Gaillard, 52; Sv.—Tessmer, 28; IP—Juden, 176.1; H—Harriger, 183; TBF—Juden, 768; R—Drews, 136; ER—Drews, 125; HR—Castillo, Bradley, 28; SH—Ramsay, 9; SF—Drews, 10; HB—Juden, 17; BB—Drews, 91; IBB—Guerra, 8; SO—Juden, 151; WP—Bradley, 23; BK—Tatis, 9.

ALL PITCHERS

*Lefthanded pitcher.

Pitcher, Team	W	L	Pct.	ERA	G	GS	CG	ShO	GF	Sv.	IP	H	TBF	R	ER	HR	SH	SF	HB	BB	IBB	SO	WP	Bk.
Adams, Willie, Paw.	4	5	.444	5.15	11	11	1	1	0	0	64.2	82	290	46	37	7	2	3	10	0	37	2	3
Adamson, Joel, Paw.*	2	4	.333	6.02	25	3	0	0	12	0	43.1	60	193	35	29	5	2	0	6	8	2	14	2	0
Alberro, Jose, Tol.	2	2	.500	5.25	14	0	0	0	5	0	24.0	28	111	16	14	4	0	2	1	11	1	21	4	1
Anderson, Matt, Tol.	0	4	.000	6.39	24	4	0	0	18	5	38.0	32	173	27	27	9	0	1	1	31	0	35	4	1
Andrews, Clayton, Syr.*	0	1	.000	7.80	3	3	0	0	0	0	15.0	10	65	14	13	5	0	1	0	13	0	9	1	0
Andujar, Luis, Char.	4	5	.444	3.00	52	0	0	0	35	16	60.0	62	252	21	20	3	4	4	3	13	0	59	3	0
Arroyo, Luis, Syr.*	0	1	.000	8.53	9	0	0	0	3	0	12.2	18	65	13	12	1	1	1	0	9	1	10	1	1

Pitcher, Team	W	L	Pct.	ERA	G	GS	CG	ShO	GF	Sv.	IP	H	TBF	R	ER	HR	SH	SF	HB	BB	IBB	SO	WP	Bk.
Atchley, Justin, Ind.*	2	1	.667	5.40	5	4	0	0	1	1	23.1	39	106	14	14	5	0	0	2	6	0	6	0	0
Baez, Kevin, Nor.	0	0	.000	3.38	2	0	0	0	2	0	2.2	5	14	1	1	1	0	0	0	1	0	0	0	0
Baez, Kevin, Nor.	0	0	.000	3.38	2	0	0	0	2	0	2.2	5	14	1	1	1	0	0	0	1	0	0	0	0
Bailey, Roger, Dur.	1	0	1.000	5.67	7	4	0	0	0	0	27.0	28	123	21	17	3	0	1	2	13	0	17	1	0
Baker, Jason, Ott.	1	0	1.000	8.53	11	0	0	0	7	0	12.2	18	69	12	12	1	1	0	0	14	0	9	4	0
Bale, John, Syr.*	0	3	.000	3.97	6	4	0	0	0	0	22.2	16	92	14	10	1	2	3	0	10	0	10	1	0
Baptist, Travis, Paw.*	4	2	.667	5.31	17	3	0	0	2	0	42.1	49	195	27	25	5	1	0	1	19	0	30	2	0
Barkley, Brian, Paw.*	0	1	.000	5.14	3	3	0	0	0	0	14.0	11	63	9	8	2	1	1	1	7	0	5	1	0
Barnett, Marty, Dur.	1	0	1.000	5.46	16	0	0	0	6	0	28.0	30	124	17	17	2	1	3	1	14	1	19	4	0
Barrios, Manny, Ind.	2	7	.222	5.28	49	8	0	0	9	0	90.1	94	399	60	53	8	3	2	7	35	0	73	9	2
Batista, Miguel, Ott.	0	1	.000	2.25	3	3	0	0	0	0	8.0	3	30	2	2	1	0	0	0	4	0	7	0	0
Bautista, Jose, Ott.-Nor.	7	5	.583	5.43	36	12	0	0	6	4	111.0	144	500	72	67	20	3	3	6	26	2	65	4	0
Beck, Greg, Lou.	0	0	.000	81.00	1	0	0	0	0	0	0.1	3	4	3	3	1	0	0	0	0	0	0	0	0
Beirne, Kevin, Char.	5	5	.500	5.42	20	20	0	0	0	0	113.0	134	495	75	68	14	1	4	2	36	0	63	12	0
Belinda, Stan, Ind.	2	0	1.000	2.38	10	0	0	0	2	0	11.1	7	47	3	3	1	0	2	0	6	0	10	0	0
Beltran, Rigo, Nor.*	2	1	.667	1.61	21	0	0	0	4	0	22.1	16	93	5	4	1	1	0	1	12	1	27	1	0
Bennett, Joel, S./W.B.	10	4	.714	4.61	20	20	1	1	0	0	127.0	134	550	71	65	10	2	6	6	47	2	125	5	0
Bennett, Shayne, Ott.	3	9	.250	5.04	38	8	0	0	17	8	89.1	96	397	53	50	12	5	4	4	37	3	70	5	1
Benz, Jake, Ott.*	2	3	.400	5.93	18	0	0	0	9	1	30.1	42	152	27	20	3	1	4	1	20	3	34	2	0
Bere, Jason, Ind.-Lou.	2	3	.400	5.36	10	9	0	0	1	0	43.2	46	196	28	26	3	2	3	0	27	0	35	1	0
Blood, Darin, Roch.	0	4	.000	8.66	12	10	0	0	0	0	43.2	53	211	43	42	3	1	4	2	38	0	21	5	1
Bochtler, Doug, Syr.	4	0	1.000	2.63	14	0	0	0	3	0	27.1	18	110	9	8	1	0	3	0	10	0	28	0	0
Bogott, Kurt, Syr.*	8	6	.571	4.62	46	4	0	0	10	1	85.2	80	392	52	44	11	3	3	8	44	4	76	9	0
Bolton, Rod, S./W.B.	11	10	.524	3.82	24	24	4	2	0	0	153.0	161	655	76	65	10	5	1	1	52	3	85	6	0
Borkowski, David, Tol.	6	8	.429	3.50	19	19	3	0	0	0	126.0	119	530	59	49	16	0	3	10	43	0	94	10	0
Borowski, Joe, Lou.	6	2	.750	5.46	58	0	0	0	28	4	89.0	94	399	59	54	7	4	6	3	44	3	70	3	1
Bovee, Mike, Syr.	0	2	.000	7.32	19	3	0	0	6	1	35.2	49	175	29	29	6	2	2	2	20	1	32	1	0
Bowie, Micah, Rich.*	4	4	.500	2.96	13	13	0	0	0	0	73.0	65	288	24	24	4	2	2	0	14	0	82	2	0
Bradford, Chad, Char.	9	3	.750	1.94	47	0	0	0	19	5	74.1	63	293	19	16	2	3	2	0	15	0	56	0	0
Bradford, Josh, Syr.	0	1	.000	18.00	1	1	0	0	0	0	4.0	9	24	8	8	2	0	0	0	3	0	2	1	0
Bradley, Ryan, Col.	5	12	.294	6.21	29	24	1	0	1	0	145.0	163	664	112	100	28	5	9	10	73	0	118	23	1
Brewer, Billy, S./W.B.*	6	1	.857	3.78	33	5	0	0	10	2	69.0	59	293	32	29	5	1	5	28	0	57	9	0	
Brooks, Antone, Rich.*	3	5	.375	3.86	43	0	0	0	18	1	56.0	57	241	28	24	2	5	5	0	21	0	39	3	0
Brower, Jim, Buf.	11	11	.500	4.73	27	27	0	0	0	0	160.0	164	689	101	84	23	6	8	8	59	6	76	9	2
Brown, Jamie, Buf.	1	0	1.000	5.40	1	0	0	0	0	0	5.0	8	23	4	3	0	1	1	0	1	0	2	0	0
Brunson, Will, Tol.*	3	1	.750	4.53	38	1	0	0	15	3	47.2	45	201	28	24	5	3	0	2	17	1	41	2	1
Buddie, Mike, Col.	9	2	.818	2.86	49	2	0	0	14	0	78.2	80	335	30	25	2	4	5	5	22	2	68	8	0
Bullinger, Kirk, Paw.	0	2	.000	2.39	35	0	0	0	30	15	37.2	37	160	14	10	3	1	1	2	13	4	27	0	0
Burrows, Terry, Roch.*	1	6	.143	3.97	17	17	0	0	0	0	93.0	74	382	49	41	9	2	6	7	39	0	75	1	2
Butler, Adam, Rich.*	0	0	.000	2.25	9	0	0	0	7	3	8.0	10	39	4	2	0	2	1	0	3	0	6	1	0
Cadaret, Greg, Buf.*	0	0	.000	2.70	10	0	0	0	2	0	6.2	6	32	3	2	0	0	1	0	7	1	8	1	0
Cairncross, Cameron, Buf.*	0	3	.000	5.21	19	0	0	0	9	0	19.0	22	86	13	11	1	2	4	2	6	0	13	1	0
Callaway, Mickey, Dur.	7	1	.875	4.20	15	15	0	0	0	0	81.1	86	350	45	38	5	0	3	8	28	0	56	6	1
Cammack, Eric, Nor.	0	0	.000	3.12	9	0	0	0	5	4	8.2	7	35	3	3	1	0	1	1	0	17	1	0	
Camp, Jared, Buf.	0	0	.000	0.84	10	0	0	0	7	1	10.2	4	51	2	1	0	1	1	13	0	14	4	0	
Carrara, Giovanni, Ind.	12	7	.632	3.47	39	21	2	1	7	0	158.0	144	660	68	61	20	7	2	7	58	3	114	3	1
Carroll, Dave, Col.*	0	0	.000	9.00	1	0	0	0	0	0	1.0	1	5	2	1	0	0	0	0	1	0	1	1	0
Castillo, Carlos, Char.	9	6	.600	5.15	20	20	5	0	0	0	136.1	150	583	88	78	28	3	4	3	30	1	105	5	3
Cather, Mike, Rich.	2	7	.222	6.78	45	0	0	0	20	1	67.2	71	308	57	51	4	8	5	1	34	2	60	5	3
Charlton, Norm, Dur.*	3	2	.600	3.69	18	0	0	0	9	1	31.2	27	132	13	13	7	1	0	3	10	1	29	1	0
Checo, Robinson, Tol.	0	0	.000	0.00	2	1	0	0	0	0	5.0	2	19	0	0	0	0	1	1	0	6	0	0	
Chen, Bruce, Rich.*	6	3	.667	3.81	14	14	0	0	0	0	78.0	73	324	36	33	10	3	4	0	26	0	90	2	2
Cho, Jin Ho, Paw.	9	3	.750	3.45	17	17	4	0	0	0	109.2	99	447	46	42	12	2	3	4	29	1	80	1	0
Clark, Howie, Rich.*	0	0	.000	9.00	2	0	0	0	2	0	2.0	4	12	2	2	0	0	2	0	0	0	0	0	
Converse, Jim, Lou.	4	3	.571	5.81	30	4	0	0	4	0	62.0	76	288	43	40	8	1	2	0	34	0	40	3	0
Coppinger, Rocky, Roch.	2	2	.500	3.66	5	5	0	0	0	0	32.0	28	133	13	13	3	0	1	0	12	0	37	1	0
Corey, Bryan, Tol.	5	2	.714	2.86	48	0	0	0	17	2	69.1	63	303	27	22	6	4	1	2	34	4	36	2	1
Corsi, Jim, Roch.	0	0	.000	3.48	10	0	0	0	8	2	10.1	12	46	4	4	0	0	0	3	0	7	0	0	
Cortes, David, Rich.	2	3	.400	3.35	47	0	0	0	42	22	45.2	50	198	19	17	2	2	1	0	14	5	42	2	0
Croghan, Andy, Syr.	0	0	.000	0.00	2	0	0	0	2	2	3.1	1	12	0	0	0	1	1	0	2	0	4	0	0
Cruz, Nelson, Tol.	7	1	.875	2.73	10	10	4	2	0	0	62.2	47	247	20	19	5	0	0	4	21	0	41	1	0
Cumberland, Chris, Paw.*	4	3	.571	4.45	36	1	0	0	16	0	62.2	56	266	33	31	4	2	3	2	30	0	35	4	0
Dale, Carl, Lou.	0	1	.000	4.63	7	0	0	0	2	1	11.2	8	48	6	6	2	0	0	5	0	8	0	0	
D'Amico, Jeff, Lou.	0	0	.000	13.50	1	1	0	0	0	0	3.1	6	18	5	5	0	0	1	2	0	1	0	0	
Daneker, Pat, Char.	4	4	.500	6.57	9	9	1	0	0	0	49.1	64	230	36	36	10	1	2	3	16	0	36	4	0
Daniels, John, Dur.	2	0	1.000	4.89	21	0	0	0	8	0	35.0	37	154	19	19	2	1	4	1	9	0	25	2	0
Darden, Tony, Nor.	0	0	.000	0.00	2	0	0	0	1	0	2.1	2	10	2	0	1	0	0	0	1	0	6	0	0
Davenport, Joe, Char.	0	0	.000	8.00	6	0	0	0	1	0	9.0	13	40	8	8	0	0	0	1	6	0	3	0	0
Davey, Tom, Syr.	1	2	.333	3.48	6	6	0	0	0	0	33.2	30	144	15	13	1	2	1	3	19	0	20	3	0
Davis, Tim, Dur.*	0	0	.000	9.00	3	0	0	0	1	0	2.0	2	11	2	2	0	0	2	1	0	1	0	0	
Dawley, Joey, Rich.	0	3	.000	5.18	7	7	1	0	0	0	40.0	43	174	26	23	5	3	2	0	12	0	31	4	0
Dedrick, Jim, Buf.	2	2	.500	4.08	30	4	0	0	7	0	46.1	49	211	23	21	5	1	2	1	27	1	26	1	1
DeHart, Rick, Ott.*	2	4	.333	4.78	15	2	0	0	5	0	26.1	33	127	19	14	3	0	3	2	11	1	22	1	0
Delahoya, Javier, Roch.	4	3	.571	5.09	14	14	0	0	0	0	81.1	88	356	49	46	14	1	3	7	26	0	58	5	2
Delgado, Ernie, Syr.	0	4	.000	9.43	14	4	0	0	2	0	27.2	38	139	29	29	3	1	1	0	19	0	15	2	0
De Los Santos, Luis, Col.	6	3	.667	4.77	12	12	0	0	0	0	66.0	81	299	42	35	11	1	0	4	24	0	45	1	0
DeLucia, Rich, Buf.	2	3	.400	4.18	44	0	0	0	33	19	47.1	39	210	24	22	6	1	1	2	29	3	46	4	0
De Paula, Sean, Buf.	0	0	.000	0.00	5	0	0	0	5	2	5.0	0	19	0	0	0	1	3	0	7	1	0	
DeSilva, John, Ott.	4	1	.800	2.89	22	15	0	0	3	0	90.1	73	377	35	29	4	6	5	2	41	1	75	5	0
Dimma, Douglas, Syr.*	0	0	.000	9.00	1	0	0	0	0	0	1.0	2	4	1	1	1	0	0	0	0	1	0	0	
Dixon, Tim, Ott.-Paw.*	0	1	.000	8.53	4	0	0	0	1	0	6.1	9	31	6	6	4	0	1	3	0	5	0	0	
Dodd, Robert, S./W.B.*	4	0	1.000	0.91	6	4	1	0	1	1	29.2	19	114	5	3	1	1	1	6	0	23	0	0	

Pitcher, Team	W	L	Pct.	ERA	G	GS	CG	ShO	GF	Sv.	IP	H	TBF	R	ER	HR	SH	SF	HB	BB	IBB	SO	WP	Bk.
Donnelly, Brendan, Dur.-Syr. ..	5	6	.455	3.03	42	1	0	0	12	2	71.1	61	286	27	24	6	2	4	4	22	2	70	6	0
Dotel, Octavio, Nor.	5	2	.714	3.84	13	13	1	0	0	0	70.1	52	293	33	30	9	1	1	2	34	1	90	3	1
Dougherty, Tony, Buf.	0	2	.000	5.63	16	1	0	0	4	0	24.0	28	112	17	15	3	0	3	1	15	2	8	1	1
Drews, Matt, Tol.	2	14	.125	8.27	28	22	0	0	3	0	136.0	171	668	136	125	21	1	10	14	91	2	70	16	2
Driskill, Travis, Buf.	9	8	.529	4.83	31	18	0	0	3	0	132.1	146	561	78	71	21	5	5	6	32	2	90	4	1
Drumright, Mike, Tol.	6	10	.375	5.97	21	21	1	0	0	0	120.2	116	535	88	80	17	2	7	7	59	2	76	8	0
Duran, Roberto, Ott.*	1	1	.500	5.25	5	2	0	0	0	0	12.0	10	59	8	7	1	1	0	1	13	0	10	3	0
Durocher, Jayson, Ott.	1	3	.250	1.51	17	0	0	0	6	4	35.2	17	146	12	6	2	3	1	1	20	2	22	3	0
Duvall, Mike, Dur.*	2	2	.500	5.40	19	1	0	0	4	2	30.0	32	131	20	18	4	0	0	0	12	1	27	0	0
Dykhoff, Radhames, Roch.*	2	0	1.000	3.94	47	0	0	0	6	1	82.1	69	341	42	36	11	3	2	3	31	0	57	1	0
Eaton, Adam, S./W.B.	1	1	.500	3.00	3	3	0	0	0	0	21.0	17	83	10	7	1	0	0	1	6	0	10	0	0
Ebert, Derrin, Rich.*	8	7	.533	4.30	25	24	2	1	0	0	150.2	173	646	79	72	13	5	6	2	44	0	82	7	0
Eiland, Dave, Dur.	5	3	.625	3.36	10	10	0	0	0	0	59.0	60	242	26	22	7	1	3	1	9	0	46	0	0
Eldred, Cal, Lou.	0	1	.000	5.30	4	4	0	0	0	0	18.2	19	86	12	11	4	0	0	0	10	0	21	0	0
Erdos, Todd, Col.	3	2	.600	6.56	27	8	0	0	3	0	59.0	70	270	47	43	10	0	5	3	25	1	53	4	0
Estrada, Horacio, Lou.*	6	6	.500	5.67	25	24	1	0	0	0	131.2	128	575	87	83	21	3	8	9	65	1	112	8	1
Etler, Todd, Ind.	2	1	.667	6.39	26	0	0	0	6	0	38.0	42	182	29	27	3	0	2	0	29	1	35	1	0
Evans, Dave, Roch.	2	11	.154	5.35	60	0	0	0	32	2	70.2	70	309	48	42	11	5	2	5	27	2	65	9	1
Evans, Keith, Ott.	2	13	.133	4.80	24	18	2	0	0	0	122.0	143	525	79	65	17	3	1	10	22	0	74	2	0
Eyre, Scott, Char.*	6	4	.600	3.82	12	11	0	0	0	0	68.1	75	291	32	29	3	1	2	1	23	1	63	5	2
Falteisek, Steve, Lou.	5	11	.313	6.84	42	4	0	0	8	0	76.1	98	359	65	58	13	2	2	4	41	4	34	7	1
Farrell, Jim, Paw.	2	3	.400	4.19	14	5	0	0	2	0	43.0	45	191	25	20	7	2	3	1	16	0	35	2	0
Fernandez, Jared, Paw.	12	9	.571	4.24	27	20	3	0	2	0	163.1	172	687	88	77	20	7	5	5	39	0	76	3	1
Fesh, Sean, S./W.B.*	4	3	.571	4.39	45	0	0	0	16	1	53.1	50	235	29	26	5	4	1	0	31	5	38	4	0
Fetters, Mike, Roch.	0	0	.000	0.00	4	0	0	0	0	0	3.2	0	14	0	0	0	0	0	0	2	0	6	0	0
Field, Nathan, Ott.	0	0	.000	3.00	2	0	0	0	1	0	3.0	4	16	1	1	0	0	0	0	4	0	4	0	0
Fiore, Tony, S./W.B.	0	0	.000	6.64	13	0	0	0	2	0	20.1	28	102	19	15	0	0	1	0	15	1	13	4	0
Fleetham, Ben, Nor.	1	2	.333	14.85	6	0	0	0	2	0	6.2	11	40	15	11	3	0	0	0	10	1	9	2	0
Flury, Pat, Ind.	1	1	.500	7.04	23	0	0	0	14	6	23.0	27	115	18	18	4	0	1	1	20	0	20	6	0
Ford, Ben, Col.	6	3	.667	4.73	53	0	0	0	23	3	70.1	69	318	42	37	4	2	1	9	39	1	40	11	0
Fordham, Tom, Char.*	4	7	.364	7.31	29	21	0	0	2	0	112.0	144	538	101	91	25	2	4	3	66	0	101	10	0
Forster, Scott, Ott.*	0	4	.000	5.16	53	0	0	0	27	2	52.1	49	249	32	30	3	2	1	2	47	2	32	8	0
Fossas, Tony, Col.*	1	0	1.000	4.05	26	0	0	0	4	0	20.0	17	83	10	9	6	0	0	2	6	0	15	0	0
Gaillard, Eddie, Dur.	3	6	.333	2.89	59	0	0	0	52	26	62.1	67	283	30	20	6	3	1	4	23	3	67	2	0
Garces, Rich, Paw.	1	0	1.000	3.25	21	0	0	0	15	7	27.2	24	117	11	10	5	1	1	0	10	0	24	1	0
Glauber, Keith, Ind.	3	3	.500	5.82	12	12	1	1	0	0	68.0	84	305	49	44	8	2	6	6	20	0	51	1	0
Glover, Gary, Syr.	4	6	.400	5.19	14	14	0	0	0	0	76.1	93	347	50	44	10	0	3	0	35	0	57	3	1
Goldsmith, Gary, Tol.	0	3	.000	6.95	6	5	0	0	1	0	22.0	29	100	21	17	5	0	0	1	9	1	14	1	0
Gonzalez, Dicky, Nor.	0	1	.000	2.70	1	1	0	0	0	0	6.2	5	23	2	2	0	0	0	0	1	0	3	0	0
Gooden, Dwight, Buf.	0	1	.000	2.45	1	1	0	0	0	0	3.2	6	19	1	1	1	0	0	0	3	1	3	0	0
Grace, Mike, S./W.B.	2	2	.500	4.44	10	9	0	0	0	0	46.2	52	202	25	23	6	2	1	2	17	0	27	1	0
Grahe, Joe, S./W.B.	3	1	.750	3.00	23	4	0	0	18	10	36.0	38	157	15	12	3	1	2	1	15	1	25	3	0
Granger, Jeff, Lou.*	1	6	.143	4.73	56	1	0	0	21	3	59.0	72	271	40	31	8	5	2	3	25	3	50	0	0
Graterol, Beiker, Tol.	3	9	.250	5.83	17	15	0	0	1	0	78.2	89	357	55	51	10	2	5	7	38	2	47	3	3
Green, Tyler, S./W.B.	4	6	.400	7.69	19	7	1	0	4	0	50.1	78	248	47	43	8	1	3	4	24	1	31	3	0
Greene, Rick, Ind.	5	7	.417	3.69	61	0	0	0	29	9	78.0	78	331	37	32	3	4	5	2	35	4	40	6	0
Greisinger, Seth, Tol.	0	1	.000	5.87	2	2	0	0	0	0	7.2	9	34	5	5	0	1	0	0	3	0	4	1	0
Gross, Kip, Paw.	1	0	1.000	5.40	10	2	0	0	2	0	21.2	24	98	14	13	3	0	1	2	12	0	16	2	0
Grzanich, Mike, Tol.	1	0	1.000	9.28	14	0	0	0	8	1	21.1	21	109	24	22	4	0	3	5	25	0	17	1	0
Guerra, Mark, Nor.	8	3	.727	2.93	63	2	0	0	11	0	89.0	90	391	45	29	5	3	2	0	39	8	70	2	0
Guthrie, Mark, Paw.*	0	0	.000	0.00	1	1	0	0	0	0	1.0	0	3	0	0	0	0	0	0	0	0	1	0	0
Hamilton, Jimmy, Buf.-Roch.*	1	2	.333	5.81	29	0	0	0	4	0	26.1	25	133	25	17	3	1	4	1	31	0	27	1	0
Hamilton, Joey, Syr.	0	1	.000	5.11	3	3	0	0	0	0	12.1	15	57	8	7	2	0	2	2	5	0	9	0	0
Haney, Chris, Buf.*	2	5	.286	3.22	13	10	0	0	0	0	58.2	50	247	25	21	4	6	3	1	22	1	37	4	1
Haney, Todd, Nor.	0	0	.000	81.00	1	0	0	0	0	0	1.0	9	13	9	9	1	0	0	0	1	0	0	0	0
Harikkala, Tim, Paw.	1	2	.333	5.40	14	1	0	0	4	0	30.0	44	141	19	18	2	0	1	2	7	1	19	0	0
Harriger, Denny, Ind.	14	6	.700	4.08	27	27	1	0	0	0	172.0	183	717	82	78	15	2	5	4	36	2	110	6	0
Harris, D.J., Syr.	0	0	.000	7.71	7	0	0	0	0	0	14.0	20	73	15	12	4	0	0	0	10	0	6	2	0
Harris, Reggie, Lou.	3	4	.429	4.73	41	0	0	0	37	16	40.0	43	182	21	21	7	0	2	3	20	1	45	5	0
Harrison, Tommy, Rich.	0	1	.000	8.10	4	0	0	0	1	0	10.0	17	52	9	9	2	0	0	0	6	1	6	1	0
Hartmann, Pete, Roch.*	1	5	.167	8.93	34	3	0	0	8	0	44.1	56	215	45	44	14	0	1	3	27	1	43	7	0
Hasselhoff, Derek, Char.	6	0	1.000	4.82	49	0	0	0	18	4	71.0	83	311	46	38	7	1	0	0	25	1	65	3	0
Heathcott, Mike, Char.	10	8	.556	5.17	32	21	1	0	5	0	139.1	177	632	89	80	14	6	4	4	64	1	77	9	0
Henderson, Rod, Lou.	7	11	.389	6.34	28	22	0	0	1	0	120.2	119	550	109	85	20	5	5	7	64	0	76	6	0
Henderson, Ryan, Lou.-Nor. ...	1	2	.333	6.84	28	2	0	0	8	0	48.2	49	231	45	37	4	0	1	4	34	3	46	9	0
Henriquez, Oscar, Nor.	3	4	.429	4.00	53	0	0	0	41	23	54.0	54	254	31	24	8	4	3	3	38	4	65	8	1
Hernandez, Santos, Dur.	0	2	.000	10.80	6	4	0	0	0	0	18.1	34	98	25	22	9	0	0	1	11	0	12	1	1
Hiljus, Erik, Tol.	2	3	.400	4.40	33	0	0	0	9	5	59.1	49	239	31	29	5	5	2	2	16	0	73	5	0
Holbert, Aaron, Dur.	0	0	.000	54.00	2	0	0	0	2	0	1.1	8	14	8	8	0	0	0	0	2	0	1	0	0
Hosey, Dwayne, Ott.	0	0	.000	0.00	1	0	0	0	1	0	0.2	1	4	0	0	0	0	0	0	1	0	0	1	0
Hudek, John, Rich.-Syr.	0	2	.000	5.83	24	0	0	0	11	1	29.1	31	131	20	19	3	3	2	0	13	1	32	2	0
Iglesias, Mike, Rich.	0	2	.000	15.75	3	0	0	0	0	0	4.0	6	22	7	7	0	0	0	0	4	1	7	0	0
Isringhausen, Jason, Nor.	3	1	.750	2.29	12	8	0	0	1	0	51.0	33	203	18	13	4	1	0	1	20	0	51	0	1
Jacquez, Thomas, S./W.B.*	0	1	.000	2.45	3	0	0	0	1	0	3.2	4	15	1	1	0	0	0	0	0	0	4	0	0
Janzen, Marty, Ind.	1	1	.500	4.86	9	1	0	0	3	0	16.2	16	73	9	9	0	1	1	2	8	2	8	1	0
Johns, Doug, Roch.*	1	1	.500	4.85	6	6	1	0	0	0	29.2	34	130	20	16	3	0	3	1	6	0	18	0	1
Johnson, Barry, S./W.B.	6	10	.375	5.02	31	18	1	1	5	0	136.1	157	602	83	76	12	1	5	1	49	2	88	7	0
Johnson, Jason, Roch.	4	2	.667	3.65	8	8	0	0	0	0	44.1	35	194	19	18	6	0	1	1	27	0	47	2	1
Johnson, Mike, Ott.	6	12	.333	5.38	28	27	0	0	1	0	147.1	174	673	105	88	24	5	4	7	63	0	120	7	0
Jones, Bobby, Nor.	2	0	1.000	2.45	2	2	0	0	0	0	11.0	11	47	3	3	2	0	0	1	3	0	8	0	0
Juden, Jeff, Col.	11	12	.478	5.56	27	26	4	1	0	0	176.1	164	768	124	109	24	6	7	17	76	2	151	14	4
Kamieniecki, Scott, Roch.	1	2	.333	5.09	4	4	0	0	0	0	23.0	23	95	13	13	5	0	1	1	6	0	14	0	0

Pitcher, Team	W	L	Pct.	ERA	G	GS	CG	ShO	GF	Sv.	IP	H	TBF	R	ER	HR	SH	SF	HB	BB	IBB	SO	WP	Bk.
Keagle, Greg, Tol.	1	4	.200	7.16	7	7	0	0	0	0	32.2	50	158	29	26	3	1	2	4	13	0	19	1	1
Kida, Masao, Tol.	0	0	.000	3.18	3	0	0	0	1	0	5.2	6	23	2	2	2	0	0	0	1	0	4	0	0
Kieschnick, Brooks, Dur.	0	0	.000	0.00	1	0	0	0	1	0	2.0	1	9	1	0	0	0	0	0	1	0	1	2	0
Klingenbeck, Scott, Ind.	4	4	.500	4.82	14	12	0	0	1	1	74.2	89	328	44	40	8	5	5	2	26	1	53	3	0
Koch, Billy, Syr.	3	0	1.000	3.86	5	5	0	0	0	0	25.2	27	111	11	11	3	0	1	2	10	0	22	0	2
Langston, Marcus, Buf.*	0	1	.000	3.86	4	4	0	0	0	0	18.2	16	77	9	8	4	0	0	0	8	0	11	0	0
Levrault, Allen, Lou.	1	3	.250	8.65	9	5	0	0	1	0	34.1	48	169	37	33	9	1	2	3	16	0	33	1	0
Lewis, Richie, Nor.	7	8	.467	5.06	20	20	3	1	0	0	122.2	128	542	82	69	19	6	2	5	49	7	101	4	1
LeBlanc, Eric, Ind.	1	2	.333	7.11	14	3	0	0	1	1	44.1	57	209	43	35	4	1	5	4	19	1	26	3	0
Lidle, Cory, Dur.	0	0	.000	4.76	3	2	0	0	0	0	5.2	9	26	3	3	0	0	0	1	6	1	0	0	0
Lilly, Ted, Ott.*	8	5	.615	3.84	16	16	0	0	0	0	89.0	81	364	40	38	12	1	2	2	23	0	78	1	2
Linton, Doug, Roch.	7	5	.583	3.65	18	18	1	0	0	0	118.1	120	510	58	48	13	3	4	10	27	1	97	3	0
Lira, Felipe, Tol.	2	11	.154	6.71	30	17	0	0	7	1	114.0	163	527	97	85	25	3	4	4	35	3	70	3	0
Looney, Brian, Tol.-S./W.B.*	4	0	1.000	5.70	50	4	0	0	11	2	71.0	70	329	47	45	10	5	4	3	50	0	64	8	1
Lopez, Johan, Nor.	3	5	.375	4.15	33	8	0	0	6	1	102.0	98	438	49	47	13	6	0	2	44	6	84	10	1
Lukasiewicz, Mark, Syr.*	4	4	.500	5.34	37	9	1	0	6	3	97.2	109	431	59	58	20	1	2	0	40	1	77	5	1
Lundquist, David, Char.	0	0	.000	0.00	3	0	0	0	1	0	3.2	3	14	0	0	0	0	0	0	1	0	4	1	0
Lyons, Mike, Nor.	0	0	.000	21.00	2	0	0	0	1	0	3.0	7	19	7	7	1	0	0	3	0	0	5	0	0
Maduro, Calvin, Roch.	11	11	.500	3.99	29	28	2	1	0	0	169.0	179	735	88	75	23	1	7	5	60	0	149	4	1
Mahomes, Pat, Nor.	4	1	.800	3.49	6	6	0	0	0	0	38.2	38	164	17	15	6	0	1	0	12	1	24	1	0
Mahoney, Mike, Rich.	0	0	.000	6.75	1	0	0	0	1	0	1.1	3	8	1	1	0	0	0	1	0	0	0	0	0
Mann, Jim, Syr.	6	5	.545	4.64	47	0	0	0	20	5	66.0	53	287	35	34	11	1	1	2	39	1	72	6	0
Marquez, Robert, Ott.	1	1	.500	4.88	18	0	0	0	7	1	27.2	33	131	19	15	3	1	1	1	14	2	16	1	1
Martin, Tom, Buf.*	1	0	1.000	3.00	5	0	0	0	1	0	6.0	5	25	2	2	1	0	0	0	1	0	6	0	0
Martinez, Pablo, Rich.	0	0	.000	45.00	1	0	0	0	1	0	1.0	3	10	5	5	1	0	0	1	3	0	2	0	0
Martinez, Ramon, Paw.	0	1	.000	9.00	2	2	0	0	0	0	9.0	10	43	9	9	4	0	0	1	6	0	7	1	0
Martinez, Romulo, Tol.	0	0	.000	5.40	6	0	0	0	3	0	6.2	7	32	5	4	0	0	0	6	0	0	2	0	0
Martinez, Willie, Buf.	2	2	.500	6.85	4	4	0	0	0	0	22.1	28	101	17	17	3	1	0	2	7	1	12	0	0
Matthews, Mike, Buf.*	1	2	.333	7.59	25	0	0	0	8	0	21.1	23	99	18	18	3	1	2	2	18	0	16	0	1
McCarthy, Greg, Col.*	2	1	.667	3.86	29	0	0	0	17	1	35.0	24	150	19	15	4	0	2	1	19	0	21	3	0
McCarty, Dave, Tol.*	0	0	.000	4.50	2	0	0	0	2	0	2.0	1	7	1	1	0	0	0	0	1	0	0	0	0
McClellan, Sean, Syr.	0	0	.000	3.86	8	0	0	0	5	2	7.0	6	34	4	3	1	0	0	4	0	5	1	0
McCommon, Jason, Roch.	7	10	.412	4.98	29	18	1	1	1	0	124.2	143	550	73	69	21	4	3	1	50	1	68	2	2
McMichael, Greg, Nor.	0	0	.000	2.70	3	1	0	0	0	0	3.1	4	16	1	1	0	0	0	3	0	4	0	0
Meacham, Rusty, Ind.	1	3	.250	6.98	16	1	0	0	6	1	29.2	38	142	27	23	6	2	3	2	15	3	19	2	0
Menhart, Paul, Buf.	2	1	.667	4.85	7	0	0	0	0	0	13.0	18	60	7	7	0	0	1	4	0	10	2	0
Mercado, Hector, Nor.*	0	0	.000	1.50	2	2	0	0	0	0	6.0	3	22	1	1	1	0	1	1	0	2	0	0
Mercedes, Jose, Nor.	2	1	.667	2.53	6	6	0	0	0	0	32.0	36	146	15	9	2	4	2	2	11	1	19	0	0
Merrell, Phil, Ind.	0	3	.000	14.73	3	3	0	0	0	0	11.0	21	59	21	18	4	0	1	4	0	6	3	1
Minor, Blas, Lou.	4	4	.500	4.58	21	17	0	0	0	0	108.0	118	466	59	55	13	1	2	4	32	2	77	1	0
Mitchell, Scott, Ott.	4	4	.500	5.63	18	9	0	0	1	0	62.1	78	282	43	39	11	1	3	3	25	0	28	0	1
Mix, Greg, Paw.	4	4	.500	3.69	46	4	0	0	13	1	85.1	89	388	45	35	9	3	5	4	40	0	79	9	1
Molina, Gabe, Roch.	2	2	.500	3.14	45	0	0	0	36	18	57.1	45	241	22	20	3	2	1	2	23	1	58	6	1
Montgomery, Steve, S./W.B.	0	0	.000	6.23	14	0	0	0	11	7	13.0	17	65	9	9	0	1	0	1	11	0	13	1	1
Moore, Marcus, Syr.	0	1	.000	11.25	7	0	0	0	5	0	12.0	14	62	15	15	2	1	0	1	13	0	12	1	0
Moraga, David, Ott.*	1	2	.333	6.19	4	0	0	0	1	0	16.0	24	76	14	11	4	1	2	0	5	0	10	1	0
Morris, Jim, Dur.*	3	1	.750	5.48	18	0	0	0	5	0	23.0	21	103	14	14	3	0	0	1	19	0	16	2	0
Mota, Guillermo, Ott.	2	0	1.000	1.89	14	0	0	0	10	5	19.0	16	76	6	4	0	2	0	1	5	0	17	0	0
Munoz, Bobby, Nor.	3	3	.500	4.39	39	3	0	0	11	5	55.1	55	251	35	27	5	2	3	1	31	1	50	7	0
Munro, Peter, Syr.	6	1	.857	3.10	18	11	0	0	3	0	69.2	70	312	29	24	6	0	3	4	33	1	68	3	0
Murray, Dan, Nor.	12	10	.545	4.97	29	27	3	1	1	0	145.0	149	650	91	80	22	7	5	7	70	5	96	11	3
Myers, Jimmy, Nor.-S./W.B.	1	1	.500	6.50	14	0	0	0	3	1	18.0	26	84	14	13	1	0	1	1	5	0	8	2	0
Naulty, Dan, Col.	2	1	.667	4.35	7	0	0	0	2	0	10.1	14	48	6	5	1	0	2	0	4	0	5	1	0
Neagle, Denny, Ind.*	2	0	1.000	4.67	3	3	0	0	0	0	17.1	11	66	9	9	2	0	1	1	2	0	9	0	0
Nelson, Joe, Rich.	2	3	.400	4.54	12	3	0	0	2	1	33.2	33	150	18	17	2	4	1	0	15	0	31	3	0
Neubart, Garrett, Nor.	0	0	.000	3.38	2	0	0	0	2	0	2.2	3	11	1	1	0	0	1	0	0	0	1	0	0
Newman, Alan, Dur.*	10	0	1.000	2.24	50	0	0	0	7	0	80.1	59	316	24	20	2	2	2	3	20	0	76	3	1
Nichting, Chris, Col.	8	5	.615	5.29	25	21	2	0	0	0	127.2	135	552	80	75	22	2	4	3	47	0	110	6	0
Nunez, Maximo, Dur.	1	0	1.000	5.40	21	0	0	0	9	2	31.2	25	147	20	19	2	1	0	5	28	0	31	6	0
Nye, Ryan, S./W.B.	5	4	.556	5.10	14	10	0	0	1	0	65.1	69	283	41	37	8	2	1	2	20	1	63	2	0
Ohka, Tomokazu, Paw.	7	0	1.000	1.58	12	12	1	1	0	0	68.1	60	274	17	12	5	1	1	0	11	0	63	1	0
Olsen, Jason, Char.	2	4	.333	7.11	22	10	0	0	2	0	62.0	84	296	59	49	12	1	5	5	29	0	49	3	0
Ontiveros, Steve, Lou.	5	1	.833	4.44	8	8	0	0	0	0	48.2	47	203	26	24	5	3	1	0	12	1	33	1	0
Ortega, Pablo, Dur.	0	1	.000	34.71	1	1	0	0	0	0	2.1	10	16	9	9	0	0	0	0	2	1	0	0	0
Palacios, Vicente, Nor.	2	1	.667	1.86	7	0	0	0	2	1	9.2	9	42	2	2	1	1	1	2	4	0	9	0	0
Pall, Donn, Ind.	1	0	1.000	8.44	4	0	0	0	1	0	5.1	9	26	7	5	2	1	0	0	1	0	1	0	0
Parker, Christian, Ott.	0	1	.000	7.59	7	0	0	0	0	0	10.2	10	49	9	9	0	1	2	7	0	5	0	0
Parris, Steve, Ind.	0	2	.000	4.04	6	6	0	0	0	0	35.2	39	148	16	16	5	0	4	1	9	1	31	0	0
Passini, Brian, Lou.*	2	3	.400	7.48	6	6	0	0	0	0	27.2	34	132	23	23	4	1	2	0	17	1	14	0	0
Pavano, Carl, Ott.	0	1	.000	9.00	2	2	0	0	0	0	5.0	7	23	5	5	1	0	1	0	0	0	3	0	0
Pavlas, Dave, Col.	4	2	.667	4.04	38	2	0	0	13	1	62.1	69	256	32	28	5	0	3	2	9	1	49	1	0
Pena, Juan, Paw.	4	2	.667	4.13	10	10	0	0	0	0	48.0	44	206	28	22	8	0	0	4	13	0	61	1	3
Pennington, Brad, Syr.*	3	0	1.000	4.24	27	0	0	0	12	1	34.0	30	158	20	16	3	0	5	2	30	0	34	4	1
Peterson, Kyle, Lou.	7	6	.538	3.55	18	18	1	1	0	0	109.0	90	466	52	43	13	3	3	6	42	1	95	5	2
Pina, Rafael, Roch.	8	10	.444	4.37	48	10	0	0	18	5	111.1	113	488	60	54	15	1	3	2	48	2	88	7	1
Pisciotta, Marc, Rich.	3	2	.600	6.06	23	0	0	0	3	0	35.2	34	153	25	24	3	2	3	0	17	3	27	3	0
Pittsley, Jim, Lou.	2	4	.333	8.77	8	8	0	0	0	0	39.0	55	187	42	38	8	1	3	2	16	0	26	4	0
Plantenberg, Erik, Dur.-Roch.*	7	5	.583	5.91	40	7	0	0	12	0	80.2	100	371	59	53	20	1	0	1	41	0	72	8	1
Pontes, Dan, Nor.	0	0	.000	9.39	14	0	0	1	0	0	23.0	36	116	25	24	5	1	0	1	11	0	14	2	0
Post, Dave, Ott.	0	0	.000	135.00	1	0	0	0	1	0	0.1	6	8	6	5	1	0	0	0	0	0	0	0	0
Powell, Jeremy, Ott.	3	5	.375	2.97	16	16	0	0	0	0	91.0	85	382	37	30	5	3	4	37	0	72	6	0
Priest, Eddie, Ind.*	6	5	.545	5.35	18	12	0	0	2	2	69.0	86	303	41	41	10	3	3	2	20	1	35	3	1

Pitcher, Team	W	L	Pct.	ERA	G	GS	CG	ShO	GF	Sv.	IP	H	TBF	R	ER	HR	SH	SF	HB	BB	IBB	SO	WP	Bk.
Probst, Alan, Syr.	0	0	.000	4.50	2	0	0	0	2	0	2.0	1	7	1	1	1	0	0	0	0	0	1	0	0
Pulsipher, Bill, Lou.*	0	2	.000	4.28	6	6	0	0	0	0	27.1	22	121	14	13	1	2	0	0	19	0	21	1	0
Quantrill, Paul, Syr.	0	0	.000	0.00	2	0	0	0	0	0	2.0	1	6	0	0	0	0	0	0	0	0	1	0	0
Quevedo, Ruben, Rich.	6	5	.545	5.37	21	21	0	0	0	0	105.2	112	444	65	63	26	2	2	1	34	0	98	4	0
Rakers, Jason, Buf.	7	8	.467	4.92	23	20	1	0	1	0	131.2	151	577	83	72	17	4	2	6	31	2	85	4	3
Ramirez, Hector, Lou.	3	3	.500	3.80	58	0	0	0	26	9	94.2	91	398	45	40	13	4	2	2	33	0	55	4	0
Ramirez, Jose, Tol.*	0	0	.000	1.80	1	1	0	0	0	0	5.0	3	23	1	1	0	0	0	1	4	1	3	0	0
Ramsay, Robert, Paw.*	6	6	.500	5.35	20	20	0	0	0	0	114.1	114	498	81	68	21	9	4	4	36	1	79	5	3
Ratliff, Jon, Rich.	5	12	.294	4.45	27	27	0	0	0	0	157.2	154	660	88	78	24	3	6	3	44	2	129	5	0
Reece, Dana, Syr.*	0	0	.000	0.00	1	0	0	0	0	0	2.0	1	9	0	0	0	0	0	0	2	0	1	0	0
Reed, Brandon, Tol.	8	5	.615	4.14	44	6	1	0	21	3	91.1	101	401	53	42	6	1	7	5	26	3	59	1	0
Reed, Rick, Nor.	0	1	.000	27.00	1	1	0	0	0	0	3.0	10	21	9	9	1	0	1	0	2	0	2	0	0
Rekar, Bryan, Dur.	4	1	.800	3.86	6	5	0	0	1	0	35.0	29	142	15	15	3	1	0	1	8	0	26	3	0
Reyes, Al, Lou.	0	2	.000	8.38	6	0	0	0	0	0	9.2	12	50	9	9	0	1	3	4	7	2	8	1	0
Riedling, John, Ind.	1	0	1.000	1.54	24	0	0	0	6	1	35.0	19	142	9	6	1	2	0	3	18	2	26	2	0
Rigdon, Paul, Buf.	7	4	.636	4.53	19	19	0	0	0	0	103.1	114	451	60	52	11	3	2	1	28	0	60	4	2
Riske, David, Rich.	3	0	1.000	0.65	23	0	0	0	19	6	27.2	14	101	3	2	0	1	0	0	7	0	22	0	0
Rizzo, Todd, Char.*	4	5	.444	4.06	53	0	0	0	16	8	71.0	68	308	37	32	5	6	5	2	31	2	46	6	0
Roach, Peter, Tol.*	1	1	.500	4.50	4	0	0	0	0	0	8.0	6	29	4	4	2	0	1	0	2	0	5	0	0
Roberts, Grant, Nor.	2	1	.667	4.50	5	5	0	0	0	0	28.0	32	122	15	14	1	0	1	0	11	2	30	3	0
Roberts, Willis, Tol.	5	8	.385	6.26	31	12	2	0	9	0	92.0	112	433	68	64	10	3	3	3	59	3	52	5	4
Robertson, Rich, Ind.*	0	0	.000	9.82	9	0	0	0	1	0	7.1	17	42	9	8	0	0	0	0	4	1	7	0	1
Rodriguez, Nerio, Syr.	10	8	.556	4.54	27	27	1	1	0	0	162.2	161	688	84	82	17	3	5	7	53	0	137	5	2
Rogers, Jason, Roch.*	0	3	.000	8.10	9	0	0	0	3	0	10.0	15	50	9	9	3	1	0	0	6	1	7	2	0
Rojas, Mel, Ott.	0	1	.000	5.14	12	0	0	0	6	2	21.0	25	99	13	12	3	0	0	1	12	0	16	3	0
Romano, Mike, Syr.	12	8	.600	4.13	29	28	2	0	0	0	174.1	160	756	90	80	21	4	4	8	84	2	104	8	1
Roque, Rafael, Lou.*	1	0	1.000	0.00	2	2	0	0	0	0	10.0	4	35	0	0	0	1	0	1	3	0	3	0	0
Rose, Brian, Paw.	2	1	.667	2.89	7	7	0	0	0	0	28.0	28	117	10	9	6	0	0	0	8	0	30	0	0
Ruebel, Matt, Nor.*	3	0	1.000	4.50	7	7	0	0	0	0	40.0	40	174	20	20	6	0	2	3	17	0	23	0	0
Runyan, Sean, Tol.*	0	0	.000	3.48	10	0	0	0	2	0	10.1	7	45	4	4	1	0	2	0	6	0	7	0	0
Ryan, B.J., Ind.-Roch.*	1	0	1.000	3.09	22	0	0	0	7	1	23.1	17	92	8	8	2	1	0	0	7	2	32	2	0
Ryan, Ken, S./W.B.	2	2	.500	5.66	31	0	0	0	18	6	41.1	54	197	30	26	2	3	3	0	19	2	33	1	0
Sager, A.J., Ind.	6	3	.667	4.67	24	7	0	0	6	0	52.0	79	254	45	27	5	3	4	1	25	1	18	0	1
Salyers, Jeremy, Ott.	0	0	.000	1.50	1	1	0	0	0	0	6.0	6	24	2	1	0	1	0	0	2	0	2	1	0
Sanders, Frankie, Buf.	1	0	1.000	9.00	1	1	0	0	0	0	5.0	6	25	5	5	2	0	0	4	0	3	0	0
Santana, Marino, Paw.	2	3	.400	2.95	25	0	0	0	10	1	39.2	28	171	15	13	5	0	3	2	17	3	45	7	3
Saunders, Tony, Dur.*	0	0	.000	2.57	1	1	0	0	0	0	7.0	8	31	3	2	0	0	1	1	2	0	7	0	0
Schrenk, Steve, S./W.B.	3	1	.750	2.93	32	0	0	0	13	2	43.0	38	185	17	14	2	3	2	0	21	6	34	2	0
Scott, Darryl, S./W.B.	7	6	.538	4.09	57	4	0	0	30	10	105.2	100	456	53	48	11	4	2	4	47	4	91	7	0
Secoda, Jason, Char.	2	5	.286	5.28	7	7	3	0	0	0	44.1	54	201	35	26	10	0	1	3	10	0	33	4	0
Seelbach, Chris, Rich.	6	1	.857	5.15	13	8	1	0	2	0	57.2	51	255	34	33	4	1	1	2	34	1	48	3	0
Sekany, Jason, Paw.	0	1	.000	4.76	1	1	0	0	0	0	5.2	7	27	4	3	2	0	0	0	4	0	1	0	0
Sexton, Jeff, Buf.	0	1	.000	6.52	23	1	0	0	11	0	29.0	47	149	24	21	3	1	2	1	14	3	22	3	0
Shuey, Paul, Buf.	0	0	.000	0.00	1	0	0	0	0	0	1.0	0	4	0	0	0	0	0	0	1	0	1	1	0
Shumaker, Anthony, S./W.B.*	3	5	.375	5.72	14	14	1	0	0	0	89.2	119	403	60	57	15	3	6	2	32	2	49	2	0
Sinclair, Steve, Syr.*	2	2	.500	2.06	34	0	0	0	30	18	39.1	24	156	11	9	3	0	0	4	12	1	31	1	0
Small, Aaron, Lou.-Dur.	5	7	.417	6.88	32	18	0	0	3	0	120.1	156	555	104	92	19	2	8	3	47	3	63	8	0
Small, Mark, Ott.	4	5	.444	5.54	42	0	0	0	10	2	66.2	85	309	50	41	9	4	0	1	32	0	43	6	0
Smart, J.D., Ott.	0	1	.000	2.61	6	4	0	0	0	0	20.2	22	90	7	6	2	0	0	1	6	0	9	1	1
Smith, Brian, Syr.	7	4	.636	3.50	29	0	0	0	23	7	46.1	45	210	22	18	7	5	1	2	24	4	46	2	0
Smith, Dan, Ott.	5	4	.556	3.68	11	11	0	0	0	0	71.0	61	298	31	29	7	3	0	7	27	0	59	3	0
Snyder, John, Char.	3	0	1.000	4.24	3	3	0	0	0	0	17.0	17	75	9	8	2	0	0	2	5	0	9	0	0
Snyder, Matt, Roch.	6	6	.500	5.21	48	3	0	0	15	1	84.2	95	380	60	49	14	3	4	4	30	4	59	6	0
Sparks, Jeff, Dur.	1	0	1.000	3.38	18	0	0	0	5	0	24.0	16	106	11	9	2	0	1	1	14	0	31	3	0
Speier, Justin, Rich.	2	4	.333	5.62	27	0	0	0	16	3	41.2	51	201	28	26	4	1	1	3	22	4	39	6	1
Spence, Cam, Col.	0	1	.000	5.14	1	1	0	0	0	0	7.0	8	30	4	4	1	0	1	0	1	0	4	0	0
Springer, Russ, Rich.	1	0	1.000	1.17	11	0	0	0	6	2	15.1	9	58	2	2	0	1	1	0	1	0	13	0	0
Stanifer, Rob, Paw.	3	1	.750	2.04	31	0	0	0	20	3	39.2	34	168	21	9	5	0	0	0	15	1	29	4	0
Stevens, Dave, Buf.	1	0	1.000	1.52	20	0	0	0	18	12	23.2	12	97	4	4	1	1	1	2	14	1	28	0	0
Stevenson, Jason, Syr.	1	2	.333	6.05	7	7	0	0	0	0	38.2	52	180	30	26	7	0	2	1	21	0	15	2	1
Stevenson, Rod, Ott.	2	1	.667	3.93	17	0	0	0	11	2	18.1	15	76	9	8	4	0	3	2	7	0	12	1	0
Stewart, Scott, Nor.*	6	4	.600	4.42	35	14	0	0	3	0	99.2	109	442	55	49	9	5	2	2	36	1	85	5	3
Strickland, Scott, Ott.	3	0	1.000	1.63	19	0	0	0	12	5	27.2	23	116	5	5	0	0	1	1	11	2	34	1	0
Strong, Joe, Dur.	0	1	.000	7.98	6	1	0	0	1	0	14.2	20	71	13	13	4	0	0	0	8	0	12	0	0
Stull, Everett, Rich.	8	8	.500	4.47	30	22	0	0	5	0	139.0	124	603	75	69	17	4	7	8	73	0	126	12	2
Sturtze, Tanyon, Char.	9	4	.692	4.05	33	14	2	1	11	3	104.1	83	433	53	47	7	1	2	1	41	1	107	2	0
Tam, Jeff, Nor.-Buf.	2	3	.400	2.53	32	0	0	0	12	3	46.1	47	193	16	13	3	1	0	1	11	2	23	0	1
Tatis, Ramon, Dur.*	12	8	.600	5.26	28	28	0	0	0	0	155.1	178	692	100	95	19	2	4	4	74	0	97	9	9
Telgheder, Dave, Buf.	8	8	.500	3.95	29	14	1	0	3	0	107.0	109	451	56	47	8	3	6	3	21	2	60	3	1
Tessmer, Jay, Col.	3	3	.500	3.34	51	0	0	0	48	28	56.2	52	232	22	21	4	5	0	1	12	1	42	3	0
Therneau, Dave, Ind.	2	0	1.000	8.17	7	7	0	0	0	0	36.1	52	172	36	33	9	1	2	1	14	0	22	4	1
Thompson, Mark, Ind.	2	6	.250	5.13	11	10	0	0	0	0	54.1	50	237	31	31	5	1	4	6	29	1	28	0	0
Tolar, Kevin, Ind.*	1	0	1.000	2.08	8	1	0	0	1	0	13.0	8	53	4	3	1	0	1	0	7	1	18	1	0
Tomberlin, Andy, Nor.*	0	0	.000	135.00	1	0	0	0	0	0	0.1	4	9	5	5	0	0	0	0	4	0	1	0	0
Tomko, Brett, Ind.	2	0	1.000	4.97	2	2	0	0	0	0	12.2	15	54	7	7	1	0	0	1	1	0	9	0	0
Treadwell, Jody, Nor.	1	2	.333	9.93	11	3	0	0	2	0	22.2	27	115	25	25	5	1	2	18	1	19	1	0
Turrentine, Rich, Nor.	0	1	.000	6.75	2	0	0	0	1	0	2.2	6	14	2	2	1	1	0	1	3	0	0	0
Urso, Sal, Paw.*	1	0	1.000	3.52	4	0	0	0	1	0	7.2	10	36	4	3	0	0	1	0	5	0	6	0	0
Valdes, Marc, Dur.	1	2	.333	5.18	9	9	0	0	0	0	40.0	39	171	25	23	3	2	0	4	12	0	23	0	0
VanEgmond, Tim, Lou.	0	5	.000	5.06	8	7	0	0	0	0	26.2	28	125	15	15	5	0	2	4	17	0	15	5	0
VanRyn, Ben, Char.*	3	2	.600	5.93	47	8	0	0	13	5	68.1	83	314	47	45	9	1	6	1	30	0	54	4	0
Vazquez, Javier, Ott.	4	2	.667	4.85	7	7	0	0	0	0	42.2	45	183	24	23	7	2	2	2	16	0	46	0	0

Pitcher, Team	W	L	Pct.	ERA	G	GS	CG	ShO	GF	Sv.	IP	H	TBF	R	ER	HR	SH	SF	HB	BB	IBB	SO	WP	Bk.
Villano, Mike, Nor.	0	0	.000	4.50	2	0	0	0	2	0	2.0	3	10	1	1	0	0	0	0	2	0	1	0	0
Villegas, Ismael, Rich.	6	7	.462	4.40	44	2	0	0	8	1	92.0	93	400	51	45	7	6	3	2	39	3	61	8	0
Villone, Ron, Ind.*	2	0	1.000	1.42	18	0	0	0	6	1	19.0	9	75	3	3	1	1	1	2	13	1	23	0	0
Virchis, Adam, Char.	0	0	.000	1.42	3	0	0	0	3	0	6.1	6	27	1	1	1	0	0	0	1	0	4	0	0
Wade, Terrell, Dur.*	1	7	.125	9.49	34	19	0	0	4	0	98.2	140	501	112	104	21	1	8	2	80	0	61	5	0
Wagner, Paul, Buf.	8	4	.667	3.82	23	23	0	0	0	0	129.2	123	559	67	55	11	1	4	4	55	2	95	11	0
Walker, Mike, Buf.	2	1	.667	5.60	29	0	0	0	11	2	35.1	43	179	29	22	4	3	2	1	26	5	15	5	0
Wallace, Derek, Nor.	2	5	.286	3.60	36	0	0	0	19	7	55.0	53	233	24	22	6	1	0	2	25	7	38	2	0
Ward, Bryan, Char.*	2	0	1.000	3.52	14	0	0	0	6	1	15.1	15	64	7	6	2	1	1	1	3	1	15	1	0
Wasdin, John, Paw.	1	1	.500	2.12	5	5	0	0	0	0	29.2	19	113	9	7	1	1	1	1	7	0	28	0	0
Watson, Allen, Col.*	0	0	.000	6.14	2	2	0	0	0	0	7.1	7	31	5	5	2	0	0	0	2	0	5	0	0
Welch, Mike, S./W.B.-Nor.	3	4	.429	5.81	37	5	0	0	16	0	66.2	78	298	47	43	8	1	4	3	26	1	28	4	0
Wengert, Don, Col.-Rich.	0	1	.000	6.75	7	3	0	0	0	0	21.1	32	98	16	16	5	1	0	2	3	1	8	2	0
Wheeler, Dan, Dur.	7	5	.583	4.92	14	14	2	1	0	0	82.1	103	369	59	45	16	1	3	4	25	0	58	1	0
Williams, Matt, Col.*	0	2	.000	3.86	13	1	0	0	3	0	21.0	15	87	9	9	1	0	0	0	11	0	22	0	1
Williams, Shad, S./W.B.	0	2	.000	19.80	2	2	0	0	0	0	5.0	17	33	11	11	0	0	2	1	3	0	2	0	0
Williams, Todd, Ind.	1	3	.250	5.10	38	0	0	0	33	24	42.1	38	174	24	24	3	2	2	5	13	0	35	7	0
Willoughby, Justin, Rich.*	0	0	.000	9.00	1	0	0	0	1	0	1.0	3	6	1	1	0	0	0	0	0	0	1	1	0
Wilson, Trevor, Col.*	3	2	.600	3.56	19	4	0	0	4	1	48.0	47	207	25	19	5	1	1	6	12	0	41	2	3
Wohlers, Mark, Ind.	0	0	.000	108.00	1	0	0	0	0	0	0.1	1	7	4	4	0	0	0	0	5	0	1	4	0
Wolcott, Bob, Paw.	6	13	.316	3.59	26	16	2	0	5	2	125.1	131	538	67	50	17	7	4	8	28	3	69	3	0
Wolf, Randy, S./W.B.*	4	5	.444	3.61	12	12	0	0	0	0	77.1	73	329	36	31	8	1	2	1	29	1	72	4	0
Wright, Jaret, Buf.	0	0	.000	0.00	1	1	0	0	0	0	3.0	0	10	0	0	0	0	0	0	0	0	4	0	0
Wunsch, Kelly, Lou.*	2	1	.667	4.75	16	2	0	0	3	0	41.2	52	189	23	22	4	0	2	6	14	0	20	3	0
Yarnall, Ed, Col.*	13	4	.765	3.47	23	23	1	1	0	0	145.1	136	611	61	56	5	3	8	3	57	0	146	2	1
Yennaco, Jay, Syr.	2	6	.250	6.86	15	15	0	0	0	0	80.0	107	373	68	61	11	2	2	1	42	1	45	2	0
Zancanaro, Dave, Col.*	7	2	.778	4.17	13	13	1	0	0	0	77.2	85	336	40	36	11	0	1	0	28	0	45	1	2
Zuber, Jon, S./W.B.*	0	0	.000	0.00	1	0	0	0	0	0	2.0	2	6	0	0	0	0	0	0	0	0	0	0	0

COMBINATION SHUTOUTS: **Buffalo (5)**—Wagner-Dougherty-Matthews, Brower-Cadaret-Stevens, Telgheder-Stevens, Brower-Hamilton-Riske, Rigdon-Tam-Riske. **Charlotte (3)**—Eyre-Heathcott, Beirne-Bradford, Sturtze-Rizzo-Andujar. **Columbus (3)**—Yarnall-Erdos-Tessmer, Juden-Ford-Tessmer, De Los Santos-Tessmer. **Durham (1)**—Eiland-Munoz-Gaillard. **Indianapolis (4)**—Carrara-Pall, Carrara-Sager-Williams, Priest-Greene-Williams, Carrara-Priest. **Louisville (6)**—Van Egmond-Converse-Ramirez-Harris, Estrada-Harris, Passini-Borowski-Harris, Minor-Ramirez-Granger, Peterson-Borowski-Granger, Roque-Harris. **Norfolk (5)**—Mercado-Lopez-Henriquez, Isringhausen-Tam-Henriquez, Murray-Guerra-Henriquez, Lewis-Tam, Bautista-Beltran-Henriquez. **Ottawa (6)**—Smith-Small-Forster-Mota, Lilly-Bautista-Small-Forster, DeSilva-Mota, Lilly-Rojas, DeSilva-Strickland-Small, Bennett-Durocher. **Pawtucket (7)**—Wasdin-Farrell-Adamson, Ramsay-Wolcott, Cho-Santana, Adamson-Santana-Mix, Ohka-Stanifer, Rose-Gross-Stanifer-Bullinger, Adams-Fernandez-Bullinger. **Richmond (7)**—Chen-Cortes-Brooks, Chen-Cather-Pisciotta-Butler, Bowie-Springer, Chen-Villegas, Brooks-Cortes, Stull-Villegas-Cortes, Stull-Cortes, Ratliff-Cortes. **Rochester (6)**—Maduro-Dykhoff-Molina, McCommon-Pina, Johnson-Dykhoff-Pina, Coppinger-Pina, McCommon-Snyder-Corsi, Pina-Dykhoff. **Scranton/Wilkes-Barre (7)**—Wolf-Schrenk-Scott, Brewer-Fiore-Montgomery, Shumaker-Scott-Brewer, Nye-Fesh-Ryan, Grace-Scott, Grahe-Dodd, Dodd-Scott. **Syracuse (3)**—Koch-Bochtler-Bovee, Romano-Bochtler, Munro-Bogott-Pennington. **Toledo (0)**—None.

NO-HIT GAMES: None.

PITCHERS WITH TWO OR MORE TEAMS

Pitcher, Team	W	L	Pct.	ERA	G	GS	CG	ShO	GF	Sv.	IP	H	TBF	R	ER	HR	SH	SF	HB	BB	IBB	SO	WP	Bk.
Bautista, Jose, Ott.	0	1	.000	5.72	16	0	0	0	5	4	28.1	33	126	19	18	6	2	2	1	5	1	24	0	0
Bautista, Jose, Nor.	7	4	.636	5.33	20	12	0	0	1	0	82.2	111	374	53	49	14	1	1	5	21	1	41	4	0
Bere, Jason, Ind.	0	2	.000	10.19	5	4	0	0	1	0	17.2	25	94	20	20	3	0	1	0	19	0	8	0	0
Bere, Jason, Lou.	2	1	.667	2.08	5	5	0	0	0	0	26.0	21	102	8	6	0	2	2	0	8	0	27	1	0
Dixon, Tim, Ott.*	0	0	.000	6.75	2	0	0	0	1	0	1.1	3	6	1	1	1	0	0	0	0	0	1	0	0
Dixon, Tim, Paw.*	0	1	.000	9.00	2	0	0	0	0	0	5.0	6	25	5	5	3	0	0	1	3	0	4	0	0
Donnelly, Brendan, Dur.	5	5	.500	3.05	37	1	0	0	10	2	62.0	53	247	23	21	5	0	4	4	18	1	61	5	0
Donnelly, Brendan, Syr.	5	1	.500	2.89	5	0	0	0	2	0	9.1	8	39	4	3	1	2	0	0	4	1	9	1	0
Hamilton, Jimmy, Buf.*	1	2	.333	5.18	26	0	0	0	4	0	24.1	24	122	22	14	3	1	3	1	27	0	25	1	0
Hamilton, Jimmy, Roch.*	0	0	.000	13.50	3	0	0	0	0	0	2.0	1	11	3	3	0	0	1	0	4	0	2	0	0
Henderson, Ryan, Lou.	1	0	1.000	6.37	21	0	0	0	7	0	35.1	35	168	32	25	2	0	1	3	25	3	34	7	0
Henderson, Ryan, Nor.	0	2	.000	8.10	7	2	0	0	0	0	13.1	14	63	13	12	2	0	1	0	9	0	12	2	0
Hudek, John, Rich.	0	0	.000	6.35	12	0	0	0	5	0	11.1	14	53	8	8	0	0	1	0	5	0	17	1	0
Hudek, John, Syr.	0	2	.000	5.50	12	0	0	0	6	1	18.0	17	78	12	11	3	3	1	0	8	1	15	1	0
Looney, Brian, Tol.*	3	0	1.000	6.22	47	1	0	0	11	2	55.0	51	255	38	38	7	5	4	2	44	0	52	7	0
Looney, Brian, S./W.B.*	1	0	1.000	3.94	3	3	0	0	0	0	16.0	19	74	9	7	3	0	0	1	6	0	12	1	1
Myers, Jimmy, Nor.	0	0	.000	17.18	3	0	0	0	1	0	3.2	11	24	8	7	0	0	0	2	2	0	2	0	0
Myers, Jimmy, S./W.B.	1	0	1.000	3.77	11	0	0	0	2	1	14.1	15	60	6	6	1	1	3	0	6	2	0		
Plantenberg, Erik, Dur.*	5	4	.556	6.02	23	7	0	0	5	0	58.1	75	270	43	39	19	1	0	1	28	0	51	3	1
Plantenberg, Erik, Roch.*	2	1	.667	5.64	17	0	0	0	7	0	22.1	25	101	16	14	1	0	0	13	0	21	5	0	
Ryan, B.J., Ind.*	1	0	1.000	4.00	11	0	0	0	4	0	9.0	9	37	4	4	0	0	0	3	1	12	1	0	
Ryan, B.J., Roch.*	0	0	.000	2.51	11	0	0	0	3	1	14.1	8	55	4	4	2	1	0	4	1	20	1	0	
Small, Aaron, Lou.	1	1	.500	9.43	11	0	0	0	2	0	21.0	38	111	23	22	3	1	0	15	1	11	4	0	
Small, Aaron, Dur.	4	6	.400	6.34	21	18	0	0	0	0	99.1	118	444	81	70	16	1	8	3	32	2	52	4	0
Tam, Jeff, Nor.	0	1	.000	3.10	16	0	0	0	9	3	20.1	24	87	7	7	1	0	3	1	10	0	1		
Tam, Jeff, Buf.	2	2	.500	2.08	16	0	0	0	8	1	26.0	23	106	9	6	2	1	0	8	1	13	0	0	
Welch, Mike, Nor.	2	2	.500	3.58	24	0	0	0	14	0	32.2	33	142	17	13	4	1	1	2	13	1	17	3	0
Welch, Mike, S./W.B.*	1	2	.333	7.94	13	5	0	0	2	0	34.0	45	156	30	30	4	0	1	3	13	0	11	1	0
Wengert, Don, Col.	0	1	.000	7.63	6	2	0	0	0	0	15.1	25	73	13	13	4	0	1	3	1	5	1	0	
Wengert, Don, Rich.	0	0	.000	4.50	1	1	0	0	0	0	6.0	7	25	3	3	1	1	0	1	0	6	1	0	

1999 FIELDING
TEAM

Team	Pct.	G	PO	A	E	TC	DP	TP	PB	Team	Pct.	G	PO	A	E	TC	DP	TP	PB
Indianapolis	.981	144	3794	1639	106	5539	171	0	19	Syracuse	.978	144	3774	1376	116	5266	113	0	10
Richmond	.979	142	3696	1322	106	5124	116	0	16	Toledo	.977	144	3723	1564	127	5414	147	1	20
Durham	.978	143	3759	1537	117	5413	154	0	19	Scranton/W.-B.	.976	144	3759	1583	132	5474	158	0	7

Team	Pct.	G	PO	A	E	TC	DP	TP	PB	Team	Pct.	G	PO	A	E	TC	DP	TP	PB
Columbus	.975	141	3690	1437	130	5257	129	0	20	Rochester	.974	144	3823	1429	142	5394	128	0	6
Buffalo	.974	144	3740	1418	135	5293	110	0	17	Ottawa	.974	144	3764	1481	142	5387	132	1	23
Louisville	.974	144	3815	1518	140	5473	144	0	10	Norfolk	.971	140	3659	1372	151	5182	122	0	25
Charlotte	.974	144	3675	1419	135	5229	116	0	11	Pawtucket	.970	144	3800	1395	162	5357	114	0	16

INDIVIDUAL

FIRST BASEMEN

NOTE: All caps denotes fielding-percentage leader based on 72 games for catchers, 96 for all other non-pitchers and 115 innings for pitchers. *Throws lefthanded.

Player, Team	Pct.	G	PO	A	E	TC	DP
Abad, Andy, Paw.*	.977	20	157	13	4	174	15
Agbayani, Benny, Nor.	.987	8	71	6	1	78	6
Alcantara, Israel, Paw.	1.000	5	37	2	0	39	4
Baerga, Carlos, Ind.	1.000	7	51	0	0	51	8
Banks, Brian, Lou.	.944	3	16	1	1	18	3
Barker, Kevin, Lou.*	.991	120	1036	88	10	1134	100
Battle, Howard, Rich.	.926	3	23	2	2	27	3
Bell, Mike, Nor.	1.000	17	90	6	0	96	9
Bellinger, Clay, Col.	1.000	3	21	4	0	25	0
Bierek, Kurt, Col.	.994	128	1082	73	7	1162	106
Blum, Geoff, Ott.	1.000	6	59	3	0	62	6
Bonnici, Jim, Tol.	1.000	4	26	2	0	28	1
Branson, Jeff, Ind.	1.000	1	8	0	0	8	2
Brooks, Jerry, Nor.	.985	38	252	17	4	273	23
Burrell, Pat, S./W.B.	1.000	6	58	1	0	59	8
Camilli, Jason, Ott.	.988	9	76	9	1	86	5
Carver, Steve, S./W.B.	.990	67	572	33	6	611	64
Chamblee, James, Paw.	1.000	3	23	4	0	27	1
Clark, Howie, Roch.	1.000	2	9	1	0	10	0
Clark, Tony, Tol.	1.000	1	10	1	0	11	0
Coolbaugh, Mike, Col.	.976	10	76	6	2	84	7
Coquillette, Trace, Ott.	1.000	1	6	0	0	6	0
Cox, Steve, Dur.*	.996	123	1125	73	5	1203	121
Cromer, D.T., Ind.*	.989	50	422	35	5	462	48
Daubach, Brian, Paw.	.969	3	30	1	1	32	3
Davis, Tommy, Roch.	.986	18	135	10	2	147	11
Depastino, Joe, Paw.	1.000	1	1	0	0	1	0
Eddie, Steve, Char.	1.000	3	25	0	0	25	4
Fernandez, Jose, Ott.	1.000	10	88	4	0	92	6
Fick, Robert, Tol.	.963	7	46	6	2	54	3
Fraraccio, Dan, Dur.	1.000	2	13	0	0	13	1
Fullmer, Brad, Ott.	.990	25	187	13	2	202	20
Garcia, Guillermo, Ind.	.986	13	138	6	2	146	10
Grifol, Pedro, Nor.	1.000	1	4	0	0	4	1
Gubanich, Creighton, Paw.	1.000	1	1	0	0	1	0
Hamelin, Bob, Tol.*	.991	13	106	5	1	112	14
Hiatt, Phil, Ind.	.997	38	319	37	1	357	51
Hollins, Dave, Char.	.985	9	62	3	1	66	7
Jefferson, Reggie, Paw.*	1.000	2	18	1	0	19	3
Kinkade, Mike, Nor.	.989	12	81	10	1	92	3
Lee, Carlos, Char.	1.000	4	33	2	0	35	4
Liefer, Jeff, Char.	.991	29	207	20	2	229	15
Livingstone, Scott, Roch.-Nor.	1.000	16	95	15	0	110	7
Lopez, Luis, Syr.	.994	82	641	55	4	700	62
Lovullo, Torey, S./W.B.	.929	5	24	2	2	28	2
Lydy, Scott, Char.	.938	3	12	3	1	16	1
Magdaleno, Ricky, Char.	1.000	1	2	0	0	2	0
Manto, Jeff, Buf.	.993	54	417	22	3	442	37
Maxwell, Jason, Tol.	1.000	1	10	1	0	11	0
McCall, Rod, Ind.	1.000	29	237	25	0	262	21
McCARTY, Dave, Tol.*	.999	115	968	104	1	1073	102
McClain, Scott, Dur.	.973	13	104	3	3	110	11
McGuire, Ryan, Ott.*	.996	34	247	14	1	262	25
McKeel, Walt, Tol.	.909	2	18	2	2	22	2
Merloni, Lou, Paw.	1.000	3	9	0	0	9	0
Miller, David, Buf.*	.996	30	232	13	1	246	20
Miller, Orlando, Buf.	1.000	3	16	3	0	19	1
Minor, Ryan, Roch.	.992	15	116	13	1	130	11
Morales, Francisco, Ott.	1.000	1	2	0	0	2	1
Mouton, Lyle, Lou.	.875	1	6	1	1	8	0
Ortiz, Luis, Lou.	1.000	23	185	14	0	199	19
Ortiz, Nick, Buf.	1.000	3	3	0	0	3	0
Paquette, Craig, Nor.	.991	16	98	8	1	107	9
Perry, Chan, Buf.	.986	53	405	32	6	443	32
Perry, Herbert, Dur.	.967	7	53	6	2	61	2
Pickering, Calvin, Roch.*	.985	97	821	45	13	879	75
Post, Dave, Ott.	1.000	10	92	7	0	99	13
Probst, Alan, Syr.	1.000	3	6	0	0	6	0
Raven, Luis, Char.	.980	14	93	5	2	100	8
Ronan, Marc, S./W.B.	1.000	1	1	0	0	1	0

Player, Team	Pct.	G	PO	A	E	TC	DP
Rumfield, Toby, Rich.	.992	49	345	18	3	366	43
Schall, Gene, Rich.	.991	74	535	36	5	576	40
Seguignol, Fernando, Ott.	.977	50	388	39	10	437	41
Simon, Randall, Rich.*	1.000	14	115	14	0	129	9
Snopek, Chris, Paw.-Ind.	1.000	2	13	2	0	15	1
Snusz, Chris, Ott.	1.000	6	34	0	0	34	2
Stenson, Dernell, Paw.*	.966	115	919	56	34	1009	78
Sweeney, Mark, Ind.*	.988	17	151	7	2	160	17
Tinsley, Lee, Ind.	1.000	1	2	0	0	2	1
Toca, Jorge, Nor.	.987	44	351	41	5	397	46
Tomberlin, Andy, Nor.*	.988	12	80	0	1	81	4
Turner, Chris, Buf.	.984	16	108	13	2	123	13
Tyler, Brad, Rich.	1.000	14	106	5	0	111	13
Valdez, Mario, Char.	.991	99	732	54	7	793	65
Vinas, Julio, Roch.	1.000	17	138	12	0	150	18
Waszgis, B.J., Col.	.882	5	29	1	4	34	6
Williamson, Antone, Lou.	1.000	3	12	1	0	13	2
Wilson, Tom, Dur.	1.000	2	1	1	0	2	0
Witt, Kevin, Syr.	.995	66	500	51	3	554	32
Wood, Jason, Tol.	.987	8	67	7	1	75	13
Zuber, Jon, S./W.B.*	.997	73	588	74	2	664	65

TRIPLE PLAYS: McCarty, Post.

FIRST BASEMEN WITH TWO OR MORE TEAMS

Player, Team	Pct.	G	PO	A	E	TC	DP
Livingstone, Scott, Roch.	1.000	3	13	0	0	13	1
Livingstone, Scott, Nor.	1.000	13	82	15	0	97	6
Snopek, Chris, Paw.	1.000	1	1	0	0	1	0
Snopek, Chris, Ind.	1.000	1	12	2	0	14	1

SECOND BASEMEN

Player, Team	Pct.	G	PO	A	E	TC	DP
Baerga, Carlos, Ind.	.978	16	34	57	2	93	14
Baez, Kevin, Ind.-Nor.	.980	36	67	76	3	146	22
Battle, Howard, Rich.	1.000	1	1	3	0	4	1
Bell, Mike, Nor.	.936	22	47	41	6	94	12
Belliard, Ronnie, Lou.	.975	29	51	66	3	120	12
Bellinger, Clay, Col.	1.000	4	6	14	0	20	3
Blum, Geoff, Ott.	.971	6	14	20	1	35	6
Boone, Aaron, Ind.	1.000	1	3	2	0	5	2
Branson, Jeff, Ind.	.875	3	4	3	1	8	1
Brito, Tilson, Char.	.965	95	183	255	16	454	53
Cabrera, Jolbert, Buf.	.968	6	15	15	1	31	2
Camilli, Jason, Ott.	.969	11	9	22	1	32	3
Carvajal, Jhonny, Ott.	.969	18	28	35	2	65	5
Cedeno, Andujar, Col.	.667	5	1	3	2	6	1
Chamblee, James, Paw.	.976	103	207	238	11	456	55
Clark, Howie, Roch.	1.000	7	6	11	0	17	3
Coquillette, Trace, Ott.	.966	85	150	196	12	358	46
Cromer, Brandon, Lou.	.985	45	92	111	3	206	29
Darden, Tony, Nor.	.000	1	0	0	0	0	0
Eddie, Steve, Ind.	.967	6	14	15	1	30	3
Fernandez, Jose, Ind.	1.000	1	3	2	0	5	1
Finn, John, S./W.B.	.973	10	19	17	1	37	6
Fonville, Chad, Paw.	.952	23	38	42	4	84	7
Forbes, P.J., Roch.	.989	35	71	102	2	175	29
Fraraccio, Dan, Dur.	1.000	6	8	14	0	22	4
Frye, Jeff, Paw.	1.000	3	1	11	0	12	1
Garcia, Jesse, Roch.	.947	21	41	48	5	94	10
Gonzalez, Jose, Char.	1.000	6	6	12	0	18	0
Graffanino, Tony, Dur.	.998	84	182	231	1	414	73
Grebeck, Craig, Syr.	.882	3	8	7	2	17	2
Guiliano, Matt, S./W.B.	.917	5	6	5	1	12	1
Hairston, Jerry, Roch.	.974	89	182	230	11	423	50
Halter, Shane, Nor.	1.000	17	23	38	0	61	10
Haney, Todd, Nor.	.967	88	172	205	13	390	43
Hardtke, Jason, Ind.	.982	51	106	160	5	271	42
Holbert, Aaron, Dur.	.977	53	100	154	6	260	38
Huff, Larry, S./W.B.	1.000	3	4	3	0	7	3
Ingram, Garey, Paw.	1.000	22	30	57	0	87	11
Jackson, Gavin, Paw.	1.000	5	3	11	0	14	1
Jimenez, D'Angelo, Col.	1.000	4	9	11	0	20	0
Lamb, David, Dur.	1.000	3	5	5	0	10	1

Player, Team	Pct.	G	PO	A	E	TC	DP
Ledesma, Aaron, Dur.	1.000	1	2	4	0	6	1
Lopez, Mickey, Lou.	.976	47	104	141	6	251	42
LOVULLO, Torey, S./W.B.	.982	132	262	390	12	664	99
Macias, Jose, Tol.	.971	107	204	339	16	559	74
Magdaleno, Ricky, Char.	.000	1	0	0	0	0	0
Malloy, Marty, Rich.	.990	65	111	172	3	286	31
Martin, Chris, Dur.	.000	1	0	0	0	0	0
Martin, Norberto, Syr.	.982	36	64	99	3	166	14
Martinez, Pablo, Rich.	.963	13	18	34	2	54	5
Maxwell, Jason, Tol.	.984	40	69	111	3	183	26
McDonald, John, Buf.	1.000	2	4	5	0	9	2
Melo, Juan, Syr.	1.000	3	4	7	0	11	2
Merloni, Lou, Paw.	.833	2	3	2	1	6	2
Miller, Orlando, Buf.	1.000	2	1	2	0	3	1
Moore, Brandon, Char.	1.000	3	6	6	0	12	2
Mora, Melvin, Nor.	1.000	1	1	2	0	3	0
Mummau, Rob, Syr.	.980	80	155	187	7	349	44
Perez, Santiago, Lou.	.941	5	8	8	1	17	2
Post, Dave, Ott.	.977	34	47	82	3	132	21
Raabe, Brian, Col.	.981	94	165	249	8	422	67
Scutaro, Marcos, Buf.	.974	123	230	331	15	576	67
Selby, Bill, Buf.	1.000	13	25	29	0	54	5
Silvestri, Dave, Dur.	1.000	1	0	3	0	3	0
Simons, Mitch, Char.	.990	49	92	116	2	210	28
Sisco, Steve, Rich.	.983	70	131	151	5	287	46
Snopek, Chris, Ind.	.976	26	45	76	3	124	18
Solano, Fausto, Syr.	1.000	1	1	4	0	5	0
Soriano, Alfonso, Col.	1.000	1	1	2	0	3	1
Stankiewicz, Andy, Col.	.983	43	69	108	3	180	21
Strange, Mike, Syr.	.977	12	18	24	1	43	4
Tyler, Brad, Rich.	1.000	3	5	5	0	10	0
Williams, Jason, Ind.	.990	40	75	120	2	197	33
Wood, Jason, Tol.	1.000	2	2	7	0	9	2
Woodward, Chris, Syr.	.949	16	30	45	4	79	8
Zosky, Eddie, Lou.	.963	26	51	53	4	108	16

TRIPLE PLAY: Macias.

SECOND BASEMEN WITH TWO OR MORE TEAMS

Player, Team	Pct.	G	PO	A	E	TC	DP
Baez, Kevin, Ind.	1.000	10	20	11	0	31	3
Baez, Kevin, Nor.	.974	26	47	65	3	115	19

THIRD BASEMEN

Player, Team	Pct.	G	PO	A	E	TC	DP
Alvarez, Gabe, Tol.	.893	86	48	160	25	233	9
Andreopoulos, Alex, Lou.	.000	1	0	0	0	0	0
Andrews, Shane, Ott.	1.000	2	1	2	0	3	0
Baerga, Carlos, Ind.	.957	31	21	69	4	94	5
Baez, Kevin, Ind.-Nor.	1.000	4	1	3	0	4	0
Barrett, Michael, Ott.	.800	2	0	4	1	5	0
Battle, Howard, Rich.	.939	84	41	114	10	165	13
Bellinger, Clay, Col.	.966	24	16	40	2	58	3
Beltre, Esteban, Roch.	1.000	13	6	27	0	33	2
BLAKE, Casey, Syr.	.967	109	94	168	9	271	13
Blum, Geoff, Ott.	.900	3	3	6	1	10	2
Boone, Aaron, Ind.	.929	9	5	21	2	28	1
Branson, Jeff, Ind.	.970	10	10	22	1	33	4
Branyan, Russell, Buf.	.921	108	63	205	23	291	11
Brito, Tilson, Char.	1.000	5	3	9	0	12	1
Brooks, Jerry, Nor.	.000	1	0	0	0	0	0
Cabrera, Jolbert, Buf.	.900	3	2	7	1	10	0
Camilli, Jason, Ott.	.929	4	4	9	1	14	1
Carvajal, Jhonny, Ott.	1.000	2	3	2	0	5	1
Cedeno, Andujar, Col.	.936	37	16	57	5	78	5
Chamblee, James, Paw.	.860	28	15	28	7	50	0
Clark, Howie, Buf.	1.000	4	3	6	0	9	0
Collier, Lou, Lou.	.951	20	10	48	3	61	4
Coolbaugh, Mike, Col.	.903	64	44	105	16	165	11
Coquillette, Trace, Ott.	.826	9	3	16	4	23	2
Cromer, Brandon, Lou.	.968	39	22	68	3	93	7
Dalesandro, Mark, Syr.	1.000	2	0	4	0	4	1
Darden, Tony, Nor.	.950	11	5	14	1	20	2
Davis, Tommy, Roch.	.900	6	3	15	2	20	0
Eddie, Steve, Char.	.942	29	20	45	4	69	4
Fernandez, Jose, Ott.	.911	113	94	223	31	348	20
Fick, Robert, Tol.	.333	1	0	1	2	3	0
Finn, John, S./W.B.	1.000	1	0	1	0	1	0
Fonville, Chad, Paw.	.824	6	4	10	3	17	1
Forbes, P.J., Roch.	.982	40	33	74	2	109	7
Fraraccio, Dan, Dur.	.857	1	3	3	1	7	1
Fryman, Travis, Buf.	.750	2	0	3	1	4	0
Garcia, Guillermo, Ind.	.857	2	3	3	1	7	1

Player, Team	Pct.	G	PO	A	E	TC	DP
Garcia, Luis, Tol.	.972	16	14	21	1	36	2
Gonzalez, Jose, Char.	.000	3	0	0	0	0	0
Gonzalez, Manny, Char.	.000	1	0	0	0	0	0
Graffanino, Tony, Dur.	1.000	1	0	2	0	2	0
Guiliano, Matt, S./W.B.	.933	8	3	11	1	15	1
Halter, Shane, Nor.	.895	14	15	19	4	38	1
Haney, Todd, Nor.	.868	32	24	55	12	91	7
Hardtke, Jason, Ind.	.933	36	31	81	8	120	10
Hiatt, Phil, Ind.	.975	16	9	30	1	40	3
Holbert, Aaron, Dur.	.889	4	1	7	1	9	0
Hollins, Dave, Char.	.904	49	30	55	9	94	2
Huff, Larry, S./W.B.	1.000	3	0	7	0	7	2
Jimenez, D'Angelo, Col.	.952	6	5	15	1	21	1
Kinkade, Mike, Nor.	.926	42	20	67	7	94	7
Krause, Scott, Lou.	1.000	1	1	0	0	1	0
Lee, Carlos, Char.	.882	13	10	20	4	34	1
Liefer, Jeff, Char.	.000	1	0	0	0	0	0
Liniak, Cole, Paw.	.941	94	66	156	14	236	17
Livingstone, Scott, Roch.-Nor.	.881	16	14	23	5	42	2
Lopez, Luis, Syr.	.969	30	17	45	2	64	2
Lovullo, Torey, S./W.B.	1.000	2	2	6	0	8	0
Lucca, Lou, S./W.B.	.960	136	76	310	16	402	27
Magdaleno, Ricky, Char.	1.000	2	0	2	0	2	1
Malloy, Marty, Rich.	.933	31	20	50	5	75	7
Martinez, Pablo, Rich.	1.000	1	0	3	0	3	0
Maxwell, Jason, Tol.	.861	15	4	27	5	36	2
McClain, Scott, Dur.	.938	83	64	162	15	241	19
McDonald, John, Buf.	1.000	3	1	9	0	10	0
McKeel, Walt, Tol.	1.000	1	0	1	0	1	0
Merloni, Lou, Paw.	.951	26	24	53	4	81	4
Miller, Orlando, Buf.	.960	8	5	19	1	25	1
Minor, Ryan, Roch.	.940	83	54	135	12	201	12
Moore, Brandon, Char.	.973	21	10	26	1	37	1
Mora, Melvin, Nor.	.000	1	0	0	1	1	0
Mummau, Rob, Syr.	.889	6	3	5	1	9	0
Oliver, Joe, Dur.	.000	1	0	0	0	0	0
Ortiz, Luis, Lou.	.871	27	19	55	11	85	5
Pachot, John, Ott.	.800	2	2	2	1	5	0
Paquette, Craig, Nor.	.941	39	26	69	6	101	5
Perry, Herbert, Dur.	1.000	4	3	6	0	9	1
Post, Dave, Ott.	.909	16	11	29	4	44	0
Raabe, Brian, Col.	.979	22	8	38	1	47	5
Raven, Luis, Char.	.889	5	1	7	1	9	0
Rust, Brian, Roch.	1.000	1	1	6	0	7	0
Salzano, Jerry, Ind.	1.000	3	0	2	0	2	0
Selby, Bill, Buf.	.929	24	14	51	5	70	2
Simons, Mitch, Char.	.960	46	27	68	4	99	2
Sisco, Steve, Rich.	.966	31	22	62	3	87	3
Smith, Bobby, Dur.	.944	54	44	126	10	180	15
Snopek, Chris, Paw.-Ind.	.907	43	17	81	10	108	13
Soriano, Alfonso, Col.	.929	5	3	10	1	14	0
Trammell, Bubba, Dur.	1.000	1	0	2	0	2	0
Tyler, Brad, Rich.	.000	1	0	0	0	0	0
Vinas, Julio, Rich.	.889	5	3	5	1	9	0
Williamson, Antone, Lou.	.864	20	5	33	6	44	1
Wood, Jason, Tol.	.974	30	20	54	2	76	6
Zosky, Eddie, Lou.	.914	59	30	108	13	151	12

TRIPLE PLAY: Alvarez.

THIRD BASEMEN WITH TWO OR MORE TEAMS

Player, Team	Pct.	G	PO	A	E	TC	DP
Baez, Kevin, Ind.	1.000	2	0	2	0	2	0
Baez, Kevin, Nor.	1.000	2	1	1	0	2	0
Livingstone, Scott, Roch.	.833	2	2	3	1	6	0
Livingstone, Scott, Nor.	.889	14	12	20	4	36	2
Snopek, Chris, Paw.	1.000	1	1	0	0	1	0
Snopek, Chris, Ind.	.907	42	16	81	10	107	13

SHORTSTOPS

Player, Team	Pct.	G	PO	A	E	TC	DP
Alvarez, Gabe, Tol.	1.000	1	2	2	0	4	1
Baez, Kevin, Ind.-Nor.	.966	32	31	83	4	118	17
Bellinger, Clay, Col.	1.000	11	17	31	0	48	7
Beltre, Esteban, Roch.-Char.	.955	116	151	319	22	492	59
Blake, Casey, Syr.	.500	1	0	1	1	2	0
Blum, Geoff, Ott.	.958	59	78	150	10	238	30
Boone, Aaron, Ind.	.900	1	3	6	1	10	1
BRANSON, Jeff, Ind.	.974	106	160	335	13	508	81
Brito, Tilson, Char.	1.000	1	1	3	0	4	0
Cabrera, Jolbert, Buf.	.956	23	29	57	4	90	9
Camilli, Jason, Ott.	.000	1	0	0	0	0	0
Carvajal, Jhonny, Ott.	.973	72	123	206	9	338	53

Player, Team	Pct.	G	PO	A	E	TC	DP
Cedeno, Andujar, Col.	.900	3	2	7	1	10	1
Collier, Lou, Lou.	1.000	3	4	11	0	15	2
Cromer, Brandon, Lou.	.875	6	9	12	3	24	1
DeRosa, Mark, Rich.	.951	102	139	249	20	408	55
Eddie, Steve, Char.	.750	4	3	6	3	12	3
Finn, John, S./W.B.	.944	28	33	85	7	125	19
Flores, Jose, S./W.B.	.960	63	90	175	11	276	38
Fonville, Chad, Paw.	.914	23	23	51	7	81	12
Forbes, P.J., Roch.	.951	11	22	36	3	61	9
Fraraccio, Dan, Dur.	1.000	2	3	8	0	11	1
Freel, Ryan, Syr.	.800	3	1	7	2	10	0
Garcia, Jesse, Roch.	.942	41	54	108	10	172	23
Garcia, Luis, Tol.	.955	72	124	235	17	376	48
Grebeck, Craig, Syr.	1.000	1	1	3	0	4	0
Guiliano, Matt, S./W.B.	.921	57	70	174	21	265	44
Hairston, Jerry, Roch.	.934	18	24	47	5	76	9
Halter, Shane, Nor.	.955	69	92	181	13	286	40
Haney, Todd, Nor.	1.000	1	1	1	0	2	0
Hardtke, Jason, Ind.	1.000	10	16	29	0	45	7
Holbert, Aaron, Dur.	.958	22	32	60	4	96	15
Huff, Larry, S./W.B.	.000	1	0	0	0	0	0
Jackson, Gavin, Paw.	.966	45	70	129	7	206	26
Jimenez, D'Angelo, Col.	.955	116	188	346	25	559	73
Lamb, David, Dur.	.897	5	8	18	3	29	1
Ledesma, Aaron, Dur.	.917	1	5	6	1	12	3
Macias, Jose, Tol.	.895	3	6	11	2	19	1
Magdaleno, Ricky, Char.	.943	23	32	50	5	87	14
Malloy, Marty, Rich.	.936	11	18	26	3	47	9
Martin, Chris, Dur.	.952	116	159	380	27	566	75
Martin, Norberto, Syr.	.955	37	48	102	7	157	11
Martinez, Gabby, Char.	.946	16	18	35	3	56	5
Martinez, Pablo, Rich.	.969	33	41	113	5	159	19
Maxwell, Jason, Tol.	.967	68	108	189	10	307	53
McDonald, John, Buf.	.953	61	82	180	13	275	36
Melo, Juan, Ind.-Syr.	.968	40	73	110	6	189	23
Merloni, Lou, Paw.	.943	31	43	72	7	122	14
Miller, Orlando, Buf.	.964	43	60	129	7	196	20
Moore, Brandon, Char.	.946	67	87	191	16	294	44
Mora, Melvin, Nor.	.928	49	63	130	15	208	23
Mummau, Rob, Syr.	.000	1	0	0	0	0	0
Ojeda, Augie, Roch.	.000	1	0	0	0	0	0
Ortiz, Nick, Buf.	.973	17	26	46	2	74	10
Paquette, Craig, Nor.	1.000	1	1	2	0	3	0
Perez, Santiago, Lou.	.935	102	142	273	29	444	51
Post, Dave, Ott.	.985	20	19	47	1	67	10
Rollins, Jimmy, S./W.B.	.960	4	9	15	1	25	4
Sadler, Donnie, Paw.	.944	36	73	96	10	179	19
Scutaro, Marcos, Buf.	.966	6	9	19	1	29	4
Simons, Mitch, Char.	.824	8	5	9	3	17	0
Sisco, Steve, Rich.	.929	4	5	8	1	14	2
Smith, Bobby, Dur.	1.000	2	2	0	0	2	0
Snopek, Chris, Paw.-Ind.	.979	51	58	130	4	192	28
Solano, Fausto, Syr.	.962	8	8	17	1	26	3
Soriano, Alfonso, Col.	.959	14	15	32	2	49	6
Soriano, Fred, Syr.	.960	5	9	15	1	25	7
Stankiewicz, Andy, Col.	1.000	1	0	2	0	2	0
Tebbs, Nate, Paw.	.750	3	2	1	1	4	0
Valentin, Jose, Lou.	1.000	6	7	17	0	24	2
Wood, Jason, Tol.	.957	6	7	15	1	23	3
Woodward, Chris, Syr.	.972	59	84	155	7	246	40
Zosky, Eddie, Lou.	.989	37	60	117	2	179	35

TRIPLE PLAY: Blum.

SHORTSTOPS WITH TWO OR MORE TEAMS

Player, Team	Pct.	G	PO	A	E	TC	DP
Baez, Kevin, Ind.	.917	4	3	8	1	12	1
Baez, Kevin, Nor.	.972	28	28	75	3	106	16
Beltre, Esteban, Roch.	.951	78	106	206	16	328	40
Beltre, Esteban, Char.	.963	38	45	113	6	164	19
Melo, Juan, Ind.	1.000	2	5	7	0	12	0
Melo, Juan, Syr.	.966	38	68	103	6	177	23
Snopek, Chris, Paw.	.969	20	27	36	2	65	7
Snopek, Chris, Ind.	.984	31	31	94	2	127	21

OUTFIELDERS

Player, Team	Pct.	G	PO	A	E	TC	DP
Abad, Andy, Paw.*	.985	68	127	3	2	132	1
Abbott, Jeff, Char.*	.979	67	136	4	3	143	1
Adolfo, Carlos, Ott.	.952	16	39	1	2	42	1
Agbayani, Benny, Nor.	.977	18	42	0	1	43	0
Alcantara, Israel, Paw.	1.000	14	25	0	0	25	0
Allensworth, Jermaine, Nor.	.975	74	155	3	4	162	2
Alvarez, Gabe, Tol.	.976	20	37	3	1	41	2
Ashby, Chris, Col.	.981	65	99	7	2	108	1
Ashley, Billy, Tol.	1.000	13	25	0	0	25	0
Banks, Brian, Lou.	1.000	2	7	0	0	7	0
Barker, Kevin, Lou.*	.000	1	0	0	0	0	0
BARTEE, Kimera, Tol.	.996	104	239	5	1	245	1
Bass, Jayson, Rich.	.969	52	92	3	3	98	0
Beamon, Trey, Char.	1.000	11	16	0	0	16	0
Bellinger, Clay, Col.	1.000	5	8	0	0	8	0
Benitez, Yamil, Lou.	.963	85	175	8	7	190	2
Bergeron, Peter, Ott.	.973	39	64	8	2	74	0
Berroa, Geronimo, Syr.	.941	5	15	1	1	17	0
Bierek, Kurt, Col.	1.000	8	10	0	0	10	0
Bradshaw, Terry, Ott.	1.000	30	50	0	0	50	0
Brito, Tilson, Char.	1.000	10	24	0	0	24	0
Buccheri, Jim, Dur.-Nor.	1.000	28	34	0	0	34	0
Budzinski, Mark, Buf.*	1.000	45	114	1	0	115	1
Burkhart, Lance, Ott.	1.000	1	1	0	0	1	0
Burrell, Pat, S./W.B.	1.000	4	4	0	0	4	0
Burton, Darren, S./W.B.	.975	98	191	8	5	204	4
Butler, Rich, Dur.	.981	79	148	3	3	154	1
Cabrera, Jolbert, Buf.	1.000	40	107	3	0	110	0
Camilli, Jason, Ott.	.000	4	0	0	0	0	0
Carpenter, Bubba, Col.*	.981	101	197	7	4	208	2
Carter, Mike, S./W.B.	1.000	6	7	0	0	7	0
Carter, Shannon, Syr.*	1.000	1	2	0	0	2	0
Carvajal, Jhonny, Ott.	1.000	5	3	0	0	3	0
Carver, Steve, S./W.B.	.000	1	0	0	0	0	0
Christensen, McKay, Char.*	1.000	1	2	0	0	2	0
Clark, Howie, Roch.	.984	70	122	4	2	128	0
Clyburn, Danny, Dur.	.976	69	116	4	3	123	0
Coleman, Michael, Paw.	.980	108	299	2	6	307	0
Collier, Lou, Lou.	1.000	2	3	0	0	3	0
Coolbaugh, Mike, Col.	.958	44	68	0	3	71	0
Cradle, Rickey, Tol.	.981	107	206	6	4	216	0
Cromer, Brandon, Lou.	1.000	4	7	0	0	7	0
Cromer, D.T., Ind.*	.957	69	85	3	4	92	0
Cruz, Jacob, Buf.*	.953	43	77	5	4	86	1
Cruz, Jose, Syr.	1.000	29	75	2	0	77	1
Dalesandro, Mark, Syr.	1.000	15	25	1	0	26	1
Darden, Tony, Nor.	1.000	1	3	0	0	3	0
Daubach, Brian, Paw.	1.000	2	1	1	0	2	0
Delgado, Alex, Syr.	1.000	2	4	0	0	4	0
Dent, Darrell, Roch.*	1.000	9	18	0	0	18	0
Dunn, Todd, Lou.-Roch.	.955	56	81	3	4	88	0
Fonville, Chad, Paw.	.950	19	37	1	2	40	0
Forbes, P.J., Roch.	1.000	8	14	0	0	14	0
Frank, Mike, Ind.*	.996	113	220	10	1	231	1
Fraraccio, Dan, Dur.	.000	1	0	0	0	0	0
Frazier, Lou, S./W.B.	.969	56	155	2	5	162	0
Freel, Ryan, Syr.	.976	16	39	2	1	42	0
Glass, Chip, Col.*	.988	52	79	4	1	84	0
Gonzalez, Manny, Char.	.987	41	71	6	1	78	0
Greene, Willie, Syr.	1.000	14	24	2	0	26	0
Guerra, Mark, Nor.	.000	1	0	0	0	0	0
Guillen, Jose, Dur.	1.000	9	19	1	0	20	0
Halter, Shane, Nor.	.950	32	56	1	3	60	0
Haltiwanger, Garrick, Nor.*	1.000	6	7	0	0	7	0
Haney, Todd, Nor.	.000	1	0	0	0	0	0
Herrera, Jose, Roch.*	.975	36	76	1	2	79	0
Hiatt, Phil, Ind.	1.000	16	33	1	0	34	0
Holbert, Aaron, Dur.	1.000	7	11	0	0	11	0
Hollins, Damon, Ind.*	.983	101	219	14	4	237	4
Hosey, Dwayne, Ott.	.980	26	47	1	1	49	0
Hunter, Scott, Nor.-Ott.	.979	126	232	6	5	243	1
Hurst, Jimmy, Syr.	.938	20	44	1	3	48	0
Hyzdu, Adam, Paw.	1.000	8	10	0	0	10	0
Iapoce, Anthony, Lou.*	.984	25	57	3	1	61	0
Inglin, Jeff, Char.	1.000	12	7	0	0	7	0
Ingram, Garey, Paw.	.969	35	58	4	2	64	0
Isom, Johnny, Roch.	1.000	33	55	4	0	59	0
Johnson, Adam, Rich.*	1.000	11	20	2	0	22	1
Jones, Chris, Syr.	.983	25	57	2	1	60	1
Jones, Terry, Ott.	.984	80	172	9	3	184	2
Kapler, Gabe, Tol.	1.000	14	33	0	0	33	0
Kieschnick, Brooks, Dur.	1.000	8	15	0	0	15	0
Kingsale, Eugene, Roch.	.975	47	118	1	3	122	0
Kinkade, Mike, Nor.	.955	11	19	2	1	22	0
Krause, Scott, Lou.	.972	123	201	8	6	215	3
Ledee, Ricky, Col.*	.953	30	59	2	3	64	0
Lee, Carlos, Char.	1.000	9	13	0	0	13	0
Lennon, Pat, Syr.-Tol.	.974	61	107	5	3	115	2
Lewis, Richie, Nor.	.500	2	1	0	1	2	0

Player, Team	Pct.	G	PO	A	E	TC	DP
Liefer, Jeff, Char.	.958	25	19	4	1	24	0
Livingstone, Scott, Roch.	1.000	1	2	0	0	2	0
Lombard, George, Rich.	.974	67	108	3	3	114	0
Long, Terrence, Nor.*	.980	75	192	8	4	204	1
Lowery, Terrell, Dur.	.992	69	129	3	1	133	0
Lydy, Scott, Char.	1.000	17	31	1	0	32	0
Macias, Jose, Tol.	1.000	5	8	1	0	9	0
Magee, Wendell, S./W.B.	.975	140	310	7	8	325	1
Malloy, Marty, Rich.	.000	1	0	0	0	0	0
Martin, Norberto, Syr.	1.000	8	12	0	0	12	0
Martinez, Greg, Lou.	.996	103	233	7	1	241	3
Martinez, Pablo, Rich.	1.000	8	8	0	0	8	0
May, Derrick, Roch.	.969	68	116	7	4	127	0
McCarty, Dave, Tol.*	.972	20	33	2	1	36	1
McGuire, Ryan, Ott.*	1.000	17	28	1	0	29	0
McKeel, Walt, Tol.	.900	5	9	0	1	10	0
McMillon, Billy, S./W.B.*	.979	129	219	11	5	235	2
McNabb, Buck, Rich.	.950	15	37	1	2	40	0
Mendoza, Carlos, Dur.*	.983	71	107	8	2	117	0
Miller, David, Buf.*	.972	56	100	4	3	107	1
Mitchell, Keith, Paw.	.987	76	148	1	2	151	1
Mitchell, Scott, Ott.	1.000	1	1	0	0	1	0
Moore, Brandon, Char.	1.000	4	6	0	0	6	0
Mora, Melvin, Nor.	1.000	30	62	2	0	64	0
Morgan, Scott, Buf.	.972	45	101	3	3	107	0
Mottola, Chad, Char.	.981	138	288	17	6	311	4
Mouton, Lyle, Roch.-Lou.	.980	109	238	7	5	250	1
Mummau, Rob, Syr.	.971	36	64	2	2	68	2
Murphy, Mike, Roch.	.976	69	158	5	4	167	2
Neubart, Garrett, Nor.	1.000	11	18	1	0	19	0
Nunnally, Jon, Paw.	.983	119	271	12	5	288	1
Otero, Ricky, Roch.*	.979	52	90	4	2	96	0
Paquette, Craig, Nor.	.979	19	43	3	1	47	0
Payton, Jay, Nor.	.984	34	59	3	1	63	1
Perry, Chan, Buf.	.967	21	28	1	1	30	1
Pickering, Calvin, Roch.*	1.000	2	1	0	0	1	0
Polonia, Luis, Tol.*	.985	36	64	2	1	67	0
Post, Dave, Ott.	.956	23	40	3	2	45	1
Powell, Alonzo, Col.	.973	41	70	2	2	74	0
Probst, Alan, Syr.	1.000	2	1	0	0	1	0
Ramirez, Alex, Buf.	.977	71	167	6	4	177	3
Ramirez, Dan, Char.	1.000	6	15	0	0	15	0
Roberts, David, Buf.*	.996	87	247	4	1	252	1
Roberts, Lonell, Rich.	.983	117	278	5	5	288	0
Robinson, Kerry, Ind.*	.977	33	83	3	2	88	0
Sanchez, Alex, Dur.*	1.000	3	8	0	0	8	0
Sanders, Anthony, Syr.	.980	123	279	17	6	302	3
Schall, Gene, Rich.	1.000	22	28	1	0	29	0
Seguignol, Fernando, Ott.	1.000	6	9	1	0	10	0
Selby, Bill, Buf.	1.000	17	26	0	0	26	0
Siddall, Joe, Tol.	1.000	3	1	0	0	1	0
Simmons, Brian, Char.	.973	78	171	6	5	182	1
Simons, Mitch, Char.	.977	25	41	2	1	44	0
Sisco, Steve, Rich.	1.000	10	23	0	0	23	0
Snopek, Chris, Ind.	1.000	1	1	0	0	1	0
Spencer, Shane, Col.	.958	13	23	0	1	24	0
Staton, T.J., Ott.*	1.000	11	20	0	0	20	0
Stowers, Chris, Ott.*	.993	114	284	11	2	297	2
Strawberry, Darryl, Col.*	1.000	8	14	0	0	14	0
Swann, Pedro, Tol.	.993	83	141	8	1	150	0
Sweeney, Mark, Ind.*	.973	53	106	2	3	111	1
Tarasco, Tony, Col.	.990	94	204	1	2	207	0
Tebbs, Nate, Paw.	1.000	1	5	0	0	5	0
Thompson, Andy, Syr.	1.000	45	89	4	0	93	0
Tinsley, Lee, Ind.	1.000	22	27	0	0	27	0
Toca, Jorge, Nor.	1.000	1	0	1	0	1	0
Tomberlin, Andy, Nor.*	.991	53	102	6	1	109	3
Toth, Dave, Char.	1.000	3	1	0	0	1	0
Trammell, Bubba, Dur.	.959	44	65	6	3	74	1
Tyler, Brad, Rich.	.977	92	206	2	5	213	2
Tyner, Jason, Nor.*	1.000	2	4	0	0	4	0
Valdez, Mario, Char.	1.000	22	30	0	0	30	0
Vinas, Julio, Roch.	.000	1	0	0	0	0	0
Wells, Vernon, Syr.	.976	33	79	2	2	83	0
Whatley, Gabe, Rich.	.992	67	118	2	1	121	0
Whiten, Mark, Buf.	.989	35	88	4	1	93	1
Whitmore, Darrell, Ind.	.977	56	83	1	2	86	0
Wilcox, Luke, Dur.	.959	28	46	1	2	49	1
Wilson, Tom, Dur.	1.000	6	8	4	0	12	0
Winn, Randy, Dur.	.966	46	113	2	4	119	0
Witt, Kevin, Syr.	.988	50	79	4	1	84	0
Wood, Jason, Tol.	1.000	2	2	0	0	2	0
Zuber, Jon, S./W.B.*	1.000	13	20	1	0	21	0

OUTFIELDERS WITH TWO OR MORE TEAMS

Player, Team	Pct.	G	PO	A	E	TC	DP
Buccheri, Jim, Dur.	1.000	3	3	0	0	3	0
Buccheri, Jim, Nor.	1.000	25	31	0	0	31	0
Dunn, Todd, Lou.	.961	32	46	3	2	51	0
Dunn, Todd, Roch.	.946	24	35	0	2	37	0
Hunter, Scott, Nor.	1.000	48	84	3	0	87	0
Hunter, Scott, Ott.	.968	78	148	3	5	156	1
Lennon, Pat, Syr.	1.000	21	39	2	0	41	1
Lennon, Pat, Tol.	.959	40	68	3	3	74	1
Mouton, Lyle, Roch.	.941	34	63	1	4	68	1
Mouton, Lyle, Lou.	.995	75	175	6	1	182	0

CATCHERS

Player, Team	Pct.	G	PO	A	E	TC	DP	PB
Alomar, Sandy, Buf.	.921	8	35	0	3	38	0	2
Alvarez, Clemente, S./W.B.	1.000	9	59	6	0	65	0	1
Andreopoulos, Alex, Lou.	.992	63	360	35	3	398	8	4
Banks, Brian, Lou.	1.000	1	6	0	0	6	0	0
Borders, Pat, Buf.	.986	54	316	25	5	346	1	2
Brito, Jorge, Lou.	1.000	4	26	1	0	27	1	0
Brooks, Jerry, Nor.	.993	23	125	8	1	134	0	4
Brown, Kevin, Syr.	.979	82	575	42	13	630	7	6
Cancel, Robinson, Lou.	.992	36	210	25	2	237	1	3
Casanova, Raul, Tol.	.985	31	173	21	3	197	3	5
Christopherson, Eric, Char.	.986	62	396	27	6	429	3	5
Cox, Darron, Ott.	1.000	3	17	2	0	19	0	0
Dalesandro, Mark, Syr.	1.000	2	7	0	0	7	0	0
Davis, James, Ind.	.966	16	75	9	3	87	0	2
Davis, Tommy, Roch.	.984	60	398	35	7	440	7	3
DeCinces, Tim, Roch.	.988	12	78	7	1	86	0	0
Delgado, Alex, Syr.	.977	34	201	12	5	218	2	1
Depastino, Joe, Paw.	.991	75	423	43	4	470	3	4
Estalella, Bobby, S./W.B.	.993	101	652	43	5	700	10	3
Fick, Robert, Tol.	.970	5	31	1	1	33	0	0
Fletcher, Darrin, Syr.	1.000	3	18	5	0	23	0	1
Foster, Jim, Roch.	.993	34	257	22	2	281	0	2
Garcia, Guillermo, Ind.	.991	50	307	22	3	332	4	7
Garcia, Neil, Dur.	.981	12	46	7	1	54	2	1
Greene, Charlie, Lou.	.994	49	306	27	2	335	9	3
Grifol, Pedro, Nor.	.993	53	382	29	3	414	5	5
Gubanich, Creighton, Paw.	.974	24	135	14	4	153	3	3
Halter, Shane, Nor.	1.000	1	1	0	0	1	0	0
Harriss, Robin, Buf.	1.000	2	10	2	0	12	1	1
Hatteberg, Scott, Paw.	1.000	9	47	4	0	51	0	3
Hughes, Bobby, Lou.	1.000	8	41	2	0	43	0	0
Johnson, Brian, Ind.	1.000	5	22	2	0	24	0	1
Kinkade, Mike, Nor.	1.000	16	89	9	1	99	0	6
LaRue, Jason, Ind.	.984	67	384	45	7	436	6	8
Levis, Jesse, Dur.	1.000	24	142	9	0	151	0	1
Machado, Robert, Char.-Ott.	.979	36	252	24	6	282	4	2
Mahoney, Mike, Rich.	.989	42	237	24	3	264	1	4
Matos, Pascual, Rich.	.990	66	456	43	5	504	2	6
McClain, Scott, Dur.	1.000	1	1	0	0	1	0	0
McKeel, Walt, Tol.	.986	45	266	25	4	295	2	8
Melhuse, Adam, Syr.	1.000	18	121	8	0	129	0	0
Millan, Adan, S./W.B.	1.000	1	8	0	0	8	0	0
Molina, Izzy, Col.	.985	95	618	52	10	680	2	10
Morales, Francisco, Ott.	.990	97	661	64	7	732	9	16
Mummau, Rob, Syr.	1.000	2	12	2	0	14	0	2
Oliver, Joe, Dur.	.984	55	399	27	7	433	2	11
Owens, Jayhawk, Ind.	.990	14	87	8	1	96	0	1
Pachot, John, Ott.	.982	16	100	11	2	113	2	3
Pohle, Ike, Syr.	1.000	1	6	1	0	7	0	0
Prince, Tom, S./W.B.	1.000	6	31	2	0	33	0	0
Probst, Alan, Syr.	1.000	16	74	6	0	80	0	0
Rodriguez, Luis, Paw.	.857	2	6	0	1	7	0	0
Rodriguez, Sammy, Nor.	1.000	5	16	0	0	16	0	2
Romero, Mandy, Paw.-Nor.	.990	69	478	30	5	513	6	9
Ronan, Marc, S./W.B.	.981	32	185	19	4	208	2	3
Rumfield, Toby, Rich.	.987	50	347	23	5	375	3	6
SIDDALL, Joe, Tol.	.998	72	410	33	1	444	5	6
Sisco, Steve, Rich.	1.000	2	1	1	0	2	0	0
Snusz, Chris, Ott.	.989	13	84	7	1	92	0	2
Soliz, Steve, Buf.	.980	39	180	19	4	203	0	7
Toth, Dave, Char.	.987	75	475	55	7	537	4	6
Turner, Chris, Buf.	.989	52	316	30	4	350	5	5
Valera, Yohanny, Nor.	.974	22	138	14	4	156	4	5
Vinas, Julio, Roch.	.978	33	253	17	6	276	1	1
Waszgis, B.J., Col.	.986	55	388	26	6	420	4	10
Webster, Lenny, Roch.	1.000	9	49	4	0	53	1	0
Wilson, Tom, Dur.	.986	60	391	41	6	438	8	6

Player, Team	Pct.	G	PO	A	E	TC	DP	PB
Wilson, Vance, Nor.	.991	14	95	11	1	107	2	0
Wood, Jason, Tol.	1.000	2	2	0	0	2	0	1

CATCHERS WITH TWO OR MORE TEAMS

Player, Team	Pct.	G	PO	A	E	TC	DP	PB
Machado, Robert, Char.	.976	16	111	12	3	126	1	0
Machado, Robert, Ott.	.981	20	141	12	3	156	3	2
Romero, Mandy, Paw.	.994	46	316	20	2	338	3	6
Romero, Mandy, Nor.	.983	23	162	10	3	175	3	3

PITCHERS

Player, Team	Pct.	G	PO	A	E	TC	DP
Adams, Willie, Paw.	1.000	11	3	13	0	16	0
Adamson, Joel, Paw.*	.947	25	1	17	1	19	2
Alberro, Jose, Tol.	1.000	14	6	1	0	7	0
Anderson, Matt, Tol.	1.000	24	2	0	0	2	0
Andrews, Clayton, Syr.*	.750	3	0	3	1	4	0
Andujar, Luis, Char.	.929	52	4	9	1	14	0
Arroyo, Luis, Syr.*	1.000	9	2	1	0	3	0
Atchley, Justin, Ind.*	1.000	5	2	5	0	7	0
Baez, Kevin, Nor.	.000	2	0	0	0	0	0
Bailey, Roger, Dur.	1.000	7	2	5	0	7	0
Baker, Jason, Ott.	1.000	11	4	1	0	5	0
Bale, Jim, Syr.*	1.000	6	2	3	0	5	0
Baptist, Travis, Paw.*	1.000	17	2	13	0	15	1
Barkley, Brian, Paw.*	1.000	3	0	3	0	3	0
Barnett, Marty, Dur.	1.000	16	1	3	0	4	0
Barrios, Manny, Ind.	.955	49	4	17	1	22	3
Batista, Miguel, Ott.	.000	3	0	0	0	0	0
Bautista, Jose, Ott.-Nor.	.966	36	11	17	1	29	2
Beck, Greg, Lou.	.000	1	0	0	0	0	0
Beirne, Kevin, Char.	.950	20	5	14	1	20	0
Belinda, Stan, Ind.	1.000	10	0	1	0	1	0
Beltran, Rigo, Nor.*	1.000	21	1	3	0	4	0
Bennett, Joel, S./W.B.	1.000	20	10	24	0	34	4
Bennett, Shayne, Ott.	1.000	38	7	13	0	20	1
Benz, Jake, Ott.*	.889	18	2	6	1	9	1
Bere, Jason, Ind.-Lou.	.714	10	4	1	2	7	0
Blood, Darin, Roch.	1.000	12	5	7	0	12	1
Bochtler, Doug, Syr.	1.000	14	3	2	0	5	0
Bogott, Kurt, Syr.*	.900	46	5	13	2	20	1
Bolton, Rod, S./W.B.	.917	24	19	14	3	36	1
Borkowski, David, Tol.	.978	19	15	30	1	46	3
Borowski, Joe, Lou.	.917	58	3	8	1	12	2
Bovee, Mike, Syr.	1.000	19	3	1	0	4	0
Bowie, Micah, Rich.*	1.000	13	6	5	0	11	1
Bradford, Chad, Char.	.909	47	5	25	3	33	1
Bradford, Josh, Syr.	.000	1	0	0	0	0	0
Bradley, Ryan, Col.	.875	29	8	13	3	24	1
Brewer, Billy, S./W.B.*	.900	33	2	7	1	10	2
Brooks, Antone, Rich.*	1.000	43	10	11	0	21	2
Brower, Jim, Buf.	.950	27	17	21	2	40	2
Brown, Jamie, Buf.	.000	1	0	0	0	0	0
Brunson, Will, Tol.*	1.000	38	3	4	0	7	0
Buddie, Mike, Col.	1.000	49	6	18	0	24	4
Bullinger, Kirk, Paw.	1.000	35	4	13	0	17	2
Burrows, Terry, Roch.*	.913	17	3	18	2	23	2
Butler, Adam, Rich.*	.667	9	0	2	1	3	0
Cadaret, Greg, Buf.*	1.000	10	1	0	0	1	0
Cairncross, Cameron, Buf.*	.857	19	3	3	1	7	0
Callaway, Mickey, Dur.	.923	15	3	9	1	13	1
Cammack, Eric, Nor.	1.000	9	0	2	0	2	0
Camp, Jared, Buf.	1.000	10	1	0	0	1	0
Carrara, Giovanni, Ind.	1.000	39	17	23	0	40	2
Carroll, Dave, Col.*	.000	1	0	0	1	1	0
Castillo, Carlos, Char.	.909	20	5	15	2	22	0
Cather, Mike, Rich.	.824	45	2	12	3	17	0
Charlton, Norm, Dur.*	1.000	18	1	4	0	5	0
Checo, Robinson, Rich.	1.000	2	0	1	0	1	0
Chen, Bruce, Rich.*	1.000	14	3	6	0	9	0
Cho, Jin Ho, Paw.	1.000	17	6	10	0	16	0
Clark, Howie, Roch.	.000	2	0	0	0	0	0
Converse, Jim, Lou.	.833	30	6	4	2	12	0
Coppinger, Rocky, Roch.	1.000	5	1	1	0	2	0
Corey, Bryan, Tol.	1.000	48	3	11	0	14	1
Corsi, Jim, Roch.	1.000	10	1	2	0	3	0
Cortes, David, Rich.	.833	47	0	5	1	6	1
Croghan, Andy, Syr.	1.000	2	0	1	0	1	0
Cruz, Nelson, Tol.	1.000	10	8	13	0	21	2
Cumberland, Chris, Paw.*	.917	36	1	10	1	12	0
Dale, Carl, Lou.	1.000	7	0	1	0	1	0
D'Amico, Jeff, Lou.	1.000	1	0	1	0	1	0

Player, Team	Pct.	G	PO	A	E	TC	DP
Daneker, Pat, Char.	1.000	9	6	5	0	11	0
Daniels, John, Dur.	1.000	21	2	3	0	5	0
Darden, Tony, Nor.	.000	2	0	0	0	0	0
Davenport, Joe, Char.	1.000	6	1	0	0	1	0
Davey, Tom, Syr.	.875	6	4	3	1	8	2
Davis, Jim, Dur.*	1.000	3	0	1	0	1	0
Dawley, Joey, Rich.	1.000	7	2	5	0	7	0
Dedrick, Jim, Buf.	.778	30	4	3	2	9	1
DeHart, Rick, Ott.*	.875	15	0	7	1	8	0
Delahoya, Javier, Roch.	1.000	14	4	10	0	14	1
Delgado, Ernie, Syr.	.875	14	2	5	1	8	1
De Los Santos, Luis, Col.	.880	12	8	14	3	25	4
DeLucia, Rich, Buf.	1.000	44	1	3	0	4	0
De Paula, Sean, Buf.	.000	5	0	0	0	0	0
DeSilva, John, Ott.	.952	22	7	13	1	21	5
Dimma, Douglas, Syr.*	.000	1	0	0	0	0	0
Dixon, Tim, Ott.-Paw.*	1.000	4	1	0	0	1	0
Dodd, Robert, S./W.B.*	1.000	6	2	3	0	5	1
Donnelly, Brendan, Dur.-Syr.	.900	42	4	5	1	10	1
Dotel, Octavio, Nor.	.882	13	3	12	2	17	1
Dougherty, Tony, Buf.	1.000	16	1	2	0	3	0
Drews, Matt, Tol.	1.000	28	8	9	0	17	0
Driskill, Travis, Buf.	1.000	31	2	9	0	11	0
Drumright, Mike, Tol.	.905	21	13	6	2	21	1
Duran, Roberto, Ott.*	.800	5	1	3	1	5	1
Durocher, Jayson, Ott.	1.000	17	2	7	0	9	0
Duvall, Mike, Dur.*	1.000	19	1	8	0	9	1
Dykhoff, Radhames, Roch.*	.900	47	7	11	2	20	2
Eaton, Adam, S./W.B.	1.000	3	1	0	0	1	0
Ebert, Derrin, Rich.*	1.000	25	3	27	0	30	2
Eiland, Dave, Char.	1.000	10	2	14	0	16	2
Eldred, Cal, Lou.	1.000	4	1	2	0	3	0
Erdos, Todd, Col.	1.000	27	6	1	0	7	0
Estrada, Horacio, Lou.*	1.000	25	7	14	0	21	0
Etler, Todd, Ind.	.875	26	2	5	1	8	0
Evans, Dave, Roch.	1.000	60	1	10	0	11	3
Evans, Keith, Ott.	.977	24	8	34	1	43	1
Eyre, Scott, Char.*	1.000	12	0	10	0	10	1
Falteisek, Steve, Lou.	.957	42	3	19	1	23	1
Farrell, Jim, Paw.	.909	14	2	8	1	11	0
Fernandez, Jared, Paw.	.980	27	6	43	1	50	2
Fesh, Sean, S./W.B.*	1.000	45	5	10	0	15	1
Fetters, Mike, Roch.	.000	4	0	0	0	0	0
Field, Nathan, Ott.	.000	2	0	0	0	0	0
Fiore, Tony, S./W.B.	.833	13	2	3	1	6	1
Fleetham, Ben, Nor.	.500	6	0	1	1	2	0
Flury, Pat, Ind.	1.000	23	4	3	0	7	0
Ford, Ben, Col.	.941	53	2	14	1	17	1
Fordham, Tom, Char.*	.923	29	4	8	1	13	0
Forster, Scott, Ott.*	1.000	53	1	11	0	12	0
Fossas, Tony, Col.*	1.000	26	2	2	0	4	0
Gaillard, Eddie, Dur.	1.000	59	5	7	0	12	0
Garces, Rich, Paw.	1.000	21	1	6	0	7	0
Glauber, Keith, Ind.	1.000	12	4	8	0	12	1
Glover, Gary, Syr.	.850	14	7	10	3	20	0
Goldsmith, Gary, Tol.	1.000	6	0	2	0	2	0
Gonzalez, Dicky, Nor.	1.000	1	1	0	0	1	0
Gooden, Dwight, Buf.	1.000	1	0	0	0	0	0
Grace, Mike, S./W.B.	1.000	10	5	10	0	15	0
Grahe, Joe, S./W.B.	1.000	23	4	8	0	12	1
Granger, Jeff, Lou.*	.800	56	5	11	4	20	2
Graterol, Beiker, Tol.	.913	17	9	12	2	23	1
Green, Tyler, S./W.B.	.800	19	7	9	4	20	1
Greene, Rick, Ind.	1.000	61	6	9	0	15	1
Greisinger, Seth, Ind.	1.000	2	1	0	0	1	1
Gross, Kip, Paw.	1.000	10	0	2	0	2	1
Grzanich, Mike, Tol.	1.000	14	5	4	0	9	3
Guerra, Mark, Nor.	.926	63	9	16	2	27	1
Guthrie, Mark, Paw.*	.000	1	0	0	0	0	0
Hamilton, Jimmy, Buf.-Roch.*	1.000	29	0	2	0	2	0
Hamilton, Joey, Syr.	.800	3	0	4	1	5	0
Haney, Chris, Buf.*	.778	13	0	7	2	9	0
Haney, Todd, Nor.	1.000	1	0	0	0	0	0
Harikkala, Tim, Paw.	1.000	14	2	10	0	12	2
HARRIGER, Denny, Ind.	1.000	27	23	18	0	41	3
Harris, D.J., Syr.	1.000	7	0	3	0	3	0
Harris, Reggie, Lou.	1.000	41	5	2	0	7	0
Harrison, Tommy, Rich.	1.000	49	4	13	0	17	1
Hartmann, Pete, Roch.*	1.000	34	1	2	0	3	0
Hasselhoff, Derek, Char.	1.000	49	4	13	0	17	1
Heathcott, Mike, Char.	.949	32	13	24	2	39	6
Henderson, Rod, Lou.	.931	28	11	16	2	29	2
Henderson, Ryan, Lou.-Nor.	1.000	28	4	4	0	8	0

Player, Team	Pct.	G	PO	A	E	TC	DP
Henriquez, Oscar, Nor.	1.000	53	6	4	0	10	1
Hernandez, Santos, Dur.	1.000	6	0	4	0	4	0
Hiljus, Erik, Tol.	.857	33	3	3	1	7	1
Holbert, Aaron, Dur.	.000	2	0	0	0	0	0
Hosey, Dwayne, Ott.	.000	1	0	0	0	0	0
Hudek, John, Rich.-Syr.	.800	24	1	3	1	5	0
Iglesias, Mike, Rich.	1.000	3	0	1	0	1	0
Isringhausen, Jason, Nor.	1.000	12	4	9	0	13	0
Jacquez, Thomas, S./W.B.*	.000	3	0	0	0	0	0
Janzen, Marty, Ind.	1.000	9	1	0	0	1	0
Johns, Doug, Roch.*	.800	6	4	8	3	15	0
Johnson, Barry, S./W.B.	.962	31	9	16	1	26	2
Johnson, Jason, Roch.	1.000	8	3	7	0	10	0
Johnson, Mike, Ott.	.857	28	15	21	6	42	4
Jones, Bobby, Nor.	1.000	2	2	0	0	2	0
Juden, Jeff, Col.	.951	27	9	30	2	41	2
Kamieniecki, Scott, Roch.	1.000	4	4	5	0	9	0
Keagle, Greg, Tol.	.750	7	1	2	1	4	0
Kida, Masao, Tol.	.000	3	0	0	0	0	0
Kieschnick, Brooks, Dur.	.000	1	0	0	0	0	0
Klingenbeck, Scott, Ind.	.882	14	5	10	2	17	1
Koch, Billy, Syr.	1.000	5	1	3	0	4	0
Langston, Mark, Buf.*	.889	4	2	6	1	9	0
LeBlanc, Eric, Ind.	.867	14	7	6	2	15	0
Levrault, Allen, Lou.	.750	9	2	1	1	4	0
Lewis, Richie, Nor.	.939	20	13	18	2	33	0
Lidle, Cory, Dur.	1.000	3	0	1	0	1	1
Lilly, Ted, Ott.*	1.000	16	3	10	0	13	2
Linton, Doug, Roch.	.840	18	8	13	4	25	1
Lira, Felipe, Tol.	.941	30	13	19	2	34	2
Looney, Brian, Tol.-S./W.B.*	.933	50	7	7	1	15	0
Lopez, Johan, Nor.	.960	33	5	19	1	25	0
Lukasiewicz, Mark, Syr.*	1.000	37	3	10	0	13	0
Lundquist, David, Char.	.000	3	0	0	0	0	0
Lyons, Mike, Nor.	.000	2	0	0	0	0	0
Maduro, Calvin, Roch.	.923	29	11	25	3	39	2
Mahomes, Pat, Nor.	.833	6	2	3	1	6	0
Mahoney, Mike, Rich.	.000	1	0	0	0	0	0
Mann, Jim, Syr.	1.000	47	5	3	0	8	0
Marquez, Robert, Ott.	.667	18	1	3	2	6	0
Martin, Tom, Buf.*	1.000	5	1	2	0	3	0
Martinez, Pablo, Rich.	.000	1	0	0	0	0	0
Martinez, Ramon, Paw.	1.000	2	0	2	0	2	0
Martinez, Romulo, Tol.	1.000	6	0	2	0	2	1
Martinez, Willie, Buf.	.667	4	0	2	1	3	0
Matthews, Mike, Buf.*	.833	25	0	5	1	6	1
McCarthy, Greg, Col.*	1.000	29	5	4	0	9	0
McCarty, Dave, Tol.*	.000	2	0	0	0	0	0
McClellan, Sean, Syr.	.000	8	0	0	1	1	0
McCommon, Jason, Roch.	1.000	29	6	17	0	23	1
McMichael, Greg, Nor.	1.000	3	0	1	0	1	0
Meacham, Rusty, Ind.	1.000	16	2	7	0	9	2
Menhart, Paul, Buf.	1.000	7	2	0	0	2	0
Mercado, Hector, Nor.*	.000	2	0	0	0	0	0
Mercedes, Jose, Nor.	.923	6	4	8	1	13	0
Merrell, Phil, Ind.	1.000	3	1	3	0	4	0
Minor, Blas, Lou.	1.000	21	14	15	0	29	2
Mitchell, Scott, Ott.	1.000	18	5	8	0	13	2
Mix, Greg, Paw.	.750	46	2	13	5	20	1
Molina, Gabe, Roch.	1.000	45	4	9	0	13	1
Montgomery, Steve, S./W.B.	1.000	14	0	2	0	2	0
Moore, Marcus, Syr.	.500	7	1	0	1	2	0
Moraga, David, Ott.*	1.000	4	2	3	0	5	0
Morris, Jim, Dur.*	1.000	18	0	3	0	3	1
Mota, Guillermo, Ott.	1.000	14	0	5	0	5	1
Munoz, Bobby, Dur.	1.000	39	3	9	0	12	0
Munro, Peter, Syr.	.895	18	6	11	2	19	2
Murray, Dan, Nor.	.861	29	10	21	5	36	0
Myers, Jimmy, Nor.-S./W.B.	.857	14	1	5	1	7	0
Naulty, Dan, Col.	1.000	7	1	1	0	2	0
Neagle, Denny, Ind.*	1.000	3	1	0	0	1	0
Nelson, Joe, Rich.	1.000	12	3	5	0	8	0
Neubart, Garrett, Nor.	1.000	2	0	1	0	1	0
Newman, Alan, Dur.*	.846	50	2	9	2	13	0
Nichting, Chris, Col.	.893	25	8	17	3	28	0
Nunez, Maximo, Dur.	1.000	21	2	1	0	3	0
Nye, Ryan, S./W.B.	.941	14	7	9	1	17	0
Ohka, Tomokazu, Paw.	1.000	12	3	7	0	10	2
Olsen, Jason, Char.	1.000	22	4	8	0	12	0
Ontiveros, Steve, Lou.	.941	8	9	7	1	17	0
Ortega, Pablo, Dur.	.000	1	0	0	0	0	0
Palacios, Vicente, Nor.	1.000	7	0	1	0	1	0
Pall, Donn, Ind.	.000	4	0	0	0	0	0
Parker, Christian, Ott.	1.000	7	2	4	0	6	0
Parris, Steve, Ind.	1.000	6	2	4	0	6	0
Passini, Brian, Lou.*	1.000	6	2	3	0	5	0
Pavano, Carl, Ott.	1.000	2	0	1	0	1	0
Pavlas, Dave, Col.	1.000	38	4	8	0	12	0
Pena, Juan, Paw.	.875	10	4	3	1	8	0
Pennington, Brad, Syr.*	1.000	27	2	1	0	3	0
Peterson, Kyle, Lou.	.967	18	7	22	1	30	1
Pina, Rafael, Roch.	.909	48	8	12	2	22	0
Pisciotta, Marc, Rich.	.923	23	2	3	0	5	0
Pittsley, Jim, Lou.	1.000	8	0	2	0	2	0
Plantenberg, Erik, Dur.-Roch.*	1.000	40	4	11	0	15	0
Pontes, Dan, Nor.	1.000	14	2	0	0	2	0
Post, Dave, Ott.	.000	1	0	0	0	0	0
Powell, Jeremy, Ott.	.938	16	7	8	1	16	1
Priest, Eddie, Ind.*	.889	18	3	5	1	9	1
Probst, Alan, Syr.	.000	2	0	0	0	0	0
Pulsipher, Bill, Lou.*	1.000	6	0	5	0	5	1
Quantrill, Paul, Syr.	.000	2	0	0	0	0	0
Quevedo, Ruben, Rich.	.929	21	4	9	1	14	0
Rakers, Jason, Buf.	1.000	23	10	11	0	21	0
Ramirez, Hector, Lou.	1.000	58	5	9	0	14	2
Ramirez, Jose, Tol.*	.000	1	0	0	0	0	0
Ramsay, Robert, Paw.*	.867	20	5	8	2	15	0
Ratliff, Jon, Rich.	.958	27	7	16	1	24	2
Reece, Dana, Syr.*	1.000	1	0	3	0	3	0
Reed, Brandon, Tol.	1.000	44	9	10	0	19	1
Reed, Rick, Nor.	.000	1	0	0	0	0	0
Rekar, Bryan, Dur.	.889	6	3	5	1	9	0
Reyes, Al, Lou.	1.000	6	0	3	0	3	0
Riedling, John, Ind.	1.000	24	5	3	0	8	0
Rigdon, Paul, Buf.	.824	19	10	4	3	17	0
Riske, David, Buf.	1.000	23	2	1	0	3	1
Rizzo, Todd, Char.*	1.000	53	1	13	0	14	1
Roach, Peter, Tol.*	1.000	4	1	0	0	1	1
Roberts, Grant, Nor.	1.000	5	2	2	0	4	0
Roberts, Willis, Tol.	.871	31	11	16	4	31	2
Robertson, Rich, Ind.*	1.000	9	0	1	0	1	0
Rodriguez, Nerio, Syr.	.958	27	3	20	1	24	0
Rogers, Jason, Roch.*	1.000	9	0	2	0	2	0
Rojas, Mel, Ott.	.000	12	0	0	0	0	0
Romano, Mike, Syr.	1.000	29	5	28	0	33	0
Roque, Rafael, Lou.*	.833	2	2	3	1	6	1
Rose, Brian, Paw.	1.000	7	2	3	0	5	0
Ruebel, Matt, Nor.*	1.000	7	0	2	0	2	0
Runyan, Sean, Tol.*	1.000	10	0	2	0	2	0
Ryan, B.J., Ind.-Roch.*	1.000	22	0	3	0	3	0
Ryan, Ken, S./W.B.	.800	31	2	2	1	5	1
Sager, J.D., Ind.	1.000	24	3	9	0	12	1
Salyers, Jeremy, Ott.	1.000	1	1	2	0	3	0
Sanders, Frankie, Buf.	.000	1	0	0	0	0	0
Santana, Marino, Paw.	1.000	25	4	2	0	6	0
Saunders, Tony, Dur.*	1.000	1	0	1	0	1	0
Schrenk, Steve, S./W.B.	.941	32	2	14	1	17	1
Scott, Darryl, S./W.B.	.905	57	7	12	2	21	0
Secoda, Jason, Char.	1.000	7	2	4	0	6	0
Seelbach, Chris, Rich.	1.000	13	1	7	0	8	0
Sekany, Jason, Paw.	1.000	1	1	1	0	2	0
Sexton, Jeff, Buf.	1.000	23	2	4	0	6	0
Shuey, Paul, Buf.	1.000	1	0	1	0	1	0
Shumaker, Anthony, S./W.B.*	.917	14	4	18	2	24	0
Sinclair, Steve, Syr.*	.714	34	2	3	2	7	0
Small, Aaron, Lou.-Dur.	1.000	32	18	14	0	32	1
Small, Mark, Ott.	1.000	42	5	11	0	16	1
Smart, J.D., Ott.	1.000	6	3	1	0	4	0
Smith, Brian, Syr.	.917	29	3	8	1	12	0
Smith, Dan, Ott.	.917	11	2	9	1	12	0
Snyder, John, Char.	1.000	3	2	4	0	6	0
Snyder, Matt, Roch.	.941	48	6	10	1	17	1
Sparks, Jeff, Dur.	1.000	18	3	0	0	3	0
Speier, Justin, Rich.	1.000	27	1	2	0	3	1
Spence, Cam, Col.	.000	1	0	0	0	0	0
Springer, Russ, Rich.	1.000	11	2	0	0	2	0
Stanifer, Rob, Paw.	1.000	31	7	6	0	13	0
Stevens, Dave, Buf.	1.000	20	0	2	0	2	0
Stevenson, Jason, Syr.	.889	7	4	4	1	9	0
Stevenson, Rod, Ott.	1.000	17	1	3	0	4	0
Stewart, Scott, Nor.*	.944	35	4	13	1	18	0
Strickland, Scott, Ott.	.833	19	2	3	1	6	0
Strong, Joe, Dur.	1.000	6	1	1	0	2	0
Stull, Everett, Rich.	1.000	30	7	16	0	23	0
Sturtze, Tanyon, Char.	.950	33	12	7	1	20	0
Tam, Jeff, Nor.-Buf.	.909	32	4	6	1	11	0

Player, Team	Pct.	G	PO	A	E	TC	DP
Tatis, Ramon, Dur.*	.929	28	8	18	2	28	1
Telgheder, Dave, Buf.	.941	29	5	11	1	17	0
Tessmer, Jay, Col.	1.000	51	5	14	0	19	1
Therneau, Dave, Ind.	1.000	7	4	3	0	7	1
Thompson, Mark, Ind.	1.000	11	6	10	0	16	0
Tolar, Kevin, Ind.*	.000	8	0	0	0	0	0
Tomberlin, Andy, Nor.*	.000	1	0	0	0	0	0
Tomko, Brett, Ind.	1.000	2	1	4	0	5	0
Treadwell, Jody, Nor.	.857	11	3	3	1	7	0
Turrentine, Rich, Nor.	.000	2	0	0	0	0	0
Urso, Sal, Paw.*	1.000	4	0	2	0	2	0
Valdes, Marc, Dur.	1.000	9	5	11	0	16	0
VanEgmond, Tim, Lou.	.875	8	2	5	1	8	1
VanRyn, Ben, Char.*	1.000	47	7	5	0	12	1
Vazquez, Javier, Ott.	1.000	7	1	12	0	13	1
Villano, Mike, Nor.	.000	2	0	0	0	0	0
Villegas, Ismael, Rich.	1.000	44	8	13	0	21	1
Villone, Ron, Ind.*	1.000	18	1	3	0	4	0
Virchis, Adam, Char.	1.000	3	1	1	0	2	0
Wade, Terrell, Dur.*	1.000	34	1	7	0	8	1
Wagner, Paul, Buf.	.963	23	12	14	1	27	0
Walker, Mike, Buf.	1.000	29	2	5	0	7	1
Wallace, Derek, Buf.	.923	36	3	9	1	13	1
Ward, Bryan, Char.*	.857	14	1	5	1	7	2
Wasdin, John, Paw.	1.000	5	1	4	0	5	0
Watson, Allen, Col.*	1.000	2	0	1	0	1	0
Welch, Mike, S./W.B.-Nor.	1.000	37	1	7	0	8	1
Wengert, Don, Col.-Rich.	1.000	7	2	5	0	7	0
Wheeler, Dan, Dur.	1.000	14	8	5	0	13	0
Williams, Matt, Col.*	1.000	13	3	3	0	6	1
Williams, Shad, S./W.B.	1.000	2	0	1	0	1	0
Williams, Todd, Ind.	1.000	38	1	16	0	17	3
Willoughby, Justin, Rich.*	.000	1	0	0	0	0	0
Wilson, Trevor, Col.*	.778	19	3	4	2	9	0
Wohlers, Mark, Ind.	.000	1	0	0	0	0	0
Wolcott, Bob, Paw.	.906	26	8	21	3	32	3
Wolf, Randy, S./W.B.*	.882	12	8	7	2	17	0
Wright, Jaret, Buf.	.000	1	0	0	0	0	0
Wunsch, Kelly, Lou.*	1.000	16	2	6	0	8	1
Yarnall, Ed, Col.*	1.000	23	7	23	0	30	0
Yennaco, Jay, Syr.	1.000	15	7	6	0	13	2
Zancanaro, Dave, Col.*	.923	13	1	11	1	13	0
Zuber, Jon, S./W.B.*	1.000	1	1	0	0	1	0

TRIPLE PLAY: Vazquez.

PITCHERS WITH TWO OR MORE TEAMS

Player, Team	Pct.	G	PO	A	E	TC	DP
Bautista, Jose, Ott.	1.000	16	2	6	0	8	0
Bautista, Jose, Nor.	.952	20	9	11	1	21	2
Bere, Jason, Ind.	.750	5	3	0	1	4	0
Bere, Jason, Lou.	.667	5	1	1	1	3	0
Dixon, Tim, Ott.*	.000	2	0	0	0	0	0
Dixon, Tim, Paw.*	1.000	2	1	0	0	1	0
Donnelly, Brendan, Dur.	1.000	37	2	3	0	5	1
Donnelly, Brendan, Syr.	.800	5	2	2	1	5	0
Hamilton, Jimmy, Buf.*	1.000	26	0	2	0	2	0
Hamilton, Jimmy, Roch.*	.000	3	0	0	0	0	0
Henderson, Ryan, Lou.	1.000	21	3	2	0	5	0
Henderson, Ryan, Nor.	1.000	7	1	2	0	3	0
Hudek, John, Rich.	.000	12	0	0	0	0	0
Hudek, John, Syr.	.800	12	1	3	1	5	0
Looney, Brian, Tol.*	.917	47	5	6	1	12	0
Looney, Brian, S./W.B.*	1.000	3	2	1	0	3	0
Myers, Jimmy, Nor.	.667	3	0	2	1	3	0
Myers, Jimmy, S./W.B.	1.000	11	1	3	0	4	0
Plantenberg, Erik, Roch.*	1.000	17	0	5	0	5	0
Plantenberg, Erik, Dur.*	1.000	23	4	6	0	10	0
Ryan, B.J., Ind.*	.000	11	0	0	0	0	0
Ryan, B.J., Roch.*	1.000	11	0	3	0	3	0
Small, Aaron, Lou.	1.000	11	2	5	0	7	1
Small, Aaron, Dur.	1.000	21	16	9	0	25	0
Tam, Jeff, Nor.	1.000	16	1	3	0	4	0
Tam, Jeff, Buf.	.857	16	3	3	1	7	0
Welch, Mike, Nor.	1.000	24	1	4	0	5	0
Welch, Mike, S./W.B.	1.000	13	0	3	0	3	1
Wengert, Don, Col.	1.000	6	2	4	0	6	0
Wengert, Don, Rich.	1.000	1	0	1	0	1	0

The following players appeared only as designated hitter, pinch-hitter or pinch runner: Bonilla, dh; Jefferires, dh; Malave, dh-ph.

LEAGUE CHAMPIONS

Year	Team	Pct.
1884—	Trenton	.520
1885—	Syracuse	.584
1886—	Utica	.646
1887—	Toronto	.644
1888—	Syracuse	.723
1889—	Detroit	.649
1890—	Detroit	.617
1891—	Buffalo (reg. season)	.727
	Buffalo (supplemental)	.680
1892—	Providence	.615
	Binghamton*	.667
1893—	Erie	.606
1894—	Providence	.696
1895—	Springfield	.687
1896—	Providence	.602
1897—	Syracuse	.632
1898—	Montreal	.586
1899—	Rochester	.624
1900—	Providence	.616
1901—	Rochester	.642
1902—	Toronto	.669
1903—	Jersey City	.742
1904—	Buffalo	.657
1905—	Providence	.638
1906—	Buffalo	.607
1907—	Toronto	.619
1908—	Baltimore	.593
1909—	Rochester	.596
1910—	Rochester	.601
1911—	Rochester	.645
1912—	Toronto	.595
1913—	Newark	.625
1914—	Providence	.617
1915—	Buffalo	.632
1916—	Buffalo	.586
1917—	Toronto	.604
1918—	Toronto	.693
1919—	Baltimore	.671
1920—	Baltimore	.719
1921—	Baltimore	.717
1922—	Baltimore	.689
1923—	Baltimore	.677
1924—	Baltimore	.709
1925—	Baltimore	.633
1926—	Toronto	.657
1927—	Buffalo	.667
1928—	Rochester	.549
1929—	Rochester	.613
1930—	Rochester	.629
1931—	Rochester	.601
1932—	Newark	.649
1933—	Newark	.622
	Buffalo (4th)†	.494
1934—	Newark	.608
	Toronto (3rd)†	.559
1935—	Montreal	.597
	Syracuse (2nd)†	.565
1936—	Buffalo‡	.610
1937—	Newark‡	.717
1938—	Newark‡	.684
1939—	Jersey City	.582
	Rochester (2nd)†	.556
1940—	Rochester	.611
	Newark (2nd)†	.594
1941—	Newark	.649
	Montreal (2nd)†	.584
1942—	Newark	.601
	Syracuse (3rd)†	.513
1943—	Toronto	.625
	Syracuse (3rd)†	.536
1944—	Baltimore‡	.553
1945—	Montreal	.621
	Newark (2nd)†	.582
1946—	Montreal‡	.649
1947—	Jersey City	.610
	Syracuse (3rd)†	.575
1948—	Montreal‡	.614
1949—	Buffalo	.584
	Montreal (3rd)†	.545
1950—	Rochester	.609
	Baltimore (3rd)†	.556
1951—	Montreal‡	.617
1952—	Montreal	.629
	Rochester (3rd)†	.619
1953—	Rochester	.630
	Montreal (2nd)†	.586
1954—	Toronto	.630
	Syracuse (4th)§	.510
1955—	Montreal	.617
	Rochester (4th)†	.497
1956—	Toronto	.566
	Rochester (2nd)†	.553
1957—	Toronto	.575
	Buffalo (2nd)†	.571
1958—	Montreal‡	.588
1959—	Buffalo	.582
	Havana (3rd)†	.523
1960—	Toronto‡	.649
1961—	Columbus	.597
	Buffalo (3rd)†	.559
1962—	Jacksonville	.610
	Atlanta (3rd)†	.539
1963—	Syracuse∞	.533
	Indianapolis‡	.562
1964—	Jacksonville	.589
	Rochester (4th)†	.532
1965—	Columbus	.582
	Toronto (3rd)†	.556
1966—	Rochester	.565
	Toronto (2nd-tied)†	.558
1967—	Richmond	.574

CLASS AAA International League

Year	Team	Pct.	Year	Team	Pct.	Year	Team	Pct.
	Toledo (3rd)†	.525	1979—	Columbus‡	.612	1991—	Columbus♦	.590
1968—	Toledo	.565	1980—	Columbus‡	.593		Pawtucket	.552
	Jacksonville (4th)†	.514	1981—	Columbus‡	.633	1992—	Columbus♦	.660
1969—	Tidewater	.563	1982—	Richmond	.590		Scr. W.B.	.592
	Syracuse (3rd)†	.536		Tidewater (3rd)†	.540	1993—	Charlotte♦	.610
1970—	Syracuse‡	.600	1983—	Columbus	.593		Rochester	.525
1971—	Rochester‡	.614		Tidewater (4th)†	.511	1994—	Richmond♦	.567
1972—	Louisville	.563	1984—	Columbus	.590		Pawtucket	.549
	Tidewater (3rd)†	.545		Pawtucket (4th)†	.536	1995—	Norfolk	.606
1973—	Charleston	.586	1985—	Syracuse	.564		Ottawa♦	.507
	Pawtuckets†	.534		Tidewater (4th)†	.540	1996—	Columbus♦	.599
1974—	Memphis	.613	1986—	Richmond‡	.571		Rochester	.511
	Rochester ∞‡	.611	1987—	Tidewater	.579	1997—	Rochester♦	.589
1975—	Tidewater‡	.610		Columbus†	.550		Columbus	.556
1976—	Rochester	.638	1988—	Rochester♦	.546	1998—	Buffalo■	.566
	Syracuse (2nd)†	.590		Tidewater	.546	1999—	Columbus	.589
1977—	Pawtucket	.571	1989—	Syracuse	.572		Charlotte▲	.569
	Charleston (2nd)‡	.557		Richmond♦	.555			
1978—	Charleston	.607	1990—	Rochester♦	.614			
	Richmond (4th)†	.511		Columbus	.596			

*Won split-season playoff. †Won four-team playoff. ‡Won championship and four-team playoff. §Defeated Havana in game to decide fourth place, then won four-team playoff. ∞League was divided into Northern, Southern divisions. ♦League divided into Eastern, Western divisions; won playoffs. ■League divided into Eastern, Northern and Southern divisions; won four-team playoff. ▲League divided into North, South and West divisions; won four-team playoff. (NOTE—Known as Eastern League in 1884, New York State League in 1885, International League in 1886-87, International Association in 1888, International League in 1889-90, Eastern Association in 1891 and Eastern League from 1892 until 1912.)

CLASS AAA *International League*

MEXICAN LEAGUE

1999 FINAL STANDINGS

FIRST HALF

NORTHERN ZONE

Team	W	L	T	Pct.	GB
Monclova	38	23	1	.623	....
Saltillo	38	24	0	.613	0.5
Monterrey	32	29	1	.525	6.0
Torreon	28	33	1	.459	10.0
Nuevo Laredo	24	37	1	.393	14.0
Reynosa	23	37	2	.383	14.5

CENTRAL ZONE

Team	W	L	T	Pct.	GB
Mexico City Tigers	43	18	1	.700	....
Mexico City Reds	36	25	0	.590	6.5
Cordoba	26	34	1	.433	16.0
Aguascalientes	26	35	1	.426	16.5
Oaxaca	24	38	0	.387	19.0

SOUTHERN ZONE

Team	W	L	T	Pct.	GB
Campeche	33	28	1	.541	....
Tabasco	33	28	1	.541	....
Yucatan	30	31	1	.492	3.0
Cancun	29	32	0	.475	4.0
Veracruz	26	36	0	.419	7.5

SECOND HALF

NORTHERN ZONE

Team	W	L	T	Pct.	GB
Saltillo	36	21	0	.632	....
Monclova	33	23	1	.589	2.5
Monterrey	32	25	0	.561	4.0
Nuevo Laredo	29	28	0	.509	7.0
Torreon	22	36	0	.379	14.5
Reynosa	19	38	1	.333	17.0

CENTRAL ZONE

Team	W	L	T	Pct.	GB
Mexico City Reds	38	18	0	.679	....
Mexico City Tigers	33	20	1	.623	3.5
Cordoba	25	32	0	.439	13.5
Oaxaca	25	22	0	.439	13.5
Aguascalientes	21	39	0	.350	19.0

SOUTHERN ZONE

Team	W	L	T	Pct.	GB
Cancun	34	25	1	.576	....
Yucatan	30	25	1	.545	2.0
Tabasco	30	29	0	.508	4.0
Campeche	25	32	0	.439	8.0
Veracruz	24	33	1	.421	9.0

COMPOSITE

NORTHERN ZONE

Team	W	L	T	Pct.	GB
Saltillo	74	45	0	.622	....
Monclova	71	46	2	.607	1.0
Monterrey	64	54	1	.542	9.5
Nuevo Laredo	53	65	1	.449	20.5
Torreon	50	69	1	.420	24.0
Reynosa	42	75	3	.359	31.0

CENTRAL ZONE

Team	W	L	T	Pct.	GB
Mexico City Tigers	75	38	2	.664	....
Mexico City Reds	74	43	0	.632	3.0
Cordoba	51	66	1	.436	26.0
Oaxaca	49	70	0	.412	29.0
Aguascalientes	47	74	1	.388	33.0

SOUTHERN ZONE

Team	W	L	T	Pct.	GB
Cancun	63	57	1	.525	....
Tabasco	63	57	1	.525	....
Yucatan	60	56	2	.517	1.0
Campeche	58	60	1	.492	4.0
Veracruz	50	69	1	.420	12.5

PLAYOFFS—Mexico City Tigers defeated Tabasco, four games to three; Monclova defeated Cancun, four games to none; Mexico City Reds defeated Monterrey, four games to one; Saltillo defeated Campeche, four games to two, in the first round; Mexico City Reds defeated Saltillo, four games to three; Mexico City Tigers defeated Monclova, four games to two, in the second round; Mexico City Reds defeated Mexico City Tigers, four games to two, in final series to capture league championship.

(Compiled by Ana Luisa Perea Talarico, League Statistician, Mexico, D.F.)

1999 BATTING

TEAM

Team	Avg.	G	TPA	AB	R	H	TB	2B	3B	HR	RBI	SH	SF	HP	BB	IBB	SO	SB	CS	GDP	LOB	ShO	Slg.	OBP
M.C. Tigers	.315	115	4620	3931	772	1240	1816	188	44	100	722	52	56	44	537	42	564	90	54	123	911	3	.462	.399
M.C. Reds	.306	117	4706	4083	735	1250	1864	210	19	122	691	22	42	44	515	38	523	70	33	148	920	4	.457	.386
Monterrey	.301	119	4722	4073	621	1226	1641	205	18	58	569	64	42	45	498	40	488	83	58	116	963	8	.403	.380
Saltillo	.294	119	4726	4016	629	1180	1611	162	28	71	569	74	33	27	576	58	537	60	53	130	1003	3	.401	.383
Torreon	.293	120	4689	3990	573	1170	1583	185	16	64	527	79	40	41	539	20	550	68	42	147	989	7	.397	.380
Oaxaca	.290	119	4691	3958	608	1149	1607	199	26	69	562	66	35	42	590	33	471	62	34	149	985	9	.406	.385
Monclova	.266	119	4721	3950	667	1139	1710	188	28	109	620	76	46	38	611	42	581	95	49	118	970	8	.433	.385
Aguascalientes	.264	122	4521	3875	632	1100	1595	167	41	82	568	47	39	48	512	19	507	65	64	142	831	10	.412	.371
Yucatan	.272	118	4492	3816	519	1037	1369	130	38	42	449	95	23	30	437	60	55	90	927	9	.359	.363
Nuevo Laredo	.272	119	4635	3940	525	1070	1451	144	15	69	458	79	29	63	524	26	475	28	35	147	976	8	.368	.364
Tabasco	.266	121	4541	3970	450	1056	1364	159	13	41	408	76	39	44	412	30	417	45	49	125	925	9	.344	.339
Reynosa	.284	120	4651	3995	513	1135	1435	147	17	67	466	95	31	48	482	34	599	40	39	129	921	7	.359	.347
Veracruz	.262	120	4427	3846	438	1006	1346	124	6	68	399	72	26	33	450	30	462	69	64	91	878	10	.350	.342
Cordoba	.260	118	4372	3781	492	982	1379	147	14	74	441	79	22	57	433	29	617	89	45	90	868	13	.365	.343
Campeche	.259	119	4427	3859	436	1000	1319	157	24	38	392	87	24	32	425	51	464	56	45	131	881	11	.342	.336
Cancun	.257	121	4401	3822	476	981	1349	147	22	59	415	73	36	45	425	28	500	50	38	113	848	7	.353	.335

CLASS AAA *Mexican League*

TOP QUALIFIERS FOR BATTING CHAMPIONSHIP

Minimum 329 plate appearances.

Player, Team	Avg.	G	TPA	AB	R	H	TB	2B	3B	HR	RBI	SH	SF	HP	BB	IBB	SO	SB	CS	GDP	Slg.	OBP
Franco, Julio, Tig.	.423	93	414	326	90	138	214	22	6	14	77	0	2	6	80	13	44	9	1	22	.656	.541
Carrillo, Garcia, Tig.	.416	112	502	421	107	175	266	27	2	20	98	3	4	3	71	7	31	3	0	7	.632	.499
Garcia, Cornelio, Tor.	.349	105	491	390	62	136	167	22	3	1	41	5	3	4	89	1	48	25	11	14	.428	.471
Rodriguez, Boi, Monc.	.342	118	550	459	99	157	278	33	5	26	105	0	7	2	82	15	81	43	15	11	.606	.438
Barron, Tony, Mex.	.341	101	438	369	67	126	189	22	1	13	83	0	4	7	58	4	45	3	3	20	.512	.436
Gainey, Ty, Sal.	.339	97	416	319	73	108	196	17	1	23	78	0	2	3	92	15	63	3	3	8	.614	.488
Gonzalez, Jesus, Tor.	.338	112	501	432	90	146	261	36	2	25	92	0	2	4	63	6	59	6	2	19	.604	.425
Gastelum, Sergio, Tig.	.337	106	491	415	92	140	180	16	3	6	61	8	2	5	61	0	28	12	10	9	.434	.427
Castellano, Pedro, Mex.	.336	115	532	455	92	153	251	28	2	22	99	0	9	7	61	4	66	4	3	17	.552	.415
Sherman, Darrell, Monc.	.336	109	523	396	93	133	174	23	3	4	41	5	4	2	116	6	35	20	13	7	.439	.485
Bullett, Scott, Cam.	.336	87	349	295	43	99	126	14	2	3	34	2	3	2	47	16	39	18	10	8	.427	.427
Munoz, Jose, Sal.	.335	93	438	358	74	120	162	11	11	3	29	6	0	1	73	9	40	20	17	4	.453	.449
Vizcarra, Roberto, Ags.-Tig.	.334	92	417	353	77	118	167	19	0	10	46	8	4	4	48	1	24	11	8	7	.473	.416
Romero, Wilfredo, Tig.-Sal.	.333	115	544	475	110	158	229	18	10	11	81	2	7	2	58	3	62	27	11	16	.482	.402
Garcia, Hector, Mont.	.328	94	425	378	67	124	157	18	0	5	35	10	2	2	33	2	26	8	5	6	.415	.383

DEPARTMENTAL LEADERS: G—Garzon, Peguero, Tellez, 120; AB—Espinosa, 509; R—W. Romero, 110; H—Carrillo, 175; TB—B. Rodriguez, 278; 2B—J. Gonzalez, 36; 3B—J. Munoz 11; HR—Meggers, 28; RBI—B. Rodriguez, 105; SH—J. Pacho, 26; SF—Castellano, G. Martinez, Salas, 9; HP—R. Zambrano, 21; BB—Sherman, 116; IBB—Bullett, 16; SO—Chance, 107; SB—B. Rodriguez, 43; CS—L. Arredondo, 18; GIDP—F. Rodriguez, 24; Slg—J. Franco, .656; OBP—J. Franco, .541.

ALL PLAYERS

Player, Team	Avg.	G	TPA	AB	R	H	TB	2B	3B	HR	RBI	SH	SF	HP	BB	IBB	SO	SB	CS	GDP	Slg.	OBP
Abrego, Jesus, Rey.	.245	97	392	306	35	75	91	8	1	2	23	14	2	9	61	4	38	1	4	9	.297	.384
Acuna, Jose, Tor.	.255	56	182	153	11	39	45	4	1	0	13	10	2	1	16	0	26	2	3	4	.294	.326
Aganza, Ruben, Monc.	.266	109	465	403	58	107	163	20	0	12	67	3	4	8	47	4	49	0	1	15	.404	.351
Aguilera, Antonio, Mont.	.302	86	310	248	53	75	100	11	1	4	25	4	2	4	52	3	36	4	5	2	.403	.428
Aguilera, Armando, Sal.	.191	50	102	89	11	17	21	4	0	0	3	1	1	1	10	1	15	1	1	6	.236	.277
Almeida, Shamar, Oax.	.285	80	210	158	30	45	66	9	0	4	21	1	1	5	45	0	25	1	1	4	.418	.455
Alvarez, Hector, Oax.	.324	100	482	404	65	131	161	17	2	3	41	5	4	3	66	1	65	6	10	6	.399	.419
Alvarez, Jorge, Cor.	.306	118	502	454	73	139	224	34	0	17	73	1	3	2	42	4	61	11	2	13	.493	.365
Amezcua, Adan, Rey.	.247	46	177	150	21	37	61	9	0	5	18	2	1	3	21	0	19	3	2	9	.407	.349
Arano, Eloy, Cor.	.238	88	359	323	31	77	87	6	2	0	28	6	1	3	26	2	29	9	5	9	.269	.300
Arano, Marco, Tab.	.195	17	45	41	4	8	9	1	0	0	2	2	1	0	1	0	8	1	0	0	.220	.209
Arano, Wilfredo, Lar.	.324	117	468	383	52	124	156	17	3	3	51	3	5	9	68	11	27	7	7	12	.407	.432
Arauz, Leobardo, Yuc.	.309	101	386	327	51	101	138	15	5	4	36	6	4	3	46	5	37	1	3	7	.422	.395
Arias, Francisco, Sal.	.252	70	191	151	27	38	44	6	0	0	17	9	1	2	28	0	27	3	2	3	.291	.374
Armenta, Cristhian, Lar.	.274	32	107	95	14	26	28	2	0	0	8	0	2	3	7	0	20	1	0	4	.295	.336
Armenta, Guillermo, Ver.	.305	82	341	282	43	86	97	11	0	0	30	10	0	3	46	0	27	13	12	8	.344	.408
Arredondo, Hernando, Can.	.246	52	128	118	12	29	35	3	0	1	15	0	2	2	6	0	14	2	0	5	.297	.289
Arredondo, Jesus, Agua.	.257	69	269	206	42	53	60	5	1	0	30	3	3	11	46	1	22	6	4	10	.291	.414
Arredondo, Luis, Yuc.	.327	114	526	462	71	151	186	15	7	2	50	8	4	4	48	6	35	20	18	6	.403	.392
Arvizu, Javier, Tor.-Tab.	.261	84	277	218	35	57	87	12	0	6	36	4	6	0	49	4	39	1	0	8	.399	.388
Avila, Ruben, Agua.	.271	94	325	280	32	76	113	12	2	7	45	4	3	1	37	2	38	0	2	12	.404	.353
Azocar, Oscar, Ver.	.263	118	500	463	58	122	170	9	0	13	60	0	5	4	28	6	15	4	2	17	.367	.308
Barrera, Nelson, Oax.	.275	102	396	346	48	95	156	16	0	15	64	1	2	5	42	4	53	4	1	16	.451	.359
Barron, Tony, Mex.	.341	101	438	369	67	126	189	22	1	13	83	0	4	7	58	4	45	3	3	20	.512	.436
Bell, Juan, Cor.	.307	114	487	420	67	129	181	23	7	5	63	3	0	3	61	7	63	20	5	5	.431	.399
Beltran, Juan, Cam.	.212	35	77	66	8	14	15	1	0	0	4	0	0	7	0	0	7	0	0	1	.227	.288
Berry, Mike, Ver.	.222	8	32	27	1	6	8	2	0	0	6	0	0	0	5	0	4	0	0	0	.296	.344
Bethea, Larry, Cor.	.285	73	294	256	40	73	123	14	0	12	36	1	0	8	29	3	80	12	6	5	.480	.375
Bojorquez, Victor, Mex.	.280	117	503	468	70	131	186	18	5	9	58	4	4	7	20	0	48	11	5	17	.397	.317
Bolado, Carlos, Ver.	.233	33	52	43	4	10	11	1	0	0	2	0	0	1	8	0	11	1	0	1	.256	.365
Brena, Jaime, Oax.	.207	14	35	29	3	6	6	0	0	0	1	1	0	1	4	0	1	1	1	2	.207	.324
Brown, Ray, Tab.	.299	104	436	355	58	106	147	21	1	6	54	0	7	5	69	8	28	4	5	8	.414	.413
Bruno, Julio, Tab.	.338	74	309	287	32	97	134	19	0	6	54	1	2	3	16	2	24	3	1	14	.467	.377
Bullett, Scott, Cam.	.336	87	349	295	43	99	126	14	2	3	34	2	3	2	47	16	39	18	10	8	.427	.427
Bustamante, Omar, Sal.-Lar.	.222	13	30	27	2	6	9	0	0	1	2	1	0	1	1	0	5	0	0	0	.333	.276
Bustillos, Luis, Rey.	.230	119	478	421	38	97	111	10	2	0	30	22	2	3	30	0	74	5	11	10	.264	.285
Camacho, Reginaldo, Rey.	.149	51	143	134	5	20	22	2	0	0	4	2	1	1	5	0	24	0	1	5	.164	.184
Canale, George, Yuc.	.222	9	42	36	6	8	10	2	0	0	5	0	0	0	6	0	5	1	0	0	.278	.333
Canizalez, Juan, Mont.	.296	106	442	392	43	116	149	22	1	3	50	3	2	2	43	4	41	5	4	13	.380	.367
Canseco, Ozzie, Mont.-Tab.	.297	48	202	158	20	47	77	7	1	7	38	0	2	2	40	3	42	2	1	4	.487	.441
Carrasco, Ernesto, Lar.	.259	109	421	367	55	95	121	15	1	3	24	9	0	2	43	4	47	3	0	4	.330	.340
Carrillo, Garcia, Tig.	.416	112	502	421	107	175	266	27	2	20	98	3	4	3	71	7	31	3	0	7	.632	.499
Carter, Michael, Tor.-Ver.	.313	64	270	243	38	76	96	10	2	2	22	4	1	3	19	2	16	17	4	7	.395	.368
Castaneda, Hector, Cor.-Yuc.	.295	102	390	312	51	92	131	9	3	8	45	4	1	2	71	6	46	2	1	16	.420	.427
Castaneda, Rafael, Oax.	.271	117	475	410	48	111	165	20	5	8	68	6	4	0	55	1	21	8	7	23	.402	.354
Castellano, Pedro, Mex.	.336	115	532	455	92	153	251	28	2	22	99	0	9	7	61	4	66	4	3	17	.552	.415
Castro, Arnoldo, Can.	.269	119	513	443	54	119	146	13	1	4	45	12	5	1	52	1	35	5	1	10	.330	.343
Castro, Carlos, Tab.	.190	42	131	126	8	24	29	2	0	1	4	2	1	1	0	1	21	1	4	5	.230	.202
Cazarin, Manuel, Can.-Cam.	.269	111	433	379	41	102	141	18	0	7	44	8	2	3	41	3	23	1	3	19	.372	.344
Cervantes, Ivan, Mex.	.248	45	112	101	22	25	37	6	0	2	19	2	0	1	8	0	16	2	0	4	.366	.309
Cervantes, Regugio, Lar.-Sal.	.333	35	52	48	6	16	20	1	0	1	10	0	0	0	4	2	6	0	0	3	.417	.385
Cervera, Francisco, Cam.	.242	112	437	363	46	88	131	18	2	7	47	5	1	7	61	5	61	7	6	15	.361	.361
Chan, Armando, Monc.-Cam.	.154	32	61	52	3	8	8	0	0	0	5	0	1	1	6	1	10	1	0	2	.154	.279
Chance, Tony, Monc.-Tab.	.249	111	489	406	60	101	181	16	3	20	81	5	5	2	71	2	107	4	4	12	.446	.360
Chimelis, Joel, Lar.	.315	115	497	447	72	141	220	22	3	17	80	3	3	7	31	1	34	0	3	18	.492	.367
Choi, Hwan, Tor.	.253	24	108	91	13	23	26	3	0	0	8	2	1	1	13	1	9	1	1	1	.286	.349
Claudio, Patricio, Tab.-Can.	.254	101	436	382	53	97	117	10	2	2	45	6	5	0	43	6	60	16	14	5	.306	.326
Cobos, Rogelio, Cam.	.236	64	238	212	24	50	72	5	3	3	20	4	2	1	19	2	49	0	0	5	.340	.299

Player, Team	Avg.	G	TPA	AB	R	H	TB	2B	3B	HR	RBI	SH	SF	HP	BB	IBB	SO	SB	CS	GDP	Slg.	OBP
Contreras, Jose, Rey.	.130	13	27	23	2	3	3	0	0	0	0	1	0	1	2	0	4	1	0	1	.130	.231
Cruz, Antonio, Lar.-Agua.	.255	75	255	212	27	54	75	9	0	4	32	6	2	7	28	0	22	0	1	9	.354	.357
Cruz, Fausto, Yuc.	.301	67	301	256	38	77	113	15	3	5	33	3	3	2	37	0	27	4	4	4	.441	.389
Cruz, Luis, Rey.	.229	19	54	48	3	11	11	0	0	0	3	3	0	0	3	1	10	0	0	1	.229	.275
Cuevas, Jorge, Agua.	.103	28	49	39	8	4	8	1	0	1	4	2	0	1	7	0	19	0	1	2	.205	.255
De la Cruz, Hector, Ver.-Yuc.	.268	21	83	71	8	19	24	3	1	0	6	0	2	0	10	1	6	4	2	6	.338	.349
De la Torre, Francisco, Oax.	.143	7	16	14	2	2	2	0	0	0	2	0	0	0	2	0	3	0	0	1	.143	.250
De Lima, Rafael, Agua.	.298	89	398	322	62	96	130	16	6	2	36	5	2	3	66	2	45	13	9	6	.404	.420
Diaz, Luis, Agua.-Tor.	.242	63	228	186	32	45	73	8	1	6	22	3	2	0	37	2	47	2	1	4	.392	.364
Diaz, Pedro, Agua.	.267	40	129	120	16	32	42	5	1	1	11	0	0	1	8	0	19	0	1	5	.350	.318
Diaz, Remigio, Mont.	.250	70	265	232	33	58	75	9	1	2	24	7	3	2	21	2	15	9	4	6	.323	.314
Dominguez, David, Can.-Lar.	.222	79	307	266	25	59	85	10	2	4	25	1	1	0	39	2	53	2	0	12	.320	.320
Duran, Felipe, Oax.-Ver.	.220	43	130	118	10	26	36	4	0	2	15	4	2	2	4	0	12	0	1	2	.305	.254
Escalante, Marclo, Can.	.263	38	88	76	7	20	20	0	0	0	4	3	0	0	9	0	15	0	0	4	.263	.341
Espino, Daniel, Mont.	.319	75	259	229	29	73	96	11	3	2	53	3	2	6	19	1	26	8	4	12	.419	.383
Espino, Omar, Lar.	.205	77	206	166	11	34	47	4	0	3	17	5	3	5	27	1	32	3	2	8	.283	.328
Espinosa, Ramon, Rey.	.322	119	547	509	79	164	222	19	6	9	62	8	3	4	23	4	33	10	7	22	.436	.354
Espinosa, Cutberto, Rey.	.000	5	3	1	1	0	0	0	0	0	0	0	0	0	2	0	0	0	0	1	.000	.667
Espinosa, Javier, Can.	.200	10	23	20	1	4	5	1	0	0	3	0	0	0	3	0	4	0	1	0	.250	.304
Espinoza, Jose, Lar.	.286	62	280	241	27	69	85	10	0	2	23	5	2	1	31	1	21	3	6	3	.353	.367
Espinoza, Ramon, Tor.	.176	24	36	34	2	6	7	1	0	0	2	0	0	1	1	0	15	0	0	1	.206	.222
Esquer, Ramon, Oax.-Mex.	.315	89	398	327	56	103	125	12	2	2	35	9	3	1	58	1	25	6	5	17	.382	.416
Estrada, Hector, Monc.	.205	102	403	347	46	71	121	7	2	13	48	2	3	9	42	7	53	0	0	10	.349	.304
Estrada, Ricardo, Can.	.212	52	119	104	8	22	26	4	0	0	6	2	1	1	11	0	27	1	0	1	.250	.291
Estrella, Isaac, Lar.	.250	12	41	32	6	8	12	1	0	1	3	1	0	0	8	0	10	1	1	1	.375	.400
Felix, Jesus, Yuc.-Rey.	.122	27	58	49	3	6	6	0	0	0	2	1	0	6	0	7	0	1	1	.122	.214
Felix, Lauro, Rey.	.240	102	433	337	60	81	108	14	2	3	26	8	3	1	84	0	81	6	3	5	.320	.391
Fentanes, Oscar, Tab.	.274	117	477	416	49	114	149	19	2	4	48	6	7	8	40	4	41	2	3	13	.358	.344
Fernandez, Daniel, Mex.	.320	81	385	331	66	106	121	13	1	0	24	1	1	3	49	2	25	14	5	3	.366	.411
Figueroa, Antonio, Cor.	.167	26	60	54	5	9	9	0	0	0	5	2	1	1	2	0	6	1	1	1	.167	.207
Figueroa, Jesus, Oax.	.190	26	59	51	2	10	12	2	0	0	2	2	0	0	6	0	16	0	0	3	.235	.281
Fink, Marc, Cor.	.300	9	35	30	3	9	15	0	0	2	4	0	0	0	5	2	8	0	0	1	.500	.400
Flores, Miguel, Mont.	.314	103	471	420	71	132	169	20	4	3	54	4	6	4	37	4	33	13	13	17	.402	.370
Fornes, Daniel, Rey.	.271	107	425	369	43	100	143	21	2	6	55	7	3	6	40	5	41	3	5	9	.388	.349
Franco, Iker, Tig.	.308	19	17	13	6	4	4	0	0	0	3	0	0	4	0	1	0	0	0	.308	.471
Franco, Julio, Tig.	.423	93	414	326	90	138	214	22	6	14	77	0	2	6	80	13	44	9	1	22	.656	.541
Gainey, Ty, Sal.	.339	97	416	319	73	108	196	17	1	23	78	0	2	3	92	15	63	3	3	8	.614	.488
Gama, Ricardo, Tab.	.288	96	409	358	46	103	128	17	4	0	28	11	2	2	36	0	31	5	2	7	.358	.354
Garcia, Carlos, Tig.	.368	56	257	239	38	88	136	18	3	8	54	0	5	0	13	3	22	13	5	8	.569	.393
Garcia, Cornelio, Tor.	.349	105	491	390	82	136	167	22	3	1	41	5	3	4	89	1	48	25	11	14	.428	.471
Garcia, Hector, Mont.	.328	94	425	378	67	124	157	18	0	5	35	10	2	2	33	2	26	8	5	6	.415	.383
Garcia, Heriberto, Ver.-Oax.	.261	92	301	261	44	68	84	10	3	0	19	6	1	1	32	0	24	3	3	10	.322	.342
Garcia, Leo, Oax.	.287	119	536	457	71	131	178	17	6	6	66	7	2	2	68	9	38	20	8	17	.389	.380
Garza, Fidel, Mont.	.316	22	21	19	3	6	7	1	0	0	2	0	0	0	3	0	0	1	0	1	.368	.316
Garza, Gerardo, Lar.	.235	103	320	268	34	63	72	7	1	0	18	21	1	1	29	0	34	0	2	14	.269	.311
Garzon, Eliseo, Tor.	.290	120	472	396	59	115	151	18	0	6	50	9	4	6	57	2	40	0	1	11	.381	.384
Gastelum, Carlos, Monc.-Cor.	.252	46	127	111	8	28	29	1	0	0	11	7	1	1	7	0	14	0	0	8	.261	.300
Gastelum, Sergio, Tig.	.337	106	491	415	92	140	180	16	3	6	61	8	2	5	61	0	28	12	10	9	.434	.427
Gavia, Jesus, Yuc.	.255	64	191	165	19	42	51	6	0	1	23	8	2	4	12	1	17	0	0	3	.309	.317
Gomez, Heber, Tab.	.291	117	517	464	64	135	174	20	2	5	35	10	0	8	35	0	43	9	6	12	.375	.351
Gonzalez, Fernando, Rey.	.120	19	28	25	0	3	4	1	0	0	1	0	0	2	1	0	4	0	0	0	.160	.185
Gonzalez, Jesus, Mont.	.338	112	501	432	90	146	261	36	2	25	92	0	2	4	63	6	59	6	2	9	.604	.425
Gonzalez, Jose, Yuc.-Agua.	.301	115	478	392	86	118	198	22	5	16	65	1	3	1	81	3	64	19	9	12	.505	.419
Gonzalez, Manuel, Ver.	.200	5	6	5	0	1	2	1	0	0	0	0	0	0	1	0	1	0	0	0	.400	.333
Gonzalez, Rene, Rey.	.293	19	86	75	14	22	31	1	1	2	10	1	2	0	8	1	6	0	0	4	.413	.353
Gonzalez, Rolando, Monc.	.271	27	53	48	6	13	13	0	0	0	5	1	0	1	3	0	13	0	0	1	.271	.327
Gonzalez, Roman, Cor.	.223	52	142	130	9	29	31	2	0	0	8	6	1	0	5	0	31	0	0	1	.238	.250
Green, Dario, Tor.	.250	13	34	32	4	8	10	2	0	0	2	2	0	0	0	0	10	0	1	0	.313	.250
Groppuso, Mike, Yuc.	.256	21	93	82	9	21	25	4	0	0	6	2	0	0	9	0	11	2	1	1	.305	.330
Guerrero, Epy, Cam.	.324	106	461	386	53	125	185	23	5	9	59	11	3	1	60	5	26	3	3	12	.479	.413
Guerrero, Francisco, Cor.	.053	8	23	19	0	1	1	0	0	0	0	0	0	0	4	0	5	0	1	1	.053	.217
Guizar, Hector, Monc.	.300	114	460	413	55	124	165	17	3	6	56	20	5	2	20	2	34	3	1	15	.400	.332
Hall, Joe, Ver.	.224	16	63	58	2	13	16	1	1	0	4	0	0	0	5	0	11	0	0	0	.276	.286
Hernandez, Cesar, Cam.	.275	117	508	454	67	125	165	16	6	4	52	3	4	5	42	1	56	17	12	8	.363	.341
Hernandez, Esteban, Mex.-Oax.	.116	20	52	43	6	5	6	1	0	0	2	3	0	0	6	0	16	1	0	0	.140	.224
Hernandez, Juan, Cor.	.353	11	22	17	3	6	6	0	0	0	3	0	1	0	4	0	3	0	0	0	.353	.455
Hernandez, Julio, Lar.	.236	106	436	365	44	86	106	11	3	1	28	13	4	10	44	0	49	3	6	17	.290	.331
Hernandez, Miguel, Ver.	.129	20	34	31	1	4	4	0	0	0	1	3	0	0	0	0	2	0	0	1	.129	.129
Herrera, Christian, Ver.	.118	9	21	17	0	2	2	0	0	0	1	0	0	0	4	0	7	0	1	0	.118	.286
Hurtado, Hector, Cam.-Can.	.184	62	186	174	8	32	38	4	1	0	9	3	0	1	8	1	19	0	1	7	.218	.224
Iglesias, Luis, Mex.-Yuc.	.286	54	227	196	25	56	90	11	1	7	31	2	1	4	24	1	36	0	0	4	.459	.373
Incaviglia, Pete, Mont.	.323	25	113	96	18	31	42	5	0	2	12	0	2	3	12	0	22	8	0	2	.438	.407
Iturbe, Pedro, Tig.	.274	83	259	230	38	63	84	8	2	3	26	3	2	2	22	5	35	4	3	8	.365	.340
Jimenez, Alfonso, Sal.	.299	108	418	361	45	108	145	23	1	4	52	10	5	0	42	6	32	3	3	19	.402	.368
Jimenez, Eduardo, Sal.	.296	83	339	260	40	77	122	12	0	11	55	0	6	4	69	8	52	0	1	8	.469	.442
Jones, Ron, Lar.	.246	16	76	57	11	14	21	4	0	1	6	0	0	3	16	1	6	0	0	3	.368	.434
Jones, Tim, Agua.	.260	29	108	77	18	20	35	1	1	4	11	1	0	1	29	1	13	3	5	1	.455	.467
Kapano, Randy, Mont.	.337	24	105	89	18	30	41	5	0	2	16	1	3	0	12	1	15	2	0	3	.461	.404
Laureano, Francisco, Agua.	.289	28	113	97	13	28	39	5	0	2	8	0	0	1	16	1	12	0	0	3	.402	.389
Leal, Guadalupe, Cam.-Monc.	.292	63	150	137	15	40	53	7	0	2	22	0	1	0	12	2	25	0	0	6	.387	.347
Lee, Derek, Yuc.-Mex.	.333	45	196	156	27	52	70	6	0	4	32	1	3	0	36	1	23	1	1	5	.449	.451
Leyva, German, Ver.	.312	114	467	391	53	122	165	19	0	8	49	10	6	3	58	5	11	4	3	12	.422	.398
Liriano, Nelson, Mex.	.313	80	391	323	78	101	151	10	5	10	54	3	3	0	62	4	43	24	6	9	.467	.420
Lopez, Carlos, Tab.	.000	7	9	8	0	0	0	0	0	0	0	0	0	0	1	0	3	0	0	0	.000	.111
Lopez, Fabian, Oax.	.282	99	373	326	39	92	115	19	2	0	35	13	7	3	24	1	29	5	5	11	.353	.331
Lopez, Gonzalo, Yuc.	.286	53	179	161	21	46	55	4	1	1	16	1	0	0	17	0	25	0	1	3	.342	.354

Player, Team	Avg.	G	TPA	AB	R	H	TB	2B	3B	HR	RBI	SH	SF	HP	BB	IBB	SO	SB	CS	GDP	Slg.	OBP
Loredo, Jorge, Oax.	.262	73	222	195	29	51	75	14	2	2	28	6	0	1	20	1	38	1	2	13	.385	.333
Machiria, Pablo, Agua.	.307	109	455	423	51	130	188	21	2	11	86	1	8	11	12	3	32	1	3	20	.444	.337
Magallanes, Everardo, Mont.	.399	62	283	228	59	91	121	15	0	5	32	8	0	1	46	7	10	7	1	5	.531	.502
Magallanes, Roberto, Tor.	.325	13	59	40	9	13	14	1	0	0	6	0	2	0	17	0	7	1	1	3	.350	.508
Malave, Jose, Lar.	.254	19	79	71	10	18	18	0	0	0	5	0	0	0	8	0	9	1	0	1	.254	.329
Malpica, Enrique, Ver.-Yuc.	.191	35	74	68	10	13	18	2	0	1	5	1	1	0	4	0	10	0	0	3	.265	.233
Martinez, Abel, Can.	.235	110	369	332	30	78	90	8	2	0	35	5	4	5	23	0	43	6	6	7	.271	.291
Martinez, Augusto, Tab.	.154	13	13	13	3	2	2	0	0	0	2	0	0	0	0	0	2	0	1	0	.154	.154
Martinez, Domingo, Mex.	.302	56	251	215	34	65	97	8	0	8	50	0	5	3	28	3	30	0	1	15	.451	.382
Martinez, Enrique, Agua.	.307	88	342	290	52	89	141	14	4	10	53	5	2	0	45	2	54	6	8	6	.486	.398
Martinez, Grimaldo, Monc.	.260	112	479	407	53	106	143	15	2	6	49	17	9	2	44	0	26	8	5	12	.351	.329
Martinez, Luis, Sal.	.307	115	481	449	58	138	167	22	2	1	42	14	1	0	17	1	26	8	4	11	.372	.332
Martinez, Raul, Ver.	.217	90	264	230	18	50	60	7	0	1	17	5	0	3	26	0	27	0	4	8	.261	.305
Martinez, Ray, Mex.	.312	96	424	359	68	112	188	19	0	19	75	1	4	6	54	6	52	3	3	17	.524	.407
Mata, Noe, Ver.	.256	62	135	117	15	30	38	2	0	2	6	4	0	4	10	0	22	2	3	3	.325	.336
May, Derrick, Mont.	.324	32	142	108	19	35	52	5	0	4	29	0	4	2	28	3	10	1	3	0	.481	.458
Medina, Ernesto, Mont.	.188	7	18	16	5	3	4	1	0	0	1	0	0	0	2	0	7	1	0	0	.250	.278
Medina, Jose, Sal.	.245	101	312	274	37	67	90	8	3	3	40	6	1	3	28	2	53	1	3	7	.328	.320
Meggers, Mike, Ver.-Tor.	.263	102	431	365	62	96	195	15	0	28	61	1	1	4	60	9	87	2	4	10	.534	.372
Mendez, Francisco, Mont.	.167	6	6	6	2	1	4	0	0	1	2	0	0	0	0	0	1	0	0	0	.667	.167
Mendez, Roberto, Oax.	.311	86	351	273	51	85	125	11	1	9	40	2	3	3	70	9	47	17	12	9	.458	.453
Mere, Pedro, Ver.	.259	88	291	239	27	62	79	8	0	3	24	10	3	2	37	1	33	2	6	7	.331	.359
Meza, Alfredo, Mont.	.248	100	335	310	23	77	91	9	1	1	29	6	2	0	17	1	43	1	3	10	.294	.286
Meza, Gonzalo, Mex.	.215	52	152	130	16	28	35	4	0	1	10	3	1	0	18	2	28	1	2	1	.269	.303
Minjares, Francisco, Agua.	.234	80	222	201	28	47	63	3	5	1	18	0	2	0	19	0	23	2	4	7	.313	.297
Miranda, Julio, Agua.	.000	2	8	7	1	0	0	0	0	0	1	1	0	0	0	0	0	0	0	1	.000	.000
Mitchel, Domingo, Yuc.-Can.	.231	33	126	104	19	24	34	3	2	1	14	0	1	0	21	2	23	0	2	3	.327	.357
Mitchel, Tony, Ver.	.268	46	191	164	15	44	71	6	0	7	25	0	1	0	26	2	43	2	1	3	.433	.366
Mitchell, Kevin, Tab.	.212	14	56	52	5	11	16	2	0	1	4	0	0	0	4	0	3	0	0	2	.308	.268
Montalvo, Ivan, Tig.	.224	104	408	331	53	74	126	13	3	11	70	6	6	7	58	7	64	2	4	12	.381	.346
Montanez, Daniel, Ver.	.187	68	221	198	20	37	43	4	1	0	7	10	1	0	12	0	35	6	4	1	.217	.232
Moore, Kerwin, Ver.	.271	40	179	140	26	38	46	5	0	1	16	3	0	2	34	1	25	12	5	0	.329	.420
Morales, Florentino, Lar.	.245	64	174	139	13	34	37	1	1	0	9	7	1	6	21	1	14	3	1	8	.266	.365
Morejon, Oswaldo, Yuc.	.252	90	373	321	42	81	99	5	5	1	26	14	0	6	32	1	28	4	6	11	.308	.331
Moreno, David, Cam.	.143	41	62	49	8	7	10	1	1	0	4	3	2	0	8	0	7	0	0	2	.204	.254
Moreno, Leonardo, Oax.-Ver.	.195	64	138	128	13	25	29	4	0	0	9	2	1	2	5	0	15	1	2	0	.227	.235
Morones, Martin, Ver.	.255	100	342	302	26	77	94	5	0	4	26	5	1	2	32	0	31	5	7	5	.311	.329
Munoz, Adan, Monc.	.348	22	52	46	4	16	21	3	1	0	7	1	0	1	4	0	8	0	0	4	.457	.412
Munoz, Jose, Sal.	.335	93	438	358	74	120	162	11	11	3	29	6	0	1	73	9	40	20	17	4	.453	.449
Munoz, Noe, Sal.	.308	108	457	383	61	118	142	12	0	4	63	6	6	4	58	4	47	2	5	17	.371	.399
Nokes, Matt, Cor.	.000	2	8	8	0	0	0	0	0	0	0	0	0	0	0	0	1	0	0	0	.000	.000
Nunez, Ray, Agua.	.289	92	385	353	52	102	152	16	5	8	68	1	5	3	23	1	46	0	2	18	.431	.333
Obando, Sherman, Oax.	.360	46	199	161	37	58	102	12	1	10	40	0	1	3	34	5	20	3	1	5	.634	.477
Ochoa, Edgar, Agua.-Ver.	.200	7	6	5	1	1	1	0	0	0	1	0	0	0	0	0	1	0	0	0	.200	.333
Ojeda, Miguel, Mex.	.275	89	375	316	60	87	138	17	2	10	45	2	4	2	51	7	35	5	2	6	.437	.375
Olivares, Roberto, Cor.	.111	7	11	9	1	1	1	0	0	0	1	0	0	0	2	0	5	0	0	0	.111	.273
Olvera, Sergio, Cam.-Can.	.140	46	109	100	10	14	17	3	0	0	7	1	1	1	6	0	8	0	1	2	.170	.194
Orantes, Ramon, Mont.	.294	84	334	309	37	91	122	20	1	3	39	4	0	6	15	2	31	4	0	7	.395	.339
Ortega, Antonio, Oax.-Mex.	.235	30	80	68	7	16	18	2	0	0	8	1	0	0	11	0	10	0	1	1	.265	.342
Ortiz, Alejandro, Lar.	.294	117	478	415	49	122	182	15	0	15	68	3	2	4	54	3	42	0	2	15	.439	.379
Osuna, Hector, Can.	.284	34	89	74	7	21	23	2	0	0	7	4	1	3	7	0	10	0	0	0	.311	.365
Pacho, Carlos, Yuc.	.191	28	57	47	2	9	11	2	0	0	6	2	0	0	8	0	9	0	0	2	.234	.336
Pacho, Juan, Yuc.	.260	110	371	308	35	80	85	5	0	0	25	26	1	2	34	1	21	0	4	8	.276	.336
Paez, Raul, Rey.-Cam.	.304	71	235	204	21	62	79	11	0	2	27	4	1	1	25	2	19	0	0	6	.387	.381
Payro, Edison, Cam.-Tab.	.219	82	279	233	18	51	55	4	0	0	12	7	0	0	39	0	39	1	6	9	.236	.331
Peguero, Julio, Can.	.269	120	510	450	57	121	165	23	3	5	44	5	0	3	52	7	54	20	13	14	.367	.349
Pena, Carlos, Tab.	.050	15	22	20	1	1	1	0	0	0	0	1	0	0	1	0	3	0	0	1	.050	.095
Peraza, Rudy, Yuc.	.000	1	2	2	0	0	0	0	0	0	0	0	0	0	0	0	0	0	0	0	.000	.000
Perez, Alejandro, Yuc.	.000	2	3	2	1	0	0	0	0	0	0	1	0	0	0	0	1	0	0	0	.000	.333
Perez, Alfredo, Cam.	.274	89	363	318	36	87	99	12	0	0	19	12	3	5	25	0	19	2	3	5	.311	.336
Perez, Francisco, Rey.	.257	92	246	218	26	56	67	5	0	2	20	2	0	6	20	5	45	6	1	4	.307	.336
Perez, Juan, Tor.	.229	23	40	35	3	8	9	1	0	0	0	0	0	0	5	0	12	0	0	0	.257	.325
Perez, Luis, Monc.	.000	1	1	1	0	0	1	0	0	0	0	0	0	0	0	0	0	0	0	0	1.000	1.000
Pinto, Placido, Mex.	.291	34	59	55	4	16	23	4	0	1	8	1	0	1	2	0	17	0	1	0	.418	.328
Poe, Charles, Tab.-Tor.	.349	74	308	269	39	94	127	8	2	7	51	0	4	5	30	2	42	4	2	7	.472	.419
Quintero, Alan, Yuc.	.287	48	144	129	18	37	51	5	3	1	15	1	0	3	11	0	19	0	1	5	.395	.357
Quintero, Edgar, Mont.	.271	62	147	118	21	32	50	7	1	3	12	2	0	2	25	1	41	5	6	5	.424	.407
Quintero, Guillermo, Cor.	.251	109	432	374	47	94	111	15	1	0	18	13	2	3	40	0	51	15	8	7	.297	.329
Ramirez, Angel, Tig.	.154	13	59	52	7	8	13	1	2	0	7	1	2	1	3	0	9	0	0	3	.250	.207
Ramirez, Efren, Cor.	.234	107	393	329	39	77	108	7	0	8	31	10	2	17	35	1	59	4	5	5	.328	.333
Ramirez, Enrique, Can.	.263	119	407	353	34	93	109	13	0	1	26	25	4	0	25	0	26	1	3	9	.309	.309
Ramirez, Jesus, Ver.-Tab.-Oax.	.273	53	169	139	18	38	47	7	1	0	13	5	3	3	19	0	13	2	8	2	.338	.366
Ramon, Reyes, Tab.-Cam.	.190	61	163	147	8	28	32	4	0	0	14	5	2	0	9	3	12	2	2	4	.218	.234
Resendez, Carlos, Monc.	.161	24	33	31	6	5	8	0	0	1	2	0	0	1	1	0	7	0	0	1	.258	.212
Reyes, Gilberto, Ver.	.243	34	125	115	6	28	38	4	0	2	13	0	2	1	7	0	15	1	0	3	.330	.289
Reyes, Jesus, Sal.	.273	9	13	11	3	3	4	1	0	0	4	0	0	2	0	1	0	0	0	0	.364	.385
Rivera, Jesus, Tab.	.188	58	130	112	11	21	21	0	0	0	6	3	0	0	15	1	7	0	2	5	.188	.283
Robles, Javier, Tig.	.291	107	466	382	74	111	176	16	5	13	80	5	8	2	69	2	55	12	5	13	.461	.399
Robles, Juan, Rey.-Can.	.246	40	77	69	9	17	20	3	0	0	5	2	0	0	6	0	8	0	1	3	.290	.307
Robles, Trinidad, Tig.	.252	50	162	135	22	34	46	3	3	1	13	3	1	3	20	0	32	2	3	3	.341	.358
Rodriguez, Armando, Tig.	.315	95	361	327	50	103	140	16	3	5	66	4	5	2	23	0	53	6	4	11	.428	.359
Rodriguez, Aurelio, Tab.	.224	21	63	58	4	13	14	1	0	0	3	1	0	0	4	0	15	0	2	2	.241	.274
Rodriguez, Boi, Monc.	.342	118	550	459	99	157	278	33	5	26	105	0	7	2	82	15	81	43	15	11	.606	.458
Rodriguez, Fernando, Cam.	.298	113	463	410	50	122	167	23	2	6	49	5	1	3	44	5	51	3	3	24	.407	.369
Rodriguez, Hector, Rey.	.225	66	189	169	18	38	46	5	0	1	15	6	2	1	11	0	34	0	1	7	.272	.273
Rojas, Francisco, Tab.	.233	17	50	43	3	10	11	1	0	0	4	2	0	4	1	0	5	1	2	0	.256	.313

Player, Team	Avg.	G	TPA	AB	R	H	TB	2B	3B	HR	RBI	SH	SF	HP	BB	IBB	SO	SB	CS	GDP	Slg.	OBP
Rojas, Homar, Oax.	.322	81	319	286	40	92	127	18	1	5	56	0	3	2	28	0	17	2	1	11	.444	.382
Romero, Marco, Sal.	.275	113	449	393	60	108	172	16	0	16	64	1	4	2	49	5	79	7	4	11	.438	.355
Romero, Oscar, Tor.	.337	50	206	178	24	60	84	10	1	4	26	1	2	1	24	0	15	1	1	6	.472	.415
Romero, Wilfredo, Tig.-Sal.	.333	115	544	475	110	158	229	18	10	11	81	2	7	2	58	3	62	27	11	16	.482	.402
Rubio, Sergio, Yuc.	.253	40	109	95	14	24	32	3	1	1	12	2	0	2	10	0	8	0	0	2	.337	.336
Ruiz, Juan, Cor.	.246	114	466	414	42	102	130	17	1	3	53	9	4	5	34	1	44	1	4	13	.314	.309
Saenz, Ricardo, Monc.	.314	119	529	420	84	132	213	30	0	17	85	4	7	1	97	6	77	7	2	10	.507	.438
Salas, Heriberto, Tor.	.269	102	414	353	46	95	116	10	1	3	46	8	9	7	37	1	41	6	3	15	.329	.342
Salazar, Carlos, Yuc.	.000	3	1	1	2	0	0	0	0	0	0	0	0	0	0	0	0	0	0	0	.000	.000
Sanchez, Armando, Cor.	.000	4	6	6	0	0	0	0	0	0	0	0	0	0	0	0	0	0	0	0	.000	.000
Sanchez, Gerardo, Lar.	.275	119	534	437	74	120	183	20	2	13	71	5	3	8	81	1	54	1	1	16	.419	.395
Sanchez, Orlando, Mont.	.309	73	242	217	32	67	85	9	3	1	35	8	1	1	15	0	30	4	2	1	.392	.355
Sanchez, Raul, Can.	.268	112	374	336	49	90	136	9	8	7	46	8	3	1	26	2	45	7	3	13	.405	.320
Sanchez, Roque, Cam.	.236	108	406	368	34	87	107	13	2	1	27	18	1	6	13	2	28	2	2	14	.291	.273
Sanchez, Wilfredo, Can.	.250	17	14	12	5	3	6	1	1	0	0	0	0	0	2	0	1	0	0	0	.500	.357
Sandez, Angel, Sal.	.000	4	2	2	1	0	0	0	0	0	0	0	0	0	0	0	1	0	0	0	.000	.000
Sandoval, Jose, Mex.	.309	112	466	418	67	129	198	29	2	12	77	2	2	1	43	4	54	1	1	19	.474	.373
Sandoval, Octavio, Tig.	.269	73	192	167	24	45	61	11	1	1	20	4	3	4	14	0	34	4	2	2	.365	.335
Santana, Mario, Mont.	.244	58	103	90	12	22	28	3	0	1	10	1	2	1	9	1	11	0	2	2	.311	.314
Santos, Andres, Lar.	.282	48	125	110	17	31	50	4	0	5	18	2	2	0	11	0	16	0	4	7	.455	.341
Saucedo, Roberto, Mont.-Rey.	.296	87	333	277	37	82	142	9	3	15	50	4	4	4	44	2	60	0	1	9	.513	.395
Sherman, Darrell, Monc.	.336	109	523	396	93	133	174	23	3	4	41	5	4	2	116	6	35	20	13	7	.439	.485
Sievers, Carlos, Yuc.	.275	104	393	335	45	92	138	19	3	7	58	3	1	9	45	4	41	4	3	8	.412	.374
So, Young, Can.	.265	11	40	34	2	9	9	0	0	0	2	0	0	0	6	0	5	0	1	1	.265	.375
Soriano, Ricardo, Cor.	.212	63	174	146	12	31	35	4	0	0	13	9	1	4	14	0	30	4	2	5	.240	.297
Soto, Saul, Mex.	.313	57	186	179	21	56	76	14	0	2	23	1	1	1	4	0	24	0	1	3	.425	.330
Sotomayor, Gilberto, Monc.	.211	15	23	19	6	4	4	0	0	0	0	0	0	0	4	0	7	0	0	1	.211	.348
Stark, Matt, Rey.-Mont.	.323	52	222	167	26	54	83	11	0	6	25	0	4	9	42	4	12	1	1	3	.497	.473
Stoner, Mike, Mont.	.293	36	161	147	21	43	70	10	1	5	33	1	3	1	9	0	12	2	2	9	.476	.331
Suarez, Luis, Tig.	.321	77	286	262	41	84	121	15	2	6	45	3	2	1	18	4	37	2	5	5	.462	.364
Tatis, Bernardo, Yuc.	.249	91	368	297	33	74	95	9	3	2	37	5	2	0	64	3	37	17	8	9	.320	.380
Tavarez, Jesus, Ver.	.331	68	285	254	25	84	102	11	2	1	20	2	1	2	26	4	12	7	3	3	.402	.396
Tellez, Alonso, Rey.	.311	120	516	447	64	139	218	22	0	19	103	1	7	3	58	8	45	2	1	17	.488	.388
Tequet, Lazaro, Tab.	.278	41	95	90	6	25	29	4	0	0	9	0	0	2	3	1	11	1	0	6	.322	.316
Tinsley, Lee, Monc.	.305	35	150	118	22	36	52	3	2	3	12	1	0	1	30	0	24	8	4	0	.441	.450
Torres, Ariel, Tor.	.000	4	2	2	2	0	0	0	0	0	0	0	0	0	0	0	2	0	0	1	.000	.000
Trafton, Todd, Oax.	.272	52	210	173	27	47	77	12	0	6	30	0	1	9	27	1	30	0	0	8	.445	.395
Trapaga, Julio, Tig.	.227	58	182	154	23	35	42	5	1	0	17	7	4	3	14	0	35	0	2	4	.273	.297
Valdez, Emmanuel, Tig.	.179	41	109	84	15	15	27	3	0	3	22	4	3	2	16	0	29	1	1	1	.321	.314
Valdez, Francisco, Tab.	.254	118	446	386	35	98	128	18	0	4	37	13	8	6	33	2	26	1	1	16	.332	.316
Valdez, Jesus, Cam.	.258	107	381	333	25	86	101	9	0	2	33	6	1	0	41	5	33	3	0	13	.303	.339
Valdez, Ramon, Cor.	.176	64	218	176	25	31	34	3	0	0	6	9	0	4	29	0	21	5	4	3	.193	.306
Valdivia, Arturo, Ver.	.000	2	2	2	0	0	0	0	0	0	0	0	0	0	0	0	1	0	0	0	.000	.000
Valencia, Carlos, Tab.	.249	98	342	301	24	75	93	13	1	1	33	9	3	1	28	1	15	0	3	8	.309	.312
Valenzuela, Irving, Monc.	.319	39	78	69	18	22	29	2	1	1	8	5	0	1	3	0	9	1	0	1	.420	.356
Valle, Cosme, Mex.	.270	30	67	63	10	17	33	5	1	3	10	1	0	1	2	0	8	0	0	3	.524	.303
Valle, Jorge, Monc.	.288	113	437	364	59	105	147	19	7	3	50	15	2	6	50	0	46	2	4	16	.404	.382
Valle, Jose, Cor.-Yuc.	.232	56	123	99	12	23	26	1	1	0	6	8	0	0	16	0	13	0	0	4	.263	.339
Valle, Roberto, Tor.	.209	51	134	115	8	24	26	2	0	0	7	3	0	0	16	0	25	2	3	6	.226	.305
Vazquez, Felipe, Lar.	.268	42	69	56	6	15	15	0	0	0	3	1	0	2	10	0	6	0	0	1	.268	.397
Vazquez, Gregorio, Tab.	.118	12	18	17	0	2	2	0	0	0	1	0	0	0	1	0	4	0	0	2	.118	.167
Vazquez, Jorge, Monc.-Tor.	.125	29	36	32	2	4	5	1	0	0	1	0	0	0	4	0	14	0	0	0	.156	.222
Vazquez, Jorge, Tig.	.000	3	4	4	0	0	0	0	0	0	0	0	0	0	0	0	2	0	0	0	.000	.000
Vega, Edgar, Agua.	.238	81	254	231	28	55	86	7	9	2	30	3	1	1	18	1	26	1	2	10	.372	.295
Velazquez, Guillermo, Mont.	.264	58	249	197	24	52	71	10	0	3	36	0	3	0	49	4	43	0	2	7	.360	.406
Velez, Manuel, Tab.-Agua.	.240	83	283	250	31	60	70	7	0	1	22	5	3	3	22	0	24	2	7	16	.280	.306
Verdugo, Sostenes, Yuc.	.000	2	5	3	1	0	0	0	0	0	0	0	0	1	1	0	0	0	0	0	.000	.400
Verdugo, Vicente, Sal.	.280	91	372	325	45	91	109	13	1	1	32	7	3	3	34	0	19	1	3	20	.335	.351
Villanueva, Hector, Yuc.-Oax.	.225	21	95	71	12	16	28	3	0	3	13	0	0	1	23	4	6	1	0	3	.394	.421
Villarreal, Alejandro, Lar.	.394	12	34	33	4	13	15	2	0	0	3	0	0	1	0	0	2	0	0	1	.455	.412
Villarreal, Salvador, Rey.	.181	55	87	72	18	13	15	2	0	0	6	5	1	1	8	0	29	0	1	4	.208	.268
Villegas, Fernando, Sal.	.290	112	471	410	54	119	148	9	7	2	53	7	3	3	48	3	57	1	4	7	.361	.366
Villegas, Ramon, Tab.	.222	4	9	9	1	2	2	0	0	0	0	0	0	0	0	0	2	0	1	0	.222	.222
Vizcarra, Marco, Sal.	.198	64	102	86	14	17	20	3	0	0	5	5	0	0	11	0	10	2	1	4	.233	.289
Vizcarra, Roberto, Ags.-Tig.	.334	92	417	353	77	118	167	19	0	10	46	8	4	4	48	1	24	11	8	7	.473	.416
Voigt, Jack, Rey.	.237	41	179	152	20	36	49	7	0	2	17	0	0	2	25	1	28	3	0	7	.322	.352
Wong, Julian, Yuc.	.217	10	28	23	4	5	7	2	0	0	1	2	0	1	2	0	3	0	0	0	.304	.308
Yan, Julian, Cor.	.298	116	489	413	76	123	227	19	2	27	79	0	5	5	66	8	97	7	2	4	.550	.397
Yuriar, Jesus, Tor.	.244	53	190	156	19	38	48	5	1	1	22	6	2	2	24	1	20	1	5	8	.308	.348
Zambrano, Eduardo, Can.	.253	117	478	419	64	106	191	26	4	17	51	0	2	4	53	5	87	1	1	10	.456	.341
Zambrano, Roberto, Can.	.254	116	478	370	68	94	168	23	0	17	67	0	7	21	80	6	51	0	1	10	.454	.408
Zamudio, Rafael, Tor.-Agua.	.240	80	228	196	20	47	63	8	1	2	25	2	0	4	26	1	35	2	2	1	.321	.341
Zazueta, Juan, Tor.	.289	116	470	415	47	120	146	16	2	2	43	20	4	4	27	1	29	2	2	17	.352	.336
Zazueta, Mauricio, Tor.	.300	115	481	426	64	128	164	20	5	2	57	7	3	0	45	3	64	6	3	18	.385	.365

GRAND SLAMS: J. Franco, Ca. Garcia, Machiria, Montalvo, B. Rodriguez, W. Romero, 2 each; Aganza, Barrera, H. Castaneda, Castellano, R. Cervantes, A. Cruz, R. Diaz, H. Estrada, Je. Gonzalez, Iglesias, D. Martinez, E. Martinez, Meggers, A. Meza, Orantes, Ef. Ramirez, F. Rodriguez, H. Rojas, M. Romero, G. Sanchez, 1 each.

AWARDED FIRST BASE ON CATCHER'S INTERFERENCE: Ab. Martinez 3 (Saucedo 2, H. Castaneda); Morones 2 (Ar. Rodriguez, Vega); A. Meza (F. Gonzalez); Payro (Cazarin).

PLAYERS WITH TWO OR MORE TEAMS

Player, Team	Avg.	G	TPA	AB	R	H	TB	2B	3B	HR	RBI	SH	SF	HP	BB	IBB	SO	SB	CS	GDP	Slg.	OBP
Arvizu, Javier, Tor.	.268	57	184	142	20	38	57	7	0	4	28	2	5	33	2	0	28	1	0	6	.401	.401
Arvizu, Javier, Tab.	.250	27	97	76	15	19	30	5	0	2	8	2	1	16	2	0	11	0	0	2	.395	.389
Bustamante, Omar, Sal.	.200	4	6	5	0	1	1	0	0	0	1	1	0	0	0	1	1	0	0	0	.200	.200
Bustamante, Omar, Lar.	.227	9	23	22	2	5	8	0	0	1	1	0	0	1	0	0	4	0	0	0	.364	.261
Canseco, Ozzie, Mont.	.297	22	94	74	7	22	34	4	1	2	19	0	1	18	1	1	17	0	1	1	.459	.436

Player, Team	Avg.	G	TPA	AB	R	H	TB	2B	3B	HR	RBI	SH	SF	HP	BB	IBB	SO	SB	CS	GDP	Slg.	OBP
Canseco, Ozzie, Tab.	.298	26	109	84	13	25	43	3	0	5	19	0	1	22	2	1	25	2	0	3	.512	.450
Carter, Michael, Tor.	.321	40	173	159	27	51	68	9	1	2	16	2	0	12	0	2	7	11	1	7	.428	.368
Carter, Michael, Ver.	.298	24	96	84	11	25	28	1	1	0	6	2	1	7	2	1	9	6	3	0	.333	.362
Castaneda, Hector, Cor.	.231	19	71	52	6	12	15	1	1	0	6	0	0	18	1	1	7	0	0	5	.288	.437
Castaneda, Hector, Yuc.	.308	83	323	260	45	80	116	8	2	8	39	4	1	53	5	1	39	2	1	11	.446	.433
Cazarin, Manuel, Can.	.283	89	346	307	35	87	113	11	0	5	34	5	1	32	1	2	20	1	3	16	.368	.352
Cazarin, Manuel, Cam.	.208	22	87	72	6	15	28	7	0	2	10	3	1	9	2	1	3	0	0	3	.389	.310
Cervantes, Regugio, Lar.	.278	17	19	18	3	5	6	1	0	0	1	0	0	1	0	0	2	0	0	1	.333	.316
Cervantes, Regugio, Sal.	.367	18	35	30	3	11	14	0	0	1	9	0	0	3	2	0	4	0	0	2	.467	.457
Chan, Armando, Monc.	.000	12	11	7	1	0	0	0	0	0	1	0	0	4	0	0	3	0	0	1	.000	.364
Chan, Armando, Cam.	.178	20	50	45	2	8	8	0	0	0	5	0	0	4	1	1	9	0	0	1	.178	.260
Chance, Tony, Monc.	.240	83	369	308	46	74	133	10	2	15	66	2	4	54	1	1	88	3	4	9	.432	.351
Chance, Tony, Tab.	.276	28	120	98	14	27	48	4	1	5	15	3	1	17	1	1	19	1	0	3	.490	.385
Claudio, Patricio, Tab.	.287	37	165	143	23	41	45	4	0	0	7	2	0	19	1	0	25	10	9	1	.315	.374
Claudio, Patricio, Can.	.234	64	277	239	30	56	72	6	2	2	18	4	5	24	5	0	35	6	5	4	.301	.311
Cruz, Antonio, Lar.	.111	3	10	9	0	1	1	0	0	0	0	0	0	1	0	1	2	0	0	0	.111	.200
Cruz, Antonio, Agua.	.261	72	238	203	27	53	74	9	0	4	32	6	2	27	0	6	20	0	1	9	.365	.345
De la Cruz, Hector, Ver.	.267	18	71	60	7	16	21	3	1	0	6	0	2	8	1	0	2	2	1	6	.350	.352
De la Cruz, Hector, Yuc.	.273	3	13	11	1	3	3	0	0	0	0	0	0	2	0	0	4	2	1	0	.273	.385
Diaz, Luis, Agua.	.242	40	149	120	24	29	47	4	1	4	15	2	2	23	2	0	30	2	0	2	.392	.367
Diaz, Luis, Tor.	.242	23	81	66	8	16	26	4	0	2	7	1	0	14	0	0	17	0	1	2	.394	.375
Dominguez, David, Can.	.228	19	64	57	5	13	16	1	1	0	4	0	0	7	0	0	9	0	0	4	.281	.313
Dominguez, David, Lar.	.220	60	245	209	20	46	69	9	1	4	21	1	1	32	2	0	44	2	0	8	.330	.328
Duran, Felipe, Oax.	.292	9	29	24	1	7	7	0	0	0	3	3	1	1	0	1	1	0	0	0	.292	.308
Duran, Felipe, Ver.	.202	34	99	94	9	19	29	4	0	2	12	1	1	3	0	1	11	0	1	2	.309	.224
Esquer, Ramon, Oax.	.332	56	247	199	31	66	78	8	2	0	24	8	2	38	0	0	15	4	5	9	.392	.435
Esquer, Ramon, Mex.	.289	33	151	128	25	37	47	4	0	2	11	1	1	20	1	1	10	2	0	8	.367	.387
Felix, Jesus, Yuc.	.125	10	19	16	0	2	2	0	0	0	0	0	1	2	0	0	0	0	1	0	.125	.211
Felix, Jesus, Rey.	.121	17	39	33	3	4	4	0	0	0	0	2	0	4	0	0	7	0	0	1	.121	.216
Garcia, Heriberto, Ver.	.162	13	46	37	5	6	6	0	0	0	2	1	0	8	0	1	2	0	2	4	.162	.311
Garcia, Heriberto, Oax.	.277	79	254	224	39	62	78	10	3	0	17	5	1	24	0	0	22	3	1	6	.348	.345
Gastelum, Carlos, Monc.	.000	5	3	3	0	0	0	0	0	0	0	0	0	0	0	0	1	0	0	0	.000	.000
Gastelum, Carlos, Cor.	.259	41	123	108	8	28	29	1	0	0	11	7	1	7	0	1	13	0	0	8	.269	.302
Gonzalez, Jose, Yuc.	.186	28	118	102	13	19	33	3	1	3	19	0	2	13	1	0	14	2	1	2	.324	.280
Gonzalez, Jose, Agua.	.341	87	362	290	73	99	165	19	4	13	46	1	1	68	2	1	50	17	8	10	.569	.468
Hernandez, Esteban, Mex.	.250	3	4	4	1	1	1	0	0	0	0	0	0	0	0	0	0	0	0	0	.250	.250
Hernandez, Esteban, Oax.	.103	17	48	39	5	4	5	1	0	0	2	3	0	6	0	0	13	1	0	0	.128	.222
Hurtado, Hector, Cam.	.196	53	170	158	8	31	37	4	1	0	9	3	0	8	1	0	15	0	1	7	.234	.240
Hurtado, Hector, Yuc.	.063	9	16	16	0	1	1	0	0	0	0	0	0	0	0	0	4	0	0	0	.063	.063
Iglesias, Luis, Mex.	.307	27	107	101	14	31	53	7	0	5	21	0	1	5	0	4	18	0	0	4	.525	.336
Iglesias, Luis, Yuc.	.263	27	117	95	11	25	37	4	1	2	10	2	0	19	1	1	18	0	0	0	.389	.391
Leal, Guadalupe, Cam.	.154	20	57	52	5	8	9	1	0	0	4	0	0	4	1	0	7	0	0	2	.173	.228
Leal, Guadalupe, Monc.	.376	43	95	85	10	32	44	6	0	2	18	0	1	8	1	0	18	0	0	4	.518	.432
Lee, Derek, Yuc.	.258	18	77	66	6	17	18	1	0	0	6	1	1	9	0	0	10	1	0	3	.273	.342
Lee, Derek, Mex.	.389	27	120	90	21	35	52	5	0	4	26	0	2	27	1	0	13	0	1	2	.578	.525
Malpica, Enrique, Ver.	.190	12	23	21	4	4	5	1	0	0	1	1	0	1	0	0	4	0	0	1	.238	.227
Malpica, Enrique, Yuc.	.191	23	51	47	6	9	13	1	0	1	4	0	1	3	0	0	6	0	0	2	.277	.235
Meggers, Mike, Ver.	.283	77	335	276	51	78	160	13	0	23	51	1	1	49	8	1	65	2	3	6	.580	.404
Meggers, Mike, Tor.	.202	25	101	89	11	18	35	2	0	5	10	0	0	11	1	3	22	0	1	4	.393	.297
Mitchel, Domingo, Yuc.	.246	22	80	65	15	16	25	2	2	1	10	0	0	14	1	0	12	0	2	0	.385	.388
Mitchel, Domingo, Can.	.205	11	48	39	4	8	9	1	0	0	4	0	1	7	0	0	11	0	0	3	.231	.333
Moreno, Leonardo, Oax.	.300	10	11	10	7	3	5	2	0	0	3	0	0	1	0	0	1	1	1	0	.500	.364
Moreno, Leonardo, Ver.	.186	54	125	118	6	22	24	2	0	0	6	2	1	4	0	2	14	0	1	0	.203	.211
Ochoa, Edgar, Agua.	.000	2	0	0	0	0	0	0	0	0	0	0	0	0	0	0	0	0	0	0	.000	.000
Ochoa, Edgar, Ver.	.200	5	6	5	1	1	1	0	0	0	0	0	0	1	0	0	1	0	0	0	.200	.333
Olvera, Sergio, Cam.	.134	41	105	97	8	13	16	3	0	0	7	1	1	6	0	0	8	0	1	2	.165	.183
Olvera, Sergio, Cam.	.333	5	3	3	2	1	1	0	0	0	0	0	0	0	0	1	0	0	0	0	.333	.333
Ortega, Antonio, Oax.	.167	16	42	36	5	6	7	1	0	0	2	0	0	6	0	0	5	0	0	1	.194	.286
Ortega, Antonio, Mex.	.313	14	38	32	2	10	11	1	0	0	6	1	0	5	0	0	5	0	0	0	.344	.405
Paez, Raul, Rey.	.321	57	184	162	17	52	65	10	0	1	21	3	0	18	1	1	16	0	0	5	.401	.392
Paez, Raul, Cam.	.238	14	52	42	4	10	14	1	0	1	6	1	1	7	1	0	3	0	0	1	.333	.353
Payro, Edison, Cam.	.168	45	131	107	8	18	21	3	0	0	5	5	0	19	0	0	25	0	3	5	.196	.294
Payro, Edison, Tab.	.262	37	148	126	10	33	34	1	0	0	7	2	0	20	0	0	14	1	3	4	.270	.363
Poe, Charles, Tab.	.289	34	139	121	10	35	43	1	2	1	15	0	3	13	2	1	19	1	1	3	.355	.360
Poe, Charles, Tor.	.399	40	166	148	29	59	84	7	0	6	36	0	1	17	0	4	23	3	1	4	.568	.458
Ramirez, Jesus, Ver.	.167	8	21	18	0	3	3	0	0	0	0	1	0	2	1	0	4	0	1	0	.167	.250
Ramirez, Jesus, Tab.	.000	1	4	2	0	0	0	0	0	0	0	1	0	1	0	0	0	0	0	0	.000	.333
Ramirez, Jesus, Oax.	.294	44	141	119	18	35	44	7	1	0	13	3	3	16	0	2	9	2	6	2	.370	.374
Ramon, Reyes, Tab.	.183	43	132	115	7	21	24	3	0	0	12	4	2	8	3	0	7	1	1	4	.209	.250
Ramon, Reyes, Cam.	.219	12	34	32	1	7	8	1	0	0	2	1	0	1	0	0	5	1	1	0	.250	.242
Robles, Juan, Rey.	.224	23	57	49	7	11	12	1	0	0	1	2	0	6	0	0	4	0	1	1	.245	.309
Robles, Juan, Can.	.300	17	20	20	2	6	8	2	0	0	4	0	0	0	0	0	4	0	0	2	.400	.300
Romero, Wilfredo, Tig.	.325	89	421	366	87	119	175	13	8	9	59	1	7	46	1	2	52	19	9	13	.478	.395
Romero, Wilfredo, Sal.	.358	26	124	109	23	39	54	5	2	2	22	1	0	12	2	0	10	8	2	3	.495	.431
Saucedo, Roberto, Mont.	.083	8	13	12	1	1	1	0	0	0	0	0	0	1	0	0	5	0	0	2	.083	.154
Saucedo, Roberto, Rey.	.306	79	318	265	36	81	141	9	3	15	50	4	4	43	2	4	55	0	1	7	.532	.407
Stark, Matt, Rey.	.345	9	37	29	3	10	11	1	0	0	2	0	0	7	1	2	2	0	0	0	.379	.486
Stark, Matt, Mont.	.319	43	180	138	23	44	72	10	0	6	23	0	4	35	3	7	10	1	1	3	.522	.456
Valle, Jose, Cor.	.250	17	57	44	5	11	12	1	0	0	3	0	0	10	0	0	6	0	0	3	.273	.389
Valle, Jose, Yuc.	.218	39	66	55	7	12	14	0	1	0	2	5	0	6	0	0	7	0	0	1	.255	.295
Vazquez, Jorge, Monc.	.167	10	8	6	1	1	1	0	0	0	0	0	0	2	0	0	2	0	0	0	.167	.375
Vazquez, Jorge, Tor.	.115	19	28	26	1	3	6	1	1	0	1	0	0	2	0	0	12	0	0	0	.154	.179
Velez, Manuel, Tab.	.163	18	57	49	4	8	8	0	0	0	1	1	0	7	0	1	5	0	2	2	.163	.268
Velez, Manuel, Agua.	.259	65	223	201	27	52	62	7	0	1	21	4	3	15	0	2	19	2	5	14	.308	.306
Villanueva, Hector, Yuc.	.128	14	66	47	3	6	12	0	0	2	9	0	0	16	3	0	4	0	0	1	.255	.379
Villanueva, Hector, Oax.	.417	7	32	24	9	10	16	3	0	1	4	0	0	7	1	1	2	1	0	2	.667	.563

Player, Team	Avg.	G	TPA	AB	R	H	TB	2B	3B	HR	RBI	SH	SF	HP	BB	IBB	SO	SB	CS	GDP	Slg.	OBP
Vizcarra, Roberto, Agua.	.345	86	386	330	72	114	162	18	0	10	42	8	4	43	1	3	23	10	8	5	.491	.418
Vizcarra, Roberto, Tig.	.174	6	28	23	5	4	5	1	0	0	4	0	0	5	0	1	1	1	0	2	.217	.321
Zamudio, Rafael, Tor.	.234	49	129	111	14	26	35	4	1	1	14	1	0	16	1	1	19	0	1	0	.315	.336
Zamudio, Rafael, Agua.	.247	31	96	85	6	21	28	4	0	1	11	1	0	10	0	3	16	2	1	1	.329	.326

1999 PITCHING

TEAM

Team	W	L	Pct.	ERA	G	CG	ShO	Sv.	IP	H	TBF	R	ER	HR	SH	SF	HB	BB	IBB	SO	WP	Bk.
Tabasco	63	57	.525	3.30	121	7	17	40	1058.2	1061	3993	461	388	57	62	39	24	355	29	454	40	4
Campeche	58	60	.492	3.31	119	15	14	33	1036.2	1003	3842	436	381	43	88	34	56	432	22	550	51	3
Monclova	71	46	.607	3.58	119	9	9	31	1044.0	1062	3961	498	415	77	55	26	32	376	25	526	42	5
Yucatan	60	56	.517	3.75	118	9	12	23	1016.0	1101	3906	486	423	44	75	41	38	425	26	519	42	0
Cancun	63	57	.525	3.81	121	12	9	32	1032.0	1046	3849	497	437	80	79	32	43	470	19	349	48	3
Veracruz	50	69	.420	4.09	120	8	13	29	1026.2	1005	3828	549	467	87	71	42	59	495	31	476	40	4
Monterrey	64	54	.542	4.14	119	11	6	23	1050.1	1024	3921	551	483	60	70	37	35	580	24	591	61	4
Reynosa	42	75	.359	4.30	120	7	2	17	1051.0	1120	3998	609	502	64	104	44	50	553	38	700	68	6
Saltillo	74	45	.622	4.38	119	7	9	45	1045.0	1103	3926	576	509	62	70	30	45	591	18	594	63	5
M.C. Reds	74	43	.632	4.44	117	11	6	32	1032.0	1173	4005	571	509	62	64	25	39	453	16	485	44	0
Cordoba	51	66	.436	4.47	118	13	6	21	997.2	1045	3779	556	495	86	84	29	50	553	63	470	42	8
M.C. Tigers	75	38	.664	4.60	115	8	5	35	995.0	1064	3802	593	509	62	53	31	33	587	31	500	74	2
Nuevo Laredo	53	65	.449	4.61	119	4	6	26	1040.1	1115	3950	603	533	81	69	34	39	642	66	571	87	5
Torreon	50	69	.420	5.10	120	3	3	32	1036.1	1237	4057	670	587	79	75	45	50	546	54	506	45	7
Oaxaca	49	70	.412	5.16	119	9	7	23	1021.0	1163	4001	660	585	77	59	29	48	508	39	473	58	9
Aguascalientes	47	74	.388	6.27	122	13	2	21	1006.1	1317	4087	770	701	112	58	45	48	483	51	428	39	2

INDIVIDUAL

TOP QUALIFIERS FOR EARNED-RUN AVERAGE TITLE

Minimum 98 innings.

Pitcher, Team	W	L	Pct.	ERA	G	GS	CG	ShO	Rel.	Sv.	IP	H	TBF	R	ER	HR	SH	SF	HB	BB	IBB	SO	WP	Bk.
Alvarez, Juan, Tab.	12	8	.600	2.20	25	25	2	1	0	0	163.1	155	670	56	40	2	5	3	4	44	3	64	3	0
Elvira, Narciso, Cam.	10	6	.625	2.25	20	20	5	3	0	0	144.0	97	578	44	36	2	9	3	3	57	0	133	8	0
Lopez, Gilberto, Can.	7	6	.538	2.29	48	6	1	1	42	18	102.1	79	417	28	26	5	10	6	6	46	5	35	2	1
Martinez, Miguel, Tab.	16	5	.762	2.33	25	25	2	1	0	0	166.1	153	669	50	43	9	7	2	3	37	2	77	2	1
Rivera, Oscar, Ver.	7	4	.636	2.54	21	18	3	2	3	0	120.1	93	509	51	34	7	4	3	8	61	1	83	4	0
Bourgeois, Steve, Sal.	14	5	.737	2.62	20	20	3	1	0	0	141.0	115	592	49	41	2	8	3	8	2	107	3	0
Palafox, Juan, Monc.	13	5	.722	2.79	23	23	6	3	0	0	171.0	163	700	64	53	9	8	0	10	44	3	100	8	0
Quinones, Enrique, Yuc.	10	9	.526	2.87	25	25	2	2	0	0	150.2	169	646	60	48	5	8	4	3	47	2	71	1	0
Manzanillo, Ravelo, Yuc.	10	5	.667	2.90	24	21	4	1	3	1	145.2	115	639	59	47	3	9	6	6	101	1	94	3	0
Meza, Leobardo, Ver.	9	5	.643	3.01	23	19	1	1	4	1	122.2	95	512	44	41	10	7	4	5	64	3	60	1	1
Acosta, Aaron, Lar.	5	4	.556	3.10	21	20	1	0	1	0	116.0	101	497	47	40	7	4	2	3	62	1	84	8	0
Alvarez, Octavio, Mex.	12	6	.667	3.12	23	22	7	0	1	0	170.0	168	697	69	59	10	12	2	4	46	1	69	4	0
Turgeon, David, Rey.	5	5	.500	3.16	17	17	1	0	0	0	111.0	106	475	46	39	6	10	3	3	42	2	71	3	1
Valenzuela, Gil, Can.	14	3	.824	3.18	20	20	3	1	0	0	124.1	132	524	46	44	9	11	1	5	39	2	28	5	0
Loaiza, Sabino, Cam.	8	7	.533	3.19	24	23	1	1	0	0	141.0	131	616	57	50	4	13	5	11	73	2	51	3	0

DEPARTMENTAL LEADERS: W—M. Martinez, Jose Navarro, 16; L—Carrasco, 15; Pct.—H. Heredia, .900; G—Ayala, E. Herrera, 61; GS—Carrasco, 27; CG—O. Alvarez, 7; ShO—Elvira, M. Munoz, Palafox, 3; Rel.—Ayala, E. Herrera, 61; Sv.—Ayala, 41; IP—Carrasco, 180.2; H—Carrasco, 217; TBF—Villegas, 798; R—Carrasco, Villegas, 117; ER—Carrasco, Villegas, 104; HR—Villegas, 20; SH—L. Perez, 16; SF—Ochoa, Pimentel, 9; HB—Ra. Rodriguez, 12; BB—Manzanillo, 101; IBB—Para, Picota, 13; SO—Elvira, 133; WP—Melendez, 18; BK—Ali, Loya, 3.

ALL PITCHERS

Pitcher, Team	W	L	Pct.	ERA	G	GS	CG	ShO	Rel.	Sv.	IP	H	TBF	R	ER	HR	SH	SF	HB	BB	IBB	SO	WP	Bk.
Acosta, Aaron, Lar.	5	4	.556	3.10	21	20	1	0	1	0	116.0	101	497	47	40	7	4	2	3	62	1	84	8	0
Acosta, Gerardo, Oax.	3	10	.231	5.48	23	18	1	0	5	0	95.1	97	444	64	58	8	5	1	3	73	3	51	12	0
Acosta, Jaciel, Monc.	0	0	.000	11.57	7	0	0	0	7	0	7.0	9	37	9	9	0	1	1	2	6	0	2	0	0
Aguilar, Jose, Tor.-Mont.	3	2	.600	6.89	50	0	0	0	50	2	32.2	43	161	27	25	3	5	2	0	20	3	21	2	2
Aguilar, Mario, Cam.	0	2	.000	11.81	13	1	0	0	12	0	10.2	18	59	14	14	1	1	0	1	11	0	7	3	0
Aguilera, Adrian, Mex.	0	1	.000	6.30	5	2	0	0	3	0	10.0	8	54	12	7	2	1	1	1	16	0	5	3	0
Aguirre, Guadencio, Tab.	4	3	.571	1.72	49	0	0	0	49	30	62.2	49	245	12	12	1	1	0	2	18	4	42	3	0
Aleman, Paulo, Cor.	2	4	.333	3.81	18	7	0	0	11	0	59.0	46	253	26	25	7	5	3	2	40	2	11	4	2
Ali, Sam, Oax.	3	8	.273	5.66	14	14	0	0	0	0	90.2	108	415	64	57	4	9	2	2	49	2	47	10	3
Almeida, Roussell, Lar.	3	1	.750	4.66	38	0	0	0	38	0	56.0	49	258	34	29	3	1	3	3	47	5	41	11	1
Alvarez, Antonio, Monc.	7	2	.778	3.20	26	13	1	1	13	0	101.1	97	433	43	36	13	2	2	2	35	3	46	4	0
Alvarez, Juan, Tab.	12	8	.600	2.20	25	25	2	1	0	0	163.1	155	670	56	40	2	5	3	4	44	3	64	3	0
Alvarez, Octavio, Mex.	12	6	.667	3.12	23	22	7	0	1	0	170.0	168	697	69	59	10	12	2	4	46	1	69	4	0
Angulo, Luis, Sal.	0	0	.000	10.13	9	0	0	0	9	0	8.2	38	10	9	0	0	1	0	6	0	1	1	0
Angulo, Victor, Tig.	0	0	.000	12.00	14	0	0	0	14	0	6.0	10	38	8	8	0	0	1	12	0	4	4	0
Arias, Joel, Mont.	0	0	.000	10.80	2	0	0	0	2	0	1.2	4	9	2	2	0	0	0	0	0	1	0	0
Armenta, Alejandro, Tig.	4	2	.667	3.53	27	4	0	0	23	2	43.1	39	202	24	17	1	3	4	2	33	2	18	7	0
Arocha, Rene, Yuc.-Mont.	1	7	.125	4.55	12	9	1	0	0	0	57.1	67	248	29	29	3	4	1	0	14	1	47	3	0
Atilano, Juan, Ver.	0	0	.000	5.68	6	0	0	0	6	0	6.1	8	31	5	4	1	0	1	6	0	3	1	0
Atondo, Sergio, Yuc.	0	0	.000	45.00	2	0	0	0	2	0	1.0	2	9	6	5	0	0	0	4	0	0	0	0
Avilez, Alejandro, Sal.	1	0	.000	9.39	7	0	0	0	7	0	7.2	14	42	11	8	1	0	0	3	2	0	4	0	0
Ayala, Luis, Sal.	7	3	.700	1.71	61	0	0	0	61	41	79.0	54	287	17	15	1	3	0	3	22	5	28	3	0
Baez, Sixto, Oak.	0	0	.000	0.00	1	0	0	0	0	0	0.0	2	3	0	0	0	0	0	0	1	0	0	0	0
Baez, Victor, Cor.	1	3	.250	3.38	32	0	0	0	32	0	37.1	25	175	21	14	2	6	3	1	37	5	13	1	1
Barraza, Ernesto, Tig.-Tor.	6	7	.462	6.17	23	22	0	0	1	0	108.0	134	531	79	74	6	8	4	1	93	2	41	14	1
Barrera, Sigfrido, Yuc.	0	0	.000	10.13	5	0	0	0	5	0	5.1	10	32	6	6	0	0	0	0	7	0	2	3	0
Barron, Avelino, Tab.	0	0	.000	10.80	4	0	0	0	7	0	3.1	8	24	5	4	0	1	1	0	7	1	3	0	0
Beltran, Alonso, Tig.	1	0	1.000	3.00	3	3	0	0	0	0	9.0	11	39	7	3	0	0	3	0	4	0	0
Bernal, Manuel, Mex.	5	2	.714	2.92	13	7	0	0	6	0	52.1	50	217	17	17	1	3	1	2	17	1	26	1	0

CLASS AAA *Mexican League*

Pitcher, Team	W	L	Pct.	ERA	G	GS	CG	ShO	Rel.	Sv.	IP	H	TBF	R	ER	HR	SH	SF	HB	BB	IBB	SO	WP	Bk.
Berumen, Andres, Mont.	0	4	.000	5.10	12	5	1	0	7	1	30.0	26	140	21	17	2	3	2	2	24	0	11	3	0
Blancas, Rigoberto, Tab.	0	0	.000	0.00	3	0	0	0	3	0	2.0	1	11	0	0	0	0	0	0	4	0	0	0	0
Bourgeois, Steve, Sal.	14	5	.737	2.62	20	20	3	1	0	0	141.0	115	592	49	41	2	8	2	3	82	2	107	3	0
Boze, Wayne, Sal.	10	6	.625	4.36	25	25	2	1	0	0	148.2	152	653	79	72	8	7	4	8	90	1	85	5	1
Burnett, Heath, Oax.	1	3	.250	5.68	4	4	0	0	0	0	19.0	21	80	12	12	3	0	0	0	8	0	10	1	0
Bustillos, Oscar, Tig.-Agua.	1	0	1.000	12.18	15	0	0	0	15	0	17.0	24	95	26	23	2	0	1	0	22	0	11	5	0
Butcher, Mike, Agua.	0	1	.000	15.00	4	0	0	0	4	0	6.0	12	35	10	10	2	1	1	1	6	1	4	2	0
Cabrales, Gabriel, Agua.	3	2	.600	4.95	56	0	0	0	56	1	91.0	120	408	55	50	8	6	3	2	27	7	43	1	0
Camara, Pedro, Cor.	3	6	.333	5.79	26	12	1	0	14	2	74.2	70	354	51	48	5	8	4	1	70	3	47	10	0
Campillo, Jorge, Tig.	1	2	.333	2.90	32	0	0	0	32	1	71.1	50	302	29	23	3	1	2	3	46	2	41	6	0
Campos, Francisco, Cam.	6	11	.353	3.71	24	24	5	0	0	0	157.2	162	668	74	65	11	15	4	5	53	6	97	7	0
Candelario, Dimas, Cor.	0	1	.000	5.06	6	0	0	0	6	0	5.1	9	26	3	3	1	0	0	0	3	0	2	0	0
Cantu, Jacobo, Tor.	0	1	.000	6.75	9	1	0	0	8	0	16.0	24	79	14	12	3	1	1	0	7	0	9	0	0
Cardenas, Faustino, Can.	0	0	.000	4.26	6	0	0	0	6	0	12.2	11	50	8	6	1	0	1	0	0	0	9	0	0
Carranza, Javier, Can.	1	5	.167	3.83	10	10	0	0	0	0	54.0	58	247	26	23	4	5	0	1	36	1	22	4	0
Carrasco, Alejandro, Oax.	12	15	.444	5.18	27	27	6	1	0	0	180.2	217	797	117	104	15	7	4	8	54	5	75	6	1
Caruso, Eugene, Lar.	6	9	.400	4.30	22	21	2	1	1	0	132.0	135	584	67	63	9	8	1	3	76	5	83	1	0
Castaneda, Aurelio, Agua.	11	9	.550	4.80	26	25	6	2	1	0	152.0	172	671	89	81	17	7	3	9	58	5	49	5	0
Castellanos, Hugo, Lar.	0	0	.000	6.94	24	1	0	0	23	0	36.1	44	176	32	28	6	1	0	1	24	1	22	3	0
Cazares, Juan, Sal.	2	1	.667	1.50	18	0	0	0	18	0	6.0	7	25	2	1	0	1	0	0	4	0	3	0	0
Cazares, Rosario, Sal.	0	0	.000	2.45	17	0	0	0	17	2	22.0	19	88	6	6	1	2	1	0	6	0	11	3	0
Cazares, Tomas, Monc.	5	1	.833	1.34	36	3	0	0	33	0	40.1	28	171	9	6	0	2	0	4	25	0	27	4	1
Cecena, Jose, Monc.	9	6	.600	4.17	24	20	1	0	4	0	116.2	109	485	64	54	11	8	4	0	38	1	69	8	0
Cerros, Juan, Rey.	4	3	.571	4.94	38	0	0	0	38	1	54.2	57	260	36	30	2	10	2	4	38	8	36	4	0
Chapa, Javier, Cam.	4	5	.444	3.92	20	15	1	1	5	0	80.1	89	366	42	35	6	4	2	3	45	1	32	7	0
Chavez, Carlos, Agua.	0	3	.000	6.57	5	5	0	0	0	0	24.2	27	126	19	18	0	2	3	1	26	0	12	1	0
Conde, Argenis, Tor.	9	6	.600	4.18	53	15	0	0	38	0	140.0	163	622	73	65	7	11	4	3	71	11	75	2	0
Cota, Marino, Oax.	3	10	.231	3.69	44	10	0	0	34	15	105.0	117	480	51	43	3	9	5	3	47	8	64	0	2
Couoh, Enrique, Yuc.-Ver.	3	8	.273	2.75	50	0	0	0	50	3	68.2	57	295	23	21	2	8	2	0	39	7	53	6	0
Cruz, Javier, Mex.	8	5	.615	2.90	48	2	0	0	46	15	77.2	71	322	26	25	6	7	2	3	22	4	60	2	0
Cruz, Juan, Yuc.	0	1	.000	4.80	21	1	0	0	20	2	15.0	19	71	8	8	0	1	1	0	8	0	13	5	0
Cruz, Luis, Tig.-Agua.	0	1	.000	10.71	16	1	0	0	15	0	21.0	37	117	25	25	3	2	1	1	17	2	11	2	0
Diaz, Alejandro, Ver.-Can.	2	2	.500	5.34	40	0	0	0	40	3	60.2	76	270	38	36	10	5	2	6	16	1	13	3	0
Diaz, Marco, Lar.	2	3	.400	5.03	20	7	0	0	13	0	53.2	56	232	34	30	5	0	3	1	21	1	25	2	1
Diaz, Rafael, Mont.	8	2	.800	2.60	36	4	2	1	32	15	86.2	50	332	27	26	3	5	1	4	32	1	74	4	0
Dominguez, Carlos, Sal.	0	0	.000	9.00	7	0	0	0	7	0	3.0	5	16	3	3	1	0	0	0	2	0	1	1	0
Dominguez, David, Mex.-Oax.	0	0	.000	14.73	3	0	0	0	3	0	3.2	5	24	6	6	0	0	0	3	5	0	3	2	0
Douglas, Osorio, Can.	0	0	.000	27.00	1	0	0	0	1	0	0.1	1	2	1	1	0	0	0	0	0	0	0	0	0
Duarte, Miguel, Sal.	4	3	.571	3.55	44	3	0	0	41	0	76.0	67	334	36	30	5	9	4	2	48	2	50	4	1
Elguezabal, Octavio, Cam.	0	1	.000	8.03	12	1	0	0	11	0	12.1	17	74	12	11	0	3	3	3	21	0	5	3	0
Elizalde, Carlos, Oax.	0	1	.000	6.35	2	1	0	0	1	0	5.2	11	27	4	4	0	1	0	0	1	0	2	0	0
Elvira, Narciso, Cam.	10	6	.625	2.25	20	20	5	3	0	0	144.0	97	578	44	36	2	9	3	3	57	0	133	8	0
Enriquez, Martin, Sal.	5	4	.556	4.12	32	6	0	0	26	2	59.0	66	265	30	27	5	7	1	2	29	4	37	6	1
Esparza, Emerson, Monc.	8	8	.500	4.74	24	23	0	0	1	0	117.2	151	543	79	62	5	6	2	4	51	2	35	4	1
Esquer, Mercedes, Rey.	0	6	.000	5.25	19	13	1	0	6	0	72.0	86	323	47	42	6	7	2	1	33	0	30	3	0
Federico, Gustavo, Agua.-Mont.	6	2	.750	4.60	34	0	0	0	34	7	43.0	52	191	23	22	4	1	1	1	18	3	17	0	0
Felix, Antonio, Agua.	0	0	.000	0.00	2	0	0	0	2	0	2.0	2	8	0	0	0	0	0	0	2	0	0	0	0
Fernandez, Osvaldo, Mont.-Sal.	3	5	.375	5.77	12	10	0	0	2	0	53.0	61	258	39	34	1	2	1	3	47	1	45	7	1
Ferrer, Jesus, Tor.	0	0	.000	14.14	5	0	0	0	5	0	7.0	12	43	11	11	1	0	0	0	9	0	1	0	0
Figueroa, Fernando, Sal.	1	0	1.000	3.18	4	3	0	0	1	0	17.0	16	78	8	6	1	3	0	1	11	0	5	0	0
Flores, Ignacio, Monc.	3	5	.375	2.85	54	1	0	0	53	2	72.2	77	318	32	23	6	5	2	1	30	7	48	1	0
Flores, Jorge, Tab.	2	0	1.000	4.12	26	1	0	0	25	1	39.1	43	180	19	18	0	4	1	2	23	5	12	2	0
Fontes, Agustin, Can.	7	5	.583	3.42	21	19	2	0	2	0	115.2	134	500	49	44	6	7	3	7	35	0	34	4	0
Fregoso, Raul, Can.	4	1	.800	4.25	13	6	1	0	7	0	48.2	43	212	26	23	6	4	1	2	29	0	20	1	0
Galvez, Rosario, Agua.-Tab.	0	2	.000	8.10	23	4	0	0	19	0	30.0	41	158	28	27	7	3	1	2	30	2	15	6	2
Gamez, Francisco, Mont.	0	0	.000	9.72	4	1	0	0	3	0	8.1	9	43	9	9	0	0	1	2	8	1	4	1	0
Garcia, Adolfo, Cam.	2	1	.667	3.02	23	0	0	0	23	1	44.2	46	182	17	15	0	4	3	3	11	1	6	2	1
Garcia, Alfredo, Mex.	9	6	.600	4.30	19	18	2	1	1	0	113.0	132	500	60	54	5	3	0	4	38	2	54	3	0
Garcia, Carlos, Mex.	12	4	.750	4.05	25	25	2	1	0	0	153.1	170	688	78	69	9	5	6	8	78	1	58	4	0
Garcia, Gerardo, Tig.	5	1	.833	4.60	22	3	0	0	19	0	45.0	55	218	30	23	0	0	3	1	31	3	25	5	0
Garcia, Jose, Sal.	0	2	.000	11.12	13	0	0	0	13	0	5.2	9	30	8	7	0	1	0	0	5	0	2	0	0
Garcia, Jose L., Tig.	6	6	.500	5.33	27	19	1	0	8	0	125.0	160	568	88	74	12	6	2	3	46	2	69	5	0
Garcia, Manuel, Tig.	0	0	.000	9.00	12	0	0	0	12	0	12.0	13	60	12	12	0	1	1	0	13	1	2	3	0
Garcia, Mike, Mex.	0	0	.000	0.75	12	0	0	0	12	8	12.0	5	42	1	1	0	0	0	0	3	0	20	0	0
Garcialuna, Francisco, Mex.	0	1	.000	11.57	2	1	0	0	1	0	4.2	9	26	6	6	0	0	1	0	4	0	1	0	0
Garibay, Daniel, Tig.	2	5	.286	5.06	16	16	1	0	0	0	89.0	91	407	62	50	6	8	1	3	56	3	59	5	0
Garibay, Roberto, Can.	7	1	.875	3.71	27	4	2	1	23	0	53.1	50	226	29	22	4	1	1	3	20	1	17	3	0
Garibay, Salvador, Lar.	3	1	.750	3.60	18	0	0	0	18	0	35.0	35	146	15	14	1	4	2	0	16	6	9	2	0
Garza, Roberto, Lar.	1	1	.500	5.40	30	1	0	0	29	1	45.0	46	207	28	27	5	3	3	5	32	3	16	1	1
Gomez, Gustavo, Rey.	2	2	.500	6.27	25	3	0	0	22	0	56.0	65	268	40	39	3	6	3	6	41	4	31	2	0
Gomez, Martin, Cor.	0	1	.000	6.75	4	0	0	0	4	0	5.1	4	22	4	4	3	1	0	0	2	0	4	0	0
Gonzalez, Arnulfo, Ver.	0	2	.000	7.13	8	2	0	0	6	0	17.2	19	88	15	14	2	2	0	1	17	1	9	0	0
Gonzalez, Arturo, Mont.	6	6	.500	4.23	15	15	2	0	0	0	87.1	92	378	46	41	7	4	4	2	30	1	31	4	0
Gonzalez, Gilberto, Tor.	3	5	.375	6.89	16	13	0	0	3	0	64.0	80	311	54	49	7	5	6	0	49	1	42	7	0
Gonzalez, Victor, Monc.	2	2	.500	4.42	33	0	0	0	33	0	59.0	66	249	33	29	5	6	3	1	17	3	20	1	1
Grajales, Norberto, Tor.	8	6	.571	3.32	27	17	1	0	10	1	116.2	121	487	51	43	5	4	3	5	29	2	49	6	0
Green, Ottis, Sa.-Tor.	0	4	.000	4.31	7	6	1	0	1	0	39.2	36	183	23	19	4	1	5	2	30	0	29	3	0
Guerica, Guillermo, Oax.	0	0	.000	6.23	8	0	0	0	8	0	13.0	21	66	13	9	1	0	0	1	6	0	6	0	1
Guerra, Pascual, Tab.	2	3	.400	3.89	9	8	0	0	1	0	44.0	52	190	22	19	1	5	2	0	14	0	9	0	0
Gutierrez, Cosme, Oax.	0	1	.000	1.69	20	0	0	0	20	0	16.0	14	71	5	3	0	1	1	1	7	1	11	0	0
Gutierrez, Marco, Mex.	4	3	.571	5.69	19	12	0	0	7	0	61.2	76	289	45	39	5	5	2	1	33	0	24	5	0
Guzman, Christian, Monc.	0	0	.000	1.93	6	0	0	0	6	0	4.2	5	20	1	1	0	0	0	0	1	0	2	0	1
Heredia, Hector, Yuc.	9	1	.900	2.78	39	3	0	0	36	14	68.0	67	290	26	21	2	4	3	1	19	5	38	1	0
Heredia, Julian, Rey.	3	9	.250	3.09	15	14	3	1	1	0	90.1	91	400	42	31	5	7	5	10	41	1	82	8	0
Heredia, Wilson, Tig.	1	1	.500	11.42	5	5	0	0	0	0	17.1	18	88	24	22	2	1	0	3	23	0	20	2	0
Hernandez, Fernando, Mont.	6	5	.545	4.55	17	17	3	1	0	0	110.2	105	495	64	56	5	10	2	3	68	2	99	11	0

Pitcher, Team	W	L	Pct.	ERA	G	GS	CG	ShO	Rel.	Sv.	IP	H	TBF	R	ER	HR	SH	SF	HB	BB	IBB	SO	WP	Bk.
Hernandez, Jose, Monc.	7	5	.583	4.49	20	19	0	0	1	0	100.1	112	428	60	50	12	4	1	3	34	1	43	1	1
Hernandez, Martin, Can.-Sal.	7	4	.636	3.76	18	18	1	1	0	0	117.1	112	502	56	49	8	12	4	3	54	0	43	6	0
Herrera, Calixto, Monc.-Tor.	2	0	1.000	4.95	27	0	0	0	27	1	40.0	39	188	27	22	3	2	1	1	37	5	31	5	0
Herrera, Enrique, Tab.	7	5	.583	2.16	61	0	0	0	61	7	83.1	71	345	23	20	1	7	3	2	35	7	42	4	0
Higuera, Teodoro, Mont.	7	2	.778	2.91	9	9	0	0	0	0	52.2	41	224	20	17	2	4	1	1	34	0	34	4	0
Hollins, Stacy, Tor.	2	5	.286	7.17	8	8	1	0	0	0	42.2	45	195	34	34	1	2	2	5	19	0	28	2	0
Huerta, Edgar, Tig.	0	0	.000	0.00	1	0	0	0	1	0	0.0	0	1	1	1	0	0	0	0	1	0	0	0	0
Huerta, Francisco, Can.	0	0	.000	27.00	2	0	0	0	2	0	0.2	0	7	2	2	0	0	0	0	5	0	0	0	0
Huerta, Luis, Lar.	4	6	.400	4.74	19	18	0	0	1	0	81.2	112	382	51	43	6	4	4	3	34	3	32	8	0
Izabal, Luis, Can.	0	1	.000	5.74	10	0	0	0	10	0	15.2	17	73	10	10	0	2	0	1	12	1	6	0	1
Jimenez, German, Lar.	4	6	.400	3.59	20	20	1	1	0	0	105.1	110	464	52	42	7	7	2	3	66	3	34	7	0
Jimenez, Isaac, Ver.	5	6	.455	4.41	19	19	1	0	0	0	102.0	104	441	56	50	5	12	2	8	42	2	37	4	0
Kamar, Emil, Can.	5	4	.556	4.77	19	9	2	1	10	1	60.1	61	269	33	32	4	3	2	4	37	0	21	5	0
Kil, Hong, Oak.	0	1	.000	0.00	1	0	0	0	1	0	0.0	1	2	2	2	0	0	0	0	1	0	0	0	0
Lara, Edy, Yuc.	1	0	1.000	4.07	26	0	0	0	26	0	42.0	53	199	24	19	4	1	3	6	18	3	17	3	0
Lara, Hugo, Ver.-Tab.	5	8	.385	3.83	24	20	1	0	4	0	105.2	118	455	55	45	7	4	2	7	28	2	38	3	0
Lara, Jorge, Sal.	13	5	.722	4.42	23	23	1	1	0	0	138.1	144	586	72	68	18	5	6	5	49	0	61	3	0
Larranaga, Miguel, Can.	2	1	.667	1.41	21	0	0	0	21	2	38.1	35	148	6	6	1	4	3	1	9	2	9	0	1
Leon, Cupertino, Mex.	1	0	1.000	4.99	21	0	0	0	21	2	30.2	40	144	21	17	2	1	2	3	13	0	6	1	0
Leon, Juan, Tor.	3	3	.500	2.53	28	6	0	0	22	0	67.2	72	308	33	19	1	1	2	7	35	1	40	4	1
Lewis, Richie, Rey.	1	3	.250	3.33	11	6	0	0	5	2	46.0	35	201	19	17	3	7	0	0	27	2	37	7	0
Leyva, Edgar, Cor.	7	4	.636	3.54	24	17	2	1	7	1	109.1	101	483	56	43	8	8	1	5	60	5	73	3	0
Lezama, Rafael, Tab.-Ver.	0	1	.000	6.75	41	0	0	0	41	1	20.0	27	100	16	15	2	3	1	1	14	0	12	0	1
Linares, Yfrain, Agua.-Cor.	1	5	.167	5.40	12	8	1	0	4	0	41.2	43	211	29	25	1	3	2	0	43	1	29	4	0
Lizarraga, Andres, Lar.	1	0	1.000	8.53	10	1	0	0	9	0	12.2	17	61	13	12	2	0	2	1	8	1	4	2	0
Loaiza, Sabino, Cam.	8	7	.533	3.19	24	23	1	1	1	0	141.0	131	616	57	50	4	13	5	11	73	2	51	3	0
Lopez, Emigdio, Cam.	9	11	.450	3.71	26	24	2	0	2	0	152.2	168	647	69	63	8	10	7	10	36	1	73	4	0
Lopez, Gilberto, Can.	7	6	.538	2.29	48	6	1	1	42	18	102.1	79	417	28	26	5	10	6	6	46	5	35	2	1
Lopez, Jesus, Oax.	0	1	.000	5.33	43	0	0	0	43	3	27.0	23	121	18	16	2	1	1	1	21	2	9	2	0
Lopez, Jonas, Yuc.	4	7	.364	6.38	16	14	1	1	2	0	67.2	100	318	49	48	4	3	2	1	21	1	18	2	0
Lopez, Jose, Tor.	0	5	.000	2.54	45	0	0	0	45	19	46.0	44	204	19	13	0	4	3	4	23	6	28	0	0
Lopez, Jose, Lar.	1	4	.200	9.22	19	5	0	0	14	0	27.1	38	146	30	28	4	0	3	1	30	1	14	8	0
Lopez, Raymundo, Monc.	0	0	.000	1.69	6	0	0	0	6	0	5.1	3	22	1	1	0	0	0	0	6	1	1	0	0
Loya, Rigoberto, Mont.	3	5	.375	4.55	28	13	1	1	15	0	93.0	93	425	58	47	2	5	2	5	65	0	41	5	3
Luevano, Juan, Ver.	4	2	.667	1.53	55	0	0	0	55	25	64.2	46	261	12	11	4	2	3	3	21	3	24	1	0
Macias, Luis, Monc.	0	0	.000	6.75	4	0	0	0	4	0	1.1	1	10	1	1	0	0	0	1	5	0	1	0	0
Manriquez, Alberto, Mont.-Agua.	2	1	.667	5.96	29	1	0	0	28	0	48.1	64	229	38	32	7	2	2	2	21	0	21	3	0
Manzanillo, Ravelo, Mont.-Yuc.	10	5	.667	2.90	24	21	4	1	3	1	145.2	115	639	59	47	3	9	6	6	101	1	94	3	0
Marquez, Isidro, Tig.	9	6	.600	2.97	54	0	0	0	54	26	66.2	69	291	28	22	5	7	2	1	31	6	36	0	0
Martinez, Cesar, Tor.	5	8	.385	6.04	30	15	0	0	15	0	89.1	117	419	65	60	13	5	6	3	46	2	33	5	0
Martinez, Francisco, Lar.	1	1	.500	4.00	15	0	0	0	15	5	18.0	19	85	8	8	0	1	0	0	14	4	13	5	0
Martinez, Jesus, Ver.	7	7	.500	3.55	23	9	0	0	14	0	88.2	75	371	37	35	5	10	3	4	40	6	31	6	1
Martinez, Juan, Mex.	0	0	.000	6.75	3	0	0	0	3	0	2.2	4	14	2	2	0	0	0	0	2	0	1	2	0
Martinez, Miguel, Tab.	16	5	.762	2.33	25	25	2	1	0	0	166.1	153	669	50	43	9	7	6	2	37	2	77	2	1
Martinez, Pedro, Oax.	5	0	1.000	1.38	11	9	0	0	2	0	58.2	51	231	11	9	3	1	0	0	17	0	30	1	0
Mascorro, David, Mex.	0	0	.000	5.48	43	0	0	0	43	2	23.0	29	102	14	14	1	6	0	0	11	0	7	1	0
Medina, Alonso, Sal.	0	0	.000	4.50	11	0	0	0	11	0	10.0	9	54	6	5	1	0	0	0	14	0	3	3	0
Mefia, Delfino, Lar.	0	0	.000	0.00	1	1	0	0	0	0	2.0	1	14	1	0	0	2	0	0	7	0	2	1	0
Melendez, Nestor, Rey.	4	5	.444	3.54	38	8	0	0	30	0	68.2	55	308	38	27	4	4	4	3	55	3	47	18	0
Mendez, Luis, Tor.	0	0	.000	3.86	2	0	0	0	2	0	2.1	3	11	1	1	0	0	0	0	1	0	0	0	0
Mendoza, Marco, Rey.	0	0	.000	6.35	6	0	0	0	6	0	5.2	8	31	4	4	1	0	0	0	7	0	0	1	0
Mere, Fernando, Ver.	0	2	.000	4.34	19	2	0	0	17	0	37.1	42	169	18	18	5	2	2	2	20	0	8	2	0
Metoyer, Tony, Can.-Lar.	3	7	.300	2.98	50	0	0	0	50	25	54.1	55	243	26	18	4	7	1	0	32	4	36	10	0
Meza, Leobardo, Ver.	9	5	.643	3.01	23	19	1	1	4	1	122.2	95	512	44	41	10	7	4	5	64	3	60	1	1
Mikkelsen, Linc, Sal.	0	1	.000	7.36	3	3	0	0	0	0	14.2	19	64	12	12	1	0	0	1	6	0	8	0	0
Miranda, Julio, Agua.	2	4	.333	5.26	43	0	0	0	43	10	49.2	63	232	35	29	6	4	2	4	23	2	29	1	0
Molina, Primitivo, Mont.	0	3	.000	5.93	23	0	0	0	23	0	27.1	37	124	18	18	0	4	1	0	10	2	8	0	0
Montano, Ignacio, Cor.	1	0	1.000	3.86	31	0	0	0	31	0	18.2	17	88	8	8	1	0	1	0	18	1	9	0	1
Montemayor, Humberto, Mont.	1	5	.167	4.87	27	8	0	0	19	1	77.2	76	350	45	42	5	5	3	4	47	1	42	7	0
Mora, Eleazar, Ver.	7	10	.412	4.19	22	21	1	0	1	0	126.2	138	533	66	59	13	7	4	3	41	2	50	1	0
Morales, Luis, Ver.	0	1	.000	5.76	25	2	0	0	23	0	29.2	34	138	21	19	4	0	0	3	19	0	27	2	0
Moreno, Claudio, Mex.	9	2	.818	5.13	53	1	0	0	52	2	79.0	104	371	50	45	5	6	2	2	46	2	35	5	0
Moreno, Leobardo, Mex.-Sal.	7	7	.500	5.94	21	18	0	0	3	0	89.1	121	425	65	59	9	4	1	0	53	0	52	7	0
Munoz, Leonardo, Mont.	3	3	.500	4.42	46	1	0	0	45	1	38.2	40	178	20	19	6	1	1	1	30	2	19	4	0
Munoz, Miguel, Cor.	9	8	.529	3.39	23	23	3	3	0	0	143.1	150	612	62	54	9	7	4	8	31	3	53	0	0
Munoz, Ricardo, Agua.	0	0	.000	3.75	5	1	0	0	4	0	12.0	17	52	5	5	2	1	1	0	1	0	3	0	0
Murillo, Felipe, Tor.	5	6	.455	4.08	49	0	0	0	49	10	57.1	64	251	31	26	4	13	2	2	25	10	21	0	0
Navarro, Joel, Mex.	2	1	.667	6.92	8	1	0	0	7	0	13.0	16	62	11	10	0	0	0	0	7	1	9	0	0
Navarro, Jose, Tig.	16	4	.800	3.62	42	10	2	0	32	2	134.1	145	582	60	54	11	11	5	6	53	5	44	3	0
Navarro, Luis, Yuc.	4	3	.571	3.92	19	9	1	1	10	0	66.2	75	288	29	29	4	8	3	2	18	1	30	1	0
Neri, Braulio, Sal.-Cam.	0	0	.000	5.14	13	0	0	0	13	0	14.0	19	74	13	8	0	3	1	4	11	0	9	2	0
Neri, Eduardo, Ver.-Yuc.	3	6	.333	3.81	45	0	0	0	45	2	52.0	51	232	28	22	6	7	2	1	25	1	31	0	0
Nieblas, Mauro, Mont.	0	0	.000	6.75	2	0	0	0	2	0	1.1	1	10	1	1	0	0	0	0	5	0	1	1	0
Nieblas, Omar, Tab.	0	1	.000	3.76	19	0	0	0	19	0	26.1	23	115	11	11	0	0	1	0	16	0	12	6	0
Nunez, Javier, Sal.-Agua.	0	0	.000	11.32	7	0	0	0	7	0	10.1	18	53	13	13	1	0	0	2	6	1	1	3	0
Nunez, Jose, Tig.	15	3	.833	3.78	26	25	3	2	1	0	157.1	154	688	73	66	9	5	5	4	84	4	72	13	0
Nunez, Jose, Oax.	5	6	.455	6.87	26	14	1	0	12	0	97.0	118	454	81	74	8	3	3	10	51	3	39	1	0
Ochoa, Pablo, Rey.	8	11	.421	3.86	24	24	2	0	0	0	142.1	136	633	81	61	4	11	9	3	78	1	128	8	1
Olague, Jesus, Mont.-Agua.	3	5	.375	6.68	22	9	0	0	13	0	60.2	78	293	49	45	1	2	6	2	41	2	38	4	0
Orea, Flavio, Cor.	2	6	.250	5.40	26	0	0	0	26	4	33.1	36	152	23	20	4	4	0	1	19	5	22	1	1
Oropeza, Eddie, Rey.	0	4	.000	7.06	7	3	0	0	4	0	21.2	32	109	19	17	3	3	1	2	16	2	8	1	0
Orozco, Jaime, Rey.	3	12	.200	6.13	20	19	0	0	1	0	101.1	151	462	85	69	13	12	5	2	14	1	27	1	0
Ortega, Raul, Yuc.-Tor.	0	0	.000	3.86	15	0	0	0	15	0	9.1	13	47	6	4	0	0	0	2	4	1	3	1	0
Ortega, Roberto, Cor.	3	6	.333	6.56	30	6	0	0	24	3	46.2	54	226	37	34	1	8	2	3	40	4	28	5	0
Ortega, Wilbert, Yuc.	1	4	.200	3.19	37	7	0	0	30	1	53.2	58	236	28	19	4	6	5	2	25	2	20	1	0
Osuna, Ricardo, Tab.	0	1	.000	4.09	2	2	0	0	0	0	11.0	14	51	7	5	0	1	2	0	4	0	4	1	1

Pitcher, Team	W	L	Pct.	ERA	G	GS	CG	ShO	Rel.	Sv.	IP	H	TBF	R	ER	HR	SH	SF	HB	BB	IBB	SO	WP	Bk.
Osuna, Roberto, Yuc.-Cor.-Sal.	0	1	.000	14.81	13	0	0	0	13	2	10.1	18	67	19	17	2	2	1	3	15	2	6	0	0
Palacios, Vicente, Rey.	5	2	.714	0.95	43	0	0	0	43	10	66.0	47	256	8	7	1	10	2	2	20	2	68	1	1
Palafox, Juan, Monc.	13	5	.722	2.79	23	23	6	3	0	0	171.0	163	700	64	53	9	8	0	10	44	3	100	8	0
Parra, Julio, Lar.	6	6	.500	3.80	55	0	0	0	55	2	64.0	66	300	30	27	2	10	1	3	47	13	48	5	0
Pena, Joel, Ver.	3	9	.250	4.60	39	5	1	0	34	1	78.1	82	365	52	40	7	11	1	4	53	7	38	6	0
Perez, Leonardo, Cor.	6	12	.333	4.80	24	24	5	1	0	0	135.0	158	598	78	72	12	16	3	4	56	9	61	3	1
Perez, Vladimir, Lar.-Oax.	0	3	.000	6.49	24	0	0	0	24	0	26.1	35	131	20	19	2	7	1	1	17	4	14	4	1
Picota, Alberto, Oax.-Lar.	10	6	.625	4.90	40	9	0	0	31	0	93.2	100	443	58	51	3	12	4	4	72	13	67	11	1
Pimentel, Roberto, Tab.	12	9	.571	3.56	25	25	3	2	0	0	161.2	161	670	72	64	11	10	9	5	46	0	61	5	0
Powell, Dennis, Cam.	5	4	.556	1.10	45	0	0	0	45	20	65.1	51	275	11	8	2	6	3	1	25	1	45	4	0
Pulido, Raymundo, Tab.	1	2	.333	6.45	15	1	0	0	14	0	22.1	32	109	25	16	2	2	0	0	8	0	13	3	0
Purata, Julio, Rey.	0	1	.000	9.00	3	1	0	0	2	0	3.0	7	22	4	3	0	0	1	2	3	0	4	0	0
Quinones, Enrique, Yuc.	10	9	.526	2.87	25	25	2	2	0	0	150.2	169	646	60	48	5	8	4	3	47	2	71	1	0
Quintanilla, Enrique, Lar.	5	8	.385	5.26	26	17	0	0	9	0	99.1	115	447	64	58	14	6	1	6	45	3	36	2	1
Quiroz, Aaron, Ver.	3	5	.375	6.58	10	9	0	0	1	0	39.2	49	185	31	29	5	1	4	1	19	2	17	3	0
Ramirez, Carlos, Oax.	0	1	.000	3.64	22	0	0	0	22	0	29.2	28	126	13	12	0	1	2	1	12	1	9	0	0
Renteria, Hilario, Can.-Tor.	1	1	.500	6.00	16	7	0	0	9	0	39.0	52	179	29	26	5	3	2	3	15	1	15	0	0
Retes, Jose, Oax.	1	0	1.000	6.55	23	0	0	0	23	2	22.0	23	106	19	16	1	1	1	3	16	1	12	6	0
Retes, Lorenzo, Mont.	2	0	1.000	3.28	31	1	0	0	30	0	35.2	38	163	13	13	1	4	3	2	21	4	14	1	0
Reyes, Nathanael, Mex.	7	7	.500	5.03	26	23	0	0	3	0	130.2	162	590	80	73	7	10	5	7	59	0	46	7	0
Reyes, Pablo, Mont.	12	7	.632	3.65	28	26	1	0	2	1	170.0	169	724	83	69	13	7	6	2	70	2	79	5	1
Rios, Alejandro, Tor.	0	0	.000	0.00	1	0	0	0	1	0	0	0	2	1	1	0	0	0	0	2	0	0	0	0
Rios, Jesus, Monc.	6	5	.545	4.12	17	17	1	0	0	0	109.1	117	466	56	50	11	4	6	2	33	0	60	5	0
Rivas, Jesus, Ver.	0	0	.000	8.68	6	0	0	0	6	0	9.1	10	46	13	9	3	1	5	0	6	0	2	1	0
Rivera, Francisco, Tor.	0	0	.000	9.53	3	0	0	0	3	0	5.2	6	29	6	6	0	0	0	0	6	0	1	1	0
Rivera, Oscar, Ver.	7	4	.636	2.54	21	18	3	2	3	0	120.1	93	509	51	34	7	4	3	8	61	1	83	4	0
Rivera, Paul, Can.	0	3	.000	4.21	55	1	0	0	54	1	36.1	25	160	22	17	3	3	1	0	28	1	19	6	0
Robles, Jorge, Cor.	4	1	.800	3.54	34	0	0	0	34	2	53.1	60	240	25	21	4	7	2	5	23	6	16	0	0
Rodriguez, Inoc, Can.	2	7	.222	3.50	24	14	0	0	10	0	79.2	86	359	45	31	11	6	1	1	45	0	28	1	0
Rodriguez, Manuel, Cor.	2	4	.333	6.50	31	6	0	0	25	1	73.1	81	353	56	53	7	2	1	4	58	8	44	7	0
Rodriguez, Raul, Tor.	4	8	.333	6.08	23	23	0	0	0	0	121.1	171	574	87	82	14	7	2	12	55	2	48	2	1
Rodriguez, Rosario, Sal.	0	0	.000	0.00	14	0	0	0	14	0	4.0	5	18	0	0	0	0	1	0	2	0	0	0	0
Rodriguez, Salvador, Yuc.	4	7	.364	3.64	19	13	1	0	6	1	94.0	110	405	42	38	4	8	2	0	25	1	55	2	0
Rojo, Oscar, Rey.	2	4	.333	5.58	28	7	0	0	21	2	61.1	75	285	41	38	6	3	2	4	30	5	42	1	1
Romero, Alejandro, Mex.	4	2	.667	4.94	41	0	0	0	41	3	74.2	81	331	45	41	6	5	1	2	37	3	42	1	0
Romero, Cesar, Lar.	0	0	.000	7.00	16	0	0	0	16	0	18.0	23	84	14	14	3	0	0	2	12	0	7	0	0
Romero, Juan, Cor.	3	2	.600	3.07	49	0	0	0	49	7	70.1	65	303	27	24	6	4	2	9	29	7	37	4	1
Romo, Rene, Agua.	0	0	.000	7.71	1	0	0	0	1	0	2.1	3	12	2	2	0	0	0	1	2	0	0	0	0
Romo, Ricardo, Mont.	0	0	.000	4.15	8	0	0	0	8	0	13.0	16	61	6	6	1	1	0	0	8	0	7	0	0
Roque, Jorge, Tor.	3	2	.600	5.37	31	4	0	0	27	0	55.1	69	258	42	33	7	3	1	1	28	3	24	2	0
Ruffin, Johnny, Oax.	0	1	.000	5.68	5	0	0	0	5	1	6.1	5	30	6	4	0	1	0	0	5	2	5	1	0
Ruiz, Cecilio, Tab.	3	8	.273	3.30	19	19	0	0	0	0	101.0	96	423	48	37	12	10	2	1	24	2	40	2	0
Ruiz, Juan, Yuc.	0	0	.000	12.00	3	0	0	0	3	0	3.0	7	19	4	4	1	0	0	0	4	0	2	0	0
Saenz, Alfredo, Can.	0	0	.000	11.12	3	0	0	0	3	0	5.2	9	30	7	7	1	0	0	1	4	1	0	1	0
Saldana, Edgardo, Yuc.	0	3	.000	3.62	37	1	0	0	36	0	69.2	72	292	31	28	3	4	7	1	26	4	32	4	0
Salgado, Eduardo, Ver.	0	0	.000	9.82	4	0	0	0	4	0	3.2	5	19	6	4	0	1	1	1	3	0	1	2	0
Salkeld, Roger, Tig.	2	1	.667	6.14	6	6	0	0	0	0	29.1	38	136	23	20	0	3	1	1	16	0	13	2	0
Sanchez, Alejandro, Can.	5	7	.417	3.59	37	13	1	0	24	0	97.2	91	410	45	39	5	8	3	2	37	2	29	5	0
Sanchez, Claudio, Oax.	5	2	.714	4.72	42	0	0	0	42	2	68.2	82	308	38	36	9	6	4	1	27	2	17	4	0
Sanchez, Efrain, Cam.	8	2	.800	2.30	38	5	1	1	33	1	86.0	82	357	26	22	2	11	0	6	30	6	39	3	0
Sanchez, Hector, Agua.	9	11	.450	7.55	24	24	1	0	0	0	112.0	171	522	102	94	13	1	6	4	32	5	31	1	0
Sanchez, Pablo, Sal.	5	4	.556	7.63	35	4	0	0	31	0	59.0	90	300	52	50	2	9	2	3	47	3	31	6	1
Sandoval, Guillermo, Sal.-Can.	4	1	.800	5.05	34	0	0	0	34	0	46.1	55	227	29	26	2	3	2	6	28	0	35	5	0
Serrato, Alvaro, Lar.	0	0	.000	0.00	1	0	0	0	1	0	1.1	1	7	1	0	0	0	1	0	1	0	1	0	0
Sierra, Abel, Yuc.-Ver.-Tab.	0	2	.000	8.53	18	2	0	0	16	0	25.1	42	134	33	24	2	1	3	1	15	0	6	2	1
Sinohui, David, Cam.	3	6	.333	4.12	48	0	0	0	48	11	63.1	63	274	31	29	3	4	1	3	25	1	33	3	0
Solarte, Jose, Monc.	5	4	.556	2.51	54	0	0	0	54	28	64.2	58	262	21	18	2	7	3	2	16	2	31	3	0
Solis, Ricardo, Cor.	8	8	.500	4.60	26	22	2	0	4	0	121.1	157	541	67	62	16	6	3	4	45	3	43	2	1
Sombra, Francisco, Agua.	2	0	1.000	4.14	51	0	0	0	51	1	37.0	36	151	17	17	3	2	1	0	14	4	21	1	0
Soto, Antonio, Can.	0	3	.000	14.25	7	4	0	0	3	0	12.0	25	73	19	19	1	0	1	2	12	0	2	2	0
Soto, Daniel, Oax.	5	4	.556	5.38	27	8	0	0	19	0	77.0	86	350	51	46	10	3	3	8	39	3	36	5	0
Soto, Jesus, Can.	0	0	.000	5.63	5	0	0	0	5	0	8.0	12	40	7	5	0	0	1	1	6	0	2	0	0
Strong, Joe, Tig.	1	1	.500	4.73	11	0	0	0	11	13	13.1	17	66	9	7	0	0	0	0	10	1	10	0	0
Sulu, Mario, Cam.	0	3	.000	3.71	25	0	0	0	25	0	43.2	47	199	20	18	2	5	2	2	26	2	16	1	2
Sung, Won, Agua.	2	5	.286	4.98	8	8	1	0	0	0	47.0	54	196	30	26	2	5	4	3	21	3	21	0	0
Tejeda, Felix, Agua.	1	3	.250	6.21	37	4	1	0	33	3	33.1	47	163	28	23	6	2	1	0	13	1	15	0	1
Tijerna, Alberto, Rey.	0	1	.000	5.05	19	1	0	0	18	0	35.2	45	182	30	20	1	2	2	6	34	2	14	2	0
Tress, Irving, Cor.	0	0	.000	3.00	3	1	0	0	2	0	3.0	2	17	1	1	0	0	0	1	8	0	1	2	0
Turgeon, David, Rey.	5	5	.500	3.16	17	17	1	0	0	0	111.0	106	475	46	39	6	10	3	3	42	2	71	3	1
Turuda, Miyoki, Mex.	1	1	.500	8.25	10	0	0	0	10	0	12.0	19	63	12	11	0	0	0	0	12	1	11	1	0
Uribe, Juan, Yuc.	2	1	.667	4.36	17	4	0	0	13	0	43.1	45	189	26	21	1	6	1	4	20	0	10	0	0
Valdez, Armando, Mont.	7	1	.875	2.34	50	0	0	0	50	2	73.0	62	314	20	19	3	10	1	3	38	6	49	3	0
Valdez, Efrain, Tig.	5	3	.625	4.15	8	8	1	0	0	0	52.0	57	220	25	24	3	3	1	3	19	1	25	2	1
Valdez, Rodolfo, Monc.	3	2	.600	2.88	21	0	0	0	21	0	25.0	22	105	9	8	2	0	0	0	11	1	13	0	0
Valencia, Jorge, Agua.	2	7	.222	5.88	34	10	0	0	24	0	90.1	105	419	69	59	11	4	2	7	47	3	47	1	1
Valenzuela, Gil, Can.	14	3	.824	3.18	20	20	3	1	0	0	124.1	132	524	46	44	9	11	1	5	39	2	28	5	0
Valenzuela, Jesus, Oax.	4	4	.500	6.72	25	9	1	0	16	0	69.2	91	338	59	52	9	4	1	3	43	2	28	4	1
Valenzuela, Jose, Tig.	1	0	1.000	7.04	15	1	0	0	14	0	23.0	29	112	21	18	4	0	1	0	17	0	16	1	1
Valerio, Julio, Monc.	3	1	.750	2.34	37	0	0	0	37	1	34.2	34	144	11	9	1	1	2	0	11	1	23	2	0
Vargas, Ignacio, Agua.-Sal.	2	3	.400	11.02	26	2	0	0	24	0	32.2	64	183	42	40	10	4	3	0	23	2	17	2	0
Vargas, Joel, Tab.	2	4	.333	6.48	30	3	0	0	27	0	50.0	62	225	36	36	7	1	2	3	19	1	29	2	0
Vargas, Juan, Ver.	0	0	.000	0.00	1	0	0	0	1	0	1.0	0	3	0	0	0	0	0	0	0	0	0	0	0
Vazquez, Adrian, Cam.	3	1	.750	3.07	9	6	0	0	3	0	29.1	24	128	13	10	2	1	0	3	17	1	9	1	0
Vega, Obed, Lar.-Rey.	3	5	.375	4.43	36	3	0	0	33	0	65.0	69	301	40	32	5	4	2	2	43	4	57	8	1
Velazquez, Ernesto, Tor.-Tab.	2	8	.200	5.72	51	1	0	0	50	1	72.1	92	346	52	46	4	8	6	2	41	7	22	4	2
Velazquez, Israel, Agua.	1	2	.333	7.86	7	6	0	0	1	0	26.1	35	128	23	23	2	2	2	3	15	3	20	1	0

Pitcher, Team	W	L	Pct.	ERA	G	GS	CG	ShO	Rel.	Sv.	IP	H	TBF	R	ER	HR	SH	SF	HB	BB	IBB	SO	WP	Bk.
Verdugo, Hugo, Sal.-Lar.	0	4	.000	6.28	13	3	0	0	10	0	28.2	33	144	26	20	2	0	1	4	22	0	19	4	0
Verdugo, Orlando, Yuc.	7	4	.636	3.72	16	16	0	0	0	0	94.1	93	426	42	39	4	5	5	10	49	0	50	9	0
Villalobos, Noe, Mont.	0	0	.000	10.80	2	0	0	0	2	0	1.2	3	9	2	2	0	0	0	0	1	0	2	0	0
Villaluna, Miguel, Mont.	0	0	.000	0.00	2	0	0	0	2	0	2.2	0	11	0	0	0	0	0	0	3	0	2	0	0
Villarreal, Antonio, Yuc.	2	0	1.000	2.45	2	2	0	0	0	0	11.0	9	47	5	3	2	0	0	1	3	1	4	1	0
Villarreal, Carlos, Tor.	0	0	.000	9.00	12	0	0	0	12	0	7.0	10	35	9	7	0	0	1	0	7	0	3	3	0
Villaverde, Jose, Ver.	0	0	.000	5.40	3	0	0	0	3	0	1.2	2	10	1	1	0	0	0	0	3	0	0	0	0
Villegas, Jose, Agua.	7	15	.318	6.25	28	26	3	0	2	0	149.2	206	707	117	104	20	11	7	9	64	6	41	5	0
Vizcarra, Enrique, Sal.	0	0	.000	32.40	2	0	0	0	2	0	1.2	6	14	7	6	0	1	0	0	3	0	0	1	0
Vizcarra, Ernesto, Agua.	0	0	.000	15.00	1	0	0	0	1	0	3.0	6	15	5	5	0	0	0	0	1	0	0	1	0
Woodson, Kerry, Sal.	0	1	.000	6.30	3	3	0	0	0	0	10.0	11	53	10	7	0	2	0	1	12	1	9	3	0
Zamudio, Jeovanni, Rey.	2	3	.400	4.80	45	3	0	0	42	2	60.0	63	278	37	32	2	8	2	0	41	1	24	2	1
Zavala, Marcos, Tig.	0	0	.000	2.37	24	0	0	0	24	2	19.0	9	80	5	5	1	0	0	1	15	0	7	1	0
Zavala, Rogelio, Can.	0	0	.000	2.45	4	0	0	0	4	0	3.2	2	17	1	1	0	0	1	0	4	0	3	0	0

COMBINATION SHUTOUTS: A total of 78 combination shutouts were pitched in the Mexican League in 1999. Tabasco led the league with 13.
NO-HIT GAMES: Elvira, Campeche, defeated Cancun, 5-0, March 20; Elvira, Campeche, defeated Laredo, 1-0, June 10.

PITCHERS WITH TWO OR MORE TEAMS

Pitcher, Team	W	L	Pct.	ERA	G	GS	CG	ShO	Rel.	Sv.	IP	H	TBF	R	ER	HR	SH	SF	HB	BB	IBB	SO	WP	Bk.
Aguilar, Jose, Tor.	2	2	.500	7.53	41	0	0	0	41	1	28.2	39	142	26	24	3	4	2	0	18	3	19	1	2
Aguilar, Jose, Mont.	1	0	1.000	2.25	9	0	0	0	9	1	4.0	4	19	1	1	0	1	0	0	2	0	2	1	0
Arocha, Rene, Yuc.	1	6	.143	5.06	9	7	1	0	2	0	42.2	47	183	24	24	2	3	0	0	11	0	38	3	0
Arocha, Rene, Mont.	0	1	.000	3.07	3	2	0	0	1	0	14.2	20	65	5	5	1	1	1	0	3	1	9	0	0
Barraza, Ernesto, Tig.	5	3	.625	6.72	16	15	0	0	1	0	73.2	90	368	59	55	5	4	1	1	70	1	30	13	0
Barraza, Ernesto, Tor.	1	4	.200	4.98	7	7	0	0	0	0	34.1	44	163	20	19	1	4	3	0	23	1	11	1	1
Bustillos, Oscar, Tig.	1	0	1.000	3.38	5	0	0	0	5	0	8.0	7	37	3	3	0	0	1	0	7	0	5	2	0
Bustillos, Oscar, Agua.	0	0	.000	20.00	10	0	0	0	10	0	9.0	17	58	23	20	2	0	0	0	15	0	6	3	0
Couoh, Enrique, Yuc.	2	5	.286	2.73	24	0	0	0	24	3	29.2	27	129	11	9	0	5	1	0	18	4	22	4	0
Couoh, Enrique, Ver.	1	3	.250	2.77	26	0	0	0	26	0	39.0	30	166	12	12	2	3	1	0	21	3	31	2	0
Cruz, Luis, Tig.	0	0	.000	54.00	1	0	0	0	1	0	0.1	2	4	2	2	0	0	0	0	1	0	0	0	0
Cruz, Luis, Agua.	0	1	.000	10.02	15	1	0	0	14	0	20.2	35	113	23	23	3	2	1	1	16	2	11	2	0
Diaz, Alejandro, Ver.	1	0	1.000	7.36	14	0	0	0	14	0	18.1	26	87	16	15	2	1	1	3	7	0	2	1	0
Diaz, Alejandro, Can.	1	2	.333	4.46	26	0	0	0	26	3	42.1	50	183	22	21	8	4	1	3	9	1	11	2	0
Dominguez, David, Mex.	0	0	.000	6.00	2	0	0	0	2	0	3.0	3	17	2	2	0	0	0	2	3	0	3	2	0
Dominguez, David, Oax.	0	0	.000	54.00	1	0	0	0	1	0	0.2	2	7	4	4	0	0	0	1	2	0	0	0	0
Federico, Gustavo, Agua.	3	1	.750	4.19	24	0	0	0	24	6	34.1	41	148	17	16	1	1	1	1	13	3	15	0	0
Federico, Gustavo, Mont.	3	1	.750	6.23	10	0	0	0	10	1	8.2	11	43	6	6	3	0	0	0	5	0	2	0	0
Fernandez, Osvaldo, Mont.	1	3	.250	6.52	4	4	0	0	0	0	19.1	21	91	14	14	0	1	0	1	16	1	12	2	0
Fernandez, Osvaldo, Sal.	2	2	.500	5.35	8	6	0	0	2	0	33.2	40	167	25	20	1	1	1	2	31	0	33	5	1
Galvez, Rosario, Agua.	0	0	.000	16.88	7	0	0	0	7	0	2.2	7	22	5	5	1	0	0	0	6	0	2	2	0
Galvez, Rosario, Tab.	0	2	.000	7.24	16	4	0	0	12	0	27.1	34	136	23	22	6	3	1	2	24	2	13	4	2
Green, Ottis, Sal.	0	1	.000	7.04	2	1	0	0	1	0	7.2	8	38	7	6	1	0	2	0	7	0	6	2	0
Green, Ottis, Tor.	0	3	.000	3.66	5	5	1	0	0	0	32.0	28	145	16	13	3	1	3	2	23	0	23	1	0
Hernandez, Martin, Can.	6	4	.600	4.48	13	13	0	0	0	0	82.1	81	355	46	41	8	9	4	3	39	0	31	4	0
Hernandez, Martin, Sal.	1	0	1.000	2.06	5	5	1	1	0	0	35.0	31	147	10	8	0	3	0	0	15	0	12	2	0
Herrera, Calixto, Monc.	0	0	.000	3.46	10	0	0	0	10	0	13.0	10	55	5	5	0	1	0	0	11	0	5	1	0
Herrera, Calixto, Tor.	2	0	1.000	5.67	17	0	0	0	17	1	27.0	29	133	22	17	3	1	1	1	26	5	26	4	0
Lara, Hugo, Ver.	3	5	.375	4.52	15	12	1	0	3	0	61.2	74	274	37	31	5	3	1	7	16	1	23	1	0
Lara, Hugo, Tab.	2	3	.400	2.86	9	8	0	0	1	0	44.0	44	181	18	14	2	1	1	0	12	1	15	2	0
Lezama, Rafael, Tab.	0	0	.000	3.38	33	0	0	0	33	1	13.1	13	59	6	5	1	2	0	0	6	0	8	0	0
Lezama, Rafael, Ver.	0	1	.000	13.50	8	0	0	0	8	0	6.2	14	41	10	10	1	1	1	1	8	0	4	0	1
Linares, Yfrain, Agua.	1	5	.167	5.63	10	8	1	0	2	0	40.0	41	201	29	25	1	3	2	0	39	1	28	4	0
Linares, Yfrain, Cor.	0	0	.000	0.00	2	0	0	0	2	0	1.2	2	10	0	0	0	0	0	0	4	0	1	0	0
Manriquez, Alberto, Mont.	1	0	1.000	6.17	16	0	1	0	16	0	23.1	31	110	22	16	4	1	0	1	9	0	7	1	0
Manriquez, Alberto, Agua.	1	1	.500	5.76	13	1	2	0	12	0	25.0	33	119	16	16	3	1	2	1	12	0	14	2	0
Manzanillo, Ravelo, Mont.	0	2	.000	4.24	5	5	1	0	0	0	23.1	22	110	18	11	2	1	3	1	22	0	14	1	0
Manzanillo, Ravelo, Yuc.	10	3	.769	2.65	19	16	3	1	3	1	122.1	93	529	41	36	1	8	3	5	79	1	80	2	0
Metoyer, Tony, Can.	0	3	.000	4.11	15	0	0	0	15	7	15.1	15	68	8	7	2	2	0	0	8	1	10	2	0
Metoyer, Tony, Lar.	3	4	.429	2.54	35	0	0	0	35	18	39.0	40	175	17	11	2	5	1	0	24	3	26	8	0
Moreno, Leobardo, Mex.	0	2	.000	17.65	5	3	0	0	2	0	8.2	26	57	20	17	4	0	0	0	6	0	6	2	0
Moreno, Leobardo, Sal.	7	5	.583	4.69	16	15	0	0	1	0	80.2	95	368	45	42	5	4	1	0	47	0	46	5	0
Neri, Braulio, Sal.	0	0	.000	3.24	8	0	0	0	8	0	8.1	11	45	7	3	0	1	0	2	9	0	5	0	0
Neri, Braulio, Cam.	0	0	.000	7.94	5	0	0	0	5	0	5.2	8	29	6	5	0	2	1	2	2	0	4	2	0
Neri, Eduardo, Ver.	0	5	.000	5.34	30	0	0	0	30	2	28.2	29	129	21	17	4	3	2	1	13	0	16	0	0
Neri, Eduardo, Yuc.	3	1	.750	1.93	15	0	0	0	15	0	23.1	22	103	7	5	2	4	0	0	12	1	15	0	0
Nunez, Javier, Sal.	0	0	.000	22.09	2	0	0	0	2	0	3.2	12	25	9	9	1	0	0	2	2	0	0	0	0
Nunez, Javier, Agua.	0	0	.000	5.40	5	0	0	0	5	0	6.2	6	28	4	4	0	0	0	0	4	1	1	3	0
Olague, Jesus, Mont.	3	4	.429	5.32	13	8	0	0	5	0	45.2	53	215	30	27	0	2	5	1	29	0	27	3	0
Olague, Jesus, Agua.	0	1	.000	10.80	9	1	0	0	8	0	15.0	25	78	19	18	1	0	1	1	12	2	11	1	0
Ortega, Raul, Yuc.	0	0	.000	2.70	5	0	0	0	5	0	3.1	5	17	3	1	0	0	0	1	0	0	1	0	0
Ortega, Raul, Tor.	0	0	.000	4.50	10	0	0	0	10	0	6.0	8	30	3	3	0	0	0	1	4	1	2	1	0
Osuna, Roberto, Yuc.	0	1	.000	18.00	3	0	0	0	3	1	3.0	7	18	6	6	1	0	1	1	3	0	1	0	0
Osuna, Roberto, Cor.	0	0	.000	12.15	7	0	0	0	7	1	6.2	8	42	11	9	0	2	0	2	10	2	5	0	0
Osuna, Roberto, Sal.	0	0	.000	27.00	3	0	0	0	3	0	0.2	3	7	2	2	1	0	0	0	2	0	0	0	0
Perez, Vladimir, Lar.	0	3	.000	8.18	10	0	0	0	10	0	11.0	18	61	11	10	1	4	1	1	9	0	8	2	1
Perez, Vladimir, Oax.	0	0	.000	5.28	14	0	0	0	14	0	15.1	17	70	9	9	1	3	0	0	8	4	6	2	0
Picota, Alberto, Oax.	2	2	.500	5.70	5	5	0	0	0	0	23.2	28	119	19	15	0	3	1	2	20	0	15	3	1
Picota, Alberto, Lar.	8	4	.667	4.63	35	4	0	0	31	0	70.0	72	324	39	36	3	9	3	2	52	13	52	8	0
Renteria, Hilario, Can.	0	1	.000	7.45	5	2	0	0	3	0	9.2	16	45	8	8	1	0	1	0	3	1	5	0	0
Renteria, Hilario, Tor.	1	0	1.000	5.52	11	5	0	0	6	0	29.1	36	134	21	18	4	3	1	3	12	0	10	0	0
Sandoval, Guillermo, Sal.	2	1	.667	6.48	27	0	0	0	27	0	33.1	42	171	27	24	2	3	2	6	21	0	27	4	0
Sandoval, Guillermo, Can.	2	0	1.000	1.38	7	0	0	0	7	0	13.0	13	58	2	2	0	0	0	0	7	0	8	1	0
Sierra, Abel, Yuc.	0	0	.000	8.53	6	0	0	0	6	0	6.1	11	39	8	6	0	1	0	0	8	0	0	0	0
Sierra, Abel, Ver.	0	2	.000	6.91	7	2	0	0	5	0	14.1	21	72	18	11	2	0	2	1	6	0	5	2	1
Sierra, Abel, Tab.	0	0	.000	13.50	5	0	0	0	5	0	4.2	10	23	7	7	0	0	1	0	1	0	1	0	0

Pitcher, Team	W	L	Pct.	ERA	G	GS	CG	ShO	Rel.	Sv.	IP	H	TBF	R	ER	HR	SH	SF	HB	BB	IBB	SO	WP	Bk.
Vargas, Ignacio, Agua.	2	3	.400	17.18	16	2	0	0	14	0	14.2	36	89	28	28	8	3	2	0	14	2	4	2	0
Vargas, Ignacio, Sal.	0	0	.000	6.00	10	0	0	0	10	0	18.0	28	94	14	12	2	1	1	0	9	0	13	0	0
Vega, Obed, Lar.	0	1	.000	5.59	6	2	0	0	4	0	9.2	8	45	8	6	1	0	1	0	10	0	6	2	0
Vega, Obed, Rey.	3	4	.429	4.23	30	1	0	0	29	0	55.1	61	256	32	26	4	4	1	2	33	4	51	6	1
Velazquez, Ernesto, Tor.	2	5	.286	7.03	28	1	0	0	27	0	39.2	52	198	31	31	2	6	2	1	28	6	13	3	2
Velazquez, Ernesto, Tab.	0	3	.000	4.13	23	0	0	0	23	1	32.2	40	148	21	15	2	2	4	1	13	1	9	1	0
Verdugo, Hugo, Sal.	0	1	.000	5.40	8	2	0	0	6	0	21.2	24	109	19	13	2	0	1	3	17	0	11	3	0
Verdugo, Hugo, Lar.	0	3	.000	9.00	5	1	0	0	4	0	7.0	9	35	7	7	0	0	0	1	5	0	8	1	0

1999 FIELDING

TEAM

Team	Pct.	G	PO	A	E	TC	DP	TP	PB	Team	Pct.	G	PO	A	E	TC	DP	TP	PB
Cancun	.979	121	3096	1354	96	4546	130	0	8	Yucatan	.975	118	3048	1331	114	4493	101	0	3
Saltillo	.978	119	3135	1536	106	4777	171	0	13	Monclova	.975	119	3132	1323	112	4567	150	1	10
Torreon	.978	120	3109	1473	102	4684	145	0	6	Nuevo Laredo	.975	119	3121	1343	113	4577	155	0	33
M.C. Reds	.977	117	3096	1514	107	4717	137	0	2	M.C. Tigers........	.974	115	2985	1359	115	4459	155	2	6
Monterrey	.977	119	3151	1451	108	4710	118	0	4	Aguascalientes ..	.974	122	3019	1406	116	4541	145	0	4
Oaxaca	.976	119	3063	1420	112	4595	144	0	7	Cordoba	.974	118	2993	1239	112	4344	119	1	11
Campeche	.976	119	3110	1332	110	4552	114	0	10	Tabasco	.973	121	3176	1548	130	4854	127	1	4
Veracruz	.975	120	3080	1527	120	4727	118	1	11	Reynosa	.965	120	3153	1325	161	4639	135	0	14

INDIVIDUAL

Note: Fielding statistics for multiple-team players are not broken down by teams. Teams listed in fielding are last clubs played by fielders.

FIRST BASEMEN

Player, Team	Pct.	G	PO	A	E	TC	DP
Aganza, Ruben, Monc.	.996	102	974	52	4	1030	114
Aguilera, Armando, Sal.	.974	8	33	4	1	38	3
Almeida, Shamar, Oax.	.990	49	398	17	4	419	45
Amezcua, Adan, Rey.	1.000	5	38	1	0	39	5
Arrendondo, Luis, Yuc.	1.000	1	1	0	0	1	1
Arvizu, Javier, Tab.	.995	22	178	6	1	185	19
Avila, Ruben, Agua.	.991	79	634	47	6	687	74
Azocar, Oscar, Ver.	.991	118	1163	110	12	1285	108
Barron, Tony, Mex.	1.000	1	4	0	0	4	0
Bethea, Larry, Cor.	.989	19	177	4	2	183	15
Brown, Ray, Tab.	.990	93	897	76	10	983	85
Canale, George, Yuc.	.986	8	66	2	1	69	8
Canseco, Ozzie, Tab.	.985	5	61	4	1	66	6
Carrillo, Garcia, Tig.	1.000	17	98	9	0	107	11
Castaneda, Hector, Yuc.	1.000	17	140	11	0	151	14
Castaneda, Rafael, Oax.	.980	6	48	1	1	50	5
Castellano, Pedro, Mex.	.994	81	779	65	5	849	84
Cervantes, Ivan, Mex.	1.000	1	2	0	0	2	0
Cervantes, Refugio, Sal.	1.000	5	13	4	0	17	1
Chan, Armando, Cam.	.903	5	27	1	3	31	1
Chimelis, Joel, Lar.	1.000	16	108	6	0	114	16
Cruz, Fausto, Yuc.	1.000	2	10	0	0	10	1
Cruz, Luis, Rey.	1.000	6	35	1	0	36	4
De la Cruz, Hector, Yuc.	1.000	3	21	6	0	27	1
Diaz, Luis, Tor.	1.000	18	168	8	0	176	17
Escalante, Marclo, Can.	1.000	1	10	1	0	11	1
Espino, Daniel, Mont.	.997	40	301	31	1	333	32
Espino, Omar, Lar.	1.000	5	26	1	0	27	4
Estrada, Ricardo, Can.	1.000	11	85	1	0	86	8
Figueroa, Antonio, Cor.	1.000	2	8	0	0	8	0
Figueroa, Jesus, Oax.	1.000	2	5	1	0	6	0
Fornes, Daniel, Rey.	.985	57	401	48	7	456	44
Franco, Julio, Tig.	.993	29	253	23	2	278	44
Gavia, Jesus, Yuc.	1.000	1	2	0	0	2	0
Gonzalez, Fernando, Rey.	1.000	1	10	1	0	11	0
Gonzalez, Jesus, Tor.	.995	92	884	67	5	956	100
Gonzalez, Jose, Agua.	1.000	1	4	1	0	5	1
Iglesias, Luis, Yuc.	.988	26	223	16	3	242	22
Iturbe, Pedro, Tig.	.995	47	378	33	2	413	47
Kapano, Randy, Mont.	1.000	13	133	6	0	139	13
Laureano, Francisco, Agua.	.982	6	51	5	1	57	5
Leal, Guadalupe, Monc.	1.000	11	80	4	0	84	9
Machiria, Pablo, Agua.	.984	16	122	3	2	127	15
Martinez, Domingo, Mex.	.989	32	329	28	4	361	31
Martinez, Enrique, Agua.	1.000	1	5	0	0	5	0
Mata, Noe, Ver.	1.000	1	2	0	0	2	0
Medina, Jose, Sal.	1.000	2	4	0	0	4	1
Meggers, Mike, Tor.	.985	8	63	3	1	67	12
Miranda, Julio, Agua.	.933	1	13	1	1	15	1
Mitchel, Domingo, Can.	.986	24	206	3	3	212	22
Montalvo, Ivan, Tig.	1.000	1	0	1	0	1	0
Moreno, Leonardo, Ver.	1.000	3	21	1	0	22	3
Munoz, Jose, Sal.	.966	8	54	3	2	59	7
Nunez, Ray, Agua.	.994	19	149	14	1	164	14
Obando, Sherman, Oax.	.995	42	359	35	2	396	40

Player, Team	Pct.	G	PO	A	E	TC	DP
Ojeda, Miguel, Mex.	1.000	7	37	5	0	42	5
Orantes, Ramon, Mont.	1.000	9	91	8	0	99	7
Ortiz, Alejandro, Lar.	.978	28	203	15	5	223	26
Paez, Raul, Cam.	.990	61	477	43	5	525	56
Peguero, Julio, Can.	1.000	4	14	0	0	14	2
Pena, Carlos, Tab.	1.000	1	8	0	0	8	0
Perez, Francisco, Rey.	1.000	11	10	0	0	10	1
Poe, Charles, Tor.	1.000	6	34	1	0	35	1
Quintero, Alan, Yuc.	1.000	3	20	3	0	23	2
Ramirez, Jesus, Oax.	1.000	1	2	0	0	2	0
Ramon, Reyes, Cam.	.974	4	33	5	1	39	7
Rivera, Jesus, Tab.	1.000	5	16	3	0	19	1
Robles, Trinidad, Tig.	1.000	2	19	1	0	20	4
Rodriguez, Armando, Tig.	1.000	2	6	0	0	6	1
Rodriguez, Boi, Monc.	.982	18	159	8	3	170	21
Rodriguez, Hector, Rey.	1.000	1	1	0	0	1	0
Rojas, Francisco, Tab.	1.000	13	108	13	0	121	13
Romero, Marco, Sal.	.993	111	987	83	8	1078	144
Sanchez, Gerardo, Lar.	.997	76	645	58	2	705	87
Sanchez, Roque, Cam.	1.000	43	380	30	0	410	32
Saucedo, Roberto, Rey.	.982	21	153	11	3	167	10
Sievers, Carlos, Yuc.	1.000	1	1	1	0	2	0
Soto, Saul, Mex.	1.000	1	1	0	0	1	0
Stark, Matt, Mont.	1.000	9	82	7	0	89	4
Suarez, Luis, Tig.	.995	24	194	11	1	206	32
Tatis, Bernardo, Yuc.	.994	36	289	21	2	312	17
Trafton, Todd, Oax.	.988	35	310	15	4	329	32
Trapaga, Julio, Tig.	1.000	7	51	3	0	54	7
Valdez, Emmanuel, Tig.	1.000	4	6	2	0	8	0
Valdez, Jesus, Cam.	.996	58	445	32	2	479	41
Valle, Cosme, Mex.	.857	2	5	1	1	7	2
Vazquez, Felipe, Lar.	1.000	1	1	0	0	1	0
Vazquez, Jorge, Tig.	1.000	1	1	0	0	1	0
Vega, Edgar, Agua.	1.000	2	4	0	0	4	0
Velazquez, Guillermo, Mont.	.995	56	533	44	3	580	51
Villanueva, Hector, Oax.	.980	16	137	9	3	149	20
Villarreal, Alejandro, Lar.	1.000	1	8	0	0	8	3
Yan, Julian, Cor.	.991	99	847	50	8	905	88
Zambrano, Eduardo, Can.	.974	4	32	5	1	38	6
ZAMBRANO, Roberto, Can.	.997	101	905	57	3	965	90
Zamudio, Rafael, Agua.	.969	8	54	8	2	64	6
Zazueta, Juan, Tor.	.952	2	18	2	1	21	1

TRIPLE PLAYS: Aganza, Azocar, Brown, Iturbe.

SECOND BASEMEN

Player, Team	Pct.	G	PO	A	E	TC	DP
Acuna, Jose, Tor.	1.000	1	1	0	0	1	0
Alvarez, Jorge, Cor.	1.000	5	9	6	0	15	1
Arias, Francisco, Sal.	.978	48	111	114	5	230	38
Armenta, Guillermo, Ver.	.969	60	118	162	9	289	29
Arredondo, Jesus, Agua.	1.000	3	3	4	0	7	2
Bell, Juan, Cor.	.977	110	300	294	14	608	83
Beltran, Juan, Cam.	1.000	1	1	1	0	2	0
Brena, James, Oax.	1.000	10	21	21	0	42	9
Bruno, Julio, Tab.	1.000	1	1	4	0	5	0
Bustillos, Luis, Rey.	.974	104	260	274	14	548	72

– 410 –

Player, Team	Pct.	G	PO	A	E	TC	DP
Camacho, Reginaldo, Rey.	.923	3	7	5	1	13	0
Carrasco, Ernesto, Lar.	.973	14	35	36	2	73	12
Castellano, Pedro, Mex.	.965	14	37	46	3	86	13
Castro, Arnoldo, Can.	.980	119	387	335	15	737	95
Cervantes, Ivan, Mex.	.952	6	9	11	1	21	2
Chimelis, Joel, Lar.	.980	86	262	239	10	511	81
Cobos, Rogelio, Cam.	.833	1	4	1	1	6	0
Contreras, Jose, Rey.	.889	4	4	4	1	9	1
Cruz, Fausto, Yuc.	1.000	1	2	1	0	3	0
Esquer, Ramon, Mex.	.984	86	243	247	8	498	66
Estrella, Isaac, Lar.	1.000	1	0	1	0	1	0
Felix, Jesus, Rey.	.929	8	12	14	2	28	6
Felix, Lauro, Rey.	1.000	1	0	2	0	2	0
Flores, Miguel, Mont.	.974	104	285	303	16	604	78
Gama, Ricardo, Tab.	.970	96	268	322	18	608	79
Garcia, Heriberto, Oax.	1.000	6	9	21	0	30	2
Garza, Fidel, Mont.	1.000	11	7	18	0	25	3
Gastelum, Sergio, Tig.	.967	71	219	227	15	461	72
Gonzalez, Rene, Rey.	1.000	1	1	1	0	2	0
Gonzalez, Rolando, Monc.	1.000	5	8	4	0	12	0
Gonzalez, Roman, Cor.	1.000	5	11	7	0	18	2
Guerrero, Epy, Cam.	.986	29	79	65	2	146	18
Hernandez, Esteban, Oax.	.600	1	5	1	4	10	0
Hernandez, Juan, Cor.	1.000	1	1	1	0	2	0
Iturbe, Pedro, Tig.	1.000	1	2	0	0	2	0
Laureano, Francisco, Agua.	1.000	4	12	10	0	22	4
Liriano, Nelson, Mex.	.988	67	185	232	5	422	62
Lopez, Fabian, Oax.	.984	43	116	127	4	247	36
Lopez, Gonzalo, Yuc.	.986	15	25	44	1	70	10
Loredo, Jorge, Oax.	1.000	9	47	52	0	99	16
Magallanes, Everardo, Mont.	.939	9	16	15	2	33	6
Malpica, Enrique, Yuc.	1.000	4	2	2	0	4	0
Martinez, Abel, Can.	1.000	4	11	6	0	17	3
Martinez, Augusto, Tab.	1.000	2	1	0	0	1	0
MARTINEZ, Grimaldo, Monc.	.986	112	288	344	9	641	99
Martinez, Ray, Mex.	.667	1	0	2	1	3	0
Mendez, Francisco, Mont.	1.000	1	4	1	0	5	0
Mere, Pedro, Ver.	.982	66	151	173	6	330	49
Minjares, Francisco, Agua.	1.000	14	23	23	0	46	8
Montanez, Daniel, Ver.	1.000	3	3	6	0	9	0
Morales, Florentino, Lar.	.979	30	69	69	3	141	16
Morejon, Oswaldo, Yuc.	.981	89	268	260	10	538	61
Pacho, Juan, Yuc.	1.000	10	17	28	0	45	4
Peraza, Rudy, Yuc.	.800	1	2	2	1	5	0
Perez, Alfredo, Cam.	.967	54	141	123	9	273	31
Quintero, Guillermo, Cor.	.929	4	9	4	1	14	2
Ramirez, Jesus, Oax.	1.000	1	5	3	0	8	1
Rivera, Jesus, Tab.	.979	23	65	73	3	141	18
Robles, Trinidad, Tig.	.979	20	48	45	2	95	18
Rodriguez, Aurelio, Tab.	1.000	2	2	3	0	5	0
Rodriguez, Hector, Rey.	.920	11	24	22	4	50	6
Romero, Wilfredo, Sal.	1.000	1	2	0	0	2	0
Sanchez, Orlando, Mont.	.980	12	30	18	1	49	7
Sanchez, Roque, Cam.	.975	48	134	98	6	238	33
Sandoval, Octavio, Tig.	1.000	1	2	0	0	2	0
Tatis, Bernardo, Yuc.	1.000	1	2	2	0	4	0
Trapaga, Julio, Tig.	.983	37	92	83	3	178	26
Valenzuela, Irving, Monc.	.976	12	24	16	1	41	5
Valle, Cosme, Mex.	1.000	1	2	0	0	2	0
Valle, Jorge, Monc.	1.000	1	0	1	0	1	0
Valle, Jose, Yuc.	1.000	2	0	3	0	3	0
Valle, Roberto, Tor.	1.000	6	7	13	0	20	4
Velez, Manuel, Agua.	.990	37	74	122	2	198	34
Verdugo, Sostenes, Yuc.	.667	1	2	0	1	3	0
Verdugo, Vicente, Sal.	.982	89	243	309	10	562	106
Villarreal, Salvador, Rey.	.000	2	0	0	1	1	0
Vizcarra, Marco, Sal.	1.000	4	6	3	0	9	0
Vizcarra, Roberto, Tig.	.972	84	215	240	13	468	70
Wong, Julian, Yuc.	.943	10	15	18	2	35	3
Zazueta, Juan, Tor.	.980	9	26	22	1	49	8
Zazueta, Mauricio, Tor.	.978	115	365	352	16	733	110

TRIPLE PLAYS: Bell, Gama, Mere, R. Vizcarra.

THIRD BASEMEN

Player, Team	Pct.	G	PO	A	E	TC	DP
Acuna, Jose, Tor.	1.000	1	0	5	0	5	0
Arano, Marco, Tab.	1.000	13	6	31	0	37	3
Arias, Francisco, Sal.	.833	4	2	3	1	6	1
Armenta, Christhian, Lar.	.600	2	0	3	2	5	0
Arredondo, Hernando, Can.	.935	4	13	30	3	46	3
Arredondo, Jesus, Agua.	1.000	1	3	3	0	6	1
Beltran, Juan, Cam.	1.000	1	3	5	0	8	0
Berry, Mike, Ver.	1.000	1	1	0	0	1	0
Bruno, Julio, Tab.	.957	72	74	170	11	255	14
Camacho, Reginaldo, Rey.	.929	38	17	61	6	84	9
Carrasco, Ernesto, Lar.	.949	79	68	137	11	216	17
Castaneda, Rafael, Oax.	.960	105	92	241	14	347	29
Castellano, Pedro, Mex.	.983	18	10	49	1	60	6
Cervantes, Ivan, Mex.	.960	16	6	42	2	50	6
Cervera, Francisco, Cam.	.955	103	75	220	14	309	3
Chimelis, Joel, Lar.	.872	14	13	28	6	47	3
Contreras, Jose, Rey.	1.000	8	3	3	0	6	1
Cruz, Fausto, Yuc.	.981	63	74	132	4	210	10
Cruz, Luis, Rey.	.333	1	0	1	2	3	0
Diaz, Pedro, Agua.	.923	28	17	43	5	65	6
Duran, Felipe, Ver.	1.000	1	1	1	0	2	0
Espinoza, Ramon, Tor.	.333	1	1	0	2	3	0
Estrella, Isaac, Lar.	1.000	1	0	1	0	1	0
Felix, Jesus, Rey.	.941	7	5	11	1	17	3
Felix, Lauro, Rey.	1.000	3	6	12	0	18	2
Fornes, Daniel, Rey.	1.000	2	5	5	0	10	1
Garcia, Heriberto, Oax.	1.000	1	3	8	0	11	0
Garza, Fidel, Mont.	1.000	3	1	5	0	6	0
Gastelum, Sergio, Tig.	.900	10	4	23	3	30	3
Gomez, Heber, Tab.	1.000	5	11	15	0	26	2
Gonzalez, Fernando, Rey.	1.000	1	1	1	0	2	0
Gonzalez, Rene, Rey.	.811	19	13	30	10	53	5
Gonzalez, Rolando, Monc.	.881	18	6	31	5	42	3
Gonzalez, Roman, Cor.	.944	5	5	12	1	18	0
Groppuso, Mike, Yuc.	.962	8	12	13	1	26	0
Guerrero, Epy, Cam.	1.000	1	1	2	0	3	0
Guizar, Hector, Monc.	1.000	1	2	0	0	2	0
Hernandez, Juan, Cor.	1.000	1	1	4	0	5	1
Hernandez, Julio, Lar.	1.000	1	1	4	0	5	1
Iglesias, Luis, Yuc.	1.000	5	8	7	0	15	1
JIMENEZ, Alfonso, Sal.	.967	109	74	216	10	300	34
Kapano, Randy, Mont.	1.000		5	35	0	40	3
Laureano, Francisco, Agua.	.945	17	15	37	3	55	5
Leyva, German, Ver.	.950	110	111	304	22	437	26
Lopez, Fabian, Oax.	.940	21	7	40	3	50	4
Lopez, Gonzalo, Yuc.	.857	8	5	13	3	21	1
Loredo, Jorge, Oax.	.917	4	4	7	1	12	0
Magallanes, Everardo, Mont.	.950	53	40	151	10	201	13
Magallanes, Roberto, Tor.	.957	6	5	17	1	23	0
Malpica, Enrique, Yuc.	.833	14	9	21	6	36	3
Mantalvo, Ivan, Tig.	.931	99	85	199	21	305	28
Martinez, Abel, Can.	.958	90	83	171	11	265	19
Martinez, Domingo, Mex.	1.000	2	23	2	0	25	3
Martinez, Luis, Sal.	1.000	1	1	4	0	5	2
Martinez, Ray, Mex.	.924	60	80	212	24	316	24
Medina, Jose, Sal.	1.000	1	3	0	0	3	0
Mere, Pedro, Ver.	1.000	7	5	18	0	23	2
Minjares, Francisco, Agua.	1.000	6	4	11	0	15	3
Montanez, Daniel, Ver.	1.000	1	0	3	0	3	0
Morales, Florentino, Lar.	1.000	1	1	0	0	1	0
Nunez, Ray, Agua.	.943	56	37	127	10	174	9
Olvera, Sergio, Can.	1.000	2	5	5	0	10	0
Orantes, Ramon, Mont.	.933	57	46	122	12	180	19
Perez, Alejandro, Yuc.	.800	1	2	2	1	5	0
Perez, Alfredo, Cam.	1.000	2	1	4	0	5	0
Quintero, Guillermo, Cor.	1.000	3	7	8	0	15	0
Ramirez, Enrique, Can.	.989	19	29	59	1	89	3
Ramon, Reyes, Cam.	.600	3	3	0	2	5	0
Rivera, Jesus, Tab.	1.000	5	1	4	0	5	0
Robles, Trinidad, Tig.	.905	13	7	31	4	42	6
Rodriguez, Aurelio, Tab.	.895	17	6	45	6	57	3
Rodriguez, Hector, Rey.	.935	47	33	67	7	107	4
Romero, Marco, Sal.	.667	1	1	1	1	3	0
Romero, Oscar, Tor.	.963	46	35	96	5	136	12
Ruiz, Juan, Cor.	.952	11	112	242	18	372	25
Salas, Heriberto, Can.	.980	0	16	33	1	50	12
Sanchez, Orlando, Mont.	1.000	1	0	1	0	1	0
Sanchez, Roque, Cam.	.971	18	10	24	1	35	2
Sanchez, Wilfredo, Can.	.875	4	4	3	1	8	1
Santos, Andres, Lar.	.855	31	14	33	8	55	4
So Young, Can.	1.000	11	7	27	0	34	3
Tatis, Bernardo, Yuc.	.884	27	19	42	8	69	1
Valenzuela, Irving, Monc.	.667	1	0	2	1	3	0
Valle, Cosme, Mex.	.900	10	5	4	1	10	0
Valle, Jorge, Monc.	.929	111	91	221	24	336	27
Valle, Roberto, Tab.	.900	8	2	16	2	20	0
Valle, Roberto, Tor.	.667	3	0	4	2	6	0
Vazquez, Gregorio, Tab.	1.000	1	0	1	0	1	0
Velez, Manuel, Agua.	.946	32	22	65	5	92	8
Verdugo, Sostenes, Yuc.	1.000	1	0	3	0	3	0
Verdugo, Vicente, Sal.	.833	1	4	1	1	6	1
Villarreal, Alejandro, Lar.	.900	9	4	14	2	20	2
Vizcarra, Enrique, Sal.	1.000	1	0	1	0	1	0
Vizcarra, Marco, Sal.	.955	41	17	47	3	67	9
Voigt, Jack, Rey.	.908	22	22	47	7	76	6
Zamudio, Rafael, Agua.	.923	7	2	10	1	13	2
Zazueta, Juan, Tor.	.962	53	39	137	7	183	13

TRIPLE PLAYS: Bruno, Leyva, J. Valle.

CLASS AAA Mexican League

SHORTSTOPS

Player, Team	Pct.	G	PO	A	E	TC	DP
Arano, Marco, Tab.	1.000	2	0	4	0	4	0
Arias, Francisco, Sal.	1.000	4	2	6	0	8	0
Armenta, Christhian, Lar.	1.000	3	3	7	0	10	0
Armenta, Guillermo, Ver.	.958	22	33	80	5	118	17
Arredondo, Hernando, Can.	.840	9	7	14	4	25	1
Arredondo, Jesus, Agua.	.977	68	111	234	8	353	49
Bell, Juan, Cor.	1.000	2	1	4	0	5	0
Beltran, Juan, Cam.	.953	30	31	70	5	106	15
Brena, Jaime, Oax.	.917	4	4	7	1	12	2
Bustillos, Luis, Rey.	.926	17	25	38	5	68	8
Camacho, Reginaldo, Rey.	1.000	1	1	1	0	2	0
Carrasco, Ernesto, Lar.	1.000	12	33	34	0	67	12
Cervantes, Ivan, Mex.	.914	15	10	22	3	35	5
Cervera, Francisco, Cam.	1.000	5	4	8	0	12	1
Cruz, Fausto, Yuc.	1.000	3	4	10	0	14	1
Diaz, Pedro, Agua.	.949	8	15	22	2	39	3
Diaz, Remigio, Mont.	.975	70	106	246	9	361	43
Duran, Felipe, Ver.	.946	38	55	104	9	168	17
Estrella, Isaac, Lar.	.963	6	10	16	1	27	4
Felix, Jesus, Rey.	.913	8	5	16	2	23	3
Felix, Lauro, Rey.	.939	99	186	303	32	521	67
Fornes, Daniel, Rey.	1.000	1	1	1	0	2	1
Garcia, Heriberto, Oax.	.965	83	135	246	14	395	58
Garza, Fidel, Mont.	.800	8	1	3	1	5	0
Gastelum, Sergio, Tig.	1.000	1	5	4	0	9	1
Gomez, Heber, Tab.	.963	111	196	429	24	649	76
Gonzalez, Roman, Cor.	1.000	1	0	4	0	4	0
Guerrero, Epy, Cam.	.946	35	49	90	8	147	11
Guizar, Hector, Monc.	.953	113	223	360	29	612	91
Hernandez, Juan, Cor.	1.000	8	5	13	0	18	2
Hernandez, Julio, Lar.	.972	106	205	360	16	581	96
Herrera, Christian, Ver.	.946	9	13	22	2	37	2
Laureano, Francisco, Agua.	1.000	3	1	5	0	6	0
Leyva, German, Ver.	.900	2	3	6	1	10	1
Lopez, Fabian, Oax.	.914	16	16	37	5	58	8
Lopez, Gonzalo, Yuc.	.900	4	3	6	1	10	1
Loredo, Jorge, Oax.	.927	45	39	138	14	191	21
Magallanes, Everardo, Mont.	1.000	3	4	4	0	8	1
Magallanes, Roberto, Tor.	1.000	1	1	3	0	4	2
Malpica, Enrique, Yuc.	.000	1	0	0	1	1	0
Martinez, Abel, Cam.	.967	13	6	23	1	30	4
Martinez, Augusto, Tab.	.900	6	2	7	1	10	2
Martinez, Luis, Sal.	.960	114	228	444	28	700	109
Medina, Ernesto, Mont.	1.000	1	0	3	0	3	0
Mere, Pedro, Ver.	.833	2	1	4	1	6	0
Minjares, Francisco, Agua.	.958	53	69	159	10	238	36
Montanez, Daniel, Ver.	.973	59	100	189	8	297	38
Morales, Florentino, Lar.	1.000	1	0	1	0	1	0
Nunez, Ray, Agua.	.600	1	0	3	2	5	0
Olvera, Sergio, Can.	.957	39	55	77	6	138	16
Orantes, Ramon, Mont.	1.000	1	2	2	0	4	1
Pacho, Juan, Yuc.	.967	104	168	305	16	489	54
Paez, Raul, Cam.	1.000	1	2	3	0	5	1
Peguero, Julio, Can.	1.000	1	3	0	0	3	0
Perez, Alfredo, Cam.	.939	33	54	101	10	165	21
Quintero, Guillermo, Cor.	.937	100	173	321	33	527	63
RAMIREZ, Enrique, Can.	.977	100	184	324	12	520	65
Rivera, Jesus, Tab.	.882	6	6	9	2	17	2
Robles, Javier, Tig.	.951	106	217	370	30	617	90
Robles, Trinidad, Tig.	.953	10	11	30	2	43	9
Rodriguez, Hector, Rey.	1.000	1	1	1	0	2	0
Rojas, Francisco, Tab.	1.000	1	2	2	0	4	0
Ruiz, Juan, Cor.	1.000	3	0	7	0	7	0
Salas, Heriberto, Tor.	.964	91	141	308	17	466	67
Sanchez, Orlando, Mont.	.940	55	78	155	15	248	21
Sanchez, Roque, Cam.	1.000	1	2	2	0	4	1
Sanchez, Wilfredo, Can.	1.000	8	3	9	0	12	0
Sandoval, Jose, Mex.	.970	112	199	389	18	606	79
Santos, Andres, Lar.	.000	1	0	0	1	1	0
Soriano, Ricardo, Cor.	1.000	1	3	0	0	3	0
Trapaga, Julio, Tig.	1.000	2	1	2	0	3	1
Valdez, Ramon, Cor.	1.000	1	2	0	0	2	0
Valenzuela, Irving, Monc.	.944	14	9	25	2	36	5
Valle, Jorge, Monc.	1.000	2	2	3	0	5	1
Valle, Jose, Yuc.	.961	38	41	81	5	127	13
Valle, Roberto, Tor.	.993	33	51	98	1	150	13
Velez, Manuel, Agua.	1.000	6	9	14	0	23	5
Verdugo, Vicente, Sal.	1.000	1	0	2	0	2	0
Vizcarra, Marco, Sal.	.905	5	8	11	2	21	2
Zazueta, Juan, Tor.	1.000	5	1	12	0	13	2

TRIPLE PLAY: J. Robles.

OUTFIELDERS

Player, Team	Pct.	G	PO	A	E	TC	DP
Abrego, Jesus, Rey.	.958	84	132	4	6	142	0
Acuna, Jose, Tor.	.977	50	84	2	2	88	0
Aguilar, Antonio, Mont.	.983	62	112	3	2	117	0
Aguilera, Armando, Sal.	1.000	5	7	2	0	9	0
Alvarez, Hector, Oax.	.976	100	241	7	6	254	2
Alvarez, Jorge, Cor.	.969	114	201	19	7	227	3
Arano, Eloy, Cor.	.975	87	189	5	5	199	1
Arano, Wilfredo, Lar.	.976	116	233	12	6	251	6
Arauz, Leobardo, Yuc.	.981	98	199	12	4	215	2
Arias, Francisco, Sal.	1.000	1	0	1	0	1	0
Armenta, Cristhian, Lar.	.926	22	42	8	4	54	1
Arredondo, Hernando, Can.	.929	12	25	1	2	28	0
Arredondo, Luis, Yuc.	.967	113	223	12	8	243	2
Avila, Ruben, Agua.	1.000	2	2	0	0	2	0
Barron, Tony, Mex.	.987	86	148	5	2	155	2
Bojorquez, Victor, Mex.	.969	114	233	16	8	257	0
Bolado, Carlos, Ver.	.950	16	18	1	1	20	0
Bullett, Scott, Cam.	.976	59	115	5	3	123	0
Canizalez, Juan, Mont.	.959	102	177	9	8	194	3
Canseco, Ozzie, Tab.	1.000	5	8	2	0	10	0
Carillo, Matias, Tig.	.989	98	174	9	2	185	3
Carter, Michael, Ver.	.977	62	122	3	3	128	1
Castro, Carlos, Tab.	.938	40	75	1	5	81	0
Cervantes, Regugio, Sal.	1.000	1	1	0	0	1	0
Chan, Armando, Cam.	1.000	8	8	0	0	8	0
Chance, Tony, Tab.	.981	105	196	12	4	212	3
Chimelis, Joel, Lar.	.500	1	0	1	1	2	0
Choi, Hwan, Tor.	.981	24	53	0	1	54	0
Claudio, Patricio, Can.	.981	100	251	9	5	265	1
Cruz, Luis, Rey.	.909	8	10	0	1	11	0
Cuevas, Jorge, Agua.	1.000	20	21	2	0	23	0
De la Cruz, Hector, Yuc.	1.000	15	30	0	0	30	0
De la Torre, Francisco, Oax.	.714	4	5	0	2	7	0
De Lima, Rafael, Agua.	.940	89	167	6	11	184	0
Diaz, Luis, Tor.	.957	27	41	3	2	46	0
Dominguez, David, Lar.	.965	74	131	6	5	142	3
Escalante, Marcelo, Can.	1.000	30	36	1	0	37	1
Espino, Daniel, Mont.	.969	21	29	2	1	32	0
Espino, Omar, Lar.	.975	57	76	2	2	80	0
Espinosa, Ramon, Rey.	.970	118	314	8	10	332	4
Espinoza, Cutberto, Rey.	1.000	1	1	0	0	1	0
Espinoza, Javier, Can.	1.000	6	6	2	0	8	1
Espinoza, Jose, Lar.	.977	57	122	5	3	130	0
Estrella, Isaac, Lar.	.750	2	3	0	1	4	0
Fentanes, Oscar, Tab.	.967	112	225	7	8	240	1
Fernandez, Daniel, Mex.	.976	80	154	7	4	165	1
Figueroa, Marco, Cor.	.964	14	26	1	1	28	0
Fink, Marc, Cor.	1.000	2	1	0	0	1	0
Fornes, Daniel, Rey.	1.000	49	71	6	0	77	1
Garcia, Carlos, Tig.	1.000	55	138	5	0	143	1
Garcia, Cornelio, Tor.	.975	103	183	13	5	201	2
Garcia, Hector, Mont.	.989	82	176	3	2	181	0
Garcia, Leo, Oax.	.970	118	218	7	7	232	0
Gastelum, Sergio, Tig.	.952	25	38	2	2	42	0
Gonzalez, Jesus, Tor.	1.000	2	2	0	0	2	0
Gonzalez, Jose, Agua.	.968	108	238	5	8	251	1
Gonzalez, Roman, Cor.	1.000	26	45	2	0	47	0
Green, Dario, Tor.	.917	11	11	0	1	12	0
Groppuso, Mike, Yuc.	.969	13	31	0	1	32	0
Hall, Joe, Ver.	.938	15	29	1	2	32	0
Hernandez, Cesar, Cam.	.980	117	273	17	6	296	5
Iglesias, Luis, Yuc.	1.000	3	5	0	0	5	0
Incaviglia, Pete, Mont.	.981	25	51	2	1	54	1
Iturbe, Pedro, Tig.	1.000	21	29	2	0	31	0
Jimenez, Eduardo, Sal.	.988	66	77	4	1	82	0
Jones, Tim, Agua.	.980	27	50	0	1	51	0
Kapano, Randy, Mont.	1.000	2	3	0	0	3	0
Leal, Guadalupe, Monc.	.909	13	18	2	2	22	0
Lee, Derek, Mex.	.926	34	46	4	4	54	0
Lopez, Fabian, Oax.	.971	17	31	2	1	34	1
Lopez, Gonzalo, Yuc.	1.000	18	39	3	0	42	1
Machiria, Pablo, Agua.	.970	36	59	6	2	67	0
Malave, Jose, Lar.	.951	19	35	4	2	41	0
Malpica, Enrique, Yuc.	1.000	2	3	0	0	3	0
Martinez, Abel, Can.	.750	1	0	3	1	4	1
Martinez, Enrique, Agua.	.964	81	153	8	6	167	1
Mata, Noe, Ver.	1.000	44	62	1	0	63	0
May, Derrick, Mont.	1.000	11	21	0	0	21	0
Medina, Ernesto, Mont.	1.000	5	4	1	0	5	0
Medina, Jose, Sal.	.980	89	137	10	3	150	2
Meggers, Mike, Tor.	.968	51	82	10	3	95	0
MENDEZ, Roberto, Oax.	.993	84	144	8	1	153	2
Meza, Gonzalo, Mex.	1.000	44	60	3	0	63	0
Mitchel, Tony, Ver.	1.000	2	2	0	0	2	0

Player, Team	Pct.	G	PO	A	E	TC	DP
Moore, Kerwin, Ver.	.977	39	83	3	2	88	1
Moreno, David, Cam.	.980	32	43	6	1	50	1
Moreno, Leonardo, Ver.	.965	36	52	3	2	57	0
Morones, Martin, Ver.	.989	87	164	11	2	177	0
Munoz, Jose, Sal.	.964	90	177	10	7	194	3
Nunez, Ray, Agua.	.800	10	8	0	2	10	0
Obando, Sherman, Oax.	1.000	3	8	1	0	9	1
Ojeda, Miguel, Mex.	1.000	19	34	2	0	36	0
Payro, Edison, Tab.	.963	74	145	11	6	162	0
PEGUERO, Julio, Can.	.993	116	273	7	2	282	0
Perez, Francisco, Rey.	1.000	54	74	6	0	80	2
Poe, Charles, Tor.	.945	48	82	4	5	91	0
Quintero, Alan, Yuc.	.973	15	36	0	1	37	0
Quintero, Edgar, Mont.	.987	38	75	2	1	78	0
Ramirez, Angel, Tig.	1.000	12	15	1	0	16	0
Ramirez, Jesus, Oax.	.976	46	81	0	2	83	0
Ramon, Reyes, Cam.	.981	34	51	0	1	52	0
Reyes, Jesus, Sal.	1.000	6	3	0	0	3	0
Rodriguez, Boi, Monc.	.875	3	7	0	1	8	0
Rodriguez, Fernando, Cam.	.962	82	162	16	7	185	5
Romero, Wilfredo, Sal.	.991	113	202	9	2	213	1
Rubio, Sergio, Yuc.	.983	35	59	0	1	60	0
Saenz, Ricardo, Monc.	.992	118	249	11	2	262	1
Salazar, Carlos, Yuc.	1.000	1	1	0	0	1	0
Sanchez, Gerardo, Lar.	.989	46	85	4	1	90	2
Sanchez, Raul, Can.	.978	107	216	5	5	226	0
Sandez, Angel, Sal.	.500	3	1	0	1	2	0
Sandoval, Octavio, Tig.	.966	58	82	4	3	89	0
Sherman, Darrell, Monc.	.985	109	254	5	4	263	3
Soriano, Ricardo, Cor.	.988	49	79	3	1	83	0
Sotomayor, Gilberto, Monc.	1.000	10	14	4	0	18	1
Stoner, Mike, Mont.	.947	31	51	3	3	57	1
Suarez, Luis, Tig.	1.000	26	47	2	0	49	2
Tatis, Bernardo, Yuc.	1.000	29	40	4	0	44	0
Tavarez, Jesus, Ver.	.979	64	137	2	3	142	1
Tellez, Alonso, Rey.	1.000	24	30	1	0	31	0
Tinsley, Lee, Monc.	.944	35	48	3	3	54	1
Tiquet, Lazaro, Tab.	1.000	8	14	0	0	14	0
Valdez, Jesus, Cam.	1.000	47	70	7	0	77	3
Valdez, Ramon, Cor.	.986	57	141	4	2	147	0
Valencia, Carlos, Tab.	1.000	67	103	4	0	107	0
Valle, Cosme, Mex.	1.000	2	2	0	0	2	0
Valle, Roberto, Tor.	1.000	2	1	1	0	2	0
Vazquez, Gregorio, Tab.	1.000	9	14	0	0	14	0
Vazquez, Jorge, Tor.	.964	19	27	0	1	28	0
Vega, Edgar, Agua.	1.000	5	14	0	0	14	0
Velez, Manuel, Agua.	1.000	2	3	0	0	3	0
Villarreal, Salvador, Rey.	.975	37	34	5	1	40	1
Villegas, Fernando, Sal.	.979	108	179	9	4	192	0
Villegas, Ramon, Tab.	1.000	2	6	0	0	6	0
Voigt, Jack, Rey.	.906	19	27	2	3	32	0
Yan, Julian, Cor.	.892	19	33	0	4	37	0
Yuriar, Jesus, Tor.	.981	50	97	9	2	108	2
Zambrano, Eduardo, Can.	.956	30	58	7	3	68	2
Zambrano, Roberto, Can.	1.000	8	15	1	0	16	0
Zamudio, Jeovanni, Rey.	1.000	1	1	0	0	1	0
Zamudio, Rafael, Agua.	.931	47	65	2	5	72	1
Zazueta, Juan, Tor.	.982	41	51	4	1	56	0

CATCHERS

Player, Team	Pct.	G	PO	A	E	TC	DP	PB
Abrego, Jesus, Rey.	.973	4	28	8	1	37	1	0
Aguilera, Armando, Sal.	.988	23	76	7	1	84	2	4
Amezcua, Adan, Rey.	.978	38	236	32	6	274	3	4
Avila, Ruben, Agua.	1.000	1	3	0	0	3	0	0
Bustamante, Omar, Lar.	1.000	10	35	3	0	38	2	3
Castaneda, Hector, Yuc.	.985	61	286	46	5	337	2	0
Castaneda, Rafael, Oax.	1.000	10	25	3	0	28	0	0
Cazarin, Manuel, Cam.	.974	109	397	91	13	501	17	9
Cervantes, Refugio, Sal.	1.000	3	5	0	0	5	0	0
Cobos, Rogelio, Cam.	.988	60	291	40	4	335	5	4
Cruz, Antonio, Agua.	.979	69	252	25	6	283	2	1
Espino, Omar, Lar.	1.000	1	1	0	0	1	0	0
Espinoza, Ramon, Tor.	1.000	16	39	0	0	39	0	1
Estrada, Hector, Monc.	.990	101	443	35	5	483	1	7
Estrada, Ricardo, Can.	1.000	1	1	0	0	1	0	0
Figueroa, Jesus, Oax.	.973	21	64	7	2	73	1	0
Fornes, Daniel, Rey.	1.000	1	10	0	0	10	1	0
Franco, Iker, Tig.	1.000	16	23	1	0	24	0	0
Garza, Gerardo, Lar.	.991	104	482	59	5	546	11	8
Garzon, Eliseo, Tor.	.980	112	490	58	11	559	6	5
Gastelum, Carlos, Cor.	.994	45	155	11	1	167	1	3
Gavia, Jesus, Yuc.	1.000	55	251	33	0	284	1	2
Gonzalez, Fernando, Rey.	1.000	15	46	5	0	51	0	0
Gonzalez, Roman, Cor.	.889	2	8	0	1	9	0	2
Hall, Joe, Ver.	1.000	1	3	1	0	4	0	0
Hernandez, Esteban, Oax.	.969	18	55	8	2	65	1	1
Hernandez, Miguel, Ver.	.969	20	53	9	2	64	1	0
Hurtado, Hector, Can.	.967	51	245	22	9	276	4	5
Lopez, Carlos, Tab.	1.000	6	8	0	0	8	0	0
Martinez, Raul, Ver.	.988	77	288	47	4	339	7	6
Meza, Alfredo, Mont.	.989	100	491	54	6	551	6	3
Meza, Gonzalo, Mex.	1.000	1	6	0	0	6	0	0
Munoz, Adan, Monc.	.958	20	61	8	3	72	1	2
Munoz, Noe, Sal.	.991	106	556	76	6	638	6	9
Ochoa, Edgar, Ver.	1.000	5	8	0	0	8	0	0
Ojeda, Miguel, Mex.	.980	68	296	43	7	346	6	1
Olivares, Roberto, Cor.	1.000	2	2	0	0	2	0	0
Ortega, Antonio, Mex.	.989	25	79	13	1	93	1	0
Osuna, Hector, Can.	.952	31	85	14	5	104	0	0
Pacho, Carlos, Yuc.	.969	25	59	3	2	64	1	1
Pena, Carlos, Tab.	1.000	14	23	4	0	27	1	1
Perez, Juan, Tor.	1.000	11	36	5	0	41	0	0
Pinto, Placido, Ver.	.983	29	55	4	1	60	0	1
Ramirez, Efren, Cor.	.983	85	369	32	7	408	5	4
Resendez, Carlos, Monc.	.967	22	52	7	2	61	5	1
Reyes, Gilberto, Ver.	.968	29	107	14	4	125	2	2
Robles, Juan, Can.	.983	34	101	16	2	119	4	3
Rodriguez, Armando, Tig.	.985	96	404	55	7	466	2	3
Rojas, Homar, Oax.	.986	76	321	36	5	362	8	6
Santana, Mario, Mont.	.960	49	129	14	6	149	1	1
Saucedo, Roberto, Rey.	.974	63	328	41	10	379	4	7
Soriano, Ricardo, Cor.	1.000	2	7	0	0	7	0	1
Soto, Saul, Mex.	.987	50	203	18	3	224	2	0
Valdez, Emmanuel, Tig.	.982	29	100	12	2	114	1	0
Valdez, Francisco, Tab.	.985	118	480	58	8	546	6	2
Valdez, Ramon, Cor.	1.000	1	1	0	0	2	0	0
Valdivia, Arturo, Ver.	1.000	2	1	0	0	1	0	0
Vazquez, Felipe, Lar.	.992	38	116	13	1	130	3	1
VEGA, Edgar, Agua.	.993	71	236	36	2	274	5	3
Villanueva, Hector, Oax.	1.000	5	16	2	0	18	0	0

PITCHERS

Player, Team	Pct.	G	PO	A	E	TC	DP
Acosta, Aaron, Lar.	.943	21	9	24	2	35	2
Acosta, Gerardo, Oax.	1.000	23	6	18	0	24	1
Acosta, Jaciel, Monc.	1.000	7	2	2	0	4	0
Aguilar, Jose, Mont.	1.000	50	0	8	0	8	0
Aguilar, Mario, Cam.	1.000	13	0	1	0	1	0
Aguilera, Adrian, Mex.	1.000	5	1	3	0	4	0
Aguirre, Guadencio, Tab.	.938	49	3	12	1	16	0
Aleman, Paulo, Cor.	1.000	18	1	9	0	10	0
Ali, Sam, Oax.	.893	4	6	19	3	28	1
Almeida, Roussell, Lar.	1.000	38	9	8	0	17	1
Alvarez, Antonio, Monc.	1.000	26	4	12	0	16	0
Alvarez, Juan, Sal.	.889	25	6	26	4	36	0
Alvarez, Octavio, Mex.	1.000	23	11	24	0	35	1
Angulo, Luis, Sal.	1.000	9	1	1	0	2	0
Angulo, Victor, Tig.	1.000	14	0	1	0	1	0
Arias, Joel, Mont.	1.000	2	0	1	0	1	0
Armenta, Alejandro, Tig.	.929	27	6	7	1	14	1
Arocha, Rene, Mont.	1.000	12	2	6	0	8	0
Atilano, Juan, Ver.	.000	6	0	0	1	1	0
Avilez, Alejandro, Sal.	1.000	7	0	1	0	1	0
Ayala, Luis, Sal.	1.000	61	4	23	0	27	4
Baez, Victor, Cor.	1.000	32	1	7	0	8	0
Barraza, Ernesto, Tor.	.967	23	9	20	1	30	2
Bernal, Manuel, Mex.	.833	13	3	2	1	6	1
Berumen, Andres, Mont.	1.000	12	1	4	0	5	0
Bourgeois, Steve, Cam.	.968	20	8	22	1	31	1
Boze, Wayne, Sal.	.969	25	13	18	1	32	0
Burnett, Heath, Oax.	1.000	4	1	1	0	2	0
Bustillos, Oscar, Agua.	1.000	15	4	2	0	6	0
Butcher, Mike, Agua.	1.000	4	1	0	0	1	0
Cabrales, Gabriel, Agua.	1.000	56	7	12	0	19	3
Camara, Pedro, Cor.	1.000	26	2	9	0	11	0
Campillo, Jorge, Tig.	1.000	32	2	8	0	10	1
Campos, Francisco, Cam.	.981	24	13	40	1	54	1
Cantu, Jacobo, Tor.	1.000	9	1	0	0	1	0
Cardenas, Faustino, Can.	.667	6	0	2	1	3	0
Carranza, Javier, Can.	.941	10	3	13	1	17	2
Carrasco, Alejandro, Can.	.978	27	9	35	1	45	2
Caruso, Eugene, Lar.	.900	22	1	17	2	20	0
Castaneda, Aurelio, Agua.	.923	26	5	31	3	39	2
Castellanos, Hugo, Lar.	1.000	24	3	6	0	9	0
Cazares, Juan, Sal.	1.000	18	0	2	0	2	0
Cazares, Rosario, Sal.	1.000	17	1	2	0	3	0
Cazares, Tomas, Monc.	1.000	36	1	9	0	10	1
Cecena, Jose, Monc.	.952	24	4	16	1	21	0
Cerros, Juan, Rey.	.909	38	5	15	2	22	0
Chapa, Javier, Cam.	1.000	20	5	11	0	16	0
Chavez, Carlos, Agua.	1.000	5	1	2	0	3	1

CLASS AAA Mexican League

Player, Team	Pct.	G	PO	A	E	TC	DP
Conde, Argenis, Tor.	.952	53	10	30	2	42	4
Cota, Marino, Oax.	1.000	44	5	25	0	30	3
Couoh, Enrique, Ver.	.875	50	2	5	1	8	0
Cruz, Javier, Mex.	1.000	48	7	17	0	24	2
Cruz, Juan, Yuc.	1.000	21	0	2	0	2	1
Cruz, Luis, Agua.	1.000	16	0	2	0	2	0
Diaz, Alejandro, Can.	1.000	40	4	13	0	17	0
Diaz, Marco, Lar.	.900	20	3	6	1	10	1
Diaz, Rafael, Mont.	1.000	36	4	13	0	17	1
Dominguez, David, Oax.	1.000	3	1	1	0	2	0
Duarte, Miguel, Sal.	.857	44	5	7	2	14	1
Elguezabal, Octavio, Cam.	1.000	12	1	5	0	6	1
Elizalde, Carlos, Oax.	1.000	2	0	2	0	2	0
Elvira, Narciso, Cam.	1.000	20	4	26	0	30	1
Enriquez, Martin, Sal.	.917	32	3	8	1	12	2
Esparza, Emerson, Monc.	.964	24	3	24	1	28	4
Esquer, Mercedes, Rey.	.824	19	2	12	3	17	2
Federico, Gustavo, Mont.	1.000	34	6	7	0	13	2
Felix, Antonio, Agua.	1.000	2	0	1	0	1	0
Fernandez, Osvaldo, Sal.	1.000	12	3	11	0	14	2
Figueroa, Fernando, Sal.	.857	4	1	5	1	7	0
Flores, Ignacio, Monc.	.938	54	2	13	1	16	1
Flores, Jorge, Tab.	.929	26	4	9	1	14	0
Fontes, Agustin, Can.	.929	21	1	12	1	14	1
Fregoso, Raul, Can.	1.000	13	0	8	0	8	0
Galvez, Rosario, Tab.	1.000	23	3	7	0	10	2
Gamez, Francisco, Mont.	1.000	4	0	1	0	1	0
Garcia, Adolfo, Cam.	1.000	23	1	9	0	10	5
Garcia, Alfredo, Mex.	.955	19	7	14	1	22	2
Garcia, Carlos, Mex.	.929	25	8	31	3	42	3
Garcia, Gerardo, Tig.	.750	22	2	4	2	8	1
Garcia, Jose, Sal.	1.000	13	0	2	0	2	0
Garcia, Jose, Tig.	.933	27	5	9	1	15	0
Garcia, Manuel, Tig.	1.000	12	3	0	0	3	0
Garcia, Mike, Mex.	1.000	12	1	0	0	1	0
Garcialuna, Francisco, Mex.	1.000	2	0	1	0	1	0
Garibay, Daniel, Tig.	1.000	16	3	19	0	22	3
Garibay, Roberto, Can.	1.000	27	2	6	0	8	1
Garibay, Salvador, Lar.	1.000	18	2	10	0	12	1
Garza, Roberto, Lar.	1.000	30	3	6	0	9	2
Gomez, Gustavo, Rey.	.938	25	6	9	1	16	1
Gomez, Martin, Can.	1.000	4	1	1	0	2	1
Gonzalez, Arnulfo, Ver.	1.000	8	2	2	0	4	0
Gonzalez, Arturo, Mont.	1.000	15	7	12	0	19	0
Gonzalez, Gilberto, Tor.	.923	6	4	8	1	13	1
Gonzalez, Victor, Monc.	.938	33	1	14	1	16	1
Grajales, Norberto, Tor.	1.000	27	7	36	0	43	3
Green, Ottis, Tor.	.875	7	1	6	1	8	0
Guerica, Guillermo, Oax.	1.000	8	1	1	0	2	1
Guerra, Pascual, Tab.	1.000	9	3	14	0	17	0
Gutierrez, Cosme, Oax.	1.000	20	2	5	0	7	0
Gutierrez, Marco, Mex.	.933	19	5	9	1	15	0
Heredia, Hector, Yuc.	.938	39	1	14	1	16	0
Heredia, Julian, Rey.	.957	15	3	19	1	23	1
Heredia, Wilson, Tor.	1.000	5	2	2	0	4	0
Hernandez, Fernando, Mont.	.905	17	7	12	2	21	0
Hernandez, Jose, Monc.	.960	20	5	19	1	25	1
Hernandez, Martin, Sal.	1.000	18	4	18	0	22	1
Herrera, Calixto, Tor.	.750	27	2	4	2	8	0
Herrera, Enrique, Tab.	.964	61	4	23	1	28	3
Higuera, Teodoro, Mont.	1.000	9	2	7	0	9	1
Hollins, Stacy, Tor.	1.000	8	4	3	0	7	0
Huerta, Luis, Lar.	.944	9	7	10	1	18	1
Izabal, Luis, Can.	.833	10	0	5	1	6	0
Jimenez, Isaac, Ver.	.868	19	9	24	5	38	0
Jinenez, German, Lar.	1.000	20	4	21	0	25	1
Kamar, Emil, Can.	.923	19	4	8	1	13	2
Lara, Edy, Yuc.	1.000	26	1	5	0	6	1
Lara, Hugo, Tab.	.929	24	12	14	2	28	0
Lara, Jorge, Sal.	.958	23	8	15	1	24	2
Larranaga, Miguel, Can.	1.000	21	5	9	0	14	1
Leon, Cupertino, Mex.	.917	21	2	9	1	12	1
Leon, Juan, Tor.	.900	28	2	7	1	10	0
Lewis, Richie, Rey.	1.000	11	8	9	0	17	0
Leyva, Edgar, Cor.	1.000	24	7	16	0	23	0
Lezama, Rafael, Ver.	1.000	41	1	2	0	3	0
Linares, Yfrain, Cor.	.700	12	3	4	3	10	0
Lizarraga, Andres, Lar.	1.000	10	1	4	0	5	0
Loaiza, Sabino, Cam.	.925	24	4	33	3	40	3
Lopez, Emigdio, Cam.	1.000	26	10	23	0	33	0
Lopez, Gilberto, Can.	1.000	48	1	15	0	16	0
Lopez, Jesus, Oax.	1.000	43	2	4	0	6	1
Lopez, Jonas, Yuc.	.875	6	1	13	2	16	1
Lopez, Jose, Lar.	1.000	19	0	2	0	2	0
Lopez, Jose, Tor.	.833	45	2	3	1	6	0
Lopez, Raymundo, Monc.	1.000	6	0	1	0	1	0
Loya, Rigoberto, Mont.	.895	28	4	13	2	19	0
Luevano, Juan, Ver.	.917	55	4	7	1	12	2
Manriquez, Alberto, Agua.	.917	29	2	9	1	12	0
Manzanillo, Ravelo, Yuc.	.957	24	12	32	2	46	3
Marquez, Isidro, Tig.	.957	54	3	19	1	23	3
Martinez, Cesar, Tor.	.909	30	0	10	1	11	0
Martinez, Francisco, Lar.	1.000	15	1	5	0	6	0
Martinez, Jesus, Ver.	.935	23	6	23	2	31	1
Martinez, Juan, Mex.	1.000	3	1	1	0	2	0
Martinez, Miguel, Tab.	.951	25	7	32	2	41	4
Martinez, Pedro, Oax.	1.000	11	1	12	0	13	0
Mascorro, David, Mex.	1.000	43	3	8	0	11	0
Medina, Alonso, Sal.	1.000	11	2	0	0	2	0
Mefia, Delfino, Lar.	1.000	1	0	2	0	2	0
Melendez, Nestor, Rey.	1.000	38	6	13	0	19	2
Mere, Fernando, Ver.	1.000	19	2	4	0	6	0
Metoyer, Tony, Lar.	1.000	50	3	6	0	9	1
Meza, Leobardo, Ver.	1.000	23	8	19	0	27	2
Mikkelsen, Linc, Sal.	1.000	3	0	2	0	2	0
Miranda, Julio, Agua.	1.000	43	3	7	0	10	0
Molina, Primitivo, Mont.	1.000	23	3	4	0	7	0
Montano, Ignacio, Cor.	1.000	31	0	2	0	2	0
Montemayor, Humberto, Mont.	1.000	27	3	16	0	19	0
MORA, Eleazar, Ver.	1.000	22	6	45	0	51	2
Morales, Luis, Ver.	1.000	25	1	1	0	2	0
Moreno, Claudio, Mex.	1.000	53	3	18	0	21	0
Moreno, Leobardo, Sal.	.944	21	3	14	1	18	0
Munoz, Leonardo, Mont.	1.000	46	0	6	0	6	0
Munoz, Miguel, Cor.	.971	23	3	31	1	35	2
Munoz, Ricardo, Agua.	1.000	5	1	1	0	2	0
Murillo, Felipe, Tor.	1.000	49	0	9	0	9	0
Navarro, Joel, Mex.	1.000	8	0	3	0	3	0
Navarro, Jose, Tig.	.929	42	8	18	2	28	1
Navarro, Luis, Yuc.	1.000	9	4	22	0	26	1
Neri, Braulio, Cam.	1.000	13	3	6	0	9	1
Neri, Eduardo, Yuc.	1.000	45	3	19	0	22	1
Nieblas, Omar, Tab.	1.000	19	1	1	0	2	0
Nunez, Javier, Agua.	1.000	7	1	2	0	3	0
Nunez, Jose, Tig.	.926	26	10	15	2	27	1
Nunez, Jose, Oax.	.917	26	6	16	2	24	2
Ochoa, Pablo, Rey.	.839	24	8	18	5	31	2
Olague, Jesus, Agua.	.909	22	6	4	1	11	0
Orea, Flavio, Cor.	1.000	26	1	7	0	8	0
Oropeza, Eddie, Rey.	.900	7	1	8	1	10	2
Orozco, Jaime, Rey.	.926	20	8	17	2	27	1
Ortega, Raul, Tor.	1.000	15	0	1	0	1	0
Ortega, Roberto, Cor.	1.000	30	2	8	0	10	2
Ortega, Wilbert, Yuc.	.909	37	1	9	1	11	0
Osuna, Ricardo, Tab.	1.000	2	1	1	0	2	0
Osuna, Roberto, Sal.	1.000	13	0	4	0	4	1
Palacios, Vicente, Rey.	1.000	43	4	15	0	19	2
Palafox, Juan, Monc.	.974	23	6	31	1	38	1
Parra, Julio, Lar.	.857	55	3	15	3	21	0
Pena, Joel, Ver.	.950	39	6	13	1	20	0
Perez, Vladimir, Oax.	.714	24	0	5	2	7	0
Perez, Leonardo, Cor.	.931	24	5	22	2	29	2
Picota, Alberto, Lar.	.875	40	3	11	2	16	0
Pimentel, Roberto, Tab.	.944	25	3	31	2	36	1
Powell, Dennis, Cam.	.889	45	3	21	3	27	2
Pulido, Raymundo, Tab.	1.000	15	1	2	0	3	0
Quinones, Enrique, Yuc.	.960	25	7	17	1	25	1
Quintanilla, Enrique, Lar.	.833	26	2	13	3	18	1
Quiroz, Aaron, Ver.	1.000	10	2	4	0	6	0
Ramirez, Carlos, Oax.	1.000	22	1	4	0	5	2
Renteria, Hilario, Tor.	1.000	16	0	6	0	6	0
Retes, Jose, Oax.	1.000	23	1	6	0	7	1
Retes, Lorenzo, Mont.	.909	31	2	8	1	11	1
Reyes, Nathanael, Mex.	.976	26	9	31	1	41	4
Reyes, Pablo, Mont.	1.000	28	5	38	0	43	1
Rios, Jesus, Monc.	.929	17	1	12	1	14	0
Rivas, Jesus, Ver.	1.000	6	0	2	0	2	0
Rivera, Francisco, Tor.	1.000	3	0	1	0	1	0
Rivera, Oscar, Ver.	.974	21	10	28	1	39	1
Rivera, Paul, Can.	.667	55	0	6	3	9	0
Robles, Jorge, Cor.	1.000	34	1	10	0	11	0
Rodriguez, Inoc, Can.	1.000	24	1	13	0	14	1
Rodriguez, Manuel, Cor.	.833	31	1	4	1	6	0
Rodriguez, Raul, Tor.	1.000	23	6	27	0	33	5
Rodriguez, Rosario, Sal.	1.000	4	1	1	0	2	1
Rodriguez, Salvador, Yuc.	.895	19	5	12	2	19	0
Rojo, Oscar, Rey.	1.000	28	0	4	0	4	2
Romero, Alejandro, Mex.	.938	41	4	11	1	16	0
Romero, Cesar, Lar.	1.000	16	0	2	0	2	0
Romero, Juan, Cor.	1.000	49	1	5	0	6	0
Romo, Ricardo, Mont.	1.000	8	1	2	0	3	0
Roque, Jorge, Tor.	1.000	31	3	9	0	12	0

Player, Team	Pct.	G	PO	A	E	TC	DP
Ruffin, Johnny, Oax.	.500	5	0	1	1	2	0
Ruiz, Cecilio, Tab.	.969	19	7	24	1	32	1
Saldana, Edgardo, Yuc.	.929	37	4	9	1	14	1
Salgado, Eduardo, Ver.	1.000	4	0	1	0	1	0
Salkeld, Roger, Tig.	1.000	6	2	4	0	6	0
Sanchez, Alejandro, Can.	1.000	37	6	16	0	22	2
Sanchez, Claudio, Oax.	1.000	42	2	9	0	11	0
Sanchez, Efrain, Cam.	.962	38	5	20	1	26	1
Sanchez, Hector, Agua.	1.000	24	11	22	0	33	1
Sanchez, Pablo, Sal.	1.000	35	2	11	0	13	1
Sandoval, Guillermo, Can.	.750	34	3	0	1	4	0
Sierra, Abel, Tab.	1.000	18	1	5	0	6	0
Sinohui, David, Cam.	1.000	48	8	8	0	16	0
Solarte, Jose, Monc.	.938	54	4	11	1	16	0
Solis, Ricardo, Cor.	.960	26	4	20	1	25	0
Sombra, Francisco, Agua.	1.000	51	5	10	0	15	0
Soto, Antonio, Can.	1.000	7	0	1	0	1	0
Soto, Daniel, Oax.	.923	27	0	12	1	13	1
Strong, Joe, Tig.	1.000	11	2	2	0	4	1
Sulu, Mario, Cam.	.941	25	3	13	1	17	1
Sung, Won, Agua.	.923	8	2	10	1	13	0
Tejeda, Felix, Agua.	.875	37	2	5	1	8	0
Tijerna, Alberto, Rey.	1.000	19	2	6	0	8	0
Turgeon, David, Rey.	1.000	17	7	22	0	29	1
Turuda, Miyoki, Mex.	1.000	10	1	4	0	5	3
Uribe, Juan, Yuc.	1.000	17	1	12	0	13	2
Valdez, Armando, Mont.	.955	50	1	20	1	22	1
Valdez, Efrain, Tig.	1.000	8	4	17	0	21	0
Valdez, Rodolfo, Monc.	1.000	21	0	3	0	3	0
Valencia, Jorge, Agua.	1.000	34	6	17	0	23	2
Valenzuela, Gil, Can.	1.000	20	9	20	0	29	2
Valenzuela, Jesus, Oax.	1.000	25	4	17	0	21	3
Valenzuela, Jose, Tig.	1.000	15	2	1	0	3	0
Valerio, Julio, Monc.	1.000	37	1	4	0	5	0
Vargas, Ignacio, Sal.	.909	26	3	7	1	11	1
Vargas, Joel, Tab.	1.000	30	2	6	0	8	1
Vazquez, Adrian, Cam.	1.000	9	6	7	0	13	1
Vega, Obed, Rey.	1.000	36	5	7	0	12	0
Velazquez, Ernesto, Tab.	.889	51	4	12	2	18	0
Velazquez, Israel, Agua.	1.000	7	4	4	0	8	1
Verdugo, Hugo, Lar.	.778	13	4	3	2	9	1
Verdugo, Orlando, Yuc.	.833	6	2	18	4	24	4
Villaluna, Miguel, Mont.	1.000	2	0	1	0	1	0
Villarreal, Antonio, Yuc.	.750	2	0	3	1	4	1
Villarreal, Carlos, Tor.	1.000	12	2	0	0	2	0
Villaverde, Jose, Ver.	1.000	3	0	1	0	1	0
Villegas, Jose, Agua.	.967	28	11	18	1	30	1
Vizcarra, Enrique, Sal.	1.000	2	1	1	0	2	0
Vizcarra, Ernesto, Agua.	1.000	1	1	0	0	1	0
Woodson, Kerry, Sal.	1.000	3	1	1	0	2	0
Zamudio, Jeovanni, Rey.	1.000	45	9	14	0	23	3
Zavala, Marcos, Tig.	1.000	24	2	2	0	4	0

TRIPLE PLAY: Robles.

LEAGUE CHAMPIONS

Year	Team	Pct.
1955—	Mexico City Tigers*	.539
1956—	Mexico City Reds	.692
1957—	Yucatan	.567
	Mex. C. Reds (2nd)†	.550
1958—	Nuevo Laredo	.625
1959—	Poza Rica	.575
	Mex. C. Reds (3rd)†	.507
1960—	Mexico City Tigers	.538
1961—	Veracruz	.575
1962—	Monterrey	.592
1963—	Puebla	.606
1964—	Mexico City Reds	.586
1965—	Mexico City Reds	.590
1966—	Mexico City Tigers‡	.614
	Mexico City Reds	.571
1967—	Jalisco	.607
1968—	Mexico City Reds	.586
1969—	Reynosa	.591
1970—	Aguila§	.580
	Mexico City Reds	.607
1971—	Jalisco§	.558
	Saltillo	.593
1972—	Saltillo	.636
	Cordoba§	.541
1973—	Saltillo	.656
	Mexico City Reds∞	.590

Year	Team	Pct.
1974—	Jalisco	.627
	Mexico City Reds∞	.551
1975—	Tampico∞	.541
	Cordoba	.649
1976—	Mexico City Reds∞	.543
	Union Laguna	.547
1977—	Mexico City Reds	.623
	Nuevo Laredo∞	.507
1978—	Aguascalientes∞	.589
	Union Laguna	.523
1979—	Saltillo	.704
	Puebla∞	.628
1980—	No champion▲	
1981—	Mexico City Reds	.615
	Reynosa	.492
1982—	Ciudad Juarez∞	.570
	Mexico City Tigers	.508
1983—	Campeche◆	.614
	Ciudad Juarez	.535
1984—	Yucatan◆	.560
	Ciudad Juarez	.509
1985—	Mexico City Reds◆	.606
	Nuevo Laredo	.5275
1986—	Puebla◆	.682
	Monclova	.598

Year	Team	Pct.
1987—	Mexico City Reds◆	.605
	Monterrey	.536
1988—	Mexico City Reds◆	.646
	Nuevo Laredo	.602
1989—	Nuevo Laredo◆	.621
	Yucatan	.539
1990—	Nuevo Laredo	.618
	Leon◆	.565
1991—	Monterrey◆	.683
	Mexico City Reds	.627
1992—	Mexico City Tigers◆	.594
	Nuevo Laredo	.538
1993—	Nuevo Laredo	.589
	Tabasco◆	.528
1994—	Mexico City Red Devils◆	.646
	Monterrey Sultans	.608
1995—	Mexico City Red Devils	.708
	Monterrey Sultans◆	.570
1996—	Monterrey Sultans	.713
	Mexico City Reds◆	.619
1997—	Mexico City Red Devils	.686
	Mexico City Tigers■	.658
1998—	Monterrey	.672
	Oaxaca■	.576
1999—	Mexico City Tigers	.664
	Mexico City Reds■	.632

*Defeated Nuevo Laredo, two games to none, in playoff for pennant. †Won four-team playoff. ‡Won split-season playoff. §League divided into Northern, Southern divisions; won two-team playoff. ∞League divided into Northern, Southern zones; sub-divided into Eastern, Western divisions, won eight-team playoff. ▲ A players strike on July 1 forced the cancellation of the regular season and playoff schedule. ◆ League divided into Northern, Southern zones; four clubs from each zone qualified for postseason play. Won final series for league championship. ■ League divided into Northern, Central and Southern zones; played split season, with top eight teams qualifying for playoffs. Won final series for league championship.

PACIFIC COAST LEAGUE

LEAGUE OFFICE

President
Branch Rickey

Address
1631 Mesa Ave.
Colorado Springs, CO 80906

Phone
719-636-3399

TEAMS

ALBUQUERQUE DUKES

General manager
Pat McKernan
Manager
Tom Gamboa
Ballpark (capacity, surface)
Albuquerque Sports Stadium (10,510, grass)
Affiliation
Dodgers
Address
Avenida Cesar Chavez SE
Albuquerque, NM 87106
Phone
505-243-1791

CALGARY CANNONS

Vice president, baseball operations
John Traub
Manager
Lynn Jones
Ballpark (capacity, surface)
Burn Stadium (8,000, grass)
Affiliation
Marlins
Address
2255 Crowchild Trail N.W.
Calgary, Alberta T2M 4S7
Phone
403-284-1111

COLORADO SPRINGS SKY SOX

General manager/president
Robert Goughan
Manager
Chris Cron
Ballpark (capacity, surface)
Sky Sox Stadium (9,000, grass)
Affiliation
Rockies
Address
4385 Tutt Blvd.
Colorado Springs, CO 80922
Phone
719-597-1449

EDMONTON TRAPPERS

General manager
Mel Kowalchuk
Manager
To be announced
Ballpark (capacity, surface)
Teluf Field (10,000; artificial infield, grass outfield)
Affiliation
Angels
Address
10233 96th Ave.
Edmonton, Alberta T5K 0A5

Phone
780-414-4450

FRESNO GRIZZLIES

Vice president/general manager
Derek Leistra
Manager
Shane Turner
Ballpark (capacity, surface)
Beinden Field (6,500, grass)
Affiliation
Giants
Address
1231 N Street
Fresno, CA 93721
Phone
209-442-1994

IOWA CUBS

General manager
Sam Bernabe
Manager
Dave Trembley
Ballpark (capacity, surface)
Sec Taylor Stadium (10,500, grass)
Affiliation
Cubs
Address
350 SW 1 St.
Des Moines, IA 50309
Phone
515-243-6111

LAS VEGAS STARS

General manager
Don Logan
Manager
Duane Espy
Ballpark (capacity, surface)
Cashman Field (9,370, grass)
Affiliation
Padres
Address
850 Las Vegas Blvd. N
Las Vegas, NV 89101
Phone
702-386-7200

MEMPHIS REDBIRDS

President/general manager
Allie Prescott
Manager
Gaylen Pitts
Ballpark (capacity, surface)
Autozone Park (14,200; grass)
Affiliation
Cardinals
Address
8 S. Third Street
Memphis, TN 38103

Phone
901-432-9900

NASHVILLE SOUNDS

General manager
Tom Moncries
Manager
Trent Jewett
Ballpark (capacity, surface)
Greer Stadium (11,500, grass)
Affiliation
Pirates
Address
534 Chestnut Street
Nashville, TN 37203
Phone
615-242-4371

NEW ORLEANS ZEPHYRS

General manager
Dan Hanrahan
Manager
Tony Pena
Ballpark (capacity, surface)
Zephyr Field (11,000, grass)
Affiliation
Astros
Address
6000 Airline Drive
Metairie, LA 70003
Phone
504-734-5155

OKLAHOMA REDHAWKS

General Manager
Tim O'Toole
Manager
DeMarlo Hale
Ballpark (capacity, surface)
Southwestern Bell Bricktown Ball Park (13,066, grass)
Affiliation
Rangers
Address
2 South Mickey Mantle
Oklahoma City, OK 73104
Phone
405-218-1000

OMAHA GOLDEN SPIKES

Vice president/general manager
Bill Gorman
Manager
John Mizerock
Ballpark (capacity, surface)
Omaha's Rosenblatt Stadium (23,000, grass)
Affiliation
Royals
Address
1202 Bert Murphy Drive
Omaha, NE 68107

SACRAMENTO RIVER CATS

Phone
402-734-2550

General Manager
Gary Arthur

Manager
Bob Geren

Ballpark (capacity, surface)
Raley Field (10,500, grass)

Affiliation
Athletics

Address
1001 Second Street
Old Sacramento, CA 95814

Phone
916-319-4700

SALT LAKE BUZZ

Assistant general manager
Dorsena Picknell

Manager
Phil Roof

Ballpark (capacity, surface)
Franklin-Covey Field (15,500, grass)

Affiliation
Twins

Address
P.O. Box 4108
Salt Lake City, UT 84110

Phone
801-485-3800

TACOMA RAINIERS

Executive vice president
Mel Taylor

Manager
Dave Myers

Ballpark (capacity, surface)
Cheney Stadium (10,106, grass)

Affiliation
Mariners

Address
P.O. Box 11087
Tacoma, WA 98411

Phone
252-752-7707

TUCSON SIDEWINDERS

Vice president of baseball operations
Mike Feder

Manager
Tom Spencer

Ballpark (capacity, surface)
Tucson Electric Park (11,000, grass)

Affiliation
Diamondbacks

Address
P.O. Box 27045
Tucson, AZ 85716

Phone
520-434-1021

1999 FINAL STANDINGS

EAST DIVISION

Team	W	L	T	Pct.	GB
Oklahoma (Rangers)	83	59	0	.585	...
Nashville (Pirates)	80	60	0	.571	2.0
Memphis (Cardinals)	74	64	0	.536	7.0
New Orleans (Astros)	55	85	0	.393	27.0

CENTRAL DIVISION

Team	W	L	T	Pct.	GB
Omaha (Royals)	81	60	0	.574	...
Colorado Springs (Rockies)	66	73	0	.475	14.0
Albuquerque (Dodgers)	65	74	0	.468	15.0
Iowa (Cubs)	65	76	0	.461	16.0

NORTH DIVISION

Team	W	L	T	Pct.	GB
Vancouver (Athletics)	84	58	0	.592	...
Tacoma (Mariners)	69	70	0	.496	13.5
Edmonton (Angels)	65	74	0	.468	17.5
Calgary (Marlins)	57	82	0	.410	25.5

SOUTH DIVISION

Team	W	L	T	Pct.	GB
Salt Lake (Twins)	73	68	0	.518	...
Fresno (Giants)	73	69	0	.514	0.5
Las Vegas (Padres)	67	75	0	.472	6.5
Tucson (Diamondbacks)	66	76	0	.465	7.5

COMPOSITE

Team	Van.	Ok.	Oma.	Nash.	Mem.	S.L.	Fres.	Tac.	C.S.	L.V.	Edm.	Alb.	Tuc.	Iowa	Cal.	N.O.	W	L	T	Pct.	GB
Vancouver (Athletics)	...	4	6	4	5	5	2	11	6	2	8	4	6	4	12	5	84	58	0	.592	...
Oklahoma (Rangers)	4	...	3	8	9	4	5	3	5	6	5	4	5	5	5	12	83	59	0	.585	1
Omaha (Royals)	2	5	...	2	5	3	2	6	12	5	6	9	3	10	6	5	81	60	0	.574	2.5
Nashville (Pirates)	4	7	6	...	8	4	5	5	6	3	5	4	4	6	3	10	80	60	0	.571	3.0
Memphis (Cardinals)	3	7	2	8	...	6	4	3	2	4	4	2	4	6	5	14	74	64	0	.536	8.0
Salt Lake (Twins)	3	4	5	4	2	...	9	6	2	6	2	6	11	3	6	4	73	68	0	.518	10.5
Fresno (Giants)	6	3	6	3	4	6	...	4	5	10	6	4	7	2	5	2	73	69	0	.514	11.0
Tacoma (Mariners)	5	5	2	2	5	1	4	...	4	6	7	8	6	3	7	4	69	70	0	.496	13.5
Colo. Springs (Rockies)	2	3	4	2	3	6	3	3	...	4	6	7	3	9	5	6	66	73	0	.475	16.5
Las Vegas (Padres)	6	2	3	5	4	10	6	2	3	...	2	7	7	3	4	3	67	75	0	.472	17.0
Edmonton (Angels)	8	3	1	3	3	6	2	7	2	6	...	3	4	5	9	3	65	74	0	.468	17.5
Albuquerque (Dodgers)	3	3	7	4	6	2	4	0	9	1	5	...	3	12	4	2	65	74	0	.468	17.5
Tucson (D'backs)	2	3	4	4	4	5	9	2	5	9	3	5	...	2	3	6	66	76	0	.465	18.0
Iowa (Cubs)	4	3	6	1	2	5	5	5	7	4	3	4	6	...	5	5	65	76	0	.461	18.5
Calgary (Marlins)	4	3	2	4	2	2	3	9	3	4	7	2	5	3	...	4	57	82	0	.410	25.5
New Orleans (Astros)	2	4	3	6	2	3	6	4	2	5	5	2	3	3	3	...	55	85	0	.393	28.0

Major league affiliations in parentheses.

PLAYOFFS: Vancouver defeated Salt Lake, three games to two; Oklahoma defeated Omaha, three games to one; Vancouver defeated Oklahoma, three games to one to win league champioship; Vancouver defeated Charlotte to win AAA World Series.

REGULAR-SEASON ATTENDANCE: Albuquerque, 319,339; Calgary, 269,002; Colorado Springs, 202,724; Edmonton, 385,913; Fresno, 311,804; Iowa, 416,804; Las Vegas, 339,702; Memphis, 397,339; Nashville, 335,901; New Orleans, 472,665; Oklahoma, 471,722; Omaha, 411,233; Salt Lake, 505,547; Tacoma, 271,026; Tucson, 254,817; Vancouver, 241,461. Total—5,606,999. Playoffs (13 games)—70,549. Class AAA All-Star Game at Metairie, La.—8,895.

MANAGERS: Albuquerque, Mike Scioscia; Calgary, Lynn Jones; Colorado Springs, Bill Hayes; Edmonton, Carney Lansford; Fresno, Ron Roenicke; Iowa, Terry Kennedy; Las Vegas, Mike Ramsey; Memphis, Gaylen Pitts; Nashville, Trent Jewett; New Orleans, Tony Pena; Oklahoma, Greg Biagini; Omaha, Ron Johnson; Salt Lake, Phil Roof; Tacoma, Dave Myers; Tucson, Chris Speier; Vancouver, Mike Quade.

ALL-STAR TEAM: 1B—J.R. Phillips, Colorado Springs; 2B—Adam Kennedy, Memphis; 3B—Kit Pellow, Omaha; SS—Scott Sheldon, Oklahoma; OF—Chad Hermansen, Nashville; Calvin Murray, Fresno; Mark Quinn, Omaha; C—Sal Fasano, Omaha; DH—David Ortiz, Salt Lake; Utility—Frank Menechino, Vancouver; RHP—Brett Laxton, Vancouver; LHP—Matt Perisho, Oklahoma; RP—David Wainhouse, Colorado Springs; Most Valuable Player—Calin Murray, Fresno; Rookie of the Year—Mark Quinn, Omaha; Manager of the Year—Greg Biagini, Oklahoma.

1999 BATTING

TEAM

Team	Avg.	G	TPA	AB	R	H	TB	2B	3B	HR	RBI	SH	SF	HP	BB	IBB	SO	SB	CS	GDP	LOB	ShO	Slg.	OBP
Colo. Springs ..	.297	139	5380	4793	793	1422	2363	303	28	194	750	46	47	57	437	17	1012	100	53	112	988	5	.493	.359
Fresno............	.294	142	5496	4857	849	1430	2276	262	37	170	784	58	56	42	483	23	883	145	61	116	963	4	.469	.360
Tucson	.292	142	5482	4885	766	1427	2204	282	36	141	705	46	49	53	449	18	941	86	46	122	1031	6	.451	.355
Salt Lake.......	.291	141	5393	4736	814	1379	2206	274	38	159	766	34	40	62	521	14	951	84	48	137	973	4	.466	.366
Omaha	.289	141	5458	4828	826	1395	2405	277	20	231	779	40	36	97	457	18	990	104	63	112	981	3	.498	.360
Nashville	.289	140	5347	4757	806	1373	2266	292	26	183	761	39	54	57	440	19	855	93	50	111	934	8	.476	.352
Albuquerque....	.284	139	5321	4703	742	1338	2134	288	32	148	694	61	38	47	472	16	979	119	83	95	949	7	.454	.353
Memphis........	.284	138	5289	4666	743	1323	2072	300	34	127	683	46	45	60	472	19	1017	110	49	95	984	2	.444	.354
Vancouver.......	.282	142	5433	4740	759	1339	2057	272	37	124	693	43	38	65	547	26	902	93	54	149	1025	3	.434	.362
Oklahoma	.282	142	5418	4819	787	1360	2153	286	27	151	738	29	46	55	469	29	970	84	46	123	963	1	.447	.350
Calgary..........	.282	139	5213	4703	716	1327	2187	315	34	159	670	32	33	42	403	17	995	73	50	121	938	7	.465	.342
Tacoma	.281	139	5466	4841	689	1359	2007	272	35	102	624	35	55	47	488	22	949	121	54	108	1089	4	.415	.349
Edmonton	.281	139	5334	4767	730	1338	2083	272	31	137	677	38	37	48	444	13	860	84	61	108	956	4	.437	.346
New Orleans....	.270	140	5276	4711	674	1270	1928	266	19	118	618	41	32	38	454	15	914	75	62	113	939	7	.409	.337
Las Vegas	.264	142	5447	4771	692	1261	2025	297	31	135	636	36	29	51	560	15	1106	105	41	123	1047	4	.424	.346
Iowa...............	.263	141	5400	4800	699	1261	2074	287	29	156	646	45	34	60	461	21	1093	116	62	89	959	4	.432	.333

INDIVIDUAL

TOP QUALIFIERS FOR BATTING CHAMPIONSHIP

Minimum 383 plate appearances. *Lefthanded batter. †Switch-hitter.

Player, Team	Avg.	G	TPA	AB	R	H	TB	2B	3B	HR	RBI	SH	SF	HP	BB	IBB	SO	SB	CS	GDP	Slg.	OBP
Quinn, Mark, Oma.	.360	107	470	428	67	154	256	27	0	25	84	0	4	10	28	3	69	7	9	9	.598	.409
Murray, Calvin, Fres.	.334	130	608	548	122	183	297	31	7	23	73	4	4	3	49	3	88	42	14	6	.542	.389
Crespo, Felipe, Fres.†	.332	112	482	385	98	128	237	27	5	24	84	5	7	7	78	6	73	17	8	10	.616	.447
Ramirez, Aramis, Nash. ...	.328	131	548	460	92	151	251	35	1	21	76	0	6	9	73	6	56	5	3	11	.546	.425
Valdes, Pedro, Okla.*	.327	110	456	394	72	129	221	27	1	21	72	0	4	6	52	6	60	1	2	6	.561	.410
Kennedy, Adam, Mem.*	.327	91	405	367	69	120	180	22	4	10	63	0	5	4	29	0	36	20	6	7	.490	.378
Woods, Ken, Fres.	.324	124	517	469	77	152	201	23	4	6	73	2	9	3	33	0	45	19	4	8	.429	.366
Wilson, Desi, Tuc.*	.323	130	491	452	65	146	205	27	7	6	62	0	3	2	34	2	76	2	3	18	.454	.371
Brinkley, Darryl, Nash.	.323	111	407	372	68	120	201	35	2	14	75	0	3	1	31	0	58	5	5	11	.540	.373
Latham, Chris, S.L.†	.322	94	443	382	93	123	208	24	8	15	51	4	2	1	54	2	95	18	13	5	.545	.405
Roskos, John, Cal.	.320	134	570	506	85	162	278	44	0	24	90	0	9	3	52	2	112	2	1	18	.549	.381
Perez, Eduardo, Mem.	.320	119	468	416	67	133	218	31	0	18	82	0	1	6	45	4	92	7	8	11	.524	.393
Vitiello, Joe, Oma.	.318	122	521	447	70	142	259	33	0	28	98	0	4	4	66	2	84	3	4	16	.579	.407
Garcia, Amaury, Cal.	.317	119	537	479	94	152	258	37	9	17	53	7	1	6	44	0	79	17	11	9	.539	.381
Grijak, Kevin, Alb.*	.317	119	428	401	58	127	211	28	1	18	80	2	3	3	19	2	50	2	6	4	.526	.350

DEPARTMENTAL LEADERS: G—Zywica, 135; AB—C. Murray, 548; R—C. Murray, 122; H—C. Murray, 183; TB—C. Murray, 297; 2B—Roskos, 44; 3B—A. Garcia, Menechino, Robinson, 9 each; HR—J.R. Phillips, 41; RBI—D. Ortiz, 110; SH—Moriarty, 11; SF—several players, 9 each; HP—Fasano, 26; BB—Seitzer, 89; IBB—Menechino, 7; SO—Quinlan, 159; SB—C. Murray, 42; CS—Riggs, Hutchins, Porter, 17 each; GIDP—Ball, 19; Slg.—Crespo, .616; OBP—Crespo, 447.

ALL PLAYERS

*Lefthanded batter. †Switch-hitter.

Player, Team	Avg.	G	TPA	AB	R	H	TB	2B	3B	HR	RBI	SH	SF	HP	BB	IBB	SO	SB	CS	GDP	Slg.	OBP
Ah Yat, Paul, Nash.	.071	13	15	14	1	1	1	0	0	0	0	0	0	0	1	0	9	0	0	1	.071	.133
Akers, Chad, Tac.	.313	48	214	192	31	60	78	9	3	1	14	1	2	1	18	1	25	7	3	3	.406	.371
Alberro, Jose, Cal.	.167	24	6	6	1	1	1	0	0	0	0	0	0	0	0	0	3	0	0	0	.167	.167
Alcala, Juan, Tac.	.000	1	1	1	0	0	0	0	0	0	0	0	0	0	0	0	0	0	0	0	.000	.000
Alexander, Chad, N.O.	.240	28	104	96	7	23	34	5	0	2	8	0	2	0	6	0	22	0	1	3	.354	.279
Allen, Dusty, L.V.	.273	128	536	454	68	124	214	30	3	18	89	0	2	1	79	0	143	3	5	5	.471	.381
Almanzar, Carlos, L.V.	.000	11	6	6	0	0	0	0	0	0	0	0	0	0	0	0	5	0	0	1	.000	.000
Almanzar, Richard, Iowa	.215	33	101	93	13	20	31	2	3	1	4	2	0	0	6	0	7	6	1	4	.333	.263
Alvarez, Rafael, S.L.†	.375	6	16	16	3	6	7	1	0	0	2	0	0	0	0	0	1	0	0	1	.438	.375
Ametller, Jesus, Mem.*	.250	2	4	4	0	1	1	0	0	0	0	0	0	0	0	0	0	0	0	0	.250	.250
Anderson, Brian, Tuc.†	.500	2	3	2	0	1	1	0	0	0	1	0	0	0	1	0	0	0	0	0	.500	.500
Anderson, Jimmy, Nash.*	.167	26	30	2	5	8	3	0	0	2	0	2	0	0	2	0	7	0	0	0	.267	.219
Ankiel, Rick, Mem.*	.286	16	23	21	3	6	8	2	0	0	4	1	1	0	0	0	3	0	0	2	.381	.273
Anthony, Eric, Alb.*	.300	7	23	20	4	6	11	2	0	1	3	0	0	0	3	1	5	0	0	0	.550	.391
Ardoin, Danny, Van.	.253	109	405	336	53	85	126	13	2	8	46	9	1	9	50	0	78	3	3	12	.375	.364
Arias, George, L.V.	.284	26	113	95	30	27	68	7	2	10	30	0	0	1	17	1	28	1	0	3	.716	.398
Arnold, Jamie, Alb.	.000	7	2	2	0	0	0	0	0	0	0	0	0	0	0	0	1	0	0	0	.000	.000
Arroyo, Bronson, Nash.	.200	5	6	5	1	1	1	0	0	0	0	0	0	0	1	0	2	0	0	0	.200	.333
Arroyo, Luis, Cal.*	.000	22	1	1	0	0	0	0	0	0	0	0	0	0	0	0	1	0	0	0	.000	.000
Baerga, Carlos, L.V.†	.286	21	101	91	15	26	39	7	0	2	9	0	0	1	9	0	5	0	0	2	.429	.356
Bailey, Cory, Fres.	.000	43	1	0	0	0	0	0	0	0	0	0	0	0	1	0	0	0	0	0	.000	1.000
Bailey, Roger, C.S.	.250	6	7	4	1	1	2	1	0	0	1	0	0	2	0	0	1	0	1	0	.500	.400
Bako, Paul, N.O.*	.191	12	49	47	2	9	17	3	1	1	4	1	0	0	1	0	11	0	0	1	.362	.208
Ball, Jeff, Van.	.309	96	397	346	50	107	157	22	2	8	51	7	4	3	37	0	57	7	2	19	.454	.377
Barker, Richie, Iowa	.250	55	5	4	0	1	1	0	0	0	1	0	0	0	0	0	2	0	0	0	.250	.250
Barkett, Andy, Okla.*	.307	132	541	486	70	149	221	32	5	10	76	0	5	6	44	4	71	7	7	18	.455	.368
Barnes, Brian, Mem.*	.154	37	18	13	1	2	3	1	0	0	1	5	0	0	0	0	5	0	0	0	.231	.154
Barry, Jeff, C.S.†	.341	64	204	185	36	63	108	15	0	10	27	0	0	2	19	2	31	6	3	6	.584	.402
Battle, Allen, Iowa	.245	35	126	110	16	27	43	7	0	3	14	1	1	0	14	1	30	2	1	1	.391	.328
Bautista, Danny, Cal.	.319	38	147	135	25	43	77	8	1	8	28	0	0	1	11	2	18	3	3	1	.570	.374
Beckett, Robbie, Alb.	.000	15	6	5	2	0	0	0	0	0	0	0	0	0	1	0	0	0	0	0	.000	.167

Player, Team	Avg.	G	TPA	AB	R	H	TB	2B	3B	HR	RBI	SH	SF	HP	BB	IBB	SO	SB	CS	GDP	Slg.	OBP
Belk, Tim, Mem.	.200	21	64	55	10	11	24	4	0	3	8	0	0	0	9	0	9	1	0	4	.436	.313
Belliard, Francisco, Tuc.†	.143	3	8	7	0	1	1	0	0	0	2	0	0	0	1	0	3	0	0	0	.143	.250
Bergman, Sean, N.O.	.000	3	1	1	0	0	0	0	0	0	0	0	0	0	0	0	0	0	0	0	.000	.000
Berkman, Lance, N.O.†	.323	64	267	226	42	73	117	20	0	8	49	0	2	0	39	1	47	7	1	10	.518	.419
Betten, Randy, Edm.	.379	12	31	29	5	11	12	1	0	0	3	2	0	0	0	0	5	0	0	0	.414	.379
Betzsold, James, N.O.	.217	63	217	198	29	43	79	15	0	7	27	0	2	3	14	0	64	3	2	1	.399	.276
Bierbrodt, Nick, Tuc.*	.250	11	9	8	3	2	2	0	0	0	1	0	0	0	1	0	1	0	0	0	.250	.333
Bieser, Steve, Nash.-Mem.* ...	.306	64	220	193	28	59	89	14	2	4	19	5	0	4	18	0	34	8	0	2	.461	.377
Billingsley, Brent, Cal.*	.136	21	23	22	0	3	4	1	0	0	1	1	0	0	0	0	4	0	0	0	.182	.136
Blanco, Henry, C.S.	.333	15	60	57	8	19	32	4	0	3	12	1	1	0	1	0	12	0	1	1	.561	.339
Blowers, Mike, Tac.	.231	3	13	13	1	3	4	1	0	0	2	0	0	0	0	0	4	0	0	0	.308	.231
Bochtler, Doug, Alb.	.000	18	1	1	0	0	0	0	0	0	0	0	0	0	0	0	1	0	0	0	.000	.000
Boskie, Shawn, Alb.	.278	15	23	18	2	5	8	3	0	0	2	5	0	0	0	0	7	0	0	0	.444	.278
Bost, Heath, C.S.	.083	38	15	12	1	1	1	0	0	0	0	3	0	0	0	0	1	0	0	0	.083	.083
Bournigal, Rafael, Okla.	.375	17	69	56	16	21	36	6	0	3	14	0	1	0	12	0	5	1	1	1	.643	.478
Boyd, Jason, Tuc.-Nash.	.167	50	7	6	0	1	1	0	0	0	1	0	1	0	0	0	1	0	0	0	.167	.143
Bridges, Kary, Iowa-Okla.*	.322	85	294	264	39	85	120	14	0	7	39	4	3	1	22	2	19	6	3	8	.455	.372
Briggs, Anthony, C.S.	.333	10	3	3	1	1	4	0	0	1	3	0	0	0	0	0	1	0	0	0	1.333	.333
Brinkley, Darryl, Nash.	.323	111	407	372	68	120	201	35	2	14	75	0	3	1	31	0	58	5	5	11	.540	.373
Brito, Juan, Oma.	.286	2	7	7	1	2	4	2	0	0	0	0	0	0	0	0	2	0	0	0	.571	.286
Brohawn, Troy, Tuc.*	.000	3	4	4	0	0	0	0	0	0	0	0	0	0	0	0	0	0	0	0	.000	.000
Brown, Adrian, Nash.†	.321	17	67	56	10	18	23	3	1	0	4	0	0	0	11	1	8	6	1	0	.411	.433
Brown, Emil, Nash.	.307	110	476	430	97	132	216	20	5	18	60	0	4	7	35	1	80	16	5	7	.502	.366
Brown, Randy, Tac.	.256	44	172	156	15	40	67	7	1	6	27	6	0	1	9	1	48	4	2	6	.429	.301
Brown, Roosevelt, Iowa*	.358	74	294	268	50	96	191	25	2	22	79	0	4	3	19	1	54	3	3	8	.713	.401
Brownson, Mark, C.S.*	.250	18	32	28	4	7	8	1	0	0	0	3	0	0	1	0	8	0	0	0	.286	.276
Brumbaugh, Cliff, Okla.	.250	4	12	12	1	3	3	0	0	0	1	0	0	0	0	0	2	0	0	0	.250	.250
Buchanan, Brian, S.L.	.297	107	431	391	67	116	172	24	1	10	60	0	3	9	28	0	85	11	2	14	.440	.355
Buhner, Shawn, Tac.	.240	43	161	146	17	35	46	8	0	1	12	0	2	3	10	0	43	0	1	9	.315	.298
Bunch, Mel, Tac.	.000	22	1	1	0	0	0	0	0	0	0	0	0	0	0	0	0	0	0	0	.000	.000
Burgus, Travis, Cal.*	.000	20	1	1	0	0	0	0	0	0	0	0	0	0	0	0	0	0	0	0	.000	.000
Burke, Jamie, Edm.	.336	46	177	149	29	50	68	9	0	3	16	2	0	3	23	0	18	0	1	2	.456	.434
Busby, Mike, Mem.	.231	29	14	13	1	3	5	2	0	0	1	0	0	0	1	0	6	0	0	0	.385	.286
Byas, Michael, Fres.†	.364	5	27	22	4	8	10	2	0	0	2	0	0	0	5	1	4	2	1	0	.455	.481
Byington, Jimmie, Oma.	.206	89	255	228	28	47	65	10	1	2	23	3	1	3	20	0	46	3	7	6	.285	.278
Cabrera, Jose, N.O.	.000	31	1	1	0	0	0	0	0	0	0	0	0	0	0	0	1	0	0	0	.000	.000
Caminiti, Ken, N.O.†	.350	6	22	20	6	7	11	4	0	0	3	0	0	0	2	0	1	0	0	0	.550	.409
Campusano, Carlos, Fres.	.283	16	52	46	2	13	15	2	0	0	3	0	1	3	2	0	9	0	0	4	.326	.346
Candaele, Casey, N.O.†	.266	126	519	467	56	124	185	34	3	7	42	2	0	3	47	1	54	3	9	7	.396	.337
Cangelosi, John, C.S.†	.330	29	136	109	22	36	46	7	0	1	13	1	1	1	24	0	16	4	3	4	.422	.452
Canizaro, Jay, Fres.	.280	106	426	364	77	102	204	20	2	26	78	2	7	3	49	3	79	16	5	9	.560	.364
Carlson, Dan, Tuc.	.269	33	30	26	2	7	10	1	1	0	3	1	0	0	3	0	8	0	0	0	.385	.345
Carlyle, Buddy, L.V.*	.139	25	45	36	6	5	6	1	0	0	3	6	0	0	3	0	10	0	0	1	.167	.205
Carr, Jeremy, Oma.	.262	73	331	275	47	72	98	12	1	4	25	9	0	5	42	1	58	15	8	4	.356	.370
Carroll, Mark, Tac.	.000	1	1	1	0	0	0	0	0	0	0	0	0	0	0	0	1	0	0	0	.000	.000
Carvajal, Jovino, Edm.†	.245	108	397	367	38	90	126	15	3	5	40	4	3	3	20	1	63	17	13	7	.343	.288
Castillo, Frank, Nash.	.087	19	30	23	2	2	3	1	0	0	1	6	0	0	1	0	9	0	0	2	.130	.125
Castro, Juan, Alb.	.274	116	467	423	52	116	170	25	4	7	51	6	4	0	34	2	70	2	3	14	.402	.325
Castro, Ramon, Cal.	.258	97	378	349	43	90	157	22	0	15	61	0	3	2	24	3	64	0	0	11	.450	.307
Cedeno, Domingo, Tac.†	.268	33	121	112	17	30	43	8	1	1	13	0	0	2	7	1	36	1	3	1	.384	.322
Cey, Dan, S.L.	.295	117	447	403	63	119	176	18	3	11	56	2	3	7	32	1	66	10	2	12	.437	.355
Chamberlain, Wes, Alb.	.307	111	410	375	53	115	194	19	3	18	78	0	3	7	24	0	66	3	7	8	.517	.357
Charles, Frank, L.V.	.246	80	287	272	25	67	96	19	2	2	28	0	2	3	10	2	61	2	0	16	.353	.279
Chavez, Raul, Tac.	.268	102	390	354	39	95	126	20	1	3	40	0	2	6	28	1	63	1	3	11	.356	.331
Checo, Robinson, Alb.	.000	16	23	19	1	0	0	0	0	0	0	3	0	0	1	0	9	0	0	1	.000	.050
Chouinard, Bobby, Tuc.	.167	12	15	12	0	2	2	0	0	0	0	3	0	0	0	0	7	0	0	0	.167	.167
Christenson, Ryan, Van.	.344	33	150	128	30	44	57	8	1	1	16	0	0	0	22	2	21	7	2	4	.445	.440
Christian, Eddie, Edm.†	.236	44	160	148	24	35	57	5	1	5	15	0	0	0	12	0	31	4	3	6	.385	.294
Clapinski, Chris, Cal.†	.322	81	303	267	51	86	143	21	6	8	35	3	1	2	30	0	53	5	1	6	.536	.393
Clapp, Stubby, Mem.*	.260	110	457	393	72	102	174	26	2	14	62	4	4	3	53	4	96	7	7	9	.443	.349
Clark, Dave, Alb.*	.324	37	134	108	19	35	53	7	1	3	17	0	0	0	26	1	26	2	0	3	.491	.455
Clayton, Royce, Okla.	.143	2	10	7	1	1	1	0	0	0	1	0	0	0	3	0	3	0	0	0	.143	.400
Clemente, Edgard, C.S.	.304	75	296	273	45	83	157	24	1	16	59	0	1	2	20	1	55	5	5	6	.575	.355
Clemons, Chris, Tuc.	.250	45	6	4	1	1	1	0	0	0	0	1	0	0	1	0	1	0	0	0	.250	.400
Cline, Pat, Iowa	.228	98	321	290	27	66	106	20	1	6	42	0	1	4	26	0	73	1	2	8	.366	.299
Clontz, Brad, Nash.	.000	12	2	1	0	0	0	0	0	0	0	0	0	0	1	0	1	0	0	0	.000	.500
Colangelo, Mike, Edm.	.362	26	121	105	13	38	47	7	1	0	9	1	0	2	13	1	18	2	1	1	.448	.442
Cole, Victor, Iowa*	.100	19	11	10	0	1	1	0	0	0	0	1	0	0	0	0	4	0	0	0	.100	.100
Connelly, Steve, Fres.	.000	55	8	6	2	0	0	0	0	0	0	0	0	0	2	0	5	0	0	0	.000	.250
Conti, Jason, Tuc.*	.290	133	590	520	100	151	217	23	8	9	57	3	6	5	55	1	89	22	8	8	.417	.360
Cookson, Brent, Alb.	.321	85	322	277	57	89	193	18	1	28	70	1	4	2	38	2	56	7	1	5	.697	.402
Coolbaugh, Scott, Tuc.	.255	74	251	212	28	54	91	14	1	7	31	1	4	2	32	3	49	1	1	4	.429	.352
Cora, Alex, Alb.*	.308	80	334	302	51	93	130	11	7	4	37	9	3	8	12	0	37	9	5	8	.430	.348
Corbin, Archie, Cal.	1.000	12	1	1	0	1	1	0	0	0	0	0	0	0	0	0	0	0	0	0	1.000	1.000
Cordova, Francisco, Nash.	.000	2	2	2	0	0	0	0	0	0	0	0	0	0	0	0	1	0	0	0	.000	.000
Cornelius, Reid, Cal.	.258	29	35	31	3	8	11	3	0	0	4	2	0	1	1	0	5	0	0	0	.355	.303
Corps, Edwin, Fres.	1.000	4	1	1	1	1	1	0	0	0	1	0	0	0	0	0	0	0	0	0	1.000	1.000
Cotton, John, C.S.*	.315	70	255	235	50	74	139	18	1	15	48	1	3	2	14	4	64	4	2	6	.591	.354
Crabtree, Robbie, Fres.	.000	22	3	2	0	0	0	0	0	0	0	1	0	0	0	0	2	0	0	0	.000	.000
Creek, Doug, Iowa*	.083	26	30	24	1	2	2	0	0	0	2	5	0	0	1	0	5	0	0	0	.083	.120
Creek, Ryan, N.O.	.167	6	8	6	1	1	4	0	0	1	2	2	0	0	0	0	2	0	0	0	.667	.167
Crespo, Felipe, Fres.†	.332	112	482	385	98	128	237	27	5	24	84	5	7	7	78	6	73	17	8	10	.616	.447

Player, Team	Avg.	G	TPA	AB	R	H	TB	2B	3B	HR	RBI	SH	SF	HP	BB	IBB	SO	SB	CS	GDP	Slg.	OBP
Croghan, Andy, Alb.	.000	35	1	1	0	0	0	0	0	0	0	0	0	0	0	0	1	0	0	0	.000	.000
Cromer, Tripp, Alb.	.267	5	17	15	1	4	6	2	0	0	1	0	0	1	1	0	3	0	1	0	.400	.353
Crow, Dean, N.O.*	.000	34	3	3	0	0	0	0	0	0	0	0	0	0	0	0	3	0	0	0	.000	.000
Cruz, Ivan, Nash.*	.326	75	304	273	57	89	186	20	1	25	81	0	9	1	21	4	56	0	2	7	.681	.365
Cummings, John, Tuc.*	.333	11	4	3	0	1	1	0	0	0	0	0	0	0	1	0	1	0	0	0	.333	.500
Cummings, Midre, S.L.*	.322	69	288	261	50	84	150	19	4	13	68	0	1	3	23	0	43	4	4	5	.575	.382
Cunnane, Will, L.V.	.000	28	1	1	0	0	0	0	0	0	0	0	0	0	0	0	1	0	0	0	.000	.000
Cuyler, Milt, Okla.†	.173	20	56	52	3	9	13	4	0	0	6	2	0	0	2	0	12	1	1	0	.250	.204
Darensbourg, Vic, Cal.*	.000	9	1	1	0	0	0	0	0	0	0	0	0	0	0	0	0	0	0	0	.000	.000
Darr, Mike, L.V.*	.298	100	438	383	57	114	178	34	0	10	62	0	1	4	50	0	103	10	3	11	.465	.384
DaVanon, Jeff, Edm.†	.326	34	155	132	35	43	75	8	3	6	19	1	1	1	20	0	27	11	4	1	.568	.416
Davis, Ben, L.V.†	.308	58	229	201	27	62	103	18	1	7	44	0	2	2	24	1	41	4	1	5	.512	.384
Davis, Kane, Nash.	.000	12	9	8	1	0	0	0	0	0	0	0	0	0	1	0	6	0	0	0	.000	.111
Decker, Steve, Edm.	.284	64	279	225	51	64	132	19	2	15	51	0	7	3	44	3	38	0	0	7	.587	.398
De La Rosa, Maximo, Tac.-C.S.	.500	23	2	2	1	1	2	1	0	0	0	0	0	0	0	0	0	0	0	0	1.000	.500
Delgado, Wilson, Fres.†	.300	57	234	213	28	64	83	10	3	1	33	3	0	0	18	1	35	4	2	8	.390	.355
Del Toro, Miguel, Fres.	.333	40	7	6	1	2	2	0	0	0	0	1	0	0	0	0	1	0	0	0	.333	.333
Demetral, Chris, Okla.*	.262	65	219	183	29	48	69	7	1	4	18	7	1	0	28	0	35	1	2	3	.377	.358
Dempster, Ryan, Cal.	.182	5	14	11	0	2	3	1	0	0	2	3	0	0	0	0	7	0	0	0	.273	.182
Dennis, Shane, L.V.	.100	34	22	20	2	2	2	0	0	0	1	2	0	0	0	0	6	0	0	1	.100	.100
Detmers, Kris, Mem.†	.120	23	25	25	2	3	4	1	0	0	2	0	0	0	0	0	13	0	0	0	.160	.120
Diaz, Edwin, Tuc.	.311	107	446	415	72	129	188	24	1	11	50	3	4	7	17	3	77	6	7	7	.453	.345
Diorio, Nate, N.O.	.000	50	2	2	0	0	0	0	0	0	0	0	0	0	0	0	1	0	0	0	.000	.000
Dishington, Nate, Mem.*	.209	72	223	196	34	41	78	11	1	8	32	0	2	0	25	1	96	1	4	1	.398	.296
Dougherty, Jim, Nash.	.000	53	6	5	1	0	0	0	0	0	0	0	0	0	1	0	1	0	0	0	.000	.167
Dransfeldt, Kelly, Okla.	.237	102	392	359	55	85	140	21	2	10	44	3	3	3	24	0	108	6	3	12	.390	.288
Drew, J.D., Mem.*	.299	25	97	87	11	26	39	5	1	2	15	0	0	2	8	0	20	6	1	0	.448	.371
Drumheller, Al, L.V.	.000	21	11	9	1	0	0	0	0	0	0	1	0	0	1	0	2	0	0	1	.000	.100
Drumright, Mike, Cal.*	.000	12	2	2	0	0	0	0	0	0	0	0	0	0	0	0	2	0	0	0	.000	.000
Duncan, Geoff, Cal.	.000	5	1	1	0	0	0	0	0	0	0	0	0	0	0	0	1	0	0	0	.000	.000
Duncan, Mariano, Cal.	.200	2	6	5	0	1	2	1	0	0	0	0	0	1	0	0	2	0	0	0	.400	.333
Dunwoody, Todd, Cal.*	.272	65	260	246	35	67	124	16	7	9	36	0	2	2	10	1	56	7	8	5	.504	.304
Durango, Ariel, Tac.†	.000	1	4	4	0	0	0	0	0	0	0	0	0	0	0	0	0	0	0	1	.000	.000
Durazo, Erubiel, Tuc.*	.407	30	134	118	27	48	85	7	0	10	28	0	1	1	14	0	18	1	0	0	.720	.470
Eischen, Joey, Tuc.*	.333	27	3	3	1	1	2	1	0	0	0	0	0	0	0	0	1	0	0	0	.667	.333
Ellis, Robert, N.O.	.139	27	39	36	3	5	5	0	0	0	1	1	0	0	2	0	8	0	0	0	.139	.184
Encarnacion, Mario, Van.	.241	39	155	145	18	35	49	5	0	3	17	0	2	2	6	0	44	5	4	7	.338	.277
Espada, Josue, Van.	.308	6	29	26	2	8	9	1	0	0	0	0	0	0	3	0	4	1	2	0	.346	.379
Estrella, Luis, Fres.	1.000	8	1	1	1	1	1	0	0	0	0	0	0	0	0	0	0	0	0	0	1.000	1.000
Evans, Tom, Okla.	.280	128	516	439	84	123	200	35	3	12	68	1	1	9	66	1	100	5	4	10	.456	.384
Eversgerd, Bryan, Mem.	.000	60	1	1	0	0	0	0	0	0	0	0	0	0	0	0	0	0	0	0	.000	.000
Faircloth, Chad, Fres.*	.000	1	1	1	0	0	0	0	0	0	0	0	0	0	0	0	0	0	0	0	.000	.000
Farmer, Michael, C.S.†	.323	29	33	31	6	10	17	3	2	0	1	0	0	1	1	0	8	1	0	0	.548	.364
Farnsworth, Kyle, Iowa	.333	6	3	3	1	1	2	1	0	0	0	0	0	0	0	0	2	0	0	0	.667	.333
Fasano, Sal, Oma.	.275	88	350	280	63	77	155	15	0	21	49	1	1	26	42	1	69	4	2	7	.554	.415
Ferguson, Jeff, S.L.	.265	95	342	298	44	79	111	16	2	4	48	5	3	8	28	0	39	7	5	12	.372	.341
Figueroa, Nelson, Tuc.†	.286	24	35	28	6	8	9	1	0	0	1	4	0	0	3	0	7	0	0	0	.321	.355
Flener, Huck, Tac.†	.000	23	1	0	0	0	0	0	0	0	0	0	0	1	0	0	0	0	0	0	.000	1.000
Flores, Jose, Tac.	.308	42	189	143	33	44	61	6	1	3	15	2	2	5	37	1	23	4	3	2	.427	.460
Floyd, Cliff, Cal.*	.387	9	33	31	6	12	22	1	0	3	8	0	0	0	2	0	8	0	1	0	.710	.424
Fontenot, Joe, Cal.	.333	8	16	15	2	5	7	2	0	0	0	1	0	0	0	0	5	0	0	1	.467	.333
Forbes, P.J., Okla.	.104	22	75	67	4	7	8	1	0	0	2	2	0	1	5	0	12	0	0	2	.119	.178
Foster, Jim, Tuc.-Edm.	.289	35	124	114	17	33	50	11	0	2	18	0	2	0	8	0	15	1	0	5	.439	.331
Franco, Raul, Cal.	.273	16	57	55	7	15	15	0	0	0	4	0	0	0	2	0	4	0	0	7	.273	.298
Freeman, Ricky, Van.	.223	61	227	202	27	45	71	14	0	4	24	2	0	3	20	0	39	0	4	5	.351	.302
Frias, Hanley, Tuc.†	.300	23	88	80	15	24	27	3	0	0	6	1	0	0	7	0	15	3	1	2	.338	.356
Fultz, Aaron, Fres.*	.233	37	35	30	4	7	7	0	0	0	3	0	0	2	1	0	1	0	0	1	.233	.281
Gajkowski, Steve, Iowa	.000	58	2	2	0	0	0	0	0	0	0	0	0	0	0	0	1	0	0	0	.000	.000
Garcia, Amaury, Cal.	.317	119	537	479	94	152	258	37	9	17	53	7	1	6	44	0	79	17	11	9	.539	.381
Garcia, Carlos, L.V.	.281	78	295	274	36	77	105	19	0	3	28	0	0	3	17	1	61	5	0	10	.383	.330
Garcia, Freddy, Nash.	.000	4	10	9	0	0	0	0	0	0	0	0	0	0	1	0	3	0	0	0	.000	.100
Garcia, Mike, Nash.	.000	23	1	0	0	0	0	0	0	0	0	1	0	0	0	0	0	0	0	0	.000	.000
Gazarek, Marty, Iowa	.320	40	135	128	13	41	68	12	0	5	16	0	1	1	5	1	13	0	1	2	.531	.348
Giambi, Jeremy, Oma.*	.346	35	161	127	31	44	87	5	1	12	28	0	2	1	31	2	30	1	1	2	.685	.472
Giard, Ken, Nash.	.000	14	1	1	0	0	0	0	0	0	0	0	0	0	0	0	1	0	0	0	.000	.000
Gibbs, Kevin, Alb.†	.286	11	27	21	4	6	9	3	0	0	1	1	0	1	4	0	6	2	2	0	.429	.423
Gibralter, Steve, Oma.	.266	110	461	417	77	111	218	21	1	28	78	2	2	13	27	1	97	6	3	9	.523	.329
Gibson, Derrick, C.S.	.275	110	423	385	68	106	188	19	6	17	67	0	2	6	30	0	82	12	6	5	.488	.336
Gil, Benji, Cal.	.279	116	453	412	74	115	197	29	1	17	64	4	3	7	27	1	101	17	5	5	.478	.332
Gilbert, Shawn, Alb.	.304	114	499	421	88	128	199	35	3	10	52	8	4	4	62	0	84	25	8	3	.473	.395
Giovanola, Ed, L.V.*	.283	36	122	106	23	30	44	6	1	2	10	0	0	0	16	1	23	2	0	3	.415	.377
Gipson, Charles, Tac.	.299	47	193	174	26	52	64	6	3	0	21	2	0	3	14	0	24	18	4	5	.368	.361
Gomez, Chris, L.V.	.333	10	31	27	3	9	10	1	0	0	4	0	0	1	2	0	6	0	0	1	.370	.400
Gonzales, Rene, N.O.	.253	27	93	79	9	20	24	4	0	0	11	2	1	0	11	0	11	1	0	3	.304	.341
Gonzalez, Gabe, Cal.*	.000	24	1	1	0	0	0	0	0	0	0	0	0	0	0	0	1	0	0	0	.000	.000
Gonzalez, Jeremi, Iowa	.000	3	3	3	0	0	0	0	0	0	0	0	0	0	0	0	2	0	0	0	.000	.000
Gonzalez, Jimmy, L.V.	.295	40	129	112	10	33	53	9	1	3	19	0	3	0	14	1	29	0	0	1	.473	.364
Gonzalez, Lariel, C.S.	.000	12	1	1	0	0	0	0	0	0	0	0	0	0	0	0	1	0	0	0	.000	.000
Gonzalez, Wiklenman, L.V.	.272	24	100	92	13	25	49	6	0	6	12	0	0	3	5	0	10	0	0	3	.533	.330
Graves, Bryan, Edm.	.400	2	7	5	2	2	3	1	0	0	1	0	0	1	1	0	2	0	0	0	.600	.571
Green, Scarborough, Okla.† ...	.248	104	403	359	68	89	126	16	6	3	29	4	3	3	34	1	86	26	12	3	.351	.316
Greene, Todd, Edm.	.243	19	75	74	10	18	39	6	0	5	14	0	0	1	0	0	12	0	0	4	.527	.253

Player, Team	Avg.	G	TPA	AB	R	H	TB	2B	3B	HR	RBI	SH	SF	HP	BB	IBB	SO	SB	CS	GDP	Slg.	OBP
Grijak, Kevin, Alb.*	.317	119	428	401	58	127	211	28	1	18	80	2	3	3	19	2	50	2	6	4	.526	.350
Grilli, Jason, Fres.-Cal.	.130	27	26	23	2	3	3	0	0	0	1	3	0	0	0	0	10	0	0	1	.130	.130
Guevara, Giomar, Tac.†	.293	32	131	116	15	34	56	13	0	3	15	1	0	2	12	0	22	0	1	3	.483	.369
Guiel, Aaron, L.V.*	.245	84	309	257	46	63	128	25	2	12	39	0	3	5	44	3	86	5	4	6	.498	.362
Guillen, Jose, Nash.	.333	35	144	132	28	44	69	10	0	5	22	0	1	2	8	0	21	0	1	4	.523	.378
Gulan, Mike, Cal.	.276	84	304	286	41	79	145	23	2	13	51	1	3	4	10	0	82	2	1	9	.507	.307
Gutierrez, Ricky, N.O.	.214	4	16	14	0	3	3	0	0	0	1	0	0	0	2	0	3	0	0	2	.214	.313
Guzman, Edwards, Fres.*	.274	90	386	358	48	98	132	13	0	7	48	4	4	3	17	0	50	6	5	11	.369	.309
Haas, Chris, Mem.*	.229	114	474	397	63	91	168	19	2	18	73	3	5	2	66	3	155	4	4	4	.423	.338
Hacker, Steve, S.L.	.150	8	26	20	2	3	9	0	0	2	3	0	0	1	5	1	7	0	1	1	.450	.346
Hackman, Luther, C.S.	.389	15	25	18	1	7	8	1	0	0	1	5	0	0	2	0	7	0	0	0	.444	.450
Hajek, Dave, C.S.	.295	127	568	533	84	157	230	43	3	8	58	3	7	0	25	0	42	13	8	12	.432	.322
Hamel, Jon, L.V.	.000	1	4	2	0	0	0	0	0	0	0	0	0	0	1	1	0	1	0	0	0	.000	.500
Hanel, Marcus, Tuc.	.067	6	19	15	1	1	1	0	0	0	0	0	0	0	4	0	2	0	0	0	.067	.263
Hansell, Greg, Nash.	.000	23	1	1	0	0	0	0	0	0	0	0	0	0	0	0	0	0	0	0	.000	.000
Hansen, Jed, Oma.	.274	54	213	175	35	48	87	8	5	7	22	3	0	3	32	2	72	8	3	2	.497	.395
Hanson, Erik, Cal.-Oma.	.000	24	7	5	0	0	0	0	0	0	1	1	0	0	1	0	3	0	0	0	.000	.167
Hastings, Lionel, Cal.	.267	34	83	75	8	20	29	4	1	1	4	2	1	0	5	1	13	2	0	4	.387	.309
Hatcher, Chris, C.S.	.344	98	372	334	63	115	206	24	2	21	69	0	5	10	23	1	89	12	4	12	.617	.398
Hemphill, Bret, Edm.†	.313	74	290	246	29	77	116	16	1	7	31	7	2	4	31	0	58	1	0	8	.472	.396
Herges, Matt, Alb.*	.121	21	35	33	0	4	5	1	0	0	2	1	0	0	1	0	11	0	0	0	.152	.147
Hermansen, Chad, Nash.	.270	125	539	496	89	134	263	27	3	32	97	0	4	4	35	1	119	19	10	9	.530	.321
Hernandez, Carlos, N.O.	.293	94	398	355	56	104	118	14	0	0	43	3	3	10	27	1	65	22	13	5	.332	.357
Hernandez, Ramon, Van.	.261	77	327	291	38	76	132	11	3	13	55	2	4	7	23	1	37	1	2	13	.454	.326
Herrick, Jason, Edm.*	.208	25	73	72	6	15	21	3	0	1	7	0	0	0	1	0	27	0	2	0	.292	.219
Hills, Rich, Tac.	.000	1	4	4	0	0	0	0	0	0	0	0	0	0	0	0	0	0	0	0	.000	.000
Hinch, A.J., Van.	.377	15	65	61	9	23	32	3	0	2	7	0	0	1	3	1	12	1	1	0	.525	.415
Hinske, Eric, Iowa*	.267	4	16	15	3	4	9	0	1	1	2	0	0	0	1	0	4	0	0	0	.600	.313
Hodges, Kevin, N.O.-Tac.	.333	19	4	3	0	1	1	0	0	0	0	1	0	0	0	0	1	0	0	0	.333	.333
Holbert, Ray, Oma.	.297	33	141	128	26	38	54	4	0	4	12	0	1	0	12	0	35	13	4	1	.422	.355
Holzemer, Mark, C.S.*	.250	41	8	8	0	2	2	0	0	0	1	0	0	0	0	0	2	0	0	0	.250	.250
Howard, Dave, Mem.†	.263	8	22	19	3	5	5	0	0	0	2	0	1	1	1	0	6	2	0	0	.263	.318
Howard, Matt, Nash.	.293	114	437	399	41	117	144	17	2	2	44	4	5	4	25	0	24	13	10	15	.361	.337
Howard, Thomas, Mem.†	.361	35	135	119	24	43	63	10	2	2	21	1	1	1	13	0	21	1	2	2	.529	.425
Hubbard, Mike, Okla.	.283	110	427	392	48	111	157	19	0	9	49	2	5	3	25	1	70	4	1	13	.401	.327
Hubbard, Trenidad, Alb.	.333	32	142	123	24	41	68	8	2	5	24	0	3	0	16	1	27	16	4	4	.553	.401
Huckaby, Ken, Tuc.	.301	107	379	355	44	107	135	20	1	2	42	4	5	2	13	2	33	0	0	11	.380	.325
Huisman, Rick, N.O.	.000	35	2	2	0	0	0	0	0	0	0	0	0	0	0	0	1	0	0	1	.000	.000
Huls, Steve, S.L.	.233	17	33	30	6	7	7	0	0	0	2	0	0	0	3	0	7	0	1	2	.233	.303
Hulse, David, Mem.*	.335	74	215	200	37	67	96	13	2	4	31	0	3	3	9	1	39	4	2	3	.480	.367
Hutchins, Norm, Edm.†	.250	126	578	521	80	130	190	27	6	7	51	4	4	8	40	1	127	25	17	8	.365	.311
Hutchinson, Chad, Mem.	1.000	2	4	2	0	2	2	0	0	0	2	1	0	0	1	0	0	0	0	0	1.000	1.000
Hyers, Tim, Cal.*	.268	51	194	179	25	48	72	12	0	4	20	0	1	0	14	1	22	1	1	6	.402	.320
Hyzdu, Adam, Nash.	.250	14	48	44	6	11	27	1	0	5	13	0	0	0	4	0	11	0	0	2	.614	.313
Ibanez, Raul, Tac.*	.355	8	32	31	6	11	21	1	0	3	5	0	0	0	1	0	7	1	0	0	.677	.375
Incaviglia, Pete, Tuc.-N.O.	.181	26	105	94	9	17	29	7	1	1	13	0	1	1	9	0	26	2	2	1	.309	.257
Jackson, Ryan, Tac.*	.308	105	454	409	57	126	179	25	2	8	62	1	7	1	36	5	64	12	3	9	.438	.360
Jacobsen, Joe, Edm.	.000	12	1	1	0	0	0	0	0	0	0	0	0	0	0	0	1	0	0	0	.000	.000
Jennings, Robin, Iowa*	.309	67	285	259	47	80	137	20	5	9	43	0	0	1	25	0	34	6	4	7	.529	.372
Jensen, Jason, Tuc.*	.000	1	1	1	0	0	0	0	0	0	0	0	0	0	0	0	0	0	0	0	.000	.000
Jensen, Marcus, Mem.†	.291	72	272	237	38	69	120	19	4	8	44	0	1	4	30	0	59	0	0	3	.506	.379
Jensen, Ryan, Fres.	.333	27	38	33	7	11	16	2	0	1	3	3	0	0	2	0	6	0	0	1	.485	.371
Jimenez, Jose, Mem.	.000	4	5	5	0	0	0	0	0	0	0	0	0	0	0	0	2	0	0	0	.000	.000
Johns, Keith, Edm.	.208	81	267	236	32	49	71	9	2	3	26	1	2	2	26	0	38	2	0	8	.301	.289
Johnson, Earl, Tac.†	.236	17	64	55	6	13	15	2	0	0	4	0	1	0	8	0	6	5	1	1	.273	.328
Johnson, Keith, Tuc.	.287	107	402	356	61	102	157	19	0	12	46	4	4	8	30	2	71	2	4	11	.441	.352
Johnson, Russ, N.O.	.351	22	94	77	17	27	36	6	0	1	12	0	0	1	16	0	13	1	3	2	.468	.468
Jones, Bobby, C.S.	.000	3	3	3	1	0	0	0	0	0	0	0	0	0	0	0	0	0	0	0	.000	.000
Jones, Jacque, S.L.*	.298	52	210	198	32	59	88	13	2	4	26	1	2	0	9	1	36	9	2	5	.444	.325
Jones, Jaime, Oma.	.246	41	148	138	12	34	40	6	0	0	7	0	0	0	10	1	30	1	3	5	.290	.297
Joyner, Wally, L.V.*	.235	6	21	17	4	4	4	0	0	0	2	0	0	1	3	0	2	0	0	2	.235	.381
Judd, Mike, Alb.	.350	21	24	20	5	7	9	2	0	0	1	3	0	0	1	0	5	0	0	0	.450	.381
Juelsgaard, Jarod, Iowa	.176	23	20	17	3	3	3	0	0	0	0	2	0	0	1	0	6	0	0	0	.176	.222
Kelly, Mike, C.S.	.277	114	465	394	69	109	169	27	3	9	50	1	2	11	57	1	93	10	7	4	.429	.381
Kennedy, Adam, Mem.*	.327	91	405	367	69	120	180	22	4	10	63	0	5	4	29	0	36	20	6	7	.490	.378
Kieschnick, Brooks, Edm.*	.314	77	319	296	54	93	188	20	3	23	73	0	2	2	19	1	60	0	1	5	.635	.357
Kim, Byung-Hyun, Tuc.	.000	11	4	4	0	0	0	0	0	0	0	0	0	0	0	0	2	0	0	0	.000	.000
King, Bill, Van.	.000	45	1	1	0	0	0	0	0	0	0	0	0	0	0	0	1	0	0	0	.000	.000
King, Brett, Iowa	.196	32	133	112	16	22	40	6	0	4	10	2	1	1	17	0	27	6	1	2	.357	.305
Kirby, Wayne, L.V.*	.300	66	190	160	29	48	91	7	3	10	31	1	1	0	28	0	36	2	4	1	.569	.402
Klassen, Danny, Tuc.	.269	64	268	245	38	66	106	16	3	6	33	0	2	1	20	1	51	5	3	5	.433	.325
Knorr, Randy, N.O.	.352	77	294	270	33	95	152	22	1	11	41	0	3	1	20	1	41	0	1	5	.563	.395
Koeyers, Ramsey, Tuc.	.128	15	44	39	6	5	6	1	0	0	1	1	0	0	4	0	7	0	0	0	.154	.209
Kolb, Brandon, L.V.	.000	42	2	0	0	0	0	0	0	0	0	0	0	1	0	0	0	0	0	0	.000	1.000
Kubenka, Jeff, Alb.	.000	51	5	4	0	0	0	0	0	0	0	1	0	0	0	0	2	0	0	0	.000	.000
Lacy, Kerry, Iowa	.143	49	8	7	0	1	1	0	0	0	0	0	0	0	1	0	5	0	0	0	.143	.250
Laker, Tim, Nash.	.269	112	441	405	48	109	180	29	3	12	65	0	3	4	29	2	68	3	0	10	.444	.322
Lamb, Mike, Okla.*	.500	2	4	2	0	1	1	0	0	0	0	0	0	1	1	0	1	0	1	0	.500	.750
Lariviere, Jason, Mem.	.286	133	558	497	90	142	210	35	3	9	47	4	3	7	47	0	64	18	4	10	.423	.354
LaRocca, Greg, L.V.	.275	14	58	51	3	14	16	2	0	0	2	0	1	4	2	0	10	2	2	3	.314	.345
Latham, Chris, S.L.†	.322	94	443	382	93	123	208	24	8	15	51	4	2	1	54	2	95	18	13	5	.545	.405
Lawrence, Sean, Van.*	.000	25	1	1	0	0	0	0	0	0	0	0	0	0	0	0	0	0	0	0	.000	.000

Player, Team	Avg.	G	TPA	AB	R	H	TB	2B	3B	HR	RBI	SH	SF	HP	BB	IBB	SO	SB	CS	GDP	Slg.	OBP
Leach, Jalal, Fres.*	.294	116	404	371	58	109	183	19	5	15	75	2	4	0	27	2	67	8	7	8	.493	.338
LeCroy, Matthew, S.L.	.303	29	127	119	23	36	72	4	1	10	30	0	2	1	5	0	22	0	1	8	.605	.331
Lee, David, C.S.	.000	6	1	1	0	0	0	0	0	0	0	0	0	0	0	0	0	0	0	0	.000	.000
Lee, Derrek, Cal.	.283	89	377	339	60	96	175	20	1	19	73	0	4	4	30	2	90	3	4	7	.516	.345
Lesher, Brian, Van.	.292	103	441	387	66	113	188	29	2	14	64	2	5	6	41	0	71	8	2	16	.486	.364
Leyritz, Jim, L.V.	.000	2	8	8	0	0	0	0	0	0	0	0	0	0	0	0	5	0	0	0	.000	.000
Lidle, Kevin, L.V.	.276	10	33	29	5	8	17	3	0	2	5	0	1	0	3	0	8	0	0	2	.586	.333
Lisanti, Bob, Iowa	.173	31	54	52	5	9	12	3	0	0	1	1	0	0	1	0	14	0	0	1	.231	.189
Little, Mark, Mem.	.296	51	215	196	40	58	88	11	5	3	22	1	1	6	10	1	48	12	5	3	.449	.347
Livingstone, Scott, Alb.*	.205	28	87	78	11	16	20	1	0	1	4	0	0	0	9	1	12	2	1	1	.256	.287
Lobaton, Jose, Cal.	.189	36	100	90	9	17	23	6	0	0	4	2	0	2	6	0	26	2	2	5	.256	.255
LoDuca, Paul, Alb.	.368	26	92	76	17	28	40	9	0	1	8	0	0	6	10	0	1	1	1	0	.526	.478
Lomon, Kevin, Edm.	.000	23	1	1	0	0	0	0	0	0	0	0	0	0	0	0	1	0	0	0	.000	.000
Long, Terrence, Van.*	.247	40	165	154	16	38	54	6	2	2	21	0	1	0	10	2	29	7	5	4	.351	.297
Lopez, Mendy, Oma.	.311	61	243	222	41	69	113	8	0	12	40	2	1	0	18	1	41	2	2	5	.509	.361
Lopez, Pedro, N.O.	.267	19	69	60	11	16	26	4	0	2	11	2	0	0	7	1	8	0	0	0	.433	.343
Lorraine, Andrew, Iowa*	.065	23	38	31	0	2	2	0	0	0	0	2	0	1	4	0	18	0	0	0	.065	.194
Lovingier, Kevin, Mem.*	.000	51	3	3	0	0	0	0	0	0	0	0	0	0	0	0	1	0	0	0	.000	.000
Lowell, Mike, Cal.	.313	24	91	83	11	26	35	3	0	2	9	0	0	0	8	0	19	0	0	0	.422	.374
Luderer, Brian, Van.	.321	10	33	28	6	9	10	1	0	0	4	0	0	1	4	0	2	0	0	0	.357	.424
Ludwick, Eric, Cal.	.000	48	2	1	1	0	0	0	0	0	0	0	0	0	1	0	1	0	0	0	.000	.500
Luebbers, Larry, Mem.	.077	25	36	26	2	2	3	1	0	0	7	0	0	3	0	8	1	0	0	1	.115	.172
Luke, Matt, Edm.*	.429	6	27	21	7	9	28	2	1	5	15	0	0	0	6	1	4	0	0	1	1.333	.556
Luuloa, Keith, Edm.	.285	115	451	396	54	113	150	23	1	4	46	4	2	5	44	0	53	7	7	14	.379	.362
Mahay, Ron, Van.*	.000	33	2	2	0	0	0	0	0	0	0	0	0	0	0	0	0	0	0	0	.000	.000
Manwaring, Kirt, C.S.	.227	7	23	22	3	5	8	0	0	1	2	0	0	0	1	0	2	0	0	1	.364	.261
Marsters, Brandon, S.L.	.200	11	27	25	4	5	9	1	0	1	8	0	0	0	2	0	6	0	0	1	.360	.259
Martinez, Felix, Oma.†	.304	8	26	23	2	7	12	5	0	0	2	1	0	0	2	0	6	0	1	0	.522	.360
Martinez, Ramon E., Fres.	.325	29	125	114	13	37	52	7	1	2	17	0	1	0	10	1	17	2	0	2	.456	.376
Martinez, Sandy, Iowa*	.232	36	132	125	8	29	41	6	0	2	18	0	2	0	5	1	29	1	0	2	.328	.258
Martins, Eric, Van.	.239	97	341	301	39	72	106	15	5	3	33	3	2	4	31	2	47	2	1	8	.352	.317
Marval, Raul, Fres.	.300	97	313	280	41	84	122	15	1	7	46	9	5	3	16	1	48	2	3	4	.436	.339
Marzano, John, Okla.	.244	44	171	160	15	39	55	10	0	2	16	1	0	2	8	0	19	0	1	7	.344	.288
Mashore, Damon, Fres.	.262	110	395	347	62	91	173	20	1	20	69	4	2	4	38	0	98	7	3	15	.499	.340
Mateo, Ruben, Okla.	.336	63	278	253	53	85	151	12	0	18	62	0	3	8	14	6	36	6	3	5	.597	.385
Mathis, Joe, Tac.*	.250	26	101	92	8	23	30	5	1	0	7	2	1	0	6	1	25	3	0	0	.326	.293
Matos, Francisco, Tac.	.310	100	423	393	43	122	161	24	3	3	33	5	5	2	18	0	41	4	6	10	.410	.340
Matthews, Gary, L.V.†	.256	121	491	422	57	108	163	23	3	9	52	0	4	7	58	0	104	17	6	13	.386	.352
Maxcy, Brian, N.O.	.000	4	1	1	0	0	0	0	0	0	0	0	0	0	0	0	0	0	0	0	.000	.000
Mayes, Craig, Fres.*	.260	62	180	169	19	44	65	12	0	3	16	2	1	0	8	1	26	1	1	9	.385	.292
McDonald, Jason, Van.†	.326	32	152	129	27	42	65	9	1	4	18	2	0	2	19	1	33	8	5	0	.504	.420
McDonald, Keith, Mem.	.301	39	136	113	20	34	56	7	0	5	27	1	2	0	20	0	25	1	0	1	.496	.400
McMullen, Mike, Fres.	.143	41	7	7	1	1	1	0	0	0	0	0	0	0	0	0	5	0	0	0	.143	.143
McNichol, Brian, Iowa*	.158	29	42	38	2	6	7	1	0	0	2	3	0	1	0	0	10	0	0	1	.184	.179
Meacham, Rusty, N.O.	.286	17	8	7	1	2	5	1	1	0	1	1	0	0	0	0	1	0	0	0	.714	.286
Meares, Pat, Nash.	.167	5	20	18	3	3	3	0	0	0	0	0	0	1	1	0	3	1	0	0	.167	.250
Medrano, Tony, Oma.	.313	33	128	112	14	35	49	6	1	2	23	3	2	1	10	0	15	0	1	3	.438	.368
Mejia, Roberto, Alb.	.146	16	42	41	6	6	9	0	0	1	5	0	0	0	1	0	8	0	1	0	.220	.167
Melo, Juan, L.V.†	.201	45	178	169	17	34	47	3	2	2	13	0	0	2	7	0	34	1	1	5	.278	.242
Mendez, Carlos, Oma.	.280	84	305	293	38	82	137	25	0	10	37	3	3	0	6	0	32	4	3	8	.468	.291
Menechino, Frankie, Van.	.309	130	589	501	103	155	249	31	9	15	88	1	5	9	73	7	97	4	5	12	.497	.403
Menhart, Paul, Edm.-Cal.	.000	17	6	4	2	0	0	0	0	0	0	0	0	0	2	0	1	0	0	0	.000	.333
Mercedes, Henry, Oma.	.244	69	226	193	27	47	73	8	0	6	32	3	1	2	27	0	63	4	1	2	.378	.341
Mercedes, Jose, L.V.-Cal.	.056	19	22	18	0	1	1	0	0	0	0	4	0	0	0	0	12	0	0	0	.056	.056
Meyers, Chad, Iowa	.354	44	210	175	39	62	79	13	2	0	16	3	0	3	29	0	20	17	7	1	.451	.454
Michalak, Chris, Edm.-Tuc.*	.231	45	19	13	2	3	4	1	0	0	5	0	0	1	0	3	0	0	0	.308	.286
Milacki, Bob, Nash.	.143	22	27	21	1	3	3	0	0	0	2	2	1	0	3	0	8	0	0	0	.143	.240
Millar, Kevin, Cal.	.301	36	155	143	24	43	77	11	1	7	26	0	1	0	11	2	19	2	0	5	.538	.348
Miller, Kurt, Iowa	.000	8	2	1	1	0	0	0	0	0	0	0	0	0	0	0	0	0	0	0	.000	.500
Miller, Ryan, N.O.	.276	64	181	174	19	48	59	8	0	1	25	0	1	1	5	0	29	0	2	3	.339	.298
Miller, Wade, N.O.	.172	26	36	29	0	5	5	0	0	0	2	4	1	0	2	0	8	0	0	0	.172	.219
Mirabelli, Doug, Fres.	.313	86	374	320	63	100	168	24	1	14	51	0	5	1	48	2	56	8	2	6	.525	.398
Mitchell, Dean, Alb.	.000	31	4	2	1	0	0	0	0	0	0	1	0	0	1	0	1	0	0	0	.000	.000
Mitchell, Mike, L.V.*	.241	27	100	87	7	21	29	5	0	1	11	0	1	0	12	0	20	0	0	3	.333	.330
Mlicki, Doug, Mem.	.500	38	6	6	0	3	4	1	0	0	0	0	0	0	0	0	1	0	0	0	.667	.500
Mohler, Mike, Mem.	.000	10	1	1	0	0	0	0	0	0	0	0	0	0	0	0	1	0	0	0	.000	.000
Molina, Ben, Edm.	.286	65	268	241	28	69	106	16	0	7	41	1	4	6	15	1	17	1	2	7	.440	.338
Molina, Jose, Oma.	.263	74	268	240	24	63	88	11	1	4	26	2	2	4	20	5	54	0	1	3	.367	.327
Monahan, Shane, Tac.*	.256	108	424	399	51	102	148	21	2	7	32	1	2	3	19	2	81	9	3	4	.371	.293
Monroe, Craig, Okla.	.250	6	18	16	2	4	5	1	0	0	1	1	0	0	1	0	4	0	0	0	.313	.294
Montgomery, Ray, Nash.	.331	90	307	272	57	90	165	23	2	16	52	1	5	5	24	0	49	5	3	5	.607	.389
Morales, Willie, Van.	.143	5	17	14	2	2	3	1	0	0	2	1	1	0	1	0	4	0	0	2	.214	.294
Moriarty, Mike, S.L.	.258	128	458	380	63	98	145	21	7	4	51	11	5	6	56	1	62	6	4	9	.382	.358
Morman, Russ, Cal.	.327	21	59	52	10	17	27	1	0	3	12	0	0	0	7	0	6	1	0	1	.519	.407
Mueller, Bill, Fres.†	.417	3	13	12	3	5	7	0	1	0	6	0	1	0	0	0	0	0	0	0	.583	.385
Murphy, Mike, Tac.	.295	38	148	129	22	38	57	7	3	2	22	1	3	2	13	0	36	10	4	2	.442	.361
Murray, Calvin, Fres.	.334	130	608	548	122	183	297	31	7	23	73	4	4	3	49	3	88	42	14	6	.542	.389
Murray, Heath, L.V.*	.250	15	17	12	1	3	3	0	0	0	0	2	0	0	3	0	3	0	0	0	.250	.400
Nathan, Joe, Fres.	.250	13	13	12	3	3	6	0	0	1	1	0	0	0	1	0	4	0	0	0	.500	.308
Neal, Mike, N.O.	.202	94	274	243	33	49	79	10	1	6	28	0	2	2	27	0	61	3	0	3	.325	.285
Neill, Mike, Van.*	.296	96	430	365	61	108	165	23	2	10	61	2	4	2	57	0	97	10	5	11	.452	.390
Nevin, Phil, L.V.	.200	3	10	10	2	2	8	0	0	2	2	0	0	0	0	0	2	0	0	1	.800	.200

Player, Team	Avg.	G	TPA	AB	R	H	TB	2B	3B	HR	RBI	SH	SF	HP	BB	IBB	SO	SB	CS	GDP	Slg.	OBP
Newfield, Marc, Van.	.143	7	29	28	1	4	4	0	0	0	1	0	0	0	1	0	2	0	0	1	.143	.172
Newhan, David, L.V.*	.286	98	411	374	49	107	176	25	1	14	49	4	1	2	30	0	84	22	4	8	.471	.342
Newson, Warren, Alb.*	.260	95	331	285	42	74	120	22	0	8	38	0	0	2	44	1	70	2	4	9	.421	.363
Nicholas, Darrell, S.L.	.293	106	393	348	55	102	140	19	2	5	44	7	1	4	33	0	76	14	7	6	.402	.360
Nieves, Jose, Iowa	.268	104	430	392	55	105	169	25	3	11	59	6	4	4	24	2	65	11	8	9	.431	.314
Nomo, Hideo, Iowa	.000	3	3	3	0	0	0	0	0	0	0	0	0	0	0	0	1	0	0	0	.000	.000
Norman, Les, Oma.	.273	89	361	333	53	91	154	20	2	13	40	3	5	5	14	0	45	7	3	6	.462	.308
Norton, Phillip, Iowa	.095	14	24	21	2	2	3	1	0	0	0	0	0	1	2	0	9	0	0	1	.143	.208
Nunez, Abraham, Nash.†	.310	15	63	58	12	18	18	0	0	0	3	0	0	0	5	0	8	1	0	2	.310	.365
Nussbeck, Mark, Mem.*	.059	36	20	17	1	1	1	0	0	0	1	1	1	0	1	0	6	0	0	1	.059	.105
Ojala, Kirt, Cal.*	.125	16	10	8	1	1	2	1	0	0	0	1	0	0	1	0	3	0	0	1	.250	.222
Ordaz, Luis, Mem.	.285	107	402	362	31	103	139	25	4	1	45	3	9	4	24	2	40	3	4	12	.384	.328
Orie, Kevin, Cal.	.319	23	86	72	10	23	41	9	0	3	8	0	0	1	13	0	7	0	0	0	.569	.430
Oropesa, Eddie, Fres.*	.136	22	26	22	0	3	3	0	0	0	0	3	0	0	1	0	6	0	0	0	.136	.174
Ortiz, David, S.L.*	.315	130	563	476	85	150	281	35	3	30	110	0	5	3	79	5	105	2	2	8	.590	.412
Ortiz, Hector, Alb.	.305	55	175	164	21	50	77	9	0	6	20	0	3	1	7	1	27	2	3	8	.470	.331
Ortiz, Jose, Van.	.284	107	422	377	66	107	167	29	2	9	45	3	4	9	29	1	50	13	4	8	.443	.346
Osik, Keith, Nash.	.091	4	12	11	0	1	1	0	0	0	0	0	0	1	0	0	1	0	0	0	.091	.167
Osteen, Gavin, Alb.	.067	34	17	15	1	1	2	1	0	0	0	2	0	0	0	0	7	0	0	0	.133	.067
Pachot, John, Tuc.	.265	35	105	102	10	27	34	4	0	1	11	0	0	0	3	0	10	1	0	5	.333	.286
Padilla, Vicente, Tuc.	.143	18	28	21	1	3	3	0	0	0	1	3	0	0	4	0	9	0	0	2	.143	.280
Patrick, Bronswell, Fres.	.132	28	40	38	1	5	5	0	0	0	4	2	0	0	0	0	14	0	0	0	.132	.132
Patterson, Jarrod, Tuc.*	.336	75	316	274	46	92	156	25	3	11	47	0	3	3	36	0	37	4	1	9	.569	.415
Patterson, John, Tuc.	.000	7	6	5	0	0	0	0	0	0	0	1	0	0	0	0	4	0	0	0	.000	.000
Patzke, Jeff, Nash.†	.220	59	210	173	20	38	51	5	1	2	14	1	2	2	32	1	29	2	3	2	.295	.344
Pelaez, Alex, L.V.	.308	5	13	13	1	4	4	0	0	0	0	0	0	0	0	0	2	0	0	1	.308	.308
Pellow, Kit, Oma.	.286	131	521	475	88	136	277	28	4	35	99	1	7	18	20	3	117	6	5	11	.583	.335
Pemberton, Rudy, Mem.	.260	25	85	73	13	19	32	7	0	2	11	0	0	6	6	1	13	1	0	1	.438	.365
Pena, Angel, Alb.	.291	34	137	127	15	37	52	10	1	1	24	0	0	0	10	0	24	3	2	1	.409	.343
Pena, Elvis, C.S.†	.163	13	47	43	5	7	8	1	0	0	1	0	0	1	3	0	7	4	1	0	.186	.234
Pennyfeather, William, Edm.	.212	34	105	99	16	21	34	5	1	2	10	1	0	0	5	0	21	3	0	1	.343	.250
Perez, Carlos, Alb.*	.333	6	7	3	1	1	1	0	0	0	0	3	0	0	1	0	2	0	0	0	.333	.500
Perez, Dario, Cal.	.150	28	21	20	0	3	4	1	0	0	2	1	0	0	0	0	11	0	0	0	.200	.150
Perez, Eduardo, Mem.	.320	119	468	416	67	133	218	31	0	18	82	0	1	6	45	4	92	7	8	11	.524	.393
Perez, Tomas, Edm.†	.260	83	322	296	31	77	108	17	1	4	40	2	3	2	19	0	43	2	2	1	.365	.306
Peters, Chris, Nash.*	.429	11	7	7	2	3	3	0	0	0	1	0	0	0	0	0	1	0	0	0	.429	.429
Petersen, Chris, C.S.	.259	107	411	370	56	96	137	21	1	6	33	3	2	7	29	1	85	4	0	12	.370	.324
Petrick, Ben, C.S.	.312	84	335	282	56	88	171	16	5	19	64	0	6	3	44	1	58	9	6	4	.606	.403
Phillips, J.R., C.S.*	.311	124	537	479	87	149	294	22	0	41	100	0	3	1	54	6	143	4	3	13	.614	.380
Phillips, Jason, Nash.	.000	1	1	1	0	0	0	0	0	0	0	0	0	0	0	0	1	0	0	0	.000	.000
Piatt, Adam, Van.	.222	6	24	18	1	4	5	1	0	0	3	0	0	0	6	0	2	0	0	2	.278	.417
Pierzynski, A.J., S.L.*	.259	67	246	228	29	59	72	10	0	1	25	2	0	0	16	0	29	0	0	11	.316	.307
Pledger, Kinnis, Tac.*	.275	43	180	153	20	42	76	8	1	8	30	1	5	2	19	1	37	0	2	4	.497	.352
Polanco, Placido, Mem.	.275	29	125	120	18	33	39	4	1	0	10	0	1	1	3	0	11	2	0	7	.325	.296
Polcovich, Kevin, Nash.	.240	80	268	233	37	56	77	10	1	3	25	7	4	4	20	1	52	6	4	4	.330	.307
Porter, Bo, Iowa	.292	111	491	414	86	121	230	24	2	27	64	1	3	8	65	0	121	15	17	7	.556	.396
Porzio, Mike, C.S.*	.000	35	3	3	0	0	0	0	0	0	0	0	0	0	0	0	1	0	0	0	.000	.000
Powell, Brian, N.O.	.100	9	13	10	1	1	1	0	0	0	1	2	1	0	0	0	3	0	0	0	.100	.091
Powell, Dante, Tuc.	.332	51	205	187	29	62	101	14	2	7	30	3	0	1	14	0	38	22	6	0	.540	.381
Prieto, Chris, L.V.*	.241	108	404	348	66	84	128	14	6	6	29	2	2	6	46	0	51	21	6	2	.368	.338
Pritchett, Chris, Edm.*	.279	96	401	348	60	97	150	15	1	12	45	1	2	3	47	3	70	1	1	7	.431	.368
Quevedo, Ruben, Iowa	.167	7	8	6	1	1	1	0	0	0	1	1	0	0	1	0	4	0	0	0	.167	.286
Quinlan, Tom, Iowa	.250	133	529	472	62	118	197	26	1	17	58	1	2	13	41	0	159	1	1	6	.417	.326
Quinn, Mark, Oma.	.360	107	470	428	67	154	256	27	0	25	84	0	4	10	28	3	69	7	9	9	.598	.409
Radmanovich, Ryan, Tac.*	.286	109	486	420	69	120	201	24	3	17	80	3	6	4	53	5	83	10	4	8	.479	.366
Raggio, Brady, Okla.	.000	30	1	1	0	0	0	0	0	0	0	0	0	0	0	0	1	0	0	0	.000	.000
Ramirez, Aramis, Nash.	.328	131	548	460	92	151	251	35	1	21	76	0	6	9	73	6	56	5	3	11	.546	.425
Ramirez, Omar, N.O.	.253	110	415	379	56	96	133	15	2	6	51	2	2	2	30	2	49	8	3	13	.351	.310
Ramirez, Roberto, C.S.	.167	10	16	12	2	2	3	1	0	0	1	3	0	0	1	0	2	1	0	0	.250	.231
Randall, Scott, C.S.	.000	9	10	7	0	0	0	0	0	0	0	3	0	0	0	0	7	0	0	0	.000	.000
Randolph, Steve, Tuc.*	.667	12	13	12	4	8	12	1	0	1	5	0	0	0	1	0	0	0	1	0	1.000	.692
Rath, Gary, S.L.*	.000	21	0	0	1	0	0	0	0	0	0	0	0	0	0	0	0	0	0	0	.000	.000
Reeder, Cory, Okla.	.190	8	23	21	3	4	6	2	0	0	1	0	0	2	0	0	6	0	0	0	.286	.261
Reese, Nate, Cal.	.250	9	21	20	4	5	6	1	0	0	2	0	0	0	1	0	5	0	0	1	.300	.286
Reeves, Glenn, Cal.	.216	91	278	236	33	51	67	8	1	2	21	0	1	4	37	0	42	3	6	10	.284	.331
Rennhack, Mike, Iowa†	.226	49	166	146	8	33	48	7	1	2	11	0	0	0	20	2	40	2	1	1	.329	.319
Richard, Chris, Mem.*	.412	4	18	17	3	7	12	2	0	1	4	0	0	0	1	0	2	0	0	1	.706	.444
Richardson, Brian, S.L.	.277	130	521	451	77	125	210	23	4	18	73	2	8	6	54	0	104	0	0	10	.466	.356
Riggs, Adam, Alb.	.292	133	584	513	87	150	232	29	7	13	81	2	5	10	54	0	114	25	17	8	.452	.368
Rios, Armando, Fres.*	.275	31	124	109	24	30	45	3	0	4	21	0	0	4	11	0	22	3	1	2	.413	.363
Rios, Eduardo, Tuc.	.375	3	9	8	1	3	7	1	0	1	2	0	1	0	0	0	3	0	0	0	.875	.333
Ritchie, Todd, Nash.	.000	1	1	1	0	0	0	0	0	0	0	0	0	0	0	0	0	0	0	0	.000	.000
Rivera, Roberto, L.V.*	.250	21	8	8	1	2	3	1	0	0	0	0	0	0	0	0	2	0	0	0	.375	.250
Roberge, J.P., Oma.	.314	116	473	437	77	137	213	31	3	13	66	5	0	5	26	0	59	16	5	15	.487	.359
Robertson, Mike, Nash.*	.309	74	237	220	34	68	113	16	1	9	31	1	3	3	10	1	32	2	1	5	.514	.343
Robertson, Rich, Okla.-Nash.*	.500	10	2	2	0	1	1	0	0	0	0	0	0	0	0	0	0	0	0	0	.500	.500
Robertson, Ryan, Cal.*	.302	59	196	169	16	51	64	10	0	1	19	0	1	0	26	0	29	0	2	2	.379	.393
Robinson, Kerry, Tac.*	.322	79	354	335	53	108	142	16	9	0	34	3	2	0	14	0	44	30	7	4	.424	.348
Rosario, Mel, Okla.†	.192	7	26	26	2	5	6	1	0	0	3	0	0	0	0	0	8	1	0	1	.231	.192
Roskos, John, Cal.	.320	134	570	506	85	162	278	44	0	24	90	0	9	3	52	2	112	2	1	18	.549	.381
Rossiter, Mike, C.S.	1.000	24	2	2	1	2	3	1	0	0	0	0	0	0	0	0	0	0	0	0	1.500	1.000
Rossy, Rico, L.V.	.255	93	308	259	42	66	108	12	0	10	29	4	2	2	41	3	27	4	1	5	.417	.359

Player, Team	Avg.	G	TPA	AB	R	H	TB	2B	3B	HR	RBI	SH	SF	HP	BB	IBB	SO	SB	CS	GDP	Slg.	OBP
Ruebel, Matt, Tuc.*	.000	6	1	0	0	0	0	0	0	0	0	0	0	0	1	0	0	0	0	0	.000	1.000
Ruffin, Johnny, Alb.	.000	46	1	1	0	0	0	0	0	0	0	0	0	0	0	0	1	0	0	0	.000	.000
Rupp, Chad, S.L.	.193	37	141	119	18	23	47	3	0	7	18	0	3	2	17	0	48	3	0	4	.395	.298
Russo, Paul, N.O.	.263	48	154	133	19	35	53	6	0	4	18	0	0	0	21	0	28	1	0	8	.398	.364
Ryan, Matt, Nash.	.000	48	9	7	0	0	0	0	0	0	0	1	0	0	1	0	3	0	0	0	.000	.125
Ryan, Rob, Tuc.*	.290	117	487	414	72	120	217	30	5	19	88	0	5	12	56	2	70	4	3	13	.524	.386
Sabel, Erik, Tuc.	.125	22	17	16	0	2	3	1	0	0	0	0	1	0	0	0	8	0	0	0	.188	.125
Sachse, Matt, Tac.*	.200	11	41	35	2	7	8	1	0	0	0	2	0	0	4	0	13	1	0	0	.229	.282
Saenz, Olmedo, Van.	.600	2	7	5	1	3	4	1	0	0	2	0	1	0	1	0	0	0	0	0	.800	.571
Sagmoen, Marc, Okla.*	.272	83	294	268	42	73	129	11	3	13	43	1	1	0	24	3	58	3	2	7	.481	.331
Saipe, Mike, C.S.	.000	11	8	6	0	0	0	0	0	0	0	2	0	0	0	0	2	0	0	0	.000	.000
Salkeld, Roger, Cal.	.400	27	5	5	0	2	4	2	0	0	0	0	0	0	0	0	0	0	0	1	.800	.400
Sanchez, Jesus, Cal.*	.000	4	1	1	0	0	0	0	0	0	0	0	0	0	0	0	1	0	0	0	.000	.000
Sanford, Chance, Alb.*	.247	77	261	227	37	56	96	14	1	8	29	2	0	1	31	1	55	6	3	5	.423	.340
Sauveur, Rich, Nash.*	.000	53	5	5	0	0	0	0	0	0	0	0	0	0	0	0	2	0	0	0	.000	.000
Saylor, Jamie, N.O.*	.224	113	373	330	38	74	110	14	5	4	36	2	4	3	34	1	83	8	10	6	.333	.299
Scanlan, Bob, N.O.	.103	28	31	29	0	3	4	1	0	0	3	1	0	0	1	0	10	0	0	0	.138	.133
Scarsone, Steve, Oma.	.172	18	66	58	9	10	26	1	0	5	7	0	1	0	7	0	21	1	0	2	.448	.258
Sealy, Scot, Tac.	.184	67	233	201	22	37	59	4	0	6	24	2	4	6	20	0	56	0	0	2	.294	.273
Secrist, Reed, Nash.*	.265	46	114	102	12	27	43	8	1	2	15	1	1	2	8	1	22	1	1	1	.422	.327
Seifert, Ryan, C.S.	.000	1	1	1	1	0	0	0	0	0	0	0	0	0	0	0	0	0	0	0	.000	.000
Seitzer, Brad, Tac.	.287	130	574	474	80	136	199	34	1	9	66	2	8	1	89	2	86	1	2	14	.420	.395
Sell, Chip, Tac.*	.357	30	92	84	12	30	42	5	2	1	18	2	0	3	3	0	14	4	3	2	.500	.400
Servais, Scott, Fres.	.273	3	11	11	3	3	6	1	1	0	2	0	0	0	0	1	0	0	0	0	.545	.273
Sexton, Chris, C.S.	.339	60	205	171	23	58	67	9	0	0	17	5	1	0	28	0	22	5	1	7	.392	.430
Sheets, Andy, Edm.	.289	12	49	45	6	13	16	1	1	0	4	2	0	0	2	0	11	0	1	0	.356	.319
Sheff, Chris, Van.	.287	118	473	421	62	121	192	24	1	15	70	3	3	1	45	1	87	9	6	15	.456	.355
Sheldon, Scott, Okla.	.311	122	519	453	94	141	266	35	3	28	97	0	7	3	56	3	112	12	2	11	.587	.385
Shoemaker, Stephen, C.S.*...	.154	18	14	13	1	2	2	0	0	0	0	1	0	0	0	0	3	0	0	0	.154	.154
Shouse, Brian, Tuc.*	.000	30	8	8	0	0	0	0	0	0	0	0	0	0	0	0	4	0	1	0	.000	.000
Shumpert, Terry, C.S.	.380	29	84	79	15	30	58	8	1	6	17	1	0	0	4	0	9	3	1	1	.734	.410
Sikorski, Brian, N.O.	.139	36	45	36	2	5	6	1	0	0	1	8	0	0	1	0	10	0	0	0	.167	.162
Silva, Jose, Nash.	.200	2	5	5	1	1	4	0	0	1	1	0	0	0	0	0	0	0	0	0	.800	.200
Silvestri, Dave, Edm.	.318	79	348	318	55	101	137	18	0	6	42	4	2	2	22	0	43	4	3	12	.431	.363
Simms, Mike, Okla.	.274	22	90	73	7	20	27	1	0	2	16	0	1	0	16	1	25	0	0	3	.370	.400
Skrmetta, Matt, L.V.†	.000	20	1	0	0	0	0	0	0	0	0	1	0	0	0	0	0	0	0	0	.000	.000
Slusarski, Joe, N.O.	.000	40	5	5	0	0	0	0	0	0	0	0	0	0	0	0	3	0	0	0	.000	.000
Smith, Jeff, S.L.*	.389	5	18	18	5	7	13	3	0	1	3	0	0	0	0	0	1	0	0	1	.722	.389
Smith, Pete, Mem.-L.V.	.259	21	32	27	1	7	8	1	0	0	3	0	0	0	2	0	10	0	0	1	.296	.310
Snellgrove, Clay, L.V.	.667	1	3	3	1	2	4	2	0	0	0	0	0	0	0	0	0	0	0	0	1.333	.667
Soderstrom, Steve, Fres.	.500	22	13	10	2	5	6	1	0	0	1	2	0	0	1	0	2	0	0	0	.600	.545
Sodowsky, Clint, Mem.*	.083	19	15	12	1	1	1	0	0	0	2	3	0	0	0	0	4	0	0	0	.083	.083
Solano, Danny, Okla.	.000	3	7	6	0	0	0	0	0	0	0	1	0	1	0	0	4	0	0	0	.000	.000
Sosa, Juan, C.S.	.393	6	28	28	3	11	17	1	1	1	5	0	0	0	0	0	1	1	0	2	.607	.393
Sparks, Jeff, Nash.	.000	34	4	3	0	0	0	0	0	0	0	1	0	0	0	0	1	0	0	0	.000	.000
Spencer, Stan, L.V.	.308	13	14	13	2	4	4	0	0	0	0	1	0	0	0	0	0	0	0	0	.308	.308
Spiezio, Scott, Van.†	.390	28	122	105	27	41	68	7	1	6	27	0	0	2	15	2	16	0	0	3	.648	.475
Stahoviak, Scott, Iowa*	.237	83	324	274	51	65	125	16	1	14	44	2	3	1	44	2	88	4	1	3	.456	.342
Stanifer, Rob, Cal.	.000	16	1	1	0	0	0	0	0	0	0	0	0	0	0	0	1	0	0	0	.000	.000
Steed, Dave, Alb.	.210	30	74	62	8	13	17	4	0	0	5	4	1	0	7	1	17	0	1	3	.274	.286
Stefanski, Mike, Mem.	.299	64	225	201	27	60	84	12	0	4	22	1	2	4	17	0	28	3	0	8	.418	.362
Stein, Blake, Van.	.000	19	2	1	0	0	0	0	0	0	0	1	0	0	0	0	0	0	0	0	.000	.000
Stephenson, Garrett, Mem. ...	.000	4	10	5	0	0	0	0	0	0	0	5	0	0	2	0	1	0	0	0	.000	.286
Stevens, Dave, Tac.	.000	7	1	1	0	0	0	0	0	0	0	0	0	0	0	0	0	0	0	0	.000	.000
Stone, Ricky, Alb.	.300	27	43	40	3	12	16	4	0	0	5	3	0	0	0	0	11	1	1	0	.400	.300
Stoner, Mike, Tuc.-Edm.	.363	36	109	102	14	37	54	6	1	3	18	0	1	0	6	0	14	0	1	2	.529	.394
Stoops, Jim, C.S.	.000	55	8	6	0	0	0	0	0	0	0	2	0	0	0	0	4	0	0	0	.000	.000
Stovall, DaRond, Cal.-Alb.†....	.207	83	304	266	40	55	106	15	3	10	34	1	4	0	33	1	109	8	4	2	.398	.290
Strange, Doug, Nash.†	.077	5	14	13	2	1	2	1	0	0	0	0	0	1	0	0	2	0	0	1	.154	.143
Strittmatter, Mark, C.S.	.215	71	229	195	16	42	66	10	1	4	31	1	4	9	20	0	45	0	0	2	.338	.313
Sullivan, Brendan, L.V.	.000	45	2	1	0	0	0	0	0	0	0	0	0	0	1	0	0	0	0	0	.000	.500
Sutton, Larry, Oma.*	.277	39	178	148	28	41	60	8	1	3	12	1	1	1	27	2	24	4	1	4	.405	.390
Sveum, Dale, Tuc.-Nash.†	.297	62	216	192	28	57	86	15	1	4	29	0	1	2	21	0	53	1	1	8	.448	.370
Swartzbaugh, Dave, Tuc.	.000	13	2	1	0	0	0	0	0	0	0	1	0	0	0	0	0	0	0	0	.000	.000
Tatum, Jim, C.S.	.313	109	441	396	57	124	191	23	1	14	64	1	8	3	33	0	85	1	2	14	.482	.364
Tavares, Jesus, Fres.†	.167	2	6	6	0	1	1	0	0	0	0	0	0	0	0	0	0	0	0	0	.167	.167
Tavarez, Julian, Fres.*	1.000	4	1	1	0	1	1	0	0	0	0	0	0	0	0	0	0	0	0	0	1.000	1.000
Tejero, Fausto, Edm.	.294	5	20	17	3	5	8	0	0	1	2	0	0	0	3	0	4	0	0	0	.471	.400
Telemaco, Amaury, Tuc.	.000	13	1	1	0	0	0	0	0	0	0	0	0	0	0	0	0	0	0	0	.000	.000
t'Hoen, E.J., Edm.	.138	9	32	29	2	4	4	0	0	0	0	1	0	0	2	0	7	0	0	0	.138	.194
Thompson, Mark, Mem.	.417	9	13	12	1	5	6	1	0	0	0	0	1	0	0	0	2	0	0	0	.500	.417
Thompson, Ryan, N.O.	.309	112	445	404	60	125	200	23	2	16	58	0	2	2	37	0	78	4	9	17	.495	.369
Thomson, John, C.S.	.000	5	5	5	0	0	0	0	0	0	0	0	0	0	0	0	1	0	0	0	.000	.000
Thrower, Jake, L.V.†	.288	72	301	267	40	77	114	17	4	4	30	3	2	2	27	2	56	4	4	6	.427	.356
Thurston, Jerry, N.O.	.220	21	66	59	7	13	13	0	0	0	4	1	0	2	4	0	15	0	1	3	.220	.292
Timmons, Ozzie, Tac.	.273	82	355	297	56	81	166	22	0	21	66	0	3	2	53	1	81	0	2	9	.559	.383
Tollberg, Brian, L.V.	.500	5	3	2	0	1	2	1	0	0	0	1	0	0	0	0	0	0	0	0	1.000	.500
Torrealba, Yorvit, Fres.	.254	17	69	63	9	16	24	2	0	2	10	0	2	4	0	0	11	0	1	2	.381	.319
Tremie, Chris, Nash.	.248	47	142	121	20	30	46	7	0	3	16	3	2	2	14	0	29	4	0	4	.380	.331
Tuttle, Dave, Tuc.	.071	36	15	14	1	1	1	0	0	0	1	0	0	0	0	0	6	0	0	0	.071	.071
Unroe, Tim, Edm.-Oma.*	.333	15	71	66	14	22	47	5	1	6	20	0	0	0	5	0	14	0	0	0	.712	.380
Valdes, Pedro, Okla.*	.327	110	456	394	72	129	221	27	1	21	72	0	4	6	52	6	60	1	2	6	.561	.410

Player, Team	Avg.	G	TPA	AB	R	H	TB	2B	3B	HR	RBI	SH	SF	HP	BB	IBB	SO	SB	CS	GDP	Slg.	OBP
Van Poppel, Todd, Nash.	.061	28	40	33	3	2	2	0	0	0	1	5	0	0	2	0	17	0	0	1	.061	.114
Vaz, Roberto, Van.*	.264	109	427	367	54	97	144	18	4	7	38	5	2	2	51	3	72	7	5	8	.392	.355
Verdugo, Jason, Fres.	.000	9	3	2	0	0	0	0	0	0	0	1	0	0	0	0	2	0	0	0	.000	.000
Villalobos, Carlos, N.O.	.283	133	564	499	82	141	203	33	1	9	50	5	4	2	54	0	100	11	3	11	.407	.352
Villano, Mike, Cal.	.000	36	3	2	0	0	0	0	0	0	0	0	0	0	1	0	0	0	0	0	.000	.333
Vitiello, Joe, Oma.	.318	122	521	447	70	142	259	33	0	28	98	0	4	4	66	2	84	3	4	16	.579	.407
Voigt, Jack, Fres.	.194	23	86	67	12	13	22	4	1	1	5	0	1	1	17	0	21	1	0	0	.328	.360
Vosberg, Ed, L.V.-Tuc.*	.000	34	2	2	0	0	0	0	0	0	0	0	0	0	0	0	1	0	0	0	.000	.000
Wainhouse, David, C.S.*	.000	38	2	2	0	0	0	0	0	0	0	0	0	0	0	0	1	0	0	0	.000	.000
Walker, Pete, C.S.	.000	48	1	1	0	0	0	0	0	0	0	0	0	0	0	0	1	0	0	0	.000	.000
Wallace, Kent, N.O.*	.143	37	8	7	4	1	1	0	0	0	0	1	0	0	0	0	2	0	0	0	.143	.143
Walton, Jerome, Cal.	.321	26	92	84	12	27	37	8	1	0	12	0	1	2	5	0	12	5	1	1	.440	.370
Ward, Daryle, N.O.*	.353	61	267	241	56	85	186	15	1	28	65	0	0	3	23	5	43	1	1	3	.772	.416
Ward, Turner, Nash.-Tuc.† ...	.318	47	155	129	24	41	60	5	1	4	25	0	0	2	23	0	18	7	2	2	.465	.429
Warner, Ron, Mem.	.290	90	282	245	35	71	120	14	1	11	33	0	2	3	32	2	70	8	2	3	.490	.376
Watkins, Pat, C.S.	.333	12	33	30	4	10	11	1	0	0	2	0	1	0	2	0	6	0	0	0	.367	.364
Watkins, Scott, Iowa*	.000	47	2	1	0	0	0	0	0	0	0	0	1	0	0	0	1	0	0	0	.000	.500
Weber, Ben, Fres.	.167	53	6	6	1	1	1	0	0	0	0	0	0	0	0	0	2	0	0	0	.167	.167
Weber, Neil, Tuc.-Alb.*	.000	18	3	0	0	0	0	0	0	0	0	1	0	0	0	0	3	0	0	0	.000	1.000
Wehner, John, Nash.	.431	17	62	58	14	25	52	3	0	8	15	0	1	0	3	0	6	0	0	1	.897	.452
West, David, Alb.*	.000	2	2	2	0	0	0	0	0	0	0	0	0	0	0	0	2	0	0	0	.000	.000
White, Derrick, Iowa	.262	132	563	503	75	132	202	31	0	13	77	0	6	7	47	5	94	10	8	11	.402	.330
White, Walt, Tuc.	.203	54	169	153	18	31	50	8	1	3	13	1	1	0	14	1	39	0	0	6	.327	.268
Whiteside, Matt, L.V.	.167	47	8	6	0	1	1	0	0	0	0	1	0	0	1	0	1	0	0	0	.167	.286
Wilkins, Marc, Nash.	.000	8	1	0	0	0	0	0	0	0	0	1	0	0	0	0	0	0	0	0	.000	.000
Wilkins, Rick, Alb.*	.253	92	334	300	39	76	110	8	1	8	33	2	2	1	29	2	87	1	8	7	.367	.319
Williams, Eddie, S.L.	.316	97	387	345	56	109	184	24	0	17	57	0	2	5	35	1	68	0	1	13	.533	.385
Williams, George, S.L.-N.O.†...	.284	103	392	328	56	93	143	21	1	9	45	0	1	8	55	4	70	1	4	15	.436	.398
Williams, Jeff, Alb.	.389	42	20	18	2	7	8	1	0	0	1	2	0	0	0	0	8	0	0	0	.444	.389
Williams, Keith, Fres.	.282	89	335	294	46	83	145	23	3	11	50	2	3	2	34	1	50	4	2	8	.493	.357
Williams, Reggie, Edm.†	.314	35	155	137	25	43	72	9	1	6	31	0	2	0	16	1	29	3	2	4	.526	.381
Wilson, Brandon, Iowa	.278	123	524	472	82	131	207	28	6	12	49	8	4	6	34	1	76	31	5	10	.439	.331
Wilson, Desi, Tuc.*	.323	130	491	452	65	146	205	27	7	6	62	0	3	2	34	2	76	2	3	18	.454	.371
Wolff, Bryan, L.V.	.049	28	46	41	3	2	3	1	0	0	2	2	0	0	3	0	21	0	0	0	.073	.114
Womack, Tony, Tuc.*	.250	4	19	16	1	4	8	1	0	1	3	1	0	0	2	0	3	0	1	2	.500	.333
Woodall, Brad, Iowa†	.077	16	15	13	0	1	1	0	0	0	0	1	0	0	1	0	4	0	0	1	.077	.143
Woods, Ken, Fres.	.324	124	517	469	77	152	201	23	4	6	73	2	9	3	33	0	45	19	4	8	.429	.366
Wright, Jamey, C.S.	.167	17	28	24	2	4	8	1	0	1	4	4	0	0	0	0	14	0	0	0	.333	.167
Young, Ernie, Tuc.	.294	126	521	453	78	133	250	25	1	30	95	0	6	5	57	1	129	4	1	9	.552	.374
Young, Travis, Nash.	.250	26	106	92	15	23	32	1	1	2	11	1	1	3	9	1	23	3	2	1	.348	.333
Zinter, Alan, Iowa†	.255	14	56	51	7	13	24	2	0	3	8	0	0	5	0	13	0	0	1	.471	.321
Zywica, Mike, Okla.	.265	13	543	495	80	131	195	31	3	9	79	1	7	7	33	0	119	4	1	13	.394	.315

GRAND SLAMS: Allen, G. Arias, Bautista, Belk, Canizaro, Carvajal, Chamberlain, Clapp, Conti, Cookson, A. Cora, I. Cruz, Decker, Diaz, Dishington, Durazo, Gibralter, Gibson, Gil, Grijak, Haas, Hermansen, G. Hyzdu, J. Jones, M. Kelly, Kennedy, Lariviere, Luke, McDonald, Mendez, Menechino, R. Montgomery, Morman, Murray, Newson, D. Ortiz, Pellow, E. Perez, Petrick, Prieto, Pritchett, Radmanovich, Riggs, Rios, Roberge, Roskos, Sealy, Simms, Sveum, R. Thompson, Timmons, Villalobos, E. Williams, E. Young, 1 each.

AWARDED FIRST BASE ON CATCHER'S INTERFERENCE: Haas (Blanco); J. Guillen (G. Williams); Chamberlain (Stefanski); Canizaro (Russo); Ward (Sealy); Hutchins (Hubbard); B. Molina (Sealy); C. Gomez (Knorr); Little (Pachot); Woods (Petrick); C. Garcia (E. Guzman); Conti (Petrick); Norman (Marzano).

PLAYERS WITH TWO OR MORE TEAMS

Player, Team	Avg.	G	TPA	AB	R	H	TB	2B	3B	HR	RBI	SH	SF	HP	BB	IBB	SO	SB	CS	GDP	Slg.	OBP
Bieser, Steve, Nash.	.231	6	16	13	3	3	4	1	0	0	3	0	0	1	2	0	4	0	0	0	.308	.375
Bieser, Steve, Mem.*	.311	58	204	180	25	56	85	13	2	4	16	5	0	3	16	0	30	8	0	2	.472	.377
Boyd, Jason, Tuc.	.167	45	7	6	0	1	1	0	0	0	1	0	1	0	0	0	1	0	0	0	.167	.143
Boyd, Jason, Nash.	.000	5	0	0	0	0	0	0	0	0	0	0	0	0	0	0	0	0	0	0	.000	.000
Bridges, Kary, Iowa*	.120	10	26	25	1	3	3	0	0	0	0	0	0	0	1	0	5	0	0	0	.120	.154
Bridges, Kary, Okla.*	.343	75	268	239	38	82	117	14	0	7	39	4	3	1	21	2	14	6	3	8	.490	.394
De La Rosa, Maximo, Tac.	.000	15	0	0	0	0	0	0	0	0	0	0	0	0	0	0	0	0	0	0	.000	.000
De La Rosa, Maximo, C.S.	.500	8	2	2	1	1	2	1	0	0	0	0	0	0	0	0	0	0	0	0	1.000	.500
Foster, Jim, Tuc.	.269	11	31	26	4	7	8	1	0	0	3	0	1	0	4	0	2	0	0	3	.308	.355
Foster, Jim, Edm.	.295	24	93	88	13	26	42	10	0	2	15	0	1	0	4	0	13	1	0	2	.477	.323
Grilli, Jason, Fres.	.105	19	21	19	1	2	2	0	0	0	1	2	0	0	0	0	10	0	0	1	.105	.105
Grilli, Jason, Cal.	.250	8	5	4	1	1	1	0	0	0	0	1	0	0	0	0	2	0	0	0	.250	.250
Hanson, Erik, Cal.	.000	10	7	5	0	0	0	0	0	0	0	1	1	0	1	0	3	0	0	0	.000	.167
Hanson, Erik, Oma.	.000	14	0	0	0	0	0	0	0	0	0	0	0	0	0	0	0	0	0	0	.000	.000
Hodges, Kevin, N.O.	.333	5	4	3	0	1	1	0	0	0	0	1	0	0	0	0	1	0	0	0	.333	.333
Hodges, Kevin, Tac.	.000	14	0	0	0	0	0	0	0	0	0	0	0	0	0	0	0	0	0	0	.000	.000
Incaviglia, Pete, Tuc.	.156	8	33	32	3	5	9	4	0	0	7	0	0	1	1	0	11	1	0	1	.281	.182
Incaviglia, Pete, N.O.	.194	18	72	62	6	12	20	3	1	1	6	0	1	1	8	0	15	1	2	0	.323	.292
Menhart, Paul, Edm.	.000	9	0	0	0	0	0	0	0	0	0	0	0	0	0	0	0	0	0	0	.000	.000
Menhart, Paul, Cal.	.000	8	6	4	2	0	0	0	0	0	0	2	0	0	2	0	1	0	0	0	.000	.333
Mercedes, Jose, L.V.	.063	15	19	16	0	1	1	0	0	0	0	3	0	0	0	0	11	0	0	0	.063	.063
Mercedes, Jose, Cal.	.000	4	3	2	0	0	0	0	0	0	0	1	0	0	0	0	1	0	0	0	.000	.000
Michalak, Chris, Edm.*	.000	24	0	0	0	0	0	0	0	0	0	0	0	0	0	0	0	0	0	0	.000	.000
Michalak, Chris, Tuc.*	.231	21	19	13	2	3	4	1	0	0	0	5	0	0	1	0	3	0	0	0	.308	.286
Robertson, Rich, Okla.*	.000	3	0	0	0	0	0	0	0	0	0	0	0	0	0	0	0	0	0	0	.000	.000
Robertson, Rich, Nash.*	.500	7	2	2	0	1	1	0	0	0	0	0	0	0	0	0	1	0	0	0	.500	.500
Smith, Pete, Mem.	.300	8	11	10	1	3	4	1	0	0	1	0	0	0	1	0	4	0	0	0	.400	.300
Smith, Pete, L.V.	.235	13	21	17	0	4	4	0	0	0	2	2	0	0	2	0	6	0	0	1	.235	.316
Stoner, Mike, Tuc.	.429	14	24	21	2	9	10	1	0	0	6	0	1	0	2	0	3	0	0	0	.476	.458
Stoner, Mike, Edm.	.346	22	85	81	12	28	44	5	1	3	12	0	0	2	2	0	4	0	1	2	.543	.376

Player, Team	Avg.	G	TPA	AB	R	H	TB	2B	3B	HR	RBI	SH	SF	HP	BB	IBB	SO	SB	CS	GDP	Slg.	OBP
Stovall, DaRond, Cal.	.189	37	119	106	10	20	38	3	3	3	13	1	1	0	11	1	44	0	0	0	.358	.263
Stovall, DaRond, Alb.†	.219	46	185	160	30	35	68	12	0	7	21	0	3	0	22	0	65	8	4	2	.425	.308
Sveum, Dale, Tuc.†	.209	20	71	67	3	14	18	1	0	1	4	0	1	0	3	0	23	0	1	3	.269	.239
Sveum, Dale, Nash.†	.344	42	145	125	25	43	68	14	1	3	25	0	0	2	18	0	30	1	0	5	.544	.434
Unroe, Tim, Edm.	.386	10	49	44	10	17	39	5	1	5	18	0	0	0	5	0	9	0	0	0	.886	.449
Unroe, Tim, Oma.	.227	5	22	22	4	5	8	0	0	1	2	0	0	0	0	0	5	0	0	0	.364	.227
Vosberg, Ed, L.V.*	.000	8	0	0	0	0	0	0	0	0	0	0	0	0	0	0	0	0	0	0	.000	.000
Vosberg, Ed, Tuc.*	.000	26	2	2	0	0	0	0	0	0	0	0	0	0	0	0	1	0	0	0	.000	.000
Ward, Turner, Nash.†	.292	35	107	89	15	26	37	3	1	2	17	0	0	1	16	0	14	3	1	1	.416	.406
Ward, Turner, Tuc.†	.375	12	48	40	9	15	23	2	0	2	8	0	0	1	7	0	4	4	1	1	.575	.479
Weber, Neil, Tuc.	.000	9	0	0	0	0	0	0	0	0	0	0	0	0	0	0	0	0	0	0	.000	.000
Weber, Neil, Alb.*	.000	9	3	0	0	0	0	0	0	0	0	1	0	0	3	0	0	0	0	0	.000	1.000
Williams, George, S.L.	.303	74	276	228	38	69	105	16	1	6	31	0	0	6	42	2	51	0	3	9	.461	.424
Williams, George, N.O.†	.240	29	116	100	18	24	38	5	0	3	14	0	1	2	13	2	19	1	1	6	.380	.336

1999 PITCHING

TEAM

Team	W	L	Pct.	ERA	G	CG	ShO	Sv.	IP	H	TBF	R	ER	HR	SH	SF	HB	BB	IBB	SO	WP	Bk.
Vancouver.........	84	58	.592	3.84	142	6	11	43	1229.0	1287	5291	617	525	103	41	39	36	436	17	925	69	4
Tacoma	69	70	.496	4.35	139	8	6	36	1231.2	1245	5346	664	595	131	30	38	76	476	20	998	62	7
Nashville	80	60	.571	4.49	140	4	1	43	1216.0	1328	5384	708	606	129	56	35	49	464	37	1042	63	3
Oklahoma..........	83	59	.585	4.65	142	16	5	43	1233.2	1349	5368	696	638	131	26	38	43	456	9	900	62	3
Iowa.................	65	76	.461	4.67	141	6	4	25	1242.1	1290	5444	716	644	152	51	37	55	495	14	1014	63	7
Omaha..............	81	60	.574	4.77	141	6	5	29	1226.0	1313	5361	744	650	177	33	36	62	438	15	957	64	8
Fresno..............	73	69	.514	4.92	142	5	2	29	1230.0	1327	5482	800	672	195	40	38	65	499	10	1107	97	12
Edmonton..........	65	74	.468	4.94	139	5	4	25	1213.1	1365	5297	746	666	157	24	43	41	421	12	936	57	6
Memphis	74	64	.536	4.98	138	3	6	37	1195.1	1298	5257	738	662	165	47	39	43	459	13	945	57	5
New Orleans	55	85	.393	5.03	140	7	6	31	1209.2	1332	5356	750	676	137	52	42	56	416	27	851	66	10
Las Vegas	67	75	.472	5.08	142	6	6	30	1230.2	1437	5509	791	695	164	41	55	57	451	13	1057	64	3
Tucson.............	66	76	.465	5.15	142	2	6	32	1222.1	1400	5471	807	700	144	55	36	57	523	38	1013	55	11
Albuquerque	65	74	.468	5.31	139	8	5	34	1206.0	1363	5403	805	711	175	41	47	67	514	21	1023	70	6
Salt Lake	73	68	.518	5.32	141	4	2	35	1203.2	1387	5441	807	711	163	36	57	54	494	17	858	75	6
Colo. Springs	66	73	.475	5.51	139	10	2	34	1193.1	1457	5409	830	730	164	49	46	67	504	28	909	61	12
Calgary.............	57	82	.410	5.84	139	4	2	22	1171.0	1424	5347	866	760	148	47	43	53	511	11	882	73	6

INDIVIDUAL

TOP QUALIFIERS FOR EARNED-RUN AVERAGE TITLE

Minimum 114 innings. *Lefthanded pitcher.

Pitcher, Team	W	L	Pct.	ERA	G	GS	CG	ShO	GF	Sv.	IP	H	TBF	R	ER	HR	SH	SF	HB	BB	IBB	SO	WP	Bk.
Bunch, Mel, Tac.	10	2	.833	3.10	21	19	1	1	0	0	125.0	112	517	53	43	11	1	1	8	40	1	117	4	1
Laxton, Brett, Van.	13	8	.619	3.46	25	25	3	1	0	0	161.1	158	662	68	62	8	5	4	6	49	0	112	10	0
Fyhrie, Mike, Edm.	9	5	.643	3.47	19	18	0	0	0	0	114.0	90	460	47	44	8	1	3	3	40	0	113	0	0
Lorraine, Andrew, Iowa*	9	8	.529	3.71	22	21	1	0	0	0	143.0	149	603	67	59	16	4	2	6	34	0	96	5	0
Creek, Doug, Iowa*	7	3	.700	3.79	25	20	0	0	3	1	130.2	116	567	66	55	20	5	6	12	62	0	140	6	0
Anderson, Jimmy, Nash.*	11	2	.846	3.84	21	21	1	0	0	0	133.2	153	579	67	57	5	6	0	3	41	0	93	8	0
Figueroa, Nelson, Tuc.	11	6	.647	3.94	24	21	1	1	0	0	128.0	128	541	59	56	16	3	1	5	41	0	106	6	0
Luebbers, Larry, Mem.	13	4	.765	4.03	21	19	1	1	0	0	129.2	134	547	61	58	15	7	3	5	33	1	84	3	0
Mercedes, Jose, L.V.-Cal.	9	3	.273	4.03	19	18	0	0	0	0	114.0	140	508	70	51	16	6	2	2	23	0	70	1	1
Mulder, Mark, Van.*	6	7	.462	4.06	22	22	1	0	0	0	128.2	152	549	69	58	13	4	5	3	31	0	81	6	0
Miller, Wade, N.O.	11	9	.550	4.38	26	26	2	0	0	0	162.1	156	704	85	79	16	6	2	4	64	0	135	10	1
Rusch, Glendon, Oma.*	4	7	.364	4.42	20	20	1	0	0	0	114.0	143	511	68	56	10	3	4	5	33	0	102	3	0
Cornelius, Reid, Cal.	10	6	.625	4.49	27	27	2	1	0	0	172.1	184	750	96	86	9	4	8	7	68	3	135	12	2
Pote, Lou, Edm.	7	9	.438	4.52	24	23	3	0	1	0	150.0	171	637	80	75	19	2	2	2	41	0	118	6	0
Barber, Brian, Oma.	9	5	.643	4.56	19	19	2	1	0	0	120.1	128	520	68	61	21	4	1	5	29	1	75	6	0

DEPARTMENTAL LEADERS: W—Perisho, 15; L—Scanlan, 15; Pct.—J. Anderson, .846; G—Brow, 64; GS—McNichol, Scanlan, Patrick, 28 each; CG—Knight, 5; ShO—Raggio, 2; GF—Ludwick, 44; Sv.—Wainhouse, 22; IP—Wolff, 177.2; H—Scanlan, 208; TBF—Wolff, 770; R—Stone, 123; ER—Stone, Scanlan, 102 each; HR—Patrick, 33; SH—Milacki, 12; SF—Scanlan, 10; HB—D. Creek, Scanlan, Sullivan, 12 each; BB—Perisho, 78; IBB—Padilla, 7; SO—Van Poppel, 157; WP—Connelly, 14; BK—Checo, Oropesa, 4 each.

ALL PITCHERS

*Lefthanded pitcher.

Pitcher, Team	W	L	Pct.	ERA	G	GS	CG	ShO	GF	Sv.	IP	H	TBF	R	ER	HR	SH	SF	HB	BB	IBB	SO	WP	Bk.
Abbott, Paul, Tac.	1	1	.500	6.43	2	2	0	0	0	0	14.0	21	63	11	10	1	1	1	4	0	10	0	0
Adamson, Joel, Tac.*	2	2	.500	5.15	14	6	0	0	3	0	36.2	48	174	25	21	4	1	3	6	15	1	15	1	1
Ah Yat, Paul, Nash.*	4	3	.571	5.71	13	11	1	0	1	0	64.2	75	291	45	41	10	3	2	4	24	1	41	1	1
Alberro, Jose, Cal.	3	2	.600	6.64	24	8	0	0	4	0	59.2	79	267	46	44	9	1	1	2	16	0	43	5	0
Almanza, Armando, Cal.*	2	2	.500	10.90	15	0	0	0	4	0	17.1	29	99	27	21	3	0	1	0	18	0	20	2	0
Almanzar, Carlos, L.V.	1	3	.250	9.53	11	3	0	0	5	0	22.2	32	107	25	24	11	0	2	2	8	1	18	1	0
Alston, Garvin, Alb.	1	2	.333	5.06	5	0	0	0	2	0	10.2	12	46	6	6	1	1	0	1	4	0	5	1	0
Alvarez, Juan, Edm.*	1	0	.000	3.49	27	0	0	0	13	0	28.1	30	123	13	11	2	1	1	1	8	0	25	0	1
Anderson, Brian, Tuc.*	0	1	.000	5.40	2	2	0	0	0	0	6.2	9	30	5	4	1	1	1	0	1	0	8	0	0
Anderson, Jimmy, Nash.*	11	2	.846	3.84	21	21	1	0	0	0	133.2	153	579	67	57	5	6	0	3	41	0	93	8	0
Ankiel, Rick, Mem.*	7	3	.700	3.16	16	16	0	0	0	0	88.1	73	385	37	31	7	1	3	7	46	1	119	6	1
Arnold, Jamie, Alb.	0	2	.000	5.59	7	2	0	0	1	0	19.1	28	91	14	12	1	1	0	2	7	0	13	3	0
Arroyo, Bronson, Nash.	0	2	.000	10.38	3	3	0	0	0	0	13.0	22	71	15	15	1	0	0	1	10	0	11	0	0
Arroyo, Luis, Cal.*	2	1	.667	6.48	22	0	0	0	8	0	33.1	42	157	33	24	6	2	2	3	17	0	26	0	1

Pitcher, Team	W	L	Pct.	ERA	G	GS	CG	ShO	GF	Sv.	IP	H	TBF	R	ER	HR	SH	SF	HB	BB	IBB	SO	WP	Bk.
Baez, Benito, Van.*	0	2	.000	3.50	11	0	0	0	4	1	18.0	18	76	7	7	2	0	0	0	7	0	19	1	1
Bailey, Cory, Fres.	2	1	.667	3.30	43	0	0	0	39	18	46.1	47	200	24	17	7	2	0	0	17	0	52	3	1
Bailey, Roger, C.S.	0	0	.000	7.06	4	4	0	0	0	0	21.2	31	105	19	17	1	1	1	0	14	0	15	1	0
Baptist, Travis, S.L.*	1	3	.250	5.35	17	6	0	0	5	1	38.2	46	174	24	23	6	0	0	1	17	0	23	3	0
Barber, Brian, Oma.	9	5	.643	4.56	19	19	2	1	0	0	120.1	128	520	68	61	21	4	1	5	29	1	75	6	0
Barker, Richie, Iowa	4	4	.500	4.26	55	2	0	0	25	7	74.0	72	326	37	35	7	3	1	6	30	2	52	7	1
Barnes, Brian, Mem.*	4	3	.571	5.50	36	10	0	0	7	0	90.0	104	393	55	55	16	4	3	3	33	1	88	5	0
Batchelor, Rich, Tuc.	0	4	.000	4.50	30	0	0	0	28	12	28.0	29	125	19	14	2	1	1	2	12	1	23	2	0
Beck, Rod, Iowa	0	0	.000	0.00	2	0	0	0	1	0	2.0	1	7	0	0	0	0	0	0	0	0	2	0	0
Beckett, Robbie, Alb.*	1	3	.250	7.57	15	5	0	0	4	0	44.0	48	211	39	37	8	0	4	3	37	0	54	2	0
Bell, Jason, S.L.	5	5	.500	6.37	18	15	0	0	0	0	76.1	96	364	58	54	12	3	4	3	35	0	72	4	1
Beltran, Rigo, C.S.*	1	0	1.000	2.25	6	0	0	0	2	0	8.0	12	41	3	2	1	0	0	1	5	1	12	1	0
Benes, Alan, Mem.	0	1	.000	3.18	3	3	0	0	0	0	5.2	8	25	3	2	0	0	0	2	0	3	0	0
Benz, Jake, Cal.*	1	0	1.000	0.00	2	0	0	0	1	0	4.0	3	18	1	0	0	0	0	3	0	4	0	0
Bergman, Sean, N.O.	0	1	.000	9.95	3	1	0	0	0	0	6.1	9	30	8	7	0	0	0	2	0	2	1	0
Bertotti, Mike, Tac.*	0	2	.000	10.29	3	3	0	0	0	0	7.0	6	43	8	8	0	1	0	17	0	6	1	0
Bierbrodt, Nick, Tuc.*	1	4	.200	7.27	11	11	0	0	0	0	43.1	57	213	42	35	9	4	0	3	30	0	43	3	0
Bieser, Steve, Mem.	0	0	.000	0.00	1	0	0	0	1	0	1.0	0	4	0	0	0	0	0	2	0	0	1	0
Billingsley, Brent, Cal.*	2	9	.182	5.55	21	21	0	0	0	0	116.2	133	522	81	72	15	9	3	1	48	0	79	8	0
Bluma, Jaime, Oma.	0	0	.000	3.22	17	0	0	0	10	2	22.1	21	92	10	8	5	1	0	4	1	19	0	0
Bochtler, Doug, Alb.	3	4	.429	3.18	18	0	0	0	9	3	22.2	16	93	9	8	3	0	0	11	1	25	5	0
Borland, Toby, Edm.	2	1	.667	7.00	21	0	0	0	10	0	27.0	31	136	24	21	5	1	3	3	23	2	34	2	0
Boskie, Shawn, Alb.	4	8	.333	5.84	15	15	0	0	0	0	86.1	111	401	66	56	14	3	4	4	37	2	62	5	0
Bost, Heath, C.S.	4	4	.556	5.53	38	6	0	0	8	0	86.1	120	378	59	53	10	2	1	4	12	2	67	0	0
Bowers, Shane, S.L.	7	4	.636	5.68	31	18	0	0	1	0	122.0	149	560	86	77	25	2	5	1	54	0	103	11	0
Boyd, Jason, Tuc.-Nash.	6	5	.545	4.26	49	0	0	0	19	5	80.1	78	339	42	38	6	2	4	3	27	2	62	6	2
Briggs, Anthony, C.S.	1	1	.500	7.64	10	1	0	0	2	0	17.2	30	95	25	15	2	3	5	1	10	1	5	0	0
Brohawn, Troy, Tuc.*	1	0	1.000	3.29	3	2	0	0	0	0	13.2	22	67	8	5	1	3	0	0	3	0	12	0	0
Bross, Terry, Tuc.	0	0	.000	11.57	2	0	0	0	1	0	2.1	6	13	3	3	1	0	0	0	1	0	0	0	0
Brow, Scott, Edm.	1	6	.143	5.70	64	0	0	0	32	15	79.0	94	352	53	50	7	3	5	1	31	2	48	6	0
Brownson, Mark, C.S.	6	6	.500	6.20	17	16	2	0	0	0	103.0	120	446	75	71	24	2	6	7	24	0	81	6	2
Bunch, Mel, Tac.	10	2	.833	3.10	21	19	1	1	0	0	125.0	112	517	53	43	11	1	1	8	40	1	117	4	1
Burgus, Travis, Cal.*	1	0	1.000	5.40	20	0	0	0	9	1	23.1	33	109	17	14	3	1	0	1	8	0	15	1	0
Burke, Jamie, Edm.	1	0	1.000	0.00	1	0	0	0	1	0	3.0	1	11	0	0	0	0	0	0	1	0	3	0	0
Busby, Mike, Mem.	3	4	.429	7.43	29	10	0	0	6	0	72.2	112	359	69	60	12	2	5	3	36	1	50	8	0
Byington, Jimmie, Oma.	0	0	.000	20.25	1	0	0	0	1	0	1.1	3	8	3	3	0	0	0	2	0	2	0	0
Byrdak, Tim, Oma.*	3	1	.750	1.81	33	0	0	0	17	4	49.2	39	216	19	10	0	2	2	6	28	2	51	2	0
Cabrera, Jose, N.O.	3	1	.750	2.82	31	0	0	0	19	7	51.0	34	201	18	16	3	2	2	2	12	3	41	2	0
Candaele, Casey, N.O.	0	0	.000	0.00	1	0	0	0	0	0	0.0	2	2	2	2	1	0	0	0	0	0	0	0	0
Carlson, Dan, Tuc.	4	9	.308	5.43	32	18	0	0	5	0	117.2	130	527	82	71	19	3	1	6	52	6	118	4	2
Carlyle, Buddy, L.V.	11	8	.579	4.89	25	25	0	0	0	0	160.0	180	690	99	87	25	5	8	6	42	1	138	6	0
Carmona, Rafael, Tac.	1	3	.250	3.53	27	0	0	0	9	2	43.1	39	185	18	17	6	1	0	1	20	0	38	2	0
Carrasco, Hector, S.L.	1	0	1.000	0.00	3	0	0	0	3	1	4.1	3	18	0	0	0	1	0	0	3	0	3	0	0
Carroll, Dave, S.L.*	1	1	.000	6.55	36	0	0	0	9	2	34.1	34	152	25	25	5	0	1	3	19	1	26	6	0
Castillo, Frank, Nash.	7	5	.583	4.68	19	19	0	0	0	0	119.1	139	520	72	62	15	2	1	6	32	4	90	5	0
Cey, Dan, S.L.	0	0	.000	36.00	1	0	0	0	0	0	1.0	3	7	4	4	1	0	0	0	1	0	0	0	0
Chavez, Anthony, Van.	4	6	.400	3.91	54	0	0	0	36	14	69.0	67	315	42	30	8	3	3	3	37	5	72	2	0
Checo, Robinson, Alb.	3	6	.333	4.33	16	15	0	0	0	0	79.0	68	342	40	38	15	1	2	3	39	1	98	5	4
Chouinard, Bobby, Tuc.	4	1	.800	4.06	12	9	0	0	1	0	62.0	70	259	33	28	8	5	1	2	13	0	63	0	0
Christiansen, Jason, Nash.*	0	0	.000	0.00	2	0	0	0	0	0	2.0	0	6	0	0	0	0	0	0	0	0	1	0	0
Clark, Terry, Van.	3	4	.429	4.79	14	7	0	0	1	0	41.1	47	180	25	22	3	1	1	3	14	0	17	3	0
Clemons, Chris, Tuc.	6	4	.600	5.93	45	3	0	0	11	1	68.1	77	329	53	45	11	6	4	4	44	3	75	8	0
Clontz, Brad, Nash.	0	2	.000	3.50	12	0	0	0	12	7	18.0	12	73	8	7	3	2	1	1	6	0	23	0	0
Cloude, Ken, Tac.	5	1	.833	2.33	6	6	2	0	0	0	38.2	19	149	11	10	3	1	1	2	15	0	33	3	0
Cole, Victor, Iowa	2	1	.667	4.69	19	2	0	0	2	0	40.1	41	188	24	21	3	2	0	3	23	1	33	5	2
Connelly, Steve, Fres.	6	4	.600	5.25	54	0	0	0	20	2	72.0	93	338	58	42	8	2	2	5	32	3	47	14	1
Cooke, Steve, L.V.*	0	0	.000	30.00	5	0	0	0	1	0	3.0	6	27	10	10	2	0	2	1	12	1	0	5	0
Coolbaugh, Scott, Tuc.	0	0	.000	3.00	1	0	0	0	0	0	3.0	3	12	1	1	0	0	0	0	0	0	0	0	0
Cooper, Brian, Edm.	2	1	.667	3.77	5	5	0	0	0	0	31.0	30	130	17	13	0	0	2	1	10	0	32	1	0
Corbin, Archie, Cal.	0	1	.000	6.75	12	0	0	0	7	0	13.1	13	61	11	10	3	0	1	0	10	0	16	3	0
Cordova, Francisco, Nash.	2	0	1.000	0.75	2	2	0	0	0	0	12.0	10	47	2	1	1	0	1	0	1	0	7	0	0
Cornelius, Reid, Cal.	10	6	.625	4.49	27	27	2	1	0	0	172.1	184	750	96	86	9	4	8	7	68	3	135	12	2
Corps, Edwin, Fres.	0	0	.000	3.86	4	0	0	0	3	0	7.0	9	33	7	3	0	0	0	0	3	0	11	1	0
Crabtree, Robbie, Fres.	1	4	.200	5.24	22	1	0	0	11	1	34.1	37	150	23	20	2	0	0	0	10	1	40	3	0
Crafton, Kevin, Mem.	0	1	.000	22.85	4	0	0	0	4	0	4.1	12	26	12	11	2	0	1	1	0	0	2	0	0
Creek, Doug, Iowa*	7	3	.700	3.79	25	20	0	0	1	0	130.2	116	567	66	55	20	5	6	12	62	0	140	6	0
Creek, Ryan, N.O.	1	2	.333	3.98	6	5	0	0	0	0	31.2	30	141	17	14	4	4	0	2	16	0	20	2	0
Croghan, Andy, Alb.	2	1	.667	2.81	35	0	0	0	9	2	41.2	43	179	16	13	5	0	2	4	14	0	31	0	0
Croushore, Rich, Mem.	1	0	1.000	6.75	7	0	0	0	5	4	6.2	8	34	5	5	1	0	1	0	6	0	11	1	0
Crow, Dean, N.O.	2	6	.250	7.04	34	0	0	0	11	5	46.0	71	217	36	36	4	5	6	2	12	4	22	2	1
Cummings, John, Tuc.*	1	1	.500	8.31	11	1	0	0	2	0	21.2	33	103	24	20	5	0	2	0	9	0	18	1	1
Cunnane, Will, L.V.	2	1	.667	0.98	28	0	0	0	21	11	36.2	30	157	5	4	0	1	0	0	16	2	54	1	0
Dale, Carl, Van.	4	3	.571	3.48	29	0	0	0	11	4	44.0	41	189	19	17	0	1	1	2	18	1	27	1	0
D'Amico, Jeff, Van.-Oma.	3	5	.375	3.53	26	0	0	0	21	5	35.2	45	163	19	14	2	1	0	1	13	1	22	5	1
Darensbourg, Vic, Cal.*	0	0	.000	4.63	9	0	0	0	2	1	11.2	13	46	6	6	0	0	1	0	12	0	0	0
Darwin, Jeff, L.V.	1	1	.500	13.50	8	0	0	0	5	0	10.0	19	55	17	15	2	0	1	0	5	0	9	1	0
Davis, Doug, Okla.*	7	0	1.000	3.00	13	11	0	0	0	0	78.0	77	330	27	26	4	3	1	2	31	0	74	2	0
Davis, Kane, Nash.	3	2	.600	6.75	12	9	0	0	1	0	49.1	65	224	38	37	8	2	1	3	17	1	31	2	0
De Jean, Mike, C.S.	0	0	.000	0.00	1	0	0	0	0	0	1.0	1	3	0	0	0	0	0	0	0	0	0	0	0
De La Maza, Roland, Van.	0	0	.000	12.00	4	0	0	0	1	0	3.0	5	16	4	4	1	0	0	0	4	0	4	0	0
De La Rosa, Max., Tac.-C.S.	0	3	.000	4.91	23	0	0	0	7	1	33.0	46	160	21	18	4	1	2	5	14	2	29	4	0
Delgado, Danny, Tac.	0	1	.000	6.00	2	0	0	0	2	0	3.0	4	14	2	2	0	1	0	0	2	1	2	0	0

Pitcher, Team	W	L	Pct.	ERA	G	GS	CG	ShO	GF	Sv.	IP	H	TBF	R	ER	HR	SH	SF	HB	BB	IBB	SO	WP	Bk.
Del Toro, Miguel, Fres.	4	2	.667	4.42	40	0	0	0	12	0	71.1	76	323	41	35	11	5	2	6	29	1	71	5	1
Dempster, Ryan, Cal.	1	1	.500	4.99	5	5	0	0	0	0	30.2	30	132	17	17	6	1	2	0	10	1	29	4	0
Dennis, Shane, L.V.*	3	10	.231	5.59	34	18	0	0	5	0	116.0	140	538	83	72	19	4	4	4	60	1	104	6	0
Detmers, Kris, Mem.*	6	8	.429	5.10	23	22	0	0	0	0	125.1	135	544	74	71	17	5	5	2	44	2	90	2	0
Dickey, R.A., Okla.	2	2	.500	4.37	6	2	0	0	1	0	22.2	23	99	12	11	1	3	0	1	7	1	17	2	0
Diorio, Mike, N.O.	2	3	.400	6.40	50	0	0	0	14	1	70.1	85	333	59	50	10	2	7	31	6	32	6	0	
Dougherty, Jim, Nash.	3	3	.500	5.43	53	0	0	0	20	10	59.2	69	274	38	36	9	3	4	0	27	5	55	0	0
Drumheller, Al, L.V.*	6	4	.600	4.90	20	7	0	0	6	0	60.2	72	266	36	33	7	1	6	2	22	0	46	6	0
Drumright, Mike, Cal.	0	2	.000	13.71	12	0	0	0	1	0	21.0	39	133	33	32	5	1	0	1	13	0	15	2	0
Dunbar, Matt, Nash.*	1	0	1.000	4.35	11	0	0	0	1	0	10.1	13	46	6	5	1	2	0	4	1	9	0	0	
Duncan, Geoff, Cal.	1	0	1.000	4.00	5	0	0	0	2	1	9.0	4	39	4	4	0	0	2	10	0	5	1	0	
Edsell, Geoff, Edm.	1	4	.200	5.01	30	0	0	0	7	0	46.2	46	208	27	26	6	1	2	2	25	2	37	1	0
Eischen, Joey, Tuc.*	1	3	.250	9.07	27	1	0	0	8	1	41.2	63	209	47	42	7	1	1	1	26	3	36	6	0
Ellis, Robert, N.O.	7	12	.368	5.43	27	27	1	0	0	0	155.2	176	690	106	94	20	5	6	51	1	105	11	2	
Estrella, Luis, Fres.	0	1	.000	12.34	8	0	0	0	7	0	11.2	23	63	16	16	4	1	1	0	7	0	5	1	0
Etherton, Seth, Edm.	0	2	.000	5.48	4	4	0	0	0	0	21.1	25	94	13	13	7	1	1	0	6	0	19	1	0
Evans, Bart, Oma.	4	5	.444	8.10	30	0	0	0	12	2	33.1	33	172	34	30	5	1	1	9	36	2	34	6	0
Eversgerd, Bryan, Mem.*	6	6	.500	2.86	59	0	0	0	27	2	66.0	56	269	26	21	9	4	0	3	15	0	46	0	0
Farmer, Michael, C.S.*	8	10	.444	7.86	25	20	2	0	1	0	113.1	170	532	111	99	24	11	1	2	44	3	75	1	3
Farnsworth, Kyle, Iowa	2	2	.500	3.20	6	6	0	0	0	0	39.1	38	157	16	14	5	3	0	0	9	0	29	1	0
Figueroa, Nelson, Tuc.	11	6	.647	3.94	24	21	1	1	0	0	128.0	128	541	59	56	16	3	1	5	41	0	106	6	0
Fiore, Tony, S.L.	2	1	.667	3.47	40	0	0	0	35	19	46.2	45	205	21	18	1	2	2	2	26	3	38	3	1
Fleetham, Ben, Tac.	2	2	.333	3.38	14	0	0	0	7	1	18.2	19	85	9	7	1	0	1	0	10	0	26	3	0
Flener, Huck, Tac.*	4	4	.500	5.45	22	5	0	0	6	1	66.0	72	292	41	40	6	2	2	3	26	2	48	5	1
Fontenot, Joe, Cal.	3	2	.600	5.11	8	8	1	1	0	0	44.0	52	193	26	25	2	4	3	3	19	0	18	1	1
Franklin, Ryan, Tac.	6	9	.400	4.71	29	19	2	1	4	2	135.2	142	574	81	71	17	2	4	9	33	1	94	1	1
Freeman, Ricky, Van.	0	0	.000	0.00	1	0	0	0	1	0	0.1	0	1	0	0	0	0	0	0	0	0	0	0	0
Frey, Steve, Okla.*	1	2	.333	4.47	30	0	0	0	19	4	44.1	51	191	25	22	7	1	1	0	15	0	38	1	0
Fultz, Aaron, Fres.*	9	8	.529	4.98	37	20	1	0	7	0	137.1	141	601	87	76	32	3	9	7	51	1	151	11	1
Fussell, Chris, Oma.	10	3	.769	3.54	14	13	1	1	1	0	81.1	66	332	35	32	11	2	0	2	27	0	80	4	0
Fyhrie, Mike, Edm.	9	5	.643	3.47	19	18	0	0	0	0	114.0	90	460	47	44	8	1	3	3	40	0	113	0	0
Gajkowski, Steve, Iowa	5	8	.385	3.73	58	0	0	0	31	9	79.2	79	334	36	33	8	5	0	0	25	0	64	4	0
Gandarillas, Gus, S.L.	2	2	.500	4.55	42	0	0	0	8	2	61.1	73	279	37	31	8	0	0	2	20	4	47	7	1
Garcia, Mike, Nash.	0	2	.000	3.95	23	0	0	0	10	2	27.1	24	114	12	12	3	3	1	1	10	2	35	0	0
Garrett, Hal, Alb.	0	0	.000	15.43	1	0	0	0	0	0	2.1	3	11	4	4	1	0	0	0	2	0	1	0	0
Giard, Ken, Nash.	0	0	.000	4.32	14	0	0	0	4	0	16.2	16	76	10	8	1	1	1	0	11	0	21	1	0
Gilbert, Shawn, Alb.	0	0	.000	13.50	1	0	0	0	1	0	1.1	2	7	2	2	1	0	0	0	1	0	0	0	0
Glynn, Ryan, Okla.	6	2	.750	3.39	16	16	2	1	0	0	90.1	81	385	46	34	7	1	4	4	36	1	55	3	0
Gonzalez, Gabe, Cal.*	1	1	.500	4.18	24	0	0	0	10	0	28.0	27	123	15	13	2	0	2	2	9	1	23	0	0
Gonzalez, Jeremi, Iowa	1	0	1.000	4.50	3	3	0	0	0	0	10.0	10	45	8	5	1	1	0	1	6	0	5	1	0
Gonzalez, Lariel, C.S.	0	1	.000	10.13	11	0	0	0	4	0	13.1	18	66	16	15	2	1	1	0	12	2	9	1	0
Gooding, Jason, Oma.*	0	1	.000	6.00	1	0	0	0	0	0	6.0	8	26	4	4	1	0	1	0	2	0	0	0	
Gregg, Kevin, Van.	1	0	1.000	3.60	1	1	0	0	0	0	5.0	6	21	2	2	0	0	0	2	0	4	2	0	
Grilli, Jason, Fres.-Cal.	8	10	.444	6.16	27	27	1	0	0	0	141.2	180	666	117	97	29	4	4	8	62	0	103	8	1
Gunderson, Eric, Okla.*	0	1	.000	8.10	5	0	0	0	2	1	6.2	11	32	6	6	2	0	0	1	0	3	1	0
Hackman, Luther, C.S.	7	6	.538	3.74	15	15	1	1	0	0	101.0	106	445	49	42	7	4	3	6	44	2	88	2	2
Hansell, Greg, Nash.	3	3	.500	2.00	22	0	0	0	10	2	27.0	18	110	8	6	2	2	3	1	9	1	36	4	0
Hanson, Erik, Cal.-Oma.	5	9	.357	5.90	24	19	0	0	3	0	108.1	126	484	75	71	15	6	3	5	48	0	85	6	1
Harris, Jeff, S.L.	4	3	.571	6.90	36	0	0	0	7	0	45.2	61	220	38	35	7	3	4	3	26	1	20	2	0
Harville, Chad, Van.	1	0	1.000	1.75	22	0	0	0	19	11	25.2	24	114	5	5	0	0	3	11	1	36	4	0	
Hawblitzel, Ryan, Edm.	4	4	.500	5.34	24	7	0	0	2	0	64.0	81	295	47	38	8	2	2	4	24	1	37	0	0
Heiserman, Rick, Mem.	2	3	.400	5.11	52	0	0	0	38	20	61.2	67	266	37	35	7	1	1	4	21	1	57	6	0
Henry, Butch, Tac.*	2	0	1.000	0.00	4	0	0	0	1	0	5.0	4	18	0	0	0	1	0	0	0	0	3	0	0
Henry, Doug, N.O.	0	0	.000	4.50	3	3	0	0	0	0	4.0	4	20	2	2	0	0	1	3	0	3	1	0	
Herges, Matt, Alb.	8	3	.727	4.73	21	21	2	0	0	0	131.1	135	563	82	69	17	7	5	7	47	1	88	4	0
Hernandez, Fernando, Tuc.	0	2	.000	8.44	5	1	0	0	1	0	16.0	22	75	16	15	3	1	0	1	4	0	14	0	0
Herrick, Jason, Edm.*	0	0	.000	0.00	1	0	0	0	1	0	0.2	0	2	0	0	0	0	0	0	1	0	0	0	0
Hinchliffe, Brett, Tac.	9	7	.563	5.15	21	21	3	0	0	0	131.0	141	563	78	75	17	4	5	5	44	1	107	9	0
Hodges, Kevin, N.O.-Tac.	4	6	.400	4.24	19	17	0	0	1	0	110.1	122	484	54	52	9	3	3	10	38	2	58	3	0
Holdridge, David, Tac.	5	6	.455	4.34	41	0	0	0	26	10	66.1	67	297	38	32	3	3	2	9	23	2	68	7	0
Holmes, Darren, Tuc.	0	0	.000	0.00	1	0	0	0	0	0	1.0	0	3	0	0	0	0	0	0	1	0	0	0	0
Holtz, Mike, Edm.*	2	1	.667	2.30	20	0	0	0	8	1	27.1	20	111	7	7	4	1	0	0	11	1	39	1	0
Holzemer, Mark, C.S.*	3	2	.600	5.69	41	1	0	0	11	1	55.1	77	268	39	35	10	2	2	6	24	1	49	2	0
Hudson, Joe, Okla.	1	1	.500	5.00	5	0	0	0	3	0	9.0	15	42	6	5	1	0	1	0	4	0	4	1	0
Hudson, Tim, Van.	4	0	1.000	2.20	8	8	0	0	0	0	49.0	38	202	16	12	2	0	1	1	21	0	61	2	0
Huisman, Rick, N.O.	3	1	.750	3.61	35	0	0	0	15	3	52.1	42	217	23	21	6	0	1	1	16	2	67	0	0
Huls, Steve, S.L.	0	0	.000	9.00	1	0	0	0	1	0	1.0	1	4	1	1	1	0	0	0	0	0	0	0	0
Hutchinson, Chad, Mem.	2	0	1.000	2.19	2	2	0	0	0	0	12.1	4	48	3	3	2	0	0	8	0	16	0	0	
Jacobsen, Joe, Edm.	0	1	.000	7.20	12	0	0	0	7	0	15.0	24	75	13	12	2	0	1	0	5	1	6	1	0
James, Mike, Edm.	1	2	.333	8.64	8	1	0	0	6	0	8.1	16	43	14	8	3	0	1	1	2	0	3	1	0
Jarvis, Kevin, Van.	10	2	.833	3.41	17	16	2	1	0	0	103.0	110	439	47	39	14	3	1	2	26	0	64	3	0
Jensen, Jason, Tuc.*	0	1	.000	3.86	1	1	0	0	0	0	4.2	6	24	6	2	0	0	0	4	1	3	0	0	
Jensen, Ryan, Fres.	11	10	.524	5.12	27	27	0	0	0	0	156.1	160	688	96	89	17	6	6	6	68	1	150	13	0
Jimenez, Jose, Mem.	2	2	.500	3.04	4	4	0	0	0	0	26.2	30	113	10	9	0	2	1	2	9	0	18	0	0
Johnson, Jonathan, Okla.	8	4	.667	6.25	21	8	0	0	5	2	67.2	91	308	53	47	9	2	3	2	23	0	38	6	0
Johnson, Keith, Tuc.	0	0	36.00		0	1	0	0	0	1	0	1.0	5	9	4	4	1	0	0	0	1	0	0	0
Jones, Bobby, C.S.*	2	1	.667	5.40	3	3	0	0	0	0	16.2	17	82	13	10	1	0	3	15	0	14	1	0	
Jones, Marcus, Van.	2	1	.667	2.40	3	3	0	0	0	0	15.0	23	73	11	4	1	0	0	5	0	5	1	0	
Jordan, Ricardo, Alb.*	4	1	.800	7.20	37	0	0	0	10	2	30.0	33	142	26	24	5	0	3	4	21	1	35	0	0
Judd, Mike, Alb.	8	7	.533	6.67	21	21	1	0	0	0	110.2	132	507	90	82	22	3	1	7	47	1	122	9	0
Juelsgaard, Jarod, Iowa	4	7	.364	5.59	23	12	2	1	3	0	83.2	92	372	57	52	12	3	4	7	26	1	54	0	2
Karchner, Matt, Iowa	0	0	.000	6.35	5	1	0	0	0	0	5.2	6	24	4	4	1	0	1	1	0	6	0	0	

Pitcher, Team	W	L	Pct.	ERA	G	GS	CG	ShO	GF	Sv.	IP	H	TBF	R	ER	HR	SH	SF	HB	BB	IBB	SO	WP	Bk.
Karp, Ryan, Okla.*	2	2	.500	7.49	8	6	1	0	0	0	39.2	62	190	34	33	5	1	1	3	14	0	28	2	0
Kim, Byung-Hyun, Tuc.	4	0	1.000	2.40	11	3	0	0	3	1	30.0	21	123	9	8	2	0	0	1	15	1	40	1	3
King, Bill, Van.	9	6	.600	3.49	45	7	0	0	14	4	98.0	105	414	52	38	11	3	4	4	22	2	60	5	0
King, Curtis, Mem.	2	2	.500	2.61	27	0	0	0	13	7	31.0	21	124	13	9	2	2	1	1	10	2	25	0	0
King, Ray, Iowa*	4	4	.500	1.88	37	0	0	0	19	2	43.0	31	183	11	9	1	2	2	2	22	3	41	2	0
Knight, Brandon, Okla.	9	8	.529	4.91	27	26	5	0	0	0	163.0	173	706	96	89	23	1	3	10	47	2	97	9	3
Kolb, Brandon, L.V.	2	1	.667	3.94	42	0	0	0	16	4	61.2	72	281	36	27	3	1	3	3	29	1	63	7	0
Kolb, Dan, Okla.	5	3	.625	5.10	11	8	0	0	2	0	60.0	74	261	35	34	4	2	0	1	27	0	21	2	0
Krivda, Rick, Oma.*	6	8	.429	5.70	21	18	0	0	0	0	115.1	154	541	94	73	17	2	3	5	41	0	70	3	3
Kroon, Marc, Tac.	3	2	.600	6.11	13	5	0	0	1	0	35.1	31	161	24	24	5	0	1	4	21	0	38	1	1
Kubenka, Jeff, Alb.*	4	4	.500	3.22	51	0	0	0	27	11	67.0	62	286	33	24	6	3	2	4	23	3	63	4	0
Kubinski, Tim, Van.*	5	3	.625	3.44	46	1	0	0	17	6	73.1	70	314	30	28	2	6	2	2	27	3	56	5	2
Lacy, Kerry, Iowa	3	8	.273	5.44	49	5	0	0	14	0	92.2	105	422	65	56	5	4	4	3	44	2	69	7	1
Lawrence, Sean, Van.*	2	2	.500	4.81	25	2	0	0	7	0	39.1	51	188	25	21	4	2	1	1	21	1	37	1	0
Laxton, Brett, Van.	13	8	.619	3.46	25	25	3	1	0	0	161.1	158	662	68	62	8	5	4	6	49	0	112	10	0
Lee, Corey, Okla.*	3	0	1.000	2.03	4	4	0	0	0	0	26.2	21	105	6	6	2	0	0	0	8	0	25	2	0
Lee, David, C.S.	0	0	.000	0.00	6	0	0	0	6	3	5.2	3	20	0	0	0	0	1	0	7	2	6	0	0
Leiter, Mark, Tac.	0	0	.000	4.50	1	1	0	0	0	0	2.0	2	7	1	1	0	0	0	0	2	0	3	0	0
Lincoln, Mike, S.L.	5	2	.714	7.78	9	9	0	0	0	0	59.0	82	274	52	51	12	1	5	2	21	0	39	2	0
Lineweaver, Aaron, Oma.	0	1	.000	6.00	1	1	0	0	0	0	6.0	6	25	4	4	0	0	1	0	3	0	3	0	0
Loaiza, Esteban, Okla.	0	0	.000	0.00	2	2	0	0	0	0	4.1	3	19	0	0	0	0	0	0	3	0	6	0	0
Lobaton, Jose, Cal.	0	1	.000	18.00	2	0	0	0	2	0	2.0	4	12	4	4	0	0	0	3	1	1	0	0	0
Lomon, Kevin, Edm.	7	8	.467	5.75	23	17	0	0	0	0	123.2	170	560	86	79	23	2	7	5	35	0	91	11	2
Long, Joey, Nash.*	2	1	.667	4.50	35	0	0	0	10	0	36.0	39	164	25	18	5	0	4	0	22	2	37	6	1
Lorraine, Andrew, Iowa*	9	8	.529	3.71	22	21	1	0	0	0	143.0	149	603	67	59	16	4	2	6	34	0	96	5	0
Lovingier, Kevin, Mem.*	3	4	.429	4.85	51	0	0	0	11	0	78.0	66	338	44	42	8	1	1	0	40	0	66	4	0
Lubozynski, Matt, Edm.*	0	0	.000	0.00	1	0	0	0	1	0	2.0	1	8	0	0	0	0	0	0	1	0	1	0	0
Luce, Robert, Tac.	0	3	.000	8.44	3	3	0	0	0	0	16.0	22	73	15	15	4	1	1	0	7	0	6	0	0
Ludwick, Eric, Cal.	11	6	.647	3.86	48	0	0	0	44	14	58.1	65	270	33	25	5	3	1	2	36	4	61	1	0
Luebbers, Larry, Mem.	13	4	.765	4.03	21	19	1	1	0	0	129.2	134	547	61	58	15	7	3	5	33	1	84	3	0
Mahaffey, Alan, S.L.*	1	2	.333	5.48	7	5	0	0	0	0	21.1	28	106	17	13	1	1	0	1	15	1	11	1	1
Mahay, Ron, Van.*	7	2	.778	4.29	32	15	0	0	4	0	107.0	116	466	57	51	12	1	5	0	45	0	73	5	0
Manning, David, Iowa	0	0	.000	4.66	7	0	0	0	2	0	9.2	9	44	6	5	2	0	3	0	8	0	7	0	0
Manwiller, Tim, Van.	4	2	.667	6.46	11	11	0	0	0	0	54.1	72	247	42	39	9	2	4	4	14	0	30	1	0
Marsters, Brandon, S.L.	0	0	.000	0.00	1	0	0	0	1	0	1.0	1	5	0	0	0	0	0	0	1	0	0	0	0
Marte, Damaso, Tac.*	3	3	.500	5.13	31	11	0	0	4	0	73.2	79	335	43	42	13	1	1	2	40	1	59	1	2
Marzano, John, Okla.	0	0	.000	0.00	1	0	0	0	0	0	0.1	0	1	0	0	0	0	0	0	0	0	0	0	0
Mathews, T.J., Van.	0	0	.000	9.00	1	1	0	0	0	0	1.0	1	4	1	1	0	0	0	0	0	0	1	0	0
Mathews, Terry, Oma.	1	0	1.000	1.65	7	0	0	0	6	0	16.1	11	60	4	3	1	0	0	0	5	0	11	2	0
Maxcy, Brian, N.O.	0	0	.000	12.38	4	1	0	0	3	0	8.0	12	39	11	11	2	1	0	1	2	0	6	0	0
McCarthy, Greg, Tac.*	0	1	.000	2.05	18	0	0	0	6	0	22.0	18	94	6	5	0	0	1	2	13	1	14	3	0
McCurry, Jeff, N.O.	0	7	.000	4.15	40	0	0	0	37	14	43.1	48	197	23	20	3	4	2	3	14	5	26	3	0
McDill, Allen, Okla.*	1	3	.250	3.72	42	0	0	0	35	18	48.1	45	207	22	20	6	1	1	2	17	0	46	4	0
McDowell, Jack, Edm.	1	0	1.000	5.73	2	2	0	0	0	0	11.0	12	47	7	7	1	1	0	0	3	0	2	0	0
McMullen, Mike, Fres.	2	2	.500	4.36	41	0	0	0	13	0	66.0	52	290	36	32	5	1	1	10	41	2	56	4	2
McNichol, Brian, Iowa*	10	11	.476	5.58	28	28	2	1	0	0	161.1	194	720	108	100	21	7	2	7	55	0	120	6	0
Meacham, Rusty, N.O.	3	4	.429	4.94	17	5	0	0	7	1	47.1	56	205	26	26	6	1	2	1	9	0	47	1	1
Meche, Gil, Tac.	2	2	.500	3.19	6	6	0	0	0	0	31.0	31	135	12	11	3	0	2	1	13	0	24	2	0
Medina, Rafael, Cal.	1	2	.333	3.34	25	0	0	0	9	1	35.0	29	153	15	13	1	1	0	2	21	0	34	3	0
Menhart, Paul, Edm.-Cal.	5	5	.500	5.89	17	17	0	0	0	0	81.0	106	375	60	53	10	1	3	1	37	1	51	2	0
Mercedes, Jose, L.V.-Cal.	3	8	.273	4.03	19	18	0	0	0	0	114.0	140	508	70	51	16	6	2	2	23	0	70	1	1
Michalak, Chris, Edm.-Tuc.*	6	0	1.000	4.29	45	6	0	0	14	3	92.1	92	400	50	44	9	2	4	7	40	2	66	2	1
Milacki, Bob, Nash.	6	8	.429	4.86	22	20	0	0	0	0	111.0	130	510	82	60	14	12	4	4	43	5	79	10	0
Miller, Kurt, Iowa	1	2	.333	5.09	8	2	0	0	2	1	17.2	17	77	10	10	3	0	1	0	8	0	23	2	0
Miller, Travis, S.L.*	1	2	.333	2.50	16	0	0	0	9	1	18.0	16	75	7	5	1	0	0	6	0	19	2	0	0
Miller, Wade, N.O.	11	9	.550	4.38	26	26	2	0	0	0	162.1	156	704	85	79	16	6	2	4	64	0	135	10	1
Mintz, Steve, Edm.	4	3	.571	2.35	31	0	0	0	27	9	30.2	31	127	11	8	2	0	1	2	6	0	17	2	0
Mitchell, Dean, Alb.	2	1	.667	7.36	31	0	0	0	15	0	47.2	61	232	41	39	9	1	3	1	28	2	42	6	0
Mlicki, Doug, Mem.	3	1	.750	5.78	38	0	0	0	12	0	67.0	78	299	48	43	16	1	1	1	26	2	26	6	0
Mohler, Mike, Mem.*	2	1	.667	3.07	10	0	0	0	2	1	14.2	16	64	5	5	0	0	0	5	1	17	0	0	0
Montgomery, Jeff, Oma.	0	0	.000	0.00	4	0	0	0	4	1	5.0	1	17	0	0	0	0	0	1	0	3	0	0	0
Montoya, Norm, Edm.*	4	1	.800	5.61	38	3	0	0	14	0	67.1	92	296	49	42	5	3	3	17	2	30	2	0	0
Moody, Eric, Okla.	7	4	.636	3.42	39	1	0	0	20	4	73.2	78	309	33	28	5	3	3	4	13	3	31	3	0
Moreno, Orber, Oma.	3	1	.750	2.10	16	0	0	0	15	0	25.2	17	97	6	6	2	0	0	4	0	30	0	0	0
Morman, Alvin, Oma.*	0	0	.000	3.14	8	1	0	0	3	1	14.1	8	51	5	5	3	1	0	1	0	15	0	0	0
Morse, Paul, Edm.	1	5	.167	7.11	10	9	0	0	1	0	49.1	64	232	44	39	10	1	1	1	34	0	30	6	1
Mounce, Tony, N.O.*	0	1	.000	2.45	14	0	0	0	2	0	11.0	10	55	3	3	0	1	0	0	13	0	10	2	0
Mulder, Mark, Van.*	6	7	.462	4.06	22	22	1	0	0	0	128.2	152	549	69	58	13	4	5	3	31	0	81	6	0
Mullen, Scott, Oma.*	6	7	.462	6.26	20	20	0	0	0	0	119.1	150	543	91	83	24	4	6	2	53	2	87	7	1
Murray, Heath, L.V.*	5	4	.556	4.26	15	15	1	1	0	0	82.1	99	366	45	39	5	1	3	2	32	0	65	4	0
Myers, Rodney, Iowa	2	4	.333	4.06	20	1	0	0	14	2	31.0	29	131	18	14	3	2	1	0	11	3	24	0	0
Nathan, Joe, Fres.	6	4	.600	4.46	13	13	1	0	0	0	74.2	68	324	44	37	11	3	1	5	36	0	82	6	1
Nomo, Hideo, Iowa	1	1	.500	3.71	3	3	0	0	0	0	17.0	12	72	7	7	1	0	0	0	12	0	18	3	0
Norton, Phillip, Iowa*	5	6	.455	6.67	14	14	0	0	0	0	79.2	98	361	63	59	20	0	2	5	33	0	61	3	1
Nunez, Vladimir, Tuc.	1	0	1.000	6.75	3	0	0	0	0	0	2.2	5	11	2	2	0	0	0	0	0	0	3	0	0
Nussbeck, Mark, Mem.	6	10	.375	8.23	36	16	0	0	6	0	101.2	145	481	100	93	23	7	4	3	37	1	82	5	1
Ohme, Kevin, S.L.*	5	3	.625	3.83	51	3	0	0	15	2	82.1	94	368	44	35	8	1	6	8	31	2	48	4	1
Ojala, Kirt, Cal.*	3	8	.273	7.21	16	14	1	0	0	0	78.2	110	381	70	63	12	4	5	2	44	0	54	6	0
Opipari, Mario, Mem.	0	0	.000	10.13	3	0	0	0	0	0	2.2	2	11	3	3	0	0	0	0	3	0	0	1	0
Oquist, Mike, Van.	0	1	.000	0.00	1	1	0	0	0	0	6.0	2	22	0	0	0	0	0	0	1	0	2	1	0
Oropesa, Eddie, Fres.*	6	5	.545	4.85	21	18	1	0	0	0	102.0	113	460	69	55	15	3	1	3	49	0	61	13	4
Ortiz, Ramon, Edm.	5	3	.625	4.05	9	9	0	0	0	0	53.1	46	224	26	24	7	0	0	2	19	0	64	6	2

Pitcher, Team	W	L	Pct.	ERA	G	GS	CG	ShO	GF	Sv.	IP	H	TBF	R	ER	HR	SH	SF	HB	BB	IBB	SO	WP	Bk.
Osteen, Gavin, Alb.*	6	8	.429	5.12	34	12	0	0	10	2	103.2	127	464	64	59	10	2	1	6	33	4	65	3	0
Padilla, Vicente, Tuc.	7	4	.636	3.75	18	14	0	0	0	0	93.2	107	405	47	39	6	5	2	7	24	7	58	0	1
Patrick, Bronswell, Fres.	14	11	.560	4.88	28	28	1	0	0	0	164.0	194	719	116	89	33	5	5	3	42	0	142	2	1
Patterson, Danny, Okla.*	1	0	1.000	0.00	2	0	0	0	1	0	3.0	1	11	0	0	0	0	0	1	0	4	0	0
Patterson, John, Tuc.	1	5	.167	7.04	7	6	0	0	0	0	30.2	43	148	26	24	3	0	0	0	18	0	29	0	0
Perez, Carlos, Alb.*	3	3	.500	5.92	6	6	2	0	0	0	38.0	46	168	28	25	6	2	1	3	10	0	14	0	1
Perez, Dario, Cal.	7	13	.350	5.73	28	21	0	0	2	0	132.0	150	563	94	84	22	7	3	7	31	0	66	3	0
Perez, Juan, Van.*	0	4	.000	6.96	20	1	0	0	7	0	32.1	42	151	25	25	3	2	2	2	15	3	22	3	0
Perisho, Matt, Okla.*	15	7	.682	4.61	27	27	2	0	0	0	156.1	160	681	86	80	14	2	5	3	78	1	150	6	0
Perkins, Dan, S.L.	0	0	.000	4.26	3	2	0	0	0	0	12.2	11	57	6	6	3	0	0	2	4	0	7	3	0
Peters, Chris, Nash.*	3	1	.750	2.19	11	9	0	0	1	1	49.1	54	214	18	12	1	0	0	1	15	1	34	3	0
Peters, Don, Tuc.	0	1	.000	3.86	3	0	0	0	2	0	4.2	1	17	2	2	0	1	1	1	2	0	2	0	0
Phillips, J.R., C.S.*	0	0	.000	0.00	2	0	0	0	2	0	3.1	2	12	0	0	0	0	0	0	0	0	1	0	0
Phillips, Jason, Nash.	0	0	.000	15.00	1	1	0	0	0	0	3.0	6	19	6	5	0	0	0	0	5	1	5	1	0
Pickett, Ricky, Okla.*	3	4	.429	8.13	29	3	0	0	11	2	55.1	77	281	53	50	12	2	3	2	43	0	55	4	0
Pisciotta, Marc, Oma.	0	1	.000	11.20	10	0	0	0	5	0	13.2	18	67	18	17	3	0	2	1	11	1	8	2	0
Porzio, Mike, C.S.*	5	1	.833	3.38	35	0	0	0	6	0	42.2	44	198	16	16	5	3	0	3	30	4	33	4	1
Pote, Lou, Edm.	7	9	.438	4.50	24	23	3	0	1	0	150.0	171	637	80	75	19	2	2	4	41	0	118	6	0
Powell, Brian, N.O.	4	4	.500	6.19	9	9	0	0	0	0	48.0	54	214	39	33	5	3	0	0	21	0	36	5	1
Quevedo, Ruben, Iowa	3	1	.750	3.45	7	7	1	1	0	0	44.1	34	185	18	17	1	2	3	0	21	0	50	0	0
Radlosky, Rob, S.L.	8	4	.667	3.91	22	20	1	0	1	0	101.1	98	440	49	44	12	2	4	6	38	1	68	2	0
Raggio, Brady, Okla.	6	11	.353	5.14	30	24	4	2	4	1	168.0	193	732	100	96	16	3	8	7	49	1	114	8	0
Rain, Steve, Iowa	0	1	.000	2.00	8	0	0	0	7	2	9.0	7	38	2	2	1	0	0	0	4	0	8	0	0
Ramirez, Roberto, C.S.*	3	2	.600	3.50	10	10	0	0	0	0	61.2	64	258	26	24	6	1	1	2	17	1	55	0	1
Ramsay, Robert, Tac.*	4	1	.800	1.08	5	5	0	0	0	0	33.1	20	130	6	4	2	0	1	0	14	1	37	1	0
Randall, Scott, C.S.	1	4	.200	7.93	9	9	0	0	0	0	42.0	62	205	41	37	5	3	1	1	22	1	25	5	1
Randolph, Steve, Tuc.*	0	7	.000	6.91	11	10	1	0	0	0	41.2	47	204	37	32	7	1	2	2	32	1	26	1	0
Rath, Fred, S.L.	7	5	.583	3.92	56	0	0	0	18	3	82.2	88	350	41	36	9	3	5	6	24	0	36	6	0
Rath, Gary, S.L.*	3	8	.273	5.62	20	18	1	0	1	0	99.1	129	454	76	62	12	7	7	1	27	1	67	7	0
Ray, Ken, Oma.	1	0	1.000	5.19	27	0	0	0	23	8	43.1	41	184	27	25	9	1	2	1	12	1	36	3	0
Redman, Mark, S.L.*	9	9	.500	5.05	24	24	1	0	0	0	133.2	141	583	87	75	12	5	4	4	51	1	114	3	0
Reichert, Dan, Oma.	9	2	.818	3.71	17	17	1	0	0	0	111.2	92	464	51	46	9	2	2	6	50	0	123	9	0
Rigby, Brad, Van.	0	1	.000	1.93	1	1	0	0	0	0	4.2	6	23	3	1	0	0	0	0	2	0	6	0	0
Rios, Dan, Oma.	10	4	.714	6.07	47	5	0	0	20	4	89.0	111	417	64	60	13	3	4	8	39	4	44	6	1
Ritchie, Todd, Nash.	0	0	.000	1.80	1	1	0	0	0	0	5.0	6	22	1	1	0	1	0	0	1	0	4	0	0
Rivera, Roberto, L.V.*	1	2	.333	10.16	20	3	0	0	7	0	33.2	61	175	39	38	6	2	3	3	14	0	25	2	0
Robertson, Rich, Okla.-Nash.*	2	4	.333	7.94	10	9	1	0	0	0	34.0	46	172	32	30	3	3	2	4	23	1	33	4	0
Rodriguez, Frank, S.L.	3	4	.429	6.70	9	9	1	0	0	0	43.0	40	191	34	32	8	1	2	6	14	0	33	2	0
Romero, J.C., S.L.*	4	1	.800	3.20	15	0	0	0	7	1	19.2	18	89	11	7	1	1	1	1	14	0	20	3	0
Rooney, Mike, Tuc.	0	0	.000	0.00	1	0	0	0	0	0	0.0	2	4	3	1	1	0	0	0	2	0	0	0	0
Rossiter, Mike, C.S.	2	0	1.000	3.89	24	0	0	0	5	0	37.0	37	166	16	16	3	2	2	5	20	0	31	3	0
Rossy, Rico, L.V.	0	0	.000	18.00	1	0	0	0	1	0	2.0	5	11	4	4	0	0	1	0	1	0	0	0	0
Ruebel, Matt, Tuc.*	1	3	.250	7.00	6	2	0	0	0	0	27.0	32	120	26	21	6	0	2	1	10	0	19	2	0
Ruffcorn, Scott, Oma.	1	0	1.000	5.02	8	0	0	0	1	0	14.1	14	63	10	8	4	0	1	0	10	0	8	1	0
Ruffin, Johnny, Alb.	1	1	.500	3.17	46	0	0	0	28	10	54.0	41	222	21	19	7	3	2	0	26	0	66	5	0
Rusch, Glendon, Oma.*	4	7	.364	4.42	20	20	1	0	0	0	114.0	143	511	68	56	10	3	4	5	33	0	102	3	0
Ryan, Jason, S.L.	4	4	.500	5.13	9	9	0	0	0	0	54.1	57	240	36	31	8	1	3	1	24	1	34	0	0
Ryan, Ken, Nash.	1	1	.500	3.86	6	0	0	0	2	0	7.0	7	33	3	3	1	1	0	1	8	1	9	1	0
Ryan, Matt, Nash.	6	5	.545	4.42	48	6	0	0	20	8	79.1	87	357	48	39	7	1	2	6	35	1	52	2	0
Sabel, Erik, Tuc.	5	2	.714	3.34	22	9	0	0	8	2	72.2	79	306	36	27	4	5	1	1	24	4	38	3	0
Saier, Matt, Oma.	4	4	.500	5.09	9	9	1	0	0	0	58.1	69	255	37	33	13	0	1	1	8	0	44	1	0
Saipe, Mike, C.S.	1	5	.167	4.83	11	11	0	0	0	0	54.0	62	232	36	29	11	0	4	1	20	0	39	3	0
Sak, Jim, L.V.	2	2	.500	3.58	23	0	0	0	17	6	27.2	22	121	11	11	5	0	3	1	17	0	32	2	0
Salkeld, Roger, Cal.	1	1	.500	4.63	27	2	0	0	10	1	35.0	37	159	21	18	5	0	3	2	20	1	32	4	0
Sampson, Benj, S.L.*	1	1	.500	8.04	3	3	0	0	0	0	15.2	25	72	16	14	3	0	2	1	1	0	7	1	0
Sanchez, Jesus, Cal.*	0	0	.000	5.79	4	1	0	0	2	1	9.1	8	40	6	6	0	0	2	5	0	14	1	0
Santiago, Jose, Oma.	0	0	.000	0.00	1	0	0	0	0	0	1.2	3	7	0	0	0	0	0	0	0	0	0	0	0
Sauveur, Rich, Nash.*	5	2	.714	1.95	53	3	0	0	18	7	64.2	62	272	21	14	6	1	0	0	16	5	61	1	0
Scanlan, Bob, N.O.	8	15	.348	5.61	28	28	2	0	0	0	163.2	208	748	116	102	12	6	10	12	55	0	78	11	2
Scheffer, Aaron, Tac.	2	3	.400	2.87	35	1	0	0	16	9	59.2	47	248	25	19	6	3	0	4	23	2	62	3	0
Schoeneweis, Scott, Edm.*	2	4	.333	7.64	9	7	0	0	0	0	35.1	58	177	35	30	6	0	1	3	12	0	29	4	0
Scott, Tim, Nash.	1	3	.250	5.09	19	0	0	0	7	0	23.0	29	105	14	13	3	0	2	7	1	21	0	0
Seifert, Ryan, C.S.	0	0	.000	4.50	1	1	0	0	0	0	4.0	4	18	2	2	1	0	0	2	0	2	0	0
Serafini, Dan, Iowa*	0	0	.000	2.77	2	2	0	0	0	0	13.0	12	56	6	4	1	1	0	0	5	0	11	0	0
Shoemaker, Stephen, C.S.	4	6	.400	6.00	16	16	0	0	0	0	81.0	100	382	59	54	8	1	5	47	1	46	8	0
Shouse, Brian, Tuc.*	3	4	.429	6.25	30	0	0	0	8	0	44.2	63	213	35	31	4	6	2	1	18	3	32	2	0
Sievert, Mark, Okla.	0	0	.000	10.32	7	0	0	0	5	0	11.1	17	57	13	13	4	0	1	8	0	5	1	0
Sikorski, Brian, N.O.	7	10	.412	4.95	28	27	1	0	0	0	158.1	169	699	92	87	25	8	1	9	58	1	122	6	2
Silva, Jose, Nash.	2	0	1.000	1.50	2	2	0	0	0	0	12.0	14	55	4	2	0	2	1	0	4	0	10	0	0
Sinclair, Steve, Tac.*	1	0	1.000	4.50	2	0	0	0	0	0	2.0	2	9	1	1	0	0	0	1	0	1	1	0
Skrmetta, Matt, L.V.	2	1	.667	3.45	20	0	0	0	11	1	28.2	20	117	13	11	4	0	1	1	11	0	25	2	0
Slocumb, Heathcliff, Mem.	0	0	.000	4.50	2	0	0	0	1	0	2.0	3	10	1	1	0	0	1	0	2	0	0	0
Slusarski, Joe, N.O.	1	4	.200	3.64	40	2	0	0	14	1	64.1	71	270	31	26	5	4	3	4	13	1	40	2	0
Smith, Chuck, Okla.	5	4	.556	2.96	32	4	2	0	13	4	85.0	73	341	28	28	7	1	3	1	28	0	76	5	0
Smith, Pete, Mem.-L.V.	6	8	.429	4.76	21	20	2	0	0	0	109.2	130	483	75	58	14	3	5	2	29	0	82	4	2
Snow, Bert, Van.	1	0	1.000	3.86	2	0	0	0	0	0	2.1	3	11	1	1	0	0	1	0	0	3	0	0
Soderstrom, Steve, Fres.	2	8	.200	6.78	22	13	0	0	3	0	71.2	90	355	64	54	16	4	4	8	35	0	58	8	0
Sodowsky, Clint, Mem.	4	5	.444	4.82	19	13	2	1	3	0	80.1	85	350	55	43	14	4	1	4	32	0	52	6	2
Sparks, Jeff, Nash.	5	3	.625	3.83	34	0	0	0	8	0	49.1	37	209	25	21	4	1	2	4	23	1	69	7	0
Spencer, Sean, Tac.*	2	1	.667	3.47	44	0	0	0	28	7	49.1	41	205	21	19	6	1	0	1	23	2	53	4	0
Spencer, Stan, L.V.	5	4	.556	5.47	12	10	0	0	0	0	54.1	69	247	35	33	8	4	2	2	15	0	50	1	0
Stanifer, Rob, Cal.	1	2	.333	12.38	16	0	0	0	8	0	16.0	32	87	23	22	7	1	1	4	6	0	15	0	0

Pitcher, Team	W	L	Pct.	ERA	G	GS	CG	ShO	GF	Sv.	IP	H	TBF	R	ER	HR	SH	SF	HB	BB	IBB	SO	WP	Bk.
Stechschulte, Gene, Mem.	0	0	.000	7.71	2	0	0	0	0	0	2.1	2	14	2	2	0	0	1	0	5	0	2	0	0
Steenstra, Kennie, Tac.	1	4	.200	5.57	13	10	0	0	1	0	51.2	60	231	40	32	5	1	7	3	15	0	24	1	0
Stein, Blake, Van.	4	2	.667	4.10	19	19	0	0	0	0	109.2	94	451	54	50	9	1	4	0	43	0	111	7	1
Stentz, Brent, S.L.	0	3	.000	11.22	23	0	0	0	15	3	25.2	43	139	34	32	6	2	2	0	21	1	23	3	1
Stephenson, Garrett, Mem.	1	1	.500	3.16	4	4	0	0	0	0	25.2	22	102	9	9	2	0	0	1	7	0	19	0	0
Stevens, Dave, Tac.	1	1	.500	12.60	7	0	0	0	1	0	10.0	14	54	14	14	2	0	0	2	6	1	8	1	0
Stone, Ricky, Alb.	6	10	.375	5.50	27	27	2	0	0	0	167.0	205	764	123	102	23	8	7	8	71	4	132	11	1
Stoops, Jim, C.S.	3	7	.300	5.18	55	5	0	0	22	3	88.2	93	400	54	51	11	6	6	4	56	2	57	7	0
Sullivan, Brendan, L.V.	2	4	.333	7.60	45	0	0	0	14	0	66.1	88	332	60	56	6	3	5	12	38	3	50	2	0
Swartzbaugh, Dave, Tuc.	0	0	.000	6.23	13	0	0	0	5	0	21.2	27	105	16	15	4	1	1	1	14	0	20	2	0
Sweeney, Brian, Tac.	0	2	.000	6.75	5	1	0	0	2	0	16.0	26	75	17	12	5	2	0	0	2	0	10	1	0
Tavarez, Julian, Fres.	0	0	.000	2.25	4	1	0	0	1	0	8.0	3	30	2	2	1	0	0	1	3	0	9	0	0
Tejera, Michael, Cal.*	0	0	.000	12.00	2	2	0	0	0	0	9.0	19	49	14	12	2	1	1	1	4	0	5	1	0
Telemaco, Amaury, Tuc.	0	3	.000	5.09	13	12	0	0	0	0	17.2	21	79	11	10	1	1	3	6	0	17	0	0
Thompson, Mark, Mem.	4	2	.667	2.94	9	8	0	0	0	0	52.0	50	225	22	17	3	4	3	0	20	0	27	1	0
Thomson, John, C.S.	0	2	.000	9.45	5	5	1	0	0	0	20.0	36	98	25	21	3	2	1	0	8	0	19	1	1
Tollberg, Brian, L.V.	1	2	.333	4.85	5	5	0	0	0	0	29.2	34	123	17	16	3	1	0	2	6	0	23	1	0
Troutman, Keith, Edm.	1	0	1.000	3.54	6	3	0	0	1	0	20.1	23	88	12	8	4	0	1	3	2	0	22	2	0
Tuttle, Dave, Tuc.	2	5	.286	6.51	35	9	0	0	11	0	84.1	100	385	62	61	8	3	6	4	48	2	55	4	1
Van Poppel, Todd, Nash.	10	6	.625	4.95	27	27	2	0	0	0	163.2	173	716	95	90	23	7	4	5	62	1	157	5	1
Vasquez, Leo, Van.*	0	0	.000	5.40	1	0	0	0	0	0	1.2	2	8	1	1	0	0	0	0	2	0	0	0	0
Venafro, Mike, Okla.*	0	0	.000	5.40	6	0	0	0	3	1	11.2	16	46	7	7	2	0	0	0	2	0	11	0	0
Veras, Dario, Oma.	1	2	.333	4.35	11	0	0	0	3	0	20.2	19	81	10	10	5	1	0	1	3	0	17	0	0
Verdugo, Jason, Fres.	1	0	1.000	4.87	9	2	0	0	2	0	20.1	19	89	14	11	5	0	0	0	9	0	29	1	0
Verplancke, Joe, Tuc.	0	0	.000	0.00	2	0	0	0	0	0	2.1	1	9	0	0	0	1	0	0	0	0	4	0	0
Villano, Mike, Cal.	1	5	.167	6.21	36	1	0	0	11	2	58.0	87	273	43	40	18	1	0	5	17	0	48	7	1
Vizcaino, Luis, Van.	0	1	.000	1.38	7	0	0	0	3	0	13.0	13	56	4	2	0	0	0	0	6	0	7	1	0
Vosberg, Ed, L.V.-Tuc.*	1	0	1.000	0.84	34	0	0	0	17	8	43.0	29	158	6	4	1	1	0	0	12	1	42	2	0
Wainhouse, David, C.S.	1	3	.250	3.19	38	0	0	0	35	22	42.1	42	175	19	15	6	1	0	2	7	1	42	0	0
Walker, Jamie, Oma.*	0	1	.000	4.67	4	0	0	0	0	0	17.1	22	79	12	9	1	1	2	2	4	0	11	0	0
Walker, Pete, C.S.	8	4	.667	4.48	48	0	0	0	23	5	62.1	64	273	37	31	9	2	2	2	28	3	57	2	1
Wallace, Jeff, Nash.*	2	2	.500	8.79	15	0	0	0	7	3	14.1	18	68	15	14	3	1	0	2	8	1	14	1	0
Wallace, Kent, N.O.	2	2	.500	4.14	36	1	0	0	11	1	58.2	61	248	30	27	9	1	2	1	13	3	43	1	0
Ward, Jeremy, Tuc.	0	0	.000	0.00	1	0	0	0	0	0	1.2	2	8	0	0	0	0	0	0	2	0	1	0	0
Warner, Ron, Mem.	0	0	.000	0.00	2	0	0	0	0	0	1.1	2	8	0	0	0	0	1	0	1	0	1	0	0
Washburn, Jarrod, Edm.*	1	1	.500	4.73	11	11	1	0	0	0	59.0	50	243	31	31	6	2	1	1	17	0	55	1	0
Watkins, Scott, Iowa*	1	2	.333	6.14	47	3	0	0	10	0	63.0	71	287	47	43	11	3	3	2	33	1	54	7	0
Weaver, Eric, Tac.	1	2	.333	3.86	16	3	0	0	5	1	25.2	22	105	11	11	4	0	1	1	7	0	22	1	0
Weber, Ben, Fres.	2	4	.333	3.34	51	0	0	0	19	8	86.1	78	358	34	32	6	3	3	5	28	2	67	9	0
Weber, Neil, Tuc.-Alb.*	1	2	.333	10.43	18	0	0	0	7	0	29.1	53	152	35	34	8	2	1	2	13	1	30	3	0
Weibl, Clint, Mem.	1	0	1.000	5.40	5	0	0	0	1	0	8.1	10	36	9	5	2	1	1	0	2	0	8	0	0
Wengert, Don, Oma.	4	1	.800	4.17	16	2	0	0	7	1	41.0	41	167	20	19	5	2	1	4	9	1	24	1	1
West, David, Alb.*	0	1	.000	6.43	2	1	0	0	1	0	7.0	9	29	5	5	1	0	1	0	0	0	7	1	0
Whiteside, Matt, L.V.	9	5	.643	5.12	44	3	0	0	23	7	89.2	99	398	59	51	13	1	4	3	29	3	88	2	0
Wilkins, Marc, Nash.	1	1	.500	0.79	8	0	0	0	6	3	11.1	9	45	3	1	0	0	2	0	3	1	8	0	0
Williams, Eddie, S.L.	0	1	.000	10.13	2	0	0	0	1	0	2.2	5	15	3	3	1	0	0	2	0	0	0	0	0
Williams, Jeff, Alb.*	9	7	.563	5.01	42	14	1	1	10	4	125.2	151	558	77	70	14	4	8	9	47	2	86	3	0
Williams, Shad, Edm.	5	3	.625	3.72	16	11	1	0	1	0	75.0	73	303	36	31	9	1	3	1	19	0	35	2	0
Williams, Todd, Tac.	0	0	.000	0.00	1	0	0	0	1	0	1.2	1	5	0	0	0	0	0	0	0	0	0	0	0
Wilson, Desi, Tuc.*	0	0	.000	0.00	1	0	0	0	1	0	1.0	0	3	0	0	0	0	0	0	1	0	0	0	0
Wilson, Kris, Oma.	0	1	.000	8.44	1	1	0	0	0	0	5.1	8	23	5	5	3	0	0	0	0	0	6	0	0
Wolff, Bryan, L.V.	8	12	.400	4.66	28	27	2	0	0	0	177.2	199	770	99	92	22	10	6	8	57	0	151	8	1
Woodall, Brad, Iowa*	2	2	.500	6.84	15	9	0	0	2	1	52.2	67	245	40	40	9	4	2	0	23	1	41	4	0
Wright, Jamey, C.S.	5	7	.417	6.46	17	16	2	0	1	0	100.1	133	463	87	72	13	1	4	10	38	2	75	9	0
Zimmerman, Jeff, Okla.	1	0	1.000	0.00	2	0	0	0	2	1	3.2	0	10	0	0	0	0	0	0	0	0	2	0	0
Zimmerman, Jordan, Tac.*	0	0	.000	5.14	9	0	0	0	2	0	7.0	13	35	4	4	1	0	0	4	1	0	4	1	0
Zito, Barry, Van.*	1	0	1.000	1.50	1	1	0	0	0	0	6.0	6	24	1	1	0	0	0	0	2	0	6	2	0

COMBINATION SHUTOUTS: **Albuquerque (4)**—Stine-Arnold-Croghan, Judd-Osteen-Jordan-Croghan, Checo-Croghan-Kubenka, Checo-Osteen-Kubenka. **Calgary (0)**—None. **Colorado Springs (1)**—Bost-Porzio-Walker. **Edmonton (4)**—Pote-Borland-Jacobsen, Ortiz-Alvarez-Edsell-Holtz, Williams-Alvarez, Cooper-James-Mintz. **Fresno (2)**—Oropesa-Connelly, Fultz-Connelly. **Iowa (1)**—Lorraine-Barker. **Las Vegas (4)**—Dennis-Whiteside-Cunnane, Wolff-Rivera-Cunnane, Carlyle-Almanzar, Smith-Dennis. **Memphis (4)**—Barnes-Mohler, Ankiel-Mohler-Lovingier, Ankiel-Barnes, Thompson-King. **Nashville (1)**—Milacki-Clontz. **New Orleans (5)**—Miller-Diorio, Miller-Cabrera, Creek-Meachem, Sikorski-Slusarski-McCurry, Miller-Slusarski-McCurry. **Oklahoma (2)**—Perisho-Smith-McDill, Knight-Frey. **Omaha (3)**—Fussell-Byrdak, Rusch-Ray, Rusch-Rios-Pisciotta. **Salt Lake (2)**—Bell-Miller-Rath, Radlosky-Ohme-Gandarillas-Romero-Fiore. **Tacoma (4)**—Marte-Carmona-Weaver, Ramsay-Carmona, Weaver-Hodges-Carmona, Ramsay-Marte-Carmona. **Tucson (5)**—Figueroa-Carlson-Batchelor, Kim-Boyd, Padilla-Tuttle-Eischen, Carlson-Vosberg, Figueroa-Sabel. **Vancouver (9)**—Clark-King-Chavez, Mulder-Dale-Kubinski-Chavez, Laxton-Mahay-Chavez, Hudson-Mahay-Perez, Stein-Lawrence-Chavez, Laxton-Lawrence, Jarvis-Kubinski-Chavez, Laxton-Dale, Jarvis-Chavez.

NO-HIT GAMES: Frank Rodriguez, Salt Lake, defeated Iowa, 2-1, May 8; Clark-King-Chavez, Vancouver, defeated New Orleans, 3-0, April 13.

PITCHERS WITH TWO OR MORE TEAMS

Pitcher, Team	W	L	Pct.	ERA	G	GS	CG	ShO	GF	Sv.	IP	H	TBF	R	ER	HR	SH	SF	HB	BB	IBB	SO	WP	Bk.
Boyd, Jason, Tuc.	6	5	.545	4.52	44	0	0	0	17	5	75.2	76	325	42	38	6	2	4	3	27	2	60	6	2
Boyd, Jason, Nash.	0	0	.000	0.00	3	0	0	0	2	0	4.2	2	14	0	0	0	0	0	0	0	0	2	0	0
D'Amico, Jeff, Tuc.	2	2	.500	2.65	14	0	0	0	11	3	17.0	16	75	6	5	1	1	0	0	10	1	10	2	0
D'Amico, Jeff, Oma.	3	9	.250	4.34	12	0	0	0	10	2	18.2	29	88	13	9	1	0	0	3	0	12	3	1
De La Rosa, Maximo, Tac.	0	2	.000	6.14	15	0	0	0	5	1	22.0	34	112	18	15	3	0	2	3	10	1	24	2	0
De La Rosa, Maximo, C.S.	0	1	.000	2.45	8	0	0	0	2	0	11.0	12	48	3	3	1	1	0	2	4	1	5	2	0
Grilli, Jason, Fres.	7	5	.583	5.54	19	19	1	0	0	0	100.2	124	461	69	62	22	2	3	6	39	0	76	3	0
Grilli, Jason, Cal.	1	5	.167	7.68	8	8	0	0	0	0	41.0	56	205	48	35	7	2	1	2	23	0	27	5	1
Hanson, Erik, Cal.	1	6	.143	7.55	10	9	0	0	0	0	47.2	68	229	43	40	4	3	1	2	26	0	42	1	0
Hanson, Erik, Oma.	4	3	.571	4.60	14	10	0	0	3	0	60.2	58	255	32	31	11	3	2	3	22	0	43	5	1
Hodges, Kevin, N.O.	1	3	.250	7.24	5	5	0	0	0	0	27.1	34	126	23	22	6	0	2	1	11	1	16	0	0
Hodges, Kevin, Tac.	3	3	.500	3.25	14	12	0	0	1	0	83.0	88	358	31	30	3	1	9	27	1	42	3	0

Pitcher, Team	W	L	Pct.	ERA	G	GS	CG	ShO	GF	Sv.	IP	H	TBF	R	ER	HR	SH	SF	HB	BB	IBB	SO	WP	Bk.
Menhart, Paul, Edm.	3	3	.500	6.80	9	9	0	0	0	0	42.1	58	190	34	32	10	1	0	1	14	1	21	0	0
Menhart, Paul, Cal.	2	2	.500	4.89	8	8	0	0	0	0	38.2	48	185	26	21	0	0	3	0	23	0	30	2	0
Mercedes, Jose, L.V.	2	6	.250	4.30	15	14	0	0	0	0	88.0	110	396	57	42	14	5	2	2	20	0	57	1	1
Mercedes, Jose, Cal.	1	2	.333	3.12	4	4	0	0	0	0	26.0	30	112	13	9	2	1	0	0	3	0	13	0	0
Michalak, Chris, Edm.*	1	0	1.000	5.72	24	0	0	0	7	0	28.1	28	125	20	18	3	0	2	1	14	0	25	1	0
Michalak, Chris, Tuc.*	5	0	1.000	3.66	21	6	0	0	7	3	64.0	64	275	30	26	6	2	2	6	26	2	41	1	1
Robertson, Rich, Okla.*	0	1	.000	7.71	3	0	0	0	0	0	4.2	7	24	5	4	0	0	1	0	3	0	4	0	0
Robertson, Rich, Nash.*	2	3	.400	7.98	7	6	0	0	0	0	29.1	39	148	27	26	3	3	1	4	20	1	29	4	0
Smith, Pete, Mem.	2	3	.400	6.87	8	8	0	0	0	0	38.0	53	182	35	29	7	1	3	1	16	0	35	1	1
Smith, Pete, L.V.	4	5	.444	3.64	13	12	2	0	1	0	71.2	77	301	40	29	7	2	2	1	13	0	47	3	1
Vosberg, Ed, L.V.*	0	0	.000	1.08	8	0	0	0	1	1	8.1	3	31	1	1	1	0	0	0	4	0	12	0	0
Vosberg, Ed, Tuc.*	1	0	1.000	0.78	26	0	0	0	16	7	34.2	26	127	5	3	0	1	0	8	1	0	30	2	0
Weber, Neil, Tuc.*	1	1	.500	10.66	9	0	0	0	3	0	12.2	23	65	16	15	2	0	0	1	4	1	16	0	0
Weber, Neil, Alb.*	0	1	.000	10.26	9	0	0	0	0	0	16.2	30	87	19	19	6	2	1	0	9	0	14	3	0

1999 FIELDING
TEAM

Team	Pct.	G	PO	A	E	TC	DP	TP	PB	Team	Pct.	G	PO	A	E	TC	DP	TP	PB
Oklahoma	.978	142	3701	1549	119	5369	169	0	11	Calgary	.972	139	3513	1452	144	5109	155	0	18
Memphis	.976	138	3586	1501	126	5213	142	0	7	Colo. Springs	.972	139	3580	1504	148	5232	166	0	16
Edmonton	.976	139	3640	1471	127	5238	139	0	14	New Orleans	.971	140	3629	1503	151	5283	109	0	10
Iowa	.976	141	3727	1540	131	5398	118	1	26	Omaha	.971	141	3678	1331	148	5157	132	0	16
Tacoma	.974	139	3695	1384	134	5213	131	0	11	Salt Lake	.971	141	3611	1548	156	5315	129	0	8
Vancouver	.974	142	3687	1434	137	5258	164	0	10	Tucson	.970	140	3667	1493	157	5317	142	0	12
Las Vegas	.974	142	3692	1396	138	5226	136	0	9	Nashville	.970	140	3648	1498	160	5306	128	0	12
Albuquerque	.973	139	3618	1469	141	5228	148	0	9	Fresno	.969	142	3690	1443	163	5296	118	0	19

INDIVIDUAL

FIRST BASEMEN

NOTE: All caps denotes fielding-percentage leader based on 71 games for catchers, 95 for all other non-pitchers and 114 innings for pitchers. *Throws lefthanded.

Player, Team	Pct.	G	PO	A	E	TC	DP
Allen, Dusty, L.V.	.985	69	507	35	8	550	58
Anthony, Eric, Alb.*	1.000	1	2	0	0	2	0
Ardoin, Danny, Van.	.975	6	35	4	1	40	8
Ball, Jeff, Van.	.989	24	172	12	2	186	20
BARKETT, Andy, Okla.*	.995	122	1003	87	6	1096	125
Belk, Tim, Mem.	.986	10	71	2	1	74	7
Berkman, Lance, N.O.*	1.000	4	29	1	0	30	1
Betzsold, James, N.O.	.992	15	119	7	1	127	11
Blowers, Mike, Tac.	1.000	3	21	0	0	21	3
Brumbaugh, Cliff, Okla.	1.000	1	3	2	0	5	0
Buhner, Shawn, Tac.	.994	20	143	13	1	157	16
Burke, Jamie, Edm.	1.000	3	25	0	0	25	1
Byington, Jimmie, Oma.	.000	1	0	0	0	0	0
Candaele, Casey, N.O.	1.000	1	1	0	0	1	0
Chamberlain, Wes, Alb.	.989	66	431	36	5	472	52
Charles, Frank, L.V.	.988	22	153	12	2	167	15
Chavez, Raul, Tac.	.000	1	0	0	0	0	0
Clark, Dave, Alb.	.976	7	41	0	1	42	5
Coolbaugh, Scott, Tuc.	.990	16	93	8	1	102	9
Cotton, John, C.S.	1.000	2	5	0	0	5	2
Crespo, Felipe, Fres.	.993	70	560	47	4	611	61
Cromer, Tripp, Alb.	1.000	1	8	1	0	9	1
Cruz, Ivan, Nash.*	.993	65	571	37	4	612	51
Decker, Steve, Edm.	.993	14	126	8	1	135	12
Dishington, Nate, Mem.	1.000	11	73	4	0	77	7
Durazo, Erubiel, Tuc.*	.996	29	241	20	1	262	31
Evans, Tom, Okla.	1.000	1	1	0	0	1	0
Fasano, Sal, Oma.	1.000	1	6	1	0	7	0
Foster, Jim, Edm.	1.000	3	7	0	0	7	2
Freeman, Ricky, Van.	.981	49	394	20	8	422	42
Garcia, Carlos, L.V.	.983	38	256	26	5	287	27
Giambi, Jeremy, Oma.*	.983	15	111	8	2	121	10
Gibralter, Steve, Oma.	.965	9	49	6	2	57	8
Gonzales, Rene, N.O.	.990	10	95	5	1	101	9
Gonzalez, Jimmy, L.V.	.667	1	2	0	1	3	0
Grijak, Kevin, Alb.	.991	28	208	13	2	223	25
Guzman, Edwards, Fres.	.935	4	27	2	2	31	3
Haas, Chris, Mem.	.996	31	256	15	1	272	30
Hatcher, Chris, C.S.	.957	13	82	7	4	93	12
Hemphill, Bret, Edm.	.975	6	36	3	1	40	4
Hernandez, Ramon, Van.	1.000	4	26	0	0	26	3
Hinske, Eric, Iowa	.947	2	17	1	1	19	1
Hubbard, Mike, Okla.	1.000	1	7	0	0	7	2
Huckaby, Ken, Tuc.	1.000	1	10	1	0	11	1
Hyers, Tim, Cal.*	1.000	17	126	7	0	133	18

Player, Team	Pct.	G	PO	A	E	TC	DP
Ibanez, Raul, Tac.	1.000	1	1	0	0	1	0
Jackson, Ryan, Tac.*	.990	91	704	55	8	767	76
Jennings, Robin, Iowa*	1.000	1	3	0	0	3	0
Johnson, Keith, Tuc.	1.000	3	17	3	0	20	1
Joyner, Wally, L.V.*	1.000	6	38	2	0	40	3
Kieschnick, Brooks, Edm.	.981	31	238	24	5	267	29
Knorr, Randy, N.O.	.939	6	41	5	3	49	5
Laker, Tim, Nash.	.972	15	65	5	2	72	5
Lee, Derrek, Cal.	.983	88	718	68	14	800	86
Lesher, Brian, Van.*	.993	63	543	35	4	582	64
Leyritz, Jim, L.V.	1.000	2	17	1	0	18	2
Livingstone, Scott, Alb.	.987	16	136	11	2	149	22
LoDuca, Paul, Alb.	1.000	2	15	4	0	19	3
Luuloa, Keith, Edm.	1.000	5	25	1	0	26	2
Marzano, John, Okla.	.000	1	0	0	0	0	0
Mayes, Craig, Fres.	1.000	2	11	2	0	13	3
McDonald, Keith, Mem.	1.000	1	12	2	0	14	0
Mendez, Carlos, Oma.	.991	44	319	12	3	334	32
Millar, Kevin, Cal.	1.000	5	21	0	0	21	2
Mirabelli, Doug, Fres.	.994	19	146	15	1	162	12
Mitchell, Mike, L.V.	.978	23	165	11	4	180	15
Montgomery, Ray, Nash.	.982	14	100	7	2	109	7
Morales, Willie, Van.	.971	4	33	0	1	34	7
Morman, Russ, Cal.	1.000	8	32	5	0	37	8
Neal, Mike, N.O.	.991	14	98	11	1	110	4
Nevin, Phil, L.V.	1.000	1	1	1	0	2	0
Ortiz, David, S.L.*	.980	111	896	77	20	993	98
Ortiz, Hector, Alb.	.973	18	99	9	3	111	11
Pellow, Kit, Oma.	1.000	2	15	1	0	16	1
Pennyfeather, William, Edm.	1.000	2	10	1	0	11	2
Perez, Eduardo, Mem.	.991	90	708	64	7	779	78
Phillips, J.R., C.S.*	.990	122	993	114	11	1118	131
Pledger, Kinnis, Tac.	.987	19	142	10	2	154	17
Pritchett, Chris, Edm.	.989	86	714	63	9	786	74
Quinlan, Tom, Iowa	.986	22	187	17	3	207	16
Richard, Chris, Mem.*	1.000	4	34	5	0	39	4
Richardson, Brian, S.L.	.971	8	30	3	1	34	3
Roberge, J.P., Oma.	.980	8	45	3	1	49	6
Robertson, Mike, Nash.*	.993	55	384	28	3	415	40
Robertson, Ryan, Cal.	1.000	1	4	0	0	4	0
Roskos, John, Cal.	1.000	31	218	14	0	232	28
Rupp, Chad, S.L.	.987	19	127	20	2	149	13
Russo, Paul, N.O.	.991	25	220	11	2	233	13
Saylor, Jamie, N.O.	.983	8	55	4	0	59	3
Sealy, Scot, Tac.	1.000	3	10	1	0	11	1
Secrist, Reed, Nash.	.921	7	34	1	3	38	6
Seitzer, Brad, Tac.	.986	6	65	6	1	72	3
Sheldon, Scott, Okla.	.978	12	82	7	2	91	11
Simms, Mike, Okla.	.969	5	29	2	1	32	2

Player, Team	Pct.	G	PO	A	E	TC	DP
Stahoviak, Scott, Iowa	.990	71	563	44	6	613	50
Steed, Dave, Alb.	1.000	10	68	4	0	72	5
Stefanski, Mike, Mem.	1.000	1	1	0	0	1	0
Strittmatter, Mark, C.S.	1.000	2	3	0	0	3	0
Sutton, Larry, Oma.*	.985	34	235	21	4	260	25
Sveum, Dale, Tuc.-Nash.	.957	12	62	4	3	69	13
Tatum, Jim, C.S.	1.000	4	41	6	0	47	6
Tavarez, Jesus, Fres.	1.000	1	14	1	0	15	0
Valdes, Pedro, Okla.*	1.000	11	107	6	0	113	8
Vitiello, Joe, Oma.	.981	43	289	21	6	316	34
Voigt, Jack, Fres.	.994	16	148	6	1	155	13
Walton, Jerome, Cal.	1.000	1	4	2	0	6	0
Ward, Daryle, N.O.*	.993	59	527	35	4	566	46
Warner, Ron, Mem.	.964	9	48	6	2	56	8
White, Derrick, Iowa	.991	48	388	33	4	425	25
Wilkins, Rick, Alb.	.962	19	118	10	5	133	9
Williams, Eddie, S.L.	1.000	16	116	10	0	126	9
Williams, George, N.O.	.974	9	69	6	2	77	4
Williams, Keith, Fres.	.964	11	74	6	3	83	2
Williams, Reggie, Edm.	1.000	2	9	1	0	10	1
Wilson, Desi, Tuc.*	.976	99	757	55	20	832	79
Woods, Ken, Fres.	.984	31	225	15	4	244	20
Zinter, Alan, Iowa	1.000	8	66	7	0	73	7

TRIPLE PLAYS: Ball, White.

FIRST BASEMEN WITH TWO OR MORE TEAMS

Player, Team	Pct.	G	PO	A	E	TC	DP
Sveum, Dale, Tuc.	.970	4	30	2	1	33	5
Sveum, Dale, Nash.	.944	8	32	2	2	36	8

SECOND BASEMEN

Player, Team	Pct.	G	PO	A	E	TC	DP
Akers, Chad, Tac.	.972	6	14	21	1	36	5
Almanzar, Richard, Iowa	.935	12	25	18	3	46	8
Ametller, Jesus, Mem.	1.000	1	1	1	0	2	1
Baerga, Carlos, L.V.	.944	2	5	12	1	18	4
Belliard, Francisco, Tuc.	1.000	2	4	6	0	10	1
Betten, Randy, Edm.	1.000	3	10	8	0	18	2
Bieser, Steve, Nash.-Mem.	1.000	5	8	9	0	17	2
Bournigal, Rafael, Okla.	1.000	7	14	30	0	44	5
Bridges, Kary, Iowa-Okla.	.991	34	44	64	1	109	20
Brown, Randy, Tac.	.961	28	64	59	5	128	20
Burke, Jamie, Edm.	1.000	1	2	2	0	4	0
Byington, Jimmie, Oma.	.950	14	16	22	2	40	4
Campusano, Carlos, Fres.	1.000	2	2	2	0	4	0
Candaele, Casey, N.O.	.976	76	124	202	8	334	41
Canizaro, Jay, Fres.	.969	99	181	263	14	458	59
Carr, Jeremy, Oma.	.875	7	5	9	2	16	2
Castro, Juan, Alb.	.986	16	28	40	1	69	8
Cedeno, Domingo, Tac.	1.000	5	14	9	0	23	3
Cey, Dan, S.L.	.967	115	235	319	19	573	76
Chavez, Raul, Tac.	.800	1	2	2	1	5	0
Clapinski, Chris, Cal.	.978	11	24	21	1	46	11
Clapp, Stubby, Mem.	.972	68	119	157	8	284	42
Cora, Alex, Alb.	1.000	1	1	1	0	2	0
Cotton, John, C.S.	1.000	13	19	40	0	59	11
Crespo, Felipe, Fres.	.886	9	14	17	4	35	2
Cromer, Tripp, Alb.	1.000	2	8	7	0	15	3
Delgado, Wilson, Fres.	1.000	1	1	0	0	1	0
Demetral, Chris, Okla.	.994	41	74	86	1	161	26
Diaz, Edwin, Tuc.	.982	58	111	165	5	281	44
Dransfeldt, Kelly, Okla.	1.000	8	11	18	0	29	6
Durango, Ariel, Tac.	1.000	1	0	1	0	1	0
Espada, Josue, Van.	.968	6	13	17	1	31	4
Ferguson, Jeff, S.L.	.969	35	66	88	5	159	20
Forbes, P.J., Okla.	.976	18	30	53	2	85	14
Frias, Hanley, Tuc.	1.000	5	12	9	0	21	3
Garcia, Amaury, Cal.	.971	119	227	308	16	551	90
Garcia, Carlos, L.V.	1.000	7	19	14	0	33	5
Gilbert, Shawn, Alb.	1.000	3	8	7	0	15	2
Giovanola, Ed, L.V.	1.000	3	8	5	0	13	1
Gipson, Charles, Tac.	1.000	4	7	9	0	16	1
Gonzales, Rene, N.O.	1.000	4	3	4	0	7	0
Guevara, Giomar, Tac.	1.000	8	15	18	0	33	5
Hajek, Dave, C.S.	.979	117	262	341	13	616	88
Hansen, Jed, Oma.	1.000	35	76	72	0	148	24
Hastings, Lionel, Cal.	1.000	8	6	19	0	25	5
Hernandez, Carlos, N.O.	.987	14	22	53	1	76	13
Holbert, Ray, Oma.	.923	8	15	9	2	26	0
Howard, Dave, Oma.	1.000	4	8	8	0	16	3
HOWARD, Matt, Nash.	.982	100	189	259	8	456	68
Huls, Steve, S.L.	.889	2	4	4	1	9	0

Player, Team	Pct.	G	PO	A	E	TC	DP
Johns, Keith, Edm.	.976	21	31	51	2	84	15
Johnson, Keith, Tuc.	.986	43	94	110	3	207	37
Johnson, Russ, N.O.	1.000	13	23	32	0	55	9
Kennedy, Adam, Mem.	.972	52	117	123	7	247	37
Klassen, Danny, Tuc.	.000	1	0	0	0	0	0
LaRocca, Greg, L.V.	.875	1	5	2	1	8	1
Lobaton, Jose, Cal.	.963	9	21	31	2	54	10
Lopez, Mendy, Oma.	.880	6	10	12	3	25	3
Luuloa, Keith, Edm.	.971	62	118	186	9	313	39
Martins, Eric, Van.	.971	82	137	197	10	344	54
Marval, Raul, Fres.	1.000	6	10	10	0	20	4
Marzano, John, Okla.	.000	1	0	0	0	0	0
Matos, Francisco, Tac.	.980	89	177	208	8	393	53
McDonald, Jason, Van.	1.000	1	2	3	0	5	1
Medrano, Tony, Oma.	.991	24	46	66	1	113	19
Menechino, Frankie, Van.	1.000	40	57	106	0	163	23
Meyers, Chad, Iowa	.980	39	95	99	4	198	28
Miller, Ryan, N.O.	.915	17	29	36	6	71	9
Monahan, Shane, Tac.	1.000	1	0	2	0	2	1
Newhan, David, L.V.	.952	95	162	233	20	415	58
Nieves, Jose, Iowa	1.000	1	1	6	0	7	0
Ortiz, Jose, Van.	1.000	4	11	12	0	23	5
Patzke, Jeff, Nash.	.981	35	75	83	3	161	15
Pelaez, Alex, L.V.	1.000	1	1	1	0	2	1
Pena, Elvis, C.S.	.917	5	12	10	2	24	3
Perez, Tomas, Edm.	1.000	11	26	34	0	60	11
Polanco, Placido, Mem.	.990	22	34	65	1	100	24
Polcovich, Kevin, Nash.	1.000	4	3	9	0	12	1
Richardson, Brian, S.L.	.000	2	0	0	0	0	0
Riggs, Adam, Alb.	.964	112	259	299	21	579	86
Rios, Eduardo, Tac.	1.000	2	4	6	0	10	2
Roberge, J.P., Oma.	.985	60	115	149	4	268	38
Rossy, Rico, L.V.	.978	10	23	21	1	45	4
Sanford, Chance, Alb.	.980	12	22	28	1	51	7
Saylor, Jamie, N.O.	1.000	6	3	6	0	9	0
Scarsone, Steve, Oma.	1.000	4	8	5	0	13	0
Sealy, Scot, Tac.	1.000	2	0	1	0	1	0
Sexton, Chris, C.S.	.933	4	14	14	2	30	5
Sheets, Andy, Edm.	1.000	2	3	2	0	5	1
Sheldon, Scott, Okla.	.997	60	99	195	1	295	49
Shumpert, Terry, C.S.	.963	5	9	17	1	27	6
Silvestri, Dave, Edm.	.975	42	65	94	4	163	23
Snellgrove, Clay, L.V.	1.000	1	0	4	0	4	0
Spiezio, Scott, Van.	.967	24	48	70	4	122	19
Strange, Doug, Nash.	.846	2	7	4	2	13	1
Sveum, Dale, Nash.	.963	9	15	11	1	27	2
t'Hoen, E.J., Edm.	1.000	6	10	24	0	34	5
Thrower, Jake, L.V.	.984	29	44	83	2	129	21
Villalobos, Carlos, N.O.	.901	26	37	45	9	91	3
Warner, Ron, Mem.	1.000	9	11	24	0	35	6
Watkins, Pat, C.S.	1.000	1	1	0	0	1	0
Wehner, John, Nash.	1.000	1	2	5	0	7	1
White, Walt, Tuc.	.980	40	88	105	4	197	24
Williams, Reggie, Edm.	1.000	1	1	0	0	1	0
Wilson, Brandon, Iowa	.975	93	187	239	11	437	44
Woods, Ken, Fres.	.789	5	6	9	4	19	1
Young, Travis, Fres.	.992	26	46	76	1	123	22

TRIPLE PLAYS: Martins, Wilson.

SECOND BASEMEN WITH TWO OR MORE TEAMS

Player, Team	Pct.	G	PO	A	E	TC	DP
Bieser, Steve, Nash.	1.000	3	7	7	0	14	1
Bieser, Steve, Mem.	1.000	2	1	2	0	3	1
Bridges, Kary, Iowa	1.000	2	0	1	0	1	0
Bridges, Kary, Okla.	.991	32	44	63	1	108	20

THIRD BASEMEN

Player, Team	Pct.	G	PO	A	E	TC	DP
Akers, Chad, Tac.	.912	14	4	27	3	34	2
Almanzar, Richard, Iowa	.906	12	6	23	3	32	2
Ardoin, Danny, Van.	.857	10	5	13	3	21	2
Arias, George, L.V.	.950	25	20	37	3	60	4
Baerga, Carlos, L.V.	.909	19	11	29	4	44	5
Ball, Jeff, Van.	.914	56	30	98	12	140	12
Barry, Jeff, C.S.	1.000	6	3	12	0	15	3
Betten, Randy, Edm.	.933	4	3	11	1	15	1
Bieser, Steve, Nash.-Mem.	.939	10	9	22	2	33	2
Bournigal, Rafael, Okla.	.800	2	2	2	1	5	1
Bridges, Kary, Iowa-Okla.	.925	21	5	32	3	40	3
Buhner, Shawn, Tac.	.905	6	7	12	2	21	1
Burke, Jamie, Edm.	.949	33	19	56	4	79	6
Byington, Jimmie, Oma.	1.000	3	1	7	0	8	2

- 433 -

CLASS AAA *Pacific Coast League*

Player, Team	Pct.	G	PO	A	E	TC	DP
Caminiti, Ken, N.O.	.700	6	2	5	3	10	0
Campusano, Carlos, Fres.	.885	11	6	17	3	26	1
Candaele, Casey, N.O.	.917	9	4	7	1	12	0
Canizaro, Jay, Fres.	.667	1	0	2	1	3	0
Castro, Juan, Alb.	.943	42	24	76	6	106	11
Charles, Frank, L.V.	.829	21	11	18	6	35	2
Chavez, Raul, Tac.	1.000	1	1	2	0	3	0
Clapinski, Chris, Cal.	1.000	36	28	64	0	92	6
Clapp, Stubby, Mem.	1.000	12	3	16	0	19	4
Coolbaugh, Scott, Tuc.	.920	40	29	75	9	113	6
Cotton, John, C.S.	.937	26	13	61	5	79	7
Crespo, Felipe, Fres.	.813	5	6	7	3	16	0
Decker, Steve, Edm.	.929	38	15	64	6	85	3
Evans, Tom, Okla.	.951	126	81	266	18	365	24
Ferguson, Jeff, S.L.	.898	37	13	66	9	88	3
Flores, Jose, Tac.	1.000	1	0	4	0	4	0
Forbes, P.J., Okla.	1.000	1	1	0	0	1	0
Frias, Hanley, Tuc.	.917	14	9	24	3	36	0
Garcia, Carlos, L.V.	.965	24	13	42	2	57	4
Garcia, Freddy, Nash.	1.000	2	1	2	0	3	0
Gilbert, Shawn, Alb.	.973	33	14	58	2	74	6
Giovanola, Ed, L.V.	.940	23	9	38	3	50	7
Gipson, Charles, Tac.	1.000	5	1	4	0	5	1
Gonzales, Rene, N.O.	.929	6	6	7	1	14	1
Gulan, Mike, Cal.	.959	67	28	114	6	148	14
Guzman, Edwards, Fres.	.915	58	26	114	13	153	11
Haas, Chris, Mem.	.953	81	56	165	11	232	25
Hajek, Dave, C.S.	1.000	4	5	3	0	8	0
Hastings, Lionel, Cal.	1.000	4	0	3	0	3	0
Hernandez, Ramon, Van.	.857	11	11	13	4	28	0
Hills, Rich, Tac.	1.000	1	0	3	0	3	0
Hinske, Eric, Iowa	1.000	1	0	2	0	2	0
Howard, Matt, Nash.	.923	7	4	8	1	13	1
Huckaby, Ken, Tuc.	.750	2	1	2	1	4	0
Huls, Steve, S.L.	1.000	5	1	4	0	5	0
Johns, Keith, Edm.	1.000	7	4	10	0	14	2
Johnson, Keith, Tuc.	.800	8	4	4	2	10	1
Kennedy, Adam, Mem.	.870	7	8	12	3	23	0
Kieschnick, Brooks, Edm.	1.000	1	0	2	0	2	0
Laker, Tim, Nash.	.500	2	1	0	1	2	0
Lamb, Mike, Okla.	.000	2	0	0	0	0	0
Lariviere, Jason, Mem.	.000	1	0	0	0	0	0
LaRocca, Greg, L.V.	.957	7	5	17	1	23	4
Livingstone, Scott, Alb.	1.000	1	0	1	0	1	0
Lopez, Mendy, Oma.	1.000	3	3	6	0	9	0
Lowell, Mike, Cal.	.939	21	11	51	4	66	6
Luuloa, Keith, Edm.	.925	37	26	72	8	106	4
Martinez, Ramon E., Fres.	1.000	1	2	1	0	3	0
Martins, Eric, Van.	.952	9	4	16	1	21	0
Marval, Raul, Fres.	.857	12	5	19	4	28	1
Marzano, John, Okla.	.000	1	0	0	0	0	0
Matos, Francisco, Tac.	.800	3	1	3	1	5	1
Mejia, Roberto, Alb.	.905	10	6	13	2	21	1
Melo, Juan, L.V.	.000	2	0	0	0	0	0
Menechino, Frankie, Van.	.964	57	34	99	5	138	12
Millar, Kevin, Cal.	.857	10	3	9	2	14	2
Miller, Ryan, N.O.	1.000	11	3	15	0	18	0
Morales, Willie, Van.	.000	2	0	0	0	0	0
Moriarty, Mike, S.L.	1.000	1	0	1	0	1	0
Mueller, Bill, Fres.	.800	3	2	10	3	15	0
Neal, Mike, N.O.	.897	13	9	26	4	39	2
Nevin, Phil, L.V.	1.000	1	1	1	0	2	0
Orie, Kevin, Cal.	.875	21	12	30	6	48	7
Patterson, Jarrod, Tuc.	.916	73	41	101	13	155	12
Pelaez, Alex, L.V.	.833	4	0	5	1	6	0
Pellow, Kit, Oma.	.901	127	78	223	33	334	18
Perez, Eduardo, Mem.	.950	16	7	31	2	40	1
Piatt, Adam, Van.	.875	5	3	11	2	16	1
Polanco, Placido, Mem.	1.000	3	5	9	0	14	1
Polcovich, Kevin, Nash.	.000	1	0	0	0	0	0
QUINLAN, Tom, Iowa	.963	116	85	257	13	355	28
Radmanovich, Ryan, Tac.	.800	5	1	3	1	5	0
Ramirez, Aramis, Nash.	.884	124	70	250	42	362	19
Richardson, Brian, S.L.	.928	110	53	203	20	276	21
Riggs, Adam, Alb.	.946	17	5	30	2	37	3
Roberge, J.P., Oma.	.893	13	6	19	3	28	2
Roskos, John, Cal.	.750	2	1	2	1	4	0
Rossy, Rico, L.V.	.750	4	3	6	3	12	1
Rupp, Chad, S.L.	.000	1	0	0	0	0	0
Saenz, Olmedo, Van.	1.000	2	1	0	0	1	0
Sanford, Chance, Alb.	.921	51	27	90	10	127	10
Saylor, Jamie, N.O.	1.000	16	8	19	0	27	0

Player, Team	Pct.	G	PO	A	E	TC	DP
Secrist, Reed, Nash.	.875	8	3	11	2	16	1
Seitzer, Brad, Tac.	.928	108	79	204	22	305	23
Sexton, Chris, C.S.	.923	18	7	17	2	26	1
Sheldon, Scott, Okla.	.889	6	6	18	3	27	2
Shumpert, Terry, C.S.	.941	11	4	12	1	17	2
Silvestri, Dave, Edm.	.968	21	9	21	1	31	1
Spiezio, Scott, Van.	1.000	3	2	3	0	5	1
Steed, Dave, Alb.	1.000	4	5	4	0	9	2
Strange, Doug, Nash.	.000	1	0	0	0	0	0
Sveum, Dale, Tuc.-Nash.	.894	14	10	32	5	47	2
Tatum, Jim, C.S.	.913	87	57	132	18	207	11
t'Hoen, E.J., Edm.	1.000	3	1	10	0	11	1
Thrower, Jake, L.V.	.933	28	13	57	5	75	8
Tremie, Chris, Nash.	1.000	1	0	2	0	2	0
Unroe, Tim, Edm.	.900	2	5	4	1	10	1
Villalobos, Carlos, N.O.	.927	100	59	244	24	327	18
Voigt, Jack, Fres.	1.000	5	1	10	0	11	0
Warner, Ron, Mem.	.923	21	17	43	5	65	3
White, Walt, Tuc.	.000	1	0	0	0	0	0
Williams, Eddie, S.L.	1.000	3	1	3	0	4	1
Williams, Reggie, Edm.	.667	1	1	1	1	3	0
Wilson, Brandon, Iowa	.926	20	6	44	4	54	1
Woods, Ken, Fres.	.877	54	29	92	17	138	12

TRIPLE PLAY: Quinlan.

THIRD BASEMEN WITH TWO OR MORE TEAMS

Player, Team	Pct.	G	PO	A	E	TC	DP
Bieser, Steve, Nash.	1.000	1	0	1	0	1	0
Bieser, Steve, Mem.	.938	9	9	21	2	32	2
Bridges, Kary, Iowa	1.000	5	0	7	0	7	0
Bridges, Kary, Okla.	.909	16	5	25	3	33	3
Sveum, Dale, Tuc.	.879	8	7	22	4	33	2
Sveum, Dale, Nash.	.929	6	3	10	1	14	0

SHORTSTOPS

Player, Team	Pct.	G	PO	A	E	TC	DP
Akers, Chad, Tac.	.976	15	29	52	2	83	12
Almanzar, Richard, Iowa	1.000	4	4	8	0	12	1
Bournigal, Rafael, Okla.	.950	6	6	13	1	20	4
Brown, Randy, Tac.	.955	17	19	45	3	67	7
Byington, Jimmie, Oma.	.883	22	34	57	12	103	15
Candaele, Casey, N.O.	.980	27	30	70	2	102	8
Canizaro, Jay, Fres.	1.000	2	3	3	0	6	2
Castro, Juan, Alb.	.953	59	74	170	12	256	42
Cedeno, Domingo, Tac.	.939	26	31	62	6	99	13
Chavez, Raul, Tac.	1.000	1	2	4	0	6	0
Clapinski, Chris, Cal.	.924	22	24	49	6	79	11
Clapp, Stubby, Mem.	.000	1	0	0	0	0	0
Clayton, Royce, Okla.	1.000	2	4	7	0	11	2
Cora, Alex, Alb.	.968	76	133	233	12	378	58
Crespo, Felipe, Fres.	1.000	2	4	4	0	8	0
Cromer, Tripp, Alb.	1.000	1	1	3	0	4	0
Delgado, Wilson, Fres.	.944	56	85	166	15	266	34
Demetral, Chris, Okla.	.977	13	16	27	1	44	6
Diaz, Edwin, Tuc.	.926	44	70	117	15	202	30
Dransfeldt, Kelly, Okla.	.958	96	151	279	19	449	72
Duncan, Mariano, Cal.	1.000	2	0	4	0	4	1
Ferguson, Jeff, S.L.	.986	24	21	47	1	69	8
Flores, Jose, Tac.	.946	41	66	126	11	203	22
Forbes, P.J., Okla.	1.000	2	2	3	0	5	1
Franco, Raul, Cal.	.943	7	8	25	2	35	7
Frias, Hanley, Tuc.	.909	4	2	8	1	11	1
Garcia, Carlos, L.V.	.889	2	2	6	1	9	1
Gil, Benji, Cal.	.943	110	173	304	29	506	75
Gilbert, Shawn, Alb.	.945	13	14	38	3	55	6
Giovanola, Ed, L.V.	.967	11	10	19	1	30	4
Gipson, Charles, Tac.	.903	24	34	50	9	93	17
Gomez, Chris, L.V.	.933	9	8	20	2	30	5
Guevara, Giomar, Tac.	.965	24	41	69	4	114	13
Gulan, Mike, Cal.	1.000	4	1	6	0	7	2
Gutierrez, Ricky, N.O.	.875	4	10	11	3	24	3
Hajek, Dave, C.S.	.947	5	7	11	1	19	4
Hansen, Jed, Oma.	.927	22	39	63	8	110	16
Hernandez, Carlos, N.O.	.963	82	123	239	14	376	39
Holbert, Ray, Oma.	.980	24	36	63	2	101	17
Howard, Dave, Mem.	1.000	2	3	3	0	6	0
Howard, Matt, Nash.	.864	4	3	16	3	22	0
Huls, Steve, S.L.	.833	1	2	3	1	6	1
Johns, Keith, Edm.	.954	48	81	145	11	237	17
Johnson, Keith, Tuc.	.964	33	49	113	6	168	24
Johnson, Russ, N.O.	.925	9	9	28	3	40	8
Kennedy, Adam, Mem.	.918	25	19	71	8	98	11

Player, Team	Pct.	G	PO	A	E	TC	DP
King, Brett, Iowa	.934	32	51	105	11	167	23
Klassen, Danny, Tuc.	.969	59	87	193	9	289	42
LaRocca, Greg, L.V.	.944	6	5	12	1	18	3
Lobaton, Jose, Cal.	.868	17	19	27	7	53	8
Lopez, Mendy, Oma.	.979	53	85	153	5	243	27
Martinez, Felix, Oma.	.963	7	8	18	1	27	4
Martinez, Ramon E., Fres.	.950	26	24	71	5	100	10
Martins, Eric, Van.	.926	4	8	17	2	27	5
Marval, Raul, Fres.	.940	59	72	146	14	232	32
Marzano, John, Okla.	.000	1	0	0	0	0	0
Matos, Francisco, Tac.	1.000	1	0	2	0	2	0
Meares, Pat, Nash.	.800	5	2	6	2	10	1
Medrano, Tony, Oma.	1.000	8	26	19	0	45	7
Melo, Juan, L.V.	.957	44	70	108	8	186	24
Menechino, Frankie, Van.	.975	42	61	136	5	202	33
Miller, Ryan, N.O.	.955	13	21	21	2	44	4
Moriarty, Mike, S.L.	.953	127	176	426	30	632	85
Newhan, David, L.V.	1.000	1	2	2	0	4	1
Nieves, Jose, Iowa	.958	101	121	309	19	449	54
Nunez, Abraham, Nash.	.971	15	23	43	2	68	10
Ordaz, Luis, Mem.	.956	103	150	346	23	519	72
Ortiz, Jose, Van.	.942	103	168	283	28	479	71
Patzke, Jeff, Nash.	.949	25	30	63	5	98	16
Pena, Elvis, C.S.	.872	8	11	23	5	39	6
Perez, Tomas, Edm.	.968	73	123	209	11	343	53
PETERSEN, Chris, C.S.	.961	106	196	340	22	558	94
Piatt, Adam, Van.	1.000	1	3	5	0	8	2
Polanco, Placido, Mem.	.933	4	4	10	1	15	1
Polcovich, Kevin, Nash.	.969	71	85	229	10	324	42
Roberge, J.P., Oma.	1.000	4	6	6	0	12	1
Rossy, Rico, L.V.	.978	72	85	186	6	277	41
Saylor, Jamie, N.O.	.915	18	23	52	7	82	9
Scarsone, Steve, Oma.	1.000	12	22	27	0	49	7
Seitzer, Brad, Tac.	1.000	1	0	1	0	1	0
Sexton, Chris, C.S.	.989	20	29	59	1	89	16
Sheets, Andy, Edm.	.977	10	10	32	1	43	9
Sheldon, Scott, Okla.	.987	33	48	103	2	153	23
Shumpert, Terry, C.S.	.842	5	9	7	3	19	2
Silvestri, Dave, Edm.	.965	15	25	30	2	57	9
Solano, Danny, Okla.	.714	3	3	7	4	14	4
Sosa, Juan, C.S.	1.000	2	6	8	0	14	3
Sveum, Dale, Nash.	.949	16	11	63	4	78	14
Thrower, Jake, L.V.	.963	16	28	49	3	80	10
Warner, Ron, Mem.	.933	16	15	41	4	60	8
Wehner, John, Nash.	.943	14	19	31	3	53	11
White, Walt, Tuc.	1.000	6	6	15	0	21	3
Wilson, Brandon, Iowa	.972	8	14	21	1	36	1
Woods, Ken, Fres.	.909	6	5	15	2	22	3

OUTFIELDERS

Player, Team	Pct.	G	PO	A	E	TC	DP
Akers, Chad, Tac.	1.000	11	23	2	0	25	0
Alexander, Chad, N.O.	.985	28	64	2	1	67	1
Allen, Dusty, L.V.	.966	57	79	6	3	88	1
Alvarez, Rafael, S.L.*	1.000	6	3	0	0	3	0
Anthony, Eric, Alb.*	1.000	5	6	0	0	6	0
Ball, Jeff, Van.	.000	1	0	0	0	0	0
Barkett, Andy, Okla.*	.000	1	0	0	0	0	0
Barry, Jeff, C.S.	1.000	44	87	3	0	90	0
Battle, Allen, Iowa	.960	13	23	1	1	25	0
Bautista, Danny, Cal.	.969	36	90	5	3	98	3
Belk, Tim, Mem.	1.000	2	2	0	0	2	0
Berkman, Lance, N.O.*	.965	56	106	5	4	115	1
Betten, Randy, Edm.	1.000	3	2	0	0	2	0
Betzsold, James, N.O.	.950	46	88	7	5	100	3
Bieser, Steve, Mem.	.973	38	69	2	2	73	1
Bridges, Kary, Okla.	.944	17	17	0	1	18	0
Brinkley, Darryl, Nash.	.969	81	118	7	4	129	2
Brown, Adrian, Nash.	.969	17	31	0	1	32	0
Brown, Emil, Nash.	.948	107	173	10	10	193	1
Brown, Roosevelt, Iowa	.959	67	107	11	5	123	1
Brumbaugh, Cliff, Okla.	.000	3	0	0	0	0	0
Buchanan, Brian, S.L.	.980	101	184	9	4	197	1
Burke, Jamie, Edm.	1.000	1	2	1	0	3	0
Byas, Michael, Fres.	1.000	5	10	1	0	11	0
Byington, Jimmie, Oma.	.988	41	80	1	1	82	1
Candaele, Casey, N.O.	1.000	16	32	1	0	33	0
Cangelosi, John, C.S.*	.980	26	47	2	1	50	0
Carr, Jeremy, Oma.	.958	66	110	5	5	120	1
Carvajal, Jovino, Edm.	.968	101	172	9	6	187	0
Chamberlain, Wes, Alb.	.900	24	18	0	2	20	0
Charles, Frank, L.V.	1.000	1	1	0	0	1	0

Player, Team	Pct.	G	PO	A	E	TC	DP
Christenson, Ryan, Van.	.978	33	88	1	2	91	0
Christian, Eddie, Edm.*	.964	33	52	1	2	55	0
Clapinski, Chris, Cal.	1.000	18	25	2	0	27	0
Clapp, Stubby, Mem.	1.000	39	50	4	0	54	0
Clark, Dave, Alb.	.970	25	31	1	1	33	0
Clemente, Edgard, C.S.	.992	63	114	8	1	123	1
Cline, Pat, Iowa	.923	18	24	0	2	26	0
Colangelo, Mike, Edm.	.941	26	29	3	2	34	0
Conti, Jason, Tuc.	.974	126	278	17	8	303	3
Cookson, Brent, Alb.	.989	81	169	4	2	175	1
Cotton, John, C.S.	.917	18	21	1	2	24	0
Crespo, Felipe, Fres.	.950	24	36	2	2	40	0
Cummings, Midre, S.L.	.954	64	101	3	5	109	1
Cuyler, Milt, Okla.	.966	19	28	0	1	29	0
Darr, Mike, L.V.	.989	97	172	11	2	185	1
DaVanon, Jeff, Edm.	1.000	33	74	6	0	80	1
Demetral, Chris, Oma.	1.000	15	11	0	0	11	0
Dishington, Nate, Mem.	1.000	34	43	3	0	46	0
Drew, J.D., Mem.	1.000	25	44	2	0	46	1
Dunwoody, Todd, Cal.*	.977	64	159	10	4	173	1
Encarnacion, Mario, Van.	.960	37	91	6	4	101	2
Eversgerd, Bryan, Mem.*	.000	1	0	0	0	0	0
Ferguson, Jeff, S.L.	1.000	4	5	0	0	5	0
Floyd, Cliff, Cal.	1.000	9	8	0	0	8	0
Franco, Raul, Cal.	1.000	3	2	0	0	2	0
Freeman, Ricky, Van.	1.000	8	10	0	0	10	0
Gazarek, Marty, Iowa	.989	38	84	5	1	90	1
Giambi, Jeremy, Oma.*	1.000	20	45	1	0	46	0
Gibbs, Kevin, Alb.	1.000	4	11	0	0	11	0
Gibralter, Steve, Oma.	.962	86	167	12	7	186	3
Gibson, Derrick, C.S.	.957	101	171	5	8	184	0
Gil, Benji, Cal.	1.000	5	10	0	0	10	0
Gilbert, Shawn, Alb.	.984	71	111	10	2	123	3
Gipson, Charles, Tac.	1.000	14	34	2	0	36	2
Green, Scarborough, Okla.	.975	103	219	13	6	238	1
Greene, Todd, Edm.	1.000	12	23	0	0	23	0
Grijak, Kevin, Alb.	.993	90	137	7	1	145	1
Guiel, Aaron, L.V.	.944	49	81	4	5	90	0
Guillen, Jose, Nash.	.939	30	57	5	4	66	1
Gulan, Mike, Cal.	.895	9	16	1	2	19	0
Hansen, Jed, Oma.	1.000	1	1	0	0	1	0
Hastings, Lionel, Cal.	.000	7	0	0	0	0	0
Hatcher, Chris, C.S.	.936	59	81	7	6	94	1
Hermansen, Chad, Nash.	.989	117	258	9	3	270	3
Herrick, Jason, Edm.*	.947	19	34	2	2	38	1
Howard, Dave, Mem.	1.000	1	1	0	0	1	0
Howard, Matt, Nash.	.000	1	0	0	0	0	0
Howard, Thomas, Mem.	.982	34	54	2	1	57	0
Hubbard, Mike, Okla.	.000	1	0	0	0	0	0
Hubbard, Trenidad, Alb.	.974	31	72	2	2	76	0
Huls, Steve, S.L.	1.000	6	8	0	0	8	0
Hulse, David, Mem.*	.946	55	66	4	4	74	1
Hutchins, Norm, Edm.*	.983	125	294	2	5	301	0
Hyers, Tim, Cal.*	.985	33	65	2	1	68	1
Hyzdu, Adam, Nash.	1.000	12	26	1	0	27	0
Ibanez, Raul, Tac.	1.000	6	12	0	0	12	0
Incaviglia, Pete, Tuc.-N.O.	.926	21	25	0	2	27	0
Jackson, Ryan, Tac.*	.917	5	10	1	1	12	0
Jennings, Robin, Iowa*	.977	61	123	7	3	133	1
Johnson, Earl, Tac.	1.000	17	49	1	0	50	1
Johnson, Keith, Tuc.	1.000	6	8	0	0	8	0
Johnson, Russ, N.O.	.000	1	0	0	0	0	0
Jones, Jacque, S.L.*	.987	52	150	2	2	154	1
Jones, Jaime, Cal.*	.961	39	68	5	3	76	1
Kelly, Mike, C.S.	.975	104	188	10	5	203	2
Kennedy, Adam, Mem.	1.000	10	16	0	0	16	0
Kieschnick, Brooks, Edm.	1.000	7	8	0	0	8	0
Kirby, Wayne, L.V.	.969	32	63	0	2	65	0
Knorr, Randy, N.O.	.000	1	0	0	0	0	0
Lariviere, Jason, Mem.	.993	131	247	18	2	267	4
Latham, Chris, S.L.	.978	94	262	9	6	277	1
Leach, Jalal, Fres.*	.975	90	153	5	4	162	0
Lesher, Brian, Van.*	1.000	37	56	2	0	58	0
Little, Mark, Mem.	.960	51	114	6	5	125	2
Livingstone, Scott, Alb.	1.000	1	1	0	0	1	0
Long, Terrence, Van.*	.961	38	95	3	4	102	1
Luke, Matt, Edm.*	1.000	3	6	0	0	6	0
Luuloa, Keith, Edm.	.952	13	20	0	1	21	0
Marzano, John, Okla.	1.000	1	1	0	0	1	0
Mashore, Damon, Fres.	.993	92	133	5	1	139	0
Mateo, Ruben, Okla.	.963	59	128	3	5	136	1
Mathis, Joe, Tac.	1.000	25	39	1	0	40	0
Matthews, Gary, L.V.	.976	120	273	7	7	287	1

CLASS AAA *Pacific Coast League*

Player, Team	Pct.	G	PO	A	E	TC	DP
McDonald, Jason, Van.	.988	32	77	3	1	81	2
Medrano, Tony, Oma.	.000	1	0	0	0	0	0
Mejia, Roberto, Alb.	1.000	3	1	0	0	1	0
Mendez, Carlos, Oma.	1.000	14	23	0	0	23	0
Mercedes, Henry, Oma.	.000	2	0	0	0	0	0
Meyers, Chad, Iowa	1.000	5	9	0	0	9	0
Millar, Kevin, Cal.	1.000	27	39	0	0	39	0
Monahan, Shane, Tac.	.995	88	205	7	1	213	2
Monroe, Craig, Okla.	1.000	6	17	0	0	17	0
Montgomery, Ray, Nash.	.953	65	80	2	4	86	0
Morman, Russ, Cal.	1.000	3	5	0	0	5	0
Murphy, Mike, Tac.	1.000	35	87	0	0	87	0
Murray, Calvin, Fres.	.980	129	284	8	6	298	0
Neal, Mike, N.O.	.983	33	56	1	1	58	0
Neill, Mike, Van.*	.967	80	136	9	5	150	2
Newfield, Marc, Van.	1.000	4	10	0	0	10	0
Newson, Warren, Alb.*	.980	77	91	5	2	98	0
Nicholas, Darrell, S.L.	.952	98	149	10	8	167	0
Norman, Les, Oma.	.996	87	215	8	1	224	1
Osik, Keith, Nash.	.000	1	0	0	0	0	0
Patzke, Jeff, Nash.	.000	1	0	0	0	0	0
Pemberton, Rudy, Mem.	1.000	20	22	2	0	24	0
Pennyfeather, William, Edm.	.942	29	46	3	3	52	0
Petrick, Ben, C.S.	.000	1	0	0	0	0	0
Phillips, J.R., C.S.*	.000	1	0	0	0	0	0
Pledger, Kinnis, Tac.	.667	1	2	0	1	3	0
Polcovich, Kevin, Nash.	.000	1	0	0	0	0	0
PORTER, Bo, Iowa	1.000	107	223	5	0	228	3
Powell, Dante, Tuc.	.952	45	94	5	5	104	0
Prieto, Chris, L.V.*	.994	94	154	6	1	161	1
Pritchett, Chris, Edm.	1.000	1	3	1	0	4	0
Quinn, Mark, Oma.	.983	101	216	13	4	233	2
Radmanovich, Ryan, Tac.	.985	92	184	12	3	199	3
Ramirez, Omar, N.O.	.995	103	188	6	1	195	3
Reeves, Glenn, Cal.	.993	78	132	9	1	142	2
Rennhack, Mike, Iowa	1.000	43	69	3	0	72	1
Richardson, Brian, S.L.	.912	15	30	1	3	34	1
Rios, Armando, Fres.*	1.000	20	28	1	0	29	0
Roberge, J.P., Oma.	.941	28	45	3	3	51	0
Robertson, Mike, Nash.*	1.000	5	4	0	0	4	0
Robinson, Kerry, Tac.*	.974	70	141	6	4	151	2
Roskos, John, Cal.	.981	85	102	1	2	105	0
Rupp, Chad, S.L.	1.000	6	4	0	0	4	0
Ryan, Rob, Tuc.*	.969	104	182	8	6	196	1
Sachse, Matt, Tac.*	1.000	11	18	1	0	19	0
Sagmoen, Marc, Okla.*	.986	81	133	4	2	139	1
Sanford, Chance, Alb.	1.000	13	8	0	0	8	0
Saylor, Jamie, N.O.	.965	55	101	8	4	113	1
Scarsone, Steve, Oma.	1.000	3	3	0	0	3	0
Secrist, Reed, Nash.	1.000	2	4	0	0	4	0
Sell, Chip, Tuc.	1.000	22	27	1	0	28	0
Sexton, Chris, C.S.	1.000	14	32	0	0	32	0
Sheff, Chris, Van.	.991	102	213	9	2	224	3
Sheldon, Scott, Okla.	.000	1	0	0	0	0	0
Shumpert, Terry, C.S.	1.000	3	1	0	0	1	0
Simms, Mike, Okla.	1.000	7	6	0	0	6	0
Sosa, Juan, C.S.	.900	4	9	0	1	10	0
Stahoviak, Scott, Iowa	.952	8	18	2	1	21	0
Stoner, Mike, Tuc.-Edm.	.931	14	26	1	2	29	0
Stovall, DaRond, Cal.-Alb.*	.981	76	151	5	3	159	0
Sutton, Larry, Oma.*	1.000	7	12	0	0	12	0
Thompson, Ryan, N.O.	.965	104	209	12	8	229	3
Timmons, Ozzie, Tac.	.973	53	106	3	3	112	1
Unroe, Tim, Edm.-Oma.	1.000	10	15	0	0	15	0
Valdes, Pedro, Okla.*	.981	29	51	2	1	54	0
Vaz, Roberto, Van.*	.957	66	103	8	5	116	2
Villalobos, Carlos, N.O.	.944	4	16	1	1	18	1
Wallace, Kent, N.O.	.000	1	0	0	0	0	0
Walton, Jerome, Cal.	.959	22	46	1	2	49	0
Ward, Daryle, N.O.*	.500	3	1	0	1	2	0
Ward, Turner, Nash.-Tuc.	.902	25	35	2	4	41	1
Warner, Ron, Mem.	.971	24	32	2	1	35	0
Watkins, Pat, C.S.	1.000	7	13	0	0	13	0
Wehner, John, Nash.	1.000	2	1	1	0	2	0
White, Derrick, Iowa	1.000	82	125	6	0	131	0
Williams, George, S.L.	1.000	5	7	1	0	8	0
Williams, Keith, Fres.	1.000	59	85	7	0	92	1
Williams, Reggie, Edm.	.979	23	44	3	1	48	0
Wilson, Desi, Tuc.*	1.000	12	18	0	0	18	0
Womack, Tony, Tuc.	1.000	4	8	1	0	9	0
Woods, Ken, Fres.	1.000	24	34	3	0	37	1
Young, Ernie, Tuc.	.987	107	142	11	2	155	0
Zywica, Mike, Okla.	.970	134	247	12	8	267	6

TRIPLE PLAY: Long.

OUTFIELDERS WITH TWO OR MORE TEAMS

Player, Team	Pct.	G	PO	A	E	TC	DP
Incaviglia, Pete, Tuc.	1.000	7	6	0	0	6	0
Incaviglia, Pete, N.O.	.905	14	19	0	2	21	0
Stoner, Mike, Tuc.	1.000	4	5	0	0	5	0
Stoner, Mike, Edm.	.917	10	21	1	2	24	0
Stovall, DaRond, Cal.	.982	32	52	3	1	56	0
Stovall, DaRond, Alb.*	.981	44	99	2	2	103	0
Unroe, Tim, Edm.	1.000	8	12	0	0	12	0
Unroe, Tim, Oma.	1.000	2	3	0	0	3	0
Ward, Turner, Nash.	.900	14	17	1	2	20	0
Ward, Turner, Tuc.	.905	11	18	1	2	21	1

CATCHERS

Player, Team	Pct.	G	PO	A	E	TC	DP	PB
Ardoin, Danny, Van.	.989	83	498	59	6	563	9	6
Bako, Paul, N.O.	.984	12	58	4	1	63	1	0
Bieser, Steve, Nash.-Mem.	1.000	4	4	1	0	5	0	1
Blanco, Henry, C.S.	.990	14	87	12	1	100	2	2
Brito, Juan, Oma.	1.000	2	16	1	0	17	0	0
Burke, Jamie, Edm.	.909	5	8	2	1	11	0	0
Candaele, Casey, N.O.	1.000	1	1	0	0	1	0	0
Castro, Ramon, Cal.	.989	90	552	67	7	626	7	9
Charles, Frank, L.V.	.990	27	195	12	2	209	1	0
Chavez, Raul, Tac.	.988	95	664	74	9	747	5	9
Cline, Pat, Iowa	.966	30	187	11	7	205	1	10
Davis, Ben, L.V.	.992	58	454	32	4	490	5	5
Decker, Steve, Edm.	1.000	4	28	0	0	28	0	0
Fasano, Sal, Oma.	.981	82	576	50	12	638	3	8
Foster, Jim, Tuc.-Edm.	.982	28	194	21	4	219	1	3
Gibralter, Steve, Oma.	.500	1	1	0	1	2	0	0
Gonzalez, Jimmy, L.V.	.991	28	200	21	2	223	4	2
Gonzalez, Wiklenman, L.V.	.984	23	175	10	3	188	3	1
Graves, Bryan, Edm.	1.000	2	13	3	0	16	0	1
Guzman, Edwards, Fres.	.957	31	229	13	11	253	1	7
Hamel, Jon, L.V.	1.000	1	4	0	0	4	0	0
Hanel, Marcus, Tuc.	1.000	6	46	3	0	49	1	1
Hastings, Lionel, Cal.	1.000	11	66	6	0	72	0	2
Hemphill, Bret, Edm.	.995	56	348	44	2	394	4	7
Hernandez, Ramon, Van.	.997	44	302	27	1	330	6	3
Hinch, A.J., Van.	.989	12	83	3	1	87	1	1
HUBBARD, Mike, Okla.	.994	105	675	47	4	726	5	9
Huckaby, Ken, Tuc.	.988	101	695	52	9	756	3	8
Jensen, Marcus, Mem.	.995	59	380	32	2	414	1	2
Knorr, Randy, N.O.	.991	67	396	35	4	435	4	1
Koeyers, Ramsey, Tuc.	.990	13	95	7	1	103	0	0
Laker, Tim, Nash.	.984	95	660	64	12	736	2	7
LeCroy, Matthew, S.L.	1.000	19	100	6	0	106	0	4
Lidle, Kevin, L.V.	1.000	10	55	7	0	62	1	1
Lisanti, Bob, Iowa	.971	11	64	4	2	70	1	2
LoDuca, Paul, Alb.	.975	17	147	11	4	162	1	0
Lopez, Pedro, N.O.	.993	19	126	15	1	142	3	3
Luderer, Brian, Van.	.984	10	60	1	1	62	0	0
Manwaring, Kirt, C.S.	1.000	4	32	0	0	32	0	0
Marsters, Brandon, S.L.	1.000	10	42	4	0	46	2	0
Martinez, Sandy, Iowa	.996	34	239	17	1	257	0	3
Marzano, John, Okla.	.978	32	170	11	4	185	6	1
Mayes, Craig, Fres.	.992	39	239	15	2	256	0	3
McDonald, Keith, Mem.	1.000	25	162	7	0	169	2	0
Mendez, Carlos, Oma.	1.000	4	12	2	0	14	0	0
Mercedes, Henry, Oma.	.998	66	382	43	1	426	5	8
Mirabelli, Doug, Fres.	.993	66	473	58	4	535	2	2
Molina, Ben, Edm.	.993	54	351	47	3	401	5	3
Molina, Jose, Iowa	.987	71	488	44	7	539	5	9
Nevin, Phil, L.V.	1.000	2	10	2	0	12	1	0
Norman, Les, Oma.	1.000	1	1	0	0	1	0	0
Ortiz, Hector, Alb.	.971	33	213	23	7	243	2	0
Osik, Keith, Nash.	1.000	4	24	3	0	27	0	0
Pachot, John, Tuc.	.974	31	159	27	5	191	6	2
Patterson, Jarrod, Tuc.	1.000	1	6	0	0	6	0	0
Pena, Angel, Alb.	.987	30	200	28	3	231	2	3
Petrick, Ben, C.S.	.980	66	411	32	9	452	4	14
Pierzynski, A.J., S.L.	.984	63	376	45	7	428	1	3
Reeder, Cory, Okla.	1.000	8	33	2	0	35	0	1
Reese, Nate, Cal.	1.000	4	17	1	0	18	0	0
Robertson, Ryan, Cal.	.975	35	220	14	6	240	5	4
Rosario, Mel, Okla.	.976	7	39	1	1	41	0	0
Roskos, John, Cal.	.951	7	53	5	3	61	1	3
Russo, Paul, N.O.	.971	14	61	5	2	68	0	3
Sealy, Scot, Tac.	.985	53	361	38	6	405	7	2
Secrist, Reed, Nash.	1.000	20	83	6	0	89	0	4
Servais, Scott, Fres.	1.000	3	23	1	0	24	0	1
Sheldon, Scott, Okla.	.955	4	19	2	1	22	0	0
Smith, Jeff, S.L.	.969	4	31	0	1	32	0	0

Player, Team	Pct.	G	PO	A	E	TC	DP	PB
Steed, Dave, Alb.	1.000	8	51	7	0	58	1	0
Stefanski, Mike, Mem.	.980	58	411	26	9	446	4	5
Strittmatter, Mark, C.S.	.995	60	379	40	2	421	6	0
Tatum, Jim, C.S.	.972	5	33	2	1	36	0	0
Tejero, Fausto, Edm.	.978	5	39	5	1	45	0	1
Thurston, Jerrey, N.O.	1.000	21	118	10	0	128	1	2
Torrealba, Yorvit, Fres.	.988	17	155	12	2	169	1	6
Tremie, Chris, Nash.	.988	42	292	29	4	325	2	0
Wilkins, Rick, Alb.	.992	59	428	39	4	471	4	6
Williams, George, S.L.-N.O.	.987	72	439	26	6	471	1	2
Zinter, Alan, Iowa	1.000	7	44	5	0	49	1	2

CATCHERS WITH TWO OR MORE TEAMS

Player, Team	Pct.	G	PO	A	E	TC	DP	PB
Bieser, Steve, Nash.	.000	2	0	0	0	0	0	1
Bieser, Steve, Mem.	1.000	2	4	1	0	5	0	1
Foster, Jim, Tuc.	.968	10	56	5	2	63	0	1
Foster, Jim, Edm.	.987	18	138	16	2	156	1	2
Williams, George, S.L.	.988	53	325	15	4	344	0	1
Williams, George, N.O.	.984	19	114	11	2	127	1	1

PITCHERS

Player, Team	Pct.	G	PO	A	E	TC	DP
Abbott, Paul, Tac.	1.000	2	2	1	0	3	0
Adamson, Joel, Tac.*	.889	14	1	7	1	9	1
Ah Yat, Paul, Nash.*	1.000	13	4	3	0	7	0
Alberro, Jose, Cal.	.889	24	7	9	2	18	1
Almanza, Armando, Cal.*	1.000	15	0	1	0	1	0
Almanzar, Carlos, L.V.	.500	11	1	0	1	2	0
Alston, Garvin, Alb.	1.000	5	0	1	0	1	0
Alvarez, Juan, Edm.*	1.000	27	1	2	0	3	0
Anderson, Brian, Tuc.*	1.000	2	0	1	0	1	0
Anderson, Jimmy, Nash.*	.950	21	12	26	2	40	3
Ankiel, Rick, Mem.*	1.000	16	8	14	0	22	1
Arnold, Jamie, Alb.	1.000	7	0	2	0	2	0
Arroyo, Bronson, Nash.	1.000	3	0	2	0	2	0
Arroyo, Luis, Cal.*	.889	22	1	7	1	9	0
Baez, Benito, Van.*	1.000	11	0	2	0	2	0
Bailey, Cory, Fres.	1.000	43	2	5	0	7	0
Bailey, Roger, C.S.	1.000	4	0	4	0	4	0
Baptist, Travis, S.L.*	1.000	17	7	11	0	18	2
Barber, Brian, Oma.	1.000	19	5	7	0	12	1
Barker, Richie, Iowa	.950	55	6	13	1	20	2
Barnes, Brian, Mem.*	.813	36	4	9	3	16	0
Batchelor, Rich, Tuc.	1.000	30	3	3	0	6	0
Beck, Rod, Iowa	.000	2	0	0	0	0	0
Beckett, Robbie, Alb.*	.750	15	0	3	1	4	0
Bell, Jason, S.L.	1.000	18	4	9	0	13	0
Beltran, Rigo, C.S.*	1.000	6	0	2	0	2	0
Benes, Alan, Mem.	.000	3	0	0	0	0	0
Benz, Jake, Cal.*	.000	2	0	0	0	0	0
Bergman, Sean, N.O.	1.000	3	1	1	0	2	0
Bertotti, Mike, Tac.*	1.000	3	0	2	0	2	0
Bierbrodt, Nick, Tuc.*	.818	11	1	8	2	11	1
Bieser, Steve, Mem.	.000	1	0	0	0	0	0
Billingsley, Brent, Cal.*	.952	21	5	15	1	21	1
Bluma, Jaime, Oma.	1.000	17	0	2	0	2	0
Bochtler, Doug, Alb.	1.000	18	1	2	0	3	0
Borland, Toby, Edm.	.857	21	2	4	1	7	0
Boskie, Shawn, Alb.	.960	15	9	15	1	25	2
Bost, Heath, C.S.	.966	38	14	14	1	29	1
Bowers, Shane, S.L.	1.000	31	8	10	0	18	0
Boyd, Jason, Tuc.-Nash.	.850	49	5	12	3	20	1
Briggs, Anthony, C.S.	1.000	10	2	1	0	3	0
Brohawn, Troy, Tuc.*	1.000	3	0	1	0	1	0
Bross, Terry, Tuc.	1.000	2	0	1	0	1	1
Brow, Scott, Edm.	.950	64	5	14	1	20	1
Brownson, Mark, C.S.	.864	17	11	8	3	22	2
Bunch, Mel, Tac.	.950	21	9	10	1	20	2
Burgus, Travis, Cal.*	1.000	20	1	2	0	3	1
Burke, Jamie, Edm.	.000	1	0	0	0	0	0
Busby, Mike, Mem.	.800	29	5	3	2	10	0
Byington, Jimmie, Oma.	.000	1	0	0	0	0	0
Byrdak, Tim, Oma.*	.923	33	4	8	1	13	1
Cabrera, Jose, N.O.	.875	31	3	4	1	8	0
Candaele, Casey, N.O.	.000	1	0	0	0	0	0
Carlson, Dan, Tuc.	1.000	32	3	11	0	14	1
Carlyle, Buddy, L.V.	.943	25	7	26	2	35	1
Carmona, Rafael, Tac.	1.000	27	3	4	0	7	1
Carrasco, Hector, S.L.	1.000	3	0	1	0	1	0
Carroll, Dave, S.L.*	1.000	36	4	8	0	12	1
Castillo, Frank, Nash.	.889	19	3	21	3	27	2

Player, Team	Pct.	G	PO	A	E	TC	DP
Cey, Dan, S.L.	.000	1	0	0	0	0	0
Chavez, Anthony, Van.	.833	54	2	8	2	12	0
Checo, Robinson, Alb.	.900	16	4	5	1	10	0
Chouinard, Bobby, Tuc.	.846	12	2	9	2	13	0
Christiansen, Jason, Nash.*	.000	2	0	0	0	0	0
Clark, Terry, Van.	1.000	14	2	4	0	6	1
Clemons, Chris, Tuc.	1.000	45	2	8	0	10	0
Clontz, Brad, Nash.	.667	12	1	1	1	3	0
Cloude, Ken, Tac.	.833	6	1	9	2	12	2
Cole, Victor, Iowa	1.000	19	1	9	0	10	0
Connelly, Steve, Fres.	1.000	54	4	12	0	16	0
Cooke, Steve, L.V.*	1.000	5	2	0	0	2	0
Coolbaugh, Scott, Tuc.	.000	1	0	0	0	0	0
Cooper, Brian, Edm.	1.000	5	3	1	0	4	1
Corbin, Archie, Cal.	.000	12	0	0	0	0	0
Cordova, Francisco, Nash.	1.000	2	0	1	0	1	0
CORNELIUS, Reid, Cal.	1.000	27	19	28	0	47	2
Corps, Edwin, Fres.	1.000	4	0	3	0	3	0
Crabtree, Robbie, Fres.	1.000	22	2	5	0	7	0
Crafton, Kevin, Mem.	1.000	4	0	1	0	1	0
Creek, Doug, Iowa*	.857	25	7	11	3	21	1
Creek, Ryan, N.O.	1.000	6	2	6	0	8	1
Croghan, Andy, Alb.	.750	35	2	4	2	8	0
Croushore, Rich, Mem.	.000	7	0	0	0	0	0
Crow, Dean, N.O.	1.000	34	2	8	0	10	0
Cummings, John, Tuc.*	.714	11	0	5	2	7	0
Cunnane, Will, L.V.	1.000	28	7	5	0	12	1
Dale, Carl, Van.	.571	29	0	4	3	7	0
D'Amico, Jeff, Van.-Oma.	1.000	26	3	2	0	5	1
Darensbourg, Vic, Cal.*	1.000	9	2	0	0	2	0
Darwin, Jeff, L.V.	1.000	8	0	2	0	2	0
Davis, Doug, Okla.*	1.000	13	6	17	0	23	1
Davis, Kane, Nash.	.857	12	3	3	1	7	0
De Jean, Mike, C.S.	.000	1	0	0	0	0	0
De La Maza, Roland, Van.	.000	4	0	0	0	0	0
De La Rosa, Maximo, Tac.-C.S.	1.000	23	1	3	0	4	0
Delgado, Danny, Tac.	.000	2	0	0	0	0	0
Del Toro, Miguel, Fres.	1.000	40	6	14	0	20	0
Dempster, Ryan, Cal.	1.000	5	4	7	0	11	0
Dennis, Shane, L.V.*	.947	34	5	13	1	19	0
Detmers, Kris, Mem.*	.941	23	4	12	1	17	2
Dickey, R.A., Okla.	1.000	6	2	4	0	6	0
Diorio, Mike, N.O.	.875	50	2	5	1	8	0
Dougherty, Jim, Nash.	.923	53	4	8	1	13	1
Drumheller, Al, L.V.*	1.000	20	2	10	0	12	3
Drumright, Mike, Cal.	.750	12	2	1	1	4	0
Dunbar, Matt, Nash.*	1.000	11	0	3	0	3	0
Duncan, Geoff, Cal.	1.000	5	0	1	0	1	1
Edsell, Geoff, Edm.	1.000	30	6	5	0	11	0
Eischen, Joey, Tuc.*	.833	27	2	8	2	12	0
Ellis, Robert, N.O.	.974	27	8	30	1	39	2
Estrella, Luis, Fres.	1.000	8	2	3	0	5	0
Etherton, Seth, Edm.	1.000	4	1	1	0	2	0
Evans, Bart, Oma.	.667	30	1	1	1	3	0
Eversgerd, Bryan, Mem.*	1.000	59	7	16	0	23	0
Farmer, Michael, C.S.*	.833	25	6	19	5	30	3
Farnsworth, Kyle, Iowa	1.000	6	4	4	0	8	0
Figueroa, Nelson, Tuc.	1.000	24	6	23	0	29	2
Fiore, Tony, S.L.	.950	40	7	12	1	20	2
Fleetham, Ben, Tac.	1.000	14	1	0	0	1	0
Flener, Huck, Tac.*	.900	22	2	7	1	10	1
Fontenot, Joe, Cal.	1.000	8	0	8	0	8	1
Franklin, Ryan, Tac.	.895	29	8	26	4	38	0
Freeman, Ricky, Van.	.000	1	0	0	0	0	0
Frey, Steve, Okla.*	1.000	30	0	2	0	2	0
Fultz, Aaron, Fres.*	.958	37	9	14	1	24	2
Fussell, Chris, Oma.	1.000	14	3	12	0	15	1
Fyhrie, Mike, Edm.	1.000	19	4	12	0	16	1
Gajkowski, Steve, Iowa	.955	58	7	14	1	22	1
Gandarillas, Gus, S.L.	1.000	42	4	8	0	12	0
Garcia, Mike, Nash.	1.000	23	0	1	0	1	0
Garrett, Hal, Alb.	.000	1	0	0	0	0	0
Giard, Ken, Nash.	1.000	14	1	1	0	2	0
Gilbert, Shawn, Alb.	.000	1	0	0	0	0	0
Glynn, Ryan, Okla.	.920	16	9	14	2	25	1
Gonzalez, Gabe, Cal.*	1.000	24	1	3	0	4	0
Gonzalez, Jeremi, Iowa	.750	3	1	2	1	4	0
Gonzalez, Lariel, C.S.	.500	12	0	1	1	2	0
Gooding, Jason, Oma.*	1.000	1	0	1	0	1	0
Gregg, Kevin, Van.	1.000	1	0	0	0	1	0
Grilli, Jason, Fres.-Cal.	.923	27	6	18	2	26	0
Gunderson, Eric, Okla.*	1.000	5	1	0	0	1	0
Hackman, Luther, C.S.	.950	15	9	10	1	20	1

Player, Team	Pct.	G	PO	A	E	TC	DP
Hansell, Greg, Nash.	1.000	22	1	2	0	3	0
Hanson, Erik, Cal.-Oma.	.880	24	10	12	3	25	1
Harris, Jeff, S.L.	1.000	36	6	10	0	16	1
Harville, Chad, Van.	1.000	22	1	1	0	2	0
Hawblitzel, Ryan, Edm.	1.000	24	6	7	0	13	0
Heiserman, Rick, Mem.	.929	52	6	7	1	14	0
Henry, Butch, Tac.*	.000	4	0	0	0	0	0
Henry, Doug, N.O.	1.000	3	0	1	0	1	0
Herges, Matt, Alb.	.889	21	4	20	3	27	1
Hernandez, Fernando, Tuc.	1.000	5	1	1	0	2	0
Herrick, Jason, Edm.*	1.000	1	0	1	0	1	1
Hinchliffe, Brett, Tac.	.923	21	3	9	1	13	2
Hodges, Kevin, N.O.-Tac.	1.000	19	14	20	0	34	1
Holdridge, David, Tac.	1.000	41	6	12	0	18	0
Holmes, Darren, Tuc.	.000	1	0	0	0	0	0
Holtz, Mike, Edm.*	1.000	20	0	2	0	2	0
Holzemer, Mark, C.S.*	1.000	41	2	8	0	10	0
Hudson, Joe, Okla.	.667	5	0	2	1	3	0
Hudson, Tim, Van.	.889	8	3	5	1	9	1
Huisman, Rick, N.O.	.875	35	3	4	1	8	0
Huls, Steve, S.L.	1.000	1	1	0	0	1	0
Hutchinson, Chad, Mem.	1.000	2	2	0	0	2	0
Jacobsen, Joe, Edm.	1.000	12	0	3	0	3	0
James, Mike, Edm.	1.000	8	1	0	0	1	0
Jarvis, Kevin, Van.	.941	17	4	12	1	17	1
Jensen, Jason, Tuc.*	1.000	1	0	1	0	1	0
Jensen, Ryan, Fres.	.967	27	10	19	1	30	0
Jimenez, Jose, Mem.	1.000	4	1	3	0	4	0
Johnson, Jonathan, Okla.	.875	21	8	13	3	24	0
Johnson, Keith, Tuc.	.000	1	0	0	0	0	0
Jones, Bobby, C.S.*	1.000	3	0	2	0	2	0
Jones, Marcus, Van.	.500	3	0	1	1	2	0
Jordan, Ricardo, Alb.*	1.000	37	1	4	0	5	0
Judd, Mike, Alb.	.857	21	9	9	3	21	2
Juelsgaard, Jarod, Iowa	.871	23	9	18	4	31	4
Karchner, Matt, Iowa	.000	5	0	0	0	0	0
Karp, Ryan, Okla.*	1.000	8	0	8	0	8	1
Kim, Byung-Hyun, Tuc.	1.000	11	4	3	0	7	0
King, Bill, Van.	.938	45	2	13	1	16	0
King, Curtis, Mem.	1.000	27	2	3	0	5	0
King, Ray, Iowa*	1.000	37	1	12	0	13	1
Knight, Brandon, Okla.	.931	27	12	15	2	29	0
Kolb, Brandon, L.V.	.857	42	2	4	1	7	2
Kolb, Dan, Okla.	.938	11	7	8	1	16	3
Krivda, Rick, Oma.*	.818	21	2	7	2	11	1
Kroon, Marc, Tac.	1.000	13	1	3	0	4	0
Kubenka, Jeff, Alb.*	1.000	51	4	9	0	13	0
Kubinski, Tim, Van.*	.969	46	9	22	1	32	2
Lacy, Kerry, Iowa	.880	49	8	14	3	25	3
Lawrence, Sean, Van.*	1.000	25	0	2	0	2	0
Laxton, Brett, Van.	.972	25	17	18	1	36	3
Lee, Corey, Okla.*	.833	4	3	2	1	6	0
Lee, David, C.S.	.000	6	0	0	0	0	0
Leiter, Mark, Tac.	1.000	1	0	1	0	1	0
Lincoln, Mike, S.L.	1.000	9	2	8	0	10	1
Lineweaver, Aaron, Oma.	.000	1	0	0	0	0	0
Loaiza, Esteban, Okla.	1.000	2	2	1	0	3	0
Lobaton, Jose, Cal.	.000	2	0	0	0	0	0
Lomon, Kevin, Edm.	.917	23	10	12	2	24	2
Long, Joey, Nash.*	1.000	35	2	5	0	7	1
Lorraine, Andrew, Iowa*	1.000	22	8	21	0	29	0
Lovingier, Kevin, Mem.*	.857	51	2	4	1	7	0
Lubozynski, Matt, Edm.*	.000	1	0	0	0	0	0
Luce, Robert, Tac.	1.000	3	1	4	0	5	0
Ludwick, Eric, Cal.	.909	48	3	7	1	11	2
Luebbers, Larry, Mem.	1.000	21	6	22	0	28	0
Mahaffey, Alan, S.L.*	1.000	7	1	2	0	3	0
Mahay, Ron, Van.*	1.000	32	4	7	0	11	1
Manning, David, Iowa	1.000	7	0	2	0	2	0
Manwiller, Tim, Van.	1.000	11	5	7	0	12	1
Marsters, Brandon, S.L.	.000	1	0	0	0	0	0
Marte, Damaso, Tac.*	1.000	31	6	6	0	12	1
Marzano, John, Okla.	1.000	1	1	0	0	1	0
Mathews, T.J., Van.	.000	1	0	0	0	0	0
Mathews, Terry, Oma.	1.000	7	1	2	0	3	1
Maxcy, Brian, N.O.	1.000	4	1	2	0	3	0
McCarthy, Greg, Tac.*	1.000	18	0	3	0	3	1
McCurry, Jeff, N.O.	.909	40	3	7	1	11	1
McDill, Allen, Okla.*	1.000	42	0	4	0	4	1
McDowell, Jack, Edm.	.750	2	1	2	1	4	1
McMullen, Mike, Fres.	.909	41	5	15	2	22	1
McNichol, Brian, Iowa*	.941	28	6	26	2	34	0
Meacham, Rusty, N.O.	1.000	17	3	7	0	10	1
Meche, Gil, Tac.	.800	6	1	3	1	5	0
Medina, Rafael, Cal.	.889	25	1	7	1	9	1
Menhart, Paul, Edm.-Cal.	.773	17	11	6	5	22	2
Mercedes, Jose, L.V.-Cal.	.955	19	7	14	1	22	0
Michalak, Chris, Edm.-Tuc.*	.946	45	9	26	2	37	0
Milacki, Bob, Nash.	.973	22	13	23	1	37	2
Miller, Kurt, Iowa	1.000	8	0	1	0	1	0
Miller, Travis, S.L.*	.667	16	1	1	1	3	0
Miller, Wade, N.O.	1.000	26	5	21	0	26	3
Mintz, Steve, Edm.	1.000	31	0	2	0	2	0
Mitchell, Dean, Alb.	1.000	31	7	5	0	12	0
Mlicki, Doug, Mem.	1.000	38	5	9	0	14	0
Mohler, Mike, Mem.*	1.000	10	0	2	0	2	0
Montgomery, Jeff, Oma.	1.000	4	1	0	0	1	0
Montoya, Norm, Edm.*	1.000	38	8	16	0	24	1
Moody, Eric, Okla.	1.000	39	6	11	0	17	2
Moreno, Orber, Oma.	1.000	16	1	3	0	4	0
Morman, Alvin, Oma.*	1.000	8	0	2	0	2	0
Morse, Paul, Edm.	.941	10	5	11	1	17	0
Mounce, Tony, N.O.*	1.000	14	0	1	0	1	0
Mulder, Mark, Van.*	1.000	22	5	13	0	18	1
Mullen, Scott, Oma.*	1.000	20	2	16	0	18	2
Murray, Heath, L.V.*	1.000	15	2	16	0	18	4
Myers, Rodney, Iowa	1.000	20	3	3	0	6	0
Nathan, Joe, Fres.	.818	13	4	5	2	11	1
Nomo, Hideo, Iowa	1.000	3	3	1	0	4	0
Norton, Phillip, Iowa*	.900	14	5	13	2	20	0
Nunez, Vladimir, Tuc.	1.000	3	0	1	0	1	0
Nussbeck, Mark, Mem.	.889	36	6	10	2	18	1
Ohme, Kevin, S.L.*	.944	51	2	15	1	18	1
Ojala, Kirt, Cal.*	.955	16	6	15	1	22	1
Opipari, Mario, Mem.	.000	3	0	0	0	0	0
Oquist, Mike, Van.	1.000	1	1	1	0	2	0
Oropesa, Eddie, Fres.*	.909	21	1	19	2	22	2
Ortiz, Ramon, Edm.	.692	9	4	5	4	13	1
Osteen, Gavin, Alb.*	1.000	34	6	11	0	17	1
Padilla, Vicente, Tuc.	.882	18	2	13	2	17	0
Patrick, Bronswell, Fres.	.970	28	13	19	1	33	1
Patterson, Danny, Okla.	1.000	2	0	1	0	1	0
Patterson, John, Tuc.	1.000	7	2	6	0	8	2
Perez, Carlos, Alb.*	.909	6	2	8	1	11	0
Perez, Dario, Cal.	.960	28	7	17	1	25	1
Perez, Juan, Van.*	1.000	20	0	1	0	1	0
Perisho, Matt, Okla.*	.875	27	4	17	3	24	2
Perkins, Dan, S.L.	1.000	3	2	0	0	2	0
Peters, Chris, Nash.*	1.000	11	0	8	0	8	0
Peters, Don, Tuc.	1.000	3	0	2	0	2	0
Phillips, J.R., C.S.*	.000	2	0	0	0	0	0
Phillips, Jason, Nash.	.000	1	0	0	0	0	0
Pickett, Ricky, Okla.*	.333	29	0	2	4	6	0
Pisciotta, Marc, Oma.	.500	10	0	1	1	2	0
Porzio, Mike, C.S.*	.800	35	0	4	1	5	0
Pote, Lou, Edm.	1.000	24	12	15	0	27	2
Powell, Brian, N.O.	1.000	9	5	9	0	14	1
Quevedo, Ruben, Iowa	1.000	7	2	1	0	3	0
Radlosky, Rob, S.L.	1.000	22	5	6	0	11	0
Raggio, Brady, Okla.	1.000	30	11	16	0	27	2
Rain, Steve, Iowa	1.000	8	0	1	0	1	0
Ramirez, Roberto, C.S.*	1.000	10	2	14	0	16	1
Ramsay, Robert, Tac.*	1.000	5	0	1	0	1	0
Randall, Scott, C.S.	1.000	9	4	6	0	10	0
Randolph, Steve, Tuc.*	1.000	11	0	4	0	4	0
Rath, Fred, S.L.	1.000	56	7	10	0	17	0
Rath, Gary, S.L.*	.964	20	5	22	1	28	0
Ray, Ken, Oma.	1.000	27	3	4	0	7	0
Redman, Mark, S.L.*	.968	24	12	18	1	31	1
Reichert, Dan, Oma.	.857	17	11	13	4	28	2
Rigby, Brad, Van.	1.000	1	2	0	0	2	0
Rios, Dan, Oma.	.842	47	6	10	3	19	2
Ritchie, Todd, Nash.	1.000	1	0	1	0	1	0
Rivera, Roberto, L.V.*	.889	20	2	6	1	9	0
Robertson, Rich, Okla.-Nash.*	1.000	10	3	7	0	10	0
Rodriguez, Frank, S.L.	1.000	9	4	4	0	8	1
Romero, J.C., S.L.*	.857	15	2	4	1	7	0
Rooney, Mike, Tuc.	.000	1	0	0	0	0	0
Rossiter, Mike, C.S.	.714	24	1	4	2	7	0
Rossy, Rico, L.V.	.000	1	0	0	0	0	0
Ruebel, Matt, Tuc.*	.800	6	1	3	1	5	0
Ruffcorn, Scott, Oma.	.000	8	0	0	0	0	0
Ruffin, Johnny, Alb.	1.000	46	8	4	0	12	0
Rusch, Glendon, Oma.*	.750	20	3	6	3	12	0
Ryan, Jason, S.L.	1.000	9	7	5	0	12	0
Ryan, Ken, Nash.	1.000	6	0	3	0	3	0
Ryan, Matt, Nash.	1.000	48	7	12	0	19	0

Player, Team	Pct.	G	PO	A	E	TC	DP
Sabel, Erik, Tuc.	1.000	22	2	15	0	17	3
Saier, Matt, Oma.	1.000	9	4	5	0	9	0
Saipe, Mike, C.S.	1.000	11	2	5	0	7	1
Sak, Jim, L.V.	1.000	23	3	4	0	7	0
Salkeld, Roger, Cal.	1.000	27	1	0	0	1	0
Sampson, Benj, S.L.*	1.000	3	1	3	0	4	0
Sanchez, Jesus, Cal.*	1.000	4	1	1	0	2	0
Santiago, Jose, Oma.	.000	1	0	0	0	0	0
Sauveur, Rich, Nash.*	1.000	53	5	5	0	10	0
Scanlan, Bob, N.O.	.921	28	14	21	3	38	1
Scheffer, Aaron, Tac.	.714	35	2	3	2	7	0
Schoeneweis, Scott, Edm.*	.833	9	3	2	1	6	0
Scott, Tim, Nash.	1.000	19	4	3	0	7	1
Seifert, Ryan, C.S.	.000	1	0	0	0	0	0
Serafini, Dan, Iowa*	1.000	2	1	0	0	1	0
Shoemaker, Stephen, C.S.	.818	16	3	6	2	11	1
Shouse, Brian, Tuc.*	.846	30	2	9	2	13	0
Sievert, Mark, Okla.	1.000	7	1	1	0	2	0
Sikorski, Brian, N.O.	.930	28	11	29	3	43	1
Silva, Jose, Nash.	1.000	2	1	1	0	2	0
Sinclair, Steve, Tac.*	.000	2	0	0	0	0	0
Skrmetta, Matt, L.V.	.000	20	0	0	0	0	0
Slocumb, Heathcliff, Mem.	.000	2	0	0	0	0	0
Slusarski, Joe, N.O.	1.000	40	4	8	0	12	1
Smith, Chuck, Okla.	.867	32	4	9	2	15	3
Smith, Pete, Mem.-L.V.	.960	21	8	16	1	25	0
Snow, Bert, Van.	1.000	2	0	1	0	1	0
Soderstrom, Steve, Fres.	.667	22	1	3	2	6	0
Sodowsky, Clint, Mem.	.909	19	12	8	2	22	0
Sparks, Jeff, Nash.	1.000	34	3	4	0	7	0
Spencer, Sean, Tac.*	1.000	44	2	5	0	7	0
Spencer, Stan, L.V.	1.000	12	4	8	0	12	0
Stanifer, Rob, Cal.	.000	16	0	0	0	0	0
Stechschulte, Gene, Mem.	.000	2	0	0	0	0	0
Steenstra, Kennie, Tac.	.917	13	1	10	1	12	1
Stein, Blake, Van.	.929	19	4	9	1	14	0
Stentz, Brent, S.L.	.667	23	1	1	1	3	0
Stephenson, Garrett, Mem.	1.000	4	0	5	0	5	1
Stevens, Dave, Tac.	1.000	7	2	1	0	3	0
Stone, Ricky, Alb.	.857	27	9	21	5	35	3
Stoops, Jim, C.S.	1.000	55	5	10	0	15	1
Sullivan, Brendan, L.V.	.933	45	3	11	1	15	1
Swartzbaugh, Dave, Tuc.	1.000	13	0	2	0	2	0
Sweeney, Brian, Tac.	.800	5	2	2	1	5	0
Tavarez, Julian, Fres.	1.000	4	0	1	0	1	0
Tejera, Michael, Cal.*	1.000	2	0	2	0	2	0
Telemaco, Amaury, Tuc.	.500	13	0	1	1	2	0
Thompson, Mark, Mem.	.857	9	3	9	2	14	0
Thomson, John, C.S.	1.000	5	3	2	0	5	1
Tollberg, Brian, L.V.	1.000	5	2	3	0	5	0
Troutman, Keith, Edm.	1.000	6	2	1	0	3	0
Tuttle, Dave, Tuc.	1.000	35	13	12	0	25	4
Van Poppel, Todd, Nash.	1.000	27	13	18	0	31	2
Vasquez, Leo, Van.*	.000	1	0	0	0	0	0
Venafro, Mike, Okla.*	1.000	6	1	5	0	6	0
Veras, Dario, Oma.	1.000	12	3	2	0	5	0
Verdugo, Jason, Fres.	1.000	9	1	0	0	1	0
Verplancke, Joe, Tuc.	.000	2	0	0	0	0	0
Villano, Mike, Cal.	1.000	36	4	6	0	10	1
Vizcaino, Luis, Van.	1.000	7	2	1	0	3	2
Vosberg, Ed, L.V.-Tuc.*	1.000	34	2	13	0	15	0
Wainhouse, David, C.S.	1.000	38	1	3	0	4	0
Walker, Jamie, Oma.*	1.000	4	4	1	0	5	2
Walker, Pete, C.S.	.938	48	8	7	1	16	1
Wallace, Jeff, Nash.*	.750	15	0	3	1	4	0
Wallace, Kent, N.O.	1.000	36	2	3	0	5	0
Ward, Jeremy, Tuc.	1.000	1	1	0	0	1	0
Warner, Ron, Mem.	.000	2	0	0	0	0	0
Washburn, Jarrod, Edm.*	.941	11	5	11	1	17	0
Watkins, Scott, Iowa*	.900	47	3	6	1	10	0
Weaver, Eric, Tac.	1.000	16	0	2	0	2	0
Weber, Ben, Fres.	.955	51	9	12	1	22	0
Weber, Neil, Tuc.-Alb.*	.667	18	0	2	1	3	0
Weibl, Clint, Mem.	1.000	5	3	1	0	4	0
Wengert, Don, Oma.	1.000	16	1	6	0	7	0
West, David, Alb.*	.000	2	0	0	0	0	0
Whiteside, Matt, L.V.	.920	47	7	16	2	25	1
Wilkins, Marc, Nash.	1.000	8	0	1	0	1	1
Williams, Eddie, S.L.	1.000	2	0	1	0	1	0
Williams, Jeff, Alb.*	.958	42	3	20	1	24	1
Williams, Shad, Edm.	.952	16	7	13	1	21	1
Williams, Todd, Tac.	1.000	1	0	1	0	1	0
Wilson, Desi, Tuc.*	.000	1	0	0	0	0	0
Wilson, Kris, Oma.	1.000	1	1	0	0	1	0
Wolff, Bryan, L.V.	.970	28	14	18	1	33	2
Woodall, Brad, Iowa*	1.000	15	6	6	0	12	1
Wright, Jamey, C.S.	.909	17	13	17	3	33	2
Zimmerman, Jeff, Okla.	1.000	2	0	1	0	1	0
Zimmerman, Jordan, Tac.*	.000	9	0	0	0	0	0
Zito, Barry, Van.*	.000	1	0	0	0	0	0

PITCHERS WITH TWO OR MORE TEAMS

Player, Team	Pct.	G	PO	A	E	TC	DP
Boyd, Jason, Tuc.	.833	44	4	11	3	18	0
Boyd, Jason, Nash.	1.000	5	1	1	0	2	1
D'Amico, Jeff, Van.	1.000	14	0	1	0	1	0
D'Amico, Jeff, Oma.	1.000	12	3	1	0	4	1
De La Rosa, Maximo, Tac.	1.000	15	1	2	0	3	0
De La Rosa, Maximo, C.S.	1.000	8	0	1	0	1	0
Grilli, Jason, Fres.	.950	19	4	15	1	20	0
Grilli, Jason, Cal.	.833	8	2	3	1	6	0
Hanson, Erik, Cal.	.917	10	3	8	1	12	1
Hanson, Erik, Oma.	.846	14	7	4	2	13	0
Hodges, Kevin, N.O.	1.000	5	4	6	0	10	0
Hodges, Kevin, Tac.	1.000	14	10	14	0	24	1
Menhart, Paul, Edm.	.727	9	5	3	3	11	1
Menhart, Paul, Cal.	.818	8	6	3	2	11	1
Mercedes, Jose, L.V.	.933	15	6	8	1	15	0
Mercedes, Jose, Cal.	1.000	4	1	6	0	7	0
Michalak, Chris, Edm.*	1.000	24	4	8	0	12	0
Michalak, Chris, Tac.*	.920	21	5	18	2	25	0
Robertson, Rich, Okla.*	.000	3	0	0	0	0	0
Robertson, Rich, Nash.*	1.000	7	3	7	0	10	0
Smith, Pete, Mem.	1.000	8	3	6	0	9	0
Smith, Pete, L.V.	.938	13	5	10	1	16	0
Vosberg, Ed, L.V.*	1.000	8	0	3	0	3	0
Vosberg, Ed, Tuc.*	1.000	26	2	10	0	12	0
Weber, Neil, Tuc.	1.000	9	0	1	0	1	0
Weber, Neil, Alb.*	.500	9	0	1	1	2	0

The following players appeared only as designated hitter, pinch-hitter or pinch runner: Alcala, ph; M. Carroll, ph; Faircloth, ph; Hacker, dh-ph.

LEAGUE CHAMPIONS

Year	Team	Pct.
1903—	Los Angeles	.630
1904—	Tacoma	.589
	Tacoma§	.571
	Los Angeles§	.571
1905—	Tacoma	.583
	Los Angeles*	.604
1906—	Portland	.657
1907—	Los Angeles	.608
1908—	Los Angeles	.585
1909—	San Francisco	.623
1910—	Portland	.567
1911—	Portland	.589
1912—	Oakland	.591
1913—	Portland	.559
1914—	Portland	.574
1915—	San Francisco	.570
1916—	Los Angeles	.601
1917—	San Francisco	.561
1918—	Vernon	.569
	Los Angeles (2nd)◆	.548
1919—	Vernon	.613
1920—	Vernon	.556
1921—	Los Angeles	.574
1922—	San Francisco	.638
1923—	San Francisco	.617
1924—	Seattle	.545
1925—	San Francisco	.643
1926—	Los Angeles	.599
1927—	Oakland	.615
1928—	San Francisco*	.630
	Sacramento∞	.626
	San Francisco∞	.626
1929—	Mission	.643
	Hollywood*	.592
1930—	Los Angeles	.576
	Hollywood*	.650
1931—	Hollywood	.626
	San Francisco*	.608
1932—	Portland	.587
1933—	Los Angeles	.610
1934—	Los Angeles▼	.786
	Los Angeles▼	.689
1935—	Los Angeles	.648
	San Francisco*	.608
1936—	Portland‡	.549
1937—	Sacramento	.573
	San Diego (3rd)†	.545
1938—	Los Angeles	.590
	Sacramento (3rd)†	.537
1939—	Seattle	.589
	Sacramento (4th)†	.500

CLASS AAA Pacific Coast League

Year	Team	Pct.
1940—	Seattle‡	.629
1941—	Seattle‡	.598
1942—	Sacramento	.590
	Seattle (3rd)†	.539
1943—	Los Angeles	.710
	S. Francisco (2nd)†	.574
1944—	Los Angeles	.586
	S. Francisco (3rd)†	.509
1945—	Portland	.622
	S. Francisco (4th)†	.525
1946—	San Francisco‡	.628
1947—	Los Angeles▲	.567
1948—	Oakland‡	.606
1949—	Hollywood‡	.583
1950—	Oakland	.590
1951—	Seattle‡	.593
1952—	Hollywood	.606
1953—	Hollywood	.589
1954—	San Diego■	.604
1955—	Seattle	.552
1956—	Los Angeles	.637
1957—	San Francisco	.601
1958—	Phoenix	.578
1959—	Salt Lake City	.552
1960—	Spokane	.601
1961—	Tacoma	.630
1962—	San Diego	.604
1963—	Spokane	.620
	Oklahoma City•	.632
1964—	Arkansas	.609
	San Diego•	.576
1965—	Oklahoma City	.628
	Portland	.547
1966—	Seattle•	.561

Year	Team	Pct.
	Tulsa	.578
1967—	San Diego•	.574
	Spokane	.541
1968—	Tulsa•	.642
	Spokane	.586
1969—	Tacoma•	.589
	Eugene	.603
1970—	Spokane•	.644
	Hawaii	.671
1971—	Salt Lake City	.534
	Tacoma	.545
1972—	Albuquerque	.622
	Eugene	.534
1973—	Tucson	.583
	Spokane•	.563
1974—	Spokane•	.549
	Albuquerque	.535
1975—	Salt Lake City	.556
	Hawaii•	.611
1976—	Salt Lake City	.625
	Hawaii•	.531
1977—	Phoenix•	.579
	Hawaii	.541
1978—	Tacoma††	.584
	Albuquerque††	.557
1979—	Albuquerque	.581
	Salt Lake City‡‡	.541
1980—	Albuquerque	.578
	Hawaii	.539
1981—	Albuquerque*	.712
	Tacoma	.561
1982—	Albuquerque*	.594
	Spokane	.545
1983—	Albuquerque	.594

Year	Team	Pct.
	Portland*	.528
1984—	Hawaii	.621
	Edmonton*	.486
1985—	Vancouver*	.522
	Phoenix	.563
1986—	Vancouver	.616
	Las Vegas*	.563
1987—	Calgary	.596
	Albuquerque*	.542
1988—	Vancouver	.599
	Las Vegas*	.529
1989—	Albuquerque	.563
	Vancouver*	.514
1990—	Albuquerque*	.641
	Edmonton	.553
1991—	Albuquerque	.580
	Tucson*	.564
1992—	Colorado Springs*	.596
	Portland	.576
1993—	Portland	.608
	Tucson*	.580
1994—	Albuquerque*	.597
	Vancouver	.542
1995—	Salt Lake	.549
	Colorado Springs*	.538
1996—	Edmonton*	.592
	Phoenix	.479
1997—	Phoenix	.615
	Edmonton*	.556
1998—	Iowa	.590
	New Orleans†	.535
1999—	Vancouver‡	.592

*Won split-season playoff. †Won four-team playoff. ‡Won pennant and four-team playoff. §Tied for second-half title with Tacoma winning playoff. ∞Tied for second-half title, with Sacramento winning playoff. ▲Ended regular season in tie with San Francisco and won one-game playoff for pennant, then won four-club playoff. ◆Won playoff from first-place Vernon and awarded championship. ■Defeated Hollywood in one-game playoff for pennant. ▼Won both halves, no playoff. •League was divided into Northern, Southern divisions in 1963, 1969-70-71, and Eastern, Western divisions in 1964 through 1968 and 1972 through 1977, won two-team playoff. ††League divided into Eastern and Western divisions, Tacoma and Albuquerque declared co-champions following cancellation of four-team playoff due to continuing rain and wet grounds. ‡‡Won second-half title and defeated Hawaii in four-team playoff.

CLASS AAA *Pacific Coast League*

EASTERN LEAGUE

LEAGUE OFFICE

President
Bill Troubh

Address
P.O. Box 9711
Portland, ME 04104

Phone
207-761-2700

TEAMS

AKRON AEROS

General manager/vice president
Jeff Auman
Manager
Eric Wedge
Ballpark (capacity, surface)
Canal Park (9,097, grass)
Affiliation
Indians
Address
300 S. Main St.
Akron, OH 44308
Phone
330-253-5151

ALTOONA CURVE

General manager
Jeff Parker
Manager
Marty Brown
Ballpark (capacity, surface)
Blair County Ballpark (6,120, grass)
Affiliation
Pirates
Address
P.O. Box 1029
Altoona, PA 16603
Phone
814-943-5400

BINGHAMTON METS

General manager
R.C. Reuteman
Manager
Doug Davis
Ballpark (capacity, surface)
Binghamton Municipal Stadium (6,012, grass)
Affiliation
Mets
Address
211 Henry Street
Binghamton, NY 13901
Phone
607-723-6387

BOWIE BAYSOX

General manager
Jon Danos
Manager
Andy Etchebarren
Ballpark (capacity, surface)
Prince George's Stadium (10,000, grass)
Affiliation
Orioles
Address
4101 NE Crain Highway
Bowie, MD 20716
Phone
301-805-6000

ERIE SEAWOLVES

General manager
Andy Minister
Manager
Garry Templeton
Ballpark (capacity, surface)
Jerry Uht Park (6,000, grass)
Affiliation
Angels
Address
110 E. 10th Street
Erie, PA 16501
Phone
814-456-1300

HARRISBURG SENATORS

General manager
Todd Vander Woude
Manager
Doug Sisson
Ballpark (capacity, surface)
RiverSide Stadium (6,300, grass)
Affiliation
Expos
Address
RiverSide Stadium/City Island
Harrisburg, PA 17101
Phone
717-231-4444

NEW BRITAIN ROCK CATS

General manager
To be announced
Manager
John Russell
Ballpark (capacity, surface)
New Britain Stadium (6,146, grass)
Affiliation
Twins
Address
South Main Street
New Britain, CT 06051
Phone
860-224-8383

NEW HAVEN RAVENS

General manager
Chris Canetti
Manager
Dan Rohn
Ballpark (capacity, surface)
Yale Field (6,200, grass)
Affiliation
Mariners
Address
252 Derby Ave.
West Haven, CT 06516
Phone
203-782-1666

NORWICH NAVIGATORS

General manager
Brian Mahoney
Manager
Dan Radison
Ballpark (capacity, surface)
Thomas J. Dodd Memorial Stadium (6,000, grass)
Affiliation
Yankees
Address
14 Stott Ave.
Norwich, CT 06360
Phone
860-887-7962

PORTLAND SEA DOGS

General manager
Charles Eshbach
Manager
Rick Renteria
Ballpark (capacity, surface)
Hadlock Field (6,850, grass)
Affiliation
Marlins
Address
271 Park Avenue
Portland, ME 04102
Phone
207-870-0317

READING PHILLIES

General manager
Chuck Domino
Manager
Gary Varsho
Ballpark (capacity, surface)
GPU Stadium (8,500, grass)
Affiliation
Phillies
Address
Route 61 South/1900 Centre Ave.
Reading, PA 19605
Phone
610-375-8469

TRENTON THUNDER

General manager
Wayne Hodes
Manager
Billy Gardner Jr.
Ballpark (capacity, surface)
Samuel J. Plumeri, Sr. Field at Mercer County Waterfront Park (6,300, grass)
Affiliation
Red Sox
Address
One Thunder Road
Trenton, NJ 08611
Phone
609-394-8326

CLASS AA *Eastern League*

NORTH DIVISION

Team	W	L	T	Pct.	GB
Trenton (Red Sox)	92	50	0	.648	...
Norwich (Yankees)	78	64	0	.549	14.0
Portland (Marlins)	65	77	0	.458	27.0
New Haven (Mariners)	65	77	0	.458	27.0
New Britain (Twins)	59	82	0	.418	32.5
Binghamton (Mets)	54	88	0	.380	38.0

SOUTH DIVISION

Team	W	L	T	Pct.	GB
Erie (Angels)	81	61	0	.570	...
Harrisburg (Expos)	76	66	0	.535	5.0
Reading (Phillies)	73	69	0	.514	8.0
Bowie (Orioles)	70	71	0	.496	10.5
Akron (Indians)	69	71	0	.493	11.0
Altoona (Pirates)	67	73	0	.479	13.0

COMPOSITE

Team	Tren.	Erie	Nor.	Har.	Read.	Bow.	Akr.	Alt.	Por.	N.H.	N.B.	Bing.	W	L	T	Pct.	GB
Trenton (Red Sox)	...	5	6	5	9	4	5	4	13	11	14	16	92	50	0	.648	...
Erie (Angels)	2	...	4	10	12	12	9	14	5	5	5	3	81	61	0	.570	11.0
Norwich (Yankees)	10	3	...	1	4	2	4	2	11	20	11	10	78	64	0	.549	14.0
Harrisburg (Expos)	9	6	6	...	13	10	6	7	5	3	3	8	76	66	0	.535	16.0
Reading (Phillies)	5	5	3	7	...	9	6	11	6	5	5	11	73	69	0	.514	19.0
Bowie (Orioles)	3	12	5	6	8	...	11	11	2	4	4	4	70	71	0	.496	21.5
Akron (Indians)	2	11	3	11	10	12	...	10	1	4	2	3	69	71	0	.493	22.0
Altoona (Pirates)	3	9	5	10	5	9	12	...	2	3	5	4	67	73	0	.479	24.0
Portland (Marlins)	4	2	9	2	1	5	6	5	...	8	14	9	65	77	0	.458	27.0
New Haven (Mariners)	5	2	4	4	2	3	3	4	15	...	11	12	65	77	0	.458	27.0
New Britain (Twins)	3	2	12	4	2	2	5	2	10	9	...	8	59	82	0	.418	32.5
Binghamton (Mets)	4	4	7	6	3	4	4	3	7	5	8	...	54	88	0	.380	38.0

Major league affiliations in parentheses.

PLAYOFFS: Harrisburg defeated Erie three games to one; Norwich defeated Trenton three games to two; Harrisburg defeated Norwich three games to two to win league championship.

REGULAR-SEASON ATTENDANCE: Akron, 522,459; Altoona, 323,932; Binghamton, 203,674; Bowie, 421,398; Erie, 234,257; Harrisburg, 253,399; New Britain, 177,026; New Haven, 197,163; Norwich, 244,442; Portland, 402,582; Reading, 448,367; Trenton, 440,033. Total—3,868,732. Playoffs (14 games)—37,309. Class AA All-Star Game at Moblie, Ala.—6,174.

MANAGERS: Akron, Joel Skinner; Altoona, Marty Brown; Binghamton, Doug Davis; Bowie, Joe Ferguson; Erie, Garry Templeton; Harrisburg, Doug Sisson (though July 5 and July 13 through end of season) and Rick Sweet (July 6-12); New Britain, John Russell; New Haven, Dan Rohn; Norwich, Lee Mazzilli; Portland, Frank Cacciatore; Reading, Gary Varsho; Trenton, Demarlo Hale.

ALL-STAR TEAM: 1B—Nick Johnson, Norwich; 2B—David Eckstein, Trenton; 3B—Andy Tracy, Harrisburg; SS—Alfonso Soriano, Norwich; C—Brian Schneider, Harrisburg; OF—Raul Gonzalez, Trenton; Pat Burrell, Reading; Scott Morgan, Akron; Julio Ramirez, Portland; DH—Chris Norton, Portland; Utility—Larry Barnes, Erie; RHP—Tony Armas, Harrisburg; Brian Cooper, Erie; LHP—Matt Riley, Bowie; Michael Tejera, Portland; RP—Eric Cammack, Binghamton; Player of the Year—Andy Tracy, Harrisburg; Pitcher of the Year—Michael Tejera, Portland; Rookie of the Year—Pat Burrell, Reading; Manager of the Year—Demarlo Hale, Trenton.

1999 BATTING

TEAM

Team	Avg.	G	TPA	AB	R	H	TB	2B	3B	HR	RBI	SH	SF	HP	BB	IBB	SO	SB	CS	GDP	LOB	ShO	Slg.	OBP
Trenton	.279	142	5449	4851	785	1352	2099	251	23	150	731	51	52	0	495	17	801	151	75	119	1033	5	.433	.342
Harrisburg	.268	142	5396	4723	714	1265	1999	256	29	140	666	51	41	38	543	25	910	119	73	96	999	10	.423	.345
Portland	.267	142	5436	4774	646	1277	1926	249	35	110	587	54	38	49	521	11	990	133	57	124	1047	10	.403	.343
Akron	.265	140	5391	4782	714	1266	1990	248	40	132	663	27	31	56	495	11	1066	84	41	81	1027	7	.416	.339
Norwich	.264	142	5535	4766	755	1259	1956	232	39	129	685	30	40	94	605	11	1129	168	85	102	1072	6	.410	.356
Reading	.263	142	5451	4710	680	1237	1907	236	43	116	628	81	40	71	549	19	839	164	86	119	1018	8	.405	.346
New Britain	.260	141	5311	4730	611	1232	1839	237	26	106	562	34	43	46	458	19	832	111	58	114	993	10	.389	.329
Bowie	.259	141	5493	4798	676	1245	1882	229	27	118	611	69	48	56	522	13	786	111	60	92	1039	7	.392	.336
Erie	.258	142	5422	4686	671	1210	1856	234	41	110	612	58	44	53	581	19	1094	180	82	96	1033	3	.396	.344
Altoona	.258	140	5435	4723	695	1218	1967	249	43	138	664	58	50	85	519	10	964	105	78	85	1008	6	.416	.339
New Haven	.256	142	5355	4754	610	1219	1782	222	25	97	566	31	30	62	478	13	1000	110	69	107	999	11	.375	.330
Binghamton	.254	142	5401	4789	635	1218	1847	224	33	113	582	52	35	55	470	17	1130	168	75	111	955	8	.386	.326

INDIVIDUAL

TOP QUALIFIERS FOR BATTING CHAMPIONSHIP

Minimum 383 plate appearances. *Lefthanded batter. †Switch-hitter.

Player, Team	Avg.	G	TPA	AB	R	H	TB	2B	3B	HR	RBI	SH	SF	HP	BB	IBB	SO	SB	CS	GDP	Slg.	OBP
Johnson, Nick, Nor.*	.345	132	581	420	114	145	230	33	5	14	87	0	1	37	123	6	88	8	6	9	.548	.525
Gonzalez, Raul, Tren.	.335	127	567	505	80	169	264	33	4	18	103	1	7	3	51	3	71	12	3	14	.523	.394
Burrell, Pat, Read.	.333	117	498	417	84	139	263	28	6	28	90	0	2	0	79	3	103	3	3	13	.631	.438
Bradley, Milton, Har.†	.329	87	385	346	62	114	182	22	5	12	50	1	2	3	33	0	61	14	11	5	.526	.391
Hyzdu, Adam, Alt.	.316	91	388	345	64	109	211	26	2	24	78	0	0	3	40	1	62	8	4	2	.612	.392
Short, Rick, Bow.	.314	112	449	392	60	123	190	19	0	16	62	0	5	9	43	2	48	6	1	9	.485	.394
Tyner, Jason, Bing.*	.313	129	590	518	91	162	191	19	5	0	33	8	1	1	62	0	46	49	16	8	.369	.387
Eckstein, David, Tren.	.313	131	615	483	109	151	201	22	5	6	52	13	5	25	89	0	48	32	13	6	.416	.440
Soriano, Alfonso, Nor.	.305	89	402	361	57	110	181	20	3	15	68	0	5	4	32	1	67	24	16	9	.501	.363
Leon, Donny, Nor.†	.302	118	502	457	69	138	239	34	2	21	100	1	7	3	34	2	102	0	0	10	.523	.349
Hacker, Steve, N.B.	.302	118	511	461	71	139	256	36	0	27	97	0	6	5	39	2	103	0	2	13	.555	.358
Gibralter, David, Tren.	.299	124	509	448	76	134	230	22	1	24	97	2	5	13	32	3	68	5	5	13	.513	.359
Rolison, Nate, Por.*	.299	124	514	438	71	131	204	20	1	17	69	0	2	6	68	3	112	0	1	16	.466	.399
Chevalier, Virgil, Tren.	.293	131	577	509	81	149	225	29	4	13	76	8	8	2	50	0	73	9	9	11	.442	.353
Almonte, Wady, Bow.	.293	124	525	482	63	141	227	27	4	17	83	0	5	7	31	1	72	10	10	12	.471	.341

DEPARTMENTAL LEADERS: G—Carroll, 141; AB—Julio Ramirez, 568; R—Nick Johnson, 114; H—Raul Gonzalez, 169; TB—Tracy, 276; 2B—Hacker, 36; 3B—Redman, 12; HR—Norton, 38; RBI—Tracy, 128; SH—Ojeda, 25; SF—Barnes, 16; HP—Nick Johnson, 37; BB—Nick Johnson, 123; IBB—Barnes, 7; SO—Gainey, 184; SB—Julio Ramirez, 64; CS—Taylor, 22; GIDP—Wilton Veras, 23; Slg.—Norton, .633; OBP—Nick Johnson, .525.

ALL PLAYERS

*Lefthanded batter. †Switch-hitter.

Player, Team	Avg.	G	TPA	AB	R	H	TB	2B	3B	HR	RBI	SH	SF	HP	BB	IBB	SO	SB	CS	GDP	Slg.	OBP
Abbott, Chuck, Erie	.239	125	501	444	70	106	139	13	1	6	46	6	2	2	47	1	138	9	10	10	.313	.313
Adolfo, Carlos, Har.	.271	76	252	221	37	60	106	16	0	10	41	1	1	4	25	2	51	3	2	8	.480	.355
Agamennone, Brandon, Har.	.286	22	8	7	3	2	3	1	0	0	2	1	0	0	0	0	3	0	0	0	.429	.286
Ah Yat, Paul, Alt.	.100	16	14	10	0	1	1	0	0	0	1	0	0	0	4	0	6	0	0	0	.100	.357
Akers, Chad, N.H.	.000	1	0	0	1	0	0	0	0	0	0	0	0	0	0	0	0	0	0	0	.000	.000
Alcantara, Israel, Tren.	.294	77	324	293	48	86	172	26	0	20	60	0	0	4	27	0	78	4	2	0	.587	.361
Alley, Charles, Bow.†	.111	5	12	9	4	1	2	1	0	0	0	0	0	0	1	0	3	0	0	0	.222	.200
Almonte, Hector, Por.	.000	47	1	1	0	0	0	0	0	0	0	0	0	0	0	0	1	0	0	0	.000	.000
Almonte, Wady, Bow.	.293	124	525	482	68	141	227	27	4	17	83	0	5	7	31	1	72	10	10	12	.471	.341
Alomar, Sandy, Akr.	.310	10	34	29	8	9	12	0	0	1	6	0	2	0	3	0	2	1	0	0	.414	.353
Alvarez, Clemente, Read.	.176	48	159	142	12	25	38	5	1	2	12	5	1	0	11	0	38	1	1	3	.268	.234
Antczak, Chuck, Read.	.000	8	19	19	0	0	0	0	0	0	0	0	0	0	0	0	6	0	0	1	.000	.000
Armas, Tony, Har.	.091	24	30	22	1	2	2	0	0	0	2	4	0	0	4	0	7	0	0	0	.091	.231
Arroyo, Bronson, Alt.	.286	26	25	21	2	6	7	1	0	0	2	3	0	0	1	0	8	0	0	0	.333	.318
Arroyo, Luis, Por.*	1.000	10	1	1	0	1	1	0	0	0	0	0	0	0	0	0	0	0	0	0	1.000	1.000
Arteaga, J.D., Bing.*	.000	11	2	1	0	0	0	0	0	0	0	1	0	0	0	0	1	0	0	0	.000	.000
Asche, Mike, Alt.	.412	7	18	17	3	7	9	2	0	0	3	0	0	0	1	0	3	1	1	0	.529	.444
Ashby, Chris, Nor.	.250	29	124	108	11	27	43	5	1	3	16	0	2	3	11	0	20	3	4	3	.398	.331
Bady, Ed, Akr.†	.243	69	269	230	42	56	81	13	3	2	33	4	2	1	32	0	68	19	5	3	.352	.336
Bailie, Matt, Read.	.000	1	2	2	0	0	0	0	0	0	0	0	0	0	0	0	0	0	0	0	.000	.000
Baker, Jason, Har.	.000	23	2	2	0	0	0	0	0	0	0	0	0	0	0	0	1	0	0	0	.000	.000
Barnes, John, N.B.	.263	129	511	452	62	119	181	21	1	13	58	1	4	5	49	3	40	10	2	15	.400	.339
Barnes, Larry, Erie*	.286	130	567	497	73	142	245	25	9	20	100	0	16	5	49	7	99	14	3	7	.493	.346
Barnett, Marty, Read.	.000	35	2	1	0	0	0	0	0	0	0	1	0	0	0	0	1	0	0	0	.000	.000
Baron, Jim, Alt.*	.071	29	14	14	0	1	1	0	0	0	0	0	0	0	0	0	4	0	0	0	.071	.071
Bass, Jayson, N.H.*	.265	123	511	431	79	114	210	23	5	21	67	0	5	3	72	1	160	34	14	3	.487	.370
Bates, Fletcher, Por.†	.253	139	590	537	72	136	209	28	9	9	55	4	8	2	39	1	109	18	6	10	.389	.302
Beamon, Trey, Bing.*	.240	71	279	246	32	59	78	13	0	2	20	1	1	2	29	0	41	13	10	12	.317	.324
Benefield, Brian, Akr.	.193	44	161	145	14	28	44	3	2	3	14	0	0	0	16	0	32	3	3	1	.303	.273
Bennett, Ryan, Bing.	.000	1	4	4	1	0	0	0	0	0	0	0	0	0	0	0	2	0	0	0	.000	.000
Benz, Jake, Por.*	.000	23	1	1	0	0	0	0	0	0	0	0	0	0	0	0	0	0	0	0	.000	.000
Bergeron, Peter, Har.*	.327	42	189	162	29	53	83	14	2	4	18	0	3	0	24	4	29	9	7	0	.512	.407
Betances, Junior, Akr.	.294	89	345	306	41	90	120	14	5	2	28	1	1	6	31	1	53	9	6	7	.392	.369
Betten, Randy, Erie	.150	7	21	20	3	3	5	0	1	0	1	1	0	0	0	0	7	3	0	0	.250	.150
Betts, Todd, Akr.*	.280	104	446	375	60	105	188	24	1	19	67	0	3	7	61	2	65	2	1	3	.501	.388
Bieser, Steve, Alt.*	.209	40	174	148	24	31	52	5	2	4	23	0	1	4	21	0	32	3	4	2	.351	.322
Blank, Matt, Har.*	.333	15	23	21	1	7	7	0	0	0	2	1	0	0	1	0	2	0	1	1	.333	.364
Bradley, Milton, Har.†	.329	87	385	346	62	114	182	22	5	12	50	1	2	3	33	0	61	14	11	5	.526	.391
Bravo, Danny, Har.†	.143	12	30	28	0	4	5	1	0	0	2	1	0	0	1	0	6	0	0	0	.179	.172
Brester, Jason, Read.*	.000	16	22	16	0	0	0	0	0	0	0	5	0	0	1	0	6	0	0	0	.000	.059
Brittan, Corey, Bing.	.200	54	6	5	0	1	1	0	0	0	3	0	1	0	0	0	3	0	0	0	.200	.167
Brosnan, Jason, N.H.*	.000	28	1	1	0	0	0	0	0	0	0	0	0	0	1	0	0	0	0	0	.000	.000
Brown, Alvin, Alt.-Erie	.000	13	4	4	1	0	0	0	0	0	1	0	0	0	0	0	2	0	0	0	.000	.000
Brown, Randy, N.H.	.257	46	189	167	30	43	78	7	5	6	22	2	0	1	19	1	37	0	4	2	.467	.337
Brown, Richard, Nor.*	.261	104	424	383	46	100	152	18	8	6	54	0	4	3	34	0	81	5	8	6	.397	.323
Brown, Vick, Nor.	.251	132	582	482	86	121	157	19	1	5	48	5	5	7	83	0	101	50	14	15	.326	.366
Bruce, Mo, Bing.	.270	133	575	500	80	135	195	25	4	9	76	5	4	6	61	2	134	33	11	9	.390	.351
Bryant, Matt, Alt.	.250	12	26	24	1	6	6	0	0	0	1	0	0	0	2	0	7	0	0	0	.250	.308
Buccheri, Jim, Bing.	.294	4	18	17	1	5	8	1	1	0	1	1	0	0	0	0	4	0	0	1	.471	.294
Budzinski, Mark, Akr.*	.283	86	352	297	58	84	131	17	6	6	46	2	0	5	48	0	63	9	4	3	.441	.391
Bump, Nate, Por.	.333	8	3	3	1	1	1	0	0	0	0	0	0	0	0	0	1	0	0	0	.333	.333
Burger, Rob, Read.	.750	10	5	4	0	3	3	0	0	0	1	0	0	0	1	0	1	0	0	0	.750	.800
Burkhart, Morgan, Tren.†	.230	66	283	239	40	55	107	14	1	12	41	0	3	10	31	1	43	3	0	2	.448	.339
Burnett, A.J., Por.	.077	26	16	13	0	1	1	0	0	0	0	1	0	0	2	0	7	0	0	0	.077	.200
Burnham, Gary, Read.*	.249	116	417	354	47	88	144	20	0	12	49	6	1	15	41	3	49	11	3	16	.407	.350
Burrell, Pat, Read.	.333	117	498	417	84	139	263	28	6	28	90	0	2	0	79	3	103	3	3	13	.631	.438
Cames, Aaron, Por.	.444	23	10	9	1	4	5	1	0	0	2	1	0	0	0	0	3	0	0	0	.556	.444
Camilli, Jason, Har.	.214	63	180	154	26	33	52	7	0	4	16	0	1	2	23	0	31	0	2	3	.338	.322
Cammack, Eric, Bing.	.000	45	1	1	0	0	0	0	0	0	0	0	0	0	0	0	1	0	0	0	.000	.000
Carroll, Jamey, Har.	.292	141	623	561	78	164	223	34	5	5	63	5	4	5	48	2	58	21	10	13	.398	.351
Casimiro, Carlos, Bow.	.221	139	578	526	73	116	195	23	1	18	64	5	5	3	39	0	101	7	12	10	.371	.276
Cedeno, Blas, Read.	.667	19	5	3	1	2	3	0	0	0	1	0	0	1	0	0	1	0	0	0	.667	.750
Censale, Silvio, Read.*	.125	16	13	8	4	1	2	1	0	0	1	2	0	0	3	0	3	0	0	0	.250	.364
Chevalier, Virgil, Tren.	.293	131	577	509	81	149	225	29	4	13	76	8	8	2	50	0	73	9	9	11	.442	.353
Christian, Eddie, Erie†	.283	53	234	205	29	58	80	11	1	3	27	8	1	0	20	0	34	14	3	5	.390	.345
Clark, Howie, Bow.*	.294	39	139	126	17	37	49	6	0	2	12	0	0	3	10	0	12	2	0	0	.389	.360
Coffie, Ivanon, Bow.*	.185	57	220	195	21	36	60	9	3	3	23	1	3	1	20	0	46	2	2	3	.308	.260
Coggin, Dave, Read.	.333	10	3	3	0	1	1	0	0	0	0	0	0	0	0	0	0	0	0	0	.333	.333
Colangelo, Mike, Erie	.339	28	127	109	24	37	56	10	3	1	13	0	0	4	14	0	22	3	3	5	.514	.433
Cordero, Wil, Akr.	.364	3	12	11	2	4	6	2	0	0	0	0	0	1	0	0	3	0	0	1	.545	.417
Corey, Mark, Bing.	.105	29	23	19	2	2	2	0	0	0	3	0	0	1	1	0	7	0	0	0	.105	.150
Cossins, Tim, Har.	.172	41	104	93	8	16	30	2	0	4	14	4	2	1	4	1	21	0	0	4	.323	.210
Cranford, Joey, N.B.	.208	57	175	159	19	33	54	4	1	5	14	3	2	1	10	0	38	0	3	1	.340	.256
Cruz, Cirilo, N.H.	.158	18	70	57	5	9	12	3	0	0	9	0	1	2	10	0	13	0	0	2	.211	.300
Cruz, Ivan, Alt.*	.154	3	14	13	1	2	3	1	0	0	3	0	0	0	1	0	8	0	0	0	.231	.214
Cummings, Midre, N.B.*	.376	24	114	93	28	35	48	7	0	2	15	0	2	2	17	1	14	3	1	1	.516	.474

- 443 -

Player, Team	Avg.	G	TPA	AB	R	H	TB	2B	3B	HR	RBI	SH	SF	HP	BB	IBB	SO	SB	CS	GDP	Slg.	OBP
Daniels, David, Alt.	.000	55	2	2	0	0	0	0	0	0	0	0	0	0	0	0	0	0	0	0	.000	.000
Darden, Tony, Bing.	.354	49	191	164	25	58	83	8	1	5	23	0	0	8	19	2	30	5	4	3	.506	.445
Davidson, Cleatus, N.B.†	.244	127	563	491	88	120	162	16	10	2	40	10	6	3	53	1	110	40	14	8	.330	.318
Davis, Kane, Alt.	.182	16	14	11	0	2	3	1	0	0	1	3	0	0	0	0	5	0	0	0	.273	.182
DeCinces, Tim, Bow.*	.260	84	313	258	38	67	118	15	0	12	36	0	1	0	54	3	52	0	2	7	.457	.387
DeHaan, Kory, Alt.*	.268	47	211	190	26	51	77	13	2	3	24	5	3	2	11	0	46	14	6	3	.405	.311
De La Rosa, Tomas, Har.	.261	135	522	467	70	122	168	22	3	6	43	7	5	1	42	2	64	28	15	10	.360	.320
Della Ratta, Pete, Bing.	.000	41	4	3	0	0	0	0	0	0	0	0	0	0	1	0	2	0	0	0	.000	.250
Dennis, Les, Nor.	.250	53	209	176	27	44	54	10	0	0	12	2	1	3	27	0	50	0	3	5	.307	.357
Dent, Darrell, Bow.*	.212	108	305	250	41	53	66	9	2	0	17	12	4	2	37	0	58	24	5	4	.264	.314
Depastino, Joe, Tren.	.217	6	27	23	5	5	12	1	0	2	5	0	0	1	3	0	3	1	0	2	.522	.333
DeShields, Delino, Bow.*	.267	4	19	15	2	4	5	1	0	0	0	0	0	1	3	0	2	0	0	0	.333	.421
Devarez, Cesar, Bow.	.265	58	220	200	25	53	76	11	0	4	29	1	1	2	16	1	24	2	2	5	.380	.324
Dewey, Jason, Erie	.223	40	156	139	17	31	50	7	0	4	14	0	0	0	17	1	50	0	1	2	.360	.308
Dina, Allen, Bing.	.229	49	204	192	25	44	60	10	3	0	15	0	2	1	9	0	46	9	3	6	.313	.265
DiSarcina, Gary, Erie	.300	5	20	20	1	6	6	0	0	0	2	0	0	0	0	0	4	0	2	0	.300	.300
Dishington, Nate, Akr.*	.237	17	68	59	12	14	31	2	0	5	14	0	0	3	6	0	30	0	0	1	.525	.338
Dixon, Tim, Har.-Tren.*	1.000	10	1	1	0	1	1	0	0	0	1	0	0	0	0	0	0	0	0	0	1.000	1.000
Dodd, Robert, Read.*	.143	42	8	7	0	1	1	0	0	0	1	1	0	0	0	0	4	0	0	0	.143	.143
Dorman, John, Akr.	.143	3	7	7	0	1	1	0	0	0	0	0	0	0	0	0	1	0	0	0	.143	.143
Dubose, Brian, Bing.*	.174	30	84	69	8	12	15	3	0	0	4	0	1	0	14	0	19	5	1	0	.217	.310
Duff, Matt, Alt.	.000	44	5	3	0	0	0	0	0	0	0	2	0	0	0	0	2	0	0	0	.000	.000
Dunbar, Matt, Alt.*	.000	49	4	4	0	0	0	0	0	0	0	0	0	0	0	0	4	0	0	0	.000	.000
Duncan, Geoff, Por.	.000	43	1	1	0	0	0	0	0	0	0	0	0	0	0	0	1	0	0	0	.000	.000
Dunn, Todd, Alt.	.167	8	32	30	0	5	7	2	0	0	2	0	0	0	2	0	10	0	1	0	.233	.219
Duran, Roberto, Har.*	.000	19	1	0	0	0	0	0	0	0	0	0	0	0	1	0	0	0	1	0	.000	1.000
Durocher, Jayson, Har.	.000	29	2	1	0	0	0	0	0	0	0	1	0	0	0	0	0	0	0	0	.000	.000
Durrington, Trent, Erie	.288	107	474	396	84	114	151	26	1	3	34	12	5	9	52	1	66	59	17	4	.381	.379
Eason, Clay, Read.	.000	10	2	2	0	0	0	0	0	0	0	0	0	0	0	0	0	0	0	0	.000	.000
Eaton, Adam, Read.	.111	12	11	9	1	1	2	1	0	0	0	0	2	0	0	0	2	0	0	0	.222	.111
Eckstein, David, Tren.	.313	131	615	483	109	151	201	22	5	6	52	13	5	25	89	0	48	32	13	6	.416	.440
Emmons, Scott, Nor.	.235	37	113	102	13	24	34	1	0	3	16	1	0	4	6	0	25	0	0	4	.333	.304
Encarnacion, Angelo, Akr.	.213	34	134	127	9	27	37	7	0	1	21	1	0	0	6	0	19	1	1	5	.291	.248
Epperson, Chad, Tren.†	.197	55	219	188	24	37	55	10	1	2	15	0	0	31	1	46	1	2	10	.293	.311
Erickson, Matt, Por.*	.269	107	425	361	38	97	121	20	2	0	35	5	5	3	51	0	65	2	3	9	.335	.360
Espinal, Juan, Tren.	.185	17	73	65	11	12	19	1	0	2	7	0	2	1	5	0	19	0	1	2	.292	.247
Estrada, Marco, N.H.†	.150	8	23	20	3	3	4	1	0	0	1	0	0	0	3	0	8	0	0	1	.200	.261
Everett, Adam, Tren.	.263	98	402	338	56	89	130	11	0	10	44	9	4	10	41	0	64	21	5	3	.385	.356
Faurot, Adam, Tren.	.250	33	115	108	11	27	33	4	1	0	8	1	0	0	6	0	20	1	1	7	.306	.289
Felston, Anthony, N.B.*	.207	36	152	135	17	28	35	3	2	0	12	1	3	0	13	1	15	12	2	0	.259	.272
Figueroa, Luis, Alt.†	.263	131	492	418	61	110	144	15	5	3	50	16	3	3	52	0	44	9	9	7	.344	.347
Finn, John, Read.	.209	40	139	115	15	24	34	8	1	0	9	3	0	1	20	0	16	7	1	1	.296	.331
Forster, Scott, Har.	.000	2	1	0	0	0	0	0	0	0	0	1	0	0	0	0	0	0	0	0	.000	.000
Foster, Jim, Erie	.250	4	18	16	2	4	8	1	0	1	3	0	0	0	2	0	0	0	0	1	.500	.333
France, Aaron, Alt.*	.167	33	8	6	1	1	4	0	0	1	1	1	0	0	1	0	5	0	0	0	.667	.286
Francia, David, Read.*	.271	107	380	339	41	92	136	22	5	4	43	6	1	13	21	3	57	13	4	5	.401	.334
Fryman, Travis, Akr.	.250	4	15	12	4	3	6	0	0	1	4	0	1	0	2	0	4	0	0	1	.500	.333
Funaro, Joe, Por.	.366	74	310	268	42	98	128	19	1	3	40	3	4	4	31	1	22	6	6	6	.478	.433
Gainey, Bryon, Bing.*	.237	137	553	502	68	119	234	28	6	25	78	0	5	6	40	2	184	1	2	9	.466	.298
Giard, Ken, Alt.	.000	38	2	2	0	0	0	0	0	0	0	0	0	0	0	0	0	0	0	0	.000	.000
Gibralter, David, Tren.	.299	124	509	448	76	134	230	22	1	24	97	2	5	13	32	3	68	5	5	13	.513	.359
Gipson, Charles, N.H.	.000	5	22	18	2	0	0	0	0	0	0	1	0	0	3	0	2	1	0	0	.000	.143
Glass, Chip, Nor.*	.251	65	271	239	36	60	93	9	3	6	34	0	0	1	31	1	49	5	5	5	.389	.339
Gonzalez, Gabe, Por.*	.000	26	2	2	0	0	0	0	0	0	0	0	0	0	0	0	1	0	0	0	.000	.000
Gonzalez, Mike, Alt.	.000	7	2	2	0	0	0	0	0	0	0	0	0	0	0	0	0	0	0	0	.000	.000
Gonzalez, Raul, Tren.	.335	127	567	505	80	169	264	33	4	18	103	1	7	3	51	3	71	12	3	14	.523	.394
Grahe, Joe, Read.	1.000	7	1	1	0	1	1	0	0	0	1	0	0	0	0	0	0	0	0	0	1.000	1.000
Graves, Bryan, Erie	.194	37	140	103	22	20	27	2	1	1	8	3	0	2	32	0	32	1	0	1	.262	.394
Guiel, Jeff, Erie*	.263	57	216	175	34	46	80	10	3	6	24	1	3	2	33	0	33	3	3	3	.457	.380
Gunderson, Shane, N.B.	.253	46	165	154	15	39	61	11	1	3	16	2	0	2	7	0	37	1	1	6	.396	.294
Haad, Yamid, Alt.	.182	43	158	137	20	25	46	3	0	6	10	1	1	0	19	0	32	7	3	4	.336	.280
Hacker, Steve, N.B.	.302	118	511	461	71	139	256	36	0	27	97	0	6	5	39	2	103	0	2	13	.555	.358
Hafer, Jeff, Bing.	1.000	7	1	1	0	1	1	0	0	0	0	0	0	0	0	0	0	0	0	0	1.000	1.000
Hage, Tom, Bow.*	.277	128	484	426	53	118	171	21	4	8	65	3	3	2	50	3	60	1	1	8	.401	.353
Haltiwanger, Garrick, Bing.	.273	4	12	11	1	3	6	0	0	1	2	0	0	1	0	1	0	0	0	0	.545	.333
Harris, Brian, Read.†	.221	119	440	380	42	84	118	13	3	5	41	7	6	1	46	1	58	9	5	10	.311	.306
Harrison, Adonis, N.H.*	.272	120	498	449	54	122	144	16	0	2	45	1	4	6	38	0	75	22	18	12	.321	.334
Harriss, Robin, Akr.	.167	17	52	48	9	8	15	1	0	2	6	1	0	2	1	0	12	1	0	0	.313	.216
Hastings, Lionel, Por.	.228	61	232	197	26	45	61	5	1	3	14	1	0	2	32	0	45	2	2	6	.310	.324
Haverbusch, Kevin, Alt.	.286	93	373	332	57	95	163	22	2	14	61	1	9	19	12	0	60	6	4	9	.491	.339
Hayes, Heath, Akr.	.266	119	472	418	51	111	178	15	2	16	68	1	5	7	41	1	111	2	1	8	.426	.338
Haynes, Nathan, Erie*	.158	5	25	19	3	3	4	1	0	0	0	0	0	0	1	5	0	0	2	.211	.304
Heinrichs, Jon, Por.	.227	49	196	176	25	40	62	11	1	3	17	1	0	3	16	0	23	4	0	7	.352	.303
Henderson, Scott, Por.	.200	46	5	5	1	1	1	0	0	0	0	0	0	0	0	0	3	0	0	0	.200	.200
Herbert, Russ, Read.	.417	26	17	12	1	5	8	0	0	1	3	4	0	0	1	0	2	0	0	1	.667	.462
Herbison, Brett, Bing.	.222	28	22	18	3	4	4	0	0	0	1	2	0	0	2	0	6	0	0	0	.222	.300
Hernaiz, Juan, Akr.	.190	7	21	21	3	4	7	0	0	1	1	0	0	0	0	0	7	0	0	1	.333	.190
Hernandez, Alexander, Alt.*	.257	126	537	475	76	122	199	26	3	15	63	3	3	2	54	1	110	11	8	3	.419	.333
Herrick, Jason, Erie*	.167	25	88	78	9	13	26	5	1	2	6	1	1	0	8	0	28	1	0	2	.333	.241
Hillenbrand, Shea, Tren.	.259	69	302	282	41	73	109	15	0	7	36	0	3	3	14	3	27	6	5	6	.387	.298
Hills, Rich, N.H.	.262	83	331	282	30	74	101	15	0	4	29	0	2	7	40	0	47	1	3	6	.358	.354
Horne, Tyrone, Read.*	.267	80	307	262	37	70	102	13	2	5	37	0	2	0	43	1	64	13	9	4	.389	.368

Player, Team	Avg.	G	TPA	AB	R	H	TB	2B	3B	HR	RBI	SH	SF	HP	BB	IBB	SO	SB	CS	GDP	Slg.	OBP
Horner, Jim, N.H.	.270	76	302	278	29	75	110	17	0	6	50	1	2	4	17	0	51	1	1	10	.396	.319
Hubbs, Dan, Read.	.000	3	1	1	0	0	0	0	0	0	0	0	0	0	0	0	0	0	0	0	.000	.000
Huelsmann, Mike, Akr.†	.277	43	195	177	20	49	59	5	1	1	10	3	0	0	15	0	30	12	3	0	.333	.333
Huff, B.J., Bing.	.249	57	227	205	26	51	83	9	1	7	32	0	2	1	19	1	46	9	2	4	.405	.313
Huff, Larry, Read.	.260	121	511	427	72	111	154	28	3	3	54	6	8	10	60	1	69	28	6	11	.361	.358
Huls, Steve, N.B.	.217	56	182	152	13	33	34	1	0	0	10	3	1	3	23	0	32	4	3	5	.224	.330
Hyzdu, Adam, Alt.	.316	91	388	345	64	109	211	26	2	24	78	0	3	3	40	1	62	8	4	2	.612	.392
Iglesias, Luis, Alt.	.281	31	104	89	13	25	49	6	0	6	16	0	1	1	14	0	26	0	1	1	.551	.385
Isom, Johnny, Bow.	.228	38	140	127	19	29	41	6	0	2	16	0	0	1	12	1	25	0	1	5	.323	.300
Jackson, Gavin, Tren.	.211	27	94	71	11	15	16	1	0	0	5	3	1	4	15	0	12	2	1	1	.225	.374
Jacquez, Thomas, Read.*	.200	38	11	10	0	2	2	0	0	0	2	1	0	0	0	0	5	0	0	0	.200	.200
James, Kenny, Har.†	.255	29	109	102	8	26	34	4	2	0	6	5	0	1	1	0	19	7	3	1	.333	.269
Johannes, Todd, Har.	.250	1	4	4	0	1	1	0	0	0	0	0	0	0	0	0	2	0	0	0	.250	.250
Johnson, Earl, N.H.†	.245	37	151	139	18	34	37	3	0	0	10	2	2	0	8	0	31	11	4	1	.266	.282
Johnson, Nick, Nor.	.345	132	581	420	114	145	230	33	5	14	87	0	1	37	123	6	88	8	6	9	.548	.525
Jones, Bobby, Bing.	1.000	3	1	1	0	1	1	0	0	0	0	2	0	0	0	0	0	0	0	0	1.000	1.000
Jones, Jaime, Por.*	.254	73	295	244	39	62	99	16	0	7	31	0	2	2	47	1	81	2	0	3	.406	.376
Jorgensen, Tim, Alt.*	.130	7	23	23	1	3	4	1	0	0	2	0	0	0	0	0	6	0	0	1	.174	.130
Kawabata, Kyle, Read.	.000	8	2	2	0	0	0	0	0	0	0	0	0	0	0	0	0	0	0	0	.000	.000
Kershner, Jason, Read.*	.333	57	4	3	1	1	1	0	0	0	0	0	0	0	0	0	0	0	0	0	.333	.500
Kilburg, Joe, Akr.*	.271	42	173	144	20	39	50	8	0	1	14	1	0	5	23	1	28	1	2	3	.347	.390
Kingman, Brendan, N.H.	.279	130	545	509	58	142	192	20	0	10	56	1	4	5	26	2	71	0	0	18	.377	.318
Kingsale, Eugene, Bow.†	.235	67	310	268	43	63	91	14	3	2	23	6	2	1	33	0	46	14	10	4	.340	.319
Kleinz, Larry, Por.	.261	94	323	276	30	72	110	21	1	5	43	3	0	5	39	2	50	2	3	12	.399	.363
Knotts, Gary, Por.	.364	12	13	11	1	4	4	0	0	0	1	2	0	0	0	0	4	0	0	0	.364	.364
Kuilan, Hector, Por.	.261	76	265	245	22	64	81	11	0	2	32	3	4	2	11	0	42	0	0	9	.331	.294
Lane, Ryan, N.B.	.286	17	58	49	6	14	25	0	1	3	6	0	0	2	7	1	10	2	2	1	.510	.397
Leese, Brandon, Por.	.125	20	10	8	0	1	2	1	0	0	1	2	0	0	0	0	3	0	0	0	.250	.125
Leggett, Adam, Erie†	.167	24	95	72	8	12	15	0	0	1	6	1	1	0	21	1	14	2	3	2	.208	.351
Leon, Donny, Nor.†	.302	118	502	457	69	138	239	34	2	21	100	1	7	3	34	2	102	0	0	10	.523	.349
Lewis, Marc, N.B.	.260	101	428	384	38	100	154	27	0	9	52	0	2	4	38	1	79	6	4	12	.401	.332
Lobaton, Jose, Alt.	.250	13	37	32	2	8	10	2	0	0	3	0	0	2	0	0	13	1	0	0	.313	.294
Lomasney, Steve, Tren.	.245	47	193	151	24	37	79	6	0	12	31	1	1	9	31	2	44	7	5	5	.523	.401
Long, Garrett, Alt.	.245	109	431	355	61	87	161	12	4	18	56	4	2	7	63	1	100	6	6	7	.454	.368
Lopez-Cao, Mike, Bow.*	.255	16	49	47	5	12	19	1	0	2	7	0	0	0	2	0	8	0	0	1	.404	.286
Lopez, Johan, Bing.	.000	2	1	1	0	0	0	0	0	0	0	0	0	0	0	0	0	0	0	0	.000	.000
Lopez, Jose, Bing.	.145	20	57	55	2	8	10	2	0	0	6	0	0	0	2	0	24	2	1	2	.182	.175
Lopez, Rafael, N.H.	.188	8	32	32	1	6	7	1	0	0	1	0	0	0	0	0	5	0	0	1	.219	.188
Lorenzana, Luis, Alt.	.216	34	97	74	9	16	26	2	1	2	8	1	3	4	14	0	17	0	0	2	.351	.358
Lyons, Mike, Bing.	.167	53	6	6	0	1	1	0	0	0	0	0	0	0	0	0	4	0	0	0	.167	.167
Mackowiak, Rob, Alt.*	.262	53	216	195	21	51	81	15	3	3	27	2	4	7	8	1	34	0	2	6	.415	.308
Magdaleno, Ricky, N.H.	.271	68	284	258	30	70	88	13	1	1	24	2	2	1	21	0	45	1	3	6	.341	.326
Malave, Jaime, Har.	.222	12	21	18	4	4	13	0	0	3	4	1	0	0	2	0	4	0	0	0	.722	.300
Maness, Dwight, N.H.	.241	27	99	87	11	21	40	2	1	5	12	0	0	1	11	0	18	9	5	3	.460	.333
Marn, Kevin, N.H.	.286	2	8	7	0	2	2	0	0	0	1	0	0	0	1	0	3	1	0	0	.286	.375
Marquez, Robert, Har.	.000	18	1	1	0	0	0	0	0	0	0	0	0	0	0	0	0	0	0	0	.000	.000
Martinez, Victor, N.H.	.000	2	6	4	0	0	0	0	0	0	0	0	0	1	1	0	3	0	0	0	.000	.333
Mashore, Justin, Tren.-Bing.	.259	18	61	58	7	15	26	4	2	1	8	1	0	1	1	1	17	2	0	2	.448	.283
Mathis, Joe, N.H.*	.271	67	267	240	29	65	94	13	5	2	30	8	1	3	15	0	45	9	5	3	.392	.320
Matos, Luis, Bow.	.237	66	310	283	41	67	107	11	1	9	36	5	6	1	15	0	39	14	5	6	.378	.272
Mattes, Troy, Har.	.000	20	12	9	1	0	0	0	0	0	0	2	0	0	1	0	4	0	0	0	.000	.100
McConnell, Sam, Alt.*	.250	13	5	4	0	1	1	0	0	0	1	0	0	0	1	0	1	0	0	0	.250	.400
McCrary, Scott, Bing.	.167	17	8	6	1	1	4	0	0	1	1	1	0	0	1	0	1	0	0	0	.667	.286
McDonald, Donzell, Nor.†	.272	137	641	533	95	145	196	19	10	4	33	11	1	6	90	0	110	54	20	5	.368	.383
McDonald, John, Bow.*	.296	55	253	226	31	67	82	12	0	1	26	2	4	2	19	0	26	7	3	5	.363	.351
McDougal, Mike, Bow.*	.000	48	1	1	0	0	0	0	0	0	0	0	0	0	0	0	0	0	0	0	.000	.000
McEntire, Ethan, Bing.*	.000	4	2	2	0	0	0	0	0	0	0	0	0	0	0	0	1	0	0	0	.000	.000
McKinley, Dan, Akr.*	.257	111	502	463	70	119	160	20	6	3	37	8	3	4	24	0	87	3	5	8	.346	.298
McLamb, Brian, Nor.†	.159	48	135	126	11	20	31	5	0	2	14	0	0	5	4	0	46	1	1	6	.246	.215
McNamara, Rusty, Read.	.249	50	202	177	26	44	70	9	1	5	20	4	0	4	17	0	22	0	4	6	.395	.328
Meggers, Mike, Bing.	.161	18	63	56	6	9	16	4	0	1	6	0	0	0	7	1	29	0	0	0	.286	.254
Mirizzi, Marc, Nor.†	.106	15	56	47	6	5	8	0	0	1	6	0	3	1	5	0	13	0	0	1	.170	.196
Mitchell, Scott, Har.	.333	3	3	3	0	1	1	0	0	0	0	0	0	0	0	0	0	0	0	0	.333	.333
Moeller, Chad, N.B.	.248	89	282	250	29	62	91	11	3	4	24	1	4	6	21	1	44	0	0	7	.364	.317
Mohr, Dustan, Akr.	.167	12	48	42	3	7	11	2	1	0	2	1	0	0	5	0	7	0	1	1	.262	.255
Moraga, David, Har.*	.000	1	1	0	1	0	0	0	0	0	0	0	0	0	0	0	0	0	0	0	.000	1.000
Morgan, Scott, Akr.	.282	88	385	344	72	97	205	26	2	26	70	0	1	2	38	5	96	6	1	4	.596	.356
Morris, Jeremy, Nor.	.247	111	429	392	50	97	142	16	1	9	52	2	2	2	31	0	91	8	2	7	.362	.304
Moss, Rick, N.B.*	.270	90	279	252	28	68	93	13	0	4	29	1	0	2	24	1	37	0	5	5	.369	.338
Mucker, Kelcey, N.B.*	.272	109	407	368	26	100	119	16	0	1	25	1	3	3	32	1	57	0	3	10	.323	.333
Murphy, Nate, Erie*	.267	104	422	359	48	96	171	17	8	14	56	4	2	3	54	3	85	6	5	7	.476	.366
Neubart, Garrett, Bing.	.288	83	299	260	36	75	106	14	4	3	21	8	1	8	22	0	40	17	5	6	.408	.361
Newfield, Marc, Tren.	.154	4	16	13	3	2	6	1	0	1	2	0	0	2	1	0	3	1	0	0	.462	.313
Niebla, Ruben, Har.*	.000	29	2	2	0	0	0	0	0	0	0	0	0	0	0	0	0	0	0	0	.000	.000
Niles, Drew, Por.†	.230	46	161	135	12	31	34	3	0	0	9	3	2	0	21	0	34	0	2	7	.252	.329
Norton, Chris, Por.	.291	120	479	406	74	118	257	25	0	38	97	0	1	1	71	2	124	1	2	15	.633	.397
Nunnari, Talmadge, Har.*	.331	83	284	239	45	79	116	17	1	6	29	2	2	1	39	3	46	7	2	3	.485	.423
O'Connor, Brian, Alt.*	.125	28	19	16	0	2	3	1	0	0	0	3	0	0	0	0	8	0	1	0	.188	.125
Ojeda, Augie, Bow.†	.267	134	558	460	73	123	179	18	4	10	60	25	4	11	57	0	47	6	2	7	.389	.359
Ortiz, Nick, Akr.	.267	55	219	195	24	52	77	15	2	2	13	0	3	4	17	0	40	1	2	5	.395	.333
Ottavinia, Paul, Nor.*	.288	59	207	191	26	55	93	11	3	7	31	0	1	1	14	1	40	5	3	5	.487	.338
Ozuna, Pablo, Por.	.281	117	538	502	62	141	201	25	7	7	46	7	3	13	13	0	50	31	16	8	.400	.315

Player, Team	Avg.	G	TPA	AB	R	H	TB	2B	3B	HR	RBI	SH	SF	HP	BB	IBB	SO	SB	CS	GDP	Slg.	OBP
Parker, Christian, Har.	.000	36	6	6	1	0	0	0	0	0	0	0	0	0	0	0	0	0	0	0	.000	.000
Patzke, Jeff, Alt.†	.298	53	235	198	31	59	79	12	1	2	25	0	2	2	33	1	45	4	2	4	.399	.400
Paz, Richard, Bow.	.286	79	340	273	39	78	100	12	2	2	20	8	2	6	51	0	35	11	3	4	.366	.407
Pena, Alex, Alt.	.500	9	2	2	1	1	4	0	0	1	2	0	0	0	0	0	0	0	0	0	2.000	.500
Penny, Brad, Por.	1.000	6	2	1	0	1	1	0	0	0	0	1	0	0	0	0	0	0	0	0	1.000	1.000
Pennyfeather, William, Erie	.205	11	45	39	4	8	9	1	0	0	4	0	1	0	5	0	13	1	2	0	.231	.289
Peoples, Danny, Akr.	.251	127	555	494	75	124	216	23	3	21	78	0	2	4	55	1	142	2	1	9	.437	.330
Perry, Chan, Akr.	.279	37	167	154	24	43	78	14	0	7	30	0	1	1	11	0	27	1	0	3	.506	.329
Peterman, Tommy, N.B.*	.262	140	606	538	68	141	229	28	0	20	84	0	4	3	61	5	84	1	2	10	.426	.338
Phelps, Tommy, Har.*	.000	13	6	6	0	0	0	0	0	0	0	0	0	0	0	0	0	0	0	0	.000	.000
Phillips, Jason, Bing.	.227	39	160	141	13	32	58	5	0	7	23	2	1	3	13	0	20	0	0	4	.411	.304
Pierce, Kirk, Read.	.259	83	312	255	37	66	103	10	0	9	40	0	5	10	42	1	56	4	4	9	.404	.378
Politte, Cliff, Read.	.222	37	10	9	1	2	2	0	0	0	2	1	0	0	0	0	4	0	0	0	.222	.222
Pontes, Dan, Bing.	.000	19	3	2	0	0	0	0	0	0	0	0	0	0	1	0	1	0	0	0	.000	.333
Post, Dave, Har.	.381	5	23	21	5	8	12	1	0	1	3	1	0	0	1	0	2	0	0	0	.571	.409
Preston, Brian, Har.	.067	6	16	15	1	1	1	0	0	0	2	0	0	0	1	0	4	0	0	1	.067	.125
Pumphrey, Ken, Bing.	.091	25	13	11	0	1	2	1	0	0	0	2	0	0	0	0	5	0	0	0	.182	.091
Pyc, David, Read.*	.125	17	11	8	1	1	1	0	0	0	2	3	0	0	0	0	5	0	0	0	.125	.125
Quezada, Edward, Har.	.000	3	1	1	1	0	0	0	0	0	0	0	0	0	0	0	0	0	0	0	.000	.000
Ramirez, Julio, Por.	.261	138	619	568	87	148	237	30	10	13	64	5	5	2	39	1	150	64	15	5	.417	.308
Rapp, Travis, Erie	.250	3	10	8	1	2	3	1	0	0	0	0	0	0	2	0	4	0	0	0	.375	.400
Raynor, Mark, Read.	.209	14	51	43	4	9	11	0	1	0	3	1	0	1	6	0	4	0	1	6	.256	.320
Rector, Bobby, Por.	.000	13	6	5	0	0	0	0	0	0	0	0	0	0	1	0	2	0	0	0	.000	.167
Redman, Tike, Alt.*	.269	136	604	532	84	143	196	20	12	3	60	6	10	3	52	1	52	29	16	6	.368	.332
Reese, Nate, Por.	.000	3	3	3	0	0	0	0	0	0	0	0	0	0	0	0	1	0	0	0	.000	.000
Reeves, Glenn, Por.	.000	6	9	9	0	0	0	0	0	0	0	0	0	0	0	0	6	0	0	0	.000	.000
Regan, Jason, N.H.	.213	45	170	150	12	32	52	9	1	3	13	1	0	2	17	1	46	2	1	1	.347	.302
Rivas, Luis, N.B.	.254	132	580	527	78	134	199	30	7	7	49	8	2	2	41	1	92	31	14	16	.378	.309
Rivera, Roberto, Bow.†	.222	9	37	36	0	8	8	0	0	0	1	0	0	0	0	0	9	2	0	1	.222	.243
Roberts, Grant, Bing.	.208	24	26	24	1	5	5	0	0	0	1	2	0	0	0	0	7	0	0	1	.208	.208
Robertson, Mike, Alt.*	.280	46	203	175	31	49	88	12	0	9	28	3	0	1	24	2	26	0	3	1	.503	.370
Robertson, Ryan, Por.*	.246	44	154	130	15	32	44	6	0	2	10	1	0	1	22	0	17	0	0	5	.338	.359
Robinson, Adam, Akr.	.277	66	262	238	37	66	101	12	4	5	30	2	0	2	20	0	49	4	1	5	.424	.338
Rodgers, Bobby, Por.	.167	26	8	6	1	1	2	1	0	0	2	1	0	0	1	0	3	0	0	0	.333	.286
Rodriguez, Luis, Tren.	.272	32	118	114	10	31	50	7	0	4	14	0	0	1	3	0	25	2	1	4	.439	.297
Rodriguez, Sammy, Bing.	.227	69	229	203	15	46	65	10	0	3	24	2	0	3	21	0	49	2	3	2	.320	.308
Rodriguez, Victor, Por.	.206	38	113	97	13	20	28	3	1	1	12	3	1	2	10	0	9	0	1	3	.289	.291
Rolison, Nate, Por.*	.299	124	514	438	71	131	204	20	1	17	69	0	2	6	68	3	112	0	1	16	.466	.399
Rollins, Jimmy, Read.†	.273	133	598	532	81	145	215	21	8	11	56	12	2	1	51	1	47	24	13	8	.404	.336
Ronca, Joe, Bow.	.242	46	168	153	12	37	66	12	1	5	25	0	1	1	13	2	43	1	3	2	.431	.304
Rosario, Mel, Alt.†	.241	26	94	87	11	21	33	9	0	1	11	0	1	0	6	0	15	0	0	5	.379	.287
Rosenkranz, Terry, Bow.*	.000	26	1	1	0	0	0	0	0	0	0	0	0	0	0	0	1	0	0	0	.000	.000
Royster, Aaron, Read.	.291	91	366	309	53	90	135	17	2	8	48	2	4	3	48	2	90	11	5	3	.437	.387
Runion, Tony, Alt.	.000	32	1	1	0	0	0	0	0	0	0	0	0	0	0	0	1	0	0	0	.000	.000
Rust, Brian, Bow.	.309	52	174	149	24	46	69	11	0	4	21	2	3	3	17	0	29	2	0	3	.463	.384
Rutherford, Mark, Read.	.000	4	3	3	1	0	0	0	0	0	0	0	0	0	0	0	0	0	0	0	.000	.000
Sachse, Matt, N.H.*	.113	27	108	97	12	11	15	1	0	1	4	1	0	0	10	0	36	1	2	3	.155	.196
Salyers, Jeremy, Har.	.000	12	4	4	0	0	0	0	0	0	0	0	0	0	0	0	3	0	0	0	.000	.000
Sanchez, Yuri, Bing.†	.231	116	429	381	43	88	115	10	1	5	30	5	4	2	37	3	135	6	5	3	.302	.300
Saylor, Ryan, Har.*	.000	28	5	4	0	0	0	0	0	0	0	0	0	0	1	0	3	0	0	0	.000	.200
Schifano, Tony, Por.	.239	29	74	67	9	16	19	1	1	0	6	1	0	1	5	0	9	0	0	3	.284	.301
Schneider, Brian, Har.*	.264	121	459	421	48	111	183	19	1	17	66	3	1	2	32	2	56	2	2	6	.435	.318
Schwab, Chris, Akr.	.000	2	7	6	0	0	0	0	0	0	0	0	0	1	0	0	3	0	0	0	.000	.143
Secrist, Reed, Alt.*	.168	36	111	95	9	16	21	5	0	0	10	1	1	1	13	1	23	0	0	6	.221	.273
Short, Barry, Bing.	.000	24	3	1	0	0	0	0	0	0	0	0	0	0	2	0	1	0	0	0	.000	.667
Short, Rick, Bow.	.314	112	449	392	60	123	190	19	0	16	62	0	5	9	43	2	48	6	1	9	.485	.390
Shumaker, Anthony, Read.* ...	.286	10	8	7	2	2	2	0	0	0	1	0	0	1	0	0	2	0	0	0	.286	.286
Shumpert, Derek, Nor.	.217	54	191	166	25	36	65	8	0	7	15	3	3	6	13	0	63	3	2	5	.392	.293
Simonton, Benji, Erie	.242	62	215	182	13	44	59	10	1	1	19	2	1	2	28	0	55	4	4	6	.324	.347
Smith, Jeff, N.B.*	.253	79	298	265	25	67	98	13	0	6	31	3	4	3	23	0	40	1	0	4	.370	.326
Smith, Rod, Nor.†	.600	1	5	5	1	3	3	0	0	0	1	0	0	0	1	2	0	0	0	.600	.600
Snusz, Chris, Har.	.308	5	14	13	2	4	5	1	0	0	3	0	0	0	1	0	3	0	0	1	.385	.357
Soliz, Steve, Akr.	.130	7	24	23	1	3	3	0	0	0	3	0	0	0	1	0	4	0	0	1	.130	.167
Soriano, Alfonso, Nor.	.305	89	402	361	57	110	181	20	3	15	68	0	5	4	32	1	67	24	16	9	.501	.363
Soriano, Jose, Tren.	.253	61	182	166	38	42	59	9	1	2	20	1	1	2	12	1	31	15	6	3	.355	.309
Stevenson, Rod, Har.	.000	37	1	1	0	0	0	0	0	0	0	0	0	0	0	0	0	0	0	0	.000	.000
Stewart, Andy, Read.	.300	54	221	190	23	57	97	19	0	7	40	3	4	7	16	1	18	0	3	8	.511	.369
Stoffels, Alex, Bing.	.000	3	11	8	0	0	0	0	0	0	0	0	0	0	3	0	4	0	0	0	.000	.273
Stoner, Mike, Erie	.339	14	64	62	10	21	34	4	0	3	15	0	0	0	2	1	8	0	1	0	.548	.359
Sweeney, Brian, N.H.	.000	24	1	1	0	0	0	0	0	0	0	0	0	0	0	0	1	0	0	0	.000	.000
Sweet, Jon, Alt.*	.257	37	121	105	15	27	40	5	1	2	13	1	3	1	11	0	15	0	1	3	.381	.325
Tamargo, John, Bing.†	.215	112	415	363	27	78	109	13	3	4	37	5	3	4	40	1	55	7	5	8	.300	.298
Taveras, Frank, Akr.*	.190	16	47	42	6	8	12	1	0	1	4	0	1	0	4	0	17	0	0	0	.286	.255
Taylor, Reggie, Read.*	.266	127	553	526	75	140	222	17	10	15	61	3	3	3	18	1	79	38	22	11	.422	.293
Tebbs, Nate, Tren.†	.271	107	417	365	49	99	127	14	1	4	35	11	7	5	29	1	67	21	10	7	.348	.328
Tejera, Michael, Por.*	.231	25	15	13	2	3	3	0	0	0	1	1	1	0	0	0	0	0	0	0	.231	.214
Tejero, Fausto, Erie	.213	62	231	211	19	45	63	9	3	0	18	4	0	3	13	0	38	0	2	7	.299	.269
Thames, Marcus, Nor.	.225	51	210	182	25	41	63	6	2	4	26	1	2	3	22	0	40	0	1	2	.346	.314
t'Hoen, E.J., Erie	.203	56	209	187	18	38	58	12	1	2	21	5	1	3	13	0	52	6	2	4	.310	.265
Thomas, Evan, Read.	.267	37	16	15	0	4	4	0	0	0	2	1	0	0	0	0	3	0	0	0	.267	.267
Thomas, Juan, N.H.	.243	71	288	267	47	65	126	13	0	16	51	0	1	6	14	1	92	0	0	6	.472	.295
Tinoco, Luis, Read.	.271	39	121	96	18	26	33	4	0	1	10	0	1	2	22	1	23	2	2	3	.344	.413

Player, Team	Avg.	G	TPA	AB	R	H	TB	2B	3B	HR	RBI	SH	SF	HP	BB	IBB	SO	SB	CS	GDP	Slg.	OBP
Toca, Jorge, Bing.	.308	75	320	279	60	86	163	15	1	20	67	0	4	5	32	3	43	5	5	9	.584	.384
Tolentino, Juan, Erie	.252	136	548	489	61	123	179	19	5	9	61	8	2	2	47	0	116	47	14	7	.366	.319
Tracy, Andy, Har.*	.274	134	573	493	96	135	276	26	2	37	128	1	3	6	70	4	139	6	1	10	.560	.369
Tucker, Jon, Har.*	.257	112	421	362	53	93	157	21	2	13	55	1	5	3	50	0	85	4	4	8	.434	.348
Tucker, T.J., Har.	.308	19	14	13	2	4	4	0	0	0	1	1	0	0	0	0	3	0	0	0	.308	.308
Turrentine, Rich, Bing.	1.000	17	1	1	0	1	1	0	0	0	0	0	0	0	0	0	0	0	0	0	1.000	1.000
Tyner, Jason, Bing.*	.313	129	590	518	91	162	191	19	5	0	33	8	1	1	62	0	46	49	16	8	.369	.387
Valencia, Victor, Nor.	.222	119	453	396	57	88	172	18	0	22	72	4	3	5	45	0	142	0	0	4	.434	.307
Valera, Yohanny, Bing.	.289	57	225	204	33	59	106	14	3	9	39	0	2	2	17	1	57	2	1	9	.520	.347
Vasquez, Leo, Bing.*	.200	27	6	5	2	1	2	1	0	0	0	0	0	0	1	0	3	0	0	0	.400	.333
Vazquez, Ramon, N.H.*	.258	127	514	438	58	113	161	27	3	5	45	6	3	5	62	4	77	8	1	11	.368	.354
Veras, Wilton, Tren.	.281	116	508	474	65	133	193	23	2	11	75	1	5	5	23	1	55	7	6	23	.407	.318
Villafuerte, Brandon, Por.	.000	23	5	3	0	0	0	0	0	0	0	2	0	0	0	0	1	0	0	0	.000	.000
Walker, Tyler, Bing.	.000	13	11	6	1	0	0	0	0	0	1	3	0	0	2	0	3	0	0	0	.000	.250
Walther, Chris, Erie	.355	9	35	31	5	11	18	2	1	1	6	0	0	0	4	0	4	0	0	3	.581	.429
Ward, Turner, Alt.†	.000	1	5	3	1	0	0	0	0	0	0	0	0	0	2	0	2	0	0	0	.000	.400
Ware, Jeremy, Har.	.262	111	431	381	57	100	154	23	2	9	56	2	5	2	41	2	79	12	5	19	.404	.333
Wathan, Dusty, N.H.	.279	96	374	333	37	93	125	16	2	4	37	4	1	12	24	1	60	4	1	11	.375	.349
Weber, Jake, N.H.*	.256	136	561	489	64	125	184	22	2	11	59	1	2	3	66	2	73	5	7	7	.376	.346
Wehner, John, Alt.	.167	4	13	12	2	2	2	0	0	0	2	0	0	1	0	0	1	1	0	0	.167	.231
Werth, Jayson, Bow.	.273	35	144	121	18	33	43	5	1	1	11	1	3	2	17	0	26	7	1	1	.355	.364
Westbrook, Jake, Har.	.042	27	30	24	0	1	1	0	0	0	0	2	0	0	4	0	11	0	0	0	.042	.179
Whitaker, Chad, Akr.*	.322	41	166	149	18	48	79	12	2	5	38	0	2	0	15	0	40	0	1	3	.530	.380
Wilkerson, Brad, Har.*	.235	138	523	422	66	99	150	21	3	8	49	1	5	7	88	3	100	3	5	3	.355	.372
Williams, Shad, Read.	.000	16	1	1	0	0	0	0	0	0	0	0	0	0	0	0	0	0	0	0	.000	.000
Wilson, Craig, Alt.	.268	111	426	362	57	97	184	21	3	20	69	1	4	19	40	0	104	1	3	8	.508	.367
Wimmer, Chris, Alt.	.252	27	120	107	9	27	39	5	2	1	6	1	0	4	8	1	12	5	2	3	.364	.328
Wolff, Mike, Erie	.248	91	376	307	43	76	133	21	3	10	40	1	0	5	63	2	85	4	6	6	.433	.384
Wooten, Shawn, Erie	.292	137	587	518	70	151	237	27	1	19	88	1	8	10	50	1	102	3	1	12	.458	.360
Wright, Ron, Alt.	.213	24	90	80	2	17	23	6	0	0	4	0	0	1	9	0	27	0	0	1	.288	.300
Zamora, Junior, Bing.	.239	67	273	255	28	61	108	17	0	10	33	0	2	3	12	1	62	2	1	13	.424	.279
Zech, Scott, Har.	.278	22	80	72	8	20	29	4	1	1	10	2	2	0	4	0	13	3	2	0	.403	.308

GRAND SLAMS: Gibralter, Leon, Rolison, Toca, Valencia, Wolff, 2 each; Abbott, Alcantara, Bieser, Brown, Burrell, Carroll, Casimiro, Clark, Dehaan, Everett, Gainey, R. Gonzalez, Haverbusch, A. Hernandez, Hyzdu, J. Jones, Norton, Ojeda, Peterman, Ronca, L. Sanchez, Stewart, Stoner, Tolentino, Tucker, Whitaker, Wilson, 1 each.

AWARDED FIRST BASE ON CATCHER'S INTERFERENCE: Gibralter, 9 (Valencia 2, J. Smith, Kuilan, Hastings, Valera, Bennett, Alvarez, Graves); Alley 2 (Dewey, Tejero); Guiel 2 (Rosario, Hastings); Redman (Schneider); Stewart (Tejero); Zamora (Tejero); Ojeda (Hastings); Nunnari (Graves); Lorenzana (Lomasney).

PLAYERS WITH TWO OR MORE TEAMS

Player, Team	Avg.	G	TPA	AB	R	H	TB	2B	3B	HR	RBI	SH	SF	HP	BB	IBB	SO	SB	CS	GDP	Slg.	OBP
Brown, Alvin, Alt.	.000	7	4	4	1	0	0	0	0	0	1	0	0	0	0	0	2	0	0	0	.000	.000
Brown, Alvin, Erie	.000	6	0	0	0	0	0	0	0	0	0	0	0	0	0	0	0	0	0	0	.000	.000
Dixon, Tim, Har.*	1.000	2	1	1	0	1	1	0	0	0	1	0	0	0	0	0	0	0	0	0	1.000	1.000
Dixon, Tim, Tren.*	.000	8	0	0	0	0	0	0	0	0	0	0	0	0	0	0	0	0	0	0	.000	.000
Mashore, Justin, Tren.	.375	5	17	16	3	6	12	2	2	0	5	0	0	0	1	1	4	1	0	0	.750	.412
Mashore, Justin, Bing.	.214	13	44	42	4	9	14	2	0	1	3	1	0	1	0	0	13	1	0	2	.333	.233

1999 PITCHING

TEAM

Team	W	L	Pct.	ERA	G	CG	ShO	Sv.	IP	H	TBF	R	ER	HR	SH	SF	HB	BB	IBB	SO	WP	Bk.
Erie	81	61	.570	3.75	142	19	7	37	1249.1	1197	5345	617	520	127	49	33	68	451	1	967	46	12
Trenton	92	50	.648	3.85	142	7	17	42	1265.1	1200	5347	603	541	105	40	34	53	453	14	986	67	9
New Haven	65	77	.458	3.86	142	10	7	36	1244.0	1215	5376	625	533	104	41	36	66	549	13	1059	80	6
Norwich	78	64	.549	3.93	142	6	6	47	1242.1	1209	5437	680	543	82	40	52	40	550	30	981	73	10
Altoona	67	73	.479	4.07	140	4	5	32	1244.2	1252	5497	680	563	99	61	44	50	570	23	935	91	18
Harrisburg	76	66	.535	4.09	142	7	10	31	1232.2	1200	5319	649	560	137	62	36	79	496	9	812	58	8
Bowie	70	71	.496	4.28	141	9	7	33	1260.2	1264	5496	670	600	156	59	31	60	534	22	989	63	19
Portland	65	77	.458	4.30	142	2	5	39	1242.0	1301	5484	708	593	130	56	31	78	520	21	1068	73	11
Binghamton	54	88	.380	4.58	142	1	8	29	1255.2	1297	5595	767	639	125	49	38	82	557	9	939	48	10
Akron	69	71	.493	4.64	140	2	6	41	1215.2	1232	5373	702	627	123	49	58	69	562	11	839	72	13
Reading	73	69	.514	4.65	142	9	4	39	1249.2	1295	5490	732	645	145	45	48	70	494	21	984	48	11
New Britain	59	82	.418	4.79	141	7	9	30	1224.1	1336	5435	759	651	126	45	51	50	500	10	982	53	7

INDIVIDUAL

TOP QUALIFIERS FOR EARNED-RUN AVERAGE TITLE

Minimum 114 innings.*Lefthanded pitcher.

Pitcher, Team	W	L	Pct.	ERA	G	GS	CG	ShO	GF	Sv.	IP	H	TBF	R	ER	HR	SH	SF	HB	BB	IBB	SO	WP	Bk.
Ahearne, Pat, N.H.	8	3	.727	2.61	17	17	4	2	0	0	124.0	114	493	41	36	6	3	1	3	27	0	80	2	0
Tejera, Michael, Por.*	13	4	.765	2.62	25	25	0	0	0	0	154.2	137	640	55	45	13	9	3	7	45	1	152	6	1
Armas, Tony, Har.	9	7	.563	2.89	24	24	2	1	0	0	149.2	123	611	62	48	10	8	1	3	55	0	106	5	1
Riley, Matt, Bow.*	10	6	.625	3.22	20	20	3	0	0	0	125.2	113	520	53	45	13	2	3	5	42	0	131	10	4
Thomas, Evan, Read.	9	5	.643	3.25	36	15	1	0	8	3	127.1	123	545	53	46	7	3	7	5	50	2	127	2	0
Etherton, Seth, Erie	10	10	.500	3.27	24	24	4	1	0	0	167.2	153	694	72	61	14	7	5	3	43	0	153	4	4
Cooper, Brian, Erie	10	5	.667	3.30	22	22	6	0	0	0	158.0	146	640	61	58	17	3	1	13	29	0	143	5	1
Sekany, Jason, Tren.	14	4	.778	3.35	27	22	3	2	1	0	161.1	143	674	65	60	8	3	4	6	64	0	116	10	1
Arroyo, Bronson, Alt.	15	4	.789	3.65	25	25	2	1	0	0	153.0	167	668	73	62	15	5	2	7	58	1	100	6	0
Beverlin, Jason, Nor.	15	9	.625	3.69	28	27	1	0	0	0	173.1	153	743	91	71	16	6	7	6	81	0	147	10	1
Towers, Josh, Bow.	12	7	.632	3.76	29	28	5	2	1	0	189.0	204	786	86	79	26	12	4	5	26	1	106	5	3

Pitcher, Team	W	L	Pct.	ERA	G	GS	CG	ShO	GF	Sv.	IP	H	TBF	R	ER	HR	SH	SF	HB	BB	IBB	SO	WP	Bk.
Westbrook, Jake, Har.	11	5	.688	3.92	27	27	2	2	0	0	174.2	180	748	88	76	14	12	3	13	63	1	90	2	1
Baron, Jim, Alt.*	9	9	.500	3.97	29	20	0	0	3	0	145.0	141	618	73	64	13	6	8	4	44	2	75	6	5
Crawford, Paxton, Tren.	7	8	.467	4.08	28	28	1	1	0	0	163.1	151	696	81	74	12	7	4	10	59	1	111	10	1
Martinez, Willie, Akr.	9	8	.529	4.09	24	24	0	0	0	0	147.1	163	639	83	67	20	5	2	3	45	0	91	8	0

DEPARTMENTAL LEADERS: W—Arroyo, Beverlin, 15 each; L—Pineiro, 15; Pct.—De La Hoya, .900; G—Lisio, 59; GS—Crawford, Towers, 28 each; CG—Cooper, 6; ShO—Several players, 2 each; GF—Lisio, 56; Sv.—Lisio, 33; IP—Towers, 189.0; H—Towers, 204; TBF—Towers, 786; R—Herbison, 115; ER—Herbison, 97; HR—Towers, 26; SH—Towers, Westbrook, 12 each; SF—Espinal, 11; HB—Pumphrey, Parker, 15 each; BB—O'Connor, 92; IBB—Deschenes, McDougal, 6 each; SO—Anderson, 162; WP—O'Connor, 21; BK—Baron, 5.

ALL PITCHERS

*Lefthanded pitcher.

Pitcher, Team	W	L	Pct.	ERA	G	GS	CG	ShO	GF	Sv.	IP	H	TBF	R	ER	HR	SH	SF	HB	BB	IBB	SO	WP	Bk.
Adams, Willie, Tren.	1	1	.500	4.63	2	2	0	0	0	0	11.2	17	53	6	6	2	0	0	0	2	0	6	2	0
Agamennone, Brandon, Har.	5	2	.714	3.10	22	4	0	0	11	5	52.1	44	210	19	18	5	3	0	2	14	0	41	2	0
Ah Yat, Paul, Alt.*	8	4	.667	3.02	16	15	0	0	0	0	95.1	86	398	41	32	6	4	4	3	30	0	90	4	1
Ahearne, Pat, N.H.	8	3	.727	2.61	17	17	4	2	0	0	124.0	114	493	41	36	6	3	1	3	27	0	80	2	0
Almanza, Armando, Por.*	0	1	.000	3.97	10	0	0	0	6	3	11.1	5	41	5	5	1	1	0	0	4	0	20	0	0
Almonte, Hector, Por.	1	4	.200	2.84	47	0	0	0	41	23	44.1	42	202	14	14	1	8	1	2	26	3	42	4	0
Alvarez, Juan, Erie*	1	2	.333	2.05	23	0	0	0	12	4	30.2	20	121	14	7	4	1	2	2	6	0	22	1	1
Anderson, Bill, Erie.	1	1	.500	5.40	5	5	0	0	0	0	18.1	20	83	12	11	2	0	0	0	8	0	12	2	0
Anderson, Ryan, N.H.*	9	13	.409	4.50	24	24	0	0	0	0	134.0	131	606	77	67	9	2	5	8	86	1	162	9	3
Armas, Tony, Har.	9	7	.563	2.89	24	24	2	1	0	0	149.2	123	611	62	48	10	8	1	3	55	0	106	5	1
Arroyo, Bronson, Alt.	15	4	.789	3.65	25	25	2	1	0	0	153.0	167	668	73	62	15	5	2	7	58	1	100	6	0
Arroyo, Luis, Por.*	0	1	.000	3.29	9	0	0	0	1	1	13.2	14	61	11	5	2	2	0	0	8	4	10	0	0
Arteaga, J.D., Bing.*	3	1	.750	5.72	11	3	0	0	1	0	28.1	32	133	21	18	3	0	2	2	14	0	24	0	0
Atkins, Ross, Akr.	6	8	.429	5.77	33	7	0	0	5	3	87.1	90	398	60	56	10	5		6	47	0	43	5	1
Ayers, Mike, Alt.*	0	0	.000	1.59	11	0	0	0	3	0	17.0	10	70	4	3	1	1		0	11	0	16	5	0
Babineaux, Darrin, N.B.	0	0	.000	6.52	5	0	0	0	3	0	9.2	14	52	10	7	1	0	1	1	4	0	7	2	0
Bacsik, Mike, Akr.*	11	11	.500	4.64	26	26	1	0	0	0	149.1	164	647	84	77	24	5	5	7	47	0	84	4	0
Bailie, Matt, Read.	1	0	1.000	0.00	1	1	0	0	0	0	6.0	3	20	0	0	0	0	0	0	0	1	6	0	0
Baker, Jason, Har.	1	3	.250	6.03	23	1	0	0	7	0	31.1	36	150	22	21	4	2	2	1	28	0	24	1	0
Barkley, Brian, Tren.*	5	0	1.000	2.55	7	7	0	0	0	0	35.1	32	135	10	10	2	0	0	2	6	0	18	0	0
Barnett, Marty, Read.	2	3	.400	2.53	35	0	0	0	19	7	53.1	43	226	19	15	2	0	0	2	24	2	33	1	1
Baron, Jim, Alt.*	9	9	.500	3.97	29	20	0	0	3	0	145.0	141	618	73	64	13	6	8	4	44	2	75	6	5
Beale, Chuck, Tren.	2	5	.286	5.95	29	1	0	0	6	1	59.0	71	276	45	39	6	4		1	36	4	41	8	0
Beaumont, Matt, Erie*	5	6	.455	4.73	32	12	0	0	6	1	106.2	97	474	64	56	13	5	3	7	59	0	76	3	3
Bell, Jason, N.B.	3	3	.500	3.42	7	7	0	0	0	0	47.1	46	198	21	18	4	2	1	2	11	0	34	0	1
Bell, Mike, Bow.*	7	7	.500	4.59	41	13	0	0	5	1	131.1	134	575	80	67	13	4	3	12	49	1	79	3	1
Belovsky, Josh, Tren.	0	0	.000	33.75	1	0	0	0	0	0	1.1	4	10	5	5	0	0	0	0	2	0	2	0	0
Beltran, Alonso, Alt.	0	2	.000	9.00	13	0	0	0	1	1	18.0	27	86	18	18	2	0	1	0	9	0	18	1	0
Benz, Jake, Por.*	1	0	1.000	4.32	23	0	0	0	11	0	33.1	33	152	19	16	6	0	2	0	23	0	24	3	1
Betancourt, Rafael, Tren.	6	2	.750	3.62	39	0	0	0	30	13	54.2	50	218	24	22	7	2		0	10	0	50	1	0
Beverlin, Jason, Nor.	15	9	.625	3.69	28	27	1	0	0	0	173.1	153	743	91	71	16	6	7	6	81	0	147	10	1
Blank, Matt, Har.*	6	3	.667	3.92	15	14	0	0	0	0	85.0	94	363	41	37	14	5	2	0	26	0	42	3	0
Blazier, Ron, Bow.	1	1	.500	7.39	19	0	0	0	6	2	31.2	40	145	27	26	6	2		2	12	0	28	1	0
Bohannon, Gary, Bing.	0	0	.000	49.50	2	0	0	0	0	0	2.0	12	23	13	11	0	1		1	3	0	0	0	0
Bovee, Mike, Erie.	1	1	.500	1.32	26	0	0	0	23	12	34.0	26	132	6	5	2	0	1	2	5	0	33	0	0
Brammer, J.D., Akr.	3	2	.600	4.76	47	0	0	0	24	8	75.2	53	349	44	40	4	4	3	9	60	0	69	11	3
Brannan, Ryan, Read.	0	0	.000	16.62	5	0	0	0	2	0	4.1	9	28	8	8	0	1		1	4	1	1	1	0
Brester, Jason, Read.*	7	5	.583	3.76	16	16	3	1	0	0	105.1	105	436	48	44	8	4	6	2	26	1	87	6	2
Brittan, Corey, Bing.	2	4	.333	2.78	54	0	0	0	27	7	90.2	84	375	36	28	6	3		1	23	0	60	3	2
Brosnan, Jason, N.H.*	3	0	1.000	2.34	28	1	0	0	15	6	50.0	32	193	14	13	4	3	1	2	15	2	44	4	0
Brown, Alvin, Alt.-Erie	4	2	.667	6.55	13	6	0	0	4	2	33.0	38	163	28	24	0	3	3	3	24	0	21	9	1
Brown, Jamie, Akr.	5	9	.357	4.57	23	23	1	0	0	0	138.0	140	586	72	70	11	7	10	13	39	1	98	2	3
Bullinger, Kirk, Tren.	1	1	.500	0.53	17	0	0	0	17	10	17.0	6	60	2	1	1	0		0	5	1	16	1	0
Bump, Nate, Por.	2	6	.250	6.07	8	8	0	0	0	0	43.0	57	203	38	29	3	1	2	5	12	0	33	1	0
Burger, Rob, Read.	0	6	.000	13.50	9	9	0	0	0	0	27.1	29	156	43	41	5	2	2	5	45	0	23	7	0
Burgos, Enrique, Alt.*	0	1	.000	2.25	5	0	0	0	2	0	4.0	1	14	1	1	0	1	0	0	3	0	2	0	0
Burgus, Travis, Por.*	0	0	.000	0.00	1	0	0	0	0	0	0.2	0	2	0	0	0	0		0	1	0	1	0	0
Burnett, A.J., Por.	6	12	.333	5.52	26	23	0	0	0	1	120.2	132	552	91	74	15	3	4	5	71	0	121	16	2
Burnham, Gary, Read.*	0	0	.000	18.00	1	0	0	0	0	0	1.0	1	5	2	2	1	0	0	0	2	0	0	0	0
Callier, Jeremy, Erie.	0	0	.000	18.00	1	0	0	0	0	0	1.0	2	7	2	2	0	0	0	0	2	0	2	0	0
Cames, Aaron, Por.	3	6	.333	5.55	23	16	1	0	2	0	95.2	110	435	64	59	17	0	3	9	46	1	66	3	1
Cammack, Eric, Bing.	4	2	.667	2.38	45	0	0	0	38	15	56.2	38	231	17	15	2	5	2	1	38	1	83	0	2
Camp, Jared, Akr.	1	2	.333	6.50	17	0	0	0	13	7	18.0	22	92	17	13	0	2		2	16	0	18	2	1
Carroll, Dave, Nor.*	0	0	.000	0.00	3	0	0	0	0	0	6.0	5	27	3	0	0	0		0	3	0	6	0	0
Cedeno, Blas, Read.	2	2	.500	4.26	19	0	0	0	5	0	31.2	30	131	16	15	5	2	1	2	13	3	18	0	0
Censale, Silvio, Read.*	1	6	.143	11.77	16	11	0	0	0	0	52.0	74	279	76	68	15	3	5	3	48	1	36	4	0
Christiansen, Jason, Alt.*	0	0	.000	0.00	2	0	0	0	2	0	3.0	1	11	0	0	0	0	0	0	2	0	2	0	0
Clark, Chris, Por.	1	0	1.000	7.50	4	0	0	0	4	0	6.0	5	29	5	5	1	1	1	0	7	0	6	0	0
Coggin, Dave, Read.	2	5	.286	7.50	9	9	0	0	0	0	42.0	55	203	37	35	8	0	3	0	20	0	21	6	0
Cooper, Brian, Erie	10	5	.667	3.30	22	22	0	0	0	0	158.0	146	640	61	58	17	3	1	13	29	0	143	5	1
Cordova, Francisco, Alt.	1	1	.500	4.66	2	2	0	0	0	0	9.2	13	48	8	5	0	0	0	0	4	1	12	1	0
Corey, Mark, Bing.	7	13	.350	5.40	29	27	0	0	0	0	155.0	175	698	108	93	18	4	1	9	64	0	111	1	1
Crawford, Paxton, Tren.	7	8	.467	4.08	28	28	1	1	0	0	163.1	151	696	81	74	12	7	4	10	59	1	111	10	1
Cressend, Jack, Tren.-N.B.	8	10	.444	4.61	28	27	2	2	0	0	160.0	171	700	91	82	13	3	6	5	57	0	136	6	2
Cumberland, Chris, Tren.*	2	0	1.000	0.43	14	0	0	0	6	1	21.0	12	84	1	1	0	0	0	1	13	1	18	1	0
Cummings, Ryan, Erie.	1	1	.500	5.09	3	3	0	0	0	0	17.2	18	81	12	10	3	0	1	3	10	0	7	0	0
Daniels, David, Alt.	2	2	.500	2.67	55	0	0	0	29	6	67.1	55	276	21	20	8	5	2	1	19	2	63	1	0
Davis, Kane, Alt.	4	6	.400	3.78	16	16	0	0	0	0	95.1	97	421	51	40	5	3	4	3	41	1	53	4	0
Dedrick, Jim, Akr.	1	0	1.000	9.00	2	0	0	0	0	0	3.0	4	13	3	3	2	0	0	0	0	0	2	0	0

Pitcher, Team	W	L	Pct.	ERA	G	GS	CG	ShO	GF	Sv.	IP	H	TBF	R	ER	HR	SH	SF	HB	BB	IBB	SO	WP	Bk.
De La Cruz, Francisco, Nor.	6	5	.545	4.59	29	19	1	0	4	0	133.1	141	603	89	68	10	2	5	2	73	0	91	11	3
Delahoya, Javier, Bow.	9	1	.900	3.36	12	12	1	0	0	0	77.2	64	310	29	29	12	2	1	1	18	1	68	4	0
De La Rosa, Maximo, N.H.	0	1	.000	2.53	10	0	0	0	9	4	10.2	9	45	4	3	1	0	0	1	3	0	7	2	0
Della Ratta, Pete, Bing.	1	4	.200	2.18	41	3	0	0	9	0	82.2	75	329	22	20	4	2	3	3	13	1	68	2	0
De Paula, Sean, Akr.	1	0	1.000	3.54	14	0	0	0	6	1	28.0	20	122	11	11	2	2	0	2	17	0	31	2	0
Deschenes, Marc, Akr.	3	2	.600	3.31	43	0	0	0	26	3	65.1	57	277	28	24	5	5	2	2	31	6	64	3	0
Dingman, Craig, Nor.	8	6	.571	1.57	55	0	0	0	21	9	74.1	56	288	16	13	2	2	0	2	12	2	90	2	0
Dixon, Tim, Har.-Tren.*	2	1	.667	3.52	10	2	0	0	1	0	23.0	19	93	10	9	3	1	1	2	8	0	14	3	0
Dodd, Robert, Read.*.............	10	2	.833	3.83	42	0	0	0	18	5	80.0	78	335	38	34	8	2	2	3	23	1	79	1	2
Donnelly, Brendan, Alt.	0	0	.000	7.71	2	0	0	0	2	1	2.1	4	12	2	2	0	1	2	0	2	0	0	0	0
Dougherty, Tony, Alt.-Tren.	0	0	.000	7.71	15	1	0	0	5	1	23.1	41	121	27	20	3	0	1	2	13	1	16	0	0
Downs, Scott, N.B.*...............	0	0	.000	8.69	6	3	0	0	1	0	19.2	33	99	21	19	5	0	0	1	10	1	22	0	0
Duff, Matt, Alt.	2	4	.333	2.81	44	0	0	0	29	12	57.2	43	241	19	18	5	4	2	2	35	4	59	4	1
Dunbar, Matt, Alt.*	3	5	.375	3.42	49	0	0	0	14	2	47.1	35	204	19	18	2	2	1	6	23	3	35	7	0
Duncan, Geoff, Por.	2	3	.400	2.85	43	0	0	0	22	4	66.1	59	276	24	21	8	1	0	2	26	2	59	3	1
Dunham, Pat, N.H.	0	1	.000	2.57	3	0	0	0	2	0	7.0	1	37	2	2	0	2	1	0	16	3	5	1	0
Duran, Roberto, Har.*	2	2	.500	8.31	19	1	0	0	7	1	21.2	15	115	20	20	1	0	1	7	31	0	20	8	0
Durocher, Jayson, Har.	1	3	.250	3.48	29	1	0	0	11	4	51.2	44	224	29	20	5	2	2	6	25	1	36	3	1
Eason, Clay, Read.	0	2	.000	10.38	10	1	0	0	5	1	13.0	14	74	15	15	4	1	0	6	14	0	13	4	0
Eaton, Adam, Read.	5	4	.556	2.92	12	12	2	0	0	0	77.0	60	317	30	25	9	1	2	5	28	1	67	1	2
Edsell, Geoff, Erie....................	2	3	.400	3.46	26	2	0	0	14	2	39.0	45	179	20	15	1	1	3	6	13	0	28	0	0
Eibey, Scott, Bow.*.................	2	0	1.000	2.63	27	4	0	0	3	0	51.1	49	222	17	15	2	1	1	1	25	2	29	5	2
Einertson, Darrell, Nor.	2	2	.500	4.97	21	0	0	0	6	0	29.0	39	141	23	16	2	4	0	1	10	5	16	4	0
Escobar, Ruben, Akr.	0	0	.000	16.20	1	0	0	0	0	0	1.2	5	11	3	3	1	0	0	0	0	0	0	0	1
Espinal, Jose, N.B.	3	12	.200	5.54	29	20	2	0	3	0	131.2	160	595	100	81	10	8	11	2	41	0	90	3	0
Etherton, Seth, Erie	10	10	.500	3.27	24	24	4	1	0	0	167.2	153	694	72	61	14	7	5	3	43	0	153	4	4
Evans, Keith, Har.	0	2	.000	3.67	5	5	0	0	0	0	27.0	29	120	14	11	5	1	0	3	5	0	21	1	0
Falkenborg, Brian, Bow.	3	6	.333	3.78	16	16	0	0	0	0	83.1	77	361	40	35	11	2	0	5	36	0	77	1	0
Farrell, Jim, Tren.	2	2	.500	3.33	7	5	0	0	0	0	27.0	26	116	13	10	1	0	1	1	9	1	26	1	0
Faurot, Adam, Tren.	1	0	1.000	0.00	1	0	0	0	0	0	1.0	0	5	0	0	0	0	0	0	2	0	1	0	0
Fernandez, Jared, Tren.	3	0	1.000	3.38	7	0	0	0	4	1	18.2	18	80	9	7	4	0	0	0	8	0	10	1	0
Fitzgerald, Brian, N.H.*	2	2	.500	3.83	29	1	0	0	13	3	54.0	58	228	24	23	2	2	2	1	18	0	37	0	0
Flores, Randy, Nor.*...............	0	1	.000	6.48	4	4	0	0	0	0	25.0	32	120	20	18	0	2	0	1	11	1	19	1	1
Forster, Scott, Har.*	0	0	.000	0.00	2	0	0	0	1	0	5.0	3	16	0	0	0	0	0	1	0	0	1	0	0
France, Aaron, Alt.	4	5	.444	3.67	33	11	0	0	7	0	95.2	79	414	50	39	8	5	3	5	48	1	70	7	3
Franco, John, Bing.*	0	0	.000	0.00	1	1	0	0	0	0	1.1	0	4	0	0	0	0	0	0	0	0	1	0	0
Fuentes, Brian, N.H.*	3	3	.500	4.95	15	14	0	0	0	0	60.0	53	272	36	33	5	2	5	11	46	0	66	1	1
Gandarillas, Gus, N.B.	1	3	.250	8.63	18	0	0	0	5	1	32.1	38	155	32	31	3	2	1	2	21	2	26	5	0
Garcia, Al, Alt.	0	0	.000	4.50	2	0	0	0	1	0	4.0	6	22	4	2	0	2	0	0	3	0	1	1	0
Garza, Alberto, Akr.	3	5	.375	9.35	10	9	0	0	0	0	42.1	54	216	46	44	5	2	0	3	41	0	38	4	0
Garza, Chris, N.B.*.................	1	0	1.000	2.08	31	0	0	0	8	0	30.1	14	129	10	7	0	2	1	4	19	0	40	4	0
Gentile, Scott, Bow.	1	2	.333	8.36	10	0	0	0	4	0	14.0	15	68	13	13	5	0	1	1	9	0	12	1	0
Giard, Ken, Alt.	2	2	.500	1.71	38	0	0	0	20	6	42.0	34	182	12	8	1	1	0	0	25	2	48	2	0
Gonzalez, Gabe, Por.*	2	4	.333	3.55	26	0	0	0	11	0	38.0	38	161	19	15	2	4	1	3	8	1	34	2	0
Gonzalez, Mike, Alt.*..............	2	3	.400	8.10	7	5	0	0	0	0	26.2	34	133	25	24	4	2	1	2	19	0	31	3	3
Gooden, Dwight, Akr.	0	0	.000	3.00	1	1	0	0	0	0	3.0	3	12	2	1	0	0	0	0	1	0	2	0	0
Grahe, Joe, Read.	0	0	.000	0.90	7	0	0	0	6	4	10.0	7	39	3	1	0	0	0	0	2	0	12	0	0
Green, Steve, Erie..................	3	1	.750	3.32	6	6	1	0	0	0	40.2	34	176	25	15	4	1	2	2	19	0	32	1	0
Gryboski, Kevin, N.H.	2	5	.286	2.89	47	0	0	0	32	10	62.1	67	267	27	20	5	5	2	3	20	4	41	3	0
Guardado, Eddie, N.B.*	0	0	.000	1.93	3	0	0	0	0	0	4.2	3	17	1	1	0	0	0	0	0	0	5	0	0
Hafer, Jeff, Bing.	0	2	.000	3.14	7	0	0	0	1	0	14.1	12	54	5	5	2	0	0	0	0	0	9	1	0
Haigler, Phil, N.B.	1	4	.200	6.32	19	6	0	0	7	0	52.2	74	252	53	37	6	2	3	5	20	0	18	0	0
Hamilton, Jimmy, Akr.*	0	2	.000	3.73	25	0	0	0	10	2	31.1	19	134	14	13	1	1	1	1	24	2	27	4	0
Hancock, Ryan, Erie...............	0	1	.000	5.27	8	0	0	0	3	1	13.2	23	63	8	8	2	0	1	0	2	0	6	1	0
Harriger, Mark, Erie...............	2	1	.667	4.70	6	6	0	0	0	0	30.2	31	135	16	16	4	0	0	0	15	0	13	4	0
Harris, Jeff, N.B.	3	1	.750	1.48	20	0	0	0	6	0	24.1	21	106	5	4	0	3	0	1	14	2	12	1	0
Hartmann, Pete, Bow.*............	1	1	.500	1.72	11	0	0	0	1	0	15.2	11	66	4	3	1	2	0	0	8	0	12	2	1
Hazlett, Andy, Tren.*	9	9	.500	4.16	27	26	2	1	1	1	164.1	155	674	84	76	15	5	2	8	41	0	123	7	3
Henderson, Ryan, Bing.	0	2	.000	7.04	5	2	0	0	1	0	7.2	9	35	6	6	1	0	0	1	6	0	8	2	0
Henderson, Scott, Por.	6	3	.667	2.96	46	1	0	0	21	7	85.0	67	343	32	28	4	4	2	8	26	4	83	7	0
Herbert, Russ, Read.	3	5	.375	4.75	26	9	0	0	7	3	83.1	90	369	53	44	7	3	6	8	32	1	55	1	3
Herbison, Brett, Bing.	5	13	.278	5.85	27	26	1	0	0	0	149.1	161	689	115	97	20	5	9	14	81	0	60	7	0
Heredia, Maximo, Bow.	6	4	.600	4.24	50	0	0	0	17	0	76.1	80	341	42	36	12	1	1	5	33	4	56	3	1
Hill, Jason, Erie*	1	2	.333	9.96	23	0	0	0	7	0	28.0	37	151	37	31	4	3	1	4	24	1	14	1	0
Hooten, David, N.B.	6	6	.500	3.56	52	5	0	0	17	1	103.2	94	450	55	41	10	3	6	1	49	2	89	3	0
Hubbs, Dan, Read.	0	0	.000	5.63	3	1	0	0	0	0	8.0	10	37	5	5	2	0	0	0	5	0	8	0	0
Iglesias, Mario, Bow.	1	4	.200	7.52	14	2	0	0	3	0	26.1	28	123	23	22	6	3	0	1	16	2	27	0	0
Jacquez, Thomas, Read.*	6	5	.545	5.28	38	14	0	0	8	1	122.2	149	555	84	72	20	3	2	11	32	1	68	1	0
Johnson, Greg, Erie*..............	0	0	.000	12.00	2	0	0	0	1	0	3.0	8	17	4	4	0	0	1	0	1	0	4	0	0
Johnson, Mark, Nor.	9	3	.750	3.68	16	15	0	0	0	0	88.0	88	393	51	36	7	1	5	4	39	0	52	6	0
Jones, Bobby, Bing.	1	2	.333	3.86	3	3	0	0	0	0	11.2	11	50	5	5	3	0	0	0	5	0	12	1	0
Kamieniecki, Scott, Bow.	0	1	.000	3.60	1	1	0	0	0	0	5.0	6	18	2	2	0	0	0	0	0	0	1	0	0
Kaufman, Brad, Nor.	3	2	.600	4.12	40	5	0	0	9	1	83.0	76	361	45	38	6	2	3	2	38	5	81	7	0
Kawabata, Kyle, Read.	0	0	.000	6.00	8	0	0	0	3	0	12.0	20	58	9	8	2	1	1	0	2	0	7	0	0
Keisler, Randy, Nor.*	3	4	.429	4.57	8	8	0	0	0	0	43.1	45	189	24	22	2	1	3	3	17	0	33	2	0
Kershner, Jason, Read.*	4	4	.500	5.73	57	2	0	0	30	8	92.2	99	412	67	59	14	3	6	5	40	3	86	5	0
Kim, Sun-Woo, Tren.	9	8	.529	4.89	26	26	1	1	0	0	149.0	160	641	86	81	16	2	5	9	44	2	130	4	0
Kinney, Matt, N.B.	4	7	.364	7.12	14	13	0	0	0	0	60.2	69	284	54	48	8	2	3	4	36	0	50	6	1
Kirkreit, Daron, N.H.	2	2	.500	2.63	5	4	0	0	1	0	24.0	33	107	8	7	0	1	1	0	7	0	15	3	0
Knotts, Gary, Por.	6	3	.667	3.75	12	12	1	1	0	0	81.2	79	358	39	34	12	4	3	8	33	0	63	4	0
Kohlmeier, Ryan, Bow.	3	7	.300	3.16	55	0	0	0	49	23	62.2	44	256	23	22	10	4	2	1	29	1	78	2	1
Lail, Denny, Nor.	5	0	1.000	1.74	6	6	0	0	0	0	41.1	24	156	12	8	1	1	0	0	11	0	29	1	1
Lara, Giovanny, Har.	0	0	.000	7.90	9	0	0	0	6	0	13.2	19	71	12	12	2	1	0	0	8	0	10	0	0

Pitcher, Team	W	L	Pct.	ERA	G	GS	CG	ShO	GF	Sv.	IP	H	TBF	R	ER	HR	SH	SF	HB	BB	IBB	SO	WP	Bk.
Larkin, Andy, Por.	1	1	.500	7.11	7	1	0	0	3	0	12.2	16	57	10	10	2	0	0	4	0	7	1	0
Leese, Brandon, Por.	4	4	.500	5.73	20	11	0	0	2	0	81.2	110	370	66	52	8	2	0	7	20	0	52	2	2
Lisio, Joe, Nor.	2	6	.250	4.13	59	0	0	0	56	33	56.2	58	245	27	26	4	2	1	1	27	1	49	2	0
Lohse, Kyle, N.B.	3	4	.429	5.89	11	11	1	0	0	0	70.1	87	311	49	46	9	3	4	5	23	0	41	2	0
Long, Joey, Alt.*	0	0	.000	5.91	8	0	0	0	4	0	10.2	16	50	8	7	3	0	0	0	4	0	5	0	0
Lopez, Johan, Bing.	0	0	.000	13.50	2	0	0	0	1	0	2.0	3	11	3	3	0	1	0	0	3	0	1	0	0
Luce, Robert, N.H.	0	0	.000	8.59	2	0	0	0	0	0	7.1	11	35	10	7	2	0	0	1	3	0	3	1	0
Lynch, Ryan, Bow.*	1	0	1.000	6.89	9	0	0	0	5	1	15.2	23	85	15	12	1	0	1	2	16	1	11	1	0
Lyons, Mike, Bing.	4	7	.364	3.40	53	0	0	0	29	5	79.1	76	358	41	30	6	6	2	12	37	2	70	4	0
Maeda, Kats, Nor.	3	2	.600	4.34	25	7	1	0	11	1	76.2	82	345	41	37	7	0	5	3	40	0	48	10	0
Mahaffey, Alan, N.B.*	8	6	.571	4.12	33	12	1	0	7	1	98.1	109	435	47	45	15	3	5	6	34	0	89	3	2
Mairena, Oswaldo, Nor.*	4	4	.571	2.67	49	0	0	0	16	2	57.1	48	252	24	17	3	4	4	1	27	4	47	4	0
Maloney, Sean, Bow.	0	0	.000	3.38	4	0	0	0	1	0	10.2	10	46	4	4	1	0	0	0	3	0	17	1	0
Marquez, Robert, Har.	2	2	.500	4.56	18	0	0	0	11	1	25.2	21	116	15	13	3	1	1	2	8	1	22	0	0
Martin, Tom, Akr.*	0	0	.000	1.00	3	3	0	0	0	0	9.0	4	34	1	1	0	1	0	1	3	0	9	0	0
Martinez, Javier, Alt.	0	0	.000	6.10	10	0	0	0	3	0	10.1	11	55	8	7	1	0	1	0	14	0	16	0	0
Martinez, Willie, Akr.	9	8	.529	4.09	24	24	0	0	0	0	147.1	163	639	83	67	20	5	2	3	45	0	91	8	0
Mathews, Del, Alt.*	1	1	.500	6.00	9	0	0	0	2	0	12.0	21	66	15	8	2	0	0	6	2	8	1	0
Mattes, Troy, Har.	5	8	.385	5.36	20	19	0	0	0	0	97.1	114	433	67	58	12	8	4	7	38	0	58	3	0
Matthews, Mike, Akr.-Tren.*	0	5	.000	7.47	9	9	0	0	0	0	37.1	47	179	37	31	8	1	4	2	24	0	18	0	2
McClaskey, Tim, N.H.	0	0	.000	2.25	4	0	0	0	2	0	8.0	4	27	2	2	1	0	0	0	1	0	7	0	0
McConnell, Sam, Alt.*	1	7	.125	6.64	13	12	1	0	0	0	62.1	82	299	52	46	7	6	3	4	33	1	40	5	1
McCrary, Scott, Bing.	1	5	.167	4.86	17	6	0	0	3	0	53.2	72	247	34	29	8	4	4	1	21	0	29	1	0
McDougal, Mike, Bow.	5	7	.417	4.26	48	0	0	0	22	8	61.1	70	285	34	29	10	7	0	4	31	6	47	2	0
McEntire, Ethan, Bing.*	0	2	.000	13.17	4	3	0	0	1	0	13.2	26	75	23	20	5	0	0	0	8	0	7	1	0
McMichael, Greg, Bing.	0	0	.000	0.00	2	2	0	0	0	0	3.0	2	13	1	0	0	0	0	1	0	0	5	0	0
McMullen, Jerry, Tren.*	1	0	1.000	6.00	3	0	0	0	1	0	3.0	4	15	2	2	0	0	0	0	2	0	2	0	0
McNatt, Josh, Bow.*	0	1	.000	5.14	2	1	0	0	0	0	7.0	8	32	5	4	0	1	0	0	6	0	1	2	0
Meche, Gil, N.H.	3	4	.429	3.05	10	10	0	0	0	0	59.0	51	250	24	20	3	2	1	0	26	0	56	4	0
Medina, Carlos, Bow.*	3	6	.333	5.54	15	15	0	0	0	0	78.0	86	350	52	48	6	2	2	7	37	0	70	6	4
Mintz, Steve, Erie	1	1	.500	2.23	26	0	0	0	14	9	32.1	26	135	12	8	3	1	1	2	12	0	33	0	0
Mitchell, Scott, Har.	2	0	1.000	4.26	3	3	1	0	0	0	19.0	16	74	9	9	5	0	1	0	3	0	10	1	1
Montane, Ivan, N.H.	4	2	.667	2.47	41	0	0	0	25	10	54.2	38	219	16	15	2	3	0	2	22	2	70	5	0
Moraga, David, Har.*	1	0	1.000	0.00	1	0	0	0	0	0	3.0	1	11	0	0	0	0	0	1	0	0	0	0	0
Moreno, Julio, Bow.	2	2	.500	5.28	10	10	0	0	0	0	44.1	46	202	29	26	9	1	2	1	27	0	25	4	0
Morse, Paul, Erie	8	6	.571	3.33	15	14	2	0	0	0	97.1	83	419	44	36	9	5	1	5	54	0	52	10	1
Mota, Danny, N.B.	0	1	.000	3.55	6	0	0	0	5	0	12.2	11	52	5	5	2	1	0	0	5	1	12	0	0
Mucker, Kelcey, N.B.	0	0	.000	9.00	1	0	0	0	1	0	1.0	1	5	2	1	1	0	0	0	1	0	1	0	0
Negrette, Richard, Akr.	1	3	.250	6.13	33	0	0	0	10	1	47.0	49	230	35	32	2	1	2	3	47	0	34	7	0
Neubart, Garrett, Bing.	0	0	.000	0.00	1	0	0	0	1	0	2.0	1	7	0	0	0	0	0	0	0	0	1	0	0
Newton, Geronimo, N.H.*	2	1	.667	3.97	31	2	0	0	8	0	59.0	60	254	32	26	8	1	1	0	26	0	48	1	0
Niebla, Ruben, Har.*	2	0	1.000	5.58	29	0	0	0	12	1	30.2	31	142	22	19	2	0	2	1	22	0	23	2	1
Niedermaier, Brad, N.B.	2	2	.500	4.35	41	0	0	0	23	9	49.2	50	222	29	24	6	2	1	1	27	0	47	7	0
Nina, Elvin, Erie	3	0	1.000	4.07	4	4	0	0	0	0	24.1	20	103	12	11	2	1	1	0	15	0	19	1	0
O'Connor, Brian, Alt.*	7	11	.389	4.70	28	27	1	0	0	0	153.1	152	698	98	80	10	11	3	6	92	2	106	21	0
Ohka, Tomokazu, Tren.	8	0	1.000	3.00	12	12	0	0	0	0	72.0	63	298	26	24	9	0	3	25	0	53	3	0
Ortiz, Ramon, Erie	9	4	.692	2.82	15	15	2	2	0	0	102.0	88	419	38	32	12	3	2	2	40	0	86	1	0
Padilla, Juan, Erie	1	1	.500	6.63	11	0	0	0	3	2	19.0	31	92	15	14	3	2	1	1	7	0	12	2	0
Pageler, Mick, Por.	4	2	.667	4.76	31	1	0	0	12	1	51.0	70	237	33	27	4	1	2	3	13	1	44	4	0
Parker, Christian, Har.	8	5	.615	3.65	36	6	0	0	16	3	88.2	86	386	39	36	11	5	0	15	37	2	45	10	2
Paronto, Chad, Bow.	0	4	.000	8.12	15	9	0	0	0	0	41.0	59	209	39	37	3	1	1	4	32	1	27	3	0
Parrish, John, Bow.*	0	2	.000	4.04	12	10	0	0	2	0	55.2	49	248	28	25	4	7	5	3	43	1	42	3	1
Pena, Alex, Alt.	1	0	1.000	3.86	9	0	0	0	2	0	21.0	22	93	12	9	2	0	3	9	0	20	2	1
Penny, Brad, Por.	1	0	1.000	3.90	6	6	0	0	0	0	32.1	28	139	15	14	3	0	1	3	14	0	35	3	2
Petroff, Daniel, Erie	0	0	.000	9.45	8	0	0	0	4	0	13.1	21	66	17	14	1	1	3	1	4	0	8	0	1
Phelps, Tommy, Har.*	3	6	.333	5.71	13	13	1	0	0	0	64.2	76	306	53	41	13	3	6	7	26	0	36	2	0
Pineiro, Joel, N.H.	10	15	.400	4.72	28	25	4	0	0	0	166.0	190	724	105	87	18	6	5	5	52	0	116	11	0
Politte, Cliff, Read.	9	8	.529	3.63	37	13	1	0	16	5	109.0	112	460	45	44	12	6	1	5	33	3	97	4	0
Pontes, Dan, Bing.	3	1	.750	5.01	19	0	0	0	5	1	32.1	29	141	18	18	7	0	2	15	1	37	1	0
Poole, Jim, Akr.*	0	0	.000	0.00	2	0	0	0	0	0	2.2	0	7	0	0	0	0	0	0	4	1	0	0	0
Pumphrey, Ken, Bing.	6	9	.400	4.80	25	23	0	0	1	0	131.1	146	617	95	70	10	4	4	15	71	0	84	5	0
Pyc, David, Read.*	5	2	.714	4.33	17	13	1	0	1	0	81.0	95	351	44	39	9	2	2	6	15	0	51	1	0
Quezada, Edward, Har.	0	0	.000	1.80	3	0	0	0	2	0	5.0	2	18	1	1	0	0	0	1	0	4	0	0
Rector, Bobby, Por.	0	4	.000	3.59	13	4	0	0	1	0	42.2	43	187	23	17	3	7	0	2	14	0	19	0	0
Reed, Rick, Bing.	0	0	.000	1.80	1	1	0	0	0	0	5.0	1	17	1	1	1	0	0	0	1	0	5	0	0
Resz, Greg, Nor.	3	2	.600	4.36	20	5	0	0	4	0	43.1	40	190	25	21	1	1	1	20	2	45	2	0
Rigdon, Paul, Akr.*	7	0	1.000	0.90	8	7	0	0	0	0	50.0	20	177	5	5	2	0	1	2	10	0	25	1	0
Riley, Matt, Bow.*	10	6	.625	3.22	20	20	3	0	0	0	125.2	113	520	53	45	13	2	3	5	42	0	131	10	4
Rincon, Ricardo, Akr.*	0	0	.000	5.40	2	0	0	0	1	0	1.2	2	8	1	1	1	0	0	0	0	2	0	0
Riske, David, Akr.	0	0	.000	1.90	23	0	0	0	22	12	23.2	5	90	6	5	1	0	2	0	13	0	33	1	0
Robbins, Jake, Nor.	3	12	.200	5.43	20	19	2	1	0	0	111.0	118	508	80	67	14	4	8	3	60	3	63	2	2
Roberts, Grant, Bing.	7	6	.538	4.87	23	23	0	0	0	0	131.1	135	576	81	71	9	6	3	12	49	0	94	8	0
Rodgers, Bobby, Por.	5	10	.333	5.43	26	22	0	0	1	0	122.2	147	576	85	74	13	4	3	6	70	0	109	8	0
Rogers, Jason, Bow.*	0	1	.000	1.54	7	0	0	0	2	0	11.2	11	53	5	2	0	2	1	0	9	1	9	0	0
Romero, J.C., N.B.*	4	4	.500	3.40	36	1	0	0	17	7	53.0	51	244	25	20	6	3	2	4	34	0	53	2	1
Rosenkranz, Terry, Bow.*	3	1	.750	3.98	26	0	0	0	9	0	43.0	36	186	20	19	5	3	3	0	26	0	36	4	0
Ruebel, Matt, Bing.*	2	0	1.000	2.73	6	5	0	0	0	0	26.1	24	114	13	8	2	0	1	8	0	25	1	0
Runion, Tony, Alt.	1	4	.200	3.59	31	0	0	0	8	2	42.2	52	184	23	17	3	2	3	1	9	0	39	4	1
Rust, Brian, Bow.	0	0	.000	0.00	2	0	0	0	2	0	2.1	1	9	0	0	0	0	1	0	1	0	0	0	0
Rutherford, Mark, Read.	1	0	1.000	0.98	4	4	0	0	0	0	18.1	11	72	3	2	1	0	0	0	9	0	10	1	0
Ryan, Jason, N.B.	2	4	.333	4.80	8	8	0	0	0	0	50.2	48	217	29	27	6	1	0	1	24	0	42	3	0
Saberhagen, Bret, Tren.	1	0	1.000	0.00	1	1	0	0	0	0	6.0	2	19	0	0	0	0	0	0	0	0	5	0	0
St. Pierre, Bob, Akr.	0	0	.000	18.00	4	0	0	0	3	0	4.0	9	25	8	8	1	0	0	0	4	0	2	0	0

Pitcher, Team	W	L	Pct.	ERA	G	GS	CG	ShO	GF	Sv.	IP	H	TBF	R	ER	HR	SH	SF	HB	BB	IBB	SO	WP	Bk.
Salter, Cody, Erie	6	2	.750	4.10	27	3	0	0	8	0	52.2	65	238	29	24	2	2	1	4	14	0	16	3	1
Salyers, Jeremy, Har.	1	0	1.000	2.81	12	1	0	0	8	0	25.2	20	105	9	8	1	1	0	2	11	0	9	1	0
Sanders, Frankie, Akr.	6	6	.500	4.85	33	13	0	0	6	2	120.2	139	546	72	65	12	6	7	6	51	2	72	9	0
Saylor, Ryan, Har.	6	1	.857	3.62	28	3	0	0	12	7	59.2	50	250	28	24	7	3	3	2	24	3	55	3	0
Scheffer, Aaron, N.H.	2	0	1.000	3.71	10	0	0	0	4	0	17.0	19	79	9	7	3	1	0	1	8	0	24	1	0
Secrist, Reed, Alt.	0	0	.000	0.00	1	0	0	0	1	0	1.0	1	4	0	0	0	0	0	0	0	0	0	0	0
Sekany, Jason, Tren.	14	4	.778	3.35	27	22	3	2	1	0	161.1	143	674	65	60	8	3	4	6	64	0	116	10	1
Sexton, Jeff, Akr.	1	0	1.000	3.60	15	0	0	0	11	2	20.0	24	89	10	8	1	2	5	1	9	0	16	1	0
Shields, Scot, Erie	4	4	.500	2.89	10	10	1	1	0	0	74.2	57	300	26	24	10	4	0	6	26	0	81	2	0
Short, Barry, Bing.	0	7	.000	3.48	24	0	0	0	12	0	41.1	43	187	29	16	3	5	2	2	16	2	22	2	1
Shumaker, Anthony, Read.*	4	3	.571	1.78	10	10	1	0	0	0	60.2	48	249	17	12	3	3	2	2	17	1	60	1	1
Smetana, Steve, Tren.*	5	4	.556	3.99	39	3	0	0	12	1	85.2	90	359	39	38	8	1	4	3	26	1	61	3	1
Smith, Cam, N.H.	1	4	.200	5.07	41	0	0	0	10	0	55.0	42	267	39	31	3	1	5	9	61	0	59	20	0
Spence, Cam, Nor.	5	5	.500	5.79	19	16	0	0	2	0	91.2	118	421	75	59	7	3	8	6	32	3	62	3	2
Spiers, Corey, N.B.*	5	2	.714	3.47	8	8	1	1	0	0	46.2	50	192	21	18	3	0	3	1	12	0	21	3	0
Stanifer, Rob, Tren.	0	0	.000	0.00	5	0	0	0	3	1	9.0	6	36	0	0	0	1	0	0	4	2	11	0	0
Stark, Dennis, N.H.	9	11	.450	4.40	26	26	2	1	0	0	147.1	151	646	82	72	14	6	2	13	62	0	103	7	1
Stentz, Brent, N.B.	0	1	.000	3.73	32	0	0	0	28	9	31.1	23	125	13	13	3	0	0	0	12	2	44	0	0
Stevenson, Rod, Har.	2	9	.182	4.38	37	0	0	0	25	4	51.1	54	224	32	25	8	2	6	1	21	1	34	5	0
Stewart, Scott, Bing.*	1	0	1.000	0.00	1	1	0	0	0	0	5.0	3	18	0	0	0	0	0	0	5	0	5	0	0
Strickland, Scott, Har.	1	1	.500	2.48	14	1	0	0	6	3	29.0	25	117	8	8	1	1	0	1	10	0	36	0	0
Sweeney, Brian, N.H.	4	6	.400	4.69	23	18	0	0	3	1	111.1	125	478	65	58	18	1	3	4	31	1	83	4	0
Taglienti, Jeff, Tren.	0	0	.000	2.79	10	0	0	0	4	2	19.1	9	72	6	6	2	1	1	0	5	0	17	0	0
Tebbs, Nate, Tren.	0	0	.000	0.00	1	0	0	0	1	0	1.0	0	3	0	0	0	0	0	0	0	0	0	0	0
Tejera, Michael, Por.*	13	4	.765	2.62	25	25	0	0	0	0	154.2	137	640	55	45	13	9	3	7	45	1	152	6	1
Thomas, Evan, Read.	9	5	.643	3.25	36	15	1	0	8	3	127.1	123	545	53	46	7	3	7	5	50	2	127	2	0
Thompson, Chris, Tren.	0	0	.000	9.00	1	0	0	0	1	0	1.0	2	6	1	1	0	0	0	0	1	0	1	1	0
Towers, Josh, Bow.	12	7	.632	3.76	29	28	5	2	1	0	189.0	204	786	86	79	26	12	4	5	26	1	106	5	3
Troutman, Keith, Erie	5	4	.556	4.12	38	0	0	0	26	6	59.0	66	257	32	27	8	7	0	0	19	0	49	3	0
Tucker, T.J., Har.	8	5	.615	4.10	19	19	1	1	0	0	116.1	110	489	55	53	12	4	1	4	38	0	85	5	1
Turnbow, Mark, Akr.	1	0	1.000	3.00	1	1	0	0	0	0	6.0	4	25	3	2	0	0	0	0	3	0	4	0	0
Turrentine, Rich, Bing.	0	2	.000	4.66	17	0	0	0	4	0	19.1	20	97	13	10	0	0	0	1	20	2	16	2	0
Tweedlie, Brad, Tren.	6	0	1.000	3.65	44	0	0	0	20	3	56.2	59	253	28	23	3	1	5	2	21	1	31	5	0
Urso, Sal, Tren.*	2	2	.500	1.86	22	0	0	0	13	5	29.0	25	123	11	6	2	1	0	0	14	0	39	2	2
Vardijan, Dan, Por.	0	1	.000	29.08	5	0	0	0	4	0	4.1	12	37	15	14	1	0	1	2	8	1	5	3	0
Vasquez, Leo, Bing.*	1	2	.333	3.43	27	0	0	0	7	1	42.1	39	190	18	18	4	0	1	2	28	0	43	2	1
Villafuerte, Brandon, Por.	6	8	.429	3.50	22	12	0	0	4	0	100.1	97	422	45	39	11	4	2	5	40	3	85	2	1
Walker, Tyler, Bing.	6	4	.600	6.22	13	13	0	0	0	0	68.0	78	306	49	47	11	3	2	2	32	0	59	4	3
Watson, Mark, Akr.*	9	8	.529	4.34	19	17	0	0	1	0	110.0	143	500	64	53	9	6	7	6	38	0	57	6	2
Westbrook, Jake, Har.	11	5	.688	3.92	27	27	2	2	0	0	174.2	180	748	88	76	14	12	3	13	63	1	90	2	1
Wilkins, Marc, Alt.	0	1	.000	1.50	4	0	0	0	2	0	6.0	4	26	2	1	0	0	0	4	1	0	5	0	0
Williams, Matt, Nor.*	1	1	.500	2.40	22	0	0	0	5	0	30.0	22	128	9	8	3	0	1	1	18	3	44	3	0
Williams, Shad, Read.	2	2	.500	3.13	16	2	0	0	5	2	31.2	30	133	17	11	3	3	2	0	10	0	19	1	0
Wise, Matt, Erie....................	8	5	.615	3.77	16	16	3	0	0	0	98.0	102	416	48	41	10	4	3	4	24	0	72	1	0
Wright, Jaret, Akr.	1	0	1.000	0.00	1	1	0	0	0	0	5.0	3	19	0	0	0	0	0	0	1	0	6	1	0
Yeskie, Nate, N.B.	5	11	.313	5.28	25	23	0	0	2	0	129.2	157	574	83	76	15	3	3	3	47	0	102	3	0
Young, Tim, Tren.*	4	4	.500	4.37	31	0	0	0	12	2	45.1	38	204	26	22	1	6	1	5	26	0	52	4	0
Zancanaro, Dave, Nor.*	6	1	.857	2.28	15	11	1	0	1	0	79.0	64	327	25	20	4	5	1	2	32	1	61	2	0
Zimmerman, Jordan, N.H.*	1	4	.200	1.08	22	0	0	0	8	2	33.1	26	149	8	4	0	0	1	2	19	0	33	1	1

COMBINATION SHUTOUTS: **Akron (6)**—Rigdon-Brammer-Riske, Rigdon-Hamilton-Brammer, Rigdon-Brammer-Hamilton, Sanders-Riske, Bacsik-Atkins, Bacsik-Atkins-Camp. **Altoona (4)**—Ah Yat-Dunbar-Daniels, Davis-Giard, O'Connor-Duff-Dunbar-Daniels-Runion, Gonzalez-O'Connor-Duff. **Binghamton (8)**—Roberts-Brittan-Cammack, Roberts-Lyons, McCrary-Lyons, Pumphrey-Brittan-Cammack, Corey-Brittan-Vasquez, Corey-Lyons-Cammack, Roberts-Della Ratta-Cammack, Della Ratta-Arteaga-Turrentine. **Bowie (5)**—Moreno-Bell, De La Hoya-Kohlmeier, De La Hoya-Bell, Riley-Kohlmeier, Riley-McDougal-Kohlmeier. **Erie (3)**—Harriger-Edsell, Salter-Troutman, Etherton-Hill-Troutman. **Harrisburg (6)**—Tucker-Durocher, Armas-Durocher, Blank-Parker, Blank-Durocher, Agamennone-Parker, Armas-Saylor-Salyers. **New Britain (6)**—Yeskie-Niedermaier, Spiers-Niedermaier-Romero, Yeskie-Niedermaier-Romero, Cressend-Gandarillas, Kinney-Romero-Niedermaier, Mahaffey-Hooten-Garza-Stentz. **New Haven (4)**—Meche-Zimmerman, Anderson-Montane-Fitzgerald, Stark-Montane-Gryboski, Sweeney-Brosnan. **Norwich (5)**—Beverlin-Dingman-Lisio, Spence-Johnson-Kaufman, Zancanaro-Dingman, Zancanaro-Spence, Lail-Dingman-Lisio. **Portland (4)**—Tejera-Villafuerte-Pageler-Almonte, Leese-Henderson-Gonzalez-Almonte, Rodgers-Almonte, Penny-Arroyo. **Reading (3)**—Coggin-Thomas-Dodd, Politte-Dodd, Bailie-Cedeno-Kershner. **Trenton (12)**—Ohka-Cumberland, Ohka-Cumberland-Beale-Bulliner, Kim-Cumberland-Bullinger, Ohka-Cumberland-Bullinger, Hazlett-Stanifer, Hazlett-Young, Dixon-Beale-Urso, Barkley-Smetana-Betancourt, Sekany-Betancourt, Crawford-Young, Barkley-Urso, Farrell-Young.

NO-HIT GAME: Eaton, Reading, lost to Norwich, 1-0, June 22.

PITCHERS WITH TWO OR MORE TEAMS

Pitcher, Team	W	L	Pct.	ERA	G	GS	CG	ShO	GF	Sv.	IP	H	TBF	R	ER	HR	SH	SF	HB	BB	IBB	SO	WP	Bk.
Brown, Alvin, Alt.	4	1	.800	6.49	7	6	0	0	0	0	26.1	29	124	22	19	0	3	3	1	17	0	15	6	1
Brown, Alvin, Erie.................	0	1	.000	6.75	6	0	0	0	4	2	6.2	9	39	6	5	0	0	0	2	7	0	6	3	0
Cressend, Jack, Tren.	1	0	1.000	7.20	3	3	0	0	0	0	15.0	19	71	12	12	3	0	1	0	7	0	11	2	0
Cressend, Jack, N.B.	7	10	.412	4.34	25	24	2	2	0	0	145.0	152	629	79	70	10	3	5	5	50	0	125	4	2
Dixon, Tim, Har.*	0	1	.000	5.79	2	0	0	0	0	0	4.2	4	20	4	3	1	0	1	0	2	0	4	1	0
Dixon, Tim, Tren.*	2	0	1.000	2.95	8	2	0	0	1	0	18.1	15	73	6	6	2	1	0	2	6	0	10	2	0
Dougherty, Tony, Alt.	0	0	.000	7.47	9	0	0	0	3	0	15.2	29	80	19	13	3	0	1	1	7	1	6	0	0
Dougherty, Tony, Tren.	0	0	.000	8.22	6	0	0	0	2	1	7.2	12	41	8	7	0	0	0	1	6	0	10	0	2
Matthews, Mike, Akr.*	0	5	.000	8.77	6	6	0	0	0	0	25.2	36	127	30	25	7	0	3	2	15	0	10	0	2
Matthews, Mike, Tren.*	0	0	.000	4.63	3	3	0	0	0	0	11.2	11	52	7	6	1	1	1	0	9	0	8	0	0

1999 FIELDING

TEAM

Team	Pct.	G	PO	A	E	TC	DP	TP	PB	Team	Pct.	G	PO	A	E	TC	DP	TP	PB
Trenton	.977	142	3796	1508	123	5427	130	0	22	Erie	.971	142	3748	1485	154	5387	128	0	10
Harrisburg	.974	142	3698	1517	140	5355	138	0	10	Portland	.969	142	3726	1462	164	5352	122	0	36
Bowie	.974	141	3782	1427	140	5349	127	0	8	New Britain	.969	141	3673	1566	169	5408	139	0	16
Reading	.972	142	3749	1515	151	5415	103	0	16	Binghamton	.966	142	3767	1563	190	5520	128	1	7
Akron	.972	140	3647	1501	148	5296	126	0	19	Altoona	.965	140	3734	1606	194	5534	126	0	25
New Haven	.972	142	3732	1538	152	5422	147	0	19	Norwich	.960	142	3727	1381	212	5320	121	1	17

INDIVIDUAL

FIRST BASEMEN

NOTE: All caps denotes fielding-percentage leader based on 71 games for catchers, 95 for all other non-pitchers and 114 innings for pitchers. *Throws lefthanded.

Player, Team	Pct.	G	PO	A	E	TC	DP
Alcantara, Israel, Tren.	1.000	15	82	6	0	88	10
Asche, Mike, Alt.	.889	1	7	1	1	9	0
Barnes, Larry, Erie*	.992	123	1047	87	9	1143	87
Betts, Todd, Akr.	1.000	18	153	7	0	160	16
Burkhart, Morgan, Tren.*	.987	25	215	7	3	225	19
Burnham, Gary, Read.*	.985	52	368	31	6	405	33
Burrell, Pat, Read.	.985	85	665	55	11	731	49
Chevalier, Virgil, Tren.	.750	3	3	0	1	4	0
Clark, Howie, Bow.	1.000	3	24	1	0	25	6
Cossins, Tim, Har.	1.000	4	17	0	0	17	2
Cranford, Joey, N.B.	1.000	1	9	1	0	10	1
Cruz, Cirilo, N.H.	1.000	6	41	2	0	43	4
Dishington, Nate, Akr.	1.000	2	12	0	0	12	2
Dubose, Brian, Bing.	1.000	5	41	2	0	43	5
Emmons, Scott, Nor.	1.000	2	9	1	0	10	2
Epperson, Chad, Tren.	.982	14	102	7	2	111	13
Gainey, Bryon, Bing.	.986	120	1004	90	16	1110	86
Gibralter, David, Tren.	.991	100	868	59	8	935	76
Hacker, Steve, N.B.	.978	5	42	2	1	45	4
Hage, Tom, Bow.	.987	101	746	59	11	816	64
Hayes, Heath, Akr.	1.000	15	135	11	0	146	15
Hernandez, Alexander, Alt.*	1.000	6	60	4	0	64	7
Huff, Larry, Read.	1.000	1	4	0	0	4	0
Hyzdu, Adam, Alt.	.974	18	176	11	5	192	16
Iglesias, Luis, Alt.	.980	6	44	4	1	49	4
Johnson, Nick, Nor.*	.983	132	1070	85	20	1175	103
Kilburg, Joe, Alt.	.980	6	46	3	1	50	3
KINGMAN, Brendan, N.H.	.993	115	943	84	7	1034	103
Long, Garrett, Alt.	.994	47	419	40	3	462	38
McNamara, Rusty, Read.	1.000	3	22	2	0	24	1
Meggers, Mike, Bing.	.935	3	27	2	2	31	2
Morris, Jeremy, Nor.	.944	5	34	0	2	36	2
Mucker, Kelcey, N.B.	1.000	1	6	0	0	6	0
Niles, Drew, Por.	1.000	1	8	0	0	8	0
Norton, Chris, Por.	.992	30	231	17	2	250	21
Nunnari, Talmadge, Har.*	.992	40	334	21	3	358	35
Ottavinia, Paul, Nor.*	.973	10	63	8	2	73	3
Peoples, Danny, Akr.	.984	91	775	81	14	870	71
Perry, Chan, Akr.	.983	12	98	16	2	116	9
Peterman, Tommy, N.B.*	.986	134	1129	110	17	1256	121
Robertson, Mike, Alt.*	.983	35	328	22	6	356	37
Rodriguez, Luis, Tren.	1.000	1	4	0	0	4	0
Rodriguez, Victor, Por.	1.000	5	11	1	0	12	3
Rolison, Nate, Por.	.987	115	920	69	13	1002	89
Rust, Brian, Bow.	.990	29	186	17	2	205	15
Schifano, Tony, Por.	1.000	1	1	0	0	1	1
Schneider, Brian, Har.	1.000	1	9	1	0	10	1
Secrist, Reed, Alt.	.981	5	46	6	1	53	2
Short, Rick, Bow.	.988	34	221	16	3	240	24
Simonton, Benji, Erie	.909	1	10	0	1	11	1
Smith, Jeff, N.B.	1.000	1	6	0	0	6	0
Snusz, Chris, Har.	1.000	1	5	1	0	6	0
Stewart, Andy, Read.	.992	15	113	10	1	124	11
Sweet, Jon, Alt.	.889	1	8	0	1	9	2
Tejero, Fausto, Erie	.833	1	4	1	1	6	1
Thomas, Juan, N.H.	.992	14	125	5	1	131	16
Toca, Jorge, Bing.	.994	22	158	13	1	172	19
Tracy, Andy, Har.	.994	18	138	18	1	157	8
Tucker, Jon, Har.*	.992	91	744	48	6	798	79
Valera, Yohanny, Bing.	1.000	1	4	1	0	5	0
Walther, Chris, Erie	1.000	1	9	0	0	9	3
Wathan, Dusty, N.H.	.989	12	85	7	1	93	11
Wilkerson, Brad, Har.*	1.000	1	1	0	0	1	0
Wilson, Craig, Alt.	.962	13	118	7	5	130	9

Player, Team	Pct.	G	PO	A	E	TC	DP
Wolff, Mike, Erie	.994	17	161	15	1	177	19
Wooten, Shawn, Erie	1.000	1	1	1	0	2	0
Wright, Ron, Alt.	.991	11	94	12	1	107	5

TRIPLE PLAY: Gainey.

SECOND BASEMEN

Player, Team	Pct.	G	PO	A	E	TC	DP
Bady, Ed, Akr.	1.000	3	1	1	0	2	0
Benefield, Brian, Akr.	.951	38	64	112	9	185	16
Betances, Junior, Akr.	.981	36	53	106	3	162	14
Betten, Randy, Erie	1.000	1	1	4	0	5	3
Bieser, Steve, Alt.	.962	11	26	24	2	52	6
Bravo, Danny, Har.	.941	4	6	10	1	17	0
Brown, Randy, N.H.	1.000	1	2	4	0	6	2
Brown, Vick, Nor.	.958	131	239	334	25	598	68
Bruce, Mo, Bing.	.963	112	255	343	23	621	74
Bryant, Matt, Alt.	1.000	3	4	4	0	8	1
Camilli, Jason, Har.	.987	20	33	41	1	75	6
Carroll, Jamey, Har.	.982	120	220	379	11	610	86
Casimiro, Carlos, Bow.	.970	136	281	331	19	631	87
Clark, Howie, Bow.	1.000	4	4	9	0	13	1
Cranford, Joey, N.B.	.906	7	12	17	3	32	1
Davidson, Cleatus, N.B.	.982	110	264	323	11	598	78
Dennis, Les, Nor.	1.000	3	0	7	0	7	1
DeShields, Delino, Bow.	1.000	3	5	5	0	10	1
Dorman, John, Akr.	1.000	3	4	6	0	10	1
Durrington, Trent, Erie	.974	107	212	312	14	538	54
ECKSTEIN, David, Tren.	.985	127	232	359	9	600	87
Erickson, Matt, Por.	.974	106	212	282	13	507	68
Faurot, Adam, Tren.	.971	12	24	44	2	70	7
Figueroa, Luis, Alt.	1.000	1	0	5	0	5	0
Finn, John, Read.	.979	14	16	31	1	48	3
Funaro, Joe, Por.	.945	11	18	34	3	55	5
Gipson, Charles, N.H.	1.000	2	8	6	0	14	2
Harris, Brian, Read.	.973	113	210	298	14	522	58
Harrison, Adonis, N.H.	.958	117	248	319	25	592	77
Hastings, Lionel, Por.	1.000	1	4	3	0	7	2
Hills, Rich, N.H.	.944	10	11	23	2	36	5
Huff, Larry, Read.	.923	16	19	41	5	65	6
Huls, Steve, N.B.	.966	19	34	52	3	89	11
Jackson, Gavin, Tren.	1.000	2	5	5	0	10	2
Kilburg, Joe, Akr.	.992	21	50	74	1	125	20
Lane, Ryan, N.B.	1.000	2	4	5	0	9	2
Leggett, Adam, Erie	1.000	21	42	67	0	109	17
Lobaton, Jose, Por.	1.000	3	5	4	0	9	1
Lorenzana, Luis, Alt.	.967	8	10	19	1	30	6
Mackowiak, Rob, Alt.	.971	52	112	158	8	278	39
Mashore, Justin, Bing.	.000	1	0	0	1	1	0
McDonald, John, Akr.	1.000	1	0	1	0	1	0
McLamb, Brian, Nor.	.922	16	18	29	4	51	10
McNamara, Rusty, Read.	1.000	3	6	10	0	16	3
Niles, Drew, Por.	.953	22	47	55	5	107	7
Ortiz, Nick, Akr.	1.000	3	3	6	0	9	2
Patzke, Jeff, Alt.	.974	46	98	129	6	233	32
Paz, Richard, Bow.	1.000	1	2	7	0	9	2
Post, Dave, Har.	1.000	1	4	1	0	5	1
Raynor, Mark, Read.	.953	9	18	23	2	43	7
Rivas, Luis, N.B.	.951	9	14	25	2	41	9
Robinson, Adam, Akr.	.968	40	67	115	6	188	29
Rodriguez, Victor, Por.	1.000	8	16	8	0	24	1
Rust, Brian, Bow.	1.000	1	0	2	0	2	0
Schifano, Tony, Por.	1.000	5	3	4	0	7	2
Short, Rick, Bow.	1.000	4	2	2	0	4	1
Tamargo, John, Bing.	.953	34	62	101	8	171	20
Tebbs, Nate, Tren.	.900	3	3	6	1	10	3
t'Hoen, E.J., Erie	.933	19	26	44	5	75	12
Vazquez, Ramon, N.H.	.953	16	34	47	4	85	15

Player, Team	Pct.	G	PO	A	E	TC	DP
Wimmer, Chris, Alt.	.965	26	42	67	4	113	6
Wolff, Mike, Erie	1.000	1	0	2	0	2	0
Zech, Scott, Har.	.944	7	19	15	2	36	3

THIRD BASEMEN

Player, Team	Pct.	G	PO	A	E	TC	DP
Benefield, Brian, Akr.	.667	4	0	2	1	3	1
Betances, Junior, Akr.	.889	21	20	28	6	54	2
Betten, Randy, Erie	1.000	2	0	3	0	3	0
Betts, Todd, Akr.	.935	77	54	134	13	201	11
Bieser, Steve, Alt.	.854	13	4	31	6	41	3
Bravo, Danny, Har.	.900	5	2	7	1	10	1
Brown, Randy, N.H.	.897	24	18	43	7	68	5
Bruce, Mo, Bing.	.979	17	17	30	1	48	4
Bryant, Matt, Alt.	.000	2	0	0	0	0	0
Camilli, Jason, Har.	.875	25	15	27	6	48	4
Casimiro, Carlos, Bow.	.667	1	0	2	1	3	0
Coffie, Ivanon, Bow.	.941	55	39	89	8	136	6
Cranford, Joey, N.B.	.915	29	14	61	7	82	5
Darden, Tony, Bing.	.939	18	10	36	3	49	4
Dennis, Les, Nor.	.000	1	0	0	0	0	0
Emmons, Scott, Nor.	.000	3	0	0	0	0	0
Espinal, Juan, Tren.	.828	16	4	20	5	29	0
Faurot, Adam, Tren.	.897	11	7	19	3	29	1
Finn, John, Read.	.906	21	19	39	6	64	4
Fryman, Travis, Akr.	1.000	1	0	2	0	2	0
Funaro, Joe, Por.	.943	47	31	101	8	140	11
Gipson, Charles, N.H.	.667	1	1	1	1	3	0
Gunderson, Shane, N.B.	.000	0	0	0	0	0	0
Hastings, Lionel, Por.	1.000	9	1	13	0	14	0
Haverbusch, Kevin, Alt.	.861	79	45	159	33	237	12
Hayes, Heath, Akr.	.895	15	8	26	4	38	0
Hills, Rich, N.H.	.909	53	26	94	12	132	9
Huff, Larry, Read.	.934	96	67	189	18	274	9
Huls, Steve, N.B.	.932	39	15	67	6	88	9
Hyzdu, Adam, Alt.	.800	10	3	13	4	20	2
Iglesias, Luis, Alt.	.875	13	9	26	5	40	0
Jorgensen, Tim, Alt.	.944	5	4	13	1	18	1
Kingman, Brendan, N.H.	.857	5	3	15	3	21	1
Kleinz, Larry, Por.	.902	76	33	123	17	173	15
Lane, Ryan, N.B.	.886	14	5	34	5	44	1
Leggett, Adam, Erie	.800	3	0	4	1	5	0
Leon, Donny, Nor.	.882	115	87	175	35	297	12
Lobaton, Jose, Por.	1.000	4	1	7	0	8	0
Lopez, Jose, Bing.	.684	7	1	12	6	19	1
Lorenzana, Luis, Alt.	.931	20	6	21	2	29	3
McLamb, Brian, Nor.	.840	18	12	30	8	50	3
McNamara, Rusty, Read.	.918	31	25	42	6	73	2
Mirizzi, Marc, Nor.	.920	11	4	19	2	25	3
Morris, Jeremy, Nor.	.786	5	3	8	3	14	1
Moss, Rick, N.B.	.904	78	40	110	16	166	11
Niles, Drew, Por.	1.000	2	0	2	0	2	0
Ojeda, Augie, Bow.	1.000	1	1	0	0	1	0
Ortiz, Nick, Akr.	.934	22	19	52	5	76	2
Paz, Richard, Bow.	.934	70	51	118	12	181	8
Raynor, Mark, Read.	.875	3	0	7	1	8	0
Regan, Jason, N.H.	.906	22	14	44	6	64	1
Rodriguez, Victor, Por.	.959	21	9	38	2	49	7
Rust, Brian, Bow.	.925	18	16	33	4	53	1
Schifano, Tony, Por.	1.000	8	8	5	0	13	2
Secrist, Reed, Alt.	.500	4	1	3	4	8	0
Short, Rick, Bow.	.917	12	5	17	2	24	1
Stewart, Andy, Read.	1.000	4	2	7	0	9	2
Sweet, Jon, Alt.	.913	9	3	18	2	23	0
Tamargo, John, Bing.	.883	43	25	81	14	120	7
Taveras, Frank, Akr.	1.000	12	3	10	0	13	0
Tebbs, Nate, Tren.	.750	2	0	3	1	4	0
t'Hoen, E.J., Erie	.884	22	11	27	5	43	3
Toca, Jorge, Bing.	1.000	2	2	1	0	3	0
Tracy, Andy, Har.	.918	110	88	182	24	294	18
Vazquez, Ramon, N.H.	.922	44	25	82	9	116	9
VERAS, Wilton, Tren.	.945	115	83	245	19	347	27
Walther, Chris, Erie	1.000	3	0	5	0	5	1
Wehner, John, Alt.	.857	3	1	5	1	7	1
Wooten, Shawn, Erie	.938	124	91	243	22	356	24
Zamora, Junior, Bing.	.926	62	47	127	14	188	9
Zech, Scott, Har.	.943	12	7	26	2	35	0

TRIPLE PLAY: Leon.

SHORTSTOPS

Player, Team	Pct.	G	PO	A	E	TC	DP
Abbott, Chuck, Erie	.945	125	185	309	29	523	72
Betances, Junior, Akr.	.946	31	45	112	9	166	23
Betten, Randy, Erie	1.000	3	2	4	0	6	0
Brown, Randy, N.H.	.957	12	19	25	2	46	3
Bryant, Matt, Alt.	.944	6	9	8	1	18	1
Camilli, Jason, Har.	1.000	1	2	3	0	5	0
Carroll, Jamey, Har.	.952	18	24	36	3	63	9
Coffie, Ivanon, Bow.	1.000	2	0	1	0	1	0
Cranford, Joey, N.B.	1.000	1	4	2	0	6	1
Davidson, Cleatus, N.B.	.943	18	31	51	5	87	14
De La Rosa, Tomas, Har.	.946	129	219	381	34	634	83
Dennis, Les, Nor.	.925	48	69	116	15	200	29
DiSarcina, Gary, Erie	1.000	5	5	12	0	17	1
Everett, Adam, Tren.	.959	98	150	273	18	441	61
Faurot, Adam, Tren.	.952	5	7	13	1	21	2
Figueroa, Luis, Alt.	.956	129	222	391	28	641	78
Finn, John, Read.	.923	3	4	8	1	13	2
Funaro, Joe, Por.	1.000	5	5	7	0	12	1
Gipson, Charles, N.H.	.000	1	0	0	0	0	0
Harris, Brian, Read.	1.000	5	10	11	0	21	2
Haverbusch, Kevin, Alt.	1.000	4	0	6	0	6	0
Huff, Larry, Read.	1.000	2	5	5	0	10	1
Jackson, Gavin, Tren.	.947	25	34	56	5	95	10
Lobaton, Jose, Por.	.909	4	2	8	1	11	0
Lorenzana, Luis, Alt.	.941	6	3	13	1	17	4
Magdaleno, Ricky, N.H.	.971	66	97	202	9	308	49
McDonald, John, Akr.	.969	55	102	152	8	262	42
McLamb, Brian, Nor.	1.000	9	19	14	0	33	5
Mirizzi, Marc, Nor.	.833	1	2	3	1	6	0
Niles, Drew, Por.	.933	20	28	42	5	75	9
OJEDA, Augie, Bow.	.969	133	210	379	19	608	79
Ortiz, Nick, Akr.	.992	28	40	78	1	119	14
Ozuna, Pablo, Por.	.946	117	179	309	28	516	53
Patzke, Jeff, Alt.	.919	7	14	20	3	37	5
Paz, Richard, Bow.	.919	9	14	20	3	37	7
Raynor, Mark, Read.	1.000	2	1	2	0	3	0
Rivas, Luis, N.B.	.933	123	150	367	37	554	78
Robinson, Adam, Akr.	.959	27	52	66	5	123	19
Rodriguez, Victor, Por.	1.000	3	1	2	0	3	0
Rollins, Jimmy, Read.	.965	133	211	392	22	625	72
Sanchez, Yuri, Bing.	.937	114	150	284	29	463	56
Schifano, Tony, Por.	.960	6	12	12	1	25	5
Soriano, Alfonso, Nor.	.937	87	160	243	27	430	53
Tamargo, John, Bing.	.932	33	45	79	9	133	19
Taveras, Frank, Akr.	.875	2	3	4	1	8	1
Tebbs, Nate, Tren.	.988	21	30	52	1	83	9
t'Hoen, E.J., Erie	.887	15	21	42	8	71	8
Vazquez, Ramon, N.H.	.945	67	98	214	18	330	43
Zamora, Junior, Bing.	.900	5	12	15	3	30	6

TRIPLE PLAY: Sanchez.

OUTFIELDERS

Player, Team	Pct.	G	PO	A	E	TC	DP
Adolfo, Carlos, Har.	.968	51	87	5	3	95	0
Alcantara, Israel, Tren.	.982	50	103	4	2	109	1
Almonte, Wady, Bow.	.959	109	195	13	9	217	5
Asche, Mike, Alt.	.875	5	6	1	1	8	0
Ashby, Chris, Nor.	1.000	16	35	3	0	38	0
Bady, Ed, Akr.	.966	49	105	8	4	117	0
Barnes, John, N.B.	.985	127	247	12	4	263	2
Bass, Jayson, N.H.*	.954	110	220	8	11	239	2
Bates, Fletcher, Por.	.969	139	208	14	7	229	2
Beamon, Trey, Bing.	.947	55	106	1	6	113	0
Bergeron, Peter, Har.	.986	40	72	1	1	74	1
Betten, Randy, Erie	1.000	2	5	1	0	6	0
Bieser, Steve, Alt.	1.000	4	1	1	0	2	0
Bradley, Milton, Har.	.971	77	166	3	5	174	3
Brown, Randy, N.H.	.500	2	1	0	1	2	0
Brown, Richard, Nor.*	.955	94	166	4	8	178	1
Bruce, Mo, Bing.	1.000	3	3	0	0	3	0
Buccheri, Jim, Bing.	1.000	3	8	0	0	8	0
Budzinski, Mark, Akr.*	.989	81	175	3	2	180	0
Burnham, Gary, Read.*	.973	40	70	2	2	74	0
Burrell, Pat, Read.	.981	27	50	1	1	52	0
Camilli, Jason, Har.	1.000	8	6	1	0	7	0
Chevalier, Virgil, Tren.	.973	129	239	12	7	258	1
Christian, Eddie, Erie*	.978	46	85	6	2	93	1
Clark, Howie, Bow.	1.000	3	3	0	0	3	0
Colangelo, Mike, Erie	.950	27	35	3	2	40	0
Cordero, Wil, Alt.	.000	2	0	0	0	0	0
Cranford, Joey, N.B.	1.000	15	27	0	0	27	0
Cummings, Midre, N.B.	1.000	24	50	2	0	52	0
Darden, Tony, Bing.	1.000	3	7	0	0	7	0
DeHaan, Kory, Alt.	.989	46	88	1	1	90	0
DENT, Darrell, Bow.*	.994	104	150	4	1	155	1

Player, Team	Pct.	G	PO	A	E	TC	DP
Devarez, Cesar, Bow.	.800	2	4	0	1	5	0
Dina, Allen, Bing.	.981	48	103	3	2	108	1
Dishington, Nate, Akr.	.000	1	0	0	0	0	0
Dubose, Brian, Bing.	1.000	4	5	0	0	5	0
Dunn, Todd, Alt.	.857	7	6	0	1	7	0
Epperson, Chad, Tren.	.000	1	0	0	0	0	0
Faurot, Adam, Tren.	.000	1	0	0	0	0	0
Felston, Anthony, N.B.*	.924	35	60	1	5	66	1
Francia, David, Read.*	.973	99	207	9	6	222	2
Funaro, Joe, Por.	1.000	19	25	0	0	25	0
Gibralter, David, Tren.	1.000	2	4	0	0	4	0
Gipson, Charles, N.H.	1.000	1	1	0	0	1	0
Glass, Chip, Nor.*	.985	65	128	7	2	137	4
Gonzalez, Raul, Tren.	.993	120	268	4	2	274	1
Guiel, Jeff, Erie	.977	46	78	6	2	86	2
Gunderson, Shane, N.B.	.907	31	34	5	4	43	1
Haltiwanger, Garrick, Bing.*	.923	4	12	0	1	13	0
Hastings, Lionel, Por.	.962	12	23	2	1	26	0
Haynes, Nathan, Erie*	1.000	5	5	1	0	6	0
Heinrichs, Jon, Por.	.948	48	68	5	4	77	1
Hernaiz, Juan, Akr.	1.000	1	2	0	0	2	0
Hernandez, Alexander, Alt.*	.976	103	189	11	5	205	1
Herrick, Jason, Erie*	.961	23	44	5	2	51	1
Hills, Rich, N.H.	1.000	23	23	1	0	24	0
Horne, Tyrone, Read.	.962	51	73	2	3	78	0
Huelsmann, Mike, Akr.	.990	43	93	3	1	97	0
Huff, B.J., Bing.	.969	55	89	5	3	97	1
Huff, Larry, Read.	1.000	7	7	4	0	11	0
Hyzdu, Adam, Alt.	.980	60	96	3	2	101	0
Iglesias, Luis, Alt.	.800	5	3	1	1	5	0
Isom, Johnny, Bow.	.981	27	49	2	1	52	0
James, Kenny, Har.	1.000	25	65	0	0	65	0
Johnson, Earl, N.H.	.986	37	64	4	1	69	2
Jones, Jaime, Por.*	.939	73	106	2	7	115	0
Kilburg, Joe, Akr.	1.000	8	16	0	0	16	0
Kingman, Brendan, N.H.	1.000	9	13	0	0	13	0
Kingsale, Eugene, Bow.	.978	67	173	2	4	179	1
Lewis, Marc, N.B.	.982	101	211	10	4	225	3
Long, Garrett, Alt.	.964	48	75	6	3	84	0
Lopez, Jose, Bing.	.889	9	8	0	1	9	0
Lopez, Rafael, N.H.	1.000	8	9	1	0	10	0
Mackowiak, Rob, Alt.	1.000	1	2	0	0	2	0
Magdaleno, Ricky, N.H.	1.000	3	4	0	0	4	0
Maness, Dwight, N.H.	.955	27	41	1	2	44	0
Marn, Kevin, N.H.	1.000	2	4	0	0	4	0
Mashore, Justin, Tren.-Bing.	1.000	17	33	4	0	37	1
Mathis, Joe, N.H.	.978	62	125	6	3	134	0
Matos, Luis, Bow.	.982	66	152	8	3	163	1
McDonald, Donzell, Nor.	.973	134	314	8	9	331	4
McKinley, Dan, Akr.	.983	111	234	2	4	240	1
McNamara, Rusty, Read.	1.000	9	20	1	0	21	0
Meggers, Mike, Bing.	.917	7	10	1	1	12	0
Mohr, Dustan, Akr.	1.000	11	28	1	0	29	1
Morgan, Scott, Akr.	.967	80	170	6	6	182	0
Morris, Jeremy, Nor.	.882	20	26	4	4	34	0
Mucker, Kelcey, N.B.	.978	104	174	4	4	182	1
Murphy, Nate, Erie*	.977	101	207	5	5	217	1
Neubart, Garrett, Bing.	1.000	65	114	11	0	125	2
Newfield, Marc, Tren.	.889	4	8	0	1	9	0
Niles, Drew, Por.	1.000	2	6	1	0	7	0
Norton, Chris, Por.	.875	6	7	0	1	8	0
Nunnari, Talmadge, Har.*	.974	22	38	0	1	39	0
Ottavinia, Paul, Nor.*	1.000	34	63	2	0	65	0
Pennyfeather, William, Erie	.952	9	19	1	1	21	1
Perry, Chan, Akr.	1.000	3	3	0	0	3	0
Peterman, Tommy, N.B.*	1.000	1	4	0	0	4	0
Post, Dave, Har.	1.000	3	6	1	0	7	0
Ramirez, Julio, Por.	.969	137	326	14	11	351	3
Redman, Tike, Alt.*	.972	133	301	12	9	322	2
Reeves, Glenn, Por.	1.000	4	2	0	0	2	0
Rivera, Roberto, Bow.	.938	9	15	0	1	16	0
Robertson, Mike, Alt.*	.750	3	3	0	1	4	0
Ronca, Joe, Bow.	.938	21	29	1	2	32	0
Royster, Aaron, Read.	1.000	71	114	4	0	118	1
Sachse, Matt, N.H.*	.957	24	43	1	2	46	0
Schifano, Tony, Por.	1.000	3	2	0	0	2	0
Schwab, Chris, Akr.*	.000	1	0	0	0	0	0
Secrist, Reed, Alt.	1.000	3	2	0	0	2	0
Short, Rick, Bow.	.984	60	119	2	2	123	1
Shumpert, Derek, Nor.	.983	30	55	2	1	58	0
Simonton, Benji, Erie	.987	41	74	2	1	77	0
Soriano, Jose, Tren.	.983	59	109	4	2	115	1
Stoner, Mike, Erie	.909	6	10	0	1	11	0
Sweet, Jon, Alt.	.000	1	0	0	0	0	0

Player, Team	Pct.	G	PO	A	E	TC	DP
Taveras, Frank, Akr.	1.000	1	1	0	0	1	0
Taylor, Reggie, Read.	.971	122	295	9	9	313	1
Tebbs, Nate, Tren.	.993	85	136	6	1	143	2
Thames, Marcus, Nor.	.929	49	84	8	7	99	1
Tinoco, Luis, Read.	.895	24	32	2	4	38	0
Toca, Jorge, Bing.	.961	49	91	8	4	103	0
Tolentino, Juan, Erie	.968	134	293	7	10	310	1
Tracy, Andy, Har.	1.000	1	1	0	0	1	0
Tucker, Jon, Har.*	.917	6	11	0	1	12	0
Tyner, Jason, Bing.*	.993	127	255	11	2	268	2
Ware, Jeremy, Har.	.977	96	201	7	5	213	1
Wathan, Dusty, N.H.	1.000	1	1	0	0	1	0
Weber, Jake, N.H.	.988	133	226	15	3	244	2
Wehner, John, Alt.	1.000	1	1	0	0	1	0
Werth, Jayson, Bow.	1.000	1	1	0	0	1	0
Whitaker, Chad, Akr.	.957	36	66	1	3	70	0
Wilkerson, Brad, Har.*	.972	123	233	11	7	251	4
Wilson, Craig, Alt.	.929	14	12	1	1	14	0
Wolff, Mike, Erie	1.000	1	2	0	0	2	0
Zech, Scott, Har.	.000	1	0	0	0	0	0

OUTFIELDERS WITH TWO OR MORE TEAMS

Player, Team	Pct.	G	PO	A	E	TC	DP
Mashore, Justin, Tren.	1.000	5	8	1	0	9	0
Mashore, Justin, Bing.	1.000	12	25	3	0	28	1

CATCHERS

Player, Team	Pct.	G	PO	A	E	TC	DP	PB
Alley, Charles, Bow.	1.000	5	31	2	0	33	1	0
Alomar, Sandy, Akr.	.929	5	12	1	1	14	0	0
Alvarez, Clemente, Read.	.992	48	326	24	3	353	2	4
Antczak, Chuck, Read.	.980	8	46	4	1	51	0	2
Asche, Mike, Alt.	1.000	1	2	0	0	2	0	0
Bennett, Ryan, Bing.	.800	1	4	0	1	5	0	0
Bieser, Steve, Alt.	.988	12	65	15	1	81	3	2
Chevalier, Virgil, Tren.	1.000	2	14	1	0	15	1	2
Clark, Howie, Bow.	.000	1	0	0	0	0	0	0
Cossins, Tim, Har.	.989	31	163	10	2	175	1	2
DeCinces, Tim, Bow.	.991	67	421	36	4	461	7	3
Depastino, Joe, Tren.	1.000	1	6	1	0	7	0	0
Devarez, Cesar, Bow.	.994	43	283	42	2	327	5	4
Dewey, Jason, Erie	.981	40	277	28	6	311	3	2
Emmons, Scott, Nor.	.984	32	164	22	3	189	2	3
Encarnacion, Angelo, Akr.	.978	34	203	24	5	232	3	4
Epperson, Chad, Tren.	1.000	12	89	11	0	100	0	1
Foster, Jim, Erie	1.000	4	30	1	0	31	1	0
Graves, Bryan, Erie	.978	37	245	23	6	274	3	3
Haad, Yamid, Alt.	.969	41	272	37	10	319	2	3
Harriss, Robin, Akr.	.981	17	98	8	2	108	2	3
Hastings, Lionel, Por.	.988	41	293	34	4	331	4	8
Hayes, Heath, Akr.	.982	87	484	69	10	563	7	10
Hillenbrand, Shea, Tren.	.987	55	337	41	5	383	7	12
Horner, Jim, N.H.	.998	68	522	49	1	572	3	15
Johannes, Todd, Har.	1.000	1	4	0	0	4	0	0
Kuilan, Hector, Por.	.984	68	472	65	9	546	6	10
Lomasney, Steve, Tren.	.970	46	355	33	12	400	1	5
Lopez-Cao, Mike, Bow.	.972	14	63	7	2	72	0	0
Malave, Jaime, Har.	1.000	7	18	2	0	20	0	1
Moeller, Chad, N.B.	.984	84	548	59	10	617	4	8
Phillips, Jason, Bing.	.984	38	271	28	5	304	1	0
Pierce, Kirk, Read.	.990	70	468	48	5	521	3	9
Preston, Brian, Har.	1.000	6	26	1	0	27	0	1
Rapp, Travis, Erie	1.000	3	16	4	0	20	0	0
Robertson, Ryan, Por.	.989	43	320	32	4	356	3	8
Rodriguez, Luis, Tren.	.995	30	192	25	1	218	4	2
Rodriguez, Sammy, Bing.	.992	59	325	34	3	362	5	2
Rosario, Mel, Alt.	.978	23	161	19	4	184	0	4
SCHNEIDER, Brian, Har.	.992	112	613	91	6	710	7	6
Secrist, Reed, Alt.	.985	19	115	16	2	133	1	2
Smith, Jeff, N.B.	.980	69	437	49	10	496	4	8
Snusz, Chris, Har.	.917	3	16	6	2	24	1	0
Soliz, Steve, Akr.	1.000	7	50	9	0	59	0	2
Stewart, Andy, Read.	1.000	29	172	24	0	196	1	1
Stoffels, Alex, Bing.	.923	1	12	0	1	13	0	0
Sweet, Jon, Alt.	1.000	21	117	15	0	132	2	2
Tejero, Fausto, Erie	.987	62	399	41	6	446	5	4
Valencia, Victor, Nor.	.983	115	822	80	16	918	4	14
Valera, Yohanny, Bing.	.967	55	363	46	14	423	3	5
Wathan, Dusty, N.H.	.989	78	562	64	7	633	5	8
Werth, Jayson, Bow.	.996	29	203	22	1	226	2	1
Wilson, Craig, Alt.	.988	34	220	33	3	256	3	7
Wooten, Shawn, Erie	1.000	2	9	2	0	11	1	3

TRIPLE PLAY: Valencia.

PITCHERS

Player, Team	Pct.	G	PO	A	E	TC	DP
Adams, Willie, Tren.	1.000	2	3	1	0	4	0
Agamennone, Brandon, Har.	1.000	22	3	9	0	12	0
Ah Yat, Paul, Alt.*	1.000	16	7	18	0	25	1
Ahearne, Pat, N.H.	1.000	17	8	32	0	40	1
Almanza, Armando, Por.*	1.000	10	0	1	0	1	1
Almonte, Hector, Por.	.889	47	2	6	1	9	0
Alvarez, Juan, Erie*	1.000	23	1	4	0	5	1
Anderson, Bill, Erie	1.000	5	0	3	0	3	0
Anderson, Ryan, N.H.*	.800	24	2	22	6	30	1
Armas, Tony, Har.	.971	24	9	24	1	34	2
Arroyo, Bronson, Alt.	.941	25	13	19	2	34	2
Arroyo, Luis, Por.*	.667	9	0	2	1	3	0
Arteaga, J.D., Bing.*	1.000	11	3	3	0	6	0
Atkins, Ross, Akr.	1.000	33	14	6	0	20	0
Ayers, Mike, Alt.*	1.000	11	1	2	0	3	0
Babineaux, Darrin, N.B.	1.000	5	1	2	0	3	0
Bacsik, Mike, Akr.*	.919	26	10	24	3	37	1
Bailie, Matt, Read.	1.000	1	1	0	0	1	0
Baker, Jason, Har.	1.000	23	4	4	0	8	0
Barkley, Brian, Tren.*	1.000	7	5	7	0	12	1
Barnett, Marty, Read.	1.000	35	4	5	0	9	0
Baron, Jim, Alt.*	1.000	29	3	29	0	32	0
Beale, Chuck, Tren.	.944	29	6	11	1	18	0
Beaumont, Matt, Erie*	.926	32	8	17	2	27	1
Bell, Jason, N.B.	.818	7	3	6	2	11	1
Bell, Mike, Bow.*	.973	41	13	23	1	37	2
Belovsky, Josh, Tren.	.000	1	0	0	0	0	0
Beltran, Alonso, Alt.	1.000	13	0	2	0	2	1
Benz, Jake, Por.*	.667	23	1	1	1	3	1
Betancourt, Rafael, Tren.	1.000	39	4	3	0	7	1
Beverlin, Jason, Nor.	.969	28	10	21	1	32	0
Blank, Matt, Har.*	.963	15	11	15	1	27	1
Blazier, Ron, Bow.	1.000	19	3	2	0	5	0
Bohannon, Gary, Bing.	1.000	2	0	1	0	1	0
Bovee, Mike, Erie	1.000	26	4	4	0	8	1
Brammer, J.D., Akr.	.933	47	6	8	1	15	1
Brannan, Ryan, Read.	.000	5	0	0	1	1	0
Brester, Jason, Read.*	.879	16	7	22	4	33	0
Brittan, Corey, Bing.	1.000	54	7	20	0	27	0
Brosnan, Jason, N.H.*	1.000	28	3	6	0	9	0
Brown, Alvin, Alt.-Erie	.800	13	1	3	1	5	0
Brown, Jamie, Akr.	.923	23	11	13	2	26	0
Bullinger, Kirk, Tren.	1.000	17	0	5	0	5	1
Bump, Nate, Por.	1.000	8	3	7	0	10	0
Burger, Rob, Read.	.714	9	2	3	2	7	0
Burgos, Enrique, Alt.*	.000	5	0	0	0	0	0
Burgus, Travis, Por.*	.000	1	0	0	1	1	0
Burnett, A.J., Por.	.958	26	10	13	1	24	0
Burnham, Gary, Read.*	.000	1	0	0	0	0	0
Callier, Jeremy, Erie	.000	1	0	0	0	0	0
Cames, Aaron, Por.	.786	23	4	7	3	14	1
Cammack, Eric, Bing.	1.000	45	6	6	0	12	2
Camp, Jared, Akr.	1.000	17	0	1	0	1	0
Carroll, Dave, Nor.*	.000	3	0	0	0	0	0
Cedeno, Blas, Read.	1.000	19	2	10	0	12	0
Censale, Silvio, Read.*	.867	16	1	12	2	15	0
Christiansen, Jason, Alt.*	.000	2	0	0	0	0	0
Clark, Chris, Por.	.000	4	0	0	0	0	0
Coggin, Dave, Read.	.917	9	7	4	1	12	0
Cooper, Brian, Erie*	1.000	22	8	22	0	30	0
Cordova, Francisco, Alt.	1.000	2	1	0	0	1	0
Corey, Mark, Bing.	.925	29	14	23	3	40	0
Crawford, Paxton, Tren.	.970	28	10	22	1	33	1
Cressend, Jack, Tren.-N.B.	1.000	28	13	22	0	35	0
Cumberland, Chris, Tren.*	1.000	14	0	4	0	4	0
Cummings, Ryan, Erie	.500	3	0	1	1	2	0
Daniels, David, Alt.	1.000	55	6	9	0	15	0
Davis, Kane, Alt.	.920	16	6	17	2	25	3
Dedrick, Jim, Akr.	.000	2	0	0	0	0	0
De La Cruz, Francisco, Nor.	.943	29	10	23	2	35	1
Delahoya, Javier, Bow.	1.000	12	2	11	0	13	1
De La Rosa, Maximo, N.H.	1.000	10	1	0	0	1	0
Della Ratta, Pete, Bing.	1.000	41	4	10	0	14	3
De Paula, Sean, Alt.	1.000	14	2	9	0	11	0
Deschenes, Marc, Akr.	1.000	43	3	4	0	7	1
Dingman, Craig, Nor.	.857	55	6	6	2	14	1
Dixon, Tim, Har.-Tren.*	1.000	10	1	2	0	3	0
Dodd, Robert, Read.*	.917	42	1	10	1	12	0
Donnelly, Brendan, Alt.	1.000	2	0	1	0	1	0
Dougherty, Tony, Alt.-Tren.	1.000	15	1	0	0	1	0
Downs, Scott, N.B.*	1.000	6	0	2	0	2	0
Duff, Matt, Alt.	1.000	44	8	11	0	19	4
Dunbar, Matt, Alt.*	1.000	49	5	11	0	16	3
Duncan, Geoff, Por.	1.000	43	4	9	0	13	0
Dunham, Pat, N.H.	1.000	3	0	2	0	2	0
Duran, Roberto, Har.*	1.000	19	1	3	0	4	1
Durocher, Jayson, Har.	1.000	29	1	3	0	4	0
Eason, Clay, Read.	1.000	10	0	1	0	1	0
Eaton, Adam, Read.	1.000	12	3	10	0	13	0
Edsell, Geoff, Erie	.875	26	5	2	1	8	0
Eibey, Scott, Bow.*	.857	27	3	3	1	7	2
Einertson, Darrell, Nor.	1.000	21	4	9	0	13	1
Escobar, Ruben, Akr.	1.000	1	1	0	0	1	0
Espinal, Jose, N.B.	.875	29	10	18	4	32	1
Etherton, Seth, Erie	.923	24	11	25	3	39	0
Evans, Keith, Har.	1.000	5	2	5	0	7	0
Falkenborg, Brian, Bow.	.923	17	7	17	2	26	1
Farrell, Jim, Tren.	1.000	7	1	2	0	3	0
Faurot, Adam, Tren.	.000	1	0	0	0	0	0
Fernandez, Jared, Tren.	1.000	7	1	4	0	5	1
Fitzgerald, Brian, N.H.*	.944	29	9	8	1	18	2
Flores, Randy, Nor.*	.867	4	3	10	2	15	1
Forster, Scott, Har.*	1.000	2	1	1	0	2	0
France, Aaron, Alt.	1.000	33	7	10	0	17	0
Franco, John, Bing.*	.000	1	0	0	0	0	0
Fuentes, Brian, N.H.*	1.000	15	0	18	0	18	0
Gandarillas, Gus, N.B.	.909	18	5	5	1	11	0
Garcia, Al, Alt.	.750	2	0	3	1	4	0
Garza, Alberto, Akr.	1.000	10	1	6	0	7	2
Garza, Chris, N.B.*	1.000	31	3	5	0	8	0
Gentile, Scott, Bow.	.000	10	0	0	0	0	0
Giard, Ken, Alt.	.833	38	3	2	1	6	0
Gonzalez, Gabe, Por.*	.889	26	2	6	1	9	0
Gonzalez, Mike, Alt.*	1.000	7	0	7	0	7	0
Gooden, Dwight, Akr.	1.000	1	0	1	0	1	0
Grahe, Joe, Read.	1.000	7	0	1	0	1	0
Green, Steve, Erie	1.000	6	4	5	0	9	0
Gryboski, Kevin, N.H.	1.000	47	4	7	0	11	0
Guardado, Eddie, N.B.*	1.000	3	1	1	0	2	0
Hafer, Jeff, Bing.	1.000	7	0	4	0	4	0
Haigler, Phil, N.B.	.905	19	5	14	2	21	1
Hamilton, Jimmy, Akr.*	1.000	25	2	3	0	5	0
Hancock, Ryan, Erie	1.000	8	3	2	0	5	0
Harriger, Mark, Erie	1.000	6	5	7	0	12	0
Harris, Jeff, N.B.	1.000	20	0	6	0	6	0
Hartmann, Pete, Bow.*	.833	11	1	4	1	6	1
Hazlett, Andy, Tren.*	1.000	27	8	29	0	37	3
Henderson, Ryan, Bing.	1.000	5	0	3	0	3	1
Henderson, Scott, Por.	.941	46	4	12	1	17	0
Herbert, Russ, Read.	.909	26	9	11	2	22	0
Herbison, Brett, Bing.	1.000	27	9	20	0	29	0
Heredia, Maximo, Bow.	1.000	50	2	5	0	7	0
Hill, Jason, Erie*	1.000	23	1	5	0	6	0
Hooten, David, N.B.	.933	52	9	19	2	30	0
Hubbs, Dan, Read.	.000	3	0	0	0	0	0
Iglesias, Mario, Bow.	1.000	14	3	1	0	4	0
Jacquez, Thomas, Read.*	.903	38	9	19	3	31	2
Johnson, Greg, Erie*	1.000	2	1	0	0	1	0
Johnson, Mark, Nor.	1.000	16	9	10	0	19	0
Jones, Bobby, Bing.	1.000	3	2	0	0	2	0
Kamienicki, Scott, Bow.	1.000	1	1	2	0	3	0
Kaufman, Brad, Nor.	.900	40	2	7	1	10	0
Kawabata, Kyle, Read.	1.000	8	0	1	0	1	0
Keisler, Randy, Nor.*	1.000	8	0	1	0	1	0
Kershner, Jason, Read.*	.875	57	9	12	3	24	2
Kim, Sun-Woo, Tren.	.906	26	5	24	3	32	2
Kinney, Matt, N.B.	1.000	14	3	6	0	9	0
Kirkreit, Daron, N.H.	1.000	5	2	2	0	4	1
Knotts, Gary, Erie	1.000	12	6	12	2	20	0
Kohlmeier, Ryan, Bow.	1.000	55	6	4	0	10	0
Lail, Denny, Nor.	1.000	6	2	6	0	8	0
Lara, Giovanny, Har.	1.000	9	3	1	0	4	0
Larkin, Andy, Por.	1.000	7	0	1	0	1	0
Leese, Brandon, Por.	.947	20	7	11	1	19	0
Lisio, Joe, Nor.	1.000	59	4	4	0	8	0
Lohse, Kyle, N.B.	.947	11	6	12	1	19	1
Long, Joey, Alt.*	.000	8	0	0	1	1	0
Lopez, Johan, Bing.	1.000	2	0	1	0	1	0
Luce, Robert, N.H.	.000	2	0	0	0	0	0
Lynch, Ryan, Bow.*	1.000	9	2	1	0	3	1
Lyons, Mike, Bing.	.923	53	10	14	2	26	1
Maeda, Kats, Nor.	1.000	25	7	12	0	19	3
Mahaffey, Alan, N.B.*	1.000	33	6	9	0	15	1
Mairena, Oswaldo, Nor.*	1.000	49	2	8	0	10	0

CLASS AA Eastern League

Player, Team	Pct.	G	PO	A	E	TC	DP
Maloney, Sean, Bow.	.667	4	1	1	1	3	0
Marquez, Robert, Har.	.875	18	4	3	1	8	0
Martin, Tom, Akr.*	.667	3	0	2	1	3	0
Martinez, Javier, Alt.	1.000	10	1	0	0	1	0
Martinez, Willie, Akr.	.860	24	17	20	6	43	2
Mathews, Del, Alt.*	1.000	9	0	2	0	2	0
Mattes, Troy, Har.	.889	20	2	14	2	18	3
Matthews, Mike, Akr.-Tren.*	.857	9	0	12	2	14	0
McClaskey, Tim, N.H.	.000	4	0	0	0	0	0
McConnell, Sam, Alt.*	.955	13	3	18	1	22	0
McCrary, Scott, Bing.	1.000	17	4	12	0	16	1
McDougal, Mike, Bow.	.955	48	5	16	1	22	2
McEntire, Ethan, Bing.*	.500	4	0	1	1	2	0
McMichael, Greg, Bing.	.000	2	0	0	0	0	0
McMullen, Jerry, Tren.*	.000	3	0	0	0	0	0
McNatt, Josh, Bow.*	1.000	2	1	0	0	1	0
Meche, Gil, N.H.	1.000	10	3	4	0	7	0
Medina, Carlos, Bow.*	.900	15	4	5	1	10	0
Mintz, Steve, Erie	.571	26	1	3	3	7	1
Mitchell, Scott, Har.	1.000	3	0	2	0	2	0
Montane, Ivan, N.H.	.889	41	4	4	1	9	1
Moraga, David, Har.*	.000	1	0	0	0	0	0
Moreno, Julio, Bow.	.700	10	1	6	3	10	0
Morse, Paul, Erie	.952	15	9	11	1	21	1
Mota, Danny, N.B.	1.000	6	2	3	0	5	0
Mucker, Kelcey, N.B.	.000	1	0	0	0	0	0
Negrette, Richard, Akr.	.833	33	3	2	1	6	0
Neubart, Garrett, Bing.	.000	1	0	0	0	0	0
Newton, Geronimo, N.H.*	.923	31	1	11	1	13	0
Niebla, Ruben, Har.*	1.000	29	3	3	0	6	0
Niedermaier, Brad, N.B.	1.000	41	2	5	0	7	0
Nina, Elvin, Erie	1.000	4	1	3	0	4	0
O'Connor, Brian, Alt.*	.938	28	9	21	2	32	1
Ohka, Tomokazu, Tren.	.917	12	5	6	1	12	1
Ortiz, Ramon, Erie	.917	15	8	14	2	24	3
Padilla, Juan, N.B.	1.000	11	1	6	0	7	0
Pageler, Mick, Por.	.857	31	5	1	1	7	0
Parker, Christian, Har.	.917	36	5	17	2	24	2
Paronto, Chad, Bow.	.917	15	4	7	1	12	1
Parrish, John, Bow.*	.880	12	5	17	3	25	0
Pena, Alex, Alt.	1.000	9	2	2	0	4	0
Penny, Brad, Por.	1.000	6	1	3	0	4	0
Petroff, Daniel, Erie	1.000	8	0	1	0	1	0
Phelps, Tommy, Har.*	.778	13	1	6	2	9	0
PINEIRO, Joel, N.H.	1.000	28	14	28	0	42	4
Politte, Cliff, Read.	1.000	37	3	20	0	23	0
Pontes, Dan, Bing.	1.000	19	2	4	0	6	0
Poole, Jim, Akr.*	.000	2	0	0	0	0	0
Pumphrey, Ken, Bing.	.861	25	12	19	5	36	0
Pyc, David, Read.*	.950	17	10	9	1	20	0
Quezada, Edward, Har.	1.000	3	1	0	0	1	0
Rector, Bobby, Por.	1.000	13	2	8	0	10	0
Reed, Rick, Bing.	1.000	1	1	4	0	5	0
Resz, Greg, Nor.	.750	20	0	3	1	4	0
Rigdon, Paul, Akr.	1.000	8	5	7	0	12	0
Riley, Matt, Bow.*	.857	20	3	15	3	21	1
Rincon, Ricardo, Akr.*	.000	2	0	0	0	0	0
Riske, David, Akr.	1.000	23	0	2	0	2	0
Robbins, Jake, Nor.	.875	20	12	23	5	40	0
Roberts, Grant, Bing.	.909	23	7	23	3	33	2
Rodgers, Bobby, Por.	.962	26	11	14	1	26	2
Rogers, James, Bow.*	1.000	7	1	3	0	4	1
Romero, J.C., N.B.*	.882	36	6	9	2	17	0
Rosenkranz, Terry, Bow.*	1.000	26	2	3	0	5	0
Ruebel, Matt, Bing.*	1.000	6	2	6	0	8	0
Runion, Tony, Alt.	.800	31	2	6	2	10	0
Rust, Brian, Bow.	1.000	2	1	1	0	2	0
Rutherford, Mark, Read.	1.000	4	2	2	0	4	0
Ryan, Jason, N.B.	1.000	8	5	10	0	15	2

Player, Team	Pct.	G	PO	A	E	TC	DP
Saberhagen, Bret, Tren.	1.000	1	0	3	0	3	0
St. Pierre, Bob, Akr.	1.000	4	0	2	0	2	0
Salter, Cody, Erie	1.000	27	5	4	0	9	1
Salyers, Jeremy, Har.	1.000	12	3	2	0	5	0
Sanders, Frankie, Akr.	.968	33	11	19	1	31	1
Saylor, Ryan, Har.	1.000	28	1	6	0	7	0
Scheffer, Aaron, N.H.	1.000	10	2	0	0	2	0
Secrist, Reed, Alt.	1.000	1	1	0	0	1	0
Sekany, Jason, Tren.	1.000	27	9	21	0	30	0
Sexton, Jeff, Akr.	1.000	15	2	2	0	4	0
Shields, Scot, Erie	.938	10	1	14	1	16	2
Short, Barry, Bing.	.933	24	4	10	1	15	1
Shumaker, Anthony, Read.*	1.000	10	4	7	0	11	0
Smetana, Steve, Tren.*	.895	39	4	13	2	19	1
Smith, Cam, N.H.	.571	41	3	1	3	7	0
Spence, Cam, Nor.	.929	19	2	11	1	14	0
Spiers, Corey, N.B.*	1.000	8	3	13	0	16	1
Stanifer, Rob, Tren.	1.000	5	0	2	0	2	0
Stark, Dennis, N.H.	.960	26	9	15	1	25	1
Stentz, Brent, N.H.	1.000	32	3	1	0	4	0
Stevenson, Rod, Har.	.917	37	5	6	1	12	2
Stewart, Scott, Bing.*	1.000	1	0	1	0	1	0
Strickland, Scott, Har.	1.000	14	1	4	0	5	0
Sweeney, Brian, N.H.	.938	23	7	8	1	16	1
Taglienti, Jeff, Tren.	1.000	10	3	1	0	4	0
Tebbs, Nate, Tren.	.000	1	0	0	0	0	0
Tejera, Michael, Por.*	.970	25	11	21	1	33	1
Thomas, Evan, Read.	.955	36	7	14	1	22	1
Thompson, Chris, Tren.	.000	1	0	0	0	0	0
Towers, Josh, Bow.	.898	29	13	31	5	49	0
Troutman, Keith, Erie	1.000	38	2	9	0	11	1
Tucker, T.J., Har.	1.000	19	5	12	0	17	0
Turnbow, Mark, Akr.	.500	1	0	1	1	2	0
Turrentine, Rich, Bing.	.667	17	2	0	1	3	0
Tweedlie, Brad, Tren.	.882	44	4	11	2	17	1
Urso, Sal, Tren.*	.909	22	1	9	1	11	0
Vardijan, Dan, Por.	.000	5	0	0	0	0	0
Vasquez, Leo, Bing.*	1.000	27	3	7	0	10	0
Villafuerte, Brandon, Por.	.913	22	9	12	2	23	1
Walker, Tyler, Bing.	1.000	13	4	3	0	7	0
Watson, Mark, Akr.*	.919	19	11	23	3	37	2
Westbrook, Jake, Har.	.967	27	19	40	2	61	6
Wilkins, Marc, Alt.	1.000	4	2	2	0	4	0
Williams, Matt, Nor.*	.750	22	1	2	1	4	0
Williams, Shad, Read.	.800	16	3	5	2	10	0
Wise, Matt, Erie	1.000	16	9	10	0	19	0
Wright, Jaret, Akr.	1.000	1	0	1	0	1	0
Yeskie, Nate, N.B.	.977	25	18	24	1	43	3
Young, Tim, Tren.*	1.000	31	1	5	0	6	0
Zancanaro, Dave, Nor.*	.909	15	7	13	2	22	1
Zimmerman, Jordan, N.H.*	1.000	22	3	3	0	6	0

TRIPLE PLAY: Roberts.

PITCHERS WITH TWO OR MORE TEAMS

Player, Team	Pct.	G	PO	A	E	TC	DP
Brown, Alvin, Alt.	.750	7	1	2	1	4	0
Brown, Alvin, Erie	1.000	6	0	1	0	1	0
Cressend, Jack, Tren.	1.000	3	3	1	0	4	0
Cressend, Jack, N.B.	1.000	25	10	21	0	31	0
Dixon, Tim, Har.*	1.000	2	0	1	0	1	0
Dixon, Tim, Tren.*	1.000	8	1	1	0	2	0
Dougherty, Tony, Alt.	.000	9	0	0	0	0	0
Dougherty, Tony, Tren.	1.000	6	1	0	0	1	0
Matthews, Mike, Akr.*	.750	6	0	6	2	8	0
Matthews, Mike, Tren.*	1.000	3	0	6	0	6	0

The following players appeared only as designated hitter, pinch-hitter or pinch runner: Akers, pr; I. Cruz, dh; Estrada, dh-pr; V. Martinez, dh-ph; Reese, ph; R. Smith, dh; Ward, dh.

LEAGUE CHAMPIONS

Year	Team	Pct.	Year	Team	Pct.	Year	Team	Pct.
1923—	Williamsport	.661	1931—	Harrisburg	.597	1937—	Elmira†	.622
1924—	Williamsport	.654	1932—	Wilkes-Barre	.561	1938—	Binghamton	.622
1925—	York§	.583	1933—	Binghamton	.690		Elmira (3rd)‡	.522
	Williamsport§	.583	1934—	Binghamton	.694	1939—	Scranton†	.571
1926—	Scranton	.627		Williamsport*	.603	1940—	Scranton	.568
1927—	Harrisburg	.630	1935—	Scranton	.657		Binghamton (2nd)‡	.554
1928—	Harrisburg	.603		Binghamton*	.580	1941—	Wilkes-Barre	.630
1929—	Binghamton	.597	1936—	Scranton*	.609		Elmira (3rd)‡	.514
1930—	Wilkes-Barre	.572		Elmira	.629	1942—	Albany	.600

Year	Team	Pct.	Year	Team	Pct.	Year	Team	Pct.
	Scranton (2nd)‡	.593	1963—	Charleston	.593	1983—	Lynn	.554
1943—	Scranton	.630	1964—	Elmira	.586		New Britain‡	.518
	Elmira (2nd)‡	.568	1965—	Pittsfield	.607	1984—	Waterbury	.543
1944—	Hartford	.723	1966—	Elmira	.633		Vermont‡	.536
	Binghamton (4th)‡	.474	1967—	Binghamton♦	.586	1985—	Albany	.540
1945—	Utica	.615		Elmira	.532		Vermont‡	.514
	Albany (3rd)‡	.564	1968—	Pittsfield	.604	1986—	Reading	.566
1946—	Scranton†	.691		Reading (2nd)‡	.579		Vermont‡	.554
1947—	Utica†	.652	1969—	York	.640	1987—	Pittsfield	.630
1948—	Scranton†	.636	1970—	Waterbury■	.560		Harrisburg‡	.550
1949—	Albany	.664		Reading■	.553	1988—	Glens Falls	.584
	Binghamton (4th)‡	.500	1971—	Three Rivers	.569		Albany‡	.522
1950—	Wilkes-Barre‡	.652		Elmira▼	.561	1989—	Albany‡	.657
1951—	Wilkes-Barre‡	.612	1972—	West Haven▼	.600		Harrisburg	.522
	Scranton (2nd)†	.562		Three Rivers	.559	1990—	Albany	.568
1952—	Albany	.603	1973—	Reading▼	.551		London‡	.547
	Binghamton (2nd)‡	.562		Pittsfield	.551	1991—	Harrisburg	.621
1953—	Reading	.682	1974—	Thetford Miners (2nd)•	.536		Albany‡	.543
	Binghamton (2nd)‡	.636		Pittsfield (2nd)	.496	1992—	Canton/Akron	.580
1954—	Wilkes-Barre	.576	1975—	Reading	.613		Binghamton‡	.572
	Albany (3rd)‡	.540		Bristol*	.587	1993—	Harrisburg‡	.681
1955—	Reading	.613	1976—	Three Rivers	.601		Canton/Akron	.543
	Allentown (2nd)‡	.565		West Haven††	.576	1994—	Harrisburg	.633
1956—	Schenectady†	.609	1977—	West Haven‡‡	.623		Binghamton‡	.582
1957—	Binghamton	.607		Three Rivers	.551	1995—	New Haven	.556
	Reading (3rd)‡	.529	1978—	Reading	.642		Reading‡	.514
1958—	Lancaster∞	.568		Bristol*	.580	1996—	Portland	.589
	Binghamton (6th)‡	.493	1979—	West Haven§§	.597		Harrisburg‡	.521
1959—	Springfield†	.607	1980—	Holyoke*	.561	1997—	Harrisburg‡	.606
1960—	Williamsport▲	.551		Waterbury	.540		Portland	.556
	Springfield (3rd)▲	.496	1981—	Glens Falls	.615	1998—	New Britain	.585
1961—	Springfield	.612		Bristol*	.577		Harrisburg‡	.514
1962—	Williamsport	.593	1982—	West Haven*	.614	1999—	Trenton	.648
	Elmira (2nd)‡	.514		Lynn	.590		Harrisburg‡	.535

*Won split-season playoff. †Won championship and four-team playoff. ‡Won four-team playoff. §Tied for pennant, York winning playoff. ∞League was divided into Northern, Southern divisions and played a split season; Lancaster was overall season leader. ▲Playoff finals canceled after one game because of rain with Williamsport and Springfield declared playoff co-champions. ♦League was divided into Eastern, Western divisions; Binghamton won playoff. ■Tied for pennant, Waterbury winning playoff. ▼League was divided into American, National divisions; won playoff. •League was divided into American and National divisions; won four-team playoff. ††League was divided into Northern, Southern divisions, won playoff. ‡‡League was divided into New England and Canadian-American divisions; won playoff. §§Won both halves of split season (no playoffs). (NOTE—Known as New York-Pennsylvania League prior to 1938.)

SOUTHERN LEAGUE

LEAGUE OFFICE

President/secretary-treasurer
Arnold Fielkow

Address
1 Depot St., Suite 300
Marietta, GA 30060

Phone
770-428-4749

TEAMS

BIRMINGHAM BARONS

General manager
Tony Ensor
Manager
To be announced
Ballpark (capacity, surface)
Hoover Metropolitan Stadium
(10,800, grass)
Affiliation
White Sox
Address
P.O. Box 360007
Birmingham, AL 35236
Phone
205-988-3200

CAROLINA MUDCATS

General manager
Joe Kremer
Manager
Ron Gideon
Ballpark (capacity, surface)
Five County Stadium (6,500, grass)
Affiliation
Rockies
Address
P.O. Drawer 1218
Zebulon, NC 27597
Phone
919-269-2287

CHATTANOOGA LOOKOUTS

President
J. Frank Burke
General manager
Rich Mozingo
Manager
Mike Rojas
Ballpark (capacity, surface)
BellSouth Park (6,100, grass)
Affiliation
Reds
Address
201 Power Alley
Chattanooga, TN 37402
Phone
423-267-2208

GREENVILLE BRAVES

General manager
Steve DeSalvo
Manager
Paul Runge
Ballpark (capacity, surface)
Greenville Municipal Stadium (7,027,
grass)
Affiliation
Braves
Address
P.O. Box 16683
Greenville, SC 29606
Phone
864-299-3456

HUNTSVILLE STARS

President/general manager
Don Mincher
Manager
Carlos Lezcano
Ballpark (capacity, surface)
Joe W. Davis Stadium (10,400, grass)
Affiliation
Brewers
Address
1201 E. Duval Street
Huntsville, AL 35804
Phone
256-882-2562

JACKSONVILLE SUNS

Vice president/general manager
Peter Bragan Jr.
Manager
Gene Roof
Ballpark (capacity, surface)
Wolfson Park (8,200, grass)
Affiliation
Tigers
Address
P.O. Box 4756
Jacksonville, FL 32201
Phone
904-358-2846

MOBILE BAYBEARS

Vice president/general manager
Bill Shanahan
Manager
Mike Basso
Ballpark (capacity, surface)
Hank Aaron Stadium (6,000, grass)
Affiliation
Padres
Address
755 Bolling Brothers Blvd.
Mobile, AL 36606
Phone
334-479-2327

ORLANDO RAYS

General manager
Tom Ramsberger
Manager
To be announced
Ballpark (capacity, surface)
Tinker Field (6,102, grass)
Affiliation
Devil Rays
Address
287 S. Tampa Ave.
Orlando, FL 32805
Phone
407-245-2827

TENNESSEE SMOKIES

General manager
Dan Rajkowski
Manager
Rocket Wheeler
Ballpark (capacity, surface)
To be announced (6,000, grass)
Affiliation
Blue Jays
Address
To be announced
Phone
865-637-9494

WEST TENN DIAMOND JAXX

Assistant general manager
Brian Cheever
Manager
Dave Bialas
Ballpark (capacity, surface)
Pringles Park (6,000, grass)
Affiliation
Cubs
Address
4 Fun Place
Jackson, TN 38305
Phone
901-664-2020

CLASS AA *Southern League*

FIRST HALF

EAST DIVISION

Team	W	L	T	Pct.	GB
Knoxville (Blue Jays)	38	32	0	.543	...
Jacksonville (Tigers)	36	34	0	.514	2.0
Greenville (Braves)	31	37	0	.456	6.0
Orlando (Devil Rays)	30	37	0	.448	6.5
Carolina (Rockies)	31	39	0	.443	7.0

WEST DIVISION

Team	W	L	T	Pct.	GB
West Tenn (Cubs)	39	32	0	.549	...
Huntsville (Brewers)	38	33	0	.535	1.0
Chattanooga (Reds)	37	33	0	.529	1.5
Moblie (Padres)	34	35	0	.493	4.0
Birmingham (White Sox)	34	36	0	.486	4.5

SECOND HALF

EAST DIVISION

Team	W	L	T	Pct.	GB
Orlando (Devil Rays)	40	31	0	.563	...
Jacksonville (Tigers)	39	32	0	.549	1.0
Knoxville (Blue Jays)	33	37	0	.471	6.5
Carolina (Rockies)	29	41	0	.414	10.5
Greenville (Braves)	27	43	0	.386	12.5

WEST DIVISION

Team	W	L	T	Pct.	GB
West Tenn (Cubs)	45	25	0	.643	...
Chattanooga (Reds)	41	29	0	.586	4.0
Birmingham (White Sox)	39	31	0	.557	6.0
Mobile (Padres)	32	38	0	.457	13.0
Huntsville (Brewers)	26	44	0	.371	19.0

COMPOSITE

Team	W.T.	Chat.	Jax.	Birm.	Orl.	Knox.	Mob.	Hun.	Car.	Gre.	W	L	T	Pct.	GB
West Tenn (Cubs)	...	8	10	9	8	12	8	9	9	11	84	57	0	.596	...
Chattanooga (Reds)	6	...	7	8	7	11	8	8	10	12	78	62	0	.557	5.5
Jacksonville (Tigers)	6	9	...	10	8	5	8	8	10	11	75	66	0	.532	9.0
Birmingham (White Sox)	7	8	6	...	9	8	8	11	9	7	73	67	0	.521	10.5
Orlando (Devil Rays)	8	8	9	7	...	8	7	9	8	6	70	68	0	.507	12.5
Knoxville (Blue Jays)	3	5	10	7	8	...	9	10	11	8	71	69	0	.507	12.5
Mobile (Padres)	8	7	7	7	7	7	...	7	8	8	66	73	0	.475	17.0
Huntsville (Brewers)	8	8	7	5	5	6	9	...	7	9	64	77	0	.454	20.0
Carolina (Rockies)	6	5	5	6	8	5	8	9	...	8	60	80	0	.429	23.5
Greenville (Braves)	5	4	5	8	8	7	7	6	8	...	58	80	0	.420	24.5

Carolina's home games played in Zebulon, N.C.; West Tenn's home games played in Jackson, Tenn.

Major league affiliations in parentheses.

PLAYOFFS: Orlando defeated Knoxville three games to one; West Tenn defeated Chattanooga three games to one; Orlando defeated West Tenn three games to one to win league championship.

REGULAR-SEASON ATTENDANCE: Birmingham, 314,010; Carolina, 238,002; Chattanooga, 218,946; Greenville, 257,171; Huntsville, 275,000; Jacksonville, 233,630; Knoxville, 119,571; Mobile, 293,147; Orlando, 81,032; West Tenn, 302,203. Total—2,332,712. Playoffs (11 games)—18,557. Class AA All-Star Game at Moblie, Ala.—6,174.

MANAGERS: Birmingham, Chris Crow; Carolina, Jay Loviglio; Chattanooga, Phillip Wellman; Greenville, Paul Runge; Huntsville, Darrell Evans; Jacksonville, Dave Anderson; Knoxville, Omar Malave; Mobile, Mike Basso; Orlando, Bill Russell; West Tenn, Dave Trembley.

ALL-STAR TEAM: 1B—Julio Zuleta, West Tenn; 2B—Dustin Carr, Orlando; 3B—Aubrey Huff, Orlando; SS—Kevin Nicholson, Mobile; OF—Brady Clark, Chattanooga; Rod Blair, Carolina; Eric Gillespie, Jacksonville; John Curl, Mobile; DH—Tim Giles, Knoxville; C—Javier Cardona, Jacksonville; Utility—Adam Melhuse, Knoxville; RHP—Jeff Yoder, West Tenn; LHP—David Darwin, Jacksonville; RP—Francisco Cordero, Jacksonville; Most Valuable Player—Brady Clark, Chattanooga; Most Outstanding Pitcher—Francisco Cordero, Jacksonville; Hustler of the Year—Ethan Faggett, Mobile; Manager of the Year—Dave Trembley, West Tenn.

1999 BATTING
TEAM

Team	Avg.	G	TPA	AB	R	H	TB	2B	3B	HR	RBI	SH	SF	HP	BB	IBB	SO	SB	CS	GDP	LOB	ShO	Slg.	OBP
Orlando	.281	138	5277	4695	686	1319	254	26	118	639	40	45	39	458	16	760	91	59	125	993	6	.422	.347
Knoxville	.278	140	5520	4717	824	1312	2097	274	29	151	755	24	55	58	666	20	860	122	79	119	1039	3	.445	.370
Chattanooga	.277	140	5473	4789	765	1327	2108	270	35	147	710	47	50	57	530	21	919	130	88	117	1005	7	.440	.353
Jacksonville	.276	141	5626	4952	792	1367	2181	305	31	149	743	14	50	49	561	9	1032	106	44	99	1087	7	.440	.352
Birmingham	.268	140	5304	4671	699	1253	1861	229	38	101	636	46	40	46	491	19	883	160	76	110	999	8	.398	.342
Mobile	.264	139	5389	4686	711	1235	1920	265	36	116	664	36	38	59	570	24	1094	139	51	103	1030	5	.410	.348
Greenville	.260	138	5144	4558	640	1186	1802	241	24	109	594	46	42	66	432	16	884	108	88	89	914	10	.395	.330
Carolina	.255	140	5157	4587	597	1169	1827	260	34	110	547	47	41	59	423	15	1017	103	58	100	956	8	.398	.323
West Tenn	.254	141	5303	4648	646	1181	1846	275	36	106	595	42	40	91	482	30	1044	144	71	86	1002	11	.397	.333
Huntsville	.252	141	5405	4698	646	1182	1735	229	24	92	582	42	44	79	542	24	915	178	72	112	1009	14	.369	.336

INDIVIDUAL
TOP QUALIFIERS FOR BATTING CHAMPIONSHIP
Minimum 378 plate appearances. *Lefthanded batter. †Switch-hitter.

Player, Team	Avg.	G	TPA	AB	R	H	TB	2B	3B	HR	RBI	SH	SF	HP	BB	IBB	SO	SB	CS	GDP	Slg.	OBP
Clark, Brady, Chat.	.326	138	608	506	103	165	261	37	4	17	75	5	5	2	89	6	58	25	17	6	.516	.425
Williams, Jason, Chat.	.319	87	389	332	65	106	158	27	2	7	45	1	4	6	46	2	40	3	4	9	.476	.407
Giles, Tim, Knox. *	.311	133	578	505	76	157	239	24	2	18	114	1	10	6	56	5	93	0	2	13	.473	.380
Cardona, Javier, Jack.	.309	108	477	418	84	129	238	31	0	26	92	0	5	8	46	0	69	4	2	16	.569	.384
Gillespie, Eric, Jack. *	.306	118	534	474	80	145	242	28	6	19	88	0	5	2	53	2	89	12	2	12	.511	.375
Smith, Demond, Gre. †	.305	132	491	416	70	127	188	20	7	9	59	8	5	7	55	1	72	31	13	5	.452	.391
Solano, Fausto, Knox.	.305	104	415	348	62	106	166	18	0	14	61	1	3	6	57	1	54	11	15	9	.477	.408
Bair, Rod, Car.	.303	125	525	472	70	143	228	34	6	13	81	0	6	16	28	0	78	14	12	11	.483	.358
Carr, Dustin, Orl.	.302	125	547	461	76	139	185	22	3	6	63	8	3	4	70	0	62	7	2	12	.401	.396

CLASS AA Southern League

Player, Team	Avg.	G	TPA	AB	R	H	TB	2B	3B	HR	RBI	SH	SF	HP	BB	IBB	SO	SB	CS	GDP	Slg.	OBP
Huff, Aubrey, Orl.*	.301	133	561	491	85	148	260	40	3	22	78	0	2	4	64	4	77	2	3	14	.530	.385
Pena, Elvis, Car.†	.301	110	420	356	57	107	149	24	6	2	31	8	2	6	48	2	64	21	6	6	.419	.391
Goodell, Steve, Gre.	.299	102	409	338	69	101	175	25	2	15	58	0	3	12	55	2	61	8	6	5	.518	.412
Nevers, Tom, Chat.	.295	111	401	380	61	112	190	23	2	17	65	2	2	2	15	0	74	3	5	14	.500	.323
Zuleta, Julio, W.T.	.295	133	545	482	75	142	250	37	4	21	97	0	8	20	35	6	122	4	3	11	.519	.361
Melhuse, Adam, Knox.†	.294	107	489	374	79	110	192	25	0	19	69	0	3	4	108	7	76	5	6	10	.513	.454

DEPARTMENTAL LEADERS: G—Clark, 138; AB—Abernathy, 577; R—Abernathy, 108; H—Abernathy, 168; TB—Clark, 261; 2B—Vieira, 44; 3B—Faggett, 11; HR—Cardona, 26; RBI—Giles, 114; SH—Sanchez, 10; SF—Giles, 10; HP—Zuleta, 20; BB—Melhuse, 108; IBB—Melhuse, 7; SO—Curl, 137; SB—Faggett, 63; CS—Alexis Sanchez, 27; GIDP—Balfe, 18; Slg.—Cardona, .569; OBP—Melhuse, .454.

ALL PLAYERS

*Lefthanded batter. †Switch-hitter.

Player, Team	Avg.	G	TPA	AB	R	H	TB	2B	3B	HR	RBI	SH	SF	HP	BB	IBB	SO	SB	CS	GDP	Slg.	OBP
Abernathy, Brent, Knox.	.291	136	650	577	108	168	251	42	1	13	62	5	7	6	55	1	47	34	15	11	.435	.355
Agosto, Stevenson, Mob.*	.250	40	11	8	1	2	2	0	0	0	0	2	0	0	1	0	1	0	0	0	.250	.333
Ahrendt, Jay, Mob.*	.200	8	19	15	2	3	4	1	0	0	2	0	0	0	4	2	8	0	0	0	.267	.368
Airoso, Kurt, Jack.	.272	134	638	536	95	146	216	28	6	10	72	0	6	5	89	1	113	10	3	8	.403	.377
Akin, Jay, Hun.*	.000	46	8	5	1	0	0	0	0	0	0	1	0	0	2	0	2	0	0	0	.000	.286
Alfano, Jeff, Hun.	.247	83	288	247	20	61	91	15	0	5	31	0	6	0	35	2	65	4	1	10	.368	.354
Almanzar, Richard, W.T.	.305	42	172	151	27	46	59	7	0	2	16	2	0	1	18	0	19	13	7	0	.391	.382
Anderson, Bill, Mob.	.167	4	6	6	0	1	1	0	0	0	0	0	0	0	0	0	4	0	0	0	.167	.167
Anthony, Brian, Car.*	.222	64	185	171	20	38	70	9	1	7	20	0	2	1	11	0	39	1	2	5	.409	.275
Atchley, Justin, Chat.*	.053	17	22	19	2	1	2	1	0	0	1	3	0	0	0	0	7	0	0	0	.105	.053
Aude, Rich, Birm.	.290	129	533	486	63	141	214	33	2	12	85	0	4	9	34	5	90	15	3	15	.440	.345
Averette, Robert, Chat.	.571	6	7	7	1	4	5	1	0	0	1	0	0	0	0	0	1	0	0	0	.714	.571
Azuaje, Jesus, Hun.	.281	119	480	391	63	110	161	21	0	10	60	0	7	11	70	0	26	34	8	13	.412	.399
Badeaux, Brooks, Orl.†	.500	3	2	2	1	1	4	0	0	1	1	0	0	0	0	0	0	0	0	0	2.000	.500
Bailey, Roger, Car.	.000	4	5	4	0	0	0	0	0	0	0	1	0	0	0	0	1	0	0	0	.000	.000
Bair, Rod, Car.	.303	125	525	472	70	143	228	34	6	13	81	0	6	16	28	0	78	14	12	11	.483	.358
Balfe, Ryan, Mob.†	.280	111	457	400	69	112	182	31	3	11	70	0	3	4	50	4	95	0	1	18	.455	.363
Barthol, Blake, Car.	.280	96	368	322	41	90	138	18	3	8	27	5	1	7	32	2	62	0	1	8	.429	.356
Beasley, Ray, Gre.	.125	50	8	8	0	1	1	0	0	0	0	0	0	0	0	0	4	0	0	0	.125	.125
Beck, Greg, Hun.	.077	26	30	26	2	2	2	0	0	0	3	4	0	0	0	0	10	0	0	1	.077	.077
Becker, Brian, Orl.	.252	129	529	480	67	121	201	24	1	18	74	0	3	4	42	2	89	0	0	16	.419	.316
Bell, Rob, Chat.	.111	12	12	9	0	1	1	0	0	0	0	3	0	0	0	0	6	0	0	0	.111	.111
Berry, Mike, Car.	.242	90	337	306	36	74	120	15	2	9	38	0	3	2	26	0	61	0	2	11	.392	.303
Bevel, Bobby, Car.*	.000	49	3	2	1	0	0	0	0	0	0	1	0	0	0	0	1	0	0	0	.000	.000
Bowers, Brent, W.T.*	.160	35	114	100	10	16	26	4	0	2	9	1	1	1	11	1	16	4	0	2	.260	.248
Bravo, Danny, Birm.†	.281	76	319	270	49	76	96	12	1	2	38	3	3	2	41	1	39	6	5	9	.356	.377
Brester, Jason, Car.*	.000	11	11	10	0	0	0	0	0	0	0	1	0	0	0	0	5	0	0	0	.000	.000
Brito, Jorge, Hun.	.299	26	73	67	11	20	33	2	1	3	7	0	0	2	4	0	15	0	0	1	.493	.356
Brock, Tarrik, Car.-W.T.*	.233	120	484	407	69	95	149	20	5	8	32	2	1	2	72	1	127	16	8	2	.366	.349
Broussard, Benjamin, Chat.*	.213	35	141	127	26	27	56	5	0	8	21	0	3	1	11	1	41	1	0	0	.441	.291
Brown, Roosevelt, W.T.*	.296	34	141	125	12	37	58	12	0	3	12	0	0	2	14	1	29	6	1	1	.464	.376
Buccheri, Jim, Orl.	.311	45	182	161	18	50	63	8	1	1	16	3	0	3	15	0	24	5	4	2	.391	.380
Bullard, Jason, Gre.	1.000	5	1	1	1	1	1	0	0	0	0	0	0	0	0	0	0	0	0	0	1.000	1.000
Burress, Andy, Chat.	.272	63	280	257	42	70	105	12	1	7	28	2	1	2	18	1	41	11	4	6	.409	.324
Butler, Adam, Gre.*	.167	27	6	6	0	1	1	0	0	0	0	0	0	0	0	0	3	0	0	0	.167	.167
Butler, Rob, Knox.*	.337	64	283	258	48	87	118	13	6	2	36	1	2	2	19	0	21	4	5	6	.457	.384
Cairo, Miguel, Orl.	.385	3	13	13	1	5	7	2	0	0	1	0	0	0	0	0	1	0	1	0	.538	.385
Cancel, Robinson, Hun.	.251	66	250	223	35	56	83	10	1	5	32	0	1	3	23	0	38	8	5	10	.372	.328
Candelaria, Ben, Jack.*	.269	120	505	464	65	125	216	31	3	18	77	0	5	1	35	3	93	6	7	13	.466	.319
Cardona, Javier, Jack.	.309	108	477	418	84	129	238	31	0	26	92	0	5	8	46	4	69	4	2	16	.569	.384
Carlyle, Ken, Gre.	.125	17	9	8	0	1	1	0	0	0	1	1	0	0	0	0	3	0	0	0	.125	.125
Carr, Dustin, Orl.	.302	125	547	461	76	139	185	22	3	6	63	8	3	4	70	0	62	7	2	12	.401	.396
Cepeda, Jose, Gre.	.276	58	215	196	19	54	69	8	2	1	17	2	3	1	13	0	15	2	3	7	.352	.319
Chavez, Carlos, Hun.	.000	13	2	2	0	0	0	0	0	0	0	0	0	0	0	0	1	0	0	0	.000	.000
Chiaffredo, Paul, Knox.	.077	11	43	39	3	3	7	1	0	1	3	2	0	2	0	0	10	0	0	2	.179	.122
Christensen, McKay, Birm.*	.290	75	337	293	53	85	114	8	6	3	28	4	1	8	31	0	46	18	6	6	.389	.363
Clark, Brady, Chat.	.326	138	608	506	103	165	261	37	4	17	75	5	5	2	89	6	58	25	17	6	.516	.425
Colina, Roberto, Orl.*	.273	99	358	315	45	86	126	20	1	6	53	0	3	3	37	4	47	0	1	8	.400	.352
Connacher, Kevin, Birm.	.222	7	20	18	1	4	4	0	0	0	2	0	0	0	2	0	5	1	0	2	.222	.300
Conner, Decomba, Chat.	.179	45	143	123	17	22	44	3	2	5	19	1	2	0	17	0	31	1	2	1	.358	.275
Converse, Jim, Hun.*	.000	16	2	1	0	0	0	0	0	0	0	0	0	0	1	0	0	0	0	0	.000	.000
Cotton, John, Car.*	.282	42	174	163	27	46	85	9	0	10	21	0	0	1	10	1	48	0	1	3	.521	.328
Crede, Joe, Birm.	.251	74	317	291	37	73	101	14	1	4	42	0	3	1	22	1	47	2	6	15	.347	.303
Cripps, Bobby, Knox.*	.172	25	96	87	13	15	27	6	0	2	9	0	1	2	6	0	37	0	0	0	.310	.240
Crowell, Jim, Chat.	.207	27	30	29	2	6	7	1	0	0	3	1	0	0	0	0	9	0	0	0	.241	.207
Cruz, Charlie, Gre.*	.000	11	2	2	0	0	0	0	0	0	0	0	0	0	0	0	1	0	0	0	.000	.000
Cruz, Luis, Orl.	.281	13	33	32	2	9	11	0	0	0	1	0	0	1	0	0	6	0	0	1	.344	.303
Curl, John, Mob.*	.285	133	560	474	79	135	237	30	3	22	76	0	8	1	77	3	137	9	5	0	.500	.380
Davis, James, Chat.	.241	16	58	54	7	13	30	5	0	4	16	0	1	2	1	0	5	0	1	3	.556	.276
Dawkins, Travis, Chat.	.364	32	145	129	24	47	60	7	0	2	13	2	0	0	14	0	17	15	5	5	.465	.427
Dawley, Joey, Gre.	.083	26	26	24	2	2	3	1	0	0	2	1	0	0	1	0	9	0	1	1	.125	.120
Dawsey, Jason, Hun.*	.333	4	4	3	0	1	1	0	0	0	1	1	0	0	0	0	0	0	0	0	.333	.333
Dellaero, Jason, Birm.†	.268	81	300	272	40	73	122	13	3	10	44	0	2	3	14	0	76	6	8	5	.449	.308
De Los Santos, Eddy, Orl.	.275	128	491	448	53	123	164	24	4	3	49	5	7	2	29	0	69	3	2	9	.366	.317
DeWitt, Scott, Car.	.500	45	2	2	0	1	1	0	0	0	0	0	0	0	0	0	0	0	0	0	.500	.500
Diaz, Alejandro, Chat.	.264	55	235	220	27	58	104	9	8	7	35	2	2	3	8	0	31	6	2	3	.473	.296
DiPace, Danny, Hun.*	.115	11	29	26	2	3	4	1	0	0	2	0	0	0	3	0	7	0	0	0	.154	.207
Dishman, Richard, Gre.	.071	30	30	28	0	2	2	0	0	0	0	2	0	0	0	0	5	0	0	1	.071	.071
Dixon, Tim, Hun.*	.000	24	5	5	0	0	0	0	0	0	0	0	0	0	0	0	3	0	0	0	.000	.000
Donaldson, Bo, Chat.	.000	38	3	3	0	0	0	0	0	0	0	0	0	0	0	0	2	0	0	1	.000	.000

Player, Team	Avg.	G	TPA	AB	R	H	TB	2B	3B	HR	RBI	SH	SF	HP	BB	IBB	SO	SB	CS	GDP	Slg.	OBP
Doughty, Brian, Mob.	.190	36	26	21	2	4	5	1	0	0	0	4	0	0	1	0	7	0	0	1	.238	.227
Downs, Scott, W.T.*	.100	13	15	10	1	1	1	0	0	0	0	2	0	0	3	0	5	0	0	0	.100	.308
Drumheller, Al, Mob.	.294	14	18	17	3	5	7	2	0	0	6	1	0	0	0	0	4	0	0	0	.412	.294
Duncan, Courtney, W.T.*	.200	11	7	5	1	1	1	0	0	0	0	0	0	0	2	0	3	0	0	0	.200	.429
Eaglin, Mike, Birm.	.227	27	82	75	7	17	19	2	0	0	8	0	2	1	4	0	17	1	2	2	.253	.268
Eberwein, Kevin, Mob.	.171	10	39	35	5	6	10	1	0	1	2	0	1	0	3	0	16	0	0	0	.286	.231
Eddie, Steve, Chat.-Birm.	.197	52	175	157	15	31	42	8	0	1	12	3	3	0	12	0	30	0	3	6	.268	.250
Elliott, Dave, Hun.	.233	123	477	404	69	94	153	23	0	12	55	1	6	7	59	2	111	11	6	5	.379	.336
Encarnacion, Angelo, W.T.	.257	30	106	101	11	26	37	6	1	1	10	0	0	1	4	0	12	2	0	1	.366	.292
Estes, Eric, Mob.	.000	8	2	2	0	0	0	0	0	0	0	0	0	0	0	0	0	0	0	0	.000	.000
Etler, Todd, Chat.	.000	14	3	2	1	0	0	0	0	0	0	0	0	0	1	0	0	0	0	0	.000	.333
Faggett, Ethan, Mob.*	.243	128	590	527	82	128	186	18	11	6	43	3	0	7	53	0	126	63	14	4	.353	.320
Faurot, Adam, Hun.	.260	22	52	50	5	13	15	2	0	0	7	0	1	0	1	0	7	1	0	3	.300	.269
Feuerstein, Dave, Car.	.220	101	311	287	27	63	81	9	3	1	18	1	2	3	18	1	43	6	2	6	.282	.271
Flach, Jason, Gre.	.000	12	4	3	1	0	0	0	0	0	0	0	0	0	1	0	1	0	0	0	.000	.250
Florez, Tim, Chat.	.252	39	161	139	24	35	60	8	1	5	22	1	3	3	15	0	23	7	2	6	.432	.331
Font, Franklin, W.T.	.344	25	107	96	14	33	40	2	1	1	17	1	1	1	8	1	14	4	4	0	.417	.396
Forney, Rick, Gre.	.357	12	19	14	2	5	6	1	0	0	2	3	0	0	2	0	2	0	0	0	.429	.438
Fraraccio, Dan, Orl.	.287	82	287	254	48	73	119	19	3	7	28	2	4	2	25	1	43	1	4	7	.469	.351
Freel, Ryan, Knox.	.283	11	55	46	9	13	23	5	1	1	9	0	1	0	8	0	4	4	2	0	.500	.382
Freire, Alejandro, Jack.	.296	66	276	243	45	72	122	20	0	10	43	0	4	6	23	0	44	2	0	8	.502	.366
Garcia, Guillermo, Chat.	.310	10	45	42	11	13	25	3	3	1	7	0	0	1	2	0	6	0	0	3	.595	.356
Garcia, Neil, Orl.†	.284	31	112	95	13	27	36	6	0	1	11	3	3	1	10	0	16	0	1	2	.379	.349
Gazarek, Marty, W.T.	.297	35	136	128	16	38	67	9	1	6	27	0	1	3	4	1	7	2	5	3	.523	.331
Giles, Tim, Knox.*	.311	133	578	505	76	157	239	24	2	18	114	1	10	6	56	5	93	0	2	13	.473	.380
Gillespie, Eric, Jack.*	.306	118	534	474	80	145	242	28	6	19	88	0	5	2	53	2	89	12	2	12	.511	.375
Giron, Isabel, Knox.-Mob.	.083	28	13	12	1	1	2	1	0	0	2	1	0	0	0	0	6	0	0	0	.167	.083
Gissell, Chris, W.T.	.125	21	18	16	1	2	2	0	0	0	0	1	0	0	1	0	6	1	0	0	.125	.176
Glauber, Keith, Chat.	.125	7	9	8	2	1	1	0	0	0	0	0	0	0	1	0	2	0	0	0	.125	.222
Glavine, Mike, Gre.*	.269	107	357	305	47	82	157	24	0	17	52	0	2	1	49	0	65	0	3	3	.515	.370
Gomez, Ramon, Birm.	.285	99	314	274	47	78	98	10	5	0	26	6	1	2	31	1	81	26	10	1	.358	.360
Gomez, Rudy, Knox.	.281	122	521	427	74	120	203	26	3	17	92	5	8	6	75	0	63	10	4	16	.475	.390
Gonzalez, Jeremi, W.T.	.000	3	1	1	0	0	0	0	0	0	0	0	0	0	0	0	0	0	0	0	.000	.000
Gonzalez, Jimmy, Mob.	.265	21	79	68	15	18	27	3	0	2	8	0	1	3	7	1	16	0	0	2	.397	.354
Gonzalez, Wiklenman, Mob.	.338	61	264	225	38	76	126	16	2	10	49	0	3	7	29	2	28	0	0	8	.560	.424
Goodell, Steve, Gre.	.299	102	409	338	69	101	175	25	2	15	58	0	3	12	55	2	61	8	6	5	.518	.412
Green, Chad, Hun.†	.246	116	475	422	56	104	162	22	3	10	46	2	3	2	46	2	109	28	13	6	.384	.321
Guzman, Domingo, Mob.	.000	41	3	3	0	0	0	0	0	0	0	0	0	0	0	0	1	0	0	0	.000	.000
Hackman, Luther, Car.	.133	11	18	15	1	2	4	2	0	0	2	0	1	0	2	0	5	0	0	0	.267	.222
Hall, Toby, Orl.	.254	46	183	173	20	44	78	7	0	9	34	1	4	1	4	1	10	1	1	7	.451	.269
Haring, Brett, Chat.	.222	7	9	9	1	2	3	1	0	0	2	0	0	0	0	0	0	0	0	0	.333	.222
Harrison, Tommy, Gre.	.111	16	11	9	0	1	1	0	0	0	0	1	0	0	1	0	7	0	0	0	.111	.200
Hartvigson, Chad, Car.*	.000	30	1	1	0	0	0	0	0	0	0	0	0	0	0	0	0	0	0	0	.000	.000
Hawkins, Al, Hun.	.091	19	26	22	0	2	2	0	0	0	0	3	0	0	1	0	6	0	0	0	.091	.130
Hawkins, Kraig, Orl.	.301	94	341	296	41	89	101	10	1	0	27	4	2	1	38	1	45	19	10	9	.341	.380
Hayes, Chris, Knox.	.287	36	152	129	25	37	56	11	1	2	16	0	0	5	18	0	29	4	4	3	.434	.395
Helmer, Chad, Hun.	.000	7	1	0	0	0	0	0	0	0	0	0	0	0	1	0	0	0	0	0	.000	1.000
Helms, Wes, Gre.	.301	30	121	113	15	34	64	6	0	8	26	0	0	1	7	1	34	1	0	3	.566	.347
Hernandez, Elvin, W.T.	.087	29	31	23	2	2	2	0	0	0	2	6	0	0	2	0	3	0	0	0	.087	.160
Herndon, Junior, Mob.	.036	26	35	28	1	1	2	1	0	0	4	5	1	0	1	0	19	0	0	1	.071	.067
Hite, Kevin, Mob.	.000	51	3	3	0	0	0	0	0	0	0	0	0	0	0	0	3	0	0	0	.000	.000
Horn, Jeff, Gre.	.229	66	189	166	19	38	50	6	0	2	27	0	3	4	16	0	28	0	1	4	.301	.307
Huff, Aubrey, Orl.*	.301	133	561	491	85	148	260	40	3	22	78	0	2	4	64	4	77	2	3	14	.530	.385
Huntsman, Scott, Hun.	.167	47	6	6	1	1	2	1	0	0	0	0	0	0	0	0	4	0	0	1	.333	.167
Hyde, Brandon, Birm.	.278	7	21	18	4	5	8	3	0	0	2	0	0	0	3	0	4	0	1	0	.444	.381
Iapoce, Anthony, Hun.†	.263	50	146	133	17	35	42	7	0	0	5	0	0	1	12	0	25	2	2	0	.316	.329
Ibarra, Jesse, Jack.†	.157	18	81	70	9	11	15	1	0	1	6	0	1	0	10	1	20	0	0	1	.214	.259
Iglesias, Mike, Gre.	.000	4	4	2	0	0	0	0	0	0	0	1	0	0	1	0	2	0	0	0	.000	.333
Inglin, Jeff, Birm.	.292	117	500	432	63	126	205	26	4	15	63	2	2	6	58	3	62	20	2	13	.475	.382
Ingram, Darron, Chat.	.221	85	296	267	42	59	109	11	3	11	40	0	1	0	28	1	95	5	7	5	.408	.294
Jacobs, Ryan, Car.	.167	28	19	18	1	3	4	1	0	0	1	1	0	0	0	0	5	0	0	0	.222	.167
Jacobsen, Buck, Hun.	.193	47	178	150	20	29	46	6	1	3	19	0	5	3	20	0	32	4	1	4	.307	.292
Janzen, Marty, Chat.	.167	30	6	6	0	1	1	0	0	0	0	0	0	0	0	0	2	0	0	0	.167	.167
Jennings, Robin, W.T.*	.321	13	61	53	11	17	35	3	0	5	17	0	2	1	5	0	7	1	0	2	.660	.377
Johnson, A.J., Mob.	.243	44	144	136	12	33	52	7	0	4	18	0	0	2	6	0	35	1	3	4	.382	.285
Johnson, Adam, Gre.*	.289	104	435	394	50	114	187	27	2	14	72	0	5	4	31	1	74	1	6	11	.475	.343
Johnston, Doug, Hun.	.095	21	23	21	1	2	2	0	0	0	1	1	0	0	1	0	7	0	0	2	.095	.136
Jones, Ryan, Jack.	.253	125	543	487	66	123	207	21	3	19	73	0	3	3	50	0	115	1	1	7	.425	.324
Jorgensen, Randy, Mob.*	.321	72	297	252	41	81	117	15	0	7	54	1	3	5	36	0	46	2	2	6	.464	.412
Keck, Brian, Car.	.200	5	19	15	0	3	5	0	1	0	2	0	0	0	4	0	3	2	1	1	.333	.368
Kelley, Rich, Hun.*	.000	25	2	1	0	0	0	0	0	0	0	0	0	0	1	0	1	0	0	0	.000	.500
Kent, Robbie, Mob.	.271	109	387	336	48	91	138	17	3	8	56	2	3	2	44	3	71	2	0	8	.411	.356
King, Brad, W.T.	.228	92	287	232	29	53	63	10	0	0	25	2	6	9	38	5	34	2	1	7	.272	.351
King, Brett, W.T.	.218	54	189	142	27	31	46	6	0	3	13	2	2	4	39	1	49	7	6	0	.324	.396
Kirgan, Chris, Car.	.222	133	540	474	55	105	175	27	2	13	84	0	4	2	60	4	115	1	0	17	.369	.309
Klimek, Josh, Hun.*	.239	123	479	431	46	103	173	28	0	14	71	2	8	4	33	6	78	3	2	5	.401	.294
Kolb, Brandon, Mob.	.000	7	1	1	0	0	0	0	0	0	0	0	0	0	0	0	0	0	0	0	.000	.000
Kominek, Toby, Hun.	.232	128	530	456	56	106	168	20	3	12	59	1	3	18	52	2	118	7	10	9	.368	.333
Lackey, Steve, Gre.	.292	80	345	315	50	92	128	18	3	4	38	6	3	0	21	0	55	9	8	7	.406	.333
Langaigne, Selwyn, Knox.*	.244	40	135	123	18	30	36	4	1	0	10	2	0	0	10	0	25	3	4	10	.293	.301
Larkin, Stephen, Chat.*	.299	104	304	264	34	79	111	16	2	4	42	3	6	0	31	3	44	7	3	3	.420	.365
Larson, Brandon, Chat.	.285	43	187	172	28	49	95	10	0	12	42	0	2	3	10	1	51	4	5	3	.552	.332
Lawrence, Joe, Knox.	.264	70	311	250	52	66	107	16	2	7	24	0	2	3	56	0	48	7	6	10	.428	.402
Lawrence, Tony, Chat.	.125	4	10	8	0	1	1	0	0	0	1	0	0	1	1	0	4	0	0	2	.125	.300
Lee, Derek, Hun.*	.100	27	35	30	2	3	4	1	0	0	1	2	0	0	3	0	5	0	0	1	.133	.182

Player, Team	Avg.	G	TPA	AB	R	H	TB	2B	3B	HR	RBI	SH	SF	HP	BB	IBB	SO	SB	CS	GDP	Slg.	OBP
Lemonis, Chris, Jack.*	.283	75	290	265	35	75	108	16	1	5	38	0	0	6	19	0	45	1	2	6	.408	.345
Levis, Jesse, Orl.*	.396	13	55	48	6	19	29	7	0	1	11	0	1	0	6	0	4	0	0	0	.604	.455
Levrault, Allen, Hun.	.238	16	23	21	2	5	9	1	0	1	2	1	0	0	1	0	3	0	0	0	.429	.273
LeBlanc, Eric, Chat.*	.133	15	18	15	2	2	3	1	0	0	1	3	0	0	0	0	4	0	0	0	.200	.133
Lidle, Kevin, Mob.	.222	63	219	180	23	40	66	8	0	6	26	2	2	5	30	2	40	1	3	4	.367	.346
Light, Tal, Car.	.185	80	284	259	26	48	93	18	0	9	30	1	1	7	16	0	121	0	3	4	.359	.251
Lindsey, Rodney, Jack.	.185	7	29	27	3	5	6	1	0	0	2	1	0	0	1	0	6	0	0	0	.222	.214
Lindstrom, David, Car.	.271	66	250	214	30	58	98	17	1	7	35	1	5	6	24	0	35	1	3	9	.458	.353
Livingston, Doug, Car.	.202	43	137	119	11	24	31	2	1	1	9	3	2	0	13	4	24	4	2	1	.261	.291
Lobaton, Jose, Hun.	.281	45	148	128	23	36	48	6	0	2	18	3	3	1	13	1	34	2	0	0	.375	.345
Long, Ryan, Orl.	.233	8	31	30	2	7	8	1	0	0	4	0	0	0	1	0	3	0	0	3	.267	.258
Lopez, Mickey, Hun.†	.298	83	373	315	58	94	135	16	5	5	40	3	4	5	46	2	46	31	4	9	.429	.392
Lopez, Rodrigo, Mob.	.086	28	38	35	0	3	3	0	0	0	1	2	0	0	1	0	19	0	0	1	.086	.111
Loyd, Brian, Knox.	.280	104	424	364	53	102	155	18	1	11	65	4	6	4	46	3	57	9	2	11	.426	.362
Lunar, Fernando, Gre.	.224	105	367	343	33	77	103	15	1	3	35	0	0	12	12	5	64	0	1	7	.300	.275
Luzinski, Ryan, Chat.-Mob.	.279	77	276	233	28	65	91	20	0	2	30	2	2	2	37	2	58	1	2	6	.391	.380
Lydy, Scott, Birm.	.265	111	472	400	74	106	193	25	1	20	65	1	1	3	67	3	61	18	3	5	.483	.374
Macalutas, Jon, Hun.	.265	93	355	306	50	81	118	20	1	5	45	0	0	11	38	2	32	4	3	11	.386	.366
MacRae, Scott, Chat.	.214	39	19	14	0	3	4	1	0	0	1	3	0	0	2	0	4	0	0	0	.286	.313
Malave, Jose, Car.	.274	44	166	146	21	40	82	10	1	10	26	0	2	2	16	0	28	0	1	3	.562	.349
Mallard, Randi, Chat.	.389	16	21	18	3	7	11	2	1	0	5	2	1	0	0	0	6	2	0	0	.611	.368
Manning, David, W.T.	.043	23	28	23	0	1	1	0	0	0	1	4	0	0	1	0	8	0	0	2	.043	.083
Manning, Nate, W.T.	.222	13	31	27	0	6	8	2	0	0	5	0	0	2	2	0	8	1	0	0	.296	.323
Manzano, Adrian, Gre.	.000	42	5	5	0	0	0	0	0	0	0	0	0	0	0	0	2	0	0	1	.000	.000
Marquis, Jason, Gre.	.000	12	8	7	0	0	0	0	0	0	0	1	0	0	0	0	6	0	0	0	.000	.000
Marrero, Oreste, Hun.*	.216	15	38	37	2	8	14	3	0	1	7	0	0	0	1	0	8	0	0	2	.378	.237
Martin, Chandler, Car.	.122	27	45	41	1	5	6	1	0	0	3	0	0	1	0	0	12	0	0	1	.146	.143
Martinez, Greg, Hun.†	.276	25	111	98	18	27	34	3	2	0	6	1	0	0	12	1	13	8	2	2	.347	.355
Martinez, Pablo, Gre.†	.237	57	253	228	28	54	72	9	3	1	19	2	3	0	20	0	41	6	8	6	.316	.295
Mathis, Jared, Hun.	.225	74	237	218	23	49	62	5	1	2	24	9	1	1	8	0	32	2	3	2	.284	.254
Maurer, Dave, Mob.	.500	54	2	2	0	1	1	0	0	0	0	0	0	0	0	0	0	0	0	0	.500	.500
McClure, Brian, Mob.*	.207	51	191	169	17	35	54	10	3	1	27	1	2	2	17	1	34	0	0	4	.320	.284
McNabb, Buck, Gre.*	.323	25	98	93	9	30	34	4	0	0	5	0	0	0	5	0	18	2	2	2	.366	.357
Melhuse, Adam, Knox.†	.294	107	489	374	79	110	192	25	0	19	69	0	3	4	108	7	76	5	6	10	.513	.454
Merrell, Phil, Chat.	.000	7	5	4	0	0	0	0	0	0	0	0	0	0	1	0	3	0	0	0	.000	.200
Meyer, Jake, Chat.	.000	20	1	1	0	0	0	0	0	0	0	0	0	0	0	0	1	0	0	0	.000	.000
Meyers, Chad, W.T.	.290	64	274	238	45	69	101	19	2	3	29	0	0	10	26	0	40	22	8	6	.424	.383
Meyers, Mike, W.T.	.000	5	6	5	0	0	0	0	0	0	1	1	0	0	0	0	1	0	0	0	.000	.000
Micucci, Mike, W.T.*	.169	52	133	124	7	21	22	1	0	0	7	1	1	0	7	1	32	1	0	4	.177	.212
Middlebrook, Jason, Mob.	.000	13	16	13	0	0	0	0	0	0	0	3	0	0	0	0	3	0	0	2	.000	.000
Milburn, Adam, Gre.	.000	14	1	1	0	0	0	0	0	0	0	0	0	0	0	0	1	0	0	0	.000	.000
Miller, Corky, Chat.	.221	33	127	104	20	23	45	10	0	4	16	0	1	11	11	0	30	0	0	3	.433	.354
Milliard, Ralph, Chat.	.294	32	128	102	19	30	47	3	1	4	23	1	2	3	20	1	13	2	3	1	.461	.417
Mitchell, Derek, Jack.	.242	124	486	422	56	102	142	17	1	7	49	4	5	2	53	0	117	4	2	3	.336	.326
Molina, Jose, W.T.	.171	14	39	35	2	6	9	3	0	0	5	1	1	0	2	0	14	0	0	1	.257	.211
Monds, Wonderful, Chat.	.260	75	335	311	48	81	132	14	2	11	32	5	1	1	17	0	49	14	8	8	.424	.300
Moore, Brandon, Birm.	.193	36	139	119	11	23	30	3	2	0	13	2	1	0	17	0	20	4	2	9	.252	.292
Morenz, Shea, Mob.*	.263	21	63	57	6	15	20	5	0	0	7	0	1	1	4	0	27	1	1	0	.351	.317
Mortimer, Mark, Gre.	.233	11	34	30	4	7	8	1	0	0	5	0	1	0	3	0	7	0	0	0	.267	.294
Mosquera, Julio, Orl.	.305	80	282	259	36	79	106	13	1	4	37	1	4	3	15	2	40	1	0	14	.409	.345
Moss, Damian, Gre.	.750	7	7	4	1	3	5	2	0	0	3	2	1	0	0	0	0	0	0	0	1.250	.662
Nelson, Bry, W.T.†	.268	129	520	471	66	126	208	24	5	16	78	1	4	2	42	4	52	10	7	13	.442	.328
Nelson, Joe, Gre.	.000	25	2	2	0	0	0	0	0	0	0	0	0	0	0	0	1	0	0	0	.000	.000
Nevers, Tom, Chat.	.295	111	401	380	61	112	190	23	2	17	65	2	2	2	15	0	74	3	5	14	.500	.323
Newman, Eric, W.T.	.333	58	7	6	0	2	2	0	0	0	0	0	0	0	1	0	1	0	0	0	.333	.429
Newstrom, Doug, Birm.*	.285	82	285	253	30	72	94	11	1	3	23	0	2	0	29	2	42	3	4	8	.372	.356
Nicholson, Kevin, Mob.†	.288	127	548	489	84	141	224	38	3	13	81	1	6	5	46	1	92	16	5	15	.458	.352
Nomo, Hideo, Hun.	.667	1	3	3	0	2	2	0	0	0	2	0	0	0	0	0	1	0	0	0	.667	.667
Norris, Dax, Gre.	.278	120	455	403	59	112	184	27	0	15	66	0	4	7	41	2	59	2	1	10	.457	.352
Norton, Phillip, W.T.	.154	14	17	13	0	2	2	0	0	0	1	3	0	0	1	0	6	0	0	0	.154	.176
Olson, Dan, Birm.*	.165	33	112	97	14	16	38	4	0	6	13	0	0	0	15	0	44	1	1	0	.392	.277
Owens, Jayhawk, Chat.	.222	47	188	153	24	34	60	6	1	6	21	0	2	2	31	1	45	3	0	9	.392	.356
Paciorek, Pete, Mob.*	.221	83	268	226	38	50	75	9	2	4	17	0	0	4	38	0	60	2	3	6	.332	.343
Paredes, Roberto, Hun.	.250	28	4	4	1	1	2	1	0	0	0	0	0	0	0	0	1	0	0	0	.500	.250
Passini, Brian, Hun.*	.333	8	11	9	0	3	3	0	0	0	2	0	0	0	2	0	0	0	0	0	.333	.333
Paul, Josh, Birm.	.279	93	360	319	47	89	126	19	3	4	42	3	4	5	29	1	68	6	6	6	.395	.345
Pearsall, J.J., Chat.	.500	32	4	4	0	2	4	2	0	0	1	0	0	0	0	0	1	0	0	0	1.000	.500
Pemberton, Rudy, Birm.	.277	85	348	307	49	85	159	14	3	18	60	0	3	11	27	2	55	8	3	8	.518	.353
Pena, Elvis, Car.†	.301	110	420	356	57	107	149	24	6	2	31	8	2	6	48	2	64	21	6	6	.419	.391
Pena, Jesus, Birm.*	.000	41	0	0	1	0	0	0	0	0	0	0	0	0	0	0	0	0	0	0	.000	.000
Pendergrass, Tyrone, Gre.†	.262	100	391	344	60	90	126	12	3	6	31	5	3	2	37	0	61	19	14	3	.366	.334
Petrick, Ben, Car.	.309	20	80	68	18	21	40	5	1	4	22	0	2	1	9	0	15	3	1	0	.588	.388
Pickler, Jeff, Hun.*	.279	51	202	183	20	51	64	8	1	1	23	2	2	0	15	0	25	9	4	11	.350	.330
Pigott, Anthony, Orl.	.250	4	8	8	0	2	3	1	0	0	0	0	0	0	0	0	2	0	0	0	.375	.250
Pimentel, Jose, Gre.	.214	106	401	364	55	78	122	18	1	8	45	4	4	5	24	3	80	20	10	9	.335	.270
Polanco, Enohel, W.T.	.240	116	386	354	44	85	125	21	5	3	30	5	3	4	20	2	89	12	8	9	.353	.286
Pomierski, Joe, Orl.*	.261	62	220	188	31	49	92	10	3	9	33	2	2	5	22	0	44	1	1	2	.489	.350
Presto, Nick, Chat.	.268	73	272	224	34	60	74	8	0	2	28	2	2	6	38	0	34	5	7	6	.330	.385
Priebe, Kevin, Hun.	.000	3	1	0	0	0	0	0	0	0	0	1	0	0	0	0	0	0	0	0	.000	.000
Priest, Eddie, Chat.	.231	12	16	13	0	3	3	0	0	0	0	1	0	0	2	0	7	0	0	0	.231	.333
Prieto, Rick, Mob.†	.287	118	427	359	61	103	143	14	4	6	43	5	1	5	57	0	55	28	5	6	.398	.391
Probst, Alan, Knox.	.212	21	74	66	5	14	20	3	0	1	7	1	2	0	5	0	23	0	0	3	.303	.260
Quatraro, Matt, Orl.	.250	1	5	4	1	1	4	0	0	1	2	1	0	0	0	0	0	0	0	0	1.000	.250
Rain, Steve, W.T.	.000	40	2	1	0	0	0	0	0	0	0	0	0	0	0	0	2	0	0	0	.000	.000
Raleigh, Matt, Car.	.209	48	140	115	13	24	44	8	0	4	12	1	0	1	23	1	60	0	0	2	.383	.345

Player, Team	Avg.	G	TPA	AB	R	H	TB	2B	3B	HR	RBI	SH	SF	HP	BB	IBB	SO	SB	CS	GDP	Slg.	OBP
Ramirez, Dan, Birm.	.197	32	132	127	16	25	30	5	0	0	10	0	1	1	3	0	31	6	4	0	.236	.220
Randall, Scott, Car.	.133	16	18	15	2	2	2	0	0	0	0	3	0	0	0	0	5	0	0	1	.133	.133
Rawitzer, Kevin, Car.*	.500	33	5	2	1	1	1	0	0	0	0	2	0	0	1	0	0	0	0	0	.500	.667
Rennhack, Mike, W.T.†	.254	66	225	189	29	48	74	11	0	5	21	0	0	2	34	0	46	4	0	6	.392	.373
Rexrode, Jackie, Birm.*	.268	70	250	213	34	57	74	7	5	0	25	5	4	0	28	0	30	14	4	1	.347	.347
Ricken, Ray, Mob.	.286	20	15	14	4	4	9	2	0	1	4	1	0	0	0	0	4	0	0	0	.643	.286
Ricketts, Chad, W.T.	.000	57	4	4	0	0	0	0	0	0	0	0	0	0	0	0	3	0	0	0	.000	.000
Riedling, John, Chat.	.000	40	1	1	0	0	0	0	0	0	0	0	0	0	0	0	1	0	0	0	.000	.000
Riley, Marquis, Jack.†	.255	54	192	161	30	41	45	4	0	0	16	0	1	0	30	0	29	16	3	1	.280	.370
Rivera, Mike, Jack.	.174	7	25	23	3	4	11	1	0	2	6	0	0	0	2	0	5	0	0	0	.478	.240
Rivers, Jonathan, W.T.	.182	35	97	88	10	16	22	3	0	1	6	0	0	1	8	0	20	5	0	2	.250	.258
Roberts, Chris, Car.	.182	44	13	11	2	2	2	0	0	0	1	2	0	0	0	0	5	0	0	0	.182	.182
Robertson, Rich, Car.*	.167	11	12	12	2	2	2	0	0	0	0	0	0	0	0	0	2	0	0	0	.167	.167
Rodriguez, Liu, Birm.†	.291	64	280	244	42	71	93	11	1	3	37	8	3	3	22	0	35	5	3	2	.381	.353
Rose, Ted, Chat.*	.000	14	2	2	0	0	0	0	0	0	0	0	0	0	0	0	0	0	0	0	.000	.000
Rossiter, Mike, Car.	.000	16	1	1	0	0	0	0	0	0	0	0	0	0	0	0	1	0	0	0	.000	.000
Rupp, Chad, Knox.	.257	67	287	241	49	62	133	19	2	16	44	0	0	2	44	0	73	7	2	1	.552	.376
Ryan, Jason, W.T.†	.083	8	13	12	0	1	1	0	0	0	0	1	0	0	0	0	3	0	0	0	.083	.083
Ryder, Derek, Birm.	.148	12	31	27	4	4	5	1	0	0	2	1	1	1	2	0	3	0	0	0	.185	.233
Sak, Jim, Mob.	.000	18	3	3	0	0	0	0	0	0	0	0	0	0	0	0	1	0	0	0	.000	.000
Salamon, John, Gre.	.000	28	3	2	0	0	0	0	0	0	0	1	0	0	0	0	0	0	0	1	.000	.000
Salzano, Jerry, Chat.	.327	72	313	263	44	86	119	19	1	4	38	2	4	5	39	1	38	14	10	5	.452	.418
Sanchez, Alex, Orl.*	.254	121	538	500	68	127	153	12	4	2	29	10	2	0	26	1	88	48	27	8	.306	.290
Santana, Pedro, Jack.	.279	120	562	512	89	143	205	35	6	5	49	8	5	3	34	0	98	34	9	8	.400	.325
Sasser, Rob, Jack.	.283	117	487	424	60	120	181	38	1	7	61	0	3	3	57	1	101	9	5	5	.427	.370
Saunders, Chris, Chat.	.315	58	256	216	31	68	104	13	1	7	35	0	5	0	34	1	42	0	1	6	.481	.400
Schifano, Tony, Knox.	.272	27	98	92	12	25	31	4	1	0	15	1	1	1	3	0	15	5	3	3	.337	.299
Schmidt, Bryan, Mob.	.188	17	37	32	7	6	7	1	0	0	3	0	0	0	5	0	8	0	0	1	.219	.297
Schutz, Carl, W.T.*	.000	41	1	1	0	0	0	0	0	0	0	0	0	0	0	0	0	0	0	0	.000	.000
Seelbach, Chris, Gre.	.000	8	10	8	0	0	0	0	0	0	0	2	0	0	0	0	4	0	0	0	.000	.000
Serrano, Wascar, Mob.	.182	7	12	11	1	2	2	0	0	0	0	1	0	0	0	0	4	0	0	0	.182	.182
Shumate, Jacob, Gre.	.000	14	11	10	0	0	0	0	0	0	0	1	0	0	0	0	9	0	0	0	.000	.000
Skrmetta, Matt, Mob.†	.000	25	2	2	0	0	0	0	0	0	0	0	0	0	0	0	0	0	0	1	.000	.000
Smith, Dan, W.T.*	.222	57	9	9	1	2	2	0	0	0	0	0	0	0	0	0	3	0	0	0	.222	.222
Smith, Demond, Gre.†	.305	132	491	416	70	127	188	20	7	9	59	8	5	7	55	1	72	31	13	5	.452	.391
Smith, Travis, Hun.	.300	9	10	10	3	3	3	0	0	0	0	0	0	0	0	0	2	0	0	0	.300	.300
Snusz, Chris, Chat.	.500	2	7	6	0	3	4	1	0	0	2	0	0	0	1	0	0	0	0	0	.667	.571
Solano, Fausto, Knox.	.305	104	415	348	62	106	166	18	0	14	61	1	3	6	57	1	54	11	15	9	.477	.408
Sollmann, Scott, Hun.*	.314	55	228	191	34	60	77	4	5	1	9	0	3	0	34	0	31	17	8	3	.403	.425
Sosa, Juan, Car.	.276	125	534	490	70	135	188	22	5	7	42	5	6	2	31	0	65	38	15	12	.384	.318
Speed, Dorian, W.T.	.267	121	455	415	70	111	190	21	8	14	57	2	1	8	27	0	106	22	11	6	.458	.324
Steenstra, Kennie, Gre.	.000	8	2	2	0	0	0	0	0	0	0	0	0	0	0	0	1	0	0	0	.000	.000
Stegall, Randy, Chat.	.207	13	33	29	0	6	6	0	0	0	1	1	1	0	2	0	5	0	0	1	.207	.250
Steinmetz, Earl, Gre.	.000	6	2	2	0	0	0	0	0	0	0	0	0	0	0	0	1	0	0	0	.000	.000
Strange, Mike, Knox.	.093	29	81	54	10	5	5	0	0	0	4	0	0	1	26	0	24	1	0	3	.093	.395
Stromsborg, Ryan, Knox.	.249	99	408	377	54	94	144	17	3	9	45	1	2	0	28	0	91	5	4	6	.382	.300
Theodile, Robert, Hun.	.444	47	9	9	0	4	4	0	0	0	0	0	0	0	0	0	3	0	0	0	.444	.444
Therneau, Dave, Chat.	.250	3	4	4	1	1	1	0	0	0	0	0	0	0	0	0	1	0	0	1	.250	.250
Thompson, Andy, Knox.	.244	67	301	254	56	62	129	16	3	15	53	0	5	8	34	2	55	7	3	2	.508	.346
Thrower, Jake, Mob.†	.242	40	172	149	15	36	58	9	2	3	26	0	1	1	21	1	26	3	3	2	.389	.337
Tolar, Kevin, Chat.	.000	47	1	1	0	0	0	0	0	0	0	0	0	0	0	0	0	0	0	0	.000	.000
Trippy, Joe, Car.*	.221	79	170	131	26	29	40	5	0	2	15	2	1	6	30	0	25	6	7	1	.305	.387
Tucci, Pete, Mob.	.250	83	343	312	45	78	126	15	0	11	35	0	1	4	26	3	83	11	6	7	.404	.315
VanEgmond, Tim, Hun.	.000	3	2	1	0	0	0	0	0	0	0	1	0	0	0	0	1	0	0	0	.000	.000
Vavrek, Mike, Car.*	.000	10	7	4	1	0	0	0	0	0	0	0	0	2	0	0	1	0	0	0	.000	.200
Vidal, Gilbert, Car.	.240	45	142	129	10	31	45	8	0	2	12	3	1	1	8	0	30	0	0	2	.349	.288
Vieira, Scott, W.T.	.292	126	523	455	63	133	215	44	4	10	58	0	3	12	53	4	126	10	6	4	.473	.379
Wakeland, Chris, Jack.*	.321	55	253	212	42	68	129	16	3	13	36	0	2	4	35	1	53	6	5	2	.608	.423
Walker, Ron, W.T.	.219	105	353	302	42	66	115	20	1	9	42	0	5	7	39	0	86	2	0	6	.381	.317
Walls, Doug, Car.*	.480	26	30	25	4	12	13	1	0	0	5	2	2	0	1	0	3	0	0	1	.520	.464
Walters, Brett, Mob.	.500	9	2	2	0	1	1	0	0	0	0	0	0	0	0	0	0	0	0	0	.500	.500
Watkins, Pat, Car.	.298	88	346	312	38	93	131	27	1	3	40	1	3	6	24	0	49	6	5	3	.420	.357
Wells, Vernon, Knox.	.340	26	120	106	18	36	55	6	3	2	17	0	2	0	12	1	15	6	2	0	.519	.400
Wilcox, Luke, Orl.*	.270	90	375	333	60	90	176	24	1	20	64	0	4	3	35	0	54	3	2	9	.529	.341
Williams, Glenn, Gre.	.225	57	217	204	19	46	69	11	0	4	15	1	1	4	7	1	58	1	4	2	.338	.264
Williams, Jason, Chat.	.319	87	389	332	65	106	158	27	2	7	45	1	4	6	46	2	40	3	4	9	.476	.407
Williamson, Antone, Hun.*	.342	12	46	38	5	13	16	3	0	0	6	0	0	1	7	0	6	3	0	1	.421	.457
Wilson, Tom, Orl.	.288	30	126	104	12	30	53	2	0	7	23	0	1	3	18	0	34	0	0	3	.510	.405
Winkelsas, Joe, Gre.	.000	55	2	2	0	0	0	0	0	0	0	0	0	0	0	0	0	0	0	0	.000	.000
Wunsch, Kelly, Hun.*	.000	22	5	5	0	0	0	0	0	0	0	0	0	0	0	0	4	0	0	0	.000	.000
Yankosky, L.J., Gre.	.160	20	25	25	1	4	5	1	0	0	0	0	0	0	0	0	6	0	0	0	.200	.160
Yoder, Jeff, W.T.*	.000	29	20	15	1	0	0	0	0	0	0	3	0	0	2	0	7	0	0	0	.000	.118
Young, Danny, W.T.	.000	27	8	7	0	0	0	0	0	0	0	1	0	0	0	0	6	0	0	0	.000	.000
Zamarripa, Mark, Car.	.000	5	3	2	1	0	0	0	0	0	0	0	0	1	0	0	1	0	0	0	.000	.333
Zuleta, Julio, W.T.	.295	133	545	482	75	142	250	37	4	21	97	0	8	20	35	6	122	4	3	11	.519	.361

GRAND SLAMS: Barthol, Becker, Berry, Cancel, Crede, J. Davis, Diaz, Florez, Glavine, Giles, W. Gonzalez, Horn, Huff, Inglin, Jennings, A. Johnson, Klimek, Kominek, Lemonis, Luzinski, Maculatus, Pemberton, Pimentel, Pomierski, Salzano, Thrower, Walker, Wilcox, 1 each.

AWARDED FIRST BASE ON CATCHER'S INTERFERENCE: Bair 3 (Morris, Cancel, Lidle); Airoso 2 (Barthol, Vidal); Speed 2 (Cancel, Alfano); Butler (Hall); Barthol (Morris); Klimek (Paul); Newstrom (Cardona); Saunders (Cancel); Goodell (King); Carr (Newstrom); Pomierski (Cardona); Clark (Cardona); Azuaje (Barthol); Nicholson (Barthol); Johnson (Lawrence).

PLAYERS WITH TWO OR MORE TEAMS

Player, Team	Avg.	G	TPA	AB	R	H	TB	2B	3B	HR	RBI	SH	SF	HP	BB	IBB	SO	SB	CS	GDP	Slg.	OBP
Brock, Tarrik, Car.	.248	66	260	218	40	54	87	10	1	7	23	1	1	1	39	0	67	7	4	2	.399	.363
Brock, Tarrik, W.T.*	.217	54	224	189	29	41	62	10	4	1	9	1	1	0	33	1	60	9	4	0	.328	.332

Player, Team	Avg.	G	TPA	AB	R	H	TB	2B	3B	HR	RBI	SH	SF	HP	BB	IBB	SO	SB	CS	GDP	Slg.	OBP
Eddie, Steve, Chat.	.190	6	22	21	2	4	4	0	0	0	2	0	1	0	0	0	3	0	0	1	.190	.182
Eddie, Steve, Birm.	.199	46	153	136	13	27	38	8	0	1	10	3	2	0	12	0	27	0	3	5	.279	.260
Giron, Isabel, Knox.	.000	17	0	0	0	0	0	0	0	0	0	0	0	0	0	0	0	0	0	0	.000	.000
Giron, Isabel, Mob.	.083	11	13	12	1	1	2	1	0	0	2	1	0	0	0	0	6	0	0	0	.167	.083
Luzinski, Ryan, Chat.	.246	55	198	171	17	42	58	10	0	2	26	1	1	1	24	2	43	1	2	4	.339	.340
Luzinski, Ryan, Mob.	.371	22	78	62	11	23	33	10	0	0	4	1	1	1	13	0	15	0	0	2	.532	.481

1999 PITCHING
TEAM

Team	W	L	Pct.	ERA	G	CG	ShO	Sv.	IP	H	TBF	R	ER	HR	SH	SF	HB	BB	IBB	SO	WP	Bk.
West Tenn	84	57	.596	3.58	141	8	9	45	1230.2	1115	5323	579	489	89	39	52	48	590	38	1133	83	7
Birmingham	73	67	.521	3.81	140	6	8	31	1207.1	1108	5158	592	511	103	27	37	69	475	4	876	76	9
Chattanooga	78	62	.557	4.23	140	3	8	35	1241.1	1308	5426	682	583	98	44	35	36	533	21	948	73	10
Jacksonville	75	66	.532	4.28	141	6	8	39	1252.1	1280	5471	710	595	126	30	42	66	466	9	877	41	10
Carolina	60	80	.429	4.32	140	8	7	38	1197.0	1249	5309	685	575	109	59	35	67	489	7	1020	78	14
Huntsville	64	77	.454	4.49	141	8	7	27	1240.2	1299	5461	724	619	146	44	42	81	503	23	833	79	12
Knoxville	71	69	.507	4.76	140	4	9	32	1222.1	1300	5401	757	646	114	35	48	54	549	8	974	68	13
Orlando	70	68	.507	4.78	138	5	11	33	1200.1	1259	5286	742	638	130	25	34	77	469	16	953	66	19
Greenville	58	80	.420	4.98	138	4	6	30	1185.2	1279	5384	763	656	129	40	48	61	588	42	920	63	12
Mobile	66	73	.475	5.09	139	7	6	30	1214.2	1334	5398	772	687	155	41	52	54	493	26	874	67	4

INDIVIDUAL

TOP QUALIFIERS FOR EARNED-RUN AVERAGE TITLE

Minimum 112 innings. *Lefthanded pitcher.

Pitcher, Team	W	L	Pct.	ERA	G	GS	CG	ShO	GF	Sv.	IP	H	TBF	R	ER	HR	SH	SF	HB	BB	IBB	SO	WP	Bk.
Yoder, Jeff, W.T.	10	5	.667	3.08	29	22	0	0	1	0	134.1	115	574	54	46	10	2	6	5	70	5	109	5	1
Roberts, Mark, Birm.	5	8	.385	3.40	33	17	0	0	7	2	124.1	108	525	64	47	11	3	7	3	41	0	84	3	0
Secoda, Jason, Birm.	8	7	.533	3.44	22	17	1	1	0	0	115.0	100	477	49	44	7	2	4	8	39	0	94	8	1
Santos, Victor, Jack.	12	6	.667	3.49	28	28	2	1	0	0	173.0	150	722	86	67	16	1	5	7	58	2	146	3	0
Chantres, Carlos, Birm.	6	8	.429	3.50	28	21	1	0	5	2	141.1	122	596	64	55	13	1	7	7	61	0	105	9	1
Darwin, David, Jack.*	14	12	.538	3.56	28	28	3	1	0	0	187.1	194	813	95	74	19	1	6	11	58	1	100	2	0
Walls, Doug, Car.	10	9	.526	3.65	26	26	2	1	0	0	150.1	159	642	74	61	14	10	4	4	44	0	140	6	1
Myette, Aaron, Birm.	12	7	.632	3.66	28	28	0	0	0	0	164.2	138	711	76	67	19	2	3	15	77	0	135	6	1
Martin, Chandler, Car.	13	8	.619	3.78	27	27	2	1	0	0	164.1	153	707	82	69	14	6	4	14	63	0	130	11	6
Lee, Derek, Hun.*	8	8	.500	3.86	26	21	4	2	0	0	140.0	143	604	70	60	16	6	2	8	51	4	77	5	1
Ortega, Pablo, Orl.	8	10	.444	3.87	22	22	1	1	0	0	130.1	147	567	77	56	14	3	9	8	47	3	74	4	3
Andrews, Clayton, Knox.*	10	8	.556	3.93	25	25	0	0	0	0	132.2	143	593	85	58	13	8	3	4	69	0	93	4	2
Manning, David, W.T.	8	5	.615	3.94	23	18	6	2	0	0	123.1	113	518	59	54	7	5	4	3	51	1	78	7	0
Dishman, Richard, Gre.	6	13	.316	4.19	30	24	0	1	0	1	139.2	146	613	76	65	19	6	4	7	58	0	131	5	0
Lopez, Rodrigo, Mob.	10	8	.556	4.41	28	28	2	1	0	0	169.1	187	728	91	83	14	4	6	7	58	3	138	5	1

DEPARTMENTAL LEADERS: W—Darwin, 14; L—Dishman, 13; Pct.—Levrault, .818; G—Enders, 60; GS—Belitz, Myette, Lopez, Santos, Darwin, 28 each; CG—Manning, 6; ShO—Manning, Lee, Herndon, 2 each; GF—Cordero, 43; Sv.—Cordero, 43; IP—Darwin, 187.1; H—Darwin, 194; TBF—Darwin, 813; R—Belitz, 114; ER—Belitz, 103; HR—Giron, 29; SH—Walls, 10; SF—Giron, Ortega, 9 each; HB—Myette, 15; BB—Crowell, 85; IBB—Manzano, Newman, Winkelsas, 6 each; SO—Santos, 146; WP—Mallard, 15; BK—Martin, 6.

ALL PITCHERS

*Lefthanded pitcher.

Pitcher, Team	W	L	Pct.	ERA	G	GS	CG	ShO	GF	Sv.	IP	H	TBF	R	ER	HR	SH	SF	HB	BB	IBB	SO	WP	Bk.
Adams, Terry, W.T.	0	0	.000	16.88	2	1	0	0	0	0	2.2	5	15	6	5	0	0	1	0	2	0	2	0	0
Agosto, Stevenson, Mob.*	3	3	.500	5.89	40	1	0	0	5	0	81.0	81	371	61	53	13	2	7	1	59	1	59	10	1
Akin, Jay, Hun.*	2	5	.286	4.18	46	1	0	0	12	0	84.0	93	374	51	39	9	3	2	4	31	3	62	1	2
Alberro, Jose, Jack.	0	0	.000	3.38	1	0	0	0	0	0	2.2	4	13	2	1	0	0	0	1	1	0	1	0	0
Anderson, Bill, Mob.	0	0	.000	7.00	4	4	0	0	0	0	18.0	20	83	14	14	2	1	1	1	13	0	19	1	0
Andrews, Clayton, Knox.*	10	8	.556	3.93	25	25	0	0	0	0	132.2	143	593	85	58	13	8	3	4	69	0	93	4	2
Aquino, Julio, Orl.	0	0	.000	18.47	5	0	0	0	2	0	6.1	18	38	15	13	3	0	1	2	0	0	4	3	0
Arroyo, Luis, Knox.*	0	0	.000	1.35	5	0	0	0	2	1	6.2	2	22	1	1	0	0	1	0	0	0	7	0	0
Atchley, Justin, Chat.*	4	9	.308	3.42	17	17	0	0	0	0	97.1	114	416	48	37	9	1	6	1	22	1	70	1	1
Averette, Robert, Chat.	2	1	.667	5.20	6	6	1	0	0	0	36.1	42	164	22	21	1	0	1	2	19	0	15	0	0
Bailey, Roger, Car.	3	0	1.000	7.00	4	4	0	0	0	0	18.0	21	86	16	14	2	2	1	2	10	0	14	2	0
Bale, John, Knox.*	2	2	.500	7.00	33	4	0	0	9	1	62.1	64	265	32	26	7	1	0	0	16	1	91	4	0
Barcelo, Lorenzo, Birm.	0	1	.000	3.60	4	4	0	0	0	0	20.0	14	79	8	8	0	1	2	1	6	0	14	0	0
Beasley, Ray, Gre.*	7	4	.636	4.63	50	0	0	0	22	3	81.2	84	349	45	42	8	2	4	3	26	5	71	3	1
Beck, Greg, Hun.	10	9	.526	4.45	26	25	0	0	1	0	151.2	157	648	79	75	24	5	7	8	48	1	93	12	0
Belitz, Todd, Orl.*	9	9	.500	5.77	28	28	0	0	0	0	160.2	169	712	114	103	23	3	6	11	65	1	118	2	4
Bell, Rob, Chat.	3	6	.333	3.13	12	12	2	1	0	0	72.0	75	293	30	25	7	2	2	0	17	0	68	1	0
Bevel, Bobby, Car.*	3	7	.300	4.43	48	0	0	0	22	7	67.0	70	294	37	33	7	4	1	2	27	2	58	9	0
Blanco, Alberto, Jack.*	3	2	.600	3.75	37	4	0	0	11	1	72.0	58	307	37	30	10	2	3	3	37	1	62	1	4
Bleazard, David, Knox.	5	3	.625	3.22	15	15	1	1	0	0	86.2	81	358	36	31	4	1	4	4	34	0	49	7	2
Bowers, Cedrick, Orl.*	6	9	.400	5.98	27	27	1	0	0	0	125.0	125	567	94	83	18	3	5	4	76	0	138	12	1
Bradford, Josh, Knox.	5	4	.556	5.31	34	12	0	0	6	2	105.0	109	465	65	62	9	1	4	5	53	1	83	11	0
Brester, Jason, Car.*	2	6	.250	5.76	11	11	0	0	0	0	59.1	71	268	45	38	8	1	1	2	26	0	44	3	3
Briggs, Anthony, Car.	0	1	.000	11.25	4	0	0	0	1	0	4.0	7	22	5	5	0	1	0	0	4	0	4	0	0
Brown, Elliot, Orl.	0	2	.000	7.71	10	1	0	0	0	0	18.2	25	89	18	16	2	0	1	0	12	0	12	3	0
Bruner, Clay, Jack.	1	3	.250	8.88	7	5	0	0	1	1	25.1	47	129	32	25	0	0	3	1	10	0	9	2	0
Bullard, Jason, Gre.	0	1	.000	18.78	5	0	0	0	1	0	7.2	16	53	18	16	2	0	1	1	12	2	5	1	0
Butler, Adam, Gre.*	1	3	.250	7.65	27	0	0	0	12	1	42.1	71	215	44	36	7	4	3	5	12	1	29	1	0
Callaway, Mickey, Orl.	1	1	.500	4.50	2	2	0	0	0	0	10.0	15	44	6	5	1	0	0	0	2	0	7	1	0
Carlyle, Ken, Gre.	1	6	.143	5.93	17	12	0	0	2	0	71.1	89	346	60	47	11	1	1	4	42	4	33	5	0
Chantres, Carlos, Birm.	6	8	.429	3.50	28	21	1	0	5	2	141.1	122	596	64	55	13	1	7	7	61	0	105	9	1

Pitcher, Team	W	L	Pct.	ERA	G	GS	CG	ShO	GF	Sv.	IP	H	TBF	R	ER	HR	SH	SF	HB	BB	IBB	SO	WP	Bk.
Chavez, Carlos, Hun.	0	3	.000	10.64	13	3	0	0	6	0	22.0	37	116	27	26	5	0	2	2	13	0	12	3	0
Cole, Victor, W.T.	3	1	.750	3.91	17	0	0	0	8	0	23.0	21	103	11	10	2	0	1	0	18	0	17	2	0
Colmenares, Luis, Car.	0	0	.000	8.10	8	0	0	0	1	0	10.0	16	52	9	9	2	2	0	0	8	0	10	1	0
Converse, Jim, Hun.	1	1	.500	2.86	16	0	0	0	15	5	22.0	14	87	8	7	2	0	2	1	7	0	25	1	0
Cordero, Francisco, Jack.	4	1	.800	1.38	47	0	0	0	43	27	52.1	35	218	9	8	3	2	0	3	22	0	58	3	0
Crowell, Jim, Chat.*	10	5	.667	5.10	27	27	0	0	0	0	148.1	173	690	98	84	12	5	6	4	85	0	80	3	0
Cruz, Charlie, Gre.*	1	0	1.000	3.45	11	0	0	0	4	1	15.2	23	77	6	6	1	0	2	1	9	1	11	0	0
D'Amico, Jeff, Hun.	0	1	.000	36.00	1	1	0	0	0	0	2.0	6	15	8	8	3	0	0	1	2	0	2	0	0
Daneker, Pat, Birm.	6	8	.429	3.22	16	16	3	0	0	0	109.0	106	451	46	39	6	2	2	2	30	1	71	4	2
Daniels, John, Orl.	3	2	.600	1.90	38	0	0	0	30	14	52.0	33	208	14	11	2	1	3	4	15	3	40	3	1
Darwin, David, Jack.*	14	12	.538	3.56	28	28	3	1	0	0	187.1	194	813	95	74	19	1	6	11	58	1	100	2	0
Davenport, Joe, Birm.	3	5	.375	3.10	40	0	0	0	33	10	49.1	43	213	26	17	3	4	3	2	19	1	24	8	0
Dawley, Joey, Gre.	5	3	.625	4.03	26	11	0	0	2	0	91.2	76	387	54	41	5	3	4	3	37	3	89	3	2
Dawsey, Jason, Hun.*	1	0	1.000	9.00	4	4	0	0	0	0	18.0	22	83	18	18	6	0	0	0	10	0	8	0	0
Delgado, Ernie, Knox.	4	1	.800	3.51	31	0	0	0	12	0	51.1	49	219	27	20	1	1	3	1	23	0	33	5	0
DeWitt, Scott, Car.*	1	2	.333	3.92	45	0	0	0	15	2	66.2	84	309	34	29	2	3	2	4	21	1	65	6	1
Dishman, Richard, Gre.	6	13	.316	4.19	30	24	1	0	1	1	139.2	146	613	76	65	19	6	4	7	58	0	131	5	0
Dixon, Tim, Hun.*	0	0	.000	2.75	24	1	0	0	15	6	39.1	33	174	16	12	3	2	2	4	19	0	43	2	0
Donaldson, Bo, Chat.	5	3	.625	2.98	38	0	0	0	19	6	51.1	30	199	18	17	2	3	1	1	16	2	67	2	1
Doughty, Brian, Mob.	8	10	.444	4.77	36	15	0	0	3	1	137.2	161	591	85	73	20	7	4	3	29	1	69	1	0
Downs, Scott, W.T.*	8	1	.889	1.35	13	12	1	0	0	0	80.0	56	319	13	12	2	1	0	1	28	0	101	1	0
Drumheller, Al, Mob.*	5	2	.714	4.33	12	12	0	0	0	0	68.2	78	304	40	33	7	4	3	2	29	2	55	4	0
Duncan, Courtney, W.T.	1	7	.125	7.13	11	8	0	0	2	0	41.2	44	210	42	33	3	2	6	2	42	4	42	8	0
Eldred, Cal, Hun.	0	1	.000	7.50	2	2	1	0	0	0	12.0	13	55	10	10	2	0	0	2	3	0	10	0	0
Enders, Trevor, Orl.*	8	2	.800	3.30	60	0	0	0	11	1	95.1	86	394	37	35	4	3	5	2	33	1	63	5	0
Estes, Eric, Mob.	0	1	.000	10.90	8	2	0	0	5	0	17.1	33	93	22	21	5	1	2	0	9	0	4	4	0
Etler, Todd, Chat.	0	0	.000	2.35	14	0	0	0	3	0	23.0	17	94	6	6	1	0	1	1	8	0	26	0	0
Fennell, Barry, W.T.*	0	0	.000	0.00	1	0	0	0	0	0	1.1	2	6	0	0	0	0	0	0	1	1	0	0	0
Flach, Jason, Gre.	1	2	.333	6.63	12	2	0	0	4	1	36.2	44	163	29	27	4	3	3	3	10	0	15	1	0
Flury, Pat, Chat.	1	1	.500	2.87	43	0	0	0	21	15	53.1	36	221	20	17	2	5	0	1	31	0	69	4	1
Fogg, Josh, Birm.	3	2	.600	5.89	10	10	0	0	0	0	55.0	66	249	37	36	8	1	2	5	18	0	40	2	1
Forney, Rick, Gre.	3	3	.500	2.99	12	12	0	0	0	0	72.1	67	291	27	24	5	4	1	2	19	1	70	0	0
Fraraccio, Dan, Orl.	0	0	.000	9.00	2	0	0	0	2	0	2.0	4	10	2	2	0	0	0	0	0	0	1	1	0
Garcia, Apostol, Jack.	0	0	.000	0.00	3	0	0	0	2	0	4.1	0	14	0	0	0	0	0	1	0	0	4	0	0
Gardner, Lee, Orl.	0	0	.000	9.00	1	0	0	0	0	0	2.0	3	9	2	2	0	0	0	1	0	0	1	0	0
Garland, Jon, Birm.	3	1	.750	4.38	7	7	0	0	0	0	39.0	39	175	22	19	4	2	1	3	18	0	27	4	0
Giron, Isabel, Knox.-Mob.	11	12	.478	5.46	28	27	0	0	0	0	158.1	168	696	108	96	29	4	9	8	54	1	126	3	1
Gissell, Chris, W.T.	3	8	.273	5.99	20	18	0	0	0	0	97.2	121	470	76	65	10	4	6	10	62	3	57	9	2
Glauber, Keith, Chat.	5	0	1.000	1.98	7	7	0	0	0	0	50.0	42	193	12	11	0	1	1	2	8	0	26	3	1
Glover, Gary, Knox.	8	2	.800	3.56	13	13	1	0	0	0	86.0	70	346	39	34	5	2	1	4	27	0	77	4	0
Goldsmith, Gary, Jack.	3	4	.429	3.87	33	5	0	0	10	2	79.0	84	337	35	34	8	3	4	6	24	0	30	4	0
Gonzalez, Jeremi, W.T.	0	0	.000	1.74	3	3	0	0	0	0	10.1	7	46	2	2	0	1	0	1	9	0	12	0	0
Gonzalez, Lariel, Car.	2	1	.667	5.29	30	0	0	0	24	14	34.0	39	167	27	20	4	4	1	1	22	0	41	8	0
Gordon, Mike, Hun.	0	1	.000	0.00	7	0	0	0	6	0	6.1	8	35	8	0	0	0	0	0	7	2	5	0	0
Guzman, Domingo, Mob.	1	2	.333	5.47	41	0	0	0	21	6	51.0	60	240	33	31	2	3	3	5	25	1	38	3	0
Hackman, Luther, Car.	4	3	.571	4.04	11	10	0	0	0	0	62.1	53	271	33	28	4	2	1	4	28	0	50	4	0
Haring, Brett, Chat.*	2	1	.667	3.72	7	4	0	0	0	0	36.1	46	159	18	15	1	3	0	0	12	0	15	2	0
Harper, Travis, Orl.	6	3	.667	5.38	14	14	1	1	0	0	72.0	73	319	45	43	10	0	5	10	26	0	68	7	0
Harris, D.J., Knox.	0	4	.333	7.05	25	4	0	0	6	0	60.0	73	283	50	47	9	0	3	2	31	0	36	3	0
Harrison, Tommy, Gre.	3	7	.300	7.39	16	12	0	0	0	0	63.1	75	311	59	52	11	2	3	7	43	1	42	5	2
Hart, Len, Mob.*	0	0	.000	3.38	2	0	0	0	1	0	2.2	4	14	1	1	0	0	0	0	2	0	4	0	0
Hartshorn, Ty, Knox.	4	1	.800	4.79	10	7	0	0	0	0	47.0	60	206	32	25	4	0	3	4	15	0	24	0	0
Hartvigson, Chad, Car.*	0	5	.000	6.28	30	0	0	0	17	1	43.0	48	193	35	30	6	2	3	0	11	1	32	1	0
Hawkins, Al, Hun.	8	9	.471	5.33	19	19	0	0	0	0	99.2	126	447	71	59	10	1	6	10	29	2	56	14	1
Helmer, Chad, Hun.	1	0	1.000	8.38	7	0	0	0	3	0	9.2	15	56	12	9	1	0	1	0	9	0	7	2	0
Henderson, Ryan, Hun.	2	0	1.000	0.63	12	0	0	0	10	6	14.1	12	59	2	1	0	0	0	6	1	13	2	0	0
Hendrickson, Mark, Knox.*	2	7	.222	6.63	12	11	0	0	0	0	55.2	73	254	46	41	4	2	0	2	21	0	39	2	1
Hernandez, Elvin, W.T.	9	9	.500	4.94	29	25	1	1	1	1	151.1	174	637	100	83	16	4	7	6	50	3	98	10	0
Hernandez, Santos, Orl.	5	4	.556	3.70	35	4	0	0	13	5	56.0	43	228	31	23	5	3	1	2	15	0	47	1	0
Herndon, Junior, Mob.	10	9	.526	4.69	26	26	2	2	0	0	163.0	172	706	96	85	24	9	1	8	52	3	87	10	0
Hibbard, Billy, Knox.	0	0	.000	8.10	3	0	0	0	0	0	3.1	7	18	3	3	1	0	0	1	0	0	0	0	0
Hiljus, Erik, Jack.	1	0	1.000	1.04	10	0	0	0	3	0	17.1	5	65	4	2	1	3	1	1	5	0	28	1	1
Hite, Kevin, Mob.	2	4	.333	4.32	51	0	0	0	39	15	58.1	71	256	30	28	6	1	4	3	17	4	52	2	1
Huntsman, Scott, Hun.	1	4	.200	3.63	47	0	0	0	20	5	69.1	72	300	33	28	8	2	2	3	25	3	31	1	0
Iglesias, Mario, Birm.	5	3	.625	4.68	23	2	0	0	4	0	50.0	51	216	29	26	8	2	1	2	21	1	29	3	0
Iglesias, Mike, Gre.	0	3	.000	7.07	4	4	0	0	0	0	14.0	19	66	11	11	2	0	1	0	6	0	5	1	0
Jacobs, Ryan, Car.*	6	12	.333	5.29	28	21	0	0	2	0	114.0	120	535	76	67	10	6	4	8	68	1	89	5	0
Janzen, Marty, Chat.	1	3	.250	4.94	30	4	0	0	7	0	54.2	54	246	32	30	6	4	1	7	29	4	41	5	0
Johnston, Doug, Hun.	7	11	.389	5.01	21	21	1	0	0	0	118.2	128	516	72	66	17	5	3	9	43	3	80	5	1
Kaufman, John, Orl.*	1	3	.250	8.83	21	2	0	0	5	0	35.2	54	172	39	35	3	2	0	14	10	0	22	0	0
Keagle, Greg, Jack.	4	2	.667	2.85	9	9	1	0	0	0	53.2	58	238	22	17	4	0	1	1	22	0	28	1	2
Kelley, Rich, Hun.*	1	3	.250	5.72	25	0	0	0	12	3	28.1	30	123	19	18	3	2	0	3	8	0	26	1	1
Kent, Nathan, Gre.	0	0	.000	18.00	1	0	0	0	0	0	1.0	1	6	2	2	1	0	0	0	2	0	2	0	0
Kolb, Brandon, Mob.	0	2	.000	0.79	7	0	0	0	6	2	11.1	8	52	4	1	0	1	0	1	4	0	14	1	0
Lakman, Jason, Birm.	0	0	.000	15.00	3	0	0	0	2	0	3.0	3	22	5	5	0	0	0	2	9	0	3	5	0
Lee, David, Car.	0	0	.000	1.04	16	0	0	0	15	10	17.1	8	63	3	2	1	0	0	1	3	0	16	0	0
Lee, Derek, Hun.*	8	8	.500	5.72	26	21	4	2	0	0	140.0	143	640	70	60	16	6	2	8	51	4	77	5	1
Levrault, Allen, Hun.	9	2	.818	3.43	16	16	2	1	0	0	99.2	77	404	44	38	11	3	2	5	33	0	82	3	3
LeBlanc, Eric, Chat.	3	3	.500	3.84	15	9	0	0	2	0	65.2	63	271	33	28	7	4	1	1	20	1	37	2	0
LeRoy, John, Orl.	0	0	.000	4.50	4	0	0	0	2	0	6.0	7	30	3	3	2	0	0	0	5	0	5	0	0
Lidle, Kevin, Mob.	0	0	.000	9.00	1	0	0	0	1	0	1.0	1	4	1	1	1	0	0	0	0	0	0	0	0
Lopez, Rodrigo, Mob.	10	8	.556	4.41	28	28	2	1	0	0	169.1	187	728	91	83	14	4	6	7	58	3	138	5	1
Lowe, Benny, Knox.*	4	6	.400	5.14	58	0	0	0	19	3	68.1	68	309	44	39	8	6	4	3	40	0	70	7	0
MacRae, Scott, Chat.	8	7	.533	4.42	39	17	0	0	6	0	128.1	139	555	76	63	18	3	2	5	49	1	81	6	0
Mallard, Randi, Chat.	4	5	.444	6.78	14	14	0	0	0	0	71.2	92	342	61	54	7	2	2	2	45	0	45	15	2

CLASS AA Southern League

Pitcher, Team	W	L	Pct.	ERA	G	GS	CG	ShO	GF	Sv.	IP	H	TBF	R	ER	HR	SH	SF	HB	BB	IBB	SO	WP	Bk.
Manias, James, Chat.*	0	0	.000	0.00	1	0	0	0	0	0	0.2	0	2	0	0	0	0	0	0	0	0	0	0	0
Mann, Jim, Knox.	1	2	.333	0.93	6	0	0	0	4	0	9.2	6	39	2	1	3	1	2	1	0	0	12	0	0
Manning, David, W.T.	8	5	.615	3.94	23	18	6	2	0	0	123.1	113	518	59	54	7	5	4	3	51	1	78	7	0
Manon, Julio, Orl.	3	3	.500	5.10	30	5	0	0	8	0	67.0	80	303	43	38	9	0	1	2	23	0	53	3	0
Manzano, Adrian, Gre.	5	2	.714	3.21	42	0	0	0	6	2	61.2	61	267	24	22	6	4	2	2	22	6	51	1	0
Maroth, Mike, Jack.*	1	2	.333	4.79	4	4	0	0	0	0	20.2	27	96	15	11	2	1	1	0	7	0	10	1	0
Marquis, Jason, Gre.	3	4	.429	4.58	12	12	1	0	0	0	55.0	52	248	33	28	7	0	1	2	29	0	35	1	0
Martin, Chandler, Car.	13	8	.619	3.78	27	27	2	1	0	0	164.1	153	707	82	69	14	6	4	14	63	0	130	11	6
Martinez, Romulo, Jack.	3	7	.300	4.98	52	0	0	0	16	1	72.1	85	325	48	40	5	6	2	3	21	2	46	2	0
Maurer, Dave, Mob.*	4	4	.500	3.63	54	0	0	0	33	3	72.0	59	301	30	29	7	1	4	3	26	5	59	6	0
McClellan, Sean, Knox.	1	0	1.000	3.48	14	0	0	0	4	1	20.2	18	88	8	8	1	1	1	0	11	0	24	0	0
Merrell, Phil, Chat.	2	2	.500	6.62	7	7	0	0	0	0	35.1	47	166	32	26	3	3	2	2	14	1	15	6	0
Meyer, Jake, Chat.	2	2	.500	5.96	20	0	0	0	10	0	22.2	24	102	17	15	1	0	1	0	14	0	16	4	0
Meyers, Mike, W.T.	4	0	1.000	1.09	5	5	0	0	0	0	33.0	21	128	5	4	1	1	1	0	10	1	51	1	0
Middlebrook, Jason, Mob.	4	6	.400	8.06	13	13	0	0	0	0	63.2	78	302	59	57	9	1	5	8	30	1	38	5	0
Milburn, Adam, Gre.*	1	0	1.000	4.74	14	0	0	0	9	0	19.0	23	85	10	10	2	0	0	1	7	1	10	1	1
Miles, Chad, Jack.*	3	2	.600	6.14	45	0	0	0	23	0	58.2	78	285	49	40	9	0	3	2	30	0	50	7	0
Miller, Matt, Jack.*	4	1	.800	4.43	7	7	0	0	0	0	40.2	43	176	23	20	3	3	1	2	12	0	25	0	0
Minor, Blas, Hun.	0	1	.000	9.39	2	2	0	0	0	0	7.2	11	39	12	8	3	0	0	0	5	0	6	1	0
Moss, Damian, Gre.*	1	3	.250	8.54	7	7	0	0	0	0	32.2	50	171	33	31	6	0	3	2	21	0	22	8	0
Myette, Aaron, Birm.	12	7	.632	3.66	28	28	0	0	0	0	164.2	138	711	76	67	19	2	3	15	77	0	135	6	1
Morris, Jim, Orl.*	0	1	.000	1.80	3	0	0	0	2	1	5.0	6	22	1	1	0	0	0	1	0	0	6	1	1
Negrette, Richard, W.T.	1	0	1.000	5.40	3	0	0	0	2	0	3.1	3	15	2	2	1	0	0	0	2	0	2	1	0
Nelson, Joe, Gre.	1	1	.500	2.37	25	0	0	0	15	8	30.1	19	130	15	8	2	2	1	3	14	2	37	0	0
Newman, Eric, W.T.	5	3	.625	3.20	58	0	0	0	15	8	84.1	61	359	37	30	5	5	2	5	49	6	90	8	0
Nomo, Hideo, Hun.	1	0	1.000	0.00	1	1	0	0	0	0	7.0	5	24	0	0	0	0	0	0	1	0	7	0	0
Norris, Dax, Gre.	0	0	.000	0.00	2	0	0	0	2	0	2.1	1	10	0	0	0	0	0	0	3	0	0	1	0
Norton, Phillip, W.T.*	7	4	.636	2.39	14	13	0	0	0	0	86.2	72	365	32	23	5	3	4	3	42	4	81	9	0
Nunez, Maximo, Orl.	0	2	.000	3.46	26	0	0	0	18	9	26.0	23	121	11	10	2	1	1	3	17	0	19	0	0
Olsen, Jason, Birm.	1	3	.250	3.82	9	4	1	0	3	0	33.0	33	138	15	14	2	1	0	1	10	0	25	3	0
Ortega, Pablo, Orl.	8	10	.444	3.87	22	22	1	1	0	0	130.1	147	567	77	56	14	3	9	8	47	3	74	4	3
Paredes, Roberto, Hun.	2	3	.400	3.96	28	0	0	0	7	1	52.1	48	237	26	23	4	1	1	5	29	1	35	8	0
Passini, Brian, Hun.*	0	4	.000	3.62	8	8	0	0	0	0	37.1	33	160	19	15	2	1	3	2	19	1	22	4	0
Pearsall, J.J., Chat.*	3	1	.750	5.90	32	0	0	0	7	0	39.2	40	184	31	26	5	0	1	0	28	3	36	2	0
Pena, Jesus, Birm.*	3	2	.600	2.36	40	0	0	0	18	5	45.2	31	183	12	12	2	1	1	0	18	1	49	2	1
Pettyjohn, Adam, Jack.*	9	5	.643	4.69	20	20	0	0	0	0	126.2	134	548	75	66	13	3	5	8	35	0	92	4	0
Piersoll, Chris, W.T.	0	0	.000	0.63	8	1	0	0	4	1	14.1	12	57	1	1	0	1	0	0	3	0	14	2	0
Priebe, Kevin, Hun.*	0	0	.000	2.57	3	0	0	0	1	0	7.0	7	29	2	2	1	1	0	1	2	0	4	0	0
Priest, Eddie, Chat.*	4	3	.571	3.97	12	12	0	0	0	0	77.0	99	337	42	34	6	3	1	3	14	0	60	1	7
Pujals, Denis, Orl.	5	3	.625	3.86	42	0	0	0	9	0	72.1	82	316	35	31	6	2	6	6	19	3	39	6	0
Rain, Steve, W.T.	3	1	.750	1.59	40	0	0	0	39	24	45.1	32	188	9	8	3	0	2	1	16	3	55	5	1
Randall, Scott, Car.	5	8	.385	3.43	16	16	3	1	0	0	99.2	101	432	52	38	6	3	5	8	34	2	102	3	0
Rawitzer, Kevin, Car.*	3	2	.600	3.60	33	4	0	0	8	1	70.0	73	304	33	28	5	3	2	4	26	0	54	3	1
Reyes, Eddy, Orl.	1	3	.250	4.08	18	0	0	0	11	2	28.2	31	133	16	13	3	1	1	6	11	2	25	2	3
Ricken, Ray, Mob.	7	7	.500	5.37	20	19	3	1	0	0	110.2	122	496	73	66	15	2	2	0	55	0	67	5	0
Ricketts, Chad, W.T.	6	4	.600	3.09	57	0	0	0	26	8	67.0	55	275	25	23	8	3	1	2	21	4	80	1	0
Riedling, John, Chat.	9	5	.643	3.43	40	0	0	0	23	5	42.0	41	186	23	16	2	1	2	1	20	3	38	7	0
Rivette, Scott, Knox.	4	7	.364	3.81	56	0	0	0	33	10	78.0	85	341	40	33	2	1	3	5	29	4	74	7	2
Roberts, Chris, Car.*	5	4	.556	3.78	43	1	0	0	17	1	81.0	76	360	46	34	10	5	2	6	36	0	52	3	0
Roberts, Mark, Birm.	5	8	.385	3.40	33	17	0	0	7	2	124.1	108	525	64	47	11	3	7	3	41	0	84	3	0
Robertson, Rich, Car.*	3	2	.600	3.21	11	7	0	0	2	0	47.2	48	201	20	17	3	1	2	4	16	0	42	2	0
Romo, Greg, Jack.	2	2	.500	8.27	8	3	0	0	2	0	20.2	29	94	20	19	4	0	0	0	7	1	15	3	0
Rose, Ted, Chat.	2	0	1.000	4.24	13	0	0	0	4	2	17.0	17	75	8	8	2	0	1	2	9	1	23	0	0
Rossiter, Mike, Car.	0	1	.000	2.08	16	0	0	0	8	2	21.2	11	80	5	5	0	1	0	1	9	0	24	2	0
Rupe, Ryan, Orl.	2	2	.500	2.73	5	5	0	0	0	0	26.1	18	109	13	8	1	0	0	2	6	0	22	1	1
Ryan, B.J., Chat.*	2	1	.667	2.59	35	0	0	0	23	6	41.2	33	172	13	12	1	2	1	0	17	0	46	2	2
Ryan, Jason, W.T.	5	0	1.000	1.41	8	7	0	0	0	0	44.2	29	185	12	7	1	1	1	4	15	1	53	1	0
Sak, Jim, Mob.	4	1	.800	1.69	18	0	0	0	5	2	26.2	15	106	11	5	1	2	0	2	15	0	37	1	0
Salamon, John, Gre.	2	4	.333	8.29	28	1	0	0	5	1	42.1	42	207	41	39	7	4	3	2	42	2	41	6	2
Santos, Victor, Jack.	12	6	.667	3.49	28	28	2	1	0	0	173.0	150	722	86	67	16	1	5	7	58	2	146	3	0
Schaffer, Trevor, Knox.	1	3	.250	5.67	38	0	0	0	19	1	54.0	69	265	43	34	10	0	5	3	38	2	23	6	0
Schmack, Brian, Birm.	4	4	.500	3.43	43	0	0	0	26	6	63.0	60	270	31	24	3	2	1	8	18	0	56	6	0
Schutz, Carl, W.T.*	3	1	.750	4.38	40	0	0	0	12	1	51.1	54	239	30	25	4	1	4	4	30	2	46	6	0
Seay, Bobby, Orl.*	1	2	.333	7.94	6	6	0	0	0	0	17.0	22	85	15	15	2	0	0	1	15	0	16	4	2
Secoda, Jason, Birm.	8	7	.533	3.44	22	17	1	1	0	0	115.0	100	477	49	44	7	4	8	4	39	0	94	8	1
Seelbach, Chris, Gre.	3	2	.600	3.89	8	6	1	0	0	0	39.1	31	170	18	17	5	1	1	2	19	2	47	2	0
Serrano, Wascar, Mob.	2	3	.400	5.53	7	7	0	0	0	0	42.1	48	196	27	26	5	1	3	6	17	1	29	1	1
Shumate, Jacob, Gre.	3	4	.429	4.74	14	12	0	0	0	0	57.0	43	270	30	30	6	1	3	5	61	1	48	9	1
Skrmetta, Matt, Mob.	1	3	.250	6.27	25	1	0	0	9	1	37.1	42	181	28	26	3	1	2	3	24	1	45	5	0
Smith, Brian, Knox.	1	2	.333	5.14	29	0	0	0	21	13	35.0	42	154	25	20	4	0	1	3	6	0	27	2	1
Smith, Dan, W.T.*	5	3	.625	4.22	56	0	0	0	21	2	74.2	70	321	38	35	9	4	4	1	31	0	78	2	0
Smith, Keilan, Jack.	1	2	.333	6.61	19	0	0	0	5	0	31.1	35	156	25	23	5	1	4	4	23	0	24	2	0
Smith, Travis, Hun.	3	2	.600	5.87	7	7	0	0	0	0	38.1	40	171	27	25	3	2	2	0	18	0	23	6	1
Smoltz, John, Gre.	0	0	.000	4.50	2	1	0	0	0	0	4.0	5	18	2	2	0	0	0	0	1	0	7	0	0
Sneed, John, Knox.	3	1	.750	5.08	6	6	0	0	0	0	28.1	33	131	17	16	2	1	1	2	21	0	28	1	0
Snyder, Bill, Jack.	1	0	1.000	2.50	14	0	0	0	8	2	18.0	16	80	6	5	0	0	3	5	1	0	17	0	0
Steensira, Kennie, Gre.	2	1	.667	3.79	8	0	0	0	0	0	19.0	25	80	8	8	1	0	1	0	9	1	12	2	0
Steinmetz, Earl, Gre.	0	2	.000	6.75	6	2	0	0	2	0	10.2	13	57	9	8	1	0	1	1	16	1	6	1	0
Stevenson, Jason, Knox.	4	7	.364	6.24	21	19	1	0	0	0	92.1	99	429	69	64	8	2	5	2	57	0	73	4	4
Strong, Joe, Orl.	1	4	.200	5.68	11	7	2	0	3	0	38.0	40	163	24	24	6	1	1	0	18	1	34	0	1
Swartzbaugh, Dave, Jack.	0	4	.000	10.25	6	6	0	0	0	0	26.1	36	127	31	30	7	0	0	1	12	1	22	0	0
Szymborski, Tom, Mob.	1	0	1.000	5.40	6	0	0	0	3	0	6.2	10	37	4	4	1	0	1	9	5	0	3	0	0
Theodile, Robert, Hun.	3	7	.300	5.75	47	0	0	0	18	0	92.1	118	449	71	59	9	7	4	9	56	1	60	8	2
Therneau, Dave, Chat.	2	0	1.000	2.57	3	3	0	0	0	0	21.0	22	88	7	6	2	0	0	1	8	0	11	0	0
Tokarse, Brian, Birm.	0	1	.000	5.06	6	0	0	0	0	0	10.2	12	46	7	6	1	1	0	0	3	0	11	1	0

Pitcher, Team	W	L	Pct.	ERA	G	GS	CG	ShO	GF	Sv.	IP	H	TBF	R	ER	HR	SH	SF	HB	BB	IBB	SO	WP	Bk.
Tolar, Kevin, Chat.*	4	4	.500	4.97	47	1	0	0	16	1	54.1	61	262	32	30	2	2	2	0	45	4	60	4	0
Trippy, Joe, Gre.*	0	0	.000	14.54	5	0	0	0	5	0	4.1	10	25	7	7	0	0	1	0	3	0	1	0	0
Tucker, Julien, Birm.	2	1	.667	5.33	37	0	0	0	22	5	49.0	52	222	30	29	6	1	0	5	22	0	32	6	0
Valdes, Marc, Orl.	0	1	.000	5.87	2	2	0	0	0	0	7.2	7	32	5	5	2	1	0	2	2	0	5	0	0
VanEgmond, Tim, Hun.	0	1	.000	3.27	3	3	0	0	0	0	11.0	11	52	6	4	3	1	0	0	6	0	9	0	0
Vavrek, Mike, Car.*	1	5	.167	7.38	10	9	0	0	0	0	46.1	71	230	42	38	11	3	1	0	19	0	41	8	0
Villafuerte, Brandon, Jack.	0	2	.000	1.88	15	0	0	0	10	5	24.0	17	101	6	5	0	2	1	1	12	0	20	1	0
Vining, Ken, Birm.*	0	2	.000	9.26	3	3	0	0	0	0	11.2	20	62	16	12	1	0	1	1	9	0	8	0	1
Virchis, Adam, Birm.	0	0	.000	0.00	1	0	0	0	0	0	3.0	3	12	0	0	0	1	0	0	0	0	1	0	0
Walls, Doug, Car.	10	9	.526	3.65	26	26	2	1	0	0	150.1	159	642	74	61	14	10	4	4	44	0	140	6	1
Walters, Brett, Mob.	0	1	.000	5.40	9	0	0	0	2	0	13.1	13	64	8	8	3	1	0	1	9	2	12	1	0
Weaver, Jeff, Jack.	0	0	.000	3.00	1	1	0	0	0	0	6.0	5	22	2	2	0	0	0	0	0	0	6	0	0
Webb, Alan, Jack.*	9	9	.500	4.95	26	22	0	0	1	0	140.0	140	605	88	77	17	1	3	8	64	0	88	4	3
Wells, Kip, Birm.	8	2	.800	2.94	11	11	0	0	0	0	70.1	49	283	24	23	5	0	4	31	0	44	1	1
Wheeler, Dan, Orl.	3	0	1.000	3.26	9	9	0	0	0	0	58.0	56	236	27	21	7	0	2	4	8	0	53	1	1
Whitley, Curtis, Birm.*	4	2	.667	5.01	36	0	0	0	14	1	50.1	58	228	31	28	4	1	1	0	25	0	24	5	0
Winkelsas, Joe, Gre.	4	4	.500	3.75	55	0	0	0	40	12	62.1	71	280	32	26	5	2	0	2	30	6	38	3	1
Wohlers, Mark, Chat.	0	0	.000	16.20	2	0	0	0	0	0	1.2	1	9	3	3	1	0	0	0	3	0	3	3	0
Wunsch, Kelly, Hun.*	4	1	.800	1.95	22	3	0	0	7	1	50.2	40	204	13	11	1	1	1	4	23	1	35	0	0
Yankosky, L.J., Gre.	5	8	.385	4.24	20	20	1	0	0	0	108.1	122	489	70	51	5	1	4	3	43	3	62	3	1
Yennaco, Jay, Knox.	3	4	.429	6.60	8	8	1	0	0	0	43.2	52	193	34	32	9	2	0	0	17	0	30	0	0
Yoder, Jeff, W.T.	10	5	.667	3.08	29	22	0	0	1	0	134.1	115	574	54	46	10	2	6	5	70	5	109	5	1
Young, Danny, W.T.*	3	5	.375	3.28	27	8	0	0	2	0	60.1	48	258	25	22	2	1	2	0	38	0	67	5	3
Zamarripa, Mark, Car.	2	1	.667	4.43	5	4	0	0	0	0	20.1	20	93	11	10	0	0	2	14	0	12	1	2
Zambrano, Victor, Orl.	4	1	.778	4.59	40	4	0	0	12	1	82.1	92	379	55	42	5	1	2	9	38	2	81	6	1

COMBINATION SHUTOUTS: **Birmingham (7)**—Myette-Davenport, Chantres-Schmack-Pena, Secoda-Pena-Schmack-Davenport, Myette-Davenport, Wells-Roberts, Myette-Tokarse-Schmack, Fogg-Roberts-Schmack. **Carolina (4)**—Hackman-Hartvigson, Martin-Bevel-Lee, Martin-DeWitt, Zamarripa-Rawitzer-Rossiter. **Chattanooga (7)**—Glauber-Etler-Ryan, MacRae-Tolar, Glauber-Flury-Riedling, Crowell-Riedling-Flury, Atchley-Donaldson-Flury, Bell-Meyer-Janzen-Donaldson-Flury. **Greenville (6)**—Forney-Winkelsas, Yankosky-Dawley-Salamon-Winkelsas, Forney-Manzano-Nelson, Iglesias-Beasley-Manzano-Steinmetz-Nelson, Dawley-Manzano-Nelson, Marquis-Beasley-Salamon-Winkelsas. **Huntsville (4)**—Nomo-Huntsman, Passini-Paredes-Dixon, Hawkins-Huntsman-Dixon, Passini-Paredes. **Jacksonville (6)**—Webb-Goldsmith-Cordero, Blanco-Smith-Cordero, Webb-Cordero, Webb-Smith-Miles, Keagle-Cordero, Miller-Villafuerte-Snyder. **Knoxville (8)**—Andrews-Delgado-Smith, Bradford-Lowe-Smith, Glover-Rivette-Harris, Glover-Lowe-Smith, Andrews-Bale, Harris-Rivette, Stevenson-McClellan-Lowe-Rivette, Hendrickson-Bradford. **New Haven (4)**—Meche-Zimmerman, Anderson-Montane-Fitzgerald, Stark-Montane-Gryboski, Sweeney-Brosnan. **Mobile (2)**—Herndon-Sak-Maurer, Herndon-Guzman-Hite. **Orlando (9)**—Rupe-Enders-Pujals, Rupe-Enders-Daniels, Strong-Hernandez-Nunez, Manon-Nunez, Zambrano-Enders-Pujals, Belitz-Pujals, Bowers-Hernandez, Bowers-Reyes, Ortega-Nunez-Hernandez. **Reading (3)**—Coggin-Thomas-Dodd, Politte-Dodd, Bailie-Cedeno-Kershner. **West Tenn (6)**—Norton-Ricketts-Rain, Gonzalez-Gissell-Rain, Manning-Young-Ricketts-Rain, Downs-Newman, Downs-Ricketts, Downs-Ricketts.

NO-HIT GAME: Manning, West Tenn defeated Jacksonville, 1-0, July 22.

PITCHERS WITH TWO OR MORE TEAMS

Pitcher, Team	W	L	Pct.	ERA	G	GS	CG	ShO	GF	Sv.	IP	H	TBF	R	ER	HR	SH	SF	HB	BB	IBB	SO	WP	Bk.
Giron, Isabel, Knox.	7	5	.583	4.89	17	16	0	0	0	0	95.2	97	423	59	52	12	3	6	7	39	0	81	1	1
Giron, Isabel, Mob.	4	7	.364	6.32	11	11	0	0	0	0	62.2	71	273	49	44	17	1	3	1	15	1	45	2	0

1999 FIELDING

TEAM

Team	Pct.	G	PO	A	E	TC	DP	TP	PB	Team	Pct.	G	PO	A	E	TC	DP	TP	PB
West Tenn	.974	141	3692	1330	135	5157	119	1	22	Carolina	.969	140	3591	1426	159	5176	102	0	17
Birmingham	.973	140	3622	1424	142	5188	119	0	14	Mobile	.968	139	3644	1449	167	5260	126	1	12
Huntsville	.972	141	3722	1525	150	5397	133	0	30	Orlando	.968	138	3601	1341	163	5105	127	0	19
Chattanooga	.972	140	3724	1583	155	5462	160	0	26	Greenville	.968	138	3557	1445	168	5170	130	2	13
Knoxville	.971	140	3667	1412	149	5228	127	0	10	Jacksonville	.966	141	3757	1553	185	5495	129	0	17

INDIVIDUAL

FIRST BASEMEN

NOTE: All caps denotes fielding-percentage leader based on 70 games for catchers, 93 for all other non-pitchers and 112 innings for pitchers. *Throws lefthanded.

Player, Team	Pct.	G	PO	A	E	TC	DP
Anthony, Brian, Car.	.968	12	85	5	3	93	8
AUDE, Rich, Birm.	.995	107	884	46	5	935	85
Becker, Brian, Orl.	.992	127	1006	57	9	1072	110
Broussard, Benjamin, Chat.*	1.000	13	113	9	0	122	12
Cepeda, Jose, Gre.	1.000	1	1	0	0	1	0
Colina, Roberto, Orl.*	.961	18	115	8	5	128	10
Cripps, Bobby, Knox.	1.000	4	36	2	0	38	5
Curl, John, Mob.	.985	22	187	13	3	203	15
Eddie, Steve, Chat.-Birm.	1.000	21	116	8	0	124	12
Freire, Alejandro, Jack.	.980	33	259	28	6	293	18
Garcia, Guillermo, Chat.	1.000	1	6	1	0	7	2
Giles, Tim, Knox.	.992	102	831	75	7	913	91
Glavine, Mike, Gre.*	.994	64	487	44	3	534	47
Goodell, Steve, Gre.	.909	2	9	1	1	11	1
Hayes, Chris, Knox.	.882	2	13	2	2	17	1
Helms, Wes, Gre.	.984	30	226	18	4	248	23
Ibarra, Jesse, Jack.	.923	2	12	0	1	13	1
Jacobsen, Buck, Hun.	.961	13	112	11	5	128	10
Johnson, Adam, Gre.*	.990	15	91	10	1	102	10
Jones, Ryan, Jack.	.991	106	963	58	9	1030	93
Jorgensen, Randy, Mob.*	.991	58	498	34	5	537	50

Player, Team	Pct.	G	PO	A	E	TC	DP
Kirgan, Chris, Car.	.989	121	1010	91	12	1113	85
Kominek, Toby, Hun.	.991	48	427	24	4	455	49
Langaigne, Selwyn, Knox.*	1.000	2	3	2	0	5	0
Larkin, Stephen, Chat.*	.993	53	428	23	3	454	48
Lemonis, Chris, Jack.	1.000	2	29	0	0	29	2
Lindstrom, David, Jack.	1.000	1	2	1	0	3	0
Luzinski, Ryan, Chat.	1.000	2	5	2	0	7	2
Lydy, Scott, Birm.	1.000	3	16	0	0	16	0
Macalutas, Jon, Hun.	.991	75	617	57	6	680	55
Marrero, Oreste, Hun.*	.985	8	62	5	1	68	3
Melhuse, Adam, Knox.	.991	27	203	15	2	220	21
Moore, Brandon, Birm.	1.000	2	21	2	0	23	2
Mortimer, Mark, Gre.	1.000	1	3	0	0	3	0
Nevers, Tom, Chat.	.991	14	94	13	1	108	13
Newstrom, Doug, Birm.	.981	19	145	10	3	158	7
Norris, Dax, Gre.	.991	47	295	18	3	316	30
Owens, Jayhawk, Chat.	1.000	1	2	0	0	2	0
Paciorek, Pete, Mob.*	.989	62	499	32	6	537	44
Presto, Nick, Chat.	.990	10	95	6	1	102	15
Raleigh, Matt, Car.	.964	8	52	2	2	56	4
Rodriguez, Liu, Birm.	1.000	5	7	1	0	8	0
Rupp, Chad, Knox.	.943	5	32	1	2	35	3
Saunders, Chris, Chat.	.993	54	502	37	4	543	47
Stegall, Randy, Chat.	1.000	4	39	3	0	42	4
Strange, Mike, Knox.	.973	5	31	5	1	37	2
Tucci, Pete, Mob.	.875	1	7	0	1	8	1

Player, Team	Pct.	G	PO	A	E	TC	DP
Vieira, Scott, W.T.	.990	36	178	14	2	194	15
Walker, Ron, W.T.	1.000	2	1	0	0	1	0
Williamson, Antone, Hun.	.960	7	45	3	2	50	3
Zuleta, Julio, W.T.	.991	120	897	63	9	969	89

TRIPLE PLAYS: Glavine, Norris.

FIRST BASEMEN WITH TWO OR MORE TEAMS

Player, Team	Pct.	G	PO	A	E	TC	DP
Eddie, Steve, Chat.	1.000	1	10	1	0	11	1
Eddie, Steve, Birm.	1.000	20	106	7	0	113	11

SECOND BASEMEN

Player, Team	Pct.	G	PO	A	E	TC	DP
Abernathy, Brent, Knox.	.976	132	292	361	16	669	89
Almanzar, Richard, W.T.	.984	41	77	104	3	184	29
Azuaje, Jesus, Hun.	1.000	4	11	7	0	18	2
Badeaux, Brooks, Orl.	.000	1	0	0	0	0	0
Berry, Mike, Car.	.987	23	34	41	1	76	10
Bravo, Danny, Birm.	.972	29	47	56	3	106	9
Cairo, Miguel, Orl.	1.000	3	2	7	0	9	2
CARR, Dustin, Orl.	.977	123	273	332	14	619	98
Cepeda, Jose, Gre.	.969	56	80	138	7	225	32
Connacher, Kevin, Birm.	.963	7	13	13	1	27	1
Cruz, Luis, Orl.	1.000	7	7	6	0	13	0
Eaglin, Mike, Birm.	.937	21	20	39	4	63	8
Eddie, Steve, Chat.-Birm.	1.000	3	4	5	0	9	1
Faurot, Adam, Hun.	.909	2	3	7	1	11	1
Florez, Tim, Chat.	.992	31	48	69	1	118	19
Font, Franklin, W.T.	.971	20	33	34	2	69	10
Fraraccio, Dan, Orl.	.977	13	19	23	1	43	4
Gomez, Rudy, Knox.	.933	6	13	15	2	30	1
Goodell, Steve, Gre.	1.000	5	8	4	0	12	1
Kent, Robbie, Mob.	.957	63	124	144	12	280	37
King, Brett, W.T.	.944	9	9	8	1	18	3
Lackey, Steve, Gre.	.975	11	15	24	1	40	1
Lemonis, Chris, Jack.	.968	25	63	57	4	124	16
Livingston, Doug, Car.	.981	35	69	84	3	156	15
Lopez, Mickey, Hun.	.973	82	208	225	12	445	49
Mathis, Jared, Hun.	.962	12	27	23	2	52	7
McClure, Brian, Mob.	.982	45	100	113	4	217	31
Meyers, Chad, W.T.	.966	63	106	148	9	263	29
Nelson, Bry, W.T.	.989	23	43	45	1	89	13
Nevers, Tom, Chat.	.967	11	20	38	2	60	12
Pena, Elvis, Car.	.970	79	166	193	11	370	43
Pickler, Jeff, Hun.	.972	51	117	124	7	248	43
Pimentel, Jose, Gre.	.985	27	57	77	2	136	19
Polanco, Enohel, W.T.	1.000	7	7	12	0	19	2
Presto, Nick, Chat.	.925	14	29	45	6	80	11
Prieto, Rick, Mob.	1.000	1	0	1	0	1	0
Rexrode, Jackie, Birm.	.958	67	129	169	13	311	43
Rodriguez, Liu, Birm.	.981	39	86	72	3	161	18
Santana, Pedro, Jack.	.969	119	277	338	20	635	85
Schmidt, Bryan, Mob.	1.000	8	9	8	0	17	3
Stegall, Randy, Chat.	1.000	5	9	8	0	17	2
Strange, Mike, Knox.	.929	3	8	5	1	14	1
Thrower, Jake, Mob.	.941	37	59	85	9	153	13
Watkins, Pat, Car.	.964	17	24	29	2	55	4
Williams, Glenn, Gre.	.976	52	112	134	6	252	33
Williams, Jason, Chat.	.988	82	159	246	5	410	73

TRIPLE PLAYS: Kent, G. Williams.

SECOND BASEMEN WITH TWO OR MORE TEAMS

Player, Team	Pct.	G	PO	A	E	TC	DP
Eddie, Steve, Chat.	1.000	2	3	3	0	6	1
Eddie, Steve, Birm.	1.000	1	1	2	0	3	0

THIRD BASEMEN

Player, Team	Pct.	G	PO	A	E	TC	DP
Anthony, Brian, Car.	.928	24	12	52	5	69	0
Azuaje, Jesus, Hun.	.930	31	15	38	4	57	3
Balfe, Ryan, Mob.	.922	108	70	213	24	307	18
Berry, Mike, Car.	.883	63	28	116	19	163	9
Bravo, Danny, Birm.	.931	47	34	87	9	130	5
Cancel, Robinson, Hun.	1.000	4	5	4	0	9	0
Clark, Brady, Chat.	.000	1	0	0	1	1	0
Cotton, John, Car.	.854	36	22	54	13	89	3
Crede, Joe, Birm.	.910	72	68	133	20	221	10
Eberwein, Kevin, Mob.	.957	10	3	19	1	23	1
Eddie, Steve, Birm.	.922	28	17	54	6	77	4
Elliott, Dave, Hun.	.923	7	0	12	1	13	2
Faurot, Adam, Hun.	1.000	6	1	6	0	7	0
Florez, Tim, Chat.	1.000	1	0	1	0	1	0
Font, Franklin, W.T.	1.000	1	1	2	0	3	0
Fraraccio, Dan, Orl.	1.000	9	5	11	0	16	1

Player, Team	Pct.	G	PO	A	E	TC	DP
Garcia, Guillermo, Chat.	1.000	1	0	3	0	3	0
Gillespie, Eric, Jack.	.902	31	18	65	9	92	6
Gomez, Rudy, Knox.	.968	43	20	71	3	94	11
Gonzalez, Jimmy, Mob.	.500	1	1	1	2	4	2
Goodell, Steve, Gre.	.880	90	69	143	29	241	13
Hayes, Chris, Knox.	.895	17	7	27	4	38	3
Horn, Jeff, Gre.	.795	20	13	18	8	39	2
HUFF, Aubrey, Orl.	.927	133	93	273	29	395	23
Keck, Brian, Car.	1.000	3	2	7	0	9	0
Kent, Robbie, Mob.	.887	32	24	39	8	71	6
King, Brett, W.T.	1.000	1	0	1	0	1	0
Klimek, Josh, Hun.	.924	100	81	197	23	301	15
Larson, Brandon, Chat.	.885	42	22	93	15	130	8
Lawrence, Joe, Knox.	.910	67	29	112	14	155	14
Lemonis, Chris, Jack.	1.000	3	0	10	0	10	0
Lobaton, Jose, Hun.	.000	1	0	0	0	0	0
Luzinski, Ryan, Chat.	.778	5	3	11	4	18	0
Lydy, Scott, Birm.	1.000	2	1	1	0	2	0
Manning, Nate, Knox.	1.000	8	4	11	0	15	1
Mathis, Jared, Hun.	.950	9	8	11	1	20	2
Melhuse, Adam, Knox.	.913	6	6	15	2	23	2
Moore, Brandon, Birm.	1.000	3	0	9	0	9	1
Nelson, Bry, W.T.	.905	92	56	134	20	210	11
Nevers, Tom, Chat.	.910	22	12	49	6	67	8
Newstrom, Doug, Birm.	.333	1	0	1	2	3	0
Pimentel, Jose, Gre.	.910	38	22	69	9	100	2
Presto, Nick, Chat.	.750	3	0	6	2	8	1
Raleigh, Matt, Car.	.863	18	8	36	7	51	5
Rodriguez, Liu, Birm.	1.000	1	2	3	0	5	1
Salzano, Jerry, Chat.	.903	71	34	152	20	206	13
Sasser, Rob, Jack.	.911	109	82	276	35	393	27
Solano, Fausto, Knox.	.909	7	3	7	1	11	0
Stegall, Randy, Chat.	.000	1	0	0	0	0	0
Strange, Mike, Knox.	.917	5	3	8	1	12	0
Stromsborg, Ryan, Knox.	.500	2	1	1	2	4	0
Walker, Ron, W.T.	.888	62	32	87	15	134	10
Williams, Glenn, Gre.	1.000	5	1	11	0	12	1
Williamson, Antone, Hun.	1.000	4	5	10	0	15	0

SHORTSTOPS

Player, Team	Pct.	G	PO	A	E	TC	DP
Azuaje, Jesus, Hun.	.974	85	133	273	11	417	61
Badeaux, Brooks, Orl.	1.000	1	2	0	0	2	0
Bravo, Danny, Birm.	.966	12	10	46	2	58	8
Cruz, Luis, Orl.	1.000	1	0	2	0	2	0
Dawkins, Travis, Chat.	.979	32	52	89	3	144	22
Dellaero, Jason, Birm.	.948	80	138	227	20	385	39
De Los Santos, Eddy, Orl.	.928	128	155	344	39	538	75
Eddie, Steve, Chat.	1.000	1	1	2	0	3	0
Faurot, Adam, Hun.	.938	5	7	8	1	16	2
Font, Franklin, W.T.	.913	8	8	13	2	23	2
Fraraccio, Dan, Orl.	.907	15	21	28	5	54	10
Gomez, Rudy, Knox.	.924	44	68	102	14	184	22
Goodell, Steve, Gre.	1.000	11	19	30	0	49	6
Keck, Brian, Car.	1.000	1	1	4	0	5	0
Kent, Robbie, Mob.	.940	13	20	27	3	50	5
King, Brett, W.T.	.962	43	54	121	7	182	25
Klimek, Josh, Hun.	1.000	1	1	8	0	9	1
Lackey, Steve, Gre.	.926	71	111	203	25	339	44
Lawrence, Joe, Knox.	1.000	2	1	2	0	3	0
Lemonis, Chris, Jack.	.911	21	28	54	8	90	10
Livingston, Doug, Car.	1.000	2	1	0	0	1	0
Lobaton, Jose, Hun.	.910	35	37	85	12	134	8
Lopez, Mickey, Hun.	1.000	1	0	2	0	2	0
Martinez, Pablo, Gre.	.961	56	90	182	11	283	39
Mathis, Jared, Hun.	.962	29	42	83	5	130	15
McClure, Brian, Mob.	.000	1	0	0	0	0	0
Milliard, Ralph, Chat.	.963	29	44	87	5	136	22
Mitchell, Derek, Jack.	.936	123	155	361	35	551	67
Moore, Brandon, Birm.	.979	31	48	93	3	144	23
Nelson, Bry, W.T.	.833	5	3	2	1	6	0
Nevers, Tom, Chat.	.954	49	70	156	11	237	40
Nicholson, Kevin, Mob.	.948	126	187	402	32	621	75
Pena, Elvis, Car.	.983	29	40	74	2	116	12
Pimentel, Jose, Gre.	.941	5	3	13	1	17	3
Polanco, Enohel, W.T.	.948	103	146	237	21	404	53
Presto, Nick, Chat.	.929	37	61	97	12	170	24
Rodriguez, Liu, Birm.	.942	27	24	73	6	103	14
Schifano, Tony, Knox.	1.000	8	12	15	0	27	5
Schmidt, Bryan, Mob.	1.000	1	0	4	0	4	0
Solano, Fausto, Knox.	.948	93	157	265	23	445	58
SOSA, Juan, Car.	.958	114	191	361	24	576	62
Thrower, Jake, Mob.	.867	4	8	5	2	15	1
Watkins, Pat, Car.	.750	2	2	4	2	8	0

TRIPLE PLAYS: King, Martinez.

OUTFIELDERS

Player, Team	Pct.	G	PO	A	E	TC	DP
Airoso, Kurt, Jack.	.987	134	362	12	5	379	3
Bair, Rod, Car.	.977	121	209	7	5	221	1
Bowers, Brent, W.T.	.988	34	80	3	1	84	0
Bravo, Danny, Birm.	1.000	1	1	0	0	1	0
BROCK, Tarrik, Car.-W.T.*	.997	113	274	8	1	283	1
Broussard, Benjamin, Chat.*	.931	19	26	1	2	29	0
Brown, Roosevelt, W.T.	.983	33	52	5	1	58	0
Buccheri, Jim, Orl.	.975	38	77	2	2	81	1
Burress, Andy, Chat.	.957	52	85	5	4	94	0
Butler, Rob, Knox.*	.975	62	111	7	3	121	1
Cancel, Robinson, Hun.	.667	1	2	0	1	3	0
Candelaria, Ben, Jack.	.964	118	180	10	7	197	1
Carr, Dustin, Orl.	.000	1	0	0	0	0	0
Christensen, McKay, Birm.*	.990	74	190	2	2	194	0
Clark, Brady, Chat.	.985	133	255	10	4	269	2
Colina, Roberto, Orl.*	.947	18	18	0	1	19	0
Conner, Decomba, Chat.	.967	33	55	3	2	60	0
Cripps, Bobby, Knox.	.667	1	2	0	1	3	0
Cruz, Luis, Orl.	1.000	1	1	0	0	1	0
Curl, John, Mob.	.955	102	190	3	9	202	1
Diaz, Alejandro, Chat.	.987	55	144	5	2	151	2
DiPace, Danny, Hun.	1.000	7	9	0	0	9	0
Elliott, Dave, Hun.	.980	111	196	5	4	205	1
Faggett, Ethan, Mob.*	.971	125	293	11	9	313	2
Faurot, Adam, Hun.	1.000	2	3	0	0	3	0
Feuerstein, Dave, Car.	.973	84	134	11	4	149	0
Fraraccio, Dan, Orl.	.957	45	67	0	3	70	0
Freel, Ryan, Knox.	1.000	11	23	1	0	24	0
Freire, Alejandro, Jack.	1.000	4	9	0	0	9	0
Gazarek, Marty, W.T.	.960	33	47	1	2	50	0
Giles, Tim, Knox.	1.000	1	2	0	0	2	0
Gillespie, Eric, Jack.	.985	64	124	6	2	132	3
Glavine, Mike, Gre.*	.959	30	46	1	2	49	1
Gomez, Ramon, Birm.	.973	92	177	6	5	188	2
Gomez, Rudy, Knox.	1.000	8	11	0	0	11	0
Green, Chad, Hun.	.984	112	240	6	4	250	1
Hawkins, Kraig, Orl.	.978	91	129	6	3	138	0
Hayes, Chris, Knox.	1.000	17	37	3	0	40	0
Iapoce, Anthony, Hun.*	.980	27	50	0	1	51	0
Inglin, Jeff, Birm.	.978	105	166	9	4	179	1
Ingram, Darron, Chat.	.989	55	83	4	1	88	0
Jacobsen, Buck, Hun.	.881	28	37	0	5	42	0
Jennings, Robin, W.T.*	1.000	13	18	1	0	19	0
Johnson, A.J., Mob.	.981	28	51	2	1	54	0
Johnson, Adam, Gre.*	.972	91	164	9	5	178	4
Keck, Brian, Car.	1.000	1	2	0	0	2	0
King, Brad, W.T.	1.000	6	4	0	0	4	0
Kominek, Toby, Hun.	.987	83	147	10	2	159	2
Langaigne, Selwyn, Knox.*	.989	38	86	3	1	90	1
Larkin, Stephen, Chat.*	.905	14	18	1	2	21	0
Lemonis, Chris, Jack.	1.000	4	6	0	0	6	0
Light, Tal, Car.	.955	60	78	7	4	89	0
Lindsey, Rodney, Jack.	.929	7	12	1	1	14	0
Lindstrom, David, Jack.	1.000	6	6	1	0	7	0
Lobaton, Jose, Hun.	.000	2	0	0	0	0	0
Long, Ryan, Orl.	.833	7	14	1	3	18	0
Lydy, Scott, Birm.	.991	108	216	9	2	227	1
Macalutas, Jon, Hun.	1.000	6	7	0	0	7	0
Malave, Jose, Car.	1.000	39	50	2	0	52	0
Martinez, Greg, Hun.	1.000	22	49	0	0	49	0
Mathis, Jared, Hun.	.857	8	5	1	1	7	1
McNabb, Buck, Gre.	.977	20	41	2	1	44	0
Melhuse, Adam, Knox.	.973	44	66	5	2	73	1
Monds, Wonderful, Chat.	.972	70	132	9	4	145	1
Morenz, Shea, Mob.	1.000	6	9	0	0	9	0
Mortimer, Mark, Gre.	1.000	8	8	0	0	8	0
Mosquera, Julio, Orl.	1.000	2	2	0	0	2	0
Nelson, Bry, W.T.	1.000	15	17	1	0	18	0
Olson, Dan, Birm.*	.966	16	28	0	1	29	0
Pemberton, Rudy, Birm.	.960	13	23	1	1	25	0
Pendergrass, Tyrone, Gre.	.975	96	230	8	6	244	4
Pigott, Anthony, Orl.	1.000	3	3	0	0	3	0
Pimentel, Jose, Gre.	.949	40	72	2	4	78	0
Pomierski, Joe, Orl.	.972	56	99	7	3	109	1
Prieto, Rick, Mob.	.979	97	182	3	4	189	1
Ramirez, Dan, Birm.	.944	31	64	3	4	71	1
Rennhack, Mike, W.T.	.965	46	81	1	3	85	1
Riley, Marquis, Jack.	.963	43	78	0	3	81	0
Rivers, Jonathan, W.T.	.923	29	33	3	3	39	0
Rodriguez, Liu, Birm.	1.000	1	1	0	0	1	0
Rupp, Chad, Knox.	.986	42	71	2	1	74	0
Sanchez, Alex, Orl.*	.958	121	314	8	14	336	2
Schifano, Tony, Knox.	1.000	20	32	2	0	34	0

Player, Team	Pct.	G	PO	A	E	TC	DP
Smith, Demond, Gre.	.991	129	211	12	2	225	2
Sollmann, Scott, Hun.*	.982	50	106	1	2	109	1
Sosa, Juan, Car.	1.000	9	11	0	0	11	0
Speed, Dorian, W.T.	.980	116	197	2	4	203	0
Stromsborg, Ryan, Knox.	.976	97	194	7	5	206	0
Thompson, Andy, Knox.	.965	66	108	3	4	115	1
Trippy, Joe, Gre.*	.958	51	66	3	3	72	0
Tucci, Pete, Mob.	.975	78	156	2	4	162	0
Vieira, Scott, W.T.	.980	101	144	4	3	151	0
Wakeland, Chris, Jack.*	.944	54	97	4	6	107	0
Watkins, Pat, Car.	.973	69	107	3	3	113	1
Wells, Vernon, Knox.	1.000	26	56	4	0	60	3
Wilcox, Luke, Orl.	.972	71	132	5	4	141	1

TRIPLE PLAYS: Pendergrass, Smith.

OUTFIELDERS WITH TWO OR MORE TEAMS

Player, Team	Pct.	G	PO	A	E	TC	DP
Brock, Tarrik, Car.	1.000	61	138	2	0	140	0
Brock, Tarrik, W.T.*	.993	52	136	6	1	143	1

CATCHERS

Player, Team	Pct.	G	PO	A	E	TC	DP	PB
Ahrendt, Jay, Mob.	.974	8	34	3	1	38	0	0
Alfano, Jeff, Hun.	.985	73	416	49	7	472	2	23
Barthol, Blake, Car.	.983	92	656	53	12	721	2	13
Bravo, Danny, Birm.	1.000	1	0	1	0	1	0	0
Brito, Jorge, Hun.	.976	17	73	9	2	84	0	2
Cancel, Robinson, Hun.	.977	51	292	48	8	348	5	5
Cardona, Javier, Jack.	.983	88	565	58	11	634	7	13
Chiaffredo, Paul, Knox.	.980	11	88	8	2	98	0	0
Cripps, Bobby, Knox.	.974	6	35	3	1	39	0	3
Davis, James, Chat.	.971	13	88	12	3	103	1	1
Encarnacion, Angelo, W.T.	.992	29	221	25	2	248	1	1
Garcia, Guillermo, Chat.	1.000	5	29	5	0	34	1	0
Garcia, Neil, Orl.	.990	23	181	26	2	209	1	5
Gonzalez, Jimmy, Mob.	.968	16	81	9	3	93	1	2
Gonzalez, Wiklenman, Mob.	.982	52	329	43	7	379	3	5
Hall, Toby, Orl.	.986	37	261	27	4	292	5	5
Horn, Jeff, Gre.	.988	28	153	18	2	173	1	2
Hyde, Brandon, Birm.	.968	7	28	2	1	31	0	5
King, Brad, W.T.	.989	85	571	49	7	627	6	9
Lawrence, Tony, Chat.	.938	3	14	1	1	16	1	1
Levis, Jesse, Orl.	.982	7	52	4	1	57	0	0
Lidle, Kevin, Mob.	.981	53	310	48	7	365	3	3
Lindstrom, David, Jack.	.988	52	306	30	4	340	5	4
Loyd, Brian, W.T.	.980	102	740	80	17	837	3	5
Lunar, Fernando, Gre.	.986	96	611	88	10	709	12	9
Luzinski, Ryan, Chat.-Mob.	.988	69	443	42	6	491	8	12
Mathis, Jared, Hun.	.967	15	55	3	2	60	1	0
Melhuse, Adam, Knox.	1.000	7	35	1	0	36	0	2
Micucci, Mike, W.T.	.993	49	267	24	2	293	2	8
Miller, Corky, Chat.	.989	33	227	35	3	265	6	8
Molina, Jose, W.T.	.982	12	97	13	2	112	0	4
Mosquera, Julio, Orl.	.988	57	374	36	5	415	0	8
Newstrom, Doug, Birm.	.988	51	281	37	4	322	4	4
Norris, Dax, Gre.	.979	26	161	24	4	189	1	2
Owens, Jayhawk, Chat.	.985	44	311	26	5	342	3	5
PAUL, Josh, Birm.	.992	85	526	66	5	597	4	7
Petrick, Ben, Car.	.992	16	113	10	1	124	0	1
Probst, Alan, Knox.	.985	16	112	16	2	130	1	0
Quatraro, Matt, Orl.	1.000	1	9	3	0	12	0	0
Rivera, Mike, Jack.	1.000	7	46	4	0	50	1	0
Ryder, Derek, Birm.	.983	12	47	10	1	58	0	3
Snusz, Chris, Chat.	1.000	2	14	1	0	15	0	0
Vidal, Gilbert, Car.	.974	42	279	17	8	304	2	3
Wilson, Tom, Orl.	.971	20	121	15	4	140	0	1

CATCHERS WITH TWO OR MORE TEAMS

Player, Team	Pct.	G	PO	A	E	TC	DP	PB
Luzinski, Ryan, Chat.	.985	47	300	30	5	335	6	10
Luzinski, Ryan, Mob.	.994	22	143	12	1	156	2	2

PITCHERS

Player, Team	Pct.	G	PO	A	E	TC	DP
Adams, Terry, W.T.	.000	2	0	0	0	0	0
Agosto, Stevenson, Mob.*	.952	40	2	18	1	21	1
Akin, Jay, Hun.*	1.000	46	3	15	0	18	0
Alberto, Jose, Jack.	.000	1	0	0	0	0	0
Anderson, Bill, Mob.	1.000	4	0	1	0	1	0
Andrews, Clayton, Knox.*	.957	25	4	18	1	23	0
Aquino, Julio, Orl.	.000	5	0	0	0	0	0
Arroyo, Luis, Knox.*	1.000	5	0	1	0	1	0
Atchley, Justin, Chat.*	.941	17	2	14	1	17	0
Averette, Robert, Chat.	1.000	6	4	8	0	12	0

Player, Team	Pct.	G	PO	A	E	TC	DP
Bailey, Roger, Car.	.909	4	4	6	1	11	1
Bale, John, Knox.*	.875	33	3	4	1	8	0
Barcelo, Lorenzo, Birm.	1.000	4	3	1	0	4	0
Beasley, Ray, Gre.*	1.000	50	4	8	0	12	1
Beck, Greg, Hun.	1.000	26	12	11	0	23	0
Belitz, Todd, Orl.*	1.000	28	7	18	0	25	1
Bell, Rob, Chat.	1.000	12	4	14	0	18	2
Bevel, Bobby, Car.*	1.000	48	3	10	0	13	0
Blanco, Alberto, Jack.*	.929	37	4	9	1	14	1
Bleazard, David, Knox.	1.000	15	11	14	0	25	2
Bowers, Cedrick, Orl.*	.750	27	1	5	2	8	1
Bradford, Josh, Knox.	1.000	34	10	12	0	22	3
Brester, Jason, Car.*	.950	11	5	14	1	20	0
Briggs, Anthony, Car.	1.000	4	0	1	0	1	0
Brown, Elliot, Orl.	1.000	10	0	1	0	1	1
Bruner, Clay, Jack.	.857	7	1	5	1	7	1
Bullard, Jason, Gre.	.667	5	0	2	1	3	0
Butler, Adam, Gre.*	.857	27	0	6	1	7	0
Callaway, Mickey, Orl.	1.000	2	0	2	0	2	0
Carlyle, Ken, Gre.	.913	17	5	16	2	23	1
Chantres, Carlos, Birm.	.966	28	9	19	1	29	0
Chavez, Carlos, Hun.	1.000	13	0	5	0	5	1
Cole, Victor, W.T.	1.000	18	1	2	0	3	1
Colmenares, Luis, Car.	1.000	8	0	1	0	1	0
Converse, Jim, Hun.	.800	16	1	3	1	5	0
Cordero, Francisco, Jack.	1.000	47	1	8	0	9	1
CROWELL, Jim, Chat.*	1.000	27	7	27	0	34	4
Cruz, Charlie, Gre.*	1.000	11	1	1	0	2	0
D'Amico, Jeff, Hun.	.000	1	0	0	0	0	0
Daneker, Pat, Birm.	.926	16	8	17	2	27	0
Daniels, John, Orl.	.857	38	3	3	1	7	0
Darwin, David, Jack.*	.960	28	17	31	2	50	2
Davenport, Joe, Birm.	1.000	40	2	7	0	9	0
Dawley, Joey, Gre.	1.000	26	6	7	0	13	0
Dawsey, Jason, Hun.*	1.000	4	2	1	0	3	0
Delgado, Ernie, Knox.	.941	31	6	10	1	17	0
DeWitt, Scott, Car.*	1.000	45	6	12	0	18	1
Dishman, Richard, Gre.	1.000	30	9	18	0	27	2
Dixon, Tim, Hun.*	1.000	24	0	5	0	5	0
Donaldson, Bo, Chat.	1.000	38	0	6	0	6	0
Doughty, Brian, Mob.	.966	36	10	18	1	29	1
Downs, Scott, W.T.*	.941	13	4	12	1	17	0
Drumheller, Al, Mob.*	.955	12	7	14	1	22	4
Duncan, Courtney, W.T.	1.000	11	1	7	0	8	1
Eldred, Cal, Hun.	1.000	2	1	1	0	2	0
Enders, Trevor, Orl.*	.900	60	6	12	2	20	0
Estes, Eric, Mob.	.000	8	0	0	0	0	0
Etler, Todd, Chat.	1.000	14	3	0	0	3	1
Fennell, Barry, W.T.*	1.000	1	0	1	0	1	0
Flach, Jason, Gre.	.800	12	3	5	2	10	1
Flury, Pat, Chat.	1.000	43	9	3	0	12	0
Fogg, Josh, Birm.	.917	10	2	9	1	12	0
Forney, Rick, Gre.	1.000	12	2	9	0	11	0
Fraraccio, Dan, Orl.	.000	2	0	0	0	0	0
Garcia, Apostol, Jack.	1.000	3	1	1	0	2	0
Gardner, Lee, Orl.	1.000	1	0	1	0	1	0
Garland, Jon, Birm.	1.000	7	2	5	0	7	0
Giron, Isabel, Knox.-Mob.	1.000	28	8	21	0	29	0
Gissell, Chris, W.T.	.889	20	7	9	2	18	0
Glauber, Keith, Chat.	.909	7	3	7	1	11	0
Glover, Gary, Knox.	.947	13	6	12	1	19	1
Goldsmith, Gary, Jack.	.941	33	4	12	1	17	1
Gonzalez, Jeremi, W.T.	1.000	3	1	0	0	1	0
Gonzalez, Lariel, Car.	1.000	30	1	2	0	3	0
Gordon, Mike, Hun.	.000	7	0	0	0	0	0
Guzman, Domingo, Mob.	.889	41	1	7	1	9	0
Hackman, Luther, Car.	.889	11	5	3	1	9	0
Haring, Brett, Chat.*	1.000	7	3	10	0	13	0
Harper, Travis, Orl.	1.000	14	2	7	0	9	2
Harris, D.J., Knox.	.938	25	7	8	1	16	0
Harrison, Tommy, Gre.	.875	16	4	3	1	8	0
Hart, Len, Mob.*	1.000	2	1	0	0	1	0
Hartshorn, Ty, Knox.	.909	10	3	7	1	11	0
Hartvigson, Chad, Car.*	1.000	30	0	4	0	4	0
Hawkins, Al, Hun.	.917	19	5	17	2	24	1
Helmer, Chad, Hun.	1.000	7	0	1	0	1	0
Henderson, Ryan, Hun.	1.000	12	1	2	0	3	0
Hendrickson, Mark, Knox.*	1.000	12	5	10	0	15	0
Hernandez, Elvin, W.T.	.972	29	17	18	1	36	0
Hernandez, Santos, Orl.	1.000	35	4	4	0	8	0
Herndon, Junior, Mob.	.961	26	14	35	2	51	7
Hibbard, Billy, Knox.	.000	3	0	0	0	0	0
Hiljus, Erik, Jack.	1.000	10	2	3	0	5	0
Hite, Kevin, Mob.	1.000	51	2	3	0	5	1
Huntsman, Scott, Hun.	.938	47	4	11	1	16	0
Iglesias, Mario, Birm.	1.000	23	1	6	0	7	1
Iglesias, Mike, Gre.	1.000	4	3	0	0	3	0
Jacobs, Ryan, Car.*	1.000	28	6	14	0	20	0
Janzen, Marty, Chat.	.929	30	2	11	1	14	1
Johnston, Doug, Hun.	.962	21	7	18	1	26	1
Kaufman, John, Orl.*	.889	21	0	8	1	9	0
Keagle, Greg, Jack.	1.000	9	4	9	0	13	1
Kelley, Rich, Hun.*	.714	25	1	4	2	7	0
Kent, Nathan, Gre.	.000	1	0	0	0	0	0
Kolb, Brandon, Mob.	1.000	7	2	1	0	3	0
Lakman, Jason, Birm.	.000	3	0	0	0	0	0
Lee, David, Car.	1.000	16	0	2	0	2	0
Lee, Derek, Hun.*	.974	26	15	22	1	38	2
Levrault, Allen, Hun.	1.000	16	4	10	0	14	0
LeBlanc, Eric, Chat.	.778	15	6	8	4	18	1
LeRoy, John, Orl.	.000	4	0	0	0	0	0
Lidle, Kevin, Mob.	.000	1	0	0	0	0	0
Lopez, Rodrigo, Mob.	.972	28	8	27	1	36	1
Lowe, Benny, Knox.*	.882	58	2	13	2	17	2
MacRae, Scott, Chat.	.935	39	13	16	2	31	1
Mallard, Randi, Chat.	.833	14	5	5	2	12	0
Manias, James, Chat.*	1.000	1	0	1	0	1	0
Mann, Jim, Knox.	.667	6	1	1	1	3	0
Manning, David, W.T.	.962	23	7	18	1	26	3
Manon, Julio, Orl.	1.000	30	3	2	0	5	0
Manzano, Adrian, Gre.	1.000	42	6	9	0	15	0
Maroth, Mike, Car.*	1.000	4	3	4	0	7	0
Marquis, Jason, Gre.	.875	12	0	7	1	8	1
Martin, Chandler, Car.	.895	27	5	29	4	38	3
Martinez, Romulo, Jack.	1.000	52	5	18	0	23	3
Maurer, Dave, Mob.*	.933	54	6	8	1	15	0
McClellan, Sean, Knox.	1.000	14	3	1	0	4	0
Merrell, Phil, Chat.	1.000	7	3	7	0	10	0
Meyer, Jake, Chat.	1.000	20	2	2	0	4	1
Meyers, Mike, W.T.	1.000	5	1	2	0	3	0
Middlebrook, Jason, Mob.	1.000	13	4	5	0	9	0
Milburn, Adam, Gre.*	1.000	14	1	1	0	2	0
Miles, Chad, Jack.*	.750	45	3	3	2	8	0
Miller, Matt, Jack.*	.750	7	1	2	1	4	0
Minor, Blas, Hun.	1.000	2	0	1	0	1	0
Moss, Damian, Gre.*	.500	7	1	2	3	6	0
Myette, Aaron, Birm.	.905	28	9	10	2	21	2
Morris, Jim, Orl.*	.000	3	0	0	0	0	0
Negrette, Richard, W.T.	.000	3	0	0	0	0	0
Nelson, Joe, Gre.	1.000	25	3	2	0	5	0
Newman, Eric, W.T.	.952	58	4	16	1	21	5
Nomo, Hideo, Hun.	.000	1	0	0	0	0	0
Norris, Dax, Gre.	1.000	2	1	0	0	1	1
Norton, Phillip, W.T.*	1.000	14	9	15	0	24	2
Nunez, Maximo, Orl.	1.000	26	2	1	0	3	0
Olsen, Jason, Birm.	1.000	9	0	4	0	4	0
Ortega, Pablo, Orl.	.909	22	7	13	2	22	3
Paredes, Roberto, Hun.	.867	28	5	8	2	15	1
Passini, Brian, Hun.*	1.000	8	0	5	0	5	1
Pearsall, J.J., Chat.*	.900	32	5	4	1	10	1
Pena, Jesus, Birm.*	.667	40	0	4	2	6	0
Pettyjohn, Adam, Jack.*	.968	20	8	22	1	31	0
Piersoll, Chris, W.T.	1.000	8	0	3	0	3	0
Priebe, Kevin, Hun.*	1.000	3	0	2	0	2	0
Priest, Eddie, Chat.*	.889	12	2	14	2	18	3
Pujals, Denis, Orl.	1.000	42	1	3	0	4	0
Rain, Steve, W.T.	1.000	40	3	4	0	7	0
Randall, Scott, Car.	.913	16	10	11	2	23	0
Rawitzer, Kevin, Car.*	.833	33	3	7	2	12	1
Reyes, Eddy, Orl.	.800	18	3	1	1	5	1
Ricken, Ray, Mob.	1.000	20	8	14	0	22	1
Ricketts, Chad, W.T.	1.000	57	0	7	0	7	0
Riedling, John, Chat.	1.000	40	2	10	0	12	0
Rivette, Scott, Knox.	.929	56	6	7	1	14	2
Roberts, Chris, Car.*	.846	43	2	9	2	13	0
Roberts, Mark, Birm.	.941	33	4	12	1	17	0
Robertson, Rich, Car.*	1.000	11	4	5	0	9	0
Romo, Greg, Jack.	1.000	8	1	2	0	3	0
Rose, Ted, Chat.	1.000	13	1	0	0	1	0
Rossiter, Mike, Car.	.000	16	0	0	0	0	0
Rupe, Ryan, Orl.	.750	5	1	2	1	4	0
Ryan, B.J., Chat.*	1.000	35	3	12	0	15	0
Ryan, Jason, W.T.	.818	8	4	5	2	11	0
Sak, Jim, Mob.	1.000	18	0	1	0	1	0
Salamon, John, Gre.	.667	28	1	3	2	6	0
Santos, Victor, Jack.	.741	28	9	11	7	27	0
Schaffer, Trevor, Knox.	.909	38	4	6	1	11	0
Schmack, Brian, Birm.	1.000	43	1	9	0	10	1
Schutz, Carl, W.T.*	.889	40	2	6	1	9	0
Seay, Bobby, Orl.*	1.000	6	0	5	0	5	1

Player, Team	Pct.	G	PO	A	E	TC	DP
Secoda, Jason, Birm.	.952	22	7	13	1	21	1
Seelbach, Chris, Gre.	1.000	8	0	4	0	4	0
Serrano, Wascar, Mob.	1.000	7	1	7	0	8	0
Shumate, Jacob, Gre.	1.000	14	6	6	0	12	1
Skrmetta, Matt, Mob.	1.000	25	1	3	0	4	0
Smith, Brian, Knox.	.923	29	4	8	1	13	0
Smith, Dan, W.T.*	.947	56	6	12	1	19	1
Smith, Keilan, Jack.	1.000	19	3	3	0	6	0
Smith, Travis, Hun.	.875	7	1	6	1	8	0
Smoltz, John, Gre.	.000	2	0	0	0	0	0
Sneed, John, Knox.	.500	6	0	1	1	2	0
Snyder, Bill, Jack.	1.000	14	2	1	0	3	1
Steenstra, Kennie, Gre.	1.000	8	0	2	0	2	0
Steinmetz, Earl, Gre.	.800	6	2	2	1	5	1
Stevenson, Jason, Knox.	1.000	21	7	9	0	16	0
Strong, Joe, Orl.	1.000	11	0	8	0	8	1
Swartzbaugh, Dave, Jack.	1.000	6	1	1	0	2	0
Szymborski, Tom, Mob.	.500	6	0	1	1	2	0
Theodile, Robert, Hun.	.947	47	6	12	1	19	1
Therneau, Dave, Chat.	1.000	3	1	2	0	3	0
Tokarse, Brian, Birm.	1.000	6	0	1	0	1	0
Tolar, Kevin, Chat.*	.857	47	2	4	1	7	0
Trippy, Joe, Gre.*	1.000	5	1	0	0	1	0
Tucker, Julien, Birm.	1.000	37	2	4	0	6	0
Valdes, Marc, Orl.	1.000	2	0	1	0	1	0
VanEgmond, Tim, Hun.	1.000	3	0	1	0	1	0
Vavrek, Mike, Car.*	1.000	10	2	8	0	10	1
Villafuerte, Brandon, Jack.	1.000	15	1	4	0	5	0
Vining, Ken, Birm.*	1.000	3	0	2	0	2	0
Virchis, Adam, Birm.	.000	1	0	0	0	0	0
Walls, Doug, Car.	.900	26	10	17	3	30	1
Walters, Brett, Mob.	1.000	9	0	4	0	4	0
Weaver, Jeff, Jack.	1.000	1	1	0	0	1	0
Webb, Alan, Jack.*	.923	26	6	30	3	39	2
Wells, Kip, Birm.	.875	11	3	4	1	8	0
Wheeler, Dan, Orl.	1.000	9	5	2	0	7	0
Whitley, Curtis, Birm.*	.917	36	4	7	1	12	0
Winkelsas, Joe, Gre.	.813	55	4	9	3	16	3
Wohlers, Mark, Chat.	.000	2	0	0	0	0	0
Wunsch, Kelly, Hun.*	.923	22	3	9	1	13	1
Yankosky, L.J., Gre.	.974	20	19	19	1	39	3
Yennaco, Jay, Knox.	1.000	8	1	3	0	4	0
Yoder, Jeff, W.T.	.938	29	3	12	1	16	3
Young, Danny, W.T.*	1.000	27	2	7	0	9	0
Zamarripa, Mark, Car.	1.000	5	1	6	0	7	0
Zambrano, Victor, Orl.	.882	40	4	11	2	17	1

TRIPLE PLAY: E. Hernandez.

PITCHERS WITH TWO OR MORE TEAMS

Player, Team	Pct.	G	PO	A	E	TC	DP
Giron, Isabel, Knox.	1.000	17	6	14	0	20	0
Giron, Isabel, Mob.	1.000	11	2	7	0	9	0

LEAGUE CHAMPIONS

Year	Team	Pct.
1904—	Macon	.598
1905—	Macon	.625
1906—	Savannah	.637
1907—	Charleston	.620
1908—	Jacksonville	.694
1909—	Chattanooga*	.738
	Augusta	.702
1910—	Columbus	.588
1911—	Columbus*	.681
	Columbia	.710
1912—	Jacksonville*	.679
	Columbus	.632
1913—	Savannah	.754
	Savannah	.593
1914—	Savannah*	.667
	Albany	.650
1915—	Macon	.588
	Columbus*	.686
1916—	Augusta*	.617
	Columbia	.631
1917—	Charleston	.741
	Columbia*	.667
1918—	Did not operate.	
1919—	Columbia	.585
1920—	Columbia	.633
1921—	Columbia	.642
1922—	Charleston	.625
1923—	Charlotte*	.653
	Macon	.580
1924—	Augusta	.612
1925—	Spartanburg	.620
1926—	Greenville	.662
1927—	Greenville	.622
1928—	Asheville	.664
1929—	Asheville	.605
	Knoxville*	.634
1930—	Greenville*	.620
	Macon	.643
1931-35—	Did not operate.	
1936—	Jacksonville	.652
	Columbus*	.650
1937—	Columbus	.572
	Savannah (3rd)†	.565
1938—	Savannah	.574
	Macon (2nd)†	.570
1939—	Columbus	.601
	Augusta (2nd)†	.597
1940—	Savannah	.627
	Columbus (2nd)†	.583
1941—	Macon	.643
	Columbia (2nd)†	.636
1942—	Charleston	.620
	Macon (2nd)†	.585
1943-45—	Did not operate.	
1946—	Columbus	.568
	Augusta (4th)†	.547
1947—	Columbus	.575
	Savannah (2nd)†	.563
1948—	Charleston	.572
	Greenville (3rd)†	.549
1949—	Macon‡	.623
1950—	Macon‡	.588
1951—	Montgomery	.607
1952—	Columbia	.649
	Montgomery (3rd)†	.558
1953—	Jacksonville	.679
	Savannah (2nd)†	.571
1954—	Jacksonville	.593
	Savannah (2nd)†	.571
1955—	Columbia	.636
	Augusta (3rd)†	.543
1956—	Jacksonville‡	.621
1957—	Augusta	.636
	Charlotte (2nd)†	.562
1958—	Augusta	.550
	Macon (3rd)†	.500
1959—	Knoxville	.557
	Gastonia (4th)†	.504
1960—	Columbia	.597
	Savannah (3rd)†	.561
1961—	Asheville	.635
1962—	Savannah	.662
	Macon (3rd)†	.576
1963—	Augusta*	.661
	Lynchburg	.662
1964—	Lynchburg	.579
1965—	Columbus	.572
1966—	Mobile	.629
1967—	Birmingham	.604
1968—	Asheville	.614
1969—	Charlotte	.579
1970—	Columbus	.569
1971—	Did not operate as league—clubs were members of Dixie Association.	
1972—	Asheville	.583
	Montgomery§	.561
1973—	Montgomery§	.580
	Jacksonville	.559
1974—	Jacksonville	.565
	Knoxville§	.533
1975—	Orlando	.587
	Montgomery§	.545
1976—	Montgomery∞	.591
	Orlando	.540
1977—	Montgomery∞	.628
	Jacksonville	.522
1978—	Knoxville∞	.611
	Savannah	.500
1979—	Columbus	.587
	Nashville∞	.576
1980—	Memphis	.576
	Charlotte∞	.500
1981—	Nashville	.566
	Orlando∞	.556
1982—	Jacksonville	.576
	Nashville∞	.535
1983—	Birmingham∞	.628
	Jacksonville	.531
1984—	Charlotte∞	.510
	Knoxville	.483
1985—	Charlotte	.545
	Huntsville∞	.542
1986—	Huntsville∞	.553
	Columbus∞	.500
1987—	Charlotte	.586
	Birmingham∞	.476
1988—	Greenville	.604
	Chattanooga∞	.566
1989—	Birmingham∞	.615
	Greenville	.504
1990—	Orlando	.590
	Memphis∞	.507
1991—	Greenville	.611
	Orlando∞	.535
1992—	Greenville∞	.699
	Chattanooga	.629
1993—	Birmingham∞	.549
	Knoxville	.500
1994—	Huntsville∞	.587
	Carolina	.529
1995—	Carolina∞	.618
	Chattanooga	.580
1996—	Chattanooga	.579
	Jacksonville∞	.543
1997—	Huntsville	.554
	Greenville∞	.529
1998—	Mobile∞	.614
	Jacksonville	.614
1999—	West Tenn.	.596
	Orlando∞	.507

*Won split season playoff. †Won four-club playoff. ‡Won championship and four-club playoff. §League was divided into Eastern and Western divisions; won playoff. ∞League was divided into Eastern and Western divisions and played split season; won playoff.

CLASS AA Southern League

TEXAS LEAGUE

LEAGUE OFFICE

President/treasurer
Tom Kayser

Address
2442 Facet Oak
San Antonio, TX 78232

Phone
210-545-5297

TEAMS

ARKANSAS TRAVELERS
Vice president/general manager
Bill Valentine
Manager
Chris Maloney
Ballpark (capacity, surface)
Ray Winder Field (6,083, grass)
Affiliation
Cardinals
Address
P.O. Box 55066
Little Rock, AR 72215
Phone
501-664-1555

EL PASO DIABLOS
President
Rick Parr
Manager
Don Wakamatsu
Ballpark (capacity, surface)
Cohen Stadium (9,765, grass)
Affiliation
Diamondbacks
Address
9700 Gateway Blvd. N.
El Paso, TX 79924
Phone
915-755-2000

MIDLAND ROCKHOUNDS
General manager
Monty Hoppel
Manager
Tony DeFrancesco
Ballpark (capacity, surface)
Christensen Stadium (5,000, grass)
Affiliation
Athletics
Address
P.O. Box 51187
Midland, TX 79710

Phone
915-683-4251

ROUND ROCK EXPRESS
General manager
Jay Miller
Manager
Jackie Moore
Ballpark (capacity, surface)
To be announced (7,500, grass)
Affiliation
Astros
Address
P.O. Box 5309
Round Rock, TX 78683
Phone
512-255-2255

SAN ANTONIO MISSIONS
President
Burl Yarbrough
Manager
Rick Burleson
Ballpark (capacity, surface)
Nelson Wolff Stadium (6,300, grass)
Affiliation
Dodgers
Address
5757 Highway 90 West
San Antonio, TX 78227
Phone
210-675-7275

SHREVEPORT CAPTAINS
General manager
Daniel Robinson
Manager
Bill Hayes
Ballpark (capacity, surface)
Fair Grounds Field (6,200, grass)
Affiliation
Giants

Address
P.O. Box 3448
Shreveport, LA 71133
Phone
318-636-5555

TULSA DRILLERS
Executive v.p./general manager
Chuck Lamson
Manager
Bobby Jones
Ballpark (capacity, surface)
Drillers Stadium (10,842, grass)
Affiliation
Rangers
Address
P.O. Box 4448
Tulsa, OK 74159
Phone
918-744-5998

WICHITA WRANGLERS
General manager
Steve Shaad
Manager
Keith Bodie
Ballpark (capacity, surface)
Lawrence-Dumont Stadium (6,111, artificial infield, grass outfield)
Affiliation
Royals
Address
P.O. Box 1420
Wichita, KS 67201
Phone
316-267-3372

1999 FINAL STANDINGS

FIRST HALF

EAST DIVISION

Team	W	L	T	Pct.	GB
Shreveport (Giants)	39	24	0	.574	...
Tulsa (Rangers)	34	34	0	.500	5.0
Arkansas (Cardinals)	31	37	0	.456	8.0
Jackson (Astros)	30	38	0	.441	9.0

WEST DIVISION

Team	W	L	T	Pct.	GB
Wichita (Royals)	38	30	0	.559	...
Midland (Athletics)	36	32	0	.529	2.0
El Paso (Diamondbacks)	34	34	0	.500	4.0
San Antonio (Dodgers)	30	38	0	.441	8.0

SECOND HALF

EAST DIVISION

Team	W	L	T	Pct.	GB
Tulsa (Rangers)	40	32	0	.556	...
Jackson (Astros)	38	34	0	.528	2.0
Shreveport (Giants)	32	40	0	.444	8.0
Arkansas (Cardinals)	28	44	0	.389	12.0

WEST DIVISION

Team	W	L	T	Pct.	GB
Wichita (Royals)	45	27	0	.625	...
Midland (Athletics)	38	34	0	.528	7.0
San Antonio (Dodgers)	37	35	0	.514	8.0
El Paso (Diamondbacks)	30	42	0	.417	15.0

COMPOSITE

Team	Wich.	Tul.	Mid.	Shre.	Jac.	S.A.	E.P.	Ark.	W	L	T	Pct.	GB
Wichita (Royals)	...	8	21	4	7	16	17	10	83	57	0	.593	...
Tulsa (Rangers)	4	...	5	16	16	6	5	22	74	66	0	.529	9.0
Midland (Athletics)	11	5	...	6	6	20	20	6	74	66	0	.529	9.0
Shreveport (Giants)	6	16	6	...	17	4	7	15	71	69	0	.507	12.0
Jackson (Astros)	3	16	6	15	...	7	6	15	68	72	0	.486	15.0
San Antonio (Dodgers)	16	6	12	6	3	...	17	7	67	73	0	.79	16.0
El Paso (Diamondbacks)	15	5	12	5	6	15	...	6	64	76	0	.457	19.0
Arkansas (Cardinals)	2	10	4	17	17	5	4	...	59	81	0	.421	24.0

Arkansas' home games played in Little Rock, Ark.

Major league affiliations in parentheses.

PLAYOFFS: Wichita won both halves to receive a bye into the final; Tulsa defeated Shreveport three games to one in semi-finals; Wichita defeated Tulsa four games to none to win league championship.

REGULAR-SEASON ATTENDANCE: Arkansas, 191,346; El Paso, 313,622; Jackson, 99,240; Midland, 176,369; San Antonio, 318,590; Shreveport, 155,416; Tulsa, 351,929; Wichita, 181,403. Total—1,787,915. Playoffs (8 games)—12,484. Class AA All-Star Game at Mobile, Ala.—6,174.

MANAGERS: Arkansas, Chris Maloney; El Paso, Don Wakamatsu; Jackson, Jim Pankovits; Midland, Tony Defrancesco; San Antonio, Jimmy Johnson; Shreveport, Shane Turner; Tulsa, Bobby Jones; Wichita, John Mizerock.

ALL-STAR TEAM: 1B—T.R. Marcinczyk, Midland and Chris Richard, Arkansas; 2B—Tom Sergio, Tulsa; 3B—Adam Piatt, Midland; SS—Julio Lugo, Jackson; OF—Jeff DaVanon, Midland; Mario Encarnacion, Midland; Tony Mota, San Antonio; C—Rod Barajas, El Paso; Utility—Josue Espada, Midland; Utility—Mike Lamb, Tulsa; RHP—Eric Gagne, San Antonio; RHP—Tony McKnight, Jackson; LHP—Rick Ankiel, Arkansas; LHP—Jason Davis, Shreveport; LHP—Corey Lee, Tulsa; Most Valuable Player—Adam Piatt, Midland; Pitcher of the Year—Eric Gagne, San Antonio; Manager of the Year—John Mizerock, Wichita.

1999 BATTING
TEAM

Team	Avg.	G	TPA	AB	R	H	TB	2B	3B	HR	RBI	SH	SF	HP	BB	IBB	SO	SB	CS	GDP	LOB	ShO	Slg.	OBP
Midland	.294	140	5522	4786	884	1406	2305	311	48	164	818	32	54	64	586	29	916	138	77	101	1044	7	.482	.374
El Paso	.284	140	5370	4835	726	1375	2091	303	46	107	675	27	40	52	416	27	986	88	55	95	1031	5	.432	.345
San Antonio	.282	140	5373	4733	710	1337	2012	265	52	102	658	53	41	30	516	17	915	171	90	97	1018	9	.425	.354
Wichita	.280	140	5321	4596	785	1286	1965	257	28	122	691	52	46	50	577	18	785	140	93	104	988	5	.428	.363
Tulsa	.265	140	5396	4798	720	1272	2028	284	38	132	657	23	37	47	491	19	910	130	46	97	1010	5	.423	.337
Jackson	.257	140	5228	4670	628	1199	1877	233	23	133	576	50	41	65	402	13	918	127	77	95	937	9	.402	.322
Arkansas	.253	140	4882	4405	527	1113	1763	207	34	125	489	44	38	67	328	7	950	79	56	106	861	10	.400	.312
Shreveport	.249	140	5195	4581	613	1140	1693	222	32	89	573	41	32	57	484	18	944	103	62	108	968	15	.370	.326

INDIVIDUAL

TOP QUALIFIERS FOR BATTING CHAMPIONSHIP

Minimum 378 plate appearances. *Lefthanded batter. †Switch-hitter.

Player, Team	Avg.	G	TPA	AB	R	H	TB	2B	3B	HR	RBI	SH	SF	HP	BB	IBB	SO	SB	CS	GDP	Slg.	OBP
Piatt, Adam, Mid.	.345	129	586	476	128	164	335	48	3	39	135	0	9	7	93	10	101	7	3	11	.704	.451
DaVanon, Jeff, Mid.†	.342	100	440	374	87	128	212	29	11	11	60	4	5	4	53	3	68	18	10	6	.567	.424
Espada, Josue, Mid.	.338	113	504	435	85	147	184	15	2	6	51	2	3	2	62	0	51	22	16	5	.423	.420
Mota, Tony, S.A.†	.325	98	392	345	65	112	192	31	2	15	75	4	2	0	41	6	56	13	5	14	.557	.394
Lamb, Mike, Tul.*	.324	137	613	544	98	176	300	51	5	21	100	1	8	7	53	5	65	4	3	11	.551	.386
Lugo, Julio, Jack.	.319	116	497	445	77	142	206	24	5	10	42	1	4	3	44	0	53	25	11	6	.463	.381
Barajas, Rod, E.P.	.318	127	548	510	77	162	249	41	2	14	95	0	6	8	24	6	73	2	0	8	.488	.354
Encarnacion, Mario, Mid.	.309	94	403	353	69	109	192	21	4	18	71	0	2	1	47	4	86	9	9	6	.544	.390
Ametller, Jesus, Ark.*	.307	116	412	397	53	122	182	26	2	10	53	1	5	4	5	0	21	2	1	13	.458	.319
Moreta, Ramon, S.A.	.305	117	428	397	56	121	146	13	3	2	42	11	2	0	18	0	66	26	16	12	.368	.333
Clark, Kevin, E.P.	.298	106	399	373	44	111	165	24	3	8	64	0	2	3	21	4	75	0	2	14	.442	.338
Maddox, Garry, E.P.*	.295	127	536	492	80	145	243	35	9	15	75	1	4	8	31	2	106	22	5	5	.494	.344
Prieto, Alejandro, Wich.	.294	114	415	360	56	106	155	23	4	6	41	13	3	1	35	1	47	12	6	10	.431	.356
McKay, Cody, Mid.*	.294	94	385	333	59	98	139	21	1	6	43	1	5	8	38	5	40	1	2	7	.417	.375
Richard, Chris, Ark.*	.294	133	500	442	78	130	249	26	3	29	94	0	6	8	43	5	75	7	7	14	.563	.363

DEPARTMENTAL LEADERS: G—Butler, Saturria, 139 each; AB—Lamb, 544; R—Piatt, 128; H—Lamb, 176; TB—Piatt, 335; 2B—Lamb, 51; 3B—Allen, 12; HR—Piatt, 39; RBI—Piatt, 135; SH—Prieto, 13; SF—Truby, 12; HP—Bocabica, 13; BB—Piatt, McNally, 93 each; IBB—Piatt, 10; SO—Gann, 141; SB—Metcalfe, 57; CS—Metcalfe, 21; GIDP—Feliz, 18; Slg.—Piatt, .704; OBP—Piatt, .451.

ALL PLAYERS

*Lefthanded batter. †Switch-hitter.

Player, Team	Avg.	G	TPA	AB	R	H	TB	2B	3B	HR	RBI	SH	SF	HP	BB	IBB	SO	SB	CS	GDP	Slg.	OBP
Alexander, Chad, Jack.	.309	84	357	317	42	98	158	27	3	9	44	0	3	3	34	1	58	9	5	4	.498	.378
Allen, Luke, S.A.*	.281	137	582	533	90	150	232	16	12	14	82	2	2	1	44	0	102	14	8	8	.435	.336
Alvarez, Victor, S.A.*	.250	9	11	8	1	2	3	1	0	0	0	1	0	0	2	0	2	0	0	0	.375	.400
Amado, Jose, Wich.	.290	121	522	459	71	133	205	29	2	13	93	0	6	3	54	4	37	5	3	15	.447	.364
Ambrose, John, Ark.	.048	34	21	21	0	1	1	0	0	0	0	0	0	0	0	0	8	0	0	1	.048	.048
Ametller, Jesus, Ark.*	.307	116	412	397	53	122	182	26	2	10	53	1	5	4	5	0	21	2	1	13	.458	.319
Andrews, Jeff, E.P.	.143	35	10	7	0	1	1	0	0	0	1	2	1	0	0	0	4	0	0	0	.143	.143
Ankiel, Rick, Ark.*	.400	8	13	10	1	4	7	0	0	1	1	2	0	0	1	0	0	0	0	0	.700	.455
Barajas, Rod, E.P.	.318	127	548	510	77	162	249	41	2	14	95	0	6	8	24	6	73	2	0	8	.488	.354
Barr, Tucker, Jack.	.252	41	124	107	8	27	42	0	0	5	15	0	0	5	12	0	20	0	0	3	.393	.355
Bautista, Juan, Tul.	.246	127	509	471	60	116	160	14	3	8	45	6	0	7	25	0	114	18	9	12	.340	.294
Bautista, Juan, E.P.	.000	2	3	3	0	0	0	0	0	0	0	0	0	0	0	0	2	0	0	0	.000	.000
Bearden, Doug, Jack.	.181	25	86	83	7	15	18	3	0	0	3	0	0	1	2	0	24	0	0	2	.217	.209
Beckett, Robbie, S.A.	.235	18	20	17	0	4	5	1	0	0	1	3	0	0	0	0	8	0	0	0	.294	.235
Bellhorn, Mark, Mid.†	.298	17	68	57	12	17	26	3	0	2	8	0	0	0	11	0	13	1	0	2	.456	.412

CLASS AA *Texas League*

Player, Team	Avg.	G	TPA	AB	R	H	TB	2B	3B	HR	RBI	SH	SF	HP	BB	IBB	SO	SB	CS	GDP	Slg.	OBP
Benes, Adam, Ark.*	.000	28	2	1	1	0	0	0	0	0	0	0	0	0	1	0	1	0	0	0	.000	.500
Benes, Alan, Ark.	.000	2	1	1	0	0	0	0	0	0	0	0	0	0	0	0	1	0	0	0	.000	.000
Bennett, Erik, Jack.	.000	20	2	2	0	0	0	0	0	0	0	0	0	0	0	0	1	0	0	0	.000	.000
Berroa, Angel, Mid.	.059	4	17	17	3	1	2	1	0	0	0	0	0	0	0	0	2	0	0	0	.118	.059
Betzsold, James, Jack.	.238	38	155	126	30	30	56	6	1	6	17	1	0	5	22	0	35	4	3	2	.444	.373
Bierbrodt, Nick, E.P.*	.000	14	12	10	0	0	0	0	0	0	0	1	0	0	1	0	2	0	0	1	.000	.091
Bocachica, Hiram, S.A.	.291	123	559	477	84	139	214	22	10	11	60	4	5	13	60	0	71	30	15	5	.449	.382
Bowles, Justin, Mid.	.286	131	542	489	73	140	243	27	8	20	73	3	4	2	44	1	122	10	7	13	.497	.345
Braswell, Bryan, Jack.*	.320	29	34	25	6	8	12	4	0	0	4	2	1	1	5	0	11	0	0	0	.480	.438
Brito, Juan, Wich.	.091	4	13	11	0	1	1	0	0	0	0	0	0	0	2	0	3	0	0	2	.091	.231
Brock, J.J., E.P.	.191	43	143	136	13	26	34	4	2	0	8	1	0	2	4	1	26	0	1	5	.250	.225
Brown, Dee, Wich.*	.353	65	276	235	58	83	139	14	3	12	56	1	2	3	35	1	41	10	8	2	.591	.440
Brown, Ray, Wich.*	.318	13	52	44	8	14	21	4	0	1	11	0	0	0	8	0	5	0	0	2	.477	.423
Brumbaugh, Cliff, Tul.	.281	135	590	513	94	144	260	35	3	25	89	0	4	2	71	1	88	5	4	5	.507	.368
Brunette, Justin, Ark.*	.000	18	1	1	0	0	0	0	0	0	0	0	0	0	0	0	0	0	0	0	.000	.000
Buckles, Bucky, Tul.	1.000	36	1	1	0	1	1	0	0	0	0	0	0	0	0	0	0	0	0	0	1.000	1.000
Bump, Nate, Shre.	.250	17	22	20	1	5	5	0	0	0	1	1	0	0	1	0	7	1	0	0	.250	.286
Burgus, Travis, E.P.*	.000	17	1	1	0	0	0	0	0	0	0	0	0	0	0	0	1	0	0	0	.000	.000
Burns, Kevin, Ark.*	.281	113	402	352	55	99	160	21	2	12	58	0	4	4	42	4	74	6	3	2	.455	.361
Butler, Brent, Ark.	.269	139	565	528	68	142	204	21	1	13	54	0	5	6	26	0	47	0	4	16	.386	.308
Byas, Michael, Shre.†	.271	129	559	487	76	132	143	9	1	0	41	3	0	1	68	0	79	31	15	7	.294	.362
Byrnes, Eric, Mid.	.238	43	189	164	25	39	56	14	0	1	22	2	3	3	17	0	32	6	3	5	.341	.316
Calloway, Ronald, E.P.*	.219	11	39	32	4	7	7	0	0	0	1	0	0	0	7	0	7	1	2	0	.219	.359
Campusano, Carlos, Shre.	.154	15	42	39	5	6	13	0	2	1	6	0	0	0	3	0	10	1	0	1	.333	.214
Castro, Jose, Mid.†	.261	119	425	368	69	96	140	17	3	7	42	9	3	7	38	1	90	21	7	5	.380	.334
Cesar, Dionys, Mid.†	.190	35	126	105	15	20	39	4	3	3	15	1	1	1	18	0	28	1	4	0	.371	.312
Chavarria, David, Shre.*	.333	10	3	3	0	1	1	0	0	0	0	0	0	0	0	0	0	0	0	0	.333	.333
Chiaramonte, Giuseppe, Shre.	.245	114	452	400	54	98	179	20	2	19	74	0	5	6	40	1	88	4	2	5	.448	.319
Chirinos, Germain, Mid.	.214	4	17	14	1	3	4	1	0	0	0	0	0	0	3	0	3	1	0	0	.286	.353
Clark, Doug, Shre.*	.220	15	54	50	6	11	17	3	0	1	6	0	0	0	4	0	11	1	1	0	.340	.278
Clark, Kevin, E.P.	.298	106	399	373	44	111	165	24	3	8	64	0	2	3	21	4	75	0	2	14	.442	.338
Cole, Eric, Jack.	.167	15	56	54	4	9	16	1	0	2	8	1	0	0	1	0	11	0	0	3	.296	.182
Collins, Michael, S.A.	.333	7	18	12	1	4	4	0	0	0	0	0	0	1	5	0	2	0	1	0	.333	.529
Coolbaugh, Scott, E.P.	.279	18	74	61	12	17	29	3	0	3	17	0	0	0	13	1	9	1	0	2	.475	.405
Corps, Edwin, Shre.	.133	24	18	15	0	2	3	1	0	0	1	0	0	0	2	0	4	0	0	0	.200	.235
Crabtree, Robbie, Shre.	.000	36	6	4	0	0	0	0	0	0	0	0	0	0	0	0	3	0	0	0	.000	.000
Crafton, Kevin, Ark.	.000	42	2	2	0	0	0	0	0	0	0	0	0	0	0	0	0	0	0	0	.000	.000
Creek, Ryan, Jack.	.111	8	12	9	0	1	1	0	0	0	0	2	0	0	0	0	3	0	0	0	.111	.111
Crews, Jason, E.P.	1.000	35	1	1	0	1	1	0	0	0	0	0	0	0	0	0	0	0	0	0	1.000	1.000
Cuevas, Trent, S.A.	.500	2	2	2	0	1	1	0	0	0	0	0	0	0	0	0	0	0	0	0	.500	.500
Cuyler, Milt, Tul.†	.326	36	159	138	30	45	57	4	4	0	13	1	0	2	18	1	29	7	6	2	.413	.411
Dace, Derek, E.P.*	.000	40	2	2	0	0	0	0	0	0	0	0	0	0	0	0	0	0	0	0	.000	.000
Dallimore, Brian, Jack.	.267	70	280	251	38	67	97	13	1	5	19	2	1	10	16	0	44	13	3	12	.386	.335
DaVanon, Jeff, Mid.†	.342	100	440	374	87	128	212	29	11	11	60	4	5	4	53	0	68	18	10	6	.567	.424
Davis, Allen, S.A.*	.000	29	20	17	2	0	0	0	0	0	0	1	0	0	2	0	6	0	0	1	.000	.105
Davis, Glenn, S.A.†	.260	134	564	492	72	128	199	33	4	10	63	1	2	0	69	4	130	6	7	12	.404	.350
Davis, Jason, Shre.*	.333	52	4	3	1	1	1	0	0	0	0	0	0	0	1	0	0	0	0	0	.333	.500
Deck, Billy, Ark.*	.061	18	36	33	1	2	3	1	0	0	0	0	0	2	1	0	16	0	0	1	.091	.139
Dewitt, Matt, Ark.	.300	26	36	30	1	9	13	1	0	1	4	3	0	0	3	0	7	0	0	0	.433	.364
Diaz, Freddie, Tul.†	.096	16	59	52	5	5	8	3	0	0	9	0	1	0	6	1	15	1	0	1	.154	.186
Diaz, Juan, S.A.	.303	66	287	254	42	77	127	21	1	9	52	0	4	3	26	1	77	0	0	4	.500	.369
Dilone, Juan, Shre.†	.253	112	395	340	52	86	132	19	6	5	44	0	1	8	46	3	87	11	7	8	.388	.354
Dodson, Jeremy, Wich.*	.257	133	506	452	63	116	201	20	1	21	58	1	0	2	51	2	95	9	5	12	.445	.335
Dubose, Brian, S.A.	.264	42	135	121	15	32	56	9	3	3	22	0	3	0	11	1	25	0	1	4	.463	.319
Dubose, Eric, Mid.*	.000	21	1	1	0	0	0	0	0	0	0	0	0	0	0	0	0	0	0	0	.000	.000
Duffy, Jim, Jack.	.133	26	65	60	5	8	8	0	0	0	2	0	1	4	0	0	15	0	0	1	.133	.200
Durazo, Erubiel, E.P.*	.403	64	275	226	53	91	157	18	3	14	55	0	3	2	44	6	37	2	1	5	.695	.498
Eckelman, Alex, Ark.	.241	41	130	116	5	28	41	4	3	1	13	2	3	4	5	0	20	0	0	4	.353	.289
Encarnacion, Mario, Mid.	.309	94	403	353	69	109	192	21	4	18	71	0	2	1	47	4	86	9	9	6	.544	.390
Escamilla, Roman, Wich.	.244	60	218	201	21	49	65	13	0	1	28	0	4	0	13	1	46	3	0	6	.323	.284
Escandon, Emiliano, Wich.*	.259	120	428	340	59	88	137	18	5	7	57	4	7	4	73	3	46	5	7	9	.403	.389
Espada, Josue, Mid.	.338	113	504	435	85	147	184	15	2	6	51	2	3	2	62	0	51	22	16	5	.423	.420
Esteves, Jake, Shre.	.235	15	21	17	2	4	6	2	0	0	2	2	0	0	2	0	3	0	0	0	.353	.316
Estrella, Luis, Shre.	.250	40	16	16	0	4	4	0	0	0	2	0	0	0	1	0	4	0	0	1	.250	.294
Faircloth, Chad, Shre.*	.216	23	39	37	4	8	10	2	0	0	3	0	0	0	2	0	14	0	0	2	.270	.256
Farley, Cordell, Ark.	.259	122	450	421	43	109	165	16	8	8	41	5	3	2	19	0	97	24	16	3	.392	.292
Feliz, Pedro, Shre.	.253	131	519	491	52	124	199	24	6	13	77	1	5	3	19	0	90	4	2	18	.405	.282
Feramisco, Derek, Ark.	.182	57	141	121	10	22	33	5	0	2	9	0	0	1	19	0	27	1	2	3	.273	.298
Foster, Kris, S.A.	.000	33	2	2	0	0	0	0	0	0	0	0	0	0	0	0	0	0	0	0	.000	.000
Franklin, Wayne, Jack.*	.000	46	3	1	0	0	0	0	0	0	0	1	0	0	1	0	1	0	0	0	.000	.500
Gagne, Eric, S.A.	.207	26	31	29	1	6	8	2	0	0	2	1	0	0	1	0	12	0	0	1	.276	.233
Gallagher, Shawn, Tul.	.283	112	484	452	61	128	218	30	3	18	78	0	2	4	26	2	84	1	0	9	.482	.326
Gann, Jamie, E.P.	.262	109	488	443	69	116	179	24	6	9	56	3	2	8	32	0	141	7	11	8	.404	.322
Garcia, Apostol, S.A.	.308	32	16	13	1	4	6	2	0	0	1	1	0	0	2	0	2	0	0	0	.462	.400
Garcia, Ossie, Ark.	.125	5	9	8	0	1	1	0	0	0	1	0	0	0	1	0	2	0	0	0	.125	.222
Garland, Tim, Mid.	.289	119	507	463	84	134	195	23	10	6	55	5	1	9	29	1	59	28	13	11	.421	.343
Garrett, Hal, S.A.	.200	42	8	5	2	1	1	0	0	0	0	0	0	0	3	0	1	0	0	0	.200	.500
Garrison, Webster, Mid.	.274	43	143	124	17	34	55	9	0	4	21	0	2	1	16	2	15	1	1	3	.444	.357
Gil, Geronimo, S.A.	.283	106	398	343	47	97	170	26	1	15	59	0	4	2	49	1	58	2	0	15	.496	.372
Ginter, Keith, Jack.	.382	9	41	34	9	13	17	1	0	1	6	0	1	2	4	0	6	0	0	1	.500	.463
Glendenning, Mike, Shre.	.264	32	120	106	14	28	49	6	0	5	19	0	1	1	12	0	30	1	1	2	.462	.342
Goodwin, David, Wich.	.300	3	11	10	3	3	3	0	0	0	0	0	0	0	1	0	3	0	0	0	.300	.364
Goodwin, Joe, Tul.	.235	30	106	98	15	23	30	7	0	0	8	1	0	0	7	0	24	0	1	1	.306	.286
Grabowski, Jason, Tul.*	.167	2	8	6	1	1	1	0	0	0	0	0	0	0	2	1	2	0	0	0	.167	.375
Green, Jason, Jack.	.000	33	3	3	0	0	0	0	0	0	0	0	0	0	0	0	1	0	0	0	.000	.000

Player, Team	Avg.	G	TPA	AB	R	H	TB	2B	3B	HR	RBI	SH	SF	HP	BB	IBB	SO	SB	CS	GDP	Slg.	OBP
Gulseth, Mark, Shre.*	.228	62	166	145	13	33	42	6	0	1	17	1	2	0	18	0	26	1	0	6	.290	.309
Gutierrez, Ricky, Jack.	.333	4	16	12	4	4	5	1	0	0	1	0	0	0	4	0	3	0	1	0	.417	.500
Hallmark, Pat, Wich.	.285	75	273	242	35	69	95	7	2	5	24	3	2	5	21	0	62	14	7	3	.393	.352
Hardge, Mike, Ark.	.227	54	170	141	15	32	52	3	1	5	11	0	0	4	25	1	43	3	3	2	.369	.359
Hartman, Ron, E.P.	.195	24	90	82	6	16	21	3	1	0	7	0	2	1	5	0	8	0	0	0	.256	.244
Heckman, Andy, Shre.	.261	23	26	23	2	6	7	1	0	0	2	2	0	1	0	0	7	0	0	1	.304	.292
Herrick, Jason, E.P.*	.301	49	189	173	23	52	90	18	1	6	20	0	0	2	14	1	45	2	5	5	.520	.360
Hodges, Kevin, Jack.	.091	8	11	11	0	1	1	0	0	0	1	0	0	0	0	0	5	0	0	0	.091	.091
Hogan, Todd, Ark.	.200	91	312	280	36	56	87	7	6	4	21	4	2	5	21	0	68	8	7	6	.311	.266
Howell, Jack, Jack.*	.375	3	8	8	2	3	10	1	0	2	3	0	0	0	0	0	2	0	0	0	1.250	.375
Hutchinson, Chad, Ark.	.227	25	28	22	2	5	5	0	0	0	2	0	0	4	0	0	11	0	0	2	.227	.346
Ibarra, Jesse, Tul.†	.222	90	375	325	32	72	117	10	1	11	49	1	3	5	41	4	88	0	0	10	.360	.316
Ireland, Eric, Jack.	.000	3	3	2	0	0	0	0	0	0	0	0	0	0	1	0	1	0	0	0	.000	.333
Jarvis, Matt, S.A.	.000	3	1	1	0	0	0	0	0	0	0	0	0	0	0	0	0	0	0	0	.000	.000
Jensen, Jason, E.P.*	.000	4	3	2	1	0	0	0	0	0	0	0	0	0	1	0	2	0	0	0	.000	.333
Johnson, A.J., Jack.	.241	63	207	187	21	45	64	7	0	4	16	1	2	8	9	0	38	4	2	3	.342	.301
Johnson, J.J., Jack.	.252	131	497	437	57	110	196	28	2	18	69	6	2	5	47	1	119	11	11	7	.449	.330
Johnson, Keith, E.P.	.300	17	76	70	17	21	42	10	1	3	15	1	1	0	4	0	17	0	1	4	.600	.333
Johnson, Ric, Jack.	.245	99	344	323	28	79	103	19	1	1	27	4	2	2	13	2	44	5	5	6	.319	.276
Karnuth, Jason, Ark.	.088	26	40	34	0	3	3	0	0	0	1	3	0	0	3	0	12	0	0	1	.088	.162
Kermode, Al, E.P.	.000	12	16	15	1	0	0	0	0	0	0	0	0	1	0	0	9	0	0	0	.000	.063
Kester, Tim, Jack.	.167	45	7	6	0	1	1	0	0	0	0	1	0	0	0	0	1	0	0	0	.167	.167
Kim, Byung-Hyun, E.P.	.500	10	3	2	1	1	1	0	0	0	0	0	0	0	1	0	0	0	0	0	.500	.667
King, Cesar, Tul.	.227	95	359	321	41	73	129	19	2	11	45	3	1	2	32	1	70	2	1	7	.402	.301
Kleiner, Stacy, Ark.	.221	85	265	235	23	52	70	8	2	2	16	2	1	3	24	0	60	2	1	10	.298	.300
Knoll, Brian, Shre.	.182	33	24	22	0	4	4	0	0	0	0	0	0	0	1	0	2	0	0	0	.182	.217
Knott, Eric, E.P.*	.080	27	29	25	1	2	2	0	0	0	0	1	0	0	3	0	13	0	0	0	.080	.179
Koeyers, Ramsey, E.P.	.208	26	82	77	6	16	28	9	0	1	10	0	0	1	4	0	20	0	0	2	.364	.256
Lamb, Mike, Tul.*	.324	137	613	544	98	176	300	51	5	21	100	1	8	7	53	5	65	4	3	11	.551	.386
Lane, Ryan, Tul.	.273	77	295	264	38	72	132	23	5	9	48	0	4	1	26	0	47	5	2	9	.500	.336
Layne, Jason, Wich.*	.217	30	109	92	13	20	30	4	0	2	12	1	0	1	15	0	24	1	2	3	.326	.333
Leon, Jose, Ark.	.233	112	368	335	37	78	149	17	0	18	54	1	1	6	25	0	114	3	3	5	.445	.297
Leyva, Julian, Mid.*	.500	13	3	2	0	1	1	0	0	0	0	1	0	0	0	0	1	0	0	0	.500	.500
Linebrink, Scott, Shre.	.300	10	10	10	0	3	4	1	0	0	0	0	0	0	0	0	2	0	0	0	.400	.300
Lopez, Pedro, Jack.	.184	81	275	255	20	47	76	11	0	6	28	4	2	2	12	0	52	1	1	2	.298	.225
Lugo, Julio, Jack.	.319	116	497	445	77	142	206	24	5	10	42	1	4	3	44	0	53	25	11	6	.463	.381
Maddox, Garry, E.P.*	.295	127	536	492	80	145	243	35	9	15	75	1	4	8	31	2	106	22	5	5	.494	.344
Magruder, Chris, Shre.†	.256	133	558	476	78	122	169	21	4	6	60	2	3	8	69	4	85	17	12	15	.355	.358
Malloy, Bill, Shre.	.000	17	2	1	0	0	0	0	0	0	0	1	0	0	0	0	0	0	0	0	.000	.000
Marcinczyk, T.R., Mid.	.279	127	559	477	87	133	243	39	1	23	111	0	7	12	62	2	109	2	0	12	.509	.371
Martin, Jared, E.P.†	.258	19	67	62	9	16	23	4	0	1	5	0	1	0	4	0	13	0	0	0	.371	.299
Martine, Chris, Ark.	.150	18	48	40	3	6	7	1	0	0	1	2	0	4	2	0	12	0	0	1	.175	.261
Martinez, Felix, Wich.†	.269	87	378	327	57	88	126	22	2	4	37	8	3	3	37	0	43	19	12	8	.385	.346
Marval, Raul, Shre.	.250	2	4	4	0	1	1	0	0	0	0	0	0	0	0	0	1	0	1	0	.250	.250
Matos, Julius, E.P.	.280	120	446	425	54	119	161	17	5	5	41	4	3	1	13	0	37	5	2	10	.379	.301
Matthews, Mike, Ark.*	.250	2	4	4	0	1	1	0	0	0	0	0	0	0	0	0	0	0	0	1	.250	.250
Mayo, Blake, S.A.-E.P.	.000	56	5	4	0	0	0	0	0	0	0	0	0	1	0	0	4	0	0	0	.000	.200
McCutcheon, Mike, E.P.*	.000	3	1	0	0	0	0	0	0	0	0	0	0	0	1	0	0	0	0	0	.000	1.000
McDonald, Keith, Ark.	.307	49	183	163	21	50	66	10	0	2	14	0	2	3	15	0	35	1	0	1	.405	.372
McKay, Cody, Mid.*	.294	94	385	333	59	98	139	21	1	6	43	1	5	8	38	5	40	1	2	11	.417	.375
McKinnon, Sandy, E.P.	.250	3	12	12	1	3	3	0	0	0	2	0	0	0	0	0	2	0	0	0	.250	.250
McKnight, Tony, Jack.*	.133	25	37	30	3	4	4	0	0	0	0	5	0	0	2	0	11	0	0	0	.133	.188
McNally, Sean, Wich.	.282	129	545	440	97	124	260	24	2	36	109	1	6	8	93	2	132	7	3	12	.591	.411
Medrano, Tony, Wich.	.339	73	293	257	45	87	119	15	1	5	32	5	6	4	21	0	23	4	2	3	.463	.389
Mendoza, Carlos, Shre.†	.202	111	386	332	35	67	100	16	4	3	34	8	4	6	36	3	65	1	4	3	.301	.288
Metcalfe, Mike, S.A.†	.293	123	542	461	78	135	175	25	3	3	57	9	4	3	65	1	47	57	21	3	.380	.381
Metzler, Rod, Wich.†	.500	3	12	10	5	5	13	2	0	2	4	1	0	1	0	0	3	0	0	1	1.300	.545
Miadich, Bart, E.P.	.000	12	2	1	0	0	0	0	0	0	0	0	0	0	1	0	1	0	0	0	.000	.500
Miller, Ryan, Jack.	.147	27	79	75	5	11	13	0	1	0	4	0	0	2	2	0	11	5	0	4	.173	.190
Minor, Damon, Shre.*	.273	136	567	473	76	129	230	33	4	20	82	0	3	8	80	6	115	1	0	10	.486	.385
Mitchell, Dean, S.A.	.000	10	7	6	0	0	0	0	0	0	0	1	0	0	0	0	2	0	0	0	.000	.000
Montgomery, Matt, S.A.	.000	59	1	1	1	0	0	0	0	0	0	0	0	0	0	0	0	0	0	1	.000	.000
Moore, Kenderick, Wich.	.251	80	279	243	36	61	72	11	0	0	27	3	2	11	20	0	55	19	10	4	.296	.333
Morales, Willie, Mid.	.280	102	379	343	43	96	171	27	0	16	71	2	4	6	24	0	54	2	0	8	.499	.334
Moreta, Ramon, S.A.	.305	117	428	397	56	121	146	13	3	2	42	11	2	0	18	0	66	26	16	12	.368	.333
Morris, Bobby, Tul.*	.333	6	26	21	0	7	9	2	0	0	2	0	0	1	4	0	1	0	0	1	.429	.462
Mota, Tony, S.A.†	.325	98	392	345	65	112	192	31	2	15	75	4	2	0	41	6	56	13	5	14	.557	.394
Mounce, Tony, Jack.*	.125	31	12	8	2	1	1	0	0	0	1	2	0	0	2	0	3	0	0	0	.125	.300
Munoz, Juan, Ark.*	.667	2	3	3	1	2	2	0	0	0	0	0	0	0	0	0	0	0	0	0	.667	.667
Myers, Adrian, Tul.	.235	99	406	357	60	84	107	12	4	1	28	1	1	3	44	0	63	33	7	14	.300	.323
Myers, Rod, S.A.*	.252	46	171	147	21	37	54	11	0	2	16	3	2	1	18	0	35	2	2	2	.367	.333
Nathan, Joe, Shre.	.500	2	2	2	0	1	2	1	0	0	1	0	0	0	0	0	1	0	0	0	1.000	.500
Neubart, Adam, E.P.	.209	13	50	43	7	9	15	3	0	1	4	2	0	0	5	0	14	0	1	0	.349	.292
Norris, Ben, E.P.*	.063	20	21	16	1	1	1	0	0	0	0	4	0	0	1	0	4	0	0	0	.063	.118
Nussbeck, Mark, Ark.*	.000	2	2	2	0	0	0	0	0	0	0	0	0	0	0	0	1	0	0	0	.000	.000
O'Malley, Paul, Jack.	.000	36	6	5	0	0	0	0	0	0	0	1	0	0	0	0	0	0	0	0	.000	.167
Opipari, Mario, Ark.†	.000	20	1	1	0	0	0	0	0	0	0	0	0	0	0	0	1	0	0	0	.000	.000
Ortega, Bill, Ark.	.377	20	80	69	10	26	41	9	0	2	10	1	0	0	10	0	9	0	0	4	.594	.456
Ortiz, Hector, S.A.	.240	40	134	121	10	29	33	4	0	0	13	0	3	0	10	0	17	0	1	2	.273	.291
Ortiz, Nick, Ark.	.175	14	43	40	4	7	8	1	0	0	2	0	0	0	3	0	7	0	0	2	.200	.233
Owens, Ryan, E.P.	.319	31	124	113	11	36	46	5	1	1	18	0	1	2	8	0	36	1	2	1	.407	.371
Patterson, Jarrod, E.P.*	.382	67	304	249	63	95	152	27	3	8	51	0	3	1	51	6	45	3	2	3	.610	.484
Patterson, John, E.P.	.059	18	17	17	0	1	1	0	0	0	0	0	0	0	0	0	3	0	0	0	.059	.059
Penny, Brad, E.P.	.267	17	16	15	2	4	4	0	0	0	2	1	0	0	0	0	3	0	0	1	.267	.267
Perez, Jhonny, Jack.	.250	76	307	276	37	69	105	16	4	4	25	6	2	1	19	0	44	7	8	8	.380	.299

Player, Team	Avg.	G	TPA	AB	R	H	TB	2B	3B	HR	RBI	SH	SF	HP	BB	IBB	SO	SB	CS	GDP	Slg.	OBP
Persails, Mark, Jack.	.000	12	3	2	1	0	0	0	0	0	0	0	0	0	1	0	1	0	0	0	.000	.333
Peters, Don, E.P.	.000	32	3	2	0	0	0	0	0	0	1	0	1	0	0	0	2	0	0	0	.000	.000
Phillips, Paul, Wich.	.267	108	427	393	58	105	138	20	2	3	56	3	3	2	26	0	38	8	9	8	.351	.314
Phoenix, Wynter, S.A.*	.249	60	198	169	22	42	65	6	1	5	22	4	2	2	21	1	41	1	2	3	.385	.335
Piatt, Adam, Mid.	.345	129	586	476	128	164	335	48	3	39	135	0	9	7	93	10	101	7	3	11	.704	.451
Piniella, Juan, Tul.	.264	124	535	458	69	121	175	23	2	9	46	1	8	7	61	0	120	15	6	6	.382	.354
Podsednik, Scott, Tul.*	.155	37	123	116	10	18	22	4	0	0	1	2	0	0	5	0	13	6	2	3	.190	.190
Priess, Matthew, Shre.	.167	5	13	12	1	2	5	0	0	1	1	0	0	0	1	0	3	0	0	0	.417	.231
Prieto, Alejandro, Wich.	.294	114	415	360	56	106	155	23	4	6	41	13	3	1	35	1	47	12	6	10	.431	.356
Prihoda, Steve, Wich.	.000	50	1	1	0	0	0	0	0	0	0	0	0	0	0	0	0	0	0	0	.000	.000
Prokopec, Luke, S.A.*	.219	27	35	32	4	7	12	3	1	0	2	1	0	0	2	0	9	0	0	0	.375	.265
Randolph, Steve, E.P.*	.250	8	10	8	0	2	2	0	0	0	1	0	0	0	2	0	2	0	0	0	.250	.400
Ransom, Cody, Shre.	.122	14	49	41	6	5	11	0	0	2	4	1	2	1	4	0	22	0	0	0	.268	.208
Reed, Steve, Ark.	.000	36	8	6	0	0	0	0	0	0	0	2	0	0	0	0	3	0	0	0	.000	.000
Rexrode, Jackie, E.P.*	.319	37	176	144	30	46	63	7	2	2	11	2	1	0	29	0	16	7	3	0	.438	.431
Ricabal, Dan, Shre.	.000	8	1	1	0	0	0	0	0	0	0	0	0	0	0	0	1	0	0	0	.000	.000
Richard, Chris, Ark.*	.294	133	500	442	78	130	249	26	3	29	94	0	6	8	43	5	75	7	7	14	.563	.363
Riley, Michael, Shre.*	.100	30	21	20	1	2	2	0	0	0	1	0	0	1	0	0	9	0	0	0	.100	.143
Rios, Eduardo, E.P.	.283	16	64	60	8	17	20	3	0	0	10	0	0	0	4	0	8	0	0	1	.333	.328
Robertson, Jeriome, Jack.*	.231	28	45	39	0	9	11	2	0	0	6	3	1	0	2	0	11	0	0	0	.282	.262
Rodriguez, Jose, Ark.*	.000	30	1	1	0	0	0	0	0	0	0	0	0	0	0	0	1	0	0	0	.000	.000
Root, Derek, Jack.*	.031	28	37	32	0	1	1	0	0	0	0	5	0	0	0	0	6	0	0	0	.031	.031
Rosario, Mel, Tul.†	.208	28	102	96	12	20	47	3	0	8	19	1	1	1	3	0	28	1	0	0	.490	.238
Rose, Mike, Jack.†	.244	15	59	45	8	11	20	0	0	3	8	1	0	0	13	1	10	0	2	1	.444	.414
Saitta, Rich, S.A.	.291	91	266	254	25	74	99	11	4	2	34	1	2	1	8	0	43	7	4	3	.390	.313
Samboy, Nelson, Jack.	.300	45	183	170	20	51	60	9	0	0	14	1	1	0	11	0	14	6	5	1	.353	.341
Sanchez, Martin, E.P.	.000	42	11	10	1	0	0	0	0	0	0	1	0	0	0	0	2	0	0	0	.000	.000
Sanchez, Victor, Jack.	.251	125	457	407	61	102	171	18	0	17	68	0	3	7	40	3	93	11	9	17	.420	.326
Sandoval, Jhensy, E.P.	.222	34	136	126	10	28	39	6	1	1	23	1	1	1	7	0	42	1	1	3	.310	.267
Sasser, Rob, Tul.	.263	5	20	19	3	5	7	2	0	0	0	0	0	0	1	0	2	0	0	0	.368	.300
Saturria, Luis, Ark.	.244	139	531	484	66	118	204	30	4	16	61	2	5	5	35	1	134	16	8	12	.421	.299
Schmidt, Dave, Ark.*	.221	48	131	113	6	25	38	4	0	3	15	1	4	2	11	0	34	1	1	4	.336	.292
Schroeffel, Scott, E.P.†	.182	42	14	11	1	2	2	0	0	0	1	1	0	0	2	0	3	0	0	0	.182	.308
Sell, Chip, E.P.*	.307	92	356	329	50	101	143	16	1	8	35	0	4	3	20	0	66	19	6	5	.435	.348
Sergio, Tom, Tul.*	.291	128	584	512	88	149	229	38	6	10	72	5	4	5	58	3	59	19	5	6	.447	.366
Skeels, Andy, S.A.*	1.000	1	1	1	0	1	1	0	0	0	0	0	0	0	0	0	0	0	0	0	1.000	1.000
Skeels, David, Mid.	.273	23	74	66	6	18	26	5	0	1	12	1	1	0	6	0	15	2	0	0	.394	.329
Snow, Casey, S.A.†	.253	61	190	170	21	43	67	8	2	4	16	2	3	2	13	1	45	0	0	4	.394	.309
Spivey, Junior, E.P.	.293	44	204	164	40	48	75	10	4	3	19	1	1	2	36	0	27	14	10	5	.457	.424
Stephenson, Garrett, Ark.	.500	1	2	2	0	1	1	0	0	0	0	0	0	0	0	0	0	0	0	0	.500	.500
Stoner, Mike, E.P.	.000	1	1	0	1	0	0	0	0	0	0	0	0	0	1	0	0	0	0	0	.000	1.000
Stovall, DaRond, S.A.†	.367	12	56	49	9	18	33	3	0	4	11	0	0	7	0	10	1	1	0	.673	.446
Stuckenschneider, Eric, Mid. .	.163	29	112	92	17	15	23	4	2	0	16	0	2	1	17	0	22	6	1	2	.250	.295
Tomlinson, Goef, Wich.*	.280	128	568	479	100	134	185	31	4	4	46	8	5	4	72	4	82	24	19	5	.386	.375
Torrealba, Yorvit, Shre.	.244	65	232	217	25	53	77	10	1	4	19	2	2	2	9	0	34	0	2	6	.355	.278
Truby, Chris, Jack.	.282	124	516	465	78	131	242	21	3	28	87	0	12	3	36	1	88	20	8	11	.520	.329
Tucker, Ben, Shre.	.000	18	1	1	0	0	0	0	0	0	0	0	0	0	0	0	1	0	0	0	.000	.000
Tyler, Josh, Shre.	.263	105	370	331	41	87	113	17	0	3	39	3	2	4	30	1	53	14	5	10	.341	.330
Urban, Jeff, Shre.	.167	14	15	12	0	2	3	1	0	0	2	0	0	1	0	7	0	0	0	.250	.231
Valdes, Pedro, Tul.*	.353	11	42	34	3	12	19	4	0	1	4	0	0	0	8	0	6	0	0	1	.559	.476
Van Rossum, Chris, E.P.*	.280	26	86	75	11	21	35	5	0	3	9	0	1	2	8	0	21	1	0	1	.467	.360
Vasquez, Leo, Mid.*	.000	13	1	1	0	0	0	0	0	0	0	0	0	0	0	0	0	0	0	0	.000	.000
Vaz, Roberto, Mid.*	.406	10	43	32	4	13	19	3	0	1	12	1	2	0	8	0	5	0	1	1	.594	.500
Verdugo, Jason, Shre.	.000	40	3	3	0	0	0	0	0	0	0	0	0	0	0	0	2	0	0	0	.000	.000
Vogelsong, Ryan, Shre.	.000	6	3	3	0	0	0	0	0	0	0	0	0	0	0	0	0	0	0	0	.000	.000
Wallace, Kent, Jack.*	1.000	13	1	1	0	1	1	0	0	0	0	0	0	0	0	0	0	0	0	0	1.000	1.000
Walter, Mike, Jack.	.200	34	5	5	0	1	1	0	0	0	0	0	0	0	0	0	2	0	0	0	.200	.200
Ward, Jeremy, E.P.	.000	19	3	3	0	0	0	0	0	0	0	0	0	0	0	0	0	0	0	0	.000	.000
Warner, Mike, S.A.*	.330	62	229	191	35	63	98	16	5	3	25	1	1	2	34	1	29	12	6	2	.513	.434
Weber, Neil, S.A.*	.286	12	7	7	0	2	2	0	0	0	1	0	0	0	0	0	1	0	0	0	.286	.286
Weibl, Clint, Ark.	.071	28	18	14	0	1	1	0	0	0	3	0	0	1	0	5	0	0	0	.071	.133
White, Walt, E.P.	.120	13	52	50	4	6	9	3	0	0	1	0	0	2	0	13	0	0	1	.180	.154
Wolff, Mike, E.P.*	.226	52	172	155	14	35	48	8	1	1	17	0	2	4	11	0	23	0	0	5	.310	.291
Woodward, Finley, Ark.	.000	5	6	5	0	0	0	0	0	0	0	1	0	0	0	0	1	0	0	0	.000	.000
Woolf, Jason, Ark.†	.272	86	363	320	46	87	137	18	4	8	15	6	1	8	28	0	86	11	3	3	.428	.329
Workman, Widd, S.A.	.111	9	10	9	1	1	1	0	0	0	0	0	0	0	1	0	4	0	0	0	.111	.200
Young, Travis, Shre.	.264	108	467	416	68	110	157	28	2	5	38	7	2	8	33	0	75	16	11	11	.377	.329
Zamora, Pete, S.A.*	.000	36	7	5	0	0	0	0	0	0	0	1	0	0	1	0	3	0	0	0	.000	.167
Zerbe, Chad, Shre.*	.375	7	9	8	0	3	4	1	0	0	0	1	0	0	0	0	2	0	0	0	.500	.375

GRAND SLAMS: Bowles, Feliz, Ibarra, McNally, Moreta, Piatt, 2 each; Amando, Ametller, Brumbaugh, Castro, Cesar, Chiaramonte, Durazo, Gallagher, Garrison, Magruder, Marcinczyk, Minor, Morales, Mota, Myers, Neubart, Patterson, Piniella, Sanchez, Sandoval, Spivey, 1 each.

AWARDED FIRST BASE ON CATCHER'S INTERFERENCE: Perez 3 (McDonald, Kleiner, Goodwin); Prieto 3 (Barajas, Snow, McKay); Minor 3 (Lopez 2, McDonald); McNally 2 (Skeels, Barajas); Richard (King); Young (Ortiz); Piatt (Barajas); Marcinczyk (Barajas); Betzsold (Rosario); Chiaramonte (Lopez).

PLAYERS WITH TWO OR MORE TEAMS

Player, Team	Avg.	G	TPA	AB	R	H	TB	2B	3B	HR	RBI	SH	SF	HP	BB	IBB	SO	SB	CS	GDP	Slg.	OBP
Mayo, Blake, S.A.	.000	41	2	2	0	0	0	0	0	0	0	0	0	0	0	0	2	0	0	0	.000	.000
Mayo, Blake, E.P.	.000	15	3	2	0	0	0	0	0	0	0	0	0	0	1	0	2	0	0	0	.000	.333

TEAM

Team	W	L	Pct.	ERA	G	CG	ShO	Sv.	IP	H	TBF	R	ER	HR	SH	SF	HB	BB	IBB	SO	WP	Bk.
Shreveport	71	69	.507	3.67	140	4	13	39	1208.1	1165	5125	585	493	102	47	35	42	410	8	851	54	12
Jackson	68	72	.486	3.76	140	2	10	39	1219.2	1183	5286	632	510	129	40	29	71	465	16	988	70	11
Tulsa	74	66	.529	4.13	140	7	10	36	1228.1	1218	5350	666	563	132	37	42	56	487	13	984	82	6
Wichita	83	57	.593	4.27	140	2	8	42	1196.2	1339	5200	643	568	118	33	37	46	377	36	772	59	8
San Antonio	67	73	.479	4.33	140	2	8	40	1212.1	1235	5363	733	583	103	51	49	64	518	19	951	65	6
Arkansas	59	81	.421	4.65	140	5	7	36	1153.0	1188	5075	690	596	139	43	39	40	521	10	876	66	8
El Paso	64	76	.457	4.69	140	8	7	31	1198.2	1352	5352	741	625	111	40	39	59	470	14	944	74	11
Midland	74	66	.529	5.67	140	3	2	35	1201.0	1448	5553	903	756	140	31	59	54	552	32	958	89	13

INDIVIDUAL

TOP QUALIFIERS FOR EARNED-RUN AVERAGE TITLE

Minimum 112 innings.*Lefthanded pitcher.

Pitcher, Team	W	L	Pct.	ERA	G	GS	CG	ShO	GF	Sv.	IP	H	TBF	R	ER	HR	SH	SF	HB	BB	IBB	SO	WP	Bk.
Gagne, Eric, S.A.	12	4	.750	2.63	26	26	0	0	0	0	167.2	122	683	55	49	17	2	2	8	64	0	185	6	0
McKnight, Tony, Jack.	9	9	.500	2.75	24	24	0	0	0	0	160.1	134	653	60	49	15	1	0	4	44	0	118	6	1
Robertson, Jeriome, Jack.*	15	7	.682	3.06	28	28	1	0	0	0	191.0	184	791	81	65	22	6	4	8	45	2	133	5	7
Knoll, Brian, Shre.	9	7	.563	3.51	33	17	1	1	6	1	128.1	117	530	54	50	15	5	4	11	34	0	91	6	0
Heckman, Andy, Shre.*	10	6	.625	4.08	23	23	1	1	0	0	132.1	142	572	67	60	11	6	5	2	43	1	70	3	0
Calero, Kiko, Wich.	9	3	.750	4.11	26	23	1	1	1	0	129.1	143	579	67	59	14	2	2	6	57	3	92	7	2
Norris, Ben, E.P.*	10	6	.625	4.16	20	20	0	0	0	0	119.0	132	535	61	55	13	3	2	8	53	0	87	6	2
Davis, Allen, S.A.*	7	10	.412	4.22	29	20	1	1	3	0	130.0	140	574	83	61	13	5	4	4	46	1	87	4	0
Dewitt, Matt, Ark.	9	8	.529	4.43	26	26	0	0	0	0	148.1	153	644	87	73	21	4	3	1	59	0	107	3	1
Lee, Corey, Tul.*	8	5	.615	4.44	22	22	0	0	0	0	127.2	132	549	76	63	11	1	1	4	40	0	121	3	1
Braswell, Bryan, Jack.*	9	10	.474	4.52	28	28	1	0	0	0	171.1	180	741	104	86	27	4	6	4	54	0	131	10	0
Knott, Eric, E.P.*	7	11	.389	4.57	27	27	3	0	0	0	161.1	198	711	95	82	11	4	5	5	42	0	83	3	2
Durbin, Chad, Wich.	8	10	.444	4.64	28	27	1	1	0	0	157.0	154	664	88	81	20	1	10	6	49	1	122	12	1
Root, Derek, Jack.*	7	16	.304	4.65	28	26	0	0	0	0	156.2	167	711	103	81	17	5	3	11	79	2	129	14	2
Hutchinson, Chad, Ark.	7	11	.389	4.72	25	25	0	0	0	0	141.0	127	624	79	74	12	8	5	4	85	0	150	20	3

DEPARTMENTAL LEADERS: W—Robertson, 15; L—Root, 16; Pct.—Esteves, .800; G—Montgomery, 58; GS—Braswell, Robertson, 28 each; CG—Knott, 3; ShO—several players tied, 1 each; GF—Montgomery, 56; Sv.—Montgomery, 26; IP—Robertson, 191.0; H—Knott, 198; TBF—Robertson, 791; R—Prokopec, 113; ER—Prokopec, 95; HR—Braswell, 27; SH—Hutchinson, Kester, 8 each; SF—Durbin, 10; HB—Walter, Beckett, 13 each; BB—Hutchinson, 85; IBB—Gorrell, 7; SO—Gagne, 185; WP—Hutchinson, 20; BK—Robertson, 7.

ALL PITCHERS

*Lefthanded pitcher.

Pitcher, Team	W	L	Pct.	ERA	G	GS	CG	ShO	GF	Sv.	IP	H	TBF	R	ER	HR	SH	SF	HB	BB	IBB	SO	WP	Bk.
Alvarez, Victor, S.A.*	4	3	.571	3.67	9	9	0	0	0	0	56.1	58	234	27	23	5	3	1	2	10	0	43	1	0
Ambrose, John, Ark.	4	12	.250	4.73	34	16	0	0	17	9	106.2	108	483	65	56	11	6	6	5	68	0	78	10	0
Anderson, Jason, Mid.*	4	9	.308	6.89	23	23	0	0	0	0	111.0	148	531	103	85	15	6	7	10	47	0	74	5	3
Andrews, Jeff, E.P.	3	8	.273	5.30	35	8	0	0	21	7	73.0	87	323	47	43	6	3	5	3	24	3	40	1	1
Ankiel, Rick, Ark.*	6	0	1.000	0.91	8	8	1	1	0	0	49.1	25	191	6	5	2	1	0	2	16	0	75	0	0
Austin, Jeffrey, Wich.	3	1	.750	4.46	6	6	0	0	0	0	34.1	40	155	19	17	1	0	1	2	11	1	21	4	0
Avrard, Corey, Ark.	1	1	.500	3.12	25	0	0	0	13	6	26.0	15	109	12	9	2	1	2	0	14	1	31	5	0
Baez, Benito, Mid.*	5	1	.833	5.47	37	0	0	0	9	3	54.1	68	243	35	33	5	3	7	0	15	2	51	2	2
Beckett, Robbie, S.A.*	7	7	.500	5.18	18	16	1	1	2	1	97.1	82	451	63	56	7	5	6	13	68	1	92	7	0
Benes, Adam, Ark.	1	1	.500	5.36	28	0	0	0	10	0	40.1	51	182	30	24	9	0	2	1	15	1	19	0	1
Benes, Alan, S.A.	0	0	.000	6.23	2	2	0	0	0	0	4.1	6	19	3	3	0	0	0	1	0	0	0	0	0
Bennett, Erik, Jack.	0	3	.000	4.13	20	0	0	0	8	1	28.1	23	122	14	13	5	3	1	4	12	3	32	0	0
Bertotti, Mike, Mid.*	2	3	.400	8.42	20	0	0	0	6	1	25.2	30	141	26	24	0	0	1	1	37	0	25	7	0
Bierbrodt, Nick, E.P.*	5	6	.455	4.62	14	14	2	1	0	0	76.0	78	341	45	39	3	2	1	8	37	0	55	5	0
Bluma, Jaime, Wich.	2	6	.250	5.40	30	0	0	0	22	6	38.1	40	169	25	23	9	0	1	0	16	3	21	0	1
Braswell, Bryan, Jack.*	9	10	.474	4.52	28	28	1	0	0	0	171.1	180	741	104	86	27	4	6	4	54	0	131	10	0
Brewer, Ryan, Wich.	5	2	.714	5.54	42	1	0	0	20	3	66.2	85	291	45	41	9	6	3	17	3	34	5	1
Brink, Jim, Mid.	1	1	.500	7.88	5	0	0	0	2	0	8.0	10	35	7	7	4	0	0	1	1	0	4	0	0
Brunette, Justin, Ark.*	1	2	.333	1.96	18	0	0	0	3	0	18.1	21	82	12	4	3	0	0	7	0	23	1	0
Buckles, Bucky, Tul.	10	4	.714	3.73	36	5	0	0	10	1	72.1	71	319	42	30	10	4	3	6	34	3	39	4	0
Bump, Nate, Shre.	4	10	.286	3.31	17	17	1	1	0	0	92.1	85	394	40	34	9	6	0	5	32	0	59	2	0
Burgus, Travis, E.P.*	1	1	.500	4.33	17	0	0	0	6	2	27.0	26	118	14	13	3	0	0	1	13	0	32	4	0
Burkett, John, Tul.	0	1	.000	2.70	2	2	0	0	0	0	6.2	7	32	5	2	0	0	0	0	3	0	3	2	0
Calero, Kiko, Wich.	9	3	.750	4.11	26	23	1	1	1	0	129.1	143	579	67	59	14	2	2	6	57	3	92	7	2
Carter, Lance, Wich.	5	2	.714	0.78	44	0	0	0	33	13	69.2	49	282	10	6	1	1	1	2	27	5	77	3	0
Chapman, Jake, Wich.*	3	0	1.000	4.39	52	0	0	0	13	3	69.2	87	316	38	34	3	5	0	3	29	6	53	4	0
Chavarria, David, Shre.	0	1	.000	7.47	10	1	0	0	8	0	15.2	24	86	22	13	4	0	1	1	9	0	16	5	0
Cobb, Trevor, Tul.*	4	5	.444	5.26	35	3	0	0	8	1	75.1	79	350	52	44	13	3	4	7	33	0	44	13	0
Cook, Derrick, Tul.	7	6	.538	5.67	21	21	2	0	0	0	114.1	137	524	81	72	12	3	6	4	45	3	71	17	0
Corps, Edwin, Shre.	4	4	.500	4.59	24	12	0	0	5	0	84.1	98	376	54	43	9	4	2	4	29	1	34	5	1
Crabtree, Robbie, Shre.	4	2	.667	2.56	36	0	0	0	14	2	63.1	50	251	21	18	2	0	1	0	18	2	65	3	0
Crafton, Kevin, Ark.	7	2	.778	7.58	42	0	0	0	14	2	46.1	57	209	41	39	9	2	1	1	16	1	41	2	0
Creek, Ryan, Jack.	3	4	.571	4.57	8	7	0	0	0	0	43.1	47	199	25	22	4	1	0	2	25	0	32	2	0
Crews, Jason, E.P.	3	4	.429	5.66	35	2	0	0	9	0	55.2	73	261	47	35	7	1	2	2	23	2	30	7	0
Dace, Derek, E.P.*	2	2	.500	5.19	40	0	0	0	14	0	52.0	58	232	33	30	4	2	3	2	23	2	34	0	0
D'Amico, Jeff, Mid.	1	2	.333	4.96	32	0	0	0	18	3	45.1	53	207	31	25	4	3	3	16	2	38	3	0
Davis, Allen, S.A.*	7	10	.412	4.22	29	20	1	1	3	0	130.0	140	574	83	61	13	5	4	4	46	1	87	4	0
Davis, Doug, Tul.*	4	4	.500	2.42	12	12	1	0	0	0	74.1	65	305	26	20	9	1	0	2	25	0	79	2	1
Davis, Jason, Shre.*	5	1	.833	1.27	52	0	0	0	38	21	64.0	42	249	9	9	1	3	0	1	22	1	54	2	2
Deck, Billy, Ark.*	0	0	.000	0.00	1	0	0	0	1	0	1.0	1	4	0	0	0	0	0	0	0	0	0	0	0

Pitcher, Team	W	L	Pct.	ERA	G	GS	CG	ShO	GF	Sv.	IP	H	TBF	R	ER	HR	SH	SF	HB	BB	IBB	SO	WP	Bk.
Dewitt, Matt, Ark.	9	8	.529	4.43	26	26	0	0	0	0	148.1	153	644	87	73	21	4	3	1	59	0	107	3	1
Dickey, R.A., Tul.	6	7	.462	4.55	35	11	0	0	21	10	95.0	105	419	60	48	13	1	4	2	40	1	59	9	0
Dubose, Eric, Mid.*	4	2	.667	5.49	21	14	0	0	3	1	77.0	89	361	57	47	10	2	4	7	44	1	68	8	0
Durbin, Chad, Wich.	8	10	.444	4.64	28	27	1	1	0	0	157.0	154	664	88	81	20	1	10	6	49	1	122	12	1
Elder, David, Tul.	1	0	1.000	8.10	3	0	0	0	1	0	6.2	8	32	7	6	0	0	0	0	6	1	7	0	0
Enochs, Chris, Mid.	3	5	.375	10.00	13	11	0	0	0	0	45.0	69	238	57	50	9	0	5	3	34	1	33	11	0
Esteves, Jake, Shre.	8	2	.800	3.63	15	14	0	0	0	0	91.2	76	373	40	37	7	2	5	4	23	1	53	3	2
Estrella, Luis, Shre.	6	4	.600	3.02	40	5	0	0	15	4	92.1	77	375	33	31	2	2	1	2	33	1	75	7	1
Foster, Kris, S.A.	0	2	.000	3.59	33	0	0	0	19	4	52.2	43	228	24	21	3	2	2	0	26	1	53	6	0
Franklin, Wayne, Jack.*	3	1	.750	1.61	46	0	0	0	40	20	50.1	31	200	11	9	3	3	4	3	16	3	40	1	0
Gagne, Eric, S.A.	12	4	.750	2.63	26	26	0	0	0	0	167.2	122	683	55	49	17	2	2	8	64	0	185	6	0
Garcia, Apostol, S.A.	7	5	.583	3.36	32	11	0	0	8	1	101.2	110	455	57	38	5	5	4	7	45	3	50	7	2
Garrett, Hal, S.A.	5	9	.357	3.61	42	4	0	0	13	2	94.2	70	404	47	38	8	7	2	1	55	4	76	9	0
Geis, John, Ark.*	2	5	.286	6.83	45	0	0	0	13	0	55.1	65	256	44	42	9	4	2	3	29	2	29	2	0
Gooding, Jason, Wich.*	13	7	.650	4.73	23	23	0	0	0	0	139.0	176	599	80	73	16	3	2	2	39	5	63	3	0
Gorrell, Chris, Mid.	2	0	1.000	7.83	30	0	0	0	12	1	56.1	92	285	63	49	7	3	1	2	23	7	41	0	1
Green, Jason, Jack.	3	3	.500	3.40	33	0	0	0	18	10	42.1	41	187	20	16	2	0	0	0	20	2	50	0	1
Gregg, Kevin, Mid.	4	7	.364	3.74	16	16	2	0	0	0	91.1	75	380	45	38	7	0	3	6	31	1	66	6	0
Hardge, Mike, Ark.	0	0	.000	22.50	3	0	0	0	2	0	2.0	7	15	5	5	2	0	0	0	2	0	3	0	0
Harville, Chad, Mid.	2	0	1.000	2.01	17	0	0	0	16	7	22.1	13	90	6	5	1	0	1	1	9	0	35	2	0
Heckman, Andy, Shre.*	10	6	.625	4.08	23	23	1	1	0	0	132.1	142	572	67	60	11	6	5	2	43	1	70	3	0
Henry, Doug, Jack.	0	1	.000	4.50	2	1	0	0	1	0	2.0	2	10	1	1	0	0	0	0	3	0	0	0	0
Hodges, Kevin, Jack.	1	4	.200	2.94	8	8	0	0	0	0	49.0	48	211	22	16	0	2	2	3	16	0	21	0	0
Hudson, Tim, Mid.	3	0	1.000	0.50	3	3	0	0	0	0	18.0	9	63	1	1	0	1	0	3	0	0	18	0	0
Hutchinson, Chad, Ark.	7	11	.389	4.72	25	25	0	0	0	0	141.0	127	624	79	74	12	8	5	4	85	0	150	20	3
Ireland, Eric, Jack.	0	1	.000	4.30	3	3	0	0	0	0	14.2	19	64	9	7	1	1	0	0	2	1	15	2	0
Jacob, Russell, E.P.	0	0	.000	6.75	3	0	0	0	2	0	2.2	5	16	4	2	1	0	0	0	2	0	3	0	0
Jarvis, Matt, S.A.*	0	1	.000	27.00	3	0	0	0	1	0	3.0	10	20	10	9	0	0	0	0	3	1	1	0	0
Jensen, Jason, E.P.*	0	1	.000	8.49	4	2	0	0	1	0	11.2	20	62	11	11	0	1	1	0	9	0	8	3	0
Johnson, Jonathan, Tul.	0	0	.000	9.53	1	1	0	0	0	0	5.2	12	28	6	3	1	1	0	0	4	0	4	0	0
Joseph, Kevin, Shre.	0	2	.000	1.42	7	0	0	0	3	0	12.2	8	52	4	2	0	1	0	1	5	0	16	0	0
Karnuth, Jason, Ark.	7	11	.389	5.22	26	26	2	0	0	0	160.1	175	696	105	93	16	5	7	11	55	0	71	2	0
Karp, Ryan, Tul.*	2	2	.500	2.78	11	9	1	0	0	0	64.2	50	259	21	20	5	4	2	3	21	0	49	2	0
Kermode, Al, E.P.	4	4	.500	3.01	12	11	1	1	0	0	71.2	68	293	31	24	7	4	4	2	12	0	56	2	0
Kester, Tim, Jack.	8	5	.615	3.72	43	2	0	0	13	1	75.0	91	342	43	31	9	8	2	10	19	2	51	4	0
Kim, Byung-Hyun, E.P.	2	0	1.000	2.11	10	0	0	0	3	0	21.1	6	81	5	5	0	3	1	3	9	0	32	0	2
Kimball, Andrew, Mid.	9	5	.643	5.44	47	0	0	0	15	2	89.1	112	412	64	54	14	2	4	2	40	4	87	13	4
Knoll, Brian, Shre.	9	7	.563	3.51	33	17	1	1	6	1	128.1	117	530	54	50	15	5	4	11	34	0	91	6	0
Knott, Eric, E.P.*	7	11	.389	4.57	27	27	3	0	0	0	161.1	198	711	95	82	11	4	5	5	42	0	83	3	2
Kolb, Dan, Tul.	1	2	.333	2.79	7	7	1	1	0	0	38.2	38	170	16	12	0	3	1	2	18	0	32	2	0
Lee, Corey, Tul.*	8	5	.615	4.44	22	22	0	0	0	0	127.2	132	549	76	63	11	1	1	4	44	0	121	3	1
Leyva, Julian, Mid.	3	4	.429	6.03	12	11	1	1	1	0	62.2	86	274	46	42	10	0	1	0	12	1	39	0	0
Linebrink, Scott, Shre.	1	8	.111	6.44	10	10	0	0	0	0	43.1	48	190	31	31	7	0	4	0	14	0	33	1	0
Lineweaver, Aaron, Wich.	4	3	.571	5.28	9	7	0	0	1	0	44.1	49	205	32	26	5	1	2	6	15	0	20	1	0
Malloy, Bill, Shre.	2	0	1.000	6.26	17	0	0	0	6	1	27.1	31	125	20	19	3	0	1	1	15	0	16	2	0
Manwiller, Tim, Mid.	6	2	.750	3.51	17	13	0	0	1	0	84.2	95	366	43	33	6	4	2	4	24	2	58	3	0
Marcinczyk, T.R., Mid.	0	0	.000	0.00	1	0	0	0	1	0	1.2	2	5	0	0	0	0	0	0	0	0	0	0	0
Martinez, Jose, Tul.	4	4	.500	5.42	33	9	0	0	10	3	98.0	112	441	69	59	16	2	6	2	36	0	70	2	1
Mathews, Terry, Wich.	0	0	.000	4.50	1	0	0	0	0	0	2.0	2	8	1	1	0	0	0	0	0	0	2	0	0
Matthews, Mike, Ark.*	2	0	1.000	0.00	2	2	1	1	0	0	12.0	3	39	0	0	0	0	0	0	1	0	10	0	0
Mayo, Blake, S.A.-E.P.	3	3	.500	5.68	56	1	0	0	18	4	76.0	104	357	56	48	5	3	2	3	33	3	49	8	0
McCutcheon, Mike, E.P.*	1	1	.500	6.23	3	1	0	0	0	0	8.2	7	41	8	6	1	1	0	0	9	0	8	1	0
McKnight, Tony, Jack.	9	9	.500	2.75	24	24	0	0	0	0	160.1	134	653	60	49	15	1	0	4	44	0	118	6	1
Medrano, Tony, Wich.	0	0	.000	0.00	1	0	0	0	0	0	1.0	3	6	0	0	0	0	0	0	0	0	0	0	0
Miadich, Bart, E.P.	0	0	.000	8.10	12	0	0	0	2	1	20.0	37	104	22	18	3	1	1	2	7	1	16	0	0
Miller, Matt, Tul.	6	4	.600	3.38	34	0	0	0	25	7	56.0	42	235	24	21	2	4	5	1	28	2	83	5	0
Mitchell, Dean, S.A.	1	2	.333	3.13	10	7	0	0	0	2	31.2	36	144	20	11	2	0	2	0	14	0	28	3	0
Montgomery, Jeff, Wich.	0	0	.000	9.00	1	0	0	0	0	0	1.0	2	5	1	1	0	0	0	0	1	0	1	0	0
Montgomery, Matt, S.A.	5	6	.455	2.60	58	0	0	0	56	26	55.1	65	254	35	16	1	3	2	3	17	2	39	5	1
Moreno, Juan, Tul.*	4	3	.571	2.30	42	0	0	0	27	3	62.2	33	255	20	16	5	2	3	3	32	2	83	6	0
Morrison, Robbie, Wich.	2	0	1.000	2.01	15	0	0	0	11	5	22.1	26	97	7	5	0	0	1	1	7	1	21	3	0
Mounce, Tony, Jack.*	5	2	.714	3.69	31	6	0	0	11	0	68.1	64	300	33	28	6	1	1	2	30	0	80	5	0
Mullen, Scott, Wich.*	4	3	.571	4.01	9	9	0	0	0	0	49.1	47	216	28	22	2	1	4	1	18	1	30	3	0
Narcisse, Tyrone, Jack.	0	0	.000	7.30	10	0	0	0	2	0	12.1	14	59	12	10	4	1	1	2	7	1	8	2	0
Nathan, Joe, Shre.	0	1	.000	3.12	2	2	0	0	0	0	8.2	5	38	4	3	0	1	1	1	7	0	7	2	1
Nelson, Chris, Mid.	1	1	.500	7.92	19	0	0	0	8	0	30.2	45	157	30	27	5	0	4	1	22	0	24	3	0
Newton, Geronimo, S.A.*	0	1	.000	3.21	11	0	0	0	3	0	14.0	17	67	6	5	1	1	0	0	10	1	14	0	1
Niebla, Ruben, S.A.*	2	1	.667	3.77	12	0	0	0	4	0	14.1	19	65	7	6	0	1	0	0	5	1	12	0	0
Niles, Randy, Mid.	4	6	.400	5.73	23	14	0	0	2	0	88.0	126	435	78	56	7	2	5	1	47	0	46	6	0
Nina, Elvin, Mid.	3	2	.600	4.80	7	4	0	0	2	0	30.0	36	140	21	16	0	1	1	2	18	0	19	1	0
Norris, Ben, E.P.*	10	6	.625	4.16	20	20	0	0	0	0	119.0	132	535	61	55	13	3	2	8	53	0	87	6	2
Nussbeck, Mark, Ark.	0	1	.000	6.17	2	2	0	0	0	0	11.2	12	54	8	8	1	0	0	0	9	0	11	2	0
O'Dell, Jake, Mid.	0	2	.000	11.31	9	3	0	0	1	0	24.2	36	125	31	31	8	0	2	2	15	1	16	3	0
O'Malley, Paul, Jack.	1	3	.250	5.60	36	7	0	0	11	0	70.2	75	329	53	44	10	2	3	5	48	0	65	10	0
Opipari, Mario, Ark.	1	0	1.000	3.51	20	0	0	0	8	0	25.2	30	112	11	10	1	1	3	1	11	2	16	2	0
Painter, Lance, Ark.*	0	0	.000	0.00	1	1	0	0	0	0	2.0	1	7	0	0	0	0	0	0	0	0	4	0	0
Patterson, John, E.P.	8	6	.571	4.77	18	18	2	0	0	0	100.0	98	429	61	53	16	3	1	0	42	0	117	3	0
Pearsall, J.J., S.A.*	0	0	.000	4.50	10	0	0	0	3	0	16.0	14	75	11	8	1	0	1	1	8	0	13	0	0
Penny, Brad, E.P.	2	7	.222	4.80	17	17	0	0	0	0	90.0	109	391	56	48	9	1	2	4	25	0	100	4	2
Perez, Juan, Mid.*	2	2	.500	6.94	23	0	0	0	11	3	35.0	47	167	29	27	2	3	2	1	18	3	30	2	2
Persails, Mark, Jack.	1	0	1.000	1.37	12	0	0	0	7	1	19.2	15	82	5	3	1	1	0	0	10	0	20	2	0
Peters, Don, E.P.	3	3	.500	5.71	32	0	0	0	18	4	41.0	57	199	36	26	3	3	3	3	16	1	29	2	0
Poland, Trey, Tul.*	5	8	.385	4.93	21	21	2	1	0	0	118.2	139	546	74	65	11	3	3	5	56	0	80	9	2
Prihoda, Steve, Wich.*	6	3	.667	4.00	49	0	0	0	15	2	78.2	91	343	43	35	8	4	2	4	15	4	51	3	0
Prokopec, Luke, S.A.	8	12	.400	5.42	27	27	0	0	0	0	157.2	172	685	113	95	18	7	8	7	46	0	128	3	1

Pitcher, Team	W	L	Pct.	ERA	G	GS	CG	ShO	GF	Sv.	IP	H	TBF	R	ER	HR	SH	SF	HB	BB	IBB	SO	WP	Bk.
Quarnstrom, Robert, Tul.*	1	0	1.000	1.98	10	0	0	0	0	0	13.2	12	58	3	3	2	1	0	0	4	0	7	0	0
Randolph, Steve, E.P.*	2	2	.500	2.64	8	8	0	0	0	0	44.1	39	186	14	13	1	2	0	1	23	0	38	1	1
Ray, Ken, Wich.	0	0	.000	5.06	14	0	0	0	13	7	21.1	23	90	12	12	2	1	0	1	10	0	18	1	1
Reed, Steve, Ark.	4	8	.333	5.42	36	9	0	0	10	0	81.1	87	355	59	49	15	1	7	2	28	1	45	5	2
Ricabal, Dan, Shre.	2	0	1.000	4.91	8	0	0	0	6	0	11.0	15	49	6	6	1	1	0	0	5	0	4	2	0
Riley, Michael, Shre.*	8	3	.727	2.11	30	13	1	1	4	1	111.0	80	456	35	26	6	2	2	1	53	0	107	2	1
Robertson, Jeriome, Jack.*	15	7	.682	3.06	28	28	1	0	0	0	191.0	184	791	81	65	22	6	4	8	45	2	133	5	7
Rodriguez, Jose, Ark.*	1	2	.333	3.25	30	0	0	0	9	0	36.0	38	173	16	13	6	2	0	0	25	0	30	4	0
Root, Derek, Jack.*	7	16	.304	4.65	28	26	0	0	0	0	156.2	167	711	103	81	17	5	3	11	79	2	129	14	2
Sabel, Erik, E.P.	0	1	.000	6.30	8	1	0	0	4	1	10.0	16	49	9	7	1	0	0	1	4	0	7	0	0
Saier, Matt, Wich.	9	7	.563	5.01	19	19	0	0	0	0	109.2	137	484	64	61	11	4	6	3	34	2	61	6	0
Sanchez, Martin, E.P.	4	4	.500	3.90	42	9	0	0	21	6	97.0	95	434	57	42	10	4	4	6	41	1	73	7	0
Santiago, Jose, Wich.	0	1	.000	2.00	4	2	0	0	1	0	9.0	8	32	2	2	0	1	0	0	0	0	0	0	0
Schroeffel, Scott, E.P.	5	4	.556	4.72	41	1	0	0	13	2	64.1	75	305	55	48	9	1	4	6	34	2	52	18	1
Sell, Chip, E.P.	0	0	.000	18.00	1	0	0	0	1	0	1.0	4	7	2	2	0	0	0	0	0	0	0	0	0
Silva, Ted, Tul.	6	3	.667	4.00	13	11	0	0	0	0	72.0	64	295	34	32	10	1	0	6	14	0	48	3	0
Skeels, David, Mid.	0	0	.000	18.00	2	0	0	0	2	0	2.0	5	12	4	4	1	0	0	1	0	2	0	0
Smith, Toby, Wich.	5	2	.714	2.94	22	13	0	0	5	1	79.2	86	336	30	26	6	1	1	3	18	1	40	3	0
Snow, Bert, Mid.	1	1	.500	1.71	21	0	0	0	21	13	21.0	14	84	4	4	3	0	0	9	3	32	1	0
Sollecito, Gabe, Tul.	5	4	.556	2.43	53	0	0	0	23	11	96.1	85	400	28	26	6	3	3	8	29	1	80	3	1
Stechschulte, Gene, Ark.	2	6	.250	3.40	39	0	0	0	33	19	42.1	41	191	26	16	4	4	1	4	20	1	41	3	0
Stephenson, Garrett, Ark.	1	0	.000	3.38	1	1	0	0	0	0	5.1	8	23	3	2	1	1	0	1	0	2	0	0
Tucker, Ben, Shre.	3	3	.500	4.18	18	0	0	0	8	1	28.0	37	128	19	13	1	4	1	1	12	1	12	1	0
Urban, Jeff, Shre.*	2	7	.222	5.81	14	14	0	0	0	0	69.2	100	319	54	45	8	5	0	1	19	0	54	3	0
Vasquez, Leo, Mid.*	3	1	.750	3.09	13	0	0	0	5	1	23.1	18	103	11	8	2	1	1	2	13	1	24	1	1
Verdugo, Jason, Shre.	2	3	.400	3.02	40	0	0	0	22	8	62.2	58	261	34	21	7	4	4	1	12	0	46	4	2
Verplancke, Joe, E.P.	0	0	.000	135.00	1	0	0	0	0	0	0.1	5	6	5	5	2	0	0	0	0	0	0	0	0
Vizcaino, Luis, Mid.	8	7	.533	5.85	25	19	0	0	1	0	104.2	120	473	74	68	18	1	3	3	48	2	88	6	0
Vogelsong, Ryan, Shre.	0	2	.000	7.31	6	6	0	0	0	0	28.1	40	137	25	23	7	0	1	2	15	0	23	1	1
Wagner, Denny, Mid.	1	2	.333	4.23	5	5	0	0	0	0	27.2	28	127	22	13	1	0	2	2	14	1	12	3	0
Wallace, Kent, Jack.	0	1	.000	2.30	13	0	0	0	12	3	15.2	13	64	4	4	1	1	1	0	6	0	16	1	0
Walter, Mike, Jack.	2	1	.667	4.81	34	0	0	0	20	4	48.2	35	221	32	26	2	0	1	13	31	0	44	6	0
Ward, Jeremy, E.P.	1	1	.500	2.45	19	0	0	0	17	5	25.2	18	101	7	7	1	0	1	0	9	1	26	1	0
Weber, Neil, S.A.*	4	2	.667	5.24	12	11	0	0	0	0	55.0	62	253	39	32	8	2	3	6	24	0	31	4	0
Weibl, Clint, Ark.	4	9	.308	4.66	28	17	1	0	2	0	110.0	121	483	59	57	11	3	0	3	49	1	75	4	1
Wilson, Kris, Wich.	5	7	.417	5.45	23	10	0	0	2	0	74.1	91	323	51	45	11	2	3	14	0	45	1	2
Woodman, Hank, Tul.	0	4	.000	5.46	6	6	0	0	0	0	29.2	27	133	24	18	4	0	1	0	19	0	25	0	0
Woodward, Finley, Ark.	0	2	.000	4.94	5	5	0	0	0	0	27.1	36	124	19	15	4	0	0	2	10	0	15	1	0
Workman, Widd, S.A.	1	5	.167	6.97	9	9	0	0	0	0	50.1	73	249	48	39	9	3	5	6	27	0	27	4	0
Zamora, Pete, S.A.*	2	1	.667	6.08	35	0	0	0	8	3	63.2	79	292	48	43	5	3	5	4	30	2	41	4	1
Zerbe, Chad, Shre.*	1	3	.250	1.96	7	6	0	0	1	0	41.1	32	164	13	9	2	1	2	3	10	0	16	0	1
Zito, Barry, Mid.*	2	1	.667	4.91	4	4	0	0	0	0	22.0	22	99	15	12	1	0	0	1	11	0	29	2	0

COMBINATION SHUTOUTS: **Arkansas (5)**—Hutchinson-Stechschulte, Ankiel-Rodriguez, Ambrose-Crafton, Hutchinson-Reed, Hutchinson-Ambrose. **El Paso (5)**—Patterson-Sanchez-Peters, Penny-Peters-Andrews, Patterson-Sanchez, Kermode-Sanchez, Norris-Ward-Peters. **Jackson (10)**—Hodges-Walter, Robertson-Walter, McKnight-Wallace-Walter, Root-Franklin, Creek-Mounce-Green-Franklin, Robertson-Green, Creek-Franklin-Green, Mounce-Bennett, McKnight-Green-Franklin, Robertson-Green-Bennett. **Midland (1)**—Manwiller-Baez. **San Antonio (6)**—Prokopec-Pearsall-Montgomery, Workman-Montgomery, Beckett-Mayo, Gagne-Mayo-Montgomery, Gagne-Foster, Prokopec-Montgomery. **Shreveport (9)**—Knoll-Estrella-Tucker, Heckman-Verdugo, Knoll-Verdugo-Davis, Bump-Tucker, Riley-Verdugo, Linebrink-Crabtree-Davis, Riley-Knoll, Zerbe-Estrella-Davis, Riley-Estrella-Davis. **Tulsa (8)**—Silva-Buckles-Dickey, Cook-Sollecito, Lee-Quarnstrom, Davis-Sollecito, Dickey-Moreno, Martinez-Sollecito, Dickey-Sollecito, Karp-Miller-Moreno. **Wichita (6)**—Calero-Chapman-Carter, Durbin-Carter, Calero-Smith-Chapman-Carter, Durbin-Prihoda-Carter-Chapman, Calero-Smith-Chapman-Morrison, Smith-Chapman-Morrison.

NO-HIT GAMES: None.

PITCHERS WITH TWO OR MORE TEAMS

Pitcher, Team	W	L	Pct.	ERA	G	GS	CG	ShO	GF	Sv.	IP	H	TBF	R	ER	HR	SH	SF	HB	BB	IBB	SO	WP	Bk.
Mayo, Blake, S.A.	2	2	.500	5.82	41	0	0	0	17	3	51.0	63	230	40	33	5	2	2	2	20	2	31	2	0
Mayo, Blake, E.P.	1	1	.500	5.40	15	1	0	0	1	1	25.0	41	127	16	15	0	1	0	1	13	1	18	6	0

1999 FIELDING

TEAM

Team	Pct.	G	PO	A	E	TC	DP	TP	PB	Team	Pct.	G	PO	A	E	TC	DP	TP	PB
West Tenn	.974	141	3692	1330	135	5157	119	1	22	Carolina	.969	140	3591	1426	159	5176	102	0	17
Birmingham	.973	140	3622	1424	142	5188	119	0	14	Mobile	.968	139	3644	1449	167	5260	126	1	12
Huntsville	.972	141	3722	1525	150	5397	133	0	30	Orlando	.968	138	3601	1341	163	5105	127	0	19
Chattanooga	.972	140	3724	1583	155	5462	160	0	25	Greenville	.968	138	3557	1445	168	5170	130	2	13
Knoxville	.971	140	3667	1412	149	5228	127	0	10	Jacksonville	.966	141	3757	1553	185	5495	129	0	17

INDIVIDUAL

FIRST BASEMEN

NOTE: All caps denotes fielding-percentage leader based on 70 games for catchers, 93 for all other non-pitchers and 112 innings for pitchers. *Throws lefthanded.

Player, Team	Pct.	G	PO	A	E	TC	DP
Anthony, Brian, Car.	.968	12	85	5	3	93	8
AUDE, Rich, Birm.	.995	107	884	46	5	935	85
Becker, Brian, Orl.	.992	127	1006	57	9	1072	110
Broussard, Benjamin, Chat.*	1.000	13	113	9	0	122	12
Cepeda, Jose, Gre.	1.000	1	1	0	0	1	0
Colina, Roberto, Orl.*	.961	18	115	8	5	128	10
Cripps, Bobby, Knox.	1.000	4	36	2	0	38	5

Player, Team	Pct.	G	PO	A	E	TC	DP
Curl, John, Mob.	.985	22	187	13	3	203	15
Eddie, Steve, Chat.-Birm.	1.000	21	116	8	0	124	12
Freire, Alejandro, Jack.	.980	33	259	28	6	293	18
Garcia, Guillermo, Chat.	1.000	1	6	1	0	7	2
Giles, Tim, Knox.	.992	102	831	75	7	913	91
Glavine, Mike, Gre.*	.994	64	487	44	3	534	47
Goodell, Steve, Gre.	.909	2	9	1	1	11	1
Hayes, Chris, Knox.	.882	2	13	2	2	17	1
Helms, Wes, Gre.	.984	30	226	18	4	248	23
Ibarra, Jesse, Jack.	.923	2	12	0	1	13	1
Jacobsen, Buck, Hun.	.961	13	112	11	5	128	10

Player, Team	Pct.	G	PO	A	E	TC	DP
Johnson, Adam, Gre.*	.990	15	91	10	1	102	10
Jones, Ryan, Jack.	.991	106	963	58	9	1030	93
Jorgensen, Randy, Mob.*	.991	58	498	34	5	537	50
Kirgan, Chris, Car.	.989	121	1010	91	12	1113	85
Kominek, Toby, Hun.	.991	48	427	24	4	455	49
Langaigne, Selwyn, Knox.*	1.000	2	3	2	0	5	0
Larkin, Stephen, Chat.*	.993	53	428	23	3	454	48
Lemonis, Chris, Jack.	1.000	2	29	0	0	29	2
Lindstrom, David, Jack.	1.000	1	2	1	0	3	0
Luzinski, Ryan, Chat.	1.000	2	5	2	0	7	2
Lydy, Scott, Birm.	1.000	3	16	0	0	16	0
Macalutas, Jon, Hun.	.991	75	617	57	6	680	55
Marrero, Oreste, Hun.*	.985	8	62	5	1	68	3
Melhuse, Adam, Knox.	.991	27	203	15	2	220	21
Moore, Brandon, Birm.	1.000	2	21	2	0	23	2
Mortimer, Mark, Gre.	1.000	1	3	0	0	3	0
Nevers, Tom, Chat.	.991	14	94	13	1	108	13
Newstrom, Doug, Birm.	.981	19	145	10	3	158	7
Norris, Dax, Gre.	.991	47	295	18	3	316	30
Owens, Jayhawk, Chat.	1.000	1	2	0	0	2	0
Paciorek, Pete, Mob.*	.989	62	499	32	6	537	44
Presto, Nick, Chat.	.990	10	95	6	1	102	15
Raleigh, Matt, Car.	.964	8	52	2	2	56	4
Rodriguez, Liu, Birm.	1.000	5	7	1	0	8	0
Rupp, Chad, Knox.	.943	5	32	1	2	35	3
Saunders, Chris, Chat.	.993	54	502	37	4	543	47
Stegall, Randy, Chat.	1.000	4	39	3	0	42	4
Strange, Mike, Knox.	.973	5	31	5	1	37	2
Tucci, Pete, Mob.	.875	1	7	0	1	8	1
Vieira, Scott, W.T.	.990	36	178	14	2	194	15
Walker, Ron, W.T.	1.000	2	1	0	0	1	0
Williamson, Antone, Hun.	.960	7	45	3	2	50	3
Zuleta, Julio, W.T.	.991	120	897	63	9	969	89

TRIPLE PLAYS: Glavine, Norris.

FIRST BASEMEN WITH TWO OR MORE TEAMS

Player, Team	Pct.	G	PO	A	E	TC	DP
Eddie, Steve, Chat.	1.000	1	10	1	0	11	1
Eddie, Steve, Birm.	1.000	20	106	7	0	113	11

SECOND BASEMEN

Player, Team	Pct.	G	PO	A	E	TC	DP
Abernathy, Brent, Knox.	.976	132	292	361	16	669	89
Almanzar, Richard, W.T.	.984	41	77	104	3	184	29
Azuaje, Jesus, Hun.	1.000	4	11	7	0	18	2
Badeaux, Brooks, Orl.	.000	1	0	0	0	0	0
Berry, Mike, Car.	.987	23	34	41	1	76	10
Bravo, Danny, Birm.	.972	29	47	56	3	106	9
Cairo, Miguel, Orl.	1.000	3	2	7	0	9	2
CARR, Dustin, Orl.	.977	123	273	332	14	619	98
Cepeda, Jose, Gre.	.969	56	80	138	7	225	32
Connacher, Kevin, Birm.	.963	7	13	13	1	27	1
Cruz, Luis, Orl.	1.000	7	7	6	0	13	0
Eaglin, Mike, Birm.	.937	21	20	39	4	63	8
Eddie, Steve, Chat.-Birm.	1.000	3	4	5	0	9	1
Faurot, Adam, Hun.	.909	2	3	7	1	11	1
Florez, Tim, Chat.	.992	31	48	69	1	118	19
Font, Franklin, W.T.	.971	20	33	34	2	69	10
Fraraccio, Dan, Orl.	.977	13	19	23	1	43	4
Gomez, Rudy, Knox.	.933	6	13	15	2	30	1
Goodell, Steve, Gre.	1.000	5	8	4	0	12	1
Kent, Robbie, Mob.	.957	63	124	144	12	280	37
King, Brett, W.T.	.944	9	9	8	1	18	3
Lackey, Steve, Gre.	.975	11	15	24	1	40	1
Lemonis, Chris, Jack.	.968	25	63	57	4	124	16
Livingston, Doug, Car.	.981	35	69	84	3	156	15
Lopez, Mickey, Hun.	.973	82	208	225	12	445	49
Mathis, Jared, Hun.	.962	12	27	23	2	52	7
McClure, Brian, Mob.	.982	45	100	113	4	217	31
Meyers, Chad, W.T.	.966	63	106	148	9	263	29
Nelson, Bry, W.T.	.989	23	43	45	1	89	13
Nevers, Tom, Chat.	.967	11	20	38	2	60	12
Pena, Elvis, Car.	.970	79	166	193	11	370	43
Pickler, Jeff, Hun.	.972	51	117	124	7	248	43
Pimentel, Jose, Gre.	.985	27	57	77	2	136	19
Polanco, Enohel, W.T.	1.000	7	7	12	0	19	2
Presto, Nick, Chat.	.925	14	29	45	6	80	11
Prieto, Rick, Mob.	1.000	1	1	0	0	1	0
Rexrode, Jackie, Birm.	.958	67	129	169	13	311	43
Rodriguez, Liu, Birm.	.981	39	86	72	3	161	18
Santana, Pedro, Jack.	.969	119	277	338	20	635	85
Schmidt, Bryan, Mob.	1.000	8	9	8	0	17	3
Stegall, Randy, Chat.	1.000	5	9	8	0	17	2
Strange, Mike, Knox.	.929	3	8	5	1	14	1

Player, Team	Pct.	G	PO	A	E	TC	DP
Thrower, Jake, Mob.	.941	37	59	85	9	153	13
Watkins, Pat, Car.	.964	17	24	29	2	55	4
Williams, Glenn, Gre.	.976	52	112	134	6	252	33
Williams, Jason, Chat.	.988	82	159	246	5	410	73

TRIPLE PLAYS: Kent, G. Williams.

SECOND BASEMEN WITH TWO OR MORE TEAMS

Player, Team	Pct.	G	PO	A	E	TC	DP
Eddie, Steve, Chat.	1.000	2	3	3	0	6	1
Eddie, Steve, Birm.	1.000	1	1	2	0	3	0

THIRD BASEMEN

Player, Team	Pct.	G	PO	A	E	TC	DP
Anthony, Brian, Car.	.928	24	12	52	5	69	0
Azuaje, Jesus, Hun.	.930	31	15	38	4	57	3
Balfe, Ryan, Mob.	.922	108	70	213	24	307	18
Berry, Mike, Car.	.883	63	28	116	19	163	9
Bravo, Danny, Birm.	.931	47	34	87	9	130	5
Cancel, Robinson, Hun.	1.000	4	5	4	0	9	0
Clark, Brady, Chat.	.000	1	0	0	1	1	0
Cotton, John, Car.	.854	36	22	54	13	89	3
Crede, Joe, Birm.	.910	72	68	133	20	221	10
Eberwein, Kevin, Mob.	.957	10	3	19	1	23	1
Eddie, Steve, Birm.	.922	28	17	54	6	77	5
Elliott, Dave, Hun.	.923	7	0	12	1	13	2
Faurot, Adam, Hun.	1.000	6	1	6	0	7	0
Florez, Tim, Chat.	1.000	1	0	1	0	1	0
Font, Franklin, W.T.	1.000	1	1	2	0	3	0
Fraraccio, Dan, Orl.	1.000	9	5	11	0	16	1
Garcia, Guillermo, Chat.	1.000	1	0	3	0	3	0
Gillespie, Eric, Jack.	.902	31	18	65	9	92	6
Gomez, Rudy, Knox.	.968	43	20	71	3	94	11
Gonzalez, Jimmy, Mob.	.500	1	1	1	2	4	2
Goodell, Steve, Gre.	.880	90	69	143	29	241	13
Hayes, Chris, Knox.	.895	17	7	27	4	38	3
Horn, Jeff, Gre.	.795	20	13	18	8	39	2
HUFF, Aubrey, Orl.	.927	133	93	273	29	395	23
Keck, Brian, Car.	1.000	3	2	7	0	9	0
Kent, Robbie, Mob.	.887	32	24	39	8	71	6
King, Brett, W.T.	1.000	1	0	1	0	1	0
Klimek, Josh, Hun.	.924	100	81	197	23	301	15
Larson, Brandon, Chat.	.885	42	22	93	15	130	8
Lawrence, Joe, Knox.	.910	67	29	112	14	155	14
Lemonis, Chris, Jack.	1.000	3	0	10	0	10	0
Lobaton, Jose, Hun.	.000	1	0	0	0	0	0
Luzinski, Ryan, Chat.	.778	5	3	11	4	18	0
Lydy, Scott, Birm.	1.000	2	1	1	0	2	0
Manning, Nate, W.T.	1.000	8	4	11	0	15	1
Mathis, Jared, Hun.	.950	9	8	11	1	20	2
Melhuse, Adam, Knox.	.913	6	6	15	2	23	2
Moore, Brandon, Birm.	1.000	3	0	9	0	9	1
Nelson, Bry, W.T.	.905	92	56	134	20	210	11
Nevers, Tom, Chat.	.910	22	12	49	6	67	4
Newstrom, Doug, Birm.	.333	1	0	1	2	3	0
Pimentel, Jose, Gre.	.910	38	22	69	9	100	2
Presto, Nick, Chat.	.750	3	0	6	2	8	1
Raleigh, Matt, Car.	.863	18	8	36	7	51	5
Rodriguez, Liu, Birm.	1.000	1	2	3	0	5	1
Salzano, Jerry, Chat.	.903	71	34	152	20	206	13
Sasser, Rob, Jack.	.911	109	82	276	35	393	27
Solano, Fausto, Knox.	.909	7	3	7	1	11	0
Stegall, Randy, Chat.	.000	1	0	0	0	0	0
Strange, Mike, Knox.	.917	5	3	8	1	12	0
Stromsborg, Ryan, Knox.	.500	2	1	1	2	4	0
Walker, Ron, W.T.	.888	62	32	87	15	134	10
Williams, Glenn, Gre.	1.000	5	1	11	0	12	1
Williamson, Antone, Hun.	1.000	4	5	10	0	15	0

SHORTSTOPS

Player, Team	Pct.	G	PO	A	E	TC	DP
Azuaje, Jesus, Hun.	.974	85	133	273	11	417	61
Badeaux, Brooks, Orl.	1.000	1	2	0	0	2	0
Bravo, Danny, Birm.	.966	12	10	46	2	58	8
Cruz, Luis, Orl.	1.000	1	0	2	0	2	0
Dawkins, Travis, Chat.	.979	32	52	89	3	144	22
Dellaero, Jason, Birm.	.948	80	138	227	20	385	39
De Los Santos, Eddy, Orl.	.928	128	155	344	39	538	75
Eddie, Steve, Chat.	1.000	1	1	2	0	3	0
Faurot, Adam, Hun.	.938	5	7	8	1	16	2
Font, Franklin, W.T.	.913	8	8	13	2	23	2
Fraraccio, Dan, Orl.	.907	15	21	28	5	54	10
Gomez, Rudy, Knox.	.924	44	68	102	14	184	22
Goodell, Steve, Gre.	1.000	11	19	30	0	49	6
Keck, Brian, Car.	1.000	1	1	4	0	5	0

Player, Team	Pct.	G	PO	A	E	TC	DP
Kent, Robbie, Mob.	.940	13	20	27	3	50	5
King, Brett, W.T.	.962	43	54	121	7	182	25
Klimek, Josh, Hun.	1.000	1	1	8	0	9	1
Lackey, Steve, Gre.	.926	71	111	203	25	339	44
Lawrence, Joe, Knox.	1.000	2	1	2	0	3	0
Lemonis, Chris, Jack.	.911	21	28	54	8	90	10
Livingston, Doug, Car.	1.000	2	1	0	0	1	0
Lobaton, Jose, Hun.	.910	35	37	85	12	134	8
Lopez, Mickey, Hun.	1.000	1	0	2	0	2	0
Martinez, Pablo, Gre.	.961	56	90	182	11	283	39
Mathis, Jared, Hun.	.962	29	42	83	5	130	15
McClure, Brian, Mob.	.000	1	0	0	0	0	0
Milliard, Ralph, Chat.	.963	29	44	87	5	136	22
Mitchell, Derek, Jack.	.936	123	155	361	35	551	67
Moore, Brandon, Birm.	.979	31	48	93	3	144	23
Nelson, Bry, W.T.	.833	5	3	2	1	6	0
Nevers, Tom, Chat.	.954	49	70	156	11	237	40
Nicholson, Kevin, Mob.	.948	126	187	402	32	621	75
Pena, Elvis, Car.	.983	29	40	74	2	116	12
Pimentel, Jose, Gre.	.941	5	3	13	1	17	3
Polanco, Enohel, W.T.	.948	103	146	237	21	404	53
Presto, Nick, Chat.	.929	37	61	97	12	170	24
Rodriguez, Liu, Birm.	.942	27	24	73	6	103	14
Schifano, Tony, Knox.	1.000	8	12	15	0	27	5
Schmidt, Bryan, Mob.	1.000	1	0	4	0	4	0
Solano, Fausto, Knox.	.948	93	157	265	23	445	58
SOSA, Juan, Car.	.958	114	191	361	24	576	62
Thrower, Jake, Mob.	.867	4	8	5	2	15	1
Watkins, Pat, Car.	.750	2	2	4	2	8	0

TRIPLE PLAYS: King, Martinez.

OUTFIELDERS

Player, Team	Pct.	G	PO	A	E	TC	DP
Airoso, Kurt, Jack.	.987	134	362	12	5	379	3
Bair, Rod, Car.	.977	121	209	7	5	221	1
Bowers, Brent, W.T.	.988	34	80	3	1	84	0
Bravo, Danny, Birm.	1.000	1	1	0	0	1	0
BROCK, Tarrik, Car.-W.T.*	.997	113	274	8	1	283	1
Broussard, Benjamin, Chat.*	.931	19	26	1	2	29	0
Brown, Roosevelt, W.T.	.983	33	52	5	1	58	0
Buccheri, Jim, Orl.	.975	38	77	2	2	81	1
Burress, Andy, Chat.	.957	52	85	5	4	94	0
Butler, Rob, Knox.*	.975	62	111	7	3	121	1
Cancel, Robinson, Hun.	.667	1	2	0	1	3	0
Candelaria, Ben, Jack.	.964	118	180	10	7	197	1
Carr, Dustin, Orl.	.000	1	0	0	0	0	0
Christensen, McKay, Birm.*	.990	74	190	2	2	194	0
Clark, Brady, Chat.	.985	133	255	10	4	269	2
Colina, Roberto, Orl.*	.947	18	18	0	1	19	0
Conner, Decomba, Chat.	.967	33	55	3	2	60	0
Cripps, Bobby, Knox.	.667	1	2	0	1	3	0
Cruz, Luis, Orl.	1.000	1	1	0	0	1	0
Curl, John, Mob.	.955	102	190	3	9	202	1
Diaz, Alejandro, Chat.	.987	55	144	5	2	151	2
DiPace, Danny, Hun.	1.000	7	9	0	0	9	0
Elliott, Dave, Hun.	.980	111	196	5	4	205	1
Faggett, Ethan, Mob.*	.971	125	293	11	9	313	2
Faurot, Adam, Hun.	1.000	2	3	0	0	3	0
Feuerstein, Dave, Car.	.973	84	134	11	4	149	0
Fraraccio, Dan, Orl.	.957	45	67	0	3	70	0
Freel, Ryan, Knox.	1.000	11	23	1	0	24	0
Freire, Alejandro, Jack.	1.000	4	9	0	0	9	0
Gazarek, Marty, W.T.	.960	33	47	1	2	50	0
Giles, Tim, Knox.	1.000	1	2	0	0	2	0
Gillespie, Eric, Jack.	.985	64	124	6	2	132	3
Glavine, Mike, Gre.*	.959	30	46	1	2	49	1
Gomez, Ramon, Birm.	.973	92	177	6	5	188	2
Gomez, Rudy, Knox.	1.000	8	11	0	0	11	0
Green, Chad, Hun.	.984	112	240	6	4	250	1
Hawkins, Kraig, Orl.	.978	91	129	6	3	138	0
Hayes, Chris, Knox.	1.000	17	37	3	0	40	0
Iapoce, Anthony, Hun.*	.980	27	50	0	1	51	0
Inglin, Jeff, Birm.	.978	105	166	9	4	179	1
Ingram, Darron, Chat.	.989	55	83	4	1	88	0
Jacobsen, Buck, Hun.	.881	28	37	0	5	42	0
Jennings, Robin, W.T.*	1.000	13	18	1	0	19	0
Johnson, A.J., Mob.	.981	28	51	2	1	54	0
Johnson, Adam, Gre.*	.972	91	164	9	5	178	4
Keck, Brian, Car.	1.000	1	2	0	0	2	0
King, Brad, W.T.	1.000	6	4	0	0	4	0
Kominek, Toby, Hun.	.987	83	147	10	2	159	2
Langaigne, Selwyn, Knox.*	.989	38	86	3	1	90	1
Larkin, Stephen, Chat.*	.905	14	18	1	2	21	0
Lemonis, Chris, Jack.	1.000	4	6	0	0	6	0

Player, Team	Pct.	G	PO	A	E	TC	DP
Light, Tal, Car.	.955	60	78	7	4	89	0
Lindsey, Rodney, Jack.	.929	7	12	1	1	14	0
Lindstrom, David, Jack.	1.000	6	6	1	0	7	0
Lobaton, Jose, Hun.	.000	2	0	0	0	0	0
Long, Ryan, Orl.	.833	7	14	1	3	18	0
Lydy, Scott, Birm.	.991	108	216	9	2	227	1
Macalutas, Jon, Hun.	1.000	6	7	0	0	7	0
Malave, Jose, Car.	1.000	39	50	2	0	52	0
Martinez, Greg, Hun.	1.000	22	49	0	0	49	0
Mathis, Jared, Hun.	.857	8	5	1	1	7	1
McNabb, Buck, Gre.	.977	20	41	2	1	44	0
Melhuse, Adam, Knox.	.973	44	66	5	2	73	1
Monds, Wonderful, Chat.	.972	70	132	9	4	145	1
Morenz, Shea, Mob.	1.000	6	9	0	0	9	0
Mortimer, Mark, Gre.	1.000	8	8	0	0	8	0
Mosquera, Julio, Orl.	1.000	2	2	0	0	2	0
Nelson, Bry, W.T.	1.000	15	17	1	0	18	0
Olson, Dan, Birm.*	.966	16	28	0	1	29	0
Pemberton, Rudy, Birm.	.960	13	23	1	1	25	0
Pendergrass, Tyrone, Gre.	.975	96	230	8	6	244	4
Pigott, Anthony, Orl.	1.000	3	3	0	0	3	0
Pimentel, Jose, Gre.	.949	40	72	2	4	78	0
Pomierski, Joe, Orl.	.972	56	99	7	3	109	1
Prieto, Rick, Mob.	.979	97	182	3	4	189	1
Ramirez, Dan, Birm.	.944	31	64	3	4	71	1
Rennhack, Mike, W.T.	.965	46	81	1	3	85	1
Riley, Marquis, Jack.	.963	43	78	0	3	81	0
Rivers, Jonathan, W.T.	.923	29	33	3	3	39	0
Rodriguez, Liu, Birm.	1.000	1	1	0	0	1	0
Rupp, Chad, Knox.	.986	42	71	2	1	74	0
Sanchez, Alex, Orl.*	.958	121	314	8	14	336	2
Schifano, Tony, Knox.	1.000	20	32	2	0	34	0
Smith, Demond, Gre.	.991	129	211	12	2	225	2
Sollmann, Scott, Hun.*	.982	50	106	1	2	109	1
Sosa, Juan, Car.	1.000	9	11	0	0	11	0
Speed, Dorian, W.T.	.980	116	197	2	4	203	0
Stromsborg, Ryan, Knox.	.976	97	194	7	5	206	0
Thompson, Andy, Knox.	.965	66	108	3	4	115	1
Trippy, Joe, Gre.*	.958	51	66	3	3	72	0
Tucci, Pete, Mob.	.975	78	156	2	4	162	0
Vieira, Scott, W.T.	.980	101	144	4	3	151	0
Wakeland, Chris, Jack.*	.944	54	97	4	6	107	0
Watkins, Pat, Car.	.973	69	107	3	3	113	1
Wells, Vernon, Knox.	1.000	26	56	4	0	60	3
Wilcox, Luke, Orl.	.972	71	132	5	4	141	1

TRIPLE PLAYS: Pendergrass, Smith.

OUTFIELDERS WITH TWO OR MORE TEAMS

Player, Team	Pct.	G	PO	A	E	TC	DP
Brock, Tarrik, Car.	1.000	61	138	2	0	140	0
Brock, Tarrik, W.T.*	.993	52	136	6	1	143	1

CATCHERS

Player, Team	Pct.	G	PO	A	E	TC	DP	PB
Ahrendt, Jay, Mob.	.974	8	34	3	1	38	0	0
Alfano, Jeff, Hun.	.985	73	416	49	7	472	2	23
Barthol, Blake, Car.	.983	92	656	53	12	721	2	13
Bravo, Danny, Birm.	1.000	1	1	0	1	1	0	0
Brito, Jorge, Hun.	.976	17	73	9	2	84	0	2
Cancel, Robinson, Hun.	.977	51	292	48	8	348	5	5
Cardona, Javier, Jack.	.983	88	565	58	11	634	7	13
Chiafredo, Paul, Knox.	.980	11	88	8	2	98	0	0
Cripps, Bobby, Knox.	.974	6	35	3	1	39	0	3
Davis, James, Chat.	.971	13	88	12	3	103	1	1
Encarnacion, Angelo, W.T.	.992	29	221	25	2	248	1	1
Garcia, Guillermo, Chat.	1.000	5	29	5	0	34	1	0
Garcia, Neil, Orl.	.990	23	181	26	2	209	1	5
Gonzalez, Jimmy, Mob.	.968	16	81	9	3	93	1	2
Gonzalez, Wiklenman, Mob.	.982	52	329	43	7	379	3	5
Hall, Toby, Orl.	.986	37	261	27	4	292	5	5
Horn, Jeff, Gre.	.988	28	153	18	2	173	1	2
Hyde, Brandon, Birm.	.968	7	28	2	1	31	0	0
King, Brad, W.T.	.989	85	571	49	7	627	6	9
Lawrence, Tony, Chat.	.938	3	14	1	1	16	1	1
Levis, Jesse, Orl.	.982	7	52	4	1	57	0	0
Lidle, Kevin, Mob.	.981	53	310	48	7	365	3	3
Lindstrom, David, Jack.	.988	52	306	30	4	340	5	4
Loyd, Brian, Knox.	.980	102	740	80	17	837	3	5
Lunar, Fernando, Gre.	.986	96	611	88	10	709	12	9
Luzinski, Ryan, Chat.-Mob.	.988	69	443	42	6	491	8	12
Mathis, Jared, Hun.	.967	15	55	3	2	60	1	0
Melhuse, Adam, Knox.	1.000	7	35	1	0	36	0	2
Micucci, Mike, W.T.	.993	49	267	24	2	293	2	8
Miller, Corky, Chat.	.989	33	227	35	3	265	6	8

Player, Team	Pct.	G	PO	A	E	TC	DP	PB
Molina, Jose, W.T.	.982	12	97	13	2	112	0	4
Mosquera, Julio, Orl.	.988	57	374	36	5	415	0	8
Newstrom, Doug, Birm.	.988	51	281	37	4	322	4	4
Norris, Dax, Gre.	.979	26	161	24	4	189	1	2
Owens, Jayhawk, Chat.	.985	44	311	26	5	342	3	5
PAUL, Josh, Birm.	.992	85	526	66	5	597	4	7
Petrick, Ben, Car.	.992	16	113	10	1	124	0	1
Probst, Alan, Knox.	.985	16	112	16	2	130	1	0
Quatraro, Matt, Orl.	1.000	1	9	3	0	12	0	0
Rivera, Mike, Jack.	1.000	7	46	4	0	50	1	0
Ryder, Derek, Birm.	.983	12	47	10	1	58	0	3
Snusz, Chris, Chat.	1.000	2	14	1	0	15	0	0
Vidal, Gilbert, Car.	.974	42	279	17	8	304	2	3
Wilson, Tom, Orl.	.971	20	121	15	4	140	0	1

CATCHERS WITH TWO OR MORE TEAMS

Player, Team	Pct.	G	PO	A	E	TC	DP	PB
Luzinski, Ryan, Chat.	.985	47	300	30	5	335	6	10
Luzinski, Ryan, Mob.	.994	22	143	12	1	156	2	2

PITCHERS

Player, Team	Pct.	G	PO	A	E	TC	DP
Adams, Terry, W.T.	.000	2	0	0	0	0	0
Agosto, Stevenson, Mob.*	.952	40	2	18	1	21	1
Akin, Jay, Hun.*	1.000	46	3	15	0	18	0
Alberro, Jose, Jack.	.000	1	0	0	0	0	0
Anderson, Bill, Mob.	1.000	4	0	1	0	1	0
Andrews, Clayton, Knox.*	.957	25	4	18	1	23	0
Aquino, Julio, Orl.	.000	5	0	0	0	0	0
Arroyo, Luis, Knox.*	1.000	5	0	1	0	1	0
Atchley, Justin, Chat.*	.941	17	2	14	1	17	0
Averette, Robert, Chat.	1.000	6	4	8	0	12	0
Bailey, Roger, Car.*	.909	4	4	6	1	11	1
Bale, John, Knox.*	.875	33	3	4	1	8	0
Barcelo, Lorenzo, Birm.	1.000	4	3	1	0	4	0
Beasley, Ray, Gre.*	1.000	50	4	8	0	12	1
Beck, Greg, Hun.	1.000	26	12	11	0	23	0
Belitz, Todd, Orl.*	1.000	28	7	18	0	25	1
Bell, Rob, Chat.	1.000	12	4	14	0	18	2
Bevel, Bobby, Car.*	1.000	48	3	10	0	13	0
Blanco, Alberto, Jack.*	.929	37	4	9	1	14	1
Bleazard, David, Knox.	1.000	15	11	14	0	25	2
Bowers, Cedrick, Orl.*	.750	27	1	5	2	8	1
Bradford, Josh, Knox.	1.000	34	10	12	0	22	3
Brester, Jason, Car.*	.950	11	5	14	1	20	0
Briggs, Anthony, Car.	1.000	4	0	1	0	1	0
Brown, Elliot, Orl.	1.000	10	0	1	0	1	1
Bruner, Clay, Jack.	.857	7	1	5	1	7	1
Bullard, Jason, Gre.	.667	5	0	2	1	3	0
Butler, Adam, Gre.*	.857	27	0	6	1	7	0
Callaway, Mickey, Orl.	1.000	2	0	2	0	2	0
Carlyle, Ken, Gre.	.913	17	5	16	2	23	1
Chantres, Carlos, Birm.	.966	28	9	19	1	29	0
Chavez, Carlos, Hun.	1.000	13	0	5	0	5	1
Cole, Victor, W.T.	1.000	18	1	2	0	3	1
Colmenares, Luis, Car.	1.000	8	0	1	0	1	0
Converse, Jim, Hun.	.800	16	1	3	1	5	0
Cordero, Francisco, Jack.	1.000	47	1	8	0	9	1
CROWELL, Jim, Chat.*	1.000	27	7	27	0	34	4
Cruz, Charlie, Gre.*	1.000	11	1	1	0	2	0
D'Amico, Jeff, Hun.	.000	1	0	0	0	0	0
Daneker, Pat, Birm.	.926	16	8	17	2	27	0
Daniels, John, Orl.	.857	38	3	3	1	7	0
Darwin, David, Jack.*	.960	28	17	31	2	50	2
Davenport, Joe, Birm.	1.000	40	2	7	0	9	0
Dawley, Joey, Gre.	1.000	26	6	7	0	13	0
Dawsey, Jason, Hun.*	1.000	4	2	1	0	3	0
Delgado, Ernie, Knox.	.941	31	6	10	1	17	0
DeWitt, Scott, Car.*	1.000	45	6	12	0	18	1
Dishman, Richard, Gre.	1.000	30	9	18	0	27	2
Dixon, Tim, Hun.*	1.000	24	0	5	0	5	0
Donaldson, Bo, Chat.	1.000	38	0	6	0	6	0
Doughty, Brian, Mob.	.966	36	10	18	1	29	1
Downs, Scott, W.T.*	.941	13	4	12	1	17	0
Drumheller, Al, Mob.*	.955	12	7	14	1	22	4
Duncan, Courtney, W.T.	1.000	11	1	7	0	8	1
Eldred, Cal, Hun.	1.000	2	1	1	0	3	0
Enders, Trevor, Orl.*	.900	60	6	12	2	20	0
Estes, Eric, Mob.	.000	8	0	0	0	0	0
Etler, Todd, Chat.	1.000	14	3	0	0	3	1
Fennell, Barry, W.T.*	1.000	1	0	1	0	1	0
Flach, Jason, Gre.	.800	12	3	5	2	10	1
Flury, Pat, Chat.	1.000	43	9	3	0	12	0
Fogg, Josh, Birm.	.917	10	2	9	1	12	0
Forney, Rick, Gre.	1.000	12	2	9	0	11	0
Fraraccio, Dan, Orl.	.000	2	0	0	0	0	0
Garcia, Apostol, Jack.	1.000	3	1	1	0	2	0
Gardner, Lee, Orl.	1.000	1	0	1	0	1	0
Garland, Jon, Birm.	1.000	7	2	5	0	7	0
Giron, Isabel, Knox.-Mob.	1.000	28	8	21	0	29	0
Gissell, Chris, W.T.	.889	20	7	9	2	18	0
Glauber, Keith, Chat.	.909	7	3	7	1	11	0
Glover, Gary, Knox.	.947	13	6	12	1	19	1
Goldsmith, Gary, Jack.	.941	33	4	12	1	17	1
Gonzalez, Jeremi, W.T.	1.000	3	1	0	0	1	0
Gonzalez, Lariel, Car.	1.000	30	1	2	0	3	0
Gordon, Mike, Hun.	.000	7	0	0	0	0	0
Guzman, Domingo, Mob.	.889	41	1	7	1	9	0
Hackman, Luther, Car.	.889	11	5	3	1	9	0
Haring, Brett, Chat.*	1.000	7	3	10	0	13	0
Harper, Travis, Orl.	1.000	14	2	7	0	9	2
Harris, D.J., Knox.	.938	25	7	8	1	16	0
Harrison, Tommy, Gre.	.875	16	4	3	1	8	0
Hart, Len, Mob.*	1.000	2	1	0	0	1	0
Hartshorn, Ty, Knox.	.909	10	3	7	1	11	0
Hartvigson, Chad, Car.*	1.000	30	0	4	0	4	0
Hawkins, Al, Hun.	.917	19	5	17	2	24	1
Helmer, Chad, Hun.	1.000	7	0	1	0	1	0
Henderson, Ryan, Hun.	1.000	12	1	2	0	3	0
Hendrickson, Mark, Knox.*	1.000	12	5	10	0	15	0
Hernandez, Elvin, W.T.	.972	29	17	18	1	36	0
Hernandez, Santos, Orl.	1.000	35	4	4	0	8	0
Herndon, Junior, Mob.	.961	26	14	35	2	51	7
Hibbard, Billy, Knox.	.000	3	0	0	0	0	0
Hiljus, Erik, Jack.	1.000	10	2	3	0	5	0
Hite, Kevin, Mob.	1.000	51	2	3	0	5	1
Huntsman, Scott, Hun.	.938	47	4	11	1	16	0
Iglesias, Mario, Birm.	1.000	23	1	6	0	7	1
Iglesias, Mike, Gre.	1.000	4	3	0	0	3	0
Jacobs, Ryan, Car.*	1.000	28	6	14	0	20	0
Janzen, Marty, Chat.	.929	30	2	11	1	14	1
Johnston, Doug, Hun.	.962	21	7	18	1	26	1
Kaufman, John, Orl.*	.889	21	0	8	1	9	0
Keagle, Greg, Jack.	1.000	9	4	9	0	13	1
Kelley, Rich, Hun.*	.714	25	1	4	2	7	0
Kent, Nathan, Gre.	1.000	1	0	0	0	0	0
Kolb, Brandon, Mob.	1.000	7	2	1	0	3	0
Lakman, Jason, Birm.	.000	3	0	0	0	0	0
Lee, David, Car.	1.000	16	0	2	0	2	0
Lee, Derek, Hun.*	.974	26	15	22	1	38	2
Levrault, Allen, Hun.	1.000	16	4	10	0	14	0
LeBlanc, Eric, Chat.	.778	15	6	8	4	18	1
LeRoy, John, Orl.	.000	4	0	0	0	0	0
Lidle, Kevin, Mob.	1.000	1	0	0	0	0	0
Lopez, Rodrigo, Mob.	.972	28	8	27	1	36	1
Lowe, Benny, Knox.*	.882	58	2	13	2	17	2
MacRae, Scott, Chat.	.935	39	13	16	2	31	1
Mallard, Randi, Chat.	.833	14	5	5	2	12	0
Manias, James, Chat.*	1.000	1	0	1	0	1	0
Mann, Jim, Knox.	.667	6	1	1	1	3	0
Manning, David, W.T.	.962	23	7	18	1	26	3
Manon, Julio, Orl.	1.000	30	3	2	0	5	0
Manzano, Adrian, Gre.	1.000	42	6	9	0	15	0
Maroth, Mike, Jack.*	1.000	4	3	4	0	7	0
Marquis, Jason, Gre.	.875	12	0	7	1	8	1
Martin, Chandler, Car.	.895	27	5	29	4	38	3
Martinez, Romulo, Jack.	1.000	52	5	18	0	23	3
Maurer, Dave, Mob.*	.933	54	6	8	1	15	0
McClellan, Sean, Knox.	1.000	14	3	1	0	4	0
Merrell, Phil, Chat.	1.000	7	3	7	0	10	0
Meyer, Jake, Chat.	1.000	20	2	2	0	4	1
Meyers, Mike, W.T.	1.000	5	1	2	0	3	0
Middlebrook, Jason, Mob.	1.000	13	4	5	0	9	0
Milburn, Adam, Gre.*	1.000	14	1	1	0	2	0
Miles, Chad, Jack.*	.750	45	3	3	2	8	0
Miller, Matt, Jack.*	.750	7	1	2	1	4	0
Minor, Blas, Hun.	1.000	2	0	1	0	1	0
Moss, Damian, Gre.*	.500	7	1	2	3	6	0
Myette, Aaron, Birm.	.905	28	9	10	2	21	2
Morris, Jim, Orl.*	.000	3	0	0	0	0	0
Negrette, Richard, W.T.	.000	3	0	0	0	0	0
Nelson, Joe, Gre.	1.000	25	3	2	0	5	0
Newman, Eric, W.T.	.952	58	4	16	1	21	5
Nomo, Hideo, Hun.	.000	1	0	0	0	0	0
Norris, Dax, Gre.	1.000	2	1	0	0	1	0
Norton, Phillip, W.T.*	1.000	14	9	15	0	24	2
Nunez, Maximo, Orl.	1.000	26	2	1	0	3	0
Olsen, Jason, Birm.	1.000	9	0	4	0	4	0
Ortega, Pablo, Orl.	.909	22	7	13	2	22	3

Player, Team	Pct.	G	PO	A	E	TC	DP
Paredes, Roberto, Hun.	.867	28	5	8	2	15	1
Passini, Brian, Hun.*	1.000	8	0	5	0	5	1
Pearsall, J.J., Chat.*	.900	32	5	4	1	10	1
Pena, Jesus, Birm.*	.667	40	0	4	2	6	0
Pettyjohn, Adam, Jack.*	.968	20	8	22	1	31	0
Piersoll, Chris, W.T.	1.000	8	0	3	0	3	0
Priebe, Kevin, Hun.*	1.000	3	0	2	0	2	0
Priest, Eddie, Chat.*	.889	12	2	14	2	18	3
Pujals, Denis, Orl.	1.000	42	1	3	0	4	0
Rain, Steve, W.T.	1.000	40	3	4	0	7	0
Randall, Scott, Car.	.913	16	10	11	2	23	0
Rawitzer, Kevin, Car.*	.833	33	3	7	2	12	1
Reyes, Eddy, Orl.	.800	18	3	1	1	5	1
Ricken, Ray, Mob.	1.000	20	8	14	0	22	1
Ricketts, Chad, W.T.	1.000	57	0	7	0	7	0
Riedling, John, Chat.	1.000	40	2	10	0	12	0
Rivette, Scott, Knox.	.929	56	6	7	1	14	2
Roberts, Chris, Car.*	.846	43	2	9	2	13	0
Roberts, Mark, Birm.	.941	33	4	12	1	17	0
Robertson, Rich, Car.*	1.000	11	4	5	0	9	0
Romo, Greg, Jack.	1.000	8	1	2	0	3	0
Rose, Ted, Chat.	1.000	13	1	0	0	1	0
Rossiter, Mike, Car.	.000	16	0	0	0	0	0
Rupe, Ryan, Orl.	.750	5	1	2	1	4	0
Ryan, B.J., Chat.*	1.000	35	3	12	0	15	0
Ryan, Jason, W.T.	.818	8	4	5	2	11	0
Sak, Jim, Mob.	1.000	18	0	1	0	1	0
Salamon, John, Gre.	.667	28	1	3	2	6	0
Santos, Victor, Jack.	.741	28	9	11	7	27	0
Schaffer, Trevor, Knox.	.909	38	4	6	1	11	0
Schmack, Brian, Birm.	1.000	43	1	9	0	10	1
Schutz, Carl, W.T.*	.889	40	2	6	1	9	0
Seay, Bobby, Orl.*	1.000	6	0	5	0	5	1
Secoda, Jason, Birm.	.952	22	7	13	1	21	1
Seelbach, Chris, Gre.	1.000	8	0	4	0	4	0
Serrano, Wascar, Mob.	1.000	7	1	7	0	8	0
Shumate, Jacob, Gre.	1.000	14	6	6	0	12	1
Skrmetta, Matt, Mob.	1.000	25	1	3	0	4	0
Smith, Brian, Knox.	.923	29	4	8	1	13	0
Smith, Dan, W.T.*	.947	56	6	12	1	19	1
Smith, Keilan, Jack.	1.000	19	3	3	0	6	0
Smith, Travis, Hun.	.875	7	1	6	1	8	0
Smoltz, John, Gre.	.000	2	0	0	0	0	0

Player, Team	Pct.	G	PO	A	E	TC	DP
Sneed, John, Knox.	.500	6	0	1	1	2	0
Snyder, Bill, Jack.	1.000	14	2	1	0	3	1
Steenstra, Kennie, Gre.	1.000	8	0	2	0	2	0
Steinmetz, Earl, Gre.	.800	6	2	2	1	5	1
Stevenson, Jason, Knox.	1.000	21	7	9	0	16	0
Strong, Joe, Orl.	1.000	11	0	8	0	8	1
Swartzbaugh, Dave, Jack.	1.000	6	1	1	0	2	0
Szymborski, Tom, Mob.	.500	6	0	1	1	2	0
Theodile, Robert, Hun.	.947	47	6	12	1	19	1
Therneau, Dave, Chat.	1.000	3	1	2	0	3	0
Tokarse, Brian, Birm.	1.000	6	0	1	0	1	0
Tolar, Kevin, Chat.*	.857	47	2	4	1	7	0
Trippy, Joe, Gre.*	1.000	5	1	0	0	1	0
Tucker, Julien, Birm.	1.000	37	2	4	0	6	0
Valdes, Marc, Orl.	1.000	2	0	1	0	1	0
VanEgmond, Tim, Hun.	1.000	3	0	1	0	1	0
Vavrek, Mike, Car.*	1.000	10	2	8	0	10	1
Villafuerte, Brandon, Jack.	1.000	15	1	4	0	5	0
Vining, Ken, Birm.*	1.000	3	0	2	0	2	0
Virchis, Adam, Birm.	.000	1	0	0	0	0	0
Walls, Doug, Car.	.900	26	10	17	3	30	1
Walters, Brett, Mob.	1.000	9	0	4	0	4	0
Weaver, Jeff, Jack.	1.000	1	1	0	0	1	0
Webb, Alan, Jack.*	.923	26	6	30	3	39	2
Wells, Kip, Birm.	.875	11	3	4	1	8	0
Wheeler, Dan, Orl.	1.000	9	5	2	0	7	0
Whitley, Curtis, Birm.*	.917	36	4	7	1	12	0
Winkelsas, Joe, Gre.	.813	55	4	9	3	16	3
Wohlers, Mark, Chat.	.000	2	0	0	0	0	0
Wunsch, Kelly, Hun.*	.923	22	3	9	1	13	1
Yankosky, L.J., Gre.	.974	20	19	19	1	39	3
Yennaco, Jay, Knox.	1.000	8	1	3	0	4	0
Yoder, Jeff, W.T.	.938	29	3	12	1	16	3
Young, Danny, W.T.*	1.000	27	2	7	0	9	0
Zamarripa, Mark, Car.	1.000	5	1	6	0	7	0
Zambrano, Victor, Orl.	.882	40	4	11	2	17	1

TRIPLE PLAY: E. Hernandez.

PITCHERS WITH TWO OR MORE TEAMS

Player, Team	Pct.	G	PO	A	E	TC	DP
Giron, Isabel, Knox.	1.000	17	6	14	0	20	0
Giron, Isabel, Mob.	1.000	11	2	7	0	9	0

LEAGUE CHAMPIONS

Year	Team	Pct.
1888—	Dallas	.671
1889—	Houston	.551
1890—	Galveston	.705
1892—	Houston	.741
	Houston	.613
1895—	Dallas	.754
	Fort Worth*	.750
1896—	Fort Worth	.757
	Houston*	.679
	Galveston	.548
1897—	San Antonio†	.657
	Galveston†	.717
1898—League disbanded.		
1899—	Galveston	.632
	Galveston	.762
1900-01—Did not operate.		
1902—	Corsicana	.866
	Corsicana	.682
1903—	Paris-Waco	.615
	Dallas*	.648
1904—	Corsicana*	.615
	Fort Worth	.800
1905—	Fort Worth	.545
1906—	Fort Worth	.677
	Cleburne∞	.609
1907—	Austin	.629
1908—	San Antonio	.664
1909—	Houston	.601
1910—	Dallas†	.586
	Houston†	.586
1911—	Austin	.575
1912—	Houston	.626
1913—	Houston	.620
1914—	Houston†	.671
	Waco†	.671
1915—	Waco	.592
1916—	Waco	.587

Year	Team	Pct.
1917—	Dallas	.600
1918—	Dallas	.584
1919—	Shreveport*	.677
	Fort Worth	.651
1920—	Fort Worth	.703
	Fort Worth	.750
1921—	Fort Worth	.691
	Fort Worth	.662
1922—	Fort Worth	.694
	Fort Worth	.711
1923—	Fort Worth	.632
1924—	Fort Worth	.689
	Fort Worth	.763
1925—	Fort Worth	.711
	Fort Worth▲	.653
1926—	Dallas	.574
1927—	Wichita Falls	.654
1928—	Houston*	.679
	Wichita Falls	.731
1929—	Dallas*	.588
	Wichita Falls	.620
1930—	Wichita Falls	.697
	Fort Worth*	.632
1931—	Houston♦	.625
	Houston	.734
1932—	Beaumont*	.640
	Dallas	.727
1933—	Houston	.623
	San Antonio (4th)§	.523
1934—	Galveston‡	.579
1935—	Oklahoma City‡	.590
1936—	Dallas	.604
	Tulsa (3rd)§	.519
1937—	Oklahoma City	.635
	Fort Worth (3rd)§	.535
1938—	Beaumont	.635

Year	Team	Pct.
1939—	Houston	.606
	Fort Worth (4th)§	.540
1940—	Houston‡	.652
1941—	Houston	.673
	Dallas (4th)§	.519
1942—	Beaumont	.605
	Shreveport (2nd)§	.576
1943-44-45—Did not operate.		
1946—	Fort Worth	.656
	Dallas (2nd)§	.591
1947—	Houston‡	.623
1948—	Fort Worth‡	.601
1949—	Fort Worth	.649
	Tulsa (2nd)§	.584
1950—	Beaumont	.595
	San Antonio (4th)§	.513
1951—	Houston‡	.619
1952—	Dallas	.571
	Shreveport (3rd)§	.522
1953—	Dallas‡	.571
1954—	Shreveport	.559
	Houston (2nd)§	.553
1955—	Dallas	.581
	Shreveport (3rd)§	.540
1956—	Houston‡	.623
1957—	Dallas	.662
	Houston (2nd)§	.630
1958—	Fort Worth	.582
	Cor. Christi (3rd)§	.507
1959—	Victoria	.589
	Austin (2nd)§	.548
1960—	Rio Grande Valley	.590
	Tulsa (3rd)	.528
1961—	Amarillo	.643
	San Antonio (3rd)§	.532
1962—	El Paso	.571
	Tulsa (2nd)§	.550

CLASS AA *Texas League*

Year	Team	Pct.	Year	Team	Pct.	Year	Team•	Pct.
1963—	San Antonio	.564	1977—	El Paso	.600	1989—	Arkansas•	.585
	Tulsa (3rd)§	.529		Arkansas•	.485		Wichita	.537
1964—	San Antonio‡	.607	1978—	El Paso•	.593	1990—	San Antonio	.582
1965—	Tulsa	.574		Jackson	.567		Shreveport•	.489
	Albuquerque■	.550	1979—	Arkansas•	.571	1991—	Shreveport•	.632
1966—	Arkansas	.579		Midland	.563		El Paso	.596
1967—	Albuquerque	.557	1980—	Arkansas•	.596	1992—	Shreveport	.566
1968—	Arkansas	.586		San Antonio	.544		Wichita•	.515
	El Paso■	.562	1981—	San Antonio	.571	1993—	El Paso	.563
1969—	Amarillo	.593		Jackson•	.507		Jackson•	.541
	Memphis■	.504	1982—	El Paso	.559	1994—	El Paso•	.647
1970—	Albuquerque◆	.615		Tulsa•	.515		Jackson	.548
	Memphis	.507	1983—	Jackson	.507	1995—	Shreveport•	.652
1971—	Did not operate as league—clubs were members of Dixie Association.			Beaumont•	.500		Midland	.485
1972—	Alexandria	.600	1984—	Beaumont	.654	1996—	Jackson•	.547
	El Paso■	.557		Jackson•	.610		Wichita	.500
1973—	San Antonio	.590	1985—	El Paso	.632	1997—	San Antonio•	.604
	Memphis■	.558		Jackson•	.537		Shreveport	.551
1974—	Victoria■	.581	1986—	El Paso•	.630	1998—	Arkansas	.571
	El Paso	.555		Jackson	.533		Tulsa•	.557
1975—	Lafayette▼	.558	1987—	Wichita•	.515	1999—	Wichita•	.593
	Midland▼	.604		Jackson	.515			
1976—	Amarillo■	.600	1988—	El Paso	.552			
	Shreveport	.515		Tulsa•	.522			

*Won split-season playoff. †Won playoff for title. ‡Finished first and won four-club playoff. §Won four-club playoff. ∞Title to Cleburne by default. ▲Tied with Dallas in second half and won playoff for championship. ◆Tied with Beaumont at end of first half and won title in best-of-five series played as part of second-half schedule. ■League divided into Eastern, Western divisions; won two-team playoff. ▼League divided into Eastern, Western divisions; declared co-champions when playoffs were not completed. •League divided into Eastern and Western divisions and played split-season; won playoffs. NOTE—Championship awarded to winner of four-team play-off, 1933-51; first-place team and playoff winner co-champions, 1952-64

CALIFORNIA LEAGUE

LEAGUE OFFICE

President
Joe Gagliardi
Address
2380 S. Bascom Ave., Suite 200
Campbell, CA 95008
Phone
408-369-8038

Teams (affiliation)
Bakersfield Blaze (Giants)
High Desert Mavericks (Diamondbacks)
Lake Elsinore Storm (Angels)
Lancaster Jethawks (Mariners)
Modesto A's (A's)
Rancho Cucamonga Quakes (Padres)

San Bernardino Stampede (Dodgers)
San Jose Giants (Giants)
Stockton Ports (Brewers)
Visalia Oaks (A's)

1999 FINAL STANDINGS

FIRST HALF

NORTHERN DIVISION

Team	W	L	T	Pct.	GB
Modesto (Athletics)	44	26	0	.629	...
San Jose (Giants)	38	32	0	.543	6.0
Bakersfield (Giants)	36	34	0	.514	8.0
Stockton (Brewers)	34	36	0	.486	10.0
Visalia (Athletics)	32	38	0	.457	12.0

SOUTHERN DIVISION

Team	W	L	T	Pct.	GB
Rancho Cucamonga (Padres)	42	28	0	.600	...
San Bernardino (Dodgers)	41	29	0	.586	1.0
Lake Elsinore (Angels)	30	40	0	.429	12.0
High Desert (Diamondbacks)	30	40	0	.429	12.0
Lancaster (Mariners)	23	47	0	.329	19.0

SECOND HALF

NORTHERN DIVISION

Team	W	L	T	Pct.	GB
Modesto (Athletics)	44	26	0	.629	...
Visalia (Athletics)	43	27	0	.614	1.0
San Jose (Giants)	37	33	0	.529	7.0
Bakersfield (Giants)	28	42	0	.400	16.0
Stockton (Brewers)	23	47	0	.329	21.0

SOUTHERN DIVISION

Team	W	L	T	Pct.	GB
San Bernardino (Dodgers)	39	32	0	.549	...
High Desert (Diamondbacks)	38	33	0	.535	1.0
Rancho Cucamonga (Padres)	34	36	0	.486	4.5
Lake Elsinore (Angels)	33	37	0	.471	5.5
Lancaster (Mariners)	32	38	0	.457	6.5

COMPOSITE

Team	Mod.	S.B.	R.C.	Vis.	S.J.	H.D.	Bak.	L.E.	Stoc.	Lan.	W	L	T	Pct.	GB
Modesto (Athletics)	...	8	9	8	13	8	12	9	12	9	88	52	0	.629	...
San Bernardino (Dodgers)	4	...	12	7	6	7	8	15	10	11	80	61	0	.567	8.5
Rancho Cucamonga (Padres)	3	8	...	5	5	12	9	12	8	14	76	64	0	.543	12.0
Visalia (Athletics)	12	5	7	...	11	9	10	5	8	8	75	65	0	.536	13.0
San Jose (Giants)	8	6	7	9	...	8	14	5	11	7	75	65	0	.536	13.0
High Desert (Diamondbacks)	4	14	8	3	4	...	4	10	9	12	68	73	0	.482	20.5
Bakersfield (Giants)	8	4	3	10	5	8	...	6	12	8	64	76	0	.457	24.0
Lake Elsinore (Angels)	3	5	8	7	7	10	6	...	7	10	63	77	0	.450	25.0
Stockton (Brewers)	7	2	4	12	9	3	9	5	...	6	57	83	0	.407	31.0
Lancaster (Mariners)	3	9	6	4	5	8	4	10	6	...	55	85	0	.393	33.0

Major league affiliations in parentheses.

High Desert plays home games in Adelanto, Calif.

PLAYOFFS: San Bernardino defeated High Desert two games to none; San Jose defeated Visalia two games to one; San Bernardino defeated Rancho Cucamonga three games to two; San Jose defeated Modesto three games to two; San Bernardino defeated San Jose three games to two to win league championship.

REGULAR-SEASON ATTENDANCE: Bakersfield, 107,747; High Desert, 146,772; Lake Elsinore, 282,533; Lancaster, 218,479; Modesto, 133,757; Rancho Cucamonga, 321,682; San Bernardino, 167,437; San Jose, 157,598; Stockton, 73,702; Visalia, 65,538. Total—1,675,245. Playoffs (20 games)—31,512. California-Carolina League All-Star Game at Lake Elsinore, Calif.—6,518.

MANAGERS: Bakersfield, Keith Comstock; High Desert, Derek Bryant; Lake Elsinore, Mario Mendoza; Lancaster, Darrin Garner; Modesto, Bob Geren; Rancho Cucamonga, Tom Levasseur; San Bernardino, Rick Burleson, San Jose, Lenn Sakata; Stockton, Bernie Moncallo (through July 23) and Carlos Ponce (from July 24 through end of season); Visalia, Juan Navarette.

ALL-STAR TEAM: 1B—Robb Gorr, San Bernardino; 2B—Belvani Martinez, High Desert; 3B—Jacques Landry, Modesto; SS—Nelson Castro, Lake Elsinore and Alex Cintron, High Desert; OF—Chin-Feng Chen, San Bernardino; Jack Cust, High Desert; Eric Byrnes, Modesto; DH—Wilbert Nieves, Rancho Cucamonga; LHP—Randey Dorame, San Bernardino; RHP—Rick Guttormson, Rancho Cucamonga; RHP—Scot Shields, Lake Elsinore; RHP—Bill Everly, San Bernardino; Most Valuable Player—Chin-Feng Chen, San Bernardino; Rookie of the Year—Chin-Feng Chen, San Bernardino; Pitcher of the Year—Randey Dorame, San Bernardino; Manager of the Year—Bob Geren, Modesto.

1999 BATTING

TEAM

Team	Avg.	G	TPA	AB	R	H	TB	2B	3B	HR	RBI	SH	SF	HP	BB	IBB	SO	SB	CS	GDP	LOB	ShO	Slg.	OBP
High Desert	.293	141	5667	4941	903	1449	2296	268	51	159	827	42	44	57	583	13	1116	140	100	97	1053	5	.465	.371
Modesto	.289	140	5628	4885	872	1410	2196	300	63	120	787	28	67	73	575	11	1075	193	88	95	1073	4	.450	.368
San Bernardino	.287	141	5616	4936	764	1416	2039	224	57	95	685	51	44	68	517	27	918	145	78	112	1085	4	.413	.360
Lancaster	.279	140	5535	4892	812	1363	2124	249	43	142	726	36	37	70	500	17	1112	137	91	87	1018	7	.434	.352
Visalia	.274	140	5671	4791	871	1312	2045	259	39	132	783	38	56	85	701	19	1044	154	88	108	1113	4	.427	.372
R. Cucamonga	.273	140	5388	4755	715	1300	1903	237	33	100	628	35	36	78	484	17	1016	136	78	142	1000	4	.400	.348
Lake Elsinore	.273	140	5469	4831	753	1320	1992	274	61	92	669	27	49	66	496	11	1034	190	91	91	985	6	.412	.346
Stockton	.268	140	5364	4787	654	1283	1826	223	43	78	596	38	58	75	406	19	991	126	95	84	987	5	.381	.331
Bakersfield	.268	140	5407	4786	685	1281	1789	224	43	66	613	23	43	77	478	12	1116	187	99	77	1017	10	.374	.341
San Jose	.264	140	5457	4780	722	1260	1948	254	26	126	649	39	33	76	529	15	1143	134	61	97	1059	7	.408	.344

TOP QUALIFIERS FOR BATTING CHAMPIONSHIP

Minimum 378 plate appearances. *Lefthanded batter. †Switch-hitter.

Player, Team	Avg.	G	TPA	AB	R	H	TB	2B	3B	HR	RBI	SH	SF	HP	BB	IBB	SO	SB	CS	GDP	Slg.	OBP
Byrnes, Eric, Mod.	.337	96	439	365	86	123	171	28	1	6	66	0	7	9	58	2	37	28	8	14	.468	.433
Cust, Jack, H.D.*	.334	125	556	455	107	152	296	42	3	32	112	0	3	2	96	2	145	1	4	5	.651	.450
Martinez, Belvani, H.D.	.333	109	511	477	84	159	224	23	9	8	55	3	4	9	18	1	69	35	30	5	.470	.366
Otero, William, S.J.	.333	96	443	402	81	134	198	28	3	10	56	1	1	2	37	0	67	20	4	5	.493	.391
Hammock, Robert, H.D.	.332	114	434	379	80	126	187	20	7	9	72	0	6	2	47	2	63	3	6	8	.493	.403
Nieves, Wilbert, R.C.	.328	120	477	427	58	140	191	26	2	7	61	1	4	5	40	1	54	2	7	12	.447	.389
Clark, Doug, Bak.*	.326	118	484	420	67	137	191	17	2	11	58	0	0	5	59	4	89	17	11	5	.455	.415
Thomas, Gary, Mod.	.323	99	398	344	69	111	154	14	4	7	38	8	4	9	33	1	45	23	6	7	.448	.392
Gorr, Robb, S.B.	.319	132	591	546	67	174	241	22	6	11	106	3	7	5	30	5	59	5	2	14	.441	.355
Gonzalez, Jimmy, S.B.	.316	111	505	471	78	149	204	28	6	5	53	5	4	5	20	2	55	9	9	8	.433	.348
Chen, Chin-Feng, S.B.	.316	131	597	510	98	161	296	22	10	31	123	0	7	5	75	6	129	31	7	7	.580	.404
Clark, Jermaine, Lan.*	.315	126	573	502	112	158	219	27	8	6	61	8	3	2	58	2	80	33	15	10	.436	.386
Gallo, Ismael, S.B.*	.314	104	401	338	66	106	133	15	3	2	42	12	4	7	40	2	30	3	1	4	.393	.393
Keith, Rusty, Vis.	.313	124	544	448	87	140	204	28	3	10	62	3	4	7	82	1	59	10	8	13	.455	.423
German, Esteban, Mod.	.311	128	620	501	107	156	208	16	12	4	52	5	7	5	102	0	128	40	16	3	.415	.428
Landry, Jacques, Mod.	.311	133	580	508	92	158	297	46	6	27	111	3	12	10	47	2	128	18	4	6	.585	.373

DEPARTMENTAL LEADERS: G—Zuniga, 136; AB—Hart, 550; R—Clark, 112; H—Gorr, 174; TB—Landry, 297; 2B—Hart, 48; 3B—Salazar, 18; HR—Cust, 32; RBI—Chen, Hart, Mensik, 123 each; SH—Cintron, 17; SF—Cridland, 16; HP—Blakely, 20; BB—German, 102; IBB—Mensik, 11; SO—Flaherty, 168; SB—Castro, 53; CS—Martinez, 30; GIDP—Pelaez, 24; Slg.—Cust, .651; OBP—Cust, .450.

ALL PLAYERS

*Lefthanded batter. †Switch-hitter.

Player, Team	Avg.	G	TPA	AB	R	H	TB	2B	3B	HR	RBI	SH	SF	HP	BB	IBB	SO	SB	CS	GDP	Slg.	OBP
Ahrendt, Jay, R.C.*	.256	40	137	121	14	31	41	5	1	1	14	0	0	16	0	44	0	1	1		.339	.343
Alcala, Juan, Lan.	.071	8	15	14	0	1	2	1	0	0	2	0	0	1	0	7	0	0	0		.143	.133
Allen, Jeff, Bak.	.265	130	541	480	80	127	195	32	3	10	65	0	4	10	47	0	130	24	5	12	.406	.340
Amador, Gerardo, Lan.	.270	19	81	74	12	20	28	3	1	1	9	2	0	2	3	0	24	2	1	0	.378	.316
Arias, George, R.C.	.190	7	23	21	1	4	9	2	0	1	4	0	0	0	2	0	9	0	0	1	.429	.261
Basabe, Jesus, Mod.	.235	95	366	310	45	73	141	21	1	15	51	1	3	16	36	0	97	12	5	5	.455	.342
Bazzani, Matt, S.J.	.237	34	102	93	18	22	49	4	1	7	12	0	1	8	0	29	0	0	1		.527	.304
Beatriz, Ramy, Stoc.*	.242	41	159	149	21	36	50	7	2	1	10	0	2	1	7	0	24	3	5	1	.336	.277
Belliard, Francisco, H.D.†	.255	16	54	47	4	12	15	1	1	0	1	2	0	1	4	0	16	1	1	0	.319	.321
Bertrand, Ben, Bak.	.190	12	25	21	3	4	5	1	0	0	0	0	0	1	3	0	7	0	0	1	.238	.320
Betten, Randy, L.E.	.327	15	56	52	11	17	22	2	0	1	7	0	0	1	3	0	10	3	0	2	.423	.375
Blair, James, S.B.	.256	25	96	78	13	20	30	2	1	2	7	0	1	1	16	0	15	3	2	4	.385	.385
Blakely, Darren, L.E.†	.251	124	571	510	88	128	222	38	10	12	63	1	4	20	36	1	159	23	13	3	.435	.323
Bledsoe, Hunter, S.B.	.265	45	178	166	17	44	62	10	1	2	13	0	1	2	9	0	27	3	0	6	.373	.309
Briones, Chris, R.C.	.184	27	82	76	3	14	20	3	0	1	6	2	0	1	3	0	23	0	0	2	.263	.225
Brown, Jason, S.B.	.218	68	267	234	28	51	84	11	2	6	28	3	0	7	23	1	64	1	2	9	.359	.307
Burns, Xavier, Bak.	.218	80	265	229	28	50	74	9	3	3	29	0	6	11	19	1	70	10	9	6	.323	.302
Burroughs, Sean, R.C.*	.435	6	27	23	3	10	16	3	0	1	5	0	0	1	3	0	3	0	1	1	.696	.519
Bush, Darren, R.C.*	.282	77	277	238	35	67	102	9	1	8	36	2	0	1	36	1	51	7	4	7	.429	.379
Byrnes, Eric, Mod.	.337	96	439	365	86	123	171	28	1	6	66	0	7	9	58	2	37	28	8	14	.468	.433
Caiazzo, Nick, Stoc.	.300	114	468	430	51	129	182	21	4	8	56	1	4	8	25	0	85	2	3	12	.423	.347
Calloway, Ronald, H.D.*	.316	60	230	196	41	62	87	14	1	3	23	2	0	2	30	0	34	22	7	3	.444	.412
Camilo, Juan, Vis.*	.284	82	324	285	58	81	153	17	2	17	52	0	1	4	34	0	89	7	6	8	.537	.367
Campusano, Carlos, S.J.-Bak.	.326	41	152	135	20	44	56	4	1	2	11	3	1	6	7	0	28	6	3	1	.415	.383
Casper, Brett, S.J.	.266	121	505	436	71	116	190	22	2	16	77	4	3	6	56	2	135	20	10	12	.436	.355
Castro, Nelson, L.E.	.250	125	495	444	68	111	154	16	12	1	50	5	4	3	36	1	75	53	19	5	.347	.308
Cepeda, Ali, S.J.	.077	9	13	13	0	1	1	0	0	0	0	0	0	0	0	0	4	0	0	0	.077	.077
Cesar, Dionys, Vis.†	.322	77	371	320	59	103	155	21	5	7	62	2	5	3	41	3	51	21	11	8	.484	.398
Chatman, Karl, L.E.	.267	79	336	300	40	80	109	13	2	4	37	1	2	4	29	2	87	13	9	9	.363	.337
Chen, Chin-Feng, S.B.	.316	131	597	510	98	161	296	22	10	31	123	0	7	5	75	6	129	31	7	7	.580	.404
Cintron, Alex, H.D.†	.307	128	542	499	78	153	195	25	4	3	64	17	4	3	19	0	65	15	8	14	.391	.333
Clark, Doug, Bak.*	.326	118	484	420	67	137	191	17	2	11	58	0	0	5	59	4	89	17	11	5	.455	.415
Clark, Jermaine, Lan.*	.315	126	573	502	112	158	219	27	8	6	61	8	3	2	58	2	80	33	15	10	.436	.386
Clifton, Rodney, Vis.	.261	110	446	371	67	97	162	30	4	9	56	2	6	4	63	1	81	12	5	6	.437	.369
Colon, Jose, Stoc.	.258	97	296	264	49	68	90	9	2	3	28	1	2	6	23	0	62	15	6	3	.341	.324
Connors, Greg, Lan.	.268	117	500	448	72	120	202	20	7	16	84	1	5	6	40	2	91	10	7	3	.451	.333
Cosbey, Chris, Mod.*	.200	39	102	90	16	18	22	4	0	0	7	1	1	1	9	0	23	9	4	1	.244	.277
Cosme, Caonabo, Mod.	.214	122	499	444	55	95	126	21	2	2	47	3	3	4	45	1	148	14	7	12	.284	.290
Cridland, Mark, Stoc.*	.261	124	497	437	51	114	189	26	5	13	87	5	16	6	33	2	64	14	7	6	.432	.311
Cromer, Tripp, S.B.	.500	4	18	18	3	9	15	3	0	1	6	0	0	0	0	0	3	0	0	0	.833	.500
Crosby, Bubba, S.B.*	.296	96	424	371	53	110	140	21	3	1	37	4	1	6	42	3	71	19	8	6	.377	.372
Cruz, Cirilo, Lan.	.249	94	378	342	51	85	135	12	1	12	44	3	1	4	28	1	73	1	1	4	.395	.312
Cruz, Hector, H.D.†	.220	14	44	41	8	9	10	1	0	0	3	0	0	1	2	0	11	0	1	0	.244	.273
Cuntz, Casey, H.D.	.265	86	301	257	46	68	111	11	1	10	39	3	1	2	38	1	61	0	2	6	.432	.362
Curtis, Matt, L.E.†	.261	126	536	460	72	120	201	26	2	17	76	0	6	2	68	3	84	2	2	8	.437	.354
Cust, Jack, H.D.*	.334	125	556	455	107	152	296	42	3	32	112	0	3	2	96	2	145	1	4	5	.651	.450
Daeley, Scott, S.J.	.222	2	9	9	1	2	2	0	0	0	0	0	0	0	0	0	2	1	0	0	.222	.222
Dean, Mike, S.J.	.284	23	96	81	16	23	34	4	2	1	12	1	2	1	11	0	15	13	3	1	.420	.368
Deardorff, Jeff, Stoc.	.266	126	485	436	59	116	172	22	2	10	47	1	2	6	40	1	150	2	7	5	.394	.335
De La Cruz, Jose, Vis.	.209	43	131	115	17	24	43	5	1	4	17	0	2	2	12	0	32	3	1	4	.374	.290
Dewey, Jason, L.E.	.322	66	276	242	48	78	131	23	0	10	31	0	2	2	30	0	62	0	0	5	.541	.399
DiSarcina, Gary, L.E.	.083	4	14	12	0	1	1	0	0	0	0	1	0	0	1	0	0	0	0	0	.083	.154
Dougherty, Jeb, L.E.	.260	115	452	381	66	99	141	13	4	7	45	4	3	10	54	0	68	35	13	11	.370	.364
Eady, Gerald, Lan.	.245	52	190	151	20	37	50	4	3	1	18	3	1	8	27	0	57	7	12	2	.331	.385

Player, Team	Avg.	G	TPA	AB	R	H	TB	2B	3B	HR	RBI	SH	SF	HP	BB	IBB	SO	SB	CS	GDP	Slg.	OBP
Eberwein, Kevin, R.C.	.259	110	475	417	69	108	200	30	4	18	69	2	2	12	42	0	139	7	5	7	.480	.342
Edmonds, Jim, L.E.*	.421	5	23	19	4	8	10	2	0	0	3	0	0	0	4	0	2	2	0	0	.526	.522
Estrada, Marco, Lan.†	.200	13	38	35	3	7	9	2	0	0	3	0	0	1	2	0	8	1	0	1	.257	.263
Faircloth, Chad, Bak.*	.262	51	162	145	14	38	52	12	1	0	16	1	2	0	14	1	35	5	4	2	.359	.323
Fernandez, Alex, Lan.*	.282	118	458	426	63	120	195	29	2	14	62	5	2	4	21	1	83	21	11	13	.458	.320
Figueroa, Luis, Lan.	.356	39	168	146	21	52	74	8	1	4	20	0	2	2	18	2	8	2	2	10	.507	.429
Flaherty, Tim, S.J.	.267	132	573	490	82	131	245	33	3	25	88	0	5	9	69	3	168	11	3	5	.500	.365
Flores, Javier, Vis.	.296	103	406	362	48	107	146	22	1	5	63	2	6	9	27	0	59	6	3	8	.403	.354
Fox, Jason, Stoc.†	.234	70	276	248	34	58	75	8	3	1	18	10	2	2	14	0	63	15	4	7	.302	.278
Freitas, Joe, L.E.	.111	3	10	9	1	1	2	1	0	0	1	0	0	0	1	0	3	0	0	0	.222	.200
French, Ron, R.C.	.150	7	26	20	2	3	5	0	1	0	3	1	0	4	1	0	5	0	0	0	.250	.320
Fuentes, Joel, Bak.†	.198	64	184	162	20	32	37	5	0	0	16	1	2	0	19	0	38	5	1	1	.228	.279
Gallo, Ismael, S.B.*	.314	104	401	338	66	106	133	15	3	2	42	12	4	7	40	2	30	3	1	4	.393	.393
German, Esteban, Mod.	.311	128	620	501	107	156	208	16	12	4	52	5	7	5	102	0	128	40	16	3	.415	.428
Glendenning, Mike, S.J.	.245	104	453	368	71	90	187	26	1	23	80	0	3	11	71	2	112	7	4	10	.508	.380
Goldfield, Josh, H.D.*	.400	5	6	5	2	2	2	0	0	0	0	0	0	0	1	0	0	0	0	0	.400	.500
Gonzalez, Jimmy, S.B.	.316	111	505	471	78	149	204	28	6	5	53	5	4	5	20	2	55	9	9	8	.433	.348
Gorr, Robb, S.B.	.319	132	591	546	67	174	241	22	6	11	106	3	7	5	30	5	59	5	2	14	.441	.355
Graham, Justin, H.D.	.100	4	10	10	0	1	1	0	0	0	1	0	0	0	0	0	4	0	0	0	.100	.100
Graves, Bryan, L.E.	.237	15	46	38	3	9	11	2	0	0	6	0	1	0	7	0	13	0	0	1	.289	.348
Greene, Clay, Bak.	.257	46	170	148	19	38	40	2	0	0	17	3	0	1	18	0	44	16	4	2	.270	.341
Grudzielanek, Mark, S.B.	.250	4	16	16	2	4	4	0	0	0	0	0	0	0	0	1	0	2	1	0	.250	.250
Guiel, Jeff, L.E.*	.328	15	69	58	12	19	36	4	2	3	12	0	0	0	11	0	18	2	1	0	.621	.435
Hagins, Steve, L.E.	.262	40	152	141	21	37	65	14	1	4	22	0	1	5	5	0	39	2	1	3	.461	.309
Halloran, Matt, R.C.	.217	95	338	309	39	67	82	11	2	0	22	4	1	7	17	0	75	15	9	17	.265	.272
Hammock, Robert, H.D.	.332	114	434	379	80	126	187	20	7	9	72	0	6	2	47	2	63	3	6	8	.493	.403
Hargrove, Harvey, Lan.	.294	130	574	510	83	150	207	20	2	11	80	4	5	3	51	0	116	17	16	5	.406	.359
Hart, Jason, Mod.	.305	135	617	550	96	168	277	48	2	19	123	0	7	4	56	1	105	2	5	18	.504	.370
Hartman, Ron, H.D.	.250	33	135	124	13	31	43	6	0	2	22	0	1	3	7	1	13	0	0	7	.347	.304
Haynes, Nathan, Vis.-L.E.*	.318	61	292	255	47	81	111	12	6	2	29	2	2	4	29	0	46	22	15	3	.435	.393
Hernandez, John, S.B.	.261	61	227	199	31	52	90	17	0	7	25	4	0	3	21	1	44	0	1	8	.452	.341
Hill, Steve, Bak.†	.266	135	581	522	78	139	167	16	6	0	60	10	2	6	40	0	99	39	13	7	.320	.325
Hollandsworth, Todd, S.B.*	.385	4	16	13	3	5	7	2	0	0	3	0	0	1	2	0	4	0	1	1	.538	.500
Hood, Jay, L.E.	.235	102	411	374	48	88	121	14	5	3	43	5	6	2	24	0	81	8	9	7	.324	.281
Howe, Matt, Vis.	.200	42	143	120	14	24	32	3	1	1	11	0	2	3	18	0	27	3	4	3	.267	.315
Huisman, Jason, L.E.	.275	91	382	346	50	95	127	17	3	3	43	0	4	8	24	0	64	10	5	8	.367	.332
Hunter, Johnny, R.C.	.217	25	116	106	11	23	27	4	0	0	9	0	2	0	8	0	32	1	2	1	.255	.267
Illig, Brett, S.B.	.236	75	309	276	33	65	86	11	2	2	25	2	3	5	23	0	74	7	3	9	.312	.303
Jacobsen, Buck, Stoc.	.250	46	182	156	22	39	62	8	0	5	22	0	1	4	21	1	40	3	3	4	.397	.352
Jaramillo, Lee, Stoc.	.229	23	54	48	4	11	18	2	1	1	10	0	0	1	5	0	13	1	2	2	.375	.315
Johnson, James, Stoc.†	.000	30	0	0	1	0	0	0	0	0	0	0	0	0	0	0	0	0	0	0	.000	.000
Johnson, Patrick, L.E.-H.D.	.266	63	210	177	22	47	62	6	0	3	21	3	1	0	29	0	53	0	2	2	.350	.367
Jones, Tim, Vis.*	.205	72	229	185	31	38	65	8	2	5	31	0	2	2	40	1	76	9	1	3	.351	.349
Keith, Rusty, Vis.	.313	124	544	448	87	140	204	28	3	10	62	3	4	7	82	1	59	10	8	13	.455	.423
Kennedy, Gus, L.E.	.204	29	109	93	13	19	33	5	0	3	13	0	1	0	15	0	25	4	2	3	.355	.312
Kirby, Scott, Stoc.	.287	60	238	202	35	58	109	15	3	10	36	0	4	7	25	2	59	3	3	7	.540	.378
Koeyers, Ramsey, H.D.	.235	5	19	17	3	4	7	0	0	1	2	1	0	1	0	0	3	0	0	1	.412	.278
Koonce, Graham, R.C.*	.285	132	569	474	76	135	210	16	1	19	79	0	6	11	76	5	110	4	1	12	.443	.392
Kraus, Jake, Stoc.	.236	25	79	72	4	17	23	4	1	0	11	0	1	0	6	0	11	0	1	2	.319	.291
Kuzmic, Craig, Lan.†	.204	32	130	108	19	22	41	4	0	5	15	0	1	1	20	1	43	3	1	1	.380	.331
Landry, Jacques, Mod.	.311	133	580	508	92	158	297	46	6	27	111	3	12	10	47	2	128	18	4	6	.585	.373
Lara, Eddie, Vis.†	.299	105	424	358	67	107	166	20	6	9	56	6	5	11	44	0	45	25	16	17	.464	.388
Leggett, Adam, L.E.†	.243	57	211	185	19	45	68	14	0	3	25	2	2	2	20	1	30	6	3	3	.368	.321
Leyritz, Jim, R.C.	.000	1	4	4	0	0	0	0	0	0	0	0	0	0	0	0	1	0	0	0	.000	.000
Leyva, Julian, Vis.*	1.000	16	1	1	0	1	1	0	0	0	0	0	0	0	0	0	0	0	0	0	1.000	1.000
Light, Tal, Stoc.	.118	4	17	17	1	2	2	0	0	0	2	0	0	0	0	0	13	0	0	1	.118	.118
Lopez, Miguel, H.D.	.200	9	22	20	1	4	5	1	0	0	3	0	1	1	0	0	7	0	0	2	.250	.227
Lopez, Norberto, L.E.	.000	2	4	4	0	0	0	0	0	0	0	0	0	0	0	0	2	0	0	0	.000	.000
Lopez, Rafael, Lan.	.287	72	270	247	37	71	102	10	3	5	28	2	1	5	15	0	36	5	4	11	.413	.340
Luderer, Brian, Mod.	.286	55	204	182	22	52	72	13	2	1	22	2	2	2	16	1	25	3	3	5	.396	.347
Ludwick, Ryan, Mod.	.275	43	198	171	28	47	76	11	3	4	34	0	5	3	19	0	45	2	1	0	.444	.348
Luke, Matt, L.E.*	.340	13	61	53	10	18	29	5	3	0	7	0	0	1	7	1	14	2	0	0	.547	.426
Luster, Jeremy, Bak.†	.201	52	207	184	26	37	47	4	3	0	19	0	1	0	22	1	54	9	4	6	.255	.285
Macalutas, Jon, Stoc.	.281	32	142	121	12	34	47	7	0	2	20	0	3	2	15	0	16	2	2	3	.388	.362
Magdaleno, Ricky, Lan.	.348	23	103	89	12	31	42	4	2	1	14	0	2	1	11	0	12	2	1	1	.472	.417
Manzueta, Roberto, H.D.*	.000	40	2	2	0	0	0	0	0	0	0	0	0	0	0	0	1	0	0	0	.000	.000
Mapes, Jake, Bak.	.176	11	18	17	3	3	5	2	0	0	3	0	0	1	0	0	7	0	0	0	.294	.222
Marchiano, Mike, Lan.	.313	47	204	182	25	57	79	11	1	3	29	0	3	3	16	1	28	4	1	5	.434	.373
Martin, Jared, H.D.†	.240	89	318	283	38	68	90	12	2	2	30	3	1	2	29	0	46	2	4	2	.318	.314
Martines, Jason, H.D.*	.000	43	2	1	0	0	0	0	0	0	0	0	0	0	1	0	1	0	0	0	.000	.500
Martinez, Belvan, H.D.	.333	109	511	477	84	159	224	23	9	8	55	3	4	9	18	1	69	35	30	7	.470	.358
Martinez, Hipolito, Vis.	.267	113	501	431	93	115	208	24	3	21	77	1	5	5	59	1	119	8	4	8	.483	.358
Mathis, Jared, Stoc.	.230	23	66	61	7	14	15	1	0	0	10	0	1	2	2	0	3	1	3	1	.246	.273
Matthews, Lamont, S.B.*	.267	4	17	15	2	4	8	1	0	1	3	0	0	0	2	0	7	1	0	0	.533	.353
Maynard, Scott, Lan.	.259	8	31	27	6	7	14	4	0	1	3	0	0	0	4	0	3	0	0	0	.519	.355
McClure, Brian, R.C.*	.224	36	148	116	26	26	39	5	1	2	15	3	2	1	26	0	22	4	1	1	.336	.366
McCorkle, Shawn, Lan.*	.275	83	340	302	45	83	134	22	1	9	52	0	2	1	35	4	97	1	1	3	.444	.350
McCrotty, Will, S.B.	.254	93	357	319	43	81	111	12	3	4	43	4	6	1	27	0	49	0	2	11	.348	.309
McDowell, Arturo, Bak.*	.222	121	510	441	66	98	140	16	10	2	37	3	6	11	49	0	140	28	23	4	.317	.312
McGowan, Sean, S.J.	.375	2	8	8	1	3	4	1	0	0	1	0	0	0	0	0	3	0	1	0	.500	.375
McKinley, Dan, S.J.*	.226	15	62	53	7	12	19	2	1	1	3	1	0	1	7	1	13	2	0	1	.358	.328
McKinnon, Sandy, H.D.	.667	1	3	3	0	2	2	0	0	0	1	0	0	0	0	0	1	0	0	0	.667	.667
Meier, Dan, H.D.*	.268	129	499	418	85	112	217	25	4	24	89	1	1	9	70	3	138	0	0	6	.519	.384
Melendez, Angel, S.J.	.222	101	411	370	32	82	116	17	1	5	41	4	3	9	24	1	100	10	8	13	.314	.283
Mensik, Todd, Vis.*	.291	134	596	505	93	147	271	29	4	29	123	0	3	9	79	11	114	5	1	8	.537	.394

Player, Team	Avg.	G	TPA	AB	R	H	TB	2B	3B	HR	RBI	SH	SF	HP	BB	IBB	SO	SB	CS	GDP	Slg.	OBP
Messner, Jake, Bak.*	.291	55	192	172	33	50	94	11	6	7	35	0	2	1	16	1	45	2	2	1	.547	.351
Montenegro, Jose, Stoc.	.164	21	59	55	1	9	12	0	0	1	5	1	0	1	2	0	8	0	1	0	.218	.207
Moon, Brian, Stoc.†	.265	116	435	385	52	102	126	14	2	2	30	2	4	7	37	4	40	6	6	9	.327	.337
Moreno, Jose, Lan.	.162	23	77	68	9	11	13	2	0	0	4	1	0	1	7	0	12	4	1	2	.191	.250
Mota, Pedro, S.J.*	.269	50	187	171	26	46	66	3	4	3	19	2	2	0	12	1	38	3	7	2	.386	.314
Mott, Bill, L.E.*	.318	25	103	88	16	28	38	5	1	1	12	2	2	1	10	0	18	6	3	1	.432	.386
Murphy, Nate, L.E.*	.355	28	121	107	21	38	63	8	1	5	20	0	1	2	11	1	27	9	4	0	.589	.421
Myers, Greg, R.C.*	.000	3	4	3	0	0	0	0	0	0	0	0	0	0	1	0	1	0	0	0	.000	.250
Neal, Steve, H.D.*	.250	6	21	20	3	5	11	0	0	2	2	0	0	0	1	0	7	0	0	2	.550	.286
Neubart, Adam, H.D.	.321	55	247	212	47	68	113	9	6	8	38	2	3	10	20	1	52	10	10	3	.533	.400
Newton, Kimani, S.B.	.245	40	158	143	19	35	46	3	4	0	16	0	0	2	13	0	39	9	3	2	.322	.316
Nieckula, Aaron, Vis.	.277	25	81	65	13	18	22	4	0	0	10	2	2	4	8	0	17	2	0	0	.338	.380
Niemet, Robert, Bak.	.263	27	75	57	7	15	19	4	0	0	7	0	1	4	13	0	9	3	1	3	.333	.427
Nieves, Wilbert, R.C.	.328	120	477	427	58	140	191	26	2	7	61	1	4	5	40	1	54	2	7	12	.447	.389
Nunez, Abraham, H.D.†	.273	130	585	488	106	133	240	29	6	22	93	1	8	2	86	2	122	40	13	10	.492	.378
Olivo, Miguel, Mod.	.305	73	268	243	46	74	126	13	6	9	42	1	1	2	21	1	60	4	5	6	.519	.363
Osborne, Mark, H.D.*	.248	113	383	335	52	83	137	15	3	11	69	2	4	2	40	0	88	1	3	9	.409	.328
Osilka, Garret, Stoc.	.255	100	316	278	43	71	96	11	1	4	28	5	2	7	24	0	60	7	9	2	.345	.328
Otero, William, S.J.	.333	96	443	402	81	134	198	28	3	10	56	1	1	2	37	0	67	20	4	5	.493	.391
Owens, Jeremy, R.C.	.158	9	41	38	2	6	7	1	0	0	1	0	1	1	1	0	13	2	1	1	.184	.195
Owens, Ryan, H.D.	.398	26	115	103	19	41	66	7	3	4	28	1	1	1	9	0	30	1	2	0	.641	.447
Pecci, Jay, Vis.†	.252	119	437	377	60	95	116	14	2	1	43	7	1	10	42	0	56	12	7	9	.308	.342
Pelaez, Alex, R.C.	.298	117	482	443	62	132	173	21	4	4	54	1	2	1	35	3	53	7	3	24	.391	.349
Pernalete, Marco, S.J.†	.238	99	412	370	50	88	116	19	0	3	32	5	2	5	30	1	105	10	3	2	.314	.302
Pernell, Brandon, R.C.	.280	133	598	529	96	148	255	30	7	21	84	5	6	8	50	1	156	33	14	14	.482	.347
Pickler, Jeff, Stoc.*	.338	80	336	311	40	105	128	14	3	1	42	1	1	0	23	2	29	7	6	6	.412	.382
Piedra, Jorge, S.B.*	.300	8	36	30	6	9	11	2	0	0	3	1	2	0	3	0	3	1	0	0	.367	.343
Pimentel, Franklin, Vis.†	.500	3	3	2	0	1	1	0	0	0	1	0	1	0	0	0	0	0	1	0	.500	.333
Priebe, Kevin, Stoc.	.000	34	1	0	0	0	0	0	0	0	0	0	1	0	0	0	0	0	0	0	.000	.000
Priess, Matthew, S.J.	.229	86	341	293	35	67	85	11	2	1	28	4	4	2	38	1	38	1	2	11	.290	.318
Pujols, Rafael, Mod.†	.236	71	261	233	28	55	80	16	0	3	32	0	2	1	24	0	34	5	6	4	.343	.308
Quintana, Wilfredo, Lan.	.297	10	40	37	7	11	23	1	1	3	8	0	0	1	2	0	14	1	0	1	.622	.350
Ramirez, Joel, Lan.	.239	106	427	376	55	90	127	17	7	2	42	4	5	13	29	0	64	10	8	3	.338	.312
Ransom, Cody, Bak.	.275	99	420	356	69	98	155	12	6	11	47	1	1	8	54	0	108	15	8	2	.435	.382
Rapp, Travis, L.E.	.176	12	37	34	2	6	8	2	0	0	1	0	0	1	2	0	14	0	0	0	.235	.243
Regan, Jason, Lan.	.255	64	273	231	50	59	123	17	1	15	45	1	2	6	33	2	77	4	1	6	.532	.360
Reynoso, Ismael, S.J.	.249	79	277	253	26	63	86	12	1	3	26	6	1	5	12	0	48	12	3	7	.340	.295
Riggs, Eric, S.B.†	.275	130	611	523	105	144	230	18	10	16	69	7	5	6	70	2	92	27	11	6	.440	.364
Rinne, James, H.D.	.280	104	302	268	45	75	118	10	0	11	39	3	3	1	27	0	66	5	5	9	.440	.344
Rodriguez, Guillermo, Bak.	.290	41	105	93	10	27	35	5	0	1	11	3	2	4	3	0	18	4	0	2	.376	.333
Rodriguez, Juan, L.E.†	.302	86	354	315	54	95	137	12	6	6	50	4	1	2	32	0	70	7	5	5	.435	.369
Rogue, Francisco, Stoc.	.333	8	17	15	2	5	6	1	0	0	3	1	0	0	1	0	0	0	1	0	.400	.375
Rosario, Carlos, Vis.†	.236	37	152	123	27	29	36	5	1	0	16	5	1	2	21	0	29	11	6	1	.293	.354
Rosario, Omar, Mod.*	.298	116	503	419	82	125	175	23	6	5	57	4	4	6	70	1	94	19	12	4	.418	.403
Ross, Justin, L.E.*	.258	22	85	66	10	17	22	3	1	0	5	0	2	0	16	0	16	2	1	2	.333	.393
Rowan, Chris, Stoc.	.237	121	479	431	53	102	168	25	4	11	55	5	4	9	30	1	142	9	5	6	.390	.297
Sachse, Matt, Lan.*	.305	69	272	236	40	72	115	18	2	7	41	1	1	1	33	0	67	5	4	1	.487	.391
Salazar, Oscar, Mod.	.295	130	574	525	100	155	271	26	18	18	105	0	9	1	39	1	106	14	6	10	.516	.342
Salmon, Tim, L.E.	.600	1	5	5	0	3	5	2	0	0	2	0	0	0	0	0	1	0	0	0	1.000	.600
Schaub, Greg, Stoc.	.251	119	459	422	51	106	149	18	5	5	43	3	8	5	21	2	71	4	7	6	.353	.289
Schneidmiller, Gary, Vis.	.276	85	296	239	56	66	78	8	2	0	22	6	2	0	49	0	57	4	2	4	.326	.397
Seal, Scott, R.C.*	.248	123	500	439	67	109	175	23	2	13	70	3	2	10	45	5	96	7	3	13	.399	.331
Serrano, Sammy, Bak.	.276	125	504	463	55	128	187	30	1	9	80	0	6	5	30	1	78	4	6	16	.404	.323
Simonton, Benji, L.E.	.370	49	217	184	39	68	110	14	2	8	48	0	2	2	29	0	52	0	0	3	.598	.456
Snellgrove, Clay, R.C.	.293	116	491	426	62	125	158	20	2	3	43	4	5	7	19	0	42	8	7	14	.371	.330
Sollmann, Scott, Stoc.*	.349	67	304	249	61	87	107	10	5	0	33	1	1	1	52	3	38	32	14	1	.430	.462
Sosa, Nicolas, Vis.	.218	100	418	339	53	74	129	14	1	13	67	0	7	7	65	1	106	4	2	7	.381	.349
Southall, Rick, Lan.*	.000	1	2	2	0	0	0	0	0	0	0	0	0	0	0	0	2	0	0	0	.000	.000
Steelmon, Wyley, H.D.*	.220	32	102	91	13	20	29	6	0	1	10	0	0	2	9	0	19	1	1	1	.319	.304
Stuart, Rich, L.E.	.186	11	45	43	3	8	11	1	1	0	3	0	0	1	1	0	11	1	2	0	.256	.222
Summers, John, Bak.†	.295	114	449	403	50	119	163	19	2	7	51	0	1	5	40	0	65	2	5	4	.404	.365
Taylor, Joshua, Lan.	.077	6	14	13	0	1	1	0	0	0	2	0	0	0	1	0	6	0	0	0	.077	.143
Theodorou, Nick, S.B.†	.310	104	441	355	57	110	129	11	4	0	44	5	1	7	72	0	62	14	14	7	.363	.434
Thomas, Gary, Mod.	.323	99	398	344	69	111	154	14	4	7	38	8	4	9	33	1	45	23	6	7	.448	.392
Thurston, Joseph, S.B.*	.000	2	4	3	0	0	0	0	0	0	0	0	0	1	0	0	1	0	0	0	.000	.250
Tommasini, Kevin, S.J.	.254	108	439	382	52	97	136	17	2	6	34	3	1	5	48	1	86	3	3	12	.356	.344
Torcato, Tony, Bak.*	.291	110	463	422	50	123	160	25	0	4	58	1	7	3	30	3	67	2	1	6	.379	.338
Torrealba, Yorvit, S.J.	.315	19	81	73	10	23	32	3	0	2	14	0	1	1	6	0	15	0	0	2	.438	.370
Trejo, Francisco, H.D.*	.000	3	1	1	0	0	0	0	0	0	0	0	0	0	0	0	1	0	0	0	.000	.000
Tsoukalas, John, S.J.*	.322	64	234	208	36	67	111	15	1	9	41	0	0	1	25	2	42	0	1	3	.534	.397
Valderrama, Carlos, S.J.	.256	26	96	90	12	23	25	2	0	0	12	2	0	0	4	0	19	8	4	1	.278	.287
Valera, Ramon, Lan.†	.185	17	66	54	10	10	11	1	0	0	1	1	0	1	10	0	10	4	4	0	.204	.323
Van Rossum, Chris, H.D.*	.311	28	103	90	13	28	47	5	1	4	16	0	2	2	9	0	27	2	1	1	.522	.379
Walker, Kevin, R.C.*	.000	28	0	0	1	0	0	0	0	0	0	0	0	0	0	0	0	0	0	0	.000	.000
Walther, Chris, L.E.	.295	100	414	380	48	112	151	26	2	3	60	1	6	0	27	3	31	3	3	15	.397	.337
Wickersham, Jack, R.C.	.282	56	198	174	28	49	59	10	0	0	14	4	1	4	15	0	37	13	5	6	.339	.351
Williams, Peanut, Lan.	.324	68	312	272	60	88	178	12	0	26	59	0	1	4	35	1	89	0	0	5	.654	.407
Wilson, Andy, R.C.	.293	105	408	351	60	103	134	18	5	1	39	3	2	4	48	1	50	26	14	8	.382	.383
Young, Eric, S.B.	.250	3	12	12	0	3	3	0	0	0	2	0	0	0	0	0	2	0	0	0	.250	.250
Zuniga, Tony, S.J.	.270	136	618	533	82	144	213	33	3	10	66	3	4	13	65	0	89	9	4	8	.400	.361

GRAND SLAMS: Curtis 3; Mensik, Riggs, 2 each; Basabe, Caiazzo, Chatman, Chen, Clifton, Connors, Cridland, Cruz, Cuntz, Flaherty, Glendenning, Hargrove, Landry, McCorkle, Neubart, Owens, Pernell, Rosario, Seal, Serrano, Simonton, Sosa, 1 each.

AWARDED FIRST BASE ON CATCHER'S INTERFERENCE: Castro 3 (Bazzani, Pujols, Serrano); Koonce 2 (Hammock, Bazzani); Macalutas (Ahrendt); Seal (Olivo); Hill (Hammock); Theodorou (Caiazzo); Pujols (Williams); Ross (Nieves); Messner (Williams); Melendez (Pujols); Hargrove (Torrealba).

PLAYERS WITH TWO OR MORE TEAMS

Player, Team	Avg.	G	TPA	AB	R	H	TB	2B	3B	HR	RBI	SH	SF	HP	BB	IBB	SO	SB	CS	GDP	Slg.	OBP
Campusano, Carlos, S.J.	.310	27	98	84	13	26	33	2	1	1	7	3	1	4	6	0	15	4	1	1	.393	.379
Campusano, Carlos, Bak.	.353	14	54	51	7	18	23	2	0	1	4	0	0	2	1	0	13	2	2	0	.451	.389
Haynes, Nathan, Vis.*	.310	35	168	145	28	45	57	7	1	1	14	2	1	3	17	0	27	12	10	1	.393	.392
Haynes, Nathan, L.E.*	.327	26	124	110	19	36	54	5	5	1	15	0	1	1	12	0	19	10	5	2	.491	.395
Johnson, Patrick, L.E.	.205	26	90	78	7	16	19	0	0	1	6	2	0	0	10	0	26	0	0	1	.244	.295
Johnson, Patrick, H.D.	.313	37	120	99	15	31	43	6	0	2	15	1	1	0	19	0	27	0	2	1	.434	.420

1998 PITCHING

TEAM

Team	W	L	Pct.	ERA	G	CG	ShO	Sv.	IP	H	TBF	R	ER	HR	SH	SF	HB	BB	IBB	SO	WP	Bk.
R. Cucamonga	76	64	.543	3.85	140	6	11	38	1232.2	1198	5242	619	527	94	30	37	58	425	13	1110	84	23
Modesto	88	52	.629	4.18	140	0	7	54	1246.0	1310	5572	734	579	82	43	48	85	544	26	1099	103	11
San Jose	75	65	.536	4.22	140	2	4	38	1227.0	1264	5409	704	575	68	40	44	67	526	2	1068	97	21
San Bernardino	80	61	.567	4.34	141	3	8	46	1266.0	1321	5531	697	611	96	36	55	62	546	16	1126	89	13
Stockton	57	83	.407	4.60	140	9	8	34	1228.0	1316	5491	802	627	129	51	51	67	523	22	1048	103	19
Lake Elsinore	63	77	.450	4.63	140	21	9	38	1239.0	1385	5531	771	637	101	44	33	64	481	30	999	83	14
Bakersfield	64	76	.457	4.81	140	3	2	33	1230.1	1329	5509	787	658	140	25	45	79	493	8	926	73	9
Visalia	75	65	.536	4.95	140	1	3	38	1235.1	1376	5634	832	680	108	33	53	55	577	21	1118	133	12
High Desert	68	73	.482	5.44	141	0	0	28	1231.0	1391	5653	890	744	144	32	49	89	621	16	1099	80	19
Lancaster	55	85	.393	5.74	140	4	4	21	1223.0	1504	5644	915	780	148	23	52	99	533	7	972	104	14

INDIVIDUAL

TOP QUALIFIERS FOR EARNED-RUN AVERAGE TITLE

Minimum 112 innings.*Lefthanded pitcher.

Pitcher, Team	W	L	Pct.	ERA	G	GS	CG	ShO	GF	Sv.	IP	H	TBF	R	ER	HR	SH	SF	HB	BB	IBB	SO	WP	Bk.
Dorame, Randey, S.B.*	14	3	.824	2.51	24	24	1	1	0	0	154.1	130	613	52	43	9	3	6	3	37	0	159	7	1
Serrano, Wascar, R.C.	9	8	.529	3.33	21	21	1	1	0	0	132.1	110	537	58	49	10	1	5	1	43	0	129	8	5
Colome, Jesus, Mod.	8	4	.667	3.36	31	22	0	0	2	1	128.2	125	564	63	48	6	1	6	9	60	2	127	13	2
Lawrence, Brian, R.C.	12	8	.600	3.39	27	27	4	3	0	0	175.1	178	723	72	66	6	7	5	10	30	1	166	7	5
Wagner, Denny, Mod.	7	4	.636	3.56	27	15	0	0	5	3	113.2	116	502	57	45	7	0	3	10	42	2	99	7	3
Kramer, Aaron, R.C.	9	9	.500	3.63	23	23	0	0	0	0	139.0	154	592	73	56	14	1	5	3	31	0	98	6	4
Zerbe, Chad, Bak.*	7	7	.500	3.64	21	21	0	0	0	0	126.0	124	533	66	51	4	0	5	2	33	0	81	6	0
Guttormson, Rick, R.C.	14	8	.636	3.72	28	28	1	0	0	0	174.1	165	714	83	72	15	4	1	9	36	0	125	6	2
Prata, Danny, Bak.*	9	9	.500	3.91	27	27	0	0	0	0	142.2	143	632	80	62	22	2	2	9	54	0	87	6	1
Green, Steve, L.E.	7	6	.538	3.95	19	19	4	4	0	0	120.2	130	526	70	53	9	4	1	6	37	2	91	1	3
Stewart, Paul, Stoc.	10	11	.476	3.96	27	25	5	1	0	0	170.1	171	733	90	75	18	6	9	4	61	0	117	7	1
Jones, Marcus, Vis.-Mod.	8	5	.615	4.02	25	20	0	0	0	0	123.0	132	538	74	55	12	5	3	7	46	1	118	4	1
Castillo, Marcos, S.B.	14	9	.609	4.10	27	27	1	1	0	0	167.0	182	720	90	76	14	2	4	8	48	1	130	6	2
Burnside, Adrian, S.B.*	10	9	.526	4.17	26	22	0	0	0	0	131.2	124	571	69	61	7	3	4	11	55	0	129	10	2
Jensen, Jared, Vis.	9	7	.563	4.20	32	22	0	0	2	0	141.1	154	607	82	66	15	2	6	3	41	2	110	9	1

DEPARTMENTAL LEADERS: W—Dorame, Castillo, Guttormson, 14 each; L—Bermudez, 14; Pct.—Dorame, .824; G—Everly, Noriega, 60 each; GS—Fish, 29; CG—Stewart, Fish, 5 each; ShO—Green, 4; GF—Everly, 57; Sv.—Everly, 34; IP—Fish, 196.2; H—Fish, 220; TBF—Fish, 876; R—Fish, 125; ER—Fish, 107; HR—Coscia, 25; SH—several players tied, 7 each; SF—Caracciolo, Farnsworth. Parker, 10 each; HB—Bermudez, 18; BB—Caracciolo, 126; IBB—Morrison, 7; SO—Fish, 180; WP—Bennett, 39; BK—Jones, Lawrence, Serrano, 5 each.

ALL PITCHERS

*Lefthanded pitcher.

Pitcher, Team	W	L	Pct.	ERA	G	GS	CG	ShO	GF	Sv.	IP	H	TBF	R	ER	HR	SH	SF	HB	BB	IBB	SO	WP	Bk.
Adkins, Jon, Mod.	9	5	.643	4.76	26	15	0	0	2	1	102.0	113	460	65	54	6	4	6	9	30	1	93	8	0
Anderson, Jason, Vis.*	2	1	.667	2.52	4	4	0	0	0	0	25.0	32	110	9	7	1	0	0	2	0	0	17	1	0
Andra, Jeff, S.J.*	4	2	.667	4.50	13	7	0	0	0	0	50.0	54	217	28	25	3	2	2	0	19	1	54	3	1
Andrews, Jeff, H.D.	0	3	.000	6.37	6	6	0	0	0	0	29.2	41	143	27	21	5	0	1	2	13	0	25	1	0
Aragon, Angel, R.C.	2	7	.222	3.54	53	0	0	0	36	19	68.2	55	291	33	27	3	4	3	6	28	3	76	6	1
Barton, Christopher, Stoc.	1	1	.500	10.31	7	2	0	0	1	0	18.1	23	90	23	21	1	1	0	3	15	0	8	4	0
Bazzani, Matt, S.J.	0	0	.000	12.00	2	0	0	0	2	0	3.0	7	15	4	4	3	0	0	0	0	0	1	0	0
Bazzell, Shane, Vis.	2	4	.333	5.13	8	8	0	0	0	0	40.1	50	182	27	23	4	1	1	0	19	0	29	0	1
Bell, Scott, S.B.	2	5	.286	6.04	28	0	0	0	13	3	50.2	66	239	40	34	4	3	6	3	22	1	37	5	0
Bello, Emerson, Lan.	0	0	.000	6.75	9	0	0	0	1	0	13.1	15	65	12	10	3	0	3	9	0	0	13	1	0
Bennett, Tom, Vis.	1	9	.100	8.01	36	8	0	0	5	0	87.2	113	463	91	78	7	3	4	2	94	1	87	39	1
Bermudez, Manny, Bak.	5	14	.263	5.99	32	22	1	0	1	0	145.2	183	687	121	97	8	7	5	18	66	1	65	7	1
Bido, Jose, H.D.	0	0	.000	12.46	11	0	0	0	5	0	13.0	23	74	19	18	3	0	1	3	9	0	14	0	0
Bieniasz, Derek, Lan.	1	8	.111	7.91	15	9	0	0	0	0	52.1	75	249	48	46	7	2	2	6	20	0	29	4	1
Bridges, Douglas, L.E.*	3	2	.600	4.33	5	5	2	0	0	0	35.1	42	156	19	17	4	2	0	0	11	0	34	3	0
Brink, Jim, Mod.	3	0	1.000	4.57	47	0	0	0	41	29	45.1	53	204	24	23	2	5	4	0	18	3	38	0	0
Brooks, Jacob, L.E.	3	3	.500	7.12	27	0	0	0	15	4	36.2	38	176	33	29	7	2	3	1	29	1	43	9	1
Burnside, Adrian, S.B.*	10	9	.526	4.17	26	22	0	0	0	0	131.2	124	571	69	61	7	3	4	11	55	0	129	10	2
Bynum, Michael, R.C.*	3	1	.750	3.29	7	7	0	0	0	0	38.1	35	159	17	14	1	1	1	2	8	0	44	2	2
Calandriello, Donato, Mod.*	4	1	.800	3.56	38	0	0	0	13	1	48.0	36	210	22	19	2	2	3	4	31	1	44	7	1
Callier, Jeremy, L.E.	5	3	.625	3.86	34	7	0	0	9	2	95.2	107	418	48	41	5	5	0	3	33	2	69	6	1
Calzada, Javier, Vis.	2	0	1.000	6.63	8	0	0	0	4	0	19.0	24	85	17	14	4	1	4	1	4	1	15	2	1
Camp, Shawn, R.C.	1	5	.167	3.95	53	0	0	0	28	6	66.0	68	285	37	29	4	4	4	1	25	3	78	7	1
Campusano, Carlos, S.J.	0	0	.000	6.75	1	0	0	0	1	0	1.1	3	7	1	1	0	0	0	0	0	0	0	0	0
Caracciolo, Lance, S.B.*	6	7	.462	5.01	28	26	0	0	0	0	140.0	124	645	90	78	9	7	10	10	126	0	98	8	1
Carmody, Brian, Lan.*	3	3	.500	3.66	16	2	0	0	3	0	39.1	43	179	22	16	2	1	0	1	18	1	45	5	1
Castillo, Marcos, S.B.	14	9	.609	4.10	27	27	1	1	0	0	167.0	182	720	90	76	14	2	4	8	48	1	130	6	2
Cepeda, Wellington, H.D.	6	6	.500	5.71	42	3	0	0	13	2	86.2	106	407	64	55	14	3	3	1	42	1	74	10	0
Cervantes, Chris, H.D.*	0	0	.000	162.00	1	0	0	0	1	0	0.1	5	7	6	6	1	0	0	1	1	0	1	0	0

Pitcher, Team	W	L	Pct.	ERA	G	GS	CG	ShO	GF	Sv.	IP	H	TBF	R	ER	HR	SH	SF	HB	BB	IBB	SO	WP	Bk.
Cervantes, Peter, S.B.	4	3	.571	4.18	40	1	0	0	12	5	79.2	92	345	38	37	4	2	3	1	21	1	89	5	0
Chavarria, David, S.J.	0	2	.000	7.58	21	0	0	0	2	0	29.2	43	145	25	25	2	2	1	3	16	0	26	11	3
Checo, Robinson, S.B.	0	0	.000	10.80	2	2	0	0	0	0	5.0	5	23	6	6	2	0	0	0	3	0	6	1	0
Childers, Jason, Stoc.	2	8	.200	3.56	12	12	1	0	0	0	73.1	78	314	39	29	12	2	2	3	11	0	73	3	1
Chung, Rocky, S.B.	1	0	1.000	1.71	9	0	0	0	2	0	21.0	13	78	5	4	2	0	1	1	3	0	23	1	1
Colome, Jesus, Mod.	8	4	.667	3.36	31	22	0	0	2	1	128.2	125	564	63	48	6	1	6	9	60	2	127	13	2
Colon, Jose, Stoc.	0	0	.000	9.00	1	0	0	0	1	0	1.0	2	6	1	1	0	0	0	1	0	0	0	0	0
Colyer, Stephen, S.B.*	7	9	.438	4.70	27	25	1	0	0	0	145.2	145	644	82	76	12	3	7	8	86	0	131	8	3
Condrey, Clay, R.C.	0	0	.000	3.68	6	0	0	0	1	0	7.1	4	29	3	3	1	0	0	3	0	0	9	0	0
Connolly, Keith, Bak.	7	8	.467	4.34	54	0	0	0	22	3	83.0	61	364	41	40	8	4	3	8	47	1	95	6	0
Correa, Elvis, S.B.	2	2	.500	4.98	40	0	0	0	14	1	68.2	87	307	42	38	7	2	6	5	17	2	40	8	0
Cosbey, Chris, Mod.*	0	1	.000	9.00	1	0	0	0	1	0	1.0	2	5	1	1	0	1	1	0	0	0	1	0	0
Coscia, Tony, Bak.	10	11	.476	4.51	28	28	1	0	0	0	171.2	186	737	100	86	25	4	7	15	38	0	133	7	3
Cowsill, Brendon, L.E.	4	10	.286	5.37	27	20	4	1	2	1	125.2	155	562	87	75	17	6	9	5	36	0	62	3	0
Cox, Ryan, Bak.	1	4	.200	4.86	7	7	0	0	0	0	33.1	46	151	22	18	6	1	0	1	3	0	30	2	0
Cummings, Ryan, L.E.	3	1	.750	3.28	7	7	0	0	0	0	46.2	43	203	19	17	3	1	0	4	15	1	41	1	0
Davis, Clint, H.D.	0	0	1.000	4.50	2	0	0	0	1	0	2.0	0	9	1	1	0	2	0	0	2	0	3	1	0
De La Rosa, Jorge, H.D.*	0	0	.000	0.00	2	0	0	0	2	0	3.0	1	12	0	0	0	0	0	0	3	0	3	0	0
Diaz, Antonio, R.C.	0	0	.000	5.11	9	0	0	0	5	0	12.1	7	52	7	7	3	0	1	0	7	0	7	0	0
Dorame, Randey, S.B.*	14	3	.824	2.51	24	24	1	1	0	0	154.1	130	613	52	43	9	3	6	3	37	0	159	7	1
Duarte, Renney, L.E.	0	1	.000	6.43	3	3	0	0	0	0	14.0	22	71	13	10	2	0	0	1	8	1	6	0	1
Dunham, Pat, Lan.	1	4	.200	7.78	9	8	0	0	0	0	39.1	49	193	40	34	5	0	2	2	28	0	33	6	2
Emanuel, Brandon, L.E.	0	2	.000	5.14	2	2	0	0	0	0	14.0	15	64	11	8	1	0	2	1	7	0	12	0	0
Enochs, Chris, Vis.	0	0	.000	4.91	4	4	0	0	0	0	18.1	24	87	10	10	4	0	1	0	10	0	19	2	0
Esteves, Jake, S.J.	6	1	.857	2.01	12	11	1	0	1	0	71.2	59	281	21	16	1	4	1	2	17	0	56	3	1
Everly, Bill, S.B.	7	4	.636	3.41	60	0	0	0	57	34	63.1	66	272	26	24	6	4	0	3	21	3	51	3	0
Fahrner, Evan, H.D.	0	1	.000	6.00	3	1	0	0	0	0	3.0	3	18	3	2	0	0	0	0	7	0	3	0	1
Farnsworth, Jeff, Lan.	3	6	.333	6.50	26	9	0	0	6	3	72.0	91	351	61	52	7	1	10	15	43	1	43	10	0
Featherstone, Deron, Bak.	0	0	.000	7.59	6	0	0	0	4	0	10.2	13	65	17	9	0	0	1	1	17	0	13	4	0
Fernandez, Ozzie, S.J.	0	1	.000	6.00	4	4	0	0	0	0	9.0	6	37	6	6	1	0	0	2	2	0	5	0	0
Fields, Brian, Bak.*	2	0	1.000	5.80	20	0	0	0	4	1	35.2	43	164	25	23	7	0	1	0	12	1	22	3	1
Fikac, Jeremy, R.C.	8	3	.727	5.08	40	6	0	0	13	0	85.0	94	381	50	48	7	0	2	4	43	0	75	8	2
Fischer, Mike, S.B.	1	0	1.000	4.91	3	3	0	0	0	0	11.0	13	47	6	6	1	0	0	0	4	0	7	1	0
Fish, Steve, L.E.	11	11	.500	4.90	32	29	5	2	0	0	196.2	220	876	125	107	17	0	8	10	72	3	180	15	2
Fitzgerald, Brian, Lan.*	1	3	.250	7.15	6	6	0	0	0	0	34.0	50	153	35	27	3	0	2	0	4	0	23	1	0
Flores, Benito, Bak.*	2	1	.667	3.67	34	6	0	0	7	0	81.0	81	357	42	33	3	1	2	2	34	2	63	6	0
Flores, Pedro, S.B.*	2	3	.400	7.61	32	0	0	0	14	1	47.1	68	236	47	40	4	2	0	4	30	4	35	6	0
Foran, John, R.C.	9	5	.643	4.80	25	20	0	0	0	0	105.0	113	482	70	56	12	0	6	10	53	0	89	13	1
Gallo, Ismael, S.B.	0	0	.000	9.00	1	0	0	0	1	0	1.0	7	11	7	1	0	0	0	0	0	0	0	1	0
Gangemi, Joe, L.E.*	3	11	.214	7.16	21	15	1	0	2	0	81.2	118	388	81	65	10	1	2	5	41	1	55	7	0
Gardner, Mark, S.J.	1	0	1.000	4.50	2	2	0	0	0	0	10.0	10	44	5	5	0	0	1	3	0	13	0	1
Goodrich, Randy, S.J.	8	8	.500	4.81	38	18	0	0	4	1	136.2	174	623	95	73	6	5	6	11	34	0	82	6	3
Gorrell, Chris, Vis.	4	3	.571	5.09	16	0	0	0	14	4	23.0	33	110	14	13	2	1	0	1	7	0	31	2	0
Green, Steve, L.E.	7	6	.538	3.95	19	19	4	4	0	0	120.2	130	526	70	53	9	4	1	6	37	2	91	1	3
Gregg, Kevin, Vis.	4	4	.500	3.80	13	11	1	1	2	1	64.0	60	271	34	27	3	1	2	4	23	0	48	7	1
Guttormson, Rick, R.C.	14	8	.636	3.72	28	28	1	0	0	0	174.1	165	714	83	72	15	4	1	9	36	0	125	6	2
Harrell, Tim, S.B.	5	2	.714	4.82	44	0	0	0	14	2	74.2	78	324	40	40	10	4	4	0	36	2	78	13	0
Hart, Len, R.C.*	2	1	.667	0.83	33	0	0	0	12	3	43.1	19	166	5	4	1	0	1	18	0	54	3	0
Hawkins, Al, Stoc.	3	0	1.000	3.60	4	4	0	0	0	0	25.0	26	105	12	10	2	1	0	1	6	0	11	2	0
Hebert, Cedric, S.B.	2	2	.500	5.89	16	5	0	0	4	1	44.1	57	203	34	29	3	0	1	3	19	0	37	3	1
Helmer, Chad, Stoc.	1	4	.200	2.86	20	4	0	0	11	6	34.2	35	157	18	11	3	2	3	3	18	2	33	5	0
Hill, Jason, L.E.*	0	0	.000	13.06	10	0	0	0	5	2	10.1	16	61	19	15	3	2	0	3	12	0	12	2	0
Hite, Kevin, R.C.	0	1	.000	4.05	7	0	0	0	7	4	6.2	6	27	3	3	1	0	0	1	0	8	0	0
Hoerman, Jared, Lan.	0	0	.000	7.04	4	0	0	0	1	0	7.2	8	36	6	6	2	0	1	0	7	0	6	1	0
Holmes, Mike, Mod.	9	6	.600	4.88	34	18	0	0	9	6	145.2	184	629	100	79	14	3	4	5	15	3	84	3	1
Horgan, Joe, Bak.*	6	10	.375	5.22	25	19	1	0	1	0	117.1	129	520	76	68	18	2	2	10	43	0	101	5	2
Huller, Mike, Bak.*	0	0	.000	18.00	1	0	0	0	1	0	1.0	2	7	2	2	0	0	0	2	0	1	0	0
Immel, Stephen, H.D.	4	1	.800	5.53	19	0	0	0	5	0	40.2	61	192	36	25	7	1	3	5	12	0	35	0	1
James, Mike, L.E.	0	0	.000	5.79	3	3	0	0	0	0	9.1	12	41	6	6	0	0	0	1	0	6	0	0
Jaramillo, Lee, Stoc.	0	0	.000	4.50	2	0	0	0	2	0	2.0	3	11	3	1	1	0	0	0	1	0	1	1	0
Jarvis, Kevin, Mod.	0	0	.000	1.29	2	2	0	0	0	0	7.0	4	26	1	1	0	1	0	0	1	0	10	0	0
Jensen, Jared, Vis.	9	7	.563	4.20	32	22	0	0	2	0	141.1	154	607	82	66	15	2	6	3	41	2	110	9	1
Jensen, Jason, H.D.*	2	2	.500	4.47	9	9	0	0	0	0	44.1	43	194	24	22	8	0	1	1	22	0	24	2	0
Johnson, Eric, Bak.	1	0	1.000	5.82	17	0	0	0	8	0	21.2	22	106	14	14	1	0	1	2	21	0	14	1	0
Johnson, Greg, L.E.*	4	4	.500	3.21	39	5	1	0	12	1	81.1	83	337	36	29	5	1	0	15	2	63	7	1
Johnson, James, Stoc.*	5	6	.455	4.73	29	23	1	1	1	0	129.1	146	568	83	68	13	6	5	2	47	1	135	23	1
Jones, Chris, S.J.*	8	12	.400	4.61	28	27	0	0	0	0	130.2	121	592	85	67	5	4	3	6	87	0	118	17	5
Jones, Marcus, Vis.-Mod.	5	8	.615	4.02	25	20	0	0	0	0	123.0	132	538	74	55	12	5	3	7	46	1	118	4	1
Joseph, Kevin, S.J.	1	2	.333	2.35	20	0	0	0	9	2	30.2	17	122	9	8	1	3	0	13	0	30	2	1
Kaye, Justin, Lan.	3	5	.375	5.75	53	0	0	0	46	14	61.0	68	289	42	39	4	2	3	5	40	1	66	6	0
Kees, Justin, H.D.	6	2	.750	5.57	30	7	0	0	7	1	85.2	89	385	60	53	10	2	3	10	51	1	68	4	3
Kendall, Phil, Stoc.	0	10	.000	5.68	18	18	1	0	0	0	103.0	113	479	71	65	12	2	5	7	63	1	60	12	2
Kenny, Seth, Mod.	0	3	.000	3.52	18	0	0	0	11	0	23.0	26	110	13	9	0	0	2	13	2	18	1	0
Kirby, Scott, Stoc.	0	0	.000	11.57	3	0	0	0	1	0	2.1	4	12	3	3	1	0	0	0	1	0	0	0	0
Kirkreit, Daron, Lan.*	4	4	.500	5.36	9	9	0	0	0	0	47.0	65	212	34	28	5	1	1	17	0	35	4	1
Kirst, Mark, Stoc.	3	7	.300	6.45	32	4	0	0	14	2	60.0	67	284	55	43	12	3	5	31	1	58	9	2
Kiyono, Masashi, S.J.	2	1	.667	7.46	32	3	0	0	13	0	56.2	87	290	62	47	5	2	3	29	0	31	10	0
Klein, Matt, Vis.	1	1	.500	5.55	11	2	0	0	1	0	24.1	35	129	24	15	2	0	3	20	0	18	5	0
Klepaski, Jose, Lan.	0	0	.000	0.00	1	0	0	0	1	0	2.0	0	7	0	0	0	0	0	0	1	0	0	0
Koehler, Russ, Lan.	0	3	.000	8.03	7	0	0	0	5	0	24.2	33	125	28	22	5	1	2	18	0	19	5	0
Kohl, Doug, H.D.	9	5	.643	7.38	30	11	0	0	3	0	89.0	114	421	79	73	13	1	5	6	40	2	74	7	0
Kramer, Aaron, R.C.	9	9	.500	3.63	23	23	0	0	0	0	139.0	154	592	73	56	14	1	5	3	31	0	98	6	4
Krawczyk, Jack, Stoc.	5	4	.556	4.68	41	1	0	0	13	2	77.0	87	331	48	40	8	5	3	1	19	2	74	3	0
Lara, Eddie, Vis.	0	0	.000	0.00	1	0	0	0	1	0	0.2	1	4	0	0	0	0	0	1	0	2	0	0
Lawrence, Brian, R.C.	12	8	.600	3.39	27	27	4	3	0	0	175.1	178	723	72	66	6	7	5	10	30	1	166	7	5

Pitcher, Team	W	L	Pct.	ERA	G	GS	CG	ShO	GF	Sv.	IP	H	TBF	R	ER	HR	SH	SF	HB	BB	IBB	SO	WP	Bk.
Leyva, Julian, Vis.	7	3	.700	4.25	15	14	0	0	1	1	82.2	87	366	50	39	9	1	4	4	25	0	67	0	0
Longo, Neil, Lan.	6	7	.462	5.71	23	19	0	0	2	0	127.2	163	576	87	81	15	2	6	9	46	0	76	5	1
Lopez, Rafael, Lan.	0	0	.000	0.00	1	0	0	0	1	0	0.1	1	2	0	0	0	0	0	0	0	0	0	0	0
Lubozynski, Matt, L.E.*	1	1	.500	2.31	30	0	0	0	15	3	39.0	35	164	12	10	1	2	0	0	17	2	18	4	1
Luque, Roger, R.C.*	0	0	.000	10.80	3	0	0	0	0	0	1.2	3	11	2	2	1	0	0	1	2	0	2	1	0
Maddux, Mike, S.B.	0	0	.000	3.00	5	0	0	0	2	2	9.0	8	35	4	3	0	0	1	0	2	0	10	2	1
Madero, Francisco, S.B.	3	2	.600	2.70	12	2	0	0	4	0	26.2	28	111	10	8	1	0	1	1	9	2	33	2	1
Malerich, Will, S.J.*	5	4	.556	4.46	45	0	0	0	14	1	72.2	95	338	43	36	5	3	2	4	38	1	59	3	0
Mallette, Brian, Stoc.	2	0	1.000	1.50	28	0	0	0	14	4	36.0	38	162	16	6	1	0	1	3	16	1	34	0	0
Malloy, Bill, S.J.	5	4	.556	4.18	17	13	0	0	1	0	79.2	87	348	45	37	4	1	0	3	37	0	66	7	4
Manzueta, Roberto, H.D.	2	2	.500	3.51	40	0	0	0	19	2	66.2	63	294	29	26	4	1	2	8	31	2	59	8	0
Martines, Jason, H.D.	9	7	.563	2.26	43	0	0	0	37	9	71.2	68	306	33	18	5	2	1	2	28	4	73	1	1
Maurer, Mike, Mod.	1	0	1.000	2.65	15	0	0	0	3	1	17.0	23	81	8	5	1	0	0	1	5	0	15	3	0
McCall, Travis, Mod.*	9	3	.750	4.54	43	0	0	0	18	3	71.1	79	322	46	36	8	5	9	1	31	4	67	6	1
McClaskey, Tim, Lan.	3	3	.500	6.36	30	0	0	0	9	0	58.0	83	260	51	41	9	1	1	6	11	0	54	3	0
McDowell, Jack, L.E.	0	1	.000	7.36	1	1	0	0	0	0	7.1	11	33	7	6	2	0	0	0	1	0	7	0	0
Mears, Chris, Lan.	3	6	.333	7.08	10	10	0	0	0	0	54.2	71	250	44	43	12	1	1	3	18	0	45	3	2
Messman, Joe, S.J.	0	0	.000	27.00	2	0	0	0	2	0	1.2	6	13	5	5	0	0	0	0	3	0	0	3	0
Messner, Jake, Bak.*	0	0	.000	0.00	1	0	0	0	1	0	1.0	0	3	0	0	0	0	0	0	1	0	0	0	0
Miadich, Bart, H.D.	3	8	.273	5.42	21	16	0	0	1	0	98.0	125	448	71	59	9	2	4	12	40	0	85	1	1
Miller, Benji, S.J.	3	2	.600	3.02	47	0	0	0	38	20	59.2	53	248	26	20	3	2	4	1	17	0	61	6	2
Miller, Jim, Stoc.	8	9	.471	4.42	28	17	1	0	7	1	124.1	137	557	91	61	13	3	4	13	44	1	101	8	4
Montenegro, Jose, Stoc.	0	0	.000	0.00	1	0	0	0	0	0	0.2	3	9	6	0	1	0	0	0	3	0	1	1	0
Moore, Brad, Mod.	3	2	.600	5.11	34	0	0	0	15	0	37.0	37	182	24	21	2	2	2	5	31	2	42	11	0
Moore, Darin, Mod.	1	1	.500	11.76	12	0	0	0	2	0	20.2	21	111	27	27	0	2	0	5	26	0	21	12	0
Morrison, Cody, L.E.	4	8	.333	5.32	45	0	0	0	27	3	67.2	65	332	57	40	2	3	1	11	50	7	64	7	1
Myers, Aaron, Stoc.	3	4	.429	4.55	22	10	0	0	2	1	83.0	88	360	52	42	7	3	6	8	25	2	81	3	4
Niebla, Ruben, S.B.*	0	1	.000	4.76	3	0	0	0	1	0	5.2	9	25	3	3	1	0	0	0	1	0	6	0	0
Niles, Randy, Mod.	3	0	1.000	3.15	8	4	0	0	3	2	34.1	39	144	13	12	2	1	0	3	8	1	35	4	0
Nina, Elvin, Mod.	5	2	.714	2.09	17	12	0	0	0	0	73.1	59	319	31	17	2	3	0	6	41	1	74	5	0
Nix, Wayne, Mod.	9	6	.600	4.22	34	18	0	0	4	2	119.1	109	532	76	56	10	3	5	9	69	2	105	8	3
Nogowski, Brandon, Vis.*	5	4	.556	4.02	33	2	0	0	11	3	65.0	71	290	40	29	4	2	3	2	19	1	60	5	0
Noriega, Ray, Vis.*	5	3	.625	4.02	60	0	0	0	34	11	69.1	67	308	36	31	6	4	4	2	32	2	62	6	0
Norris, Ben, H.D.*	2	2	.500	4.43	8	8	0	0	0	0	40.2	39	181	27	20	4	0	3	4	24	0	45	0	0
O'Dell, Jake, Mod.	1	0	1.000	2.57	3	0	0	0	1	0	7.0	7	31	2	2	0	0	0	0	3	0	10	0	0
Oleksik, George, H.D.	0	2	.000	3.86	4	0	0	0	2	0	7.0	14	39	11	3	1	0	0	0	6	0	5	2	0
O'Reilly, John, H.D.	1	4	.200	7.24	21	4	0	0	6	1	46.0	53	230	46	37	5	4	2	2	36	0	47	4	2
Oropesa, Eddie, Bak.*	2	0	1.000	3.60	2	1	0	0	0	0	10.0	13	41	5	4	2	0	0	0	1	0	10	2	0
Osuna, Antonio, S.B.	0	0	.000	2.33	13	4	0	0	0	0	19.1	19	82	6	5	0	1	1	1	6	0	27	0	0
Ozias, Todd, Bak.	5	5	.500	2.56	52	0	0	0	49	26	56.1	47	235	21	16	6	0	2	1	25	1	67	6	0
Padilla, Vicente, H.D.	4	1	.800	3.73	9	9	0	0	0	0	50.2	50	220	27	21	3	1	2	1	17	0	55	2	2
Padua, Geraldo, R.C.	3	3	.500	4.65	7	7	0	0	0	0	40.2	43	174	21	21	4	0	0	0	18	0	41	6	0
Paredes, Roberto, Stoc.	1	3	.250	7.41	12	6	0	0	3	0	34.0	31	159	28	28	7	0	2	3	27	0	30	1	1
Parker, Brandon, Lan.	9	7	.563	5.09	27	27	0	0	0	0	139.2	164	640	95	79	12	5	10	14	67	0	147	5	3
Pasqualicchio, Mike, Stoc.*	0	1	.000	5.27	4	4	0	0	0	0	13.2	15	56	9	8	3	2	0	0	4	0	12	0	0
Pena, Juan, Vis.*	9	5	.643	5.76	33	18	0	0	4	1	131.1	168	609	106	84	10	3	3	0	61	2	107	9	3
Perozo, Felix, L.E.	0	5	.000	5.70	32	0	0	0	23	2	36.1	44	172	26	23	3	2	1	2	18	1	23	5	0
Pipes, Joey, L.E.	1	0	1.000	1.69	2	2	1	0	0	0	16.0	16	64	3	3	1	1	0	0	4	0	19	0	1
Pourron, Joe, S.J.	2	0	1.000	6.17	14	0	0	0	7	0	23.1	17	118	18	16	0	2	2	2	32	0	23	8	0
Prata, Danny, Bak.*	9	9	.500	3.91	27	27	0	0	0	0	142.2	143	632	80	62	22	2	2	9	54	0	87	6	1
Priebe, Kevin, Stoc.*	3	2	.600	2.76	34	0	0	0	24	6	42.1	40	185	20	13	1	4	0	0	22	4	46	6	1
Pujols, Rafael, Mod.	0	0	.000	0.00	1	0	0	0	1	0	1.0	0	3	0	0	0	0	0	0	0	0	0	0	0
Rajotte, Jason, Bak.*	1	1	.500	5.23	47	0	0	0	22	2	53.1	63	248	35	31	4	4	4	1	26	1	43	3	0
Ramirez, Erasmo, S.J.*	2	0	1.000	2.67	31	0	0	0	12	5	57.1	42	219	18	17	2	2	4	1	8	0	52	2	0
Ramos, Juan, Lan.	1	4	.200	6.28	42	0	0	0	29	1	61.2	82	309	58	43	9	2	1	8	36	0	41	13	1
Ricabal, Dan, S.J.	1	0	1.000	4.91	7	0	0	0	5	1	7.1	13	39	7	4	0	0	0	0	5	0	1	0	0
Rice, Nathan, Bak.*	0	0	.000	22.85	3	0	0	0	1	0	4.1	11	36	14	11	1	0	0	1	10	0	3	1	0
Rodriguez, Juan, L.E.*	0	0	.000	0.00	1	0	0	0	1	0	1.0	0	4	0	0	0	0	0	0	1	0	0	0	0
Rubio, Miguel, H.D.	2	5	.286	6.14	27	11	0	0	7	1	77.2	96	368	61	53	8	4	5	8	33	0	53	5	0
Salter, Cody, L.E.	1	0	1.000	4.91	7	2	0	0	0	0	22.0	27	98	12	12	0	0	0	2	8	1	9	3	1
Sanchez, Duaner, H.D.	0	0	.000	7.53	3	3	0	0	0	0	14.1	15	63	13	12	2	0	1	1	9	0	9	0	0
Sanchez, Simon, H.D.	3	5	.375	5.27	40	1	0	0	26	7	71.2	79	330	45	42	8	3	3	8	31	3	53	4	0
Santos, Josh, S.J.*	3	6	.333	4.32	13	13	1	0	0	0	66.2	75	308	47	32	6	2	4	8	29	0	47	2	0
Schmidt, Donnie, Lan.	1	2	.333	3.50	21	0	0	0	8	0	36.0	46	178	20	14	1	0	4	3	25	0	21	4	1
Schubmehl, Brian, Stoc.	6	6	.500	4.07	43	1	0	0	18	9	77.1	81	360	52	35	4	7	2	3	47	3	71	5	1
Schultz, Jeff, Mod.	2	9	.182	5.44	23	11	0	0	4	3	82.2	90	388	58	50	5	5	2	5	49	0	63	7	0
Seaver, Mark, Mod.	12	4	.750	4.30	34	17	0	0	5	2	134.0	158	606	85	64	10	3	3	8	57	2	112	7	0
Serrano, Wascar, R.C.	9	8	.529	3.33	21	21	1	1	0	0	132.1	110	537	58	49	10	1	5	1	43	0	129	8	5
Sheets, Ben, Stoc.	1	0	1.000	3.58	5	5	0	0	0	0	27.2	23	115	11	11	1	0	1	1	14	0	28	1	0
Shepherd, Alvie, L.E.	0	0	.000	15.88	5	0	0	0	2	0	5.2	11	32	11	10	2	0	0	2	3	0	6	2	0
Shields, Scot, L.E.	10	3	.769	2.52	24	9	2	1	6	1	107.1	91	443	37	30	1	4	4	5	39	4	113	6	1
Simonson, Chris, Stoc.	2	1	.667	3.16	15	1	0	0	6	2	31.1	31	136	13	11	0	2	1	1	12	2	31	0	1
Simpson, Allan, Lan.	0	0	.000	6.33	9	0	0	0	0	0	21.1	17	96	16	15	4	0	2	2	14	0	25	2	1
Smith, Travis, Stoc.	0	2	.000	6.14	3	3	0	0	0	0	7.1	9	35	6	5	1	1	0	1	3	0	8	0	0
Snellgrove, Clay, R.C.	0	0	.000	18.00	1	0	0	0	1	0	1.0	2	5	2	2	1	0	0	0	0	0	0	0	0
Snow, Bert, Vis.	3	2	.600	5.15	31	3	0	0	14	5	64.2	55	298	43	37	4	4	4	4	40	3	90	10	1
Stark, Zac, Lan.*	1	2	.333	3.99	49	0	0	0	15	2	79.0	75	345	44	35	9	2	0	4	29	2	72	4	0
Stephens, Jason, L.E.	3	3	.500	4.19	15	11	1	0	0	0	68.2	84	310	39	32	6	3	1	2	24	2	66	2	0
Stewart, Paul, Stoc.	10	11	.476	3.96	27	25	5	1	0	0	170.1	171	733	90	75	18	6	9	4	61	0	117	7	1
Sundbeck, Cody, H.D.	4	5	.444	7.08	14	14	0	0	0	0	67.1	81	311	59	53	5	1	1	7	35	0	68	12	2
Sweeney, Brian, Lan.	0	0	.000	6.75	5	0	0	0	1	0	9.1	14	44	7	7	4	0	0	0	3	0	14	1	0
Szymborski, Tom, R.C.	1	2	.333	4.78	28	0	0	0	6	0	43.1	48	191	26	23	5	2	0	3	23	2	33	5	0
Tavarez, Julian, S.J.	0	0	.000	0.00	1	1	0	0	0	0	4.0	1	12	0	0	0	0	0	0	1	0	3	0	0
Thompson, Eric, Vis.	9	6	.600	5.61	31	20	0	0	5	1	126.2	150	595	91	79	9	2	6	11	56	2	110	10	1
Travis, Jesse, Bak.	2	5	.286	8.74	14	9	0	0	0	0	45.1	71	218	47	44	8	0	2	1	20	0	27	3	0

Pitcher, Team	W	L	Pct.	ERA	G	GS	CG	ShO	GF	Sv.	IP	H	TBF	R	ER	HR	SH	SF	HB	BB	IBB	SO	WP	Bk.
Trejo, Francisco, H.D.*	0	0	.000	6.75	3	0	0	0	2	0	6.2	5	32	6	5	1	0	0	1	7	0	6	3	0
Tsoukalas, John, S.J.	0	0	.000	0.00	1	0	0	0	1	0	1.0	0	3	0	0	0	0	0	0	0	0	0	0	0
Tucker, Ben, S.J.	4	6	.400	4.57	16	15	0	0	0	0	82.2	106	380	46	42	7	1	1	12	26	0	65	5	0
Turman, Jason, Lan.	4	10	.286	5.20	31	12	1	0	9	1	97.0	116	436	66	56	12	1	2	6	35	1	78	14	0
Urban, Jeff, S.J.*	8	5	.615	3.76	15	13	0	0	2	0	81.1	78	336	41	34	7	0	2	4	18	0	89	0	0
Valenti, Jon, Bak.	4	1	.800	5.12	46	0	0	0	13	1	84.1	85	378	55	48	15	0	8	5	39	1	69	4	1
Valera, Ramon, Lan.	0	0	.000	27.00	1	0	0	0	1	0	0.2	1	4	2	2	1	0	0	0	1	0	0	0	0
Verplancke, Joe, H.D.	1	0	1.000	10.38	3	0	0	0	0	0	4.1	5	22	5	5	1	1	1	0	4	0	5	0	0
Victery, Joe, Lan.	1	4	.200	8.51	10	5	0	0	3	0	30.2	51	156	35	29	4	0	1	3	13	0	15	2	0
Vogelsong, Ryan, S.J.	4	4	.500	2.45	13	13	0	0	0	0	69.2	37	274	26	19	3	1	2	3	27	0	86	3	0
Volkman, Keith, R.C.*	2	2	.500	5.40	49	0	0	0	16	2	53.1	59	254	38	32	4	4	2	4	37	1	41	5	0
Wagner, Denny, Mod.	7	4	.636	3.56	27	15	0	0	5	3	113.2	116	502	57	45	7	0	3	10	42	2	99	7	3
Waites, David, Vis.	1	4	.200	5.87	32	0	0	0	22	7	38.1	30	180	25	25	2	2	3	8	29	3	28	8	1
Walker, Kevin, R.C.*	1	1	.500	3.46	27	1	0	0	9	4	39.0	35	169	19	15	2	1	2	3	19	3	35	1	0
Ward, Jeremy, H.D.	0	0	.000	2.08	4	4	0	0	0	0	8.2	5	35	2	2	0	0	0	1	3	0	12	0	4
Wells, Matt, S.J.	8	5	.615	3.67	57	0	0	0	24	4	90.2	73	400	41	37	4	4	8	1	65	0	100	6	0
Wells, Zach, Bak.	0	0	.000	3.00	4	0	0	0	3	0	6.0	6	27	4	2	2	0	0	2	1	0	3	0	0
White, Matt, H.D.	2	8	.200	5.79	31	17	0	0	4	1	91.2	101	418	70	59	15	2	3	3	49	1	78	5	0
Wilson, Jeff, H.D.*	7	4	.636	4.31	32	17	0	0	2	1	110.2	106	494	66	53	12	2	4	3	67	2	122	8	2
Wooten, Greg, Lan.	10	4	.714	4.33	17	17	3	0	0	0	114.1	123	489	62	55	13	2	3	6	30	1	72	5	0
Worrell, Tim, Mod.	0	0	.000	0.00	1	1	0	0	0	0	2.0	0	6	0	0	0	0	0	0	0	0	1	0	0
Yates, Tyler, Vis.	2	5	.286	5.47	47	1	0	0	19	4	82.1	98	382	64	50	12	3	2	4	35	3	74	12	0
Zapata, Juan, Stoc.	1	4	.200	6.67	30	0	0	0	12	1	54.0	65	267	52	40	7	1	2	4	33	2	35	9	0
Zerbe, Chad, Bak.*	7	7	.500	3.64	21	21	0	0	0	0	126.0	124	533	66	51	4	0	5	2	33	0	81	6	0
Zito, Barry, Vis.*	3	0	1.000	2.45	8	8	0	0	0	0	40.1	21	157	13	11	3	0	1	0	22	0	62	3	0

COMBINATION SHUTOUTS: **Bakersfield (2)**—Bermudez-Connolly-Rajotte, Horgan-Flores-Rajotte. **High Desert (0)**—None. Lake Elsinore (1)—Bridges-Lubozynski-Perozo. **Lancaster (4)**—Fitzgerald-Sweeney-Stark-Kaye, Parker-McClaskey-Ramos-Stark-Kaye, Parker-Kaye, Wooten-Farnsworth. **Modesto (7)**—Adkins-Niles, Nix-Wagner, Nina-Colome, Colome-Nina-O'Dell, Jarvis-Adkins-Calandriello-Moore, Nina-Colome-Moore, Jones-Schultz. **Rancho Cucamonga (7)**—Guttormson-Szymborski-Hart-Hite, Guttormson-Aragon-Hite, Lawrence-Volkman, Foran-Walker-Hart, Walker-Aragon, Foran-Aragon, Kramer-Walker-Volkman. **San Bernardino (6)**—Dorame-Maddux, Burnside-Cervantes, Caraccioli-Flores, Caraccioli-Harrell-Everly, Colyer-Cervantes-Everly, Checo-Osuna-Chung-Bell. **San Jose (4)**—Esteves-Ramirez-Wells, Goodrich-Malerich-Miller, Vogelsong-Ramirez-Wells, Tucker-Malerich-Miller. **Stockton (6)**—Schubmehl-Kirst, Stewart-Kirst-Schubmehl, Childers-Schubmehl, Pasqualicchio-Myers-Simonson, Childers-Simonson, Sheets-Helmer. **Visalia (2)**—Gregg-Waites-Noriega, Anderson-Noriega.

NO-HIT GAME: Castillo, San Bernardino defeated Lake Elsinore, 4-0, June 14.

PITCHERS WITH TWO OR MORE TEAMS

Pitcher, Team	W	L	Pct.	ERA	G	GS	CG	ShO	GF	Sv.	IP	H	TBF	R	ER	HR	SH	SF	HB	BB	IBB	SO	WP	Bk.
Jones, Marcus, Vis.	6	4	.600	4.45	18	15	0	0	0	0	91.0	103	401	56	45	7	3	3	4	32	1	82	3	1
Jones, Marcus, Mod.	2	1	.667	2.81	7	5	0	0	0	0	32.0	29	137	18	10	5	2	0	3	14	0	36	1	0

1999 FIELDING
TEAM

Team	Pct.	G	PO	A	E	TC	DP	TP	PB	Team	Pct.	G	PO	A	E	TC	DP	TP	PB
San Bernardino	.972	141	3798	1440	151	5389	112	1	25	Visalia	.963	140	3706	1507	199	5412	106	0	41
R. Cucamonga	.970	140	3698	1510	163	5371	122	0	12	Stockton	.962	140	3684	1392	202	5278	113	0	19
San Jose	.967	140	3681	1584	182	5447	122	0	29	Modesto	.960	140	3738	1540	219	5497	111	0	27
Lancaster	.967	140	3669	1440	177	5286	138	0	23	Bakersfield	.959	140	3691	1514	225	5430	123	0	14
Lake Elsinore	.964	140	3717	1613	197	5527	137	0	28	High Desert	.958	141	3693	1427	225	5345	125	1	20

INDIVIDUAL

FIRST BASEMEN

NOTE: All caps denotes fielding-percentage leader based on 70 games for catchers, 93 for all other non-pitchers and 112 innings for pitchers. *Throws lefthanded.

Player, Team	Pct.	G	PO	A	E	TC	DP
Betten, Randy, L.E.	1.000	1	11	2	0	13	0
Bledsoe, Hunter, S.B.	.948	10	54	1	3	58	7
Brown, Jason, S.B.	1.000	7	41	3	0	44	5
Caiazzo, Nick, Stoc.	.978	55	413	29	10	452	26
Connors, Greg, Lan.	1.000	11	95	4	0	99	11
Cridland, Mark, Stoc.	1.000	5	37	1	0	38	1
Cromer, Tripp, S.B.	1.000	1	6	0	0	6	1
Cruz, Cirilo, Lan.	.985	26	177	15	3	195	15
Cuntz, Casey, H.D.	.979	15	85	8	2	95	10
Curtis, Matt, L.E.	.984	48	397	36	7	440	43
Deardorff, Jeff, Stoc.	1.000	2	6	0	0	6	1
De La Cruz, Jose, Vis.	1.000	2	3	0	0	3	0
Eberwein, Kevin, R.C.	1.000	3	21	2	0	23	1
Flaherty, Tim, S.J.	.985	127	1116	85	18	1219	103
GORR, Robb, S.B.	.994	126	995	114	7	1116	83
Hagins, Steve, L.E.	1.000	1	1	0	0	1	0
Hart, Jason, Mod.	.989	127	1148	76	13	1237	88
Hartman, Ron, H.D.	1.000	7	40	1	0	41	3
Howe, Matt, Vis.	1.000	1	2	0	0	2	0
Jacobsen, Buck, Stoc.	.952	2	17	3	1	21	1
Jaramillo, Lee, Stoc.	1.000	2	2	0	0	2	1
Jones, Tim, Vis.	1.000	1	1	0	0	1	0
Keith, Rusty, Vis.	1.000	1	5	0	0	5	0
Kirby, Scott, Stoc.	.969	39	327	17	11	355	35
Koonce, Graham, R.C.*	.986	126	1136	55	17	1208	100
Kraus, Jake, Stoc.	1.000	16	92	5	0	97	7

Player, Team	Pct.	G	PO	A	E	TC	DP
Kuzmic, Craig, Lan.	1.000	2	17	3	0	20	1
Landry, Jacques, Mod.	1.000	1	10	0	0	10	0
Light, Tal, Stoc.	1.000	2	22	1	0	23	6
Luster, Jeremy, Bak.	.989	48	423	31	5	459	39
Macalutas, Jon, Stoc.	.984	28	217	22	4	243	19
McCorkle, Shawn, Lan.	.985	59	495	33	8	536	48
Meier, Dan, H.D.*	.993	113	782	47	6	835	67
Mensik, Todd, Vis.*	.986	78	646	41	10	697	56
Messner, Jake, Bak.*	1.000	3	14	1	0	15	2
Neal, Steve, H.D.*	.976	5	38	2	1	41	4
Niemet, Robert, Bak.	.986	14	69	4	1	74	8
Osborne, Mark, H.D.	.960	14	91	6	4	101	9
Pelaez, Alex, R.C.	.991	14	93	12	1	106	9
Pujols, Rafael, Mod.	.973	15	102	8	3	113	12
Rodriguez, Guillermo, Bak.	1.000	3	4	0	0	4	0
Rodriguez, Juan, L.E.*	.979	44	347	24	8	379	37
Salazar, Oscar, Mod.	1.000	1	9	0	0	9	0
Simonton, Benji, L.E.	.958	3	23	0	1	24	1
Sosa, Nicolas, Vis.	.978	66	536	30	13	579	45
Steelmon, Wyley, H.D.	.984	18	112	8	2	122	13
Summers, John, Bak.	.984	86	695	52	12	759	64
Tsoukalas, John, S.J.	.993	17	129	10	1	140	10
Walther, Chris, L.E.	.991	52	498	27	5	530	38
Williams, Peanut, Lan.	.991	51	394	26	4	424	58

SECOND BASEMEN

Player, Team	Pct.	G	PO	A	E	TC	DP
Belliard, Francisco, H.D.	1.000	2	8	2	0	10	1
Betten, Randy, L.E.	1.000	8	14	20	0	34	6

Player, Team	Pct.	G	PO	A	E	TC	DP
Cesar, Dionys, Vis.	.947	76	148	189	19	356	45
Cintron, Alex, H.D.	1.000	5	9	5	0	14	2
CLARK, Jermaine, Lan.	.983	122	243	346	10	599	92
Cromer, Tripp, S.B.	1.000	1	3	3	0	6	2
Cruz, Hector, H.D.	1.000	5	10	7	0	17	1
Cuntz, Casey, H.D.	.975	21	24	53	2	79	14
Fuentes, Joel, Bak.	.962	49	114	113	9	236	30
Gallo, Ismael, S.B.	1.000	40	78	98	0	176	23
German, Esteban, Mod.	.932	110	201	321	38	560	45
Gonzalez, Jimmy, S.B.	.957	43	69	85	7	161	17
Hargrove, Harvey, Lan.	1.000	1	2	1	0	3	0
Hill, Steve, Bak.	.955	107	222	263	23	508	58
Hood, Jay, L.E.	.962	82	159	243	16	418	60
Howe, Matt, Vis.	1.000	3	3	5	0	8	1
Huisman, Jason, L.E.	.956	17	32	33	3	68	12
Illig, Brett, S.B.	.982	27	56	53	2	111	11
Landry, Jacques, Mod.	1.000	2	1	0	0	1	0
Lara, Eddie, Vis.	.959	28	58	82	6	146	13
Leggett, Adam, L.E.	.975	42	102	129	6	237	25
Martin, Jared, H.D.	.892	16	29	29	7	65	4
Martinez, Belvani, H.D.	.933	106	186	274	33	493	58
Mathis, Jared, Stoc.	.956	11	15	28	2	45	3
McClure, Brian, R.C.	.993	32	49	100	1	150	15
McCrotty, Will, S.B.	1.000	1	2	4	0	6	0
Montenegro, Jose, Stoc.	.911	12	9	32	4	45	8
Moreno, Jose, Lan.	.950	6	10	9	1	20	1
Osilka, Garret, Stoc.	.957	53	102	118	10	230	22
Otero, William, S.J.	.979	92	196	279	10	485	59
Pecci, Jay, Vis.	1.000	8	9	14	0	23	1
Pelaez, Alex, R.C.	.956	17	34	53	4	91	9
Pernalete, Marco, S.J.	.973	50	94	159	7	260	31
Pickler, Jeff, Stoc.	.962	76	133	172	12	317	38
Pimentel, Franklin, Vis.	1.000	2	2	2	0	4	0
Ramirez, Joel, Lan.	.958	11	18	28	2	48	6
Regan, Jason, Lan.	.875	4	8	6	2	16	2
Riggs, Eric, S.B.	1.000	30	66	68	0	134	17
Rodriguez, Juan, L.E.*	1.000	1	1	0	0	1	0
Rosario, Carlos, Vis.	.953	35	86	96	9	191	19
Salazar, Oscar, Mod.	.971	33	48	87	4	139	16
Snellgrove, Clay, R.C.	.981	49	107	148	5	260	31
Taylor, Joshua, Lan.	1.000	4	2	8	0	10	1
Theodorou, Nick, S.B.	.895	6	6	11	2	19	2
Valera, Ramon, Lan.	.944	5	5	12	1	18	2
Wickersham, Jack, R.C.	.948	45	78	105	10	193	26
Wilson, Andy, R.C.	1.000	2	2	1	0	3	0
Young, Eric, S.B.	.833	3	3	7	2	12	1

TRIPLE PLAYS: Illig, Martinez.

THIRD BASEMEN

Player, Team	Pct.	G	PO	A	E	TC	DP
Arias, George, R.C.	.800	4	1	3	1	5	0
Belliard, Francisco, H.D.	.846	7	2	9	2	13	0
Betten, Randy, L.E.	.920	6	5	18	2	25	2
Blair, James, S.B.	1.000	21	12	31	0	43	2
Bledsoe, Hunter, S.B.	.000	1	0	0	0	0	0
Burns, Xavier, Bak.	.867	61	33	117	23	173	12
Burroughs, Sean, R.C.	1.000	2	2	5	0	7	1
Connors, Greg, Lan.	1.000	6	5	6	0	11	0
Cromer, Tripp, S.B.	1.000	1	0	1	0	1	1
Cruz, Cirilo, Lan.	.911	30	20	52	7	79	4
Cruz, Hector, H.D.	1.000	3	1	3	0	4	0
Cuntz, Casey, H.D.	.909	36	35	65	10	110	11
Curtis, Matt, L.E.	.804	18	6	31	9	46	3
Deardorff, Jeff, Stoc.	.889	122	91	197	36	324	17
Eberwein, Kevin, R.C.	.933	91	63	188	18	269	16
Figueroa, Luis, Lan.	.929	32	16	62	6	84	5
Flores, Javier, Vis.	.923	9	2	22	2	26	1
Fuentes, Joel, Bak.	.800	9	7	9	4	20	1
Gallo, Ismael, S.B.	1.000	2	0	1	0	1	0
Gonzalez, Jimmy, S.B.	.916	58	53	110	15	178	11
Hammock, Robert, H.D.	1.000	1	0	3	0	3	0
Hargrove, Harvey, Lan.	1.000	1	1	1	0	2	1
Hartman, Ron, H.D.	.903	23	12	44	6	62	5
Hill, Steve, Bak.	1.000	2	1	1	0	2	0
Hood, Jay, L.E.	.000	1	0	0	0	0	0
Howe, Matt, Vis.	.876	35	16	83	14	113	7
Huisman, Jason, L.E.	.879	70	44	152	27	223	15
Illig, Brett, S.B.	.938	46	37	68	7	112	10
Jaramillo, Lee, Stoc.	.000	1	0	0	1	1	0
Kirby, Scott, Stoc.	.833	13	7	23	6	36	4
Kuzmic, Craig, Lan.	.900	10	4	14	2	20	3
Landry, Jacques, Mod.	.898	111	60	223	32	315	12

Player, Team	Pct.	G	PO	A	E	TC	DP
Lara, Eddie, Vis.	.967	32	25	62	3	90	8
Leggett, Adam, L.E.	.857	5	5	7	2	14	0
Magdaleno, Ricky, Lan.	.833	3	2	8	2	12	0
Martin, Jared, H.D.	.950	60	28	106	7	141	12
Martinez, Belvani, H.D.	.000	1	0	0	0	0	0
McClure, Brian, R.C.	1.000	1	0	1	0	1	0
Montenegro, Jose, Stoc.	1.000	5	0	5	0	5	0
Moreno, Jose, Lan.	1.000	2	0	3	0	3	0
Niemet, Robert, Bak.	.000	1	0	0	1	1	0
Osilka, Garret, Stoc.	1.000	14	6	16	0	22	2
Owens, Ryan, H.D.	.845	25	12	37	9	58	4
Pelaez, Alex, R.C.	.960	41	19	78	4	101	8
Pujols, Rafael, Mod.	1.000	7	0	9	0	9	0
Ramirez, Joel, Lan.	.750	2	2	4	2	8	0
Regan, Jason, Lan.	.938	62	45	107	10	162	12
Salazar, Oscar, Mod.	.840	28	16	47	12	75	4
Schneidmiller, Gary, Vis.	.881	76	47	145	26	218	8
Snellgrove, Clay, R.C.	.957	10	2	20	1	23	2
Summers, John, Bak.	.857	4	1	5	1	7	0
Taylor, Joshua, Lan.	1.000	2	0	2	0	2	0
Theodorou, Nick, S.B.	.957	17	12	33	2	47	3
Torcato, Tony, Bak.	.886	82	54	164	28	246	14
Tsoukalas, John, S.J.	.944	7	4	13	1	18	1
Walther, Chris, L.E.	.921	47	26	103	11	140	17
Wickersham, Jack, R.C.	1.000	1	0	1	0	1	0
ZUNIGA, Tony, S.J.	.929	135	82	312	30	424	33

SHORTSTOPS

Player, Team	Pct.	G	PO	A	E	TC	DP
Belliard, Francisco, H.D.	.941	4	10	6	1	17	1
Campusano, Carlos, S.J.-Bak.	.930	40	57	116	13	186	21
CASTRO, Nelson, L.E.	.962	123	210	370	23	603	74
Cintron, Alex, H.D.	.950	125	223	308	28	559	73
Cosme, Caonabo, Mod.	.932	122	185	362	40	587	73
Cromer, Tripp, S.B.	1.000	1	0	4	0	4	0
Cruz, Hector, H.D.	.852	7	8	15	4	27	1
Cuntz, Casey, H.D.	.889	9	6	18	3	27	2
DiSarcina, Gary, L.E.	.857	3	1	5	1	7	2
Eberwein, Kevin, R.C.	1.000	1	0	2	0	2	0
Estrada, Marco, Lan.	.974	13	12	26	1	39	7
Fuentes, Joel, Bak.	1.000	3	5	1	0	6	0
Gallo, Ismael, S.B.	.958	41	66	118	8	192	22
Grudzielanek, Mark, S.B.	1.000	4	1	11	0	12	1
Halloran, Matt, R.C.	.940	91	115	277	25	417	57
Hargrove, Harvey, Lan.	1.000	6	7	5	0	12	2
Hill, Steve, Bak.	.890	32	35	78	14	127	14
Hood, Jay, L.E.	.977	21	25	60	2	87	12
Lara, Eddie, Vis.	.901	45	51	94	16	161	11
Magdaleno, Ricky, Lan.	.978	19	29	60	2	91	17
Martin, Jared, H.D.	.885	9	9	14	3	26	2
Mathis, Jared, Stoc.	1.000	5	5	8	0	13	1
Moreno, Jose, Lan.	.875	5	9	12	3	24	1
Osilka, Garret, Stoc.	.911	20	36	36	7	79	5
Otero, William, S.J.	.833	2	2	3	1	6	0
Pecci, Jay, Vis.	.942	111	138	298	27	463	53
Pernalete, Marco, S.J.	.913	45	51	117	16	184	20
Ramirez, Joel, Lan.	.954	95	161	274	21	456	68
Ransom, Cody, Bak.	.938	99	133	318	30	481	49
Reynoso, Ismael, S.J.	.958	76	111	229	15	355	43
Riggs, Eric, S.B.	.945	101	151	265	24	440	44
Rowan, Chris, Stoc.	.919	121	187	324	45	556	67
Salazar, Oscar, Mod.	.926	20	27	48	6	81	11
Snellgrove, Clay, R.C.	.943	49	71	127	12	210	30
Thurston, Joseph, S.B.	1.000	1	2	1	0	3	0
Valera, Ramon, Lan.	.913	12	16	26	4	46	5
Wickersham, Jack, R.C.	1.000	3	3	5	0	8	0

TRIPLE PLAY: Riggs.

SHORTSTOPS WITH TWO OR MORE TEAMS

Player, Team	Pct.	G	PO	A	E	TC	DP
Campusano, Carlos, S.J.	.940	26	43	82	8	133	13
Campusano, Carlos, Bak.	.906	14	14	34	5	53	8

OUTFIELDERS

Player, Team	Pct.	G	PO	A	E	TC	DP
Allen, Jeff, Bak.	.981	123	250	10	5	265	2
Amador, Gerardo, Lan.	.964	17	26	1	1	28	0
Basabe, Jesus, Mod.	.935	84	150	8	11	169	3
Beatriz, Ramy, Stoc.*	.989	39	86	6	1	93	0
Belliard, Francisco, H.D.	.000	1	0	0	0	0	0
Blakely, Darren, L.E.	.986	121	209	8	3	220	1

Player, Team	Pct.	G	PO	A	E	TC	DP
Bledsoe, Hunter, S.B.	1.000	2	2	0	0	2	0
Brown, Jason, S.B.	.951	22	39	0	2	41	0
Bush, Darren, R.C.	.971	61	97	2	3	102	0
Byrnes, Eric, Mod.	.960	96	133	10	6	149	1
Caiazzo, Nick, Stoc.	.500	1	1	0	1	2	0
Calloway, Ronald, H.D.*	.962	49	76	0	3	79	0
Camilo, Juan, Vis.	.952	60	109	11	6	126	1
Casper, Brett, S.J.	.971	121	226	7	7	240	2
Cepeda, Ali, S.J.	1.000	3	1	0	0	1	0
Chatman, Karl, S.B.	.963	69	152	2	6	160	0
Chen, Chin-Feng, S.B.	.971	117	195	7	6	208	1
Clark, Doug, Bak.	.956	109	194	3	9	206	0
Clifton, Rodney, Vis.	.979	105	176	7	4	187	1
Colon, Jose, Stoc.	.979	87	129	8	3	140	2
Connors, Greg, Lan.	.952	6	18	2	1	21	0
Cosbey, Chris, Mod.*	.981	32	52	1	1	54	0
Cridland, Mark, Stoc.	.942	80	138	9	9	156	3
Crosby, Bubba, S.B.*	.975	90	191	7	5	203	0
Cruz, Cirilo, Lan.	.943	33	48	2	3	53	0
Cuntz, Casey, H.D.	1.000	8	7	1	0	8	0
Curtis, Matt, L.E.	1.000	4	3	0	0	3	0
Cust, Jack, H.D.	.922	114	136	5	12	153	0
Daeley, Scott, S.J.	1.000	2	5	0	0	5	0
Dean, Mike, S.J.	.889	6	8	0	1	9	0
Dougherty, Jeb, L.E.	.962	112	171	7	7	185	1
Eady, Gerald, Lan.	.855	46	65	6	12	83	0
Faircloth, Chad, Bak.	.967	39	55	3	2	60	0
Fernandez, Alex, Lan.*	.936	114	179	12	13	204	2
Fox, Jason, Stoc.	.985	63	125	3	2	130	1
Glendenning, Mike, S.J.	.969	55	83	10	3	96	1
Gonzalez, Jimmy, S.B.	1.000	4	2	0	0	2	0
Graham, Justin, Mod.	1.000	3	2	1	0	3	0
Greene, Clay, Bak.	.938	31	59	1	4	64	0
Guiel, Jeff, L.E.	1.000	15	31	2	0	33	0
Hammock, Robert, H.D.	1.000	2	1	0	0	1	0
Hargrove, Harvey, Lan.	.956	123	273	11	13	297	1
Haynes, Nathan, Vis.-Lak.*	.970	61	124	5	4	133	0
Hollandsworth, Todd, S.B.*	1.000	4	3	1	0	4	0
Hunter, Johnny, R.C.	.978	25	39	5	1	45	0
Jacobsen, Buck, Stoc.	1.000	14	14	0	0	14	0
Jones, Tim, Vis.	.915	31	41	2	4	47	0
KEITH, Rusty, Vis.	.995	114	206	8	1	215	1
Kennedy, Gus, L.E.	.976	20	38	2	1	41	0
Kirby, Scott, Stoc.	.000	1	0	0	0	0	0
Light, Tal, Stoc.	.800	2	4	0	1	5	0
Ludwick, Ryan, Mod.*	1.000	40	69	2	0	71	0
Luke, Matt, L.E.*	1.000	9	15	2	0	17	0
Macalutas, Jon, Stoc.	1.000	2	2	1	0	3	0
Marchiano, Mike, Lan.	.961	33	46	3	2	51	1
Martinez, Hipolito, Vis.	.977	102	158	13	4	175	3
Mathis, Jared, Stoc.	1.000	5	6	0	0	6	0
Matthews, Lamont, S.B.*	.000	1	0	0	0	0	0
McDowell, Arturo, Bak.*	.971	116	260	8	8	276	1
McKinley, Dan, S.J.	1.000	15	32	0	0	32	0
McKinnon, Sandy, H.D.	.500	1	1	0	1	2	0
Meier, Dan, H.D.*	1.000	8	8	0	0	8	0
Melendez, Angel, S.J.	.955	100	162	6	8	176	0
Messner, Jake, Bak.*	.977	30	41	2	1	44	1
Moreno, Jose, Lan.	.000	1	0	0	0	0	0
Mota, Pedro, S.J.*	.950	46	74	2	4	80	1
Murphy, Nate, L.E.*	.978	25	43	1	1	45	0
Neubart, Adam, H.D.	.984	52	122	5	2	129	0
Newton, Kimani, S.B.	.930	40	100	6	8	114	2
Nunez, Abraham, H.D.	.951	130	254	20	14	288	1
Owens, Jeremy, R.C.	.957	9	20	2	1	23	1
Pernell, Brandon, R.C.	.979	132	273	6	6	285	2
Piedra, Jorge, S.B.*	1.000	8	18	2	0	20	0
Quintana, Wilfredo, Lan.	1.000	3	9	0	0	9	0
Rinne, James, H.D.	.983	64	110	5	2	117	0
Rodriguez, Juan, L.E.*	.935	41	70	2	5	77	0
Rosario, Omar, Mod.*	.953	98	152	9	8	169	3
Ross, Justin, L.E.*	.909	17	20	0	2	22	0
Sachse, Matt, Lan.*	.993	69	137	2	1	140	0
Salazar, Oscar, Mod.	.000	1	0	0	0	0	0
Schaub, Greg, Stoc.	.963	117	219	16	9	244	3
Seal, Scott, R.C.*	.954	118	179	7	9	195	1
Simonton, Benji, L.E.	.969	37	61	1	2	64	0
Snellgrove, Clay, R.C.	1.000	3	6	0	0	6	0
Sollmann, Scott, Stoc.*	.982	55	108	3	2	113	0
Stuart, Rich, L.E.	.929	11	12	1	1	14	0
Theodorou, Nick, S.B.	.978	77	170	6	4	180	2
Thomas, Gary, Mod.	.971	97	193	9	6	208	0

Player, Team	Pct.	G	PO	A	E	TC	DP
Tommasini, Kevin, S.J.	.989	67	84	5	1	90	0
Valderrama, Carlos, S.J.	1.000	21	32	4	0	36	1
Van Rossum, Chris, H.D.*	.948	28	52	3	3	58	0
Williams, Peanut, Lan.	1.000	2	1	0	0	1	0
Wilson, Andy, R.C.	.956	85	122	9	6	137	0

OUTFIELDERS WITH TWO OR MORE TEAMS

Player, Team	Pct.	G	PO	A	E	TC	DP
Haynes, Nathan, Vis.*	.972	35	65	5	2	72	0
Haynes, Nathan, L.E.*	.967	26	59	0	2	61	0

CATCHERS

Player, Team	Pct.	G	PO	A	E	TC	DP	PB
Ahrendt, Jay, R.C.	.965	16	105	6	4	115	0	1
Alcala, Juan, Lan.	1.000	7	25	2	0	27	1	0
Bazzani, Matt, S.J.	.948	29	156	9	9	174	1	10
Bertrand, Ben, Bak.	1.000	10	50	1	0	51	0	0
Briones, Chris, R.C.	.974	16	70	5	2	77	0	2
Brown, Jason, S.B.	1.000	5	29	4	0	33	0	0
Bush, Darren, R.C.	.000	1	0	0	0	0	0	0
Caiazzo, Nick, Stoc.	.993	21	134	13	1	148	1	7
Connors, Greg, Lan.	.989	55	398	39	5	442	2	6
Curtis, Matt, L.E.	.986	11	64	6	1	71	1	0
Dean, Mike, S.J.	.960	17	110	10	5	125	0	3
De La Cruz, Jose, Vis.	.976	41	251	29	7	287	0	15
Dewey, Jason, L.E.	.984	62	443	45	8	496	4	9
Flaherty, Tim, S.J.	1.000	1	2	0	0	2	0	0
Flores, Javier, Vis.	.987	97	678	98	10	786	1	23
French, Ron, R.C.	1.000	2	14	0	0	14	0	0
Goldfield, Josh, H.D.	1.000	3	6	0	0	6	0	0
Graves, Bryan, L.E.	.970	13	80	17	3	100	0	1
Hagins, Steve, L.E.	.960	31	165	26	8	199	2	12
Hammock, Robert, H.D.	.975	89	593	100	18	711	11	12
Hernandez, John, S.B.	.981	55	429	45	9	483	6	15
Illig, Brett, S.B.	1.000	1	6	0	0	6	0	0
Jaramillo, Lee, Stoc.	.958	10	42	4	2	48	0	3
Johnson, Patrick, L.E.-H.D.	.980	55	361	34	8	403	6	6
Koeyers, Ramsey, H.D.	.978	5	42	3	1	46	1	1
Kuzmic, Craig, Lan.	1.000	14	87	12	0	99	1	3
Lopez, Miguel, H.D.	.942	8	44	5	3	52	0	2
Lopez, Norberto, L.E.	1.000	2	9	0	0	9	0	0
Lopez, Rafael, Lan.	.989	63	421	50	5	476	5	9
Luderer, Brian, Mod.	.981	48	327	40	7	374	1	5
Mapes, Jake, Bak.	1.000	7	14	0	0	14	0	0
Mathis, Jared, Stoc.	1.000	1	6	1	0	7	0	2
Maynard, Scott, Lan.	1.000	8	43	5	0	48	0	0
McCrotty, Will, S.B.	.982	90	676	79	14	769	2	10
Montenegro, Jose, Stoc.	1.000	5	15	5	0	20	1	0
Moon, Brian, Stoc.	.991	115	833	129	9	971	11	10
Myers, Greg, R.C.	1.000	2	7	1	0	8	0	0
Nieckula, Aaron, Vis.	1.000	25	171	14	0	185	0	3
NIEVES, Wilbert, R.C.	.995	117	902	107	5	1014	8	9
Olivo, Miguel, Mod.	.974	71	509	50	15	574	2	15
Osborne, Mark, H.D.	.962	37	226	30	10	266	1	4
Priess, Matthew, S.J.	.979	86	634	56	15	705	2	15
Pujols, Rafael, Mod.	.982	40	280	43	6	329	4	7
Rapp, Travis, L.E.	.989	11	79	8	1	88	2	1
Rodriguez, Guillermo, Bak.	.967	36	155	21	6	182	3	3
Rogue, Francisco, Stoc.	.963	6	21	5	1	27	0	0
Serrano, Sammy, Bak.	.984	114	721	91	13	825	7	11
Tommasini, Kevin, S.J.	1.000	1	1	0	0	1	0	0
Torrealba, Yorvit, S.J.	.975	19	176	16	5	197	2	1
Williams, Peanut, Lan.	.864	4	18	1	3	22	0	3

CATCHERS WITH TWO OR MORE TEAMS

Player, Team	Pct.	G	PO	A	E	TC	DP	PB
Johnson, Patrick, L.E.	.969	25	168	17	6	191	4	5
Johnson, Patrick, H.D.	.991	30	193	17	2	212	2	1

PITCHERS

Player, Team	Pct.	G	PO	A	E	TC	DP
Adkins, Jon, Mod.	.926	26	5	20	2	27	2
Anderson, Jason, Vis.*	.857	4	2	4	1	7	0
Andra, Jeff, S.J.*	1.000	13	2	5	0	7	0
Andrews, Jeff, H.D.	.778	6	4	3	2	9	0
Aragon, Angel, R.C.	.900	53	2	7	1	10	0
Barton, Christopher, Stoc.	1.000	7	0	4	0	4	0
Bazzani, Matt, S.J.	.000	2	0	0	0	0	0
Bazzell, Shane, Vis.	1.000	8	3	4	0	7	0
Bell, Scott, S.B.	.923	28	7	5	1	13	2
Bello, Emerson, Lan.	.500	9	0	1	1	2	0

Player, Team	Pct.	G	PO	A	E	TC	DP
Bennett, Tom, Vis.	.917	36	1	10	1	12	1
Bermudez, Manny, Bak.	.929	32	6	33	3	42	1
Bido, Jose, H.D.	1.000	11	1	0	0	1	0
Bieniasz, Derek, Lan.	.929	15	4	9	1	14	1
Bridges, Douglas, L.E.*	.857	5	1	5	1	7	0
Brink, Jim, Mod.	.923	47	4	8	1	13	0
Brooks, Jacob, L.E.	.667	27	1	3	2	6	0
Burnside, Adrian, S.B.*	.972	26	5	30	1	36	1
Bynum, Michael, R.C.*	.875	7	2	5	1	8	1
Calandriello, Donato, Mod.*	1.000	38	2	7	0	9	1
Callier, Jeremy, L.E.	.900	34	9	18	3	30	1
Calzada, Javier, Vis.	.833	8	0	5	1	6	0
Camp, Shawn, R.C.	.938	53	4	11	1	16	0
Campusano, Carlos, S.J.	1.000	1	1	0	0	1	0
Caraccioli, Lance, S.B.*	.838	28	3	28	6	37	0
Carmody, Brian, Lan.*	.750	16	0	3	1	4	0
CASTILLO, Marcos, S.B.	1.000	27	15	18	0	33	2
Cepeda, Wellington, H.D.	.944	42	6	11	1	18	1
Cervantes, Chris, H.D.*	.000	1	0	0	0	0	0
Cervantes, Peter, S.B.	1.000	40	0	12	0	12	1
Chavarria, David, S.J.	1.000	21	0	3	0	3	0
Checo, Robinson, S.B.	.000	2	0	0	0	0	0
Childers, Jason, Stoc.	1.000	12	5	9	0	14	0
Chung, Rocky, S.B.	1.000	9	1	1	0	2	0
Colome, Jesus, Mod.	.939	31	11	20	2	33	0
Colon, Jose, Stoc.	.000	1	0	0	0	0	0
Colyer, Stephen, S.B.*	.955	27	5	16	1	22	0
Condrey, Clay, R.C.	1.000	6	2	0	0	2	0
Connolly, Keith, Bak.	.917	54	4	7	1	12	1
Correa, Elvis, S.B.	.889	40	10	6	2	18	1
Cosbey, Chris, Mod.*	.000	1	0	0	0	0	0
Coscia, Tony, Bak.	.897	28	9	17	3	29	2
Cowsill, Brendon, L.E.	.960	27	15	33	2	50	2
Cox, Ryan, Bak.	1.000	7	4	2	0	6	0
Cummings, Ryan, L.E.	1.000	7	3	6	0	9	0
Davis, Clint, H.D.	.500	2	0	1	1	2	0
De La Rosa, Jorge, H.D.*	.000	2	0	0	0	0	0
Diaz, Antonio, R.C.	1.000	9	1	2	0	3	0
Dorame, Randey, S.B.*	.941	24	5	27	2	34	0
Duarte, Renney, L.E.	.833	3	2	3	1	6	0
Dunham, Pat, Lan.	.500	9	0	3	3	6	0
Emanuel, Brandon, L.E.	1.000	2	2	4	0	6	0
Enochs, Chris, Vis.	1.000	4	3	3	0	6	0
Esteves, Jake, S.J.	.952	12	4	16	1	21	2
Everly, Bill, S.B.	1.000	60	2	12	0	14	2
Fahrner, Evan, H.D.	1.000	3	0	1	0	1	0
Farnsworth, Jeff, Lan.	.833	26	2	8	2	12	0
Featherstone, Deron, Bak.	1.000	6	0	1	0	1	0
Fernandez, Ozzie, S.J.	1.000	4	1	0	0	1	0
Fields, Brian, Bak.*	1.000	20	3	7	0	10	1
Fikac, Jeremy, R.C.	.929	40	5	8	1	14	1
Fischer, Mike, S.B.	1.000	3	2	2	0	4	0
Fish, Steve, L.E.	.902	32	17	20	4	41	3
Fitzgerald, Brian, Lan.*	1.000	6	2	8	0	10	0
Flores, Benito, Bak.*	.926	34	6	19	2	27	1
Flores, Pedro, S.B.*	.889	32	1	7	1	9	1
Foran, John, R.C.	.952	25	10	10	1	21	1
Gallo, Ismael, S.B.	.000	1	0	0	0	0	0
Gangemi, Joe, L.E.*	1.000	21	2	9	0	11	1
Gardner, Mark, S.J.	.000	2	0	0	1	1	0
Goodrich, Randy, S.J.	.846	38	11	22	6	39	0
Gorrell, Chris, Vis.	1.000	16	0	4	0	4	0
Green, Steve, L.E.	.929	19	1	25	2	28	1
Gregg, Kevin, Vis.	.875	13	2	5	1	8	1
Guttormson, Rick, R.C.	.903	28	9	19	3	31	0
Harrell, Tim, Vis.	1.000	44	8	12	0	20	0
Hart, Len, R.C.*	1.000	33	2	4	0	6	0
Hawkins, Al, Stoc.	.909	4	3	7	1	11	0
Hebert, Cedric, S.B.	.857	16	4	2	1	7	0
Helmer, Chad, Stoc.	1.000	20	2	6	0	8	0
Hill, Jason, L.E.*	1.000	10	1	3	0	4	0
Hite, Kevin, R.C.	1.000	7	1	3	0	4	0
Hoerman, Jared, Lan.	1.000	4	1	1	0	2	0
Holmes, Mike, Mod.	.975	34	14	25	1	40	3
Horgan, Joe, Bak.*	.842	25	3	13	3	19	0
Huller, Mike, Bak.*	.000	1	0	0	0	0	0
Immel, Stephen, H.D.	1.000	19	2	11	0	13	1
James, Mike, L.E.	1.000	3	1	0	0	1	0
Jaramillo, Lee, Stoc.	.000	2	0	0	0	0	0
Jarvis, Kevin, Mod.	1.000	2	1	2	0	3	0
Jensen, Jared, Vis.	.964	32	10	17	1	28	1
Jensen, Jason, H.D.*	1.000	9	1	5	0	6	0
Johnson, Eric, Bak.	.800	17	2	2	1	5	0
Johnson, Greg, L.E.*	.826	39	3	16	4	23	1
Johnson, James, Stoc.*	.960	29	8	16	1	25	0
Jones, Chris, S.J.*	.917	28	4	18	2	24	0
Jones, Marcus, Vis.-Mod.	.893	25	8	17	3	28	2
Joseph, Kevin, S.J.	1.000	20	0	3	0	3	0
Kaye, Justin, Lan.	1.000	53	5	6	0	11	0
Kees, Justin, H.D.	.870	30	4	16	3	23	1
Kendall, Phil, Stoc.	.957	18	10	12	1	23	1
Kenny, Seth, Mod.	1.000	18	1	2	0	3	0
Kirby, Scott, Stoc.	.000	3	0	0	0	0	0
Kirkreit, Daron, Lan.	1.000	9	2	2	0	4	0
Kirst, Mark, Stoc.	1.000	32	4	7	0	11	0
Kiyono, Masashi, S.J.	.889	32	4	4	1	9	0
Klein, Matt, Vis.	.600	11	3	0	2	5	0
Klepaski, Jose, Lan.	.000	1	0	0	0	0	0
Koehler, Russ, Lan.	.900	7	1	8	1	10	0
Kohl, Doug, H.D.	1.000	30	5	9	0	14	2
Kramer, Aaron, R.C.	.760	23	2	17	6	25	3
Krawczyk, Jack, Stoc.	.917	41	4	7	1	12	0
Lara, Eddie, Vis.	.000	1	0	0	0	0	0
Lawrence, Brian, R.C.	.936	27	7	37	3	47	3
Leyva, Julian, Vis.	1.000	15	6	13	0	19	0
Longo, Neil, Lan.	.931	23	14	13	2	29	3
Lopez, Rafael, Lan.	.000	1	0	0	0	0	0
Lubozynski, Matt, L.E.*	1.000	30	3	8	0	11	1
Luque, Roger, R.C.*	1.000	3	0	2	0	2	0
Maddux, Mike, S.B.	1.000	5	1	4	0	5	0
Madero, Francisco, S.B.	1.000	12	2	3	0	5	1
Malerich, Will, S.J.*	1.000	45	2	12	0	14	1
Mallette, Brian, Stoc.	.875	28	4	3	1	8	1
Malloy, Bill, S.J.	.778	17	3	4	2	9	2
Manzueta, Roberto, H.D.	.846	40	1	10	2	13	0
Martines, Jason, H.D.	1.000	43	0	9	0	9	0
Maurer, Mike, Mod.	1.000	15	1	3	0	4	0
McCall, Travis, Mod.*	1.000	43	5	9	0	14	0
McClaskey, Tim, Lan.	.700	30	5	2	3	10	0
McDowell, Jack, L.E.	1.000	1	0	1	0	1	0
Mears, Chris, Lan.	1.000	10	2	2	0	4	0
Messman, Joe, S.J.	.000	2	0	0	0	0	0
Messner, Jake, Bak.*	.000	1	0	0	0	0	0
Miadich, Bart, H.D.	.903	21	8	20	3	31	1
Miller, Benji, S.J.	1.000	47	4	8	0	12	0
Miller, Jim, Stoc.	.913	28	7	14	2	23	1
Montenegro, Jose, Stoc.	.000	1	0	0	0	0	0
Moore, Brad, Mod.	1.000	34	0	5	0	5	0
Moore, Darin, Mod.	1.000	12	0	2	0	2	0
Morrison, Cody, L.E.	.929	45	2	11	1	14	0
Myers, Aaron, Stoc.	.929	22	7	6	1	14	0
Niebla, Ruben, S.B.*	1.000	3	0	3	0	3	0
Niles, Randy, Mod.	1.000	8	1	4	0	5	0
Nina, Elvin, Mod.	.913	17	5	16	2	23	0
Nix, Wayne, Mod.	1.000	34	2	11	0	13	1
Nogowski, Brandon, Vis.*	1.000	33	1	8	0	9	0
Noriega, Ray, Vis.*	1.000	60	3	11	0	14	1
Norris, Ben, H.D.*	.833	8	1	4	1	6	0
O'Dell, Jake, Mod.	1.000	3	1	0	0	1	0
Oleksik, George, H.D.	1.000	4	1	2	0	3	0
O'Reilly, John, H.D.	.900	21	1	8	1	10	0
Oropesa, Eddie, Bak.*	1.000	2	1	0	0	1	0
Osuna, Antonio, S.B.	.625	13	2	3	3	8	1
Ozias, Todd, Bak.	1.000	52	4	7	0	11	1
Padilla, Vicente, H.D.	1.000	9	5	7	0	12	0
Padua, Geraldo, R.C.	1.000	7	0	3	0	3	0
Paredes, Roberto, Stoc.	1.000	12	4	4	0	8	1
Parker, Brandon, Lan.	.760	27	8	11	6	25	1
Pasqualicchio, Mike, Stoc.*	1.000	4	1	3	0	4	0
Pena, Juan, Vis.*	.923	33	3	21	2	26	2
Perozo, Felix, L.E.	.875	32	2	5	1	8	0
Pipes, Joey, L.E.	1.000	2	1	2	0	3	0
Pourron, Joe, S.J.	.750	14	1	2	1	4	1
Prata, Danny, Bak.*	.889	27	3	21	3	27	0
Priebe, Kevin, Stoc.*	.800	34	0	4	1	5	0
Pujols, Rafael, Mod.	.000	1	0	0	0	0	0
Rajotte, Jason, Bak.*	.889	47	3	5	1	9	0
Ramirez, Erasmo, S.J.*	1.000	31	2	14	0	16	0
Ramos, Juan, Lan.	.600	42	2	4	4	10	0
Ricabal, Dan, S.J.	1.000	7	0	1	0	1	0
Rice, Nathan, Bak.*	1.000	3	0	2	0	2	0
Rodriguez, Juan, L.E.*	.000	1	0	0	0	0	0
Rubio, Miguel, H.D.	.900	27	4	5	1	10	0
Salter, Cody, L.E.	1.000	7	0	3	0	3	0

Player, Team	Pct.	G	PO	A	E	TC	DP
Sanchez, Duaner, H.D.	1.000	3	1	2	0	3	0
Sanchez, Simon, H.D.	1.000	40	2	7	0	9	0
Santos, Josh, S.J.*	1.000	13	3	13	0	16	1
Schmidt, Donnie, Lan.	.933	21	5	9	1	15	1
Schubmehl, Brian, Stoc.	.944	43	2	15	1	18	1
Schultz, Jeff, Mod.	.929	23	4	9	1	14	0
Seaver, Mark, Mod.	1.000	34	7	15	0	22	3
Serrano, Wascar, R.C.	.851	21	10	30	7	47	0
Sheets, Ben, Stoc.	1.000	5	3	5	0	8	2
Shepherd, Alvie, L.E.	.000	5	0	0	0	0	0
Shields, Scot, L.E.	.960	24	4	20	1	25	1
Simonson, Chris, Stoc.	.800	15	0	4	1	5	0
Simpson, Allan, Lan.	1.000	9	1	2	0	3	1
Smith, Travis, Stoc.	1.000	3	0	1	0	1	0
Snellgrove, Clay, R.C.	.000	1	0	0	0	0	0
Snow, Bert, Vis.	.625	31	3	2	3	8	0
Stark, Zac, Lan.*	.938	49	3	12	1	16	1
Stephens, Jason, L.E.	.929	15	0	13	1	14	0
Stewart, Paul, Stoc.	1.000	27	11	19	0	30	1
Sundbeck, Cody, H.D.	.818	14	3	6	2	11	1
Sweeney, Brian, Lan.	.000	5	0	0	0	0	0
Szymborski, Tom, R.C.	.750	28	4	2	2	8	1
Tavarez, Julian, S.J.	1.000	1	2	0	0	2	1
Thompson, Eric, Vis.	1.000	31	13	17	0	30	0
Travis, Jesse, Bak.	.900	14	3	6	1	10	1
Trejo, Francisco, H.D.*	1.000	3	0	1	0	1	0
Tsoukalas, John, S.J.	.000	1	0	0	0	0	0
Tucker, Ben, S.J.	.958	16	8	15	1	24	3

Player, Team	Pct.	G	PO	A	E	TC	DP
Turman, Jason, Lan.	1.000	31	5	12	0	17	0
Urban, Jeff, S.J.*	1.000	15	5	18	0	23	0
Valenti, Jon, Bak.	.867	46	6	7	2	15	0
Valera, Ramon, Lan.	.000	1	0	0	0	0	0
Verplancke, Joe, H.D.	.000	3	0	0	0	0	0
Victery, Joe, Lan.	.889	10	6	2	1	9	1
Vogelsong, Ryan, S.J.	1.000	13	5	5	0	10	0
Volkman, Keith, R.C.*	1.000	49	5	10	0	15	1
Wagner, Denny, Mod.	.960	27	0	24	1	25	0
Waites, David, Vis.	1.000	32	3	8	0	11	0
Walker, Kevin, R.C.*	.900	27	2	7	1	10	0
Ward, Jeremy, H.D.	.000	4	0	0	0	0	0
Wells, Matt, S.J.	.857	57	5	7	2	14	0
Wells, Zach, Bak.	.000	4	0	0	0	0	0
White, Matt, H.D.	.765	31	4	9	4	17	0
Wilson, Jeff, H.D.*	.875	32	6	15	3	24	1
WOOTEN, Greg, Lan.	1.000	17	12	21	0	33	1
Worrell, Tim, Mod.	.000	1	0	0	0	0	0
Yates, Tyler, Vis.	.947	47	7	11	1	19	0
Zapata, Juan, Stoc.	.889	30	2	6	1	9	0
Zerbe, Chad, Bak.*	.978	21	11	34	1	46	2
Zito, Barry, Vis.*	.857	8	4	2	1	7	0

PITCHERS WITH TWO OR MORE TEAMS

Player, Team	Pct.	G	PO	A	E	TC	DP
Jones, Marcus, Vis.	.900	18	6	12	2	20	2
Jones, Marcus, Mod.	.875	7	2	5	1	8	0

The following players appeared only as designated hitter, pinch-hitter or pinch runner: Edmonds, dh; Freitas, dh; Leyritz, dh; McGowan, dh; Mott, dh-ph-pr; Salmon, dh; Southall, dh.

LEAGUE CHAMPIONS

Year	Team	Pct.
1914—	Fresno	.571
1915—	Modesto	.857
1916-40—	Did not operate.	
1941—	Fresno	.643
	Santa Barbara (2nd)*	.597
1942—	Santa Barbara†	.642
1943-44-45—	Did not operate.	
1946—	Stockton‡	.600
1947—	Stockton‡	.679
1948—	Fresno	.607
	Santa Barbara (3rd)*	.529
1949—	Bakersfield	.612
	San Jose (4th)*	.543
1950—	Ventura	.607
	Modesto (2nd)*	.586
1951—	Santa Barbara‡	.599
1952—	Fresno‡	.629
1953—	San Jose‡	.664
1954—	Modesto‡	.623
1955—	Stockton	.733
	Fresno§	.718
1956—	Fresno§	.650
1957—	Visalia∞	.622
	Salinas (4th)*	.504
1958—	Fresno*	.639
	Bakersfield	.672
1959—	Bakersfield	.592
	Modesto§	.643
1960—	Reno	.614
	Reno	.657
1961—	Reno	.743
	Reno	.643
1962—	San Jose§	.686
	Reno	.587
1963—	Modesto	.589
	Stockton§	.687
1964—	Fresno	.638

Year	Team	Pct.
	Fresno	.600
1965—	San Jose	.586
	Stockton§	.614
1966—	Modesto	.577
	Modesto	.671
1967—	San Jose§	.676
	Modesto	.586
1968—	San Jose	.629
	Fresno§	.623
1969—	Stockton§	.600
	Visalia	.614
1970—	Bakersfield	.667
	Bakersfield	.671
1971—	Visalia§	.583
	Fresno	.500
1972—	Modesto§	.547
	Bakersfield	.629
1973—	Lodi§	.657
	Bakersfield	.571
1974—	Fresno§	.607
	San Jose	.579
1975—	Reno	.614
	Reno	.614
1976—	Salinas	.650
	Reno§	.547
1977—	Salinas	.564
	Lodi§	.579
1978—	Visalia§	.698
	Lodi	.607
1979—	San Jose§	.636
	Reno	.525
1980—	Stockton§	.638
	Visalia	.507
1981—	Visalia	.621
	Lodi§	.521
1982—	Modesto§	.671

Year	Team	Pct.
	Visalia	.586
1983—	Visalia	.621
	Redwood§	.529
1984—	Modesto§	.597
	Bakersfield	.486
1985—	Fresno§	.575
	Stockton	.566
1986—	Palm Springs‡	.613
	Stockton§	.585
1987—	Fresno§	.559
	Reno	.535
1988—	Stockton	.657
	Riverside§	.599
1989—	Stockton	.627
	Bakersfield§	.577
1990—	Visalia	.638
	Stockton§	.582
1991—	San Jose	.676
	High Desert§	.537
1992—	Stockton§	.610
	Visalia	.551
1993—	High Desert§	.620
	Modesto	.529
1994—	Modesto	.706
	Rancho Cucamonga§	.566
1995—	San Bernardino§	.612
	San Jose	.550
1996—	San Jose	.636
	Lake Elsinore‡	.550
1997—	High Desert▲	.593
	San Bernardino	.486
1998—	San Jose▲	.593
	Rancho Cucamonga	.550
1999—	Modesto	.629
	San Bernardino▲	.567

*Won four-club playoff. †League disbanded June 28. ‡Won championship and four-club playoff. §Won split-season playoff. ∞Won both halves of split season. ▲Played split season and won six-club playoff.

CAROLINA LEAGUE

LEAGUE OFFICE

President/treasurer
John Hopkins

Address
P.O. Box 9503
Greensboro, NC 27429

Phone
336-691-9030

Teams (affiliation)
Frederick Keys (Orioles)
Kinston Indians (Indians)
Lynchburg Hillcats (Pirates)
Myrtle Beach Pelicans (Braves)
Prince William Cannons (Cardinals)
Salem Avalanche (Rockies)

Wilmington Blue Rocks (Royals)
Winston-Salem Warthogs (White Sox)

1999 FINAL STANDINGS
FIRST HALF

NORTHERN DIVISION

Team	W	L	T	Pct.	GB
Wilmington (Royals)	39	30	0	.565	...
Frederick (Orioles)	37	33	0	.529	2.5
Lynchburg (Pirates)	35	34	0	.507	4.0
Potomac (Cardinals)	24	45	0	.348	15.0

SOUTHERN DIVISION

Team	W	L	T	Pct.	GB
Kinston (Indians)	37	32	0	.536	...
Winston-Salem (White Sox)	36	33	0	.522	1.0
Myrtle Beach (Braves)	35	34	0	.507	2.0
Salem (Rockies)	34	36	0	.486	3.5

SECOND HALF

NORTHERN DIVISION

Team	W	L	T	Pct.	GB
Wilmington (Royals)	38	31	0	.551	...
Frederick (Orioles)	30	38	0	.441	7.5
Potomac (Cardinals)	30	40	0	.429	8.5
Lynchburg (Pirates)	29	39	0	.426	8.5

SOUTHERN DIVISION

Team	W	L	T	Pct.	GB
Myrtle Beach (Braves)	44	26	0	.629	...
Kinston (Indians)	42	26	0	.618	1.0
Salem (Rockies)	35	33	0	.515	8.0
Winston-Salem (White Sox)	27	42	0	.391	16.5

COMPOSITE

Team	Kin.	M.B.	Wil.	Sal.	Fred.	Lyn.	W.S.	Poto.	W	L	T	Pct.	GB
Kinston (Indians)	...	10	9	11	14	11	10	14	79	58	0	.577	...
Myrtle Beach (Braves)	10	...	11	14	12	11	12	9	79	60	0	.568	1.0
Wilmington (Royals)	11	9	...	12	10	11	11	13	77	61	0	.558	2.5
Salem (Rockies)	9	6	8	...	12	9	12	13	69	69	0	.500	10.5
Frederick (Orioles)	4	8	10	8	...	13	12	12	67	71	0	.486	12.5
Lynchburg (Pirates)	8	9	9	9	7	...	11	11	64	73	0	.467	15.0
Winston-Salem (White Sox)	10	7	8	8	8	9	...	13	63	75	0	.457	16.5
Potomac (Cardinals)	6	11	6	7	8	9	7	...	54	85	0	.388	26.0

Major league affiliations in parentheses.

PLAYOFFS: Myrtle Beach defeated Kinston two games to one; championship series was tied two games apiece when the seres was cancelled due to Hurricane Floyd. Myrtle Beach and Wilmington declared Co-Carolina League champions.

REGULAR-SEASON ATTENDANCE: Frederick, 313,603; Kinston, 124,010; Lynchburg, 110,937; Myrtle Beach, 232,619; Potomac, 209,168; Salem, 206,012; Wilmington, 321,143; Winston-Salem, 134,764. Total—1,652,256. Playoffs (7 games)—14,561. Carolina-California League All-Star Game at Lake Elsinore, Calif.—6,518.

MANAGERS: Frederick, Andy Etchebarren; Kinston, Eric Wedge; Lynchburg, Scott Little; Myrtle Beach, Brian Snitker; Potomac, Joe Cunningham; Salem, Ron Gideon; Wilmington, Jeff Garber; Winston-Salem, Jerry Terrell.

ALL-STAR TEAM: 1B—Eddy Furniss, Lynchburg; 2B—Marcus Giles, Myrtle Beach; 3B—Mike Edwards, Kinston; SS—Eddy Martinez, Frederick; Utility INF—Joe Dillon, Wilmington; OF—Jody Gerut, Salem; Derrick Lankford, Lynchburg; Aaron Rowand, Winston-Salem; Utility OF—Brandon Berger, Wilmington; C—Chris Heintz, Winston-Salem; DH—Andy Bevins, Potomac; SP—Josh Kalinowski, Salem; RP—Travis Thompson, Salem; Most Valuable Player—Marcus Giles, Myrtle Beach; Pitcher of the Year—Josh Kalinowski, Salem; Manager of the Year—Eric Wedge, Kinston.

1999 BATTING
TEAM

Team	Avg.	G	TPA	AB	R	H	TB	2B	3B	HR	RBI	SH	SF	HP	BB	IBB	SO	SB	CS	GDP	LOB	ShO	Slg.	OBP
Frederick	.264	138	5408	4667	699	1232	1751	222	30	79	623	43	53	56	589	10	952	171	72	106	1041	8	.375	.350
Wilmington	.260	138	5301	4641	653	1208	1738	209	33	85	583	52	43	83	482	16	950	143	71	97	1015	9	.374	.338
Lynchburg	.259	137	5298	4568	680	1182	1838	228	40	116	614	38	38	72	582	14	1146	126	71	106	977	9	.402	.349
Kinston	.252	137	5170	4492	644	1132	1721	241	36	92	561	42	29	53	554	18	1088	142	59	82	1007	8	.383	.339
Winston-Salem	.251	138	5219	4623	635	1159	1741	242	29	94	571	43	35	60	458	14	1037	174	77	80	948	11	.377	.324
Myrtle Beach	.250	139	5317	4763	637	1193	1846	240	49	105	578	31	40	56	427	21	1190	108	54	93	964	7	.388	.317
Salem	.247	138	5110	4521	574	1116	1579	206	37	61	511	77	37	45	430	14	915	126	62	85	919	10	.349	.316
Potomac	.243	139	5255	4610	619	1120	1671	221	30	90	573	42	40	88	475	8	1051	138	81	99	972	9	.362	.323

CLASS A Carolina League

TOP QUALIFIERS FOR BATTING CHAMPIONSHIP

Minimum 378 plate appearances. *Lefthanded batter. †Switch-hitter.

Player, Team	Avg.	G	TPA	AB	R	H	TB	2B	3B	HR	RBI	SH	SF	HP	BB	IBB	SO	SB	CS	GDP	Slg.	OBP
Giles, Marcus, M.B.	.326	126	560	497	80	162	255	40	7	13	73	0	5	4	54	5	89	9	6	9	.513	.393
Ortega, Bill, Pot.	.306	110	472	421	66	129	191	27	4	9	74	6	3	4	38	2	69	7	7	17	.454	.367
May, Freddy, Lyn.*	.295	126	534	441	61	130	182	20	4	8	56	0	5	3	85	0	105	17	11	12	.413	.408
Berger, Brandon, Wil.	.293	119	515	450	73	132	215	27	4	16	73	6	6	8	45	0	93	29	7	3	.478	.363
Heintz, Chris, W.S.	.293	118	466	417	55	122	180	33	2	7	60	3	2	4	40	1	72	6	3	7	.432	.359
Lankford, Derrick, Lyn.*	.292	123	521	456	80	133	237	28	8	20	88	0	6	7	52	1	124	4	0	7	.520	.369
Martinez, Eddy, Fred.	.291	127	491	416	68	121	150	21	1	2	55	5	5	13	52	1	99	8	4	6	.361	.383
Edwards, Mike, Kin.	.289	133	567	456	76	132	213	25	4	16	89	0	9	9	93	6	117	8	3	12	.467	.413
Gerut, Jody, Sal.*	.289	133	567	499	80	144	232	33	11	11	63	1	3	3	61	4	65	25	12	10	.465	.367
Sears, Todd, Sal.*	.281	109	448	385	58	108	171	21	0	14	59	0	1	4	58	1	99	11	2	9	.444	.379
Mohr, Dustan, Kin.	.280	112	458	429	46	120	179	29	3	8	60	1	1	1	26	2	104	6	1	13	.417	.322
Rowand, Aaron, W.S.	.279	133	565	512	96	143	258	37	3	24	88	2	5	13	33	2	94	15	10	13	.504	.336
Hamilton, Jon, Kin.*	.279	131	544	473	74	132	210	29	5	13	65	5	4	1	61	1	114	9	4	3	.444	.360
Bevins, Andy, Pot.	.277	138	576	513	92	142	251	30	2	25	97	3	4	11	44	2	128	6	2	11	.489	.344
Rivera, Roberto, Fred.	.274	118	505	460	70	126	191	21	4	12	53	0	3	3	39	0	89	18	9	4	.415	.333

DEPARTMENTAL LEADERS: G—Bevins, 138; AB—Garabito, 539; R—Rowand, Furniss, 96 each; H—Giles, 162; TB—Rowand, 258; 2B—Giles, 40; 3B—Ross, 13; HR—Bevins, 25; RBI—Bevins, 97; SH—Figgins, Keck, 14 each; SF—Garabito, 10; HP—Radcliff, 18; BB—Brown, Edwards, 6 each; SO—Pointer, 146; SB—Pratt, 47; CS—Garabito, 18; GIDP—Figueroa, 21; Slg.—Lankford, .520; OBP—Edwards, .413.

ALL PLAYERS

*Lefthanded batter. †Switch-hitter.

Player, Team	Avg.	G	TPA	AB	R	H	TB	2B	3B	HR	RBI	SH	SF	HP	BB	IBB	SO	SB	CS	GDP	Slg.	OBP
Albert, Rashad, W.S.	.111	21	58	54	3	6	9	1	1	0	1	0	0	0	4	0	23	0	2	1	.167	.172
Alley, Charles, Fred.†	.227	41	157	132	21	30	39	6	0	1	12	1	0	1	23	1	27	0	1	1	.295	.346
Allison, Cody, Kin.*	.215	43	143	121	15	26	33	4	0	1	11	4	0	1	17	0	32	1	0	3	.273	.317
Alviso, Jerome, Sal.†	.251	128	538	491	48	123	151	16	3	2	43	12	4	3	28	0	67	5	6	4	.308	.293
Anderson, Frank, Lyn.	.171	12	41	35	4	6	6	0	0	0	3	2	1	0	3	0	12	0	1	0	.171	.231
Anthony, Brian, Sal.*	.242	36	138	128	13	31	47	7	0	3	13	1	1	0	8	0	28	0	2	4	.367	.285
Arias, Rogelio, Sal.	.259	76	284	263	28	68	83	11	2	0	24	6	0	0	15	2	33	3	0	12	.316	.299
Bass, Jayson, M.B.†	.220	44	183	164	20	36	55	7	3	2	19	1	1	2	15	1	45	8	3	1	.335	.291
Benham, David, Pot.	.154	9	30	26	2	4	5	1	0	0	1	1	0	2	1	0	7	0	0	2	.192	.241
Benham, Jason, Fred.*	.148	16	31	27	3	4	4	0	0	0	2	1	1	0	2	0	2	0	0	1	.148	.200
Berger, Brandon, Wil.	.293	119	515	450	73	132	215	27	4	16	73	6	6	8	45	0	93	29	7	3	.478	.363
Berger, Matt, W.S.	.225	90	372	329	41	74	121	17	0	10	49	1	6	2	34	1	86	1	3	4	.368	.296
Bevins, Andy, Pot.	.277	138	576	513	92	142	251	30	2	25	97	3	4	11	44	2	128	6	2	11	.489	.344
Bone, Billy, Lyn.	.250	38	130	104	17	26	34	5	0	1	13	2	1	1	22	0	35	3	1	1	.327	.383
Brignac, Junior, M.B.	.228	64	288	254	32	58	90	7	2	7	35	2	4	4	24	3	84	11	10	6	.354	.301
Brito, Juan, Wil.	.283	14	47	46	3	13	14	1	0	0	1	0	0	0	1	0	11	0	0	1	.304	.298
Britt, Bryan, Pot.	.192	11	27	26	1	5	8	0	0	1	3	0	0	0	1	0	11	0	0	2	.308	.222
Bronowicz, Scott, M.B.*	.143	21	63	56	9	8	11	1	1	0	4	0	0	1	6	0	12	0	0	0	.196	.238
Brown, Dee, Wil.*	.308	61	269	221	49	68	121	10	2	13	46	0	4	0	44	6	56	20	8	10	.548	.431
Bryant, Matt, Lyn.	.284	26	114	102	9	29	33	4	0	0	11	1	0	0	11	0	12	4	1	3	.324	.354
Bultmann, Kurt, Lyn.	.195	30	110	87	7	17	22	3	1	0	3	3	0	3	17	0	15	0	0	3	.253	.346
Campbell, Wylie, Wil.	.241	45	166	137	22	33	40	4	0	1	17	2	0	2	25	1	29	6	5	3	.292	.366
Caradonna, Brett, W.S.*	.251	128	564	505	68	127	190	28	4	9	62	4	5	2	48	2	108	18	7	5	.376	.316
Caruso, Joe, Wil.	.235	102	412	361	60	85	125	13	6	5	37	6	3	8	34	0	68	6	4	7	.346	.313
Cepeda, Jose, Wil.-M.B.	.306	60	268	232	36	71	82	7	2	0	25	6	3	5	22	0	20	5	8	9	.353	.374
Coffie, Ivanon, Fred.*	.283	73	311	276	35	78	137	18	4	11	53	0	3	4	28	3	62	7	4	5	.496	.354
Combs, Chris, Lyn.*	.154	37	14	13	1	2	4	0	1	0	1	0	0	0	1	0	3	0	0	0	.308	.214
Connacher, Kevin, W.S.	.259	121	483	413	60	107	161	14	5	10	48	6	0	1	63	0	101	27	13	7	.390	.358
Conner, Decomba, Wil.	.304	48	198	171	27	52	66	7	2	1	17	1	0	5	21	1	26	9	1	2	.386	.396
Correa, Miguel, Sal.†	.255	100	407	373	48	95	159	19	6	11	79	1	6	2	25	1	72	11	12	5	.426	.300
Cortez, Santos, Lyn.	.224	48	177	161	19	36	45	6	0	1	10	4	1	3	8	0	34	1	3	4	.280	.272
Cruz, Edgar, Kin.	.150	35	145	133	13	20	37	11	0	2	14	1	0	2	9	0	46	0	0	1	.278	.215
Currens, Tim, W.S.*	.000	16	3	0	0	0	0	0	0	0	0	1	0	0	2	0	0	0	0	0	.000	1.000
Curry, Mike, Wil.*	.230	54	240	200	31	46	57	4	2	1	16	3	2	1	34	1	39	24	9	2	.285	.342
Daedelow, Craig, Fred.	.100	16	56	50	6	5	6	1	0	0	2	2	0	0	4	0	7	0	0	0	.120	.167
Deck, Billy, Pot.*	.260	71	282	235	35	61	90	12	4	3	32	3	2	11	31	1	54	4	2	6	.383	.369
DeHaan, Kory, Lyn.*	.325	78	340	295	55	96	146	19	5	7	42	4	1	4	36	3	63	32	10	4	.495	.405
Dellaero, Jason, W.S.†	.223	54	209	184	22	41	60	13	0	2	19	4	0	3	18	1	59	9	4	2	.326	.302
Depippo, Jeff, Kin.	.213	68	231	174	33	37	53	8	1	2	19	8	3	17	29	0	51	3	1	1	.305	.372
DeShields, Delino, Fred.*	.125	2	8	8	1	1	4	0	0	1	0	0	0	0	0	0	1	0	0	0	.500	.125
Dillon, Joe, Wil.	.264	134	576	503	73	133	216	31	2	16	90	2	5	7	59	4	124	9	6	12	.429	.347
Downs, Brian, W.S.	.180	20	63	61	7	11	15	1	0	1	5	0	0	0	2	0	13	1	0	3	.246	.206
Eckelman, Alex, Pot.	.193	52	180	161	20	31	52	5	2	4	14	1	0	5	13	0	39	3	3	2	.323	.274
Edwards, Mike, Kin.	.289	133	567	456	76	132	213	25	4	16	89	0	9	9	93	6	117	8	3	12	.467	.413
Escalante, Jaime, Fred.†	.333	5	3	3	0	1	2	1	0	0	1	0	0	0	0	0	1	0	0	0	.667	.333
Evans, Lee, Lyn.†	.225	117	465	413	44	93	148	18	2	11	58	2	8	5	37	2	129	3	6	4	.358	.292
Evans, Pat, Fred.†	.333	1	4	3	2	1	2	1	0	0	1	0	0	0	1	0	0	0	0	0	.667	.500
Figgins, Chone, Sal.†	.239	123	504	444	65	106	124	12	3	0	22	14	2	3	41	0	86	27	13	5	.279	.306
Figueroa, Franky, Fred.	.250	132	571	527	59	132	209	20	3	17	78	0	5	7	32	0	138	2	3	21	.397	.299
Fitzgerald, Jason, Kin.*	.239	82	338	310	26	74	109	17	3	4	39	1	3	1	22	1	77	15	7	5	.352	.289
Freeman, Brad, Pot.	.234	109	408	342	36	80	107	17	2	2	37	3	3	15	45	1	75	9	13	3	.313	.346
Furcal, Rafael, M.B.†	.293	43	204	184	32	54	69	9	3	0	12	6	0	0	14	0	42	23	8	3	.375	.343
Furniss, Eddy, Lyn.*	.261	128	549	444	96	116	220	33	1	23	87	0	5	6	94	5	113	5	4	13	.495	.393
Garabito, Eddy, Fred.†	.256	132	613	539	76	138	188	24	4	6	77	8	10	4	52	1	68	38	18	7	.349	.321
Garrick, Matt, Pot.	.167	70	252	216	17	36	57	10	1	3	17	3	1	0	32	0	57	1	5	4	.264	.273
Gentry, Aaron, Pot.	.159	66	155	138	13	22	31	4	1	1	8	1	2	1	13	0	54	4	3	4	.225	.234

Player, Team	Avg.	G	TPA	AB	R	H	TB	2B	3B	HR	RBI	SH	SF	HP	BB	IBB	SO	SB	CS	GDP	Slg.	OBP
Gerut, Jody, Sal.*	.289	133	567	499	80	144	232	33	11	11	63	1	3	3	61	4	65	25	12	10	.465	.367
Giles, Marcus, M.B.	.326	126	560	497	80	162	255	40	7	13	73	0	5	4	54	5	89	9	6	9	.513	.393
Gonzales, Jose, Sal.	.170	44	159	141	9	24	30	6	0	0	18	3	3	0	12	0	35	1	0	1	.213	.231
Gonzalez, Luis, Kin.	.000	1	1	1	0	0	0	0	0	0	0	0	0	0	0	0	0	0	0	0	.000	.000
Gutierrez, Victor, Lyn.	.234	114	479	428	55	100	130	11	8	1	33	11	0	3	37	0	68	23	9	10	.304	.299
Guzman, Wilson, Lyn.*	.500	35	2	2	0	1	1	0	0	0	2	0	0	0	0	0	1	0	0	0	.500	.500
Haad, Yamid, Lyn.	.254	59	248	209	31	53	81	11	1	5	33	2	3	1	33	1	42	5	2	8	.388	.354
Hamilton, Jon, Kin.*	.279	131	544	473	74	132	210	29	5	13	65	5	4	1	61	1	114	9	4	3	.444	.360
Hamlin, Mark, Sal.	.248	103	411	363	45	90	137	20	3	7	48	3	2	8	35	2	111	4	3	5	.377	.326
Hammond, Joey, Fred.	.290	79	309	245	41	71	96	14	1	3	37	5	2	0	57	0	66	3	3	8	.392	.421
Heintz, Chris, W.S.	.293	118	466	417	55	122	180	33	2	7	60	3	2	4	40	1	72	6	3	7	.432	.359
Hemme, Justin, Sal.*	.192	22	88	78	8	15	25	4	0	2	4	2	1	0	7	1	22	0	1	1	.321	.256
Hessman, Mike, M.B.	.247	103	426	365	62	90	184	25	0	23	54	0	3	11	47	3	135	0	3	3	.504	.347
Hill, Jeremy, Wil.	.234	92	358	304	37	71	97	12	1	4	27	8	2	6	38	0	75	2	0	15	.319	.329
Huelsmann, Mike, Kin.†	.305	58	215	177	35	54	74	6	4	2	22	8	0	1	29	0	19	14	3	0	.418	.406
Hughes, Brian, Fred.	.246	90	324	272	38	67	93	14	3	2	26	4	1	2	45	0	67	5	4	12	.342	.356
Jackson, Jeremy A., Sal.*	.246	36	131	122	12	30	39	7	1	0	5	3	0	1	5	0	36	4	1	1	.320	.281
Jacobs, Dwayne, W.S.	.000	47	2	0	0	0	0	0	0	0	0	0	0	0	0	0	2	0	0	0	.000	.000
Jones, Jay, Sal.*	.150	18	67	60	4	9	12	3	0	0	8	0	2	1	4	0	9	0	0	0	.200	.209
Jorgensen, Tim, Lyn.*	.278	64	262	230	32	64	103	21	3	4	34	0	2	3	26	2	47	0	1	6	.448	.356
Keck, Brian, Sal.	.242	103	404	347	54	84	109	10	3	3	30	14	5	1	37	1	53	14	2	9	.314	.313
Kilburg, Joe, Kin.*	.299	42	173	137	34	41	60	8	1	3	17	3	0	4	29	1	19	3	3	1	.438	.435
Kim, Dave, Pot.	.259	123	496	440	68	114	196	23	1	19	72	2	6	6	42	1	107	7	6	16	.445	.328
Klee, Chuck, W.S.	.211	73	216	199	19	42	65	11	0	4	24	1	0	2	14	0	50	3	0	4	.327	.270
Lackey, Steve, M.B.	.273	53	238	216	24	59	73	10	2	0	16	1	2	4	15	0	33	13	4	1	.338	.329
Lankford, Derrick, Lyn.*	.292	123	521	456	80	133	237	28	8	20	88	0	6	7	52	1	124	4	0	7	.520	.369
Lee, Jason, Pot.*	.212	44	137	113	15	24	31	4	0	1	9	2	1	3	18	0	35	11	0	1	.274	.333
Lehr, Ryan, M.B.	.255	109	474	423	59	108	176	18	4	14	68	0	1	5	45	1	63	3	2	15	.416	.333
Leon, Alfredo, Fred.	.214	6	16	14	3	3	3	0	0	0	1	1	0	0	1	0	3	1	0	1	.214	.267
Lindsey, John, Sal.	.208	75	291	260	32	54	83	15	1	4	35	3	1	7	20	1	69	2	1	3	.319	.281
Livingston, Doug, Sal.	.258	64	276	233	33	60	77	13	2	0	24	6	4	3	30	0	39	10	2	6	.330	.344
Lopez-Cao, Mike, Fred.*	.239	29	99	88	12	21	31	4	0	2	11	1	1	0	9	0	16	1	0	1	.352	.306
Lorenzana, Luis, Lyn.	.256	49	172	156	15	40	53	7	0	2	14	0	1	4	11	0	37	2	3	5	.340	.320
Mackowiak, Rob, Lyn.*	.304	74	291	263	51	80	116	7	4	7	30	4	0	6	18	0	57	9	4	5	.441	.362
Maier, T.J., Pot.	.263	102	415	353	53	93	114	15	0	2	38	0	4	3	55	0	61	12	7	6	.323	.364
Manning, Brian, W.S.	.240	106	407	350	45	84	127	20	4	5	47	3	5	10	32	1	55	24	4	7	.363	.317
Martine, Chris, Pot.	.206	42	159	136	11	28	42	7	2	1	14	3	2	2	16	0	42	1	2	3	.309	.295
Martinez, Eddy, Fred.	.291	127	491	416	68	121	150	21	1	2	55	5	5	13	52	1	99	8	4	6	.361	.383
Martinez, Louis, M.B.	.133	5	16	15	1	2	3	1	0	0	0	0	0	0	1	0	2	0	0	0	.200	.188
Matos, Luis, Fred.	.297	68	302	273	40	81	119	15	1	7	41	2	5	2	20	1	35	27	6	6	.436	.343
Maxwell, Keith, Lyn.	.250	35	142	132	10	33	50	6	1	3	16	0	0	4	6	0	29	0	2	3	.379	.303
May, Freddy, Lyn.*	.295	126	534	441	61	130	182	20	4	8	56	0	5	3	85	0	105	17	11	12	.413	.408
MaCrory, Bob, Pot.	.233	114	469	434	52	101	126	15	2	2	29	5	1	5	24	0	70	27	10	8	.290	.280
McDonald, Darnell, Fred.	.266	130	587	507	81	135	186	23	5	6	73	7	7	5	61	0	92	26	9	13	.367	.347
McGee, Tom, Fred.	.200	7	32	30	2	6	7	1	0	0	3	0	1	0	1	0	6	0	0	2	.233	.219
Medrano, Steve, Wil.†	.251	98	402	362	41	91	101	4	3	0	24	8	1	1	30	1	66	12	10	5	.279	.310
Mitchell, Andres, Sal.	.183	33	125	109	10	20	28	3	1	1	11	2	1	2	11	0	35	7	2	3	.257	.268
Mohr, Dustan, Kin.	.280	112	458	429	46	120	179	29	3	8	60	1	1	1	26	2	104	6	6	13	.417	.322
Montas, Ricardo, Wil.	.246	98	406	349	46	86	107	15	0	2	31	5	2	3	47	0	60	4	2	7	.307	.339
Moore, Griffin, Wil.	.059	6	19	17	1	1	2	1	0	0	4	0	0	1	1	0	7	0	0	0	.118	.158
Mortimer, Mark, Wil.	.276	73	290	250	29	69	91	13	0	3	31	3	4	5	28	0	48	1	0	6	.364	.355
Munoz, Billy, Kin.*	.254	106	429	378	46	96	150	25	1	9	55	1	1	1	48	2	108	3	2	9	.397	.339
Ndungidi, Ntema, Fred.*	.266	60	236	192	40	51	67	10	3	0	18	1	1	3	39	0	43	4	2	6	.349	.396
Olson, Dan, W.S.*	.319	64	262	216	36	69	112	16	0	9	41	0	1	6	39	4	80	1	1	0	.519	.435
Ortega, Bill, Pot.	.306	110	472	421	66	129	191	27	4	9	74	6	3	4	38	2	69	7	7	17	.454	.367
Pagan, Carlos, Wil.	.000	4	8	8	0	0	0	0	0	0	0	0	0	0	0	0	3	0	0	0	.000	.000
Paxton, Chris, Fred.*	.249	58	210	169	26	42	68	8	0	6	28	1	1	5	34	1	54	0	0	5	.402	.388
Paz, Richard, Fred.	.252	54	220	163	27	41	50	9	0	0	18	3	5	2	47	0	27	15	6	2	.307	.415
Pointer, Corey, Lyn.	.180	108	389	327	55	59	124	18	1	15	44	2	2	14	44	0	147	13	12	3	.379	.302
Pratt, Scott, Kin.*	.247	133	573	486	86	120	186	27	6	9	54	1	3	6	77	3	95	47	11	6	.383	.355
Pugh, Josh, M.B.	.165	41	130	115	4	19	21	2	0	0	12	1	2	1	10	0	32	0	0	2	.183	.234
Quaccia, Luke, Pot.*	.247	125	493	429	46	106	175	26	2	13	80	2	6	14	42	0	112	4	5	7	.408	.330
Radcliff, Vic, Wil.	.265	114	448	393	62	104	163	22	8	7	56	3	6	18	28	1	69	13	3	5	.415	.337
Ramirez, Dan, W.S.	.267	85	394	360	56	96	109	4	3	1	19	2	1	2	29	0	58	44	17	7	.303	.324
Reyes, Jose, Lyn.	.154	30	77	65	7	10	17	4	0	1	4	0	0	1	11	0	28	1	0	1	.262	.286
Rivera, Roberto, Fred.	.274	118	505	460	70	126	191	21	4	12	53	0	3	3	39	0	89	18	9	4	.415	.333
Rodriguez, Jeff, M.B.	.000	1	1	1	0	0	0	0	0	0	0	0	0	0	0	0	0	0	0	0	.000	.000
Ross, Jason, M.B.	.268	133	536	482	80	129	214	23	13	12	64	1	2	8	43	2	136	31	5	11	.444	.336
Rowand, Aaron, W.S.	.279	133	565	512	96	143	258	37	3	24	88	2	5	13	33	2	94	15	10	13	.504	.336
Rupert, Bryan, Pot.	.190	40	133	121	11	23	38	7	1	2	16	1	1	1	9	0	42	0	0	3	.314	.250
Rust, Brian, Fred.	.148	9	34	27	7	4	5	1	0	0	1	0	0	2	5	0	7	0	0	0	.185	.324
Ryder, Derek, W.S.	.208	39	131	120	11	25	29	4	0	0	8	3	2	1	5	0	17	0	3	2	.242	.242
Salargo, Steven, Fred.	.100	3	10	10	0	1	1	0	0	0	0	0	0	0	0	0	5	0	0	1	.100	.100
Santana, Osmany, Kin.*	.241	43	155	145	16	35	52	8	0	3	20	1	0	1	8	0	26	7	0	2	.359	.286
Scharrer, Jim, M.B.	.260	119	507	466	52	121	160	18	0	7	54	3	4	3	30	4	120	0	1	7	.343	.306
Schwartzbauer, Brad, Sal.*	.257	58	217	179	21	46	57	3	1	2	19	5	1	6	26	0	44	1	3	3	.318	.368
Sears, Todd, Sal.*	.281	109	448	385	58	108	171	21	0	14	59	0	1	4	58	1	99	11	2	9	.444	.379
Sheppard, Greg, W.S.	.201	79	252	224	22	45	71	5	0	7	27	1	1	5	21	2	74	6	2	5	.317	.283
Smith, Casey, Kin.	.163	39	146	129	15	21	33	6	0	2	15	0	0	3	14	0	48	0	1	2	.256	.260
Smothers, Stewart, M.B.	.151	56	205	185	19	28	45	4	2	3	14	0	5	0	15	1	71	2	2	3	.243	.210
Snead, Esix, Pot.†	.181	67	291	249	37	45	63	8	5	0	14	3	3	4	32	0	57	35	12	2	.253	.281
Sorensen, Zach, Kin.†	.238	130	582	508	79	121	172	16	7	7	59	8	2	2	62	1	126	24	12	6	.339	.322
Spencer, Jeff, M.B.	.247	111	437	397	59	98	167	28	4	11	42	0	4	2	34	1	126	2	6	4	.421	.307
Suarez, Luis, W.S.	.203	74	273	241	20	49	66	7	2	2	26	5	3	2	22	0	66	3	2	4	.274	.272
Taveras, Frank, Kin.*	.234	31	114	107	11	25	37	7	1	1	11	0	0	1	6	0	27	0	0	4	.346	.281

Player, Team	Avg.	G	TPA	AB	R	H	TB	2B	3B	HR	RBI	SH	SF	HP	BB	IBB	SO	SB	CS	GDP	Slg.	OBP
Taylor, Adam, Kin.	.188	6	18	16	2	3	6	0	0	1	2	0	0	0	2	0	7	0	1	0	.375	.278
Terhune, Mike, M.B.†	.224	92	346	312	24	70	89	10	3	1	26	6	1	0	27	0	51	3	2	11	.285	.285
Terrell, Jim, W.S.*	.271	119	506	436	74	118	168	31	5	3	47	7	4	7	52	0	79	16	6	9	.385	.355
Torrealba, Steve, M.B.	.211	52	193	175	23	37	64	9	0	6	23	3	0	2	13	0	47	1	0	4	.366	.274
Torres, Rafael, Wil.	.242	76	276	252	15	61	71	7	0	1	20	2	2	5	15	0	51	0	4	3	.282	.296
Ullery, Dave, Wil.*	.231	60	223	199	20	46	70	18	0	2	27	0	4	2	18	1	70	0	0	3	.352	.296
Vidal, Gilbert, Sal.	.196	13	55	46	6	9	15	3	0	1	6	1	0	1	7	1	12	1	0	4	.326	.315
Washington, Rico, Lyn.*	.283	57	242	205	31	58	86	7	0	7	32	1	2	4	30	0	45	4	1	8	.420	.382
Werth, Jayson, Fred.	.305	66	279	236	41	72	93	10	1	3	30	1	2	3	37	2	37	16	3	4	.394	.403
Whitaker, Chad, Kin.*	.239	76	304	280	34	67	108	14	0	9	36	0	2	1	21	1	62	2	3	14	.386	.293
Whitlock, Brian, Kin.	.250	13	35	32	3	8	9	1	0	0	3	0	1	1	1	0	10	0	2	0	.281	.286
Willis, Dave, Wil.	.261	116	475	441	58	115	191	26	1	16	72	0	7	7	20	0	84	4	4	10	.433	.299
Wilson, Jack, Pot.	.296	64	281	257	44	76	94	10	1	2	18	3	1	1	19	1	31	7	4	2	.366	.345
Wong, Jerrod, M.B.*	.224	58	218	201	27	45	79	11	4	5	31	4	2	4	6	0	52	1	2	7	.393	.258

GRAND SLAMS: Bevins 3; Berger 2; Alviso, Caradonna, Cruz, Edwards, Fitzgerald, Lehr, Matos, McDonald, Ortega, Paxton, Sheppard, Smith, Washington, Willis, Wong, 1 each.

AWARDED FIRST BASE ON CATCHER'S INTERFERENCE: Manning 7 (Rupert 2, Martine 2, Depippo, Taylor, Evans); Wong (Brito); Bevins (Werth); Scharrer (Gonzales); Jorgensen (Allison); Pugh (Gonzales); Fitzgerald (Hill).

PLAYERS WITH TWO OR MORE TEAMS

Player, Team	Avg.	G	TPA	AB	R	H	TB	2B	3B	HR	RBI	SH	SF	HP	BB	IBB	SO	SB	CS	GDP	Slg.	OBP
Cepeda, Jose, Wil.	.313	59	263	227	35	71	82	7	2	0	25	6	3	5	22	0	19	5	8	9	.361	.381
Cepeda, Jose, M.B.	.000	1	5	5	1	0	0	0	0	0	0	0	0	0	0	0	1	0	0	0	.000	.000

1999 PITCHING

TEAM

Team	W	L	Pct.	ERA	G	CG	ShO	Sv.	IP	H	TBF	R	ER	HR	SH	SF	HB	BB	IBB	SO	WP	Bk.
Myrtle Beach	79	60	.568	3.50	139	0	10	41	1248.2	1056	5271	552	486	95	48	35	31	559	17	1159	88	3
Kinston	79	58	.577	3.63	137	4	11	47	1184.0	1031	5062	569	478	83	51	35	86	492	13	1092	82	4
Salem	69	69	.500	3.83	138	6	8	38	1205.1	1152	5189	600	513	73	46	30	67	468	6	1078	89	4
Wilmington	77	61	.558	3.99	138	1	9	40	1221.0	1165	5252	607	541	78	39	33	60	503	11	1090	73	5
Winston-Salem ...	63	75	.457	4.05	138	7	10	29	1209.1	1155	5348	675	544	70	54	36	83	568	21	1065	123	5
Frederick	67	71	.486	4.32	138	8	8	26	1219.0	1269	5381	714	585	118	45	44	69	479	26	943	80	6
Lynchburg	64	73	.467	4.38	137	6	7	24	1206.0	1271	5265	706	587	102	37	46	44	431	8	1008	81	10
Potomac	54	85	.388	4.59	139	3	8	26	1209.0	1243	5323	718	617	103	48	56	73	497	13	894	98	4

INDIVIDUAL

TOP QUALIFIERS FOR EARNED-RUN AVERAGE TITLE

Minimum 112 innings. *Lefthanded pitcher.

Pitcher, Team	W	L	Pct.	ERA	G	GS	CG	ShO	GF	Sv.	IP	H	TBF	R	ER	HR	SH	SF	HB	BB	IBB	SO	WP	Bk.
Kalinowski, Josh, Sal.*	11	6	.647	2.11	27	27	1	0	0	0	162.1	119	659	47	38	3	4	2	6	71	0	176	11	1
Lewis, Derrick, M.B.	8	4	.667	2.40	24	23	0	0	0	0	131.0	100	551	44	35	9	1	3	3	81	0	102	6	1
Sobkowiak, Scott, M.B.	9	4	.692	2.84	27	26	0	0	1	0	139.1	100	572	50	44	10	3	2	2	63	1	161	12	1
Garland, Jon, W.S.	5	7	.417	3.33	19	19	2	1	0	0	119.0	109	500	57	44	7	4	5	8	39	2	84	7	0
Scott, Brian, W.S.	8	8	.500	3.41	25	25	1	0	0	0	147.2	135	637	75	56	7	7	3	5	60	3	132	17	0
George, Chris, Wil.*	9	7	.563	3.60	27	27	0	0	0	0	145.0	142	618	65	58	8	3	4	5	53	0	142	5	1
Drew, Tim, Kin.	13	5	.722	3.73	28	28	2	0	0	0	169.0	154	713	79	70	12	5	3	10	60	0	125	7	0
Austin, Jeffrey, Wil.	7	2	.778	3.77	18	18	0	0	0	0	112.1	108	473	52	47	10	5	3	2	39	0	97	5	0
Shiell, Jason, M.B.	6	7	.462	3.77	26	17	0	0	1	0	114.2	118	485	51	48	5	4	2	3	36	0	90	9	0
Difelice, Mark, Sal.	8	12	.400	3.86	27	23	3	0	1	0	156.1	142	642	71	67	20	4	6	4	36	0	142	3	1
Gonzalez, Mike, Lyn.*	10	4	.714	4.02	20	20	0	0	0	0	112.0	98	478	55	50	10	2	1	4	63	0	119	10	0
Woodward, Finley, Pot.	6	7	.462	4.10	24	18	1	0	1	0	120.2	126	511	61	55	14	4	6	1	28	0	82	5	0
Lanfranco, Otoniel, Pot.	8	6	.571	4.29	21	21	0	0	0	0	115.1	105	475	59	55	13	4	3	9	35	0	83	4	1
Lakman, Jason, W.S.	9	8	.529	4.36	20	20	2	0	0	0	119.2	108	531	69	58	4	3	4	8	55	1	110	14	0
Bauer, Rick, Fred.	10	9	.526	4.56	26	26	4	0	0	0	152.0	159	662	85	77	17	3	11	12	54	2	123	11	1

DEPARTMENTAL LEADERS: W—Drew, 13; L—Bausher, 15; Pct.—Drew, .722; G—DeLeon, 59; GS—Drew, 28; CG—McConnell, Bauer, 4 each; ShO—McConnell, 2; GF—Thompson, 52; Sv.—Thompson, 27; IP—Price, 171.2; H—Price, 198; TBF—Price, 762; R—Price, 102; ER—Price, 94; HR—DiFelice, 20; SH—Matcuk, 8; SF—Bauer, 11; HB—Matcuk, 20; BB—Lewis, 81; IBB—Milburn, 6; SO—Kalinowski, 176; WP—Jacobs, 28; BK—Alvarado, 4.

ALL PITCHERS

*Lefthanded pitcher.

Pitcher, Team	W	L	Pct.	ERA	G	GS	CG	ShO	GF	Sv.	IP	H	TBF	R	ER	HR	SH	SF	HB	BB	IBB	SO	WP	Bk.
Abreu, Winston, M.B.	3	2	.600	3.28	13	12	0	0	0	0	68.2	53	290	26	25	7	2	4	0	41	0	76	3	1
Achilles, Matt, Fred.	5	8	.385	4.31	16	15	1	0	1	0	94.0	103	413	57	45	6	2	6	5	32	2	77	5	0
Alvarado, Carlos, Lyn.	4	6	.400	4.57	20	18	0	0	0	0	90.2	89	400	52	46	4	0	1	2	46	0	75	8	4
Alviso, Jerome, Sal.	0	0	.000	0.00	1	0	0	0	0	0	1.0	0	4	0	0	0	0	0	0	1	0	0	0	0
Aracena, Juan, Kin.-Fred.	1	1	.500	2.00	7	0	0	0	4	0	9.0	9	35	3	2	1	0	0	1	0	7	1	0
Austin, Jeffrey, Wil.	7	2	.778	3.77	18	18	0	0	0	0	112.1	108	473	52	47	10	5	3	2	39	0	97	5	0
Avrard, Corey, Pot.	2	2	.500	4.41	28	0	0	0	11	0	32.2	32	157	19	16	2	1	1	4	26	1	40	7	0
Ayers, Mike, Lyn.*	1	2	.333	2.70	27	0	0	0	14	2	36.2	34	153	13	11	1	2	2	1	16	0	28	4	0
Bauer, Rick, Fred.	10	9	.526	4.56	26	26	4	0	0	0	152.0	159	662	85	77	17	3	11	12	54	2	123	11	1
Bausher, Andy, Lyn.*	6	15	.286	4.83	25	24	1	0	0	0	143.1	165	648	98	77	12	4	4	6	52	1	89	7	2
Bautista, Martin, Kin.	6	1	.857	2.76	20	0	0	0	6	2	42.1	31	179	16	13	3	5	3	3	20	1	44	2	0
Benes, Alan, Pot.	0	0	.000	1.80	2	2	0	0	0	0	5.0	1	18	1	1	0	0	1	0	4	0	2	0	0
Borne, Matt, W.S.	1	2	.333	7.02	10	1	0	0	3	0	16.2	21	83	14	13	0	1	2	2	13	3	8	1	0
Breitenstein, Keith, Lyn.*	1	2	.333	2.65	33	8	0	0	4	0	85.0	85	362	37	25	4	5	4	5	25	0	62	5	0
Brewington, Jamie, Kin.	1	10	.091	3.87	36	5	0	0	15	4	81.1	74	353	42	35	6	2	4	2	37	0	81	8	1

Pitcher, Team	W	L	Pct.	ERA	G	GS	CG	ShO	GF	Sv.	IP	H	TBF	R	ER	HR	SH	SF	HB	BB	IBB	SO	WP	Bk.
Brown, Derek, Fred.	6	5	.545	4.03	43	0	0	0	37	14	51.1	49	232	31	23	6	4	1	4	20	1	36	4	1
Brueggemann, Dean, Sal.*	3	3	.500	5.90	37	0	0	0	17	2	61.0	64	288	46	40	7	6	1	4	43	1	52	13	2
Cairncross, Cameron, Kin.*	2	0	1.000	0.00	6	0	0	0	4	2	9.2	5	35	1	0	0	0	0	1	4	0	11	1	0
Camp, Jared, Kin.	3	2	.600	1.98	18	6	1	0	7	4	54.2	48	224	15	12	2	0	3	4	16	0	59	4	0
Cardona, Steve, W.S.	1	0	1.000	6.23	17	0	0	0	10	1	26.0	29	126	20	18	1	0	2	1	17	0	24	4	1
Carrasco, Danny, Lyn.	0	1	.000	6.35	2	0	0	0	0	0	5.2	9	29	8	4	0	1	0	0	3	0	4	0	0
Chacon, Shawn, Sal.	5	5	.500	4.13	12	12	0	0	0	0	72.0	69	316	44	33	3	1	3	2	34	0	66	5	0
Christman, Tim, Sal.*	1	2	.333	2.42	38	0	0	0	7	2	48.1	38	188	18	13	0	1	2	2	12	0	64	1	0
Colmenares, Luis, Sal.	5	3	.625	4.64	26	7	0	0	7	0	75.2	80	341	43	39	6	2	3	3	34	0	65	5	0
Combs, Chris, Lyn.	5	3	.625	6.52	32	13	0	0	8	0	89.2	112	415	73	65	18	3	5	5	40	0	69	4	1
Coogan, Patrick, Pot.	4	7	.364	5.79	19	19	2	0	0	0	101.0	112	457	73	65	14	4	5	7	43	0	67	5	0
Corey, Michael, M.B.	2	1	.667	4.78	22	0	0	0	17	6	32.0	32	139	19	17	4	3	0	0	11	0	31	1	0
Currens, Tim, W.S.	1	1	.500	2.49	14	0	0	0	8	0	21.2	21	98	8	6	1	2	0	1	13	2	17	5	0
Daedelow, Craig, Fred.	0	0	.000	0.00	1	0	0	0	1	0	1.0	0	4	0	0	0	1	0	0	0	0	0	0	0
Delaney, Donnie, Wil.	0	3	.000	5.40	23	0	0	0	14	3	25.0	25	125	17	15	2	2	2	2	28	2	26	2	0
De Leon, Jose, Kin.	5	6	.455	5.48	59	0	0	0	31	5	70.2	68	316	48	43	4	4	4	0	42	2	47	11	0
Delgado, Joseph, Wil.	0	1	.000	4.70	2	1	0	0	0	0	7.2	6	32	4	4	1	0	0	1	2	0	5	2	0
De Paula, Sean, Kin.	4	2	.667	2.28	23	0	0	0	14	7	51.1	36	208	17	13	6	0	0	3	17	0	75	4	0
Difelice, Mark, Kin.	8	12	.400	3.86	27	23	3	0	1	0	156.1	142	642	71	67	20	4	6	4	36	0	142	3	1
Douglass, Sean, Fred.	5	6	.455	3.32	16	16	1	0	0	0	97.2	101	425	48	36	9	4	3	5	35	0	89	3	0
Drese, Ryan, Kin.	5	4	.556	4.93	15	15	1	0	0	0	69.1	46	310	47	38	2	3	1	10	52	0	81	7	1
Drew, Tim, Kin.	13	5	.722	3.73	28	28	2	0	0	0	169.0	154	713	79	70	12	5	3	10	60	0	125	7	0
Duff, Matt, Lyn.	2	3	.400	5.08	7	7	0	0	0	0	39.0	41	169	22	22	6	1	1	0	13	0	40	0	1
Eibey, Scott, Fred.*	0	2	.000	3.72	15	0	0	0	6	0	29.0	26	120	14	12	2	0	1	0	10	1	27	0	0
Embry, Byron, M.B.	0	0	.000	0.00	2	0	0	0	1	0	6.0	1	19	0	0	0	0	1	0	5	0	5	0	0
Emiliano, Jamie, Sal.	5	1	.833	3.52	45	0	0	0	23	7	53.2	50	240	26	21	4	3	2	5	29	1	47	8	0
Felix, Miguel, W.S.	1	0	1.000	1.93	9	0	0	0	4	1	14.0	11	62	8	3	1	0	1	5	7	0	7	2	0
Figueroa, Juan, W.S.	2	5	.286	5.27	10	10	1	0	0	0	56.1	67	252	47	33	2	3	2	2	19	0	50	3	0
Fischer, Sean, Fred.*	0	1	.000	13.50	3	0	0	0	0	0	4.2	10	29	7	7	0	0	0	6	1	3	2	0
Flach, Jason, M.B.	9	4	.692	3.07	24	14	0	0	4	0	108.1	101	460	50	37	8	5	2	3	37	1	63	3	0
Fleck, Will, M.B.	10	10	.500	6.48	40	0	0	0	17	0	75.0	67	342	56	54	14	5	1	3	52	3	72	9	0
Fogg, Josh, W.S.	10	5	.667	2.96	17	17	1	1	0	0	103.1	93	441	44	34	3	1	1	11	33	0	109	2	0
Frachiseur, Zach, M.B.	7	3	.700	2.76	37	5	0	0	9	2	98.0	75	397	34	30	5	2	4	2	31	1	93	5	0
Franks, Lance, Pot.	5	1	.833	2.63	54	0	0	0	6	0	78.2	63	308	25	23	5	2	2	3	17	0	61	2	0
Freeman, Ryan, W.S.	2	6	.250	4.91	32	8	0	0	5	1	95.1	100	417	58	52	13	6	4	5	32	1	64	1	1
Garland, Jon, W.S.	5	7	.417	3.33	19	19	2	1	0	0	119.0	109	502	57	44	7	4	5	8	39	2	84	7	0
Garza, Alberto, Kin.	2	3	.400	3.62	6	6	0	0	0	0	27.1	25	128	13	11	2	1	0	3	17	0	27	1	0
Gentile, Scott, Fred.	0	0	.000	0.00	2	0	0	0	2	0	2.0	0	6	0	0	0	0	0	0	0	0	4	0	0
Gentry, Aaron, Pot.	0	0	.000	0.00	2	0	0	0	2	0	2.0	3	11	2	0	0	0	1	0	1	0	1	0	0
George, Chris, Wil.*	9	7	.563	3.60	27	27	0	0	0	0	145.0	142	618	65	58	8	3	4	5	53	0	142	5	1
Gonzales, Rick, Pot.	3	4	.429	6.13	47	3	0	0	7	0	72.0	88	337	58	49	8	4	7	5	38	3	39	11	1
Gonzalez, Edwin, Wil.	1	1	.500	6.55	5	0	0	0	1	0	11.0	14	52	12	8	3	1	0	0	4	0	8	0	0
Gonzalez, Mike, Lyn.*	10	4	.714	4.02	20	20	0	0	0	0	112.0	98	478	55	50	10	2	1	4	63	0	119	10	0
Greene, Ryan, M.B.	3	5	.375	3.40	44	0	0	0	29	16	82.0	65	339	32	31	7	5	1	2	29	1	85	11	0
Gross, Rafael, Kin.	1	0	1.000	3.12	4	0	0	0	2	0	8.2	9	34	3	3	0	0	1	0	1	0	5	1	0
Guerrero, Junior, Wil.	4	2	.667	1.40	9	9	0	0	0	0	51.1	30	206	10	8	2	1	1	0	26	0	68	4	0
Guerrier, Matt, W.S.	0	0	.000	5.40	4	0	0	0	4	2	3.1	3	15	2	2	0	0	0	1	0	0	5	2	0
Guillory, Dan, Kin.	1	3	.250	5.12	25	0	0	0	15	5	31.2	36	152	20	18	2	3	1	2	16	4	32	6	1
Guy, Brad, Lyn.	6	6	.500	4.11	49	0	0	0	27	10	72.1	77	308	35	33	2	5	2	1	17	2	60	7	1
Guzman, Wilson, Lyn.*	1	2	.333	3.44	35	0	0	0	13	2	65.1	70	283	35	25	3	0	4	1	12	0	78	2	0
Halla, Ryan, Lyn.	2	7	.222	5.13	46	0	0	0	29	7	54.1	60	246	34	31	5	5	4	2	20	1	56	7	0
Halpin, Jeremy, Fred.	5	3	.625	3.56	45	1	0	0	22	2	83.1	95	359	44	33	7	2	4	3	18	2	53	4	0
Held, Travis, Pot.	2	10	.167	5.40	24	21	0	0	1	0	111.2	140	500	76	67	11	6	4	10	25	0	85	6	1
Huffaker, Mike, Pot.	1	5	.167	3.86	54	0	0	0	13	0	67.2	59	322	33	29	5	5	2	9	51	3	79	11	0
Huntsman, Brandon, Fred.	4	4	.500	6.85	11	10	0	0	0	0	44.2	58	207	37	34	8	0	0	4	19	0	29	4	0
Izquierdo, Hansel, W.S.	3	5	.375	4.14	18	13	0	0	4	0	82.2	76	371	46	38	5	5	2	8	46	1	72	13	1
Jacobs, Dwayne, W.S.	1	3	.250	5.03	46	1	0	0	20	4	59.0	33	286	38	33	4	3	0	6	79	0	76	28	1
Jerue, Tristan, Pot.	0	1	.000	7.36	4	3	0	0	0	0	14.2	18	67	12	12	0	1	1	8	0	9	2	0
Johnson, D.J., Sal.	0	0	.000	3.00	4	0	0	0	4	0	6.0	4	26	2	2	1	0	0	0	2	0	6	0	0
Johnson, Solomon, W.S.*	1	2	.333	3.33	17	0	0	0	4	0	24.1	25	114	11	9	1	4	1	2	15	1	22	1	0
Kalinowski, Josh, Sal.*	11	6	.647	2.11	27	27	1	0	0	0	162.1	119	659	47	38	3	4	2	6	71	0	176	11	1
Kamienecki, Scott, Fred.	0	0	.000	0.00	1	1	0	0	0	0	4.0	0	14	0	0	0	0	0	1	0	3	0	0
Kringen, Jake, Sal.*	0	1	1.000	6.62	8	0	0	0	4	0	17.2	30	93	14	13	0	1	0	9	0	17	0	0
Lakman, Jason, W.S.	9	8	.529	4.36	20	20	2	0	0	0	119.2	108	531	69	58	4	3	4	8	55	1	110	14	0
Lamber, Justin, Wil.*	5	3	.625	3.67	39	2	0	0	18	6	68.2	68	304	29	28	2	1	0	2	33	2	67	8	0
Lambert, Kris, Lyn.*	1	3	.250	2.60	13	5	0	0	3	0	45.0	43	183	16	13	1	0	0	1	12	0	37	2	0
Lanfranco, Otoniel, Pot.	8	6	.571	4.29	21	21	0	0	0	0	115.1	105	475	59	55	13	4	3	9	35	0	83	4	1
Lee, Garrett, M.B.	1	1	.500	5.09	3	3	0	0	0	0	17.2	21	77	12	10	1	1	0	0	3	0	12	0	1
Lewis, Derrick, M.B.	8	4	.667	2.40	24	23	0	0	0	0	131.0	100	551	44	35	9	1	3	3	81	0	102	6	1
Lineweaver, Aaron, Wil.	8	6	.571	3.55	17	16	0	0	0	0	101.1	96	425	45	40	5	6	2	4	36	0	75	4	0
Lopez, Jose, W.S.	0	1	.000	4.73	19	0	0	0	5	1	26.2	38	138	22	14	0	1	0	4	14	0	10	3	0
Lynch, Ryan, Fred.*	1	1	.500	4.87	12	1	0	0	3	0	20.1	18	104	12	11	2	4	1	2	20	2	23	4	0
Maloney, Sean, Fred.	1	0	1.000	1.42	15	0	0	0	8	2	25.1	21	109	10	4	2	0	1	1	10	1	22	0	0
Manning, Brian, W.S.	0	0	.000	3.00	2	0	0	0	1	0	3.0	4	14	1	1	0	0	0	0	2	0	2	0	0
Marquis, Jason, M.B.	3	0	1.000	0.28	6	6	0	0	0	0	32.0	22	134	2	1	0	0	1	1	17	0	41	2	0
Marr, Jason, Pot.	1	6	.143	5.26	50	0	0	0	45	21	53.0	57	237	36	31	5	2	3	1	21	3	40	6	0
Martin, Jeff, Lyn.	2	1	.667	5.58	10	3	0	0	2	0	30.2	34	143	27	19	2	0	1	1	13	1	27	3	0
Martinez, Lionel, M.B.	1	0	1.000	0.00	1	0	0	0	1	0	1.0	1	5	0	0	0	0	0	0	1	0	1	0	0
Mastrolonardo, David, Fred.	0	0	.000	7.88	8	0	0	0	1	1	8.0	6	37	7	7	0	0	0	2	6	0	5	1	0
Matcuk, Steve, Sal.	8	11	.421	5.07	26	26	1	0	0	0	152.2	157	672	100	86	10	8	1	20	64	0	103	6	0
Mays, Jarrod, Kin.	5	5	.500	2.09	45	1	0	0	32	19	73.1	48	293	23	17	5	7	2	6	18	2	75	4	0
McConnell, Sam, Lyn.*	7	3	.700	3.19	15	15	4	2	0	0	101.2	84	402	41	36	8	3	5	5	27	1	70	6	0

Pitcher, Team	W	L	Pct.	ERA	G	GS	CG	ShO	GF	Sv.	IP	H	TBF	R	ER	HR	SH	SF	HB	BB	IBB	SO	WP	Bk.
McNatt, Josh, Fred.*	2	3	.400	6.00	19	6	0	0	3	0	45.0	41	219	36	30	5	2	5	3	44	2	29	12	0
Medina, Carlos, Fred.*	4	0	1.000	1.72	5	5	0	0	0	0	31.1	22	127	6	6	1	2	0	3	13	0	30	1	1
Milburn, Adam, M.B.*	2	4	.333	4.20	39	0	0	0	32	15	45.0	53	195	27	21	5	4	6	1	14	6	27	0	0
Miller, Justin, Sal.	1	2	.333	4.14	8	8	0	0	0	0	37.0	35	159	18	17	3	0	0	5	11	0	35	5	0
Minter, Matt, Lyn.*	3	2	.600	5.03	41	0	0	0	22	3	62.2	67	272	40	35	5	3	4	1	16	1	55	5	0
Montas, Ricardo, Wil.	0	0	.000	18.00	1	0	0	0	1	0	1.0	4	7	2	2	0	0	1	0	1	0	1	0	0
Morrison, Robbie, Wil.	2	5	.286	2.27	28	0	0	0	22	6	43.2	31	173	13	11	2	2	1	4	13	1	47	0	1
Murphy, Brian, Fred.	1	2	.333	4.22	26	0	0	0	11	3	53.1	51	224	36	25	6	1	0	3	10	0	39	0	0
Nation, Joey, M.B.*	5	4	.556	4.39	19	17	0	0	0	0	96.1	88	401	51	47	7	2	4	2	37	0	87	4	0
Navarro, Jason, Pot.*	5	13	.278	6.06	39	14	0	0	3	0	111.1	134	508	82	75	12	3	6	5	49	0	66	7	1
Opipari, Mario, Pot.	0	1	.000	3.12	7	0	0	0	4	0	8.2	12	41	7	3	0	1	1	0	3	0	9	0	0
Pacheco, Delvis, M.B.	6	5	.545	3.44	40	3	0	0	16	2	99.1	87	429	47	38	9	5	2	6	42	3	87	7	0
Padilla, Roy, Kin.*	0	0	.000	4.15	8	0	0	0	2	1	13.0	9	57	6	6	1	0	0	2	10	0	7	0	0
Paredes, Carlos, Wil.	6	0	1.000	4.09	36	0	0	0	12	3	55.0	47	253	31	25	3	0	2	2	48	2	49	9	0
Paronto, Chad, Fred.	5	5	.375	4.73	13	13	1	0	0	0	72.1	81	323	46	38	7	2	1	5	26	1	55	2	0
Parrish, John, Fred.*	2	2	.500	4.17	6	6	0	0	0	0	36.2	34	151	17	17	4	1	2	0	12	0	44	5	0
Paxton, Chris, Fred.	0	0	.000	1.59	6	0	0	0	6	0	5.2	4	23	2	1	0	0	1	0	1	0	1	0	0
Pederson, Justin, Wil.	4	4	.500	4.54	34	4	0	0	8	2	77.1	67	349	46	39	4	0	4	9	40	1	67	6	0
Percell, Brody, Kin.*	0	0	.000	4.50	5	5	0	0	0	0	23.0	25	101	12	11	3	0	0	0	11	0	22	1	0
Perez, Randy, Fred.*	0	1	.000	9.00	2	1	0	0	1	0	7.0	14	35	8	7	0	1	0	0	4	1	0	0	0
Pirkl, Greg, Kin.	0	1	.000	7.11	6	0	0	0	6	2	6.1	11	32	6	5	0	1	1	0	3	0	5	0	0
Prempas, Lyle, Lyn.*	2	3	.400	5.68	6	6	0	0	0	0	25.1	27	112	19	16	3	0	2	0	7	0	25	3	0
Price, Ryan, Sal.	10	12	.455	4.93	28	27	1	0	0	0	171.2	198	762	102	94	13	6	5	8	57	0	143	22	0
Pugmire, Robert, Kin.	7	1	.875	3.66	16	16	0	0	0	0	96.0	85	396	44	39	8	4	1	8	25	0	89	3	0
Rauch, Jon, W.S.	0	0	.000	3.00	1	1	0	0	0	0	6.0	4	26	3	2	1	0	0	0	3	0	7	1	0
Reames, Britt, Pot.	3	2	.600	3.19	10	8	0	0	0	0	36.2	34	163	21	13	2	2	1	3	21	0	22	4	0
Reyes, Jose, Lyn.	0	0	.000	22.50	1	0	0	0	1	0	2.0	5	12	5	5	1	0	0	1	0	0	2	0	0
Richardson, Kasey, Fred.*	5	2	.714	5.31	38	0	0	0	15	2	61.0	63	277	38	36	7	6	2	6	32	5	44	4	0
Riley, Matt, Fred.*	3	2	.600	2.61	8	8	0	0	0	0	51.2	34	200	19	15	5	3	0	1	14	0	58	1	1
Rivera, Luis, M.B.	0	0	.000	3.11	25	13	0	0	2	0	66.2	45	292	25	23	3	2	1	1	23	0	81	7	0
Roberts, Mike, Wil.	0	0	.000	1.74	9	0	0	0	6	1	10.1	10	42	2	2	1	1	0	0	1	0	6	0	0
Romero, Jordan, Fred.-Kin.	0	0	.000	3.31	10	0	0	0	3	0	16.1	12	75	10	6	1	1	0	1	14	1	13	2	0
Rosa, Cristy, Sal.	1	1	.500	2.91	8	2	0	0	3	0	21.2	27	99	13	7	0	0	1	1	7	0	12	3	0
Sabathia, C.C., Kin.*	3	3	.500	5.34	7	7	0	0	0	0	32.0	30	143	22	19	3	3	3	1	19	0	29	6	0
Scott, Brian, W.S.	8	8	.500	3.41	25	25	1	0	0	0	147.2	135	637	75	56	7	7	3	5	60	3	132	17	0
Sedlacek, Shawn, Wil.	4	6	.400	5.28	17	17	1	0	0	0	92.0	111	411	61	54	7	6	3	6	26	0	69	4	0
Seifert, Ryan, Sal.	3	5	.375	3.50	24	0	0	0	5	0	46.1	40	196	24	18	0	2	2	3	21	0	51	0	0
Shepherd, Alvie, Fred.	0	0	.000	11.81	3	2	0	0	0	0	5.1	7	33	7	7	2	0	0	0	10	0	6	1	0
Sheredy, Kevin, Pot.	5	5	.500	3.98	41	12	0	0	12	0	104.0	100	462	58	46	6	3	6	6	53	1	69	13	0
Shiell, Jason, M.B.	6	7	.462	3.77	26	17	0	0	1	0	114.2	118	485	51	48	5	4	2	3	36	0	90	9	0
Shumate, Jacob, M.B.	3	3	.500	7.15	20	0	0	0	9	0	22.2	15	116	19	18	0	3	1	1	33	0	31	8	0
Sido, Wilson, Kin.	1	2	.333	5.94	9	7	0	0	0	0	36.1	33	163	26	24	4	1	1	5	22	1	22	6	0
Sims, Ken, Fred.	4	4	.500	4.17	35	1	0	0	11	2	69.0	83	312	38	32	7	3	1	4	19	3	41	1	0
Smith, Robert, Pot.*	4	9	.308	2.96	18	18	0	0	0	0	103.1	91	433	47	34	2	3	2	9	32	0	93	4	0
Sobkowiak, Scott, M.B.	9	4	.692	2.84	27	26	0	0	1	0	139.1	100	572	50	44	10	3	2	2	63	1	161	12	1
Sonnier, Shawn, Wil.	1	2	.333	2.88	44	0	0	0	38	13	59.1	46	237	20	19	1	2	0	1	19	2	73	2	0
Sparks, Steve, Lyn.	2	3	.400	6.23	5	5	1	0	0	0	26.0	36	124	20	18	3	0	2	1	15	0	20	2	0
Spenser, Kaipo, Kin.	3	4	.429	3.25	35	5	0	0	7	1	72.0	65	316	33	26	4	2	1	14	22	0	46	3	0
Spiegel, Mike, Kin.*	5	3	.625	3.09	18	18	0	0	0	0	96.0	69	405	46	33	8	6	4	7	51	0	103	11	0
Spurgeon, Jay, Fred.	6	9	.400	4.75	26	26	1	0	0	0	146.0	176	659	99	77	14	4	4	4	53	2	87	12	2
Terhune, Mike, M.B.	0	0	.000	36.00	1	0	0	0	1	0	1.0	5	8	4	4	0	0	1	0	0	0	1	0	0
Thompson, John, W.S.-Wil.	2	2	.500	3.48	22	2	0	0	11	4	44.0	39	182	21	17	3	1	3	2	20	0	34	6	0
Thompson, Travis, Sal.	3	3	.500	1.74	56	0	0	0	52	27	62.0	54	267	19	12	1	7	1	2	24	4	53	5	0
Thomson, John, Sal.	0	1	.000	9.00	1	1	0	0	0	0	2.0	4	10	2	2	0	0	0	0	0	0	2	0	0
Thorn, Todd, Wil.*	8	5	.615	5.61	34	13	0	0	6	2	126.2	143	559	85	79	14	4	4	9	44	1	89	6	2
Thurman, Corey, Wil.	8	11	.421	4.88	27	27	0	0	0	0	149.1	160	667	89	81	11	4	5	9	64	0	131	11	1
Tokarse, Brian, W.S.	5	4	.556	2.31	40	0	0	0	37	14	46.2	37	201	15	12	2	4	1	3	22	3	55	2	0
Turnbow, Mark, Kin.	5	4	.556	6.41	12	12	0	0	0	0	60.1	76	279	48	43	5	2	4	4	25	0	42	1	0
Vavrek, Mike, Sal.*	3	1	.750	1.85	10	5	0	0	3	0	48.2	32	191	10	10	2	1	2	13	0	38	1	0
Virchis, Adam, W.S.	3	5	.375	4.73	33	7	0	0	7	1	78.0	82	347	50	41	9	5	3	4	33	0	59	4	0
Voyles, Brad, M.B.	1	1	.500	2.25	5	0	0	0	2	0	12.0	7	50	3	3	1	1	0	0	9	1	13	1	0
Wagner, Ken, Kin.	1	1	.500	6.75	14	0	0	0	6	0	26.2	31	122	25	20	4	0	0	0	12	0	21	1	0
Watson, Mark, Kin.	6	0	1.000	1.04	11	4	0	0	1	0	43.1	28	163	7	5	1	0	0	0	10	0	40	1	1
Weidert, Chris, Kin.	4	3	.571	2.58	27	2	0	0	13	0	52.1	49	223	15	15	2	5	2	1	22	5	42	3	0
Wells, Kip, W.S.	5	6	.455	3.57	14	14	0	0	0	0	85.2	78	353	39	34	4	2	2	6	34	1	95	7	0
Weymouth, Marty, W.S.	5	6	.455	4.71	41	0	0	0	16	2	57.1	62	257	35	30	1	3	1	1	21	3	42	3	1
Whitley, Curtis, W.S.*	0	0	.000	4.50	9	0	0	0	3	2	8.0	9	34	4	4	3	0	1	0	4	0	4	0	0
Williams, Larry, Lyn.	4	4	.500	3.55	34	3	0	0	8	0	63.1	58	269	36	25	9	1	4	2	21	1	51	4	0
Wilson, Kris, Wil.	8	1	.889	1.13	14	4	0	0	1	0	48.0	25	169	7	6	0	0	0	11	0	45	1	0
Wimberly, Larry, Lyn.*	5	3	.625	5.04	11	10	0	0	0	0	55.1	77	257	40	31	5	2	0	5	13	0	41	2	1
Woodward, Finley, Pot.	6	7	.462	4.10	24	18	1	0	1	0	120.2	126	511	61	55	14	4	6	1	28	0	82	5	0
Wrigley, Jase, Sal.	2	0	1.000	0.96	8	0	0	0	5	0	9.1	9	36	1	1	0	0	0	0	6	0	6	1	0
Yen, Buddy, Wil.	0	0	.000	45.00	2	0	0	0	1	0	1.0	3	11	5	5	0	0	0	1	4	0	1	0	0

COMBINATION SHUTOUTS: **Frederick (8)**—McNatt-Halpin-Brown, Riley-Murphy, Riley-Sims-Lynch, Huntsman-Eibey-Brown, Douglass-Sims-Brown, Paronto-Lynch-Brown, Spurgeon-Richardson-Brown, Bauer-Maloney-Richardson. **Kinston (11)**—Brew-Cairncross, Watson-Guillory-Wagner, Turnbow-Camp, Garza-DePaula-Mays, Garza-DePaula-Mays, Weidert-Bautista-Mays, Drew-Brewington-Weidert, Pugmire-Bautista-Mays, Drew-Aracena, Drese-Padilla, Spenseer-Weidert-Brewington. **Lynchburg (5)**—Duff-Guzman-Halla, Alvarado-Breitenstein-Halla, Bausher-Guy, Wimberly-Guy, Breitenstein-Guzman. **Myrtle Beach (10)**—Marquis-Flach-Corey, Marquis-Fleck-Shumate-Flach, Marquis-Pacheco-Fleck, Lewis-Shumate-Greene, Marquis-Frachiseur-Milburn, Lewis-Rivera-Greene, Rivera-Sobkowiak, Lewis-Pacheco, Abreu-Frachiseur-Greene, Abreu-Frachiseur-Corey. **Potomac (8)**—Navarro-Huffaker-Opipari, Held-Franks-Huffaker-Avrard-Marr, Smith-Gonzales-Franks-DeLeon, Coogan-Sheredy, Benes-Reames-Franks-Huffaker, Smith-Franks-Sheredy-Marr, Lanfranco-Navarro-Gonzales, Gonzales-DeLeon. **Salem (8)**—Price-Emiliano-Kringen, DiFelice-Thompson, Price-Brueggemann-Emiliano-Thompson, Kalinowski-Brueggemann, Kalinowski-Thompson, Vavrek-Colmenares-Brueggemann, Vavrek-Thompson, Price-Thmpson. **Wilmington (9)**—Lineweaver-Sonnier, Wilson-Lamber-Sonnier, Lineweaver-Sonnier, George-Thorn-Sonnier, George-Pederson-Sonnier, Sedlacek-Lineweaver-Delaney, Guerrero-Thompson-Sonnier, Thurman-Thompson, Guerrero-Lamber-Sonnier. **Winston-Salem (8)**—Scott-Tokarse, Scott-Tokarse, Fogg-Virchis, Scott-Tokarse, Fogg-Weymouth, Garland-Freeman-Tokarse, Virchis-Tokarse, Fogg-Weymouth-Freeman-Tokarse.

NO-HIT GAMES: None.

PITCHERS WITH TWO OR MORE TEAMS

Pitcher, Team	W	L	Pct.	ERA	G	GS	CG	ShO	GF	Sv.	IP	H	TBF	R	ER	HR	SH	SF	HB	BB	IBB	SO	WP	Bk.
Aracena, Juan, Kin.	1	1	.500	2.57	5	0	0	0	2	0	7.0	7	28	2	2	0	1	0	0	1	0	7	1	0
Aracena, Juan, Fred.	0	0	.000	0.00	2	0	0	0	2	0	2.0	2	7	1	0	0	0	0	0	0	0	0	0	0
Romero, Jordan, Fred.	0	0	.000	2.93	9	0	0	0	2	0	15.1	11	70	9	5	1	1	0	1	13	1	11	2	0
Romero, Jordan, Kin.	0	0	.000	9.00	1	0	0	0	1	0	1.0	1	5	1	1	0	0	0	1	0	1	0	0	0
Thompson, John, W.S.	0	1	.000	7.00	2	2	0	0	0	0	9.0	10	43	9	7	1	0	1	0	8	0	9	3	0
Thompson, John, Wil.	2	1	.667	2.57	20	0	0	0	11	4	35.0	29	139	12	10	2	1	2	2	12	0	25	3	0

1999 FIELDING
TEAM

Team	Pct.	G	PO	A	E	TC	DP	TP	PB	Team	Pct.	G	PO	A	E	TC	DP	TP	PB
Wilmington	.975	138	3663	1450	132	5245	123	0	20	Lynchburg	.969	137	3618	1477	165	5260	113	0	25
Myrtle Beach	.973	139	3746	1346	143	5235	95	0	20	Salem	.969	138	3616	1489	166	5271	125	0	22
Kinston	.970	137	3552	1462	156	5170	92	0	26	Frederick	.964	138	3657	1530	193	5380	129	0	16
Potomac	.969	139	3627	1420	162	5209	122	0	11	Winston-Salem	.960	138	3628	1469	211	5308	132	1	30

INDIVIDUAL

FIRST BASEMEN

NOTE: All caps denotes fielding-percentage leader based on 70 games for catchers, 93 for all other non-pitchers and 112 innings for pitchers. *Throws lefthanded.

Player, Team	Pct.	G	PO	A	E	TC	DP
Allison, Cody, Kin.	.993	30	245	27	2	274	17
Benham, Jason, Fred.	1.000	3	10	0	0	10	1
Berger, Matt, W.S.	.992	77	687	51	6	744	61
Bone, Billy, Lyn.	.000	1	0	0	0	0	0
Britt, Bryan, Pot.	1.000	3	26	0	0	26	2
Bryant, Matt, Lyn.	1.000	3	16	3	0	19	0
Deck, Billy, Pot.*	.990	36	285	23	3	311	38
Dillon, Joe, Wil.	.991	13	104	9	1	114	7
Downs, Brian, W.S.	1.000	4	36	1	0	37	2
Figueroa, Franky, Fred.	.993	132	1144	98	9	1251	107
Furniss, Eddy, Lyn.*	.989	87	735	59	9	803	61
Gentry, Aaron, Pot.	.000	2	0	0	0	0	0
Haad, Yamid, Lyn.	.982	5	52	3	1	56	5
Hammond, Joey, Fred.	1.000	2	8	0	0	8	1
Heintz, Chris, W.S.	.989	10	78	9	1	88	12
Hemme, Justin, Sal.*	.957	17	149	6	7	162	10
Jorgensen, Tim, Lyn.	.000	3	0	0	0	0	0
Keck, Brian, Sal.	1.000	15	119	5	0	124	13
Kilburg, Joe, Kin.	1.000	3	22	1	0	23	1
Klee, Chuck, W.S.	1.000	9	65	5	0	70	6
Lankford, Derrick, Lyn.	.997	34	264	22	1	287	23
Lehr, Ryan, M.B.	.980	59	454	41	10	505	37
Lindsey, John, Sal.	.986	47	384	28	6	418	33
Maxwell, Keith, Lyn.	.972	19	166	10	5	181	13
Montas, Ricardo, Wil.	1.000	16	135	11	0	146	14
Munoz, Billy, Kin.*	.987	104	861	77	12	950	64
Olson, Dan, W.S.*	.973	31	247	9	7	263	30
Paxton, Chris, Fred.	.970	7	60	4	2	66	11
QUACCIA, Luke, Pot.	.995	110	885	69	5	959	68
Rupert, Bryan, Pot.	.000	1	0	0	0	0	0
Scharrer, Jim, M.B.	.988	74	599	42	8	649	44
Schwartzbauer, Brad, Sal.	.985	17	123	8	2	133	13
Sears, Todd, Sal.	.989	47	410	26	5	441	36
Sheppard, Greg, W.S.	.985	18	128	6	2	136	5
Taveras, Frank, Kin.	.936	5	42	2	3	47	3
Ullery, Dave, Wil.	1.000	5	4	0	0	4	0
Willis, Dave, Wil.	.989	113	948	88	11	1047	90
Wong, Jerrod, M.B.*	1.000	7	54	6	0	60	3

FIRST BASEMEN (continued)

Player, Team	Pct.	G	PO	A	E	TC	DP
Jorgensen, Tim, Lyn.	.000	1	0	0	0	0	0
Keck, Brian, Sal.	1.000	7	9	17	0	26	2
Kilburg, Joe, Kin.	.960	5	11	13	1	25	3
Klee, Chuck, W.S.	.902	22	31	61	10	102	12
Livingston, Doug, Sal.	.976	17	31	50	2	83	8
Lorenzana, Luis, Lyn.	.978	25	35	55	2	92	15
Mackowiak, Rob, Lyn.	.996	62	99	157	1	257	34
Maier, T.J., Lyn.	.943	22	39	43	5	87	11
Martinez, Louis, M.B.	1.000	2	4	5	0	9	0
MaCrory, Bob, Pot.	.973	113	209	293	14	516	70
Montas, Ricardo, Wil.	.991	25	47	64	1	112	18
Moore, Griffin, Wil.	1.000	1	2	4	0	6	0
Pratt, Scott, Kin.	.958	130	219	310	23	552	55
Taveras, Frank, Kin.	1.000	1	2	0	0	2	0
Terhune, Mike, M.B.	.962	19	30	46	3	79	9
Terrell, Jim, W.S.	1.000	1	0	2	0	2	0
Washington, Rico, Lyn.	.926	11	16	34	4	54	7
Whitlock, Brian, Kin.	1.000	1	3	2	0	5	0

TRIPLE PLAY: Connacher.

SECOND BASEMEN

Player, Team	Pct.	G	PO	A	E	TC	DP
Alviso, Jerome, Sal.	.977	117	261	331	14	606	84
Benham, Jason, Fred.	1.000	1	0	1	0	1	1
Bone, Billy, Lyn.	.947	14	32	40	4	76	8
Bryant, Matt, Lyn.	1.000	5	10	12	0	22	1
Bultmann, Kurt, Lyn.	.974	30	51	62	3	116	13
Campbell, Wylie, Wil.	.975	22	24	55	2	81	11
Caruso, Joe, Wil.	.977	64	130	165	7	302	37
Cepeda, Jose, Wil.	.982	35	60	102	3	165	23
Connacher, Kevin, W.S.	.977	121	189	356	13	558	79
Daedelow, Craig, Fred.	.714	1	2	3	2	7	0
DeShields, Delino, Fred.	1.000	2	5	5	0	10	2
Eckelman, Alex, Pot.	.985	17	24	40	1	65	10
Garabito, Eddy, Fred.	.960	117	237	309	23	569	74
GILES, Marcus, M.B.	.985	121	222	291	8	521	41
Hammond, Joey, Fred.	.964	26	32	48	3	83	14

THIRD BASEMEN

Player, Team	Pct.	G	PO	A	E	TC	DP
Anthony, Brian, Sal.	.983	25	12	47	1	60	3
Benham, Jason, Fred.	.800	8	1	7	2	10	0
Berger, Matt, W.S.	.885	15	4	19	3	26	3
Bone, Billy, Lyn.	.842	23	17	31	9	57	5
Bryant, Matt, Lyn.	.615	5	1	7	5	13	1
Cepeda, Jose, Wil.	1.000	9	5	13	0	18	1
Coffie, Ivanon, Fred.	.905	54	29	114	15	158	9
Daedelow, Craig, Fred.	.000	1	0	0	0	0	0
Dillon, Joe, Wil.	.918	111	94	209	27	330	20
Eckelman, Alex, Pot.	.915	20	11	32	4	47	2
Edwards, Mike, Kin.	.910	127	56	226	28	310	8
Freeman, Brad, Pot.	.940	34	26	53	5	84	6
Gentry, Aaron, Pot.	.925	40	19	67	7	93	9
Haad, Yamid, Lyn.	.000	1	0	0	0	0	0
Hammond, Joey, Fred.	.922	28	19	52	6	77	3
HESSMAN, Mike, M.B.	.941	97	74	132	13	219	8
Jorgensen, Tim, Lyn.	.927	63	38	126	13	177	13
Keck, Brian, Sal.	.977	55	28	97	3	128	10
Kilburg, Joe, Kin.	.750	3	1	2	1	4	0
Klee, Chuck, W.S.	.810	17	8	26	8	42	1
Lankford, Derrick, Lyn.	.842	9	6	10	3	19	1
Leon, Alfredo, Fred.	.778	3	2	5	2	9	0
Livingston, Doug, Sal.	.973	12	9	27	1	37	6
Lorenzana, Luis, Lyn.	.929	19	7	32	3	42	0
Maier, T.J., Pot.	.930	61	30	117	11	158	8
Martinez, Louis, M.B.	.900	3	3	6	1	10	0
Maxwell, Keith, Lyn.	1.000	2	1	1	0	2	0
Montas, Ricardo, Wil.	.962	21	14	37	2	53	4
Moore, Griffin, Wil.	.000	1	0	0	0	0	0
Mortimer, Mark, M.B.	.833	7	1	4	1	6	0
Paz, Richard, Fred.	.913	50	28	109	13	150	10
Rust, Brian, Fred.	.813	6	3	10	3	16	1
Schwartzbauer, Brad, Sal.	.872	19	9	32	6	47	4
Sears, Todd, Sal.	.724	32	12	43	21	76	4
Taveras, Frank, Kin.	.875	11	5	16	3	24	1
Terhune, Mike, M.B.	.923	36	17	55	6	78	2
Terrell, Jim, W.S.	.894	112	76	185	31	292	17
Washington, Rico, Lyn.	.943	33	21	61	5	87	3
Whitlock, Brian, Kin.	1.000	2	0	5	0	5	0

CLASS A Carolina League

SHORTSTOPS

Player, Team	Pct.	G	PO	A	E	TC	DP
Alviso, Jerome, Sal.	1.000	8	12	24	0	36	3
Bone, Billy, Lyn.	.667	2	0	4	2	6	0
Bryant, Matt, Lyn.	.951	15	18	40	3	61	6
Campbell, Wylie, Wil.	.884	21	27	57	11	95	8
Cepeda, Jose, Wil.-M.B.	.939	15	9	37	3	49	9
Coffie, Ivanon, Fred.	.904	13	22	25	5	52	7
Daedelow, Craig, Fred.	.769	2	3	7	3	13	3
Dellaero, Jason, W.S.	.932	54	89	170	19	278	42
Eckelman, Alex, Pot.	.973	9	17	19	1	37	3
Figgins, Chone, Sal.	.925	122	172	381	45	598	67
Freeman, Brad, Pot.	.927	66	110	168	22	300	36
Furcal, Rafael, M.B.	.975	43	48	109	4	161	26
Gentry, Aaron, Pot.	1.000	5	6	9	0	15	0
GUTIERREZ, Victor, Lyn.	.966	114	185	334	18	537	63
Hammond, Joey, Fred.	.000	1	0	0	0	0	0
Hessman, Mike, M.B.	1.000	6	5	18	0	23	4
Keck, Brian, Sal.	.980	10	15	33	1	49	5
Klee, Chuck, W.S.	.940	23	20	43	4	67	9
Lackey, Steve, M.B.	.941	53	100	138	15	253	26
Lorenzana, Luis, Lyn.	.961	11	12	37	2	51	2
Martinez, Eddy, Fred.	.941	124	189	386	36	611	80
Medrano, Steve, Wil.	.963	98	142	253	15	410	62
Montas, Ricardo, Wil.	1.000	11	11	19	0	30	3
Paz, Richard, Fred.	1.000	1	2	6	0	8	4
Sorensen, Zach, Kin.	.963	129	175	399	22	596	68
Suarez, Luis, W.S.	.905	74	118	206	34	358	52
Taveras, Frank, Kin.	1.000	8	6	27	0	33	1
Terhune, Mike, M.B.	.948	38	55	90	8	153	16
Terrell, Jim, W.S.	1.000	1	1	0	0	1	0
Whitlock, Brian, Kin.	.750	2	2	7	3	12	2
Wilson, Jack, Pot.	.941	64	98	187	18	303	44

TRIPLE PLAY: Suarez.

SHORTSTOPS WITH TWO OR MORE TEAMS

Player, Team	Pct.	G	PO	A	E	TC	DP
Cepeda, Jose, Wil.	.938	14	9	36	3	48	9
Cepeda, Jose, M.B.	1.000	1	0	1	0	1	0

OUTFIELDERS

Player, Team	Pct.	G	PO	A	E	TC	DP
Albert, Rashad, W.S.	.969	20	30	1	1	32	1
Bass, Jayson, M.B.	.986	41	70	2	1	73	0
Berger, Brandon, Wil.	.964	76	130	2	5	137	0
Bevins, Andy, Pot.	.935	56	85	1	6	92	0
Brignac, Junior, M.B.	.974	64	146	4	4	154	0
Britt, Bryan, Pot.	.000	3	0	0	0	0	0
Bronowicz, Scott, M.B.	1.000	1	4	0	0	4	0
Brown, Dee, Wil.	.979	57	91	4	2	97	0
Caradonna, Brett, W.S.	.969	127	153	5	5	163	0
Caruso, Joe, Wil.	.968	38	61	0	2	63	0
Conner, Decomba, Wil.	.942	44	63	2	4	69	0
Correa, Miguel, Sal.	.964	94	183	3	7	193	1
Cortez, Santos, Lyn.	.976	38	39	1	1	41	0
Curry, Mike, Wil.	1.000	54	86	3	0	89	2
Daedelow, Craig, Fred.	1.000	7	10	1	0	11	0
Deck, Billy, Pot.*	.986	41	70	1	1	72	1
DeHaan, Kory, Wil.	.976	78	164	2	4	170	2
Eckelman, Alex, Pot.	.000	1	0	0	0	0	0
Evans, Lee, Lyn.	1.000	1	1	0	0	1	0
Fitzgerald, Jason, Kin.*	.000	1	0	0	0	0	0
Freeman, Brad, Pot.	1.000	3	3	0	0	3	0
Gentry, Aaron, Pot.	1.000	4	10	0	0	10	0
Gerut, Jody, Sal.*	.970	128	218	7	7	232	2
Haad, Yamid, Lyn.	.500	2	1	0	1	2	0
Hamilton, Jon, Kin.*	.979	127	219	11	5	235	1
Hamlin, Mark, Sal.	.980	97	143	6	3	152	2
Hammond, Joey, Fred.	.833	3	5	0	1	6	0
Huelsmann, Mike, Wil.	.987	49	74	3	1	78	1
Hughes, Brian, Fred.	.992	76	129	2	1	132	1
Jackson, Jeremy A., Sal.	1.000	26	45	4	0	49	0
Keck, Brian, Sal.	.917	9	11	0	1	12	0
Kilburg, Joe, Kin.	.923	19	23	1	2	26	0
Kim, Dave, Pot.	.947	115	185	10	11	206	1
Lankford, Derrick, Lyn.	.962	79	121	6	5	132	1
Lee, Jason, Pot.	.988	44	81	3	1	85	0
Livingston, Doug, Sal.	.978	32	43	1	1	45	0
Mackowiak, Rob, Lyn.	1.000	11	18	1	0	19	1
Maier, T.J., Pot.	1.000	2	5	0	0	5	0
Manning, Brian, W.S.	.963	65	101	3	4	108	0
Matos, Luis, Fred.	.987	66	143	6	2	151	1

Player, Team	Pct.	G	PO	A	E	TC	DP
Maxwell, Keith, Lyn.	.962	12	25	0	1	26	0
May, Freddy, Lyn.*	.959	122	209	4	9	222	1
McDonald, Darnell, Fred.	.956	110	207	9	10	226	4
Mitchell, Andres, Sal.	.959	33	68	3	3	74	1
Mohr, Dustan, Kin.	.973	108	207	13	6	226	4
Moore, Griffin, Wil.	.000	1	0	0	0	0	0
Mortimer, Mark, M.B.	.000	1	0	0	0	0	0
Ndungidi, Ntema, Fred.	.934	54	107	6	8	121	0
Olson, Dan, W.S.*	.957	15	21	1	1	23	0
ORTEGA, Bill, Pot.	.989	109	252	11	3	266	2
Paz, Richard, Fred.	1.000	1	1	0	0	1	0
Pointer, Corey, Lyn.	.946	104	202	10	12	224	3
Radcliff, Vic, Wil.	.962	110	191	12	8	211	2
Ramirez, Dan, W.S.	.949	85	189	15	11	215	2
Rivera, Roberto, Fred.	.973	112	205	9	6	220	1
Ross, Jason, M.B.	.972	131	234	11	7	252	1
Rowand, Aaron, W.S.	.973	99	172	9	5	186	3
Salargo, Steven, Fred.	.000	2	0	0	0	0	0
Santana, Osmany, Kin.*	1.000	43	79	2	0	81	0
Scharrer, Jim, M.B.	.000	1	0	0	0	0	0
Sheppard, Greg, W.S.	.941	18	15	1	1	17	0
Smothers, Stewart, M.B.	.993	56	131	3	1	135	2
Snead, Esix, Pot.	.989	67	179	4	2	185	1
Spencer, Jeff, M.B.	.956	99	189	5	9	203	1
Taveras, Frank, Kin.	.769	9	8	2	3	13	0
Torres, Rafael, Kin.	.971	56	98	4	3	105	1
Whitaker, Chad, Kin.	.979	60	90	3	2	95	0
Whitlock, Brian, Kin.	1.000	7	12	0	0	12	0
Wong, Jerrod, M.B.*	.944	35	66	1	4	71	0

CATCHERS

Player, Team	Pct.	G	PO	A	E	TC	DP	PB
Alley, Charles, Fred.	.984	41	277	31	5	313	1	8
Allison, Cody, Kin.	.833	3	5	0	1	6	0	0
Anderson, Frank, Lyn.	.988	11	73	8	1	82	1	1
Arias, Rogelio, Sal.	.987	76	588	77	9	674	6	13
Brito, Juan, Wil.	.984	14	117	7	2	126	0	0
Bronowicz, Scott, M.B.	.983	18	106	8	2	116	1	0
Cruz, Edgar, Kin.	.984	30	218	28	4	250	0	10
Daedelow, Craig, Fred.	1.000	1	2	1	0	3	0	1
Depippo, Jeff, Kin.	.991	68	521	51	5	577	3	14
Downs, Brian, W.S.	1.000	12	87	4	0	91	1	2
Escalante, Jaime, Fred.	1.000	5	10	0	0	10	0	0
Evans, Lee, Lyn.	.982	79	528	66	11	605	5	13
Garrick, Matt, Pot.	.986	70	429	54	7	490	6	4
Gonzales, Jose, Sal.	.981	44	327	28	7	362	2	9
Haad, Yamid, Lyn.	1.000	31	240	18	0	258	1	7
Heintz, Chris, W.S.	.981	92	716	74	15	805	5	19
HILL, Jeremy, Wil.	.991	92	703	87	7	797	5	14
Jones, Jay, Sal.	1.000	17	128	16	0	144	1	0
Leon, Alfredo, Fred.	.600	2	2	1	2	5	0	0
Lopez-Cao, Mike, Fred.	.983	22	107	8	2	117	1	1
Martine, Chris, Pot.	.994	42	281	43	2	326	3	3
McGee, Tom, Fred.	.985	7	57	9	1	67	2	0
Mortimer, Mark, M.B.	.992	45	357	34	3	394	1	5
Pagan, Carlos, Wil.	.923	4	23	1	2	26	0	0
Paxton, Chris, Fred.	.958	14	57	11	3	71	0	1
Pugh, Josh, M.B.	.983	41	325	25	6	356	5	6
Reyes, Jose, Lyn.	.984	10	52	10	1	63	0	2
Rodriguez, Jeff, M.B.	.000	1	0	0	0	0	0	0
Rupert, Bryan, Pot.	.949	37	186	18	11	215	2	4
Ryder, Derek, W.S.	.982	39	254	25	5	284	4	8
Samuel, Tomas, Sal.	.000	1	0	0	0	0	0	0
Sheppard, Greg, W.S.	1.000	4	22	3	0	25	0	1
Smith, Casey, Kin.	.988	39	319	20	4	343	1	2
Taylor, Adam, Kin.	.977	6	40	2	1	43	0	0
Torrealba, Steve, M.B.	.978	50	378	57	10	445	2	9
Ullery, Dave, Wil.	.996	37	247	32	1	280	4	6
Vidal, Gilbert, Sal.	1.000	5	36	2	0	38	1	0
Washington, Rico, Lyn.	.991	14	95	14	1	110	2	2
Werth, Jayson, Fred.	.981	61	453	56	10	519	4	5

TRIPLE PLAY: Heintz.

PITCHERS

Player, Team	Pct.	G	PO	A	E	TC	DP
Abreu, Winston, M.B.	1.000	13	2	7	0	9	0
Achilles, Matt, Fred.	.960	16	9	15	1	25	1
Alvarado, Carlos, Lyn.	.917	20	5	17	2	24	1
Alviso, Jerome, Sal.	.000	1	0	0	0	0	0
Aracena, Juan, Kin.-Fred.	1.000	7	2	2	0	4	0
Austin, Jeffrey, Wil.	.917	18	5	17	2	24	0
Avrard, Corey, Pot.	1.000	28	0	6	0	6	1

Player, Team	Pct.	G	PO	A	E	TC	DP
Ayers, Mike, Lyn.*	1.000	27	0	5	0	5	0
Bauer, Rick, Fred.	.959	26	15	32	2	49	4
Bausher, Andy, Lyn.*	.795	25	4	27	8	39	0
Bautista, Martin, Kin.	.882	20	5	10	2	17	0
Benes, Alan, Pot.	.000	2	0	0	0	0	0
Borne, Matt, W.S.	1.000	10	1	0	0	1	0
Breitenstein, Keith, Lyn.*	.800	33	3	9	3	15	1
Brewington, Jamie, Kin.	1.000	36	1	12	0	13	0
Brown, Derek, Fred.	.938	43	8	7	1	16	0
Brueggemann, Dean, Sal.*	1.000	37	6	16	0	22	1
Cairncross, Cameron, Kin.*	.889	6	0	8	1	9	0
Camp, Jared, Kin.	.889	18	2	6	1	9	0
Cardona, Steve, W.S.	.667	17	1	1	1	3	1
Carrasco, Danny, Lyn.	.500	2	0	2	2	4	0
Chacon, Shawn, Sal.	.800	12	3	5	2	10	1
Christman, Tim, Sal.*	.667	38	1	5	3	9	0
Colmenares, Luis, Sal.	1.000	26	3	8	0	11	0
Combs, Chris, Lyn.	.958	32	9	14	1	24	0
Coogan, Patrick, Pot.	.882	19	6	9	2	17	0
Corey, Michael, M.B.	.909	22	1	9	1	11	0
Currens, Tim, W.S.	1.000	14	1	6	0	7	0
Daedelow, Craig, Fred.	.000	1	0	0	0	0	0
Delaney, Donnie, Wil.	1.000	23	1	4	0	5	1
De Leon, Jose, Pot.	.917	59	4	7	1	12	0
Delgado, Joseph, Wil.	1.000	2	1	1	0	2	0
De Paula, Sean, Kin.	1.000	23	2	6	0	8	0
Difelice, Mark, Sal.	1.000	27	10	13	0	23	2
Douglass, Sean, Fred.	.867	16	5	8	2	15	2
Drese, Ryan, Kin.	.909	15	13	7	2	22	2
Drew, Tim, Kin.	.979	28	17	30	1	48	1
Duff, Matt, Lyn.	1.000	7	3	6	0	9	1
Eibey, Scott, Fred.*	1.000	15	1	4	0	5	1
Embry, Byron, M.B.	.000	2	0	0	0	0	0
Emiliano, Jamie, Sal.	1.000	45	2	9	0	11	0
Felix, Miguel, W.S.	1.000	9	0	2	0	2	0
Figueroa, Juan, W.S.	1.000	10	3	6	0	9	0
Fischer, Sean, Fred.*	.000	3	0	0	0	0	0
Flach, Jason, M.B.	.972	24	12	23	1	36	1
Fleck, Will, M.B.	.917	40	4	7	1	12	1
Fogg, Josh, W.S.	.885	17	9	14	3	26	0
Frachiseur, Zach, M.B.	.947	37	3	15	1	19	1
Franks, Lance, Pot.	1.000	54	7	15	0	22	2
Freeman, Kai, W.S.	.926	32	6	19	2	27	2
Garland, Jon, W.S.	.973	19	13	23	1	37	2
Garza, Alberto, Kin.	.667	6	0	2	1	3	0
Gentile, Scott, Fred.	.000	2	0	0	0	0	0
Gentry, Aaron, Pot.	1.000	2	0	1	0	1	0
George, Chris, Wil.*	.973	27	8	28	1	37	0
Gonzales, Rick, Pot.	.938	47	4	11	1	16	0
Gonzalez, Edwin, Wil.	1.000	5	1	3	0	4	0
Gonzalez, Mike, Lyn.*	.938	20	7	23	2	32	1
Greene, Ryan, M.B.	.909	44	5	15	2	22	0
Gross, Rafael, Kin.	1.000	4	0	1	0	1	0
Guerrero, Junior, Wil.	.818	9	8	1	2	11	0
Guerrier, Matt, W.S.	1.000	4	1	0	0	1	0
Guillory, Dan, Kin.	.857	25	0	6	1	7	0
Guy, Brad, Lyn.	1.000	49	7	18	0	25	1
Guzman, Wilson, Lyn.*	.667	35	2	8	5	15	0
Halla, Ryan, Lyn.	.938	46	4	11	1	16	1
Halpin, Jeremy, Fred.	.952	45	7	13	1	21	0
Held, Travis, Pot.	.727	24	5	11	6	22	1
Huffaker, Mike, Pot.	.923	54	4	8	1	13	0
Huntsman, Brandon, Fred.	1.000	11	3	7	0	10	1
Izquierdo, Hansel, W.S.	.900	18	6	12	2	20	0
Jacobs, Dwayne, W.S.	.900	46	5	4	1	10	1
Jerue, Tristan, Pot.	1.000	4	4	2	0	6	0
Johnson, D.J., Sal.	.000	4	0	0	0	0	0
Johnson, Solomon, W.S.*	.833	17	2	3	1	6	0
Kalinowski, Josh, Sal.*	.955	27	8	34	2	44	3
Kamieniecki, Scott, Fred.	1.000	1	0	1	0	1	0
Kringen, Jake, Sal.*	.714	8	1	4	2	7	1
Lakman, Jason, W.S.	.800	20	7	13	5	25	0
Lamber, Justin, Wil.*	1.000	39	8	8	0	16	1
Lambert, Kris, Lyn.*	1.000	13	5	4	0	9	0
Lanfranco, Otoniel, Pot.	.818	21	8	10	4	22	0
Lee, Garrett, M.B.	1.000	3	3	2	0	5	0
Lewis, Derrick, M.B.	.914	24	7	25	3	35	2
Lineweaver, Aaron, Wil.	.963	17	7	19	1	27	2
Lopez, Jose, W.S.	.727	19	4	4	3	11	0
Lynch, Ryan, Fred.*	.857	12	0	6	1	7	0
Maloney, Sean, Fred.	1.000	15	3	2	0	5	0
Manning, Brian, W.S.	1.000	2	1	2	0	3	1
Marquis, Jason, M.B.	1.000	6	5	9	0	14	1
Marr, Jason, Pot.	.769	50	6	4	3	13	0
Martin, Jeff, Lyn.	1.000	10	2	3	0	5	0
Martinez, Lionel, M.B.	.000	1	0	0	0	0	0
Mastrolonardo, David, Fred.	1.000	8	0	1	0	1	0
Matcuk, Steve, Sal.	1.000	26	9	26	0	35	0
Mays, Jarrod, Kin.	.944	45	3	14	1	18	1
McConnell, Sam, Lyn.*	1.000	15	5	22	0	27	0
McNatt, Josh, Fred.*	.929	19	3	10	1	14	0
Medina, Carlos, Fred.*	.875	5	1	6	1	8	1
Milburn, Adam, M.B.*	.895	39	4	13	2	19	2
Miller, Justin, Sal.	.778	8	2	5	2	9	0
Minter, Matt, Lyn.*	1.000	41	2	4	0	6	0
Montas, Ricardo, Wil.	1.000	1	0	1	0	1	1
Morrison, Robbie, Wil.	1.000	28	0	5	0	5	2
Murphy, Brian, Fred.	1.000	26	5	9	0	14	1
Nation, Joey, M.B.*	.955	19	3	18	1	22	2
Navarro, Jason, Pot.*	1.000	39	6	17	0	23	0
Opipari, Mario, Pot.	.000	7	0	0	0	0	0
Pacheco, Delvis, M.B.	1.000	40	4	20	0	24	2
Padilla, Roy, Kin.*	1.000	8	0	9	0	9	0
Paredes, Carlos, Wil.	1.000	36	6	7	0	13	0
Paronto, Chad, Fred.	1.000	13	7	11	0	18	0
Parrish, John, Fred.*	1.000	6	2	3	0	5	0
Paxton, Chris, Fred.	.000	6	0	0	0	0	0
Pederson, Justin, Wil.	.929	34	5	8	1	14	0
Percell, Brody, Kin.*	.909	5	0	10	1	11	0
Perez, Randy, Fred.*	1.000	2	0	2	0	2	0
Pirkl, Greg, Kin.	.500	6	0	2	2	4	0
Prempas, Lyle, Lyn.*	1.000	6	2	5	0	7	0
Price, Ryan, Sal.	.972	28	8	27	1	36	0
Pugmire, Robert, Kin.	1.000	16	8	15	0	23	1
Rauch, Jon, W.S.	.000	1	0	0	0	0	0
Reames, Britt, Pot.	1.000	10	2	1	0	3	0
Reyes, Jose, Lyn.	.000	1	0	0	0	0	0
Richardson, Kasey, Fred.*	1.000	38	5	11	0	16	0
Riley, Matt, Fred.*	.875	8	3	11	2	16	0
Rivera, Luis, M.B.	.900	25	2	7	1	10	0
Roberts, Mike, Wil.	1.000	9	1	0	0	1	0
Romero, Jordan, Fred.-Kin.	1.000	10	2	2	0	4	0
Rosa, Cristy, Sal.	1.000	8	2	4	0	6	0
Sabathia, C.C., Kin.*	1.000	7	0	10	0	10	1
SCOTT, Brian, W.S.	1.000	25	12	31	0	43	2
Sedlacek, Shawn, Wil.	1.000	17	7	11	0	18	1
Seifert, Ryan, Sal.	.889	24	1	7	1	9	1
Shepherd, Alvie, Fred.	.500	3	1	0	1	2	0
Sheredy, Kevin, Pot.	.885	41	11	12	3	26	0
Shiell, Jason, M.B.	.921	26	9	26	3	38	4
Shumate, Jacob, M.B.	1.000	20	1	3	0	4	0
Sido, Wilson, Kin.	.857	9	2	10	2	14	0
Sims, Ken, Fred.	.857	35	3	9	2	14	1
Smith, Robert, Pot.*	1.000	18	5	25	0	30	0
Sobkowiak, Scott, M.B.	.864	27	9	10	3	22	0
Sonnier, Shawn, Wil.	.857	44	2	4	1	7	0
Sparks, Steve, Lyn.	1.000	5	0	7	0	7	0
Spenser, Kaipo, Kin.	.941	35	9	7	1	17	0
Spiegel, Mike, Kin.*	.800	18	6	14	5	25	1
Spurgeon, Jay, Fred.	.897	26	6	20	3	29	1
Terhune, Mike, M.B.	.000	1	0	0	0	0	0
Thompson, John, W.S.-Wil.	1.000	22	4	8	0	12	2
Thompson, Travis, Sal.	.958	56	9	14	1	24	1
Thomson, John, Sal.	1.000	1	0	1	0	1	0
Thorn, Todd, Wil.*	.952	34	16	24	2	42	1
Thurman, Corey, Wil.	.909	27	13	17	3	33	2
Tokarse, Brian, W.S.	1.000	40	1	4	0	5	0
Turnbow, Mark, Kin.	.882	12	5	10	2	17	0
Vavrek, Mike, Sal.*	1.000	10	4	8	0	12	0
Virchis, Adam, W.S.	.958	33	6	17	1	24	0
Voyles, Brad, M.B.	1.000	5	0	3	0	3	0
Wagner, Ken, Kin.	1.000	14	4	2	0	6	0
Watson, Mark, Kin.*	1.000	11	4	11	0	15	1
Weidert, Chris, Kin.	.929	27	4	9	1	14	0
Wells, Kip, W.S.	.842	14	4	12	3	19	1
Weymouth, Marty, W.S.	.846	41	7	4	2	13	0
Whitley, Curtis, W.S.*	1.000	9	1	0	0	1	0
Williams, Larry, Lyn.	.933	34	8	6	1	15	0
Wilson, Kris, Wil.	1.000	14	4	10	0	14	1
Wimberly, Larry, Lyn.*	1.000	11	0	6	0	6	0
Woodward, Finley, W.S.	.952	24	4	16	1	21	0
Wrigley, Jase, Sal.	1.000	8	2	1	0	3	0
Yen, Buddy, Wil.	.000	2	0	0	0	0	0

PITCHERS WITH TWO OR MORE TEAMS

Player, Team	Pct.	G	PO	A	E	TC	DP
Aracena, Juan, Kin.	1.000	5	2	1	0	3	0
Aracena, Juan, Fred.	1.000	2	0	1	0	1	0
Romero, Jordan, Fred.	1.000	9	2	2	0	4	0
Romero, Jordan, Kin.	.000	1	0	0	0	0	0
Thompson, John, W.S.	1.000	2	0	2	0	2	0
Thompson, John, Wil.	1.000	20	4	6	0	10	2

The following players appeared only as designated hitter, pinch-hitter or pinch runner: D. Benham, ph; P. Evans, dh; L. Gonzalez, ph.

LEAGUE CHAMPIONS

Year	Team	Pct.	Year	Team	Pct.	Year	Team	Pct.
1945—	Danville	.681	1965—	Peninsula§	.597	1982—	Alexandria‡	.597
1946—	Greensboro	.599		Durham§	.580		Durham	.588
	Raleigh (2nd)†	.563		Tidewater†	.528	1983—	Lynchburg‡	.691
1947—	Burlington	.613	1966—	Kinston§	.547		Winston-Salem	.529
	Raleigh (3rd)†	.574		Winston-Salem§	.586	1984—	Lynchburg‡	.645
1948—	Raleigh	.592		Rocky Mount†	.533		Durham	.486
	Martinsville (2nd)†	.570	1967—	Durham∞(West.)	.536	1985—	Lynchburg	.679
1949—	Danville	.601		Raleigh (East.)	.542		Winston-Salem‡	.417
	Burlington (4th)†	.500	1968—	Salem (West.)	.607	1986—	Hagerstown	.655
1950—	Winston-Salem*	.693		Ral-Dur (East.)	.597		Winston-Salem‡	.594
1951—	Durham	.600		HP-Thom.▲(W.)	.493	1987—	Salem‡	.576
	Winston-Salem (2nd)†	.583	1969—	Rocky M (East.)	.569		Kinston	.536
1952—	Raleigh	.581		Salem (West.)	.542	1988—	Kinston§	.629
	Reidsville (4th)†	.536		Ral-Dur◆(East.)	.560		Lynchburg	.486
1953—	Raleigh	.593	1970—	Winston-Salem‡	.586	1989—	Durham	.609
	Danville (2nd)†	.572		Burlington	.597		Prince William‡	.522
1954—	Fayetteville*	.628	1971—	Peninsula‡	.647	1990—	Kinston	.652
1955—	HP-Thomasville	.580		Kinston	.623		Frederick‡	.544
	Danville (2nd)†	.533	1972—	Salem‡	.657	1991—	Kinston‡	.645
1956—	HP-Thomasville	.591		Burlington	.632		Lynchburg	.482
	Fayetteville (4th)§	.523	1973—	Lynchburg	.588	1992—	Lynchburg	.570
1957—	Durham	.632		Winston-Salem‡	.557		Peninsula‡	.536
	HP-Thomasville	.622	1974—	Salem	.671	1993—	Wilmington	.532
1958—	Danville	.576		Salem	.582		Winston-Salem‡	.514
	Burlington (4th)†	.511	1975—	Rocky Mount	.667	1994—	Wilmington‡	.681
1959—	Raleigh	.600		Rocky Mount	.614		Winston-Salem	.555
	Wilson (2nd)†	.550	1976—	Winston-Salem	.618	1995—	Wilmington	.601
1960—	Greensboro‡	.636		Winston-Salem	.551		Kinston‡	.591
	Burlington	.586	1977—	Lynchburg	.591	1996—	Wilmington▼	.571
1961—	Wilson	.594		Peninsula‡	.556		Kinston	.551
1962—	Durham	.636	1978—	Peninsula	.696	1997—	Kinston	.621
	Wilson	.600		Lynchburg‡	.614		Lynchburg†	.586
	Kinston (2nd)†	.593	1979—	Winston-Salem■	.607	1998—	Wilmington▼	.614
1963—	Kinston§	.538	1980—	Peninsula‡	.714		Winston-Salem	.568
	Greensboro§	.590		Durham	.600	1999—	Kinston	.577
	Wilson (2nd)†	.535	1981—	Peninsula	.522		Myrtle Beach•	.568
1964—	Kinston§	.572		Hagerstown‡	.507		Wilmington•	.568
	Winston-Salem§†	.590						

*Won championship and four-club playoff. †Won four-club playoff. ‡Won split-season playoff. §League was divided into Eastern, Western divisions. ∞Won eight-club, two-division playoff. ▲Won eight-club, two-division playoff against Raleigh-Durham. ◆Won eight-club, two-division playoff against Burlington. ■Won both halves of split season (no playoffs). ▼League divided into Northern and Southern divisions and played a split-season, won playoffs. •Declared co-champions after final series cancelled due to hurricane.

CLASS A *Carolina League*

FLORIDA STATE LEAGUE

LEAGUE OFFICE

President
Chuck Murphy

Address
P.O. Box 349
Daytona Beach, FL 32115

Phone
904-252-7479

Teams (affiliation)
Brevard County Manatees (Marlins)
Charlotte Rangers (Rangers)
Clearwater Phillies (Phillies)
Daytona Cubs (Cubs)
Dunedin Blue Jays (Blue Jays)
Fort Myers Miracle (Twins)
Jupiter Hammerheads (Expos)

Kissimmee Cobras (Astros)
Lakeland Tigers (Tigers)
St. Lucie Mets (Mets)
St. Petersburg Devil Rays (Devil Rays)
Sarasota Red Sox (Red Sox)
Tampa Yankees (Yankees)
Vero Beach Dodgers (Dodgers)

1999 FINAL STANDINGS

FIRST HALF

EAST DIVISION

Team	W	L	T	Pct.	GB
Jupiter (Expos)	39	29	0	.574	...
St. Lucie (Mets)	31	37	0	.456	8.0
Kissimmee (Astros)	30	37	0	.448	8.5
Daytona (Cubs)	30	38	0	.441	9.0
Brevard County (Marlins)	27	40	0	.403	11.5
Vero Beach (Dodgers)	26	42	0	.382	13.0

WEST DIVISION

Team	W	L	T	Pct.	GB
Clearwater (Phillies)	46	23	0	.667	...
Dunedin (Blue Jays)	45	24	0	.652	1.0
Tampa (Yankees)	39	29	0	.574	6.5
St. Petersburg (Devil Rays)	39	29	0	.574	6.5
Sarasota (Red Sox)	39	30	0	.565	7.0
Lakeland (Tigers)	33	36	0	.478	13.0
Charlotte (Rangers)	29	40	0	.420	17.0
Fort Myers (Twins)	25	44	0	.362	21.0

SECOND HALF

EAST DIVISION

Team	W	L	T	Pct.	GB
Kissimmee (Astros)	41	29	0	.586	...
St. Lucie (Mets)	37	33	0	.529	4.0
Brevard County (Marlins)	34	34	0	.500	6.0
Jupiter (Expos)	34	36	0	.486	7.0
Daytona (Cubs)	33	37	0	.471	8.0
Vero Beach (Dodgers)	22	43	0	.338	16.5

WEST DIVISION

Team	W	L	T	Pct.	GB
Dunedin (Blue Jays)	41	27	0	.603	...
Tampa (Yankees)	39	29	0	.574	2.0
Charlotte (Rangers)	40	30	0	.571	2.0
St. Petersburg (Devil Rays)	35	34	0	.507	6.5
Fort Myers (Twins)	35	35	0	.500	7.0
Lakeland (Tigers)	32	37	0	.464	9.5
Clearwater (Phillies)	31	36	0	.463	9.5
Sarasota (Red Sox)	28	42	0	.400	14.0

COMPOSITE

Team	Dun.	Tam.	Cle.	StP	Jup.	Kis.	Char.	StL	Sar.	Lak.	Day.	B.C.	F.M.	V.B.	W	L	T	Pct.	GB
Dunedin (Blue Jays)	...	6	6	9	5	6	7	5	5	8	7	5	9	8	86	51	0	.628	...
Tampa (Yankees)	6	...	10	4	3	5	5	6	8	7	7	5	8	4	78	58	0	.574	7.5
Clearwater (Phillies)	9	4	...	5	4	5	9	7	7	9	6	5	3	4	77	59	0	.566	8.5
St. Petersburg (Devil Rays)	3	7	7	...	6	2	6	2	8	7	6	5	9	6	74	63	0	.540	12.0
Jupiter (Expos)	3	5	4	2	...	7	4	7	4	4	10	8	6	9	73	65	0	.529	13.5
Kissimmee (Astros)	2	3	3	6	9	...	3	7	5	4	5	9	5	10	71	66	0	.518	15.0
Charlotte (Rangers)	5	7	3	6	4	5	...	3	10	5	5	2	9	5	69	70	0	.496	18.0
St. Lucie (Mets)	3	2	1	6	9	7	5	...	5	6	5	7	3	9	68	70	0	.493	18.5
Sarasota (Red Sox)	7	4	5	7	4	3	6	3	...	6	4	5	7	6	67	72	0	.482	20.0
Lakeland (Tigers)	6	8	4	5	4	4	7	2	6	...	1	5	7	6	65	73	0	.471	21.5
Daytona (Cubs)	1	1	2	2	4	11	3	9	4	7	...	9	4	6	63	75	0	.457	23.5
Brevard County (Marlins)	3	3	3	3	6	4	6	7	3	3	7	...	4	9	61	74	0	.452	24.0
Fort Myers (Twins)	3	4	9	7	2	3	6	5	5	5	4	4	...	3	60	79	0	.432	27.0
Vero Beach (Dodgers)	0	4	2	1	5	4	3	7	2	2	8	5	5	...	48	85	0	.361	36.0

Brevard County played home games in Melbourne, Fla.; Charlotte played home games in Port Charlotte, Fla.

Major league affiliations in parentheses.

PLAYOFFS: Kissimmee defeated Jupiter two games to one; Dunedin defeated Clearwater two games to one; Kissimmee defeated Dunedin three games to one to win league championship.

REGULAR-SEASON ATTENDANCE: Brevard County, 115,145; Charlotte, 42,119; Clearwater, 70,147; Daytona, 62,491; Dunedin, 51,819; Fort Myers, 108,074; Jupiter, 105,037; Kissimmee, 33,789; Lakeland, 36,092; St. Lucie, 40,928; St. Petersburg, 82,631; Sarasota, 45,844; Tampa, 91,603; Vero Beach, 50,838. Total—936,557. Playoffs (10 games)—4,343. All-Star Game at Lakeland, Fla.—4,146.

MANAGERS: Brevard County, Dave Huppert; Charlotte, Jim Byrd; Clearwater, Bill Dancy; Daytona, Nate Oliver; Dunedin, Rocket Wheeler; Fort Myers, Mike Boulanger; Jupiter, Luis Dorante; Kissimmee, Manny Acta; Lakeland, Mark Meleski; St. Lucie, Howie Freiling; St. Petersburg, Roy Silver; Sarasota, Butch Hobson; Tampa, Tom Nieto; Vero Beach, Alvaro Espinoza.

ALL-STAR TEAM: 1B—Eric Hinske, Daytona; 2B—Jason Romano, Charlotte; 3B—Jason Grabowski, Charlotte; SS—Cesar Izturis, Dunedin; Utility INF—Mike Young, Dunedin; OF—Quincy Foster, Brevard County; Clearwater, Vernon Wells, Dunedin; Eric Valent, Clearwater; Utility OF—Allen Dina, St. Lucie; C—Michael Rivera, Lakeland; Matt LeCroy, Fort Myers; DH—Josh Phelps, Dunedin; RHP—Eric Ireland, Kissimmee; RHP—John Sneed, Dunedin; RHP—Mike Myers, Daytona; LHP—Wilfredo Rodriguez, Kissimmee; RP—Jason Ellison, Tampa; RP—Bob File, Dunedin; Most Valuable Player—Vernon Wells, Dunedin; Manager—Rocket Wheeler, Dunedin; Coach—Luis Dorante, Jupiter; Coach—Manny Acta, Kissimmee.

CLASS A *Florida State League*

TEAM

Team	Avg.	G	TPA	AB	R	H	TB	2B	3B	HR	RBI	SH	SF	HP	BB	IBB	SO	SB	CS	GDP	LOB	ShO	Slg.	OBP
Dunedin	.288	137	5239	4659	760	1341	2064	285	39	120	695	51	45	70	414	12	835	159	74	103	944	7	.443	.352
Clearwater	.281	136	5415	4653	756	1307	1896	232	48	87	691	42	66	75	579	24	811	103	48	110	1078	2	.407	.365
Fort Myers	.270	139	5283	4635	686	1251	1809	221	32	91	626	32	48	61	507	16	801	95	54	111	1022	11	.390	.346
Sarasota	.269	139	5323	4649	693	1250	1868	238	31	106	608	49	39	88	498	16	841	121	58	94	1053	7	.402	.348
Charlotte	.269	139	5254	4583	702	1232	1820	215	53	89	636	39	40	71	521	18	914	180	101	70	978	10	.397	.350
Brevard County	.264	135	5085	4541	591	1201	1615	174	33	58	537	39	47	62	396	12	842	140	68	89	958	10	.356	.329
Lakeland	.264	138	5151	4623	638	1221	1726	231	41	64	570	27	42	66	393	10	911	173	71	111	921	9	.373	.328
Tampa	.264	136	5226	4577	622	1208	1807	219	55	90	561	25	52	61	511	18	991	79	48	99	1051	3	.395	.342
St. Lucie	.261	138	5174	4595	625	1199	1774	203	39	98	557	49	43	68	419	15	971	143	75	98	953	7	.386	.329
St. Petersburg	.258	137	5001	4491	579	1160	1581	174	29	63	519	45	36	62	367	10	851	93	58	97	896	10	.352	.321
Daytona	.258	138	4986	4452	589	1147	1650	206	30	79	526	35	40	81	378	18	795	128	76	104	896	11	.371	.324
Vero Beach	.253	133	4842	4262	531	1079	1479	181	21	59	451	48	33	71	428	13	884	125	110	76	882	11	.347	.329
Kissimmee	.252	137	5170	4554	652	1149	1807	227	34	121	589	27	31	72	486	14	1051	118	82	80	942	8	.397	.332
Jupiter	.252	138	5119	4471	579	1126	1537	184	28	57	513	85	49	86	428	16	895	206	102	87	931	11	.344	.326

INDIVIDUAL

TOP QUALIFIERS FOR BATTING CHAMPIONSHIP

Minimum 378 plate appearances. *Lefthanded batter. †Switch-hitter.

Player, Team	Avg.	G	TPA	AB	R	H	TB	2B	3B	HR	RBI	SH	SF	HP	BB	IBB	SO	SB	CS	GDP	Slg.	OBP
Dina, Allen, St.L.	.344	85	381	343	65	118	178	16	4	12	47	4	3	6	25	0	54	34	10	2	.519	.395
Phelps, Josh, Dun.	.328	110	448	406	72	133	228	27	4	20	88	2	4	8	28	0	104	6	3	13	.562	.379
Grabowski, Jason, Char.*	.313	123	507	434	68	136	215	31	6	12	87	1	2	5	65	3	66	13	10	8	.495	.407
Young, Mike, Dun.	.313	129	566	495	86	155	212	36	3	5	83	1	5	4	61	2	78	30	6	10	.428	.389
Romano, Jason, Char.	.312	120	522	459	84	143	237	27	14	13	71	4	7	13	39	2	72	34	16	4	.516	.376
Izturis, Cesar, Dun.†	.308	131	590	536	77	165	226	28	12	3	77	17	9	6	22	4	58	32	16	9	.422	.337
Michaels, Jason, Cle.	.306	122	529	451	91	138	223	31	6	14	65	1	6	3	68	2	103	10	7	7	.494	.396
Punto, Nick, Cle.†	.305	106	478	400	65	122	155	18	6	1	48	3	5	3	67	3	53	16	7	13	.388	.404
Bolivar, Papo, F.M.	.305	114	468	433	54	132	168	21	3	3	37	3	1	4	27	1	56	8	9	10	.388	.351
Johnson, Rontrez, Sar.	.300	132	591	494	97	148	210	30	4	8	59	8	7	8	74	0	63	18	15	7	.425	.395
Moreno, Juan, St.L.	.300	120	488	424	64	127	167	18	5	4	47	7	4	2	51	0	70	28	11	10	.394	.374
Espinal, Juan, Sar.	.299	111	469	441	78	123	179	26	0	10	67	1	4	6	47	0	83	12	4	9	.436	.376
Kiil, Skip, Cle.	.298	86	390	305	74	91	164	15	8	14	55	5	3	7	70	0	101	24	5	2	.538	.436
Cuddyer, Michael, F.M.	.298	130	560	466	87	139	219	24	4	16	82	2	6	10	76	0	91	14	4	20	.470	.403
Gload, Ross, B.C.*	.298	133	556	490	80	146	208	26	3	10	74	2	5	5	53	3	76	3	1	8	.424	.369
Garcia, Douglas, Char.*	.298	112	419	386	57	115	139	14	5	0	34	3	1	3	26	0	69	14	8	4	.360	.346

DEPARTMENTAL LEADERS: G—Butler, 137; AB—Foster, 568; R—Peeples, 100; H—Foster, 167; TB—Peeples, 262; 2B—Young, Butler, 36 each; 3B—Romano, 14; HR—Burkhart, 23; RBI—Valent, 106; SH—Izturis, Mateo, 17 each; SF—Pond, 11; HP—Graham, 19; BB—Cuddyer, Jones, 76 each; IBB—Baker, Hinske, Rodriguez, 7 each; SO—Pena, 135; SB—Lindsey, 61; CS—Randolph, 26; GIDP—Cuddyer, 20; Slg.—Phelps, .562; OBP—Kiil, .436.

ALL PLAYERS

*Lefthanded batter. †Switch-hitter.

Player, Team	Avg.	G	TPA	AB	R	H	TB	2B	3B	HR	RBI	SH	SF	HP	BB	IBB	SO	SB	CS	GDP	Slg.	OBP
Abreu, Dennis, Day.	.257	105	393	374	44	96	116	10	2	2	30	2	1	3	13	0	69	29	9	10	.310	.286
Acevedo, Carlos, Cle.	.286	12	45	42	4	12	16	2	1	0	6	0	0	0	3	0	7	2	1	0	.381	.333
Acevedo, Inocencio, Char.	.000	1	4	3	1	0	0	0	0	0	0	0	0	1	0	0	1	0	0	0	.000	.250
Alamo, Efrain, St.P.	.138	8	29	29	1	4	5	1	0	0	0	0	0	0	0	0	9	0	0	0	.172	.138
Albert, Rashad, Jup.	.224	76	292	245	25	55	71	3	5	1	21	9	1	3	34	2	74	14	16	6	.290	.325
Alevras, Chad, Sar.	.143	2	8	7	2	1	4	0	0	1	2	1	0	0	0	0	0	0	0	1	.571	.143
Almonte, Erick, Tam.	.257	61	257	230	36	59	86	8	2	5	25	5	2	2	18	0	49	3	1	6	.374	.313
Alvarez, Aaron, B.C.	.667	1	3	3	1	2	5	0	0	1	1	0	0	0	0	0	0	0	0	0	1.667	.667
Alvarez, Rafael, F.M.†	.293	83	350	304	47	89	149	22	4	10	58	1	3	4	38	4	48	8	4	8	.490	.375
Amrhein, Mike, Day.	.278	127	502	449	55	125	184	27	1	10	58	3	6	13	31	1	67	1	1	14	.410	.339
Antczak, Chuck, Cle.	.258	15	35	31	3	8	10	2	0	0	4	0	0	2	2	0	6	0	0	1	.323	.343
August, Brian, Tam.	.270	92	375	318	40	86	124	21	1	5	42	4	10	2	41	0	72	1	0	9	.390	.348
Auterson, Jeff, V.B.	.206	104	403	349	39	72	101	19	2	2	27	7	3	10	34	0	118	5	18	6	.289	.293
Backe, Brandon, St.P.	.197	41	164	132	21	26	37	6	1	1	11	6	2	3	21	0	34	0	3	4	.280	.316
Badeaux, Brooks, St.P.†	.284	96	406	342	68	97	105	6	1	0	19	5	0	2	57	1	44	2	7	4	.307	.389
Bagley, Lorenzo, Dun.	.280	90	321	275	46	77	128	11	2	12	44	0	5	6	35	1	70	9	7	6	.465	.368
Baker, Derek, Char.*	.260	119	493	419	69	109	150	16	2	7	55	0	4	12	58	7	83	3	2	9	.358	.363
Barr, Clint, Tam.	.154	7	16	13	1	2	2	0	0	0	0	0	0	1	2	0	6	0	0	0	.154	.313
Batista, Angel, St.P.*	.250	6	18	16	4	4	4	0	0	0	0	1	0	0	1	0	0	0	1	0	.250	.294
Bautista, Rayner, Lak.	.228	96	333	303	35	69	91	11	4	1	32	4	2	3	21	0	75	7	3	10	.300	.283
Bearden, Doug, Kis.	.268	45	164	149	19	40	55	7	1	2	16	4	1	2	8	0	35	1	4	3	.369	.313
Bell, Ricky, V.B.	.234	100	416	376	37	88	131	26	1	5	46	4	4	4	27	0	81	1	3	13	.348	.290
Belliard, Fernando, St.P.	.167	6	12	12	1	2	2	0	0	0	0	0	0	0	0	0	6	0	0	0	.167	.167
Benham, David, Sar.	.238	33	114	105	10	25	39	5	0	3	11	0	1	3	5	0	18	0	0	3	.371	.289
Bennett, Ryan, St.L.	.224	56	193	165	19	37	41	4	0	0	12	3	3	1	19	0	32	2	1	5	.248	.303
Berns, Robert, St.P.	.209	14	50	43	4	9	12	3	0	0	7	0	2	2	3	0	2	0	1	1	.279	.280
Berroa, Geronimo, Dun.	.200	4	8	5	1	1	2	1	0	0	2	0	0	1	2	0	1	0	0	0	.400	.500
Besco, Derek, Lak.	.287	122	500	456	70	131	194	26	4	9	66	1	3	3	37	4	88	10	7	12	.425	.343
Bly, Derrick, Day.	.235	41	171	149	22	35	60	13	0	4	15	1	1	3	16	1	34	1	1	2	.403	.320
Bolivar, Papo, F.M.	.305	114	468	433	54	132	168	21	3	3	37	3	1	4	27	1	56	8	9	10	.388	.351
Borrego, Ramon, F.M.†	.221	27	94	86	9	19	22	3	0	0	6	0	0	1	7	0	15	4	0	1	.256	.287
Boughton, Mike, Char.†	.179	14	43	39	5	7	7	0	0	0	4	0	1	0	3	0	9	2	1	1	.179	.233
Bravo, Danny, Jup.†	.300	7	24	20	5	6	12	3	0	1	3	2	0	1	1	0	5	0	0	1	.600	.364
Brosius, Scott, Tam.	.333	1	3	3	0	1	1	0	0	0	0	0	0	0	0	0	0	0	0	0	.333	.333

CLASS A *Florida State League*

Player, Team	Avg.	G	TPA	AB	R	H	TB	2B	3B	HR	RBI	SH	SF	HP	BB	IBB	SO	SB	CS	GDP	Slg.	OBP
Buckley, Brandon, Kis.	.199	51	161	146	13	29	37	5	0	1	11	3	1	0	11	1	29	1	3	4	.253	.253
Bunkley, Antuan, Lak.	.272	133	554	493	52	134	172	26	0	4	69	0	4	8	49	2	69	1	1	14	.349	.345
Burkhart, Lance, Jup.	.214	45	148	131	19	28	51	8	0	5	21	0	2	2	13	1	35	1	1	1	.389	.291
Burkhart, Morgan, Sar.†	.363	68	295	245	56	89	176	18	0	23	67	0	7	6	37	6	33	5	2	4	.718	.447
Burns, Pat, St.L.†	.238	133	542	488	54	116	164	26	2	6	54	1	1	2	50	3	122	6	3	15	.336	.311
Bush, Homer, Dun.	.357	4	17	14	3	5	7	2	0	0	0	1	0	1	1	0	1	1	0	1	.500	.438
Butler, Allen, F.M.*	.253	137	565	491	73	124	206	36	2	14	73	3	3	3	65	4	121	3	3	8	.420	.342
Butler, Garrett, St.P.†	.249	94	354	329	36	82	108	14	3	2	31	5	1	2	17	0	61	16	6	3	.328	.289
Cairo, Miguel, St.P.	.385	3	14	13	2	5	5	0	0	0	0	0	0	0	1	0	2	1	1	0	.385	.429
Calloway, Ronald, Jup.*	.270	54	232	211	30	57	82	8	4	3	25	4	0	2	15	0	45	5	6	9	.389	.325
Capellan, Rene, Lak.	.177	34	119	113	14	20	25	2	0	1	9	2	0	1	3	0	10	2	2	4	.221	.205
Capista, Aaron, Sar.†	.264	130	578	518	64	137	176	18	3	5	47	8	4	3	45	2	60	25	10	9	.340	.325
Carreno, Jose, Jup.	.000	2	6	6	0	0	0	0	0	0	0	0	0	0	0	0	2	0	0	0	.000	.000
Carter, Charley, Kis.	.274	115	451	416	62	114	173	19	2	12	56	0	4	3	28	2	77	0	3	7	.416	.322
Carter, Quincy, Day.	.000	1	3	3	0	0	0	0	0	0	0	0	0	0	0	0	1	0	0	0	.000	.000
Casanova, Raul, Lak.†	.500	4	13	12	3	6	11	2	0	1	6	0	0	1	0	0	1	0	0	0	.917	.538
Casillas, Uriel, Cle.	.283	32	144	113	23	32	37	5	0	0	24	4	1	9	17	0	10	4	2	2	.327	.414
Castellano, John, V.B.	.444	6	21	18	3	8	8	0	0	0	0	1	0	0	2	0	0	0	0	1	.444	.500
Chambliss, Russ, Tam.*	.000	5	6	6	0	0	0	0	0	0	0	0	0	0	0	0	2	0	0	0	.000	.000
Chavera, Arnie, Kis.*	.277	62	246	213	29	59	114	13	0	14	43	0	0	7	26	3	59	1	0	2	.535	.374
Chavez, Endy, St.L.*	.311	45	208	183	33	57	77	8	3	2	18	2	1	0	22	2	22	9	3	5	.421	.383
Cheek, Shawn, Sar.	.080	15	29	25	1	2	2	0	0	0	1	0	1	1	2	0	10	0	0	0	.080	.172
Chiaffredo, Paul, Dun.	.253	88	298	261	39	66	101	22	2	3	21	4	4	12	17	0	44	1	4	12	.387	.323
Clarke, Jason, Day.†	.240	81	285	254	24	61	75	6	1	2	29	2	3	1	25	0	27	8	3	2	.295	.307
Cole, Eric, Kis.	.265	120	510	460	62	122	198	27	5	13	67	0	4	7	39	3	120	23	13	12	.430	.329
Collier, Lamonte, Cle.	.264	104	383	318	50	84	101	11	3	0	28	6	5	5	49	1	60	4	3	12	.318	.366
Collins, Michael, V.B.	.267	101	403	356	37	95	118	10	2	3	31	9	3	1	34	0	68	8	12	7	.331	.330
Connally, Christopher, Day.	.233	29	96	90	10	21	24	3	0	0	9	0	0	1	5	0	19	2	1	0	.267	.281
Connell, Jerry, Cle.	.289	25	101	90	11	26	38	4	1	2	18	0	2	1	8	0	27	2	0	3	.422	.347
Copeland, Brandon, St.L.	.128	16	44	39	3	5	9	1	0	1	4	1	0	0	4	1	18	2	0	1	.231	.209
Craig, Benny, Kis.†	.077	4	13	13	0	1	1	0	0	0	0	0	0	0	0	0	6	0	0	1	.077	.077
Cranford, Joey, F.M.	.242	38	149	124	18	30	45	4	1	3	14	0	6	2	17	0	22	3	2	4	.363	.329
Crespo, Cesar, B.C.†	.286	115	500	427	63	122	161	17	2	6	40	7	2	1	62	2	86	22	8	4	.377	.376
Cripps, Bobby, Dun.*	.063	5	17	16	1	1	1	0	0	0	1	0	0	0	1	0	7	0	0	1	.063	.118
Cruz, Luis, St.P.	.220	58	233	218	25	48	59	5	0	2	17	3	1	1	10	0	38	1	2	5	.271	.257
Cuddyer, Michael, F.M.	.298	130	560	466	87	139	219	24	4	16	82	2	6	10	76	0	91	14	4	20	.470	.403
Dallimore, Brian, Kis.	.270	19	83	74	12	20	22	2	0	0	3	1	1	3	4	0	10	2	1	1	.297	.329
De Leon, Jorge, Sar.	.274	66	248	219	33	60	78	11	2	1	18	5	0	0	24	0	33	3	2	5	.356	.346
Delgado, Alex, Dun.	.170	13	50	47	6	8	14	0	0	2	4	0	0	2	1	0	6	0	0	2	.298	.220
Dennis, Les, Tam.	.303	23	106	89	20	27	32	3	1	0	7	1	1	0	15	0	20	0	1	2	.360	.400
Diaz, Miguel, Jup.	.000	2	4	4	0	0	0	0	0	0	0	0	0	0	0	0	2	0	0	0	.000	.000
Dina, Allen, St.L.	.344	85	381	343	65	118	178	16	4	12	47	4	3	6	25	0	54	34	10	2	.519	.395
Dito, Robert, Jup.	.000	1	2	2	0	0	0	0	0	0	0	0	0	0	0	0	2	0	0	0	.000	.000
Dominique, Andy, Cle.	.255	130	577	487	77	124	205	29	5	14	92	3	8	10	69	4	84	3	3	13	.421	.354
Duffy, Jim, Kis.	.248	60	173	149	26	37	58	8	2	3	25	3	1	3	17	0	48	5	5	3	.389	.335
Ellis, John, Char.	.270	48	165	152	15	41	50	7	1	0	17	1	0	1	11	0	21	0	1	2	.329	.323
Ensberg, Morgan, Kis.	.239	123	508	427	72	102	176	25	2	15	69	1	3	9	68	0	90	17	6	9	.412	.353
Epperson, Chad, Sar.†	.242	26	102	99	9	24	36	1	1	3	14	0	0	0	3	0	18	2	1	2	.364	.265
Escobar, Alex, St.L.	.667	1	5	3	1	2	5	0	0	1	3	0	1	0	1	0	1	1	1	0	1.667	.600
Espinal, Juan, Sar.	.299	111	469	411	78	123	179	26	0	10	67	1	4	6	47	0	83	12	4	9	.436	.376
Estalella, Bobby, Cle.	.423	8	29	26	3	11	17	3	0	1	8	0	0	0	3	0	3	0	0	0	.654	.483
Estrada, Johnny, Cle.†	.277	98	376	346	35	96	138	15	0	9	52	6	8	2	14	3	26	1	0	12	.399	.303
Feliciano, Jesus, V.B.*	.254	98	407	370	44	94	107	13	0	0	21	2	2	4	29	1	38	20	10	4	.289	.314
Feliz, Joselyn, B.C.	.200	11	27	25	0	5	7	2	0	0	2	0	0	1	1	0	8	0	0	0	.280	.259
Felston, Anthony, F.M.*	.296	81	377	311	66	92	118	11	3	3	47	4	1	9	52	0	41	21	10	2	.379	.410
Feramisco, Derek, V.B.	.208	18	65	53	7	11	17	3	0	1	4	0	0	1	11	0	12	0	2	0	.321	.354
Fischer, Mark, Sar.	.253	106	393	359	42	91	126	14	3	5	40	4	1	1	28	0	85	11	6	11	.351	.308
Fleming, Ryan, Dun.*	.228	51	141	123	17	28	37	7	1	0	9	3	1	4	10	1	19	4	3	3	.301	.304
Font, Franklin, Day.	.295	87	349	315	48	93	114	7	4	2	33	8	3	2	21	0	38	14	6	10	.362	.340
Forbush, Nate, Lak.†	.288	84	295	250	38	72	101	14	0	5	28	0	2	0	43	2	62	1	3	7	.404	.390
Foster, Quincy, B.C.*	.294	134	616	568	78	167	201	13	6	3	54	2	2	8	36	1	96	56	23	4	.354	.344
Franco, Raul, B.C.	.239	111	456	426	41	102	124	17	1	1	43	3	10	3	13	0	48	4	6	14	.291	.261
Freeman, Terrance, Lak.†	.278	101	437	381	64	106	129	19	2	0	47	3	3	7	43	0	59	37	12	2	.339	.359
Freire, Alejandro, Lak.	.220	13	56	41	6	9	15	3	0	1	5	1	1	3	10	0	7	0	0	1	.366	.400
Frick, Matt, B.C.	.221	35	128	113	8	25	30	5	0	0	12	1	1	2	11	0	27	0	1	2	.265	.299
Fuentes, Javier, Sar.	.290	64	224	176	28	51	55	4	0	0	13	3	3	6	33	0	17	6	1	2	.313	.413
Fuentes, Omar, Tam.	.246	19	62	57	4	14	14	0	0	0	8	0	1	1	3	0	7	0	0	1	.246	.290
Garcia, Douglas, Char.*	.298	112	419	386	57	115	139	14	5	0	34	3	1	3	26	0	69	14	8	4	.360	.346
Gibbons, Jay, Dun.*	.311	60	238	212	34	66	107	14	0	9	39	0	1	0	25	0	38	2	1	4	.505	.382
Ginter, Keith, Kis.	.263	103	453	376	66	99	161	15	4	13	46	2	2	12	61	1	90	9	10	7	.428	.381
Gload, Ross, B.C.*	.298	133	556	490	80	146	208	26	3	10	74	2	5	5	53	3	76	3	1	8	.424	.369
Gomes, Tony, V.B.	.000	37	1	1	0	0	0	0	0	0	0	0	0	0	0	0	1	0	0	0	.000	.000
Goodwin, Tom, Char.*	.364	3	12	11	2	4	5	1	0	0	0	0	0	0	1	0	4	0	0	0	.455	.417
Grabowski, Jason, Char.*	.313	123	507	434	68	136	215	31	6	12	87	1	2	5	65	3	66	13	10	8	.495	.407
Graham, Jess, Sar.*	.268	129	538	462	66	124	188	33	5	7	65	6	2	19	49	3	77	5	4	8	.407	.361
Green, Kevin, B.C.	.167	11	26	24	1	4	4	0	0	0	2	1	0	0	1	0	10	0	1	0	.167	.200
Grimmett, Ryan, Lak.	.203	50	165	133	32	27	42	4	1	3	16	1	1	5	25	0	41	24	4	1	.316	.348
Haas, Danny, Sar.*	.241	87	273	241	18	58	76	8	5	0	24	2	2	6	22	1	54	4	3	5	.315	.317
Hall, Doug, Day.*	.248	31	106	101	9	25	33	8	0	0	8	2	1	0	2	0	11	2	0	1	.327	.260
Hall, Noah, Jup.	.236	119	468	398	57	94	134	10	3	8	49	6	7	8	49	1	60	32	11	12	.337	.327
Hall, Toby, St.P.	.297	56	235	212	24	63	90	13	1	4	36	1	3	2	17	0	9	0	2	7	.425	.350
Haltiwanger, Garrick, St.L.	.265	111	472	423	67	112	172	18	6	10	71	0	5	13	31	3	77	20	12	6	.407	.331
Hargreaves, Brad, Day.	.168	39	107	101	6	17	20	3	0	0	6	2	0	0	4	0	27	1	0	8	.198	.200
Harper, Brandon, B.C.	.268	81	320	280	35	75	96	9	0	4	40	4	3	3	30	2	31	1	1	4	.343	.342
Harrell, Ken, Tam.	1.000	1	1	1	1	1	1	0	0	0	1	0	0	0	0	0	0	0	0	0	1.000	1.000

Player, Team	Avg.	G	TPA	AB	R	H	TB	2B	3B	HR	RBI	SH	SF	HP	BB	IBB	SO	SB	CS	GDP	Slg.	OBP
Harrison, Jamal, F.M.	.189	30	114	95	6	18	25	1	0	2	11	0	2	1	16	0	24	0	2	1	.263	.307
Hatteberg, Scott, Sar.*	1.000	1	2	1	0	1	1	0	0	0	1	0	0	1	0	0	0	0	0	0	1.000	1.000
Hayes, Chris, Dun.	.305	60	230	190	42	58	95	15	2	6	41	4	1	9	26	1	37	12	4	3	.500	.412
Heinrichs, Jon, B.C.	.250	67	279	252	40	63	93	12	0	6	44	0	4	1	22	1	34	7	2	6	.369	.308
Henson, Drew, Tam.	.280	69	284	254	37	71	122	12	0	13	37	0	3	1	26	0	71	3	1	6	.480	.345
Hernandez, Michel, Sar.	.246	82	307	281	26	69	87	10	1	2	23	3	2	3	18	0	49	2	2	8	.310	.296
Hill, Nakia, V.B.	.180	19	55	50	6	9	15	0	3	0	4	1	0	0	4	0	12	0	1	0	.300	.241
Hinske, Eric, Day.*	.297	130	518	445	76	132	229	28	6	19	79	1	5	5	62	7	90	16	10	5	.515	.385
Honeycutt, Heath, B.C.	.285	103	413	376	58	107	156	18	8	5	50	0	3	9	25	1	78	6	1	10	.415	.341
Hook, Kevin, Jup.	.239	34	112	88	16	21	29	5	0	1	6	3	1	4	16	0	21	3	1	1	.330	.376
Hoover, Paul, St.P.	.272	118	482	408	66	111	160	13	6	8	54	0	4	16	54	3	81	23	7	13	.392	.376
Husted, Brent, V.B.	.000	47	1	1	0	0	0	0	0	0	0	0	0	0	0	0	1	0	0	0	.000	.000
Izturis, Cesar, Dun.†	.308	131	590	536	77	165	226	28	12	3	77	17	9	6	22	4	58	32	16	9	.422	.337
James, Kenny, Jup.†	.237	99	419	372	68	88	105	9	1	2	32	8	1	6	31	2	57	37	7	8	.282	.305
Jaramillo, Frank, Char.	.216	12	38	37	1	8	8	0	0	0	4	0	0	1	1	0	9	1	1	0	.216	.237
Jaramillo, Milko, V.B.†	.203	99	353	320	26	65	74	4	1	1	31	10	1	8	14	1	67	15	5	4	.231	.254
Jefferson, Reggie, Sar.*	.429	3	15	14	4	6	11	2	0	1	2	0	0	0	1	0	2	0	0	0	.786	.467
Jimenez, Felipe, Day.	.196	18	57	51	5	10	10	0	0	0	7	0	0	2	4	0	13	2	1	2	.196	.281
Johnson, Gary, Day.	.229	108	380	323	46	74	113	16	1	7	38	3	5	10	39	1	53	4	6	10	.350	.326
Johnson, Rontrez, Sar.	.300	132	591	494	97	148	210	30	4	8	59	8	7	8	74	0	63	18	15	7	.425	.395
Johnson, Tom, St.L.	.256	56	227	199	25	51	66	12	0	1	10	2	4	1	21	0	57	12	5	1	.332	.324
Jones, Aaron, Tam.*	.278	132	537	454	50	126	185	25	11	4	57	1	2	4	76	3	92	6	5	18	.407	.384
Jones, Jeremy, Char.	.194	11	35	31	4	6	10	1	0	1	4	0	0	0	4	0	10	1	0	1	.323	.286
Jorgensen, Randy, St.P.*	.219	26	102	96	6	21	30	6	0	1	5	0	1	0	5	1	11	0	0	7	.313	.255
Joyce, Jesse, Kis.	.143	4	7	7	2	1	1	0	0	0	0	0	0	0	0	0	2	0	0	0	.143	.143
Kawabata, Kyle, Cle.	.000	34	1	1	0	0	0	0	0	0	0	0	0	0	0	0	0	0	0	0	.000	.000
Kellner, Ryan, V.B.	.207	54	194	179	21	37	46	1	1	2	14	3	0	2	10	0	51	1	1	5	.257	.257
Kelly, Kenny, St.P.	.277	51	228	206	39	57	84	10	4	3	21	0	0	4	18	0	46	14	5	1	.408	.346
Key, Jeff, Sar.*	.234	25	88	77	9	18	29	6	1	1	13	0	1	0	11	0	12	4	2	4	.377	.318
Kiil, Skip, Cle.	.298	86	390	305	74	91	164	15	8	14	55	5	3	7	70	0	101	24	5	2	.538	.436
Kleinz, Larry, B.C.	.227	11	50	44	8	10	13	3	0	0	6	0	0	1	4	0	8	0	0	0	.295	.306
Knupfer, Jason, Cle.	.289	15	60	45	13	13	15	2	0	0	3	3	0	0	12	0	5	1	0	0	.333	.439
Kofler, Eric, Tam.*	.358	15	60	53	7	19	29	6	2	0	14	0	1	1	5	1	10	1	0	2	.547	.417
Langaigne, Selwyn, Dun.*	.294	62	223	201	35	59	76	9	1	2	25	3	3	0	16	0	29	5	5	2	.378	.341
Lauterhahn, Dan, Lak.	.270	63	168	152	19	41	56	7	1	2	14	2	1	0	13	0	22	4	3	1	.368	.325
Lawton, Matt, F.M.*	.571	4	17	14	3	8	9	1	0	0	2	0	0	0	3	0	1	1	0	0	.643	.647
Leach, Nick, V.B.*	.283	128	520	449	58	127	208	21	0	20	74	0	3	6	62	3	73	10	5	6	.463	.375
Ledesma, Aaron, St.P.	.143	2	8	7	0	1	2	1	0	0	0	0	0	0	1	0	1	0	0	1	.286	.250
Lentz, Ryan, Jup.*	.207	114	436	362	39	75	111	16	1	6	35	4	3	17	50	2	84	1	3	5	.307	.329
Leon, Carlos, Sar.†	.156	47	174	154	16	24	27	1	1	0	14	5	0	3	12	0	16	9	1	3	.175	.231
LeCroy, Matthew, F.M.	.279	89	380	333	54	93	175	20	1	20	69	0	1	3	42	3	51	0	1	10	.526	.364
Lindsey, Rodney, Lak.	.266	120	537	485	81	129	186	20	8	7	51	4	5	18	25	0	129	61	20	6	.384	.323
Logan, Kyle, Kis.*	.291	113	439	399	57	116	184	33	7	7	62	1	3	3	33	4	62	16	5	5	.461	.347
Lomasney, Steve, Sar.	.270	55	223	189	35	51	85	10	0	8	28	0	0	8	26	0	57	5	2	2	.450	.381
Lopez, Mendy, Sar.	.244	86	331	291	44	71	88	7	2	2	26	5	2	2	30	1	58	7	5	11	.302	.317
Lorenzo, Juan, F.M.†	.257	119	444	421	51	108	130	11	1	3	48	4	4	6	9	0	68	8	3	8	.309	.283
Lough, Aaron, F.M.	.143	5	14	14	0	2	2	0	0	0	0	0	0	0	0	0	3	0	0	0	.143	.143
Lutz, Manuel, Lak.*	.288	46	188	177	19	51	75	15	0	3	23	0	1	1	9	0	45	0	2	6	.424	.324
Machado, Anderson, Cle.†	.000	1	2	2	0	0	0	0	0	0	0	0	0	0	0	0	1	0	0	0	.000	.000
Maduro, Remy, B.C.*	.231	29	104	91	14	21	32	5	0	2	8	0	2	3	8	0	17	1	0	2	.352	.308
Mahoney, Sean, St.P.	.152	35	131	112	8	17	26	6	0	1	8	1	2	3	13	0	32	2	0	2	.232	.254
Malave, Jaime, Jup.	.400	3	13	10	2	4	6	2	0	0	2	0	1	0	2	0	1	0	0	0	.600	.462
Malone, Nate, Day.	.156	15	36	32	3	5	7	2	0	0	2	0	0	0	4	0	5	0	0	3	.219	.250
Manning, Nate, Day.	.252	110	439	393	48	99	161	23	3	11	57	2	4	7	33	1	83	2	2	10	.410	.318
Marsh, Roy, Sar.	.375	7	25	24	6	9	11	1	0	0	3	0	0	0	1	0	5	3	0	0	.458	.400
Marsters, Brandon, F.M.	.237	54	198	173	18	41	58	11	0	2	28	0	5	1	19	0	33	1	0	7	.335	.308
Marzano, John, Char.	.000	1	4	4	0	0	0	0	0	0	0	0	0	0	0	0	0	0	0	1	.000	.000
Mashore, Justin, Sar.-St.L.	.196	45	169	153	19	30	50	7	2	3	14	1	1	2	12	1	38	2	4	4	.327	.262
Mateo, Henry, Jup.*	.260	118	524	447	69	116	169	27	7	4	58	17	6	10	44	3	112	32	16	4	.378	.335
Matranga, David, Kis.	.231	124	563	472	70	109	155	20	4	6	48	9	2	12	68	0	118	17	10	3	.328	.341
Maxwell, Vernon, Tam.	.085	23	51	47	4	4	4	0	0	0	1	0	0	1	3	0	14	0	0	1	.085	.157
McBride, Gator, Sar.	.360	36	146	136	25	49	92	10	3	9	29	1	0	2	7	3	13	2	1	1	.676	.400
McConnell, Jason, F.M.†	.238	48	176	151	23	36	42	6	0	0	13	3	2	0	20	0	24	5	0	2	.278	.324
McGrath, Sean, St.L.	.222	35	80	72	7	16	17	1	0	0	6	3	1	1	3	0	17	0	0	1	.236	.260
McNamara, Rusty, Cle.	.321	69	316	274	40	88	113	12	2	3	43	2	2	9	29	1	22	5	3	8	.412	.401
Mejia, Maximiliano, V.B.	.218	28	100	87	14	19	26	4	0	1	20	2	1	2	8	0	25	4	2	1	.299	.296
Mejias, Erick, Char.†	.500	1	4	4	0	2	2	0	0	0	1	0	0	0	0	0	1	0	0	0	.500	.500
Melconian, Alex, B.C.	.263	58	243	205	26	54	74	6	1	4	20	4	1	9	24	0	48	11	9	5	.361	.364
Melian, Jackson, Tam.	.283	128	535	467	65	132	193	17	13	6	61	1	8	10	49	1	98	11	8	8	.413	.358
Mento, Alfredo, St.L.	.000	1	1	1	0	0	0	0	0	0	0	0	0	0	0	0	1	0	0	0	.000	.000
Michaels, Jason, Cle.	.306	122	529	451	91	138	223	31	6	14	65	1	6	3	68	2	103	10	7	7	.494	.396
Miller, Kenny, St.L.	.237	93	334	304	32	72	96	13	1	3	24	5	1	6	18	0	50	3	5	6	.316	.292
Mirizzi, Marc, Tam.†	.239	90	378	330	40	79	119	16	3	6	30	4	2	5	37	1	87	1	0	8	.361	.324
Monroe, Craig, Char.	.260	130	536	480	77	125	199	21	1	17	81	3	7	4	42	2	102	40	16	8	.415	.321
Montilla, Miguel, Tam.	.121	12	42	33	2	4	4	0	0	0	0	0	0	0	8	0	10	0	0	1	.121	.310
Moore, Kevin, V.B.†	.500	2	8	6	0	3	3	0	0	0	0	0	0	0	2	0	1	0	1	0	.500	.625
Moore, Lacarlo, Lak.*	.245	36	104	94	15	23	29	4	1	0	6	1	0	1	8	0	18	6	3	3	.309	.308
Moore, Ryan, Jup.*	.200	5	11	10	2	2	5	0	0	1	1	0	0	0	1	0	5	0	0	0	.500	.273
Mora, Juan, Lak.*	.125	3	9	8	1	1	2	1	0	0	0	0	1	0	0	0	3	0	0	0	.250	.125
Moreno, Justin, St.L.	.300	120	488	424	64	127	167	18	5	4	47	7	4	2	51	0	70	28	11	10	.394	.374
Morillo, Luis, Dun.*	.000	4	3	3	1	0	0	0	0	0	0	0	0	0	0	0	1	0	0	0	.000	.000
Morrison, Greg, Dun.*	.265	81	279	260	31	69	94	17	1	2	34	1	2	0	15	1	32	2	1	6	.362	.303
Moskau, Ryan, V.B.-B.C.	.000	26	3	2	1	0	0	0	0	0	0	0	1	0	0	0	1	0	0	0	.000	.000
Munson, Eric, Lak.*	.333	2	7	6	0	2	2	0	0	0	1	0	0	0	1	0	1	0	0	0	.333	.429
Nelson, Reggie, Lak.	.286	3	7	7	0	2	2	0	0	0	0	0	0	0	0	0	1	0	0	0	.286	.286

Player, Team	Avg.	G	TPA	AB	R	H	TB	2B	3B	HR	RBI	SH	SF	HP	BB	IBB	SO	SB	CS	GDP	Slg.	OBP
Neuberger, Scott, St.P.	.260	127	481	442	55	115	165	14	3	10	63	1	6	8	24	0	104	1	2	12	.373	.306
Newton, Kimani, V.B.	.265	62	242	211	29	56	67	7	2	0	18	0	1	1	29	0	67	7	5	4	.318	.355
Niles, Drew, B.C.†	.171	40	135	117	12	20	26	1	1	1	12	0	2	1	15	0	30	0	0	2	.222	.267
Nina, Amuarys, Char.	.265	112	481	426	65	113	144	15	5	2	29	5	2	3	45	0	101	24	12	9	.338	.338
Nunnari, Talmadge, Jup.*	.356	71	293	261	41	93	127	17	1	5	44	1	0	3	27	1	36	10	0	5	.487	.423
Olmeda, Jose, Sar.†	.269	53	171	160	20	43	66	12	1	3	20	1	2	2	6	0	39	1	3	3	.413	.300
Ozarowski, Rich, Lak.†	.272	52	196	173	24	47	73	8	6	2	23	4	2	3	14	0	23	4	1	4	.422	.333
Pagan, Felix, F.M.	.083	7	28	24	2	2	2	0	0	0	1	0	0	0	4	0	10	1	0	0	.083	.214
Parker, Chris, Lak.	.125	3	8	8	1	1	2	1	0	0	0	0	0	0	0	0	3	0	0	1	.250	.125
Patton, Cory, St.L.	.077	9	18	13	3	1	1	0	0	0	0	0	0	0	3	0	8	0	0	0	.077	.250
Payton, Jay, St.L.	.346	7	30	26	3	9	12	1	1	0	3	0	0	0	4	0	5	0	1	1	.462	.433
Peeples, Mike, Dun.	.288	132	607	541	100	156	262	34	6	20	68	5	5	7	49	1	80	20	11	7	.484	.352
Pena, Carlos, Char.*	.255	136	597	501	85	128	229	31	8	18	103	0	6	16	74	2	135	2	5	7	.457	.365
Pena, Jose, Char.	.230	64	208	187	39	43	64	9	3	2	24	2	1	1	17	0	32	8	7	1	.342	.296
Perez, Jersen, St.L.	.256	128	515	468	60	120	170	15	7	7	45	9	3	8	27	0	117	7	5	10	.363	.306
Perez, Josue, V.B.-Cle.†	.269	85	330	294	39	79	103	16	1	2	28	1	4	3	28	0	46	20	12	8	.350	.334
Perez, Nestor, St.P.	.264	111	391	364	33	96	106	8	1	0	23	14	1	2	10	0	53	4	5	8	.291	.286
Peters, Tony, Dun.	.244	116	374	316	58	77	135	12	2	14	50	4	3	6	44	1	97	15	4	3	.427	.344
Phelps, Josh, Dun.	.328	110	448	406	72	133	228	27	4	20	88	2	4	8	28	0	104	6	3	13	.562	.379
Phillips, Jason, St.L.	.258	81	318	283	36	73	114	12	1	9	48	0	4	8	23	0	28	0	1	10	.403	.327
Phoenix, Wynter, V.B.*	.347	62	254	202	43	70	99	10	2	5	31	1	1	8	42	4	30	6	5	1	.490	.474
Piedra, Jorge, V.B.*	.288	15	67	59	13	17	25	3	1	1	6	0	1	0	7	1	9	2	2	0	.424	.358
Pigott, Anthony, St.P.	.268	105	358	339	41	91	114	9	4	2	33	3	1	4	11	0	84	16	8	5	.336	.299
Pinto, Rene, Tam.	.229	22	76	70	9	16	28	5	2	1	6	1	1	1	3	0	19	0	0	3	.400	.267
Poeck, Chad, Char.	.000	10	2	2	0	0	0	0	0	0	0	0	0	0	0	0	1	0	0	0	.000	.000
Polidor, Wil, Cle.†	.238	52	165	151	18	36	45	9	0	0	14	0	1	2	11	2	18	1	0	4	.298	.297
Pond, Simon, Jup.*	.256	127	508	434	47	111	168	25	1	10	77	1	11	14	48	3	83	4	8	10	.387	.341
Prince, Tom, Cle.	.364	9	38	33	5	12	18	0	0	2	9	1	0	1	3	0	3	1	0	1	.545	.432
Punto, Nick, Cle.†	.305	106	478	400	65	122	155	18	6	1	48	3	5	3	67	3	53	16	7	13	.388	.404
Quatraro, Matt, St.P.	.261	73	235	218	20	57	84	14	2	3	23	2	0	1	14	1	47	3	1	6	.385	.309
Quero, Pedro, Jup.	.239	114	445	419	36	100	132	16	2	4	52	1	7	2	16	1	83	13	12	12	.315	.266
Quinones, Marcus, Char.†	.261	7	25	23	2	6	7	1	0	0	3	0	0	1	1	0	5	0	1	0	.304	.320
Ramos, Kelly, St.L.†	.188	24	95	80	6	15	26	3	1	2	11	4	3	0	8	1	16	0	0	4	.325	.253
Ramsey, Brad, Day.	.212	105	394	330	47	70	112	15	0	9	44	2	6	16	40	1	67	1	3	17	.339	.321
Randolph, Jaisen, Day.	.272	130	566	511	70	139	171	16	5	2	37	4	0	8	43	1	86	25	26	4	.335	.338
Reding, Josh, Jup.	.263	121	457	415	54	109	129	10	2	2	31	12	6	1	22	0	73	30	9	6	.311	.297
Reed, Brian, B.C.	.214	19	60	56	3	12	14	2	0	0	1	0	0	1	3	0	20	2	1	2	.250	.267
Reese, Nate, B.C.	.266	70	264	237	25	63	96	12	0	7	38	2	5	2	18	0	44	0	0	7	.405	.317
Relaford, Desi, Cle.†	.286	2	8	7	1	2	2	0	0	0	1	0	0	0	1	0	1	0	0	0	.286	.375
Rhodes, Nicholas, St.P.	.500	1	3	2	2	1	4	0	0	1	1	0	0	0	1	0	0	0	0	0	2.000	.667
Richards, Rowan, Char.	.265	9	35	34	5	9	13	1	0	1	5	0	1	0	0	0	8	0	1	0	.382	.257
Rico, Diego, Day.*	.282	100	383	344	50	97	141	22	5	4	42	3	4	6	26	2	66	10	4	6	.410	.339
Riggan, Jerrod, St.L.	.000	44	1	1	0	0	0	0	0	0	0	0	0	0	0	0	1	0	0	0	.000	.000
Rigsby, Randy, B.C.*	.262	106	408	362	41	95	129	16	6	2	37	3	3	6	34	2	76	6	3	6	.356	.333
Rios, Brian, Lak.	.281	119	465	430	60	121	180	27	7	6	44	0	6	5	24	1	47	7	3	13	.419	.323
Rivera, Juan, Tam.	.263	109	466	426	50	112	178	20	2	14	77	0	8	5	26	3	67	5	4	13	.418	.308
Rivera, Mike, Lak.	.278	104	401	370	44	103	169	20	2	14	72	0	8	3	20	0	59	1	1	10	.457	.314
Roach, Jason, St.L.	.215	115	457	409	51	88	154	21	0	15	62	3	6	9	30	0	122	6	0	11	.377	.280
Rodriguez, John, Tam.*	.305	71	317	269	37	82	126	14	3	8	43	1	3	3	41	7	52	2	5	5	.468	.399
Rodriguez, Luis, Sar.	.289	31	126	114	19	33	50	8	0	3	14	1	2	1	8	0	17	5	1	2	.439	.336
Rodriguez, Mike, Dun.	.281	80	282	260	36	73	104	17	1	4	30	3	0	2	17	0	40	3	2	9	.400	.330
Rodriguez, Ronny, Sar.	.250	4	13	12	4	3	4	1	0	0	0	1	0	0	0	0	2	0	0	1	.333	.250
Rolls, Damian, V.B.	.297	127	533	474	68	141	198	26	2	9	54	4	5	14	36	2	66	24	13	6	.418	.361
Romano, Jason, Char.	.312	120	522	459	84	143	237	27	14	13	71	4	7	13	39	2	72	34	16	4	.516	.376
Rose, Mike, Kis.†	.277	95	367	303	61	84	137	16	2	11	32	0	2	3	59	0	64	12	6	7	.452	.398
Ross, David, V.B.	.227	114	435	375	47	85	127	19	1	7	39	1	6	7	46	1	111	5	10	10	.339	.318
Royster, Aaron, Cle.	.317	11	44	41	6	13	19	2	2	0	5	0	0	0	3	0	10	1	0	3	.463	.364
Rupp, Chad, Dun.	.308	4	18	13	4	4	9	2	0	1	7	0	0	0	5	0	4	0	0	0	.692	.500
Ryan, Mike, F.M.*	.274	131	585	507	85	139	199	26	5	8	71	4	6	5	63	2	60	3	4	11	.393	.356
Salazar, Jeremy, Cle.	.300	2	10	10	1	3	4	1	0	0	1	0	0	0	0	0	2	0	0	0	.400	.300
Salinas, Trey, St.P.	.250	10	32	32	5	8	14	6	0	0	2	0	0	0	0	0	6	0	0	1	.438	.250
Sandberg, Jared, St.P.	.276	136	570	504	73	139	231	24	1	22	96	1	5	9	51	0	133	8	2	12	.458	.350
Sandusky, Scott, Jup.	.254	108	390	354	31	90	104	9	1	1	22	7	0	8	20	0	72	4	5	6	.294	.309
Sapp, Damian, Sar.	.197	86	347	289	38	57	109	11	1	13	48	0	2	12	44	0	102	0	0	8	.377	.326
Schifano, Tony, B.C.	.248	45	160	141	21	35	46	3	1	2	15	3	2	2	12	0	36	2	2	1	.326	.312
Simms, Mike, Char.	.220	12	51	41	7	9	16	1	0	2	9	0	1	1	8	0	3	0	0	3	.390	.353
Smalls, Terrence, B.C.*	.208	32	87	77	5	16	17	1	0	0	5	2	0	2	6	0	8	5	2	1	.221	.282
Smith, Jason, Day.*	.261	39	158	142	22	37	61	5	2	5	26	0	1	3	12	3	29	9	3	2	.430	.329
Smith, Nestor, F.M.†	.283	96	360	329	39	93	131	14	6	4	34	2	5	8	16	1	67	8	7	3	.398	.327
Smith, Rod, Tam.†	.264	126	591	507	92	134	201	33	8	6	45	3	1	11	69	0	102	38	18	1	.396	.364
Solano, Danny, Char.	.271	116	513	421	64	114	161	18	4	7	44	12	0	6	74	0	74	21	13	3	.382	.387
Soriano, Fred, Dun.	.213	46	149	136	21	29	46	5	0	4	17	3	0	1	9	0	35	3	4	5	.338	.267
Soules, Ryan, Tam.*	.254	22	89	71	12	18	31	5	1	2	12	0	3	1	14	0	22	0	0	0	.437	.371
Stanton, Tom, St.L.*	.171	37	98	82	10	14	28	6	1	2	5	1	0	3	12	0	38	1	1	2	.341	.299
Steele, Alex, Lak.	.212	16	59	52	3	11	14	3	0	0	3	0	0	1	6	0	17	0	0	0	.269	.305
Stocker, Kevin, St.P.†	.091	3	12	11	2	1	1	0	0	0	0	0	0	0	1	0	2	0	0	0	.091	.167
Stodgel, Jeff, V.B.†	.211	44	135	123	14	26	31	1	2	0	8	1	0	1	10	0	24	3	4	3	.252	.276
Strange, Mike, Dun.	.375	3	9	8	2	3	6	0	0	1	3	0	0	0	1	0	3	0	0	0	.750	.444
Stromsborg, Ryan, Dun.	.224	20	80	76	5	17	30	10	0	1	9	0	1	0	3	0	17	1	1	1	.395	.250
Taveras, Luis, Char.	.263	95	348	308	36	81	125	18	4	6	46	3	4	3	30	0	69	10	4	6	.406	.330
Terrell, Jeff, Cle.*	.283	109	440	385	63	109	141	18	4	2	45	3	5	5	42	2	44	13	8	8	.366	.357
Thames, Marcus, Tam.	.244	69	307	266	47	65	118	12	4	11	38	1	2	3	33	1	58	3	0	1	.444	.332
Thomas, J.J., Kis.	.230	88	314	287	36	66	129	15	0	16	44	1	4	2	20	0	109	0	0	4	.449	.281
Thompson, Nick, Cle.	.111	9	33	27	4	3	4	1	0	0	1	0	0	2	4	0	12	0	1	0	.148	.273
Tinoco, Luis, Cle.	.182	32	123	110	15	20	23	3	0	0	6	0	1	4	8	0	23	1	0	1	.209	.260

Player, Team	Avg.	G	TPA	AB	R	H	TB	2B	3B	HR	RBI	SH	SF	HP	BB	IBB	SO	SB	CS	GDP	Slg.	OBP
Tomberlin, Andy, St.L.*	.379	9	35	29	4	11	15	1	0	1	4	0	0	2	4	0	8	2	0	0	.517	.486
Torres, Gabby, F.M.	.221	22	75	68	7	15	21	3	0	1	6	1	1	2	3	0	8	0	0	5	.309	.270
Torres, Jaime, Tam.	.273	9	36	33	1	9	10	1	0	0	3	0	0	2	1	0	4	1	0	4	.303	.333
Tucker, Jon, Jup.*	.400	3	11	10	0	4	4	0	0	0	0	0	0	0	1	0	1	0	2	0	.400	.455
Twombley, Dennis, Tam.	.243	15	43	37	3	9	10	1	0	0	3	0	0	0	6	0	11	0	0	1	.270	.349
Uccello, Jeff, Sar.	.281	10	36	32	4	9	13	4	0	0	2	1	0	0	3	0	6	0	0	0	.406	.343
Ugueto, Luis, B.C.†	.133	12	38	30	1	4	4	0	0	0	3	1	0	0	7	0	5	1	0	3	.133	.297
Urquhart, Derick, Jup.*	.182	23	51	44	5	8	9	1	0	0	5	0	0	0	7	0	7	2	0	0	.205	.294
Valent, Eric, Cle.*	.288	134	594	520	91	150	259	31	9	20	106	1	10	5	58	5	110	5	3	10	.498	.359
Van Iten, Robert, Cle.*	.264	98	391	345	48	91	124	16	1	5	51	4	7	4	31	1	63	3	4	7	.359	.326
Vargas, Arias, Lak.	.122	21	47	41	2	5	5	0	0	0	2	1	0	1	4	0	13	0	0	0	.122	.217
Vasquez, Alejandro, Kis.*	.236	79	291	275	31	65	91	6	4	4	29	0	1	1	14	0	40	3	5	8	.331	.275
Velazquez, Jose, St.P.*	.260	112	453	404	43	105	133	15	2	3	69	2	7	3	37	4	46	2	5	5	.329	.322
Vento, Mike, Tam.	.259	70	277	255	37	66	99	10	1	7	28	0	2	3	17	1	69	2	3	1	.388	.310
Vessel, Andrew, Day.	.208	20	80	77	7	16	26	4	0	2	8	0	0	1	2	0	15	1	0	1	.338	.238
Wakeland, Chris, Lak.*	.412	4	17	17	3	7	8	1	0	0	7	0	0	0	0	0	0	1	0	0	.471	.412
Ware, Jeremy, Jup.	.320	7	27	25	5	8	16	2	0	2	11	0	0	0	2	0	5	3	0	0	.640	.370
Ware, Ryan, Char.	.182	67	212	181	16	33	39	3	0	1	15	5	3	1	22	1	40	6	3	3	.215	.271
Washington, Kelley, B.C.	.269	57	216	197	30	53	79	6	4	4	30	4	2	2	11	0	56	13	7	4	.401	.311
Wells, Vernon, Dun.	.343	70	293	265	43	91	144	16	2	11	43	0	1	1	26	0	34	13	2	6	.543	.403
Wesson, Barry, Kis.	.216	115	386	352	32	76	105	15	1	4	34	2	2	4	26	0	84	8	7	3	.298	.276
Whitby, Cory, Sar.*	.200	3	7	5	0	1	1	0	0	0	0	0	0	0	2	0	1	0	0	0	.200	.429
Wigginton, Ty, St.L.	.292	123	522	456	69	133	229	23	5	21	73	4	2	4	56	4	82	9	12	5	.502	.373
Winrow, Gary, Tam.*	.429	3	7	7	1	3	3	0	0	0	0	0	0	0	0	0	0	0	0	1	.429	.429
Wood, Jason, Lak.	.235	5	22	17	0	4	4	0	0	0	1	0	0	1	4	1	2	0	1	0	.235	.409
Yates, Chris, Kis.	.250	16	41	36	2	9	10	1	0	0	4	0	0	1	4	0	8	3	4	1	.278	.341
Young, Mike, Dun.	.313	129	566	495	86	155	212	36	3	5	83	1	5	4	61	2	78	30	6	10	.428	.389
Zapata, Alexis, Lak.	.245	115	444	404	52	99	139	15	5	5	45	3	2	2	33	0	116	7	5	16	.344	.304
Zech, Scott, Jup.	.281	68	250	203	28	57	73	13	0	1	18	10	3	5	29	0	30	15	5	1	.360	.373

GRAND SLAMS: Chavera, Ensberg, Fischer, Gload, Johnson, Ware, 2 each; Bautista, Bearden, Cole, Grabowski, Hall, Haltiwanger, Harper, Jaramillo, Kiil, LeCrow, Logan, Manning, Matranga, Melian, Neuberger, Olmeda, Pond, Rios, Romano, Rupp, Ryan, Sapp, Thames, Vessel, Wigginton, 1 each.

AWARDED FIRST BASE ON CATCHER'S INTERFERENCE: Fuentes 3 (Taveras, Kellner, Hoover); Patton 2 (Forbush 2); Bennett 2 (Ellis, Sandusky); Thames 2 (Bennett, Taveras); Kleinz (Forbush); Bell (Forbush); Nunnari (Sapp); Reding (Quatraro); LeCroy (Rose); Rivera (Ellis); Crespo (Lomasney); James (Taveras); Morrison (Fuentes); Franco (Sandusky); Peters (Taveras); Lopez (Harper); Gload (Rodriguez); Sandusky (Kellner).

PLAYERS WITH TWO OR MORE TEAMS

Player, Team	Avg.	G	TPA	AB	R	H	TB	2B	3B	HR	RBI	SH	SF	HP	BB	IBB	SO	SB	CS	GDP	Slg.	OBP
Mashore, Justin, Sar.	.163	17	55	49	6	8	17	3	0	2	4	1	0	0	5	0	13	1	0	1	.347	.241
Mashore, Justin, St.L.	.212	28	114	104	13	22	33	4	2	1	10	0	1	2	7	1	25	1	4	3	.317	.272
Moskau, Ryan, V.B.	.000	17	3	2	1	0	0	0	0	0	0	1	0	0	0	0	0	0	0	0	.000	.000
Moskau, Ryan, B.C.	.000	9	0	0	0	0	0	0	0	0	0	0	0	0	0	0	0	0	0	0	.000	.000
Perez, Josue, V.B.†	.279	62	227	201	24	56	78	14	1	2	22	1	2	2	21	0	29	14	11	5	.388	.350
Perez, Josue, Cle.†	.247	23	103	93	15	23	25	2	0	0	6	0	2	1	7	0	17	6	1	3	.269	.301

1999 PITCHING
TEAM

Team	W	L	Pct.	ERA	G	CG	ShO	Sv.	IP	H	TBF	R	ER	HR	SH	SF	HB	BB	IBB	SO	WP	Bk.
Jupiter	73	65	.529	3.17	138	6	13	32	1209.2	1056	5041	509	426	65	40	44	69	402	12	885	65	9
Tampa	78	58	.574	3.43	136	4	9	42	1194.2	1154	5113	561	455	60	46	33	42	415	26	1002	57	6
St. Petersburg	74	63	.540	3.69	137	3	12	40	1177.1	1227	5065	585	483	57	41	37	2	362	9	805	75	7
Kissimmee	71	66	.518	3.72	137	9	8	31	1190.2	1143	5093	595	492	80	41	39	62	416	21	918	97	11
St. Lucie	68	70	.493	3.83	138	7	7	31	1201.0	1177	5240	637	511	71	52	32	56	533	29	957	67	13
Dunedin	86	51	.628	3.88	137	6	9	42	1195.2	1131	5117	592	515	86	33	78	475	11	967	60	10
Charlotte	69	70	.496	4.16	139	10	8	34	1189.2	1275	5245	669	550	83	39	58	75	481	7	816	70	16
Clearwater	77	59	.566	4.18	136	5	11	44	1204.2	1323	5302	690	559	85	42	44	51	406	20	798	77	14
Daytona	63	75	.457	4.25	138	10	9	34	1164.2	1151	5134	694	550	103	44	41	42	73	540	12	981	91	7
Lakeland	65	73	.471	4.38	138	7	3	28	1192.2	1243	5230	681	581	106	44	49	58	471	13	843	57	9
Sarasota	67	72	.482	4.44	139	3	7	38	1189.0	1311	5311	709	586	88	37	50	2	443	24	929	93	6
Brevard County	61	74	.452	4.44	135	13	7	27	1171.1	1228	5153	686	578	96	43	45	84	430	11	789	66	9
Fort Myers	60	79	.432	4.55	139	5	9	20	1187.2	1307	5263	716	601	79	44	54	63	469	6	884	89	11
Vero Beach	48	85	.361	4.67	133	5	5	32	1126.0	1145	4985	679	584	122	47	51	79	482	11	819	77	16

INDIVIDUAL

TOP QUALIFIERS FOR EARNED-RUN AVERAGE TITLE
Minimum 112 innings. *Lefthanded pitcher.

Pitcher, Team	W	L	Pct.	ERA	G	GS	CG	ShO	GF	Sv.	IP	H	TBF	R	ER	HR	SH	SF	HB	BB	IBB	SO	WP	Bk.
!reland, Eric, Kis.	10	7	.588	2.06	24	24	5	2	0	0	170.1	145	684	59	39	12	7	1	8	30	1	133	13	2
Comer, Scott, B.C.*	9	4	.692	2.35	19	19	5	1	0	0	130.0	120	502	38	34	3	3	4	3	5	0	85	0	1
Lundberg, Dave, Char.	14	7	.667	2.83	30	21	4	1	1	0	156.0	162	656	63	49	4	2	6	9	44	1	81	4	4
Gonzalez, Dicky, St.L.	14	9	.609	2.83	25	25	3	0	0	0	168.2	156	673	66	53	11	4	0	6	30	1	143	4	1
Flores, Randy, Tam.*	11	4	.733	2.87	21	20	1	1	1	0	135.0	118	555	56	43	4	4	4	7	38	0	99	5	0
Navarro, Scott, Kis.*	8	3	.727	2.88	37	11	1	1	5	0	112.2	108	452	39	36	4	5	5	3	17	3	86	7	2
Rodriguez, Wilfredo, Kis.*	15	7	.682	2.88	25	24	0	0	1	0	153.1	108	624	55	49	8	2	5	13	62	0	148	5	1
Estrella, Leo, Dun.	14	7	.667	3.21	27	24	2	2	0	0	168.0	166	696	74	60	11	6	5	17	47	0	116	6	1
Sneed, John, Dun.	11	2	.846	3.45	21	20	0	0	0	0	125.1	107	511	53	48	10	3	4	6	36	1	143	5	0
Moskau, Ryan, V.B.-B.C.*	9	8	.529	3.60	26	26	2	0	0	0	167.2	149	704	76	67	12	7	4	8	61	0	108	6	4
Moraga, David, Jup.*	8	6	.571	3.66	23	23	2	2	0	0	137.2	124	575	63	56	8	4	0	4	44	0	91	6	0
Brea, Lesli, St.L.	1	7	.125	3.73	32	18	0	0	9	3	120.2	95	515	64	50	4	2	2	4	68	1	136	7	3

Pitcher, Team	W	L	Pct.	ERA	G	GS	CG	ShO	GF	Sv.	IP	H	TBF	R	ER	HR	SH	SF	HB	BB	IBB	SO	WP	Bk.
Fisher, Peter, F.M.	5	10	.333	3.74	25	24	0	0	0	0	146.2	171	639	74	61	10	3	6	9	38	0	91	14	3
McClellan, Matt, Dun.	13	5	.722	3.79	26	25	1	0	0	0	147.1	114	612	69	62	15	1	5	10	61	0	146	6	3
Flohr, Adam, St.P.*	6	6	.500	3.80	31	18	0	0	2	0	135.0	164	587	78	57	10	6	1	9	30	0	64	9	2

DEPARTMENTAL LEADERS: W—Rodriguez, 15; L—Lynch, Richards, Taczy, 14 each; Pct.—Sneed, .846; G—Nickle, 60; GS—Thomas, 27; CG—Comer, Ireland, 5 each; ShO—several players tied, 2 each; GF—Nickle, 50; Sv.—Ellison, 35; IP—Ireland, 170.1; H—Garrett, 189; TBF—Moskau, 704; R—Teut, 113; ER—Teut. Mills, 94; HR—Johnson, 20; SH—Carnes, 8; SF—Taczy, 10; HB—Lampley, 18; BB—Mills, 87; IBB—Cubillan, 6; SO—Rodriguez, 148; WP—Mills, 20; BK—Lundberg, Moskau, 4 each.

ALL PITCHERS

*Lefthanded pitcher.

Pitcher, Team	W	L	Pct.	ERA	G	GS	CG	ShO	GF	Sv.	IP	H	TBF	R	ER	HR	SH	SF	HB	BB	IBB	SO	WP	Bk.
Adair, Derek, Cle.	1	0	1.000	3.21	9	0	0	0	4	3	14.0	16	58	5	5	0	0	0	0	1	0	9	0	0
Adams, Willie, Sar.	1	1	.500	1.98	2	2	0	0	0	0	13.2	14	58	5	3	1	0	0	1	1	0	6	0	0
Agamennone, Brandon, Jup.	4	2	.667	3.15	16	9	0	0	0	0	65.2	51	268	31	23	4	2	4	3	15	0	41	1	2
Akin, Aaron, B.C.	5	8	.385	5.13	27	15	1	0	5	0	108.2	149	496	79	62	17	4	6	12	34	0	55	3	1
Albin, Scott, Jup.	0	1	.000	4.50	2	0	0	0	2	1	2.0	4	12	4	1	0	0	1	0	1	1	3	0	0
Alvarez, Victor, V.B.*	4	4	.500	1.97	12	12	1	0	0	0	73.0	56	280	21	16	4	1	1	2	16	0	57	1	1
Antczak, Chuck, Cle.	0	0	.000	0.00	1	0	0	0	1	0	3.0	3	15	2	0	1	0	1	1	0	0	0	0	0
Arrojo, Rolando, St.P.	0	1	.000	4.50	2	2	0	0	0	0	10.0	11	43	6	5	0	0	1	0	1	0	10	0	0
Arteaga, J.D., St.L.*	0	1	.000	3.60	1	1	0	0	0	0	5.0	3	19	2	2	1	0	1	0	2	0	0	0	0
Avery, Paul, V.B.*	2	7	.222	4.83	32	7	0	0	10	0	78.1	82	369	51	42	5	5	9	4	46	2	57	9	3
Baginski, Jr., Thomas, Lak.*	0	0	.000	6.43	6	0	0	0	2	0	7.0	10	37	5	5	1	0	1	0	7	0	5	0	0
Bailie, Matt, Cle.	0	0	.000	3.00	2	0	0	0	2	0	3.0	2	14	1	1	0	0	0	0	3	0	5	0	0
Barkley, Brian, Sar.*	1	0	1.000	0.00	1	0	0	0	0	0	3.0	2	12	0	0	0	0	0	0	1	0	2	0	0
Barnsby, Scott, V.B.	0	0	.000	8.22	4	0	0	0	0	0	7.2	12	39	10	7	1	0	0	0	2	0	7	2	0
Barry, Shawn, St.L.*	3	4	.429	6.99	46	0	0	0	11	0	37.1	35	199	33	29	4	4	2	6	46	3	40	12	0
Bauder, Mike, Lak.*	1	3	.250	4.40	28	0	0	0	12	1	43.0	56	201	22	21	1	6	1	2	19	3	30	4	0
Beech, Matt, Cle.*	0	0	.000	7.71	2	2	0	0	0	0	4.2	7	24	5	4	0	0	1	0	2	0	3	0	0
Belcher, B.J., Char.	2	2	.500	4.62	15	4	0	0	3	0	37.0	48	173	22	19	4	1	2	2	19	0	15	0	1
Belovsky, Josh, Sar.	6	2	.750	2.36	48	0	0	0	43	20	53.1	42	223	15	14	1	7	0	4	23	5	53	5	0
Benoit, Joaquin, Char.	7	4	.636	5.31	22	22	0	0	0	0	105.0	117	483	67	62	5	1	7	11	50	0	83	3	2
Berger, Craig, St.L.	1	3	.250	4.89	36	0	0	0	26	9	38.2	49	188	22	21	2	3	0	3	25	3	21	3	0
Betancourt, Rafael, Sar.	0	0	.000	0.00	6	0	0	0	5	4	7.0	5	25	0	0	0	0	0	0	1	0	6	0	0
Black, Brett, Cle.	3	3	.500	5.16	34	0	0	0	19	3	45.1	55	194	30	26	5	2	4	2	6	4	27	0	1
Blank, Matt, Jup.*	9	5	.643	2.40	14	14	3	1	0	0	90.0	64	348	26	24	5	3	3	2	19	1	66	1	2
Bleazard, David, Dun.	6	6	.500	2.28	14	13	1	0	1	0	90.2	73	374	36	23	1	2	1	2	30	1	58	5	1
Blevins, Jeremy, Tam.	0	0	.000	0.00	1	0	0	0	0	0	1.2	4	11	3	0	0	0	0	1	1	0	0	0	0
Bohannon, Gary, St.L.	6	6	.500	4.42	32	12	1	0	8	2	108.0	131	480	66	53	4	7	5	8	30	2	58	5	1
Bond, Aaron, Char.	2	4	.333	6.45	8	7	0	0	1	0	37.2	54	183	34	27	1	2	2	3	23	0	18	3	0
Booker, Chris, Day.	2	5	.286	3.95	42	0	0	0	29	6	73.0	72	328	45	32	6	2	3	3	37	1	68	5	0
Bowe, Brandon, B.C.	2	0	1.000	3.15	9	0	0	0	3	1	20.0	18	86	7	7	4	0	0	0	10	0	21	3	1
Box, John, St.P.*	2	2	.500	5.05	42	0	0	0	16	0	57.0	71	259	34	32	6	3	4	4	15	0	39	9	0
Brackeen, Colin, Dun.*	2	1	.667	3.88	40	0	0	0	14	3	53.1	60	247	29	23	4	0	0	8	28	0	33	3	0
Brannan, Ryan, Cle.	4	4	.500	4.89	28	13	0	0	11	0	77.1	86	370	63	42	8	1	4	13	40	0	39	10	1
Brea, Lesli, St.L.	1	7	.125	3.73	32	18	0	0	9	3	120.2	95	516	64	50	4	2	2	4	68	1	136	7	3
Bridges, Donald, Jup.	4	6	.400	4.09	18	18	1	1	0	0	99.0	116	429	53	45	5	3	8	2	36	0	63	7	0
Brown, Elliot, St.P.	5	3	.625	2.67	38	0	0	0	15	3	57.1	44	230	20	17	1	2	1	3	14	1	42	5	0
Buller, Sean, Lak.*	0	0	.000	9.00	1	0	0	0	1	0	3.0	4	15	3	3	0	0	1	0	2	0	2	0	0
Bullinger, Jim, V.B.	0	2	.000	7.58	6	6	0	0	0	0	19.0	23	90	17	16	5	1	1	0	10	0	18	1	0
Burger, Rob, Cle.	1	2	.333	3.00	6	5	0	0	0	0	24.0	15	114	10	8	1	1	0	2	24	0	23	5	0
Cames, Aaron, B.C.	2	0	1.000	0.77	4	4	0	0	0	0	23.1	17	92	3	2	0	1	0	3	5	0	23	0	0
Campos, David, B.C.*	0	2	.000	6.75	13	0	0	0	7	0	25.1	25	121	24	19	3	0	3	2	16	0	17	2	0
Cannon, Jon, Day.*	3	5	.375	4.42	33	11	1	0	12	0	95.2	83	424	55	47	8	7	5	10	66	3	77	6	2
Carnes, Matt, F.M.	4	4	.500	3.67	52	1	0	0	20	4	81.0	74	343	48	33	4	8	7	2	26	0	67	6	1
Carrasco, Hector, F.M.	0	0	.000	4.50	1	1	0	0	0	0	2.0	2	8	1	1	0	0	0	0	1	0	1	0	0
Carroll, Dave, Tam.*	0	0	.000	2.08	2	1	0	0	1	0	4.1	6	22	1	1	0	0	0	0	2	0	5	0	0
Castillo, Jose, Lak.	2	1	.667	2.63	8	0	0	0	6	0	13.2	7	54	4	4	1	0	1	0	5	2	11	0	0
Castro, Eleuterio, Sar.	1	0	1.000	4.15	3	1	0	0	2	0	13.0	13	55	6	6	2	0	1	0	6	1	8	0	0
Cedeno, Blas, Cle.	4	4	.500	4.21	34	0	0	0	8	1	57.2	63	243	33	27	5	2	4	1	17	1	42	4	0
Cedeno, Jovanny, Char.	1	0	1.000	5.40	1	1	0	0	0	0	5.0	7	24	3	3	1	0	0	1	1	0	5	0	0
Cepeda, Victor, Lak.	0	6	.000	7.07	11	3	0	0	0	0	28.0	41	139	27	22	4	2	1	1	15	0	23	1	0
Cerros, Juan, St.L.	2	0	1.000	0.00	5	0	0	0	2	0	7.2	5	32	1	0	0	0	0	1	4	0	6	0	1
Cheek, Andrew, Sar.*	0	0	.000	13.50	2	0	0	0	1	0	4.0	8	25	6	6	0	1	0	0	6	0	0	1	0
Cheek, Shawn, Sar.	0	0	.000	9.00	1	0	0	0	1	0	1.0	1	5	1	1	0	0	0	0	1	0	0	0	0
Chiavacci, Ron, Jup.	4	4	.500	2.23	8	8	0	0	0	0	48.1	36	198	15	12	5	0	0	5	17	0	32	3	0
Choate, Randy, Tam.*	2	2	.500	4.50	47	0	0	0	17	1	50.0	51	224	25	25	4	4	0	2	24	5	62	4	0
Christensen, Benjamin, Day.	1	3	.250	6.35	4	4	0	0	0	0	22.2	25	106	16	16	4	1	1	3	11	0	18	1	1
Clark, Chris, B.C.	3	8	.273	5.55	28	12	0	0	10	1	86.0	93	395	60	53	5	3	5	6	48	1	48	12	0
Clark, Mark, Char.	0	0	.000	1.29	2	2	0	0	0	0	7.0	5	26	1	1	0	0	1	0	1	0	2	0	0
Coco, Pasqual, Dun.	4	6	.400	5.64	13	13	2	0	0	0	75.0	81	338	50	47	7	3	3	6	36	0	59	7	2
Collier, Lamonte, Cle.	0	0	.000	108.00	1	0	0	0	0	0	0.1	2	8	4	4	0	0	0	0	5	0	0	1	0
Comer, Scott, B.C.*	9	4	.692	2.35	19	19	5	1	0	0	130.0	120	502	38	34	3	3	4	3	5	0	85	0	1
Cordova, Jorge, B.C.	1	0	1.000	4.38	6	0	0	0	1	0	12.1	9	52	6	6	1	0	1	2	6	0	11	1	0
Cosgrove, Mike, F.M.	0	1	.000	3.38	7	0	0	0	4	1	10.2	12	52	8	4	2	1	1	0	6	1	9	0	0
Cotton, Joe, Cle.	5	3	.625	1.95	38	3	0	0	5	1	69.1	41	263	17	15	5	1	3	1	15	2	43	1	0
Creek, Ryan, Kis.	2	4	.333	4.08	7	7	0	0	0	0	35.1	36	153	19	16	4	1	2	4	12	0	23	0	0
Cubillan, Darwin, Tam.	7	4	.636	2.51	55	0	0	0	28	3	75.1	57	311	27	21	6	4	1	3	32	6	76	2	0
Cutchins, Todd, St.L.*	6	7	.462	3.96	25	25	1	0	0	0	129.2	127	579	68	57	10	4	4	5	82	0	106	4	1
Darrell, Tommy, Sar.	4	10	.286	4.99	30	12	1	0	6	3	101.0	118	455	75	56	8	5	7	5	30	5	67	11	0
Davies, Bob, F.M.	10	10	.500	4.59	25	23	1	1	1	0	137.1	156	594	82	70	13	3	7	5	38	1	105	6	2
Davis, Keith, Tam.-Lak.	5	1	.833	3.04	36	0	0	0	2	0	50.1	53	219	24	17	2	1	2	6	15	0	39	10	0
Davis, Tim, St.P.*	0	0	.000	27.00	1	0	0	0	0	0	0.2	3	6	2	2	0	0	0	0	1	0	1	1	0
Delacruz, Luis, Tam.	2	0	1.000	2.08	5	0	0	0	0	0	8.2	9	40	2	2	0	0	0	0	5	0	1	1	1

Pitcher, Team	W	L	Pct.	ERA	G	GS	CG	ShO	GF	Sv.	IP	H	TBF	R	ER	HR	SH	SF	HB	BB	IBB	SO	WP	Bk.
Dorame, Randey, V.B.*	0	2	.000	5.73	3	0	0	0	0	0	11.0	15	48	9	7	2	0	0	0	1	0	5	0	0
Dotel, Melido, V.B.	6	5	.545	4.46	31	6	0	0	14	1	72.2	56	344	45	36	6	1	1	5	73	0	57	8	1
Dougherty, Tony, Sar.	0	1	.000	3.00	4	0	0	0	2	0	3.0	3	13	1	1	1	0	0	1	1	0	2	0	0
Downs, Scott, F.M.-Day.*	5	1	.833	1.56	9	9	1	1	0	0	57.2	48	230	15	10	2	0	1	1	17	0	50	5	1
Duchscherer, Justin, Sar.	7	7	.500	4.49	20	18	0	0	0	0	112.1	101	475	62	56	14	2	5	12	30	0	105	5	0
Duckworth, Brandon, Cle.	11	5	.688	4.84	27	17	0	0	1	1	132.0	164	602	84	71	13	5	7	5	40	0	101	10	1
Duncan, Courtney, Day.	4	5	.444	5.54	15	11	1	1	3	1	65.0	70	300	60	40	6	3	2	4	34	1	48	5	0
Duncan, Sean, Char.*	7	6	.538	3.15	45	0	0	0	25	8	80.0	71	360	38	28	4	4	6	2	52	3	65	9	2
Duran, Roberto, Jup.*	0	2	.000	4.13	7	6	0	0	0	0	24.0	13	110	15	11	3	0	2	6	29	1	24	3	0
Durkovic, Peter, Lak.*	1	1	.500	4.71	17	0	0	0	8	3	21.0	19	88	12	11	4	1	1	2	5	0	11	1	1
Eason, Clay, Cle.	1	1	.500	4.00	18	0	0	0	3	0	27.0	26	125	18	12	3	3	2	0	17	3	31	4	1
Eaton, Adam, Cle.	5	5	.500	3.91	13	13	0	0	0	0	69.0	81	308	39	30	2	2	2	4	24	0	50	1	2
Einertson, Darrell, Tam.	0	0	.000	1.93	2	1	0	0	0	0	4.2	1	19	1	1	0	0	0	1	1	0	3	0	0
Elder, David, Char.	4	2	.667	2.84	24	1	0	0	16	4	44.1	33	186	15	14	2	4	0	2	25	0	42	4	0
Ellison, Jason, Tam.	0	2	.000	2.15	49	0	0	0	42	35	54.1	42	226	15	13	0	4	2	4	19	1	56	0	0
Estrella, Leo, Dun.	14	7	.667	3.21	27	24	2	2	0	0	168.0	166	696	74	60	11	6	5	17	47	0	116	6	1
Fennell, Barry, Day.*	1	2	.333	4.99	22	0	0	0	14	5	30.2	33	140	21	17	1	3	1	18	1	0	21	3	0
File, Bob, Dun.	4	1	.800	1.70	47	0	0	0	42	26	53.0	30	203	13	10	2	3	0	4	14	0	48	1	1
Fisher, Louis, Day.	3	8	.273	5.56	40	0	0	0	21	9	69.2	63	321	59	43	5	3	1	2	50	2	64	13	0
Fisher, Peter, F.M.	5	10	.333	3.74	25	24	0	0	0	0	146.2	171	639	74	61	10	3	6	9	38	0	91	14	3
Fleming, Emar, Char.	9	9	.500	4.30	24	22	1	1	1	0	142.1	138	608	81	68	19	4	6	10	62	0	100	4	3
Flohr, Adam, St.P.*	6	6	.500	3.80	31	18	0	0	2	0	135.0	164	587	78	57	10	6	1	9	30	0	64	9	2
Flores, Randy, Tam.*	11	4	.733	2.87	21	20	1	1	1	0	135.0	118	555	56	43	4	4	7	38	0	99	5	0
Florie, Bryce, Lak.	0	0	.000	0.00	1	1	0	0	0	0	3.0	0	9	0	0	0	0	0	0	0	0	7	0	0
Foster, Kris, V.B.	1	1	.500	1.76	8	0	0	0	3	0	15.1	10	59	5	3	1	0	2	0	2	0	15	0	0
Franklin, Wayne, Kis.*	3	0	1.000	1.53	12	0	0	0	7	1	17.2	11	69	4	3	0	1	0	1	6	0	22	0	0
Freehill, Mike, Char.	2	2	.500	3.57	17	0	0	0	16	8	17.2	15	79	11	7	1	1	0	2	9	0	18	5	0
Frey, Chris, Char.	0	1	.000	6.75	2	0	0	0	1	0	4.0	10	22	3	3	0	1	0	2	1	3	3	0	0
Gagliano, Steve, B.C.	2	5	.286	4.62	15	7	0	0	5	0	48.2	59	227	38	25	6	0	4	4	14	0	29	3	0
Gandy, Josh, F.M.*	4	3	.571	3.67	47	1	0	0	24	3	73.2	75	324	33	30	2	4	3	0	36	0	64	3	0
Garcia, Gabe, Kis.	0	1	.000	13.50	1	0	0	0	1	0	2.0	5	10	3	3	1	0	0	0	1	0	0	0	0
Gardner, Lee, St.P.	2	0	1.000	1.96	20	0	0	0	13	7	23.0	20	96	7	5	1	1	1	2	5	0	22	0	0
Garibaldi, Cecilio, St.P.	6	6	.500	4.36	21	15	0	0	1	0	99.0	109	429	56	48	7	3	4	12	28	2	52	6	1
Garrett, Josh, Sar.	8	10	.444	4.59	26	26	0	0	0	0	149.0	189	683	87	76	9	1	6	17	50	2	95	7	0
Garvin, Robert, B.C.	0	0	.000	0.00	1	0	0	0	0	0	2.2	2	12	0	0	0	0	2	0	3	0	0	0	0
Garza, Chris, F.M.*	1	2	.333	3.12	21	1	0	0	10	2	40.1	36	169	16	14	1	1	1	3	18	0	30	3	1
Gaskill, Derek, St.L.	2	0	1.000	8.04	22	0	0	0	6	0	28.0	34	145	30	25	2	3	1	3	24	0	28	6	0
Geary, Geoff, Cle.	10	5	.667	3.95	24	19	2	0	0	0	139.0	175	611	77	61	11	6	4	5	31	1	77	6	3
German, Yon, St.L.*	1	7	.125	5.40	10	9	0	0	1	0	55.0	67	250	41	33	5	2	0	21	3	40	4	3	
Glick, David, Kis.*	0	3	.000	4.70	32	0	0	0	10	0	44.0	47	206	29	23	1	2	2	4	22	2	41	3	0
Gomes, Tony, V.B.	4	5	.444	6.28	37	0	0	0	17	2	61.2	67	285	45	43	7	7	2	2	32	3	70	5	1
Gonzalez, Dicky, St.L.	14	9	.609	2.83	25	25	3	0	0	0	168.2	156	673	66	53	11	4	0	6	30	1	143	4	1
Gonzalez, Jeremi, Day.	0	0	.000	0.00	2	2	0	0	0	0	4.2	2	16	0	0	0	0	0	0	4	0	0	0	0
Grace, Bryan, Tam.	2	0	1.000	2.04	9	0	0	0	4	0	17.2	17	91	7	4	0	2	0	2	18	3	10	3	1
Greisinger, Seth, Lak.	0	0	.000	3.86	1	1	0	0	0	0	4.2	2	17	2	2	1	0	0	0	1	0	2	0	0
Gulin, Lindsay, Day.*	2	0	1.000	0.00	3	1	0	0	0	0	13.2	7	53	0	0	0	1	0	0	7	0	19	0	0
Guzman, Leiby, Char.	5	6	.455	5.88	19	18	0	0	1	0	93.1	114	420	67	61	16	0	5	9	40	0	45	5	0
Hafer, Jeff, St.L.	4	2	.667	3.22	36	2	0	0	21	5	67.0	74	306	43	24	3	3	3	2	16	4	51	3	2
Haigler, Phil, F.M.	6	3	.667	4.25	11	9	1	0	2	0	53.0	68	228	27	25	3	2	2	10	1	24	1	0	
Haines, Talley, St.P.	0	0	.000	0.00	2	0	0	0	1	0	4.1	1	13	0	0	0	2	0	0	4	0	0	0	
Hammons, Matt, Day.	2	4	.333	4.98	15	11	0	0	3	1	59.2	54	262	36	33	6	4	3	4	32	0	53	6	0
Hargreaves, Brad, Day.	0	0	.000	10.80	1	0	0	0	0	0	1.2	3	10	2	2	1	0	0	1	1	0	1	0	0
Harper, Travis, St.P.	5	4	.556	3.43	14	14	0	0	0	0	81.1	82	347	36	31	4	1	4	10	23	0	79	8	0
Hartshorn, Ty, Dun.	3	1	.750	6.68	7	7	0	0	0	0	31.0	43	150	25	23	3	0	3	2	16	0	30	1	0
Heath, Woody, Dun.	6	4	.600	5.00	22	14	0	0	1	0	102.2	109	462	67	57	11	1	5	3	47	1	89	3	1
Hebert, Cedric, V.B.	1	0	1.000	3.12	7	0	0	0	3	0	8.2	8	41	3	3	1	0	0	1	7	0	6	0	0
Hebson, Bryan, Jup.	7	6	.538	2.00	17	16	0	0	1	0	103.1	85	414	33	23	5	2	3	5	26	0	79	3	0
Hibbard, Billy, Dun.	3	2	.600	4.72	31	1	0	0	4	0	55.1	54	235	29	29	4	4	2	2	18	0	34	2	0
Hiljus, Erik, Lak.	0	0	.000	2.25	3	0	0	0	1	0	4.0	4	15	1	1	0	0	0	0	0	0	9	0	1
Hill, Kendall, F.M.	2	5	.286	6.41	39	4	0	0	12	0	80.0	99	378	68	57	8	3	1	4	42	0	55	11	3
Hostetler, Jim, Lak.	0	0	.000	8.49	31	0	0	0	17	0	41.1	51	201	44	39	5	0	7	0	31	1	27	3	0
Howard, Tom, F.M.*	1	2	.333	5.06	22	0	0	0	14	0	42.2	43	194	28	24	3	1	3	2	25	0	22	4	0
Huggins, David, Dun.	2	3	.400	3.09	42	3	0	0	12	1	70.0	72	325	29	24	3	2	0	1	52	4	57	3	1
Hughes, Mike, Jup.*	1	2	.333	4.70	17	2	0	0	6	0	30.2	41	145	17	16	2	1	3	16	0	22	2	0	
Hurtado, Victor, B.C.	0	2	.000	9.43	4	4	0	0	0	0	21.0	28	99	22	22	2	0	2	1	7	1	6	2	0
Husted, Brent, V.B.	2	4	.333	4.17	47	0	0	0	44	27	54.0	42	222	30	25	9	2	3	1	17	0	41	2	0
Infante, Asdrubal, Lak.	0	1	.000	4.50	1	1	0	0	0	0	6	4	21	2	2	1	0	0	3	0	3	0	0	
Ireland, Eric, Kis.	10	7	.588	2.06	24	24	5	2	0	0	170.1	145	684	59	39	12	7	1	8	30	1	133	13	2
James, Delvin, St.P.	3	0	1.000	3.18	3	2	0	0	1	0	17.0	18	71	6	6	0	0	0	3	4	0	6	1	0
Jimenez, Jason, St.P.*	4	4	.500	2.38	41	1	0	0	19	5	56.2	46	229	23	15	2	2	0	3	21	2	47	2	0
Johnson, Craig, Lak.	11	11	.500	5.13	26	25	0	0	1	0	144.0	176	638	93	82	20	6	7	6	31	0	98	2	0
Johnson, Mark, Tam.	1	0	1.000	1.50	1	0	0	0	0	0	6.0	4	22	1	1	1	0	0	0	1	0	6	0	0
Johnston, Sean, Day.*	2	5	.286	5.00	26	3	0	0	6	0	68.1	91	338	54	38	5	3	3	6	39	1	28	7	0
Julio, Jorge, Jup.	4	8	.333	3.92	23	22	0	0	1	0	114.2	116	491	62	50	6	3	5	3	34	0	80	11	1
Kaufman, John, St.P.*	1	2	.333	3.57	16	0	0	0	5	0	22.2	29	101	10	9	3	2	0	2	6	2	22	0	0
Kawabata, Kyle, Cle.	3	1	.750	1.15	33	0	0	0	18	7	47.0	36	191	11	6	2	2	1	2	10	0	37	3	0
Keagle, Greg, Lak.	1	3	.250	4.50	6	6	0	0	0	0	36.0	35	153	19	18	5	2	2	4	13	0	26	1	3
Keisler, Randy, Tam.*	10	3	.769	3.30	15	15	1	0	0	0	90.0	67	375	43	33	2	3	1	3	40	0	77	4	1
Kessel, Kyle, St.L.*	1	2	.333	4.63	8	8	0	0	0	0	35.0	35	157	22	18	4	2	1	1	16	0	24	0	0
Kirsten, Rick, Lak.	2	0	1.000	0.54	2	2	1	1	0	0	16.2	7	60	1	1	0	0	0	0	6	0	8	1	0
Knotts, Gary, B.C.	9	6	.600	4.60	16	16	3	2	0	0	94.0	101	402	52	48	7	1	3	8	29	0	65	1	0
LaChapelle, Yan, Dun.	2	3	.400	5.24	15	7	0	0	2	1	44.2	46	205	28	26	3	3	3	7	22	0	36	5	0
Lail, Denny, Tam.	1	3	.250	2.08	22	4	0	0	6	2	60.2	45	237	17	14	2	0	1	1	16	0	53	1	0
Lamarsh, Robert, Char.*	0	0	.000	2.70	1	1	0	0	0	0	3.1	9	18	1	1	0	0	0	0	0	0	0	0	0
Lampley, Daniel, Sar.	10	8	.556	4.55	25	25	2	1	0	0	140.1	152	623	85	71	13	1	5	18	54	1	126	7	0

Pitcher, Team	W	L	Pct.	ERA	G	GS	CG	ShO	GF	Sv.	IP	H	TBF	R	ER	HR	SH	SF	HB	BB	IBB	SO	WP	Bk.
Lanzetta, Tobin, V.B.	0	1	.000	3.38	4	0	0	0	3	0	5.1	3	23	2	2	0	1	0	1	3	1	2	1	0
Lara, Giovanny, Jup.	3	1	.750	2.76	33	0	0	0	15	0	65.1	59	264	24	20	1	7	2	0	18	2	42	2	1
Larkin, Andy, B.C.	0	1	.000	2.40	4	4	0	0	0	0	15.0	16	66	5	4	0	0	2	3	3	0	7	0	0
Lawrence, Clint, Dun.*	1	2	.333	7.61	15	3	0	0	7	1	23.2	29	115	23	20	5	1	0	0	20	0	16	3	0
Levan, Matt, B.C.*	2	3	.400	4.07	35	2	0	0	14	2	66.1	52	291	39	30	6	4	2	1	39	3	84	9	0
Lewis, Craig, Tam.	0	1	.000	5.27	5	1	0	0	0	0	13.2	18	62	9	8	1	2	0	3	0	12	2	1	0
Lidge, Bradley, Kis.	0	2	.000	3.38	6	6	0	0	0	0	21.1	13	82	8	8	0	0	0	11	0	19	2	0	
Lidle, Cory, St.P.	0	0	.000	0.00	2	2	0	0	0	0	5.0	2	19	0	0	0	0	0	0	2	0	0	0	0
Lira, James, St.P.	4	1	.800	3.05	36	0	0	0	13	0	44.1	45	191	18	15	1	2	2	2	17	1	25	4	0
Loewer, Carlton, Cle.	0	2	.000	7.71	3	3	0	0	0	0	7.0	10	31	6	6	0	0	0	1	0	5	2	0	
Lohrman, Dave, St.L.	4	0	1.000	3.08	43	1	0	0	16	0	76.0	64	325	33	26	3	4	1	4	46	4	75	5	0
Lohse, Kyle, Day.-F.M.	7	6	.538	3.90	16	16	1	1	0	0	94.2	95	397	49	41	9	4	5	4	25	0	74	2	0
Lopez, Albie, St.P.	0	0	.000	5.40	2	1	0	0	0	0	3.1	7	17	5	2	0	0	0	0	3	0	3	0	0
Loux, Shane, Lak.	6	5	.545	4.05	17	17	0	0	0	0	91.0	92	412	48	41	8	2	5	10	47	0	52	7	1
Love, Jeff, Kis.	2	3	.400	6.66	15	0	0	0	7	0	25.2	34	120	24	19	2	1	1	1	9	2	20	1	0
Lundberg, Dave, Char.	14	7	.667	2.83	30	21	4	1	1	0	156.0	162	656	63	49	4	2	6	9	44	1	81	4	4
Lynch, Jim, Kis.	3	14	.176	4.93	28	21	3	0	2	0	129.2	131	588	82	71	14	4	5	10	61	2	99	12	0
Lyons, Jonathan, Sar.	1	2	.333	5.92	23	0	0	0	7	0	24.1	44	131	25	16	2	1	1	1	11	2	18	2	0
Madero, Francisco, V.B.	2	6	.250	5.09	12	10	1	0	2	0	69.0	75	302	43	39	9	4	1	3	25	1	45	3	1
Maldonado, Esteban, Kis.	0	0	.000	3.38	8	1	0	0	3	0	10.2	6	50	6	4	1	0	0	2	12	0	4	6	0
Malko, Bryan, F.M.	7	9	.438	4.49	30	18	2	1	4	1	110.1	120	492	60	55	8	2	3	9	48	0	102	5	0
Maroth, Mike, Sar.-Lak.*	13	7	.650	3.94	23	22	0	0	0	0	128.0	142	568	72	56	4	7	4	10	42	1	75	13	2
Marquez, Robert, Jup.	3	0	1.000	0.00	13	0	0	0	9	3	15.2	5	60	2	0	0	2	0	1	6	0	15	0	1
Marrero, Darwin, Jup.	0	0	.000	13.50	2	0	0	0	0	0	1.1	1	7	2	2	0	0	0	0	2	0	4	1	0
Marriott, Mike, B.C.	1	5	.167	9.00	8	8	0	0	0	0	34.0	50	172	36	34	5	4	1	4	21	0	22	6	1
Marshall, Lee, F.M.	2	2	.500	1.47	28	0	0	0	18	5	36.2	32	144	10	6	1	4	3	0	5	0	25	1	0
Marsonek, Sam, Char.	3	9	.250	5.54	15	15	2	0	0	0	91.0	111	420	69	56	8	4	14	27	0	61	4	1
Marsters, Brandon, F.M.	0	0	.000	0.00	1	0	0	0	1	0	1.0	1	5	0	0	0	0	0	1	0	0	0	0	
Martinez, Jesus, Sar.*	1	2	.333	5.23	16	2	0	0	8	0	32.2	36	151	20	19	2	2	6	3	17	1	20	5	0
Martinez, Ramon, Sar.	1	0	1.000	3.00	3	3	0	0	0	0	12.0	11	54	7	4	1	2	1	2	7	0	9	1	0
Mattes, Troy, Jup.	3	0	1.000	3.70	5	5	0	0	0	0	24.1	27	103	11	10	2	1	1	3	7	0	12	0	0
Matz, Brian, Jup.*	5	2	.714	2.36	41	1	0	0	17	7	91.1	77	375	30	24	3	7	0	6	31	1	46	4	1
McClellan, Matt, Dun.	13	5	.722	3.79	26	25	1	0	0	0	147.1	114	612	69	62	15	1	5	10	61	0	146	6	3
McClellan, Sean, Dun.	0	0	.000	6.00	3	0	0	0	0	0	3.0	1	11	2	2	1	0	0	0	1	0	5	0	0
McConnell, Jason, F.M.	0	0	.000	0.00	1	0	0	0	1	0	1.0	1	4	0	0	0	0	0	0	0	0	1	0	0
McCurtain, Paul, B.C.	3	2	.600	3.43	40	0	0	0	32	12	57.2	59	261	32	22	1	0	1	2	25	0	49	2	1
McDonald, Jon, St.P.*	1	0	1.000	6.00	10	0	0	0	2	0	15.0	19	70	12	10	1	0	1	6	0	10	1	0
McEntire, Ethan, St.L.*	8	10	.444	3.84	22	21	0	0	0	0	129.0	130	562	68	55	8	5	6	5	62	0	63	4	0
McLeary, Marty, Sar.	1	0	1.000	12.08	8	0	0	0	0	0	12.2	29	73	20	17	1	2	1	1	7	0	11	2	0
McMullen, Jerry, Sar.*	1	3	.250	2.85	41	0	0	0	15	2	47.1	47	206	21	15	4	0	1	0	19	0	56	4	0
Mercedes, Carlos, Kis.	2	4	.333	4.92	41	1	0	0	10	2	75.0	82	340	51	41	5	2	6	2	31	3	39	8	2
Messman, Joe, Kis.	3	4	.429	2.43	45	0	0	0	40	15	59.1	38	251	20	16	4	0	4	0	35	2	47	6	2
Meyers, Mike, Day.	10	3	.769	1.93	19	17	2	0	2	0	107.1	68	436	30	23	9	2	3	9	40	0	122	4	0
Miller, Matt, Char.	1	2	.333	3.03	22	0	0	0	20	8	29.2	27	132	12	10	0	0	1	1	13	1	39	2	0
Miller, Matt, Lak.*	4	9	.308	4.15	19	19	1	0	0	0	108.1	108	473	58	50	9	5	2	2	45	0	82	0	1
Mills, Ryan, F.M.*	3	10	.231	8.87	27	21	0	0	3	0	95.1	121	499	107	94	6	0	6	16	87	1	70	20	0
Mlodik, Kevin, Char.	0	4	.000	4.07	25	0	0	0	13	0	48.2	52	229	29	22	2	5	4	3	30	0	33	12	0
Mobley, Kevin, Lak.	7	4	.636	3.82	46	5	0	0	12	2	96.2	107	444	48	41	11	5	8	3	26	1	73	5	0
Montgomery, Steve, V.B.	0	0	.000	2.43	9	6	0	0	1	0	37.0	28	145	12	10	5	0	0	4	10	0	33	4	0
Moody, Eric, Char.	0	0	.000	9.00	1	1	0	0	0	0	2.0	2	9	2	2	0	0	1	0	0	0	1	0	0
Moore, Chris, B.C.	0	0	.000	5.40	13	0	0	0	5	0	28.1	20	125	20	17	5	2	1	2	20	0	16	1	2
Moraga, David, Jup.*	8	6	.571	3.66	23	23	2	2	0	0	137.2	124	575	63	56	8	4	0	4	44	0	91	6	0
Mori, Kazuma, Jup.	1	0	1.000	7.36	3	0	0	0	3	0	3.2	3	19	4	3	0	0	1	1	2	0	2	1	0
Moskau, Ryan, V.B.-B.C.*	9	8	.529	3.60	26	26	2	0	0	0	167.2	149	704	76	67	12	7	4	8	61	0	108	6	4
Mota, Danny, F.M.	1	1	.500	2.41	11	0	0	0	3	0	18.2	19	79	5	5	0	1	1	0	5	0	22	0	0
Nakamura, Micheal, F.M.	2	0	1.000	1.83	14	0	0	0	6	2	19.2	9	74	5	4	1	2	2	0	5	0	18	1	0
Narcisse, Tyrone, Kis.	0	0	.000	6.75	4	0	0	0	3	0	5.1	10	29	4	4	0	0	1	2	0	3	0	0	
Nation, Joey, Day.*	2	0	1.000	1.38	2	2	0	0	0	0	13.0	8	47	2	2	0	0	0	2	0	11	0	0	
Navarro, Scott, Kis.*	8	3	.727	2.88	37	11	1	1	5	0	112.2	108	452	39	36	4	5	5	3	17	3	86	7	2
Nelson, Jeff, Tam.	0	0	.000	0.00	3	3	0	0	0	0	3.0	1	12	0	0	0	0	0	2	0	5	0	0	
Nicholson, John, Jup.	0	4	.000	21.60	4	4	0	0	0	0	8.1	9	60	21	20	1	1	1	6	19	0	3	4	0
Nickle, Douglas, Cle.	2	4	.333	2.29	60	0	0	0	50	28	70.2	60	299	25	18	1	1	1	4	23	3	70	6	0
Niebla, Ruben, V.B.*	0	0	.000	0.00	1	0	0	0	0	0	2.0	1	7	0	0	0	0	0	0	0	0	4	0	0
Noel, Todd, Tam.	3	7	.300	4.34	17	17	0	0	0	0	93.1	101	415	56	45	3	2	9	4	33	1	80	7	2
Ohman, Will, Day.*	2	5	.286	5.05	11	11	0	0	0	0	57.0	70	253	37	32	8	1	1	1	13	0	45	3	0
Olsen, Kevin, B.C.	2	5	.286	5.05	11	11	0	0	0	0	57.0	70	253	37	32	8	1	1	1	13	0	45	3	0
Ortega, Pablo, St.P.	1	2	.333	1.93	4	1	0	0	0	0	9.1	9	39	6	2	1	0	0	1	5	0	5	1	0
Padilla, Juan, F.M.	2	2	.500	3.48	22	0	0	0	11	0	33.2	32	146	14	13	1	3	2	1	17	2	28	3	0
Partenheimer, Brian, Sar.-B.C.*	3	3	.500	2.07	38	0	0	0	14	4	74.0	55	297	21	17	4	4	3	6	17	1	57	4	0
Pena, Juan, Sar.	0	1	.000	7.11	2	2	0	0	0	0	6.1	12	28	6	5	0	0	0	0	5	0	5	1	0
Persails, Mark, Kis.	1	1	.500	2.21	10	0	0	0	2	0	20.1	26	92	9	5	1	0	1	0	4	0	15	3	0
Person, Robert, Dun.	0	0	.000	3.00	1	1	0	0	0	0	3.0	4	12	1	1	0	0	0	1	0	3	0	0	
Pettitte, Andy, Tam.*	1	0	1.000	0.00	1	1	0	0	0	0	5.0	4	20	0	0	0	0	0	2	0	8	0	0	
Pettyjohn, Adam, Lak.*	3	4	.429	3.77	9	9	2	0	0	0	59.2	62	255	35	25	2	2	1	1	11	0	51	2	0
Phelps, Travis, St.P.	10	8	.556	4.24	24	23	1	1	0	0	133.2	148	574	70	63	6	4	4	11	39	0	101	2	0
Piersoll, Chris, Day.	7	3	.700	3.72	33	4	0	0	20	5	67.2	68	296	30	28	7	1	0	7	24	2	74	9	0
Pineda, Isauro, Sar.	2	1	.667	5.23	11	8	0	0	2	0	51.2	56	230	32	30	3	1	3	24	0	32	0	0	
Pineda, Luis, Lak.	1	0	1.000	1.04	8	0	0	0	8	0	8.2	6	39	2	1	0	0	0	7	0	8	0	0	
Poeck, Chad, Char.	0	0	.000	1.20	9	0	0	0	3	1	15.0	10	59	3	2	0	0	0	6	0	12	2	0	
Poland, Trey, Char.*	2	2	.500	0.84	5	5	1	1	0	0	32.1	16	120	4	3	1	0	1	0	8	0	28	0	0
Pontes, Dan, St.L.	0	0	.000	2.70	4	0	0	0	0	0	6.2	7	28	2	2	0	0	0	0	2	0	7	1	0
Pyc, David, Cle.*	3	0	1.000	0.00	7	0	0	0	5	0	10.0	7	35	0	0	0	0	0	1	0	9	0	0	
Quantrill, Paul, Dun.	0	1	.000	4.50	5	4	0	0	0	0	6.0	5	22	3	3	1	0	0	1	0	2	0	0	
Quarnstrom, Robert, Char.*	2	2	.500	3.51	30	0	0	0	16	4	59.0	68	260	30	23	3	2	5	2	16	0	38	3	1
Quezada, Edward, Jup.	2	6	.250	4.38	34	1	0	0	14	0	63.2	64	273	34	31	4	1	1	7	17	0	25	6	1

Pitcher, Team	W	L	Pct.	ERA	G	GS	CG	ShO	GF	Sv.	IP	H	TBF	R	ER	HR	SH	SF	HB	BB	IBB	SO	WP	Bk.
Quintal, Craig, Lak.	1	11	.083	4.84	26	16	2	0	4	2	109.2	129	490	74	59	10	3	3	10	27	3	45	2	0
Ramirez, Jose, Lak.*	5	5	.500	5.00	29	6	0	0	7	0	84.2	79	370	53	47	9	1	2	2	46	2	62	5	1
Rangel, Julio, Tam.	3	3	.500	2.93	12	9	0	0	1	1	55.1	48	225	23	18	1	1	2	2	17	1	36	4	0
Regalado, Maximo, V.B.	2	12	.143	5.80	20	19	1	0	0	0	90.0	110	429	65	58	16	5	3	12	49	0	58	7	0
Reith, Brian, Tam.	9	9	.500	4.70	26	23	0	0	0	0	139.2	174	616	87	73	12	7	4	4	35	1	101	4	0
Reitsma, Chris, Sar.	4	10	.286	5.61	19	19	0	0	0	0	96.1	116	440	71	60	11	1	4	10	31	1	79	7	3
Reyes, Eddy, St.P.	0	2	.000	1.88	37	0	0	0	33	25	38.1	31	172	13	8	0	4	1	6	23	1	30	0	0
Richards, Mark, B.C.	6	14	.300	6.13	26	24	2	0	2	2	133.2	171	624	107	91	14	7	5	13	51	0	54	5	2
Rico, Diego, Day.*	0	0	.000	0.00	1	0	0	0	1	0	1.0	0	4	0	0	0	0	0	0	2	0	0	0	0
Riggan, Jerrod, St.L.	5	5	.500	3.33	44	0	0	0	26	12	73.0	69	305	33	27	4	6	1	5	24	5	66	4	0
Roach, Jason, St.L.	0	0	.000	0.00	2	0	0	0	1	0	2.0	1	7	0	0	0	0	0	0	0	0	5	0	0
Robbins, Jake, Tam.	3	3	.500	4.75	7	7	0	0	0	0	41.2	44	187	30	22	3	1	2	2	19	2	31	5	0
Roberts, Rick, V.B.*	1	4	.200	6.04	11	10	0	0	1	0	44.2	54	208	35	30	7	3	2	2	25	0	29	6	0
Rodney, Fernando, Lak.	1	0	1.000	1.42	4	0	0	0	4	2	6.1	7	25	1	1	0	0	0	1	1	0	5	0	0
Rodriguez, Wilfredo, Kis.*	15	7	.682	2.88	25	24	0	0	1	0	153.1	108	624	55	49	8	2	5	13	62	0	148	5	1
Rogers, Brian, Tam.	8	10	.444	3.83	25	23	1	1	0	0	134.0	141	577	62	57	13	2	1	2	43	1	129	7	0
Roller, Adam, Sar.	0	0	.000	16.88	1	0	0	0	1	0	2.2	5	14	5	5	1	0	0	0	2	0	2	0	0
Romo, Greg, Lak.	8	4	.667	3.49	25	15	1	1	4	2	105.2	90	445	46	41	8	1	1	4	46	1	89	3	0
Rosario, Juan, St.P.	5	3	.625	2.67	15	15	0	0	0	0	94.1	80	391	34	28	2	5	3	11	25	0	37	2	1
Rose, Brian, Sar.	1	0	1.000	6.14	5	0	0	0	2	1	7.1	10	36	5	5	0	0	0	0	5	0	9	2	0
Rose, Johnathan, Cle.*	0	1	.000	6.75	8	0	0	0	4	0	9.1	12	44	7	7	3	0	0	0	6	0	7	1	0
Ruhl, Nathan, St.P.	2	0	1.000	2.57	4	0	0	0	4	0	7.0	9	32	2	2	0	0	1	3	0	5	0	0
Rutherford, Mark, Cle.	0	4	.000	9.20	9	9	0	0	0	0	46.0	64	228	57	47	6	2	6	2	25	3	23	1	1
Salamon, John, Tam.	0	0	.000	0.00	2	0	0	0	1	0	1.2	3	11	2	0	0	0	0	2	0	2	0	0
Sams, Aaron, Day.*	2	5	.286	4.75	10	10	1	0	0	0	55.0	53	239	31	29	4	0	1	4	26	0	41	5	1
Saylor, Ryan, Jup.	1	0	1.000	0.40	21	0	0	0	21	10	22.1	15	92	1	1	1	0	0	6	0	21	0	0
Schaffer, Trevor, Dun.	3	1	.750	1.98	8	0	0	0	4	0	13.2	8	51	3	3	1	0	0	6	0	10	2	0
Schuldt, Matt, St.P.	2	0	1.000	4.83	19	2	0	0	7	0	31.2	36	147	19	17	5	1	1	3	16	0	23	5	1
Schultz, Eric, Char.	2	2	.500	5.36	19	1	0	0	4	1	45.1	56	196	30	27	3	4	1	2	9	0	44	4	1
Seabury, Jaron, Dun.	4	3	.571	5.37	35	0	0	0	18	3	53.2	59	231	33	32	1	3	0	3	19	1	34	5	0
Seaman, John, B.C.	5	2	.714	4.45	25	0	0	0	7	0	54.2	47	238	32	27	3	2	2	5	27	1	47	7	0
Seay, Bobby, St.P.*	2	6	.250	3.00	12	11	0	0	1	0	57.0	56	238	25	19	0	2	2	4	23	0	45	2	0
Seo, Jae, St.L.	2	0	1.000	1.84	3	3	0	0	0	0	14.2	8	55	3	3	0	0	1	0	2	0	14	0	0
Serrano, Jim, Jup.	8	5	.615	2.13	44	1	0	0	24	8	93.0	59	365	25	22	4	2	5	7	27	4	118	8	0
Sessions, Doug, Kis.	3	0	1.000	1.97	35	0	0	0	27	13	45.2	35	183	11	10	1	1	0	1	14	1	55	2	0
Shearn, Tom, Kis.	10	6	.625	3.90	24	24	0	0	0	0	145.1	144	624	75	63	11	5	5	4	53	2	107	15	1
Sheldon, Kyle, Jup.	1	1	.500	3.34	20	0	0	0	12	1	29.2	37	133	13	11	2	0	2	3	7	1	22	0	0
Shipp, Kevin, Cle.	7	4	.636	5.51	32	7	0	0	2	0	83.1	108	374	56	51	5	4	1	3	22	1	54	3	2
Short, Barry, St.L.	2	2	.500	4.32	10	0	0	0	4	0	16.2	19	72	8	8	0	0	0	4	1	9	1	0
Silva, Doug, Char.	4	4	.500	3.90	24	12	0	0	6	0	94.2	103	404	58	41	8	2	2	1	25	1	55	5	1
Simon, Ben, V.B.	7	4	.636	3.45	38	5	0	0	12	2	88.2	79	382	44	34	5	4	2	10	29	2	89	7	1
Smith, Clint, Lak.	3	2	.600	5.06	7	7	0	0	0	0	37.1	42	170	29	21	3	1	2	0	18	0	32	5	1
Sneed, John, Dun.	11	2	.846	3.45	21	20	0	0	0	0	125.1	107	511	53	48	10	3	4	6	36	1	143	5	0
Snyder, Bill, Lak.	4	1	.800	1.92	47	0	0	0	42	16	51.2	34	197	13	11	0	4	2	1	18	0	39	0	0
Spear, Russell, Lak.	0	0	.000	9.24	8	2	0	0	1	0	12.2	15	77	17	13	1	0	1	4	24	0	8	5	0
Spence, Cam, Tam.	3	0	1.000	1.93	7	7	1	0	0	0	46.2	32	185	13	10	2	0	1	1	11	0	36	1	0
Spinelli, Mike, Sar.*	2	2	.500	3.14	38	0	0	0	16	2	80.1	73	352	36	28	4	1	2	5	44	1	58	9	1
Standridge, Jason, St.P.	4	4	.500	3.91	8	8	0	0	0	0	48.1	49	208	21	21	0	1	0	4	20	0	26	6	1
Stodgel, Jeff, V.B.	0	0	.000	0.00	1	0	0	0	1	0	0.1	0	1	0	0	0	0	0	0	0	0	0	0	0
Strickland, Scott, Jup.	1	1	.500	3.51	12	1	0	0	7	2	25.2	21	103	11	10	1	1	1	2	4	1	33	1	0
Sullivan, Shane, Day.	0	1	.000	6.75	4	0	0	0	0	0	12.0	17	55	10	9	3	0	1	0	7	0	5	0	0
Swiatkiewicz, Chris, Tam.	0	0	.000	0.00	2	0	0	0	1	0	2.1	1	9	0	0	0	0	0	0	0	0	1	0	0
Taczy, Craig, V.B.*	5	14	.263	4.66	28	25	2	0	1	0	160.1	172	701	93	83	12	3	10	14	50	0	83	6	1
Taglienti, Jeff, Sar.	1	1	.500	3.00	14	0	0	0	5	3	30.0	26	128	12	10	1	2	2	12	1	27	4	0
Tam, Jeff, St.L.	0	0	.000	3.38	2	0	0	0	0	0	2.2	4	13	1	1	0	0	0	0	0	0	3	0	0
Teut, Nate, Day.*	5	12	.294	6.38	26	26	1	0	0	0	132.2	180	613	113	94	16	3	9	9	41	0	91	13	1
Thomas, Brad, F.M.*	8	11	.421	4.78	27	27	1	1	0	0	152.1	182	666	99	81	11	4	3	6	46	0	108	8	1
Thomas, Don, Kis.*	8	6	.571	6.95	18	18	0	0	0	0	90.2	129	413	77	70	8	4	3	2	28	2	44	11	1
Thompson, Chris, Sar.	2	5	.286	5.61	28	2	0	0	15	1	43.1	48	202	33	27	3	1	0	6	22	3	41	7	0
Tovar, Angel, Tam.	1	1	.500	10.80	3	0	0	0	3	0	1.2	5	10	2	2	0	0	0	1	0	1	0	0
Tucker, T.J., Jup.	5	1	.833	1.23	7	7	0	0	0	0	44.0	24	171	7	6	2	0	1	0	16	0	35	1	0
Urdaneta, Lino, V.B.	5	4	.556	4.84	27	5	0	0	6	0	67.0	74	292	42	36	10	4	3	6	20	1	43	3	3
Van Gilder, Ryan, Jup.	0	1	.000	7.50	5	0	0	0	2	0	6.0	5	26	5	5	1	0	0	0	3	0	6	0	0
Vardijan, Dan, B.C.	3	1	.750	2.60	34	0	0	0	27	7	45.0	43	198	14	13	1	4	1	5	20	4	33	4	0
Vigeland, William, Char.	0	0	.000	7.27	5	0	0	0	2	0	8.2	14	41	7	7	0	0	1	4	0	9	0	0
Wade, Travis, Kis.	0	0	.000	0.00	1	0	0	0	1	0	1.0	1	4	0	0	0	0	0	0	0	0	0	0	0
Walker, Adam, Cle.*	9	7	.563	3.93	26	25	3	2	1	0	149.0	156	646	80	65	7	6	3	3	52	0	100	9	2
Walker, Tyler, St.L.	6	5	.545	2.94	13	13	2	0	0	0	79.2	64	329	31	26	6	3	2	3	29	2	64	4	1
Wallace, Chris, Tam.	3	4	.429	5.06	30	0	0	0	6	0	37.1	46	166	24	21	4	6	2	0	15	2	21	1	0
Wedel, Jeremy, Cle.	0	0	.000	1.69	4	0	0	0	1	0	5.1	4	21	1	1	0	0	0	1	0	3	1	0
Weimer, Matt, Dun.	6	3	.667	2.89	46	0	0	0	26	6	65.1	60	273	23	21	5	2	1	5	20	3	37	3	0
Westmoreland, Ken, Cle.	8	4	.667	4.20	20	20	0	0	0	0	111.1	130	484	59	52	7	4	0	3	40	2	40	9	0
White, Matt, St.P.	9	7	.563	5.18	21	20	2	0	0	0	113.0	125	498	75	65	6	2	6	8	33	0	92	10	1
Whitesides, Johnny, Kis.	1	1	.500	4.26	14	0	0	0	9	0	25.1	34	119	20	12	1	2	3	1	6	1	11	3	0
Williams, Randy, Day.*	3	4	.429	4.75	14	9	0	0	3	1	53.0	55	243	36	28	5	4	1	1	30	0	47	3	0
Willis, Jason, Tam.	2	0	1.000	2.03	3	3	0	0	0	0	13.1	9	55	3	3	0	1	0	0	7	0	10	0	0
Wood, Stanton, Tam.	4	1	.800	3.75	50	0	0	0	19	0	81.2	89	355	43	34	2	3	2	2	23	3	66	4	0
Woodman, Hank, Char.	2	2	.500	4.11	6	6	2	0	0	0	30.2	33	137	19	14	1	0	2	1	9	0	18	0	0
Workman, Widd, V.B.	1	1	.500	7.35	25	3	0	0	10	0	56.1	79	275	53	46	9	3	7	5	25	1	32	6	0
Yan, Esteban, St.P.	0	0	.000	0.00	2	2	0	0	0	0	4.0	3	15	1	0	0	0	0	1	0	0	0	0
Yennaco, Jay, Dun.	2	0	1.000	0.82	3	2	0	0	0	0	11.0	10	44	2	1	0	1	0	2	0	11	0	0
Yoder, Jeff, Day.	0	0	.000	0.84	5	0	0	0	2	1	10.2	8	44	2	1	0	1	0	5	0	11	0	0
Zambrano, Victor, St.P.	0	2	.000	4.00	2	0	0	0	1	0	9.0	10	43	6	4	1	0	1	5	0	15	1	0

COMBINATION SHUTOUTS: **Brevard County (4)**—Knotts-Levan-McCurtain, Comer-McCurtain, Akin-Partenheimer-McCurtain, Cames-Levan-Clark-Vardijan. **Charlotte (5)**—Fleming-Schultz-Duncan, Poland-Miller, Guzman-Duncan, Benoit-Elder-Duncan, Lundberg-Poeck-Freehill. **Clearwater (9)**—Westmoreland-Shipp-Cotton-Cedeno-

Kawabata, Westmoreland-Cedeno-Nickle, Shipp-Kawabata, Walker-Cedeno-Kawabata, Eaton-Eason-Nickle, Brannan-Eason-Nickle, Westmoreland-Cotton, West-moreland-Nickle, Burger-Cotton-Nickle. **Daytona (4)**—Teut-Fisher, Hammons-Williams, Gulin-Booker, Nation-Ohman. **Dunedin (7)**—Bleazard-File, Sneed-Hibbard-Seabury, Bleazard-Huggins-Brackeen, Sneed-Brackeen-File, Sneed-Huggins, McClellan-Huggins-Hibbard-Lawrence, McClellan-Weimer-Files. **Fort Myers (6)**—Fisher-Garza-Carnes-Cosgrove, Mills-Carnes, Davies-Gandy, Fisher-Davies, Garza-Gandy, Fisher-Howard-Marshall. **Jupiter (9)**—Tucker-Quezada-Strickland, Julio-Matz-Serrano, Tucker-Serrano-Saylor, Tucker-Agamennone-Strickland, Blank-Serrano-Marquez, Matz-Hughes-Serrano, Duran-Matz, Chiavacci-Hughes-Sheldon-Albin. **Kissimmee (5)**—Creek-Franklin, Ireland-Franklin, Shearn-Mercedes-Lynch, Lidge-Rodriguez, Rodriguez-Messman. **Lakeland (1)**—Miller-Bauder-Snyder. **St. Lucie (7)**—Walker-Hafer, Walker-Berger, McEntire-Hafer, Gonzalez-Riggan, Kessel-Lohrman, Brea-Bohannon, Gonzalez-Cerros. **St. Petersburg (11)**—White-Zambrano-Reyes, Seay-Zambrano-Reyes, Ortega-Brown-Box, Seay-Zambrano-Reyes, Seay-Schuldt-Box-Lira-Reyes, White-Brown, Phelps-Schuldt-Box-Reyes, Flohr-Reyes, White-Gardner-Kaufman-Reyes, Garibaldi-Jimenez-Gardner, Lidle-James. **Sarasota (6)**—Darrell-McMullen, Maroth-Belovsky, Duchscherer-Belovsky, Duchscherer-Spinelli-Belovsky, Maroth-Thompson-Spinelli-Belovsky, Lampley-McMullen-Dougherty. **Tampa (7)**—Lail-Wood, Rangel-Wallace, Reith-Wood, Reith-Lail-Ellison, Einertson-Delacruz-Wood-Cubillan, Willis-Lail, Spence-Cubillan. **Vero Beach (5)**—Moskau-Husted, Simon-Foster, Regalado-Gomes, Simon-Gomes-Husted, Taczy-Husted.

NO-HIT GAMES: Ireland, Kissimmee, defeated St. Petersburg, 5-0, June 23; Thomas, Fort Myers, defeated Charlotte, 9-0, July 12.

PITCHERS WITH TWO OR MORE TEAMS

Pitcher, Team	W	L	Pct.	ERA	G	GS	CG	ShO	GF	Sv.	IP	H	TBF	R	ER	HR	SH	SF	HB	BB	IBB	SO	WP	Bk.
Davis, Keith, Tam.	2	1	.667	2.25	11	0	0	0	1	0	16.0	17	75	9	4	0	1	1	5	0	15	2	0
Davis, Keith, Lak.	3	0	1.000	3.41	25	0	0	0	7	0	34.1	36	144	15	13	2	1	1	5	10	0	24	8	0
Downs, Scott, F.M.*	0	1	.000	0.00	2	2	0	0	0	0	9.2	7	45	3	0	0	0	1	0	6	0	9	2	0
Downs, Scott, Day.*	5	0	1.000	1.88	7	7	1	1	0	0	48.0	41	185	12	10	2	0	0	1	11	0	41	3	1
Lohse, Kyle, Day.	5	3	.625	2.89	9	9	1	1	0	0	53.0	48	217	21	17	4	2	1	0	16	0	41	1	0
Lohse, Kyle, F.M.	2	3	.400	5.18	7	7	0	0	0	0	41.2	47	180	28	24	5	2	4	4	9	0	33	1	0
Maroth, Mike, Sar.*	11	6	.647	4.04	20	19	0	0	0	0	111.1	124	497	65	50	3	6	4	10	35	1	64	11	2
Maroth, Mike, Lak.*	2	1	.667	3.24	3	3	0	0	0	0	16.2	18	71	7	6	1	1	0	0	7	0	11	2	0
Moskau, Ryan, Sar.*	5	5	.500	4.15	17	17	0	0	0	0	104.0	99	443	54	48	8	3	4	7	40	0	68	6	4
Moskau, Ryan, B.C.*	4	3	.571	2.69	9	9	2	0	0	0	63.2	50	261	22	19	4	4	0	1	21	0	40	0	0
Partenheimer, Brian, Sar.*	1	0	1.000	1.80	17	0	0	0	6	2	30.0	26	117	8	6	3	1	2	0	3	0	28	2	0
Partenheimer, Brian, B.C.*	2	3	.400	2.25	21	0	0	0	8	2	44.0	29	180	13	11	1	3	1	6	14	1	29	2	0

1999 FIELDING

TEAM

Team	Pct.	G	PO	A	E	TC	DP	TP	PB	Team	Pct.	G	PO	A	E	TC	DP	TP	PB
Jupiter	.973	138	3629	1489	140	5258	91	0	19	Kissimmee	.967	137	3572	1483	175	5230	123	0	22
St. Petersburg	.973	137	3532	1499	141	5172	116	0	24	Sarasota	.966	139	3567	1488	179	5234	103	0	28
Dunedin	.972	137	3587	1612	152	5351	150	0	17	Charlotte	.965	139	3569	1397	179	5145	131	0	35
Lakeland	.969	138	3578	1550	162	5290	132	0	36	Vero Beach	.965	138	3378	1407	173	4958	104	0	29
Brevard County	.967	135	3514	1494	169	5177	104	0	32	Daytona	.964	138	3494	1338	183	5015	110	0	23
Fort Myers	.967	139	3563	1583	174	5320	134	0	22	St. Lucie	.963	138	3603	1571	199	5373	118	0	16
Tampa	.967	136	3584	1429	173	5186	93	0	15	Clearwater	.962	136	3614	1557	204	5375	119	1	32

INDIVIDUAL

FIRST BASEMEN

NOTE: All caps denotes fielding-percentage leader based on 70 games for catchers, 93 for all other non-pitchers and 112 innings for pitchers. *Throws lefthanded.

Player, Team	Pct.	G	PO	A	E	TC	DP
Alamo, Efrain, St.P.	1.000	1	7	0	0	7	0
Amrhein, Mike, Day.	.995	50	411	20	2	433	33
August, Brian, Tam.	1.000	5	24	0	0	24	2
Auterson, Jeff, V.B.	1.000	1	2	0	0	2	0
Backe, Brandon, St.P.	1.000	1	1	0	0	1	0
Bearden, Doug, Kis.	1.000	1	4	1	0	5	2
Benham, David, Sar.	.969	16	117	7	4	128	8
Berns, Derrick, St.P.*	1.000	10	72	6	0	78	6
Bly, Derrick, Day.	1.000	9	76	3	0	79	7
Boughton, Mike, Char.	1.000	1	9	0	0	9	1
Bunkley, Antuan, Lak.	.982	102	891	53	17	961	87
Burkhart, Morgan, Sar.*	.992	57	488	32	4	524	44
Burns, Pat, St.L.*	.981	125	1080	66	22	1168	94
BUTLER, Allen, F.M.	.995	137	1260	108	7	1375	116
Carreno, Jose, Jup.	1.000	1	1	0	0	1	0
Carter, Charley, Kis.	.989	107	949	46	11	1006	66
Collins, Michael, V.B.	1.000	1	10	1	0	11	1
Dominique, Andy, Cle.	.991	34	304	17	3	324	31
Ensberg, Morgan, Kis.	1.000	1	2	1	0	3	0
Epperson, Chad, Sar.	1.000	9	74	6	0	80	7
Espinal, Juan, Sar.	.992	17	125	7	1	133	9
Feliciano, Jesus, V.B.*	1.000	1	2	0	0	2	0
Feramisco, Derek, V.B.	.000	1	0	0	0	0	0
Forbush, Nate, Lak.	.986	36	264	17	4	285	28
Freire, Alejandro, Lak.	.986	6	65	4	1	70	5
Frick, Matt, B.C.	1.000	2	21	2	0	23	1
Gibbons, Jay, Dun.*	.991	57	527	33	5	565	57
Gload, Ross, B.C.*	.993	133	1200	83	9	1292	90
Grabowski, Jason, Char.	1.000	3	22	0	0	22	2
Harrison, Jamal, F.M.	.875	1	7	0	1	8	2
Hayes, Chris, Dun.	.990	13	95	6	1	102	6
Hinske, Eric, Day.	.991	57	422	41	4	467	38
Hoover, Paul, St.P.	1.000	4	18	5	0	23	1
Jefferson, Reggie, Sar.*	1.000	3	30	4	0	34	1

Player, Team	Pct.	G	PO	A	E	TC	DP
Jones, Aaron, Tam.*	.989	128	1079	49	12	1140	76
Jorgensen, Randy, St.P.*	.996	25	212	15	1	228	18
Kellner, Ryan, V.B.	1.000	2	4	0	0	4	0
Key, Jeff, Sar.	.990	10	90	8	1	99	7
Leach, Nick, V.B.	.984	123	1018	71	18	1107	88
Lentz, Ryan, Jup.	1.000	1	1	0	0	1	0
Lomasney, Steve, Sar.	1.000	1	7	0	0	7	1
Lutz, Manuel, Lak.	.960	3	22	2	1	25	2
Manning, Nate, Day.	.985	27	193	8	3	204	19
McGrath, Sean, St.L.	1.000	1	4	0	0	4	0
McNamara, Rusty, Cle.	.984	28	227	21	4	252	20
Mirizzi, Marc, Tam.	1.000	2	19	2	0	21	1
Morrison, Greg, Dun.*	.985	46	362	29	6	397	43
Nunnari, Talmadge, Jup.*	.988	43	383	24	5	412	21
Pena, Carlos, Char.*	.986	135	1056	83	16	1155	121
Peters, Tony, Dun.	1.000	24	150	7	0	157	13
Phoenix, Wynter, V.B.*	.981	5	47	4	1	52	2
Pinto, Rene, Tam.	1.000	1	1	0	0	1	1
Polidor, Wil, Cle.	1.000	1	2	1	0	3	0
Pond, Simon, Jup.	.998	50	440	39	1	480	32
Quatraro, Matt, St.P.	.986	11	63	10	1	74	7
Quero, Pedro, Jup.	.995	49	401	15	2	418	35
Rigsby, Randy, B.C.*	.958	4	20	3	1	24	2
Rios, Brian, Lak.	1.000	1	6	0	0	6	0
Roach, Jason, St.L.	.971	13	125	9	4	138	9
Rodriguez, Luis, Sar.	1.000	2	10	2	0	12	1
Rodriguez, Mike, Dun.	.989	23	161	11	2	174	14
Ross, David, V.B.	.953	5	39	2	2	43	4
Rupp, Chad, Dun.	1.000	4	30	2	0	32	2
Sapp, Damian, Sar.	.977	30	237	16	6	259	19
Soules, Ryan, Tam.	1.000	4	35	2	0	37	2
Stodgel, Jeff, V.B.	1.000	1	1	0	0	1	0
Strange, Mike, Dun.	1.000	1	2	0	0	2	1
Thomas, J.J., Kis.	.975	38	303	13	8	324	39
Tomberlin, Andy, St.L.*	.933	3	14	0	1	15	1
Torres, Gabby, F.M.	1.000	5	0	5	0	5	0
Tucker, Jon, Jup.*	1.000	2	10	0	0	10	1
Uccello, Jeff, Sar.	1.000	1	1	0	0	1	0

Player, Team	Pct.	G	PO	A	E	TC	DP
Van Iten, Robert, Cle.	.988	78	686	45	9	740	55
Velazquez, Jose, St.P.*	.991	92	838	62	8	908	75
Vento, Mike, Tam.	1.000	1	5	0	0	5	1
Wood, Jason, Lak.	1.000	1	6	1	0	7	0
Zech, Scott, Jup.	1.000	1	1	1	0	2	0

TRIPLE PLAY: Van Iten.

SECOND BASEMEN

Player, Team	Pct.	G	PO	A	E	TC	DP
Abreu, Dennis, Day.	.953	103	218	225	22	465	50
Acevedo, Inocencio, Char.	1.000	1	4	5	0	9	1
Backe, Brandon, St.P.	1.000	2	3	1	0	4	1
Badeaux, Brooks, St.P.	.983	80	164	238	7	409	46
Bearden, Doug, Kis.	1.000	11	19	28	0	47	6
Bell, Ricky, V.B.	.971	67	142	187	10	339	37
Borrego, Ramon, F.M.	.852	6	9	14	4	27	1
Bravo, Danny, Jup.	1.000	2	4	6	0	10	1
Bush, Homer, Dun.	1.000	3	7	7	0	14	3
Cairo, Miguel, St.P.	.958	3	8	15	1	24	4
Capellan, Rene, Lak.	.956	13	30	35	3	68	7
Casillas, Uriel, Cle.	.938	6	14	16	2	32	2
Clarke, Jason, Day.	.979	36	53	86	3	142	24
Cole, Eric, Kis.	.986	17	25	44	1	70	10
Collins, Michael, V.B.	.977	45	97	118	5	220	25
Crespo, Cesar, B.C.	.958	97	227	272	22	521	55
Cruz, Luis, St.P.	.964	55	104	162	10	276	30
Dallimore, Brian, Kis.	.956	9	20	23	2	45	9
De Leon, Jorge, Sar.	.972	53	107	139	7	253	28
Font, Franklin, Day.	.977	10	16	26	1	43	4
Franco, Raul, B.C.	.974	37	74	110	5	189	18
Freeman, Terrance, Lak.	.967	100	220	300	18	538	72
Fuentes, Javier, Sar.	.955	15	26	37	3	66	4
Ginter, Keith, Kis.	.959	102	209	281	21	511	75
Haas, Danny, Sar.	.000	1	0	0	0	0	0
Hill, Nakia, V.B.	.980	13	18	32	1	51	5
Hook, Kevin, Jup.	.900	9	13	14	3	30	3
Izturis, Cesar, Dun.	.980	45	96	146	5	247	41
Jaramillo, Milko, V.B.	.000	1	0	0	0	0	0
Joyce, Jesse, Kis.	.875	1	3	4	1	8	3
Knupfer, Jason, Cle.	.946	15	30	40	4	74	11
Lauterhahn, Dan, Lak.	.938	7	7	8	1	16	4
Leon, Carlos, Sar.	.966	47	102	124	8	234	23
Malone, Nick, Sar.	.950	4	6	13	1	20	2
Mateo, Henry, Jup.	.962	100	193	235	17	445	45
McConnell, Jason, F.M.	.932	9	20	21	3	44	5
McGrath, Sean, St.L.	.981	15	12	39	1	52	3
Mejias, Erick, Char.	1.000	1	4	4	0	8	2
Mirizzi, Marc, Tam.	.949	9	13	24	2	39	5
Montilla, Miguel, Tam.	.929	3	4	9	1	14	2
Moore, Ryan, Jup.	1.000	2	3	6	0	9	1
Nelson, Reggie, Lak.	1.000	2	6	5	0	11	1
Olmeda, Jose, Sar.	.921	24	42	51	8	101	15
Ozarowski, Rich, Lak.	.955	23	47	60	5	112	9
Peeples, Mike, Dun.	.969	7	15	16	1	32	5
Perez, Jersen, St.L.	.968	13	25	35	2	62	7
Polidor, Wil, Cle.	.967	31	49	68	4	121	15
Pond, Simon, Jup.	1.000	2	1	2	0	3	1
Quinones, Marcus, Char.	.889	6	8	8	2	18	2
Rodriguez, Ronny, Sar.	1.000	3	2	5	0	7	2
Rolls, Damian, V.B.	1.000	1	3	3	0	6	0
Romano, Jason, Char.	.957	112	232	282	23	537	74
Ryan, Mike, F.M.	.949	126	257	395	35	687	81
Schifano, Tony, B.C.	1.000	1	0	1	0	1	1
Smalls, Terrence, B.C.	1.000	4	2	5	0	7	0
Smith, Rod, Tam.	.950	126	270	319	31	620	59
Soriano, Fred, Dun.	.986	17	22	49	1	72	10
Stodgel, Jeff, V.B.	.964	20	36	44	3	83	9
Terrell, Jeff, Cle.	.950	100	224	275	26	525	56
Ware, Ryan, Char.	.985	24	66	63	2	131	17
WIGGINTON, Ty, St.L.	.974	118	270	321	16	607	70
Wood, Jason, Lak.	.000	1	0	0	0	0	0
Young, Mike, Dun.	.976	74	113	219	8	340	44
Zech, Scott, Jup.	.976	32	41	82	3	126	11

THIRD BASEMEN

Player, Team	Pct.	G	PO	A	E	TC	DP
August, Brian, Tam.	.919	54	25	111	12	148	7
Bearden, Doug, Kis.	.925	16	9	28	3	40	3
Bell, Ricky, V.B.	.872	17	6	28	5	39	1
Bly, Derrick, Day.	.893	14	5	20	3	28	1
Brosius, Scott, Tam.	1.000	1	2	0	0	2	0
Capellan, Rene, Lak.	.750	7	5	13	6	24	3

Player, Team	Pct.	G	PO	A	E	TC	DP
Carter, Charley, Kis.	.778	3	2	5	2	9	0
Casillas, Uriel, Cle.	.976	17	8	32	1	41	2
Clarke, Jason, Day.	.950	8	4	15	1	20	1
Collier, Lamonte, Cle.	.862	84	48	152	32	232	18
Collins, Michael, V.B.	1.000	6	4	9	0	13	1
Cuddyer, Michael, F.M.	.921	128	81	245	28	354	25
Dallimore, Brian, Kis.	.882	7	2	13	2	17	1
De Leon, Jorge, Sar.	.857	5	2	10	2	14	1
Ellis, John, Char.	1.000	2	0	2	0	2	0
Ensberg, Morgan, Kis.	.902	115	68	235	33	336	19
Espinal, Juan, Sar.	.899	90	56	167	25	248	13
Font, Franklin, Day.	.750	3	1	2	1	4	0
Franco, Raul, B.C.	.953	28	21	60	4	85	4
Fuentes, Javier, Sar.	.879	44	13	74	12	99	3
Fuentes, Omar, Tam.	1.000	1	0	1	0	1	0
Grabowski, Jason, Char.	.911	117	78	199	27	304	10
Hayes, Chris, Dun.	.969	28	17	78	3	98	8
Henson, Drew, Tam.	.864	51	29	79	17	125	5
Hinske, Eric, Day.	.878	60	32	97	18	147	9
Honeycutt, Heath, B.C.	.923	97	73	213	24	310	17
Hoover, Paul, St.P.	1.000	3	0	7	0	7	1
Izturis, Cesar, Dun.	1.000	2	0	4	0	4	0
James, Kenny, Jup.	.000	1	0	0	0	0	0
Jaramillo, Frank, Char.	.889	3	0	8	1	9	0
Kleinz, Larry, B.C.	1.000	1	1	2	0	3	0
Leach, Nick, V.B.	1.000	1	0	1	0	1	0
Ledesma, Aaron, St.P.	.667	1	0	2	1	3	1
Lentz, Ryan, Jup.	.921	87	68	166	20	254	10
Lutz, Manuel, Lak.	.850	7	2	15	3	20	0
Manning, Nate, Day.	.901	61	49	124	19	192	17
McConnell, Jason, F.M.	.926	12	8	17	2	27	4
McGrath, Sean, St.L.	.857	6	1	11	2	14	0
McNamara, Rusty, Cle.	.887	31	27	59	11	97	8
Miller, Kenny, St.L.	.906	45	39	96	14	149	6
Mirizzi, Marc, Tam.	.926	33	24	63	7	94	7
Moore, Ryan, Jup.	1.000	3	1	1	0	2	1
Olmeda, Jose, Sar.	.867	8	7	6	2	15	1
Ozarowski, Rich, Lak.	.966	10	6	22	1	29	1
Peeples, Mike, Dun.	.899	49	33	109	16	158	8
Peters, Tony, Dun.	.929	6	3	10	1	14	1
Polidor, Wil, Cle.	.881	13	16	21	5	42	0
Pond, Simon, Jup.	.937	22	14	45	4	63	3
Quatraro, Matt, St.P.	.000	1	0	0	0	0	0
Richards, Rowan, Char.	1.000	1	2	3	0	5	0
RIOS, Brian, Lak.	.947	117	87	232	18	337	23
Roach, Jason, St.L.	.928	94	66	190	20	276	23
Rodriguez, Mike, Dun.	.912	37	12	71	8	91	6
Rolls, Damian, V.B.	.923	113	88	210	25	323	21
Salinas, Trey, St.P.	1.000	1	1	0	0	1	0
Sandberg, Jared, St.P.	.913	134	102	284	37	423	25
Schifano, Tony, B.C.	.818	4	5	4	2	11	0
Smalls, Terrence, B.C.	.970	13	7	25	1	33	3
Soriano, Fred, Dun.	.863	25	10	34	7	51	1
Stodgel, Jeff, V.B.	.000	1	0	0	0	0	0
Strange, Mike, Dun.	1.000	2	0	11	0	11	0
Taveras, Luis, Char.	1.000	1	0	1	0	1	0
Terrell, Jeff, Cle.	.600	4	0	3	2	5	0
Van Iten, Robert, Cle.	.750	6	1	11	4	16	1
Ware, Ryan, Char.	.953	20	11	30	2	43	2
Wood, Jason, Lak.	.000	1	0	0	0	0	0
Zech, Scott, Jup.	.978	34	19	72	2	93	6

SHORTSTOPS

Player, Team	Pct.	G	PO	A	E	TC	DP
Almonte, Erick, Tam.	.938	61	88	217	20	325	23
August, Brian, Tam.	.900	4	6	12	2	20	3
Backe, Brandon, St.P.	.930	11	14	26	3	43	6
Badeaux, Brooks, St.P.	.939	15	23	39	4	66	5
Bautista, Rayner, Lak.	.954	93	132	284	20	436	56
Bearden, Doug, Kis.	.902	14	14	41	6	61	8
Borrego, Ramon, F.M.	.889	2	1	7	1	9	0
Boughton, Mike, Char.	.919	8	12	22	3	37	5
Bravo, Danny, Jup.	.938	4	3	12	1	16	2
Capista, Aaron, Sar.	.958	128	180	419	26	625	70
Casillas, Uriel, Cle.	.915	11	19	35	5	59	4
Clarke, Jason, Day.	.933	29	30	67	7	104	13
Collier, Lamonte, Cle.	.903	18	23	42	7	72	5
Collins, Michael, V.B.	.951	36	55	121	9	185	20
De Leon, Jorge, Sar.	1.000	4	3	8	0	11	1
Dennis, Les, Tam.	.978	23	27	63	2	92	11
Ensberg, Morgan, Kis.	.833	2	3	7	2	12	1
Font, Franklin, Day.	.936	76	111	195	21	327	34

Player, Team	Pct.	G	PO	A	E	TC	DP
Franco, Raul, B.C.	.857	4	2	4	1	7	1
Hill, Nakia, V.B.	.667	1	3	3	3	9	1
Hook, Kevin, Jup.	.920	22	17	52	6	75	5
Izturis, Cesar, Dun.	.963	84	128	287	16	431	64
Jaramillo, Frank, Char.	.889	7	12	20	4	36	2
Jaramillo, Milko, V.B.	.937	98	145	270	28	443	39
Kellner, Ryan, V.B.	.000	1	0	0	0	0	0
Lauterhahn, Dan, Lak.	.913	47	42	158	19	219	22
Ledesma, Aaron, St.P.	1.000	1	3	2	0	5	0
Lorenzo, Juan, F.M.	.951	119	141	381	27	549	73
Machado, Anderson, Cle.	.000	1	0	0	0	0	0
Malone, Nick, Sar.	.933	5	5	9	1	15	3
Matranga, David, Kis.	.954	122	160	427	28	615	72
McConnell, Jason, F.M.	.960	26	35	62	4	101	14
McGrath, Sean, St.L.	.944	12	13	21	2	36	3
Miller, Kenny, St.L.	.917	33	40	81	11	132	17
Mirizzi, Marc, Tam.	.935	42	73	127	14	214	19
Montilla, Miguel, Tam.	.886	8	12	27	5	44	6
Niles, Drew, B.C.	.947	40	43	119	9	171	15
Olmeda, Jose, Sar.	.930	11	12	28	3	43	5
Ozarowski, Rich, Lak.	1.000	6	10	18	0	28	6
Perez, Jersen, St.L.	.937	106	159	317	32	508	50
Perez, Nestor, St.P.	.965	111	142	303	16	461	60
Polidor, Wil, Cle.	.971	8	8	25	1	34	3
Punto, Nick, Cle.	.958	106	168	380	24	572	68
Quinones, Marcus, Char.	1.000	1	0	2	0	2	0
Reding, Josh, Jup.	.950	118	183	393	30	606	48
Relaford, Desi, Cle.	.800	2	3	1	1	5	1
Schifano, Tony, B.C.	.960	31	54	89	6	149	11
Smith, Jason, Day.	.953	39	66	75	7	148	20
SOLANO, Danny, Char.	.972	116	218	339	16	573	95
Soriano, Fred, Dun.	.846	3	3	8	2	13	3
Stocker, Kevin, St.P.	1.000	3	5	10	0	15	2
Stodgel, Jeff, V.B.	1.000	2	2	1	0	3	1
Ugueto, Luis, B.C.	.958	12	19	27	2	48	4
Ware, Ryan, Char.	.887	14	16	31	6	53	5
Washington, Kelley, B.C.	.924	57	87	182	22	291	26
Wood, Jason, Lak.	.882	3	8	7	2	17	2
Young, Mike, Dun.	.936	53	50	156	14	220	41
Zech, Scott, Jup.	1.000	3	5	8	0	13	2

TRIPLE PLAY: Punto.

OUTFIELDERS

Player, Team	Pct.	G	PO	A	E	TC	DP
Acevedo, Carlos, Cle.	.875	12	19	2	3	24	1
Alamo, Efrain, St.P.	1.000	5	10	1	0	11	1
Albert, Rashad, Jup.	.988	75	151	9	2	162	1
Alvarez, Rafael, F.M.*	.967	78	133	14	5	152	2
Antczak, Chuck, Cle.	.800	2	3	1	1	5	0
Auterson, Jeff, V.B.	.976	74	160	4	4	168	2
Backe, Brandon, St.P.	1.000	30	53	3	0	56	0
Badeaux, Brooks, St.P.	1.000	1	1	0	0	1	0
Bagley, Lorenzo, Dun.	.950	69	93	3	5	101	1
Batista, Angel, St.P.*	.923	6	10	2	1	13	0
Berroa, Geronimo, Dun.	.500	2	1	0	1	2	0
Besco, Derek, Lak.	.950	94	129	5	7	141	0
Bly, Derrick, Day.	1.000	18	31	0	0	31	0
Bolivar, Papo, F.M.	.984	70	121	5	2	128	0
Borrego, Ramon, F.M.	1.000	15	18	2	0	20	0
Boughton, Mike, Char.	1.000	3	5	0	0	5	0
Butler, Garrett, St.P.	1.000	85	178	7	0	185	1
Calloway, Ronald, Jup.*	1.000	51	134	13	0	147	1
Capellan, Rene, Lak.	1.000	3	3	2	0	5	0
Carter, Quincy, Char.	1.000	1	1	0	0	1	0
Chambliss, Russ, Tam.	1.000	3	3	0	0	3	0
Chavez, Endy, St.L.*	.980	39	95	3	2	100	1
Cheek, Shawn, Sar.	.000	1	0	0	0	0	0
Cole, Eric, Kis.	.982	89	154	6	3	163	3
Collier, Lamonte, Cle.	1.000	6	7	0	0	7	0
Collins, Michael, V.B.	1.000	7	9	0	0	9	0
Connally, Christopher, Day.	1.000	11	14	1	0	15	0
Connell, Jerry, Cle.	.933	21	35	7	3	45	1
Copeland, Brandon, St.L.	.857	12	15	3	3	21	0
Craig, Benny, Kis.	1.000	2	5	1	0	6	0
Cranford, Joey, F.M.	.917	29	31	2	3	36	1
Dallimore, Brian, Kis.	.600	3	3	0	2	5	0
Dina, Allen, St.L.	.967	84	191	11	7	209	0
Duffy, Jim, Kis.	.979	47	91	3	2	96	0
Epperson, Chad, Sar.	1.000	1	1	0	0	1	0
Escobar, Alex, St.L.	1.000	1	2	0	0	2	0
Feliciano, Jesus, V.B.*	.979	95	179	4	4	187	1
Felston, Anthony, F.M.*	.973	79	174	3	5	182	0

Player, Team	Pct.	G	PO	A	E	TC	DP
Feramisco, Derek, V.B.	1.000	17	32	4	0	36	0
Fischer, Mark, Sar.	.953	92	176	7	9	192	0
Fleming, Ryan, Dun.*	.982	47	55	0	1	56	0
Foster, Quincy, B.C.	.951	133	276	13	15	304	0
Franco, Raul, B.C.	.911	27	39	2	4	45	0
Fuentes, Javier, Sar.	1.000	1	1	0	0	1	0
Garcia, Douglas, Char.*	.959	107	219	12	10	241	1
Goodwin, Tom, Char.	1.000	3	8	0	0	8	0
Graham, Jess, Sar.*	.963	120	162	19	7	188	2
Green, Kevin, B.C.	.923	10	11	1	1	13	0
Grimmett, Ryan, Lak.	.987	45	73	3	1	77	1
Haas, Danny, Sar.	.984	46	61	2	1	64	0
Hall, Doug, Day.*	1.000	12	16	0	0	16	0
Hall, Noah, Jup.	.972	113	202	10	6	218	0
Haltiwanger, Garrick, St.L.*	.951	90	124	12	7	143	4
Hayes, Chris, Dun.	1.000	5	6	0	0	6	0
Heinrichs, Jon, B.C.	.992	64	114	4	1	119	0
Hinske, Eric, Day.	1.000	6	4	2	0	6	0
James, Kenny, Jup.	.991	96	227	4	2	233	0
Jaramillo, Frank, Char.	.750	1	2	1	1	4	0
Jimenez, Felipe, Day.	.923	17	23	1	2	26	0
Johnson, Gary, Day.	.976	105	230	12	6	248	4
Johnson, Rontrez, Sar.	.975	132	303	5	8	316	2
Johnson, Tom, St.L.	.938	51	89	1	6	96	0
Jones, Jeremy, Char.	.800	2	3	1	1	5	0
Joyce, Jesse, Kis.	1.000	3	4	0	0	4	0
Kelly, Kenny, St.P.	.970	51	121	9	4	134	2
Key, Jeff, Sar.	1.000	14	24	2	0	26	0
Kiil, Skip, Cle.	.988	83	154	9	2	165	0
Kofler, Eric, Tam.*	1.000	1	1	0	0	1	0
Langaigne, Selwyn, Dun.*	.976	61	117	7	3	127	0
Lawton, Matt, F.M.	1.000	4	8	0	0	8	0
Lindsey, Rodney, Lak.	.973	117	282	7	8	297	2
Logan, Kyle, Kis.	.958	106	154	5	7	166	1
Lopez, Manny, F.M.	.981	68	97	9	2	108	2
Lutz, Manuel, Lak.	1.000	30	37	0	0	37	0
Maduro, Remy, B.C.	.967	26	28	1	1	30	0
Mahoney, Sean, St.P.	.950	33	36	2	2	40	1
Malone, Nick, Sar.	.000	1	0	0	0	0	0
Manning, Nate, Day.	.923	19	22	2	2	26	1
Marsh, Roy, Sar.	1.000	7	15	0	0	15	0
Mashore, Justin, Sar.-St.L.	.987	39	67	8	1	76	3
Maxwell, Vernon, Tam.	.962	16	24	1	1	26	0
McBride, Gator, Sar.	1.000	17	41	1	0	42	0
McNamara, Rusty, Cle.	.955	11	20	1	1	22	0
Mejia, Maximiliano, V.B.	.918	27	53	3	5	61	0
Melconian, Alex, B.C.	.991	57	106	7	1	114	1
Melian, Jackson, Tam.	.965	126	268	7	10	285	1
Michaels, Jason, Cle.	.996	90	247	12	1	260	2
Mirizzi, Marc, Tam.	.000	1	0	0	0	0	0
Monroe, Craig, Char.	.980	130	326	13	7	346	3
Montilla, Miguel, Tam.	.000	1	0	0	0	0	0
Moore, Kevin, V.B.	1.000	2	4	0	0	4	0
Moore, Lacarlo, Lak.	.978	28	43	2	1	46	0
Mora, Juan, Lak.*	1.000	3	3	0	0	3	0
Moreno, Juan, St.L.	.957	98	144	11	7	162	2
Morillo, Luis, Dun.*	.000	3	0	0	0	0	0
Morrison, Greg, Dun.*	1.000	26	28	1	0	29	0
Neuberger, Scott, St.P.	.965	122	254	18	10	282	5
Newton, Kimani, V.B.	.971	52	66	1	2	69	0
Nina, Amuarys, Char.	.983	112	228	7	4	239	1
Nunnari, Talmadge, Jup.*	.900	7	8	1	1	10	0
Pagan, Felix, F.M.	1.000	4	7	0	0	7	0
Patton, Cory, St.L.	1.000	7	13	0	0	13	0
Payton, Jay, St.L.	.955	7	20	1	1	22	0
Peeples, Mike, Dun.	.958	78	110	5	5	120	0
Pena, Jose, Char.	.949	59	92	2	5	99	0
Perez, Josue, V.B.-Cle.	.989	85	174	4	2	180	0
Peters, Tony, Dun.	.968	85	108	12	4	124	5
Phoenix, Wynter, V.B.*	.953	47	76	5	4	85	0
Piedra, Jorge, V.B.*	.933	15	28	0	2	30	0
Pigott, Anthony, St.P.	.975	84	148	5	4	157	0
Poeck, Chad, Char.	1.000	1	2	0	0	2	0
Quatraro, Matt, St.P.	.913	14	19	2	2	23	0
Quero, Pedro, Jup.	.974	67	107	5	3	115	0
Randolph, Jaisen, Day.	.962	130	264	14	11	289	1
Reed, Brian, B.C.	.939	16	30	1	2	33	0
Richards, Rowan, Char.	1.000	9	13	0	0	13	0
Rico, Diego, Day.*	.993	93	132	7	1	140	1
Rigsby, Randy, B.C.*	.952	78	132	7	7	146	1
Rivera, Juan, Tam.	.979	93	181	8	4	193	3
Roach, Jason, St.L.	1.000	6	7	1	0	8	0

Player, Team	Pct.	G	PO	A	E	TC	DP
Rodriguez, John, Tam.*	.966	69	109	6	4	119	0
Rodriguez, Mike, Dun.	.000	1	0	0	0	0	0
Ross, David, V.B.	.000	1	0	0	0	0	0
Royster, Aaron, Cle.	1.000	6	9	0	0	9	0
Rupp, Chad, Dun.	.000	1	0	0	0	0	0
Schifano, Tony, B.C.	.947	10	17	1	1	19	0
Smalls, Terrence, B.C.	1.000	1	1	0	0	1	0
Smith, Nestor, F.M.	.960	86	160	7	7	174	1
Soules, Ryan, Tam.	1.000	1	4	0	0	4	0
Stodgel, Jeff, V.B.	1.000	21	30	1	0	31	1
Stromsborg, Ryan, Dun.	1.000	20	22	1	0	23	0
Thames, Marcus, Tam.	.974	48	104	8	3	115	1
Thomas, J.J., Kis.	1.000	14	22	1	0	23	0
Thompson, Nick, Cle.	1.000	3	4	0	0	4	0
Tinoco, Luis, Cle.	.976	28	38	2	1	41	1
Tomberlin, Andy, St.L.*	1.000	5	6	0	0	6	0
Urquhart, Derick, Jup.*	1.000	22	20	1	0	21	0
Valent, Eric, Cle.*	.969	129	265	17	9	291	3
Van Iten, Robert, Cle.	.833	7	5	0	1	6	0
Vasquez, Alejandro, Kis.*	.991	60	107	1	1	109	0
Vento, Mike, Tam.	.989	57	85	6	1	92	0
Vessel, Andrew, Day.	1.000	17	28	1	0	29	0
Wakeland, Chris, Lak.*	1.000	4	4	0	0	4	0
Ware, Jeremy, Jup.	1.000	6	17	0	0	17	0
Ware, Ryan, Char.	.833	3	5	0	1	6	0
Wells, Vernon, Dun.	.993	69	130	3	1	134	1
WESSON, Barry, Kis.	.992	113	245	7	2	254	2
Winrow, Gary, Tam.*	1.000	2	1	0	0	1	0
Yates, Chris, Kis.*	.913	15	20	1	2	23	0
Zapata, Alexis, Lak.	.992	107	232	6	2	240	2
Zech, Scott, Jup.	1.000	1	1	0	0	1	0

OUTFIELDERS WITH TWO OR MORE TEAMS

Player, Team	Pct.	G	PO	A	E	TC	DP
Mashore, Justin, Sar.	1.000	12	24	2	0	26	0
Mashore, Justin, St.L.	.980	27	43	6	1	50	3
Perez, Josue, V.B.	.984	62	120	4	2	126	0
Perez, Josue, Cle.	1.000	23	54	0	0	54	0

CATCHERS

Player, Team	Pct.	G	PO	A	E	TC	DP	PB
Alevras, Chad, Sar.	1.000	1	7	0	0	7	0	0
Alvarez, Aaron, B.C.	1.000	1	5	1	0	6	0	0
Amrhein, Mike, Day.	.992	45	336	32	3	371	5	5
Antczak, Chuck, Cle.	1.000	8	39	2	0	41	0	1
Barr, Clint, Tam.	.972	6	34	1	1	36	0	1
Benham, David, Sar.	.974	16	99	12	3	114	0	3
Bennett, Ryan, St.L.	.983	46	261	36	5	302	1	7
Buckley, Brandon, Kis.	.997	50	277	37	1	315	2	8
Burkhart, Lance, Jup.	.987	35	203	22	3	228	1	8
Carreno, Jose, Jup.	1.000	2	10	1	0	11	0	0
Casanova, Raul, Lak.	1.000	3	14	2	0	16	0	3
Castellano, John, V.B.	1.000	6	37	4	0	41	1	1
Chavera, Arnie, Kis.	1.000	8	47	1	0	48	0	3
Cheek, Shawn, Sar.	.960	10	41	7	2	50	0	0
CHIAFFREDO, Paul, Dun.	.992	88	565	68	5	638	6	14
Cripps, Bobby, Dun.	.944	2	16	1	1	18	0	1
Delgado, Alex, Dun.	.988	10	71	13	1	85	2	0
Dominique, Andy, Cle.	.977	46	270	27	7	304	0	12
Ellis, John, Char.	.966	47	247	41	10	298	0	7
Epperson, Chad, Sar.	.975	10	69	9	2	80	0	0
Estalella, Bobby, Cle.	.976	6	37	4	1	42	0	0
Estrada, Johnny, Cle.	.989	75	417	54	5	476	0	17
Feliz, Joselyn, B.C.	1.000	10	41	7	0	48	1	5
Forbush, Nate, Lak.	.963	34	165	17	7	189	2	12
Frick, Matt, B.C.	.987	24	138	13	2	153	2	5
Fuentes, Omar, Tam.	.972	18	121	18	4	143	0	1
Hall, Toby, St.P.	.980	30	173	27	4	204	0	5
Hargreaves, Brad, Day.	.972	38	219	28	7	254	2	7
Harper, Brandon, B.C.	.984	75	445	57	8	510	6	14
Hatteberg, Scott, Sar.	1.000	1	3	1	0	4	0	0
Hernandez, Michel, Tam.	.989	81	580	67	7	654	2	8
Hoover, Paul, St.P.	.992	87	551	63	5	619	3	14
Jones, Jeremy, Char.	1.000	9	47	5	0	52	0	2
Kellner, Ryan, V.B.	.978	35	200	25	5	230	0	10
Lentz, Ryan, Jup.	1.000	1	2	0	0	2	0	0
LeCroy, Matthew, F.M.	.983	66	406	48	8	462	4	11
Lomasney, Steve, Sar.	.973	47	277	46	9	332	1	5
Lough, Aaron, F.M.	.967	5	28	1	1	30	0	2
Malave, Jaime, Jup.	1.000	2	11	2	0	13	0	0
Marsters, Brandon, F.M.	.971	53	355	45	12	412	9	8
Melconian, Alex, B.C.	1.000	1	2	0	0	2	0	0

Player, Team	Pct.	G	PO	A	E	TC	DP	PB
Parker, Chris, Lak.	1.000	3	13	3	0	16	0	1
Peters, Tony, Dun.	.946	8	34	1	2	37	0	1
Phelps, Josh, Dun.	.994	27	161	13	1	175	4	0
Phillips, Jason, St.L.	.992	68	457	64	4	525	3	5
Pinto, Rene, Tam.	.993	19	139	9	1	149	0	2
Prince, Tom, Cle.	.981	9	47	4	1	52	0	2
Quatraro, Matt, St.P.	.984	25	111	12	2	125	1	5
Ramos, Kelly, St.L.	.973	24	176	37	6	219	3	2
Ramsey, Brad, Day.	.971	65	434	29	14	477	1	11
Reese, Nate, B.C.	.973	34	198	21	6	225	1	8
Rhodes, Nicholas, St.P.	1.000	1	4	0	0	4	0	0
Rivera, Mike, Lak.	.989	94	588	104	8	700	6	19
Rodriguez, Luis, Sar.	.983	27	206	30	4	240	2	6
Rodriguez, Mike, Dun.	.975	25	146	10	4	160	0	1
Rodriguez, Ronny, Sar.	1.000	1	7	2	0	9	0	0
Rose, Mike, Kis.	.981	88	599	76	13	688	5	11
Ross, David, V.B.	.980	96	592	97	14	703	5	18
Salazar, Jeremy, Cle.	1.000	2	15	1	0	16	0	0
Sandusky, Scott, Jup.	.979	107	671	82	16	769	4	10
Sapp, Damian, Sar.	.985	29	177	19	3	199	0	14
Schifano, Tony, B.C.	.000	1	0	0	0	0	0	0
Stanton, Tom, St.L.	1.000	8	47	7	0	54	1	2
Stodgel, Jeff, V.B.	1.000	4	3	1	0	4	0	0
Taveras, Luis, Char.	.966	95	546	81	22	649	4	26
Thompson, Nick, Cle.	1.000	1	6	0	0	6	0	0
Torres, Gabby, F.M.	.985	21	115	15	2	132	1	1
Torres, Jaime, Tam.	1.000	9	60	5	0	65	1	1
Twombley, Dennis, Tam.	.988	14	75	6	1	82	0	2
Uccello, Jeff, Sar.	1.000	7	52	4	0	56	0	0
Vargas, Arias, Lak.	1.000	18	68	11	0	79	2	1
Whitby, Cory, Sar.	1.000	3	13	0	0	13	0	0
Zech, Scott, Jup.	1.000	1	1	0	0	1	0	0

PITCHERS

Player, Team	Pct.	G	PO	A	E	TC	DP
Adair, Derek, Cle.	.833	9	0	5	1	6	0
Adams, Willie, Sar.	.750	2	1	2	1	4	0
Agamennone, Brandon, Jup.	1.000	16	7	7	0	14	1
Akin, Aaron, B.C.	1.000	27	6	24	0	30	2
Albin, Scott, Jup.	.000	2	0	0	0	0	0
Alvarez, Victor, V.B.*	1.000	12	3	12	0	15	0
Antczak, Chuck, Cle.	1.000	1	0	1	0	1	0
Arrojo, Rolando, St.P.	1.000	2	1	2	0	3	0
Arteaga, J.D., St.L.*	1.000	1	0	1	0	1	0
Avery, Paul, V.B.*	1.000	32	0	6	0	6	0
Baginski, Jr., Thomas, Lak.*	1.000	6	0	0	0	0	0
Bailie, Matt, Cle.	.000	2	0	0	0	0	0
Barkley, Brian, Sar.*	.000	1	0	0	0	0	0
Barnsby, Scott, V.B.	.000	4	0	0	0	0	0
Barry, Shawn, St.L.*	1.000	46	0	7	0	7	0
Bauder, Mike, Lak.*	1.000	28	4	9	0	13	1
Beech, Matt, Cle.*	.000	2	0	0	0	0	0
Belcher, B.J., Char.	.625	15	0	5	3	8	0
Belovsky, Josh, Sar.	.875	48	1	13	2	16	0
Benoit, Joaquin, Char.	.933	22	6	8	1	15	0
Berger, Craig, St.L.	.875	36	2	12	2	16	1
Betancourt, Rafael, Sar.	.000	6	0	0	0	0	0
Black, Brett, Cle.	1.000	34	1	5	0	6	0
Blank, Matt, Jup.*	1.000	14	5	13	0	18	0
Bleazard, David, Dun.	.957	14	8	14	1	23	2
Blevins, Jeremy, Tam.	1.000	1	1	0	0	1	0
Bohannon, Gary, St.L.	.926	32	6	19	2	27	0
Bond, Aaron, Char.	1.000	8	0	4	0	4	0
Booker, Chris, Day.	1.000	42	4	6	0	10	0
Bowe, Brandon, B.C.	1.000	9	4	2	0	6	1
Box, John, St.P.*	1.000	42	2	3	0	5	0
Brackeen, Colin, Dun.*	1.000	40	8	9	0	17	1
Brannan, Ryan, Cle.	1.000	28	3	11	0	14	1
Brea, Lesli, St.L.	.840	32	3	18	4	25	3
Bridges, Donald, Jup.	.917	18	6	16	2	24	3
Brown, Elliot, St.P.	.833	38	2	8	2	12	0
Buller, Sean, Lak.*	.000	1	0	0	0	0	0
Bullinger, Jim, V.B.	.857	6	3	3	1	7	0
Burger, Rob, Cle.	1.000	6	2	1	0	3	0
Cames, Aaron, B.C.	.833	4	3	2	1	6	0
Campos, David, B.C.*	1.000	13	0	1	0	1	0
Cannon, Jon, Day.*	.872	33	8	33	6	47	1
Carnes, Matt, F.M.	.941	52	8	8	1	17	0
Carrasco, Hector, F.M.	.000	1	0	0	0	0	0
Carroll, Dave, Tam.*	1.000	2	0	1	0	1	0
Castillo, Jose, Lak.	1.000	8	1	0	0	1	0
Castro, Eleuterio, Sar.	.000	3	0	0	0	0	0

Player, Team	Pct.	G	PO	A	E	TC	DP
Cedeno, Blas, Cle.	.938	34	6	9	1	16	0
Cedeno, Jovanny, Char.	1.000	1	0	1	0	1	0
Cepeda, Victor, Lak.	1.000	11	2	4	0	6	1
Cerros, Juan, St.L.	.000	5	0	0	0	0	0
Cheek, Andrew, Sar.*	1.000	2	0	2	0	2	0
Cheek, Shawn, Sar.	.000	1	0	0	0	0	0
Chiavacci, Ron, Jup.	1.000	8	1	5	0	6	0
Choate, Randy, Tam.*	.947	47	4	14	1	19	1
Christensen, Benjamin, Day.	1.000	4	1	4	0	5	0
Clark, Chris, B.C.	1.000	28	2	9	0	11	0
Clark, Mark, Char.	1.000	2	2	2	0	4	1
Coco, Pasqual, Dun.	.875	13	3	11	2	16	1
Collier, Lamonte, Cle.	.000	1	0	0	0	0	0
Comer, Scott, B.C.*	1.000	19	8	17	0	25	2
Cordova, Jorge, B.C.	1.000	6	0	1	0	1	0
Cosgrove, Mike, F.M.	1.000	7	0	1	0	1	0
Cotton, Joe, Cle.	1.000	38	0	17	0	17	1
Creek, Ryan, Kis.	.714	7	1	4	2	7	0
Cubillan, Darwin, Tam.	1.000	55	6	13	0	19	0
Cutchins, Todd, St.L.*	.882	25	7	23	4	34	1
Darrell, Tommy, Sar.	.920	30	5	18	2	25	0
Davies, Bob, F.M.	.944	25	10	24	2	36	1
Davis, Keith, Tam.-Lak.	1.000	36	2	5	0	7	0
Davis, Tim, St.P.*	.000	1	0	0	0	0	0
Delacruz, Luis, Tam.	1.000	5	1	2	0	3	1
Dorame, Randey, V.B.*	.000	3	0	0	1	1	0
Dotel, Melido, V.B.	.773	31	4	13	5	22	0
Dougherty, Tony, Sar.	.000	4	0	0	0	0	0
Downs, Scott, F.M.-Day.*	.958	9	4	19	1	24	1
Duchscherer, Justin, Sar.	.944	20	6	11	1	18	0
Duckworth, Brandon, Cle.	.929	27	9	17	2	28	1
Duncan, Courtney, Day.	1.000	15	6	8	0	14	0
Duncan, Sean, Char.*	1.000	45	8	8	0	16	2
Duran, Roberto, Jup.*	1.000	7	0	4	0	4	1
Durkovic, Peter, Lak.*	1.000	17	2	3	0	5	1
Eason, Clay, Cle.	.750	18	0	3	1	4	0
Eaton, Adam, Cle.	.813	13	5	8	3	16	2
Einertson, Darrell, Tam.	1.000	2	0	1	0	1	0
Elder, David, Char.	.857	24	2	4	1	7	0
Ellison, Jason, Tam.	1.000	49	5	7	0	12	1
Estrella, Leo, Dun.	.870	27	11	29	6	46	4
Fennell, Barry, Day.*	1.000	22	1	5	0	6	0
File, Bob, Dun.	.952	47	4	16	1	21	0
Fisher, Louis, Day.	.870	40	2	18	3	23	1
Fisher, Peter, F.M.	.912	25	10	21	3	34	2
Fleming, Emar, Char.	.935	24	10	19	2	31	3
Flohr, Adam, St.P.*	.974	31	5	32	1	38	2
Flores, Randy, Tam.*	1.000	21	0	24	0	24	1
Florie, Bryce, Lak.	.000	1	0	0	0	0	0
Foster, Kris, V.B.	1.000	8	1	1	0	2	0
Franklin, Wayne, Kis.*	1.000	12	3	3	0	6	0
Freehill, Mike, Char.	1.000	17	0	1	0	1	0
Frey, Chris, Char.	1.000	2	0	1	0	1	0
Gagliano, Steve, B.C.	.875	15	1	6	1	8	1
Gandy, Josh, F.M.*	.882	47	3	12	2	17	1
Garcia, Gabe, Kis.	.000	1	0	0	0	0	0
Gardner, Lee, St.P.	1.000	20	6	2	0	8	0
Garibaldi, Cecilio, St.P.	.842	21	5	11	3	19	1
Garrett, Josh, Sar.	.971	26	11	22	1	34	4
Garvin, Robert, B.C.	.000	1	0	0	0	0	0
Garza, Chris, F.M.*	1.000	21	2	8	0	10	0
Gaskill, Derek, St.L.	.800	22	0	4	1	5	0
Geary, Geoff, Cle.	.864	24	3	16	3	22	0
German, Yon, St.L.*	.900	10	3	6	1	10	0
Glick, David, Kis.*	1.000	32	5	2	0	7	0
Gomes, Tony, V.B.	.778	37	2	5	2	9	0
Gonzalez, Dicky, St.L.	.972	25	12	23	1	36	1
Gonzalez, Jeremi, Day.	.000	2	0	0	0	0	0
Grace, Bryan, Tam.	1.000	9	4	3	0	7	1
Greisinger, Seth, Lak.	1.000	1	0	2	0	2	0
Gulin, Lindsay, Day.*	1.000	3	0	4	0	4	0
Guzman, Leiby, Char.	1.000	19	5	7	0	12	2
Hafer, Jeff, St.L.	.923	36	4	8	1	13	0
Haigler, Phil, F.M.	.944	11	5	12	1	18	1
Haines, Talley, St.P.	1.000	2	1	0	0	1	1
Hammons, Matt, Day.	.882	15	3	12	2	17	1
Hargreaves, Brad, Day.	.000	1	0	0	0	0	0
Harper, Travis, St.P.	.909	14	4	6	1	11	1
Hartshorn, Ty, Dun.	1.000	7	2	2	0	4	0
Heath, Woody, Dun.	.833	22	8	7	3	18	0
Hebert, Cedric, V.B.	1.000	7	0	4	0	4	0
Hebson, Bryan, Jup.	.857	17	2	16	3	21	1
Hibbard, Billy, Dun.	1.000	31	4	8	0	12	0
Hiljus, Erik, Lak.	.000	3	0	0	0	0	0
Hill, Kendall, F.M.	.842	39	3	13	3	19	1
Hostetler, Jim, Lak.	.857	31	4	2	1	7	0
Howard, Tom, F.M.*	.857	22	0	6	1	7	0
Huggins, David, Dun.	.938	42	3	12	1	16	1
Hughes, Mike, Jup.*	1.000	17	0	4	0	4	0
Hurtado, Victor, B.C.	1.000	4	0	3	0	3	0
Husted, Brent, V.B.	.950	47	7	12	1	20	1
Infante, Asdrubal, Lak.	1.000	1	0	1	0	1	0
Ireland, Eric, Kis.	.830	24	15	24	8	47	2
James, Delvin, St.P.	1.000	3	2	1	0	3	1
Jimenez, Jason, St.P.*	.947	41	3	15	1	19	0
Johnson, Craig, Lak.	.964	26	11	16	1	28	1
Johnson, Mark, Tam.	1.000	1	1	0	0	1	1
Johnston, Sean, Day.*	.944	26	5	12	1	18	1
Julio, Jorge, Jup.	.909	23	8	12	2	22	0
Kaufman, John, St.P.*	1.000	16	1	4	0	5	0
Kawabata, Kyle, Cle.	.909	33	5	5	1	11	1
Keagle, Greg, Lak.	1.000	6	1	2	0	3	0
Keisler, Randy, Tam.*	.941	15	6	10	1	17	0
Kessel, Kyle, St.L.*	1.000	8	1	8	0	9	0
Kirsten, Rick, Lak.	1.000	2	0	2	0	2	1
Knotts, Gary, B.C.	.923	16	4	8	1	13	0
Lail, Denny, Tam.	1.000	22	3	5	0	8	0
Lamarsh, Robert, Char.*	1.000	1	0	1	0	1	0
Lampley, Daniel, Sar.	.895	25	5	12	2	19	0
Lanzetta, Tobin, V.B.	1.000	4	2	2	0	4	0
Lara, Giovanny, Jup.	1.000	33	1	8	0	9	0
Larkin, Andy, B.C.	1.000	4	1	2	0	3	0
Lawrence, Clint, Dun.*	.400	15	1	1	3	5	0
LaChapelle, Yan, Dun.	1.000	15	4	4	0	8	0
Levan, Matt, B.C.*	.900	35	2	7	1	10	0
Lewis, Craig, Tam.	.875	5	1	6	1	8	0
Lidge, Bradley, Kis.	.000	6	0	0	0	0	0
Lidle, Cory, St.P.	.000	2	0	0	1	1	0
Lira, James, St.P.	1.000	36	4	3	0	7	0
Loewer, Carlton, Cle.	1.000	3	0	2	0	2	1
Lohrman, Dave, St.L.	.813	43	5	8	3	16	3
Lohse, Kyle, Day.-F.M.	1.000	16	6	10	0	16	0
Lopez, Albie, St.P.	.000	2	0	0	1	1	0
Loux, Shane, Lak.	.955	17	8	13	1	22	2
Love, Jeff, Kis.	.500	15	0	2	2	4	0
LUNDBERG, Dave, Char.	1.000	30	15	22	0	37	4
Lynch, Jim, Kis.	.800	28	3	17	5	25	1
Lyons, Jonathan, Sar.	1.000	23	2	4	0	6	0
Madero, Francisco, V.B.	.818	12	4	5	2	11	0
Maldonado, Esteban, Kis.	1.000	8	2	0	0	2	0
Malko, Bryan, F.M.	1.000	30	10	12	0	22	0
Maroth, Mike, Sar.-Lak.*	1.000	23	9	21	0	30	0
Marquez, Robert, Jup.	.667	13	1	1	1	3	0
Marrero, Darwin, Jup.	.000	2	0	0	0	0	0
Marriott, Mike, B.C.	.786	8	6	5	3	14	0
Marshall, Lee, F.M.	.923	28	4	8	1	13	0
Marsonek, Sam, Char.	1.000	15	3	15	0	18	0
Marsters, Brandon, F.M.	.000	1	0	0	0	0	0
Martinez, Jesus, Sar.*	1.000	16	1	3	0	4	0
Martinez, Ramon, Sar.	1.000	3	1	3	0	4	0
Mattes, Troy, Jup.*	1.000	5	1	2	0	3	1
Matz, Brian, Jup.*	.957	41	4	18	1	23	1
McClellan, Matt, Dun.	.938	26	13	17	2	32	1
McClellan, Sean, Dun.	.000	3	0	0	0	0	0
McConnell, Jason, F.M.	.000	1	0	0	0	0	0
McCurtain, Paul, B.C.	1.000	40	4	3	0	7	0
McDonald, Jon, St.P.*	.800	10	3	1	1	5	1
McEntire, Ethan, St.L.*	.970	22	8	24	1	33	2
McLeary, Marty, Sar.	.600	8	1	2	2	5	0
McMullen, Jerry, Sar.*	1.000	41	0	3	0	3	0
Mercedes, Carlos, Kis.	.929	41	2	11	1	14	0
Messman, Joe, Kis.	1.000	45	4	9	0	13	2
Meyers, Mike, Day.	.933	19	2	12	1	15	1
Miller, Matt, Lak.*	.909	19	6	14	2	22	0
Miller, Matt, Char.	.750	22	2	1	1	4	0
Mills, Ryan, F.M.*	.917	27	2	9	1	12	0
Mlodik, Kevin, Char.	1.000	25	1	5	0	6	0
Mobley, Kevin, Lak.	1.000	46	4	8	0	12	2
Montgomery, Steve, V.B.	1.000	9	1	6	0	7	1
Moody, Eric, Char.	.000	1	0	0	0	0	0
Moore, Chris, B.C.	1.000	13	3	2	0	5	0
Moraga, David, Jup.*	.966	23	10	18	1	29	1
Mori, Kazuma, Jup.	1.000	3	1	0	0	1	0
Moskau, Ryan, V.B.-B.C.*	.978	26	12	32	1	45	2

Player, Team	Pct.	G	PO	A	E	TC	DP
Mota, Danny, F.M.	1.000	11	2	2	0	4	0
Nakamura, Micheal, F.M.	1.000	14	3	3	0	6	0
Narcisse, Tyrone, Kis.	1.000	4	0	1	0	1	0
Nation, Joey, Day.*	1.000	2	1	2	0	3	0
Navarro, Scott, Kis.*	1.000	37	6	13	0	19	1
Nelson, Jeff, Tam.	1.000	3	0	1	0	1	0
Nicholson, John, Jup.	1.000	4	0	1	0	1	0
Nickle, Douglas, Cle.	1.000	60	4	14	0	18	0
Niebla, Ruben, V.B.*	.000	1	0	0	0	0	0
Noel, Todd, Tam.	.966	17	11	17	1	29	1
Ohman, Will, Day.*	.882	31	1	14	2	17	2
Olsen, Kevin, B.C.	1.000	11	2	7	0	9	1
Ortega, Pablo, St.P.	1.000	4	1	1	0	2	0
Padilla, Juan, F.M.	1.000	22	9	6	0	15	0
Partenheimer, Brian, Sar.-B.C.*	1.000	38	6	16	0	22	1
Pena, Juan, Sar.	1.000	2	1	0	0	1	0
Persails, Mark, Kis.	1.000	10	2	4	0	6	1
Person, Robert, Dun.	1.000	1	0	1	0	1	0
Pettitte, Andy, Tam.*	.000	1	0	0	0	0	0
Pettyjohn, Adam, Lak.*	1.000	9	3	11	0	14	0
Phelps, Travis, St.P.	1.000	24	10	22	0	32	2
Piersoll, Chris, Day.	.818	33	1	8	2	11	0
Pineda, Isauro, Sar.	1.000	11	1	7	0	8	1
Pineda, Luis, Lak.	1.000	8	2	1	0	3	0
Poeck, Chad, Char.	1.000	9	1	3	0	4	0
Poland, Trey, Char.*	1.000	6	2	3	0	5	0
Pontes, Dan, St.L.	1.000	4	1	0	0	1	0
Pyc, David, Cle.*	.500	7	0	1	1	2	0
Quantrill, Paul, Dun.	1.000	5	0	1	0	1	0
Quarnstrom, Robert, Char.*	.667	30	1	7	4	12	0
Quezada, Edward, Jup.	.933	34	4	10	1	15	2
Quintal, Craig, Lak.	.955	26	6	15	1	22	0
Ramirez, Jose, Lak.*	1.000	29	4	13	0	17	2
Rangel, Julio, Tam.	1.000	12	2	6	0	8	0
Regalado, Maximo, V.B.	.875	20	5	9	2	16	0
Reith, Brian, Tam.	.957	26	5	17	1	23	0
Reitsma, Chris, Sar.	.938	19	9	6	1	16	1
Reyes, Eddy, St.P.	.889	37	3	5	1	9	0
Richards, Mark, B.C.	.941	26	14	18	2	34	0
Rico, Diego, Day.*	.000	1	0	0	0	0	0
Riggan, Jerrod, St.L.	1.000	44	5	18	0	23	1
Roach, Jason, St.L.	.000	2	0	0	0	0	0
Robbins, Jake, Tam.	.750	7	1	8	3	12	0
Roberts, Rick, V.B.*	1.000	11	2	9	0	11	1
Rodney, Fernando, Lak.	.000	4	0	0	0	0	0
Rodriguez, Wilfredo, Kis.*	.833	25	6	14	4	24	1
Rogers, Brian, Tam.	.913	25	4	17	2	23	0
Roller, Adam, Sar.	1.000	1	1	0	0	1	0
Romo, Greg, Lak.	.917	25	5	17	2	24	0
Rosario, Juan, St.P.	.905	15	9	10	2	21	1
Rose, Brian, Sar.	1.000	5	2	0	0	2	0
Rose, Johnathan, Cle.*	.750	8	1	2	1	4	0
Ruhl, Nathan, St.P.	.000	4	0	0	0	0	0
Rutherford, Mark, Cle.	.875	9	4	3	1	8	1
Salamon, John, Tam.	.000	2	0	0	1	1	0
Sams, Aaron, Day.*	1.000	10	2	13	0	15	0
Saylor, Ryan, Jup.	1.000	21	1	1	0	2	0
Schaffer, Trevor, Dun.	1.000	8	0	1	0	1	0
Schuldt, Matt, St.P.	1.000	19	2	2	0	4	0
Schultz, Eric, Char.	1.000	19	5	5	0	10	1
Seabury, Jaron, Dun.	1.000	35	4	13	0	17	2
Seaman, John, B.C.	.923	25	4	8	1	13	0
Seay, Bobby, St.P.*	1.000	12	1	13	0	14	0
Seo, Jae, St.L.	.000	3	0	0	0	0	0
Serrano, Jim, Jup.	.944	44	5	12	1	18	0

Player, Team	Pct.	G	PO	A	E	TC	DP
Sessions, Doug, Kis.	1.000	35	1	6	0	7	0
Shearn, Tom, Kis.	1.000	24	2	23	0	25	0
Sheldon, Kyle, Jup.	1.000	20	1	3	0	4	1
Shipp, Kevin, Cle.	.931	32	9	18	2	29	3
Short, Barry, St.L.	.800	10	1	3	1	5	0
Silva, Doug, Char.	.800	24	8	4	3	15	0
Simon, Ben, V.B.	1.000	38	8	10	0	18	2
Smith, Clint, Lak.	1.000	7	2	5	0	7	0
Sneed, John, Dun.	.957	21	6	16	1	23	0
Snyder, Bill, Lak.	.909	47	1	9	1	11	2
Spear, Russell, Lak.	1.000	8	0	2	0	2	1
Spence, Cam, Tam.	1.000	7	2	5	0	7	0
Spinelli, Mike, Sar.*	.556	38	1	4	4	9	0
Standridge, Jason, St.P.	1.000	8	12	5	0	17	1
Stodgel, Jeff, V.B.	.000	1	0	0	0	0	0
Strickland, Scott, Jup.	1.000	12	0	3	0	3	0
Sullivan, Shane, Day.	1.000	4	0	2	0	2	0
Swiatkiewicz, Chris, Tam.	.000	2	0	0	0	0	0
Taczy, Craig, V.B.*	.848	28	12	16	5	33	1
Taglienti, Jeff, Sar.	1.000	14	2	4	0	6	0
Tam, Jeff, St.L.	.000	2	0	0	0	0	0
Teut, Nate, Day.*	.816	26	7	24	7	38	0
THOMAS, Brad, F.M.*	1.000	27	10	27	0	37	1
Thomas, Don, Kis.*	1.000	18	2	10	0	12	0
Thompson, Chris, Sar.	.909	28	3	7	1	11	0
Tovar, Angel, Tam.	.000	3	0	0	0	0	0
Tucker, T.J., Jup.	.938	7	5	10	1	16	2
Urdaneta, Lino, V.B.	.933	27	2	12	1	15	0
Van Gilder, Ryan, Jup.	1.000	5	0	1	0	1	0
Vardijan, Dan, B.C.	.875	34	4	10	2	16	0
Vigeland, William, Char.	1.000	5	1	1	0	2	0
Wade, Travis, Kis.	.000	1	0	0	0	0	0
Walker, Adam, Cle.*	.870	26	9	11	3	23	2
Walker, Tyler, St.L.	.895	13	7	10	2	19	0
Wallace, Chris, Tam.	1.000	30	2	10	0	12	1
Wedel, Jeremy, Cle.	.000	4	0	0	0	0	0
Weimer, Matt, Dun.	.964	46	8	19	1	28	4
Westmoreland, Ken, Cle.	.897	20	5	23	3	29	0
White, Matt, St.P.	.864	21	6	13	3	22	0
Whitesides, Johnny, Kis.	1.000	14	1	1	0	2	0
Williams, Randy, Day.*	1.000	14	4	8	0	12	0
Willis, Jason, Tam.	1.000	3	0	2	0	2	0
Wood, Stanton, Tam.	1.000	50	0	11	0	11	1
Woodman, Hank, Char.	.900	6	4	5	1	10	1
Workman, Widd, V.B.	1.000	25	3	4	0	7	0
Yan, Esteban, St.P.	.000	2	0	0	0	0	0
Yennaco, Jay, Dun.	.500	3	1	0	1	2	0
Yoder, Jeff, Day.	1.000	5	0	1	0	1	0
Zambrano, Victor, St.P.	.667	7	0	2	1	3	0

PITCHERS WITH TWO OR MORE TEAMS

Player, Team	Pct.	G	PO	A	E	TC	DP
Davis, Keith, Tam.	1.000	11	0	2	0	2	0
Davis, Keith, Lak.	1.000	25	2	3	0	5	0
Downs, Scott, F.M.*	1.000	2	0	5	0	5	0
Downs, Scott, Day.*	.947	7	4	14	1	19	1
Lohse, Kyle, Day.	1.000	9	1	5	0	6	0
Lohse, Kyle, F.M.	1.000	7	5	5	0	10	0
Maroth, Mike, Sar.*	1.000	20	9	19	0	28	0
Maroth, Mike, Lak.*	1.000	3	0	2	0	2	0
Moskau, Ryan, V.B.*	.966	17	8	20	1	29	2
Moskau, Ryan, B.C.*	1.000	9	4	12	0	16	0
Partenheimer, Brian, Sar.*	1.000	17	3	6	0	9	0
Partenheimer, Brian, B.C.*	1.000	21	3	10	0	13	1

The following players appeared only as designated hitter, pinch-hitter or pinch runner: Baker, dh-ph; Belliard, dh-ph; Diaz, dh-ph; Dito, dh-ph; Harrell, ph; Marzano, dh; Mento, ph; Munson, dh; Simms, dh; Steele, dh.

LEAGUE CHAMPIONS

Year	Team	Pct.	Year	Team	Pct.	Year	Team	Pct.
1919—	Sanford*	.605		Lakeland	.683	1937—	Gainesville§	.616
	Orlando*	.703	1925—	St. Petersburg	.667	1938—	Leesburg	.626
1920—	Tampa	.654		Tampa†	.696		Gainesville (2nd)‡	.615
	Tampa	.722	1926—	Sanford	.647	1939—	Sanford§	.787
1921—	Orlando	.635		Sanford	.623	1940—	Daytona Beach	.619
1922—	St. Petersburg	.503	1927—	Orlando†	.600		Orlando (4th)‡	.507
	St. Petersburg	.618		Miami	.661	1941—	St. Augustine	.659
1923—	Orlando	.667	1928-35—Did not operate.				Leesburg (4th)‡	.488
	Orlando	.678	1936—	Gainesville	.542	1942-45—Did not operate.		
1924—	Lakeland	.695		St. Augustine (4th)†	.492	1946—	Orlando§	.681

Year	Team	Pct.
1947—	St. Augustine	.625
	Gainesville (2nd)‡	.584
1948—	Orlando	.643
	Daytona Beach (2nd)‡	.616
1949—	Gainesville	.635
	St. Augustine (3rd)‡	.556
1950—	Orlando	.629
	DeLand (3rd)‡	.590
1951—	DeLand§	.643
1952—	DeLand∞	.704
	Palatka (3rd)‡	.569
1953—	Daytona Beach†	.657
	DeLand	.703
1954—	Jacksonville Beach	.629
	Lakeland†	.594
1955—	Orlando	.671
	Orlando	.643
1956—	Cocoa	.614
	Cocoa	.671
1957—	Palatka	.629
	Tampa†	.681
1958—	St. Petersburg	.732
	St. Petersburg	.681
1959—	Tampa	.591
	St. Petersburg†	.612
1960—	Lakeland	.731
	Palatka†	.614
1961—	Tampa†	.710
	Sarasota	.696
1962—	Sarasota	.689
	Fort Lauderdale†	.623
1963—	Sarasota	.645
	Sarasota	.667
1964—	Fort Lauderdale†	.629
	St. Petersburg	.594
1965—	Fort Lauderdale	.627
		.634
1966—	Leesburg†	.781
	St. Petersburg	.700
1967—	St. Petersburg▲	.691
	Orlando	.638
1968—	Miami	.613
	Orlando♦	.579
1969—	Miami■	.606
	Orlando	.606
1970—	Miami▼	.662
	St. Petersburg	.600
1971—	Miami▼	.667
	Daytona Beach	.586
1972—	Miami•	.562
	Daytona Beach	.606
1973—	St. Petersburg††	.575
	West Palm Beach	.580
1974—	West Palm Beach††	.598
	Fort Lauderdale	.626
1975—	St. Petersburg††	.652
	Miami	.581
1976—	Tampa	.559
	Lakeland††	.536
1977—	Lakeland††	.616
	West Palm Beach	.583
1978—	Lakeland	.565
	Miami§	.539
1979—	Fort Lauderdale	.643
	Winter Haven‡‡	.577
1980—	Daytona Beach	.628
	Fort Lauderdale††	.606
1981—	Fort Myers	.554
	Daytona Beach§§	.504
1982—	Fort Lauderdale§§	.621
	Tampa	.546
1983—	Daytona Beach	.634
	Vero Beach§§	.515
1984—	Tampa	.532
	Fort Lauderdale§§	.521
1985—	Fort Myers∞∞	.590
	Fort Lauderdale	.550
1986—	St. Petersburg∞∞	.647
	West Palm Beach	.593
1987—	Fort Lauderdale∞∞	.616
	Osceola	.576
1988—	Osceola	.606
	St. Lucie▲▲	.532
1989—	Port Charlotte▲▲	.540
	St. Petersburg	.540
1990—	West Palm Beach	.697
	Vero Beach▲▲	.585
1991—	Clearwater	.623
	West Palm Beach▲▲	.550
1992—	Sarasota	.639
	Lakeland♦♦	.530
1993—	St. Lucie	.600
	Clearwater§§	.556
1994—	Tampa§§	.606
	Brevard County	.561
1995—	Daytona§§	.644
	Fort Myers	.577
1996—	Tampa	.627
	St. Lucie§§	.534
1997—	St. Petersburg■ ■	.591
	Vero Beach	.511
1998—	Charlotte	.594
	St. Lucie■ ■	.515
1999—	Dunedin	.628
	Kissimmee■ ■	.578

*Split-season playoff abandoned after each team won three games. †Won split-season playoff. ‡Won four-club playoff. §Won championship and four-club playoff. ∞Won both halves of split season. ▲League divided into Eastern and Western divisions with split season. St. Petersburg and Orlando won both halves of split season; St. Petersburg won playoff. ♦League divided into Eastern and Western divisions. Miami won regular-season pennant on basis of highest won-lost percentage. Orlando won four-club playoff involving first two teams in each division. ■ League divided into Southern and Central divisions. Miami won playoff between division leaders. (NOTE—Pennant awarded to playoff winner in 1936.) ▼League divided into Eastern and Western divisions. Miami won regular-season pennant on basis of highest won-loss percentage, and also won four-club playoff involving first two teams in each division. •League divided into Eastern and Western divisions. Won four-club playoff involving first two teams in each division. ††League divided into Northern and Southern divisions. Won four-club playoff involving first two teams in each division. ‡‡League divided into Northern and Southern divisions. Same two clubs won both halves; won playoffs. §§Won split-season playoff. ∞∞League divided into Western, Central and Southern divisions. Won four-club playoff. ▲▲League divided into Eastern, Western and Central divisions; played split-season. Won six-club playoff. ♦♦League divided into Eastern, Western and Central divisions; played split-season. Won eight-club playoff. ■ ■ League divided into East and West divisions and played split season; won four-club playoff.

MIDWEST LEAGUE

LEAGUE OFFICE

President
George H. Spelius

Address
P.O. Box 936
Beloit, WI 53512

Phone
608-364-1188

Teams (affiliation)
Beloit Snappers (Brewers)
Burlington Bees (White Sox)
Cedar Rapids Kernels (Angels)
Clinton Lumber Kings (Reds)
Fort Wayne Wizards (Padres)
Kane County Cougars (Marlins)
Lansing Lugnuts (Cubs)

Michigan Battle Cats (Astros)
Peoria Chiefs (Cardinals)
Quad City River Bandits (Twins)
Dayton Dragons (Reds)
South Bend Silver Hawks
(Diamondbacks)
West Michigan Whitecaps (Tigers)
Wisconsin Timber Rattlers (Mariners)

1999 FINAL STANDINGS

FIRST HALF

EASTERN DIVISION

Team	W	L	T	Pct.	GB
Lansing (Cubs)	38	32	0	.543	...
Michigan (Astros)	35	34	0	.507	2.5
South Bend (Diamondbacks)	32	37	0	.464	5.5
West Michigan (Tigers)	29	41	0	.414	9.0
Fort Wayne (Padres)	29	41	0	.414	9.0

CENTRAL DIVISION

Team	W	L	T	Pct.	GB
Rockford (Reds)	45	24	0	.652	...
Kane County (Marlins)	40	27	0	.597	4.0
Peoria (Cardinals)	37	32	0	.536	8.0
Wisconsin (Mariners)	32	36	0	.471	12.5
Beloit (Brewers)	25	44	0	.362	20.0

WESTERN DIVISION

Team	W	L	T	Pct.	GB
Clinton (Reds)	41	27	0	.603	...
Quad City (Twins)	38	31	0	.551	3.5
Burlington (White Sox)	31	38	0	.449	10.5
Cedar Rapids (Angels)	30	38	0	.441	11.0

SECOND HALF

EASTERN DIVISION

Team	W	L	T	Pct.	GB
Michigan (Astros)	41	28	0	.594	...
West Michigan (Tigers)	39	31	0	.557	2.5
South Bend (Diamondbacks)	36	34	0	.514	5.5
Lansing (Cubs)	35	35	0	.500	6.5
Fort Wayne (Padres)	32	38	0	.457	9.5

CENTRAL DIVISION

Team	W	L	T	Pct.	GB
Wisconsin (Mariners)	40	30	0	.571	...
Kane County (Marlins)	38	32	0	.543	2.0
Beloit (Brewers)	34	36	0	.486	6.0
Rockford (Reds)	31	39	0	.443	9.0
Peoria (Cardinals)	26	44	0	.371	14.0

WESTERN DIVISION

Team	W	L	T	Pct.	GB
Burlington (White Sox)	40	30	0	.571	...
Quad City (Twins)	39	31	0	.557	1.0
Cedar Rapids (Angels)	31	39	0	.443	9.0
Clinton (Reds)	27	42	0	.391	12.5

COMPOSITE

Team	K.C.	Q.C.	Mch.	Rck.	Wis.	Lan.	Burl.	Clin.	S.B.	W.M.	Peo.	C.R.	F.W.	Bel.	W	L	T	Pct.	GB
Kane County (Marlins)	...	4	5	11	6	5	5	3	5	5	6	5	4	14	78	59	0	.569	...
Quad City (Twins)	4	...	5	3	6	5	13	11	6	5	2	9	3	5	77	62	0	.554	2.0
Michigan (Astros)	3	3	...	4	5	11	4	4	9	4	4	10	6	6	76	62	0	.551	2.5
Rockford (Reds)	5	5	4	...	8	4	4	4	5	7	14	6	3	7	76	63	0	.547	3.0
Wisconsin (Mariners)	11	2	2	8	...	4	5	4	3	5	9	3	5	11	72	66	0	.522	6.5
Lansing (Cubs)	3	3	6	4	4	...	3	4	10	10	6	5	10	5	73	67	0	.521	6.5
Burlington (White Sox)	3	6	4	4	3	5	...	12	4	3	4	15	4	4	71	68	0	.511	8.0
Clinton (Reds)	5	9	3	4	3	4	8	...	4	5	7	9	5	2	68	69	0	.496	10.0
South Bend (Diamondbacks)	2	2	7	3	5	7	4	4	...	5	4	5	14	6	68	71	0	.489	10.5
West Michigan (Tigers)	3	3	9	1	3	7	5	3	12	...	6	3	7	6	68	72	0	.486	11.5
Peoria (Cardinals)	10	6	4	4	8	2	4	1	4	2	...	5	6	7	63	76	0	.453	16.0
Cedar Rapids (Angels)	3	11	4	2	5	3	5	10	3	5	3	...	4	3	61	77	0	.442	17.5
Fort Wayne (Padres)	4	5	7	5	3	7	4	3	4	9	2	4	...	4	61	79	0	.436	18.5
Beloit (Brewers)	3	3	2	10	7	3	4	6	2	2	9	4	4	...	59	80	0	.424	20.0

Quad City's home games played in Davenport, Iowa; Kane County's home games played in Geneva, Ill.; Michgan's home games played in Battle Creek, Mich.; West Michigan's home games played in Comstock Park, Mich.

Major league affiliations in parentheses.

PLAYOFFS: Lansing defeated Michigan two games to none; Wisconsin defeated Rockford two games to none; Burlington defeated Clinton two games to one; Kane County defeated Quad City two games to one; Wisconsin defeated Lansing two games to none; Burlington defeated Kane County two games to one; Burlington defeated Wisconsin three games to two to win league championship.

REGULAR-SEASON ATTENDANCE: Beloit, 54,689; Burlington, 66,178; Cedar Rapids, 127,612; Clinton, 61,485; Fort Wayne, 201,395; Kane County, 451,145; Lansing, 462,515; Michigan, 108,033; Peoria, 150,254; Quad City, 145,734; Rockford, 63,705; South Bend, 200,518; West Michigan, 457,350; Wisconsin, 223,814. Total—2,774,427. Playoffs (20 games)—23,349. All-Star Game at Lansing, Mich.—10,034.

MANAGERS: Beloit, Don Money; Burlington, Nick Capra; Cedar Rapids, Mitch Seoane; Clinton, Freddie Benavides; Fort Wayne, Dan Simonds; Kane County, Rick Renteria; Lansing, Oscar Acosta; Michigan, Al Pedrique; Peoria, Brian Rupp; Quad City, Jose Marzan; Rockford, Mike Rojas; South Bend, Mike Brumley; West Michigan, Bruce Fields; Wisconsin, Steve Roadcap.

ALL-STAR TEAM: 1B—Aaron McNeal, Burlington; 2B—Aaron Miles, Michigan; 3B—Sean Burroughs, Fort Wayne; SS—Travis Dawkins, Rockford; OF—Corey Patterson, Lansing; Michael Restovich, Quad City; Juan Silvestre, Wisconsin; C—Jeff Goldbach, Lansing; DH—Eric Munson, West Michigan; LHP—David Noyce, Kane County; RHP—Juan Rincon, Quad City; LHR—Clint Chrysler, Wisconsin; RHR—Brandon Puffer, Clinton; Most Valuable Player—Aaron McNeal, Michigan; Prospect of the Year—Corey Patterson, Lansing; Manager of the Year—Rick Renteria, Kane County.

TEAM

Team	Avg.	G	TPA	AB	R	H	TB	2B	3B	HR	RBI	SH	SF	HP	BB	IBB	SO	SB	CS	GDP	LOB	ShO	Slg.	OBP
Michigan	.284	138	5295	4747	810	1350	2158	277	54	141	741	31	55	61	401	13	873	105	67	97	928	4	.455	.344
Lansing	.274	140	5423	4670	822	1278	2127	288	60	147	752	10	54	70	619	12	1031	133	61	108	1025	8	.455	.363
Kane County	.270	137	5398	4681	777	1263	1852	251	40	86	674	32	48	83	554	14	1010	166	67	88	1034	3	.396	.354
Wisconsin	.268	138	5371	4645	721	1243	1812	247	26	90	650	28	37	52	609	9	1027	122	72	116	1066	6	.390	.356
Rockford	.266	139	5202	4587	700	1221	1898	243	43	116	621	28	52	84	451	22	975	227	123	89	908	4	.414	.339
Burlington	.263	139	5372	4604	734	1213	1827	239	39	99	661	39	51	68	610	13	1023	155	65	87	1068	7	.397	.355
Beloit	.263	139	5290	4664	680	1227	1808	231	34	94	606	46	40	49	491	15	1056	94	39	104	979	10	.388	.337
South Bend	.262	139	5258	4712	642	1236	1744	229	45	63	578	9	43	47	447	11	986	108	73	96	972	14	.370	.330
Fort Wayne	.259	140	5417	4668	672	1209	1689	221	38	61	593	44	53	81	571	20	1102	225	100	96	1038	7	.362	.346
Quad City	.258	139	5496	4655	743	1203	1841	252	28	110	658	51	52	80	658	21	893	96	58	122	1103	7	.395	.356
Clinton	.255	137	5095	4542	648	1159	1694	234	38	75	579	28	43	57	455	11	1045	157	76	91	895	4	.373	.324
Cedar Rapids	.255	138	5272	4627	666	1178	1753	235	35	90	573	37	39	63	506	17	901	152	63	90	1017	11	.379	.334
Peoria	.254	139	5237	4634	641	1178	1695	228	41	69	552	45	29	74	455	9	1049	125	79	90	969	14	.366	.329
West Michigan	.253	140	5355	4688	696	1186	1751	260	43	73	627	38	43	65	521	10	1091	197	73	91	995	8	.374	.333

INDIVIDUAL

TOP QUALIFIERS FOR BATTING CHAMPIONSHIP

Minimum 378 plate appearances. *Lefthanded batter. †Switch-hitter.

Player, Team	Avg.	G	TPA	AB	R	H	TB	2B	3B	HR	RBI	SH	SF	HP	BB	IBB	SO	SB	CS	GDP	Slg.	OBP
Urquiola, Carlos, S.B.*	.362	93	415	384	66	139	158	13	3	0	35	1	3	5	22	0	32	20	14	2	.411	.401
Burroughs, Sean, F.W.*	.359	122	521	426	65	153	204	30	3	5	80	2	5	14	74	7	59	17	15	10	.479	.464
Robinson, Bo, Wis.	.329	138	619	499	101	164	259	50	3	13	102	0	8	4	108	4	75	4	1	18	.519	.446
Valenzuela, Mario, Burl.	.323	122	533	477	89	154	227	31	6	10	70	3	3	6	44	0	77	13	6	16	.476	.385
Patterson, Corey, Lan.*	.320	112	509	475	94	152	281	35	17	20	79	0	4	5	25	1	85	33	9	5	.592	.358
Miles, Aaron, Mich.†	.317	112	513	470	72	149	223	28	8	10	71	6	7	2	28	3	33	17	12	8	.474	.353
Restovich, Michael, Q.C.	.312	131	585	493	91	154	253	30	6	19	107	0	5	13	74	4	100	7	9	9	.513	.412
McNeal, Aaron, Mich.	.310	133	581	536	95	166	315	29	3	38	131	0	3	2	40	4	121	7	1	13	.588	.358
Turnquist, Tyler, Mich.	.309	118	531	456	89	141	213	25	7	11	67	1	7	5	62	1	69	5	4	14	.467	.392
Merriman, Terrell, Burl.*	.306	109	469	382	77	117	198	18	9	15	85	2	6	2	70	3	84	27	4	2	.518	.411
Darula, Bobby, Bel.*	.304	120	512	438	63	133	185	24	8	4	75	1	4	7	62	4	57	19	5	7	.422	.395
Hill, Willy, K.C.*	.303	127	605	535	85	162	199	19	6	2	57	10	8	8	44	0	56	38	24	4	.372	.360
Gomez, Richard, W.M.	.303	130	544	479	89	145	219	26	12	8	81	0	1	10	54	1	122	66	10	1	.457	.384
Meadows, Tydus, Lan.	.301	126	530	449	80	135	230	32	6	17	74	0	4	11	66	2	85	18	10	13	.512	.400
Williams, P.J., Wis.	.299	115	433	371	65	111	141	14	5	2	46	5	3	6	48	0	63	22	7	5	.380	.386

DEPARTMENTAL LEADERS: G—Robinson, 138; AB—McNeal, 536; R—Owens, 111; H—McNeal, 166; TB—McNeal, 315; 2B—Robinson, 50; 3B—Patterson, 17; HR—McNeal, 38; RBI—McNeal, 131; SH—Rodriguez, 13; SF—Wise, 14; HP—Schaeffer, Miller, 20 each; BB—Robinson, 108; IBB—Burroughs, 7; SO—Owens, 153; SB—Gomez, 66; CS—Hill, Perez, 24 each; GIDP—McMillin, 18; Slg.—Patterson, .592; OBP—Burroughs, .464.

ALL PLAYERS

*Lefthanded batter. †Switch-hitter.

Player, Team	Avg.	G	TPA	AB	R	H	TB	2B	3B	HR	RBI	SH	SF	HP	BB	IBB	SO	SB	CS	GDP	Slg.	OBP
Abreu, Miguel, K.C.	.000	3	7	7	0	0	0	0	0	0	1	0	0	0	0	0	6	0	0	0	.000	.000
Acevas, Jonathan, Burl.	.188	65	251	202	28	38	63	9	2	4	23	5	1	8	35	3	52	3	2	9	.312	.329
Adams, John, S.B.	.288	74	299	285	38	82	133	19	1	10	38	0	3	0	11	1	66	10	5	5	.467	.311
Aguila, Chris, K.C.	.244	122	484	430	74	105	185	21	7	15	78	3	2	9	40	2	127	14	4	9	.430	.320
Ahlers, Steve, C.R.	.265	74	297	260	27	69	79	5	1	1	29	3	3	1	30	0	44	15	9	6	.304	.340
Alfaro, Jason, Mich.	.271	118	509	473	74	128	176	25	4	5	50	5	7	1	23	0	62	5	5	10	.372	.302
Alleyne, Roberto, Mich.	.291	95	361	323	61	94	149	25	3	8	60	1	7	5	25	2	59	9	2	4	.461	.344
Almonte, Claudio, Q.C.	.213	46	174	150	19	32	40	4	2	0	12	3	1	1	19	0	41	4	3	4	.267	.304
Alvarez, Jimmy, Q.C.†	.253	121	534	435	69	110	150	20	1	6	48	7	5	6	81	3	112	15	10	9	.345	.374
Araujo, Danilo, Peo.	.277	105	416	361	53	100	117	10	2	1	36	6	3	3	43	0	75	21	16	5	.324	.356
Baderdeen, Kevin, Clin.	.252	113	444	405	47	102	159	22	4	9	49	0	2	2	35	0	128	9	6	9	.393	.313
Bailey, Jeff, K.C.	.278	76	322	277	49	77	128	19	1	10	53	0	5	6	34	2	77	1	1	8	.462	.363
Battersby, Eric, Burl.	.290	132	568	472	78	137	222	27	2	18	93	0	9	4	83	1	90	13	2	8	.470	.394
Bautista, Jorge, K.C.	.220	61	216	186	30	41	62	12	0	3	30	1	4	4	21	0	54	2	1	4	.333	.307
Beatriz, Ramy, Bel.*	.296	70	273	243	43	72	99	14	2	3	26	1	0	0	29	3	39	5	3	5	.407	.371
Beattie, Andrew, Clin.†	.230	108	411	335	58	77	112	11	3	6	41	8	5	3	60	1	75	18	4	6	.334	.347
Belliard, Francisco, S.B.†	.249	70	289	265	28	66	79	11	1	0	15	2	0	2	20	0	64	3	2	7	.298	.307
Berroa, Cristian, F.W.†	.240	119	469	442	49	106	134	12	3	4	40	5	5	3	14	0	71	25	11	9	.308	.265
Bly, Derrick, Lan.	.295	63	234	220	36	65	99	14	4	4	29	0	2	3	9	0	48	1	1	8	.450	.329
Bolling, Kirk, S.B.	.184	16	56	49	6	9	17	5	0	1	6	0	0	1	6	0	18	1	0	0	.347	.286
Boone, Matt, W.M.	.242	116	459	421	46	102	155	24	1	9	50	1	5	3	29	0	119	8	7	8	.368	.293
Bordenick, Ryan, Bel.	.270	73	281	248	40	67	106	19	1	6	36	3	4	2	25	1	60	2	0	7	.427	.338
Bowers, Jason, Peo.	.263	112	461	414	53	109	145	14	8	2	49	5	1	9	32	1	78	10	9	6	.350	.329
Brito, Obispo, Bel.	.234	101	387	364	44	85	132	24	1	7	48	4	3	3	13	1	76	7	0	7	.363	.264
Brock, J.J., S.B.	.221	48	189	172	19	38	55	8	3	1	13	2	2	1	12	0	27	2	2	6	.320	.273
Broussard, Benjamin, Clin.*...	.550	5	23	20	8	11	23	4	1	2	6	0	0	3	2	0	4	0	0	1	1.150	.609
Buck, John, Mich.	.100	4	12	10	1	1	2	1	0	0	0	0	0	0	2	0	3	0	0	0	.200	.250
Burns, Kevan, S.B.*	.318	43	171	157	22	50	66	8	1	2	25	0	0	0	14	0	27	3	4	5	.420	.374
Burress, Andy, Rock.	.304	72	293	270	45	82	122	24	4	4	32	1	3	2	17	1	45	17	6	4	.452	.346
Burroughs, Sean, F.W.*	.359	122	521	426	65	153	204	30	3	5	80	2	5	14	74	7	59	17	15	10	.479	.464
Bush, Ron, W.M.	.255	118	506	444	56	113	147	23	4	1	60	10	3	5	44	0	57	14	10	5	.331	.327
Caceres, Wilmy, Clin.†	.261	117	512	476	77	124	155	18	5	1	30	2	2	2	30	1	65	52	22	6	.326	.306
Callahan, David, K.C.†	.245	124	515	457	65	112	148	22	4	2	53	1	2	4	39	0	105	2	1	7	.324	.305
Campbell, Sean, F.W.*	.265	102	381	343	48	91	137	17	4	7	54	4	4	3	27	2	71	10	4	6	.399	.321
Candela, Frank, Bel.	.299	30	121	107	15	32	36	4	0	0	13	0	2	0	9	0	12	14	6	1	.336	.364

Player, Team	Avg.	G	TPA	AB	R	H	TB	2B	3B	HR	RBI	SH	SF	HP	BB	IBB	SO	SB	CS	GDP	Slg.	OBP
Castillo, Ruben, Wis.	.205	20	49	44	7	9	9	0	0	0	4	0	0	0	5	0	9	1	1	3	.205	.286
Cedeno, Jesus, W.M.	.236	47	168	157	14	37	55	9	0	3	18	1	1	3	6	0	34	3	3	3	.350	.275
Chapman, Scott, Mich.	.270	64	248	226	37	61	113	17	1	11	36	0	1	7	14	0	32	1	2	7	.500	.331
Choi, Hee, Lan.*	.321	79	344	290	71	93	177	18	6	18	70	0	2	2	50	0	68	2	1	8	.610	.422
Christensen, Mike, C.R.	.282	127	558	504	68	142	236	36	2	18	71	0	4	5	42	3	102	1	2	12	.468	.341
Clark, Greg, Peo.	.214	68	265	229	26	49	69	11	0	3	23	1	4	2	29	0	76	0	4	6	.301	.303
Closser, J.D., S.B.†	.241	52	212	174	29	42	59	8	0	3	27	0	3	1	34	0	37	0	1	3	.339	.363
Condon, Mike, C.R.	.122	13	45	41	2	5	5	0	0	0	1	0	0	1	3	0	7	0	0	0	.122	.200
Conley, Brian, Rock.	.228	89	316	285	39	65	84	7	3	2	22	6	2	4	19	0	69	13	8	3	.295	.284
Cook, Jon, F.W.	.213	107	376	315	60	67	87	12	1	2	32	4	3	0	54	0	94	39	11	3	.276	.325
Copley, Travis, Clin.*	.200	4	18	15	3	3	3	0	0	0	0	0	0	0	3	0	0	0	0	1	.200	.333
Cosentino, Tony, F.W.	.244	37	151	127	11	31	36	5	0	0	11	0	1	1	22	0	33	1	1	3	.283	.358
Croud, Will, C.R.†	.231	87	337	281	39	65	92	11	5	2	31	3	5	2	46	0	44	5	5	8	.327	.338
Cutshall, Pat, Mich.	.238	8	24	21	3	5	5	0	0	0	2	1	0	0	2	0	3	0	1	0	.238	.304
Da Luz, Craig, W.M.	.264	87	343	314	36	83	116	14	5	3	49	2	4	3	20	0	46	3	1	6	.369	.311
Daigle, Leo, W.M.	.276	108	453	406	59	112	165	36	1	5	60	1	6	7	33	0	121	3	0	9	.406	.336
Darula, Bobby, Bel.*	.304	120	512	438	63	133	185	24	8	4	75	1	4	7	62	4	57	19	5	7	.422	.395
Davis, James, Clin.	.200	3	12	10	0	2	2	0	0	0	0	0	0	1	1	0	2	1	0	0	.200	.333
Dawkins, Travis, Rock.	.272	76	342	305	56	83	129	10	6	8	32	1	1	0	35	2	38	38	13	5	.423	.346
De La Cruz, Erickson, Bel.	.215	95	290	260	19	56	64	8	0	0	13	8	0	3	19	0	35	1	4	7	.246	.277
De La Cruz, Henry, Lan.	.215	71	243	209	26	45	77	14	0	6	31	1	1	3	29	0	75	7	4	6	.368	.318
Delgado, Ariel, C.R.*	.259	102	402	359	52	93	131	27	1	3	47	4	5	5	29	0	63	14	1	8	.365	.319
Diaz , Alejandro, Clin.	.285	55	239	221	39	63	101	14	3	6	41	0	4	2	12	1	35	28	11	6	.457	.322
Diaz, Angel, C.R.	.242	81	321	281	43	68	111	11	1	10	42	0	0	6	34	0	85	0	3	4	.395	.336
Diaz, Michael, C.R.*	.181	25	90	72	12	13	14	1	0	0	6	1	3	0	14	0	22	3	1	1	.194	.303
Diaz, Miguel, Peo.	.254	105	365	343	44	87	126	18	6	3	34	6	1	7	8	0	59	10	6	6	.367	.284
Dimmick, Josh, Mich.-Q.C.†	.292	77	298	264	36	77	117	16	3	6	40	0	3	2	27	2	37	2	1	8	.443	.358
Dorsett, Chris, Lan.	.231	57	173	130	20	30	44	8	0	2	19	1	4	1	37	0	24	2	2	7	.338	.395
Downing, Brad, C.R.*	.234	13	51	47	7	11	20	3	0	2	7	0	0	1	3	0	10	0	0	1	.426	.294
Downing, Lance, S.B.*	.289	118	484	439	65	127	158	18	5	1	51	0	7	3	35	3	69	7	3	9	.360	.341
Dunaway, Jason, F.W.	.216	85	290	255	34	55	72	10	2	1	17	1	1	6	27	0	58	12	6	11	.282	.304
Dunn, Adam, Rock.*	.307	93	372	313	62	96	149	16	2	11	44	0	3	10	46	3	64	21	10	6	.476	.409
Durham, Chad, Burl.	.200	7	29	25	3	5	6	1	0	0	0	0	0	0	4	0	6	2	3	1	.240	.310
Dusan, Joe, F.W.*	.293	53	221	184	29	54	83	10	2	5	37	1	4	2	29	0	50	1	3	4	.451	.388
Dyt, Darren, Peo.*	.237	81	279	253	30	60	80	15	1	1	24	1	0	1	24	0	55	4	2	13	.316	.306
Elliott, Dawan, Rock.*	.133	19	35	30	3	4	7	0	0	1	6	0	1	0	4	0	10	0	1	0	.233	.229
Encarnacion, Bienvenido, C.R.†	.262	57	225	206	28	54	64	3	2	1	23	6	2	0	11	0	33	4	2	8	.311	.297
Escalona, Felix, Mich.	.288	116	452	396	78	114	169	29	4	6	47	7	3	17	29	0	60	7	7	4	.427	.360
Escobar, Gustavo, Peo.	.319	24	103	94	11	30	38	2	3	0	18	2	1	0	6	0	14	2	2	5	.404	.356
Espino, Fernando, Wis.	.293	130	532	481	71	141	203	29	0	11	69	1	3	9	38	0	91	5	8	16	.422	.354
Faison, Vince, F.W.*	.208	11	56	48	10	10	12	2	0	0	1	1	0	1	6	0	18	7	1	0	.250	.309
Farnsworth, Troy, Peo.	.250	134	571	500	76	125	221	33	3	19	78	0	4	12	55	4	124	3	2	10	.442	.336
Fatheree, Danny, Mich.	.203	38	131	118	13	24	36	5	2	1	18	0	1	1	11	0	19	2	1	3	.305	.275
Fennell, Jason, Burl.†	.279	114	487	398	78	111	171	28	7	6	79	1	8	5	75	5	56	22	6	8	.430	.393
Ferrand, Francisco, K.C.*	.255	16	58	51	6	13	17	4	0	0	4	0	0	0	7	0	8	0	2	0	.333	.345
Fick, Robert, W.M.*	.273	3	13	11	2	3	3	0	0	0	0	0	0	0	2	0	0	1	0	0	.273	.385
Figueroa, Eduardo, Bel.*	.253	70	274	233	38	59	99	19	0	7	43	2	7	3	29	1	72	0	0	7	.425	.335
Folkers, Brandon, Peo.*	.249	86	312	257	35	64	104	15	2	7	36	2	1	6	45	2	96	6	3	5	.405	.372
Fox, Jason, Bel.†	.221	41	176	163	18	36	44	3	1	1	6	1	0	1	11	0	34	8	3	2	.270	.274
Freeman, Corey, Wis.	.190	18	67	63	6	12	18	6	0	0	9	2	0	1	1	0	18	0	0	1	.286	.215
French, Ron, F.W.	.269	65	257	219	24	59	82	11	0	4	31	4	4	7	23	1	58	0	3	3	.374	.352
Frese, Nate, Lan.	.265	107	445	373	68	99	146	27	4	4	49	1	8	5	58	2	67	10	4	13	.391	.365
Frick, Matt, K.C.	.275	21	92	80	14	22	36	5	0	3	10	0	2	1	9	0	27	0	1	1	.450	.348
Fukuhara, Pete, Lan.	.311	60	269	235	39	73	129	19	2	11	40	3	2	5	24	1	31	7	5	3	.549	.383
Garcia, Alex, F.W.	.209	71	232	201	27	42	59	9	1	2	26	2	4	0	25	0	62	5	2	2	.294	.291
Garcia, Tony, Burl.	.235	73	271	230	35	54	70	10	0	2	20	5	1	13	22	0	76	3	4	4	.304	.335
Garrett, Scott, Rock.	.200	8	24	20	4	4	5	1	0	0	1	0	0	1	3	0	7	0	0	0	.250	.333
Garza, Rolando, Burl.	.209	40	164	148	13	31	38	4	0	1	8	3	1	0	12	0	30	4	3	5	.257	.267
Gastelum, Carlos, C.R.	.227	19	73	66	8	15	16	1	0	0	8	1	0	0	6	0	5	2	2	1	.242	.292
Gay, Dennis, C.R.	.191	16	55	47	4	9	12	3	0	0	8	1	1	2	4	0	14	0	0	0	.255	.278
German, Franklin, Lan.	.242	84	316	281	49	68	99	12	2	5	31	1	3	7	23	0	75	12	4	3	.352	.312
Godfrey, Tim, Rock.†	.247	34	89	77	10	19	24	2	0	1	7	2	1	0	9	0	23	3	3	1	.312	.322
Goldbach, Jeff, Lan.	.271	112	475	399	82	108	195	27	3	18	72	0	5	7	64	2	66	1	4	5	.489	.377
Gomez, Richard, W.M.	.303	130	544	479	89	145	219	26	12	8	81	0	1	10	54	1	122	66	10	1	.457	.384
Gonzalez, Jose, Burl.	.278	70	297	266	36	74	98	11	2	3	28	2	3	7	19	0	52	13	8	3	.368	.339
Gordon, Brian, S.B.*	.212	48	195	184	21	39	54	9	3	0	17	0	1	1	9	0	35	8	3	3	.293	.251
Goudie, Jaime, Clin.	.321	84	365	340	56	109	146	20	4	3	50	0	2	2	21	2	46	16	6	8	.429	.362
Griffin, Matt, Lan.	.182	5	12	11	0	2	3	1	0	0	1	0	0	0	1	0	4	0	0	0	.273	.250
Guillen, Jose, Bel.†	.268	76	287	228	45	61	79	7	4	1	20	7	2	2	48	0	65	12	4	5	.346	.396
Guzman, Elpidio, C.R.*	.274	130	577	526	74	144	208	26	13	4	48	5	3	2	41	4	84	52	17	11	.395	.327
Hall, Doug, Lan.*	.278	33	108	90	16	25	39	8	0	2	18	0	2	0	16	1	23	3	2	3	.433	.380
Hammond, Derry, Bel.	.229	107	433	380	65	87	159	17	2	17	50	0	5	5	43	0	141	1	1	7	.418	.312
Hankins, Ryan, Burl.	.294	129	591	487	93	143	232	36	4	15	74	2	8	3	91	1	118	11	6	8	.476	.402
Hawthorne, Kyle, Q.C.	.238	84	356	315	44	75	99	14	2	2	31	4	4	5	27	1	61	14	5	6	.314	.305
Haynes, Larry, Wis.	.261	67	199	176	36	46	79	5	5	6	23	4	0	1	18	0	58	9	3	0	.449	.333
Hazen, Mike, F.W.	.203	72	269	222	23	45	62	8	0	3	24	1	3	6	37	0	62	6	5	8	.279	.328
Hemmings, Scot, F.W.	.111	12	42	36	3	4	5	1	0	0	4	0	0	1	5	0	18	1	0	1	.139	.238
Hernandez, Orlando, Wis.	.231	15	27	26	3	6	7	1	0	0	1	0	0	1	0	0	8	0	0	1	.269	.259
Hill, Jason, C.R.	.287	111	447	390	59	112	161	22	0	9	52	4	5	12	36	4	59	3	2	5	.413	.361
Hill, Willy, K.C.*	.303	127	605	535	85	162	199	19	6	2	57	10	8	8	44	0	56	38	24	4	.372	.360
Hodge, Kevin, Q.C.	.240	125	520	425	65	102	177	30	3	13	73	1	8	7	78	1	85	6	6	12	.416	.361
Howard, Jason, Clin.	.162	25	71	68	5	11	14	3	0	0	6	0	0	0	3	0	17	0	0	2	.206	.197
Hyde, Brandon, Burl.	.286	65	253	210	33	60	93	15	0	6	40	1	3	6	33	0	60	1	1	4	.443	.393
Incantalupo, Todd, Bel.*	.000	40	1	1	0	0	0	0	0	0	0	0	0	0	0	0	0	0	0	0	.000	.000
Inge, Brandon, W.M.	.244	100	402	352	54	86	142	25	2	9	46	2	6	3	39	0	87	15	3	7	.403	.320

Player, Team	Avg.	G	TPA	AB	R	H	TB	2B	3B	HR	RBI	SH	SF	HP	BB	IBB	SO	SB	CS	GDP	Slg.	OBP
Ingram, Darron, Clin.	.355	22	90	76	15	27	47	5	0	5	18	0	0	0	14	0	20	1	1	0	.618	.456
Jaramillo, Frank, Bel.	.307	65	272	244	48	75	127	12	2	12	40	1	2	1	24	0	41	6	2	9	.520	.369
Jenkins, Corey, Burl.	.195	32	130	113	8	22	36	5	0	3	12	0	0	1	16	0	51	1	0	4	.319	.300
Jimenez, Carlos, W.M.	.228	87	326	272	57	62	87	12	2	3	24	2	1	2	49	0	78	14	5	3	.320	.349
Johnerson, Ryan, Clin.	.208	40	133	120	17	25	38	5	1	2	16	1	1	2	9	0	37	3	3	2	.317	.273
Jordan, Kevin, Mich.	.252	116	443	413	60	104	162	21	2	11	66	1	3	8	18	1	98	17	6	8	.392	.294
Jordan, Yustin, Q.C.	.200	47	182	150	28	30	62	11	0	7	30	1	1	4	26	0	42	0	1	8	.413	.331
Joyce, Jesse, Mich.	.167	8	26	24	4	4	10	1	1	1	1	0	0	0	2	0	5	0	1	0	.417	.231
Kasper, Todd, S.B.*	.188	34	114	101	7	19	20	1	0	0	9	0	1	0	12	0	37	1	1	2	.198	.272
Kata, Matthew, S.B.†	.261	78	352	318	40	83	116	14	5	3	33	1	1	4	28	0	46	5	6	5	.365	.328
Kearns, Austin, Rock.	.258	124	488	426	72	110	195	36	5	13	48	0	3	9	50	3	120	21	8	9	.458	.346
Kelly, Chris, Peo.	.169	18	67	59	5	10	11	1	0	0	7	0	0	1	7	0	18	0	0	0	.186	.269
Kelly, Heath, K.C.	.249	69	233	189	34	47	62	8	2	1	31	1	3	4	36	1	69	7	3	6	.328	.375
Kelton, Dave, Lan.	.269	124	553	509	75	137	201	17	4	13	68	0	3	2	39	1	121	22	9	11	.395	.322
Kidwell, Tommy, Peo.	.257	50	177	167	23	43	53	6	2	0	15	2	1	2	5	0	27	2	1	2	.317	.286
Kielty, Bobby, Q.C.†	.294	69	296	245	52	72	126	13	1	13	43	2	3	3	43	1	56	12	3	7	.514	.401
Kirby, Scott, Bel.	.304	68	300	247	54	75	142	14	1	17	47	0	3	3	47	0	59	3	1	5	.575	.417
Kison, Robbie, Rock.-Clin.	.229	27	87	70	10	16	23	2	1	1	6	0	1	4	12	0	16	0	1	2	.329	.368
Knight, Marcus, C.R.†	.216	132	532	462	69	100	161	20	7	9	52	1	2	6	61	2	97	21	8	5	.348	.315
Kuzmic, Craig, Wis.†	.238	91	390	323	48	77	127	18	1	10	55	2	2	2	61	0	84	7	4	10	.393	.361
Larson, Brandon, Rock.	.300	69	281	250	38	75	134	18	1	13	52	0	3	3	25	1	67	12	2	7	.536	.367
Lawrence, Tony, F.W.-Rock.	.192	56	206	177	13	34	46	10	1	0	13	2	0	4	23	0	57	1	1	4	.260	.299
Layton, Blane, Clin.-Rock.*	.283	76	256	219	38	62	100	16	5	4	32	3	2	1	31	3	58	9	5	3	.457	.372
Leatherman, Dan, Q.C.*	.259	74	298	255	41	66	84	12	0	2	31	4	1	3	35	3	28	2	5	5	.329	.354
Lee, Jason, Peo.*	.232	66	256	224	31	52	72	14	0	2	26	1	3	4	24	1	58	5	3	2	.321	.314
Loggins, Joshua, F.W.	.297	136	601	522	75	155	240	29	7	14	85	2	5	12	60	4	119	24	12	13	.460	.379
Lopez, Jose, S.B.	.165	26	95	91	5	15	21	3	0	1	8	0	0	1	3	0	19	0	0	2	.231	.200
Lopez, Luis, Mich.	.266	95	376	335	55	89	159	22	3	14	48	3	1	4	33	0	96	7	5	9	.475	.338
Lopez, Norberto, C.R.	.167	2	7	6	0	1	1	0	0	0	1	0	0	0	1	0	2	0	0	0	.167	.286
Lough, Aaron, Q.C.	.250	3	13	12	1	3	3	0	0	0	1	0	0	0	1	0	4	0	0	0	.250	.308
Mackiewitz, Richard, Bel.*	.262	102	391	355	44	93	138	19	1	8	57	2	3	3	28	2	57	1	0	9	.389	.319
Maldonado, Carlos, Wis.	.308	92	349	302	35	93	106	13	0	0	33	2	2	0	43	1	32	4	6	10	.351	.392
Marciniak, Dave, Q.C.	.261	47	191	165	20	43	59	7	0	3	19	1	0	5	20	0	19	2	1	3	.358	.358
Markray, Thad, Clin.-Rock.	.189	62	220	190	22	36	54	6	0	4	22	3	4	1	22	0	49	3	4	6	.284	.272
Martinez, Victor, Wis.	.224	69	288	254	41	57	82	10	3	3	28	3	4	6	21	0	37	3	2	7	.323	.295
Matan, James, Rock.	.254	116	442	393	39	100	147	17	0	10	56	0	6	5	38	2	90	5	6	10	.374	.324
Mauck, Matt, Lan.*	.221	107	352	298	37	66	107	9	4	8	59	1	1	7	45	0	100	2	1	5	.359	.336
Maynard, Scott, Wis.	.200	50	147	135	16	27	37	4	0	2	15	1	1	0	10	0	29	1	3	3	.274	.253
McAffee, Josh, S.B.	.246	68	274	232	32	57	88	16	0	5	24	0	2	5	35	0	76	0	1	3	.379	.354
McConnell, Jason, Q.C.†	.212	27	109	99	12	21	24	1	1	0	3	1	2	0	7	0	24	3	3	1	.242	.259
McMillin, Brian, Q.C.	.266	116	478	414	69	110	194	21	3	19	74	4	3	4	53	1	75	19	4	18	.469	.352
McNaughton, Troy, Peo.*	.273	125	529	484	57	132	211	25	6	14	84	0	4	4	37	1	123	5	4	11	.436	.327
McNeal, Aaron, Mich.	.310	133	581	536	95	166	315	29	3	38	131	0	3	2	40	4	121	7	1	13	.588	.358
Meadows, Tydus, Lan.	.301	126	530	449	80	135	230	32	6	17	74	0	4	11	66	2	85	18	10	13	.512	.400
Medosch, Keith, C.R.	.125	20	50	40	4	5	5	0	0	0	0	0	0	0	1	0	15	0	1	0	.125	.300
Medrano, Jesus, K.C.	.274	118	491	445	64	122	173	26	5	5	46	1	5	4	36	1	92	42	11	3	.389	.331
Meran, Jorge, W.M.	.197	44	163	152	18	30	53	9	4	2	23	1	2	1	7	0	38	1	3	1	.349	.235
Merriman, Terrell, Burl.*	.306	109	469	382	77	117	198	18	9	15	85	2	6	2	70	3	84	27	4	2	.518	.411
Miles, Aaron, Mich.†	.317	112	513	470	72	149	223	28	8	10	71	6	7	2	28	3	33	17	12	8	.474	.353
Miller, Corky, Rock.	.287	66	250	195	43	56	98	10	1	10	40	1	1	20	33	1	42	3	6	5	.503	.438
Montenegro, Jose, Bel.	.333	2	8	6	1	2	5	1	1	0	1	0	0	0	2	0	1	0	0	0	.833	.500
Moore, Lacarlo, W.M.*	.299	43	182	164	27	49	55	4	1	0	17	1	0	1	16	1	26	8	3	7	.335	.365
Morales, Stephen, K.C.†	.271	28	103	96	12	26	37	5	0	2	11	2	0	1	4	0	16	0	0	2	.385	.307
Moreno, Jose, Wis.	.000	3	4	4	0	0	0	0	0	0	0	0	0	0	0	0	0	0	1	1	.000	.000
Moreno, Mikel, Lan.	.158	5	19	19	1	3	8	0	1	1	2	0	0	0	0	0	2	1	0	0	.421	.158
Morrow, Alvin, Bel.	.233	82	347	296	29	69	89	11	0	3	41	0	3	1	47	0	121	0	0	8	.301	.337
Mounts, J.R., Burl.	.212	95	360	326	40	69	103	14	1	6	32	1	2	6	25	0	129	11	7	1	.316	.279
Moye, Melvin, S.B.	.254	72	271	244	33	62	86	13	1	3	30	1	2	5	19	0	75	4	2	10	.352	.319
Munson, Eric, W.M.*	.266	67	299	252	42	67	127	16	1	14	44	0	1	9	37	3	47	3	1	4	.504	.378
Navarro, Ibrahim, Lan.	.199	55	176	156	19	31	43	7	1	1	18	0	3	2	15	0	39	2	0	7	.276	.273
Neal, Steve, S.B.*	.281	69	293	249	41	70	109	14	2	7	53	0	3	1	40	2	72	6	2	3	.438	.379
Nelson, Brian, Wis.	.205	58	195	171	17	35	54	10	0	3	21	0	0	2	22	0	54	2	1	4	.316	.303
Neubart, Adam, S.B.	.231	27	105	91	14	21	29	3	1	1	9	0	2	6	6	0	20	4	4	2	.319	.314
Nicholson, Derek, Mich.*	.319	66	250	216	40	69	96	8	5	3	39	1	2	1	30	0	25	3	4	6	.444	.402
Noboa, Joel, S.B.	.179	11	39	39	2	7	9	2	0	0	3	0	0	0	0	0	17	0	0	2	.231	.179
Nykoluk, Kevin, Peo.	.260	55	194	177	24	46	67	13	1	2	19	0	1	2	14	0	25	0	1	6	.379	.320
O'Connor, Brian, Mich.	.156	21	76	64	8	10	12	2	0	0	5	2	1	0	9	0	29	0	1	2	.188	.257
Oliver, Bill, C.R.	.082	21	70	61	6	5	9	1	0	1	1	0	0	3	6	0	28	0	0	1	.148	.200
Oliver, Brian, C.R.	.274	66	292	252	43	69	105	16	1	6	29	4	4	6	26	0	30	12	1	3	.417	.351
Oliver, Johnny, Clin.	.115	17	57	52	7	6	9	0	0	1	2	0	0	0	5	0	16	0	2	3	.173	.193
Owens, Jeremy, F.W.	.281	129	595	513	111	144	221	26	12	9	66	4	6	9	63	2	153	65	14	5	.431	.365
Padgett, Matt, K.C.*	.333	45	181	159	34	53	77	9	0	5	23	0	1	1	20	0	40	1	0	4	.484	.409
Parker, Clark, Burl.*	.156	32	96	77	13	12	15	1	1	0	4	1	0	2	16	0	24	6	2	2	.195	.316
Patten, Chris, Bel.	.285	124	528	478	69	136	187	16	7	7	65	8	4	8	30	1	100	6	5	9	.391	.335
Patterson, Corey, Lan.*	.320	112	509	475	94	152	281	35	17	20	79	0	4	5	25	1	85	33	9	5	.592	.358
Perez, Antonio, Rock.	.288	119	452	385	69	111	158	20	3	7	41	8	3	13	43	0	80	35	24	3	.410	.376
Peters, Samone, Clin.	.221	83	312	290	32	64	124	13	1	15	46	0	2	3	17	0	131	0	2	5	.428	.269
Pinero, Juan, Lan.†	.293	27	101	82	19	24	32	5	0	1	8	1	1	4	13	0	14	1	2	0	.390	.410
Pond, Ryan, C.R.	.246	44	184	167	18	41	65	12	0	4	21	3	1	2	11	1	34	2	1	2	.389	.298
Porter, Colin, Mich.*	.291	127	524	453	91	132	232	28	9	18	68	3	8	7	53	2	123	23	13	4	.512	.369
Price, Corey, Rock.†	.000	6	9	9	0	0	0	0	0	0	0	0	0	0	0	0	2	0	0	0	.000	.000
Price, Duane, Clin.	.167	37	111	96	8	16	17	1	0	0	5	3	2	1	9	1	30	4	2	3	.177	.241
Rapp, Travis, C.R.	.189	14	42	37	6	7	13	3	0	1	8	0	1	2	2	0	16	0	0	0	.351	.262
Restovich, Michael, Q.C.	.312	131	585	493	91	154	253	30	6	19	107	0	5	13	74	4	100	7	9	9	.513	.412
Reyes, Deurys, W.M.*	.246	46	154	134	23	33	65	11	3	5	27	2	0	2	16	3	53	8	1	1	.485	.336

Player, Team	Avg.	G	TPA	AB	R	H	TB	2B	3B	HR	RBI	SH	SF	HP	BB	IBB	SO	SB	CS	GDP	Slg.	OBP
Rich, Billy, W.M.	.251	108	449	394	64	99	148	20	1	9	50	1	2	5	47	1	87	6	4	8	.376	.337
Rios, Fernando, Rock.-Clin.	.278	99	396	356	45	99	128	23	0	2	50	2	4	2	32	3	43	5	5	4	.360	.338
Rivera, Francisco, Clin.*	.320	15	54	50	7	16	24	6	1	0	6	0	0	0	4	0	10	0	0	1	.480	.370
Robinson, Bo, Wis.	.329	138	619	499	101	164	259	50	3	13	102	0	8	4	108	4	75	4	1	18	.519	.446
Rodriguez, Hernandez, Clin.	.252	28	123	115	10	29	40	4	2	1	6	1	2	1	4	0	17	6	0	3	.348	.279
Rodriguez, Luis, Q.C.†	.270	119	513	434	63	117	146	20	0	3	50	13	9	4	53	0	49	8	4	10	.336	.348
Roneberg, Brett, K.C.*	.288	132	600	511	88	147	211	32	4	8	68	0	5	4	79	4	82	3	2	11	.413	.384
Rosamond, Michael, Mich.	.100	4	13	10	0	1	1	0	0	0	2	0	1	0	2	0	3	0	1	0	.100	.231
Ross, Justin, C.R.*	.288	51	238	184	43	53	76	14	0	3	23	0	0	1	53	2	30	10	3	5	.413	.450
Ruiz, Randy, Clin.	.625	2	10	8	3	5	7	2	0	0	2	0	1	0	1	0	0	0	0	1	.875	.600
Runnells, T.J., W.M.	.229	88	329	288	35	66	78	10	1	0	32	5	6	1	29	0	42	5	4	15	.271	.296
Sanchez, Marcos, Rock.†	.246	20	61	57	6	14	23	2	2	1	7	0	1	0	3	0	23	4	1	1	.404	.279
Sanchez, Wellington, Bel.	.261	71	294	261	35	68	88	14	3	0	23	4	0	4	25	0	58	9	3	5	.337	.334
Sandoval, Danny, Burl.†	.227	76	280	255	34	58	74	5	1	3	37	6	2	0	17	0	39	8	5	7	.290	.274
Santamarina, Juan, Burl.*	.179	29	109	95	12	17	22	2	0	1	10	0	0	0	14	0	15	5	0	0	.232	.284
Santiago, Daniel, Rock.†	.000	1	2	2	0	0	0	0	0	0	0	0	0	0	0	0	2	0	0	0	.000	.000
Santonocito, Justin, Clin.*	.180	26	67	61	5	11	16	2	0	1	5	1	0	0	5	0	12	0	0	1	.262	.242
Santos, Jose, K.C.	.270	128	564	459	93	124	221	30	5	19	105	0	5	17	83	2	130	18	4	6	.481	.397
Sassanella, Jeremy, W.M.†	.073	14	42	41	2	3	4	1	0	0	6	0	0	0	1	0	18	0	0	1	.098	.095
Scanlon, Matt, Q.C.*	.189	16	58	53	8	10	17	2	1	1	5	1	1	1	2	0	8	0	0	1	.321	.228
Schaeffer, Jon, Q.C.	.290	116	509	390	97	113	205	33	4	17	65	2	5	20	92	1	69	2	3	12	.526	.444
Schaffer, Jake, Mich.	.130	7	24	23	2	3	3	0	0	0	2	0	0	0	1	0	8	0	0	0	.130	.167
Scheschuk, John, F.W.*	.252	66	294	242	35	61	84	14	0	3	36	1	6	2	43	4	34	3	1	4	.347	.362
Schill, Vaughn, Wis.	.354	25	96	79	13	28	32	4	0	0	7	1	2	1	13	0	16	7	1	2	.405	.442
Schmidt, Bryan, F.W.	.238	67	259	227	23	54	63	7	1	0	13	6	1	5	20	0	49	2	4	8	.278	.312
Schrager, Tony, Lan.	.270	122	509	392	83	106	193	31	4	16	73	1	8	5	103	2	101	8	3	8	.492	.421
Secoda, Joe, Peo.	.253	116	478	400	61	101	125	14	2	2	30	6	1	9	62	0	97	15	9	2	.313	.364
Selander, Craig, Q.C.*	.226	100	374	345	41	78	107	17	3	2	32	6	2	0	21	2	56	2	1	6	.310	.269
Shrum, Allen, Q.C.	.236	68	213	191	14	45	60	12	0	1	22	1	2	3	16	0	52	0	0	8	.314	.302
Silvestre, Juan, Wis.	.288	137	595	534	89	154	259	34	4	21	107	0	8	6	47	1	124	5	4	17	.485	.348
Singletary, Dan, S.B.*	.235	95	366	306	47	72	107	8	6	5	43	0	5	1	54	2	53	15	9	7	.350	.347
Smalls, Terrence, K.C.*	.227	8	25	22	2	5	7	0	1	0	2	1	1	0	1	0	2	1	0	1	.318	.250
Snead, Esix, Peo.†	.193	59	226	181	35	35	50	7	1	2	18	7	1	2	35	0	42	29	9	3	.276	.329
Snusz, Chris, Rock.-Clin.	.176	23	80	74	8	13	20	2	1	1	5	1	0	1	4	0	21	1	0	1	.270	.228
Southall, Rick, Wis.*	.246	102	383	337	47	83	134	19	1	10	51	0	0	4	42	1	101	4	1	5	.398	.337
Stegall, Randy, Clin.-Rock.	.268	97	390	351	53	94	132	16	5	4	62	2	2	5	30	0	84	6	6	6	.376	.332
Stuart, Rich, C.R.	.288	67	282	250	46	72	137	16	2	15	55	0	0	2	30	1	53	8	4	5	.548	.369
Suarez, Luis, Burl.	.243	51	200	173	24	42	64	10	0	4	25	3	2	3	19	0	32	5	4	1	.370	.325
Suarez, Marc, Clin.-Rock.	.194	37	133	108	12	21	33	3	0	3	11	1	4	1	19	0	33	2	3	3	.306	.311
Sykes, Jamie, S.B.	.286	127	541	479	75	137	236	34	10	15	83	1	4	4	53	1	111	17	8	9	.493	.359
Thorpe, A.D., Clin.-Rock.†	.300	13	23	20	5	6	8	2	0	0	1	1	0	1	1	0	2	2	3	1	.400	.364
Ticen, Kevin, C.R.	.284	27	100	88	8	25	32	4	0	1	10	1	0	3	8	0	24	0	1	4	.364	.364
Toomey, Chris, Clin.	.261	100	369	307	51	80	119	19	1	6	41	2	4	15	41	0	87	5	3	7	.388	.371
Torres, Andres, W.M.†	.236	117	523	407	72	96	132	20	5	2	34	9	5	10	92	1	116	39	18	2	.324	.385
Torres, Bernie, Burl.	.257	65	291	268	40	69	95	12	4	2	21	4	2	2	15	0	32	7	2	4	.354	.300
Treanor, Matt, K.C.	.286	86	363	308	56	88	141	21	1	10	53	2	2	15	36	0	65	4	1	9	.458	.385
Tucent, Francisco, Bel.†	.186	38	105	102	9	19	26	4	0	1	10	1	1	1	0	0	26	0	1	4	.255	.192
Turnquist, Tyler, Mich.	.309	118	531	456	89	141	213	25	7	11	67	1	7	5	62	1	69	5	4	14	.467	.392
Urquiola, Carlos, S.B.*	.362	93	415	384	66	139	158	13	3	0	35	1	3	5	22	0	32	20	14	2	.411	.401
Valenzuela, Mario, Burl.	.323	122	533	477	89	154	227	31	6	10	70	3	3	6	44	0	77	13	6	16	.476	.385
Valera, Greg, S.B.	.156	53	197	186	18	29	37	4	2	0	10	1	0	1	9	0	46	1	2	6	.199	.199
Valera, Ramon, Wis.†	.270	99	463	382	72	103	131	14	4	2	33	4	1	1	75	1	92	42	19	3	.343	.390
Vandemore, Anthony, F.W.*	.278	5	19	18	0	5	7	2	0	0	0	0	0	0	1	0	5	0	0	0	.389	.316
Van Rossum, Chris, S.B.*	.167	2	9	6	2	1	1	0	0	0	1	0	0	0	3	0	1	0	0	0	.167	.444
Vaughn, Clint, Clin.	.238	104	406	374	45	89	131	25	4	3	54	1	5	8	18	1	87	2	2	8	.350	.284
Vessel, Andrew, Lan.	.308	13	56	52	7	16	24	4	2	0	11	0	1	1	2	0	3	1	0	3	.462	.339
Vina, Fernando, Bel.*	.200	2	10	10	1	2	3	1	0	0	0	0	0	0	0	0	2	0	1	0	.300	.200
Wagner, Mike, F.W.	.261	13	56	46	10	12	19	1	0	2	8	0	1	1	8	0	15	0	0	0	.413	.375
Wathan, Derek, K.C.†	.254	125	540	469	71	119	148	18	4	1	49	10	3	5	53	2	54	33	12	13	.316	.334
Welsh, Eric, Rock.*	.280	101	394	368	52	103	174	23	0	16	64	0	2	1	23	3	57	3	2	9	.473	.322
Whitehead, Braxton, Clin.	.298	82	308	272	41	81	109	19	0	3	38	0	1	5	30	1	42	0	0	7	.401	.377
Wickersham, Jack, F.W.	.236	39	160	140	24	33	42	7	1	0	20	4	0	4	12	0	28	6	6	4	.300	.314
William, Jovany, Peo.	.204	67	268	240	30	49	81	8	0	8	27	3	3	8	14	0	59	2	3	6	.338	.268
Williams, P.J., Wis.	.299	115	433	371	65	111	141	14	5	2	46	5	3	6	48	0	63	22	7	5	.380	.386
Williams, Peanut, Wis.	.250	9	37	32	6	8	15	1	0	2	7	0	0	1	4	0	12	0	0	0	.469	.351
Williford, Dan, S.B.*	.083	8	27	24	1	2	2	0	0	0	0	0	0	1	2	0	10	0	0	0	.083	.185
Wilson, Jack, Peo.	.343	64	271	251	47	86	125	22	4	3	28	3	0	2	15	0	23	11	5	2	.498	.384
Wise, Dewayne, Rock.*	.253	131	570	502	70	127	206	20	13	11	81	5	14	7	42	2	81	35	13	6	.410	.312
Wolff, Mike, S.B.*	.291	66	267	237	31	69	104	18	1	5	45	0	4	4	20	2	28	1	4	5	.439	.351
Woodward, Mattson, Wis.	.213	58	175	150	15	32	33	1	0	0	9	0	0	1	24	0	45	0	3	5	.220	.326
Zambrano, Alan, Wis.†	.202	90	323	282	33	57	86	14	0	5	30	3	3	6	29	1	79	6	7	5	.305	.288
Zeber, Ryan, Rock.-Clin.	.250	41	120	108	11	27	35	6	1	0	10	0	1	3	8	1	21	1	5	3	.324	.317

GRAND SLAMS: Restovich 3; Battersby, Figueroa, McMillin, McNeal, 2 each; Adams, Aguila, Beattie, Boone, Campbell, Downing, Espino, Fennell, Folkers, Fukuhara, Goldbach, Gomez, Haynes, Hill, Inge, Jordan, Kelton, Kielty, Kirby, Larson, Miles, Neal, Patten, Peters, Porter, Robinson, Santos, Schaeffer, Suarez, Sykes, William, Wise, Wolff, 1 each.

AWARDED FIRST BASE ON CATCHER'S INTERFERENCE: Merriman 7 (Diaz, Dimmick, Hill, Lopez, Suarez, Whitehead, William); Christiansen 3 (Cosentino, Hyde, McAffee); Dimmick 2 (Goldbach, Lawrence); Wolff 2 (Goldbach, Hill); Folkers (Nelson); German (Whitehead); Hawthorne (Nelson); Hodge (Diaz); Roneberg (Garcia).

PLAYERS WITH TWO OR MORE TEAMS

Player, Team	Avg.	G	TPA	AB	R	H	TB	2B	3B	HR	RBI	SH	SF	HP	BB	IBB	SO	SB	CS	GDP	Slg.	OBP
Dimmick, Josh, Mich.†	.306	53	203	180	27	55	82	11	2	4	28	0	3	1	17	0	25	2	1	5	.456	.363
Dimmick, Josh, Q.C.†	.262	24	95	84	9	22	35	5	1	2	12	0	0	1	10	2	12	0	0	3	.417	.347
Kison, Robbie, Rock.	.200	7	21	15	3	3	3	0	0	0	1	0	0	2	4	0	4	0	0	0	.200	.429
Kison, Robbie, Clin.	.236	20	66	55	7	13	20	2	1	1	5	0	1	2	8	0	12	0	1	2	.364	.348

Player, Team	Avg.	G	TPA	AB	R	H	TB	2B	3B	HR	RBI	SH	SF	HP	BB	IBB	SO	SB	CS	GDP	Slg.	OBP
Lawrence, Tony, F.W.	.197	46	169	142	11	28	38	8	1	0	8	2	0	4	21	0	45	1	1	2	.268	.317
Lawrence, Tony, Rock.	.171	10	37	35	2	6	8	2	0	0	5	0	0	2	0	0	12	0	0	2	.229	.216
Layton, Blane, Clin.*	.294	42	138	109	19	32	48	6	2	2	12	3	0	1	25	3	31	5	2	1	.440	.430
Layton, Blane, Rock.*	.273	34	118	110	19	30	52	10	3	2	20	0	2	0	6	0	27	4	3	2	.473	.305
Markray, Thad, Clin.	.100	3	11	10	1	1	1	0	0	0	0	0	0	0	1	0	2	0	0	0	.100	.182
Markray, Thad, Rock.	.194	59	209	180	21	35	53	6	0	4	22	3	4	1	21	0	47	3	4	6	.294	.277
Rios, Fernando, Rock.	.284	24	94	81	9	23	30	7	0	0	8	0	1	1	11	3	9	2	3	2	.370	.372
Rios, Fernando, Clin.	.276	75	302	275	36	76	98	16	0	2	42	2	3	1	21	0	34	3	2	2	.356	.327
Snusz, Chris, Rock.	.170	19	58	53	6	9	13	1	0	1	2	1	0	1	3	0	13	1	0	1	.245	.228
Snusz, Chris, Clin.	.190	4	22	21	2	4	7	1	1	0	3	0	0	0	1	0	8	0	0	0	.333	.227
Stegall, Randy, Clin.	.250	71	287	252	39	63	95	12	4	4	44	2	2	4	27	0	64	3	2	3	.377	.330
Stegall, Randy, Rock.	.313	26	103	99	14	31	37	4	1	0	18	0	0	1	3	0	20	3	4	3	.374	.340
Suarez, Marc, Clin.	.158	33	117	95	8	15	23	2	0	2	10	1	4	1	16	0	31	0	3	3	.242	.276
Suarez, Marc, Rock.	.462	4	16	13	4	6	10	1	0	1	1	0	0	0	3	0	2	2	0	0	.769	.563
Thorpe, A.D., Clin.†	.333	6	14	12	2	4	6	2	0	0	1	1	0	1	0	0	2	1	2	0	.500	.385
Thorpe, A.D., Rock.†	.250	7	9	8	3	2	2	0	0	0	0	0	0	0	1	0	0	1	1	1	.250	.333
Zeber, Ryan, Rock.	.255	39	117	106	11	27	35	6	1	0	10	0	1	3	7	1	21	1	5	3	.330	.316
Zeber, Ryan, Clin.	.000	2	3	2	0	0	0	0	0	0	0	0	0	0	1	0	0	0	0	0	.000	.333

1999 PITCHING

TEAM

Team	W	L	Pct.	ERA	G	CG	ShO	Sv.	IP	H	TBF	R	ER	HR	SH	SF	HB	BB	IBB	SO	WP	Bk.
Clinton	68	69	.496	3.91	137	6	5	37	1180.2	1093	5131	643	513	96	48	40	72	516	19	964	92	14
Quad City	77	62	.554	3.94	139	2	10	31	1220.2	1139	5339	649	534	78	31	32	69	569	32	1103	90	10
West Michigan	68	72	.486	4.04	140	10	9	30	1219.2	1170	5332	682	548	80	41	50	65	570	12	1033	111	23
Kane County	78	59	.569	4.07	137	6	11	29	1206.0	1247	5241	617	545	82	36	46	60	466	5	955	63	12
Wisconsin	72	66	.522	4.09	138	12	10	29	1197.2	1194	5219	653	544	90	40	50	60	434	12	1110	91	29
Rockford	76	63	.547	4.23	139	16	18	32	1204.1	1232	5323	690	566	72	37	36	67	524	33	1046	97	13
South Bend	68	71	.489	4.38	139	0	6	36	1214.1	1222	5339	702	591	90	30	40	65	482	1	1003	107	13
Cedar Rapids	61	77	.442	4.49	138	21	7	35	1195.2	1242	5287	741	596	117	43	64	70	459	7	976	102	16
Lansing	73	67	.521	4.73	140	5	4	32	1198.2	1312	5314	750	630	83	31	51	60	528	7	893	92	12
Peoria	63	76	.453	4.74	139	2	4	26	1201.0	1240	5326	748	633	104	35	51	70	511	6	978	65	18
Burlington	71	68	.511	4.79	139	9	4	35	1194.0	1291	5386	763	635	89	26	46	77	519	23	953	87	21
Michigan	76	62	.551	4.82	138	5	5	30	1192.0	1264	5245	732	639	96	26	47	62	483	15	1055	102	19
Beloit	59	80	.424	4.85	139	8	9	30	1201.2	1261	5419	770	648	120	20	39	74	582	10	1002	106	17
Fort Wayne	61	79	.436	4.98	140	2	5	33	1224.1	1237	5540	812	678	115	22	47	63	675	13	991	86	16

INDIVIDUAL

TOP QUALIFIERS FOR EARNED-RUN AVERAGE TITLE

Minimum 112 innings. *Lefthanded pitcher.

Pitcher, Team	W	L	Pct.	ERA	G	GS	CG	ShO	GF	Sv.	IP	H	TBF	R	ER	HR	SH	SF	HB	BB	IBB	SO	WP	Bk.
Averette, Robert, Rock.	9	5	.643	2.58	19	19	2	2	0	0	125.2	117	521	54	36	2	4	3	4	40	3	98	9	0
Hayden, Terry, Clin.-Rock.*	8	6	.571	2.70	38	14	1	0	6	0	116.2	108	503	57	35	10	10	3	6	42	0	79	6	0
Rincon, Juan, Q.C.	14	8	.636	2.92	28	28	0	0	0	0	163.1	146	683	67	53	8	1	3	2	66	3	153	11	0
Palma, Ricardo, Lan.*	7	7	.500	2.94	22	22	2	0	0	0	134.2	134	571	61	44	6	1	4	3	44	0	79	8	4
Almonte, Edwin, Burl.	9	12	.429	3.03	37	5	2	0	16	5	115.2	107	480	48	39	5	2	1	2	28	4	85	6	1
Figueroa, Juan, Burl.	8	4	.667	3.12	17	16	2	0	0	0	115.1	100	491	51	40	8	0	6	5	44	0	139	4	1
Cervantes, Chris, S.B.*	8	5	.615	3.13	38	10	0	0	14	3	115.0	109	490	49	40	9	5	1	4	34	0	89	10	1
Anderson, Wes, K.C.	9	5	.643	3.21	23	23	2	1	0	0	137.1	111	565	55	49	8	3	5	5	51	0	134	4	0
Haring, Brett, Rock.*	10	3	.769	3.34	25	18	3	3	1	1	124.0	113	516	53	46	7	4	3	4	42	0	94	5	0
Hoard, Brent, Q.C.*	12	7	.632	3.43	28	28	1	0	0	0	149.2	143	643	68	57	9	4	3	2	64	1	139	7	1
Bridges, Douglas, C.R.*	15	5	.750	3.59	22	22	3	2	0	0	150.1	136	628	67	60	12	7	4	7	45	0	128	7	2
Sismondo, Bobby, W.M.*	9	5	.643	3.67	27	27	1	1	0	0	169.1	153	708	86	69	12	4	5	7	62	2	135	8	1
Cornejo, Nate, W.M.	9	11	.450	3.71	28	28	4	1	0	0	174.2	173	750	87	72	4	10	9	12	67	0	125	11	5
Acevedo, Jose, Clin.	8	6	.571	3.77	24	24	1	1	0	0	133.2	119	553	65	56	14	2	3	0	43	0	136	5	3
Davis, Lance, Rock.*	7	5	.583	3.82	22	20	1	0	0	0	127.1	135	550	62	54	9	5	2	4	49	1	95	2	0

DEPARTMENTAL LEADERS: W—Bridges, 15; L—Shibilo, 13; Pct.—Mears, .909; G—Rivera, 60; GS—several players tied, 28 each; CG—Hundley, 6; ShO—Merrell, Haring, 3 each; GF—Puffer, 55; Sv.—Puffer, 34; IP—Cornejo, 174.2; H—Wuertz, 191; TBF—Cornejo, 750; R—Shibilo, 105; ER—Stemle, 90; HR—Duarte, Matos, 19 each; SH—Cornejo, Hayden, 10 each; SF—Torres, 14; HB—Jacobs, 15; BB—Howard, 110; IBB—Giuliano, 7; SO—Rincon, 153; WP—Mendoza, 20; BK—several players tied, 6 each.

ALL PITCHERS

*Lefthanded pitcher.

Pitcher, Team	W	L	Pct.	ERA	G	GS	CG	ShO	GF	Sv.	IP	H	TBF	R	ER	HR	SH	SF	HB	BB	IBB	SO	WP	Bk.
Acevedo, Jose, Clin.	8	6	.571	3.77	24	24	1	1	0	0	133.2	119	553	65	56	14	2	3	0	43	0	136	5	3
Almonte, Edwin, Burl.	9	12	.429	3.03	37	5	2	0	16	5	115.2	107	480	48	39	5	2	1	2	28	4	85	6	1
Altman, Gene, Rock.-Clin.	2	8	.200	5.61	14	14	0	0	0	0	67.1	70	314	50	42	4	1	3	6	41	0	70	6	0
Anderson, Wes, K.C.	9	5	.643	3.21	23	23	2	1	0	0	137.1	111	565	55	49	8	3	5	5	51	0	134	4	0
Atchison, Scott, Wis.	4	5	.444	3.42	15	13	0	0	0	0	81.2	67	326	34	31	4	2	2	3	25	1	85	4	1
Averette, Robert, Rock.	9	5	.643	2.58	19	19	2	2	0	0	125.2	117	521	54	36	2	4	3	4	40	3	98	9	0
Bailey, Ben, Clin.	1	0	1.000	5.06	9	2	0	0	1	0	21.1	20	88	12	12	3	0	0	2	8	0	16	2	0
Balbuena, Caleb, Wis.	1	3	.250	5.32	8	8	0	0	0	0	44.0	48	201	33	26	6	2	1	1	16	0	37	4	2
Balfour, Grant, Q.C.	8	5	.615	3.53	19	14	0	0	2	1	91.2	66	368	39	36	7	1	1	6	37	0	95	1	0
Barcelo, Lorenzo, Burl.	1	0	1.000	3.60	1	1	0	0	0	0	5.0	3	18	2	2	1	1	0	0	0	0	6	0	0
Barton, Christopher, Bel.	0	1	.000	5.46	16	0	0	0	3	2	28.0	31	143	27	17	5	0	0	7	16	0	18	9	1
Bartosh, Cliff, F.W.*	5	12	.294	4.44	35	20	1	1	0	0	129.2	136	567	76	64	14	0	4	10	49	0	100	7	2
Bauer, Ryan, F.W.	4	9	.308	4.89	36	15	1	0	12	5	110.1	111	495	75	60	10	2	5	7	55	0	86	6	0
Bautista, Jorge, K.C.	1	0	1.000	0.00	1	0	0	0	0	0	1.0	1	5	0	0	0	1	0	0	2	0	1	0	0

CLASS A Midwest League

Pitcher, Team	W	L	Pct.	ERA	G	GS	CG	ShO	GF	Sv.	IP	H	TBF	R	ER	HR	SH	SF	HB	BB	IBB	SO	WP	Bk.
Bell, Casey, F.W.	0	0	.000	6.75	2	0	0	0	0	0	6.2	8	28	5	5	1	0	0	0	1	0	3	1	0
Bernero, Adam, W.M.	8	4	.667	2.54	15	15	2	1	0	0	95.2	75	386	36	27	8	0	2	4	23	0	80	3	3
Berroa, Oliver, Wis.	1	0	1.000	1.84	21	0	0	0	10	1	29.1	22	124	8	6	1	2	1	4	17	0	28	6	0
Berryman, Brian, F.W.	4	2	.667	4.05	9	9	0	0	0	0	46.2	43	205	25	21	2	0	2	2	24	0	19	0	2
Bess, Stephen, W.M.	1	1	.500	0.93	12	0	0	0	7	3	19.1	12	76	2	2	0	0	0	0	7	0	23	1	0
Birdsong, Tim, Clin.	5	8	.385	4.27	24	23	0	0	0	0	128.2	131	555	75	61	9	0	8	4	50	0	95	7	0
Blackmore, John, Mich.	3	4	.429	7.48	37	0	0	0	25	7	49.1	64	241	44	41	9	4	3	2	29	2	43	10	4
Bloomer, Chris, S.B.	1	2	.333	3.99	43	0	0	0	39	21	49.2	44	210	28	22	3	2	1	2	16	0	54	8	1
Book, Jeremy, Peo.	6	5	.545	5.33	27	16	0	0	1	0	103.0	110	458	70	61	9	2	3	11	32	0	67	6	6
Borges, Reece, Mich.	6	2	.750	5.04	37	1	0	0	6	2	64.1	74	295	45	36	4	2	2	6	23	2	37	5	1
Borne, Matt, Burl.	2	4	.333	4.75	22	0	0	0	14	2	30.1	35	149	20	16	3	1	1	5	22	3	24	5	2
Brewer, Clint, Clin.-Rock.	9	2	.818	4.53	34	9	0	0	9	0	91.1	80	390	56	46	12	5	1	2	37	1	55	5	1
Bridges, Douglas, C.R.*	15	5	.750	3.59	22	22	3	2	0	0	150.1	136	628	67	60	12	7	4	7	45	0	128	7	2
Brown, Tighe, Burl.	0	0	.000	7.71	4	0	0	0	1	0	4.2	3	25	4	4	1	0	0	0	6	0	8	1	0
Brown, Zay, Clin.	0	1	.000	4.15	3	0	0	0	1	0	4.1	4	20	2	2	0	0	0	0	3	1	1	1	0
Bruback, Matt, Lan.	9	8	.529	5.40	25	25	0	0	0	0	135.0	151	633	92	81	15	5	3	10	87	0	118	10	1
Brunette, Justin, Peo.*	3	1	.750	1.81	38	0	0	0	12	2	44.2	34	181	9	9	2	2	1	1	16	1	44	2	1
Buehrle, Mark, Burl.*	7	4	.636	4.10	20	14	1	1	4	3	98.2	105	412	49	45	8	2	2	5	16	1	91	3	6
Buller, Sean, W.M.*	10	10	.500	4.94	31	17	2	0	2	0	120.1	133	528	78	66	11	3	6	5	55	1	72	9	0
Cardona, Steve, S.B.	1	2	.333	6.23	14	0	0	0	10	0	21.2	31	103	18	15	3	2	1	1	5	0	26	4	0
Cento, Anthony, Q.C.*	1	0	1.000	1.08	11	0	0	0	3	0	8.1	6	34	2	1	0	1	1	3	1	1	11	1	0
Cervantes, Chris, S.B.*	8	5	.615	3.13	38	10	0	0	14	3	115.0	109	490	49	40	9	5	1	4	34	0	89	10	1
Chighisola, Louis, Clin.*	0	1	.000	2.77	7	1	0	0	5	0	13.0	11	55	4	4	1	0	1	0	7	0	8	1	0
Childers, Matt, Bel.	3	10	.231	5.94	20	19	0	0	0	0	100.0	129	448	72	66	9	1	5	5	30	1	52	0	2
Christenson, Ryan, Peo.	4	4	.500	5.32	29	8	0	0	2	0	89.2	101	410	63	53	9	2	5	5	42	0	84	5	0
Chrysler, Clint, Wis.*	5	7	.417	2.06	51	0	0	0	28	8	56.2	47	243	22	13	4	4	4	3	22	3	59	5	1
Clackum, Scott, K.C.	4	4	.500	3.30	47	1	0	0	29	10	71.0	82	306	32	26	0	2	1	1	14	1	53	4	0
Condrey, Clay, F.W.	2	3	.400	3.78	42	0	0	0	39	20	47.2	40	202	24	20	5	0	2	0	19	4	47	4	1
Cooper, Eric, Clin.-Rock.	3	6	.333	6.93	16	14	1	0	1	0	61.0	70	295	53	47	10	2	5	5	47	1	43	16	2
Cordova, Jorge, K.C.	1	0	1.000	0.47	12	0	0	0	3	0	19.1	6	73	2	1	0	0	0	0	10	0	17	1	0
Cornejo, Nate, W.M.	9	11	.450	3.71	28	28	4	1	0	0	174.2	173	750	87	72	4	10	9	12	67	0	125	11	5
Correa, Cristobal, Peo.	0	2	.000	10.35	5	5	0	0	0	0	20.0	26	99	24	23	4	2	2	0	14	0	15	3	1
Cosgrove, Mike, Q.C.	7	7	.500	4.74	42	0	0	0	15	1	62.2	71	276	37	33	9	2	2	1	24	3	46	2	3
Crews, Jason, S.B.	0	2	.000	2.08	9	0	0	0	8	1	13.0	11	56	6	3	0	1	1	1	2	0	14	2	0
Cummings, Ryan, C.R.	5	8	.385	4.39	19	19	3	1	0	0	121.0	104	511	69	59	14	4	10	6	35	0	97	18	2
Currens, Tim, Burl.	1	3	.250	6.68	22	0	0	0	10	0	33.2	50	163	31	25	1	1	1	2	14	1	26	3	0
D'Amico, Jeff, Bel.	1	0	1.000	0.00	2	2	0	0	0	0	8.0	7	31	0	0	0	0	0	1	0	0	6	0	0
Dant, Larry, Lan.	1	1	.750	4.97	43	0	0	0	31	12	54.1	54	244	35	30	5	2	4	7	19	2	52	2	0
Darnell, Paul, Clin.*	3	2	.600	3.06	6	6	0	0	0	0	35.1	35	152	19	12	4	0	3	13	0	23	1	0
Darr, Jay, F.W.	3	1	.250	5.87	7	4	0	0	1	0	23.0	27	116	19	15	2	0	2	2	12	0	12	1	1
Davis, Lance, Rock.*	7	5	.583	3.82	22	20	1	0	0	0	127.1	135	550	62	54	9	5	2	4	49	1	95	2	0
Dehart, Casey, Clin.*	2	0	1.000	3.38	24	0	0	0	4	0	21.1	16	97	10	8	1	1	0	16	0	17	7	0
Delano, Mike, Lan.*	1	0	.000	3.48	2	2	0	0	0	0	10.1	7	38	5	4	0	0	0	2	0	10	1	0
Delatori, Keola, Lan.	3	5	.375	7.63	15	4	0	0	4	1	30.2	34	144	28	26	1	0	1	2	20	0	27	1	1
Demouy, Chris, C.R.*	2	1	.667	2.40	46	0	0	0	28	16	48.2	39	212	18	13	3	7	3	0	28	2	51	8	0
Dent, Doug, F.W.	4	1	.800	3.51	8	8	0	0	0	0	48.2	43	201	23	19	2	0	1	1	17	0	32	4	1
Diaz, Antonio, F.W.	6	3	.667	4.17	28	9	0	0	7	0	75.1	77	330	41	35	5	2	3	1	28	0	54	7	1
Dobis, Jason, Q.C.	5	1	.833	5.05	23	4	0	0	4	1	57.0	67	249	36	32	5	1	1	1	17	2	36	5	0
Dobson, Dwayne, C.R.	1	7	.125	8.51	22	6	0	0	2	0	61.1	94	329	75	58	6	1	5	9	43	0	31	7	2
Dobson, Mark, F.W.	2	0	1.000	4.50	41	0	0	0	13	0	80.1	92	376	65	58	10	1	0	48	1	83	2	0
Donaldson, Bo, Rock.	2	1	.667	1.20	19	0	0	0	7	1	30.0	17	119	7	4	0	4	0	12	3	50	2	1
Duarte, Renney, C.R.	6	11	.353	4.75	31	18	3	2	4	1	132.2	145	561	81	70	19	4	4	2	33	0	102	5	1
Dunham, Pat, Wis.	0	1	.000	7.53	12	0	0	0	4	1	14.1	23	74	15	12	1	1	1	2	7	0	13	4	0
Dunning, Justin, Wis.	4	4	.500	5.61	25	8	0	0	12	2	69.0	79	329	50	43	8	2	1	8	36	0	76	17	0
Emanuel, Brandon, C.R.	7	12	.368	4.47	23	23	5	0	0	0	153.0	173	678	92	76	16	2	10	4	50	0	88	9	1
Escamilla, Paco, Clin.	1	6	.143	5.24	12	9	0	0	1	0	55.0	56	244	36	32	4	2	6	20	0	52	4	0
Eyre, Willie, Q.C.	1	0	1.000	4.26	2	2	0	0	0	0	12.2	8	51	6	6	0	0	1	1	6	0	10	1	0
Fahrner, Evan, S.B.	3	1	.750	6.08	20	1	0	0	9	1	37.0	39	172	27	25	3	0	0	1	21	0	45	5	2
Fahs, Paul, Peo.	1	0	1.000	0.00	2	0	0	0	1	0	2.1	3	10	0	0	0	0	0	0	0	2	0	0
Farizo, Brad, K.C.	4	7	.364	5.27	34	12	0	0	9	1	112.2	143	509	81	66	10	5	3	4	37	0	80	7	2
Fauske, Josh, Burl.	0	0	.000	5.14	5	0	0	0	2	0	7.0	6	35	6	4	0	0	1	1	7	0	6	3	1
Felix, Miguel, Burl.	0	2	.000	7.86	30	0	0	0	11	0	44.2	60	237	52	39	3	0	4	7	39	0	29	15	1
Ferguson, Tony, Mich.	0	2	.000	7.71	5	0	0	0	1	0	4.2	8	24	4	4	1	0	0	0	6	0	2	1	0
Ferrier, Shayne, C.R.	0	0	.000	5.06	7	0	0	0	4	0	10.2	11	54	10	6	1	0	2	8	0	8	3	1
Figueroa, Juan, Burl.	8	4	.667	3.12	17	16	2	0	0	0	115.1	100	491	51	40	8	0	6	5	44	0	139	4	1
Fischer, Eric, Burl.*	10	11	.476	5.19	25	25	2	1	0	0	137.0	160	614	89	79	11	4	3	8	50	1	78	4	2
Fitts, Brian, Q.C.	6	4	.600	5.58	37	12	0	0	5	1	100.0	109	448	73	62	15	4	4	10	32	0	71	11	0
Folkers, Brandon, Peo.*	0	0	.000	4.50	5	0	0	0	5	0	6.0	6	27	3	3	0	0	1	0	3	0	5	0	0
Foote, Joe, Q.C.	7	5	.583	3.93	44	18	1	1	7	2	135.0	131	582	72	59	6	4	5	4	49	2	111	9	1
Forbes, Keith, F.W.	4	8	.429	6.18	42	2	0	0	16	3	67.0	60	329	52	46	11	3	2	9	65	3	70	7	3
Frasor, Jason, W.M.	2	1	.667	2.63	4	4	1	1	0	0	24.0	17	97	10	7	2	2	0	9	0	33	0	3
Frazier, Brad, Q.C.	1	3	.250	5.40	33	0	0	0	6	1	48.1	52	243	37	29	1	3	3	9	39	5	26	9	2
Freehill, Mike, C.R.	0	0	.000	11.57	2	0	0	0	1	0	2.1	4	15	3	3	0	0	0	0	4	0	2	0	1
Fuller, Jody, S.B.	7	4	.636	4.49	36	11	0	0	10	0	116.1	133	524	68	58	6	1	7	4	43	0	83	7	0
Gagliano, Steve, Bel.	5	3	.625	4.10	15	9	1	1	2	1	74.2	71	314	40	34	8	4	1	6	23	0	45	9	0
Gallo, Michael, Mich.*	2	3	.400	5.85	12	12	0	0	0	0	60.0	76	268	47	39	6	1	2	1	23	0	32	1	0
Gangemi, Joe, C.R.*	1	2	.333	3.58	5	5	0	0	0	0	27.2	37	128	17	11	4	0	4	1	13	0	23	2	0
Garcia, Gabe, Mich.	5	3	.625	4.63	38	8	0	0	11	3	89.1	100	393	49	46	11	0	1	5	37	1	79	8	0
Gardner, Nathan, Rock.	3	2	.600	5.09	34	0	0	0	15	2	46.0	51	219	31	26	1	1	3	31	3	27	8	0
Geitz, Scott, Bel.	1	3	.250	5.19	52	0	0	0	17	3	69.1	75	315	44	40	5	3	1	7	31	0	56	4	0
Gilich, Denny, C.R.	3	7	.300	4.22	51	0	0	0	19	2	64.0	62	290	36	30	5	4	1	11	31	0	79	4	2
Ginter, Matt, Burl.	4	2	.667	4.05	9	9	0	0	0	0	40.0	38	173	20	18	3	1	0	3	19	0	29	1	0
Giuliano, Joe, Rock.	3	4	.429	4.03	43	1	0	0	11	2	73.2	79	348	51	33	6	3	5	8	39	7	54	8	1
Glick, David, Mich.*	1	0	1.000	0.55	10	0	0	0	3	1	16.1	7	66	2	1	0	0	3	5	1	20	2	0
Goetz, Geoff, K.C.*	5	3	.625	4.26	16	12	0	0	0	0	50.2	52	223	28	24	4	0	4	6	24	0	43	7	0

– 530 –

Pitcher, Team	W	L	Pct.	ERA	G	GS	CG	ShO	GF	Sv.	IP	H	TBF	R	ER	HR	SH	SF	HB	BB	IBB	SO	WP	Bk.
Gold, J.M., Bel.	6	10	.375	5.40	21	21	2	0	0	0	111.2	120	505	82	67	16	3	5	4	54	2	93	13	2
Gomer, Jeramy, Lan.*	2	1	.667	5.86	7	5	0	0	1	0	27.2	27	121	18	18	3	1	1	3	12	0	21	2	0
Gooch, Arnie, Clin.	1	1	.500	4.50	2	2	0	0	0	0	8.0	8	36	5	4	1	0	0	0	3	0	5	0	0
Good, Andrew, S.B.	11	10	.524	4.10	27	27	0	0	0	0	153.2	160	662	80	70	9	3	9	9	42	0	146	7	0
Gooden, Derek, Peo.	3	2	.600	4.82	38	0	0	0	34	12	37.1	41	162	20	20	1	0	1	5	12	1	21	1	0
Grater, Kevin, Bel.	5	3	.625	2.39	9	8	1	1	1	0	60.1	47	240	17	16	3	1	0	6	17	0	65	2	3
Greeny, Burdette, Bel.	0	0	.000	5.79	19	0	0	0	12	3	28.0	38	126	20	18	2	0	0	3	7	0	22	2	1
Griffin, Kirk, Peo.	3	4	.429	3.60	57	0	0	0	37	11	65.0	42	258	28	26	4	5	3	1	22	2	53	3	1
Gunderson, Matt, Lan.	0	0	.000	9.61	13	0	0	0	3	0	19.2	28	97	23	21	2	0	3	1	11	0	11	6	1
Gutierrez, Lazaro, W.M.*	2	1	.667	4.66	35	0	0	0	17	1	46.1	50	220	26	24	5	3	2	1	40	0	49	3	0
Hamulack, Tim, Mich.*	3	0	1.000	3.04	25	0	0	0	12	0	26.2	23	112	9	9	0	1	2	0	11	0	32	2	1
Hand, Jon, Peo.	3	3	.500	3.64	58	0	0	0	17	1	81.2	90	352	43	33	4	1	5	5	22	2	55	3	3
Harber, Ryan, K.C.*	3	5	.375	3.57	24	14	0	0	4	0	98.1	110	438	50	39	10	6	7	3	33	0	77	5	2
Haring, Brett, Rock.*	10	3	.769	3.34	25	18	3	3	1	1	124.0	113	516	53	46	7	4	3	4	42	0	94	5	0
Harris, Josh, F.W.	2	5	.286	7.43	17	7	0	0	3	0	53.1	67	255	52	44	6	2	3	4	28	1	28	0	2
Hart, Damien, Clin.*	2	5	.286	5.45	26	0	0	0	8	0	34.2	34	160	25	21	3	3	4	2	18	3	20	5	0
Harwas, Oliver, C.R.	3	4	.429	5.61	37	0	0	0	16	2	51.1	50	240	40	32	3	4	1	9	29	1	37	12	0
Hayden, Terry, Clin.-Rock.*	8	6	.571	2.70	38	14	1	0	6	0	116.2	108	503	57	35	10	10	3	6	42	0	79	6	0
Heams, Shane, W.M.	5	4	.556	2.35	51	0	0	0	30	10	69.0	41	294	26	18	1	3	4	1	39	2	101	15	1
Heaverlo, Jeff, Wis.	1	0	1.000	2.55	3	3	1	1	0	0	17.2	15	75	6	5	1	1	0	1	7	0	24	0	1
Hecht, Brian, Mich.	4	1	.800	3.15	27	0	0	0	13	1	34.1	42	152	13	12	0	1	1	2	10	2	26	2	0
Held, Travis, Peo.	1	0	1.000	2.53	2	2	0	0	0	0	10.2	14	47	3	3	1	1	0	0	4	0	7	1	1
Henriquez, Hector, K.C.*	2	5	.286	7.59	14	10	0	0	1	0	53.1	65	255	47	45	4	0	4	4	40	0	31	3	2
Hoard, Brent, Q.C.*	12	7	.632	3.43	28	28	1	0	0	0	149.2	143	643	68	57	9	4	3	2	64	1	139	7	1
Hodge, Kevin, Q.C.	0	0	.000	0.00	2	0	0	0	2	0	0.2	3	5	0	0	0	0	0	0	0	0	0	0	0
Howard, Ben, F.W.	6	10	.375	4.73	28	28	0	0	0	0	144.2	123	666	100	76	17	4	3	5	110	0	131	19	1
Howard, Tom, Q.C.*	2	1	.667	1.53	15	1	0	0	4	0	29.1	26	118	6	5	1	0	0	0	4	0	22	2	0
Hundley, Jeff, C.R.*	9	9	.500	4.04	25	25	6	1	0	0	158.0	163	698	99	71	17	5	8	8	62	0	140	10	2
Incantalupo, Todd, Bel.*	4	4	.500	6.04	40	7	0	0	8	1	95.1	115	443	71	64	7	3	5	7	40	1	62	4	0
Jacobs, Greg, C.R.*	2	5	.286	4.44	36	10	0	0	10	1	105.1	108	457	62	52	7	2	7	5	37	2	106	8	1
Jacobs, Jake, Q.C.	0	3	.000	4.79	48	0	0	0	21	0	71.1	63	347	52	38	7	3	4	15	55	4	70	6	0
Jacobson, Andrew, Burl.	1	1	.500	6.05	13	1	0	0	6	0	19.1	28	96	19	13	1	0	2	1	12	1	10	3	0
Jensen, Jason, S.B.*	2	3	.400	2.64	18	2	0	0	6	2	44.1	26	179	19	13	1	1	2	1	21	0	22	1	0
Johnson, Solomon, Burl.*	3	2	.600	4.92	19	8	0	0	3	0	53.0	70	249	38	29	2	0	5	1	17	1	39	1	1
Jones, Charlie, S.B.	2	3	.400	2.70	7	6	0	0	0	0	30.0	27	130	13	9	4	0	0	0	19	1	25	3	0
Jones, Fontella, Bel.	4	3	.571	4.34	36	5	0	0	19	4	76.2	84	347	44	37	10	0	1	2	35	0	76	11	1
Jones, Greg, C.R.	2	4	.333	3.83	34	0	0	0	29	13	40.0	37	165	18	17	5	2	0	0	13	2	41	5	0
Jones, Travis, F.W.*	8	2	.800	3.15	41	7	0	0	6	0	91.1	90	409	42	32	6	2	5	4	57	0	72	7	2
Kalita, Tim, W.M.*	4	1	.800	4.18	9	9	0	0	0	0	47.1	46	213	26	22	2	1	1	5	27	0	35	4	1
Kane, Kyle, Burl.	1	0	1.000	13.50	12	0	0	0	5	1	18.0	28	100	29	27	3	0	2	3	12	0	17	5	1
Keller, Kris, W.M.	5	3	.625	2.92	49	0	0	0	28	8	77.0	63	324	28	25	6	4	3	3	36	1	87	11	2
Kelly, Heath, K.C.	0	1	.000	9.00	1	0	0	0	1	0	1.0	1	4	1	1	1	0	0	0	0	0	2	0	0
Key, Scott, Rock.	0	0	.000	27.00	1	0	0	0	0	0	0.2	0	4	2	2	0	0	0	0	2	0	0	0	0
Koplove, Mike, S.B.	5	2	.714	2.04	45	0	0	0	19	7	84.0	70	351	23	19	5	3	0	11	29	0	98	4	0
Koutrouba, Tom, W.M.*	3	2	.600	5.40	31	11	0	0	7	0	85.0	110	381	56	51	5	1	4	2	24	1	46	1	1
Koziara, Matt, Rock.	1	2	.333	4.08	8	3	0	0	0	0	28.2	39	131	19	13	1	1	0	1	13	1	15	2	0
Krawczyk, Jack, Bel.	0	0	.000	0.00	6	0	0	0	6	3	6.1	5	24	0	0	0	0	0	0	1	0	11	0	0
Krug, Dustin, Lan.	3	7	.300	3.36	46	0	0	0	23	5	59.0	75	278	34	22	1	4	5	4	25	0	32	9	0
Kuzmic, Craig, Wis.	0	0	.000	0.00	1	0	0	0	1	1	1.0	1	4	0	0	0	0	0	0	0	0	1	0	0
Lambert, Jeremy, Peo.	2	1	.667	8.91	21	0	0	0	1	0	34.1	48	175	36	34	5	0	2	2	27	0	27	3	0
Lara, Nelson, K.C.	3	2	.600	6.06	46	0	0	0	34	10	52.0	50	257	38	35	5	3	3	7	47	1	45	8	0
Laroche, Jeff, K.C.*	1	4	.200	4.65	17	0	0	0	6	0	31.0	32	144	18	16	3	3	1	3	20	0	15	1	0
Levy, Tye, Clin.*	1	1	.500	4.15	7	0	0	0	2	1	8.2	12	43	4	4	2	1	2	0	4	0	6	0	1
Lewis, Rickey, Bel.	5	6	.455	6.02	16	14	0	0	1	0	64.1	70	315	59	43	9	0	7	2	55	0	42	10	2
LeBlanc, Eric, Rock.	0	0	.000	1.86	2	1	0	0	1	1	9.2	5	38	2	2	0	0	0	1	4	0	9	0	0
Longo, Neil, Wis.	2	2	.500	0.96	5	5	3	1	0	0	37.2	24	140	9	4	0	1	1	0	8	0	18	1	1
Looper, Aaron, Wis.	9	6	.600	4.10	38	7	0	0	10	3	90.0	89	391	47	41	8	1	3	6	26	0	73	6	1
Lopez, Javier, S.B.*	4	6	.400	6.00	20	20	0	0	0	0	99.0	122	458	74	66	9	1	4	3	43	0	70	9	0
Loux, Shane, W.M.	1	3	.250	6.27	8	8	0	0	0	0	47.1	55	215	39	33	5	1	2	8	16	1	43	4	0
Lovingood, Ray, Rock.*	1	0	1.000	4.85	16	1	0	0	9	0	29.2	27	133	16	16	2	0	1	2	16	0	24	3	0
Lowery, Phil, K.C.*	1	0	1.000	1.80	1	1	0	0	0	0	5.0	5	19	1	1	0	0	0	0	0	0	3	0	0
Luque, Roger, F.W.*	4	5	.444	3.84	46	3	0	0	20	2	77.1	67	337	39	33	2	3	5	2	40	3	79	4	1
Mackiewitz, Richard, Bel.*	0	0	.000	27.00	1	0	0	0	1	0	1.0	2	7	3	3	0	0	0	0	2	0	1	0	0
Madson, Will, W.M.	1	2	.333	10.13	8	0	0	0	3	0	8.0	15	44	10	9	3	0	1	0	6	1	7	0	0
Majewski, Gary, Burl.	0	0	.000	37.80	2	0	0	0	0	0	3.1	11	28	14	14	3	1	0	2	4	0	1	0	0
Mallard, Randi, Clin.	0	1	.000	6.89	6	1	0	0	1	0	15.2	18	70	12	12	0	0	0	3	3	0	21	4	0
Mallory, Andrew, Lan.	0	0	.000	13.50	5	0	0	0	1	0	4.2	12	31	11	7	2	0	0	2	4	0	2	1	0
Manias, James, Rock.*	9	7	.563	3.67	30	10	4	1	1	0	90.2	84	391	46	37	5	1	1	2	36	2	103	5	0
Mateo, Julio, Wis.	1	3	.250	4.34	20	0	0	0	10	4	29.0	31	131	18	14	2	2	1	1	8	2	27	2	0
Mathews, Dan, Bel.	3	4	.429	8.69	19	3	0	0	9	3	29.0	41	156	34	28	5	0	0	2	25	0	26	5	0
Matos, Josue, Wis.	9	9	.500	4.63	25	22	2	1	0	0	138.0	143	596	78	71	19	1	5	4	42	1	136	4	6
Maynard, Scott, Wis.	0	0	.000	0.00	2	0	0	0	2	0	2.0	0	6	0	0	0	0	0	0	0	0	2	0	0
McCutcheon, Mike, S.B.*	6	2	.750	4.00	28	8	0	0	6	0	87.2	87	384	48	39	5	2	2	1	36	0	74	3	1
McEvoy, Casey, Clin.-Rock.	1	3	.250	8.47	13	5	1	0	1	0	34.0	44	166	38	32	2	0	0	5	18	1	34	4	2
McGowan, Brian, W.M.	2	5	.286	5.05	39	0	0	0	8	0	62.1	66	309	58	35	4	7	2	2	47	1	40	16	2
Mears, Chris, Wis.	10	1	.909	2.43	13	13	2	1	0	0	89.0	76	359	33	24	1	2	3	5	16	0	78	1	0
Mendoza, Geronimo, Burl.	9	8	.529	4.63	28	28	0	0	0	0	157.1	186	713	96	81	10	3	3	8	60	5	119	7	0
Mendoza, Hatuey, S.B.	3	9	.250	8.27	13	11	0	0	2	0	57.2	64	283	57	53	5	0	1	8	45	0	36	20	2
Merrell, Phil, Clin.	8	3	.727	2.20	16	16	3	3	0	0	102.1	75	402	32	25	3	3	1	5	31	0	87	10	0
Meyer, Jake, Rock.	3	2	.600	2.54	33	0	0	0	31	16	46.0	40	197	16	13	1	4	0	3	18	4	51	2	0
Miller, Aaron, Q.C.*	6	6	.500	4.32	25	18	0	0	1	1	83.1	55	378	53	40	3	2	3	8	73	2	87	6	0
Miller, Jim, Bel.	0	1	.000	3.77	6	1	0	0	2	0	14.1	13	59	6	6	4	0	0	0	5	0	9	2	0
Minaya, Pedro, Clin.	4	6	.400	5.57	36	11	0	0	10	0	84.0	88	397	65	52	4	4	2	7	58	0	74	11	4
Miniel, Roberto, Bel.	0	0	.000	9.37	10	0	0	0	3	0	16.1	23	87	19	17	5	0	0	0	16	0	11	3	0
Montane, Ivan, Wis.	0	0	.000	0.71	10	0	0	0	9	3	12.2	5	49	1	1	0	0	0	0	5	0	18	2	0

Pitcher, Team	W	L	Pct.	ERA	G	GS	CG	ShO	GF	Sv.	IP	H	TBF	R	ER	HR	SH	SF	HB	BB	IBB	SO	WP	Bk.
Moore, Chris, K.C.	3	0	1.000	2.15	25	0	0	0	7	5	46.0	41	198	12	11	1	1	0	8	23	1	52	3	1
Murphy, Matt, Lan.*	3	1	.750	3.50	25	2	0	0	10	2	46.1	50	198	22	18	2	1	1	1	16	0	39	1	1
Nannini, Mike, Mich.	4	10	.286	4.43	15	15	0	0	0	0	87.1	107	398	56	43	8	2	7	4	31	1	68	3	0
Neal, Blaine, K.C.	4	2	.667	2.32	26	0	0	0	18	6	31.0	21	117	8	8	2	2	0	0	10	0	31	1	0
Neu, Michael, Rock.	0	1	.000	4.50	9	0	0	0	2	1	18.0	17	84	10	9	1	0	1	2	12	1	23	4	0
Neugebauer, Nickolas, Bel.	7	5	.583	3.90	18	18	0	0	0	0	80.2	50	372	41	35	4	2	3	6	80	0	125	10	2
Noyce, David, K.C.*	7	3	.700	3.30	16	16	2	2	0	0	101.0	82	419	43	37	5	3	5	3	29	0	86	6	1
Nykoluk, Kevin, Peo.	0	0	.000	0.00	1	0	0	0	1	0	1.0	0	4	0	0	0	0	0	1	0	0	0	0	0
Oleksik, George, Rock.	0	1	.000	6.35	21	0	0	0	9	2	28.1	32	133	22	20	4	1	0	5	12	2	24	5	0
Olsen, Kevin, K.C.	5	2	.714	3.38	10	9	0	0	0	0	61.1	65	257	25	23	3	0	3	2	16	0	52	2	0
O'Reilly, John, S.B.	0	1	.000	8.74	4	2	0	0	1	0	11.1	17	56	11	11	4	0	0	0	5	0	15	1	0
Ortiz, Omar, F.W.	1	2	.333	6.75	4	4	0	0	0	0	18.2	17	91	16	14	0	0	0	2	20	0	9	1	0
Oswalt, Roy, Mich.	13	4	.765	4.46	22	22	2	0	0	0	151.1	144	643	78	75	8	2	5	7	54	0	143	8	4
Padilla, Juan, Q.C.	2	2	.000	2.40	12	0	0	0	4	0	15.0	18	69	8	4	0	0	1	0	6	2	16	4	1
Palma, Ricardo, Lan.*	7	7	.500	2.94	22	22	2	0	0	0	134.2	134	571	61	44	6	1	4	3	44	0	79	8	4
Parker, Allan, C.R.	0	0	.000	54.00	1	0	0	0	0	0	1.0	7	10	6	6	1	0	0	0	0	0	0	0	0
Parker, Clark, Burl.	0	0	.000	18.00	1	0	0	0	1	0	1.0	2	7	2	2	0	0	1	1	1	0	0	0	0
Peguero, Darwin, Mich.*	7	7	.500	4.11	24	20	0	0	2	0	114.0	115	483	58	52	7	2	2	5	35	1	88	6	3
Penney, Mike, Bel.	9	12	.429	4.24	27	27	4	2	0	0	170.0	171	740	94	80	16	2	3	7	70	2	109	11	2
Perry, Tim, F.W.	2	5	.286	5.08	10	10	0	0	0	0	51.1	50	241	39	29	4	1	4	3	34	0	46	5	0
Pesqueira, Omar, F.W.	4	5	.444	5.08	47	2	0	0	15	2	78.0	84	344	49	44	7	2	3	2	30	1	56	3	0
Pidgeon, Matt, K.C.	7	6	.538	4.95	40	7	0	0	8	0	100.0	126	447	59	55	6	3	2	8	36	2	64	3	1
Pine, Chris, Bel.	0	1	.000	3.14	7	0	0	0	4	0	14.1	13	65	7	5	1	0	2	1	10	0	17	2	0
Pineda, Jairo, Mich.	0	2	.000	8.84	4	4	0	0	0	0	19.1	30	91	24	19	1	0	2	5	6	0	9	0	0
Pineda, Luis, W.M.	0	2	.000	3.57	24	3	0	0	19	7	40.1	30	175	18	16	2	2	5	1	26	2	55	5	0
Pipes, Joey, C.R.	4	1	.800	2.95	7	6	1	0	1	0	42.2	45	184	24	14	1	1	1	4	11	0	23	2	1
Poe, Ryan, Bel.	6	10	.375	3.56	49	5	0	0	28	9	96.0	94	398	46	38	9	1	2	3	16	3	108	5	1
Polanco, Elvis, Lan.	0	4	.000	6.45	25	0	0	0	16	4	37.2	54	187	34	27	3	2	2	3	16	2	29	0	0
Prather, Scott, Peo.*	9	10	.474	3.85	27	27	0	0	0	0	147.1	134	642	81	63	10	4	4	11	77	0	132	5	0
Prinz, Bret, S.B.	6	10	.375	4.48	30	23	0	0	3	0	138.2	129	594	82	69	16	5	7	8	52	0	98	10	4
Puffer, Brandon, Clin.	1	2	.333	1.99	59	0	0	0	55	34	63.1	53	277	20	14	2	2	2	11	24	3	60	4	1
Purvis, Robert, Burl.	0	0	.000	2.38	6	0	0	0	3	1	11.1	10	50	5	3	1	0	0	1	4	0	8	0	1
Redding, Tim, Mich.	8	6	.571	4.97	43	11	0	0	24	14	105.0	84	470	69	58	4	6	5	3	76	1	141	19	2
Rincon, Juan, Q.C.	14	8	.636	2.92	28	28	0	0	0	0	163.1	146	683	67	53	8	1	3	2	66	3	153	11	0
Rivera, Saul, Q.C.	4	1	.800	1.42	60	0	0	0	54	23	69.2	42	283	12	11	0	2	0	6	36	5	102	2	0
Roberts, Rick, W.M.*	0	0	.000	12.00	1	1	0	0	0	0	3.0	5	16	5	4	1	0	1	0	2	0	1	1	0
Robertson, Nathan, K.C.*	6	1	.857	2.29	8	8	1	1	0	0	51.0	42	197	14	13	1	0	2	0	12	0	33	0	0
Robinson, Dustin, Clin.	3	6	.333	4.76	44	1	0	0	11	0	70.0	67	312	51	37	8	7	6	4	29	3	53	4	0
Rodgers, Marcus, Burl.	0	0	.000	33.75	4	0	0	0	2	0	2.2	10	22	10	10	2	0	1	1	3	0	5	1	0
Rodriguez, Jose, Peo.*	2	3	.400	3.31	15	0	0	0	2	0	16.1	14	74	7	6	1	3	0	0	8	0	15	0	0
Rosado, Juan, Bel.*	0	0	.000	9.90	8	0	0	0	3	0	10.0	11	54	12	11	1	0	0	1	14	0	4	2	0
Rose, Brian, Clin.-Rock.	11	2	.846	2.94	48	1	0	0	26	6	67.1	65	283	24	22	7	3	1	3	23	3	64	3	0
Royer, Jason, S.B.	7	7	.500	4.69	32	18	0	0	6	1	119.0	135	531	77	62	6	2	1	6	43	0	62	8	1
Sams, Aaron, Lan.*	6	4	.600	4.67	17	17	0	0	0	0	96.1	99	428	57	50	6	1	4	3	52	0	83	12	0
Santana, Johan, Mich.*	8	8	.500	4.66	27	26	1	0	0	0	160.1	162	688	94	83	14	1	6	10	55	0	150	10	1
Santonocito, Justin, Clin.	0	0	.000	0.00	2	0	0	0	1	0	2.1	2	14	2	0	0	0	0	2	3	0	0	0	0
Schmidt, Donnie, Wis.	0	1	.000	4.50	5	0	0	0	3	0	8.0	5	39	6	4	0	2	0	1	9	1	8	1	1
Schoening, Brent, Q.C.	0	1	.000	2.45	6	1	0	0	1	1	11.0	7	45	3	3	1	0	0	0	5	0	11	1	1
Schurman, Ryan, Clin.	3	3	.500	3.54	44	3	0	0	15	2	86.1	74	380	41	34	8	6	2	7	50	6	83	7	2
Seaman, John, K.C.	1	2	.333	5.57	13	0	0	0	6	0	21.0	27	95	15	13	1	1	1	2	4	0	12	4	1
Sequea, Jacobo, Rock.	4	6	.400	4.92	16	16	2	1	0	0	89.2	88	393	52	49	6	2	5	7	44	0	67	9	6
Sergent, Joe, K.C.*	2	1	.667	7.11	8	0	0	0	2	0	12.2	17	59	10	10	1	1	1	1	4	1	9	0	0
Sessions, Doug, Mich.	0	0	.000	0.69	12	0	0	0	12	5	13.0	6	44	1	1	1	0	1	1	0	0	18	0	0
Shepherd, Alvie, C.R.	0	0	.000	4.70	6	0	0	0	3	0	7.2	4	36	5	4	0	0	2	0	8	0	5	0	0
Shibilo, Andy, Peo.	4	13	.235	5.11	27	24	2	0	0	0	135.2	157	621	105	77	10	3	8	14	41	0	96	6	2
Shields, Drew, K.C.	1	0	1.000	5.48	14	0	0	0	2	0	23.0	30	110	14	14	3	0	3	9	0	0	20	2	0
Simpson, Allan, Wis.	2	9	.182	4.38	24	13	1	0	3	0	90.1	83	402	56	44	4	4	8	3	48	0	88	4	1
Sismondo, Bobby, W.M.*	9	12	.429	3.67	27	27	1	1	0	0	169.1	153	708	86	69	12	4	5	7	62	2	135	8	1
Smith, Brandon, Mich.	1	2	.333	6.66	18	0	0	0	10	0	24.1	25	117	19	18	2	0	1	1	20	1	19	5	0
Smith, Clint, W.M.	4	7	.364	4.23	20	14	0	0	1	0	87.1	88	397	60	41	6	2	3	8	48	0	73	13	4
Smith, Justin, Wis.*	1	1	.500	4.82	7	7	0	0	0	0	37.1	41	163	22	20	6	2	1	3	10	0	29	0	1
Smith, Robert, Peo.*	4	1	.800	2.83	9	9	0	0	0	0	54.0	53	219	20	17	4	1	3	2	16	0	59	2	1
Smyth, Steve, Lan.*	5	3	.625	6.93	10	10	0	0	0	0	50.2	68	238	40	39	5	0	2	2	30	0	46	6	0
Soriano, Gabriel, Rock.	0	2	.000	13.97	8	0	0	0	3	0	9.2	18	64	21	15	1	0	0	1	16	2	10	4	0
Spykstra, Dave, Mich.	0	0	.000	6.75	5	0	0	0	1	0	5.1	2	30	7	4	0	0	2	0	10	0	9	6	0
Stemle, Steve, Peo.	7	10	.412	5.47	28	28	0	0	0	0	148.0	177	688	104	90	11	3	5	6	67	0	113	14	0
Stewart, Joshua, Burl.*	2	0	1.000	7.28	16	0	0	0	3	1	29.2	38	138	25	24	6	2	2	21	0	35	1	0
Stumm, Jason, Burl.	3	3	.500	5.32	10	10	0	0	0	0	44.0	47	199	31	26	4	0	1	1	27	1	33	4	2
Sturdy, Tim, Q.C.	2	7	.222	6.27	13	13	0	0	0	0	60.1	85	282	48	42	4	3	0	5	16	0	39	2	1
Suarez, Luis, C.R.	1	1	.500	7.00	4	4	0	0	0	0	18.0	25	91	19	14	3	0	1	9	0	15	2	0
Sullivan, Shane, Lan.	2	0	1.000	8.15	13	0	0	0	3	0	17.2	28	95	20	16	1	0	1	1	13	0	9	3	1
Therneau, Dave, Rock.	12	3	.800	3.41	16	16	2	2	0	0	100.1	95	422	41	38	6	2	3	4	33	1	106	5	2
Thornton, Matt, Wis.*	0	0	.000	4.91	25	1	0	0	3	1	29.1	39	154	19	16	1	4	1	0	25	0	34	5	0
Torres, Leo, Lan.*	2	0	1.000	2.74	51	0	0	0	20	3	62.1	51	259	22	19	2	2	1	3	28	1	47	1	1
Torres, Manny, Rock.	1	6	.143	6.05	8	7	1	0	0	0	38.2	48	177	33	26	2	0	2	1	11	0	29	1	1
Torres, Melqui, Wis.	13	9	.591	4.51	27	27	3	2	0	0	171.2	185	736	99	86	9	3	14	10	45	0	129	12	6
Ulloa, Enmanuel, Wis.	7	3	.700	4.60	35	10	0	0	17	5	88.0	90	384	50	45	9	1	0	1	36	2	98	8	6
Valdez, Jose, Clin.	0	1	.000	15.88	3	1	0	0	0	0	5.2	16	35	10	10	0	0	0	2	3	0	5	2	0
Valverde, Jose, S.B.	0	0	.000	0.00	2	0	0	0	1	0	2.2	2	11	0	0	0	0	0	1	2	0	3	1	1
Van De Weg, Ryan, F.W.	3	4	.429	6.71	13	8	0	0	3	1	53.2	71	257	46	40	6	0	2	7	28	0	41	7	0
Vargas, Claudio, K.C.	5	5	.500	3.88	19	19	1	0	0	0	99.2	97	426	47	43	8	0	3	0	41	0	88	2	2
Verplancke, Joe, S.B.	2	2	.500	4.81	18	0	0	0	6	0	33.2	16	145	22	18	4	2	3	4	24	0	43	4	0
Viator, Dustin, F.W.	0	1	.000	17.18	5	0	0	0	2	0	3.2	7	18	7	7	2	0	0	0	2	0	0	0	0
Victoria, Lester, Q.C.*	1	1	.500	4.03	41	0	0	0	8	0	51.1	41	235	30	23	2	1	1	3	42	2	58	10	0
Viles, Jeff, Peo.	3	5	.375	5.35	58	0	0	0	15	0	70.2	59	307	47	42	15	3	1	4	34	0	79	3	0

Pitcher, Team	W	L	Pct.	ERA	G	GS	CG	ShO	GF	Sv.	IP	H	TBF	R	ER	HR	SH	SF	HB	BB	IBB	SO	WP	Bk.
Wade, Travis, Mich.	0	0	.000	9.64	10	0	0	0	5	2	14.0	22	78	18	15	2	0	0	2	11	1	9	1	0
Waligora, Tom, Lan.	2	6	.250	4.28	50	1	0	0	20	5	82.0	78	365	44	39	8	5	5	4	38	1	56	8	0
Walrond, Les, Peo.*	7	10	.412	5.70	21	20	0	0	0	0	109.0	115	489	77	69	12	2	5	3	59	0	78	6	0
Ward, Matt, K.C.*	3	1	.750	5.06	5	5	0	0	0	0	26.2	41	118	17	15	6	0	0	4	0	0	7	0	0
Watkins, Steve, F.W.	0	3	.000	8.47	4	4	0	0	0	0	17.0	24	83	17	16	3	1	0	2	9	0	21	1	0
Whatley, Brannon, Burl.	3	5	.375	3.47	45	0	0	0	37	20	57.0	48	254	29	22	3	6	1	1	34	4	52	9	0
Whitesides, Johnny, Rock.	1	1	.500	8.04	13	1	0	0	4	0	15.2	24	82	19	14	0	0	2	3	10	0	11	2	0
Whitney, Jacob, Mich.*	9	8	.529	4.61	33	19	2	0	3	1	136.2	152	570	81	70	15	2	7	3	29	1	121	10	3
Williams, Mike, Burl.	6	7	.462	4.45	37	16	2	0	12	2	127.1	119	573	78	63	9	4	6	14	65	1	83	11	2
Willis, Craig, Wis.	2	2	.500	5.90	39	1	0	0	17	0	61.0	81	293	47	40	6	3	3	4	26	2	49	5	1
Winchester, Scott, Rock.	1	1	.500	2.79	6	6	0	0	0	0	19.1	19	82	7	6	2	1	0	0	3	0	11	0	0
Wohlers, Mark, Rock.	0	0	.000	4.50	2	0	0	0	0	0	2.0	1	9	1	1	0	0	0	2	0	0	4	0	0
Wooten, Shane, Bel.*	0	0	.000	3.09	33	0	0	0	10	1	35.0	29	162	16	12	1	0	3	4	25	1	35	2	0
Wright, Daniel, Burl.	0	0	.000	6.00	2	0	0	0	0	0	6.0	5	26	4	4	1	0	0	1	3	0	3	0	0
Wuertz, Mike, Lan.	11	12	.478	4.80	28	28	1	0	0	0	161.1	191	716	104	86	11	2	10	1	44	0	127	11	0
Wylie, Mitch, Burl.	1	0	1.000	1.97	6	6	0	0	0	0	32.0	28	134	11	7	0	0	3	2	11	0	27	0	0
Yates, Chad, Peo.	1	2	.333	2.59	22	0	0	0	9	0	24.1	16	103	8	7	2	1	0	2	14	0	26	4	2
Yount, Andy, W.M.	2	3	.400	5.61	24	3	0	0	8	1	43.1	38	199	31	27	3	0	0	4	36	0	28	6	0
Zamarripa, Tony, Lan.	2	0	1.000	7.20	11	0	0	0	1	0	15.0	21	68	13	12	1	0	0	5	0	7	0	0
Zambrano, Carlos, Lan.	13	7	.650	4.17	27	24	2	1	2	0	153.1	150	663	87	71	9	5	4	10	62	1	98	10	2
Zapata, Juan, Bel.	0	2	.000	8.03	7	0	0	0	2	0	12.1	22	68	16	11	0	0	1	1	9	0	9	0	0
Zyskowski, Garrett, Mich.*	2	0	1.000	7.71	14	0	0	0	5	1	16.1	21	78	14	14	3	1	1	3	12	1	12	3	0

COMBINATION SHUTOUTS: **Beloit** (5)—Gold-Wooten-Krawczyk, Neugebauer-Incantalupo-Geitz, Poe-Jones, Jones-Barton-Poe, Gagliano-Wooten. **Burlington** (2)—Figueroa-Johnson-Felix, Ginter-Almonte. **Cedar Rapids** (1)—Bridges-Gilich-Jones. **Clinton** (1)—Darnell-Minaya. **Fort Wayne** (4)—Diaz-Bauer, Jones-Pesqueria-Dobson, Jones-Luque-Condrey, Bartosh-Bauer. **Kane County** (7)—Goetz-Shields-Clackum, Henriquez-Laroche-Shields-Pidgeon-Bautista, Vargas-Neal-Lara, Anderson-Lara, Anderson-Neal, Anderson-Neal. **Lansing** (3)—Wuertz-Torres-Waligora, Sams-Murphy-Waligora-Krug, Murphy-Krug. **Michigan** (5)—Santana-Borges, Oswalt-Redding, Santana-Hecht-Redding, Borges-Hamulack, Gallo-Borges. **Peoria** (4)—Smith-Brunette-Gooden, Prather-Hand-Book-Viles, Shibilo-Brunette, Prather-Griffin. **Quad City** (9)—Foote-Howard-Rivera, Sturdy-Victoria-Miller, Hoard-Victoria, Rincon-Foote-Rivera, Rincon-Cosgrove-Rivera, Balfour-Rivera, Dobis-Jacobs-Fitts, Eyre-Jacobs, Hoard-Balfour. **Rockford** (9)—Altman-Haring-Meyer, Therneau-Whitesides-Hayden, Averette-Meyer, Therneau-Meyer, Haring-Gardner, Davis-Donaldson-Meyer, Manias-Gardner-Meyer, Averette-Wohlers-Meyer, Davis-Oleksik. **South Bend** (6)—Jones-Jensen-Koplove, Good-Koplove, Jensen-Koplove, Royer-Koplove, Fuller-Fahrner, Prinz-Verplancke-Cervantes. **West Michigan** (5)—Cornejo-Yount, Buller-Pineda, Sismondo-Heams-Pineda, Sismondo-Keller, Yount-Gutierrez. **Wisconsin** (4)—Mears-Simpson-Ulloa, Torres-Simpson, Ulloa-Looper-Chrysler, Torres-Chrysler.

NO-HIT GAMES: Ireland, Kissimmee, defeated St. Petersburg, 5-0, June 23; Thomas, Fort Myers, defeated Charlotte, 9-0, July 12.

PITCHERS WITH TWO OR MORE TEAMS

Pitcher, Team	W	L	Pct.	ERA	G	GS	CG	ShO	GF	Sv.	IP	H	TBF	R	ER	HR	SH	SF	HB	BB	IBB	SO	WP	Bk.
Altman, Gene, Rock.	2	6	.250	6.08	11	11	0	0	0	0	53.1	63	254	41	36	4	1	3	3	34	0	51	6	0
Altman, Gene, Clin.	0	2	.000	3.86	3	3	0	0	0	0	14.0	7	60	9	6	0	0	0	3	7	0	19	0	0
Brewer, Clint, Clin.	8	2	.800	4.15	24	9	0	0	4	0	73.2	61	308	41	34	10	4	1	2	28	0	39	2	0
Brewer, Clint, Rock.	1	0	1.000	6.11	10	0	0	0	5	0	17.2	19	82	15	12	2	1	0	0	9	1	16	3	1
Cooper, Eric, Clin.	2	5	.286	6.08	12	10	1	0	1	0	47.1	49	226	38	32	8	2	3	2	36	1	37	9	2
Cooper, Eric, Rock.	1	1	.500	9.88	4	4	0	0	0	0	13.2	21	69	15	15	2	0	2	3	11	0	6	7	0
Hayden, Terry, Clin.*	8	6	.571	2.38	33	14	1	0	4	0	109.2	98	470	51	29	9	8	3	6	39	0	72	6	0
Hayden, Terry, Rock.*	0	0	.000	7.71	5	0	0	0	2	0	7.0	10	33	6	6	1	2	0	0	3	0	7	0	0
McEvoy, Casey, Clin.	0	1	.000	10.24	7	0	0	0	1	0	9.2	12	48	12	11	1	0	0	2	8	1	13	2	1
McEvoy, Casey, Rock.	1	2	.333	7.77	6	5	1	0	0	0	24.1	32	118	26	21	1	0	3	3	10	0	21	2	1
Rose, Brian, Clin.	7	0	1.000	0.55	24	1	0	0	4	0	32.2	27	129	2	2	1	3	0	1	11	1	24	0	0
Rose, Brian, Rock.	4	2	.667	5.19	24	0	0	0	22	4	34.2	38	154	22	20	5	2	2	2	12	2	40	3	0

1999 FIELDING

TEAM

Team	Pct.	G	PO	A	E	TC	DP	TP	PB	Team	Pct.	G	PO	A	E	TC	DP	TP	PB
Kane County......	.971	137	3618	1514	155	5287	147	0	24	South Bend	.962	139	3643	1639	208	5490	109	0	26
Michigan	.970	138	3576	1376	153	5105	124	2	21	West Michigan ..	.962	140	3659	1626	209	5494	115	0	27
Quad City	.966	139	3662	1517	185	5364	133	0	24	Fort Wayne	.961	140	3673	1384	203	5260	124	0	29
Peoria..............	.965	139	3603	1484	183	5270	117	0	26	Rockford	.961	139	3613	1536	208	5357	113	0	15
Beloit...............	.965	139	3605	1407	184	5196	106	0	20	Burlington.........	.958	139	3582	1538	222	5342	116	0	35
Wisconsin	.964	138	3593	1401	184	5178	91	0	14	Clinton.............	.958	137	3542	1476	220	5238	127	1	25
Lansing............	.964	140	3596	1503	193	5292	145	0	40	Cedar Rapids.....	.958	138	3587	1585	229	5401	137	0	22

INDIVIDUAL

FIRST BASEMEN

NOTE: All caps denotes fielding-percentage leader based on 70 games for catchers, 93 for all other non-pitchers and 112 innings for pitchers. *Throws lefthanded.

Player, Team	Pct.	G	PO	A	E	TC	DP
Baderdeen, Kevin, Clin.	.947	4	34	2	2	38	3
BATTERSBY, Eric, Burl.*	.987	93	807	60	11	878	66
Bautista, Jorge, K.C.	1.000	16	143	4	0	147	17
Bly, Derrick, Lan.	.988	29	232	14	3	249	17
Bolling, Kirk, S.B.	1.000	1	6	0	0	6	1
Bordenick, Ryan, Bel.	.979	17	134	8	3	145	9
Broussard, Benjamin, Clin.*	1.000	3	18	0	0	18	2
Callahan, David, K.C.*	.987	123	1050	64	15	1129	116
Choi, Hee, Lan.*	.976	79	694	50	18	762	80
Da Luz, Craig, W.M.	.991	39	313	30	3	346	31
Daigle, Leo, W.M.	.980	72	610	62	14	686	41
De La Cruz, Henry, Lan.	.818	2	8	1	2	11	1
Delgado, Ariel, C.R.*	.981	97	848	63	18	929	82

Player, Team	Pct.	G	PO	A	E	TC	DP
Diaz, Angel, C.R.	.995	18	179	10	1	190	15
Downing, Lance, S.B.	1.000	1	8	0	0	8	0
Dusan, Joe, F.W.*	.984	51	407	22	7	436	39
Dyt, Darren, Peo.	.968	12	58	3	2	63	5
Farnsworth, Troy, Peo.	.984	42	359	19	6	384	36
Fatheree, Danny, Mich.	1.000	5	25	0	0	25	5
Fennell, Jason, Burl.	1.000	6	47	7	0	54	5
Fick, Robert, W.M.	.933	1	13	1	1	15	2
Figueroa, Eduardo, Bel.*	.996	34	264	19	1	283	20
Folkers, Brandon, Peo.*	.987	81	655	41	9	705	55
Garcia, Tony, Burl.	.938	4	27	3	2	32	0
Garza, Rolando, Burl.	.991	34	320	16	3	339	23
Griffin, Matt, Lan.	1.000	2	11	1	0	12	1
Hankins, Ryan, Burl.	1.000	6	49	1	0	50	4
Hawthorne, Kyle, Q.C.	1.000	11	76	6	0	82	11
Hyde, Brandon, Burl.	1.000	2	21	2	0	23	1
Johnson, Ryan, Clin.	.981	8	51	1	1	53	4

Player, Team	Pct.	G	PO	A	E	TC	DP
Jordan, Yustin, Q.C.	.971	25	184	18	6	208	27
Kelly, Chris, Peo.	.972	9	66	3	2	71	3
Kelly, Heath, K.C.	1.000	1	2	0	0	2	0
Kirby, Scott, Bel.	1.000	1	8	2	0	10	0
Kuzmic, Craig, Wis.	1.000	1	1	0	0	1	0
Lawrence, Tony, F.W.	1.000	7	47	2	0	49	4
Leatherman, Dan, Q.C.*	.988	64	566	30	7	603	48
Loggins, Joshua, F.W.	.949	7	53	3	3	59	9
Lopez, Jose, S.B.	.909	2	10	0	1	11	0
Mackiewitz, Richard, Bel.*	.995	89	715	63	4	782	62
Marciniak, Dave, Q.C.	.959	14	109	8	5	122	11
Markray, Thad, Clin.-Rock.	.900	2	8	1	1	10	1
Matan, James, Rock.	.988	55	461	25	6	492	38
Mauck, Matt, Lan.	.970	37	278	15	9	302	31
McNeal, Aaron, Mich.	.985	129	1013	111	17	1141	101
Munson, Eric, W.M.	.990	33	281	27	3	311	31
Navarro, Ibrahim, Lan.	1.000	1	4	0	0	4	1
Neal, Steve, S.B.*	.993	69	608	58	5	671	45
Nelson, Brian, Wis.	.944	4	33	1	2	36	3
Nicholson, Derek, Mich.	.974	6	35	3	1	39	4
Nykoluk, Kevin, Peo.	1.000	10	65	4	0	69	5
Oliver, Bill, C.R.	.977	15	118	7	3	128	10
Robinson, Bo, Wis.	.994	19	137	20	1	158	14
Roneberg, Brett, K.C.*	1.000	3	24	0	0	24	2
Ross, Justin, C.R.*	1.000	5	40	4	0	44	3
Ruiz, Randy, Clin.	1.000	2	13	0	0	13	2
Santonocito, Justin, Clin.	1.000	2	14	2	0	16	1
Sassanella, Jeremy, W.M.	.000	1	0	0	0	0	0
Schaeffer, Jon, Q.C.	.994	42	313	12	2	327	27
Scheschuk, John, F.W.*	.991	66	515	40	5	560	56
Schmidt, Bryan, F.W.	1.000	7	32	3	0	35	3
Selander, Craig, Q.C.	.857	1	6	0	1	7	0
Southall, Rick, Wis.	.983	69	555	37	10	602	42
Stegall, Randy, Clin.-Rock.	.989	23	166	9	2	177	11
Ticen, Kevin, C.R.	.977	10	82	4	2	88	12
Turnquist, Tyler, Mich.	1.000	3	13	2	0	15	1
Vaughn, Clint, Clin.	.979	101	905	56	21	982	92
Welsh, Eric, Rock.*	.983	93	736	70	14	820	61
Whitehead, Braxton, Clin.	1.000	3	26	2	0	28	4
Wickersham, Jack, F.W.	1.000	9	71	3	0	74	2
William, Jovany, Peo.	1.000	4	26	4	0	30	2
Williams, Peanut, Wis.	1.000	4	23	3	0	26	1
Williford, Dan, S.B.*	1.000	1	20	1	0	21	0
Wolff, Mike, S.B.*	.987	66	617	60	9	686	52
Woodward, Mattson, Wis.	.982	56	397	35	8	440	21

TRIPLE PLAYS: Johnson, McNeal.

FIRST BASEMEN WITH TWO OR MORE TEAMS

Player, Team	Pct.	G	PO	A	E	TC	DP
Markray, Thad, Clin.	.875	1	6	1	1	8	1
Markray, Thad, Rock.	1.000	1	2	0	0	2	0
Stegall, Randy, Clin.	.994	20	153	9	1	163	11
Stegall, Randy, Rock.	.929	3	13	0	1	14	0

SECOND BASEMEN

Player, Team	Pct.	G	PO	A	E	TC	DP
Ahlers, Steve, C.R.	.980	24	47	53	2	102	17
Alvarez, Jimmy, Q.C.	.953	14	24	37	3	64	8
Araujo, Danilo, Peo.	.957	101	187	214	18	419	51
Beattie, Andrew, Clin.	.941	52	84	141	14	239	30
Belliard, Francisco, S.B.	.941	55	97	143	15	255	22
Bowers, Jason, Peo.	.966	18	32	52	3	87	14
Brock, J.J., S.B.	.963	41	97	112	8	217	26
Bush, Ron, W.M.	.957	64	114	156	12	282	31
Condon, Mike, C.R.	.948	13	25	30	3	58	7
Conley, Brian, Rock.	.971	70	120	186	9	315	41
Downing, Lance, S.B.	.974	8	11	27	1	39	2
Dunaway, Jason, F.W.	.954	49	83	124	10	217	24
Encarnacion, Bienvenido, C.R.	.937	20	49	55	7	111	18
Escalona, Felix, Mich.	.978	63	118	152	6	276	35
Escobar, Gustavo, Peo.	.958	7	10	13	1	24	1
French, Ron, F.W.	1.000	1	0	1	0	1	0
Garcia, Alex, F.W.	.968	54	78	133	7	218	29
Gastelum, Carlos, C.R.	1.000	11	26	34	0	60	6
Gay, Dennis, C.R.	.872	9	18	16	5	39	5
German, Franklin, Lan.	.923	15	22	26	4	52	5
Godfrey, Tim, Rock.	.933	21	27	43	5	75	2
Gonzalez, Jose, Burl.	.963	55	108	153	10	271	34
Goudie, Jaime, Clin.	.957	58	114	151	12	277	32
Griffin, Matt, Lan.	1.000	1	4	4	0	8	3
Guillen, Jose, Bel.	.900	16	26	28	6	60	3
Hankins, Ryan, Burl.	1.000	11	12	32	0	44	2

Player, Team	Pct.	G	PO	A	E	TC	DP
Hawthorne, Kyle, Q.C.	.981	11	22	31	1	54	12
Hodge, Kevin, Q.C.	.977	10	13	29	1	43	8
Kelly, Heath, K.C.	.966	28	51	64	4	119	19
Kidwell, Tommy, Peo.	.981	24	47	59	2	108	14
Kison, Robbie, Rock.-Clin.	.918	18	40	49	8	97	14
Kuzmic, Craig, Wis.	.000	1	0	0	0	0	0
Marciniak, Dave, Q.C.	.955	9	16	26	2	44	5
Martinez, Victor, Wis.	.934	31	46	82	9	137	6
McConnell, Jason, Q.C.	.939	11	12	19	2	33	2
Medosch, Keith, C.R.	.971	8	14	19	1	34	5
Medrano, Jesus, K.C.	.970	116	246	309	17	572	79
Miles, Aaron, Mich.	.964	73	131	164	11	306	46
Navarro, Ibrahim, Lan.	.981	12	21	32	1	54	9
Oliver, Brian, C.R.	.990	20	49	52	1	102	9
Parker, Clark, Burl.	.906	29	49	57	11	117	13
Patten, Chris, Bel.	.973	118	259	307	16	582	59
Perez, Antonio, Rock.	.934	58	97	144	17	258	30
Pond, Ryan, C.R.	.953	38	86	116	10	212	33
Price, Corey, Rock.	1.000	3	4	2	0	6	1
RODRIGUEZ, Luis, Q.C.	.984	93	171	271	7	449	67
Runnells, T.J., W.M.	.958	83	165	181	15	361	50
Santamarina, Juan, Burl.	.900	2	3	6	1	10	1
Santonocito, Justin, Clin.	.969	10	9	22	1	32	3
Schaffer, Jake, Mich.	1.000	2	3	4	0	7	1
Schmidt, Bryan, F.W.	.990	21	41	59	1	101	17
Schrager, Tony, Lan.	.983	122	198	325	9	532	81
Secoda, Joe, Peo.	.000	1	0	0	0	0	0
Smalls, Terrence, K.C.	.938	5	4	11	1	16	4
Stegall, Randy, Clin.-Rock.	.947	12	18	36	3	57	7
Thorpe, A.D., Clin.	.900	2	5	4	1	10	2
Torres, Bernie, Burl.	.985	56	97	159	4	260	30
Tucent, Francisco, Bel.	.902	11	17	20	4	41	3
Turnquist, Tyler, Mich.	.778	2	3	4	2	9	1
Urquiola, Carlos, S.B.	.967	38	65	110	6	181	25
Valera, Ramon, Wis.	.959	36	54	110	7	171	20
Vina, Fernando, Bel.	.500	1	0	2	2	4	0
Wickersham, Jack, F.W.	.987	26	69	83	2	154	20
Zambrano, Alan, Wis.	.959	83	126	203	14	343	33

TRIPLE PLAY: Beattie.

SECOND BASEMEN WITH TWO OR MORE TEAMS

Player, Team	Pct.	G	PO	A	E	TC	DP
Kison, Robbie, Rock.	1.000	3	4	5	0	9	2
Kison, Robbie, Clin.	.909	15	36	44	8	88	12
Stegall, Randy, Clin.	.952	9	15	25	2	42	5
Stegall, Randy, Rock.	.933	3	3	11	1	15	2

THIRD BASEMEN

Player, Team	Pct.	G	PO	A	E	TC	DP
Ahlers, Steve, C.R.	.938	5	2	13	1	16	1
Alfaro, Jason, Mich.	.833	5	3	7	2	12	2
Baderdeen, Kevin, Clin.	.906	100	53	198	26	277	16
Bautista, Jorge, K.C.	.821	11	1	31	7	39	4
Beattie, Andrew, Clin.	1.000	4	1	1	0	2	0
Belliard, Francisco, S.B.	.818	10	6	21	6	33	1
Bly, Derrick, Lan.	1.000	6	2	14	0	16	1
Bolling, Kirk, S.B.	.815	10	3	19	5	27	0
Boone, Matt, W.M.	.900	105	74	223	33	330	13
Bordenick, Ryan, Bel.	.000	1	0	0	1	1	0
Bowers, Jason, Peo.	.944	26	20	64	5	89	7
Brock, J.J., S.B.	.750	1	0	3	1	4	0
Burroughs, Sean, F.W.	.898	120	96	230	37	363	19
Bush, Ron, W.M.	.000	1	0	0	0	0	0
Christensen, Mike, C.R.	.917	125	68	306	34	408	39
Conley, Brian, Rock.	.862	11	9	16	4	29	2
Cutshall, Pat, Mich.	1.000	5	2	7	0	9	1
Da Luz, Craig, W.M.	.956	39	34	95	6	135	6
Downing, Lance, S.B.	.907	99	58	243	31	332	15
Escalona, Felix, Mich.	.891	22	10	39	6	55	6
Escobar, Gustavo, Peo.	.894	13	10	32	5	47	3
Farnsworth, Troy, Peo.	.917	89	57	197	23	277	14
Garcia, Alex, F.W.	1.000	11	12	14	0	26	2
Garcia, Tony, Burl.	1.000	3	0	5	0	5	0
Garza, Rolando, K.C.	.714	5	1	4	2	7	1
Gastelum, Carlos, C.R.	.909	3	3	7	1	11	1
Gay, Dennis, C.R.	1.000	5	1	5	0	6	0
German, Franklin, Lan.	.692	7	1	8	4	13	1
Godfrey, Tim, Rock.	.667	5	0	2	1	3	0
Gonzalez, Jose, Burl.	.500	3	0	2	2	4	0
Goudie, Jaime, Clin.	.882	6	3	12	2	17	1
HANKINS, Ryan, Burl.	.925	106	65	208	22	295	14
Hawthorne, Kyle, Q.C.	.909	13	6	14	2	22	3

Player, Team	Pct.	G	PO	A	E	TC	DP
Hodge, Kevin, Q.C.	.920	104	61	249	27	337	26
Howard, Jason, Clin.	.000	1	0	0	1	1	0
Jaramillo, Frank, Bel.	.902	49	37	92	14	143	10
Johnerson, Ryan, Clin.	.857	4	1	5	1	7	0
Jordan, Kevin, Mich.	.000	1	0	0	1	1	0
Jordan, Yustin, Q.C.	.500	1	0	1	1	2	0
Joyce, Jesse, Mich.	1.000	1	1	3	0	4	0
Kelly, Heath, K.C.	.500	3	0	2	2	4	1
Kelton, Dave, Lan.	.893	113	59	207	32	298	12
Kidwell, Tommy, Peo.	.879	18	20	38	8	66	9
Kirby, Scott, Bel.	.920	67	60	136	17	213	14
Kison, Robbie, Clin.	1.000	1	1	1	0	2	0
Kuzmic, Craig, Wis.	.963	58	20	85	4	109	6
Larson, Brandon, Rock.	.912	69	43	153	18	204	10
Marciniak, Dave, Q.C.	.000	1	0	0	0	0	0
Markray, Thad, Clin.-Rock.	.937	60	31	118	10	159	14
Martinez, Victor, Wis.	.895	5	2	15	2	19	1
Matan, James, Rock.	1.000	1	0	1	0	1	0
Mauck, Matt, Lan.	.800	11	3	9	3	15	0
Maynard, Scott, Wis.	1.000	4	0	3	0	3	0
McConnell, Jason, Q.C.	.920	6	2	21	2	25	2
Medosch, Keith, C.R.	.800	3	1	3	1	5	1
Montenegro, Jose, Bel.	1.000	2	0	4	0	4	0
Moreno, Jose, Wis.	.000	1	0	0	1	1	0
Moye, Melvin, S.B.	.766	13	2	34	11	47	2
Navarro, Ibrahim, Lan.	.944	13	1	16	1	18	0
Nicholson, Derek, Mich.	1.000	3	1	10	0	11	0
Noboa, Joel, S.B.	.868	9	8	25	5	38	2
Patten, Chris, Bel.	.870	6	4	16	3	23	0
Price, Corey, Rock.	.250	2	0	1	3	4	0
Restovich, Michael, Q.C.	.000	1	0	0	0	0	0
Robinson, Bo, Mich.	.932	83	48	144	14	206	8
Rodriguez, Luis, Q.C.	.909	12	13	27	4	44	1
Santamarina, Juan, Burl.	.837	28	13	59	14	86	3
Santonocito, Justin, Clin.	.000	1	0	0	0	0	0
Santos, Jose, K.C.	.905	125	104	277	40	421	26
Scanlon, Matt, Q.C.	.944	13	2	32	2	36	2
Schmidt, Bryan, F.W.	.913	19	13	29	4	46	2
Stegall, Randy, Clin.-Rock.	.925	37	21	77	8	106	10
Ticen, Kevin, C.R.	.688	4	4	7	5	16	3
Torres, Bernie, Burl.	.900	8	1	8	1	10	0
Tucent, Francisco, Bel.	.881	22	9	28	5	42	2
Turnquist, Tyler, Mich.	.924	105	77	201	23	301	15
Vaughn, Clint, Clin.	1.000	1	1	1	0	2	0

TRIPLE PLAY: Baderdeen.

THIRD BASEMEN WITH TWO OR MORE TEAMS

Player, Team	Pct.	G	PO	A	E	TC	DP
Markray, Thad, Clin.	.800	2	1	3	1	5	0
Markray, Thad, Rock.	.942	58	30	115	9	154	14
Stegall, Randy, Clin.	.933	25	12	58	5	75	7
Stegall, Randy, Rock.	.903	12	9	19	3	31	3

SHORTSTOPS

Player, Team	Pct.	G	PO	A	E	TC	DP
Ahlers, Steve, C.R.	.874	47	64	130	28	222	27
Alfaro, Jason, Mich.	.954	109	161	270	21	452	60
Alvarez, Jimmy, Q.C.	.927	100	148	257	32	437	59
Baderdeen, Kevin, Clin.	.000	1	0	0	0	0	0
Beattie, Andrew, Clin.	.892	19	24	50	9	83	11
Belliard, Francisco, S.B.	.933	5	10	18	2	30	5
Berroa, Cristian, F.W.	.930	118	175	314	37	526	60
Bowers, Jason, Peo.	.946	71	79	204	16	299	36
Brock, J.J., S.B.	.939	9	12	19	2	33	2
Bush, Ron, Mich.	.920	57	83	158	21	262	33
Caceres, Wilmy, Clin.	.925	110	179	340	42	561	62
Castillo, Ruben, Wis.	.840	19	23	45	13	81	7
Conley, Brian, Rock.	1.000	7	6	16	0	22	1
Dawkins, Travis, Rock.	.950	75	120	206	17	343	33
Dunaway, Jason, F.W.	.925	16	20	29	4	53	10
Encarnacion, Bienvenido, C.R.	.910	37	50	112	16	178	20
Escalona, Felix, Mich.	.933	31	31	94	9	134	16
Escobar, Gustavo, Peo.	1.000	4	4	18	0	22	5
Freeman, Corey, Wis.	.919	18	26	42	6	74	10
Frese, Nate, Lan.	.963	104	176	371	21	568	85
Gastelum, Carlos, C.R.	.917	5	2	9	1	12	1
Gay, Dennis, C.R.	1.000	2	7	7	0	14	3
German, Franklin, Lan.	.894	21	22	54	9	85	7
Godfrey, Tim, Rock.	.875	2	4	3	1	8	0
Griffin, Matt, Lan.	.900	1	3	6	1	10	1
Guillen, Jose, Bel.	.901	57	72	138	23	233	29
Hankins, Ryan, Burl.	1.000	9	11	31	0	42	4

Player, Team	Pct.	G	PO	A	E	TC	DP
Hawthorne, Kyle, Q.C.	.917	39	40	115	14	169	19
Jaramillo, Frank, Bel.	.970	21	35	63	3	101	7
Jimenez, Carlos, W.M.	.915	87	138	282	39	459	47
Kata, Matthew, S.B.	.937	75	95	230	22	347	31
Kelly, Heath, K.C.	.932	25	21	48	5	74	13
Kelton, Dave, Lan.	.000	1	0	0	0	0	0
Kidwell, Tommy, Peo.	.870	6	10	10	3	23	2
Kison, Robbie, Rock.-Clin.	.857	2	1	5	1	7	1
Kuzmic, Craig, Wis.	1.000	1	0	1	0	1	0
Martinez, Victor, Wis.	.909	22	36	64	10	110	13
McConnell, Jason, Q.C.	.946	7	13	22	2	37	4
Medosch, Keith, C.R.	.880	5	4	18	3	25	1
Moreno, Jose, Wis.	1.000	2	1	3	0	4	1
Navarro, Ibrahim, Lan.	.925	22	36	75	9	120	16
Oliver, Bill, C.R.	1.000	1	1	1	0	2	0
Oliver, Brian, C.R.	.940	47	53	136	12	201	22
Perez, Antonio, Rock.	.925	59	78	155	19	252	26
Sanchez, Wellington, Bel.	.951	69	86	183	14	283	32
Sandoval, Danny, Burl.	.929	75	104	236	26	366	41
Schaffer, Jake, Mich.	1.000	3	2	5	0	7	3
Schill, Vaughn, Wis.	.948	24	34	57	5	96	10
Schmidt, Bryan, F.W.	.899	17	23	39	7	69	14
Stegall, Randy, Clin.	.891	13	17	32	6	55	12
Suarez, Luis, Burl.	.927	51	78	151	18	247	25
Thorpe, A.D., Rock.	.833	2	0	5	1	6	0
Torres, Bernie, Burl.	.976	10	14	27	1	42	4
Tucent, Francisco, Bel.	.000	2	0	0	1	1	0
Valera, Greg, S.B.	.940	53	75	192	17	284	39
Valera, Ramon, Wis.	.918	63	90	156	22	268	22
WATHAN, Derek, K.C.	.963	125	185	394	22	601	90
Wilson, Jack, Peo.	.943	64	84	182	16	282	31

TRIPLE PLAY: Alfaro.

SHORTSTOPS WITH TWO OR MORE TEAMS

Player, Team	Pct.	G	PO	A	E	TC	DP
Kison, Robbie, Rock.	1.000	1	0	2	0	2	0
Kison, Robbie, Clin.	.800	1	1	3	1	5	1

OUTFIELDERS

Player, Team	Pct.	G	PO	A	E	TC	DP
Abreu, Miguel, K.C.	1.000	2	1	0	0	1	0
Adams, John, S.B.	.993	72	134	5	1	140	1
Aguila, Chris, K.C.	.977	121	194	19	5	218	3
Alleyne, Roberto, Mich.	.960	81	114	6	5	125	0
Almonte, Claudio, Q.C.	.942	40	48	1	3	52	1
Baderdeen, Kevin, Clin.	1.000	4	4	0	0	4	0
Battersby, Eric, Burl.*	.985	41	61	3	1	65	1
Bautista, Jorge, K.C.	.000	2	0	0	0	0	0
Beatriz, Ramy, Bel.*	.940	68	118	7	8	133	2
Beattie, Andrew, Clin.	.962	14	23	2	1	26	0
Bly, Derrick, Lan.	.857	11	18	0	3	21	0
Bordenick, Ryan, Bel.	1.000	2	0	1	0	1	0
Broussard, Benjamin, Clin.*	.778	3	7	0	2	9	0
Burns, Kevan, S.B.*	1.000	40	83	1	0	84	0
Burress, Andy, Rock.	.976	63	77	5	2	84	1
Candela, Frank, Bel.	1.000	13	29	0	0	29	0
Cedeno, Jesus, W.M.	.984	34	61	2	1	64	0
Cook, Jon, F.W.	.966	94	162	11	6	179	1
Croud, Will, C.R.	.970	76	120	8	4	132	2
Da Luz, Craig, W.M.	.000	2	0	0	0	0	0
Darula, Bobby, Bel.	.960	64	95	2	4	101	0
De La Cruz, Erickson, Bel.	.960	94	159	9	7	175	3
De La Cruz, Henry, Lan.	.969	62	117	10	4	131	1
Diaz , Alejandro, Clin.	.961	55	119	5	5	129	2
Diaz, Michael, C.R.*	1.000	21	26	2	0	28	0
Diaz, Miguel, Peo.	.955	100	184	8	9	201	2
Downing, Brad, C.R.	1.000	11	14	0	0	14	0
Downing, Lance, S.B.	1.000	1	2	0	0	2	0
Dunaway, Jason, F.W.	1.000	2	1	0	0	1	0
Dunn, Adam, Rock.	.918	70	85	5	8	98	0
Durham, Chad, Burl.	1.000	6	16	1	0	17	0
Dyt, Darren, Peo.	.947	25	36	0	2	38	0
Elliott, Dawan, Rock.*	1.000	8	6	0	0	6	0
Espino, Fernando, Wis.	.958	123	194	11	9	214	1
Faison, Vince, F.W.	.967	11	29	0	1	30	0
Fennell, Jason, Burl.	.956	41	83	4	4	91	0
Ferrand, Francisco, K.C.*	.955	11	21	0	1	22	0
Folkers, Brandon, Peo.*	1.000	1	1	0	0	1	0
Fox, Jason, Bel.	.940	25	60	3	4	67	1
Freeman, Corey, Wis.	.000	1	0	0	0	0	0
Fukuhara, Pete, Lan.	.980	58	142	2	3	147	0
Garcia, Tony, Burl.	.000	2	0	0	0	0	0

Player, Team	Pct.	G	PO	A	E	TC	DP
German, Franklin, Lan.	.915	28	39	4	4	47	2
Gomez, Richard, W.M.	.951	115	162	12	9	183	3
Gordon, Brian, S.B.	.926	46	63	0	5	68	0
Goudie, Jaime, Clin.	1.000	1	1	0	0	1	0
Guillen, Jose, Bel.	1.000	1	1	0	0	1	0
Guzman, Elpidio, C.R.*	.953	130	256	9	13	278	2
Hall, Doug, Lan.*	.931	18	26	1	2	29	1
Hammond, Derry, Bel.	.974	105	178	12	5	195	1
Hawthorne, Kyle, S.B.	.000	1	0	0	0	0	0
Haynes, Larry, Wis.	.979	66	93	2	2	97	1
Hazen, Mike, F.W.*	.974	46	75	0	2	77	0
Hemmings, Scot, F.W.	1.000	7	10	0	0	10	0
Hernandez, Orlando, Wis.	1.000	15	10	1	0	11	0
Hill, Willy, K.C.*	.982	126	263	5	5	273	2
Hodge, Kevin, Q.C.	1.000	7	12	1	0	13	0
Howard, Jason, Clin.	1.000	1	1	0	0	1	0
Ingram, Darron, Clin.	1.000	14	13	4	0	17	0
Jenkins, Corey, Burl.	.953	27	39	2	2	43	1
Johnerson, Ryan, Clin.	.963	25	24	2	1	27	0
Jordan, Kevin, Mich.	.968	103	143	7	5	155	0
Jordan, Yustin, Q.C.	.826	16	18	1	4	23	0
Joyce, Jesse, Mich.	1.000	3	1	0	0	1	0
Kearns, Austin, Rock.	.939	121	185	14	13	212	4
Kelly, Heath, K.C.	.909	13	9	1	1	11	0
Kielty, Bobby, Q.C.	.977	56	125	4	3	132	0
Kison, Robbie, Clin.	1.000	1	4	0	0	4	0
Knight, Marcus, C.R.	.964	130	228	10	9	247	2
Kuzmic, Craig, Wis.	1.000	36	26	1	0	27	1
Layton, Blane, Clin.-Rock.*	.968	54	86	5	3	94	1
Leatherman, Dan, Q.C.*	.500	4	1	0	1	2	0
Lee, Jason, Peo.	.984	63	120	1	2	123	0
Loggins, Joshua, F.W.	.973	128	273	11	8	292	2
Lopez, Luis, Mich.	.973	91	176	6	5	187	2
Mackiewitz, Richard, Bel.*	1.000	1	1	0	0	1	0
Martinez, Victor, Wis.	.909	10	10	0	1	11	0
Matan, James, Rock.	1.000	4	5	0	0	5	0
Maynard, Scott, Wis.	.000	1	0	0	0	0	0
McConnell, Jason, Q.C.	1.000	1	3	0	0	3	0
McMILLIN, Brian, Q.C.	1.000	103	167	5	0	172	2
McNaughton, Troy, Peo.*	.952	71	110	9	6	125	2
Meadows, Tydus, Lan.	.965	121	185	7	7	199	0
Medosch, Keith, C.R.	1.000	1	1	0	0	1	0
Merriman, Terrell, Burl.*	.948	104	179	5	10	194	1
Moore, Lacarlo, W.M.	.982	30	52	3	1	56	0
Moreno, Mikel, Lan.	1.000	5	14	2	0	16	1
Morrow, Alvin, Bel.	.931	78	122	0	9	131	0
Mounts, J.R., Burl.	.935	90	157	2	11	170	0
Moye, Melvin, S.B.	1.000	33	38	4	0	42	0
Nelson, Brian, Wis.	.000	2	0	0	1	1	0
Neubart, Adam, S.B.	.959	27	44	3	2	49	0
Nicholson, Derek, Mich.	.956	22	41	2	2	45	1
Nykoluk, Kevin, Peo.	1.000	3	1	0	0	1	0
Oliver, Johnny, Clin.	1.000	16	23	2	0	25	0
Owens, Jeremy, F.W.	.951	128	309	18	17	344	2
Padgett, Matt, K.C.*	.970	24	29	3	1	33	0
Patterson, Corey, Lan.	.965	102	244	7	9	260	3
Peters, Samone, Clin.	.920	50	73	7	7	87	0
Pinero, Juan, Lan.	.976	22	37	3	1	41	0
Porter, Colin, Mich.*	.987	122	303	10	4	317	3
Price, Duane, Clin.	.969	37	60	3	2	65	1
Restovich, Michael, Q.C.	.958	124	200	6	9	215	0
Reyes, Deurys, W.M.*	.954	37	62	0	3	65	0
Rich, Billy, W.M.	.976	101	154	11	4	169	1
Rios, Fernando, Rock.-Clin.	.980	78	140	7	3	150	2
Robinson, Bo, Wis.	1.000	1	1	0	0	1	0
Rodriguez, Hernandez, Clin.	1.000	28	67	1	0	68	0
Roneberg, Brett, K.C.*	.987	126	214	10	3	227	1
Rosamond, Michael, Mich.	1.000	3	9	0	0	9	0
Ross, Justin, C.R.*	.982	32	53	2	1	56	0
Schmidt, Bryan, F.W.	1.000	1	2	1	0	3	0
Secoda, Joe, Peo.	.953	115	173	10	9	192	2
Selander, Craig, Q.C.	.953	82	110	11	6	127	2
Silvestre, Juan, Wis.	.917	99	135	9	13	157	0
Singletary, Dan, S.B.*	.951	49	94	4	5	103	0
Snead, Esix, Peo.	.975	59	153	4	4	161	1
Southall, Rick, Wis.	.000	1	0	0	0	0	0
Stegall, Randy, Clin.-Rock.	.909	12	20	0	2	22	0
Stuart, Rich, C.R.	.919	21	30	4	3	37	0
Sykes, Jamie, S.B.	.987	123	219	11	3	233	4
Thorpe, A.D., Clin.	.000	1	0	0	0	0	0
Toomey, Chris, Clin.	.987	88	139	10	2	151	0
Torres, Andres, W.M.	.972	112	233	9	7	249	2

Player, Team	Pct.	G	PO	A	E	TC	DP
Tucent, Francisco, Bel.	.000	2	0	0	0	0	0
Turnquist, Tyler, Mich.	1.000	4	3	0	0	3	0
Urquiola, Carlos, S.B.	.977	30	41	2	1	44	0
Valenzuela, Mario, Burl.	.959	118	170	16	8	194	6
Vandemore, Anthony, F.W.	.875	4	5	2	1	8	1
Van Rossum, Chris, S.B.*	1.000	2	1	0	0	1	0
Vessel, Andrew, Lan.	.963	13	26	0	1	27	0
Wagner, Mike, F.W.	.833	11	14	1	3	18	0
Williams, P.J., Wis.	.977	111	247	8	6	261	1
Williford, Dan, S.B.*	1.000	3	2	2	0	4	0
Wise, Dewayne, Rock.*	.975	131	294	16	8	318	2
Zambrano, Alan, Wis.	.000	2	0	0	0	0	0

OUTFIELDERS WITH TWO OR MORE TEAMS

Player, Team	Pct.	G	PO	A	E	TC	DP
Layton, Blane, Clin.*	.959	32	44	3	2	49	1
Layton, Blane, Rock.*	.978	22	42	2	1	45	0
Rios, Fernando, Rock.	1.000	6	11	1	0	12	1
Rios, Fernando, Clin.	.978	72	129	6	3	138	1
Stegall, Randy, Clin.	.000	1	0	0	0	0	0
Stegall, Randy, Rock.	.909	11	20	0	2	22	0

CATCHERS

Player, Team	Pct.	G	PO	A	E	TC	DP	PB
Acevas, Jonathan, Burl.	.979	61	412	51	10	473	0	10
Bailey, Jeff, K.C.	.982	21	147	14	3	164	1	6
Bordenick, Ryan, Bel.	.991	44	284	37	3	324	2	1
Brito, Obispo, Bel.	.984	100	722	99	13	834	3	19
Buck, John, Mich.	1.000	4	28	3	0	31	0	0
CAMPBELL, Sean, F.W.	.995	79	498	53	3	554	1	15
Chapman, Scott, Mich.	.979	54	401	22	9	432	3	14
Christensen, Mike, C.R.	1.000	1	2	0	0	2	0	1
Clark, Greg, Peo.	.988	66	430	63	6	499	2	13
Closser, J.D., S.B.	.951	34	202	29	12	243	2	12
Cosentino, Tony, F.W.	.975	27	182	17	5	204	1	2
Darula, Bobby, Bel.	1.000	2	10	1	0	11	0	0
Davis, James, Clin.	1.000	3	25	2	0	27	0	0
Diaz, Angel, C.R.	.980	32	214	28	5	247	2	4
Dimmick, Josh, Mich.-Q.C.	.987	60	485	43	7	535	2	6
Dorsett, Chris, Lan.	.992	39	224	28	2	254	1	8
Fatheree, Danny, Mich.	.991	28	206	12	2	220	3	1
Fennell, Jason, Burl.	.000	1	0	0	0	0	0	0
Fick, Robert, W.M.	.875	1	5	2	1	8	0	0
French, Ron, F.W.	.987	21	140	12	2	154	0	5
Frick, Matt, K.C.	.992	16	112	11	1	124	0	2
Garcia, Tony, Burl.	.976	64	446	35	12	493	3	19
Garrett, Scott, Rock.	.953	8	38	3	2	43	0	0
Goldbach, Jeff, Lan.	.985	85	524	53	9	586	2	23
Hill, Jason, C.R.	.983	96	641	91	13	745	4	15
Howard, Jason, Clin.	.984	22	111	10	2	123	1	4
Hyde, Brandon, Burl.	.983	19	113	4	2	119	2	6
Inge, Brandon, W.M.	.990	95	703	114	8	825	5	16
Kasper, Todd, S.B.	.996	32	210	21	1	232	1	6
Kuzmic, Craig, Wis.	1.000	6	38	8	0	46	0	0
Lawrence, Tony, F.W.-Rock.	.968	38	252	22	9	283	1	11
Lopez, Jose, S.B.	.979	23	167	16	4	187	0	3
Lopez, Norberto, C.R.	1.000	2	16	1	0	17	0	0
Lough, Aaron, Q.C.	1.000	1	5	2	0	7	0	1
Maldonado, Carlos, Wis.	.994	88	718	64	5	787	3	7
Mauck, Matt, Lan.	.973	36	166	11	5	182	2	9
Maynard, Scott, Wis.	1.000	45	264	29	0	293	0	3
McAffee, Josh, S.B.	.979	59	421	52	10	483	2	5
Meran, Jorge, W.M.	.982	40	284	43	6	333	2	11
Miller, Corky, Rock.	.975	66	497	60	14	571	6	2
Morales, Stephen, K.C.	.982	23	145	20	3	168	2	2
Munson, Eric, W.M.	1.000	5	38	2	0	40	0	0
Nelson, Brian, Wis.	.966	18	109	4	4	117	1	0
Nykoluk, Kevin, Peo.	.982	20	144	18	3	165	2	4
O'Connor, Brian, Mich.	.993	20	129	14	1	144	2	3
Rapp, Travis, C.R.	1.000	8	47	6	0	53	0	0
Rivera, Francisco, Clin.	.992	15	111	9	1	121	1	4
Sanchez, Marcos, Rock.	1.000	20	118	12	0	130	0	3
Santiago, Daniel, Rock.	1.000	1	4	1	0	5	1	0
Schaeffer, Jon, Q.C.	.983	73	528	43	10	581	3	11
Shrum, Allen, Q.C.	.991	65	410	38	4	452	2	9
Snusz, Chris, Rock.-Clin.	.978	23	150	29	4	183	0	5
Suarez, Marc, Clin.	.969	33	215	31	8	254	3	5
Ticen, Kevin, C.R.	.952	6	37	3	2	42	0	2
Treanor, Matt, K.C.	.988	81	595	48	8	651	6	14
Whitehead, Braxton, Clin.	.991	71	481	46	5	532	3	11
William, Jovany, Peo.	.982	55	389	53	8	450	2	9
Zeber, Ryan, Rock.-Clin.	.970	40	210	13	7	230	0	2

CATCHERS WITH TWO OR MORE TEAMS

Player, Team	Pct.	G	PO	A	E	TC	DP	PB
Dimmick, Josh, Mich.	.988	42	313	24	4	341	2	3
Dimmick, Josh, Q.C.	.985	18	172	19	3	194	0	3
Lawrence, Tony, F.W.	.965	28	177	18	7	202	1	7
Lawrence, Tony, Rock.	.975	10	75	4	2	81	0	4
Snusz, Chris, Rock.	.972	19	115	22	4	141	0	4
Snusz, Chris, Clin.	1.000	4	35	7	0	42	0	1
Zeber, Ryan, Rock.	.969	38	203	13	7	223	0	2
Zeber, Ryan, Clin.	1.000	2	7	0	0	7	0	0

PITCHERS

Player, Team	Pct.	G	PO	A	E	TC	DP
Acevedo, Jose, Clin.	.800	24	4	8	3	15	1
Almonte, Edwin, Burl.	.906	37	10	19	3	32	1
Altman, Gene, Rock.-Clin.	.941	14	3	13	1	17	1
Anderson, Wes, K.C.	.958	23	10	13	1	24	2
Atchison, Scott, Wis.	1.000	15	4	12	0	16	1
Averette, Robert, Rock.	.923	19	7	17	2	26	1
Bailey, Ben, Clin.	1.000	9	1	2	0	3	0
Balbuena, Caleb, Wis.	1.000	8	5	6	0	11	0
Balfour, Grant, Q.C.	1.000	19	5	11	0	16	1
Barcelo, Lorenzo, Burl.	1.000	1	0	1	0	1	0
Barton, Christopher, Bel.	.750	16	5	1	2	8	1
Bartosh, Cliff, F.W.*	.889	35	4	12	2	18	0
Bauer, Ryan, F.W.	.889	36	6	10	2	18	2
Bautista, Jorge, K.C.	1.000	1	0	2	0	2	0
Bell, Casey, F.W.	1.000	2	0	1	0	1	0
Bernero, Adam, W.M.	1.000	15	10	15	0	25	0
Berroa, Oliver, Wis.	.667	21	2	2	2	6	0
Berryman, Brian, F.W.	.833	9	3	2	1	6	0
Bess, Stephen, W.M.	1.000	12	1	4	0	5	0
Birdsong, Tim, Clin.	.952	24	3	17	1	21	2
Blackmore, John, Mich.	.846	37	3	8	2	13	0
Bloomer, Chris, S.B.	1.000	43	6	4	0	10	0
Book, Jeremy, Peo.	.864	27	4	15	3	22	0
Borges, Reece, Mich.	1.000	37	7	9	0	16	0
Borne, Matt, Burl.	1.000	22	2	1	0	3	0
Brewer, Clint, Clin.-Rock.	.933	34	6	8	1	15	0
Bridges, Douglas, C.R.*	.920	22	4	19	2	25	2
Brown, Tighe, Burl.	.000	4	0	0	0	0	0
Brown, Zay, Clin.	.000	3	0	0	0	0	0
Bruback, Matt, Lan.	.905	25	8	11	2	21	1
Brunette, Justin, Peo.*	1.000	38	3	9	0	12	1
Buehrle, Mark, Burl.*	.889	20	9	23	4	36	0
Buller, Sean, W.M.*	1.000	31	4	22	0	26	2
Cardona, Steve, S.B.	1.000	14	0	4	0	4	0
Cento, Anthony, Q.C.*	1.000	11	0	1	0	1	0
Cervantes, Chris, S.B.*	.947	38	15	21	2	38	0
Chighisola, Louis, Clin.*	1.000	7	0	2	0	2	0
Childers, Matt, Bel.	.923	20	9	15	2	26	1
Christenson, Ryan, Peo.	.875	29	6	8	2	16	2
Chrysler, Clint, Wis.*	.875	51	4	3	1	8	0
Clackum, Scott, K.C.	.963	47	6	20	1	27	2
Condrey, Clay, F.W.	.778	42	4	3	2	9	0
Cooper, Eric, Clin.-Rock.	.800	16	0	8	2	10	0
Cordova, Jorge, F.W.	1.000	12	0	2	0	2	0
Cornejo, Nate, W.M.	.900	28	14	40	6	60	2
Correa, Cristobal, Peo.	1.000	5	1	1	0	2	0
Cosgrove, Mike, Q.C.	.938	42	2	13	1	16	0
Crews, Jason, S.B.	1.000	9	0	1	0	1	0
Cummings, Ryan, C.R.	.889	19	8	16	3	27	1
Currens, Tim, Burl.	1.000	22	4	4	0	8	0
D'Amico, Jeff, Bel.	1.000	2	0	1	0	1	0
Dant, Larry, Lan.	1.000	43	3	4	0	7	0
Darnell, Paul, Clin.*	.714	6	1	4	2	7	0
Darr, Jay, F.W.	1.000	7	1	3	0	4	0
Davis, Lance, Rock.*	.933	22	12	30	3	45	3
Dehart, Casey, Clin.*	.857	24	1	5	1	7	0
Delano, Mike, Lan.*	1.000	2	0	1	0	1	0
Delatori, Keola, Lan.	.800	15	1	3	1	5	0
Demouy, Chris, C.R.*	.929	46	3	10	1	14	0
Dent, Doug, F.W.	1.000	8	3	7	0	10	0
Diaz, Antonio, F.W.	.870	27	6	14	3	23	0
Dobis, Jason, Q.C.	.938	23	8	7	1	16	1
Dobson, Dwayne, C.R.	1.000	22	1	4	0	5	0
Dobson, Mark, F.W.	1.000	41	1	8	0	9	0
Donaldson, Bo, Rock.	1.000	19	3	3	0	6	0
Duarte, Renney, C.R.	.909	31	12	28	4	44	2
Dunham, Pat, Wis.	.800	12	1	3	1	5	0
Dunning, Justin, Wis.	.909	25	6	4	1	11	0
Emanuel, Brandon, C.R.	.893	23	8	17	3	28	0

Player, Team	Pct.	G	PO	A	E	TC	DP
Escamilla, Paco, Clin.	.923	12	1	11	1	13	1
Eyre, Willie, Q.C.	1.000	2	1	1	0	2	0
Fahrner, Evan, S.B.	1.000	20	5	2	0	7	0
Fahs, Paul, Peo.	1.000	2	1	0	0	1	0
Farizo, Brad, K.C.	.947	34	5	13	1	19	1
Fauske, Josh, Burl.	.000	5	0	0	0	0	0
Felix, Miguel, Burl.	.714	30	2	3	2	7	0
Ferguson, Tony, Mich.	1.000	5	1	2	0	3	0
Ferrier, Shayne, C.R.	1.000	7	1	3	0	4	1
Figueroa, Juan, Burl.	.824	17	5	9	3	17	0
Fischer, Eric, Burl.*	.913	25	7	35	4	46	0
Fitts, Brian, Q.C.	.958	37	6	17	1	24	2
Folkers, Brandon, Peo.*	1.000	5	1	0	0	1	0
Foote, Joe, Q.C.	.889	44	4	12	2	18	1
Forbes, Keith, F.W.	.875	42	4	3	1	8	0
Frasor, Jason, W.M.	1.000	4	0	3	0	3	0
Frazier, Brad, Q.C.	.714	33	1	4	2	7	0
Freehill, Mike, C.R.	.000	2	0	0	0	0	0
Fuller, Jody, S.B.	1.000	36	6	20	0	26	2
Gagliano, Steve, Bel.	1.000	15	5	9	0	14	2
Gallo, Michael, Mich.*	.933	12	5	9	1	15	1
Gangemi, Joe, C.R.*	.889	5	0	8	1	9	0
Garcia, Gabe, Mich.	.923	38	2	10	1	13	2
Gardner, Nathan, Rock.	1.000	34	2	4	0	6	0
Geitz, Scott, Bel.	1.000	52	5	16	0	21	2
Gilich, Denny, C.R.	1.000	51	3	7	0	10	0
Ginter, Matt, Burl.	.857	9	3	3	1	7	0
Giuliano, Joe, Rock.	.933	43	5	9	1	15	1
Glick, David, Mich.*	1.000	10	1	0	0	1	0
Goetz, Geoff, K.C.*	1.000	16	2	14	0	16	1
Gold, J.M., Bel.	.960	21	10	14	1	25	0
Gomer, Jeramy, Lan.*	1.000	7	0	5	0	5	0
Gooch, Arnie, Clin.	1.000	2	1	2	0	3	0
Good, Andrew, S.B.	.926	27	9	16	2	27	0
Gooden, Derek, Peo.	1.000	38	5	7	0	12	0
Grater, Kevin, Bel.	1.000	9	3	4	0	7	0
Greeny, Burdette, Bel.	1.000	19	1	2	0	3	0
Griffin, Kirk, Peo.	1.000	57	6	11	0	17	0
Gunderson, Matt, Lan.	1.000	13	1	1	0	2	0
Gutierrez, Lazaro, W.M.*	1.000	35	0	12	0	12	1
Hamulack, Tim, Mich.*	1.000	25	0	3	0	3	0
Hand, Jon, Peo.	.857	58	2	10	2	14	0
Harber, Ryan, K.C.*	.909	24	1	19	2	22	1
HARING, Brett, Rock.*	1.000	25	5	26	0	31	2
Harris, Josh, F.W.	1.000	17	3	2	0	5	0
Hart, Damien, Clin.*	.600	26	0	3	2	5	0
Harwas, Oliver, C.R.	.800	37	3	9	3	15	0
Hayden, Terry, Clin.-Rock.*	.920	38	6	17	2	25	0
Heams, Shane, W.M.	.813	51	5	8	3	16	0
Heaverlo, Jeff, Wis.	1.000	3	0	1	0	1	0
Hecht, Brian, Mich.	1.000	27	1	6	0	7	1
Held, Travis, Peo.	.750	3	1	2	1	4	0
Henriquez, Hector, K.C.*	.938	14	4	11	1	16	0
Hoard, Brent, Q.C.*	.963	28	5	21	1	27	0
Hodge, Kevin, Q.C.	.000	2	0	0	0	0	0
Howard, Ben, F.W.	.679	28	8	11	9	28	0
Howard, Tom, Q.C.*	1.000	15	1	5	0	6	0
Hundley, Jeff, C.R.*	.889	25	6	42	6	54	2
Incantalupo, Todd, Bel.*	.933	40	5	9	1	15	1
Jacobs, Greg, C.R.*	1.000	36	6	20	0	26	3
Jacobs, Jake, Q.C.	.714	48	2	8	4	14	0
Jacobson, Andrew, Burl.	1.000	13	3	2	0	5	0
Jensen, Jason, S.B.*	1.000	18	7	10	0	17	1
Johnson, Solomon, Burl.*	1.000	19	2	6	0	8	0
Jones, Charlie, S.B.	.857	7	4	2	1	7	1
Jones, Fontella, Bel.	1.000	36	8	8	0	16	0
Jones, Greg, C.R.	1.000	34	3	10	0	13	0
Jones, Travis, F.W.*	.867	41	3	10	2	15	1
Kalita, Tim, W.M.*	.875	9	3	11	2	16	0
Kane, Kyle, Burl.	.000	12	0	0	0	0	0
Keller, Kris, W.M.	1.000	49	5	7	0	12	0
Kelly, Heath, K.C.	.000	1	0	0	0	0	0
Key, Scott, Rock.	1.000	1	0	1	0	1	0
Koplove, Mike, S.B.	.967	45	13	16	1	30	1
Koutrouba, Tom, W.M.*	1.000	31	8	12	0	20	0
Koziara, Matt, Rock.	1.000	8	3	4	0	7	0
Krawczyk, Jack, Bel.	.000	6	0	0	0	0	0
Krug, Dustin, Lan.	1.000	46	2	7	0	9	2
Kuzmic, Craig, Wis.	.000	1	0	0	0	0	0
Lambert, Jeremy, Peo.	1.000	21	4	2	0	6	0
Lara, Nelson, K.C.	1.000	46	4	6	0	10	0
Laroche, Jeff, K.C.*	1.000	17	0	5	0	5	0

Player, Team	Pct.	G	PO	A	E	TC	DP
Levy, Tye, Clin.*	1.000	7	1	0	0	1	0
Lewis, Rickey, Bel.	1.000	16	3	4	0	7	0
LeBlanc, Eric, Rock.	1.000	2	0	1	0	1	0
Longo, Neil, Wis.	1.000	5	4	9	0	13	1
Looper, Aaron, Wis.	.957	38	11	11	1	23	1
Lopez, Javier, S.B.*	.926	20	6	19	2	27	0
Loux, Shane, W.M.	.889	8	4	4	1	9	1
Lovingood, Ray, Rock.*	.750	16	1	2	1	4	0
Lowery, Phil, K.C.*	.000	1	0	0	0	0	0
Luque, Roger, F.W.*	.875	46	3	4	1	8	0
Mackiewitz, Richard, Bel.*	.000	1	0	0	0	0	0
Madson, Will, W.M.	1.000	8	1	0	0	1	0
Majewski, Gary, Burl.	1.000	2	0	1	0	1	0
Mallard, Randi, Clin.	1.000	6	0	2	0	2	0
Mallory, Andrew, Lan.	.000	5	0	0	0	0	0
Manias, James, Rock.*	1.000	30	7	8	0	15	0
Mateo, Julio, Wis.	1.000	20	3	7	0	10	0
Mathews, Dan, Bel.	1.000	19	2	3	0	5	0
Matos, Josue, Wis.	.960	25	10	14	1	25	0
Maynard, Scott, Wis.	.000	2	0	0	0	0	0
McCutcheon, Mike, S.B.*	.893	28	5	20	3	28	2
McEvoy, Casey, Clin.-Rock.	1.000	13	4	6	0	10	1
McGowan, Brian, W.M.	.900	39	4	23	3	30	3
Mears, Chris, Wis.	1.000	13	2	11	0	13	2
Mendoza, Geronimo, Burl.	.946	28	13	22	2	37	2
Mendoza, Hatuey, S.B.	.929	13	7	6	1	14	2
Merrell, Phil, Clin.	.900	16	6	12	2	20	1
Meyer, Jake, Rock.	.889	33	1	7	1	9	0
Miller, Aaron, Q.C.*	.813	25	4	9	3	16	0
Miller, Jim, Bel.	1.000	6	2	1	0	3	0
Minaya, Pedro, Clin.	.963	36	6	20	1	27	2
Miniel, Roberto, Bel.	.000	10	0	0	0	0	0
Montane, Ivan, Wis.	1.000	10	1	1	0	2	0
Moore, Chris, K.C.	.917	25	4	7	1	12	1
Murphy, Matt, Lan.*	1.000	25	1	6	0	7	0
Nannini, Mike, Mich.	.950	15	6	13	1	20	1
Neal, Blaine, K.C.	1.000	26	2	4	0	6	0
Neu, Michael, Rock.	1.000	9	2	2	0	4	0
Neugebauer, Nickolas, Bel.	.900	18	6	3	1	10	0
Noyce, David, K.C.*	.913	16	4	17	2	23	1
Nykoluk, Kevin, Peo.	1.000	1	1	0	0	1	0
Oleksik, George, Rock.	.875	21	4	3	1	8	0
Olsen, Aaron, K.C.	1.000	10	2	4	0	6	0
O'Reilly, John, S.B.	1.000	4	1	0	0	1	0
Ortiz, Omar, F.W.	1.000	4	1	2	0	3	1
Oswalt, Roy, Mich.	.971	22	11	22	1	34	0
Padilla, Juan, Q.C.	1.000	12	3	3	0	6	2
Palma, Ricardo, Lan.*	.946	22	9	26	2	37	2
Parker, Allan, C.R.	.000	1	0	0	0	0	0
Parker, Clark, Burl.	.000	1	0	0	0	0	0
Peguero, Darwin, Mich.*	.905	24	6	13	2	21	0
Penney, Mike, Bel.	.947	27	30	24	3	57	5
Perry, Tim, F.W.	.900	10	3	6	1	10	1
Pesqueira, Omar, F.W.	1.000	47	3	5	0	8	1
Pidgeon, Matt, K.C.	1.000	40	6	13	0	19	1
Pine, Chris, Bel.	1.000	7	1	1	0	2	0
Pineda, Jairo, Mich.	.750	4	1	2	1	4	0
Pineda, Luis, W.M.	.750	24	1	2	1	4	0
Pipes, Joey, C.R.	.909	7	2	8	1	11	0
Poe, Ryan, Bel.	1.000	49	4	5	0	9	0
Polanco, Elvis, Lan.	.833	25	3	2	1	6	1
Prather, Scott, Peo.*	.955	27	5	16	1	22	1
Prinz, Bret, S.B.	.970	30	16	16	1	33	1
Puffer, Brandon, Clin.	.952	59	3	17	1	21	0
Purvis, Robert, Burl.	1.000	6	1	2	0	3	0
Redding, Tim, Mich.	.815	43	11	11	5	27	0
Rincon, Juan, Q.C.	.972	28	11	24	1	36	0
Rivera, Saul, Q.C.	1.000	60	2	8	0	10	0
Roberts, Rick, W.M.*	.000	1	0	0	0	0	0
Robertson, Nathan, K.C.*	1.000	8	1	3	0	4	0
Robinson, Dustin, Clin.	.900	44	2	7	1	10	0
Rodgers, Marcus, Burl.	.000	4	0	0	1	1	0
Rodriguez, Jose, Peo.*	1.000	15	0	2	0	2	0
Rosado, Juan, Bel.*	1.000	8	0	2	0	2	0
Rose, Brian, Clin.-Rock.	.955	48	8	13	1	22	1
Royer, Jason, S.B.	.889	32	10	14	3	27	3
Sams, Aaron, Lan.*	.926	17	6	19	2	27	3
Santana, Johan, Mich.*	.969	27	13	50	2	65	1

Player, Team	Pct.	G	PO	A	E	TC	DP
Santonocito, Justin, Clin.	.000	2	0	0	0	0	0
Schmidt, Donnie, Wis.	.750	5	0	3	1	4	0
Schoening, Brent, Q.C.	1.000	6	2	0	0	2	0
Schurman, Ryan, Clin.	.923	44	1	11	1	13	0
Seaman, John, K.C.	1.000	13	0	6	0	6	0
Sequea, Jacobo, Rock.	.862	16	4	21	4	29	0
Sergent, Joe, K.C.*	1.000	8	0	3	0	3	0
Sessions, Doug, Mich.	1.000	12	0	2	0	2	0
Shepherd, Alvie, C.R.	1.000	6	1	0	0	1	0
Shibilo, Andy, Peo.	.935	27	9	20	2	31	0
Shields, Drew, K.C.	1.000	14	2	2	0	4	0
Simpson, Allan, Wis.	.938	24	11	19	2	32	1
Sismondo, Bobby, W.M.*	.907	27	5	34	4	43	0
Smith, Brandon, Mich.	.889	18	2	6	1	9	1
Smith, Clint, W.M.	.941	20	11	5	1	17	1
Smith, Justin, Wis.*	.857	7	3	3	1	7	1
Smith, Robert, Peo.*	1.000	9	2	10	0	12	0
Smyth, Steve, Lan.*	1.000	10	2	8	0	10	0
Soriano, Gabriel, Rock.	1.000	8	3	0	0	3	0
Spykstra, Dave, Mich.	.000	5	0	0	0	0	0
Stemle, Steve, Peo.	.971	28	11	22	1	34	2
Stewart, Joshua, Burl.*	1.000	16	4	4	0	8	0
Stumm, Jason, Burl.	.625	10	0	5	3	8	0
Sturdy, Tim, Q.C.	.813	13	4	9	3	16	0
Suarez, Luis, C.R.	1.000	4	0	3	0	3	0
Sullivan, Shane, Lan.	1.000	13	0	5	0	5	0
THERNEAU, Dave, Rock.	1.000	16	9	22	0	31	2
Thornton, Matt, Wis.*	1.000	25	2	4	0	6	0
Torres, Leo, Lan.*	1.000	51	0	12	0	12	4
Torres, Manny, Rock.	1.000	8	2	6	0	8	0
Torres, Melqui, Wis.	.952	27	13	27	2	42	1
Ulloa, Enmanuel, Wis.	.952	35	8	12	1	21	1
Valdez, Jose, Clin.	.000	3	0	0	0	0	0
Valverde, Jose, S.B.	.000	2	0	0	0	0	0
Van De Weg, Ryan, F.W.	1.000	13	4	7	0	11	1
Vargas, Claudio, K.C.	.882	19	4	11	2	17	0
Verplancke, Joe, S.B.	.875	18	4	3	1	8	0
Viator, Dustin, F.W.	.000	5	0	0	0	0	0
Victoria, Lester, Q.C.*	1.000	41	5	8	0	13	0
Viles, Jeff, Peo.	.917	58	6	5	1	12	1
Wade, Travis, Mich.	1.000	10	2	2	0	4	0
Waligora, Tom, Lan.	.769	50	5	5	3	13	0
Walrond, Les, Peo.*	.957	21	5	17	1	23	0
Ward, Matt, K.C.*	1.000	5	0	4	0	4	0
Watkins, Steve, F.W.	1.000	4	1	2	0	3	0
Whatley, Brannon, Burl.	.909	45	6	14	2	22	1
Whitesides, Johnny, Rock.	.833	13	0	5	1	6	0
Whitney, Jacob, Mich.*	1.000	33	6	23	0	29	1
Williams, Mike, Burl.	.800	37	7	25	8	40	2
Willis, Craig, Wis.	.923	39	6	6	1	13	1
Winchester, Scott, Rock.	1.000	6	3	1	0	4	0
Wohlers, Mark, Rock.	.000	2	0	0	0	0	0
Wooten, Shane, Bel.*	.667	33	1	3	2	6	0
Wright, Daniel, Burl.	1.000	2	1	3	0	4	1
Wuertz, Mike, Lan.	.929	28	10	16	2	28	1
Wylie, Mitch, Burl.	.857	6	0	6	1	7	0
Yates, Chad, Peo.	.800	22	0	4	1	5	0
Yount, Andy, W.M.	.938	24	4	11	1	16	0
Zamarripa, Tony, Lan.	1.000	11	0	1	0	1	0
Zambrano, Carlos, Lan.	.852	27	8	15	4	27	4
Zapata, Juan, Bel.	.600	7	1	2	2	5	0
Zyskowski, Garrett, Mich.*	1.000	14	2	3	0	5	1

TRIPLE PLAYS: B. Smith, Zyskowski.

PITCHERS WITH TWO OR MORE TEAMS

Player, Team	Pct.	G	PO	A	E	TC	DP
Altman, Gene, Rock.	.941	11	3	13	1	17	1
Altman, Gene, Clin.	.000	3	0	0	0	0	0
Brewer, Clint, Clin.	.933	24	6	8	1	15	0
Brewer, Clint, Rock.	.000	10	0	0	0	0	0
Cooper, Eric, Clin.	.800	12	0	8	2	10	0
Cooper, Eric, Rock.	.000	4	0	0	0	0	0
Hayden, Terry, Clin.*	.913	33	6	15	2	23	0
Hayden, Terry, Rock.*	1.000	5	0	2	0	2	0
McEvoy, Casey, Clin.	1.000	7	1	1	0	2	1
McEvoy, Casey, Rock.	1.000	6	3	5	0	8	0
Rose, Brian, Clin.	1.000	24	5	7	0	12	0
Rose, Brian, Rock.	.900	24	3	6	1	10	1

The following player appeared only as designated hitter, pinch-hitter or pinch runner: Copley, dh.

LEAGUE CHAMPIONS

Year	Team	Pct.	Year	Team	Pct.	Year	Team	Pct.
1947—	Belleville	.667	1966—	Fox Cities◆	.689	1983—	Appleton•	.635
	Belleville	.672		Cedar Rapids	.762		Springfield	.576
1948—	West Frankfort*	.708	1967—	Wisconsin Rapids	.685	1984—	Appleton•	.640
1949—	Centralia	.627		Appleton◆	.587		Springfield	.504
	Paducah (4th)†	.454	1968—	Decatur	.656	1985—	Kenosha▼	.568
1950—	Centralia‡	.675		Quad Cities◆	.648		Peoria	.536
1951—	Paris§	.700	1969—	Appleton	.648	1986—	Springfield	.621
	Danville (4th)†	.432		Appleton	.690		Waterloo▼	.557
1952—	Danville∞	.685	1970—	Quincy◆	.691	1987—	Springfield	.671
	Decatur (3rd)†	.584		Quad Cities	.581		Kenosha▼	.586
1953—	Decatur*	.576	1971—	Appleton	.642	1988—	Cedar Rapids■	.621
1954—	Decatur	.587		Quad Cities■	.548		Kenosha	.579
	Danville (2nd)‡	.528	1972—	Appleton	.598	1989—	South Bend■	.644
1955—	Dubuque*	.587		Danville■	.584		Springfield	.541
1956—	Paris▲	.656	1973—	Wisconsin Rapids■	.562	1990—	Cedar Rapids	.657
	Dubuque	.603		Danville	.537		Quad City■	.579
1957—	Decatur▲	.683	1974—	Appleton	.593	1991—	Clinton■	.583
	Clinton	.623		Danville■	.517		Madison	.558
1958—	Michigan City	.623	1975—	Waterloo■	.727	1992—	Quad City	.664
	Waterloo◆	.613		Quad Cities	.624		Cedar Rapids■	.594
1959—	Waterloo	.613	1976—	Waterloo■	.600	1993—	Clinton	.597
	Waterloo	.613		Cedar Rapids	.595		South Bend■	.566
1960—	Waterloo	.629	1977—	Waterloo	.580	1994—	Rockford	.640
	Waterloo	.677		Burlington■	.511		Cedar Rapids■	.554
1961—	Waterloo	.613	1978—	Appleton■	.708	1995—	Beloit††	.633
	Quincy◆	.594		Burlington	.500		Michigan	.543
1962—	Dubuque◆	.667	1979—	Waterloo	.600	1996—	Wisconsin	.570
	Waterloo	.625		Quad Cities■	.579		West Michigan††	.558
1963—	Clinton	.710	1980—	Waterloo■	.610	1997—	Kane County	.507
	Clinton	.629		Quad Cities	.532		Lansing**	.504
1964—	Clinton	.667	1981—	Wausau■	.636	1998—	West Michigan††	.593
	Fox Cities◆	.667		Quad Cities	.570	1999—	Kane County	.569
1965—	Burlington	.667	1982—	Madison	.626		Burlington**	.511
	Burlington	.677		Appleton▼	.579			

*Won championship and four-club playoff. †Won four-club playoff. ‡Playoff finals canceled because of bad weather. §Won both halves of split season. ∞Won first half of split season and tied Paris for second-half title. ▲Won first-half title and four-team playoff. ◆Won split season playoff. ■League divided into Northern and Southern divisions and played split season. Playoff winner. ▼League divided into Northern, Central and Southern divisions. Playoff winner. •League divided into Northern, Central and Southern divisions; regular season and playoff winner. ††League divided into Eastern, Central and Western divisions; regular season and playoff winner. **League divided into Eastern, Central and Western divisions, playoff winner. (NOTE—Known as Illinois State League in 1947-48 and Mississippi-Ohio Valley League from 1949 through 1955.)

CLASS A *Midwest League*

NEW YORK-PENN LEAGUE

LEAGUE OFFICE

President
Bob Julian

Address
1629 Oneida St.
Utica, NY 13501

Phone
315-733-8036

Teams (affiliation)
Auburn Doubledays (Astros)
Batavia Muck Dogs (Phillies)
Hudson Valley Renegades (Devil Rays)
Jamestown Jammers (Braves)
Lowell Spinners (Red Sox)
Mahoning Valley Scrappers (Indians)
New Jersey Cardinals (Cardinals)

Oneonta Tigers (Tigers)
Pittsfield Mets (Mets)
St. Catharines Stompers (Blue Jays)
Utica Blue Sox (Marlins)
Vermont Expos (Expos)
Staten Island Yankees (Yankees)
Williamsport Crosscutters (Pirates)

1999 FINAL STANDINGS

McNAMARA DIVISION

Team	W	L	T	Pct.	GB
Utica (Marlins)	42	33	0	.560	...
Hudson Valley (Devil Rays)	42	34	0	.553	0.5
Oneonta (Tigers)	41	34	0	.547	1.0
Pittsfield (Mets)	41	35	0	.539	1.5
Staten Island (Yankees)	39	34	0	.527	2.5
Lowell (Red Sox)	34	42	0	.447	8.5
Vermont (Expos)	33	43	0	.434	9.5
New Jersey (Cardinals)	30	46	0	.395	12.5

PINCKNEY DIVISION

Team	W	L	T	Pct.	GB
Mahoning Valley (Indians)	43	33	0	.566	...
Batavia (Phillies)	42	34	0	.553	1.0
Auburn (Astros)	39	37	0	.513	4.0
Jamestown (Braves)	38	38	0	.500	5.0
St. Catharines (Blue Jays)	34	42	0	.447	9.0
Williamsport (Pirates)	32	44	0	.421	11.0

COMPOSITE

Team	M.V.	Uti.	H.V.	Bat.	One.	Pit.	S.I.	Aub.	Jam.	StC	Low.	Ver.	Wpt.	N.J.	W	L	T	Pct.	GB
Mahoning Valley (Indians)	...	0	0	7	0	0	0	9	8	8	0	0	11	0	43	33	0	.566	...
Utica (Marlins)	0	...	5	0	5	7	4	0	0	0	8	8	0	5	42	33	0	.560	0.5
Hudson Valley (Devil Rays)	0	6	...	0	8	5	5	0	0	0	6	6	0	6	42	34	0	.553	1.0
Batavia (Phillies)	8	0	0	...	0	0	0	5	8	10	0	0	11	0	42	34	0	.553	1.0
Oneonta (Tigers)	0	6	3	0	...	7	4	0	0	0	6	7	0	8	41	34	0	.547	1.5
Pittsfield (Mets)	0	4	6	0	4	...	6	0	0	0	8	6	0	7	41	35	0	.539	2.0
Staten Island (Yankees)	0	6	6	0	5	5	...	0	0	0	6	6	0	5	39	35	0	.527	3.0
Auburn (Astros)	6	0	0	11	0	0	0	...	7	8	0	0	7	0	39	37	0	.513	4.0
Jamestown (Braves)	8	0	0	7	0	0	0	8	...	6	0	0	9	0	38	38	0	.500	5.0
St. Catharines (Blue Jays)	7	0	0	5	0	0	0	7	9	...	0	0	6	0	34	42	0	.447	9.0
Lowell (Red Sox)	0	3	4	0	5	3	5	0	0	0	...	6	0	8	34	42	0	.447	9.0
Vermont (Expos)	0	2	5	0	4	5	5	0	0	0	5	...	0	7	33	43	0	.434	10.0
Williamsport (Pirates)	4	0	0	4	0	0	0	8	6	10	0	0	...	0	32	44	0	.421	11.0
New Jersey (Cardinals)	0	6	5	0	3	3	6	0	0	0	3	4	0	...	30	46	0	.395	13.0

Major league affiliations in parentheses.

PLAYOFFS: Mahoning Valley defeated Batavia two games to none; Hudson Valley defeated Utica two games to one; Hudson Valley defeated Mahoning Valley two games to one to win league championship.

REGULAR-SEASON ATTENDANCE: Auburn, 57,933; Batavia, 39,357; Hudson Valley, 161,678; Jamestown, 62,428; Lowell, 180,077; Mahoning Valley, 203,073; New Jersey, 135,802; Oneonta, 51,047; Pittsfield, 80,131; St. Catharines, 46,905; Staten Island, 117,765; Utica, 64,468; Vermont, 112,842; Williamsport, 57,548. Total—1,371,054. Playoffs (8 games)—22,376.

MANAGERS: Auburn, Lyle Yates; Batavia, Greg Legg; Hudson Valley, Edwin Rodriguez; Jamestown, Jim Saul; Lowell, Luis Aguayo; Mahoning Valley, Ted Kubiak; New Jersey, Jeff Shireman; Oneonta, Kevin Bradshaw; Pittsfield, Tony Tijerina; St. Catharines, Eddie Rodriguez; Staten Island, Joe Arnold; Utica, Ken Joyce; Vermont, Tony Barbone; Williamsport, Curtis Wilkerson.

ALL-STAR TEAM: 1B—Jason Lane, Auburn and Daniel Grummitt, Hudson Valley; 2B—Nick Green, Jamestown and Joe Kerrigan, Lowell; 3B—Asdrubal Oropez, Jamestown and Andrew Beinbrink, Hudson Valley; SS—Brandon Jackson, St. Catharines and Seth Taylor, Staten Island; Res. INF—Tony Alvarez, Williamsport and Andy Phillips, Staten Island; OF—Michael Rosamond, Auburn; Valentino Pascucci, Vermont; Marlon Byrd, Batavia; Matt Cepicky, Vermont; Jewell Williams, Mahoning Valley; Matt Watson, Vermont; Michael Hill, Auburn; Carlos Rodriguez, Lowell; C—John Buck, Auburn; Eliezer Alfonzo, New Jersey; Victor Martinez, Mahoning Valley; Chairon Isenia, Hudson Valley; RHP—Aaron Dean, St. Catharines; Dave Walling, Staten Island; Mike Mannini, Auburn; Jason Frasor, Oneonta; LHP—Mark Outlaw, Batavia; Todd Moser, Utica; Frank Brooks, Batavia; Joseph Kennedy, Hudson Valley; DH—Jason Landreth, Williamsport and Tony Lucca, Utica; Most Valuable Player (Pinckney Division)—Tony Alvarez, Williamsport; Most Valuable Player (McNamara Division)—Andrew Beinbrink, Hudson Valley.

1999 BATTING

TEAM

Team	Avg.	G	TPA	AB	R	H	TB	2B	3B	HR	RBI	SH	SF	HP	BB	IBB	SO	SB	CS	GDP	LOB	ShO	Slg.	OBP
Vermont	.273	76	3044	2680	400	732	1041	126	24	45	352	12	25	38	289	9	577	94	46	53	594	7	.388	.349
Auburn	.262	76	2943	2567	399	673	991	120	33	44	343	7	25	45	299	6	585	191	64	43	534	5	.386	.346
Utica	.259	75	2911	2530	357	655	957	136	29	36	310	22	27	53	279	6	570	69	44	52	558	2	.378	.342
Lowell	.256	76	2984	2620	379	671	994	137	27	44	323	20	21	40	283	8	574	81	33	56	572	4	.379	.335
Staten Island	.255	74	2818	2457	372	626	951	126	23	51	332	16	27	40	278	9	597	67	34	39	516	2	.387	.337
Jamestown	.251	76	2836	2520	365	632	946	117	16	55	321	13	26	42	235	2	599	101	28	45	503	4	.375	.322
Mahoning Val.	.250	76	2824	2429	406	607	911	119	19	49	350	13	32	45	305	2	623	115	49	45	487	2	.375	.340
Pittsfield	.249	76	2896	2536	368	631	933	137	21	41	317	29	15	46	270	5	591	125	49	34	510	5	.368	.330
Batavia	.248	76	2915	2589	379	643	968	115	33	48	329	14	27	46	239	4	633	125	33	34	544	3	.374	.320
Hudson Valley	.247	76	2930	2620	340	647	982	132	22	53	292	18	23	36	233	6	644	74	36	44	547	2	.375	.315
St. Catharines	.246	76	2855	2455	332	604	877	115	16	42	292	23	35	56	286	4	655	96	46	28	566	3	.357	.334
Williamsport	.244	76	2866	2522	329	616	870	120	13	36	289	13	16	45	270	5	617	108	42	51	554	10	.345	.326
Oneonta	.241	75	2839	2523	313	607	836	112	21	25	267	17	21	42	236	6	637	131	29	30	554	7	.331	.314
New Jersey	.233	76	2785	2494	320	582	862	94	39	36	271	28	14	57	192	2	635	97	66	44	447	5	.346	.301

TOP QUALIFIERS FOR BATTING CHAMPIONSHIP

Minimum 205 plate appearances. *Lefthanded batter. †Switch-hitter.

Player, Team	Avg.	G	TPA	AB	R	H	TB	2B	3B	HR	RBI	SH	SF	HP	BB	IBB	SO	SB	CS	GDP	Slg.	OBP
Watson, Matthew, Ver.*	.380	70	323	284	55	108	147	12	3	7	47	2	4	3	30	1	27	17	7	6	.518	.439
Pascucci, Valentino, Ver.	.351	72	328	259	62	91	140	26	1	7	48	0	2	14	53	3	46	17	2	5	.541	.482
Beinbrink, Andrew, H.V.	.339	76	343	292	46	99	160	24	2	11	51	0	4	8	39	2	49	13	4	4	.548	.426
Jackson, Brandon, St.C.	.332	62	255	214	37	71	92	13	1	2	25	0	5	8	28	0	45	3	8	4	.430	.420
Phillips, Andy, S.I.	.322	64	276	233	35	75	121	11	7	7	48	0	3	3	37	1	40	3	3	4	.519	.417
Alvarez, Antonio, Wil.	.321	58	240	196	44	63	100	14	1	7	45	1	6	16	21	1	36	38	9	2	.510	.418
Lucca, Tony, Uti.*	.321	67	285	240	35	77	120	20	1	7	47	0	2	7	36	3	47	7	2	6	.500	.421
Santana, Pedro, S.I.	.321	67	247	237	35	76	123	18	1	9	41	1	0	0	9	2	57	5	4	6	.519	.346
Grindell, Nate, M.V.	.315	71	299	267	42	84	123	20	2	5	47	0	4	4	24	1	39	6	5	3	.461	.375
Landreth, Jason, Mil.	.314	62	248	210	35	66	100	14	1	6	37	0	2	2	34	0	35	5	5	3	.476	.411
Kerrigan, Joseph, Low.*	.314	63	289	242	38	76	88	6	3	0	19	1	1	2	43	1	52	5	6	3	.364	.420
Cepicky, Matthew, Ver.*	.307	74	344	323	50	99	160	15	5	12	53	0	0	1	20	1	49	10	9	6	.495	.349
Nye, Rodney, Pit.	.306	70	296	255	45	78	133	30	2	7	48	0	4	5	32	1	36	10	4	5	.522	.389
Moore, Frank, H.V.*	.304	74	346	319	53	97	125	12	5	2	20	2	2	2	21	1	68	24	9	1	.392	.349
Dominguez, Luis, Aub.	.298	63	256	218	34	65	80	11	2	0	27	2	3	0	33	0	28	6	3	4	.367	.386
Batson, Thomas, Bat.	.298	65	288	245	52	73	115	10	4	8	33	2	3	3	35	1	36	11	5	3	.469	.388

DEPARTMENTAL LEADERS: G—Beinbrink, 76; AB—Cepicky, 323; R—Pascucci, 62; H—Watson, 108; TB—Beinbrink, Cepicky, 160 each; 2B—Nye, 30; 3B—Bailey, Carvajal, 8 each; HR—Grummitt, 22; RBI—Lane, 59; SH—Wright, 6; SF—Moreno, Bernhardt, 7 each; HP—Alvarez, 16; BB—Holliday, 63; IBB—Dwyer, Lucca, Pascucci, 3 each; SO—Martin, 107; SB—Requena, 44; CS—Lemon, 16; GIDP—Goodman, 10; Slg.—Beinbrink, .548; OBP—Pascucci, .482.

ALL PLAYERS

*Lefthanded batter. †Switch-hitter.

Player, Team	Avg.	G	TPA	AB	R	H	TB	2B	3B	HR	RBI	SH	SF	HP	BB	IBB	SO	SB	CS	GDP	Slg.	OBP
Acuna, Ronald, Pit.	.225	22	83	71	7	16	19	3	0	0	6	2	1	1	8	0	26	8	6	0	.268	.309
Alfieri, Frank, Aub.	.237	23	85	76	9	18	34	4	0	4	12	2	0	0	7	0	22	2	0	1	.447	.301
Alfonzo, Eliezer, N.J.	.326	46	187	178	14	58	83	12	2	3	28	1	1	4	3	0	39	3	4	5	.466	.349
Alvarez, Antonio, Wil.	.321	58	240	196	44	63	100	14	1	7	45	1	6	16	21	1	36	38	9	2	.510	.418
Ambres, Chip, Uti.	.267	28	129	105	24	28	58	3	6	5	15	0	2	1	21	0	25	11	4	1	.552	.388
Anderson, Dennis, Uti.	.188	30	108	96	10	18	24	1	1	1	8	3	1	1	7	0	28	2	0	1	.250	.248
Anderson, Jon, Low.†	.266	35	141	124	20	33	38	5	0	0	11	2	2	0	13	0	10	7	4	1	.306	.331
Arias, Jeison, H.V.	.143	17	52	49	5	7	8	1	0	0	2	0	0	0	3	0	20	0	1	0	.163	.192
Armstrong, Christopher, Aub.	.325	22	85	77	17	25	31	4	1	0	11	0	0	4	4	0	9	7	1	3	.403	.388
Avila, Rob, Bat.	.148	10	35	27	3	4	7	3	0	0	2	0	0	2	6	0	6	0	0	0	.259	.343
Bailey, Travis, N.J.	.228	66	265	241	37	55	104	9	8	8	31	1	1	4	17	1	81	6	2	2	.432	.289
Barns, B.J., Wil.*	.400	14	65	50	10	20	27	4	0	1	11	0	0	3	12	0	11	0	2	0	.540	.538
Batcheller, Chris, Wil.	.148	23	86	81	2	12	16	1	0	1	9	1	1	2	1	0	31	1	0	3	.198	.176
Batista, Angel, H.V.*	.183	53	193	164	19	30	35	5	0	0	12	3	3	1	22	0	46	8	4	1	.213	.279
Batson, Thomas, Bat.	.298	65	288	245	52	73	115	10	4	8	33	2	3	3	35	1	36	11	5	3	.469	.388
Beam, Dusty, One.	.170	50	184	165	20	28	33	5	0	0	3	2	0	0	17	0	45	2	1	3	.200	.247
Beinbrink, Andrew, H.V.	.339	76	343	292	46	99	160	24	2	11	51	0	4	8	39	2	49	13	4	4	.548	.426
Bernhardt, Jossephany, St.C.	.243	70	284	267	20	65	92	10	1	5	35	1	7	1	8	1	67	2	1	3	.345	.261
Beverly, Shomari, Bat.	.243	65	286	267	35	65	101	13	7	3	34	0	1	2	16	0	75	19	4	2	.378	.290
Blake, Casey, St.C.	.667	1	4	3	0	2	2	0	0	0	0	0	0	0	1	0	0	0	0	0	.667	.750
Bonifay, Joshua, Wil.	.260	52	228	200	42	52	78	10	2	4	17	1	0	2	25	0	55	2	2	1	.390	.348
Bost, Tom, M.V.*	.186	23	83	70	11	13	30	0	1	5	13	0	1	1	11	0	35	0	0	0	.429	.301
Brazeal, Spencer, S.I.	.100	8	12	10	3	1	1	0	0	0	1	0	0	1	1	0	4	0	0	0	.100	.250
Brett, Jason, Pit.	.211	42	128	109	20	23	26	3	0	0	7	4	0	5	10	0	20	12	2	0	.239	.306
Brown, Andy, S.I.*	.214	67	246	215	38	46	85	8	5	7	22	0	2	2	27	0	97	5	2	1	.395	.305
Buck, John, Aub.	.245	63	267	233	36	57	83	17	0	3	29	1	2	5	25	1	48	7	1	7	.356	.328
Burke, Paul, Jam.	.178	34	115	101	5	18	23	1	0	1	8	3	2	0	9	0	27	1	0	0	.228	.241
Byrd, Marlon, Bat.	.296	65	279	243	40	72	130	7	6	13	50	0	3	5	28	1	70	8	2	3	.535	.376
Calais, Ian, Jam.	.210	68	254	224	19	47	57	8	1	0	20	4	1	2	23	0	47	4	5	6	.254	.288
Cantu, Jorge, H.V.	.260	72	308	281	33	73	97	17	2	1	33	4	1	2	20	0	59	3	4	8	.345	.313
Caracciolo, Anthony, Ver.	.200	7	23	15	2	3	4	1	0	0	3	0	0	2	6	0	5	1	0	0	.267	.478
Carter, Shannon, St.C.*	.279	61	230	215	38	60	76	5	4	1	16	1	1	2	11	0	54	15	6	1	.353	.319
Carvajal, Ramon, N.J.†	.250	65	259	240	35	60	103	9	8	6	30	4	1	1	13	0	59	12	7	3	.429	.290
Celli, Mike, Jam.†	.272	72	290	246	39	67	91	16	1	2	33	1	6	5	32	1	55	8	0	6	.370	.360
Centile, Raul, M.V.†	.239	25	95	88	15	21	33	5	2	1	13	1	1	0	5	0	17	3	1	2	.375	.277
Cepicky, Matthew, Ver.*	.307	74	344	323	50	99	160	15	5	12	53	0	0	1	20	1	49	10	9	6	.495	.349
Close, James, Uti.	.181	59	208	188	23	34	52	7	1	3	26	1	3	0	16	0	60	6	7	3	.277	.242
Cody, Ryan, Bat.	.111	3	10	9	1	1	2	1	0	0	0	0	0	0	1	0	4	0	0	0	.222	.200
Collazo, Julio, Bat.	.250	5	19	16	0	4	4	0	0	0	2	1	0	0	2	0	6	0	0	0	.250	.333
Correa, Dominic, S.I.	.208	56	165	144	17	30	50	8	0	4	22	3	0	4	14	1	36	1	2	3	.347	.296
Cotten, Jeremy, Wil.	.200	50	195	175	16	35	53	13	1	1	24	0	1	1	18	0	67	0	0	4	.303	.277
Cox, Brian, Jam.	1.000	18	1	1	1	1	1	0	0	0	0	0	0	0	0	0	0	0	0	0	1.000	1.000
Cripps, Bobby, St.C.*	.290	10	34	31	3	9	15	0	0	2	7	0	1	0	2	0	9	0	0	0	.484	.324
Daggett, Jesse, Wil.	.222	5	22	18	1	4	7	3	0	0	1	0	0	0	4	0	3	0	0	0	.389	.364
Dalton, David, Jam.	.317	27	116	104	23	33	45	1	4	1	15	2	1	0	9	0	20	14	3	1	.433	.368
Davis, Jermaine, St.C.	.158	33	106	101	7	16	29	5	1	2	11	0	3	2	1	0	36	1	2	0	.287	.198
Day, Paul, M.V.	.219	9	38	32	4	7	10	1	1	0	5	0	1	0	5	0	6	0	0	2	.313	.316
De Aza, Modesto, Aub.	.220	61	244	223	38	49	70	7	4	2	18	0	2	8	11	0	73	34	10	5	.314	.279
DeGroote, Casey, S.I.*	.095	7	23	21	3	2	3	1	0	0	3	1	0	0	2	0	12	0	0	0	.143	.174
Deitrick, Jeremy, Bat.	.265	26	91	83	16	22	38	10	0	2	13	0	1	2	5	0	21	0	0	0	.458	.319
Deschenes, Pat, Pit.*	.313	5	21	16	7	5	8	0	0	1	3	0	1	0	4	0	2	0	0	1	.500	.429
Diaz, Diogenes, Wil.	.300	9	35	30	3	9	15	3	0	1	3	0	0	1	4	0	7	1	2	1	.500	.400
Diaz, Matt, H.V.	.245	54	224	208	22	51	73	15	2	1	20	2	2	6	6	0	43	6	2	5	.351	.284
Dominguez, Luis, Aub.	.298	63	256	218	34	65	80	11	2	0	27	2	3	0	33	0	28	6	3	4	.367	.386

CLASS A New York-Pennsylvania League

Player, Team	Avg.	G	TPA	AB	R	H	TB	2B	3B	HR	RBI	SH	SF	HP	BB	IBB	SO	SB	CS	GDP	Slg.	OBP
Drobiak, Jayson, One.*	.225	31	107	102	10	23	33	8	1	0	14	0	1	0	4	1	23	2	3	2	.324	.252
Duarte, Justin, Bat.	.250	45	154	140	15	35	46	8	0	1	20	1	2	3	8	0	36	0	0	4	.329	.301
Dwyer, Mike, Low.*	.247	71	311	271	24	67	88	12	0	3	41	1	3	2	34	3	50	3	2	6	.325	.332
Dyer, Matthew, Pit.	.500	2	4	4	0	2	2	0	0	0	2	0	0	0	0	0	1	0	0	0	.500	.500
Eberly, Rodney, Bat.*	.205	50	194	171	17	35	46	5	0	2	18	1	5	2	15	0	26	0	0	4	.269	.269
Elzy, Steven, Pit.	.244	40	145	131	16	32	44	10	1	0	18	2	1	2	9	0	15	2	0	4	.336	.301
Escobar, Gustavo, N.J.	.271	31	104	96	17	26	34	2	3	0	12	0	0	1	7	0	22	5	2	2	.354	.327
Espino, Jose, N.J.	.199	42	147	136	12	27	35	4	2	0	10	0	2	0	9	0	44	5	4	3	.257	.245
Espinoza, Andres, Ver.	.211	29	76	71	9	15	18	3	0	0	2	0	0	1	4	0	15	1	1	1	.254	.263
Estevez, Domingo, St.C.†	.255	61	245	212	31	54	88	21	2	3	28	2	4	6	21	0	32	12	9	1	.415	.333
Ewan, Bry, Jam.	.193	31	127	109	9	21	27	3	0	1	15	1	2	2	13	0	33	0	0	1	.248	.286
Ewing, Byron, M.V.	.273	15	53	44	7	12	17	2	0	1	6	0	0	0	9	0	9	1	0	2	.386	.396
Ewing, Chris, N.J.	.130	26	65	54	5	7	10	1	1	0	0	0	0	2	9	0	25	1	1	0	.185	.277
Faigin, Jason, S.I.	.000	20	0	0	0	0	0	0	0	0	0	0	0	0	0	0	0	0	0	0	.000	.000
Feliz, Joselyn, Uti.	.230	25	89	87	7	20	32	4	1	2	18	0	0	0	2	0	19	1	0	1	.368	.247
Ferrand, Francisco, Uti.*	.293	63	253	229	26	67	89	16	0	2	27	5	3	1	15	0	38	3	1	7	.389	.335
Floyd, Mike, N.J.	.219	38	146	137	17	30	41	8	0	1	16	2	1	2	4	0	40	4	1	1	.299	.250
Ford, Lew, Low.	.280	62	277	250	48	70	116	17	4	7	34	0	3	5	19	1	35	15	2	6	.464	.339
Fowler, Ben, M.V.†	.210	17	65	62	5	13	25	3	0	3	15	0	1	0	2	0	21	0	1	1	.403	.231
Francisco, Joseph, Jam.	.199	42	157	146	17	29	45	10	0	2	10	0	0	2	9	0	37	9	1	3	.308	.255
Fuentes, Omar, S.I.	.279	50	154	129	15	36	54	7	1	3	21	2	1	3	19	0	18	0	1	2	.419	.382
Gallaher, T.T., M.V.	.316	6	24	19	7	6	12	1	1	1	5	0	0	0	5	0	2	0	0	2	.632	.458
Gay, Curtis, M.V.*	.231	65	265	234	34	54	77	13	2	2	24	1	2	4	24	0	98	3	2	5	.329	.311
Geisbush, David, Jam.	.232	26	75	69	11	16	29	2	1	3	12	1	0	0	5	0	25	2	0	1	.420	.284
Gomez, Jose, Uti.	.173	25	84	75	6	13	18	3	1	0	6	2	0	2	5	0	27	2	0	1	.240	.244
Gonzalez, Santos, St.C.†	.233	42	165	150	14	35	49	3	1	3	14	1	1	0	13	0	41	9	2	1	.327	.293
Goodeill, Harold, H.V.	.174	8	26	23	3	4	7	1	1	0	2	0	0	1	2	0	6	0	0	0	.304	.269
Goodman, Scott, Uti.*	.262	68	275	221	38	58	96	15	1	7	29	0	0	11	43	2	43	4	7	10	.434	.407
Gordon, Johnny, One.*	.155	44	124	110	13	17	27	4	3	0	5	0	0	0	14	0	30	4	1	1	.245	.250
Green, Jason, S.I.	.200	25	33	25	6	5	6	1	0	0	1	0	0	1	7	0	3	0	0	1	.240	.394
Green, Nick, Jam.	.297	73	306	273	52	81	129	15	0	11	41	0	3	4	26	0	66	14	4	4	.473	.363
Gregg, Neal, S.I.*	.212	17	42	33	4	7	13	3	0	1	8	0	1	3	5	0	14	0	0	1	.394	.357
Griffin, Justin, M.V.	.111	5	11	9	2	1	1	0	0	0	0	0	0	0	2	0	5	0	0	0	.111	.273
Grindell, Nate, M.V.	.315	71	299	267	42	84	123	20	2	5	47	0	4	4	24	1	39	6	5	3	.461	.375
Grummitt, Dan, H.V.	.254	73	324	287	44	73	154	13	1	22	58	0	2	5	30	1	78	3	1	4	.537	.333
Hamilton, Josh, H.V.*	.194	16	75	72	7	14	17	3	0	0	7	0	1	1	1	0	14	1	1	2	.236	.213
Hart, Bo, N.J.	.184	50	188	163	23	30	48	3	3	3	15	3	0	12	10	0	38	4	2	1	.294	.281
Hernandez, Johnny, N.J.†	.394	10	43	33	4	13	14	1	0	0	2	0	0	0	10	0	9	1	4	0	.424	.535
Hernandez, Jose, Wil.	.237	35	125	118	5	28	32	4	0	0	9	2	0	2	3	0	20	1	1	7	.271	.268
Hill, Michael, Aub.	.297	69	303	269	44	80	113	11	2	6	39	0	2	3	29	1	65	22	6	2	.420	.370
Hitchcox, Brian, Bat.*	.223	54	197	166	22	37	50	5	1	2	18	1	3	8	19	0	14	7	1	2	.301	.327
Hlousek, Robert, One.	.220	36	126	109	15	24	27	3	0	0	3	3	1	1	12	1	11	9	1	3	.248	.301
Holliday, Joshua, St.C.†	.255	71	299	216	50	55	100	13	1	10	37	5	4	11	63	2	57	1	2	2	.463	.439
Hooper, Kevin, Uti.	.280	73	337	289	52	81	111	18	6	0	22	2	3	4	39	0	35	14	8	2	.384	.370
Hoover, Steven, Aub.	.202	32	106	94	4	19	28	2	2	1	5	0	0	4	8	0	18	2	2	0	.298	.292
House, J.R., Wil.	.300	26	109	100	11	30	39	6	0	1	13	0	0	0	9	0	21	0	1	2	.390	.358
Hudson, Daniel, Wil.	.214	37	142	117	14	25	35	6	2	0	9	1	1	1	22	0	41	5	3	1	.299	.340
Isenia, Chairon, H.V.	.263	33	125	118	17	31	49	9	0	3	16	0	2	1	4	0	22	0	1	4	.415	.288
Jackson, Brandon, St.C.	.332	62	255	214	37	71	92	13	1	2	25	0	5	8	28	0	45	3	8	4	.430	.420
Jackson, Kevin, One.	.216	38	140	125	11	27	41	5	0	3	20	0	4	0	11	0	48	2	0	0	.328	.271
Jarvais, Kregg, Low.	.193	36	118	109	13	21	29	6	1	0	9	1	0	1	8	0	31	3	0	1	.266	.254
Jaworowski, Aaron, S.I.*	.200	11	35	30	2	6	8	2	0	0	4	0	0	2	3	1	8	0	0	0	.267	.314
Johannes, Todd, Ver.	.298	24	96	84	5	25	27	2	0	0	11	0	2	0	10	0	15	1	0	2	.321	.365
Johnson, Eric, M.V.	.257	28	125	105	23	27	36	4	1	1	10	0	0	2	18	0	17	12	1	3	.343	.376
Johnson, Gabe, N.J.	.194	35	136	124	12	24	48	5	2	5	14	1	1	1	9	0	49	1	1	4	.387	.252
Johnson, Reed, St.C.	.241	60	225	191	24	46	64	8	2	2	23	4	4	2	24	1	31	5	5	4	.335	.326
Johnson, Tony, Pit.†	.202	63	224	178	31	36	67	8	4	5	28	2	1	4	39	1	59	14	2	2	.376	.356
Joyce, Jesse, Aub.	.300	18	76	70	11	21	36	5	2	2	10	0	0	2	4	0	13	1	2	1	.514	.355
Kerrigan, Joseph, Low.*	.314	63	289	242	38	76	88	6	3	0	19	1	1	2	43	1	52	5	6	3	.364	.420
Laflair, Jay, M.V.	.200	16	39	30	8	6	9	3	0	0	3	1	0	3	5	0	6	2	0	2	.300	.368
Landreth, Jason, Wil.	.314	62	248	210	35	66	100	14	1	6	37	0	2	2	34	0	35	5	5	3	.476	.411
Lane, Jason, Aub.	.279	74	329	283	46	79	146	18	5	13	59	0	4	3	38	2	46	6	4	2	.516	.366
Langlois, J.-Sebastien, Jam.	.245	59	248	220	24	54	74	7	2	3	20	0	3	25	1	54	10	2	4	.336	.331
Langston, James, Wil.†	.275	54	207	200	15	55	68	8	1	1	20	0	1	6	1	40	2	1	6	.340	.300
Lara, Balmes, One.	.276	63	255	232	30	64	103	10	4	7	37	2	3	4	14	1	63	9	1	5	.444	.324
Leal, Jaeme, Jam.	.273	33	113	99	16	27	56	5	0	8	28	0	3	3	8	0	37	0	0	3	.566	.336
Leaumont, Jeff, S.I.*	.241	67	240	212	35	51	65	12	1	0	20	1	5	1	21	0	61	7	4	4	.307	.305
Lebron, Francisco, Pit.	.289	75	313	266	46	77	121	17	0	9	43	0	0	1	46	1	53	6	1	8	.455	.396
Lebron, Hector, H.V.*	.250	17	60	56	3	14	20	3	0	1	6	0	1	0	3	0	13	0	0	1	.357	.283
Lebron, Jesus, St.C.	.239	65	252	218	37	52	83	11	1	6	29	1	4	2	27	0	90	15	4	2	.381	.323
Ledesma, Phil, Low.	.270	30	98	74	19	20	30	3	2	1	12	2	1	5	16	0	15	8	2	1	.405	.427
Lee, Monte, N.J.	.223	38	144	121	20	27	31	4	0	0	10	0	0	5	18	0	25	14	6	1	.256	.347
Lemon, Tim, N.J.	.198	72	276	242	25	48	71	5	3	4	29	4	2	6	22	0	62	16	16	4	.293	.279
Lopez, Samuel, Pit.	.429	2	7	7	0	3	3	0	0	0	0	0	0	0	0	0	3	0	0	0	.429	.429
Lotterhos, Chris, M.V.	.210	41	150	124	21	26	40	7	2	1	9	0	1	2	23	0	33	5	6	2	.323	.340
Lowe, Steve, M.V.	.232	33	118	95	19	22	31	3	0	2	11	1	1	9	12	0	26	4	3	0	.326	.368
Lucca, Tony, Uti.*	.321	67	285	240	35	77	120	20	1	7	47	0	2	7	36	3	47	7	2	6	.500	.421
Ludvigsen, Marc, Pit.*	.220	30	108	100	11	22	35	5	1	2	13	2	1	0	5	0	43	0	1	0	.350	.255
Lugo, Felix, Ver.†	.206	46	188	170	19	35	62	6	3	5	25	2	1	3	12	0	67	3	2	3	.365	.269
MacMillan, Chris, M.V.	.167	7	28	24	2	4	5	1	0	0	4	0	0	0	4	0	9	1	1	0	.208	.286
Malave, Dennis, M.V.*	.244	12	50	41	11	10	13	0	0	1	8	0	1	1	7	0	9	1	1	0	.317	.360
Malone, Nick, Low.	.250	6	19	16	3	4	6	2	0	0	1	1	1	0	1	0	5	0	0	0	.375	.278
Martin, Brian, H.V.	.195	70	311	262	34	51	85	7	6	5	27	2	5	40	1	107	12	5	4	.324	.311
Martin, Justin, Wil.†	.248	31	133	109	26	27	29	2	0	0	8	2	1	0	21	0	26	16	1	1	.266	.366

Player, Team	Avg.	G	TPA	AB	R	H	TB	2B	3B	HR	RBI	SH	SF	HP	BB	IBB	SO	SB	CS	GDP	Slg.	OBP
Martinez, Victor, M.V.†	.277	64	269	235	37	65	86	9	0	4	36	0	6	1	27	0	31	0	1	4	.366	.346
Maule, Jason, Aub.*	.221	35	109	86	12	19	22	3	0	0	11	0	1	1	21	0	20	10	1	3	.256	.376
McArthur, Kennon, Bat.	.194	31	112	103	13	20	36	10	0	2	4	0	0	4	5	0	31	0	0	1	.350	.259
McKinley, Josh, Ver.†	.251	69	323	283	47	71	101	12	3	4	32	3	3	1	33	0	52	9	5	7	.357	.328
McKinney, Antonio, One.	.249	68	257	229	36	57	74	9	1	2	20	1	1	8	18	0	60	26	4	1	.323	.324
Meadows, Mike, Pit.	.261	48	157	134	23	35	60	10	0	5	24	0	1	1	21	1	57	3	0	0	.448	.363
Meadows, Randy, Ver.	.200	9	34	30	4	6	6	0	0	0	2	1	0	0	3	0	7	1	2	0	.200	.273
Melucci, Lou, Ver.	.195	33	135	123	13	24	29	3	1	0	7	1	0	1	10	0	34	6	1	2	.236	.261
Mendez, Donaldo, Aub.	.209	25	94	86	9	18	21	1	1	0	10	0	2	4	2	0	23	10	5	3	.244	.255
Mento, Alfredo, Pit.	.251	72	311	275	42	69	93	12	3	2	23	5	2	5	24	0	55	24	11	2	.338	.320
Merhoff, Aaron, Bat.	.137	16	58	51	3	7	11	2	1	0	6	0	0	0	6	0	16	0	0	0	.216	.228
Miley, Perry, Low.	.245	46	173	147	19	36	50	6	1	2	19	4	1	3	18	0	29	9	3	4	.340	.337
Minus, Stephen, Low.	.249	66	279	237	32	59	91	13	2	5	26	0	2	1	39	2	67	6	1	6	.384	.355
Mitchell, Todd, S.I.	.270	65	271	248	34	67	85	13	1	1	23	1	0	1	21	1	39	11	2	3	.343	.330
Mize, Matt, Pit.†	.263	69	307	281	32	74	102	15	2	3	27	3	0	1	22	0	78	22	7	2	.363	.319
Moore, Frank, H.V.*	.304	74	346	319	53	97	125	12	5	2	20	2	2	2	21	1	68	24	9	1	.392	.349
Moore, Ryan, Ver.*	.262	26	119	103	16	27	39	4	1	2	12	0	1	2	13	1	21	1	3	1	.379	.353
Moraga, Omar, M.V.*	.230	67	276	248	35	57	94	21	2	4	37	2	4	1	21	0	69	3	2	5	.379	.288
Morales, Victor, St.C.†	.220	43	152	132	10	29	33	4	0	0	16	4	0	5	11	0	24	7	0	5	.250	.304
Moreno, Jorge, One.	.257	69	275	230	38	59	100	10	2	9	38	2	7	5	31	0	61	15	7	4	.435	.348
Murch, Jeremy, H.V.*	.214	39	145	131	18	28	54	7	2	5	18	0	1	1	12	1	36	1	2	2	.412	.283
Muthig, Dean, Bat.	.262	31	114	107	16	28	42	7	2	1	18	0	3	0	4	0	28	1	0	1	.393	.281
Nelson, Reggie, One.	.237	67	293	249	44	59	79	11	3	1	20	4	1	3	36	0	42	32	8	4	.317	.339
Nicolas, Jose, Wil.	.202	29	107	99	8	20	31	6	1	1	11	0	0	1	7	0	32	2	2	4	.313	.262
Niles, Drew, Uti.†	.227	18	77	66	4	15	18	3	0	0	7	2	0	0	9	0	15	0	3	1	.273	.320
Norrell, Troy, Bat.	.250	28	109	100	16	25	54	7	2	6	21	0	0	1	8	1	45	1	0	1	.540	.312
Nunez, Hector, One.	.284	33	111	102	6	29	42	9	2	0	15	0	0	2	6	0	13	0	0	1	.412	.336
Nunez, Jose, N.J.	.306	45	182	157	29	48	64	11	1	1	13	3	0	2	20	1	18	6	3	4	.408	.391
Nye, Rodney, Pit.	.306	70	296	255	45	78	133	30	2	7	48	0	4	5	32	1	36	10	4	5	.522	.389
Ochoa, Javier, Aub.	.277	15	52	47	5	13	17	2	1	0	11	0	2	0	3	0	7	0	1	2	.362	.308
O'Neill, Daniel, Bat.†	.189	34	122	106	11	20	25	2	0	1	8	1	0	1	14	0	27	7	2	2	.236	.289
Oropeza, Asdrubal, Jam.	.293	74	310	266	56	78	134	12	1	14	46	0	6	6	32	0	60	10	2	3	.504	.374
Ortega, Jose, N.J.	.190	30	108	100	12	19	20	1	0	0	8	1	1	5	1	0	32	4	0	1	.200	.234
Ortiz, Juan, Ver.	.235	32	124	115	16	27	32	0	1	1	9	1	0	2	9	0	29	6	1	2	.278	.285
Padilla, Jorge, Bat.	.252	65	270	238	28	60	81	10	1	3	30	1	2	7	22	1	79	2	1	3	.340	.331
Parker, Chris, One.	.198	38	133	116	10	23	34	5	0	2	17	0	2	3	12	0	38	0	1	3	.293	.286
Pascucci, Valentino, Ver.	.351	72	328	259	62	91	140	26	1	7	48	0	2	14	53	3	46	17	2	5	.541	.482
Pass, Patrick, Uti.	.000	1	3	2	1	0	0	0	0	0	0	0	0	0	1	0	1	0	0	0	.000	.333
Pelfrey, Brice, Wil.	.120	14	54	50	1	6	8	0	1	0	2	0	0	3	1	0	12	1	0	1	.160	.185
Pemberthy, Aaron, N.J.	.250	15	54	48	6	12	18	4	1	0	6	0	0	3	3	0	17	0	0	2	.375	.333
Perez, Deivi, Wil.	.189	48	169	148	20	28	44	7	0	3	9	2	0	1	18	1	35	2	0	5	.297	.281
Perini, Mike, S.I.*	.186	43	105	97	11	18	30	4	1	2	13	0	2	0	6	1	40	1	0	0	.309	.229
Perkins, Kevin, Uti.	.287	60	237	202	35	58	83	11	4	2	23	3	5	8	19	0	41	2	3	4	.411	.363
Phillips, Andy, S.I.	.322	64	276	233	35	75	121	11	7	7	48	0	3	3	37	1	40	3	3	4	.519	.417
Pichardo, Henry, M.V.	.400	2	5	5	0	2	3	1	0	0	1	0	0	0	0	0	1	0	0	0	.600	.400
Piercy, Mike, Wil.*	.192	8	32	26	3	5	8	0	0	1	5	0	0	0	6	0	7	0	3	0	.308	.344
Pohle, Ike, St.C.	.239	46	170	142	19	34	56	10	0	4	20	1	2	4	21	0	47	0	1	2	.394	.344
Postell, Matthew, Uti.*	.264	45	172	148	15	39	51	8	2	0	21	1	3	2	18	0	50	4	2	5	.345	.345
Poulsen, Christopher, Jam.	.220	37	129	123	19	27	41	8	0	2	14	0	1	3	2	0	22	2	2	4	.333	.248
Preston, Brian, Ver.	.214	28	122	103	14	22	36	8	0	2	16	0	4	2	13	0	25	2	0	2	.350	.303
Ramirez, Edgar, H.V.	.192	34	133	120	14	23	37	6	1	2	6	2	0	1	10	0	46	2	1	1	.308	.260
Ravelo, Manuel, Wil.	.214	55	222	201	27	43	50	2	1	1	10	2	2	0	17	1	43	23	7	2	.249	.273
Requena, Alexander, M.V.†	.234	61	261	214	44	50	62	6	3	0	18	4	1	6	36	0	64	44	12	0	.290	.358
Reyes, Ambiorix, Bat.	.234	25	81	77	4	18	19	1	0	0	5	1	0	3	0	0	7	6	2	1	.247	.263
Reyes, Dadny, Uti.†	.256	30	86	78	9	20	27	3	2	0	3	0	1	1	6	0	17	2	1	4	.346	.314
Reyes, Deurys, One.*	.342	12	44	38	8	13	24	3	1	2	9	0	1	0	5	0	12	3	0	0	.632	.409
Rhodes, Dusty, S.I.*	.249	45	210	169	28	42	56	11	0	1	13	2	2	4	33	0	42	3	5	2	.331	.380
Richardson, Corey, One.	.264	41	156	125	25	33	37	2	1	0	9	1	1	4	25	1	34	19	4	1	.296	.400
Richardson, Juan, Bat.	.125	7	27	24	1	3	6	0	0	1	2	0	0	1	2	0	8	0	1	0	.250	.222
Rickon, Jim, M.V.	.200	8	28	25	3	5	8	0	0	1	4	1	0	0	2	0	7	0	0	2	.320	.259
Riepe, Andrew, Low.	.310	31	113	100	16	31	46	12	0	1	15	3	2	2	6	0	14	0	0	3	.460	.355
Riggins, Auntwan, St.C.†	.238	44	122	105	16	25	30	3	1	0	11	0	0	5	12	0	34	12	2	0	.286	.344
Rivera, Luis Jr., M.V.	.227	31	113	97	14	22	33	6	1	1	12	0	1	1	14	1	28	0	2	3	.340	.327
Rodriguez, Carlos, Low.	.250	60	243	228	37	57	116	13	5	12	46	0	0	2	13	0	66	17	3	5	.509	.296
Rodriguez, Felix, S.I.	.000	1	2	2	0	0	0	0	0	0	0	0	0	0	0	0	1	0	0	0	.000	.000
Rodriguez, Jeff, Jam.	.287	48	191	174	23	50	60	10	0	0	14	1	0	5	11	0	27	3	0	2	.345	.347
Rojas, Alex, Bat.	.284	45	196	176	38	50	62	6	3	0	16	2	0	3	15	0	37	39	7	4	.352	.351
Rosamond, Michael, Aub.	.265	61	257	230	34	61	96	9	4	6	24	0	1	3	23	0	63	22	6	5	.417	.339
Ryden, Karl, Aub.	.333	31	142	117	24	39	56	8	0	3	15	0	2	4	19	0	19	10	4	1	.479	.437
Saba, Cesar, Low.†........	.275	69	318	284	38	78	106	16	3	2	30	2	0	4	28	0	49	1	3	9	.373	.348
St. Pierre, Maxim, One.	.251	51	190	175	12	44	54	7	0	1	22	0	1	3	11	0	29	9	0	2	.309	.305
Sampson, Christopher, Aub.	.239	51	184	159	23	38	54	7	3	1	19	1	1	1	22	1	49	21	5	2	.340	.333
Santana, Pedro, S.I.	.321	67	247	237	35	76	123	18	1	9	41	1	0	0	9	2	57	5	4	6	.519	.346
Santiago, Ramon, One.†	.340	12	54	50	9	17	25	1	2	1	8	1	0	1	2	0	12	5	0	0	.500	.377
Santos, Juan, St.C.†	.172	43	152	128	16	22	31	6	0	1	8	1	0	3	20	0	38	1	1	1	.242	.298
Sarabia, Eliot, Wil.	.200	34	119	100	12	20	23	1	1	0	10	1	0	4	14	0	12	7	1	2	.230	.322
Sassanella, Jeremy, One.†	.271	54	189	170	16	46	53	7	0	0	13	0	2	2	13	0	57	1	0	1	.312	.326
Schell, Barry, Uti.*	.179	33	105	95	13	17	27	2	1	2	10	0	2	1	7	0	37	2	0	1	.284	.238
Schley, Joseph, Bat.	.197	36	91	71	15	14	22	3	1	1	7	3	0	1	16	0	24	8	3	1	.310	.352
Schneider, Matthew, Wil.*	.197	24	87	76	10	15	27	4	1	2	11	0	0	3	8	0	27	1	0	1	.355	.276
Schumacher, Shawn, N.J.*	.227	47	174	154	14	35	50	6	0	3	23	0	3	4	11	0	8	2	3	9	.325	.291
Segura, Rolando, Wil.	.333	29	122	108	20	36	58	10	0	4	24	0	0	2	12	1	26	1	1	4	.537	.410
Sherrill, J.J., M.V.†	.375	3	9	8	1	3	3	0	0	0	1	0	0	0	1	0	4	0	0	0	.375	.444
Shipp, Brian, Pit.	.238	65	264	240	25	57	78	10	4	1	19	2	2	2	18	0	56	8	6	2	.325	.294

Player, Team	Avg.	G	TPA	AB	R	H	TB	2B	3B	HR	RBI	SH	SF	HP	BB	IBB	SO	SB	CS	GDP	Slg.	OBP
Sickles, Jeremy, Wil.	.160	27	100	94	4	15	20	2	0	1	1	0	0	2	4	0	19	0	1	1	.213	.210
Siegfried, Jason, One.	.164	24	68	61	6	10	13	3	0	0	3	1	0	0	6	0	28	0	0	1	.213	.239
Simmons, Jerry, Jam.	.216	62	257	232	37	50	81	9	5	4	27	0	0	5	20	0	46	19	6	2	.349	.292
Sitzman, James, Bat.*	.296	49	183	169	33	50	71	5	5	2	22	0	4	1	9	0	37	15	5	2	.420	.328
Smith, Fred, St.C.	.223	40	160	130	10	29	37	3	1	1	12	2	2	4	22	0	50	13	3	2	.285	.348
Smith, Ryan, Pit.	.143	12	36	35	1	5	8	0	0	1	5	0	0	1	0	0	5	0	0	0	.229	.167
Stockam, Travis, Pit.	.219	41	148	128	19	28	46	4	1	4	19	1	0	11	8	1	32	1	3	1	.359	.320
Stoffels, Alex, Pit.	.114	26	79	70	5	8	9	1	0	0	9	0	0	3	6	0	19	6	2	3	.129	.215
Suriel, Miguel, H.V.	.231	33	132	121	15	28	36	8	0	0	7	2	0	1	8	0	15	1	1	6	.298	.285
Sutter, Chad, S.I.	.130	36	92	77	8	10	17	1	0	2	7	2	2	2	0	11	0	18	1	0	1	.221	.233
Taylor, Seth, S.I.	.293	74	331	283	57	83	111	11	1	5	36	2	3	8	35	1	40	23	6	8	.392	.383
Terni, Chaz, Low.	.202	38	136	119	10	24	32	6	1	0	7	2	2	3	10	0	35	1	2	1	.269	.276
Thames, Damon, N.J.	.228	47	197	180	22	41	48	5	1	0	16	4	1	4	7	0	42	10	5	1	.267	.271
Thomas, Mark, Ver.*	.316	44	182	152	23	48	62	5	3	1	23	0	2	1	27	1	28	10	3	3	.408	.418
Ticehurst, Brad, S.I.*	.253	63	255	221	29	56	102	12	5	8	39	0	6	6	22	1	51	4	3	2	.462	.333
Topolski, Jon, Aub.*	.243	67	311	255	46	62	91	11	6	2	38	0	3	3	50	1	72	27	13	2	.357	.370
Ugueto, Luis, Uti.†	.276	56	239	217	33	60	78	11	2	1	26	3	0	1	18	0	46	9	4	4	.359	.335
Ust, Brant, One.	.261	58	250	226	23	59	92	12	3	5	34	1	3	4	16	2	54	3	4	3	.407	.317
Valdez, Angel, S.I.	.211	34	79	71	11	15	21	3	0	1	13	2	0	1	5	0	16	3	2	1	.296	.273
Valdez, Castulo, H.V.	.231	12	33	26	4	6	6	0	0	0	0	1	0	1	5	0	4	0	0	0	.231	.375
Valdez, Wilson, Ver.	.246	36	138	130	19	32	42	7	0	1	10	0	1	0	7	0	21	4	3	3	.323	.323
Van Pareren, Tim, Ver.†	.207	30	100	82	9	17	19	2	0	0	3	1	2	3	12	0	23	4	1	1	.232	.323
Vazquez, Carlos, H.V.	.198	29	100	91	3	18	19	1	0	0	7	0	2	0	7	0	18	0	0	1	.209	.250
Villar, Jose, Jam.	.248	39	147	133	14	33	53	6	1	4	17	0	1	2	11	0	43	5	3	5	.398	.319
Waldron, Jeffrey, Low.*	.176	39	145	125	17	22	30	3	1	1	13	0	0	6	14	1	22	0	1	4	.240	.290
Walker, Javon, Uti.	.000	8	12	11	0	0	0	0	0	0	0	0	0	0	1	0	7	0	0	0	.000	.083
Warren, Chris, Low.	.223	56	234	215	29	48	82	13	3	5	25	2	3	2	12	0	69	3	2	5	.381	.267
Washington, Mo, Wil.	.125	5	19	16	0	2	2	0	0	0	0	0	0	1	2	0	11	0	0	0	.125	.263
Watson, Matthew, Ver.*	.380	70	323	284	55	108	147	12	3	7	47	2	4	3	30	1	27	17	7	6	.518	.439
Wiese, Brian, Low.	.316	21	90	79	16	25	46	4	1	5	18	0	0	2	9	0	25	2	2	1	.582	.400
Williams, Charles, N.J.†	.244	28	114	90	16	22	40	4	4	2	8	4	0	1	19	0	25	3	5	2	.444	.382
Williams, Clyde, Ver.*	.234	63	276	256	23	60	84	14	2	2	37	1	2	1	16	1	85	1	4	6	.328	.280
Williams, Jewell, M.V.	.273	62	258	220	37	60	93	9	0	8	42	0	1	6	31	1	60	14	7	7	.423	.376
Williamson, Casey, One.*	.245	48	161	139	19	34	45	8	0	1	15	1	0	7	14	0	38	5	1	0	.324	.344
Woody, Dominic, Uti.	.276	48	212	181	26	50	73	11	0	4	22	0	2	13	16	1	34	0	2	1	.403	.373
Wright, Brad, Pit.*	.258	63	265	236	38	61	79	9	3	1	23	6	1	4	18	0	31	9	4	4	.335	.320
Zapata, Juan, Aub.	.227	16	45	44	7	10	13	0	0	1	5	1	0	0	0	0	10	4	0	0	.295	.227

GRAND SLAMS: Leal, Phillips, Stockam, 2 each; Alfonzo, Bailey, Carvajal, Gay, Gonzalez, Landreth, Langlois, Ludvigsen, Norrell, Pascucci, Parker, Rodriguez, Sampson, Ticehurst, Valdez, 1 each.

AWARDED FIRST BASE ON CATCHER'S INTERFERENCE: Sassanella, 2 (Rivera, Feliz); Schumacher, 2 (Suriel, Rivera); Buck (Hernandez); Bailey (Preston); Lane (Rodriguez); Merhoff (Hernandez); Nunez (Feliz); Thames (Anderson).

1999 PITCHING

TEAM

Team	W	L	Pct.	ERA	G	CG	ShO	Sv.	IP	H	TBF	R	ER	HR	SH	SF	HB	BB	IBB	SO	WP	Bk.
Oneonta	41	34	.547	3.13	75	3	5	25	660.2	565	2832	302	230	41	23	28	35	306	9	609	70	14
Hudson Valley	42	34	.553	3.35	76	1	8	20	687.0	585	2873	308	256	25	25	16	60	240	3	632	51	10
Utica	42	33	.560	3.69	75	4	6	20	670.1	631	2828	338	275	54	18	13	42	219	3	622	56	8
Pittsfield	41	35	.539	3.69	76	0	6	20	675.0	655	2903	336	277	32	24	21	39	247	5	540	51	7
Auburn	39	37	.513	3.69	76	3	5	18	670.0	607	2905	364	275	41	19	25	60	258	1	616	41	12
Batavia	42	34	.553	3.84	76	4	6	15	668.0	629	2881	341	285	36	14	33	51	277	10	602	74	13
Williamsport	32	44	.421	3.89	76	7	4	16	656.1	622	2877	372	284	41	10	35	58	276	5	565	44	22
Staten Island	39	35	.527	3.95	74	1	3	20	647.1	660	2797	333	284	35	19	18	23	207	9	670	60	16
Lowell	34	42	.447	4.06	76	0	3	10	674.0	675	2986	395	304	48	17	31	44	262	7	639	58	21
Mahoning Valley .	34	42	.447	4.19	76	1	2	19	648.0	650	2840	363	302	44	19	27	36	243	1	638	45	9
New Jersey	30	46	.395	4.25	76	2	2	16	665.1	656	2919	377	314	51	17	20	43	277	6	540	68	12
Jamestown	38	38	.500	4.48	76	3	4	23	656.1	630	2851	377	327	50	11	25	41	263	1	638	64	8
St. Catharines	34	42	.447	4.49	76	0	6	21	649.1	637	2888	393	324	62	10	16	33	317	5	653	69	16
Vermont	33	43	.434	4.82	76	1	1	19	676.0	724	3076	460	362	45	19	26	66	302	9	573	67	15

INDIVIDUAL

TOP QUALIFIERS FOR EARNED-RUN AVERAGE TITLE
Minimum 61 innings. *Lefthanded pitcher.

Pitcher, Team	W	L	Pct.	ERA	G	GS	CG	ShO	GF	Sv.	IP	H	TBF	R	ER	HR	SH	SF	HB	BB	IBB	SO	WP	Bk.
Moser, Todd, Uti.*	8	2	.800	1.53	14	14	3	1	0	0	88.0	63	343	20	15	2	1	1	2	24	0	86	4	2
Leek, Randy, One.*	6	3	.667	1.56	21	3	1	0	4	1	63.1	58	249	16	11	0	1	1	2	9	1	66	2	0
Nannini, Mike, Aub.	5	3	.625	1.90	11	11	2	1	0	0	75.2	55	295	19	16	2	3	3	4	17	0	86	1	0
Dean, Aaron, St.C.*	4	0	1.000	2.34	17	8	0	0	6	1	61.2	50	243	18	16	3	1	1	5	13	1	68	7	2
Kennedy, Joe, H.V.*	6	5	.545	2.65	16	16	1	1	0	0	95.0	78	376	33	28	2	1	1	4	26	0	101	7	1
Pineda, Jairo, Aub.	9	2	.818	2.88	15	15	1	0	0	0	84.1	70	360	35	27	5	0	3	8	31	0	67	3	2
Brooks, Frank, Bat.*	7	3	.700	2.91	16	12	1	1	2	0	77.1	64	312	26	25	2	0	1	2	33	0	58	2	6
Graman, Alex, S.I.*	6	3	.667	2.99	14	14	0	0	0	0	81.1	74	324	30	27	7	3	1	1	16	0	85	1	1
Hendricks, John, Pit.*	5	4	.556	3.04	15	14	0	0	0	0	80.0	78	340	38	27	4	4	2	3	19	0	64	2	1
Walling, Dave, S.I.	8	2	.800	3.14	14	14	0	0	0	0	80.1	76	331	31	28	3	1	2	2	18	1	82	1	3
Queen, Mike, Pit.*	5	3	.625	3.26	15	15	0	0	0	0	77.1	68	322	33	28	5	0	4	5	24	0	69	3	3
Chipperfield, Calvin, One.	4	4	.500	3.28	15	15	0	0	0	0	79.2	55	332	32	29	5	2	4	5	33	0	83	9	0

Pitcher, Team	W	L	Pct.	ERA	G	GS	CG	ShO	GF	Sv.	IP	H	TBF	R	ER	HR	SH	SF	HB	BB	IBB	SO	WP	Bk.
Weslowski, Robert, Pit.	4	4	.500	3.33	14	14	0	0	0	0	83.2	79	344	35	31	2	1	2	5	22	1	62	1	0
Claussen, Brandon, S.I.*	6	4	.600	3.38	12	12	1	0	0	0	72.0	70	295	30	27	4	3	0	3	12	2	89	4	4
Glaser, Eric, Low.	4	5	.444	3.43	14	14	0	0	0	0	78.2	65	324	37	30	7	2	1	2	26	0	82	1	0
Rowe, Casey, One.	3	4	.429	3.43	15	15	1	1	0	0	76.0	76	330	42	29	6	2	3	1	30	0	50	5	9

DEPARTMENTAL LEADERS: W—Pineda, 9; L—Orloski, 9; Pct.—Pineda, .818; G—Watson, Peck, 31 each; GS—Kennedy, 16; CG—Moser, 3; ShO—Pautz, 2; GF—Watson, Ortiz, 27 each; Sv.—Watson, 19; IP—Kennedy, 95.0; H—Encarnacion, 102; TBF—Madson, 383; R—Riccobono, 63; ER—Markwell, 50; HR—Ward, Chisnall, Cowie, Curtis, 10 each; SH—Pruett, Rivera, 6 each; SF—Wilson, Vinton, 8 each; HB—Riccobono, Rojas, 43 each; BB—Rojas, Madson, 43 each; IBB—Rivera, Harris, Seale, 3 each; SO—Kennedy, 101; WP—Thomas, 16; BK—Rowe, 9.

ALL PITCHERS

*Lefthanded pitcher.

Pitcher, Team	W	L	Pct.	ERA	G	GS	CG	ShO	GF	Sv.	IP	H	TBF	R	ER	HR	SH	SF	HB	BB	IBB	SO	WP	Bk.
Abreu, Miguel, Uti.	1	0	1.000	6.45	15	0	0	0	6	0	22.1	23	102	16	16	7	0	1	1	17	0	12	3	0
Albin, Scott, Ver.	4	2	.667	2.62	26	0	0	0	16	6	55.0	50	226	22	16	3	0	1	1	11	1	57	3	0
Alcala, Jason, Wil.	0	0	.000	4.38	6	0	0	0	4	0	12.1	11	56	7	6	1	0	0	2	6	0	11	0	0
Alston, Travis, Bat.	1	0	1.000	4.22	15	3	0	0	3	0	32.0	35	149	19	15	1	0	3	1	17	0	29	6	0
Andersen, Derek, H.V.*	2	3	.400	2.60	20	5	0	0	5	0	55.1	46	220	19	16	0	2	1	2	14	0	56	2	2
Anderson, Travis, Aub.	1	5	.167	5.22	9	8	0	0	0	0	39.2	42	175	31	23	2	0	2	3	17	0	29	5	0
Andujar, Jesse, Ver.	0	0	.000	18.69	5	0	0	0	1	0	4.1	2	31	11	9	0	0	1	4	10	0	2	2	0
Baginski, Jr., Thomas, One.*...	1	1	.500	4.50	3	0	0	0	2	1	6.0	8	29	4	3	0	1	1	0	4	0	6	0	0
Bailie, Matt, Bat.	2	2	.500	4.15	10	0	0	0	8	3	17.1	15	72	8	8	1	1	0	2	4	1	23	4	0
Baker, Christopher, St.C.	2	4	.333	6.20	12	10	0	0	0	0	49.1	61	221	37	34	6	1	0	1	14	1	55	7	2
Baldassano, Joseph, Ver.	0	1	.000	6.75	6	0	0	0	4	0	8.0	9	45	7	6	0	0	0	2	9	0	11	4	1
Barnett, Aaron, One.*	5	0	1.000	5.05	23	0	0	0	6	0	35.2	35	161	21	20	2	3	1	0	22	1	35	5	0
Barrett, Scott, Aub.*	0	0	.000	3.18	5	2	0	0	0	0	11.1	8	49	5	4	0	0	2	0	6	0	13	1	1
Bazan, Juan, Wil.	4	3	.571	3.02	8	8	1	0	0	0	47.2	37	191	17	16	4	0	2	1	16	0	33	2	0
Behn, Brendan, Pit.*	2	2	.500	3.15	15	1	0	0	10	1	40.0	39	172	18	14	3	3	0	2	11	1	39	2	0
Bess, Stephen, One.	0	0	.000	1.06	7	1	0	0	2	2	17.0	9	67	2	2	1	1	0	0	7	2	23	1	0
Biddlestone, Jason, Wil.	0	1	.000	9.00	1	1	0	0	0	0	5.0	7	26	6	5	0	0	1	0	3	0	2	0	0
Blitstein, Jeffrey, Aub.	4	5	.444	4.31	17	5	0	0	6	1	54.1	58	234	33	26	4	2	2	4	9	0	29	2	2
Bluma, Marc, St.C.	3	4	.429	5.92	24	0	0	0	23	13	24.1	22	106	16	16	3	1	0	1	7	1	32	2	0
Bonner, Luke, M.V.	4	3	.571	4.74	19	1	0	0	5	0	38.0	46	170	20	20	4	2	1	4	8	0	37	2	1
Bost, Ronald, St.C.*	0	0	.000	7.36	4	0	0	0	1	0	3.2	2	16	3	3	1	0	0	0	3	0	2	0	0
Bottenfield, Jason, Low.	1	2	.333	5.70	23	0	0	0	2	0	36.1	36	166	29	23	3	3	2	2	17	0	24	2	3
Bowe, Brandon, Uti.	2	0	1.000	2.92	6	0	0	0	1	0	12.1	14	54	6	4	0	0	0	0	2	0	24	1	0
Brookman, Ryan, Bat.	1	0	1.000	0.46	14	0	0	0	5	1	19.2	17	83	5	1	0	0	2	0	7	2	13	3	1
Brooks, Frank, Bat.*	7	3	.700	2.91	16	12	1	1	2	0	77.1	64	312	26	25	2	0	1	2	33	0	58	2	6
Brown, Craig, M.V.*	1	1	.500	6.14	18	0	0	0	7	1	29.1	34	136	20	20	0	1	1	2	15	0	33	4	1
Brown,, Stephen, Aub.	3	2	.600	5.30	18	7	0	0	4	1	52.2	57	243	40	31	4	0	3	4	21	1	43	5	0
Burke, Erick, One.*	1	1	.500	8.82	15	0	0	0	6	0	16.1	28	107	26	16	2	2	3	3	25	0	15	8	2
Butler, Mark, N.J.	2	0	1.000	7.32	18	0	0	0	5	0	19.2	22	111	18	16	1	0	0	9	22	0	8	3	0
Byrd, Mike, M.V.	2	0	1.000	2.70	9	0	0	0	2	1	20.0	17	89	12	6	0	0	0	1	10	0	23	1	0
Byron, Terence, Uti.	3	0	1.000	1.24	6	6	1	1	0	0	29.0	17	110	7	4	0	0	0	3	7	0	31	2	2
Calvo, Jose, Aub.	0	2	.000	5.14	5	0	0	0	1	1	7.0	9	36	9	4	0	0	1	1	4	0	5	2	0
Caple, Chance, N.J.	0	4	.000	4.38	7	7	0	0	0	0	37.0	35	164	24	18	4	0	1	2	18	0	36	2	1
Carlson, Jeff, S.I.	0	0	.000	2.70	6	0	0	0	3	0	6.2	2	29	2	2	0	0	0	2	3	0	6	2	0
Carpenter, Chris, St.C.	0	0	.000	4.50	1	1	0	0	0	0	4.0	5	18	2	2	0	0	0	0	1	0	6	1	0
Carrasco, Danny, Wil.	4	2	.667	2.96	18	4	0	0	6	0	51.2	43	212	20	17	2	1	3	3	23	0	49	7	4
Chipperfield, Calvin, One.	4	4	.500	3.28	15	15	0	0	0	0	79.2	55	332	32	29	5	2	4	5	33	0	83	9	0
Chisnall, Wesley, Ver.	2	5	.286	8.64	9	9	0	0	0	0	41.2	57	214	57	40	10	3	2	10	20	0	26	5	1
Classen, Ender, Wil.	0	0	.000	3.12	3	1	0	0	0	0	8.2	9	37	3	3	0	0	0	3	2	0	5	0	1
Claussen, Brandon, S.I.*	6	4	.600	3.38	12	12	1	0	0	0	72.0	70	295	30	27	4	3	0	3	12	2	89	4	4
Collins, Patrick, Ver.	2	4	.333	3.48	12	11	0	0	0	0	54.1	57	243	35	21	3	0	3	6	21	0	39	5	1
Colon, Roman, Jam.	7	5	.583	4.54	15	15	1	0	0	0	77.1	77	329	48	39	4	1	3	2	25	0	61	7	2
Cook, Brent, N.J.	5	1	.833	2.84	9	8	0	0	0	0	44.1	42	189	19	14	2	0	0	1	16	0	42	5	2
Correa, Cristobal, N.J.	3	3	.500	2.94	9	9	0	0	0	0	52.0	41	217	20	17	5	0	2	1	26	0	59	3	1
Cowie, Stephen, M.V.	2	5	.286	4.67	12	10	0	0	0	0	61.2	66	262	38	32	10	2	1	5	7	0	83	2	1
Cox, Brian, Jam.	1	1	.500	4.82	17	1	0	0	5	1	28.0	23	128	17	15	1	0	1	2	18	0	29	6	0
Crawford, Chris, H.V.	0	0	.000	0.00	1	0	0	0	0	0	1.0	0	4	0	0	0	0	1	0	1	0	2	2	0
Crumpton, Chuck, Ver.	1	2	.333	1.93	19	0	0	0	13	5	23.1	24	102	11	5	0	1	1	3	6	0	24	2	1
Cummings, Jeremy, N.J.	6	6	.500	3.60	14	14	1	0	0	0	85.0	88	341	42	34	5	3	0	5	7	0	62	4	4
Curtis, Daniel, Jam.	5	6	.455	4.58	15	15	1	1	0	0	74.2	74	323	41	38	10	1	1	6	24	0	61	7	1
Dagley, Corey, Bat.	5	5	.500	4.27	15	12	0	0	1	0	65.1	77	287	35	31	1	0	4	6	19	0	44	5	1
Dailey, Matt, H.V.*	0	1	.000	7.08	14	0	0	0	3	0	20.1	27	100	19	16	3	0	0	1	12	0	17	2	1
Dansby, Justin, Jam.	1	4	.200	6.57	24	0	0	0	13	4	38.1	45	187	29	28	3	0	2	4	24	0	43	5	1
Dean, Aaron, St.C.*	4	0	1.000	2.34	17	8	0	0	6	1	61.2	50	243	18	16	3	1	1	5	13	1	68	7	2
DeLaCruz, Andres, S.I.	0	2	.000	13.50	5	0	0	0	5	2	4.0	7	21	6	6	0	0	0	1	2	0	3	2	0
Denney, Kyle, M.V.	1	0	1.000	1.80	1	1	0	0	0	0	5.0	5	16	1	1	1	0	0	0	0	0	5	0	0
Detwiler, James, St.C.*	2	4	.333	3.27	14	6	0	0	3	0	44.0	45	199	23	16	3	0	0	1	25	0	45	2	4
Dimma, Douglas, St.C.*	3	1	.750	3.78	17	2	0	0	5	1	47.2	48	214	29	20	1	1	0	3	28	1	42	4	2
Dinkel, Aaron, N.J.	0	0	.000	9.58	13	0	0	0	5	0	10.1	16	63	13	11	0	0	0	0	15	0	6	3	0
Dorn, Grant, Ver.	3	3	.500	3.15	23	1	0	0	8	3	54.1	55	234	23	19	4	2	1	2	19	0	54	5	0
Dreier, Tom, St.C.	1	0	1.000	2.53	4	0	0	0	0	0	10.2	6	46	3	3	0	0	0	0	9	0	15	1	0
Drese, Ryan, M.V.	0	2	.000	2.65	5	5	0	0	0	0	17.0	8	66	6	5	1	0	2	1	7	0	26	0	1
Eavenson, Clay, S.I.	0	0	.000	6.75	1	0	0	0	1	0	1.1	2	6	1	1	0	0	0	1	0	0	0	1	0
Encarnacion, Orlando, Pit.	3	6	.333	4.81	15	15	0	0	0	0	86.0	102	365	51	46	6	3	4	4	13	0	61	2	1
Escobar, Ruben, M.V.	2	0	1.000	3.67	17	0	0	0	8	1	41.2	47	175	20	17	5	4	2	0	5	0	22	2	0
Espina, Rendy, Bat.*	0	1	.000	36.00	1	0	0	0	0	0	1.0	5	9	4	4	1	0	0	0	1	0	1	0	0
Everett, Matt, M.V.	0	0	.000	4.50	3	0	0	0	1	0	4.0	4	15	2	2	0	1	0	0	1	0	5	0	0
Fahs, Paul, N.J.	1	2	.333	3.38	30	0	0	0	15	7	34.2	25	149	17	13	1	0	3	4	19	1	21	6	0
Faigin, Jason, S.I.	1	1	.500	3.18	18	0	0	0	9	1	22.2	22	96	9	8	1	1	0	2	5	0	27	0	1
Fereira, Ramon, Aub.	2	4	.333	5.33	21	3	0	0	7	1	49.0	42	235	41	29	7	2	1	8	28	0	49	8	1
Ferguson, Tony, Aub.	0	0	.000	1.29	3	0	0	0	2	1	7.0	3	26	1	1	0	0	0	1	1	0	8	1	0

Pitcher, Team	W	L	Pct.	ERA	G	GS	CG	ShO	GF	Sv.	IP	H	TBF	R	ER	HR	SH	SF	HB	BB	IBB	SO	WP	Bk.
Finnegan, Mike, Ver.	1	1	.500	5.74	14	0	0	0	3	0	26.2	38	128	18	17	1	0	1	0	18	0	17	0	1
Fossum, Casey, Low.*	0	1	.000	1.26	5	5	0	0	0	0	14.1	6	56	2	2	1	0	2	5	0	16	0	4
Franco, Jose, S.I.	3	3	.500	2.83	30	0	0	0	18	5	41.1	29	171	14	13	1	3	1	1	14	1	58	3	1
Fraser, Joe, Ver.	0	1	.000	24.75	4	0	0	0	0	0	4.0	9	31	14	11	0	0	1	3	7	0	2	4	0
Frasor, Jason, One.	3	3	.500	1.69	12	11	0	0	0	0	58.2	36	229	16	11	3	0	1	1	22	0	69	3	2
Frendling, Neal, H.V.	3	1	.750	3.10	9	9	0	0	0	0	49.1	39	195	21	17	2	0	3	4	10	0	50	3	0
Fry, Justin, Bat.	4	0	1.000	1.35	25	0	0	0	20	6	33.1	18	127	5	5	1	0	0	2	10	2	59	6	1
Gallo, Michael, Aub.*	1	0	1.000	1.23	3	3	0	0	0	0	14.2	13	63	4	2	0	0	0	0	7	0	11	0	0
Gamble, Jerome, Low.	1	0	1.000	1.75	5	5	0	0	0	0	25.2	18	101	7	5	1	0	0	9	0	37	0	0
Garcia, Ramon, Low.	0	0	.000	3.60	5	0	0	0	5	2	5.0	5	22	2	2	0	0	2	0	2	0	5	1	1
Garcia, Rosman, S.I.	2	6	.250	4.26	18	10	0	0	1	1	69.2	86	310	40	33	3	3	3	4	14	2	40	4	1
Gargano, Mike, N.J.	1	4	.200	5.69	21	7	0	0	0	0	49.0	57	233	34	31	3	1	2	8	27	0	20	6	0
Garvin, Robert, Uti.	3	5	.375	3.95	23	3	0	0	0	0	54.2	58	224	29	24	4	1	2	0	8	0	39	2	0
Gawer, Matt, Jam.*	2	1	.667	3.30	21	0	0	0	13	6	30.0	24	128	12	11	1	0	2	2	18	0	44	4	0
George, Christopher, Aub.	2	1	.667	1.48	21	0	0	0	15	2	30.1	28	129	9	5	1	0	1	3	9	0	41	3	0
Getz, Cody, H.V.*	5	1	.833	2.85	11	11	0	0	0	0	60.0	56	247	22	19	4	2	0	7	17	0	69	3	0
Giese, Daniel, Low.	3	0	1.000	1.83	18	0	0	0	8	2	34.1	17	131	8	7	2	1	1	2	10	1	27	2	0
Glaser, Eric, Low.	4	5	.444	3.43	14	14	0	0	0	0	78.2	65	324	37	30	7	2	1	2	26	0	82	1	0
Glaser, Scott, Wil.*	0	1	.000	4.50	3	0	0	0	2	0	4.0	5	18	2	2	0	0	0	1	0	6	0	0
Good, Eric, Ver.*	5	5	.500	5.79	15	15	0	0	0	0	70.0	77	319	49	45	3	1	2	8	30	0	59	3	2
Gordon, Kevin, Uti.	1	0	1.000	6.75	1	0	0	0	0	0	1.1	3	7	1	1	0	0	0	0	1	0	1	0	0
Gorman, Pat, Pit.	3	2	.600	3.21	19	0	0	0	9	1	33.2	30	152	17	12	3	4	1	2	20	1	40	5	0
Gourlay, Matt, St.C.	1	1	.500	5.21	14	0	0	0	2	0	19.0	14	95	17	11	4	0	1	4	18	0	24	4	0
Grace, Bryan, S.I.	0	4	.000	5.68	8	1	0	0	3	0	12.2	13	63	14	8	2	0	2	1	9	0	11	3	2
Gracesqui, Franklyn, St.C.*	2	3	.400	5.05	15	10	0	0	1	1	46.1	44	220	30	26	4	0	2	3	41	0	45	6	2
Graman, Alex, S.I.*	6	3	.667	2.99	14	14	0	0	0	0	81.1	74	324	30	27	7	3	1	1	16	0	85	1	1
Hancock, Rodney, Wil.*	1	2	.333	1.69	8	4	0	0	4	0	32.0	27	136	13	6	0	1	1	2	13	1	35	3	1
Harris, Silas, Ver.*	0	5	.000	7.20	23	1	0	0	7	0	30.0	32	158	24	24	3	1	2	5	30	3	32	6	0
Hawkins, Barry, Pit.	1	2	.333	3.86	16	0	0	0	4	0	37.1	39	159	20	16	1	1	1	4	12	0	24	5	0
Hendricks, John, Pit.*	5	4	.556	3.04	15	14	0	0	0	0	80.0	78	340	38	27	4	4	2	3	19	0	64	2	1
Henriquez, Hector, Uti.*	1	1	.500	6.19	12	1	0	0	1	0	16.0	16	74	12	11	2	0	1	1	13	0	12	2	1
Hickman, Benjaman, Uti.	3	2	.600	2.13	24	0	0	0	19	7	38.0	36	149	12	9	1	4	0	1	4	0	38	0	1
Hoover, Steven, Aub.	0	0	.000	9.00	1	0	0	0	1	0	1.0	1	5	1	1	0	0	0	0	0	0	0	0	0
Hubbel, Travis, St.C.	0	0	.000	1.80	5	3	0	0	2	1	20.0	16	83	5	4	1	0	0	1	7	0	19	0	0
Humrich, Christopher, Ver.	1	1	.500	3.97	22	0	0	0	7	0	45.1	45	199	29	20	2	3	0	2	20	0	52	3	0
Hutchinson, Brian, Jam.*	1	2	.333	6.35	14	0	0	0	4	0	22.2	24	103	19	16	3	1	1	5	12	0	22	5	0
Jackson, Brian, M.V.	6	4	.600	3.44	14	13	0	0	0	0	70.2	75	321	38	27	1	2	4	4	30	0	51	2	2
Jamison, Ryan, Aub.	5	3	.625	4.11	15	15	0	0	0	0	87.2	83	374	45	40	7	1	3	6	36	0	83	5	4
Janke, Cheyenne, N.J.	2	5	.286	3.67	15	14	0	0	0	0	83.1	85	356	40	34	8	2	1	1	20	0	63	8	2
Johnston, Michael, Wil.*	3	2	.600	4.25	14	2	0	0	3	2	42.1	46	193	26	20	5	0	3	0	18	0	33	3	1
Johnston, Rikki, One.*	1	6	.143	4.05	12	12	1	0	0	0	60.0	57	256	33	27	2	1	4	2	30	0	36	7	0
Joseph, Jake, Pit.	3	2	.600	2.91	11	6	0	0	1	1	43.1	35	189	19	14	1	0	1	0	27	0	26	7	1
Kalita, Tim, One.*	0	0	.000	0.00	3	3	0	0	0	0	12.1	3	44	1	0	0	0	0	5	0	15	1	0
Kearney, Ryan, M.V.	3	0	1.000	1.44	11	2	0	0	4	0	25.0	23	100	4	4	0	0	0	1	5	0	26	1	0
Keelin, Chris, Bat.	1	0	1.000	5.06	14	0	0	0	5	0	21.1	19	103	18	12	2	0	2	5	16	0	27	3	1
Kelley, Chris, M.V.	3	4	.429	5.63	13	11	0	0	0	0	48.0	44	228	40	30	2	1	3	4	34	0	54	9	0
Kennedy, Joe, H.V.*	6	5	.545	2.65	16	16	1	1	0	0	95.0	78	376	33	28	2	1	1	4	26	0	101	7	1
Kent, Nathan, Jam.	3	3	.500	4.13	14	11	0	0	1	1	52.1	57	225	31	24	2	0	0	0	11	0	49	1	0
Klein, Cody, S.I.*	0	0	.000	3.57	16	0	0	0	4	0	22.2	17	89	9	9	2	0	1	0	6	0	23	5	0
Klepacki, Edward, Ver.	5	4	.556	4.73	14	14	1	0	0	0	78.0	92	347	54	41	1	0	4	5	18	1	40	10	2
Knowles, Michael, S.I.	0	0	.000	14.21	3	2	0	0	0	0	6.1	15	37	12	10	0	0	1	0	4	0	5	2	1
Kremer, John, S.I.	3	0	1.000	2.84	23	0	0	0	4	0	38.0	31	162	14	12	5	1	0	0	17	1	59	5	0
Lane, Jason, Aub.*	0	0	.000	0.00	1	0	0	0	0	0	1.0	0	3	0	0	0	0	0	0	0	0	1	0	0
Langen, Brian, N.J.*	1	3	.250	4.60	26	0	0	0	6	0	29.1	26	138	20	15	2	2	0	3	21	2	24	4	0
Langston, David, S.I.	0	0	.000	20.25	2	0	0	0	0	0	1.1	3	10	3	3	0	0	0	3	0	1	0	0
Laroche, Jeff, Uti.*	3	3	.500	8.03	26	0	0	0	9	1	37.0	62	187	37	33	5	1	2	5	15	0	29	3	0
Law, Keith, One.	2	2	.500	3.40	22	1	0	0	10	2	45.0	35	199	23	17	5	1	1	5	28	0	32	10	0
Lawson, Jarrod, Bat.	0	4	.000	8.31	4	4	0	0	0	0	17.1	27	90	19	16	2	2	2	1	12	0	11	9	0
Layfield, Scotty, N.J.	2	2	.500	3.15	23	3	0	0	15	8	34.1	27	150	16	12	3	1	1	2	21	1	26	4	0
Layne, Roger, M.V.	0	0	.000	5.40	4	0	0	0	1	0	6.2	8	35	4	4	1	0	1	0	7	0	9	0	0
Leach, Bryan, Low.	5	2	.714	3.57	13	4	0	0	1	0	45.1	41	194	23	18	4	0	1	0	18	0	52	2	0
Ledden, Ryan, H.V.	3	1	.750	6.53	20	0	0	0	4	0	30.1	33	148	23	22	1	0	1	4	27	0	16	10	3
Ledesma, Phil, Low.	0	0	.000	8.10	3	0	0	0	2	0	3.1	6	20	3	3	0	0	1	1	5	0	3	1	0
Lee, Andy, Low.*	2	1	.667	3.51	26	1	0	0	6	0	48.2	52	216	22	19	7	1	3	3	16	0	58	6	3
Lee, Garrett, Jam.	4	3	.571	4.07	13	13	1	0	0	0	77.1	79	323	39	35	8	1	5	6	16	0	47	0	2
Leek, Randy, One.*	6	3	.667	1.56	21	3	1	0	4	1	63.1	58	249	16	11	0	1	1	2	9	1	66	2	0
Lewis, Peyton, St.C.	2	1	.667	1.31	15	1	0	0	3	2	41.1	26	164	8	6	2	1	2	2	15	0	54	2	1
Lopez, Gustavo, Uti.	4	2	.667	3.53	13	13	0	0	0	0	63.2	59	261	28	25	5	0	1	1	17	0	46	5	0
Lowe, Matt, Pit.	3	5	.375	4.57	16	11	0	0	4	2	69.0	67	309	42	35	3	3	2	7	37	0	33	11	1
Lowery, Phil, Uti.*	1	0	1.000	6.00	2	0	0	0	0	0	6.0	7	26	4	4	1	0	0	1	1	0	5	0	0
Macias, Jose, M.V.	1	0	1.000	1.80	1	1	0	0	0	0	5.0	2	19	1	1	0	0	1	0	2	0	1	0	0
Madson, Ryan, Bat.	5	5	.500	4.72	15	15	0	0	0	0	87.2	80	383	51	46	5	2	4	10	43	0	75	10	0
Maleski, Eric, M.V.	4	1	.800	4.82	22	0	0	0	17	8	37.1	42	158	21	20	3	2	0	2	6	0	32	3	0
Manning, Mike, M.V.	2	1	.667	2.67	20	0	0	0	14	3	33.2	25	138	11	10	0	0	1	1	12	0	34	7	0
Marin, Willy, H.V.	2	3	.400	3.34	23	1	0	0	11	2	56.2	43	237	23	21	2	2	1	9	13	1	47	1	0
Marini, Anthony, M.V.*	5	3	.625	3.60	13	11	0	0	1	0	65.0	64	281	31	26	4	1	4	3	25	1	56	4	3
Markwell, Diegomar, St.C.*	3	4	.429	7.58	14	13	0	0	0	0	59.1	72	295	55	50	8	1	1	4	38	0	54	6	0
Marrero, Darwin, Ver.	3	3	.500	5.28	14	14	0	0	0	0	76.2	86	343	53	45	7	4	3	5	27	0	74	5	2
Martinez, Anastacio, Low.	3	0	.000	3.68	11	11	0	0	0	0	51.1	61	234	36	21	4	0	4	18	0	43	9	2
Martinez, Ramon, Low.	0	0	.000	0.00	1	0	0	0	0	0	2.0	0	7	0	0	0	0	0	0	0	0	1	0	0
Marx, Tommy, One.*	2	1	.667	3.22	6	4	0	0	0	0	22.1	20	98	14	8	2	0	1	0	13	0	19	1	0
Matew, Francisco, N.J.	1	1	.500	3.58	19	0	0	0	1	0	32.2	34	135	17	13	0	0	2	1	8	0	28	1	0
Mattson, John, Pit.	1	3	.250	9.00	11	0	0	0	3	0	18.0	32	95	20	18	1	1	1	1	10	0	20	5	0
McCarter, Jason, Pit.	4	0	1.000	3.34	21	0	0	0	14	2	35.0	33	160	17	13	1	0	1	2	25	0	36	5	0
McClain, Jeremy, Low.	3	6	.333	5.40	16	7	0	0	0	0	51.2	59	230	41	31	4	1	3	2	17	1	53	4	3

Pitcher, Team	W	L	Pct.	ERA	G	GS	CG	ShO	GF	Sv.	IP	H	TBF	R	ER	HR	SH	SF	HB	BB	IBB	SO	WP	Bk.
McClendon, Matthew, Jam.	1	1	.500	3.91	7	7	0	0	0	0	23.0	18	94	11	10	2	0	0	1	11	0	24	2	0
McCormick, Terry, H.V.*	3	1	.750	3.94	9	6	0	0	0	0	29.2	22	134	15	13	2	2	0	6	15	0	23	3	0
McDonald, Corey, One.*	3	3	.500	4.67	19	0	0	0	8	0	34.2	34	153	18	18	5	1	4	0	23	0	30	8	0
McKoin, Heath, H.V.*	2	7	.222	6.28	15	14	0	0	0	0	57.1	67	272	52	40	4	0	3	6	33	0	51	6	0
Minix, Travis, H.V.	2	2	.500	1.44	27	0	0	0	19	7	56.1	36	221	11	9	2	5	2	2	12	2	68	3	0
Montilla, Felix, Wil.	1	2	.333	3.99	23	0	0	0	21	10	29.1	29	126	14	13	3	0	1	1	11	0	29	0	2
Moore, Bryan, Uti.	2	1	.667	1.54	26	0	0	0	23	9	35.0	29	146	13	6	1	0	0	4	5	1	36	2	0
Morse, Bryan, Uti.*	3	5	.375	3.45	14	14	0	0	0	0	78.1	73	324	41	30	5	2	1	3	19	0	74	6	1
Moser, Todd, Uti.*	8	2	.800	1.53	14	14	3	1	0	0	88.0	63	343	20	15	2	1	1	2	24	0	86	4	2
Murray, Steve, St.C.*	1	4	.200	5.68	12	8	0	0	2	1	57.0	68	252	46	36	7	0	4	1	16	0	46	5	0
Nannini, Mike, Aub.	5	3	.625	1.90	11	11	2	1	0	0	75.2	55	295	19	16	2	3	3	4	17	0	86	1	0
Needle, Chad, St.C.	1	2	.333	5.85	15	0	0	0	7	0	20.0	18	86	13	13	5	1	1	2	5	0	20	0	0
Norris, Shon, Low.	4	4	.500	5.05	27	0	0	0	25	3	41.0	41	179	25	23	2	2	2	2	13	0	29	7	0
Novits, Carey, M.V.*	2	4	.333	5.45	12	3	0	0	3	1	34.2	46	166	30	21	5	2	2	1	19	0	33	4	0
Nunley, Robert, St.C.	0	0	.000	3.12	7	0	0	0	3	0	8.2	8	35	3	3	1	0	1	1	2	0	10	0	1
Oase, Ryan, H.V.	0	0	.000	6.75	1	0	0	0	0	0	1.1	3	8	1	1	0	0	0	0	1	0	1	0	0
Oliver, Scott, S.I.	0	1	.000	9.95	2	2	0	0	0	0	6.1	9	33	9	7	1	0	0	0	4	0	4	2	1
Orloski, Joe, St.C.	3	9	.250	4.59	17	7	0	0	3	1	64.2	80	290	48	33	9	0	1	1	22	0	57	7	0
Ortiz, John, Aub.*	1	2	.333	4.66	23	0	0	0	8	0	36.2	39	168	25	19	1	2	1	4	22	0	28	1	0
Ortiz, Jose, H.V.	4	3	.571	1.74	29	0	0	0	27	9	46.2	31	183	14	9	0	2	0	3	14	0	35	1	1
Outlaw, Mark, Bat.*	1	1	.500	1.62	23	0	0	0	10	4	33.1	26	134	10	6	1	2	3	0	9	2	45	5	0
Parra, Christian, Jam.	1	2	.333	3.10	9	9	0	0	0	0	49.1	46	207	21	17	2	0	0	1	19	0	62	1	1
Pautz, Brad, Bat.	8	4	.667	4.06	13	13	2	2	0	0	77.2	77	326	37	35	4	2	1	1	30	1	58	4	1
Pearce, Josh, N.J.	3	7	.300	4.98	14	14	1	1	0	0	77.2	78	336	45	43	8	2	6	5	20	0	78	14	1
Peck, Brandon, N.J.*	1	4	.200	4.04	31	0	0	0	16	0	35.2	37	147	17	16	3	4	0	0	11	0	29	0	1
Peguero, Radhame, H.V.	2	1	.667	2.42	4	4	0	0	0	0	26.0	13	96	8	7	0	0	0	3	11	0	24	2	0
Pierce, Tony, Jam.	0	1	.000	2.70	17	0	0	0	14	8	26.2	14	107	9	8	0	0	1	2	12	0	44	1	0
Pilato, Chris, Bat.	0	0	.000	4.50	11	0	0	0	5	0	14.0	15	69	8	7	0	3	0	3	9	1	18	7	1
Pineda, Jairo, Aub.	9	2	.818	2.88	15	15	1	0	0	0	84.1	70	360	35	27	5	0	3	8	31	0	67	3	2
Prater, Andy, Wil.	2	4	.333	6.10	10	10	1	0	0	0	38.1	45	183	36	26	8	0	3	6	18	0	21	2	0
Pruett, Jason, H.V.*	4	2	.667	1.99	25	0	0	0	5	1	40.2	32	166	13	9	1	6	1	1	8	0	29	1	1
Queen, Mike, Pit.*	5	3	.625	3.26	15	15	0	0	0	0	77.1	68	322	33	28	5	0	4	5	24	0	69	3	3
Reece, Dana, St.C.*	1	0	1.000	2.70	5	0	0	0	3	0	6.2	4	27	2	2	1	0	0	1	3	0	7	0	0
Reid, Justin, Wil.	2	6	.250	4.62	16	11	0	0	4	1	62.1	71	277	41	32	4	0	3	3	23	0	68	0	4
Renwick, Tyler, St.C.	2	4	.333	5.31	16	5	0	0	6	0	39.0	35	182	28	23	2	1	2	1	33	0	32	10	0
Riccobono, Rick, Low.	4	6	.400	5.24	15	14	0	0	0	0	77.1	93	368	63	45	4	3	5	11	30	0	54	9	0
Ridenour, Ryan, S.I.*	0	0	.000	4.50	2	0	0	0	1	0	2.0	2	8	1	1	0	0	0	0	0	0	4	1	0
Riggins, Auntwan, St.C.	0	0	.000	0.00	1	0	0	0	1	0	1.0	2	5	0	0	0	0	0	0	0	0	1	0	1
Rivera, Homero, One.*	5	2	.714	2.72	23	0	0	0	7	0	49.2	44	218	19	15	3	6	4	4	22	3	47	5	1
Roberts, Phil, M.V.	0	0	.000	6.23	3	0	0	0	1	0	4.1	6	25	5	3	0	0	0	1	4	0	4	0	0
Robertson, Nathan, Uti.*	2	0	1.000	2.77	5	5	0	0	0	0	26.0	22	101	9	8	0	1	2	0	8	0	26	0	0
Rodriguez, Anthony, S.I.	1	0	1.000	6.87	13	0	0	0	5	0	18.1	24	89	15	14	1	0	2	0	13	0	19	8	0
Rojas, Chris, Wil.	5	7	.417	4.87	15	15	1	1	0	0	81.1	72	374	57	44	4	1	3	11	43	0	85	10	1
Roller, Adam, Low.	4	5	.444	2.54	23	0	0	0	23	2	39.0	30	186	16	11	1	3	2	9	29	2	41	7	1
Roque, Darryll, Ver.	2	3	.400	4.63	12	7	0	0	0	0	44.2	44	191	27	23	4	1	3	9	12	0	37	1	0
Rosengren, Phil, M.V.	2	3	.400	5.07	11	9	0	0	1	0	49.2	40	215	30	28	4	0	1	1	24	0	41	3	0
Rowe, Casey, One.	3	4	.429	3.43	15	15	1	1	0	0	76.0	76	330	42	29	6	2	3	1	30	0	50	5	9
Rupp, Michael, Low.	1	5	.167	5.81	18	8	0	0	1	0	57.1	72	275	46	37	2	0	4	3	33	2	48	4	1
Sabathia, C.C., M.V.*	0	0	.000	1.83	6	6	0	0	0	0	19.2	9	77	5	4	0	0	2	0	12	0	27	0	0
Sabens, Mike, Wil.	1	1	.500	10.80	5	0	0	0	1	0	6.2	8	39	8	8	1	1	2	2	9	1	6	1	1
Sadler, Carl, M.V.*	0	1	.000	31.50	1	1	0	0	0	0	2.0	8	17	7	7	0	0	0	0	3	0	3	1	0
Saladin, Miguel, Aub.	1	4	.200	7.13	8	0	0	0	3	0	17.2	23	92	19	14	1	2	0	7	7	0	10	1	2
Samadani, Ali, Jam.	3	1	.750	5.36	22	0	0	0	5	1	40.1	41	178	28	24	6	0	3	0	17	0	37	6	1
Sansom, Trevor, N.J.	1	3	.250	7.71	20	0	0	0	7	0	23.1	34	121	28	20	3	1	1	1	16	2	18	4	0
Santana, Humberto, Pit.*	1	0	1.000	0.00	4	0	0	0	1	0	9.1	7	38	2	0	1	0	0	0	2	1	12	0	0
Satterfield, Jeremy, Jam.	2	2	.500	4.28	23	0	0	0	13	1	33.2	25	148	17	16	0	2	4	4	22	0	36	7	0
Satterfield, Troy, Wil.*	2	1	.667	1.70	17	0	0	0	5	0	37.0	33	150	11	7	1	3	0	1	11	2	28	0	0
Seale, Dustin, St.C.-Ver.*	2	2	.500	0.76	17	0	0	0	9	2	23.2	15	101	2	2	0	2	0	0	15	3	20	6	3
Sergent, Joe, Uti.*	0	0	.000	1.40	10	0	0	0	1	1	19.1	9	74	4	3	2	0	0	0	7	1	23	0	0
Serrano, Elio, Bat.	0	4	.000	4.12	19	3	0	0	2	1	39.1	38	176	22	18	3	0	2	3	20	1	29	2	0
Shields, Drew, Uti.	2	3	.400	8.51	13	2	0	0	3	0	24.1	30	126	28	23	2	3	0	6	17	1	33	5	0
Sirianni, Jay, M.V.*	2	0	1.000	2.70	3	2	1	1	0	0	13.1	15	56	6	4	1	1	0	0	4	0	16	0	0
Smith, Chad, Bat.	0	0	.000	10.80	3	0	0	0	0	0	5.0	9	28	8	6	1	0	0	0	1	0	8	3	0
Smuin, Shane, Uti.	1	3	.250	3.98	23	0	0	0	6	1	43.0	33	179	20	19	3	3	0	5	21	0	51	5	0
Solano, Alexander, Low.	1	2	.333	5.61	6	6	0	0	0	0	33.2	40	150	23	21	6	1	3	1	7	1	26	2	3
Southard, Lee, St.C.	0	0	.000	10.38	5	0	0	0	3	0	4.1	2	29	5	5	0	0	0	0	14	0	6	4	0
Spencer, Corey, Low.*	1	0	1.000	2.48	19	0	0	0	3	1	29.0	33	127	12	8	0	0	0	0	7	0	38	1	0
Spille, Ryan, St.C.*	1	0	1.000	0.00	1	1	0	0	0	0	5.0	2	17	0	0	0	0	0	1	0	0	5	0	1
Stine, Justin, St.C.*	2	0	1.000	1.08	2	1	0	0	0	0	8.1	5	29	1	1	1	0	0	0	1	0	4	0	0
Sullivan, Ted, M.V.	1	1	.500	6.57	13	0	0	0	9	4	12.1	14	57	9	9	2	0	1	3	1	0	13	0	0
Sunderman, Nick, M.V.*	0	0	.000	4.50	2	0	0	0	1	0	4.0	2	18	2	2	0	0	0	2	2	0	4	0	0
Swiatkiewicz, Chris, S.I.	0	0	.000	6.23	6	0	0	0	5	2	8.2	13	43	8	6	2	0	0	0	3	0	6	0	0
Terry, Mike, Pit.*	2	1	.667	5.34	18	0	0	0	11	1	32.0	33	142	19	19	1	3	2	4	14	0	24	0	0
Thomas, Gaige, Uti.	0	5	.000	5.40	13	11	0	0	1	1	40.0	41	193	34	24	4	1	2	8	30	0	32	16	0
Toriz, Steve, Ver.	2	2	.500	4.58	21	4	0	0	9	3	39.1	34	180	25	20	4	3	1	1	31	2	31	4	1
Truitt, Derrick, Jam.	2	3	.400	4.63	18	0	0	0	3	1	35.0	28	149	20	18	3	3	1	4	18	0	30	4	0
Tucker, Bradley, Bat.	0	1	.000	3.81	17	1	0	0	9	0	26.0	24	112	15	11	4	0	1	3	11	0	15	0	1
Valera, Nelson, H.V.	0	1	.000	16.88	2	1	0	0	0	0	2.2	4	16	5	5	1	0	1	1	2	0	3	0	0
Vanhekken, Andrew, One.*	4	2	.667	2.15	11	10	0	0	0	0	50.1	44	210	17	12	3	0	0	3	16	0	50	1	0
Vinton, Drew, Wil.	1	4	.200	4.16	17	7	1	0	5	0	62.2	58	283	43	29	1	1	8	7	33	0	49	11	4
Viole, Paul, Pit.	3	0	1.000	0.00	18	0	0	0	14	11	23.0	7	83	0	0	0	0	0	0	7	1	28	2	0
Wade, Travis, Aub.	1	1	.500	2.39	26	0	0	0	23	11	37.2	25	150	10	10	0	3	0	2	13	0	53	0	0
Wallace, Chris, S.I.	0	1	.000	4.02	14	0	0	0	11	8	15.2	9	70	7	7	0	2	2	0	13	0	12	3	0
Wallace, Justin, Wil.*	0	0	.000	5.40	19	0	0	0	8	2	31.2	35	143	22	19	2	0	4	2	16	1	23	1	2
Walling, Dave, S.I.	8	2	.800	3.14	14	14	0	0	0	0	80.1	76	331	31	28	3	1	2	2	18	1	82	1	3

Pitcher, Team	W	L	Pct.	ERA	G	GS	CG	ShO	GF	Sv.	IP	H	TBF	R	ER	HR	SH	SF	HB	BB	IBB	SO	WP	Bk.
Ward, Matt, Uti.*	2	1	.667	4.00	8	6	0	0	1	0	36.0	36	148	17	16	10	1	0	1	3	0	24	0	0
Watson, Gregory, One.	1	2	.333	3.21	31	0	0	0	27	19	33.2	23	150	18	12	2	2	0	9	17	2	33	4	0
Weslowski, Robert, Pit.	4	4	.500	3.33	14	14	0	0	0	0	83.2	79	344	35	31	2	1	2	5	22	1	62	1	0
Whiteley, Shad, S.I.	3	4	.429	4.96	12	12	0	0	0	0	61.2	69	279	39	34	1	1	3	2	26	0	71	9	0
Whitesides, Johnny, Aub.	1	0	1.000	2.51	6	0	0	0	2	0	14.1	13	66	12	4	2	3	1	0	8	0	13	0	0
Wilkerson, Byron, Aub.	3	3	.500	3.75	9	7	0	0	1	0	48.0	38	202	25	20	5	1	2	5	22	0	47	3	0
Williams, David, Wil.*	4	2	.667	2.56	7	7	1	1	0	0	45.2	33	180	17	13	2	0	0	2	11	0	47	0	0
Williamson, Brian, Pit.	1	1	.500	4.91	6	0	0	0	5	1	7.1	6	33	5	4	0	1	0	0	4	0	2	1	0
Willis, Jason, S.I.	1	2	.333	4.09	7	7	0	0	0	0	33.0	45	157	18	15	0	1	0	3	12	1	27	2	1
Willoughby, Justin, Jam.*	5	3	.625	5.29	19	5	0	0	2	0	47.2	55	222	35	28	5	2	1	2	16	1	49	8	0
Wilson, Mike, Bat.	5	3	.625	3.64	13	13	1	0	0	0	84.0	66	349	42	34	7	1	8	10	29	0	73	5	0
Witte, Lou, S.I.	5	2	.714	3.05	25	0	0	0	4	1	41.1	42	174	21	14	2	0	0	1	12	1	39	1	0
Wright, Barrett, H.V.	4	2	.667	3.70	10	9	0	0	1	1	58.1	55	250	29	24	1	3	1	7	24	0	40	5	1
Wright, Shane, Wil.	2	6	.250	2.81	17	6	2	0	6	1	57.2	53	253	29	18	3	2	4	9	19	0	38	4	1
Yates, Chad, N.J.	1	1	.500	3.71	12	0	0	0	4	1	17.0	9	69	7	7	3	1	0	0	10	0	20	1	0
Zipser, Mike, Bat.	2	1	.667	2.76	9	0	0	0	2	0	16.1	17	72	9	5	0	0	2	9	5	0	16	0	0

COMBINATION SHUTOUTS: **Auburn (4)**—Nannini-Ortiz, Nannini-George, Jamison-George, Pineda-Fereira. **Batavia (3)**—Dagley-Outlaw, Dagley-Fry, Pautz-Zipser-Outlaw. **Hudson Valley (7)**—McKoin-Minix-Ortiz, Kennedy-Minix, Peguero-Minix, Getz-Marin-Ortiz, Getz-Anderson-Ortiz, Frendling-Pruett, Frendling-Pruett. **Jamestown (3)**—McClendon-Hutchinson-Gawer, Lee-Willoughby, Curtis-Dansby. **Lowell (0)**—None. **Mahoning Valley (1)**—Jackson-Novits. **New Jersey (1)**—Cook-Peck-Gargano-Fahs. **Oneonta (4)**—Rowe-Barnett-Rivera-Burke, Chipperfield-Bess, Frasor-Watson, Marx-Baginski. **Pittsfield (6)**—Hendricks-Hawkins-Williamson, Queen-McCarter-Terry, Weslowski-Terry-McCarter, Hendricks-McCarter, Encarnacion-Viole, Queen-Lowe. **St. Catharines (6)**—Spille-Dimma, Stine-Hubbel, Detwiler-Dean, Dean-Lewis, Renwick-Orloski, Gracesqui-Gourlay-Reese-Bluma. **Staten Island (3)**—Graman-Swiatkiewicz, Willis-Garcia-Faigin, Whiteley-Witte-Franco. **Utica (4)**—Moser-Moore, Byron-Smuin-Moore, Morse-Henriquez, Byron-Smuin-Moore. **Vermont (1)**—Good-Dorn. **Williamsport (2)**—Bazan-Hancock, Hancock-Johnston.

NO-HIT GAMES: None.

PITCHERS WITH TWO OR MORE TEAMS

Pitcher, Team	W	L	Pct.	ERA	G	GS	CG	ShO	GF	Sv.	IP	H	TBF	R	ER	HR	SH	SF	HB	BB	IBB	SO	WP	Bk.
Seale, Dustin, St.C.*	0	1	.000	2.70	3	0	0	0	2	0	3.1	2	16	1	1	0	2	0	0	2	1	4	1	0
Seale, Dustin, Ver.*	2	1	.667	0.44	14	0	0	0	7	2	20.1	13	85	1	1	0	0	0	0	13	2	16	5	3

1999 FIELDING

TEAM

Team	Pct.	G	PO	A	E	TC	DP	TP	PB	Team	Pct.	G	PO	A	E	TC	DP	TP	PB
Hudson Valley	.967	76	2061	857	101	3019	66	0	9	Batavia	.960	76	2004	769	117	2890	63	0	14
Staten Island	.965	74	1942	740	96	2778	45	0	21	St. Catharines	.959	76	1948	699	112	2759	61	0	21
Utica	.965	75	2011	824	102	2937	74	0	31	Mahoning Valley	.957	76	1944	757	120	2821	58	0	14
Jamestown	.964	76	1969	753	101	2823	46	0	10	Williamsport	.955	76	1969	815	132	2916	69	0	11
Pittsfield	.963	76	2025	856	112	2993	75	0	24	Lowell	.954	76	2022	736	134	2892	53	0	18
Oneonta	.961	75	1982	751	110	2843	56	1	12	Vermont	.953	76	2028	771	138	2937	39	0	23
New Jersey	.961	76	1996	855	116	2967	65	0	16	Auburn	.946	76	2010	775	160	2945	49	0	8

INDIVIDUAL

FIRST BASEMEN

NOTE: All caps denotes fielding-percentage leader based on 38 games for catchers, 51 for all other non-pitchers and 61 innings for pitchers. *Throws lefthanded.

Player, Team	Pct.	G	PO	A	E	TC	DP
Alvarez, Antonio, Wil.	1.000	1	10	2	0	12	4
Armstrong, Christopher, Aub.	.975	5	39	0	1	40	3
Avila, Rob, Bat.	.909	2	10	0	1	11	0
Bailey, Travis, Wil.	.982	49	457	33	9	499	35
Bernhardt, Jossephang, St.C.	.973	6	35	1	1	37	2
Burke, Paul, Jam.	.994	17	149	7	1	157	7
Cotten, Jeremy, Wil.	.983	45	373	29	7	409	34
Dominguez, Luis, Aub.	1.000	1	1	0	0	1	0
Duarte, Justin, Bat.	.987	40	291	15	4	310	31
Dwyer, Mike, Low.*	.987	68	544	50	8	602	43
Eberly, Rodney, Bat.	.978	30	204	15	5	224	16
Ewan, Bry, Jam.	.970	28	218	7	7	232	12
Ewing, Byron, M.V.	1.000	9	85	4	0	89	4
Fuentes, Omar, S.I.	1.000	4	17	1	0	18	0
Gay, Curtis, M.V.*	.988	65	535	24	7	566	38
Geisbush, David, Jam.	1.000	1	3	0	0	3	0
Gregg, Neal, S.I.	.983	8	51	6	1	58	3
Grindell, Nate, M.V.	1.000	2	9	0	0	9	0
Grummitt, Dan, H.V.	.984	68	620	44	11	675	53
Holliday, Joshua, St.C.	.987	19	138	13	2	153	19
House, J.R., Wil.	.986	8	67	4	1	72	5
Jackson, Kevin, One.	.980	30	213	26	5	244	13
Jaworowski, Aaron, S.I.	.975	6	36	3	1	40	3
Landreth, Jason, Wil.	.974	24	173	17	5	195	15
Lane, Jason, Aub.*	.986	72	577	41	9	627	39
Leal, Jaeme, Jam.	.983	33	215	15	4	234	19
Leaumont, Jeff, S.I.*	.994	65	461	59	3	523	34
LEBRON, Francisco, Pit.	.998	60	538	40	1	579	56
Lebron, Hector, H.V.	.985	7	61	6	1	68	5
Lucca, Tony, Uti.*	.987	61	565	41	8	614	61
Ludvigsen, Marc, Pit.*	.857	1	6	0	1	7	0

Player, Team	Pct.	G	PO	A	E	TC	DP
Meadows, Mike, Pit.	.971	5	30	4	1	35	1
Minus, Stephen, Low.	.988	12	81	2	1	84	3
Morales, Victor, St.C.	.994	23	168	6	1	175	17
Muthig, Dean, Bat.	1.000	18	105	8	0	113	9
O'Neill, Daniel, Bat.*	1.000	1	1	0	0	1	0
Ortega, Jose, N.J.	.983	30	272	15	5	292	23
Postell, Matthew, Uti.	.993	15	127	9	1	137	10
Poulsen, Christopher, Jam.	.979	7	45	2	1	48	7
Reyes, Dadny, Uti.	.000	1	0	0	0	0	0
Rickon, Jim, M.V.	1.000	1	7	0	0	7	0
Riggins, Auntwan, St.C.	.987	25	145	6	2	153	12
Rivera, Luis J., Ver.	.875	2	7	0	1	8	1
Santos, Juan, St.C.	.969	15	88	7	3	98	6
Sassanella, Jeremy, One.	.982	54	393	32	8	433	30
Suriel, Miguel, H.V.	1.000	1	6	0	0	6	0
Thomas, Mark, Ver.*	.975	31	219	17	6	242	10
Valdez, Angel, S.I.	1.000	4	10	2	0	12	0
Vazquez, Carlos, H.V.	1.000	2	7	1	0	8	0
Williams, Clyde, Ver.*	.981	47	380	32	8	420	17
Wright, Brad, Pit.*	.986	14	131	6	2	139	6

TRIPLE PLAYS: Eberly, Lucca.

SECOND BASEMEN

Player, Team	Pct.	G	PO	A	E	TC	DP
Alvarez, Antonio, Wil.	.938	7	17	13	2	32	4
Anderson, Jon, Low.	.977	26	51	74	3	128	14
Batson, Thomas, Bat.	.980	33	66	79	3	148	24
Bonifay, Joshua, Wil.	.945	37	86	87	10	183	26
Brett, Jason, Pit.	.953	20	29	53	4	86	10
Caracciolo, Anthony, N.J.	.963	56	105	156	10	271	26
Carvajal, Ramon, N.J.	1.000	1	2	2	0	4	0
Centile, Raul, M.V.	1.000	2	3	0	0	3	0
Correa, Dominic, S.I.	.924	18	32	29	5	66	7
Dalton, David, Jam.	1.000	2	1	4	0	5	0

Player, Team	Pct.	G	PO	A	E	TC	DP
De Aza, Modesto, Aub.	.938	50	88	110	13	211	15
Drobiak, Jayson, One.	.867	4	4	9	2	15	2
Estevez, Domingo, St.C.	.952	58	110	127	12	249	39
Geisbush, David, Jam.	1.000	6	6	6	0	12	2
Green, Nick, Jam.	.955	73	141	174	15	330	37
Hart, Bo, N.J.	.954	19	37	46	4	87	16
Hlousek, Robert, One.	.945	33	54	67	7	128	14
HOOPER, Kevin, Uti.	.989	73	145	215	4	364	50
Jackson, Brandon, St.C.	.939	10	14	17	2	33	4
Kerrigan, Joseph, Low.	.944	48	77	126	12	215	20
Lopez, Samuel, Pit.	.875	2	3	4	1	8	0
Lotterhos, Chris, M.V.	.897	7	14	12	3	29	3
Martin, Justin, Wil.	.952	19	45	55	5	105	13
Maule, Jason, Aub.	.971	29	43	57	3	103	11
McKinley, Josh, Ver.	1.000	16	36	27	0	63	7
Melucci, Lou, Ver.	.946	32	58	82	8	148	9
Mendez, Donaldo, Aub.	1.000	1	3	5	0	8	2
Mitchell, Todd, S.I.	.975	61	99	137	6	242	29
Mize, Matt, Pit.	.955	58	103	176	13	292	32
Moore, Frank, H.V.	.954	74	148	182	16	346	48
Moore, Ryan, M.V.	.857	2	1	5	1	7	0
Moraga, Omar, M.V.	.979	66	133	153	6	292	35
Morales, Victor, St.C.	.971	10	19	15	1	35	3
Nelson, Reggie, One.	.966	44	83	114	7	204	16
Nunez, Jose, N.J.	.889	2	3	5	1	9	1
Pelfrey, Brice, Wil.	.946	14	26	27	3	56	8
Pichardo, Henry, M.V.	1.000	2	2	2	0	4	1
Ramirez, Edgar, H.V.	1.000	4	4	3	0	7	2
Reyes, Dadny, Uti.	.882	4	7	8	2	17	5
Riggins, Auntwan, St.C.	1.000	2	3	1	0	4	1
Rojas, Alex, Bat.	.951	45	70	86	8	164	13
Schley, Joseph, Bat.	.923	9	7	17	2	26	3
Taylor, Seth, S.I.	1.000	1	2	3	0	5	0
Terni, Chaz, Low.	.875	4	3	11	2	16	2
Valdez, Wilson, Ver.	1.000	6	15	19	0	34	3
Van Pareren, Tim, Ver.	.956	24	34	52	4	90	6

TRIPLE PLAYS: Batson, Hooper, Nelson.

THIRD BASEMEN

Player, Team	Pct.	G	PO	A	E	TC	DP
Alfieri, Frank, Aub.	.867	20	15	24	6	45	0
Alvarez, Antonio, Wil.	.838	33	22	71	18	111	6
Avila, Rob, Bat.	.778	5	2	5	2	9	0
Bailey, Travis, N.J.	.960	18	12	36	2	50	3
Batson, Thomas, Bat.	.909	31	19	51	7	77	3
Beam, Dusty, One.	1.000	4	3	3	0	6	1
BEINBRINK, Andrew, H.V.	.952	75	52	185	12	249	15
Bernhardt, Jossephang, St.C.	.887	63	32	94	16	142	7
Blake, Casey, St.C.	1.000	1	1	3	0	4	0
Bonifay, Joshua, Wil.	1.000	6	1	9	0	10	1
Caracciolo, Anthony, Ver.	.909	2	3	7	1	11	0
Carvajal, Ramon, N.J.	.000	1	0	0	0	0	0
Centile, Raul, M.V.	.600	2	1	2	2	5	0
Correa, Dominic, S.I.	.909	4	3	7	1	11	1
Dalton, David, Jam.	1.000	1	1	1	0	2	0
DeGroote, Casey, S.I.	1.000	6	4	11	0	15	1
Dominguez, Luis, Aub.	.884	57	39	113	20	172	1
Drobiak, Jayson, One.	.882	14	9	21	4	34	1
Eberly, Rodney, Bat.	.886	20	11	28	5	44	1
Escobar, Gustavo, N.J.	.875	15	9	26	5	40	2
Geisbush, David, Jam.	1.000	1	0	1	0	1	0
Gomez, Jose, Uti.	.884	20	9	29	5	43	2
Gonzalez, Santos, St.C.	.000	2	0	0	0	0	0
Griffin, Justin, M.V.	.000	1	0	0	0	0	0
Grindell, Nate, M.V.	.894	67	29	156	22	207	13
Hart, Bo, N.J.	1.000	8	12	21	0	33	5
Hitchcox, Brian, Bat.	.900	10	3	24	3	30	6
Holliday, Joshua, St.C.	.750	4	0	9	3	12	2
Jackson, Brandon, St.C.	1.000	1	2	1	0	3	0
Joyce, Jesse, Aub.	.833	2	1	4	1	6	0
Langston, James, Wil.	.837	17	11	25	7	43	8
Lugo, Felix, Ver.	.893	46	34	100	16	150	4
MacMillan, Chris, M.V.	.947	7	3	15	1	19	1
McKinley, Josh, Ver.	.900	3	3	6	1	10	0
Meadows, Mike, Pit.	.906	13	12	17	3	32	0
Meadows, Randy, Ver.	1.000	8	5	12	0	17	0
Minus, Stephen, Low.	.895	50	26	76	12	114	6
Mitchell, Todd, S.I.	1.000	3	2	4	0	6	0
Moore, Ryan, Ver.	.875	16	14	21	5	40	0
Morales, Victor, St.C.	.905	10	7	12	2	21	1
Muthig, Dean, Bat.	.970	16	9	23	1	33	3
Nunez, Hector, One.	.796	17	10	33	11	54	4

Player, Team	Pct.	G	PO	A	E	TC	DP
Nunez, Jose, N.J.	.931	38	29	93	9	131	5
Nye, Rodney, Pit.	.888	65	49	118	21	188	9
Oropeza, Asdrubal, Jam.	.928	74	41	179	17	237	10
Perkins, Kevin, Uti.	.918	32	18	49	6	73	5
Phillips, Andy, S.I.	.904	63	38	113	16	167	10
Postell, Matthew, Uti.	.893	18	22	28	6	56	4
Ramirez, Edgar, H.V.	1.000	1	0	2	0	2	0
Reyes, Dadny, Uti.	.902	18	6	31	4	41	2
Richardson, Juan, Bat.	.789	7	3	12	4	19	2
Riggins, Auntwan, St.C.	.500	1	0	2	2	4	0
Rodriguez, Jeff, Jam.	1.000	2	1	1	0	2	0
Sampson, Christopher, Aub.	.000	1	0	0	0	0	0
Segura, Rolando, Wil.	.901	24	10	54	7	71	5
Shipp, Brian, Pit.	1.000	2	0	2	0	2	0
Terni, Chaz, Low.	.924	29	30	55	7	92	2
Ust, Brant, One.	.908	48	35	93	13	141	4
Van Pareren, Tim, Ver.	.800	4	1	3	1	5	0

TRIPLE PLAY: Muthig.

SHORTSTOPS

Player, Team	Pct.	G	PO	A	E	TC	DP
Alvarez, Antonio, Wil.	.000	1	0	0	0	0	0
Anderson, Jon, Low.	.625	2	2	3	3	8	1
Batson, Thomas, Bat.	.964	9	7	20	1	28	3
Beam, Dusty, One.	.944	45	80	104	11	195	23
Brett, Jason, Pit.	.891	17	23	34	7	64	11
CALAIS, Ian, Jam.	.946	68	95	166	15	276	31
Cantu, Jorge, H.V.	.928	72	111	210	25	346	40
Caracciolo, Anthony, Ver.	.800	4	11	9	5	25	1
Centile, Raul, M.V.	.866	17	25	33	9	67	8
Collazo, Julio, Bat.	.952	5	5	15	1	21	3
Dalton, David, Jam.	.933	8	4	24	2	30	1
De Aza, Modesto, Aub.	.778	9	15	20	10	45	3
Escobar, Gustavo, N.J.	.952	15	12	48	3	63	5
Geisbush, David, Jam.	.846	4	5	6	2	13	2
Gonzalez, Santos, St.C.	.890	40	40	105	18	163	16
Hart, Bo, N.J.	.943	20	30	52	5	87	5
Hitchcox, Brian, Bat.	.933	46	74	134	15	223	22
Jackson, Brandon, St.C.	.959	41	53	110	7	170	26
Kerrigan, Joseph, Low.	.923	3	3	9	1	13	2
Lotterhos, Chris, M.V.	.919	34	49	88	12	149	13
Lowe, Steve, M.V.	.891	28	31	83	14	128	10
Malone, Nick, Low.	.850	4	7	10	3	20	3
Maule, Jason, Aub.	1.000	1	1	1	0	2	1
McKinley, Josh, Ver.	.907	46	90	106	20	216	13
Mendez, Donaldo, Aub.	.868	22	34	58	14	106	9
Mitchell, Todd, S.I.	1.000	4	3	1	0	4	0
Morales, Victor, St.C.	.000	1	0	0	0	0	0
Nelson, Reggie, One.	.976	20	41	39	2	82	7
Niles, Drew, Uti.	.943	18	19	47	4	70	5
Perez, Deivi, Wil.	.939	48	76	139	14	229	28
Perkins, Kevin, Uti.	1.000	2	4	4	0	8	1
Ramirez, Edgar, H.V.	.765	4	3	10	4	17	1
Reyes, Ambiorix, Bat.	.946	25	36	70	6	112	6
Reyes, Dadny, Uti.	1.000	3	0	1	0	1	0
Saba, Cesar, Low.	.876	69	87	161	35	283	32
Sampson, Christopher, Aub.	.890	48	68	150	27	245	24
Santiago, Ramon, One.	.979	12	18	28	1	47	6
Sarabia, Eliot, Wil.	.952	33	45	93	7	145	18
Shipp, Brian, Pit.	.938	64	101	217	21	339	46
Taylor, Seth, S.I.	.915	73	96	172	25	293	24
Thames, Damon, N.J.	.887	46	71	126	25	222	32
Ugueto, Luis, Uti.	.940	56	84	180	17	281	38
Valdez, Wilson, Ver.	.945	30	53	85	8	146	16

TRIPLE PLAYS: Beam, Ugueto.

OUTFIELDERS

Player, Team	Pct.	G	PO	A	E	TC	DP
Acuna, Ronald, Pit.	.980	22	46	2	1	49	0
Alvarez, Antonio, Wil.	.875	5	7	0	1	8	0
Ambres, Chip, Uti.	.956	28	43	0	2	45	0
Arias, Jeison, H.V.	1.000	15	28	2	0	30	0
Barns, B.J., Wil.	.967	14	29	0	1	30	0
Batcheller, Chris, Wil.	.955	22	21	0	1	22	0
Batista, Angel, H.V.*	.949	52	92	2	5	99	0
Beverly, Shomari, Bat.	.930	57	103	3	8	114	1
Bonifay, Joshua, Wil.	.000	1	0	0	0	0	0
Bost, Tom, M.V.	1.000	9	15	0	0	15	0
Brown, Andy, S.I.*	.937	59	97	7	7	111	0
Byrd, Marlon, Bat.	.926	44	82	5	7	94	1
Carter, Shannon, St.C.*	.966	49	51	6	2	59	0

Player, Team	Pct.	G	PO	A	E	TC	DP
Celli, Mike, Jam.*	.986	61	64	7	1	72	0
Cepicky, Matthew, Ver.	.978	53	84	5	2	91	0
Close, James, Uti.	.965	54	76	7	3	86	3
Davis, Jermaine, St.C.	.839	29	24	2	5	31	1
Diaz, Matt, H.V.	.972	54	92	12	3	107	2
Dwyer, Mike, Low.*	.000	2	0	0	0	0	0
Espino, Jose, N.J.	.923	39	66	6	6	78	1
Espinoza, Andres, Ver.	.951	25	39	0	2	41	0
Ewing, Chris, N.J.	1.000	20	23	2	0	25	1
Ferrand, Francisco, Uti.*	.964	62	122	10	5	137	3
Floyd, Mike, N.J.	.953	35	55	6	3	64	1
Ford, Lew, Low.	.993	55	130	4	1	135	0
Francisco, Joseph, Jam.	.951	26	35	4	2	41	0
Gallaher, T.T., M.V.	.875	5	5	2	1	8	0
Geisbush, David, Jam.	1.000	2	1	0	0	1	0
Goodeill, Harold, H.V.	1.000	3	3	1	0	4	0
Goodman, Scott, Uti.*	.920	59	76	5	7	88	1
Gordon, Johnny, One.*	.878	31	40	3	6	49	2
Griffin, Justin, M.V.	1.000	2	1	1	0	2	0
Grindell, Nate, M.V.	1.000	2	1	0	0	1	0
Hamilton, Josh, H.V.*	1.000	16	51	1	0	52	0
Hernandez, Johnny, N.J.	1.000	10	13	2	0	15	0
Hill, Michael, Aub.	.959	67	110	6	5	121	0
Hoover, Steven, Aub.	.960	23	21	3	1	25	1
Hudson, Daniel, Wil.	.933	37	64	6	5	75	0
Johnson, Eric, M.V.	.907	25	46	3	5	54	2
Johnson, Reed, St.C.	.976	57	114	9	3	126	2
Johnson, Tony, Pit.	.943	57	77	5	5	87	1
Joyce, Jesse, Aub.	1.000	1	1	0	0	1	0
Landreth, Jason, Wil.	.975	25	39	0	1	40	0
Langlois, Jean-sebastien, Jam.	.961	54	96	3	4	103	0
Langston, James, Wil.	.965	37	52	3	2	57	0
Lara, Balmes, One.	.962	57	93	7	4	104	1
Lebron, Francisco, Pit.	1.000	5	4	1	0	5	0
Lebron, Hector, H.V.	.000	1	0	0	0	0	0
LEBRON, Jesus, St.C.	.993	60	133	9	1	143	1
Ledesma, Phil, Low.	.946	23	34	1	2	37	0
Lee, Monte, N.J.*	.969	35	59	3	2	64	1
Lemon, Tim, N.J.	.969	70	120	6	4	130	1
Ludvigsen, Marc, Pit.*	1.000	23	30	1	0	31	1
Malave, Dennis, M.V.*	1.000	12	25	1	0	26	1
Martin, Brian, H.V.	.989	69	86	5	1	92	0
Martin, Justin, Wil.	.938	7	15	0	1	16	0
McKinney, Antonio, One.	.969	62	119	4	4	127	1
Meadows, Mike, Pit.	1.000	12	12	1	0	13	0
Mento, Alfredo, Pit.	.965	70	162	3	6	171	2
Merhoff, Aaron, Bat.	1.000	7	7	0	0	7	0
Miley, Perry, Low.	.965	40	82	0	3	85	0
Mize, Matt, Pit.	1.000	9	11	0	0	11	0
Moreno, Jorge, M.V.	.959	66	63	7	3	73	3
Murch, Jeremy, H.V.*	.909	9	9	1	1	11	0
Nicolas, Jose, Wil.	.848	21	27	1	5	33	0
O'Neill, Daniel, Bat.*	.950	21	36	2	2	40	1
Ortiz, Juan, Ver.	.962	31	75	0	3	78	0
Padilla, Jorge, Bat.	.955	56	119	7	6	132	3
Pascucci, Valentino, Ver.	.956	66	121	9	6	136	0
Pass, Patrick, Uti.	.000	1	0	0	0	0	0
Perini, Mike, S.I.	.000	6	0	0	1	1	0
Perkins, Kevin, Uti.	.958	24	23	0	1	24	0
Piercy, Mike, Wil.*	.941	8	16	0	1	17	0
Ramirez, Edgar, H.V.	.913	18	20	1	2	23	0
Ravelo, Manuel, Wil.	.960	49	118	2	5	125	2
Requena, Alexander, M.V.	.966	56	111	4	4	119	1
Reyes, Deurys, One.*	.938	9	14	1	1	16	0
Rhodes, Dusty, S.I.	1.000	44	110	6	0	116	3
Richardson, Corey, One.	.976	37	78	3	2	83	0
Riggins, Auntwan, St.C.	.857	7	5	1	1	7	0
Rodriguez, Carlos, Low.	.934	52	92	7	7	106	0
Rosamond, Michael, Aub.	.960	61	160	6	7	173	1
Ryden, Karl, Aub.	1.000	9	14	1	0	15	0
Santana, Pedro, S.I.	.933	55	55	1	4	60	0
Schell, Barry, Uti.*	.944	14	17	0	1	18	0
Schley, Joseph, Bat.	1.000	16	22	0	0	22	0
Schneider, Matthew, Wil.	1.000	13	17	1	0	18	0
Sherrill, J.J., M.V.	1.000	3	8	0	0	8	0
Simmons, Jerry, Jam.	.990	52	99	1	1	101	0
Sitzman, James, Bat.*	1.000	38	74	2	0	76	0
Smith, Fred, St.C.	.959	39	89	5	4	98	0
Ticehurst, Brad, S.I.	.925	58	72	2	6	80	1
Topolski, Jon, Aub.	.926	64	81	6	7	94	2
Valdez, Angel, S.I.	.971	25	32	1	1	34	0
Villar, Jose, Jam.	.988	38	81	2	1	84	0
Waldron, Jeffrey, Low.	.000	1	0	0	0	0	0
Walker, Javon, Uti.	.000	3	0	0	0	0	0

Player, Team	Pct.	G	PO	A	E	TC	DP
Warren, Chris, Low.	.974	46	71	5	2	78	1
Washington, Mo, Wil.	.889	4	8	0	1	9	0
Watson, Matthew, Ver.	.959	63	133	6	6	145	2
Wiese, Brian, Low.	.955	16	20	1	1	22	0
Williams, Charles, N.J.*	.930	28	39	1	3	43	0
Williams, Clyde, Ver.*	.667	2	2	0	1	3	0
Williams, Jewell, M.V.	.940	53	91	3	6	100	1
Williamson, Casey, One.*	1.000	45	57	1	0	58	0
Wright, Brad, Pit.*	.986	47	70	3	1	74	0
Zapata, Juan, Aub.	.733	13	10	1	4	15	0

TRIPLE PLAY: Gordon.

CATCHERS

Player, Team	Pct.	G	PO	A	E	TC	DP	PB
Alfonzo, Eliezer, N.J.	.969	23	158	31	6	195	2	8
Alvarez, Antonio, Wil.	1.000	1	1	0	0	1	0	0
Anderson, Dennis, Uti.	.976	29	223	24	6	253	1	5
Brazeal, Spencer, S.I.	.946	8	30	5	2	37	0	4
Buck, John, Aub.	.974	63	549	52	16	617	5	7
Burke, Paul, Jam.	.987	13	132	15	2	149	0	3
Cody, Ryan, Bat.	1.000	3	24	2	0	26	0	1
Cripps, Bobby, St.C.	1.000	1	3	0	0	3	0	0
Daggett, Jesse, Wil.	.931	3	27	0	2	29	0	1
Deitrick, Jeremy, Bat.	.985	26	183	17	3	203	0	4
Diaz, Diogenes, Wil.	1.000	9	55	6	0	61	0	0
Dyer, Matthew, Pit.	1.000	2	4	0	0	4	0	0
ELZY, Steven, Pit.	.989	38	248	27	3	278	3	13
Feliz, Joselyn, Uti.	.984	19	158	30	3	191	1	8
Fowler, Ben, M.V.	.988	10	76	6	1	83	1	0
Fuentes, Omar, S.I.	.989	48	308	39	4	351	3	13
Green, Jason, S.I.	.988	25	73	7	1	81	0	0
Hernandez, Jose, Wil.	.977	35	229	24	6	259	2	8
Holliday, Joshua, St.C.	.995	18	169	15	1	185	1	6
House, J.R., Wil.	.984	14	113	10	2	125	1	0
Isenia, Chairon, H.V.	.989	33	233	30	3	266	3	4
Jarvais, Kregg, Low.	.980	35	259	33	6	298	4	8
Johannes, Todd, Ver.	.985	23	170	24	3	197	1	3
Johnson, Gabe, N.J.	.993	20	118	23	1	142	1	6
Laflair, Jay, M.V.	.970	16	78	19	3	100	0	2
Martinez, Victor, M.V.	.984	51	427	56	8	491	4	10
McArthur, Kennon, Bat.	.969	28	204	18	7	229	1	5
Norrell, Troy, Bat.	.969	24	197	23	7	227	3	4
Ochoa, Javier, Aub.	.973	15	98	11	3	112	0	1
Parker, Chris, One.	.977	36	268	34	7	309	1	1
Pemberthy, Aaron, N.J.	1.000	9	54	5	0	59	1	0
Pohle, Ike, St.C.	.986	38	268	17	4	289	2	6
Poulsen, Christopher, Jam.	.981	24	186	25	4	215	1	2
Preston, Brian, Ver.	.973	28	187	29	6	222	2	15
Rickon, Jim, M.V.	.982	6	49	5	1	55	2	2
Riepe, Andrew, Low.	.975	30	213	18	6	237	0	7
Rivera, Luis J., Ver.	.977	29	219	33	6	258	0	5
Rodriguez, Felix, S.I.	1.000	1	5	0	0	5	0	1
Rodriguez, Jeff, Jam.	.980	40	322	29	7	358	0	5
St. Pierre, Maxim, One.	.985	42	293	35	5	333	5	9
Santos, Juan, St.C.	.991	29	213	17	2	232	0	9
Schumacher, Shawn, N.J.	.991	31	203	22	2	227	1	2
Sickles, Jeremy, Wil.	.987	19	135	13	2	150	1	2
Siegfried, Jason, One.	1.000	8	39	3	0	42	0	2
Smith, Ryan, Pit.	.984	12	59	4	1	64	0	2
Stockam, Travis, Pit.	.976	12	78	5	2	85	2	4
Stoffels, Alex, Pit.	.989	26	159	14	2	175	3	5
Suriel, Miguel, Wil.	.988	32	276	46	4	326	1	4
Sutter, Chad, S.I.	.993	34	238	28	2	268	1	3
Valdez, Castulo, H.V.	.977	12	79	6	2	87	2	0
Vazquez, Carlos, H.V.	.977	6	39	4	1	44	0	1
Waldron, Jeffrey, Low.	.974	23	168	20	5	193	1	3
Woody, Dominic, Uti.	.985	30	233	28	4	265	2	18

TRIPLE PLAY: St. Pierre.

PITCHERS

Player, Team	Pct.	G	PO	A	E	TC	DP
Abreu, Miguel, Uti.	1.000	15	1	0	0	1	0
Albin, Scott, Ver.	1.000	26	3	9	0	12	0
Alcala, Jason, Wil.	1.000	6	2	1	0	3	0
Alston, Travis, Bat.	1.000	15	2	4	0	6	1
Andersen, Derek, H.V.*	1.000	20	2	9	0	11	1
Anderson, Travis, Aub.	1.000	9	4	10	0	14	1
Andujar, Jesse, Ver.	.000	5	0	0	0	0	0
Baginski, Jr., Thomas, One.*	.000	3	0	0	1	1	0
Bailie, Matt, Bat.	1.000	10	1	2	0	3	0
Baker, Christopher, St.C.	1.000	12	1	7	0	8	1
Baldassano, Joseph, Ver.	.000	6	0	0	0	0	0

Player, Team	Pct.	G	PO	A	E	TC	DP	Player, Team	Pct.	G	PO	A	E	TC	DP
Barnett, Aaron, One.*	1.000	23	0	3	0	3	0	Gourlay, Matt, St.C.	1.000	14	0	1	0	1	0
Barrett, Scott, Aub.*	.500	5	0	1	1	2	0	Grace, Bryan, S.I.	.750	8	3	0	1	4	0
Bazan, Juan, Wil.	1.000	8	3	9	0	12	0	Gracesqui, Franklyn, St.C.*	.750	15	1	5	2	8	0
Behn, Brendan, Pit.*	1.000	15	2	5	0	7	0	Graman, Alex, S.I.*	.947	14	7	11	1	19	1
Bess, Stephen, One.	.333	7	0	1	2	3	0	Hancock, Rodney, Wil.*	1.000	8	2	11	0	13	0
Biddlestone, Jason, Wil.	.000	1	0	0	0	0	0	Harris, Silas, Ver.*	.833	23	0	5	1	6	0
Blitstein, Jeffrey, Aub.	.882	17	4	11	2	17	0	Hawkins, Barry, Pit.	1.000	16	6	6	0	12	0
Bluma, Marc, St.C.	.750	24	2	1	1	4	1	Hendricks, John, Pit.*	.917	15	2	20	2	24	0
Bonner, Luke, M.V.	.857	19	0	6	1	7	1	Henriquez, Hector, Uti.*	.714	12	1	4	2	7	0
Bost, Ronald, St.C.*	.000	4	0	0	0	0	0	Hickman, Benjamin, Uti.	1.000	24	2	3	0	5	0
Bottenfield, Jason, Low.	.875	23	2	5	1	8	0	Hoover, Steven, Aub.	.000	1	0	0	0	0	0
Bowe, Brandon, Uti.	1.000	6	0	1	0	1	0	Hubbel, Travis, St.C.	1.000	5	2	4	0	6	0
Brookman, Ryan, Bat.	1.000	14	1	8	0	9	0	Humrich, Christopher, Ver.	.500	22	1	2	3	6	0
Brooks, Frank, Bat.*	1.000	16	1	13	0	14	3	Hutchinson, Brian, Jam.*	1.000	14	0	7	0	7	0
Brown, Craig, M.V.*	1.000	18	1	4	0	5	0	Jackson, Brian, M.V.	.727	14	1	7	3	11	0
Brown,, Stephen, Aub.	.765	18	2	11	4	17	2	JAMISON, Ryan, Aub.	1.000	15	9	16	0	25	2
Burke, Erick, One.*	1.000	15	1	3	0	4	0	Janke, Cheyenne, N.J.	.917	15	6	5	1	12	0
Butler, Mark, N.J.	1.000	18	0	1	0	1	0	Johnston, Michael, Wil.*	1.000	15	0	8	0	8	0
Byrd, Mike, M.V.	1.000	9	1	0	0	1	0	Johnston, Rikki, One.*	.929	12	2	11	1	14	0
Byron, Terence, Uti.	1.000	6	1	3	0	4	0	Joseph, Jake, Pit.	1.000	11	0	4	0	4	0
Calvo, Jose, Aub.	.000	5	0	0	0	0	0	Kalita, Tim, One.*	.750	3	1	2	1	4	0
Caple, Chance, N.J.	1.000	7	1	6	0	7	0	Kearney, Ryan, M.V.	1.000	11	1	2	0	3	0
Carlson, Jeff, S.I.	1.000	6	3	0	0	3	0	Keelin, Chris, Bat.	.500	14	0	1	1	2	0
Carpenter, Chris, St.C.	.000	1	0	0	0	0	0	Kelley, Chris, M.V.	.900	13	2	7	1	10	0
Carrasco, Danny, Wil.	.765	18	0	13	4	17	0	Kennedy, Joe, H.V.*	.958	16	5	18	1	24	1
Chipperfield, Calvin, One.	1.000	15	4	12	0	16	1	Kent, Nathan, Jam.	.667	14	0	2	1	3	0
Chisnall, Wesley, Ver.	.875	9	2	5	1	8	1	Klein, Cody, S.I.*	1.000	16	4	4	0	8	0
Classen, Ender, Wil.	.500	3	0	1	1	2	0	Klepacki, Edward, Ver.	1.000	14	7	8	0	15	1
Claussen, Brandon, S.I.*	.958	12	7	16	1	24	0	Knowles, Michael, S.I.	1.000	3	1	0	0	1	0
Collins, Patrick, Ver.	1.000	12	3	6	0	9	0	Kremer, John, S.I.	.800	23	1	3	1	5	0
Colon, Roman, Jam.	.923	15	2	10	1	13	0	Lane, Jason, Aub.*	.000	1	0	0	0	0	0
Cook, Brent, N.J.	.889	9	4	4	1	9	0	Langen, Brian, N.J.*	1.000	26	3	8	0	11	0
Correa, Cristobal, N.J.	1.000	9	2	7	0	9	0	Langston, David, S.I.	.000	2	0	0	0	0	0
Cowie, Stephen, M.V.	1.000	12	1	7	0	8	0	Laroche, Jeff, Uti.*	1.000	26	1	2	0	3	0
Cox, Brian, Jam.	1.000	17	2	2	0	4	0	Law, Keith, One.	1.000	22	2	2	0	4	1
Crawford, Chris, H.V.	.000	1	0	0	0	0	0	Lawson, Jarrod, Bat.	1.000	4	1	1	0	2	1
Crumpton, Chuck, Ver.	.714	19	1	4	2	7	0	Layfield, Scotty, N.J.	1.000	23	2	5	0	7	0
Cummings, Jeremy, N.J.	.882	14	3	12	2	17	0	Layne, Roger, M.V.	1.000	4	0	1	0	1	0
Curtis, Daniel, Jam.	.875	15	6	8	2	16	1	Leach, Bryan, Low.	1.000	13	0	5	0	5	0
Dagley, Corey, Bat.	.938	15	6	9	1	16	1	Ledden, Ryan, H.V.	.875	20	2	5	1	8	1
Dailey, Matt, H.V.*	.833	14	2	3	1	6	0	Ledesma, Phil, Low.	.000	3	0	0	0	0	0
Dansby, Justin, Jam.	.800	24	2	2	1	5	0	Lee, Andy, Low.*	.667	26	0	2	1	3	0
Dean, Aaron, St.C.*	.875	17	1	6	1	8	0	Lee, Garrett, Jam.	.889	13	1	7	1	9	0
Denney, Kyle, M.V.	.000	1	0	0	0	0	0	Leek, Randy, One.*	.882	21	3	12	2	17	0
Detwiler, James, St.C.*	.875	14	2	5	1	8	0	Lewis, Peyton, St.C.	.833	15	3	7	2	12	1
DeLaCruz, Andres, S.I.	1.000	5	1	1	0	2	0	Lopez, Gustavo, Uti.	.625	13	4	1	3	8	0
Dimma, Douglas, St.C.*	.545	17	1	5	5	11	1	Lowe, Matt, Pit.	.810	16	6	11	4	21	1
Dinkel, Aaron, N.J.	.500	13	0	2	2	4	0	Lowery, Phil, Uti.*	.000	2	0	0	0	0	0
Dorn, Grant, Ver.	.900	23	1	8	1	10	1	Macias, Jose, M.V.	.000	1	0	0	0	0	0
Dreier, Tom, St.C.	1.000	4	0	1	0	1	0	Madson, Ryan, Bat.	.941	15	2	14	1	17	2
Drese, Ryan, M.V.	1.000	5	1	4	0	5	0	Maleski, Eric, M.V.	1.000	22	2	6	0	8	0
Eavenson, Clay, S.I.	.000	1	0	0	0	0	0	Manning, Mike, M.V.	1.000	20	2	1	0	3	0
Encarnacion, Orlando, Pit.	.862	15	7	18	4	29	2	Marin, Willy, H.V.	.913	23	7	14	2	23	1
Escobar, Ruben, M.V.	.889	17	2	6	1	9	1	Marini, Anthony, M.V.*	.875	13	3	4	1	8	0
Espina, Rendy, Bat.*	.000	1	0	0	0	0	0	Markwell, Diegomar, St.C.*	.882	14	3	12	2	17	1
Everett, Matt, M.V.	.500	3	0	1	1	2	0	Marrero, Darwin, Ver.	.900	14	4	5	1	10	0
Fahs, Paul, N.J.	.500	30	1	0	1	2	0	Martinez, Anastacio, Low.	.765	11	7	6	4	17	1
Faigin, Jason, S.I.	.000	18	0	0	0	0	0	Martinez, Ramon, Low.	1.000	1	0	1	0	1	0
Fereira, Ramon, Aub.	1.000	21	5	6	0	11	0	Marx, Tommy, One.*	1.000	6	0	2	0	2	0
Ferguson, Tony, Aub.	1.000	3	0	1	0	1	0	Matew, Francisco, N.J.	1.000	19	2	3	0	5	0
Finnegan, Mike, Ver.	1.000	14	1	5	0	6	0	Mattson, John, Pit.	.857	11	2	4	1	7	0
Fossum, Casey, Low.*	1.000	5	0	2	0	2	0	McCarter, Jason, Pit.	1.000	21	0	5	0	5	1
Franco, Jose, S.I.	1.000	30	5	3	0	8	0	McClain, Jeremy, Low.	.929	16	5	8	1	14	1
Fraser, Joe, Ver.	.000	4	0	0	0	0	0	McClendon, Matthew, Jam.	1.000	7	3	1	0	4	0
Frasor, Jason, One.	1.000	12	4	8	0	12	0	McCormick, Terry, H.V.*	.750	9	0	3	1	4	0
Frendling, Neal, H.V.	1.000	9	5	2	0	7	0	McDonald, Corey, One.*	1.000	18	3	4	0	7	0
Fry, Justin, Bat.	1.000	25	2	1	0	3	0	McKoin, Heath, H.V.*	.846	15	3	8	2	13	0
Gallo, Michael, Aub.*	1.000	3	1	0	0	1	0	Minix, Travis, H.V.	.800	27	4	4	2	10	1
Gamble, Jerome, Low.	1.000	5	2	2	0	4	0	Montilla, Felix, Wil.	1.000	23	1	2	0	3	0
Garcia, Ramon, Low.	.000	5	0	0	0	0	0	Moore, Bryan, Uti.	.857	26	1	5	1	7	1
Garcia, Rosman, S.I.	.923	18	10	14	2	26	1	Morse, Bryan, Uti.*	.950	14	6	13	1	20	0
Gargano, Mike, N.J.	.905	21	6	13	2	21	2	Moser, Todd, Uti.*	.909	14	6	14	2	22	1
Garvin, Robert, Uti.	.917	23	2	9	1	12	0	Murray, Steve, St.C.*	.800	12	0	8	2	10	0
Gawer, Matt, Jam.*	1.000	21	3	3	0	6	1	Nannini, Mike, Aub.	1.000	11	4	9	0	13	1
George, Christopher, Aub.	1.000	21	0	3	0	3	0	Needle, Chad, St.C.	1.000	15	1	6	0	7	0
Getz, Cody, H.V.*	1.000	11	3	11	0	14	0	Norris, Shon, Low.	.857	27	1	5	1	7	0
Giese, Daniel, Low.	1.000	18	5	1	0	6	0	Novits, Carey, M.V.*	.889	12	1	7	1	9	0
Glaser, Eric, Low.	1.000	14	0	5	0	5	0	Nunley, Robert, St.C.	1.000	7	0	1	0	1	0
Glaser, Scott, Wil.*	1.000	3	0	2	0	2	0	Oase, Ryan, H.V.	.000	1	0	0	0	0	0
Good, Eric, Ver.*	.818	15	4	14	4	22	1	Oliver, Scott, S.I.	.750	2	1	2	1	4	0
Gordon, Kevin, Uti.	.000	1	0	0	0	0	0	Orloski, Joe, St.C.	1.000	17	2	11	0	13	0
Gorman, Pat, Pit.	.667	19	0	2	1	3	1	Ortiz, John, Aub.*	.944	23	3	14	1	18	1

Player, Team	Pct.	G	PO	A	E	TC	DP
Ortiz, Jose, H.V.	1.000	29	1	9	0	10	0
Outlaw, Mark, Bat.*	1.000	23	0	5	0	5	0
Parra, Christian, Jam.	.909	9	1	9	1	11	0
Pautz, Brad, Bat.	1.000	13	1	14	0	15	0
Pearce, Josh, N.J.	.933	14	3	11	1	15	1
Peck, Brandon, N.J.*	.933	31	3	11	1	15	0
Peguero, Radhame, H.V.	1.000	4	4	0	0	4	0
Pierce, Tony, Jam.	.333	17	0	1	2	3	0
Pilato, Chris, Bat.	1.000	11	2	4	0	6	0
Pineda, Jairo, Aub.	.850	15	6	11	3	20	0
Prater, Andy, Wil.	1.000	10	1	4	0	5	1
Pruett, Jason, H.V.*	1.000	25	1	10	0	11	0
Queen, Mike, Pit.*	.938	15	3	12	1	16	2
Reece, Dana, St.C.*	.000	5	0	0	1	1	0
Reid, Justin, Wil.	.944	16	5	12	1	18	0
Renwick, Tyler, St.C.	1.000	16	3	4	0	7	1
Riccobono, Rick, Low.	.913	15	8	13	2	23	0
Ridenour, Ryan, S.I.*	1.000	2	0	1	0	1	0
Riggins, Auntwan, St.C.	.000	1	0	0	0	0	0
Rivera, Homero, One.*	.929	23	1	12	1	14	0
Roberts, Phil, M.V.	.000	3	0	0	0	0	0
Robertson, Nathan, Uti.*	1.000	5	2	5	0	7	0
Rodriguez, Anthony, S.I.	.889	13	3	5	1	9	0
Rojas, Chris, Wil.	.941	15	3	13	1	17	1
Roller, Adam, Low.	.857	23	3	3	1	7	0
Roque, Darryll, Ver.	.625	12	2	3	3	8	0
Rosengren, Phil, M.V.	.700	11	3	4	3	10	0
Rowe, Casey, One.	.950	15	12	7	1	20	2
Rupp, Michael, Low.	.882	18	9	6	2	17	1
Sabathia, C.C., M.V.*	1.000	6	1	2	0	3	1
Sabens, Mike, Wil.	1.000	5	1	1	0	2	0
Sadler, Carl, M.V.*	.000	1	0	0	0	0	0
Saladin, Miguel, Aub.	1.000	8	1	3	0	4	0
Samadani, Ali, Jam.	1.000	22	4	2	0	6	0
Sansom, Trevor, N.J.	1.000	20	1	1	0	2	0
Santana, Humberto, Pit.*	1.000	4	1	3	0	4	0
Satterfield, Jeremy, Jam.	.857	23	2	4	1	7	0
Satterfield, Troy, Wil.*	1.000	17	2	15	0	17	2
Seale, Dustin, St.C.-Ver.*	1.000	17	0	3	0	3	0
Sergent, Joe, Uti.*	1.000	10	1	2	0	3	0
Serrano, Elio, Bat.	1.000	19	3	2	0	5	1
Shields, Drew, Uti.	1.000	13	1	4	0	5	0
Sirianni, Jay, M.V.*	1.000	3	0	4	0	4	1
Smith, Chad, Bat.	1.000	3	1	0	0	1	0
Smuin, Shane, Uti.	1.000	23	3	5	0	8	0
Solano, Alexander, Low.	.667	6	0	2	1	3	0
Southard, Lee, St.C.	1.000	5	1	0	0	1	0
Spencer, Corey, Low.*	1.000	19	0	4	0	4	0
Spille, Ryan, St.C.*	1.000	1	0	1	0	1	0
Stine, Justin, St.C.*	1.000	2	1	2	0	3	0
Sullivan, Ted, M.V.	1.000	13	0	2	0	2	0
Sunderman, Nick, M.V.*	1.000	2	0	3	0	3	0
Swiatkiewicz, Chris, S.I.	1.000	6	2	2	0	4	0
Terry, Mike, Pit.*	1.000	18	1	5	0	6	0
Thomas, Gaige, Uti.	.667	13	2	2	2	6	0
Toriz, Steve, Ver.	.800	21	3	5	2	10	0
Truitt, Derrick, Jam.	.714	18	2	8	4	14	1
Tucker, Bradley, Bat.	1.000	17	3	5	0	8	1
Valera, Nelson, H.V.	.000	2	0	0	0	0	0
Vanhekken, Andrew, One.*	.889	11	1	7	1	9	1
Vinton, Drew, Wil.	1.000	17	2	10	0	12	1
Viole, Paul, Pit.	.833	18	0	5	1	6	0
Wade, Travis, Aub.	1.000	26	1	4	0	5	0
Wallace, Chris, S.I.	1.000	14	0	4	0	4	0
Wallace, Justin, Wil.*	.778	19	3	4	2	9	1
Walling, Dave, S.I.	1.000	14	7	11	0	18	0
Ward, Matt, Uti.*	.833	8	0	5	1	6	0
Watson, Gregory, One.	1.000	31	4	4	0	8	0
Weslowski, Robert, Pit.	.931	14	10	17	2	29	0
Whiteley, Shad, S.I.	.889	12	2	6	1	9	0
Whitesides, Johnny, Aub.	.500	6	0	2	2	4	1
Wilkerson, Byron, Aub.	1.000	9	2	4	0	6	0
Williams, David, Wil.*	.889	7	3	5	1	9	0
Williamson, Brian, Pit.	1.000	6	0	2	0	2	0
Willis, Jason, S.I.	1.000	7	4	4	0	8	0
Willoughby, Justin, Jam.*	.889	19	0	8	1	9	0
Wilson, Mike, Bat.	.600	13	2	4	4	10	0
Witte, Lou, S.I.	.941	25	7	9	1	17	0
Wright, Barrett, H.V.	1.000	10	2	7	0	9	0
Wright, Shane, Wil.	1.000	17	6	13	0	19	0
Yates, Chad, N.J.	1.000	13	2	2	0	4	0
Zipser, Mike, Bat.	.600	9	2	1	2	5	0

PITCHERS WITH TWO OR MORE TEAMS

Player, Team	Pct.	G	PO	A	E	TC	DP
Seale, Dustin, St.C.*	1.000	3	0	2	0	2	0
Seale, Dustin, Ver.*	1.000	14	0	1	0	1	0

The following players appeared only as designated hitter, pinch-hitter or pinch runner: Day, dh; Deschenes, dh.

LEAGUE CHAMPIONS

Year	Team	Pct.
1939—	Olean*	.631
1940—	Olean*	.625
1941—	Jamestown	.618
	Bradford (2nd)†	.549
1942—	Jamestown*	.672
1943—	Lockport	.591
	Wellsville (3rd)†	.532
1944—	Lockport	.608
	Jamestown (2nd)†	.565
1945—	Batavia*	.677
1946—	Jamestown‡	.672
	Batavia‡	.672
1947—	Jamestown*	.690
1948—	Lockport*	.603
1949—	Bradford*	.635
1950—	Hornell	.653
	Olean (2nd)†	.568
1951—	Olean	.622
	Hornell (3rd)†	.568
1952—	Hamilton	.659
	Jamestown (2nd)†	.643
1953—	Jamestown*	.704
1954—	Corning*	.621
1955—	Hamilton*	.656
1956—	Wellsville*	.617
1957—	Wellsville	.632
	Erie (2nd)†	.598
1958—	Wellsville	.556
	Geneva (2nd)†	.548
1959—	Wellsville†	.635
1960—	Erie	.643
	Wellsville (2nd)†	.535
1961—	Geneva	.616
	Olean (4th)†	.512
1962—	Jamestown	.580
	Auburn (3rd)†	.521
1963—	Auburn	.585
	Batavia (3rd)†	.485
1964—	Auburn§	.622
1965—	Binghamton	.677
	Binghamton	.607
1966—	Auburn∞	.620
	Binghamton	.646
1967—	Auburn	.667
1968—	Auburn	.645
	Oneonta (2nd)*	.558
1969—	Oneonta	.662
1970—	Auburn	.623
1971—	Oneonta	.662
1972—	Niagara Falls	.686
1973—	Auburn	.667
1974—	Oneonta	.768
1975—	Newark	.688
	Newark	.714
1976—	Elmira	.727
	Elmira	.703
1977—	Oneonta▲	.671
	Batavia	.600
1978—	Oneonta	.729
	Geneva◆	.718
1979—	Geneva	.725
	Oneonta◆	.618
1980—	Oneonta▲	.662
	Geneva	.649
1981—	Oneonta▲	.658
	Jamestown	.649
1982—	Oneonta	.566
	Niagara Falls▲	.553
1983—	Utica▲	.649
	Newark	.649
1984—	Newark	.622
	Little Falls▲	.587
1985—	Oneonta*	.705
	Auburn	.603
1986—	Oneonta	.766
	St. Catharines◆	.632
1987—	Geneva▲	.632
	Watertown	.579
1988—	Oneonta▲	.632
	Jamestown	.618
1989—	Pittsfield	.697
	Jamestown▲	.579
1990—	Oneonta■	.667
	Geneva	.662
1991—	Pittsfield	.662
	Jamestown■	.654
1992—	Hamilton	.737
	Geneva▼	.547
1993—	Niagara Falls▼	.603
	Pittsfield	.533

CLASS A New York-Pennsylvania League

Year	Team	Pct.	Year	Team	Pct.	Year	Team	Pct.
1994—	Auburn	.592	1997—	St. Catharines	.579	1999—	Auburn††	.573
	New Jersey▼	.573		Batavia	.635		Mahoning Valley	.566
1995—	Vermont	.645		Pittsfield▼	.568		Hudson Valley‡‡	.553
	Watertown▼	.630	1998—	Hudson Valley	.658			
1996—	Vermont▼	.649		Oneonta††	.592			

*Won championship and four-club playoff. †Won four-club playoff. ‡Jamestown and Batavia declared co-champions; Batavia defeated Jamestown in final of four-club playoff. §Won championship and two-club playoff. ∞Won split-season playoff. ▲League divided into Eastern and Western divisions; won playoff. League divided into Wrigley and Yawkey divisions; won playoff. ■League divided into Eastern, Western and Stedler divisions; won playoff. ▼League divided into McNamara, Pinckney and Stedler divisions; won playoff. ††Named co-champions due to final series being rained out. (NOTE—Known as Pennsylvania-Ontario-New York League from 1939 through 1956.) ‡‡League divided into McNamara and Pinckney divisions; won playoff.

NORTHWEST LEAGUE

LEAGUE OFFICE

President/treasurer
Bob Richmond
Address
P.O. Box 1645
Boise, ID 83701
Phone
208-429-1511

Teams (affiliation)
Boise Hawks (Angels)
Eugene Emeralds (Cubs)
Everett AquaSox (Mariners)
Portland Rockies (Rockies)

Salem-Keizer Volcanoes (Giants)
Southern Oregon Timberjacks (A's)
Spokane Indians (Royals)
Yakima Bears (Dodgers)

1999 FINAL STANDINGS

NORTH DIVISION

Team	W	L	T	Pct.	GB
Spokane (Royals)	44	32	0	.579	...
Boise (Angels)	43	33	0	.566	1.0
Everett (Mariners)	41	35	0	.539	3.0
Yakima (Dodgers)	33	43	0	.434	11.0

SOUTH DIVISION

Team	W	L	T	Pct.	GB
Portland (Rockies)	39	37	0	.513	...
Southern Oregon (Athletics)	38	38	0	.500	1.0
Salem-Keizer (Giants)	37	39	0	.487	2.0
Eugene (Cubs)	29	47	0	.382	10.0

COMPOSITE

Team	Spo.	Boi.	Ever.	Port.	S.O.	S.K.	Yak.	Eug.	W	L	T	Pct.	GB
Spokane (Royals)	...	5	7	5	6	7	8	6	44	32	0	.579	...
Boise (Spokane)	7	...	8	5	4	7	6	6	43	33	0	.566	1.0
Everett (Mariners)	5	4	...	7	7	4	9	5	41	35	0	.539	3.0
Portland (Rockies)	5	5	3	...	8	5	6	7	39	37	0	.513	5.0
Southern Oregon (Athletics)	4	6	3	4	...	5	6	10	38	38	0	.500	6.0
Salem-Keizer (Giants)	3	3	6	7	7	...	4	7	37	39	0	.487	7.0
Yakima (Dodgers)	4	6	3	4	4	6	...	6	33	43	0	.434	11.0
Eugene (Cubs)	4	4	5	5	2	5	4	...	29	47	0	.382	15.0

Major league affiliations in parentheses.

Southern Oregon played home games in Medford, Ore.

PLAYOFFS: Spokane defeated Portland three games to none to win league championship.

REGULAR-SEASON ATTENDANCE: Boise, 132,885; Eugene, 122,500; Everett, 103,455; Portland, 206,136; Salem-Keizer, 124,527; Southern Oregon, 69,495; Spokane, 187,315; Yakima, 74,977. Total—1,021,390. Playoffs (3 games)—11,264.

MANAGERS: Boise, Tom Kotchman; Eugene, Bob Ralston; Everett, Terry Pollreisz; Portland, Alan Cockrell; Salem-Keizer, Frank Reberger; Southern Oregon, Greg Sparks; Spokane, Kevin Long; Yakima, Dino Ebel.

ALL-STAR TEAM: 1B—Sean McGowan, Salem-Keizer; 2B—Alfredo Amezaga, Boise; 3B—G.J. Raymundo, Spokane; SS—Mark Ellis, Spokane; OF—Chris Snelling, Everett; Michael O'Keefe, Boise; Kirk Asche, Southern Oregon; C—Gerald Laird, Southern Oregon; DH—Ken Harvey, Spokane; LHP—Craig Anderson, Everett; RHP—Cam Esslinger, Portland; LHRP—Tony Cogan, Spokane and Bryan Mazur, Southern Oregon; RHRP—Jay Gehrke, Spokane; Most Valuable Player—Robb Quinlan, Boise; Manager of the Year—Kevin Long, Spokane and Greg Sparks, Southern Oregon.

1999 BATTING

TEAM

Team	Avg.	G	TPA	AB	R	H	TB	2B	3B	HR	RBI	SH	SF	HP	BB	IBB	SO	SB	CS	GDP	LOB	ShO	Slg.	OBP
Boise	.302	76	3166	2697	556	814	1162	167	17	49	495	13	31	44	381	11	515	77	32	56	625	2	.431	.393
Spokane	.283	76	3050	2648	477	749	1105	138	16	62	408	32	22	45	303	15	476	110	40	61	573	3	.417	.363
S. Oregon	.269	76	3142	2631	489	708	1115	136	26	73	434	15	37	58	401	9	631	101	44	39	641	2	.424	.373
Everett	.268	76	2990	2589	423	693	1031	139	17	55	369	18	33	40	310	9	563	83	46	40	588	2	.398	.351
Eugene	.266	76	2888	2576	390	684	1006	123	14	57	341	12	15	59	226	2	556	83	51	56	512	1	.391	.337
Portland	.263	76	2980	2630	416	692	1088	142	22	70	369	15	24	32	279	10	684	71	38	41	560	3	.414	.338
Salem-Keizer	.262	76	2985	2582	426	677	964	117	13	48	373	30	14	47	312*	12	544	128	54	35	575	1	.373	.351
Yakima	.260	76	2962	2517	418	654	967	126	11	55	362	48	20	63	314	13	582	103	70	43	530	1	.384	.354

INDIVIDUAL

TOP QUALIFIERS FOR BATTING CHAMPIONSHIP

Minimum 205 plate appearances. *Lefthanded batter. †Switch-hitter.

Player, Team	Avg.	G	TPA	AB	R	H	TB	2B	3B	HR	RBI	SH	SF	HP	BB	IBB	SO	SB	CS	GDP	Slg.	OBP
Harvey, Kenneth, Spo.	.397	56	235	204	49	81	122	17	0	8	41	0	0	8	23	4	30	7	3	3	.598	.477
Lockwood, Mike, S.O.*	.361	69	308	255	48	92	141	18	5	7	51	0	6	8	39	1	49	6	5	5	.553	.451
Barski, Chris, Boi.*	.348	53	221	184	39	64	96	14	0	6	39	0	3	4	30	1	44	1	0	3	.522	.443
Medina, Luis, Eug.	.337	56	216	202	30	68	83	6	0	3	31	1	0	2	11	0	21	2	1	7	.411	.377
McGowan, Sean, S.K.	.335	63	278	257	40	86	145	12	1	15	62	0	0	1	20	4	56	3	1	6	.564	.385
Johnstone, Benjamin, Eug.	.333	54	208	186	34	62	74	9	0	1	11	3	0	10	9	0	30	16	14	1	.398	.395
Ellis, Mark, Spo.	.327	71	340	281	67	92	127	14	0	7	47	5	4	3	47	3	40	21	7	1	.452	.424
O'Keefe, Michael, Boi.*	.326	72	329	264	52	86	128	13	1	9	70	0	5	6	54	2	41	4	1	7	.485	.444
Raymundo, Gregg, Spo.	.323	67	295	254	44	82	133	16	1	11	44	2	3	4	32	4	37	1	1	9	.524	.403
Quinlan, Robb, Boi.	.322	73	335	295	51	95	144	20	1	9	77	0	1	4	35	2	52	5	3	5	.488	.400
Amezaga, Alfredo, Boi.	.322	48	237	205	52	66	86	6	4	2	29	3	1	5	23	2	29	14	3	7	.420	.402
Sledge, Terrmel, Ever.*	.318	62	273	233	43	74	103	8	3	5	32	2	2	9	27	0	35	9	8	2	.442	.406

Player, Team	Avg.	G	TPA	AB	R	H	TB	2B	3B	HR	RBI	SH	SF	HP	BB	IBB	SO	SB	CS	GDP	Slg.	OBP
Wren, Cliff, Yak.	.315	64	281	254	46	80	131	21	0	10	44	5	0	4	18	2	39	11	5	5	.516	.370
Johnson, Gary, Boi.*	.314	71	303	264	56	83	108	17	1	2	48	0	3	2	34	3	44	6	2	6	.409	.393
Gripp, Ryan, Eug.	.308	73	306	266	40	82	138	18	1	12	48	0	3	10	27	0	65	2	1	7	.519	.389

DEPARTMENTAL LEADERS: G—Gsell, 76; AB—Quinlan, 295; R—Ellis, Jester, 67 each; H—Quinlan, 95; TB—Asche, 146; 2B—Burford, Bikowski, 22 each; 3B—Forbes, 6; HR—Asche, Matthews, 17 each; RBI—Quinlan, 77; SH—Shanks, 11; SF—Henderson, 7; HP—Thurston, 21; BB—O'Keefe, 54; IBB—McGowan, Harvey, Raymundo, 4 each; SO—Lincoln, 102; SB—Rosario, 31; CS—Thurston, 18; GIDP—Baker, 14; Slg.—Harvey, .598; OBP—Harvey, .477.

ALL PLAYERS

*Lefthanded batter. †Switch-hitter.

Player, Team	Avg.	G	TPA	AB	R	H	TB	2B	3B	HR	RBI	SH	SF	HP	BB	IBB	SO	SB	CS	GDP	Slg.	OBP
Abate, Michael, Ever.	.254	57	206	185	34	47	77	15	0	5	23	2	0	2	17	1	57	1	2	2	.416	.324
Alcala, Juan, Ever.	.207	17	59	58	4	12	19	4	0	1	8	1	0	0	0	0	17	1	0	0	.328	.207
Aldrup, Morey, Eug.	.169	31	68	65	6	11	15	1	0	1	4	1	0	0	2	0	17	2	0	1	.231	.194
Allen, Shane, Yak.	.243	33	124	111	15	27	37	10	0	0	11	3	0	4	6	0	25	4	2	1	.333	.306
Alou, Felipe, Spo.	.238	17	47	42	4	10	13	1	1	0	4	0	0	0	5	0	12	2	0	1	.310	.319
Amador, Gerardo, Ever.	.293	14	66	58	10	17	26	3	0	2	12	0	0	2	6	1	12	3	1	3	.448	.379
Amezaga, Alfredo, Boi.	.322	48	237	205	52	66	86	6	4	2	29	3	1	5	23	2	29	14	3	7	.420	.402
Asche, Kirk, S.O.	.288	66	302	260	53	75	146	14	3	17	67	0	6		34	3	56	10	0	7	.562	.381
Baker, Jacob, Spo.	.282	65	269	234	34	66	94	15	2	3	39	0	2	1	32	2	46	9	4	14	.402	.368
Barnett, Nathan, Ever.*	.225	18	45	40	4	9	13	4	0	0	5	1	0	1	3	0	12	0	0	0	.325	.295
Barski, Chris, Boi.*	.348	53	221	184	39	64	96	14	0	6	39	0	3	4	30	1	44	1	0	3	.522	.443
Bass, Kevin, Eug.†	.191	59	222	188	23	36	72	8	2	8	30	1	3	5	25	0	79	4	4	1	.383	.299
Bikowski, Scott, Boi.*	.297	65	301	246	59	73	101	22	0	2	45	3	1	5	46	1	42	11	4	3	.411	.416
Bloomquist, William, Ever. ...	.287	42	202	178	35	51	73	10	3	2	27	0	1	1	22	0	25	17	5	1	.410	.366
Boeth, Timothy, Boi.	.296	51	201	169	36	50	71	11	2	2	22	0	4	4	24	0	21	9	6	3	.420	.388
Burford, Kevin, Port.*	.306	64	275	216	55	66	113	22	2	7	33	0	2	5	52	3	45	9	6	3	.523	.447
Carroll, Mark, Ever.	.228	45	161	147	22	29	38	6	0	1	14	0	4	1	29	0	39	0	0	3	.299	.366
Castillo, Ruben, Ever.	.288	62	251	226	38	65	85	10	2	2	27	3	1	2	19	0	48	11	2	3	.376	.347
Catalanotte, Greg, Port.†	.282	68	281	245	38	69	123	8	2	14	47	1	3	2	30	2	75	4	2	1	.502	.361
Cepeda, Ali, S.K.	.250	24	55	44	9	11	13	2	0	0	5	0	0	0	11	0	15	4	2	1	.295	.400
Christianson, Ryan, Ever.	.280	30	124	107	19	30	61	7	0	8	17	0	0	3	14	1	31	3	1	1	.570	.379
Clay, Michael, Spo.	.151	31	93	86	9	13	20	4	0	1	4	0	1	2	4	0	15	1	0	4	.233	.204
Clements, Jason, S.O.†	.181	36	123	105	20	19	24	2	0	1	8	2	1	2	13	0	32	0	3	1	.229	.281
Cohens, Derrick, Eug.	.212	43	136	118	14	25	30	5	0	0	11	0	0	1	15	0	29	3	5	4	.254	.306
Cook, Joshua, S.K.	.241	35	129	112	16	27	39	9	0	1	16	0	1	5	11	0	24	5	6	2	.348	.333
Cordido, Julio, S.K.	.264	70	278	242	36	64	81	10	2	1	28	2	1	4	29	0	44	8	4	3	.335	.351
Cordova, Ben, Spo.*	.250	4	19	16	4	4	12	0	1	2	7	0	0	0	3	0	5	0	0	1	.750	.368
Covington, Kevin, Yak.	.302	43	185	169	24	51	72	13	1	2	23	2	3	0	7	1	37	3	4	4	.426	.324
Curry, Christopher, Eug.	.227	41	140	132	18	30	42	6	0	2	9	0	3	0	5	0	35	0	2	3	.318	.271
Dalton, Joshua, Yak.†	.251	59	259	203	33	51	66	12	0	1	28	6	3	5	42	3	45	11	5	2	.325	.387
Dealey, Scott, S.K.	.246	69	321	268	42	66	80	12	1	0	22	6	3	1	43	0	29	29	9	3	.299	.349
Declet, Miguel, S.O.	.380	14	55	50	13	19	32	7	0	2	6	0	1	1	3	0	16	1	0	0	.640	.418
De La Cruz, Jose, S.O.	.157	18	61	51	7	8	15	4	0	1	8	0	1	0	9	0	16	0	0	1	.294	.295
Deschaine, James, Eug.	.298	73	302	272	49	81	123	12	0	10	48	1	0	0	29	0	59	7	7	8	.452	.365
Doudt, Anthony, Boi.	.242	23	71	62	9	15	25	4	0	2	12	0	3	0	6	0	17	0	0	2	.403	.296
Dunn, Casey, Spo.	.294	58	245	218	34	64	106	7	1	11	49	1	3	4	19	2	28	0	1	5	.486	.357
Duplissea, William, Yak.	.152	13	42	33	5	5	9	2	0	1	4	1	0	3	5	0	7	2	1	1	.303	.303
Durango, Ariel, Ever.†	.269	25	103	93	19	25	38	5	1	2	9	0	0	4	9	0	25	11	5	3	.409	.340
Dzurilla, Michael, Eug.	.291	70	300	278	43	81	114	14	2	5	44	2	1	3	16	0	33	12	4	3	.410	.336
Ellis, Mark, Spo.	.327	71	340	281	67	92	127	14	0	7	47	5	4	3	47	3	40	21	7	1	.452	.424
Estrella, Gorky, Ever.	.250	28	115	84	15	21	30	4	1	1	11	0	0	0	31	3	22	2	2	1	.357	.452
Forbes, Matt, S.O.	.279	63	294	258	50	72	113	17	6	4	34	1	1	0	34	0	77	13	6	0	.438	.362
Gasparino, Billy, Port.	.260	62	292	242	48	63	94	9	2	6	23	5	1	4	40	1	57	10	8	4	.388	.373
Gay, Dennis, Boi.	.242	19	38	33	5	8	10	2	0	0	5	0	1	1	3	0	6	0	0	0	.303	.316
Gipson, Charles, Ever.	.500	1	4	2	0	1	3	0	1	0	1	0	0	0	2	0	1	0	0	0	1.500	.750
Glassey, Josh, Yak.*	.228	28	116	92	13	21	31	4	0	2	14	4	1	0	19	0	24	0	1	5	.337	.337
Goelz, Jim, Yak.	.282	42	161	142	19	40	48	3	1	1	17	3	2	2	12	0	22	2	5	4	.338	.342
Gonzalez, Julian, Spo.	.250	16	61	52	5	13	20	2	1	1	6	0	0	0	9	0	17	1	3	0	.385	.361
Gregorio, Thomas, Boi.	.296	52	201	186	29	55	82	10	1	5	36	0	2	2	11	0	33	0	1	3	.441	.338
Gripp, Ryan, Eug.	.308	73	306	266	40	82	138	18	1	12	48	0	3	10	27	0	65	2	1	7	.519	.389
Grochol, Bryan, S.K.*	.241	28	86	79	9	19	23	1	0	1	10	0	0	0	7	1	15	2	3	2	.291	.302
Gsell, Tony, Eug.	.250	76	312	276	50	69	128	21	1	12	43	0	2	11	23	1	69	12	5	3	.464	.330
Gundrum, Kristoffer, Ever.*	.297	29	104	91	13	27	37	4	0	2	15	0	2	1	10	1	27	5	0	0	.407	.365
Hall, Justin, S.K.	.300	5	24	20	2	6	9	3	0	0	2	1	1	1	1	0	4	1	0	0	.450	.348
Hart, Dickie, Boi.	.000	4	2	2	0	0	0	0	0	0	0	0	0	0	0	0	2	0	0	0	.000	.000
Harvey, Kenneth, Spo.	.397	56	235	204	49	81	122	17	0	8	41	0	8		23	4	30	7	3	3	.598	.477
Healy, Liam, Eug.	.240	17	62	50	8	12	23	2	0	3	12	2	0	6	12	0	12	0	1	1	.460	.345
Hemme, Justin, Port.*	.276	71	311	275	48	76	136	16	1	14	59	1	3		29	1	56	2	1	3	.495	.348
Henderson, Bradley, S.O.	.269	57	236	197	30	53	79	9	1	5	36	0	7	5	27	0	33	3	1	4	.401	.360
Hertel, Brian, Ever.	.357	5	17	14	5	5	6	1	0	0	0	0	0	0	3	0	0	0	0	0	.429	.471
Hochgesang, Joshua, S.O.	.155	21	90	71	10	11	16	2	0	1	3	0	0	4	14	0	23	0	1	1	.225	.326
Holst, Micah, S.K.	.289	57	220	204	37	59	83	8	2	4	28	0	3	3	6	0	32	20	5	1	.407	.315
Howe, Matt, S.O.	.301	64	284	229	44	69	127	12	2	14	45	0	2	4	48	2	49	9	2	3	.555	.428
Jaroncyk, Ryan, Yak.†	.355	8	38	31	6	11	15	4	0	0	4	0	3	0	5	0	10	2	1	1	.484	.444
Jester, Joe, S.K.	.300	72	329	263	67	79	124	19	1	8	40	7	2	7	50	3	57	13	6	2	.471	.422
Johnson, Brian, Spo.	.248	41	162	137	18	34	44	7	0	1	22	1	0	9	12	0	20	4	3	0	.321	.342
Johnson, Gary, Boi.*	.314	71	303	264	56	83	108	17	1	2	48	0	3	2	34	3	44	6	2	6	.409	.393
Johnstone, Benjamin, Eug. ...	.333	54	208	186	34	62	74	9	0	1	11	3	0	10	9	0	30	16	14	1	.398	.395
Kelleher, Pat, Boi.*	.176	9	27	17	4	3	5	2	0	0	2	2	0	0	8	0	4	3	0	0	.294	.440
Keller, G.W., S.K.	.242	28	122	95	10	23	28	5	0	0	13	2	6	0	17	0	10	5	1	2	.295	.383
Kelley, Casey, Boi.*	.307	61	239	205	45	63	104	12	4	7	37	0	1	1	32	0	60	2	1	3	.507	.402
Kluver, Hayden, Yak.*	.203	25	88	79	9	16	21	2	0	1	6	0	0	0	6	0	26	0	1	1	.266	.256
Koen, Nate, Eug.	.185	23	31	27	1	5	8	3	0	0	3	0	0		4	0	6	0	1	0	.296	.290

Player, Team	Avg.	G	TPA	AB	R	H	TB	2B	3B	HR	RBI	SH	SF	HP	BB	IBB	SO	SB	CS	GDP	Slg.	OBP
Kopitzke, Casey, Eug.	.209	37	131	110	19	23	26	3	0	0	12	0	2	4	15	0	25	3	3	6	.236	.321
Laird, Gerald, S.O.	.285	60	265	228	45	65	82	7	2	2	39	2	5	2	28	0	43	10	5	4	.360	.361
Leone, Justin, Ever.	.263	62	245	205	34	54	90	14	2	6	35	1	5	2	32	0	49	5	3	5	.439	.361
Lincoln, Justin, Port.	.241	68	287	253	36	61	97	14	2	6	44	0	2	4	28	0	102	6	2	6	.383	.324
Lockwood, Mike, S.O.*	.361	69	308	255	48	92	141	18	5	7	51	0	6	8	39	1	49	6	5	5	.553	.451
Lombardi, Dominick, Boi.	.292	6	26	24	1	7	9	2	0	0	5	0	0	0	2	0	3	0	0	1	.375	.346
Longmire, Marcel, Eug.	.000	1	2	2	0	0	0	0	0	0	1	0	0	0	0	0	1	0	0	0	.000	.000
Lopez, Norberto, Boi.	.231	5	15	13	1	3	4	1	0	0	0	0	0	0	2	0	5	0	0	0	.308	.333
Lucas, Kevin, Spo.	.256	38	135	121	28	31	36	3	1	0	11	5	0	5	4	0	12	5	1	2	.298	.329
Luster, Jeremy, S.K.†	.219	39	166	146	22	32	44	7	1	1	14	1	0	3	16	0	48	7	1	0	.301	.309
Luther, Ryan, S.K.	.300	61	249	220	34	66	92	12	1	4	38	0	2	9	18	1	35	12	4	5	.418	.373
Mahoney, Ricardo, Port.	.252	63	248	226	31	57	86	13	2	4	28	1	3	1	17	0	33	4	2	4	.381	.304
Mapes, Jake, S.K.	.172	12	32	29	2	5	7	2	0	0	4	0	0	1	2	0	11	0	2	0	.241	.250
Marquez, Eduardo, Eug.	.205	32	80	73	9	15	19	2	1	0	8	1	0	5	1	0	15	3	1	2	.260	.266
Martinez, Victor, Ever.	.212	28	121	113	9	24	31	2	1	1	15	1	2	1	4	0	24	1	3	0	.274	.242
Mattern, Erik, S.K.	.220	17	63	41	11	9	15	1	1	1	6	2	0	4	16	0	9	1	1	1	.366	.475
Matthews, Lamont, Yak.*	.225	66	290	249	46	56	122	11	2	17	52	2	2	2	34	1	87	4	4	1	.490	.321
McAuley, James, Spo.	.143	12	46	35	7	5	9	1	0	1	6	1	0	1	9	0	10	2	0	0	.257	.333
McGowan, Sean, S.K.	.335	63	278	257	40	86	145	12	1	15	62	0	0	1	20	4	56	3	1	6	.564	.385
McQueen, Eric, Port.	.255	46	169	153	14	39	52	8	1	1	14	0	3	3	10	0	52	0	1	3	.340	.308
Medina, Luis, Eug.	.337	56	216	202	30	68	83	6	0	3	31	1	0	2	11	0	21	2	1	7	.411	.377
Messner, Jake, S.K.*	.263	8	24	19	4	5	8	0	0	1	5	0	0	0	5	0	4	0	0	0	.421	.417
Moore, Chris, Port.*	.265	63	281	260	39	69	104	19	2	4	38	3	2	1	15	2	64	0	3	1	.400	.306
Moreno, Omar, Yak.†	.195	44	175	133	30	26	27	1	0	0	8	6	1	2	33	0	28	11	8	4	.203	.361
Nelson, Eric, Spo.†	.277	69	322	285	51	79	129	18	4	8	52	1	2	1	33	0	65	12	2	6	.453	.352
Nieckula, Aaron, S.O.	.260	15	62	50	11	13	20	4	0	1	9	0	1	2	9	0	12	2	1	2	.400	.387
Niemet, Robert, S.K.	.214	18	63	56	8	12	13	1	0	0	4	0	0	1	6	0	5	1	2	1	.232	.302
O'Keefe, Michael, Boi.*	.326	72	329	264	52	86	128	13	1	9	70	0	5	6	54	2	41	4	1	7	.485	.444
Ortega, Sixto, Port.	.250	1	4	4	1	1	1	0	0	0	0	0	0	0	0	0	1	0	0	0	.250	.250
Palmieri, Jon, Boi.	.325	48	178	151	34	49	69	10	2	2	31	0	4	6	17	0	10	4	4	3	.457	.404
Parnell, Sean, Ever.	.244	36	147	131	25	32	40	8	0	0	18	1	2	1	12	0	24	5	3	3	.305	.308
Pene, Ryan, S.K.	.192	40	146	125	18	24	35	5	0	2	21	0	0	1	19	1	40	1	0	0	.280	.313
Phillips, Dan, Port.	.286	71	303	280	38	80	137	19	4	10	53	0	3	6	14	1	72	8	4	9	.489	.330
Pinero, Juan, Eug.†	.235	10	41	34	5	8	11	1	1	0	6	0	0	3	4	0	4	5	1	1	.324	.366
Porter, Jamie, S.O.	.240	44	146	129	30	31	44	5	1	2	16	2	1	3	11	0	32	9	4	1	.341	.313
Proctor, Jerry, Yak.†	.194	10	42	36	4	7	9	2	0	0	3	0	0	1	5	0	15	0	0	0	.250	.310
Quinlan, Robb, Boi.	.322	73	335	295	51	95	144	20	1	9	77	0	1	4	35	2	52	5	3	5	.488	.400
Quintana, Wilfredo, Ever.	.161	19	64	62	6	10	16	3	0	1	5	0	2	0	0	0	21	0	1	2	.258	.156
Ramirez, Charlie, Spo.	.263	54	196	179	34	47	66	7	3	2	15	2	1	0	14	0	30	8	3	6	.369	.314
Ramirez, Oscar, Ever.	.308	6	18	13	4	4	7	3	0	0	5	0	0	0	4	0	3	0	0	0	.538	.471
Ransom, Troy, S.K.	.140	26	60	50	6	7	12	1	2	0	6	3	1	1	5	0	19	1	2	2	.240	.228
Raymundo, Gregg, Spo.	.323	67	295	254	44	82	133	16	1	11	44	2	3	4	32	4	37	1	1	9	.524	.403
Robles, Kevin, Ever.	.262	62	240	214	27	56	83	12	0	5	32	0	5	5	16	0	44	0	0	5	.388	.324
Rodriguez, Guillermo, S.K.	.254	33	126	114	16	29	52	5	0	6	34	0	0	3	9	1	28	1	3	2	.456	.325
Rosario, Carlos, S.O.†	.227	63	313	260	51	59	84	9	5	2	27	4	3	2	44	0	56	31	13	2	.323	.340
Rosario, Melvin, Port.*	.243	50	201	185	29	45	56	5	3	0	8	1	0	0	15	0	46	12	2	3	.303	.300
Rozich, John, Yak.	.231	40	159	134	20	31	46	5	2	2	16	2	0	0	23	0	41	1	3	2	.343	.344
Ruiz, Ramon, Yak.	.293	46	194	167	34	49	85	10	1	8	32	1	0	2	24	3	33	6	2	3	.509	.389
Ruiz, Willy, Spo.	.273	6	12	11	3	3	4	1	0	0	0	0	0	0	1	0	3	2	1	0	.364	.333
Ryan, Jeff, Eug.	.275	45	170	149	26	41	63	6	5	2	16	2	2	0	17	0	39	9	1	4	.423	.345
Sanchez, Tino, Port.†	.168	31	114	101	10	17	25	3	1	1	9	2	1	1	9	2	11	0	0	2	.248	.241
Santos, Jose, Boi.	.000	1	1	1	0	0	0	0	0	0	0	0	0	0	0	0	0	0	0	0	.000	.000
Scheid, Jeremy, S.O.*	.254	60	248	213	28	54	74	9	1	3	35	0	2	1	32	2	60	0	0	6	.347	.351
Seever, Brian, Boi.	.320	36	127	103	32	33	40	5	1	0	7	1	1	1	21	0	27	14	3	1	.388	.437
Shaffer, Joshua, Boi.*	.209	66	259	225	46	47	61	11	0	1	21	4	0	0	30	0	65	3	4	6	.271	.302
Shanks, James, Spo.	.258	69	294	260	41	67	76	9	0	0	29	11	1	3	19	0	52	19	5	6	.292	.314
Shearin, Jarrett, Spo.	.251	51	219	183	37	46	71	14	1	3	20	1	2	2	31	0	42	16	5	3	.388	.362
Shipp, Charles, Eug.	.267	6	16	15	3	4	5	1	0	0	1	0	0	0	1	0	3	0	0	2	.333	.313
Sledge, Terrmel, Ever.*	.318	62	273	233	43	74	103	8	3	5	32	2	9	2	27	0	35	9	8	2	.442	.406
Snelling, Christopher, Ever.* ..	.306	69	312	265	46	81	132	15	3	10	50	3	5	6	33	2	24	8	9	4	.498	.388
Sosa, Jorge, Port.†	.204	35	127	113	15	23	32	3	0	2	8	0	0	1	13	0	57	2	3	0	.283	.291
Soto, Jorge, S.O.	.244	45	210	160	37	39	81	9	0	11	30	0	2	10	38	1	63	1	2	0	.506	.414
Taylor, Joshua, Ever.	.211	42	114	90	11	19	23	1	0	1	8	3	2	2	17	0	21	0	1	2	.256	.342
Thurston, Joseph, Yak.*	.285	71	334	277	48	79	95	10	3	0	32	6	3	21	27	1	34	27	18	3	.343	.387
Ticen, Kevin, Boi.	.292	14	55	48	5	14	19	5	0	0	9	0	1	3	3	0	10	1	0	3	.396	.364
Turco, Paul, S.K.*	.181	44	133	116	8	21	24	3	0	0	5	6	0	1	10	0	27	3	1	2	.207	.252
Valderrama, Carlos, S.K.	.291	40	149	134	27	39	50	3	1	2	18	3	0	0	12	0	34	17	2	0	.373	.349
Valdez, Eladio, Yak.	.243	39	150	136	20	33	50	5	0	4	21	4	2	4	4	0	18	1	2	3	.368	.281
Vasquez, Sandy, Yak.	.262	75	329	271	46	71	102	11	1	6	44	0	1	13	44	2	91	18	8	3	.376	.389
Vilorio, Miguel, Port.	.338	21	88	77	14	26	32	3	0	1	5	1	1	1	7	0	14	13	4	2	.416	.395
Wren, Cliff, Yak.	.315	64	281	254	46	80	131	21	0	10	44	5	0	4	18	2	39	11	5	5	.516	.370
Wright, Michael, S.K.	.270	24	83	63	14	17	24	4	0	1	7	0	1	2	17	0	12	0	0	2	.381	.434
Zoccolillo, Peter, Eug.*	.235	64	209	183	20	43	55	7	1	1	15	0	2	2	22	1	26	3	2	2	.301	.321

GRAND SLAMS: Catalanotte, Dunn, Quinlan, 2 each; Burford, De La Cruz, Deschaine, Forbes, Jester, Lockwood, Matthews, Rodriguez, Snelling, 1 each.

AWARDED FIRST BASE ON CATCHER'S INTERFERENCE: Covington 4 (Alcala, Sanchez 3); Holst, 4 (Alcala 2, Carroll, Sanchez); Cohens, 2 (Alcala 2); Healy 2 (Wright 2); Howe (Luther); Matthews (Luther); Pene (Nieckula); Ramirez (Gregorio); Vilorio (Luther).

1999 PITCHING

TEAM

Team	W	L	Pct.	ERA	G	CG	ShO	Sv.	IP	H	TBF	R	ER	HR	SH	SF	HB	BB	IBB	SO	WP	Bk.
Spokane............	44	32	.579	4.17	76	0	1	19	672.2	669	2970	383	312	57	28	13	55	298	10	624	50	9
Everett...............	41	35	.539	4.29	76	4	4	18	662.2	626	2954	395	316	55	27	19	36	355	13	640	70	7

Team	W	L	Pct.	ERA	G	CG	ShO	Sv.	IP	H	TBF	R	ER	HR	SH	SF	HB	BB	IBB	SO	WP	Bk.
Portland	39	37	.513	4.74	76	1	1	24	668.2	672	3082	443	352	42	26	29	66	354	8	607	53	16
Salem-Keizer	37	39	.487	4.87	76	2	1	21	663.2	705	2998	432	359	54	24	26	49	319	5	570	58	19
Boise	43	33	.566	4.89	76	3	2	17	669.1	738	2993	451	364	65	17	16	37	254	14	554	63	9
S. Oregon	38	38	.500	5.17	76	0	1	12	672.1	742	3101	486	386	59	28	28	47	333	18	484	53	13
Yakima	33	43	.434	5.62	76	1	1	17	667.1	746	3065	504	417	74	15	33	46	319	5	476	68	5
Eugene	29	47	.382	5.85	76	0	4	12	650.1	773	3017	501	423	63	18	32	52	294	8	596	63	14

INDIVIDUAL

TOP QUALIFIERS FOR EARNED-RUN AVERAGE TITLE

Minimum 61 innings. *Lefthanded pitcher.

Pitcher, Team	W	L	Pct.	ERA	G	GS	CG	ShO	GF	Sv.	IP	H	TBF	R	ER	HR	SH	SF	HB	BB	IBB	SO	WP	Bk.
Crawford, Wesley, Boi.*	5	1	.833	2.21	11	9	2	0	0	0	61.0	52	251	23	15	3	0	1	1	17	0	54	6	0
Soriano, Rafael, Ever.	5	4	.556	3.11	14	14	0	0	0	0	75.1	56	323	34	26	8	1	0	4	49	0	83	2	0
Anderson, Craig, Ever.*	10	2	.833	3.20	15	15	2	1	0	0	90.0	81	360	42	32	7	3	2	3	13	1	82	5	1
Lopez, Aquilino, Ever.	7	6	.538	3.80	15	15	1	0	0	0	87.2	76	365	44	37	8	1	2	2	30	2	93	2	0
Esslinger, Cam, Port.	6	3	.667	3.83	14	14	0	0	0	0	80.0	76	351	37	34	1	4	2	10	35	1	68	3	2
King, James, Spo.*	6	2	.778	3.88	17	7	0	0	2	0	72.0	60	295	38	31	8	1	0	0	29	0	63	5	1
Devey, Phil, Yak.*	5	4	.556	3.91	13	13	1	0	0	0	78.1	70	330	43	34	6	2	0	9	27	0	56	6	1
Pacheco, Enemencio, Port.	4	3	.571	3.95	12	12	1	0	0	0	73.0	73	327	43	32	7	2	3	7	21	1	44	4	1
Surkont, Keith, S.O.	5	3	.625	4.48	17	13	0	0	4	1	74.1	85	332	45	37	5	4	3	2	35	2	39	6	1
Cozier, Vance, S.K.	5	4	.556	4.57	15	10	0	1	0	1	61.0	61	260	34	31	4	3	1	2	24	1	46	1	0
Baerlocher, Ryan, Spo.	7	2	.778	4.70	15	15	0	0	0	0	74.2	78	326	43	39	7	2	0	6	32	0	68	0	0
Hadden, Randy, Yak.	6	5	.545	4.78	16	11	0	0	3	1	86.2	94	371	51	46	7	0	4	3	25	1	53	6	1
Medrano, Juan, Spo.	3	5	.375	4.85	15	15	0	0	0	0	68.2	77	301	46	37	10	4	1	7	25	1	30	7	2
Walton, Sam, Ever.*	3	3	.500	4.94	14	14	0	0	0	0	62.0	55	292	39	34	7	0	1	2	60	0	59	16	0
Lackey, John, Boi.	6	2	.750	4.98	15	15	1	0	0	0	81.1	81	372	59	45	7	5	2	8	50	1	77	14	1

DEPARTMENTAL LEADERS: W—Anderson, 10; L—Gomer, 11; Pct.—Anderson, .833; G—Gehrke, Garcia, 32 each; GS—DePaula, 16; CG—Crawford, Anderson, 2 each; ShO—Williams, Barnes, Anderson, 1 each; GF—Gehrke, 32; Sv.—Gehrke, 13; IP—Anderson, 90.0; H—Gomer, 106; TBF—DePaula, 392; R—Gomer, 70; ER—Gomer, 67; HR—Rijo, 14; SH—Delgado, 7; SF—Gomer, 7; HB—Vracar, 13; BB—Walton, 60; IBB—Burton, 5; SO—Lopez, 93; WP—Walton, 16; BK—Lee, 6.

ALL PITCHERS

*Lefthanded pitcher.

Pitcher, Team	W	L	Pct.	ERA	G	GS	CG	ShO	GF	Sv.	IP	H	TBF	R	ER	HR	SH	SF	HB	BB	IBB	SO	WP	Bk.
Abate, Michael, Ever.	0	0	.000	0.00	1	0	0	0	1	0	1.0	0	3	0	0	0	0	0	0	1	0	1	0	0
Acosta, Jhon, Eug.	1	0	1.000	6.62	13	3	0	0	0	0	35.1	39	156	29	26	7	0	1	1	14	1	43	0	0
Adams, Christopher, Eug.	1	1	.500	5.30	17	0	0	0	14	4	18.2	24	94	14	11	0	0	1	0	14	1	17	5	0
Ainsworth, Kurt, S.K.	3	3	.500	1.61	10	10	1	0	0	0	44.2	34	187	18	8	1	3	2	3	18	0	64	3	0
Aldrup, Morey, Eug.	0	0	.000	0.00	1	0	0	0	1	0	0.2	0	2	0	0	0	0	0	0	0	0	0	0	0
Anderson, Craig, Ever.*	10	2	.833	3.20	15	15	2	1	0	0	90.0	81	360	42	32	7	3	2	3	13	1	82	5	1
Baerlocher, Ryan, Spo.	7	2	.778	4.70	15	15	0	0	0	0	74.2	78	326	43	39	7	2	0	6	32	0	68	0	0
Barnes, Pat, Ever.*	3	3	.500	5.66	15	10	1	1	0	0	49.1	59	236	40	31	4	4	1	5	26	0	39	8	1
Barnett, Nathan, Ever.*	0	0	.000	0.00	1	0	0	0	1	0	2.0	2	9	0	0	0	0	0	0	1	0	3	0	0
Bazzell, Shane, S.O.	3	1	.750	1.86	5	5	0	0	0	0	29.0	27	126	15	6	1	0	2	1	9	0	18	0	4
Beltran, Francis, Eug.	0	2	.000	8.36	16	0	0	0	7	0	28.0	41	142	32	26	2	0	1	3	14	0	28	6	0
Bergman, Dusty, Boi.*	5	5	.500	6.54	15	15	0	0	0	0	74.1	102	340	58	54	12	1	1	1	18	2	46	6	0
Berry, Jonathan, Yak.	1	6	.143	8.69	16	10	0	0	1	0	58.0	81	299	68	56	3	1	4	3	46	0	31	15	0
Berryman, Chad, Boi.	1	1	.500	2.35	24	0	0	0	11	1	46.0	34	181	16	12	4	0	1	2	13	1	42	8	2
Brummett, Sean, Boi.*	1	2	.333	6.68	17	3	0	0	2	0	32.1	41	148	25	24	3	1	0	1	12	1	26	1	0
Burgos, Ricardo, Yak.	2	3	.333	4.32	18	0	0	0	17	4	41.2	50	194	31	20	6	3	0	1	9	1	24	3	0
Burton, Timothy, Ever.	2	3	.400	3.72	26	0	0	0	13	1	38.2	40	181	25	16	2	3	1	0	21	5	28	6	0
Cameron, Ryan, Port.	1	0	1.000	0.00	4	0	0	0	3	1	5.0	1	18	0	0	0	0	1	1	4	0	0		
Carreras, Marino, Ever.*	1	4	.200	7.18	22	0	0	0	9	2	31.1	37	157	29	25	4	2	1	4	24	1	30	2	1
Castillo, Wilson, Yak.	1	0	1.000	8.10	8	0	0	0	2	0	20.0	26	110	25	18	3	2	1	4	22	0	11	6	1
Cercy, Richard, Port.	1	2	.333	5.34	13	1	0	0	2	0	28.2	29	137	19	17	0	0	3	6	17	0	25	6	0
Chiasson, Scott, S.O.	2	2	.500	5.22	15	13	0	0	2	0	69.0	80	318	52	40	6	3	2	5	39	0	51	3	0
Christensen, Benjamin, Eug. ..	0	2	.000	5.91	5	5	0	0	0	0	21.1	21	100	14	14	2	0	1	0	14	0	21	2	0
Cogan, Anthony, Spo.*	1	3	.250	1.36	27	0	0	0	11	4	39.2	26	160	10	6	0	6	1	2	14	2	37	3	1
Conroy, Ken, Eug.	5	3	.625	4.37	11	11	0	0	0	0	59.2	75	274	37	29	5	1	3	2	23	0	48	4	0
Cox, Ryan, S.K.	2	1	.667	3.15	8	8	0	0	0	0	34.1	39	139	13	12	1	2	1	1	10	0	20	0	2
Cozier, Vance, S.K.	5	4	.556	4.57	15	10	0	1	0	1	61.0	61	260	34	31	4	3	1	2	24	1	46	1	0
Crawford, Jeremy, S.O.*	2	1	.667	3.96	19	0	0	0	14	2	38.2	40	174	20	17	2	1	1	3	14	1	24	2	0
Crawford, Wesley, Boi.*	5	1	.833	2.21	11	9	2	0	0	0	61.0	52	251	23	15	3	0	1	1	17	0	54	6	0
Crowder, Chuck, Port.*	2	1	.667	4.33	6	6	0	0	0	0	27.0	24	119	14	13	2	0	0	2	16	0	39	2	0
Cruz, Juan, Eug.	5	6	.455	5.94	15	15	0	0	0	0	80.1	97	374	59	53	11	1	4	9	33	0	65	4	0
Cueto, Jose, Eug.	0	2	.000	4.50	4	4	0	0	0	0	24.0	26	101	13	12	2	2	1	4	5	0	21	1	0
Cunningham, Jeremy, S.K.	0	0	.000	4.70	7	5	0	0	1	1	15.1	25	76	11	8	0	0	1	6	9	0	13	0	0
Delgado, Danny, Eug.	2	3	.400	3.05	17	1	0	0	9	3	38.1	35	164	18	13	3	7	4	0	12	1	35	1	0
De Paula, Julio, Port.	6	6	.500	6.01	16	16	0	0	0	0	85.1	97	392	67	57	8	5	4	5	43	0	77	7	1
Devey, Phil, Yak.*	5	4	.556	3.91	13	13	1	0	0	0	78.1	70	330	43	34	6	2	0	9	27	0	56	6	1
Diaz, Zachary, Boi.*	1	2	.333	2.43	17	0	0	0	4	2	29.2	36	133	11	8	0	1	1	1	7	1	24	1	0
Douglass, Ryan, Spo.	0	1	.000	4.43	4	4	0	0	0	0	20.1	24	87	13	10	0	0	1	6	0	14	3	0	
Duprey, Pete, Ever.*	3	1	.750	1.00	22	0	0	0	12	3	36.0	26	143	7	4	0	2	1	3	12	0	32	1	0
Ebanks, Victor, Boi.	6	3	.667	3.94	27	0	0	0	13	3	48.0	44	209	23	21	4	0	2	3	22	2	53	2	0
Eppeneder, James, Eug.*	3	1	.750	2.87	20	0	0	0	15	1	31.1	21	137	10	10	3	1	0	1	22	1	42	1	0
Esslinger, Cam, Port.	6	3	.667	3.83	14	14	0	0	0	0	80.0	76	351	37	34	1	4	2	10	35	1	68	3	2
Featherstone, Deron, S.K.	0	1	.000	46.29	2	0	0	0	1	0	2.1	7	22	12	12	0	0	1	2	6	0	1	0	0
Ferrier, Shayne, Boi.	0	0	.000	27.00	4	0	0	0	3	0	3.1	9	24	10	10	2	0	1	4	0	2	1	0	
Fields, Brian, S.K.*	2	3	.400	3.12	24	0	0	0	17	5	34.2	30	146	14	12	5	3	2	1	14	1	38	4	0
Franco, Edwin, Spo.*	0	0	.000	2.08	3	1	0	0	1	0	4.1	5	20	1	1	0	1	0	0	2	0	6	1	1
Gage, Matthew, S.O.	8	7	.533	5.68	18	5	0	0	7	0	65.0	78	292	49	41	11	4	3	4	16	3	39	4	1

CLASS A *Northwest League*

Pitcher, Team	W	L	Pct.	ERA	G	GS	CG	ShO	GF	Sv.	IP	H	TBF	R	ER	HR	SH	SF	HB	BB	IBB	SO	WP	Bk.
Garcia, Raul, Spo.	9	2	.818	2.39	32	0	0	0	7	1	52.2	47	222	18	14	5	1	1	2	21	2	64	3	2
Garner, Brandon, Port.	0	0	.000	9.00	1	0	0	0	0	0	1.0	2	6	1	1	0	0	0	0	1	0	1	0	0
Gehrke, Jay, Spo.	0	3	.000	5.59	32	0	0	0	32	13	29.0	34	143	21	18	3	1	0	3	21	0	33	3	0
German, Franklyn, S.O.	3	5	.375	5.99	15	15	0	0	0	0	73.2	89	344	52	49	10	0	4	4	45	1	58	4	0
Gilfillan, Jason, Spo.	4	1	.800	5.71	25	0	0	0	7	1	34.2	31	161	23	22	6	3	4	6	22	0	37	3	1
Glysch, Craig, Boi.	3	4	.429	3.62	22	0	0	0	11	2	32.1	30	132	15	13	1	1	1	2	7	2	28	0	0
Gomer, Jeramy, Eug.*	2	11	.154	7.32	16	15	0	0	0	0	82.1	106	368	70	67	9	4	7	3	28	0	52	7	0
Gomez, Diogenes, Port.	3	2	.600	2.30	24	0	0	0	17	7	27.1	25	122	12	7	3	2	2	1	13	3	17	0	0
Gordon, Kevin, Port.	0	1	.000	9.31	8	0	0	0	0	0	9.2	14	55	18	10	2	1	0	0	7	0	11	1	0
Grezlovski, Benjamin, Boi.	0	1	.000	2.16	14	0	0	0	14	7	16.2	11	65	5	4	2	1	0	0	3	1	20	0	0
Grunwald, Erik, Ever.	0	0	.000	2.25	4	0	0	0	3	1	4.0	5	22	1	1	0	0	0	4	0	4	1	0
Gunderson, Matt, Eug.	1	3	.250	5.11	8	0	0	0	4	1	12.1	16	58	11	7	2	1	1	0	6	2	15	1	1
Haase, Frank, Port.*	0	1	.000	6.62	14	0	0	0	5	0	17.2	18	87	20	13	2	0	1	1	14	1	10	2	2
Hadden, Randy, Yak.	6	5	.545	4.78	16	11	0	0	3	1	86.2	94	371	51	46	7	0	4	3	25	1	53	6	1
Haworth, Brent, Boi.	0	0	.000	6.75	15	0	0	0	4	0	20.0	30	106	26	15	2	0	1	1	14	0	14	4	1
Heaverlo, Jeff, Ever.	1	0	1.000	2.08	3	0	0	0	1	0	8.2	5	35	5	2	1	1	0	1	2	0	9	1	0
Henderson, Bradley, S.O.	0	0	.000	27.00	1	0	0	0	1	0	0.1	1	2	1	1	1	0	0	0	0	0	0	0	0
Herrera, Pedro, Spo.	1	0	1.000	6.30	16	0	0	0	3	0	20.0	27	100	18	14	1	0	0	3	14	0	14	5	0
Hills, Mark, S.K.*	0	2	.000	6.71	16	7	0	0	1	0	51.1	70	253	49	39	3	3	3	1	27	0	41	4	1
Hilton, Nathan, S.O.	2	4	.333	6.82	16	14	0	0	0	0	67.1	80	324	63	51	7	3	1	6	28	0	50	7	0
Hoffman, Matt, Port.	4	1	.800	6.27	23	0	0	0	8	1	33.0	35	161	27	23	2	4	1	3	23	0	22	3	0
House, Craig, Port.	2	1	.667	2.08	26	0	0	0	19	11	34.2	28	154	14	8	0	1	0	5	14	0	58	4	2
Huller, Mike, S.K.*	0	0	.000	12.00	3	0	0	0	2	0	3.0	6	21	5	4	0	0	1	2	3	0	4	1	1
Hurtado, Ed, Boi.	0	0	.000	18.00	4	0	0	0	0	0	4.0	8	25	9	8	2	0	0	0	3	0	3	2	0
Jackson, Jonathan, Spo.	0	2	.000	5.60	19	0	0	0	3	0	35.1	49	166	27	22	6	2	1	5	18	1	32	0	0
Jackson, Stosh, Eug.*	0	2	.000	3.24	10	0	0	0	5	1	16.2	20	76	12	6	0	0	0	0	5	0	24	2	1
Jennings, Jason, Port.	1	0	1.000	1.00	2	2	0	0	0	0	9.0	5	33	1	1	0	0	0	0	2	0	11	0	0
Jimenez, Reinaldo, S.K.	2	5	.714	5.54	24	0	0	0	4	0	37.1	44	184	29	23	7	4	2	5	27	0	23	8	2
Johnson, Eric, S.K.	1	1	.500	7.71	15	1	0	0	3	0	16.1	18	86	15	14	1	0	2	17	0	18	5	1
Jones, Craig, Spo.	1	1	.500	6.23	2	2	0	0	0	0	8.2	11	42	8	6	0	0	4	1	0	4	0	0
Junge, Eric, Yak.	5	7	.417	5.82	15	15	0	0	0	0	82.0	98	363	60	53	10	3	6	0	31	0	55	3	0
Kent, Steven, Ever.*	3	2	.600	5.35	21	0	0	0	8	4	37.0	31	168	24	22	2	1	1	2	26	1	43	6	0
Kibler, Ryan, Port.	0	0	.000	21.60	1	1	0	0	0	0	3.1	8	21	8	8	1	0	0	4	0	4	0	0
Kidd, Jake, Port.	2	1	.667	2.65	11	0	0	0	6	0	17.0	10	67	6	5	1	1	1	2	5	0	17	2	0
King, James, Spo.*	7	2	.778	3.88	17	7	0	0	2	0	72.0	60	295	38	31	8	1	0	0	29	0	63	5	1
Klepaski, Jose, Ever.	0	0	.000	6.75	3	0	0	0	0	0	5.1	6	29	4	4	0	0	1	5	0	5	1	0
Kurtz-Nicholl, Jesse, Spo.*	5	2	.714	3.08	24	0	0	0	4	0	38.0	39	165	19	13	0	2	0	0	14	2	38	4	0
Labitzke, Jesse, Port.*	1	1	.500	3.67	18	0	0	0	5	3	27.0	24	121	15	11	0	1	0	1	17	0	30	2	0
Lackey, John, Boi.	6	2	.750	4.98	15	15	1	0	0	0	81.1	81	372	59	45	7	5	2	8	50	1	77	14	1
Lacorte, Vincent, Boi.	2	6	.250	5.40	11	9	0	0	1	0	50.0	64	224	38	30	5	1	1	3	15	2	32	5	1
Lavery, Timothy, Eug.*	3	2	.600	3.63	15	2	0	0	4	3	39.2	42	169	21	16	2	0	0	0	17	0	43	2	3
Lee, Fletcher, S.K.	2	1	.667	3.11	26	0	0	0	16	5	37.2	33	166	15	13	3	1	1	2	20	1	34	5	6
Lehr, Charles, S.O.	2	6	.250	5.95	14	4	0	0	7	0	42.1	62	207	36	28	3	5	1	2	17	3	40	9	0
Little, Rodney, Port.	0	0	1.000	13.00	6	0	0	0	0	0	9.0	12	55	15	13	0	0	2	1	17	1	4	4	0
Little, Roger, Port.	4	0	.000	6.21	12	4	0	0	3	0	33.1	41	160	27	23	2	0	1	3	15	0	21	2	0
Lopez, Aquilino, Ever.	7	6	.538	3.80	15	15	1	0	0	0	87.2	76	365	44	37	8	1	2	2	30	2	93	2	0
MacDougal, Robert, Spo.	2	2	.500	4.47	11	11	0	0	0	0	46.1	43	196	25	23	3	1	1	6	17	0	57	8	1
Mazur, Bryan, S.O.*	5	2	.714	3.35	23	0	0	0	20	8	40.1	36	172	20	15	5	2	3	1	17	2	29	3	0
Meagher, Brian, S.K.*	3	2	.600	4.88	17	6	0	0	3	0	51.2	56	236	32	28	2	0	4	28	0	41	2	3
Medrano, Juan, Spo.	3	5	.375	4.85	15	15	0	0	0	0	68.2	77	311	46	37	10	4	1	7	25	1	30	7	2
Meeks, Eric, S.O.	0	0	.000	9.00	6	3	0	0	1	0	19.0	21	91	22	19	2	0	1	3	11	0	10	0	1
Mendoza, Mario, Boi.	8	2	.800	5.49	15	15	0	0	0	0	78.2	93	355	58	48	5	4	2	7	29	1	47	9	2
Miller, Corey, S.O.	1	1	.500	2.25	5	0	0	0	1	0	12.0	5	44	4	3	1	0	0	1	2	0	10	1	0
Monzon, Yoel, Port.	3	4	.429	4.74	17	7	0	0	3	1	57.0	65	272	43	30	3	3	6	7	29	0	37	2	4
Moore, Darin, S.O.	1	0	1.000	1.42	5	2	0	0	0	0	12.2	9	55	4	2	0	1	0	2	6	1	14	1	0
Moore, Gregory, Boi.	2	2	.500	5.02	10	4	0	0	2	0	28.2	39	132	22	16	6	1	0	1	6	0	24	1	1
Negron, Jose, S.O.	0	4	.000	5.61	13	1	0	0	5	1	25.2	16	124	21	16	2	3	1	6	23	0	25	1	3
Ohm, Joe, Eug.	0	5	.000	6.31	21	1	0	0	7	0	41.1	50	196	31	29	3	4	2	2	19	0	32	7	1
Ojeda, Joseph, S.K.	2	3	.400	6.55	16	0	0	0	2	0	33.0	39	155	27	24	3	0	2	5	17	1	20	6	1
Olore, Kevin, Ever.	0	0	.000	4.88	22	0	0	0	12	2	31.1	31	141	21	17	5	0	0	2	21	1	31	4	2
Oyler, Scott, S.O.	0	0	.000	15.43	4	0	0	0	1	0	7.0	11	39	14	12	0	0	1	2	6	1	4	2	2
Pacheco, Enemencio, Port.	4	3	.571	3.95	12	12	1	0	0	0	73.0	73	327	43	32	7	2	3	7	21	1	44	4	1
Padilla, Charly, Boi.	1	0	1.000	7.23	10	0	0	0	4	0	18.2	21	92	16	15	4	0	1	0	13	0	14	0	1
Parker, Beau, Yak.	0	0	.000	0.00	3	1	0	0	0	0	6.2	6	27	0	0	0	0	0	4	0	6	0	0
Parrish, Wade, Yak.*	4	3	.571	4.05	17	8	0	0	5	0	60.0	57	261	30	27	4	0	2	1	24	0	48	2	0
Pichardo, Carlos, Spo.	1	2	.333	3.77	4	4	0	0	0	0	14.1	14	70	15	6	0	1	0	1	10	0	10	0	0
Polanco, Elvis, Eug.	0	0	.000	8.22	10	0	0	0	6	1	15.1	22	77	16	14	0	1	1	3	9	0	13	0	0
Pomar, Jason, S.O.	2	0	1.000	3.81	16	1	0	0	6	0	49.2	55	232	31	21	2	0	1	2	25	1	42	5	0
Pourron, Joe, S.K.	0	0	.000	11.57	8	0	0	0	2	0	7.0	13	40	10	9	1	0	2	0	6	0	6	2	0
Proctor, Scott, Yak.	4	2	.667	7.20	16	6	0	0	5	0	50.0	57	235	45	40	4	1	4	5	26	0	41	7	1
Putz, Joseph, Ever.	0	0	.000	4.84	10	0	0	0	3	2	22.1	23	99	13	12	2	1	4	2	11	1	17	0	1
Rijo, Fernando, Yak.	1	4	.200	7.69	18	4	0	0	10	2	57.1	63	271	57	49	14	0	5	9	31	0	39	9	0
Roberts, Rick, Yak.*	1	3	.250	7.27	11	6	0	0	1	0	34.2	52	176	34	28	5	0	3	0	23	0	26	4	1
Rodriguez, Francisco, Boi.	1	0	1.000	5.40	1	1	0	0	0	0	5.0	3	22	4	3	0	0	1	0	1	0	6	0	0
Russo, Mike, Spo.	2	2	.333	3.40	21	1	0	0	4	0	41.2	39	190	19	16	4	0	3	6	23	1	29	2	0
Sabino, Miguel, S.K.	1	2	.333	6.44	10	6	0	0	0	0	43.1	48	193	35	31	5	1	0	3	18	1	29	3	0
Sanches, Brian, Spo.	1	1	.500	4.76	9	9	0	0	0	0	34.0	32	146	19	18	2	0	0	1	12	0	51	0	0
Sanchez, Cade, S.O.	0	1	.000	3.80	9	0	0	0	4	0	21.1	20	103	15	9	0	0	3	21	0	15	4	1
Schreyer, Brett, Boi.	0	0	.000	1.08	6	0	0	0	4	2	8.1	6	40	5	1	0	0	0	1	7	0	8	0	0
Shaffar, Benjamin, Eug.	4	5	.444	5.79	14	13	0	0	0	0	65.1	79	311	54	42	5	0	1	9	27	1	76	6	5
Smith, Justin, Ever.*	1	0	1.000	3.18	2	0	0	0	1	0	5.2	3	21	3	2	1	0	0	1	0	8	0	0
Smyth, Steve, Eug.*	1	1	.500	4.38	5	5	0	0	0	0	24.2	29	110	17	12	1	1	3	0	7	0	14	2	1
Snyder, Kyle, Spo.	1	0	1.000	4.13	7	7	0	0	0	0	24.0	20	103	13	11	1	2	1	2	7	0	25	1	0
Soriano, Rafael, Ever.	5	4	.556	3.11	14	14	0	0	0	0	75.1	56	323	34	26	8	1	0	4	49	0	83	2	0
Springston, Adam, Yak.	0	0	.000	4.00	6	0	0	0	5	0	9.0	8	42	6	4	1	0	2	1	7	0	4	0	0

Pitcher, Team	W	L	Pct.	ERA	G	GS	CG	ShO	GF	Sv.	IP	H	TBF	R	ER	HR	SH	SF	HB	BB	IBB	SO	WP	Bk.
Stephenson, Brian, Eug.	0	1	.000	4.50	2	2	0	0	0	0	4.0	4	22	5	2	0	0	1	4	0	4	0	0
Suarez, Felipe, Boi.	1	2	.333	6.07	5	5	0	0	0	0	29.2	32	135	26	20	2	1	1	4	11	0	33	2	0
Sullivan, Luke, Boi.*	0	0	.000	13.50	2	0	0	0	0	0	1.1	2	7	2	2	1	0	0	2	0	1	1	0
Surkont, Keith, S.O.	5	3	.625	4.48	17	13	0	0	4	1	74.1	85	332	45	37	5	4	3	2	35	2	39	6	1
Taschner, Jack, S.K.*	3	2	.600	2.51	7	6	0	0	0	0	28.2	26	118	12	8	1	0	0	0	10	0	36	0	0
Tauscher, Ryan, S.O.*	2	1	.667	6.84	12	0	0	0	6	0	25.0	27	122	22	19	1	2	1	3	19	3	16	1	0
Turner, Kyle, Spo.*	0	1	.000	4.40	8	0	0	0	2	0	14.1	13	67	7	7	1	1	0	0	10	1	12	2	0
Ugas, Juan, Yak.	3	5	.375	4.62	20	2	0	0	12	3	50.2	55	237	32	26	7	3	0	5	26	1	45	2	0
Vargas, Derrick, Port.*	1	0	1.000	3.98	18	0	0	0	3	0	31.2	26	158	17	14	0	0	1	7	32	0	33	5	4
Vent, Kevin, S.K.	2	3	.400	5.03	17	6	0	0	10	3	39.1	44	174	25	22	4	2	2	1	18	0	31	2	1
Vracar, Paul, Eug.	1	0	1.000	10.69	20	0	0	0	8	0	32.0	46	177	45	38	5	1	4	13	26	2	26	10	2
Waldrum, Kevin, Eug.	0	0	.000	6.14	4	0	0	0	1	0	7.1	10	34	6	5	2	0	1	1	3	0	1	1	0
Wallace, Jeffrey, Yak.	0	1	.000	3.28	11	0	0	0	7	0	24.2	20	110	12	9	2	0	0	3	14	2	26	3	0
Walters, Jason, Yak.	0	1	.000	8.22	8	0	0	0	7	3	7.2	9	39	10	7	2	0	2	2	7	0	13	2	0
Walton, Sam, Ever.*	3	3	.500	4.94	14	14	0	0	0	0	62.0	55	292	39	34	7	0	1	2	60	0	59	16	0
Wayne, Hawkeye, Ever.	0	2	.000	8.29	15	7	0	0	0	0	33.2	47	186	39	31	1	2	1	5	32	0	34	13	0
Webb, John, Eug.	1	0	1.000	0.00	2	0	0	0	2	1	4.0	1	14	0	0	0	0	0	0	1	0	3	0	0
Wells, Roy, Ever.	0	2	.000	19.29	2	0	0	0	0	0	2.1	5	15	5	5	0	0	1	0	4	0	3	0	1
Wells, Zach, S.K.	4	1	.800	3.48	15	0	0	0	6	1	20.2	17	91	13	8	2	2	2	3	8	0	13	0	0
Wiggins, Daniel, Eug.	1	0	1.000	6.00	3	0	0	0	1	0	6.0	4	25	5	4	1	1	0	0	3	0	8	2	0
Williams, Jerome, S.K.	1	1	.500	2.19	7	7	1	1	0	0	37.0	29	151	13	9	1	0	1	3	11	0	34	1	0
Yacco, Anthony, S.K.	0	1	.000	13.15	9	4	0	0	1	1	13.0	16	73	19	19	1	0	1	5	14	0	12	4	1
Young, Colin, Port.*	2	5	.286	4.88	15	13	0	0	1	0	59.0	59	266	39	32	8	1	2	5	28	0	74	4	0
Zimmerman, Jordan, Ever.*	0	0	.000	27.00	1	0	0	0	0	0	0.2	3	5	2	2	0	0	0	0	0	1	1	0
Zirelli, Michael, S.K.	1	4	.200	4.41	25	0	0	0	4	2	51.0	50	227	31	25	9	0	2	3	17	0	47	6	0

COMBINATION SHUTOUTS: **Boise (2)**—Crawford-Brummett-Haworth, Mendoza-Glysch-Diaz. **Eugene (4)**—Shaffar-Lavery-Adams, Smyth-Polanco, Cueto-Eppeneder, Shaffar-Beltran. **Everett (2)**—Anderson-Putz-Kent, Soriano-Carreras-Kent. **Portland (1)**—Esslinger-House-Lebitzke-Cameron. **Salem-Keizer (0)**—None. **Southern Oregon (1)**—Hilton-Pomar-Surkont. **Spokane (1)**—Medrano-Garcia-Cogan. Yakima (1)—Hadden-Ugas.

NO-HIT GAMES: None.

1999 FIELDING

TEAM

Team	Pct.	G	PO	A	E	TC	DP	TP	PB	Team	Pct.	G	PO	A	E	TC	DP	TP	PB
Spokane	.961	76	2019	858	118	2995	59	0	13	Yakima	.957	76	2002	890	129	3021	74	0	21
Salem-Keizer	.959	76	1991	808	119	2918	70	0	22	S. Oregon	.955	76	2017	901	139	3057	55	0	27
Boise	.958	76	2008	879	126	3013	65	0	11	Everett	.952	76	1988	788	139	2915	71	0	18
Eugene	.958	76	1951	727	117	2795	67	0	21	Portland	.949	76	2006	782	150	2938	51	0	17

INDIVIDUAL

FIRST BASEMEN

NOTE: All caps denotes fielding-percentage leader based on 38 games for catchers, 51 for all other non-pitchers and 61 innings for pitchers. *Throws lefthanded.

Player, Team	Pct.	G	PO	A	E	TC	DP
Abate, Michael, Ever.	.000	1	0	0	0	0	0
Aldrup, Morey, Eug.	.000	1	0	0	0	0	0
Baker, Jacob, Spo.	1.000	34	297	24	0	321	24
Barnett, Nathan, Ever.*	.989	16	83	3	1	87	7
Clay, Michael, Spo.	1.000	6	38	4	0	42	5
Curry, Christopher, Eug.	1.000	1	4	0	0	4	0
De La Cruz, Jose, S.O.	.947	4	17	1	1	19	2
Estrella, Gorky, Ever.	.973	10	69	4	2	75	4
Gundrum, Kristoffer, Ever.*	.956	20	139	12	7	158	13
Harvey, Kenneth, Spo.	.984	37	289	22	5	316	18
Healy, Liam, Spo.	.952	6	56	4	3	63	9
Hemme, Justin, Port.*	.976	69	579	28	15	622	40
Hertel, Brian, Ever.	1.000	5	32	4	0	36	2
KELLEY, Casey, Boi.	.994	53	420	41	3	464	41
Koen, Nate, Eug.	1.000	3	6	0	0	6	1
Longmire, Marcel, Eug.	.750	1	3	0	1	4	0
Luster, Jeremy, S.K.	.975	35	284	25	8	317	29
Mahoney, Ricardo, Port.	.947	8	68	3	4	75	4
Martinez, Victor, Ever.	.959	10	69	1	3	73	5
McGowan, Sean, S.K.	.983	32	274	18	5	297	29
Medina, Luis, Eug.	.977	34	199	17	5	221	19
Niemet, Robert, S.K.	.966	10	77	7	3	87	2
Palmieri, Jon, Boi.	.984	31	284	16	5	305	20
Pene, Ryan, S.K.	.909	5	19	1	2	22	2
Quinlan, Robb, Boi.	1.000	2	12	2	0	14	1
Robles, Kevin, Ever.	.983	34	218	17	4	239	32
Scheid, Jeremy, S.O.*	.989	53	477	43	6	526	32
Soto, Jorge, S.O.	.978	24	215	6	5	226	14
Vasquez, Sandy, Yak.	.976	23	192	12	5	209	14
Wren, Cliff, Yak.	.993	55	536	32	4	572	52
Wright, Michael, S.K.	1.000	1	4	0	0	4	0
Zoccolillo, Peter, Eug.	.987	47	356	23	5	384	35

SECOND BASEMEN

Player, Team	Pct.	G	PO	A	E	TC	DP
Aldrup, Morey, Eug.	1.000	3	2	4	0	6	2
Amezaga, Alfredo, Boi.	.955	40	83	110	9	202	28
Bloomquist, William, Ever.	.953	37	63	79	7	149	19
Boeth, Timothy, Boi.	.933	29	46	79	9	134	14
Cook, Joshua, S.K.	.969	23	47	47	3	97	17
Dalton, Joshua, Yak.	.951	46	89	105	10	204	25
Durango, Ariel, Ever.	.949	22	47	64	6	117	22
DZURILLA, Michael, Eug.	.966	68	138	148	10	296	35
Gasparino, Billy, Port.	.915	11	24	19	4	47	5
Gay, Dennis, Boi.	.905	6	9	10	2	21	2
Goelz, Jim, Yak.	.962	30	50	78	5	133	28
Gsell, Tony, Eug.	.944	7	18	16	2	36	3
Hart, Dickie, Boi.	1.000	3	2	0	0	2	0
Henderson, Bradley, S.O.	.946	40	74	101	10	185	14
Jester, Joe, S.K.	.991	26	46	66	1	113	20
Keller, G.W., S.O.	.976	7	18	22	1	41	6
Lucas, Kevin, Spo.	.950	8	8	30	2	40	7
Luther, Ryan, S.K.	.967	15	23	35	2	60	4
Martinez, Victor, Ever.	1.000	3	2	3	0	5	0
Mattern, Erik, S.K.	1.000	13	15	19	0	34	3
Moore, Chris, Port.	.945	48	98	124	13	235	15
Nelson, Eric, Spo.	.935	66	130	189	22	341	34
Quinlan, Robb, Boi.	.862	6	13	12	4	29	1
Ransom, Troy, S.K.	1.000	1	0	5	0	5	1
Rosario, Carlos, S.O.	.946	35	85	108	11	204	17
Ruiz, Ramon, Yak.	.857	1	2	4	1	7	2
Ruiz, Willy, Spo.	1.000	3	5	3	0	8	0
Ryan, Jeff, Eug.	1.000	7	6	3	0	9	1
Soto, Jorge, S.O.	.000	1	0	0	0	0	0
Taylor, Joshua, Ever.	.955	20	31	33	3	67	6
Thurston, Joseph, Yak.	1.000	1	3	0	0	3	0
Turco, Paul, S.K.	.919	15	16	18	3	37	4
Vilorio, Miguel, Port.	.918	20	40	38	7	85	11

THIRD BASEMEN

Player, Team	Pct.	G	PO	A	E	TC	DP
Aldrup, Morey, Eug.	.000	1	0	0	0	0	0
Baker, Jacob, Spo.	1.000	3	1	1	0	2	0
Boeth, Timothy, Boi.	.600	3	0	3	2	5	0
Clay, Michael, Spo.	.957	20	11	33	2	46	1
Cook, Joshua, S.K.	.842	6	5	11	3	19	0
Cordido, Julio, S.K.	.922	70	60	128	16	204	8
Durango, Ariel, Ever.	.000	1	0	0	0	0	0
Estrella, Gorky, Ever.	.870	19	11	36	7	54	1
Gasparino, Billy, Port.	.905	43	28	86	12	126	6
Goelz, Jim, Yak.	1.000	11	7	16	0	23	1
GRIPP, Ryan, Eug.	.938	70	52	130	12	194	21
Henderson, Bradley, S.O.	.800	5	2	6	2	10	0
Hochgesang, Joshua, S.O.	.870	9	6	14	3	23	0
Howe, Matt, S.O.	.883	53	27	124	20	171	10
Keller, G.W., S.O.	.927	10	10	28	3	41	1
Leone, Justin, Ever.	.906	40	29	86	12	127	8
Lincoln, Justin, Port.	1.000	2	0	4	0	4	0
Lucas, Kevin, Spo.	.900	10	6	12	2	20	1
Luther, Ryan, S.K.	1.000	3	2	5	0	7	0
Mahoney, Ricardo, Port.	.850	22	20	48	12	80	2
Martinez, Victor, Ever.	.757	14	7	21	9	37	1
Mattern, Erik, S.K.	1.000	1	0	2	0	2	0
Medina, Luis, Eug.	.769	13	2	18	6	26	2
Moore, Chris, Port.	.829	12	11	23	7	41	2
Nieckula, Aaron, S.O.	.000	1	0	0	0	0	0
Quinlan, Robb, Boi.	.889	64	38	147	23	208	13
Ramirez, Oscar, Ever.	.800	5	3	1	1	5	0
Raymundo, Gregg, Spo.	.893	52	26	74	12	112	5
Robles, Kevin, Ever.	.000	1	0	0	0	0	0
Ruiz, Ramon, Yak.	.883	35	22	84	14	120	9
Ruiz, Willy, Spo.	.500	2	0	1	1	2	0
Santos, Jose, Boi.	1.000	1	0	2	0	2	0
Taylor, Joshua, Ever.	.813	9	7	19	6	32	1
Ticen, Kevin, Boi.	.813	11	7	19	6	32	0
Valdez, Eladio, Yak.	.848	32	14	81	17	112	9

SHORTSTOPS

Player, Team	Pct.	G	PO	A	E	TC	DP
Aldrup, Morey, Eug.	.800	3	0	4	1	5	1
Amezaga, Alfredo, Boi.	.945	10	18	34	3	55	4
Castillo, Ruben, Ever.	.946	62	122	178	17	317	41
Clay, Michael, Spo.	.000	1	0	0	0	0	0
Clements, Jason, S.O.	.848	33	37	91	23	151	17
Cook, Joshua, S.K.	.893	7	11	14	3	28	4
Dalton, Joshua, Yak.	.884	9	14	24	5	43	6
Declet, Miguel, S.O.	.898	13	20	24	5	49	3
Deschaine, James, Eug.	.773	15	17	34	15	66	2
Durango, Ariel, Ever.	.857	2	4	2	1	7	1
ELLIS, Mark, Spo.	.958	71	138	230	16	384	41
Gasparino, Billy, Port.	.857	10	9	27	6	42	1
Gay, Dennis, Boi.	1.000	4	7	10	0	17	1
Gipson, Charles, Ever.	1.000	1	0	4	0	4	1
Goelz, Jim, Yak.	1.000	1	1	3	0	4	0
Gsell, Tony, Eug.	.943	62	92	174	16	282	29
Hall, Justin, S.O.	.852	5	8	15	4	27	1
Jester, Joe, S.K.	.940	48	57	132	12	201	27
Leone, Justin, Ever.	.921	18	28	42	6	76	9
Lincoln, Justin, Port.	.913	66	77	184	25	286	24
Lucas, Kevin, Spo.	.958	8	5	18	1	24	4
Luther, Ryan, S.K.	.714	1	2	3	2	7	1
Moore, Chris, Port.	1.000	3	4	10	0	14	3
Rosario, Carlos, S.O.	.951	31	55	99	8	162	8
Shaffer, Joshua, Boi.	.926	66	101	225	26	352	34
Taylor, Joshua, Ever.	1.000	1	1	0	0	1	0
Thurston, Joseph, Yak.	.924	68	108	246	29	383	43
Turco, Paul, S.K.	.910	25	32	79	11	122	19

OUTFIELDERS

Player, Team	Pct.	G	PO	A	E	TC	DP
Abate, Michael, Ever.	.930	44	48	5	4	57	0
Aldrup, Morey, Eug.	1.000	20	21	0	0	21	0
Allen, Shane, Yak.	.943	25	47	3	3	53	1
Alou, Felipe, Spo.	.900	15	9	0	1	10	0
Amador, Gerardo, Ever.	1.000	14	15	1	0	16	0
Asche, Kirk, S.O.	.991	63	107	2	1	110	1
Baker, Jacob, Spo.	1.000	16	24	0	0	24	0
Bass, Kevin, Eug.	.895	39	65	3	8	76	0
Bikowski, Scott, Boi.*	.991	61	98	8	1	107	1
Bloomquist, William, Ever.	1.000	1	2	0	0	2	0
Boeth, Timothy, Boi.	1.000	4	2	0	0	2	0
Burford, Kevin, Port.*	.857	11	11	1	2	14	1
Catalanotte, Greg, Port.	.969	67	111	12	4	127	3

Player, Team	Pct.	G	PO	A	E	TC	DP
Cepeda, Ali, S.K.	.864	15	17	2	3	22	0
Cohens, Derrick, Eug.	.967	36	57	1	2	60	1
Cordova, Ben, Spo.*	1.000	4	4	0	0	4	0
Covington, Kevin, Yak.	.942	35	64	1	4	69	1
Dealey, Scott, S.K.	.988	69	158	8	2	168	3
Deschaine, James, Eug.	.935	26	40	3	3	46	1
Dunn, Casey, Spo.	1.000	1	2	0	0	2	0
Forbes, Matt, S.O.	.965	61	130	6	5	141	0
Gonzalez, Julian, Spo.	.867	16	25	1	4	30	0
Grochol, Bryan, S.K.*	1.000	6	5	0	0	5	0
Gundrum, Kristoffer, Ever.*	.875	9	7	0	1	8	0
Healy, Liam, Spo.	1.000	7	9	1	0	10	0
Holst, Micah, S.K.	.977	52	78	6	2	86	0
Jaroncyk, Ryan, Yak.	1.000	8	18	1	0	19	0
Johnson, Gary, Boi.*	.957	69	108	3	5	116	1
Johnstone, Benjamin, Eug.	.974	48	112	1	3	116	0
Kelleher, Pat, Boi.	1.000	6	11	1	0	12	0
Keller, G.W., S.O.	1.000	10	14	2	0	16	0
Kluver, Hayden, Yak.*	.923	15	23	1	2	26	1
Lockwood, Mike, S.O.*	.969	65	113	10	4	127	3
Lucas, Kevin, Spo.	.947	12	16	2	1	19	1
Luther, Ryan, S.K.	.935	21	29	0	2	31	0
Mahoney, Ricardo, Port.	.889	16	16	0	2	18	0
Marquez, Eduardo, Eug.	.871	30	26	1	4	31	1
Martinez, Victor, Ever.	1.000	4	2	0	0	2	0
Matthews, Lamont, Yak.*	.976	66	160	5	4	169	0
Moreno, Omar, Yak.	.986	36	69	2	1	72	0
Niemet, Robert, S.K.	.889	6	8	0	1	9	0
O'Keefe, Michael, Boi.*	.990	72	91	4	1	96	0
Parnell, Sean, Ever.	.976	29	39	2	1	42	0
Pene, Ryan, S.K.	.945	30	49	3	3	55	1
Phillips, Dan, Port.	.973	68	104	3	3	110	0
Pinero, Juan, Eug.	1.000	9	15	1	0	16	1
Porter, Jamie, S.O.	.938	38	56	4	4	64	1
Quintana, Wilfredo, Ever.	.941	16	14	2	1	17	0
Ramirez, Charlie, Spo.	.913	53	61	2	6	69	0
Ransom, Troy, S.K.	1.000	21	20	0	0	20	0
Rosario, Melvin, Port.*	.968	48	116	4	4	124	1
Ryan, Jeff, Eug.	.930	40	58	8	5	71	1
Seever, Brian, Boi.	.983	33	54	3	1	58	0
Shanks, James, Spo.	.945	67	130	7	8	145	1
Shearin, Jarrett, Spo.	.943	51	75	8	5	88	1
Shipp, Charles, Eug.	1.000	4	2	1	0	3	0
Sledge, Terrmel, Ever.*	.958	62	92	0	4	96	0
SNELLING, Christopher, Ever.*	.993	69	138	6	1	145	0
Sosa, Jorge, Port.	.940	26	45	2	3	50	0
Turco, Paul, S.K.	.000	1	0	0	0	0	0
Valderrama, Carlos, S.K.	.971	36	60	7	2	69	0
Vasquez, Sandy, Yak.	.978	51	83	6	2	91	0
Zoccolillo, Peter, Eug.	1.000	10	18	0	0	18	0

CATCHERS

Player, Team	Pct.	G	PO	A	E	TC	DP	PB
Alcala, Juan, Ever.	.954	15	125	21	7	153	2	6
Barski, Chris, Boi.	1.000	6	35	0	0	35	0	0
Carroll, Mark, Ever.	.980	44	336	48	8	392	2	7
Christianson, Ryan, Ever.	.981	13	98	4	2	104	1	0
CURRY, Christopher, Eug.	.991	38	285	36	3	324	6	9
De La Cruz, Jose, S.O.	1.000	15	91	13	0	104	0	6
Doudt, Anthony, Boi.	.992	17	109	12	1	122	0	3
Dunn, Casey, Spo.	.996	33	241	36	1	278	0	3
Duplissea, William, Yak.	.985	12	51	15	1	67	0	5
Glassey, Josh, Yak.	.981	28	180	24	4	208	2	5
Gregorio, Thomas, Boi.	.987	51	332	55	5	392	2	8
Johnson, Brian, Spo.	.980	39	303	43	7	353	1	8
Koen, Nate, Eug.	1.000	18	61	5	0	66	0	1
Kopitzke, Casey, Eug.	.987	37	259	35	4	298	4	11
Laird, Gerald, S.O.	.972	51	305	70	11	386	4	19
Lombardi, Dominick, Boi.	.907	6	40	9	5	54	1	0
Lopez, Norberto, Boi.	1.000	5	32	0	0	32	0	0
Luther, Ryan, S.K.	.970	22	137	24	5	166	0	10
Mahoney, Ricardo, Port.	.944	3	33	1	2	36	0	1
Mapes, Jake, S.K.	.929	11	57	8	5	70	1	3
McAuley, James, Spo.	.961	8	68	5	3	76	0	2
McQueen, Eric, Port.	.988	46	347	53	5	405	7	9
Nieckula, Aaron, S.O.	.975	14	99	16	3	118	3	2
Ortega, Sixto, Port.	1.000	1	7	0	0	7	0	0
Robles, Kevin, Ever.	.968	13	82	8	3	93	0	5
Rodriguez, Guillermo, S.K.	.982	31	248	26	5	279	1	4
Rozich, John, Yak.	.971	40	231	35	8	274	4	11
Sanchez, Tino, Port.	.966	31	230	28	9	267	4	7
Wright, Michael, S.K.	.960	22	118	27	6	151	2	5

PITCHERS

Player, Team	Pct.	G	PO	A	E	TC	DP
Abate, Michael, Ever.	.000	1	0	0	0	0	0
Acosta, Jhon, Eug.	1.000	13	2	3	0	5	0
Adams, Christopher, Eug.	1.000	17	0	4	0	4	1
Ainsworth, Kurt, S.K.	1.000	10	0	5	0	5	0
Aldrup, Morey, Eug.	.000	1	0	0	0	0	0
Anderson, Craig, Ever.*	1.000	15	5	15	0	20	2
Baerlocher, Ryan, Spo.	.941	15	4	12	1	17	0
Barnes, Pat, Ever.*	.750	15	0	6	2	8	0
Barnett, Nathan, Ever.*	.000	1	0	0	0	0	0
Bazzell, Shane, S.O.	1.000	5	1	6	0	7	0
Beltran, Francis, Eug.	1.000	16	1	3	0	4	0
Bergman, Dusty, Boi.*	.882	15	5	10	2	17	1
Berry, Jonathan, Yak.	.895	16	7	10	2	19	1
Berryman, Chad, Boi.	1.000	24	4	3	0	7	0
Brummett, Sean, Boi.*	1.000	17	3	4	0	7	1
Burgos, Ricardo, Yak.	1.000	18	2	9	0	11	0
Burton, Timothy, Ever.	1.000	26	2	4	0	6	0
Cameron, Ryan, Port.	.500	4	0	1	1	2	1
Carreras, Marino, Ever.*	.500	22	0	1	1	2	1
Castillo, Wilson, Yak.	.800	8	0	4	1	5	0
Cercy, Richard, Port.	1.000	13	2	4	0	6	1
Chiasson, Scott, S.O.	1.000	15	6	9	0	15	1
Christensen, Benjamin, Eug.	1.000	5	1	0	0	1	0
Cogan, Anthony, Spo.*	.889	27	2	14	2	18	0
Conroy, Ken, Eug.	.900	11	2	7	1	10	0
Cox, Ryan, S.K.	.833	8	1	4	1	6	1
Cozier, Vance, S.K.	1.000	15	0	9	0	9	1
Crawford, Jeremy, S.O.*	.923	19	5	7	1	13	0
Crawford, Wesley, Boi.*	.889	11	3	5	1	9	1
Crowder, Chuck, Port.*	.800	6	1	3	1	5	0
Cruz, Juan, Eug.	.889	15	2	6	1	9	0
Cueto, Jose, Eug.	.750	4	1	2	1	4	0
Cunningham, Jeremy, S.K.	1.000	7	1	2	0	3	0
De Paula, Julio, Port.	.900	16	3	6	1	10	0
Delgado, Danny, Ever.	.778	17	2	5	2	9	0
Devey, Phil, Yak.*	1.000	13	4	21	0	25	0
Diaz, Zachary, Boi.*	1.000	17	0	4	0	4	0
Douglass, Ryan, Spo.	1.000	4	2	4	0	6	0
Duprey, Pete, Ever.*	1.000	22	1	8	0	9	2
Ebanks, Victor, Boi.	.875	27	2	5	1	8	0
Eppeneder, James, Eug.*	1.000	20	1	1	0	2	0
Esslinger, Cam, Port.	1.000	14	3	14	0	17	1
Featherstone, Deron, S.K.	.000	4	0	0	0	0	0
Ferrier, Shayne, Boi.	.000	4	0	0	0	0	0
Fields, Brian, S.K.*	1.000	24	1	4	0	5	0
Franco, Edwin, Spo.	1.000	3	0	2	0	2	0
Gage, Matthew, S.O.	1.000	18	5	2	0	7	0
Garcia, Raul, Spo.	.889	32	5	3	1	9	0
Garner, Brandon, Port.	.000	1	0	0	0	0	0
Gehrke, Jay, Spo.	1.000	32	2	1	0	3	0
German, Franklyn, S.O.	.941	15	4	12	1	17	0
Gilfillan, Jason, Spo.	1.000	25	2	2	0	4	0
Glysch, Craig, Boi.	.889	22	5	3	1	9	0
Gomer, Jeramy, Eug.*	.882	16	5	10	2	17	3
Gomez, Diogenes, Port.	1.000	24	2	5	0	7	0
Gordon, Kevin, Port.	.500	8	0	1	1	2	0
Grezlovski, Benjamin, Boi.	.500	14	0	2	2	4	0
Grunwald, Erik, Ever.	.000	4	0	0	0	0	0
Gunderson, Matt, Eug.	1.000	8	1	2	0	3	0
Haase, Frank, Port.*	1.000	14	0	2	0	2	0
Hadden, Randy, Yak.	.955	16	4	17	1	22	1
Haworth, Brent, Boi.	.600	15	0	3	2	5	0
Heaverlo, Jeff, Ever.	1.000	3	1	1	0	2	0
Henderson, Bradley, S.O.	.000	1	0	0	0	0	0
Herrera, Pedro, Spo.	1.000	16	1	4	0	5	0
Hills, Mark, S.K.*	.833	16	1	9	2	12	0
Hilton, Nathan, S.O.	.857	16	2	10	2	14	0
Hoffman, Matt, Port.	1.000	23	1	7	0	8	1
House, Craig, Port.	.857	26	0	6	1	7	0
Huller, Mike, S.K.*	.000	3	0	0	0	0	0
Hurtado, Ed, Boi.	.000	4	0	0	0	0	0
Jackson, Jonathan, Spo.	.875	19	2	5	1	8	1
Jackson, Stosh, Eug.*	.667	10	0	2	1	3	0
Jennings, Jason, Port.	1.000	2	1	1	0	2	0
Jimenez, Reinaldo, S.K.	.800	24	2	6	2	10	0
Johnson, Eric, S.K.	1.000	15	0	2	0	2	0
Jones, Craig, Spo.	1.000	2	0	1	0	1	0
Junge, Eric, Yak.	.900	15	3	6	1	10	0
Kent, Steven, Ever.*	1.000	21	1	3	0	4	0
Kibler, Ryan, Port.	1.000	1	1	0	0	1	0
Kidd, Jake, Port.	1.000	11	1	3	0	4	0
KING, James, Spo.*	1.000	17	7	24	0	31	0
Klepaski, Jose, Ever.	1.000	3	0	2	0	2	0
Kurtz-Nicholl, Jesse, Spo.*	.833	24	0	5	1	6	2
Labitzke, Jesse, Port.*	1.000	18	0	4	0	4	0
Lackey, John, Boi.	1.000	15	10	6	0	16	0
Lacorte, Vincent, Boi.	1.000	11	6	10	0	16	0
Lavery, Timothy, Eug.*	1.000	15	4	6	0	10	0
Lee, Fletcher, S.K.	1.000	26	1	5	0	6	1
Lehr, Charles, S.O.	.923	14	4	8	1	13	0
Little, Rodney, Port.	1.000	6	1	1	0	2	0
Little, Roger, Port.	.667	12	0	2	1	3	0
Lopez, Aquilino, Ever.	.727	15	5	11	6	22	0
MacDougal, Robert, Spo.	.857	11	1	5	1	7	0
Mazur, Bryan, S.O.*	1.000	23	2	8	0	10	1
Meagher, Brian, S.K.*	1.000	17	2	10	0	12	0
Medrano, Juan, Spo.	.882	15	9	6	2	17	0
Meeks, Eric, S.O.	1.000	6	3	1	0	4	0
Mendoza, Mario, Boi.	.737	15	6	8	5	19	1
Miller, Corey, S.O.	1.000	5	3	0	0	3	0
Monzon, Yoel, Port.	.909	17	6	4	1	11	0
Moore, Darin, S.O.	1.000	5	0	4	0	4	0
Moore, Gregory, Boi.	1.000	10	4	4	0	8	0
Negron, Jose, S.O.	1.000	13	2	1	0	3	0
Ohm, Joe, Eug.	.889	21	3	5	1	9	0
Ojeda, Joseph, S.K.	.917	16	5	6	1	12	0
Olore, Kevin, Ever.	.750	22	0	3	1	4	0
Oyler, Scott, S.O.	1.000	4	0	4	0	4	0
Pacheco, Enemencio, Port.	.947	12	5	13	1	19	0
Padilla, Charly, Boi.	1.000	10	1	2	0	3	0
Parker, Beau, Yak.	1.000	3	0	1	0	1	0
Parrish, Wade, Yak.*	.923	17	1	11	1	13	0
Pichardo, Carlos, Spo.	.500	4	1	1	2	4	0
Polanco, Elvis, Eug.	1.000	10	1	2	0	3	0
Pomar, Jason, S.O.	.889	16	3	5	1	9	0
Pourron, Joe, S.K.	.000	8	0	0	0	0	0
Proctor, Scott, Yak.	1.000	16	2	6	0	8	1
Putz, Joseph, Ever.	1.000	10	3	5	0	8	1
Rijo, Fernando, Yak.	.929	18	8	5	1	14	0
Roberts, Rick, Yak.*	1.000	11	1	8	0	9	1
Rodriguez, Francisco, Boi.	1.000	1	1	0	0	1	0
Russo, Mike, Spo.	.800	21	2	6	2	10	1
Sabino, Miguel, S.K.	.750	10	2	1	1	4	0
Sanches, Brian, Spo.	.800	9	0	4	1	5	0
Sanchez, Cade, S.O.	1.000	9	2	1	0	3	0
Schreyer, Brett, Boi.	.500	9	0	1	1	2	0
Shaffar, Benjamin, Eug.	.900	14	6	3	1	10	0
Smith, Justin, Ever.*	1.000	2	0	1	0	1	0
Smyth, Steve, Eug.*	.667	5	1	3	2	6	0
Snyder, Kyle, Spo.	.800	7	1	7	2	10	0
Soriano, Rafael, Ever.	1.000	14	3	8	0	11	0
Springston, Adam, Yak.	1.000	6	2	0	0	2	0
Stephenson, Brian, Eug.	1.000	2	1	0	0	1	0
Suarez, Felipe, Boi.	1.000	5	4	4	0	8	0
Sullivan, Luke, Boi.*	1.000	2	2	0	0	2	0
Surkont, Keith, S.O.	.875	17	6	15	3	24	2
Taschner, Jack, S.K.*	1.000	7	3	5	0	8	2
Tauscher, Ryan, S.O.*	1.000	12	3	3	0	6	0
Turner, Kyle, Spo.*	1.000	8	1	2	0	3	0
Ugas, Juan, Yak.	.750	20	3	3	2	8	0
Vargas, Derrick, Port.*	.667	18	0	2	1	3	0
Vent, Kevin, S.K.	1.000	17	4	5	0	9	2
Vracar, Paul, Eug.	.750	20	5	1	2	8	0
Waldrum, Kevin, Eug.	.000	4	0	0	0	0	0
Wallace, Jeffrey, Yak.	1.000	11	1	10	0	11	0
Walters, Jason, Yak.	.500	8	0	1	1	2	0
Walton, Sam, Ever.*	.857	14	0	6	1	7	0
Wayne, Hawkeye, Ever.	.714	15	2	3	2	7	0
Webb, John, Eug.	1.000	2	0	1	0	1	0
Wells, Roy, Ever.	.000	2	0	0	0	0	0
Wells, Zach, S.K.	.714	15	3	2	2	7	0
Wiggins, Daniel, Eug.	1.000	3	0	0	0	0	0
Williams, Jerome, S.K.	1.000	7	3	3	0	6	1
Yacco, Anthony, S.K.	.000	9	0	0	0	0	0
Young, Colin, Port.*	.750	15	1	5	2	8	1
Zimmerman, Jordan, Ever.*	.000	1	0	0	0	0	0
Zirelli, Michael, S.K.	1.000	25	4	4	0	8	0

The following players appeared only as designated hitter, pinch-hitter or pinch runner: Messner, dh-ph; Proctor, dh.

Year	Team	Pct.
1901—	Portland	.675
1902—	Butte	.608
1903—	Butte	.578
1904—	Boise	.625
1905—	Vancouver	.586
	Everett*	.667
1906—	Tacoma	.600
1907—	Aberdeen	.625
1908—	Vancouver	.578
1909—	Seattle	.653
1910—	Spokane	.596
1911—	Vancouver	.628
1912—	Seattle	.600
1913—	Vancouver	.600
1914—	Vancouver	.632
1915—	Seattle	.564
1916—	Spokane	.622
1917—	Great Falls	.592
1918—	Seattle	.588
1919—	Seattle	.590
1920—	Victoria	.600
1921—	Yakima	.710
	Yakima	.660
1922—	Calgary‡	.600
1923-36—Did not operate.		
1937—	Wenatchee	.603
	Tacoma*	.627
1938—	Yakima	.583
	Bellingham (2nd)†	.511
1939—	Wenatchee	.601
	Tacoma (2nd)†	.533
1940—	Spokane	.587
	Tacoma (4th)†	.500
1941—	Spokane	.669
1942—	Vancouver	.594
1943-45—Did not operate.		
1946—	Wenatchee	.622
1947—	Vancouver	.566
1948—	Spokane	.614
1949—	Yakima	.660
	Vancouver (2nd)†	.615
1950—	Yakima	.613
1951—	Spokane	.655
1952—	Victoria	.631
1953—	Salem	.635
	Spokane*	.590

Year	Team	Pct.
1954—	Vancouver*	.636
	Lewiston	.629
1955—	Salem	.646
	Eugene*	.639
1956—	Yakima	.691
	Yakima	.619
1957—	Eugene	.576
	Wenatchee*	.647
1958—	Lewiston	.621
	Yakima*	.594
1959—	Salem	.623
	Yakima*	.563
1960—	Yakima	.638
	Yakima	.562
1961—	Lewiston*	.621
	Yakima	.600
1962—	Wenatchee*	.574
	Tri-City	.580
1963—	Lewiston	.594
	Yakima*	.613
1964—	Eugene	.636
	Yakima*	.611
1965—	Lewiston	.667
	Tri-City*	.681
1966—	Tri-City	.679
1967—	Medford	.607
1968—	Tri-City	.600
1969—	Rogue Valley	.633
1970—	Lewiston§	.538
	Coos Bay-No. Bend	.563
1971—	Tri-City§	.625
	Bend	.538
1972—	Lewiston§	.675
	Walla Walla	.513
1973—	Walla Walla∞	.638
	Portland	.563
1974—	Bellingham	.619
	Eugene▲	.571
1975—	Portland	.545
	Eugene◆	.684
1976—	Portland	.556
	Walla Walla◆	.639
1977—	Bellingham■	.618
	Portland	.667
1978—	Grays Harbor▼	.671
	Eugene	.514

Year	Team	Pct.
1979—	Central Oregon◆	.606
	Walla Walla	.571
1980—	Bellingham•	.643
	Eugene•	.529
1981—	Medford◆	.600
	Bellingham	.557
1982—	Medford	.757
	Salem◆	.486
1983—	Medford††	.735
	Bellingham	.588
1984—	Tri-Cities††	.622
	Medford	.608
1985—	Everett††	.541
	Eugene	.541
1986—	Bellingham††	.608
	Eugene	.608
1987—	Spokane▲	.711
	Everett	.653
1988—	Southern Oregon	.605
	Spokane◆	.553
1989—	Southern Oregon	.600
	Spokane◆	.547
1990—	Boise	.697
	Spokane◆	.645
1991—	Boise◆	.658
	Yakima	.579
1992—	Bellingham◆	.566
	Bend	.566
1993—	Bellingham	.579
	Boise◆	.539
1994—	Yakima	.645
	Boise◆	.579
1995—	Boise◆	.640
	Bellingham	.566
1996—	Eugene	.645
	Yakima§	.526
1997—	Boise	.671
	Portland◆	.579
1998—	Spokane	.618
	Boise	.618
	Salem-Keizer◆	.566
1999—	Spokane◆	.579

*Won split-season playoff. †Won four-club playoff. ‡League disbanded June 18. §League divided into Northern and Southern divisions, declared champion under league rules. ∞League divided into Eastern and Western divisions, declared champion under league rules. ▲League divided into Eastern and Western divisions; won two-team playoff. ◆League divided into North and South divisions; won two-team playoff. ■ League divided into Affiliate and Independent divisions; won two-team playoff. ▼Declared league champion after winning one-game playoff. Balance of playoff canceled due to rain and wet grounds. •Declared co-champion after winning one game. Balance of playoff canceled due to rain and wet grounds. ††League divided into Washington and Oregon divisions; won two-team playoff. (NOTE—Known as Pacific Northwest League 1901-02, Pacific National League 1903-04, Northwestern League 1905-18, Pacific Coast International League 1919-22 and Western International League 1937-54.)

SOUTH ATLANTIC LEAGUE

LEAGUE OFFICE

President/secretary-treasurer
John Moss

Address
P.O. Box 38
Kings Mountain, NC 28086

Phone
704-739-3466

Teams (affiliation)
Asheville Tourists (Rockies)
Augusta Greenjackets (Red Sox)
Capital City Bombers (Mets)
Charleston (S.C.) Riverdogs (Devil Rays)
Charleston (W.Va.) Alley Cats (Royals)
Columbus Redstixx (Indians)
Delmarva Shorebirds (Orioles)

Cape Fear Crocks (Expos)
Greensboro Bats (Yankees)
Hagerstown Suns (Blue Jays)
Hickory Crawdads (Pirates)
Macon Braves (Braves)
Piedmont Bollweevils (Phillies)
Savannah Sand Gnats (Rangers)

1999 FINAL STANDINGS

FIRST HALF

NORTHERN DIVISION

Team	W	L	T	Pct.	GB
Hagerstown (Blue Jays)	48	23	0	.676	...
Cape Fear (Expos)	38	33	0	.535	10.0
Charleston, W.Va. (Royals)	30	42	0	.417	18.5
Delmarva (Orioles)	26	44	0	.371	21.5

CENTRAL DIVISION

Team	W	L	T	Pct.	GB
Columbia (Mets)	44	27	0	.620	...
Greensboro (Yankees)	37	35	0	.514	7.5
Piedmont (Phillies)	36	35	0	.507	8.0
Hickory (Pirates)	35	35	0	.500	8.5
Charleston, S.C. (Devil Rays)	32	40	0	.444	12.5
Asheville (Rockies)	29	42	0	.408	15.0

SOUTHERN DIVISION

Team	W	L	T	Pct.	GB
Columbus (Indians)	44	27	0	.620	...
Macon (Braves)	40	30	0	.571	3.5
Augusta (Red Sox)	29	40	0	.420	14.0
Savannah (Rangers)	28	43	0	.394	16.0

SECOND HALF

NORTHERN DIVISION

Team	W	L	T	Pct.	GB
Cape Fear (Expos)	37	32	0	.536	...
Hagerstown (Blue Jays)	36	33	0	.522	1.0
Delmarva (Orioles)	32	36	0	.471	4.5
Charleston, W.Va. (Royals)	31	38	0	.449	6.0

CENTRAL DIVISION

Team	W	L	T	Pct.	GB
Greensboro (Yankees)	40	29	0	.580	...
Columbia (Mets)	39	31	0	.557	1.5
Hickory (Pirates)	35	35	0	.500	5.5
Asheville (Rockies)	35	35	0	.500	5.5
Piedmont (Phillies)	33	36	0	.478	7.0
Charleston, S.C. (Devil Rays)	33	37	0	.471	7.5

SOUTHERN DIVISION

Team	W	L	T	Pct.	GB
Augusta (Red Sox)	40	30	0	.571	...
Macon (Braves)	34	34	0	.500	5.0
Savannah (Rangers)	34	35	0	.493	5.5
Columbus (Indians)	26	44	0	.371	14.0

COMPOSITE

Team	Hag.	C'bia	Gbr.	Mac.	C.F.	Hic.	C'bus	Aug.	Pied.	CSC	Ash.	Sav.	CWV	Del.	W	L	T	Pct.	GB
Hagerstown (Blue Jays)	...	5	5	4	10	4	6	5	5	6	7	4	10	13	84	56	0	.600	...
Columbia (Mets)	3	...	7	3	5	8	6	5	12	10	8	4	5	7	83	58	0	.589	1.5
Greensboro (Yankees)	3	7	...	3	5	7	7	3	7	9	12	7	2	5	77	64	0	.546	7.5
Macon (Braves)	4	5	5	...	3	4	11	9	3	4	5	11	7	3	74	64	0	.536	9.0
Cape Fear (Expos)	10	3	3	5	...	5	4	5	4	5	4	3	12	5	75	65	0	.536	9.0
Hickory (Pirates)	4	9	10	4	3	...	2	3	9	8	7	5	1	5	70	70	0	.500	14.0
Columbus (Indians)	2	2	1	12	4	6	...	8	2	6	3	14	4	6	70	71	0	.496	14.5
Augusta (Red Sox)	3	3	5	10	3	4	10	...	2	3	5	12	5	4	69	70	0	.496	14.5
Piedmont (Phillies)	3	4	6	4	4	7	6	6	...	8	6	4	5	6	69	71	0	.493	15.0
Charleston, S.C. (Devil Rays)	2	5	9	4	3	5	2	5	8	...	6	5	6	5	65	77	0	.458	20.0
Asheville (Rockies)	1	7	4	3	4	7	5	3	10	10	...	1	6	3	64	77	0	.454	20.5
Savannah (Rangers)	4	4	1	7	4	3	6	11	4	3	7	...	4	4	62	78	0	.443	22.0
Charleston, W.Va. (Royals)	9	3	6	0	11	7	4	3	3	2	2	4	...	7	61	80	0	.433	23.5
Delmarva (Orioles)	8	1	2	5	6	3	2	4	2	3	5	4	13	...	58	80	0	.420	25.0

Major league affiliations in parentheses.

PLAYOFFS: Augusta defeated Columbus two games to none; Hickory defeated Macon two games to none; Cape Fear defeated Hagerstown two games to none; Columbia defeated Greensboro two games to one; Augusta defeated Hickory two games to one; Cape Fear defeated Columbia two games to none; Augusta defeated Cape Fear two games to one to win league championship.

REGULAR-SEASON ATTENDANCE: Asheville, 137,836; Augusta, 156,685; Cape Fear, 72,856; Charleston, S.C., 238,184; Charleston, W.Va., 92,738; Columbia, 133,273; Columbus, 104,153; Delmarva, 296,004; Greensboro, 156,270; Hagerstown, 105,380; Hickory, 188,531; Macon, 115,897; Piedmont, 119,637; Savannah, 132,017. Total—2,049,461. Playoffs (17 games)—15,428. All-Star Game at Salisbury, Md.—4,685.

MANAGERS: Asheville, Jim Eppard; Augusta, Billy Gardner Jr.; Cape Fear, Frank Kremblas; Charleston, S.C., Charlie Montoyo; Charleston, W.Va., Tom Poquette; Columbia, Dave Engle; Columbus, Brad Komminsk; Delmarva, Butch Davis; Greensboro, Stan Hough; Hagerstown, Rolando Pino; Hickory, Tracy Woodson; Macon, Jeff Treadway; Piedmont, Ken Oberkfell; Savannah, Paul Carey.

ALL-STAR TEAM: 1B—Travis Hafner, Savannah; 2B—Javier Colina, Asheville; 3B—Scott Seabol, Greensboro; SS—Rafael Furcal, Macon; Utility INF—Travis Wilson, Macon; OF—Aljereau Benjamin, Cape Fear; Juan Pierre, Asheville; Brian Cole, Columbia; Utility OF—Mike Curry, Charleston, W.Va.; C—Rico Washington, Hickory; DH—Jay Gibbons, Hagerstown; RHP—Jason Standridge, Charleston, S.C.; LHP—Jimmy Osting, Macon; Manager—Rolando Pino, Hagerstown; Coach—Tommy Gregg, Macon; Coach—Carlos Arroyo, Piedmont; Most Valuable Player—Scott Seabol, Greensboro; Most Valuable Pitcher—Jason Standridge, Charleston, S.C.; Most Outstanding Major League Prospect—Rafael Furcal, Macon; General Manager of the Year—Todd Parnall, Piedmont.

TEAM

Team	Avg.	G	TPA	AB	R	H	TB	2B	3B	HR	RBI	SH	SF	HP	BB	IBB	SO	SB	CS	GDP	LOB	ShO	Slg.	OBP
Asheville	.278	141	5338	4869	701	1352	1973	263	20	106	609	43	30	76	320	4	956	149	64	92	987	7	.405	.330
Columbus	.263	141	5278	4679	688	1231	1863	222	40	110	608	33	43	70	453	11	1005	179	88	92	928	10	.398	.334
Greensboro	.262	141	5263	4756	733	1245	1954	251	46	122	650	26	44	7	430	7	1232	106	62	83	983	9	.411	.321
Macon	.261	138	5175	4633	661	1210	1852	235	31	115	584	23	35	69	415	8	1169	199	94	69	946	7	.400	.329
Columbia	.258	141	5246	4682	688	1209	1980	238	34	155	626	31	54	73	406	6	1089	167	68	72	927	5	.423	.324
Hickory	.256	140	5432	4781	705	1222	1900	226	25	134	641	39	35	79	498	15	1119	96	62	90	987	11	.397	.334
Cape Fear	.255	140	5085	4553	616	1161	1702	222	38	81	536	37	27	71	397	9	1109	173	155	65	839	9	.374	.323
Hagerstown	.254	140	5502	4826	731	1225	1857	234	34	110	646	28	42	44	562	9	1076	179	65	86	1031	6	.385	.334
Augusta	.245	139	5150	4657	626	1140	1667	198	40	83	532	30	33	3	427	5	1064	139	71	116	975	9	.358	.307
Piedmont	.244	140	5049	4548	528	1111	1653	214	38	84	481	31	29	81	360	4	993	145	58	90	964	10	.363	.309
Charleston, W.V.	.244	141	5312	4661	593	1135	1627	227	35	65	509	50	27	75	499	5	1138	270	105	78	963	7	.349	.325
Savannah	.242	140	5174	4621	607	1118	1688	203	41	95	556	35	36	58	424	7	1197	82	57	81	918	12	.365	.311
Delmarva	.240	138	5330	4557	627	1092	1518	203	41	47	556	46	39	73	615	12	1175	163	80	101	1035	10	.333	.337
Charleston, S.C.	.237	142	5325	4719	634	1118	1647	207	29	88	546	48	39	69	450	13	1117	132	64	105	940	9	.349	.310

INDIVIDUAL

TOP QUALIFIERS FOR BATTING CHAMPIONSHIP

Minimum 383 plate appearances. *Lefthanded batter. †Switch-hitter.

Player, Team	Avg.	G	TPA	AB	R	H	TB	2B	3B	HR	RBI	SH	SF	HP	BB	IBB	SO	SB	CS	GDP	Slg.	OBP
Furcal, Rafael, Mac.†	.337	83	382	335	73	113	133	15	1	1	29	1	0	5	41	1	36	73	22	4	.397	.417
Benjamin, Al, C.F.	.322	128	527	488	66	157	229	38	2	10	77	0	5	7	27	2	110	14	17	9	.469	.362
Rivera, Carlos, Hick.*	.322	119	488	457	63	147	218	30	1	13	86	0	4	11	15	2	45	2	1	13	.477	.355
Pierre, Juan, Ash.*	.320	140	648	585	93	187	228	28	5	1	55	11	6	8	38	2	37	66	19	12	.390	.366
Cole, Brian, C'bia	.316	125	545	500	97	158	261	41	4	18	71	1	5	2	37	0	77	50	16	8	.522	.362
Seabol, Scott, Gre.	.315	138	608	543	86	171	283	55	6	15	89	0	11	9	45	1	91	6	5	9	.521	.370
Curry, Mike, C.W.Va.*	.311	85	384	318	70	99	118	13	3	0	25	6	3	9	48	0	58	61	13	4	.371	.413
Wilson, Travis, Mac.	.309	90	390	363	65	112	173	20	4	11	63	0	3	15	9	1	66	14	8	4	.477	.349
Colina, Javier, Ash.	.302	124	556	516	70	156	217	37	3	6	81	2	6	6	26	0	101	12	11	12	.421	.339
Castillo, Geramel, Sav.†	.301	114	430	405	42	122	160	21	4	3	40	2	2	2	19	0	94	4	4	7	.395	.334
Brown, Billy, Gre.	.294	134	606	520	102	153	250	28	6	19	62	2	1	12	71	0	144	21	10	9	.481	.391
Hafner, Travis, Sav.*	.292	134	563	480	94	140	262	30	4	28	111	0	5	11	67	6	151	5	4	11	.546	.387
Jenkins, Brian, C'bia	.290	107	444	400	69	116	205	15	7	20	79	4	6	4	30	2	69	19	7	7	.513	.341
Giron, Alejandro, Pied.	.287	99	410	387	43	111	162	15	6	8	59	2	3	3	15	0	75	12	6	8	.419	.316
Goodwin, David, C.W.Va.	.286	128	554	490	68	140	208	29	6	9	73	2	4	13	45	0	123	10	5	10	.424	.359
Mulvehill, Chase, C'bia	.286	116	478	427	65	122	184	23	6	9	58	5	5	12	29	0	97	29	13	6	.431	.345

DEPARTMENTAL LEADERS: G—Pierre, 140; AB—Pierre, 585; R—Nunez, 116; H—Pierre, 187; TB—Seabol, 283; 2B—Seabol, 55; 3B—Nunez, Minges, 11 each; HR—Hafner, Snyder, 28; RBI—Hafner, 111; SH—Mann, 12; SF—Seabol, 11; HP—Schreimann, 19; BB—Machado, 102; IBB—Washington, 7; SO—Zapp, 163; SB—Furcal, 73; CS—Machado, 28; GIDP—Carnes, 18; Slg.—Hafner, .546; OBP—Furcal, .417.

ALL PLAYERS

*Lefthanded batter. †Switch-hitter.

Player, Team	Avg.	G	TPA	AB	R	H	TB	2B	3B	HR	RBI	SH	SF	HP	BB	IBB	SO	SB	CS	GDP	Slg.	OBP
Acevedo, Carlos, Pied.	.282	56	201	188	22	53	66	10	0	1	19	0	2	0	11	0	30	7	2	3	.351	.318
Acevedo, Luis, Sav.	.000	6	18	15	1	0	0	0	0	0	0	0	0	0	3	0	5	0	0	0	.000	.167
Ackerman, Scott, C.F.	.268	67	246	224	30	60	92	14	0	6	31	1	3	2	16	1	58	5	2	4	.411	.318
Ahumada, Alejandro, Aug.	.259	125	521	455	72	118	180	24	4	10	57	5	4	16	41	0	107	9	7	16	.396	.339
Alamo, Efrain, C.S.C.	.246	97	375	346	46	85	145	14	8	10	53	4	2	7	16	0	96	4	6	6	.419	.291
Aldridge, Cory, Mac.*	.251	124	488	443	48	111	174	19	4	12	65	1	5	6	33	2	123	9	6	9	.393	.308
Alevras, Chad, Aug.	.294	5	19	17	2	5	6	1	0	0	3	0	0	0	2	0	6	0	0	0	.353	.368
Alou, Felipe, C.W.Va.	.195	57	204	185	18	36	46	8	1	0	13	2	2	2	13	0	50	11	4	1	.249	.252
Alvarez, Carlos, C'bus	.257	96	374	319	56	82	146	18	2	14	49	0	6	16	33	0	70	9	7	5	.458	.350
Anderson, Frank, Hick.	.194	38	141	129	15	25	41	4	0	4	11	1	0	3	8	1	52	0	2	4	.318	.257
Arias, Jeison, C.S.C.	.148	30	89	81	9	12	18	2	2	0	6	0	0	1	7	0	34	1	0	3	.222	.225
Avila, Rob, Pied.	.222	3	9	9	1	2	3	1	0	0	0	0	0	0	0	0	4	0	0	0	.333	.222
Ayres, Yancy, C.W.Va.	.169	25	72	65	4	11	11	0	0	0	2	0	0	0	7	0	17	0	0	2	.169	.250
Backe, Brandon, C.S.C.	.232	84	322	292	43	63	105	11	2	9	40	6	3	6	35	1	81	3	5	8	.386	.309
Baez, Ernies, Sav.†	.000	3	4	3	1	0	0	0	0	0	0	0	0	0	1	0	2	0	0	0	.000	.250
Barns, B.J., Hick.*	.230	52	202	174	16	40	74	8	4	6	25	1	0	2	25	0	47	5	3	5	.425	.333
Bastardo, Angel, C'bus	.245	19	59	53	6	13	26	0	2	3	9	0	0	1	5	0	13	0	0	3	.491	.322
Benefield, Brian, C'bia	.274	81	361	303	60	83	144	14	1	15	51	2	5	8	43	1	67	18	12	4	.475	.373
Benham, David, Aug.	.000	3	9	9	0	0	0	0	0	0	0	0	0	0	0	0	7	0	0	0	.000	.000
Benham, Jason, Del.*	.095	7	24	21	1	2	4	2	0	0	3	0	0	0	3	1	6	0	0	0	.190	.208
Benjamin, Al, C.F.	.322	128	527	488	66	157	229	38	2	10	77	0	5	7	27	2	110	14	17	9	.469	.362
Beverly, Shomari, Pied.	.197	50	187	173	18	34	59	7	0	6	12	1	0	2	11	0	62	4	2	1	.341	.253
Bigbie, Larry, Del.*	.279	43	197	165	18	46	65	7	3	2	27	0	3	0	29	0	42	3	1	4	.394	.381
Blalock, Hank, Sav.*	.240	7	28	25	3	6	10	1	0	1	2	0	1	1	1	0	3	0	0	0	.400	.286
Bone, Billy, Hick.	.200	7	29	20	7	4	9	2	0	1	3	1	0	1	7	0	6	0	0	1	.450	.429
Bonilla, Juan, Del.	.273	6	12	11	1	3	3	0	0	0	0	0	0	0	1	0	4	0	0	1	.273	.333
Boscan, Jean, Mac.	.226	105	401	368	40	83	112	17	0	4	38	2	3	2	26	0	94	2	4	10	.304	.278
Boughton, Mike, Sav.†	.267	26	103	90	7	24	28	4	0	0	12	0	0	0	12	0	22	1	2	4	.311	.353
Brett, Jason, C'bia	.242	32	111	95	11	23	26	3	0	0	1	3	0	1	12	0	25	4	2	2	.274	.333
Brignac, Junior, Mac.	.299	69	283	268	35	80	125	18	3	7	38	0	2	2	11	0	68	17	5	2	.466	.329
Brito, Juan, C.W.Va.	.240	61	223	208	14	50	56	6	0	0	19	3	0	1	11	0	37	1	2	8	.269	.282
Brown, Andy, Gre.*	.176	29	118	108	14	19	41	5	1	5	15	0	0	0	10	0	49	0	1	0	.380	.246
Brown, Billy, Gre.	.294	134	606	520	102	153	250	28	6	19	62	2	1	12	71	0	144	21	10	9	.481	.391

Player, Team	Avg.	G	TPA	AB	R	H	TB	2B	3B	HR	RBI	SH	SF	HP	BB	IBB	SO	SB	CS	GDP	Slg.	OBP
Brown, Tonayne, Aug.	.261	135	607	541	82	141	191	24	7	4	45	8	4	8	46	0	89	25	22	14	.353	.326
Bultmann, Kurt, Hick.	.356	13	54	45	4	16	18	2	0	0	9	2	1	0	6	0	4	1	1	3	.400	.423
Bundy, Ryan, Hag.	.222	46	179	153	19	34	56	5	1	5	17	3	0	5	18	0	62	5	3	0	.366	.324
Burkhart, Lance, C.F.	.167	2	8	6	2	1	2	1	0	0	0	0	0	0	2	0	4	0	0	0	.333	.375
Bush, Brian, Pied.	.233	38	142	129	12	30	33	3	0	0	7	1	0	5	7	0	32	4	5	0	.256	.298
Caballero, Antonio, Hick.*	.079	13	41	38	3	3	3	0	0	0	2	0	0	0	3	0	13	0	1	0	.079	.146
Calderon, Henry, C.W.Va.	.227	130	502	459	49	104	156	29	1	7	56	9	4	9	21	1	106	33	14	9	.340	.272
Calzado, Napolean, Del.	.278	6	19	18	2	5	6	1	0	0	1	0	1	0	0	0	4	0	0	1	.333	.263
Cameron, Troy, Mac.†	.238	130	542	462	71	110	208	28	2	22	77	0	6	6	68	0	161	7	9	6	.450	.339
Carnes, Shayne, Pied.*	.268	106	426	396	45	106	164	28	0	10	55	0	2	2	26	1	78	1	1	18	.414	.315
Carreno, Jose, C.F.	.221	41	148	140	11	31	33	2	0	0	10	1	1	1	5	0	16	4	3	3	.236	.252
Casillas, Uriel, Pied.	.227	73	283	225	30	51	66	11	2	0	20	2	1	7	48	0	33	4	5	7	.293	.377
Castaneda, Cesar, Sav.	.202	103	366	331	33	67	120	13	2	12	47	0	1	5	29	0	105	2	4	8	.363	.276
Castillo, Geramel, Sav.†	.301	114	430	405	42	122	160	21	4	3	40	2	2	2	19	0	94	4	4	7	.395	.334
Castri, Andrea, Gre.	.239	78	304	264	35	63	97	14	1	6	33	2	1	12	25	0	91	2	3	1	.367	.331
Castro, Martires, C.F.	.290	9	31	31	1	9	13	2	1	0	3	0	0	0	0	0	7	1	0	0	.419	.290
Castro, Ramon, Mac.†	.260	105	385	350	32	91	120	12	4	3	33	7	2	2	24	0	55	13	5	4	.343	.310
Chavez, Endy, C'bia*	.253	73	290	253	40	64	74	8	1	0	15	2	1	0	34	0	36	20	12	3	.292	.340
Cheek, Shawn, Aug.	.375	5	16	16	3	6	8	2	0	0	2	0	0	0	0	0	1	0	0	0	.500	.375
Chwan, Brian, C.S.C.*	.221	49	151	136	16	30	47	8	0	3	9	0	3	1	10	0	29	0	0	2	.346	.273
Cleto, Ambioris, Hick.	.106	24	84	66	6	7	8	1	0	0	6	1	0	0	17	0	23	0	2	1	.121	.289
Cody, Ryan, Pied.	.333	1	4	3	1	1	1	0	0	0	0	0	0	0	1	0	1	0	0	0	.333	.500
Cole, Brian, C'bia	.316	125	545	500	97	158	261	41	4	18	71	1	5	2	37	0	77	50	16	8	.522	.362
Colina, Javier, Ash.	.302	124	556	516	70	156	217	37	3	6	81	2	6	6	26	0	101	12	11	12	.421	.339
Connell, Jerry, Pied.	.239	31	121	109	9	26	46	9	1	3	15	0	1	1	10	0	46	1	1	0	.422	.306
Copeland, Brandon, C'bia	.198	33	123	101	14	20	39	4	0	5	17	1	1	5	15	0	39	5	1	2	.386	.328
Cordero, Willy, Sav.	.246	101	406	366	51	90	136	20	4	6	37	7	2	4	27	0	70	11	6	4	.372	.303
Cota, Humberto, C.S.C.-Hick.	.277	122	520	469	70	130	201	32	3	11	81	1	7	2	41	2	71	4	2	9	.429	.333
Cruz, Edgar, C'bus	.216	62	253	232	22	50	72	10	0	4	23	0	1	0	20	1	54	0	0	3	.310	.277
Cruz, Rafael, Sav.	.065	23	70	62	0	4	5	1	0	0	3	0	0	1	7	0	30	1	1	1	.081	.171
Curry, Mike, C.W.Va.*	.311	85	384	318	70	99	118	13	3	0	25	6	3	9	48	0	58	61	13	4	.371	.413
Daedelow, Craig, Del.	.313	45	203	160	28	50	57	3	2	0	21	2	3	3	35	0	26	1	3	3	.356	.438
Dalton, David, Mac.	.288	39	151	132	19	38	56	7	1	3	12	0	1	4	14	0	34	3	3	0	.424	.371
Dampeer, Kelly, C'bus	.258	94	335	299	37	77	115	13	5	5	39	5	3	3	25	0	52	10	4	12	.385	.318
Darjean, John, Gre.	.249	113	435	398	47	99	131	18	4	2	43	7	3	8	19	0	80	20	11	4	.329	.294
Davies, Justin, Hag.*	.197	127	499	396	69	78	86	6	1	0	23	7	1	2	86	1	55	36	15	7	.217	.342
Davis, J.J., Hick.	.265	86	367	317	58	84	169	26	1	19	65	0	2	4	44	3	99	2	5	3	.533	.360
Davison, Ashanti, Del.	.159	53	210	170	20	27	35	5	0	1	13	2	0	7	31	0	45	8	6	7	.206	.313
Derosso, Tony, Aug.	.297	36	147	128	19	38	65	7	1	6	27	0	2	1	16	0	21	0	0	3	.508	.374
DeShields, Delino, Del.*	.286	2	8	7	1	2	5	0	0	1	2	0	0	0	1	0	1	0	1	0	.714	.375
Diaz, Diogenes, Hick.	.205	13	41	39	1	8	10	2	0	0	1	1	0	0	1	0	12	0	0	1	.256	.225
Diaz, Maikell, Del.	.276	91	381	322	45	89	109	8	3	2	34	5	1	11	42	0	68	31	15	9	.339	.378
Diaz, Miguel, C.F.	.000	1	3	2	0	0	0	0	0	0	0	0	0	0	1	0	2	0	0	0	.000	.333
DiPace, Danny, C.W.Va.*	.224	65	233	192	23	43	60	11	0	2	19	1	0	6	34	1	67	8	3	3	.313	.358
Duck, Kevin, Ash.*	.225	105	384	338	37	76	115	15	0	8	36	2	1	1	42	0	98	0	2	10	.340	.312
Duncan, Carlos, Pied.	.217	73	308	276	41	60	114	15	3	11	40	1	4	8	19	0	88	15	4	4	.413	.283
Dusan, Joe, Hag.*	.239	69	274	243	26	58	96	14	0	8	37	0	1	2	28	0	82	3	1	3	.395	.321
Elder, Rick, Del.*	.083	11	47	36	7	3	9	0	0	2	4	1	0	0	10	1	15	0	0	0	.250	.283
Elwood, Brad, Gre.	.232	81	293	259	35	60	84	11	2	3	30	2	3	5	24	1	72	3	2	2	.324	.306
Erickson, Corey, C'bia	.236	129	491	424	64	100	192	21	1	23	57	0	6	14	46	0	120	9	3	4	.453	.327
Escalante, Jaime, Del.†	.191	45	164	141	15	27	37	4	0	2	14	0	0	3	20	0	45	0	0	3	.262	.305
Espy, Nate, Pied.	.254	83	345	295	37	75	130	18	2	11	38	0	1	1	48	2	56	3	1	7	.441	.359
Esquerra, Marques, C'bus†	.256	122	454	403	53	103	134	14	4	3	44	7	3	8	32	1	65	9	8	14	.333	.321
Ewing, Byron, C'bus	.243	47	191	173	19	42	62	11	0	3	19	0	0	2	16	0	41	10	1	2	.358	.314
Fajardo, Alejandro, Pied.	.243	118	515	444	66	108	154	16	6	6	43	10	3	6	52	0	91	44	10	7	.347	.329
Felix, Hersy, C.W.Va.	.288	23	83	80	6	23	33	7	0	1	4	0	0	0	3	0	17	2	0	2	.413	.313
Fleming, Ryan, Hag.*	.335	61	256	227	34	76	101	9	2	4	35	2	4	0	23	1	26	7	6	4	.445	.390
Fowler, Ben, C'bus†	.258	28	103	97	12	25	38	4	0	3	11	1	0	0	5	0	23	2	2	0	.392	.294
Freeman, Choo, Ash.	.274	131	534	485	82	133	205	22	4	14	66	1	2	7	39	1	132	16	4	3	.423	.336
Freitas, Jeremy, C.W.Va.*	.247	85	344	300	38	74	137	20	2	13	52	1	2	4	37	1	80	3	0	3	.457	.335
Frey, Chris, Sav.	.000	31	1	1	0	0	0	0	0	0	0	0	0	0	0	0	1	0	0	0	.000	.000
Fuentes, Javier, Aug.	.254	39	159	130	16	33	42	4	1	1	13	1	1	4	22	0	13	6	1	0	.323	.376
Furcal, Rafael, Mac.†	.337	83	382	335	73	113	133	15	1	1	29	1	0	5	41	1	36	73	22	4	.397	.417
Garcia, Oscar, C'bus	.241	8	33	29	3	7	9	2	0	0	1	0	0	0	4	0	11	1	1	0	.310	.333
Gettis, Byron, C.W.Va.	.295	43	170	149	19	44	61	7	2	2	13	4	1	6	10	0	36	10	3	3	.409	.361
Gibbons, Jay, Hag.*	.305	71	330	292	53	89	161	20	2	16	69	0	5	1	32	1	56	3	0	12	.551	.370
Giron, Alejandro, Pied.	.287	99	410	387	43	111	162	15	6	8	59	2	3	3	15	0	75	12	6	8	.419	.316
Gonzalez, Luis, C'bus	.294	83	339	299	41	88	131	18	2	7	50	4	5	5	26	0	40	6	5	5	.438	.355
Goodwin, David, C.W.Va.	.286	128	554	490	68	140	208	29	6	9	73	2	4	13	45	0	123	10	5	10	.424	.359
Gordnier, Aaron, C'bus	.254	64	203	177	30	45	83	10	2	8	29	0	1	2	23	0	49	3	2	5	.469	.345
Green, Nick, Mac.	.200	3	10	10	1	2	5	0	0	1	3	0	0	0	0	0	4	1	0	0	.500	.200
Greene, Claude, Gre.†	.247	115	486	437	74	108	182	16	5	16	68	0	6	17	26	2	118	7	2	10	.416	.311
Gregg, Neal, Gre.*	.208	11	25	24	1	5	5	0	0	0	2	0	0	1	0	0	7	0	0	0	.208	.240
Grummitt, Dan, C.S.C.	.133	8	33	30	6	4	8	1	0	1	4	0	0	2	1	0	12	0	0	0	.267	.212
Guerrero, Pedro, Sav.	.183	42	156	131	20	24	41	2	3	3	12	11	2	1	11	0	39	11	0	4	.313	.248
Gutierrez, Derrick, Del.	.262	30	108	103	12	27	36	6	0	1	14	0	0	2	3	0	28	1	1	3	.350	.296
Guzman, Carlos, Pied.*	.163	16	52	49	5	8	10	2	0	0	5	0	0	0	3	0	17	2	0	0	.204	.212
Hafner, Travis, Sav.*	.292	134	563	480	94	140	262	30	4	28	111	0	5	11	67	6	151	5	4	11	.546	.387
Haman, Mack, Del.	.220	68	269	246	27	54	80	9	4	3	37	1	1	7	14	1	67	4	2	6	.325	.280
Hammond, Joey, Del.	.259	21	94	81	10	21	29	1	2	1	7	0	0	0	13	0	22	0	0	4	.358	.362
Hannahan, Buzz, Pied.	.123	22	71	65	5	8	8	0	0	0	3	0	0	0	6	0	12	3	1	0	.123	.197
Harris, Kevin, Sav.	.161	59	189	180	15	29	47	5	2	3	11	3	0	3	3	0	72	8	6	0	.261	.188
Harris, Willie, Del.*	.265	66	301	272	42	72	97	13	3	2	32	4	4	1	20	0	41	17	11	4	.357	.313
Hart, Corey, C.W.Va.†	.190	92	365	295	43	56	78	16	3	0	39	4	5	3	58	1	62	13	7	3	.264	.324
Hart, Keith, Aug.	.262	86	358	336	29	88	121	14	2	5	50	0	5	5	12	0	72	2	0	15	.360	.293

Player, Team	Avg.	G	TPA	AB	R	H	TB	2B	3B	HR	RBI	SH	SF	HP	BB	IBB	SO	SB	CS	GDP	Slg.	OBP
Harts, Jeremy, Hick.†	.132	22	80	68	8	9	10	1	0	0	1	1	0	1	10	0	24	1	0	1	.147	.253
Hazelton, Justin, Sav.	.154	4	14	13	0	2	3	1	0	0	1	0	0	0	1	0	8	0	0	0	.231	.214
Heine, Kyle, Gre.	.254	19	67	59	5	15	20	5	0	0	7	2	0	1	5	0	14	0	1	1	.339	.323
Hendricks, Jason, C.F.	.263	82	308	270	42	71	121	13	2	11	38	0	2	10	26	0	84	8	4	0	.448	.347
Hernandez, Jesus, C'bus*	.306	70	291	255	43	78	142	22	3	12	56	0	2	4	30	3	53	8	2	6	.557	.385
Hill, Bobby, C'bia*	.245	86	305	278	31	68	95	12	3	3	14	5	4	2	16	0	57	12	3	5	.342	.287
Hobbs, Jay, Hick.*	.252	124	498	409	60	103	190	22	1	21	73	5	6	3	75	0	116	5	5	8	.465	.367
Hoch, Corey, Del.	.209	36	142	115	7	24	26	2	0	0	12	1	0	3	23	0	27	0	2	2	.226	.355
Hodges, Scott, C.F.*	.258	127	507	449	62	116	175	31	2	8	59	1	9	3	45	2	105	8	15	11	.390	.324
Holliday, Matt, Ash.	.264	121	511	444	76	117	193	28	0	16	64	0	5	9	53	0	116	10	3	8	.435	.350
Hook, Kevin, C.F.	.063	5	18	16	1	1	1	0	0	0	0	0	0	0	2	0	4	0	0	0	.063	.167
Hooper, Daren, Del.	.244	24	95	90	13	22	33	7	2	0	5	0	2	3	0	0	30	0	1	6	.367	.284
Hopper, Norris, C.W.Va.	.500	5	22	22	3	11	15	0	2	0	2	0	0	0	0	0	1	1	0	0	.682	.500
House, J.R., Hick.	.273	4	11	11	1	3	3	0	0	0	0	0	0	0	0	0	3	0	0	0	.273	.273
Hudson, Orlando, Hag.†	.267	132	563	513	66	137	206	36	6	7	74	1	5	2	42	3	85	8	6	10	.402	.322
Ishida, Takehito, Pied.	.242	10	34	33	2	8	11	1	1	0	0	0	0	0	1	0	7	0	1	0	.333	.265
Isturiz, Maicer, C'bus†	.300	57	245	220	46	66	89	5	3	4	23	1	3	1	20	0	28	14	2	2	.405	.357
Jackson, Jeremy A., Ash.*	.250	17	56	52	6	13	17	4	0	0	3	0	0	1	3	0	14	2	0	0	.327	.304
James, Drue, Mac.	.185	40	137	119	10	22	27	2	0	1	8	1	0	2	15	0	37	0	0	3	.227	.287
James, Tony, Aug.	.224	55	187	170	17	38	52	8	0	2	19	1	1	5	10	0	35	3	3	7	.306	.285
Jenkins, Brian, C'bia	.290	107	444	400	69	116	205	15	7	20	79	4	6	4	30	2	69	19	7	7	.513	.341
Joffrion, Jack, C.S.C.	.209	83	308	292	32	61	93	15	1	5	28	1	4	2	9	0	89	7	3	3	.318	.235
Johnson, Eric, Del.	.234	11	54	47	5	11	16	5	0	0	7	0	0	1	6	0	15	1	2	1	.340	.333
Johnson, Erik, Ash.	.293	87	335	311	40	91	142	20	2	9	43	1	1	4	18	0	34	7	2	6	.457	.338
Johnson, Jason, Pied.	.264	111	484	447	51	118	152	21	5	1	31	5	2	8	22	0	61	27	11	7	.340	.309
Johnson, Tom, Ash.	.333	2	9	9	1	3	3	0	0	0	1	0	0	0	0	0	4	1	1	0	.333	.333
Jones, Jay, Ash.*	.297	43	158	148	22	44	64	8	0	4	20	0	0	2	8	0	16	2	0	1	.432	.342
Jones, Jeremy, Sav.	.241	43	154	133	18	32	42	6	2	0	16	2	3	1	15	0	27	0	1	2	.316	.316
Katz, Glenn, C.S.C.	.246	55	192	179	18	44	51	7	0	0	17	4	1	2	6	0	24	6	7	2	.285	.277
Keaveney, Jeff, Aug.	.205	23	92	78	10	16	31	3	0	4	18	0	0	4	10	0	31	0	0	1	.397	.326
Kerrigan, Joseph, Aug.*	.200	9	41	35	7	7	8	1	0	0	1	0	0	0	6	0	6	1	2	1	.229	.317
Key, Jeff, Aug.*	.212	78	295	255	32	54	81	9	3	4	27	0	1	10	29	1	61	11	1	2	.318	.315
Kidd, Scott, Gre.	.274	115	499	463	74	127	211	31	4	15	84	0	5	6	25	0	103	4	2	17	.456	.317
Kremblas, Mike, Hag.	.206	58	196	165	22	34	41	7	0	0	7	1	1	14	15	0	28	2	0	5	.248	.323
Landaeta, Luis, Ash.*	.280	117	481	453	61	127	163	22	1	4	51	5	1	2	20	1	80	9	7	9	.360	.313
Langerhans, Ryan, Mac.*	.268	121	511	448	66	120	179	30	1	9	49	2	2	7	52	2	99	19	11	8	.400	.352
Larned, Andrew, Aug.	.258	34	109	93	8	24	31	4	0	1	13	2	0	2	12	0	18	1	1	4	.333	.355
LaForest, Pete, C.S.C.*	.256	125	515	445	64	114	180	21	3	13	53	6	3	5	55	6	97	9	3	11	.404	.343
Lebron, Francisco, C'bia	.222	10	42	36	4	8	14	0	0	2	2	0	0	0	6	0	9	0	0	1	.389	.333
Lebron, Hector, C.S.C.*	.229	57	207	188	26	43	53	3	2	1	21	3	2	6	8	0	42	7	2	5	.282	.279
Leon, Carlos, Aug.†	.233	60	244	210	34	49	59	7	0	1	19	0	1	10	23	0	42	13	4	2	.281	.336
Leon, Richy, Ash.	.245	62	234	212	28	52	77	10	0	5	31	9	2	5	6	0	29	2	3	5	.363	.280
Ligons, Merrell, C.W.Va.†	.203	87	281	232	37	47	73	10	2	4	18	3	0	1	45	0	82	17	6	6	.315	.335
Llanos, Alex, C.S.C.*	.000	5	15	13	1	0	0	0	0	0	0	0	0	0	2	0	4	1	0	1	.000	.133
Logan, Matt, Hag.*	.243	119	493	453	55	110	160	21	1	9	57	2	4	2	32	1	130	3	2	6	.353	.293
Lopez-Cao, Mike, Del.*	.167	2	8	6	2	1	4	0	0	1	3	0	1	0	1	0	0	0	0	0	.667	.250
Lopez, Felipe, Hag.†	.277	134	607	537	87	149	226	27	4	14	80	0	6	3	61	0	157	21	14	7	.421	.351
Machado, Albenis, C.F.†	.247	124	550	434	84	107	139	16	5	2	34	7	1	6	102	2	77	19	28	1	.320	.396
Machado, Anderson, Pied.†	.233	20	69	60	7	14	22	4	2	0	7	1	0	1	7	0	20	2	1	0	.367	.324
Malave, Dennis, C'bus*	.267	44	167	150	16	40	57	6	1	3	15	2	0	1	14	0	44	8	8	5	.380	.333
Malinowski, Scott, C'bia*	.208	100	332	313	30	65	74	2	2	1	20	3	1	0	15	0	51	3	3	7	.236	.243
Maloney, Jeff, Hag.†	.233	88	339	305	36	71	111	17	1	7	37	2	2	4	26	0	70	8	4	6	.364	.300
Maluchnik, Gregg, Mac.	.206	57	161	131	18	27	33	3	0	1	9	3	1	5	21	0	35	2	3	2	.252	.335
Mann, Derek, C.S.C.*	.283	124	545	449	86	127	164	20	1	5	45	12	4	9	71	0	88	22	10	6	.365	.388
Manning, Patrick, Mac.	.259	43	191	170	25	44	71	11	2	4	19	4	0	3	14	1	42	3	1	3	.418	.326
Marciante, Frank, Sav.†	.290	84	309	286	36	83	112	12	1	5	37	0	4	3	16	0	50	1	2	8	.392	.330
Martin, Billy, C'bia	.236	64	253	220	38	52	97	19	1	8	30	0	3	6	24	0	82	1	1	3	.441	.324
Martin, Brian, C.S.C.	.172	40	156	145	9	25	39	1	2	3	13	0	1	1	9	0	70	1	2	5	.269	.224
Martin, Justin, Hag.†	.294	23	104	85	14	25	26	1	0	0	5	1	0	1	17	0	19	12	2	0	.306	.417
Massucco, Scott, Gre.	.000	3	4	4	0	0	0	0	0	0	0	0	0	0	0	0	2	0	0	1	.000	.000
Maxwell, Keith, Hick.	.262	62	234	206	26	54	91	11	1	8	39	0	0	9	19	0	49	2	2	3	.442	.350
McGee, Tom, Del.	.271	71	264	218	37	59	91	16	2	4	27	2	5	4	34	2	52	0	4	5	.417	.372
McGrath, Sean, C'bia	.179	30	104	95	13	17	25	6	1	0	13	0	5	3	1	0	31	0	0	2	.263	.202
McKinley, Josh, C.F.†	.262	48	185	168	18	44	56	12	0	0	17	0	1	0	16	0	38	9	6	3	.333	.324
Meadows, Randy, C.F.	.227	50	157	141	18	32	39	5	1	0	9	4	0	5	7	0	35	2	5	2	.277	.288
Meliah, David, Sav.*	.296	93	379	358	53	106	157	21	3	8	49	0	2	3	16	0	80	3	6	8	.439	.330
Melo, Ramon, C.W.Va.	.273	3	12	11	0	3	3	0	0	0	1	0	0	0	1	0	4	0	0	0	.273	.333
Mench, Kevin, Sav.	.304	6	25	23	4	7	16	1	1	2	8	0	0	0	2	0	4	0	0	1	.696	.360
Mendoza, Angel, Aug.	.263	119	473	429	58	113	157	7	8	7	46	1	2	7	34	0	97	19	8	8	.366	.320
Mento, Alfredo, C'bia	.333	3	12	12	5	4	5	1	0	0	2	0	0	0	0	0	2	2	0	0	.417	.333
Metzler, Rod, C.W.Va.†	.264	130	525	462	64	122	180	23	7	7	60	5	1	9	48	0	98	29	14	7	.390	.344
Mikels, Jason, Mac.	.000	5	1	1	0	0	0	0	0	0	0	0	0	0	0	0	1	0	0	0	.000	.000
Minges, Tyler, C'bus	.242	127	524	492	64	119	196	25	11	10	62	3	6	4	19	0	113	23	7	12	.398	.273
Mirizzi, Marc, Gre.†	.265	9	40	34	5	9	14	0	1	1	3	0	0	1	5	0	9	0	0	1	.412	.375
Moore, Eric, Sav.	.000	23	1	1	0	0	0	0	0	0	0	0	0	0	0	0	1	0	0	0	.000	.000
Moore, Griffin, C.W.Va.	.217	40	121	106	10	23	28	3	1	0	6	1	1	3	8	0	13	2	2	4	.264	.288
Mulvehill, Chase, C'bia	.286	116	478	427	65	122	184	23	6	9	58	5	5	12	29	0	97	29	13	6	.431	.345
Myers, Tootie, C.F.	.223	137	567	515	61	115	183	19	8	11	52	6	1	10	35	1	147	30	16	9	.355	.285
Na, Jim, C.F.*	.217	67	246	221	24	48	69	10	4	1	18	2	0	6	17	0	45	7	5	3	.312	.291
Ndungidi, Ntema, Del.*	.194	64	271	217	33	42	54	8	2	0	24	1	1	3	49	2	54	18	2	7	.249	.348
Nieves, Juan, Hag.	.146	47	149	130	14	19	27	3	1	1	14	3	2	2	12	0	28	7	1	3	.208	.226
Nolasco, Regino, Del.	.119	23	68	59	10	7	7	0	0	0	6	2	1	1	5	0	16	1	1	1	.119	.197
Novak, John, Sav.	.251	66	250	215	38	54	93	13	1	8	36	0	2	5	28	0	65	3	2	3	.433	.348
Nowlin, Cody, Sav.*	.181	56	228	204	25	37	57	6	1	4	26	0	3	2	19	0	58	1	2	3	.279	.254
Nunez, Jorge, Hag.	.268	133	609	564	116	151	243	28	11	14	61	1	2	2	40	1	103	51	8	8	.431	.317

Player, Team	Avg.	G	TPA	AB	R	H	TB	2B	3B	HR	RBI	SH	SF	HP	BB	IBB	SO	SB	CS	GDP	Slg.	OBP
Olivares, Teuris, Gre.	.279	110	490	451	78	126	189	18	6	11	52	3	4	6	26	0	78	14	7	10	.419	.324
Oliver, Johnny, Aug.	.208	33	132	120	9	25	29	4	0	0	7	1	0	1	10	0	36	1	0	3	.242	.275
Olmeda, Jose, C'bus†	.264	30	120	106	16	28	44	3	2	3	16	0	1	2	11	0	32	5	1	3	.415	.342
Ortiz, Juan, C.F.	.159	16	55	44	7	7	8	1	0	0	2	3	0	1	7	0	21	1	1	0	.182	.288
Ottevaere, Derek, Sav.	.273	97	375	337	45	92	134	11	5	7	43	0	3	8	27	0	70	3	1	2	.398	.339
Padilla, Jorge, Pied.	.208	44	178	168	13	35	56	10	1	3	17	0	1	4	5	0	44	0	0	5	.333	.247
Pagan, Carlos, C.W.Va.	.227	50	169	154	19	35	62	9	0	6	21	0	2	0	13	0	40	2	2	1	.403	.284
Pena, Jose, Aug.	.226	49	183	168	23	38	63	8	1	5	24	0	3	2	10	0	50	1	2	2	.375	.273
Pena, Rodolfo, Aug.	.238	99	348	320	35	76	102	15	1	3	37	4	1	7	16	0	79	1	1	8	.319	.288
Perez, Deivi, Hick.	.205	25	97	83	13	17	27	4	0	2	9	0	0	0	14	0	26	2	0	0	.325	.320
Piercy, Brad, C.F.*	.232	90	345	323	40	75	109	12	2	6	23	3	0	2	17	0	111	17	11	5	.337	.275
Piercy, Mike, Hick.*	.167	8	23	18	7	3	3	0	0	0	0	1	0	1	3	0	2	1	1	0	.167	.318
Pierre, Juan, Ash.*	.320	140	648	585	93	187	228	28	5	1	55	11	6	8	38	2	37	66	19	12	.390	.366
Pinto, Rene, Gre.	.259	19	64	58	9	15	24	1	1	2	6	0	0	1	5	0	13	0	1	2	.414	.328
Pittman, Thomas, C.F.	.283	131	545	505	74	143	241	26	3	22	97	0	4	11	25	0	146	12	17	9	.477	.328
Polidor, Wil, Pied.†	.221	26	98	95	7	21	26	3	1	0	7	1	0	0	2	0	15	0	1	1	.274	.237
Powers, Jeff, C'bus*	.266	76	268	233	34	62	78	10	0	2	30	3	4	4	24	2	24	2	3	0	.335	.340
Pressley, Josh, C.S.C.*	.243	118	495	437	50	106	155	22	0	9	64	0	4	5	49	5	80	1	4	11	.355	.323
Price, Corey, Del.†	.244	22	92	82	8	20	24	4	0	0	9	1	1	0	8	0	24	0	0	2	.293	.308
Prieto, Jonathan, Hick.*	.303	61	272	244	42	74	88	9	1	1	21	3	1	2	22	0	55	10	7	4	.361	.364
Purkiss, Matt, Del.*	.210	107	430	366	44	77	125	15	0	11	46	0	1	6	57	0	124	0	0	8	.342	.326
Pursell, Mike, C'bus*	.217	18	76	69	9	15	21	4	1	0	6	0	1	0	6	0	11	1	0	3	.304	.276
Quinones, Marcus, Sav.†	.203	37	143	123	17	25	34	9	0	0	9	4	1	1	14	0	28	2	1	4	.276	.288
Raines, Tim, Del.	.248	117	496	415	80	103	149	24	8	2	49	3	4	3	71	1	130	49	16	1	.359	.359
Ralph, Brian, Hick.*	.167	16	56	48	7	8	11	3	0	0	2	1	0	1	6	0	8	3	2	0	.229	.273
Ramirez, Charlie, C.W.Va.	.200	28	79	70	5	14	14	0	0	0	4	1	1	0	7	1	16	1	2	3	.200	.269
Ramos, Kelly, C'bia†	.256	82	284	262	31	67	111	14	0	10	34	2	1	10	9	0	52	4	2	5	.424	.305
Reed, Keith, Del.	.258	61	269	240	36	62	94	14	3	4	25	2	2	3	22	0	53	3	2	4	.392	.326
Reyes, Ambiorix, Pied.	.245	78	277	257	30	63	76	7	3	0	15	3	0	6	11	0	23	14	5	5	.296	.292
Reyes, Jose, Hick.	.275	23	88	80	11	22	43	4	1	5	15	0	0	4	4	0	18	3	1	3	.538	.341
Reyes, Rene, Ash.†	.350	40	167	160	26	56	73	6	1	3	19	0	0	1	6	0	22	1	0	1	.456	.377
Rhodes, Dusty, Gre.*	.295	67	289	234	43	69	97	10	3	4	44	2	5	5	43	2	57	7	5	3	.415	.408
Rhodes, Nicholas, C.S.C.	.239	19	52	46	6	11	15	0	2	0	0	0	0	1	5	0	11	0	0	2	.326	.327
Ribaudo, Mike, C'bia	.246	58	207	199	22	49	82	12	0	7	33	3	1	0	4	0	53	0	1	5	.412	.260
Richardson, Juan, Pied.	.167	4	14	12	0	2	3	1	0	0	2	1	0	0	1	0	5	0	0	1	.250	.231
Riordan, Matthew, Del.	.289	54	237	204	22	59	88	12	4	3	38	1	3	5	24	2	46	6	5	0	.431	.373
Risinger, Ben, Hick.	.249	124	512	449	56	112	150	20	3	4	44	9	3	12	39	0	80	2	4	12	.334	.324
Rivera, Carlos, Hick.*	.322	119	488	457	63	147	218	30	1	13	86	0	4	11	15	2	45	2	1	13	.477	.355
Roberts, Brian, Del.†	.240	47	201	167	22	40	54	12	1	0	21	5	1	1	27	0	42	17	5	0	.323	.347
Rodriguez, Carlos, Aug.	.193	33	131	119	14	23	40	6	1	3	8	1	0	3	8	0	41	1	2	4	.336	.262
Rodriguez, Junior, Gre.	.188	69	237	191	28	36	60	3	3	5	25	4	1	4	37	0	75	1	2	2	.314	.330
Rojas, Mo, C.W.Va.	.091	18	37	33	4	3	4	1	0	0	3	0	0	1	3	0	12	1	2	1	.121	.189
Rollins, Antwon, Sav.	.242	8	38	33	7	8	8	0	0	0	1	1	0	0	4	0	14	3	0	0	.242	.324
Romano, Jimmie, Sav.	.201	44	140	134	13	27	35	2	0	2	14	1	0	0	5	0	26	1	0	2	.261	.230
Ross, Donovan, C.W.Va.*	.176	6	23	17	1	3	4	1	0	0	0	1	0	1	4	0	6	0	0	1	.235	.364
Ruan, Wilken, C.F.	.224	112	428	397	43	89	116	16	4	1	47	7	0	6	18	0	79	29	17	5	.292	.268
Ruiz, Willy, C.W.Va.	.304	57	229	191	31	58	66	6	1	0	19	4	0	0	34	0	44	24	14	1	.346	.409
Rumfield, Brock, Del.	.228	119	485	421	60	96	123	13	1	4	56	7	3	7	47	1	101	3	0	13	.292	.314
Rust, Brian, Del.	.260	21	87	77	11	20	34	9	1	1	16	1	3	0	6	1	27	0	0	5	.442	.302
Ryan, Kelvin, C.S.C.	.236	128	525	478	63	113	175	20	3	12	66	4	5	7	30	0	107	12	4	10	.366	.288
Salazar, Jeremy, Pied.	.252	98	384	345	37	87	134	17	0	10	36	1	4	7	27	0	90	1	0	9	.388	.316
Santana, Osmany, C'bus*	.323	38	146	133	23	43	49	6	0	0	17	1	1	1	10	1	21	15	6	0	.368	.372
Santos, Angel, Aug.†	.270	130	538	466	83	126	205	30	2	15	55	2	3	5	62	4	88	25	10	12	.440	.360
Schreimann, Eric, Pied.	.241	78	296	257	35	62	118	10	5	12	37	1	3	19	16	0	77	1	1	5	.459	.329
Schwab, Chris, C'bus	.288	54	203	177	25	51	90	10	1	9	26	0	0	0	26	2	54	13	6	4	.508	.379
Scioneaux, Damian, C.S.C.*	.111	5	20	18	1	2	2	0	0	0	0	0	0	0	2	0	3	2	0	2	.111	.200
Seabol, Scott, Gre.	.315	138	608	543	86	171	283	55	6	15	89	0	11	9	45	1	91	6	5	9	.521	.370
Seestedt, Michael, Del.	.263	27	95	80	8	21	24	3	0	0	3	5	0	0	10	0	20	0	0	1	.300	.344
Segura, Rolando, Hick.	.303	40	156	142	23	43	69	8	0	6	21	0	0	2	12	0	30	0	3	3	.486	.365
Shackelford, Brian, C.W.Va.*	.200	73	289	260	25	52	100	14	2	10	30	1	1	1	26	0	80	1	1	3	.385	.274
Shelley, Jason, Hick.	.259	20	58	54	8	14	19	2	0	1	6	0	2	1	1	0	14	0	1	0	.352	.276
Sienko, Ryan, Sav.	.151	37	97	86	7	13	19	3	0	1	6	0	1	2	8	0	25	0	0	2	.221	.237
Skrehot, Shaun, Hick.	.234	115	493	461	53	108	138	17	5	1	37	7	4	5	16	0	72	12	8	8	.299	.265
Smith, Casey, C'bus	.235	47	190	153	21	36	45	6	0	1	13	1	1	7	28	0	48	0	2	1	.294	.376
Smith, Ryan, C'bia	.000	1	3	3	0	0	0	0	0	0	0	0	0	0	0	0	1	0	0	0	.000	.000
Smith, Sam, Ash.	.272	87	338	316	42	86	126	16	0	8	39	0	0	10	12	0	79	7	2	4	.399	.320
Smothers, Stewart, Mac.	.283	63	242	219	32	62	95	12	0	7	39	2	5	0	16	0	61	2	3	2	.434	.325
Snyder, Earl, C'bia	.267	136	552	486	73	130	247	25	4	28	97	0	9	2	55	0	117	2	2	5	.508	.339
Soler, Ramon, C.S.C.†	.237	108	456	389	74	92	116	17	2	1	28	6	1	4	56	0	93	46	14	5	.298	.338
Soriano, Jose, Aug.	.345	38	163	148	28	51	83	7	5	5	28	0	3	2	10	0	37	12	5	5	.561	.387
Sosa, Jovanny, Hick.	.209	108	451	402	61	84	168	16	1	22	53	0	4	8	37	1	145	2	2	9	.418	.286
Stewart, Colin, Mac.	.208	29	78	72	8	15	19	4	0	0	3	0	0	1	5	0	16	3	1	3	.264	.269
Stratton, Robert, C'bia	.274	95	374	318	58	87	173	17	3	21	60	0	3	5	48	4	112	7	1	1	.544	.374
Strickland, Greg, Mac.*	.261	86	343	314	58	82	132	13	8	7	34	0	1	2	26	1	74	27	12	1	.420	.321
Suriel, Miguel, C.S.C.	.226	80	293	257	24	58	85	18	0	3	22	1	1	3	31	0	35	2	1	9	.331	.315
Taveras, Jose, C.W.Va.	.245	91	361	335	41	82	112	14	2	4	29	2	0	5	19	0	78	38	10	2	.334	.295
Taylor, Adam, C'bus	.296	8	29	27	4	8	13	2	0	1	4	0	0	0	2	0	9	0	0	0	.481	.345
Taylor, Seth, Gre.	.300	4	13	10	1	3	4	1	0	0	1	1	0	1	1	0	0	1	0	0	.400	.417
Terni, Chaz, Aug.	.179	36	134	123	10	22	36	3	4	1	10	0	0	2	9	0	36	1	1	3	.293	.246
Thompson, Andy, C'bia*	.227	61	213	185	14	42	53	11	0	0	17	0	0	6	22	0	45	0	0	4	.286	.329
Thompson, Eric, C'bus*	.250	74	315	280	48	70	79	9	0	0	15	3	0	1	31	0	83	22	9	3	.282	.327
Thompson, Tyler, Hag.	.261	130	530	440	84	115	200	28	3	17	81	2	5	4	79	0	122	20	3	7	.455	.375
Torres, Jason, Sav.*	.167	43	137	126	6	21	28	3	2	0	8	0	1	0	10	0	31	2	1	4	.222	.226
Twombley, Dennis, Gre.	.239	44	167	142	19	34	61	6	0	7	22	1	2	5	17	0	44	0	0	4	.430	.337
Umbria, Jose, Hag.	.290	62	214	186	24	54	68	5	0	3	20	0	2	0	26	0	36	2	2	4	.366	.374

Player, Team	Avg.	G	TPA	AB	R	H	TB	2B	3B	HR	RBI	SH	SF	HP	BB	IBB	SO	SB	CS	GDP	Slg.	OBP
Uribe, Juan, Ash.	.267	125	471	430	57	115	176	28	3	9	46	11	4	6	20	0	79	11	7	12	.409	.307
Urquhart, Derick, C.F.*	.308	54	198	169	31	52	73	4	4	3	18	2	0	1	26	1	19	6	8	1	.432	.403
Valdez, Angel, Gre.	.272	35	132	125	11	34	41	4	0	1	14	0	0	5	2	0	32	2	3	2	.328	.311
Valdez, Jerry, Pied.	.222	39	141	126	11	28	39	5	0	2	13	1	2	1	11	1	26	0	0	2	.310	.286
Vann, Eric, C.W.Va.†	.074	14	32	27	1	2	2	0	0	0	1	0	0	1	4	0	11	2	1	1	.074	.219
Velazquez, Gil, C'bia	.227	21	84	75	9	17	23	4	1	0	6	2	3	1	3	0	14	0	1	2	.307	.256
Vento, Mike, Gre.	.250	40	165	148	20	37	59	11	1	3	16	0	1	2	14	1	46	3	1	1	.399	.321
Warren, Chris, Aug.	.170	42	170	153	16	26	45	4	0	5	16	3	1	2	11	0	53	4	0	4	.294	.230
Warriax, Brandon, Sav.	.153	43	163	144	10	22	30	3	1	1	13	2	2	0	15	0	43	7	1	1	.208	.230
Washington, Dion, Gre.	.218	84	322	284	46	62	101	14	2	7	34	0	1	6	30	0	107	15	6	4	.356	.305
Washington, Rico, Hick.*	.355	76	349	287	70	102	158	15	1	13	50	0	6	8	48	7	45	5	1	4	.551	.453
Weichard, Paul, Hick.†	.225	89	349	316	44	71	99	7	3	5	37	4	0	0	28	0	92	23	7	4	.313	.288
Whitby, Cory, Aug.*	.214	35	91	70	12	15	22	4	0	1	5	0	0	3	18	0	20	2	1	0	.314	.396
Whitehurst, Tom, Ash.	.240	33	109	100	15	24	28	1	0	1	6	1	1	5	2	0	23	3	2	1	.280	.287
Wiese, Brian, Aug.	.118	23	84	68	7	8	10	2	0	0	2	1	1	4	10	0	18	1	0	2	.147	.265
Wilder, Paul, C.S.C.*	.173	44	174	150	15	26	42	4	0	4	13	0	0	3	21	0	61	7	1	3	.280	.287
Wilson, Travis, Mac.	.309	90	390	363	65	112	173	20	4	11	63	0	3	15	9	1	66	14	8	8	.477	.349
Winchester, Jeff, Ash.	.232	86	347	310	45	72	146	18	1	18	48	0	1	9	27	0	92	0	1	8	.471	.311
Winter, Jon, C.S.C.	.250	13	41	32	3	8	10	2	0	0	3	0	0	2	7	0	10	0	1	2	.313	.404
Wright, Corey, Sav.*	.263	95	387	316	61	83	111	15	5	1	23	1	1	5	64	1	73	13	13	2	.351	.394
Zapp, A.J., Mac.*	.229	119	479	428	60	98	190	24	1	22	65	0	4	7	40	0	163	4	1	4	.444	.300
Zech, Scott, C.F.	.300	3	13	10	1	3	3	0	0	0	1	0	0	0	3	0	1	1	0	0	.300	.462
Zepeda, Jesse, Hag.†	.225	89	271	222	26	50	75	8	1	5	34	4	2	1	42	1	36	3	0	4	.338	.348

GRAND SLAMS: Cameron, 3; Davis, Gordnier, Pressley, 2 each; Ahumada, Alamo, Backe, Copeland, Diaz, Duncan, Freeman, Hafner, Hendricks, Holliday, Jenkins, Johnson, Keaveney, Landaeta, Lebron, Minges, Nunez, Pena, Perez, Pierre, Pittman, Rivera, Rumfield, Smothers, Stratton, Uribe, Washington, Wright, 1 each.

AWARDED FIRST BASE ON CATCHER'S INTERFERENCE: Merriman, 7 (Diaz, Dimmick, Hill, Lopez, Suarez, Whitehead, William); Christiansen, 3 (Cosentino, Hyde, McAffee); Dimmick, 2 (Goldbach, Lawrence); Wolff, 2 (Goldbach, Hill); Folkers (Nelson); German (Whitehead); Hawthorne (Nelson); Hodge (Diaz); Roneberg (Garcia).

PLAYERS WITH TWO OR MORE TEAMS

Player, Team	Avg.	G	TPA	AB	R	H	TB	2B	3B	HR	RBI	SH	SF	HP	BB	IBB	SO	SB	CS	GDP	Slg.	OBP
Cota, Humberto, C.S.C.	.280	85	364	336	42	94	144	21	1	9	61	1	5	2	20	1	51	1	1	9	.429	.320
Cota, Humberto, Hick.	.271	37	156	133	28	36	57	11	2	2	20	0	2	0	21	1	20	3	1	0	.429	.365

1999 PITCHING

TEAM

Team	W	L	Pct.	ERA	G	CG	ShO	Sv.	IP	H	TBF	R	ER	HR	SH	SF	HB	BB	IBB	SO	WP	Bk.
Piedmont	69	71	.493	3.02	140	16	12	42	1187.1	1099	4995	540	399	73	42	26	53	352	7	1041	58	8
Augusta............	69	70	.496	3.35	139	3	14	35	1216.2	1157	5180	585	453	86	30	29	54	407	13	1170	71	11
Cape Fear	75	65	.536	3.57	140	5	4	32	1216.0	1172	5209	613	483	96	33	43	71	441	7	952	83	9
Macon	74	64	.536	3.59	138	1	5	40	1193.0	1083	5111	585	476	101	31	40	67	466	10	1128	90	22
Hagerstown.......	84	56	.600	3.63	140	2	11	43	1262.0	1138	5350	616	509	78	44	26	12	440	8	1049	82	15
Columbia...........	83	58	.589	3.64	141	3	11	37	1220.2	1115	5205	611	494	94	30	30	76	448	6	1103	103	14
Charleston, S.C. .	65	77	.458	3.83	142	6	9	33	1243.1	1192	5321	651	529	87	44	40	59	430	17	1010	88	16
Greensboro	77	64	.546	3.98	141	7	6	36	1223.1	1204	5283	646	541	100	25	33	64	406	6	1186	141	15
Hickory	70	70	.500	3.99	140	2	9	33	1247.1	1243	5444	702	553	129	39	33	88	470	18	1130	75	12
Charleston, W.V..	61	80	.433	4.02	141	6	10	28	1245.0	1252	5462	689	556	72	47	45	75	532	16	1078	96	19
Delmarva...........	58	80	.420	4.33	138	7	7	27	1213.0	1214	5289	705	583	109	47	34	63	479	2	1134	82	20
Columbus	70	71	.496	4.38	141	3	7	34	1220.1	1207	5320	703	594	132	25	32	88	443	3	1182	94	15
Savannah	62	78	.443	4.53	140	6	12	34	1206.2	1262	5339	749	608	117	31	49	71	450	0	1113	97	16
Asheville	64	77	.454	4.66	141	6	4	35	1211.0	1231	5370	743	627	121	32	53	7	492	2	1163	109	22

INDIVIDUAL

TOP QUALIFIERS FOR EARNED-RUN AVERAGE TITLE

Minimum 114 innings.*Lefthanded pitcher.

Pitcher, Team	W	L	Pct.	ERA	G	GS	CG	ShO	GF	Sv.	IP	H	TBF	R	ER	HR	SH	SF	HB	BB	IBB	SO	WP	Bk.
Standridge, Jason, C.S.C.	9	1	.900	2.02	18	18	3	3	0	0	116.0	80	455	35	26	5	5	5	7	31	0	84	9	2
Gonzalez, Edwin, C.W.Va.	7	6	.538	2.24	27	13	3	2	4	2	120.1	101	479	37	30	6	5	4	5	28	0	136	13	1
Baisley, Brad, Pied.	10	7	.588	2.26	23	23	3	2	0	0	147.2	116	606	56	37	5	5	5	14	55	1	110	6	2
Norton, Jason, Aug.	9	6	.600	2.32	30	17	2	1	5	0	136.0	106	544	50	35	11	1	2	4	28	1	150	7	0
Kubes, Greg, Pied.*	11	12	.478	2.62	27	27	4	0	0	0	164.2	162	705	65	48	4	8	3	47	0	147	4	0
Strange, Patrick, C'bia	12	5	.706	2.63	28	21	2	0	1	1	154.0	138	627	57	45	4	4	3	10	29	1	113	7	0
Hughes, Travis, Sav.	11	7	.611	2.81	30	23	1	0	5	2	157.0	127	646	60	49	9	3	3	11	54	0	150	9	2
Cook, Andy, C'bia	12	7	.632	2.83	27	26	0	0	1	1	149.2	150	628	66	47	16	4	4	3	42	0	124	10	1
Padua, Geraldo, Gre.	9	4	.692	2.84	21	21	1	1	0	0	139.2	120	569	53	44	12	0	1	2	35	0	155	13	1
Osting, Jimmy, Mac.*	14	4	.778	2.88	27	22	0	0	5	2	147.0	130	581	52	47	13	2	1	5	30	0	131	2	0
Miller, Greg, Aug.*	10	6	.625	3.10	25	25	1	0	0	0	136.2	109	558	54	47	8	1	0	5	56	0	146	4	3
Silva, Carlos, Pied.	11	8	.579	3.12	26	26	3	1	0	0	164.1	176	708	79	57	6	8	6	9	41	2	99	8	2
Dunn, Keith, Gre.	9	9	.500	3.13	35	18	1	0	14	5	135.1	134	561	61	47	7	5	4	12	16	1	109	14	0
Vega, Rene, C'bia*	11	7	.611	3.14	29	22	1	0	2	1	146.0	101	593	57	51	8	3	2	12	50	1	148	6	4
Stephens, John, Del.	10	8	.556	3.22	28	24	4	2	0	0	170.1	148	702	75	61	10	5	4	10	36	0	217	4	0

DEPARTMENTAL LEADERS: W—Osting, 14; L—Stewart, Casteel, McGill, Casey, 14 each; Pct.—Coco, .917; G—Kingrey, Pavlovich, 56 each; GS—Casey, Van Buren, Smith, 28 each; CG—Turnbow, Kubes, Stephens, 4 each; ShO—Standridge, 3; GF—Kingrey, Bell, 48 each; Sv.—Kingrey, Cisar, 27 each; IP—Smith, 171.1; H—Silva, 176; TBF—Smith, 724; R—Cook, Casey, Stewart, 99 each; ER—Cook, Tynan, 87 each; HR—Tynan, Stewart, 19 each; SH—Affeldt, James, 9 each; SF—Van Buren, 13; HB—Cassidy, 21; BB—Affeldt, 80; IBB—Haines, Lee, Mancha, Pavlovich, 4 each; SO—Stephens, 217; WP—Casey, 25; BK—several pitchers tied, 7 each.

ALL PITCHERS

*Lefthanded pitcher.

Pitcher, Team	W	L	Pct.	ERA	G	GS	CG	ShO	GF	Sv.	IP	H	TBF	R	ER	HR	SH	SF	HB	BB	IBB	SO	WP	Bk.
Abreu, Winston, Mac.	7	2	.778	1.69	14	14	0	0	0	0	69.1	41	272	17	13	3	0	2	4	26	0	95	7	1
Adair, Derek, Pied.	2	4	.333	4.70	8	6	1	0	2	0	38.1	44	166	28	20	4	0	1	0	6	0	15	2	2
Affeldt, Jeremy, C.W.Va.*	7	7	.500	3.83	27	24	2	1	1	0	143.1	140	637	78	61	4	9	4	8	80	0	111	14	4
Ammons, Cary, C.W.Va.*	8	5	.615	2.98	16	16	0	0	0	0	90.2	80	371	41	30	3	4	2	2	34	0	92	5	0
Andrade, Jancy, Del.	2	5	.286	5.52	26	8	0	0	3	0	75.0	73	339	61	46	8	1	2	4	44	0	63	8	2
Aracena, Juan, C'bus.	2	0	1.000	3.28	32	0	0	0	30	18	35.2	32	138	13	13	7	1	0	1	3	0	30	1	0
Aramboles, Ricardo, Gre.	1	2	.333	2.34	6	6	1	0	0	0	34.2	25	136	9	9	1	1	1	0	12	0	34	5	0
Arthurs, Shane, C.F.	7	8	.467	4.16	25	21	2	0	2	0	136.1	144	596	77	63	8	7	5	7	52	1	87	10	0
Babula, Shaun, Del.*	0	2	.000	3.29	16	0	0	0	7	2	13.2	17	65	7	5	3	5	2	0	5	0	16	1	1
Bailie, Matt, Pied.	0	0	.000	1.47	6	1	0	0	4	1	18.1	13	75	5	3	0	0	0	7	0	24	1	0
Baisley, Brad, Pied.	10	7	.588	2.26	23	23	3	2	0	0	147.2	116	606	56	37	5	5	5	14	55	1	110	6	2
Bautista, Francisco, C.W.Va.	0	1	.000	4.35	7	0	0	0	4	0	10.1	11	54	7	5	1	0	0	1	12	1	5	2	0
Bautista, Martin, C'bus	6	3	.667	4.95	15	12	0	0	0	0	67.1	80	311	46	37	5	1	2	6	20	0	51	5	0
Bechler, Steven, Del.	8	12	.400	3.54	26	26	1	1	0	0	152.1	137	642	69	60	12	5	2	4	58	0	139	9	0
Becks, Ryan, C.F.*	10	6	.625	3.84	34	6	0	0	11	0	93.2	96	408	52	40	10	2	2	6	32	1	62	5	0
Behn, Brendan, C'bia*	0	0	.000	36.00	1	0	0	0	1	0	1.0	4	8	4	4	0	0	0	1	0	1	2	0
Beimel, Joe, Hick.*	5	11	.313	4.43	29	22	0	0	3	0	130.0	146	570	81	64	12	4	5	12	43	0	102	10	2
Beitey, Jason, Sav.	1	3	.250	5.36	21	1	0	0	9	2	48.2	54	228	38	29	4	1	5	6	28	0	38	5	2
Bell, Heath, C'bia	1	7	.125	2.60	55	0	0	0	48	25	62.1	47	251	23	18	3	2	0	0	17	0	68	3	1
Bellhorn, Todd, C'bia*	4	5	.444	4.30	38	0	0	0	10	0	58.2	55	265	38	28	3	2	2	3	32	0	46	6	0
Bello, Jilberto, Del.	6	4	.600	3.97	38	0	0	0	21	4	65.2	68	292	36	29	4	5	1	2	29	0	46	5	1
Bennett, Jeff, Hick.	2	2	.500	5.91	8	6	0	0	2	0	35.0	48	161	25	23	5	2	0	1	9	0	16	2	0
Blanco, Roger, Mac.	1	3	.250	9.71	19	6	0	0	5	0	38.0	63	199	46	41	8	0	1	5	16	0	28	3	3
Blazier, Ron, Del.	1	0	1.000	3.60	2	0	0	0	2	1	5.0	4	20	2	2	1	0	0	1	0	0	7	0	0
Blevins, Jeremy, Gre.	10	5	.667	4.05	19	19	0	0	0	0	106.2	105	449	56	48	7	1	3	3	30	0	81	8	0
Blythe, Billy, Mac.	0	0	.000	9.00	1	0	0	0	1	0	1.0	2	5	1	1	0	0	0	0	0	0	1	2	0
Bong, Jung, Mac.*	6	5	.545	3.98	26	20	0	0	2	1	108.2	111	484	61	48	8	5	1	11	50	0	100	9	4
Boublis, Dan, Sav.	7	3	.700	6.32	30	9	2	0	14	0	84.0	116	399	66	59	10	0	5	4	35	0	59	9	1
Boughton, Mike, Sav.	0	0	.000	0.00	1	0	0	0	1	0	0.2	2	5	3	0	1	0	0	0	0	0	1	0	0
Bowles, Brian, Hag.	6	2	.750	3.97	48	1	0	0	22	3	79.1	73	355	41	35	4	3	4	12	39	3	80	9	0
Box, John, C.S.C.*	1	0	1.000	0.00	2	0	0	0	1	0	2.0	2	6	0	0	0	0	0	0	0	0	1	0	0
Brantley, Brian, Ash.	6	6	.500	5.88	34	3	0	0	13	3	90.1	89	406	65	59	6	7	2	11	44	0	100	13	1
Bravo, Franklin, Hick.	7	1	.875	3.22	34	8	0	0	6	0	95.0	82	415	47	34	11	6	3	9	42	2	81	3	2
Brazoban, Melvin, Sav.	1	2	.333	7.09	29	5	0	0	11	2	66.0	72	335	63	52	6	1	3	2	60	0	75	13	2
Bridges, Donald, C.F.	1	6	.857	2.28	8	8	1	1	0	0	47.1	37	189	12	12	2	2	0	5	17	0	44	5	0
Buchanan, Brian, Gre.*	4	3	.571	3.00	48	0	0	0	14	1	51.0	41	238	21	17	1	2	3	6	40	0	58	8	1
Buirley, Matt, Hick.	8	4	.667	3.76	46	0	0	0	33	11	55.0	44	253	34	23	4	2	0	9	32	3	63	7	1
Burch, Matt, C.W.Va.	3	11	.214	6.35	21	15	0	0	2	0	73.2	95	355	62	52	14	3	3	6	41	1	43	7	2
Cameron, Ryan, Ash.	3	1	.750	2.34	17	0	0	0	5	2	34.2	18	140	10	9	1	0	0	1	18	1	40	4	0
Carpenter, Justin, Gre.	3	2	.600	4.06	40	0	0	0	17	0	57.2	57	258	39	26	6	0	3	3	29	0	45	9	0
Carr, Tim, C'bia.	6	4	.600	1.58	45	0	0	0	18	0	68.1	58	280	18	12	4	3	0	7	20	2	64	4	0
Carter, Justin, Ash.*	13	6	.684	3.56	27	26	2	1	1	0	144.0	138	639	79	57	10	5	4	12	72	0	146	8	3
Carter, Roger, C.S.C.*	0	3	.000	8.76	12	1	0	0	4	1	12.1	11	65	15	12	2	0	2	17	0	14	1	0
Casey, Joe, Hag.	7	14	.333	4.69	28	28	0	0	0	0	142.0	150	637	99	74	10	4	3	10	64	0	79	25	3
Cassidy, Scott, Hag.	13	7	.650	3.27	27	27	1	0	0	0	170.2	151	694	78	62	13	2	1	21	30	0	178	3	2
Casteel, Ricky, Del.	3	14	.176	5.01	29	21	2	0	6	0	134.2	152	591	92	75	13	4	8	4	53	0	100	4	1
Castelli, Robert, C.F.	2	2	.500	3.71	29	0	0	0	18	5	43.2	39	204	30	18	4	0	3	2	35	0	46	5	3
Chavez, Christopher, Mac.	1	2	.333	3.52	13	0	0	0	10	3	15.1	14	64	9	6	1	1	1	0	6	2	18	1	0
Chiavacci, Ron, C.F.	5	3	.625	3.59	20	8	0	0	6	1	62.2	60	295	39	25	5	3	3	6	34	0	67	1	0
Cisar, Mark, Aug.	3	6	.333	2.24	52	0	0	0	47	27	68.1	57	288	22	17	0	3	2	4	22	3	64	4	0
Clark, Mark, Sav.	0	0	.000	0.00	1	0	0	0	0	0	4.0	2	14	0	0	0	0	0	0	1	0	1	0	0
Claussen, Brandon, Gre.*	0	1	.000	10.50	1	1	1	0	0	0	6.0	8	29	7	7	1	0	0	0	2	0	5	1	1
Coco, Pasqual, Hag.	11	1	.917	2.21	14	14	0	0	0	0	97.2	67	384	29	24	4	1	1	8	25	1	83	2	0
Cook, Aaron, Ash.	4	12	.250	6.44	25	25	2	0	0	0	121.2	157	561	99	87	17	2	1	9	42	0	73	15	0
Cook, Andy, C'bia	12	7	.632	2.83	27	26	0	0	1	1	149.2	150	628	66	47	16	4	4	3	42	0	124	10	1
Corcoran, Tim, C'bia.	0	3	.000	4.44	40	3	0	0	10	3	75.0	62	332	43	37	5	4	3	9	41	0	89	8	1
Corey, Michael, Mac.	1	1	.500	0.53	21	0	0	0	17	7	33.2	18	126	7	2	1	0	1	7	0	39	6	0
Cornejo, Jesse, C.S.C.*	5	4	.556	3.50	51	0	0	0	16	2	72.0	66	313	35	28	5	2	1	33	3	75	4	2
Crawford, Danny, Hick.	6	4	.600	4.07	16	9	0	0	3	0	59.2	66	260	35	27	7	1	1	21	1	39	1	1
Crumpton, Chuck, C.F.	2	1	.667	0.47	13	0	0	0	13	7	19.0	15	74	3	1	0	0	1	3	0	15	0	0
Daedelow, Craig, Del.	0	0	.000	9.00	1	0	0	0	1	0	1.0	3	7	2	1	0	0	0	1	0	0	0	0	0
Dampeer, Kelly, C'bus.	0	0	.000	0.00	2	0	0	0	2	0	2.0	0	8	0	0	0	0	0	1	0	2	0	0
Dansby, Justin, Mac.	0	2	.000	7.50	4	0	0	0	2	0	6.0	7	31	5	5	1	0	0	6	0	7	0	1
Day, Zach, Gre.	0	1	.000	2.25	2	2	0	0	0	0	8.0	14	42	11	2	0	1	1	1	4	0	0
DeLaCruz, Andres, Gre.	0	0	.000	10.13	3	0	0	0	1	0	2.2	5	16	3	3	0	0	1	2	0	2	3	0
Delgado, Joseph, C.W.Va.	3	4	.429	4.60	11	11	0	0	0	0	45.0	53	208	29	23	1	0	3	4	21	0	31	3	3
Dent, Doug, Mac.	4	5	.444	3.44	17	17	0	0	0	0	89.0	78	375	42	34	8	1	3	2	30	0	64	5	1
Douglass, Ryan, C.W.Va.	4	4	.429	4.71	10	9	0	0	0	0	42.0	55	188	28	22	1	1	2	2	13	0	22	5	0
Dreier, Tom, Hag.	0	0	.000	6.75	4	0	0	0	4	0	9.1	12	50	11	7	2	0	0	1	8	0	10	4	0
Drese, Ryan, C'bus.	0	2	.000	4.50	2	2	0	0	0	0	12.0	9	49	6	6	2	0	0	4	0	15	3	0
Duchscherer, Justin, Aug.	4	0	1.000	0.22	6	6	0	0	0	0	41.0	21	150	1	1	0	0	0	8	0	39	1	0
Dunn, Keith, Gre.	9	9	.500	3.13	35	18	1	0	14	5	135.1	134	561	61	47	7	5	4	12	16	1	109	14	0
Eason, Clay, Pied.	0	1	.000	2.18	10	0	0	0	5	2	20.2	13	86	5	5	2	0	0	1	11	1	33	0	0
Eavenson, Clay, Gre.	0	1	.000	3.38	5	1	0	0	1	0	10.2	12	47	7	4	1	0	1	0	3	0	5	1	0
Embry, Byron, Mac.	5	2	.714	2.38	25	0	0	0	4	0	45.1	35	194	17	12	3	2	0	25	0	42	5	1
Espina, Rendy, Pied.*	0	2	.000	4.63	15	0	0	0	7	3	35.0	35	143	20	18	1	2	1	10	1	31	3	1
Evans, Mike, Ash.*	5	6	.455	4.29	38	0	0	0	22	7	84.0	81	367	52	40	12	1	5	9	35	0	70	5	2
Everett, Matt, C'bus.	2	4	.333	4.55	18	0	0	0	8	1	31.2	30	135	17	16	5	1	0	2	14	0	19	2	0
Fenus, Justin, Pied.	2	0	1.000	2.43	10	4	0	0	2	0	37.0	29	150	14	10	3	1	1	2	10	0	27	0	0
Field, Nathan, C.F.	4	8	.333	5.40	42	0	0	0	21	2	65.0	75	300	49	39	8	2	3	7	22	2	55	4	0
Figueroa, Carlos, Sav.*	0	0	.000	5.85	10	0	0	0	2	1	20.0	19	97	14	13	2	0	3	16	0	30	5	1
Fleming, Travis, Del.	2	1	.667	4.70	14	1	0	0	4	1	38.1	36	159	24	20	4	1	1	1	14	0	33	3	0

Pitcher, Team	W	L	Pct.	ERA	G	GS	CG	ShO	GF	Sv.	IP	H	TBF	R	ER	HR	SH	SF	HB	BB	IBB	SO	WP	Bk.
Frachiseur, Zach, Mac.	0	1	.000	6.75	4	0	0	0	2	0	4.0	5	21	3	3	1	0	0	0	2	0	6	0	0
Frey, Chris, Sav.	2	0	1.000	2.44	31	0	0	0	12	5	59.0	53	247	27	16	1	1	0	2	15	0	55	7	0
Garcia, Rosman, Gre.	2	3	.400	6.38	9	9	0	0	0	0	42.1	60	204	33	30	4	0	1	2	20	0	31	12	3
Garcia, Sonny, Del.	3	5	.375	5.81	13	12	0	0	0	0	62.0	68	271	46	40	6	1	2	8	19	0	44	5	0
Gaskill, Derek, C'bia	2	1	.667	3.10	12	0	0	0	6	0	20.1	13	79	7	7	1	0	0	0	9	0	23	3	0
German, Yon, C'bia*	8	2	.800	2.26	14	14	0	0	0	0	87.2	82	352	33	22	9	1	2	0	15	0	68	3	1
Giese, Daniel, Aug.	1	0	1.000	2.08	9	0	0	0	1	0	17.1	15	71	4	4	1	1	0	3	5	0	11	1	0
Gilfillan, Jason, C.W.Va.	0	1	.000	14.66	8	0	0	0	1	0	11.2	22	66	21	19	2	0	0	1	6	0	9	1	0
Glaser, Eric, Aug.	1	0	1.000	0.00	1	1	0	0	0	0	5.0	2	17	0	0	0	0	0	0	1	0	7	0	0
Glaser, Scott, Hick.*	1	1	.500	4.43	17	0	0	0	7	0	20.1	23	90	12	10	3	0	1	1	3	0	10	0	0
Gonzalez, Edwin, C.W.Va.	7	6	.538	2.24	27	13	3	2	4	2	120.1	101	479	37	30	6	5	4	5	28	0	136	13	1
Gordon, Kevin, Ash.	0	1	.000	2.57	2	1	0	0	0	0	7.0	7	31	4	2	1	0	1	0	3	0	4	0	0
Gorman, Pat, C'bia	1	1	.500	11.78	15	0	0	0	8	0	18.1	28	106	27	24	4	0	1	0	19	0	19	4	0
Gourlay, Matt, Hag.	0	1	.000	13.50	7	0	0	0	3	0	6.2	10	42	10	10	0	0	1	2	13	0	5	0	0
Grabow, John, Hick.*	9	10	.474	3.80	26	26	0	0	0	0	156.1	152	654	82	66	16	3	3	5	32	0	164	3	0
Granadillo, Adel, C'bus	0	1	.000	15.00	2	0	0	0	0	0	3.0	3	14	5	5	1	1	1	0	3	0	1	1	0
Gray, Michael, Mac.*	5	4	.556	3.65	46	1	0	0	22	9	81.1	88	349	45	33	6	3	2	7	12	1	57	2	1
Gross, Rafael, C'bus	6	1	.857	2.60	42	0	0	0	31	7	62.1	51	249	19	18	3	2	0	1	14	0	62	0	0
Guerrero, Junior, C.W.Va.	7	3	.700	2.76	19	19	0	0	0	0	104.1	90	441	39	32	6	4	5	3	45	0	113	10	2
Guillory, Dan, C'bus	1	1	.500	1.93	15	0	0	0	8	0	32.2	21	130	9	7	3	0	0	0	10	0	43	0	0
Guzman, Ambiorix, Sav.	3	7	.300	4.40	29	1	0	0	18	6	71.2	71	301	37	35	10	6	4	5	16	0	73	2	2
Guzman, Juan, Del.	9	5	.643	3.55	29	18	0	0	8	3	124.1	124	531	51	49	10	2	2	7	44	0	134	6	4
Haines, Talley, C.S.C.	3	2	.600	3.25	47	0	0	0	34	18	61.0	51	248	33	22	2	2	0	3	12	4	68	5	1
Hancock, Joshua, Aug.	6	8	.429	3.80	25	25	0	0	0	0	139.2	154	607	79	59	12	4	2	4	46	0	106	10	1
Hebson, Bryan, C.F.	0	1	.000	2.67	6	6	0	0	0	0	33.2	22	142	13	10	2	1	1	3	17	0	34	2	0
Heffernan, Greg, C'bia	0	0	.000	5.14	5	0	0	0	3	0	7.0	7	31	8	4	2	0	0	0	5	0	5	0	0
Herndon, Eric, Mac.	5	4	.556	4.00	27	2	0	0	5	1	72.0	72	314	42	32	9	1	1	1	27	0	75	2	2
Hertzel, Patrick, C.S.C.	7	7	.500	3.98	35	16	0	0	7	0	126.2	142	559	66	56	10	1	3	3	46	1	96	7	0
Hiles, Cary, Pied.	3	2	.600	2.21	44	0	0	0	40	26	61.0	52	255	20	15	3	6	0	3	12	0	84	9	0
Hill, Terrance, Aug.*	3	6	.333	2.73	53	0	0	0	15	1	92.1	77	383	30	28	6	5	3	3	25	2	95	11	0
Houser, Kyle, Ash.	0	1	.000	8.18	4	3	0	0	0	0	11.0	14	51	12	10	5	0	1	0	3	0	19	2	1
Hudson, Luke, Ash.	6	5	.545	4.30	21	20	1	0	1	0	88.0	89	372	47	42	10	2	2	8	24	0	96	3	3
Hughes, Mike, C'bus*	0	0	.000	4.50	6	2	0	0	3	1	18.0	15	71	11	9	2	0	1	0	3	0	22	1	1
Hughes, Travis, Sav.	11	7	.611	2.81	30	23	1	0	5	2	157.0	127	646	60	49	9	3	3	11	54	0	150	9	2
Huntsman, Brandon, Del.	1	1	.500	4.43	7	2	0	0	3	0	22.1	20	96	12	11	3	1	1	0	9	0	25	0	0
Jackson, Jer. D., C.W.Va.-C'bia*	5	5	.500	3.69	24	17	0	0	4	0	109.2	104	461	57	45	5	2	1	6	33	0	91	9	0
James, Delvin, C.S.C.	8	8	.500	3.64	25	25	1	0	0	0	158.1	142	654	76	64	13	9	4	8	33	1	106	8	1
Jennings, Jason, Ash.	2	2	.500	3.70	12	12	0	0	0	0	58.1	55	242	27	24	3	2	6	8	69	4	0		
Jodie, Brett, Gre.	9	6	.600	3.81	25	20	2	0	3	1	120.1	125	497	59	51	10	0	1	1	18	0	106	9	0
Johnston, Clint, Hick.*	5	6	.455	4.73	34	10	0	0	4	0	93.1	92	420	63	49	12	2	1	6	49	0	94	7	0
Kanovich, Jason, C.F.*	4	2	.667	3.19	36	0	0	0	16	2	62.0	52	267	28	22	3	1	3	3	28	1	46	9	2
Kearney, Ryan, C'bus	0	1	.000	5.65	6	0	0	0	1	0	14.1	17	67	10	9	2	0	4	5	0	6	0	1	
Keelin, Chris, Pied.	1	0	1.000	3.00	4	0	0	0	3	0	6.0	9	32	6	2	1	0	0	0	4	0	4	0	0
Keisler, Randy, Gre.*	1	1	.500	2.38	4	4	0	0	0	0	22.2	12	91	6	6	1	0	1	10	0	42	0	0	
Kidd, Jake, Ash.	2	1	.667	1.48	9	1	0	0	4	2	24.1	16	94	7	4	2	2	3	3	0	21	0	0	
Kingrey, Jarrod, Hag.	3	2	.600	3.10	56	0	0	0	48	27	61.0	49	259	24	21	5	1	0	6	26	0	69	0	4
Knowles, Michael, Gre.	1	1	.500	8.23	11	2	0	0	5	0	27.1	45	137	27	25	1	0	0	2	10	0	27	5	1
Kofler, Ed, C.S.C.	9	11	.450	4.00	27	27	0	0	0	0	157.1	153	661	85	70	10	4	7	11	37	0	136	10	4
Kosderka, Matt, Sav.	12	9	.571	3.81	31	20	1	1	8	4	134.2	133	577	69	57	14	3	8	3	50	0	114	9	2
Kubes, Greg, Pied.*	11	12	.478	2.62	27	27	4	0	0	0	164.2	162	705	65	48	4	8	3	47	0	147	4	0	
Labitzke, Jesse, Ash.*	0	2	.000	8.07	14	1	0	0	8	0	32.1	40	159	29	29	2	1	3	2	25	0	35	3	0
Lamattina, Ryan, Ash.*	3	4	.429	3.50	38	0	0	0	25	9	79.2	68	334	36	31	10	2	2	6	29	1	78	5	0
Layne, Roger, C'bus	1	0	1.000	1.50	1	1	0	0	0	0	6.0	4	21	1	1	0	0	0	2	0	7	0	0	
LaRosa, Tom, Hag.	0	0	.000	4.76	12	0	0	0	4	1	11.1	9	60	8	6	0	0	1	2	16	0	18	8	0
Lee, Wayne, C.W.Va.	7	2	.778	3.96	48	0	0	0	22	6	88.2	82	366	45	39	11	3	3	3	26	4	77	4	2
Leon, Richy, Ash.	0	0	.000	0.00	1	0	0	0	1	0	1.0	0	3	0	0	0	0	0	0	0	0	0	0	0
Lewis, Craig, Gre.	4	0	1.000	2.66	9	5	0	0	1	1	47.1	42	197	17	14	3	1	2	2	7	1	51	3	0
Lewis, Peyton, Hag.	0	0	.000	0.00	2	0	0	0	2	0	2.0	0	8	0	0	0	0	0	1	0	5	2	0	
Ligons, Merrell, C.W.Va.	0	0	.000	0.00	2	0	0	0	2	0	2.0	6	6	0	0	0	0	0	0	0	0	1	0	0
Lontayo, Alejandro, Aug.*	2	0	1.000	4.30	40	0	0	0	14	0	58.2	55	255	31	28	7	1	2	4	26	0	80	3	1
Lowe, Matt, C'bia	0	0	.000	9.00	1	0	0	0	1	0	2.0	3	9	2	2	1	0	0	0	2	0	0	0	0
Lynch, Pat, Hag.-Ash.	11	6	.647	3.48	26	20	0	0	2	1	139.2	141	577	59	54	10	7	4	7	24	0	120	1	2
Lyons, Jonathan, Aug.	1	1	.500	2.15	19	0	0	0	10	2	29.1	26	123	9	7	1	1	2	1	9	0	32	0	1
Maas, Steve, C.W.Va.	0	4	.000	5.20	21	0	0	0	13	2	27.2	28	118	17	16	1	0	1	0	12	0	33	0	0
Macias, Jose, C'bus	0	0	.000	4.50	1	0	0	0	1	0	2.0	1	7	1	1	0	0	0	0	0	0	2	0	0
Madison, Scott, C'bus*	2	2	.500	4.60	10	4	0	0	2	0	31.1	37	140	19	16	6	1	0	1	13	0	22	1	0
Maluchnik, Gregg, Mac.	0	0	.000	9.00	1	0	0	0	1	0	1.0	1	5	1	1	0	0	0	0	1	0	2	0	
Mancha, Tony, C.W.Va.	4	3	.571	5.23	40	3	0	0	24	2	82.2	89	370	50	48	6	1	3	9	38	4	76	2	2
Maness, Nick, Gre.	5	6	.455	4.45	23	22	0	0	0	0	107.1	92	469	74	59	8	3	5	6	57	0	99	20	2
Mangum, Mark, C.F.	10	11	.476	3.50	26	26	1	0	0	0	159.1	156	677	85	62	14	1	7	16	54	0	107	15	0
Marietta, Ron, C'bus*	3	6	.333	8.25	11	11	0	0	0	0	48.0	71	244	48	44	9	1	0	8	19	0	40	7	0
Martin, Jeff, Hick.	0	2	.000	1.88	13	0	0	0	3	0	24.0	19	97	6	5	1	1	0	3	8	1	23	1	0
Martinez, Anastacio, Aug.	4	4	.333	6.30	10	10	0	0	0	0	40.0	44	188	37	28	7	0	0	2	18	0	36	1	3
Martinez, Javier, Hick.	0	0	.000	3.52	6	0	0	0	0	0	7.2	6	36	6	3	0	1	0	0	6	0	13	1	0
Martinez, Obispo, C.F.	0	0	.000	10.13	7	0	0	0	4	0	8.0	12	40	10	9	1	0	0	2	5	0	8	1	0
Matsko, Rick, C'bus	7	5	.583	4.55	42	0	0	0	8	0	85.0	70	374	49	43	8	2	6	11	43	1	93	13	0
Mattson, John, C'bia	0	0	.000	9.00	1	0	0	0	0	0	3.0	6	16	3	3	1	0	0	2	0	2	1	0	
McDonald, Jon, C.S.C.*	0	0	.000	6.97	14	0	0	0	8	0	20.2	26	97	19	16	3	0	0	5	1	19	1	0	
McDougal, Mike, Del.	1	0	1.000	0.00	1	0	0	0	0	0	2.0	3	9	0	0	0	0	0	0	3	0	0		
McGill, Frankie, Sav.	8	14	.364	5.22	26	26	0	0	0	0	141.1	163	645	92	82	13	4	2	9	56	0	128	13	0
McLeary, Marty, Aug.	5	6	.455	3.12	35	9	0	0	16	3	80.2	73	338	34	28	8	3	2	4	25	1	90	5	2
Mikels, Jason, Mac.	0	1	.000	3.00	5	0	0	0	2	1	12.0	9	48	7	4	2	1	1	0	4	0	6	0	0
Miller, Greg, Aug.*	10	6	.625	3.10	25	25	1	0	0	0	136.2	109	558	54	47	8	1	0	5	56	0	146	4	3
Mlodik, Kevin, Sav.	2	2	.500	0.90	14	0	0	0	14	5	20.0	12	81	5	2	1	1	0	0	8	0	32	2	1
Montero, Francisco, Pied.	4	3	.571	3.05	25	9	0	0	7	2	85.2	84	365	48	29	13	2	0	2	20	0	70	2	0

Pitcher, Team	W	L	Pct.	ERA	G	GS	CG	ShO	GF	Sv.	IP	H	TBF	R	ER	HR	SH	SF	HB	BB	IBB	SO	WP	Bk.
Montilla, Felix, Hick.	0	0	.000	5.40	2	0	0	0	0	0	3.1	6	16	2	2	0	0	0	0	0	0	1	0	1
Moore, Eric, Sav.	1	1	.500	2.86	23	0	0	0	17	1	34.2	38	148	16	11	0	1	1	6	7	0	28	4	0
Moss, Damian, Mac.*	0	3	.000	4.32	12	12	0	0	0	0	41.2	33	172	20	20	8	1	0	4	15	0	49	2	1
Mowel, Mike, Aug.	5	13	.278	4.90	21	21	0	0	0	0	101.0	131	459	68	55	9	1	2	4	40	1	76	9	0
Mundy, Mike, Ash.	3	3	.500	5.90	37	0	0	0	22	2	58.0	65	286	43	38	6	0	4	4	42	0	59	10	2
Nation, Joey, Mac.*	1	1	.500	2.96	6	6	0	0	0	0	27.1	27	118	10	9	1	0	1	1	9	0	31	2	1
Norton, Jason, Aug.	9	6	.600	2.32	30	17	2	1	5	0	136.0	106	544	50	35	11	1	2	4	28	1	150	7	0
Nunez, Franklin, Pied.	4	8	.333	3.39	13	13	1	0	0	0	77.0	69	326	39	29	4	4	1	6	25	0	88	2	1
Ochoa, Pablo, C'bia	0	0	.000	0.00	3	0	0	0	2	1	5.2	2	19	0	0	0	0	0	0	1	0	4	0	0
Oliver, Scott, Gre.	1	1	.500	3.71	7	7	1	0	0	0	43.2	42	182	22	18	3	2	1	1	8	0	37	2	2
Ormond, Rodney, Del.	1	2	.333	2.89	17	1	0	0	7	3	37.1	29	156	16	12	1	0	0	4	19	0	38	5	2
Osting, Jimmy, Mac.*	14	4	.778	2.88	27	22	0	0	5	2	147.0	130	581	52	47	13	2	1	5	30	0	131	2	0
Pacheco, Enemencio, Ash.	3	9	.250	5.29	15	15	1	0	0	0	85.0	98	383	60	50	4	2	7	4	29	0	59	4	2
Padilla, Roy, C'bus*	2	2	.500	3.02	30	0	0	0	11	3	59.2	53	263	27	20	3	0	2	10	27	0	56	9	0
Padua, Geraldo, Gre.	9	4	.692	2.84	21	21	1	1	0	0	139.2	120	569	53	44	12	0	1	2	35	0	155	13	1
Pamus, Javier, C.W.Va.	3	3	.500	2.79	44	0	0	0	17	4	90.1	87	398	37	28	1	5	0	5	34	2	81	3	0
Paradis, Michael, Del.	0	1	.000	15.00	2	2	0	0	0	0	3.0	3	16	5	5	0	1	0	0	4	0	6	0	1
Parra, Christian, Mac.	1	1	.500	3.31	6	6	0	0	0	0	32.2	33	139	15	12	3	0	1	3	12	0	37	1	1
Parrish, John, Del.*	0	1	.000	7.20	4	0	0	0	1	0	10.0	9	47	8	8	1	0	0	1	6	1	10	3	0
Pavlovich, Tony, Hick.	5	1	.833	2.33	56	0	0	0	39	20	73.1	55	287	29	19	8	1	3	1	16	4	78	1	0
Peguero, Radhame, C.S.C.	0	4	.000	4.15	11	11	0	0	0	0	56.1	61	249	31	26	2	3	2	3	25	0	29	3	0
Pena, Alex, Hick.	0	4	.000	6.60	22	7	0	0	7	0	46.1	68	244	42	34	6	1	2	8	31	2	37	7	0
Percell, Brody, C'bus*	1	3	.250	4.30	6	6	0	0	0	0	29.1	22	116	15	14	3	1	1	1	10	0	30	0	0
Perez, Norberto, Del.	0	4	.000	6.15	25	2	0	0	10	1	41.0	43	188	31	28	7	3	2	5	17	0	39	4	1
Perez, Randy, Del.*	0	2	.000	7.11	21	0	0	0	11	2	25.1	28	118	22	20	4	2	0	2	15	0	9	2	0
Phillips, Matthew, Aug.	2	5	.286	4.76	39	1	0	0	14	1	73.2	85	326	55	39	7	3	4	4	23	3	69	3	0
Pichardo, Carlos, C.W.Va.	2	3	.400	2.57	10	8	0	0	0	0	42.0	44	187	19	12	1	2	2	3	22	0	24	3	0
Pierce, Tony, Mac.	0	0	.000	1.80	8	0	0	0	3	0	15.0	11	63	3	3	1	0	1	0	7	0	23	4	0
Pilato, Chris, Pied.	1	2	.333	4.50	4	4	0	0	0	0	22.0	20	92	12	11	0	0	1	0	8	0	15	2	0
Pineda, Isauro, Aug.	2	1	.667	3.38	8	8	0	0	0	0	42.2	51	195	24	16	0	2	3	3	15	0	36	5	0
Place, Eric, Hag.*	6	4	.600	3.13	40	0	0	0	13	0	72.0	55	306	34	25	2	8	3	2	38	1	56	3	1
Prater, Andy, Hick.	2	3	.400	5.80	15	12	0	0	0	0	63.2	71	284	46	41	14	5	2	4	18	0	52	1	1
Pratt, Andy, Sav.*	4	4	.500	2.89	13	13	1	1	0	0	71.2	66	299	30	23	4	4	2	4	16	0	100	4	0
Prokop, Michael, C'bia	5	2	.714	3.83	37	0	0	0	23	4	40.0	51	189	21	17	1	2	1	5	17	1	33	5	0
Pugmire, Robert, C'bus	6	1	.857	2.65	10	10	0	0	0	0	57.2	43	229	20	17	4	1	1	2	14	0	71	1	1
Rakers, Aaron, Del.	4	1	.800	1.42	18	0	0	0	16	8	25.1	9	97	6	4	0	0	1	0	13	0	38	1	1
Ramirez, Horacio, Mac.*	6	3	.667	2.67	17	14	1	1	0	0	77.2	70	316	30	23	6	2	5	2	25	0	43	1	1
Ramos, Fernando, Pied.	3	6	.333	2.88	38	0	0	0	25	4	68.2	61	286	31	22	12	3	1	1	19	1	73	4	0
Reinike, Chris, C'bus	3	4	.429	4.31	11	11	0	0	0	0	48.0	55	222	28	23	3	0	1	4	21	0	41	1	1
Ridenour, Ryan, Gre.*	0	2	.000	9.58	17	1	0	0	6	0	31.0	33	163	35	33	3	2	1	7	31	0	32	20	1
Rivera, Carlos, Hick.*	0	0	.000	9.00	1	0	0	0	1	0	1.0	2	5	1	1	0	0	0	0	0	0	0	0	0
Robinson, Jeremy, C.S.C.*	5	8	.385	4.41	29	16	0	0	3	0	116.1	144	499	59	57	9	5	2	6	29	2	67	2	1
Rodriguez, Cristobal, C.F.	5	8	.385	4.17	26	25	0	0	1	0	121.0	100	525	68	56	12	2	4	7	65	0	128	12	3
Rodriguez, Jose, C.S.C.	0	1	.000	6.57	7	0	0	0	4	1	12.1	20	67	15	9	1	2	1	0	7	0	11	3	0
Romero, Jordan, Del.	3	7	.300	4.74	24	9	0	0	11	2	76.0	87	359	55	40	10	6	3	6	38	0	61	11	1
Rosa, Cristy, Ash.	0	2	.000	6.45	7	4	0	0	2	1	22.1	26	105	21	16	5	1	1	4	9	0	11	3	0
Rosado, Juan, Sav.*	0	1	.000	4.86	20	0	0	0	12	4	33.1	35	161	29	18	2	2	3	2	23	0	35	2	0
Rose, Johnathan, Pied.*	0	5	.000	6.30	21	1	0	0	12	1	30.0	40	147	24	21	5	1	1	1	17	1	34	5	0
Ruhl, Nathan, C.S.C.	4	4	.500	2.93	36	0	0	0	13	2	55.1	31	234	20	18	3	2	3	1	34	1	82	9	1
Russo, Mike, C.W.Va.	0	2	.000	13.94	10	0	0	0	5	0	10.1	18	60	18	16	1	0	2	1	10	1	10	4	0
Sabathia, C.C., C'bus*	2	0	1.000	1.08	3	3	0	0	0	0	16.2	8	64	2	2	1	1	0	1	5	0	20	1	0
Saenz, Jason, C'bia*	10	8	.556	5.44	27	27	0	0	0	0	134.0	147	617	89	81	16	0	5	18	68	0	125	16	2
Salyers, Jeremy, C.F.	2	3	.400	2.29	22	7	0	0	6	1	63.0	62	257	22	16	3	3	2	3	18	0	37	2	0
Sanchez, Willmen, C'bus*	1	1	.500	6.45	13	0	0	0	5	1	22.1	29	108	23	16	4	0	2	1	10	0	19	5	0
Sandoval, Marcos, Hag.	4	3	.571	4.55	27	10	0	0	5	4	83.0	89	368	47	42	6	2	1	15	32	0	53	8	1
Santana, Humberto, C'bia*	3	1	.750	3.24	10	2	0	0	1	1	25.0	19	101	12	9	2	0	1	0	4	0	19	3	0
Schuldt, Matt, C.S.C.	1	4	.200	4.91	26	1	0	0	15	1	33.0	31	149	24	18	2	2	3	1	20	0	26	3	0
Schwager, Matthew, Del.	0	1	.000	5.48	10	0	0	0	2	0	21.1	32	99	15	13	2	0	0	0	6	0	20	1	1
Seale, Dustin, C.F.*	1	0	1.000	1.80	3	0	0	0	3	0	5.0	3	19	1	1	0	0	1	0	1	0	4	0	0
Seberino, Ronni, C.S.C.*	6	2	.750	2.65	50	0	0	0	11	0	74.2	57	315	29	22	5	0	4	1	38	3	73	10	1
Sequea, Jacobo, Del.	0	2	.000	3.90	6	6	0	0	0	0	30.0	35	134	19	13	4	1	0	2	16	0	25	3	3
Sheldon, Kyle, C.F.	5	1	.833	2.05	26	0	0	0	23	9	44.0	39	175	13	10	3	3	0	1	10	2	30	2	0
Siciliano, Jess, Hick.	0	2	.000	9.53	6	0	0	0	3	0	5.2	11	35	8	6	0	0	0	2	6	0	4	2	0
Sido, Wilson, C'bus	3	7	.300	7.35	13	12	0	0	0	0	49.0	63	232	43	40	5	2	2	3	23	0	51	4	3
Silva, Carlos, Pied.	11	8	.579	3.12	26	26	3	1	0	0	164.1	176	708	79	57	6	8	6	9	41	2	99	8	2
Silva, Doug, Sav.	0	1	.000	2.04	7	0	0	0	4	1	17.2	15	72	5	4	2	0	0	0	3	0	18	1	0
Simontacchi, Jason, Hick.	4	6	.400	4.02	23	7	0	0	8	1	69.1	71	297	34	31	8	2	1	6	19	1	66	5	3
Simpson, Cory, Mac.	3	5	.375	6.04	14	9	0	0	0	0	50.2	37	229	37	34	4	2	5	2	44	0	40	3	1
Smith, Taylor, Hag.	7	10	.412	3.78	28	28	1	1	0	0	171.1	158	724	87	72	11	3	4	12	51	0	119	5	0
Smith, Toby, C.W.Va.	0	1	.000	2.08	2	1	0	0	0	0	4.1	1	18	4	1	0	0	0	0	3	0	4	0	0
Solano, Alexander, Aug.	1	2	.333	4.82	9	5	0	0	1	0	28.0	32	126	25	15	5	0	2	2	7	0	18	3	1
Solano, Francisco, C.W.Va.	1	6	.143	5.52	32	6	1	0	12	4	89.2	100	414	63	55	8	2	3	13	37	1	52	3	1
Sparks, Steve, Hick.	4	6	.400	4.47	25	12	1	1	2	0	88.2	97	407	60	44	3	3	3	5	51	0	72	7	0
Spencer, Corey, Aug.*	1	0	1.000	4.63	7	1	0	0	2	1	11.2	13	49	6	6	1	0	0	0	5	0	13	0	0
Spiegel, Mike, C'bus*	2	0	1.000	2.83	7	7	0	0	0	0	35.0	27	145	13	11	4	1	0	1	14	0	38	2	2
Spille, Ryan, Hag.*	7	1	.875	2.20	14	11	0	0	0	0	69.2	49	263	20	17	3	3	1	4	15	0	49	1	1
Spooneybarger, Tim, Mac.	0	1	.000	3.60	7	0	0	0	3	0	10.0	7	47	4	4	1	1	0	0	10	1	17	2	0
Spurling, Chris, Gre.	4	6	.400	3.66	49	0	0	0	26	4	76.1	78	332	34	31	8	4	9	2	23	3	68	7	0
Stabile, Paul, Hick.*	3	3	.500	4.00	46	0	0	0	14	1	74.1	70	335	42	33	9	1	3	4	42	0	87	6	1
Stafford, Mike, Hag.*	3	2	.600	2.70	39	0	0	0	18	5	50.0	37	194	15	15	2	3	0	1	10	0	40	1	1
Standridge, Jason, C.S.C.	9	1	.900	2.02	18	18	3	3	0	0	116.0	80	455	35	26	5	5	5	7	31	0	84	9	2
Stephens, John, Del.	10	8	.556	3.22	28	27	4	2	0	0	170.1	148	702	75	61	10	5	4	10	36	0	217	4	0

Pitcher, Team	W	L	Pct.	ERA	G	GS	CG	ShO	GF	Sv.	IP	H	TBF	R	ER	HR	SH	SF	HB	BB	IBB	SO	WP	Bk.
Stewart, John, Sav.*	6	14	.300	5.04	30	20	1	0	7	1	130.1	144	576	99	73	19	4	8	7	24	0	79	5	2
Stine, Justin, Hag.*	0	0	.000	3.86	17	0	0	0	5	0	28.0	30	125	13	12	1	1	2	3	7	0	20	3	0
Strange, Patrick, C'bia	12	5	.706	2.63	28	21	2	0	1	1	154.0	138	627	57	45	4	4	3	10	29	1	113	7	0
Surridge, Lance, Aug.	9	5	.643	3.05	37	10	0	0	5	0	106.1	102	459	52	36	3	3	1	3	38	1	88	4	0
Suttles, Donnie, C'bus	4	6	.400	4.56	16	16	1	0	0	0	77.0	86	349	55	39	6	1	1	11	29	0	66	11	1
Sylvester, Billy, Mac.	5	4	.556	3.12	44	1	0	0	21	2	83.2	78	373	37	29	3	5	5	6	37	2	75	5	1
Tapia, Rafael, Del.	3	0	1.000	2.35	7	2	0	0	1	0	23.0	18	92	7	6	2	0	0	1	6	0	16	3	1
Taylor, Aaron, Mac.	6	7	.462	4.88	27	8	0	0	6	1	79.1	86	360	56	43	9	2	5	7	27	2	78	17	0
Tetz, Kristofer, C.F.	3	3	.500	4.35	10	9	0	0	0	0	49.2	54	209	25	24	5	0	1	1	12	0	36	3	0
Theodile, Simeon, Del.	1	2	.333	5.83	33	1	0	0	17	0	54.0	68	259	44	35	4	4	3	1	27	1	45	4	0
Thompson, Andy, C'bia	0	0	.000	12.00	2	0	0	0	2	0	3.0	5	16	5	4	2	0	0	0	1	0	3	0	0
Thompson, Doug, Ash.	3	3	.500	4.34	25	0	0	0	12	3	56.0	56	250	29	27	9	1	2	6	18	0	72	5	3
Toriz, Steve, C.F.	0	1	.000	6.75	1	1	0	0	0	0	4.0	2	15	3	3	0	0	1	0	2	0	1	0	0
Torres, Luis, Hick.	3	2	.600	3.26	7	7	0	0	0	0	38.2	40	168	17	14	3	2	2	4	20	1	26	6	0
Turnbow, Derrick, Pied.	12	8	.600	3.35	26	26	4	1	0	0	161.0	130	651	67	60	10	1	2	7	53	0	149	8	0
Turnbow, Mark, C'bus	3	4	.429	3.72	13	13	1	0	0	0	72.2	78	304	38	30	7	0	3	13	0	75	4	2
Tynan, Chris, Sav.	4	10	.286	6.99	21	21	0	0	0	0	112.0	140	512	96	87	19	0	5	7	38	0	97	7	1
Vael, Rob, C'bus.	5	4	.556	4.86	42	7	0	0	16	0	92.2	89	422	59	50	14	3	2	5	53	1	91	12	1
Van Buren, Jermaine, Ash.	7	10	.412	4.91	28	28	0	0	0	0	143.0	143	640	87	78	16	1	13	19	70	0	133	19	2
Van Gilder, Ryan, C.F.	0	1	.000	54.00	1	0	0	0	0	0	0.2	2	6	4	4	0	0	0	0	2	0	0	0	0
Vargas, Jose, C'bus	2	5	.286	4.66	34	6	0	0	5	2	85.0	88	374	47	44	10	1	2	5	29	0	103	1	1
Vega, Rene, C'bia*	11	7	.611	3.14	29	22	1	0	2	1	146.0	101	593	57	51	8	3	2	12	50	1	148	6	4
Viole, Paul, C'bia	0	0	.000	0.00	2	0	0	0	0	0	2.0	1	10	1	0	0	0	0	2	0	1	0	0
Vogtli, Robb, Gre.	3	2	.600	5.17	25	0	0	0	7	1	38.1	39	169	25	22	7	2	0	1	18	1	38	2	0
Voyles, Brad, Mac.	3	3	.500	2.98	38	0	0	0	26	14	51.1	27	226	21	17	0	1	2	5	39	2	65	7	2
Waldron, Brad, C.F.	3	2	.600	3.38	25	9	0	0	9	5	93.1	104	397	40	35	6	4	3	0	20	0	72	4	0
Wamback, Trevor, C.F.	6	3	.667	2.84	24	14	1	0	2	1	104.2	98	414	39	33	10	2	2	3	14	0	77	3	1
Ward, Monty, C.W.Va.	2	9	.182	2.88	42	3	0	0	24	7	84.1	74	370	42	27	1	7	7	3	40	2	93	9	2
Weber, Brett, Gre.	8	4	.667	1.97	52	0	0	0	38	23	73.0	56	295	24	16	2	3	1	5	17	0	83	5	1
Wedel, Jeremy, Pied.	5	3	.625	2.16	23	0	0	0	17	3	50.0	46	202	19	12	2	1	1	3	8	0	40	2	0
Weslowski, Robert, C'bia	1	0	1.000	6.45	9	0	0	0	0	0	22.1	22	102	18	16	3	1	1	3	13	1	21	1	2
White, Matt, C'bus*	3	10	.231	5.29	19	18	1	0	0	0	95.1	99	414	67	56	12	3	5	31	0	75	7	1
Whiteley, Shad, Gre.	1	9	.100	7.64	15	8	0	0	1	0	55.1	67	276	52	47	7	1	0	6	42	0	62	5	4
Wiggins, Scott, Gre.*	7	1	.875	3.95	17	17	0	0	0	0	93.1	84	395	45	41	15	1	0	6	32	0	110	7	0
Williams, David, Hick.*	3	1	.750	3.20	9	9	1	1	0	0	59.0	42	228	22	21	5	0	2	6	11	0	46	2	0
Wimberly, Larry, Hick.*	3	1	.750	1.51	17	5	0	0	3	0	47.2	32	182	8	8	2	2	1	1	11	3	57	3	0
Woodards, Orlando, Hag.	7	4	.636	4.15	44	3	0	0	12	2	80.1	66	352	45	37	5	6	1	7	43	3	79	7	1
Wright, Barrett, C.S.C.	2	6	.250	5.37	13	13	0	0	0	0	63.2	67	299	55	38	5	3	4	7	41	0	34	8	1
Wright, Chris, C.S.C.	5	12	.294	4.02	38	14	0	0	20	8	105.1	108	451	54	47	10	4	0	5	22	1	89	5	2
Wrigley, Jase, Ash.	3	2	.600	3.09	28	0	0	0	18	6	58.1	63	259	32	20	2	2	2	2	16	0	58	6	2
Zallie, Chris, Aug.*	2	1	.667	4.32	9	0	0	0	6	0	8.1	4	44	4	4	0	1	2	4	10	1	14	0	0
Zamarripa, Mark, C'bus	4	0	1.000	3.45	15	0	0	0	7	1	28.2	26	120	13	11	3	0	2	12	1	31	2	0

COMBINATION SHUTOUTS: **Asheville (3)**—Carter-Gordon-Bradley, Jennings-Thompson, Jennings-Cameron. **Augusta (13)**—Duchscherer-Phillips, Hancock-Norton-Cisar, Duchscherer-Cisar, Duchscherer-Hill, Miller-Phillips-Lontayo-Cisar, Norton-McLeary, Surridge-McLeary-Lontayo, Miller-McLeary, Norton-Lyons-McLeary, Miller-Lyons-Hill-Cisar, Hancock-Hill-Cisar, Norton-Spencer-Lyons-Hill, Lontayo-Glaser-Giese-Hill. **Cape Fear (3)**—Waldron-Sheldon, Chiavacci-Kanovich-Field, Becks-Arthurs. **Charleston, S.C. (6)**—James-Cornejo-Carter-Wright, James-Haines-Wright, James-Wright, Wright-Robinson-Haines, Kofler-Seberino-Schuldt, Kofler-Seberino-Schuldt. **Charleston, W.Va. (7)**—Ammons-Ward, Ammons-Russo-Lee, Guerrero-Gonzalez-Lee, Ammons-Solano, Burch-Ward, Delgado-Pichardo-Pamus-Maas, Delgado-Mancha-Pamus. **Columbia (11)**—Cook-Corcoran-Bellhorn-Carr, Cook-Strange, Saenz-Corcoran-Bell, Strange-Carr, Saenz-Bellhorn, Saenz-Cook, Saenz-Bellhorn-Bell, Strange-Carr, Vega-Bell, Vega-Carr-Corcoran, Cook-Santana-Bell. **Columbus (7)**—Pugmire-Zamarripa, Pugmire-Hughes, Reinike-Vael-Zamarripa, Suttles-Bautista-Padilla, Marietta-Padilla-Matsko, Sido-Padilla, Vael-Guillory. **Delmarva (4)**—Garcia-Rakers, Andrade-Ormond, Bechler-Babula-Ormond, Stephens-Bello. **Greensboro (5)**—Padua-Dunn, Blevins-Spurling-Dunn, Blevins-Buchanan-Weber-Dunn, Dunn-Jodie-Weber, Aramboles-Vogtli-Weber. **Hagerstown (10)**—Smith-Woodards-Bowles-Place, Casey-Place, Spille-Sandoval-Kingrey, Spille-Sandoval-Kingrey, Casey-Stine, Spille-Sandoval-Bowles, Cassidy-Place, Lynch-Woodards, Spille-Sandoval-Stafford. **Hickory (7)**—Grabow-Simontacchi, Beimel-Sparks-Wimberly, Grabow-Buirley-Bravo-Pavlovich, Beimel-Simontacchi-Buirley, Grabow-Pavlovich-Pena, Bravo-Stabile-Buirley, Grabow-Stabile. **Macon (4)**—Bong-Osting, Moss-Simpson-Gray-Voyles, Ramirez-Herndon-Voyles, Taylor-Ramirez-Chavez. **Piedmont (8)**—Nunez-Fenus-Hiles, Silva-Ramos, Nunez-Rose-Eason, Silva-Hiles, Kubes-Wedel, Baisley-Hiles, Turnbow-Hiles, Montero-Espina. **Savannah (10)**—Brazoban-Figueroa-Mlodik, Hughes-Brazoban, McGill-Beitey-Mlodik, Hughes-Frey-Kosderka, McGill-Frey-Brazoban, Boublis-Guzman, McGill-Guzman, Hughes-Stewart, Boublis-Frey, Clark-Stewart.

NO-HIT GAME: Standridge, Charleston, S.C., defeated Columbia, 3-0, June 28; Baisley, Piedmont, defeated Hagewstown, 3-0, August 12.

PITCHERS WITH TWO OR MORE TEAMS

Pitcher, Team	W	L	Pct.	ERA	G	GS	CG	ShO	GF	Sv.	IP	H	TBF	R	ER	HR	SH	SF	HB	BB	IBB	SO	WP	Bk.
Jackson, Jeremy D., C.W.Va.*.	4	5	.444	4.41	19	13	0	0	4	0	81.2	82	356	52	40	4	1	1	6	30	0	65	8	0
Jackson, Jeremy D., C'bia*	1	0	1.000	1.61	5	4	0	0	0	0	28.0	22	105	5	5	1	1	0	0	3	0	26	1	0
Lynch, Pat, Hag.	10	5	.667	3.52	24	18	0	0	2	1	127.2	133	529	55	50	10	7	3	6	22	0	106	1	1
Lynch, Pat, Ash.	1	1	.500	3.00	2	2	0	0	0	0	12.0	8	48	4	4	0	0	1	2	0	14	0	1

1999 FIELDING
TEAM

Team	Pct.	G	PO	A	E	TC	DP	TP	PB	Team	Pct.	G	PO	A	E	TC	DP	TP	PB
Hagerstown	.969	140	3786	1593	174	5553	124	0	29	Delmarva	.962	138	3639	1386	196	5221	88	0	27
Charleston, W.V.	.964	141	3735	1607	197	5539	122	0	22	Charleston, S.C.	.962	142	3730	1569	211	5510	133	0	29
Hickory	.964	140	3742	1443	194	5379	107	0	48	Asheville	.961	141	3633	1524	211	5368	113	0	35
Cape Fear	.964	140	3648	1477	192	5317	111	0	26	Columbia	.960	141	3662	1584	219	5465	123	0	22
Augusta	.964	139	3650	1423	192	5265	105	0	25	Savannah	.959	140	3620	1407	216	5243	110	0	19
Macon	.963	138	3579	1293	186	5058	95	0	22	Columbus	.958	141	3661	1454	227	5342	107	0	19
Greensboro	.963	141	3670	1486	199	5355	98	0	51	Piedmont	.955	140	3562	1474	235	5271	102	0	25

FIRST BASEMEN

NOTE: All caps denotes fielding-percentage leader based on 71 games for catchers, 95 for all other non-pitchers and 114 innings for pitchers. *Throws lefthanded.

Player, Team	Pct.	G	PO	A	E	TC	DP
Alevras, Chad, Aug.	.857	1	6	0	1	7	2
Alvarez, Carlos, C'bus	.988	12	76	4	1	81	5
Backe, Brandon, C.S.C.	1.000	5	38	2	0	40	1
Benham, David, Aug.	1.000	1	6	1	0	7	2
Brito, Juan, C.W.Va.	1.000	1	1	0	0	1	0
Carnes, Shayne, Pied.*	.992	57	480	34	4	518	29
Castaneda, Cesar, Sav.	1.000	2	8	0	0	8	1
Castri, Andrea, Gre.	.994	55	457	26	3	486	40
Cota, Humberto, C.S.C.	1.000	2	16	0	0	16	2
Dampeer, Kelly, C'bus	.968	8	56	5	2	63	6
Derosso, Tony, Aug.	.992	15	115	3	1	119	10
DiPace, Danny, C.W.Va.	1.000	4	28	3	0	31	7
Duck, Kevin, Ash.*	.985	105	912	49	15	976	78
Dusan, Joe, Hag.*	.983	40	370	32	7	409	25
Elder, Rick, Del.*	.950	11	90	6	5	101	6
Escalante, Jaime, Del.	.833	2	5	0	1	6	1
Espy, Nate, Pied.	.993	74	637	39	5	681	50
Esquerra, Marques, C'bus	.990	39	292	19	3	314	14
Ewing, Byron, C'bus	.995	46	380	32	2	414	25
Fowler, Ben, C'bus	1.000	1	11	0	0	11	1
Freitas, Jeremy, C.W.Va.	.984	19	180	10	3	193	9
Gettis, Byron, C.W.Va.	1.000	1	4	0	0	4	1
Gibbons, Jay, Hag.*	.978	22	213	12	5	230	18
Goodwin, David, C.W.Va.	.988	119	1013	86	13	1112	90
Gordnier, Aaron, C'bus	1.000	2	15	1	0	16	3
Greene, Claude, Gre.	.990	22	192	12	2	206	12
Gregg, Neal, Gre.	1.000	3	16	1	0	17	0
Grummitt, Dan, C.S.C.	.973	4	35	1	1	37	2
Hafner, Travis, Sav.	.988	108	881	58	11	950	73
Hannahan, Buzz, Pied.	1.000	1	5	0	0	5	0
Hart, Keith, Aug.	.987	85	718	27	10	755	56
Hernandez, Jesus, C'bus*	1.000	1	6	1	0	7	1
Hobbs, Jay, Hick.*	.972	19	128	13	4	145	9
Hoch, Corey, Del.	.972	9	67	3	2	72	3
Jenkins, Brian, C'bia	.968	6	25	5	1	31	3
Keaveney, Jeff, Aug.	.963	15	117	12	5	134	10
Key, Jeff, Aug.	.972	27	195	12	6	213	16
Lebron, Francisco, C'bia	.987	9	74	3	1	78	6
Lebron, Hector, C.S.C.	.984	37	287	23	5	315	24
Logan, Matt, Hag.	.989	80	719	60	9	788	69
Maluchnik, Gregg, Mac.	1.000	21	134	7	0	141	14
Marciante, Frank, Sav.	.991	29	210	5	2	217	22
Martin, Billy, C'bia	1.000	3	20	0	0	20	5
Maxwell, Keith, Hick.	.992	16	112	6	1	119	10
McGee, Tom, Del.	.800	1	4	0	1	5	1
McGrath, Sean, C'bia	.966	6	42	3	0	45	6
Meadows, Randy, C.F.	.966	11	79	6	3	88	3
Moore, Griffin, C.W.Va.	1.000	1	15	0	0	15	5
Na, Jim, C.F.	.966	14	105	8	4	117	10
Ottevaere, Derek, Sav.	.962	9	50	1	2	53	4
Pena, Rodolfo, Aug.	.929	2	11	2	1	14	0
Pittman, Thomas, C.F.	.986	119	975	76	15	1066	82
Pressley, Josh, C.S.C.	.986	100	926	44	14	984	88
Purkiss, Matt, Del.	.975	84	629	42	17	688	40
Pursell, Mike, C'bus	.979	18	171	13	4	188	20
Reyes, Rene, Ash.	1.000	4	20	1	0	21	1
Risinger, Ben, Hick.	1.000	9	11	2	0	13	1
Rivera, Carlos, Hick.*	.985	114	932	75	15	1022	76
Romano, Jimmie, Sav.	.667	1	2	0	1	3	0
Rumfield, Brock, Del.	.980	31	229	14	5	248	15
Rust, Brian, Del.	.973	10	66	7	2	75	4
Schreimann, Eric, Pied.	1.000	9	70	6	0	76	6
Schwab, Chris, C'bus*	.967	26	190	14	7	211	17
Sienko, Ryan, Sav.	.960	6	23	1	1	25	0
Smith, Sam, Ash.	.983	44	329	23	6	358	22
SNYDER, Earl, C'bia	.993	126	1106	80	8	1194	96
Suriel, Miguel, C.S.C.	1.000	4	12	2	0	14	2
Umbria, Jose, Hag.	.923	4	11	1	1	13	1
Washington, Dion, Gre.	.976	67	567	51	15	633	41
Wilson, Travis, Mac.	1.000	10	48	8	0	56	5
Zapp, A.J., Mac.	.981	115	877	63	18	958	64

Player, Team	Pct.	G	PO	A	E	TC	DP
Benefield, Brian, C'bus	.940	68	106	208	20	334	39
Benham, Jason, Del.	1.000	4	8	8	0	16	2
Bone, Billy, Hick.	1.000	5	3	19	0	22	2
Boughton, Mike, Sav.	.970	13	27	37	2	66	5
Brett, Jason, C'bia	.917	8	17	16	3	36	6
Bultmann, Kurt, Hick.	.967	13	24	35	2	61	6
Casillas, Uriel, Pied.	.933	6	9	19	2	30	2
Castaneda, Cesar, Sav.	1.000	1	0	2	0	2	0
Castro, Ramon, Mac.	.974	39	68	82	4	154	15
Colina, Javier, Ash.	.967	118	198	304	17	519	63
Cordero, Willy, Sav.	.956	21	34	53	4	91	7
Daedelow, Craig, Del.	.954	20	32	51	4	87	9
Dalton, David, Mac.	.971	28	57	76	4	137	16
Dampeer, Kelly, C'bus	.964	34	62	73	5	140	9
DeShields, Delino, Del.	1.000	2	4	5	0	9	0
Diaz, Maikell, Del.	1.000	6	10	14	0	24	3
Erickson, Corey, C'bia	.963	126	230	335	22	587	71
Fajardo, Alejandro, Pied.	.922	116	249	304	47	600	60
Fuentes, Javier, Aug.	.875	2	3	4	1	8	1
Garcia, Oscar, C'bus	1.000	6	10	11	0	21	1
Gonzalez, Luis, C'bus	.944	22	28	57	5	90	11
Gordnier, Aaron, C'bus	1.000	1	1	0	0	1	0
Green, Nick, Mac.	1.000	2	2	1	0	3	0
Guerrero, Pedro, Sav.	.928	42	73	95	13	181	17
Gutierrez, Derrick, Del.	1.000	4	8	8	0	16	1
Hammond, Joey, Del.	1.000	5	7	10	0	17	1
Hannahan, Buzz, Pied.	1.000	3	5	8	0	13	2
Harris, Willie, Del.	.965	64	126	175	11	312	36
Hart, Corey, C.W.Va.	1.000	3	5	8	0	13	2
Hoch, Corey, Del.	.974	8	19	19	1	39	3
Hopper, Norris, C.W.Va.	.929	5	10	16	2	28	1
Hudson, Orlando, Hag.	1.000	2	1	4	0	5	1
Ishida, Takehito, Pied.	.816	6	16	15	7	38	4
James, Tony, Aug.	.969	33	53	105	5	163	24
Joffrion, Jack, C.S.C.	.987	17	35	42	1	78	11
Kerrigan, Joseph, Aug.	.941	4	3	13	1	17	2
Kidd, Scott, Gre.	.956	115	186	330	24	540	58
LaForest, Pete, C.S.C.	1.000	1	0	1	0	1	1
Leon, Carlos, Aug.	.963	59	128	159	11	298	30
Leon, Richy, Ash.	.990	25	27	70	1	98	14
Ligons, Merrell, C.W.Va.	.947	9	15	21	2	38	4
Llanos, Alex, C.S.C.	.000	2	0	0	0	0	0
Machado, Albenis, C.F.	1.000	2	3	6	0	9	0
Malinowski, Scott, C'bia	1.000	6	12	12	0	24	3
MANN, Derek, C.S.C.	.977	117	219	375	14	608	74
Martin, Justin, Hick.	.959	15	30	40	3	73	6
McGrath, Sean, C'bia	1.000	8	10	19	0	29	4
Meadows, Randy, C.F.	1.000	4	5	7	0	12	2
Meliah, David, Sav.	.960	66	133	182	13	328	42
Metzler, Rod, C'bia	.962	113	220	290	20	530	59
Mirizzi, Marc, Gre.	1.000	3	8	8	0	16	5
Myers, Tootie, C.F.	.942	136	263	358	38	659	63
Nolasco, Regino, Del.	.958	18	31	37	3	71	5
Nunez, Jorge, Hag.	.952	122	225	349	29	603	71
Olivares, Teuris, Gre.	.857	1	4	2	1	7	1
Perez, Deivi, Hick.	1.000	1	0	1	0	1	0
Powers, Jeff, C'bus	.972	16	29	40	2	71	10
Price, Corey, Del.	.945	16	38	48	5	91	7
Prieto, Jonathan, Hick.	.950	61	94	133	12	239	26
Quinones, Marcus, Sav.	.955	4	9	12	1	22	2
Reyes, Ambiorix, Pied.	.960	10	20	28	2	50	4
Risinger, Ben, Hick.	.990	24	51	50	1	102	15
Rodriguez, Junior, Gre.	.919	20	31	48	7	86	5
Romano, Jimmie, Sav.	1.000	2	1	0	0	1	0
Ruiz, Willy, C.W.Va.	.982	21	44	64	2	110	17
Rumfield, Brock, Del.	1.000	1	1	2	0	3	0
Santos, Angel, Aug.	.955	48	73	117	9	199	19
Skrehot, Shaun, Hick.	.963	29	54	75	5	134	20
Taylor, Seth, Gre.	.938	3	6	9	1	16	2
Wilson, Travis, Mac.	.970	72	134	154	9	297	35
Winter, Jon, C.S.C.	1.000	7	11	12	0	23	3
Zepeda, Jesse, Hag.	.981	27	36	68	2	106	5

THIRD BASEMEN

Player, Team	Pct.	G	PO	A	E	TC	DP
Acevedo, Luis, Sav.	1.000	3	1	2	0	3	0
Ahumada, Alejandro, Aug.	.923	32	18	54	6	78	10
Backe, Brandon, C.S.C.	.000	1	0	0	1	1	0
Benefield, Brian, C'bus	.800	2	3	5	2	10	1

SECOND BASEMEN

Player, Team	Pct.	G	PO	A	E	TC	DP
Acevedo, Luis, Sav.	1.000	2	2	3	0	5	0
Backe, Brandon, C.S.C.	.917	8	11	22	3	36	3

Player, Team	Pct.	G	PO	A	E	TC	DP
Benham, Jason, Del.	1.000	2	2	4	0	6	0
Blalock, Hank, Sav.	.762	7	3	13	5	21	1
Brett, Jason, C'bia	1.000	2	1	0	0	1	0
Calderon, Henry, C.W.Va.	.875	8	6	15	3	24	0
Calzado, Napolean, Del.	.800	6	2	6	2	10	0
Cameron, Troy, Mac.	.890	118	84	190	34	308	15
Casillas, Uriel, Pied.	.911	37	26	76	10	112	10
Castaneda, Cesar, Sav.	.921	100	62	183	21	266	19
Castri, Andrea, Gre.	1.000	1	0	1	0	1	0
Castro, Ramon, Mac.	.906	16	13	16	3	32	3
Chwan, Brian, C.S.C.	1.000	1	2	0	0	2	1
Colina, Javier, Ash.	.800	3	2	6	2	10	0
Cordero, Willy, Sav.	.815	19	8	36	10	54	2
Dalton, David, Mac.	.889	7	3	13	2	18	1
Dampeer, Kelly, C'bus	.880	31	25	48	10	83	4
Diaz, Maikell, Del.	.940	28	17	46	4	67	4
Duncan, Carlos, Pied.	.906	43	40	86	13	139	13
Erickson, Corey, C'bia	1.000	2	0	2	0	2	0
Esquerra, Marques, C'bus	.862	80	44	131	28	203	11
Fuentes, Javier, Aug.	.913	28	16	47	6	69	4
Gonzalez, Luis, C'bus	.930	23	10	43	4	57	5
Hafner, Travis, Sav.	.500	5	0	4	4	8	0
Hammond, Joey, Del.	.926	13	11	14	2	27	1
Hannahan, Buzz, Pied.	.921	17	7	28	3	38	1
Hart, Corey, C.W.Va.	.906	84	44	158	21	223	17
Hill, Bobby, C'bia	.958	9	2	21	1	24	1
Hoch, Corey, Del.	.833	5	3	7	2	12	0
Hodges, Scott, C.F.	.932	123	105	225	24	354	26
Holliday, Matt, Ash.	.871	108	57	192	37	286	9
House, J.R., Hick.	.000	1	0	0	0	0	0
HUDSON, Orlando, Hag.	.940	103	93	235	21	349	15
Ishida, Takehito, Pied.	.909	4	4	6	1	11	2
James, Drue, Mac.	.000	1	0	0	0	0	0
James, Tony, Aug.	.968	13	6	24	1	31	1
Joffrion, Jack, C.S.C.	.500	1	1	1	2	4	0
Kerrigan, Joseph, Aug.	1.000	1	1	4	0	5	0
Kremblas, Mike, Hag.	1.000	1	1	3	0	4	0
LaForest, Pete, C.S.C.	.893	118	84	225	37	346	22
Leon, Richy, Ash.	1.000	11	4	26	0	30	3
Ligons, Merrell, C.W.Va.	.897	27	8	53	7	68	7
Llanos, Alex, C.S.C.	.000	1	0	0	0	0	0
Malinowski, Scott, C'bia	.942	68	26	136	10	172	14
Maluchnik, Gregg, Mac.	1.000	3	0	4	0	4	0
Martin, Billy, C'bia	.829	56	31	114	30	175	9
Maxwell, Keith, Hick.	1.000	1	0	1	0	1	0
McGee, Tom, Del.	.667	1	1	1	1	3	1
McGrath, Sean, C'bia	.750	11	7	20	9	36	2
Meadows, Randy, C.F.	.927	21	12	39	4	55	0
Meliah, David, Sav.	.896	22	12	31	5	48	2
Moore, Griffin, C.W.Va.	.897	25	18	43	7	68	2
Na, Jim, C.F.	.833	2	2	3	1	6	0
Nunez, Jorge, Hag.	1.000	2	0	4	0	4	0
Polidor, Wil, Pied.	.885	23	13	41	7	61	2
Powers, Jeff, C'bus	.949	14	9	28	2	39	2
Quinones, Marcus, Sav.	1.000	1	0	4	0	4	0
Reyes, Ambiorix, Pied.	.833	8	4	11	3	18	1
Richardson, Juan, Pied.	1.000	4	2	8	0	10	1
Risinger, Ben, Hick.	.931	83	54	135	14	203	13
Rodriguez, Junior, Gre.	.938	6	5	10	1	16	1
Romano, Jimmie, Sav.	1.000	2	1	0	0	1	0
Ruiz, Willy, C.W.Va.	.932	18	9	32	3	44	3
Rumfield, Brock, Del.	.941	80	76	114	12	202	5
Rust, Brian, Del.	.964	8	5	22	1	28	0
Santos, Angel, Aug.	.888	34	25	62	11	98	6
Schreimann, Eric, Pied.	.700	6	3	4	3	10	1
Seabol, Scott, Gre.	.936	138	79	274	24	377	25
Segura, Rolando, Hick.	.925	39	18	68	7	93	7
Shelley, Jason, Hick.	.895	18	9	25	4	38	2
Sienko, Ryan, Sav.	.000	1	0	0	1	1	0
Skrehot, Shaun, Hick.	.944	9	2	15	1	18	2
Smith, Sam, Ash.	.863	21	12	32	7	51	3
Snyder, Earl, C'bia	.800	9	6	14	5	25	0
Suriel, Miguel, C.S.C.	.918	24	14	42	5	61	6
Terni, Chaz, Aug.	.794	36	24	57	21	102	7
Umbria, Jose, Hag.	1.000	1	0	1	0	1	0
Washington, Rico, Hick.	.909	5	0	10	1	11	0
Zech, Scott, C.F.	1.000	1	0	4	0	4	1
Zepeda, Jesse, Hag.	.935	63	31	84	8	123	8

SHORTSTOPS

Player, Team	Pct.	G	PO	A	E	TC	DP
Acevedo, Luis, Sav.	1.000	1	1	2	0	3	0
Ahumada, Alejandro, Aug.	.937	94	132	227	24	383	45

Player, Team	Pct.	G	PO	A	E	TC	DP
Backe, Brandon, C.S.C.	.882	3	7	8	2	17	3
Boughton, Mike, Sav.	.929	11	14	25	3	42	5
Brett, Jason, C'bia	.888	20	18	69	11	98	10
Calderon, Henry, C.W.Va.	.938	121	193	353	36	582	68
Cameron, Troy, Mac.	.800	1	0	4	1	5	0
Casillas, Uriel, Pied.	.933	30	46	94	10	150	16
Castro, Ramon, Mac.	.939	29	30	63	6	99	11
Cleto, Ambioris, Hick.	.921	24	34	71	9	114	12
Colina, Javier, Ash.	.000	1	0	0	0	0	0
Cordero, Willy, Sav.	.924	61	74	182	21	277	29
Dalton, David, Mac.	1.000	1	1	0	0	1	0
Dampeer, Kelly, C'bus	.926	11	9	16	2	27	4
Diaz, Maikell, Del.	.947	59	79	136	12	227	14
Duncan, Carlos, Pied.	.909	30	43	87	13	143	16
Fuentes, Javier, Aug.	.923	4	6	6	1	13	0
Furcal, Rafael, Mac.	.912	74	117	192	30	339	36
Garcia, Oscar, C'bus	1.000	2	3	3	0	6	0
Gonzalez, Luis, C'bus	.924	35	42	103	12	157	15
Gutierrez, Derrick, Del.	.953	26	29	52	4	85	5
Hannahan, Buzz, Pied.	.750	1	0	3	1	4	0
Hart, Corey, C.W.Va.	.000	1	0	0	0	0	0
Hill, Bobby, C'bia	.931	76	92	218	23	333	50
Hoch, Corey, Del.	1.000	10	13	20	0	33	5
Hook, Kevin, C.F.	.889	2	3	5	1	9	2
Isturiz, Maicer, C'bus	.939	45	76	109	12	197	16
Joffrion, Jack, C.S.C.	.907	48	64	132	20	216	23
Kidd, Scott, Gre.	.000	1	0	0	0	0	0
Leon, Richy, Ash.	.926	19	24	51	6	81	13
Ligons, Merrell, C.W.Va.	1.000	10	17	25	0	42	2
Lopez, Felipe, Hag.	.943	133	182	352	32	566	62
MACHADO, Albenis, C.F.	.964	108	177	334	19	530	57
Machado, Anderson, Pied.	.910	20	22	59	8	89	5
Malinowski, Scott, C'bia	.926	27	35	78	9	122	17
Mann, Derek, C.S.C.	1.000	1	1	1	0	2	0
Manning, Patrick, Mac.	.927	38	51	113	13	177	15
McGrath, Sean, C'bia	.733	4	2	9	4	15	1
McKinley, Josh, C.F.	.840	22	31	53	16	100	7
Meadows, Randy, C.F.	.957	11	21	24	2	47	5
Melo, Ramon, C.W.Va.	.857	3	4	8	2	14	2
Mirizzi, Marc, Gre.	.923	6	4	8	1	13	1
Nolasco, Regino, Del.	.941	5	3	13	1	17	1
Nunez, Jorge, Hag.	.949	17	24	34	3	59	8
Olivares, Teuris, Gre.	.930	109	156	321	36	513	55
Olmeda, Jose, C'bus	.904	29	33	89	13	135	16
Perez, Deivi, Hick.	.915	25	40	68	10	118	12
Powers, Jeff, C'bus	.937	34	46	72	8	126	23
Quinones, Marcus, Sav.	.943	30	47	85	8	140	17
Reyes, Ambiorix, Pied.	.906	60	87	164	26	277	26
Risinger, Ben, Hick.	.947	22	31	40	4	75	5
Roberts, Brian, Del.	.964	46	76	138	8	222	28
Rodriguez, Junior, Gre.	.901	28	31	69	11	111	6
Romano, Jimmie, Sav.	1.000	1	0	2	0	2	0
Ruiz, Willy, C.W.Va.	.924	17	26	35	5	66	7
Santos, Angel, Aug.	.933	45	65	131	14	210	21
Shelley, Jason, Hick.	.000	1	0	0	0	0	0
Skrehot, Shaun, Hick.	.939	82	123	228	23	374	35
Soler, Ramon, C.S.C.	.908	91	116	279	40	435	48
Taylor, Seth, Gre.	.714	3	2	2	2	7	1
Uribe, Juan, Ash.	.938	125	187	390	38	615	72
Velazquez, Gil, C'bia	.950	21	27	69	5	101	10
Warriax, Brandon, Sav.	.926	40	51	99	12	162	19
Winter, Jon, C.S.C.	.957	6	5	17	1	23	3

OUTFIELDERS

Player, Team	Pct.	G	PO	A	E	TC	DP
Acevedo, Carlos, Pied.	.932	53	89	7	7	103	2
Alamo, Efrain, C.S.C.	.946	92	168	7	10	185	2
Aldridge, Cory, Mac.	.963	116	176	4	7	187	0
Alou, Felipe, C.W.Va.	.971	57	94	7	3	104	1
Alvarez, Carlos, C'bus	.967	65	105	11	4	120	2
Arias, Jeison, Gre.	.919	26	32	2	3	37	1
Backe, Brandon, C.S.C.	.973	63	103	7	3	113	2
Baez, Ernies, Sav.	.000	2	0	0	0	0	0
Barns, B.J., Hick.	.966	51	84	2	3	89	1
Bastardo, Angel, C'bus	.000	1	0	0	0	0	0
Benjamin, Al, C.F.	.948	89	158	5	9	172	1
Beverly, Shomari, Pied.	.922	49	79	4	7	90	0
Bigbie, Larry, Del.*	.950	32	54	3	3	60	2
Brignac, Antoine, Mac.	.974	69	145	5	4	154	1
Brown, Andy, Gre.*	.938	29	30	0	2	30	0
Brown, Billy, Gre.	.968	110	180	3	6	189	0
Brown, Tonayne, Aug.*	.986	126	270	9	4	283	1

– 574 –

Player, Team	Pct.	G	PO	A	E	TC	DP
Bush, Brian, Pied.	.966	38	56	1	2	59	1
Caballero, Antonio, Hick.*	.913	11	21	0	2	23	0
Carnes, Shayne, Pied.*	.963	13	25	1	1	27	0
Castillo, Geramel, Sav.	.933	99	160	8	12	180	2
Castro, Martires, C.F.	1.000	8	13	1	0	14	0
Castro, Ramon, Mac.	1.000	3	1	0	0	1	0
Chavez, Endy, C'bia*	.967	72	140	8	5	153	3
Cole, Brian, C'bia	.988	118	227	10	3	240	0
Connell, Jerry, Pied.	.960	13	23	1	1	25	1
Copeland, Brandon, C'bia	.919	21	33	1	3	37	0
Curry, Mike, C.W.Va.	.994	85	165	5	1	171	0
Dampeer, Kelly, C'bus	1.000	1	2	0	0	2	0
Darjean, John, Gre.	.978	107	179	1	4	184	0
Davies, Justin, Hag.	.977	123	240	12	6	258	2
Davis, J.J., Hick.	.950	51	73	3	4	80	1
Davison, Ashanti, Del.	.946	50	81	7	5	93	0
DiPace, Danny, C.W.Va.	.857	26	28	2	5	35	0
Elwood, Brad, Gre.	1.000	2	1	0	0	1	0
Esquerra, Marques, C'bus	1.000	2	5	0	0	5	0
Fajardo, Alejandro, Pied.	1.000	2	8	0	0	8	0
Fleming, Ryan, Hag.*	.983	58	109	6	2	117	2
Freeman, Choo, Ash.	.975	130	229	8	6	243	2
Freitas, Jeremy, C.W.Va.	.909	13	10	0	1	11	0
Gettis, Byron, C.W.Va.	.944	43	63	5	4	72	0
Gibbons, Jay, Hag.*	.917	11	11	0	1	12	0
Giron, Alejandro, Pied.	.963	90	123	7	5	135	2
Gordnier, Aaron, C'bus	1.000	38	44	2	0	46	0
Greene, Claude, Gre.	.968	58	86	4	3	93	0
Guzman, Carlos, Pied.*	.857	15	17	1	3	21	0
Haman, Mack, Del.	.944	55	97	5	6	108	0
Hammond, Joey, Del.	1.000	1	1	0	0	1	0
Harris, Kevin, Sav.	.951	54	76	1	4	81	0
Harris, Willie, Del.	1.000	3	2	1	0	3	0
Harts, Jeremy, Hick.*	.947	22	51	3	3	57	0
Hazelton, Justin, Sav.	1.000	4	7	0	0	7	0
Hendricks, Jason, C.F.	.971	70	124	9	4	137	1
Hernandez, Jesus, C'bus*	.939	65	88	4	6	98	1
Hobbs, Jay, Hick.*	.976	81	151	15	4	170	2
Hook, Kevin, C.F.	.000	1	0	0	0	0	0
Hooper, Daren, Del.	1.000	7	17	0	0	17	0
Hudson, Orlando, Hag.	1.000	22	30	2	0	32	1
Jackson, Jeremy A., Ash.	1.000	13	19	0	0	19	0
Jenkins, Brian, C'bia	.929	70	99	5	8	112	0
Johnson, Eric, Del.	1.000	9	20	3	0	23	0
Johnson, Jason, Pied.	.956	111	166	7	8	181	1
Johnson, Tom, Ash.	1.000	2	2	0	0	2	0
Katz, Glenn, C.S.C.	.990	52	90	7	1	98	1
Key, Jeff, Aug.	.900	22	26	1	3	30	0
Landaeta, Luis, Ash.*	.957	112	162	17	8	187	3
Langerhans, Ryan, Mac.*	.976	112	193	7	5	205	0
Lebron, Hector, C.S.C.	.875	10	6	1	1	8	0
Leon, Richy, Ash.	.909	8	10	0	1	11	0
Ligons, Merrell, C.W.Va.	.944	41	64	4	4	72	1
Malave, Dennis, C'bus*	.986	44	65	4	1	70	0
Malinowski, Scott, C'bia	1.000	1	1	0	0	1	0
Maloney, Jeff, Hag.	.949	69	110	2	6	118	1
Maluchnik, Gregg, Mac.	.875	6	7	0	1	8	0
Martin, Billy, C'bia	.000	1	0	0	0	0	0
Martin, Brian, C.S.C.	.967	31	55	3	2	60	1
Martin, Justin, Hick.	1.000	7	9	1	0	10	0
Maxwell, Keith, Hick.	.903	23	28	0	3	31	0
Meliah, David, Sav.	1.000	7	12	0	0	12	0
Mench, Kevin, Sav.	.900	6	17	1	2	20	0
Mendoza, Angel, Aug.	.964	100	172	13	7	192	1
Mento, Alfredo, C'bia	1.000	3	3	0	0	3	0
Metzler, Rod, C.W.Va.	1.000	12	16	0	0	16	0
Minges, Tyler, C'bus	.957	113	192	8	9	209	1
Mulvehill, Chase, C'bia	.938	108	158	9	11	178	2
Na, Jim, C.F.	.952	36	58	2	3	63	0
Ndungidi, Ntema, Del.	.952	57	75	4	4	83	0
Nieves, Juan, Hag.	.949	46	53	3	3	59	0
Novak, John, Sav.	.957	64	107	4	5	116	0
Nowlin, Cody, Sav.	.962	34	51	0	2	53	0
Oliver, Johnny, Aug.	.914	22	31	1	3	35	0
Ortiz, Juan, C.F.	.929	16	21	5	2	28	0
Ottevaere, Derek, Sav.	.937	71	89	0	6	95	0
Padilla, Jorge, Pied.	.963	42	76	2	3	81	0
Pena, Jose, Aug.	.950	40	53	4	3	60	0
Piercy, Brad, C.F.	.990	48	97	4	1	102	1
Piercy, Mike, Hick.*	.909	7	10	0	1	11	0
Pierre, Juan, Ash.*	.981	140	193	13	4	210	4
Price, Corey, Del.	.923	4	12	0	1	13	0
Raines, Tim, Del.	.961	115	237	8	10	255	3

Player, Team	Pct.	G	PO	A	E	TC	DP
Ralph, Brian, Hick.*	1.000	14	27	2	0	29	2
Ramirez, Charlie, C.W.Va.	1.000	28	28	1	0	29	0
Reed, Keith, Del.	.926	58	83	5	7	95	1
Rhodes, Dusty, Gre.	.982	62	107	5	2	114	0
Ribaudo, Mike, C'bia	.000	1	0	0	0	0	0
Riordan, Matthew, Del.	.957	26	44	1	2	47	0
Rodriguez, Carlos, Aug.	.909	29	38	2	4	44	0
Rodriguez, Junior, Gre.	.750	6	6	0	2	8	0
Rojas, Mo, C.W.Va.	.955	17	19	2	1	22	0
Rollins, Antwon, Sav.	.933	8	13	1	1	15	0
Romano, Jimmie, Sav.	1.000	4	3	1	0	4	0
Ruan, Wilken, C.F.	.986	112	263	18	4	285	4
Ruiz, Willy, C.W.Va.	1.000	3	3	0	0	3	0
Ryan, Kelvin, C.S.C.	.973	125	242	8	7	257	2
Santana, Osmany, C'bus*	.974	35	75	1	2	78	0
Schwab, Chris, C'bus*	.900	10	7	2	1	10	0
Scioneaux, Damian, C.S.C.	.857	5	6	0	1	7	0
Shackelford, Brian, C.W.Va.*	.948	53	67	6	4	77	1
Sienko, Ryan, Sav.	1.000	1	2	1	0	3	0
Smothers, Stewart, Mac.	.969	62	120	6	4	130	0
Soriano, Jose, Aug.	.986	37	66	7	1	74	3
Sosa, Jovanny, Hick.	.943	89	143	5	9	157	0
Stewart, Colin, Mac.	1.000	27	49	1	0	50	0
Stratton, Robert, C'bia	.939	52	60	2	4	66	0
Strickland, Greg, Mac.*	.973	42	73	0	2	75	0
Suriel, Miguel, C.S.C.	.909	13	19	1	2	22	0
Taveras, Jose, C.W.Va.	.955	89	166	4	8	178	0
Thompson, Eric, C'bus*	.963	71	126	3	5	134	1
THOMPSON, Tyler, Hag.	.989	124	177	8	2	187	2
Torres, Jason, Sav.	.800	3	4	0	1	5	0
Urquhart, Derick, C.F.*	.990	52	94	4	1	99	0
Valdez, Angel, Gre.	.910	34	59	2	6	67	0
Vann, Eric, C.W.Va.	1.000	11	10	0	0	10	0
Vento, Mike, Gre.	.938	23	29	1	2	32	0
Warren, Chris, Aug.	.943	31	48	2	3	53	1
Washington, Dion, Gre.	1.000	2	1	0	0	1	0
Weichard, Paul, Hick.*	.957	88	213	9	10	232	1
Whitehurst, Tom, Ash.	.865	29	30	2	5	37	1
Wiese, Brian, Aug.	.958	19	23	0	1	24	0
Wilder, Paul, C.S.C.	.938	31	45	0	3	48	0
Wright, Corey, Sav.*	.984	94	181	2	3	186	1

CATCHERS

Player, Team	Pct.	G	PO	A	E	TC	DP	PB
Ackerman, Scott, C.F.	.983	61	405	60	8	473	5	17
Alevras, Chad, Aug.	1.000	3	28	2	0	30	0	1
Anderson, Frank, Hick.	.976	38	259	29	7	295	1	10
Avila, Rob, Pied.	.923	2	10	2	1	13	0	1
Ayres, Yancy, C.W.Va.	.986	25	121	16	2	139	1	3
Bastardo, Angel, C'bus	.978	12	83	8	2	93	1	1
Benham, David, Aug.	1.000	3	8	3	0	11	0	0
Bonilla, Juan, Del.	1.000	5	21	2	0	23	0	3
Boscan, Jean, Mac.	.986	95	798	95	13	906	4	15
Brito, Juan, C.W.Va.	.991	59	476	61	5	542	1	10
Bundy, Ryan, Hag.	.983	43	295	44	6	345	4	12
Burkhart, Lance, C.F.	1.000	2	16	0	0	16	0	1
Carreno, Jose, C.F.	.967	41	285	38	11	334	5	4
Cheek, Shawn, Aug.	.976	5	35	5	1	41	0	3
Chwan, Brian, C.S.C.	.980	40	218	24	5	247	2	6
Cody, Ryan, Pied.	1.000	1	9	2	0	11	0	0
Cota, Humberto, C.S.C.-Hick.	.988	91	662	83	9	754	2	17
Cruz, Edgar, C'bus	.984	50	385	43	7	435	1	13
Cruz, Rafael, Sav.	.990	23	172	26	2	200	3	2
Daedelow, Craig, Del.	.966	19	129	12	5	146	0	1
Diaz, Diogenes, Hick.	.984	11	56	5	1	62	0	2
Diaz, Miguel, C.F.	1.000	1	10	0	0	10	0	1
Elwood, Brad, Gre.	.985	76	564	77	10	651	1	33
Escalante, Jaime, Del.	.989	39	322	42	4	368	5	8
Felix, Hersy, C.W.Va.	.977	23	156	17	4	177	2	1
Fowler, Ben, C'bus	.988	27	222	20	3	245	0	0
Heine, Kyle, C.W.Va.	.976	19	155	11	4	170	1	5
James, Drue, Mac.	.977	31	192	18	5	215	0	3
Johnson, Erik, Ash.	.970	44	357	35	12	404	1	9
Jones, Jay, Ash.	.989	33	237	25	3	265	1	8
Jones, Jeremy, Sav.	.989	42	317	33	4	354	0	3
Kremblas, Mike, Hag.	.983	54	355	56	7	418	5	5
Larned, Andrew, Aug.	.981	32	222	33	5	260	1	7
Lopez-Cao, Mike, Del.	.950	2	18	1	1	20	0	0
Maluchnik, Gregg, Mac.	.980	22	133	16	3	152	1	4
Massucco, Scott, Gre.	.800	3	4	0	1	5	0	0
McGee, Tom, Del.	.987	63	466	59	7	532	5	14
Pagan, Carlos, C.W.Va.	.977	48	324	55	9	388	5	8

Player, Team	Pct.	G	PO	A	E	TC	DP	PB
PENA, Rodolfo, Aug.	.993	96	706	125	6	837	5	11
Piercy, Brad, C.F.	.989	40	237	34	3	274	0	3
Pinto, Rene, Gre.	.975	15	143	16	4	163	0	4
Ramos, Kelly, C'bia	.988	75	553	80	8	641	3	7
Reyes, Jose, Hick.	.984	14	103	19	2	124	2	5
Rhodes, Nicholas, C.S.C.	.969	15	85	10	3	98	0	2
Ribaudo, Mike, C'bia	.979	39	251	33	6	290	0	8
Romano, Jimmie, Sav.	.971	38	238	34	8	280	2	4
Salazar, Jeremy, Pied.	.985	92	731	104	13	848	3	13
Schreimann, Eric, Pied.	.989	27	164	17	2	183	0	2
Seestedt, Michael, Del.	.986	24	197	14	3	214	0	1
Sienko, Ryan, Sav.	.976	21	114	8	3	125	1	4
Smith, Casey, C'bus	.966	47	401	50	16	467	5	5
Smith, Ryan, C'bia	1.000	1	5	5	0	10	0	1
Suriel, Miguel, C.S.C.	.997	38	281	37	1	319	1	9
Taylor, Adam, C'bus	.985	8	56	10	1	67	0	0
Thompson, Andy, C'bia	.994	37	276	30	2	308	0	6
Torres, Jason, Sav.	.977	37	266	31	7	304	0	6
Twombley, Dennis, Gre.	.985	38	300	31	5	336	0	9
Umbria, Jose, Hag.	.991	55	409	40	4	453	3	12
Valdez, Jerry, Pied.	.986	20	129	17	2	148	2	9
Washington, Rico, Hick.	.984	54	471	36	8	515	2	26
Whitby, Cory, Aug.	.993	20	129	9	1	139	0	3
Winchester, Jeff, Ash.	.978	72	559	62	14	635	1	18

CATCHERS WITH TWO OR MORE TEAMS

Player, Team	Pct.	G	PO	A	E	TC	DP	PB
Cota, Humberto, C.S.C.	.986	61	427	61	7	495	1	12
Cota, Humberto, Hick.	.992	30	235	22	2	259	1	5

PITCHERS

Player, Team	Pct.	G	PO	A	E	TC	DP
Abreu, Winston, Mac.	1.000	14	6	5	0	11	1
Adair, Derek, Pied.	.917	8	4	7	1	12	0
Affeldt, Jeremy, C.W.Va.*	.963	27	2	24	1	27	1
Ammons, Cary, C.W.Va.*	1.000	16	6	25	0	31	0
Andrade, Jancy, Del.	.867	26	5	8	2	15	0
Aracena, Juan, C'bus	1.000	32	1	5	0	6	0
Aramboles, Ricardo, Gre.	.857	6	3	3	1	7	0
Arthurs, Shane, C.F.	.763	25	6	23	9	38	1
Babula, Shaun, Del.*	.750	16	1	2	1	4	0
Bailie, Matt, Pied.	1.000	6	0	2	0	2	0
Baisley, Brad, Pied.	.971	23	15	18	1	34	0
Bautista, Francisco, C.W.Va.	1.000	7	0	1	0	1	0
Bautista, Martin, C'bus	.895	15	7	10	2	19	0
Bechler, Steven, Del.	.857	26	4	20	4	28	0
Becks, Ryan, C.F.*	1.000	34	6	16	0	22	0
Behn, Brendan, C'bia*	.000	1	0	0	0	0	0
Beimel, Joe, Hick.*	1.000	29	4	26	0	30	1
Beitey, Jason, Sav.	.750	21	1	5	2	8	0
Bell, Heath, C'bia	.909	55	2	8	1	11	0
Bellhorn, Todd, C'bia*	1.000	38	5	11	0	16	1
Bello, Jilberto, Del.	.875	38	7	14	3	24	1
Bennett, Jeff, Hick.	.909	8	3	7	1	11	1
Blanco, Roger, Mac.	.833	19	3	2	1	6	0
Blazier, Ron, Del.	.000	2	0	0	0	0	0
Blevins, Jeremy, Gre.	.929	19	6	20	2	28	0
Blythe, Billy, Mac.	.000	1	0	0	0	0	0
Bong, Jung, Mac.*	.929	26	5	21	2	28	3
Boublis, Dan, Sav.	.833	30	8	7	3	18	0
Boughton, Mike, Sav.	.000	1	0	0	0	0	0
Bowles, Brian, Hag.	.950	48	3	16	1	20	2
Box, John, C.S.C.*	1.000	2	1	1	0	2	0
Brantley, Brian, Ash.	.963	34	4	22	1	27	1
Bravo, Franklin, Hick.	.938	34	4	11	1	16	2
Brazoban, Melvin, Sav.	.857	29	3	3	1	7	1
Bridges, Donald, C.F.	1.000	8	6	12	0	18	0
Buchanan, Brian, Gre.*	.929	48	2	11	1	14	1
Buirley, Matt, Hick.	.900	46	4	5	1	10	0
Burch, Matt, C.W.Va.	.913	21	9	12	2	23	1
Cameron, Ryan, Ash.	1.000	17	4	3	0	7	1
Carpenter, Justin, Gre.	1.000	40	3	6	0	9	1
Carr, Tim, C'bia	.800	45	4	4	2	10	2
Carter, Justin, Ash.*	.914	27	6	26	3	35	1
Carter, Roger, C.S.C.	.800	12	3	1	1	5	0
Casey, Joe, Hag.	.925	28	13	24	3	40	0
Cassidy, Scott, Hag.	.974	27	13	24	1	38	1
Casteel, Ricky, Del.	.814	29	6	29	8	43	2
Castelli, Robert, C.F.	1.000	29	3	3	0	6	0
Chavez, Christopher, Mac.	1.000	13	1	0	0	1	0
Chiavacci, Ron, C.F.	.667	20	1	1	1	3	0
Cisar, Mark, Aug.	.944	52	5	12	1	18	1

Player, Team	Pct.	G	PO	A	E	TC	DP
Clark, Mark, Sav.	1.000	1	0	1	0	1	0
Claussen, Brandon, Gre.*	.000	1	0	0	0	0	0
Coco, Pasqual, Hag.	.929	14	4	9	1	14	1
Cook, Aaron, Ash.	.878	25	7	29	5	41	1
Cook, Andy, C'bia	.892	27	9	24	4	37	1
Corcoran, Tim, C'bia	.813	40	3	10	3	16	0
Corey, Michael, Mac.	.900	21	3	6	1	10	0
Cornejo, Jesse, C.S.C.*	1.000	51	3	7	0	10	1
Crawford, Danny, Hick.	1.000	16	6	8	0	14	2
Crumpton, Chuck, C.F.	1.000	13	2	2	0	4	0
Daedelow, Craig, Del.	.000	1	0	0	0	0	0
Dampeer, Kelly, C'bus	1.000	2	0	1	0	1	0
Dansby, Justin, Mac.	1.000	4	1	0	0	1	0
Day, Zach, Gre.	1.000	2	0	1	0	1	0
Delgado, Joseph, C.W.Va.	1.000	11	6	3	0	9	0
Dent, Doug, Mac.	1.000	17	7	13	0	20	1
DeLaCruz, Andres, Gre.	1.000	3	0	1	0	1	0
Douglass, Ryan, C.W.Va.	1.000	10	3	6	0	9	0
Dreier, Tom, Hag.	1.000	8	0	1	0	1	0
Drese, Ryan, C'bus	.000	2	0	0	2	2	0
Duchscherer, Justin, Aug.	1.000	6	5	2	0	7	0
DUNN, Keith, Gre.	1.000	35	13	24	0	37	1
Eason, Clay, Pied.	1.000	10	1	3	0	4	0
Eavenson, Clay, Gre.	.000	5	0	0	1	1	0
Embry, Byron, Mac.	1.000	25	2	2	0	4	0
Espina, Rendy, Pied.*	1.000	15	0	5	0	5	1
Evans, Mike, Ash.*	.935	38	7	22	2	31	3
Everett, Matt, C'bus	.778	18	2	5	2	9	0
Fenus, Justin, Pied.	.917	10	4	7	1	12	0
Field, Nathan, C.F.	1.000	42	5	3	0	8	0
Figueroa, Carlos, Sav.*	.500	10	1	0	1	2	0
Fleming, Travis, Del.	.800	14	2	2	1	5	0
Frachiseur, Zach, Mac.	1.000	4	0	1	0	1	0
Frey, Chris, Sav.	1.000	31	4	7	0	11	1
Garcia, Rosman, Gre.	.875	9	1	6	1	8	0
Garcia, Sonny, Del.	.962	13	8	17	1	26	3
Gaskill, Derek, C'bia	1.000	12	0	1	0	1	0
German, Yon, C'bia*	.941	14	3	13	1	17	2
Giese, Daniel, Aug.	.750	9	1	2	1	4	0
Gilfillan, Jason, C.W.Va.	.000	8	0	0	0	0	0
Glaser, Eric, Aug.	.000	1	0	0	0	0	0
Glaser, Scott, Hick.*	.875	17	1	6	1	8	1
Gonzalez, Edwin, C.W.Va.	1.000	27	3	24	0	27	2
Gordon, Kevin, Ash.	1.000	2	0	3	0	3	0
Gorman, Pat, C'bia	.714	15	3	2	2	7	0
Gourlay, Matt, Hag.	.000	7	0	0	0	0	0
Grabow, John, Hick.*	.857	26	1	17	3	21	0
Granadillo, Adel, C'bus	1.000	2	1	0	0	1	0
Gray, Michael, Mac.*	.889	46	6	10	2	18	1
Gross, Rafael, C'bus	.917	42	3	8	1	12	0
Guerrero, Junior, C.W.Va.	.880	19	8	14	3	25	1
Guillory, Dan, C'bus	1.000	15	1	5	0	6	0
Guzman, Ambiorix, Sav.	1.000	29	3	15	0	18	0
Guzman, Juan, Del.	.958	29	8	15	1	24	0
Haines, Talley, C.S.C.	1.000	47	5	9	0	14	0
Hancock, Joshua, Aug.	1.000	25	12	11	0	23	0
Hebson, Bryan, C.F.	.833	6	2	3	1	6	0
Heffernan, Greg, C'bia	1.000	5	1	1	0	2	0
Herndon, Eric, Mac.	.889	27	1	15	2	18	0
Hertzel, Patrick, C.S.C.	.871	35	8	19	4	31	2
Hiles, Cary, Pied.	.857	44	1	11	2	14	0
Hill, Terrance, Aug.*	.857	53	5	13	3	21	0
Houser, Kyle, Ash.	.667	4	1	1	1	3	0
Hudson, Luke, Ash.	1.000	21	1	11	0	12	0
Hughes, Mike, C'bia*	1.000	6	1	0	0	1	0
Hughes, Travis, Sav.	.828	30	7	17	5	29	0
Huntsman, Brandon, Del.	.000	7	0	0	0	0	0
Jackson, Jeremy D., C.W.Va.-C'bia*	.969	24	7	24	1	32	1
James, Delvin, C.S.C.	.933	25	9	19	2	30	3
Jennings, Jason, Ash.	1.000	12	2	5	0	7	0
Jodie, Brett, Gre.	1.000	25	4	17	0	21	1
Johnston, Clint, Hick.*	.952	34	5	15	1	21	0
Kanovich, Jason, C.F.*	.889	36	3	5	1	9	0
Kearney, Ryan, C'bus	1.000	6	1	2	0	3	0
Keelin, Chris, Pied.	.000	4	0	0	0	0	0
Keisler, Randy, Gre.*	1.000	4	1	1	0	2	0
Kidd, Jake, Ash.	.833	9	2	8	2	12	0
Kingrey, Jarrod, Hag.	.824	56	4	10	3	17	0
Knowles, Michael, Gre.	1.000	11	1	3	0	4	1
Kofler, Ed, C.S.C.	.971	27	15	18	1	34	4
Kosderka, Matt, Sav.	.962	31	10	15	1	26	3
Kubes, Greg, Pied.*	.867	27	3	23	4	30	0

Player, Team	Pct.	G	PO	A	E	TC	DP
Labitzke, Jesse, Ash.*	1.000	14	2	7	0	9	0
Lamattina, Ryan, Ash.*	1.000	38	6	15	0	21	2
Layne, Roger, C'bus.	.000	1	0	0	0	0	0
LaRosa, Tom, Hag.	1.000	12	2	0	0	2	0
Lee, Wayne, C.W.Va.	.875	48	3	11	2	16	1
Leon, Richy, Ash.	.000	1	0	0	0	0	0
Lewis, Craig, Gre.	1.000	9	6	9	0	15	0
Lewis, Peyton, Hag.	.000	2	0	0	0	0	0
Ligons, Merrell, C.W.Va.	.000	2	0	0	0	0	0
Lontayo, Alejandro, Aug.*	.857	40	2	10	2	14	0
Lowe, Matt, C'bia.	.000	1	0	0	0	0	0
Lynch, Pat, Hag.-Ash.	.786	26	14	8	6	28	0
Lyons, Jonathan, Aug.	1.000	19	1	0	0	1	0
Maas, Steve, C'bus.	1.000	21	1	3	0	4	0
Macias, Jose, C'bus.	.000	1	0	0	0	0	0
Madison, Scott, C'bus*	.923	10	2	10	1	13	0
Maluchnik, Gregg, Mac.	.000	1	0	0	0	0	0
Mancha, Tony, C.W.Va.	.882	40	2	13	2	17	2
Maness, Nick, C'bus.	.848	23	10	18	5	33	0
Mangum, Mark, C.F.	1.000	26	17	19	0	36	1
Marietta, Ron, C'bus*	1.000	11	2	5	0	7	0
Martin, Jeff, Hick.	1.000	13	3	6	0	9	0
Martinez, Anastacio, Aug.	1.000	10	1	3	0	4	0
Martinez, Javier, Hick.	1.000	6	0	1	0	1	0
Martinez, Obispo, C.F.	.667	7	1	1	1	3	0
Matsko, Rick, C'bus.	.923	42	4	8	1	13	2
Mattson, John, C'bia	.000	1	0	0	0	0	0
McDonald, Jon, C.S.C.*	1.000	14	2	7	0	9	0
McDougal, Mike, Del.	.000	1	0	0	0	0	0
McGill, Frankie, Sav.	.962	26	3	22	1	26	2
McLeary, Marty, Aug.	.905	35	3	16	2	21	1
Mikels, Jason, Mac.	.000	5	0	0	1	1	0
Miller, Greg, Aug.*	.947	25	8	10	1	19	1
Mlodik, Kevin, Sav.	1.000	14	1	1	0	2	0
Montero, Francisco, Pied.	.920	25	6	17	2	25	3
Montilla, Felix, Hick.	.000	2	0	0	0	0	0
Moore, Eric, Sav.	1.000	23	2	2	0	4	0
Moss, Damian, Mac.*	1.000	12	0	5	0	5	0
Mowel, Mike, Aug.	1.000	21	14	16	0	30	2
Mundy, Mike, Ash.	1.000	37	3	5	0	8	0
Nation, Joey, Mac.*	1.000	6	2	3	0	5	0
Norton, Jason, Aug.	.917	30	5	17	2	24	0
Nunez, Franklin, Pied.	.900	13	5	4	1	10	1
Ochoa, Pablo, C'bia	1.000	3	0	1	0	1	0
Oliver, Scott, Gre.	.833	7	3	7	2	12	0
Ormond, Rodney, Del.	1.000	17	5	10	0	15	1
Osting, Jimmy, Mac.*	.974	27	7	30	1	38	0
Pacheco, Enemencio, Ash.	.917	15	6	16	2	24	0
Padilla, Roy, C'bus*	1.000	30	8	17	0	25	2
Padua, Geraldo, Gre.	.760	21	13	6	6	25	0
Pamus, Javier, C.W.Va.	.905	44	7	12	2	21	2
Paradis, Michael, Del.	1.000	2	0	1	0	1	0
Parra, Christian, Mac.	.889	6	2	6	1	9	0
Parrish, John, Del.*	1.000	4	1	3	0	4	0
Pavlovich, Tony, Hick.	.818	56	3	6	2	11	1
Peguero, Radhame, C.S.C.	1.000	11	1	17	0	18	1
Pena, Alex, Hick.	.750	22	4	5	3	12	0
Percell, Brody, C'bus*	1.000	6	3	1	0	4	0
Perez, Norberto, Del.	.875	25	2	5	1	8	0
Perez, Randy, Del.*	.700	21	3	4	3	10	0
Phillips, Matthew, Aug.	1.000	39	6	8	0	14	1
Pichardo, Carlos, C.W.Va.	.944	10	5	12	1	18	1
Pierce, Tony, Mac.	1.000	8	1	2	0	3	0
Pilato, Chris, Pied.	1.000	4	3	3	0	6	0
Pineda, Isauro, Aug.	.889	8	1	7	1	9	0
Place, Eric, Hag.*	.958	40	5	18	1	24	0
Prater, Andy, Hick.	.750	15	0	9	3	12	0
Pratt, Andy, Sav.*	.923	13	2	10	1	13	0
Prokop, Michael, C'bia.	1.000	37	2	8	0	10	2
Pugmire, Robert, C'bus*	1.000	10	4	7	0	11	3
Rakers, Aaron, Del.	.667	18	1	1	1	3	1
Ramirez, Horacio, Mac.*	.833	17	6	9	3	18	1
Ramos, Fernando, Pied.	1.000	38	2	10	0	12	0
Reinike, Chris, C'bus	.786	11	6	5	3	14	0
Ridenour, Ryan, Gre.*	.500	17	0	1	1	2	0
Rivera, Carlos, Hick.*	.000	1	0	0	0	0	0
Robinson, Jeremy, C.S.C.*	.958	29	1	22	1	24	0
Rodriguez, Cristobal, C.F.	.958	26	8	15	1	24	0
Rodriguez, Jose, C.S.C.	1.000	7	0	1	0	1	0
Romero, Jordan, Del.	.871	24	8	19	4	31	0
Rosa, Cristy, Ash.	1.000	7	1	6	0	7	2
Rosado, Juan, Sav.*	.889	20	3	5	1	9	0
Rose, Johnathan, Pied.*	1.000	21	0	6	0	6	0
Ruhl, Nathan, C.S.C.	.714	36	2	3	2	7	0
Russo, Mike, C.W.Va.	1.000	10	0	1	0	1	0
Sabathia, C.C., C'bus*	1.000	3	0	3	0	3	0
Saenz, Jason, C'bia*	.938	27	4	11	1	16	0
Salyers, Jeremy, C.F.	1.000	22	6	11	0	17	2
Sanchez, Willmen, C'bus*	1.000	13	2	3	0	5	0
Sandoval, Marcos, Hag.	1.000	27	5	7	0	12	2
Santana, Humberto, C'bia*	.857	10	3	3	1	7	1
Schuldt, Matt, C.S.C.	.833	26	2	3	1	6	0
Schwager, Matthew, Del.	1.000	10	1	4	0	5	0
Seale, Dustin, C.F.*	.000	3	0	0	0	0	0
Seberino, Ronni, C.S.C.*	.929	50	2	11	1	14	0
Sequea, Jacobo, Del.	1.000	6	2	3	0	5	0
Sheldon, Kyle, C.F.	.917	26	2	9	1	12	1
Siciliano, Jess, Hick.	.000	6	0	0	0	0	0
Sido, Wilson, C'bus.	1.000	13	1	6	0	7	0
Silva, Carlos, Pied.	.979	26	16	31	1	48	0
Silva, Doug, Sav.	1.000	7	1	1	0	2	0
Simontacchi, Jason, Hick.	1.000	23	8	21	0	29	2
Simpson, Cory, Mac.	1.000	14	6	4	0	10	0
Smith, Taylor, Hag.	.953	28	15	26	2	43	3
Smith, Toby, C.W.Va.	.000	2	0	0	0	0	0
Solano, Alexander, Aug.	.750	9	2	1	1	4	0
Solano, Francisco, C.W.Va.	.750	32	2	10	4	16	1
Sparks, Steve, Hick.	1.000	25	8	10	0	18	2
Spencer, Corey, Aug.*	1.000	7	0	1	0	1	0
Spiegel, Mike, C'bus*	.875	7	2	5	1	8	1
Spille, Ryan, Hag.*	.947	14	4	14	1	19	1
Spooneybarger, Tim, Mac.	1.000	7	1	3	0	4	0
Spurling, Chris, Gre.	.938	49	7	8	1	16	0
Stabile, Paul, Hick.*	.800	46	0	8	2	10	0
Stafford, Mike, Hag.*	1.000	39	2	5	0	7	0
Standridge, Jason, C.S.C.	1.000	18	6	17	0	23	0
Stephens, John, Del.	.923	28	2	22	2	26	0
Stewart, John, Sav.*	1.000	30	10	18	0	28	0
Stine, Justin, Hag.*	1.000	17	1	3	0	4	0
Strange, Patrick, C'bia	.900	28	11	25	4	40	3
Surridge, Lance, Aug.	1.000	37	3	11	0	14	0
Suttles, Donnie, C'bus.	.905	16	2	17	2	21	0
Sylvester, Billy, Mac.	1.000	44	6	8	0	14	0
Tapia, Rafael, Del.	1.000	7	1	4	0	5	0
Taylor, Aaron, Mac.	.824	27	7	7	3	17	0
Tetz, Kristofer, C.F.	.889	10	4	4	1	9	0
Theodile, Simeon, Del.	1.000	33	5	14	0	19	0
Thompson, Andy, C'bia	1.000	2	0	1	0	1	0
Thompson, Doug, Ash.	.875	25	4	3	1	8	0
Toriz, Steve, C.F.	.000	1	0	0	0	0	0
Torres, Luis, Hick.	1.000	7	2	3	0	5	0
Turnbow, Derrick, Pied.	.939	26	7	24	2	33	1
Turnbow, Mark, C'bus.	1.000	13	3	4	0	7	0
Tynan, Chris, Sav.	1.000	21	5	10	0	15	0
Vael, Rob, C'bus	.952	42	5	15	1	21	0
Van Buren, Jermaine, Ash.	.829	28	4	25	6	35	1
Van Gilder, Ryan, C.F.	.000	1	0	0	0	0	0
Vargas, Jose, C'bus.	.833	34	4	6	2	12	0
Vega, Rene, C'bia*	.921	29	9	26	3	38	2
Viole, Paul, C'bia	1.000	2	0	1	0	1	0
Vogtli, Robb, Gre.	1.000	25	5	1	0	6	1
Voyles, Brad, Mac.	.750	38	0	3	1	4	0
Waldron, Brad, C.F.	.857	25	4	8	2	14	0
Wamback, Trevor, C.F.	.960	24	10	14	1	25	0
Ward, Monty, C.W.Va.	.882	42	3	12	2	17	1
Weber, Brett, Gre.	.963	52	6	20	1	27	2
Wedel, Jeremy, Pied.	1.000	23	2	10	0	12	3
Weslowski, Robert, C'bia	1.000	9	2	5	0	7	0
White, Matt, C'bus*	.750	19	6	9	5	20	0
Whiteley, Shad, Gre.	.875	15	2	5	1	8	1
Wiggins, Scott, Gre.*	.900	17	5	13	2	20	0
Williams, David, Hick.*	.909	9	1	9	1	11	0
Wimberly, Larry, Hick.*	1.000	17	1	9	0	10	0
Woodards, Orlando, Hag.	.960	44	8	16	1	25	2
Wright, Barrett, C.S.C.	.818	13	5	4	2	11	0
Wright, Chris, C.S.C.	.944	38	4	13	1	18	1
Wrigley, Jase, Ash.	.700	28	3	11	6	20	1
Zallie, Chris, Aug.*	.000	9	0	0	1	1	0
Zamarripa, Mark, C'bus	.700	15	1	6	3	10	1

PITCHERS WITH TWO OR MORE TEAMS

Player, Team	Pct.	G	PO	A	E	TC	DP
Jackson, Jeremy D., C.W.Va.*	.960	19	5	19	1	25	0
Jackson, Jeremy D., C'bia*	1.000	5	2	5	0	7	1
Lynch, Pat, Hag.	.786	24	14	8	6	28	0
Lynch, Pat, Ash.	.000	2	0	0	0	0	0

The following player appeared only as designated hitter, pinch-hitter or pinch runner: Ross, ph.

LEAGUE CHAMPIONS

Year	Team	Pct.
1948—	Lincolnton*	.627
1949—	Newton-Conover	.667
	Rutherford Co. (2nd)†	.627
1950—	Newton-Conover	.627
	Lenoir (2nd)†	.626
1951—	Morganton	.645
	Shelby (2nd)†	.604
1952—	Lincolnton	.649
	Shelby (2nd)†	.645
1953-59—	League inactive.	
1960—	Lexington	.707
	Salisbury (2nd)†	.650
1961—	Salisbury	.627
	Shelby (4th)†	.481
1962—	Statesville	.563
	Statesville	.700
1963—	Greenville†	.576
	Salisbury	.631
1964—	Rock Hill	.672
	Salisbury‡	.631
1965—	Salisbury	.641
	Rock Hill‡	.603
1966—	Spartanburg	.682
	Spartanburg	.767
1967—	Spartanburg	.730
	Spartanburg	.567
1968—	Spartanburg	.597
	Greenwood‡	.597
1969—	Greenwood‡	.587
	Shelby	.565

Year	Team	Pct.
1970—	Greenville	.576
	Greenville	.619
1971—	Greenwood	.631
	Greenwood	.759
1972—	Spartanburg‡	.788
	Greenville	.652
1973—	Spartanburg‡	.646
	Gastonia	.619
1974—	Gastonia	.606
	Gastonia	.672
1975—	Spartanburg	.543
	Spartanburg	.614
1976—	Asheville	.544
	Greenwood‡	.600
1977—	Greenwood	.557
	Gastonia‡	.590
1978—	Greenwood	.614
	Greenwood	.565
1979—	Greenwood‡	.565
	Spartanburg	.525
1980—	Greensboro	.590
	Charleston	.561
1981—	Greensboro‡	.695
	Greenwood	.549
1982—	Greensboro‡	.681
	Florence	.546
1983—	Columbia	.620
	Gastonia‡	.587
1984—	Charleston	.549
	Asheville‡	.510

Year	Team	Pct.
1985—	Florence‡	.599
	Greensboro	.540
1986—	Columbia‡	.682
	Asheville	.643
1987—	Asheville	.655
	Myrtle Beach‡	.597
1988—	Charleston (S.C.)	.616
	Spartanburg‡	.500
1989—	Gastonia	.657
	Augusta‡	.535
1990—	Columbia	.580
	Charleston (W.Va.)‡	.538
1991—	Charleston (W.Va.)	.648
	Columbia‡	.614
1992—	Columbia	.572
	Myrtle Beach‡	.522
1993—	Savannah‡	.662
	Greensboro	.603
1994—	Columbus	.630
	Savannah‡	.599
1995—	Piedmont	.586
	Augusta‡	.551
1996—	Delmarva	.585
	Savannah†	.511
1997—	Delmarva§	.543
	Greensboro	.536
1998—	Columbia§	.638
	Hagerstown	.574
1999—	Hagerstown	.600
	Augusta§	.496

*Won championship and four-club playoff. †Won four-club playoff. ‡Won split-season playoff. §Won split season, eight-club playoff. (NOTE—Known as Western Carolina League from 1948 through 1962 and known as Western Carolinas League through 1979.)

CLASS A *South Atlantic League*

APPALACHIAN LEAGUE

LEAGUE OFFICE

President
Lee Landers
Address
283 Deerchase Circle
Statesville, NC 28625
Phone
704-873-5300

Teams (affiliation)
Bluefield Orioles (Orioles)
Bristol White Sox (White Sox)
Burlington Indians (Indians)
Danville Braves (Braves)
Elizabethton Twins (Twins)
Johnson City Cardinals (Cardinals)

Kingsport Mets (Mets)
Martinsville Astros (Astros)
Princeton Devil Rays (Devil Rays)
Pulaski Rangers (Rangers)

1999 FINAL STANDINGS

NORTH DIVISION

Team	W	L	T	Pct.	GB
Martinsville (Astros)	41	29	0	.586	...
Danville (Braves)	38	31	0	.551	2.5
Bluefield (Orioles)	25	43	0	.368	15.0
Princeton (Devil Rays)	25	45	0	.357	16.0
Burlington (Indians)	21	49	0	.300	20.0

SOUTH DIVISION

Team	W	L	T	Pct.	GB
Pulaski (Rangers)	48	21	0	.696	...
Bristol (White Sox)	45	24	0	.652	3.0
Elizabethton (Twins)	40	30	0	.571	8.5
Kingsport (Mets)	34	36	0	.486	14.5
Johnson City (Cardinals)	30	39	0	.435	18.0

COMPOSITE

Team	Pul.	Bri.	Mar.	Eliz.	Dan.	King.	J.C.	Blu.	Pri.	Burl.	W	L	T	Pct.	GB
Pulaski (Rangers)	...	3	6	3	4	3	4	9	8	8	48	21	0	.696	...
Bristol (White Sox)	3	...	2	7	2	6	9	5	5	6	45	24	0	.652	3.0
Martinsville (Astros)	4	4	...	3	5	5	2	2	9	7	41	29	0	.586	7.5
Elizabethton (Twins)	3	5	3	...	3	8	7	5	3	3	40	30	0	.571	8.5
Danville (Braves)	1	4	5	3	...	3	3	5	4	10	38	31	0	.551	10.0
Kingsport (Mets)	3	5	1	3	3	...	8	5	3	3	34	36	0	.486	14.5
Johnson City (Cardinals)	2	2	4	4	3	4	...	2	4	5	30	39	0	.435	18.0
Bluefield (Orioles)	1	0	4	1	5	1	3	...	8	2	25	43	0	.368	22.5
Princeton (Devil Rays)	2	1	1	3	2	3	2	6	...	5	25	45	0	.357	23.5
Burlington (Indians)	2	0	3	3	4	3	1	4	1	...	21	49	0	.300	27.5

Major league affiliations in parentheses.

PLAYOFFS: Martinsville defeated Pulaski two games to none to win league championship.

REGULAR-SEASON ATTENDANCE: Bluefield, 32,392; Bristol, 22,194; Burlington, 43,718; Danville, 57,044; Elizabethton, 11,823; Johnson City, 15,193; Kingsport, 55,457; Martinsville, 43,309; Princeton, 33,017; Pulaski, 16,370. Total—330,517. Playoffs (2 games)—1,716.

MANAGERS: Bluefield, Duffy Dyer; Bristol, Gary Pellant; Burlington, Jack Mull; Danville, J.J. Cannon; Elizabethton, Jon Mathews; Johnson City, Steve Turco; Kingsport, Guy Conti; Martinsville, Brad Wellman; Princeton, Bobby Ramos; Pulaski, Bruce Crabbe.

ALL-STAR TEAM: C—Frederick Torres, Pulaski; 1B—Chris Delgado, Bristol; 2B—Ruben Salazar, Elizabethton; 3B—Matthew Scanlow, Elizabethton; SS—Wilson Betemit, Danville; Utility INF—Eric Sandberg, Elizabethton; OF—Josh Hamilton, Princeton; Kevin Mench, Pulaski; Chad Durham, Bristol; DH—Rick Elder, Bluefield; RHP—Aaron Harang, Pulaski; LHP—Randy Perez, Bluefield; RP—Santiago Ramirez, Martinsville; Player of the Year—Ruben Salazar, Elizabethton; Pitcher of the Year—Aaron Harang, Pulaski; Manager of the Year—Bruce Crabbe, Pulaski.

1999 BATTING

TEAM

Team	Avg.	G	TPA	AB	R	H	TB	2B	3B	HR	RBI	SH	SF	HP	BB	IBB	SO	SB	CS	GDP	LOB	ShO	Slg.	OBP
Elizabethton	.297	70	2938	2515	505	748	1171	148	28	73	449	8	17	52	346	8	589	74	31	54	615	1	.466	.391
Pulaski	.289	69	2717	2356	475	681	1079	141	16	75	409	24	28	40	269	5	545	86	20	37	514	0	.458	.368
Bristol	.275	69	2665	2309	392	635	909	108	14	46	329	20	21	40	275	6	478	131	47	47	523	3	.394	.359
Kingsport	.272	70	2723	2373	378	646	912	110	18	40	313	35	17	61	237	5	566	130	57	37	509	2	.384	.351
Danville	.269	69	2729	2343	408	631	898	121	28	30	340	15	18	49	304	3	594	85	45	36	541	3	.383	.363
Princeton	.265	70	2676	2411	384	640	968	137	16	53	322	7	13	36	209	4	703	86	44	36	476	6	.401	.332
Bluefield	.259	68	2749	2375	445	616	964	111	30	59	372	6	19	39	310	5	587	51	21	37	529	3	.406	.352
Martinsville	.254	70	2639	2318	366	589	879	131	24	37	297	4	16	48	253	1	611	159	55	27	458	4	.379	.338
Johnson City	.241	69	2717	2357	366	569	839	98	20	44	309	29	19	46	266	6	674	123	50	38	506	4	.356	.328
Burlington	.228	70	2686	2318	336	529	744	85	14	34	281	15	20	62	271	3	624	82	36	45	499	2	.321	.323

INDIVIDUAL

TOP QUALIFIERS FOR BATTING CHAMPIONSHIP

Minimum 189 plate appearances. *Lefthanded batter. †Switch-hitter.

Player, Team	Avg.	G	TPA	AB	R	H	TB	2B	3B	HR	RBI	SH	SF	HP	BB	IBB	SO	SB	CS	GDP	Slg.	OBP
Salazar, Ruben, Eliz.	.401	64	318	262	66	105	175	24	2	14	65	1	2	5	48	3	43	11	4	8	.668	.498
Brazell, Craig, King.*	.385	59	239	221	27	85	121	16	1	6	39	2	1	8	7	4	34	6	5	5	.548	.422
Mench, Kevin, Pul.	.362	65	295	260	63	94	166	22	1	16	60	0	5	2	28	0	48	12	2	2	.638	.420
Jones, Jason, Pul.†	.355	69	307	262	65	93	152	24	1	11	58	0	5	7	33	1	55	1	2	5	.580	.433
Scanlon, Matt, Eliz.*	.354	57	284	240	54	85	129	16	5	6	48	1	1	6	36	0	45	8	0	5	.538	.449
Cadiente, Brett, Pul.*	.354	68	319	274	69	97	148	16	7	7	48	1	3	3	38	1	51	18	3	3	.540	.434
Hamilton, Josh, Prin.*	.347	56	252	236	49	82	140	20	4	10	48	1	2	0	13	0	43	17	3	0	.593	.378
Fiore, Curt, Dan.	.333	53	230	198	35	66	88	13	0	3	24	0	1	7	22	1	39	0	5	5	.444	.417
Johnson, Ben, J.C.	.330	57	240	203	38	67	108	9	1	10	51	1	2	5	29	1	57	14	6	0	.532	.423

Player, Team	Avg.	G	TPA	AB	R	H	TB	2B	3B	HR	RBI	SH	SF	HP	BB	IBB	SO	SB	CS	GDP	Slg.	OBP
Elder, Rick, Blue.*	.329	46	194	158	35	52	98	8	4	10	40	0	3	3	30	1	57	2	0	2	.620	.438
Durham, Chad, Bris.	.324	68	320	278	66	90	106	12	2	0	36	2	3	4	33	2	44	57	13	1	.381	.399
Betemit, Wilson, Dan.†	.320	67	291	259	39	83	120	18	2	5	53	1	3	1	27	1	63	6	3	4	.463	.383
Crawford, Carl, Prin.*	.319	60	279	260	62	83	105	14	4	0	25	1	3	1	13	0	47	17	4	5	.404	.350
Garbe, Brandon, Eliz.	.316	41	192	171	33	54	71	8	0	3	32	0	0	1	20	0	34	4	1	3	.415	.391
West, Kevin, Eliz.	.314	63	269	229	43	72	132	12	6	12	55	0	2	16	22	2	68	4	2	3	.576	.409
Almonte, Claudio, Eliz.	.314	45	197	172	32	54	79	15	2	2	23	0	2	2	21	0	41	4	6	1	.459	.391

DEPARTMENTAL LEADERS: G—J. Jones, 69; AB—D. Jones, 284; R—Cadiente, 69; H—Salazar, 105; TB—Salazar, 175; 2B—Salazar, J. Jones, 24 each; 3B—Cadinete, Huffman, 7 each; HR—Mench, 16; RBI—Salazar, 65; SH—Crisp, 8; SF—Garcia, 6; HP—Sherrill, 22; BB—Forbes, 53; IBB—Brazell, 4; SO—Osorio, 79; SB—Durham, 57; CS—Durham, 13; GIDP—Torres, 10; Slg.—Salazar, .498.

ALL PLAYERS

*Lefthanded batter. †Switch-hitter.

Player, Team	Avg.	G	TPA	AB	R	H	TB	2B	3B	HR	RBI	SH	SF	HP	BB	IBB	SO	SB	CS	GDP	Slg.	OBP
Aaron, Oginga, Prin.	.000	2	4	4	0	0	0	0	0	0	0	0	0	0	0	0	2	0	0	0	.000	.000
Abreu, David, King.†	.438	5	25	16	5	7	7	0	0	0	1	1	0	0	8	0	2	3	1	0	.438	.625
Acevedo, Luis, Pul.	.087	9	32	23	4	2	2	0	0	0	1	0	0	0	9	0	9	4	0	0	.087	.344
Acosta, Emilio, J.C.	.243	36	121	107	11	26	39	6	2	1	16	1	0	5	8	2	16	2	0	3	.364	.325
Acuna, Ronald, King.	.285	38	143	123	26	35	46	8	0	1	24	2	1	3	14	0	32	15	5	3	.374	.369
Aguirregaviria, Frank, Bris.	.239	17	49	46	3	11	16	2	0	1	3	0	0	3	0	0	16	0	0	1	.348	.386
Albertson, Justin, J.C.	.234	41	146	128	17	30	48	1	1	5	16	0	0	1	17	0	60	11	2	4	.375	.329
Almonte, Claudio, Eliz.	.314	45	197	172	32	54	79	15	2	2	23	0	2	2	21	0	41	4	6	1	.459	.391
Alvarez, Nell, King.	.270	53	190	159	32	43	73	5	2	7	27	6	1	7	17	0	43	9	7	5	.459	.364
Andrianoff, Jonathan, Mar.	.218	24	68	55	8	12	13	1	0	0	6	1	1	2	9	0	29	4	3	0	.236	.343
Argento, Shaun, Dan.	.233	16	46	43	5	10	13	3	0	0	8	0	1	0	2	0	10	0	0	1	.302	.261
Baez, Ernies, Pul.†	.192	8	30	26	3	5	11	0	0	2	5	0	0	0	4	0	6	1	0	1	.423	.300
Banez, Marco, J.C.*	.200	2	5	5	1	1	1	0	0	0	0	0	0	0	0	0	1	0	0	0	.200	.200
Bastardo, Angel, Burl.	.262	17	65	61	7	16	19	3	0	0	4	0	0	0	4	0	13	1	0	2	.311	.308
Batista, Angel, Prin.*	.138	7	30	29	4	4	5	1	0	0	1	0	0	0	1	0	8	0	0	0	.172	.167
Batista, Carlos, Burl.	.234	45	180	171	16	40	57	8	0	3	29	0	1	0	8	0	49	0	2	6	.333	.267
Berrien, Samuel, Blue.*	.239	30	114	92	13	22	27	3	1	0	9	0	0	4	18	0	22	1	1	1	.293	.386
Betemit, Wilson, Dan.†	.320	67	291	259	39	83	120	18	2	5	53	1	3	1	27	1	63	6	3	4	.463	.383
Bigbie, Larry, Blue.*	.267	8	35	30	3	8	8	0	0	0	4	0	1	1	3	0	8	1	3	1	.267	.343
Blankenship, Anthony, Bris.	.103	12	34	29	4	3	3	0	0	0	1	0	0	0	5	0	16	0	1	0	.103	.235
Bonilla, Juan, Blue.	.240	34	114	100	12	24	32	5	0	1	17	0	1	1	12	0	23	0	0	3	.320	.325
Brazell, Craig, King.*	.385	59	239	221	27	85	121	16	1	6	39	2	1	8	7	4	34	6	5	5	.548	.422
Buckley, Chris, J.C.	.251	47	186	171	19	43	64	8	2	3	23	1	0	1	13	0	68	10	4	0	.374	.308
Cabrera, Raymond, Blue.	.274	31	127	117	21	32	47	9	0	2	9	0	1	3	6	0	14	1	3	4	.402	.323
Cadiente, Brett, Pul.*	.354	68	319	274	69	97	148	16	7	7	48	1	3	3	38	1	51	18	3	3	.540	.434
Calzado, Napolean, Blue.	.291	52	223	199	46	58	91	11	2	6	31	0	1	3	20	1	32	9	1	3	.457	.363
Candelario, Luis, Prin.	.130	13	56	54	3	7	11	1	0	1	8	0	1	0	1	0	18	1	0	4	.204	.143
Carrillo, Robert, Mar.	.224	49	199	174	21	39	67	7	0	7	28	0	3	7	15	0	56	5	2	5	.385	.307
Centeno, Edwin, Blue.†	.250	5	8	8	1	2	2	0	0	0	0	0	0	0	0	0	2	1	0	0	.250	.250
Centile, Raul, Burl.†	.167	9	28	24	2	4	4	0	0	0	1	0	0	0	4	0	7	1	0	0	.167	.286
Ciarrachi, Kevin, King.	.000	2	2	1	0	0	0	0	0	0	0	0	0	0	1	0	1	0	0	0	.000	.500
Collura, Todd, Eliz.	.313	23	78	67	13	21	31	4	0	2	18	0	1	3	7	0	20	0	0	0	.463	.397
Colmenter, Jesus, Burl.†	.243	36	147	140	15	34	40	6	0	0	12	0	1	0	6	0	39	4	2	1	.286	.272
Crawford, Carl, Prin.*	.319	60	279	260	62	83	105	14	4	0	25	1	3	1	13	0	47	17	4	5	.404	.350
Crisp, Covelli, J.C.†	.258	65	285	229	55	59	81	5	4	3	22	8	2	2	44	0	41	27	6	0	.354	.379
Crocker, Nickolas, Dan.*	.256	63	281	242	52	62	92	15	3	3	32	0	2	6	31	0	56	5	4	4	.380	.352
Cruz, Rafael, Pul.	.222	15	60	54	7	12	15	3	0	0	8	1	0	1	4	0	18	0	0	2	.278	.288
Cubillan, Jose, Pul.†	.100	5	15	10	4	1	1	0	0	0	1	0	1	2	2	0	8	0	0	0	.100	.333
De Caster, Yurendell, Prin.	.257	48	212	183	37	47	92	12	0	11	36	1	2	6	20	0	65	4	2	4	.503	.344
De La Cruz, Ruddi, King.	.225	54	196	160	30	36	52	6	2	2	12	3	1	7	25	0	47	10	5	4	.325	.352
Delgado, Chris, Bris.	.300	61	257	217	36	65	119	10	1	14	54	1	3	3	33	2	64	1	0	7	.548	.395
De Los Santos, Santo, J.C.	.214	55	186	159	22	34	43	2	2	1	10	6	1	4	16	0	58	3	5	2	.270	.300
Deschenes, Pat, King.*	.377	40	183	151	30	57	80	8	3	3	30	1	1	5	25	0	18	6	2	4	.530	.478
Diaz, Aneuris, J.C.	.229	56	223	205	30	47	72	9	2	4	27	2	1	4	10	0	55	6	2	3	.351	.277
Diaz, Johnny, J.C.	.111	3	11	9	0	1	1	0	0	0	1	0	1	1	0	0	0	0	0	0	.111	.182
Dillard, Thomas, Eliz.	.264	34	120	110	17	29	40	6	1	1	17	1	1	4	4	0	28	4	2	2	.364	.311
Donato, Gregorio, Dan.	.288	53	242	215	30	62	89	15	3	2	37	2	5	1	19	0	45	13	6	6	.414	.342
Duncan, Chris, J.C.*	.214	55	230	201	23	43	71	8	1	6	34	0	3	1	25	0	62	3	1	4	.353	.300
Durham, Chad, Bris.	.324	68	320	278	66	90	106	12	2	0	36	2	3	4	33	2	44	57	13	1	.381	.399
Dyer, Matthew, King.	.200	22	43	40	2	8	10	2	0	0	3	0	0	0	3	0	10	0	0	1	.250	.256
Edge, Michael, Burl.	.207	29	107	92	9	19	20	1	0	0	9	3	2	1	9	0	26	1	2	0	.217	.279
Elder, Rick, Blue.*	.329	46	194	158	35	52	98	8	4	10	40	0	3	3	30	1	57	2	0	2	.620	.438
Fafard, Mathias, King.	.353	9	21	17	4	6	10	1	0	1	6	1	0	2	1	0	3	0	0	0	.588	.400
Finnerty, Francis, Burl.†	.237	37	146	131	12	31	36	2	0	1	15	0	1	2	12	0	34	0	2	3	.275	.301
Fiore, Curt, Dan.	.333	53	230	198	35	66	88	13	0	3	24	0	1	7	22	1	39	0	5	5	.444	.417
Forbes, Michael, Dan.*	.280	58	265	207	47	58	80	11	4	1	34	0	5	0	53	0	47	1	4	1	.386	.438
Franco, Pascual, J.C.	.310	18	64	58	12	18	26	2	0	2	14	0	1	2	3	0	22	1	0	0	.448	.359
Garbe, Brandon, Eliz.	.316	41	192	171	33	54	71	8	0	3	32	0	0	1	20	0	34	4	1	3	.415	.391
Garcia, Kevys, Mar.	.255	50	217	192	36	49	70	9	3	2	18	1	0	4	20	0	65	16	4	2	.365	.338
Garcia, Oscar, Burl.	.289	56	242	194	39	56	82	9	1	5	41	1	6	8	33	0	42	17	4	6	.423	.402
Garcia, Yosnel, Burl.	.253	29	95	83	7	21	25	2	1	0	11	2	0	1	9	0	12	4	1	1	.301	.333
Garza, Rolando, Bris.	.253	62	225	198	30	50	63	8	1	1	17	0	3	3	21	0	32	3	3	5	.318	.329
Gentry, Garett, Mar.*	.239	33	128	117	16	28	42	4	2	2	14	0	0	2	9	0	26	4	0	1	.359	.305
Gordon, Alexis, Blue.*	.333	27	121	105	26	35	74	4	4	9	32	0	1	2	13	1	35	4	1	0	.705	.413
Green, Kevin, Dan.	.174	44	177	149	24	26	49	6	1	5	16	2	2	11	13	0	68	4	2	1	.329	.286
Griffin, Justin, Burl.	.179	14	42	39	7	7	9	2	0	0	1	0	0	2	1	0	13	0	1	0	.231	.238
Griswold, Matthew, Blue.*	.275	40	184	149	30	41	69	8	1	6	26	0	1	2	32	1	50	2	1	0	.463	.408
Guerrero, Pedro, Pul.	.216	63	282	218	57	47	73	2	5	5	22	6	3	6	49	1	59	19	7	3	.335	.370
Gutierrez, Derrick, Blue.	.203	34	147	123	18	25	39	2	3	2	15	3	0	1	20	0	44	3	1	0	.317	.319

Player, Team	Avg.	G	TPA	AB	R	H	TB	2B	3B	HR	RBI	SH	SF	HP	BB	IBB	SO	SB	CS	GDP	Slg.	OBP
Gutierrez, Fernando, Blue.	.269	23	83	78	5	21	28	7	0	0	11	0	0	1	4	0	19	0	1	0	.359	.313
Guyton, Eric, King.	.263	59	203	186	17	49	68	11	1	2	28	3	1	2	11	0	39	6	1	2	.366	.310
Hambrick, Marcus, Dan.*	.258	38	136	120	21	31	40	4	1	1	9	1	1	0	14	0	39	9	3	0	.333	.333
Hamilton, Josh, Prin.*	.347	56	252	236	49	82	140	20	4	10	48	1	2	0	13	0	43	17	3	0	.593	.378
Harrelson, Casey, Bris.*	.150	18	46	40	3	6	7	1	0	0	1	0	0	1	5	0	11	0	1	0	.175	.261
Harris, Willie, Blue.*	.273	5	27	22	3	6	7	1	0	0	3	0	1	0	4	0	2	1	0	1	.318	.370
Hartley, Will, Burl.†	.159	48	197	151	19	24	39	3	0	4	14	0	0	5	41	0	51	3	0	0	.258	.355
Heffernan, Christian, Dan.*	.109	23	68	55	10	6	10	0	2	0	2	1	0	0	11	0	25	4	0	0	.182	.258
Helena, Roberto, Prin.	.274	61	236	223	31	61	71	7	0	1	14	1	1	1	10	0	44	4	6	1	.318	.306
Helquist, Jonathan, Mar.	.301	49	193	173	33	52	85	15	3	4	17	0	0	2	18	0	50	5	5	1	.491	.373
Hernandez, Carlos, King.	.000	5	5	4	1	0	0	0	0	0	0	0	0	0	1	0	2	0	0	0	.000	.200
Hernandez, Johnny, J.C.†	.262	60	270	225	45	59	80	12	3	1	32	0	5	2	38	3	45	23	7	9	.356	.367
Holt, Todd, Bris.	.292	36	125	113	14	33	44	8	0	1	13	3	0	1	8	0	33	4	5	2	.389	.344
Huffman, Royce, Mar.	.296	53	235	196	39	58	94	16	7	2	36	0	4	4	31	0	29	18	2	2	.480	.396
Hunter, David, King.*	.250	19	35	32	5	8	15	1	0	2	4	1	0	0	2	0	10	0	0	0	.469	.294
Ide, Antoine, Blue.	.224	24	95	85	17	19	25	2	2	0	8	1	0	2	7	0	10	2	1	1	.294	.298
Isenia, Chairon, Prin.	.275	30	113	102	19	28	45	7	2	2	12	0	1	2	8	0	16	5	2	2	.441	.336
Jackson, Chris, Burl.	.153	22	71	59	8	9	11	2	0	0	5	0	0	2	10	0	16	0	0	1	.186	.296
Jacobs, John, Prin.	.257	65	278	241	39	62	95	19	1	4	36	0	0	8	29	3	72	15	6	4	.394	.356
Jaramillo, Tony, Pul.*	.185	25	94	81	10	15	19	4	0	0	11	1	1	0	11	1	25	0	0	1	.235	.280
Jimenez, Jonathan, Pul.	.239	61	238	213	25	51	73	11	1	3	27	1	2	5	17	0	65	3	2	2	.343	.308
Johnson, Ben, J.C.	.330	57	240	203	38	67	108	9	1	10	51	1	2	5	29	1	57	14	6	0	.532	.423
Johnson, Eric, Burl.	.231	39	180	147	26	34	54	9	1	3	22	0	1	7	25	0	29	13	1	3	.367	.367
Jones, Damien, Dan.*	.296	68	330	284	56	84	103	6	5	1	29	6	0	3	37	0	58	27	11	4	.363	.383
Jones, Jason, Pul.†	.355	69	307	262	65	93	152	24	1	11	58	0	5	7	33	1	55	1	2	5	.580	.433
Jordan, Yustin, Eliz.	.371	11	40	35	7	13	27	5	0	3	8	0	0	0	5	0	7	0	0	1	.771	.450
Kane, Patrick, Mar.	.204	35	119	98	15	20	28	5	0	1	8	0	0	5	16	0	33	4	3	0	.286	.345
Kessick, Jonathan, Blue.	.204	28	101	93	13	19	34	3	0	4	14	0	1	3	4	0	33	0	0	0	.366	.257
Lama, Jesus, Prin.	.262	20	77	65	16	17	36	5	1	4	13	0	0	0	12	0	26	4	1	1	.554	.377
Lantigua, Denys, Burl.	.133	14	49	45	7	6	7	1	0	0	2	0	0	0	4	0	8	1	0	0	.156	.204
Ledesma, Luis, Mar.	.183	26	98	93	10	17	20	3	0	0	7	0	0	0	5	0	26	1	2	2	.215	.224
Lockridge, Sherwin, Eliz.	.235	21	17	17	1	4	4	0	0	0	2	0	0	0	0	0	6	0	1	0	.235	.235
Lopez, Aristides, Mar.	.220	41	137	132	13	29	35	4	1	0	8	0	0	0	5	0	31	9	6	2	.265	.248
Lopez, Guuillermo, Dan.	.083	14	51	36	6	3	4	1	0	0	2	0	0	1	14	0	15	0	0	0	.111	.353
Lough, Aaron, Eliz.	.220	32	115	100	14	22	35	3	2	2	9	0	0	3	12	1	33	0	0	3	.350	.322
Lugo, Carlos, Burl.	.141	25	77	71	5	10	12	0	1	0	5	2	0	3	1	0	31	1	1	1	.169	.187
Lugo, Roberto, King.*	.179	25	42	39	5	7	11	1	0	1	4	0	0	1	2	0	8	0	0	1	.282	.238
Lynn, Brody, Burl.†	.140	37	145	121	17	17	23	0	0	2	9	1	2	2	19	0	56	2	4	5	.190	.264
Maduro, Jorge, Prin.	.241	24	89	83	5	20	24	4	0	0	6	1	0	1	4	0	20	1	2	0	.289	.284
Mansfield, Doug, Prin.*	.145	22	77	69	9	10	12	2	0	0	8	0	0	3	5	0	30	0	0	2	.174	.234
Manuel, Marcellous, Bris.*	.300	66	273	240	38	72	105	13	1	6	48	1	5	4	23	0	37	8	3	7	.438	.364
Maya, Johan, Mar.†	.239	42	152	138	22	33	45	7	1	1	12	1	1	5	7	0	15	9	5	3	.326	.298
Mejias, Aureliano, J.C.†	.227	33	88	75	9	17	22	3	1	0	5	0	1	2	10	0	29	2	2	3	.293	.330
Mench, Kevin, Pul.	.362	65	295	260	63	94	166	22	1	16	60	0	5	2	28	0	48	12	2	2	.638	.420
Milton, Prinz, Dan.	.173	36	141	127	20	22	28	4	1	0	15	0	0	5	9	0	31	6	1	5	.220	.255
Monzon, Francisco, Blue.	.244	24	92	82	14	20	27	4	0	1	7	0	0	1	9	0	20	1	1	3	.329	.326
Morla, Gilberto, Burl.	.111	5	11	9	0	1	1	0	0	0	0	0	0	1	1	0	6	0	1	0	.111	.273
Moyer, Kyle, Burl.*	.265	38	154	132	15	35	43	5	0	1	10	0	1	0	21	2	40	0	0	2	.326	.364
Nanita, Manny, Eliz.	.230	38	145	135	20	31	45	6	1	2	19	0	0	1	9	0	40	1	0	1	.333	.283
Nelson, Timothy, Blue.	.226	33	127	115	19	26	42	3	2	3	16	0	1	5	6	0	35	0	0	0	.365	.291
Nolasco, Regino, Blue.	.202	58	221	198	35	40	54	5	3	1	26	2	0	2	19	0	49	5	1	6	.273	.279
Nowlin, Cody, Pul.*	.278	58	255	227	45	63	99	10	1	8	49	1	3	3	21	1	34	5	0	4	.436	.343
O'Connor, Brian, Mar.	.184	13	46	38	3	7	11	1	0	1	2	0	0	0	8	0	4	2	3	1	.289	.326
Ortiz, Daniel, Prin.	.156	43	161	141	15	22	31	4	1	1	11	0	0	4	16	0	74	0	3	4	.220	.261
Osorio, Isrrael, Prin.	.278	60	247	205	36	57	112	15	2	12	50	0	2	3	37	1	79	8	4	3	.546	.393
O'Sullivan, Patrick, King.	.267	51	177	161	22	43	63	8	0	4	23	4	1	1	10	1	42	4	2	3	.391	.312
Pemberthy, Aaron, J.C.	.000	1	2	2	0	0	0	0	0	0	0	0	0	0	0	0	0	0	0	1	.000	.000
Perez, Jay, Mar.†	.273	42	172	139	25	38	53	9	0	2	36	0	2	7	24	0	47	17	4	2	.381	.401
Perez, Juan, J.C.	.234	46	199	171	31	40	56	11	1	1	11	5	0	5	18	0	41	13	7	1	.327	.325
Pichardo, Henry, Burl.	.262	62	254	233	44	61	91	12	3	4	32	2	3	2	14	0	30	8	5	8	.391	.306
Pimentel, Hector, J.C.	.300	3	10	10	0	3	4	1	0	0	2	0	0	0	0	0	0	0	0	1	.400	.300
Poe, Adam, Pul.	.298	49	197	171	26	51	69	12	0	2	31	3	3	4	16	0	30	11	3	1	.404	.366
Quintero, Humberto, Bris.	.277	48	173	155	30	43	52	5	2	0	15	3	0	6	9	0	19	11	1	8	.335	.341
Ramirez, Anthony, Mar.*	.344	22	75	64	13	22	41	7	0	4	20	0	1	1	9	0	11	1	2	0	.641	.427
Rayborn, Kris, J.C.*	.000	14	1	1	0	0	0	0	0	0	0	0	0	0	0	0	0	0	0	0	.000	.000
Redman, Prentice, King.	.295	58	231	200	40	59	93	14	1	6	29	3	2	2	24	0	42	16	11	0	.465	.373
Reed, Keith, Blue.	.188	4	17	16	2	3	3	0	0	0	0	0	0	0	1	0	3	0	1	0	.188	.235
Rickon, Jim, Burl.	.302	31	116	96	16	29	46	5	0	4	17	0	0	1	19	0	25	2	1	2	.479	.422
Rincon, Carlos, Mar.	.239	55	201	180	29	43	68	12	2	3	21	0	2	3	16	0	59	24	6	2	.378	.308
Riordan, Matthew, Blue.	.333	5	24	21	2	7	13	1	1	1	6	0	0	0	3	0	3	1	1	0	.619	.417
Rivas, Justo, Dan.	.312	60	243	215	35	67	96	11	6	2	42	1	2	4	21	0	44	10	5	3	.447	.380
Roman, Junior, Bris.†	.260	44	150	131	21	34	42	8	0	0	12	2	0	1	16	0	22	15	2	1	.321	.345
Rummel, Jason, Bris.	.267	56	248	191	39	51	87	10	1	8	36	1	3	5	48	1	32	11	2	3	.455	.421
Salargo, Steven, Blue.	.306	50	212	170	46	52	81	12	1	5	45	0	4	1	37	0	28	8	2	3	.476	.425
Salas, Juan, Prin.	.259	53	211	193	19	50	65	9	0	2	15	1	1	3	13	0	50	1	7	1	.337	.314
Salazar, Erick, Mar.	.195	17	49	41	6	8	8	0	0	0	0	1	0	5	3	0	15	3	0	1	.195	.327
Salazar, Ruben, Eliz.	.401	64	318	262	66	105	175	24	2	14	65	1	2	5	48	3	43	11	4	8	.668	.498
Sandberg, Eric, Eliz.*	.306	67	307	255	60	78	143	16	2	15	62	1	4	2	45	2	51	3	2	9	.561	.408
Santamarina, Juan, Bris.*	.254	60	231	213	36	54	81	10	1	5	22	1	1	0	16	1	41	5	5	5	.380	.304
Santillan, Manuel, Mar.	.181	21	77	72	13	13	24	3	1	2	9	1	0	0	4	0	21	2	2	2	.333	.224
Santini, Travis, Burl.	.284	44	182	169	17	48	70	6	2	4	29	1	1	1	10	1	45	0	1	5	.414	.326
Scanlon, Matt, Eliz.*	.354	57	284	240	54	85	129	16	5	6	48	1	1	6	36	0	45	8	0	5	.538	.449
Schmitt, Brian, Mar.*	.267	51	210	180	27	48	73	11	1	4	26	0	1	0	29	1	48	4	4	1	.406	.367
Schuda, Justin, Prin.*	.315	33	126	111	17	35	56	9	0	4	19	0	0	1	14	0	44	0	0	0	.505	.397
Seale, Marvin, King.†	.233	63	237	210	46	49	68	7	3	2	20	2	1	0	24	0	75	22	4	1	.324	.311

Player, Team	Avg.	G	TPA	AB	R	H	TB	2B	3B	HR	RBI	SH	SF	HP	BB	IBB	SO	SB	CS	GDP	Slg.	OBP
Serrano, Yalian, Prin.	.000	7	10	10	0	0	0	0	0	0	0	0	0	0	0	0	8	0	0	0	.000	.000
Sherrill, J.J., Burl.†	.206	64	293	233	55	48	80	11	6	3	24	5	0	26	29	0	64	28	9	0	.343	.358
Smith, Ryan, King.	.186	31	94	86	8	16	20	2	1	0	9	0	0	1	7	0	20	1	1	1	.233	.255
Southward, Deshawn, Eliz..	.249	50	206	173	34	43	60	10	2	1	25	1	2	2	28	0	30	16	4	4	.347	.356
Sowers, Douglas, Blue.*	.249	53	219	181	32	45	85	14	1	8	35	0	3	2	33	1	54	2	1	0	.470	.365
Spooner, Brent, J.C.	.214	42	145	126	17	27	39	9	0	1	10	0	3	16	0	24	0	3	2	.310	.317
Stanley, Derek, Bris.	.230	39	158	135	20	31	45	5	3	1	9	3	0	3	17	0	31	6	6	3	.333	.329
Teilon, Nilson, Bris.	.296	68	281	240	43	71	114	12	2	9	51	1	3	8	29	0	68	6	4	3	.475	.386
Terveen, Bryce, Dan.*	.242	50	188	157	21	38	62	9	0	5	27	1	0	5	25	1	44	0	1	2	.395	.364
Thompson, Alva, Dan.	.361	11	43	36	7	13	24	3	1	2	10	0	1	0	6	0	10	0	0	0	.667	.442
Torres, Franklin, Eliz.	.251	52	223	187	44	47	81	7	3	7	30	0	0	4	32	0	60	12	3	3	.433	.372
Torres, Frederick, Pul.	.304	60	254	240	35	73	116	19	0	8	45	4	0	3	7	0	53	1	0	10	.483	.332
Torres, Gabby, Eliz.	.250	7	30	24	5	6	10	1	0	1	3	1	0	1	4	0	1	1	1	3	.417	.379
Torres, Jason, Pul.*	.277	25	78	65	18	18	36	4	1	4	8	0	0	1	12	0	16	0	0	0	.554	.397
Torres, Reynaldo, J.C.	.152	36	116	105	8	16	25	6	0	1	10	0	2	3	6	0	52	1	0	1	.238	.216
Tucker, Mamon, Blue.	.253	58	264	233	52	59	78	9	5	0	18	0	0	2	29	0	44	7	1	9	.335	.341
Vasquez, Geraldo, J.C.	.228	49	190	167	28	38	59	6	0	5	25	5	0	5	13	0	43	7	5	4	.353	.303
Velazquez, Gil, King.	.262	62	253	225	24	59	70	8	0	1	19	2	4	3	19	0	43	4	1	5	.311	.324
Volquez, Bolivar, Prin.	.272	58	219	202	23	55	68	8	1	1	20	1	0	3	13	0	57	9	4	5	.337	.326
Wandall, Chad, Eliz.	.247	65	321	271	56	67	87	12	1	2	27	1	2	1	46	0	71	6	4	6	.321	.356
Warriax, Brandon, Pul.	.254	65	261	232	44	59	99	9	2	9	35	6	2	3	18	0	68	11	1	3	.427	.314
West, Kevin, Eliz.	.314	63	269	229	43	72	132	12	6	12	55	0	2	16	22	2	68	4	2	3	.576	.409
Williamson, Bryan, Eliz.	.254	24	76	67	6	17	22	3	1	0	6	1	0	1	7	0	11	0	1	2	.328	.343
Wright, Gavin, Mar.	.309	61	263	236	37	73	102	17	3	2	29	0	1	1	25	0	46	31	2	0	.432	.376
Yancy, Michael, King.	.284	65	247	215	36	61	79	6	3	2	29	2	2	13	15	0	50	24	7	2	.367	.343
Zaragoza, Anthony, King.	.155	36	105	84	8	13	17	2	1	0	3	1	1	4	15	0	27	4	2	0	.202	.308
Zardis, Alex, King.	.116	33	52	43	10	5	9	4	0	0	3	1	0	1	7	0	18	0	3	0	.209	.255

GRAND SLAMS: Delgado, Salargo, 2 each; Acuna, Baez, Betemit, DeSchenes, Dillard, Gordon, Manuel, Nolasco, Perez, Sandberg, Schuda, 1 each.

AWARDED FIRST BASE ON CATCHER'S INTERFERENCE: Fiore 2 (Collura, Rickon); Crawford (Collura); Diaz (Jackson); Heffernan (Quintero).

1999 PITCHING

TEAM

Team	W	L	Pct.	ERA	G	CG	ShO	Sv.	IP	H	TBF	R	ER	HR	SH	SF	HB	BB	IBB	SO	WP	Bk.
Martinsville	41	29	.586	3.58	70	2	3	23	610.1	556	2632	323	243	44	20	13	62	245	1	646	70	12
Bristol	45	24	.652	3.89	69	4	4	25	592.1	596	2625	346	256	42	17	14	38	242	7	662	60	15
Pulaski	48	21	.696	4.01	69	4	8	20	590.0	579	2611	343	263	49	6	21	53	262	3	589	50	15
Kingsport	34	36	.486	4.32	70	2	2	12	612.0	595	2747	369	294	40	21	21	49	314	15	603	76	10
Elizabethton	40	30	.571	4.35	70	1	3	16	612.0	658	2799	390	296	51	18	18	47	258	4	602	79	5
Danville	38	31	.551	4.48	69	0	2	15	597.0	611	2690	398	297	39	15	16	52	248	1	614	66	15
Burlington	21	49	.300	4.66	70	1	1	9	602.1	634	2744	429	312	54	26	25	33	269	7	617	90	14
Johnson City	30	39	.435	4.77	69	1	5	12	611.1	637	2744	408	324	46	16	16	38	268	5	584	58	17
Bluefield	25	43	.368	5.76	68	1	0	9	584.2	696	2767	505	374	62	14	17	50	291	0	571	68	10
Princeton	25	45	.357	6.30	70	0	0	13	594.1	722	2885	544	416	64	10	27	51	343	3	483	128	15

INDIVIDUAL

TOP QUALIFIERS FOR EARNED-RUN AVERAGE TITLE

Minimum 56 innings. *Lefthanded pitcher.

Pitcher, Team	W	L	Pct.	ERA	G	GS	CG	ShO	GF	Sv.	IP	H	TBF	R	ER	HR	SH	SF	HB	BB	IBB	SO	WP	Bk.
Lewis, Colby, Pul.	7	3	.700	1.95	14	11	1	1	0	0	64.2	46	280	24	14	3	0	3	7	27	0	84	3	4
Harang, Aaron, Pul.	9	2	.818	2.30	16	16	1	1	6	1	78.1	64	309	22	20	5	2	3	4	17	1	87	2	1
Dittfurth, Ryan, Pul.	7	2	.778	2.60	14	14	1	0	0	0	83.0	66	361	35	24	4	0	1	15	42	0	85	6	2
Stanford, Derek, Mar.	4	4	.500	2.87	11	9	0	0	1	0	59.2	39	250	28	19	2	3	1	11	25	0	75	8	0
Valera, Nelson, Prin.	5	2	.714	2.91	23	1	0	0	3	0	58.2	55	242	26	19	7	0	3	2	15	0	52	7	1
Simpson, Andre, Bris.	7	1	.875	3.00	13	13	1	0	0	0	72.0	69	297	33	24	2	2	3	1	22	0	79	6	0
Majewski, Gary, Bris.	7	1	.875	3.05	13	13	1	1	0	0	76.2	67	325	34	26	4	4	1	7	37	0	91	1	0
Chenard, Kenneth, King.	6	3	.667	3.07	14	13	1	0	0	0	76.1	64	317	32	26	6	1	4	3	25	1	80	8	2
Sprague, Kevin, J.C.*	5	3	.625	3.23	11	11	0	0	0	0	64.0	47	264	27	23	4	3	2	2	27	0	73	3	4
Mendez, David, Dan.*	6	3	.667	3.25	12	12	0	0	0	0	61.0	61	273	32	22	6	2	0	2	28	0	74	5	0
Griffiths, Jeremy, King.	3	5	.375	3.30	14	14	1	0	0	0	76.1	68	321	40	28	6	1	3	1	36	1	74	5	1
Sturdy, Tim, Eliz.	6	1	.857	3.31	12	12	0	0	0	0	73.1	71	311	33	27	2	3	1	4	17	0	64	9	1
Graham, Frank, King.	3	3	.500	3.71	14	14	0	0	0	0	80.0	69	348	42	33	4	1	1	7	33	0	79	7	1
Nunez, Jose, King.*	3	4	.429	3.75	13	13	0	0	0	0	69.2	75	296	36	29	6	0	2	4	15	0	63	4	0
Parker, Daniel, Mar.	6	4	.600	3.91	14	13	1	0	0	0	73.2	77	324	47	32	5	1	1	6	30	0	71	19	0

DEPARTMENTAL LEADERS: W—Harang, 9; L—Vandermeer, Whitecotton, 8 each; Pct.—Majewski, Simpson, .875; G—Stokes, 33; GS—several players tied, 14 each; CG—several players tied, 1 each; ShO—several players tied, 1 each; GF—Stokes, 27; Sv.—Ramirez, 17; IP—Dittfurth, 83.0; H—Pridie, 93; TBF—Caraballo, 352; R—Knapp, 77; ER—Knapp, 63; HR—Knapp, 14; SH—Rosario, 7; SF—Houle, 6; HB—Dittfurth, 15; BB—Veras, 50; IBB—Chivers, Christ, Polk, 3 each; SO—Majewski, 91; WP—Waechter, 21; BK—Caraballo, 5.

ALL PITCHERS

*Lefthanded pitcher.

Pitcher, Team	W	L	Pct.	ERA	G	GS	CG	ShO	GF	Sv.	IP	H	TBF	R	ER	HR	SH	SF	HB	BB	IBB	SO	WP	Bk.
Andrade, Jancy, Blue.	1	0	1.000	2.87	3	3	0	0	0	0	15.2	17	65	8	5	1	1	1	1	0	0	16	1	0
Armstrong, Charles, Prin.*	0	0	.000	13.50	3	0	0	0	0	0	2	7	18	5	4	0	0	1	0	3	0	2	0	1
Babula, Shaun, Blue.*	1	0	1.000	1.13	4	0	0	0	0	0	8.0	4	33	2	1	0	0	0	5	10	0	10	0	0
Backsmeyer, Justin, Pul.	3	1	.750	6.75	12	7	0	0	0	0	42.2	55	211	41	32	8	0	0	5	30	0	31	10	2
Banez, Marco, J.C.*	0	0	.000	36.00	1	0	0	0	0	0	1.0	4	8	4	4	1	0	0	0	1	0	1	0	0
Barr, Adam, Burl.*	0	4	.000	7.50	9	7	0	0	0	0	18.0	21	105	22	15	0	1	0	4	28	0	21	2	0

Pitcher, Team	W	L	Pct.	ERA	G	GS	CG	ShO	GF	Sv.	IP	H	TBF	R	ER	HR	SH	SF	HB	BB	IBB	SO	WP	Bk.
Barrett, Jimmy, Mar.	0	1	.000	4.42	6	3	0	0	1	0	18.1	15	82	9	9	0	1	1	4	10	1	12	2	1
Belisle, Matthew, Dan.	2	5	.286	4.67	14	14	0	0	0	0	71.1	86	329	50	37	3	0	2	8	23	0	60	6	2
Bonilla, Juan, Blue.	0	0	.000	18.00	1	0	0	0	1	0	1.0	2	8	3	2	1	0	0	1	1	0	1	0	0
Brewer, Dustin, Blue.	0	0	.000	0.00	1	0	0	0	0	0	1.0	2	6	1	0	0	0	0	0	1	0	0	0	0
Brown, Graeme, King.	4	3	.571	3.50	18	3	0	0	3	1	46.1	47	203	24	18	6	3	1	4	19	1	46	5	0
Brown, Tighe, Bris.	1	2	.333	10.24	7	0	0	0	4	1	9.2	18	52	12	11	1	1	1	0	5	1	11	0	0
Bullock, Jeremiah, Pul.*	2	3	.400	5.72	13	13	0	0	0	0	67.2	78	315	60	43	7	1	3	6	31	0	39	10	3
Button, Sammy, Burl.*	1	5	.167	5.19	13	12	0	0	0	0	50.1	55	236	38	29	3	1	2	5	26	0	44	8	0
Campbell, Jarrett, Prin.	4	2	.667	5.05	11	9	0	0	0	0	46.1	51	215	35	26	3	1	3	5	15	0	29	7	3
Caraballo, Angel, Bris.	8	2	.800	4.00	13	13	1	0	0	0	81.0	88	352	40	36	11	2	0	4	27	0	88	10	5
Cenate, Joshua, Blue.*	1	5	.167	4.46	9	9	0	0	0	0	38.1	45	183	32	19	1	3	2	3	20	0	55	5	2
Cento, Anthony, Eliz.*	1	2	.333	1.86	18	0	0	0	14	5	19.1	22	90	6	4	1	1	0	1	6	1	35	1	0
Chavez, Christopher, Dan.	1	1	.500	3.75	11	0	0	0	10	4	12.0	9	50	5	5	0	0	1	5	0	15	1	1
Chenard, Kenneth, King.	6	3	.667	3.07	14	13	1	0	0	0	76.1	64	317	32	26	6	1	4	3	25	1	80	8	2
Chivers, Jason, King.*	3	1	.750	4.26	20	1	0	0	10	0	25.1	29	137	18	12	0	2	2	3	29	3	30	2	1
Christ, John, Burl.	3	4	.429	4.08	23	0	0	0	19	4	35.1	35	158	19	16	3	3	1	1	18	3	36	2	0
Clifton, Derek, Dan.	4	4	.500	6.60	13	13	0	0	0	0	60.0	81	273	52	44	3	1	1	2	16	0	46	4	3
Colon, Jose, Burl.	2	0	1.000	3.24	13	0	0	0	4	0	25.0	19	107	14	9	4	1	2	1	6	1	29	8	1
Cooke, Andrew, Eliz.*	1	4	.200	5.27	16	9	0	0	0	0	54.2	65	246	44	32	8	3	2	2	9	0	58	6	0
Cromer, Jason, Prin.*	1	5	.167	7.46	11	8	0	0	1	0	41.0	69	204	45	34	6	2	0	3	14	0	26	9	0
Cromer, Nathan, Prin.*	0	4	.000	11.44	13	7	0	0	0	0	39.1	72	228	69	50	7	1	2	1	33	1	28	10	1
Crudale, Mike, J.C.	0	1	.000	3.27	24	0	0	0	8	1	33.0	29	142	15	12	1	1	0	1	14	0	36	5	0
Cullen, Ryan, Pul.*	1	2	.333	3.54	19	0	0	0	12	6	40.2	33	169	20	16	1	1	0	1	17	0	47	7	0
Curreri, Joseph, Bris.	1	0	1.000	2.92	16	0	0	0	12	5	24.2	17	103	10	8	2	0	1	3	9	0	24	0	0
Curtis, Tom, Dan.*	2	2	.500	4.45	18	0	0	0	10	3	32.1	35	143	25	16	1	2	0	1	9	0	48	6	0
Daboin, Jorge, Burl.	1	1	.500	3.73	15	0	0	0	7	1	31.1	29	130	16	13	2	1	2	1	9	0	26	3	1
Dailey, Matt, Prin.*	0	0	.000	1.29	4	0	0	0	1	0	7.0	5	30	1	1	0	0	0	2	3	0	6	0	1
Denney, Kyle, Burl.	3	4	.429	3.44	12	3	0	0	4	1	34.0	26	143	17	13	7	4	1	2	15	0	37	2	3
Dittfurth, Ryan, Pul.	7	2	.778	2.60	14	14	1	1	0	0	83.0	66	361	35	24	4	0	1	15	42	0	85	6	2
Dittmer, Greg, Prin.*	1	3	.250	3.27	28	0	0	0	7	1	44.0	48	202	28	16	2	0	2	5	16	0	32	0	1
Dukeman, Gregory, Dan.	0	1	.000	3.38	17	0	0	0	6	2	24.0	30	113	16	9	2	0	0	2	6	1	21	3	1
Ennis, John, Dan.	4	3	.571	5.07	13	13	0	0	0	0	65.2	71	296	46	37	7	3	2	9	21	0	60	3	2
Eyre, Willie, Eliz.	6	3	.667	4.53	16	10	1	0	1	0	57.2	60	270	38	29	4	2	0	4	34	0	59	7	1
Ferguson, Tony, Mar.	0	2	.000	2.20	15	0	0	0	13	3	32.2	27	131	12	8	1	1	1	2	6	0	32	4	1
Fiora, Chris, J.C.	0	3	.000	8.69	18	0	0	0	11	2	19.2	27	103	21	19	4	0	1	1	14	0	31	3	0
Fischer, Sean, Blue.*	1	2	.333	6.89	17	1	0	0	5	0	32.2	38	164	37	25	3	3	2	1	24	0	32	10	0
Fitzgerald, Ryan, Mar.	1	1	.500	5.11	12	0	0	0	2	0	24.2	24	111	20	14	4	0	1	0	6	0	22	1	0
Flock, Rick, Eliz.	2	3	.400	4.55	22	0	0	0	9	3	27.2	30	122	19	14	4	0	1	1	7	1	37	2	0
Foster, John, Dan.*	4	1	.800	1.38	18	0	0	0	7	1	39.0	28	148	10	6	0	5	2	6	0	36	4	0
Frendling, Neal, Prin.	2	1	.667	2.50	4	3	0	0	0	0	18.0	16	76	8	5	1	0	0	2	5	0	18	2	0
Frias, Juan, Prin.	2	2	.500	5.84	30	0	0	0	16	2	37.0	40	175	28	24	3	0	0	1	18	0	38	6	0
Gomez, Rafael, King.	3	3	.500	4.66	25	0	0	0	11	4	36.2	35	163	21	19	1	3	3	2	20	2	23	2	1
Graham, Frank, King.	3	3	.500	3.71	14	14	0	0	0	0	80.0	69	348	42	33	4	1	1	7	33	0	79	7	1
Graves, Donovan, J.C.	3	1	.750	3.71	19	5	0	0	5	1	43.2	40	187	24	18	3	2	2	1	17	0	51	2	0
Griffiths, Jeremy, King.	3	5	.375	3.30	14	14	1	0	0	0	76.1	68	321	40	28	6	1	3	1	36	1	74	5	1
Grippo, Mike, J.C.*	0	1	.000	8.35	14	0	0	0	1	1	18.1	21	88	18	17	2	1	4	1	12	0	18	1	1
Guerrier, Matt, Bris.	5	0	1.000	1.05	21	0	0	0	19	10	25.2	18	109	9	3	1	0	2	1	14	2	37	1	1
Harang, Aaron, Pul.	9	2	.818	2.30	16	10	1	1	6	1	78.1	64	309	22	20	5	2	3	4	17	1	87	2	1
Hee, Aaron, King.*	0	4	.000	7.58	12	12	0	0	0	0	48.2	64	250	48	41	4	1	0	8	37	0	38	10	0
Hernandez, Carlos, Mar.*	5	1	.833	1.79	13	9	0	0	0	0	55.1	36	227	21	11	2	1	1	6	23	0	82	6	0
Hollingsworth, Scott, Pul.	0	1	.000	5.49	12	0	0	0	5	0	19.2	24	95	18	12	3	0	1	1	4	0	20	2	0
Houle, Marc, Blue.	0	3	.000	7.16	20	0	0	0	7	0	44.0	57	212	44	35	5	0	6	5	27	0	36	10	4
James, Nicholas, King.	0	0	.000	0.00	2	0	0	0	1	0	1.0	1	5	0	0	0	0	0	0	1	0	2	1	0
Johnson, Derrick, Mar.*	2	2	.500	4.18	21	0	0	0	11	0	47.1	32	198	23	22	6	2	0	6	32	0	46	2	2
Jones, Sean, Blue.	1	3	.250	6.12	13	11	0	0	0	0	60.1	82	302	54	41	3	0	5	33	0	52	3	0
Kane, Kyle, Bris.	2	0	1.000	2.57	5	5	0	0	0	0	28.0	19	112	8	8	2	2	0	2	11	0	23	3	0
Kann, Kristopher, Mar.	0	2	.000	7.82	9	6	0	0	1	0	25.1	36	129	26	22	2	1	2	4	16	0	16	5	0
Knapp, Ben, Blue.	4	6	.400	9.24	14	14	0	0	0	0	61.1	88	320	77	63	12	2	1	13	40	0	50	10	1
Koeth, Mark, Burl.	3	4	.429	5.32	20	2	0	0	4	1	47.1	55	222	40	28	8	3	2	3	19	0	51	12	0
Kolb, Jason, Prin.*	0	0	.000	10.13	2	0	0	0	1	0	2.2	4	14	3	3	2	0	0	1	0	1	0	0
Latham, Jason, Mar.	3	3	.500	5.20	15	6	0	0	3	0	45.0	51	208	35	26	7	1	1	3	19	0	45	3	1
Layne, Roger, Burl.	1	2	.333	4.50	11	0	0	0	2	1	30.0	36	142	23	15	4	1	2	1	8	1	22	6	0
Lelless, Alexander, Dan.	1	0	1.000	7.07	18	0	0	0	4	1	28.0	35	137	26	22	1	0	2	18	0	20	5	1
Lewis, Colby, Pul.	7	3	.700	1.95	14	11	1	1	0	0	64.2	46	280	24	14	3	0	3	7	27	0	84	3	4
Lockridge, Sherwin, Eliz.	1	1	.500	6.11	16	0	0	0	4	0	17.2	18	91	17	12	3	2	0	5	16	0	21	3	0
Lugo, Carlos, Burl.	0	1	.000	0.00	3	0	0	0	3	0	3.0	2	14	1	0	0	0	0	0	2	0	1	1	1
Macias, Jose, Burl.	0	2	.000	8.73	26	0	0	0	4	1	28.2	30	139	28	25	3	0	0	25	0	37	10	1
Majewski, Gary, Bris.	7	1	.875	3.05	13	13	1	1	0	0	76.2	67	325	34	26	4	4	1	7	37	0	91	1	0
Manning, Mike, Burl.	0	2	.000	4.50	4	0	0	0	1	0	8.0	9	39	6	4	0	2	1	0	4	2	9	2	0
Mansfield, Doug, Prin.	0	0	.000	0.00	1	0	0	0	0	0	2.0	4	10	0	0	0	0	0	2	0	0	0	0
Mastrolonardo, David, Blue.	0	0	.000	0.00	1	0	0	0	0	0	1.2	0	5	0	0	0	0	0	0	0	2	1	0
Mazur, Graham, Bris.*	2	2	.500	2.05	10	0	0	0	3	0	22.0	17	87	7	5	0	1	0	3	0	34	3	0
McClung, Michael, Prin.	2	4	.333	7.69	13	10	0	0	0	0	45.2	53	244	47	39	3	0	1	9	48	0	46	20	0
McGinnis, Johnny, Dan.	6	5	.545	5.01	14	14	0	0	0	0	70.0	70	312	48	39	4	0	1	8	23	0	70	8	0
McKey, Dustin, Prin.	1	1	.500	8.73	26	0	0	0	9	0	44.1	62	221	49	43	10	1	1	5	18	1	31	8	2
McWhirter, Kristopher, Bris.	0	1	.000	4.21	12	1	0	0	5	2	25.2	25	116	16	12	2	1	1	12	0	23	2	5
Melson, Nate, Eliz.	3	1	.750	2.48	22	0	0	0	5	2	36.1	40	166	22	10	2	2	0	4	10	1	23	3	0
Mendez, David, Dan.*	6	3	.667	3.25	12	12	0	0	0	0	61.0	61	273	32	22	6	2	0	2	28	0	74	5	0
Mikels, Jason, Dan.	1	2	.333	2.65	16	3	0	0	5	1	37.1	32	168	20	11	4	0	2	4	16	0	42	4	4
Mikkola, Shaun, King.	0	0	.000	10.64	9	0	0	0	5	0	11.0	17	62	13	13	1	0	1	12	0	10	4	0
Mozingo, Daniel, Bris.*	4	7	.364	6.04	13	13	1	0	0	0	67.0	79	323	59	45	3	0	1	7	32	0	68	14	1
Nowakowski, Brian, Eliz.	1	0	1.000	3.05	16	0	0	0	5	0	20.2	17	99	12	7	3	0	2	4	11	0	26	3	0
Nunez, Jose, King.*	3	4	.429	3.75	13	13	0	0	0	0	69.2	75	296	36	29	6	0	4	6	13	0	63	4	0
Olivo, Carlos, J.C.	2	1	.667	4.22	6	6	0	0	0	0	32.0	35	144	19	15	2	0	4	13	1	31	4	1
Ormond, Rodney, Blue.	1	0	1.000	0.00	4	0	0	0	4	0	9.1	2	36	4	0	0	0	1	0	3	0	11	1	0

Pitcher, Team	W	L	Pct.	ERA	G	GS	CG	ShO	GF	Sv.	IP	H	TBF	R	ER	HR	SH	SF	HB	BB	IBB	SO	WP	Bk.
Parker, Daniel, Mar.	6	4	.600	3.91	14	13	1	0	0	0	73.2	73	324	47	32	5	1	1	6	30	0	71	19	0
Parker, Matt, J.C.	1	1	.500	2.59	23	0	0	0	15	2	31.1	22	124	13	9	3	1	0	0	11	2	43	2	0
Perez, Elvis, Dan.	2	1	.667	9.82	21	0	0	0	4	0	29.1	37	157	42	32	6	0	3	6	22	0	28	5	1
Perez, Randy, Blue.*	4	3	.571	2.70	14	5	1	0	4	0	50.0	51	211	26	15	4	0	1	2	12	0	39	4	0
Perkins, Mike, J.C.	6	1	.857	4.09	15	11	0	0	1	0	61.2	71	270	34	28	2	0	2	2	19	0	50	1	2
Plank, Terry, Blue.	1	3	.250	6.68	20	1	0	0	6	0	32.1	42	152	26	24	6	1	0	2	12	0	46	4	2
Polk, Scott, King.	4	5	.444	3.19	23	0	0	0	11	4	48.0	32	207	24	17	2	3	1	3	30	3	70	9	2
Polo, Bienvenido, J.C.	0	5	.000	12.96	20	0	0	0	5	0	25.0	47	147	47	36	3	0	1	6	19	0	11	5	1
Poplin, Paul, Eliz.	6	3	.667	4.38	21	0	0	0	11	3	37.0	50	174	25	18	4	1	1	1	11	1	37	5	0
Price, Kevin, Prin.	0	0	.000	9.00	4	0	0	0	1	0	5.0	9	34	14	5	1	0	0	1	5	0	6	2	0
Pridie, Jon, Eliz.	5	6	.455	4.48	14	14	0	0	0	0	76.1	93	347	44	38	4	1	5	5	33	0	64	10	1
Pruitt, Jason, Blue.*	2	4	.333	6.00	17	8	0	0	5	1	54.0	56	245	41	36	9	1	1	1	31	0	57	8	0
Rakers, Aaron, Blue.	0	0	.000	2.57	3	0	0	0	1	0	7.0	5	28	2	2	1	0	0	0	3	0	12	0	0
Ramirez, Enrique, Blue.	0	1	.000	3.07	13	0	0	0	11	1	14.2	18	74	9	5	0	0	1	4	9	0	14	1	0
Ramirez, Santiago, Mar.	2	1	.667	1.45	25	0	0	0	25	17	31.0	26	127	9	5	1	1	0	0	14	1	35	7	1
Rauch, Jon, Bris.	4	4	.500	4.45	14	9	0	0	3	2	56.2	65	264	44	28	4	1	2	3	16	1	66	6	2
Rayborn, Kris, J.C.*	1	7	.125	5.79	13	13	0	0	0	0	65.1	79	301	54	42	2	2	3	8	33	0	34	11	2
Regilio, Nick, Pul.	4	2	.667	1.63	11	8	1	1	0	0	49.2	30	194	12	9	2	0	1	3	16	0	58	4	1
Reynolds, Jacob, Burl.	0	2	.000	9.00	3	3	0	0	0	0	10.0	13	52	14	10	1	0	0	1	8	0	7	2	0
Riveles, Mike, J.C.	0	0	.000	4.91	4	0	0	0	1	0	7.1	12	40	10	4	1	0	0	0	4	0	4	1	0
Rivera, Leyson, Burl.	0	1	.000	7.71	17	0	0	0	10	0	23.1	29	126	30	20	5	2	0	1	19	0	25	6	0
Riviere, Rhett, Eliz.	1	0	1.000	2.25	7	0	0	0	2	0	8.0	7	37	3	2	0	0	1	0	4	0	6	0	0
Rizo, Miguel, J.C.	2	3	.400	3.16	20	0	0	0	4	1	31.1	26	133	12	11	2	0	1	1	14	1	22	5	0
Roberts, Nick, Mar.	4	2	.667	1.90	10	7	1	0	1	1	47.1	43	188	11	10	0	1	0	1	6	0	56	2	3
Rochez, Angel, Pul.	2	1	.667	8.24	18	3	0	0	4	3	39.1	54	191	40	36	8	1	2	2	20	0	29	1	0
Rodriguez, Alfredo, Pul.	0	1	.000	9.72	6	0	0	0	2	0	8.1	13	44	10	9	2	0	1	2	5	0	5	0	2
Rodriguez, Luis, Pul.	0	0	.000	0.00	1	0	0	0	1	0	1.0	2	4	0	0	0	0	0	0	0	0	1	0	0
Rogers, Devin, Burl.	0	2	.000	7.52	8	6	0	0	1	0	20.1	26	99	23	17	0	0	2	0	15	0	21	6	3
Rogers, Lionel, King.	3	1	.750	1.84	14	0	0	0	11	2	29.1	17	121	7	6	1	2	1	1	17	2	34	5	0
Rohling, Stuart, Bris.	0	2	.000	4.41	16	1	0	0	5	1	32.2	34	147	19	16	3	1	0	2	17	0	44	5	0
Rosario, Rodrigo, Mar.	5	5	.500	4.69	14	14	0	0	0	0	78.2	78	345	46	41	9	7	3	11	32	0	86	7	0
Ryba, Jason, Blue.	1	3	.250	5.94	18	3	0	0	2	0	47.0	55	225	40	31	5	2	0	3	23	0	42	5	0
Sadler, Carl, Burl.*	1	0	1.000	3.13	5	5	0	0	0	0	23.0	18	93	10	8	0	1	0	0	10	0	22	5	0
Saladin, Miguel, Mar.	1	1	.500	5.06	11	0	0	0	4	1	16.0	24	79	12	9	1	0	0	4	4	0	19	0	1
Samora, Santo, J.C.	2	0	1.000	2.48	18	2	0	0	4	1	32.2	26	133	12	9	2	1	0	1	11	0	17	2	1
Sanchez, Willmen, Burl.*	0	1	.000	3.22	10	0	0	0	2	1	22.1	26	93	8	8	4	1	0	2	3	0	26	0	1
Schmidt, Pat, Dan.*	0	1	.000	4.76	13	0	0	0	6	0	17.0	9	96	11	9	0	2	3	2	37	0	16	7	0
Schwager, Matthew, Blue.	3	1	.750	3.60	22	0	0	0	21	7	30.0	31	127	19	12	2	0	1	1	5	0	29	2	0
Scuglik, Mike, Pul.*	2	2	.500	3.10	18	0	0	0	8	3	29.0	36	129	15	10	2	0	1	2	10	2	36	1	0
Sents, Marcus, Eliz.	5	1	.833	6.14	13	13	0	0	0	0	63.0	56	295	48	43	8	1	1	7	48	0	60	15	1
Sheets, Matt, Eliz.	3	3	.500	4.79	12	12	0	0	0	0	62.0	69	276	40	33	4	2	1	7	20	0	55	7	0
Shepherd, Alvie, Blue.	1	1	.500	4.00	2	2	0	0	0	0	9.0	11	44	8	4	0	0	1	4	0	0	7	3	0
Silverthorn, Will, Prin.*	0	0	.000	1.86	7	0	0	0	4	0	9.2	16	52	10	2	0	0	0	1	7	0	9	5	0
Simpson, Andre, Bris.	7	1	.875	3.00	13	13	1	0	0	0	72.0	69	297	33	24	2	3	1	22	0	79	6	0
Sirianni, Jay, Burl.*	1	5	.167	4.50	11	10	1	0	0	0	56.0	62	245	36	28	6	2	1	3	12	0	66	3	0
Smith, Brandon, Mar.	2	0	1.000	1.35	8	0	0	0	5	0	13.1	6	52	3	2	1	0	1	0	10	0	10	2	0
Smith, Matthew, King.	1	1	.500	10.88	18	0	0	0	4	0	24.0	33	132	35	29	2	0	3	5	20	1	28	8	2
Spooneybarger, Tim, Dan.	3	0	1.000	2.22	12	0	0	0	2	0	24.1	15	103	11	6	0	0	2	14	0	36	5	0
Sprague, Kevin, J.C.*	5	3	.625	3.23	11	11	0	0	0	0	64.0	47	264	27	23	4	3	2	27	0	73	3	4
Stanford, Derek, Mar.	4	4	.500	2.87	11	9	0	0	1	0	59.2	39	250	28	19	2	3	1	11	25	0	75	8	0
Stewart, Joshua, Bris.*	1	0	1.000	1.50	5	0	0	0	2	1	18.0	13	71	5	3	0	1	0	2	5	0	25	0	0
Stokes, Brian, Prin.	2	3	.400	3.89	33	0	0	0	27	9	37.0	33	163	20	16	2	2	1	1	21	0	39	8	1
Sturdy, Tim, Eliz.	6	1	.857	3.31	12	12	0	0	0	0	73.1	71	311	33	27	2	3	1	4	17	0	64	9	1
Sunderman, Nick, Burl.*	1	0	1.000	3.60	16	0	0	0	2	0	30.0	30	135	17	12	1	1	1	3	15	0	42	3	3
Sweeney, Mike, King.	1	3	.250	5.64	19	0	0	0	8	1	30.1	34	136	20	19	1	2	0	4	11	1	20	2	0
Teekel, Josh, J.C.	2	3	.400	5.35	8	8	0	0	0	0	33.2	41	157	26	20	4	0	0	4	8	0	42	2	3
Tejeda, Franklin, J.C.	2	1	.667	3.08	14	2	0	0	4	1	26.1	24	115	15	9	0	2	1	7	0	28	3	1
Tomaszewski, Eliot, Blue.	0	0	.000	7.20	1	1	0	0	0	0	5.0	8	23	5	4	0	0	1	1	0	1	0	0
Tommassi, Carlos, Burl.	1	1	.500	3.55	12	0	0	0	5	0	25.1	29	119	22	10	0	1	2	1	9	0	24	6	0
Underhill, Ray, Eliz.	0	1	.000	7.20	17	0	0	0	6	0	25.0	36	128	24	20	2	0	2	1	15	0	18	5	1
Valdez, Domingo, Pul.	0	0	.000	6.75	3	3	0	0	0	0	16.0	20	74	14	12	2	0	1	2	7	0	14	2	0
Valentine, Joseph, Bris.	0	0	.000	7.02	11	0	0	0	7	0	16.2	27	90	17	13	2	0	3	3	9	0	14	1	1
Valera, Nelson, Prin.	5	2	.714	2.91	23	1	0	0	3	1	58.2	55	242	26	19	7	0	3	15	0	52	7	1
Vandermeer, Scott, Prin.	2	8	.200	6.63	14	11	0	0	0	0	58.1	58	269	54	43	10	2	4	2	36	0	32	13	2
Vasquez, Luis, Mar.*	6	1	.857	2.79	13	3	0	0	1	1	42.0	46	181	21	13	3	0	0	4	12	0	39	2	2
Veras, Enger, Prin.	3	5	.375	7.12	14	14	0	0	0	0	60.2	74	299	57	48	5	1	4	7	50	1	48	10	1
Veronie, Shanin, Dan.	2	2	.500	0.70	18	0	0	0	15	3	25.2	12	92	4	2	2	0	0	1	4	0	42	0	0
Vincentq, Matt, J.C.*	1	2	.333	3.81	24	0	0	0	8	2	28.1	24	127	14	12	3	2	1	1	18	1	36	1	1
Wade, Matt, Burl.	3	3	.500	1.09	7	7	0	0	0	0	33.0	26	130	10	4	1	0	1	1	3	0	33	2	0
Waechter, Doug, Prin.	0	5	.000	9.77	11	7	0	0	0	0	35.0	46	189	45	38	2	0	5	4	35	0	38	21	1
Wallace, Shane, Burl.*	1	5	.167	5.25	12	12	0	0	0	0	48.0	58	217	35	28	2	1	5	3	15	0	38	1	0
Weaver, Joseph, Pul.	6	0	1.000	6.43	18	0	0	0	8	0	21.0	30	107	17	15	1	0	0	1	5	0	17	1	0
Weis, John, Eliz.*	0	1	.000	2.16	26	0	0	0	12	3	33.1	24	147	15	8	2	0	1	1	17	0	39	3	0
Wessel, Travis, Pul.*	5	1	.833	4.03	21	0	0	0	19	7	29.0	28	128	15	13	1	1	4	2	11	0	36	1	0
West, Brian, Bris.	1	2	.333	10.50	8	1	0	0	2	2	18.0	26	98	25	21	4	1	0	1	14	2	17	5	0
Wheeler, David, King.	0	0	.000	4.00	7	0	0	0	4	0	9.0	10	49	9	4	0	2	0	3	9	0	6	4	0
Whitecotton, Billy, Blue.	3	8	.273	7.22	15	10	0	0	0	0	62.1	82	304	67	50	9	1	0	6	37	0	60	19	1
Wright, Daniel, Bris.	2	0	1.000	1.00	10	0	0	0	3	1	18.0	14	79	8	2	1	0	0	1	9	1	18	3	0
Zazueta, Peter, J.C.	3	6	.333	5.72	11	11	1	0	0	0	56.2	62	261	43	36	7	1	0	4	26	0	56	7	0

COMBINATION SHUTOUTS: **Bluefield (0)**—None. **Bristol (2)**—Simpson-Rohling-McWhirter, Majewski-Curreri. **Burlington (1)**—Wallace-Denny-Sanchez. **Danville (2)**—McGinnis-Perez-Foster, McGinnis-Dukeman-Veronie. **Elizabethton (3)**—Sturdy-Lockridge-Flock, Pridie-Cento, Sturdy-Riviere-Underhill-Lockridge. **Johnson City (4)**—Zazueta-Grippo-Parker, Teekel-Grippo, Perkins-Rizo-Vincent-Parker, Sprague-Grippo-Fiora. **Kingsport (2)**—Griffiths-Chivers, Nunez-Rogers. **Martinsville (3)**—Roberts-Hernandez-Ferguson, Hernandez-Kann-Roberts, Hernandez-Smith-Ramirez. **Princeton (0)**—None. **Pulaski (4)**—Harang-Wessel, Harang-Cullen, Harang-Rochez, Dittfurth-Scuglik.

NO-HIT GAMES: None.

TEAM

Team	Pct.	G	PO	A	E	TC	DP	TP	PB
Kingsport	.957	70	1836	744	117	2697	55	0	14
Martinsville	.956	70	1831	754	118	2703	59	1	12
Pulaski	.956	69	1770	684	113	2567	50	0	26
Bristol	.951	69	1777	692	128	2597	48	0	9
Johnson City	.949	69	1834	782	141	2757	48	0	18
Elizabethton	.947	70	1836	805	148	2789	42	0	24
Danville	.944	69	1791	725	150	2666	49	0	21
Princeton	.937	70	1783	774	173	2730	52	0	35
Bluefield	.933	68	1754	708	178	2640	58	0	21
Burlington	.931	70	1807	687	185	2679	44	0	17

INDIVIDUAL

FIRST BASEMEN

NOTE: All caps denotes fielding-percentage leader based on 35 games for catchers, 47 for all other non-pitchers and 56 innings for pitchers. *Throws lefthanded.

Player, Team	Pct.	G	PO	A	E	TC	DP
Acosta, Emilio, J.C.	.667	2	2	0	1	3	0
Aguirregaviria, Frank, Bris.	1.000	2	5	0	0	5	1
Albertson, Justin, J.C.	1.000	1	1	0	0	1	0
Alvarez, Nell, King.	.667	3	2	0	1	3	0
Banez, Marco, J.C.*	1.000	2	12	1	0	13	0
Batista, Carlos, Burl.	.974	44	348	28	10	386	22
Berrien, Samuel, Blue.*	.965	23	151	14	6	171	17
Bonilla, Juan, Blue.	.959	25	172	15	8	195	24
Brazell, Craig, King.	.986	30	257	15	4	276	17
Carrillo, Robert, Mar.	.997	42	356	27	1	384	28
CROCKER, Nickolas, Dan.*	.992	52	446	30	4	480	33
Delgado, Chris, Bris.	.978	58	456	22	11	489	37
Deschenes, Pat, King.	.995	25	176	7	1	184	11
Diaz, Aneuris, J.C.	1.000	1	1	0	0	1	1
Duncan, Chris, J.C.	.977	53	497	24	12	533	36
Elder, Rick, Blue.*	.964	23	182	7	7	196	10
Finnerty, Francis, Burl.	1.000	2	18	5	0	23	1
Fiore, Curt, Dan.	.986	16	133	9	2	144	9
Garza, Rolando, Bris.	.983	8	58	0	1	59	6
Griffin, Justin, Burl.	1.000	1	2	0	0	2	1
Guyton, Eric, King.	.939	6	29	2	2	33	2
Harrelson, Casey, Bris.	1.000	8	35	1	0	36	1
Hunter, David, King.*	.978	18	86	5	2	93	10
Jones, Jason, Pul.	.980	67	551	30	12	593	42
Jordan, Yustin, Eliz.	1.000	2	9	1	0	10	0
Lough, Aaron, Eliz.	1.000	6	28	4	0	32	2
Lugo, Roberto, King.*	.986	20	69	3	1	73	10
Moyer, Kyle, Burl.*	.967	28	189	17	7	213	12
Nanita, Manny, Eliz.	1.000	2	10	0	0	10	0
Nelson, Timothy, Blue.	.950	4	16	3	1	20	2
Ortiz, Daniel, Prin.	.945	21	162	9	10	181	13
Osorio, Isrrael, Prin.	.967	51	434	39	16	489	31
O'Sullivan, Patrick, King.	1.000	1	3	0	0	3	0
Ramirez, Anthony, Mar.	1.000	1	8	2	0	10	0
Redman, Prentice, King.	.000	1	0	0	0	0	0
Salas, Juan, Prin.	1.000	1	1	0	0	1	0
Sandberg, Eric, Eliz.*	.986	66	586	39	9	634	36
Santamarina, Juan, Bris.	1.000	1	10	0	0	10	1
Schmitt, Brian, Mar.*	.981	29	250	10	5	265	27
Schuda, Justin, Prin.	1.000	2	10	0	0	10	2
Terveen, Bryce, Dan.	1.000	1	9	0	0	9	2
Torres, Jason, Pul.	1.000	3	15	1	0	16	1
Torres, Reynaldo, J.C.	.979	18	134	3	3	140	7
Guyton, Eric, King.	.000	1	0	0	0	0	0
Harris, Willie, Blue.	.966	5	15	13	1	29	4
Hernandez, Carlos, King.	1.000	1	1	2	0	3	0
Huffman, Royce, Mar.	1.000	3	1	9	0	10	0
Isenia, Chairon, Prin.	.750	1	2	1	1	4	0
Jaramillo, Tony, Pul.	.962	12	23	28	2	53	3
Kane, Patrick, Mar.	.951	34	40	96	7	143	16
Kann, Kristopher, Mar.	1.000	1	0	1	0	1	0
Lockridge, Sherwin, Eliz.	1.000	4	6	7	0	13	1
Lopez, Aristides, Mar.	1.000	1	1	0	0	1	0
Maya, Johan, Mar.	.964	23	28	53	3	84	15
NOLASCO, Regino, Blue.	.957	50	121	124	11	256	31
Pichardo, Henry, Burl.	.933	60	80	130	15	225	22
Roman, Junior, Bris.	1.000	1	1	1	0	2	0
Rummel, Jason, Bris.	.981	25	44	57	2	103	17
Salas, Juan, Prin.	.906	22	52	54	11	117	16
Salazar, Ruben, Eliz.	.939	27	53	86	9	148	13
Sowers, Douglas, Blue.	.905	17	35	32	7	74	8
Teilon, Nilson, Bris.	.918	46	68	100	15	183	15
Torres, Franklin, Eliz.	.925	40	68	117	15	200	20
Vasquez, Geraldo, J.C.	.923	11	18	18	3	39	2
Velazquez, Gil, King.	1.000	3	3	8	0	11	1
Zaragoza, Anthony, King.	.910	26	38	43	8	89	12
Zardis, Alex, King.	.857	5	3	3	1	7	0

TRIPLE PLAY: K. Garcia.

SECOND BASEMEN

Player, Team	Pct.	G	PO	A	E	TC	DP
Aaron, Oginga, Prin.	1.000	1	2	1	0	3	0
Abreu, David, King.	.952	5	11	9	1	21	2
Acevedo, Luis, Pul.	1.000	1	1	0	0	1	0
Andrianoff, Jonathan, Mar.	.000	1	0	0	1	1	0
Blankenship, Anthony, Bris.	.944	4	10	7	1	18	2
Centeno, Edwin, Blue.	.000	1	0	0	0	0	0
Centile, Raul, Burl.	.833	5	5	5	2	12	1
Colmenter, Jesus, Burl.	.857	2	2	4	1	7	0
Crisp, Covelli, J.C.	.912	64	101	149	24	274	23
De Caster, Yurendell, Prin.	.942	48	131	144	17	292	26
De La Cruz, Ruddi, King.	.952	48	70	108	9	187	23
Donato, Gregorio, Dan.	.914	30	54	74	12	140	15
Fafard, Mathias, King.	1.000	2	0	4	0	4	0
Garcia, Kevys, Mar.	.922	15	30	41	6	77	11
Garcia, Oscar, Burl.	.962	7	11	14	1	26	4
Green, Kevin, Dan.	.974	41	88	103	5	196	25
Griffin, Justin, Burl.	.800	1	2	2	1	5	1
Guerrero, Pedro, Pul.	.951	60	93	142	12	247	30

THIRD BASEMEN

Player, Team	Pct.	G	PO	A	E	TC	DP
Acevedo, Luis, Pul.	.923	7	6	18	2	26	4
Acosta, Emilio, J.C.	1.000	2	0	1	0	1	0
Aguirregaviria, Frank, Bris.	.800	7	4	8	3	15	0
Blankenship, Anthony, Bris.	.900	4	2	7	1	10	0
Calzado, Napolean, Blue.	.871	23	20	41	9	70	5
Deschenes, Pat, King.	.919	14	11	23	3	37	4
Diaz, Aneuris, J.C.	.914	54	29	110	13	152	6
Diaz, Johnny, J.C.	1.000	2	1	4	0	5	0
Donato, Gregorio, Dan.	.833	5	4	6	2	12	0
Fafard, Mathias, King.	.786	6	1	10	3	14	1
Finnerty, Francis, Burl.	.708	34	19	32	21	72	3
Fiore, Curt, Dan.	.951	30	19	58	4	81	8
Forbes, Michael, Dan.	.785	37	16	68	23	107	3
Garcia, Kevys, Mar.	.918	18	15	41	5	61	3
Garcia, Oscar, Burl.	1.000	1	0	2	0	2	0
Garza, Rolando, Bris.	.846	15	4	18	4	26	0
GUYTON, Eric, King.	.925	51	40	83	10	133	2
Helquist, Jonathan, Mar.	.952	18	9	31	2	42	0
Hernandez, Carlos, King.	.000	3	0	0	2	2	0
Huffman, Royce, Mar.	.892	25	19	47	8	74	5
Jacobs, John, Prin.	.867	60	44	126	26	196	11
Jaramillo, Tony, Pul.	1.000	5	2	13	0	15	2
Jimenez, Jonathan, Pul.	.906	60	40	95	14	149	4
Jordan, Yustin, Eliz.	1.000	1	0	2	0	2	0
Lough, Aaron, Eliz.	.500	1	0	1	1	2	0
Lynn, Brody, Burl.	.783	37	24	48	20	92	6
Maya, Johan, Mar.	.900	3	4	5	1	10	0
Nelson, Timothy, Blue.	.844	26	19	35	10	64	2
Pimentel, Hector, J.C.	.833	3	6	4	2	12	0
Ramirez, Anthony, Mar.	.818	8	5	13	4	22	1
Rummel, Jason, Bris.	.833	7	4	11	3	18	2
Salas, Juan, Prin.	.792	9	5	14	5	24	1
Salazar, Ruben, Eliz.	.889	16	16	32	6	54	3
Santamarina, Juan, Bris.	.879	42	24	78	14	116	5
Scanlon, Matt, Eliz.	.894	53	32	112	17	161	4
Sowers, Douglas, Blue.	.754	26	17	29	15	61	1
Torres, Franklin, Eliz.	.000	1	0	0	0	0	0
Torres, Reynaldo, J.C.	1.000	1	0	1	0	1	0
Vasquez, Geraldo, J.C.	.895	16	9	25	4	38	2
Velazquez, Gil, King.	.000	1	0	0	0	0	0

SUMMER CLASS A *Appalachian League*

Player, Team	Pct.	G	PO	A	E	TC	DP
Volquez, Bolivar, Prin.	.667	2	0	2	1	3	0
Zaragoza, Anthony, King.	1.000	1	0	1	0	1	0
Zardis, Alex, King.	.786	17	5	17	6	28	1

SHORTSTOPS

Player, Team	Pct.	G	PO	A	E	TC	DP
Acevedo, Luis, Pul.	.800	2	1	3	1	5	0
Andrianoff, Jonathan, Mar.	.931	18	28	39	5	72	11
Betemit, Wilson, Dan.	.899	67	92	201	33	326	30
Blankenship, Anthony, Bris.	1.000	3	0	6	0	6	0
Calzado, Napolean, Blue.	.912	29	42	93	13	148	14
Centile, Raul, Burl.	.889	2	5	3	1	9	0
Colmenter, Jesus, Burl.	.878	22	25	61	12	98	9
De La Cruz, Ruddi, King.	.857	7	8	16	4	28	1
De Los Santos, Santo, J.C.	.913	55	69	173	23	265	26
Donato, Gregorio, Dan.	.000	1	0	0	0	0	0
Fiore, Curt, Dan.	.750	2	2	4	2	8	0
Franco, Pascual, J.C.	.000	1	0	0	0	0	0
Garcia, Kevys, Mar.	.883	15	35	33	9	77	8
Garcia, Oscar, Burl.	.865	47	74	124	31	229	19
Garza, Rolando, Bris.	.897	6	12	14	3	29	2
Griffin, Justin, Burl.	1.000	1	1	1	0	2	0
Guerrero, Pedro, Pul.	.800	3	4	8	3	15	0
Gutierrez, Derrick, Blue.	.854	34	45	84	22	151	21
Helquist, Jonathan, Mar.	.877	25	32	68	14	114	13
Jimenez, Jonathan, Pul.	.667	1	1	1	1	3	1
Lockridge, Sherwin, Eliz.	.833	1	0	5	1	6	1
Maya, Johan, Mar.	.968	19	16	45	2	63	6
Nolasco, Regino, Blue.	.946	7	8	27	2	37	5
Roman, Junior, Bris.	.894	42	56	88	17	161	18
Rummel, Jason, Bris.	.829	8	10	24	7	41	4
Salas, Juan, Prin.	.938	18	22	54	5	81	9
Teilon, Nilson, Bris.	.902	20	31	52	9	92	13
Torres, Franklin, Eliz.	.870	7	10	10	3	23	0
Vasquez, Geraldo, J.C.	.866	28	37	47	13	97	9
VELAZQUEZ, Gil, King.	.950	59	87	181	14	282	38
Volquez, Bolivar, Prin.	.932	53	57	164	16	237	24
Wandall, Chad, Eliz.	.891	63	83	204	35	322	26
Warriax, Brandon, Pul.	.920	64	87	189	24	300	31
Zaragoza, Anthony, King.	.870	9	10	10	3	23	1

OUTFIELDERS

Player, Team	Pct.	G	PO	A	E	TC	DP
Acuna, Ronald, King.	.966	35	52	4	2	58	2
Albertson, Justin, J.C.	.935	26	29	0	2	31	0
Almonte, Claudio, Eliz.	.898	34	53	0	6	59	0
Baez, Ernies, Pul.	1.000	8	12	2	0	14	1
Batista, Angel, Prin.*	1.000	7	14	1	0	15	0
Bigbie, Larry, Blue.*	1.000	5	7	1	0	8	0
Blankenship, Anthony, Bris.	.000	1	0	0	0	0	0
Buckley, Chris, J.C.	.800	19	24	0	6	30	0
Cabrera, Raymond, Blue.	.946	23	33	2	2	37	1
Cadiente, Brett, Pul.*	.946	66	121	2	7	130	0
Candelario, Luis, Prin.	.933	7	13	1	1	15	1
Centeno, Edwin, Blue.	.800	2	3	1	1	5	0
Crawford, Carl, Prin.*	.934	58	112	2	8	122	0
Crocker, Nickolas, Dan.*	1.000	1	1	0	0	1	0
Deschenes, Pat, King.	1.000	5	2	1	0	3	0
Durham, Chad, Bris.	.977	67	122	5	3	130	0
Edge, Michael, Burl.	.933	29	40	2	3	45	1
Elder, Rick, Blue.*	.000	1	0	0	0	0	0
Fafard, Mathias, King.	.000	1	0	0	0	0	0
Garbe, Brandon, Eliz.	.883	40	52	1	7	60	0
Garza, Rolando, Bris.	.964	32	27	0	1	28	0
Gordon, Alexis, Blue.*	.878	23	35	1	5	41	0
Griffin, Justin, Burl.	.947	8	16	2	1	19	0
Griswold, Matthew, Blue.	.875	32	48	1	7	56	0
Hambrick, Marcus, Dan.*	.949	37	53	3	3	59	1
Hamilton, Josh, Prin.*	.962	55	96	6	4	106	0
Heffernan, Christian, Dan.	.958	18	22	1	1	24	0
Helena, Roberto, Prin.	.934	59	80	5	6	91	1
Hernandez, Johnny, J.C.*	.961	57	112	10	5	127	0
Holt, Todd, Bris.	.923	36	46	2	4	52	0
Huffman, Royce, Mar.	.889	17	15	1	2	18	0
Ide, Antoine, Blue.	.956	21	41	2	2	45	0
Jackson, Chris, Burl.	.882	10	15	0	2	17	0
Jacobs, John, Prin.	.875	4	7	0	1	8	0
Johnson, Ben, J.C.	.978	54	84	5	2	91	2
Johnson, Eric, Dan.	.971	39	91	8	3	102	1
Jones, Damien, Dan.*	.890	68	99	6	13	118	0
Jones, Jason, Pul.	1.000	3	2	0	0	2	0
Jordan, Yustin, Eliz.	1.000	6	2	1	0	3	1
Kane, Patrick, Mar.	1.000	1	1	0	0	1	0

Player, Team	Pct.	G	PO	A	E	TC	DP
Lama, Jesus, Prin.	.800	7	8	0	2	10	0
Ledesma, Luis, Mar.	.944	26	32	2	2	36	0
Lopez, Aristides, Mar.	.982	36	49	7	1	57	3
Lugo, Carlos, Burl.	.952	22	34	6	2	42	0
Mansfield, Doug, Prin.	.900	16	24	3	3	30	1
Manuel, Marcellous, Bris.*	.955	46	60	3	3	66	0
Mejias, Aureliano, J.C.	1.000	24	31	2	0	33	0
MENCH, Kevin, Pul.	.989	51	85	6	1	92	0
Milton, Prinz, Dan.	.933	35	52	4	4	60	1
Nanita, Manny, Eliz.	.923	14	12	0	1	13	0
Nowlin, Cody, Pul.	.946	48	65	5	4	74	1
Ortiz, Daniel, Prin.	1.000	3	1	0	0	1	0
O'Sullivan, Patrick, King.	1.000	16	27	0	0	27	0
Perez, Juan, J.C.	1.000	41	71	2	0	73	0
Pichardo, Henry, Burl.	1.000	3	9	1	0	10	1
Poe, Adam, Pul.	.977	36	38	4	1	43	1
Redman, Prentice, King.	.938	48	59	1	4	64	0
Reed, Keith, Blue.	.667	3	2	0	1	3	0
Rincon, Carlos, Mar.	.881	54	52	0	7	59	0
Riordan, Matthew, Blue.	1.000	5	13	2	0	15	0
Rivas, Justo, Dan.	.917	60	74	14	8	96	1
Salargo, Steven, Blue.	.918	47	83	7	8	98	0
Salazar, Erick, Mar.	1.000	16	24	1	0	25	0
Santini, Travis, Burl.	.932	44	50	5	4	59	0
Schmitt, Brian, Mar.*	.917	16	10	1	1	12	0
Seale, Marvin, King.	.938	57	86	5	6	97	1
Sherrill, J.J., Burl.	.966	64	139	2	5	146	1
Southward, Deshawn, Eliz.	.951	50	72	5	4	81	1
Stanley, Derek, Bris.	.977	38	40	3	1	44	1
Tucker, Mamon, Blue.	.903	50	52	4	6	62	0
West, Kevin, Eliz.	.951	63	90	7	5	102	1
Williamson, Bryan, Eliz.	1.000	18	12	0	0	12	0
Wright, Gavin, Mar.	.958	61	107	6	5	118	1
Yancy, Michael, King.	.957	59	82	6	4	92	1

CATCHERS

Player, Team	Pct.	G	PO	A	E	TC	DP	PB
Acosta, Emilio, J.C.	.976	29	192	49	6	247	0	9
Aguirregaviria, Frank, Bris.	.917	3	10	1	1	12	0	0
Alvarez, Nell, King.	.973	42	295	66	10	371	2	7
Argento, Shaun, Dan.	.975	15	108	11	3	122	0	3
Bastardo, Angel, Burl.	.981	17	140	16	3	159	0	8
Bonilla, Juan, Blue.	.960	3	23	1	1	25	0	3
Collura, Todd, Eliz.	.970	19	116	12	4	132	2	4
Cruz, Rafael, Pul.	.961	7	64	9	3	76	0	0
Dillard, Thomas, Eliz.	.976	34	249	38	7	294	0	8
Dyer, Matthew, King.	.981	21	93	12	2	107	1	5
Franco, Pascual, J.C.	.968	9	52	9	2	63	0	1
Garcia, Yosnel, Bris.	.967	29	219	46	9	274	0	8
Gentry, Garett, Mar.	.984	18	176	14	3	193	0	4
Gutierrez, Fernando, Blue.	.944	23	144	23	10	177	1	7
Hartley, Will, Burl.	1.000	4	16	3	0	19	0	0
Isenia, Chairon, Prin.	.974	26	155	29	5	189	1	7
Jackson, Chris, Burl.	.977	11	73	12	2	87	0	4
Kessick, Jonathan, Blue.	.983	27	216	20	4	240	3	4
Lantigua, Denys, Burl.	1.000	14	94	22	0	116	1	1
Lopez, Guillermo, Dan.	.982	14	97	13	2	112	0	5
Lough, Aaron, Eliz.	.963	26	188	21	8	217	0	11
Maduro, Jorge, Prin.	.984	24	166	22	3	191	1	12
Monzon, Francisco, Blue.	.986	23	177	36	3	216	2	7
Morla, Gilberto, Burl.	.971	5	25	8	1	34	0	1
O'Connor, Brian, Mar.	1.000	12	90	7	0	97	0	1
Osorio, Isrrael, Prin.	.875	3	11	3	2	16	1	0
Pemberthy, Aaron, J.C.	1.000	1	6	0	0	6	0	0
Perez, Jay, Mar.	.981	22	194	16	4	214	0	6
QUINTERO, Humberto, Bris.	.987	46	401	64	6	471	1	1
Rickon, Jim, Burl.	.971	30	239	30	8	277	0	3
Santillan, Manuel, Mar.	.981	19	177	35	4	216	1	1
Schuda, Justin, Prin.	.954	21	122	22	7	151	0	15
Serrano, Yalian, Prin.	.941	6	16	0	1	17	0	1
Smith, Ryan, King.	1.000	27	194	17	0	211	0	2
Spooner, Brent, J.C.	.977	42	292	43	8	343	3	8
Terveen, Bryce, Dan.	.980	39	301	40	7	348	0	12
Thompson, Alva, Dan.	.988	10	80	3	1	84	0	1
Torres, Frederick, Pul.	.981	50	410	43	9	462	6	20
Torres, Gabby, Eliz.	1.000	6	44	5	0	49	0	1
Torres, Jason, Pul.	.977	17	113	12	3	128	0	6

PITCHERS

Player, Team	Pct.	G	PO	A	E	TC	DP
Andrade, Jancy, Blue.	1.000	3	0	1	0	1	0
Armstrong, Charles, Prin.*	1.000	3	1	0	0	1	0
Babula, Shaun, Blue.*	1.000	4	0	2	0	2	0
Backsmeyer, Justin, Pul.	.941	12	6	10	1	17	0

Player, Team	Pct.	G	PO	A	E	TC	DP
Banez, Marco, J.C.*	.000	1	0	0	0	0	0
Barr, Adam, Burl.*	1.000	9	0	2	0	2	0
Barrett, Jimmy, Mar.	.750	6	1	2	1	4	0
Belisle, Matthew, Dan.	.909	14	5	5	1	11	0
Bonilla, Juan, Blue.	1.000	1	1	0	0	1	0
Brewer, Dustin, Blue.	.000	1	0	0	0	0	0
Brown, Graeme, King.	1.000	18	4	8	0	12	0
Brown, Tighe, Bris.	1.000	7	0	2	0	2	0
Bullock, Jeremiah, Pul.*	.864	13	4	15	3	22	0
Button, Sammy, Burl.*	.800	13	3	5	2	10	0
Campbell, Jarrett, Prin.	.846	11	5	6	2	13	0
Caraballo, Angel, Bris.	1.000	13	5	3	0	8	1
Cenate, Joshua, Blue.*	1.000	9	2	7	0	9	0
Cento, Anthony, Eliz.*	1.000	18	0	3	0	3	0
Chavez, Christopher, Dan.	.000	11	0	0	0	0	0
Chenard, Kenneth, King.	.900	14	6	12	2	20	1
Chivers, Jason, King.*	1.000	20	2	4	0	6	0
Christ, John, Burl.	.875	23	0	7	1	8	0
Clifton, Derek, Dan.	.857	13	2	10	2	14	0
Colon, Jose, Burl.	.500	13	1	0	1	2	0
Cooke, Andrew, Eliz.*	.867	16	5	8	2	15	0
Cromer, Jason, Prin.*	.813	11	2	11	3	16	2
Cromer, Nathan, Prin.	.692	13	2	7	4	13	0
Crudale, Mike, J.C.	1.000	24	2	4	0	6	1
Cullen, Ryan, Pul.*	1.000	19	1	8	0	9	1
Curreri, Joseph, Bris.	1.000	16	0	1	0	1	0
Curtis, Tom, Dan.*	.692	18	3	6	4	13	0
Daboin, Jorge, Burl.	1.000	15	1	10	0	11	0
Dailey, Matt, Prin.*	1.000	4	1	0	0	1	0
Denney, Kyle, Burl.	.857	12	1	5	1	7	0
Dittfurth, Ryan, Pul.	.737	14	6	8	5	19	1
Dittmer, Greg, Prin.*	1.000	28	3	10	0	13	1
Dukeman, Gregory, Dan.	.857	17	1	5	1	7	0
Ennis, John, Dan.	.938	13	7	8	1	16	1
Eyre, Willie, Eliz.	.944	16	7	10	1	18	1
Ferguson, Tony, Mar.	1.000	15	0	6	0	6	0
Fiora, Chris, J.C.	.667	18	2	0	1	3	0
Fischer, Sean, Blue.*	.833	17	1	4	1	6	0
Fitzgerald, Ryan, Mar.	1.000	12	1	4	0	5	0
Flock, Rick, Eliz.	.750	22	1	2	1	4	0
Foster, John, Dan.*	1.000	18	4	9	0	13	1
Frendling, Neal, Prin.	.333	4	0	1	2	3	0
Frias, Juan, Prin.	1.000	30	2	0	0	2	0
Gomez, Rafael, King.	1.000	25	1	7	0	8	1
Graham, Frank, King.	.800	14	9	11	5	25	0
Graves, Donovan, J.C.	1.000	19	2	7	0	9	0
Griffiths, Jeremy, King.	.909	14	3	7	1	11	1
Grippo, Mike, J.C.*	1.000	14	0	3	0	3	0
Guerrier, Matt, Bris.	.667	21	1	1	1	3	0
Harang, Aaron, Pul.	.944	16	4	13	1	18	1
Hee, Aaron, King.*	.500	12	0	3	3	6	0
Hernandez, Carlos, Mar.*	.889	13	1	7	1	9	0
Hollingsworth, Scott, Pul.	1.000	12	0	1	0	1	0
Houle, Marc, Blue.	.818	20	3	6	2	11	0
James, Nicholas, King.	.000	2	0	0	0	0	0
Johnson, Derrick, Mar.*	.917	21	2	9	1	12	1
Jones, Sean, Blue.	.909	13	4	16	2	22	0
Kane, Kyle, Bris.	1.000	5	2	4	0	6	0
Kann, Kristopher, Mar.	.000	9	0	0	0	0	0
Knapp, Ben, Blue.	.765	14	2	11	4	17	0
Koeth, Mark, Burl.	.750	20	2	7	3	12	0
Kolb, Jason, Prin.*	.000	2	0	0	0	0	0
Latham, Jason, Mar.	.857	15	6	6	2	14	0
Layne, Roger, Burl.	.667	11	0	4	2	6	0
Lelless, Alexander, Dan.	1.000	18	3	2	0	5	0
Lewis, Colby, Pul.	.857	14	1	5	1	7	0
Lockridge, Sherwin, Eliz.	.800	16	1	3	1	5	0
Lugo, Carlos, Burl.	.000	3	0	0	0	0	0
Macias, Jose, Burl.	1.000	12	3	1	0	4	0
Majewski, Gary, Bris.	.857	13	1	17	3	21	1
Manning, Mike, Burl.	.500	4	0	1	1	2	0
Mansfield, Doug, Prin.	.000	1	0	0	0	0	0
Mastrolonardo, David, Blue.	.000	1	0	0	0	0	0
Mazur, Graham, Eliz.	1.000	10	0	3	0	3	0
McClung, Michael, Prin.	.500	13	0	2	2	4	0
McGinnis, Johnny, Dan.	.750	14	5	10	5	20	0
McKey, Dustin, Prin.	1.000	26	3	9	0	12	0
McWhirter, Kristopher, Bris.	1.000	12	3	3	0	6	0
Melson, Nate, Eliz.	.917	22	2	9	1	12	0
Mendez, David, Dan.*	.692	12	2	7	4	13	0
Mikels, Jason, Dan.	.857	16	3	3	1	7	0
Mikkola, Shaun, King.	1.000	8	0	3	0	3	0
Mozingo, Daniel, Bris.*	.833	13	2	8	2	12	0
Nowakowski, Brian, Eliz.	1.000	16	0	3	0	3	0
Nunez, Jose, King.*	.929	13	0	13	1	14	1
Olivo, Carlos, J.C.	.800	6	2	6	2	10	0
Ormond, Rodney, Blue.	.750	4	1	2	1	4	1
PARKER, Daniel, Mar.	1.000	14	5	18	0	23	1
Parker, Matt, J.C.	.923	23	2	10	1	13	0
Perez, Elvis, Dan.	1.000	21	1	4	0	5	0
Perez, Randy, Blue.*	.917	14	4	7	1	12	0
Perkins, Mike, J.C.	1.000	15	2	8	0	10	1
Plank, Terry, Blue.	1.000	20	2	3	0	5	0
Polk, Scott, King.	.909	23	7	3	1	11	0
Polo, Bienvenido, J.C.	1.000	20	0	1	0	1	0
Poplin, Paul, Eliz.	.875	21	2	5	1	8	0
Price, Kevin, Prin.	.000	4	0	0	0	0	0
PRIDIE, Jon, Eliz.	1.000	14	7	16	0	23	0
Pruitt, Jason, Blue.*	.889	17	1	7	1	9	0
Rakers, Aaron, Blue.	1.000	3	1	1	0	2	0
Ramirez, Enrique, Blue.	1.000	13	1	2	0	3	0
Ramirez, Santiago, Mar.	.778	25	1	6	2	9	0
Rauch, Jon, Bris.	1.000	14	2	3	0	5	0
Rayborn, Kris, J.C.*	.909	13	0	20	2	22	1
Regilio, Nick, Pul.	.778	11	3	4	2	9	1
Reynolds, Jacob, Burl.	1.000	3	1	0	0	1	0
Riveles, Mike, J.C.	1.000	4	0	2	0	2	0
Rivera, Leyson, Burl.	.571	17	1	3	3	7	0
Riviere, Rhett, Eliz.	1.000	7	1	0	0	1	0
Rizo, Miguel, J.C.	1.000	20	0	4	0	4	0
Roberts, Nick, Mar.	.900	10	3	6	1	10	0
Rochez, Angel, Pul.	1.000	18	6	3	0	9	0
Rodriguez, Alfredo, Pul.	1.000	6	1	3	0	4	0
Rodriguez, Luis, Pul.	.000	1	0	0	0	0	0
Rogers, Devin, Burl.	.333	8	1	2	6	9	0
Rogers, Lionel, King.	.800	14	1	3	1	5	0
Rohling, Stuart, Bris.	1.000	16	0	6	0	6	0
Rosario, Rodrigo, Mar.	.882	14	1	14	2	17	2
Ryba, Jason, Blue.	1.000	18	5	8	0	13	1
Sadler, Carl, Burl.*	.909	5	3	7	1	11	0
Saladin, Miguel, Mar.	1.000	11	0	2	0	2	0
Samora, Santo, J.C.	.786	18	4	7	3	14	1
Sanchez, Willmen, Burl.*	1.000	10	1	8	0	9	0
Schmidt, Pat, Dan.*	.833	13	1	4	1	6	0
Schwager, Matthew, Blue.	1.000	22	2	7	0	9	1
Scuglik, Mike, Pul.*	1.000	18	1	0	0	1	0
Sents, Marcus, Eliz.	.900	13	4	5	1	10	0
Sheets, Matt, Eliz.	1.000	12	2	7	0	9	0
Shepherd, Alvie, Blue.	.000	2	0	0	0	0	0
Silverthorn, Will, Prin.*	.667	7	0	2	1	3	0
Simpson, Andre, Bris.	.875	13	1	13	2	16	1
Sirianni, Jay, Burl.*	.917	11	0	11	1	12	0
Smith, Brandon, Mar.	.800	8	2	2	1	5	0
Smith, Matthew, King.	1.000	18	0	4	0	4	0
Spooneybarger, Tim, Dan.	.800	12	3	1	1	5	0
Sprague, Kevin, J.C.*	.857	11	4	8	2	14	0
Stanford, Derek, Mar.	.933	11	3	11	1	15	1
Stewart, Joshua, Bris.*	1.000	5	0	1	0	1	0
Stokes, Brian, Prin.	.727	33	4	4	3	11	0
Sturdy, Tim, Eliz.	.960	12	9	15	1	25	0
Sunderman, Nick, Burl.*	1.000	16	1	3	0	4	1
Sweeney, Mike, King.	1.000	19	1	3	0	4	0
Teekel, Josh, J.C.	.833	8	3	2	1	6	0
Tejeda, Franklin, J.C.	1.000	14	0	7	0	7	0
Tomaszewski, Eliot, Blue.	1.000	1	1	0	0	1	0
Tommassi, Carlos, Burl.	.667	12	2	4	3	9	0
Underhill, Ray, Eliz.	.857	17	3	3	1	7	0
Valdez, Domingo, Pul.	.000	3	0	0	0	0	0
Valentine, Joseph, Bris.	.000	11	0	0	0	0	0
Valera, Nelson, Prin.	1.000	23	7	3	0	10	1
Vandermeer, Scott, Prin.	.923	14	4	8	1	13	0
Vasquez, Luis, Mar.*	.733	13	1	10	4	15	0
Veras, Enger, Prin.	.818	14	2	7	2	11	0
Veronie, Shanin, Dan.	1.000	18	1	3	0	4	0
Vincentq, Matt, J.C.*	1.000	24	0	1	0	1	0
Wade, Matt, Burl.	.714	7	0	5	2	7	0
Waechter, Doug, Prin.	.500	11	0	2	2	4	0
Wallace, Shane, Burl.*	.818	12	0	9	2	11	0
Weaver, Joseph, Pul.	1.000	18	2	1	0	3	0
Weis, John, Eliz.*	1.000	26	1	6	0	7	0
Wessel, Travis, Pul.*	.750	21	1	2	1	4	0
West, Brian, Bris.	1.000	8	1	3	0	4	0
Wheeler, David, King.	1.000	7	2	1	0	3	0
Whitecotton, Billy, Blue.	.692	15	3	6	4	13	1
Wright, Daniel, Bris.	.857	10	0	6	1	7	0
Zazueta, Peter, J.C.	1.000	11	1	12	0	13	0

The following players appeared only as designated hitter, pinch-hitter or pinch runner: Ciarrachi, ph; Cubillan, dh-pr.

Year	Team	Pct.
1921—	Greenville	.608
	Johnson City*	.627
1922—	Bristol	.557
1923—	Knoxville	.635
1924—	Knoxville*	.642
	Bristol	.607
1925—	Greenville	.667
1926-36—	Did not operate.	
1937—	Elizabethton	.559
	Pennington Gap*	.580
1938—	Elizabethton	.664
	Greenville (3rd)†	.571
1939—	Elizabethton‡	.597
1940—	Johnson City§	.726
	Elizabethton	.750
1941—	Johnson City	.614
	Elizabethton*	.661
1942—	Bristol	.667
	Bristol∞	.660
1943—	Bristol	.755
	Bristol▲	.617
1944—	Kingsport‡	.575
1945—	Kingsport‡	.670
1946—	New River‡	.675
1947—	Pulaski	.648
	New River (3rd)†	.516
1948—	Pulaski‡	.680
1949—	Bluefield‡	.721
1950—	Bluefield	.600
	Bluefield◆	.745
1951—	Kingsport‡	.659
1952—	Johnson City	.595
	Welch (3rd)†	.509
1953—	Welch*	.705
	Johnson City	.672

Year	Team	Pct.
1954—	Bluefield‡	.619
1955—	Salem■	.689
1956—	Did not operate.	
1957—	Bluefield	.701
1958—	Johnson City	.662
1959—	Morristown	.603
1960—	Wytheville	.614
1961—	Middlesboro	.591
1962—	Bluefield	.671
1963—	Bluefield	.652
1964—	Johnson City	.662
1965—	Salem	.614
1966—	Marion	.623
1967—	Bluefield	.627
1968—	Marion	.583
1969—	Pulaski▼	.576
	Johnson City	.544
1970—	Bluefield	.638
1971—	Bluefield▼	.609
	Kingsport	.559
1972—	Bristol▼	.588
	Covington	.586
1973—	Kingsport	.757
1974—	Bristol▼	.754
	Bluefield	.536
1975—	Marion	.515
	Johnson City▼	.603
1976—	Johnson City▼	.714
	Bluefield	.600
1977—	Kingsport	.623
1978—	Elizabethton	.594
1979—	Paintsville	.800
1980—	Paintsville	.657
1981—	Paintsville	.657

Year	Team	Pct.
1982—	Bluefield▼	.681
	Johnson City	.478
1983—	Paintsville	.653
1984—	Elizabethton•	.580
	Pulaski	.536
1985—	Bristol††	.638
1986—	Johnson City	.667
	Pulaski•	.621
1987—	Burlington•	.729
	Johnson City	.609
1988—	Kingsport•	.644
	Burlington	.529
1989—	Elizabethton•	.691
	Pulaski	.618
1990—	Elizabethton	.761
1991—	Pulaski•	.662
	Burlington	.597
1992—	Elizabethton	.742
	Bluefield•	.597
1993—	Burlington•	.647
	Elizabethton	.552
1994—	Princeton•	.621
	Johnson City	.618
1995—	Bluefield	.754
	Kingsport•	.727
1996—	Kingsport	.716
	Bluefield▼	.618
1997—	Pulaski	.632
	Bluefield•	.580
1998—	Bristol•	.636
	Princeton	.559
1999—	Pulaski•	.696
	Martinsville•	.586

*Won split-season playoff. †Won four-team playoff. ‡Won championship and four-team playoff. §Johnson City, first-half winner, won playoff involving six clubs. ∞Won both halves and defeated second-place Elizabethton in playoff. ▲Won both halves, but Erwin won four-team playoff. ◆Won both halves, but Bristol won two-club playoff. ■Salem and Johnson City declared playoff co-champions when weather forced cancellation of final series. ▼League was divided into Northern, Southern divisions; declared league champion based on highest won-lost percentage. •League was divided into North and South divisions; won playoff. ††Bristol declared league champion based on regular-season record.

ARIZONA LEAGUE

LEAGUE OFFICE

President/treasurer
Bob Richmond
Address
P.O. Box 1645
Boise, ID 83701
Phone
208-429-1511

Teams*
Athletics
Cubs
Diamondbacks
Mariners
Mexico All-Stars
Padres

Rockies
White Sox

*Teams play their games in Mesa, Peoria, Phoenix, Tucson and other Arizona sites to be announced.

1999 FINAL STANDINGS
COMPOSITE

Team	Ath.	Mar.	Pad.	Roc.	Mex.	Dia.	W.S.	Cubs	W	L	T	Pct.	GB
Athletics	...	10	9	2	2	2	1	13	39	17	0	.696	...
Mariners	6	...	8	1	2	1	2	12	32	24	0	.571	7.0
Padres	7	8	...	1	2	2	2	9	31	24	0	.564	7.5
Rockies	0	1	1	...	7	9	9	1	28	28	0	.500	11.0
Mexico	0	0	0	9	...	9	9	1	28	28	0	.500	11.0
Diamondbacks	0	1	0	7	7	...	8	1	24	32	0	.429	15.0
White Sox	1	0	0	7	7	8	...	0	23	33	0	.411	16.0
Cubs	3	4	6	1	1	1	2	...	18	37	0	.327	20.5

NOTE: Certain portions of the July 28th game between the White Sox and Mexico and the August 30th game between the Rockies and Mexico were unattainable. Due to these unavoidable circumstances, individual Mexico player statistics do not match Mexico team statistics.

Club names are major league affiliations.

Games played in Mesa, Peoria, Phoenix and Tucson.

PLAYOFFS: Athletics defeated Mexico one game to none to win league championship.

REGULAR-SEASON ATTENDANCE: No total official attendance figures reported.

MANAGERS: Athletics, John Kuehl; Cubs, Carmelo Martinez; Diamondbacks, Roly De Armas; Mariners, Gary Thurman; Mexico, Jose Ortiz; Padres, Randy Whisler; Rockies, P.J. Carey; White Sox, Jerry Hairston.

ALL-STAR TEAM: 1B—Casey Rogowski, White Sox; 2B—Juan Ventura, Rockies; 3B—Joel Noboa, Diamondbacks; SS—Angel Berroa, Athletics; OF—Vincent Faison, Padres; Luis Garcia, Mexico; Michael Wenner, Athletics; C—Ventura Cisneros, Mexico; DH—Luis Garcia, Mexico and Oscar Ramirez, Mariners; LHP—Claudio Galva, Athletics; RHP—Ryan Kilber, Rockies and Jacob Peavey, Padres; LHRP—Geoff Jones, Padres; RHRP—Corey Miller, Athletics; Most Valuable Player—Michael Wenner, Athletics; Manager of the Year—Gary Thurman, Mariners and Randy Whisler, Padres.

1999 BATTING
TEAM

Team	Avg.	G	TPA	AB	R	H	TB	2B	3B	HR	RBI	SH	SF	HP	BB	IBB	SO	SB	CS	GDP	LOB	ShO	Slg.	OBP
Rockies	.290	56	2218	1929	346	559	759	97	29	15	290	4	24	51	210	3	450	157	45	29	431	2	.393	.370
Mariners	.285	56	2186	1940	342	553	800	118	24	27	275	20	14	30	182	1	414	78	43	41	382	3	.412	.353
Diamondbacks	.283	56	2133	1924	292	545	745	83	18	27	252	4	17	23	165	3	437	40	15	47	403	3	.387	.344
White Sox	.270	56	2139	1864	287	504	692	81	37	11	238	22	13	31	209	1	387	76	42	40	412	3	.371	.351
Athletics	.266	56	2269	1920	384	511	778	106	34	31	323	11	18	48	272	6	516	77	37	30	434	1	.405	.368
Padres	.262	55	2147	1861	323	488	689	70	28	25	273	7	21	33	225	5	482	123	38	30	391	1	.370	.349
Cubs	.261	55	2112	1887	249	493	724	88	25	31	214	8	13	40	164	2	442	44	36	46	389	2	.384	.331
Mexico	.260	56	2102	1845	263	480	675	58	25	25	204	28	13	27	189	6	455	41	21	36	428	2	.366	.336

INDIVIDUAL

TOP QUALIFIERS FOR BATTING CHAMPIONSHIP

Minimum 151 plate appearances. *Lefthanded batter. †Switch-hitter.

Player, Team	Avg.	G	TPA	AB	R	H	TB	2B	3B	HR	RBI	SH	SF	HP	BB	IBB	SO	SB	CS	GDP	Slg.	OBP
Ventura, Juan, Rock.	.399	46	212	193	35	77	94	9	4	0	23	0	5	2	12	0	24	25	9	2	.487	.429
Wenner, Michael, Ath.	.386	49	235	207	56	80	112	12	7	2	28	4	2	5	17	0	31	36	12	4	.541	.442
Cisneros, Ventura, Mex.	.349	46	190	172	24	60	87	9	6	2	27	2	2	2	12	1	26	3	2	3	.506	.394
Flores, Ralph, W.S.	.337	55	222	193	30	65	88	9	7	0	30	3	1	2	23	0	26	10	5	6	.456	.411
Tomshack, Steven, Dia.	.333	44	169	144	21	48	68	9	1	3	22	0	3	3	19	2	24	0	0	1	.472	.414
Garcia, Luis, Mex.	.330	50	212	188	35	62	122	9	6	13	40	0	1	0	22	1	31	1	2	2	.649	.398
Ramirez, Oscar, Mar.	.327	47	196	159	44	52	74	15	2	1	26	0	3	3	28	0	28	9	4	2	.465	.430
Presichi, Cristian, Mex.	.321	52	213	190	29	61	93	8	6	4	23	3	3	1	16	0	37	4	1	4	.489	.371
Lowe, Ernesto, W.S.	.320	50	204	181	29	58	72	8	3	0	23	1	2	9	11	0	42	7	4	2	.398	.384
McCarty, Brock, Dia.	.319	53	201	191	28	61	73	5	2	1	18	1	0	2	7	0	41	5	3	4	.382	.350
Wagner, Mike, Pad.	.313	34	156	128	27	40	72	9	4	5	27	0	4	3	21	1	37	13	4	3	.563	.410
Noboa, Joel, Dia.	.312	52	226	215	31	67	116	11	1	12	41	0	2	3	6	0	60	5	1	3	.540	.336
Gearlds, Aaron, Rock.	.311	51	209	180	37	56	71	4	4	1	29	0	5	6	18	0	43	22	2	3	.394	.383
Faison, Vince, Pad.*	.309	44	201	178	40	55	85	6	6	4	28	0	2	3	18	0	45	30	4	0	.478	.378
Martinez, Guillermo, Mar.†	.306	42	172	160	24	49	59	7	0	1	19	3	2	3	4	0	33	3	6	5	.369	.331
Espinoza, Efren, Mex.	.306	48	200	183	32	56	87	9	5	4	30	1	2	2	12	1	41	8	2	2	.475	.352

DEPARTMENTAL LEADERS: G—Kail, Flores, 55 each; AB—Kail, 220; R—Wenner, 56; H—Wenner, 80; TB—Garcia, 122; 2B—Samuel, 18; 3B—Reyes, 8; HR—Garcia, 13; RBI—Chirinos, 56; SH—Rodriguez, 5; SF—Gearlds, Klatt, Ventura, 5 each; HP—Londono, 10 each; BB—Mulqueen, 42; IBB—Bellhorn, Londono, Tomshack, 2 each; SO—Perez, Felix, 64 each; SB—Wenner, 36; CS—Wenner, 12; GIDP—Kail, Solorzano, 8 each; Slg.—Garcia, .649; OBP—Wenner, .442.

ALL PLAYERS

*Lefthanded batter. †Switch-hitter.

Player, Team	Avg.	G	TPA	AB	R	H	TB	2B	3B	HR	RBI	SH	SF	HP	BB	IBB	SO	SB	CS	GDP	Slg.	OBP
Anderson, Syketo, Cubs*	.295	37	145	139	16	41	58	11	3	0	14	0	0	1	5	0	22	8	9	2	.417	.324
Battle, Allen, Cubs	.308	3	15	13	2	4	6	0	1	0	0	0	0	1	1	0	4	1	0	1	.462	.400
Beckman, Jacob, Ath.	.000	13	0	0	0	0	0	0	0	0	0	0	0	0	0	0	0	0	0	0	.000	.000
Bellhorn, Mark, Ath.†	.233	12	54	43	11	10	13	3	0	0	5	0	0	0	11	2	9	0	0	1	.302	.389
Bernard, Dagoberto, Rock. ...	.325	34	128	117	14	38	43	5	0	0	21	0	2	3	6	1	17	7	6	5	.368	.367
Berroa, Angel, Ath.	.290	46	194	169	42	49	74	11	4	2	24	0	2	7	16	0	26	11	4	1	.438	.371
Betts, Dewayne, Ath.	.129	34	80	70	13	9	12	3	0	0	6	0	1	1	8	0	25	0	0	2	.171	.225
Blankenship, Anthony, W.S. ..	.348	9	27	23	7	8	12	0	2	0	4	0	0	0	4	0	4	1	1	1	.522	.444
Cash, Lavalroe, Cubs	.268	49	208	194	29	52	91	10	1	9	29	0	2	2	10	0	46	4	3	0	.469	.308
Castillo, Carlos, Ath.	.205	31	94	88	9	18	27	4	1	1	13	0	1	2	3	0	23	0	0	2	.307	.245
Chirinos, German, Ath.	.271	54	230	199	34	54	91	9	5	6	56	0	1	2	28	1	47	13	4	3	.457	.365
Christianson, Ryan, Ath.	.263	11	40	38	3	10	18	8	0	0	7	0	0	0	2	0	12	2	0	0	.474	.300
Cisneros, Ventura, Mex.	.349	46	190	172	24	60	87	9	6	2	27	2	2	2	12	1	26	3	2	3	.506	.394
Clark, Jamie, Mar.*	.344	26	116	96	26	33	51	3	3	3	17	2	0	1	17	1	29	5	2	2	.531	.447
Clark, Kevin, Mar.	.286	17	10	7	1	2	3	1	0	0	0	0	0	0	3	0	1	1	0	0	.429	.500
Cochrane, Mark, W.S.	.220	29	96	82	13	18	25	5	1	0	2	2	0	2	10	0	19	0	0	4	.305	.319
Cordova, Alfredo, Mex.*	.071	14	47	42	2	3	4	1	0	0	0	0	0	0	5	0	17	0	0	1	.095	.170
Cruz, Hector, Dia.†	.176	24	97	85	9	15	18	1	1	0	8	0	1	0	11	0	23	2	0	1	.212	.268
Cruz, Israel, Mar.	.286	13	31	28	4	8	9	1	0	0	4	1	0	0	2	0	6	1	0	1	.321	.333
Daly, Sean, Rock.	.182	25	89	77	12	14	17	3	0	0	8	0	0	0	12	0	35	3	0	1	.221	.292
Delgado, Jorge, Dia.	.294	20	76	68	11	20	30	5	1	1	6	0	0	2	6	0	14	1	0	1	.441	.368
Diaz, Jose, Mar.	.182	23	76	66	7	12	14	2	0	0	7	4	1	0	5	0	16	0	2	4	.212	.229
Doakes, Schuyler, Mar.†	.254	34	153	138	21	35	48	7	3	0	11	0	1	1	13	0	30	9	1	2	.348	.320
Duenas, Manuel, Pad.	.192	45	177	156	28	30	45	8	2	1	20	1	3	2	15	0	60	4	0	1	.288	.267
Durango, Ariel, Mar.†	.312	21	90	77	20	24	37	5	1	2	12	3	0	2	8	0	7	6	2	0	.481	.391
Egly, John, Dia.†	.254	51	210	197	25	50	63	8	1	1	20	0	0	1	12	1	54	1	1	5	.320	.300
Ellis, Alvyn, Ath.	.216	34	121	102	13	22	31	5	2	0	12	1	2	8	8	0	45	0	0	0	.304	.317
Encarnacion, Santos, Pad.	.283	52	210	187	31	53	63	2	4	0	23	1	0	1	21	1	40	22	2	2	.337	.359
Espinoza, Efren, Mex.	.306	48	200	183	32	56	87	9	5	4	30	1	2	2	12	1	41	8	2	2	.475	.352
Faison, Vince, Pad.*	.309	44	201	178	40	55	85	6	6	4	28	0	2	3	18	0	45	30	4	0	.478	.378
Felix, Osvaldo, Mex.*	.240	50	223	196	29	47	59	5	2	1	16	1	0	3	23	1	64	3	5	2	.301	.329
Figueroa, Carlos, Rock.*	.221	49	211	181	29	40	54	10	2	0	28	0	2	5	23	0	30	10	5	2	.298	.322
Figueroa, Luis, Mar.	.500	3	10	10	2	5	6	1	0	0	1	0	0	0	0	0	0	0	0	1	.600	.500
Flores, Ralph, W.S.	.337	55	222	193	30	65	88	9	7	0	30	3	1	2	23	0	26	10	5	6	.456	.411
Freeman, Corey, Mar.	.272	28	113	103	20	28	37	9	0	0	13	0	0	2	8	0	25	8	2	1	.359	.336
Fulse, Sheldon, Mar.†	.247	31	119	97	15	24	35	11	0	0	9	0	0	0	22	0	34	12	8	1	.361	.387
Gallegos, Alejandro, Mex.*	.162	44	168	136	14	22	34	5	2	1	16	4	1	2	25	0	57	2	2	1	.250	.299
Garcia, Luis, Mex.	.330	52	212	188	35	62	122	9	6	13	40	0	1	0	22	1	31	1	2	2	.649	.398
Gauch, Barry, W.S.	.230	26	77	61	7	14	17	3	0	0	11	1	0	4	11	0	7	1	0	2	.279	.382
Gearlds, Aaron, Rock.	.311	51	209	180	37	56	71	4	4	1	29	0	5	6	18	0	43	22	2	3	.394	.383
Gil, Eric, Mex.	.194	22	72	62	8	12	15	1	1	0	4	2	0	0	8	0	24	0	1	3	.242	.286
Goldfield, Josh, Dia.*	.333	2	5	3	3	1	1	0	0	0	0	0	0	0	2	0	0	0	0	0	.333	.600
Goolsby, Kevin, W.S.	.252	45	185	155	28	39	52	5	1	2	17	4	2	2	22	0	35	7	1	3	.335	.348
Gould, Elliotte, Pad.	.196	21	67	56	7	11	12	1	0	0	4	2	0	4	5	0	19	6	3	1	.214	.299
Gregg, Mitch, Ath.*	.237	37	152	118	21	28	42	9	1	1	16	0	1	1	32	1	40	4	2	3	.356	.401
Gutierrez, Said, Pad.	.316	7	22	19	2	6	9	0	0	0	1	6	0	1	0	2	0	0	0	0	.474	.409
Guzman, Javier, Rock.†	.367	13	50	49	11	18	32	4	2	2	11	0	0	0	1	0	12	5	0	1	.653	.380
Halgren, Chris, Ath.	.182	10	27	22	4	4	4	0	0	0	1	0	1	3	0	0	11	0	0	1	.182	.308
Hall, Justin, Ath.	.350	7	28	20	5	7	8	1	0	0	4	0	1	2	5	0	5	0	1	0	.400	.500
Hall, Victor, Dia.*	.365	27	123	104	19	38	42	2	1	0	14	3	1	2	13	0	25	10	5	1	.404	.442
Hamel, Jon, Pad.	.175	27	107	80	9	14	16	2	0	0	7	0	2	7	18	0	23	2	2	0	.200	.364
Hernandez, Orlando, Mar.	.245	27	114	106	17	26	38	7	1	1	19	1	1	1	5	0	17	1	2	2	.358	.283
Hertel, Brian, Mar.	.280	33	136	125	22	35	51	5	1	3	19	1	2	2	6	0	20	1	0	2	.408	.319
Hines, Derek, Cubs	.236	36	138	123	14	29	43	4	5	0	9	1	1	2	11	0	39	6	1	1	.350	.307
Johnstone, Benjamin, Cubs ...	.429	2	7	7	1	3	3	0	0	0	1	0	0	0	0	0	2	0	0	0	.429	.429
Jorgenson, Chris, Dia.*	.000	3	3	3	1	0	0	0	0	0	0	0	0	0	0	0	2	0	0	0	.000	.400
Kail, Tom, Dia.	.305	55	243	220	33	67	103	15	3	5	41	0	4	3	16	0	48	1	0	8	.468	.354
Kashirsky, Michael, W.S.	.125	15	41	32	5	4	4	0	0	0	1	0	0	0	9	0	7	0	2	3	.125	.317
Kent, Mat, Mar.*	.227	34	128	119	18	27	45	3	3	3	15	0	0	4	5	0	28	1	0	3	.378	.281
Klassen, Danny, Dia.	.235	6	18	17	2	4	5	1	0	0	1	0	0	1	0	0	4	0	0	1	.294	.294
Klatt, Jason, Pad.	.293	47	206	174	34	51	76	7	3	4	38	0	5	2	25	0	19	12	9	7	.437	.379
Knorr, Mario, Dia.*	.233	50	202	193	16	45	54	5	2	0	21	0	2	1	6	0	32	2	0	5	.280	.257
Lagana, Shawn, Dia.	.258	39	173	159	28	41	51	8	1	0	21	0	3	1	10	0	33	5	3	5	.321	.301
Lara, Franklin, Mar.	.288	30	116	104	17	30	36	4	1	0	6	0	3	0	9	0	13	1	2	6	.346	.362
Londono, Alex, Rock.	.268	38	165	142	29	38	63	7	3	4	28	1	1	10	11	2	46	10	3	0	.444	.386
Lopez, Orlando, Mar.	.254	42	158	138	18	35	45	6	2	0	10	3	0	1	16	0	27	11	7	4	.326	.335
Lowe, Ernesto, W.S.	.320	50	204	181	29	58	72	8	3	0	23	1	2	9	11	0	42	7	4	2	.398	.384
Mallory, Michael, Cubs	.242	42	168	149	20	36	54	6	4	0	15	0	1	6	12	0	48	2	2	5	.362	.321
Marchiano, Mike, Mar.	.444	3	12	9	2	4	7	0	0	1	5	0	1	0	2	0	0	1	1	0	.778	.500
Martinez, Dionnar, Cubs†	.254	41	144	126	13	32	37	5	0	0	11	1	1	1	15	1	20	5	2	3	.294	.336
Martinez, Guillermo, Mar.†	.306	42	172	160	24	49	59	7	0	1	19	3	2	3	4	0	33	3	6	5	.369	.331
McCall, Gerard, W.S.	.268	46	191	168	33	45	76	12	5	3	26	2	0	1	20	0	36	6	3	5	.452	.349
McCarty, Brock, Dia.	.319	53	201	191	28	61	73	5	2	1	18	1	0	2	7	0	41	5	3	4	.382	.350
McClure, Trey, Cubs	.268	47	188	164	30	44	78	5	2	7	25	0	0	3	21	0	25	3	0	6	.476	.362
Mendez, Hector, Mex.	.067	7	15	15	0	1	1	0	0	0	0	0	0	0	0	0	6	0	0	0	.067	.067
Morency, Vernand, Rock.	.294	44	182	160	36	47	68	7	4	2	18	0	1	2	19	0	49	25	5	3	.425	.370
Morenz, Shea, Pad.*	.417	4	16	12	5	5	9	2	1	0	3	0	1	0	3	0	2	0	0	0	.750	.500
Morrissey, Adam, Cubs	.296	44	196	169	23	50	69	7	3	2	23	2	2	2	21	0	28	4	7	6	.408	.376
Mulqueen, Dave, Rock.†	.249	53	217	169	32	42	60	9	3	1	17	0	2	3	42	0	63	6	3	2	.355	.403
Noboa, Joel, Dia.	.312	52	226	215	31	67	116	11	1	12	41	0	2	3	6	0	60	5	1	3	.540	.336
Oglesby, Travis, Dia.	.220	35	130	109	20	24	44	8	0	4	13	0	0	2	19	0	40	0	0	3	.404	.346
Ortega, Sixto, Rock.	.232	25	90	82	8	19	22	3	0	0	14	1	0	3	4	0	20	3	2	0	.268	.292

Player, Team	Avg.	G	TPA	AB	R	H	TB	2B	3B	HR	RBI	SH	SF	HP	BB	IBB	SO	SB	CS	GDP	Slg.	OBP
Ortiz, Jorge, Ath.	.192	22	68	52	6	10	11	1	0	0	5	1	0	2	13	0	29	1	1	0	.212	.373
Pagan, Andres, Pad.	.187	27	101	91	15	17	23	3	0	1	6	0	0	1	9	0	25	3	0	1	.253	.267
Palafox, Sergio, Mex.	.270	42	171	148	29	40	49	5	2	0	17	2	1	3	17	0	16	10	1	6	.331	.355
Paredes, Reny, Cubs	.279	35	126	122	16	34	50	10	0	2	17	1	0	1	2	0	32	2	3	1	.410	.296
Paulino, Robert, Cubs..........	.208	21	57	53	3	11	12	1	0	0	4	0	1	0	3	0	22	1	1	3	.226	.246
Pellerano, Cristi, Ath.	.275	48	197	178	34	49	71	11	1	3	29	0	2	5	11	0	45	1	1	3	.399	.332
Pena, Pelagio, Mar.	.364	21	83	77	11	28	35	5	1	0	14	0	1	1	4	0	13	3	1	1	.455	.398
Pena, Wilton, Ath.	.240	41	153	129	18	31	62	14	1	5	21	0	1	9	14	0	39	0	0	3	.481	.353
Peralta, Marco, Mex.	.190	5	21	21	1	4	5	1	0	0	1	0	0	0	0	0	6	0	0	0	.238	.190
Perez, Rafael, W.S.*	.207	51	206	179	26	37	63	7	5	3	22	3	2	2	20	0	64	11	5	1	.352	.291
Pimentel, Francisco, Cubs......	.289	29	97	83	13	24	37	4	3	1	8	1	0	3	10	0	27	3	0	2	.446	.385
Pimentel, Franklin, Ath.†......	.276	54	216	174	40	48	82	6	2	8	40	1	2	1	38	1	36	6	4	3	.471	.405
Pina, Emmanuel, Cubs..........	.216	18	57	51	3	11	12	1	0	0	3	0	1	1	4	0	11	2	2	1	.235	.281
Pines, Gregory, Mar.	.299	31	109	97	14	29	49	7	2	3	17	2	1	1	8	0	15	0	0	1	.505	.355
Presichi, Cristian, Mex.	.321	52	213	190	29	61	93	8	6	4	23	3	3	1	16	0	37	4	1	4	.489	.371
Puccinelli, John, Pad.	.266	50	203	177	34	47	62	12	0	1	20	1	0	3	22	0	35	3	2	3	.350	.356
Quezada, Juan, Mex.	.200	20	70	55	8	11	13	2	0	0	3	2	0	4	9	1	19	0	0	3	.236	.353
Quintana, Wilfredo, Mar.	.379	16	62	58	10	22	36	8	0	2	18	0	1	1	2	0	11	2	2	2	.621	.403
Ramirez, Oscar, Mar.	.327	47	196	159	44	52	74	15	2	1	26	0	3	3	28	0	28	9	4	2	.465	.430
Reyes, Christian, Ath.†.........	.283	49	216	187	39	53	83	11	8	1	39	1	1	1	26	1	54	3	1	4	.444	.372
Reyes, Guillermo, W.S.†	.250	54	227	200	27	50	61	5	3	0	15	0	3	4	20	0	25	18	10	1	.305	.326
Reyes, Julio, W.S.*	.307	33	137	127	23	39	59	8	3	2	20	0	0	3	7	0	16	1	2	1	.465	.358
Reyes, Rene, Rock.†	.361	22	103	97	21	35	50	4	4	1	20	0	0	2	4	0	14	6	1	2	.515	.398
Richardson, Miguel, Mar.	.273	37	145	128	26	35	67	3	4	7	26	0	0	4	13	0	49	1	1	1	.523	.359
Robinson, Coby, Cubs...........	.188	30	97	80	12	15	26	1	2	2	9	0	0	6	11	0	25	0	1	4	.325	.330
Rodriguez, Erick, Mex.	.283	39	141	127	17	36	36	0	0	0	10	5	0	0	9	1	13	2	1	3	.283	.331
Roehler, Trent, W.S.	.067	9	16	15	1	1	2	1	0	0	0	0	0	0	1	0	6	0	0	0	.133	.125
Rogowski, Casey, W.S.*........	.288	52	191	160	23	46	57	7	2	0	27	1	3	1	26	1	34	2	1	2	.356	.384
Rohena, Omar, Cubs	.250	20	65	60	11	15	20	2	0	1	5	0	0	1	4	0	21	0	0	1	.333	.308
Romero, Nicholas, Pad.	.293	45	201	181	31	53	72	4	3	3	23	1	1	2	16	1	59	16	4	2	.398	.355
Rosa, Ivan, Ath.*	.194	32	85	72	18	14	24	4	0	2	11	0	1	1	11	0	30	0	2	0	.333	.306
Rowden, Monte, Cubs...........	.189	15	42	37	4	7	12	0	1	1	7	0	0	3	2	0	8	0	0	2	.324	.286
Samuel, Tomas, Rock.	.288	42	192	170	30	49	75	18	1	2	35	0	3	8	11	0	48	6	1	2	.441	.354
Sanchez, Jose, Mar.*	.243	39	155	136	20	33	35	2	0	0	9	4	3	0	12	0	27	6	2	3	.257	.298
Schmidt, J.P., Ath.*	.278	34	120	90	20	25	31	2	2	0	14	2	0	0	28	0	21	2	5	0	.344	.449
Sing, Brandon, Cubs	.265	17	74	68	4	18	30	4	1	2	12	0	1	0	5	0	16	1	1	2	.441	.311
Sobet, Renato, Pad.	.225	39	143	129	11	29	41	4	1	2	13	0	0	1	13	1	28	3	1	6	.318	.301
Solorzano, Lenin, W.S.	.267	51	196	180	21	48	67	6	5	1	30	0	1	1	13	0	45	5	5	8	.372	.320
Sprowl, Jon, Cubs*...............	.392	31	118	97	19	38	51	9	2	0	14	0	2	1	18	1	14	1	1	4	.526	.483
Tapia, Roman, W.S.	.300	21	60	50	7	15	19	4	0	0	6	3	0	0	7	0	12	0	3	1	.380	.386
Testa, Chris, Rock.*	.292	47	197	168	22	49	64	10	1	1	22	0	1	4	24	0	27	11	6	3	.381	.391
Thornton-Murray, Jan., Cubs† .	.205	34	127	112	12	23	27	2	1	0	4	2	0	4	9	0	24	0	3	1	.241	.288
Tomshack, Steven, Dia.	.333	44	169	144	21	48	68	9	1	3	22	0	3	3	19	2	24	0	0	1	.472	.414
Trzesniak, Nicholas, Pad.	.241	29	126	108	17	26	31	3	1	0	16	1	0	3	14	0	39	7	1	1	.287	.344
Vandemore, Anthony, Pad.*...	.276	50	211	185	32	51	73	7	3	3	39	0	2	1	23	1	51	2	6	3	.395	.355
Van Horn, Ryan, Cubs...........	.150	18	43	40	4	6	8	2	0	0	4	0	1	2	0	0	8	1	0	1	.200	.186
Van Rossum, Chris, Dia.*	.250	6	17	16	1	4	4	0	0	0	0	0	0	0	1	0	3	1	0	0	.250	.294
Ventura, Juan, Rock.	.399	46	212	193	35	77	94	9	4	0	23	0	5	2	12	0	24	25	9	2	.487	.429
Vizcaino, Maximo, Dia.	.283	12	53	46	7	13	15	0	1	0	4	0	1	2	4	0	3	1	0	4	.326	.358
Wagner, Mike, Pad.	.313	34	156	128	27	40	72	9	4	5	27	0	4	3	21	1	37	13	4	3	.563	.410
Warren, Chris, Rock.†...........	.257	40	174	144	30	37	46	4	1	1	16	2	2	3	23	0	22	18	2	3	.319	.366
Wenner, Michael, Ath.	.386	49	235	207	56	80	112	12	7	2	28	4	2	5	17	0	31	36	12	4	.541	.442
Wheat, Trey, W.S.	.293	16	63	58	7	17	18	1	0	0	4	0	0	0	5	0	9	7	0	0	.310	.349
Yakopich, Joseph, Dia.*........	.305	47	185	154	37	47	58	5	3	0	22	0	0	1	30	0	31	6	2	5	.377	.422
Zavala, Juan, Mex.	.150	36	131	107	9	16	19	1	1	0	8	2	0	10	12	0	50	2	1	3	.178	.295

GRAND SLAMS: Londono, McClure, Noboa, Quintana, Wagner, 1 each.

AWARDED FIRST BASE ON CATCHER'S INTERFERENCE: Ramirez 3 (Pina 3); Garcia (Delgado); McQueen (Cisneros); Pellerano (Pena).

1999 PITCHING

TEAM

Team	W	L	Pct.	ERA	G	CG	ShO	Sv.	IP	H	TBF	R	ER	HR	SH	SF	HB	BB	IBB	SO	WP	Bk.
Athletics...............	39	17	.696	3.55	56	0	2	21	497.0	497	2112	250	196	21	8	19	17	172	3	416	37	13
Padres.................	31	24	.564	4.24	55	1	3	15	482.0	492	2161	291	227	37	14	14	41	220	0	472	26	16
White Sox	23	33	.411	4.42	56	1	0	10	474.2	519	2142	301	233	22	13	20	34	204	15	461	53	24
Diamondbacks ...	24	32	.429	4.50	56	1	3	16	474.1	513	2184	330	237	14	14	23	41	216	0	449	66	15
Mariners	32	24	.571	4.60	56	0	2	16	492.2	498	2193	310	252	24	15	15	41	211	3	503	38	14
Mexico	28	28	.500	4.65	56	5	4	11	470.1	522	2073	289	243	20	5	12	30	177	3	397	28	20
Rockies	28	28	.500	4.85	56	3	2	8	480.1	551	2197	336	259	20	23	14	33	191	2	392	50	20
Cubs	18	37	.327	5.52	55	1	1	11	480.2	541	2250	379	295	34	12	16	46	225	1	493	39	14

INDIVIDUAL

TOP QUALIFIERS FOR EARNED-RUN AVERAGE TITLE

Minimum 45 innings.*Lefthanded pitcher.

Pitcher, Team	W	L	Pct.	ERA	G	GS	CG	ShO	GF	Sv.	IP	H	TBF	R	ER	HR	SH	SF	HB	BB	IBB	SO	WP	Bk.
Peavy, Jacob, Pad.	7	1	.875	1.34	13	11	1	0	0	0	73.2	52	286	16	11	4	2	0	3	23	0	90	5	3
Nantkes, Kurt, Ath.	5	4	.556	2.19	15	11	0	0	0	0	70.0	55	287	25	17	3	0	1	5	18	0	64	6	3
Galva, Claudio, Ath.*	6	2	.750	2.38	14	11	0	0	0	0	68.0	64	275	23	18	0	3	2	2	16	0	59	4	1
Ovalles, Juan, Dia.	7	2	.778	2.40	14	7	0	0	3	3	60.0	48	257	25	16	1	3	3	8	25	0	36	4	1

Pitcher, Team	W	L	Pct.	ERA	G	GS	CG	ShO	GF	Sv.	IP	H	TBF	R	ER	HR	SH	SF	HB	BB	IBB	SO	WP	Bk.
Calzada, Javier, Ath.	5	1	.833	2.54	10	8	0	0	1	0	46.0	32	177	19	13	4	0	2	1	11	0	30	3	1
Kibler, Ryan, Rock.	6	2	.750	2.55	14	14	2	0	0	0	81.1	77	337	35	23	3	2	0	10	14	1	55	2	0
Wells, Roy, Mar.	3	0	1.000	2.70	10	9	0	0	0	0	46.2	39	199	22	14	0	1	0	1	22	0	52	1	2
Cueto, Jose, Cubs	3	4	.429	2.86	11	9	0	0	1	0	56.2	49	247	32	18	1	1	3	4	22	0	66	2	1
Martinez, Juan, Mex.	5	5	.500	3.27	15	13	3	1	2	1	85.1	76	346	36	31	3	2	2	1	27	0	86	2	2
Hughes, Rocky, W.S.*	3	3	.500	3.33	13	6	0	0	2	1	46.0	53	202	23	17	2	3	1	0	20	2	47	2	0
Garner, Brandon, Rock.	4	5	.444	3.63	14	13	1	0	0	0	79.1	74	327	37	32	1	4	3	6	5	0	67	6	3
Villarreal, Oscar, Dia.	1	5	.167	3.78	14	11	0	0	1	0	64.1	64	286	39	27	1	2	3	10	25	0	51	6	4
Vitek, Joshua, Pad.	6	2	.750	3.99	12	10	0	0	0	0	47.1	43	212	22	21	3	0	4	8	24	0	48	2	0
Cordero, Frangil, Cubs*	2	6	.250	4.02	14	13	0	0	1	0	69.1	68	317	48	31	6	1	2	6	31	0	78	6	4
Beltre, Sandy, W.S.	5	4	.556	4.12	13	10	0	0	2	0	67.2	85	305	38	31	5	2	1	3	21	0	58	7	1

DEPARTMENTAL LEADERS: W—Ovalles, Peavey, 7 each; L—Thompson, Mendoza, 7 each; Pct.—Peavey, .875; G—Diaz, 22; GS—Kibler, 14; CG—Martinez, 3; ShO—several players tied, 1 each; GF—Moreno, 18; Sv.—Miller, 11; IP—Martinez, 85.1; H—Chavez, 89; TBF—Martinez, 346; R—Mendoza, 64; ER—Pate, 52; HR—Knapp, 14; SH—Granados, 5; SF—Mendoza, 6; HB—Patten, 11; BB—Simpson, Chavez, Cordero, Mendoza, 31 each; IBB—Hollifield, Sanders, 3 each; SO—Peavey, 90; WP—Mendoza, 14; BK—Granados, 5.

ALL PITCHERS

*Lefthanded pitcher.

Pitcher, Team	W	L	Pct.	ERA	G	GS	CG	ShO	GF	Sv.	IP	H	TBF	R	ER	HR	SH	SF	HB	BB	IBB	SO	WP	Bk.
Acosta, Jhon, Cubs	1	0	1.000	0.00	5	0	0	0	2	1	9.0	7	35	1	0	0	1	1	2	0	0	9	0	0
Alvarez, Larry, Cubs	2	0	1.000	3.18	8	0	0	0	1	0	17.0	17	74	7	6	0	0	0	1	8	0	10	0	0
Arauz, Alexis, Dia.	2	3	.400	4.41	16	8	0	0	3	1	51.0	60	246	40	25	1	2	4	1	26	0	38	12	2
Asencio, Domingo, W.S.	1	0	1.000	10.97	11	0	0	0	5	0	10.2	24	56	13	13	1	0	0	0	4	0	5	4	1
Baek, Cha, Mar.	3	0	1.000	3.67	8	4	0	0	1	0	27.0	30	112	13	11	2	0	0	0	6	0	25	2	3
Bailey, David, Cubs	0	0	.000	9.45	4	0	0	0	3	1	6.2	8	29	7	7	2	0	0	0	2	0	10	0	0
Barcelo, Lorenzo, W.S.	2	1	.667	1.69	9	9	0	0	0	0	42.2	36	171	14	8	0	1	0	1	6	0	57	3	2
Baxter, Gerik, Pad.	3	0	1.000	1.50	8	7	0	0	0	0	36.0	27	153	7	6	0	3	0	5	15	0	45	2	0
Beckman, Jacob, Ath.	4	1	.800	3.81	12	2	0	0	4	1	28.1	31	126	16	12	2	0	0	2	10	0	19	4	1
Beltran, Francis, Cubs	0	1	.000	0.00	7	0	0	0	6	2	10.2	5	38	3	0	0	0	0	1	1	0	8	0	0
Beltre, Sandy, W.S.	5	4	.556	4.12	13	10	0	0	2	0	67.2	85	305	38	31	5	2	1	3	21	0	58	7	1
Benitez, Angel, Cubs	0	3	.000	7.76	16	0	0	0	6	0	26.2	37	132	24	23	2	2	2	3	11	0	15	0	1
Blumenstock, Brad, Ath.	0	0	.000	5.40	3	2	0	0	0	0	5.0	10	28	4	3	0	0	0	0	6	0	4	2	0
Briggs, Anthony, Rock.	0	0	.000	2.45	3	3	0	0	0	0	7.1	11	33	3	2	0	0	0	0	1	0	5	0	0
Calzada, Javier, Ath.	5	1	.833	2.54	10	8	0	0	1	0	46.0	32	177	19	13	4	0	2	1	11	0	30	3	1
Castellano, Jonathan, Mex.	5	3	.625	4.58	16	12	1	0	2	0	76.2	86	336	45	39	2	0	3	5	30	0	71	9	3
Chavez, Wilton, Cubs	5	5	.500	5.88	14	13	1	1	0	0	67.1	89	328	57	44	5	2	1	6	31	0	68	4	2
Christensen, Benjamin, Cubs	0	1	.000	3.00	3	3	0	0	0	0	9.0	8	39	3	3	0	0	0	1	5	0	10	1	1
Christensen, Deryck, Rock.	2	1	.667	3.55	18	0	0	0	5	0	25.1	33	125	14	10	1	3	0	1	18	0	20	2	1
Clark, Kevin, Mar.	2	0	1.000	5.72	16	0	0	0	3	0	28.1	34	138	22	18	1	3	1	2	20	1	22	4	1
Cordero, Frangil, Cubs*	2	6	.250	4.02	14	13	0	0	1	0	69.1	68	317	48	31	6	1	2	6	31	0	78	6	4
Cortez, Martin, Mex.*	3	1	.750	3.62	20	2	0	0	5	2	27.1	32	122	13	11	1	0	1	1	11	0	22	0	3
Cueto, Jose, Cubs	3	4	.429	2.86	11	9	0	0	1	0	56.2	49	247	32	18	1	1	3	4	22	0	66	2	1
Cyr, Eric, Pad.*	2	1	.667	3.26	11	5	0	0	1	0	38.2	34	159	19	14	2	2	1	1	15	0	39	0	0
De La Rosa, Jorge, Dia.*	0	0	.000	3.21	8	0	0	0	6	2	14.0	12	56	5	5	1	0	0	0	3	0	17	2	1
Deveraux, Dale, Dia.	3	2	.600	10.41	16	0	0	0	5	0	27.2	42	146	38	32	2	1	5	4	20	0	17	6	1
Diaz, Alexander, Ath.	2	1	.667	3.19	22	0	0	0	17	5	42.1	54	184	21	15	2	0	1	2	10	1	26	1	0
Diaz, Eddy, Cubs	0	6	.000	8.39	17	2	0	0	6	2	34.1	47	180	44	32	4	2	0	6	23	1	30	7	0
Dowell, Brian, Pad.	0	0	.000	45.00	2	0	0	0	0	0	1.0	2	14	8	5	0	0	0	1	6	0	0	1	0
Drain, Bradley, Mar.	6	5	.545	4.27	13	11	0	0	0	0	65.1	63	273	38	31	3	1	1	7	13	0	71	9	0
Dunham, Pat, Mar.	0	2	.000	9.58	7	0	0	0	5	3	10.1	13	50	11	11	0	0	0	1	7	0	11	1	0
Dunphy, Micah, Ath.*	2	1	.667	3.19	16	1	0	0	3	1	31.0	35	143	18	11	2	1	2	1	17	1	34	4	0
Earle, Scott, Mar.	1	1	.500	1.46	7	0	0	0	1	0	12.1	14	54	4	2	0	0	1	0	2	0	13	0	0
Ellis, Alvyn, Ath.	0	0	.000	0.00	1	0	0	0	1	0	1.0	1	3	0	0	0	0	0	0	0	0	0	0	0
Encarnacion, Luis, Mar.	0	0	.000	10.88	15	0	0	0	9	1	22.1	26	123	30	27	1	0	1	4	24	0	25	1	1
Ericks, Dave, Cubs	1	3	.250	8.38	16	1	0	0	6	0	29.0	35	156	31	27	3	0	1	3	29	0	22	7	1
Espinal, Juan, Mar.	3	3	.500	7.12	15	5	0	0	2	0	43.0	56	206	38	34	6	2	3	4	20	0	31	2	0
Ferrand, Dario, W.S.	2	5	.286	4.46	13	13	1	0	0	0	72.2	80	321	46	36	4	0	1	7	25	1	44	9	2
Ferrand, Julian, Rock.	0	1	.000	8.27	13	0	0	0	5	1	20.2	25	99	22	19	2	0	1	1	15	0	14	7	1
Figueroa, Nelson, Dia.	0	1	.000	0.00	1	1	0	0	0	0	3.0	3	11	1	0	0	0	0	0	0	0	2	0	0
Galva, Claudio, Ath.*	6	2	.750	2.38	14	11	0	0	0	0	68.0	64	275	23	18	0	3	2	2	16	0	59	4	1
Garcia, Joaquin, Mar.	4	3	.571	4.61	12	7	0	0	2	0	52.2	64	235	33	27	1	1	5	6	13	0	51	1	0
Garner, Brandon, Rock.	4	5	.444	3.63	14	13	1	0	0	0	79.1	74	327	37	32	1	4	3	6	5	0	67	6	3
Ginter, Matt, W.S.	1	0	1.000	3.24	3	0	0	0	1	1	8.1	5	33	4	3	0	0	1	0	3	0	10	0	0
Goldfield, Josh, Dia.	0	1	.000	4.91	1	1	0	0	0	0	3.2	6	19	6	2	0	0	0	0	2	0	2	0	0
Gonzalez, Miguel, Rock.	0	1	.000	6.61	10	1	0	0	4	0	16.1	24	90	18	12	1	0	0	3	12	0	15	6	1
Granados, Bernie, Rock.	1	1	.500	5.60	16	0	0	0	7	0	27.1	38	140	28	17	2	5	1	3	12	1	25	1	5
Grunwald, Erik, Mar.	3	2	.600	2.63	18	0	0	0	15	3	24.0	22	101	10	7	0	3	1	0	9	1	23	3	0
Herrera, Jose, Mar.	3	5	.375	5.83	12	11	0	0	0	0	54.0	56	252	46	35	7	1	2	10	29	0	48	5	4
Hoerman, Jared, Mar.	1	0	1.000	1.41	11	1	0	0	5	2	32.0	24	126	6	5	0	0	0	1	6	0	46	1	0
Hoff, Steve, Cubs*	0	1	.000	4.50	3	3	0	0	0	0	6.0	6	29	4	3	1	0	0	0	5	0	9	0	0
Hollifield, Alec, W.S.	1	5	.167	6.87	16	0	0	0	7	0	18.1	29	99	19	14	2	2	4	3	11	3	14	2	1
Holmes, Darren, Dia.	0	0	.000	0.00	2	2	0	0	0	0	2.2	1	9	0	0	0	0	0	0	0	0	4	0	0
Hughes, Rocky, W.S.*	3	3	.500	3.33	13	6	0	0	2	1	46.0	53	202	23	17	2	3	1	0	20	2	47	2	0
Jackson, Stosh, Cubs*	0	1	.000	1.69	6	0	0	0	0	0	10.2	8	45	5	2	0	0	1	0	4	0	23	0	0
Jacobs, Frankey, Ath.	1	2	.333	5.48	12	0	0	0	2	0	21.1	20	90	14	13	0	0	4	0	11	0	15	3	0
Jimenez, Julio, Mex.*	3	5	.375	4.70	13	10	0	0	1	0	61.1	75	277	40	32	3	1	0	4	28	0	38	5	0
Johnson, Roney, Rock.	2	3	.400	8.64	9	8	0	0	0	0	33.1	48	163	34	32	4	0	1	1	18	0	22	2	4
Jones, Geoffrey, Pad.*	4	2	.667	4.15	14	0	0	0	7	2	39.0	38	176	25	18	5	0	5	3	18	0	32	1	0
Kesten, Michael, Mar.*	2	0	1.000	6.55	13	0	0	0	2	0	22.0	17	104	18	16	0	1	0	2	20	0	17	4	0
Kibler, Ryan, Rock.	6	2	.750	2.55	14	14	2	0	0	0	81.1	77	337	35	23	3	2	0	10	14	1	55	2	0
Kim, Byung-Hyun, Dia.	0	0	.000	0.00	1	1	0	0	0	0	2.0	1	7	0	0	0	0	0	0	1	0	2	0	0
Knorr, Mario, Dia.	0	0	.000	0.00	1	0	0	0	1	0	0.1	0	4	0	0	0	0	0	1	2	0	0	1	0
Koehler, Russ, Mar.	1	2	.333	0.96	4	4	0	0	0	0	18.2	16	79	5	2	0	1	0	1	5	0	21	0	0

Pitcher, Team	W	L	Pct.	ERA	G	GS	CG	ShO	GF	Sv.	IP	H	TBF	R	ER	HR	SH	SF	HB	BB	IBB	SO	WP	Bk.
Kroon, Marc, Mar.	0	0	.000	3.86	4	4	0	0	0	0	7.0	5	27	3	3	2	0	0	0	0	0	12	0	0
Kusiewicz, Mike, Rock.*	1	3	.250	5.47	6	6	0	0	0	0	24.2	26	112	16	15	0	1	1	2	9	0	27	1	1
Lopez, Juan, W.S.*	2	2	.500	7.33	14	2	0	0	6	2	27.0	32	132	27	22	2	1	4	1	16	1	27	2	4
Lorenzo, Javier, Rock.	6	4	.600	4.28	20	1	0	0	14	2	33.2	36	159	23	16	3	0	0	1	19	0	41	2	0
Malone, Corwin, W.S.*	0	2	.000	8.00	10	0	0	0	3	0	18.0	16	90	19	16	1	0	0	1	16	0	24	5	4
Martinez, Daniel, W.S.*	2	0	1.000	2.35	13	0	0	0	6	1	15.1	18	75	6	4	0	2	1	1	10	1	20	3	1
Martinez, Juan, Mex.	5	5	.500	3.27	15	13	3	1	2	1	85.1	76	346	36	31	3	2	2	1	27	0	86	2	2
Matos, Jesus, Rock.	2	1	.667	5.50	18	3	0	0	4	0	36.0	48	165	28	22	1	3	2	1	9	0	31	3	0
Maurer, Mike, Ath.	0	0	.000	1.23	7	0	0	0	6	2	7.1	4	26	1	1	1	0	0	0	1	0	8	0	0
Mendoza, Hatuey, Dia.	2	7	.222	5.65	13	13	0	0	0	0	71.2	83	338	64	45	3	1	6	5	31	0	69	14	3
Meyer, John, Pad.	3	1	.250	6.06	21	0	0	0	14	6	32.2	34	163	29	22	2	1	1	3	30	0	31	6	0
Middlebrook, Jason, Pad.	1	0	1.000	7.20	1	1	0	0	0	0	5.0	9	25	5	4	0	0	0	1	3	0	3	0	0
Miller, Corey, W.S.	2	0	1.000	0.78	18	0	0	0	17	11	23.0	15	90	3	2	1	0	0	1	9	1	28	0	3
Minaya, Edwin, Ath.	5	3	.625	6.18	14	11	0	0	0	0	59.2	76	274	49	41	1	1	3	1	24	0	41	4	3
Montenegro, Christopher, Mar. .	0	1	.000	3.00	19	0	0	0	11	7	27.0	19	114	11	9	1	1	0	2	15	1	35	4	3
Montoya, Saul, Mex.	2	1	.667	4.03	17	0	0	0	4	1	29.0	33	132	14	13	3	0	1	1	11	0	39	5	1
Moore, Joel, Rock.	0	0	.000	13.06	4	3	0	0	0	0	10.1	25	60	19	15	1	0	0	2	1	0	9	1	0
Morel, Francis, Dia.	2	1	.667	8.04	7	0	0	0	2	1	15.2	23	78	15	14	1	1	0	2	5	0	18	1	0
Moreno, Edgar, Mex.	4	2	.667	2.61	18	0	0	0	18	3	20.2	23	93	13	6	0	0	2	5	0	22	0	2
Moreno, Victor, Dia.	1	2	.333	9.90	7	0	0	0	4	2	10.0	17	53	13	11	0	1	0	0	6	0	7	1	0
Munoz, Arnaldo, W.S.*	0	2	.000	5.25	14	0	0	0	7	1	12.0	13	61	10	7	1	0	0	2	8	0	12	1	1
Myers, Todd, Dia.	0	0	.000	1.69	3	0	0	0	2	0	5.1	6	26	3	1	0	0	1	3	0	4	0	0
Nantkes, Kurt, Ath.	5	4	.556	2.19	15	11	0	0	0	0	70.0	55	287	25	17	3	0	1	5	18	0	64	6	3
Navarro, Hector, Mex.	3	1	.750	7.71	11	1	0	0	2	0	25.2	35	123	24	22	2	1	1	2	12	1	15	2	4
Ovalles, Juan, Dia.	7	2	.778	2.40	14	7	0	0	0	0	60.0	48	257	25	16	1	3	3	8	25	0	36	4	1
Pate, Dustin, Cubs	1	5	.167	9.62	12	11	0	0	0	0	48.2	70	233	53	52	2	0	3	5	21	0	42	8	1
Patten, Michael, W.S.	0	4	.000	4.19	15	5	0	0	3	0	38.2	27	174	22	18	0	0	2	11	30	1	27	11	0
Peavy, Jacob, Pad.	7	1	.875	1.34	13	11	1	0	0	0	73.2	52	286	16	11	4	2	0	3	23	0	90	5	3
Perez, Oliver, Pad.*	1	2	.333	5.08	15	2	0	0	7	3	28.1	28	133	20	16	1	1	0	1	16	0	37	0	2
Perkins, Gregory, Dia.	0	0	.000	6.75	4	3	0	0	0	0	12.0	13	58	11	9	0	1	0	1	8	0	11	1	0
Puga, Sergio, Mex.	1	1	.500	6.00	13	3	1	0	9	0	30.0	33	141	23	20	4	0	0	6	12	0	20	1	3
Purvis, Robert, W.S.	0	1	.000	4.00	4	0	0	0	3	2	9.0	12	48	10	4	0	0	0	6	0	7	1	4
Randolph, Steve, Dia.*	0	0	.000	4.50	2	2	0	0	0	0	6.0	5	25	3	3	0	0	0	2	0	7	0	0
Renovato, Nestor, Mex.	3	3	.500	6.89	9	9	0	0	0	0	47.0	62	217	39	36	3	1	1	4	14	0	41	6	2
Reyes, Junior, Cubs*	0	1	.000	19.41	7	0	0	0	2	0	10.2	24	69	24	23	6	0	0	1	13	0	5	0	0
Romo, Eduardo, Mex.	0	5	.000	8.07	12	3	0	0	1	0	29.0	46	152	35	26	0	0	1	3	17	0	17	1	0
Rosario, Hipolito, Pad.	0	1	.000	9.82	16	0	0	0	9	1	25.2	47	137	34	28	4	0	0	4	13	0	16	1	4
Rossiter, Mike, Rock.	0	0	.000	0.00	1	0	0	0	0	0	2.0	6	6	0	0	0	0	0	0	0	0	5	0	0
Rubio, Miguel, Dia.	0	1	.000	6.00	2	2	0	0	0	0	3.0	6	15	2	2	0	0	0	0	3	0	3	0	0
Ruiz, Juan, Mex.	0	0	.000	2.25	1	1	0	0	0	0	4.0	5	17	1	1	0	0	0	0	1	0	3	0	0
Sanders, David, W.S.*	1	0	1.000	1.10	7	1	0	0	2	1	16.1	12	66	3	2	0	1	0	1	6	3	26	1	0
Serrano, Alex, Rock.	3	2	.600	1.20	18	0	0	0	13	5	30.0	21	126	10	4	1	3	0	1	14	0	23	5	0
Simpson, Joe, Rock.	1	3	.250	6.11	14	3	0	0	0	0	35.1	39	166	28	24	0	4	1	31	0	21	8	2
Sobchuk, Justin, Ath.	3	1	.750	5.77	15	6	0	0	2	1	48.1	51	216	34	31	3	3	4	1	28	0	47	4	0
Soto, Darwin, Pad.	2	2	.500	3.69	15	4	0	0	4	1	39.0	39	176	22	16	3	3	0	6	16	0	32	3	3
Stephenson, Brian, Cubs........	0	0	.000	0.00	1	0	0	0	0	0	2.0	1	6	0	0	0	0	0	0	0	0	2	0	0
Stottlemyre, Todd, Dia.	2	0	1.000	0.53	3	3	1	0	0	0	17.0	11	64	1	1	0	0	0	1	3	0	25	0	0
Stumm, Jason, W.S.	0	0	.000	3.27	3	2	0	0	0	0	11.0	13	47	8	4	2	0	1	1	3	0	9	1	0
Thompson, Michael, Pad.	1	7	.125	6.09	13	13	0	0	0	0	65.0	78	300	52	44	8	2	3	4	27	0	62	3	4
Tollberg, Brian, Pad.	0	0	.000	4.50	2	2	0	0	0	0	4.0	4	16	2	2	0	0	0	0	0	0	6	0	0
Trask, Cody, Rock.	0	0	.000	8.31	9	1	0	0	1	0	17.1	26	89	21	16	0	2	1	0	13	0	12	4	2
Trejo, Francisco, Dia.*	0	2	.000	3.18	17	0	0	0	6	1	28.1	28	131	18	10	0	2	0	1	19	0	30	10	1
Ulacia, Dennis, W.S.*	3	2	.600	3.79	8	8	0	0	0	0	38.0	36	157	19	16	2	0	1	1	11	1	52	0	2
Valentine, Joseph, W.S.	0	0	.000	0.00	3	0	0	0	1	0	4.1	2	14	0	0	0	0	0	0	2	0	0	0	0
Valera, Greg, Dia.	1	2	.333	3.79	13	2	0	0	4	0	19.0	17	85	11	8	0	0	1	2	13	0	20	2	0
Valverde, Jose, Dia.	1	2	.333	4.08	20	0	0	0	17	8	28.2	34	138	21	13	1	0	0	4	10	0	47	1	1
Velazquez, Elih, Ath.*	4	1	.800	3.70	16	4	0	0	1	0	41.1	44	175	18	17	1	0	1	1	10	0	38	1	1
Velazquez, Ernesto, Pad.	2	3	.400	3.71	18	0	0	0	11	2	34.0	44	144	19	14	3	0	0	3	15	0	15	0	0
Villarreal, Oscar, Dia.	1	5	.167	3.78	14	11	0	0	1	0	64.1	64	286	39	27	1	2	3	10	25	0	51	6	4
Vitek, Joshua, Pad.	6	2	.750	3.99	12	10	0	0	0	0	47.1	43	212	22	21	3	0	4	8	24	0	48	2	0
Vizcarra, Enrique, Mex.	0	1	.000	1.80	11	0	0	0	5	3	15.0	9	60	3	3	0	1	2	7	2	15	2	0
Webb, John, Cubs	0	0	.000	3.58	18	0	0	0	14	3	32.2	33	147	20	13	0	1	1	3	8	0	39	2	2
Webster, Jeremy, Pad.*	1	0	1.000	4.26	7	0	0	0	1	0	12.2	13	67	11	6	2	0	0	2	13	0	16	2	0
Weinberg, Todd, Ath.*	0	0	.000	4.15	6	0	0	0	2	0	4.1	5	18	5	2	1	0	0	0	0	0	3	1	0
Wells, Roy, Mar.	3	0	1.000	2.70	10	9	0	0	0	0	46.2	39	199	22	14	0	1	0	1	22	0	52	1	2
West, Brian, W.S.	0	1	.000	13.50	2	0	0	0	1	0	4.2	10	25	7	7	0	1	2	0	2	0	3	0	0
Wiggins, Daniel, Cubs...........	3	0	1.000	2.88	17	0	0	0	6	2	34.1	29	146	16	11	2	2	1	4	11	0	47	2	1
Yepiz, Heriberto M., Mex.	0	2	.000	2.76	15	0	0	0	6	1	29.1	24	112	10	9	2	0	0	6	0	28	0	1
Zorrilla, Reinaldo, W.S.	0	1	.000	7.07	14	0	0	0	6	1	14.0	16	66	13	11	0	0	1	5	2	1	17	1	1

COMBINATION SHUTOUTS: **Athletics (2)**—Minaya-Velazquez-Maurer-Miller, Galva-Sobchuk-Weinberg. **Cubs (0)**—None. **Diamondbacks (3)**—Stottlemyre-Ovalles-Montoya, Ovalles-Montoya-Valverde, Ovalles-Montoya-Valverde. **Mariners (2)**—Espinal-Kesten-Montenegero-Grunwald, Wells-Clark-Grunwald. **Mexico (3)**—Renovato-Vizcarra, Jimenez-Yepiz, Navarro-Cortez. **Padres (3)**—Peavey-Velazquez, Peavey-Velazquez-Meyer, Cyr-Meyer. **Rockies (2)**—Kusiewicz-Gonzalez-Serrano, Garner-Matos-Serrano. **White Sox (0)**—None.

NO-HIT GAMES: None.

1999 FIELDING
TEAM

Team	Pct.	G	PO	A	E	TC	DP	TP	PB	Team	Pct.	G	PO	A	E	TC	DP	TP	PB
Mexico	.960	56	1411	532	81	2024	48	0	6	Padres..............	.946	55	1446	505	111	2062	46	0	15
Mariners............	.957	56	1478	497	89	2064	42	0	19	Cubs................	.946	55	1442	485	110	2037	22	0	18
Athletics	.953	56	1491	619	105	2215	69	0	25	Diamondbacks ..	.942	56	1423	599	125	2147	39	0	16
White Sox	.947	56	1424	584	112	2120	44	0	15	Rockies	.940	56	1441	606	130	2177	51	0	18

FIRST BASEMEN

NOTE: All caps denotes fielding-percentage leader based on 28 games for catchers, 37 for all other non-pitchers and 45 innings for pitchers. *Throws lefthanded.

Player, Team	Pct.	G	PO	A	E	TC	DP
Blankenship, Anthony, W.S.	1.000	1	1	0	0	1	1
Cisneros, Ventura, Mex.	.981	19	143	8	3	154	12
Daly, Sean, Rock.	.978	10	85	2	2	89	9
Egly, John, Dia.	.980	50	456	29	10	495	32
Ellis, Alvyn, Ath.	.965	31	242	9	9	260	31
Encarnacion, Santos, Pad.	.986	47	314	31	5	350	37
Garcia, Luis, Mex.	.985	15	129	3	2	134	16
Gauch, Barry, W.S.	1.000	1	9	0	0	9	0
Gregg, Mitch, Ath.	.995	25	202	12	1	215	27
Hertel, Brian, Mar.	.988	32	233	8	3	244	19
Kashirsky, Michael, W.S.*	1.000	14	70	3	0	73	7
Kent, Alan, Rock.	.957	10	66	1	3	70	3
Klatt, Jason, Pad.	.971	10	64	4	2	70	3
Londono, Alex, Rock.	.974	5	36	1	1	38	3
Lowe, Ernesto, W.S.	1.000	1	2	0	0	2	0
McCLURE, Trey, Cubs	.986	42	321	25	5	351	17
Mulqueen, Dave, Rock.	.980	27	236	9	5	250	21
Noboa, Joel, Dia.	.882	2	14	1	2	17	2
Oglesby, Travis, Dia.	.971	5	31	3	1	35	2
Pagan, Andres, Pad.	.906	5	24	5	3	32	2
Pena, Wilton, Ath.	.955	5	21	0	1	22	5
Pines, Gregory, Mar.	.992	18	125	4	1	130	14
Reyes, Christian, Ath.	1.000	6	29	2	0	31	2
Reyes, Rene, Rock.	.989	18	163	10	2	175	13
Rodriguez, Erick, Mex.	.989	22	163	13	2	178	14
Rogowski, Casey, W.S.*	.969	46	381	27	13	421	30
Rohena, Omar, Cubs	.963	11	72	5	3	80	1
Sprowl, Jon, Cubs*	.978	8	41	4	1	46	1
Tapia, Roman, W.S.	.944	3	17	0	1	18	4
Wheat, Trey, W.S.	1.000	1	1	0	0	1	0

SECOND BASEMEN

Player, Team	Pct.	G	PO	A	E	TC	DP
Bellhorn, Mark, Ath.	1.000	7	22	17	0	39	6
Bernard, Dagoberto, Rock.	.949	14	27	29	3	59	5
Berroa, Angel, Ath.	1.000	10	31	27	0	58	9
Blankenship, Anthony, W.S.	1.000	3	3	6	0	9	1
Cruz, Hector, Dia.	.905	11	21	36	6	63	5
Doakes, Schuyler, Mar.	.938	29	68	69	9	146	15
Duenas, Manuel, Pad.	.937	38	92	72	11	175	26
Durango, Ariel, Mar.	.931	12	31	23	4	58	5
Flores, Ralph, W.S.	1.000	1	1	2	0	3	1
Gil, Eric, Mex.	.955	17	27	37	3	67	6
Hall, Justin, Ath.	1.000	1	2	2	0	4	0
Klatt, Jason, Pad.	.956	21	33	32	3	68	10
Martinez, Dionnar, Cubs	.000	1	0	0	0	0	0
Martinez, Guillermo, Mar.	.933	12	20	22	3	45	4
Mendez, Hector, Mex.	.857	4	5	7	2	14	0
Morrissey, Adam, Cubs	.925	44	84	88	14	186	18
Palafox, Sergio, Mex.	.987	35	67	90	2	159	27
Pimentel, Francisco, Cubs	.833	2	2	3	1	6	0
Pimentel, Franklin, Ath.	.950	44	96	112	11	219	35
Ramirez, Oscar, Mar.	1.000	6	17	18	0	35	5
REYES, Guillermo, W.S.	.964	52	108	130	9	247	31
Schmidt, J.P., Ath.	1.000	1	3	3	0	6	1
Tapia, Roman, W.S.	1.000	1	1	1	0	2	0
Thornton-Murray, Jandin, Cubs	.923	13	20	16	3	39	0
Ventura, Juan, Rock.	.939	45	90	109	13	212	25
Vizcaino, Maximo, Dia.	1.000	4	6	9	0	15	1
Yakopich, Joseph, Dia.	.938	44	58	93	10	161	19

THIRD BASEMEN

Player, Team	Pct.	G	PO	A	E	TC	DP
Berroa, Angel, Ath.	.889	9	7	17	3	27	3
Blankenship, Anthony, W.S.	1.000	1	1	2	0	3	0
Cruz, Hector, Dia.	.900	4	0	9	1	10	0
Duenas, Manuel, Pad.	.875	6	3	4	1	8	0
Durango, Ariel, Mar.	1.000	2	2	8	0	10	1
Encarnacion, Santos, Pad.	.667	4	1	1	1	3	0
Espinoza, Efren, Mex.	.900	8	7	11	2	20	3
Figueroa, Luis, Mar.	1.000	1	0	1	0	1	1
Gil, Eric, Mex.	.667	2	1	1	1	3	0
Klatt, Jason, Pad.	.818	3	7	2	2	11	0
Lara, Franklin, Mar.	.910	26	18	43	6	67	4
Mulqueen, Dave, Rock.	.879	19	5	24	4	33	2

SHORTSTOPS

Player, Team	Pct.	G	PO	A	E	TC	DP
Noboa, Joel, Dia.	.919	51	42	94	12	148	2
Ortiz , Jorge, Ath.	.857	13	4	14	3	21	2
Paulino, Robert, Cubs	1.000	3	2	4	0	6	0
Pimentel, Francisco, Cubs	.864	23	19	32	8	59	0
Pimentel, Franklin, Ath.	1.000	6	3	6	0	9	1
Pines, Gregory, Mar.	1.000	1	0	1	0	1	0
PRESICHI, Cristian, Mex.	.920	49	47	102	13	162	14
Puccinelli, John, Pad.	.884	48	35	87	16	138	11
Ramirez, Oscar, Mar.	.868	30	19	40	9	68	6
Reyes, Christian, Ath.	.902	41	16	67	9	92	11
Sing, Brandon, Cubs	.918	16	12	33	4	49	2
Solorzano, Lenin, W.S.	.914	48	32	107	13	152	11
Tapia, Roman, W.S.	.941	12	7	9	1	17	0
Thornton-Murray, Jandin, Cubs.	.872	17	5	29	5	39	2
Vizcaino, Maximo, Dia.	.875	3	0	7	1	8	0
Warren, Chris, Rock.	.900	40	35	82	13	130	5

SHORTSTOPS

Player, Team	Pct.	G	PO	A	E	TC	DP
Bernard, Dagoberto, Rock.	.898	21	38	68	12	118	17
Berroa, Angel, Ath.	.903	31	46	93	15	154	28
Blankenship, Anthony, W.S.	.750	1	0	3	1	4	1
Cordova, Alfredo, Mex.	.808	7	10	11	5	26	5
Cruz, Hector, Dia.	.870	10	10	37	7	54	6
Durango, Ariel, Mar.	.957	5	7	15	1	23	4
Espinoza, Efren, Mex.	.857	15	25	35	10	70	8
Figueroa, Carlos, Rock.	.881	39	46	125	23	194	17
Flores, Ralph, W.S.	.925	53	74	137	17	228	24
Freeman, Corey, Mar.	.933	27	43	54	7	104	8
Gil, Eric, Mex.	.000	1	0	0	0	0	0
Hall, Justin, Ath.	.667	3	1	3	2	6	0
Klassen, Danny, Dia.	.962	6	4	21	1	26	1
Klatt, Jason, Pad.	.961	13	13	36	2	51	5
Lagana, Shawn, Dia.	.882	39	40	110	20	170	21
Martinez, Dionnar, Cubs	.942	40	42	88	8	138	15
Martinez, Guillermo, Mar.	.909	29	38	72	11	121	13
Paulino, Robert, Cubs	.917	17	14	19	3	36	1
Puccinelli, John, Pad.	.833	1	1	4	1	6	0
Romero, Nicholas, Pad.	.878	43	59	106	23	188	23
SANCHEZ, Jose, Mex.	.945	38	56	82	8	146	15
Schmidt, J.P., Ath.	.919	33	29	85	10	124	14
Solorzano, Lenin, W.S.	.889	4	3	5	1	9	2
Thornton-Murray, Jandin, Cubs	.842	4	7	9	3	19	0
Vizcaino, Maximo, Dia.	.897	6	10	16	3	29	3
Warren, Chris, Rock.	1.000	1	0	3	0	3	0

OUTFIELDERS

Player, Team	Pct.	G	PO	A	E	TC	DP
Anderson, Syketo, Cubs	.857	27	29	1	5	35	0
Berroa, Angel, Ath.	1.000	2	2	0	0	2	0
Betts, Dewayne, Ath.	.966	33	28	0	1	29	0
Cash, Lavalroe, Cubs	.955	39	59	5	3	67	0
Chirinos, German, Ath.	.931	50	87	7	7	101	1
Clark, Jamie, Mar.*	.967	24	27	2	1	30	0
Clark, Kevin, Mar.	1.000	2	4	0	0	4	0
Encarnacion, Santos, Pad.	1.000	6	10	1	0	11	0
Faison, Vince, Pad.	.975	42	75	4	2	81	0
Felix, Osvaldo, Mex.*	.966	50	105	9	4	118	3
Fulse, Sheldon, Mar.	.981	26	52	1	1	54	0
Gallegos, Alejandro, Mex.	.951	44	76	2	4	82	0
Garcia, Luis, Mex.	.937	37	54	5	4	63	2
Gearlds, Aaron, Rock.	.886	47	69	1	9	79	1
Gil, Eric, Mex.	.000	1	0	0	0	0	0
Goolsby, Kevin, W.S.	.930	42	60	6	5	71	1
Gould, Elliotte, Pad.	.886	15	31	0	4	35	0
Guzman, Javier, Rock.	.842	12	16	0	3	19	0
Hall, Victor, Dia.*	1.000	27	48	0	0	48	0
Hernandez, Orlando, Mar.	.957	27	43	1	2	46	0
Hines, Derek, Cubs	1.000	33	42	0	0	42	0
Johnstone, Benjamin, Cubs	1.000	2	2	0	0	2	0
Jorgenson, Chris, Dia.	.000	1	0	0	1	1	0
Kail, Tom, Dia.	.931	47	52	2	4	58	1
Knorr, Mario, Dia.	.952	44	73	6	4	83	2
Londono, Alex, Rock.	.846	24	30	3	6	39	0
Lopez, Orlando, Mar.	.952	41	58	1	3	62	0
Lowe, Ernesto, W.S.	.935	38	70	2	5	77	0
Mallory, Michael, Cubs	.926	33	62	1	5	68	0
Marchiano, Mike, Mar.	1.000	1	2	0	0	2	0
McCall, Gerard, W.S.	.000	1	0	0	0	0	0

Player, Team	Pct.	G	PO	A	E	TC	DP
McCarty, Brock, Dia.	.904	44	64	2	7	73	0
McClure, Trey, Cubs	1.000	1	2	1	0	3	0
Morency, Vernand, Rock.	.974	42	75	1	2	78	0
Morenz, Shea, Pad.	1.000	3	4	0	0	4	0
Palafox, Sergio, Mex.	.000	1	0	0	0	0	0
Paredes, Reny, Cubs	.920	28	46	0	4	50	0
Pellerano, Cristi, Ath.	.959	45	69	2	3	74	0
Perez, Rafael, W.S.	.827	50	63	4	14	81	1
Pines, Gregory, Mar.	1.000	4	4	0	0	4	0
Quintana, Wilfredo, Mar.	.933	16	23	5	2	30	1
Ramirez, Oscar, Mar.	.000	1	0	0	0	0	0
Reyes, Julio, W.S.	.906	28	29	0	3	32	0
Richardson, Miguel, Mar.	.925	35	59	3	5	67	0
Robinson, Coby, Cubs	1.000	15	25	1	0	26	0
Rogowski, Casey, W.S.*	.000	1	0	0	0	0	0
Rohena, Omar, Cubs	1.000	4	5	3	0	8	0
Rosa, Ivan, Ath.*	.871	21	24	3	4	31	0
Sobet, Renato, Pad.	.906	34	46	2	5	53	0
Testa, Chris, Rock.*	.938	47	83	7	6	96	2
Tomshack, Steven, Dia.	1.000	8	7	0	0	7	0
Van Rossum, Chris, Dia.*	.909	4	8	2	1	11	1
VANDEMORE, Anthony, Pad.	.977	46	81	5	2	88	2
Wagner, Mike, Pad.	.979	28	40	6	1	47	0
Wenner, Michael, Ath.	.956	48	81	6	4	91	1
Wheat, Trey, W.S.	.893	14	24	1	3	28	0
Yakopich, Joseph, Dia.	.000	1	0	0	0	0	0
Zavala, Juan, Mex.	.935	35	37	6	3	46	0

CATCHERS

Player, Team	Pct.	G	PO	A	E	TC	DP	PB
Castillo, Carlos, Ath.	.975	31	171	24	5	200	4	8
Christianson, Ryan, Mar.	1.000	6	45	7	0	52	0	1
Cisneros, Ventura, Mex.	.971	19	146	21	5	172	2	2
Cochrane, Mark, W.S.	.959	22	146	17	7	170	0	7
Daly, Sean, Rock.	1.000	6	40	4	0	44	0	1
Delgado, Jorge, Dia.	.977	18	150	19	4	173	0	4
Diaz, Jose, Mar.	.991	15	93	16	1	110	2	7
Gauch, Barry, W.S.	.976	14	104	18	3	125	0	2
Goldfield, Josh, Dia.	.889	1	5	3	1	9	0	2
Gutierrez, Said, Pad.	.939	7	37	9	3	49	0	3
Halgren, Chris, Ath.	1.000	7	36	2	0	38	0	2
Hamel, Jon, Pad.	.975	21	176	20	5	201	0	3
Kent, Mat, Mar.	.979	22	160	28	4	192	1	6
McCall, Gerard, W.S.	.974	25	189	32	6	227	0	5
Oglesby, Travis, Dia.	.959	18	124	18	6	148	0	8
Ortega, Sixto, Rock.	.957	24	135	20	7	162	1	6
Pagan, Andres, Pad.	.962	19	137	15	6	158	1	7
Pena, Pelagio, Mar.	.978	18	160	15	4	179	3	5
PENA, Wilton, Ath.	.980	33	207	33	5	245	3	15
Peralta, Marco, Mex.	.947	4	35	1	2	38	0	1
Pina, Emmanuel, Cubs	.950	18	153	19	9	181	0	2
Pines, Gregory, Mar.	1.000	6	47	4	0	51	1	0
Quezada, Juan, Mex.	.992	17	104	14	1	119	1	2
Rodriguez, Erick, Mex.	.991	15	101	15	1	117	1	1
Roehler, Trent, W.S.	1.000	4	8	3	0	11	0	1
Rowden, Monte, Cubs	.980	13	88	8	2	98	0	4
Samuel, Tomas, Rock.	.963	29	204	30	9	243	0	11
Sprowl, Jon, Cubs*	.987	18	133	17	2	152	0	7
Tomshack, Steven, Dia.	.944	21	167	19	11	197	0	2
Trzesniak, Nicholas, Pad.	.986	13	132	11	2	145	0	2
Van Horn, Ryan, Cubs	.972	18	115	22	4	141	0	5

PITCHERS

Player, Team	Pct.	G	PO	A	E	TC	DP
Acosta, Jhon, Cubs	1.000	5	2	3	0	5	0
Alvarez, Larry, Cubs	1.000	8	0	4	0	4	0
Arauz, Alexis, Dia.	.857	16	2	10	2	14	1
Asencio, Domingo, W.S.	1.000	11	0	2	0	2	0
Baek, Cha, Mar.	1.000	8	1	2	0	3	0
Bailey, David, Cubs	1.000	4	1	2	0	3	0
Barcelo, Lorenzo, W.S.	1.000	9	1	7	0	8	0
Baxter, Gerik, Pad.	1.000	8	1	3	0	4	0
Beckman, Jacob, Ath.	1.000	12	2	4	0	6	0
Beltran, Francis, Cubs	1.000	7	0	2	0	2	0
Beltre, Sandy, W.S.	1.000	13	3	12	0	15	1
Benitez, Angel, Cubs	.889	16	4	4	1	9	0
Blumenstock, Brad, Ath.	.833	3	1	4	1	6	0
Briggs, Anthony, Rock.	.000	3	0	0	0	0	0
Calzada, Javier, Ath.	.800	10	4	4	2	10	0
Castellano, Jonathan, Mex.	.833	16	4	6	2	12	0
Chavez, Wilton, Cubs	.700	14	11	3	6	20	0

Player, Team	Pct.	G	PO	A	E	TC	DP
Christensen, Benjamin, Cubs	1.000	3	0	1	0	1	0
Christensen, Deryck, Rock.	.833	18	1	4	1	6	1
Clark, Kevin, Mar.	1.000	16	0	1	0	1	0
Cordero, Frangil, Cubs*	.900	14	2	7	1	10	0
Cortez, Martin, Mex.*	1.000	20	1	3	0	4	0
Cueto, Jose, Cubs	.538	11	5	2	6	13	0
Cyr, Eric, Pad.*	.833	11	2	8	2	12	1
De La Rosa, Jorge, Dia.*	1.000	8	0	1	0	1	0
Deveraux, Dale, Dia.	1.000	16	2	2	0	4	0
Diaz, Alexander, Ath.	1.000	22	3	5	0	8	0
Diaz, Eddy, Cubs	.889	17	2	6	1	9	0
Dowell, Brian, Pad.	1.000	2	1	0	0	1	0
Drain, Bradley, Mar.	.818	13	2	7	2	11	1
Dunham, Pat, Mar.	1.000	7	0	1	0	1	0
Dunphy, Micah, Ath.*	.800	16	2	2	1	5	0
Earle, Scott, Mar.	.000	7	0	0	0	0	0
Ellis, Alvyn, Mar.	.000	1	0	0	0	0	0
Encarnacion, Luis, Mar.	.667	15	1	3	2	6	0
Ericks, Dave, Cubs	1.000	16	3	2	0	5	0
Espinal, Juan, Mar.	.889	15	3	5	1	9	2
Ferrand, Dario, W.S.	.875	13	4	10	2	16	0
Ferrand, Julian, Rock.	1.000	13	3	1	0	4	0
Figueroa, Nelson, Dia.	.667	1	0	2	1	3	0
Galva, Claudio, Ath.*	.950	14	6	13	1	20	0
Garcia, Joaquin, Mar.	.714	12	1	4	2	7	1
GARNER, Brandon, Rock.	1.000	14	3	16	0	19	3
Ginter, Matt, W.S.	1.000	3	1	0	0	1	0
Goldfield, Josh, Dia.	1.000	1	0	3	0	3	0
Gonzalez, Miguel, Rock.	1.000	10	2	1	0	3	0
Granados, Bernie, Rock.	1.000	16	1	3	0	4	0
Grunwald, Erik, Mar.	1.000	18	0	3	0	3	0
Herrera, Jose, Mar.	1.000	12	2	2	0	4	0
Hoerman, Jared, Mar.	1.000	11	0	2	0	2	0
Hoff, Steve, Cubs*	1.000	3	0	1	0	1	0
Hollifield, Alec, W.S.	.200	16	1	0	4	5	0
Holmes, Darren, Dia.	.000	2	0	0	0	0	0
Hughes, Rocky, W.S.*	1.000	13	2	10	0	12	1
Jackson, Stosh, Cubs*	.667	6	1	1	1	3	0
Jacobs, Frankey, Ath.	1.000	12	1	4	0	5	1
Jimenez, Julio, Mex.*	1.000	13	1	14	0	15	0
Johnson, Roney, Rock.	.889	9	4	4	1	9	0
Jones, Geoffrey, Pad.*	1.000	14	0	1	0	1	1
Kesten, Michael, Mar.*	.667	13	1	1	1	3	0
Kibler, Ryan, Rock.	.931	14	5	22	2	29	1
Kim, Byung-Hyun, Dia.	.000	1	0	0	0	0	0
Knorr, Mario, Dia.	.000	1	0	0	0	0	0
Koehler, Russ, Mar.	1.000	4	2	1	0	3	0
Kroon, Marc, Mar.	.000	4	0	0	0	0	0
Kusiewicz, Mike, Rock.*	.714	6	0	5	2	7	0
Lopez, Juan, W.S.*	.800	14	0	4	1	5	0
Lorenzo, Javier, Rock.	.667	20	0	4	2	6	0
Malone, Corwin, W.S.*	1.000	10	1	3	0	4	0
Martinez, Daniel, W.S.*	.500	13	0	1	1	2	0
Martinez, Juan, Mex.	1.000	15	1	15	0	16	2
Matos, Jesus, Rock.	1.000	18	1	4	0	5	0
Maurer, Mike, Ath.	1.000	7	1	0	0	1	0
Mendoza, Hatuey, Dia.	.857	13	6	12	3	21	0
Meyer, John, Pad.	1.000	21	3	1	0	4	0
Middlebrook, Jason, Pad.	.000	1	0	0	0	0	0
Miller, Corey, Ath.	1.000	18	2	6	0	8	3
Minaya, Edwin, Ath.	.929	14	3	10	1	14	0
Montenegro, Christopher, Mar.	1.000	19	0	2	0	2	0
Montoya, Saul, Dia.	1.000	17	2	1	0	3	0
Moore, Joel, Rock.	1.000	4	1	2	0	3	0
Morel, Francis, Dia.	1.000	7	0	2	0	2	0
Moreno, Edgar, Mex.	.800	18	1	3	1	5	0
Moreno, Victor, Dia.	.000	7	0	0	2	2	0
Munoz, Arnaldo, W.S.*	1.000	14	0	1	0	1	0
Myers, Todd, Dia.	1.000	3	0	2	0	2	0
Nantkes, Kurt, Ath.	.692	15	2	7	4	13	1
Navarro, Hector, Mex.	1.000	11	1	2	0	3	1
Ovalles, Juan, Dia.	.857	14	8	4	2	14	0
Pate, Dustin, Cubs	.889	12	4	4	1	9	0
Patten, Michael, W.S.	.667	15	1	3	2	6	0
Peavy, Jacob, Pad.	.857	13	4	8	2	14	0
Perez, Oliver, Pad.*	.750	15	1	2	1	4	0
Perkins, Gregory, Dia.	1.000	4	1	3	0	4	0
Puga, Sergio, Mex.	1.000	13	1	2	0	3	0
Purvis, Robert, W.S.	1.000	4	2	2	0	4	0
Randolph, Steve, Dia.*	1.000	2	1	2	0	3	0
Renovato, Nestor, Mex.	1.000	9	2	3	0	5	0
Reyes, Junior, Cubs*	1.000	7	1	0	0	1	0

SUMMER CLASS A *Arizona League*

Player, Team	Pct.	G	PO	A	E	TC	DP
Romo, Eduardo, Mex.	1.000	12	1	4	0	5	0
Rosario, Hipolito, Pad.	1.000	16	6	4	0	10	0
Rossiter, Mike, Rock.	.000	1	0	0	0	0	0
Rubio, Miguel, Dia.	1.000	2	0	1	0	1	0
Ruiz, Juan, Mex.	1.000	1	0	2	0	2	0
Sanders, David, W.S.*	1.000	7	0	2	0	2	0
Serrano, Alex, Rock.	.889	18	2	6	1	9	0
Simpson, Joe, Rock.	1.000	14	3	3	0	6	0
Sobchuk, Justin, Ath.	.909	15	4	6	1	11	1
Soto, Darwin, Pad.	1.000	15	2	5	0	7	0
Stephenson, Brian, Cubs	1.000	1	1	0	0	1	0
Stottlemyre, Todd, Dia.	1.000	3	1	2	0	3	0
Stumm, Jason, W.S.	1.000	3	3	3	0	6	0
Thompson, Michael, Pad.	.800	13	3	9	3	15	0
Tollberg, Brian, Pad.	.000	2	0	0	0	0	0
Trask, Cody, Rock.	.833	9	2	3	1	6	0
Trejo, Francisco, Dia.*	.800	17	0	4	1	5	0
Ulacia, Dennis, W.S.*	1.000	8	1	4	0	5	0
Valentine, Joseph, W.S.	1.000	3	0	1	0	1	0
Valera, Greg, Dia.	1.000	13	0	3	0	3	0
Valverde, Jose, Dia.	1.000	20	5	0	0	5	0
Velazquez, Elih, Ath.*	.889	16	1	7	1	9	0
Velazquez, Ernesto, Pad.	.700	18	4	3	3	10	0
Villarreal, Oscar, Dia.	.933	14	5	9	1	15	1
Vitek, Joshua, Pad.	1.000	12	4	2	0	6	1
Vizcarra, Enrique, Mex.	.833	11	2	3	1	6	0
Webb, John, Cubs	.889	18	1	7	1	9	0
Webster, Jeremy, Pad.*	1.000	7	0	2	0	2	0
Weinberg, Todd, Ath.*	1.000	6	0	1	0	1	0
Wells, Roy, Mar.	.667	10	1	1	1	3	0
West, Brian, W.S.	1.000	2	0	1	0	1	0
Wiggins, Daniel, Cubs	1.000	17	2	3	0	5	0
Yepiz, Heriberto Martinez, Mex.	1.000	15	1	2	0	3	0
Zorrilla, Reinaldo, W.S.	1.000	14	0	3	0	3	0

The following players appeared only as designated hitter, pinch-hitter or pinch runner: Battle, dh; I. Cruz, dh-ph-pr.

LEAGUE CHAMPIONS

Year	Team	Pct.	Year	Team	Pct.	Year	Team	Pct.
1988—	Peoria Brewers	.690	1992—	Scottsdale A's	.607	1996—	Padres	.643
1989—	Peoria Brewers	.732	1993—	Scottsdale A's	.636	1997—	Cubs	.618
1990—	Peoria Brewers	.679	1994—	Chandler Cardinals	.607	1998—	Rockies	.750
1991—	Scottsdale A's	.650	1995—	Scottsdale A's	.661	1999—	Athletics	.696

SUMMER CLASS A *Arizona League*

GULF COAST LEAGUE

LEAGUE OFFICE

President
Tom Saffell

Address
1503 Clower Creek Dr., H-262
Sarasota, FL 34231

Phone
941-966-6407

Teams*
Braves
Expos
Marlins
Orioles
Phillies
Pirates
Rangers
Reds
Red Sox
Royals

Tigers
Twins
Yankees

*Teams play their games in Bradenton, Clearwater, Fort Charlotte, Fort Myers, Haines City, Jupiter, Lakeland, Melbourne, Orlando, Sarasota and Tampa.

1999 FINAL STANDINGS

EASTERN DIVISION

Team	W	L	T	Pct.	GB
Mets	39	21	0	.650	...
Expos	29	31	0	.483	10.0
Braves	27	33	0	.450	12.0
Marlins	25	35	0	.417	14.0

NORTHERN DIVISION

Team	W	L	T	Pct.	GB
Royals	33	27	0	.550	...
Yankees	32	28	0	.533	1.0
Tigers	29	31	0	.483	4.0
Phillies	26	34	0	.433	7.0

WESTERN DIVISION

Team	W	L	T	Pct.	GB
Rangers	37	23	0	.617	...
Twins	33	26	1	.559	3.5
Orioles	31	28	1	.525	5.5
Red Sox	30	29	1	.508	6.5
Pirates	24	35	1	.407	12.5
Reds	23	37	0	.383	14.0

COMPOSITE

Team	Mets	Rang.	Twins	Roy.	Yank.	Ori.	R.S.	Tig.	Exp.	Brav.	Phi.	Mar.	Pir.	Reds	W	L	T	Pct.	GB
Mets	...	0	0	0	0	0	0	0	13	14	0	12	0	0	39	21	0	.650	...
Rangers	0	...	8	0	0	8	8	0	0	0	0	0	7	6	37	23	0	.617	2.0
Twins	0	4	...	0	0	9	5	0	0	0	0	0	7	8	33	26	1	.559	5.5
Royals	0	0	0	...	13	0	0	9	0	0	11	0	0	0	33	27	0	.550	6.0
Yankees	0	0	0	7	...	0	0	12	0	0	0	13	0	0	32	28	0	.533	7.0
Orioles	0	4	3	0	0	...	7	0	0	0	0	0	8	9	31	28	1	.525	7.5
Red Sox	0	4	6	0	0	5	...	0	0	0	0	0	9	6	30	29	1	.508	8.5
Tigers	0	0	0	11	8	0	0	...	0	0	10	0	0	0	29	31	0	.483	10.0
Expos	7	0	0	0	0	0	0	0	...	11	0	11	0	0	29	31	0	.483	10.0
Braves	6	0	0	0	0	0	0	0	9	...	0	12	0	0	27	33	0	.450	12.0
Phillies	0	0	0	9	7	0	0	10	0	0	...	0	0	0	26	34	0	.433	13.0
Marlins	8	0	0	0	0	0	0	0	9	8	0	...	0	0	25	35	0	.417	14.0
Pirates	0	5	5	0	0	3	3	0	0	0	0	0	...	8	24	35	1	.407	14.5
Reds	0	6	4	0	0	3	6	0	0	0	0	0	4	...	23	37	0	.373	16.0

Games played in Bradenton, Dunedin, Fort Myers, Melbourne, Osceola, Port Charlotte, St. Lucie County, Sarasota, Tampa and West Palm Beach, Fla.

TIES: Orioles at Pirates, August 17 (8-8, eighth inning). Twins at Red Sox, August 17 (3-3, sixth inning).

FORFEIT: Expos forfeited to Braves, June 24 (Braves won 9-0).

Club names are major league affiliations.

PLAYOFFS: Mets defeated Royals one game to none; Twins defeated Rangers one game to none; Mets defeated Twins two games to none to win league championship.

REGULAR-SEASON ATTENDANCE: No total official attendance figures reported.

MANAGERS: Braves, Rock Albert; Expos, Bill Masse; Marlins, Jon Deeble; Mets, John Stephenson; Orioles, Jesus Alfaro; Phillies, Ramon Aviles; Pirates, Woody Huyke; Rangers, Darryl Kennedy; Red Sox, John Sanders; Reds, Donnie Scott; Royals, Andre David; Tigers, Gary Green; Twins, Al Newman; Yankees, Ken Dominguez.

ALL-STAR TEAM: 1B—Steve Rodriguez, Tigers; 2B—Leandro Arias, Mets; 3B—Hank Blalock, Rangers; SS—Enrique Cruz, Mets; OF—Chip Ambres, Marlins; Yhency Brazoban, Yankees; Gary Withrow, Yankees; C—Mike Jacobs, Mets; SP—David Tavarez, Orioles; RP—Buddy Yen, Royals; Manager of the Year—John Stephenson, Mets.

1999 BATTING

TEAM

Team	Avg.	G	TPA	AB	R	H	TB	2B	3B	HR	RBI	SH	SF	HP	BB	IBB	SO	SB	CS	GDP	LOB	ShO	Slg.	OBP
Mets	.266	60	2298	1971	324	525	729	94	19	24	273	21	18	39	249	4	455	58	29	49	431	1	.370	.357
Twins	.262	60	2164	1838	295	481	620	77	16	10	236	34	18	33	241	11	356	75	32	33	438	2	.337	.354
Yankees	.260	60	2246	1922	292	500	730	98	18	32	268	11	19	39	255	3	486	44	33	37	453	4	.380	.355
Orioles	.258	60	2161	1896	303	490	707	90	20	29	246	26	22	30	187	6	368	141	48	30	359	1	.373	.331
Tigers	.254	60	2101	1851	240	470	655	98	15	19	209	17	16	27	190	2	463	96	41	33	386	9	.354	.330
Pirates	.250	60	2232	1990	274	497	679	84	16	22	231	12	21	32	177	3	431	82	27	37	397	2	.341	.318
Phillies	.248	60	2168	1860	248	461	634	93	10	20	202	19	18	43	228	7	450	94	33	40	430	3	.341	.341
Rangers	.247	60	2231	1909	302	471	680	91	26	22	250	21	21	42	238	13	460	85	31	35	421	2	.356	.340

Team	Avg.	G	TPA	AB	R	H	TB	2B	3B	HR	RBI	SH	SF	HP	BB	IBB	SO	SB	CS	GDP	LOB	ShO	Slg.	OBP
Royals	.247	60	2314	1939	305	478	683	89	16	28	259	22	24	25	304	0	507	101	25	37	466	1	.352	.352
Braves	.244	60	2298	2018	265	493	687	86	9	30	233	13	8	34	225	2	482	55	26	29	454	5	.340	.329
Marlins	.241	60	2298	2015	239	486	654	95	20	11	196	10	15	40	218	3	456	100	45	33	465	3	.325	.325
Red Sox	.241	60	2207	1915	279	461	640	72	19	23	232	10	20	36	226	1	401	65	45	44	388	4	.334	.329
Expos	.238	60	2132	1898	215	451	561	66	10	8	186	11	15	28	180	2	348	73	24	51	396	5	.296	.311
Reds	.225	60	2092	1861	220	418	569	75	17	14	180	13	12	34	172	4	427	87	28	36	380	4	.306	.300

INDIVIDUAL

TOP QUALIFIERS FOR BATTING CHAMPIONSHIP

Minimum 162 plate appearances. *Lefthanded batter. †Switch-hitter.

Player, Team	Avg.	G	TPA	AB	R	H	TB	2B	3B	HR	RBI	SH	SF	HP	BB	IBB	SO	SB	CS	GDP	Slg.	OBP
Blalock, Hank, Rang.*	.361	51	222	191	34	69	107	17	6	3	38	0	5	1	25	4	23	3	2	7	.560	.428
Ambres, Chip, Marl.	.353	37	168	139	29	49	71	13	3	1	15	0	2	2	25	0	19	22	3	0	.511	.452
Jacobs, Michael, Mets*	.333	44	168	147	18	49	73	12	0	4	30	0	5	1	14	2	30	2	0	3	.497	.383
Brazoban, Yhency, Yan.	.320	56	219	200	33	64	91	14	5	1	26	1	2	4	12	0	47	7	3	2	.455	.367
Sandoval, Michael, Twi.	.320	55	214	194	30	62	81	13	3	0	34	0	3	2	15	3	21	5	7	1	.418	.369
Lutz, David, Exp.*	.318	44	172	154	21	49	59	8	1	0	15	0	1	3	14	0	14	4	1	4	.383	.384
Winrow, Gary, Yan.*	.317	46	202	180	31	57	72	9	3	0	28	0	1	0	21	0	28	5	1	2	.400	.386
Castillo, Victor, Yan.	.314	42	183	153	24	48	58	8	1	0	16	2	1	5	22	0	38	9	8	1	.379	.414
Cruz, Enrique, Mets	.306	54	213	183	34	56	86	14	2	4	24	0	1	1	28	0	41	0	0	3	.470	.399
Rauls, Ian, Phi.*	.303	51	219	175	31	53	61	8	0	0	17	4	0	6	34	0	32	27	8	3	.349	.433
Hawes, Bobby, Reds	.302	45	178	162	23	49	70	11	5	0	18	1	1	1	13	1	22	11	2	4	.432	.358
Arias, Leandro, Mets†	.301	47	201	173	38	52	93	14	6	5	33	2	0	3	23	1	30	10	9	6	.538	.392
Kawabata, Kenichiro, R.S.†	.297	46	185	145	35	43	58	4	4	1	15	0	3	6	31	1	34	15	4	1	.400	.432
Phillips, Brandon, Exp.	.290	47	187	169	23	49	69	11	3	1	21	0	0	3	15	0	35	12	3	6	.408	.358
Rogers, Edward, Ori.	.288	53	210	177	34	51	61	5	1	1	19	4	2	4	23	0	22	20	3	2	.345	.379

DEPARTMENTAL LEADERS: G—Angell, 60; AB—Machado, 223; R—Morban, Machado, 45 each; H—Blalock, 69; TB—Blalock, 107; 2B—Blalock, 17; 3B—Blalock, Arias, Gordon, Harris, 6 each; HR—Dees, 9; RBI—Blalock, 38; SH—Machado, Watkins, 7 each; SF—Blalock, Jacobs, Nettles, 5 each; HP—Fowler, 4; BB—Cordova, 51; IBB—Blalock, 4; SO—Morban, 70; SB—Rauls, 27; CS—Morban, 14; GIDP—Hattig, 8; Slg.—Blalock, .560; OBP—Cordova, Ambres, .452.

ALL PLAYERS

*Lefthanded batter. †Switch-hitter.

Player, Team	Avg.	G	TPA	AB	R	H	TB	2B	3B	HR	RBI	SH	SF	HP	BB	IBB	SO	SB	CS	GDP	Slg.	OBP
Abreu, Cesar, Reds	.197	26	83	76	4	15	20	2	0	1	6	0	0	2	5	1	23	2	1	1	.263	.265
Abreu, David, Mets†	.327	32	124	98	25	32	37	3	1	0	9	3	0	3	20	0	10	13	2	1	.378	.455
Acevedo, Inocencio, Rang.	.217	27	125	115	23	25	35	4	3	0	9	0	0	2	8	0	18	16	1	2	.304	.280
Acuna, Ronald, Yan.	.250	5	21	20	1	5	6	1	0	0	3	0	0	0	1	0	4	2	0	1	.300	.286
Alley, Charles, Ori.†	.000	2	6	3	2	0	0	0	0	0	0	0	0	0	3	0	0	0	0	0	.000	.400
Almonte, Erick, Yan.	.300	9	35	30	5	9	17	2	0	2	9	0	2	0	3	0	10	1	0	1	.567	.343
Altagen, Matthew, Tig.	.250	3	11	8	0	2	2	0	0	0	2	0	0	2	1	0	4	2	0	0	.250	.455
Alvarez, Aaron, Marl.	.257	24	78	74	7	19	24	5	0	0	4	0	1	0	3	0	12	0	1	1	.324	.282
Alvarez, Henrry, Roy.	.183	29	111	104	10	19	31	8	2	0	11	0	1	5	1	0	37	2	0	1	.298	.225
Ambres, Chip, Marl.	.353	37	168	139	29	49	71	13	3	1	15	0	2	2	25	0	19	22	3	0	.511	.452
Ambrosini, Dominick, Exp.*	.161	19	71	62	5	10	11	1	0	0	0	1	0	0	8	0	19	1	0	4	.177	.257
Anderson, Jon, R.S.†	.182	3	12	11	1	2	3	1	0	0	1	0	0	0	1	0	3	0	1	0	.273	.250
Anderson, Nat, Tig.*	.130	19	59	46	6	6	8	2	0	0	3	1	1	0	11	0	16	5	0	2	.174	.293
Angell, Rick, Rang.	.251	60	232	203	35	51	73	12	2	2	32	1	3	5	20	3	30	14	3	5	.360	.329
Araujo, Victor, Pir.	.286	51	211	199	30	57	77	8	0	4	32	0	2	2	8	0	29	13	5	4	.387	.318
Arias, Leandro, Mets†	.301	47	201	173	38	52	93	14	6	5	33	2	0	3	23	1	30	10	9	6	.538	.392
Avila, Rob, Phi.	.328	16	64	58	6	19	28	3	0	2	5	0	0	2	4	0	10	2	0	1	.483	.391
Baez, Ernies, Rang.†	.286	12	48	42	4	12	16	1	0	1	8	2	0	1	3	0	15	2	1	0	.381	.348
Baez, Fleming, Rang.	.000	4	9	9	0	0	0	0	0	0	0	0	0	0	0	0	5	0	0	0	.000	.000
Baker, Casey, Mets	.192	35	126	104	12	20	23	3	0	0	9	1	1	1	18	0	20	4	2	3	.221	.315
Barnowski, Bryan, R.S.	.227	32	101	88	13	20	27	5	1	0	4	1	0	2	10	0	23	3	1	0	.307	.320
Barr, Clint, Yan.	.136	11	25	22	2	3	4	1	0	0	2	0	0	1	2	0	8	0	0	1	.182	.240
Barrow, Corey, Reds	.171	54	208	175	19	30	49	7	3	2	19	1	1	5	26	1	56	10	1	3	.280	.295
Batcheller, Chris, Pir.	.261	6	26	23	3	6	7	1	0	0	3	1	0	0	2	0	4	1	0	0	.304	.320
Bell, Josh, Mets	.222	31	110	90	14	20	20	0	0	0	7	6	0	3	11	0	27	4	3	0	.222	.327
Bishop, Bennie, Phi.	.232	28	90	82	9	19	25	4	1	0	9	0	1	0	7	0	23	4	1	3	.305	.289
Blalock, Hank, Rang.*	.361	51	222	191	34	69	107	17	6	3	38	0	5	1	25	4	23	3	2	7	.560	.428
Boitel, Ronald, R.S.†	.286	45	182	161	23	46	56	6	2	0	14	1	1	1	18	3	39	6	4	1	.348	.359
Bone, Billy, Pir.	.125	7	28	24	4	3	4	1	0	0	3	1	1	0	2	0	3	0	0	2	.167	.185
Borjas, Henry, R.S.†	.191	49	173	152	18	29	40	5	3	0	11	0	1	4	16	0	26	3	4	5	.263	.283
Bowen, Rob, Twi.†	.260	29	101	77	10	20	24	4	0	0	11	1	3	0	20	0	15	2	2	0	.312	.400
Boyer, Bret, Exp.	.172	32	99	93	6	16	17	1	0	0	8	0	0	0	6	0	20	6	1	3	.183	.222
Bradley, Wade, Phi.*	.000	2	5	5	0	0	0	0	0	0	0	0	0	0	0	0	3	0	0	0	.000	.000
Brazeal, Spencer, Yan.	.206	26	88	68	13	14	17	3	0	0	5	2	0	1	17	0	19	1	1	0	.250	.372
Brazoban, Yhency, Yan.	.320	56	219	200	33	64	91	14	5	1	26	1	2	4	12	0	47	7	3	2	.455	.367
Brito, Justo, Mets	.219	43	151	128	18	28	41	4	0	3	20	1	2	5	15	0	26	0	1	6	.320	.320
Brown, Matthew, Exp.	.162	31	111	99	11	16	26	1	0	3	11	0	0	0	11	0	38	3	0	1	.263	.252
Bryan, Jason, Rang.	.350	6	23	20	3	7	9	2	0	0	3	0	0	0	3	0	9	1	1	0	.450	.435
Cabrera, Raymond, Ori.	.310	16	62	58	8	18	25	3	2	0	12	0	1	2	1	0	6	4	0	1	.431	.339
Cabrera, Yoelmis, Pir.	.282	27	93	78	17	22	29	7	0	0	6	0	1	3	10	0	15	8	0	2	.372	.380
Caceres, Wilmy, Reds†	.333	2	9	9	2	3	3	0	0	0	0	0	0	0	0	0	1	0	0	0	.333	.333
Camarero, Rafael, Reds	.210	31	92	81	4	17	22	2	0	1	10	0	2	0	9	0	17	1	2	1	.272	.283
Campana, Wandel, Reds	.239	17	74	71	12	17	27	5	1	1	10	1	0	1	1	0	12	1	1	1	.380	.326
Campos, Juan, Tig.†	.218	43	175	147	23	32	38	6	0	0	12	3	1	7	17	0	29	12	7	1	.259	.326
Cardona, Raynier, Pir.†	.216	14	46	37	2	8	11	3	0	0	4	0	0	0	9	0	19	1	0	2	.297	.370
Caridi, Tony, R.S.†	.167	25	82	72	9	12	14	2	0	0	3	0	1	0	9	0	19	1	0	2	.194	.250
Casanova, Raul, Tig.†	.800	2	5	5	1	4	7	0	0	1	1	0	0	0	0	0	0	0	1	0	1.400	.800

Player, Team	Avg.	G	TPA	AB	R	H	TB	2B	3B	HR	RBI	SH	SF	HP	BB	IBB	SO	SB	CS	GDP	Slg.	OBP
Castellanos, Jose, Brav.	.229	23	83	70	11	16	24	3	1	1	11	1	0	4	8	0	18	1	1	1	.343	.341
Castillo, Jose, Pir.	.266	47	193	173	27	46	67	9	0	4	30	3	3	3	11	1	23	8	0	4	.387	.316
Castillo, Victor, Yan.	.314	42	183	153	24	48	58	8	1	0	16	2	1	5	22	0	38	9	8	1	.379	.414
Castro, Martires, Exp.	.237	11	40	38	5	9	16	2	1	1	7	0	0	1	1	0	9	1	0	1	.421	.275
Castro, Vicente, Pir.	.280	43	170	161	21	45	63	9	0	3	21	0	1	2	6	0	30	3	0	1	.391	.312
Cates, Jr, Gary, Ori.	.268	45	156	127	20	34	44	7	0	1	20	5	4	5	15	1	20	11	2	0	.346	.358
Centeno, Edwin, Ori.†	.272	33	99	92	22	25	41	4	3	2	15	1	1	1	4	0	26	12	3	0	.446	.306
Clark, Tommy, Brav.	.170	38	146	112	18	19	39	8	0	4	13	0	1	3	30	1	46	5	3	3	.348	.356
Cleveland, Russell, Tig.	.311	37	142	132	13	41	46	5	0	0	13	0	3	2	5	0	33	2	2	4	.348	.338
Collazo, Julio, Phi.	.256	52	218	176	34	45	48	3	0	0	7	3	0	6	33	0	36	25	1	5	.273	.391
Copley, Travis, Reds*	.208	7	28	24	5	5	7	2	0	0	1	0	0	0	4	0	6	0	0	0	.292	.321
Cordova, Ben, Roy.*	.286	52	223	168	36	48	76	9	2	5	26	2	1	1	51	0	50	12	3	2	.452	.452
Corporan, Elvis, Yan.†	.278	56	233	212	29	59	90	13	3	4	30	0	1	1	19	1	41	3	1	6	.425	.339
Cortes, Jorge, Pir.*	.301	32	109	93	14	28	34	4	1	0	14	0	2	0	14	0	19	2	1	2	.366	.385
Cruz, Enrique, Mets	.306	54	213	183	34	56	86	14	2	4	24	0	1	1	28	0	41	0	0	3	.470	.399
Cruz, Orlando, Rang.	.184	46	162	136	12	25	34	5	2	0	11	5	1	5	15	0	44	0	2	1	.250	.287
Damato, Gabriel, Reds	.200	5	13	10	0	2	2	0	0	0	0	0	0	2	1	0	0	0	1	0	.200	.385
Davis, Daniel, Tig.*	.184	45	171	147	14	27	36	6	0	1	11	0	0	1	23	1	59	2	2	3	.245	.298
Davis, Quian, Marl.	.191	26	54	47	1	9	12	1	1	0	4	1	0	3	2	0	13	1	0	0	.255	.269
Davison, Ashanti, Ori.	.258	8	35	31	5	8	11	3	0	0	3	0	0	1	3	0	7	6	1	0	.355	.343
Dees, Charlie, Ori.	.215	56	210	186	21	40	81	12	1	9	32	0	3	1	20	0	41	5	6	6	.435	.290
DeGroote, Casey, Yan.*	.150	7	23	20	1	3	3	0	0	0	2	0	0	0	3	0	6	1	0	0	.150	.261
Deitrick, Jeremy, Phi.	.353	5	17	17	3	6	10	2	1	0	3	0	0	0	0	0	2	0	1	0	.588	.353
Delgado, Dario, Phi.	.324	19	79	71	12	23	34	3	1	2	17	0	1	2	5	0	16	1	2	0	.479	.380
De Los Santos, Hector, R.S.	.243	56	241	218	36	53	70	8	0	3	21	4	3	1	15	0	38	11	8	1	.321	.291
Del Rosario, Emmanuel, Ori.†	.244	40	152	123	19	30	32	2	0	0	8	4	1	2	22	0	10	10	5	2	.260	.365
Demarco, Matt, Marl.*	.218	46	170	156	12	34	42	8	0	0	10	1	0	2	11	0	19	1	3	5	.269	.278
Dennis, Les, Yan.	.250	3	9	8	2	2	2	0	0	0	0	0	0	0	1	0	0	1	0	0	.250	.333
Derosso, Tony, R.S.	.278	5	21	18	3	5	11	3	0	1	7	0	1	0	2	0	2	0	1	1	.611	.333
Deschenes, Pat, Mets*	.380	24	99	79	16	30	36	3	0	1	12	0	2	2	15	0	8	4	2	3	.456	.480
Deshetler, Chris, Tig.*	.298	33	132	114	17	34	49	5	2	2	21	0	1	2	15	1	15	1	1	2	.430	.386
Devanez, Noel, Mets	.286	44	166	147	31	42	64	8	1	4	26	0	1	2	15	0	41	2	2	2	.435	.358
Diaz, David, Pir.	.184	17	39	38	4	7	9	2	0	0	1	0	0	0	1	0	10	0	0	1	.237	.205
Diaz, Miguel, Exp.	.179	20	63	56	7	10	14	2	1	0	5	0	0	1	6	0	12	2	0	1	.250	.270
Dito, Robert, Exp.	.229	18	54	48	5	11	14	0	0	1	9	0	0	1	5	0	13	0	0	1	.292	.315
Dolton, Odis, Reds	.177	32	105	96	11	17	24	2	1	1	12	0	0	4	5	0	43	3	0	4	.250	.248
Dorsey, Ryan, Pir.	.175	14	46	40	4	7	10	1	1	0	2	0	0	0	6	0	18	0	0	0	.250	.283
Douglas, Mo, Pir.*	.161	26	98	87	6	14	21	2	1	1	7	2	0	1	8	0	33	1	0	3	.241	.240
Doumit, Ryan, Pir.†	.282	29	105	85	17	24	32	5	0	1	7	0	1	4	15	0	14	4	2	0	.376	.410
Driggers Jr, Richard, Phi.	.229	17	50	48	6	11	13	2	0	0	3	1	0	0	1	0	11	1	0	0	.271	.245
Dyer, Matthew, Mets	.000	2	3	1	0	0	0	0	0	0	0	0	0	1	1	0	0	0	0	0	.000	.667
Eagle, Todd, Phi.	.128	14	41	39	1	5	6	1	0	0	3	0	0	1	1	0	5	1	0	1	.154	.171
Eberly, Rodney, Phi.*	.192	7	30	26	4	5	6	1	0	0	3	0	0	0	4	0	5	1	0	2	.231	.300
Edwards, John, Twi.	.230	33	115	100	17	23	31	2	0	2	16	1	2	3	9	1	20	3	1	4	.310	.307
Elder, Rick, Ori.*	.600	3	12	10	2	6	14	2	0	2	4	0	0	0	2	0	1	0	0	0	1.400	.667
Encarnacion, Arismendy, Marl.	.278	46	161	151	21	42	55	9	2	0	14	3	0	4	3	0	24	5	6	4	.364	.310
Escobar, Alex, Mets	.375	2	9	8	1	3	5	2	0	0	1	0	0	0	1	0	2	0	0	0	.625	.444
Essian, James, Roy.†	.197	30	98	71	13	14	20	4	1	0	8	2	0	1	24	0	26	3	1	1	.282	.406
Evans, Mitch, Yan.	.182	24	63	44	11	8	8	0	0	0	4	2	1	0	16	0	10	1	1	2	.182	.393
Fafard, Mathias, Mets	.182	5	14	11	4	2	5	0	0	1	2	0	0	2	1	0	0	0	0	0	.455	.357
Fernandez, Alejandro, Yan.	.214	12	34	28	2	6	9	3	0	0	3	0	0	0	6	0	8	0	0	0	.321	.353
Fernandez, Medardo, Marl.†	.306	39	152	134	20	41	51	6	2	0	16	1	0	2	15	0	30	10	4	1	.381	.384
Fick, Robert, Tig.*	.333	3	11	9	2	3	4	1	0	0	2	0	0	0	2	0	0	1	0	0	.444	.455
Foltynowicz, Roger, Reds	.250	22	74	68	1	17	22	5	0	0	7	0	0	2	4	0	11	2	0	4	.324	.311
Fowler, David, Yan.	.251	57	225	187	28	47	72	9	2	4	25	1	0	10	27	0	63	6	5	2	.385	.375
Frazier, Charles, Marl.	.288	35	142	125	12	36	42	6	0	0	9	0	0	4	13	0	31	5	1	3	.336	.373
Frye, Jeff, R.S.	.400	6	22	20	4	8	9	1	0	0	1	0	0	0	2	0	2	0	0	0	.450	.455
Gajewski, Matt, Rang.†	.210	52	207	162	31	34	55	7	1	4	26	2	0	9	34	2	41	1	0	3	.340	.376
Garabito, Vianney, Reds	.284	35	144	141	11	40	53	4	0	3	16	1	0	1	1	0	9	7	2	2	.376	.294
Garcia, Kenji, Mets	.083	32	91	72	9	6	11	2	0	1	6	0	0	2	17	0	46	0	0	2	.153	.275
Garcia, Nicolas, Ori.	.229	21	79	70	12	16	30	5	0	3	15	0	3	2	4	0	10	1	2	1	.429	.278
Geisbush, David, Brav.	.231	23	91	78	12	18	28	4	0	2	11	1	0	4	8	0	21	1	1	1	.359	.333
Gettis, Byron, Roy.	.316	28	118	95	20	30	55	6	2	5	21	0	3	3	17	0	21	3	2	2	.579	.424
Gomez, Alexis, Roy.*	.276	56	249	214	44	59	88	12	1	5	31	1	1	1	32	0	48	13	5	1	.411	.371
Gonzalez, Felix, Exp.	.209	44	136	115	11	24	30	4	1	0	12	2	2	3	14	0	13	5	3	4	.261	.306
Gonzalez, Reggie, Twi.	.301	44	158	143	17	43	58	6	3	1	14	5	2	1	7	0	20	3	3	2	.406	.333
Gordon, Alexis, Ori.*	.360	36	140	125	25	45	82	7	6	6	34	0	1	0	14	2	37	12	2	1	.656	.421
Goudie, Jaime, Reds	.500	1	2	2	0	1	1	0	0	0	1	0	0	0	0	0	0	0	0	0	.500	.500
Green, Ricky, Ori.	.000	2	1	1	0	0	0	0	0	0	0	0	0	0	0	0	1	0	0	0	.000	.000
Griswold, Matthew, Ori.*	.346	10	36	26	4	9	12	3	0	0	4	1	2	1	6	0	4	0	1	0	.462	.457
Guerrero, James, R.S.	.196	22	54	46	3	9	10	1	0	0	4	0	0	1	7	0	20	0	1	2	.217	.315
Guerrero, Julio, R.S.	.207	32	130	116	17	24	27	1	1	0	11	1	1	2	10	0	18	8	5	2	.233	.279
Guilliams, Earl, Brav.	.114	18	39	35	1	4	5	1	0	0	0	0	0	0	4	0	7	0	0	1	.143	.205
Guzman, Jonathan, Roy.	.241	43	167	141	23	34	46	4	1	2	14	2	2	1	21	0	46	11	2	5	.326	.339
Guzman, Juan, Roy.†	.167	30	113	96	11	16	20	4	0	0	7	3	3	1	10	0	36	7	0	2	.208	.245
Hamn, Larnell, Mets	.117	32	65	60	6	7	9	2	0	0	4	0	0	2	3	0	22	0	2	0	.150	.185
Harper, Shaun, Brav.	.246	51	204	191	20	47	61	8	0	2	16	1	1	2	9	0	61	6	1	1	.319	.286
Harrell, Ken, Yan.	.600	1	5	5	0	3	4	1	0	0	0	0	0	0	0	0	0	0	0	0	.800	.600
Harris, Corey, Mets	.259	49	206	185	26	48	74	11	6	1	28	1	1	0	18	0	27	6	0	5	.400	.324
Harris, Karl, Exp.	.202	28	95	89	4	18	22	4	0	0	6	1	0	1	4	0	19	0	1	2	.247	.245
Harts, Jeremy, Pir.†	.295	28	133	122	20	36	49	3	2	2	15	0	1	2	8	0	21	8	3	5	.402	.346
Hatteberg, Scott, R.S.*	.400	6	22	15	4	6	11	2	0	1	6	0	0	0	7	0	1	0	0	1	.733	.591
Hattig, John, R.S.†	.270	50	183	163	28	44	60	7	3	1	17	0	3	1	16	1	20	1	1	8	.368	.333
Hawes, Bobby, Reds	.302	45	178	162	23	49	70	11	5	0	18	1	1	1	13	1	22	11	2	4	.432	.356
Helms, Wes, Brav.	.455	9	39	33	1	15	17	2	0	0	10	0	0	1	5	0	4	0	1	1	.515	.538

Player, Team	Avg.	G	TPA	AB	R	H	TB	2B	3B	HR	RBI	SH	SF	HP	BB	IBB	SO	SB	CS	GDP	Slg.	OBP
Henley, Bob, Exp.	.250	2	6	4	0	1	1	0	0	0	1	0	1	0	1	0	1	0	0	0	.250	.333
Herbert, Keith, Marl.	.215	29	87	79	8	17	29	3	3	1	8	0	0	1	7	0	20	1	0	0	.367	.287
Hernandez, Argenis, Ori.*	.178	39	131	118	10	21	30	3	0	2	15	3	0	1	9	1	20	0	1	3	.254	.242
Hernandez, Nicolas, Exp.†	.143	4	8	7	0	1	1	0	0	0	1	0	0	0	1	0	0	0	0	3	.143	.250
Herrera, Elvis, Pir.	.111	7	23	18	5	2	2	0	0	0	1	0	1	0	4	0	6	0	0	0	.111	.261
Holbert, Ray, Roy.	.188	5	18	16	5	3	5	2	0	0	1	1	0	0	1	0	4	1	0	1	.313	.235
Hopper, Norris, Roy.	.257	46	204	179	33	46	53	3	2	0	13	2	4	0	19	0	20	22	6	2	.296	.322
House, J.R., Pir.	.327	33	127	113	13	37	67	9	3	5	23	0	1	2	11	0	23	1	0	1	.593	.394
Hudnall, Joshua, Pir.	.195	25	88	82	6	16	19	3	0	0	6	1	1	0	4	0	28	1	2	0	.232	.230
Hudson, Daniel, Pir.	.211	7	25	19	5	4	7	1	1	0	3	0	0	3	3	0	3	4	1	1	.368	.400
Hunter, David, Mets*	.220	25	88	82	12	18	22	2	1	0	8	0	1	0	5	0	26	1	1	0	.268	.261
Ide, Antoine, Ori.	.280	15	58	50	12	14	19	2	0	1	5	2	1	0	5	0	12	8	2	0	.380	.339
Infante, Juan, Exp.†	.254	26	80	67	5	17	17	0	0	0	3	2	0	1	10	0	11	2	3	1	.254	.359
Infante, Omar, Tig.	.268	25	102	97	11	26	30	4	0	0	7	0	1	0	4	0	11	4	0	1	.309	.294
Ishida, Takehito, Phi.	.318	27	96	85	8	27	41	11	0	1	14	0	1	1	9	0	11	1	1	1	.482	.385
Jacobs, Michael, Mets*	.333	44	168	147	18	49	73	12	0	4	30	0	5	1	14	2	30	2	0	3	.497	.383
Jaile, Chris, Rang.	.173	39	165	139	16	24	35	5	0	2	14	1	2	1	22	1	32	0	0	6	.252	.287
Jenkins, Neil, Tig.	.297	33	130	111	18	33	58	13	3	2	15	1	0	2	16	0	37	2	1	1	.523	.395
Jenkins, Robert, Reds	.059	6	19	17	1	1	1	0	0	0	1	0	1	0	1	0	11	0	0	0	.059	.105
Jewson, Benjamin, Phi.	.238	31	112	101	5	24	27	3	0	0	11	0	0	2	9	0	32	1	0	3	.267	.313
Johnerson, Ryan, Reds	.478	7	32	23	7	11	12	1	0	0	3	1	1	1	6	0	3	3	1	0	.522	.581
Johnson, Kareem, Twi.	.266	40	145	128	20	34	40	2	2	0	15	2	0	2	13	0	39	5	1	3	.313	.343
Jones, Albert, Twi.	.151	33	82	73	11	11	11	0	0	0	4	1	0	3	5	0	18	4	1	3	.151	.235
Jones, Garrett, Brav.*	.241	46	188	170	17	41	53	3	0	3	18	0	1	1	16	0	47	1	2	1	.312	.309
Jones, Jason, Rang.	.206	11	37	34	1	7	9	2	0	0	3	0	0	1	2	0	12	1	0	0	.265	.270
Kanaya, Takeshi, R.S.	.313	14	37	32	6	10	14	1	0	1	9	1	0	1	3	0	4	1	0	2	.438	.389
Kawabata, Kenichiro, R.S.†	.297	46	185	145	35	43	58	4	4	1	15	0	3	6	31	1	34	15	4	1	.400	.432
King, Jason, Brav.	.196	45	185	168	15	33	46	4	3	1	11	2	1	1	13	0	40	5	2	3	.274	.257
Kison, Robbie, Reds	.273	7	11	11	2	3	3	0	0	0	2	0	0	0	0	0	0	1	0	0	.273	.273
Kofler, Eric, Yan.*	.667	1	4	3	1	2	6	1	0	1	4	0	0	0	1	0	0	0	0	0	2.000	.750
Laidlaw, Jacob, Marl.	.264	56	232	201	24	53	79	9	4	3	32	1	3	5	22	0	49	3	4	3	.393	.346
Lane, Richard, Exp.*	.222	41	158	144	16	32	40	5	0	1	14	0	0	4	10	0	30	4	2	6	.278	.291
Lawson, Forrest, Mets	.250	37	139	116	15	29	34	3	1	0	11	0	1	5	17	1	36	1	1	4	.293	.367
Lawton, Matt, Twi.*	.250	1	4	4	0	1	1	0	0	0	1	0	0	0	0	0	2	0	0	0	.250	.250
Leed, Adam, Rang.	.273	12	48	44	5	12	20	2	0	2	8	0	1	0	3	0	12	1	1	1	.455	.313
Leer, David, Tig.	.271	32	121	107	12	29	36	3	2	0	12	1	1	5	7	0	26	11	4	3	.336	.342
Leflore, Alex, Reds	.175	19	72	63	5	11	14	1	1	0	2	1	0	0	8	0	24	5	2	2	.222	.268
Leon, Alfredo, Ori.	.327	29	116	107	18	35	50	6	3	1	15	0	0	3	6	1	11	11	3	2	.467	.379
Leonardo, Santos, Tig.	.258	38	136	120	16	31	39	6	1	0	13	1	0	1	14	0	31	12	7	1	.325	.341
Liriano, Ruddy, Reds	.203	22	77	69	10	14	18	2	1	0	9	1	2	1	4	0	9	4	0	0	.261	.250
Llamas, Juan, Yan.	.500	4	6	4	1	2	2	0	0	0	0	0	0	0	2	0	1	0	0	0	.500	.667
Lopez, Mendy, Roy.	.200	3	10	5	0	1	2	1	0	0	2	0	1	1	3	0	1	0	0	0	.400	.500
Lopez, Youanny, R.S.	.243	51	205	181	18	44	67	10	2	3	26	0	1	2	21	1	41	3	5	7	.370	.327
Lora, Thomas, Roy.†	.274	47	213	175	31	48	62	3	4	1	17	3	1	3	31	0	37	20	2	2	.354	.390
Louwsma, Chris, Marl.	.176	55	211	182	20	32	44	7	1	1	8	0	2	3	24	1	56	3	3	7	.242	.280
Lugo, Felix, Exp.†	.368	6	23	19	6	7	14	2	1	1	4	0	1	0	3	0	4	2	0	0	.737	.435
Lugo, Roberto, Mets*	.286	14	26	21	1	6	8	2	0	0	2	4	0	0	1	0	3	0	1	3	.381	.318
Lundquist, Ryan, Reds	.667	1	4	3	1	2	2	0	0	0	2	0	0	0	1	0	0	1	0	0	.667	.750
Lutz, David, Exp.*	.318	44	172	154	21	49	59	8	1	0	15	0	1	3	14	0	14	4	1	4	.383	.384
Lutz, Kenneth, Reds	.000	12	0	0	0	0	0	0	0	0	0	0	0	0	0	0	0	1	0	0	.000	.000
Lydon, Wayne, Mets	.183	37	69	60	13	11	14	3	0	0	5	1	0	1	7	0	13	0	1	1	.233	.279
Machado, Aleyandro, Brav.	.278	56	252	223	45	62	73	11	0	0	14	2	2	5	20	1	22	19	6	3	.327	.348
Machado, Anderson, Phi.†	.259	43	168	143	26	37	55	6	3	2	12	7	1	2	15	1	38	6	3	5	.385	.335
Mack, Antonio, Ori.	.247	48	192	170	36	42	50	6	1	0	5	5	0	0	17	0	46	20	7	1	.294	.316
Malone, Nick, R.S.	.120	12	30	25	4	3	5	2	0	0	1	1	0	1	3	0	8	2	1	0	.200	.241
Manning, Patrick, Brav.	.416	24	105	89	21	37	60	9	1	4	19	1	0	1	14	0	14	4	1	2	.674	.500
Manning, Ricky, Twi.*	.196	19	71	51	12	10	10	0	0	0	7	3	0	3	14	0	13	5	1	1	.196	.397
Marbury, Ben, R.S.	.170	20	61	53	5	9	15	3	0	1	6	1	0	3	4	0	20	1	1	0	.283	.267
Martin, Kyle, Ori.	.268	29	93	82	11	22	28	4	1	0	8	0	0	2	9	1	20	3	2	2	.341	.355
Martinez, Edgar, R.S.	.239	33	123	113	12	27	33	3	0	1	20	0	0	1	9	0	13	1	2	1	.292	.301
Martinez, Louis, Brav.	.309	26	112	97	10	30	37	5	1	0	16	2	0	1	12	0	14	0	2	1	.381	.391
Martinez, Octavio, Ori.	.237	36	122	114	11	27	37	8	1	0	15	0	2	2	4	0	11	8	1	5	.325	.270
Martinez, Orlando, Reds	.308	4	14	13	4	4	7	1	1	0	1	0	0	1	0	0	2	0	0	0	.538	.357
Massucco, Scott, Yan.	.154	6	15	13	1	2	2	0	0	0	1	0	0	0	2	0	0	0	1	1	.154	.267
Matos, Angel, Rang.	.279	36	141	122	21	34	56	12	2	2	22	0	1	0	18	0	36	2	1	3	.459	.369
Maxwell, Vernon, Yan.	.500	1	4	4	0	2	2	0	0	0	0	0	0	0	0	0	1	0	0	0	.500	.500
Maza, Luis, Twi.	.262	25	75	61	11	16	20	4	0	0	10	1	0	3	10	0	15	1	1	1	.328	.392
McIntyre, Robert, Mets	.304	32	124	102	18	31	33	2	0	0	15	2	3	2	15	0	19	7	2	1	.324	.393
McMillan, Andrew, Exp.	.210	31	111	100	11	21	25	4	0	0	2	1	0	2	8	0	19	2	1	1	.250	.282
Mejias, Erick, Rang.†	.258	56	227	194	35	50	62	7	1	1	23	2	1	8	22	0	36	11	3	3	.320	.356
Mendieta, Enrique, Marl.	.163	30	62	49	2	8	11	3	0	0	6	0	1	1	9	0	14	1	1	0	.224	.300
Mercado, Wilkins, Roy.	.266	41	147	128	17	34	50	5	1	3	15	0	1	1	17	0	23	1	0	7	.391	.354
Merhoff, Aaron, Phi.	.321	22	91	78	10	25	38	6	2	1	12	1	2	0	10	1	15	2	1	2	.487	.389
Miller, Josh, Pir.*	.091	6	22	22	0	2	4	2	0	0	0	0	0	0	0	0	6	0	0	0	.182	.091
Moncrief, Kyle, Reds*	.175	39	122	97	11	17	25	3	1	1	7	1	0	2	22	0	41	3	1	2	.258	.339
Morban, Jose, Rang.	.283	54	245	205	45	58	90	10	5	4	18	4	3	2	31	2	70	19	14	1	.439	.378
Morneau, Justin, Twi.*	.302	17	58	53	3	16	21	5	0	0	9	1	1	1	2	0	6	0	1	2	.396	.333
Morris, Jeremy, Yan.	.400	5	22	15	7	6	12	0	0	2	7	0	0	1	6	0	5	0	0	1	.800	.591
Nettles, Jeff, Yan.	.275	44	166	142	24	39	67	8	1	6	31	1	5	3	15	0	27	1	2	4	.472	.345
Nunez, Edward, Twi.*	.233	29	55	43	9	10	13	1	1	0	5	1	1	0	10	1	9	3	2	0	.302	.370
Nunez, Hector, Tig.	.308	10	30	26	4	8	12	4	0	0	6	0	0	0	4	0	3	4	1	0	.462	.400
Olmedo, Ranier, Reds	.236	54	211	195	30	46	63	12	1	1	19	1	2	1	12	0	28	13	7	1	.323	.281
O'Neill, Daniel, Phi.	.333	10	38	27	6	9	14	3	1	0	4	0	0	1	10	0	7	2	0	0	.519	.526
Osborn, Jason, Mets	.667	1	3	3	0	2	3	1	0	0	2	0	0	0	0	0	0	0	0	0	1.000	.667
Paulino, David, Marl.	.199	46	161	141	21	28	28	0	0	0	4	1	0	1	18	1	24	22	7	2	.199	.294

Player, Team	Avg.	G	TPA	AB	R	H	TB	2B	3B	HR	RBI	SH	SF	HP	BB	IBB	SO	SB	CS	GDP	Slg.	OBP
Paulino, Ronny, Pir.	.253	29	95	83	6	21	34	2	4	1	13	1	2	1	8	0	19	1	2	0	.410	.319
Pelfrey, Brice, Pir.	.241	31	126	108	19	26	27	1	0	0	7	2	3	5	8	0	15	6	3	3	.250	.315
Pena, Jose, R.S.	.375	12	40	32	9	12	16	1	0	1	7	0	0	6	2	0	7	2	1	0	.500	.500
Pena, Wily, Yan.	.247	45	186	166	21	41	74	10	1	7	26	0	1	7	12	0	54	3	2	2	.446	.323
Perea, Carlos, Roy.	.000	4	9	8	1	0	0	0	0	0	0	0	0	0	1	0	1	0	0	0	.000	.111
Perich, Joshua, Mets	.272	47	184	158	21	43	50	5	1	0	22	1	1	4	20	0	37	6	2	6	.316	.366
Phillips, Brandon, Exp.	.290	47	187	169	23	49	69	11	3	1	21	0	0	3	15	0	35	12	3	6	.408	.358
Pickering, Kelvin, Ori.	.194	23	77	72	8	14	19	2	0	1	3	0	0	1	4	0	25	0	0	3	.264	.247
Piercy, Mike, Pir.*	.314	10	42	35	6	11	12	1	0	0	3	0	0	0	7	0	7	3	1	1	.343	.429
Podsednik, Scott, Rang.*.	.412	5	19	17	6	7	9	2	0	0	5	0	0	0	2	0	3	1	0	1	.529	.474
Presto, Nick, Reds	.375	3	9	8	2	3	5	2	0	0	0	0	0	0	1	0	1	1	0	0	.625	.444
Prince, Tom, Phi.	.238	7	26	21	3	5	8	3	0	0	3	0	0	1	4	1	0	0	0	0	.381	.385
Quickstad, Barry, Twi.*	.240	32	119	96	20	23	34	4	2	1	9	0	0	1	21	1	29	11	0	3	.354	.381
Ramos, Eddy, Rang.†	.200	55	208	180	20	36	40	0	2	0	16	4	2	1	21	1	54	12	1	2	.222	.284
Rasmussen, Wes, Brav.	.221	36	145	122	16	27	37	5	1	1	15	1	1	2	19	0	40	2	2	1	.303	.333
Rauls, Ian, Phi.*	.303	51	219	175	31	53	61	8	0	0	17	4	0	6	34	0	32	27	8	3	.349	.433
Reed, Matthew, Twi.	.185	27	73	65	8	12	13	1	0	0	7	2	1	1	4	0	10	1	1	0	.200	.239
Reyes, Ivan, Yan.	.131	45	150	122	15	16	23	5	1	0	12	1	1	1	25	0	55	1	4	2	.189	.282
Reyes, Manuel, Mets	.182	11	23	22	3	4	4	0	0	0	3	0	0	0	1	0	5	0	0	2	.182	.217
Reynolds, Dusty, Tig.†	.241	19	66	54	5	13	17	2	1	0	5	1	1	0	10	0	6	1	2	0	.315	.354
Richards, Rowan, Rang.	.267	10	36	30	4	8	12	1	0	1	8	0	1	3	2	0	8	0	0	0	.400	.361
Richardson, Juan, Phi.	.226	46	184	164	27	37	66	14	0	5	23	1	3	5	11	1	46	7	6	5	.402	.290
Riek, Clifford, Pir.	.226	24	90	84	10	19	24	2	0	1	6	0	0	0	6	1	22	1	0	1	.286	.278
Riordan, Matthew, Ori.	.250	8	27	24	4	6	7	1	0	0	3	0	1	0	2	0	2	2	1	0	.292	.296
Rivera, Erick, Phi.	.150	31	107	100	8	15	25	4	0	2	10	0	2	1	4	0	32	0	2	3	.250	.187
Rivera, Juan, Yan.	.333	5	22	18	7	6	9	0	0	1	4	0	0	0	4	0	1	0	0	1	.500	.455
Rodeheaver, Roger, Phi.	.236	40	146	123	14	29	41	7	1	1	14	0	1	6	16	1	36	4	1	1	.333	.349
Rodgers, Mackeel, Roy.†	.200	31	114	105	10	21	27	3	0	1	14	2	0	2	4	0	30	3	2	2	.257	.243
Rodriguez, John, Yan.*	.286	3	10	7	1	2	4	0	1	0	1	0	0	0	3	0	0	0	0	0	.571	.500
Rodriguez, Ronny, R.S.	.247	54	189	170	19	42	52	5	1	1	13	1	1	3	14	0	32	7	2	5	.306	.314
Rodriguez, Steve, Tig.	.275	50	191	178	18	49	75	14	0	4	29	0	2	0	11	0	50	2	2	6	.421	.314
Rogers, Edward, Ori.	.288	53	210	177	34	51	61	5	1	1	19	4	2	4	23	0	22	20	3	2	.345	.379
Rollins, Antwon, Rang.	.250	1	4	4	1	1	2	1	0	0	2	0	0	0	0	0	0	0	0	0	.500	.250
Rombley, Danny, Exp.	.246	45	149	134	20	33	39	4	1	0	15	0	2	1	12	0	29	8	4	4	.291	.309
Romero, Gabriel, Brav.	.200	13	38	35	4	7	8	1	0	0	2	1	0	0	2	0	12	0	0	0	.229	.243
Rooi, Vince, Exp.	.189	36	137	111	17	21	25	4	0	0	10	0	2	2	22	0	24	3	2	4	.225	.328
Rosado, Omar, Exp.	.236	41	155	140	12	33	40	7	0	0	22	0	3	3	9	0	10	4	1	3	.286	.290
Rosario, Vicente, Mets	.200	3	5	5	0	1	1	0	0	0	0	0	0	0	0	0	2	0	0	0	.200	.200
Ross, Cody, Tig.	.218	42	163	142	19	31	57	8	3	4	18	2	1	2	16	0	28	3	1	3	.401	.304
Ross, Donovan, Roy.*	.253	31	122	91	12	23	33	10	0	0	19	2	3	1	25	0	34	1	1	1	.363	.408
Ruiz, Randy, Reds	.284	33	119	102	12	29	46	8	0	3	9	0	1	4	12	0	33	5	2	5	.451	.378
Sadler, Donnie, R.S.	.385	4	15	13	2	5	7	2	0	0	1	0	0	0	2	0	1	0	0	0	.538	.467
\Salas, Jose, Brav.†	.271	42	155	140	19	38	50	7	1	1	16	0	0	1	14	0	27	2	1	1	.357	.342
Sandoval, Michael, Twi.	.320	55	214	194	30	62	81	13	3	0	34	0	3	2	15	3	21	5	7	1	.418	.369
Santana, Emmanuel, Roy.*.	.157	26	104	83	8	13	16	3	0	0	14	0	1	0	19	0	18	1	1	2	.193	.311
Santana, Gamalier, Twi.*	.341	20	53	44	7	15	18	1	1	0	6	1	0	0	8	0	4	3	0	1	.409	.442
Santiago, Daniel, Reds†	.108	24	79	65	7	7	7	0	0	0	2	1	1	3	9	1	20	2	1	1	.108	.244
Santiago, Ramon, Tig.†	.321	35	151	134	25	43	56	9	2	0	11	4	3	1	9	0	17	20	7	3	.418	.361
Santonocito, Justin, Reds*	.100	3	10	10	1	1	1	0	0	0	0	0	0	0	0	0	1	0	0	0	.100	.100
Santoro, Patrick, R.S.	.174	8	25	23	2	4	8	1	0	1	3	0	0	0	2	0	6	0	1	0	.348	.240
Santos, Chad, Roy.*	.271	48	192	177	20	48	69	9	0	4	35	1	1	1	12	0	54	1	0	4	.390	.319
Schnall, Kevin, Reds	1.000	1	1	1	0	1	1	0	0	0	0	0	0	0	0	0	0	0	0	0	1.000	1.000
Seestedt, Michael, Ori.	.200	6	15	15	0	3	4	1	0	0	4	0	0	0	0	0	1	0	0	0	.267	.200
Seiber, Antron, R.S.	.261	13	51	46	6	12	16	0	2	0	10	0	1	0	4	0	11	2	2	1	.348	.314
Sein, Javier, Yan.*	.211	37	132	114	9	24	34	4	0	2	15	0	2	1	15	1	39	0	1	6	.298	.303
Senegal, Terence, Reds	.203	50	164	148	17	30	32	2	0	0	9	3	0	2	11	0	36	8	1	3	.216	.267
Serrano, Elio, Phi.	.200	2	9	5	2	1	1	0	0	0	1	0	1	0	3	0	1	0	0	0	.200	.444
Serrano, Hector, Phi.†	.115	10	32	26	0	3	3	0	0	0	1	1	0	1	4	0	14	0	0	1	.115	.258
Serrano, Raymond, Brav.	.258	38	112	97	14	25	46	6	0	5	21	1	1	0	13	0	15	1	0	0	.474	.342
Sheffield, Jeff, Yan.†	.000	3	4	4	0	0	0	0	0	0	0	0	0	0	0	0	1	0	0	0	.000	.000
Shelley, Jason, Pir.	.000	8	20	17	0	0	0	0	0	0	1	0	1	0	2	0	4	0	0	0	.000	.100
Shier, Peter, Ori.	.346	9	30	26	6	9	10	1	0	0	1	1	0	0	3	0	4	3	4	0	.385	.414
Smiley, Jermaine, Roy.*	.067	5	16	15	0	1	1	0	0	0	1	0	1	0	0	0	6	0	0	0	.067	.063
Smith, Toebius, Brav.	.191	29	105	94	11	18	21	3	0	0	7	0	0	1	10	0	24	6	0	1	.223	.276
Smith, Tony, Reds*	.246	21	71	65	12	16	22	2	2	0	11	0	0	0	6	0	10	3	0	2	.338	.310
Soriano, Alfonso, Yan.	.263	5	22	19	7	5	10	2	0	1	5	0	1	1	1	0	3	0	0	1	.526	.318
Soto, Jose, Marl.†	.229	49	195	175	17	40	60	8	0	4	20	1	1	3	14	1	56	10	8	0	.343	.295
Sowers, Douglas, Ori.*	.286	4	14	14	0	4	4	0	0	0	1	0	0	0	0	0	1	1	0	0	.286	.286
Stenson, Dernell, R.S.*	.217	6	26	23	2	5	11	0	0	2	7	0	0	0	3	0	5	0	0	0	.478	.308
Storke, Jonathan, Ori.	.155	25	85	71	13	11	16	3	1	0	5	0	0	2	12	0	28	4	1	1	.225	.294
Sutton, Larry, Roy.*	.258	9	39	31	7	8	13	2	0	1	6	0	0	1	7	0	6	0	0	1	.419	.410
Tamburrino, Brett, Twi.†	.209	14	51	43	9	9	9	0	0	0	5	1	0	0	7	0	10	1	0	2	.209	.320
Taylor, Corey, Reds	.667	1	3	3	2	2	2	0	0	0	0	0	0	0	0	0	0	0	0	0	.667	.800
Thompson, Alva, Brav.	.224	27	91	76	11	17	29	3	0	3	11	0	0	2	13	0	22	1	1	2	.382	.352
Tolli, Barry, Tig.	.241	43	155	137	19	33	48	7	1	2	17	2	0	1	15	0	39	12	3	1	.350	.320
Tope, Stephen, Twi.	.200	18	69	55	14	11	14	3	0	0	10	1	0	4	9	0	10	2	1	0	.255	.353
Torres, Digno, Twi.*	.277	53	199	166	20	46	58	7	1	1	26	1	2	4	26	1	36	10	2	4	.349	.384
Torres, Jaime, Yan.	.333	11	34	30	5	10	15	2	0	1	3	0	0	2	2	1	1	0	1	0	.500	.412
Tosca, Daniel, Phi.*	.236	50	184	157	19	37	57	8	0	4	22	0	3	2	22	1	38	3	1	1	.363	.332
Tyson, Torre, R.S.†	.105	10	24	19	4	2	2	0	0	0	3	0	0	0	4	0	2	1	1	1	.105	.250
Ugueto, Luis, Marl.†	.000	1	5	3	0	0	0	0	0	0	0	0	0	0	2	0	1	0	1	0	.000	.200
Valdez, Darlin, Exp.	.271	14	52	48	3	13	17	2	1	0	4	0	0	0	4	0	10	0	0	1	.354	.327
Valdez, Toribio, Rang.†	.037	10	29	27	0	1	1	0	0	0	1	0	0	0	2	0	5	0	0	0	.037	.103
Valdez, Wilson, Exp.	.293	22	90	82	12	24	26	2	0	0	7	2	1	0	5	0	7	10	0	1	.317	.330
Van Vark, Wade, Phi.†	.208	34	122	106	6	22	23	1	0	0	6	1	1	2	12	0	26	4	2	1	.217	.298

Player, Team	Avg.	G	TPA	AB	R	H	TB	2B	3B	HR	RBI	SH	SF	HP	BB	IBB	SO	SB	CS	GDP	Slg.	OBP
Vargas, Inakel, Tig.	.400	5	11	10	2	4	7	0	0	1	2	0	0	1	0	1	0	0	0	.700	.455
Venales, Luis, Marl.	.090	28	85	67	6	6	8	2	0	0	5	0	0	18	0	27	1	2	2	.119	.282
Villegas, Ernest, Rang.	.286	11	44	35	6	10	15	1	2	0	5	0	1	3	5	0	7	1	1	0	.429	.409
Wade, Mike, Ori.	.000	2	4	4	0	0	0	0	0	0	0	0	0	0	0	0	2	0	0	0	.000	.000
Wakeland, Chris, Tig.*	.071	4	14	14	2	1	1	0	0	0	1	0	0	0	0	0	4	0	0	0	.071	.071
Walker, Keronn, Roy.†	.324	18	49	37	4	12	16	1	0	1	4	1	0	2	9	0	9	0	0	1	.432	.479
Wallis, Jacob, Reds	.128	15	55	47	3	6	7	1	0	0	2	0	0	1	7	0	8	0	3	0	.149	.255
Ware, Anthony, Tig.	.186	33	110	102	11	19	27	2	0	2	8	1	1	0	6	0	48	0	0	2	.265	.229
Washington, Kelley, Marl.	.133	4	17	15	2	2	2	0	0	0	2	0	0	0	2	0	9	0	0	0	.133	.235
Watkins, Thomas, Twi.	.263	49	190	152	30	40	53	10	0	1	12	7	1	2	28	1	21	4	4	5	.349	.383
Watson, Brandon, Exp.*	.303	33	135	119	15	36	38	2	0	0	12	2	2	1	11	2	11	4	2	0	.319	.361
Weston, Aron, Pir.*	.218	33	140	119	26	26	30	2	1	0	5	0	0	1	20	0	36	14	5	1	.252	.336
Wigand, Tom, Phi.	.148	15	40	27	8	4	4	0	0	0	2	0	1	2	10	1	11	2	3	2	.148	.400
Williams, Brady, R.S.	.256	39	155	121	19	31	54	4	2	5	25	0	3	2	29	0	45	3	3	4	.446	.400
Wilson, Josh, Marl.	.266	53	237	203	29	54	71	9	4	0	27	1	4	5	24	0	36	14	2	4	.350	.352
Winrow, Gary, Yan.*	.317	46	202	180	31	57	72	9	3	0	28	0	1	0	21	0	28	5	1	2	.400	.386
Wrenn, Michael, Twi.	.256	42	151	129	24	33	55	8	1	4	21	4	1	2	15	0	19	6	0	0	.426	.340
Yingling, Joe, Tig.	.091	5	15	11	2	1	2	1	0	0	0	0	0	1	3	0	6	0	0	0	.182	.333
Young, Walter, Pir.*	.231	37	138	130	9	30	40	6	2	0	15	1	0	3	4	1	34	2	2	4	.308	.270
Zapey, Winton, Marl.	.216	29	85	74	8	16	25	6	0	1	10	0	0	4	7	0	17	1	0	1	.338	.318
Zeber, Ryan, Reds	.167	3	7	6	1	1	1	0	0	0	0	0	0	0	1	0	0	0	0	0	.167	.286
Zumwalt, Sean, Brav.	.207	51	208	188	19	39	53	3	1	3	22	0	0	5	15	0	48	1	2	6	.282	.284

GRAND SLAMS: Angell, 2; Delgado, Devanez, Fowler, Geibush, Hatteberg, Jacobs, Morris, Rodgers, Serrano, Wrenn, Zumwalt, 1 each.

AWARDED FIRST BASE ON CATCHER'S INTERFERENCE: Mendieta 2 (Salas 2); Alley (Wrenn); Devanez (Dito); Davis (Dito); Harris (Salas); Jacobs (Dito); Quickstad (Paulino); Rodgers (Evans); Santana (Tosca); Soto (Deschenes).

1999 PITCHING

TEAM

Team	W	L	Pct.	ERA	G	CG	ShO	Sv.	IP	H	TBF	R	ER	HR	SH	SF	HB	BB	IBB	SO	WP	Bk.
Red Sox	30	29	.508	3.03	60	0	3	12	511.0	465	2216	273	172	22	15	11	28	198	6	472	40	15
Mets	39	21	.650	3.10	60	1	2	15	522.2	473	2257	247	180	9	10	13	34	216	1	486	51	13
Rangers	37	23	.617	3.10	60	2	4	16	510.1	441	2148	221	176	27	14	13	28	179	3	385	30	24
Braves	27	33	.450	3.49	60	0	4	7	525.2	479	2258	258	204	23	12	17	30	214	5	440	33	16
Tigers	29	31	.483	3.65	60	2	3	14	490.1	427	2149	239	199	23	21	15	28	275	4	462	31	7
Royals	33	27	.550	3.68	60	1	5	18	519.0	498	2242	263	212	24	7	18	41	197	4	441	33	8
Pirates	24	35	.407	3.73	60	1	1	8	514.0	467	2199	275	213	19	16	25	46	196	0	383	37	12
Yankees	32	28	.533	3.78	60	3	5	16	502.2	468	2205	265	211	23	24	17	30	243	3	565	50	5
Marlins	25	35	.417	3.78	60	3	5	11	528.2	522	2303	274	222	21	13	11	36	201	4	428	42	2
Orioles	31	28	.525	3.82	60	0	2	14	504.0	472	2224	300	214	17	13	15	44	242	17	413	59	21
Expos	29	31	.483	3.99	60	1	3	17	504.2	481	2216	264	224	20	20	15	41	241	1	387	45	11
Twins	33	26	.559	4.03	60	10	6	9	480.2	490	2084	276	215	21	21	23	29	165	7	403	33	23
Reds	23	37	.383	4.73	60	1	2	8	491.0	483	2218	328	258	14	37	27	32	261	7	387	49	15
Phillies	26	34	.433	4.85	60	0	4	13	491.2	516	2235	318	265	29	17	27	35	262	1	438	38	5

INDIVIDUAL

TOP QUALIFIERS FOR EARNED-RUN AVERAGE TITLE

Minimum 48 innings. *Lefthanded pitcher.

Pitcher, Team	W	L	Pct.	ERA	G	GS	CG	ShO	GF	Sv.	IP	H	TBF	R	ER	HR	SH	SF	HB	BB	IBB	SO	WP	Bk.
Colton, Kyle, Brav.	2	1	.667	1.79	13	10	0	0	0	0	50.1	35	207	11	10	1	0	0	3	27	0	30	2	3
Evert, Brett, Brav.	5	3	.625	2.03	13	10	0	0	1	0	48.2	37	195	17	11	0	2	2	4	9	1	39	3	4
Tavarez, David, Ori.	9	0	1.000	2.14	12	9	0	0	0	0	67.1	60	277	22	16	2	2	1	7	12	2	55	4	2
Lopez, Rafael, Mets	7	1	.875	2.17	12	8	0	0	1	0	58.0	43	245	20	14	1	0	3	3	29	0	42	4	1
Song, Seung, R.S.	5	5	.500	2.30	13	9	0	0	2	0	54.2	47	233	29	14	2	0	2	4	20	0	61	2	4
Roman, Orlando, Mets	6	0	1.000	2.36	12	11	1	1	1	0	61.0	41	254	20	16	0	0	4	5	21	0	64	3	0
Richardson, Jason, Twi.	2	2	.333	2.37	12	10	0	0	0	0	49.1	46	211	21	13	2	2	1	9	23	1	54	3	0
Barreto, Joel, Twi.	4	3	.571	2.56	11	9	3	1	1	0	56.1	45	222	18	16	2	3	0	0	17	0	41	4	2
Lopez, Ignacio, Rang.	7	2	.778	2.50	12	9	0	0	2	1	56.2	60	235	22	17	2	1	1	5	5	0	31	1	0
Sauer, Marc, Marl.	5	4	.556	2.71	13	13	1	1	0	0	69.2	75	284	28	21	2	0	0	7	1	0	57	0	0
Torres, Luis, Exp.	5	3	.625	2.85	12	9	1	1	0	0	60.0	55	259	28	19	1	1	1	3	28	1	36	8	0
Martinez, David, Yan.*	5	3	.625	2.97	12	11	2	1	0	0	66.2	52	273	29	22	2	5	1	3	22	0	67	8	1
Arias, Pablo, Tig.	3	2	.600	3.02	12	12	1	0	0	0	65.2	57	282	31	22	2	1	2	8	22	1	60	2	0
Martinez, Carlos, Roy.*	4	3	.571	3.04	11	7	1	1	1	0	50.1	40	197	20	17	5	0	1	1	7	0	36	0	1
Targac, Matthew, Marl.*	1	7	.125	3.05	12	11	1	0	0	0	56.0	53	237	32	19	2	1	2	0	16	0	55	8	1

DEPARTMENTAL LEADERS: W—Tavarez, 9; L—White, 8; Pct.—Tavarez, 1.000; G—Yen, 25; GS—Sauer, 13; CG—Barreto, Romero, 3 each; ShO—several players tied, 1 each; GF—Yen, 21; Sv.—Yen, 10; IP—Sauer, 69.2; H—Sauer, 75; TBF—Sauer, White, 284; R—Ortega, 48; ER—Levesque, 36; HR—Rahrer, Mead, Tejeda, C. Martinez, Romero, 5 each; SH—D. Martinez, E. Martinez, Tate, Valdez, 5 each; SF—Levesque, Staples, 6 each; HB—White, 12; BB—Levesque, 40; IBB—De La Rosa, Tate, 3 each; SO—Martinez, 67; WP—Anez, 13; BK—Morel, 6.

ALL PITCHERS

*Lefthanded pitcher.

Pitcher, Team	W	L	Pct.	ERA	G	GS	CG	ShO	GF	Sv.	IP	H	TBF	R	ER	HR	SH	SF	HB	BB	IBB	SO	WP	Bk.
Abreu, Cesar, Reds	0	0	.000	6.75	1	0	0	0	1	0	1.1	0	7	1	1	0	0	1	1	2	0	0	1	0
Advincola, Jose, Ori.*	1	1	.500	5.46	12	5	0	0	4	0	28.0	37	131	20	17	1	1	0	2	16	0	23	8	1
Albertus, Roberto, Brav.*	4	2	.333	6.06	13	4	0	0	0	0	32.2	36	146	23	22	1	1	2	0	17	1	27	1	0
Alcala, Jason, Pir.	0	1	.000	1.23	10	0	0	0	9	2	14.2	12	59	7	2	0	1	1	0	0	0	9	1	1
Alcantara, Over, Marl.	0	0	.000	0.90	4	0	0	0	3	0	10.0	7	40	1	1	0	1	0	0	3	0	4	1	0

Pitcher, Team	W	L	Pct.	ERA	G	GS	CG	ShO	GF	Sv.	IP	H	TBF	R	ER	HR	SH	SF	HB	BB	IBB	SO	WP	Bk.
Aldridge, Mike, Yan.	2	0	1.000	8.59	7	0	0	0	0	0	7.1	6	34	7	7	0	0	1	0	5	0	12	3	0
Almonte, Erick, Yan.	0	0	.000	0.00	1	0	0	0	1	0	1.0	1	5	0	0	0	0	1	0	1	0	1	0	0
Altman, Gene, Reds.	1	0	1.000	1.80	3	3	0	0	0	0	10.0	6	41	2	2	0	0	0	0	4	0	10	0	0
Anderson, Antwoine, Marl.*	2	1	.667	3.45	13	0	0	0	6	2	28.2	28	123	13	11	1	1	1	1	9	0	26	1	0
Anez, Omar, Ori.	1	6	.143	8.33	14	6	0	0	2	0	31.1	38	161	38	29	2	0	0	2	29	0	23	13	3
Angell, Rick, Rang.	1	0	1.000	1.80	1	0	0	0	1	0	1.0	1	4	0	0	0	0	0	0	0	0	0	0	0
Aramboles, Ricardo, Yan.	2	3	.400	3.89	9	7	0	0	2	0	34.2	35	149	18	15	1	3	4	1	14	0	42	6	0
Arias, Pablo, Tig.	3	2	.600	3.02	12	12	1	0	0	0	65.2	57	282	31	22	2	1	2	8	22	1	60	2	0
Arteaga, J.D., Mets*	0	0	.000	6.75	2	1	0	0	0	0	4.0	4	15	3	3	1	0	0	0	3	0	3	0	0
Ascencio, Miguel, Phi.	1	4	.200	5.97	9	5	0	0	3	0	28.2	35	137	24	19	1	0	4	2	16	0	14	1	0
Baginski, Jr., Thomas, Tig.*	2	0	1.000	1.80	10	0	0	0	1	0	20.0	11	74	4	4	2	0	1	1	4	0	24	0	0
Baker, Brad, R.S.	1	0	1.000	0.79	4	3	0	0	0	0	11.1	10	48	3	1	0	1	0	1	2	0	10	0	1
Baldassano, Joseph, Exp.	1	2	.333	9.15	12	0	0	0	7	4	19.2	27	101	22	20	1	1	3	0	13	0	20	6	0
Baranowski, Brannon, Roy.	1	2	.333	2.83	24	0	0	0	9	1	35.0	27	151	14	11	1	1	0	1	19	2	53	3	0
Barker, Billy, Exp.*	2	2	.500	3.14	10	0	0	0	7	3	14.1	13	61	6	5	2	1	0	0	8	0	10	2	0
Barreto, Joel, Twi.	4	3	.571	2.56	11	9	3	1	1	0	56.1	45	222	18	16	2	3	0	0	17	0	41	4	2
Bedard, Erik, Ori.*	2	1	.667	1.86	8	6	0	0	1	0	29.0	20	117	7	6	1	0	0	0	13	0	41	3	0
Bell, Rob, Reds	0	0	.000	1.13	2	2	0	0	0	0	8.0	3	26	1	1	0	1	0	0	0	0	11	1	0
Bell, Tom, Marl.	1	0	1.000	4.01	13	0	0	0	9	3	24.2	21	105	11	11	2	0	1	1	7	0	9	0	0
Benitez, Fabricio, R.S.	4	4	.500	3.28	13	8	0	0	2	1	57.2	55	241	34	21	0	3	1	0	14	0	40	4	2
Bennett, Jeff, Pir.	3	4	.429	4.23	8	8	0	0	0	0	44.2	53	191	27	21	1	2	1	0	9	0	28	2	3
Berube, Martin, Ori.	0	0	.000	0.53	11	0	0	0	8	2	17.0	8	69	5	1	0	0	1	2	10	1	11	0	0
Biddlestone, Jason, Pir.	4	1	.800	2.91	12	4	0	0	3	0	46.1	39	195	19	15	1	0	2	4	16	0	45	0	0
Bowyer, Travis, Twi.	1	0	1.000	0.00	1	0	0	0	0	0	1.0	0	3	0	0	0	0	0	0	0	0	1	0	0
Boyanich, Vincent, Twi.	2	5	.286	7.56	15	0	0	0	10	2	33.1	45	159	33	28	1	3	1	3	11	1	38	6	2
Bradley, Robert, Pir.	1	1	.500	2.90	6	6	0	0	0	0	31.0	31	128	13	10	2	0	2	2	4	0	31	5	0
Brewer, Dustin, Ori.	1	1	.500	2.89	4	0	0	0	0	0	9.1	13	47	11	3	0	1	2	2	2	0	8	1	1
Brito, Eude, Phi.*	0	0	.000	5.02	12	3	0	0	3	0	28.2	39	139	22	16	0	2	2	0	19	0	23	4	1
Brown, Andrew, Brav.	1	1	.500	2.34	11	11	0	0	0	0	42.1	40	183	15	11	4	1	0	3	16	0	57	4	4
Brown, Paul, Reds*	0	3	.000	4.31	14	4	1	0	4	1	48.0	53	204	30	23	2	4	4	1	13	0	20	1	0
Buckles, Bucky, Rang.	1	0	1.000	4.50	1	1	0	0	0	0	2.0	4	10	2	1	0	0	0	0	1	0	1	0	0
Bumatay, Mike, Pir.*	2	1	.667	2.90	11	3	0	0	6	2	40.1	35	154	16	13	4	0	1	8	0	39	2	0
Burch, Matt, Roy.	0	2	.000	4.50	5	4	0	0	0	0	14.0	17	67	10	7	0	0	3	10	0	9	1	0
Bureau, Stephen, Brav.	0	0	.000	10.03	11	0	0	0	5	0	11.2	13	66	17	13	0	1	6	14	0	8	6	0
Burger, Rob, Phi.	1	1	.500	2.78	9	2	0	0	4	0	22.2	19	102	8	7	0	1	0	3	15	0	31	7	0
Burrows, Terry, Ori.*	0	0	.000	0.00	2	2	0	0	0	0	5.0	0	17	1	0	0	0	1	1	0	4	0	1
Burruezo, Joseph, Pir.	0	1	.000	4.82	7	0	0	0	3	0	9.1	6	40	6	5	0	0	1	9	0	8	0	0
Butler, Mattaues, Brav.	2	4	.333	4.03	11	10	0	0	0	0	38.0	36	168	20	17	4	1	2	22	0	38	4	0
Cabaj, Christopher, Roy.	6	0	1.000	2.66	11	2	0	0	3	0	44.0	42	179	15	13	1	0	1	2	6	0	38	4	0
Cabrera, Yunior, Mets*	2	3	.400	3.81	13	11	0	0	0	0	54.1	58	249	35	23	0	1	4	26	0	59	7	1
Campos, David, Marl.*	3	1	.750	4.19	8	0	0	0	4	0	19.1	20	84	9	9	1	1	0	2	6	0	20	3	0
Carey, Ben, Phi.*	2	2	.500	3.66	17	4	0	0	3	0	39.1	40	172	20	16	1	0	1	4	15	0	35	2	0
Casadiego, Gerardo, Exp.	1	1	.500	2.79	9	4	0	0	2	0	19.1	19	84	10	6	1	2	0	2	8	0	8	1	0
Castillo, Ramon, Marl.	1	2	.333	3.46	11	10	0	0	0	0	52.0	56	222	21	20	3	1	1	4	12	1	34	2	0
Castro, Eleuterio, R.S.	0	1	.000	3.60	6	0	0	0	2	0	15.0	15	64	7	6	1	1	0	0	4	1	8	1	0
Cavazos, Andy, Rang.	2	0	1.000	3.72	10	7	0	0	0	0	36.1	35	151	16	15	3	3	1	0	12	0	15	1	1
Cedeno, Jovanny, Rang.	3	0	1.000	0.33	6	6	1	1	0	0	27.1	13	101	3	1	0	0	2	4	0	32	1	0
Cespedes, Rafael, Brav.	1	5	.167	3.45	14	0	0	0	5	0	28.2	19	124	16	11	2	1	4	4	11	1	24	1	0
Cetani, Bryan, Brav.*	1	3	.250	4.57	13	9	0	0	0	0	41.1	48	185	27	21	1	1	4	15	0	17	3	1
Chacon, Ernesto, Yan.	4	0	1.000	3.09	18	1	0	0	4	1	35.0	30	156	14	12	1	2	1	3	21	0	55	3	0
Charron, Eric, Exp.	2	6	.250	5.86	9	8	0	0	0	0	43.0	44	189	32	28	3	1	3	2	19	0	25	5	0
Cheek, Andrew, R.S.*	2	1	.667	3.41	18	0	0	0	9	2	29.0	27	125	16	11	2	1	1	17	1	20	2	0
Chighisola, Louis, Reds*	1	2	.333	3.86	7	0	0	0	5	3	9.1	9	38	4	4	0	4	0	0	4	1	11	1	0
Chisnall, Wesley, Exp.	0	2	.000	7.36	4	4	0	0	0	0	14.2	20	72	13	12	1	1	0	6	0	8	2	0
Classen, Ender, Pir.	3	1	.750	1.82	6	6	0	0	0	0	34.2	21	139	13	7	1	1	2	7	9	0	28	0	0
Claussen, Brandon, Yan.*	0	1	.000	3.18	2	2	0	0	0	0	11.1	7	42	4	4	2	0	0	0	2	0	16	0	0
Coa, Jesus, Roy.	1	1	.500	5.74	7	2	0	0	3	0	26.2	36	129	22	17	1	0	2	4	13	0	11	3	1
Coffey, Todd, Reds	1	1	.500	3.38	5	2	0	0	0	0	16.0	9	78	12	6	1	0	1	1	14	0	14	2	2
Cole, Joseph, Mets	5	1	.833	4.41	13	8	0	0	0	0	51.0	52	234	30	25	1	0	2	11	23	0	55	9	1
Colton, Kyle, Brav.	2	1	.667	1.79	13	10	0	0	0	0	50.1	35	207	11	10	1	0	3	27	0	30	2	3
Cooper, Eric, Reds	0	2	.000	7.84	3	2	0	0	0	0	10.1	13	48	12	9	0	0	1	5	0	5	2	0
Cordova, Jorge, Marl.	1	0	1.000	1.29	7	0	0	0	5	1	14.0	8	51	3	2	0	0	0	1	6	0	18	2	0
Crowther, Jackson, Exp.	2	2	.500	3.12	13	0	0	0	4	1	34.2	30	144	14	12	0	1	0	3	11	0	26	1	2
Curtice, John, R.S.*	0	5	.000	7.36	8	6	0	0	0	0	14.2	16	80	22	12	1	1	0	6	12	0	19	3	0
Davis, Quian, Marl.	0	0	.000	9.00	1	0	0	0	1	0	2.0	3	10	2	2	0	0	0	0	0	1	0	0
Day, Zach, Yan.	1	1	.500	3.78	5	4	0	0	0	0	16.2	20	74	10	7	1	0	1	4	0	17	0	0
Dehart, Casey, Reds	0	1	.000	7.71	2	2	0	0	0	0	4.2	7	22	4	4	0	0	0	2	0	6	0	0
Delacruz, Luis, Yan.	0	0	.000	0.00	3	0	0	0	1	1	3.0	2	13	0	0	0	0	2	0	2	0	0
De La Rosa, Cristian, Ori.	1	3	.250	6.52	15	0	0	0	8	0	19.1	30	103	19	14	0	2	1	3	16	3	13	1	0
Delgado, Joseph, Roy.	1	0	1.000	0.00	1	1	0	0	0	0	6.0	2	20	0	0	0	0	0	0	1	0	4	0	0
De Los Santos, Luis, Yan.	0	0	.000	0.00	2	2	0	0	0	0	8.0	5	28	0	0	0	0	1	0	0	7	0	0
Diaz, Luis, Tig.	1	2	.333	1.99	22	0	0	0	9	2	31.2	24	135	9	7	1	3	0	2	20	2	36	1	2
Dubuc, Charles, Exp.*	1	2	.333	2.70	16	5	0	0	3	0	46.2	39	200	21	14	0	4	0	7	27	0	34	4	1
Earl, Ryan, Tig.*	3	2	.600	4.58	7	7	0	0	0	0	37.1	34	160	20	19	4	1	2	1	18	0	20	7	2
Echols, Justin, Rang.	2	2	.500	2.60	14	4	0	0	3	0	34.2	27	144	14	10	1	1	2	1	21	1	32	0	3
Einertson, Darrell, Yan.	0	1	.000	0.00	1	0	0	0	1	0	2.0	3	11	3	0	0	0	0	1	0	4	0	0
Espina, Rendy, Phi.*	1	0	1.000	0.00	2	0	0	0	2	1	1.0	1	4	0	0	0	0	0	0	1	0	0
Espinal, Jose, Yan.	4	3	.571	6.90	10	4	0	0	3	0	30.0	35	140	29	23	3	2	3	2	13	0	23	4	2
Essian, James, Roy.	0	1	.000	18.00	1	0	0	0	1	0	1.0	0	7	3	2	0	1	1	3	0	0	0	0
Evert, Brett, Brav.	5	3	.625	2.03	13	10	0	0	1	0	48.2	37	195	17	11	0	2	4	9	1	39	3	4
Falkenborg, Brian, Ori.	1	0	1.000	2.00	3	2	0	0	0	0	9.0	6	37	2	2	0	0	0	0	1	0	10	0	0
Farren, Dave, Ori.	1	1	.500	0.95	10	1	0	0	4	2	19.0	17	81	6	2	1	0	0	2	7	0	12	1	1
Figueroa, Carlos, Rang.*	4	0	1.000	0.84	5	0	0	0	2	0	10.2	5	39	1	1	0	0	0	1	3	0	17	0	4
Finnegan, Mike, Exp.	1	0	1.000	0.00	1	0	0	0	0	0	2.0	5	11	0	0	0	0	0	0	0	1	0	0
Flanagan, Ryan, Twi.	1	2	.333	3.92	8	4	0	0	3	0	20.2	10	91	11	9	0	3	0	4	16	0	14	3	3

Pitcher, Team	W	L	Pct.	ERA	G	GS	CG	ShO	GF	Sv.	IP	H	TBF	R	ER	HR	SH	SF	HB	BB	IBB	SO	WP	Bk.
Fleming, Travis, Ori.	1	1	.500	1.13	4	3	0	0	0	0	16.0	12	62	2	2	0	0	0	2	0	0	21	1	1
Francisco, Franklin, R.S.	2	4	.333	4.56	12	7	0	0	1	0	53.1	58	252	39	27	3	1	1	4	35	0	48	7	3
Franco, Edwin, Roy.*	0	0	.000	0.00	2	0	0	0	0	0	3.0	1	9	0	0	0	0	0	0	0	0	4	0	0
Fraser, Joe, Exp.	0	0	.000	0.00	4	0	0	0	1	0	5.2	1	23	0	0	0	0	0	2	9	0	4	4	0
Frederick, Kevin, Twi.	0	0	.000	15.43	2	0	0	0	0	0	2.1	6	14	5	4	0	0	1	0	1	0	3	0	0
Fuell, Jerrod, Tig.	0	3	.000	8.05	6	6	0	0	0	0	19.0	29	95	19	17	1	0	1	1	13	0	8	1	0
Gamboa, Javier, Roy.	0	0	.000	3.60	3	3	0	0	0	0	5.0	6	22	2	2	1	0	0	0	2	0	4	0	0
Garcia, Abel, Roy.*	1	2	.333	4.20	3	2	0	0	0	0	15.0	17	63	9	7	1	0	0	2	2	0	13	4	0
Garcia, Rafael, Roy.	4	2	.667	4.61	9	5	0	0	0	0	41.0	44	184	24	21	2	1	4	5	13	0	44	2	0
Garcia, Ramon, R.S.	2	0	1.000	2.96	21	0	0	0	18	5	24.1	24	116	10	8	0	1	0	1	15	2	26	3	0
Garcia, Reynaldo, Rang.	4	4	.500	3.23	12	11	0	0	0	0	64.0	55	268	30	23	3	2	4	0	26	0	42	4	3
Gardea, Mario, Yan.	1	3	.250	2.84	14	0	0	0	2	0	19.0	11	84	10	6	1	0	0	3	13	0	34	6	0
Garris, Antonio, Exp.	3	2	.600	4.02	15	1	0	0	7	1	40.1	32	169	19	18	2	2	1	4	19	0	33	3	1
Gauger, Michael, Mets*	2	0	1.000	3.30	18	0	0	0	10	3	30.0	27	127	17	11	1	0	2	2	8	0	30	1	1
Girdley, Joshua, Exp.*	0	2	.000	3.32	12	11	0	0	1	1	43.1	41	182	19	16	2	0	1	3	16	0	49	3	0
Gobble, Jimmy, Roy.*	0	0	.000	2.70	4	1	0	0	0	0	6.2	6	32	3	2	0	0	0	0	5	0	8	1	1
Gooch, Arnie, Reds	1	1	.500	1.13	2	2	0	0	0	0	8.0	5	32	2	1	0	0	1	1	0	0	6	0	0
Grantham, Ryan, Exp.	2	0	1.000	3.42	8	5	0	0	0	0	26.1	24	126	10	10	1	1	1	5	18	0	30	4	0
Guerrero, Neftali, Mets	1	2	.333	1.66	15	0	0	0	14	5	21.2	16	87	6	4	1	2	0	5	5	0	17	2	0
Guillen, Elvin, Reds	0	0	.000	9.00	7	0	0	0	4	0	8.0	9	42	9	8	0	0	1	1	11	0	7	3	2
Guzman, Leiby, Rang.	0	0	.000	0.00	1	1	0	0	0	0	3.0	2	11	0	0	0	0	0	0	0	0	1	0	0
Halisky, Scott, Ori.	0	0	.000	7.20	3	0	0	0	2	0	5.0	7	23	4	4	1	0	0	3	1	0	3	2	0
Halvorson, Greg, Mets	1	2	.333	3.86	5	3	0	0	1	0	21.0	22	95	14	9	0	1	0	1	9	0	20	3	1
Harrell, Scott, Reds	0	0	.000	6.75	2	0	0	0	0	0	4.0	6	20	4	3	1	0	0	1	1	0	2	0	0
Haynes, Brad, Marl.	1	4	.200	4.08	11	11	0	0	0	0	46.1	45	214	31	21	1	1	1	6	30	0	40	4	0
Herrera, Carlos, Phi.	0	3	.000	4.37	12	5	0	0	0	0	45.1	46	209	30	22	4	3	1	6	25	0	40	2	0
Herrera, Pedro, Roy.	0	0	.000	0.00	5	0	0	0	4	3	6.0	1	22	0	0	0	0	0	2	3	0	5	0	0
Hill, Jaime, Rang.*	2	0	1.000	2.35	21	1	0	0	12	2	46.0	32	181	12	12	0	2	0	1	20	0	38	0	2
Hill, Ryan, Roy.	0	0	.000	81.00	1	0	0	0	0	0	0.1	0	5	3	3	0	0	0	1	3	0	1	0	0
Hines, Carlos, Reds	0	0	.000	8.10	5	0	0	0	0	0	10.0	15	53	12	9	0	2	0	0	8	1	7	5	1
Hlodan, George, Pir.	0	0	.000	3.60	4	0	0	0	3	1	10.0	11	43	4	4	1	1	0	3	3	0	3	0	0
Hopper, Joshua, Mets*	3	1	.750	1.62	16	2	0	0	4	2	44.1	42	190	13	8	0	1	0	1	19	0	50	4	2
Hughes, Mike, Exp.*	0	0	.000	0.00	2	2	0	0	0	0	8.0	4	28	1	0	0	0	0	0	0	0	9	0	0
Igualada, Eric, Yan.	1	3	.250	3.80	11	0	0	0	1	0	23.2	16	98	10	10	4	1	2	1	12	0	30	3	0
Infante, Asdrubal, Tig.	3	0	1.000	1.09	15	2	1	0	9	2	33.0	17	135	5	4	0	1	0	1	20	0	51	2	0
Jelovcic, Rich, Yan.	1	1	.500	3.12	14	0	0	0	2	0	17.1	12	78	6	6	0	0	0	2	15	0	10	0	0
Jimenez, Ronal, Phi.	6	2	.750	3.51	20	0	0	0	13	4	33.1	29	144	13	13	2	0	3	1	16	0	30	1	1
Johnson, Jonathan, Rang.	0	0	.000	1.80	1	1	0	0	0	0	5.0	3	18	1	1	0	0	0	0	0	0	5	0	0
Johnson, Mark, Yan.	0	3	.000	8.18	3	2	0	0	0	0	11.0	15	53	11	10	1	1	1	0	5	1	10	0	0
Johnston, Dave, Marl.	1	2	.333	4.85	12	0	0	0	7	0	26.0	35	116	17	14	4	0	1	5	5	1	20	3	0
Joseph, Glen, Reds	1	0	1.000	7.20	2	0	0	0	1	0	5.0	8	22	4	4	0	0	0	1	0	0	3	0	0
Josephson, Jared, Pir.	1	0	1.000	1.80	8	0	0	0	7	1	10.0	8	40	2	2	0	0	0	2	0	0	8	0	1
Kessel, Kyle, Mets*	0	1	.000	3.38	3	3	0	0	0	0	8.0	5	29	4	3	0	0	0	1	2	0	11	1	0
Kinney, Matt, Twi.	0	1	.000	4.76	3	3	0	0	0	0	5.2	6	24	4	3	0	0	0	3	0	0	8	0	0
Kirsten, Rick, Tig.	1	1	.500	5.26	11	4	0	0	4	0	25.2	18	112	15	15	2	3	2	2	17	0	27	1	0
Koronka, John, Reds*	3	3	.500	1.69	7	7	0	0	0	0	37.1	25	148	11	7	1	1	3	1	14	0	27	1	1
Koziara, Matt, Reds	3	2	.600	2.05	13	1	0	0	6	0	26.1	24	123	15	6	0	3	0	2	16	2	26	2	0
Kozlowski, Benjamin, Brav.	1	1	.500	1.87	15	0	0	0	7	3	33.2	28	132	9	7	0	0	0	6	29	0	29	2	0
La Rosa, Dancy, Twi.	5	2	.714	3.66	11	11	2	0	0	0	59.0	66	258	30	24	2	3	0	20	1	0	42	4	1
Lajara, Eudy, Marl.*	1	2	.333	2.08	8	2	0	0	2	0	21.2	13	93	6	5	0	0	2	0	14	0	23	4	0
Lamarsh, Robert, Rang.*	2	0	1.000	2.00	3	0	0	0	1	0	9.0	7	35	2	2	1	0	0	1	1	0	6	0	0
Lankford, Frank, Yan.	0	0	.000	4.50	1	1	0	0	0	0	2.0	2	8	1	1	0	0	0	0	1	0	2	1	0
Laplante, Reggie, Yan.	1	2	.333	5.21	8	7	0	0	0	0	38.0	40	165	25	22	3	1	1	2	15	0	40	2	0
Leach, Bryan, R.S.	0	0	.000	0.00	1	0	0	0	1	0	2.0	2	9	1	0	0	0	0	0	1	0	1	0	0
Leahy, Bart, Marl.	0	1	.000	8.47	8	0	0	0	1	1	17.0	22	94	19	16	2	1	1	5	18	0	16	2	0
Ledezma, Wilfredo, R.S.*	5	1	.833	3.30	13	6	0	0	2	1	57.1	51	242	28	21	2	1	1	1	20	0	52	3	1
Legette, Richard, Phi.	2	1	.667	7.26	12	6	0	0	1	0	31.0	34	144	26	25	2	0	2	3	23	0	23	2	1
Lesner, Kenneth, Twi.	0	2	.000	4.70	13	0	0	0	4	1	23.0	32	109	16	12	0	1	2	1	9	1	13	1	0
Levesque, Benjamin, Pir.	2	7	.222	7.53	11	11	1	0	0	0	43.0	38	210	44	36	1	2	6	6	40	0	20	6	0
Lewis, Jeremy, Tig.*	4	5	.444	2.70	10	10	0	0	0	0	40.0	34	181	16	12	1	2	1	2	28	0	31	2	0
Lewter, John, Pir.	2	1	.667	5.63	13	0	0	0	8	1	24.0	28	116	20	15	2	3	0	2	8	0	14	4	0
Lima, Frank, Tig.	1	2	.333	4.85	20	3	0	0	3	0	48.1	48	206	28	23	1	2	1	0	14	0	53	1	2
Linarelli, Tom, R.S.	0	0	.000	13.50	1	1	0	0	0	0	1.1	2	9	3	2	0	1	0	0	2	0	1	0	0
Lockwood, Luke, Exp.*	1	2	.333	4.57	11	7	0	0	4	0	41.1	46	184	21	21	3	0	2	2	13	0	32	0	0
Loewer, Carlton, Phi.	0	0	.000	0.00	1	1	0	0	0	0	2.0	2	8	0	0	0	0	0	0	0	0	2	1	0
Lopez, Ignacio, Rang.	7	2	.778	2.70	12	9	0	0	2	1	56.2	60	235	22	17	2	1	1	5	5	0	31	1	0
Lopez, Jorge, Reds	1	1	.500	6.12	10	0	0	0	2	0	25.0	31	112	19	17	2	1	2	2	9	0	17	2	1
Lopez, Jose, Mets	0	2	.000	8.53	2	2	0	0	0	0	6.1	12	37	8	6	0	0	2	8	0	0	4	1	2
Lopez, Rafael, Mets	7	1	.875	2.17	12	8	0	0	1	0	58.0	43	245	20	14	1	0	3	3	29	0	42	4	1
Loudon, Gary, Reds.	1	2	.333	6.44	15	5	0	0	5	1	36.1	34	176	27	26	3	3	4	2	33	0	45	3	1
Love, Brandon, Reds	0	4	.000	7.66	7	6	0	0	0	0	24.2	30	118	21	21	0	2	1	4	9	0	17	1	1
Lutz, Kenneth, Reds	0	4	.000	6.50	12	9	0	0	0	0	44.1	58	210	40	32	1	3	3	3	20	0	37	0	0
Lyons, Curt, Yan.	0	0	.000	0.00	1	0	0	0	1	0	2.0	1	9	0	0	0	0	0	0	2	0	3	0	0
Maloney, Sean, Ori.	0	0	.000	0.00	1	0	0	0	1	0	2.0	1	7	0	0	0	0	0	1	0	0	3	0	0
Martinez, Carlos, Roy.*	4	3	.571	3.04	11	7	1	1	0	0	50.1	42	197	20	17	5	0	1	1	7	0	36	0	1
Martinez, David, Yan.*	5	3	.625	2.97	12	11	2	1	0	0	66.2	52	273	29	22	2	5	1	3	22	0	67	8	1
Martinez, Eddy, Reds.	3	3	.500	3.71	17	0	0	0	9	1	26.2	27	124	14	11	0	5	2	3	16	2	17	2	0
Martinez, Lionel, Brav.	2	1	.667	3.42	12	0	0	0	1	0	26.1	28	109	16	10	1	1	0	1	8	0	16	2	0
Martinez, Oscar, Yan.	2	1	.667	1.85	23	0	0	0	19	9	24.1	23	103	8	5	0	1	0	8	2	0	29	2	0
Martinez, Ramon, R.S.*	1	0	1.000	1.38	4	4	0	0	0	0	13.0	9	51	4	2	1	1	1	1	3	0	15	0	1
Marx, Tommy, Tig.*	3	2	.600	3.43	8	8	0	0	0	0	42.0	35	191	24	16	0	3	1	3	32	0	39	3	0
Mastrolonardo, David, Ori.	2	0	1.000	2.08	3	0	0	0	0	0	4.1	2	16	1	1	0	0	0	2	0	0	9	0	0
Mathews, Terry, Roy.	0	0	.000	0.00	1	1	0	0	0	0	2.0	0	6	0	0	0	0	0	0	0	0	2	0	0
McCloud, Josh, Yan.	0	0	.000	27.00	3	0	0	0	1	0	2.2	9	21	8	8	0	0	1	0	3	0	4	0	1
McGinnis, Ronald, Phi.	0	0	.000	22.50	4	0	0	0	2	0	4.0	9	30	10	10	0	0	0	0	8	0	2	0	0

Pitcher, Team	W	L	Pct.	ERA	G	GS	CG	ShO	GF	Sv.	IP	H	TBF	R	ER	HR	SH	SF	HB	BB	IBB	SO	WP	Bk.
McNatt, Josh, Ori.*	1	0	1.000	0.00	2	0	0	0	0	0	2.0	1	7	0	0	0	0	0	1	0	0	2	0	0
Mead, David, Rang.	1	3	.250	5.00	11	7	0	0	1	0	36.0	40	163	23	20	5	2	1	2	11	0	34	3	4
Mejia, Juan, Brav.	0	3	.000	5.90	16	0	0	0	9	0	29.0	40	143	23	19	3	2	0	3	8	1	24	4	1
Mendible, Franklin, Pir.	0	1	.000	1.59	4	0	0	0	1	0	5.2	4	22	1	1	0	0	0	0	4	0	3	0	0
Merrill, Darren, Exp.	2	0	1.000	3.09	6	0	0	0	3	0	11.2	13	49	4	4	0	2	0	0	2	0	5	0	3
Messenger, Randall, Marl.	0	3	.000	7.52	13	2	0	0	6	2	26.1	28	122	25	22	1	0	1	3	19	0	23	1	0
Messer, Brian, Pir.	0	1	.000	4.50	3	2	0	0	1	0	6.0	7	25	3	3	0	0	0	1	0	0	5	0	0
Mikkola, Shaun, Mets	1	0	1.000	4.13	5	4	0	0	0	0	24.0	28	111	14	11	0	0	0	0	15	0	9	2	2
Minaya, Richard, Reds	2	2	.500	4.61	16	0	0	0	10	0	27.1	25	124	19	14	1	0	4	0	16	1	19	7	2
Miniel, Rene, R.S.	1	2	.333	4.06	21	0	0	0	13	1	37.2	40	175	28	17	2	1	1	1	16	0	37	7	0
Morel, Jesus, Twi.	0	1	.000	4.55	14	0	0	0	6	1	31.2	34	156	26	16	2	0	4	5	15	0	31	2	6
Morel, Ramon, Exp.	0	1	.000	27.00	2	2	0	0	0	0	2.0	7	17	8	6	0	0	0	4	0	1	1	0
Moreno, Julio, Ori.	1	0	1.000	1.80	4	2	0	0	0	0	10.0	8	39	4	2	1	0	1	0	1	0	5	0	0
Moreno, Orber, Roy.	0	0	.000	0.00	1	1	0	0	0	0	1.0	0	3	0	0	0	0	0	0	0	0	1	0	0
Musser, Neal, Mets*	0	0	.667	2.01	8	7	0	0	0	0	31.1	26	134	13	7	1	0	0	0	18	0	22	4	0
Myers, Brett, Phi.	2	1	.667	2.33	7	5	0	0	0	0	27.0	17	105	8	7	0	0	0	2	7	0	30	2	0
Myers, Taylor, Roy.	0	2	.000	18.00	3	3	0	0	0	0	4.0	10	24	8	8	1	0	0	2	2	0	3	0	0
Nanninga, Matthew, Reds	1	1	.500	9.60	6	2	0	0	0	0	15.0	17	73	19	16	1	2	1	2	10	0	4	3	3
Nelson, Jeff, Yan.	0	0	.000	0.00	2	2	0	0	0	0	2.0	1	8	0	0	0	0	0	0	1	0	3	0	0
Nichols, Brian, Mets	3	1	.750	4.95	9	0	0	0	0	0	20.0	22	85	12	11	1	0	0	0	8	0	11	1	2
Nicholson, John, Exp.	0	0	.000	0.00	2	0	0	0	1	0	3.0	0	11	0	0	0	0	0	1	2	0	4	0	0
Obando, Omar, Yan.	1	0	1.000	0.00	2	0	0	0	0	0	4.0	5	20	4	0	1	3	0	0	3	0	3	0	0
Obermueller, Wes, Roy.	2	1	.667	2.58	11	7	0	0	2	0	38.1	33	159	16	11	2	0	1	1	12	1	39	2	1
Ochsner, Alan, Yan.	1	1	.500	5.79	4	0	0	0	1	0	4.2	4	21	4	3	1	1	0	0	4	0	6	0	0
Odom, Lance, Twi.	0	2	.000	5.79	20	0	0	0	17	5	23.1	33	113	18	15	0	1	0	3	7	1	13	2	2
Oliver, Scott, Yan.	4	1	.800	1.65	6	5	0	0	0	0	32.2	28	133	7	6	0	2	0	2	8	0	31	2	0
Ortega, Jose, Roy.	1	5	.167	5.91	12	9	0	0	0	0	53.1	67	257	48	35	1	2	5	5	30	0	27	3	1
Ortega, Jose, Roy.*	2	1	.667	3.62	17	0	0	0	7	3	37.1	41	166	17	15	3	0	0	3	18	0	32	3	0
Ortiz, Javier, Yan.	3	2	.600	5.68	12	10	1	0	0	0	50.2	63	246	40	32	4	1	1	4	35	0	46	2	0
Palki, Jeromy, Twi.	0	0	.000	0.00	3	1	0	0	0	0	5.0	0	16	0	0	0	0	0	1	0	3	0	0
Parkerson, Michael, Pir.*	0	0	.000	3.27	14	0	0	0	5	1	33.0	25	141	14	12	1	3	1	2	21	0	31	3	5
Paz, Rolando, Ori.	1	1	.500	8.64	13	0	0	0	3	0	25.0	23	124	28	24	1	1	2	2	25	1	23	6	1
Peeples, Jim, Yan.*	0	0	.000	4.96	16	0	0	0	4	0	16.1	21	87	13	9	0	1	0	1	16	0	21	3	0
Pena, Juan, R.S.	0	0	.000	0.00	1	1	0	0	0	0	2.0	0	7	0	0	0	0	0	0	0	0	4	0	0
Pepen, Robert, Mets	3	1	.750	1.47	19	0	0	0	16	2	30.2	20	119	7	5	0	2	0	0	7	0	34	2	0
Perez, Franklin, Phi.	3	4	.429	6.31	12	7	0	0	3	0	41.1	44	192	36	29	2	1	2	5	27	0	35	6	0
Phillips, James, Ori.	1	1	.500	3.90	15	0	0	0	6	2	27.2	25	123	16	12	1	0	1	3	17	1	16	6	0
Pidgeon, Chip, Mets*	0	0	.000	10.38	4	0	0	0	0	0	4.1	5	27	6	5	0	1	0	3	6	0	4	3	0
Rahrer, Josh, Rang.	4	5	.500	4.36	15	0	0	0	4	0	33.0	29	143	18	16	5	0	1	1	12	0	16	1	0
Ramirez, Enrique, Ori.	0	0	.000	2.45	9	0	0	0	9	5	11.0	9	46	3	3	0	0	0	1	3	0	7	0	0
Rasmussen, Brent, Roy.	2	1	.667	2.25	17	0	0	0	7	0	32.0	28	130	8	8	3	1	1	2	11	0	16	0	0
Reisinger, Justin, Yan.	1	0	1.000	11.05	8	0	0	0	1	0	7.1	11	42	12	9	1	0	1	3	6	0	7	5	1
Rhea, Thad, Pir.	0	1	.000	3.38	2	0	0	0	1	0	2.2	2	13	1	1	0	0	0	1	3	0	1	0	0
Rice, Scott, Ori.*	1	4	.200	10.38	9	6	0	0	0	0	17.1	26	101	34	20	2	1	0	3	20	1	14	3	1
Ridenour, Ryan, Yan.*	0	0	.000	2.08	3	1	0	0	0	0	8.2	5	36	5	2	0	0	1	0	5	0	13	0	2
Rijo, Hector, Exp.*	1	1	.500	3.42	15	0	0	0	9	3	26.1	25	116	11	10	1	2	2	2	12	0	16	0	3
Rivera, Erick, Phi.	0	0	.000	27.00	1	0	0	0	0	0	1.0	3	7	3	3	0	0	0	0	2	0	0	0	0
Rivera, Samuel, Tig.	1	0	1.000	2.35	7	1	0	0	1	1	15.1	9	66	6	4	1	0	0	1	11	0	19	4	0
Rodney, Fernando, Tig.	3	3	.500	2.40	22	0	0	0	20	9	30.0	20	129	8	8	1	3	2	3	21	0	39	1	1
Rodriguez, Alejandro, Phi.	1	1	.500	2.63	5	5	0	0	0	0	24.0	24	101	9	7	2	1	0	1	8	0	22	3	2
Rodriguez, Alfredo, Rang.	0	1	.000	2.19	9	0	0	0	6	3	12.1	14	55	6	3	0	0	0	1	1	0	8	0	0
Rodriguez, Jose, Brav.	1	2	.333	3.61	16	6	0	0	5	1	42.1	33	180	22	17	2	0	0	0	21	0	38	3	2
Rodriguez, Luis, Rang.	4	2	.667	3.47	17	5	1	1	3	1	49.1	46	217	24	19	2	1	2	6	18	0	26	7	1
Rogers, Bradley, Ori.	1	1	.500	1.69	6	0	0	0	2	0	10.2	11	46	3	2	0	0	3	1	3	1	8	2	1
Roman, Orlando, Mets	6	3	.667	2.36	12	11	1	1	1	0	61.0	41	254	20	16	0	4	5	21	0	64	3	0
Romero, Josmir, Twi.	5	3	.625	3.22	11	11	3	1	0	0	67.0	61	267	33	24	5	1	4	1	7	1	40	0	5
Roque, Darryll, Exp.	1	0	1.000	0.00	1	0	0	0	1	0	0.2	1	4	0	0	0	1	0	0	0	0	0	0	0
Rose, Johnathan, Phi.*	2	1	.667	2.50	5	2	0	0	0	0	18.0	15	74	5	5	1	0	0	7	10	1	17	1	0
Rose, Ted, Reds	0	0	.000	9.00	1	0	0	0	1	0	2.0	4	11	2	2	0	0	0	1	3	0	1	0	0
Ross, Donovan, Roy.	0	0	.000	0.00	1	0	0	0	0	0	2.0	1	9	0	0	0	0	0	2	2	0	2	0	0
Roundtree, Monte, Reds*	1	1	.500	2.42	7	3	0	0	1	0	22.1	16	96	8	6	0	0	2	11	0	19	5	0
Rundles, Richard, R.S.*	1	0	1.000	2.13	5	1	0	0	0	0	12.2	13	53	3	3	1	0	1	0	1	0	11	2	0
Rusch, Glendon, Roy.*	0	0	.000	1.50	2	2	0	0	0	0	6.0	3	25	1	1	0	0	0	3	0	9	1	0
Russo, Dennis, Reds	0	0	.000	4.50	2	0	0	0	0	0	4.0	6	19	3	2	0	0	0	2	0	1	1	1
Sabens, Mike, Pir.	0	1	.000	3.38	7	0	0	0	5	0	8.0	6	35	4	3	0	1	0	4	0	3	0	0
Sager, A.J., Reds	0	1	.000	4.50	1	1	0	0	0	0	2.0	4	9	1	1	0	0	0	1	0	1	0	0
Salazar, Luis, Marl.	5	3	.625	3.34	14	0	0	0	7	1	32.1	26	148	14	12	0	3	1	1	23	1	27	6	1
Santana, Humberto, Mets*	1	0	1.000	0.00	2	0	0	0	0	0	3.0	0	9	0	0	0	0	0	0	0	0	2	0	0
Santiago, Jose, Roy.	0	0	.000	1.80	3	3	0	0	0	0	5.0	1	16	1	1	0	0	0	0	4	0	0	0
Sauer, Marc, Marl.	5	4	.556	2.71	13	13	1	1	0	0	69.2	75	284	28	21	2	4	0	7	1	57	0	0
Sawvell, Matthew, Mets*	0	0	.000	6.30	8	0	0	0	1	0	10.0	14	49	7	7	1	0	0	4	0	13	1	0
Sclafani, Anthony, Brav.	3	2	.600	2.57	17	0	0	0	15	0	28.0	21	111	9	8	1	0	1	9	0	22	0	0
Searles, Jonathan, Pir.	1	0	1.000	4.15	8	0	0	0	1	0	13.0	14	65	10	6	1	0	2	1	9	0	9	3	0
Seo, Jung Min, R.S.	3	2	.600	2.81	13	0	0	0	6	1	32.0	29	137	14	10	2	1	1	3	10	1	26	4	0
Sequea, Jacobo, Reds	0	0	.000	4.50	1	1	0	0	0	0	2.0	2	7	1	1	0	0	0	0	3	0	0
Serrano, Willy, Tig.	0	3	.000	6.39	6	5	0	0	0	0	25.1	30	113	19	18	4	0	0	0	13	0	14	2	0
Shelley, Jason, Pir.	0	0	.000	0.00	2	0	0	0	1	0	1.1	2	6	0	0	0	0	0	0	0	0	3	0	0
Silverio, Carlos, Phi.	1	0	1.000	5.59	5	1	0	0	2	0	9.2	12	46	6	6	1	0	0	5	0	8	1	0
Smith, Chad, Phi.	3	5	.375	2.88	22	2	0	0	20	8	34.1	29	143	19	11	2	2	1	1	9	1	31	1	0
Solano, Alexander, R.S.	1	3	.250	2.39	5	5	0	0	0	0	26.1	30	118	12	7	1	1	0	2	7	0	15	1	1
Sollenberger, Matt, Mets*	1	5	.167	3.58	18	0	0	0	7	2	27.2	30	118	16	11	1	0	1	6	1	27	3	0
Song, Seung, R.S.	5	5	.500	2.33	13	9	0	0	2	0	54.2	42	233	29	14	2	0	2	4	20	0	61	2	4
Sopkin, Josh, Roy.	3	1	.750	5.70	16	1	0	0	2	0	30.0	37	145	22	19	0	0	1	23	0	19	4	0
Spears, Ricky, Yan.	0	0	.000	0.84	7	1	0	0	4	0	10.2	5	42	1	1	0	0	0	0	7	0	8	0	0

Pitcher, Team	W	L	Pct.	ERA	G	GS	CG	ShO	GF	Sv.	IP	H	TBF	R	ER	HR	SH	SF	HB	BB	IBB	SO	WP	Bk.
Stamm, Steve, Rang.*	1	2	.333	1.74	20	0	0	0	16	8	31.0	15	127	11	6	3	1	1	2	15	2	30	6	0
Staples, Dave, Phi.*	0	3	.000	7.12	15	2	0	0	2	0	36.2	45	174	31	29	4	0	6	6	13	0	38	3	0
Stiles, Brad, Roy.*	0	1	.000	1.80	4	0	0	0	2	1	5.0	3	20	3	1	0	1	0	1	3	0	5	0	0
Storke, Jonathan, Ori.	0	0	.000	9.00	1	0	0	0	1	0	2.0	3	11	3	2	0	0	0	2	0	2	0	2	0
Story, Aaron, Pir.*	2	2	.500	3.58	12	1	0	0	2	0	27.2	26	120	14	11	0	0	0	1	13	0	27	3	0
Sweeney, Mike, Mets	1	0	1.000	0.00	1	0	0	0	0	0	2.0	1	7	0	0	0	0	0	0	0	0	2	0	0
Swiatkiewicz, Chris, Yan.	1	0	1.000	0.82	9	0	0	0	8	5	11.0	5	38	1	1	0	0	2	0	2	0	13	0	0
Tankersley, Jr., Dennis, R.S.	1	0	1.000	0.76	11	6	0	0	2	1	35.2	14	133	7	3	2	0	0	3	9	1	57	0	0
Targac, Matthew, Marl.*	1	7	.125	3.05	12	11	1	0	0	0	56.0	53	237	32	19	2	1	2	0	16	0	55	8	1
Tate, Matthew, Ori.	2	2	.500	3.59	11	11	0	0	0	0	57.2	40	241	26	23	3	5	2	6	26	3	44	3	4
Tavarez, David, Ori.	9	0	1.000	2.14	12	9	0	0	0	0	67.1	60	277	22	16	2	2	1	7	12	2	55	4	2
Taylor, Jason, Tig.	3	5	.375	2.97	18	1	0	0	7	0	33.1	33	147	15	11	2	2	0	1	17	1	26	2	0
Tejeda, Robinson, Phi.	1	3	.250	4.27	12	9	0	0	2	0	46.1	47	206	27	22	5	3	1	2	27	0	39	1	1
Terry, Mike, Mets*	0	0	.000	0.00	2	0	0	0	2	1	2.0	1	6	0	0	0	0	0	0	0	0	0	0	0
Tetz, Kristofer, Exp.	0	0	.000	2.25	1	0	0	0	0	0	4.0	1	15	1	1	0	0	0	1	1	0	4	0	0
Thompson, Matthew, R.S.	0	0	.000	1.20	5	2	0	0	1	0	15.0	7	53	3	2	0	0	0	4	4	0	12	0	0
Thrasher, Jesse, Phi.	0	1	.000	15.12	5	1	0	0	0	0	8.1	15	57	16	14	1	0	2	2	15	0	6	0	0
Tomaszewski, Eliot, Ori.	3	1	.750	1.85	10	6	0	0	3	2	43.2	35	183	22	9	0	0	2	3	19	1	36	3	2
Torres, Alex, Tig.*	1	1	.500	7.23	13	1	0	0	4	0	23.2	28	123	20	19	1	0	2	2	25	0	15	2	0
Torres, Luis, Exp.	5	3	.625	2.85	12	9	1	1	1	0	60.0	55	259	28	19	1	1	1	3	28	1	36	8	0
Torres, Luis, Pir.	1	2	.333	1.69	8	8	0	0	0	0	42.2	24	157	9	8	0	1	2	5	7	0	33	4	1
Tovar, Angel, Yan.	0	1	.000	8.22	8	0	0	0	4	0	7.2	12	42	8	7	0	0	0	1	5	0	7	2	0
Trevino, Chris, Brav.*	1	3	.250	5.95	11	0	0	0	5	1	19.2	28	90	17	13	1	1	1	0	5	0	17	0	0
Trinidad, Fernando, Ori.	0	4	.000	5.09	15	0	0	0	7	1	35.1	40	155	23	20	1	1	0	3	9	2	19	1	0
Turner, Jess, Twi.	6	0	1.000	4.11	17	2	0	0	6	0	35.0	38	148	18	16	2	3	2	0	13	1	39	2	0
Turner, Kyle, Roy.*	1	0	1.000	0.00	2	1	0	0	0	0	4.0	2	15	0	0	0	0	0	0	0	0	3	0	0
Turrentine, Rich, Mets	0	0	.000	1.13	5	0	0	0	1	0	8.0	4	30	2	1	0	0	0	2	0	7	0	0
Urbina, Ulmer, Exp.	3	2	.600	6.39	14	0	0	0	9	2	25.1	22	123	19	18	1	1	1	3	24	0	20	1	1
Vail, Garett, R.S.	1	1	.500	3.21	7	0	0	0	1	0	14.0	15	63	10	5	2	0	1	0	6	0	5	0	2
Valdez, Domingo, Rang.	0	1	.000	4.91	8	7	0	0	0	0	29.1	29	138	22	16	2	0	1	5	18	0	34	4	2
Valdez, Jose, Reds	3	3	.500	1.96	12	6	0	0	2	0	41.1	20	167	12	9	0	5	1	2	25	0	36	3	0
Veras, Dario, Roy.	0	0	.000	0.00	3	2	0	0	0	0	4.0	3	15	0	0	0	0	0	0	0	0	3	0	0
Villamil, William, Rang.*	0	1	.000	4.94	14	0	0	0	6	1	23.2	24	108	14	13	0	1	1	0	12	0	17	2	4
Villanueva, Bill, Marl.	2	5	.286	3.86	11	11	1	0	0	0	58.1	58	251	29	25	0	0	1	4	21	0	42	1	0
Vogt, Robert, Pir.*	0	0	.000	12.00	3	0	0	0	3	0	3.0	5	16	4	4	0	0	1	0	2	0	3	1	0
Walker, Adrian, Brav.*	0	2	.000	4.18	13	0	0	0	3	0	23.2	22	104	11	11	2	0	3	0	15	0	30	3	0
Walker, Jamie, Roy.*	1	0	1.000	3.38	2	2	0	0	0	0	8.0	10	35	3	3	1	0	0	0	1	0	9	1	0
Walker, Keronn, Roy.	0	0	.000	0.00	1	1	0	0	0	0	3.0	2	10	0	0	0	0	0	0	1	0	4	0	0
Wamback, Trevor, Exp.	1	0	1.000	2.92	2	2	0	0	0	0	12.1	12	48	5	4	1	0	0	0	1	0	12	0	0
Wasdin, John, R.S.	0	0	.000	0.00	1	1	0	0	0	0	2.0	1	7	0	0	0	0	0	0	0	0	4	0	0
Washington, Porter, Reds	0	0	.000	9.26	10	0	0	0	4	0	11.2	17	68	19	12	1	1	1	1	13	0	13	3	0
Watkins, David, Brav.	5	0	1.000	0.92	13	0	0	0	4	2	29.1	15	115	5	3	0	0	1	11	1	24	2	1
White, James, Pir.	2	8	.200	4.86	13	11	0	0	0	0	63.0	70	284	44	34	4	1	3	12	24	0	35	3	1
Willis, Jason, Yan.	1	1	.500	2.20	4	4	0	0	0	0	16.1	13	64	4	4	0	1	0	0	6	0	17	2	0
Wolfe, Brian, Twi.	4	0	1.000	2.84	9	5	2	0	0	0	38.0	33	153	14	12	2	1	1	1	9	0	40	2	0
Wykoff, Jarred, Marl.	1	0	1.000	3.63	11	0	0	0	6	1	22.1	20	99	11	9	1	1	0	2	8	0	12	3	0
Yen, Buddy, Roy.	3	2	.600	2.40	25	0	0	0	21	10	30.0	18	120	11	8	1	0	1	5	6	1	34	1	3
Zapey, Winton, Marl.	0	0	.000	9.00	1	0	0	0	0	0	2.0	4	10	2	2	1	0	0	0	3	0	2	0	0
Zgoda, Derek, Yan.	0	0	.000	3.60	2	0	0	0	1	0	5.0	5	22	2	2	1	0	0	0	5	0	5	0	0
Zipser, Mike, Phi.	0	1	.000	4.00	6	0	0	0	2	0	9.0	11	41	5	4	1	1	2	0	5	0	6	0	0

COMBINATION SHUTOUTS: **Braves (4)**—Albertus-Rodriguez, Cetani-Waykins-Sclafani, Brown-Evert, Colton-Albertus-Watkins. **Expos (2)**—Charron-Rijo, Torres-Girdley. **Marlins (4)**—Targac-Salazar-Bell, Sauer-Lajara-Messenger, Castillo-Campos, Haynes-Anderson-Bell. **Mets (1)**—Musser-Gauger. **Orioles (2)**—Tavarez-Phillips-Ramirez, Bedard-Berube. **Phillies (4)**—Perez-Carcy, Carey-Jimenez, Rose-Smith, Loewer-Myers-Jimenez. **Pirates (1)**—Classen-Bumatay. **Rangers (2)**—Cedeno-Figueroa-Stamm-Rodriguez, Cavazos-Echols. **Red Sox (3)**—Curtice-Ledezma-Miniel, Benitez-Vail, Curtice-Benitez. **Reds (2)**—Altman-Brown-Valdez, Love-Valdez. **Royals (4)**—Gamboa-Martinez-Baranowski-Yen, Veras-Cabaj-Rasmussen, Obermueller-Cabaj-Rasmussen, Obermueller-Sopkin-Baranowski-Rasmussen. **Tigers (3)**—Lewis-Baginski-Rivera, Lewis-Baginski, Earl-Diaz-Rodney. **Twins (4)**—Larosa-Barreto-Turner, Flanagan-Boyanich-Turner-Odom, Barreto-Palki-Lesner-Turner, Barreto-Morel-Boyanich. **Yankees (4)**—De Los Santos-Aramboles, Oliver-Jelovic-Martinez, Oliver-De La Cruz-Martinez, Chacon-Obando-Martinez.

NO-HIT GAME: D. Martinez, Yankees, defeated Tigers, 5-0, August 24 (First game).

1999 FIELDING

TEAM

Team	Pct.	G	PO	A	E	TC	DP	TP	PB	Team	Pct.	G	PO	A	E	TC	DP	TP	PB
Tigers	.969	60	1471	553	65	2089	47	0	21	Phillies	.956	60	1475	573	95	2143	53	0	31
Rangers	.966	60	1531	648	76	2255	41	0	12	Pirates	.953	60	1542	693	109	2344	48	0	11
Royals	.965	60	1557	586	78	2221	55	0	24	Twins	.949	60	1442	600	109	2151	53	0	16
Marlins	.961	60	1586	654	91	2331	52	0	19	Reds	.948	60	1473	666	117	2256	52	0	24
Yankees	.961	60	1508	602	86	2196	41	0	14	Mets	.948	60	1568	639	121	2328	46	0	10
Expos	.960	60	1514	670	90	2274	41	0	8	Red Sox	.945	60	1533	629	125	2287	50	0	25
Braves	.958	60	1577	660	97	2334	51	0	37	Orioles	.944	60	1512	675	129	2316	58	0	16

INDIVIDUAL

FIRST BASEMEN

NOTE: All caps denotes fielding-percentage leader based on 30 games for catchers, 40 for all other non-pitchers and 48 innings for pitchers. *Throws lefthanded.

Player, Team	Pct.	G	PO	A	E	TC	DP
Abreu, Cesar, Reds	.935	11	83	4	6	93	10
Alvarez, Aaron, Marl.	.952	4	18	2	1	21	0
Ambrosini, Dominick, Exp.*	1.000	3	22	1	0	23	2
Anderson, Nat, Tig.	.965	13	77	6	3	86	7
Angell, Rick, Rang.	1.000	4	26	1	0	27	1
Baez, Ernies, Rang.	1.000	1	3	0	0	3	0
Borjas, Henry, R.S.	.971	33	249	17	8	274	20
Camarero, Rafael, Reds	.953	11	57	4	3	64	3
Caridi, Tony, R.S.	.966	15	105	10	4	119	6
Castellanos, Jose, Brav.	.981	5	48	3	1	52	3

Player, Team	Pct.	G	PO	A	E	TC	DP
Davis, Quian, Marl.	.979	12	45	1	1	47	2
Dees, Charlie, Ori.	.968	25	176	6	6	188	15
Delgado, Dario, Phi.	.972	16	129	10	4	143	10
Demarco, Matt, Marl.	.987	26	206	14	3	223	26
Derosso, Tony, R.S.	.923	1	12	0	1	13	1
Deschenes, Pat, Mets	1.000	6	51	2	0	53	4
DeGroote, Casey, Yan.	1.000	1	1	0	0	1	0
Douglas, Mo, Pir.*	.571	1	4	0	3	7	1
Eberly, Rodney, Phi.	1.000	6	44	2	0	46	5
Essian, James, Roy.	.986	11	67	5	1	73	10
Fick, Robert, Tig.	1.000	1	12	4	0	16	2
Gajewski, Matt, Rang.	.989	43	420	21	5	446	27
Garcia, Kenji, Mets	.941	31	201	6	13	220	19
Geisbush, David, Brav.	.977	11	84	1	2	87	8
Gonzalez, Felix, Exp.	1.000	1	1	0	0	1	0
Guerrero, James, R.S.	.949	17	109	3	6	118	10
Guerrero, Julio, R.S.	1.000	1	7	0	0	7	1
Harris, Karl, Exp.	1.000	24	206	8	0	214	19
Helms, Wes, Brav.	1.000	3	27	0	0	27	2
Hernandez, Argenis, Ori.*	.985	39	304	21	5	330	34
House, J.R., Pir.	.988	16	159	12	2	173	11
Hunter, David, Mets*	.986	25	209	6	3	218	15
Ide, Antoine, Ori.	.833	1	5	0	1	6	0
Jacobs, Michael, Mets	.889	4	23	1	3	27	2
Jewson, Benjamin, Phi.	.957	8	57	9	3	69	9
Johnson, Kareem, Twi.	1.000	1	8	0	0	8	0
Jones, Garrett, Brav.*	.981	45	384	30	8	422	32
Laidlaw, Jacob, Marl.	.935	3	27	2	2	31	3
Leon, Alfredo, Ori.	.950	3	37	1	2	40	2
Louwsma, Chris, Marl.	.992	29	242	9	2	253	15
Lugo, Felix, Exp.	1.000	1	5	0	0	5	0
Lugo, Roberto, Mets*	1.000	14	65	2	0	67	5
Lutz, David, Exp.	.994	18	149	10	1	160	9
Mack, Antonio, Ori.	1.000	1	2	0	0	2	0
Matos, Angel, Rang.	1.000	2	20	2	0	22	2
Mejias, Erick, Rang.	1.000	1	10	0	0	10	1
Mendieta, Enrique, Marl.	1.000	2	8	0	0	8	0
Moncrief, Kyle, Reds*	.986	35	274	14	4	292	16
Nettles, Jeff, Yan.	.996	29	228	17	1	246	16
Quickstad, Barry, Twi.	1.000	3	20	0	0	20	0
Reyes, Manuel, Mets	1.000	1	6	0	0	6	0
Riek, Clifford, Pir.	.990	11	94	2	1	97	4
Rodeheaver, Roger, Pir.	.983	31	208	18	4	230	19
RODRIGUEZ, Steve, Tig.	.989	48	324	31	4	359	31
Rosado, Omar, Exp.	.983	19	163	12	3	178	9
Ross, Donovan, Roy.	1.000	1	12	1	0	13	0
Ruiz, Randy, Reds	.985	14	128	6	2	136	18
Sandoval, Michael, Twi.	1.000	1	6	1	0	7	1
Santos, Chad, Roy.*	.979	47	358	20	8	386	37
Sein, Javier, Yan.	.996	35	256	17	1	274	20
Stenson, Dernell, R.S.*	.947	2	16	2	1	19	3
Storke, Jonathan, Brav.	.917	3	11	0	1	12	2
Sutton, Larry, Roy.*	.977	6	42	0	1	43	2
Tamburrino, Brett, Twi.	.970	12	85	11	3	99	13
Thompson, Alva, Brav.	1.000	3	8	0	0	8	1
Torres, Digno, Twi.*	.995	24	174	8	1	183	17
Vargas, Inakel, Tig.	1.000	2	12	4	0	16	0
Villegas, Ernest, Rang.	.981	11	101	3	2	106	6
Wade, Mike, Ori.	.900	1	8	1	1	10	0
Wrenn, Michael, Twi.	.989	26	172	9	2	183	14
Young, Walter, Pir.	.988	35	299	20	4	323	26
Zapey, Winton, Marl.	1.000	2	4	0	0	4	1

TRIPLE PLAY: Louwsma.

Player, Team	Pct.	G	PO	A	E	TC	DP
De Los Santos, Hector, R.S.	.917	13	41	36	7	84	8
Del Rosario, Emmanuel, Ori.	.937	40	90	104	13	207	27
Demarco, Matt, Marl.	1.000	5	13	11	0	24	1
Dennis, Les, Yan.	1.000	3	4	9	0	13	2
Deshetler, Chris, Tig.	1.000	17	20	33	0	53	5
Frye, Jeff, R.S.	1.000	5	3	12	0	15	0
Garabito, Vianney, Reds	.971	12	31	36	2	69	8
Gonzalez, Reggie, Twi.	.925	17	19	30	4	53	4
Goudie, Jaime, Reds	1.000	1	2	1	0	3	0
Guzman, Juan, Roy.	1.000	1	0	1	0	1	0
Harris, Corey, Mets	1.000	1	1	1	0	2	0
Herbert, Keith, Marl.	.951	27	31	46	4	81	11
Herrera, Elvis, Pir.	.864	5	5	14	3	22	3
Hopper, Norris, Roy.	.966	27	46	67	4	117	24
Hudnall, Joshua, Pir.	.500	1	0	1	1	2	0
Infante, Juan, Exp.	.912	10	13	18	3	34	4
Ishida, Takehito, Phi.	.905	15	26	41	7	74	4
Kison, Robbie, Reds	1.000	3	6	10	0	16	1
Lora, Thomas, Roy.	.981	32	71	87	3	161	19
Machado, Aleyandro, Brav.	.983	56	117	176	5	298	36
Machado, Anderson, Phi.	.955	35	59	88	7	154	22
Malone, Nick, R.S.	1.000	2	1	2	0	3	1
Martinez, Louis, Brav.	1.000	4	5	5	0	10	1
Maza, Luis, Twi.	.969	6	15	16	1	32	6
MEJIAS, Erick, Rang.	.990	47	80	115	2	197	20
Nunez, Hector, Tig.	.000	1	0	0	0	0	0
Olmedo, Ranier, Reds	.972	27	58	80	4	142	18
Paulino, David, Marl.	.973	40	81	100	5	186	23
Pelfrey, Brice, Pir.	.935	28	61	83	10	154	11
Perea, Carlos, Roy.	1.000	1	1	2	0	3	0
Presto, Nick, Reds	1.000	2	4	6	0	10	1
Rasmussen, Wes, Brav.	.833	4	6	4	2	12	2
Reed, Matthew, Twi.	1.000	1	1	3	0	4	0
Rodriguez, Ronny, R.S.	.954	31	50	74	6	130	15
Rogers, Edward, Ori.	1.000	4	6	15	0	21	4
Rosado, Omar, Exp.	.947	18	28	43	4	75	10
Santana, Gamalier, Twi.	.900	15	15	21	4	40	2
Santonocito, Justin, Reds	1.000	2	4	7	0	11	0
Santoro, Patrick, R.S.	.905	7	6	13	2	21	1
Tyson, Torre, R.S.	.963	7	7	19	1	27	3
Valdez, Wilson, Exp.	1.000	9	19	26	0	45	5
Watkins, Thomas, Twi.	.958	36	69	91	7	167	21
Wigand, Tom, Phi.	1.000	14	16	18	0	34	3

TRIPLE PLAY: Demarco.

THIRD BASEMEN

Player, Team	Pct.	G	PO	A	E	TC	DP
Abreu, Cesar, Reds	.727	8	2	6	3	11	1
Abreu, David, Mets	.767	13	10	23	10	43	1
Angell, Rick, Rang.	1.000	2	0	1	0	1	0
Araujo, Victor, Pir.	.934	39	25	89	8	122	5
Arias, Leandro, Mets	.500	1	0	1	1	2	0
Bell, Josh, Mets	.887	20	5	42	6	53	2
Blalock, Hank, Rang.	.914	48	24	103	12	139	7
Bone, Billy, Pir.	.778	4	3	11	4	18	0
Borjas, Henry, R.S.	1.000	2	1	1	0	2	1
Brown, Matthew, Exp.	.911	17	10	31	4	45	2
Camarero, Rafael, Reds	.700	8	3	11	6	20	1
Cates, Jr, Gary, Ori.	.894	15	14	28	5	47	2
Centeno, Edwin, Ori.	.000	1	0	0	0	0	0
Corporan, Elvis, Yan.	.893	53	32	68	12	112	5
Cruz, Enrique, Mets	.920	21	13	33	4	50	1
Dees, Charlie, Ori.	.900	3	2	7	1	10	1
Derosso, Tony, R.S.	.667	4	2	2	2	6	0
Deschenes, Pat, Mets	.933	15	9	33	3	45	1
Deshetler, Chris, Tig.	.886	11	7	24	4	35	1
DeGroote, Casey, Yan.	.889	4	2	6	1	9	1
Fafard, Mathias, Mets	.857	3	1	5	1	7	0
Foltynowicz, Roger, Reds	.714	1	0	5	2	7	0
Gajewski, Matt, Rang.	.000	1	0	0	0	0	0
Garabito, Vianney, Reds	.923	23	5	43	4	52	1
Garcia, Nicolas, Ori.	1.000	4	1	4	0	5	0
Geisbush, David, Brav.	.889	10	2	22	3	27	3
Gettis, Byron, Roy.	1.000	2	0	3	0	3	0
Hattig, John, R.S.	.889	38	29	83	14	126	5
Hawes, Bobby, Reds	1.000	2	1	1	0	2	0
Herrera, Elvis, Pir.	1.000	2	1	2	0	3	1
House, J.R., Pir.	.833	3	1	4	1	6	1
Hudnall, Joshua, Pir.	.800	1	1	3	1	5	0
Infante, Juan, Exp.	1.000	5	2	16	0	18	1
Jenkins, Neil, Tig.	.889	22	13	35	6	54	5
Jewson, Benjamin, Phi.	.767	19	7	26	10	43	2
King, Jason, Brav.	.918	35	24	77	9	110	7
Kison, Robbie, Reds	1.000	1	0	3	0	3	0

SECOND BASEMEN

Player, Team	Pct.	G	PO	A	E	TC	DP
Abreu, David, Mets	.946	10	10	25	2	37	10
Acevedo, Inocencio, Rang.	1.000	11	22	25	0	47	5
Anderson, Jon, R.S.	1.000	3	4	12	0	16	1
Angell, Rick, Rang.	1.000	2	2	7	0	9	1
Araujo, Victor, Pir.	.750	3	4	2	2	8	1
Arias, Leandro, Mets	.962	45	86	90	7	183	16
Baker, Casey, Yan.	.976	33	49	73	3	125	13
Bell, Josh, Mets	.907	9	21	18	4	43	5
Bone, Billy, Pir.	1.000	3	4	11	0	15	2
Borjas, Henry, R.S.	.941	4	9	7	1	17	3
Boyer, Bret, Exp.	.941	29	48	63	7	118	8
Caceres, Wilmy, Reds	1.000	1	2	2	0	4	0
Campana, Wandel, Reds	1.000	15	24	43	0	67	9
Campos, Juan, Tig.	.985	43	91	106	3	200	26
Castillo, Jose, Pir.	.939	23	58	49	7	114	15
Castillo, Victor, Yan.	.944	31	41	93	8	142	14
Cates, Jr, Gary, Ori.	1.000	19	27	49	0	76	11
Collazo, Julio, Phi.	.900	3	3	6	1	10	1

Player, Team	Pct.	G	PO	A	E	TC	DP
Laidlaw, Jacob, Marl.	.862	36	26	80	17	123	3
Leon, Alfredo, Ori.	.918	16	15	41	5	61	3
Liriano, Ruddy, Reds	.880	21	11	33	6	50	4
Llamas, Juan, Yan.	.000	2	0	0	1	1	0
Louwsma, Chris, Marl.	.928	23	17	47	5	69	10
Lugo, Felix, Exp.	.917	4	4	7	1	12	1
Lutz, David, Exp.	.769	8	4	16	6	26	1
Machado, Anderson, Phi.	1.000	1	1	4	0	5	1
Malone, Nick, R.S.	.857	3	2	4	1	7	0
Martinez, Louis, Brav.	.951	13	6	33	2	41	4
Martinez, Octavio, Ori.	1.000	1	1	0	0	1	0
Matos, Angel, Rang.	.667	1	1	1	1	3	0
Mejias, Erick, Rang.	.909	5	5	15	2	22	0
Mercado, Wilkins, Roy.	.913	41	23	61	8	92	5
Nettles, Jeff, Yan.	1.000	2	1	4	0	5	0
Nunez, Hector, Tig.	.765	9	2	11	4	17	2
Olmedo, Ranier, Reds	1.000	2	1	7	0	8	0
Paulino, David, Marl.	.947	6	7	11	1	19	0
Rasmussen, Wes, Brav.	.333	2	0	1	2	3	0
RICHARDSON, Juan, Phi.	.914	43	37	59	9	105	6
Riek, Clifford, Pir.	.864	9	3	16	3	22	0
Rodriguez, Ronny, R.S.	.800	1	2	2	1	5	0
Rogers, Edward, Ori.	.900	10	11	16	3	30	0
Romero, Gabriel, Brav.	.667	2	1	1	1	3	1
Rooi, Vince, Exp.	.915	30	15	71	8	94	4
Ross, Donovan, Roy.	.873	23	22	33	8	63	3
Sandoval, Michael, Twi.	.865	48	36	86	19	141	8
Santonocito, Justin, Reds	.800	1	3	1	1	5	0
Shelley, Jason, Pir.	.933	6	6	8	1	15	0
Sowers, Douglas, Ori.	.714	3	3	7	4	14	2
Storke, Jonathan, Ori.	.824	15	7	21	6	34	3
Tope, Stephen, Twi.	.846	3	1	10	2	13	1
Valdez, Toribio, Rang.	.882	7	3	12	2	17	0
Ware, Anthony, Tig.	.841	19	12	25	7	44	4
Watkins, Thomas, Twi.	.946	13	9	26	2	37	2
Williams, Brady, R.S.	.857	22	14	28	7	49	1
Wrenn, Michael, Twi.	.000	1	0	0	1	1	0

SHORTSTOPS

Player, Team	Pct.	G	PO	A	E	TC	DP
Abreu, David, Mets	.875	2	3	4	1	8	1
Acevedo, Inocencio, Rang.	.926	15	21	54	6	81	8
Almonte, Erick, Yan.	.931	7	4	23	2	29	3
Arias, Leandro, Mets	.833	1	1	4	1	6	1
Bell, Josh, Mets	.667	2	1	3	2	6	1
Borjas, Henry, R.S.	.895	15	16	35	6	57	8
Caceres, Wilmy, Reds	1.000	1	1	2	0	3	0
Campana, Wandel, Reds	.923	2	5	7	1	13	2
Castillo, Jose, Pir.	.908	24	46	62	11	119	11
Castillo, Victor, Yan.	.862	9	6	19	4	29	1
Cates, Jr, Gary, Ori.	.846	5	5	6	2	13	3
COLLAZO, Julio, Phi.	.956	49	54	121	8	183	28
Cruz, Enrique, Mets	.928	36	48	107	12	167	17
De Los Santos, Hector, R.S.	.924	24	36	49	7	92	9
Demarco, Matt, Marl.	.974	16	21	53	2	76	5
Dorsey, Ryan, Pir.	.926	14	25	38	5	68	9
Garcia, Nicolas, Ori.	.920	17	31	61	8	100	7
Geisbush, David, Brav.	.909	1	1	9	1	11	3
Gonzalez, Reggie, Twi.	.909	28	40	60	10	110	12
Guerrero, James, R.S.	1.000	1	3	0	0	3	0
Guzman, Juan, Roy.	.955	25	40	65	5	110	16
Hawes, Bobby, Reds	.874	34	43	96	20	159	16
Holbert, Ray, Roy.	1.000	3	7	7	0	14	3
Hudnall, Joshua, Pir.	.931	23	29	66	7	102	9
Infante, Juan, Exp.	.966	10	6	22	1	29	1
Infante, Omar, Tig.	.932	25	34	76	8	118	11
Ishida, Takehito, Phi.	.000	1	0	0	0	0	0
King, Jason, Brav.	.912	11	13	39	5	57	2
Leon, Alfredo, Ori.	.000	1	0	0	1	1	0
Lopez, Mendy, Roy.	1.000	2	2	4	0	6	0
Lora, Thomas, Roy.	1.000	2	5	8	0	13	3
Machado, Anderson, Phi.	.969	9	12	19	1	32	2
Malone, Nick, R.S.	.875	4	2	5	1	8	0
Manning, Patrick, Brav.	.931	19	27	40	5	72	12
Martinez, Louis, Brav.	.922	9	11	36	4	51	6
Maza, Luis, Twi.	.927	19	38	38	6	82	12
McIntyre, Robert, Mets	.929	26	36	68	8	112	10
Mejias, Erick, Rang.	.000	1	0	0	0	0	0
Morban, Jose, Rang.	.949	44	81	144	12	237	22
Nettles, Jeff, Yan.	1.000	1	0	1	0	1	0
Olmedo, Ranier, Reds	.880	26	31	57	12	100	9
Pelfrey, Brice, Pir.	.857	2	3	9	2	14	1
Perea, Carlos, Roy.	.750	2	3	0	1	4	1
Phillips, Brandon, Exp.	.915	40	55	127	17	199	20

Player, Team	Pct.	G	PO	A	E	TC	DP
Rasmussen, Wes, Brav.	.893	21	17	50	8	75	8
Reed, Matthew, Twi.	.840	24	28	35	12	75	6
Reyes, Ivan, Yan.	.921	44	53	110	14	177	22
Richardson, Juan, Phi.	1.000	3	5	11	0	16	1
Rodgers, Mackeel, Roy.	.879	30	53	63	16	132	14
Rodriguez, Ronny, R.S.	.930	22	32	61	7	100	13
Rogers, Edward, Ori.	.950	32	44	88	7	139	16
Romero, Gabriel, Brav.	1.000	3	0	1	0	1	0
Sadler, Donnie, R.S.	.950	4	7	12	1	20	1
Santana, Gamalier, Twi.	.000	1	0	0	0	0	0
Santiago, Ramon, Tig.	.974	35	55	93	4	152	19
Shier, Peter, Ori.	.870	9	15	25	6	46	7
Soriano, Alfonso, Yan.	.929	4	2	11	1	14	2
Storke, Jonathan, Ori.	.833	3	1	4	1	6	0
Tamburrino, Brett, Twi.	.000	1	0	0	0	0	0
Tyson, Torre, R.S.	1.000	1	0	3	0	3	0
Valdez, Toribio, Rang.	.667	1	1	1	1	3	0
Valdez, Wilson, Exp.	.952	13	24	36	3	63	6
Washington, Kelley, Marl.	1.000	3	4	9	0	13	3
Watkins, Thomas, Twi.	1.000	2	3	0	0	3	0
Wigand, Tom, Phi.	.500	1	0	1	1	2	1
Williams, Brady, R.S.	.875	2	3	4	1	8	0
Wilson, Josh, Marl.	.911	45	56	139	19	214	24

OUTFIELDERS

Player, Team	Pct.	G	PO	A	E	TC	DP
Abreu, Cesar, Reds	1.000	3	2	0	0	2	0
Acuna, Ronald, Mets	1.000	5	13	1	0	14	0
Altagen, Matthew, Tig.*	1.000	1	2	1	0	3	0
Ambres, Chip, Marl.	.939	35	59	3	4	66	0
Ambrosini, Dominick, Exp.*	.857	14	12	0	2	14	0
Angell, Rick, Rang.	.971	50	95	7	3	105	1
Araujo, Victor, Pir.	1.000	1	1	0	0	1	0
Baez, Ernies, Rang.	1.000	6	12	0	0	12	0
Barrow, Corey, Reds	.980	54	94	5	2	101	2
Batcheller, Chris, Pir.	.857	4	6	0	1	7	0
Bishop, Bennie, Phi.	.986	28	65	3	1	69	0
Boitel, Rafael, Twi.	.976	44	78	5	2	85	3
Borjas, Henry, R.S.	.000	1	0	0	1	1	0
Bradley, Wade, Phi.*	.000	2	0	0	0	0	0
Brazoban, Yhency, Yan.	.984	50	56	6	1	63	0
Brown, Matthew, Exp.	1.000	8	13	0	0	13	0
Bryan, Jason, Rang.	.900	6	9	0	1	10	0
Cabrera, Raymond, Ori.	.941	13	15	1	1	17	0
Cabrera, Yoelmis, Pir.	.973	22	33	3	1	37	0
Camarero, Rafael, Reds	.938	10	15	0	1	16	0
Caridi, Tony, R.S.	.000	2	0	0	0	0	0
Castellanos, Jose, Brav.	.900	16	26	1	3	30	0
Castro, Martires, Exp.	.950	10	18	1	1	20	0
Castro, Vicente, Pir.	.981	38	44	7	1	52	0
Cates, Jr, Gary, Ori.	1.000	6	11	0	0	11	0
Centeno, Edwin, Ori.	.917	29	42	2	4	48	0
Clark, Tommy, Brav.	.914	36	50	3	5	58	1
Cordova, Ben, Roy.*	.990	51	93	4	1	98	1
Cortes, Jorge, Pir.*	.979	25	45	1	1	47	1
Cruz, Orlando, Rang.	.968	44	60	1	2	63	0
Davis, Daniel, Tig.*	1.000	37	40	1	0	41	0
Davis, Quian, Marl.	.889	9	7	1	1	9	0
Davison, Ashanti, Ori.	.923	8	11	1	1	13	0
De Los Santos, Hector, R.S.	1.000	25	35	0	0	35	0
Dees, Charlie, Ori.	.969	30	29	2	1	32	1
Devanez, Noel, Mets	.930	39	60	6	5	71	2
Dolton, Odis, Reds	1.000	32	38	1	0	39	0
Douglas, Mo, Pir.*	.933	20	25	3	2	30	1
Driggers Jr, Richard, Phi.	1.000	14	21	1	0	22	1
Dyer, Matthew, Mets	.000	1	0	0	0	0	0
Edwards, John, Twi.	1.000	1	0	1	0	1	0
Elder, Rick, Ori.*	.000	1	0	0	0	0	0
Encarnacion, Arismendy, Marl.	.945	43	81	5	5	91	1
Escobar, Alex, Mets	1.000	1	1	0	0	1	0
Essian, James, Roy.	.889	8	8	0	1	9	0
Fernandez, Medardo, Marl.	.933	30	40	2	3	45	0
FOWLER, David, Yan.	1.000	55	79	4	0	83	0
Frazier, Charles, Marl.	1.000	32	45	3	0	48	1
Gettis, Byron, Roy.	.970	19	28	4	1	33	0
Gomez, Alexis, Roy.*	.986	56	131	7	2	140	0
Gonzalez, Felix, Exp.	1.000	40	62	5	0	67	0
Gordon, Alexis, Ori.*	.912	28	30	1	3	34	1
Griswold, Matthew, Ori.	1.000	8	12	1	0	13	0
Guerrero, Julio, R.S.	.939	31	45	1	3	49	1
Guzman, Jonathan, Roy.	.989	43	86	7	1	94	2
Guzman, Juan, Roy.	1.000	3	3	0	0	3	0
Hamn, Larnell, Mets	1.000	28	17	1	0	18	0
Harper, Shaun, Brav.	.959	50	112	5	5	122	0

Player, Team	Pct.	G	PO	A	E	TC	DP
HARRIS, Corey, Mets	1.000	46	81	2	0	83	0
Harts, Jeremy, Pir.*	1.000	28	52	2	0	54	0
Hernandez, Nicolas, Exp.	1.000	4	5	0	0	5	0
Hudson, Daniel, Pir.	1.000	5	5	1	0	6	0
Ide, Antoine, Ori.	1.000	13	21	2	0	23	0
Jenkins, Robert, Reds	1.000	6	6	1	0	7	0
Jewson, Benjamin, Phi.	.000	1	0	0	0	0	0
Johnerson, Ryan, Reds	1.000	7	13	0	0	13	0
Johnson, Kareem, Twi.	.948	38	53	2	3	58	2
Jones, Albert, Twi.	.977	27	37	6	1	44	0
Jones, Jason, Rang.*	.750	7	6	0	2	8	0
Kawabata, Kenichiro, R.S.*	.919	46	72	7	7	86	1
Lane, Richard, Exp.*	.986	34	63	5	1	69	2
Lawson, Forrest, Mets	.981	34	49	4	1	54	0
Lawton, Matt, Twi.	1.000	1	1	0	0	1	0
Leed, Adam, Rang.	1.000	9	12	0	0	12	0
Leer, David, Tig.	1.000	23	31	1	0	32	0
Leflore, Alex, Reds	.925	19	34	3	3	40	0
Leon, Alfredo, Ori.	.667	2	2	0	1	3	0
Leonardo, Santos, Tig.	.962	36	72	3	3	78	1
Liriano, Ruddy, Reds	1.000	1	1	0	0	1	0
Lopez, Youanny, R.S.	.973	47	70	3	2	75	0
Lutz, David, Exp.	.923	12	11	1	1	13	0
Lydon, Wayne, Mets	.923	28	24	0	2	26	0
Mack, Antonio, Ori.	.976	47	70	10	2	82	0
Manning, Ricky, Twi.*	.962	18	23	2	1	26	1
Marbury, Ben, R.S.	1.000	19	25	0	0	25	0
Martinez, Orlando, Reds	1.000	4	4	0	0	4	0
Matos, Angel, Rang.	.500	4	1	0	1	2	0
Maxwell, Vernon, Yan.	1.000	1	0	1	0	1	0
Mejias, Erick, Rang.	1.000	2	3	0	0	3	0
Mendieta, Enrique, Marl.	.950	23	18	1	1	20	0
Merhoff, Aaron, Phi.	.941	22	31	1	2	34	0
Miller, Josh, Pir.	.833	3	5	0	1	6	0
Nettles, Jeff, Yan.	1.000	6	6	0	0	6	0
Nunez, Edward, Twi.	.960	24	22	2	1	25	1
O'Neill, Daniel, Phi.*	1.000	10	14	1	0	15	1
Osborn, Jason, Mets	1.000	1	1	0	0	1	0
Pena, Jose, R.S.	1.000	10	7	0	0	7	0
Pena, Wily, Yan.	.947	24	35	1	2	38	0
Perich, Joshua, Mets	.911	37	39	2	4	45	0
Piercy, Mike, Pir.*	1.000	9	12	0	0	12	0
Podsednik, Scott, Rang.*	1.000	3	1	0	0	1	0
Quickstad, Barry, Twi.	1.000	21	23	1	0	24	0
Ramos, Eddy, Rang.	.946	53	85	3	5	93	0
Rauls, Ian, Phi.*	.979	47	90	3	2	95	2
Richards, Rowan, Rang.	1.000	7	7	0	0	7	0
Riordan, Matthew, Ori.	1.000	7	14	0	0	14	0
Rivera, Erick, Phi.	.932	30	53	2	4	59	1
Rivera, Juan, Yan.	1.000	5	1	0	0	1	0
Rodriguez, John, Yan.*	1.000	3	8	0	0	8	0
Rollins, Antwon, Rang.	1.000	1	3	0	0	3	0
Rombley, Danny, Exp.	.975	42	71	7	2	80	1
Romero, Gabriel, Brav.	1.000	6	6	0	0	6	0
Rosario, Vicente, Mets	.000	3	0	0	0	0	0
Ross, Cody, Tig.*	.980	41	95	4	2	101	2
Ross, Donovan, Roy.	.000	1	0	0	0	0	0
Ruiz, Randy, Reds	.500	3	1	0	1	2	0
Seiber, Antron, R.S.	.952	13	20	0	1	21	0
Senegal, Terence, Reds	.890	48	66	7	9	82	3
Sheffield, Jeff, Yan.	1.000	3	1	0	0	1	0
Smiley, Jermaine, Roy.*	.818	5	8	1	2	11	0
Smith, Toebius, Brav.	1.000	29	44	1	0	45	1
Soto, Jose, Marl.	.971	34	64	3	2	69	1
Storke, Jonathan, Ori.	.833	4	5	0	1	6	0
Sutton, Larry, Roy.*	1.000	1	1	0	0	1	0
Taylor, Corey, Reds	1.000	1	1	0	0	1	0
Tolli, Barry, Tig.	.968	41	57	4	2	63	1
Torres, Digno, Twi.*	.957	33	42	3	2	47	0
Valdez, Toribio, Rang.	1.000	2	3	0	0	3	0
Van Vark, Wade, Phi.	.938	34	55	6	4	65	2
Wakeland, Chris, Tig.*	1.000	4	6	0	0	6	0
Watson, Brandon, Exp.	.986	31	65	3	1	69	0
Weston, Aron, Pir.*	.957	32	65	2	3	70	0
Williams, Brady, R.S.	1.000	3	1	0	0	1	0
Winrow, Gary, Yan.*	1.000	42	46	4	0	50	1
Zumwalt, Sean, Brav.	.975	48	73	5	2	80	0

CATCHERS

Player, Team	Pct.	G	PO	A	E	TC	DP	PB
Alley, Charles, Ori.	.889	1	7	1	1	9	0	0
Alvarez, Aaron, Marl.	1.000	19	111	12	0	123	2	4
Alvarez, Henrry, Roy.	.976	28	172	31	5	208	2	13
Avila, Rob, Phi.	1.000	9	72	14	0	86	0	5

Player, Team	Pct.	G	PO	A	E	TC	DP	PB
Baez, Fleming, Rang.	1.000	2	7	3	0	10	0	0
Barnowski, Bryan, R.S.	.981	25	146	10	3	159	0	7
Barr, Clint, Yan.	.987	11	70	7	1	78	0	4
Bowen, Rob, Twi.	.959	24	161	27	8	196	2	9
Brazeal, Spencer, Yan.	.968	24	225	18	8	251	1	2
Brito, Justo, Mets	.974	41	295	41	9	345	0	4
Cardona, Raynier, Pir.	1.000	11	62	6	0	68	0	2
Caridi, Tony, R.S.	.980	10	39	9	1	49	0	7
Casanova, Raul, Tig.	1.000	2	7	0	0	7	0	1
CLEVELAND, Russell, Tig.	.987	36	273	32	4	309	4	16
Damato, Gabriel, Reds	1.000	5	24	5	0	29	0	1
Deitrick, Jeremy, Phi.	1.000	5	37	0	0	37	0	1
Deschenes, Pat, Mets	1.000	1	4	0	0	4	0	0
Diaz, David, Phi.	.985	16	61	4	1	66	0	1
Diaz, Miguel, Exp.	.983	17	103	13	2	118	2	2
Dito, Robert, Exp.	.954	17	94	10	5	109	0	3
Doumit, Ryan, Pir.	.975	13	63	15	2	80	1	0
Dyer, Matthew, Mets	.000	1	0	0	0	0	0	0
Eagle, Todd, Phi.	.911	7	48	3	5	56	1	7
Edwards, John, Twi.	.955	30	157	33	9	199	4	5
Essian, James, Roy.	1.000	2	7	1	0	8	0	0
Evans, Mitch, Yan.	.988	24	155	9	2	166	1	1
Fernandez, Alejandro, Yan.	.962	4	22	3	1	26	0	0
Fick, Robert, Tig.	1.000	1	1	0	0	2	0	0
Foltynowicz, Roger, Reds	.976	20	109	11	3	123	1	9
Gajewski, Matt, Rang.	1.000	9	58	3	0	61	0	2
Green, Ricky, Ori.	1.000	2	4	0	0	4	0	0
Guilliams, Earl, Brav.	.973	17	67	4	2	73	0	9
Harrell, Ken, Yan.	1.000	1	13	1	0	14	0	2
Hatteberg, Scott, R.S.	1.000	4	37	4	0	41	3	0
Henley, Bob, Exp.	.750	1	3	0	1	4	0	0
House, J.R., Pir.	1.000	5	50	10	0	60	0	2
Jacobs, Michael, Mets	.973	22	122	24	4	150	1	6
Jaile, Chris, Rang.	.980	30	214	31	5	250	2	6
Kanaya, Takeshi, R.S.	.961	8	42	7	2	51	1	4
Leon, Alfredo, Ori.	1.000	1	2	1	0	3	1	0
Lydon, Wayne, Mets	1.000	1	6	0	0	6	0	0
Martin, Kyle, Ori.	.977	27	149	21	4	174	2	6
Martinez, Edgar, R.S.	.948	26	200	20	12	232	3	7
Martinez, Octavio, Ori.	.958	31	187	42	10	239	3	5
Massucco, Scott, Yan.	.879	5	25	4	4	33	0	4
Matos, Angel, Rang.	.969	26	114	11	4	129	2	4
McMillan, Andrew, Exp.	.985	28	170	21	3	194	1	2
Paulino, Ronny, Pir.	.974	26	150	38	5	193	3	6
Pickering, Kelvin, Ori.	.907	8	38	1	4	43	0	4
Prince, Tom, Phi.	1.000	5	19	6	0	25	0	0
Reyes, Manuel, Mets	.975	8	35	4	1	40	0	0
Reynolds, Dusty, Tig.	.982	19	154	12	3	169	1	3
Salas, Jose, Brav.	.956	26	160	14	8	182	2	27
Santana, Emmanuel, Roy.	1.000	24	160	30	0	190	1	10
Santiago, Daniel, Reds	.976	24	142	18	4	164	3	9
Schnall, Kevin, Reds	1.000	1	1	0	0	1	0	0
Seestedt, Michael, Ori.	.968	6	26	4	1	31	1	1
Serrano, Elio, Phi.	1.000	2	15	2	0	17	0	3
Serrano, Hector, Phi.	.985	9	57	9	1	67	0	6
Serrano, Raymond, Brav.	.994	26	155	11	1	167	2	1
Thompson, Alva, Brav.	1.000	15	69	11	0	80	0	0
Torres, Jaime, Yan.	.955	9	58	6	3	67	1	1
Tosca, Daniel, Phi.	.986	31	206	12	3	221	4	9
Valdez, Darlin, Exp.	.946	6	30	5	2	37	0	1
Vargas, Inakel, Tig.	1.000	2	9	0	0	9	0	1
Venales, Luis, Marl.	.990	27	182	24	2	208	3	7
Walker, Keronn, Roy.	.989	14	83	7	1	91	1	1
Wallis, Jacob, Reds	.955	15	106	20	6	132	1	5
Wrenn, Michael, Twi.	.968	15	83	8	3	94	0	2
Yingling, Joe, Tig.	1.000	5	41	2	0	43	0	0
Zapey, Winton, Marl.	.994	26	144	12	1	157	0	8
Zeber, Ryan, Reds	1.000	3	14	0	0	14	0	0

PITCHERS

Player, Team	Pct.	G	PO	A	E	TC	DP
Abreu, Cesar, Reds	.000	1	0	0	0	0	0
Advincola, Jose, Ori.*	.800	12	0	8	2	10	0
Albertus, Roberto, Brav.*	1.000	13	1	3	0	4	0
Alcala, Jason, Pir.	1.000	10	1	2	0	3	1
Alcantara, Over, Marl.	.500	4	0	1	1	2	0
Aldridge, Mike, Yan.	.000	7	0	0	0	0	0
Almonte, Erick, Yan.	.000	1	0	0	0	0	0
Altman, Gene, Reds	1.000	3	0	1	0	1	0
Anderson, Antwoine, Marl.*	.875	13	1	6	1	8	0
Anez, Omar, Ori.	.400	14	0	2	3	5	0
Angell, Rick, Rang.	.000	1	0	0	0	0	0
Aramboles, Ricardo, Yan.	.667	9	0	6	3	9	0
Arias, Pablo, Tig.	.929	12	2	11	1	14	1

Player, Team	Pct.	G	PO	A	E	TC	DP
Arteaga, J.D., Mets*	.000	2	0	0	0	0	0
Ascencio, Miguel, Phi.	.667	9	2	4	3	9	0
Baginski, Jr., Thomas, Tig.*	.000	10	0	0	0	0	0
Baker, Brad, R.S.	1.000	4	1	2	0	3	0
Baldassano, Joseph, Exp.	1.000	12	1	3	0	4	0
Baranowski, Brannon, Roy.	1.000	24	0	2	0	2	0
Barker, Billy, Exp.*	1.000	10	0	4	0	4	0
Barreto, Joel, Twi.	.900	11	4	5	1	10	1
Bedard, Erik, Ori.*	1.000	8	1	4	0	5	0
Bell, Rob, Reds	1.000	2	2	2	0	4	0
Bell, Tom, Marl.	.833	13	1	4	1	6	1
Benitez, Fabricio, R.S.	.846	13	5	6	2	13	1
Bennett, Jeff, Pir.	1.000	8	1	10	0	11	0
Berube, Martin, Ori.	1.000	11	0	1	0	1	0
Biddlestone, Jason, Pir.	.846	12	4	7	2	13	0
Bowyer, Travis, Twi.	.000	1	0	0	0	0	0
Boyanich, Vincent, Twi.	.889	15	4	4	1	9	1
Bradley, Robert, Pir.	1.000	6	1	7	0	8	1
Brewer, Dustin, Ori.	1.000	4	0	2	0	2	0
Brito, Eude, Phi.*	.923	12	3	9	1	13	2
Brown, Andrew, Brav.	1.000	11	1	2	0	3	0
Brown, Paul, Reds*	.958	14	1	22	1	24	0
Buckles, Bucky, Rang.	.000	1	0	0	0	0	0
Bumatay, Mike, Pir.*	.889	11	2	6	1	9	0
Burch, Matt, Roy.	.750	5	1	2	1	4	0
Bureau, Stephen, Brav.	.667	11	0	2	1	3	0
Burger, Rob, Phi.	1.000	9	0	3	0	3	0
Burrows, Terry, Ori.*	1.000	2	1	3	0	4	0
Burruezo, Joseph, Pir.	1.000	7	1	2	0	3	0
Butler, Mattaues, Brav.	1.000	11	1	8	0	9	0
Cabaj, Christopher, Roy.	1.000	11	1	7	0	8	0
Cabrera, Yunior, Mets*	.700	13	0	7	3	10	2
Campos, David, Marl.*	1.000	8	1	1	0	2	0
Carey, Ben, Phi.*	.750	17	2	4	2	8	0
Casadiego, Gerardo, Exp.	.778	9	1	6	2	9	1
Castillo, Ramon, Marl.	.833	11	2	3	1	6	0
Castro, Eleuterio, R.S.	.667	6	0	2	1	3	0
Cavazos, Andy, Rang.	.923	10	3	9	1	13	1
Cedeno, Jovanny, Rang.	1.000	6	1	3	0	4	0
Cespedes, Rafael, Brav.	.714	14	3	2	2	7	0
Cetani, Bryan, Brav.*	1.000	13	2	8	0	10	0
Chacon, Ernesto, Yan.	1.000	18	2	2	0	4	0
Charron, Eric, Exp.	.875	9	3	4	1	8	0
Cheek, Andrew, R.S.*	1.000	18	3	5	0	8	1
Chighisola, Louis, Reds*	1.000	7	0	3	0	3	0
Chisnall, Wesley, Exp.	.500	4	0	1	1	2	0
Classen, Ender, Pir.	.917	6	1	10	1	12	1
Claussen, Brandon, Yan.*	.000	2	0	0	0	0	0
Coa, Jesus, Roy.	.889	7	3	5	1	9	0
Coffey, Todd, Reds.	1.000	5	1	1	0	2	0
Cole, Joseph, Mets	.800	13	2	6	2	10	0
Colton, Kyle, Brav.	1.000	13	7	6	0	13	0
Cooper, Eric, Reds	.000	3	0	0	0	0	0
Cordova, Jorge, Marl.	1.000	7	1	1	0	2	0
Crowther, Jackson, Exp.	.800	13	0	8	2	10	0
Curtice, John, R.S.*	1.000	8	1	1	0	2	0
Davis, Quian, Marl.	.000	1	0	0	0	0	0
Day, Zach, Yan.	1.000	5	1	3	0	4	0
De La Rosa, Cristian, Ori.	1.000	15	0	3	0	3	1
De Los Santos, Luis, Yan.	1.000	2	1	3	0	4	0
Dehart, Casey, Reds*	1.000	2	1	1	0	2	0
Delacruz, Luis, Yan.	.000	3	0	0	0	0	0
Delgado, Joseph, Roy.	.000	1	0	0	0	0	0
Diaz, Luis, Tig.	1.000	22	4	7	0	11	1
Dubuc, Charles, Exp.*	.875	16	2	5	1	8	0
Earl, Ryan, Tig.*	1.000	7	1	3	0	4	0
Echols, Justin, Rang.	1.000	14	1	4	0	5	1
Einertson, Darrell, Yan.	.000	1	0	0	0	0	0
Espina, Rendy, Phi.*	.000	2	0	0	0	0	0
Espinal, Jose, Twi.	1.000	10	1	3	0	4	1
Essian, James, Roy.	1.000	1	0	1	0	1	0
Evert, Brett, Brav.	.909	13	0	10	1	11	0
Falkenborg, Brian, Ori.	1.000	3	0	3	0	3	0
Farren, Dave, Ori.	1.000	10	0	1	0	1	0
Figueroa, Carlos, Rang.*	.000	6	0	0	0	0	0
Finnegan, Mike, Exp.	.000	1	0	0	0	0	0
Flanagan, Ryan, Twi.	1.000	9	0	5	0	5	0
Fleming, Travis, Ori.	1.000	4	1	3	0	4	0
Francisco, Franklin, R.S.	.778	12	1	6	2	9	0
Franco, Edwin, Roy.*	1.000	2	1	1	0	2	0
Fraser, Joe, Exp.	1.000	4	1	1	0	2	0
Frederick, Kevin, Twi.	1.000	2	0	1	0	1	0
Fuell, Jerrod, Tig.	1.000	6	3	2	0	5	0
Gamboa, Javier, Roy.	1.000	3	0	1	0	1	0
Garcia, Abel, Roy.*	1.000	3	1	2	0	3	0

Player, Team	Pct.	G	PO	A	E	TC	DP
Garcia, Rafael, Roy.	.714	9	0	5	2	7	0
Garcia, Ramon, R.S.	1.000	21	2	2	0	4	0
Garcia, Reynaldo, Rang.	.938	12	2	13	1	16	0
Gardea, Mario, Yan.	1.000	14	1	3	0	4	0
Garris, Antonio, Exp.	1.000	15	1	4	0	5	0
Gauger, Michael, Mets*	.000	18	0	1	1	1	0
Girdley, Joshua, Exp.*	.857	12	3	9	2	14	0
Gobble, Jimmy, Roy.*	1.000	4	1	0	0	1	0
Gooch, Arnie, Reds	1.000	2	0	2	0	2	1
Grantham, Ryan, Exp.	1.000	8	2	2	0	4	1
Guerrero, Neftali, Mets	1.000	15	0	2	0	2	0
Guillen, Elvin, Reds	1.000	7	1	3	0	4	0
Guzman, Leiby, Rang.	.000	1	0	0	0	0	0
Halisky, Scott, Ori.	1.000	3	0	2	0	2	0
Halvorson, Greg, Mets	.800	5	1	3	1	5	0
Harrell, Scott, Reds	1.000	2	0	2	0	2	0
Haynes, Brad, Marl.	.800	11	6	2	2	10	0
Herrera, Carlos, Phi.	.923	12	3	9	1	13	0
Herrera, Pedro, Roy.	1.000	5	1	0	0	1	1
Hill, Jaime, Rang.*	1.000	21	3	8	0	11	0
Hill, Ryan, Roy.	.000	1	0	0	0	0	0
Hines, Carlos, Reds	1.000	5	1	4	0	5	1
Hlodan, George, Pir.	1.000	5	1	2	0	3	0
Hopper, Joshua, Mets*	1.000	16	2	10	0	12	1
Hughes, Mike, Exp.*	.500	2	0	1	1	2	0
Igualada, Eric, Yan.	1.000	11	0	1	0	1	0
Infante, Asdrubal, Tig.	1.000	15	2	1	0	3	0
Jelovcic, Rich, Yan.	1.000	14	3	3	0	6	1
Jimenez, Ronal, Phi.	1.000	20	4	1	0	5	0
Johnson, Jonathan, Rang.	.000	1	0	0	1	1	0
Johnson, Mark, Yan.	.500	3	0	1	1	2	0
Johnston, Dave, Marl.	1.000	12	1	1	0	2	0
Joseph, Glen, Reds	.667	2	1	1	1	3	1
Josephson, Jared, Pir.	1.000	8	0	2	0	2	0
Kessel, Kyle, Mets*	.000	3	0	0	0	0	0
Kinney, Matt, Twi.	1.000	3	0	1	0	1	0
Kirsten, Rick, Tig.	1.000	11	2	2	0	4	0
Koronka, John, Reds*	1.000	7	1	9	0	10	1
Koziara, Matt, Reds	1.000	13	0	4	0	4	0
Kozlowski, Benjamin, Brav.	.900	15	4	5	1	10	0
LA ROSA, Dancy, Twi.	1.000	11	3	12	0	15	0
Lajara, Eudy, Marl.*	1.000	8	0	4	0	4	0
Lamarsh, Robert, Rang.*	1.000	3	2	1	0	3	0
Lankford, Frank, Yan.	.000	1	0	0	0	0	0
Laplante, Reggie, Yan.	.667	8	0	4	2	6	0
Leach, Bryan, R.S.	.000	1	0	0	0	0	0
Leahy, Bart, Marl.	1.000	8	0	3	0	3	1
Ledezma, Wilfredo, R.S.*	.800	13	0	8	2	10	0
Legette, Richard, Phi.	1.000	12	5	8	0	13	0
Lesner, Kenneth, Twi.	.750	13	1	2	1	4	0
Levesque, Benjamin, Pir.	.667	11	1	5	3	9	1
Lewis, Jeremy, Tig.*	.778	10	3	4	2	9	1
Lewter, John, Pir.	.818	13	4	5	2	11	0
Lima, Frank, Tig.	.857	20	2	4	1	7	0
Linarelli, Tom, R.S.	1.000	1	0	1	0	1	0
Lockwood, Luke, Exp.*	1.000	11	1	12	0	13	0
Loewer, Carlton, Phi.	1.000	1	0	2	0	2	0
Lopez, Ignacio, Rang.	.933	13	0	14	1	15	0
Lopez, Jorge, Reds	.667	10	0	2	1	3	1
Lopez, Jose, Mets	1.000	2	1	2	0	3	0
Lopez, Rafael, Mets	.857	12	1	11	2	14	0
Loudon, Gary, Reds	.867	15	3	10	2	15	1
Love, Brandon, Reds	1.000	7	2	7	0	9	0
Lutz, Kenneth, Reds	.923	12	4	8	1	13	1
Lyons, Curt, Yan.	1.000	1	0	1	0	1	0
Maloney, Sean, Ori.	.000	1	0	0	0	0	0
Martinez, Carlos, Roy.*	.938	11	5	10	1	16	0
Martinez, David, Yan.*	.778	12	3	18	6	27	0
Martinez, Eddy, Reds	1.000	17	1	8	0	9	0
Martinez, Lionel, Brav.	1.000	12	2	2	0	4	1
Martinez, Oscar, Yan.	.909	23	1	9	1	11	0
Martinez, Ramon, R.S.	1.000	4	1	2	0	3	0
Marx, Tommy, Tig.*	1.000	8	2	2	0	4	0
Mastrolonardo, David, Ori.	.000	3	0	0	0	0	0
Mathews, Terry, Roy.	1.000	1	0	0	0	0	0
McCloud, Josh, Yan.	.000	3	0	0	0	0	0
McGinnis, Ronald, Phi.	.000	4	0	0	0	0	0
McNatt, Josh, Ori.*	.000	1	0	0	0	0	0
Mead, David, Rang.	.800	11	2	2	1	5	0
Mejia, Juan, Brav.	.667	16	1	5	3	9	0
Mendible, Franklin, Pir.	1.000	4	0	3	0	3	0
Merrill, Darren, Exp.	1.000	6	1	9	0	10	0
Messenger, Randall, Marl.	1.000	13	1	2	0	3	0
Messer, Brian, Pir.	1.000	3	2	2	0	4	1
Mikkola, Shaun, Mets	.857	5	2	4	1	7	1

SUMMER CLASS A Gulf Coast League

Player, Team	Pct.	G	PO	A	E	TC	DP
Minaya, Richard, Reds	.600	16	0	3	2	5	0
Miniel, Rene, R.S.	.917	21	4	7	1	12	0
Morel, Jesus, Twi.	1.000	14	1	5	0	6	1
Morel, Ramon, Exp.	1.000	2	1	1	0	2	0
Moreno, Julio, Ori.	1.000	4	0	2	0	2	0
Moreno, Orber, Roy.	.000	1	0	0	0	0	0
Musser, Neal, Mets*	.857	8	1	5	1	7	0
Myers, Brett, Phi.	1.000	7	4	6	0	10	0
Myers, Taylor, Roy.	1.000	3	0	1	0	1	0
Nanninga, Matthew, Reds	.889	6	1	7	1	9	0
Nelson, Jeff, Yan.	1.000	2	0	1	0	1	0
Nichols, Brian, Mets	1.000	9	1	3	0	4	0
Nicholson, John, Exp.	.000	2	0	0	0	0	0
Obando, Omar, Yan.	1.000	2	0	1	0	1	0
Obermueller, Wes, Roy.	.857	11	1	5	1	7	0
Ochsner, Alan, Yan.	.000	4	0	0	0	0	0
Odom, Lance, Twi.	1.000	20	1	3	0	4	0
Oliver, Scott, Yan.	.923	6	3	9	1	13	0
Ortega, Jose, Roy.*	1.000	17	2	7	0	9	0
Ortega, Jose, Roy.	.889	12	4	4	1	9	1
Ortiz, Javier, Yan.	1.000	12	7	7	0	14	2
Palki, Jeromy, Twi.	1.000	3	1	2	0	3	0
Parkerson, Michael, Pir.*	.923	14	2	10	1	13	1
Paz, Rolando, Ori.	.857	13	1	5	1	7	0
Peeples, Jim, Yan.*	1.000	16	0	3	0	3	0
Pena, Juan, R.S.	1.000	1	1	0	0	1	0
Pepen, Robert, Mets	.889	19	4	4	1	9	0
Perez, Franklin, Phi.	.714	12	1	4	2	7	0
Phillips, James, Ori.	.833	15	3	2	1	6	0
Pidgeon, Chip, Mets*	1.000	4	0	3	0	3	0
Rahrer, Josh, Rang.	1.000	15	2	3	0	5	0
Ramirez, Enrique, Ori.	1.000	9	1	0	0	1	0
Rasmussen, Brent, Roy.	1.000	17	2	6	0	8	0
Reisinger, Justin, Yan.	.667	8	2	0	1	3	0
Rhea, Thad, Pir.	.000	2	0	0	0	0	0
Rice, Scott, Ori.*	.571	9	0	4	3	7	0
Richardson, Jason, Twi.	1.000	12	0	3	0	3	0
Ridenour, Ryan, Yan.*	.500	3	0	1	1	2	0
Rijo, Hector, Exp.*	1.000	15	0	5	0	5	0
Rivera, Erick, Phi.	.000	1	0	0	0	0	0
Rivera, Samuel, Tig.	1.000	7	1	1	0	2	0
Rodney, Fernando, Tig.	1.000	22	0	2	0	2	1
Rodriguez, Alejandro, Phi.	.800	5	3	1	1	5	0
Rodriguez, Alfredo, Rang.	1.000	9	0	2	0	2	0
Rodriguez, Jose, Brav.	.909	16	3	7	1	11	0
Rodriguez, Luis, Rang.	.889	17	2	14	2	18	0
Rogers, Bradley, Ori.	.000	6	0	0	0	0	0
Roman, Orlando, Mets	.933	12	4	10	1	15	0
Romero, Josmir, Twi.	.938	11	4	11	1	16	0
Roque, Darryll, Exp.	.000	1	0	0	0	0	0
Rose, Johnathan, Phi.*	.800	5	0	4	1	5	0
Rose, Ted, Reds.	.000	1	0	0	0	0	0
Ross, Donovan, Roy.	1.000	1	0	1	0	1	0
Roundtree, Monte, Reds*	1.000	7	1	4	0	5	0
Rundles, Richard, R.S.*	1.000	5	1	3	0	4	0
Rusch, Glendon, Roy.*	1.000	2	0	1	0	1	0
Russo, Dennis, Reds	1.000	2	1	0	0	1	0
Sabens, Mike, Pir.	1.000	7	0	4	0	4	0
Sager, A.J., Reds	.000	1	0	0	0	0	0
Salazar, Luis, Marl.	.833	14	2	3	1	6	0
Santana, Humberto, Mets*	1.000	2	0	3	0	3	0
Santiago, Jose, Roy.	1.000	3	0	1	0	1	0
Sauer, Marc, Marl.	1.000	13	2	9	0	11	0
Sawvell, Matthew, Mets*	1.000	8	0	1	0	1	0
Sclafani, Anthony, Brav.	1.000	17	1	6	0	7	1
Searles, Jonathan, Pir.	.400	8	1	1	3	5	0
Seo, Jung Min, R.S.	1.000	13	1	5	0	6	0
Sequea, Jacobo, Reds	.000	1	0	0	0	0	0
Serrano, Willy, Tig.	.800	6	1	3	1	5	0
Shelley, Jason, Pir.	1.000	2	0	1	0	1	0
Silverio, Carlos, Phi.	.500	5	0	1	1	2	0
Smith, Chad, Phi.	.900	22	1	8	1	10	0
Solano, Alexander, R.S.	1.000	5	0	5	0	5	0
Sollenberger, Matt, Mets*	1.000	18	1	4	0	5	0
Song, Seung, R.S.	1.000	13	1	9	0	10	1
Sopkin, Josh, Roy.	.000	16	0	0	0	0	0
Spears, Ricky, Yan.	1.000	7	3	2	0	5	0
Stamm, Steve, Rang.*	1.000	20	2	4	0	6	0
Staples, Dave, Phi.*.	1.000	15	1	7	0	8	0
Stiles, Brad, Roy.*	.000	4	0	0	0	0	0
Storke, Jonathan, Ori.	.000	1	0	0	0	0	0
Story, Aaron, Pir.*	.875	12	1	6	1	8	0
Sweeney, Mike, Mets	1.000	1	0	1	0	1	0
Swiatkiewicz, Chris, Yan.	1.000	9	0	3	0	3	1
Tankersley, Jr., Dennis, R.S.	1.000	11	2	4	0	6	1
Targac, Matthew, Marl.*	.947	12	5	13	1	19	1
Tate, Matthew, Ori.	.818	11	4	14	4	22	2
Tavarez, David, Ori.	.938	12	7	8	1	16	2
Taylor, Jason, Tig.	.600	18	1	2	2	5	0
Tejeda, Robinson, Phi.	.786	12	5	6	3	14	0
Terry, Mike, Mets*	.000	2	0	0	0	0	0
Tetz, Kristofer, Exp.	1.000	1	0	1	0	1	0
Thompson, Matthew, R.S.	1.000	5	0	3	0	3	0
Thrasher, Jesse, Phi.	.000	5	0	0	1	1	0
Tomaszewski, Eliot, Ori.	.667	10	0	4	2	6	0
Torres, Alex, Tig.*	.000	13	0	0	1	1	0
Torres, Luis, Exp.	.929	12	1	12	1	14	0
Torres, Luis, Pir.	.889	8	3	5	1	9	0
Tovar, Angel, Yan.	1.000	8	1	4	0	5	0
Trevino, Chris, Brav.*	.800	11	2	2	1	5	0
Trinidad, Fernando, Ori.	1.000	15	2	9	0	11	2
Turner, Jess, Twi.	.889	17	3	5	1	9	1
Turner, Kyle, Roy.*	.000	2	0	0	0	0	0
Turrentine, Rich, Mets	.667	5	1	1	1	3	0
Urbina, Ulmer, Exp.	1.000	14	2	3	0	5	0
Vail, Garett, R.S.	1.000	7	2	1	0	3	0
Valdez, Domingo, Rang.	1.000	8	1	2	0	3	0
Valdez, Jose, Reds.	.750	12	1	5	2	8	0
Veras, Dario, Roy.	1.000	3	1	0	0	1	0
Villamil, William, Rang.*	.833	10	0	5	1	6	0
Villanueva, Bill, Marl.	.846	11	4	7	2	13	1
Vogt, Robert, Pir.*	.000	3	0	0	0	0	0
Walker, Adrian, Brav.*	.857	13	2	4	1	7	0
Walker, Jamie, Roy.*	1.000	2	1	2	0	3	0
Walker, Keronn, Roy.	.000	1	0	0	0	0	0
Wamback, Trevor, Exp.	1.000	2	0	1	0	1	0
Wasdin, John, R.S.	.000	1	0	0	0	0	0
Washington, Porter, Reds	.500	10	0	1	1	2	0
Watkins, David, Brav.	.818	13	4	5	2	11	0
WHITE, James, Pir.	1.000	13	6	9	0	15	0
Willis, Jason, Yan.	1.000	4	1	0	0	1	1
Wolfe, Brian, Twi.	1.000	9	0	3	0	3	0
Wykoff, Jarred, Marl.	1.000	11	2	4	0	6	0
Yen, Buddy, Roy.	.600	25	0	3	2	5	0
Zapey, Winton, Marl.	.000	1	0	0	0	0	0
Zgoda, Derek, Yan.	1.000	2	0	2	0	2	0
Zipser, Mike, Phi.	.000	6	0	0	1	1	0

The following players appeared only as designated hitter, pinch-hitter or pinch runner: Copley, dh; Kofler, dh; Lundquist, dh; Morneau, dh; Morris, dh-ph; Tony Smith, dh-pr; Ugueto, dh.

LEAGUE CHAMPIONS

Year	Team	Pct.
1964—	Sarasota Braves	.610
1965—	Bradenton Astros	.632
1966—	New York AL	.667
1967—	Kansas City	.614
1968—	Oakland	.650
1969—	Montreal	.585
1970—	Chicago AL	.600
1971—	Kansas City	.755
1972—	Chicago NL*	.651
	Kansas City*	.651
1973—	Texas	.732
1974—	Chicago NL	.702
1975—	Texas	.774
1976—	Texas	.704

Year	Team	Pct.
1977—	Chicago AL	.731
1978—	Texas	.600
1979—	Houston	.635
1980—	Kansas City-Blue	.635
1981—	Kansas City-Gold	.688
1982—	New York AL	.667
1983—	Texas	.645
	Los Angeles†	.617
1984—	White Sox	.651
	Rangers†	.571
1985—	Yankees§	.705
	Rangers	.532
1986—	Reds	.548
	Dodgers†	.541

Year	Team	Pct.
1987—	Dodgers†	.683
	Royals	.635
1988—	Yankees†	.714
	Royals	.619
1989—	Yankees‡	.651
	Dodgers	.635
1990—	Expos	.635
	Dodgers‡	.603
1991—	Orioles	.593
	Expos∞	.533
1992—	Royals∞	.695
	Expos	.593
1993—	Rangers▲	.667
	Astros	.593

Year	Team	Pct.	Year	Team	Pct.	Year	Team	Pct.
1994—	Royals◆	.797	1996—	Yankees◆	.638	1998—	Marlins	.633
	Astros	.695		Rangers	.617		Rangers◆	.567
1995—	Royals■	.649	1997—	Mets▼	.700	1999—	Mets◆	.650
	Tigers	.579		Rangers	.567			

*Declared co-champions; no playoff. †League divided into Northern and Southern divisions; won one-game playoff for league championship. ‡League divided into Northern and Southern divisions; won best-of-three playoff for league championship. §Yankees declared champion based on winning percentage when one-game playoff against Rangers was rained out. ∞League divided into Northern, Southern and Central divisions; won best-of-three playoff for league championship. ▲League divided into Eastern, Central and Western divisions; won three-team playoff. ◆League divided into Eastern, Northern and Western divisions; won three-team playoff. ■League divided into Eastern, Northern, Northwest and Southwest divisions; won four-team playoff. ▼League divided into Eastern, Western and Northwest divisions; won four-club playoff. (Note—Known as Sarasota Rookie League in 1964 and Florida Rookie League in 1965.)

PIONEER LEAGUE

LEAGUE OFFICE

President
Jim McCurdy
Address
P.O. Box 2564
Spokane, WA 99220
Phone
509-456-7615

Teams (affiliation)
Billings Mustangs (Reds)
Butte Copper Kings (Angels)
Great Falls Dodgers (Dodgers)
Helena Brewers (Brewers)

Idaho Falls Padres (Padres)
Missoula Osprey (Diamondbacks)
Medicine Hat Blue Jays (Blue Jays)
Ogden Raptors (Brewers)

1999 FINAL STANDINGS

FIRST HALF

NORTH DIVISION

Team	W	L	T	Pct.	GB
Missoula (Diamondbacks)	28	10	0	.737	...
Helena (Brewers)	21	17	0	.553	7.0
Medicine Hat (Blue Jays)	16	22	0	.421	12.0
Great Falls (Dodgers)	14	24	0	.368	14.0

SOUTH DIVISION

Team	W	L	T	Pct.	GB
Idaho Falls (Padres)	24	14	0	.632	...
Billings (Reds)	22	16	0	.541	4.0
Butte (Angels)	17	21	0	.447	7.0
Ogden (Brewers)	10	28	0	.263	14.0

SECOND HALF

NORTH DIVISION

Team	W	L	T	Pct.	GB
Helena (Brewers)	26	11	0	.703	...
Missoula (Diamondbacks)	17	21	0	.447	9.5
Medicine Hat (Blue Jays)	17	21	0	.447	9.5
Great Falls (Dodgers)	15	23	0	.395	11.5

SOUTH DIVISION

Team	W	L	T	Pct.	GB
Idaho Falls (Padres)	24	13	0	.649	...
Billings (Reds)	20	17	0	.541	4.0
Ogden (Brewers)	16	22	0	.421	8.5
Butte (Angels)	15	22	0	.405	9.0

COMPOSITE

Team	I.F.	Hel.	Miss.	Bil.	M.H.	But.	G.F.	Ogd.	W	L	T	Pct.	GB
Idaho Falls (Padres)	...	2	4	7	6	12	6	11	48	27	0	.640	...
Helena (Brewers)	5	...	6	7	10	5	9	5	47	28	0	.627	1.0
Missoula (Diamondbacks)	4	10	...	4	9	3	8	7	45	31	0	.592	3.5
Billings (Reds)	7	1	4	...	5	8	7	10	42	33	0	.560	6.0
Medicine Hat (Blue Jays)	2	4	5	3	...	7	7	5	33	43	0	.434	15.5
Butte (Angels)	2	3	5	7	1	...	4	10	32	43	0	.427	16.0
Great Falls (Dodgers)	2	5	6	1	9	4	...	2	29	47	0	.382	19.5
Ogden (Brewers)	5	3	1	4	3	4	6	...	26	50	0	.342	22.5

Club names are major league affiliations.

PLAYOFFS: Billings defeated Idaho Falls two games to none; Missoula defeated Helena two games to none; Missoula defeated Billings two games to none to win league championship.

REGULAR-SEASON ATTENDANCE: Billings, 92,147; Butte, 20,119; Great Falls, 87,687; Helena, 25,979; Idaho Falls, 64,134; Medicine Hat, 26,852; Missoula, 56,099; Ogden, 81,345. Total—454,362. Playoff (6 games)—10,459.

MANAGERS: Billings, Russ Nixon; Butte, Joe Urso; Great Falls, Tony Harris; Helena, Carlos Lezcano; Idaho Falls, Don Werner; Medicine Hat, Paul Elliott; Missoula, Joe Almaraz; Ogden, Jon Pont (through August 4) and Ed Sedar (August 5 through end of season).

ALL-STAR TEAM: 1B—Lyle Overbay, Missoula; 2B—Brian Ward, Idaho Falls; 3B—Cordell Lindsey, Butte; SS—Jason Repko, Great Falls; OF—Ben Broussard, Billings; Cristian Guerrero, Ogden; Ryan Knox, Helena; C—J.D. Closser, Missoula; DH—Casey Brookout, Billings; RHP—Jose Mieses, Helena; LHP—Gustavo Chacin, Medicine Hat; RP—Brain Matzenbacher, Missoula; Most Valuable Player—Lyle Overbay, Missoula; Manager of the Year—Russ Nixon, Billings.

1999 BATTING

TEAM

Team	Avg.	G	TPA	AB	R	H	TB	2B	3B	HR	RBI	SH	SF	HP	BB	IBB	SO	SB	CS	GDP	LOB	ShO	Slg.	OBP
Butte	.290	75	3027	2641	529	765	1118	132	34	51	446	22	26	54	284	6	585	109	43	48	548	3	.423	.367
Billings	.288	75	3029	2645	489	761	1177	152	27	70	433	26	23	43	292	4	613	50	27	53	567	1	.445	.365
Idaho Falls	.285	75	3076	2653	546	755	1194	165	35	68	467	9	28	52	334	5	646	153	39	54	558	0	.450	.372
Missoula	.284	76	3131	2668	552	759	1144	142	33	59	472	21	26	40	376	4	658	150	47	60	564	0	.429	.378
Helena	.281	75	2922	2545	468	715	1040	129	11	58	381	19	21	54	283	4	490	143	45	52	529	2	.409	.362
Ogden	.280	75	2991	2631	437	737	1077	137	19	55	373	24	19	52	265	3	561	122	54	54	538	4	.409	.355
Great Falls	.268	76	2968	2637	438	708	996	106	31	40	353	39	26	42	224	3	498	108	49	46	518	1	.378	.333
Medicine Hat	.255	76	2914	2536	389	647	941	123	18	45	323	18	19	31	310	2	530	86	36	50	563	3	.371	.341

TOP QUALIFIERS FOR BATTING CHAMPIONSHIP

Minimum 205 plate appearances. *Lefthanded batter. †Switch-hitter.

Player, Team	Avg.	G	TPA	AB	R	H	TB	2B	3B	HR	RBI	SH	SF	HP	BB	IBB	SO	SB	CS	GDP	Slg.	OBP
Bookout, Casey, Bil.*	.363	50	234	204	49	74	129	14	1	13	63	0	1	3	26	1	37	0	1	5	.632	.440
Knox, Ryan, Hel.	.349	72	311	275	58	96	121	17	1	2	25	3	4	4	25	1	27	44	11	1	.440	.406
Overbay, Lyle, Mis.*	.343	75	352	306	66	105	180	25	7	12	101	0	4	2	40	2	53	10	3	14	.588	.418
Lindsey, Cordell, But.	.341	63	284	255	72	87	154	23	7	10	58	0	1	4	23	0	46	13	5	5	.604	.403
Ford, Will, Og.*	.341	53	206	179	38	61	98	14	4	5	46	0	3	2	22	1	27	5	5	6	.547	.413
Brooks, Jeff, Mis.	.339	73	317	295	48	100	162	18	4	12	60	0	0	5	17	0	77	6	2	10	.549	.385
Schader, Troy, I.F.	.336	68	312	268	61	90	177	16	7	19	69	0	5	4	35	1	75	2	2	0	.660	.413
White, Gregory, But.	.327	55	238	205	37	67	113	15	2	9	47	0	3	4	26	1	50	1	2	5	.551	.408
Burnett, Mark, Bil.*	.326	60	279	224	56	73	102	13	2	4	29	3	2	4	46	0	32	12	9	3	.455	.446
Closser, J.D., Mis.†	.324	76	355	275	73	89	141	22	0	10	54	1	6	2	71	2	57	9	3	8	.513	.458
Orgill, Peter, But.*	.323	58	257	217	43	70	95	8	1	5	36	0	2	12	26	1	38	0	0	6	.438	.420
Curtis, William, But.†	.319	66	280	238	40	76	114	18	1	6	46	0	2	5	35	4	58	0	2	4	.479	.414
Ward, Brian, I.F.	.317	68	326	287	50	91	139	23	2	7	60	0	4	3	32	2	46	6	3	7	.484	.387
Guerrero, Cristian, Og.	.310	65	252	226	51	70	98	7	3	5	28	0	1	2	23	0	59	26	2	3	.434	.377
Truitt, Steve, Hel.	.308	54	231	185	51	57	102	10	1	11	50	0	4	5	37	0	40	19	5	6	.551	.429

DEPARTMENTAL LEADERS: G—Closser, 76; AB—Overbay, 306; R—Terrero, 74; H—Overbay, 105; TB—Overbay, 180; 2B—Overbay, 25; 3B—Repko, Huth, 9 each; HR—Schader, 19; RBI—Overbay, 101; SH—Juarez, 7; SF—Rizzo, 7; HP—Orgill, 12; BB—Closser, 71; IBB—Curtis, 4; SO—Terrero, 91; SB—Knox, 44; CS—Knox, 11; GIDP—Overbay, 14; Slg.—Schader, .660; OBP—Closser, .458.

ALL PLAYERS

*Lefthanded batter. †Switch-hitter.

Player, Team	Avg.	G	TPA	AB	R	H	TB	2B	3B	HR	RBI	SH	SF	HP	BB	IBB	SO	SB	CS	GDP	Slg.	OBP
Amezaga, Alfredo, But.	.294	8	40	34	11	10	12	2	0	0	5	0	0	1	5	0	5	6	2	0	.353	.400
Ayala, Elio, Og.	.267	66	267	240	41	64	81	14	0	1	19	2	1	4	20	0	27	8	3	5	.338	.332
Bookout, Casey, Bil.*	.363	50	234	204	49	74	129	14	1	13	63	0	1	3	26	1	37	0	1	5	.632	.440
Boykin, Paul, I.F.*	.248	45	165	149	30	37	48	6	1	1	10	0	0	0	14	0	44	24	9	3	.322	.313
Brazoban, Jose, Hel.	.234	45	182	158	28	37	47	5	1	1	18	1	1	4	18	0	43	18	5	2	.297	.326
Brooks, Jeff, Mis.	.339	73	317	295	48	100	162	18	4	12	60	0	0	5	17	0	77	6	2	10	.549	.385
Broussard, Benjamin, Bil.*	.407	38	184	145	39	59	116	11	2	14	48	0	1	4	34	2	30	1	0	0	.800	.527
Buccheri, Joe, Hel.-Og.	.198	31	98	86	9	17	19	2	0	0	14	1	0	2	9	0	20	4	5	3	.221	.289
Burnett, Mark, Bil.*	.326	60	279	224	56	73	102	13	2	4	29	3	2	4	46	0	32	12	9	3	.455	.446
Burns, Kevan, Mis.*	.364	16	61	55	15	20	29	2	2	1	14	0	0	0	6	0	10	3	0	2	.527	.426
Bystrowski, Robby, I.F.	.297	44	189	155	37	46	69	8	3	3	19	1	0	6	27	0	44	19	5	1	.445	.420
Campana, Wandel, Bil.	.268	45	170	157	27	42	59	10	2	1	20	5	0	1	7	0	22	6	4	3	.376	.303
Castellano, John, G.F.	.246	37	149	134	13	33	44	6	1	1	25	0	4	2	9	0	8	3	2	4	.328	.295
Ceriani, Matt, Hel.	.302	57	184	162	22	49	63	11	0	1	25	2	1	4	15	0	23	4	0	5	.389	.374
Chighisola, Louis, Bil.*	.000	17	1	1	0	0	0	0	0	0	0	0	0	0	0	0	1	0	0	0	.000	.000
Clark, Chivas, M.H.*	.270	70	313	267	56	72	114	18	3	6	29	1	1	6	38	1	78	12	5	1	.427	.372
Closser, J.D., Mis.†	.324	76	355	275	73	89	141	22	0	10	54	1	6	2	71	2	57	9	3	8	.513	.458
Conyer, Darryl, Mis.*	.263	49	245	190	55	50	72	9	2	3	23	6	1	5	43	0	56	20	7	0	.379	.410
Cornett, Robert, M.H.	.289	49	198	166	26	48	72	9	3	3	36	0	3	4	25	0	31	1	1	9	.434	.389
Correa, Jose, Og.*	.288	50	181	156	25	45	85	9	2	9	34	0	2	6	17	0	30	2	2	2	.545	.376
Cosby, Robert, M.H.†	.270	46	194	178	22	48	68	9	1	3	25	0	4	0	12	0	29	10	3	3	.382	.309
Cosentino, Tony, I.F.	.375	20	96	88	14	33	48	5	2	2	30	0	2	0	6	1	11	0	0	5	.545	.404
Cruz, Hector, Mis.†	.184	15	57	49	10	9	10	1	0	0	4	0	0	0	8	0	13	2	2	0	.204	.298
Curry, Jesse, I.F.*	.264	47	182	159	28	42	85	12	5	7	35	0	0	1	22	0	53	5	0	2	.535	.357
Curry, Zane, G.F.	.244	27	107	90	10	22	25	3	0	0	8	0	1	1	15	0	16	1	3	0	.278	.355
Curtis, William, But.†	.319	66	280	238	40	76	114	18	1	6	46	0	2	5	35	4	58	0	2	4	.479	.414
Dehner, Matthew, Bil.	.307	61	263	225	34	69	91	11	1	3	25	3	2	10	23	0	73	7	2	5	.404	.392
De Los Santos, Nelson, Og.†	.252	48	152	131	27	33	53	4	2	4	23	1	1	3	16	0	39	9	3	3	.405	.344
Detienne, Dave, G.F.	.216	47	173	153	22	33	39	3	0	1	16	2	2	5	11	0	34	9	5	5	.255	.287
Devore, Doug, Mis.*	.235	32	135	115	22	27	48	4	4	3	22	0	2	4	14	0	36	2	0	2	.417	.333
Diaz, Michael, But.*	.327	14	65	49	22	16	17	1	0	0	2	0	0	1	15	0	7	11	2	1	.347	.492
Donovan, Todd, I.F.	.298	53	233	198	57	59	79	11	3	1	22	1	3	6	25	1	39	40	5	1	.399	.388
Doucet, Brandon, Hel.	.239	48	152	134	20	32	39	7	0	0	11	1	1	1	15	0	31	4	0	2	.291	.318
Dunn, Scott, Bil.	.000	9	1	1	0	0	0	0	0	0	0	0	0	0	0	0	0	0	0	0	.000	.000
Duran, Francisco, But.	.249	53	247	209	39	52	66	6	1	2	43	3	6	3	26	0	40	8	4	1	.316	.331
Duverge, Alcides, But.	.213	26	97	89	12	19	29	3	2	1	7	1	0	2	5	0	28	1	1	1	.326	.271
Ernster, Mark, Og.	.227	5	25	22	3	5	8	1	1	0	2	1	0	1	1	0	1	1	0	1	.364	.292
Escalera, Jose, G.F.	.254	32	122	114	14	29	39	4	0	2	10	0	0	0	6	0	20	1	2	4	.342	.292
Fera, Aaron, M.H.	.221	61	238	213	26	47	77	10	1	6	29	1	1	5	18	0	58	3	2	6	.362	.295
Fierro, Robert, M.H.	.237	22	79	59	10	14	16	2	0	0	10	0	1	3	16	0	9	0	0	1	.271	.418
Ford, Will, Og.*	.341	53	206	179	38	61	98	14	4	5	46	0	3	2	22	1	27	5	5	6	.547	.413
Forelli, Anthony, Og.	.294	64	254	228	22	67	93	17	0	3	37	1	2	5	18	0	51	3	3	5	.408	.356
Foster, Brian, Hel.	.152	20	54	46	4	7	7	0	0	0	2	1	0	2	5	0	16	0	0	3	.152	.264
Frank, Nick, Og.	.300	59	239	203	35	61	86	13	0	4	40	3	1	7	25	0	44	13	5	5	.424	.394
Freeman, Thomas, Mis.*	.238	16	50	42	3	10	15	1	2	0	6	0	0	1	7	0	15	1	1	0	.357	.360
Garcia, Hector, Hel.	.307	68	285	264	48	81	143	10	2	16	62	0	1	8	12	0	46	8	1	3	.542	.354
Garrett, Shawn, I.F.†	.307	53	219	192	46	59	96	14	1	7	33	0	2	4	21	0	46	5	3	11	.500	.384
Gastelum, Carlos, But.	.261	58	244	211	37	55	71	12	2	0	28	4	3	4	22	0	28	11	5	6	.336	.338
Geraldo, Anulfo, Hel.	.261	45	186	161	28	42	56	8	0	2	22	4	1	0	20	0	26	2	3	7	.348	.341
Godbolt, Keith, G.F.	.267	43	169	150	26	40	52	7	1	1	18	3	1	3	12	0	24	2	3	5	.347	.331
Goldfield, Josh, Mis.*	.254	35	138	122	15	31	35	4	0	0	23	1	0	2	13	0	31	2	0	2	.287	.326
Gosewisch, Ian, But.	.246	55	224	207	29	51	68	10	2	1	30	1	3	1	12	0	43	0	2	6	.329	.287
Graham, Justin, Mis.	.226	23	74	62	12	14	21	2	1	1	5	0	1	1	10	0	19	0	0	0	.339	.338
Guerrero, Cristian, Og.	.310	65	252	226	51	70	98	7	3	5	28	0	1	2	23	0	59	26	2	3	.434	.377
Gutierrez, Roberto, M.H.	.150	7	22	20	1	3	5	0	1	0	1	0	0	0	2	0	2	0	0	2	.250	.227

Player, Team	Avg.	G	TPA	AB	R	H	TB	2B	3B	HR	RBI	SH	SF	HP	BB	IBB	SO	SB	CS	GDP	Slg.	OBP
Gutierrez, Said, I.F.	.310	26	93	87	10	27	35	5	0	1	11	0	0	3	3	0	14	0	1	2	.402	.355
Guzman, Alexis, M.H.†	.215	47	172	149	28	32	42	8	1	0	10	1	3	1	18	0	39	3	1	3	.282	.298
Hall, Victor, Mis.*	.279	34	168	147	27	41	45	4	0	0	11	1	1	4	15	0	30	18	7	1	.306	.359
Hall, William, Og.	.289	69	300	280	41	81	118	15	2	6	31	2	1	2	15	1	61	19	8	6	.421	.329
Haver, Lance, Bil.	.343	11	39	35	5	12	16	4	0	0	4	1	1	2	0	0	15	0	1	0	.457	.368
Hills, Christopher, But.	.217	31	109	92	15	20	23	3	0	0	13	2	2	5	8	0	30	2	1	0	.250	.308
Howard, Jason, Bil.	.190	6	23	21	2	4	5	1	0	0	3	0	0	1	1	0	7	0	0	0	.238	.261
Huff, Jake, I.F.	.315	30	128	108	25	34	53	7	0	4	29	0	1	2	17	0	25	0	0	1	.491	.414
Hurtado, Omar, Bil.	.260	60	248	223	33	58	96	18	4	4	35	0	5	0	19	0	56	3	1	4	.430	.312
Huth, Jason, Bil.†	.279	59	282	251	52	70	103	12	9	1	29	4	1	1	25	0	53	3	3	4	.410	.345
Ienni, Gregory, I.F.	.228	53	214	193	34	44	75	13	0	6	29	2	0	7	12	0	58	10	6	2	.389	.297
Jackson, Brandon, But.	.279	22	83	68	16	19	32	2	1	3	13	2	0	3	10	0	28	3	1	1	.471	.395
Jaramillo, Lee, Og.	.308	43	171	143	20	44	68	11	2	3	18	1	3	3	21	1	27	2	3	1	.476	.400
Juarez, Jonny, M.H.*	.255	29	119	102	11	26	30	1	0	1	10	7	2	0	8	0	14	8	2	2	.294	.304
Kalczynski, Joseph, Mis.	.197	23	74	61	12	12	19	4	0	1	8	0	0	2	11	0	17	2	0	2	.311	.338
Kenney, Jeff, Hel.	.261	48	202	153	40	40	64	8	2	4	29	1	2	9	37	0	33	8	4	3	.418	.428
King, Brennan, G.F.	.291	61	284	247	37	72	93	13	1	2	30	6	3	4	24	0	45	9	6	7	.377	.360
Kison, Robbie, Bil.	.148	9	34	27	4	4	4	0	0	0	2	0	0	1	6	0	4	0	0	1	.148	.324
Knox, Ryan, Hel.	.349	72	311	275	58	96	121	17	1	2	25	3	4	4	25	1	27	44	11	1	.440	.406
Koronka, John, Bil.*	.000	8	3	1	0	0	0	0	0	0	0	1	0	0	1	0	0	0	0	0	.000	.500
Leflore, Ronald, Bil.	.000	2	7	6	0	0	0	0	0	0	0	0	0	1	0	0	1	0	0	2	.000	.143
Lindsey, Cordell, But.	.341	63	284	255	72	87	154	23	7	10	58	0	1	4	23	0	46	13	5	5	.604	.403
Liriano, Ruddy, Bil.	.352	17	62	54	10	19	24	2	0	1	8	1	0	1	6	0	12	1	0	1	.444	.426
Lopez, Jose, Mis.	.571	5	18	14	5	8	17	4	1	1	3	0	1	1	2	0	1	0	0	0	1.214	.611
Lopez, Norberto, But.	.118	8	18	17	1	2	2	0	0	0	0	0	0	1	0	0	8	0	0	0	.118	.167
Martin, Brandon, But.*	.246	45	169	142	22	35	50	4	4	1	21	2	1	1	23	0	40	11	4	3	.352	.353
Martinez, Alejandro, Hel.†	.289	38	146	128	14	37	50	7	0	2	16	0	0	0	18	1	20	1	0	3	.391	.377
Martinez, Candido, G.F.	.234	69	296	265	43	62	88	8	3	4	42	2	1	6	22	0	87	11	2	3	.332	.306
Mayo, Terry, Hel.	.163	36	113	104	5	17	23	3	0	1	12	2	0	1	6	0	47	0	3	0	.221	.216
Mitchell, Brian, M.H.	.226	30	99	84	13	19	31	4	1	2	11	1	0	2	12	0	20	1	3	2	.369	.337
Montenegro, Jose, Og.	.259	18	57	54	8	14	17	3	0	0	4	0	0	1	2	0	8	0	0	3	.315	.298
Moore, Jason, I.F.†	.270	64	305	252	54	68	108	16	3	6	43	1	3	6	43	0	54	16	1	6	.429	.385
Motley, Brittan, I.F.†	.235	41	172	153	23	36	45	6	0	1	20	0	0	1	16	0	40	11	1	6	.294	.312
Myers, Corey, Mis.	.276	66	297	272	43	75	107	13	2	5	44	0	1	2	22	0	65	6	3	9	.393	.333
Noboa, Joel, Mis.	.111	5	19	18	1	2	2	0	0	0	2	0	0	0	1	0	9	1	0	0	.111	.158
Oglesby, Travis, Mis.	.000	3	5	5	0	0	0	0	0	0	0	0	0	0	0	0	2	0	0	0	.000	.000
Orgill, Peter, But.*	.323	58	257	217	43	70	95	8	1	5	36	0	2	12	26	1	38	0	0	6	.438	.420
Ortiz, Miguel, But.	.387	31	127	124	24	48	80	8	3	6	29	1	0	0	2	0	19	3	3	3	.645	.397
Overbay, Lyle, Mis.*	.343	75	352	306	66	105	180	25	7	12	101	0	4	2	40	2	53	10	3	14	.588	.418
Palomares, Luis, Og.	.247	66	249	223	40	55	88	4	1	9	34	5	2	1	18	0	59	10	5	6	.395	.303
Paterson, Joe, Og.	.245	35	105	94	11	23	33	4	0	2	20	1	1	0	9	0	26	0	2	3	.351	.308
Peters, Samone, Bil.	.225	29	119	111	13	25	55	3	0	9	23	0	2	1	5	0	57	0	0	0	.495	.261
Pichardo, Gilberto, But.	.234	41	152	137	32	32	54	6	2	4	16	2	1	3	9	0	39	2	0	4	.394	.293
Pregnalato, Bob, Og.	.331	42	159	130	34	43	61	7	1	3	14	3	1	7	18	0	19	14	4	2	.469	.436
Price, Duane, Bil.	.207	10	38	29	6	6	6	0	0	0	7	1	2	0	6	0	5	2	1	1	.207	.324
Quiroz, Guillermo, M.H.	.221	63	232	208	25	46	80	7	0	9	28	2	0	4	18	0	55	0	2	4	.385	.296
Ramirez, Frankelis, G.F.*	.292	74	316	281	39	82	106	9	3	3	42	4	5	3	22	3	34	7	4	5	.377	.344
Reimers, Cameron, M.H.	.000	13	1	1	0	0	0	0	0	0	0	0	0	0	0	0	0	0	0	0	.000	.000
Repko, Jason, G.F.	.304	49	233	207	51	63	114	9	9	8	32	1	1	3	21	0	43	12	5	1	.551	.375
Rewers, Nathan, Bil.†	.067	3	16	15	3	1	2	1	0	0	2	0	0	0	1	0	2	1	0	1	.133	.125
Reyes, Eduardo, Hel.	.291	66	253	223	51	65	101	12	3	6	33	1	2	8	19	0	38	13	4	3	.453	.365
Rios, Alexis, M.H.	.269	67	252	234	35	63	76	7	3	0	13	0	0	1	17	0	31	8	4	6	.325	.321
Rivera, Francisco, Bil.*	.214	31	121	112	11	24	31	1	0	2	15	1	2	2	4	0	14	2	0	5	.277	.250
Rizzo, Jeff, I.F.*	.206	29	131	97	19	20	33	3	2	2	19	1	7	5	21	0	28	3	0	0	.340	.354
Rodriguez, Hernandez, Bil.	.293	33	157	150	30	44	59	13	1	0	13	3	1	1	2	0	23	2	0	2	.393	.305
Rojas, Eliser, Hel.	.278	43	169	151	26	42	57	4	1	3	20	2	1	1	14	0	21	7	1	4	.377	.341
Roper, Douglas, M.H.	.248	45	160	137	20	34	45	7	2	0	10	2	0	0	20	0	25	8	2	0	.328	.344
Sampson, Jacob, G.F.	.265	37	118	102	17	27	41	6	1	2	17	1	0	3	12	0	24	7	3	1	.402	.359
Santora, Jack, Mis.†	.262	51	239	195	46	51	65	9	1	1	31	6	2	2	34	0	33	36	7	3	.333	.373
Santos, Luis, Mis.	.244	43	153	123	19	30	33	3	0	0	15	3	1	0	26	0	24	5	2	4	.268	.373
Scales, Bobby, I.F.†	.290	44	203	169	47	49	78	14	6	1	30	2	1	2	29	0	31	7	2	6	.462	.398
Scarborough, Steve, Og.-Hel.	.303	48	179	152	36	46	77	14	1	5	24	0	1	3	23	2	26	9	4	0	.507	.402
Schader, Troy, I.F.	.336	68	312	268	61	90	177	16	7	19	69	0	5	4	35	1	75	2	2	0	.660	.413
Schilling, Chris, Og.	.303	16	38	33	3	10	11	1	0	0	2	1	0	1	3	0	8	0	1	1	.333	.378
Schnall, Kevin, Bil.	.315	18	76	54	22	17	27	4	0	2	14	0	0	2	20	0	10	0	0	2	.500	.513
Sharp, Preston, But.†	.327	26	113	98	25	32	46	3	4	1	12	2	1	1	11	0	15	9	2	0	.469	.396
Sherlock, Brian, M.H.	.291	73	318	265	43	77	111	16	0	6	50	2	2	3	46	0	49	17	5	3	.419	.399
Snow, Christopher, G.F.	.275	12	41	40	9	11	13	0	1	0	2	0	0	0	1	0	4	2	1	1	.325	.293
Snyder, Michael, M.H.*	.209	62	228	196	30	41	57	7	0	3	19	0	0	1	31	1	47	3	4	3	.291	.320
Spoerl, Josh, Bil.	.287	66	289	258	43	74	115	15	1	8	45	0	1	6	24	0	64	1	0	9	.446	.360
Stone, Jonathon, I.F.†	.204	28	112	98	11	20	26	6	0	0	8	1	0	2	11	0	38	5	1	1	.265	.297
Story-Harden, Thomari, G.F.	.200	13	53	45	7	9	17	2	0	2	6	0	0	3	5	0	17	2	0	0	.378	.321
Stryhas, Paul, Hel.	.285	37	139	123	18	35	49	8	0	2	14	0	2	1	13	0	24	1	1	4	.398	.353
Templeton, Garry, But.	.204	33	107	93	16	19	19	0	0	0	11	2	1	3	8	0	28	4	1	0	.204	.286
Terrero, Luis, Mis.	.287	71	318	272	74	78	129	13	7	8	40	3	6	5	32	1	91	27	10	2	.474	.365
Thomas, Charles, G.F.	.253	54	223	194	32	49	77	11	4	3	23	4	1	2	22	0	48	10	2	1	.397	.333
Tindell, Matt, Hel.	.280	29	109	100	20	28	40	6	0	2	11	0	0	2	7	0	24	4	1	3	.400	.339
Tomaszewski, Dane, G.F.	.298	34	141	131	22	39	65	9	1	5	24	2	0	1	5	0	25	3	2	2	.496	.328
Trout, Casey, Og.	.246	49	158	142	14	35	43	5	0	1	11	1	0	1	14	0	26	2	3	1	.303	.318
Truitt, Steve, Hel.	.308	54	231	185	51	57	102	10	1	11	50	0	4	5	37	0	40	19	5	6	.551	.429
Van Buizen, Rodney, G.F.	.286	69	292	259	43	74	95	9	0	4	33	6	4	6	17	0	38	9	4	4	.367	.339
Victorino, Shane, G.F.	.280	55	254	225	53	63	88	7	6	2	25	6	3	0	20	0	31	20	5	3	.391	.335
Wagner, Jeffrey, But.	.382	8	34	34	7	13	23	4	0	2	10	0	0	0	0	0	5	0	0	2	.676	.382
Wallis, Jacob, Bil.	.234	26	104	94	10	22	28	6	0	0	12	0	1	1	8	0	31	0	0	3	.298	.298
Ward, Brian, I.F.	.317	68	326	287	50	91	139	23	2	7	60	0	4	3	32	2	46	6	3	7	.484	.387

Player, Team	Avg.	G	TPA	AB	R	H	TB	2B	3B	HR	RBI	SH	SF	HP	BB	IBB	SO	SB	CS	GDP	Slg.	OBP
Ward, Corey, Bil.	.269	49	184	167	24	45	69	7	4	3	19	3	1	1	12	0	49	8	4	0	.413	.320
Warren, Tom, Og.†	.149	35	107	87	14	13	18	5	0	0	3	2	0	5	13	0	34	5	2	1	.207	.295
Weber, Jon, Bil.*	.238	22	96	80	16	19	40	6	0	5	17	0	0	0	16	1	15	1	1	2	.500	.365
Weekly, Christopher, M.H.*	.300	71	290	257	43	77	117	18	2	6	42	1	2	1	29	0	43	12	2	6	.455	.370
Welch, Edward, But.*	.344	31	140	122	29	42	50	4	2	0	19	0	0	0	18	0	30	24	6	0	.410	.429
White, Gregory, But.	.327	55	238	205	37	67	113	15	2	9	47	0	3	4	26	1	50	1	2	5	.551	.408
Williford, Dan, Mis.*	.140	16	56	50	6	7	14	4	0	1	6	0	0	2	4	0	19	0	0	1	.280	.232

GRAND SLAMS: Ienni, Overbay, Terrero, 2 each; Bookout, Broussard, Castellano, Detienne, Huff, Schader, Spoerl, Victorino, Ward, Weber, 1 each.

AWARDED FIRST BASE ON CATCHER'S INTERFERENCE: Boykin 2 (Castellano, Closser); Motley 2 (De Los Santos, Schnall); Tomaszewski 2 (Ceriani, De Los Santos); Hurtado (Stone); Lindsey (Wallis); Ramirez (Rivera); Roper (Wallis).

PLAYERS WITH TWO OR MORE TEAMS

Player, Team	Avg.	G	TPA	AB	R	H	TB	2B	3B	HR	RBI	SH	SF	HP	BB	IBB	SO	SB	CS	GDP	Slg.	OBP
Buccheri, Joe, Hel.	.200	21	71	65	6	13	15	2	0	0	13	1	0	2	3	0	15	4	4	3	.231	.257
Buccheri, Joe, Og.	.190	10	27	21	3	4	4	0	0	0	1	0	0		6	0	5	0	1	0	.190	.370
Scarborough, Steve, Og.	.231	16	44	39	7	9	14	3	1	0	6	0	0	1	4	0	10	3	2	0	.359	.318
Scarborough, Steve, Hel.	.327	32	135	113	29	37	63	11	0	5	18	0	1	2	19	2	16	6	2	0	.558	.430

1999 PITCHING

TEAM

Team	W	L	Pct.	ERA	G	CG	ShO	Sv.	IP	H	TBF	R	ER	HR	SH	SF	HB	BB	IBB	SO	WP	Bk.
Helena	47	28	.627	4.31	75	6	3	22	651.1	633	2856	404	312	49	25	12	47	264	7	509	69	12
Missoula	45	31	.592	4.49	76	1	4	21	678.0	719	3034	457	338	53	23	11	51	255	6	593	73	10
Idaho Falls	48	27	.640	4.62	75	0	1	20	668.0	700	3001	440	343	44	25	23	39	299	2	634	87	10
Billings	42	33	.560	4.66	75	1	2	18	658.1	702	2959	444	341	43	19	28	49	275	3	577	53	13
Medicine Hat	33	43	.434	4.76	76	0	2	21	648.2	739	2949	449	343	69	25	28	34	264	2	586	77	16
Ogden	26	50	.342	5.56	76	3	1	11	663.1	787	3090	541	410	64	15	27	41	336	8	577	70	6
Great Falls	29	47	.382	5.84	76	4	1	9	663.0	755	3054	511	430	60	23	28	42	327	0	533	87	11
Butte	32	43	.427	6.66	75	1	0	12	647.2	812	3125	602	479	64	23	31	65	348	4	572	115	10

INDIVIDUAL

TOP QUALIFIERS FOR EARNED-RUN AVERAGE TITLE

Minimum 61 innings. *Lefthanded pitcher.

Pitcher, Team	W	L	Pct.	ERA	G	GS	CG	ShO	GF	Sv.	IP	H	TBF	R	ER	HR	SH	SF	HB	BB	IBB	SO	WP	Bk.
Mieses, Jose, Hel.	10	2	.833	2.67	15	15	3	1	0	0	108.0	79	425	36	32	5	1	0	28	0	87	6	3	
Robinson, Jeff, Og.-Hel.	5	2	.714	2.77	10	9	2	1	1	0	62.1	49	254	29	19	3	1	0	5	19	0	65	6	0
Chacin, Gustavo, M.H.*	4	3	.571	3.09	15	9	0	0	2	1	64.0	68	280	33	22	6	4	4	7	23	0	50	4	3
Sanchez, Duaner, Mis.	5	3	.625	3.13	13	11	0	0	0	0	63.1	54	269	34	22	3	1	1	3	23	0	51	8	0
Olean, Chris, Og.-Hel.	6	1	.857	3.50	16	8	2	0	5	4	61.2	60	260	36	24	3	5	4	0	15	2	30	2	0
Martin, Scott, G.F.	4	4	.500	3.86	16	15	2	0	0	0	102.2	115	435	55	44	11	3	4	3	23	0	69	1	1
Arieta, Corey, Hel.*	6	3	.667	3.86	15	15	1	0	0	0	88.2	83	386	51	38	5	2	2	6	27	0	60	7	1
Wood, Brandon, Mis.	6	0	1.000	3.88	19	9	0	0	3	0	72.0	69	325	46	31	4	3	0	11	31	1	71	4	2
Hamann, Robert, M.H.	2	8	.200	3.93	15	13	0	0	1	0	75.2	95	337	54	33	9	3	4	2	17	0	45	7	0
Stewart, Steve, Og.*	2	3	.400	3.95	13	10	0	0	1	0	70.2	73	310	47	31	6	1	2	3	27	0	50	6	0
Franke, Aaron, But.	4	5	.444	4.35	15	14	0	0	0	0	78.2	76	343	52	38	6	6	2	2	32	0	69	8	1
Williams, Adam, G.F.*	7	2	.778	4.36	15	14	0	0	0	0	88.2	70	370	45	43	6	1	2	8	35	0	95	8	1
Watkins, Steve, I.F.	5	2	.714	4.40	12	11	0	0	0	0	61.1	60	272	39	30	5	4	3	4	25	0	75	9	0
Miniel, Roberto, Og.	5	4	.556	4.41	15	14	1	0	0	0	85.2	98	387	58	42	5	3	5	5	34	0	77	7	1
Bevis, P.J., Mis.	6	2	.750	4.62	15	15	0	0	0	0	85.2	83	357	51	44	11	1	0	7	30	0	69	6	2

DEPARTMENTAL LEADERS: W—Mieses, 10; L—Harris, 9; Pct.—Wood, 1.000; G—Verdugo, 33; GS—Harris, 16; CG—Mieses, 3; ShO—several players tied, 1 each; GF—Verdugo, 32; Sv.—Verdugo, 13; IP—Mieses, 108.0; H—Harris, 132; TBF—Martin, 435; R—Harris, 95; ER—Harris, 76; HR—McClain, Hall, 13 each; SH—Franke, Hall, 6 each; SF—Darr, 6; HB—Gordon, 12; BB—Gomez, 50; IBB—House, 4; SO—Williams, 95; WP—Harris, Bowen, 15 each; BK—Burns, Cordero, 4 each.

ALL PITCHERS

*Lefthanded pitcher.

Pitcher, Team	W	L	Pct.	ERA	G	GS	CG	ShO	GF	Sv.	IP	H	TBF	R	ER	HR	SH	SF	HB	BB	IBB	SO	WP	Bk.
Aponte, Carlos, Hel.	2	3	.400	5.75	21	1	0	0	10	1	36.0	36	155	24	23	4	3	1	1	17	2	28	2	0
Arellan, Felix, G.F.*	1	2	.333	8.42	15	3	0	0	6	0	31.0	32	156	31	29	1	0	2	2	32	0	38	11	1
Arieta, Corey, Hel.*	6	3	.667	3.86	15	15	1	0	0	0	88.2	83	386	51	38	5	2	2	6	27	0	60	7	1
Baker, Christopher, M.H.	0	1	.000	3.12	3	1	0	0	1	0	8.2	8	37	4	3	0	0	0	1	2	0	9	1	1
Barbarossa, Joshua, I.F.*	1	0	1.000	2.89	3	3	0	0	0	0	9.1	8	39	4	3	1	0	0	0	4	0	7	0	0
Baxter, Gerik, I.F.	2	0	1.000	4.81	5	5	0	0	0	0	24.1	21	110	15	13	3	1	0	2	17	0	29	1	0
Bell, Casey, I.F.	3	6	.333	4.71	15	13	0	0	1	0	78.1	85	362	57	41	3	4	2	1	39	1	37	11	0
Bevis, P.J., Mis.	6	2	.750	4.62	15	15	0	0	0	0	85.2	83	357	51	44	11	1	0	7	30	0	69	6	2
Bowen, Patrick, But.	2	2	.500	7.64	20	7	0	0	0	0	55.1	81	287	59	47	9	3	5	8	35	0	48	15	0
Bradley, David, Bil.	5	4	.556	4.87	17	9	0	0	0	0	64.2	69	292	43	35	3	2	3	5	24	0	51	4	1
Brazoban, Jose, Hel.	0	0	.000	9.00	1	0	0	0	1	0	4	1	4	1	1	0	0	0	0	0	0	1	0	0
Briceno, Pablo, Hel.	1	4	.200	4.46	12	6	0	0	1	0	42.1	36	182	26	21	6	1	0	2	21	0	23	4	0
Bridenbaugh, Christian, G.F.*	0	6	.000	7.29	17	12	0	0	1	0	79.0	114	384	77	64	11	3	2	4	25	0	54	2	2
Brown, Zay, Bil.	3	3	.500	3.70	18	7	1	0	4	0	56.0	60	253	30	23	6	4	2	5	21	0	36	2	0
Brunet, Michael, But.	1	0	1.000	1.69	9	0	0	0	6	3	10.2	8	43	2	2	1	0	0	0	4	0	12	1	0
Bukowski, Stanislaw, But.	1	2	.333	3.21	10	5	0	0	1	0	28.0	26	124	13	10	0	1	3	3	16	0	29	1	1
Burkhart, B.J., Og.-Hel.*	2	1	.667	4.55	18	0	0	0	9	0	29.2	40	134	25	15	10	0	3	1	6	0	17	1	1
Burns, Casey, I.F.	1	2	.333	3.63	12	9	0	0	0	0	39.2	44	181	24	16	1	0	1	2	22	0	48	4	4
Bynum, Michael, I.F.*	1	0	1.000	0.00	5	3	0	0	0	0	17.0	7	60	0	0	0	1	0	0	4	0	21	0	0
Cardwell, Brian, M.H.	2	1	.667	5.16	10	4	0	0	2	1	29.2	34	137	22	17	5	1	1	4	8	0	26	3	1

Pitcher, Team	W	L	Pct.	ERA	G	GS	CG	ShO	GF	Sv.	IP	H	TBF	R	ER	HR	SH	SF	HB	BB	IBB	SO	WP	Bk.
Carmona, Cesarin, I.F.	4	1	.800	4.92	25	0	0	0	7	0	53.0	58	237	33	29	1	2	1	24	0	47	7	1
Castillo, Wilson, G.F.	1	3	.250	4.50	5	0	0	0	3	0	10.0	11	45	6	5	1	1	1	1	3	0	8	4	0
Chacin, Gustavo, M.H.*	4	3	.571	3.09	15	9	0	0	2	1	64.0	68	280	33	22	6	4	4	7	23	0	50	4	3
Charles, Juan, Og.	0	1	.000	11.88	6	0	0	0	5	0	8.1	18	45	11	11	2	0	0	0	4	0	8	0	0
Chighisola, Louis, Bil.*	0	2	.000	5.14	16	0	0	0	6	0	21.0	25	105	23	12	2	3	0	4	12	0	19	4	0
Childers, Jason, Og.	0	0	.000	1.38	3	0	0	0	0	0	13.0	10	50	4	2	1	0	0	1	3	0	14	1	0
Cooper, Eric, Bil.	1	1	.500	9.00	2	2	0	0	0	0	8.0	11	37	8	8	2	0	0	3	6	1	6	1	0
Cordero, Jesus, G.F.	0	5	.000	10.43	11	6	0	0	3	0	29.1	51	161	43	34	5	1	3	5	24	0	20	12	0
Cordero, Victor, Hel.	5	3	.625	6.92	22	0	0	0	7	1	40.1	45	193	39	31	6	2	2	6	22	1	41	7	4
Curtis, Mark, M.H.*	1	3	.250	6.89	10	5	0	0	1	0	31.1	47	152	29	24	7	1	1	0	15	0	36	10	1
Cyr, Eric, I.F.*	1	0	1.000	1.80	1	1	0	0	0	0	5.0	5	19	1	1	0	0	0	1	0	3	1	0
Darnell, Paul, Bil.*	3	3	.500	5.21	9	9	0	0	0	0	48.1	55	226	37	28	5	1	4	3	22	0	39	4	0
Darr, Jay, I.F.	2	1	.667	6.79	19	0	0	0	1	0	57.0	80	273	48	43	6	3	6	4	20	0	62	6	0
Davis, Billy, G.F.	0	0	.000	46.29	5	0	0	0	0	0	1.2	4	25	12	12	0	0	1	1	14	0	0	9	0
De Hart, Blair, I.F.	3	1	.750	3.20	10	10	0	0	0	0	56.1	50	237	28	20	4	3	3	2	17	0	43	2	2
De La Rosa, Jorge, Mis.*	0	1	.000	7.98	13	0	0	0	6	2	14.2	22	75	17	13	2	0	0	0	9	0	14	4	0
Detienne, Dave, G.F.	0	0	.000	18.00	1	0	0	0	0	0	1.0	3	7	2	2	0	0	0	1	1	0	0	0	0
Detwiler, James, M.H.*	0	0	.000	4.91	3	2	0	0	0	0	11.0	10	48	6	6	2	0	2	0	6	0	14	0	0
Devine, Travis, I.F.	1	2	.333	4.26	8	4	0	0	0	0	25.1	32	113	17	12	0	3	0	0	9	0	13	7	0
Dunn, Scott, Bil.	1	3	.250	4.31	9	8	0	0	0	0	39.2	36	178	24	19	3	0	1	3	24	0	36	3	2
Durkee, Jeremy, Og.*	2	3	.400	4.06	16	1	0	0	5	2	31.0	31	140	19	14	0	1	1	5	13	0	32	3	1
Eames, Todd, Mis.	2	1	.667	2.95	19	1	0	0	3	1	39.2	37	174	19	13	3	1	2	1	17	1	28	9	1
Easton, Eric, But.	0	1	.000	12.00	16	0	0	0	5	0	18.0	29	107	37	24	3	0	1	0	20	0	18	4	0
Erazo, Rafael, Bil.	2	1	.667	8.18	9	2	0	0	1	1	22.0	32	99	23	20	2	0	0	2	6	0	16	3	3
Escamilla, Paco, Bil.	3	0	1.000	3.54	5	5	0	0	0	0	28.0	18	113	11	11	0	1	0	2	9	0	33	2	0
Flading, Cameron, But.	1	0	1.000	7.24	20	0	0	0	4	0	27.1	39	140	26	22	0	3	7	17	0	19	6	0
Forbes, Derek, Mis.	3	1	.750	5.64	13	12	0	0	0	0	59.0	77	273	45	37	4	2	2	3	20	0	63	6	0
Ford, Matthew, M.H.*	4	1	.800	2.05	13	7	0	0	0	0	48.1	31	193	11	11	0	0	0	23	0	68	1	0
Franke, Aaron, But.	4	5	.444	4.35	15	15	0	0	0	0	78.2	76	343	52	38	6	6	2	2	32	0	69	8	1
Gaud, Perfecto, M.H.*	0	1	.000	8.27	14	2	0	0	4	0	20.2	23	103	22	19	3	0	1	4	16	1	26	4	0
Gentile, Mark, Mis.*	7	4	.636	5.88	15	14	0	0	0	0	78.0	100	361	62	51	5	3	3	2	25	0	45	5	2
Gomera, Rafael, G.F.	2	5	.286	11.05	19	2	0	0	7	3	36.2	64	200	54	45	1	0	4	6	24	0	23	10	2
Gomez, Odalis, But.	2	7	.222	10.22	22	5	0	0	6	0	37.0	44	211	58	42	3	0	1	5	50	1	42	11	3
Gordon, Justin, Hel.*	1	2	.333	6.03	15	4	0	0	5	0	31.1	31	160	31	21	3	0	0	12	29	0	36	13	1
Grater, Kevin, Hel.	1	1	.500	4.40	6	5	0	0	0	0	30.2	34	126	16	15	2	2	0	1	7	0	30	1	1
Greeny, Burdette, Og.	0	3	.000	9.00	5	0	0	0	4	0	12.0	20	62	13	12	2	0	0	1	6	0	7	2	0
Hamann, Robert, M.H.	2	8	.200	3.93	15	13	0	0	1	0	75.2	95	337	54	33	9	3	4	2	17	0	45	7	0
Hanson, David, M.H.	1	2	.333	5.32	14	7	0	0	2	0	45.2	64	217	33	27	1	2	1	2	21	0	35	2	2
Harris, J.T., But.	3	4	.429	4.35	23	0	0	0	8	0	39.1	43	173	25	19	3	2	0	2	13	0	34	5	0
Harris, Julian, But.*	2	9	.182	8.38	17	16	0	0	0	0	81.2	132	409	95	76	7	1	4	2	36	0	67	15	0
Harris, Toby, Mis.	1	3	.250	5.04	22	4	1	0	7	1	60.2	80	277	48	34	5	1	0	2	14	0	43	5	1
Haworth, Brent, But.	0	0	.000	10.38	5	0	0	0	3	1	4.1	4	23	6	5	0	0	1	2	4	0	3	0	0
Horne, Travis, Hel.*	1	0	1.000	7.94	3	2	0	0	0	0	5.2	5	27	5	5	1	0	0	0	9	0	2	1	0
Horney, Michael, Bil.	4	1	.800	2.81	8	0	0	0	5	1	16.0	15	67	6	5	0	0	0	4	4	0	11	2	1
Hosford, Clinton, G.F.	1	0	1.000	6.11	10	0	0	0	6	1	17.2	18	78	13	12	2	1	0	0	11	0	12	5	1
House, Jefferson, Og.	1	3	.250	8.18	17	0	0	0	8	0	33.0	47	169	41	30	3	3	2	3	19	4	31	7	0
Houston, Ryan, M.H.	3	4	.429	6.70	14	7	0	0	1	1	45.2	61	216	41	34	4	1	3	3	19	0	30	6	2
Hunter, Johnny, I.F.	3	4	.429	5.51	29	0	0	0	14	3	49.0	55	240	41	30	5	1	0	4	34	0	54	10	0
Kelley, Jason, Og.	2	3	.400	6.00	15	3	0	0	7	1	45.0	70	215	37	30	6	0	3	2	12	0	34	5	0
Koronka, John, Bil.*	2	3	.400	5.58	7	7	0	0	0	0	40.1	41	173	26	25	1	2	2	2	17	0	34	1	0
Krismer, Jeremy, Hel.	4	3	.571	4.86	12	9	0	0	1	0	46.1	49	198	26	25	5	1	1	5	17	0	27	4	0
Landkamer, Michael, Bil.	2	2	.500	7.06	20	0	0	0	10	1	21.2	23	104	17	17	0	0	2	1	19	0	19	1	0
Levy, Tye, Bil.*	0	0	.000	5.79	9	0	0	0	8	0	9.1	11	41	8	6	2	0	1	0	3	0	10	1	0
Lewis, Rickey, Og.	1	7	.125	7.24	11	11	0	0	0	0	59.2	75	284	53	48	4	2	1	5	44	0	35	4	0
Lugo, Ruddy, Og.	1	2	.333	7.88	6	6	0	0	0	0	24.0	35	117	23	21	2	1	0	1	12	0	26	1	0
Martin, Kelly, Bil.	2	0	1.000	4.66	5	3	0	0	0	0	19.1	16	81	13	10	4	0	3	0	8	0	25	1	0
Martin, Scott, G.F.	4	4	.500	3.86	16	15	2	0	0	0	102.2	115	435	55	44	11	3	4	3	23	0	69	1	1
Martinez, Luis, Og.*	0	7	.000	6.97	15	7	0	0	4	1	50.1	66	259	65	39	3	1	3	3	34	0	43	13	0
Matias, Adalberto, But.	3	5	.375	7.85	17	7	0	0	0	0	47.0	68	233	47	41	3	2	4	10	23	0	27	11	2
Matzenbacher, Brian, Mis.	3	3	.500	3.12	24	0	0	0	22	11	26.0	22	113	13	9	0	1	0	1	13	2	28	1	1
McClain, Kevin, But.	4	5	.444	8.95	18	11	0	0	1	0	58.1	85	297	67	58	13	2	2	10	28	1	51	9	0
McConnell, Gary, Og.	1	2	.333	5.24	17	0	0	0	7	0	34.1	38	166	24	20	5	1	3	2	28	2	34	5	0
McCullem, Ryan, M.H.*	2	1	.667	6.08	9	5	0	0	2	0	23.2	34	114	17	16	1	2	0	0	11	0	19	3	1
McEvoy, Casey, Hel.	4	0	1.000	2.18	5	5	0	0	0	0	33.0	28	133	10	8	1	0	0	2	7	0	35	2	1
McGee, Christopher, Og.	3	1	.750	3.00	17	0	0	0	17	7	24.0	18	97	8	8	0	0	2	1	7	1	28	2	0
Mendoza, Hatuey, Mis.	0	0	.000	0.00	1	0	0	0	1	0	3.0	3	15	5	0	0	0	0	2	0	3	3	0
Meyer, John, I.F.	0	1	.000	14.40	2	1	0	0	0	0	5.0	13	35	13	8	1	0	1	2	3	0	1	7	0
Mieses, Jose, Hel.	10	2	.833	2.67	15	15	3	1	0	0	108.0	79	425	36	32	5	1	0	1	28	0	87	6	3
Miniel, Roberto, Og.	5	4	.556	4.41	15	14	1	0	0	0	85.2	98	387	58	42	5	3	5	5	34	0	77	7	1
Montero, Oscar, Og.	2	7	.222	5.31	13	0	0	0	1	0	61.0	67	285	47	36	8	0	1	2	42	0	63	6	1
Mosher, Andy, Hel.	1	1	.500	5.61	24	0	0	0	21	12	25.2	25	118	17	16	3	0	0	15	2	30	4	0
Mowday, Chris, M.H.	2	6	.250	5.97	16	1	0	0	7	1	28.2	34	137	25	19	3	4	2	2	12	0	28	7	1
Myers, Todd, Mis.	0	0	.000	12.86	5	1	0	0	1	0	7.0	12	44	11	10	1	1	1	3	6	0	4	1	0
Nall, Thomas, G.F.	3	8	.273	4.95	15	14	2	0	0	0	92.2	115	401	60	51	13	6	3	5	13	0	70	2	0
Nanninga, Matthew, Bil.	1	3	.250	7.81	14	0	0	0	1	0	27.2	40	132	30	24	2	2	5	2	10	0	19	2	1
Neal, Brian, G.F.*	0	2	.000	5.79	15	4	0	0	7	1	32.2	32	156	23	21	1	2	1	2	29	0	23	7	1
Nebel, Jeffrey, But.	3	2	.600	4.06	29	0	0	0	23	5	31.0	34	139	15	14	2	0	0	4	12	0	26	7	0
Newman, Timothy, M.H.	1	0	1.000	4.73	23	0	0	0	7	2	26.2	26	121	21	14	5	1	0	13	1	29	5	0
Olean, Chris, Og.-Hel.	6	1	.857	3.50	16	8	2	0	5	4	61.2	60	260	36	24	3	6	0	15	2	30	2	0
Ortega, Carlos, G.F.*	3	3	.500	2.30	17	6	0	0	8	2	54.2	45	232	25	14	0	0	2	2	13	0	52	5	0
Ortiz, Omar, I.F.	2	1	.667	3.41	6	5	0	0	0	0	29.0	25	127	18	11	2	0	1	3	13	0	24	5	1
Pearson, Dale, G.F.*	1	1	.500	4.50	7	0	0	0	7	1	16.0	16	74	10	8	2	1	0	0	8	0	11	0	1
Peavy, Jacob, I.F.	2	0	1.000	1.64	3	0	0	0	2	0	11.0	5	40	0	0	0	0	0	0	1	0	13	0	0
Perez, George, M.H.	2	2	.500	5.79	15	8	0	0	3	1	56.0	65	258	46	36	9	3	0	4	26	0	41	8	0
Piedra, Alex, G.F.	3	2	.600	5.64	18	0	0	0	10	0	30.1	22	147	21	19	1	3	2	1	36	0	25	9	0

Pitcher, Team	W	L	Pct.	ERA	G	GS	CG	ShO	GF	Sv.	IP	H	TBF	R	ER	HR	SH	SF	HB	BB	IBB	SO	WP	Bk.
Pike, Thomas, Bil.	2	2	.500	3.00	26	0	0	0	24	12	27.0	31	127	18	9	1	1	0	1	12	0	28	6	0
Porter, Scott, M.H.	1	3	.250	5.49	18	0	0	0	17	8	19.2	23	95	16	12	1	0	0	1	10	0	29	2	0
Poturnicki, Adam, Hel.	3	0	1.000	4.79	16	2	0	0	4	0	35.2	37	167	27	19	2	2	1	3	16	0	32	5	1
Reece, Dana, M.H.*	2	1	.667	7.71	13	0	0	0	4	0	11.2	19	66	11	10	4	0	0	8	0	14	1	0
Reimers, Cameron, M.H.	1	5	.167	3.25	13	5	0	0	3	2	44.1	39	184	21	16	2	1	3	2	12	0	29	7	3
Robinson, Jeff, Og.-Hel.	5	2	.714	2.77	10	9	2	1	1	0	61.2	49	254	29	19	3	1	0	5	19	0	65	6	0
Rodriguez, Francisco, But.	1	1	.500	3.31	12	9	1	0	0	0	51.2	33	211	21	19	1	3	0	3	21	1	69	10	3
Rosario, Hipolito, I.F.	0	0	.000	4.50	2	0	0	0	1	0	4.0	3	17	2	2	0	0	0	0	2	0	2	1	0
Ross, Lew, Mis.*	4	3	.571	2.79	20	0	0	0	10	4	38.2	27	160	21	12	1	3	1	2	13	0	50	4	1
St. Amand, Reuben, M.H.	0	1	.000	6.11	15	0	0	0	4	0	28.0	31	133	23	19	5	0	2	1	17	0	24	4	1
Salmon, Bradley, Bil.	2	2	.500	7.48	16	6	0	0	2	1	49.1	67	239	46	41	2	2	4	6	19	1	43	2	3
Sampson, Jacob, G.F.	0	0	.000	9.00	1	0	0	0	1	0	1.0	2	6	1	1	0	0	0	0	0	0	0	0	0
Sanchez, Duaner, Mis.	5	3	.625	3.13	13	11	0	0	0	0	63.1	54	269	34	22	3	1	1	3	23	0	51	8	0
Sanchez, Sinuhe, But.*	3	3	.500	5.94	27	0	0	0	5	2	36.1	52	171	36	24	5	3	5	3	11	1	33	5	0
Schreyer, Brett, But.	0	0	.000	2.53	10	0	0	0	7	0	10.2	9	48	3	3	0	0	0	9	0	6	4	0
Sheets, Ben, Og.	0	1	.000	5.63	2	2	0	0	0	0	8.0	8	33	5	5	2	0	0	1	2	0	12	0	0
Shiyuk, Todd, I.F.*	5	0	1.000	5.67	23	0	0	0	10	4	39.2	46	184	30	25	5	2	1	5	17	1	49	2	1
Silverio, Marcelino, I.F.	7	3	.700	6.80	23	0	0	0	5	0	46.1	47	199	38	35	4	1	1	1	20	0	41	5	0
Simonson, Chris, Hel.	3	0	1.000	1.95	6	6	0	0	0	0	37.0	34	160	21	8	2	0	0	3	8	0	29	0	0
Smith, Jesse, Hel.	2	3	.400	4.35	19	1	0	0	9	3	31.0	37	149	23	15	0	1	4	16	1	29	5	0
Smith, Travis, Og.	0	0	.000	0.00	1	1	0	0	0	0	1.0	0	5	1	0	0	0	1	0	3	0	0
Springston, Adam, G.F.	1	1	.500	2.08	4	0	0	0	3	0	8.2	4	32	4	2	1	0	0	0	3	0	12	0	0
Stanley, Cody, Bil.	1	2	.333	3.65	26	0	0	0	10	2	37.0	43	186	36	15	2	0	4	1	24	2	35	7	1
Stanton, Timothy, Mis.*	3	3	.500	3.90	21	0	0	0	7	0	32.1	35	146	19	14	5	0	0	3	9	0	35	1	0
Stevens, Josh, M.H.	5	1	.833	2.45	23	0	0	0	17	4	29.1	27	121	14	8	2	2	1	5	0	34	2	0
Stewart, Cory, Bil.*	2	0	1.000	3.14	10	10	0	0	0	0	48.2	50	217	25	17	2	0	3	3	21	0	37	1	0
Stewart, Steve, Og.*	2	3	.400	3.95	13	10	0	0	1	0	70.2	73	310	47	31	6	1	2	3	27	0	50	6	0
Thompson, Travis, Bil.	1	0	1.000	0.00	8	0	0	0	3	0	20.2	14	72	1	0	0	0	3	0	27	4	0
Toropov, Alexandre, G.F.	0	0	.000	6.75	2	0	0	0	2	0	1.1	2	7	1	1	0	0	0	2	0	1	0	0
Torres, Manny, Bil.	1	1	.500	3.48	7	2	0	0	0	0	20.2	17	84	9	8	3	0	0	7	0	18	0	0
Verdugo, Oswaldo, I.F.	5	1	.833	2.35	33	0	0	0	32	13	38.1	34	155	13	10	2	0	3	2	9	0	54	4	1
Wagner, Frank, Hel.*	0	1	.000	12.71	11	0	0	0	1	1	11.1	18	70	19	16	0	1	0	2	16	0	6	5	1
Wakefield, Doug, Bil.*	0	0	.000	4.15	3	0	0	0	3	0	4.1	5	18	2	2	2	0	0	0	1	0	3	0	0
Walker, Josh, Hel.	0	0	.000	5.40	3	0	0	0	0	0	6.2	10	30	4	4	0	1	0	0	4	0	3	1	0
Wallace, Ben, Og.*	0	1	.000	9.78	16	2	0	0	7	0	23.0	37	124	33	25	3	1	1	0	25	0	13	3	2
Wallace, Jeffrey, G.F.*	0	0	.000	3.86	4	0	0	0	3	0	4.2	5	24	2	2	0	0	1	0	5	0	5	0	1
Warren, Joshua, But.	2	0	1.000	10.93	14	0	0	0	2	1	28.0	44	148	38	34	6	0	4	16	0	16	3	0
Watkins, Steve, I.F.	5	2	.714	4.40	12	11	0	0	0	0	61.1	60	272	39	30	5	4	3	4	25	0	75	9	0
Webster, Jeremy, I.F.*	0	2	.000	6.63	12	0	0	0	4	0	19.0	22	101	19	14	1	0	6	18	0	11	5	0
Williams, Adam, G.F.*	7	2	.778	4.36	15	14	0	0	0	0	88.2	70	370	45	43	6	1	2	8	35	0	95	8	1
Williams, Joel, G.F.	2	3	.400	8.34	13	0	0	0	4	1	22.2	30	114	26	21	3	1	0	1	16	0	15	2	0
Williamson, Charles, Mis.	2	2	.500	2.52	25	0	0	0	13	2	35.2	33	160	16	10	1	3	0	5	12	1	34	5	0
Wollscheid, James, Mis.	3	5	.375	5.78	18	9	0	0	2	0	62.1	65	285	50	40	8	3	1	8	31	1	55	11	0
Wood, Brandon, Mis.	6	3	.667	3.88	19	9	0	0	3	0	72.0	69	325	46	31	4	3	0	11	31	1	71	4	2

COMBINATION SHUTOUTS: Billings (2)—Escamilla-Chighisola, Bradley-Landkamer. Butte (0)—None. Great Falls (1)—Martin-Ortega. Helena (2)—Krismer-Aponte-Olean, Mieses-Gordon. Idaho Falls (1)—Barbarossa-Silverio-Shiyuk. Medicine Hat (2)—Hanson-Newman-Stevens, Hamann-Stevens. Missoula (4)—Sanchez-Matzenbacher, Sanchez-Stanton, Wood-Williamson-Harris-Ross-Matzenbacher. Ogden (0)—None.

NO-HIT GAMES: None.

PITCHERS WITH TWO OR MORE TEAMS

Pitcher, Team	W	L	Pct.	ERA	G	GS	CG	ShO	GF	Sv.	IP	H	TBF	R	ER	HR	SH	SF	HB	BB	IBB	SO	WP	Bk.
Burkhart, B.J., Og.*	1	0	1.000	4.98	10	0	0	0	5	0	21.2	27	102	21	12	9	0	3	1	5	0	13	0	1
Burkhart, B.J., Hel.*	1	1	.500	3.38	8	0	0	0	4	0	8.0	13	32	4	3	1	0	0	1	0	4	1	0
Olean, Chris, Og.	0	0	.000	18.00	2	0	0	0	1	0	3.0	4	17	6	6	0	0	0	3	1	3	0	0
Olean, Chris, Hel.	6	1	.857	2.76	14	8	2	0	4	4	58.2	56	243	30	18	3	5	4	0	12	1	27	2	0
Robinson, Jeff, Og.	5	2	.714	2.96	9	8	2	1	1	0	54.2	45	223	25	18	3	1	0	4	16	0	51	5	0
Robinson, Jeff, Hel.	0	0	.000	1.29	1	1	0	0	0	0	7.0	4	31	4	1	0	0	1	3	0	14	1	0

1999 FIELDING

TEAM

Team	Pct.	G	PO	A	E	TC	DP	TP	PB	Team	Pct.	G	PO	A	E	TC	DP	TP	PB
Great Falls	.953	76	1989	860	139	2988	74	0	15	Medicine Hat	.951	76	1946	810	142	2898	57	0	18
Helena	.953	75	1954	819	136	2909	57	0	21	Butte	.947	75	1943	721	150	2814	53	0	19
Idaho Falls	.953	75	2004	829	139	2972	75	0	18	Missoula	.942	76	2034	896	179	3109	54	0	19
Billings	.952	75	1975	797	139	2911	73	0	21	Ogden	.938	76	1990	799	185	2974	90	0	24

INDIVIDUAL

FIRST BASEMEN

NOTE: All caps denotes fielding-percentage leader based on 38 games for catchers, 51 for all other non-pitchers and 61 innings for pitchers. *Throws lefthanded.

Player, Team	Pct.	G	PO	A	E	TC	DP
Bookout, Casey, Bil.	.987	41	363	9	5	377	29
Broussard, Benjamin, Bil.*	.976	8	75	6	2	83	11
Ceriani, Matt, Hel.	1.000	2	0	1	0	1	0
Cornett, Robert, M.H.	.995	21	175	17	1	193	16
Correa, Nelson, Og.*	.978	36	290	15	7	312	27
Curry, Jesse, I.F.*	.971	47	384	19	12	415	29

Player, Team	Pct.	G	PO	A	E	TC	DP
Dehner, Matthew, Bil.	1.000	1	11	0	0	11	2
Forelli, Anthony, Og.	.976	42	342	22	9	373	48
Frank, Nick, Og.	1.000	4	32	2	0	34	3
Freeman, Thomas, Mis.*	1.000	2	22	2	0	24	3
Garcia, Hector, Hel.	.980	67	596	39	13	648	48
Garrett, Shawn, I.F.	.969	32	266	19	9	294	31
Gosewisch, Ian, But.	.929	3	12	1	1	14	0
Huff, Jake, I.F.	.950	2	18	1	1	20	1
Huth, Jason, Bil.	.955	6	38	4	2	44	3
Juarez, Jonny, M.H.*	1.000	1	2	0	0	2	0

Player, Team	Pct.	G	PO	A	E	TC	DP
Kenney, Jeff, Hel.	1.000	2	17	0	0	17	3
Martin, Brandon, But.	.000	2	0	0	0	0	0
Martinez, Alejandro, Hel.	.965	10	79	3	3	85	4
Orgill, Peter, But.	.986	43	314	30	5	349	22
Ortiz, Miguel, But.	1.000	4	13	1	0	14	2
OVERBAY, Lyle, Mis.*	.986	68	641	46	10	697	43
Ramirez, Frankelis, G.F.*	.981	71	624	59	13	696	64
Rivera, Francisco, Bil.	.968	4	29	1	1	31	6
Rizzo, Jeff, I.F.	1.000	1	1	0	0	1	0
Sharp, Preston, But.	.000	1	0	0	0	0	0
Sherlock, Brian, M.H.	.981	57	481	30	10	521	36
Spoerl, Josh, Bil.	.970	17	151	9	5	165	12
Story-Harden, Thomari, G.F.	.000	1	0	0	0	0	0
Tomaszewski, Dane, G.F.	.982	6	52	3	1	56	5
Trout, Casey, Og.	1.000	2	7	1	0	8	1
White, Gregory, But.	.986	32	260	12	4	276	23
Williford, Dan, Mis.*	1.000	7	48	4	0	52	4

SECOND BASEMEN

Player, Team	Pct.	G	PO	A	E	TC	DP
Amezaga, Alfredo, But.	1.000	6	9	12	0	21	1
Ayala, Elio, Og.	.935	61	123	150	19	292	41
Buccheri, Joe, Hel.-Og.	.978	12	13	31	1	45	5
Burnett, Mark, Bil.	.963	52	105	153	10	268	38
Cruz, Hector, Mis.	.911	12	16	35	5	56	5
Detienne, Dave, G.F.	.955	5	6	15	1	22	1
Duran, Francisco, But.	.937	35	64	84	10	158	19
Ernster, Mark, Og.	1.000	5	6	13	0	19	3
Geraldo, Anulfo, Hel.	.967	40	78	99	6	183	22
Gosewisch, Ian, But.	.947	6	11	7	1	19	1
Huth, Jason, Bil.	.880	7	10	12	3	25	2
Kenney, Jeff, Hel.	.967	6	18	11	1	30	1
Kison, Robbie, Bil.	.884	9	12	26	5	43	5
Liriano, Ruddy, Bil.	.875	6	7	21	4	32	2
Mitchell, Brian, M.H.	.873	15	23	32	8	63	5
Montenegro, Jose, Og.	1.000	1	1	2	0	3	1
Ortiz, Miguel, But.	.906	9	8	21	3	32	1
Rewers, Nathan, Bil.	.917	3	3	8	1	12	4
Rizzo, Jeff, I.F.	1.000	3	6	2	0	8	1
Rojas, Eliser, Hel.	.992	29	52	77	1	130	19
Sampson, Jacob, G.F.	.963	8	8	18	1	27	5
Santora, Jack, Mis.	.918	51	93	132	20	245	18
Santos, Luis, Mis.	.974	18	38	38	2	78	11
Scales, Bobby, I.F.	.950	38	79	110	10	199	20
Sharp, Preston, But.	.848	10	10	18	5	33	2
Templeton, Garry, But.	.911	20	19	32	5	56	7
Trout, Casey, Og.	.951	9	23	16	2	41	6
VAN BUIZEN, Rodney, G.F.	.991	67	139	197	3	339	47
Ward, Brian, I.F.	.950	38	81	111	10	202	28
Weekly, Christopher, M.H.	.939	66	139	169	20	328	36

SECOND BASEMEN WITH TWO OR MORE TEAMS

Player, Team	Pct.	G	PO	A	E	TC	DP
Buccheri, Joe, Hel.	.958	5	8	15	1	24	2
Buccheri, Joe, Og.	1.000	7	5	16	0	21	3

THIRD BASEMEN

Player, Team	Pct.	G	PO	A	E	TC	DP
Ayala, Elio, Og.	.600	3	1	2	2	5	1
Brooks, Jeff, Mis.	.828	70	51	141	40	232	6
Burnett, Mark, Bil.	.800	4	3	5	2	10	0
Cosby, Robert, M.H.	.909	32	20	60	8	88	4
Dehner, Matthew, Bil.	.902	33	15	59	8	82	6
Detienne, Dave, G.F.	.969	9	7	24	1	32	0
Duran, Francisco, But.	.913	8	8	13	2	23	1
Frank, Nick, Og.	.895	37	29	65	11	105	5
Garrett, Shawn, I.F.	.905	9	4	15	2	21	0
Geraldo, Anulfo, Hel.	.882	6	4	11	2	17	1
Gutierrez, Roberto, M.H.	1.000	4	1	8	0	9	0
Guzman, Alexis, M.H.	1.000	1	2	1	0	3	0
Huth, Jason, Bil.	.914	33	24	61	8	93	10
Jaramillo, Lee, Og.	.878	14	10	26	5	41	1
Kenney, Jeff, Hel.	.867	8	6	20	4	30	2
King, Brennan, G.F.	.907	53	42	95	14	151	9
LINDSEY, Cordell, But.	.910	57	45	96	14	155	9
Mitchell, Brian, M.H.	.857	1	2	4	1	7	0
Montenegro, Jose, Og.	1.000	4	2	5	0	7	0
Myers, Corey, Mis.	.800	6	5	15	5	25	0
Noboa, Joel, Mis.	1.000	1	3	3	0	6	1
Ortiz, Miguel, But.	.783	10	6	12	5	23	0
Reyes, Eduardo, Hel.	.860	43	20	91	18	129	8

Player, Team	Pct.	G	PO	A	E	TC	DP
Rizzo, Jeff, I.F.	.865	12	7	25	5	37	1
Rojas, Eliser, Hel.	.846	7	4	7	2	13	0
Roper, Douglas, M.H.	.909	7	3	7	1	11	1
Santos, Luis, Mis.	.000	2	0	0	1	1	0
Scarborough, Steve, Og.	.800	8	9	15	6	30	7
Schader, Troy, I.F.	.862	35	12	44	9	65	2
Snyder, Michael, M.H.	.862	38	20	61	13	94	5
Spoerl, Josh, Bil.	.769	6	1	9	3	13	1
Stryhas, Paul, Hel.	.809	20	14	24	9	47	1
Thomas, Charles, G.F.	.800	12	11	21	8	40	3
Trout, Casey, Og.	.894	22	18	24	5	47	3
Van Buizen, Rodney, G.F.	.750	3	4	2	2	8	0
Ward, Brian, I.F.	.868	23	15	44	9	68	6
White, Gregory, But.	1.000	5	4	8	0	12	0

SHORTSTOPS

Player, Team	Pct.	G	PO	A	E	TC	DP
Amezaga, Alfredo, But.	1.000	2	6	6	0	12	2
Buccheri, Joe, Hel.	.900	5	3	6	1	10	2
Burnett, Mark, Bil.	.000	1	0	0	0	0	0
Campana, Wandel, Bil.	.941	44	79	129	13	221	26
Dehner, Matthew, Bil.	.905	23	34	90	13	137	25
Detienne, Dave, G.F.	.939	30	49	89	9	147	25
Duran, Francisco, But.	.915	18	26	39	6	71	4
Gastelum, Carlos, But.	.906	58	93	158	26	277	29
Guzman, Alexis, M.H.	.931	44	54	121	13	188	19
Hall, William, Og.	.894	65	115	204	38	357	48
Huth, Jason, Bil.	.884	9	10	28	5	43	1
Kenney, Jeff, Hel.	.917	20	30	58	8	96	10
Lindsey, Cordell, But.	1.000	3	2	6	0	8	0
Moore, Jason, I.F.	.890	58	91	177	33	301	40
MYERS, Corey, Mis.	.919	58	76	196	24	296	27
Repko, Jason, G.F.	.859	49	88	144	38	270	24
Reyes, Eduardo, Hel.	.906	22	42	64	11	117	6
Rizzo, Jeff, I.F.	.000	1	0	0	0	0	0
Roper, Douglas, M.H.	.953	38	60	121	9	190	17
Sampson, Jacob, G.F.	.500	1	1	0	1	2	0
Santos, Luis, Mis.	.940	23	31	63	6	100	10
Scarborough, Steve, Og.-Hel.	.934	40	60	111	12	183	20
Schader, Troy, I.F.	.918	19	30	59	8	97	17
Snyder, Michael, M.H.	.000	1	0	0	0	0	0
Trout, Casey, Og.	.818	10	12	24	8	44	6

SHORTSTOPS WITH TWO OR MORE TEAMS

Player, Team	Pct.	G	PO	A	E	TC	DP
Scarborough, Steve, Og.	.917	8	2	9	1	12	2
Scarborough, Steve, Hel.	.936	32	58	102	11	171	18

OUTFIELDERS

Player, Team	Pct.	G	PO	A	E	TC	DP
Boykin, Paul, I.F.	.980	41	45	4	1	50	2
Brazoban, Jose, Hel.	.955	44	59	4	3	66	0
Broussard, Benjamin, Bil.*	.942	31	47	2	3	52	1
Buccheri, Joe, Hel.	1.000	3	2	1	0	3	0
Burns, Kevan, Mis.*	1.000	7	12	0	0	12	0
Bystrowski, Robby, I.F.	.949	38	56	0	3	59	0
Castellano, John, G.F.	1.000	2	1	0	0	1	0
Clark, Chivas, M.H.*	.927	69	99	3	8	110	1
Conyer, Darryl, Mis.*	.924	45	70	3	6	79	0
Curtis, William, But.	.953	38	40	1	2	43	0
De Los Santos, Nelson, Og.	.500	2	1	0	1	2	0
Devore, Doug, Mis.*	.929	31	37	2	3	42	0
Diaz, Michael, But.*	.957	14	19	3	1	23	0
Donovan, Todd, I.F.	.978	48	81	6	2	89	2
Doucet, Brandon, Hel.	.965	41	53	2	2	57	0
Duverge, Alcides, But.	.000	1	0	0	0	0	0
Escalera, Jose, G.F.	.929	26	36	3	3	42	0
Fera, Aaron, M.H.	.963	52	73	4	3	80	1
Ford, Will, Og.*	.972	44	67	2	2	71	0
Frank, Nick, Og.	1.000	2	3	0	0	3	0
Garrett, Shawn, I.F.	1.000	8	11	0	0	11	0
Godbolt, Keith, G.F.	.911	29	40	1	4	45	0
Goldfield, Josh, Mis.	.926	16	22	3	2	27	0
Graham, Justin, Mis.	.913	15	20	1	2	23	0
Guerrero, Cristian, Og.	.942	61	95	3	6	104	1
Gutierrez, Roberto, M.H.	1.000	2	1	0	0	1	0
Hall, Victor, Mis.*	.937	34	56	3	4	63	1
Hills, Christopher, Bil.	.942	29	46	3	3	52	1
Hurtado, Omar, Bil.	.972	59	98	5	3	106	3
Huth, Jason, Bil.	.750	4	6	0	2	8	0
Ienni, Gregory, I.F.	.954	52	91	12	5	108	2

SUMMER CLASS A *Pioneer League*

Player, Team	Pct.	G	PO	A	E	TC	DP
Jackson, Brandon, But.*	.923	22	48	0	4	52	0
Juarez, Jonny, M.H.*	.862	28	23	2	4	29	0
Knox, Ryan, Hel.	.942	69	110	3	7	120	1
Leflore, Ronald, Bil.	1.000	2	1	0	0	1	0
Liriano, Ruddy, Bil.	.857	10	5	1	1	7	1
Martin, Brandon, But.	.928	41	85	5	7	97	1
Martinez, Candido, G.F.	.899	66	81	8	10	99	1
Mayo, Terry, Hel.	.939	36	46	0	3	49	0
Mitchell, Brian, M.H.	1.000	12	12	1	0	13	1
Motley, Brittan, I.F.	.986	41	70	1	1	72	0
Noboa, Joel, Mis.	.000	3	0	0	0	0	0
Overbay, Lyle, Mis.*	1.000	5	6	0	0	6	0
Palomares, Luis, Og.	.944	65	95	7	6	108	1
Paterson, Joe, Og.	.939	23	30	1	2	33	0
Peters, Samone, Bil.	.935	16	26	3	2	31	0
Pichardo, Gilberto, But.	.956	39	59	6	3	68	1
Pregnalato, Bob, Og.	.909	35	49	1	5	55	0
Price, Duane, Bil.	1.000	9	13	1	0	14	0
Ramirez, Frankelis, G.F.*	1.000	3	1	0	0	1	0
Reyes, Eduardo, Hel.	.000	1	0	0	0	0	0
Rios, Alexis, M.H.	.955	67	123	3	6	132	0
Rizzo, Jeff, I.F.	1.000	5	2	1	0	3	0
Rodriguez, Hernandez, Bil.	.943	30	63	4	4	70	0
Rojas, Eliser, Hel.	.000	1	0	0	0	0	0
Sampson, Jacob, G.F.	.900	26	26	1	3	30	0
Sharp, Preston, But.	1.000	15	21	1	0	22	0
Snow, Christopher, G.F.	1.000	9	15	0	0	15	0
Snyder, Michael, M.H.	.900	8	9	0	1	10	0
Spoerl, Josh, Bil.	1.000	2	1	0	0	1	0
Stone, Jonathon, I.F.	1.000	1	1	0	0	1	0
Story-Harden, Thomari, G.F.	1.000	1	1	0	0	1	0
Templeton, Garry, But.	.867	13	11	2	2	15	0
Terrero, Luis, Mis.	.928	71	129	12	11	152	2
Thomas, Charles, G.F.	.976	27	33	7	1	41	0
Trout, Casey, Og.	1.000	4	1	0	0	1	0
Truitt, Steve, Hel.	.963	52	98	7	4	109	1
VICTORINO, Shane, G.F.	.986	55	125	14	2	141	3
Ward, Corey, Mis.	.951	48	96	2	5	103	0
Warren, Tom, Og.	.793	28	23	0	6	29	0
Weber, Jon, Bil.*	.951	22	35	4	2	41	0
Welch, Edward, But.	.962	31	75	1	3	79	0
White, Gregory, But.	1.000	6	9	0	0	9	0
Williford, Dan, Mis.*	.750	3	3	0	1	4	0

CATCHERS

Player, Team	Pct.	G	PO	A	E	TC	DP	PB
Castellano, John, G.F.	.987	35	267	31	4	302	1	7
CERIANI, Matt, Hel.	.984	56	328	42	6	376	2	6
Closser, J.D., Mis.	.964	65	492	74	21	587	4	16
Cornett, Robert, M.H.	1.000	2	11	0	0	11	0	0
Cosentino, Tony, I.F.	1.000	10	84	10	0	94	0	1
Curry, Zane, G.F.	.984	24	162	17	3	182	2	3
De Los Santos, Nelson, Og.	.965	36	219	30	9	258	1	8
Duverge, Alcides, But.	.945	23	174	15	11	200	1	7
Fierro, Robert, M.H.	.986	20	127	12	2	141	2	3
Foster, Brian, Hel.	.937	12	51	8	4	63	0	8
Goldfield, Josh, Mis.	.984	6	53	8	1	62	0	1
Gosewisch, Ian, But.	.979	37	256	21	6	283	2	3
Gutierrez, Said, I.F.	.996	26	210	32	1	243	4	2
Haver, Lance, Bil.	1.000	8	64	6	0	70	3	3
Howard, Jason, Bil.	.975	6	34	5	1	40	1	2
Huff, Jake, I.F.	.983	19	155	17	3	175	2	8
Jaramillo, Lee, Og.	.969	28	186	30	7	223	2	11
Kalczynski, Joseph, Mis.	1.000	8	39	5	0	44	0	0
Lopez, Jose, Mis.	.917	2	10	1	1	12	0	2
Lopez, Norberto, But.	.966	8	53	3	2	58	1	3
Montenegro, Jose, Og.	.972	15	91	12	3	106	2	5
Oglesby, Travis, Mis.	1.000	3	5	0	0	5	0	0
Orgill, Peter, But.	.956	15	97	11	5	113	1	6
Quiroz, Guillermo, M.H.	.981	61	452	58	10	520	4	15
Rivera, Francisco, Bil.	.976	24	150	14	4	168	2	4
Schilling, Chris, Og.	.947	16	74	15	5	94	1	0
Schnall, Kevin, Bil.	.973	17	130	14	4	148	0	3
Stone, Jonathon, I.F.	.971	26	176	23	6	205	1	7
Tindell, Matt, Hel.	.962	23	139	12	6	157	0	7
Tomaszewski, Dane, G.F.	.979	17	124	17	3	144	1	5
Wallis, Jacob, Bil.	.971	26	208	24	7	239	1	9

PITCHERS

Player, Team	Pct.	G	PO	A	E	TC	DP
Aponte, Carlos, Hel.	.800	21	1	3	1	5	0
Arellan, Felix, G.F.*	.875	15	4	3	1	8	0

Player, Team	Pct.	G	PO	A	E	TC	DP
Arieta, Corey, Hel.*	.944	15	2	15	1	18	1
Baker, Christopher, M.H.	1.000	3	1	0	0	1	0
Barbarossa, Joshua, I.F.*	1.000	3	1	0	0	1	0
Baxter, Gerik, I.F.	1.000	5	1	3	0	4	0
Bell, Casey, I.F.	.947	15	3	15	1	19	0
Bevis, P.J., Mis.	.923	15	7	17	2	26	2
Bowen, Patrick, But.	1.000	20	5	9	0	14	1
Bradley, David, Bil.	.692	17	2	7	4	13	0
Brazoban, Jose, Hel.	.000	1	0	0	0	0	0
Briceno, Pablo, Hel.	.833	12	1	4	1	6	0
Bridenbaugh, Christian, G.F.*	1.000	17	1	12	0	13	0
Brown, Zay, Bil.	.941	18	4	12	1	17	0
Brunet, Michael, But.	1.000	9	0	2	0	2	0
Bukowski, Stanislaw, But.	1.000	10	3	4	0	7	0
Burkhart, B.J., Og.-Hel.*	.857	18	4	2	1	7	0
Burns, Casey, I.F.	.800	12	1	3	1	5	1
Bynum, Michael, I.F.*	1.000	5	2	2	0	4	0
Cardwell, Brian, M.H.	.800	10	0	4	1	5	0
Carmona, Cesarin, I.F.	1.000	25	3	12	0	15	1
Castillo, Wilson, G.F.	1.000	5	0	1	0	1	0
Chacin, Gustavo, M.H.*	.958	15	6	17	1	24	1
Charles, Juan, Og.	.000	6	0	0	0	0	0
Chighisola, Louis, Bil.*	.333	16	0	1	2	3	0
Childers, Jason, Og.	1.000	3	0	2	0	2	0
Cooper, Eric, Bil.	.000	2	0	0	0	0	0
Cordero, Jesus, G.F.	.833	11	0	5	1	6	0
Cordero, Victor, Hel.	1.000	22	1	9	0	10	0
Curtis, Mark, M.H.*	.600	10	0	6	4	10	0
Cyr, Eric, I.F.*	.000	1	0	0	0	0	0
Darnell, Paul, Bil.*	1.000	9	1	8	0	9	0
Darr, Jay, I.F.	.929	19	2	11	1	14	0
Davis, Billy, G.F.	.667	5	2	0	1	3	0
De Hart, Blair, I.F.	1.000	10	1	6	0	7	1
De La Rosa, Jorge, Mis.*	1.000	13	2	1	0	3	0
Detienne, Dave, G.F.	.000	1	0	0	0	0	0
Detwiler, James, M.H.*	1.000	3	2	2	0	4	1
Devine, Travis, I.F.	1.000	8	1	6	0	7	1
Dunn, Scott, Bil.	1.000	9	3	7	0	10	1
Durkee, Jeremy, Og.*	1.000	16	0	7	0	7	0
Eames, Todd, Mis.	.875	19	3	4	1	8	0
Easton, Eric, But.	1.000	16	1	1	0	2	0
Erazo, Rafael, Bil.	.500	9	0	1	1	2	0
Escamilla, Paco, Bil.	1.000	5	3	4	0	7	0
Flading, Cameron, But.	1.000	20	3	1	0	4	0
Forbes, Derek, Mis.	.750	13	3	9	4	16	1
Ford, Matthew, M.H.*	1.000	13	1	1	0	2	0
Franke, Aaron, But.	.895	15	2	15	2	19	0
Gaud, Perfecto, M.H.*	1.000	14	0	3	0	3	0
Gentile, Mark, Mis.*	.960	15	5	19	1	25	3
Gomera, Rafael, G.F.	.786	19	5	6	3	14	0
Gomez, Odalis, But.	.818	22	2	7	2	11	0
Gordon, Justin, M.H.*	.727	15	1	7	3	11	0
Grater, Kevin, Hel.	1.000	6	4	3	0	7	0
Greeny, Burdette, Og.	1.000	5	1	2	0	3	0
Hamann, Robert, M.H.	.647	15	3	8	6	17	0
Hanson, David, M.H.	.929	14	6	7	1	14	0
Harris, J.T., But.	.833	23	1	4	1	6	0
Harris, Julian, But.*	.905	17	4	15	2	21	1
Harris, Toby, Mis.	.875	22	5	16	3	24	1
Haworth, Brent, But.	1.000	5	0	1	0	1	0
Horne, Travis, Hel.*	1.000	3	0	3	0	3	0
Horney, Michael, Bil.	1.000	8	1	4	0	5	1
Hosford, Clinton, G.F.	.800	10	1	3	1	5	0
House, Jefferson, Og.	.250	17	0	1	3	4	0
Houston, Ryan, M.H.	.833	14	2	8	2	12	0
Hunter, Johnny, I.F.	.846	29	3	8	2	13	2
Kelley, Jason, Og.	.857	15	2	4	1	7	1
Koronka, John, Bil.*	1.000	7	0	4	0	4	0
Krismer, Jeremy, Hel.	1.000	12	4	8	0	12	0
Landkamer, Michael, Bil.	1.000	20	1	1	0	2	0
Levy, Tye, Bil.*	1.000	9	1	0	0	1	0
Lewis, Rickey, Og.	.923	11	4	8	1	13	1
Lugo, Ruddy, Og.	.750	6	1	2	1	4	0
Martin, Kelly, Bil.	1.000	5	1	4	0	5	0
MARTIN, Scott, G.F.	1.000	16	9	12	0	21	1
Martinez, Luis, Og.*	1.000	15	0	4	0	4	0
Matias, Adalberto, But.	.867	17	6	7	2	15	1
Matzenbacher, Brian, Mis.	1.000	24	1	1	0	2	0
McClain, Kevin, But.	.714	18	1	4	2	7	0
McConnell, Gary, Og.	.857	17	4	2	1	7	1
McCullem, Ryan, M.H.*	1.000	9	0	4	0	4	0
McEvoy, Casey, Bil.	1.000	5	1	4	0	5	0
McGee, Christopher, Og.	1.000	17	3	3	0	6	0
Mendoza, Hatuey, Mis.	1.000	1	2	1	0	3	1

Player, Team	Pct.	G	PO	A	E	TC	DP
Meyer, John, I.F.	.750	2	0	3	1	4	0
Mieses, Jose, Hel.	.935	15	9	20	2	31	2
Miniel, Roberto, Og.	.739	15	2	15	6	23	3
Montero, Oscar, Og.	.824	13	2	12	3	17	0
Mosher, Andy, Hel.	1.000	24	2	7	0	9	0
Mowday, Chris, M.H.	.714	16	3	2	2	7	1
Myers, Todd, Mis.	1.000	5	1	3	0	4	0
Nall, Thomas, G.F.	.909	15	4	16	2	22	1
Nanninga, Matthew, Bil.	1.000	14	0	3	0	3	0
Neal, Brian, G.F.*	1.000	15	2	6	0	8	0
Nebel, Jeffrey, But.	.857	29	3	3	1	7	1
Newman, Timothy, M.H.	1.000	23	1	1	0	2	0
Olean, Chris, Og.-Hel.	.923	16	5	7	1	13	1
Ortega, Carlos, G.F.*	.917	17	3	8	1	12	1
Ortiz, Omar, I.F.	1.000	6	0	3	0	3	0
Pearson, Dale, G.F.*	.857	7	1	5	1	7	0
Peavy, Jacob, I.F.	1.000	2	0	2	0	2	0
Perez, George, M.H.	1.000	15	3	12	0	15	0
Piedra, Alex, G.F.	.857	18	4	2	1	7	0
Pike, Thomas, Bil.	1.000	26	1	2	0	3	0
Porter, Scott, M.H.	1.000	18	1	2	0	3	0
Poturnicki, Adam, Hel.	1.000	16	3	5	0	8	1
Reece, Dana, M.H.*	.500	13	1	1	2	4	0
Reimers, Cameron, M.H.	.846	13	2	9	2	13	0
Robinson, Jeff, Og.-Hel.	1.000	10	3	8	0	11	0
Rodriguez, Francisco, But.	.941	12	6	10	1	17	0
Rosario, Hipolito, I.F.	.500	2	0	1	1	2	0
Ross, Lew, Mis.*	1.000	20	1	5	0	6	0
St. Amand, Reuben, M.H.	.667	15	1	3	2	6	0
Salmon, Bradley, Bil.	.929	16	4	9	1	14	1
Sampson, Jacob, G.F.	.000	1	0	0	0	0	0
Sanchez, Duaner, Mis.	.947	13	9	9	1	19	3
Sanchez, Sinuhe, But.*	1.000	27	2	4	0	6	1
Schreyer, Brett, But.	1.000	10	0	1	0	1	0
Sheets, Ben, Og.	1.000	2	0	1	0	1	0
Shiyuk, Todd, I.F.*	1.000	23	4	7	0	11	1
Silverio, Marcelino, I.F.	.875	23	1	6	1	8	1
Simonson, Chris, Hel.	1.000	6	2	11	0	13	1
Smith, Jesse, Hel.	1.000	19	2	6	0	8	1
Smith, Travis, Og.	.000	1	0	0	0	0	0
Springston, Adam, G.F.	.000	4	0	0	0	0	0
Stanley, Cody, Bil.	.900	26	5	4	1	10	0
Stanton, Timothy, Mis.*	1.000	21	2	5	0	7	1
Stevens, Josh, M.H.	.875	23	1	6	1	8	2
Stewart, Cory, Bil.*	1.000	10	0	3	0	3	0
Stewart, Steve, Og.*	1.000	13	4	13	0	17	4
Thompson, Travis, Bil.	.833	8	0	5	1	6	1
Toropov, Alexandre, G.F.	.000	2	0	0	0	0	0
Torres, Manny, Bil.	.000	7	0	0	0	0	0
Verdugo, Oswaldo, I.F.	1.000	33	0	2	0	2	0
Wagner, Frank, Hel.*	.667	11	1	1	1	3	0
Wakefield, Doug, But.*	1.000	3	1	0	0	1	0
Walker, Josh, Hel.	1.000	3	0	2	0	2	0
Wallace, Ben, Og.*	.400	16	0	2	3	5	0
Wallace, Jeffrey, G.F.*	1.000	4	1	1	0	2	0
Warren, Joshua, But.	.833	14	0	5	1	6	0
Watkins, Steve, I.F.	.900	12	4	5	1	10	0
Webster, Jeremy, I.F.*	1.000	12	1	2	0	3	0
Williams, Adam, G.F.*	.895	15	6	11	2	19	0
Williams, Joel, G.F.	1.000	13	3	3	0	6	0
Williamson, Charles, Mis.	1.000	25	3	4	0	7	0
Wollscheid, James, Mis.	.909	18	6	4	1	11	0
Wood, Brandon, Mis.	.944	19	6	11	1	18	1

PITCHERS WITH TWO OR MORE TEAMS

Player, Team	Pct.	G	PO	A	E	TC	DP
Burkhart, B.J., Og.*	.800	10	3	1	1	5	0
Burkhart, B.J., Hel.*	1.000	8	1	1	0	2	0
Olean, Chris, Og.	1.000	2	1	0	0	1	0
Olean, Chris, Hel.	.917	14	4	7	1	12	1
Robinson, Jeff, Og.	1.000	9	2	8	0	10	0
Robinson, Jeff, Hel.	1.000	1	1	0	0	1	0

The following player appeared only as designated hitter, pinch-hitter or pinch runner: J. Wagner, dh.

LEAGUE CHAMPIONS

Year	Team	Pct.
1939—	Twin Falls*	.581
1940—	Salt Lake City	.608
	Ogden (4th)*	.492
1941—	Boise	.623
	Ogden (2nd)*	.598
1942—	Pocatello†	.690
	Boise	.683
1943-44-45—	Did not operate.	
1946—	Twin Falls‡	.585
	Salt Lake City†	.585
1947—	Salt Lake City	.618
	Twin Falls†	.600
1948—	Pocatello	.611
	Twin Falls (2nd)*	.595
1949—	Twin Falls	.624
	Pocatello (3rd)*	.595
1950—	Pocatello	.635
	Billings (3rd)*	.571
1951—	Salt Lake City	.618
	Great Falls (3rd)*	.559
1952—	Pocatello	.595
	Idaho Falls (2nd)*	.573
1953—	Ogden	.679
	Salt Lake City (4th)*	.527
1954—	Salt Lake City	.595
	Great Falls (4th)*	.530
1955—	Boise	.588
	Magic Valley (4th)*	.489
1956—	Boise	.561
1957—	Salt Lake City	.650
	Billings†	.582
1958—	Great Falls	.582
	Boise†	.615
1959—	Boise	.633
	Billings (2nd)*	.523
1960—	Boise†	.686
	Idaho Falls	.650
1961—	Boise	.638
	Great Falls*	.571
1962—	Boise§	.565
	Billings†	.706
1963—	Boise	.702
	Magic Valley†	.643
1964—	Treasure Valley	.615
1965—	Treasure Valley	.530
1966—	Ogden	.591
1967—	Ogden	.621
1968—	Ogden	.609
1969—	Ogden	.620
1970—	Idaho Falls	.629
1971—	Great Falls	.643
1972—	Billings	.694
1973—	Billings	.629
1974—	Idaho Falls	.569
1975—	Great Falls	.577
1976—	Great Falls	.577
1977—	Lethbridge	.629
1978—	Billings∞	.735
1979—	Helena	.623
	Lethbridge▲	.559
1980—	Lethbridge▲	.743
	Billings	.629
1981—	Calgary	.657
	Butte▲	.557
1982—	Medicine Hat▲	.629
	Idaho Falls	.600
1983—	Billings▲	.614
	Calgary	.600
1984—	Billings	.691
	Helena▲	.647
1985—	Great Falls	.771
	Salt Lake City▲	.657
1986—	Salt Lake City◆	.643
	Great Falls	.571
1987—	Salt Lake City◆	.700
	Helena	.657
1988—	Great Falls◆	.754
	Butte	.629
1989—	Great Falls◆	.791
	Butte	.621
1990—	Great Falls◆	.706
	Salt Lake	.618
1991—	Salt Lake City◆	.700
	Great Falls	.657
1992—	Salt Lake	.697
	Billings◆	.697
1993—	Billings◆	.653
	Helena	.589
1994—	Billings◆	.694
	Helena	.611
1995—	Billings	.710
	Helena■	.690
1996—	Helena■	.597
	Ogden	.583
1997—	Great Falls	.556
	Billings■	.549
1998—	Medicine Hat	.622
	Idaho Falls■	.618
1999—	Idaho Falls	.640
	Missoula■	.592

*Won four-club playoff. †Won split-season playoff. ‡Ended first half in tie with Salt Lake City and won one-game playoff. §Ended first half in tie with Billings and Great Falls and won playoff. ∞Billings (first place) defeated Idaho Falls (second place) in first place-second place playoff. ▲League divided into Northern and Southern divisions; won two-club playoff. ◆Won two-club playoff. ■League divided into Northern and Southern divisions; won four-club playoff.

SUMMER CLASS A Pioneer League

MINOR LEAGUE INDEX

TEAMS AND CITIES

MINOR LEAGUE INDEX